The A-Z of Contract Clauses

Seventh Edition

The A-Z of Contract Clauses

Seventh Edition

The A-Z of Contract Clauses

Seventh Edition

Deborah Fosbrook, BA (Hons)
Barrister of the Honourable Society of Gray's Inn

and

Adrian C Laing, LLB (Exon)
Legal and Commercial Consultant

Bloomsbury Professional

LONDON • DUBLIN • EDINBURGH • NEW YORK • NEW DELHI • SYDNEY

Bloomsbury Professional

Bloomsbury Publishing Plc

50 Bedford Square, London, WC1B 3DP, UK

1385 Broadway, New York, NY 10018, USA

29 Earlsfort Terrace, Dublin 2, Ireland

BLOOMSBURY and the Diana logo are trademarks of Bloomsbury Publishing Plc

First Edition 1996

Second Edition 2003

Third Edition 2006

Fourth Edition 2008

Fifth Edition 2010

Sixth Edition Bloomsbury Professional 2014

Seventh Edition Bloomsbury Professional 2022

© Deborah Fosbrook and Adrian C Laing 1996–2022

A CIP catalogue number for this book is available from the British Library.

ISBN: HB: 978 1 52651 215 4

ePDF: 978 1 52651 217 8

ePub: 978 1 52651 216 1

Typeset by Evolution Design & Digital Ltd (Kent)

Printed in the UK by CPI Group (UK) Ltd, Croydon, CR0 4YY

With love to Katie, David, William, George, Peter, Charlotte and Sebastian

Preface

The A-Z of Contract Clauses Seventh Edition is a major new edition which has taken over two years to be extensively revised and updated. There have been many changes in the strategies and methods used across commercial and media industries. There have been massive shifts in the way that intellectual property rights and material are produced, licensed and exploited.

There is a far more multi-layered approach to selling, promoting and marketing products, services and brands. There are now more opportunities for companies, charities and individuals to generate revenue due to the incredible advances in technology.

The sequence and manner in which material is released and used has changed with streaming, play back archives, apps, podcasts, audios files, interactive games, theme parks, product placement and endorsements; the licensing of logos, images and characters, competitions and gambling, sponsored events and themed collaborations for arts, sports and music festivals used by a wide range of types of businesses.

The authors have a natural bias to all forms of publication, media and entertainment; the commissioning and licensing of films and television series; contributors and presenters agreements for programmes and podcasts; publishing contracts for books and other formats; sub-licensing and merchandising; the production, supply and distribution of products and services; sponsorship; acquiring the rights to original artwork or the services of the product of the work of a consultant; and the development and creation of material for exploitation over the internet and social media by means of websites, apps, blogs, downloads and other platforms.

This book is an essential legal, corporate and business affairs reference book which combines contracts, intellectual property and practical realistic legal issues into clear and comprehensive clauses for you to edit and adapt.

There are key main clause headings from A to Z which include, for example: Assignment, Accounting Provisions, Budget, Buy-Out, Consultation, Copyright Clearance, Disclaimer, Editorial Control, Force Majeure, Gross Receipts, Jurisdiction, Liability, Marketing, Moral Rights, Net Receipts, Payment, Rejection, Rights, Royalties and Termination.

The key main clause headings are then sub-divided broadly into: Film, Television and Video, General Business and Commercial, Internet,

Websites and Apps, Merchandising and Distribution, Publishing, Services, Sponsorship, University, Charity and Educational.

The clauses are written in plain English with a deliberate avoidance of references to legislation and archaic language. The intention is that these clauses can used in contracts, licences and other documents worldwide.

The use of this book will help you review and select clauses on a very wide range of vital topics. You will able to examine clauses on the same subject and understand how they can be varied and amended.

The clauses are not all drafted for the benefit of the same party. Some clauses are very definitely deliberately weighed in favour of one party over another whilst others seek to maintain a balance between the parties.

You will be able to improve your understanding of how editing, adding to or deleting a clause can have real consequences in the future. Some of the terms may be on subjects in which you wish to expand your knowledge and drafting skills. It will assist and encourage you to identify and list vital topics which should be discussed and clarified in negotiations. The aim is to raise matters which may cause conflict and which if agreed in advance will assist in the avoidance of disputes and litigation.

The book and the accompanying electronic files provide access to hundreds of clauses, definitions and terms which can be adapted for a great many agreements.

The first edition of this book was first published in 1996 at a time when electronic contracts were still under debate and this book was used by researchers to create contract management cycles based on the fact that the text for each clause could be encapsulated in a single unit. The developers acknowledged the contribution of this work to the creation of online electronic contracts.

This book has always looked beyond the legislation to take account of the means by which rights and material are exploited in the literary, artistic, charitable, educational, media and commercial world.

Every person will define and draft the terms of an agreement differently based on their knowledge, experience and the resources they have available. Whether you currently start with your own personal library of precedents and sample documents which you have accumulated over the years or have access and use of a pro forma archive licensed from a third party or you use a series of in-house ready made documents which have been approved by senior management. This book and the accompanying electronic files will make a very useful addition to your work as it provides access to hundreds more clauses.

It is important to review every contract and to include new clauses which create the most advantageous agreement for a company or person based on the time period allowed for negotiation and drafting and the strength of the bargaining position of the parties. Where possible every single clause in an agreement should be examined to see whether it can be improved.

Where companies constantly reissue for years the same format of contracts without any deletions of terms or addition of new clauses, these agreements invariably rapidly become inadequate and are not able to cover all the factors that may need to be covered as a priority. There are then created blank spaces where an issue has not been addressed and which becomes a potential matter for dispute at a later date.

This book and the electronic files to which you personally have access under the authorised terms of the licence is an invaluable toolkit of hundreds of individual contract clauses, rights, definitions and terms.

The clauses are drafted by established experts who understand the legal, commercial and practical aspects of negotiating, drafting and concluding agreements worldwide, as well as the methods by which copyright and intellectual property rights can be used, licensed and assigned to achieve revenue streams in different markets and medium.

Every business is filled with a wealth of contracts, licences, terms and conditions of trading, contracts for services and products; commissioning of artwork, logos, films and marketing, licensing and exploitation of copyright or other intellectual property rights and agreements for partnerships or joint ventures.

The aim with every new edition of this book is to create new contract clauses across a broad spectrum of subjects. The acquisition of the ownership of the copyright and other intellectual property rights in an image, logo, sound recording, film or other material whether it relates to the marketing or exploitation of an individual, product, service or a brand creates a financial asset for that business.

The process of negotiation and drafting of agreements as a skill is usually acquired as a result of actual practice in industry or a law firm rather than as part of a degree course or subsequent qualification. This book allows you to grasp the essence of the contents of agreements and understand the meaning and purpose of a large range of different clauses.

This book is intended to encourage you to create your own style of drafting – the clauses are a starting point for you to edit and adapt to suit the facts and circumstances. The book and the index will assist in recognising subject areas which have not been covered in a contract.

This book will provide inspiration, save time and effort and increase your ability to work through issues in difficult agreements. It will be useful to those with more advanced levels of drafting as you will find new and innovative clauses.

If you are studying contract or business law at an academic institute or university this book will enable you to see actual drafted clauses which apply across many industries.

Complete beginners who wish to develop a new knowledge base and understand clauses will be able to use the main clause headings in the book and index as a master reference checklist for different types of clauses.

You will be able to more quickly establish what might be missing from an agreement you have been asked to review. This book will help you identify the clauses which you need in a document. If you are able to create your own clauses in draft form and send these to the other party rather than just raise a series of requests then you are at a distinct commercial advantage. It allows you to respond effectively to a third party with actual clauses that can be added when reviewing a contract.

It will allow you to suggest amendments to a licence which reduce the financial consequences of an indemnity. You may insist on a procedure to be followed in order for a claim to be made.

There are clauses which reduce or confirm the liability of one party; establish who bears the cost of insurance; sets a limit on costs, the proposed budget or expenses so as to ensure that you are not expected to meet any unauthorised overspend.

It will enable you to develop stronger negotiating skills and improve your ability to adapt clauses. You can create your own list of key points to ask for to be included in a document and will be able to put more terms to the other party than you actually want. So that you have the scope to conclude terms by a process of concessions to your benefit.

It will assist you in how to structure agreements and improve your financial awareness and increase the depth of your knowledge of how to exploit material and rights.

It is intended to provide inspiration and solid background material for you to be able to decide which clauses would be relevant to your negotiations and enable you to try to achieve the most favourable result as reflected in the contract.

You may maximise your potential revenue by not granting rights which you should retain or only granting a very short licence period. You may also reserve all other rights which are not specified in the document so that they are retained and so avoid ambiguity in the future.

You will have a better understanding of how different types of clauses can be varied to either to licence more narrowly or to acquire more widely depending on your circumstances. There are clauses for both these perspectives. The clauses are drafted from many different angles depending on the intended outcome.

It will encourage you to protect your brand, trade mark, logos, copyright and intellectual property rights by making sure that certain clauses are always included in your agreements.

Conversely if you are the creator of artwork or images or text you will not want the company to use the material you have supplied in other formats without your consent and the payment of additional fees and royalties.

You may for instance not want to concede editorial control but are willing to add a number of clauses concerning consultation to satisfy a creator of material. It is important to clarify the terms which apply to the quality of material, products or services which are to be delivered and how they are to be accepted and rejected. There are main clause headings related to Acceptance, Consultation, Editorial Control, Quality Control and Rejection. There may be a prototype or sample which needs to be approved first or a detailed specification as to the content and functions. Failure to include these types of clauses may mean that you will have paid for something that does not fulfil the original criteria you envisaged.

You can use the book to update your existing contracts and ensure that you are not assigning ownership of new technologies or rights or formats which do not exist now but may be created in the future.

You can grant an option, acquire, commission, license and exploit rights in respect of archive material, films, television series, books, online text, images, logos and multi-platform content, websites, mobiles, apps, music and sound recordings or other media.

You may be supplied services by a developer, creator or consultant and then aim to acquire the rights to the product of their work. Whether it is a new computer generated logo, an image for a product or a character or a report. Failure to acquire ownership from the third party may have serious consequences. Conversely you may wish prevent a company from acquiring additional rights in your original material outside those which are specifically authorised.

It is important to clarify who owns new material that is commissioned or being designed, whether it is marketing material for social media or a new collaboration with a third party.

This book will help you in your aim to create the best working relationship. That means discussing and agreeing issues in negotiations so that they are covered in the final agreement.

You can use the clauses to grant an exclusive licence, distribution agreement or sub-licence merchandising rights. It can be used to conclude a location access arrangement or a book deal for a range of formats both in print and in electronic form or to engage a series of contributors for a development project for a film, video, website, app, podcast or other event.

There are terms relating to Option, Legal Proceedings, Termination and Novation. There are Third Party Transfer clauses which state that an agreement cannot be transferred to a third party without your prior consent. There are also diametrically opposed clauses which allow one or both parties to transfer a contract to a third party provided that certain conditions are fulfilled.

There are terms relating to Copyright Clearance, Delivery, Material and Title. You will be able to select a variety of clauses which can be edited to clarify the issue of ownership and who pays any fees, costs and other sums that may be due for supply, reproduction, performance, transmission or other exploitation.

This book and the accompanying electronic files are an excellent training and reference resource to help those who need to learn what matters in a contract and how the terms may be edited and the basic fundamentals which must be covered in order to maintain control of a project.

Since the first edition was published in 1996 this book has been used by lawyers, law societies, university libraries, institutes and trade organisations, copyright owners, agents, publishing and distribution companies, film, television and production companies, literary and advertising agents, authors, sport organisations, government, brand, product and media companies. Copies have been sold worldwide including the UK, Europe, India, Malaysia, Switzerland, Australia, Canada, Germany, Hong Kong, Norway and America.

Note this book falls within the classifications of: Contract, Media, Intellectual Property and Business. There is an extensive Legal, Commercial and Business Development directory; a new section on Codes of Practice, Policies and Guidance. As well as a selection of detailed articles on contract related matters.

Sometimes you are keen to get a contract signed and it is easy to rush ahead. Even minor changes in a contract can have advantages and affect the generation of advances and royalties you receive in the future.

You will be able to improve your drafting skills and put forward the actual words of clauses which you wish to have incorporated in a contract. It is much easier to start with a ready made clause which can be edited or added to than with a blank page. It is an obvious advantage to be able to propose a real draft clause rather than just discuss a topic in broad terms. The nuances of the final draft may have a significant impact.

When confronted with a contract in a new field it will increase your confidence to meet the challenge to break it down into component parts and restructure it in a manner which suits your purposes.

Jurisdiction: UK, Commonwealth and worldwide.

Deborah Fosbrook
Adrian C. Laing
November 2021

A

ABSENCE

General Business and Commercial

A.001
If without the prior approval of the [Company] any absence by the [Employee] lasts for [number] consecutive working days or more. The [Employee] must provide a document to the [Company] on the third day or as soon as reasonably practicable thereafter which sets out the reason for the absence and the date by which the [Employee] expects to be able to return to full-time work. On the [number] consecutive working day of absence and at weekly intervals thereafter. The [Employee] shall be obliged to supply at their own cost such medical certificates from a qualified [Doctor/other] in [country] as may be required which verifies the cause of the absence and/or illness for the full period of any absence from work.

A.002
In the event of the inability of the [Employee] to work for the [Company] due to the [Employee's] illness, injury and/or other medical reason after the completion of [number] months of the contract. Then the [Employee] shall be entitled to the sickness and/or health and/or personal injury benefits in accordance with the [Company's] staff handbook. Provided that medical certificates and/or detailed medical reports are supplied to the [Company] upon request as may be required which confirm the medical reason provided by the [Employee]. The [Company] agrees to pay such statutory sick pay to the [Employee] in the [United Kingdom] as may be required by legislation. The [Employee] acknowledges receipt of the staff handbook dated [date] which forms part of this agreement.

A.003
[Name] agrees that their position as [specify role/title] is part-time temporary work and that in the event that [Name] does not attend and/or complete all the work for any reason whatsoever. That [Name] shall not be entitled to either claim and/or be paid any sum where [Name] is absent. Nor shall [Name] be entitled to seek to be provided with alternative work and/or dates to complete any work.

1

ABSENCE

A.004

Where [Name] is absent on unauthorised leave on more than [number] days in any [one] month period at any time during this agreement. It is agreed that the [Company] may decide at its absolute discretion that [Name] may be verbally warned that their attendance must be improved and given a fixed period with an end date to do so. The [Company] may then decide after the expiry of the period of warning if there has been no improvement that a written warning notice be sent to [Name] by email or letter. This document should set out the full details of the complaint by the [Company] for [Name] to consider and the nature of the change or improvement that the [Company] requires. The [Company] agrees that [Name] shall then be asked to attend a meeting to discuss the matter with the [Company]. Although there is no obligation that [Name] should do so. In the event that the attendance of [Name] does not comply with the contract as required by the [Company]. Then the [Company] may decide at its own discretion to terminate the contract with [Name] without further notice. The [Company] shall only be obliged to pay those sums due under the contract up to the date of termination where [Name] has fulfilled the work.

A.005

The [Company] accepts and agrees that there may be occasions when the [Employee] may be absent due to domestic, family, dental, health, transport, weather conditions or due to some unforeseen emergency. The [Company] agrees that failure to give advance notice shall not in those circumstances be sufficient grounds to give a written warning regarding absence. Provided that the [Employee] contacts the [Company] as soon as reasonably possible to advise them of the position. The [Employee] shall then have the choice to either substitute alternative hours at a later date or allocate the absence as part of their annual holiday leave. The [Company] agrees that in such event the [Employee] shall still be paid for the period of absence.

A.006

If the [Employee] is absent from work due to sickness, ill-health or incapacity for [number] days in any [12] month period (whether continuous or not). The [Company] shall have the right to decide that it can no longer continue to make the position available to the [Employee] and shall have the right to terminate the contract by notice in writing. The [Company] shall only be liable to pay any salary due to the date of termination of the contract unless to dos so would be contrary to some existing legislation in [country] which applies to the [Employee] and the circumstances. The [Employee] agrees that there shall be no sums due as compensation for loss of the position, damage to reputation and/or other financial loss which may arise unless a previously stated it would be contrary to any existing legislation. The [Company] may at its discretion agree to provide a reference for the

[Employee] which shall explains that the contract ended due to absence due to [health/other] reasons and was not connected to the standard and quality of the work of the [Employee].

A.007

1.1 The [Executive] shall provide his/her exclusive services to the best of their skill and ability on a full-time basis and normal working days shall be [specify days/hours/breaks].

1.2 The [Executive] shall perform all his/her duties in a professional and diligent manner and shall not supply services of the same or similar nature to the job description under this agreement to any third party without the prior written consent of the [Company] at any time during the Term of the Agreement.

A.008

In the event of absence from work the [Executive] must notify the [Company] as soon as possible, in person wherever possible or by the best available means at his/her disposal in the circumstances. In any event the [Executive] agrees to provide the [Company] with as much notice as possible in the event that the [Executive] is unable whether as a result of sickness or general circumstances beyond the control of the [Executive] to perform any of his/her obligations under this agreement.

A.009

If the [Executive] is absent from duty without permission and without a reason acceptable to the [Company]. The [Company] reserves the right to withhold payment and to deduct from the [Executive's] salary a day's pay for each day of unauthorised absence. Disciplinary action may also be taken in accordance with the Disciplinary Procedure in Schedule B which is attached to this agreement.

A.010

In the event that there is repeated unauthorised absence for all and/or part of the day when the [Employee] is expected to be at the [office/other] of the [Company]. Then the [Company] shall arrange for a meeting to discuss the matter with the [Employee]. Where the situation does not improve and the absences continue then the [Company] shall be entitled to give written notice of the termination of the contract of employment.

A.011

In the event that a person on a temporary and/or fixed term contract whether paid or not is unable for any reason whether through illness, family problems, loss of a close relative, and/or a hospital, dentist, eye and/or other appointment relating to their health and/or any other reason does not attend work to fulfil their duties under this agreement for more than [number] consecutive days at any time. Then the [Charity] shall be entitled but no obliged to give written notice of termination of the agreement which shall have immediate effect. No compensation for any loss of any nature shall be due and the liability of the [Charity] shall be limited to any sums due for those days of work completed.

A.012

The Company agrees that the [Employee] shall be able to take such leave for dental, hospital, school and such other personal and family commitments which may be required during normal working hours. Provided that:

1.1 The [Employee] as far as possible notifies the Line Manager in advance by text, mobile or email. It is accepted that where there is an emergency notification will be after the event and

1.2 The [Employee] works additional hours to compensate for the absence and/or allocates the period as holiday leave.

A.013

It is agreed by both parties that any leave of absence which is not notified in advance shall not automatically be deemed a breach of this agreement. Where the absence is due to a genuine emergency, delay and/or failure to attend arising from a matter relating to the [Employee] and his/her family. Provided that upon return to work the [Employee] provides an explanation in writing and agrees not to be paid for those dates where the [Employee] was absent.

A.014

1.1 The [Expert] agrees that he/she shall attend and appear as a specialist on the topic of [subject] on the following [dates/times/location] at the following hearing of [specify reason].

1.2 The [Expert] agrees to write a [number] page report which analyses the data and material provided by the [Company] and makes value judgements as to the evidence and statements and their validity.

1.3 The [Specialist] accepts that it is vital that he/she is not absent for any reason unless prevented by an emergency, serious medical grounds, death and/or an Act of God.

A.015

[Name] agrees and undertakes that he/she shall be required to attend the [Exhibition] from [date] to [date] in the role of [specify role] from [–] to [–]

hours with only short breaks. In consideration of such agreement and the undertaking not to be absent for any reason [Name] shall receive the fee of [number/currency] which shall be paid within [number] days of completion of the work.

A.016

Any absence of any nature must be notified to [Human Resources/other] by email or telephone by you personally on the actual day itself specifying the reason and when you expect to be able to attend. Any absence will result in no payment for that day. An absence of more than [fourteen] working days in any month will mean that the position is no longer available to you. The contract will be automatically terminated and you will only be paid for work completed to the date of termination.

A.017

The [Company] agrees that in any year [Name] shall be permitted to take [number] days of unpaid leave of absence in additional to their annual holiday to carry out public duties, jury service, union work, academic research, training and/or for some other reason to develop their skills and career.

A.018

The [Client] agrees that once the [booking/appointment] has been confirmed and a date, time and reference allocated and agreed. If the [Client] wishes to cancel the [booking/appointment] half the fee shall be due if the [booking/appointment] is cancelled more than [seven] days in advance. Otherwise the [Company] shall be entitled to be paid whether or not the [Client] attends the [booking/appointment].

A.019

Absence and/or failure to attend all and/or any part of the [seminars/workshops] at the specified dates and times agreed between the [Company] and the [Client] shall not entitle the [Client] to any refund, reimbursement and/or otherwise of the fees paid.

A.020

Any absence and/or failure to attend on the dates specified in the agreement shall not automatically entitle the [Company] to terminate the agreement and/or to withhold any sums which may be due for other work which has been completed. The [Company] agrees that [Name] shall be provided with the opportunity to rectify the matter within [number] days. Failure to do so shall mean that the [Company] shall have the right to take such steps as it thinks fit in the circumstances.

A.021

Where the [Consultant] is absent and/or out of [country] for more than [number] days for any reason whether due to holidays, health or otherwise. He/she shall ensure that there is a nominated contact at the [Consultant Company] at all times who has the same level of expertise and knowledge who is able to advise the [Charity]. Failure to provide this alternative shall be deemed a breach of this agreement.

A.022

1.1　It is a specific requirement of this agreement that the following persons are involved in this [Project] and fulfil the roles described in full in appendix A which forms part of this agreement. [specify name/role/job description].

1.2　The funding for the [Project] is provided solely upon the basis that the personnel in 1.1 are involved in the [Project] and no substitution and/or absence may be covered by a third party and/or any other personnel.

1.3　The [Company] agrees and undertakes that all the persons specified in Appendix A are available and shall not be absent and have been engages by the [Company] for the [Project].

A.023

The [Agency] shall be obliged to notify the [Author] in the event that there is to be a major change of the management of the company and/or the Chief Executive decides to leave at any time and work elsewhere. In such event the [Author] shall have the choice as to whether they wish to end the agreement. If the agreement is terminated all the rights granted and/or assigned under the contract shall revert to the [Author]. The [Agency] shall only be paid until the date of termination and shall not be entitled to any commission after that date.

A.024

The absence of any key personnel involved in the development, production, marketing and distribution of the [Product/Service] shall not entitle the [Licensor] to cancel, terminate and/or amend the agreement. Provided that the [Licensee] can ensure and is able to establish that the quality, content, promotion and sales of the [Product/Service] shall not be damaged, harmed and/or diminished in any way.

A.025

Where the [Author/Assignor] is unable to attend any of the [dates/events] under the agreement and/or is absent for any reason such as ill -health, bereavement, transport delays, and other prior commitments. Then such failure to attend shall not be considered reasonable grounds for the reduction and/or delay of any payments and/or for the termination of the agreement. Where feasible both parties shall endeavour to agree alternative [dates/events] upon the same and/or similar terms. Further no sums shall be due in compensation for any such absence and/or failure to attend at any time by the [Author/Assignor] to the [Promoter].

A.026
Where the [Licensor] is unable to fulfil all and/or any substantial part (namely more than [number] per cent of the appearances, promotions and marketing) of the terms of the licence granted to the [Licensee] due to the absence and/or failure of [name] to attend for any reason whatsoever. Then the [Licensor] agrees that, for each date and/or event, the [Licensee] shall be entitled to retain [number] [currency] from the sums due to the [Licensor] under this agreement.

A.027
The absence of any member of the current [Management Team] specified in Schedule A whether permanent or temporary shall not entitle the [Company] to seek to terminate this agreement on the grounds of breach of contract. The [Management Team] shall have the right to substitute any person with another in the short or long term provided they are of a similar level of skill and technical ability.

A.028
The [Agency] agrees that in the event that any of the persons which it has supplied to perform the required services to the [Company] are absent, fail to attend and/or are otherwise late and/or unavailable at any time. Then the [Company] shall not be obliged to pay the [Agency] for the use of their services in respect of each such person for any such period.

A.029

1.1 The [Company] agrees that the [Consultant] shall not be required to be available at all times, and may be absent from meetings, presentations and/or unable to review documents due to prior work commitments, holidays and/or for medical reasons.

1.2 However in the event that the [Consultant] is unavailable for a continuous period of more than [number] [days/weeks]. The [Company] shall be entitled if it so decides to terminate the agreement by giving [ten] days written notice to the [Consultant].

A.030
Where there is a complete absence of a normal service provided by the [Company] to the [Client] for a period of more than [number] [days/weeks/

months]. Then the [Client] shall be entitled to be paid with immediate effect the sum of [number/currency] for each [day/week/month] in which there is a complete absence of service. No sums will be due where a partial service is achieved.

A.031

Where the [Studio] is unable to supply the agreed [Artist/Photographer] for the work and/or the person does not appear on the agreed dates and is absent for any reason. Then the [Client] shall be entitled to cancel the entire contract and to be refunded all sums that have been paid less any expenses which were agreed which have been incurred by the [Studio] with third parties.

A.032

Where the original [Artist/Photographer/Performer] for the [Event] is unable to attend and/or is to be absent for any reason. Then the [Client] agrees that the [Company] shall have the absolute discretion to book another person of suitable quality and calibre who may be available at short notice.

A.033

The [Consultant] agrees that he/she shall provide his/her services for the [Project] [specify days/hours] from [date] to [date] and shall not be entitled to any period of absence during that time except for short breaks or real emergencies. The [Consultant] agrees to be available at all other times to be contacted by mobile or email as follows: [specify contact details/availability].

A.034

The [Presenter] shall be required to attend at [location] to prepare, present, and promote the [Programme/Series] in accordance with the hours and days specified in the Work Schedule in Appendix A. There shall be no obligation to attend at the location on days or dates not specified unless agreed at least [number] days in advance between the parties. The [Company] agrees that it shall take account of the pre-existing work commitments of the [Presenter] which shall take priority.

A.035

The [Artist] shall provide his/her services to the best of their technical and artistic skill and ability and perform his/her services to a standard and in a manner which is required to ensure the completion of the [Project]. The [Artist] shall only be required to attend on such days as may be scheduled from [date] to [date] and at the times specified by the [Company] which are agreed verbally or by email in advance. Where the [Artist] has other work to complete with a third party then the [Company] accepts that other dates must be offered to complete the [Project].

A.036

The [Sponsor] agrees that the Sponsorship Fee shall still be paid in full to [Name] even if [Name] is unable to provide his/her services under this agreement due to illness, injury and/or any other issue such as mental health. On the basis that [Name] is able and willing to supply a medical certificate from a qualified medical practitioner which verifies the reason.

A.037

1.1 In the event that [Name] is absent from any of the scheduled races, promotions and/or meetings set out in the Work Schedule in Appendix A. This shall not affect any of the sums due under this agreement where it is caused by genuine medical, dental, health and/or family reasons. Nor shall it be affected where absence is due to sporting commitments which were not known at the time of concluding this agreement.

1.2 Where [Name] fails to attend for another reason which is not accepted by the [Company] then the parties shall enter into negotiations to agree either alternative work to compensate and/or a reduction in the sums due to [Name].

A.038

1.1 The attendance of [Name] at each of the following events set out in Appendix A which forms part of this agreement is a fundamental term.

1.2 If [Name] fails to attend and take part in any of the specified events. Then for each such event where [Name] does not attend and take part the [Company] shall be entitled to deduct the sum of [number/ currency] from payments due under this agreement to [Name].

1.3 In the event that [Name] fails to attend and take part in more than [four] events. Then the [Company] may at its discretion bring the contract to an end by serving written notice of termination effective immediately. In such instance the [Company] shall only be liable to pay for work which has actually been completed.

1.4 [Name] agrees that if the contract is terminated that no additional sums shall be due in compensation and/or for damages and/or losses

A.039

In the event that any and/or all of the key players [specify names] are absent from the [Event/Team] at any time. That this fact shall not be grounds to seek to terminate the contract and/or withhold payment and/or seek a reduction in the sums due. The [Company] accepts that there may be many reasons for changes in the [Event/Team] by the [Sports Organisation] and that other persons may be substituted at any time.

A.040

The [Company] has agreed to sponsor the [Festival] and agrees that it shall not be entitled to terminate the agreement, withhold and/or reduce the payments and/or otherwise alter the terms due to the alteration of the dates, venue, exhibitors, participants and/or the absence of the appearance of any persons that were expected to appear on stage at the venue.

A.041

If any of the [Performers/Sportspersons] set out in Schedule A are absent from the from the [Event/Programme] and/or the coverage, recording and distribution on radio, television and live streaming does not take place. The [Sponsor] agrees that it shall still be bound to pay the sums due under this agreement in full to the [Company].

A.042

The [Company] agrees that the [Sponsor] shall be entitled to withhold and shall not be liable to pay [number/currency] of the [Sponsorship Fee] if [specify name] does not attend and perform at the [Event].

A.043

There shall be no refund and/or reduction of fees due to the absence of [Name] at any time and/or the failure of [Name] to arrive on time and/or to complete the [course]. This condition shall apply regardless of whether the reason is due to a medical problem, transport delays, a family crisis or otherwise.

A.044

Where [thirty] days prior to the commencement of the [course] the [Client] notifies the [Institute] of any problem. Then the [Institute] may agree at its absolute discretion allow a later date to be substituted for the same course if available. Where there is no substitution then the fees paid in advance shall not be refunded and the [Institute] shall not be under any obligation to return any payment.

A.045

1.1 Where any student is unable to attend and/or complete their stipulated modules and/or course due to mental health problems, disability and/or illness. The [University] may at its sole discretion decide to refund all and/or part of the sums paid in advance and/or cancel any future fees that may fall due.

1.2 The student and/or their family and/or a nominated person must notify the [University] by email or telephone as soon as reasonably possible explaining the information known at that time.

1.3 In order for the [University] to consider the matter the student will be required to submit a document which supports their case from a qualified medical practitioner. The document should specify the start date that the issue arose if known; the facts and nature of the problem and the long term prognosis if possible.

1.4 Where it is feasible for the student to start the course a year later and/or to complete a module in another term. Then the student should specify those requirements that may need to be met to assist the student in coping with their disability and/or other issues which it would like the [University] to implement if possible.

1.5 The [University] agrees to consider each case on its merits and as far as reasonably possible to encourage students to continue their studies and to provide such support and equipment and other changes as may be necessary to adapt the environment to meet their needs. Provided that the [University] does not have to make arrangements which it cannot afford due to the high cost.

A.046

Failure by any person to attend the [lectures/tutorials/seminars], and/or to complete requested [coursework/essays/presentations] by the dates and times specified during any [degree/programme/course] may result in the refusal by the [University/Institute] to award the relevant [qualification/certificate] due to lack of compliance and fulfilment of the conditions required.

A.047

The [College/University] may at its sole entire discretion agree to the delay of the commencement start date for the [Course], the substitution of an alternative course and/or the refund of part and/or all of the fees paid to date. Where the [Applicant] relies on medical grounds then a letter from the persons own Doctor shall be required in support.

A.048

1.1 In the event that you are unable to take part in the [Festival/Run] for any reason. Then you agree that the [Charity] shall not be obliged to refund the fees paid to take part.

1.2 It is agreed by you that whatever the reason for your absence that you will not be allowed to substitute another person in your place.

1.3 You also agree that if for any reason the [Charity] has to cancel the [Festival/Run] for any reason that no refund of the fees paid shall be due. That you agree that the fees may be carried forward and for you to be allocated a place on the new date for the [Festival/Run]. Provided that where you cannot attend you may nominate another person to take your place instead.

ACCEPTANCE

Film, Television and Video

A.049

1.1 The [Licensee] agrees to reject or accept the [Master Material] within [one] month of delivery date set out in this agreement.

1.2 If the [Master Material] is delivered late for any reason then the [Licensee] may automatically reject the material.

1.3 Where the material is delivered on time but is not accepted for another reason whether technical or otherwise. The [Licensee] shall provide specific details for the failure to accept the [Master Material] to the [Licensor].

1.4 The [Licensee] agrees that the [Licensor] shall have the opportunity to provide another copy or to make a substitution which is agreed between the parties.

1.5 All material which is not accepted shall be collected by the [Licensor] or returned at the [Licensor's] expense.

A.050

1.1 The [Company] shall deliver the [DVDs/Units/other format] only if payment has been made in advance.

1.2 The [Client] shall be deemed to have accepted the [DVDs/Units/other format] once it is delivered to the address specified in the Order form. You shall not be entitled to return the [DVDs/Units/other format] once opened from the packaging unless there is a defect and/or damage to the [DVDs/Units/other format].

1.3 Where the wrong material has been delivered then the [DVDs/Units/other format] should be returned unopened and unused to the [Supplier].

1.4 None of these conditions are intended by the [Company] to supersede your statutory legal rights as a consumer in [country.]

A.051

1.1 Delivery of the [Software/Unit] to the [Company] shall not be deemed to be acceptance of the material. The [Company] shall have [number] days to assess, test and review the content of the [Software/Unit] from the date of delivery.

1.2 The [Company] agrees that within [number] days of delivery it shall notify the [Supplier] as to whether it has accepted or rejected the [Software/Unit]. In the event that the [Software/Unit] is accepted then the [Company] shall authorise the payment under clause [–].

1.3 Where the [Software/Unit] is rejected then the [Company] shall return the [Software/Unit] and all copies to the [Supplier].

1.4 Where the parties do not intend to pursue the matter and the order has been rejected. The [Company] shall arrange for all reproductions of any nature in any medium of the [Software/Unit] to be deleted, destroyed and/or erased which are in its possession and/or control which are derived from the [Software/Unit]. The [Company] shall confirm this fact to the [Supplier].

A.052

1.1 The [Company] agrees to supply the [Client] with; [specify exact material/title/duration/format]. This shall be all the master material and/or copies of the images, interviews, films, videos, sound recordings and/or any other material which the [Company] organised to be taken, filmed and/or recorded at the [Event]. All reproduction costs, delivery and other charges shall be at the [Company's] expense.

1.2 The [Company] agrees and undertakes that neither the [Company] nor any nominated crew, photographer and/or presenter shall edit, adapt, distribute and/or supply any such material in 1.1 to a third party. That any other copies in the possession and/or under the control of the [Company] shall be deleted and/or destroyed and no such material shall be retained by the [Company] unless written authority is provided otherwise by the [Client].

A.053

The [Company] shall endeavour to ensure that all subjects that may require approval and/or acceptance shall be carried out as quickly as possible and shall not delay the [Project]. The parties shall operate by allowing each other at least [number] days [excluding weekends and bank holidays] to respond to any request. All requests of any nature shall be sent for the attention of [name] at the [Company] by email to [email address] and copied to [name/email address].

A.054

1.1 The [Distributor] shall be deemed to have accepted the [Material] if no notice of rejection on quality and/or technical grounds is received by the [Licensor] within [number] days of delivery.

1.2 The ownership of the physical material shall not be transferred to the [Distributor] until payment in full has been received by the [Licensor] for the reproduction and delivery of the [Material] including any taxes, customs duties, import and/or export charges, storage costs and/or otherwise.

1.3 All risks shall pass to the [Distributor] upon delivery in respect of any losses, damages and/or destruction of the [Material]. Where any [Material] needs to be replaced then the [Distributor] agrees to reimburse the [Licensor] in respect of the full cost of any replacement that may be necessary.

A.055

1.1 The unauthorised delivery of any [Script/Proposal/Synopsis] to the [Company] by any person in any format does not mean that the material will be treated as confidential and/or private by the [Company]. No unsolicited material sent to the {Company] shall be deemed in any way accepted by the [Company] and no undertakings shall apply.

1.2 The [Company] does not accept any responsibility and/or liability for any loss, damage and/or any incident where for any reason the material is reproduced and/or distributed to third parties.

1.3 The [Company] may create its own original programmes on the same generic subject at any time. If you wish to keep your material confidential then do not send unsolicited material to the [Company].

A.056

1.1 Where [Material] is submitted to the [Company] then it shall not be deemed to be accepted at the point of delivery.

1.2 The [Company] may take whatever time its thinks necessary to assess the [Material] and to decide whether it is suitable for exploitation. If no decision is reached within a [three] month period then the [Company] shall return the [Material] at its sole cost.

1.3 The [Company] agrees that once a decision has been made to use the [Material] that it shall notify the [Agency] and issue a licence document setting out the proposed terms for the [Agency] to accept or reject.

1.4 The [Material] will not be used by the [Company] unless and/or until a licence is concluded with the [Agency].

General Business and Commercial

A.057

1.1 Delivery of any service and/or material under this agreement does not constitute acceptance of the technical quality and/or content by the [Company].

1.2 There is no time limit set on the period permitted for the [Company] to accept and/or reject the service and/or any material.

1.3 Where the service and/or material is delivered and no decision to reject the service and/or material has been made after [four] months. Then the [Company] agrees to pay for the cost of the service for a period of [one] year and/or the material up to a total value of [number/currency].

A.058

1.1 The [Client] is deemed to have accepted the [quote/written offer] when they verbally and/or in writing agree to pay the full sums specified by the [Company].

1.2 The [Client] shall then have [fourteen] days in which to change their mind and cancel the contract. If the contract is cancelled by the [Client] no further sums shall be due. A full refund shall be made of any deposit that may have been paid in advance.

A.059
Completion of the work, delivery of the products and/or signature of a receipt form shall not constitute acceptance under this agreement. The [Client] shall have a period of [twenty-eight] days in which to inspect the [Products/Services/Work] and to provide written confirmation by email, letter and/or text message of acceptance. Where for any reason the [Products/Services/Work] is not accepted then the [Client] must advise the [Company] and arrange for the cancellation of the agreement and the collection at the [Company's] cost of all products and/or material.

A.060
Any tender, quotation or exchange of letters setting out the proposed terms in respect of [Products/Work/Services/Maintenance] to be provided to the [Company/Government Department] shall not be deemed and should not be considered a contractual acceptance by the [Company/Government Department]. All proposals must be approved by the [Board of Directors/Chief Executive] and adhere to the [Company's/Government Department] authorised policies and Codes of Practice. Any letter, email or other document is an acceptance in principle and as such is subject to contract and conditional upon the signature and conclusion of a formal document setting out in detail all the rights and obligations of both the parties.

A.061
Acceptance of the [Artwork/Product/Designs/Drawings] shall take place when the full fee is paid by the [Client]. The [Client] shall have been provided with the opportunity to view the [Work/Product/Designs/Drawings]

in the exact form and content in which it is to be sold to the [Client] by the [Company]. The [Client] shall not be entitled after acceptance to seek a refund based on artistic, design and/or colour grounds.

Internet, Websites and Apps

A.062
Any person who would like to use this [Website/App/Platform] must agree to be bound by the terms and conditions of the [Company] and you are deemed to have accepted such terms when you access and use the [Website/App/Platform].

A.063
I agree that by ticking the box [and logging my details] that I have confirmed my acceptance that I will access, order products and/or services and use the [Website/App/Platform] in accordance with those terms and conditions specified in the [Terms and Conditions] pdf set out below. That I agree that I shall not be entitled to continue to use the [Website/App/Platform] if I no longer wish to be bound by such terms and conditions. Provided that I shall still be obliged to pay any sums that may be due or owing to the [Company] and the [Company] shall deliver any products and/or services that may have been ordered.

A.064
Important – please read this document carefully before [using this website/ breaking the seal to release the disc] as by doing so you are agreeing to be bound by the following conditions: [attached appendix A/ specific location of terms and conditions].

A.065
By breaking the seal you agree in full to the terms and conditions for the use of the [Disc] set out in the Licence Agreement which is contained in the [Package/other].

A.066
When you access and use this [Website/App] whether for browsing, research, placing orders, playing games, or using any forum for exchanges between individuals you are bound by the terms and conditions for access and use which you accept by either confirming your acceptance of the terms or by going beyond the first front page of the [Website/App] to other pages and links.

A.067
When you enter this [Website/App/Platform] you must accept the access and use contract which is displayed by the [Owner] and [Operator]. You are

not authorised to use any of the material including text, data, images, films, logos, databases and/or any other material and/or content other than for your own personal use at home in residential private premises. Any supply to a third party of any material and/or content which has been and/or is placed on this [Website/App/Platform] for any reason requires the prior consent of the [Owner] and [Operator]: [specify contact details].

A.068

By installing the software which is on the [Disc/USB/other format] into your computer you accept that you will be required to fulfil and be bound by the terms and conditions of the Licence Agreement which sets out the terms of trading and supply of the [Company]. If you do not wish to accept these terms then do not install or load the [Disc/USB/other format].

A.069

1.1 There are no contractual terms and conditions which you must accept to use this [Website/App/Platform]. However we expect you to recognise and respect that material is displayed which is owned by other people. if you wish to use any of it for private home use and/ or educational research and reports then you must provide a proper credit of their name and our [Website/App/Platform] as the source on which you found it.

1.2 No authorisation is provided for any commercial use of any nature and prior written consent of the copyright owner is required in each case. Any person who acts in an unreasonable manner and/or is defamatory and/or is in breach of the rights of any nature of a third party and/or the [Company] may be excluded by the [Company] from the [Website/ App/Platform]. The [Company] may also seek to be indemnified for all costs and expenses incurred and/or sums paid in settlement and/ or as a result of legal proceedings. Further the [Company] shall have the right to recover all its own legal, in-house management and other professional experts' costs and legal expenses that may be incurred as well as to those sums due in respect of a claim for damages, losses, interest and/or any to other sums.

A.070

The use and access to the software is subject to the [User] agreeing to the terms and conditions displayed on this [Website/App/Platform] [reference] and the [User] will be deemed to have accepted and entered into agreement with the [Company] by downloading the software from the [Website/App/ Platform].

A.071

If you proceed further than the first page of this [Website/App/Platform], then you accept and agree that any information, data, images, music, recordings, text, films, directory, databases, trade marks, logos, banners, advertisements and products may only be viewed and stored on your computer, hardware, software, discs, USB or any other device or equipment on a temporary basis for no more than [specify duration] and for your own private and non-commercial purposes. There is no implied or express licence granted to use any part of this [Website/App/Platform] or anything on it for commercial, educational and/or any other purpose. In the event that you wish to do so then please email [contact details/name] setting out the details of your request. Failure to adhere to the terms of the use of the [Website/App/Platform] could result in the issue of legal proceedings against you without further notice.

A.072

This is a commercial [Website/App/Platform] which is owned and controlled by [Company]. All trademarks, logos, videos, films, images, text, databases, photographs, graphics, audio files, sound recordings, blogs, downloads, uploads, podcasts, music and any other material in any other format whether for television, radio, mobile phone content, interactive games and/or otherwise on this [Website/App/Platform] are owned and/or controlled by the [Company] and/or licensed from the copyright owner by the [Company]. You accept by your use and access to this [Website/App/Platform] that you agree to be bound by the following terms and conditions;

1.1 That as a visitor to this [Website/App/Platform] you have no right to copy, store, and retrieve, reproduce, supply, transfer, distribute and/or authorise the use of any such material by a third party.

1.2 That any copies made by you on your laptop, computer, and/or any storage and/or retrieval and/or interactive device such as a USB, mobile phone, gadget, disc and/or otherwise shall be temporary and only for your own personal use for no more than [number] [hours/days/months].

1.3 That you agree after that period to delete all copies of any material. You agree that failure to do so could result in the threat of legal proceedings and/or a claim by the [Company] and/or any other copyright owner against you personally for damages, losses and costs and/or any other remedy at any time.

A.073

Access and use of this [Website/App/ Platform] is subject to the laws of the country in which you are living as well as where this site is used. Acceptance by the [Company] of your use of this site does not absolve you from a personal legal liability for the material and content that you submit and/or display and/or supply to third parties. The [Company] does not accept any responsibility for any costs, losses, damages, fines, expenses and/or otherwise that you may incur through a criminal and/or civil action against you by any person, body or other local, government and/or national entity.

A.074
The acceptance by you of any email, image, download, advertisement and marketing, product, links, newsletter, cookies, software and/or otherwise through this site shall not mean that the [Company] which owns and controls this site and/or the [Enterprise] who operate it on their behalf shall be able to provide any reassurance as to whether it is genuine and/or a scam.

Merchandising and Distribution

A.075
The [Retailer] shall be deemed to have accepted all [Articles/Products/Units] which are not returned within [seven] days of delivery.

A.076
The [Distributor] shall endeavour to ensure that all the agents, retailers and wholesalers agree to be bound by and accept the terms and conditions relating to the marketing and sales of the [Product] set out in this agreement.

A.077
The [Author] shall not be bound to accept and/or to agree to the marketing of any [Products] as follows:

1.1 Where the [Products] are not be suitable in style and/or content for the [children's/other] market.

1.2 The sample or prototype is not of an acceptable quality and/or standard and/or does not accurately reflect the artwork and/or text in the [Books].

1.3 There is no additional advance to be paid to the [Author] and/or the estimated revenue is less than [number/currency] per year.

1.4 The proposed licensee and/or manufacturer is not an established business and has no market presence in [country].

A.078
There shall be no obligation on the [Illustrator/Creator] of the [Artwork/Material] who has collaborated with the [Author/Company] to create the [Book] to accept any of the terms for the merchandising and commercial

19

exploitation in any other media except in [hardback, paperback, audiotape and audio files]. The financial arrangements proposed by the [Author/ Company] for any such agreement must ensure that the [Illustrator] receives no less sums than the [Author] and equal prominence as regards credits in all the products and marketing material.

A.079

The [Author/Artist] accept and agree that the [Distributor] shall be entitled to develop, adapt, produce, distribute and market toys, food related products, clothes, stationery, audiotapes, audio files, computer games, DVDs, a programme or series for television, and any other item or product based on the [Book/Script] and/or any character. The [Author/Artist] accept and agree that the artwork, text, names, and storylines may be different and not necessarily an accurate reflection of the [Book/Script].

A.080

The [Company] agrees that it shall be deemed to have accepted the [Products] if they have not notified the [Distributor] by [email/letter/order form] within [three] days of the delivery of the [Products] in accordance with the confirmed [email/letter/order form].

A.081

Provided that the merchandising material supplied by the [Company] is in exact accordance with the sample products. Then the merchandising material shall be accepted by the [Client] on the day of delivery and the fee paid for the balance on the same day. Where there is an error, omission and/ or delay in the design, quality, number, delivery and/or any other reason why the merchandising material fails to match the sample and the order. Then the [Client] shall be entitled to reject all the order as a result of such failure and request a full refund to be paid immediately.

A.082

The parties agree that there may be colour, technical, material and layout variations between the samples provided before manufacture and the finished product. The [Manufacturer] agrees to notify the [Company] of any discrepancies and to provide a new sample on each occasion so that the [Company] can decide whether to proceed with the production. The [Company] shall not be bound to accept delivery of the order unless it is in accordance with any such agreed samples.

A.083

The acceptance shall be deemed by the execution and return of the Acknowledgement Copy of the Purchase Order by the [Supplier] or the

[Supplier's] execution or commencement of work or commencement of delivery pursuant to the Purchase Order.

A.084

The [Purchaser] shall have the right to conduct at its sole expense an incoming inspection of the products at the destination specified in the Bill of Lading in accordance with the inspection procedures set forth in Appendix A which is attached and is part of this agreement. The [Purchaser] shall notify the [Company] of the result of the inspection judgment (acceptance or rejection) in accordance with the said inspection procedures by [method] within [one] month after the date of arrival of the products at the destination. In the event that the [Purchaser] fails to notify the [Company] within the [one] month period. Then the [Purchaser's] right of rejection of the products shall lapse and the products shall be deemed to have been accepted by the [Purchaser].

A.085

The [Company] agrees to accept or reject the [Products] and pay the sum due in full provided that they are delivered as follows:

1.1 Delivery date: [specify date/time].

1.2 Type of Products: [colour/code reference/language on packaging/ contents/other].

1.3 Quantity: [number].

1.4 All [Products] shall be of premium quality in accordance with the [Sample Prototype] and shall not be damaged or otherwise not fit or suited to the specified purpose.

1.5 Specified purpose of the [Products]: [state purpose/type of use].

1.6 All [Products] are to bear the trade marks, slogan, image, credits, copyright notices and safety warnings specified in the [Sample/ Prototype] and packaging as described and represented in the attached Schedule A.

A.086

We accept no liability for any [Products] delivered and/or services supplied to the [Company] unless the Order has been authorised by a senior executive of the [Company].

A.087

Signature of the invoice by the [Purchaser] shall be acceptance of the [Product] [and the terms and conditions of the invoice].

A.088

The [Customer] accepts the quotation and agrees to pay the sums specified by signing the Order Form setting out the terms and conditions and the Delivery and Completion dates.

A.089

The delivery of the [Products] to the [Company] shall constitute acceptance unless upon receipt of the [Products] the [Company] specifies the grounds of rejection or dissatisfaction.

A.090

The [Company] shall be given a period of [number] [weeks/months] from receipt of the [Products] in which to inspect the products and associated packaging. During that period the [Company] shall be entitled to either accept or reject the [Products] for any reason which is due to the quality and/or content and/or fitness for purpose. At the end of that review period unless the [Supplier] has received a written response in any form rejecting the [Products] then they shall be deemed to have been accepted by the [Company] and subject to payment of the sums due shall become the property of the [Company].

A.091

The [Agent] shall at all times adhere to and follow the [Company's] price lists, sale instructions and conditions and terms of business. The [Agent] shall not have the right under any circumstances to change and/or otherwise vary and/or alter the terms of business and/or prices of the [Products] specified by the [Company]. The [Agent] shall not accept and/or agree to discounts, allowances, deferments in payment, issue credit notes and/or agree to swap and/or combine [Products] and/or agree to adopt any other similar exchange and/or reduction without the prior [verbal/written] consent of the [Company].

A.092

The [Agent] agrees that the [Company] shall at its sole discretion be entitled to accept and/or reject any Order obtained by the [Agent] for any reason including poor credit rating of the client, bad payment record, unavailability of materials or textiles, conflict of interest with existing clients. The [Agent] shall not be entitled to receive any payment for any Order so rejected.

A.093

Any catalogue, advertisement, leaflets, flyers, website, app and/or other data, information, quotes, promotional offers and prices are purely for guidance only and may be amended, updated and varied at any time by the [Company]. The [Customer] may make an offer to the [Company] to order the [Goods/Services] and the [Company] will then decide whether to accept the order or not and enter into an agreement for delivery.

A.094

The submission of the order and/or request to purchase the [Products/ Services] displayed in the brochure, catalogue, flyer and/or on the website, app and/or platform whether by telephone, email, in writing and/or otherwise shall be considered an offer by the [Customer]. The contract shall be accepted by the [Company] when a purchase invoice is raised setting out the terms agreed and payment has been received in full.

A.095

The [Company] agrees that the Order and/or [Products] shall be considered to have been accepted when one of the following events has taken place:

1.1   The payment for the [Products] has been received and the funds have transferred to and retained by the [Company].

1.2   The [Company] has issued a confirmation form allocating a reference and details of the contract.

1.3   The Order has been fulfilled and the [Products] delivered as specified.

A.096

The [Customer] shall be deemed to have accepted the terms and conditions of trading of the business set out in the [catalogue/brochure/flyer] when an order is placed and payment is made for the [Products/Services].

A.097

Without affecting your statutory rights the [Company] agrees to accept returns of any [Product] within [twenty-eight days] of purchase provided that there is a receipt as proof of purchase and the [Product] and packaging is undamaged and has not been used and/or worn. You shall be entitled to a full refund and/or to substitute another item. There are a number of exceptions for hygiene and safety reasons which will not be exchanged or refunded unless they are faulty and/or defective namely: [specify items not to be returned]. Where there is no receipt and some other proof of purchase is provided then the item can only be exchanged and/or payment for the refund made in [credit vouchers].

A.098

There shall be no obligation on the [Company] to accept the alteration, cancellation, postponement and/or other modifications to this agreement whether or not arising from circumstances which could not be reasonably foreseen at the time of negotiation and conclusion of the agreement. An increase in demand, conflict of orders or work is not sufficient and the [Company] reserves the right to claim any losses, costs and/or expenses from the [Supplier] which arise as a direct and/or indirect result where the contract has to be transferred to a third party, and/or delays occur and/or the [Company] has to cancel work or orders and/or the [Supplier] cannot fulfil the work required.

A.099
The [Client] shall not be deemed to have accepted delivery where the actual delivery is not to the address specified in the [agreement/invoice].

A.100
Where the [Product] packaging has clearly been opened and/or damaged prior to delivery to the [Client]. Then delivery shall not have taken place and the [Client] shall not be bound to accept the [Product]. The [Client] shall be entitled to cancel the order and/or arrange for a new delivery date and new [Product].

A.101
There shall be a period of [number] days for the [Client] to decide whether to accept or reject the [Product/Service/other] after all the components have arrived and before it is installed by a third party. The [Client] may accept and/or reject the [Product/Service/other] but acceptance shall be deemed to have taken place once [number] days have expired after the last delivery date by the [Company].

Publishing

A.102
The [Publisher] agrees to either accept and/or provide written reasons for the rejection of the [Manuscript] of the [Book] within [two] calendar months of delivery. The [Publisher] agrees that it shall only use valid substantial reasons relating to the writing, content and style which an independent third party would find to be relevant criticism. Minor additions, deletions and changes required for less than [number] pages shall not be considered sufficient grounds not to accept the [Manuscript].

A.103
The [Publisher] agrees to accept and/or to provide written reasons for its rejection of the [Work] within [number] [weeks/months] of delivery. The [Publisher] agrees that any rejection of the [Work] shall be limited to the following grounds namely the failure by the [Author] to meet the required professional writing standards agreed and/or failure to comply with the specifics of the summary synopsis.

A.104
In the event that the [Author] shall deliver the [Work] by the specified delivery date and in the form and with the content agreed between the parties. The

[Publisher] shall be allowed [number] days to provide written confirmation of acceptance or rejection of the [Work/Manuscript/Images]. In the event there is no such confirmation either way to the [Author] then [number] days after the specified delivery date of the [Work/Manuscript/Images]. Then the [Work/Manuscript/Images] shall be deemed to have been accepted by the [Publisher].

A.105
The [Distributor] agrees that it shall accept the [Book/Sound Recording] for publication and sale. Provided that the [Book/Sound Recording] is delivered in full by [date] in [format] and is a true reflection of the agreed summary in content and style and the quality of the [text/words] are sufficient to meet the [Distributors'] required subjective standards.

A.106
The [Publisher/Distributor] shall not be entitled to refuse to accept the [Book/Manuscript/Artwork] if the reason for the delay in delivering the manuscript is due to ill-health and/or personal injury of the [Author]. Provided that the delivery date shall only be extended by a maximum of [twelve] calendar months. After that amended date the [Publishers/Distributors'] may terminate the agreement by notice in writing at any time. It is agreed that the parties shall resolve the issue of repayment of the sums due by negotiation and that in any event the [Author] shall be entitled to a repayment period scheduled over at least [three] years.

A.107
The [Unit] and all the data included on it is supplied to you the [Purchaser] by the [Publisher] based entirely on the [Book/Resource]. If you do not wish to be bound by the terms and conditions of the use of the [Unit] and data please do not remove the seal from the wallet. The following terms set out in the attached Licence shall apply to the use of the [Book/Resource], [Unit] and data whilst it is in the possession and/or under the control of the [Purchaser].

A.108
The approval by the [Publisher/Distributor] of one chapter or section of the [Book/Manuscript/Images] does not constitute acceptance of the complete [Book/Manuscript/Images] as required under clause [–].

A.109
After the complete manuscript has been delivered to the [Publisher/Distributor] in the agreed format. The [Publishers/Distributors] agree that within [twenty-eight] working days excluding weekends and bank holidays. That they shall notify the [Author] as to whether they accept or reject the

[Work/Material]. If the [Work/Material] is accepted then the [Publisher/Distributor] shall immediately arrange for payment of any sums due on delivery without delay.

A.110

In the event that the [Book/Manuscript/Images] is not accepted then the [Publisher/Distributor] shall specify the reasons in writing by email with a letter attached. The [Publisher/Distributor] agrees that it shall enter into negotiations with the [Author] to permit the [Author] to have the opportunity to resubmit the [Book/Manuscript/Images] after it has been amended by the [Author] to take account of the grounds of rejection specified by the [Publisher/Distributor]. In the event that the [Book/Manuscript/Images] is not accepted after it is resubmitted. The [Publisher/Distributor] agrees to ensure that all rights in the [Book/Manuscript/Images] of any nature shall revert to the [Author]. Further that despite the second rejection the [Author] shall not be obliged to repay any sums paid by the [Publisher/Distributor].

A.111

The [Publisher/Distributor] agrees that it shall accept the [Book/Manuscript/Sound Recordings] provided that it is [written/spoken] to the standard and in accordance with the original synopsis and chapter outline and is factually accurate and true and does not make any allegations and/or statements which are misleading and/or inaccurate.

A.112

The [Publisher/Distributor] shall not be bound to accept any delivery of the [Manuscript/Artwork] of the [Book] and/or pay any further sums to the [Author] where since signature of the agreement the [Publisher/Distributor] has discovered that the [Author] has deliberately and actively misled the [Publisher/Distributor] as to their true identity, background, qualifications, expertise and/or history of professional writing.

Services

A.113

The [Company] shall be deemed to have accepted that they shall provide the [Services/Maintenance/Support] stated in the quotation at the agreed price once they have retained the cleared funds of the deposit.

A.114

The [Agent] shall not be obliged to accept any new terms or amendments in relation to the services of the [Artist] under this agreement unless the [Company] agrees to pay further sums in consideration.

A.115

[Name] agrees and undertakes that his/her final consent to the acceptance, signature and conclusion of any commercial agreement negotiated by the [Manager] under this agreement shall not be unreasonably withheld or delayed.

A.116

The [Company] agrees that where any material whether images, text, music, products, services, interviews and/or other material are included in, added to, deleted from or edited in a particular style at the request of the [Company] to any [Report/Film/Advertisement/Project]. That the [Company] shall be obliged to accept such material and shall not be entitled to use any such material which has been included, deleted or edited in a certain manner as grounds for rejection and non-payment of the fees.

A.117

The [Company] agrees that where the cost of the [Service] is to increase at any time during the Term of the Agreement. That the [Client] shall have the right to provide [one months'/immediate] notice by [email/telephone] that they do not accept the increase cost and no longer require the [Service] from the date of the increase cost.

A.118

The [Client] agrees that the [Company] shall have the right to increase the cost charged for the [Service] at any time and may therefore charge the [Client] at the higher rate provided that the [Client] has been notified by [email/letter] whether or not payment is through direct debit and/or otherwise.

A.0119

[Name] accepts that the [Company] may increase the annual cost of the [Service] after the first year. [Name] shall not be obliged to accept and pay the higher rate for the second year and may terminate the agreement at the end of the first year.

Sponsorship

A.120

The acceptance and rejection of any the products, displays, banners, clothes, stickers, bags, advertisements and other material and any associated name, text, trade mark, logo and image supplied by the [Sponsor] under this agreement shall be entirely at the discretion of the following persons and Board: [specify names of persons]. In the event that any of the material is deemed to be unsuitable for any reason and/or offensive and/or to contravene any relevant rules, legislation and/or Codes

27

of Practice and/or guidelines and/or policies in force at that time and/or due to come into force. Then the [Association] shall be entitled to reject all and/or part of any such material and to specify the reason for such rejection in writing to the [Managing Director] of the [Sponsor]. The rejection of all and/or any such material shall not be grounds for termination of the agreement by the [Sponsor] and/or a claim for repayment of any sums. Provided that the [Association] adheres to clause [–] for the display of the [Sponsor's] name and logo at the [Event].

A.121
The [Association] accepts that if the [Event] is cancelled and/or the attendance figures do not exceed [number] visitors in total. That the [Association] shall not be entitled to receive the final payment due on [date]. The [Sponsor] accepts and agrees that no claim shall be made by the [Sponsor] against the [Association] which may relate to loss of sales, advertising and/or marketing of the [Sponsor's] business, brand and/or products and/or services.

A.122
The [Participant] accepts and agrees that the [Sponsor] shall be able to withdraw its support for the [Event/Club/Festival] at any time during the development of the [Programme/Schedule/Running Order] by notice in writing to the [Chair/Managing Director]. That in such case the [Sponsor] shall only be liable to pay for those contributions, expenses and payments due to the date of termination of the agreement. The [Sponsor] shall not bear any liability and/or responsibility for any direct and/or indirect losses, damages and/or expenses that may arise as a result of the withdrawal of the [Sponsor's] support and the termination of the agreement.

A.123
The [Institute/Company] agrees and accepts that it has approved the samples of the [Sponsor's] [Product/Services] and the proposed [Sponsorship Plan] in advance of the signature of this agreement. That copies of approved samples of the [Sponsor's] [Product/Services] and the proposed [Sponsorship Plan] .are attached as Schedule A and form part of this agreement. That neither party shall change and/or amend anything in Schedule A without the written consent of the other party. That all copies of the [Products/Services] to be distributed and/or marketed by the [Sponsor] under this agreement shall be exact copies of the samples.

A.124
The [Company] accepts that it is not the sole sponsor and that it has no right to act on behalf of [Enterprise/Name] and/or to hold itself out as having the authority to grant access to and/or any rights to third parties in respect of

the [Event/Programme/Festival] except those specified as follows: [specify scope of authority].

A.125

The [Sponsor] agrees and undertakes that it shall not have final control in respect of the decisions relating to the [Event/Programme]. The [Sponsor] accepts that it must follow the directions, guidance and requests of the [Company] in respect of all aspects of the development, preparation for, scheduling, marketing and/or filming of the [Event/Programme]. That where the [Company] requires the [Sponsor] to supply different formats of the name, trade mark, images and/or slogans of the [Sponsor] and/or their products and/or services. That the [Sponsor] shall pay all the costs of any such reproductions and/or any adaptations that may need to be commissioned by the [Company].

University, Charity and Educational

A.126

The [Institute/Library] shall be entitled to accept and/or reject the [Product/Service] within [number] [days/months] of [delivery/connection/supply] by the [Company] without any liability to pay any sums due provided that all the material associated with the [Product/Service] is returned to the [Company]. The [Institute/Library] may reject the [Product/Service] on any reasonable grounds including but not limited to:

1.1 That the [Product/Service] does not comply with the description, quality, content, fitness for purpose that was ordered and/or offered.

1.2 That the [Product/Service] is incompatible with the existing and/or proposed system, process, schedule, plans and/or development by the [Institute/Library].

1.3 That [delivery/connection/supply] was delayed, incomplete and/or not carried out by suitably qualified personnel and/or did not fulfil the function which was expected.

1.4 That the [Institute/Library] was misled as to the total cost of the installation and/or the maintenance costs and/or the cost of the [Product/Service].

A.127

Delivery of the [Manuscript/Painting/Work] to the [Institute/Charity] shall not be deemed acceptance of the authenticity of the authorship of the [Manuscript/Painting/Work] nor confirmation that the [Fee] shall be paid to the [Agent]. The [Institute/Charity] shall be allowed [number] [days] to carry out a full review and to engage an expert to verify the authorship. The expert shall, subject to the prior written approval of the [Agent], be authorised to examine the [Manuscript/Painting/Work] and to carry out such sample tests as are normal practice in order to test the veracity of the authorship. In the event that the [Institute/Charity] has not accepted and/or rejected the [Manuscript/Painting/Work] by [date]. Then the [Agent] shall be entitled to serve written notice either that the [Manuscript/Painting/Work] has been deemed accepted and/or that the agreement is terminated and that all rights to buy the [Manuscript/Painting/Work] by the [Institute/Charity] have ceased.

A.128

The [Institute/Charity] agrees that where the [Consultant] carries out the work and performs the services required in accordance with the terms of this agreement. That unless the [Consultant] has received written notice that the work is unsatisfactory and/or incomplete by [date]. That the [Institute/Charity] shall pay the sums due in clause [–] within [number] days of invoice by the [Consultant].

A.129

1.1 The [Charity] accepts donations of the following [Products] as follows: [state procedure]. The [Charity does not accept: [state listed of excluded material].

1.2 Financial donations to the [Charity] may be made as follows: [specify method/options].

1.3 You may leave a legacy of money and/or a gift of an object in a will. If there is a dispute with any other beneficiary and/or claimant on the estate the [Charity] will take legal actions to claim the bequest.

1.4 You must be the legal owner of any donation that you make to the [Charity] whether money and/or an object and/or any other donation.

ACCESS

Film, Television and Video

A.130

The [Licensor] agrees that it shall not have an automatic right of access and entry to the [Premises/Factory] where the [DVDs/Discs] are produced. The [Licensor] and its professional advisors shall no more than [twice] in each year be entitled upon written request to the [Distributor] to have a tour of all the [Premises/Factory]; to inspect the warehouse and storage facilities and to be shown all certificates and/or records to confirm compliance with current health and safety and employee working conditions legislation in [country].

A.131
The [Author] of the [Disc/Unit] shall have no right of access and/or entry to the [Company's] premises and offices at any time. The [Author] shall only be entitled to attend if invited to do so by the [Company].

A.132
In the event that the [Distributor]:

1.1   Fails to account for any royalties and/or make payments for any sums due to the [Company] for the exploitation of the rights in the [Film/ Game] granted under this agreement and/or

1.2   Operates where financially insolvent and/or is likely to be placed in receivership, administration and/or is unable to meet its financial commitments.

Then the [Distributor] agrees that the [Company] shall have the right to enter the premises, offices and warehouses [without prior written notice/within [number] hours of prior written notice] and to recover and remove all master material relating to the [Film/Game], all packaging, marketing and stock which either belong to the [Company] and/or compensate for the value of the sums which are due and have not been paid to the [Company].

A.133
Where the [Company] fails to return the [Master Material] to the [Client]. Then the [Company] agrees that the [Client] shall have the right to make an appointment and/or to have access without prior consent to the [warehouse/ offices] at any address where the [Company] may be located in order to collect the [Master Material] and any copies.

A.134
The [Company] shall not be allowed unlimited access to the [Premises] and shall have no automatic right of entry. The [Company] shall only be permitted to use the locations marked in red specified on the attached Site Map in Appendix A and in accordance with the Time and Date Schedule in Appendix B. In addition to the Licence Fee charged for access from [date] to [date] the [Company] shall also be liable to pay to the [Licensor] additional electricity, gas, water, rates, drainage, sewer and other charges and expenses that arise and/or become due as a result of the [Company's] access to and/or use of the [Premises] and any losses and/or damages. The

[Licensor] shall be entitled to reinstate the [Premises] to the condition it was in prior to the access and/or use by the [Company]. Where it is necessary to replace old with new as the old version cannot be repaired then [Company] shall be responsible for the additional cost.

A.135

The [Company] shall be allowed non-exclusive access for the production of the [Film/Programme/Series] in accordance with the agreed Schedule A and the [Land/Premises] marked out on the map in Schedule B. Copies of both Schedules are attached to and form part of this agreement. The [Landowner] agrees that there shall be no obstruction and/or restriction of the access required by the [Company] at any time.

A.136

The [Company] shall be permitted unlimited access to and use of the [Premises] at any time and may store, park, film and use the [Premises] in such manner as it thinks fit for the purpose of making the [Film]. The [Company] agrees that it shall be obliged to pay the [Owner] for any damages, losses, maintenance, repairs, costs, expenses, fees and liability that may arise as a direct and/or indirect result of its access to and use of the [Premises]. The [Company] agrees that it shall pay any demand for payment within [number] days of submission of the invoice by the [Owner] and that where the cost of any work exceeds [number/currency] that the [Company] shall pay some money in advance.

A.137

Access to the location by the crew, actors, transport, lighting, catering and other personnel engaged in the [Film] shall be in accordance with the route/ markings and maps in Schedule A. The [Company] agrees that they shall ensure that noise levels do not exceed [number] decibels after [time] each day and that no access route shall be blocked and/or obstructed at any time.

General Business and Commercial

A.138

There is no automatic right of access to the premises and land owned or controlled by the [Company]. You are only entitled to enter the building specified in your contract of employment during your normal hours of work. No access is permitted at other times without the prior consent of [Name]. The [Company] reserves the right to deny access at any time for any reason. The [Company] reserves the right to request that you leave the building, premises or land whether during your normal working day or not and may require that you be escorted by a representative from security.

A.139
Your terms of employment require that you accept and adhere to the health, safety and security measures in force at the premises, buildings and land of the [Company]

A.140
The [Employee] shall have access at any time to the premises of the [Company] for the sole purpose of fulfilling the duties and responsibilities set out in the job description. There is no right to use the facilities, premises and/or resources for any other purpose, nor to enter the premises outside the hours of [specify working hours].

A.141
The [Executive] shall be entitled to gain access to any part of the premises of the [Company] at any time without restriction provided that they show their [security pass/code] and to use the facilities, resources and organise their office staff as may be required in the circumstances. The [Executive] shall be entitled to send and receive personal emails using the equipment owned by the [Company] and to use the facilities, resources and staff to organise his/her personal and family matters.

A.142
Access to the site is restricted to authorised personnel of the [Company] who have been vetted and provided with security passwords and codes. Any such personnel who facilitate access of a third party of any nature without following the proper procedure for access in accordance with [Company] [specify document/policy] shall be escorted off the premises and dismissed with immediate effect as such conduct is deemed to constitute a flagrant breach of the security protocol for the site and the [Company].

A.143
There are no restrictions and/or limitations on access to any part of the [Land/Building] provided that you do not cause any damage to the wildlife, buildings and/or use any equipment and/or products which will cause contamination of the soil, water and/or air. Photography is permitted but not filming without prior arrangement and consent with the [Owner].

A.144
The [Company] reserves the right to withdraw the right of entry, exclude, expel, remove and/or suspend any person who in their reasonable opinion is using offensive or threatening language, acts and/or behaves in a manner which is unacceptable and/or is believed to be drunk, on illegal drugs or other substances or carrying an offensive weapon or an item which is considered a danger to the safety of others and/or who has been warned that

their conduct on previous occasions is unacceptable and/or for any other reason. The decision of the [Company] is final. There shall be no obligation to refund any sums paid for membership and/or any other fees and/or to carry out any further investigations and/or to disclose confidential sources. The [Company] reserve the right to report any matter to the [police/other].

A.145

Access to and use of this [location/activity] is entirely at your own risk and we expect you to take all reasonable precautions to protect your property and to act in a reasonable manner. There are health and safety signs and warnings displayed for your guidance which relate to age, height, equipment and conduct which you are strongly advised to follow as they are a mandatory requirement.

A.146

The [Customer] must allow access at any reasonable time which is agreed in advance in order for the [system/equipment/other] to be installed, repaired, inspected and/or removed at [address]. Access shall include the use of all necessary land, buildings and facilities including internet, water, electricity, gas, and light at the [Customer's] expense as may be necessary to carry out and complete the work required. After the completion of the work all rights to such material shall be owned by the [Customer/Company].

A.147

There is no right of access at any time to the [Premises] and the [Company] may refuse entry or vary the terms or restrict access to all or any parts without notice.

A.148

There is only limited access to the [Land/Premises] and where an area has been excluded, fenced off and/or locked then you are not permitted to enter. There is no automatic right of entry to all areas of this site.

Internet, Websites and Apps

A.149

Access to and use of the services on the [Website/Platform] are based on your agreement to the following terms with the [Company] which is the [Owner/Host Packager] of the [Website/Platform]: [specify terms].

A.150

You agree to be bound by the terms and conditions of access to and use of the [Website/App/Platform] and all conditions that apply to any films, videos, sound recordings, blogs, podcasts, data, information, text, images, trade marks, logos, sound, music, graphics, slogans, banners, links, chatrooms, games, databases and any other material at any time.

A.151

You agree that you will not use any material derived from and/or based on this [Website/App/Platform] for any purpose without providing a full credit to the copyright owner of the material and a credit to the [Website/App/Platform] as the reference source.

A.152

You agree that where any material is to be used for commercial purposes or any other purpose other than your own personal use that you will not use any such material without first contacting [specify name] at [specify email/contact method] for confirmation of the copyright position and prior written consent together with such financial arrangement as may be appropriate.

A.153

That you may not edit, adapt, alter, modify, or otherwise interfere with the [Website] and its contents and nor may you exploit, license, supply, or distribute copies in any form to third parties whether for commercial gain or not unless specifically permitted to do so on that section of the [Website] or written consent is obtained in advance.

A.154

You accept that there is material and services on the [Website/App/Platform] which are supplied by third parties which effectively act as independent businesses on the [Website/App/Platform]. You accept that the [Company] cannot supervise or control these third party businesses and that if you enter into a contract with such third parties for services or make payments to such third parties that the [Company] shall not be party to that agreement and/or liable in any form. You shall not be able to claim against the [Company] in the event that the third parties fail to fulfil the agreement they have made with you directly.

A.155

That the [Company] is not responsible for any material supplied, displayed and/or added to the [Website/App/Platform] including any email exchanges, attachments, or other material by text, images, logos or otherwise by any third parties. The [Company] endeavours to monitor the [Website/App/Platform] on a regular basis, and will correct or remove material which is found to be inaccurate, offensive or misleading.

A.156

The [Company] is not responsible for third parties which are on or connected to this [Website/App/Platform] by any links, databases or references and these must be accessed and used at your own risk. We do not endorse, approve of or review the content of these third parties and cannot accept any liability for any costs, losses, damages and/or otherwise that you may incur and/or suffer as a result of their use.

A.157

You accept that there may be delays, interruptions, failures, errors, omissions, defects, inaccuracies and other inconsistencies in access to and use of the [Website/App/Platform] and the material displayed in any form. That you shall not be entitled to make a claim against the [Company] or any third party engaged by the [Company] for any loss, damage, expenses, costs or otherwise of any nature whether direct or indirect including but not limited to personal, business, or property from your access and use of the [Website/App/Platform] and any liability shall be limited to the total value of any Order for products or services which has been paid for and not supplied or delivered.

A.158

That you agree not to use access to this [Website/App/Platform] to promote, incite, post or send any material or content which poses a serious threat to the safety of any individuals, or members of the public in any country in the world.

A.159

You agree that you shall not use access to the [Website/App/Platform] or any part to supply, upload, post, transfer, promote and/or distribute any virus, spam, software, program, file, code or any other system, method, content, instructions and/or other material and/or algorithm which would interrupt, corrupt, destroy, delay, interrupt, edit, misuse and/or affect detrimentally in any form the [Website/App/Platform] including but not limited to its functionality, operational ability, software, emails to and/or from its visitors, databases, its supply and distribution systems and/or any other matter.

A.160

You may access and view the contents of this [Website/App/Platform] for your own personal use for research, to order goods, participate in games, and use its facilities. You shall have no right to copy, download, reproduce, store and/or retrieve material whether text, logos, images, slogans, news feeds, databases, formats, music, sounds and graphics on your laptop, computer, gadget or other device or system except for your own private personal use at home while you are using the [Website/App/Platform]. Once you have left the [Website/App/Platform] then no copies should be stored of any material which you have viewed except a purchase order of products and/or services purchased. All copies should be destroyed, deleted, or erased unless you have been given specific authority under a non-exclusive licence by the [Company]. Nor shall you be entitled to supply, distribute, market or commercially exploit all or any part of the [Website/App/Platform] and its content to any other person, business or third party whether on the internet, in printed form or in any other medium and/or format unless the prior authorisation and consent of the [Company] has been obtained and a licence issued.

A.161
Access and use of this site is entirely on the basis that all subsequent downloading, printing, e-mail and exchanges with others shall be purely for non-commercial purposes and that you shall not interfere with the material or its content and shall provide a suitable credit to the copyright owner and also this site as the source.

A.162
The [Subscriber/User] has been permitted access to the services and facilities on this [Website/App/Platform] for a free trial period of [three] months in such case all standard terms and conditions shall still apply except those as to payment of subscription fees. At the end of the trial period the [Subscriber/User] shall be required to subscribe or shall cease to use the service and facilities and remove, delete or erase the software from their computer and any discs or back up material in any format.

A.163
The use of and access to this [Website/App/Platform] does not provide any consent, licence and/or right to use, reproduce, store, supply, distribute and/or exploit any of the material in any format which may be displayed. The copyright and intellectual property rights in the content of this [Website/App/Platform], the trade marks, the computer software and the databases are owned or controlled by the [Company]. There is no consent provided to store, print, download, reproduce, quote, supply, distribute and/or exploit any part of this [Website/App/Platform] whether for private use at home, for research or educational purposes, for publication and/or other media purposes and/or any other exploitation in any form whether commercial or not.

A.164
Access and use of any of the material on this [Website/App/Platform] is entirely at your own discretion, cost and liability. You may at your own discretion reproduce, store, supply and/or distribute any material provided that you acknowledge the [Website/App/Platform] as the source as follows [Name of Company/reference]. All copyright ownership, intellectual property rights, computer software rights, trade marks or other rights which are specified on

the [Website/App/Platform] should be reproduced with the relevant material in the exact same form. The absence of a copyright notice and/or other credit in respect of any material does not mean that the copyright or any other intellectual property and/or computer software rights are not held by a third party or the [Company]. You use any material entirely at your own risk and no indemnity is provided or liability accepted by the [Company].

A.165

If you are registering details on the [Website/App/Platform] on behalf of a business and/or company. You undertake and agree that:

1.1 You have the authority to do so from an officer of the business and/or company.

1.2 That if so requested by the [Website/app/Platform] that confirmation in writing of this authorisation could be provided.

1.3 That the information provided is accurate and that in the event that it should change then updated details will be provided.

1.4 That the business and/or company is a bona fide operation and adheres to all applicable legal requirements in any country.

A.166

The [Company] reserves the right as its sole discretion to refuse access to the [Website/App/Platform] and any part without any reason at any time whether before and/or after registration and/or during the operation of the [Website/App/Platform]. This may take place as a result of a direct email, notice on the [Website/App/Platform], a press release, shut down of the whole and/or part of the [Website/App/Platform] and/or by any other means that the [Company] deems fit in the circumstances. Any such refusal, cancellation, interruption, delay or denial of access shall not incur any liability on the part of the [Company] and/or any other third parties connected with the [Website/App/Platform] for any direct and/or indirect losses, financial commitments, damages and/or consequences of any nature that may arise whether reasonably foreseeable or not. The [Website/App/Platform] is used entirely at your own risk and cost and no reliance should be placed on continuous access and/or service. [Where a subscription fee has been paid then the total liability of the [Company] shall be limited to the repayment of the total subscription cost of the period for which access has been denied.]

A.167

This [Disc/Unit] is supplied to you the [Purchaser] by the [Distributor/Company] based on the following terms and conditions which you must agree to before you remove the seal and install the [Disc/Unit] [and load the software].

1.1   That the [Purchaser] is granted a non-exclusive and non-transferable licence by the [Distributor/Company] to use the [Disc/Unit] for the purpose which it is intended in conjunction with the [Work/Content] namely [specify purpose, the method and the type of use]. This right is personal to you the [Purchaser] and shall also permit you to make a copy of the files on the hard drive of your [computer/laptop/other gadget] and one back up copy of the [Disc/Unit].

1.2   There is no right granted to copy the [Disc/Unit] whether directly and/or indirectly in any format and/or medium for supply to third parties in whole and/or part at any time. All such third parties should be advised to purchase their own [disc/unit] as a licence is required.

1.3   There is no right to make additional copies and/or to reproduce the [Work/Content] for any other reason and/or to add the [Disc/Unit] and/or [Work/Content] to any centralised database, library and/or storage and retrieval system.

1.4   You shall not have the right to develop further works based upon the [Work/Content] and/or [Disc/Unit] and/or to make any adaptation. You shall not have the right to display, supply, transmit, reproduce, license, exploit, adapt and/or translate the [Work/Content] and/or the [Disc/Unit] on the internet and/or any over telecommunication system and/or to create any new format and/or other version.

A.168

The use and access to the sealed software package is subject to the [Purchaser] agreeing to the following terms and conditions and the [Purchaser] will be deemed to have accepted the agreement by opening and installing the software:

1.1   That the [Company] granted the [Purchaser] the non-exclusive license in respect of this software package to install and use the software on a [number workstations/single laptop] for [home/residential/office/business] use only.

1.2   That you may make one backup hard copy for your own use.

1.3   That the [Purchaser] shall not modify, adapt, alter or change in any manner or form any part of any data, material, logos, copyright notices or otherwise on the disc, software or packaging.

1.4   The [Purchaser] shall not make any additional copies to keep on a disc or other format or send or download in any media [including but not limited to the internet, mobile phone, television or other gadget] nor supply, transfer, authorise, license or distribute the contents of the disc, the software or any part to any third party whether for commercial gain or not. If in doubt contact the copyright owner for permission at [reference] or log on to [Website/App] and read the list of examples of permitted types of use.

A.169

There is a legal requirement that as this [Website/App/Platform] uses cookies that your consent is required for their use. Please do not access this [Website/App/Platform] if you do not want our cookies to collect and/or store your data and/or to track your usage of the material on and/or linked to this business and its associated partners. Either provide consent through the link below or do not enter as cookies are operated on this [Website/App/Platform].

A.170

The [Podcast Series] is owned and controlled by [Name]. No fee is charged for viewing the [Podcast Series] but you are not permitted to copy and reproduce material for distribution to third parties except extracts of up to [number] minutes on your own personal accounts on the following: [specify permitted accounts/resources]. You must credit the [Podcast Series] as follows: [specify credit] and provide a link as follows: [specify link]. You are not permitted to do so if you charge third parties to endorse and promote products and/or services on any of your accounts. You are not entitled to charge any fee to a third party for the use of the extract.

Merchandising and Distribution

A.171

The [Licensee] shall ensure that the [Licensor] shall be able with prior notice to access, tour, inspect and/or be provided with copies of:

1.1 The prototypes and/or samples and the completed products relating to the [Work/Product] licensed under this agreement at the offices of the [Licensee] and/or any manufacturing factory, storage and/or packaging warehouse and/or any other premises and/or location that may be used at any time.

1.2 Any associated labels, shop and/or outdoor posters, social media promotions, film, videos, advertising, marketing, sound recordings and/or any other medium.

1.3 Any supporting documents, licences, contracts, surveys, test results, health and safety reports, legal compliance assessments, insurance or otherwise that may relate to the [Work/Product].

A.172

The [Licensor] shall not have any right of access and/or authority to enter the [Studio/Factory/Land] which may be used by the [Licensee] to develop, produce, design, and manufacture the [Product] under this agreement. Nor shall the [Licensee] be required to provide any documents, financial records, insurance, and/or any other the information and/or data to the [Licensor] regarding any third party involved in the [Project/Product].

A.173
This non-exclusive licence does not grant and/or authorise any right of access to and/or use of and/or association with the [Licensors] business and/or brand name and/or product names and/or any trade marks, logos, slogans, graphics, head office, retail premises, website, app, channel, tours, competitions, promotions, advertising and/or otherwise by the [Licensee]. The [Licensee] is only authorised to the extent specified in this agreement.

A.174
The [Company] has authorised the use of their name, logo, image and slogan for the [Event] and for all the associated merchandising which is to be developed, distributed and/or supplied for free to the public. The [Company] shall be permitted access to the [Event] in order to arrange for films, videos, photographs and/or sound recordings to be made which focus on the use of the [Company's] name and the promotion of the [Company's] [Products/ Services] in association with the [Event]. Provided that any arrangements are notified and agreed in advance with the [Agent] and any access is for less than [number] [hours/days] in total.

A.175
There is no right granted which permits and/or authorises access and/or the right to inspect the following locations under this agreement [specify addresses]. These locations shall remain and continue to be the sole and exclusive responsibility of the [Distributor/Company]. In the event that any health and safety and/or legal and/or other issue arises in respect of the locations which materially affects the production, delivery and/or supply of the [Products]. The [Distributor/Company] shall provide regular reports by [method/email] to the [Copyright Owner] assessing the impact if any and shall provide details of any legal notices and/or other proceedings which may have been served on the [Distributor/Company].

A.176
1.1 The [Supplier] shall ensure that the [Purchaser] shall be able to access and inspect all the analysis, processes, production, manufacture and packaging involved at the [factory/land/warehouse] of the [Products] on no less than [number] occasions [in each year] during the continuance of this agreement.

1.2 The [Purchaser] shall be entitled to have a qualified expert in attendance to carry out an independent study who may take samples if the circumstances permit.

1.3 The [Supplier] shall upon request by the independent expert and/or the [Purchaser] also make available for inspection and supply copies of all original documents and certificates in order to ensure compliance with all legislation that may be applicable to the content, production, storage. Packaging and/or marketing of the [Products].

A.177
Where the [Company] notifies the [Manufacturer/Distributor] that they have concerns as to the source of the materials and/or water and/or energy, content, packaging, working conditions of the employees, health and/or safety compliance in respect of the [Products] and/or part and/or any associated person and /or factor of any nature. Then the [Manufacturer/Distributor] shall be obliged to provide unlimited access to any professional and expert advisors and/or executives of the [Company] that the [Company] may stipulate in order to investigate any concerns and/or allegations which may arise at any time. Whether this shall arise before, during and/or after delivery of any [Products] and/or completion of any order by the [Company] up to a period of [number/months/years] thereafter.

Sponsorship

A.178
The [Sponsor] shall not be entitled to authorise and/or grant access to the [Event/Festival] to any third parties unless it is through the use and/or purchase of valid tickets specified in clause [–]. Where the [Sponsor] is setting up a stand to give away and/or sell its [Products/Services] then the [Sponsor] must abide by the same rules of access as any other vendor. The [Company] reserves the right to withdraw the right of entry, exclude, expel, remove and/or suspend any person who in their opinion behaves in a manner which is unacceptable. The decision of the [Company] is final. There shall be no obligation to refund any sums paid for sponsorship and/or otherwise.

A.179
Sponsorship of [Name] does not permit the [Company] and/or its directors and/or employees and/or consultants to have any direct access by telephone, email and/or letter to [Name]. All requests, payments and/or other matters must be directed to and/or made to the [Agent].

A.180
The [Sponsor] shall be permitted unlimited access subject to requesting permission in advance to film, video, record, photograph, interview and

visit the following locations, persons and material at the [Club/Association] whether to be used to advertise the [Sponsor's] products and/or for any marketing and/or for publication in an article and/or for incorporation in a documentary and/or podcast:

1.1 Training ground, gym, track, stage, hospitality venue, award ceremonies, archive and museum and [specify other].

1.2 Corporate brochures and programmes, promotional material, history and designs of the brand name, trade mark and logo;

1.3 Management: [specify names of persons] for [number] hour in total

1.4 Sports Personnel/Athletes: [specify names of persons]. [Excluding family members and private homes] for [number] hours in total.

A.181
Where the [Athlete/Name] fails to attend any requested medical, drug and/or other tests by the governing national and/or international body known as [specify]. Where this results in the [Athlete/name] being disqualified after an event and/or having an award withdrawn. Then the [Sponsor] shall not be entitled to have access to any such medical records, proceedings and/or test results which may arise at any time except those disclosed in formal public documents. The [Sponsor] shall however have the right to terminate the sponsorship agreement with immediate effect and shall not be liable to pay any further sums under the agreement after the date of termination.

A.182
[Name] agrees that for the purposes of promotion and marketing the [Product/Service] on behalf of the [Sponsor]. That Name] shall allow access by any film and/or sound crews and/or photographers nominated by the [Sponsor] and agreed with [Name] to their family home at [address] for a maximum total of [number/hours] between [date and [date]. Provided that no filming, sound recordings and/or photographs shall be of any of the children of [Name] and it shall be limited to the following locations in the house and garden [specify exact locations/background].

A.183
The [Sponsor] shall be permitted early access to the {Event] and have the opportunity to choose the location of their [stands/exhibition] and the position of their marketing at the entrance and on the internal perimeter. The [Company] shall have the final decision as to the suitability of the request and may make other arrangements.

University, Charity and Educational

A.184

1.1 Access to the [Collection/Archive] shall be entirely at the sole discretion of the [Institute/Charity] and there shall be no automatic right of entry and/or use of all and/or any part any of the material in the [Collection/Archive].

1.2 The [Institute/Charity] reserves the right to deny, withdraw and/or refuse entry and/or to request that any person leave the premises for any reason and without providing any grounds and/or justification for doing so.

1.3 The [Institute/Charity] has terms and conditions for access that must be adhered to by any visitors, researchers and/or any other person. The [Institute/Charity] reserves the right to amend and/or alter these terms and conditions at any time without notice.

1.4 No liability is accepted by the [Institute/Charity] for any losses, damages, costs, expenses and/or any other sums that may arise directly and/or indirectly as a consequence of there being no access to the [Collection/Archive] at any time for any commercial, academic and/or other projects.

1.5 Access to the [Collection/Archive] shall be entirely at the risk, cost and/or liability of the person and/or company except where any personal injury and/or death is directly caused by the negligence of the [Institute/Charity].

A.185

Access to the [Library] shall be subject to the production of a current [readership/student] identity pass. The [Library] shall be entitled to refuse access to the use of the facilities, services and/or books and/or other material based on any grounds including:

1.1 A health and safety risk to the building and/or its contents and/or that a person and/or their belongings are a threat to the safety of the public and/or that a person is under the influence of drink and/or drugs and/or otherwise appears unwell.

1.2 That there are staff shortages and/or that the premises are not open for business.

1.3 That a public disturbance and/or alleged crime has been committed and/or that any person has failed to comply with the terms and condition of the [Right of Access Policy].

A.186

1.1   The [Company] shall not have any automatic right of access to the [Premises/Land] specified in Schedule A. The [Institute/Charity] grants the [Company] a non-exclusive licence to use the [Premises/Land] from [date] to [date] for the purpose of the [Event] described in Schedule B.

1.2   The [Company] agrees that it shall not be entitled to make any permanent alterations and/or additions to the [Premises/Land]. That the [Company] shall pay all the cost and expenses of any damages, losses and/or expenses incurred by the [Institute/Charity] as a direct result of the [Company's] use of the [Premises/Land] up to a maximum of [number/currency].

ACCURACY

General Business and Commercial

A.187

The measurements, fabric, sizes and colours of the [Products] may vary from both the catalogue, website, app, samples and/or within each batch which has been ordered. The [Company] cannot provide any assurances as to the accuracy of these factors as there is considerable variation in the original material.

A.188

It is important that all the information, data and material supplied is accurate and correct and exactly fits all the specifications required for the [Project]. Where the [Company] becomes aware that any part is inaccurate, or not as specified or defective then they undertake to alert the [Client] to this fact as a matter of urgency.

A.189

It is agreed that the [Proposal] is in its early stages of development, and that therefore the sales projections and revenue are not accurate, but merely an estimate. The products, figures and details may change, but at this time are provided on the basis as being correct to the best of the knowledge and belief of [Name].

A.190

The data, information and content provided in this [Website/App/Platform/ brochure] are for guidance and are not intended to be accurate and may be amended, varied or updated at any time.

A.191

The [Manufacturer] agrees to produce and supply the [Products] in accordance with the sample and specifications agreed in advance with the [Client]. In the event that there are to be any variations, alterations or change of materials, labels, images, packaging, style, content or otherwise of any nature however minor. Then the [Manufacturer] agrees that the [Client] shall be consulted in advance and that the production shall not proceed unless prior approval has been provided by the [Client].

A.192

[Name] agrees and undertakes that the information you have supplied regarding your personal and financial details are true and accurate as at [date]. That you have not been deceptive, fraudulent or dishonest and that the information does not relate to a third party. That you are over the age of [18/21 years] and that there is no consent required from any third party [whether parent, guardian, bank, court or otherwise] for you to disclose and/or whose authority and permission is required prior to entering into this contract.

A.193

[Name] agrees and undertakes that the personal information and qualifications which he/she has supplied to the [Company] can be verified and are true, accurate and up to date and that he/she is suitably qualified and experienced to carry out the duties and specialist role of: [specify title] at the[Company].

A.194

The [Institute] reserves the right to change, amend or vary any part of the [course/seminar] and/or the [lecturers/speakers] at any time without notice. The [brochure/catalogue] are for guidance only and may not be a true reflection of the total [course/seminar]. The qualification to be attained at the end of the [course/seminar] shall not be affected.

A.195

The agreement was entered into by the [Purchaser] due to the disclosure of the following documents: [specify title of document and list]. The facts and figures disclosed in the documents determined the price paid for the assets of the [Company] by the [Purchaser]. In the event that within a period of [number] years the documents are discovered to contain information, data, facts and/or figures which have material and significant errors [of more than [number] per cent overall] in favour of the [Company]. Then the [Company] shall be obliged to repay such proportion of the price paid for the assets of the [Company] as may be deemed by an independent expert to be appropriate in the circumstances. The cost of the appointment of any such expert shall be paid for by agreement in advance between the parties. This clause does not affect any rights and remedies of either party to take legal action and/or seek costs, losses, damages, interest, expenses and/or legal costs for any reason.

A.196
It is recognised by both parties that the accuracy of the financial information, sales figures, assets and liabilities are an important part of the consideration for the acquisition of the [Business/Products]. In the event that it becomes clear at a later date that the [Company] failed to disclose information which would have resulted in a lower price being negotiated then the [Company] shall be obliged to repay the sum which was overpaid due to their non-disclosure of material facts.

A.197
Both parties agree that they are each expected to take due care and attention before entering into this Agreement and shall seek such legal advice as may be necessary and engage such professional experts as may be required to protect their interests. Where any corporate documents, data, financial reports, audit reports, staff lists, stock reports, sales figures, expenditure, and/or other facts are later found to be wrong. Then it is agreed that no sums shall be repaid to either party under this Agreement provided that the error and/or inaccuracies did not arise as a result of dishonesty, fraud, and/or were deliberately altered, changed and/or amended with the intention of misleading the other party.

A.198
The [Accountant/Bank/Agent/other] agrees and undertakes that it shall keep accurate computer software data records and back-up copies of all sums received and paid from any source in any part of the world for and on behalf of [Name/Business]. That no sums shall be paid to any third party which exceed [number/currency] without the written authority and signature of [Name] as authorisation. Further that no more than [number/currency] shall be held in any one bank and that upon request full details of all bank and holding accounts together with all statements shall be supplied to [Name] at the expense of the [Accountant/Bank/Agent/other].

A.199
It is agreed between the parties that it is the [Purchaser's] responsibility and liability to assess and investigate the accuracy and reliability of all the data, information and disclosures, maps, charts and other material being sold by the [Seller]. That the [Purchaser] agrees that the acquisition is entirely at his/her own risk and that no reliance can be made in respect of any aspect of any part of the [Project/Material].

A.200

The draft information, accounts, background and forecast estimates supplied by the [Professional Advisor] are for rough guidance only and entirely based on the current financial data and disclosures supplied by [Name]. No undertakings can be provided by the [Professional Advisor] in respect of the accuracy of the feedback to [Name] as regard any liability to third parties and/or otherwise.

A.201

The [Company] agrees that it shall use its reasonable endeavours to produce accurate and detailed data and market research which can be verified if required by supplying copies of the original material and responses whether in the form of telephone marketing, online surveys, street interviews and/or otherwise. The [Company] shall retain and make available such original material to the [Distributor] for a period of up to [number] [months/years] after the final date of completion of the market research.

ACCOUNTING PERIOD

General Business and Commercial

A.202

'The Accounting Period' shall mean each period of a calendar month for the full duration of the Licence Period. Provided that the first Accounting Period shall commence on [date] and end on the final day of that calendar month.

A.203

'The Accounting Period' shall mean each calendar year from [date] until [date] and shall be treated as comprising of four quarterly three month periods ending with 31 March, 30 June, 30 September and 31 December and shall continue until the expiry, or termination of the agreement or the date upon which all manufacture, sale, rental, disposal and/or otherwise of the [Units] is accounted for to the [Licensor] whichever is the later.

A.204

'The Accounting Period' shall be as follows:

1.1   Start date: [specify date].

1.2   End date: [specify date] or such earlier or later date that shall be agreed between the parties in writing, but in any event until such time as all units and sums due have been accounted for and all sums due have been paid.

1.3 Regular weekly accounting periods beginning Monday and ending Sunday. A comprehensive accounting statement to be provided at the end of each such period.

1.4 Payment of the sums due to be made at the end of each [four] week period to the [Licensee].

A.205
'The Pilot Accounting Period' shall start on [date] and be for a period of [six/twelve] months in respect the sums received by the [Distributor] from third parties for payment for the [Products/Services].

A.206
The [Distributor] shall be entitled to vary, alter or change the accounting period by providing the [Company] with [three] months written notice. Where the new accounting period will result in delays in payments to the [Company] then the prior written consent of the [Company] shall be required.

A.207
'The Accounting Periods' shall mean the following three consecutive four months in each year during the Term of this Agreement: 1 January to 30 April, 1 May to 31 August and 1 September to 31 December. By the last day of each such period the [Company] shall provide a full and comprehensive statement of all the sums or benefits received, credited to and/or due to the [Company], any parent or associated company or any third party of any nature from the exploitation of the [Services/Content/Product] licensed under this agreement.

A.208
The [Company] agrees that it shall provide a statement to the [Creator] of the [App/Product] and pay any sums due in full by direct debit on a regular basis which shall be not less than once every [number] [weeks/months]. Where there have been no sums received then the [Company] shall still provide a statement to that effect. Otherwise payment shall be made at the same time as the statement is issued. Where the [App/Product] is very successful and the [App/Product] sells more than [number] [copies/units] then the [Company] agrees to account to the [Creator] more frequently namely once every [number] [weeks/months] and to make payment more frequently at the same time as the statement.

A.209
The [Distributor] shall provide at its own cost to [Name] at any time upon request by [Name]. A copy of the latest costs of any advertising and/

or marketing and/or details of the number of units manufactured and/or produced and/or the details of the formats and/or countries in which they have been sold and/or distributed and/or the sums deducted as costs and/or received from sales and/or credited in any currency in any part of the world whether through the [Distributor] and any other third party agent and/or sub-licensee through which it has exploited any part of the [Product/Work].

A.210
Where the [Company] does not intend to adhere to the accounting period and/or wishes to amend the dates. Then the [Company] must notify [Name] in advance and obtain their prior written consent.

ACCOUNTING PROVISIONS
Film, Television and Video

A.211
The [Licensee] undertakes that it and its sub-agents and/or sub-licensees shall keep comprehensive, accurate and complete accounting records both on computer software and as a hard copy in printed form including invoices, sums received from third parties, licences and other agreements; and details of stock which has been distributed and stock which is unsold. The [Licensee] shall provide evidence and copies of all records and documents which will verify the Gross Receipts and therefore the calculation of the royalties which shall fall due to the [Licensor].

A.212
The [Licensee] undertakes that it shall pay the [Licensor's] Royalties on [dates] in each year during the Term of this Agreement and thereafter within [number/days] of receipt of payment until all sums due and/or owing are accounted for to the [Licensor].

A.213
The [Licensee] shall at all times maintain true and accurate books, records and accounts with respect to all [DVDs/Videos/Units] which are produced, manufactured, sold, leased, licensed, lost, damaged, stolen, rented and/or otherwise exploited in respect of this agreement. The [Licensee] will provide to the [Licensor] twice a year in accordance with the Accounting Period a true and accurate statement of all sums due to the [Licensor]. Such statement shall be accompanied by a remittance of the amount shown to be due to the [Licensor].

50

A.214

The [Licensee] may withhold from amounts otherwise due reasonable reserves against anticipated returns. No monies paid to the [Licensee] and thereafter refunded and/or credited to a person shall be included in the Gross Receipts or if they are included for some reason the amount may be deducted from subsequent Gross Receipts.

A.215

Any statement submitted by the [Licensee] shall be deemed true and correct and binding upon the [Licensor] unless the [Licensor] submits to the [Licensee] in writing specific grounds of dispute as to the statement within [three] months of the date upon which any such statement is received by the [Licensor].

A.216

The [Licensor] shall have the right to examine the software, accounting records, agreements, invoice and payment records of the [Licensee] to the extent they specifically relate to the [Units/Discs] for the purpose of determining the accuracy of Accounting Statements supplied by the [Licensee]. Such examination shall be made during reasonable business hours upon reasonable advance notice at the regular place of business of the [Licensee] where such material is stored and updated. The review shall be conducted on the [Licensor's] behalf and at the [Licensor's expense] by a [certified public accountant/finance director/professional accountants and legal advisors]. Such examination shall not be made more frequently than once in any year between the 1st January and 31st December and for no more than [number] [days/weeks]. The [Licensee] agrees and undertakes to co-operate with the [Licensee] and to supply copies of such material and documents as may be relevant to the enquiry upon request.

A.217

Each statement and the accompanying remittance will be made to a nominated account specified by the [Licensor] at [bank] in [country]. If any foreign receipts are frozen or cannot be transferred to the country where the [Licensee] has its nominated account. Then the [Licensor] shall open an account in such foreign country and notify the [Licensee]. Upon the [Licensor's] written request and upon condition that the same shall be permitted by the authorities of such foreign country the [Licensee] shall transfer to the [Licensor] in such foreign country and in that foreign currency at the [Licensor's/Licensee's] cost such sums as are owed to the [Licensor]. Such transfer shall discharge the [Licensee] of its obligation in respect of those specific sums.

A.218

On the first day of March, June, September, and December in each year the [Assignee] undertakes that it shall pay the [Assignor's] Royalties due from the Gross Receipts to the [Assignor] by [specify method] in [currency] to the agreed nominated bank account held in the name of the [Assignor].

A.219

On the first day of March, June, September and December in each year the [Assignee] shall provide a detailed report to the [Assignor] with a full breakdown of the exploitation of the [Series of Discs/DVDs/Units] setting out the Gross Receipts and the [Assignor's] Royalties together with copies of all significant documentation to support the accounts. Where any sum is withheld and/or converted into another currency and charges incurred and/or there is some other delay for failure to pay any sum then there should be a statement as to the background information and the reasons.

A.220

The [Licensee] agrees and undertakes that the [Licensee] shall not be entitled to recover more than [number/currency] costs and expenses as Distribution Expenses in any one accounting period. Any excess incurred in any such period shall be at the liability of the [Licensee] and shall not be carried forward to the next period. The [Licensee] agrees that it shall be bound to pay the excess sums and not seek to reclaim them under this agreement.

A.221

The [Licensee] agrees and undertakes that it shall not fail to disclose to the [Licensor] any sums in any currency received by the [Licensee] which relate to the licensing, distribution, sale and exploitation of the [Film/Game] and [Units]. In the event that in any accounting period the [Licensee] fails to disclose any sums and this results in the [Licensor] not receiving a related royalty payment. Then the [Licensee] shall pay an additional penalty of [number] per cent of that sum to the [Licensor] when the late payment is made. No interest shall be due on the late payment.

A.222

The [Licensee] agrees that the accounting report shall provide copies of supporting documents and records to substantiate the figures for any payment or expense in excess of [number/currency] at any time.

A.223

The cost and expense of all currency conversions shall be stated in full and any charges itemised and the exchange rates and the date stipulated.

A.224

The [Licensee] shall not be liable in any way for any financial losses incurred by the [Licensor] caused by fluctuation in the rate of exchange because of any failure to convert and/or to remit any particular funds to the [country] at any particular time or at a more favourable cost or rate of exchange than the cost or rate of exchange at which such conversion and remittance was accomplished. It is agreed that the [Licensor] shall be bound by whatever arrangements the [Licensee] may make for the conversion and remittance of foreign funds and by whatever costs are incurred or rates of exchange are used for such conversion and remittance. If the laws of any jurisdiction require that taxes on such remittance be withheld for any reason then the remittance to the [Licensor] shall also be reduced accordingly. The [Licensor] shall be entitled to receive full details of the calculation of the exchange rate, the costs and expenses and the reason for withholding any sums for taxes.

A.225

The [Distributor] shall pay all the sums due to the [Licensor] under this agreement by the dates set out at the latest and where there is any delay and/or failure to pay at any time the [Distributor] shall pay an additional payment in compensation and as a penalty of [number/currency] per [day/month] to the [Licensor].

A.226

The [Company] agrees and undertakes that it shall provide a summary royalty statement to [Name] by the end of [December/March] in each year during the continuation of this agreement which shall set out the sums received from the sales, supply and exploitation of the [DVDs/Videos/Units] and the calculation of the royalty payments due to [Name]. The statement shall be accompanied by a payment by [method] for the full sum due to [Name] or the funds shall be electronically transferred to an account specified and authorised by [Name whichever has been agreed in advance. The [Company] shall not be obliged to account for any sums which fall within the following circumstances until such sums have been received, cleared and retained by the [Company]:

1.1 The sums have been received or credited, but have not been cleared by the bank.

1.2 The sums were paid, but then subsequently returned to a purchaser, wholesaler or other third party as a refund.

1.3 The sums have been received, but then offset or discounted for lost and/or damaged [DVDs/Videos/Units].

1.4 The sums have been credited in a foreign country, but have not been actually received and cleared to the [Company's] main office at [address].

1.5 The acts, omissions, fraud or dishonesty of a third party has resulted in the sums not being paid to and/or received by the [Company] including but not limited to accountants, licensees, distributors, wholesalers, retailers. This exclusion shall not apply to directors, officers or employees of the [Company].

1.6 The sums have been reduced by the costs, charges and expenses incurred relating to the exchange of currencies.

1.7 That no interest or benefits arising from the sums shall be due to be added to the royalty payments.

1.8 That stock has been destroyed or sold at below cost price.

A.227

The [Licensee] confirms and agrees that it shall be obliged to report, account, verify and pay to the [Licensor] all the sums which may be due which have been received by, credited to and/or benefited the [Licensee] in any form from the exploitation of the [Film] by the [Licensee] and/or any persons and/or third parties which they have appointed and/or requested to exploit the [Film] at any time. This obligation shall continue after the expiry and/or termination of this agreement until such time as all sums due have been reported, accounted for and paid by the [Licensee]. The [Licensee] agrees and undertakes to comply with the following conditions:

1.1 That all royalty and advance statements shall be full and comprehensive and disclose all relevant information including the contract reference, the date the sums were received by the [Licensee], any exchange rates which were applied and how they were calculated. Together with details of the percentage used for the calculation of the royalties or advances due to the [Licensor].

1.2 That the [Licensee] shall include in the accounting statement details of all sums of any nature which have been withheld, discounted, set-off, written off and/or deducted as costs, expenses, losses and/or other sums and shall state the specific reasons in each case.

1.3 That the [Licensor] shall be entitled to receive copies of all licences, manufacturing and/or supply agreements and/or any other contracts, order forms, invoices, computer software, bank statements, stock, sales records, receipts and payment records in any format and/or any other material owned and/or controlled by the [Licensee] at the [Licensees] expense for each such period for up to [three/six] years after the date of the last accounting statement by the [Licensor] relating to the [Film].

1.4 That the [Licensee] shall ensure that all third parties to be appointed or engaged by the [Licensee] to supply, produce, distribute, market or otherwise be involved in the exploitation of the [Film] under this agreement shall be of good financial standing and shall agree to pay, account and report to the [Licensee] in sufficient detail for the [Licensee] to fulfil its obligations to the [Licensor].

A.228

That where sums are not accounted for and/or paid to the [Company] due to the error, omission, fraud, dishonesty, financial difficulties, bankruptcy and/or winding up of a third party and/or the [Distributor] for any reason. Then the [Parent Company] agrees to pay all such sums as may be due to the [Company] together with such legal and accountancy fees which may be incurred in verifying and claiming the sums due up to a maximum limit of [number/currency] [in any one calendar year].

A.229

The [Company] agrees that all sums relating to the exploitation of the [DVD/Video/Disc] of the [Film] under this agreement whether as funds, income, receipts, payments, expenses or costs must be kept in a separate business account in the name of [specify name of account] with the following authorised signatories [specify authorised persons]. The following parties shall be sent a bank statement relating to the account each calendar month: [specify persons who are to receive copies of accounts/method].

A.230

The [Licensee/Distributor] shall not be obliged to pay any royalties and/or other sums to the [Licensor] where any copies of the [Work/Film] has been provided to a third party for promotional, marketing and advertising purposes. Provided that the [Licensee/Distributor] has not received any payment and no more than [number] copies have been used for such purposes in any [number] calendar months. Where that number is exceeded then the [Licensee/Distributor] shall pay the [Licensor] a fixed sum of [number/currency] per copy. The [Licensee/Distributor] shall ensure that they keep a full and accurate records of all such copies supplied to third parties for any reason.

A.231

The [Licensee] agrees and undertakes that it and its sub-agents and sub-licensees shall keep full and accurate accounting records, statements, costs and contracts which shall clearly establish and identify the Gross Receipts, the Distribution Expenses, the Net Receipts, any taxes, exchange rate conversions, and government levies and set out the calculation and final figures of the [Licensee's] Commission and the [Licensor's] Royalties in respect of the exploitation of the [Series] under this agreement.

A.232

The [Licensee] agrees that it shall pay the [Licensor's] Royalties on or by dates: [specify dates] in every year until all sums due to the [Licensee] have been paid [during the Term of this Agreement/until the expiry or termination of this agreement].

A.233

1.1 The [Licensee] shall provide a detailed report to the [Licensor] by [date] and [date] in each year with a full breakdown of the exploitation of the [Series] together with copies of all relevant documents and records for any sum in excess of [number/currency].

1.2 The [Licensee] agrees and undertakes to keep the funds and receipts relating to the [Series] separate from all other monies in the business of the [Licensee] so that they are clearly identifiable.

1.3 The [Licensee] agrees that the [Licensor] shall be entitled to arrange for an audit at its own cost at any time to inspect and make copies of the accounting records in any format, stock and/or any other relevant material in order to verify the sums due to the [Licensor] within [number] [days/months] of receipt of each report. Such audit to be at the [Licensor's] cost and by such reputable advisor as the [Licensor] may decide.

A.234

Prior to any audit the [Licensor] may be required to provide a written confidentiality undertaking to the [Licensee] in respect of any aspect of the [Licensees'] business which may be disclosed in the audit which does not directly relate to the [Licensor].

A.235

The [Licensee] agrees that all sums relating to the Gross Receipts for the [Series] shall be kept in a separate bank account and not mixed with any other monies of the [Licensee]. Nor shall a charge, lien, or other security be given in respect of the agreement or the Gross Receipts or the bank account by the [Licensee].

A.236

The [Assignee] shall provide the [Assignor] with a statement within [one] month of the end of every financial year by [date] which specifies the full details of the exploitation of the [Film] in each country, and the sums received and the costs, expenses, commission, agents' fees or other sums incurred and deducted.

A.237

The [Distributor] will provide an account in writing to the [Company] so that there shall be one account in each period of [three] months starting with the date of delivery of the first complete master copy of the [Programme] to the [Distributor]. Such account shall show particulars of all sums paid or payable by any person, company or third party who have or shall acquire any rights in any media and/or format in the [Programme] and/or any parts and all commission, remuneration and Distribution Expenses. Each such account shall be conclusive as between the [Distributor] and the [Company] as to:

1.1   The amounts of commission and any other sums due, paid or deducted by the [Distributor].

1.2   The sums due to be paid by the [Distributor] to the [Company].

1.3   Details of all sums due to the [Company] which have not been transferred by the [Distributor] to the [United Kingdom/other]. If for any reason monies due from any person, company or third party cannot be transferred by the [Distributor] to the [United Kingdom/other]. Then any such money shall be paid by the [Distributor] into a separate bank account in such country and held in the joint names of the [Company] and the [Distributor] and full details of the bank account shall be provided to the [Company].

1.4   Details of all sums due to the [Company] which have not been paid due to the default of a third party which has failed to pay the [Distributor]. The [Distributor] shall not be obliged to make any payment in respect of such sums not received provided that it shall use all reasonable endeavours to recover such sums.

A.238

The [Licensee] undertakes that it shall agree to the following terms in respect of the [Film] in respect of the accounts, audits and reports to the [Licensor]:

1.1   That the [Licensee] shall open a separate bank account and keep professional and accurate financial records, data, contracts, invoices and receipts both in paper form, and on computer software. No such material shall be destroyed, deleted, erased and/or disposed of without the prior written consent of the [Licensor] for a period of [seven] years.

1.2   That funds, production costs, advances or royalty payments from the [Licensor] or any third parties which may be received or credited to the [Licensee] shall not be used, mixed or offset in any way whatsoever with the account of any other film at any time for any reason.

1.3   The [Licensor] may carry out up to [four] audits of all financial, contractual and business records in any one calendar year during office hours. Provided that [number] [days/months] written notice is given to the [Licensee]. In the event such audits reveal errors and/or omissions prejudicial to the [Licensor] all the sums which may be due to the [Licensor] as a result of such errors and/or omissions will be paid immediately and the total cost of any such audit including accountants, legal advice and administrative charges shall be paid for in full by the [Licensee].

1.4 The [Licensee] shall undertake immediately or whenever necessary to obtain permission for remittance of any sums due to the [Licensor]. Upon the [Licensor's] request and particularly in the event of difficulties in remitting the sums due the [Licensor] shall open an account in that territory in which the [Licensee] shall pay any sums due to the [Licensor]. The [Licensor] shall then bear sole responsibility for accounting and remitting the sums to the [United Kingdom/other].

A.239

The [Assignee] undertakes that it and its sub-agents and sub-licensees shall keep full and accurate books of account, records and contracts showing the Gross Receipts, the Distribution Expenses, the Sales Tax, the Net Receipts and the Assignor's Royalties in respect of the exploitation of the [Film].

A.240

The [Assignee] shall provide a detailed report to the [Assignor] with a full breakdown of the exploitation of the [Film] showing the Gross Receipts, the Distribution Expenses, the Sales Tax, the Net Receipts and the [Assignors] Royalties by [date] and [date] in each year. The report shall include details of all units sold, licensed, lost, stolen, damaged or given away, currency conversion costs and documentation to support any deduction of Distribution Expenses. No documentation shall be shredded or disposed of without first offering to make it available to the [Assignor].

A.241

The [Assignee] undertakes that it shall pay the [Assignor's] Royalties to the [Assignor] by [cheque/direct debit/other] by [date] and [date] in each year during the continuance of this agreement and until such time whether after the end of the Term of this Agreement or not all sums due to the [Assignor] under this agreement shall have been reported, accounted for and paid.

A.242

The cost and expense of all currency conversions and bank charges shall be stated in full and such sums itemised and the exchange rate, cost, source and date stipulated.

A.243

1.1   The [Licensee] agrees that it shall disclose all sums received and/or credited to the [Licensee] and/or any other benefits allocated to them from a third party including but not limited to advances, royalties and one off payments.

1.2   The [Licensee] agrees that it shall also disclose any sums paid and/or credited to and/or benefits provided to a third party by the [Licensee]. This shall include any sub-agent, sub-licensee and/or any other person or company acting on behalf of the [Licensee].

1.3   The [Licensee] agrees and undertakes that the financial statement to be supplied by the [Licensee] in respect of the [Film] by [date] in each year shall cover all aspects of the exploitation of the [Film] and/or any part in any media including but not limited to: all forms of television cable. terrestrial, satellite and digital; free playback archive service; pay per view and/or any subscription service over the internet and/or any telecommunication system; licensing for DVDs, services and/or products, books and merchandising.

1.4   The [Licensee] agrees and undertakes that the financial statement to supplied by the [Licensee] in respect of the [Film] by [date] in each year shall cover all aspects of the deductions, distribution expenses, reproduction costs and supply of copies of master material, marketing, payments to artistes and/or performers and/or other third parties, fees to collecting societies and/or other rights holders and/or any other sums due for copyright clearance, consents, waivers, and/or monies deducted for cancellations, discounts, losses, damages, refunds and/or hospitality, travel and/or for any other reason.

A.244

Where an error, omission, default and/or failure is found and/or later disclosed whether by the [Licensor] and/or the [Licensee]. The [Licensee] shall not be entitled to a refund of any overpayment to the [Licensor]. Nor shall the [Licensor] be entitled to any interest, compensation and/or damages for an error, omission, default and/or failure by the [Licensee] provided that it was not deliberate or fraudulent and payment is made immediately it is clear that it is due. An error and/or omission arising from an audit by the [Licensor] shall result in the [Licensee] paying all costs of the accountants and legal advisors up to a maximum of [number/currency] for each such audit.

A.245

The [Licensee] shall pay all sums due to the [Licensor] by [cheque/electronic transfer to a notified bank account/in cash] in [currency].

A.246

Nothing contained in this agreement shall create or impose upon the [Company] any fiduciary obligations to the [Writer] or be deemed to mean that any monies due or payable to the [Writer] shall be held in trust by the [Company] for the [Writer]. It is the intention of the parties that the [Company] shall have the right to mix the monies or any portion of the sums payable to the [Writer] out of or on account of the Gross Receipts received in respect of the [Work/Film] with any other such receipts or sums received. It is agreed between the parties that all such receipts or sums received shall be held in a separate account at the bank designated for the [Film] only.

A.247

The [Company] agrees to ensure the provision to the [Writer] of statements relating to the receipts or other sums received in respect of the [Film] and showing the relevant details. Such statements shall be rendered not less frequently than quarterly for a period of twelve months from and after the date of first public release of the [Film] and thereafter twice a year. At the same time as the delivery of such statements the [Company] shall deliver the remittance to the [Writer] of any sums to which he/she may be entitled. The public release of the [Film] shall be when the earliest of one of the following events takes place:

1.1 The [Film] is released in cinemas whether at a premier or to the public in [country/any part of the world].

1.2 The [Film] is broadcast or transmitted on terrestrial, cable, satellite or digital television in [country/any part of the world].

1.3 The [Film] is released, sold, rented or supplied on DVD and/or offered in an electronic download format over the internet to the public in [country/any part of the world].

A.248

The [Writer] shall have the right to employ a firm of chartered accountants to examine the books of account of the [Company] relevant to the [Film] but neither the [Writer] nor the chartered accountants shall be entitled to enquire into or challenge any statement which was despatched by the [Company] to the [Writer] more than [three] years previously. It is agreed between the parties that after each such period of [three years] has expired all such statements shall be final and conclusive accounts unless written objections shall have been made within the [three] year period setting out the grounds of complaint.

A.249

The [Company] shall not be bound to pay to the [Writer] any royalty and/or other sum due where the money has not actually been received by the

[Company] by reason of force majeure and/or an embargo, banking and/or any other legal restriction. The [Company] shall be bound to inform the [Writer] of the problem and subject to the laws of the country or territory concerned may assist the [Writer] to receive payment in another manner at the [Writer's] expense.

A.250

The [Company] agrees and undertakes that:

1.1 There shall be an obligation to keep professional, complete and accurate books of account, records, contracts, computer data and other material showing all the Gross Receipts, the Distribution Expenses and the Authors Royalties in respect of the commercial exploitation of the [Film] or parts anywhere in the world [at any time/for [number] years/until no further sums are due to the [Author].

1.2 In all its contracts with its sub-agents, sub-licensees, distributors and any third parties involved in the exploitation of the [Film] or any part in any media that the same obligation in 1.1 above shall apply.

1.3 That the [Author] may serve notice to carry out an audit [once/number] in any financial year of the [Company] and shall be allowed access to all such material to verify the sums due to the [Author].

1.4 That in the event in any audit there is a deficit to the [Author] of [number/currency] then the [Company] shall pay to the [Author] [twice the total/other] of the deficit and all reasonable costs of such audit. No additional penalty, surcharge or interest shall be due on such sums. or any claim for costs.

A.251

The [Company] shall not be obliged to keep contracts, books of account, computer records or other material relating to the exploitation of the [Film] more than [six/number] [months/years] unless there are sums still due to the [Agent] or there are legal proceedings or any dispute relating to the [Film]. If the [Company] decides to destroy any material then the [Company] agrees that it shall first notify the [Agent] of their intention to destroy such material and offer them the opportunity of making copies or of purchasing such material.

A.252

The [Distributor] shall send to the [Company] an accounting statement and payments for the sums due under this agreement by [date] in each year during the Term of this Agreement. The statement shall specify how the sums due are calculated, but there shall be no obligation to provide further details in the statement. In the event that the [Company] wishes to dispute the statement or payment and believes for any reason that it has been underpaid. Then the [Company] shall notify the [Distributor] as soon as reasonably possible, but in any event within [six] months of receipt of the statement. The [Distributor] shall disclose such evidence and documents as may be relevant to satisfy the [Company] that the statement is accurate. There shall be no obligation to permit the [Company] to carry out an internal audit of the [Distributor] unless ordered to do so by a court of law. The parties shall agree a suitable venue for all the documents and records that are relevant to be displayed and inspected. In the event that the matter cannot be resolved then no part of this clause is intended to prejudice the [Company's] right to take legal action whether civil and/or criminal for any reason including for breach of contract, non-payment, to gain a court order for full disclosure and/or an audit and/or to make an allegation of fraud and/or false accounting against the [Distributor] and/or any sub-agent, sub-licensee or other third party.

A.253

There shall be [no obligation/an obligation] for the [Company] to bear the cost of any errors, omissions, fraud, dishonesty, non-disclosure or failure to transfer or pay any sums of any sub-agent, sub-licensee or any other third parties which affect or reduce the sums due to [Name] under the terms of this agreement.

A.254

1.1 The [Company] shall be liable for the acts, omissions, errors, failure to account and report and/or allow inspection, and/or non-payment of any sums due to the [Artist] which any agent, representative, manufacturer, distributor or other third party engaged or authorised by the [Company] is required to fulfil in respect of the exploitation of the services and product of the work of the [Artist].

1.2 The [Company] shall be responsible for the adherence to the accounting provisions whether the work is sub-contracted out to professional accountants or not or any other advisor. In the event that there are errors, withholding of information, non-disclosure, failure to pay and/or any other default and/or failure. Then the [Company] agrees that the [Artist] shall be entitled to be paid interest at [number] per cent from the date the sum was due. This shall only apply where the sum due is in excess of [number/currency] in each case. In addition the [Company] shall also pay all the costs of professional legal and accountancy advisors, including court fees, counsel, administration, telephone, travel and accommodation which may have been incurred by the [Artist] in pursuance of any such claim and/or dispute.

A.255

The [Production Company] agrees and undertakes to hold all funds and sums of any nature received by them in respect of and/or relating to the [Film/Project] at [Name Bank] in [country] and that the signatories to the account shall be [specify persons]. Further that all sums received from the exploitation of the rights associated with the [Film/Project] by the [Production Company] shall be deposited in that account in [currency].That no third party shall be entitled to withdraw and/or charge and/or hold any lien over that account. That no additional bank account and/or deposit account shall be set up at any time. That the [Production Company] shall ensure that no payments and/or direct debits are made from that bank account which do not directly arise from the production [and exploitation] of the [Film/Project]. That the [Production Company] shall not be entitled to use the account to pay any office, administration costs and salaries and/or other liabilities relating to the normal business of the [Production Company].

A.256

Both parties agree that they shall appoint [Advisor] as the [Accountant/ Legal/other] for the [Project] and that all such costs and expenses shall be paid for out of the existing Budget in Schedule A up to a maximum of [number/currency]. That the [Advisor] shall act for both parties and keep them both informed of the progress of the [Project]. Further that the parties shall take out joint insurance with a reputable company to cover [specify scope of cover] and any legal action that may be necessary. The cost of such insurance shall also be paid for out of the Budget.

General Business and Commercial

A.257

The [Assignor] shall provide a full report to the [Company] of the costs and expenses incurred in respect of the [Commissioned Work] upon request. The [Assignor] shall keep full and accurate records and accounts of all costs and expenses incurred in respect of the [Commissioned Work] and agrees that the [Company] shall be entitled to inspect such records and material upon request. The [Assignor] shall not be obliged to keep any such financial records beyond [date].

A.258

The [Company] shall provide a full and detailed financial record and statement to the [Copyright Owner] of all sums received directly and/or indirectly by the [Company] and/or any associated business and/or enterprise from the exploitation of the [Product/Service/Work] at any time in any part of the universe in any medium. All records, documents, accounts, contracts, invoices, receipts and bank statements whether paper, software or some other medium shall be retained and not destroyed by the [Company] for a minimum of [six] years. The [Copyright Owner] and/or its professional advisors shall upon written notice be able to inspect all such material [once] in each year during the Term of this Agreement and/or for any period thereafter until the [six] years has expired.

A.259
The [Company] shall employ a professional accountant to verify and audit the accounts at a maximum cost of [number/currency] in each year.

A.260
The [Company] shall make any payments due to [Name] within [14/28/30] [days] of receipt of any sums in excess of [number/currency]. All other sums shall be allowed to accrue until they reach that same level at which point payment shall be made. In any event all sums shall be accounted for in a statement every [three/six/twelve] months from the start date of the contract to the end of that accounting period. The accounting statement shall include sums due and not yet received which shall be marked accordingly.

A.261
The [Company] shall ensure that any person who is engaged to work on this [Project] is suitably qualified and will be able to provide [national insurance, tax references/other] which may be required for accounting purposes and to comply with the legal requirements of [country].

A.262
No expense or cost or other sum shall be deducted from the accounts which cannot be verified by a receipt or other supporting documentation.

A.263
Any error by the [Company] in the final accounts which is later revealed to the detriment of [Name] shall result in a penalty payment of [number/currency] for each such mistake and it shall be paid immediately it is confirmed together with all directly-related accountant and legal costs which [Name] incurred in order to prove the error.

A.264
The [Licensee] agrees and undertakes to the [Licensor] to:

1.1 Act in good faith and disclose any errors and/or omissions in the accounts and/or the calculation of the costs, deductions, payments and/or other sums as soon as they are noticed.

1.2 Ensure that professional accounting practices according to [specify institute] are followed by the [Licensee] in respect of the accounts and the calculation of any sums due to the [Licensor] under this agreement.

1.3 Ensure prompt payment of any sums due to the [Licensor] and agrees that failure to do so shall be considered a breach of this agreement.

A.265

Both parties shall be entitled to full disclosure of all facts whether financial, stock, audit reports, company records, third party contracts and records relating to the business. Together with any material of any nature that may be required to establish the costs incurred, the sums expended and the sums due to be paid to each party.

A.266

All calculations shall be in [currency] and where conversion is necessary the date and exchange rate and costs clearly stated. Each party shall bear the costs of its own bank charges and commissions.

A.267

All payments and records shall be kept and made in [currency] by [Name].

A.268

In the event that the [Company] decides to take legal proceedings or institute any action or claim against the [Licensee] because of the failure of the [Licensee] to provide accounts, royalty statements and/or make payment of the sums due under this agreement. The [Licensee] agrees to indemnify the [Company] in respect of the cost and expense of legal and accountancy fees up to a maximum of [number//currency] in total for the duration of this agreement. This clause shall not apply where the fault lies with a third party and not the [Licensee].

A.269

It is agreed that the [Company] shall preserve and safeguard all relevant invoices, records, letters, accounts, contracts, licences, software, discs, microfilm, sales brochures, publicity and marketing material and any other material or medium on which information about [specify project] is held for a period of not less than [number] years after the expiry or termination of the agreement. The material shall be offered to [Name] before destruction or shredding at any time.

A.270

It is agreed between the parties that any inspection of the material relating to the exploitation of the [Product] or any part shall require:

1.1 That the [Company] give [number] days written notice to [Name] at the [Distributor].

1.2 That the material be made available in normal business hours from [specify hour] to [specify hour] on working days at [specify premises] with the use of a telephone and photocopier machine at the [Distributor's] cost.

1.3 That there is a time limit on each occasion of no more than [number] days unless for any reason documents or material are not available.

1.4 That senior executives of the [Distributor] will agree to meet to answer any outstanding questions that may arise.

1.5 That the [Distributor] will co-operate fully to make available any material in its possession or control relating directly or indirectly to the [Product].

A.271

The [Company] shall not be obliged to disclose the names, addresses and personal details of clients and customers, nor any confidential business information relating to third parties or the parent company as part of the accounting process.

A.272

The [Company] agrees to pay the sums due to [Name] as follows:

1.1 within [28] days of the last days of March, June, September and December in each year for the first two years;

1.2 within [28] days of the last days of June and December for the third, fourth and fifth year; and

1.3 thereafter within [28] days of the last day of December.

A.273

Where an audit is being carried out there shall be no obligation to release the confidential and private details of a parent company, associated company or any third parties who have not provided their consent to the disclosure of the information, data, financial records, documents or otherwise. The [Company] may arrange for portions of documents, files and software to be copied in order to only disclose the relevant parts.

Internet, Websites and Apps

A.274

The [Company] shall provide an annual report to [Name] which sets out details of the amount of [users/subscribers] in that period and who clicked on or accessed the [specify material] on the [Website/Platform/ Channel] relating to [Name]. The [Company] shall pay [Name] the sum of [number/currency] if more than [number] persons click on or access the [specify material]. Where the [Company] has ceased to display the material relating to [Name] then no report or payment shall be due to [Name].

A.275
The [Company] shall not be obliged to provide any report or pay any sums in respect of copying, transfer, exploitation or reproduction of material which may arise relating to the use and/or reproduction of material relating to [Name] by unauthorised third parties.

A.276
The [Company] shall provide a full and detailed disclosure of the subscriptions, payments, fees and other sums received by the [Company] or any third party engaged to process payments in respect of the display, use, sale and exploitation of the [Material/Content] of [Name] on the [Website/Platform/Channel]. Whilst the [Company] shall not be obliged to provide personal customer details and financial records the [Company] should provide a list of numbers, country, type of payment, reason for payment and where refunds, cancellations or returns of any nature are made the reason. The [Company] agrees that the statement shall be accompanied by payment of all sums due to that date to [Name].

A.277
The [Company] agrees to pay the [Copyright Owner] the sum of [number/currency] [also specify in words] for each completed electronic format downloaded by the public and third parties of the [Film/Music/Text/Photograph] described as follows: [brief description].

The [Company] shall provide a statement to the [Copyright Owner] at the end of each period of [three] months specifying the [dates/number of downloads/source of access/country] of the [gadget/device/mobile/internet location] used to access the electronic format download but not any personal data which might identify an individual.

A.278
The [Company] agrees to pay to [Name] a fee of [number/currency] for every transaction which is completed (except not where the sums are refunded by the [Company] and/or otherwise are not retained) when the [Client] has followed the link from the [Affiliate] to the [Company] to place the order for the [Product/Holiday/Service]. The [Company] agrees to credit the account of the [Affiliate] by direct debit with any sums due at the end of each fixed period of [number] [weeks/months] starting on [date]. In addition the [Company] shall supply [Name] with a brief statement by email which sets out how the sum paid has been calculated.

A.279

1.1 The [Company] shall supply a simple statement of account of the total number of unit sales and the sums received in respect of the sub-licences granted and/or other exploitation of the [Work/Artwork/Material] in any format whether as an electronic download, an app, in print in hardback and/or paperback, on a product, merchandising and/or any other adaptation.

1.2 The same fee shall be paid to the [Contributor] for each unit of any completed transaction which shall be [number/currency] for any format. All sums due to the [Contributor] shall be paid within [number] [days] by direct debit to the nominated bank account in the name of [specify account name for the Contributor]. No bank charges and/or costs shall be attributed and/or made to the [Contributor] by the [Company] in respect of such payment method.

1.3 Where for any reason a unit is not the best method of accounting for sales and/or sums received. Then the parties shall agree another method of attributing payment to the [Contributor] based on the facts in each case.

A.280

The [Company] shall provide at its own cost and expense to the [Licensor] full and detailed statements and records by email and in paper form of all exploitation of the [Work/Logo/Image] by the [Company] to any third party of any nature in any part of the world in every [six] month period starting [date]. The [Company] shall ensure that all statements and records are supported by any documents, invoices, bank records and/or other material no matter how it is stored and/or processed by the [Company] so that it is easily verified by the [Licensor]. Any additional documents and/or data and/or detail that the [Licensor] may request in order to assess the validity of the reports shall be supplied by the [Company]. Failure to comply with any request by the [Licensor] shall be deemed to be a breach of this agreement and entitle the [Licensor] to terminate the agreement with immediate effect.

A.281

[Name] has appeared in and contributed to the [Podcast Series] owned by the [Company]. [Name] has received an fee of [number/currency] for the product of his/her work and assigned all rights to the [Company]. The [Company] has agreed to pay [Name] and additional escalating fee based on the number of views of the [Podcast Series] but not for any other forms of exploitation. The [Company] shall notify [Name] when the views in total of the [Podcast Series] exceed [number] and [Name] shall be paid an additional fee of [number/currency] within [ten] days subject to an invoice. When the [Podcast Series] total views exceed [number] then the [Company] shall notify [Name] and pay a further additional fee of [number/currency] within [ten] days subject to an invoice. No other notifications shall be required to [Name] and not further sums shall be due to be paid.

A.282

[Name] has performed on the [Film/Video] which has been posted and distributed on the channel known as: [specify channel name/reference] by the [Company]. [Name] has been paid a buyout fee for all the product of his/her work and services and no other sums are due to be paid to [Name]. [Name] has assigned all the rights to the [Company]. The [Company] is under no obligation to report and/or to account to [Name] and/or to pay any royalties for any form of exploitation in any media and/or format whether in existence now and/or created in the future.

A.283

1.1   The parties have agreed that the [Company] which owns the [Website/ App/other] shall pay {Name} the originator of the [idea/concept] an annual fixed fee of [number/currency] from [date] to [date] in each year of [number/currency].

1.2   When the total net revenue before tax exceed [number/currency] then the [Company] shall notify [Name] and the annual fixed fee shall increase to [number/currency] from the date of notification. Where the increase falls in part of a year then the first part shall be paid at the earlier rate and the second part at the increased rate.

1.3   When the total [net revenue before tax/gross receipts/sums received/ other] exceed [number/currency] then the [Company] shall notify [Name] and the annual fixed fee shall increase to [number/currency] from the date of notification. Where the increase falls in part of a year then the first part shall be paid at the earlier rate and the second part at the increased rate.

Merchandising and Distribution

A.284

The [Agent] acknowledges that the [Company] shall be entitled upon request to be provided with a copy of any record, software , data, agreements, documents or other material in the possession and/or under the control of the [Agent] relating to the [Company] including samples, garments, artwork, labels, logos, trade marks, stock, reproduction and delivery costs, insurance, sales and marketing.

A.285

You shall within [30] days after 31 March, 30 June, 30 September and 31 December in each year provide accounts for each month showing the [Units/Products] which have been supplied, distributed and sold to third parties. In addition with each such accounts you will payment the sums due to us. We shall have the right to reasonable access during ordinary business hours to inspect such of your books of account and other records as are relevant to verify the accounts and the sums paid.

A.286

The [Distributor] shall endeavour to prepare accurate and complete records and accounts relating to the number of [Units] supplied, sold, lost and/or damaged during each Accounting Period. The [Company] or its duly authorised representative may during the period of this agreement and for up to [six] months thereafter give no less than [21] days' notice to the [Distributor] that they wish to visit the premises of the [Distributor] during normal business hours to carry out an inspection.

The right of inspection shall not be more frequently than once in any [twelve] month period. The [Company] shall be entitled to inspect and make copies but shall not be entitled to make copies of any records containing names and addresses of clients and/or their personal data and/or any other information which is confidential. The [Company] shall cause as little disruption as possible during any such inspection to [Distributor's] business. The [Company's] right of inspection shall be exercised by the [Company] at its own expense and cost.

A.287

The [Distributor] and the [Company] agree that the following terms shall apply in respect of accounting and payment:

1.1   In the event that any inspection discloses that the total amount which should have been accounted for by the [Distributor] has omitted and/or is in error by [10] per cent or more of the actual total amount that was accounted during any individual accounting period. Then if the [Distributor's] auditor will certify that such error or omission exists then the [Distributor] shall upon invoice reimburse the [Company] for the reasonable costs of the [Company's] inspection as well as paying the sum due plus interest at [number] per cent from the date when the money should have been paid.

1.2   If the [Company] shall not have disputed the accuracy and/or otherwise of any accounts and/or payment within [one/two/six] years from the date of receipt by the [Company] then it shall be deemed complete and accurate.

1.3 If any inspection reveals that the [Distributor] has underreported the amount payable to the [Company] the [Distributor] agrees to make immediate payment to the [Company] of the proper amount due. If any inspection reveals that the [Distributor] has miscalculated and paid more than the amount due to the [Company] then the [Company] shall make an immediate refund of such sum to the [Distributor].

A.288

1.1 The [Licensee] shall send to the [Licensor] a statement on or before the [30th] day of the month following each of the quarterly periods ending on respectively the last days of June, September, December and March ('Accounting Statement') with full details of the computation of Royalties for the preceding quarter including without limitation the Gross Receipts received from the distribution and exploitation of the [Products/Services] during the relevant period; the Distribution Expenses incurred and the amount of Royalties payable.

1.2 At the same time as a statement is sent to the [Licensor] in 1.1 the [Licensee] shall also make payment of the Royalties shown to be due.

1.3 The first Accounting Statement will be sent by the [Licensee] in respect of the period from the beginning of the Licence Period to the last days of June, September, December or March thereafter whether or not a payment is due in respect of such period and shall continue until such time as the [Licensee] is not dealing in or exploiting any rights under this agreement and shall have accounted for all sums due. The parties shall endeavour to ensure that a final and conclusive payment shall be made at the expiration of [six] months from the end of the Licence Period or the date of termination of the agreement if earlier. If sums continue to accrue after that period then arrangements shall be made for all the monies to be paid direct to the [Licensor]. The [Licensee] shall not be entitled to any commission and/or other sums unless agreed otherwise between the parties.

A.289

1.1 The [Licensee] undertakes to the [Licensor] that it shall keep at its main place of business comprehensive and complete books of account, records and any other material, software, data and/or stock and/or sales records as may be reasonably necessary for the purpose of verifying the Accounting Statements.

1.2 The [Licensee] agrees that not more than [twice] per year during the Licence Period and for a period of one year thereafter that the [Licensor] or its duly authorised officer, agent or representative upon reasonable notice shall during normal business hours and at the [Licensor's/Licensee's] expense be entitled to inspect and take copies of such books of account and/or other material in 1.1 whether located at the main premises or elsewhere under the control or possession of the [Licensee].

A.290

The [Licensor] agrees that any information, data, sales figures and/or other records in any form supplied to the [Licensor] are provided only for the purposes of verifying the Accounting Statements and on the basis that it is confidential. The [Licensor] agrees and undertakes not to disclose any confidential facts and/or information and/or material to any third party. The [Licensor] accepts that any release of information, data and/or other material shall require the prior written approval of the [Licensee]. The [Licensee] accepts that the [Licensor] shall be entitled to disclose the information, data and material to professional legal and accounting advisors. This clause shall no longer apply after [date].

A.291

The Statement of Accounts rendered to the [Company] by the [Licensee] shall disclose such information and data as [Company] may request by notice in writing. The statement shall be clear and include details of the number of the [Products/Units] which are manufactured; the number of sales and the price allocated per {Product/Unit] and the level of unsold stock. Together with the costs and expenses itemised which have been deducted and/or set-off and/or recouped and the method of calculation of all royalties due to the [Company] and the amount which is due and the date upon which it shall be paid.

A.292

In respect of the production, manufacture, distribution, sale and disposal of the [Products/Units] the [Licensee] agrees and undertakes:

1.1 To keep professional, comprehensive and complete records and books of account relating to all dealings of any nature whether supply, disposal, transfer and/or sale of the [Products/Units] as may be necessary to enable the amount of the royalties and any other sums due to the [Company] to be accurately stated, accounted for, paid and audited.

1.2 To permit the [Company] or their duly authorised accountant or other professional advisors upon written notice to inspect and audit and take copies or extracts from the relevant records and accounts in any format required to enable the amount of the royalties and any other sums to be verified whether during the Term of this Agreement or not and shall also cover a period of up to [six years] thereafter. In the event of any inspection and/or audit revealing an error, omission and/or default in excess of [five] per cent [5]% of the royalties or other sums accrued due during the period for which such inspection and audit was made. The [Licensee] shall subject to verification of the claim by their own professional or legal advisors reimburse the [Company] with the full accountancy, legal and administration costs of such inspection and/or audit in each case. The [Licensee] will pay to the [Company] any sums shown to be due by such inspection and/or audit together with interest on the sum due at [four] per cent [4%] per annum above the base lending rate from time to time of [specify name of Bank] from the dates on which any such sums should have been paid to the [Company].

1.3 To preserve all relevant invoices, records, contracts, licences, accounts and computer software, discs, microfilm and any other material and/or medium on which relevant information, data and/or material is held for a period of no less than [six] years after the expiry and/or end of the Agreement whichever is the earlier.

A.293

The [Designer] agrees to be responsible for the collection and safeguarding of the Gross Receipts and to pay the [Licensee's] Royalties within [two] calendar months of receipt of all such money to the [Licensee]. The Designer agrees to open a bank account at [specify name of Bank] for the specific purpose of depositing and dealing in all monies received from the commercial exploitation, supply, distribution and sale of the [Licensed Articles] and the payment of any third party commission and/or other remunerations. The [Designer] agrees that the signature of both the [Designer] and the [Licensee] shall be required for the payment of any monies out of the bank account.

A.294

The [Designer] undertakes that it and its sub-agents, sub-licensees and distributors shall keep full and accurate books of account, records, contracts and prices showing all dealings of the [Licensed Articles] including the number of units manufactured, supplied, distributed and sold whether by wholesale, retail or distributed without charge for promotional purposes and all units lost, damaged, stolen and/or destroyed for any reason. Together with details of the sums which form the basis of the calculation of the [Designer's] Royalties and the [Licensee's] Royalties in respect of the [Licensed Articles].

A.295

The [Designer] agrees that the [Licensee] shall be entitled to arrange for an audit to inspect and make copies of the [Designer's] books of account, records, software, data, information, stock, contracts and any other material in any form or medium in order to verify the sums due to the [Licensee]. In the event that in any audit there is a discrepancy of more than [number/currency] in any one year to the detriment of the [Licensee] then the [Designer] shall be responsible for the reasonable costs incurred in respect of such audit up to maximum of [number/currency].

A.296

The [Licensee] confirms that the minimum [retail/wholesale/unit] selling price for the [Product] shall be not less than [number/currency] for each item in [country].

A.297

1.1 The [Licensee] shall keep competent, accurate and comprehensive books of account, records, contracts and prices showing all dealings in respect of the [Licensed Article] manufactured, supplied, distributed and/or sold whether by wholesale or retail prices and details of units distributed without charge for promotional purposes and all units lost, damaged or stolen or any other reason why no royalty is to be paid to the [Licensor].

1.2 All the information, data and facts in 1.1 shall be accurately reflected in the statements sent to the [Licensor] at the same time that the royalties are paid. Each stamen shall clearly show how the royalties have been calculated and where necessary supporting documentation and/or facts shall be provided to verify these sums.

1.3 The [Licensee] agrees to pay the royalties due to the [Licensor] as follows:

   a. Within [thirty] days of the last day of March, June, September and December in each year for the first [three] years.

   b. Within [thirty] days of the last day of June and December for the fourth, fifth and sixth year and

   c. Thereafter within [thirty] days of the last day of December thereafter.

A.298

By [date] and [date] in each year the [Licensee] shall provide a written report to the [Licensor] showing all data, information, dealings and exploitation of the [Products] including the total number of units of the [Products] manufactured, distributed, supplied and/or sold and the price whether wholesale and/or retail prices and/or discounted and/or otherwise. Together with full disclosure of sums received and/or credited whether to the

[Licensee], any sub-agent sub-licensee and/or other third party engaged by the [Licensee]. Verification must also be provided of details of the units distributed without charge for promotional purposes, and/or which are lost, damaged, stolen, returned, destroyed and/or not included in the accounts for any other reason. The report shall cover the calculation of all royalties which may be due to the [Licensor's] and state the sum upon which the royalty is derived and what percentage is being used and then the payment due to the [Licensor] in respect of the [Products]. Where any royalty to be paid exceeds [number/currency] then supporting documentation should be provided in the report. A bankers' draft in favour of the [Licensor] should be sent with each report for the sum stated to be due to the [Licensor]. The reports and the payments must be delivered by a secure method and signed for by the [Licensor].

A.299
In the event it is established by the [Licensor] that there are errors, omissions and/or defaults by the [Licensee] in excess of [number/currency] in any accounting period, Then for each such period the [Licensee] shall pay the sum due in full plus another [number/currency] in compensation. If there is an overpayment of the royalties then no refund shall be due from the [Licensor] and an adjustment and/or correction shall be made in the next accounting period from the sums due to the [Licensor]. There shall be no right to any interest.

A.300
In the event in any audit an error and/or omission and/or failure is found to be to the detriment of the [Licensor] in respect of the amount to be paid by the [Company] which is in excess of [number/currency]. The [Company] shall be obliged to repay the sum due immediately together with interest and all the fees of the [Licensor] for its accountants up to a limit of [number/currency] for any audit, but not for legal advisors or other administration costs incurred.

A.301
Each statement shall be supplied by the [Licensee] within [thirty/sixty/ninety] days following the end of each accounting period. Any statement submitted by the [Licensee] shall conclusively be deemed true and correct and binding upon the [Company] unless the [Company] notifies the [Licensee] within [twelve] months from the date any such statement has been received by the [Company] specific written grounds for disputing any such statement.

A.302
The [Company] shall have the right to examine the books and accounting records of the [Licensee] in any medium and/or format including software

75

and/or storage devices and/or online storage accounts to the extent they pertain to the [Units/Products/Services] relating to the [Project/Character]. The sole purpose of any inspection shall be to assess and verify the veracity and accuracy of the statements supplied and royalties paid by the [Licensee]. The [Company] may at its sole discretion appoint an independent chartered accountant at the [Company's] expense and subject to at least [thirty] days written notice the third party representative shall be entitled to examine the [Licensee's] books and accounting records. The [Company] shall not be entitled to examine any books or records of the [Licensee] which do not relate to the production, manufacture, distribution and exploitation of the [Units] in respect of the [Project/Character]. If the [Company's] inspection and/or audit has not been completed within [ten] days. The [Licensee] may require the [Company] to end the examination at any time upon [three] days written notice to the [Company]. The [Licensee] shall not be required to permit the [Company] to continue the examination after the end of that [three] day period unless documents or records have been unavailable for inspection and/or access has been restricted and/or barred for any reason.

A.303
The [Licensee] shall supply to the [Licensor] a quarterly written [royalty/accounting] statement no later than [/ten/twenty-one/sixty] days following the end of each quarter. Such quarters shall end on 31 March, 30 June, 30 September and 31 December in each year during the continuance of this agreement and thereafter. Each statement shall show the latest information received by the [Licensee] during each such period as to:

1.1 The number and price of any [Units] supplied, hired, played back, subscribed to and/or sold by the [Licensee].

1.2 Full details of all royalties due and/or payable to the [Licensor].

1.3 Full details of all sums received by the [Licensee] in respect of the exploitation of the [Units].

1.4 There is no requirement to account for those units lost, damaged, stolen and/or otherwise destroyed.

1.5 There is no requirement to account for those units give away for free for promotional, marketing and/or product placement and/or endorsement purposes.

The [royalty/accounting] statement shall be accompanied by a remittance for the full amount shown to be due to the [Licensor]. In the event that in any one quarter there are no sums received by the [Licensee]. Then the [Licensor] shall not be under any obligation to supply a full statement to the [Licensor], but shall merely confirm this fact by [letter/email]. The [Licensee] shall continue to provide such statements during the Licence Period and thereafter until such time as all [Units] supplied, hired, played back, and sold for any sum are accounted for by the [Licensee] to the [Licensor].

A.304

1.1 The [Licensee] shall keep secure and store at its main business address [specify details] in [country] professional accounting records of the highest standards as required by [specify organisation] which are an accurate and true record of all relevant matters. The software, data, information, agreements, contracts, permissions, clearances and records and other material shall be a true reflection of all the development, production, distribution, supply, sales, reproduction and/or commission charges and exploitation costs incurred and/or expended by the [Licensee] and/or any agent, sub-licensee and/or other third party.

1.2 The [Licensor] and/or an authorised representative may examine, inspect and request copies of or take excerpts from any such material in 1.1 and may request further information from senior executives or officers of the [Licensee] who deal or have dealt with such matters in any field either in meetings or in the form of written questions.

A.305
The [Licensor] shall also have the right to examine and take copies of the financial records, software and agreements of any sub-licensees, sub-distributors, agents or other third parties appointed by the [Licensee] to exploit, promote or market the [Units/Products/Services]. The [Licensee] shall ensure that all third parties engaged in respect of the [Units/Products/Services] in any capacity have a contractual obligation in such agreements and contracts to allow access to all relevant business dealings by the [Licensor] at the [Licensor's] cost.

A.306
The [Licensee] shall deliver to the [Licensor] at [address] commencing with the month in which the [Units] are first manufactured, a duplicate written statement in respect of the Gross Receipts. Such statements shall be supplied at the end of each period of [three] calendar months until the expiry and/or end of the agreement and/or the [Licensee] ceases permanently manufacturing the [Units] whichever is the later. In any event the [Licensee] shall be obliged to account for the manufacture, distribution, exploitation and destruction of all [Units] whether sold for the full value or not or otherwise. Each such statement shall show reasonable details relating to the period to which it refers including the specific sources, description and breakdown of the Gross Receipts.

A.307

The [Licensee] shall accompany each such statement with a remittance to the [Licensor] or its assignees of such sums as may be due to the [Licensor] under the terms of this agreement. The delivery to the [Licensor] of such remittance at the time stipulated by this agreement is to be adhered to and is of the essence of this agreement.

A.308

Each statement shall also include a complete recent list month by month of the number of [Units] manufactured or produced by the [Licensee] or its sub-licensees since the start of the agreement, and the number lost, destroyed or given away, and the number sold or marketed together with all the sums received by or credited as due to the [Licensee]. It shall not show information and data where the sums have not been remitted form any agent, sub-licensee, distributor and/or other third party.

A.309

If the [Licensor] should notify the [Licensee] in writing to pay any sum due direct to a third party The [Licensee] shall be entitled to refuse to do so. If it the [Licensee] does agree then the Licensee shall pay the amount to which the Licensor is entitled to any other third party designated by the [Licensor]. The payment by the [Licensee] to such third party in accordance with such written request shall be deemed payment to the [Licensor] and the [Licensee] shall be under no further liability to the [Licensor] in respect of such amount.

A.310

The [Licensee] shall use its best efforts to send the remittance to the [Licensor] pursuant to the terms of this agreement at the then prevailing rate of exchange. If for any reason the [Licensee] finds it impossible to have such monies transmitted to the [Licensor] or an authorised agent as agreed. Then the [Licensor] shall have the right at any time by giving written notice to the [Licensee] to require the [Licensee] to deposit such monies in the [Licensor's] name in any bank or other depository designated by the [Licensor] in any country of the Territory in which such monies are located.

A.311

The [Licensor] may at its own expense use its own staff and officers and/or appoint a qualified accountant, lawyer, professional advisor and/or other agent to inspect and examine the financial and business records in any form of the [Licensee], its directors and any associated company in its possession or control which contain information, data, records and/or accounts relating directly or indirectly to the exploitation of the [Units/Character/Trade Mark/Image] under this agreement; the expenditure and/or calculation of the costs and expenses; the prices charged and/or discounts permitted and the total sums received and therefore the sums due and/or paid to the [Licensor].

A.312

Such inspection shall be made at the main premises of the [Licensee] on a minimum of [seven] days' written notice and during normal business hours on such dates to be agreed with the [Licensee]. The [Licensor] shall be entitled to take any copies in the form of images on a mobile phone and/ or camera and/or some other gadget and/or device. The prior consent of the [Licensee] shall not be required. Where the [Licensor] requires services and/or office space on site these shall be provided at cost price.

A.313

The right to inspect may not be exercised more than once in any period of [six/twelve] months and shall not extend beyond a period of [one] year from the end of the accounting period to which such inspection relates.

A.314

If the [Licensee] shall be found as a result of such inspection to have withheld for any reason save as provided for in this agreement sums due to the [Licensor]. Then the [Licensee] shall pay the sums to the [Licensor] within [seven] days subject to invoice. In the event that such inspection reveals an error and/or omission and/or failure to the detriment of the [Licensor] in excess of [number/currency] in any one inspection the [Licensee] shall pay all reasonable costs directly incurred by the [Licensor] up to a maximum of [number/currency]. The [Licensor] shall be entitled to reserve the right to pursue any other rights and/or remedies available to the [Licensor] arising out of such error, omission and/or failure which shall include criminal and/or civil proceedings.

A.315

The [Licensee] shall not be obliged to provide any business, commercial or other details relating to the distribution and sales of the [Product/Character/ Logo] except those set out below which shall be shown in each accounting statement and supplied to the [Licensor] together with payment for any sums due:

1.1 The number of items sold at full retail and/or wholesale and/or other price in each [country/market].

1.2 The commission charges and costs of each agent, distributor and/or sub-licensee and/or any other costs deducted at any stage including costs of reproduction of master material.

1.3 The number of items sold, supplied and/or disposed of at a discount, destroyed, lost, given away, loaned, damaged, rejected as below standard, disposed of below manufacture cost price and/or for which the sum paid was refunded.

1.4 The value of total expenditure on artwork, filming, marketing and promotions.

1.5 Copies of all reviews, lists of product placements and/or paid for marketing, promotional material in any format, examples of items sold in any country including labels and packaging.

1.6 Business strategy and marketing plans for exploitation and sales the following year.

A.316

The [Distributor] agrees that it shall pay the [Assignor] an annual fee of [number/currency] per [number] of copies of the [Logo/Artwork/Image] that the [Distributor] supplies, sells and/or licenses to any third party for any reason whether at no cost, cost price, full price and/or otherwise at any time. No pro rata payment shall be made and any such balance of copies shall be carried to the next report period. All sums received from the exploitation of the [Logo/Artwork/Image] shall belong to the [Distributor] including any right of resale, and sums due from any collecting society and/or any other form of exploitation in the future.

A.317

The [Supplier] agrees that it shall provide the [Seller/Retailer] with a full list of:

1.1 The Product and Value including wholesale and retail price;

1.2 Number, dimensions, weight content and description; including comprehensive ingredients; label and packaging information and data.

1.3 Method of transport together with shipment, carriage and storage costs;

1.4 Import/export taxes and duties; and

1.5 Insurance policy cost.

A.318

The [Supplier] shall provide a [delivery statement/order form] with each consignment of the [Products] which shall be accepted and/or amended and/or rejected by the [Seller] and returned to the [Supplier] on each occasion.

A.319

The [Seller] warrants and confirms that it will keep true and accurate records of all orders from the public and shall meet such requests promptly and will pay the [Supplier] for all the [Products] delivered.

A.320

The [Seller] agrees that its orders for the [Products] shall be in the quantity, specification and dates set out in Schedule A. That all repeat or additional orders shall be in writing to the [Supplier] in the agreed format.

A.321

The [Seller] agrees that the dates specified in this agreement are an important part of the terms which have to be fulfilled. The [Seller] agrees to provide detailed orders for any request for the [Products] and shall sign and retain a copy of the delivery invoice with each order.

A.322

The [Factory] shall only reproduce and manufacture the exact number of the [Articles/Units] requested by [Name] in accordance with the written instructions on each occasion. The [Factory] shall ensure that full details are kept of all [Articles/Units] produced, manufactured, distributed, destroyed, lost, or otherwise disposed of and/or returned to the [Factory]. The records kept shall include the dates, the codes and any other method of identification, the suppliers of the materials used of any nature however small; the packaging and an example of each type of item to be kept for reference purposes.

A.323

The [Supplier] shall only engage, order supplies from or enter into a contract with any business or third party which have been in operation for at least [three] year]; has provided evidence of compliance with government health and safety regulations; has filed company accounts for at least [two] consecutive years and whose quality of work is of a suitable professional standard.

A.324

1.1   There shall be no obligation on the [Company/Distributor/Manufacturer] to produce, supply and/or to allow access to any accounting and/ or financial records of the business and/or any health and safety documents and/or other agreements, records and/or any other material relating to the production, supply and/or distribution of the [Products/ Services/Material under this agreement at any time.

1.2   Where there is an allegation of piracy and copying, fraud, failure to pay and/or non-compliance with health and safety regulations and policies and/or any other default under the agreement. Then the [Company/

Distributor/Manufacturer] agrees to cooperate and provide copies of all directly relevant documents, material stored on computer, discs and software, accounts and financial records and/or any other material which is in its possession provided that the cost of such administration is agreed in advance and will be paid by the [Enterprise].

A.325

The [Company/Distributor/Manufacturer] shall retain all records, documents, contracts, letters, storage devices, online storage accounts, data, software, receipts, invoices, bank statements and paying in records and any other material directly relevant to the creation, supply, distribution and exploitation of the [Product] under this agreement for up to [six years] after the expiry and/or end of this agreement including:

1.1 All development and supplier data, information and agreements for resources; production methods and storage; freight, customs and import and export duties and any taxes or levies.

1.2 All manufacture processes, methods and procedures; costs and expenses; interim tests and assessments to ensure compliance with health and safety legislation, regulations and policies, tests, trials, samples and final [Product]

1.3 All labels, packaging, storage, distribution, marketing and promotion; costs and expenses; client lists, databases, discounts, paid for advertising costs, insurance, invoices and payment records.

The [Company/Distributor/Manufacturer] agrees to provide a summary list of all such material and to allow access to and copies to be taken upon reasonable request by the [Name] at [Name's] sole cost.

A.326

The terms and conditions of trading and/or operation and/or access in respect of the [Company] whether in the brochure in printed form and as a download, the website, app and any other relevant associated material may be varied and amended at any time without notice. The actual price to be paid for any order will be that quoted by the [Company] at the time for a fixed period. The prices, costs and charges may be increased at any time and these will be reflected in any quote which you can either accept or reject. The samples and products delivered may be different from the images portrayed in the brochure and on the website and/or app due to natural variations in the source material. You will be advised at the time of the quotation whether the [Company] can complete an order or whether there is limited stock. Where an order is confirmed but payment is not received by the date requested by the [Company]. Then the order will automatically be cancelled by the [Company] the following day due to non-payment.

A.327

The [Company] shall not be entitled to deduct from any payment due to the [Licensor] any cost of currency conversions, bank charges, commission, expenses, marketing material, travel, insurance, mobile phones and/or other gadgets, software, administration, office, staff, photography, filming, hotel, clothes, freight and/or the cost of any professional and/or legal and/or health advisors and/or publicity agents and/or distributors and/or any other third party and/or any other matter of any nature which the [Company] may incur at any time.

A.328

The [Company] shall ensure that the manufacturer of the [Products] maintains full and accurate records of the method, procedure and content of the [Products] so that the date and time of production can be verified and the source of the material from which it has been derived can be traced if required. In addition the [Company] shall ensure that any manufacturer complies with all health and safety legislation and/or policies and/or guidelines that may be in force at any time. That the manufacturer shall be required to notify the [Company] if there is any serious allegation, complaint, investigation and/or prosecution by any government and/or local authority environmental and/or health and safety department and/or officer. The [Company] agrees to keep the [Licensor] informed and to assist in obtaining copies of such records as may be kept by the manufacturer in any format and/or medium for the [Licensor] if requested to do so at any time.

Publishing

A.329

The [Publishing Company] shall pay to [Television Company] the consideration set out in Schedule A which forms part of this agreement. Any royalty which may be due shall be calculated on the date at which payment should have been made for the sale or disposal from the third party to the [Publishing Company]. The royalty shall at that point be due regardless of whether the [Publishing Company] has actually received the money. Similarly the [Television Company] shall be obliged to pay the [Publishing Company] any advance and/or royalty payment which is due from any third party sub-licensee to the [Television Company] for the [Series] whether or not the sums have been received.

A.330

By [specify date] and [specify date] in each year of this agreement the [Publishing Company] shall deliver to the [Television Company] a true, accurate, detailed and informative report showing full details of all matters necessary to enable the [Television Company] to calculate the actual royalties due to the [Television Company]. The report shall include the number of copies of the [Work/Book] reproduced, supplied, distributed and sold in any format; the wholesale, retail and/or discounted price and the sums received and the date of payment. Where any sums are deducted under the agreement for any reason those expenses and/or costs must be itemised and be clearly identifiable as to the reason for the expenditure. The percentage royalty used in the calculation must be stated. It should be clear from which sum any percentage has been derived and calculated. Each separate royalty payment should be listed for each format which has been exploited. There should be a remittance of the payment due to the [Television Company] for the amount due for each such period. The [Publishing Company] shall also deliver a copy of any accountants and/or auditor's report for the annual accounts for each such year.

A.331
Any royalty payable to the [Television Company] shall be paid in [sterling] without deduction of any bank commission, charges, currency conversion costs or otherwise.

A.332

1.1 The [Publisher/Distributor] shall follow professional accounting practices and guidelines in respect of the maintenance and compilation of its account and records. agreements, invoices, costs and deductions which shall all be held on computer software and/or in an online storage account and/or in printed form in a secure location.

1.2 The [Publisher/Distributor] agrees and undertakes to ensure that all the necessary information, payments, receipts, data and documents are recorded in such a manner that they are a complete reflection of all dealings, sales, disposals and/or exploitation of the [Work/Film/Characters] by the [Publisher/Distributor] and/or any sub-agent, sub-distributor, sub-licensee and/or otherwise.

1.3 That no data and/or information shall be hidden, deleted and/or destroyed until a period of [six] years has expired from [date].

1.4 That the [Publisher/Distributor] shall disclose in the royalty statement supplied to the [Television Company] the number of sales and/or other forms of exploitation of the [Work/Film/Characters] with any third party including but not limited to merchandising products and/or services; and the sources of revenue; the dates sums were received and any authorised deductions including commission, expenses, marketing and/or reproduction costs. Together with the royalty percentage used to calculate the sums due to the [Television Company] and the revenue basis upon which the sum due in payment was reached.

1.5 The [Television Company] agrees and undertakes to permit the [Publisher/Distributor] the right to have access to take copies and inspect all financial records and resources and stock data and information which relates to the [Work/Film/Characters] within [number] months of each new report and payment of royalties at the [Publishers'/Distributors'] sole cost.

A.333

The [Publisher/Distributor] shall keep and preserve such books of account and records for a period of [three] years after the termination and/or expiry of the licence agreement for whatever reason and/or for so long as a dispute shall in the opinion of either party exist between the parties in respect of this agreement. In the event that any inspection carried out by or on behalf of the [Television Company] shows that any royalty statement issued by the [Publisher/Distributor] is shown to be in error to the detriment of the [Television Company] by more than [five/ten/fifteen] [per cent] then the costs of such inspection shall be paid for by the [Publisher/Distributor] up to a maximum of [number/currency] in any one financial year.

A.334

No royalties shall be payable by the [Publisher/Distributor] to the [Television Company] in respect of the following:

1.1 Copies of the [Work] presented to the [Television Company] or any third party for promotional purposes either without charge or at cost.

1.2 Copies of the Work destroyed by fire, water, enemy action, in transit or otherwise. Provided that if any such copies shall have a salvage value other than as paper pulp which is realised in whole or in part whether by the [Publishing Company] or by any other third party. Then the [Television Company] shall receive the royalty which would have been payable on the sums actually received by the [Publisher/Distributor].

A.335

1.1 The [Company] agrees and undertakes that the individual accounts shall be prepared and delivered every six months up to 30 June and 31 December respectively. All payments which may be due to the end of such accounting period shall be paid within [three calendar months/thirty days] after each of those dates. No payment shall be due to the [Author] in any period which is less than [number] pounds or less in which case that sum shall be carried forward to the next accounting date.

1.2 The [Company] agrees and undertakes that where the [specify rights/format] is exploited by the [Company]. The [Company] shall notify the [Author] within [seven] days of the conclusion of the agreement and shall pay the [Author] the percentage of any advance due within [number] days. The future royalties due under any such agreements shall be accounted for in the normal manner as stated in 1.1.

A.336

The [Author] and/or his/her authorised representative and/or agent shall have the right upon written request to examine and take copies and arrange an audit of the financial and accounting records in any medium of the [Publisher/Distributor] and/or any sub-agent, sub-distributor and/or sub-licensee in respect of the sales, receipts and disposals of the [Work/Manuscript/Book] and/or any adaptations in any format. Any such inspection and/or audit shall be at the [Author's] sole cost unless it is established that the [Publisher/Distributor] has underpaid [Author] in any accounting period by [number/currency] or more. In which case the [Publisher/Distributor] shall be obliged to pay the [Author] the sum of [number/currency] at the same time that it pays the outstanding sum due. This additional payment shall increase to [number/currency] if the outstanding sum not paid is discovered to be [number/currency] or more. No other costs and/or interest shall be paid to the [Author] for any reason.

A.337

Any overpayments made by the [Publisher/Distributor] to the [Author] in respect of the [Work/Manuscript/Book] and/or any adaptation shall be recovered and deducted from any sums subsequently due to the [Author] by the [Publisher/Distributor] whether under this agreement and/or some other agreement concluded between the parties.

A.338

1.1 The [Publisher/Distributor] undertakes that it shall supply comprehensive and complete accounting records [twice] in each year as at 30 June and 31 December which shows the sales of the [Work/Book] in hardback and paperback and any other formats including translations. audio files, e books in electronic format as downloads and/or any access a subscription service and/or any other adaptation and/or format in any medium. No account shall be made for copies which are for promotional purposes and/or below cost price.

1.2 The [Publisher/Distributor] shall pay the [Author] all royalties due within [14/30/60/90 days] of the last day of June and December in each year. The [Publisher/Distributor] shall not be obliged to make any royalty payments to the [Author] if the amount due in any accounting period is less than [ten] pounds sterling in which case such sums shall be carried forward to the next accounting period.

1.3 The [Publisher/Distributor] shall only account to the [Author] on sums which it actually receives and retains. The default and/or failure of a third party to pay any sums due shall not be the responsibility and/or liability of the [Publisher/Distributor]. The [Publisher/Distributor] shall be entitled to deduct currency conversion costs but not bank charges.

A.339

The [Publisher/Distributor] agrees and undertakes that it shall store and keep accurate and detailed business and accounting records for no less than [number] years from [date] of the following material which may be relevant to the verification of the sums due to [Name] from the exploitation of the [Work/Manuscript/Characters]:

1.1 All financial records, accounts, contracts, invoices, production and/or manufacturing costs, supply and delivery agreements and costs, sales and refund prices and data, agent and/or distribution commission charges and agreements, accountancy, legal, copyright and intellectual property advice costs and the costs and expense of clearance of rights, consents, waivers, licences and other documents of any nature. Together licences, consents and payments due to any collecting society and/or rights holder.

1.2 The costs of artwork, any cover, labels, podcasts, advertising and product placement, packaging, promotional and marketing material of the original initial [Work/Manuscript/Characters] and any other adaptation in any form and any image, text, logo, trade mark, character, music, costumes and/or any other product, service and/or other format. Together with two samples of any actual item.

A.340

By [date] and [date] in each year the [Publisher/Distributor] shall supply by email a short summary report to the [Author] with a short breakdown of the exploitation of the [Work] setting out the total sales. Where possible the report shall also state the number of copies of the [Work] used for publicity, promotional or review purposes and/or which have been lost, damaged, destroyed, pulped or remaindered and/or for any other reason no royalty payment is due to the [Author]. A payment shall be made by electronic bank transfer of the full amount due to the [Author] by the same dates.

A.341

The [Publisher/Distributor] agrees that the [Author] shall be entitled to arrange and/or personally carry out an annual audit to inspect and make copies of the [Publisher's] books of account, records, contracts and any other relevant material, data, software and/or documents in order to verify the sums due to the [Author]. The [Publisher] shall only be obliged to provide access to material, data, software and/or documents which are directly relevant to the sums calculated to be due to the [Author]. The [Author] shall be obliged to undertake not to disclose any business plans of the [Company] that may be confidential which are revealed as a result of the audit. In the event that in any audit there is an error to the detriment of the [Author] in respect of the amount paid by the [Publisher] which is in excess of [number/currency]. Then the [Publisher] shall pay the [Author] [number/currency] as compensation for the error of each such audit. In addition interest shall be due on the sums found not to have been paid at [number] per cent from the date upon which the sum should have been paid until the final date upon which the [Author] is actually paid.

A.342
The [Publisher/Distributor] agrees to open a bank account in [country] at [specify bank] with the following account name and signatories: [specify details] for the specific and sole purpose of depositing and dealing with all money relating to the exploitation of the [Work].

A.343
The [Publisher] and its sub-agents, sub-licensees and distributors shall keep for a minimum of [specify period] all material on which information is held relating to the [Work], books of account, records, invoices, discs, microfilm, computer software, letters and contracts showing the development, production, distribution and sale of the [Work] and all dealings of any nature, disposal, or transfer and all sums received by the [Publisher] in respect of the [Work].

A.344
The [Publisher] undertakes to the [Author] that a professional, comprehensive and complete history of the [Work] being exploited by the [Publisher] will be kept and recorded so that an accurate audit can be carried out by all the parties.

A.345
By [specify dates] in each year during the existence of this agreement the [Publisher/Distributor] shall provide a detailed, accurate and complete statement and report to the [Author] with a full breakdown of the exploitation of the [Work] including the number of copies lost through damage, theft or any other reason. The statement and report shall be accompanied by a [method of payment] payable to [Name] for the full amount in [currency] shown to be due to the [Author].

A.346
The [Publisher] agrees and undertakes that it shall make supply an updated statement of account twice in each yearly as at 31 March and 30 September.

The [Publishers] shall pay any sums shown to be due to the [Author] as royalties which are not set-off and recouped against the advance within [number] days of 31st March and 30th September in each year. A statement of account shall be provided to the [Author] whether any money is due or not. The [Publisher] shall not have the right to withhold any royalty payments which are due for any reason.

A.347

The [Publisher] undertakes and agrees in respect of the [Work/Manuscript/Sound Recording] and/or any part and/or any form of exploitation in any media in any part of the world at any time:

1.1 That the [Publisher] shall keep full and accurate financial records and accounting statements in a manner which complies with the standards of [specify organisation]. Together with all receipts, invoices, contracts, letter agreements, bank statements and other material in any format which shows and/or can verify the sums received by or credited to the [Publisher] and/or its parent company and/or subsidiaries and any sub-agents, sub-licensees, distributors and/or joint venture partners.

1.2 This material shall be preserved and kept secure by the [Publisher] for a minimum of [three/five/seven] years after the expiry or termination of the agreement or in the event there is a dispute between the parties for such longer period as may be necessary until it is resolved. In any event any such material shall not be destroyed without prior written notice to the [Author] of the [Publisher's] intention to do so and the opportunity for the [Author] to make copies and/or to collect the material.

1.3 That the [Publisher] shall provide copies of and/or access to inspect such background details, contracts, receipts, currency conversion records and other information, data, software and documents that the [Author] may request in order to verify whether the [Publisher] has complied with all the terms of this agreement in respect of the publication and exploitation of the [Work/Manuscript/Sound Recordings] and the accounting statements to the [Author] and the sums paid.

A.348

In the event that any sums which are in fact due under this agreement are deducted, withheld, credited but not cleared, have not been transferred by a third party, are delayed, inaccurate or omitted then the [Publisher] agrees to provide satisfactory evidence of the reason to the [Author] as soon as reasonably possible and make immediate payment where appropriate.

A.349

The [Publisher/Distributor] will only be liable for and account for those sums actually received from the publication and exploitation of the [Book] which are authorised under this agreement and is not responsible for the acts, omissions, defaults and/or failures to account and/or pay of third parties including but not limited to agents, distributors, wholesalers, retailers or otherwise.

A.350

The [Distributor] agrees and undertakes to provide to the [Author] and his/her agent and/or nominate representative all the sales, figures, receipts, information and data required in respect of the sales and exploitation of each unit of the [Book] in hardback, paperback and/or as an ebook and/or in any other electronic format in the manner set out in the specimen accounting statement attached as Appendix A and forming part of this agreement.

A.351

The [Company] agrees to provide regular updates to the [Author/Artist] as to the pre-publication marketing and actual terms of exploitation and licensing and sales of all formats of the [Work] throughout the world. The [Company] shall advise the [Author/Artist] of the name and nature of the role of any third parties including sub-agents, distributors, publicity companies, printers, suppliers, merchandising, music, food and drink, and other product companies and manufacturers who may be licensed and/or engaged for their services. The [Company] shall endeavour to ensure at all times that no third party is authorised who may bring the reputation of the [Author/Artist] and/or any of their brands and/or work into disrepute by association due to the failure of that third party to adhere to basic health and safety protection and testing, living wage employment conditions and/or their business does not have an account with a reputable bank and/or adhere to environmentally friendly and sustainable policies.

Services

A.352

The [Manager] shall as far as possible keep the [Sportsperson] fully informed on a regular basis as regards any negotiations with any third party and agrees that the [Manager] shall not be entitled to conclude any agreement or sign any document or other record or conclude any financial, business or other arrangement on behalf of the [Sportsperson] without their prior consent and authority of the [Sportsperson] by email and/or text message and/or verbally in person and/or by mobile phone.

A.353

The [Manager] agrees and undertakes that:

1.1   The [Sportsperson] shall be entitled upon request at the [Managers] cost to be provided with copies of all email exchanges in negotiations, draft documents, budgets, contracts, licences, stored software, data and information, copyright and intellectual property clearance and payment records, information relating to any application for a trade mark and/or other rights registration in any format, any lists and databases, photographs, artwork, sound recordings, films, videos, invoices and receipts, sales revenue, deductions, commission and/or other expenses, financial records and accounting statements, bank statements, marketing and publicity reports and/or any other material in the possession or under the control of the [Manager] directly and/or indirectly relating to the [Sportsperson] in any country.

1.2   The [Manager] shall retain and keep in a secure and safe manner all the material set out in 1.1 until [date].

1.3   The [Manager] shall not destroy, deliberately damage or shred any such material in 1.1 without the prior written consent and authorisation of the [Sportsperson].

A.354

The [Manager] agrees that he/she shall not be entitled to any payment and/or commission in respect of any work which have been complete and/or has been booked and/or arranged and/or agreed by the [Sportsperson] prior to [date] whether that work is performed during the Term of this Agreement or not. A brief summary of the excluded work and/or agreements is listed in Appendix A.

A.355

1.1   The [Manager] shall keep full, accurate and separate financial, business and accounting records both in paper form and on computer software showing the Gross Receipts, the Manager's Commission, the Authorised Expenses, the Net Receipts and [Name] Fees and any other sums received and/or paid out under this agreement. Together with all original contracts, licences, letter agreements, and other documents, receipts, invoices, statements and databases.

1.2   The [Manager] agrees that he/she shall not destroy any such material during the Term of this Agreement which may be needed for tax purposes and/or to verify the sums paid and due to [Name] by the authorised professional advisors of [Name].

1.3   No charges or administration costs shall be made by the [Manager] for inspection of, auditing and/or making copies of such material by [Name] and/or any authorised representative.

1.4 The [Manager] shall have the right to required that a confidentiality agreement be concluded with the authorised representative prior to access in respect of information, data and accounts which may be disclosed relating to his/her other clients.

A.356

The [Manager] agrees to pay the [Sportspersons'] Fees on the last day of each calendar month in the first [two] years and thereafter on a quarterly basis during the Term of this Agreement. Any sums still outstanding which are received after the termination and/or expiry of this agreement by the [Manager] shall be accounted for and paid to the [Sportsperson] within [seven] days of receipt by the [Manager.

A.357

1.1 By [date] and [date] in each year the [Manager] agrees to provide the [Sportsperson] with a detailed written report containing a full breakdown of the Gross Receipts, the Authorised Expenses, the Manager's Commission, the Net Receipts and the fees and payments due to the [Sportsperson]. The [Manager] shall also report to the [Sportsperson] a full list of all other travel, hospitality, accommodation, clothes, gadgets and /or other benefits and/or other costs and expenses and other sums paid f to the [Manager] and/or the [Sportsperson] relating to the services and/or work of the [Sportsperson].

1.2 The [Manager] agrees and acknowledges that he/she shall not be entitled to any sums received from the exploitation of any gesture, slogan, trade marks, logos, music, lyrics, films, sound recordings, podcasts, online internet accounts and/or any other intellectual property rights and/or material in any medium which were in existence prior to [date] which are owned and/or controlled by the [Sportsperson]. Any such sums shall be paid directly to the [Sportsperson] and not to the [Manager].

A.358

1.1 The [Manager] agrees that the [Sportsperson] shall be entitled to arrange for an audit once in each financial year from [date] to [date] to inspect and take copies of the [Managers] and any associated companies or businesses' financial and accounting records, contracts, licences, software, online cloud storage accounts and/or any other relevant material in order to verify the sums due under this agreement.

1.2 In the event that in any audit there is an error, mistake, overpayment and/or omission the parties agree that any such sum shall be paid within [seven] days.

1.3 The [Sportsperson] agrees that he/she pay all his/her own legal and accountancy costs and fees in respect of such audit if no discrepancy is found. The [Manager] agrees to pay all sums due to the [Sportsperson] within [number] days. If the sum due to the [Sportsperson is more than [number/currency] in any one audit then the [Manager] shall ensure the sum is paid immediately together with interest at [number] per cent from the date upon which the sum due should have been paid.

A.359

The [Manager] agrees to assist the [Sportsperson] in general with the financial management of all the [Sportsperson's] Fees and financial affairs generally when requested to do so including tax, value added tax, national insurance, pension, personal, health, dental and medical insurance and contributions. The [Sportsperson] shall seek the benefit of independent specialist advice where appropriate and shall not seek to rely on the [Manager] to arrange and pay for the cost of such matters.

A.360

The [Manager] agrees to open a bank account at [bank] for the specific purpose of depositing and dealing in all monies received from the exploitation of the product of the services of the [Sportsperson]. The account shall be called: [specify name] and the following persons: [specify names] shall be the sole signatory for the deposit, withdrawal and/or transfer of any funds. This arrangement shall not be changed without the prior written consent of the [Sportsperson]. The [Manager] shall not be entitled to use the account to create a charge, lien or in any way affect the claim to the sums by the [Sportsperson].

A.361

The [Agent] shall keep full and accurate books of account, records and contracts showing the Gross Receipts, the [Agent's] Commission and the Net Receipts under this agreement. All sums relating to the [Artiste] shall be kept separate and apart from all other monies received by the [Agent]. The sums received shall be deposited at [bank] within one working day of payment. There shall be two signatories to the account and no sums may be withdrawn for any reason except with the required signature of the [Artiste] and the [Agent]. Both parties shall be entitled to receive statements and other transaction records and documents from the [bank].

A.362

The [Agent] agrees to pay the Net Receipts to the [Artiste] on the last day of each calendar month in each year during the Term of this Agreement and thereafter on a quarterly basis. On the last day of [dates] the [Agent] agrees to provide a detailed report containing the breakdown of all sums received or credited together with all expenses and costs incurred, due and/or paid, the calculation of and the sum received in commission by the [Agent] and the Net Receipts due to the [Artiste].

A.363

The [Author] authorises the [Agent] to collect all sums due to the [Author] in respect of the [Work/Book/Rights] from any source throughout the [Territory/world] from [date] to date] and at any time thereafter relating to any agreement negotiated and concluded by the [Agent] during that period. Provided that the agreement is not terminated by the [Author] prior to [date] due to the default and/or breach of this agreement by the [Agent]. In such event all authority to collect any sums is withdrawn and all payments shall be paid direct to the [Author].

A.364

The [Record Company] shall send to the [Artiste] within [ninety] days after March 31, June 30, September 30 and December 31 in each year a statement showing any royalties which have become due in the preceding quarterly period together with the amount shown to be due. The [Record Company] shall, however, be entitled to deduct from royalty payments any sums which may be demanded by any government in respect of such payments. The [Record Company's] liability to remit to the [Artiste] in [United Kingdom/ other country] any royalty which is due shall not apply to countries where currency restrictions are in force which prevents the sums being transferred to the [Record Company]. The liability of the [Record Company] shall be limited to the amounts actually received by the [Record Company] in the [United Kingdom/other country]. If such currency restrictions in any countries including the United Kingdom should for any reason prevent the remittance of the whole or part of any sums and/or royalty due to the [Artiste]. Then any such royalty not paid shall be held in an account to be nominated by the [Artiste] in the country concerned if legally possible.

A.365

The [Company] shall not be entitled to:

1.1 Withhold any sums due to the [Artiste] for any reason.

1.2 Withhold any sums as a reserve against returns.

1.3 Withhold any sums against existing and/or future liability whether or not legal proceedings have been instituted by a third party.

1.4 Withhold any sums to meet the claim and/or demand for payment to any agent and/or manager who has been and/or is engaged by the [Artiste].

1.5 Withhold any sums due to the delay of the transfer of funds between connected and/or associated companies and/or businesses whether parent, subsidiary or otherwise of the [Company].

A.366

The [Agent] and the [Company] both undertake and agree that all accounts, records, contracts, letters, computer records, software and electronic storage and retrieval systems and any other material in any medium owned and/or controlled by the [Agent] and/or the [Company] relating to the exploitation of [Name/Work/Product/Rights] shall be kept and retained in a secure and safe environment in [country] for no less than [number] years from [date]. That no such material of any nature shall be destroyed and/or erased and/or deleted before [date] in any event.

A.367

1.1 That the [Company/Distributor] agrees and undertakes that it shall follow and adhere to the recommended accounting and financial practices and policies of the [specify institute] in respect of the maintenance, reporting, auditing and accounting for the sums received in respect of this agreement and the supply of reports and the payment of the sums due to [Name] under this agreement.

1.2 That the [Company/Distributor] agrees and undertakes to adhere to all legislation, regulations, guidelines, Codes of Conduct and/or any other matter which affects financial accounting practices, methods and/or verification procedures in [country].

A.368

The [Consultant] may claim a monthly expenses fee from the [Company] of up to [number/currency] without production of any receipts and/or invoices based on a written invoice by the [Consultant].

A.369

The [Consultant] shall be paid a total fee of [number/currency] for completion of the [Work/Project] and shall not be obliged to provide a detailed account of the dates, times and nature of the work that he/she has completed. Provided that the [Work/Project] is completed and carried out in accordance with the agreed work schedule and timeline in Appendix A which is attached.

Sponsorship

A.370

1.1 The [Company] shall at the end of every [three] calendar month period for the duration of the Term of this Agreement and thereafter until all sums have been settled send an accounting statement and business report to [Name]. This report shall include all sums received and/or deducted as commission and/or expenses and/or due to [Name].

1.2 The [Company] agrees that upon request by [Name] it shall provide a copy of any contract, licence, letter agreement, record, document, receipt, invoice, marketing material, labels, software, health and safety assessments, samples, reports and tests and/or any other data, information and/or material which may assist [Name] in understanding the work completed by the [Company] and/or the establishing the validity and accuracy of the information provided in the accounts and the sums due to [Name]. Disclosure shall be as specific and full as known to the [Company] itself and no information and/or data shall be withheld for any reason.

A.371

The [Sponsor] confirms that the [Organisers/Association] shall be entitled to retain all sums received from the exploitation of the [Festival/Event] including ticket and programme sales, advertising, merchandising, sound recordings, DVD, video, television and film and/or podcasts, blogs, archive playback, streaming and/or transmission over the internet and/or by means of any telecommunication system to be received through a computer, mobile, gadget and/or some other device in any manner and/or any other medium and/or format and any associated logos, images, graphics, music, lyrics, promotional material, products and/or service.

A.372

The [Promoter] undertakes that it and its sub-agents and/or sub-distributors shall keep full and accurate books of account, records, contracts, software, data, information and other material showing all sums received from the [Company] and how it has been spent in respect of the [Promoter's] Budget. The [Company] accepts that when all the budget has been spent and the [Promoter] has completed its reports to the [Company] as to the outcome. Provided that the [Company] is satisfied and agrees all copies of such material may be destroyed.

A.373

The [Promoter] agrees that the [Organisers/Association] shall be entitled to retain all copyright and intellectual property rights and sums received from the commercial and non-commercial exploitation of the [Event/Online Project] and any associated activities, rights, material, revenue and payments received including but not limited to entry charges, sales and/or receipts from any official programme and/or fundraising, advertising, sponsorship, merchandising, films, videos, sound recordings, podcasts, blogs and/or the exploitation in any form on radio, television, the internet and/or any telecommunication system and reception by mobile phones, computers, gadgets and/or other devices; DVDs, CDs, discs and/or any associated image, name, slogan, character, trade mark, logo, music and/or other means of adaptation whether in existence now or created in the future. The [Promoter] agrees and undertakes that it shall not be entitled to any sums of any nature at any time from the [Organisers/Association] and/or to register any rights and/or claim. The [Promoter] agrees and undertakes that it shall only be entitled to the fees for its services in clause [–].

A.374

The parties agree to disclose to each other all sums received in the form of payment, benefits, expenses or goods for the sponsorship, promotion, endorsement of any person, company, goods or services at any time in any form. All parties shall however be entitled to retain whatever they have received and/or are due.

A.375

In the event that the number of tickets sold and/or the attendance of the public at the [Sports Event/Music Festival] do not reach the figures which the parties predicted prior to this agreement and/or the event is cancelled due to circumstances beyond the reasonable control of the [Association]. The [Sponsor] agrees that it shall not be entitled to a reduction of the [Sponsorship Fees] due to the [Association] and shall still be obliged to pay all such sums in full.

A.376

The [Association/Company] shall provide details of the public attendance figures and admission tickets of the [Event] to the [Sponsor] within [twenty-eight] days of the [Event]. Where the figures are [fifty] per cent lower than predicted in clause [–] then the [Sponsor] shall not be obliged to pay the final payment under Clause [–] due to the [Association/Company].

A.377

The [Company] undertakes to the [Sponsor] that it shall comply with the following procedures in respect of the [Sponsorship Payment] by the [Sponsor] for the [Event/Festival/Film]:

1.1   That the [Company] shall open a new bank account for the purpose of holding the [Sponsorship Payment] to which only the following persons shall be designated signatories: [specify names].

1.2   That the [Sponsorship Payment] shall only be spent and allocated in accordance with the agreed [Budget] which is attached in Schedule A.

1.3   That no part of the [Sponsorship Payment] shall be used to pay any administration costs and/or reduce any debts and/or liability of

97

the [Company] in respect of any other matter and no funds shall be transferred outside [country].

1.4 That by [date] the [Company] shall provide to the [Sponsor] a full breakdown of all sums paid from the new bank account together with copies of the bank statements and supporting invoices and/or receipts in respect of the payments.

A.378

The [Sponsor] shall not be entitled to any accounts, press reports, admission details and/or any other data, records and/or marketing and/or any other material in any medium and/or format in respect of the [Event] from [Name/Association]. The [Sponsor] shall be obliged to use its own resources to analyse, assess, and/or gather marketing, ratings, admission and/or other details which would enable the [Sponsor] to reach a conclusion as to the value and extent of the advertising, television, press and media exposure.

A.379

The [Sponsor] shall not be entitled to copies of and/or access to any documents and any other material which are not already available to the public at any time including but not limited to the draft and audited accounts, financial records, projected forecasts and budgets, data, sales figures, losses, expenses, advertising and marketing costs, donations, personal data and payment records.

A.380

The [Club] shall as far as reasonably possible provide the [Sponsor] with details of the estimated number of people who took part in the [Event] together with details of any marketing, local and national press and media coverage whether on television, radio and/or over the internet through websites, podcasts, personal blogs and/or newsfeeds.

University, Charity and Educational

A.381

1.1 The [Company] shall ensure that comprehensive and professional accounts are created and recorded in each [six] month] period from 1 January to 30 June and from 1 July to 31 December. That within [thirty] days after each of those dates the accounts shall be supplied to the [Institute/Charity] and any sum due shall be paid which is over [ten] pounds sterling. If it is less, then that sum shall be carried forward to the next accounting date unless specifically requested by the [Institute/Charity].

1.2 The [Institute/Charity] shall be entitled to appoint a representative from the management, board and/or legal and/or financial advisors to examine the accounting records in any medium of the [Company] in respect of the exploitation of the [Work/Material/Project]. Any such inspection shall be at the [Institute's/ Charity's] sole cost and shall be subject to written notice to the [Company] and shall occur no more than twice in any year. Where an error is established the [Company] shall be obliged to pay the interest on the sum from the date it should have been paid at [number] per cent.

A.382

The [Licensee] agrees and undertakes that:

1.1 It shall provide the [Institute/Charity] with thorough and accurate financial reports and accounts audited by an accredited professional firm of accountants once in each calendar year during the Term of this Agreement and thereafter at the end of each [three/six] month period until all sums are accounts for, received and verified.

1.2 It shall keep comprehensive, clear and accurate financial, accounting and business records, receipts, invoices, contracts, letter agreements, client databases, sub-licensee, sub-agent and/or sub-distributor agreements, reports and accounts and/or other data, software, discs, online internet storage accounts and any other method of storing financial records, statements and/or payments in respect of all matters in respect of the sums received and/or paid by the [Licensee] and/or its parent company and/or subsidiaries and/or any associated companies and any sub-agent, sub-licensee, distributor or joint venture partners.

1.3 That all such material in 1.1 and 1.2 shall be preserved and kept secure by the [Licensee] for a minimum of [six] years after the expiry or termination of this agreement or in the event there is a dispute between the parties for such longer period as may be necessary until it is resolved. In any event any such material shall not be destroyed without prior written notice to the [Institute/Charity] of the [Licensee's] intention to do so and the opportunity for the [Institute/Charity] to collect and retain the material.

A.383

1.1 The [Distributor] undertakes and agrees during the Term of this Agreement to keep and provide to the [Licensor] detailed accounts and records in respect of all exploitation of the [Work/Service/Product].

1.2 The [Distributor] shall provide a detailed written report containing a full breakdown and a complete statement of accounts to the [Licensor] at the end of each [three/six/twelve] calendar month period which shall set out all sums received and/or credited, and any sums paid out and/or material distributed. The [Distributor] shall pay the [Licensor] all sums that may be due at the same time in [currency] by [direct debit/other method of payment] at the [Distributors] cost and expense. Any sums still outstanding which are not received by the [Distributor until after the expiry and/or termination of the agreement] shall be paid to the [Licensor] within [seven/thirty/sixty] days of receipt.

1.3 Where requested by the [Licensor] to do so, the [Distributor] shall provide copies of all and/or any contracts, licences, letter agreements, and other documents, receipts, invoices, databases, bank statements, computer related records, samples of the [Work/Service/Product], and any other the material that the [Licensor] may require to verify the accounts, financial records, licences granted to third parties and the sums claimed as commission, or expenses and sums due to the [Licensor].

1.4 The [Distributor] agrees that it shall not destroy any of the material relating to the [Work/Service/Product] in paragraph 1.1 to 1.3 above without the prior written consent of the [Licensor].

1.5 The [Distributor] agrees that all sums relating to the [Work/Service/Product] shall be kept separate and apart from all other monies received by the [Distributor].

A.384

1.1 The [Institute/Charity] undertakes that it and its sub-agents, and sub-licensees shall keep full and accurate books of account, records and contracts showing the [Gross Receipts/sums received] and the calculation of the [Licensor's] Royalties.

1.2 The [Institute/Charity] agrees to account to the [Licensor] and pay the [Licensor's] Royalties by [date] in each year during the Term of this Agreement and thereafter within [number] months of receipt of payment until all sums due and/or owing are accounted for to the [Licensor].

1.3 The [Institute/Charity] may withhold from amounts otherwise due reasonable reserves against anticipated returns. No monies paid to the [Institute/Charity] and thereafter refunded or credited shall be included in the Gross Receipts or if included the amount shall be deducted from subsequent Gross Receipts. No payments shall be due for anything which is lost, damaged, stolen and/or in respect of any sums due to the [Institute/Charity] and/or the [Licensor] where the sums are not actually received from a third party.

A.385
The [Institute/Charity] shall not be obliged to provide any accounts, financial information, costs and/or budget details to the [Company] at any time. Nor shall the [Company] be entitled to any control over and/or right of approval in respect of any matter relating to any sums to be spent and/or received in respect of the [Project] by the [Institute/Charity]. The [Company] shall not have any right of approval over whether a third party is to be accepted to participate in the cost of the [Project] and/or to provide sponsorship and/or some other contribution at any time.

A.386
The [Distributor] acknowledges and agrees that [Name] shall have the right to be provided with a full and frank disclosure regarding the exploitation of the [Work/Product/Material] by the Distributor. The [Distributor] shall ensure that a written report is sent to [Name] by email at the end of each month from [date]. Details shall include the nature of all agreements concluded with a third party in respect of the [Work/Product/Material] and where an agreement has been signed then a copy shall be supplied. As well as full details of any sums received from third parties and the date of payment and currency conversion costs if any incurred by the [Distributor].

ACT OF GOD

General Business and Commercial

A.387
In the event that this agreement cannot be performed and/or its obligations fulfilled for any reason beyond the reasonable control of either party to this agreement. Then any such failure to perform and/or default in respect of any obligations required under this agreement by either party due to that reason shall be deemed not to be a breach of this agreement. The reasons may include but are not limited to: war, fire, lockdowns imposed by a government, national and/or local industrial action by third parties, blockades, floods, national power failures; plaques and/or a national epidemic and/or pandemic and/or an Act of God.

A.388
For the purpose of this agreement, references to 'Act of God' shall include all uncontrollable natural forces and natural disasters whether flood, avalanche, storms, fire, drought, tsunami, cliff falls, earthquakes and/or any other unforeseeable environmental and/or climate incidents on land, sea, air and/or underground which affect the operation of the [Company]

and prevent the agreement being fulfilled until the cause has abated and/ or the damage caused has been repaired and/or is replaced. It shall not however include equipment failure caused by the negligence and/or riots, marches, acts of vandalism, acts of terrorism, war, industrial action and any acts and/or omissions by any director, employee and/or agent and/or any other third party.

A.389
This agreement shall not be considered binding on either party in the event that an Act of God shall mean that the terms of the agreement cannot be properly fulfilled and carried out whether in whole or part. Both parties agree that in such event they shall as far as possible reach an amicable settlement to resolve the matter. Each party shall bear its own losses and costs and all the terms of the agreement shall end immediately except for payment relating to work which has already been fulfilled or concluded and transfer of ownership of material which shall only be concluded subject to receipt of payment.

A.390
The term 'Act of God' shall be defined as those acts or circumstances which could not reasonably have been predicted or guarded against which are beyond the control of the parties. Examples include but are not limited to: lightning, floods, extreme weather conditions, defects in equipment, accidents, terrorism, war, violent outbursts, nationwide power failures.

The following types of acts or omissions are not applicable:

1.1 negligent and/or malicious and/or fraudulent acts and/or omissions by employees, consultants and/or sub-contractors and/or other third parties engaged to carry out work.

1.2 industrial action, strikes, walkouts and/or any other local and/or national form of protest relating to working conditions.

1.3 acts of vandalism, sabotage, damage caused by trespassers and/or visitors.

A.391
Neither party shall be responsible to the other party in circumstances where the obligations under this agreement cannot be completed due to circumstances outside the foreseeable reasonable control of the [Assignor] and/or the [Assignee]. In the event that this agreement is not completed by [date] then it will terminate with immediate effect and any payments made by the [Assignee] shall be refunded and all material and rights supplied by the [Assignor] shall be returned to the [Assignor]. There shall be no transfer and/or assignment of ownership from the [Assignor] to the [Assignee].

A.392

Where the [Website/App] is unable to function consistently and/or is interrupted and/or suffers a technical fault and/or some other unforeseen default and/or the supply of electricity, the internet service and/or some other key component is not available for any period. Then the [Advertiser/ Sponsor] shall not be entitled to reclaim any sum and/or decline to pay any sum which is due under this agreement. Provided that the problem does not continue for more than [number] days and the [Advertiser/Sponsor] is offered other dates and/or bookings as a substitute for those which have been missed.

A.393

The [Designer] acknowledges that the [Company] shall not be obliged to set up and/or exploit and/or use the [Website/app/Channel] in the event of an Act of God which significantly and materially effects the supplies, operation and/or services of the [Company] and/or any distributor, bank or joint venture partner associated with it.

A.394

Any party which is unable in whole and/or part to carry out its obligations under this agreement shall promptly give written notice to that effect to the other party stating in detail the circumstances and the estimated time it is believed will be needed to remedy the situation.

A.395

There shall be no obligation to fulfil the terms of this agreement in the event that any of the following unforeseen circumstances shall occur in respect of the [Company], its suppliers, distributors and packagers:

1.1   A war is declared and/or a state of national emergency and/or the national energy supplies are not functioning for more than [three] [weeks/months] in [country].

1.2   The [Website/App/Channel] is not functioning due to technical problems, viruses, hackers or spam for more than [four] months.

1.3   Floods, hurricanes, storms, tsunami, earthquakes, landslides and/or other extreme weather conditions occur in [country].

1.4   The [Company] is suspended and/or barred from the [Stock Market/ other].

1.5   There is a major product recall of its [Products] and/or a criminal investigation and/or coroner's inquest relating to the content and/ or some other aspect of the [Product] related to health and safety reasons.

The agreement shall either be suspended indefinitely until the conditions improve and/or the problems cease and/or shall be terminated and a settlement reached between the parties to resolve the matter.

A.396
Where the [Institute/Charity] is unable to fulfil the terms and conditions of all and/or any part of this agreement due to circumstances beyond its reasonable control which were not reasonably foreseeable and/or which are due to an Act of God and/or some other force majeure including but not limited to: lightning, floods, hurricanes, extreme weather conditions, defects in equipment, damage and/or accidents due to vandalism, acts of terrorism, war, lockdowns, epidemics, pandemics, national power failures and/or an interruption of the supply of electricity, water, gas, heating and/or blockades and/or riots which affect deliveries of supplies and/or industrial action and/or closure of any third party supplier associated with the [Institute/Charity]. Then the agreement shall be suspended until such time as it can be fulfilled by the [Institute/Charity] provided that it shall be for no more than a period of [one] year. Thereafter either party shall be entitled to serve notice to terminate the agreement and the parties shall then be obliged to negotiate a settlement to resolve any outstanding matters.

A.397
Both parties agree that the following acts, failures, defects and matters are specifically excluded and are not an Act of God:

1.1 Defects in any equipment provided by either party.

1.2 A major recall of its products and/or services for health and safety reasons, failure to comply with legislation and/or any other reason.

1.3 The technical failure and/or interruption of the the [Website/App] and/or any failure to deliver and/or to receive payment whether caused by hackers, spam, viruses and/or computer software and/or national power failure.

1.4 The default of the [Company] due to financial difficulties and its inability to pay its creditors.

1.5 Strikes, lockdowns, industrial action, riots, marches, protests, and all other civil unrest.

1.6 Vandalism, robberies, damage to property, deliberate actions by trespassers and/or visitors and/or negligent acts, omissions and errors by employees, consultants, sub-contractors, agents, licensees, directors or other third parties engaged who for any reason carry out work and/or provide services.

A.398
Where the [Event/Programme] is cancelled by the [Institute/Charity] due to circumstances which are beyond its reasonable control and could not reasonably have been foreseen. Then the [Sponsor] agrees that it shall not withdraw its funding, but shall agree to the [Event/Festival] being rescheduled as soon as possible. Where the [Event/Programme] cannot be rescheduled, then the [Institute/Charity] shall not be obliged to return the [Sponsorship Fees] paid to the date of cancellation. Provided that the [Institute/Charity] arranges a substitute online event which can be attended virtually online over the internet. The [Sponsor] shall not obliged to pay any further sums that may be due under the agreement. Subject to completion of the virtual substitute event the [Sponsor] shall not have any further rights and the agreement shall be terminated. The [Association/Charity] shall then be entitled to enter into a new sponsorship agreement with a third party for another [Event/Programme] which may be in the same format and/or have the same contributors.

A.399
The [Sponsor] and the [Company] agree that the following matters shall constitute grounds for a claim of force majeure by either party where it has a direct impact on the provision of their services and/or fulfilment of the terms of this agreement in respect of the [Film/Event].

1.1 Interruption and/or suspension of national and/or local supplies and/or the failure to work due to a defect including electricity, gas, water, sewage, air conditioning, computer hardware and/or software and/or bank transactions to process ticket sales and/or payments.

1.2 A national and/or local situation including war, threat of invasion, attacks, terrorism, strike, industrial action, blockades, protests, marches, threats of criminal action which would pose a serious threat, explosions, riot, suspension of public transport, a public announcement by the government that there is a state of crisis and/or a severe health risk to the public and/or any lockdown, epidemic, pandemic and/or closing of borders.

1.3 Major defects and/or health and safety problems with any building, equipment, stage and/or any major product recall of the [Products/Services] of the [Sponsor] and/or [Company] and/or any third party key suppliers.

1.4 Political, financial, and/or personnel problems at the [Sponsor/Company] which would have a severe and detrimental effect on the manufacture, production, investment in promotions, marketing and/or sales.

1.5 Extreme weather including lightning, floods, hurricanes, heavy snow, strong winds, tsunami, drought, landslides and earthquakes.

Where a valid assertion of force majeure is made by either and/or both parties which prevents the terms of this agreement being fulfilled in any significant manner. Both parties agree that the defaulting party who is relying on an assertion of force majeure shall be allowed a period of [three] months to remedy the situation and/or to allow the situation to change. In the event that the agreement cannot be fulfilled then the parties agree to enter into negotiations to reach an amicable settlement in respect of the matter. In any event neither party shall be obliged to pay any further sums to the other which may fall due under this agreement as soon as a reliance on force majeure is made by either party.

A.400
Where the [Licensee] is unable to fulfil any of the terms of this agreement due to force majeure which is beyond its reasonable control and/or for any other reason and this continues for a period of [number] months. Then the [Licensor] shall have the right to terminate the agreement immediately by notice in writing and all rights granted to the [Licensee] shall revert to the [Licensor]. The [Licensee] shall be obliged to return all master material provided under this agreement and to account for and pay any sums due under clauses [–].

A.401
Where any situation arises which relates to this agreement which prevents the main terms being fulfilled due to circumstances beyond the control of either party. Then as soon as that situation becomes clear and/or either party has received notice to that effect from the other party. Then either party shall have the right to terminate the agreement without any further liability and/or payments to the other party. Where a party has been paid for work and/or services which they have not fulfilled then the sums paid must be returned to the other party. No interest shall be due however.

A.402
Where the [Licensee] is unable to fulfil and/or perform any and/or all of [this agreement/clause numbers [–] for [number] [days/months] due to circumstances beyond the [Licensee's] reasonable control which are due to force majeure. Then the [Licensee] shall be obliged to notify the [Licensor] of the nature of the force majeure and the terms which the [Licensee] is unable to perform and/or fulfil. At the same time the [Licensee] must provide an estimated date by which the matter is expected to be remedied. In any event upon receipt of any such notification from the [Licensee] the [Licensor] shall have the right to terminate the agreement by notice is writing. It shall be entirely at the [Licensor's] discretion as to whether the [Licensee] is permitted the opportunity to remedy the situation. In the event

that the agreement is terminated by the [Licensor] then the termination provisions in clause [–] shall apply.

A.403

The [Licensor] and the [Licensee] agree that the following circumstances shall be accepted as grounds for force majeure. Provided that the force majeure occurs in the country in which the head office of the [Licensee] is situated namely [specify] and/or in which the manufacture and/or production of the [Product/Services] take place namely [specify location]. Force majeure shall include war, threat of invasion, attacks, terrorism, strike, blockades, explosions, riot, fire, industrial action, floods, hurricanes, interruption and/or suspension of national but not local electricity, gas, and water supplies; a declaration of a state of national crisis and the suspension of any of the major services upon which the [Licensee] relies whether airlines, shipping, postal service, freight and/or other transport.

A.404

The [Licensor] and the [Licensee] agree that the following circumstances shall not be deemed and/or accepted as grounds for force majeure:

1.1 Snow, strong winds.

1.2 Defects in any equipment, material and/or packaging.

1.3 Technical failure of the [Website/App/Platform] of the [Licensee].

1.4 Suspension and/or exclusion of the [Licensee] from the [Stock Market/Institute/other trading zone].

1.5 Computer hardware and software failures and/or defects.

1.6 Malicious, deliberate, negligent acts, omissions and errors by employees, consultants, sub-contractors, agents, directors and/or other third parties engaged to carry out work and/or to provide services to and/or by the [Licensee].

1.7 Protests, marches, arson, and/or criminal acts.

1.8 Malicious, deliberate, negligent acts, omissions and errors by trespassers and/or visitors.

A.405

Both parties agree that where one party to this agreement is unable and/or unwilling to fulfil its terms due to circumstances which could not have been predicted at the time of the original signature of the agreement. That the party who wishes to default may terminate the agreement with immediate effect provided that it pays the sum of [currency/number] to the other party as compensation in addition to any other sums that may be due as a consequence of termination.

A.406

The parties agree that the following circumstances shall constitute force majeure under this agreement:

1.1 A local protest, riot, fire and/or explosion in the vicinity of the manufacturer who produces the [Product/other item] for the [Distributor].

1.2 A political uprising, declaration of war, and/or an assassination of a major political figure either in that [country] and/or a neighbouring country.

1.3 A police and/or military and/or government lockdown of an area and/or the whole of a [country] which restricts movement of the public and/or transport and/or forces closure of the business.

1.4 Delays and cancellation of aeroplanes, ships and/or trains due to extreme weather conditions, rising water and floods, high temperatures and drought, extreme wind, falling objects, tremors, earthquakes, volcanoes, tsunamis, obstruction of roads, power failures and/or lightning.

1.5 The above list is not intended to be exhaustive and any circumstance where there is violence, fear, distress and/or the threat of loss of life and/or a severe reduction in services may constitute a relevant factor and be deemed a situation covered by force majeure.

A.407

Neither party shall be entitled to rely on a force majeure circumstance which relates to a third party. Where a third party manufacturer and/or distributor is effected for more than [specify duration of period]. Then the [Licensee] shall be obliged to find an effective alternative who can take over the work at the [Licensees'] cost. Failure to do so with a period of [number/months] from the first date of the force majeure shall be deemed a breach of this agreement.

A.408

Both parties agree that where it is clear that this agreement cannot be performed and/or carried out in the terms stated due the same circumstances which affects both parties. That the parties may either agree to delay the start of the agreement and/or cancel the arrangement. Provided that all sums paid by one party to the other prior to the date of cancellation [are refunded in full/shall not be returned].

A.409
Both parties agree and accept that in the event that either party should seek to rely upon any reason or circumstances which they submit constitutes force majeure and provides notice to that effect to the other non-defaulting party. That the non-defaulting party shall have the absolute discretion to refuse to accept the delay and/or non-performance and as a direct result serve notice to the defaulting party that the agreement is terminated with immediate effect. Provided that in such circumstances the non-defaulting party shall not be entitled to seek any refund and/or repayment of any advance payment from the defaulting party.

A.410
Both parties agree that where a circumstance arises which is due to the actions, omissions, delays, error, omission, default, negligence and/or otherwise of a third party and/or which arises due to weather, air, sea and/or land conditions and/or changes which impedes or delays the performance of this agreement within the dates specified in clause [–]. That, whether or not the circumstances constitute force majeure, the parties agree to resolve the matter by discussions between the parties to as far as possible extend the agreement. Where any matter cannot be resolved then the parties agree to appoint a mutually acceptable person to endeavour to assist the parties to reach an amicable resolution which avoids litigation. The cost of such person shall be paid for [equally by both parties/by the defaulting party].

A.411
In the event that the world market in [specify market/product/service/other subject] should fall in value dramatically in the next [specify duration of period] due to circumstances beyond the control of the [Company] whether due to an Act of God and/or some other reason beyond the control of the [Company] which could not reasonably have been predicted and anticipated. Then the [Company] shall be able to terminate the contract with [Name] with immediate effect by written notice provided that the [Company] is willing to undertake to pay [number/currency] in full within [number] [days/weeks/months] and [specify other conditions].

A.412
If in the first year of sales of [Product/Service/Game] it is clear that there is no real demand in any one or more of the licensed countries and/or there are adverse conditions due to extreme weather, failure of the economy, war, food and/or energy shortages, political unrest and/or rule by an unelected armed force and/or other organisation. Then the [Company] may cease to sell in that country, suspend the contract for up to [specify duration] and/or terminate the entire contract on one or more of those grounds. Provided that the [Company] shall permit the [Licensor] to retain all the advance paid

and revert all the rights granted to the [Licensor] and ownership of all the master material and stock that has been created and/or developed shall be transferred on terms to be agreed between the parties.

A.413

In the event that the [Institute/Charity] decides in its absolute discretion that there are circumstances which amount to force majeure and/or an Act of God which restrict and/or prevent the fulfilment of the agreement and/or that the budget and/or the criteria as to the value of the [Project] have changed to such an extent that the [Project] is no longer financially viable and/or the key personnel are no longer available. Then the [Institute/Charity] shall have the right to terminate the [Project] at any time by notice in writing to the [Company]. All rights granted by the [Institute/Charity] to the [Company] shall revert to the [Institute/Charity], and the [Institute/Charity] shall only be obliged to pay such sums as are due to the date of termination.

A.414

Where for any reason the [Project/Event] is not produced and/or completed before [date] by the [Company] in [country] for any reason due to an Act of God and/or other force majeure. Then the [Licensor] shall have the right to choose to either agree to an extension of the licence period and/or to serve notice of the termination of the agreement. In the event that the agreement is terminated then the [Company] shall be obliged to repay to the [Licensor] all sums relating to the agreed budget which have not already been expended and/or committed for the [Project]. The [Company] shall still be entitled to be paid the agreed fixed fee despite the fact the [Project] was not completed.

ADAPTATION

General Business and Commercial

A.415

The [Company] shall without limitation be entitled to edit, adapt, alter, vary, change, translate, develop, add to and/or delete from the [Work/Product/Content] and all the text, images, films, sound recordings, logos, graphics, music, slogans and any other material in any format together with all packaging, advertising and marketing material which may be supplied by [Name]. All copyright, intellectual property and trade mark rights in any such new versions, adaptations, sequels, translations, and/or associated merchandising shall belong to [specify owner of new material and rights].

5

A.416

1.1 [Name] has not provided any authority to the [Company] and the [Company] agrees and undertakes that it shall not be entitled to adapt, edit, amend, add to, delete from, change, and/or alter the [Work/Artwork/Product] and/or to combine any part of the [Work/Artwork/Product] with any other material of any nature.

1.2 The [Company] must on each occasion make a written request for the prior written approval and consent of [Name] before any work and/or changes are carried out. The failure by the [Company] to fulfil the terms of this clause shall be a serious breach of this agreement. [Name] shall not be obliged to consent to any request that may be made. Where [Name] agrees to provide written consent then this may be subject to further terms and conditions that may be imposed including additional payments and/or the condition that there be a new agreement where there is a different work, product and/or format of any nature which the [Company] wishes to be exploit.

A.417

The [Company/Distributor] agrees and undertakes that it shall not develop, adapt, revise, edit, delete from and/or add to, translate and/or otherwise change the title, layout, content, format, text, images, graphics, credits, copyright notices, trade marks, logos, moral rights assertions and/or any part of the [Work] at any time without the prior written approval in each case of the [Author]. The [Company/Distributor] agrees and undertakes not to license and/or authorise any third party to change the [Work] and/or any material associated with it including the cover, index, packaging and marketing without the prior written consent of the [Author].

A.418

The [Company/Distributor] agrees and undertakes that it does not have any right of first refusal and/or any option and/or any other rights over the [Work] and/or any part in respect of any adaptation and/or sequel and/or any right to develop, reproduce and/or exploit any material in any medium and/or format which is a new updated version and/or similar and/or based upon the same concept, characters, format, layout and/or title.

A.419

The [Company] shall be entitled to edit and adapt the [Work/Artwork/Film] and all the text and images, for the purpose of developing a format which is suitable to be downloaded and stored on a [mobile phone/gadget/computer]. The [Company] shall be able to reduce the size of the trade marks, logos and graphics, but not their location nor their colour and/or shape. All copyright, intellectual property and trade marks rights in any such new versions and/or adaptations, sequels, translations, and/ or associated merchandising shall be assigned to and belong to the [Licensor]. The [Company] agrees that it shall not hold and/or control any rights in any such new material and shall execute all such documents as may be requested by the [Licensor] to ensure the assignment of all such rights to the [Licensor].

A.420

The [Licensee] shall be entitled to edit, delete from and add to the [Sound Recordings/Audio File/Music] licensed by the [Company] under this agreement. Provided that the [Licensee] shall provide a complete copy of the final version of the proposed [Work/Product] derived from the [Sound Recordings/Audio File/Music] for the written approval of the [Company] prior to any commercial and/or non-commercial distribution to any third party. Where the final version is rejected by the [Company] for any reason. Then the [Licensee] shall be obliged to incorporate the proposed changes requested by the [Company] at the [Licensee's] sole cost. Where the parties are unable and/or unwilling to reach agreement then the [Licensee] and/or the [Company] shall be entitled to terminate this agreement by notice in writing provided that the party who serves notice of termination agrees to return all sums they have received under the agreement back to the other party.

A.421

The [Institute/Charity] shall not be entitled to adapt, develop and/or alter the credit, slogan, name, logo, image and/or trade mark of the [Sponsor/ Company] in respect of any material, packaging, advertising and/or marketing which is created, reproduced, supplied, distributed, displayed and/or posted on any product, service, website, app, platform and/or elsewhere for any reason for the purposes of this agreement.

A.422

The [Author] accepts and agrees that the [Distributor] and/or any sub-licensee may need to adapt the title, images, text, credits, acknowledgements, index and the cover for the purpose of marketing the [Work/Book/E Book/Audio File/other] outside [country]. Wherever possible the [Distributor] and/or any sub-licensee shall consult with the [Author] in order to seek their views and advice so that integrity of the [Work] is maintained. The [Distributor] and/ or sub-licensee shall not be entitled to engage a third party to re-write the [Work] and any adaptation must be as far as possible a strict translation of the original [Work]. Any rights in any development and/or adaptation shall be assigned by the [Distributor] and/or sub-licensee to the [Author]. The [Distributor] shall be responsible for the cost of any expenses that may be incurred to ensure the assignment of all such rights in all material in any format to the [Author].

A.423

The [Creator] agrees that the [Company] may be edit, adapt, add to and/or delete from the prototype software and/or the [Work] for the [App] provided that the [Company] accepts that this does not entitle the [Company] to seek to claim any joint ownership and/or copyright, design, patent, trade mark, image and or other rights of any nature in any medium at any time in the software and/or the [Work] and/or any part.

A.424

The [Author] has not authorised the [Company] to make any changes, deletions from and/or to add to the [Work/Manuscript/Article] whether in the form of a new headline, title, images, preface, footnotes, maps, photographs and/or otherwise. Every part of the finished product shall be written and/or created and/or decided upon by the [Author]. Nor shall any name of any third party except [specify permitted person/material] be present on any part of the finished product.

A.425

Any adaptations and/or new versions must be authorised by the [Licensor] and there is no implied and/or express consent provided to permit any other colour variations, additions and/or deletions and/or any other subsequent products, services and/or material to be produced based on the [Logo/Image] except those specifically authorised in Schedule A which is attached.

A.426

The [Licensor] permits the public to download this free [App] to store on their own personal device and any other gadget they may personally own for use at home but not as a business and/or other free service for any reason. There is no authority granted to edit, adapt, change and/or delete any part of the [App] and to use it in another format and/or medium in whole and/or in part. Nor is there any right granted for any person to supply and/or promote the [App] for use for any unauthorised purpose.

A.427

Where you are granted a licence by the [Licensor] to add the [Logo/Image/Slogan/Trade Mark] to your [Product/Website/Marketing] as part of a joint collaboration and partnership. Any adaptation and/or changes of the [Logo/Image/Slogan/Trade Mark] for any reason which may be made by the [Licensee] and/or a third party must be assigned to the [Licensor]. No commission, request for services, work and/or creation of software and/or electronic material, photographs, films, videos, podcasts and/or otherwise by the [Licensee] and/or a third party in respect of the [Logo/Image/Slogan/Trade Mark] should allow the [Licensee] and/or any third party to seek to claim any copyright and/or intellectual property rights of any nature in any format and/or medium at a later date. It is a condition of the grant of any rights that all adaptations, developments, changes, alterations and variations must be assigned to the [Licensor] by any such third party and the [Licensee].

A.428

The [Consultant] is engaged to create a translation of the [Work/Book/Manuscript] in [language] which shall be delivered to the [Company] in the following form: [specify format in which it is to be delivered]. The Consultant agrees and undertakes that:

1.1 He/she shall transfer all copyright and all intellectual property and//or other rights and translation rights of any nature in the product of the services of the [Consultant] to the [Company]. That he/she undertakes to conclude a comprehensive and detailed assignment of all rights in the adaptation and translation of the [Work/Book/Manuscript] for a fee of [number/currency] which shall be organised and drafted by the [Company].

1.2 That where the translation differs from the original text due to adaptation and changes requested by the [Author] of the [Work] and/or the [Company] due to cultural, religious, interpretation and/or other issues. Whether or not the [Consultant] is the originator he/she agrees not to make any claim to be the author of those changes, variations and/or adaptations. Further that where necessary the [Consultant] shall assign all rights including copyright and any other intellectual property rights to the [Company] so that absolutely none are held by the [Consultant].

1.3 That the [Consultant] shall not at any time hold himself/herself as the author, originator and/or copyright owner and/or assert any moral rights to be identified. That the [Consultant] accepts that he/she shall not be entitled to any copyright notice at any time and only the words specified as follows: Translated by [Consultant]may appear but there is no obligation to add such a credit.

1.4 The [Consultant] agrees that at later date the [Company] shall be entitled to engage and/or use any other third party that it should wish to choose at its sole discretion for any additions, changes, translations and/or alterations. That there is no obligation to use the [Consultant].

1.5 The [Company] shall be entitled at any time to add another credit to another consultant who assists with the translation and/or any other aspect of the adaptation.

1.6 The [Consultant] shall not be entitled to any additional fee, royalty and/or other payment where the translation is used by the [Company] in any other format and/or medium at any time.

1.7   The [Consultant] shall not seek to register any name, word, title, image and/or other material directly and/or indirectly associated with the [Work] and/or the translation and/or any parts in any part of the world.

ADVERTISING

Film, Television and Video

A.429

The [Assignee] shall be entitled to use and permit the use of the [DVDs/Videos/CDs] of the [Film/Series/Sound Recordings] for trade exhibitions, in-store demonstrations, conferences and festivals for the purpose of advertisement, promotions and publicity.

A.430

The [Assignee] shall be entitled to include short extracts of the [Film/Series] of less than [specify minutes of duration] in total of the same section in images, text, sound or vision or both in all media for the purpose of advertisement, promotion and publicity including but not limited to radio and/or television programmes, DVDs, podcasts, banner advertisements, pop-ups, websites, apps, newsfeeds and/or other electronic formats over the internet and/or through any telecommunication system for access via a computer, mobile, gadget and/or any other device related gadgets and/or as part of trailer in a cinema and/or outdoor advertising as posters and/or moveable images.

A.431

The [Licensee] agrees to provide copies and/or exact samples of any publicity, promotional, advertising, labels and/or packaging material in respect of the [DVD/Discs/Electronic Download Format] of the [Film/Sound Recordings] at the [Licensee's] cost upon request by the [Licensor] at any time.

A.432

The [Licensee] shall not advertise the availability for sale of the [Units] in any format in the [Territory/world] earlier than [date].

A.433

The [Company] shall not be under any obligation to use the [Text/Images] and/or exploit it in any format at any time and the failure of the [Company] to do shall not give rise to any claim by the [Writer] for loss of publicity and/or reputation and/or loss of opportunity to enhance his/her reputation.

A.434

The [Licensee] shall not use the name, trade mark and/or slogan of the [Distributor] for any purpose in connection with the distribution, advertising and/or promotion of the [Film/Video/Series] without the prior written consent of the [Distributor].

A.435

The [Licensor] shall from time to time promptly after receipt of the [Licensee's] written request send to the [Licensee] a copy of any press and social media reviews and/or advertising material with respect to the [Film/Video/Series]. This shall be limited to the material that the [Licensor] may have available and/or be willing to supply and may only be used by the [Licensee] in connection with the exploitation of the [DVDs/Discs/Electronic Download Format] under this agreement. The [Licensee] shall pay the [Licensor] for the cost of the reproduction and/or delivery of all such material in advance upon receipt of an invoice.

A.436

The [Licensee] may design, create and manufacture solely at its own expense advertising and promotional material with respect to the [Videos/DVDs/Discs] for use in connection with the rights granted under this agreement. The [Licensee] agrees to adhere to all contractual obligations, moral rights and legal obligations of the [Licensor] of which the [Licensee] shall have received notice. The [Licensee] shall make available to the [Licensor] copies all such original material manufactured by the [Licensee] upon request at no charge to the [Licensor] except for the cost of postage, packaging and insurance.

A.437

The [Licensee] shall have sole and absolute discretion to make decisions regarding the production, manufacture, distribution, supply, advertising, marketing and other exploitation of all [Videos/DVDs/Discs] of the [Film/Series] and/or any associated packaging. The [Company] agrees that it shall rely on the judgment of the [Licensee] and its sub-distributors in regard to any matter affecting the production manufacture, distribution and/or marketing including the quantity to be released. The [Licensee] shall have the right for the purpose of increasing the sales, rental and/or exposure of the [Videos/DVDs/Discs] to permit the same short extract of less than [two] minutes in sound, vision, images and/or text of the [Film/Series] to be used on other DVDs, discs, and/or banner advertisements over the internet and/or in pop-ups, and/or on any podcast, website, app and/or blog and/or in any other format over the internet and/or through any telecommunication system to a mobile, computer, gadget, watch and/or other device and/or any terrestrial, cable and/or satellite television and/

or radio channel and/or on any trailer in a cinema and/or closed circuit television system and/or on an outdoor moving screen used for promotional purposes in any location.

A.438
The [Licensor] shall provide the [Licensee] with a detailed list of all contractual, moral and legal requirements that must be adhered to in the final version to be produced in any format and/or in any advertising, marketing and/or packaging material. This list shall include credits for the actors and all other relevant personnel, copyright notices, moral rights, legal disclaimers, trade marks, logos, images and slogans. The [Licensee] agrees and undertakes to comply with the list which have been notified. The [Licensee] shall also only use the summary biographical details and/or images of the [Artists] and/or other personnel and/or contributors the [Licensee] on any website and/or platform provided they are approved by the [Licensor].

A.439
The [Distributor] agrees to be bound by any restrictions, prohibitions, conditions and/or other requirements in respect of any legislation and/or laws, codes of conduct and/or policies relating to standards, and/or guidelines, competitions, gambling, betting, children, social media, advertising, sponsorship, product placement, affiliations, health and safety regulations, labels and compliance, product liability and/or other any other matter which may affect the design, production, sales, marketing and/or promotion of the [Unit/Product] which is an adaptation of the [Film/Series].

A.440
The [Licensee] shall be entitled to promote the [Film/Video] in the form of [DVDs/Discs] by banner advertisements and promotions on the internet, in newspapers and magazines, by text to mobile phones, recorded advertisements on the radio and television, by competitions and offers through arrangements with reputable food companies and/or supermarkets. Provided that no costs incurred are attributed to the [Licensor] and none take place before [date] or after [date].

A.441
The [Licensee] shall not be entitled to use and/or promote, market, exploit and/or authorise and/or permit the [Film/Series/Sound Recordings] and/or any parts and/or the [DVD/Disc/Electronic Download Format] to be used and/or connected with and/or association with any product, game, service, person and/or otherwise which supplies, sells, markets and/or promotes [specify subject] at any time. Any failure to adhere to this requirement shall be a breach of this agreement by the [Licensee].

A.442

For the purpose of the [Licensee] exploiting the rights granted under this agreement and/or to promote the [Licensee's] business the [Licensee] shall be entitled to:

1.1 Disseminate, reproduce, print and publish the name, likeness and biography of the artistes, performers, directors, producers, editors, writers, composers, musicians, choreographer and any other persons and/or company and/or other enterprise who are credited as connected with the development, production, editing and distribution of the [Film] for the sole purpose of the advertisement, marketing and promotion the [Film]. Such arrangement is subject to the crucial term that the [Licensee] strictly adheres to all conditions, restrictions and requirements notified in writing by the [Licensor] to the [Licensee] at any time relating to any such persons and/or other third parties.

1.2 Advertise, market and promote the [Film] which shall include the sound track in conjunction with the [Film] but not separately. The [Licensee] and any sub-licensee, sub-agent and/or other authorised person, company and/or third party shall have the sole discretion as to the manner and method to be employed in the publicity, advertising, marketing and promotion of the [Film] and the amount to be expended and the choice of advertising agencies, consultants, directors and associated material.

1.3 Produce and distribute promotional short trailers for the [Film] which shall include the soundtrack which shall be approximately [number] [seconds/minutes] in length and shall not use in total extracts of more than [number] minutes in duration of the [Film]. The [Licensee] shall also be entitled to use and/or arrange for the exhibition, display and/or otherwise of the trailer in order to promote and/or advertise the [Film] and/or for broadcast, transmission and/or distribution on television, radio, theatres, conferences and/or on any website, app and/or channel over the internet and/or by means of any telecommunication system to any computer, gadget, device and/or mobile in any programme and/or as part of a review and/or in association with an interview of any person who has featured in the [Film]. Provided that at all times the intended purpose is to promote and advertise the [Film] whether for criticism, review and/or promotional purposes.

1.4 Use any trailers supplied by the [Licensor] but the [Licensee] shall not be under any obligation to do so.

1.5 Create such material as the [Licensee] shall decide at its sole discretion to advertise, promote and market the {Film]. The [Licensor] shall not be entitled to any prior approval of the content of any such material.

However the [Licensee] undertakes and agrees that nothing shall be created and/or supplied and/or distributed by the [Licensee] which is offensive and/or derogatory to the [Film] and/or any persons that appeared and/or contributed to the making of the [Film] and/or the [Author]. o

A.443
The [Licensee] shall provide the [Licensor] at the [Licensee's] sole cost with a report listing all the advertising, promotional and/or marketing material designed, created and/or distributed by the [Licensee]. The [Licensee] shall also supply sample copies of each version for retention by the [Licensor].

A.444
In the event that there is any significant error, omission and/or other matter which needs to be remedied in any advertising, marketing and/or promotional material. The [Licensee] agrees and undertakes to withdraw, amend, change and/or reissue any such material at its sole cost.

A.445
This agreement shall not permit or allow the [Licensee] to license, arrange and/or otherwise enter into any commitment in respect of any form of endorsement, sponsorship, product placement, cross promotion and/or collaborative partnership and/or association with any political campaign and/or activist group and/or with any with any other third party in respect of the [Film] and/or parts in any format whether a charity, educational institute and/or for a commercial enterprise.

A.446
The parties agree that all the press and social media statements, interviews, strategies, marketing, advertising and promotion of the [Film] and/or parts and/or any other related content shall be the sole responsibility of the [Company]. Any requests and/or other related matter which shall arise shall be referred to: [specify title/name]. Failure to adhere to this clause shall be considered by both parties as a significant breach of this agreement. All advisors, financiers and other persons involved in the [Film] shall agree to this term as part of their terms of engagement and confirm their acceptance in writing.

A.447
The [Licensee] may use prior to the broadcast and/or transmission of the [Film] use the names, images and profiles of the actors, performers and others persons credited as contributors to the [Film] in any free and/or paid for advertising and/or promotional material. Provided that such use by

119

the [Licensee] shall be made in such a manner as not to constitute either an implied and/or a direct endorsement of any product, services and/or campaign and/or business of any kind of a third party.

A.448

The [Licensor] shall make available to the [Licensee] without any extra charge any copies of any promotional and marketing material including trailers and stills that may be available which shall be retained by the [Licensee] for the duration of the agreement. In the event that trailers for any of the [Films] shall not be available. Then the [Licensee] may transmit and/or broadcast short sequences of not more than [two] minutes in duration from each of the [Films] for the purpose of programme announcements and promotional purposes as trailers. The [Licensee] shall be liable for the cost of any damage caused to any of the master copies of the [Films] for any reason.

A.449

The [Television Company] shall be entitled to broadcast, transmit and/or supply short extracts of the [Programme] and to authorise others to do so whether on its own channel [specify channel name/reference] and/or on any website, app, newsfeed, online account and/or podcast on the internet and/or by means of any telecommunication service to any mobile and/or other device. The extracts shall not be for more than [number] [seconds] in total of the material of the [Programme] which shall not be accumulative. Any such use to promote, advertise and trail the [Programme] shall not be placed where the surrounding material is obscene, derogatory, offensive and/or defamatory and/or degrading. A marketing report shall be supplied to the [Licensor] detailing the date, frequency, type and length of any such use of extracts of the [Programme] when so requested by the [Licensor] provided that it is required no more than [once] in any [six] month period.

A.450

The [Licensee] agrees that no third party shall be entitled to sponsor the [Film] and/or be included in any advertisements and/or promotional film extracts, videos, podcasts, images and/or sound recordings. The [Licensee] agrees and undertakes that it shall not add any products, services, trade marks, service marks, logos, slogans, images, jingles and/or any other material of such third parties to any trailer and/or front and/or end credits and/or any other part of the [Film] and/or any adaptation without the prior written consent of the [Licensor] except [specify permitted third parties/products/services].

A.451

The [Licensee] agrees not to arrange and/or commit to any sponsorship, advertisements, product placement and/or endorsement of products, services, music, slogans, sounds, noises, logos, trade marks, images and/ or text of a third party before or after or in any part of the [Film] without prior notification to and consent of the [Licensor].

A.452
The [Licensee] agrees and undertakes that it shall not use the [Film] and/ or any parts for the purpose of advertisement, sponsorship, endorsement, promotion, and/or marketing of any other product, service, person, company, business, charity and/or other third party except with the prior written approval of the [Licensor] in each case. The [Licensor] shall not be obliged to provide consent to any such use and the [Licensor] shall be entitled to conclude a separate agreement and payment terms with the [Licensee] in each case.

A.453
There shall be no limit as to the nature and extent of the marketing, promotion and advertising of the [Film] by the [Distributor] provided that it is intended to increase ratings and/or revenue; does not involve granting a licence to a third party and is not a misrepresentation of the [Film] and/or its content. Provided that where the [Licensor] requests the [Distributor] to withdraw and/or not use a particular method that the [Distributor] shall comply with all such requests within [number/hours/days].

A.454
The [Company] may market and promote the [Film] for Channel [specify name/reference] only by the use of the authorised and approved promotional advert supplied by the [Licensor]. The [Company] may not use any part of the [Film] in any other programme of any nature in any medium. The [Company] shall not be entitled to authorise any third party to use any title, character, still, name, logo, words, images, slogan or theme.

A.455
The [Company] shall be entitled to market and promote the [Programme] using its name, logo, music, slogan and content in any form of collaboration and/or partnerships that it may seek to use and by nay method including competitions on websites and/or such as mobile telephones, scratch cards, supermarket product tie ins and competitions, advertisements, paid for and free articles and features, indoor and outdoor posters and promotions, merchandising, whether on radio, television, the internet, in print and/ or in some other medium and/or format in any part of the world. Provided that no third party is granted any sub-licence to exploit the rights and the sole and primary purpose is to raise the ratings and viewing figures of the [Programme] by the [Company]. In addition where any sums are generated which result in payments to the [Company] by any such third parties, that

all such sums shall be equally shared between the Company] and the [Licensor]. All payments shall reported to and made to the [Licensor] at the end of each [three] calendar month period at any time.

General Business and Commercial

A.456
The [Assignor] acknowledges that the [Assignee] shall have the sole discretion as to the manner and method to be used in marketing, promoting and advertising the [Product/Service/Work] and any adaptation and/or development. That the [Assignor] shall not have any rights to be consulted and/or any rights of approval and/or any editorial control at any time.

A.457

1.1 The [Distributor] shall endeavour to keep the [Company] regularly updated in respect of the marketing, advertising and exploitation of the [Units] in each of the markets in which the [Units] is made available and/or sold.

1.2 The [Distributor] shall offer the [Company] the opportunity at the [Distributors] cost to attend publicity, promotional and trade events, exhibitions and fairs in [specify countries].

1.3 The [Distributor] shall provide details of and where available copies and samples of all brochures, flyers, advertisements and other marketing material which are made available to the trade and/or general public in respect of the [Units].

A.458
The [Assignor] agrees that from [date] it shall not have any rights and/or interest in the advertising, promotion, marketing and/or exploitation of the [Work] of any nature provided that the Assignment Fee is paid in full and the name, image, logo and trade mark of the [Assignor] does not appear on any copies of the [Work] in any format in any media.

A.459
Your appearance in the [Exhibition/Show/Competition] does not and/or shall not permit you to wear, hold, display, discuss and/or promote any brand, garment, campaign, products, services and/or other matter for the purpose of advertising or promotion which is not scripted and/or authorised by the [Company] from [date] to [date] while filming is taking place for the pre-recorded [Programme]. This condition shall apply whether you have and/or will receive money in payment and/or some other benefit and/or discount and/or free services and/or products for you and/or family member.

A.460

No reference is to be made to the terms and conditions of this agreement in any advertising, publicity, marketing and/or promotional material of any nature including any blog, podcast, paid advertisement and/or article without the express agreement of all the parties.

A.461

Subject to prior consultation [Name] agrees that the [Company] shall be entitled to use his/her name, profile and/or biographical summary details, a specially commissioned photograph and/or image and/or signature in the advertising, marketing and exploitation of the [specify product/service/other]. Provided that the [Company] agrees and undertakes that any such material shall not be used for any product endorsement and/or to promote and/or market any other [product/film/services] and/or sub-licensed to a third party. [Name] shall be provided at the [Company's] cost with a sample of each item of any nature which has any reference to [Name] created pursuant to this agreement prior to any use or exploitation of such item. [Name] shall therefore be provided with an opportunity to comment and make recommendations before it is marketed and/or distributed. The [Company] agrees to incorporate all reasonable changes requested within [number] days of receipt by [Name].

A.462

It is a condition that no logos and/or images other than [specify Name/Brand] in respect of [specify type of Product] may be displayed at this [Event] whilst filming of the [Programme] is in progress by the [Company].

A.463

It is agreed that no changes shall be made to the layout, design, colour, size, shape and/or otherwise of the range of marketing formats of the [Logo/Name/Image] provided by the [Licensor] to the [Licensee]. That all proposed samples shall be first submitted to the [Licensor] prior to production and/or distribution to any third party. That all requests and changes by the [Licensor] shall be adhered to and complied with by the [Licensee]. That the [Licensee] shall ensure strict quality control standards in respect of reproduction of the [Logo/Name/Image].

A.464

[Name] and the [Company] agree that the [Company] may use the [Photographs/Films/Sound Recordings] which were commissioned by the [Company] and taken at [location] of [Name] on [date] for the sole purpose of [specify purpose]. Where the [Company] seeks to use the material for any other reason and/or to grant a licence to a third party. Then the prior consent of [Name] shall be required and an additional fee to [Name] must be negotiated and agreed. If consent is refused by [Name] then the material cannot be used for the unauthorised purpose.

A.465

[Name] agrees that there are no limitations on how the material commissioned and created by the [Company] of [Name] whether images, videos, sound recordings, and/or films which are created and developed during the filming of the [Programme]. May be used, sub-licensed, adapted, distributed and/or marketed. Provided that no such use of any nature shall at any time expose [Name] to ridicule, embarrassment and/or impugn their reputation and/or expose them to criminal and/or civil proceedings in any country. The prior authorisation and consent of [Name] should be sought where there is any doubt as to whether the use is authorised under this agreement.

Internet, Websites and Apps

A.466

1.1 The [Advertiser/Promoter/Sponsor/Name] agrees that all advertisers, promoters, sponsors and other users of the [Website/App/Platform] including the public shall be informed in advance and be subject to conditions of access and use of the [Website/App/Platform] by the [Company].

1.2 The [Advertiser/Promoter/Sponsor/Name] agrees and undertakes that one of the conditions shall be that no product, services and/or any emails, films, sound recordings, graphics and/or any other material shall be permitted on the [Website/App/Platform] which is offensive, defamatory, obscene, derogatory and rude, dangerous, fraudulent, dishonest, misleading, harmful and/or may amount to an allegation of a criminal act and/or an allegation of breach of any legislation and/or is likely to be and/or does in fact pose a threat to children and/or health and safety of any person and/or is otherwise deemed unacceptable at the sole discretion of the [Company].

1.3 In any such circumstances without any notice whatsoever the [Company] shall be entitled to ensure that all such material is removed, deleted and/or otherwise erased from the [Website/App/Platform] and any associated marketing and advertising. The person, company or entity shall not be entitled to any further access to and/or use of the [Website/App/Platform] and shall not be entitled to be refunded any sums paid under this agreement to the [Company]. The [Company] shall not be liable for any direct and/or indirect losses suffered and/or incurred of any nature to any such person, company or entity whose material has been deleted, erased and/or removed and/or is blocked from using this [Website/App/Platform].

A.467

The [Advertiser] shall not be entitled to place material [in the Banner/on the Website] which in the view of the [Company]:

1.1 Contains subliminal advertising in text, words, images, music or any other medium; and/or

1.2 Refers to [service/goods] offered which are not available and/or are not supplied and/or are not of the same standard; and/or

1.3 Contains political, religious or controversial content which is not acceptable; and/or

1.4 Offers services such as gambling, bingo and/or other products and does not make it clear that there is an age requirement and/or does not comply with existing guidelines as to warnings; and/or

1.5 Poses a risk to health and safety and/or

1.6 Causes offence following the response from the users of the [Banner/ Website].

The [Advertiser] agrees that if it is no longer permitted to advertise on the [Banner/Website] the [Company] will refund any outstanding sums paid in advance by the [Advertiser], but that no sums shall be due and/or paid by the [Company] as compensation for removal of material, termination of any agreement, loss of reputation, sales and/or revenue.

A.468

The [Company] agrees that it shall advertise the [Products] of the [Distributor] on the [Name of Website/App/Channel/reference] as follows:

1.1 As the primary and most important advertiser other than [Name] for its own products and services. Such [Products] of the [Distributor] to feature on all the main pages together with the [Distributor's] name, image, trade mark and slogan as set out in Schedule A.

1.2 No other advertiser or associated company shall be entitled to be displayed or featured on any such main pages where there is a direct conflict of interest resulting from being the same type of business, products or services.

1.3 In any associated publicity, advertising, promotional literature, emails, text messages or marketing material by the [Company]. Where appropriate the [Distributor] shall be given due credit and recognition as the main advertiser on the [Website/App/Channel].

1.4 In any flotation of the [Company] on any stock market the [Distributor] shall similarly feature in the documentation and publicity as the main advertiser.

1.5   The [Company] shall have the final editorial decision in respect of the position and size of the [Products] and the [Distributor's] name, image, trade mark and slogan as set out in Schedule A on the [Website/ App/Channel] and any updates and changes that may be necessary. Provided that the [Company] agrees that it shall take account as far as possible of the notified details of the [Products] and other requests of the [Distributor] to ensure that no details are misleading and that they are sufficiently described and the images are accurate.

A.469

The [Company] agrees to display the [Animated Film] of the [Product] on the [Website/Channel] which is supplied by the [Distributor] at the [Distributor's] cost and expense provided that:

1.1   The master material and/or copy which is supplied of the [Animated Film] is of suitable quality and fit for its intended purpose. Where any new format and/or changes and/or deletions are required they shall be entirely at the [Distributor's] cost.

1.2   The [Animated Film] and the [Product] does not contain anything which is offensive, defamatory, dangerous and/or poses a health and safety risk and/or is likely to be in breach of any criminal and/or civil law in any part of the world and/or in breach of any relevant code, guidelines, regulation and/or any other matter.

1.3   The [Distributor] has cleared and/or obtained all rights in the [Animated Film] including any music and/or sound recording and is able to provide supporting documentation if required from any rights holder and/or collecting society.

1.4   The [Distributor] undertakes and agrees that there has been no threat of any legal proceedings and/or any legal action taken within the last [two] years against the [Distributor] in respect of the [Animated Film] which has not been settled.

1.5   The [Distributor] agrees and undertakes to indemnify the [Company] up to [number/currency] in total for any losses, damages, expenses and/or costs which are incurred by the [Company] directly arising from the display, reproduction, transmission and/or distribution of the [Animated Film] on the [Website/Channel] and any claim and/or allegation by any third party of any nature.

1.6   The [Distributor] agrees that it holds product liability insurance for the [Product] as follows: [specify cover and name of insurer].

A.470

The [Distributor] agrees that it shall monitor the [Website/App/Channel] [specify reference] on which it is intended that the [Material/Content] shall be available on a pay per view basis and/or as a downloadable app and/or otherwise. In the event that other films, text, images, music, apps and/or otherwise are being displayed which are not suitable for [specify market/age group]. Then the [Distributor] agrees that the [Author] shall have the right to insist that the [Material/Content] is no longer made available from that [Website/App/Channel]. The parties shall agree which other means may be used to promote, market and exploit the [Material/Content].

A.471
The [Distributor] agrees that it shall only market and promote [Product/Name] in a manner which is compatible with the market at which it is aimed [specify subject/market/language/demographics] for persons age [specify details] and under. No promotions, advertisements, banner links or other marketing shall be placed and/or directed at the following markets [specify excluded zones]. The [Distributor] agrees that it shall try to ensure that no unsuitable images and text are placed near and/or with the [Product/Name] and shall only use any companies and businesses for which the approval of the [Licensor] has been provided and the manner and format to be used agreed in each case.

A.472
There shall be no authority granted for any person and/or company to use the [Podcast Series] for the purpose of transmission, broadcast and/or other form of exploitation whether paid and/or unpaid in any format and/or medium without the prior written consent of [Name].

A.473
The [Company] shall be entitled to reproduce and distribute the main profile image and surname of [specify person] who has an account of this site for the purpose of search engines, archive retrieval systems and/or some other form of promotion of the site.

A.474
The [Distributor] shall have the right to use any extracts of the [Series] for the purpose of marketing the supply and/or transmission and/or streaming of any episode of the [Series] on [Channel]. There shall be no obligation to show the front and/or end credits except the following opening title credits and parties: [specify title and credits to be shown] on each occasion.

Merchandising and Distribution

A.475
The [Agent] agrees that he/she is not permitted to advertise, promote, market and/or exploit the [Character] outside the [Territory/country] unless specifically agreed in advance with the [Licensor] on each occasion.

A.476

The [Licensee] shall be entitled to use the [Licensor's] name, profile, photograph and image, but not signature in the promotion, advertising, packaging and marketing of the [Character]. The [Licensee] shall bear all the costs of the development, production, reproduction and supply of any such material. The [Licensee] agrees to consult with the [Licensor] as to the choice of photograph, text, and any associated graphics, logo, image and/or slogan. The [Licensee] shall provide a draft final copy to the [Licensor] in the colour and layout in which it is proposed to use the material in each case prior to the production and distribution of the promotion, advertising, packaging and marketing of the [Character].

A.477

The [Licensee] agrees that the [Licensor] shall have the right to approve all publicity, promotional and/or advertising material in any format in all media and the label and packaging material in respect of the [Products]. The [Licensee] acknowledges that such approval must be obtained in writing by email prior to manufacture, production and distribution of any such material so that any changes or alterations requested by the [Licensor] must be incorporated.

A.478

The [Licensee] is not entitled to grant, agree to and/or authorise either by consent and/or by omission the right of any third party and/or any director, officer, employee, consultant and/or freight company and/or insurer and/or other associates to create and/or develop and/or use any material of any nature which bears the title, logo, image and/or any associated characters or otherwise of the [Book] and/or the [Product] at any time.

A.479

The [Licensee] shall sell and market the [Product] from the [Website/Platform/Channel] known as [specify name and reference] and not through any other outlet, retailer, wholesaler and/or otherwise without the prior written approval of the [Licensor].

A.480

The [Licensee] shall not have the right to create and/or develop any app and/or any other software, article, text, image, trade mark, logo, game, betting, lottery, quiz, scratch card, competition, radio and/or television programmes and/or advertisements and create any sponsorship partnership, cartoon, banner advertisements, posters, artwork, greetings cards, food and/or drink and/or any other household and/or business products using any part of the [Image/Logo/Material] for which a licence is granted under this agreement. All promotion, marketing and authorised exploitation is limited to the [Licensee's] website, packaging of the [Product], direct marketing by the [Licensee] and all material of any nature that is to be distributed must be submitted to the [Licensor] in advance for approval.

A.481

The [Agent] confirms that the [Advertising Copy] complies with all rules, guidelines, regulations, directives and codes in force which apply to the [Company] at any time including [list requirements/organisations/guidelines] prior to or at the time of use of the Advertisement for [specify how it is to be reproduced and used].

A.482

The [Company] confirms that it shall ensure that the [Advertisement] will conform to all statutes, rules, directives, guidelines, practices and codes of advertising, marketing, product placement and/or sponsorship in relation to the exercise and exploitation by the [Distributor] of the [specify authorised rights] in the [Product].

A.483

'The Company's Products' shall mean the [Products] of the [Company] which are briefly described as follows: [brief title/summary]. A two-dimensional copy of the [Products] is attached to and forms a part of this agreement in Schedule A setting out all intellectual property rights including copyright, trade marks, service marks, logos, designs, designers and/or other creators, slogans, text, title, recordings, scripts, music, photographs, artwork, graphics, computer generated material and all consents, releases, moral rights, contractual obligations obtained, paid for and/or due.

A.484

The [Promoter] confirms that the principle aims of this agreement are to:

1.1   Promote and increase the sales of the [Company's] [Products/Services].

1.2   Raise public awareness of the [Company's] existence throughout the [Territory/country].

1.3   Inform the general public of the [Company's] positive track record within its industry.

1.4   Improve the consumer image of the [Company] throughout the [Territory/country].

1.5   Create a favourable image of the [Company] to the public in general and in particular for the purpose of recruiting potential future employees.

1.6   Increase and improve the [Company's] goodwill and understanding amongst its present customers and increase significantly the number of purchasers of its [Products/Services] in general.

A.485

The [Licensee] agrees that the [Licensor] shall be entitled to approve the appointment of any sub-agent, sub-licensee and/or any other third party in respect of the manufacture, distribution, supply, marketing and advertising and/or other exploitation of the [Units] under this agreement.

A.486

The [Licensor] agrees to attend such meetings, exhibitions and promotional events is may reasonably be required by the [Licensee] subject to sufficient prior notice and the payment of an additional fee on each occasion. The [Licensee] agrees and undertakes to pay the [Licensor] in advance the agreed fee and all costs and expenses which may be necessary which will be incurred by the [Licensor] for any attendance.

A.487

The [Purchaser] agrees that this agreement relates solely to the purchase and sale of the [Garment] for personal use and that the [Designs] and the [Garment] are not to be commercially exploited by the [Purchaser] in any form and/or used to endorse, advertise and/or promote any goods, products and/or services and/or otherwise without the prior written consent of the [Designer] and payment of a licence fee and/or royalties.

A.488

The [Company] agrees that the [Assignee] shall be entitled to commercially exploit the [Commissioned Work] in all media and/or any format at any time in the world and shall be able to organise associated sponsorship, product placement and/or advertising. That the [Company] shall not be entitled to receive any further payment of any nature for any reason in respect of any adaptation and/or development.

A.489

1.1 The [Company] agrees and undertakes that it shall arrange a major launch of the [Product] with a budget of: [specify number/currency]. That it shall arrange social media, radio, television and national press coverage; organise a publicity brochure, and a national advertising campaign of not less than [state duration] in a leading magazine or newspaper. That in addition there will be promotions by means of banner advertising on [the internet, outdoor advertising, paid for promotions on blogs, websites and podcasts. As well as display stands and promotions at national trade exhibitions. The [Company] shall supply a draft plan for the use of the budget which shall be agreed with [Name]. Any changes to the agreed launch plan must be authorised by [Name].

1.2   The [Company] shall regularly update [Name] on the work completed by the [Company] and the dates upon which the [Product] is to be promoted and/or advertised by third parties. The [Company] shall supply a review report of the launch and marketing of the [Product] to [Name] by [date].

1.3   The budget shall be paid for by [Name]. The [Company] shall only be entitled to be paid the fixed fee of [number/currency] for their work. All costs and expenses incurred by the [Company] shall be at their sole cost unless specified as agreed in the budget by [Name].

A.490

The [Supplier] agrees that the [Seller] may engage any persons to endorse and/or advertise the [Product] on the [Seller's] website, app and/or by any other means of promotion. The [Supplier] agrees that such marketing is entirely at the discretion and cost of the [Seller] provided that the persons behave in a professional manner in their public life and do not bring the [Supplier] and/or its products into disrepute and/or detrimentally affect their reputation and goodwill.

A.491

The [Artist] agrees that the [Distributor] shall be entitled to use the [Work/Image] in any manner it thinks fit and in any format and/or medium for the purpose of increasing sales and revenue and marketing including but not limited to postcards, greetings cards, T shirts, wristbands, posters, reproduction on articles and/or collaborations and partnerships with other products and brands, in books, on film, on platforms, podcasts, blogs and/or websites, in the form of licensed software; exhibitions, festivals and/or other events in any location.

A.492

The [Distributor] agrees that the [Product/Unit/Article] is a limited edition and that it is not authorised to make, supply and/or authorise any copies of any nature for any purpose at any time in any form. That the only material which can be used by the [Distributor] are the agreed details: [Name/Logo/Title/Description] set out in Schedule A which may only be used on its website and in the marketing catalogue for the event.

A.493

There are no limitations placed by the [Licensor] as to how the [Licensee] may market and raise awareness of the [Work/Product/Service] provided that:

1.1   It does not damage the reputation of the [Licensor] in anyway.

1.2   It does not seek to associate the [Work/Product/Service] with any other material which is offensive, of poor quality, does not comply with any legal requirements and/or creates an association with any company, charity and/or business which has been in existence for less than [number] and/or any political and/or activist campaign.

1.3 In the event that the [Licensor] notifies the [Licensee] that they do not like any marketing for any reason. That the [Licensee] shall take the objections into account in any future plans.

Publishing

A.494
The [Company] agrees that it shall not incorporate and/or include any advertisement, promotion, sponsorship and/or endorsement by any other third party without the prior consent of the [Author] within the [Work] and/or or on its cover and/or dust jacket and/or on any profile and/or listing for the [Work] on any website and/or platform and/or in any brochure, flyer and/or poster

A.495
The [Author] agrees that the [Agent/Company] shall be entitled to use and authorise the use of his/her name, photograph, image, biographical details, signature and any other material supplied by the [Author] or organised and commissioned by the [Agent/Company] in respect of the advertising, promotion and commercial exploitation of the [Work/Book] subject to:

1.1 The prior written approval of the [Author] of an exact copy of the draft and final proof or sample in each case.

1.2 No use of any material shall be made which would be offensive, and/or derogate from the reputation of the [Author] and/or would offend the [Author's] religion and/or beliefs and/or cause distress to the [Author's] family and/or effect the [Author's] career in a negative way.

1.3 Where an independently appointed [adjudicator/expert] agrees that sub-clause 1.2 has been breached. Then the [Agent/Company] shall pay the [Author] [number/currency] as a fixed agreed form of compensation and damages in full and final settlement of any claim under sub-clause 1.2.

A.496
In the event that the [Satellite Company] or any subsidiary or associated company launches its own magazine for subscribers. Then the [Satellite Company] agrees to provide the [Company] with promotional space in such magazine for the purposes of advertising the [specify products/services] at the [Satellite Company's] cost to the value of [number/currency] at the commercial rates.

A.497
The [Company] agrees that it shall provide a budget of [number/currency] for the advertising, promotion and publicity of the first edition of the [Work/Book] in hardback and paperback] in [country].

A.498
The [Company] agrees that all advertising, publicity, packaging and promotional material shall be provided to the [Presenter] in the exact form in which it is intended that it should be used by the [Company]. That the prior written approval of the [Presenter] shall be required prior to the use of any such advertising, publicity, packaging and promotional material. In the event that the approval of the [Presenter] is refused then such material shall not be used by the [Company].

A.499
The [Company] undertakes that it shall use its best endeavours to advertise, market and promote the [Work/Book/Sound Recordings] and that on all occasions that the agreed credit and copyright notice to the [Author] shall be used.

A.500
Where the [Author] is required to attend any interview, recording, filming and/or event in respect of the advertising, promotion or marketing of the [Work/Book/Audio File] in any form. The [Company] agrees that it shall arrange for and bear the full cost and expense of all first-class accommodation, travel and meals and reimburse any other reasonable expenses incurred by the [Author] arising directly as a result of any such contribution and attendance. On each occasion an advance against the anticipated costs shall be made to the [Author].

A.501
The [Author] shall be available as reasonably required by the [Publisher] for the promotion and advertising of the [Work/Book/Audio File] provided that the [Publisher] pays all the costs and expenses. This shall include [number] appearances and interviews in the period up to [number] months after the date of publication in [country] of [hardback/paperback/other].

A.502
The [Licensor] agrees to arrange one photographic session: [duration/date] with the [Licensee] at the [Licensee's] sole cost for the purpose of photographs to be used in the [periodical] in association with the [Extracts]. Together with one interview [duration/date]. Provided that the [Licensee] agrees and undertakes to assign the copyright and all other rights in the photographs and the interview and any material in any medium including

sound recordings and/or film and/or images which are created and/or produced arising from such sessions to the [Licensor].

A.503

The [Company] shall have the right to use extracts of the [Author's] [Work/Book] in other books and publications up to a limit of [specify number] words without payment to the [Author]. Provide that the extracts are used for the purposes of advertising, promotion and publicity and no payment is received by the [Company]. This shall not apply to use of any such extract on the internet and/or by means of any telecommunication system which shall require the prior written consent of the [Author] in each case.

A.504

The [Company] shall as far as possible send the [Author] regular copies of all publicity, advertising and promotional material for the [Work/Book] including listings on websites, bookshops, catalogues, flyers, posters and/or otherwise. Where the [Author] reports an inaccuracy and/or error then the [Company] agrees that it shall try to make sure that the in accuracy and/or error is not repeated. Further the [Company] agrees to consider all relevant promotional and/or marketing and recommendations by the [Author].

A.505

The [Company] shall advise the [Author] of the advertising and marketing budget for the [Project] and shall fully disclose all intended major expenditure. The [Author] shall be given the opportunity to comment and recommend other factors to be considered. The [Company] shall however make the final decision on the matter.

A.506

The [Distributor] shall provide a short marketing report to the [Author] before [date] listing the release dates, and the different methods of marketing which are proposed. The [Distributor] agrees to consult with the [Author] in each case and to provide a draft copy of each format and/or item upon which the [Author] can comment and make a contribution in respect of all forms of packaging, advertising, marketing and/or promotion including but not limited to catalogues, brochures, flyers, inserts, websites, videos, podcasts, blogs and/or direct marketing.

A.507

The [Author] shall not be obliged to promote, market and/or advertise the [Product/Film/DVD] and/or to attend any launch parties, readings, television and/or radio interviews and programmes and/or make any sound recordings and/

or go to any other event and/or create any additional material. All such matters shall be entirely at the personal discretion of the [Author] and there shall be no contractual requirement to make any contribution of any nature to that effect. Where the [Author] is requested to attend any event and/or create any new material then the terms and conditions of the attendance and/or contribution of the [Author] shall be subject to a separate contract on each occasion.

A.508
The [Publisher] shall be entitled to promote, market and advertise the [Work/Book/Sound Recording] by means of listings of a brief summary of the content on its own and third party websites, printed catalogues, posters, flyers, email attachments and in any other format provided that the primary purpose is to increase prepublication and post publication sales of the [Work/Book/Sound Recording].

A.509
In the event that the [Publisher] wishes to display more than a brief summary of the [Book/Audio File/eBook] on its own and/or any other website, app and/or platform. Then it is agreed that it must not to exceed more than [number pages/words] of the same identical material on all websites, apps and platforms which can be viewed on line by the public prior to purchase of the [Book/Audio File/eBook]. That any other use of the material and/or any additional material must be approved on each occasion with the [Author] and that the [Author] shall have the right to refuse consent.

A.510
The [Author] agrees that the [Publisher] and any distributor, sub-licensee and marketing company shall be authorised to reproduce, supply and distribute all images and films of the [Author] which the [Author] may supply to the [Publisher] and/or which may be commissioned by the [Publisher] during the Term of this Agreement. That if this agreement shall be terminated and/or shall expire that the authority and right to use any such images and films shall cease. The [Author] shall have the rights in the event that the agreement expires to request that the [Publisher] and any distributor, sub-licensee and marketing company supply a complete list of all the master material which they own and/or control relating to the [Author]. That the [Author] shall have the right to request that all master material and/or copies in any format are returned to the [Author] at the [Author's/other party's] cost.

A.511
The [Distributor] agrees and undertakes that it shall not acquire any copyright and/or any other intellectual property rights and/or computer software rights in any format of any nature in any material, text, articles, instructions, designs, artwork, photographs, slogan, logos, trade marks,

music, maps, charts, films, videos, podcasts and/or otherwise which the [Publisher] may supply for any purpose during the course of this agreement. That where in the course of creating marketing, advertising and promotional material the [Distributor] develops any new material of any nature which results in copyright, intellectual property rights and/or any other rights of any nature belonging to the [Distributor]. That the [Distributor] shall transfer any such rights back to the [Publisher] for a nominal fee of [number/currency] for each such transfer and sign any assignment that may be requested.

Services

A.512

The [Company] agrees to appoint the [Promoter] as the sole and exclusive advertising, marketing and promotions agent for the purpose of [specify scope of project] as set out and described in Appendix A throughout the [Territory/world] for the Term of the Agreement in accordance with the terms of this agreement.

A.513

In consideration of the [Fees and Expenses] the [Promoter] agrees to provide its non-exclusive services to the [Company] to act as agent for [specify theme of project] the [Company] and the [Company's Products] throughout the [specify countries] from [date] to [date] in accordance with the conditions set out in this contract.

A.514

The [Company] agrees that the use of the name, photograph, image and/or other material relating to [Name] supplied or created under this agreement shall require his/her specific consent and approval of each and every example to be used in each case for any endorsement, sponsorship, advertising, promotional and/or marketing purposes and/or any other charitable and/or commercial exploitation.

A.515

The [Promoter] agrees and undertakes to endeavour to ensure that as far as reasonably possible that all third parties engaged to produce material by the [Promoter] shall agree to assign the product of their services and work in all media throughout the world to the [Company]. So that neither the [Promoter] nor any third party retain any copyright, intellectual property rights, computer software rights, trade mark, domain names and/or other rights whatsoever.

A.516

The [Agent] agrees to consult with the [Actor] in respect of any artwork, stills, photographs, films, profiles and biographical background material, social media and/or other press releases and statements and any other material in any medium which may be used to advertise, market and promote the [Actor].

A.517
The [Agent] acknowledges that he/she shall be solely responsible for all administration, office and/or other costs and expenses incurred by him/her in respect of his/her services under this agreement including the advertising, promotion and marketing of [Name]. That the [Agent] shall not be able to recoup any such sums from monies due to [Name].

A.518
[Name] agrees that he/she agrees to supply all such consent and authority as may be required by the [Company]:

1.1 To arrange and/or commission, to sub-license and/or exploit images, photographs films and sound recordings of [Name] under this agreement including for broadcast and/or transmission on terrestrial, cable, satellite or digital television, radio, in DVDs, by means of telecommunications systems to mobiles and/or the internet on podcasts, online accounts, websites, apps and/or in electronic download formats and/or audio files, in competitions and/or games, discs and/or to third parties including distributors, newspapers, magazines or periodicals.

1.2 To use, adapt and/or authorise the reproduction and distribution of the professional name of [Name] and their stage name identity logo and slogan, image, caricatures, photographs, films, sound and/or other recordings, signature, profile and short biographical background in connection with the advertisement, publicity, exhibition and commercial exploitation of the [Programme/Series].

1.3 To use all such material specified in 1.1 and 1.2 above in connection with any endorsement, advertisements, promotions and/or corporate advertising of the [Company] and/or any of its products and/or services in any manner.

A.519
The [Company] agrees that [Name] shall be the sole and exclusive personality to feature in connection with and/or to endorse, appear as the main presenter, promote and/or advertise the [Product/Service] throughout the [Territory/country] from [date] to [date].

A.520
[Name] agrees and undertakes that he/she shall not provide his/her services to any third party for the support, endorsement, advertisement and/or promotion of any other product and/or service and/or game and/or lottery and/

or gambling site of any type whether it directly competes with the [Company's] Product or not other than services of a charitable nature throughout the Term of this Agreement without the prior written consent of the [Company]. The current services which [Name] already provides to [specify name of enterprise] as part of their existing career shall be excluded from this clause.

A.521

In consideration of the fees and expenses to be paid by the [Company] to [Name]. [Name] agrees to provide his/her non-exclusive services to the [Company] to endorse, promote, and advertise the [Company's] Product by personal interviews and appearances at events, performances in tours and/or exhibitions, blogs, podcasts, films, paid for articles and images and/or other material and work arranged and agreed between [Name] and the [Company]. This agreement shall start on [date and end on [date]. [Name] agrees and undertakes to assign all rights in all material created and/or commissioned by the [Company] in all media subject to payment of all the sums due under this agreement and/or subsequently agreed. Attached is a copy of the work schedule A agreed between the parties for the first [number] months and the payments listed that shall be due subject to completion of the work by [Name]. All future work shall be subject to the agreement of the payment terms and work proposed between the parties.

A.522

The [Company] acknowledges that [Name] is already committed and has entered into prior agreements for the following: [specify details/parties/dates].

A.523

The [Company] agrees that it shall not be entitled to use, transfer, exploit and/or license any of the material produced and/or created for the purpose of this agreement in which [Name] appears in sound and/or vision and/or by any other reference for any purpose other than the endorsement, promotion and advertising of the [Company's] [Product/Service] during the existence of this agreement. Where the [Company] wishes to use any such material at any time for any purpose not permitted or to license a third party then the prior written consent of [Name] is required and the settlement of a new agreement for each such permission.

A.524

The [Company] agrees that the [Agent] shall be entitled upon request to be provided at the [Company's] cost with a copy of any material in any medium produced under this agreement which it is intended and/or has been released to the public which is in the possession and/or under the control of the [Company] and/or any sub-agents, sub-licensees and/or any other third parties engaged by the [Company] featuring or including any reference to the [Artiste].

A.525

In accordance with the [Work Schedule] [name] agrees to provide the following specific services:

1.1 Presentation and performance in [number] advertisements described as follows [specify details].

1.2 Presentation and performance in a corporate video of no more than [number] minutes in duration and no more than [number] production days filmed in [country].

1.3 Attendance at not less than [number] official functions and promotional events organised by the [Company] in [country].

1.4 [Number] days for photographic sessions, sound recordings, videos, films, podcasts and/or other material.

A.526

The [Company] shall not have the right to use the benefit of the [Presenter's] association and participation in the [Programme] to endorse or promote or advertise any other products, services or programmes sold or exploited by the [Company] without the prior written consent of the [Presenter] and the payment of an additional sum to be agreed in each case.

A.527

The [Company] shall engage the services of [Name] who agrees to be available on the following terms and conditions in consideration of the payment terms set out in clause [–]:

1.1 [Name] shall appear in [number] advertisements to be transmitted on regional and national television in [country] no later than [date].

1.2 The number of recording days shall be [specify details] and include appearances in the studio for filming and recording in sound and vision. Additional days shall be paid at [specify terms and payment rate].

1.3 [Name] shall not be required to perform any words or act in any manner which could be deemed prejudicial to their career or image and/or to appear in conjunction with any material and/or person who could by association damage their career.

1.4 The [Company] shall only be entitled to use and repeat the advertisements within the [first three years] from [date]. Thereafter further additional payments and a new agreement are required for any use.

1.5 The use of the advertisements in any medium outside the authorised Territory shall be subject to the payments set out in Schedule A.

A.528

The [Company] shall not license, reproduce, permit, transfer, sell, supply, distribute and/or exploit any material which is created in the production of the [Advertisement] except the final approved Advertisement. All other material not used shall be destroyed.

A.529

[Name] agrees that his/her name, image and company email shall be exhibited on the [Company] website during the Term of this Agreement. That the [Company] shall have the right to reproduce that image in any marketing and promotional material, on any security card and in internal personnel records for that period. The [Company] shall not have the right to supply any images and/or personal data relating to [Name] to any third party at any time without the prior written consent of [Name] [except for compliance with legislation and/or under a court order].

A.530

Where [Name] has provided services to the [Company] which has resulted in the creation of new material which mentions and/or features [Name] in any format including photographs, films, DVD, blu-ray, apps, books, articles, radio and television programmes and/or interviews. Then the [Company] agrees to supply to [Name] a copy of the material that it uses in the final work at the [Company's] cost if so requested but not a copy of all the original master material that was completed.

A.531

Where a photographer and/or any third party is commissioned by the [Distributor] to work with [Name] as part of his/her service to the [Distributor] to market and/or promote the business. [Name] agrees that he/she shall not have the right to approve that person. [Name] agrees that he/she may decide to terminate the agreement with the [Distributor] and in such event that [Name] shall not be entitled to claim any further sums which may be due after the date of termination.

Sponsorship

A.532

The [Manager] agrees to ensure that the following [credit/copyright notice/ trade mark/logo/image/link] of the [Company] appears on the [item/article] of the [Sportsperson] in any arrangements with a third party and as far as possible in all publicity, advertising, promotional and packaging material as follows: [detailed description/colour/order/location].

A.533

The [Sportsperson] agrees to wear and/or display and/or endorse any item or service including clothing, equipment and/or other products provided by the [Manager] under this agreement where a contract has been concluded with a third party to do so at all exhibitions, sports events, promotional and television appearances, press calls and/or other occasions during the Term of this Agreement. The [Sportsperson] shall not be obliged to do so where in his/her own judgement it would not be appropriate for health and safety reasons, weather conditions, rules of the event and/or otherwise not be suitable and/or in his/her best interests to do so.

A.534

[Name] agrees to provide his/her exclusive services in a professional and competent manner in order to achieve the best he/she is capable of in the [specify sport/project]. [Name] agrees to provide the following services at the events set out below: [List type of appearance and precisely the contribution to be made at each event. Competitions/promotions/appearances/press conferences/exhibitions].

A.535

The [Sponsor] agrees to provide the [Sportsperson] with reasonable notice of all promotional events and other meetings which they are required to attend. It is accepted by the [Sponsor] that no attendance shall be definite if there is less than [one] calendar months' notice or there is a training schedule, competition, medical and/or family matter which is likely to conflicts with the proposed dates.

A.536

The [Sponsor] acknowledges that this agreement does not oblige the [Sportsperson] to make any personal appearances in corporate and/or charity events, in any films and/or in any interviews on television, radio, in any DVD and/or podcast in sound and/or vision at any time in respect of the [Sponsor] and/or its products and/or services. Any additional work shall require a separate fee and agreement to be concluded in each case.

A.537

The [Company] agrees that no other sponsor, logo, image, person, service, product and/or enterprise shall be used to endorse the [Unit/Project] without the prior written consent of the [Licensor] which shall not be unreasonably withheld or delayed.

141

A.538

The [Sponsor] agrees that the [Radio Company] shall be entitled to advertise, promote and endorse any third party products in the [Programme/Series] and/or in conjunction with it whether or not it directly competes with the [Sponsor's] business, products and/or services.

A.539

In consideration of the Sponsorship Fee the [Radio Station] grants to the [Sponsor] the non-exclusive right to sponsor the [Programme/Series] and agrees to promote the [Sponsor's] [Product/Service] in conjunction with it and to have the [Sponsor's] [name/logo/trade mark/jingle] incorporated into the [Programme/Series] as specified in Schedule A [describe how it is to be used/before/after and in any material] throughout the Territory for the duration of the Sponsorship Period.

A.540

The [Sponsor] agrees that the [Radio Company] shall have the right to advertise promote and endorse any third party products and/or services and/or trade marks, logos and/or slogans in the [Programme/Series] and/or in conjunction with it whether it directly competes with the [Sponsor's] business products and/or services or not.

A.541

The [Sponsor] acknowledges that the [Organisers] are entitled to arrange for, license and/or authorise third parties to advertise, sponsor and/or supply equipment, gifts, prizes, products, services, hospitality, catering and/or marketing at the [Festival]. That there are no restrictions imposed by this agreement as to the direct competitors and/or the same type of material.

A.542

The [Sponsor] agrees that the [Radio Station] shall have the sole discretion as to the manner and method to be used concerning:

1.1   The content of the advertising, sponsorship and other material before, after or in the [Programme/Series].

1.2   The title of the [Programme/Series], the presenter, any main regular contributors and the scheduling.

1.3   The marketing, promotion and advertising of the [Programme/Series].

1.4   Any personnel, content, script, guests, music, endorsements, prizes, phone-ins and competitions, merchandising or otherwise.

1.5   Any cross promotion or advertising with respect to any events, exhibitions and/or marketing in any media including products, magazines, newspapers, websites, apps, podcasts and/or otherwise.

A.543

The [Sponsor] agrees to be bound by any sponsorship, advertising or other rules, directives, legislation, regulations, guidelines, standards, practices, codes and licences which apply to the [Company] in respect of the use and transmission of the [Company's] [Products/Services] and any associated trade mark, logo, image, jingle and/or other material in the [Series] and/or any marketing and/or promotional material.

A.544

The [Company] agrees and undertakes that it shall not be entitled to use, exploit and/or promote the title of the [Programme] or any script, artist, music, slogan or any other parts of any nature in conjunction with any products or services of the [Company] under any circumstances. This agreement is not a sub-licence and does not grant any authority for any use of the material in the [Programme] to the [Company].

A.545

The [Association] accepts that the [Sponsor] shall be entitled to promote, advertise, display, publicise and otherwise commercially exploit to its own advantage the [Sponsor's] involvement in the [Event] in respect of its own products, goodwill, merchandise, advertisements, marketing material or otherwise for the duration of the [License Period].

A.546

The [Company] agrees that the [Organisers] have granted to the [Sponsor] the right to veto the advertising at the [Event] and in any tickets, brochures, advertising, equipment, uniforms, flags, banners and marketing material of any third party whose business or products directly compete or conflict with the following products or business of the [Sponsor]: [specify details].

A.547

The [Licensee] will ensure that the use of the [Licensor's Logo/Trade Mark] will not infringe any sponsorship, advertising, promotional, gambling, religious, political, health and safety and/or marketing laws, regulations, codes and practices in force at the time of production of the [Film/Podcast/Event] in [country] which may apply.

A.548

The [Company] agree and undertakes that the [Sponsor] shall be the main and primary sponsor of the [Event/Film] and that shall be made clear at the [Event/Film] and in all radio, film and media coverage; on the [Company's] website and app; in any reports and in all advertising, marketing, packaging and merchandising which is directly and indirectly associated with the [Event/Film].

A.549
The [Sponsor] shall not be entitled to advertise, promote and/or market the [Event/Film] either to promote the [Sponsors'] business and/or in association with any of its products and/or services without the written approval of the [Company] in each case. The [Sponsor] shall supply the [Company] with a sample copy of the material for approval in advance. The [Sponsor] shall be obliged to make such changes and/or alterations as the [Company] may require in order to give approval.

A.550
The [Sponsor] of the [Event/Festival] shall be entitled to market and promote its funding and support provided that it does not mislead anyone as to the extent of its sponsorship and that the images, logos, names, products, performers and any other material of any third party in any medium associated with the [Event/Festival] is not used by the [Sponsor] in anyway.

A.551
The [Agency] shall not be entitled to disclose the value of the funding by any of the [Sponsors] in any marketing and/or advertising relating directly and/or indirectly to the [Programme]. Nor shall the [Agency] have the right to reproduce any logo, trade marks, images, slogans, products and/or any other material associated with the [Sponsor] in any press release, blog, website, app, podcast and/or other content in any medium at any time.

A.552
The [Sponsor] agrees that there is no obligation by the [Company] to ensure that the name, image, logo of the [Sponsor] is listed in all marketing and promotional material distributed and/or supplied by the [Company] and/or in any television, radio, newspaper, magazine, media and digital electronic internet coverage at any time.

University, Charity and Educational

A.553
The [Company] agrees that it shall be solely responsible for all costs and expenses incurred in respect of the advertising, promotion and marketing of the [Work/Service/Product] under this agreement and shall not be able to recoup such sums from those due to the [Institute/Charity] nor shall the [Institute/Charity] be liable for any such costs and expenses.

A.554
The [Company] agrees and undertakes to ensure that the following [credit/copyright notice/trade mark/logo/image] of the [Institute/Charity] shall appear on all products, publicity, advertising, promotional, packaging and other material which is supplied, reproduced, distributed and/or licensed in

respect of the [Project] [detailed description, order and position]. A copy of which is attached in Appendix A.

A.555
The [Company] shall not have the right to use the name, logo and image of the [Institute/Charity] in the [Project/Work/Product] to endorse or promote or advertise any other products, services or work sold, licensed and/or exploited by the [Company] without the prior written consent of the [Institute/Charity] and any such arrangement shall be the subject of a separate contract.

A.556
The [Company] agrees and undertakes to follow and adhere to the legislation, regulations, standards, guidelines, codes and policies which apply to the [Institute/Charity] in respect of the advertising, marketing, promotion, packaging and exploitation of the [Work/Service/Product] and the use of the [Institutes'/Charity's] name, logo, material and premises. The [Company] agrees to provide an exact sample and/or proposed draft of all material for prior written approval by the [Institute/Charity] in each case.

A.557
The parties agree that no document, media statement and/or any other material shall be distributed, displayed on a website and/or supplied to a third party concerning the [Project] unless a draft copy has been circulated for approval by all parties to this agreement.

A.558
The [Licensee] agrees that the [Author] shall be consulted in respect of the content of any marketing and promotional material in printed form, by email in electronic form and on any website and/or app, and/or any other material in any format and/or medium. The [Licensee] shall provide the [Author] with a draft copy and take reasonable account of the requests for any changes by the [Author].

A.559
All final decisions in respect of the marketing and promotion of the [Event/Project] shall be at the discretion of the [Charity/Institute].

AFFILIATES

General Business and Commercial

A.560
'Affiliates' of the [Company] shall mean any legal entity or other business organisation anywhere in the world in which the [Company's] main holding

company [specify name] holds a [twenty-five/fifty/other] per cent or higher equity interest whether directly or indirectly, and whether the interest is shares, debentures or otherwise, voting or non-voting.

A.561

For the avoidance of doubt, the term 'Affiliate' shall have the same meaning as 'Subsidiary' throughout this agreement.

A.562

The term 'Affiliate' shall not mean 'Subsidiary' but shall mean any company, organisation or other body to which the Company is legally connected to or associated with whether directly or not in the family tree to form part of the structure of an international or national corporate organisation or by a duplication of the named directors although not linked in a corporate legal structure.

A.563

The [Affiliate] agrees that it shall have no claim and/or rights over any part of the business and/or interests and/or rights of any nature of the [Company]. That the arrangement is solely an agreement for payments by the [Company] which is contingent on the [Affiliate] creating a link or connection to the [Company] where new clients can be offered and purchase the [Products/Services] of the [Company] through the [Website/App/Platform] known as [specify name/reference]. That payment by the [Company] is only made where a purchase is made by an client and not otherwise.

A.564

The [Company] shall be entitled to cancel and/or terminate the agreement with [Name] that they may be affiliated to the [Company] as a source of customers. In the event that the [Company] cancels and/or terminates the agreement then no additional sums shall be due and/or paid to [Name] for expenses, losses, compensation and/or otherwise except those due prior to the date of cancellation and/or termination.

A.565

The [Affiliate] shall bear all its own costs and expenses which it may incur and ensure that it has suitable insurance cover for third party public liability. At no time shall the [Affiliate] be entitled to claim and/or seek to recover any of its costs of administration of its business from the [Company]. Nor shall the [Affiliate] be entitled to use the name of the [Company] and/or its trade, slogan, jingle , products and/or services except in the specified authorised manner confirmed by the [Company].

A.566

The parties agree that the [Channel/Platform/Website] shall solely be used for the [Project] and that no affiliation and/or marketing programme shall be established with any third party without the express consent of all the parties in advance.

A.567

Any Affiliate which is engaged by the [Company] must follow all the declared codes of practice, guidelines, policies and other instructions of the [Company] including in respect of the reproduction of any [Company] trade mark, slogan, image and/or otherwise and/or any marketing. Any Affiliate must not be involved in any political and/or activist campaign of any nature unless it strictly adheres to the same ethos of the [Company]. The [Company shall have the right to terminate any agreement with any Affiliate at any time without stating a reason with immediate effect upon notification. The [Company] shall pay all sums due to the Affiliate but shall not be obliged to enter into any justification for the termination of the agreement.

AGENCY

Film, Television and Video

A.568

1.1 In consideration of the Advance and the [Licensor's] Royalties the [Licensor] grants to the [Licensee] the sole and exclusive DVD and Non-Theatric Rights in the [Film] including the soundtrack [excluding any parts] throughout the [Territory/country] in [language] for the duration of the Licence Period.

1.2 This licence shall not include the right to sub-license the rights granted to the [Licensee] to any third party.

1.3 The [Licensee] shall be entitled to engage an agent and/or distributor provided that they do not acquire any rights in the [Film] and/or any marketing material.

A.569

The [Licensee] agrees and undertakes that all other rights [and/or technology] not specifically specified in clause [–] are retained by the [Licensor] and are specifically excluded from this agreement whether in existence now and/or created in the future.

A.570

[Name] appoints [Company] to act as his/her exclusive agent to market, distribute and exploit the [Film/Work] in the [rights/formats]: [specify details DVD/Videos/CDs/Discs/Audiotapes/Electronic Download Formats] and in the countries listed in Appendix A from [date] to [date]. No other formats and/or rights are granted to the [Company] and all rights shall revert to [Name] on [date].

A.571

1.1 The [Copyright Owner] appoints the [Consultant] to represent his/her interests and to advise on the best business strategy to license, adapt, develop, market, distribute and/or otherwise exploit the [Film/Work] in respect of the rights, formats and/or characters listed and described in Schedule A which forms part of this agreement in the [Territory/country/world] which shall commence on the start date of: [date] end on the expiry date of: [date] and/or shall earlier end date if the agreement shall be terminated on valid grounds and/or shall be terminated on the grounds of force majeure.

1.2 The [Copyright Owner] shall have the sole and absolute discretion as to whether any agreement is concluded with any third parties at any time.

1.3 The [Consultant] agrees that he/she does not have any authority and/or right to commit to and/or conclude and/or sign any agreement, contract and/or letter which may be legally binding upon the [Copyright Owner].

1.4 The [Consultant] agrees that he/she shall not be entitled to any present and/or future payments, royalties and/or other sums from any agreement concluded by the [Copyright Owner] in respect of the [Film/Work] and/or adaptation and/or any rights formats and/or character. The [Consultant] agrees and accepts that he/she shall only be entitled to the fixed fees set out in clause [–].

A.572

The [Trustees] appoint the [Agent] to seek to negotiate the best agreements as it can to exploit all the [Material/Archive] listed in the attached Schedule A. The [Agent] shall be appointed for a period of [one] year from [date] but shall not have the authority to conclude and sign any agreements on behalf of the [Trustees]. The [Agent] shall not acquire any rights and/or interest in any of the [Material/Archive] and/or seek to enter into any arrangement at any time to benefit from his/her access to the [Material]. The [Agent] shall not supply any copies of the [Material/Archive] to any third party. The [Agent] shall only be entitled to distribute the agreed list of titles of the [Material/Archive] with the express prior approval of the [Trustees].

A.573

The [Agent Company] shall be entitled to store, reproduce, supply and/or distribute copies of the [Images/Artwork] for use in any format including as artwork for book covers, DVDs, CDs, and for use in software for mobile phones, apps, websites, games and any other format and/or medium. Provided that no third party shall be authorised to use and/or adapt any of the [Images/Artwork] without a minimum fee of [number/currency] in each case and the conclusion of a licence agreement a copy of which can be supplied to the [Author/Artist].

A.574

The [Agent] agrees that it does not have sole and exclusive rights and that the [Licensor] may also grant the exact same rights to a third party at any time. That the [Agent] is only authorised to act as the administrator for the [Company] from [date] to [date] and that no transfer of any copyright and/or other intellectual property and/or any other rights of any type whether known now and/or developed at a later date are granted and/or assigned to the [Agent] either now and/or during the course of this agreement. That the [Agent] shall not be able to insist upon any credit and/or copyright notice and/or seek to grant and/or license and/or assign any part of the [Film/Manuscript/Book] to any third party.

A.575

In consideration of the payment of the non-returnable Advance and the [Licensor's] Royalties the [Licensor] grants to the [Licensee] the sole and exclusive [Cable, Satellite, Terrestrial and Digital Electronic Television Rights/DVD and Video Rights/Digital Electronic Archive Playback Right / Non-Theatric Rights] throughout the [Territory/country/world] for the duration of the Licence Period and the right to authorise third parties to exploit and/or exercise such rights.

A.576

The [Licensee] agrees that all other rights are specifically excluded from this agreement and are retained by the [Licensor] including but not limited to: [specify excluded rights/ Merchandising Rights/Publication Rights/Games/ Lottery/Theme Park Rights/other].

A.577

The [Copyright Owner] appoints the [Company] to act and represent the [Copyright Owner] solely in relation to the exploitation of the following rights in the [Synopsis/Manuscript/Film/Series] in the [Territory/country] from the start date of: [date] and to end date of: [date]:

1.1 All forms of television and/or radio in any language including broadcast and/or transmission and/or download and/or playback

149

and/or distribution by means of terrestrial, cable, satellite and/or digital in electronic form over the internet and/or by means of any telecommunication system for reception by computer, mobile and/or some other gadget and/or device.

1.2 All forms of Merchandising Rights and/or Publication Rights in any language directly associated with the [Synopsis/Manuscript/Film/Series].

A.578

1.1 The [Agent] shall not have any right to any sums of any nature from the exploitation of the rights in clause [–] which have not been received by the [Agent] before the end date of: [date].

1.2 The [Agent] shall not be entitled to any sums received from any agreements after the end date of this agreement: [date]. This shall be the case regardless of whether any such agreement was concluded by the [Agent] and signed during the [Agency Period] and/or the sums were due but had not been received.

A.579

The [Agent] agrees and acknowledges that it shall not be entitled to any royalties, payments, commission and/or other sums from any new work by the [Copyright Owner] and/or any option in respect of any sequel of the [Work] and/or any adaptation at any time.

A.580

The [Agent] agrees and acknowledges that it shall not be entitled to register and/or claim the rights to and/or ownership of any title, characters, logos, trade marks, design rights, graphics, computer generated material, music, slogan, format and/or any other rights of any nature in any media at any time.

A.581

The [Distributor] is acting as an authorised agent of [Name] with respect to the [Programme/Film] from [date] to [date]. During that period the [Distributor] may enter into discussions, negotiations and agreements on behalf of [Name] to license, sell supply and/or distribute copies of the [Programme/Film] for all forms of transmission and/or broadcast of television including satellite, cable, terrestrial, free, pay per view, video on demand and in the form of transmissions for play back at a later date and/or downloading and/or streaming and/or viewing in electronic form by means of the internet and/or by means of any telecommunication system on a computer, mobile and/or other gadget and/or device. Together with the right to exploit the [Programme/Film] in the form of viewings at exhibitions, by clubs, schools, on aeroplanes, in cinemas, theatres and/or festivals whether free and/or with an entry charge. The rights are limited to the original version in [specify language] and do not apply any translation and/or sub-titled version and/or any animated version and/or sequel. Nor does the [Distributor[acquire any right to edit, adapt and/or alter the [Programme/Film] and/or to license and/or grant any rights and/or option relating to any of the characters, music, costumes, script, content and/or otherwise.

A.582
The [Agent] may market the [Author] and their [Synopsis/Manuscript/Book/Audio File] and any associated material in which the [Author] owns the rights. Provided that the [Agent] agrees and undertakes that the [Author] shall have the final right to either consent and/or refuse to finalise any agreement proposed by the [Agent]. In addition the [Agent] shall only seek to negotiate with any business and/or enterprise and/or individual which has a sound financial record which can be verified of more than [number] years.

General Business and Commercial

A.583
The [Agent] shall mean the following [Company/individual] whose address is at [address] who is authorised to act on behalf of [Name] in respect of the following areas [list exact subjects] in [country] from [date] to [date].

A.584
The [Agent] shall not be entitled and is not authorised to sign any agreement, consent form, release and/or other document and/or to commit [Name] to any interview and/or booking. The [Agent] is merely permitted to negotiate and agree proposed terms, but the consent required for appearances, signature of any contracts or otherwise must be completed by [Name] in each case.

A.585
The [Agent] shall keep [Name] at the [Company] fully informed on a regular basis as regards any negotiations with any third party and agrees that he/she shall not have the right to conclude any agreement and/or make any commitment and/or supply any consent relating to [specify Project/Material] and/or the [Company] without the prior [verbal/written] consent of [Name].

A.586
The [Agent] agrees and undertakes that he/she does not have the right to negotiate and/or promote in any manner the commercial interests of the [Company] outside the [country] unless specifically agreed in advance on each occasion. Any consent given does not mean that there is a waiver of consent for any subsequent matter.

A.587
It is the intention of both parties that all products of the business services of the [Name] should be dealt with by the [Agent] whether performances, appearances, recordings, endorsements, publishing or otherwise and whether for financial gain or not from [date] to [date].

A.588
[Name] agrees that [Company] shall be his/her exclusive agent for all business work in any media for the Term of the Agreement throughout the Territory. The [Company] agrees to provide its first-class services as far as reasonably possible and attend at such locations, dates and times as agreed in advance with [Name].

A.589
[Name] confirms that he/she shall regularly advise the [Agent] in advance in writing of any dates when he/she shall not be available. That [Name] confirms that he/she is and shall be available [specify details] days a week except [specify details] each month until the end of the contract.

A.590
[Name] shall ensure at all times that he/she keeps the [Company] informed of his landline and mobile telephone number, address, email and online accounts [specify details]. [Name] undertakes to notify any changes as soon as possible.

A.591
In consideration of the payment of [number/currency] by [date] the [Company] grants the [Agent] the sole and exclusive [specify exact detailed rights] and the right to authorise any third party to exercise such rights throughout the [Territory/country/area] from [start date] to [end date].

A.592
The [Company] shall not be entitled to use the name of the [Agent] and/or profile and/or statements made by the [Agent] in any marketing and/or promotional material and/or on any podcast, website, app, platform and/or in any exhibition, conference, products and/or corporate documents without the prior approval of the [Agent] in each case.

A.593
The [Agent] shall be entitled to receive payment in accordance with the agreement in respect of all contracts negotiated by him/her during the Term of the Agreement but which are not actually signed until after the expiry of the agreement.

A.594

The [Agent] shall only be entitled to receive its commission in respect of any sums which are received by the [Agent] and/or the [Copyright Owner] for agreements relating to the exploitation of the rights in clause [–] which are signed and concluded between [start date] and [end date]. The [Agent] shall be entitled to be paid commission on all such agreements even if the payments are received after the [end date]. The [Agent] shall not however be entitled to commission on any period for which an agreement is renewed and/or extended beyond the original term of the agreement.

A.595

The [Agent] agrees that it shall not be entitled to any commission on any advance, royalties, payments, commission and/or other sums from any new work by the [Copyright Owner] whether or not derived from and/or based on the [Work]. Further the [Agent] agrees that it shall not be entitled to any commission on any advance, royalties, payments, commission and/or other sums from any sequel and/or later adaptation of the [Work] and/or part at any time.

A.596

The [Agent] agrees that it shall not be entitled to register and/or claim the rights to and/or ownership of any title, characters, logos, trade marks, domain names, design rights, graphics, computer generated material, typography, music, slogan, map, table, data, software, invention, patent and/or any other rights of any nature in any media at any time. That all rights in the [Work] and any development drafts, prototypes and/or variations, translations, adaptations and/or rights which can be registered with any collecting society shall be held in the name of the [Copyright Owner/other].

A.597

The [Agent] shall not seek to hold the [Author] responsible for any expense, cost and/or other sum which is in excess of [number/currency] which has not been specifically authorised in advance by the [Author].

A.598

The [Agent] agrees that the [Authors'] professional accountancy and legal advisors shall be entitled to have access to and to inspect and make copies of all records, data, agreements, documents, invoices, expenses, costs whether on computer, paper, in a storage device and/or gadget, at a bank and/or other financial institution and/or at one of the residential homes of the staff and/or business and/or a personal laptop and/or other device and/or storage account in order to seek to verify the accuracy of the statements from the [Agent] and the sums due and/or paid.

Internet, Websites and Apps

A.599

The [Agent] shall act for and on behalf of the [Company] in relation to all matters relating to the internet, websites, apps, podcasts and/or any telecommunication system whether accessed or received on computers, television or mobiles or some other gadget in consideration of the sums set out in clause [–]. The [Agent] shall only be on a short term contract of [specify number] months and during that period shall advise and be involved in the setting up of:

1.1 The budget, development, creation, legal protection of and marketing for a website, domain name and app.

1.2 The promotion and establishment of the website and app in [country] through a major advertising campaign including online accounts and podcasts.

1.3 To carry out a comprehensive survey and report on competing companies worldwide which exist or are setting up on the internet and to analyse their operations and marketing.

1.4 To carry out a detailed evaluation of the website and app to examine the benefits and negative factors and its effect on the [Company]. To look at this development in conjunction with the overall strategy of the [Company].

A.600

The [Agent] shall act on behalf of the [Company] on a non-exclusive basis in order to provide reports, updates and recommendations to enhance the [Company's] marketing strategy and development of its websites, apps, online accounts, podcasts and the accompanying registration of domain names; trade marks; search engine listings and brand internet strategy.

A.601

In consideration of the mutual promises and representations made by one party to the other under this agreement including payments agreed to be made by the [Company] to the [Designer]. The [Company] agrees to engage the non-exclusive services of the [Designer] to design, develop, integrate and support the [Company's] [Website/App/Platform] in accordance with the terms of this agreement.

A.602

The [Designer] agrees and undertakes that it shall perform its obligations under this agreement to the best of its skill and ability and shall maintain such high standards as are reasonably expected by the [Company] to create a fully functional [Website/App/Platform] for the [Company's] commercial and marketing purposes on or before the [date] in accordance with the Budget in Appendix A and the agreed outline proposal in Appendix B.

A.603
The [Designer] acknowledges that the [Company] shall be entitled to terminate the agreement at any stage of the development and shall not be obliged to set up, exploit or use the [Website/App/Platform]. That in the event of the termination for any reason the [Designer] shall only be entitled to be paid for the work completed to the date of termination.

A.604
The [Designer] agrees that the [Company] may at any time engage any other third party at its sole discretion to carry out work and/or to deliver services and/or to create new material for the [Website/App/Platform] and/ or any other internet and/or any other telecommunication project for the [Company]. This shall include the right of the [Company] to use any third party to provide support, maintenance and/or any other services at any time.

A.605
The [Designer] agrees that the [Company] may decide at any time not to use the services of the [Designer] and to give notice of the end of the agreement. Provided that the [Company] agrees and undertakes to pay the [Designer] for all work completed up to the end date plus an additional sum of [number/currency]. Such sums to be paid within [number] days of receipt by the [Company] of an invoice from the [Designer].

A.606
All work, expenses, costs and developments shall at all times be subject to the prior written approval of [Name] at the [Company]. The decision of the [Company] in any matter shall be final. The [Company] shall be entitled to make minor amendments to the [Project] as described in Appendix A without additional costs being charged.

A.607
The [Software Company] are not authorised to act as agents for the [Supplier] nor can they authorise the purchase of any material, services and/or market and/or hold themselves out as being entitled to do so for any reason.

A.608
The [Software Company] may as required engage such other persons and companies for the [Project] as may be needed in order to meet the delivery date and cost and content targets set out in Schedule A. The [Software

Company] is acting as agent for the [Supplier] and all terms of engagement shall require that the invoice for payment is sent to [specify name/party].

A.609
The [Company] agrees to promote and market the club known as [specify details] and its [Website/Channel] [specify references] as non-exclusive agents for a period of [number] [months/years] from [date]. The [Company] shall charge a fee of [number/currency] per calendar month and in addition the charges set out in Appendix A for printed flyers, wristbands, telephone marketing, online articles and content display and otherwise up to a maximum of [number/currency] per month.

Merchandising and Distribution

A.610
In consideration of the [Agent's] Commission the [Agent] agrees to provide his/her non-exclusive services to the [Licensor] for the Licence Period throughout the [Territory/country/world] and to fulfil the following role and responsibilities: [specify exact duties/targets/areas of media].

A.611
In consideration of the Net Receipts the [Licensor] agrees to engage the exclusive services of the [Agent] for the Licence Period throughout the Territory and grants to the [Agent] the sole and exclusive right to negotiate agreements on behalf of the [Licensor] for the production, manufacture, supply, distribution, sale, exploitation and marketing of the [Licensed Articles/Products/Services] for the Licence Period throughout the Territory.

A.612
The [Agent] acknowledges and agrees that there is only a non-exclusive right granted in respect of the negotiation of agreements for the associated trade marks and logos which are on the packaging and/or marketing material of the [Licensed Articles/Products/Services].

A.613
The [Agent] agrees that he/she shall not have the right to commit the [Licensor] to any agreement whether in writing or not without the prior written consent of the [Licensor] and that all licence agreements must be in writing and signed by or authorised by the [Licensor].

A.614
The [Agent] shall provide a professional and efficient service during normal working hours to ensure that as far as reasonably possible the [Character] is

commercially exploited and released in the following format [specify details] in [country] by [date].

A.615
The [Agent] shall disclose to the [Licensor] any other business relationship and/or client which may exist and/or be created at any time which conflicts with and/or competes with and/or could be potentially damaging to the interests of the [Licensor]. In the event that as a result of the disclosure the [Licensor] considers that the reputation of the [Licensor] and/or its business is likely to be damaged, harmed and/or suffer losses. Then the [Licensor] shall have the right to serve written notice of the termination of this agreement without further liability to the [Agent].

A.616
The [Agent] agrees that he/she shall be entirely responsible for all costs and expenses which he/she may incur in respect of the provision of his/her services under this agreement.

A.617
The [Agent] agrees and undertakes that he/she shall not have the right to negotiate, conclude, promote and/or market the commercial interests of the [Character] in any form outside the [Territory/country] unless specifically agreed in advance with the [Licensor].

A.618

1.1 The [Agent] agrees that it shall only be entitled to receive sums from contracts which are negotiated, concluded and signed in full during the continuance of the agreement.

1.2 The right to receive commission shall be for the duration of the licence agreements which relates to the exploitation of the rights. This shall mean that the [Agent] is entitled to commission after the expiry of the agreement with the [Agent].

1.3 Where any agreement is not signed until after the agreement with the [Agent] has expired. Then the [Agent] shall not be entitled to any sums despite having developed and prepared the project.

A.619

1.1 The [Agent] agrees that the [Copyright Owner] shall be entitled to terminate the agreement for the services of the [Agent] at any time at the [Copyright Owners'] sole discretion.

1.2 The [Agent] shall only be entitled to receive commission on any sums received to the date of termination. The [Agent] shall not be entitled to receive commission on any sums which accrue but are not paid before the date of termination. The [Agent] shall not be entitled to be paid any commission after the date of termination which has not been received whether or not the agreement was signed before that date of termination.

A.620

The [Agent] shall be obliged to take out an insurance cover and policy for the benefit of [Name] for public liability and/or loss of funds due to [Name] which may be due but not paid by the [Agent] for any reason whether due to management failures, theft, fire, and/or any other reason. So that in the event that [Name] is not paid by the [Agent] then [Name] can make a claim against the insurance policy. The [Agent] shall provide a copy of the policy to [Name] and proof that all premiums have been paid.

A.621

The [Agent] shall not seek to withhold from [Name] any sums which he/she receives from any [Licensee] into an account outside [country]. The [Agent] agrees to advise [Name] of the receipt of the funds and the method and date by which it is intended it shall be transferred to [country] and paid to [Name].

A.622

The [Agent] may appoint sub-agents in other countries to carry out duties and arrangements in respect of the [Work] but the [Agent] shall not be entitled to recoup the cost of any commission, charges, fees and/or other costs from the sums due to the [Company].

A.623

The [Distributor] shall be the [Agent] and not the principal in any negotiations, agreements, consents or contract under this agreement.

A.624

The [Distributor] shall be permitted to appoint sub-agents and/or sub-licensees to carry out all or any of its responsibilities under this contract. The [Distributor] shall forward to the [Company] a copy of any such contract within [one month] of the date of conclusion of a signed agreement.

A.625

Each [Licensee] undertakes that it is not the agent acting on behalf of any undisclosed company or third party whose business or products compete with or conflict with the business interests of the [Licensor].

A.626

The [Supplier] agrees to deliver the [Products] to the [Seller] for sale on the [Seller's] website on a non-exclusive basis from [date] to [date] in consideration of the payments to be made by the [Seller].

A.627
The [Supplier] confirms that it has not and shall not enter into any arrangement which has and/or might conflict with this agreement.

A.628
The [Seller] agrees that the [Products] shall only be sold from [specify website/retailer/other] and not from any other website or premises unless the [Supplier's] prior [verbal/written] approval has been obtained, such approval not to be unreasonably withheld or delayed.

A.629
The [Seller] agrees that no other product or advertisement or service shall be displayed on or featured on the [Seller's] [Website] where there is a direct conflict of interest which would directly compete with any product supplied under this agreement.

A.630
The [Seller] agrees that it shall not be entitled to adapt and/or alter the [Product] including the packaging in any way without the prior consent of the [Supplier].

A.631
The [Seller] agrees that the [Supplier] shall be entitled to supply the [Product] to any third party whether on the internet or otherwise. Provided that where the [Supplier] intends to supply the [Product] to any of the following businesses [specify names]. Then the [Supplier] shall notify the [Seller] of its intentions.

A.632
Both parties agree that this agreement is not intended to restrict, prohibit, prevent and/or effect the supply, distribution, use, endorsement and/or right of either party to act on behalf of another in respect of any other similar, competing and/or associated products, services, content and/or other material.

A.633
There is no authority provided to any agent, distributor, supplier and/or otherwise to alter, add to, change, vary, adapt and/or develop any part of the [Product/Article] and/or packaging as submitted by the [Company] in its final form prior to production.

A.634
There is no form of agency, partnership, joint venture and/or other legal arrangement created by the agreement of the [Organisers] to include the [Products/Images/Project] in its [Festival/Event/Shop/Website]. The

[Organisers] reserve the right at any time to withdraw their agreement and to remove the [Company] and the [Products/Images/Project] from the [Festival/Event/Shop/Website]. In such circumstances the [Company] agree that the [Organisers] will not have to provide a reason and shall not be liable for any resulting losses, damages and/or other consequences. The [Company] agrees that it accepts this risk and potential cost.

Publishing

A.635

In consideration of the [Agent's] Commission the [Agent] agrees to provide his/her non-exclusive services to the [Author] as a literary agent for the [Manuscript/all the written and other work of the [Author]] from [date] to [date] in [country/Territory/world] in all languages and shall fulfil the following services: [specify details of duties].

A.636

In consideration of the Net Receipts the [Author] agrees to engage the exclusive services of the [Agent] as a literary agent for the [Manuscript/future works of the [Author]] for the following period which start on: [date] and continue until the end date of; [date] throughout the [country/Territory/world] for the purpose of the commercial and/or non-commercial exploitation and/or adaptation of the [Manuscript/future works of the Author] in all media and/or in any format in whole and/or part including any associated title, name, character and/or trade mark.

A.637

The [Agent] shall provide his/her services to the [Author] and use his/her skill and knowledge to perform his/her duties to endeavour to ensure that an agreement is negotiated with a reputable publisher in respect of the [Manuscript/Synopsis] for the publication in hardback by [year] and in paperback by [year] in [language] in [specify countries/Territory].

A.638

The [Agent] shall use his/her expertise to commercially exploit and promote the [Author] and his/her writing and manuscripts in all forms of the media throughout [specify countries/Territory] including hardback and paperback books, radio and television appearances and adaptations of any written work, serialisations in newspapers and magazines, promotional articles on websites and podcasts, readings and reviews, translations, films, videos, DVDs and merchandising.

A.639

The [Agent] shall regularly keep the [Author] fully informed and updated on a regular basis as regards any discussions, negotiations, strategies, accounting statements, reports and/or documents concerning the [Author], his/her published books, audio files, online accounts and/or any unpublished material, manuscripts, licensing agreements and/or marketing. The [Agent] agrees that he/she shall not have the right to commit the [Author] and/or to conclude any agreement and/or to provide any consent without the prior approval of the [Author] based on full disclosure of the facts in each case.

A.640

This agreement does not appoint the [Agent] as an agent or partner or otherwise with the [Company] at any time. The services of the [Agent] are only engaged to advise, negotiate and act on behalf of the [Company] in respect of [specify subject matter/Project] from [date] to [date] for the agreed fixed sum of [specify number/currency]. The [Agent] shall not be entitled to any additional royalty, commission, costs and/or other sums in respect of the development, adaptation and/or exploitation of the [subject matter/Project].

A.641

All sums due to be paid under this agreement to the [Author] by the [Company] shall be paid to [Agent] of [address]. The [Author] agrees and authorises the [Company] to pay all sums due to the [Author] to the [Agent]. The [Author] agrees that the receipt by the [Agent] shall be a good and valid discharge of the sums due under this agreement. That the [Company] shall not be liable if the [Agent] does not pay the [Author] for any reason.

A.642

The [Authors] confirm that neither party has entered into and/or is bound by any option and/or other agreement with an agent in respect of their [Manuscript/Synopsis/Services]. The [Authors] agree that an agent shall not be appointed for the purpose of negotiating a publishing agreement or any other form of exploitation without the knowledge and consent of both parties.

A.643

The [Agent] agrees and undertakes as follows:

1.1 To act in the best commercial interests of the [Author] at all times.

1.2 To keep the [Author] fully informed regarding any discussion with any third parties.

1.3 To accept the final decision of the [Author] as to which third parties are acceptable and which agreements are to be concluded.

1.4 To ensure that the [Author] receives copies of all licences, agreements sand other documents. Together with copies of monthly financial reports setting out the sums received and/or accrued and/or due to be paid by third parties.

1.5   That all expenses, costs and commission deducted from any sums received by the [Agent] shall be clearly stated and disclosed in the monthly financial reports.

1.6   That the [Agent] shall not become involved in any political and/or activist campaign which damage the reputation and/or career of the [Author].

1.7   That the [Agent] shall not disclose any personal and/or family information and/or other material regarding the [Author] and/or his/her family without the prior consent of the [Author].

A.644
[Name] agrees that the [Company] shall have the right to negotiate, conclude and exploit the [Work/Product] in any media in order to achieve the most financial return and profit to [Name]. Provided that no agreement shall assign any rights and all licences concluded are limited to a maximum of [number] years for each licence.

A.645
The [Publisher] agrees and undertakes that no sub-agents, sub-licensees and/or distributors shall be entitled to edit, adapt, revise and translate the [Work]. That all such proposals are subject to the prior agreement of [Name] in writing and/or his/her agent.

Services

A.646
The [Agent] agrees that [Name] has not appointed the [Agent] to act on his/her behalf in any form whether in relation to the [Work/Services] or not outside [country]. That [Name] may appoint any person he/she thinks fit to exploit any rights in the [Work/Services] outside [country] and that the [Agent] shall not be entitled to any part of any sums received from such exploitation.

A.647
In consideration of the [Manager's] Commission the [Manager] agrees to provide his/her non-exclusive services to the [Sportsperson] to act as agent and manager in in respect of the duties and role and areas of the media described in Appendix A which forms part of this agreement from [date] to [date] in [country/world].

A.648
In consideration of the [Sportsperson's] Fees the [Sportsperson] agrees to engage the exclusive services of the [Manager] from [date] to [date]

in [country/Territory] in respect of the following specific genre and forms of commercial and non-commercial exploitation: television, radio, DVDs, videos, films, game shows and/or reality shows, sound recordings, musical contributions and theatre including appearances in any pantomime , the internet including websites, app, podcasts and channels, computer games and software, newspapers, periodicals, fiction, non-fiction books, biography and other memoire books and any other publication; interviews, public appearances, sponsorship, endorsements, promotions, competitions, charitable events, exhibitions; trade mark applications and registrations, merchandising and licensing of any products and/or services.

A.649
The [Manager] agrees to provide the [Sportsperson] with reasonable notice of meetings, events, filming, interviews and/or otherwise that he/she is required to attend by [text/email/written format] at least [seven/thirty] days in advance.

A.650
The [Agent] shall provide his/her services to the best of his/her skill and ability and shall perform all services diligently to ensure that [Name] is regularly engaged by third parties on the best possible financial terms.

A.651

1.1 The [Agent] shall use his/her knowledge and expertise to promote and market [Name] in the following areas of the media: television, radio, podcasts, websites, newsfeeds, film, newspapers, magazines, books, interviews and appearances at events.

1.2 The [Agent] shall endeavour to conclude agreements with third parties for guest appearances on television programmes; endorsement of beauty products and clothing; product placement agreements for household and other items for inclusion in films recorded at the home of [Name] and/or some other location; brand collaboration agreements to market services, products and/or some other media by [Name].

A.652

1.1 In consideration of the [Agent's] Commission, the [Agent] agrees to provide his/her non-exclusive services to the [Actor] for the Term of this Agreement throughout the Territory.

1.2 In consideration of the Net Receipts the [Actor] agrees to engage the non-exclusive services of the Agent for the Term of this Agreement throughout the Territory in all media including but not limited to appearances, performances, recordings in sound and vision in all forms of television, film, theatre, radio, videos, DVDs, corporate videos, advertisements, the internet, telephone and mobile phones, promotional events and exhibitions, features and articles in newspapers and magazines, publishing in any format, sponsorship, and merchandising, promotional, conference and exhibition appearances, product placement and/or endorsements and/or any other matter which may be agreed between the parties.

1.3 The [Actor] shall not be obliged to accept any proposal for work and/or services from the [Agent] and shall be entitled to refuse at any time.

1.4 The [Actor] shall be entitled to terminate the agreement at any time provided that he/she agrees and undertakes to pay all sums due to the date of termination.

A.653

In consideration of the Net Receipts the [Name] agrees to engage the exclusive services of the [Agent] for the Term of the Agreement throughout the [country/Territory/world]. The [Agent] shall use his/her reasonable endeavours to arrange for the engagement and commercial exploitation of [Name] in all media in any format whether in existence now or created during the existence of this agreement including but not limited to: all forms of contributions to and other roles in films, videos, podcasts, radio and/or television programmes, game shows, reality programmes, theatre productions and musicals, licensing and/or merchandising, books for the children's market, a biography and/or memoire, paid for interviews for magazines and newspapers, promotional appearances, product promotion and endorsements online on the internet and at events and/or exhibitions. Appearances and promotional work related to digital and electronic material on the internet, websites, apps and through any telecommunication system and/or any other interactive multi-media and/or computer software.

A.654

The [Agent] agrees that the [Actor] shall not be obliged to provide his/her services to any third party and that prior to any detailed negotiations by the [Agent] the prior approval of the [Actor] shall be required in each case. The [Actor] shall be entitled to refuse consent to proceed with discussions for any reason and shall not be expected to justify the decision.

A.655

The [Agent] agrees that any form of exploitation of the product of the [Artiste's] services shall require the prior consent of the [Artiste]. The [Artiste] shall be entitled to refuse to carry out any work for any reason whether or not the [Agent] will suffer a financial or other loss. The [Agent] shall not be entitled to seek any compensation, loss or damages which arises from the failure or refusal of the [Artiste] to provide consent or to perform any work.

A.656

1.1 The [Author] appoints the [Agent] to represent him/her and to endeavour to conclude agreements with third parties for the exploitation of works proposed and/or written by the [Author] during the Term of the Agreement in the [country/Territory/world] in all languages in respect of the following rights:

a. All forms of publications whether digital and in electronic form and/or in print form; hardback, paperback, e books, audio files, magazines, digests, periodicals, newspapers, pull-outs and articles.

b. All forms of films, videos and sound recordings by means of television, whether terrestrial, cable, satellite, digital and over the internet in electronic form and/or through any telecommunication system for reception by computer, mobile phone and/or some other gadget and/or device; playback archive access for free, pay on demand, subscription and/or pay per view.

c. All forms of mechanical reproduction and distribution including DVDs; computer software, discs, animated and/or interactive content; games, gambling, betting and lotteries in any format.

d. All forms of merchandising and/or sub-licensing in any format and/or medium and/or any adaptation and/or other development including any sequel of any work.

1.2 The [Agent] shall be entitled to receive commission in respect of all agreements concluded and signed by the [Author] with the third parties before the termination and/or expiry of this agreement in respect of the rights and countries stated in 1.1 above. Where there is any ambiguity then the presumption is that the rights are reserved by the [Author]. The [Agent] shall be entitled to receive the commission for the duration of each such third party agreement despite the fact that this main agreement may have expired and/or be terminated.

A.657

The [Agent] agrees to act in the best interests of the [Author] at all times and to provide the [Author] with details of any conflict of interest that may arise at any time due to the appointment of another client and/or other business interests. The [Agent] shall also provide advice and guidance on the commercial aspects of the agreements, liaise with any collecting societies and organise registration for the [Author] and collect any sums due in respect of the rights and territory granted under this agreement.

A.658

Until the expiry and/or termination of this agreement the [Agent] is entitled to collect and be paid any sums due under any agreement from any third party provided that the sums are held in a separate and clearly identifiable account to which both parties are joint signatories and both must sign to issue any payments.

After the expiry and/or termination of the Agreement then the [Author] shall be responsible for collecting all sums due and shall ensure that the [Agent] is paid any commission that may be due.

A.659

Where the [Agent] owes any sums which are outstanding to the [Author]. The [Agent] agrees that the [Author] may set-off and claim any such sums from those due to the [Agent] from the sums received by the [Author].

A.660

The [Agent] shall not be entitled to exploit rights not specifically set out above and agrees and undertakes not to do any of the following without the prior written consent of the [Author].

1.1   Set up a fan website and/or any other website relating to the [Writer].

1.2   To register the name of the [Author] as a domain name.

1.3   To sign any documents, agreements and/other apply for any trade mark and/or other rights which are owned and/or controlled by the [Author] and/or relate to the [Author's] work in any media.

A.661

The [Agent] is engaged to represent [Name] to book music venues for performances but is not entitled to deal and/or represent that he/she has any ownership and/or rights as regards the content of any music and/or lyrics which may be performed created and/or owned by [Name].

A.662

The [Author/Artist] may cease to engage the services of the [Agent] at any time and the [Agent] shall have no right to seek to claim any sums, rights and/or other interest from the [Author/Artist] after the date of termination whether the material and/or work was created and/or developed and/or booked during the contract or not.

A.663

[Name] agrees that the [Agent] may engage the services of third parties to create new material and/or develop and market the services of [Name]. Provided that all proposals are discussed and agreed with [Name] in advance and that the [Agent] agrees to pay [number] per cent of the costs and expenses.

Sponsorship

A.664

1.1 The [Company] agrees to appoint the [Promoter] as the non-exclusive agent for the [Company] to advise upon, identify, arrange and develop a sponsorship, advertising and promotions campaign for the [Company] and the [Products/Services] for primarily [country] but also the global market from [date] to [date] which focuses on social media, television, radio and magazines.

1.2 The [Promoter] shall deliver a strategy proposal report with sample material to the [Company] by [date]. Together with a recommended budget for expenditure which sets out all the costs to be incurred in developing new material, logos, images, films and/or other costs of performers and/or contributors. Together with a n estimated budget of payments to third parties and the methods as to how the material is to be used.

A.665

1.1 In consideration of the Promotion Fee and the Promotion Expenses the [Promoter] agrees to provide its non-exclusive services to the [Company] to act as agent to promote, advertise and arrange sponsorship for the [Company] and the [Products/Services] for primarily throughout [country] but also the global market from [date] to date].

1.2 The [Promoter] acknowledges and agrees that the [Company] may appoint any other person and/or company to carry out the same and/or similar work at any time and the [Promoter] agrees to assist and cooperate where necessary.

A.666

The [Promoter] acknowledges and confirms that the principal aims of this agreement are to:

1.1 Promote and increase the sales of the [Products/Services].

1.2 Raise the identity, image and brand of the [Company] and the [Products/Services] throughout the [country/Territory/world].

1.3 Negotiate and conclude sponsorship agreements with high profile events and/ exhibitions and/or to conclude product and/or service placement agreements with third parties which will enhance the media coverage and increase sales.

1.4 Any other specific aims: [–].

A.667

1.1 The [Sponsor] agrees that the sponsorship of the [Tournament/Event/ Auction] does not provide the [Sponsor] with the right to use the [Company's] name, logo, the title, slogan or other material associated with the [Tournament/Event/Auction owned or controlled by the [Company] in any advertising, promotion, marketing, service and/or product owned or controlled by the [Sponsor].

1.2 The only permitted use is as follows: [specify exact format/media/style/ duration].

A.668

The [Agency] confirms that it has not and shall not enter into any arrangement with any person, enterprise and/or business and/or for any service and/or product which has and/or might conflict with this agreement. The [Agency] agrees to provide the [Company] with details of any conflict of interest that may arise at any time due to the appointment of other clients and/or other business interests. The [Agency] agrees and undertakes to provide written notice of any conflict within [seven] days of the conclusion of any agreement. Where a conflict arises which the [Company] finds unacceptable then the [Agency] agrees that the [Company] may at its sole discretion serve written notice of the termination of the agreement. In such event the [Company] shall only owe and/or pay to the [Agency] such sums as are due to the date of termination. The [Agency] agrees that no sums and/or commission shall be paid to the [Agency] in respect of any agreement which exists after the termination date.

A.669

The [Company] agrees that the [Sponsor] shall have the [final decision/right to be consulted] in respect of the content, operation and organisation of the [Event/Programme]. The [Company] agrees to seek the prior approval of the [Sponsor] at all stages of the development, production, marketing and advertising of the [Event/Programme] prior to any final commitments and/or agreements being concluded.

A.670

The [Company] shall not have the right to sign any agreement which requires the use of the [Sponsors] trade mark, logo and/or slogan by any third party whether for any commercial and/or non-commercial purpose. The prior written consent of the [Sponsor] shall be requested by the [Company] in each case. Any such company and/or person shall be required by the [Sponsor] to sign a trade mark user licence agreement and to assign all rights in all media throughout the universe to the [Sponsor] in any such new development and/or variation.

A.671

Neither the [Sponsor] nor the [Company] shall delegate responsibility for any work and/or contribution to this [Film/Festival] to any agent and/or third party unless both parties have agreed that is the best course of action and have both approved the proposal.

A.672

Where the [Sponsor] appoints an agent and/or other third party to carry out its duties under this agreement and the [Company] agrees and supports that decision. Such consent by the [Company] does not mean absolve the [Sponsor] of liability. The [Sponsor] shall still remain directly responsible and there is no consent provide to any transfer of liability and/or other obligations under this agreement to a third party.

University, Charity and Educational

A.673

1.1 In consideration of the [Commission] the [Agent] agrees to provide his/her non-exclusive services to the [Institute/Charity] from [date to [date] for the following purpose [specify scope and extent of Project/describe in attached appendix].

1.2 The [Institute/Charity] agrees to engage the services of the [Agent] as set out in 1.1 above.

1.3 The [Agent] acknowledges that the [Institute/Charity] shall have the right to appoint another agent and/or third party in respect of any matter including the [Project] and that this is not an exclusive agreement.

1.4 The [Agent] agrees that there is no right granted to the [Agent] to commit the [Institute/Charity] to any agreement whether in writing or not without the prior written consent of the [Institute/Charity]. Further that all agreements must be in writing and signed by the [Institute/Charity].

1.5 The [Agent] agrees that he/she shall be responsible for all his/her own costs and expenses which may be incurred in respect of the provision of his/her services under this agreement. That there is no arrangement for the [Institute/Charity] to pay any expenses.

A.674

1.1 The [Agent] agrees and undertakes to keep the [Institute/Charity] fully informed on a regular basis as regards any negotiations in respect of the [Project] and shall provide copies of all correspondence, emails, proposals, samples and any other material to the [Institute/Charity] on a regular basis.

1.2 The services of the [Agent] are only engaged to advise and negotiate but not to conclude any agreement on behalf of the [Institute/Charity] in respect of the [Project] from [date] to [date] for the agreed fixed sum of [number/currency].

1.3 The [Agent] agrees that he/she shall not be entitled to any additional expenses, costs, royalties and/or other sums from the exploitation of the [Project] either during the Term of the Agreement and/or after it has ended of any nature.

A.675

The [Agency] shall perform its obligations under this agreement to the best of its skill and ability and shall ensure that its personnel, contractors and consultants are professionally qualified and shall maintain high standards in accordance with the requirements specified by the [Company/Institute] for the following purpose and aim [specify Project]. A summary of which is attached to, and forms part of this agreement.

A.676

The [Enterprise] acts as a non-exclusive agent to promote, market and distribute via its website, short films, photographs, events, exhibitions and online marketing details of the [Students] and their [Projects].

A.677

The [Charity] does not act as a representative of any third party person and/ or business associated with its organisations. Nor is any such third party person and/or business entitled to represent directly and/or indirectly that they are authorised to make social media statements, issue press releases, and/or commit to work and/or services on behalf of the [Charity].

AMENDMENTS

General Business and Commercial

A.678

This agreement contains the full understanding of the parties with respect to the subject matter and supersedes any previous agreements between the parties regarding such subject matter. This agreement may not be amended and/or any of its provisions waived except in writing executed by the relevant party which is agreeing to any such change.

A.679

This agreement supersedes all prior agreements and arrangements and embodies the entire understanding and all the terms agreed between the parties relating to the Licence. Both parties accept and agree that no previous oral and/or written representations, promises, projections, estimates and/or other information and/or disclosures shall constitute implied terms of this agreement.

A.680

This agreement may be only be amended by a single [instrument/document] which is in writing and the same document in duplicate is signed on behalf of both parties. This shall not include any exchange by email and/or text message and/or any other electronic method.

A.681

The General Terms and the Special Conditions constitutes the whole agreement between the parties. Neither party shall seek to rely on any representation other than that which is set out in writing as a provision. No variation and/or waiver of any term shall be effective and binding unless committed to writing and agreed and signed by both parties as an amendment to this agreement.

A.682

This agreement sets out the entire and complete agreement between the parties and any amendment, waiver, transfer, assignment, variation and/or other change must be in writing and signed by an authorised signatory of both the [Company] and the [Agent].

A.683

This new agreement sets out all the terms agreed between the parties. This agreement supersedes all prior agreements, practices, arrangements and conditions whether verbally agreed and/or in the form of documents. This agreement cannot be unilaterally altered by one party. This agreement may not be amended, altered and/or added to without the consent in writing of both parties to the exact terms of the new variation.

A.684

The [Licensee] acknowledges that it cannot rely on any prior representations made by the [Company] and/or any of its officers, servants, agents, employees or other representatives at any time. That the [Licensee] accepts that such representations cannot be implied in any manner. That the terms of this agreement are the only conditions which shall apply between the parties. Further that the waiver and/or variation of any term by the [Company] at any time shall not mean that the term shall be waived and/or varied on other occasions.

A.685

The contractual terms between the [Company] and the [Purchaser] are contained exclusively within this document and in no circumstances will the [Company] be bound by any purported addition to, or other variation of these terms whether oral or in writing. That any addition and/or variation must be in writing and be signed on behalf of the [Company] as a clear amendment to the main agreement. The parties agree that any representation made by any agent and/or person before or at the time the contract is entered into is expressly excluded unless the [Purchaser] was actively misled and/or would not have entered into the agreement without such assurance.

A.686

This agreement may not be changed, modified, amended and/or added to in any manner except in a written document signed by both parties. Each of the parties acknowledges and agrees that the other has not made any representations, warranties and/or undertakings of any kind which are binding except those terms expressly set out in this agreement. This agreement constitutes and contains the entire scope of the terms of the agreement between the parties with respect to the subject matter. This agreement supersedes any prior or contemporaneous agreements whether by email, text, verbally and/or in writing. Nothing contained in this agreement shall be binding upon the parties until a copy of this agreement has been executed by an officer of each party and has been delivered to the other party. This agreement may be executed in counterparts each of which shall be deemed an original but all of which shall together be one and the same instrument. Paragraph headings are inserted for convenience only and do not constitute a part of this agreement.

A.687

This agreement may not be altered, changed and/or modified except by written instrument duly executed by both the [Licensor] and the [Licensee] and this provision may not be waived except by written instrument duly executed by both the [Licensor] and the [Licensee]. This agreement is complete and embraces the entire understanding between the parties. All prior understandings whether oral or written having been incorporated as far as agreed herein. No representations, undertakings and/or warranties of any kind and/or nature have been made by either of the parties to the other to induce the making of this agreement except as specifically set out in this agreement and each of the parties agrees not to assert to the contrary.

A.688

This agreement which has been signed by all parties is the final and absolute statement of the terms and conditions to which everyone has agreed to be bound. All matters discussed, written, offered, waivered, inducements or otherwise in negotiations or prior to the signature of this agreement of any nature are only relevant to the extent that they are specified in this agreement. Neither party shall seek to imply additional terms and conditions at a later date nor seek to imply additional terms, facts or other matters which have not been specified in the agreement.

A.689
This agreement sets out the entire terms agreed between the parties and supersedes all previous discussions, representations, disclosures and/or assurances (whether in writing or not) previously made between the parties. Any amendments, additions or alterations to this agreement shall not be made except in writing and signed by a duly authorised representative of both parties.

A.690
This document constitutes the entire agreement between the parties relating to the [Service] and supersedes and operates to the exclusion of all previous arrangements, representations, practices or otherwise made by and/or on behalf of the [Company]. No amendments shall be binding and valid unless in writing and signed by the [Company].

A.691
This agreement represents the entire agreement between the parties and supersedes all previous agreements, promises, and representations made by either party to the other. Any amendment or alteration to this agreement shall be in writing and signed by an authorised senior executive from each of the parties.

A.692
This agreement sets out the full and complete terms agreed between the parties. No prior promise written and/or verbal shall be taken into account unless specified in this agreement. Any amendment and/or variation must be in writing on a document signed by the [Agent] and the [Actor].

A.693
This agreement supersedes all previous agreements, representations, undertakings and assurances given prior to this agreement and sets out all the terms agreed between the parties. Any amendment and/or alteration to this agreement must be in writing and signed by the [Company] and [Name].

A.694
Any amendment, waiver and/or alteration to this agreement must be in writing and signed by both parties.

A.695

Any amendment of any nature to this agreement must be in writing and signed by an authorised signatory of each of the parties.

A.696

This agreement sets out all matters agreed between the parties relating to the [subject matter]. It is agreed between the parties that no earlier documents, records or conversations shall be relied upon at a later date to supersede these terms. All future amendments to this agreement must be in writing and the document signed by both parties.

A.697

This agreement sets out the entire and complete understanding of the terms agreed between the parties. The terms may be changed and/or superseded by an exchange of emails with a written document attached to which both parties provide their consent that it shall constitute an amendment to the main agreement.

A.698

This agreement sets out the entire and complete agreement between the parties. The parties agree that all previous arrangements written and/or otherwise relating to [subject matter] between the parties have been and/or are now terminated so that they no longer apply. This agreement may be altered, amended and/or changed by an exchange of written signed documents in which the terms agreed are specified. There can be no oral binding amendment or signature by only one party.

A.699

This Agreement must not be changed, modified, amended and/or supplemented except in a written document signed by both parties in each case.

A.700

Amendments, waivers, alterations, additions and/or changes to this document may be in writing and/or verbally agreed provided that both parties agree and there is no ambiguity as to the amendment.

A.701

Any representations, disclosures, facts, inducements, promises and/or other matters which were raised by either party in order for the agreement to be entered into by the other party shall still be binding at a later date whether specified in this agreement or not.

A.702

All the representations, documents, statements and material supplied and put forward as [fact/background material/projected figures] by both parties shall form part of this agreement.

A.703

This agreement can be amended by any one of the following methods:

1.1 An exchange of emails confirming agreement on the new terms and conditions.

1.2 A side letter which is signed by one party and agreed to in a responding letter.

1.3 A formal new amending document which both parties sign and date.

A.704

The [Institute/Charity] and the [Company] agree that this agreement cannot be amended by emails, invoices, receipts and/or verbal exchanges. That the formal notification of any amendment must be agreed between parties and authorised by the [Chief Executive] of both parties and/or a delegated authority in the senior management.

A.705

The following documents and representations made by the [Company] which are attached in Appendix A form part of this agreement. No other information, data, representations and/or disclosures shall be deemed and/or are intended to be part of this agreement. Both parties agree and undertake that any prior exchanges of any nature not in Appendix A are specifically excluded. No amendments and/or additions to this agreement can be made by email, telephone, text, voicemail and/or other medium of any nature except in writing on paper and signed by an authorised representative of each party.

A.706

1.1 Both parties agree that this document is intended to be updated, amended and varied as required to suit the circumstances and the business requirements of the parties. Either party may send the other proposed amendments by email, letter and any other written form except text message.

1.2 All proposed amendments should be sent to [Name] on behalf of the [Distributor] and [Name] on behalf of the [Company]. Either the [Distributor] and/or the [Company] shall be entitled to reject any such proposed amendments as not feasible on cost grounds and/or for any other reason. There shall be no time limit for the rejection and/ or acceptance of any proposed amendment unless specified in the proposal.

1.3 All additions and/or amendments to the agreement shall be bound by all the terms of the existing agreement. Where any term of the existing agreement is to be deleted then both parties agree to specify the exact clause in the proposed amendment.

A.707

The [Sponsor] agrees that if for any reason the terms of the agreement are to be amended. Then the amendment must be in the form of a written document signed by the [Managing Director] of each party. The [Sponsor] agrees and undertakes that clauses [–] relating to the [Sponsorship Fee] and the [Payment Schedule] shall not be amended at any time.

A.708

The [Sub-Licensee] shall not have any right and/or authority to amend, delete from, vary and/or deviate from the terms of this agreement. No attempt by the [Sub-Licensee] whether by letter, email, phone call, text and/or by representations to third parties outside the agreed terms and/or otherwise shall be legally binding upon the [Licensor] and/or the [Licensee]. Where the [Sub-Licensee] is found to be acting outside its authority and/or on the basis by its actions that the agreement has been changed, amended and/ or varied. Then in such event the [Sub-Licensee] shall be in breach of the terms of this agreement and the [Licensor] and/or the [Licensee] shall have the right to give written notice of the termination of the agreement with the [Sub-Licensee] with immediate effect.

A.709

No amendment, change, variation and/or deletion from the agreement between the [Licensee] and the [Sub-Licensee] shall be outside the rights and/or terms granted by the [Copyright Owner/Licensor] to the [Licensee]. The [Licensee] shall have the final decision as to whether to agree to any amendment of the agreement with the [Sub-Licensee]. Any amendment must be in writing signed by a director of both parties, dated and subject to the laws of [specify country].

A.710

Both parties agree that any part of this agreement can be amended, changed, altered and/or cancelled and/or terminated. This can be by any choice of method that either party should so choose including advertisements in the press, email to the account, by letter and/or marketing flyer and/or without any prior notice and/or warning. This shall include price increases and additional costs and charges except that the party due to pay the additional sums shall have the right to refuse to do so and may cancel and/or terminate the agreement.

A.711
It is agreed between the parties that the terms and conditions shall not be altered and/or amended for any reason during each [number] period of [month/years].

A.712
Where one of the parties is in unable and/or unwilling to fulfil the terms of this agreement. Then the terms may be varied to permit another third party to assume some and/or all of the liabilities and/or responsibilities provided that [Project/Work] is still completed to the same standard and delivery date is not altered and/or varied.

A.713
Where the [Company] is unable to provide a consistent service and/or supply of the personnel at times due to reasons which it cannot control. Then the [Company] reserves the right to amend and/or alter this agreement subject to adjustments in the total price. Where the [Company] is obliged to make amendments and/or changes which effect more than [number] per cent of the service and/or personnel. Then the [Distributor] shall have the right to terminate the agreement and shall have the right to go to a third party to complete the [Project].

A.714
It is agreed that no documents relating to this [Work/Service] upon which either party would seek to rely in a court of law shall be capable of being amended by email, text and/or any other method which is not in written form on paper and signed by a person who has the authority and capacity to bind that party.

ARBITRATION

General Business and Commercial

A.715
In the event of any dispute, allegation and/or claim between the parties then both the parties agree and undertake to enter into arbitration, dispute resolution and/or some other method of resolving the matter prior to

commencing any legal action. Where one party refuses to co-operate and/ or to enter into discussions in good faith. Then the other party who has tried to avoid litigation shall have fulfilled this clause.

A.716

Either party may at its own cost request access to third party agreements held, owned, controlled and/or possessed by the other party who is believed and/ or is alleged to have failed to account, disclose information and/or carried out the terms of this agreement. The party seeking access shall send a written request to the other party stating that within [fourteen] days including weekends of the date of receipt of the request that the other defaulting party shall permit an expert who shall be a nominated independent accountant, auditor or economist access to and the right to make copies of such third party agreements.

A.717

The [Expert's] decision shall be final and binding on the parties and both parties agree to be bound by and to carry out the decision. The party who has been found by the [Expert] to be at fault shall within [seven] days of receipt of the [Expert's] decision pay to the other party the amount due together with interest at [number] per cent per annum above the base rate of [specify Bank plc] from the date on which such sums according to the decision of the [Expert] should have been paid.

A.718

The costs and expenses of the [Expert] shall be apportioned between both parties in such proportions as the [Expert] shall in her decision consider appropriate and the [Expert's] allocation of the costs shall be binding.

A.719

If at any time any question, dispute or difference shall arise between the [Purchaser] and the [Contractor] in relation to the contract or in any way connected with the work proposed or to be carried out which cannot be settled by negotiation. Then either party shall as soon as reasonably practicable give to the other notice of the existence of such question, dispute or difference specifying its nature and the point at issue and the matter shall be referred to the arbitration of a person with suitable qualifications. The arbitrator who will consider evidence from both parties and then provide a decision and both parties agree to be bound by that decision.

A.720

1.1   In the event that the parties cannot agree as to the name of the person with suitable qualifications and expertise to act as an expert who is to consider the facts and reach a recommendation and authoritative decision. Where an [Expert] is engaged by the parties and he/she identifies an issue which is not resolved between the parties. Then any such matter shall not automatically be referred to arbitration.

1.2   If the decision of the expert does not resolve all the issues and/or no expert is appointed then either party shall have the option to notify the other party that they intend to apply for an arbitration to be conducted by a professional and suitably qualified person appointed by [specify organisation].

1.3   The performance of the contract shall as far as possible continue while the arbitration proceedings are in progress unless the expert and/or one of the parties have ordered the suspension of the contract.

1.4   Where due to the seriousness of the dispute the contract has been suspended and any additional costs which may be incurred as a consequence. The parties must reach a settlement in respect of those additional costs if it is proposed that the contract should be restarted.

1.5   No payment due under the contract shall be withheld if the contract continues while the arbitration is in progress. If the contract is suspended then there shall be a right to also freeze and halt any payments until a settlement is reached between the parties and/or the binding decision of the arbitration is decided and agreed between the parties.

A.721
All disputes, differences of opinion regards quality of work and/or costs and payments and/or any other matter whatsoever arising from or relating to this agreement shall be referred to a single arbitrator to be agreed upon by the parties and/or in the event of the failure of the parties to agree then an arbitrator nominated by [specify organisation/governing body] shall be accepted by both parties. The arbitrator shall be obliged to follow all laws, legislation, regulations and/or codes of practice and/or guidelines and/or policies in in force in [country].

A.722
If any dispute and/or difference of opinion shall arise between the parties on any subject matter relating to this main agreement and/or any other matter related to any associated agreement. Then the parties agree to appoint an arbitrator upon such terms as shall be agreed between the parties. In the event that no person can be approved by both parties then it is agreed that an arbitrator may be selected and agreed from a list provided by [specify organisation].

A.723

In the event of any dispute between the parties concerning the interpretation, purpose and/or the scope of the rights granted under of this agreement. Then both parties agree to refer the dispute to the following parties whose joint decision shall be binding on both parties:

1.1   [specify individual/body/company]; and

1.2   [specify individual/body/company].

A.724

Either party to this agreement may elect for any reason not to resolve any allegation, claim, difference of opinion and/or dispute via arbitration. In such event either party may try to resolve the matter by any other method that they should so decide to follow including but not limited to mediation, alternative dispute resolution and litigation.

A.725

I agree to act as an official arbitrator for the purpose of any disputes relating to this agreement if requested to do so by both the above named parties and subject to agreement as to my fees, costs and expenses. Both parties must agree that my decision shall be binding on both parties. Signed by [Arbitrator] [Name] [Title] [date].

A.726

In the event of any dispute, disagreement as to the facts and/or any other costs, expenses losses and/or damages and/or default and/or failure being alleged and/or claimed by either party relating to this agreement then it is agreed that:

1.1   Each party shall specify the grounds of its complaint or defence in writing to the other to provide them with an opportunity of resolving the matter.

1.2   In the event that if after [specify period] any matter is still outstanding then either party may refer the issue to [specify name] of [specify organisation] to act as a conciliation service to resolve the matter. Provided that both parties reach agreement as to who is to be responsible for the cost of the conciliation service. That the conciliation service consider all the evidence of both parties and shall endeavour to assist the parties to reach a settlement. In the event that this method fails then either party may choose to exercise their own legal rights and remedies as they may decide in the circumstances.

A.727

Any dispute, disagreement, claim and/or inability to resolve differences of opinion regarding the terms, meaning and/or consequences of this agreement arising directly and/or indirectly shall be submitted to the arbitration rules and procedures of [specify name of organisation]. All documents and proceedings shall be in [specify] language.

A.728
Both parties agree and undertake that the final decision of [name] appointed under this agreement to settle disputes shall [not] be binding and may not be appealed and/or ignored.

A.729
There shall be no obligation and/or right of either party to insist that any dispute or problem and/or interpretation of the contract shall be referred to arbitration or any other form of procedure. If any matter is referred however both parties agree that the decision of the arbitrator shall be final and binding and the allocation and payment of costs shall be as follows: [specify costs allocation of role of arbitrator].

A.730
In the event of any dispute and/or any disagreement in respect of the interpretation of the clauses and/or any allegation of breach of contract and/or some other allegation of default which is unresolved between the parties which relates to the agreement. Then both parties agree to refer the dispute to an independent arbitrator whose cost shall be paid for by [specify who pays costs of arbitrator]. The arbitrator shall be appointed by arrangement with [specify organisation]. The parties agree that the decision shall not be considered binding. Both parties agree not to commence legal proceedings during the arbitration process and shall not do so until after it has ended. Either party shall have the option after completion of the arbitration process and/or within [one year] whichever is the earliest to commence legal proceedings.

A.731
Where there is any dispute of any nature regarding this agreement then the [Licensor] shall have the right to notify the [Licensee] in writing that it wishes to enter into arbitration, mediation and/or some other procedure to resolve matter the prior to taking any legal action against the [Licensee]. The written notification shall specify the reason for the request and the steps required to remedy the matter. The [Licensee] agrees to enter into arbitration, mediation and/or some other procedure if so notified in writing provided that the [Licensor] shall bear the cost for the appointment of the third party.

A.732
There shall be no obligation on either party to agree to enter into any mediation, arbitration and/or alternative dispute resolution at any time. Where

the [Licensor] has grounds for complaint and/or alleges breach of contract on any grounds including failure to pay any advance and/or royalties and/or produce and/or market the [DVD/Disc/Film]. Then the [Distributor] agrees to arrange to meet with the [Licensor] and its legal representatives to discuss the complaint and/or the allegations in each case. The [Distributor] agrees to provide a written response within [one] week of any such complaint and/or allegations.

A.733

In the event of any dispute and/or allegation of breach of contract and/or default by either party arising from the terms of this agreement. Then it is agreed that each party shall specify the grounds of its complaint and/or the allegations in writing to the other party and shall set out the proposed terms upon which the matter could be resolved. The party against whom the allegations are made and/or who is alleged to have defaulted shall within [one] calendar month of such notification provide a detailed response in writing addressing each of the allegations. In the event that the parties cannot resolve any dispute they both agree that prior to any legal proceedings being issued that they shall consider the option of arbitration in order to save costs. In the event that both parties agree to pursue the option of arbitration then they agree that the cost of the arbitrator shall be paid for [equally between the parties/as ordered by the arbitrator]. The arbitrator shall be chosen by the parties from a recommended list issued by [specify institute]. The parties agree and undertake that if they enter into arbitration at any time that the decision of the arbitrator shall not be a full and final settlement of the dispute and the costs unless a formal settlement document has been drawn up by the relevant legal advisors and is signed by a director of each party. In the event that this system of settlement fails then either party may choose to exercise their legal rights and remedies.

A.734

Where there are more than [number] parties involved in this [Project] it is agreed that where more than [number] per cent wish to refer the matter to arbitration. That all the parties shall endeavour to agree the terms of arbitration and shall bear the costs in equal proportions. Provided that the arbitration shall take place in the [specify] language in [country] and be held within [number/months] of the dispute arising and be subject to the following legislation and policy [specify details].

A.735

Where any disputes, errors, omissions, claims and/or damages, expenses, costs and/or other issues shall arise between the [Company] and [Name]. Then the parties agree that they shall be entitled to try to reach agreement through any method including mediation, arbitration, dispute resolution but there is no obligation to do so. The parties agree that they shall disclose all relevant data, plans, invoices and other information and material which may support their case and shall set out a statement in detail of the facts prior to taking any legal action.

A.736

Where a serious dispute arises between the parties which involves a claim for more than [number/currency] by one and/or more parties. Then it is agreed that the [Licensor/Licensee] shall try to settle the matter through arbitration and/or mediation using [specify method/institute] for which each party shall bear its own initial costs until a final decision is reached by the person appointed to act as arbitrator. The parties agree that the decision of the arbitrator shall be binding as to the dispute and costs.

A.737

The parties agree that where the total sum in dispute is less than [number/ currency] that there shall be no obligation to take the matter to arbitration. Further than any legal action by either party shall be in the [specify name] courts under the [quick claims process/other method] in [country].

A.738

There shall be no obligation to enter any form of mediation, arbitration and/ or alternative dispute resolution prior to the start of any legal proceedings. Any such agreement shall be subject to the terms of a separate document agreed between and signed by both parties.

A.739

Where there is a dispute between the parties and/or disagreement as to the terms, the rights and/or any payments made and/or due. Then the parties agree to negotiate and conclude an arbitration procedure with an independent third party who can review that facts and make a recommendation as to the settlement of any such matter.

A.740

Both the [Licensor] and the [Licensee] shall be bound by the rules, terms and conditions of [specify institute] in respect of any process in place to resolve disputes and/or disagreements as to interpretation. Both parties agree that they shall endeavour to follow the dispute settlement process subject to the cost of administration and legal representation.

A.741

The [Supplier] agrees that where the [Client] is in dispute with the [Supplier] regarding the source and/or content of any [Product/Article] that the [Supplier] has manufactured and/or supplied. That the [Supplier] accepts and agrees that a written report which identifies and specifies failures by the [Supplier] to adhere to [international] health and safety standards and/or content supported by scientific tests, site visits and recommendations by a recognised government department in [country] known as [specify details] and/or a private inspector engaged by the [Client] shall be regarded as conclusive evidence against the [Supplier].

A.742

Where the [Supplier] is based outside [country] which is the main office of the [Client]. In the event that the parties agree to enter into arbitration to resolve a matter. Then the [Supplier] agrees that the arbitration shall take place in [country] in [city] in [specify] language according to the procedure and process set out by [specify organisation] as at the time of the dispute. Failure to reach terms of arbitration within a period of [number] months of the dispute arising and/or being notified to the other party shall mean that either party may take legal action as they think fit in any country of the world.

A.743

Both the [Author] and the [Publisher] agree to resolve any disputes concerning this agreement either through referral to arbitration under the rules of [specify institute or other organisation] or to the Informal Disputes Settlement Procedure of the [specify organisation] in [country].

A.744

If any difference of opinion and/or a dispute shall arise between the [Publishers] and the [Author] regarding the interpretation of this agreement including in respect of the ownership of the rights and/or liabilities of either of the parties. Such matters shall be referred to the arbitration of two persons one named by either party and the cost to be paid for by [specify costs allocation between parties].

A.745

Any dispute arising in respect of this contract shall be settled in accordance with the procedure for the settlement of disputes set out in the agreement between [specify organisation] and the Company.

A.746

Any disputes arising from the interpretation and/or performance of this contract shall be settled through negotiations by both parties and if that shall fail then a conciliation process and if that shall fail arbitration by an agreed organisation or individual. The parties reserve the right to issue legal proceedings at any time however unless a matter has been finally resolved to the satisfaction of both parties.

A.747
All disputes which may at any time arise between the [Author] and the [Publishing Company] in respect of the agreement and/or the subject matter and/or as to construction and/or otherwise shall be referred to a [joint committee/other] composed of a nominee of the [Author] and a nominee of the [Publishing Company] whose unanimous decision shall be binding. Where there is no unanimous decision then any dispute shall then be referred to a sole arbitrator to be agreed upon by the parties and/or nominated by [specify institute or organisation]. Any such arbitrator shall be required to follow the existing laws, procedures and policies relating to arbitration at that time.

A.748
If any disagreement, dispute, allegation and/or threat of legal action shall arise between the [Publisher] and the [Company] concerning any aspect of this agreement and/or its interpretation, the scope of the rights and/or any responsibilities, indemnity and/or liability of either party. Each case shall be referred to either alternative dispute resolution, mediation, conciliation or arbitration or such other method as may be agreed in writing between the parties in order to minimise the costs of the dispute and resolve the matter quickly.

A.749
The parties agree that arbitration, mediation and formal dispute resolution may be considered and proposed prior to taking legal action but there is no obligation to do so. The parties agree that the [Work/Material/Rights] supplied by the [Licensor] have been made available worldwide by the [Company] and that the business and premises of the [Company] are international. The [Company] agrees that any legal action, arbitration, mediation and/or formal dispute resolution shall be limited to the legislation of [country] and take place in [specify city/country].

A.750
The [Manager] and the [Sportsperson] agree that prior to the commencement of any legal proceedings in the event of a dispute, allegations, claims, defaults, failures and/or other problems which arise pursuant to this agreement which cannot be resolved by negotiation between the parties. That without prejudice to any legal rights of either party the parties agree to refer the matter to the [specify organisation] for their advice and guidance, but which shall not be binding, in order to try to resolve the matter.

A.751
If any dispute, allegation. Failure. Default, complaint and/or otherwise of any nature shall arises and/or occurs in respect of this agreement and/or any associated document is not resolved within [specify period] of the issue

arising between the parties. Then both parties agree that in order to try to void litigation the parties agree to appoint an [arbitrator/other] from a recommended list of persons issued by [specify organisation] at the cost of both parties on the basis of a [50/50] split to resolve the matter. The decision shall not be binding on either party, but the parties must agree in advance to be bound by the allocation and liability of the cost.

A.752

In the event that there is are any complaints, allegations, threats and/or disputes arising from the performance and/or other otherwise any other terms of this agreement between the parties then the following procedures shall apply:

1.1 There shall be a meeting between a representative of the [Company] and an agent and/or legal representative of [Name] which [Name] shall also attend if he/she so wishes. In the event of a failure to agree at the above meeting a further second meeting shall be held between the parties to seek to resolve the dispute.

1.2 In the event of a further failure to agree a solution and resolve the matter. The parties shall consider some other method of dispute resolution, conciliation and/or arbitration in [country]. There is no obligation to follow any such method prior to the commencement of any legal proceedings.

1.3 It is expressly agreed and understood that this disputes procedure does not constitute a contractual obligation for parties to this agreement to follow and that it is included to help regulate and settle any difficulties and dispute that may arise in the spirit and intention of maintaining good relations between the parties to the agreement.

A.753

There is no obligation on [Name] and/or the [Company] to refer any dispute, alleged breach and/or otherwise under this agreement to arbitration, mediation or dispute resolution. All proposals to resolve any matter by any of these methods will need the prior written consent of both parties in a document which states the procedure, the time-scale, the cost and the effect of the decision.

A.754

The [Company] agrees to act in a reasonable manner in the event of a dispute or other inability to resolve any important issue in respect of the contract which has or will arise. The parties agree to meet with a fixed agenda with a list of issues set out by each party at a suitable venue with [specify name of person] whose role will be to act as an unofficial mediator and/or arbitrator between the parties. No legal representative shall attend this meeting unless both parties agree that they may do so.

A.755
All disputes, complaints or otherwise shall be referred to [organisation/role] whether related to the fulfilment of the terms of this agreement and/or the quality of the [Products/Services].

A.756
As far as possible the parties agree not to take legal action without exploring all other avenues of settlement including discussions, alternative dispute resolution, mediation, arbitration, set-off and/or other methods reasonably available. The appointment and allocation of cost shall be agreed in advance by the parties, but may reimbursed as part of a final settlement.

A.757
Where services have been and/or are provided by any person through the [Supplier] who has failed to provide a reasonable quality of work according to the order placed by the [Company]. Then the [Supplier] agrees to substitute an alternative person to complete the work at no extra cost to the [Company]. Where the work is still not completed and/or fulfilled then the [Company] may engage a third party and seek to recover all the cost from the [Supplier] for such work as may be required. Provided that the [Supplier] is given the opportunity before the third party starts the work to complete the work on the exact same terms at the [Suppliers]' cost.

A.758
The [Sponsor] agrees and undertakes that in the event there is any allegation by the [Sponsor] and/or dispute with the [Company] for any reason. That the [Sponsor] will not automatically issue legal proceedings, but will explore all available non-litigious avenues to resolve the matter. That prior to the issue of any writ the [Sponsor] will consider and attempt all the following methods:

1.1   Amicable discussions.

1.2   A written exchange of the basis of the allegations and the defence.

1.3   Arbitration and/or the appointment of an independent expert approved by both parties by [specify institute/organisation] with a remit which is to be on terms to be agreed between the parties.

A.759
The [Sponsor] and the [Distributor] agree and undertake to resolve all disputes, complaints, allegations of breach of contract and/or non-payment of any sums and/or any other failure and/or default by means of arbitration.

Both parties agree that the arbitrator should be a member of [specify institute] and qualified as [specify profession]. The appointment of the arbitrator shall be subject to the prior written approval of both parties. The arbitrator shall decide who shall bear the cost and expenses of the arbitration based on the facts of the case. Both parties agree and undertake to be bound by the final decision of the arbitrator.

A.760

In the event that the parties cannot agree upon any matter concerning the interpretation, exercise and/or performance of the obligations, liability and/or any other issue concerning this agreement. Then the parties shall endeavour to reach heads of agreement as to how to resolve the problem. Both parties reserve the right unless otherwise agreed in writing at any stage to take such legal steps as may be necessary to protect their interests.

A.761

The parties agree that any arbitration, legal proceedings and/or other procedures shall be taken in [country] by either party. Both agree and waive the right to do so in any other part of the world at any time in respect of this agreement and/or any other matter that may arise either directly and/or indirectly as a result of this agreement.

A.762

The [Institute] and the [Contributor] agree that in the event that there are any disputes, complaints, and/or allegations made by one party against the other arising from the interpretation, performance, fulfilment, rights and/or any other matter relating to this agreement. That in the first instance the parties shall try to resolve the matter through negotiations by both parties. If that shall not succeed to resolve the matter in each case then the parties agree to consider the option of entering into arbitration prior to any litigation. There shall be no obligation on either party to enter into arbitration and both parties reserve the right to commence legal proceedings at any time.

A.763

The [Institute/Charity] and the [Author] agree to resolve any disputes, allegations, complaints, and other problems of any nature arising under this agreement which cannot be resolved between the parties by one of the following procedures either arbitration, mediation, or informal disputes settlement. Both parties agree that they shall endeavour to resolve any matter through one of these procedures prior to the commencement of any legal proceedings.

A.764

The [Institute/Charity] and the [Company] agree that where there is any dispute, and/or difference of opinion as to interpretation of the terms and/

or there are allegations that one party has failed to perform their part of the agreement and/or other problems which arise pursuant to this agreement. That in the first instance both parties agree that they shall endeavour to resolve the problems by negotiation between the parties. In any event the parties shall not be obliged to do this for more than [one] calendar month from the date on which one party has notified the other of the problem in each case. That without prejudice to any legal rights of either party the parties agree to then refer the matter to an independent [arbitrator/mediator] in [country] in accordance with the rules and regulations of [specify organisation] governed by [specify country] law. The parties agree that the decision of the [arbitrator/mediator] shall not be binding unless agreed in advance between the parties in writing that it shall be so.

A.765

In the event that the parties cannot agree upon the interpretation, rights, performance, obligations, liability and/or any other issue concerning this agreement. Then both parties agree to refer the dispute to the following [organisations/body/person] [specify detail]. The parties shall reach agreement as to the terms of reference, whether the decision is to be binding and the allocation of costs. Both parties reserve the right unless otherwise agreed in writing at any stage to take legal action against the other at any stage.

A.766

The [Consortium] and each party to it agree that where there is a dispute relating to this [Project] between the parties and/or between the [Consortium] and any third party. That the legal advice of [specify name of person/firm] shall be sought for a total budget of no more than [number/currency] which shall be paid for out of the sums held by [Name] under this agreement. There shall be no obligation on any party to pay additional legal costs and/or to make a contribution to any arbitration and/or mediation costs and/or to take legal action where any such party does not wish to proceed either due to the legal advice and/or because of the financial cost and risk involved.

ASSIGNMENT

Film, Television and Video

A.767

1.1 In consideration of the Budget for the production of the [Series] by the [Assignor] based on a [Script/Project] created by [Name]. The [Assignor] agrees to assign to the [Assignee] the sole and exclusive

[DVD Rights/Videogram Rights/Non-Theatric Rights/other rights] in the [Series] including the soundtrack which shall be developed in the future throughout the [Territory/country/world] for the assignment period which shall start on [date] and end on [date].

1.2 When the agreement has expired on [date] then all the rights assigned to the [Assignee] shall cease and al rights shall be reverted back to be held jointly between the [Assignor] and the [Assignee] as joint copyright owners of all the rights.

1.3 The [Assignee] agrees and undertakes that it shall account for and pay the [Assignor] all the [Assignor's] Royalties defined in clause [–] in respect of the exploitation of the [DVD Rights/Videogram Rights/Non-Theatric Rights/other rights] in the [Series] including the soundtrack.

A.768

Subject to the above clause [–] the [Assignor] and the [Assignee] both agree that they shall hold joint present and future copyright and all other rights in the [Series] and parts including the soundtrack in all media whether in existence now and/or created in the future throughout the world for the full period of copyright and any extensions and/or renewals and/or any other period of ownership. Further that the consent of both parties shall be required to exploit and/or register any such rights which shall be the subject of separate agreements in each case.

A.769

In consideration of the payment of the Budget and the Assignment Fee the [Assignor] assigns to the [Assignee] All Media Rights as defined in clause [–] in the [Film/Series/Script/Format] and/or parts throughout the [specify countries/Territory/world] for the full period of copyright and any extensions and/or renewals [and such period to continue indefinitely in perpetuity.]

A.770

In consideration of the payment of the Assignment Fee the [Company] assigns to the [Distributor] the sole and exclusive [DVD Rights/other rights] in the [Film] including the soundtrack and/or any parts throughout the [country/Territory/world] for the [full period of copyright and any extensions and renewals/from [date] to [date].]

A.771

1.1 In consideration of the [Fee] the [Author] assigns the right to reproduce and/or exploit the [Manuscript/Book/Film/Sound Recordings] to the [Distributor] in [country/world] from [date] to [date] in the following formats: [DVD/VHS/Audiotapes/Discs/other formats] which shall be accessed and used by means of a computer, laptop, gadget and/or any machine which plays back such formats.

1.2 All other formats and methods not specifically mentioned above are excluded.

1.3 No rights are granted and/or assigned in respect of any rights owned and/or controlled by the [Author] in respect of the exploitation of rights on the internet including through any audio file, website, app and/or other electronic format and/or by means of any telecommunication system by mobile phones and/or some other device and/or through any storage and retrieval playback archive and/or any download of any nature.

1.4 There is no right granted and/or assigned by the [Author] which authorises, permits and/or allows the [Distributor] to register any copyright, domain and/or app and/or podcast name, business name and/or company based on and/or derived from any character, title, slogan and/or any other content and/or new material directly and/or indirectly arising from the [Manuscript/Book/Film/Sound Recordings].

A.772
In consideration of the [Fee] which shall be due on [date] that [Name] shall pay to the [Assignor] in full by electronic transfer direct to their notified bank account. The [Assignor] assigns to [Name] all copyright and intellectual property rights and interest and any other rights which may exist now and/or at any time in the future in any part of the world [and universe] in the [Archive Material/Sound Recordings/Films] and any associated title, logo, image, slogan, promotional, marketing and/or other documents and/or matter listed in Schedule A which is attached to and forms part of this agreement.

A.773
The [Assignor] agrees and accepts that this assignment shall prohibit any future claim by the estate [and/or beneficiaries of the estate] of the [Assignor] and/or any trustees. That the [Assignor] shall specifically not mention any such [Archive Material/Diaries/Images] in their will and/or inheritance documents once it has been assigned to [Name].

A.774
That the [Assignor] agrees that [Name] may register the title, logo, personal name, signature, image and other material listed in Appendix A and/or any adaptation in the name of the [Assignee] with any type of body to record and register their ownership, interest and/or rights in any part of the world. That the [Assignor] shall have no entitlement to be mentioned in any form in any such application.

A.775

1.1 In consideration of the payment of the Advance and the [Assignor's] Royalties the [Assignor] assigns to the [Company] the sole and exclusive rights to the [Work/Script/Film and any soundtrack] in all media throughout the [country/Territory/world] for the full period of copyright and any extensions and/or renewals and forever without any limit on the duration of time except the following which are retained by the [Assignor]: [specify excluded formats/rights/countries].

1.2 The [Assignor] agrees and undertakes to assist the [Company] in respect of the transfer of any copyright ownership and/or other rights to the [Company] and/or the collection of any sums due in respect of the rights assigned to the [Company]. The [Assignor] and/or an authorised representative shall sign and/or complete such affidavits, documents, registration forms and collecting society forms that may be necessary.

1.3 In the event that the [Company] fails to pay the Advance and/or the [Assignor's] Royalties by the dates set out in this agreement. Then if after notification of any such failure and/or default the [Company] has not remedied the problem within [number] days of receipt of notification. Then the [Assignor] shall have the right to serve written notice on the [Company] to terminate this agreement with immediate effect and all rights in the [[Work/Script/Film and any soundtrack] and any new developments and/or adaptations including ownership of any material shall revert to the [Assignor].

A.776

In consideration of the [Presenter's] Fee the [Presenter] assigns to the [Company] all present and future copyright, and all trade marks, domain names and any other intellectual property rights in all media throughout the world and universe in the product of his/her services and any other material created and/or developed for the purpose of this agreement for the full period of copyright and any extensions and/or renewals and in perpetuity including but not limited to: films, videos, programme titles, slogans, podcasts, voice-overs, sound recordings, formats, scripts, books, catalogues and other publications, merchandising, advertisements, material for websites and/or apps and/or for use on the internet and/or by means of any telecommunication system, newsfeed material, jingles, music, images and/or photographs, DVDs, CDs, marketing material, scripts, competitions, promotions and/or interactive material, software and/or discs.

A.777

The [Presenter] agrees that any present and/or future copyright and/or intellectual property rights, trade marks, inventions and patents, computer software rights, design rights, service marks, logos, images, titles, slogans, music, lyrics, domain names, films, videos, sound recordings, promotional and/or merchandising and/or any other rights or material held by the [Company] and/or which are created or developed in conjunction with the services of the [Presenter] shall be the sole and exclusive property of the [Company]. The [Presenter] shall not acquire any rights and/or interest nor does this agreement purport to grant, assign and/or transfer any such rights in the product of the services to the [Presenter] in any form.

A.778

In consideration of the Fee and the Repeat Fees [Name] assigns to the [Company] all present and future copyright and any other rights in all media throughout the [Territory/world] in the product of his/her services and any other material created under this agreement in the product of the services of [Name] and/or any adaptation t for the full period of copyright and any extensions and/or renewals and/or any such further period of time which may be permitted under any law. This assignment is subject to clause [–] set out below.

A.779

The [Company] agrees and undertakes that it shall not be entitled to use, exploit and/or license any of the material produced and/or created for the purposes of this agreement in which [Name] appears in sound and/or vision and/or by any other reference for any purpose at any time other than the endorsement, promotion and/or advertising of the [Company] and/or the [Company's] [Product/Services] during the Term of the Agreement. Where the [Company] wishes to use any such material at any time for any other purpose and/or to license a third party then it is clear that the prior written consent of the [Name] is required and the terms shall be agreed in writing for each such use by both parties and shall require an additional payment and/or royalties to [Name].

A.780

In consideration of the fees the [Contributor] assigns to the [Company] the sole and exclusive rights in all media whether now known and/or hereinafter invented in the [Film] and/or parts including the soundtrack and in any other product of the services of the [Contributor] under this agreement throughout the [Territory/world/universe] for the full period of copyright and any extensions and renewals [and in perpetuity] including but not limited to: all forms of television, satellite, cable, digital and terrestrial; all forms of video, DVD, CD, CD-Rom, games and computer software; merchandising, publishing, interactive multi-media in any text, sound, vision or otherwise; the storage, retrieval or dissemination of information; websites, app, platforms and the internet; mobile phones and any other device for telecommunication systems; theme parks, holograms and any interactive adaptation and the right to authorise, reproduce, license and transfer any such rights to third parties and to exploit any such rights at any time in any format and in any form in whole or in part in any medium.

A.781

The [Contributor] agrees on request to execute and sign any other documents which may be required at a later date to effect the assignment to the [Company] as required under this agreement. It is not the intention of this agreement that the [Contributor] should retain any rights whether in existence now and/or created in the future.

A.782

In consideration of the Assignment Fee the [Director] assigns all present and future copyright and any other intellectual property and/or other rights in all media throughout the world in the product of his/her services and in the filming material and the finished [Programme] and/or any other material created during the existence of this agreement to the [Company] for the full period of copyright and any extensions and/or renewals. For the avoidance of doubt all media shall include but not be limited to all forms of television, radio, any electronic format over the internet and/or any telecommunication system, videos and DVDs, computer software, games, publishing, merchandising and/or any other adaptation in any format.

A.783

In consideration of the [Presenter's] Fees the [Presenter] assigns to the [Company] the [Television Rights/the Internet, Telecommunication and Electronic Download Format Rights/other rights] in the product of his/her services to the [Company] which shall include the [Series/Films], the scripts, sound recordings and any promotional material provided under this agreement throughout the [Territory/world] for the full period of copyright and any extensions and/or renewals. The [Company] agrees that all rights not specifically assigned to the [Company] in this clause [–] are reserved by the [Presenter].

A.784

1.1   The [Assignor] and the [Company] agree that in consideration of the [Company] funding the full cost of the [Pilot] the [Company] shall become the joint copyright owner of the [Pilot] with the [Assignor].

1.2   The [Assignor] assigns to the [Company] the joint copyright ownership with the [Assignor] in the [Pilot] whether in existence now or created in the future in all the Media Rights as defined in clause [–] throughout the [world/country] for the full period of copyright and any extensions and renewals. The only exception shall be the following excluded rights: [specify excluded rights]. The [Company] acknowledges and agrees that the excluded rights shall remain entirely owned by the [Assignor].

A.785
In consideration of the provision of the Budget by the [Assignee] to the [Assignor] to make the [Film/Series]. The [Assignor] assigns all present and future copyright in respect of the [Television Rights/DVD and Video Rights/ the Non-Theatric Rights and the Theatric Rights/other rights] in the [Film/ Series] and parts throughout the Territory for the duration of the Assignment Period which shall commence on the date of this agreement and continue until [date]. This agreement specifically excludes any rights in respect of any electronic format, the internet and/or by means of any telecommunication system and/or any rights not specifically covered by the partial assignment.

A.786
The [Assignee] agrees that all other rights in the [Film/Series] not specifically assigned under this agreement shall remain the property of the [Assignor] including but not limited to any merchandising, publication rights, theme park rights, computer software and/or interactive animated games.

A.787
The [Assignee] undertakes that at the end of the Assignment Period it will execute any document or do anything required by the [Assignor] to confirm the reversion of all the rights to the [Assignor]. So that no rights in the [Film/ Series] are held by the [Assignee] after that time.

A.788
In consideration of the payment of the Approved Budget by the [Distributor] and the payment of the royalties due to the [Production Company]. The [Producer] assigns to the [Distributor] the sole and exclusive All Media Rights which are defined in clause [–] in the [Series] and/or parts including the soundtrack [but excluding any music and/or lyrics] throughout the [country/world] for the full period of copyright and any extensions, renewals and/or other further periods in perpetuity and without limitation.

A.789
[Name] assigns to the [Company] all copyright and/or other intellectual property rights and/or other rights of ownership, interest and/or control of any nature which may exist now and/or be created by law, technological developments and/or otherwise in the future in the [Project/Material]. [Name] agrees that the assignment shall be for the full period of copyright and any extensions and/or renewals and continue indefinitely without limitation in respect of all rights regardless of when those rights may arise. [Name]

agrees that the consideration shall be limited to a payment of [number/currency] by the [Company] to [Name] by [date]. No delay in payment shall effect the transfer of this assignment unless payment is not received by [Name] by [later date].

A.790

In consideration of the payments under this agreement the [Marketing Company] assigns to the [Distributor] all copyright, intellectual property rights and any other rights in all media throughout the universe in the following material which it has been commissioned to develop, create, to supply and/or promote and the [Marketing Company] shall not retain any rights whatsoever to exploit any such material at any time in any format and/or any medium:

1.1 Surveys, data and sources; call centre responses.

1.2 Podcasts, advertisements, images, posters and marketing campaigns. Competition rules, terms of entry and responses.

1.3 Website, app, mobile and other images, messages, sound recordings and films. Stills, photographs, sketches, caricatures, cartoons, jingles and music.

1.4 Press and social media releases, rights documents, and any other material stored in any form and/or medium.

A.791

The [Agent] agrees and undertakes that they are authorised by [Name] to assign all the copyright and any other intellectual property rights to the [Company] in respect of the performance of [Name] in the [Programme] and any associated promotional material for the full period of copyright and in perpetuity throughout the universe. That where at a later date the signature of [Name] is required for any reason to effect such transfer to the [Company] that the [Agent] shall arrange for [Name] to sign any such documents provided that the [Company] agrees to pay any expenses and costs that [Name] may incur.

General Business and Commercial

A.792

The [Executive] acknowledges and agrees that all intellectual property rights, domain names, inventions and patents, copyright, design rights, rights to data and/or databases, trade marks, service marks, community marks and any other rights in the services and/or any product of the work at any time of the [Executive] in the course of or in connection with his/her employment shall remain and be the sole and exclusive property of the

[Company]. This agreement does not purport to assign, grant, or transfer any such rights to the [Executive].

A.793
The [Executive] may not reproduce, distribute and/or otherwise exploit any copyright, intellectual property rights and/or other rights and/or material, data and/or any other matter which is created and/or developed in the course of his/her employment at the [Company] without the prior written consent of the [Company] in each case.

A.794
Without prejudice to the statutory and/or legal rights and remedies of the [Executive], The [Executive] agrees that he /she shall during the course of his/her employment [and/or after the end of the agreement if there is a dispute] at the request and cost of the [Company] execute and sign any document which may be required to complete the assignment to the [Company] of any rights, domain names, invention, patent, discovery and/or otherwise that may be required to protect the rights of the [Company]. The [Company] shall pay the full cost and expense of an independent legal advisor for the [Executive] in such circumstances together with an agreed sum for the [Executive] for his/her services when the assignment in each case has been completed.

A.795
It is agreed between the [Company] and the [Employee]:

1.1 That the [Employee] shall not acquire, obtain, register in his/her name, own, exploit and/or transfer any intellectual property rights, patents, inventions, copyright, computer software, trade marks, logos, service marks, community marks, design rights, database rights, domain names, music, lyrics, slogan in any material, text, images, artwork, maps, diagrams, computer generated material, films, sound recordings and/or any development, concept, format, service and/or product created during the course of their employment at any time in any media and/or on any subject.

1.2 That the [Employee] undertakes to assign and authorise any documentation required by the [Company] which may be necessary to transfer, register or confirm the position set out in 1.1 above to the [Company] and/or a third party in any [country]. Provided that where personal expenses, costs and legal fees are to be incurred by the [Employee] for that purpose then the [Company] agrees to pay such sums.

A.796
The [Employee] assigns to the [Company] all rights, copyright, intellectual property rights, interest, claims and/or title of any nature in all media in any

format and/or medium which may exist now or be developed at any time in the planning, production, and completion of any work and/or services that he/she may fulfil as part of their existing and/or future duties at the [Company] [whether at the premises of the [Company], at the offices of a [Client] and/or at home.] for the full period of copyright and any extended periods that may be permitted in any country of the world and for infinity and beyond.

A.797

[Name] agrees and accepts that there shall be no right to any sums from the exploitation and/or licensing and/or assignment and/or registration of any ideas, concepts, formats, proposals, development projects, research, surveys, data, images, text, sound recordings and/or films, taxonomy, index, music, logo, artwork, photographs, maps, website, app and/or mobile phone content, texts, games, quizzes, competitions, gambling, books, DVDs and/or any other material in any format and/or medium originated and/or contributed to by [Name] during office hours and/or at home while in the employment of the [Company] which arise directly and/or indirectly from the employment of [Name] by the [Company].

A.798

1.1 In consideration of the payment of the Assignment Fee by the [Assignee] to the [Assignor] the [Assignor] assigns the defined All Media Rights in 1.2 below which are in existence now or may be created in the future in the [Work] and/or parts and/or any adaptation to the [Assignee] for the Assignment Period throughout the [country/Territory/world/and universe].

1.2 'All Media Rights' shall mean all intellectual property rights and other rights of whatever nature including without limitation all copyright, trade marks, service marks, community marks, design rights, trade secrets, moral rights, confidential information, any related titles, character names, domain and/or app names. The sole and exclusive right to adapt, vary, delete from and add to, use, copy, license, authorise, print, transmit, broadcast, disseminate, store and/or retrieve, display, process, record, playback, rent, lend, supply, sell, distribute, market, use for sponsorship or for any endorsement of any material, services or person and/or the right to use any part for promotional purposes or otherwise and/or to exploit by any method, medium or process whether created in the future and/or in existence now of any nature and any developments or variations or adaptations whether videos, films, sound recordings, sound effects, text, visual images, photographs, drawings, plans, sketches, computer generated art, graphics and/or other electronic material in any format, music, lyrics, computer software, interactive material, logos, maps and slogans including but not limited to:

a. All forms of radio and television including terrestrial, cable, satellite and digital;

b. All forms of mechanical reproduction including videograms, lasers, discs, cassettes and DVDs;

c. All forms of non-theatric audiences whether for business and/ or commercial use, educational, cultural, religious and/or social, schools, colleges, universities, museums, readings, plays, addresses, speeches, lectures, seminars, conferences, or discussions;

d. All forms of theatric exploitation including cinemas;

e. All forms of publishing in printed form, hardback and/or paperback books, digests, serialisations, reproduction of extracts in newspapers and/or magazines, comics, periodicals, quotations, anthologies and/or translations in any such format in any language, sub-titles and/or braille; all rights in any title, series name and/or theme, chapter heading, format, characters, storylines, fictional locations; competitions, rules and entry conditions.

f. All forms of reproduction, display, supply, distribution, licence and/or sale through any collecting society and/or management rights collective.

g. All forms of reproduction, display, supply, distribution, licence and/or sale through any electronic format and/or method over the internet and/or through any telecommunication system and/ or any payback and/or retrieval archive and/or any streaming method and/or any website, app, download, E book, audio file, blog, podcast, newsfeed and/or blockchain and/or other algorithm, and/or any method of exchanging data, images, films, videos and/or other material in any medium and/or however it is received whether by television, radio, computer, laptop, mobile and/or some other gadget or device.

h. All forms of computer software and interactive multi-media such as compact discs, CD-Roms, computer games and all other material and/or method where there is an element of interactivity and/or a combination of sound, text, vision, graphics and/or otherwise;

i. Films, advertisements, banner advertisements, podcasts, sponsorship, endorsements and associated merchandising and sub-licensing; all forms of merchandising, toys, clothing, mugs,

199

stationery, games, posters, shoes, games, and any other two or three dimensional representation whether related to a title, logo, trade mark, image, name, character, brand name and/or some other matter; quiz questions, game formats, equipment, costumes and layout; theatre plays, musicals; readings, tours, theme and sports parks, lottery, gambling and betting, holograms and statues.

j.   All forms of storage and retrieval in any form in any medium and all database rights; rights in any index, taxonomy and /or search engine words.

k.   All forms of reproduction and/or methods of delivery of all and/or any part in any medium including photocopying, scanning, and document delivery.

l.   All forms of exploitation of the sound, music, lyrics, words, titles and/or sound recordings whether as audio files, ringtones, downloads, CDs, audiotapes, sheet music or any some other form and/or performance and/or method of exploitation.

A.799
In consideration of the [Assignment Fee] the [Assignor] assigns to the [Assignee] all intellectual property rights including copyright and any other rights in the [Work] and the [Work Material] which are owned and/or controlled by the [Assignor] for the full period of copyright including any extensions and renewals to continue indefinitely in perpetuity throughout the [Territory/world/universe].

A.800
In consideration of the [Assignment Fee] the [Assignor] assigns to the [Assignee] all intellectual property rights and any other rights in the [Work] and the [Work Material] which are owned or controlled by the [Assignor] for the assignment period which shall start on: [date] and end on: [date] in [country]. After the end date of [date] all the intellectual property rights and any other rights in the [Work Material] and any development and/or adaptation shall be assigned by the [Assignee] to the [Assignor] for a nominal fee of [number/currency].

A.801
'The Work Material' shall mean all material of the [Work] in the possession and/or under the control of the [Assignor] [excluding accounts and/or financial records relating to sums received but not expenses incurred for creating and exploiting material] including:

1.1   All copies of any master material in any format and/or medium; Together with a list of locations as to where any such material is held together with access letters giving irrevocable authority for the [Assignee] to remove such material;

1.2 All documents, records, data in any form and other material of any nature including contracts, licences, data, and databases, invoices relating to material expenses, consents, waivers, lists, proofs, scripts, publicity, advertising material, computer software, photographs, negatives, posters, catalogues, drawings, plans, sketches, electronically generated material, audio files, music, computer generated art, podcasts, videos, DVDs, films and sound recordings.

The [Assignor] agrees that it shall not retain any rights or interest in the [Work] and/or the [Work Material] after the assignment to the [Assignee].

A.802
In addition to the assignment by the [Assignor] to the [Assignee] of the defined All Media Rights in the [Work] and the [Work Material] in clause [–]. The [Assignor] agrees and undertakes that it has and/or will also assign all the following rights and/or ownership including any associated goodwill [except those matters which are identified as owned and/or controlled by a third party at the time of the assignment] as follows:

1.1 All registered trade marks, community marks, service marks and/ or any logos, images and/or slogans described and represented in Appendix A.

1.2 All design rights as described in Appendix B.

1.3 All domain names and apps as described in Appendix C.

1.4 All trade secrets and confidential information listed in Appendix D.

1.5 All sound tracks, music and sound recordings associated with any of the assigned material as listed in Appendix E.

A.803
The [Assignor] undertakes and agrees that he/she is the original creator and the sole owner of all copyright, intellectual property rights and/or any other rights in the [Script/Image/Project/Material] which are assigned under this agreement. That the [Assignor] has not exploited the [Script/Image/ Project/Material] in any form except those listed in Schedule A attached to this agreement.

A.804
That the [Assignor] undertakes and agrees that he/she is the sole owner of all intellectual property rights including copyright and any other rights in the [Work/ Material] which are bound by the following obligations, payments,

credits and moral rights a complete list of which is set out in Schedule A to this agreement. The [Assignor] shall be responsible for all sums due and other obligations up to [date/time] and the [Assignee] shall bear all payments, costs, liabilities and obligations owed to any third party from the [date/time] of this agreement.

A.805
In consideration of the payment of the Assignment Fee in full by the agreed date the [Assignor] assigns to the [Assignee] all present and future copyright and all other rights in all media whether in existence now and/or developed at a later date by new technology and/or by changes in the law in the [Work] including any parts and the [Work Material Package] throughout the [Territory/country/world] for the full period of copyright and any extensions and renewals and/or any additional periods of time as may be permitted including but not limited to:

1.1   All forms of exploitation through the medium of television and radio whether the transmission is terrestrial, by cable, digital, satellite, microwave, over the air; whether free, pay per view, encrypted or not or otherwise;

1.2   All forms of exploitation by electronic means over the internet and/or through any telecommunication systems and/or computer software and/or any mechanical reproduction including by means of computers, gadgets, mobile phones, watches and/or other devices, DVDs, audio files, electronic downloads,

1.3   All forms of exploitation through videos, cassettes, lasers, discs, merchandising, cinemas, non-paying audiences in educational, cultural, religious and social establishments, clubs, universities, and/or commercial use by businesses;

1.4   All forms of publishing whether in printed or electronic form; and/or all forms of exploitation not covered above in any medium.

A.806
The [Assignor] and the [Assignee] agree that the assignment in clause [–] is subject to the following existing agreements described and listed in Appendix A. Copies of the existing agreements are attached to and form part of this agreement as Appendix B.

A.807

1.1   The [Company] acknowledges and agrees that this agreement is not intended and does not constitute an assignment of the rights in the [Work] and/or any part to the [Company].

1.2 Where for any reason new material is created in the future by any third party commissioned by the [Company] and/or the [Company] creates and/or develops any new material based on and/or derived from the [Work]. Then the [Company] agrees and undertakes to assign and/or to ensure the assignment of all rights in all media in the [Work] and/or parts throughout the world to the [Author] so that the [Author] owns and/or controls all rights in any such new material.

A.808

No rights of any nature are intended to be transferred and/or assigned by virtue of this summary and/or proposal document which is subject to the conclusion and signature of the main agreement by all the parties.

A.809

[Name] agrees and undertakes that he/she shall on request by the [Company] at the [Company's] sole cost and expense conclude and sign such documents and/or forms as may reasonably be required by the [Company] on the advice of their professional legal advisors to vest and assign all the rights in the products of the services and/or work of [Name] under this agreement to the [Company]. Such assignment shall include but not be limited to all copyright and/or intellectual property rights and/or other rights, patents, inventions, titles, domain names, computer software, logos, graphics, films, videos, images, text and /or any other development created and/or carried out by [Name].

A.810

1.1 The [Distributor] agrees and undertakes that it shall assign all the copyright, intellectual property rights and any other rights in any new material, names, titles and/or formats based on and/or derived from and/or associated with the [Work/Product/Service] of any nature in any medium to the [Author/Copyright Owner]. This shall be the case regardless of whether the new material is commissioned from a third party and/or created by an employee and/or consultant.

1.2 The [Distributor] agrees and undertakes that the assignment in clause [–] above shall include but not be limited to any new marketing material, packaging, labels, domain names, online accounts, hashtags and/or other marketing tools; translations, newspaper, television, radio an pop-up banner advertisements, links, logos, slogans, images, text and trade marks.

1.3 That the [Distributor] agrees and undertakes to bear all the legal and administrative expenses that may be incurred by the [Distributor] in order to ensure the effective transfer of all such rights to the [Author/

Copyright Owner]. The [Author/Copyright] shall be liable for his/her own legal and administrative costs.

A.811

The parties agree that this assignment is intended to be a full and effective transfer to the [Company] of all rights in all media in all formats throughout the universe in the [Work] and any parts and all associated material listed in Schedule A for the full period of copyright and any extensions and/or renewals and/or any other further periods that may be permitted. If for any reason a new right is created by the development of new technology and/or new legislation and/or an existing right has to be registered. Then the [Author/Contributor] agrees and undertakes to sign and execute any additional legal documents and/or forms that may be required to ensure that all rights are held, owned and controlled by the [Company]. Provided that the [Company] agrees and undertakes to pay for all legal, administrative and other costs that may be incurred by both parties and also pays the [Author/Contributor] an additional fee of [number/currency] in each such case.

A.812

It is agreed between the participants of the [Consortium] that where there is to be any assignment, transfer and/license of any rights and/or other legal lien and/or claim and/or registration made in respect of any material and/or rights created, commissioned, developed, designed and/or adapted under this agreement. That it is agreed between the parties that the owner of all shall material and/or rights shall be all participants of the [Consortium] as joint owners with each party holding a portion. The name, address and director of each participant shall be recorded. All participants shall be supplied with a copy of any such documents.

A.813

Where the [Company] fails and/or delays more than [specify period] to pay the Advance Fee [and/or any royalties] due to [Name] under this agreement at any time. Then [Name] shall be entitled to serve notice that the consideration under this agreement has not been complied with in full and that the assignment clause fails to take effect due to such circumstances. [Name] may therefore also serve notice that the agreement is terminated with immediate effect and that all copyright and any other rights in the [Work] shall revert to and be assigned back to [Name].

A.814

It agreed that [Name] shall assign to the [Company] all copyright and intellectual property rights in the [Script/Work] which may exist in any media including but not limited to television, film, animation and cartoons, Blu-ray, DVD, publishing, online business, advertising and marketing, mobiles phones and computers, games, food and drink and other household and commercial products and merchandising, audio, radio, wireless and other forms of communication and exploitation, development and adaptation of any nature which exist in [year] and/or thereafter in any time and/or on any land, sub-terrain, sea, air and/or planet and/or space.

Internet, Websites and Apps

A.815

1.1 You shall not acquire and you are not granted the right to use, assign, license, exploit and/or adapt any copyright, intellectual property rights, trade marks, logos, slogans, artwork, text, emails, films, videos, podcasts, blogs, news feeds, television, radio and/or audio material, sound recordings, domain names, databases, computer software, taxonomy, sitemap and/or any electronic material and/or any other rights and/or content of any nature.

1.2 All rights in all media of any nature belong to [Company] unless stated otherwise.

1.3 It is a condition of your use of this [Website/App/Platform] that any person and/or company that registers to gain access must agree to assign to the [Company] all copyright and other intellectual property rights which they may own and/or control in any email, film, video, advertisement, photograph and/or other material which is sent by them to be displayed on the [Website/App/Platform] for the full period of copyright including any extensions and renewals to continue indefinitely in perpetuity throughout the world and universe.

A.816

1.1 The [Company] shall not acquire any copyright and/or any other rights in any emails, text, film, video, podcast, photographs, images and/or any other material which is submitted, sent, displayed, sold and/or or supplied by any member of the public and/or any business and/or or charity and/or educational establishment to any section of this [Website/Platform/Channel]. There shall be no obligation to assign any rights to the [Company] and/or to pay any royalty percentage of any sums received.

1.2 The [Company] shall however acquire a non-exclusive licence as set out in Appendix A which must be agreed to and accepted as a condition of access and/or use of this [Website/Platform/Channel].

A.817

The [Artist] agrees and undertakes:

1.1 That he/she is the sole and original creator of the [Artwork/Design].

1.2 That the [Artwork/Design] is owned by the [Artist].

1.3 That the [Artwork/Design] has not been licensed, registered, exploited and/or adapted in any format in any medium by the [Artist] and/or any third party at any time.

1.4 In consideration of the payment of the Assignment Fee the [Artist] assigns to the [Website Company] all present and future copyright and all other intellectual property rights [and trade marks, service marks and community marks and/or any other forms of registration of rights] in all media and in all [formats/medium] whether in existence now or developed by new technology or by changes in the law or otherwise in the [Artwork/Design] throughout the [world/universe] for the full period of copyright and any extensions and renewals and forever without limit of time.

For the avoidance of doubt it is agreed that 'all media' shall include but not be limited to terrestrial, cable, digital and satellite television and radio; whether free, pay per view, encrypted or not. All methods of exploitation by the internet and/or by means of any telecommunication system and/or any electronic means for access via computer, laptop, mobile phones, watches and/or other devices; websites, apps, audio files; computer software; mechanical reproduction including DVDs, and audiocassettes. All forms of publishing whether in printed and/or electronic form, and the right to supply and distribute copies in any format by any means such as merchandising for clothes and household items; tours, musicals, gambling, betting and lotteries.

1.5 The [Artist] agrees and acknowledges that the [Website Company] shall be entitled to register ownership of the [Artwork/Design] with any third party and/or any rights management collecting society and/or other organisation and shall have the right to reproduce, license, and exploit the [Artwork/Design] in any manner that it thinks fit. The [Website Company] shall not be obliged to consult with and/or seek the approval of the [Artist]. Nor shall the [Artist] be entitled to receive any additional payment, royalties and/or other sums.

1.6 The [Artist] agrees and acknowledges that the [Website Company] shall be entitled to adapt, translate, vary, develop, add to and/or delete from the [Artwork/Design] at any time. Further the [Website Company] shall be entitled to sell, dispose of, transfer, assign and/or create a charge over the [Artwork/Design]. The [Artist] waives all rights to any additional royalties, payments and/or other sums that may become due at any time including resale and any other form of reproduction.

1.7 The [Artist] agrees that the [Website Company] shall have the right to register the [Artwork/Design] as part of a trade mark, community mark, design right, service mark, and/or domain name and which is to be registered as owned and/or controlled by the [Website Company].

A.818

There shall be no transfer of rights and/or assignment in the [Musical Works/Lyrics] and/or the [Sound Recordings/Audio Files] to any person who may have access to and/or use this [Website/Platform] and listen to and/or download and/or store any material which is available. Any person who reproduces, stores and retrieves, exploits, supplies and/or the distributes the [Musical Works/Lyrics] and/or the [Sound Recordings/Audio Files] to a third party whether for commercial, educational and/or non-commercial purposes shall be in breach of copyright and legal proceedings may be taken against them without further notice.

A.819

1.1 The [Company] has engaged the [Consultant/Supplier] to carry out the [Work/Project] set out in Schedule A to develop, design and create suitable computer software, electronic and other material for the [Website/App/Podcast Series].

1.2 The [Consultant/Supplier] agrees and undertakes to assign to the [Company] all intellectual property rights and copyright, computer software rights, design rights, future design rights, patents, trade marks, service marks, domain names and any other rights in the [Work/Project] and any other material designed, developed and/or created under this agreement throughout the world and universe for the full period of copyright and any extensions and/or renewals and for such other periods as may be assigned to the [Company] without limit of time in perpetuity.

1.3 The [Consultant/Supplier] agrees that it shall not be entitled to register any claim and/or interest and/or to receive any additional payment of any nature from the exploitation and/or reproduction of any copies in any format and/or medium at any time of the [Work/Project] in 1.1 and 1.2. The [Company] shall be entitled to use, license, exploit and adapt the [Work/Project] and any material as it thinks fit and to engage such third parties as it shall decide shall be required at any time.

A.820

The [Enterprise] has been engaged by the [Company] to design, create and develop a name, logo and image known as the [Project] for the [Company's]

[Website/Podcast Series/Platform] in accordance with the specifications in Appendix A. The [Enterprise] agrees and undertakes:

1.1 To ensure that all persons who contribute to the [Project] at any time who are employees shall assign all the copyright and any other rights to the [Company] and/or if they are freelance that their terms of engagement ensure that all rights shall be assigned to the [Company].

1.2 That no person requested to contribute to any part of the [Project] by the [Enterprise] shall acquire any rights and/or interest and/or be entitled to receive any payments, royalties and/or other benefits from the assignment, registration and exploitation of their contribution and/or work of any nature whether original or not.

1.3 That all rights to any acknowledgement, credit, copyright notice and/or moral rights are and/or will be waived.

1.4 To assign to the [Company] all intellectual property rights and copyright, computer software rights and source code, design rights, future design rights, patents, trade marks, service marks, domain names and any other rights in the [Project] and/or the] [Website/Podcast Series/Platform] and/or any other material created under this agreement in all medium, methods and/or formats throughout the world and the universe for the full period of copyright and any extensions and renewals and for the full period of all other rights and forever without limitation of time.

1.5 That the [Enterprise] shall not be entitled to register any claim and/or interest and/or to receive any additional payments of any nature from the exploitation and/or reproduction of any copies in any format and/or medium at any time.

1.6 That the [Company] shall be entitled to use, license, exploit and adapt the [Project] and/or] the [Website/Podcast Series/Platform] and/or any other material as it thinks fit and to engage such third parties as it shall decide shall be required at any time.

A.821

1.1 The [Designer] has and/or will design, develop, create and deliver a prototype and finished [App/Podcast Series Format/Promotional Banners] based on all the [Logos/Image/Brands/Products] of the [Company] which are listed in Appendix A and on the proposed target outcomes in terms of achievable targets in Appendix B and the budget in Appendix C.

1.2 The [Designer] agrees to and does assign in this document any future copyright and/or intellectual property rights, trade marks, design rights, computer software rights, patents, music, sounds, shapes, images, text, characters, codes and any other material and/or data and/or charts that he/she may acquire and/or bring into existence as a direct result of the development of the [App/Podcast Series Format/ Promotional Banners] to the [Company] for the full period of copyright and any extensions and renewals and for the full period of the life of any other rights without limit. At no time shall the assignment period end so that any rights of any nature revert to the [Designer].

1.3 The [Designer] agrees to retain and deliver to the [Company] all development material of any nature and any copies of the final version together with any documents and records held and/or controlled by them in any format and/or medium which can be held by the [Company] for use as archive material in respect of the [App/Podcast Series Format/Promotional Banners]. The [Company] agrees to pay the cost of such delivery.

A.822

[Name] does not grant any assignment to the [Company] of any of the rights in the [Image/Text/Logo] where it is displayed and/or exhibited on the [Website/Podcast/Platform]. Nor does [Name] grant the [Company] any right to authorise any third party to use and/or adapt any part of the [Image/Text/Logo] whether or not it is for the purpose of marketing, promotion and/or review. The prior consent of [Name] must be sought in each case and may be refused.

A.823

In consideration of the payment for their services the [Company] assigns all intellectual property rights including copyright, computer software rights, trade marks and/or any other rights and/or interest in the [App/Podcast Series/Audio Files] {in whole and/or any parts and/or any adaptation} and the material which may have been designed, created and/or developed during the production of the [App/Podcast Series/Audio Files] to the [Distributor] for the full period of copyright and any extensions and/or renewals together such any other additional periods in which rights may be assigned but in any event such assignment shall continue indefinitely without limit of time in perpetuity. The [Company] acknowledges that there can be no assignment of any computer software which is owned by a third party.

A.824

The [Contributor] assigns all intellectual property rights including present and future copyright and/or any other rights in his/her work, scripts, performance and/or any other material created and/or supplied for the purpose of the [Podcast Series] to the [Company] for the full period of copyright as may be permitted under any legislation and/or for such additional periods as may come into existence at a later date throughout the world. Provided that the [Company] shall pay the [Contributor] the agreed buy-out fee of [number/ currency] which shall be in addition to the appearance fee of [number/ currency]. The [Contributor] agrees and undertakes that from [date] all rights of any nature in any medium in his/her work, scripts, performance and/or any other material created and/or supplied for the purpose of the [Podcast Series] by the [Contributor] shall belong to the [Company].

A.825

The [Audio File] has been commissioned and created by the [Distributor] based on a [Sound Recording] of the [Book/Work/Script] owned by [Name]. The [Distributor] agrees and undertakes that the [Audio File] and the [Sound Recording] which has been created shall be jointly owned by the [Distributor] and [Name]. That the [Distributor] shall ensure that no rights in the [Sound Recording]and/or [Audio File] are acquired by a third party. That where this agreement is terminated and/or expires and the [Distributor] no longer exploits the [Audio File]. That at the request of [Name] the [Distributor] shall sign any document to assign all rights in all media and all medium to [Name] in consideration of a nominal sum.

A.826

1.1 The [Developer] agrees and undertakes to assign to the [Company] any rights in the [App/Website/Podcast] which it may own and/or control as a result of the commission by the [Company] and the payment of the budget in Appendix A.

1.2 The [Developer] agrees that it is not the intention of the parties that the [Developer] should acquire and/or retain any rights of any type in any medium and/or format.

1.3 The [Developer] assigns all intellectual property rights including copyright, trade marks, service marks, community marks, logos, images, films, videos, graphics, slogan, sound recordings and/or computer software and/or any other rights and/or associated material which it owns and/or controls in the [App/Website/Podcast] whether in existence now and/or created in the future to the [Company] for the full period of copyright and any extensions and/or renewals and/or any other further period that may be allowed at any time which shall continue indefinitely.

A.827

1.1 The parties agree that the [Images/Sound Recordings/Videos] commissioned and paid for by [Name] under this agreement from the [Company] shall be owned by [Name].

1.2 That no ownership of any rights and/or material shall pass to [Name] until the agreed Fee and Budget in clause [–] has been paid if full to the [Company].

1.3 That in the event the work is completed by the Fee and/or Budget is not paid within [six] months. Then the [Company] shall have the right to sell and/or sub-license the rights and/or material of the commissioned work to third party without further notice to [Name].

1.4 Subject to the payment of the Fee and Budget the [Company] assigns all copyright and intellectual property rights in the commissioned work namely the [Images/Sound Recordings/Videos] and all related prototypes, samples, draft material, final version and/or otherwise to [Name] for the full period of copyright and any extensions and/or renewals and for such further periods as may be permitted at any time throughout the world in all media and/or formats and/or in respect of any adaptation, translation, merchandising and/or other form of exploitation.

Merchandising and Distribution

A.828
The [Licensee] acknowledges that it is not acquiring any copyright and/or any other intellectual property rights in the [Work/Character] and/or any [Licensed Articles] and/or any sequel and/or any logo, trade mark, title, name, character or otherwise which shall remain with and belong solely to the [Licensor] [except as specifically authorised under this agreement.]

A.829
In consideration of the payment of the Assignment Fee the [Company] assigns to the [Distributor] all present and future copyright and all other rights in all media in the [Work/Film/Project] and/or parts whether in existence now or created in the future throughout the [Territory/world/universe] for the full period of copyright and any extensions or renewals to continue in perpetuity including but not limited to:

1.1 All forms of exploitation through the medium of television and radio including reception and transmission by standard terrestrial, cable, satellite, digital television, regardless of the method of payment and/or whether it is free and/or the technical method of delivery whether encrypted and/or otherwise.

1.2 All forms of exploitation through the medium of a machine, television, watch and/or other product and/or device whether capable of being downloaded, recorded, stored and/or played by computer, laptop, cassette, disc, laser, DVD whether free and/or any method of payment and/or whether sold, for hire, under subscription, rental and/or otherwise.

1.3　All forms of television and video and non-theatric audiences including but not limited to: businesses and commercial use, educational, cultural, religious and social establishments, schools, churches, prisons, hospitals, camps, garages, workshops, film groups, professional and trade bodies, private and public libraries, colleges, universities, hotels, airlines and airports, clubs, shops, ships.

1.4　All forms of theatric exploitation including cinemas.

1.5　All forms of publication whether text, images and/or words and/or music in any medium whether printed, sound recordings, audio file and/or in electronic form as a download.

1.6　All forms of telecommunication, electronic, internet, intranet and multimedia exploitation and interactive scenarios including CD-Roms, computer games, challenges and any other methods of combining the use of sound, text, music, graphics and vision.

1.7　All forms of merchandising and commercial exploitation whether based on character, logo, images, theme, format, rules and/or otherwise including toys, games, clothing, accessories, household items, badges, sweets, stationery, theme parks and/or otherwise.

1.8　All forms of exploitation of the sound, music, lyrics, words, titles whether as audio files, ringtones, downloads, CDs, audiotapes, sheet music or any other form.

1.9　All forms of adaptation, translation, variation and/or development of the original version and/or any sequel. Together with the right to assign, sub-license, sell, supply, reproduce, distribute and exploit in any market and in any format and/or medium whether for the educational, charitable, commercial and/or non-commercial purposes.

A.830
The [Distributor/Agent] agrees and undertakes that this agreement does not transfer and/or assign any intellectual property rights, copyright, computer software rights, design rights and future design rights, trade marks, service marks, community marks or any other rights in the [Work/Character] and/or in any [Licensed Articles] and/or in any development, variation and/or adaptation and/or sequel to the [Distributor/Agent] and all rights shall remain with and belong to the [Licensor]. [Except as set out specifically in this agreement for the Licence Period].

A.831
The [Distributor] agrees and undertakes to assign to the [Licensor] all present and future copyright and any other rights in the product of the services of the [Distributor] and/or any third party relating to the development, production,

supply and sale of the [Licensed Articles] and/or the [Work/Character] and/or any associated packaging, marketing and promotional material in all media throughout the world for the full period of copyright and any extensions and renewal.

A.832

The [Distributor] agrees and undertakes that the name of the [Work/Character] and any goodwill and reputation created in respect of any trade mark, service mark, community mark, business name or logo whether existing and/or developed for the [Licensed Articles] shall remain the sole and exclusive property of the [Licensor] and/or is and/or shall be assigned to the [Licensor]. That no part of this agreement is intended to assign, transfer or vest any such rights in the [Work/Character] and/or the [Licensed Articles] and/or any associated packaging, marketing and promotional material to the [Distributor].

A.833

The [Distributor] agrees and undertakes that it is not the intention of this agreement that the [Distributor] and/or any of its designers, employees and/or consultants should acquire any intellectual property rights and/or copyright and/or any other rights in any of the products, articles and/or other material commissioned and/or developed through the [Distributor]. Where any new rights of any nature and/or medium are created and held by the [Distributor] and/or any of its designers, employees and/or consultants. Then the [Distributor] agrees that they shall be bound to sign and authorise the assignment of all such rights in all media and any format to the [Company] in consideration of a nominal sum of less than [number/currency] in each case.

A.834

The [Artist] assigns all copyright, intellectual property rights and any other rights and/or interest in any media and/or format and/or medium and in any adaptation and/or development to the [Company] which may exist now and/or be created at any time in the [Image/Logo/Work] in consideration of the payment of [number/currency] on [date] each year for a period of [number] years. In the event that the fee is not paid in any year then the [Artist] shall have the right to serve notice that unless the fee is paid within [number] days that the [Company] shall be obliged to pay the [Artist] an additional sum of [number/currency] for that period.

A.835

The [Supplier] agrees that it shall not acquire any rights or interest in the [Company's] [Website/App/Podcast/Online digital account] except those rights and/or material which directly relate to the development and/or variation of the [Supplier's] existing [Products] and/or trade marks, logos, slogans, texts, images recordings. films, jingles and/or sound recordings which have been adapted by the [Company].

A.836

[Name] agrees that it shall not acquire any patent, copyright, design rights, trade mark, service mark or logo, slogan, text, image, music or other intellectual property rights in the [Product] and/or any other marketing material and it shall be the sole and exclusive property of the [Supplier] together with any goodwill. That [Name] shall not acquire any rights in any adaptation, variation and/or otherwise. Further [Name] agrees and undertakes that where necessary it shall provide to the [Supplier] any necessary documentation to support and/or transfer any such rights and/or interest to the [Supplier] at the [Supplier's] cost and expense.

A.837

The [Promoter] assigns to the [Company] all present and future intellectual property rights including copyright and any other rights which may exist and/or be created by itself and/or any third party engaged by them to assist in respect of the [Company] and the [Company's] Products within its possession and/or control throughout the [world/universe] for the full period of copyright and any extensions or renewals and in perpetuity.

A.838

The [Distributor] agrees that all present and future copyright, design rights and intellectual property rights and patents in the [Designs], the [Licensed Articles], the [Prototypes] and the [Complete Set] are and shall remain the sole property of the [Company] and this agreement does not purport to transfer and/or assign any rights to the [Distributor].

A.839

The [Purchaser] confirms and agrees that this agreement relates solely to the sale and purchase of the [Garment/Unit] based on the [Designs] for personal use and does not assign any copyright, design rights and/or otherwise and does not authorise the [Purchaser] to commercially exploit the [Garment/Unit] and/or [Designs] in any form.

A.840

The [Production Company] agrees to ensure that anyone engaged in the development, creation, design, testing and/or creation of the samples, models and/or the production any part of the [Product/Project] and/or any associated packaging shall not acquire any rights. That all such persons shall for a nominal fee be obliged to complete an assignment of all rights that they may technically hold including all copyright and/or intellectual property rights, computer software rights, design rights, trade marks, patents, images and/or text, processes, mechanisms and/or inventions to [Name].

Publishing

A.841

The [Company] agrees that it shall not acquire any rights and/or interest in the [Work] and/or any part including but not limited to any character, title, location and/or phrase at any time save as set out in the short form permission in appendix A. That any developments, variation and/or sequel of the [Work], title, text, artwork and of any other material relating to the [Work] and/or the [Author] shall be vested in, transferred to and belong to the [Author]. No rights of any nature shall be acquired by and/or belong to the [Company] and the [Company] agrees and undertakes that it shall transfer and assign all rights, interest and copyright in all media to the [Author] at the end of this agreement which may have been created or acquired by the [Company] relating to the [Author] and the [Work].

A.842

The [Researcher] agrees to assign to the [Company] all present and future copyright and any other rights in the product of his/her services relating to [Project] and in all associated material throughout the world for the full period of copyright and any extensions and renewals.

A.843

In consideration of the payment of the [Ghost-writer's] Fee the [Ghost-writer] assigns to the [Name] all present and future copyright and all other intellectual property rights, computer software rights, trade marks and/or any other rights in the product of his/her services including: all scripts, drafts, notes, photographs, images, videos, sound recordings and/or other material which is created by him/her under this agreement and in the [Work] in all media whether in existence now and/or created in the future throughout the [country/Territory/world] for the full period of copyright and any extensions and renewals [and any further additional periods]. All media shall be defined to include but not be limited to: the title, all forms of publication such as hardback and paperback, anthology, quotations, serialisations, translations, dramatic and non-dramatic adaptations for radio and/or television and/or films, adaptations and performances for the theatre, mechanical reproduction such as DVDs, electronic formats for streaming over the internet and/or by means any telecommunication system by means of downloads, audio files and/or merchandising in the form of products and/or services.

A.844

In consideration of the Assignment Fee the [Author] assigns to the [Assignee] all present and future copyright and All Media Rights and any other rights of any nature whether in existence now and/or created later either by

215

technology and/or changes and developments in the law in the [Work] and parts including the [Artwork] and the material in Schedule A throughout the [Territory/world] for the full period of any copyright and any extensions and renewals and in perpetuity.

The [Artwork] shall mean any photograph, drawing, sketch, picture, diagram, map, chart plan and any other illustration or any engraving, lithograph, image or other material listed in Schedule A which forms part of this [Work].

'All Media Rights' shall mean the sole and exclusive right to produce, manufacture, supply, rent, sell, distribute, license, market and exploit the [Work] and any parts including the [Artwork] and the material in Schedule A in all forms of the media whether in existence now or created in the future either by developments in the law or technology including but not limited to: all forms of publication; hardback, paperback; all forms of radio, television and video; cable, digital, satellite, terrestrial, cassette, disc, any technical method of delivery; any method of payment, charging, subscription, rental, lease and for free; all forms of telecommunication systems; sound, vision, graphics, text, icons, images; all forms of theatric and non-theatric exploitation; all forms of mechanical and electronic reproduction, dissemination or otherwise, internet, intranet and multimedia exploitation; all methods of merchandising and any other developments, adaptations and/or sequels of any nature.

A.845
In consideration of the Fee the [Name] agrees and undertakes that he/she shall assign all rights so that the [Publisher] owns all present and future intellectual property rights including copyright and all other rights in the [Articles/Scripts] and the [Sound Recordings] and the [Photographs/Images] in all media whether in existence now or created in the future throughout the [Territory/world] for the full period of copyright and any extensions or renewals [and thereafter]. [Name] shall not be entitled to any additional payment and/or royalties after the date of assignment to the [Company].

A.846
The [Publisher] [Name] and the [Interviewee] agree and undertake not to commercially exploit the [Articles/Text], the [Sound Recordings] and/or the [Photographs/Images] and/or the [Artwork] in any media other than for the publication in the Periodical on the publication dates without the prior consent of all parties. The [Publisher] agrees that an additional payment on each occasion shall be due to the [Interviewee] and [Name] in the event that the parties agree to some other further forms of exploitation.

A.847
The [Author] assigns all copyright in the [Work/Review] to the [Company] for the full period of copyright and any extensions and renewals throughout the

world and universe for use on the [website/platform] [specify reference] and in any associated online service, newspapers, periodicals and subscription and/or newsfeed of the [Company] and by any other manner in all media by the [Company] and/or any sub-licensee. Provided that the [Company] pays the fee due promptly by [date] and provides a credit to the [Author] as follows: [specify credit] and that the [Company] undertakes to pay the additional fees set out in appendix A for any new forms of exploitation.

A.848
The [Author] assigns all copyright, intellectual property rights and any other rights in the [Work] including the title, headings, cover, images, index and preface to the [Company] for the full period of copyright and any other period in which ownership of rights of any nature may exist at any time throughout the [world/country] subject to the following conditions:

1.1   That the [Company] credits the [Author] as the creator as follows: [specify credit]

1.2   That all sums due under this agreement are paid in full.

1.3   That the [Company] does not go into insolvency and/or administration and/or fails to publish and/or exploit the [Work] in any form by [date].

Where the [Company] fails to fulfil any of the above conditions then the [Company] agrees that the consideration for the assignment has not been fulfilled.

Services

A.849
The [Agent] agrees that the name of the [Actor] and any goodwill and reputation created in respect of any trade mark, business name, logo, slogan, word, shape and/or gesture shall remain the sole and exclusive property of the [Actor] whether in existence now or created in the future during the Term of this Agreement. That no part of this agreement is intended to assign, transfer and/or vest any rights owned and/or controlled by the [Actor] in the [Agent].

A.850
The [Designer] in consideration of the payment of the sums set out in clause [–] assigns to the [Company] the sole and exclusive rights in all media and in all formats and/or by any method and/or means including the internet, any telecommunication system and/or any electronic means and/or computer software; any password and source code rights in any rights owned or controlled by the [Designer] in the Product Specification, domain name, website and software and any other rights and/or documents, programs,

formats and/or material of any nature which may arise in pursuance of this agreement; whether in existence now and/or created in the future throughout the universe for the full period of copyright and any other rights and any other extensions renewals and/or otherwise.

A.851

The [Designer] shall not acquire any rights and/or interest in the [Website/App/Platform] except the [specify source code/other]. Nor shall the [Designer] be entitled at any time to register, renew and/or claim any rights, interest and/or equity in the domain name and/or any logo, service mark, trade mark and/or other image, text and/or slogan which has been created and/or developed for the purpose of the [Company's] [Website/App/Platform] and/or any promotional, advertising and/or marketing material of any nature which is to be used generally in the [Company's] business.

A.852

The [Contributor] agrees and undertakes that all present and future copyright as may exist in the product of the [Contributor's] work which is provided to the [Enterprise] and/or material which is created during the course of this agreement is assigned to the [Enterprise] in all media and for exploitation in all medium for the full period of copyright including any extensions and renewals throughout the [Territory/world]. That the [Contributor] shall not retain any rights and/or interest of any in any work and/or material. That where necessary the [Contributor] shall sign such additional documents and forms as may be required by the [Enterprise] to assign any rights and/or to confirm ownership.

A.853

The [Contributor] acknowledges that such copyright and any other rights of any nature as may exist now and/or be created in the future with respect to any element of the [Website/App/Podcast] and any associated material to which he/she is providing his/her skill, services and/or work shall belong absolutely to the [Company].

A.854

1.1 In consideration of the [Basic Fee] the [Company] agrees to provide the services of [Name]. Both the [Company] and [Name] agree and undertake to assign to the [Enterprise] all copyright and intellectual property rights, computer software rights, title, trade mark and domain name rights and any other rights in the product of the services of [Name] under this agreement and any material which may be created in any form including logos, slogans, images, films, sound recordings, scripts; whether such rights are in existence now and/or created in the future in all media throughout the [country/Territory/world/universe] for the full period of copyright and any extensions and renewals and any other period of ownership that may exist.

1.2 The [Enterprise] shall not however acquire any rights and/or interest in any material in which the copyright already exists which is owned or controlled by the [Company] and/or [Name] and/or is licensed to a third party and/or is not provided as part of this agreement including but not limited to: hardback and/or paperback books, an authorised biography, a registered trade mark and/or domain name; online digital accounts; merchandising.

A.855

1.1 The [Distributor] agrees that it shall not be entitled to exploit any product of the services of the [Contributor] and/or any material created as a result outside the [Engagement Period] in any media and/or format either directly and/or by means of sub-licenses to third parties.

1.2 Any further use of the rights and/or material by the [Distributor] and/or for licensing and/or any other form of exploitation shall require the parties to agree the terms of the scope of new authorised format and additional payments to the [Contributor] in each case. Additional sums shall be due to the [Contributor] for each different type and method and period of exploitation. Both parties shall use their endeavours to reach agreement in good faith based on full disclosure of the facts.

1.3 In the event that there is no further exploitation of the rights and/material by the [Distributor] for a period of [number] years then the [Contributor] may request a full assignment of all the rights and material provided that the [Contributor] pays an assignment fee of [number/currency].

A.856

In consideration of the [Fees] the [Consultant] assigns all intellectual property rights including copyright; trade mark rights; computer software rights; rights in any data, charts, maps, diagrams, reports, images, films, videos and/or electronic material; and any other rights in any other material of any nature written, designed, developed, created and/or supplied by the [Consultant] in respect of the [Project] and/or his/her services which is owned and/or controlled by the [Consultant] to the [Company] in all media throughout the world, universe and outer space for the full period of copyright and any extensions and renewals and/or any other additional period and forever in perpetuity. This assignment relates both to rights which are in existence now and to those which may come into creation at a later date due to new legislation, technology and/or methods of adaptation which had not been envisaged at the date of this agreement.

A.857

In consideration of the [Photographer's] Fee and the [Authorised Expenses] the [Photographer] assigns to the [Company] all copyright and intellectual property rights in the [Commissioned Work] in all media and/or all forms of adaptation in any medium whether in existence now and/or created in the future due changes in the law and/or developments in new technology throughout the [world] for the full period of copyright and any extensions and renewals. This assignment shall include but not be limited to: by means of all electronic formats over the internet and/or any telecommunication system for transmission, broadcast and/or download to any computer, mobile phone and/or other gadget and/or device; any book, article and/or other form of publication; any series, film, podcast and/or product and/or service and/or other form of merchandising, theme park, endorsement and/or exploitation of any nature.

A.858

1.1   The [Supplier] agrees and undertakes that it has developed, created and delivered the computer software, computer hardware, data, source code and any other material set out in Appendix A the specification for the [Project].

1.2   The [Supplier] agrees and acknowledges that all work and contributions by the [Supplier] to the [Project] shall be original except to the extent specified in Appendix A.

1.3   The [Supplier] acknowledges that the [Company] shall own all rights in the computer software, computer hardware, data, source code and any other material set out in Appendix A the specification for the [Project]. That the [Supplier] shall not have the right to exploit any such material in any form and/or licensed the rights to any third party.

A.859

The [Company] has engaged the services of the [Supplier] to develop, create and deliver the computer software, computer hardware, data, source code and any other material set out in Appendix A the specification for the [Project]. The [Supplier] agrees and acknowledges that it is a key term and condition of this agreement that all intellectual property, patent, computer software and/or any other rights in respect of the computer software, data, source code, passwords and any other material set out in Appendix A and/or delivered under this agreement by the [Supplier] which are owned by the [Supplier] and/or rights which may come into existence in the future should belong to and/or be assigned to the [Company].

A.860

1.1 In consideration of the payment of the [Assignment Fee] and the [Project Fee] by the [Company] to the [Supplier] the [Supplier] assigns to the [Company] all present and future copyright, intellectual property rights, patents, inventions, computer software rights, source codes, passwords, trade marks, logos, rights to domain names, database rights, service marks, community marks, design rights, future design rights, trade secrets, moral rights, confidential information and/or any other rights in the [Project] and/or the material which is developed and/or created which is owned by the [Supplier] in all media and by all medium, means and processes whether in existence now and/or created in the future throughout the world and the universe for the full period of copyright and any extensions and renewals and in perpetuity.

1.2 The assignment in 1.1 shall include the sole and exclusive right to register any interest and/or rights as the owner and/or to adapt, vary, delete from and add to, use, copy, license, authorise, print, transmit, disseminate, store, retrieve, display, process, record, playback, rent, lend, supply, sell, distribute, market and/or otherwise exploit all the rights and/or material. Together with the right to do so for any developments, variations and/or adaptations. Whether text, logos, images, data, charts, maps, tables, drawings, plans, sketches, graphics, film, video, podcasts, a two dimensional and/or three dimensional representation, prototype, electronically generated material of any nature and/or medium, sound recordings, music, interactive computer generated material and/or characters, holograms and/or competitions including but not limited to: all forms of transmission, broadcast and/or exploitation on terrestrial, cable, digital and satellite radio and/or television; non-theatric and/or theatric exploitation; publications in newspapers, magazines and books in printed and/or electronic form; all forms of exploitation over the internet and/or any telecommunication system and/or by any electronic means and/or method including audio files, downloads, subscription services, websites, apps, platforms, podcasts, news feeds, gambling, betting, lotteries and/or games to any computer, gadget, device and/or mobile phone; all forms of mechanical reproduction and/or performance; translations, merchandising, endorsement, product placement and/or adaptations in any language;

A.861

Any assignment of any rights under this Agreement is solely limited to the appearance and performance of [Name] at [Event] and any filming and photographs that may be taken and/or commissioned by the [Company] from third parties. It shall not include the right to develop and/or adapt and/

or distort, and/or alter and/or license the material to another third party in a different medium.

Sponsorship

A.862

1.1 The [Sponsor] agrees and undertakes that this agreement does not transfer and/or assign any intellectual property rights, copyright, computer software rights, design rights and future design rights, trade marks, service marks, community marks, patents, know how or any other rights in anything owned and/or controlled by the [Company] to the [Sponsor] whether in existence at the time of this agreement and/or developed in the future.

1.2 The [Sponsor] agrees and undertakes that all rights shall remain with and belong to the [Company] in any adaptations, merchandising, films, sound recordings and/or any other material designed in house and/or commissioned and/or developed under this agreement by the [Company] whether or not the [Sponsor] has been consulted and/or has made any contribution to the development and/or final version.

A.863

Where the [Company] engages the services of third parties in order to fulfil the terms of its agreement with the [Institute] for the [Event/Project] as follows:

a. The design and develop of an operational website, app and other online accounts; to organise a social media campaign and/or endorsements by artists who may appear and/or attend; to develop and print digital brochures, posters, flyers, and other material; to design new slogans, logos, artwork and/or to film podcasts, interviews and/or otherwise. The [Company] agrees and undertakes to ensure that such third parties shall not be entitled to exploit and/or sub-license any product of their services to the [Company] and/or [Sponsor] to any third party in any media at any time.

b. That where a person is engaged as a presenter at the [Event/Project] by the [Company]. That such person shall not acquire any rights in the product of their services and shall be required to complete an assignment form of all rights in all media without any further payment.

A.864

The [Company] agrees and undertakes to ensure that such third parties shall not be entitled to acquire any rights in any patents, know how, copyright, design rights, trade marks, service marks, logos, slogan, text, images, films, sound recordings, computer software and/or any other intellectual property rights in the products and/or services, computer generated and/or electronic material and/or marketing and/or any other material and/or contribution of the [Sponsor]. That the [Sponsor] shall be the sole and exclusive owner of all such rights including any developments, variations or otherwise.

A.865

The [Company] agrees and undertakes to ensure that such third parties who may be commissioned shall complete any documentation and/or assignment required by the [Sponsor] to transfer and/or assign any rights and/or interest to the [Sponsor] of any adaptation which may be created and/or developed of original material and/or rights owned by the [Sponsor] at the [Sponsor's] cost and expense.

A.866

The [Company] agrees that all trade marks, business names, domain names, community marks, service marks, logos, design rights, present and future copyright and all other intellectual property rights in respect of the [Sponsor's] business and/or its products and/or services and/or any other material provided by the [Sponsor] under this agreement shall remain the sole and exclusive property of the [Sponsor] whether in existence now and/or developed in the future. That it is not the intention of either party to transfer, assign and/or create any interest of any nature in any rights in the [Sponsor's] business and/or its products and/or services to the [Company].

A.867

1.1 The [Agent] and the [Sportsperson] agree and undertake that they shall not acquire any rights and/or interest and/or attempt to register any right and/or interest in the trade marks, brand names, domain names, community marks, service marks, logos, slogans, images, design rights, present and/or future copyright and/or any other intellectual property rights in any material and/or rights owned and/or controlled by the [Sponsors] and/or adaptation whether in existence now and/or created in the future. This shall include but not be limited to any of its businesses and/or its products and/or services and/or packaging, advertising, marketing and/or other material in any media and/or format owned and/or controlled by the [Sponsor] and/or provided by the [Sponsor] under this agreement.

1.2 The [Agent] and the [Sportsperson] agree that the trade marks, business names, domain names, community marks, service marks, logos, design rights, present and future copyright and all other intellectual property rights owned and/or controlled by the [Sponsors'] and/or any development and/or adaptation whether in existence now

223

and/or created in the future shall be owned by the [Sponsor]. That no part of this agreement is intended to assign, transfer and/or vest any such rights in the [Agent] and/or the [Sportsperson]. That this undertaking shall also apply to any abbreviation and/or parody and/or imitation at any time.

A.868

The [Sponsor] agrees that where a new and original logo, design, trade mark, domain name and/or other material and/or registration is created and developed as a direct result of the joint collaboration of the [Sponsor] and the [Sportsperson]. That the parties shall hold the new and original material and/or registration as joint owners of all such rights and shall each receive an equal credit, recognition in any copyright notice and make any registration of the rights in the names of both parties. The [Sponsor] agrees to bear the total cost of any such legal, administrative and registration costs. The signature of both parties shall be required to assign any rights and to grant any sub-licence.

A.869

The [Sponsor] agrees that it has not acquired and/or been assigned and/or granted any right and/or option by the [Organiser] to attend, sponsor and/or take part in any future [Festivals/Events]. Nor has the [Sponsor] been assigned and/or granted any right to use and/or adapt the name, image, slogan and/or any other matter of the [Organiser] and/or [Festival/Event] in any future social media campaign, product development, marketing and/or promotions.

A.870

Neither the [Sponsor] nor the [Company] shall be entitled to assign, transfer and/or exploit the [Logo/Name/Image/Slogan/Initial] which they have jointly created for this [Project] without the written consent and agreement of both parties.

A.871

1.   The [Sponsor] and the [Company] acknowledge and agree that [Name] already owns and/or controls the following trade marks, domain names, social media digital accounts, slogans, clothing brands and publications: [specify and list].

1.2 All the parties agree that no part of this agreement is intended to assign, transfer and/or sub-license any such rights and/or registrations and/or material owned and/or controlled by [Name] to the [Sponsor] and/or the [Company].

University, Charity and Educational

A.872

The [Author/Contributor] agrees and undertakes that he/she has created and developed the original [Work/Product] and is the sole owner of all copyright, design rights, computer software, and any other intellectual property rights in the [Work/Product] which are assigned under this agreement to the [Institute]. That the [Author/Contributor] has not exploited the [Work/Product] in any form and/or licensed the rights to any third party.

A.873

In consideration of the payment of the Assignment Fee in full by the agreed date the [Author/Contributor] assigns to the [Institute/Charity] all present and future copyright and all other intellectual property rights, computer software rights, rights in any computer generated and/or electronic format, patent, inventions, design rights in the [Work/Product] including any parts and the [Material] whether in existence now and/or created in the future in all media and/or by any means and/or formats throughout the world, universe and outer space for the full period of copyright and any extensions and renewals and forever without limit of time including but not limited to:

1.1 all forms of transmission, broadcast and/or dissemination by radio, television, the internet and/or telecommunication system including terrestrial, cable, satellite, microwave, over the air, wireless and/or electronic distribution in any form; website, app, platform, download, audio file, archive playback and/or otherwise.

1.2 whether free, pay per view, streamed, archive playback, downloaded and/or encrypted or otherwise.

1.3 All forms of exploitation through computers, mobile phones, watches, DVDs interactive games, lottery, gambling and/or betting format, theme park, musical, videos, audiocassettes, lasers, discs, merchandising, exhibition and/or distribution through cinemas, educational, cultural, religious and social establishments, clubs, universities and/or commercial use by businesses.

1.4 All forms of publication whether in printed in magazines, newspapers, pull-outs, digests, serialisations and/or any electronic format.

1.5 All forms of exploitation not already covered above in any medium. All forms of adaptation, translation, variation and/or development of any nature.

1.6 The right to register any computer software, trade mark, community mark, design right, service mark, logo, domain and/or app name, and any associated goodwill, trade secret and confidential information.

A.874

The [Company] agrees that the name of the [Institute/Charity] and the [Work/Material] and any goodwill and reputation created in respect of any trade mark, business name, domain and/or app name, logo, initial, image and/or slogan shall remain the sole and exclusive property of the [Institute/Charity] whether in existence now or created in the course of the agreement. That no part of this agreement is intended to assign, transfer and/or vest any such rights and/or right to register any right in the [Company].

A.875

In consideration of the [Fee] the [Company] agrees to assign to the [Institute/Charity] all present and future copyright, intellectual property rights, trade marks, names, logos, images, films, podcasts, sound recordings and/or any other material in any format which is created and developed in respect of this [Project] by the [Company] whether in existence now or created in the future in all media throughout the [Territory/world/country/universe] for the full period of copyright and any extensions and renewals and in perpetuity. No rights and/or interest of any nature shall remain vested in the [Company] [and/or any employee and/or consultant.]

A.876

The [Institute] agrees that the [Student] shall not be obliged to assign any rights in the [Work/theses] to the [Institute] and that all rights of any nature in any medium including copyright and intellectual property rights are retained and owned by the [Student] the original creator and writer. That where the [Institute] wishes to use, display and/or archive the [Work/theses] for any reason they shall be obliged to seek the prior written approval of the [Student].

A.877

[Name] agrees to assign to the [Charity/Trust] all the written text and images which he/she shall submit to the [Charity/Trust] for the purpose of the promotion of the contribution of [Name] in the [Event]. Such assignment shall be in respect of all media and all rights of any nature and/or in any format throughout the world and without any limitation of time. [Name] accepts that the [Charity/Trust] may use the texts and images on any marketing and/or promotional material including the website, advertisements and/or publications. That no payment shall be due to [Name] at any time.

A.878

It is a condition of entry to the [Event] that any participant accept that filming, photographs and other recordings will be taken by members of the public, other participants, the media and the [Charity/Organisers] at the [Event]. It is a condition of entry that you provide your consent to such matters and accept that any material may be used for marketing, promotion and/or any other form of exploitation. That it is accepted that the [Charity/Organisers] cannot control how any material is exploited at a later date.

A.879

1.1 [Name] assigns to the [Charity/Institute] ownership of the physical material of [Manuscript/Book/Archive].

1.2 [Name] does not assign any copyright and/or intellectual property rights and/or trade marks and/or any rights of exploitation in any media in the physical material in 1.1. These shall remain with and belong to [Name]. This fact is accepted and agreed by the [Charity/Institute].

1.3 The [Charity/Institute] agree and undertake to notify all persons allowed access to the physical material of [Manuscript/Book/Archive]. That they are not permitted and/or authorised to make any copies and/or to film, record and/or make any images. Further that all rights and forms of exploitation are owned by [Name].

ASSIGNMENT FEE

General Business and Commercial

A.880
'The Assignment Fee' shall be the sum of [number/currency] [words].

A.881
'The Assignment Fee' means the fee of [number/currency] [words] payable by the [Assignee] to the [Company] in respect of the rights to be assigned by the [Company] to the [Assignee] in clause [–].

A.882
The Assignment Fee shall be paid as follows:

1.1 [number/currency] [words] paid on [date] (receipt of which is acknowledged).

1.2 [number/currency] [words] to be paid on or by [date] subject to delivery and acceptance of the [Products/Material/other].

A.883
'The Assignment Fee' shall mean the total fee of [number/currency] which shall be paid by the [Company] to the [Distributor] in respect of the [specify rights] to be assigned under this agreement.

A.884

The Assignment Fee shall be paid as follows:

1.1 [number/currency] to be paid within [number] [days/weeks/months] of the technical acceptance of the [delivery items/master material/format] in respect of the [Film/Series].

1.2 [number/currency] to be paid on or by [date] subject to the technical acceptance of the [delivery items/master material/format] in respect of the [Film/Series] in 1.1.

1.3 [number/currency] to be paid on or by [date] subject to the first transmission and/or broadcast of the first episode of the [Film/Series] on channel [specify channel name].

1.4 [number/currency] to be paid on or by [date] subject to the first transmission and/or broadcast of the first episode of the [Film/Series] [website/platform] [specify name] in the form of streaming under a subscription service and/or for free under an archive playback service.

A.885

'The Assignment Fee' shall be the sum of [number/currency] which the [Assignee] shall pay to the [Author] [in consideration of the rights assigned by the [Author]] as follows:

1.1 [number/currency] within [number] days of signature of this agreement by both parties and subject to invoice by the [Author].

1.2 [number/currency] upon delivery of the [Manuscript/Images] by the [Author] and the acceptance of the quality of the work by the [Assignee].

1.3 [number/currency] on or before [date] subject to the successful completion of 1.1 and 1.2 by both parties.

A.886

'The [Contributor's] Fee' shall mean total sum of [number/currency] which shall be due subject to completion of the work and the assignment of the rights.

A.887

You will be paid in the following manner [direct debit/cheque/other] in accordance with your agreed monthly fees.

A.888

The [Company] shall pay the [Name] the Agreed Fees as follows:

1.1 [number/currency] subject to signature of this agreement by both parties and within [number] days of an invoice from [Name].

1.2   [number/currency] on or before [date] subject to the completion and delivery of the services, work and material specified in Appendix A to this agreement.

A.889

In consideration of the services and product of the work provided by [Name] to the [Company] and the rights assigned to the [Company]. The [Company] agrees and undertakes to pay the sum of [number/currency] by [date] by [method] to [Name] which shall be in full and final settlement. No further expenses, costs, royalties and/or other payments of any nature for any reason shall be due to [Name]. The [Company] shall be entitled to exploit all rights and/or material as it thinks fit and shall not be obliged to consult with [Name] and/or seek his/her approval for any reason.

A.890

'The Serialisation Fee' shall be the sum of [number/currency] which shall be paid:

1.1   [number/currency] on or before [date] to the [Author/Company] subject to the supply of the [Extract] of the [Work/Book].

1.2   number/currency] on or before [date] to the [Author/Company] subject to the publication of the [Extract] in the magazine entitled: [specify name].

1.3   number/currency] with [number] days of the publication of the [Extract] in the magazine entitled: [specify name] in the event that the sales of the magazine exceed [number] copies in printed form in [country] and/or viewing numbers on the digital version on the website [reference] exceed [number].

A.891

'The Payment Schedule' shall be the details of the payment of [specify total amount] by the [Assignee] to the [Assignor]. A copy of the Payment Schedule is attached to and forms part of this agreement as Schedule A.

A.892

'The Presenter's Fee' shall be the following sums to be paid by [Company] to [Name]:

1.1   [number/currency] for the first [twelve] calendar months;

1.2   [number/currency] for the second period of [twelve] calendar months;

1.3   [number/currency] for the final period of [six] months.

A.893

1.1 The Novation Price shall be the total sum of [number/currency].

1.2 The [Company] shall pay the Novation Price to the [Publisher/ Distributor] in the following manner [specify method of payment] on or before [date].

1.3 In the event that the [Company] fails to make payment as specified in 1.1 and 1.2 above then this agreement shall have no effect whatsoever and no assignment of rights shall take effect.

A.894

'The Fee' of [number] shall be in [currency] and paid by [direct debit] to the nominated account of [Name] within [number] hours of acceptance and delivery of the [Work/Service/Product].

A.895

The Assignment Fee shall be paid in instalments on the following dates [specify dates] in equal instalments subject to the delivery of [specify amount] of the [Material] by date and the balance by [date]. Where there is a delay in delivery the payments shall also be delayed accordingly.

A.896

The [Company] shall pay [Name] a nominal fee of [one] [currency] for the assignment of all the rights in clause [–] under this agreement.

A.897

The [Company] shall pay [Name] a total fee of [number/currency] within [number days] of the completion of each [Podcast]. No additional sums shall be due to [Name] for any costs and/or expenses and/or the assignment of all rights in all media. [Name] shall not be entitled to any additional payments and/or royalties for any form of exploitation and/or sub-licensing by the [Company] at a later date.

A.898

The [Enterprise] agrees and undertakes to pay a fixed fee of [number/ currency] for each [Image/Film/Sound Recording] which it decides to use and/or exploit. This fixed fee shall be subject to the completion of a buyout assignment document by you which assigns all the rights in all media to the [Enterprise]. This document is not negotiable and in the event that it is not signed no fee will be paid and the material will not be used.

A.899

It is accepted that no part of this fee is payment for any assignment of the rights in any media. In the event that the [Company/Charity] wishes to acquire any assignment of rights they shall pay an additional fee of [number/currency] subject to completion of the buy-out document.

ASSIGNMENT PERIOD

General Business and Commercial

A.900

'The Assignment Period' shall be for a fixed period of [five/ten/twenty] [months/years] which shall commence from [date] subject to the completion and signature of this agreement.

A.901

'The Assignment Period' shall commence on [date] and shall continue until [date]. It may be extended under the option provisions in clause [–] of this agreement and/or as subsequently varied by all the parties in writing as an amendment to this agreement.

A.902

'The Assignment Period' shall commence on the date of this agreement and shall be for the full period of copyright and shall include any extensions and/or renewals and shall continue as far as possible without limit of time in perpetuity.

A.903

'The Assignment Period' shall mean be for the full period of copyright including any extensions, renewals and/or other periods which may come into effect and/or arise in the future. It is not intended that there should be any limitation as to the time period.

A.904

'The Term of this Agreement' shall commence on the [date] of this agreement and shall continue until [date].

A.905

'The Assignment Period' shall commence on full execution of this agreement by both parties and shall continue forever without limitation of time. This shall include but not limited to the full period of copyright and any extensions and/or renewals in respect of all rights, material, adaptations, developments, translations and/or otherwise at any time in any territory.

A.906

'The Assignment Period' shall commence on acceptance of the [Work/Material] by the [Company] which shall be confirmed in writing and shall continue for a period of [number] years from such date of acceptance. Provided that the [Company] shall continue during that assignment period continue to sell, license, market and and exploit the [Work/Material] and make payments to [Name].

A.907

'The Assignment Period' shall start on [date] and shall continue for the full period of copyright and any extensions and renewals and for the full period of all other rights and forever without limitation of time.

A.908

'The Term' shall mean for the full period of copyright and any extensions, renewals and/or other additional periods.

A.909

The assignment period shall start on [date] and end on [date]. At the end of the assignment period the [Company] may either negotiate a new annual assignment fee or all the rights which were assigned will revert to [Name] and/or any beneficiaries of their estate and/or to the control of any trustees.

A.910

'The Assignment Fee' shall be the annual sum of [number/currency] to be paid by the [Company] to [Name] and/or his/her estate and/or beneficiaries indefinitely for the assignment of the rights in clause [–].

A.911

'The Assignment Fee' shall be paid in addition to any other fees and/or expenses to [Name] in the event [Name] is requested by the [Company] to complete any assignment document to buy-out all the rights in the product of the services of [Name] at any time.

A.912

'The Assignment Fee' shall be the fixed monthly fee of [number/currency] to be paid by the [Company] to [Name] for the assignment of the rights and material which is created and/or owned by [Name] as a result of his/her contribution to the development, writing, performance and filming of the [Podcast Series].

AUDIO FILES

General Business and Commercial

A.913

'The Audio File' shall mean the storage of the sound recording of the [Work] and/or any part in any medium by electronic means [regardless of the medium on which the sound recording is made and/or the method by which the sounds are produced and/or reproduced] and to make it available to the public by means of an electronic retrieval system.

A.914

'The Audio File' shall mean to store by any electronic means and to make available to the public by means of an electronic retrieval system the reproduction of the recording of the whole and/or any part of a literary, dramatic and/or musical work from which sounds reproducing the work may be produced. This shall include but not be limited to the spoken version of the text of a book, music, singing, interviews, discussions, and other sounds. Regardless of the medium upon which the recording is made and/or the method by which the sounds are produced and/or reproduced.

A.915

'The Audio File' shall mean the digital electronic files created and developed by the [Company] which are in the following format [specify format] which are held by and/or stored in a system known as [specify method] which has been reproduced from the following work and/or material [List name of material, source and copyright owner]. The files are to be used as part of database and a storage and retrieval system and supplied as reproductions of the digital electronic files on the following [websites/apps/platforms]: [specify name/reference].

A.916

'The Exclusive Audio File and Publication Rights' shall mean

1.1 The exclusive right to store the sound recording of the [Work] and/ or any part in any medium by electronic means [regardless of the medium on which the sound recording is made and/or the method by which the sounds are produced and/or reproduced] and to make it available to the public by means of an electronic retrieval system and/ or as reproductions of the digital electronic files.

1.2 The sole and exclusive right to the exclusion of all third parties and the copyright owner to control, exploit, license, reproduce, supply, distribute and/or authorise the reproduction by a third party of all and/ or any part of the [Work] by means of a sound recording in electronic form which is stored as a file and made available to the public [by means of an electronic retrieval system].

1.3 The right to the sole and exclusive publication rights as the first publisher of a previously unpublished work when copies of that work are made available by means of an electronic retrieval system and/or in electronic form by some other method.

A.917

'The Audio File' shall of the [specify work/material] shall mean the sound recording which is stored in an electronic file in [format] created by [Name] and stored on [specify site] in [format].

AUTHORISATION

General Business and Commercial

A.918

We accept no liability for any products, services and/or material supplied, delivered and/or provided unless the Purchase Order has been agreed to and/or amended by a duly authorised officer of the [Company].

A.919

The [Company] warrants that it has good title and full right and authority to grant the rights set out in this agreement and undertakes that it is and it will remain fully entitled to give the warranties and undertakings and make the representations concerning the [Products/Services/Material] and/or parts in this agreement.

A.920

Nothing contained in this document shall grant the [Agent] and/or his/her employees the power to bind and/or commit the [Company] and/or to transact any business in the [Company's] name and/or to make any representations and/or incur any obligations on the [Company's] behalf. The [Agent] agrees and undertakes that he/she may only represent that they are an independent entity who has been engaged to act as an agent in the Territory subject to the terms of this agreement.

A.921

The [Author] authorises the [Agent] to collect all sums due to the [Author] in respect of the [Manuscript/Book/Rights] from any source throughout the [Territory/world] during the Term of the Agreement and at any time thereafter relating to any agreement negotiated and concluded by the [Agent] during the Term of this Agreement.

A.922

1.1   The [Artist] provides his/her consent to the [Agent] to collect and be paid all monies due to the [Artist] under the following [agreements/ categories or types of work] for the period starting [date] and ending [date].

1.2   The [Agent] is not permitted to collect monies and/or payments from any other agreements and/or work and/or rights concerning the [Artist] at any time.

1.3   Nor shall the [Agent] be entitled to collect monies and/or payments direct outside the specified dates whether or not the [Agent] negotiated or concluded the contract.

1.4   Further, all sums so collected by the [Agent] at any time shall be held in a separate account for the benefit of the [Artist] and shall not be mixed with and/or offset against any other sums and/or have a charge created over it in any manner.

A.923

The [Company] authorises the [Distributor] to take instructions and carry out work on its behalf in respect of all matters relating to the internet and/ or any electronic form and/or exploitation over any telecommunication system including the collection of sums due, registration of any domain names, development of international strategy, creation of websites and/or apps, podcasts, and/or audio files and/or any associated advertising and/ or promotional marketing. Provided that all work shall be agreed in advance and authorised by the [Company] in detail. The [Distributor] shall not have the right to act independently without prior approval. The [Distributor] shall not be entitled to commit the [Company] in any manner to any agreement and all documents must be signed by the [Company].

A.924

[Name] shall be entitled to rely on the authorisation of the [Company] where an instruction, request, agreement or consent is provided by any method in writing or verbally by an officer and/or director of the [Company].

A.925

This agreement does not permit [Name] to make any arrangements and/or commit the [Company] to any undertaking and/or agreement which is binding at any time. [Name] has no authority to act on behalf of the [Company] and/or to represent that he/she is entitled to do so.

A.926

The [Sponsor] agrees and undertakes that it shall not have any power, authority and/or right to authorise, make representations to third parties and/or to commit to and/or to incur any expense, cost and/or liability in respect of any work, material, publicity, contracts, rights, commissions, facilities, marketing, tickets and/or otherwise for any reason in respect of the [Company] and/or the [Event/Name]. The [Sponsor] agrees and undertakes that where they have acted outside the scope of this agreement without authority. That the [Sponsor] shall bear all the costs and expenses, losses and/or damages that both parties may be incur whether directly and/or indirectly which relate to the consequences of the breach of this agreement by the [Sponsor].

A.927

The [Distributor] shall not have any authority, right and/or power to delegate the development, production, distribution and/or exploitation of the [Character] and/or any associated material and/or rights to any third party. Where the [Distributor] is found and/or alleged by the [Licensor] to have acted, committed and/or made representations outside the terms of this agreement to third parties. Then the [Licensor] shall have the right to serve notice of termination of the agreement upon such terms as may be determined by the [Licensor].

A.928

The [Consultant] is authorised by the [Company] to act upon behalf of the [Company] for the purpose of preparing, writing and delivering a report on the subject of [state topic/theme]. The [Consultant] may contact and interview a list of businesses, persons and contacts which must be agreed in advance with the [Managing Director]. The [Consultant] shall keep a full record and log of all emails, letters and discussions which shall be made available to the [Company] upon request. No authority is provided to the [Consultant] to make any representations, commitments, disclosures and/or to sign any agreement which may bind the [Company] at any time.

A.929

The parties agree that any approvals, amendments and/or authorisations which may be required under this agreement require the written and/or verbal approval of [specify person] at the [Company] and [Name] not his/her agent. Where there is likely to be a delay and/or loss incurred there is no authority granted to proceed without the necessary approval.

A.930

[Name] will permit and allow the [Agent] to make such decisions and expend such funds as may be required during each calendar month up to a maximum of [number/currency] in total. Provided that the proposal has already been discussed in detail with [Name] and all relevant information disclosed.

B

BANK HOLIDAYS

General Business and Commercial

B.001
'Bank Holidays' shall mean all recognised public holidays which are observed by banks, businesses and services each year in [England and Wales/Northern Ireland/the United Kingdom excluding Scotland and Northern Ireland/country].

B.002
'Bank Holidays' shall mean those days recognised as public holidays by the [government/law courts] whether at the conclusion of and/or subsequently during the existence of this Agreement.

B.003
[Name] shall be entitled to take off as [paid/unpaid] leave any days which are bank and/or public holidays which may be applicable in the [Territory] whether recognised at the time of the Agreement or created at a later date by royal proclamation, legislation or otherwise.

B.004
[Name] shall be entitled to take as paid leave the following bank holidays [specify dates and names] in [country] which shall be in addition to any holiday entitlement specified in clause [–]. Any other religious festivals, celebrations or otherwise shall be arranged to be taken as part of annual leave or as unpaid absence subject to advance consent.

B.005
Where a bank holiday falls on a day upon which [Name] is not normally working there shall be no automatic entitlement to an additional day off in lieu.

B.006
In the [United Kingdom and the Republic of Ireland] the following bank holidays shall apply in [year] and in any subsequent year of this Agreement, subject to variation in date in each year:

239

1.1   New Year's Day [United Kingdom and Republic of Ireland] [date]

1.2   St David's Day [Wales] [date]

1.3   St Patrick's Day [Northern Ireland and Republic of Ireland] [date]

1.4   Good Friday [United Kingdom] [date]

1.5   Easter Monday [United Kingdom and Republic of Ireland] [date]

1.6   St George's Day [England] [date]

1.7   May Day [United Kingdom and Republic of Ireland] [date]

1.8   Spring Bank Holiday (United Kingdom] [date]

1.9   St Stephen's Day [Republic of Ireland] [date]

1.10 Bank Holiday [Northern Ireland] [date]

1.11 Summer Holiday [United Kingdom] [date]

1.12 Orangemen's Day Holiday [Northern Ireland] [date]

1.13 St Andrew's Day [Scotland] [date]

1.14 Christmas Day [date]

1.15 Boxing Day Bank Holiday [date]

1.16 New Year's Day Bank Holiday [date].

B.007

1.1   'Bank Holidays' shall mean all recognised bank and public holidays in [country] as specified according to the legislation and guidance of [specify government website] but shall not include any other days which are celebrated as part of any other religious body, belief or political organisation.

1.2   It is however acceptable to substitute alternative dates off in lieu provided that [Name] is able to carry out their duties at the [Company] on the recognised bank or public holidays or other suitable arrangements can be made in advance.

B.008

1.1   The [Company] agrees that the [Name] shall be entitled to the Annual Holiday Entitlement in addition to any Bank Holidays.

1.2   The [Company] agrees that [Name] shall be entitled to be paid at his/her full rate of pay at any time whilst they are not working due to Annual Holiday Entitlement and/or Bank Holidays. However where [Name] is for any reason required to work on any of those dates then they shall not be paid additional sums but provided with the opportunity to be absent on other dates.

B.009

The [Company] confirms that in the event that the [Executive] is requested to work on Bank Holidays or on those days which have been agreed as the Executive's Holidays. Then such work shall be paid for on an ad hoc basis on terms to be agreed between the parties as to the additional remuneration, but at no less than the existing rate of payment.

B.010

This position does not entitle you to receive any payments for public or national holidays and all sums shall only be paid for and subject to completion of the required work. Nor shall there be any additional leave of absence in lieu of work on any of such days.

B.011

Your entitlement to bank, public or other extra days shall be as follows [specify] and you shall be paid in full for each such day. Any such paid leave shall be in addition to your annual leave allowance in paragraph [–].

B.012

1.1   The [Consultant] shall not be obliged to provide his/her services and shall not be paid any sums by the [Company] for any dates where the [Consultant] is absent due to public holidays, religious or other festivals or other occasions which arise due to any reason whether due to family, medical or other emergencies.

1.2   Where the absence continues for [number] consecutive days which were scheduled to be work days. Then the [Company] shall be entitled to terminate the contract by written notice in accordance with clause [–] and shall not be liable to pay any further sums due under the contract.

B.013

There shall be no obligation under this Agreement to be available to provide the services of the [Agency] and/or [Name] on any weekend and/or bank holidays and/or annual leave and/or [specify dates] during the Term of this Agreement.

B.014

In the calculation of the days of notification and/or payment under this Agreement it is agreed that all weekends and Bank Holidays shall [not] be included in the number of days.

B.015

For the purpose of this Agreement it is irrelevant whether or not any day is a bank holiday and/or weekend and/or other festival, celebration and/or religious day for any faith. All days of the week shall be treated as the same and any notice period and/or calculation shall include all the days in sequence regardless of whether it is a weekend and/or bank holiday.

BANK RATE

General Business and Commercial

B.016

Unless both parties agree to the contrary in writing all references in this Agreement to 'Bank Rate' shall mean [number] per cent above the prevailing bank rate of [specify bank] in [country] on the relevant date.

B.017

1.1   Any party claiming interest under this agreement in respect of any sum due and/or owing must provide supporting evidence as to the reason for the calculation of the rate set.

1.2   Neither party shall be entitled to seek to claim more interest as a penalty payment.

B.018

1.1   The [Company] shall be entitled to charge a varied bank rate of interest depending upon the circumstances at any time and shall not be bound to continue to charge the existing rate set out in the agreement.

1.2   Where applicable an additional sum may be charged by way of a penalty and/or further interest at a higher rate if when served with notice to remedy a serious breach and/or default the other party does not rectify the matter within [one] calendar month of receipt of notice setting out all the details relating to the default.

B.019

'Bank Rate' shall be the relevant percentage figures as shall be published by the [Bank of England/other] on the relevant dates. It is accepted that the interest rate may rise and fall over a period of time. In such instance the average interest rate over the relevant period shall be used.

B.020

'The Bank Rate' shall be fixed at [number] per cent [–] % on [figure/sum] from [start date] to [end date]. The bank rate of interest shall be fixed. There shall be no additional interest due and/or added nor shall any penalty and/or additional charges, costs or other sums be due for any reason except legal costs which may be incurred in order to obtain payment.

B.021

1.1 There shall be no interest, penalties, charges, or other additional sums due under the terms of this Agreement at any time where any payment or undertaking is delayed for a period of [three] months.

1.2 After the expiry of a period of [three] months from the due date then the [Company] shall be entitled to charge a fixed sum of [number] [currency] as a penalty each [month] for the failure to comply with clause [specify] in this Agreement.

1.3 At the end of each calendar month an invoice issued for the penalty payments for the previous month and payment shall be due immediately upon receipt of an invoice.

B.022

1.1 The [Bank] shall loan the [Customer] the following sum [figure/currency] for the following purpose [specify].

1.2 The [Bank] shall not be entitled to any charge, lien or control over the assets or interests of the [Customer] and/or its business and/or property and shall only be entitled to charge the following rate of interest [number] per cent [–] % on [sum/currency] from [date] to [date]. Thereafter the [Bank] may charge the following [higher/lower] rate of [specify].

1.3 No additional sums may be added for administration, currency conversion, legal costs or otherwise unless the [Customer] defaults on the loan for [six] months and makes no payment during that period.

B.023

1.1 The [Consultant] shall be entitled to charge the [Company] an additional sum of [figure/currency] for each occasion on which the sums due under this agreement are not paid according to the specified dates.

1.2 The additional payment in 1.1 shall be in lieu of charging interest and/or imposing a penalty, but shall be without prejudice to the [Consultant's] right to take legal action.

B.024

1.1 The [Company] shall be entitled to charge interest at [number] per cent [figure] % above the bank base rate of [specify reference] in [country].

1.2 The [Company] can calculate and charge the interest from the day after any sum has not been received until the sum due has been paid in full.

1.3 The [Company] shall notify the [Client] that interest is payable, and the [Client] is in default. Where payment is received within [seven days] of the default the [Company] may decide to waive the interest at its absolute discretion.

B.025
The [Company] agrees and undertakes that the maximum amount that it shall be entitled to claim in interest on any default in payment by the [Distributor] shall be limited to the sum of [figure] [words/currency].

B.026

1.1 The parties both agree that neither shall be entitled to claim any interest, penalty or additional charges or costs in respect of any sums due under the terms of this Agreement which may not be paid by the due date and/or are not accounted for and/or some other error and/or omission. Provided that the matter is resolved within [number] months of the date the default is identified.

1.2 If after the expiry of [number] months from the default the matter is not resolved. Then either party may claim interest, penalty charges, administrative, legal and accountants' costs against the other for any reason. The parties both agree that any interest claimed by either party shall be at the fixed rate of [number] per cent from the first date the default arose until the sum is paid.

B.027
The [Company] agrees the interest rate that it shall be entitled to charge in respect of the sums owed under this Agreement shall not exceed [number] per cent [figure] % at any time. This shall be the case whether or not the bank rate set by the [specify] bank exceeds this rate or not.

B.028
The rate of interest shall be fixed at [number] per cent from [date] to [date] and shall not be dependent and/or adjusted by any changes in the bank rate; economy and/or other variations in the financial sector in any part of the world. The rate of interest cannot be increased and/or decreased by either party.

B.029

The rate of interest to be charged on the sums owed by [Name] shall be as follows:

1.1 [date] to [date] [number] per cent.

1.2 After [date] the interest rate may be varied based on the interest rates set by [specify bank or institute] but may not exceed [number] per cent.

BANNER ADVERTISEMENTS

Internet, Websites and Apps

B.030

'Banner' shall mean the advertisement [specify size/shape/position] on the [web page/app] site [reference]. The banner shall contain the following content supplied by the [Licensee] [specify] which shall have the purpose of encouraging any user of the [website/app] to click to another site linked through the banner.

B.031

1.1 The [Website/App] Company shall not acquire any intellectual property rights, trade marks and/or other ownership and/or interest in any material in any medium supplied by the [Product Company] and/or developed in pursuance of this Agreement.

1.2 The [Website/App] Company agrees that it shall not attempt to register any rights and/or to license and/or assign and/or transfer any rights to any third party relating to the material supplied by the [Product Company] and/or any developments. This prohibition shall apply to anything of any nature relating to the [Product Company] or any of its products, services, marketing, music, logs and trade marks and slogans created at any time.

B.032

The [Website/App] Distributor shall not acquire any intellectual property rights, interest or patent or the right to license third parties or any rights of exploitation in any media [except those set out in this document] in any material supplied under this Agreement to appear in the banner or associated site and links, meta tags or advertisements. This shall apply to all the original material and any variations, adaptations and developments of

245

the [Product Company] and its products, services and marketing including but not limited to any characters, trade marks, service marks, community marks, both registered and unregistered, logos, words, phrases, letters or artwork, images, sounds, sound recordings, music, lyrics, films, computer software or any other material in any medium and/or media of any nature which are supplied by or commissioned or created for or for which use is consented to by the [Product Company] at any time.

B.033

'Banner' shall mean the advertisement created by the [Website/App] Company on [Website/App] [reference] [position/size] and linked to promote the products and services of the [Product Company].

B.034

The [Company] agrees that the [Supplier] shall be able to place its banner advertisement on the [Website/App] [reference] which is owned and controlled by the [Company] on the following terms and conditions:

1.1   That the banner advertisement shall be in the form and style described as follows [specify] and a representational copy with all the content, words, slogans, artwork, computer-generated material, music, sound recordings, links and any other material of any nature which is to be displayed, appear or be connected in any form is attached and forms part of this Agreement.

1.2   That the [Supplier] shall own or control all the material set out in 1.1 and accepts full responsibility for any loss, damage, or other direct or indirect consequences financial or otherwise arising from the placement of the banner advertising on the [Website/App] of the [Company].

1.3   That the [Supplier] shall indemnify the [Company] against any claim, action or loss made or incurred by the [Company] or by a third party which arises as a direct or indirect result of the banner advertisement on the [Website/App] or any link.

1.4   The [Supplier] agrees that it shall not be entitled to use the name, logo, trade marks, community marks, products, services or any artwork, text, slogan or information or data from the [Company's] [Website/App] or business to promote, market or advertise the [Supplier] or any of its products or services or to provide or supply any such material to third parties in any form without the prior written consent of the [Company].

1.5   That the [Company] shall be entitled to nominate the jurisdiction to which this Agreement shall be bound at a later date depending on the facts of the case on each occasion. Prior to any legal proceedings being issued by either party both parties agree that they shall endeavour to resolve any dispute by the appointment of an agreed mediator the cost of which shall be shared equally between both parties.

B.035

There shall be no obligation to provide banner advertisement, or additional display details of any nature in respect of products or services which the [Company] agrees that it shall sell, distribute or supply on its [Website/App].

B.036

In consideration of the banner advertisement the [Company] shall be paid the following sums by the [Distributor]:

1.1 The [Company] shall be paid a fixed fee of [figure/currency] for the display of the banner advertisement on its [website/app] reference [–] from [date] to [date]. The fee shall be paid in full by the [Supplier] by [date].

1.2 The [Company] shall also be entitled to be paid a click through fee of [figure/currency] for every click on the banner advertisement where the persons then purchased any products or services which are not subsequently refunded for any reason. These sums shall be paid in full to the [Company] by the [Distributor] at the end of each [six] month accounting period.

1.3 The [Company] shall not be entitled to be paid a royalty of the total value of all sales or orders or other business directly arising from the click through banner advertisement.

B.037

The [Company] shall not be entitled or have the right to receive any payments, royalty, click through fee or other sums of any nature including any percentage of sales or other business income from the [Distributor] which arises as a result of the placement of the banner advertisements on the [Company] [Website/App]. The [Distributor] shall only be obliged to pay the placement fee specified in clause [–].

B.038

1.1 The [Company] shall not be obliged to display the banner advertisement and/or any related promotion on the [Website/App] in the event that the [Distributor] and/or the [Products/Services] which the business promotes are the subject of a product recall, health and safety investigation and/or any other matter which may prejudice the business of the [Company].

1.2 In such case the [Company] shall be entitled to remove the banner advertisement without further notice. The [Company] shall be entitled to retain all sums paid by the [Distributor] to the [Company] and shall not be required to return any payments in such circumstances.

B.039

1.1 The banner advertisements must be comply with the Guidance and Code of Practice issued by [specify name] and adhere to [specify code].

1.2 The banner advertisements must adhere to the advertising and promotional policy of the [Website/App] Company which may be different depending on the primary language of the market or be changed from time to time. A copy of the current policy is attached.

1.3 The [Advertising Company] agrees that it shall be obliged to adapt, develop, change and/or edit any part of the banner advertisements at its own cost and expense which may be required by the [Website/App] Company.

B.040
All copyright and any other intellectual property rights and ownership in the [Products/Services] shall belong to the [Supplier]. The banner advertisements and any associated sound recordings and links which are created, developed and produced by the [Website/App] Company for the [Supplier] shall be assigned by the [Website/App] Company or any relevant third party to the [Supplier] for a nominal sum.

B.041
The [Supplier] shall have the option to purchase the copyright and other rights in the banner advertisement created by the [Website/App] Company for the [Supplier]. Provided that the [Supplier] pays all the costs and expenses which have been incurred and/or are due in respect of the creation, development, production, clearance and acquisition of rights, staff costs and any other sums which arise directly and/or indirectly which have and/or are due to be paid by the [Website/App] Company.

B.042

1.1 The [Supplier] agrees and undertakes that no banner advertisements and/or the content of any links and/or references to and/or the content of any text services, mobile services, premium rate line services and/or otherwise of any nature which are referred to in the banner advertisements shall contain any material which is defamatory, pornographic, offensive, unsuitable for children and/or is contrary to any existing laws and/or code of practice and/or policy in [country].

1.2 The [Supplier] agrees and undertakes that every effort shall be made at the first opportunity to delete, amend, erase, correct and/or remove any material from the banner advertisements and/or any associated service which is requested by the [Company] on the grounds that its content is not acceptable and is contrary to its [Company's] policy as to the suitability of the content.

B.043

The [Advertiser] agrees and undertakes that:

1.1 It has cleared and owns and/or controls all copyright, music, logos, trademarks, text, films, sound recordings, videos, blogs, text messages and mobile services, photographs, images, links, competitions, promotions, products and/or services and any other intellectual property rights and/or material which is contained within and/or associated with the [Banner Adverts] on the [Website/App] and the associated service to send text messages to a premium rate phone line and/or any associated link and/or other [website/app].

1.2 That the [Company] that operates and/or owns the [Website/App] shall not be responsible and/or liable for any sums due for the use and/or exploitation of such rights and/or material in sub-clause 1.1 above to any copyright owner, collecting society and/or any other third party for the display of the [Banner Adverts] on the [Website/App] and/or the associated text message and/or any link and/or any other form of exploitation that may arise.

1.3 The [Advertiser] shall indemnify the [Company] in respect of any direct claim, costs and/or expenses that may be due and/or paid to any third party by the [Company] to settle any matter where in the opinion of the [Company] sufficient evidence has been produced to justify the payment of the sum claimed and/or where as a result of legal action by a third party an award of damages and/or costs is made against the [Company].

1.4 In addition the [Advertiser] shall pay to the [Company] all legal and administrative costs that may be incurred as a result of seeking legal advice from a solicitor and/or barrister and/or other expert outside the [Company] in order to seek an opinion and/or to defend a claim made against the [Company].

B.044

The [Licensee] agrees that it shall not be entitled to authorise, license, supply, adapt and/or reproduce and/or alter, distort and/or make a caricature of any part of the [Licensor's] names, images, logos, films, and associated products which may be in any banner links, advertisements, blogs, newsfeeds and/or any other material supplied by the [Licensor] to the [Licensee] at any time. The [Licensee] agrees that all material must be used in the exact media and form it is delivered by the [Licensor] for display, broadcast, transmission and use on the [Licensees] [Website/App] known as [specify].

B.045

1.1 The [Company] reserves the right not to display any banner links, advertisements, promotions, marketing newsfeed and/or any other material supplied by the [Advertiser] which in the opinion of the [Company] will result in the threat of a legal action, have a negative effect on the main business of the [Company] and/or may give rise to involvement in adverse publicity and/or news reports in any part of the world.

1.2 In such event where the [Company] on any grounds does not display any material as previously agreed and expected. The total liability of the [Company] shall be limited to [number/currency] and the Advertiser agrees to this limitation and agrees that it shall have no claim for loss of sales and/or defamation and/or any effect on its business.

B.046

The [Company] agrees to display the banner links of the [Licensor] in respect of the [Product] on the [Website/App] [specify] from [date] to [date]. Together with an editorial review by [Name] on page [number] of the site. The [Company] agrees that the banner links shall not appear next to any material on the site associated with [specify subjects].

B.047

There is no agreement by the parties which places any restriction and/or prohibition on the display, promotion, marketing, editorial and/or features of any competing and/or rival products, brands, names, logos, images, text or otherwise of any type of material in any medium directly next to, before, after and/or with any material and/or banner link supplied by the [Licensor] for the [Website/App].

B.048

1.1 Where the display, use, broadcast, transmission and/or promotion of the banner links and any associated content, logo, text, image, film and music results in a claim and/or legal action and/or liability against the parent company owner of the [Website/App] and/or any associated company and/or distributor by a collecting society, copyright owner and/or any other third party who has a valid claim and provides evidence in support to that effect.

1.2 Then the [Supplier] of all such material agrees that the claim may be settled without any legal proceedings having been started. In addition that the [Supplier] shall be obliged to pay to the parent company owner and/or associated company and/or distributor all such sums, administrative costs, expenses, legal fees and costs and other sums that they may have to pay to resolve the matter up to a maximum of [number/currency] in total [in each case/for the duration of this Agreement].

BEST ENDEAVOURS

General Business and Commercial

B.049

'Best Endeavours' shall mean taking every step which a [government institution/company/partnership] would be expected to take in achieving the objectives as if it were acting in its own best interests and taking into account its size, resources, financial position and the seriousness and consequences of the obligations.

B.050

The parties agree that where the expression 'Best Endeavours' is used throughout this Agreement the onus on such party shall be to use all endeavours to achieve the specified aim within legal, financial and ethical restraints at that time.

B.051

'Best Endeavours' shall mean taking every step that could be taken even at considerable expense and cost which a large public company would take to achieve its stated objectives and aims based on sound and informed legal, financial and corporate advice.

B.052

1.1 The [Name] shall perform their obligations under this Agreement to the best of their skill and ability and shall supply such standards of work as may be reasonably required by the [Company] in accordance with the terms of this Agreement.

1.2 Provided that the [Company] shall ensure that the [Name] shall be supplied with such technical material, facilities and support as may be necessary to fulfil the required standard of work at the [Company's] sole cost.

B.053

1.1   The [Company] agrees and undertakes that it shall provide its services to the best of its professional skill and ability providing highly qualified and specialist experienced persons to carry out the work and provide advice, guidance, research and recommendations to the [Enterprise].

1.2   The [Company] shall not supply trainees, unqualified or inexperienced personnel.

1.3   The [Enterprise] shall be entitled to request copies of the professional qualifications and curriculum vitae of each of the persons proposed for any work and shall be entitled to reject them on the grounds that they lack the necessary expertise, knowledge or experience.

B.054

1.1   Neither party shall be obliged to use their best endeavours to fulfil the terms of this Agreement and shall instead act in a commercially prudent and reasonable manner in accordance with the circumstances.

1.2   Where any part of the agreement cannot be performed due to the high costs involved or where the performance of the contract would be delayed and therefore be too late. Then a financial settlement in compensation shall be agreed between the parties which shall be by negotiation or alternative dispute resolution prior to any legal proceedings.

B.055

Both parties agree that they shall act in good faith and shall be bound by the following undertakings:

1.1   To carry out the performance of the work to be undertaken to a professional and competent standard until such time as the Agreement is ended, suspended or terminated for any reason.

1.2   That where due to unforeseen circumstances additional costs and expenses arise which directly relate to the completion of the work. That no additional costs or expenses shall be incurred or committed without the written consent of both parties.

1.3   Both parties agree to obtain and bear the cost of such consents, clearances, materials, facilities, documentation, personnel, or other matters which are being relied upon by the other party based on the terms of this Agreement provided that some unforeseen expense, cost, defect or restriction shall not arise which would fundamentally affect the economic viability of the [Project].

1.4 That where defects, errors, accounting or financial irregularities or any other material changes arise in relation to either party, or the work or their financial stability which affect the fulfilment of the terms of this Agreement. That the party who becomes aware of such matters should notify the other in writing of such problems as soon as reasonably possible.

B.056

1.1 There shall be no obligation on either party to provide the services and work under this contract to the best of their endeavours.

1.2 In the event that the details specified in Schedule [–] cannot be fulfilled, then either party shall have the right to cancel the contract by notice in writing with immediate effect. In such event the party who has cancelled the contract shall not have any further liability to the other of any nature whether as to costs already incurred or in respect of future payments under the contract.

B.057

The [Licensee] shall use its best endeavours to ensure that the [Product] is promoted and advertised in the following manner [specify catalogue/ magazine/trade fair/Website/App/festival] in [country] by [date]. In the event that this clause is not fulfilled then the [Licensee] agrees to pay the [Licensor] the additional sum of [figure/currency] in the next accounting period.

B.058

1.1 The [Licensee] shall use its reasonable endeavours to make not less than [number] of the [Product] available in the following countries [specify] by [date] at the following [retail outlets/distributors/trade shows].

1.2 The [Licensee] shall provide the [Licensor] with a report of the wholesale and trade availability of the [Product] in each country together with details and the exact samples of the [Product], packaging, marketing, and advertising.

B.059

1.1 The [Sponsor] agrees to use its best endeavours to ensure that the [Company] is provided with all the items listed in Schedule [A] for the [Sports Event/Festival] by [date].

1.2 In the event that the [Sponsor] is unable to provide any items by that date then the [Sponsor] agrees to provide a suitable alternative substitute at its own cost.

B.060

The [Company] agrees that it shall endeavour to ensure that no product and/or service is made available to [Athletes/Public] at the [Sports Event] within the confines of the official grounds specified in [Appendix A] which would directly conflict with and/or compete with the products and/or services of the [Sponsor] and specifically not the following companies and/or types of products and services [specify].

B.061

Each party agrees and undertakes that subject to the financial constraints of the need by the business to make a profit for this [Project]. That each party shall use its best endeavours to ensure that the best people within its business who are available are allocated as far as possible to work on the [Project].

B.062

Each party agrees and undertakes that it shall use its best endeavours to ensure the management, content and delivery of the [Project] shall be in accordance with the attached Schedules [–] and that no changes and/or variations of any nature, however minor, will made without the prior consent of all the parties.

BILL OF LADING

General Business and Commercial

B.063

'Bill of Lading' shall mean the written evidence in whatever form of the contract for the carriage and delivery of goods sent under the terms of this Agreement by [sea/other] whether such contract is referred to as a Contract for Bailment or any other term.

B.064

'The Bill of Lading' shall be the terms and conditions specified in writing between the parties between the [Owner] of the [Products] and the [Merchant Company] as to the liability, insurance, risk, indemnities, rights, responsibilities and cost of transport and delivery of the [Products] and their container from [the port of loading on to a vessel/address of receipt] to [the port of discharge when they are discharged/delivery address when they are delivered].

B.065

The 'Bill of Lading' may be made up of one and/or more printed documents, email attachments, texts and/or other written material which set out the basis upon which the parties have agreed terms and conditions for the movement of the [Material/Products] from one location to another in any part of the world. In the event that any terms and conditions are incomplete, inaccurate and/or not finalised. Then it is agreed between the parties that the presumption shall be that the person and/or company who has ordered the [Material/Products] shall not attain full ownership until all sums due for the purchase price of full title to the [Material/Products] and freight, insurance, taxes, imports and export duties and any other associated costs have been paid in full to the other party.

BLOG

Internet, Websites and Apps

B.066

'The Blog' shall be defined as the text, images, films, sound recordings, photographs, designs, logos, music, lyrics, slogans, trade marks, quotes, links, copyright notices and credits and other material of any nature in any medium which is provided by the [Influencer/Contributor] to the [Company] to host and display the contents on the [Website/App] [specify name] [reference].

B.067

1.1 The [Website/App] is monitored regularly by the [Company], but the [Company] does not accept any responsibility and/or liability for any material and content that is placed on the [Website/App] on and/or linked to the [Blog] which may be in breach of copyright, trade marks, intellectual property, contract, confidentiality, defamatory and/or offensive and/or for any other reason an infringement and/or breach of a third parties rights and/or contrary to any legislation in any country in any part of the world.

1.2 You are strongly advised not to supply, upload, reproduce, exploit and/or distribute any material and/or content on the [Blog/Forum] in which you have not acquired permission from the copyright owner and/or cleared the material and/or rights and/or which is likely to result in a legal action and/or claim for damages and/or costs.

B.068

1.1 I am the copyright owner of the following work [title/pages/ISBN reference]. I consent to the following extract of my work being displayed on the [Website/App/Blog] [specify reference] from [date] to [date].

1.2 After [date] you agree to delete and/or erase the extract in 1.1.

1.3 I accept that you cannot control third parties making copies of the extract and reproducing them elsewhere without consent.

1.4 I accept that you shall not be obliged to take legal action against any third parties who may make such copies of the extract and exploit the material for their own benefit.

B.069

1.1 The [Company] undertakes and agrees that it shall not acquire any rights, interest and/or intellectual property rights in the content of the [Blog] created and/or supplied by [Name] except as set out in 1.2 below.

1.2 [Name] grants the [Company] the non-exclusive right to display, promote and exploit the [Blog] in association with the [Website/App] by means of marketing. The parties agree that any form of commercial exploitation shall be subject to the terms of a separate licence agreement.

B.070

1.1 The [Contributor] shall own and/or control all copyright, intellectual property rights, trade marks, interest and goodwill in all media in any media in the [Blog] and/or parts which are supplied and/or developed and/or uploaded by the [Contributor].

1.2 The supply of the material for the [Blog] does not constitute an assignment of copyright and other rights to the [Company] of the original material and/or any developments.

B.071

The [Company] agrees that it shall not acquire any rights or interest in the [Blog] by the [Contributor] of any nature except [specify].

B.072

The [Contributor] agrees and undertakes that it shall not be entitled to register and/or claim any rights, interest and/or equity in the domain name of the [Website/App] and/or any trade marks, logos, slogans, music, sound recordings, lyrics. films, photographs, stills, images, caricatures and/or any other content which is owned and/or controlled by the [Company] in respect of the [Website/App] except that which relates specifically to the content of the [Blog] supplied by the [Contributor].

B.073

1.1 The [Contributor] shall either be the original copyright owner and creator or the [Contributor] shall be responsible for the clearance and payment for the use of all content for the [Blog] on the [Website/App] and any associated exploitation and/or marketing.

1.2 The [Contributor] shall be liable to ensure that all the content for the [Blog] is cleared and paid for and that there are no legal and/or moral rights issues outstanding for the use of the content in the manner agreed between the parties.

B.074

The [Distributor] agrees and undertakes that it shall be responsible for all intellectual property rights and copyright clearances and payments. As well as any consents and payments due for any recordings, reproductions, performances, contracts, licensing and any other form of exploitation that may be required and/or payments due to third parties arising from the supply, display, marketing, distribution and exploitation of the [Blog] by the [Distributor] at any time.

B.075

1.1 The [Company] disclaims any responsibility and/or liability for any consequences arising from your access to or use of this [Website/App] or any links in order to upload, display, amend, edit, update and/or delete the [Blog].

1.2 All content of the [Blog] may be reviewed, amended, deleted, erased, and/or edited at any time entirely at the sole discretion of the [Company].

1.3 In the event that permission to display and/or upload the [Blog] is denied for any reason. Then no compensation and/or costs and/or other sums shall be due to the [Contributor] at any time.

B.076

1.1 You use this [Website/App] and view, access, respond and download the contents of any [Blogs/Content] and/or links and/or associated material entirely at your own discretion and risk.

1.2 The [Company] is not responsible for and does not originate and/or contribute to the contents of the [Blogs/Content] and/or any links, premium rate phone lines, and/or other services, products and/or other material.

1.3 No reliance can be placed on the accuracy, truth, advice, information, opinions, and/or contents of the [Blogs/Content]. The [Company] does not recommend, endorse, agree with and/or support the views, opinions and/or contents of the [Blogs/Content]. Listing should not be taken as an endorsement of any kind nor as a recommendation as to the reliability, quality, or otherwise of the [Blogs/Content] and/or any links and/or associated material.

1.4 Any views expressed and/or images displayed on any blog and/or forum are entirely those of the author and not the [Company].

B.077

1.1 The [Company] relies on the [Contributors] to the [Blogs] on this [Website/App] to act in good faith and to provide accurate up-to-date information, data, images, text and records. All dates, prices, special offers, and other details are subject to availability and may be changed at any time. No responsibility or liability can be accepted for any errors, omissions, damages, losses, and/or expenses and/or any other sums that may arise from your use of, reliance on and/or connected to in anyway with any [Blogs].

1.2 The [Company] only permits access to browse, order goods and services and access information for private and personal use. The [Website/App] and/or the [Blogs] and content may not be reproduced, published and/or commercially exploited without the prior written consent of the [Company] and the [Contributors].

B.078

The [Parent Company], the [Subsidiary], the [Distributor] cannot accept liability for your reliance on any [Blog/Article/Content] on this [Website/App] of any nature and this site must be used for guidance only and may not accurate, complete or up to date. You are advised to take independent advice from a third party to review and advise on your particular circumstances and facts. You accept as a condition of your access to and use of any [Blogs/Articles/Content] on this [Website/App] that you do so at your own risk and cost and [Parent Company], the [Subsidiary], and/or the [Distributor] shall not be responsible and/or liable for:

1.1 Any losses, damages and/or other consequent direct or indirect costs, expenses and/or liability that may arise from your use or reliance on any material in any medium on any [Blog/Article/Content].

1.2 Any directions, advice, views and/or otherwise which are misleading and/or any error, omission and/or failure of any systems, processes or functions, viruses or destruction and/or interference with software, equipment, and/or any security lapse or breach.

1.3 Any defamatory, offensive, derogatory material or statements on any part of the site whether temporary or permanent.

1.4 Any trade descriptions, quality of goods or services, fitness for purpose, prices, payment, delivery, delay or failure to deliver or provide a service..

1.5 Any infringement or breach of copyright, design rights, moral rights, trade marks, service marks or any other intellectual property rights, or any rights, interests and/or other contractual obligations and/or otherwise of any nature.

1.6 Any links, advertisements, promotions, competitions, lotteries, premium rate phone lines, sponsorship, endorsements and/or other marketing, promotional and other material.

B.079

1.1 The [Blogs/Forums] on this [Website/App] rely on users to act in good faith and in a reasonable manner. Where material is displayed or accessible which has been provided by such third party users for [Blogs/Forums] then the [Company] does not accept responsibility for any material which is defamatory, offensive, inaccurate, unavailable, unlawful or misleading.

1.2 The [Company] have a policy of dealing with complaints. In the first instance email [specify] stating in detail the reasons. The [Company] shall then decide whether the complaint is justified and if so arrange for the deletion of any material which it concludes should be removed for any reason.

B.080

1.1 The [Writer] agrees that he/she shall try to ensure that no material which is owned and/or controlled by a third party is included in the [Blog/Article/Content] without a sufficient acknowledgement of copyright and/or other form of ownership.

1.2 That the [Writer] shall not seek to represent that any material is original to him/her which is directly derived from the work of someone else.

1.3 Nor shall the [Writer] seek to review and/or endorse and/or promote any work, product and/or service of a third party who is a business associate and/or member of their family and/or friend and/or a third party who has paid them a fee and/or supplied them free services and/or products without proper disclosure of that fact in the [Blog/Article/Content]. It is agreed by the [Writer] that all paid product placement and other forms of remuneration for marketing and promotional work must be declared in the [Blog/Article/Content].

B.081

1.1   The [Company] agrees that it shall bear all the risk and liability of the costs, expenses, damages and sums which may be due in any form from any allegations, claims, legal actions, writs, summons, orders for contempt of court and/or any other matter which may arise directly and/or indirectly from the display, use, adaptation distribution and/or exploitation of the [Blog/Article/Content] in any part of the world at any time for any material which has been supplied by the [Writer].

1.2   The undertaking by the [Company] in 1.1 shall also include any threat, claim action and/or proceedings taken against the [Writer] and/or any associated licensee, distributor and/or otherwise. The [Company] agrees to use its own in house legal team and/or any other third party legal services that may be necessary to defend, settle and/or set aside any such matters at its sole cost and expense and no liability of any nature shall be attributed to the [Writer]. Further the [Company] agrees to pay the [Writer] any loss of fees, expenses, costs and/or other sums which he/she may incur which arise due to such matters where the [Company] has requested the co-operation of the [Writer].

B.082

1.1   The [Writer] has created, designed and developed the [Blog/Features/Series] known as [specify details] which comprises regular [sport/fashion/political] commentary in [text/sound recordings/films].

1.2   In consideration of the payment of a monthly fee of [specify] on the first day of each month by direct debit. The [Writer] grants a non-exclusive worldwide licence to the [Company] to use, adapt and distribute to the public for free content from the [Blog/Features/Series] provided that there is a credit to the [Writer] as follows [specify].

1.3   The [Company] agrees that the non-exclusive licence in 1.2 is provided by the [Writer] on the basis that the [Company] uses the material entirely at its own risk and that there are no undertakings and/or indemnities of any nature given by the [Writer] and the [Company] agrees that the [Writer] is not liable for any future claim and/or legal action by a third party.

B.083

1.1 The [Company] commissions [Name] to prepare, create and develop a new blog for its websites as part of its online marketing. [

1.2 Name] shall create an original and innovative name for the blog together with a logo, slogan and image which [Name] shall assign to the [Company] for the sum of [number/currency] so that [Name] has no control, ownership, rights and/or interest in any media and/or medium at any time.

1.3 [Name] shall sign all such documents and registration forms as may be required to effect the assignment of all intellectual property rights and any other rights including trade marks to the [Company] of any material created by [Name] associated with the new blog in any format.

B.084

1.1 The [Company] agrees that the [Contributor] may deliver such material and articles, photographs and films as she/he would like to offer to the [Company] to be considered for the column and blog known as [specify].

1.2 The [Contributor] agrees that no payment shall be due to the [Contributor] unless the [Company] decides to use any part and/or all of the material, articles, photographs and films and/or any concept, idea and/or theme which arises from any of the proposals.

1.3 The [Company] agrees to pay the [Contributor] in accordance with the payment rates set put in Schedule [–] which is dependent on the type of use by the [Company]. All payments shall be made within [number] days of invoice by the [Contributor] direct to a notified bank account by electronic transfer at no cost to the [Contributor].

1.4 Where the [Contributor] creates and develops a new slogan, title, name, logo, image and/or any other material in any medium and/or format which is original to the [Contributor] and then used by the [Company]. Then the [Company] and the [Contributor] agree that both parties shall be joint copyright owners of any such new rights that may be created and/or developed. Further that the [Contributor] and [Company] shall share equally all sums received from the exploitation of such new rights and both shall be registered equally as the joint owners.

1.5 Either party may assign and/or transfer their share to a third party at any time provided that the other party is notified in advance and provided with [number] days to make a better offer.

B.085

1.1 The [Artist] has not granted any rights and/or agreement to any use by any person who views these [Images].

1.2 You are specifically advised that you are not permitted to use the [Images] for reviews, for educational purposes and/or to reproduce, copy, supply and/or distribute copies of the [Images] displayed and available for viewing on [specify website/app] without the prior written consent of [Name].

1.3 The [Artist] is the copyright owner and owns and controls all copyright, intellectual property rights, trade marks, rights of resale, design rights and all rights to reproduce, adapt, license, distort the [Images] and any associated titles, words, slogans and marketing in any format and any medium whether it exists now and/or is discovered, created, developed and/or brought into existence in the future.

B.086

In consideration of access to and use of the [website/other] and any associated material for posting and linking a blog by [Name]. [Name] agrees and assigns to the [Company]:

1.1 All copyright, computer software, intellectual property rights and the right to register and/or to receive any revenue from the exploitation of any titles, names, domain names, trade marks, slogans, images, logos, sound recordings, sounds, smells, films, text, sub-titles, photographs, stills, caricatures, emojis, lyrics, music, light sequences and any other material supplied and/or displayed on the blog known as [specify].

1.2 The assignment shall include the right by the [Company] to permit, authorise and develop any adaptation and/or variation in any medium and/or format including the right to sub-license to a third party and/or to transfer all rights owned and/or controlled by the [Company] in full to a third party.

1.3 Provided that the [Company] agrees that [Name] shall be entitled to be paid [number] per cent of all the gross sums received and retained by the [Company] at any time from the exploitation and/or assignment of the blog and/or any part and/or any associated adaptation and/or variation of any part.

B.087

1,1 The parent company and the subsidiary company which controls the [Website/App] on which the material originated by [Name] is to be supplied, distributed and promoted accept all legal and financial risk and liability arising from the use and exploitation of all such material.

1.2   The parent company and the subsidiary company agree that they shall not seek to take any civil and/or criminal proceedings and/or action against [Name] and/or his estate at any time nor to recover and/or be reimbursed in respect of any sums which they have lost, expended and/or paid to a third party for any reason.

B.088

It is agreed between the parties that in the event that [Name] shall decide to cease writing for the [Blog/Podcast] and/or creating material. That the following conditions shall apply:

1.1   That [Name] shall not hold any rights and/or interest in the title, slogan and/or trade mark for the [Blog/Podcast] and/or any other rights and/or intellectual property rights and/or right to any domain name and/or other location and/or platform relating to the [Blog/Podcast]. That all such rights and material shall belong entirely to [Company].

1.2   That [Name] shall not be entitled to any royalties and/or other payments for the use, repeats, licensing and/or other exploitation of the [Blog/Podcast] and any of its content by [Company] and/or any third party at any time.

1.3   The [Company] shall not be obliged to identify [Name] in relation to the [Blog/Podcast] for any reason. [Name] waives all moral rights and agrees that [Company] shall be entitled to edit, adapt, distort, mutilate and change the [Blog/Podcast] as it thinks fit without any consultation with [Name].

1.4   [Name] agrees to complete such documents as [Company] may request to facilitate the assignment of any rights in all media in all formats forever to [Company]. [Name] accepts that he/she shall have no claim and/or rights in respect of the ownership of the [Blog/Podcast] and any related material, music, lyrics, sound recordings, films, characters and/or otherwise at any time. That [Company] shall be entitled to develop a new version and/or series without the use of the services of [Name].

BOARD

General Business and Commercial

B.089

'The Board' means the Board of [Directors/Trustees] for the time being of the [Company/Trust] formally appointed by resolution and notified to [Companies House/other] in the [United Kingdom/other].

B.090

'The Board' shall mean the Directors of the [Company] appointed under the current legislation [specify] who have been legally appointed to the Board as either Executive or Non-Executive Directors. The Directors may vary from time to time and any new appointment shall be valid from the start date stipulated by resolution by the Board of Directors and not from any notification to comply with any legal formality.

B.091

'The Board of Directors' shall be:

1.1 The Non-Executive Directors and the employed Executive Directors of the [Company].

1.2 These persons are all jointly and severally liable for the acts, omissions and errors of the [Company].

1.3 This is the current list [specify] at the date of this Agreement of those who have the status of Directors of the Board who have been appointed by formal resolution and completed the formal statutory returns required by law to [Companies House/other].

1.4 Any resignation, dismissal or change shall take effect from the date of such action or receipt by the Board and not the time at which it is formally notified to the authorities.

1.5 Each Director shall continue to be liable after departure from the [Company] for any consequences arising from his/her period of office and shall be entitled to the benefit of such insurance cover as have may have been arranged to cover such liability for the benefit of the Board.

B.092

'The Board of Trustees' shall mean such individuals as may be appointed from time to time for periods of office to operate, administer and fulfil the terms and conditions of the charity registration number [specify name/number].

B.093

1.1 The [Executive] shall only be obliged to report to and follow the management directions of the main Board of the [Company] and shall fulfil the following duties and areas of responsibility [specify description].

1.2 The [Executive] shall not be obliged to carry out any instruction and/or action and/or to order others to do so which would be offensive or prejudicial to his/her reputation and/or in breach of any of his/her professional qualifications and codes of conduct and practice and/or which may lead to an infringement and/or breach of the laws of any country in which the [Executive] resides and/or works.

B.094
'The Directors of the Companies' shall mean all Executive and Non-Executive Directors of the main board of the Parent Company [specify] and any subsidiary, associate, holding or directly or indirectly related company whether due to a connection by shares, management, control, joint venture contract, the provision of financial support or bank guarantees [whether in existence at the time of this agreement or purchased or created thereafter] including the following companies [–].

B.095
'The Directors of the Companies' shall mean all Directors of the Group known as [specify] which shall include the Parent Company [specify] and any subsidiary, associate, holding or directly related company and shall include all the following companies: [list].

B.096
'The Board of Directors of the Company' shall be [name/status/title] [together with such other names as may be added at a later date.] All appointed Directors of the Board shall be jointly and severally liable until such time as they shall resign or be removed. Thereafter they shall only be liable for matters which may have arisen during their term as Director but shall not include [specify].

B.097
'The Board of Trustees' shall mean the Trustees of the [Trust] as may from time to time be notified to the [Charities Commission] and shall not include casual and/or full-time employees, volunteers and/or any other professional advisors. The dates of appointment and dates of departures as a Trustee shall be those recorded in the Minutes of the Board meetings.

B.098

1.1   The parties agree that the board of the [Consortium] shall comprise the following persons: [specify].

1.2   That in the event that any person is unable and/or unwilling to continue to fulfil that role. Then it is agreed that new members shall be recommended for appointment by agreement between [Name] and [Name] in the capacity of a sub- committee of the board.

1.3 All proposed appointments of any persons to the Board of the [Consortium] shall be subject to final approval of all members of the [Board] by an open vote at a meeting.

B.099

1.1 The [Directors/Trustees] of the Board agrees that they shall all be jointly and severally liable for all decisions that are taken at any time by the Board while they are on the Board.

1.2 That 1.1 shall apply regardless of whether a [Director/Trustee] took part in any decision or not.

1.3 There shall be no distinction between the roles and duties of any [Director/Trustee] except the Chairman. All parties owe a duty of care and are expected to take due care and attention and to apply due diligence to any proposal.

1.4 After the resignation and/or death and/or departure of any [Director/Trustee]. The legal obligations to the [Company/Trust] shall continue for a period of [specify].

B.100

1.1 [Name] is appointed on [date] to the Board of [Company].

1.2 This appointment does not mean that he/she is also appointed to associated and/or related businesses.

1.3 The [Company] shall arrange and pay comprehensive indemnity insurance cover for [Name] for a period of [number] years at the [Company's] sole cost with [Name] specified as the sole beneficiary. In order that [Name] be indemnified over [excess] for any claims, actions, allegations, threats, losses, expenses and/or costs, which may arise against [Name] at any time as a result of the failures, errors, actions, decisions, services and products of the [Company] and/or the [Board].

BONA FIDE

General Business and Commercial

B.101
'Bona Fide' shall mean that the parties shall act in good faith, with due regard to accuracy, honesty, and disclosure of material facts to fulfil the terms of this Agreement.

B.102

'Bona Fide' shall mean that the parties shall:

1.1   act in good faith.

1.2   disclose all material facts accurately.

1.3   not omit crucial information.

1.4   not fail to disclose that they are acting act in concert with third parties.

1.5   intend to fulfil and perform the terms of the Agreement.

1.6   be solvent and financially sound and able to meet the commitments required.

B.103

1.1   The [Licensee] shall carry out sufficient due diligence on any manufacturer, wholesaler, distributor, freight company, publicity, promotions or other business, company or person who is to be engaged to produce, supply, distribute, promote or otherwise assist in the exploitation of the [Product/services/other].

1.2   The [Licensee] shall endeavour to ensure that they are satisfied that the company or person will act in a bona fide manner and meet all the necessary criteria which may be stipulated and deliver as required and is capable of handling the finances in a fit and proper manner and to account and make payments on time.

B.104

The parties shall both act in a bone fide manner and use their reasonable endeavours to fulfil the terms of this Agreement. There is however no obligation to reveal corporate, financial and/or marketing details except as set out in the marketing and accounting provisions in paragraphs [–].

B.105

There is no bona fide provision and it is agreed:

1.1   That each party is responsible for carrying out its own background research as to the viability of the proposed [Project].

1.2   That each party shall be entitled to act in its own best interests in all the circumstances.

1.3   Each party must carry out its own investigation as to the financial stability, reliability as to deliveries, and the status, conduct and credit worthiness of the business of the other party to this Agreement.

267

1.4 Both parties accept that there is no obligation on either party to disclose facts, information, data or business plans to the other of any nature whether or not any such material may subsequently be shown to be relevant to the conclusion of this Agreement.

B.106

The [Licensee] agrees to ensure that all persons connected with the production, distribution, and marketing of the [Product] are bona fide and genuine businesses which have operated for a minimum of [number] years and are based in [country].

B.107

The [Company] shall endeavour to ensure that any other company, person and/or business associated with the [Event/Programme] shall:

1.1 act in good faith.

1.2 be solvent and have three years of audited accounts.

1.3 be capable and have appropriate professional expertise for the work required.

1.4 engage staff and personnel who comply with all current legal requirements in [country] as to health and safety and food hygiene.

1.5 not engage, employ and/or contract the services of any person who is not legally entitled to work in [country].

B.108

Where the [Company] at a later date discovers and/or finds out that it has been [actively] misled by one or more parties to this Agreement in respect of sales projections, historic data and/or the financial stability and/or who owns and/or controls any products, services and/or other material relating to this Agreement. Then the [Company] reserves the right to terminate the Agreement with immediate effect without notice and to seek to be repaid all sums which have been paid to date to any party under this Agreement.

B.109

It is agreed and accepted by all parties that no responsibility can be accepted for the failure to act and/or conduct themselves and/or to supply any material including data in a professional honest and bone fide manner by any third party including consultants, legal and financial advisors, auditors, software suppliers, publicity and marketing agents and/or otherwise. That where a problem is later identified which has an effect on the terms and conditions of the Agreement that all the parties agree to enter into mediation to resolve the matter.

BONUS

Film, Television and Video

B.110

In the event that the [Video/Film/Unit] achieves any of the following target levels: [specify [total revenue/net receipts] [awards] [audience ratings] [followers]. Then the corresponding financial bonus shall be payable within [in the next accounting period/within one calendar month of such event in each case] to the [Artist]:

1.1 For sales of [figure] copies of the [Video/Film/Unit] in [world/country]. Bonus: [figure/currency] and thereafter a bonus of [figure/currency] for every [figure] copies sold.

1.2 For subscription and/or downloads of [figure] copies of the [Video/Film] in [world/country]. Bonus: [figure/currency] and thereafter a bonus of [figure/currency] for every [figure] copies sold.

1.3 In [country] for winning [award] [Video/Film. Bonus: [figure/currency].

1.4 For [Amazon/other website] best-selling [Video/Film] list. Bonus: [figure/currency].

1.5 For completion of attendance at [number] opening premiers of the [Video/Film]. Bonus: [figure/currency].

1.6 For completion of front cover interview and image of [specify] magazine in [country]. Bonus: [Figure/currency].

B.111

1.1 In the event that the total [revenue/gross receipts/net receipts] of the [Video/Film/Unit] in [specify Territory] exceeds [specify].

1.2 Then for every additional [number/currency] received by the [Company] in respect of the [Video/Film/Unit] thereafter. The [Artist] shall receive an additional sum as a bonus of [figure/currency] on each occasion from the [Company].

1.3 There shall be no upper limit on the bonuses and such sums shall be due to be paid in respect of the accounting period in which they arise and fall due.

B.112

1.1 There shall be no performance-related, bonus or other additional payments to the [Artist]. The [Company] shall only be responsible for the payment to the [Artist] of such royalties as may arise from the sales, subscription, downloads, mechanical reproduction, performance and other exploitation] of the content of the [Video/Film] as set out in clause [–] of this Agreement except for those matters set out in 1.2 below.

1.2 Where a new method and/or process and/or other form of technology, format and/or gadget is developed at a later date which does not fall within any of the existing royalties and payments. Then it is agreed that the [Artist] shall be entitled to additional royalties and payments in each case on terms to be agreed between the parties. If no terms are agreed between the parties then the [Company] may not exploit the new development.

B.113

The [Presenter/Agent] shall only be entitled to be paid those payments set in clause [–] and shall not be entitled to receive any additional sums under this Agreement including but not limited to any of the following:

1.1 any performance-related bonus in respect of ratings, sales, gross receipts or net receipts.

1.2 any registration and/or exploitation of any intellectual property rights and/or associated logos and/or trade marks, service marks and/or domain names.

1.3 any sums collected for any performance, recording, mechanical reproduction, license and/or assignment of any rights in any format and/or medium.

1.4 no compensation for any termination and/or delay of the [Project].

1.5 no payments and/or allowances for travel, hotels, clothes, hair, makeup, photography and/or otherwise.

B.114

The [Distributor] agrees that the [Artist/Choreographer/Performer] shall be entitled to the following bonuses or additional payments in respect of the exploitation of the [Film/Video/Installation] if any or all of the following matters occur:

1.1 The [Video/Film] wins the following award [specify] Then the payment shall be [number/currency] which shall be paid as directed within [number] days.

1.2 The [Video/Film] reaches number [one] in the chart on [specify]. Then the payment shall be [number/currency] which shall be paid as directed within [number] days.

1.3 The [Video/Film] is nominated for [specify prize] in [country] in [year]. Then the payment shall be [number/currency] which shall be paid in the next accounting period which shall fall due.

B.115

The [Company] shall be entitled to the following bonuses as target-related payments set out below. All such sums shall be paid by the [Distributor] to the [Company] within [28] days of any such target being achieved and recorded by the [Distributor].

1.1 That the [Distributor] shall achieve sales of the [Film/Video/Unit] in excess of [number] in [country] by [date]. Then a one off payment of [number/currency] shall be due to the [Company].

1.2 [specify internet company] achieves total [gross/net] [sales/revenue] of [number/currency] of the [Film/Video/Unit] whether through subscription, play per view, downloads and/or otherwise. Then a one off payment of [number/currency] shall be due to the [Company].

1.3 On each occasion that a contract is concluded with a third party for the sub-license of the [Film/Video/Unit] to a third party for exploitation of the rights outside [country]. Then on each occasion a payment shall be made to the [Company] of [number/currency] in respect of each licence.

B.116

It is agreed between the [Company] and the [Distributor] that in the event that more than [number] copies of the [Work/Unit/Image] are sold and supplied to the public for more than [figure/currency] in any [three/six] month period. That the [Distributor] agrees that it shall pay the [Company] a fixed sum of [number/currency] for each copy sold and/or supplied to the public in excess of [number] for that period.

B.117

The [Writer/Company] agree and accept that even where sales exceed projections in any market and/or the [Distributor] is awarded a financial prize linked to sales as an industry award in any country and/or for any other reasons exceeds expectations. No additional sums and/or payments shall be due and/or owed to the [Writer] except those set out in this Agreement.

B.118

It is agreed that in the event that the sums received by the [Distributor] exceed the figures set out in the attached Schedule A for each of the countries specified from [date] to [date]. That the [Presenter] shall be entitled to be paid the additional sums specified in the Schedule A. All such sums shall be paid to the [Presenter] within [specify period] of the achievement of the target and the receipt of the sums by the [Distributor].

B.119

1.1 Where more than [number] copies of the complete [Work/Unit/Video] are accessed by subscription, downloaded, sold, supplied and /or licensed to any third party at any time by the [Company] in any one month period.

1.2 The [Company] agrees to pay [Name] an additional payment of [figure/currency] in arrears each calendar month by direct debit as an additional advance against future royalties for each month that the target in 1.1 is exceeded.

B.120
The following specified individuals shall receive an additional payment of a bonus in the event that the [Film] is completed by [date] in accordance with the Production Schedule and Budget: [specify name/sum/due date].

B.121

1.1 If the [Company] receives gross receipts of [number/currency] from the exploitation of the [Film/Video] worldwide within [one] year] from the date of first distribution to the paying public anywhere in the world. [Name] shall be entitled to receive a bonus of [figure/currency] within [three calendar months] of the achievement and financial verification of the target.

1.2 If the [Company receives gross receipts of [number/currency] from the exploitation of the [specify rights] in the [Film/Video] in [country]. Then [Name] shall be paid an additional fee of [number/currency] in the next accounting period that may fall due but in any event within [six] months of the achievement of the target figure.

1.3 In both 1.1 and 1.2 the [Company] shall be under a legal obligation to notify [Name] that the financial targets have been achieved as soon as this information and data is known by the Chief Executive of the [Company].

B.122
The following additional sums shall be paid by the [Company] to the [Agent] in respect of the [Artist] which shall be due and paid in the accounting period in which they shall arise:

1.1 The [Film/Video] achieves rating viewing figures of [number] on [channel/country]: [specify]. Bonus: [number/currency].

1.2 In excess of [number] people use the premium rate line phone in association with the promotion and marketing of the [Film/Video] in [country]. Bonus: [number/currency].

1.3 In excess of [number] copies of the [Film/Video] are sold, supplied and/or distributed through [specify method and company] in [specify language. Bonus payment: [figure/currency].

1.4   In excess of the target figures set out below are achieved as gross revenue is by the [Company] in the following merchandising categories:

1.4.1 toys, board games, household items, clothes, stationary, clothes, books, magazines and comics:

Target: [–] Bonus: [–].

1.4.2 mobile games, gambling, downloads, electronic devices, software, play on demand and subscription, theme parks, sales, licensing of music and sound recordings, downloads, licensed musicals and stage shows, tours, performances, sales, rental and supply of CDs, tapes, films, videos and podcasts, premium rate phone line or text message service, sports, promotional and corporate events:

Target: [–] Bonus: [–].

1.4.3 all other methods, forms and means of reproducing, supplying, distributing and/or exploiting the [Film/Video] and any associated content, image, logo, trade mark, music and/or sound recording whether in existence now and/or created at a later date:

Target: [–] Bonus: [–].

B.123
If the [Distributor] successfully concludes contracts with the following companies: [specify companies] in respect of [Film/Programme/Series] by [date]. [Name] shall be entitled to additional payments of [figure/currency] as a bonus for each contract which shall be paid within [one] month of the conclusion of each such agreement.

B.124
In the event that the [Video/Unit] achieves any of the following target levels of sales, receipts or awards then the corresponding bonus shall be payable within in the next accounting period of such event in each case to the [Artist]:

1.1   For sales of more than [number] copies of the [Video/Unit] in [world/country] in [format]. Bonus: [number/currency] and thereafter a bonus of [number/currency] for every [number] copies sold.

1.2   For [country] best-selling [Video/Unit] nominee of [specify award] list. Bonus: [number/currency].

1.3   For [Amazon/other website] top ten bestsellers list for [Video/Unit]. Bonus: [figure/currency].

1.4   For endorsement and/or reviews by [specify] as recommended. Bonus: [number/currency].

B.125

1.1 There shall be no repeat fees, royalties, bonus or any other sums due to the [Artist] for the exploitation of the [Content/Film/Image]. The [Company] shall only be responsible for the payment to the [Artist] of the fee and expenses set out in clause [–].

1.2 The [Artist] agrees that he/she shall have no claim to any royalties and/or other sums from the exploitation of the [Content/Film/Image] in any format and/or in any medium whether in existence now and/or created in the future.

B.126

The [Distributor] agrees that the [Artist/Choreographer/Performer] shall be entitled to the following bonuses in respect of the exploitation of the [Unit/Film] if any or all of the following matters occur:

1.1 The [Unit/Film] wins the following award [specify]. Then the payment shall be [number/currency] which shall be paid within one month of invoice.

1.2 The [Unit/Film] reaches number [one] in the chart on [specify]. Then the payment shall be [number/currency] which shall be paid within two months of invoice.

B.127

The [Artist] shall be entitled to the following additional payments as a bonus if the [Film/Video/Unit] achieves commercial success and/or wins the following awards. All the sums set out below shall be paid by the [Company] to the [Artist] within [six months] of any such event.

1.1 The total number of sales of complete copies of the [Film/Video/Unit] in [format] by [specify] worldwide for which revenue is received by the [Company/Distributor] are in excess of [number/words].

1.2 The [Company/Distributor] shall be obliged to notify the [Artist] that the target in 1.1 has been achieved. The [Artist] shall be entitled to be paid the sum of [figure/currency] [words].

1.3 In the event that the total advertising, merchandising, music and sub-licensing gross receipts received by the [Company/Distributor] are in excess of [figure/currency] [words].

1.4 The [Company/Distributor] shall be obliged to notify the [Artist] that the target in 1.3 has been achieved. The [Artist] shall be entitled to be paid the sum of [number/currency].

1.5 The [Film/Video/Unit] wins all and/or any of the following awards [specify awards]. Then the payment for each such award win but not for any nomination shall be [number/currency] to the [Artist].

B.128

If the [Series] is nominated for and/or wins any of the following awards [specify] whilst [Name] is the main presenter during the term of this Agreement. The [Distributor] agrees to pay [Name] an additional fee of [specify] within [one month] that the nomination and/or award is made to any of the parties involved in the [Series] including the [Distributor], production company [specify] and/or the parent company [specify] and/or any other person listed [specify].

B.129

1.1 There shall be no obligation for the [Company] to pay any additional sums, bonuses and/or an increased royalty and/or advance at any time to any persons and/or company involved in any capacity in respect of the [Film/Video/Podcast].

1.2 All parties agree that any award, prize, products, medals, statues, sums and/or other benefits may be retained by the [Company] and that there is no obligation to share and/or allocate any part to any other person and/or company.

General Business and Commercial

B.130

'Bonus' shall mean a discretionary gratuity which is over and above the [Employee's] agreed remuneration under the terms of this Agreement and shall be treated as a goodwill payment on behalf of the [Employer] and no rights of enforcement shall arise against the [Employer] in the event of non-payment of the Bonus.

B.131

'Bonus' shall mean those sums to which the [Employee] is entitled as of right under the terms of the Bonus Scheme and payment of such Bonus shall be treated as an enforceable contractual term.

B.132

'Additional Remuneration' shall mean such financial rewards, options or benefits in kind or payments by the [Company] to which the [Executive] shall be or shall become entitled or be awarded during the course of his/her employment including but not limited to:

BONUS

1.1 Any annual bonus which may be payable in the event the Executive achieves either personal targets and/or the [Company] achieves specified turnover, profit and/or cash flow targets as specified in the Executive Bonus Scheme attached as Schedule [–].

1.2 Any Executive Share Option Schemes details of which are attached as Schedule [–] which may be granted or exercised.

B.133

1.1 The [Executive] shall only be entitled to receive any payments under the bonus scheme and/or exercise an option for the share scheme and/ or receive any payments relating to the performance related targets which are achieved, exercised and/or allocated during the existence of this Agreement.

1.2 When the Agreement has been terminated and/or expired then the [Executive] shall not have any further rights in respect of those matters set out in 1.1 except where a sum should have been paid and was not received by the [Executive].

B.134

1.1 The [Employee] shall not have any right to any bonus, performance-related pay, additional sums, remuneration, options, benefits or rewards other than those set out under the terms of this Agreement.

1.2 This shall be the case whether or not someone else at a comparable level or job description in the [Company] receives or is awarded any additional sums, shares, rewards or otherwise at the discretion of the [Company].

B.135

The [Company] undertakes and agrees that it shall ensure that the [Employee] is awarded or is entitled to receive share options, bonuses, performance related pay, expenses, relocation costs, executive benefits and any other sums or privileges on the same scale and level as any other person employed in a comparative position or salary in the company at any time provided that the [Employee] shall fulfil the stipulated criteria.

B.136

The [Company] agrees that the bonuses which are to be provided to the [Executive] under this Agreement form an important part of the agreed financial package and are not discretionary and shall not lapse upon the expiry or termination of this Agreement unless it can be shown that the [Executive] was dismissed for gross misconduct.

B.137

The award of a bonus, additional payment, additional leave, an all-expenses-paid holiday, car, sporting event tickets or other products or items at any time by the [Company] to an [Employee] shall not incorporate this into the contract nor place any obligation on the [Company] to continue to provide at a later date other similar or equal in value rewards and bonuses.

B.138

The [Company] agrees and undertakes that it shall be obliged to provide to the [Executive] the same standard of benefits, rights and payments as would be available to any other person at the same level in the [Company] either before or after the [Executive] joined the [Company].

This shall apply in respect of the salary, bonuses, performance-related pay, share options, pension rights, health care and dental cover, life insurance, expenses, travel, accommodation, car, telephone, credit cards, gadgets, relocation costs and any other sums. Although the position of the [Executive] may be improved due to this clause, the [Company] shall not have the right to use it to reduce payments or otherwise to the [Executive].

B.139

1.1 The [Company] agrees and undertakes that every year the [Executive] shall be set an agreed Budget for their department which shall be the maximum expenditure for the year.

1.2 In the event that the [Executive] delivers the target set. The [Company] shall pay to the [Executive] the additional sum of [number/currency] for each year that the target is attained and/or not exceeded. The payment to the [Executive] shall be made within [two months] of the end of each financial year.

B.140

The [Company] agrees that it shall pay the [Executive] the bonus set out in this Agreement provided that he/she achieves the performance targets which have been set in appendix [–] and:

1.1 is not the subject of pending and/or ongoing disciplinary proceedings for misconduct by the [Company].

1.2 is not the subject of a serious investigation by a regulatory and/or government body which has not been concluded.

1.3 is not the subject of criminal proceedings which could result in a prison sentence.

B.141

The payment of the bonus under this agreement to the [Executive] is not based on the [Company] being in profit overall as a business but merely the achievement of the targets set for the [Executive].

B.142

The [Company] shall not be entitled to receive any additional sums, bonuses, performance related payments, royalties, contingency, residual or repeat fees or other benefits, shares, or stock or interest of any nature under the terms of this Agreement under any circumstances.

B.143

The [Executive] agrees and undertakes that he/she has freely negotiated this Agreement and shall not be entitled to claim that he/she should receive the same standard of benefits, rights and payments as would be available to any other person at the same level in the [Company] either before or after the [Executive] joined the [Company]. This shall apply in respect of the salary, bonuses, performance related pay, share options, pension rights, health care and dental cover, life insurance, expenses, travel, accommodation, car, telephone, relocation costs and any other sums. The [Executive] agrees that such matters are entirely at the sole discretion of the [Company]. Provided that the [Company] does not give preference to one gender over another as a policy which is not disclosed at the time of this agreement.

B.144

The [Company] may at its absolute discretion decide at any time to award bonuses or other additional benefits to its employees by way of a reward for hard work, recognised effort and dedication or a particular achievement for the [Company]. However there no legal obligations to do so and this reward system may be discontinued at any time, and is not related to status in the [Company] or any other particular criteria.

B.145

The award of a bonus, additional payment, or products or items at any time to any person, business or company shall not incorporate this into a term of any contract nor place any obligation on the [Company] to continue to provide at a later date other payments or rewards of a similar nature or equal in value.

B.146

Where in any part of this Agreement the [Company] agrees to pay a bonus and/or other fee which relates to completion of a task and/or targets. This shall only be due and/or payable to [Name] where the parent company [specify] and the subsidiary who is party to this Agreement is financially solvent and able to pay any sums due to [Name]. In the event that it is unable to pay the sums due then [Name] agrees that he/she shall not be entitled to place any lien and/or charge over the parent company only the subsidiary.

B.147

The [Company] agrees that where any bonus is due to [Name] due to the financial success of the [Project]:

1.1 That any such sums shall be kept in a separate bank account which is clearly identifiable and not mixed with other funds of the [Company].

1.2 That no lien, charge and/or other claim shall be made over these funds which are due to be paid as a bonus.

1.3 That [Name] shall be provided with confirmation as to where the funds are held and the date and method by which they are to be transferred to [Name].

Internet, Websites and Apps

B.148

The [Artist/Consultant] has been paid a fee for the supply of their services, any material and the product of their work for the [Website/App]. No additional sums shall be due at any time for any reason for any exploitation, licensing, sale, reproduction, distribution or otherwise of all or any part of the [Website/App] and/or any adaptation and/or variation. There shall be no bonus, performance related fees, share options, stock or additional sums due of any nature.

B.149

The [Company] shall not be entitled to any additional payment or bonus from the [Advertiser] in the event that the [Website/App] receives in excess of the target [hits/subscribers/links/downloads]. Nor shall the [Advertiser] be entitled to reduce the fee, withhold payment or request a refund of any nature if the target is not achieved.

B.150

In the event that the [Website/App] is successful and achieves in excess of [figure] [followers/subscribers/gross turnover] in the period from [date] to [date]. Then thereafter the [Advertiser/Promoter] agrees to pay to the [Company] an additional bonus payment of [figure/currency] at the end of each [six] month period thereafter starting [date] whilst those figures are maintained or exceeded.

B.151

The [Artist/Presenter] shall be entitled to the following additional sums under this Agreement in respect of the provision of their services and the use of such material on the [Website/App/other forum or account] of the [Company] and/or any associated business or partnership under this Agreement as follows:

1.1 Where the annual [gross/net receipts] of the [Company] is equal to or more than [figure/currency] in any period from [specify start and end date] then a payment of [figure/currency] shall be due for each such period.

1.2 Banner advertising receipts exceed [figure/currency] on [specify Website/App/other] then a one off payment of [figure/currency] shall be paid.

1.3 If any films, books, products and/or any merchandising material is produced and distributed by the [Company] or sub-licensed by the [Company] to a third party based on the [Website/App/other]. Then a percentage royalty of [number] per cent of the sums received by the [Company] shall be due to the [Artist/Presenter] which shall be paid within [one] calendar month of the sums received by the [Company].

1.4 Where sponsorship, product placement and endorsement fess for the following programmes and series [specify] which are received by the [Company] are in excess of [number/currency] during the existence and term of this agreement. Then the [Company] shall pay the [Artist/Presenter] a single payment of [number/currency] within [three] months of the fulfilment of that target.

B.152

The parties both agree that where the [Company] and [website/app/business] is valued by a reputable bank and/or other financial institution of international recognition at a figure of no less than [number/currency] and/or is listed on the [specify] market. That the following parties set out in Schedule [–] shall be entitled to be paid a one off bonus payment set out in that document. Provided that at the time of the achievement of either of those targets any such person is still employed in the role specified by their name and/or is a director, shareholder and/or consultant to the [Company].

B.153

No additional fees, expenses, costs, royalties, bonuses and/or other payments shall be made to the [Consultant] for any work and/or contribution to any of the websites, apps, software, products, business plans, projects, brands, marketing and/or otherwise for any new intellectual property rights, trade marks and other content and material in any medium that may be created and/or developed at any time.

B.154

1.1   In consideration of the [Project Fee] the [Design Company] shall be obliged to assign all copyright, intellectual property rights and all other rights of any nature in any media and/or any adaptation to the [Distributor] which arise directly and/or indirectly as a result of the work of the [Design Company] and/or any employee, freelance and/or consultant engaged by them on the [Project]. Such assignment shall include any ideas, concepts, formats, logos, trade marks, images, software and hardware developments, codes, patents and inventions, films and sound recordings, apps, music, lyrics, characters, games, merchandising, prototypes, samples and any supporting documents, information and data and/or other electronic form of reproduction or telecommunication whether recognised by any law in any country at the time of the [Project] or not.

1.2   The [Distributor] agrees and undertakes that where they receive in total in excess of [number/currency] from the exploitation of any of the rights set out in 1.1 by [date]. The [Design Company] shall be entitled a single additional payment of [number/currency] as a bonus [but not a royalty] which shall be paid to them by the end of the year in which such sum is received and/or achieved by the [Distributor].

Merchandising and Distribution

B.155
The [Licensor/Distributor] shall not be entitled to any additional payment and/or bonus from the [Licensee] in the event that the [Product] wins an award, exceeds the projected sales, is sold out in any country and/or exceeds [figure/currency] in total retail sales in any year.

B.156
In the event that the [Product/Book/Series] and/or any sequel is adapted and/or exploited in any form. The [Contributor] agrees that he/she shall not be entitled to receive any additional payments, royalties, bonuses, expenses, or other benefits or interest of any nature under the terms of this Agreement at any time.

B.157
The [Licensee] shall pay the [Licensor] the following bonus payments in the event that the [Work/Product] achieves any of the following targets. All sums shall be paid by the [Licensee] to the [Licensor] within [two months] of achievement of the target:

1.1   [number/currency] in the event that the [first/any edition] of the [Work/Product] sells [number] [hardback/paperback/download/audio version] copies in [country] in [year].

1.2 [number/currency] if the [Work/Product] wins any of the following awards [specify].

1.3 [number/currency] in the event that an agreement is concluded for an option for the [Work/Product] to be made into a [Film/Animated cartoon/Game].

1.4 [number/currency] where the Gross Receipts received by the [Licensee] exceed [number/currency] in any financial accounting year during the term of this agreement.

B.158

1.1 Where the [Licensee] receives more than [number/currency] in any one accounting period from the sales and exploitation of the [Product/Work]. The [Licensee] agrees to pay the [Author] an additional bonus of [number/currency] for that accounting period which shall not be considered an advance against royalties.

1.2 The [Licensee] agrees that each such bonus sum in 1.1 will be due to the [Author] for each accounting period in which the target is achieved.

B.159
The [Licensor] agrees and accepts that no additional fees, bonus and/or other sums shall be due even if the sales and/or exploitation of the [Work] exceeds the projections and/or the [Distributor] negotiates and/or receives additional fees from a form of exploitation which was not predicted at the time of the conclusion of the agreement.

B.160
The [Distributor] agrees to pay additional fees to the [Author] in the form of bonuses set out in Schedule [–] which are not an advance. The [Distributor] agrees to pay the sums within [number] days of when the target specified is achieved.

B.161
The [Supplier/Contractor] shall not be entitled to any bonus and shall not have the right to retain any sums which are under spent on the [Budget/Cost] at any time. All sums which cannot be verified by supporting documentation as to their allocation and use must be returned to the [Company].

B.162
The [Supplier] and any third parties engaged by them to [complete this Project/supply the Products] shall not be entitled to withhold the repayment of any unused funds and/or have the right to claim any bonus and/or

other costs and expenses and/or any rights and/or interest in the [Project/Products] and/or any associated material.

B.163

In the event that the [Contractor] delivers all the [Products/Services] on time and in accordance with the requirements and costs set out in this contract. Then the [Contractor] shall be awarded a bonus/satisfactory service reward of [number/currency] by the [Company] payable within [three calendar months] of the final completion of the contract and compliance with all the terms and conditions.

B.164

It is agreed between the parties that where the [Supplier] meets all the delivery dates and has fully complied with all requirements in respect of the [Articles] ordered by the [Company] from [date] to [date]. That the [Company] may at its entire discretion decide to make an additional one-off payment to the [Supplier] as a form of bonus of [number/currency] within [two months] of the end of that period. The [Supplier] acknowledges that the [Company] is under no obligation to pay the bonus to the [Supplier].

B.165

The [Distributor] may from time to time add additional content to the [Products] by way of a bonus and/or promotional offer for a limited period. The [Distributor] shall not be obliged to continue to supply the additional content after the expiry of any such period.

B.166

Where the [Distributor] requires the [Supplier] to fulfil an order and/or increase production which incurs additional unforeseen costs in any month to the [Supplier] in excess of [number/currency]. Then the [Distributor] agrees that it shall pay the [Supplier] an additional fixed bonus of [number/currency] for that month.

Publishing

B.167

The [Publisher] shall pay the [Author] the following extra sums as a bonus in the event that the [Novel/Work] achieves any of the following specified levels. All sums shall be paid by the [Company] within [28] days of an invoice subject to completion of the stated aim:

1.1 [number/currency] in the event that the [first edition] of the [Novel/Work] sells [number] [hardback/paperback/audio version/download] copies worldwide in the first year in which any version is released.

1.2 [number/currency] if the [Novel/Work] is nominated for [specify award] in [country] before [date].

1.3 [number/currency] if the [Author] is announced the winner of the [specify award] by [date] for the [Novel/Work].

1.4 [number/currency] if the [Publisher] achieves gross sales in [country] of [format] of the [Novel/Work] within [number] years of first publication of the [hardback/paperback] in [country].

1.5 [number/currency] in the event that an agreement is concluded for the [Novel/Work] to be made into a [Film/Video/Cartoon/Television Series].

1.6 [number/currency] in the event that the [Author] agrees to a repackaging deal to collate [two novels/works] into [one paperback] for distribution primarily in supermarkets.

1.7 [number/currency] if the [Novel/Work] achieves any top ten bestselling list from the following sources [specify website/newspaper/magazine/ television programme].

B.168

The [Distributor] shall pay the [Author] the following performance related sums in the event that the [Work] achieves any of the following stated targets. These sums shall not be an advance against royalties nor shall they be set-off against other agreements or sums. The obligation shall be on the [Distributor] to notify the [Author] that the target has been met and all sums shall be paid by the [Distributor] in the next accounting period following achievement of the target:

1.1 [number/currency] in the event that the [first edition] of the [Work] sells [number] [hardback/paperback/other] copies in [country] by [date] or within [six months] of publication whichever is the later.

1.2 [number/currency] if the [Work] wins the award [specify].

1.3 [number/currency] in the event that the [Work] is translated and published commercially into [specify languages] worldwide by [date].

1.4 [number/currency] if the gross receipts received or credited to the [Distributor] exceed [number/currency] from exploitation of the [Work] in any form.

1.5 [number/currency] on each occasion that any agreement is concluded for the merchandising and/or other exploitation of the [Work] where the advance to the [Distributor] exceeds [number/currency].

1.6 [number/currency] in the event that the [Author] agrees to a repackaging deal to collate the [Work] in a format not stipulated under this agreement.

1.7 [number/currency] in the event that the [Author] attends [number] or more events, book signings, literary festivals and/or other promotional and marketing events at the request of the [Distributor] during the term of this agreement.

B.169

The [Publisher] and the [Distributor] and/or any sub-agent and/or sub-licensee shall not be under obligation to pay the [Author] any sums other than those stated in this agreement. No bonus and/or other additional sums shall be due in the event that the [Book/Work] appears in any bestsellers list, wins or is nominated for any award, or is reprinted more frequently than predicted, or the sales of the [Book/Work] generate far more revenue than expected.

B.170

Where in any financial year during the term of this Agreement the total receipts from the exploitation of the [Work] exceeds [number/currency] by the [Publisher]. The [Publisher] agrees to pay the [Author] [number/currency] as a performance related payment. Any sum due shall be paid within [three calendar months] of the end of each such financial year.

B.171

1.1 The [Company] agrees that where it concludes a serialisation agreement with one or more [national newspapers/magazines] in [country] and/or any part of the world. Where the [Company] receives [number/currency] or more for each such serialisation. That the [Author] shall be entitled to an additional bonus fee of [number/currency] in respect of each such serialisation which shall not be offset against future royalties.

1.2 All sums due to the [Author] in 1.1 shall be paid within [one] calendar month of invoice by the [Author]. The [Company] agrees that it shall be obliged to notify the [Author] of the achievement of any of the proposed targets in 1.1 in any country in each case.

B.172

The [Publisher] agrees that where the [Artwork] for the cover and marketing is licensed by the [Publisher] for reproduction and commercial exploitation in any form at any time. That the [Artist] shall be entitle to an additional payment of [number/currency] as a bonus. Provided that the [Artist] does not seek to have any right to any royalty and/or other claim in respect of the [Artwork].

B.173

1.1 The [Distributor] agrees that where in the first [two] calendar months from the first date of publication the [Work] is in one and/or all of the bestseller lists of [specify]. That the [Distributor] shall pay the [Author] a one-off bonus of [number/currency] regardless of the volume of sales at that time.

1.2 The bonus in 1.1 shall be set-off against future royalties by the [Distributor] and shall be paid to the [Author] within [number] days of the event subject to invoice.

Services

B.174
'Bonus Fee' shall mean a one-off fee of [number/currency] which is separate and additional to the Basic Fee and Contributors Expenses which shall be payable to the [Contributor] by the [Company] in the next accounting period in the event that the [Contributor] meets all the proposed targets set out below:

1.1 adheres to all the time schedules stipulated for the completion and delivery of material;

1.2 completes and supplies all the documentation and other material requested; and

1.3 attends all meetings, production, filming and marketing dates.

B.175
No additional sums of any nature shall be due to the [Contributor] at any time. The [Company] shall be entitled to exploit the material and/or rights created under this Agreement at any time in any media and to assign, transfer and sub-license the material and/or rights provided the [Fee] has been paid.

B.176
In the event that the [licence/research project] known as [reference] is awarded to the [Company] by [specify enterprise] for the next [five] years. Then the [Company] agrees to pay the [Consultant] the sum of [number/currency] as a bonus payment for the granting of the [licence/research project]. Payment shall be made to the [Consultant] within [six] months of receipt of confirmation of the award and subject to the conclusion of the final award agreement.

B.177
The award of the tender, licence, research project, or government contract, renewal, sale or transfer of any interest in the business shall not result in any additional sums, royalties, benefits, products, bonuses, stock or shares being due to [Name].

B.178
There shall be no entitlement under this Agreement to any additional form of payment by way of a bonus, royalty and/or performance related fee at any

time to the [Consultant] and/or any other party whom he/she may engage for the purpose of this Agreement.

B.179

Where any application for funding by the [Consortium] is approved and paid to them by a third party and the [Consultant] has played an integral part in the preparation of the documentation, presentation and application. Then the [Consortium] agree in respect of each such successful application where the funds awarded exceed [number/currency]. That the [Consortium] shall pay the [Consultant] an additional fixed bonus of [number/currency] for each such receipt of funds from each application.

Sponsorship

B.180

'The Performance-related Fee' shall be the sums to be paid by the [Sponsor] to the [Sportsperson] in the event that the [Sportsperson] wins or achieves any of the events, records or other matters which are set out in the [Performance-related Schedule: specify target achievement/payment/date due] which is attached to and forms part of this Agreement.

B.181

In addition to the Sponsorship Fee the [Sponsor] agrees to pay to the [Sportsperson] any sums set out in the [Performance-related Schedule] within [specify period] of the event or occasion upon which the [Sportsperson] becomes entitled to any such payment.

B.182

In the event that the [Athlete/Sportsperson] achieves any of the events, records or other matters set out in Schedule A related to bonus payments, but is subsequently found to be disqualified and/or tests positive for drugs and/or is found to be using illegal and/or banned products which enhance performance. Then the [Sponsor] shall be entitled to refuse payment of any sum to which the allegation and/or proof relates to the [Athlete/Sportsperson]. Where the [Athlete/Sportsperson] is banned by its [athletics/sports] organisation and/or suspended then the [Sponsor] shall also be entitled to terminate the agreement. In such event no payments under Schedule A which have not already been paid shall be due.

B.183

The [Sponsor] agrees that where the accumulative viewing ratings for any programme in the [Series] achieves [number] or more in [country] whether through broadcast, transmission, play back and on demand television and/or viewing on a computer and/or other gadget in any one week from [date] to

[date]. That the [Sponsor] shall pay the [Company] and each of the following members of the cast [specify] a one-off fee as a bonus each of [number/currency]. Total payment of [number/currency] which cannot be recouped by the [Sponsor] under any other agreement with the [Company].

B.184

In the event that the [Sponsor's] name of [specify] and product [specify] appear in the [Programme] in full shot and are used by one of the main characters in the cast. Then an additional bonus fee of [number/currency] shall be paid to the [Company] for each different character that uses the product. The [Company] agrees that payment shall not be due for more than [number] characters in the [Programme].

B.185

1.1   No bonus, additional sum, advance, royalty, assignment fee and/or other sum shall be due to be paid by the [Licensee] in respect of the rights licensed under this agreement.

1.2   1.1 above shall not apply to any development, adaptation and/or new version which may be created at any time whether in existence at the time of this agreement or created as a new technology, method and/or right in the future.

University, Charity and Educational

B.186

The [Supplier/Contractor] shall not be entitled to any bonus, performance related payments, products, stock, shares, rights, interest or otherwise. Nor shall the [Supplier/Contractor] be entitled to save costs and retain any sums which are under spent on the [Budget/Cost/Price] at any time as an additional benefit. All sums not expended and accounted for from the allocated Budget must be returned to the [Institute/Charity].

B.187

In the event that the [Contractor] delivers all the [Products/Services] exactly in accordance with the delivery dates, costs and quality set out in this contract and complies with all the other terms and conditions. The [Institute/Charity] agrees that the [Contractor] shall be supplied with a letter of recommendation that it may use as a reference for future customers. The [Institute/Charity] also agrees that the [Contractor] may use a quote from the [Institute/Charity] which shall be agreed between the parties on its [website/app/trade directory] and in its promotional and marketing material together with an agreed link, logo and image to the [Institute/Charity].

B.188

1.1 The [Company] shall only be entitled to the sums set out in clauses [–] and the attached documents. There shall be no additional sums, benefits, products, stock shares, rights, royalties, bonuses or other interest due to the [Company].

1.2 The [University/Charity] shall be entitled to exploit the software and material, products, data, patents, copyright and any other rights or interest created or developed by the [Company] under this Agreement relating to the [Project] at any time in any media and to assign, transfer and sub-license any part of the [Project].

1.3 In the event that there is a subsequent project, licence, or government contract or the [Project] or any part is sold or transferred no additional sum shall be due to the [Company] and there shall be no right to be kept informed and/or consulted.

B.189

The [Enterprise] shall pay the [Consultant] the following performance-related sums as a bonus in the event that the [Work/Project] achieves any of the following targets. The sums shall be due within [thirty days] upon invoice by the [Consultant] provided that the target has been completed:

1.1 [number/currency] in the event that the first research and report to the [Enterprise] is completed, delivered and accepted by [date].

1.2 [number/currency] if the [Work/Project] results in the award of the tender for [specify] to the [Enterprise] by [date].

1.3 [number/currency] if the [Work/Project] is to be developed into a second phase and the [Consultant] is not to be engaged as a main contributor under a new agreement.

1.4 [number/currency] if the contribution of the [Consultant] to the [Work/Project] results in the creation of new patents, intellectual property rights, computer software rights, trade marks and/or other registrations which the [Enterprise] is able to register and/or claim as the owner anywhere in the world. In return for the payment the [Consultant] agrees to sign and execute any documents that may be required at the [Enterprise's] sole cost.

B.190

'Bonus Fee' shall mean a single payment of the fee of [figure/currency] which shall be due to be paid to the [Fundraiser] by the [Library/Charity] if the [Library/Charity] receives sponsorship and endorsement funds in excess of [number/currency] from new donors arranged by the [Fundraiser] by [date].

B.191

Where the [Institute/Charity] seeks to commercially exploit the [Concept] with a third party as a joint venture. Then the [Institute/Charity] agrees that [Name] shall be entitled to be party to that Agreement as the original creator of the [Concept] and to receive both his/her own advance and percentage royalty of any sums that may be negotiated and/or due. As well as [number] per cent of all sums due and/or paid to the [Institute/Charity] as an additional bonus payment for continued work on the [Concept] at the [Institute/Charity].

BOOKS

General Business and Commercial

B.192

'Books' shall be defined to mean any form of material comprising title, text and/or images which is produced by printing or other form of reproduction which forms a collection of pages and has a main cover whether hardback, paperback or otherwise. A copy of which is required to be lodged with the [British Library] and which is allocated an ISBN for the purposes of reference. The pages may be made of paper, plastic or fabric or other material. There may also be some interactive or other component, but it shall not form the main part of the book. The following types of books shall fall within this definition:

1.1 Hardback.

1.2 Paperback.

1.3 Anthology.

1.4 Children's annuals, plastic and fabric books; books with interactive buttons or other gadgets.

1.5 Educational editions.

1.6 Translations in any language worldwide.

1.7 The licensing of quotations from the text up to [number] pages.

1.8 Straight readings from the text up to [number] pages by means of sound recordings and performances for the purpose of marketing and promotion of the Book on radio and television, on blogs, apps, at festivals and trade exhibitions.

1.9 Large prints versions and braille versions.

1.10 Book Club editions.

1.11 The right to sub-license any of the above rights shall be included.

B.193

The following shall not be covered by and is specifically excluded from the definition of 'Books' in clause [–] above in this agreement:

1.1 Serialisation, one-shot digest, publication in newspapers, magazines and other periodicals and/or downloads of any text or images on mobiles, gadgets websites, apps and from blogs whether as a complete text and/or sound recordings.

1.2 Mechanical reproductions, computer software, PC and game consoles, discs, audiocassettes, DVDs, CDs, CD-Rom and other gadgets and devices and methods of reproduction and performance.

1.3 Adaptation for film and sound recordings to be transmitted via cable, satellite, digital and/or terrestrial television or radio and/or computer, mobile and other method of delivery over the internet and/or via any new format.

1.4 Telecommunication and wireless systems in any form, games, gambling, ringtones, animations and cartoons, theme parks, theatre and cinema and any other form of exhibition or performance.

1.5 Merchandising and formats which are not set out as permitted. Sponsorship, product placement, endorsement, advertisements, premium rate phone line competitions and trade and magazine promotions.

1.6 Photographs, stills, images, emojis, storage and retrieval system of any data or other material in any media and any development and/or variation in any medium which is not expressly permitted.

B.194

'Books' shall be defined as printed paper hardback and paperback only; all other formats, methods of reproduction or exploitation are specifically reserved by the [Company] and excluded from this Agreement. It shall not include any packaging, disc, free gift, advertising, vouchers, or promotional inserts.

B.195

'The Book' shall mean the Front cover, Preface, Contents and Index described as follows:

ISBN: [specify]

Title: [specify]

Author [name]

Length [number] pages

Photographs: [specify and list]

Copyright Notice: © [year] [name]

B.196

'The Work' shall mean the [original] work to be produced and delivered by the [Author] based on the [Synopsis and Summary] provisionally entitled [–] which is attached to and forms part of this Agreement.

The Work when complete and printed shall include the front and back cover, any reviews and endorsements, the preface, artwork and graphics, the index and any associated material.

B.197

'The E Book' shall mean a reproduction of a digital file of an exact copy of the original first edition of the [Work] [including the cover, front pages, and index] by the [Authors] which has the ISBN reference [number] and which is in the [English/other] language in [hardback/paperback]. Together with any illustrations, photographs, images, trade marks and copyright notice.

B.198

'The Audiobook' shall mean a reproduction of a sound recording of one or more persons reading and/or acting an adapted version in [language] of the text of the original first edition of the [Work] by the [Author] which has the ISBN reference [number]. This method shall include the right to add sub-titles and/or to make a braille version available to follow the text of the sound recording.

B.199

'The Digital Book' shall mean the reproduction in electronic form for the purpose of supply and /or reproduction by any telecommunication and/or electronic system to a third party in whole and/or in part of the cover, content and index of the [Work] by [Author] which has a printed ISBN of [number].

Such form of reproduction to include supply in the form of a pdf, email attachment, and/or download onto a computer, mobile and/or other gadget. It shall not include reproduction and/or adaptation for a film, television, games, betting or any other type of service or any method not currently created and/or developed.

B.200

1.1 The 'Work' shall mean the project entitled [specify] written by [specify names] as joint contributors and which it is proposed shall consist of [number] A4 pages, [number] images in [format] together with a cover, index and preface all to be supplied to the [Company] by [Name].

1.2 The copyright and all other rights in the [Work] and any developments shall be held by [specify names].

B.201

'The Book' shall mean the [number] edition of the work entitled [title] written by the Authors [full names] of [number] pages and [number][photographs/plates/engravings]. The copyright owners are [specify names] and the work was first published in [date]. A copy of the cover and the first pages of the work are attached to and form part of this Agreement in Appendix A.

B.202

'The Out of Copyright Book' shall mean the loose cover, the binding, preface, text, images, drawings, photographs and index by [author] which is out of copyright as it was published in [date] and for whom the estate of the author cannot be traced at this time.

B.203

1.1 'The Manuscript' shall be the final proof copy submitted by the [Student] to the [Institute] for the [Dissertation] which is based on a research title supplied by the [Institute] as follows [specify].

1.2 In accordance with the policy of the [Institute] the copyright in the [Dissertation] shall belong to the [Institute] and may be reproduced and/or distributed by them.

B.204

'The Book' is the work of facts and information originated, developed, written and delivered by [Name] on the subject of [specify] which comprises approximately [number] draft pages in [specify] font. Together with approximately [numbers] images designed and created by [Name] to support and enhance the text.

B.205

'The Diary' is the private diary of [name] dated [specify] which was deposited in the archive in [date]. There is no copyright in the diary which exists and the estate of [name] cannot be discovered.

BRAND

General Business and Commercial

B.206

1.1 The [Company] manufactures, develops, markets and supplies types of [generic product] and [owns/controls] the title and rights in the following brands and styles 'The Brand' shall mean the following [Products/Services] which are described as follows:

[specify product/colour/shape/images/sounds/music/smell/words/ phrases/logo/trade marks/design rights/packaging/advertising/ marketing][photographs/images] of which are attached in Schedule 1 and form part of this Agreement.

1.2 In the event that the [Advertising Agency] is required to arrange or commission any new logos, words, phrases, slogans, images, sounds, smells, scents, music or any other material of any nature by the [Company] or deriving from their work for the [Company]. The [Advertising Company] shall ensure that neither themselves nor their employees nor any third party shall acquire any rights or interest in any such new material in any form or medium and that all copyright, design rights, trade marks, community marks or any other rights, patents, inventions and computer software shall be transferred entirely to the [Company]. Further that the [Advertising Company] shall assist in the arrangements for the signature of all such legal documents as the [Company] may reasonably request in order to transfer, assign or register any rights or interest at the [Company's] cost.

B.207

1.1 Where in the course of the [Project] the [Consultant] is required to arrange, commission and/or contribute to the research, development, packaging, reproduction and/or any other use and/or exploitation in any format or media of any nature of any material including but not limited to any new logos, words, phrases, slogans, text, films, recordings, computer software, music, trials, tests, prototypes. The [Consultant] shall ensure that neither the [Consultant] nor shall employees, agents, freelance contributors or any other third party acquire any rights or interest in any material.

1.2 The [Consultant] undertakes and agrees that any rights or interest in any material in any form or medium shall be entirely owned by the [Company] and shall be transferred and assigned to the [Company] including all copyright, design rights, trade marks, community marks, patents, inventions, computer software and any other intellectual property rights and ownership of any material. Provided that the [Company] agrees to bear the reasonable cost of the legal and administrative costs and expenses of any such documents, applications and registrations that may be required and those of the [Consultant] and any third party that may be reasonably incurred.

B.208

1.1 The [Website/App Company] agrees that it shall not acquire any interest in any part of the brand of the [Advertiser] or its business whether in existence now or created in the future including trade names, slogans, text, characters, images, music, packaging, products or any other material in any medium.

1.2 All original artwork, computer-generated material, and any other content supplied by the [Advertiser] or created by any employee, consultant and/or third party engaged by the [Website/App Company] shall be returned to and belong to the [Advertiser].

1.3 The [Website/App Company] and any other person or business shall not be entitled to acquire any and/or register any rights and the [Website/App Company] shall co-operate in ensuring that all intellectual property and other rights are transferred to the [Advertiser] at the [Advertiser's] cost.

B.209

1.1 The [Consultant/Contractor] shall not be responsible for the protection, registration and/or monitoring of the trade marks, logos, slogans, copyright, patents, inventions, computer software or other intellectual property rights or any other interests of the [Enterprise] under this Agreement.

1.2 The [Consultant/Contractor] agrees and undertakes to assign to the [Enterprise] all rights of any nature in any media in any material which may be created or commissioned by the [Enterprise] for the purposes of this Agreement.

B.210

1.1 The [Website/App Company] agrees that it shall not acquire any interest or rights in any part of the [Charity] or any part of the [website/app/podcasts/downloads] and/or any other material of any nature which is in existence now or created in the future under this agreement for the benefit of the [Charity].

1.2 All original artwork, computer-generated material, films, sound recordings, images and any other material supplied by the [Charity] and/or created and developed as a variation by any volunteer, contributor, executive or third party engaged by the [Website/App Company] shall be returned to and owned by the [Charity].

1.3 Neither the [Website/App Company] nor any third party engaged by them shall be entitled to acquire any rights or interest and/or exploit and/or use and/or post and/or distribute without the prior written consent of the [Charity].

1.4 The [Website/App Company] shall co-operate in ensuring that all intellectual property and other rights including trade names, slogans, text, characters, images, music, packaging, products or other material in any medium are assigned and transferred to the [Charity] at the [Charity's] sole cost prior to the payment of the final fee under clause [–] to the [Website/App Company].

B.211

The [Company] agrees and undertakes that:

1.1 It shall not acquire any copyright, intellectual property rights, trade marks, computer software rights, patents, design rights or any other rights and/or interest in the development, production, manufacture and exploitation of the [Product/Programme/Event] and/or any associated material, images, drawings, maps, characters, music, computer-generated material,, marketing and/or packaging of any nature which is in existence now or created in the future.

1.2 That all original artwork, prototypes, sample material and any other material supplied by the [Charity/Enterprise] shall be owned and controlled by the [Charity/Enterprise].

1.3 Where any database is created by the [Company] for the purpose of marketing and promotion, sales and otherwise for the [Product/Programme/Event]. That the [Company] shall ensure that the data, information and personal details can all be shared, transferred and stored by the [Charity/Enterprise] for use by them in the future for fundraising and promotional purposes and that any person and/or third party has consented to such use.

B.212

1.1 The [Author/Creator] is not assigning any copyright, intellectual property rights, computer software rights, trade marks and/or any other rights to register any ownership and/or interest in any form and/or to collect funds from any collecting society and/or to register a domain name and/or any other right for any type of use and distribution on the internet to the [Distributor] in respect of the [Project/Work] and/or any related title, name and/or content.

1.2 The [Author] shall at all times own and control the title and all the content and associated marketing, packaging and rights regarding the exploitation of the [Project/Work] in any medium including the original names of the characters, places and the right to license and/or exploit a sequel based on the same main characters. No right to own and/or control any part of the [Project/Work] and/or the title and/or content is assigned to the [Distributor].

B.213

The [Distributor] agrees and undertakes that it does not own and shall not register any copyright, intellectual property rights, computer software rights, trade marks, logos, domain name and/or any other right and/or interest with any organisation and/or with any collecting society in the name of the [Distributor] in respect of the [Project/Work] and/or any development and/or adaptation and any associated title, name and/or other content in any format and/or medium in any part of the world and/or universe.

B.214

The [Sponsor] shall not acquire any rights in respect of the copyright and intellectual property rights in the title of the [Event/Festival] and any associated logo, trade mark, slogan, image, and/or music and/or lyrics that may be developed, produced and/or distributed by the [Company] and/or the [Sponsor]. If for any reason the [Sponsor] inadvertently acquires any such rights then the [Sponsor] agrees to assign all such rights to the [Company] at the [Company's] cost.

B.215

The [Licensee] agrees that it shall have no right and/or authority to use, reproduce and/or adapt any other product, article, logo, trade mark, image and/or brand owned and/or controlled by the [Licensor] and/or any associated companies, suppliers and/or manufacturers at any time. That the licence granted under this agreement is limited solely to the logo and image and product listed and reproduced in Appendix [–] for the period from [date] to [date].

B.216

After the end of this Agreement provided that there is no dispute and/or legal proceedings pending and/or in action. The [Licensee] shall ensure that all master copies of the [Licensors'] logos and image held by the [Licensee] in any form shall be returned to the [Licensor] at the [Licensee's] cost. That the [Licensee] shall offer the [Licensor] the opportunity to acquire any further material which it has within its possession and/control which bears the logo and/or image of the [Licensor] prior to any plan to destroy such material.

B.217

Where a new brand image, name and/or logo arises through the license to the [Licensee] which is developed from and/or adapted from the original [Logo/Image] for which rights are granted under this Agreement. The

[Licensee] agrees that all copyright, trade marks, service marks, and any other intellectual property rights and any other rights and interest shall belong to and be assigned by the [Licensee] and/or any third party from whom work has been commissioned to the [Licensor]. That the [Licensee] shall not have any claim to any funds from any exploitation except under this Agreement and/or any right to register any image, name, logo and/or use in the [Licensee's] name in any country or part of the world.

B.218

1.1 [Name] agrees to pay the [Artist] the sum of [number/currency] for the creation, design and supply of a draft and final logo, image and layout for the new business of [Name].

1.2 In consideration of an additional fee of [number/currency] the [Artist] agrees to waive all moral rights of any nature and agrees that [Name] shall be entitled to put a copyright notice in the following form [specify] and/or in any other manner next to the logo, image and layout.

1.3 That the [Artist] agrees that he/she shall not in future be entitled to reproduce, use and/or adapt the logo, image and/or layout and/or authorise others to do so for any reasons including review, articles, merchandising and/or for display on the internet to provide examples of past work.

1.4 That the [Artist] agrees to assign all intellectual property rights, copyright and the sole rights of ownership including but not limited to trade marks, service marks, rights of reproduction on film, television, radio, in computer software and on any hardware and/or gadgets, as merchandising and in the form of sponsorship and in any other form to [Name] in all media and in any format and for any purpose which exists at the time of the creation of the logo, image and layout and/or may come into existence at some future date and/or due to a new format of the work being created throughout time and space and in all countries, languages, forms of representation, reproduction and rights of registration and/or ownership and/or control at any time without further payment to the [Artist].

BREAK CLAUSES

General Business and Commercial

B.219

The [Company] shall have the right at its sole discretion to end the contract by [one month's] notice anytime during the term of this contract. Payments shall only be due for services provided to that end date. No sums shall be due as a penalty, charge, for disconnection, early termination or for any period after the end date.

B.220

If the [Company] repays the sums due under this Agreement at an earlier date than set out and the contract or the scheme is brought to an end. There shall be no additional payments to be made by the [Company] to compensate for the loss of interest, fees or commission or imposed as an early redemption charge, cost or penalty.

B.221

The Agreement shall not automatically continue and be renewed on a rolling basis, and every period of a calendar year shall be a separate agreement. The agreement shall only continue if the [Supplier/Contractor] receives written confirmation from the [Company] or payment is made for work for the next period.

B.222

This Agreement may be ended by [Name] by [method] on or by the following dates [specify]. No reason is required and no sums are due to the [Distributor] after the end date either as compensation for early termination, or for any losses or expenses which may arise either directly or indirectly as a result.

B.223

Either party shall have the right to terminate this Agreement after the expiry of a period of [six] months from the [start date] of the Agreement. Written notice to that effect must be received at least [seven] days before the expiry of the [six] month period. No reason for the termination is required and no sums shall be due in compensation and/or as damages for any losses. The only payments which shall be made are those which are still due to the date of termination. No sums shall be paid for any agreements and/or other arrangements which exist and/or were due to be signed after the date of termination.

B.224

Where the [Agent] for the [Company] acts in such a manner and/or makes such allegations which are untrue, inaccurate and likely to affect the reputation of [Name]. Then [Name] shall be entitled to terminate this Agreement with immediate effect and shall not be liable to pay any further sums due to the [Agent] and/or [Company] under this Agreement which may fall due for work after that date.

B.225
Where in the first [three] month period of this agreement either party shall fail to fulfil and perform the terms in accordance with the agreement. Then the party who has not complied with all the terms may be served notice by the other party that the agreement will end on any date that they shall decide to notify and there shall be no obligation to continue with any part of the agreement after that end date.

BUDGET

Film, Television and Video

B.226
'The Budget' shall mean the Budget for the [Film/Video/Series] which shall set out in detail all the fees, costs, charges, copyright clearance payments, mechanical reproduction and performing rights payments for any music, insurance costs, expenses, reproduction costs, and contractual obligations and liabilities connected with the development, production, completion, distribution and exploitation of the [Film/Video/Series] in accordance with the Production Schedule. A copy of the following documents are attached to and form part of this Agreement: [Budget/Production Schedule/Marketing Report].

B.227
In consideration of the production of the [Film/Video/Podcast] by the [Production Company] and the supply, assignment to and exploitation by the [Distributor].The Distributor agrees to pay the total sum set out in the attached Budget to the [Production Company] in accordance with the payment dates specified subject to completion of work. The Budget is attached and forms part of this Agreement. Where the Budget is exceeded the [Production Company] shall not be entitled to any additional sums without verification as to the reason an audit as to the sums expended and the written consent of the [Distributor].

B.228
Without prejudice to the [Production Company's] entitlement to receive a share of the proceeds of exploitation of the [Film/Video]. The Budget shall be accepted as consideration by the [Production Company] and shall be paid by the [Distributor] in full satisfaction of the amounts due to the [Production Company] in respect of all costs incurred by the [Production Company] in making, completing and supplying a technically acceptable

first class quality master copy of the [Film/Video]. The Budget shall include but not be limited to the following matters:

1.1 Directors', actors', musicians', writers', performers', composers' and contributors' fees, expenses and costs to the date of completion and a schedule for any sums due thereafter.

1.2 All intellectual property and trade mark rights [but not registration], copyright clearances and payments, consents, scriptwriters, directors and producers fees.

1.3 All costs and expenses for development, reproduction, editing, front titles and credits.

1.4 Legal, administrative, insurance, location access, accommodation, meals, travel, freight, stationery, gadgets, packaging, telephone and mobile costs.

1.5 Music clearance and payments, any sums due to any collecting societies or union members or any other person or company for recordings, reproduction, performances, distribution and exploitation.

B.229

The [Production Company] shall deliver to the [Television Company] by [the end of each month] from the date of this Agreement a written statement of the pre-production, production and post-production costs of the [Series] on an accrued cost basis. Each statement shall show the final estimated cost of the production of the [Series] against the Budget and shall contain a full and proper explanation of any variances from the Budget.

B.230

1.1 The [Production Company] shall deliver to the [Distributor] within [three] calendar months of the [delivery/acceptance] of the Master Copy of the [Film/Video] a report which provides a detailed statement of expenditure of all costs and expenses incurred and which may still be due. Wherever possible, copies of supporting receipts and invoices will be provided.

1.2 If there is a dispute between the parties as to the validity of all the sums in 1.1 then there shall be an audit carried out by an independent firm of chartered accountants approved by both the parties at the [Distributors] cost and expense. The [Production Company] shall not be entitled to retain any sums not expended and shall only be entitled to receive any sums in excess of the Budget if there has been written authorisation in advance by the [Distributor].

B.231

'The Approved Budget' shall be the agreed cost of making the [Film/Video] whether direct or indirect inclusive of all locations, facilities, technical and skilled consultants, companies and personnel, products, insurance, music, artwork, computer-generated material, permissions and consents, licences, agency fees, transport, hotel and telephone costs and expenses necessary for the development, pre-production, production, editing and supply of the [Film/Video]. A copy of which is attached and forms part of this Agreement.

B.232

[Name] agrees that he/she is not entitled to order any goods or services or to pledge, commit or authorise any payment, credit or other matter without the prior consent of [specify] in the [Company].

B.233

1.1 The [Assignor] undertakes that it shall produce the [Film/Video] using the Key Personnel in accordance with the Artistic Concept, the Approved Budget and the Production Schedule.

1.2 In the event of the Approved Budget being exceeded by up to [number/currency/percentage] the [Assignor] agrees to inform the [Assignee] in advance and provide the [Assignee] with a statement of costs incurred to date and details of the anticipated additional costs.

B.234

In the event of the Approved Budget being exceeded by more than [specify amount] the [Assignor] agrees that the prior written approval of the [Assignee] shall be required in an order to authorise any further expenditure and any further payment shall be at the [Assignee's] sole discretion.

B.235

The [Assignor] undertakes that all sums due in respect of the production of the [Series] will be paid as set out in the Budget. That in the event that it is expected that the Budget will be exceeded, the [Assignee] shall be notified immediately in writing. That no additional costs or expenses shall be incurred without the prior written consent of the [Assignee]. That the Budget only sets out the cost of clearance and payments for the following rights [–] in [country] and not all other media.

B.236

'The Budget' shall be the total cost of making the [Programmes] and all associated marketing and promotional material whether direct or indirect, inclusive of all personnel, contributors, crew, locations, equipment, facilities and other matters necessary for the development, pre-production, filming, post-production, comprehensive insurance and delivery of the completed material which is technically suitable for transmission in [format] on [medium]. The [Programmes] shall only be cleared for use in the following countries [specify] and formats [specify]. A copy of the Budget is attached to and forms part of this Agreement as Schedule A.

B.237
The [Company] undertakes that all sums due in respect of the production and exploitation of the [Film/Video/Series] and any sound recordings will be paid as set out in the Budget and that the [Distributor] is not and will not be liable for any such payments except in respect of the [specify person] and the Musical Work which are not included in the Budget.

B.238
The parties agree that [Unit] of the [Film] is only intended to be sold and exploited in [country] at first for [market] so the Budget does not cover the cost of clearance and payments for the exploitation of any other countries or rights. These may be cleared and acquired by the [Company] at their own cost at a later date.

B.239
'The Budget' shall be no more than [figure/currency] in total. This sum shall be used for the preparation, development and production of the master sound recordings for the [Disc] prior to manufacture, distribution and exploitation. The Budget shall be used to arrange clearance of and payment of any the music and/or lyrics, payment and buyout of any session and other background musicians, and/or the conclusion of any relevant contracts with musicians, artists and performers and any advance, use of any studios and/or location, and/or facilities and all relevant technical support to produce the master sound recordings to a technical standard for use in [specify format and medium].

B.240
'The Short Film Pilot Budget' shall be the sum of [number/currency] to be paid by the [Trust] to [Name] to film and edit a short film of no more than [duration] minutes based on the topic of [subject] in the form of the synopsis attached to this Agreement to be delivered by [date] in [format].

B.241
[Name] is not authorised by the [Company] to exceed the budget allocated to the [Project/Film] at any time. The [Company] will not and does not accept any liability in respect of any commitment to pay and/or expenditure incurred in excess of the agreed budget of [number/currency].

B.242

It is accepted by both parties that the sums specified is a provisional and estimated budget and may be exceeded due to additional costs and expenses which may arise directly and/or indirectly from the development, production, reproduction and distribution of the [Film/Video/Series] in different formats including artwork, advertising, packaging, music, merchandising, promotions and marketing. The [Company] and the [Distributor] agree that [specify which party] shall pay all the cost of the budget up to a maximum of [number/currency].

B.243

'The Approved Budget' shall mean the agreed direct and indirect costs of making the [Advertisement/Podcast/Film] inclusive of all performers, personnel, locations, travel and hotel costs and other benefits supplied and all other matters and costs and expenses necessary for the development, pre-production, production, sound recordings and post-production and delivery of the [Advertisement/Podcast/Film] and shall include a contingency allowance and full insurance cover for performers, personnel and delivery of the [Advertisement/Podcast/Film] Material. A copy of the Approved Budget is attached to and forms part of this Agreement as Appendix A.

B.244

'The Budget' shall be the total cost of making the [Pilot/Film] which the [Company] and [Name] have agreed in order to develop, produce and deliver [specify material] of the [Pilot/Film] by [date] based on the [Synopsis/Script] suitable for viewing on [format]. It is agreed that the [Pilot/Film] will not be suitable for transmission and/or broadcast on television but will be suitable to be posted on [specify site]. A copy of the Budget is set out in Appendix B which is attached to and forms part of this Agreement.

B.245

1.1 In the event of the Budget being exceeded the [Name] agrees to inform the [Company] in advance and provide a statement of costs incurred to date and details of the proposed additional costs. [Name] agrees not to commit to additional work and/or costs without the prior authorisation of the [Company].

1.2 That if the additional expenditure is refused by the [Company] that [Name] shall deliver all the material and documents completed to date to the [Company]. {Name] acknowledges that the [Company] shall have the right to ask a third party to complete and/or take over the [Project].

B.246

'The Series Budget' shall be the total of the sums to be paid by the [Television Company] excluding the cost of any of the Television Company's employees or consultants in respect of the production of the [Series] to the [Production Company] which shall include but not be limited to the following cost and expenses to be incurred to enable the transmission and exploitation of the [Series] in the following medium worldwide: [specify formats/methods]:

1.1 Any payments due to any contributor, performer, agent, film, television, video, radio or other third party.

1.2 Any payments as a one off and/or contained in the agreements with any collecting societies for the mechanical reproduction, performance and/or otherwise of any material including music and sound recordings.

1.3 Any payments arising as a result of contractual obligations whether to an estate of a deceased person, insurance premiums, audit fees, travel, hotel and entertainment, mobile phone and other communication costs.

1.4 Any sum due for the use and/or adaptation of any literary, dramatic, artistic or musical material and any library or other film or sound recordings incorporated into or synchronised with or otherwise forming part of the [Series] and/or any marketing.

1.5 A contingency of [number/currency].

The final total expenditure for the Series Budget as shown by the final cost statement of the actual production costs by the [Television Company].

B.247

'The Budget' shall mean the fixed sum of [figure/currency] (exclusive of taxes) which both parties to this Agreement acknowledge and agree to be the entire cost of development, pre-production, production, post-production and delivery of the [Series/Films/Videos] in accordance with the terms of this Agreement. For the avoidance of doubt the Budget shall include in particular but not by way of limitation provision for:

1.1 The original fees and clearance fees for any additional exploitation in any format to be paid to the artist, musicians, performers and all other contributors to the [Series/Films/Videos].

1.2 The cost of any location and studio hire, parking, access, transport, meals, telephone, internet, accommodation, security and other personnel. The cost of the supply of any stage, lighting, costumes, sound system and other equipment. As well as the cost of rehearsals, filming, editing, the addition of credits and title, storage and delivery of the correct formats required.

1.3 The fees paid and/or due for any person, company and/or consultant for the [Series/Films/Videos] who in some form provide a contribution whether artistic, photographic, graphic, creative, computer-generated, technical, health and safety, legal and compliance advice and services and/or facilities.

1.4 The cost of acquiring the rights in any material owned and/or controlled by third parties. Together with the cost of any insurance policies which relate to the [Series/Films/Videos].

B.248

'The Budget' shall mean the fixed sum of [figure/currency] (exclusive of specify tax) which shall be the entire cost of the development, pre-production, production, post-production and delivery of the [Film/Video] in accordance with the terms of this Agreement. A copy of the Budget is attached to and forms part of this Agreement as Schedule A. For the avoidance of doubt the Budget shall include:

1.1 The fees and exploitation fees to be paid to all performers, artists, contributors or other persons who appear in sound/or vision;

1.2 The cost of film and/or studio, location, equipment, set costs such as costumes, lighting, furniture, development, processing, editing, reproduction, credits and titles, freight and storage costs;

1.3 The cost of any personnel, director, crew, support staff, legal, accounting, graphics or other artwork, computer and software, photographic, music, technical, insurance cover and completion guarantee;

1.4 The cost of all materials such as telephone, stationery, internet use, transport and travel accommodation, food and drink, clothing, makeup, props.

1.5 The arrangement of and obtaining of all necessary consents, clearances, releases, moral rights, contracts, copyright, software, trademarks, logos, images, formats in any material or of any person or company.

B.249

The [Assignee] agrees that it shall not be entitled to offset the Budget from the Gross Receipts which shall be limited to the defined Distribution Expenses.

B.250

The [Assignor] shall set up a separate bank account for the Budget and the administration of the production, marketing, distribution and sales of the [Film/Video] at bank [specify] in [country] under the name [specify] with the following parties as authorised signatories [specify].

B.251

The [Consortium] agrees to release [number/currency] to be held in a bank account at [bank] opened for the purpose of funding the pilot development of the [Film/Video] in the name of a limited company where the two directors and signatories to the bank account are [specify]. Subject to the provision that the funds must only be used for the purpose of developing a script and pilot film as set out in the attached documents in Schedule A.

B.252

It is agreed by both parties that where the budget is exceeded and the additional costs cannot be met by either party. That subject to the consent of both parties a third person and/or company may contribute to the cost in return for the allocation of rights to exploit the [Film/Video].

B.253

1.1 The [Artist] agrees that the [Company] has awarded a budget of [number/currency] as the total budget to produce, direct and collaborate on a creative [Film/Video/Installation] on the subject of [specify].

1.2 That any additional costs and expenses shall be the responsibility of the [Artist] and not the [Company] including any sums due for music, collecting societies, copyright, rights clearance, technical, reproduction, manufacturing and marketing costs.

General Business and Commercial

B.254

The [Company] agrees that it shall bear its own costs in respect of [specify] and these are not intended to be recouped as part of the allocated Budget.

B.255

In the event that it is anticipated that the Budget is to be or is exceeded then the prior written consent of the [Parent Company] is required before the [Distributor] incurs and/or commits to any additional costs and expenses. In the event that there is no consent provided to such costs and expenses then any such sums shall be the sole responsibility of the [Distributor].

B.256

The [Company] agrees that the Budget is a statement of the total cost of the [Project] and is not for guidance, but the maximum price agreed between the parties.

B.257

1.1   The [Company] agrees and undertakes that it shall only use and pay for items for the [Project] set out in the Approved Budget and that no such sums shall be used to fund other material and/or matters.

1.2   That the [Company] shall pay for all of the [Project] out of the Approved Budget and that the [Fund Provider/Government Body] shall not be liable for any additional payments or costs once the Approved Budget has been paid to the [Company].

B.258

In the event of that it is expected that the Budget will be and/or has been exceeded by [number/currency] including the contingency provision. The [Company] agrees to inform the [Client] as soon as possible and to not delay notifying them. The [Company] will supply the [Client] with a statement of costs incurred to date and details of the additional costs and expenses which have been and/or need to be incurred.

B.259

In the event of the Budget being exceeded by more than [five] per cent then the [Company] agrees that the prior written approval of the [Client] shall be required in order to authorise any further expenditure which shall be at the [Client's] sole discretion.

B.260

'The Promotion Budget' shall be the combined costs of the Promotion Fee and the Promotion Expenses of [number/currency] which the [Promoter] is not authorised to exceed for any reason.

B.261

The parties have agreed that the total budget for the [Installation] shall be [number/currency] in accordance with the attached budget plan and the deadlines for the delivery. Both parties accept and agree that where any cost is expected to increase at any time that provided that it falls within the additional [ten] per cent contingency that it shall be permitted without prior authorisation.

B.262

1.1   The [Company] has provided a quote of [number/currency] as the proposed budget for the work to [specify purpose] and create and deliver [specify] to [Name].

1.2   The [Company reserves the right to adjust and increase the cost due to additional changes requested by [Name] at any time, delay in placing the order and/or any other matter resulting from variations and changes to the order at any time and/or increase in supply and reproduction costs of materials, insurance and/or delivery costs.

Internet, Websites and Apps

B.263
The [Design Company] shall not be entitled to any additional sums of any nature from [Name] unless agreed in writing in advance. The total liability and budget for designing, creating and setting up the [Website/App] shall be limited to [number/currency]. The sums due shall be paid in stages according to the development and completion of the [Website/App] as follows [specify].

B.264
Authorisation for additional expenditure for the budget may be by email exchanges, letters or phone call and the [Client] agrees to pay all such sums subject to completion of the authorised additional work.

B.265
'The Budget' shall be the total cost of creating, developing and delivering a functioning [Website/App] for the [Company]. The Budget shall only include the costs specified in the attached Schedule A which is attached to and forms part of this Agreement. Any further work and/or sums must be authorised in advance by the [Company].

B.266

1.1 'The Budget' shall be the total cost of creating, developing, marketing, setting up and delivering a functioning [Website/App/Project] for the [Company] specified in the attached Schedule A which is for guidance only. The total cost may be amended due to changes in the requirements specified by the [Company]. In any event the Budget shall not exceed [number/currency] unless the prior written approval of the [Company] has been obtained in advance.

1.2 The Budget shall include all the costs which directly relate to the design, development, testing, functioning, consumer and market research and establishment of the [Website/App/Project] on the internet which operates in the manner specified by the [Company].

1.3 The costs shall include of all location hire, facilities, personnel, third party presenters and contributors, performers, insurance, computer software, computer hardware, source codes and licences. As well as the cost of the acquisition and clearance of any text, artwork, photographs, archive images, trade marks, logos, music, sound recordings, films and videos. Any registrations of domain names, blogs, downloads, links, listings and/or advertisements, marketing and promotions.

B.267

The [Development Company] has agreed and undertaken to design, create, develop and deliver a finished [Website/App] in accordance with the description in Appendix A and the Budget in Appendix B. The Budget shall also include all the costs, expenses and payments that may be necessary for the [Website/App] to be used and exploited by the [Distributor] indefinitely on the internet and for the [Website/App] to fulfil the functions and operate in the manner set out in the objectives and targets in Appendix C. Where any annual registration is required then the Budget shall allocate the cost for the next [five] years.

B.268

1.1 The [Designer] confirms that the price quoted for the production of the [website/app/project] for the [Company] may be increased due to additional work and changes requested by the [Company].

1.2 That where the production and/or development is stopped due to the [Company] being unwilling and/or unable to pay any further costs to finish the [website/app/project]. That the [Designer] agrees that the [Company] shall have the right to develop, adapt and finish the [website/app/project] on its own and/or with a third party. Provided that the [Designer] has been paid in full for all work up to the date of termination of the [website/app/project by the [Company].

B.269

1.1 The [Designer] agrees that the [Company] may at its sole discretion decide not to further engage the services of the [Designer] to work on and/or complete the [Project] at any time.

1.2 The [Company] shall have the right to end the agreement with the [Designer] whether or not all of the budget has been spent and whether or not any work is not completed.

1.3 The [Company] may appoint a third party to work on the [Project] with the [Designer] and no approval and/or consent of that person and/or company is required.

B.270

1.1 Where the original budget has been exceeded and the [Design Company] and the [Trust] cannot agree terms regarding the additional costs to complete the [Project/Website/App].

1.2   Then provided that the [Design Company] has been paid for all their
      work under the original budget and any other work authorised by the
      [Trust]. Then the [Design Company] agrees that it shall have no right
      to refuse to permit the [Trust] to arrange for the collection of all the
      original material, copies of all software related to the [Project/Website/
      App], development plans and work and any associated material in
      any format and/or medium required by the [Trust] in order for them to
      transfer the work to a third party. Provided that where copies have to be
      made for any reason that the [Trust] shall pay the cost provided it has
      authorised the reproduction in each case.

B.271

[Name] acknowledges and agrees that the [Designer] has only provided a rough
quotation for the purposes of guidance of the cost of development of the [App/
Download]. That additional costs and expenses may be required to complete
the project so that it functions as requested by [Name]. [Name] agrees that
all changes, variations and adaptations requested by [Name] at any stage of
development will incur additional costs and charges by the [Designer].

B.272

The [Designer] agrees to keep [Name] regularly informed as to the costs and
expenses and charges which may be incurred beyond the original quotation
for the work. That authorisation shall be sought in advance for any sum in
excess of [number/currency]. That in any event the [Designer] agrees that
the maximum liability of [Name] to the [Designer] for the [Project] shall not
exceed [number/currency]. That any sum in excess of that figure shall be at
the [Designer's] sole cost.

B.273

1.1   The [Distributor] has engaged the services of [Name] to create and
      develop an [App/Project] for the purpose of [specify].

1.2   It is agreed between the parties that the functionality and accessibility
      of the [App/Project] by the [clients/public] is a fundamental key
      element.

1.3   A fixed price Budget has been agreed for the development, production
      and delivery of the [App/Project] by [Name] the details of which are set
      out in appendix A and form part of this agreement.

Merchandising and Distribution

B.274

The [Company] agrees that it shall provide at its sole cost a Budget of
[number/currency] for the purpose of promoting, marketing and creating paid

advertisements, articles and sponsorship and endorsement opportunities for the [Product].

B.275

The [Company] agrees that it shall allocate and spend an annual budget of [number/currency] in [country] for each year for the duration of the first [three] years of the Agreement in order to advertise, promote and market the [Product] in the following formats and medium: [specify details].

B.276

The [Distributor] agrees and undertakes that the following sums shall be spent by the [Distributor] in developing, testing, marketing, promoting and exhibiting the [Service/Product/Work]:

1.1   Development budget [number/currency] from [date] to [date].

1.2   Testing of prototypes for health, safety and quality [number/currency] before [date].

1.3   Marketing, promotion and exhibitions budget [number/currency] from [date] to [date].

B.277

The [Licensee] agrees and undertakes that it shall not be entitled to deduct any costs, expenses and/or any other sums arising from any liability directly and/or indirectly relating to the development, production, manufacture, exploitation and/or marketing of any products which are based on the [Work] from the Gross Receipts and/or the Net Receipts. That the cost of all such payments shall be entirely the responsibility of the [Licensee].

B.278

1.1   The [Distributor] agrees to advise the [Licensor] of the annual marketing and promotional budget which is being allocated to the [Project].

1.2   The [Distributor] agrees to consult with the [Licensor] as to the potential and most effective use of the funds for the purpose of reaching the target market.

1.3   The [Licensor] agrees that any use of such budget is at the [Distributor's] sole discretion and choice, and that it may be withdrawn without any reason being provided.

B.279

The [Licensee] agrees and undertakes to provide a total budget of not less than [number/currency] in the first two calendar years from [date] for the purpose of advertising, marketing, selling and raising the profile and the brand of the [Products].

B.280

The [Company] agrees and undertakes:

1.1 To design, develop, make and produce a fully functional [Prototype Product] using the key personnel in accordance with the Approved Budget agreed with the [Author]. A copy of the Approved Budget which specifies the key personnel and the functionality of the Prototype Product is attached to and forms part of this Agreement in Schedule A.

1.2 That no authority and/or consent is provided by the [Author] to exceed the Approved Budget and that any additional costs and/or expenses incurred shall be the responsibility and liability of the [Company].

1.3 Upon delivery of the completed [Prototype Product] the [Company] shall supply an itemised breakdown of the Approved Budget which confirms which sums have been spent. Where not all the sums have been spent then the [Author] shall pay the lower sum rather than the agreed Approved Budget.

B.281

The [Market Consultants] agree and undertake that they shall not have any right under this Agreement to authorise and/or commit the [Company] and reach agreement by email, verbally and/or in any written form with any other person and/or business in respect of the brand [specify] unless the exact terms and conditions have specifically been agreed with the [Executive] of the [Company] in advance in each case. This shall include but not be limited to any advertising and/or sponsorship campaign whether in print, on line and/or through events, product placement and films, radio, television, games, apps and other software, images, photographs, and any associated venue hire, catering, music and/or other expenditure and/or obligations.

B.282

1.1 The [Distributor] agrees and undertakes that they shall develop and produce the [Article/Product] in the exact from and content as the [sample/prototype] and with all the material and packaging sourced by the means and method specified in Schedule B which forms part of this Agreement.

1.2 That if at any time there is any proposal to change, vary and/or adapt any part however small the [Distributor] will notify the [Company] immediately and not commence any production with such changes, variations and/or adaptation until it has been approved by [Name] at the [Company] or his/her delegated officer.

B.283

The [Distributor] reserves the right to:

1.1 increase the cost of development, production, supply and delivery due to the [Company] at any time for any reason.

1.2 change the content and source of any ingredient and material.

1.3 cancel and/or terminate any order and/or part for any reason including the fact that production has ended.

1.4 change the packaging, text, image, logo, shape, weight, language, labels and instructions.

1.5 change the health and safety guidelines, test procedures and warning notices.

1.6 be unable to supply spare parts and/or replacements due to discontinuance of the [Product/Article].

B.284

The [Company] agrees that it has provided a fixed quote of [number/currency] for [order] provided that it is confirmed by [Name] by [date] and [time] and the price quoted is paid in advance in full together with all costs of secure and registered delivery to the notified address.

B.285

'The Authorised Budget' shall be the agreed cost of producing and supplying the [Commissioned Work] which shall include:

1.1 Material which shall be of the following quality and description [specify in detail].

1.2 Travel and accommodation costs incurred in making the Commissioned Work up to a limit of [number/currency] [in total/or for a fixed period] subject to receipts.

1.3 The costs of storage, packaging, security, insurance, freight and delivery of the Commissioned Work.

B.286

'The Budget' shall be the maximum total payment to be made by the [Company] to the [Assignor] in respect of the [Commissioned Work] which shall not exceed [number/currency] and shall include the cost and expenses for:

1.1 all preparatory artwork and designs.

1.2 all raw materials [including the hiring of locations].

1.3   the development, production, manufacture or supply.

1.4   travel and accommodation costs.

1.5   computer-generated software and graphics.

1.6   insurance, security, freight and delivery.

1.7   copyright, contract, clearance, collecting society and other third party payments for services and/or other work.

B.287
The [Assignor] undertakes that it will produce the [Commissioned Work] in accordance with the Budget. In the event that the Budget is to be exceeded, the [Assignor] agrees that the prior written approval of the [Company] shall be required in order to authorise any further expenditure and that any further payment shall be at the [Company's] sole discretion.

B.288
The [Assignor] shall provide a full report to the [Company] of the costs incurred in respect of the [Commissioned Work] upon request. In the event that the costs incurred in respect of the [Commissioned Work] are less than the Budget, then the [Assignor] agrees that the [Company] shall only be obliged to pay the lesser sum. In the event that the Budget is exceeded, the [Company] agrees to pay such additional costs provided that it has given prior written approval of the expenditure to the [Assignor].

B.289

1.1   The [Company] agrees that the Budget of [Name and Title] a copy of which is attached hereto and forms part of this Agreement is a statement of the total cost for the supply of the [Product] by the Delivery Date to the [Purchaser].

1.2   The Budget is not for guidance, but the final agreed price between the parties. Any additional costs to be incurred in order to fulfil this Agreement shall be the sole responsibility of the [Company].

B.290

1.1   The [prices/delivery charges] quoted on this [website/app] are for guidance only and may be varied at any time. Please contact the [Company] and obtain a quote for the [wholesale/retail] supply of the [products/services].

1.2   All prices are quoted exclusive of any taxes, custom duties, currency conversion costs and bank charges, freight and insurance costs which may be due to be paid by the [Client]. All costs, charges and sums due must be paid in full in advance before any products will be sent to the designated delivery address.

B.291
'The Budget' shall be the estimated cost of all the source materials, tools and machinery, transport, insurance, staff and the artist fee and the agency fee for the production of the [Article/Work] by [Name] and delivery of the completed form of the [Article/Work] to the [Company] at [address] by [date].

B.292
The [Company] agrees to pay all the costs, expenses and fees which may arise for any reason as a result of late delivery, changes in content, design, material, production schedule, location, compliance with health and safety and/or security and/or planning controls which may be necessary in respect of the installation of the [Article/Work].

B.293
'The Budget 'shall set out the fixed costs for the [Project] of [number/ currency] which may not be exceeded for any reason and shall be paid by the [Company] to [Name]. The costs shall include:

1.1 reproduction and preparation of artwork, logos and material together with all editing, changes and amendments.

1.2 supplying a sample proof copy and/or prototype (together with packaging) which is in the exact form it is proposed to reproduce it.

1.3 adding changes to and varying the sample and/or prototype (and any packaging) prior to reproduction.

1.4 supplying [number] of [format] of the final sample and/or prototype (and any packaging) in boxes of [number] in each.

1.5 all costs of delivery, freight, insurance, taxes, custom duties and any other charges and costs.

Services

B.294
There shall be a [monthly/annual] agreed budget for the services of [Name] which shall be paid in regular instalments on [dates] subject to completion of work.

B.295
The budget shall not be amended, increased, varied or reduced at any time without agreement in writing in a formal document signed by both parties.

316

B.296
The [Company] agrees that the [Consultant] shall be entitled to be repaid by the [Company] for the following sums [without receipts and/or itemised bills] which will be allocated in the budget for his/her expenditure each calendar month as follows:

1.1 car hire, petrol and/or diesel and associated costs, travel by bus, train, rail, plane and helicopter at a maximum of [number/currency].

1.2 landline, mobile, wifi and internet charges and costs at a maximum of [number/currency].

1.3 hotels, accommodation, clothes, magazines and newspaper subscriptions, marketing and print costs, entertainment and hospitality at a maximum of [number/currency].

B.297
The [Company] shall not be liable for any administration, telephone, travel, marketing and/or any other costs and/or expenses and/or commitments of the [Consultant] at any time. Nor shall the [Consultant] have the authority to agree any budget and/or expenditure on behalf of the [Company] to a third party and/or to represent that he/she has the power to authorise any such commitment.

B.298
Where either party makes such significant changes to the terms of the services to be supplied and/or to be charged under this Agreement It is agreed that this Agreement shall be terminated by both parties and new terms and conditions agreed. That there is no right by either party to make such changes and insist that the present Agreement continues.

Sponsorship

B.299
The [Sponsor] agrees and undertakes that it shall bear the cost of and pay for the Sponsorship Budget set out in Appendix A for the [Festival/Conference/Event]. Provided that the sums paid to the [Charity/Company] shall not be used for any other purpose than authorised under this agreement. Nor shall the [Sponsor] shall be liable for any additional payments or costs which may be incurred and/or due arising from the [Festival/Conference/Event].

B.300
Where the Sponsorship Budget is estimated to be insufficient for the completion of the [Tournament/Event]. Then in the event that the [Official Sponsor] decides not to pay any such additional anticipated costs and expenses that may need to be incurred and/or which will arise in order to complete the [Tournament/Event].

The [Official Sponsor] agrees that the [Company/Organisers] may seek and appoint a second corporation, enterprise and/or other additional persons and/or businesses as secondary level supporters of the [Tournament/Event]. Provided that the [Company/Organisers] agree not to appoint any second level supporter whose interests and/or business directly conflicts with that of the [Official Sponsor] in the [specify] industry and/or which would have a detrimental effect on the reputation of the [Official Sponsor].

B.301
'The Budget' shall be the maximum total payment to be made by the [Sponsor] to the [Association/Charity] which shall not exceed [number/ currency] and shall include the completion and delivery of the following work for the [Event/Project/Race]:

1.1 The cost of all preparatory artwork, designs, development, production, manufacture and supply of the [T-shirts, bottles, balloons, posters, banners, timing chips, stalls, markers and barriers, free gifts and bags].

1.2 The cost of access to and use of the location and all parking, security, electricity, water, sewage and facilities for toilets and changing rooms. As well as any risk assessment, insurance, first aid and other health and safety measures required.

1.3 The cost of any software, graphics, photographs, text, music and sound recordings, films and other material for the creation, development and functioning of an app and website known as [specify].

1.4 The cost of marketing, promoting and supplying articles and interviews; social media and other internet and platform accounts. As well as managing requests, registrations and all other matters regarding organising the [Event/Project/Race].

B.302
In the event that it is likely that the Budget is to be exceeded the [Club/ Company] agrees to contact the [Sponsor] at the earliest opportunity and to provide them with a revised costing of proposed expenditure. The prior written approval of the [Sponsor] shall be required in order for the [Club/ Company] to be authorised to incur additional costs and expenses. The [Sponsor's] shall not be obliged to agree to pay such further costs and expenses and shall have the right to refuse.

B.303
The [Club/Company/Charity] shall not be obliged to set up a separate bank account for the deposit and expenditure of sums received from the [Sponsor] in respect of the Budget for the [Event/Project/Race].

B.304

The [Sponsor] agrees that it shall provide the following budget and pay for the costs and expenses for the [Event] as set out below:

1.1 Flags, banners, tents, stands, displays and products [specify layout/ number/name].

1.2 Freelance qualified catering and bar staff, security and other persons in the following roles [–].

1.3 Rubbish removal and waste disposal, support equipment, generators, transport and lighting [–].

1.4 Security and identity tags, uniforms, transport and safety barriers and perimeter fencing.

1.5 Health and safety liability and risk assessment together with comprehensive public liability insurance of not less than [number/ currency] for [cover].

1.6 Training and procedures for emergencies, first aid cover and security checks.

1.7 All other costs and expenses that may arise directly and/or indirectly to reinstate the land, access route and use of the venue allocated to and/ or used by the [Sponsor] back to the condition it was in prior to its use or better.

B.305

The [Company] may at its absolute discretion increase the cost of sponsorship and/or funding and/or process for the [Event] at any time before an offer is accepted. The current prices displayed are for guidance only and not binding.

B.306

1.1 [Name] and [Name] have agreed to collaborate to create and develop a [Festival/Conference/Event] on the theme of [subject].

1.2 The parties agree that they shall share responsibility and liability for any sums incurred and due jointly where both parties have agreed to the expenditure in advance.

1.3 Where one party commits to the payment of costs and expenses without seeking the prior approval of the other then there shall be no joint liability.

1.4 The parties agree to create a new legal entity of which they shall each own 50%.

1.5   The parties agree to open a new account with a bank and/or building society in both their names where all sponsorship and other fundraising shall be deposited. No sums received shall be mixed with their own personal monies at any time. Both parties must jointly authorise any withdrawal of sums and/or payments from the new account.

University, Charity and Educational

B.307

The [Company] agrees that it shall bear its own expenses, insurance, staff and administrative costs in respect of the [Project/Event] and these sums are not intended to be recouped as part of the allocated Budget. Nor shall the [Institute/Charity] be responsibility if for any reason the [Company] is unable and/or unwilling to pay any sums in has incurred and/or owes which relate to the [Project/Event].

B.308

In the event that it is anticipated that the Budget allocated is insufficient to complete the work and/or to provide the services agreed. The [Distributor] must halt all work and expenditure and seek the prior written consent of the [Institute/Charity] before the [Distributor] incurs and/or commits to any further expenses and/or costs in excess of the Budget. If no consent or approval provided by the [Institute/Charity] then the [Distributor] shall be liable to pay such sums where they have acted without authority.

B.309

1.1   The [Company] agrees that the Budget in Appendix A is a comprehensive statement of the total fixed cost of all the work, materials and rights required to complete the work, services and aims set out in Appendix A.

1.2   That the [Company] agrees to adhere to the Budget and shall only be permitted to authorise expenditure in respect of those items in the Budget.

1.3   The [Company] agrees and undertakes that it shall not be authorised to incur or commit the [Institute/Charity] to any other sums and/or matters.

B.310

If the development schedule changes, the proposed aims and functions and/or the layout, colour and content of the [Website/App] are altered at the request of the [Institute/Charity] and impact on the total cost of the Budget in appendix A. The [Company] agrees to send the [Institute/Charity] a revised Budget with the higher cost in advance in writing specifying the reason for the new expenses and costs before any work is undertaken.

B.311

1.1 'The Budget' shall be the estimated costs of [number/currency] for the [Project] a copy of which is attached in Schedule A and forms part of this Agreement.

1.2 The Budget shall be paid by the [Company] and the [Charity] equally and split between them. A limit shall be set which shall be a maximum of [number/currency] which be shared equally between the [Company] and the [Institute/Charity].

B.312

'The Budget' shall be the agreed cost of [number/currency] in total to be paid by [Company] to [Name] for completion of the [Work] in [format] by [date] and delivery in full to the [Company].

B.313

The [Consortium] agree that until the budget for the [Project] is finalised and approved by the sub-committee comprising [specify]. That no steps and/or action and/or commitment shall be made by any party in respect of the work to be completed and/or the expenditure of the budget.

BUSINESS DAY

General Business and Commercial

B.314

'Business Day' means a day (other than a Saturday or Sunday) on which banks are generally open for business in [city/country].

B.315

'Business Day' shall mean any day from Monday to Friday which is not a bank or public holiday of [country].

B.316

All days of the week including weekends and bank holidays shall be counted as a day for the purposes of the calculation of any delay and/or notice and/or for any other reason.

BUY-OUT

General Business and Commercial

B.317

'Buy-out of all rights' shall mean the complete assignment and transfer of all ownership of the physical material of the prototype, developments, drafts, packaging, labels and formats and all copyright, trade marks, patents, intellectual property rights, computer software rights which are held or controlled by the [Owner] in the [Product] and/or parts in all media whether in existence now or created in the future throughout the world and universe for the full period of copyright and any extensions or renewals and in perpetuity to the [Company]. Thereafter the [Owner] shall not hold or control any rights or interest whatsoever in the [Product] and/or parts and shall not be entitled to receive any payments, sums or royalties from any exploitation in any form.

B.318

In consideration of the payment of the [Assignment Fee] by the [Company] to the [Assignor]. The [Assignor] assigns all media rights which are in existence now or which may be created in the future in the [Work] and/or parts and all the Material in any language to the [Company] from [date] for the full period of copyright and any extensions and renewals throughout the [world/universe].

B.319

'All Media Rights' shall mean:

1.1 All copyright, intellectual property rights, computer software and any other rights or interest of any nature in [Product/Work/Service] and in the physical property throughout the [country/world/universe] whether in existence now or developed in the future in any language, format or medium.

1.2 The sole and exclusive right to license, assign, transfer, copy, reproduce, lend, supply, adapt, translate, authorise, hire, sell, record, store in any form, recreate or develop in another format, disseminate or otherwise exploit by any method or medium whether it exists in technology and/or law at the time of the acquisition of the rights or is created in the future which shall include but not be limited to all matters set out in 1.1 to 1.12.

1.3 All trade marks, service marks, logos, characters and animated versions and all words, phrases, colour, shape, noise and scent associated with or part of them and/or adapted from them and any design rights and future design rights.

1.4 All database rights, trade secrets, moral rights and waivers, confidential information, and patents.

1.5 All forms of film, television, radio and interactive material including analogue, digital, terrestrial, cable or satellite received by television or transmitted or received via the internet on a PC, mobile phone or via other gadgets or devices or methods and/or played back and/or downloaded at a later date and/or pay per view, free and/or subscription.

1.6   All mechanical forms of reproduction including discs, tapes, cassettes and other means of storage and reproduction and all methods of performance and performing rights, together with the right to retain all sums due from any collecting society in any country at any time.

1.7   All text, data, index, titles, rules, images, photographs, drawings, plans, maps, sketches, marketing, packaging, posters, flyers.

1.8   All computer-generated material whether on screen or software and any material created for use with computers, hand held devices, watches, discs or any gadgets and/or storage mechanisms.

1.9   All music, lyrics, sound recordings, sounds and effects, noises.

1.10 All printed forms including books, magazines, brochures, serialisations.

1.11 All forms of merchandising, and exploitation of any kind, including toys, games, clothes, household products and gambling.

1.12 All forms of wireless and telecommunication services in respect of any part of the electromagnetic spectrum whether national, local, private or commercial and reception or transmission or broadband, ultra-wide band or otherwise which shall include but not be limited to mobile phones, two way radios, paging, data networks, public access radio, private business radio, common base stations, fixed wireless access, scanning telemetry, fixed terrestrial links, broadcasting, satellite, space science.

1.13 For the avoidance of doubt all means of access, registration, ownership and use of the internet, any domain name, platform, website, download, app and/or blockchain.

B.320

The [Assignor] assigns to the [Assignee] all copyright, trade marks, computer software, domain names and intellectual property rights of any nature in any media in any format whether in existence now or created in the future in the [Work/Material] and the [Website/App] and/or any part and any other form of reproduction and/or adaptation for the full period of copyright and any other rights and without limit of time indefinitely including but not limited to the following:

1.1   All scripts, title, text, content, codes and passwords, trade marks, logos, images, slogans, films and videos.

1.2   All promotional material, labels, packaging, sales, marketing and distribution material, data, records, agreements, licences, consents, documents, databases, invoices, sales reports, accounts and financial records whether in print form, stored in a computer or other gadget and/or stored in another format.

1.3 All drawings, designs, artwork, graphics, maps, computer-generated material, inventions, patents and technological developments.

1.4 All radio, television, film, sound recordings, recordings, advertisements, music, lyrics, jingles, telephone, internet, website, apps and downloads and electronic versions, sponsorship, endorsement, product placement, merchandising, performing rights and mechanical reproduction rights.

1.5 The right to retain all royalties and other sums received at any time from the exploitation, reproduction, performance, transmission, broadcast and/or any other type of use in any country of the world on land, sea and/or in the air and/or any part of the universe.

1.6 The right to adapt, vary, amend, alter, add to and/or delete from the [Work/Material] at any time at the [Assignee's] sole discretion.

1.7 The right to represent that the [Assignee] owns and controls the copyright and all other rights and to register any claim and/or interest and/or to assign all and/or part of those rights to a third party.

B.321

1.1 In consideration of the Buy-out Fee the [Contributor] assigns to the [Company] all copyright, intellectual property rights, and any other rights in the [Contributor's] work and the product of the [Contributor's] services and the [Film/Video/Podcast] to the [Company] in all media and in any format and/or means of exploitation whether in existence now and/or created in the future for the full period of copyright and any extensions and/or renewals and in perpetuity throughout the world and universe. This shall include the right to transmit, broadcast, display, license, supply, distribute and/or exploit the [Contributor's] work and/or the [Film/Video/Podcast] and/or any parts on the internet, via a website and/or app, at festivals and events, on television, radio, in print, via mobiles or any other format whether by text, images, sound and/or any adaptation.

1.2 The [Contributor] shall not be entitled to receive any additional payments of any nature from any exploitation of the [Contributor's] work and the product of the [Contributor's] services and the [Film/Video/Podcast] by the [Company] and/or any third party in all format and/or in any media whether in existence now and/or created in the future at any time.

B.322

In consideration of the payment of the Assignment Fee, the [Assignor] assigns to the [Assignee] all present and future copyright and all intellectual property rights, trade marks, domain names, computer software rights and any other rights in all media in any medium in the Artwork and the Artwork Material and/or any parts and any adaptation and/or development whether in existence now or created in the future throughout the world on land, sea, in the air and in the sub-terrain [and throughout the universe] for the full period of copyright and any extensions and renewals as far as possible in perpetuity including but not limited to:

1.1   All forms of exploitation through television and radio whether terrestrial, cable, satellite, and/or digital and any method on the internet, platform, website, app and/or other means of supplying and accessing material whether through a television set, radio, mobile, laptop, mobile, watch or other gadget and/or device.

1.2   All forms of exploitation through the medium of videos, discs, lasers, cassettes and/of other methods of storage and reproduction.

1.3   All forms of television, video and non-theatric audiences including but not limited to businesses and commercial use, educational, cultural, religious and social establishments, schools, churches, prisons, hospitals, camps, workshops, film societies, professional and trade bodies, private and public libraries, colleges, universities, hotels, clubs, shops, airlines.

1.4   All forms of theatric exploitation including cinemas.

1.5   All forms of publishing whether in printed or electronic form, hardback, paperback, e books, downloads and/or interactive material and/or games.

1.6   All forms of telecommunication systems and/or electronic storage, retrieval and/or distribution and/or display over the Internet, websites, apps, downloads, banners, links, pop-ups, emojis and/or otherwise and the transfer and storage of data, images, logos, text, films, videos and sound recordings to any computer, laptop, ipad, watch, mobile and/or other device.

1.7   All forms of adaptations, variations and sequels, merchandising, products and charitable and commercial exploitation including tours, theme parks, musicals, costumes, tie ins with food products and other matters.

B.323
The [Assignor] agrees that:

1.1   he/she shall only be entitled to be paid the Assignment Fee and shall not be entitled to receive any additional sums, royalties and/or otherwise that may arise directly and/or indirectly at any time from the exploitation of the Artwork and/or the Artwork Material and/or any development and/or variation exploited by the [Assignee] and/or any third party.

1.2 that all developments, variations, changes, marketing and exploitation of the Artwork and the Artwork Material shall be at the [Assignee's] sole discretion and cost.

1.3 that the [Assignee] shall be entitled to be registered as the copyright owner of the Artwork and/or the Artwork Material and to apply and register for any trade mark, service mark, community mark and/or other right and/or interest associated with any part.

B.324

The [Assignee] agrees and undertakes that it shall be responsible for any sums due in respect of the development, distribution, marketing and exploitation of the Artwork and/or the Artwork Material in any media at any time and that the Assignor shall not be liable for any such sums.

B.325

In consideration of the payment of the [Assignment Fee] by the [Company] to the [Assignor]. The [Assignor] assigns all copyright, intellectual property rights, computer software and any other rights or interest of any nature in the [Music/Lyrics/Sound Recordings] and all original and master material and/or parts to the [Company [specified in Schedule A which is attached to and forms part of this Agreement] from [date] for the full period of copyright and any extensions and renewals throughout the [country/world/universe] whether in existence now or developed in the future in any language, format or medium.

For the avoidance of doubt this shall include in respect of the assignment above in respect of the [Music/Lyrics/Sound recordings] and the original and master material:

1.1 the sole and exclusive right to license, assign, transfer, copy, reproduce, lend, supply, adapt, translate, authorise, hire, sell, record, store in any form, recreate or develop in another format, distribute or otherwise exploit by any method or medium whether it exists in technology and/ or law now and/or is created in the future.

1.2 all forms of text, messaging, paging, transmission of information and data, images, logos, sound recordings, films, videos, cable. analogue, digital, satellite, terrestrial television, radio and interactive and playback material, computer-generated material whether on screen or software and any material created for use with computers or software programs, the internet, electronic and telecommunications systems, storage, transfer and distribution devices, gadgets and watches, the internet, websites, platforms, apps, blockchain and/or any other method.

1.3 all mechanical forms of reproduction and all methods of performance and performing rights, together with the right to retain all sums due from any collecting society and/or trade organisation at any time.

1.4 all forms of publications and merchandising, recordings, compilations and adaptations. Sponsorship, advertising, promotion and other exploitation by any means and/or method and/or in any form.

B.326

In consideration of the payment of the [Budget] by the [Enterprise] to the [Development Company]. The [Development Company] agrees and assigns all copyright, intellectual property rights, computer software rights, database rights and any other rights or interest of any nature whether in existence now or developed in the future in any language, format, process, system and/or method in all media and medium in the Computer Software, the Source Code and the physical Master Material specified in Appendix A [which is attached to and forms part of this agreement] to the [Enterprise] for the full period of copyright and any extensions and renewals and in perpetuity throughout the [country/world/universe]. For the avoidance of doubt this shall include:

1.1 The sole and exclusive right for the [Enterprise] to license, assign, transfer, copy, reproduce, lend, supply, adapt, translate, authorise, hire, sell, record, store in any form, recreate or develop in another format, disseminate or otherwise exploit by any method or medium whether it exists in technology and/or law at the time of the acquisition of the rights or is created in the future.

1.2 The right to retain all royalties and other sums received at any time from the reproduction, supply, transmission, download, distribution and/or any other type of use.

1.3 The right to adapt, vary, amend, alter, add to and/or delete and/or sub-license and/or assign any part at any time at the [Enterprise's] sole discretion.

1.4 The right to represent that the [Enterprise] owns and controls the copyright and all other rights and to register any claim and/or interest.

B.327

1.1 In consideration of the payment of the [Fee] the [Contributor] assigns to the [Company] all present and future copyright and all intellectual property rights, trade marks, domain names, computer software rights, database rights and any other rights in all media in any medium in the [Database/Taxonomy/Index] and the development and master material and any copies and/or any parts described in Schedule A in whether in existence now or created in the future (either in law and/or technology) throughout the world and universe for the full period of copyright and any extensions and renewals and to continue throughout time in perpetuity.

1.2 The [Contributor] shall not have the right to receive any further sums received at any time from the reproduction, supply, transmission, download, distribution and/or any other type of use.

1.3 The [Company] shall have the right to adapt, vary, amend, alter, add to and/or delete and/or sub-license and/or assign any part at any time at the [Company's] sole discretion. The [Company] shall have the right to represent that the [Company] owns and controls the copyright and all other rights and to register any rights and/or interest in the name of the [Company] and/or any other third party.

1.4 The [Contributor] has waived all right to be identified in clause [–] and waived all moral rights in clause [–]. The [Contributor] agrees that the right of ownership may be attributed to [specify].

B.328

1.1 In consideration of the payment of the [Fee] the [Author] assigns to the [Company] the right to exploit the [Work] and/or any parts such as the title, characters, storyline and script in the form of merchandising products by the following methods and formats from [date] until [date]:

Greetings and birthday cards, postcards, posters, clothing for children, accessories, badges, playing cards, sweets, stickers, games, stationery, hardback, paperback audio and other formats of children's books, toys, food products which are marketed to children, household items and products used for children's bedrooms.

1.2 The assignment of rights in 1.1 shall not include exploitation in the form of films, television, tapes, discs, videos, radio, analogue, digital, terrestrial, cable or satellite, computer generated material whether on screen or software, animation and/or via the internet and/or any website, app and/or download, and/or storage and retrieval system, mobile phone or other devices or methods, interactive game, gambling, theme park, musical and/or performances as a play. The right to register with any collecting society and to receive any sums from the broadcast, transmission, performing rights, and/or other form of exploitation from any collecting society in any country at any time. All forms of publication and/or products for persons over the age of [number] in any format and any means of exploitation not in existence at the date of this agreement.

1.3 The following items are specifically not authorised under this agreement to be reproduced and exploited by the [Company]: [specify excluded items].

B.329

In consideration of the payment of the [Advance and the Royalties] the [Author] assigns to the [Distributor] all present and future copyright and all intellectual property rights in the [Work] [and the Work Material] throughout the [Territory] in the [English/other] language for the full period of copyright and any extensions in all printed forms of publishing whether hardback, paperback, co-editions and packaging, large print, serialisation in newspapers or magazines and/or children's plastic books.

B.330

The assignment in clause [–] by the [Company] shall not include television, radio whether terrestrial, cable, satellite, and/or digital, videos, films, sound recordings, lasers, discs, dvds, cassettes, ebooks, downloads, an electronic storage and retrieval and/or telecommunication system whether over the internet, website, app and/or any computer, laptop and/or mobile phone and/or other device. All other forms of adaptation, variation, development and/or any sequel not specifically assigned.

B.331

1.1 In consideration of the payment of the [Assignment Fee] by the [Institute/Charity] to the [Contributor].

1.2 The [Contributor] assigns all rights, interest and ownership, and the right to license, supply, distribute and/or exploit the [Work/Service/Product] and any parts or subsequent developments of any nature in any material and/or format whether they are in existence now or created in the future for the full period of copyright and any extensions and renewals throughout the [world/universe].

1.3 This assignment in 1.2 shall include, but not be limited to copyright, intellectual property rights, computer software, patents, trade marks, service marks, logos, characters, design rights, future design rights, database rights, moral rights, all printed forms including hardback and paperback books, text, index, titles, rules, images, photographs, engravings, drawings, plans, maps, sketches, marketing, packaging, posters, flyers, brochures, toys, games, household products, music, sound recordings, wireless and telecommunication services, mobile phones, two way radios, analogue, digital, terrestrial, cable and satellite television, film, radio, the internet, websites, apps and any electronic, digital or electromagnetic form, computers, CD-Rom, DVDs, videos, CDs, and any other form of mechanical reproduction or performance. The sole and exclusive right to license, assign, transfer, copy, reproduce, lend, supply, adapt, translate, authorise, hire, sell, record, store and retrieve in any form, or otherwise exploit by any method or medium.

B.332

The [Consultant] assigns to the [Institute/Charity] all copyright, trade marks, computer software, domain names and intellectual property rights of any nature in any media in any format whether in existence now or created in the future in the [Work/Project] and any part and any other form of reproduction and/or adaptation and any technological developments for the full period of copyright and any extensions or renewals including but not limited to the following:

1.1 The completed report, drafts, questionnaires and responses, correspondence, any material stored on discs, USB, hard drive and in any cloud or other account relating to the [Project] which shall be copied for supply to the [Institute/Charity].

1.2 All research, marketing, financial, scientific, and distribution material, data, records, agreements, licences, consents, documents, databases, invoices, sales reports, accounts and financial records whether in print form, stored in a computer or other gadget and/or stored in another format.

1.3 All images, photographs, drawings, designs, logos, artwork, graphics, maps, computer-generated material, formulae, processes, inventions, patents, codes, passwords or access data or information.

B.333

The [Institute/Charity] shall have the right to:

1.1 retain all sums or benefits received including royalties at any time from the exploitation, reproduction, performance, transmission, sale, supply and distribution of the [Work/Project] or any part. No further sums or payments shall be due to the [Consultant].

1.2 develop, adapt, vary, amend, alter, exploit, add to and/or delete from the [Work/Project] and/or register any right and/or interest at any time at the [Institute's/Charity's] sole discretion. No consent or approval shall be required from the [Consultant].

B.334

The [Artist] agrees:

1.1 to supply to [Name] at [Names'] cost all original draft and final sketches, drawings, software and any other reproductions and/or copies of the artwork, images, photographs, recordings, text, words and logos which have been created and developed for [Name] for the [Project].

1.2 that no material shall be retained by the [Artist].

1.3 to assign all copyright and intellectual property rights and the right to copy, license, sell, supply, distribute and to register any rights and/

or receive any sums from the exploitation in any of the material in 1.1 above to [Name] for the full period of copyright and any period thereafter indefinitely without limit throughout the universe, galaxy, world in any form and/or medium. Provided that the [Artist] has been paid the [Fee] and [Budget] in full by [Name].

1.4 that any part of the material in 1.1 may be adapted, edited, changed and/or credited to a third party and/or person. That the [Artist] agrees that he/she has waived all moral rights and/or any right to have a copyright notice, credit and/or be attributed as the creator of the material.

B.335

[Name] has agreed to carry out filming for the [Distributor] on various dates to be agreed between the parties. [Name] agrees and assigns to the [Distributor] all copyright and future copyright and intellectual property rights throughout the land, sea and air of the planet Earth in the [films] and [sound recordings] to be made by [Name] including the right to make feature and documentary films and/or license parts for satellite, cable, and terrestrial television, internet and websites, apps, blogs, online television and video distribution, publishing, merchandising and any other exploitation of any adaptation which may exist now or be invented, created and/or developed in the future.

B.336

1.1 [Name] has agreed to be interviewed by [Company/person] for [specify medium/publication] on subject [specify].

1.2 In return for a fee of [number/currency] [Name] assigns to the [Company] the copyright in the words spoken and in all sound and other recordings made in the interview on [date] and the photograph taken on [date] by [specify] for the purpose of publication and reproduction as an article in [country] and to use and/or adapt the material on the online website of the [Company] and to supply to third parties as part of their news service.

1.3 The [Company] agrees that where a third party wishes to use and adapt the material in any form that [Name] shall be notified and an additional fee negotiated for [Name] for any such use. [Name] accepts that he/she does not have a right of refusal over any exploitation of the material by the [Company].

B.337

1.1 [Name] is the designer and creator of an original concept and format and prototype for an [App] which he/she has developed using the following [materials/software] [specify].

1.2   In consideration of a non-returnable fee of [number/currency], a royalty on all sales of not less than [number] per cent and [number] shares in [specify].

[Name] agrees that he/she shall assign to the [Company] all copyright, computer software, design rights, trade marks, service marks, film, sound recordings, music and lyrics, noises, animation, characters, logos and any intellectual property rights and interest and/or to reproduce, exploit, license and/or assign such rights and material which may exist now or be created at some time in the future throughout the [world/universe]. As well as for all those additional periods that such rights of any nature may start, be renewed and/or extended.

B.338

1.1   [Name] agrees that the [Company] can buy the Asset specified in Appendix A which is attached to and forms part of this agreement for a fixed fee of [number/currency] to be paid by [date] to [Name].

1.2   [Name] agrees and undertakes to transfer, assign, execute any document and provide support in the form of an affidavit if required that all title, ownership and control of the Asset has passed and been assigned to the [Company] upon receipt of the fixed fee. Further that once the Asset is assigned that [Name] shall have no rights and/or interest and/or claim and/or any right to license, exploit, sell and/or receive any money from the Asset.

B.339

Where the [Company] has paid a fee for rights and/or an assignment which it later discovers cannot be granted and/or assigned by [Name]. Then the [Company] shall be entitled to a full refund by [Name] of all sums paid together with interest at [number] per cent and to enter on the premises of the business of [Name] and to seek to recover the sum by removing any items of value which can be sold to recoup the sum due plus any additional costs that may be incurred.

B.340

1.1   [Name] has developed a [script/manuscript] for a [play/film/video/series] which has been commissioned by the [Company] on the subject of [specify].

1.2   [Name] acknowledges and agrees that he/she was not the originator of the concept, format and/or project.

1.3   [Name] agrees that except for the payment of the fee in clause [–] for the preparation and development of the [script/manuscript], meetings, travel, editing and delivery of a final draft. That [Name] shall have no right to any further sums from the exploitation of the [script/manuscript] and/or [play/film/video/series] in any form, medium and/or any adaptation at any time by the [Company].

1.4 Further, [Name] agrees and waives all rights to any form of moral rights and/or credit except as [specify] and accepts that the [Company] may omit this credit at its sole discretion where circumstances require it to do so.

1.5 [Name] assigns all present and future copyright, intellectual property rights, trade marks, rights in any characters and all media rights in all formats, medium, developments and adaptations in the [script/manuscript] and/or any rights in the [play/film/video/series] including the title to the [Company] throughout the world for the full period of copyright and any extensions.

C

CANCELLATION

General Business and Commercial

C.001
Both parties shall have the right to cancel the contract without reason provided that send written notice to the other party at least [three] calendar months prior to [date]. This right shall not be the same as ending the contract under the termination provisions due to failure to carry out the terms of the contract.

C.002

1.1　The [Supplier/Company] agrees that the [Governing Body/Institute] shall have the right at its sole discretion to cancel this agreement at any time without any reason and/or on grounds of the failure to provide the quality of the service and/or work required and/or a change in the financial circumstances of the [Governing Body/Institute] to make the payments required.

1.2　Where the [Governing Body/Institute] wishes to cancel the agreement they shall be required to give [two] months] notice of cancellation of the agreement to the [Supplier/Company] and to make all payments until the end date.

1.3　This clause shall be in addition to any other rights under this agreement including the right of termination, rejection and/or force majeure.

C.003
There shall be no right of cancellation under this agreement and the parties agree that the terms shall be fulfilled and the expenditure and payments made by the [Company] for the duration of the agreement. This shall not affect the other rights of termination where there has been a serious and material default and/or breach of the agreement by either party and/or there are circumstances which amount to force majeure which delay and/or cause the agreement to be suspended for more than [number] [months/years].

C.004

It may be necessary for the [Client] to cancel the [booking/break/activity] due to injury, medical reasons, accident, family bereavement, and other unexpected circumstances. In such cases the [Company] should be contacted by [telephone/email/text message] as soon as possible. The [Client] shall not be entitled to a refund of any sums already incurred in respect of the ordering of goods and/or services from third parties which have already been ordered, invoiced and/or fulfilled where payments are due and/or have been made by the [Company] on behalf of the [Client]. The following sums shall be refunded and shall be dependent on the period of notice given in each case less deductible costs which shall include the deposit, any insurance premiums and any third party costs:

1.1 More than [number] [days'/months'] notification. A full refund of the total agreed amount less deductible costs.

1.2 Between [number] and [number] [days'/months'] notification. A refund of [number] per cent of the total agreed amount less deductible costs.

1.3 Between [number] and [number] [days'/months'] notification. A refund of [number] per cent of the total agreed amount less deductible costs.

1.4 Less than [number] [days'/months'] notification. There shall be no refund.

1.5 Any refund shall not include repayment of any taxes, premiums, charges and fees which may have been paid which the [Company] shall be obliged to pay and/or has paid to a third party.

C.005

There may be a cancellation of the Order by the [Client] at any time until payment has been made in full for the [Products/Services] to the [Company].

C.006

There shall be no fees, charges, costs and/or other additional sums to be invoiced and/or paid as a penalty and/or for any direct and/or indirect losses, damages and/or damage to and/or loss of reputation arising from the cancellation of this agreement by [Name].

C.007

The parties have agreed that the booking, dates, arrangements and details of the [Event] shall not be released, supplied and/or disclosed by the [Company] and/or any of its employees, sub-contractors and/or any other individuals and/or businesses engaged to provide their services at any time until after [date]. That if it is established that information, photographs and/or details were disclosed to newspapers, magazines, television, news and/or media organisations from such a source without permission from the [Client] before [date]. That the [Client] shall have the right to cancel the booking based on those grounds. If the [Client] cancels the booking for that reason then the [Client] shall only be obliged to pay [number/currency] in total.

C.008

If you should fail to pay your annual registration fee and/or such other sums as advised before the date on which your registration of your [Domain Name/Membership/other] is due to lapse or expire in each year. Then the registration shall be cancelled by the [Company] and shall end on the final date. The [Company] shall not be responsible for and/or liable to you for any reason for any losses, damages, costs and/or other consequences which may arise as a result of your failure to renew and/or extend the registration.

C.009

If you wish to cancel the service at any time then you must give at least [one] month's notice to the [Company]. You shall only be obliged to pay any subscription fee to the end of that period of notice. Any payments made for any period after the cancellation date shall be refunded on a pro rata basis.

C.010

The [Client] shall not be entitled to cancel the Order unless the [Company] advises that it cannot deliver the quantity requested and/or is unable to meet the delivery date and/or the specifications of the [Products] are different. If the Order is cancelled for any of these reasons a full refund shall be provided to the [Client] of all sums paid on account in respect of the Order.

C.011

The [Customer] may cancel the [service/subscription] within [fourteen] days of the [signature of the agreement/start of the [Service/Subscription] and shall be entitled to be paid a refund of all sums paid for the [Service/Subscription]. The refund shall be paid by the [Company] within [thirty] days of the receipt of notice of cancellation.

C.012

Where an Order is cancelled then no deposits and/or other advance payments shall be refunded. Where an Order is available for collection but is unclaimed for more than [three/six] months. Then the [Products/Units] may be destroyed and/or sold off. No sums shall be due to the [Customer] in such circumstances as a refund, compensation and/or otherwise.

C.013

The [Governing Body/Company] may cancel the [Participant's/Exhibitor's] right of access to the [premises] for any of the following reasons:

1.1 There has been a failure to comply with rules relating to health and safety, security, installation and/or repair of electrical equipment and/or failure to comply with the prohibited list of products.

1.2 The conduct, behaviour, language, gestures, and/or appearance of employees, agents and/or others invited by them to the [premises] has resulted in serious complaints and caused disruption.

1.3 There has been a failure to pay the sums due under this agreement by the specified deadlines.

C.014

In the event the [Company] is required to cancel the [Event/Holiday/Concert] for any reason then the [Client] shall be entitled to a full refund of the cost of the [Event/Holiday/Concert]. Where possible the [Company] shall try to offer an alternative arrangement for the [Client] to consider but which the [Client] shall not be obliged to accept. Nor shall the [Client] be obliged to accept vouchers and/or any other cash alternative from the [Company]. The [Company] shall not be liable for any additional costs, expenses, losses, damages and/or other sums that may and/or have been incurred by the [Client] as a result of the cancellation.

C.015

1.1 The [Agent] acknowledges that the [Artist] is under [eighteen] years of age at the time of the signature and conclusion of this agreement. That the [parents/guardian] have signed on behalf of the [Artist] who will be bound until the [Artist] is [eighteen] years old provided that the [Agent] performs the terms of the agreement and the agreement is not terminated and/or ended for any reason.

1.2 When the [Artist] reaches the age of [eighteen] years, the [Artist] shall in that year from [date] to [date] be entitled to exercise the right to terminate the agreement without providing any reason and/or grounds by notice in writing to the [Agent] to end on the [Artist's] [nineteenth birthday]. After the termination date all sums, advances and royalties arising from any agreement, contract and/or other work by the [Agent] for or on behalf of the [Artist] shall be paid direct to the [Artist] and the [Agent] shall not be entitled to any further commission, royalties, expenses, fees and/or other sums for any reason in respect of the [Artist] and/or any rights and/or in respect of any documents concluded prior to the termination date.

C.016

The [Company] reserves the right to cancel the [Service/Order/Right of Entry] at any time and for any reason. The total liability shall be limited to refund the payment made if any for the [Service/Order/Right of Entry] which has not been fulfilled by the [Company] for any period after the date of cancellation.

C.017
Where the [Client] is unable and/or unwilling to use the [Tickets/Service/ Order] and/or changes their decision and cancels the [booking/purchase] for any reason which is not due to any breach and/or default by the [Company]. Then the [Company] shall not be obliged to refund and/or make repayment of any sums paid by the [Client] up to and including the date of cancellation.

C.018
Where the [Company] is obliged to substitute another product and/or colour to fulfil any order under this agreement. Then the [Client] shall be entitled to cancel such part of the order and purchase as relates to such proposed substitution. The [Client] agrees that any such cancellation of one part of any order shall not affect those which the [Company] is able to fulfil according to the specification and delivery date which are in respect of unrelated products and/or services.

C.019
Where in any circumstances the [Client] has waived his and/or her rights to any cancellation of any part of this agreement. The [Company] agrees that any such waiver shall only relate to the specific part of the [Service/Order] and shall not prevent the [Client] from exercising their rights of cancellation in respect of another matter at a later date.

C.020
In the event that the [Client/Subscriber/Customer] does not adhere to the agreed terms and conditions of use and access to the [Website/App/ Platform]. Then the [Company] may at any time cancel the [Service/Channel/ Content] and/or block access and/or refuse to permit access to and/or use of the [Website/App/Platform] without providing any advance notice and/or reasons for taking such action. The [Company] shall not be obliged to justify the cancellation nor shall the [Client/Subscriber/Customer] be entitled to be paid any compensation, damages, losses, sums for damage to reputation and/or any other monies which arise as a direct and/or indirect result of such action by the [Company]. The [Company] shall refund any sum paid by the [Client/Subscriber/Customer] for any period where access is blocked and/ or the [Service/Channel/Content] is not available after the end date.

C.021
1.1 The [Client/Subscriber/Customer] accepts and agrees that its use and access to the [Website/App/Channel] is entirely at its own risk and

cost and agrees that no responsibility and/or liability shall be attached to and be accepted by the [Company] which arise from the [Client/Subscriber/Customer's] reliance on the supply, accuracy, reliability and/or otherwise of the [Website/App/Channel] and/or any service and/or content and/or data.

1.2 The [Client/Subscriber/Customer] accepts and agrees that the [Company] may at any time cancel, interrupt, alter, adapt, add to, delete from and/or otherwise change the service and/or content and/or data and/or block access and/or refuse to permit access to and/or use of the [Website/App/Channel] without providing any advance notice and/or reasons for taking such action. The [Client/Subscriber/Customer] accepts and agrees that it shall not be entitled to any compensation, damages, losses and/or other sums which arise as a direct and/or indirect result of such action by the [Company].

C.022
The [Customer] may cancel their access and use of the [Service/Newsletter] by sending an email to [specify] and/or unsubscribing by clicking on the relevant [box/other] on the site. The [Company] agrees and undertakes to delete the [Customer] from their database records and to cease providing the [Service/Newsletter].

C.023
Where the [Company] decides that the email address and [User/Supplier] which is uploading images, film, text, and/or any other material to the [Website/Platform] is supplying material which in the opinion of the [Company] is in breach of contract and/or an infringement of copyright and/or in breach of a third party's trade marks, services marks, name and/or logo and/or which is defamatory, offensive, inaccurate, dangerous, and/or in any other manner unacceptable and not in keeping with the theme and/or spirit and/or operation of the [Website/Platform]. Then the [Company] may without notice cancel, terminate and/or block the email address and/or the supply of any further material by the [User/Supplier] to the [Website/Platform]. The [Company] shall also delete and erase all material supplied and/or uploaded to the [Website/Platform] and/or all references to the email address and [User/Supplier].

C.024
The [Company] reserves the right to cancel your right to use any account opened at any time on any grounds without notice if it discovers and/or receives reports that the [account holder] is using the account for any illegal, immoral and/or fraudulent purpose by the laws of any country in the world which the [Company] may decide at its absolute discretion are appropriate.

C.025

The [Company] reserves the right, if it should cancel your right to access the account, to hold the account and permit access to it by any international and national authorities such as the police and intelligence which may exist to prevent crime, money laundering and any other unlawful purpose.

C.026

Where the [Client] fails to pay the fees for the account by the due date on any occasion. Then the [Company] shall have the absolute right without further notice to cancel the subscription service with effect from the actual date for which no sums have been received.

C.027

Where any party to this agreement cancels all and/or any part of their contribution to the [Site/Project] for any reason. Then it is agreed that the non-defaulting party shall have the right to cancel the whole of the agreement in its entirety with immediate effect by notice by email to the [Managing Director] of the party who has cancelled. Where the non-defaulting party has incurred expenses and costs in reliance on the contribution to be made by the other party. Then the party which has cancelled shall be liable for all such sums up to a maximum of [number/currency].

C.028

The [Company] shall have the right to cancel the order to manufacture the [Product] where the [Sample/Prototype] supplied by the [Manufacturer] does not adhere to and/or is in breach of any and/or all of the following criteria:

1.1 The health and safety standards and product quality controls required in the [United Kingdom/country].

1.2 The size, colour, content and function specifications stipulated and supplied by the [Company].

1.3 The product name, logo, packaging, labels, inserts and/or additional material is inaccurate, offensive, and/or misleading as to the content and/or quality and/or purpose.

C.029

The [Licensor] may cancel the non-exclusive licence at any time by [one] month's written notice to the [Licensee] without a requirement to specify any reason. The [Licensee] shall cease to arrange the manufacture of any new stock after the end date but shall have the right to sell-off existing stock for a period of [three] months from the date of cancellation.

C.030

Where the payment under clause [–] is not received by the [Company] by [date] then the [Company] shall have the right to cancel the agreement which shall take immediate effect by the [Company] sending a [email/letter/written notice] to the [Distributor]. The [Distributor] shall then have no right to reproduce, distribute and/or supply any products and/or services with the [Name/Logo/Trade Mark] at any time. The [Distributor] agrees that the contract shall be ended immediately and the [Distributor] shall have no right of action and/or claim against the [Company] for any sums, losses and/or damages which may arise and/or are due as a result of the cancellation at any time. Nor shall the [Distributor] be entitled to pay the sum due as a late payment and be entitled to then rely on the continuance of the contract.

C.031

The [Licensor] agrees that where he/she has approved samples of the products he/she shall not be entitled to delay and/or cancel the production of the [Units/Products] unless there have been significant changes in the quality of the materials to be used and/or colour and/or design and/or the name to be used and/or packaging.

C.032

The [Client] agrees that the manufacturer shall not be required to make any further changes to the sample and/or artwork for production once it has been agreed within the original price quote. That all additional changes and/or alterations shall be subject to a further cost and expense to be paid by the [Client].

C.033

1.1   Both parties agree that they shall not have the right to cancel the agreement once the following stages of the [Project] have been completed: [specify stages to be completed].

1.2   The parties shall however have the right to reach an arrangement for the substitution of a third party to carry out the agreement on their behalf and with their authority. Provided that the main party remains obliged to fulfil all the duties, obligations and undertakings and continues to monitor and comply with the terms of the agreement for the [Project].

C.034

The [Sponsor] shall not be entitled to cancel funding for the [Project] and shall be obliged to pay all the sums due in clause [–]. Where the [Project] is delayed and/or behind schedule and/or altered in any material form for any reason. The [Company] may agree to delay the payment of the funding by the [Sponsor]. Any such changes shall not entitle the [Sponsor] to cancel and/or withdraw the funds at any time.

C.035

The [Sponsor] reserves the right to cancel the funding of the [Event/Project/Film] in the event that the [Company] commits any act and/or takes any action and/or associates with any person and/or organisation which the [Sponsor] considers would affect the reputation of the [Sponsor] and/or any of its products and/or services and/or other partnerships and/or collaborations. The [Sponsor] shall be entitled to cancel the funding of the [Event/Project/Film] with immediate effect by written notice to [Name] at [address/email]. The [Sponsor] shall not be obliged to specify in detail the nature of the reason for the cancellation.

C.036

In the event that the [Sponsor] cancels the funding, the [Sponsor] shall not be entitled to a refund of any sums already paid and/or due prior to the date of cancellation. The [Company] shall be entitled to retain all such sums, but shall not be paid any further sums by the [Sponsor] whether the costs and/or expenses have already been incurred by the [Company] or not.

C.037

The [Sponsor] may cancel the use and authorisation of their name, trade marks, logos, slogans and [Products/Services] in connection with the [Enterprise] and/or [Event] but shall not be entitled to withdraw from funding for any reason after [date]. This shall be the case regardless of the conduct any personnel at the [Enterprise] and/or any social media reports and/or any other matter. The [Sponsor] shall be obliged to pay all sums due under this agreement to the [Enterprise]. The [Sponsor] shall not be liable for any additional costs and expenses which may be incurred by the [Enterprise] as a consequence of such action.

C.038

The [Sponsor] may cancel the agreement by notice by email to [specify person] at [specify email address] or text to [specify person] at [specify number] at any time where:

1.1   The [Company] has not acquired an official licence for the use of the [Site].

1.2   The [Site] has been made unusable due to weather conditions, floods, contamination and/or otherwise.

1.3   Health and safety, security and/or waste disposal and access to water have not been resolved to comply with the minimum standards required by any relevant local and/or government authority.

C.039

Where the [Sponsor] decides to cancel the agreement the [Sponsor] agrees that it shall not be entitled to seek to recover any sums paid to the date of cancellation and/or termination whether the [Event] has taken place or not.

C.040

The [Institute] shall have the right to cancel the agreement with the [Company/Consultant] at any time as it thinks fit provided that the [Company/Consultant] is either given [two] calendar months written notice or payment is made of [two] calendar months fee in lieu of notice. In either event the [Company/Consultant] shall not be entitled to any additional sums, costs and/or compensation from such cancellation and/or termination.

C.041

Where the [Board/Chief Executive] of the [Institute/Enterprise] reaches the conclusion that the [Company/Consultant] is not fulfilling the terms of the agreement to the standard and quality which was specified. Then the [Company/Consultant] shall be notified of the alleged breach of the agreement and provided with the opportunity to remedy the situation by a particular date. Failure to comply with all the terms of the steps required to remedy the alleged breach shall entitle the [Institute/Enterprise] to cancel and/or terminate the agreement by notice in writing with immediate effect. The [Institute/Enterprise] shall be liable to pay for all work and/or services as have been fulfilled and completed regardless of whether it fell below the required standard and/or was completed to the satisfaction of the [Board/Chief Executive] prior to the end date. Any outstanding matters shall then either be resolved by negotiation between the parties or referred to an independent [mediator] at the equal cost of both parties.

C.042

Where the [Institute] due to a reduction in its annual budget decides that it no longer requires the [Service/Products/Project] at any time. Then the [Institute] shall be entitled to cancel the agreement with [number] months' written notice to the [Company]. The [Company] agrees that no further sums shall be due to the [Company] for any reason after the expiry of the cancellation period.

C.043

Where the [Company] has not performed and/or carried out the standard and/or quality of service and/or work and/or has incurred delays which are not attributable to force majeure. The [Institute] shall not be obliged to permit the [Company] to remedy the situation but may cancel the agreement at any time and all liability shall end and no further sums shall be due to the [Company] from the [Institute].

C.044

Once payment has been made in full for the [Order/Booking] by the [Client] and [number] days have expired without cancellation by the [Client]. The [Company] shall have the right to refuse to accept any attempt at a later date to cancel by the [Client]. If the [Client] fails to attend and/or make use of the [Order/Booking] the [Company] shall not be under any obligation to offer any compensation, refund and/or substitution and/or voucher.

CAPACITY

Film, Television and Video

C.045
The [Licensor] confirms that it has and will continue to have the authority and right to conclude this agreement and fulfil its terms and that no previous agreement of any nature has been signed and/or exists and/or is pending which concerns any part of the [specify rights] in the [Film/Video/Series].

C.046
The [Author] undertakes to the [Distributor] that he/she owns and controls the [DVD/Video Rights] in the [Book] entitled: [specify title] ISBN reference [–] and these have not been granted and/or assigned to the [Publishers] and/or any other third party at any time.

C.047
That the [Artist] is age [specify] and has taken the advice of his/her agent, parents and professional advisors before concluding and signing this agreement. That there is no medical, physical and/or mental reason and/or inability to read and write which would impair the [Artist's] ability to understand the terms and/or the consequences of carrying out the terms of this agreement.

C.048

1.1 That there is no undertaking regarding the background, status, finances and/or experience of [Name/Company].

1.2 There is no undertaking provided in respect of any previous agreements, licences and/or other exploitation of rights before [date] which may conflict with this agreement.

C.049
The [Company] agrees that it shall not permit and/or encourage through marketing and promotional material the use of the [Service/Channel/VOD] by anyone under [number] years of age.

C.050

The [Licensor] warrants and undertakes that it holds all the rights granted to the [Licensee] under this agreement and that it is not aware of any legal proceedings and/or claims which would affect the grant of those rights in any part of the world. Further that the [Licensor] has not entered into and/or committed any part of those rights to a third party which would prevent them being exercised and/or exploited by the [Licensee].

C.051

The [Licensor] confirms that he/she possesses full power and authority to enter into and perform this agreement and that there are not nor will there be any liens, encumbrances and/or other restrictions against the [Work/Film/Series] and/or any part and/or any form of exploitation which would derogate from and/or be inconsistent with the rights granted to the [Distributor] in this agreement as at [date].

C.052

The [Assignor] agrees that he/she has full power and authority to enter into this agreement and that the [Assignor] has not exploited the [Work/Video/Sound Recordings] in any form except those matters specified in Schedule A which is attached and forms part of this agreement.

C.053

[Name] confirms that he/she is a member of [union/organisation] and is registered as: [specify name] registration number: [number]. That all membership fees have been paid to [date] and that [Name] shall continue as a member for the duration of this agreement.

C.054

The [Licensor] confirms that it has good title and authority to enter into this agreement and that it is not bound by any conflicting and/or prior agreement which would be detrimental to and/or conflict with and/or derogate from this agreement.

C.055

The [Company] confirms that the following copyright and other intellectual property rights have [not] been exploited [in country/worldwide]: [list subjects].

C.056

The [Distributor] undertakes that the following rights have not been granted in [Europe/Asia/other] to any third party: [specify rights].

C.057

[Name] agrees that they shall not have any right and/or authority to represent to any third party that he/she is the agent for the [Actor] at any time. [Name] agrees and accepts that their role is limited to [specify activities] and that this does not include negotiating and/or concluding any type of agreement and/or receiving payments and/or gifts on behalf of and/or for the [Actor].

General Business and Commercial

C.058

The [Executive] confirms that he/she has correctly and accurately disclosed his/her [qualifications/references/education/business experience] and has the authority to enter into this agreement and is not bound by any previous agreements, undertakings and/or any other matter which would adversely affect this agreement.

C.059

The [Executive] agrees that there are no existing agreements, undertakings, restrictions and/or court orders which would prevent him/her from entering into and/or being available to carry out the duties required under this agreement from [date].

C.060

The [Employee] confirms that he/she is a national of [country] and is aged [number] years and holds a valid passport for [country] [reference number] and a [work/other] permit to work as [specify authorisation] until [date] issued on [date] by [government body]. That the [Employee] holds a valid national insurance number [reference number]. That the [Company] shall be entitled to view all original documents and to retain a copy for their own personnel records and for compliance with any legal requirements.

C.061

The [Employee] holds the following qualifications and membership of professional bodies: [list organisations]. That by the start date of this agreement the [Employee] shall be available to carry out the duties of [role/title] at the [Company] and there shall be no restrictions from a previous employee and/or other third party which would interfere with and/or prevent the [Employee] entering into and/or performing the terms of this agreement.

C.062

That the [Employee] is over [age] years and is available to work the days and hours required by the [Company] in the general position of [specify role] at [premises/address] from [date] to [date].

C.063

The [Company/Supplier] agrees and undertakes that it shall not engage anyone under the age of [number] years to work on any part of the [Project/Products].

C.064

[Name] confirms that he/she is a qualified [specify profession] and shall comply with all the policies, guidelines and/or codes of practice specified by their professional body: [specify organisation] which may be issued at any time.

C.065

All members of the [Group] confirm that they are [eighteen] years of age or older at the date of signing this agreement. Any member who is not [eighteen] years of age at the date of this agreement must have this document signed on his/her behalf by a parent or guardian who is responsible for their welfare, and with whom they live.

C.066

[Name] confirms that he/she has been advised to take separate legal advice in respect of this agreement and [has taken specialist legal advice/ or decided of his/her own free will not to do so] and fully comprehends the consequences of signing this agreement and agrees to be bound by its terms.

C.067

Both parties to this agreement confirm that they are aged [eighteen/twenty-one] years or over at the date of signing this agreement.

C.068

Unless the parties agree to the contrary in writing the term 'Full Age' shall mean the age of [twenty-one] years or over.

C.069

That the [Company] is a legal entity registered in [country] as [type/reference] and is able to meet the terms and obligations set out in this agreement.

C.070

There are no representations, undertakings and/or any form of verification provided as to the capacity of either party to enter into this agreement. Each party must carry out its own background research as to the authority, reliability and financial stability of the other party.

C.071
Upon request by any member of the [Consortium] the [Company] agrees to provide copies of legal documents, agreements and other material in respect of any licensee with which the [Company] may conclude terms relating to the [Service/Channel/Material/Rights].

C.072
Where the [Company] is not able to recruit the quality of personnel needed to fulfil the terms of this agreement by [date]. Then the [Company] shall be obliged to notify the [Consortium] of that fact and set out the reasons and the date by which they expect the situation to be remedied.

Internet, Websites and Apps

C.073
You are granted access and use of this [Website/App/Channel] upon the condition that you are over [eighteen] years of age, and have the authority of the person who owns and/or controls the [computer/mobile/television/gadget/other] that you are using and the person who pays the cost of the internet access service and any telephone charges and other sums that may be incurred.

C.074
The [Company] does not wish and prohibits persons under [number] years of age the right to use and/or access this [Website/App/Channel]. Any person under [number] years and/or any other person who permits and/or allows these facilities and service to be used in any manner by someone who is not over the legal age limit shall be served immediate notice to end their access to and use of the [Website/App/Channel] and their account shall be closed. The service shall be cancelled and any such person shall lose all right to any repayment, refunds or compensation and all future access by that person and/or household at the same address shall be denied.

C.075
This [Website/App/Channel] may only be used and/or accessed by any persons over [number] years of age with the consent of the parent and/or guardian in each case. Together with the approval and/or consent of the person and/or company that is paying the phone, wifi, broadband and/or other access point for the [Website/App/Channel] who will accept responsibility and liability for any additional costs and other sums that may be incurred relating to use of the [Website/App/Channel] at any time including but not limited to ordering products and/or services, premium rate telephone line costs, video and/or film services and/or messaging.

C.076

Where an adult who holds the account for the [Service] authorises a person under [age] years to have access to the code for the account and to use any part of the service and/or games. Then the adult account holder shall be liable for all costs, charges and expenses that may be incurred by the other person whether the other person acted without their knowledge where they have requested additional services and/or products and/or used any other matter which incurred further sums to be paid.

C.077

1.1 [Name] confirms and undertakes that he/she is entitled to enter into this agreement to provide regular articles, podcasts and other material to the [Company] on the subject of [specify theme] in accordance with the schedule set out in appendix A.

1.2 That there is no previous and/or existing agreement and/or other agency, sponsorship and/or other arrangement with any third party of any nature which restricts and/or prohibits [Name] from signing this agreement and/or which would conflict with this agreement.

C.078

The [Contributor] agrees and undertakes that:

1.1 he/she has the ability and authority to enter into this agreement to be interviewed for a series of [Podcasts/Videos] by [Name].

1.2 there is no reason for any third party to object to this agreement of which the [Contributor] is aware which would cause legal problems for the [Company].

1.3 the existing third parties for whom the [Contributor] provides services and/or other work have consented to his/her participation in the [Podcasts/Videos].

1.4 any existing agreements and/or commissions for a book, film and/or other material by a third party with the [Contributor] do not prohibit and/or restrict the [Contributor] from participating in this series of [Podcasts/Videos].

C.079

1.1 [Name] confirms that he/she has been commissioned by the [Company] to design, create and photograph a series of [Images/Stills] for a new marketing campaign.

1.2 [Name] undertakes that he/she has the necessary skill and experience to produce the agreed material to be supplied to the quality and standard required in accordance with the proposed outline synopsis in appendix A. That all the material produced by [Name] shall be original and shall not be copied and/or derived from any third party.

C.080

1.1 There is no confirmation as to the ownership of the [Sound Recording] and all copyright clearance and/or other sums due in respect of the use, performance, broadcast, transmission, licensing, adaptation and/or other exploitation of the [Sound Recordings] shall be the responsibility and solely at the liability of the [Company].

1.2 This agreement is entered into entirely on the basis of the possession and control of the physical master material of the [Sound Recordings] described in appendix A.

C.081

In order to access and use this [Website/App/Forum] you must comply with the following conditions and terms. Failure to do so in any manner will result in the blocking, deletion and/or cancellation of your account and all the related content and material.

1.1 You must be [number] years of age and/or over.

1.2 You must have the mental capacity to enter into this agreement and have personal control over your own finances and be able to pay your financial commitments to the [Company].

1.3 You must have resided at the address which you provide to the [Company] for more than [number] months.

Merchandising and Distribution

C.082

The [Licensor] agrees and undertakes that it has the full title and authority to enter into this agreement and is not bound by any previous agreement which adversely affects this agreement as at [date].

C.083

The [Author] undertakes that he/she owns and/or controls the [specify type of Rights] in [country/Territory/world] and that the publishing agreement with [Company] does not contain any clauses and/or undertakings which would prohibit, restrict and/or conflict with the terms of this agreement with the [Distributor].

C.084

The [Licensor] confirms that he/she possesses full power and authority to enter into and perform this agreement and that there are not nor will there be any liens, encumbrances and/or other restrictions against the [Work/Images] and/or any part and/or any other form of licence to a third party to exploit any such rights which would impact in any manner on this agreement.

C.085
The [Distributor] confirms and undertakes:

1.1 that it has an agreement with [specify copyright owner] for the exclusive licence for the exploitation of the [Film/Product/Sound Recordings] in [format] in [country].

1.2 that it has the right to authorise a sub-licence to a third party in respect of 1.1.

1.3 That the [Distributor] has not licensed and/or exploited the [Film/Product/Sound Recordings] in [format] in [country] at any time prior to [date] in any language.

C.086
The [Distributor] confirms and undertakes that to the best of its knowledge and belief the [Distributor] is legally entitled to gran the rights in this agreement and is not bound by any prior agreement and/or undertaking and/or arrangement in respect of the [Series/Products/Service] which would jeopardise and/or be detrimental to the rights granted and terms agreed under this agreement with the [Enterprise].

C.087
There are no undertaking and/or warranties provided by [Name] in respect of this [Work/Product] and [Name] does not purport to be the copyright owner of the [Work/Product] and/or a licensee. [Name] owns a physical copy of the [Work/Product] which he/she is willing to make available to the [Company] at the [Company's] risk and expense for the purpose of this agreement.

C.088
The [Licensee] agrees to investigate, verify and report back on to the [Licensor] in respect of any proposed distributor, agent and/or other third party to be engaged by the [Licensee] to exploit the [Work/Product/Service] including but not limited to their financial track record, their compliance with health and safety requirements and other legal matters and their employee, sustainability, waste recycling policies and the source of materials provided by suppliers.

C.089
[Name] is the copyright owner of the [Manuscript] including the title, character names, locations and all the accompanying images. [Name] has

not previously granted and/or assigned and/or disposed of any rights of any nature in the [Manuscript] to any third party. There are no pre-existing agreements.

Publishing

C.090

The [Company] warrants and represents that [Name] is not subject to any undertakings, restriction and/or prohibition as a result of any contract nor is there any physical and/or mental issues which would prevent [Name] being able to carry out the terms of this agreement.

C.091

1.1 The [Company] is a private limited liability company incorporated in [country] with the following identification [reference number] and is trading and solvent as at [date]. The [Company] has an established reputation in [subject] and is not in any litigation with any persons and/or firms to whom they may owe any sums.

1.2 The [Company] has the full power, legal capacity and authority to enter into this agreement and is capable of meeting the cost of fulfilling all terms, responsibilities and liabilities.

C.092

The [Company] agrees and undertakes that will not have the authority and/or right to represent that it may act on behalf of the [Publisher] and/or enter into any commitment, contract and/or other collaboration at any time with any other person, enterprise and/or other third party.

C.093

The [Distributor] confirms and agrees with the [Publisher] that:

1.1 it is able to carry out the terms of this agreement to a high standard and to meet the quality controls of the [Publisher].

1.2 it has not concluded an agreement and/or licence with a third party for the development of products and/or services and/or the exploitation of rights which the [Publisher] would deem to be offensive, obscene, political and/or only suitable for adults. That the [Distributor] only specialises in the [children's /other] market.

1.3 it is not aware of any threat of legal actions and/or investigations by trading standards and/or any product recalls relating to the [Distributor] and/or any part of its business which would affect the decision of the [Publisher] to enter into this agreement.

C.094

The [Author] warrants that he/she has full authority to enter into this agreement and that he/she is not bound by any previous agreement which adversely affects this agreement.

C.095

The [Artist] warrants that he has not concealed another name or withheld details of his professional career and that at the time of signing this contract he/she is not and will not be bound by any other commitment, contract and/or memorandum which would prevent him/her fulfilling this agreement.

C.096

The [Author] undertakes to the [Publisher] that the [Author] has the capacity and right to enter this agreement. That there is no other matter which has not been disclosed relating to the [Synopsis/Work] that would prevent, prohibit and/or restrict the ability of the [Author] to be party to this agreement.

C.097

The [Author] confirms that the [specify type] Rights in the [Synopsis/Work] have not been previously licensed and/or otherwise exploited in any form in any medium throughout the [country] except as previously disclosed in writing to the [Publisher], a copy of which is attached to and forms part of this agreement in schedule A.

C.098

The [Proprietor] warrants that it has and will retain good title and authority to enter into this agreement.

C.099

The [Author] and the [Illustrator] undertake that they jointly and severally have created, developed, written and illustrated the [Work/Manuscript and Images] and that they have not granted, assigned and/or licensed any part of the copyright and/or other intellectual property rights and/or any electronic rights of any nature at any time to any third party. That there is no document or contract in existence to their knowledge which would affect their ability to enter in to this agreement.

C.100

That the [Publisher] has not concluded any agreement with another author and/or artist which is on the same subject of [specify subject/theme] which is due to be published within [two] months either before and/or after of the [Author's] [Work/Book/Sound Recordings] which would adversely affect potential sales.

C.101

The [Author] and the [Agent] confirm that no agreement which has been signed by and/or on behalf of the [Author] concerning the publication of the [Work/Book/Sound Recordings] by the [Author] will adversely affect and/or restrict the grant of the rights in this agreement by the [Author] to the [Distributor].

C.102

The [Authors] confirm that neither party has entered into or is bound by an agreement with an agent in respect of the [Work/Book/Sound Recordings].

C.103

1.1 [Name] is the authorised representative of the estate of the late [specify person] and agrees that he/she has full authority of the estate to enter into and bind the estate to this agreement with the [Company].

1.2 That [Name] agrees to supply at his/her sole cost a letter of confirmation of that authority to grant such rights under this agreement from the following members [specify names] of the family who are legally authorised to manage the estate of the late author [specify person].

Services

C.104

The [Manager] shall keep the [Group] informed on a regular basis as regards any negotiations with any third party and agrees that he/she shall not commit the [Group] and/or its members to any agreement, recording contract, tours, interviews, filming and/or otherwise without the prior [written] consent of each member of the [Group] based on full disclosure of all the relevant facts.

C.105

The [Company] warrants and confirms that it has the power and authority to execute and perform this agreement and to grant the rights to the [Distributor]. That there is no contract with any other person, firm, corporation and/or organisation which will in any way undermine, conflict with and/or adversely affect this agreement.

C.106

The [Artist] agrees and undertakes that where a previous contract and/or other arrangement prejudices his/her right to enter into this agreement. That prior to the conclusion of the agreement the [Artist] will obtain the consent of any such third party to this agreement. The [Artist] agrees and undertakes to produce the written consent document for inspection by the [Company] upon request.

C.107

1.1 The [Agent] agrees that the [Agent] shall not be entitled to commit the [Author] and/or agree final terms with any third party at any time without the express consent of the [Author].

1.2 The [Agent] agrees that the [Author] shall have the final decision in respect of all agreements of any nature (whether as to the terms or whether to sign or not) relating to the exploitation of the [Work/Future Work] in any format in any medium.

1.3 No authority is granted to the [Agent] under this agreement to sign any undertaking, document and/or agreement on behalf of the [Author].

C.108

The [Sportsperson] confirms that he/she has full title and authority to enter into this agreement and is not bound by any previous agreement, professional rules, codes of conduct and/or decisions of a governing body which adversely affect this agreement.

C.109

1.1 The [Agent] confirms that he/she has good title and authority to enter into and perform this agreement and is not bound by any other agreement which prejudices and/or adversely affects this agreement.

1.2 The [Agent] confirms that in particular there is an agreement between the [Agent] and [Advertiser] which fully authorises the [Agent] to act on the [Advertiser's] behalf and to conclude the agreement.

C.110

The [Agent] confirms that the [Author] shall have the final decision to conclude and sign any contract and/or any other document with any third party relating to the licensing, assignment, registration and/or exploitation of the [Work/Future Work]. The [Agent] agrees that no authority is granted under this agreement for the [Agent] to sign and/or enter into any contract and/or other arrangement with third parties on behalf of the [Author].

C.111

The [Author] authorises the [Agent] to collect all sums due to the [Author] in respect of the [Work/Future Work] from any source throughout the [Territory/country/world] during the Term of the Agreement [and/or any time thereafter relating to any agreement negotiated by the [Agent] during the Term of the Agreement].

C.112

The [Designer/Developer] shall perform its obligations under this agreement to the best of its skill and ability and shall achieve professional standards to create a fully functional [Website/App/Audio File/Podcast] for the [Company's] commercial and marketing purposes on or before [date] in accordance with the agreed project outlines and budget set out in Appendix A which form part of this agreement.

C.113

The [Designer/Developer] shall at all times have suitably qualified and experienced [staff/consultants/freelancers] who are able to effectively contribute to the successful completion of the [Project] and who will undertake to be bound by the terms of a confidentiality agreement prior to the commencement of any work.

C.114

The [Contributor] has expertise and experience in the design, planning and production of [websites/apps/podcasts] and agrees to be engaged on a freelance basis from [date] to date] in the role of [specify role] to [specify task] on the [Project].

C.115

The [Actor] agrees to provide his/her services and perform his/her duties at such times, dates and locations and in such manner as may reasonably be agreed with the [Company] and any other third party which may be involved in the development of the [Tour/Film/Series].

C.116

The [Actor] confirms that he/she shall make himself/herself available for all work arranged by the [Agent] except for the following dates: [specify dates not available] in [year]. Thereafter the [Actor] shall not be available for no less than [number] days in any year during the continuance of this agreement.

C.117

The [Company] confirms that [Name] and/or the [Company] have the full authority and power to enter in this agreement and that neither is bound by any prior contract, undertaking and/or restriction which has not been disclosed except for the following commitments: [specify agreements/work/dates].

C.118

The [Consultant] is a professional registered [specify title] and a member of the following bodies: [specify organisations/registration details]. The

[Consultant's] academic, professional qualifications and publications are set out in appendix A and form part of this agreement. [Name] is a recognised and acknowledged expert in the field of: [specify specialist subject].

C.119
[Name] agrees and undertakes that he/she has no physical and/or mental impairment and/or ill health and/or other symptoms which would prevent the provision of his/her services and/or completion of the agreed work and/or which would increase the premiums significantly for any insurance cover for the [Project].

C.120
[Name] agrees and undertakes not to drink alcohol and/or to take any medication for the duration of the [Project] except in an emergency which would affect his/her capacity to safely perform the tasks set out in this agreement.

Sponsorship

C.121
The [Sportsperson] confirms that he/she is a full member of the following sports organisations: [specify bodies] and is not banned, prohibited and/or restricted from practising his/her sport in [subject] in any part of the world as at [date]. That all previous reprimands, fines, suspensions and/or otherwise have expired and no longer apply.

C.122
The [Sportsperson] agrees to conduct himself/herself in a fit, proper and professional manner at all times during the Term of the Agreement. Both while participating in the sport, posting material on social media and in his/her public and private life.

C.123
[Name] confirms that he/she is [number] years of age and is permanently resident in [country] and is entitled to work and/or provides services to any company. That [Name] has full title and authority to enter into this agreement and is not bound by any previous agreement and/or professional rules and/or codes of conduct and/or policies of any governing body and/or any national organisation in [specify sport] which would affect, prohibit and/or restrict the terms and/or performance of this agreement by [Name].

C.124
The [Sponsor] agrees and undertakes that it has and will retain authority to enter into this agreement and is not bound by any other document and/or

collaboration and/or partnership with any other third party which will have and/or might have any adverse effect on the terms this agreement and/or be a conflict of interest as at [date].

C.125

The [Athlete] and [Agent] confirm that there is no arrangement, licence, contract and/or other commitment to any advertiser, manufacturer, television company, radio company, news organisation, newspaper, magazine, internet, media and/or other third party for the services of the [Athlete], endorsements of products and/or services and/or the use of products and/or services by the athlete and/or for the display of trade marks, service marks, logos, images and/or slogans which would prevent and/or prohibit and/or conflict with the [Athlete] carrying out and/or being bound by the terms of this agreement with the [Company]. This clause shall not apply to family members and/or other persons associated with the [Athlete].

C.126

The [Athlete] is a [amateur/professional] and bound by the governing body [specify] which permits the [Athlete] to enter into [sponsorship/endorsement/promotional] agreements. The [Athlete] already has agreements with the companies listed in Appendix [–], but they do not prevent the [Athlete] entering into this Agreement.

C.127

The [Company] agrees to sponsor the [Event/Project] provided that the following individuals will appear in the schedule programme: [specify persons]. In the event that more than two of these persons decide at a later date not to appear then the [Sponsor] shall have the right to nominate who the [Enterprise] should consider as an alternative.

University, Charity and Educational

C.128

The [Charity] is registered with the [Charities Commission/other organisation] number [specify registration number] and its Board of Trustees have and will comply with all the legal requirements and codes of practice which exist in [country] at any time from [date] to [date].

C.129

1.1   [Name] confirms that the organisation and/or entity known as [specify name] is a [specify type]. It is not registered as a company in any country and/or as a charity. The persons who organise and plan the activities and/or spend the money relating to [specify name] are not known as a matter of public record.

1.2 There is no confirmation as to compliance and/or adherence with any legal requirements in any country and/or any guidelines, codes of practice and/or policies of any government and/or organisation and/or governing body.

C.130

The [Consultant/Company] agrees and undertakes that:

1.1 There is no conflict of interest of which they are aware which if known to the [Institute/Charity] would affect their decision to enter into this agreement.

1.2 That there is no arrangement, contract and/or commitment to any other university, publisher, newspaper, television, radio and/or media company and/or any political and/or campaigning organisation and/or other third party for the services and/or support and/or endorsement of the [Consultant/Company] which would directly conflict with and/or have an adverse effect on this agreement and/or have a negative impact on the [Institute's/Charity's] reputation and potential to raise funds for its building and/or research projects.

C.131

1.1 [Name] [Title] of [Institute/Charity] agrees and undertakes that he/she has the authority and/or has been authorised by the [Board/Trustee] to sign this agreement on behalf of the [Institute/Charity].

1.2 That the [Institute/Charity] is permitted by its [Charter/Trust Deed/ Terms of Reference/Articles and Memorandum] to enter into such an agreement with a third party and that there is no restriction and/or prohibition on its power and/or right to do so.

C.132

The [Company] and the [Institute/Charity] both agree and undertake that they have the power and authority to enter into this agreement. That neither is bound by any prior contract, undertaking and/or restriction which has not been disclosed except for the following commitments: [specify in detail the exceptions].

C.133

The [Company] confirms that it is currently solvent, and that its accounts are audited by [specify name of auditors/ accountants] and that it is not forecast to make a loss in the next [two] years.

C.134

The [Company] agrees that it shall only use suitably qualified and professional personnel for this [Project] who have the following skills: [specify skills required]. That all such personnel shall be current members of one of the following [unions/trade/professional organisations]: [list organisations].

C.135
Where the [Consortium] have set up a new company for the [Project] which is independent from the [Institute/Charity]. Then the [Consortium] agrees that the [Institute/Charity] shall hold not less than [number] per cent of the [shares] and control [51]% of the new company. In addition it shall be entitled to [number] [non-executive] directors.

CARRIAGE COSTS

General Business and Commercial

C.136
The method of carriage shall be determined by the [Company] at its sole discretion and the [Customer] shall pay and be responsible for all carriage costs. In the event that the material is ordered less than [five days] (exclusive of Saturday, Sunday and Bank Holidays) prior to the Dispatch Date the [Customer] shall pay the [Company's] express surcharge then in force and any additional carriage costs incurred.

C.137
The method and cost of post, packaging and insurance shall be agreed with and paid for by the [Client] in advance of delivery.

C.138
The [Company] and the [Client] shall agree the method of sending and/or delivering any goods and/or products in advance and the cost of any insurance cover and additional charges. However as a minimum charge the cost payable by the [Client] shall be:

1.1 Recorded delivery post in [country] shall be not less than [number/currency].

1.2 Recorded airmail and postage outside the [country] shall be not less than [number/currency].

1.3 Personal delivery by courier in [country] shall be not less than: [number/currency].

C.139
The cost of delivery, insurance, storage, customs duties, taxes and/or any other additional matter are not included in the quoted price and will be an

additional charge which may vary according to the destination and the order required.

C.140

The [Client] shall be required to pay in advance all the costs for the delivery of the [Units/Products] to the nominated address on the order form as confirmed by the [Client]. The actual choice of the form of delivery shall be at the discretion of the [Company] in accordance with their usual business practices. After the order has been confirmed no other address may then be nominated for delivery unless the [Client] agrees to an additional administration charge.

COLLECTING SOCIETIES

General Business and Commercial

C.141

1.1 The [Company] shall be responsible for registration with any collecting societies in respect of the [Project] and any new material in any format and/or medium which may be created and/or developed. All revenues and sums received from such sources shall be shared between the parties as follows: [specify allocation of percentage/name of party].

1.2 The [Company] shall be responsible for ensuring that all material in any format and/or medium which needs to be cleared and/or acquired for the {Project] shall be the subject of authorised consent and/or a licence from the legal owner of the rights. That the [Company] shall ensure that any usage reports and/or any payments due are made whether to any individual and/or a collecting society in respect of the use, adaptation and/or exploitation of the material. That any such clearance and other payments shall be included in the main budget and not deducted from any sums due under this agreement to [Name].

C.142

Both parties agree that they shall register the [Book/Music/DVD/other] with the [collecting/trade organisation] [specify name] in the following manner:

1.1 Copyright owner to be listed as [specify names].

1.2 Allocation and payment of sums received from such registration of rights to be [split between the parties equally/other]. All sums to be paid directly to the following manner: [name/specify person to receive payments].

1.3 No authorisation is to be permitted from only one person to grant a sub-licence and/or transfer any rights and/or for the authorisation of any adaptation at any time. Both parties must agree the terms and/or conditions. Where one party is deceased then their estate shall assume and be assigned their beneficial interest.

C.143

The [Company] agrees that [Name] shall have the sole right to register with any [collecting societies/trade bodies/other] and to receive payment of all the sums received by them at any time for any adaptation, exploitation, reproduction, performance, transmission, broadcast and/or any other type of use of the [Work/Music/Film/DVD/Sound Recordings/Lyrics] and/or any parts in any country in the world on land, sea and/r in the air in any format and/or medium of any nature whether in existence now or developed in the future.

C.144

1.1 The [Company] and the [Author] agree that the [Book/Audio File] shall not be registered with [specify organisations] and/or any other trade and/or collecting body but shall be listed as an excluded work.

1.2 All requests for permission to copy, reproduce, adapt, transmit, perform, to sub-license and/or otherwise exploit the [Book/Audio File] in any form shall be referred for the approval and written consent of the [Author]. That the [Company] shall only be entitled to exercise the specific rights granted under this agreement and that this does not include the right to grant consents and/or transfer, assign and/or sub-license any rights and/or enter into any brand and/or other collaboration with any third party at any time without the prior express authorisation of the [Author].

C.145

1.1 [Name] and [Name] agree that they shall register as joint owners of the [Film/Music Composition/Sound Recordings] in respect of any copyright, intellectual property rights, associated trade marks rights, computer software and any other rights with any trade, industry, commercial and/or collecting societies in any country in the world.

1.2 The following registration details shall be provided to for [Name] and [Name] as follows: [specify in detail name/contact information/address/other].

1.3 Both parties agree that all sums received by any such organisations and/or companies in 1.1 and 1.2 shall be equally split between the parties on the basis of fifty per cent each. All currency conversion charges and other costs shall be deducted prior to payment to either party.

C.146
The [Licensee] shall be solely responsible for the clearance of all copyright and other intellectual property rights and/or any other rights and for the payment of all sums which may be due to any collecting societies, trade organisations, copyright organisations, and/or any other person and/or company which may arise from the exercise and/or exploitation of the rights granted under this agreement. The [Licensor] shall not be liable for any such sums. Not shall the [Licensee] be entitled to deduct and/or recoup any such sums from the advances and/or royalties due to the [Licensor].

C.147
Where there are collecting societies for which the parties may register rights for any part and/or all of the rights in the [Work] in any format, medium whether text, sounds, images, designs, sound recordings, film, music scores, lyrics or any other material. It is agreed that both parties shall be registered as joint owners and that both shall share the sums received and/or due equally. That where one has to be nominated that the other party shall account immediately for any sums received and pay any funds so received to the other party.

C.148
The parties agree that they shall seek to exclude the [Work/Project] from any control and/or registration with the following collecting societies: [specify organisations]. That all sub-licensing and exploitation shall be subject to the prior written approval and agreement of the [Company] and [Name]. That where both parties fail to agree that there shall be no obligation to provide consent to any proposal even where this results in loss of future revenue.

C.149
The [Assignor] agrees that the [Company] shall have the right to register with any collecting societies and/or in any legal system and with any other authority and with any other third parties as the copyright owner and the holder of all other rights in the [Work] including the name, title, logo, trade mark and any adaptation and exploitation that may be derived from the [Work] in any form. The [Assignor] agrees that they shall have no right to make any objection and/or to register a complaint in respect of any such registration in any part of the world from [date].

C.150
Where a new collecting society is created in the future which does not exist at the time of this agreement which creates a new source of revenue to the

[Company] from the exploitation of the [Work]. Then the [Company] agrees that any sums so received shall be include in the accounts and reports to [Name] and/or their estate and/or beneficiaries and/or heirs.

C.151
The parties shall discuss and agree any registration with any collecting society in any part of the world at any time. No registration shall be made without the consent of both parties and agreement as to the basis on which the funds received shall be distributed.

COLLECTIVE WORKS

General Business and Commercial

C.152
'Collective Work' shall mean any encyclopaedia, dictionary, yearbook or similar work, a newspaper, review, magazine or similar periodical and any work written in distinct parts by different authors or in which works or part of works of different authors are incorporated.

C.153
'Collective Work' shall mean a work of joint authorship or a work in which there are distinct contributions by different authors or in which works or parts of works of different authors are included.

C.154
'The Collective Work' shall mean the periodical entitled; [specify title] in the [specify language] published in [countries] by the [Company].

C.155
'The Collective Works' shall mean the original research papers, articles, talks and/or works of the authors which already exist in a separate and independent form (whether or not they have been published) and which are collated and published together as a single periodical, hardback or paperback book and/or in the form of a disc and/or as a download in electronic form with the original text, images, data, and references which are described in appendix A. [list title/description/author].

C.156
In consideration of the payment of the [Advance Fee] and the additional [unit/royalty] fees. The [Author] grants the [Company] the non-exclusive

365

right to incorporate the [Extract/Article/Report] in the [Periodical] known as [title/reference] and on the website and app [reference] from [date] to [date] on the following conditions:

1.1 That the name of the [Author] shall be displayed in the contents list with the title, and at the beginning and end of the [Extract/Article/Report] with a copyright notice and the year [number]. That the following contact details shall also be included so that any third party may seek permission for any further use [specify email] at the end.

1.2 That the [Company] agrees and undertakes not to authorise any third party to exploit, reproduce and/or adapt the [Extract/Article/Report] and the [Company] shall be limited to sales, marketing and distribution of the [Periodical] and access and use of its website and/or app.

1.3 That the [Company] shall not be entitled to translate, delete, add to, change, amend and/or alter any part of the title and content of the [Extract/Article/Report] unless submitted to the [Author] for approval and agreed by the [Author] in advance.

1.4 No part of this agreement is intended to transfer, assign and/or vest any intellectual property rights including copyright, software, trade marks, logos and/or format, formulae, data, patents, inventions, technological developments and/or any other rights of any nature in the [Company] nor in any adaptation, variation and/or amended version. Nor shall the [Company] seek to register and/or represent to third parties and/or display any trade mark, copyright notice or warning which states that the [Company] owns any of these rights.

C.157

The [Author] does not grant nor authorise the [Company] the right to sub-license the [Work/Extracts] to third parties in any form whether part of the [Collective Work] or not. The prior written approval of the [Author], an additional fee and a separate agreement shall be required in the event that the [Company] wishes to sub-license and/or assign the whole of the [Collective Work] to a third party. The [Author] shall not be under any obligation to provide any consent and may request the exclusion of the [Work/Extract] from any such form of assignment and/or exploitation.

C.158

Where the [Company] uses sections and/or parts of the [Work] of less than [number] [words/pages] and includes them with material from other authors in a compilation work which is under a different title. Then the [Author] accepts that he/she shall not be entitled to the royalty payments set out in clause [–]. The [Company] agrees that it shall be obliged and the [Author] agrees to negotiate either a complete buyout fee or a royalty fee based on

General Business and Commercial

the new project. The parties agree that where they fail to agree terms for any such use that they shall engage a mediator at the [Company's] sole cost to resolve the matter.

General Business and Commercial

C.159

There shall be no commission, agency fees, expenses, charges and/or other costs deducted from the [Sale Price] and all sums due to [Name] by the [Company] shall be paid in full within [seven] days of receipt. The [Company] acknowledges that [Name] has already paid an advanced fixed fee of [specify number/currency] for their services.

C.160

Where the transaction is arranged, negotiated and/or agreed, but no final document is signed and/or no payment is received by the [Seller] then no commission shall be paid to the [Company].

C.161

The [Company] shall have the right to deduct the agreed commission, expenses and costs due to the [Company] by [Name] under this agreement prior to the payment of any sums due to [Name].

C.162

[Name] shall be obliged to pay commission to the [Company] where any person, or company is introduced to [Name] and that person or third party subsequently concludes an agreement with [Name] in respect of [specific type of transaction/rights] directly. This clause shall apply [at any time/for duration of this Agreement/from [date] to [date]].

C.163

The [Company] shall only be entitled to receive commission on any sums actually received and paid to [Name] and retained by [Name]. Any commission paid to the [Company] may be claimed back by [Name] within [two years] of payment where the sum on which the commission is calculated is repaid to a third party by [Name] due to an error, omission, refund, overpayment, breach of contract, legal action or any other reason.

C.164

When commission has been paid to the [Company] then no sum can be reclaimed, refunded and/or returned to [Name] unless due to an error, an omission, negligence and/or fraud and/or some other criminal conduct of the [Company] and/or its directors and/or employees.

C.165
The commission payments due to [Name] shall be subject to a maximum annual limit of [number/currency] from [date] to [date].

C.166
'The Commission' shall be paid to [Name] on the actually sums received from the [purchasers/customers/retailers/distributors] and paid to the [Company] for acquisition of the following [Services/Products/Benefits]: [detailed description]. Payment to [Name] shall be in accordance with the rates set out below:

1.1   From [0] to [number] [currency]: [number] per cent payable at the end of each [six] month period.

1.2   From [50,000] to [100,000] [currency]: [number] per cent payable at the end of each year by [date].

C.167
[Name] shall be paid commission for the number of [tickets/products] which are sold by [Name] through their recommendation, links, website, articles and blogs and purchased by the public from the [Company] for which payment is received in [country] and not refunded at any time using the [code number/reference] [specify] from [date] to [date].

C.168
No commission shall be due to [Name] after [date] even if sums are received by the [Company] from the work and/or contribution of [Name] of any nature. [Name] agrees that he/she shall not be entitled to any commission after [date] even if it relates to work completed by [Name] before that date which has not yet been received by the [Company].

C.169
Commission payable to [Name] shall be based on the net sums received by the [Company] after the deduction of all marketing and administration costs, agency fees, telephone and mobile phones costs, bank charges, currency conversion costs, travel and accommodation costs, cost of supply of equipment, insurance cover and staff costs and any other mater directly related to the sums received.

C.170
There shall be no agency fees, commission, royalties, costs, expenses and/ or other payments due to any third party who links to, accesses, downloads

from, supplies material to and/or promotes this [Website/App/Platform] as a [subscriber/user].

C.171
The [Service Company] agrees to pay the [Website/App/Distribution Company] commission of [number] per cent of the total amount of the [Subscription Fees] received without any deductions for costs and expenses for the [three] years. This shall be in respect of any person, body and/or company that enters into a [Service Contract] with the [Service Company] as a direct result of a referral, link, service promotional segment and/or video and/or article and/or other material on the [Website/App/Channel] and who uses the quote reference [specify code].

C.172
The [Promoter/Distributor] shall pay the [Website/App/Platform Company] a fixed unit commission of [number/currency] for every [number] customers which follow the banner link and provide their personal details to the [Promoter/Distributor] and purchase the [Products/Services] from [date] to [date].

C.173
The [Supplier] agrees that the [Distributor] may market, promote and sell the [Products] at any price and may discount, cross-promote and/or offer such reductions as it deems fit on the [Seller's] website, app, channels and/or elsewhere in any medium. Provided that the [Distributor] shall be obliged to pay the [Fixed Unit Price] to the [Supplier] in each case for each unit supplied and/or sold to a third party regardless of the sum received.

C.174
This [Website/App/Platform] does not pay commission in money but allocates [vouchers/credits] which can be redeemed against other products, services and benefits on the [Website/App/Platform]. There is no cash alternative available at any time and failure to redeem and/or use the commission and the [vouchers/credits] within the allocated period and expiry date will not entitle you to make a claim for any financial and/or other losses and/or damages. It is a condition of your participation in this [Scheme/Project] that you agree and accept this term and condition. In the event that it is not acceptable then do not proceed and sign up to the [Scheme/Project].

C.175
The [Company] does not pay a percentage fee based on sales and/or sums received. All payments in respect of remuneration for our agents are based on achieving a target of revenue based on purchase of [products/services/other] by our [Clients] in each [six] month calendar period. Where you have

reached your target of [specify number/currency] in any [six] month period then you will receive a one off fee of [number/currency] for each such period which will be paid direct to your nominated bank account by direct debit within [one] calendar month of your successful completion of the target.

C.176

The [Licensor] agrees that the [Licensee] shall be entitled to receive commission of [number] per cent [figure] % on any sums actually received by the [Licensee] in respect of the exploitation of the [Product//Series/Podcast] and/or any adaptation for the duration of this agreement.

C.177

The [Licensee] shall not be entitled to receive commission and/or any other sums on any monies received by the [Licensee] and/or the [Licensor] after the termination and/or expiry of this agreement. This shall also apply to any contracts concluded by the [Licensee] during the term of this agreement. Any sums received by the [Licensee] after the expiry and/or termination of the agreement shall belong entirely to the [Licensor] and shall be paid directly to the [Licensor].

C.178

The [Licensee] shall be entitled to be paid and calculate their commission at the end of [calendar month/accounting period]. The [Licensee] shall disclose all commission deducted and received by the [Licensee] in the relevant accounting statements to the [Licensor].

C.179

All commission shall be paid in [sterling/dollars/other] and shall be calculated after conversion from another currency. All payments to the [Licensee] shall be directly to a bank account in [country] and no additional bank charges shall be deducted.

C.180

The [Licensee] shall not be entitled to commission on sums which are due and/or owing where the sums are not paid by the third parties. No payments shall be due to be made by the [Licensor] for any loss of commission.

C.181

The [Company] shall be entitled to receive commission on all agreements which it negotiates and concludes which are signed by [Name] in respect of the exploitation of the rights specified in this agreement. The [Company] shall be entitled to receive commission from those agreements even after the expiry of this agreement on all sums which are received by [Name] from those agreements. The right of the [Company] to receive commission shall cease either on the expiry and/or termination of the agreements in each case [and the completion of the accounting procedures] and/or by [date] whichever is the earliest.

C.182
The [Licensee] agrees and undertakes that it shall not agree and commit to pay any commission and/or agency fees which are in excess of [number] per cent and/or [number/currency] to any third party at any time. That it shall seek the approval and advice of the [Licensor] in any case where it would like to conclude and/or commit to any arrangement which is in excess of these levels. Failure to seek approval will mean that in any accounts and sums received the [Licensee] shall bear all the cost of the excess levels of commission and shall not share the costs and/or recoup them before payment to the [Licensor].

C.183
The [Licensee] shall ensure that all agents, distributors and third parties that receive commission to promote and sell the [Service/Product/Material] do not acquire any copyright and/or any other rights of any nature in any medium in the original [Service/Product/Material] and/or in any adaptation and/or variation. That where new formats and/or means of adaptation and/or exploitation is to be created and developed that the [Licensee] shall ensure that before any such parties are paid any commission they shall assign all rights in any new versions to the [Licensor].

C.184
The [Company] shall be paid a commission of [number] per cent in respect of the total value of each order placed by a wholesaler, retail outlet, online retailer and/or wholesaler and/or any other third party purchaser at the end of each [six] month period starting [date]. Any payment of commission shall be subject to payment for any such order being received and no refund, discount and/or returns being made. In such event the lower value will be applied.

C.185
The [Company] shall be paid a fixed sum of [number/currency] for each unit of [Products] which are purchased by members of the public, retailers and distributors at above [price] from [date] to [date] in [country] which directly relate to the promotions and/or marketing by the [Company] through: [specify method].

C.186
The [Sales Representative] shall be entitled to retain [fifteen] per cent of the [Retail/Wholesale Price] of each of the items sold provided that the [Retail/

Wholesale Price] in any event shall not with respect to each item be less than [number/currency].

C.187

Commission for the purposes of this agreement shall only be paid to [Name] for their work in promoting and marketing the products, services and name of the [Company] from [date] to [date]. Commission shall only be due and paid to [Name] where a person and/or other business purchases and pays in full for any of the following products and/or services which are described in detail in appendix A and forms part of this agreement. In order for [Name] to qualify for the commission the purchaser must have at the time of purchase and payment either provided a [voucher/code/other] which has been supplied by [Name] and/or they have followed a link from a blog and/or article written by [Name] which refers to the [Company] and some of its products and/or services.

C.188

Commission shall only be calculated by the [Company] on the total [retail/wholesale/net receipts] of the orders made and paid full in each calendar month which derive from the services of [Name]. The [Company] shall pay [Name] on the total amount of the [retail/wholesale/net receipts] received by the [Company] as follows:

1.1   up to and including [number/currency] at the rate of [number] per cent.

1.2   from [number/currency] to [number/currency] at the rate of [number] per cent.

1.3   no commission shall be due if the payment for the order has not been fulfilled and no ownership has passed to the [Customer].

1.4   where the [Company] incurs legal and/or administrative costs which arise from a dispute relating to any order. Then the [Company] shall be entitled to set aside a reasonable sum and not pay any commission on that sum until the matter has been resolved.

1.5   payment to [Name] shall be within [one] calendar month of the completion of any [three] calendar month period of orders by [Name].

C.189

The commission paid to [Name] shall not exceed [number/currency] in any event in any one accounting period. If any further commission is still due it shall be carried forward to the next accounting period for payment.

C.190

'The [Agent's] Commission' shall be [number] per cent of the [Gross Receipts/Net Receipts/sums received after deductions] by the [Agent] which shall commence on [date] and end on [date]. No commission shall be due to the

[Agent] after [date] regardless of whether the [Agent] was involved in the negotiation of any of the agreements and/or other documents.

C.191

1.1   The [Agent] shall be paid varying rates of commission dependent on the type of work, services and/or rights which are being exploited and/ or adapted at any time from [date] to [date].

1.2   The rates of commission and the type pf work, services and rights is listed in appendix A and forms part of this agreement. [specify type of work/services/rights and set different rates of commission which may rise and/or fall dependent on value].

1.3   Where the agreement expires and/or is terminated and/or cannot be carried out due to force majeure. Then no commission shall be due except in relation to matters which have already been completed. Any right to commission shall end on the expiry date of the agency agreement. If the agreement is terminated on valid ground then no commission shall be due from the date of termination. In the event of circumstances which amount to force majeure then either party may service notice to end the agreement on a fixed date.

C.192

In consideration of the [Agent's] Commission the [Agent] agrees to provide his non-exclusive services to the [Artiste] for the Term of the Agreement throughout the Territory.

C.193

The [Company] engages the services of [Name] as a [photographer/other] to create a series of images on [theme] in accordance with the synopsis attached in Schedule A. [specify detail of work required and format in which it is to be delivered]. [Name] accepts the commission and agrees to provide his/her services to the best of their professional ability.

C.194

The [Company] agrees to pay the [Agent's] Commission to the [Agent] by the last day of each three-month period starting on [date] throughout the Term of the Agreement. Such payment to be made in [currency] of the sum due after deduction of any bank and/or currency exchange costs by such method as the [Company] shall decide.

C.195

'The [Licensee's] Commission' shall be the [number] per cent of the Net Receipts during the continuance of this agreement. It shall not be paid if the agreement expires and/or is terminated for any reason except for sums due for work prior to those dates.

C.196

'The [Manager's] Commission' shall be [number] per cent of the Gross Receipts after deduction of the Authorised Expenses which shall apply to any agreement concluded during the existence of this main agreement. The commission shall be due to the [Manager] whether this main agreement expires and/or is terminated until such time as the third party agreements concluded by the [Agent] no longer continue in existence and/or no further sums are received.

C.197

'The [Agent's] Commission' shall mean the following percentage of the [Gross Receipts/Net Receipts/sums received after deduction of costs and expenses] in respect of any form of exploitation and/or adaptation of the [Work/Manuscript/Series] and any related appearances, interviews, tours and/or other services provided by [Name] in conjunction with the [Work/Manuscript/Series] in the [Territory/specify countries/world]:

1.1 [number] per cent [–] % in respect of all hardback, paperback and digital and /or e book copies for reading over the internet in electronic form as a download, pdf and/or otherwise on a mobile, gadget and/or computer. It shall include any discounted, reduced price, overstock, remainder, premium offer, book clubs, educational editions, anthologies, quotations and/or translations.

1.2 [number] per cent [–] % in respect of any electronic version for use over the internet and downloaded to any mobile, gadget and/or computer such an e book, pdf, audio recording and/or audio file which is used solely for listening and not reading.

1.3 [number] per cent [–] % for any serialisation of the [Work/Manuscript/Series] in any newspaper, magazine and/or periodical both in printed format and/or on any website, app and/or platform at the same time in electronic form.

1.4 [number] per cent [–] % in respect of DVDs, CDs, audiotapes, videos and other forms of mechanical reproduction and/or in respect of any option and/or exercise of any form of film, television, radio, and/or theatre rights including digital, cable, terrestrial and satellite, theatric and/or non-theatric and/or any sums due from collecting societies and/or any form of exploitation on the internet including podcasts, films, series, archive playback and/or any electronic material not covered in 1.1 to 1.3. This shall include where the material is also shown at the same time and/or as an archive replay as part of any service in respect of accessing electronic material over the internet and/or any website, app and/or platform, mobile phone, computer, and/other gadget.

1.5 [number] per cent [–] % in respect of forms of merchandising and/ or exploitation in relation to gambling sites, bingo, racing, sports, betting, theme parks, holograms, product placement, art installations, brand collaborations, premium rate phone lines, tours, animation and/ or comic strips and/or cartoon characters, computer games and any other method and/or format of exploitation whether in existence now and/or developed in the future.

C.198

'The Agent's Commission' shall be the following percentage of the [Gross Receipts/Net Receipts/sums received] in respect of the following forms of exploitation of the services and/or work of [Name] received by the Agent during the continuance of this agreement from [date]:

1.1 number] per cent [–] % of all hardback and paperback copies of any [Book] of any manuscript delivered by the [Author] to any [Publisher/ Distributor] which is sold in the United Kingdom of Great Britain and Northern Ireland, the Republic of Ireland, the Channel Islands, the Isle of Man.

1.2 [number] per cent [–] % of all hardback and paperback copies of any [Book] of any manuscript delivered by the [Author] to any [Publisher/ Distributor] sold throughout the [Territory/world] excluding the United Kingdom of Great Britain, Northern Ireland, the Republic of Ireland, the Channel Islands, the Isle of Man, the United States of America and Canada.

1.3 [number] per cent [–] % of all hardback and paperback copies of the [Book] of any manuscript delivered by the [Author] to any [Publisher/ Distributor] which is sold in the United States of America and Canada.

1.4 [number] per cent [–] % of all copies of any [Book] of any manuscript delivered by the [Author] to any [Publisher/Distributor] which are disposed of to a third party at a discount of more than [number] per cent and/or at a reduced price of more than [number/currency] per copy and/or as remainder and/or overstock.

1.5 [number] per cent [–] % of all copies of any [Book] which are disposed of as a premium offer, book club and/or educational editions.

1.6 [number] per cent [–] % of all copies of any anthologies and quotations.

1.7 [number] per cent [–] % of all translations.

1.8 [number] per cent [–] % of all straight non-dramatic radio and television reading.

1.9 [number] per cent [–] % of the first serialisation of any [Book] of any manuscript delivered by the [Author] to any [Publisher/Distributor] in any newspaper, magazine and/or periodical in printed format. [number] per cent [–] % of second and subsequent serialisations.

1.10 [number] per cent [–] % of strip cartoon and/or other similar representations.

1.11 [number] per cent [–] % of all merchandising excluding the image, name and trade mark rights of [Name] in person in private and/or public.

1.12 [number] per cent [–] % of all non-theatric rights.

1.13 [number] per cent [–] % of all merchandising, developments, and/ or adaptations, associated with and/or derived from any [Book] and/ or manuscript delivered by the [Author] [and/or any exploitation in the form of film, television, radio, video, DVD, audiotapes, computer discs, CD-Roms, computer software and/or in electronic form for use over the internet as a download, e book, audio file, game, podcast whether accessed by mobile phones, computers and/or any other gadget and/or any sums received from the registration of rights and/or from collecting societies. This shall include but not be limited to theme parks, collaborations with gambling, betting and bingo companies, lotteries and/or sports promotion, interactive competitions and games, products, services and/or any other medium and/or format and/or rights not listed above whether invented now and/or created in the future.

C.199
'The Agent's Commission' shall be the following percentage of the Gross Receipts: [number] per cent [–] %.

C.200
'The Manager's Commission' shall be the following percentage of the Net Receipts: [number] per cent [–] %.

C.201
The [Sportsperson] agrees to refer all requests of a commercial nature to the [Manager/Agent] and agrees that the [Manager/Agent] shall have the sole and exclusive right to negotiate with third parties for the commercial services of the [Sportsperson] during the Term of the Agreement.

C.202
The [Agent] confirms that the [Author] shall not be responsible for any costs and/or expenses incurred by the [Agent] and that the [Agent] shall only be entitled to receive the [Agent's Commission].

C.203

The [Manager] acknowledges that he/she shall not be entitled to any commission in respect of any work done and/or agreed to be done by the [Sportsperson] prior to the date of this agreement whether that work is performed during the Term of the Agreement or not.

C.204

1.1 The [Manager] acknowledges that he/she shall be solely responsible for his/her own expenses, costs and/or other liabilities in providing his/her services to the [Sportsperson] under this agreement.

1.2 That the [Manager] shall only be entitled to receive the [Manager's Commission] from [date] to [date].

1.3 That where the [Sportsperson] terminates this agreement early due to the default and/or failures of the [Manager] that any commission shall be suspended and any sums shall be held separately from the other funds of the [Manager] until the matter has been resolved.

1.4 That no commission shall be due after [date] to the [Manager] on any agreement and/or other arrangement regardless of whether it was negotiated and/or concluded during the Term of the Agreement by the [Manager].

1.5 That where it is shown at a later date that the [Manager] has retained sums to which he/she was not entitled. Then interest shall be due on the sum from the date of the breach until the date the sum is paid to the [Sportsperson] at [number] per cent.

C.205

The [Sportsperson] acknowledges that the [Manager] shall be entitled to the [Manager's Commission] after the expiry of this agreement in respect of all agreements negotiated by the [Manager] and concluded during the Term of this Agreement.

C.206

1.1 The [Company] confirms that all rights in any [material] supplied to the [Designer] under this agreement shall be owned and/or controlled by the [Company] unless expressly stated to belong to a third party.

1.2 The [Designer] shall at all times employ suitably qualified and experienced [staff/artists/manufacturers] who are able to contribute to the successful completion of the [Project] and the proper fulfilment of the obligations under this agreement.

1.3 The [Company] may at any time decide not to use and/or continue to use the services of the [Designer] for the [Project] and shall be entitled to terminate the agreement with [one] calendar months notification to the [Designer]. The [Company] shall only be obliged to pay such sums as may be due to the date of termination. No additional payment shall be due in compensation and/or to cover any losses and/or damages which may be incurred by the [Designer].

1.4 The [Designer] agrees that the [Company] may at any time engage any third party at its sole discretion to carry out any work and/or services on the [Project]. No prior consultation and/or approval of the [Designer] is required.

C.207

The [Agent] agrees that any form of exploitation of the product of the [Artiste's] services shall require the prior consent of the [Artiste]. The [Artiste] shall be entitled to refuse to carry out any work and/or services and/or to create any material and/or contribute in any form for any reason whether or not the [Agent] will suffer a financial or other loss. The [Agent] shall not be entitled to seek any compensation, loss and/or damages from the [Artiste] which arises from such failure to provide consent.

C.208

The [Agent] confirms that the [Author] shall have the final decision to conclude and sign any agreement, contract or other document relating to the exploitation of the [Series/Manuscript] and that no authority is granted under this agreement for the [Agent] to do so.

C.209

'The Commissioned Work' shall be the [Project/Object] to be designed, created, reproduced and delivered by the [Assignor] to the [Company] which is described in full in appendix A which is attached to and forms part of this agreement. [specify title/duration/format/content/copyright notice/ credits in detail].

C.210

The [Assignor] undertakes that it shall produce the [Commissioned Work] in accordance with the Budget, in the following format [–] by [date].

C.211

'The Commissioned Work' shall be the following series of [Sound Recordings] based on the summary in Schedule B a copy of which is attached setting out in detail the theme, style of music, instruments, persons, lyrics and songs to be created, edited, produced, and delivered by [Name] to the [Company] in [format] together with relevant music cue sheets and list of credits and copyright notices.

C.212

[Name] agrees that he/she shall produce the [Commissioned Work] in accordance with the summary in Schedule B and deliver the following agreed material by [date].

C.213

1.1 The [Company] engages and commissions the [Consultant] to carry out a [market /data survey] and to analyse and assess and report back on the topic of [specify theme/context] with the following aims [specify purpose].

1.2 The [Consultant] agrees to provide [number] copies of an A4 bound report written in [language] of no less than [number] pages together with [number] copies in [format] at the [Consultant's] sole cost by [date].

1.3 The [Consultant] agrees to also provide copies of all the [market/data survey] material, supporting material, research and data analysis to the [Company] upon request.

1.4 The [Consultant] agrees that the [Fee] shall be the total limit of the liability of the [Company] and there shall be no additional charges, costs and expenses attributed and/or claimed by the [Consultant] for any part of the work and/or services supplied under this agreement.

1.5 The [Consultant] agrees to ensure that in any [market/data survey] the contributors are age [number] and/or over and have the option to agree that can be contacted at a later date by the [Company].

1.6 The [Consultant] agrees to assign any and all rights including copyright, database rights and any other intellectual property rights in any part of the world to the [Company] in consideration of the [Fee] and also waives all moral rights and the right to be attributed as the copyright owner and/or author of the report. The [Consultant] agrees and accepts that the [Company] may edit, adapt and revise the report and/or data in any manner and also engage a third party to do so. That in any such circumstance the prior approval and/or consent of the [Consultant] shall not be required. Nor shall the [Consultant] have any claim for loss of reputation and/or otherwise.

C.214

The [Company] agrees that where [Name] has commissioned the development, design and production of a [Website/App/Podcast series] from the [Company] based on an original quote and that sum has now been exceeded whether caused by [Name] or not. That [Name] shall have the right to terminate the agreement with the [Company] and to be delivered and have ownership transferred of all originals and copies of all material including drawings, software and codes and passwords, animation, film, video, images, text, music and/or any other material as has been developed to the date of termination which relate to the [Website/App/Podcast series] commissioned by [Name] provided that the [Company has been paid in total [number/currency] by [Name]

C.215

[Name] agrees to the following terms in respect of sponsorship and/or other commercial funding of [Project/Event]:

1.1 To refer all matters relating to sponsorship and/or other commercial funding of [Project/Event] to the [Company].

1.2 That the [Company] shall have the sole and exclusive right to negotiate with third parties for the sponsorship and/or other commercial funding of [Project/Event] from [date] to [date].

1.3 That [Name] shall not be responsible for any costs, expenses and/or other sums incurred by the [Company] at any time.

1.4 The [Company] shall only be entitled to receive the [number] per cent of the monies received by [Name] in the form of sponsorship and/or other commercial funding in respect of the [Project/Event] which have been negotiated and/or concluded from [date] to [date] by the [Company].

1.5 The [Company] shall not be entitled to any commission in respect of any sum received from sponsorship and/or other commercial funding of [Project/Event/other] before [date] and/or after [date] whether or not negotiations and/or agreements were made and/or concluded during that period.

C.216

It is agreed that no agency fees and/or commission, and/or other payments and/or deductions shall be made to any third party in respect of the Sponsorship Fees being provided by the [Sponsor] for the [Event]. All the sums paid by the [Sponsor] shall be used by the [Company] for the sole purpose of the [Project] as specified in the Budget in Schedule A.

C.217

1.1 The [Company] agrees that any form of sponsorship of the [Event/Project] which involves the [Artwork/Performance] of the [Artist] shall be notified to the [Artist] before it is concluded.

1.2 The [Company] shall provide a list of sponsors and the method by which they are using and/or promoting their products and/or services.

1.3 The [Artist] shall have the right to refuse to be involved with the [Event/ Project] and/or to attend and/or provide any additional work and/or services if the [Artist] does not agree with the choice of sponsorship and/or the method. The [Artist] shall be entitled to notify the [Company] to that effect without any liability as to the losses, damages, costs, expenses and/or any other sums that may be incurred as a result.

C.218

The [Company] agrees that where any new artwork, text, logo, name and/ or other material is commissioned by them which relates to the [Sponsor], the [Event] and/or any of the services, products and/or marketing relating to the [Sponsor]. That the [Company] shall ensure that any new material shall be assigned to the [Company] and then to the [Sponsor] so that no such rights are owned and/or controlled by a third party. Where the [Company] fails to do so and the [Sponsor] is at a later date required to take legal action then the [Company] shall be obliged to bear [number] per cent of the costs incurred by the [Sponsor] and their legal and other professional advisors engaged for that purpose.

C.219

The [Company] agrees that after the [Event/Project] has been completed it shall conduct market research and gain feedback from the public, performers and others involved in order to assess how to improve and develop for the next year. The [Company] agrees to provide the [Sponsor] with a copy of any such report and/or any other new related commissioned material.

C.220

The [Sponsor] acknowledges and agrees that it shall not have any copyright, intellectual property rights in any material in any medium including but not limited to names, titles, places, logos, images, music, sound recordings, films, photographs, websites, apps, promotional games, trade marks and/or merchandising commissioned and/or developed by the [Company] which relates to the [Event/Project]. That the [Sponsor] shall not have the right to use and/or exploit and/or authorise others to reproduce, adapt, supply and/ or license any part of such material and/or rights at any time and that there is no licence granted either express or implied to do so.

C.221

1.1 'The Commissioned [Work/Project]' is called: [title] to be prepared, produced and delivered by the [Institute/Enterprise]. A summary is attached as Appendix A and forms part of this agreement. [describe in detail content/schedule/personnel/aim and purpose/proposed outcome/material].

1.2 The [Company] agrees that the [Institute/Enterprise] may at its sole discretion cancel the agreement for the use of the [Company's] services and/or engage a third party to carry out work on the [Work/Project].

C.222

The [Institute/Charity] shall have the right and be entitled to refuse to carry out work for and/or to collaborate with and/or be involved with the [Company] where at a later date it becomes aware that to do so would seriously affect the reputation of the [Institute/Charity] and/or is likely to result in legal proceedings by a third party. The [Company] shall not be entitled to seek any compensation, losses, damages and/or any other sums from the [Institute/Charity] which may arise from such a decision and notification to terminate the agreement.

C.223

The [Consultant] agrees that the [Institute/Charity] shall have the final decision in respect of all matters and that there is no consent, authority and/or implication under this commission that the [Consultant] is entitled to represent the [Institute/Charity] and/or to act as their agent and/or to sign any document and/or to enter into any other commitment.

C.224

That the [Institute/Charity] may at any time decide to cease engaging the services of the [Company] whether the [Project] has been completed or not. The [institute/Charity] shall only be required to provide [twenty-one] days' written notice to the [Company] and to pay such sums as may be due for work completed to that date.

C.225

There shall be no commission, agency fees, expenses, charges and/or costs due to the [Company]. The [Company] acknowledges that the [Institute/Charity] has already agreed a fixed fee of [number/currency] for their services. No additional payments shall be authorised by the [Institute/Charity] unless agreed in advance in writing by [name/title].

C.226

Where the [Institute/Charity] commissions a report, photograph, data analysis and any other work from [Name] during the course of their unpaid internship at the [Institute/Charity]. It is a condition of that internship that all copyright and any other rights of any nature shall belong to the [Institute/Charity].

[Name] agrees to sign and execute for [one/currency] any documents that may be required at a later date to effect transfer provided that no rights shall be sought to be transferred by the [Institute/Charity] that [Name] was already working on and/or developing in any form prior to the internship.

C.227

The [Institute/Charity] authorises the [Consortium] to commission work and engage consultants, researchers and such other persons as may be required for the [Project] provided that:

1.1 The agreed budget is not exceeded.

1.2 The [Project] terms of reference are adhered to at all times.

1.3 Regular monthly reports detailing progress; completion of tasks and expenditure are provided to [Name] at the [Institute/Charity] by the [Consortium].

1.4 That where there are to be any variations from the original proposal for the [Project]; terms of reference and/or costs that no commitment may be made without obtaining the prior written approval of [Name] at the [Institute/Charity] based on a full disclosure of the facts.

COMPANY

General Business and Commercial

C.228

'The Company' shall be [full name/registered address/company reference/ trading name] and any assignees and/or successors in title in whole and/or part. It shall not include any parent, associated or other company whether related directly and/or indirectly through directors, companies, bodies, shareholdings or otherwise.

C.229

'The Company' shall mean [Name Ltd/plc] whose main place of business is at [address] and shall not include any associated holding or other person or corporation whether connected directly and/or indirectly with the [Company]. Nor shall it include any assignees, licensees and/or successors in title.

C.230

'The Agency' shall mean the company known as: [specify] which is registered in [country] with the reference [code/number] and is authorised to act on behalf of [Name/Enterprise]. The registered office is at: [address] and the main office is at: [address].

C.231

'The Enterprise' shall be [registered company/ limited liability company/ unlimited liability company/general partnership/limited partnership/ trust/ unincorporated association/ joint venture/ joint-stock company/other] known as: [specify registered name] [specify any reference details] which operates under the name: [specify trading/other name]. The registered is at [address] and the main place of business is [address].

C.232

[Name of charity/business] who is registered as [specify tax/company/ charity status] in [address/country] and which operates under the name [specify trading name]. [referred to for the purposes of this agreement as [specify name]].

C.233

This agreement is purely between [specify details of parties] and there is no right to assign, license, authorise and/or transfer any rights, obligations, responsibilities and/or liabilities to any person, body, company and/or other third party. In order to do so the express written consent of all the parties shall be required in advance. Any party to this agreement shall have the right to refuse their consent.

C.234

'The [Publisher/Distributor]' shall mean: [specify full name of company] of [address] which is a subsidiary of the parent company [specify full name of company] of [address]. It shall include not include any assignees and/or successors in title.

C.235

'The Company' shall be the company [specify full name] which has signed this agreement together with any other directly related entity and/or body whether a parent company, subsidiary and/or part of a group structure and/ or acting together and/or trading under a group name.

C.236

'The Companies' shall be defined as follows:

1.1 The subsidiary known as [specify trading name] incorporated in the name of [specify registered legal name] in [country] registration reference [specify number] whose registered office is at [address]; and

1.2 The parent company known as [trading name] incorporated in the name of [specify registered legal name] in [country] registration reference [specify number] who registered office is at [address].

C.237
'The Company' shall be defined as [specify official name] which is a [limited company/partnership/plc/other] trading as [specify operational brand name] with official registered address [specify address] and main warehouses and/or premises in [country] at [address]. The definition shall [include/exclude] any parent company, subsidiary, affiliate, joint venture partner, consortium, associate, distributor, sub-licensee, assignees and/or successors in business and/or title in whole and/or part.

C.238
'The Company' shall be defined as the limited liability company [specify official name] owned entirely by the directors [specify names] and any assets, contracts, intellectual property rights, patents, domain names, trade marks, brand names, databases, documents, computer records and/or software and/or any other material stored at any address and/or other rights related to the business.

C.239
'The Company' shall be [specify official name] of [address] which is a [sole trader] which provides the services of [Name] as [specify role/duties].

C.240
'The Parent Company' is [specify registered official name] which is known commercially as [specify operational/trading name. Its official registered office is at [address] but it trades as a global company through many offices, premises and warehouses. It shall include any subsidiary but not any associated, partnership, affiliate, distributors, agents and/or licensees. It shall also include any assignees of the whole [and/or part] of the assets of the business and/or any successor in title.

C.241
All references to the [Company] in this agreement shall not include any parent company, associated company, subsidiary, partnership, business associates, agents, distributors, trusts, and/or any other entity.

C.242
The Parent Company of the [Sponsor] in this agreement agrees and undertakes to be bound by any terms, obligations, liability and/or indemnity which the [Sponsor] is unable and/or unwilling to perform and/or fulfil and/or pay where the [Sponsor] is alleged to be and/or is in actual in breach and/

or default of this agreement. [Provided that the total liability of the parent company shall be limited to [number/currency].]

C.243

This agreement has been reached with you the [Licensee] as a specific company and there is no right and/or permission provided that allows and/or permits the [Licensee] to assign, transfer and/or delegate any part of this agreement to a third party whether or not that other company is associated with and/or connected to the [Licensee]. Any attempt and/or evidence that you intend to do so shall entitle [Name] to terminate this agreement with immediate effect by notice by [email/other].

C.244

1.1   [Name] writes and contributes to a blog entitled: [specify name of blog] on [specify website/app/platform] [reference]. The non-exclusive services of [Name] are provided through a company known as [specify name of company] which is [specify legal status] at [address/country].

1.2   All invoices and payments relating to [Name] shall be through the company in 1.1 Payment to the company shall be fulfilment of payment to [Name].

C.245

[Name] creates, develops and operates a [channel/podcast] known as: [full name of channel/podcast]. The [channel/podcast] is legally owned and controlled by a [company/other] called: [specify legal name in full] who own all copyright, performing rights, trade marks and all intellectual property rights and assets. [Name] provides his/her exclusive services to that [company/other]. No other third party has any interest, shareholding, lien and/or charge as at [date].

C.246

The [Website/App/Platform] called: [specify name] is owned and controlled by the [Company/Enterprise] known as: [specify legal name] which is registered in [country] with [reference]. The [Company/Enterprise] is owned and controlled by [number] [shareholders/investors/other] as at [date] who are represented as follows: [specify and list names].

C.247

The [Sound Recording] is legally owned by [Name] who has authorised the following collecting societies to license and collect payments on his/her behalf from [date: [list collecting societies/addresses].

C.248

'The [Global Business]' shall be defined as the following parent company, subsidiary, associated companies, partners, associates, affiliates, distributors, suppliers and agents as at [date]: [specify name/address/registration/trading name/legal status].

C.249

All health and safety compliance documents, licences, planning permissions and authorisations and insurance for the [Company] are held and registered in the name of [specify] at [address] in [country].

C.250

'The [Charity]' shall mean: [specify legal name of charity] which trades under the names: [list trading/operating names] which is registered as: [specify legal status] with the following governing, regulatory organisations and tax authorities: [list names].The trustees of the charity may change from time to time but as at [date] are the following persons: [list names/role].

C.251

'The Institute/Archive' is the organisation known as: [specify common name] which has the legal name: [specify registered/other name] which has the website: [reference] and the app: [reference]. Its primary place of business is [specify main address] and it owns and/or control the following properties, assets and material: [list resources].

COMPETITIONS

General Business and Commercial

C.252

You the entrant [Name] of: [address] age: [specify age] years and date of birth: [specify date/month/year] contact details: [telephone/email/mobile] agree and undertake that you shall be bound by and comply with the terms and conditions for entry to the [Competition]. That in the event that you fail to comply and/or breach the terms and conditions of entry for any reason that your entry shall not be eligible and shall be disqualified from the [Competition].

C.253

In order to be able to enter the [Competition] and to be eligible to comply with the terms and conditions of entry. It is a condition that any person who enters the [Competition] must be a resident of the [United Kingdom/Channel Islands/Isle of Man] and [eighteen/other] years of age or older.

C.254

Any person who is an employee of any of the following companies [specify list of names] and/or any other agent, promoter and/or other person connected with the [Competition] and/or a member of their [immediate/ extended/other] family shall not be allowed to enter the [Competition] and shall be ineligible to participate. If any such person should enter then they will be automatically disqualified and not entitled to claim and/or be awarded any prize.

C.255

The [Company] shall be entitled at its sole discretion to declare that any entry is not to be entered for the [Competition] and is disqualified and/or invalid and/or some other reason due to a breach and/or default and/or error and/or omission on the part of the person who has submitted the entry (whether or not the answer is correct). In such event the [Company] shall not be obliged to notify the person who has entered of their decision and/or to provide a reason unless requested to do so by the person who has been rejected.

C.256

The [Company] shall be entitled at its sole discretion to decide that any entry is disqualified from the [Competition] due to the fact that it is in breach of the terms and conditions of entry. Where an entrant is disqualified the [Company] shall provide a written reason for the disqualification if so requested by the entrant.

C.257

All decisions of any nature made by the Directors and/or officers of the [Company] and/or other authorised third parties shall be final and not subject to any appeal process. The [Company] shall not enter into any correspondence, dialogue and/or otherwise with any person and/or entrant regarding any aspect of the [Competition].

C.258

All parts of the procedure of the [Competition], the decisions as to eligibility and the correctness of any answers and the award of prizes and any other matter of any nature shall be entirely at the sole discretion of the [Company/ Judges/Panel] whose decision shall be final. The results of the [Competition] shall be available [from [address] by sending a stamped address envelope marked [specify words] and/or on the [Website] [reference] after [date].

C.259

All entries must be original and the work of the person named as the entrant. No entry should be abusive, defamatory, offensive, derogatory, degrading and/or otherwise not acceptable due to the nature of the material submitted. The [Company] may at its sole discretion decide that any entry is not eligible due to the nature of the content of the entry and may disqualify a person from the [Competition] [and any such future competitions].

C.260

1.1 The prizes shall consist of: [specify sequence/prize/value in detail].

1.2 The prize(s) shall not include [specify matters not included].

1.3 The following costs and expenses shall not be part of the prizes and shall be the responsibility of the person who is selected to be awarded a prize: [specify costs and expenses not covered].

1.4 Where a specific prize is not available for any reason then the prize winner shall be awarded a prize which is similar in value and of a similar type.

C.261

The [Competition] starts on [date] and ends on [date]. All entries must be received by [time] on [date]. All entries received and/or made after that time shall not be eligible to be entered into the [Competition]. There may be a charge incurred even though the entry is not accepted as valid.

C.262

All costs of entry are the responsibility of the person entering the [Competition]. There are no refunds for any entries which are received by the [Company] which are ineligible, illegible, damaged, lost, delayed and/or received after the deadline. Only the following methods of entry to the Competition will be accepted by the [Company] [specify modes of application/formal requirements/documents and forms/any specific formats].

C.263

All entries by post shall be on an original official entry form from the [Product] accompanied by [number] of original official vouchers which have been collected from the [Product] together with a receipt and/or other proof of purchase. No photocopies are accepted. No more than [number] entries will be accepted by the [Company] from each [household/address]. All entries must have arrived at the [address] post paid by the deadline of [date/time]. No acknowledgement of the entry will be provided by the [Company].

C.264

All entries by telephone and/or mobiles shall be by phone calls to [specify telephone number] and then follow the instructions provided which will be in the [English] language and to leave your answer and personal contact details. No more than [number] entries will be accepted by the [Company] from each mobile and/or landline. All entries must be completed by the deadline [specify]. Each call shall be charged at [number/currency] from any landline in the [United Kingdom]. Calls from mobile phones and/or other networks and/or by any other method may be charged at a much higher rate. All persons who enter by telephone and/or mobile must have the permission of the person in whose name the telephone and/or mobile is held and/or who pays the bill. No acknowledgement of the entry will be provided by the [Company].

C.265

All entries by text messages from mobile phones and/or other gadgets shall be in [English/other] to [telephone number] and send your answer and [specify details required]. No more than [number] entries will be accepted by the [Company] from each mobile and/or gadget. All entries must be completed by the deadline. Each text will be charged at [number/currency] from a mobile in the [United Kingdom] plus the network rate which is charged by their network for sending a text message. Texts by any other method may be charged at a much higher level. All persons who enter by text must have the permission of the person in whose name the mobile is held and/or who pays the bill. All entries by text before the deadline will receive a text confirming their entry.

C.266

All entries online on the [Website/App] known as: [specify name] [reference] shall be made by filling in all the details required in the entry form online in [English/other] and confirming your acceptance of the terms and conditions of entry and completing the answer and sending it to the [Company]. No more than [number] entries will be accepted by the [Company] from each person. All entries must be completed by the deadline. All persons who enter by this method must have the permission of the person in whose name the computer is held and/or who pays the bill. An acknowledgement of entry will be sent by the [Company] to the email address which you provide within [number] days.

C.267

No responsibility can be accepted by the [Company] for any entries which are lost, incomplete, are delayed beyond the deadlines, fail to arrive, are damaged, are illegible, inaudible, are not transmitted, do not arrive and/or for any other reason are not received by the deadline and/or are ineligible and/or invalid.. Proof of posting is not accepted as proof of delivery to the [Company]. Proof of submitting an email and/or sending a text message is not accepted as proof of delivery to the [Company]. If the details of entry are not received by the [Company] for any reason then it is not accepted as a valid entry.

C.268

No responsibility and/or liability can be accepted by the [Company] for any costs, expenses and/or charges incurred in respect of any entries by any method. The [Company] shall not be liable for any reason to any person who may enter the [Competition] and/or any third party whose facilities and/or equipment may be used and each person enters at their own risk and cost.

C.269

The prizes will be awarded in the order that they are drawn. The winning entries will be drawn at random [in order from first to last] selected by [explain method of selection] by [date] from all eligible entrants who have provided the correct answer.

C.270

The prizes will be awarded in order of merit. The winning entries shall be selected by a panel of judges appointed by the [Company] by [date]. The [Company] may at any time appoint, withdraw and/or substitute any of the judges on the panel. The decision of the judges shall be final and there shall be no right of appeal.

C.271

Independent supervision of all valid entries received shall be made by: [specify person/company].

C.272

1.1   There shall be no independent supervision of the [Competition] and all decisions are at the sole discretion of the [Company].

1.2   The decision of the [Company] as to the winners of the [Competition] shall be final.

C.273

No entrant can be awarded more than one prize in the [Competition].

C.274

Entrants can be awarded more than one prize and for more than one category in the [Competition/Event].

C.275

The winners will be notified by [specify method of contacting winners] within [number] [days/weeks] unless the [Company] decides at its sole discretion that the timescale for notification needs to be extended for any reason.

C.276

Notification to the winners shall be by first class post by letter to the address provided by the person when they entered the [Competition] within [one] calendar month of final date of the [Competition].

C.277

Notification of the winners shall be by email to the email address provided by the person when they entered the [Competition] [within number days of the date of/after] the close of the [Competition].

C.278

Notification of the winners shall be by text to the mobile number provided by the person when they entered the [Competition] within [twenty-four] hours of the winners being announced. This notification may be delayed where necessary for any reason.

C.279

Any prize has to be accepted and taken by the person who is awarded the prize before [date/time]. After that date no prize shall be available to that person and at the [Company's] sole discretion another eligible person may be selected for the prize.

C.280

1.1   The prize can only be awarded and/or collected and/or paid to the person whose name is provided at the time of entry to the [Competition]. There is no cash available as an alternative to any prize. The [Company] is not obliged to exchange and/or transfer any prize to another person.

1.2   The list of winners will be available on [specify website/app] [reference] from [date] until [date]. No written request for details of the [Competition] results will be responded to by the [Company].

C.281

The [Company] reserves the right at its sole discretion to withdraw and/or substitute any prize at any time for any reason. The [Company] may replace and/or substitute any prize with any products, goods, services and/or cash which the [Company] decides [is appropriate/of equal value/similar] in the circumstances.

C.282

The [Company] may at any time decide to change, cancel, amend, vary, delete, add to and/or otherwise alter the terms and conditions of entry, the prizes, the criteria by which winners are chosen and/or selected and/or any other part of the [Competition]. The [Company] shall not be required to send separate notification by email, text and/or any other method to each person who has and/or may enter the [Competition]. It shall be sufficient that details shall be highlighted and available on the [Company's] [website/app] at [reference].

C.283

It is a condition of entry that the person entering the [Competition] agrees and undertakes to assign to the [Company] the sole and exclusive intellectual property rights including copyright whether in existence now and/or created in the future and any other rights in all media throughout the world and universe in all the material entered for the [Competition] (except their personal details) [including but limited to any text, film, images, photographs, and/or otherwise] for the full period of copyright and any extensions and/or renewals and in perpetuity. The [Company] shall have the right to assign, license, adapt and/or commercially exploit the material in any form and the person shall not be entitled to receive any sums. No rights of any nature shall be retained by the person who has entered the [Competition] except the right to be identified as the author by the name on the entry.

C.284

The [entrant/author] grants the [Company] the exclusive right to reproduce, distribute, supply and otherwise exploit the material submitted for the [Competition] for a period of [ten/other] years from [date/the date of entry] in all intellectual property rights including copyright, trade marks, computer software rights, database rights, design rights, patents and/or any other rights and/or interest which may exist and/or be created in the future in all media [throughout the world and universe/in country] (except their personal details) including but not limited to film, television, merchandising, publishing, the internet and downloads, mobiles, marketing and advertising. The [Company] shall also have the right to sub-license, add to, delete from, adapt and/or otherwise exploit the material without the payment of any advance, royalty and/or other sum to the [entrant/author].

C.285

The person who entered the [Competition] waives the right to be identified as the author of the material submitted for the [Competition]. It is agreed that the [Company] may be credited as the copyright owner and may assign, license and/or commercially exploit the material in any form and the person shall not be entitled to receive any sums.

C.286

The person who entered the [Competition] shall have the right to be identified as the author of the material submitted for the [Competition] and credited as the copyright owner on all copies of the material used and/or exploited by the Company] in the following form wherever possible: © [year] [name of entrant].

C.287

The personal details which have been submitted for the [Competition] will be held by the [Company] and [specify name of third party]. This information will only be shared with third parties involved with the administration of the [Competition] and/or the supply and delivery of the prizes. The personal details will only be held for [number/months/years] after the period necessary to complete the administration of the [Competition]. All personal details will then be destroyed and/or deleted after [date].

C.288

Where for any reason beyond the reasonable control of the [Company] the [Competition] cannot be carried out and/or completed as planned and/or advertised. Then the [Company] reserve the right to cancel the [Competition] at any time and in such event shall not be liable to any person who, for any reason, may have entered the [Competition]. The total liability shall be the cost of refund of the entry cost for each person.

C.289

The terms and conditions of this [Competition] shall be subject to the Laws of [country].

C.290

The governing law of this [Competition] and all matters related to it shall be [specify state/country/other].

C.291

All winners shall have their name and answer [announced/displayed/printed] on [specify website/magazine/newspaper/programme].

C.292

All winners agree to the following publicity and marketing:

1.1 in person as follows: [specify in detail use of personal names, images, photographs, filming podcast and/or programme, interviews, appearances] and

1.2 for the use of their material as follows: [specify forms of exploitation].

1.3   The [Company] agrees to pay for the costs and expenses that may be incurred by any winner provided that these are authorised and agreed with the [Company] in advance. No additional fees and/or other sums shall be due.

C.293

All winners agree to participate in such reasonable marketing and photographic shoots as may reasonably be requested by the [Company [subject to the payment of travel costs].

C.294

You agree that you enter this [race/competition/event] at your own risk and that the [Organisers] cannot accept any responsibility for any loss of any equipment, injury to any part of your body, death and/or permanent disability. You have been advised that this [race/competition/event is very dangerous and that the [Organisers] do not hold any insurance cover nor is any provided by any governing body associated with the sport. You waive all claims against the [Organisers] and the volunteers and the support services which arise from your own errors, judgement and actions. You agree that the only exception is where injury or death is caused by the negligence and/or material failure of the [Organisers] to take sufficient precautions which are within a reasonable cost with respect to any material adverse conditions.

C.295

Only one entry is permitted per person. If at a later date any person is found to have entered more than once then the [Company] reserves the right to exclude them from any further participation in the competition and they shall not be entitled to be considered in any process and/or decision to assess the winners and award prizes.

C.296

This competition is only open to those age [number] years as at [date] and under who live in [country] and have purchased a promotional copy of [specify product] from [store] between [date and [date].

C.297

The [Company] shall announce the winners of the competition of its [website/app/platform] known as: [specify name] [reference] on [date]. All winners are obliged/agree to have a promotional photograph taken and to agree that it may be used by the [Company] to promote and market the [Product] in any media at any time. The [Company] agrees to provide each winner with a copy of their promotional photograph in a frame. The [Company] agrees that where additional photographs, filming and/or appearances may be required that the [Company] shall pay the winners a reasonable fee and expenses for their services on each occasion.

C.298

Where the [Company] offer any product as a prize for any reason. They reserve the right to substitute another product of similar value at any time where the other product cannot be supplied for any reason. No cash alternative will be offered.

C.299

1.1 All decisions regarding the merit of the material submitted for the [Competition] shall be made by a carefully selected panel of experts in the field of [subject].

1.2 No communication and/or correspondence with be entered into with any entrant of the [Competition].

1.3 Where it is clear that the material submitted is not original then it shall be ineligible and not entered into the final round of submissions to be considered by the panel.

1.4 If the entrant has professional status and is not an amateur then they shall be ineligible.

1.5 If the material submitted has been displayed, published and/or distributed over the internet by the entrant then it shall be ineligible.

C.300

Where any [entrant/participant] is found by the [Institute/Charity] to have committed any of the following acts, conduct and/or otherwise they shall be banned and/or not eligible to enter and/or rejected as an [entrant/participant] from the [Competition]:

1.1 to have entered under a false name.

1.2 deliberately provided false information, data and/or material.

1.3 not be age [number] years and over.

1.4 not have complied with all the requirements of entry including the stated deadline.

1.5 have intended to falsely represent that they created the material supplied and that it is original.

COMPLIANCE

Film, Television and Video

C.301

The [Assignor] confirms that the [DVD/Film/Podcast] shall not contain any music, text and/or sound effects other than the [Musical Work] unless there is prior written consent in advance by the [Assignee].

C.302

The [Company] undertakes that the [Film/Video/Archive Playback/Electronic Download Format] shall adhere to all the following criteria set out in Appendix A [specify title, duration, performers, scenes, locations, music, product placement, script, production crew, director].

C.303

That the production, manufacture, reproduction and distribution of the [Film/Video/Archive Playback/Electronic Download Format] shall be in accordance with any legal, censorship, programming, health and safety and/or other union requirements, practices and agreements in [country/other] in existence at the time of signing this agreement and/or which may come in to effect at any time until [date].

C.304

Both parties agree and undertake that they shall endeavour to comply with all legislation, regulations, directives, codes, policies and guidelines which may exist and/or be created in respect of the production, reproduction, supply, licensing and distribution of the [Content/Material] in the [country/Territory/world] during the Term of this Agreement.

C.305

The [Licensee] agrees and undertakes to ensure that the following terms and conditions are fulfilled in respect of the reproduction, distribution and/or supply of the [Film/Video/Sound Recordings] in [Format/Unit]:

1.1 That the [Format/Unit] shall not contain any other material except the [Film/Video/Sound Recordings] without the prior written consent in advance of the [Licensor].

1.2 That the [Format/Unit] shall only be an exact reproduction of the [Film/Video/Sound Recordings] from the original master material supplied by the [Licensor] under this agreement in clause [–]. That no additional text, word, lyrics, music, films, trade marks, products, services and/or other material shall be added in anyway.

1.3 That the [Licensee] shall ensure compliance at all times with all product liability, health and safety and/or legal requirements, regulations, directives, government and trade organisations codes of practice, policies and guidelines [in country/worldwide].

1.4 That the sound track of the [Film/Video/Sound Recordings] shall not be edited, adapted, added to and/or in any way changed and/or altered without the prior written consent in advance of the [Licensor].

C.306

That the [Licensee] shall ensure that the [Format/type of Units] do not breach and/or infringe any legislation, guidelines, codes of practices, standards and/or policies relating to packaging, advertisement, sponsorship, marketing and/or commercial exploitation [in country/worldwide].

C.307

The [Licensee] shall be ensure that the manufacturer, packaging, marketing and advertising companies involved in the reproduction, distribution, supply and promotion of the [Discs/Format] are financially viable and able to fulfil the work required according to the proposed schedule and to the professional standard necessary.

C.308

The [Licensee] agrees not to distribute, market and/or promote the [DVD/Disc/CD/other Format] on any website, app and/or otherwise over the internet and/or on radio, television and/or in any other manner and/or form and/or in association with any other products and/or services which is not suitable for the [children's] market for persons age [years] and below.

C.309

The [Licensee] agrees and undertakes that it shall not alter, adapt, add to, delete and/or change any part of the [Film/Video/other Format] and/or sound track and/or any credits and/or copyright notices and/or sequence in respect of the reproduction of the material supplied by the [Licensor] as the master copy and/or the exploitation of the rights granted under this agreement. Further the [Licensee] agrees and undertakes that the where the [Licensor] requests that the [Licensee] use any different title, sound recordings and/or sub-titles in any country that the [Licensee] shall comply with all such requests.

C.310

The [Licensor] agrees that where due to legal requirements, codes of practice and/or policies of any government and/or governing body and/or other institute which regulates any relevant industry the [Licensee] is required to exclude and/or add material to the final version of any [DVD/ Disc/other Format/Units]. That the [Licensor] shall not object provided that such alterations and/or additions are notified in advance to the [Licensor] and supported by evidence of the need for such exclusions and/or additions in each case and are made at the [Licensee's] sole cost.

C.311

The [Company/Distributor] agrees to ensure that the [Programme/Series] shall not infringe and/or breach any terms of the transmission and/or broadcasting licence of the [Company/Distributor] and/or any other regulations, codes of practice, legislation and/or other matters which may apply to the [Television Company] in [specify countries] in respect of sponsorship, endorsements, advertising, product placement, competitions, gambling, betting, lotteries, prizes, children and/or any other relevant issues which apply now or may come into existence during the Licence Period.

C.312

Prior to the broadcast and/or transmission of the [Film/Video/Sound Recording] in [country] by the [Company/Distributor] it shall use its [best/reasonable] endeavours to ensure that the [Film/Video/Sound Recording] complies with all the regulations and codes of practice of: [specify organisation] and/or any internal policies and/or guidelines of the [Company/Distributor] and/ or is not likely to result in a criminal and/or civil proceedings and/or an allegation of defamation and/or any other legal action and/or claim and/or complaint by a third party. All these matters shall be the responsibility of the [Company/Distributor] and not the [Production Company]. The [Production Company] shall still be bound by the terms set out in this agreement with the [Company/Distributor] despite the compliance and legal role of the [Company/Distributor].

C.313

The [Company] confirms that the [Work/Content/Material] shall comply fully at all times with all laws, regulations, directives, existing contractual relationships and obligations, codes of practice and guidelines issued by all relevant regulatory and other related trade organisations including but not limited to those matters listed in Appendix A which may be issued before [date] [list codes/guidelines/policies/organisations].

C.314

The [Production Company] confirms that it shall ensure that the [Advertisements/Promotions] to be developed and produced listed in Appendix A will conform to all legislation and/or laws in [country] and codes of practice and guidelines issued by [specify organisations] in respect of the advertising and marketing of products and/or services for cable, satellite, terrestrial, and/or digital television , radio, archive playback services and/or electronic download formats and/or in any other manner over the internet.

C.315

The [Assignor] shall not without the prior written approval of the [Assignee] inform any person and/or company except those absolutely necessary for the production of the [Film/Video/type of format] of any content of the scripts, budget, performers, presenters, location schedules, advisors and/or director and/or other personnel. Nor shall the [Assignor] issue any press and/or media statements and/or promotional material regarding the development, production, marketing, sales and/or otherwise of the [Film/Video/type of format] without the prior written consent of the [Assignee].

C.316

The [Production Company] undertakes as far as reasonably possible that all production personnel, artistes and musicians involved in the production of the [Advertisement/Promotion] shall be members of recognised trade and/or craft unions.

C.317

The [Licensee] is permitted to edit, adapt and change the [Film/Video/Work] subject to the prior approval of the [Licensee] by [email] where it is necessary in order to comply with any policies, standards and codes by [specify organisations] in respect of the broadcast and/or transmission in [country] for the purposes of the exercise of the rights granted in this agreement.

C.318

The [Licensee] agrees that the burden shall be on the [Licensee] to take advice and consider whether any changes, edits and/or deletions shall be necessary in any part of the world where the [Film/Video/type of format] is to be exploited in order not to be subject to any complaint, claim, fine and/or investigation by a regulatory and/or government body and/or any civil and/or criminal proceedings. The [Licensee] shall only be authorised by the [Licensor] to the extent that any changes, edits and/or deletions are absolutely necessary and the detail of which must be agreed in advance.

C.319

1.1 The [Licensee] agrees that it shall not have any right to authorise and/or grant any rights to third parties for any use and/or exploitation of the [Film/Video/Sound Recordings/Format] and/or parts and/or any associated soundtrack including but not limited to by an archive playback service which is free and/or under a subscription service and/

or for a one off payment for access and/or as an electronic download and/or through access over the internet by means of a website, app and/or platform by the use of a mobile, gadget, television, computer and/or any other method and/or medium.

1.2 The [Licensee] agrees and undertakes that it shall only be entitled to license the non-exclusive rights to the [Film/Video/Sound Recordings] in its entirety as supplied by the [Licensor] for performance and/or exhibition at the following festivals; [specify names] cinemas [specify names] and university film clubs: [specify names] and/or the following clubs and associations: [specify names] in [country] from [date] to [date].

C.320

It shall be the duty of the [Licensor] to ensure that the [Series/Videos/Discs] which it supplies to the [Licensee] for reproduction and exploitation under this agreement do not have any legal problems and that there is no threat of civil and/or criminal proceedings. That the [Series/Videos/Discs] comply are not in breach of any laws, contract, licence, copyright and/or other rights and adhere to any relevant guidelines, codes of practice and/or obligations regarding compliance which may be necessary for the transmissions, publications, merchandising and/or other forms of exploitation in respect of the master material supplied by the [Licensor]. It shall be the responsibility of the [Licensee] to carry out such matters in respect of each new format and/or medium which is developed by the [Licensee].

General Business and Commercial

C.321

The [Employee] agrees to abide by the [Staff Handbook/Code of Conduct/Policies] supplied by the [Company] which are included as part of the main agreement. This shall include the right of the [Company] to refuse access to any premises to an employee who is believed in the reasonable opinion of the [security staff/other] to be under the influence of drink and/or drugs.

C.322

The [Employee] agrees to be abide by all existing procedures and practices relating to the operation of the business and any future company policies and directions relating to clothing, conduct and behaviour, how to deal with clients, use of equipment, personal telephone calls and emails, use of the internet and/or otherwise which may be notified and/or supplied to the [Employee].

C.323

The [Executive] shall not be bound by any practices, directions, policies and/or procedures of the [Company] which have not been raised in negotiations and incorporated as a term of this agreement.

C.324

The [Company] agrees that failure to comply the following policies and/or authorisation procedures and/or codes of practice shall not be a ground to suspend and/or terminate this agreement: [specify policies/authorisation procedures/codes of practice].

C.325

The [Employee] acknowledges that in the event the [Employee] breaches any of the codes of conduct, policies and/or procedures of the [Company] set out in Appendix A which form part of this agreement. That the [Company] shall have the right to terminate the employment of the [Employee] by notice in writing with immediate effect after the [Employee] has ignored a first initial verbal warning as to their conduct and/or actions.

C.326

The [Employee] agrees and undertakes to comply with [Staff/Corporate Handbook] and such additional policies and guidelines as may be issued by the [Parent Company], the subsidiary, and/or any associated company for which the [Employee] may from time to time carry out work and/or fulfil functions which are notified that the time of this agreement and/or at a later date to the [Employee] either directly in the post, by email [and/or on any relevant corporate website.]

C.327

The [Company] agrees to supply the [Employee] with a copy of any new policies, guidelines and/or company procedures from [date] the start of the contract. All existing policies, guidelines and procedures are supplied with this agreement. The [Employee] will not be expected to be bound by any policies and/or guidelines which have not been drawn to the attention of the [Employee].

C.328

The [Employee] agrees and undertakes to wear such protective clothes and head gear and/or carry out and/or fulfil such health and safety measures and/or precautions as the [Company] may require in order to comply with all existing and/or future legislation, laws, regulations, codes of practice, guidelines and/or other stipulations that may be necessary. Where the [Employee] refuses to comply for any reason then the parties must review the matter and decide how to proceed based on the facts. In any event the [Company] shall be entitled to refuse to allow the [Employee] to carry out the work and shall reallocate the [Employee] to a similar level position in a different role if possible if both parties agree to that decision.

C.329

The [Company] agrees and undertakes to ensure that the conditions of work for the [Employee] comply with any existing and/or future legislation, laws, regulations, codes of practice, guidelines and/or otherwise and in particular that all health and safety procedures are of a sufficiently high standard to ensure that there is only an acceptable and low health and/or safety risk to the [Employee].

C.330

The [Employee] agrees and undertakes to ensure that he/she will not make any commitment on behalf of the [Company] which exceeds his and/or her authority and/or job designation without the prior consent of an officer and/or director of the [Company].

C.331

The [Employee] agrees and undertakes to ensure that he/she will not exceed the [Budget/Expenditure] which he/she may from time to time be allocated by the [Company] to use as a total target without the prior consent of an officer and/or director of the [Company].

C.332

The [Employee] agrees to attend such training courses, staff sessions, network events and/or conferences, trade shows and other matters that the [Company] may from time to time specify as part of the professional development of the [Employee] and/or marketing of the [Company]. Provided that the [Company] agrees to ensure that the [Employee] is paid for such attendance and also paid in advance for any additional costs and expenses.

C.333

[Name] agrees that he/she shall adhere to all reasonable requests, policies, codes of conduct and guidelines issued by the [Company] and/or its parent company which relates to:

1.1 The use of the [Company] name, products and/or services in emails, blogs and social media outside of business hours: [specify policy].

1.2 The purchase of discounted products and/or services for friends and family: [specify policy].

1.3 The wearing of jewellery and other body adornments such as earrings and piercings at the [Company]: [specify policy]

1.4 The use of [Company] laptops, telephones, mobiles and other resources during business hours which are for private use and not related to the [Company] and/or your business role: [specify policy]

C.334

Where the [Employee] has breached and/or not complied with any policy and/or code of conduct and/or directions of the [Company]. Then the [Company] agrees that it shall not have any right to subject the [Employee] to a disciplinary hearing and/or dismiss them where it can be shown that the [Employee] was not personally supplied with a copy of any such policy and/or code of conduct at the time of the conclusion of their terms of employment and/or within [number] months thereafter and/or the directions were misleading and/or not mandatory The [Company] agrees that it cannot enforce a new policy and/or code of conduct which it has introduced against an employee who has not been notified by the [Company].

C.335

The [Company] shall from time to time create and develop new policies, practices and systems including but not limited to new rosters, hours and days of work, security access and codes, fire and health and safety, absences and ill health, disposal of damaged products and waste, purchase of products by employees, uniforms, appearance and protective clothing, religion and ethical issues. All such details shall be:

a.   displayed on the [Company] [HR resources/other] section; and

b.   notified by email to all individuals; and

c.   a printed copy may be supplied upon request; and

d.   all such material as amended from time to time shall be applicable to all staff and must be complied with as part of your terms and conditions of employment with the [Company].

C.336

The [Management Contractor] shall immediately comply with and/or ensure compliance with all instructions. In the event that any instruction requires a [Works Contract] to be altered the [Management Contractor] before compliance shall submit to the [Architect] any written objection, consent or otherwise. The [Management Contractor] need not comply and/or ensure compliance with such instruction to the extent that the instruction is unreasonable, unsafe and/or not competent.

C.337

The [Company] agrees and undertakes that it shall comply and ensure the continual compliance and adherence to all legislation and health and safety, product, service and legal requirements, codes of practice, policies and any other matter that may be relevant to the [Project]. In particular any requirements of: [specify organisation/government department/trade organisation/other] and the following laws and documents: [specify and list].

C.338

The [Company] confirms that it shall not make nor authorise or permit copies of the [Work/Product/Material] to be made at any time for any purpose whilst the [Work/Product/Material] is in its possession and/or control.

C.339

The [Company] will use its reasonable endeavours to ensure that the [Project/ Material] is at all times kept in a safe and secure manner and all reasonable steps will be taken to ensure that no unauthorised person may gain access and/or take images of and/or copy any part of the [Project/Material].

C.340

The [Purchaser] may take copies for its own private records but must return to the [Seller] as soon as reasonably practicable all original documentation regarding the provenance of the [Work/Material]. The [Purchaser] shall not be entitled to use the documents for commercial purposes and/or for any form of programme unless the prior consent of the [Seller] has been provided.

C.341

The [Company] undertakes that its employees, agents, contractors and/or distributors will be suitably qualified and/or registered with a recognised trade body and/or have sufficient experience industry to carry out and perform the standard and quality of work required. That the [Company] will be able to produce any necessary documentation, assessments and/or tests which may be required by the [Client] to verify facts and information which may be requested by any regulatory, governing and/or government agency.

C.342

The [Consortium] agrees that all arrangements with [Name] are subject to the fact that [Name] is obliged to comply with the governing body [specify organisation] and cannot carry out any act, conduct, activity and/ or marketing which would lead to and/or cause him/her to be removed as a member of that organisation. That where such an issue would arise then [Name] shall be entitled not to agree to the request from the [Consortium] and that such refusal by [Name] shall not be a breach of this agreement.

C.343

The [Assignor] does not provide any confirmation and/or undertaking and/ or warranty that any part of the [Work/Project] complies with any codes, regulations, policies and/or industry guidelines which may exist now and/or at a later date. The [Company] agrees that they accept the [Work/Project] at their own risk and cost and that any failure, deficiency and/or non-compliance which is revealed shall be the sole responsibility and liability of the [Company].

C.344

You are hereby notified that you are expected to comply with all the following policies of the [Company] which are not only for guidance but form part of your terms of engagement: [specify list of policies]. Copies of the policies are attached to and form part of this agreement in Schedule A. The [Company] reserves the right to revise and update the policies and will ensure that you will be sent a copy of any new policy by [email/other method]. The [Company] recognises that there may be personal circumstances where the [Company] may need to agree to minor adjustments to any policy. You are asked to notify [Name] by [email] or by appointment to discuss any such requests.

Internet, Websites and Apps

C.345

The [Company] agrees that:

1.1 the [Name's] [personal/stage] name, image and endorsement of the [Website/App/Product/Service] which is to be filmed and recorded under the terms of this agreement shall not be used for any sub-licensing arrangement with a third party and/or to create any merchandising.

1.2 the material and/or associated rights which are created as a result of the filming and/or recording of [Name] under this agreement may only be used by the [Company] from [date] to [date].

1.3 no assignment and/or transfer of any rights is permitted and/or authorised to a third party.

1.4 none of the material shall be edited in such a way as to cause offence and/or affect the reputation of [Name].

C.346

1.1 The [Designer] agrees and undertakes that the [Website/App/ Podcast] shall be consistent with and to the standard and functionality specified in the detailed plan, budget and synopsis in Schedule A. [provide extensive detail of format/layout/purpose/how it is to be used and operate/comparison to similar sites/timescale/final material to be delivered/budget.]

1.2 The [Designer] shall use its [best/reasonable] endeavours to ensure that the [Website/App/Podcast] is completed to a high standard and is fully operational in accordance with [specify standard/organisation].

1.3 The [Designer] agrees and undertakes that where the work is delayed due to the [Designer] and/or force majeure that an additional fee shall not be charged. That the [Designer] shall only be entitled to the agreed fee of [number/currency].

1.4 That where additional alterations, changes and/or developments are added which were not part of the original agreed quotation and/or budget at the request of the [Company]. That the [Designer] shall be entitled to charge additional fees and costs provided that these are agreed in advance prior to the commencement of the relevant work.

C.347

The [Company] shall not without the prior written approval of [Name] inform any person and/or third party of the development and production of the content of [Website/App/Platform/Podcast] and/or the details relating to the contributors, presenters, launch date, budget and/or any other information, data and/or material supplied by [Name]. The [Company] shall ensure that all personnel are aware of the condition that no person is entitled to supply and/or distribute any information, data and/or material regarding the project to third parties, any competitor and/or the media and/or newspapers.

C.348

The [Company] shall not be responsible for ensuring that the [Website], the domain name and/or any content which is delivered to [Name] shall not infringe any copyright, trade marks, and/or any other intellectual property rights, computer software rights and/or whether the [Website] exposes [Name] to the threat of criminal and/or civil proceedings and/or complaint by the public to any regulatory organisation and/or is defamatory of any person and/or in breach any legislation, laws, regulations, codes of practices, industry guidelines, trade standards, product liability and/or otherwise which apply to and/or regulate the internet and websites, products, services, premium phone services, downloads and/or supply of images, text, music, films, sponsorship, endorsements, promotions, advertising, and/or competitions which may apply now and/or which may come into existence in the future. All such matters shall be the responsibility and at the liability of [Name] and the [Company] shall not be held liable for any reason except that caused by negligence relating to personal injury and/or death directly caused by the [Company] up until [date].

C.349

The [Company] agrees and undertakes that:

1.1 it will only use and/or employ suitably qualified personnel to create, design, develop and deliver the [Website/App/Podcast] for [Name].

1.2 all the technical content of the [Website/App/Podcast] shall comply with the latest technology so that it able to fulfil all the requirements specified in the [Website/App/Podcast] Summary] in Appendix A.

1.3 all the software which is to be used is the latest current version and that in the opinion of the [Company] is the best available on the market for the allocated budget.

1.4 all the required source codes and any other data, master copies, computer software and/or information and/or other material will be provided at no additional cost so that the [Website/App/Podcast] can easily be updated and amended by [Name] and/or any other third party.

C.350

The [Company] agrees that it shall not enter into any agreement, arrangement and/or partnership and/or permit the use of the [Website/App/Podcast] advertising and/or other promotions by any third party connected and/or associated with [specify theme/subject] from [date to [date].

C.351

The [Company] shall have the right and authority to remove, delete and/or pass to any international enforcement agency, police and/or regulatory and/or compliance body any data, images, text, sound recordings, film, video, passwords, codes and/or content of any accounts which in its opinion show that the person who opened the account and/or who is using it poses a risk to children under [age] years and/or is likely to have committed a criminal offence in any part of the [world/country].

C.352

The [Company] reserves the right to delete any material from this [Website/Platform] which is posted by any person and/or company at any time. No notice shall be required and no reason shall need to be provided. The total limit of the liability of the [Company] to any such person and/or company shall be [number/currency].

C.353

[Name] agrees and undertakes to comply with the following conditions regarding the articles and/or other material for the [Blog] for the [Company];

1.1 All articles submitted shall be no longer than [number] words.

1.2 All material shall be the original work of [Name] and not copied and/or adapted from any other source.

1.3 Where any material relating to a third party is relied upon as the main source of any information and/or data and/or text. Then the third party source must be acknowledged whether the material is still in copyright or not.

1.4 No material shall be submitted by [Name] which likely to result in civil and/or criminal proceedings against the [Company] and/or a complaint to a regulatory organisation and/or may give rise to an allegation of defamation.

1.5 That no misleading information and/or material shall be deliberately included and/or any product and/or service and/or person and/or other third party promoted which [Name] has been paid to advertise, promote and/or endorse and for which [Name] has received some other benefit in kind.

C.354

The [Contributor] to the [Podcast/Videos] agrees and undertakes that they shall:

1.1 follow the directions and scripts provided by [Name].

1.2 provide their services to the best of their skill and ability.

1.3 not wear any product, display any trade mark, insignia and/or other logo and/or make any gesture and/or mention any political organisation and/or promote any activist campaign. That where [Name] requires the [Contributor] to remove any jewellery they agree to do so and/or replace any item of clothing with a non-branded product.

1.4 at all times act in a professional manner and shall not cause offence and/or make defamatory allegations and/or mock any person and/or complain about any organisation and/or government policy and/or other matter which is not the subject of the agreed scripts provided by [Name].

C.355

All images and/or messages supplied and/or posted to this [Website/ Platform] must comply with the stated policy of the [Company] set out in Document A. You are advised to read this document carefully and you will be obliged to agree to the terms in order to send and/or post material. The [Company] reserves the right to delete any messages and/images which it deems do not adhere to the policy with immediate effect and may also close your account. You will not receive any notification from the [Company] if such a decision is taken and your account will be blocked. You will not be permitted to open another account under another name. The [Company] shall not enter into any communication with you regarding the matter and the decision of the [Company] is final. There is no right of appeal.

Merchandising and Distribution

C.356

The [Supplier] accepts and agrees that it shall be responsible for ensuring that the [Products] comply with all relevant statutes, laws, regulations, guidelines, directives, health and safety requirements, tests, assessments, standards, practices, codes and/or any other matter in the [Territory/country/

world] at any time in which the [Products] are delivered to the [Distributor] and/or sold. If at any time the [Supplier] becomes aware of any matter which affects the [Products] which may pose a risk and/or which have not complied with as required then the [Supplier] shall immediately notify the [Distributor] of the situation.

C.357

The [Supplier] agrees and undertakes that the [Products] shall comply and continue to comply with all the provisions relating to design, content and material, manufacture, supply, use, and packaging of any unit of the [Products] relating to any legislation, regulation, product liability, trade practices and/or guidelines issued by any regulatory organisation and/or shall comply with all necessary tests, assessments, labels and/or other requirements which may be in force in [country] at the time of production and prior to delivery to the [Distributor].

C.358

The [Distributor] agrees that no other product and/or service, advertisement, banner, logo, trade mark, domain name, slogan, music, text, image, review, criticism, praise or comparison shall be displayed or featured in any circumstance on the [Website/App/Platform] which is in direct competition with and is a similar type of product and/or service to those supplied under this agreement by [Name].

C.359

That the [Product/Service] provided by the [Company] will be of first class technical quality and comply with the standards, safety tests, codes of practice and guidelines of [specify organisation as follows: [list title of documents].

C.360

The [Distributor] shall be obliged to arrange its own insurance cover to protect itself against any claims, fines, actions, losses, damages, legal costs and/or other consequences including the temporary closure and/or the end of trading of the [Distributor] that may arise directly and/or indirectly as a result of the failure of the [Company] to have ensured that the [Products/Services] adhere to any minimum standards, tests, criteria, quality control, health and safety and/or other requirements in any country at any time.

C.361

The parties agree they must both actively assess whether they and/or any third party they may engage as a manufacturer, supplier, distributor and/or agent have and/or will comply with any health and safety legislation, labelling, ingredient and warning notices and/or any other tests, assessments, analysis of risks to children and/or any other legal requirement and/or with any standards and compliance policies and mandatory requirements issued by the following organisations: [specify organisation and documents].

C.362

That the [Licensee] shall ensure that each [Product] shall conform in all respects to the quality, design, packaging and materials of the sample submitted to and approved by the [Licensor]. That the workmanship or materials shall not be defective and/or of a different standard and/or quality and/or in any way different in shape, size, format and/or content.

C.363

The [Licensor] agrees to attend such meetings, exhibitions and promotional events as may reasonably be required by the [Company] subject to sufficient prior notice at the [Company's] cost and expense.

C.364

In the event that the [Products] manufactured and distributed by the [Distributor] do not comply with all the product liability, health, safety, packaging and any other legislation, regulations, directives, codes, guidelines, policies and/or industry practices which may exist at the date of this agreement and/or which may come into effect thereafter. Then the [Distributor] shall be solely liable for any losses, damages, fines, expenses, costs and charges that may be incurred as a result of a product recall, replacement and/or refunds in respect of the {Products] and/or any other related matter. The [Licensor] shall not be liable for any such sums.

C.365

That the [Distributor] shall ensure that the [Product/Service/Work] shall comply with the description and purpose set out in the attached Schedule A and the sample prototype approved by the [Licensor]. The [Distributor] shall not be entitled to alter, add to, delete from and/or amend the quality, design, content, colours, packaging and materials approved by the [Licensor] without the prior written consent of the [Licensor].

C.366

The [Distributor] agrees and undertakes that the [Product/Service/Work] shall comply with all the product liability, health, safety, packaging and any other legislation, regulations, directives, codes, guidelines, policies and/or industry practices which may exist at the date of this agreement or which may come into effect thereafter [during the Licence Period/at any time].

C.367

That the [Distributor] shall ensure that testing takes place of the prototype and/or sample to ensure that it is not defective, is fit for the purpose and does not contain any materials which are toxic or unsuitable for use by [specify group/age category]. That there shall be regular reviews of the quality and content of the [Product] to ensure that the standard has not fallen and that no new substances and/or other material has been added. The results of all such tests and reviews shall be made available on request to the [Licensor] at the [Distributor's] cost.

C.368

Where after a product is available to the public it is subsequently discovered that the content is not as represented on the label and packaging. Then the [Supplier] agrees that it shall be responsible for all the costs that the [Distributor] may incur in recalling all products sold to the public including online and print advertisements, posters and other marketing, laboratory tests and analysis and other costs up to a maximum [f [number/currency]. The [Distributor] shall be responsible for its own administrative and legal costs and/or the services of any expert consultants which it may engage.

C.369

The [Manufacturer] does not accept any responsibility for compliance with any codes, guidelines, policies and/or legal requirements in any part of the world relating to the [Products]. The [Products] have been made to the specification, design and content requested by the [Company]. The [Company] agrees that it shall be solely liable to ensure that the [Products] are safe, of suitable quality for their intended use and do not pose a danger to the public.

Publishing

C.370

The [Agent] agrees that the artistic and editorial control of the [Book/Audio File/Merchandising] shall be at the sole discretion and decision of the [Author] and/or [Publisher].

C.371

The [Ghostwriter] agrees to provide regular reports to the [Company] and to make available all material in any format and/or medium which he/she has obtained, recorded and/or has access to so that copies can be made and/or inspected.

C.372

The [Distributor] agrees and undertakes to endeavour to ensure that:

1.1 all third parties and/or any sub-licensees shall comply with the contractual obligations to the [Author] set out in this agreement and that any such obligations are incorporated in their contracts.

1.2 the [Author] shall have a right of inspection and auditing of accounts of all third parties and/or sub-licensees who are required to pay any sums to the [Distributor].

1.3 no agreement with a third party and/or any sub-licence shall extend beyond [date].

1.4 no third party and/or any sub-licensee shall acquire any copyright, title, character, format, plot, packaging, domain name and/or any other intellectual property rights and/or interest in the [Work] and/or any part and/or in any adaptation, translation, merchandising and/or any option and/or right to exploit the [Work] in any format in any medium by any means without the prior approval and consent of the [Author] on each occasion.

C.373

The [Author] agrees that the cover, layout, typography and index shall be required to adhere to the [Publishers] standard policies which may be in existence at any time. That the final decision shall be with the [Publisher] although the [Author] shall be consulted.

C.374

The [Author] agrees that where any content in the [Work] and in any associated marketing, promotions and appearances he/she makes recommendations and/or provides advice to the public. That the [Author] shall ensure that the public is made aware in that the [Author] is not a qualified and expert [subject/profession] and that guidance should be sought from a professional [specify status] before they follow any proposals.

C.375

The [Publisher] agrees that the [Author] shall not be obliged to register either themselves and/or the [Work] with the following trade organisations and/or collecting societies and that the [Author] and the [Work] may be listed as excluded: [list organisations].

C.376

The [Publisher] agrees that the [Author] shall not be obliged to use the house style of the [Publisher] for the [Work] and that the cover, font, layout, index and content shall be entirely at the [Authors'] choice and discretion.

C.377

1.1 The [Author] agrees and undertakes that all his/her work shall be original except where the resource is stated and referenced in the [Manuscript/Work].

1.2 That where the [Author] records and/or films a third party in any interviews. That all such material shall be made available to the [Publisher] at no additional cost on loan if there are any legal problems and/or complaints from any such person regarding the content of the [Manuscript/Work] which is reproduced in the final edited book.

C.378
The [Publisher] agrees and undertakes that where it is necessary to engage the services of a third party to create, develop and produce any drawings, illustrations, images, infographics, maps and/or other formats for use in conjunction with the [Manuscript/Work] for the final edited book. That the [Publisher] shall ensure that all copyright and/or any other trade mark and/or intellectual property rights are held by the [Publisher/Author/both the Publisher and the Author]. That the [Publisher] shall not engage the services of any third party who will not agree to these terms.

C.379
The [Author/Illustrator] agree and undertake to:

1.1 deliver the [Work/Manuscript] in the following language [specify language] and format: [specify format] in accordance with the brief synopsis in appendix A.

1.2 that none of the [Work/Manuscript] shall contain any contribution and/or material from a third party.

1.3 that the [Work/Manuscript] shall be of such a standard and quality that it is suitable for publication in: [specify format] for the [adult/children's/other] market.

1.4 that the [Work/Manuscript] shall have been developed and produced as a result of the skill and efforts of the [Author/Illustrator] and not be derived and/or adapted from unpublished and/or published works of a third party.

Services

C.380
That the [Artiste] agrees to keep the [Agent] informed of his/her mobile and home telephone number, email, home address, business and work schedule and holidays at all reasonable times during the Term of this Agreement.

C.381

The [Artiste] agrees that to the best of his/her knowledge and belief that he/she is not now nor has at any time been subject to and/or suffered from any injury or illness which would prevent him/her from providing his/her services. The [Artiste] will at all times do all that is reasonably necessary to attain and maintain a good state of health, physical fitness and appearance as will enable him/her to fully fulfil the terms of this contract.

C.382

The [Actor] confirms that he/she is a full current member of [specify union/organisation] and will continue to be so until [date].

C.383

All information, advice and material provided by the [Consultant] to the [Company] shall to the best of his/her knowledge and belief be true and accurate and based on factual evidence unless otherwise stated.

C.384

The [Consultant] is a professional [specify status] and a member of the following organisations and/or regulatory bodies: [list]. The [Consultant's] qualifications are set out in appendix A] and he/she is an expert in the field of: [specify subject].

C.385

The [Researcher] agrees to observe all directions, policies, guidelines and safety and security requirements in force at any location at which he/she is required to work by the [Company] and shall adhere to any instructions to wear safety equipment and/or to follow procedures.

C.386

[Name] acknowledges and agrees that the licence issued to the [Company] by [specify authority] for the operation of their business as a [specify type of licence] at [address] has the following conditions attached: [specify conditions/set out in appendix A]. [Name] agrees and undertakes not to breach these conditions in the production of the [Series/Podcasts] and/or to promote and/or market the [Series/Podcasts] in any way which would damage the reputation of the [Company] and/or be detrimental to their business.

C.387

The [Consultant] shall provide an independent assessment and report on [subject matter] to the [Company] by [date] in [format]. The scope of the report shall cover the following matters: [specify subject area]. The [Consultant] shall not cover the following matters: [specify excluded matters].

Where the [Consultant] makes any reference to any legislation, guidelines, codes, health and safety assessments, test and other material and/or data. The reference must be quoted in full and the source itemised. This report is confidential and shall not be released to any third party for any reason.

C.388

The [Services/Products] to be provided by the [Supplier] must adhere to the following conditions:

1.1 comply with the original order form which was agreed between the parties.

1.2 there is no right to make a substitution and/or alteration without consent.

1.3 There must be no suspension and/or delay and/or interruptions and the agreed schedule must be completed in accordance with the timescale.

Sponsorship

C.389

The [Licensee] agrees that no sponsorship, logo, image, music, text, product, service, person and/or other third party shall be used to endorse, appear in and/or be used in any way in conjunction with the [Series] and/ or the soundtrack without the prior written approval of the [Licensor] which shall not be unreasonably withheld or delayed.

C.390

The [Sponsor] agrees to ensure that the size, shape, layout, format and use of the [Sponsor's Logo] and the [Sponsor's Product] will not infringe any legislation, laws, protocols, guidelines, codes of practice and/or regulations and/or otherwise currently in existence in [country] including any issued by the regulatory authority known as: [specify organisation] and the sports organisation: [specify organisation].

C.391

The [Association] shall ensure that the use of the [Promotional Logo] and the [Sponsor's Logo] will not infringe any sponsorship, advertising and/or promotional standards, practices and policies currently in existence with regard to the [specify governing bodies and government agencies] in [country/Territory].

C.392

The [Company] agrees to ensure that the broadcast and/or transmission of the [Sponsor's] name, trade mark, logo, images, [products/services], music and premium rate number telephone and text message service will not infringe any sponsorship, competition, advertising and/or product placement and/or any other policies and guidelines issued by [Ofcom/other] and/or any legislation and/or licence which applies to the [Company] whether relating to size, colour, words, position and/or general nature.

C.393

The [Sponsor] agrees to be bound by the requirements of the [Company] in respect of any sponsorship, promotion and/or advertising standards, practices, codes, directives, statutes and/or otherwise which apply to the [Film/Series] and/or the exploitation of the any rights relating to it.

C.394

The [Promoter] will ensure that all material produced under this agreement will comply with any sponsorship, advertising, product placement, product safety standards and rules, legislation, regulations, directives and/or any guidelines currently in existence now and/or created during the Term of this Agreement including: [European Union/ Ofcom/Oftel/ Advertising Standards Authority/Trading Standards/other organisation/government body].

C.395

The [Agent] confirms that the [Material] supplied to the [Company]:

1.1 complies with all the policies, guidelines and requirements of any regulatory organisation which governs the transmission of advertisements, promotions and/or sponsorship arrangements over the radio and/or television in [country].

1.2 does not infringe the copyright, trade marks and/or any other intellectual property rights of any third party.

1.3 will not give rise to any claim and/or allegation by a third party and/or any civil and/or criminal proceedings. That there is no defamatory content and that all the content of the [Material] has been cleared and paid for by the [Agent].

1.4 That the [Material] does not contain any subliminal content and/or any gesture, image, text and/or sound recording which could be construed as offensive, derogatory, political and/or any type of incitement, threat and/or misleading and/or contrary to any legislation in [country].

C.396

1.1 The [Sportsperson] confirms that he/she is a bona fide and current member of the following sports organisations: [list organisations/ reference].

1.2 That those organisations in 1.1 are governed by the policies and guidelines of the following governing authorities: [list governing organisations].

C.397

The [Sportsperson] agrees to conduct himself/herself in a fit proper and professional manner at all times during the Term of the Agreement at sports events, public appearances, filmed and recorded interviews for television, radio, podcasts and the internet.

C.398

The [Sponsor] acknowledges that the sponsorship of the [Programme/Series] does not give the [Sponsor] the right to use the [Company's] name, trade mark, logo, slogan, the title of the programme and/or series and/or the names of the presenter and/or performers and/any other material in any promotion, advertising, marketing, product, service and/or otherwise.

C.399

The [Sponsor] agrees that the [Radio Station] shall be entitled at its sole discretion to:

1.1 replace the [Presenter] with a person of [similar quality/reputation/ratings].

1.2 change the content at any time.

1.3 alter the title of the programme.

1.4 enter into a sponsorship and/or product promotion arrangement with another third party for the same programme.

C.400

The [Radio Station] confirms that the [Presenter] is contractually bound to the [Radio Station] to be the on-air host of the [Series] for the duration of this Agreement until [date].

C.401

The [Sponsor] undertakes that the specific products or services being promoted under this agreement together with all other products and services owned or controlled by the [Sponsor] which the public would reasonably associate with the [Sponsor's] [trade mark, logo, images, product, service, music, slogans, ringtones, and premium rate number telephone and text line] shall be safe and fit for their intended use and comply with all statutes, regulations, directives, laws and standards and codes in force in [country].

C.402

The [Company] agrees and undertakes to ensure that all third parties involved with the [Event] and any sub-licensees shall comply with the contractual obligations to the [Sponsor] set out in clauses [–] of this agreement and that such clauses are incorporated as a condition in their letters of engagement and/or other documents.

C.403

The [Company] agrees and undertakes that:

1.1   no sub-licence shall extend beyond [date].

1.2   no sub-licensee shall be assigned any rights in respect of the [Event] and/or any material and/or rights owned and/or controlled by the [Sponsor].

1.3   that no person who enters the [Event], any business partner, sub-licensee, advertising agent, publicity agency and/or any other third party shall acquire any ownership of the title of the [Event], the domain name for the website and/or any other copyright, intellectual property rights and/or any other rights in the [Event].

1.4   That no other person, business, licensee, distributor, product, advertisement, banner, logo, trade mark, domain name, slogan, music, text, image, film, photograph or otherwise shall be displayed or featured on the website, on any merchandising material, in any film, on any participant, on any marketing and publicity and/or other material of any nature which appears to give the impression and/or is credited as the [primary/main] sponsor, promoter and/or source of funding for the [Event].

1.5   That no products and/or services shall be used at the [Event] which are not supplied by the [Sponsor] in the following categories: [specify and list].

C.404

The [Sponsor] agrees that the all health and safety compliance, insurance, fire regulations, police, stewards, sanitation, artistic and editorial control of the [Event], the programme, the schedule, the layout and location, access routes, parking, facilities, marketing, publicity, and merchandising shall be at the sole discretion and cost of the [Company]. There shall be no obligation to consult with and/or seek the prior approval of the [Sponsor] for any changes, amendments and/or delays that may be necessary.

C.405

Where in the sole opinion of the [Company] the [Sponsor] and/or it business and/or its presence at the [Event] pose such a threat due to recent adverse publicity associated with them. The [Company] shall be entitled to take the view and reach the conclusion that all reference to the [Sponsor] and/or its' business and/or its involvement in the [Event] may be deleted without notice. Provided that the [Company] agrees to refund to the [Sponsor] [number] per cent of the sums paid by the [Sponsor] to date. The [Sponsor] agrees in such instance that such action shall be accepted by the [Sponsor] and that all rights to any legal claim and/or action are waived.

C.406

The [Sponsor] agrees and accepts that all staff, officers and other agents associated with the [Sponsor] at [location] from [date] to [date] must accept the instruction, orders and directions of [Name] and/or his /her nominated substitute at the [Festival]. This shall be the case whether or not it is contrary to the prior arrangements with the [Sponsor] in this agreement. Where despite a request the [Sponsor] and its staff, officers and agents fail to comply then [Name] [and/or the substituted person] may at his/her sole discretion use of the services of the security staff at the [location] to ensure compliance as a last resort and remove all such persons from the [location].

C.407

The [Sponsor] agrees and accepts that the [Company] may due to unforeseen circumstances and/or excessive crowds and/or lack of facilities and/or resources and/or any accident and/or other reason alter the duration of the booking for the [Sponsor] and/or the display of their signs and banners, and/or location of their tents and stalls. The [Sponsor] agrees to comply with all directions made by authorised employees of the [Company] and to make such changes as may be required at no additional cost to the [Company].

C.408

The [Company] agrees and undertakes that:

1.1   the [Sponsor] shall not be required to change the number, location and/or layout of its planned stalls, exhibitions and/or promotions at the [Event] unless required to do so as a result of some emergency, power failure, flood and/or some other reason due to force majeure which could not reasonably be foreseen.

1.2   the [Company] shall not enter into an agreement with another third party to sponsor the [Event] which is in the [specify industry] and/or sells [specify product/services].

1.3   that all third parties who may fund and/or sponsor the [Event] and/or enter into product placement and/ promotion arrangements with the [Company] shall be subject to the prior approval of the [Sponsor].

University, Charity and Educational

C.409

The [Company] recognises that the [Charter/Terms of Reference] of the [Institute/Charity] must be adhered to and its integrity, reputation and rights not derogated from and/or transferred to a third party. The [Company] agrees that no other company, person, product, service, advertisement, promotion, logo, trade mark, slogan, music, text, image, electronic and/or computer generated material, review, criticism and/or comparison shall be displayed, featured in and/or used in connection with the [Work/Project/Event] without the prior written consent of the [Institute/Charity].

C.410

The [Consultant/Company] agrees and undertakes to comply with all reasonable directions and instructions by senior personnel, codes of practice and/or quality control guidelines, management procedures and/or policies which the [Institute/Charity] may require to be adhered to during the Term of this Agreement.

C.411

The [Company] shall have the right to terminate this agreement at any time. Where the [Company] fails to comply with the terms and conditions of the attached [Handbook/Code of Practice/Professional Standards] when carrying out the terms of this agreement. Then the [Institute/Charity] shall have the right to terminate the agreement without providing any notice and/or the opportunity to remedy the situation. The [Institute/Charity] shall not be responsible for any losses, damages, costs and/or expenses that may arise as a result of the termination provided that the [Company] is paid up to the date of termination.

C.412

The [Researcher] acknowledges and agrees that the [Institute/Charity] and the [Researcher] shall be obliged to comply with all the protocols, regulations, codes and guidelines laid down by [specify organisation] in the [Project] including [specify and list subjects]. The [Researcher] agrees to notify the [Institute/Charity] in the event that there is any proposal not to follow these procedures in any part of the [Project]. In such event the [Institute/Charity] shall have the right to either insist that the procedures be followed and/or to agree that they be waived. The [Researcher] agrees that the decision shall be at the sole discretion of the [Institute/Charity] and that any such decision shall be final.

C.413

The [Institute/Charity] may from time to time issue new policies and guidelines for [specify subject] which shall be posted and displayed on its website [reference] under [section]. There shall be no obligation on the [Institute/ Charity] to notify each person individually and you are expected to review the terms and conditions at the start of each new academic term. Where you have a problem with any of the policies and guidelines then please contact [Name] at [specify].

C.414
The [Charity/Institute] is:

1.1 registered with: [specify organisation] as [specify status] registration number: [–] as from [date].

1.2 subject to the governing law of [country/state].

1.3 subject to the policies, guidelines and codes of practice issued by the following organisations and regulatory authorities: [specify and list].

COMPUTER-GENERATED

General Business and Commercial

C.415
'Computer-Generated' in relation to a work shall mean that the work is generated by computer in circumstances such that there is no human author of the work.

C.416
'Computer-Generated' in relation to a design means that the design is generated by computer in circumstances such that there is no human designer.

C.417
All work and designs generated by computer under this agreement shall belong to the [Distributor] and not the [Company] which owns and/or controls the computer. The [Company] agrees and undertakes to sign any document and assign any rights in the work and designs which it does or will hold under this agreement to the [Distributor] at the [Distributor's] cost.

C.418
Where any material is created, developed, designed and/or produced by [Name] in relation to this [Project] whether it is used in the final version or not including but not limited to the websites, links, banners, images, text,

titles, apps, blogs, films, videos, podcasts, sound recordings, music, lyrics, photographs, electronic material, mobile telephones and other telecommunications, ringtones, software programmes and hardware, supply and use of data, messaging, and/or any other means in any format at any time. [Name] agrees and undertakes that the [Consortium] shall hold [number] per cent of any interest and/or rights of any nature without limitation. This shall not apply to anything owned and/or controlled by [Name] prior to [date].

CONFIDENTIALITY

Film, Television and Video

C.419

Each party undertakes to keep confidential and not disclose to any third party confidential information supplied by the other under this agreement. Except both parties agree in writing that the information and/or data and/or material should be shared with a third party and/or otherwise released in order to increase sales, improve marketing and/or to permit an arrangement to reached for the distribution of the [DVDs/Units/Products].

C.420

Both parties agree and undertake that they shall not and shall ensure that their employees, agents and associated companies, agents and/or distributors shall not, disclose and/or communicate to any third party any information, data, material and/or documents relating to the other party which are not available to the public and/or are not otherwise released to an entity where the public may have access and which have been acquired during the course of this agreement in circumstances which inferred and/or were marked and/or were stated at the time to be confidential.

C.421

The [written/verbal] consent of both parties shall be required in the event that a statement, press and/or social media release, conference, video, podcast, sound recording and/or other material is to be distributed to the media and/or public which is not consistent with and/or contradicts the agreed marketing plan and/or which would in any way have a negative impact and/or or detrimental effect on the businesses of either party.

C.422

The [Assignor] and the [Assignee] shall not disclose, convey, distribute and/or communicate to any third party any confidential information of the other party at any time. This term shall not apply to professional legal, financial, tax and accounting advisors and/or the police and/or any other regulatory body for the purpose of carrying out any obligation which is a legal requirement and/or to commence civil and/or criminal proceedings. All publicity, advertising, promotional and social media material as well as press releases shall be agreed between the parties in each case. The production details of the [DVD/Discs/Units], the work and private life and performance of the [Artiste] and the release date are all confidential.

C.423

The parties agree to keep all documents, data and information confidential except for the purpose of informing their agents, legal and other professional advisors and/or government and/or compliance organisations and/or authorities as may be legally required. Neither party shall communicate and/or distribute any material on social media and/or in any newspaper, magazine and/or to any other third party without the prior approval and consent of the other party in each case.

C.424

Prior to the development, production and exploitation of the [Project] in the [DVD/Film/Video] market in [country]. It is agreed by [Name] who appears as the main performer that he/she shall not inform, discuss and/or post on any website, platform, blog and/or podcast any part of the detailed plans in respect of the [Project] at any time before [date] except the following agreed details [specify agreed information set out in appendix A].

C.425

The [Assignor] and the [Company] shall not disclose to any third party except professional legal advisors, accountants or companies or persons involved in the [Pilot] any confidential information regarding [specify topics] acquired before and/or during the course of this agreement except strictly on a need to know basis and an understanding that it is confidential and must remain so.

C.426

The [Licensor] and the [Licensee] agree that any information, data and/or documents which either may disclose to the other in circumstances in which it is made clear that it is confidential shall not be disclosed to any third party without prior authority. This term shall not apply to the professional advisors of either party who provide financial, legal corporate and insurance advice. Where one or both parties releases and/or authorises the disclosure of all and/or part of their own confidential information, data and/or documents to the media and/or any other third party so that they are no longer confidential. Then this clause shall no longer apply to such material. This clause shall no longer apply to either party after [date/time].

C.427

Any script, pilot, film, budget, document, email and/or other communication circulated by the [Company] relating to its programmes, schedules, content and exploitation of any material on Channel [specify name] prior to broadcast and/or transmission and/or release to the press, media and/or public is to be treated as confidential and is not to be supplied, reproduced and/or distributed by any person without the prior consent of the [Chief Executive] of the [Company] except to legal advisors, personal agents and managers and/or such third parties directly involved in the completion of any necessary arrangements who may be informed of a limited amount of information to fulfil their task.

C.428

The [Company] will consider and review any programme idea submitted by a member of the public by the following procedure [specify method of application/assessment/response]. However no assurance can be provided that any matter is confidential, and/or will not be supplied to third parties. Any submission is entirely at your own risk. The [Company] may already be working and/or have drawn up a list of ideas and projects which may be similar and/or exactly the same prior to receipt of your idea. There is no commitment and/or agreement by the [Company] to reach an agreement for the use and/or exploitation of any idea submitted.

C.429

No information, idea, project, pilot, game and/or merchandising, developed, created and/or proposed by any employee, researcher, consultant, agent and/or any other third party will be considered and/or deemed confidential by the [Company]. There shall be no restriction and/or prohibition which prevents by the [Company] from creating, developing and exploiting a television and/or radio programme, podcast and/or feature film and/or any other project based on the same generic topic and/or theme and/or notable person

C.430

The parties agree that the attached synopsis supplied by the [Company] in schedule A is confidential and shall remain so until [date]. Thereafter the confidentiality restriction shall not apply.

General Business and Commercial

C.431

The [Executive] shall not divulge nor communicate to any person (other than those who need to know and/or with proper authority) any of the business plans, trade secrets and/or other confidential information relating to the [Company] which he/she may have received and/or obtained while in the service of the [Company]. This restriction shall continue to apply after the termination of his/her engagement for a period of [specify duration] but shall cease to apply to information and/or knowledge which may come into the public domain otherwise than through the default of the [Executive] and/or which has been received by the [Executive] from a third party not entitled to disclose the material.

C.432

The [Executive] is not permitted to distribute and/or communicate and/or post any information, data, documents, statements, letters and/or articles purporting to represent the opinion and/or strategy of the [Company] unless prior authorisation and consent is obtained from the [Chief Executive] of the [Company]

C.433

The [Executive] must not contact and/or communicate with any member of the press and/or media and/or anyone so connected on behalf of the [Company] without the prior [verbal/written] consent of [position/name].

C.434

When the [Executive] ceases to be employed by the [Company] for any reason then the [Executive] shall only be obliged to keep confidential information which was not already and/or does not become placed in the public domain by the [Company], by its reports, marketing and/or other employees. Any restriction as to the use of confidential information shall only apply for [three] years. It is then presumed to be out of date and no longer confidential.

C.435

The [Employee] agrees not to disclose at any time in the future any ingredients, formula, content, recipe, data, manufacturing processes and/ or reproduction methods and/or any other trade secrets and/or confidential information relating to the [Products] which are not on the label, packaging and/or available to distributors and/or the public by the [Company].

C.436

The [Company] agrees that there are no confidentiality restrictions imposed on [Name] by virtue of this agreement. That [Name] shall not be prohibited from sharing and/or distributing any information, data and/or documents which relates to the [Company] and/or its business at any time.

C.437

[Name] accepts and agrees that the [Company] may reproduce and distribute copies of the agreement with [Name] to any third party and that the agreement and/or his/her fee and expenses is not confidential and/or private.

C.438

The [Company] agrees that the [Employee] will be notified in each case if any information, data, report, research, material and/or other matter is confidential to the [Company]. Further the [Company] agrees to also provide the [Employee] with a notified expiry date where it is no longer confidential and the [Employee] will be released from the obligation.

C.439

The [Employee] agrees that where he/she is informed that any material to which the [Company] has access to and/or which is supplied by a third party is confidential and/or under an embargo and/or likely to prejudice civil and/or criminal proceedings and/or the subject of a legal action. Then the [Employee] agrees and undertakes not to copy, film, record, supply, reproduce and/or distribute any such material to any person including their immediate family members and/or to communicate the contents to any third party.

C.440

No reference is to be made to the terms of this agreement by either party in any media at any time without the prior written consent of the other party in each case.

C.441

Each party undertakes to keep private and confidential and not disclose and/or communicate and/or supply to any third party any data, reports, background information and/or otherwise supplied by the other during the negotiation of and/or conclusion of this agreement.

C.442

Both parties to this agreement agree that they shall maintain the following matters in the utmost secrecy and confidence as follows:

1.1 the terms of this agreement.

1.2 all verbal communications, representations and information of any nature made by the parties and/or their advisors pursuant to the conclusion and fulfilment of this agreement.

1.3 all documents, data, research reports, accounts, financial records, projections, budgets, recordings, records, films, videos, software, formula, processes, inventions, information and/or any other material and/or facts of any nature in any media which were supplied and/or conveyed prior to and/or pursuant to this agreement.

1.4 further that all such matters shall be restricted to the knowledge of [the Board of Directors/other] of either party, and any statutory and/or regulatory body which may have the right to request any details and/or any professional advisers. In such cases all persons shall be required to abide by a request of confidentiality.

1.5 no further disclosures shall be made without the prior written consent of both parties.

1.6 this clause shall survive the termination and/or expiry of this agreement and shall continue until matters are in public domain or until such time as the parties mutually agree to release each other from the undertaking.

C.443

1.1 The [Company] and [specify party] shall not disclose to any third party any confidential business and/or future plans and/or marketing strategies and/or future products and/or future services of the other party at any time acquired during the existence of this agreement.

1.2 No reference is to be made to the terms of this agreement by either party in any advertising, marketing and/or corporate promotional events and/or documents and/or any other material of any nature before [date] without the prior consent of the other party.

1.3 In the event that both parties agree to hold a press and/or media conference and/or issue a statement then the following material shall be included: [specify].

1.4 It is accepted that both parties may need to release material in the strictest confidence to advisors and/or consultants who are providing professional advice and guidance to the [Company].

C.444

The [Licensor] and the [Licensee] shall not disclose to any third party (except professional legal advisors, consultants and accountants) any confidential information, business and/or future plans of the other party at any time which is acquired pursuant to this agreement. Both parties agree that no reference is to be made to the terms, or discussions relating to this agreement in any advertising, promotional, publicity and/or other material in any media for distribution to the general public and/or any media companies without the prior written approval of the [Managing Director] of the other party.

C.445

I acknowledge receipt of [identify document] supplied to me by [Name] and confirm that the sole purpose of being granted access is [specify use/ permission].

C.446

I confirm that I shall not make nor authorise nor permit any copies of the [Work] to be made at any time for any purpose whilst it is in my possession. I shall keep the [Work] in a safe and secure manner and take all reasonable steps to ensure that no unauthorised party gains access to the [Work].

C.447

I shall keep the existence and content of the [Work] strictly confidential and will only disclose the existence and content of the [Work] to [specify third parties]. In the event that the existence and contents of the [Work] are disclosed for some unexpected reason to other senior executives of the [Company] then I shall advise [Name] immediately and I shall ensure that any such persons are made fully aware of this agreement and undertake to maintain strict confidentiality.

C.448

I will immediately return the [Work] to [Name] upon request and in any event shall deliver it in a safe and secure manner no later than [date]. I shall confirm in writing that no further copies or reproductions of any part of the [Work] are in my possession or control and that none were made or supplied to other persons.

C.449

1.1   The [Company] agrees to release copies of the following documents to [Name] of [firm/company] who act as [specify role] for the [Consortium] for the purpose of due diligence on the sole basis that all the content is confidential and private to the [Company]: [specify and list documents by title].

1.2   The [Consortium] agrees and undertakes not to release, reproduce, distribute and/or supply copies of any part of the documents in 1.1 in any medium and/or form at any time to any person and/or third party except [specify authorised persons].

1.3   The [Consortium] agrees that where for any reason they are at a later date shown to be in breach of 1.2 that the [Company] shall be entitled to financial compensation of [number/currency] regardless of whether any loss and/or damage can be shown to have been suffered.

C.450

No material shall be deemed to be confidential where it is already available on the [Company] website, app, social media, in any public corporate documents, marketing material and/or that of any parent and/or associated business and/or it is available upon request and supplied to any member of the public and/or has been reproduced in a report and/or statement by the [Company] and/or a third party in any part of the world.

Internet, Websites and Apps

C.451

You are permitted access to information, reports and/or data on this [Website/App/Platform] by using your personal [identity code/password] on the condition that you agree that you are bound by the terms and conditions of access, and will not attempt to interfere with, reproduce, supply, distribute and/or otherwise use any such material without the prior written consent of the [Company] which controls this [Website/App/Platform]. No content is confidential but that does not mean that you are entitled to exploit any material and/or rights without authority and consent. There is no licence and/or authority provided to you for any reason in any manner to exploit any material and/or rights.

C.452

You will be denied access to any material, data and/or information which is deemed confidential on this [Platform] by the [Company] unless you have signed a confidentiality document and been allocated a password and user name.

C.453

The [Contributor] agrees and undertakes not to disclose, supply, reproduce, communicate and/or distribute (except to his/her own professional legal advisors, agent and/or accountant) any discussions, representations, emails, documents, data, reports, recordings, films, images, records, business plans, marketing strategies, databases, computer software, inventions, technology and/or any material and/or facts and/or products and/or services of any nature in any media which is supplied in circumstances where it is made clear by the [Company] and/or its directors, officers, consultants and/or professional advisors that it is confidential. Both parties agree that no reference is to be made to the terms of this agreement to any third party except where either party may be required to do so as a legal and/or compliance matter.

C.454

There shall be no requirement that either party is bound to treat as confidential and/or private any disclosure, plans, information and/or other material which is disclosed at any time during the conclusion of this agreement and/or thereafter by either party.

C.455

No information, comments, images, videos and/or other material which is supplied to this [App/Platform/Channel] can be treated as confidential except for your personal details and password which will not be disclosed to any third party except at the request of the police and/or under a court order. All other material which you submit and/or disclose on any blog, forum, chatroom and/or other section of this [App/Platform/Channel] is at your own risk and no assurance can be provided that it cannot be read by third parties who are not in your connected group.

C.456

Where the [Company] inadvertently releases confidential and/or private personal details and/or images, films, videos and/or comments due to theft, hacking, fraud, failure of the technological systems and/or for any other reason. Then you agree that the total liability of the [Company] to you shall be limited to [number/currency] in total.

C.457

Data, personal details, passwords and other information which is entered by you on this [Website/App] shall be treated as exclusive to your account provided that it is not later released by you to the public and/or found to be associated with an intention to commit and/or you have committed a criminal act using this [Website/App] and/or any of its facilities to arrange, commission and/or convey details to other third parties. In any such cases there shall be no duty of confidentiality and/or privacy and the [Company] may at its sole discretion supply all such material to the police and/or any other law enforcement agency in any part of the world.

C.458

The [Company] reserves the right to allow any law enforcement and/or government agency access to your account, password, data, information and other material if there are reasonable grounds to believe that you have acted in a fraudulent manner and/or committed a crime and/or posted material related to a crime and/or have actively misled the [Company] to your age and/or identity. If you wish to keep any material either private and/or confidential then do not use this [Platform/Channel]. All material and contributions can be accessed and viewed for free by the general public.

Merchandising and Distribution

C.459

The [Company] and the [Supplier] both agree and undertake that they shall be required to maintain secrecy and not to disclose any confidential information, methods, processes, ingredients, knowledge, documents, prices, plans, forecasts, tests, data, software and/or computer records and/or any other material which the [Company] and/or the [Supplier] have communicated and/or provided to the other as confidential. This obligation shall remain binding on both parties save in the event of written and prior authorisation of the other party.

C.460

The [Supplier] and the [Distributor/Agent] shall not disclose at any stage to any third party (except their respective professional legal advisors, accountants and banks) any confidential information, products, services, business forecasts, details of any contracts and/or licences, future promotions and marketing, financial data, safety reports and assessments, complaints and/or discussions with regulatory organisations and/or any other material of the other party made during the negotiation of this agreement and/or at any time thereafter. This clause does not apply to anything already in and/or subsequently released into the public domain by either party relating to their own material and/or an independent third party.

C.461

The [Purchaser/Distributor] will act in good faith at all times and shall only use the [specify and refer to as confidential information] for the purpose for which it is intended namely [specify authorised use] and for no other purpose. Nor will the [Purchaser/Distributor] under any circumstances seek to take commercial advantage over the [Supplier] by virtue of acquiring the confidential information. The [Supplier] agrees that this does not apply once the material and/or associated product is released by a third party and/or sold by the [Supplier] and/or made available to purchase by the public.

C.462

The [Purchaser/Distributor] will only disclose the confidential information to such employees, professional and financial advisors and/or consultants on a need to know basis. Every person permitted access shall be shown this letter of confidentiality and each person shall provide a written undertaking to be bound by the terms. A list of names of such persons shall be provided to the [Supplier] if so requested for any reason.

C.463

The [Purchaser/Distributor] agrees and undertakes that it shall to bound by the following conditions in respect of all the [material/Information/other] described in appendix A:

1.1 That the [Purchaser/Distributor] shall not to make any copies in any format and/or medium unless specifically authorised to do so under this agreement.

1.2 That the [material/information/other] described in appendix A shall be kept in a secure, safe and fire proof location at [address]. That it shall be returned to the [Company] by secure courier at the [Purchasers'/Distributors'] cost by [date] in the same condition that it was supplied.

1.4 That no title, intellectual property rights and/or any other rights of ownership of any nature are intended to be transferred to and/or vested in and/or acquired by the [Purchaser/Distributor] at this time. This is a temporary loan.

1.5 The [Purchaser/Distributor] shall not make lucrative offers, entice, poach and/or solicit employees, consultants, customers, suppliers and/or other third parties involved with the business of the [Company] to transfer their work and/or services from the [Company] to the [Purchaser/Distributor].

1.6 The [Purchaser/Distributor] shall indemnify the [Company] for any damages, losses, costs and expenses including loss of sales, damage to reputation and/or any other matter suffered by the [Company] and/or arising as a direct and/or indirect result of any breach and/or alleged breach and/or default by the [Purchaser/Distributor] of this agreement. This indemnity shall only relate to any claim made by the [Company] by [date]. The indemnity shall end on [date/time].

C.464

1.1 The [Manufacturer] agrees that all the work to be completed for the [Company] shall be treated by the [Manufacturer] and its employees and others engaged by them involved in the process of production, packaging and delivery of any products as confidential and private as far as possible.

1.2 That in event that any third party should contact the [Manufacturer] at any time requesting any information, data, documents, samples and/or any other material of any nature. That the [Manufacturer] shall refer any such request to [name] at the [Company] and also notify [name] to that effect.

1.3 That the [Manufacturer] shall ensure that all business plans, product proposals, samples, test results, final products, details of processes and any other material are held in a secure location and that where any material is held on a hard drive and/or in any other software that access is restricted.

C.465

Where in the course of developing and/or producing any product and/or method of packaging and/or manufacturing process the [Company] specifies the use of a system, method, mechanism, technique and/or other new advance which is not already carried out by the [Manufacturer] which

433

is innovative, original and new. Than the [Manufacturer] agrees that all rights including inventions, copyright, design rights and any other rights in any such creation, material and/or development shall belong entirely to the [Company] who shall be the sole owners and shall have the right to insist that it be kept confidential by the [Manufacturer].

C.466

The [Licensor] and the [Licensee] shall not disclose to any third party any confidential information, data, decisions and/or future business plans of the other party at any time acquired pursuant to the conclusion of and/or during the existence of this agreement. Where direct access is required to confidential information a separate confidentiality agreement for that purpose may be requested to be signed.

C.467

[Name] agrees and undertakes not to disclose any script, text, title, content, format, music, artiste and/or other production, contract and/or scheduling details and/or any other matter which relates to the [Series] and/or any associated licensing of rights, merchandising and/or any related sponsorship and/or product placement arrangements at any time before [date] without the prior written consent of the [Company]. Failure to adhere to this clause shall be a breach of this agreement and shall result in the removal of [Name] from the [Series] and the termination of this agreement.

C.468

Both parties shall maintain the following issues in the utmost secrecy and confidence:

1.1 The terms of this agreement.

1.2 All representations, data, material, documents, emails, text messages and recordings viewed, made and/or exchanged prior to and/or after this agreement relating to the products and/or services of the [Company] which are not yet on sale to the public and/or any proposed plans, marketing strategy and/or new developments. Disclosure shall only be made on the agreed basis of this agreement or with the prior approval of the other party.

C.469

The [Licensee] agrees that it and/or its agents and/or distributors shall not disclose and/or reproduce, supply, distribute and/or release to the public and/or the media any business plans, launch dates, financial data, contract details, management policies, audit reports, verbal representations made in private meetings and/or any other material and/or information which is made available by the [Licensor] under this agreement to the [Licensee] regardless of whether it is confidential. That where the [Licensee] and/or its agents and/

434

or distributors are considered by the [Licensor] to be in breach of this clause [–] that they shall be provided with the opportunity to refute the allegations and resolve the matter. Where the [Licensees'] failure to adhere to this clause is not resolved and has resulted in a financial loss and/or damage to the reputation of the [Licensor]. The [Licensor] shall have the right to terminate this agreement by [one] month's notice by written notice to that effect.

C.470

Where the [Company] provides proposals for new products, recipes, business plans, samples and /or any other material and/or data and/or information in meetings and/or by email and/or any other form of exchanges and supply to the [Distributor] and its executives, management and employees and consultants. Then the [Distributor] agrees that it shall be assumed that it is confidential and not for public release and/or reproduction and/or use by the [Distributor] in any manner and/or form at any time without the prior written approval of [Name] at the [Company].

C.471

The [Licensee] shall not be entitled to have access and/or use of any films, videos, sound recordings, scripts, drawings, photographs, posters, manuscripts and/or other material held by [Name] in respect of the [state subject] except for [specify material/format] copies of which are to be reproduced by the [Licensor] and delivered by [date] to the [Licensee]. The [Licensee] shall pay all costs of any reproduction, insurance and delivery.

Publishing

C.472

The [Ghostwriter] undertakes not to disclose any material of any nature to any third party nor make any statement (whether true or not) concerning the private, sexual, personal and public life and/or views and/or life story and/or childhood of [Name] to any third party acquired directly and/or indirectly during the course of the preparation of the [Work/Book/other] or from any other source of any nature. The [Ghostwriter] further agrees that such non-disclosure shall operate during the course of the Term of this Agreement and any time thereafter [indefinitely/until such material and/or information is released to the public by [Name].

C.473

The [Company] acknowledges and agrees that the [Originator] shall be entitled to exploit any material and/or rights created entirely by him/her under this agreement. Provided that all references to and any confidential information and material supplied by the [Company] shall be deleted and/or the prior written approval of the [Company] obtained in each case.

C.474

The [Author] and the [Company/Distributor] agree that:

1.1 they shall not disclose to any third party except their respective professional agents, legal, audit, insurance and accounting advisors any confidential, business, future plans and/or data of the other party at any time acquired before and/or during the existence of this agreement.

1.2 they shall not make any reference to any part of this agreement except those agreed for the credits, moral rights and marketing of the [Work/Book/Material] in any advertising, promotional, corporate and/or exhibition material without the prior [written] consent of the other party.

1.3 the parties shall issue a joint press, media and social media release to announce this agreement. That the [Author] shall agree to be filmed for a short podcast and/or promotional video of no more than [number] minutes for the announcement at the [Company/Distributors'] sole cost.

1.4 the [Company/Distributor] shall not release, inform and/or disclose any details of the [Work/Book/Material] or its contents to another writer or third party prior to the publication date where the purpose is to create a competing and/or similar work.

1.5 this clause shall not be applicable where the information, data and/or contents are available to the public in general.

1.6 this clause shall only apply until one year after the termination and/or expiry of this agreement.

C.475

The [Contributor] shall not disclose and/or release at any stage to any third party any confidential business, future plans, information, data, software, artwork, scripts and/or other material of the [Company] and/or the commercial terms of this agreement except to [specify agreed persons].

C.476

In the event that a press, television, radio and/or social media statement, video, podcast, film and/or sound recording is to be released by either the [Author] and/or the [Agent] it shall be limited to the following matters: [description of the parties and backgrounds].

C.477

After the expiry and/or termination of this agreement all parties undertake not to disclose to the press and/or any other media company, publisher and/or otherwise information relating to events, conversations, finance, documents and/or general behaviour of the other party which arose from private meetings and were not intended for public knowledge.

C.478

The [Trustees] of the estate of [Name] agree that where access to diaries, documents, photographs, sound recordings, films, videos and/or any other material in any form is requested by the [Publisher] in order to defend and/or refute an allegation by a third party of defamation in respect of the [Work/Book/other]. That the [Trustees] shall provide copies of such original confidential material as may be necessary in order to support the allegations and also provide an affidavit in support to the legal advisors of the [Publishers] at the [Publishers'] sole cost.

C.479

No unsolicited submission in any format by an author to the [Company] shall be treated at any time as confidential whether marked to that effect or not. The only circumstances where the [Company] agrees to treat material as confidential will be where an author, agent and/or other person has agreed terms and conditions of confidentiality in advance prior to the submission of any such material and the [Company] has signed a confidentiality agreement authorised by the [Managing Director] of the [Company].

Services

C.480

The [Designer] and the [Company] shall not disclose at any stage to any third party any confidential, business and/or future plans and/or documents and/or images and/or sound recordings of the other party including but not limited to the commercial terms of this agreement unless a public disclosure, press statement or similar release or any advertising, promotional or corporate document or other material has been specifically agreed by both parties.

C.481

1.1 Where the [Designer] is approaching third parties for contributions and/or assistance in respect of the [App/Platform/Project] then the information to be disclosed shall be kept to a minimum and a representative of the [Company] shall be provided with the opportunity to attend all such meetings with the [Designer].

1.2 The [Designer] shall keep a proper record of all discussions with all third parties relating to the [App/Platform/Project].

C.482

The [Contributor] shall not issue any statement in public, on social media and/or to any media company and/or freelance third party including the press, radio, television and/or any internet business such as a podcast, blog and/or news supplier concerning any confidential business and/or future developments and/or financial forecasts and/or proposed purchases of the [Company] without the prior consent of [Name] [Director/role].

C.483

[Name] shall not disclose and/or supply to any third party [unless] authorised to do so] any confidential information, data and/or documents and/or other material of the [Company] and/or any employee, presenter, consultant and/or supplier connected with the [Company] which has been and/or will be acquired as a result of this agreement at any time. No reference is to be made to the terms of this agreement by either party in any social media, promotional material, press and media releases, interviews and/or in any other medium before [date].

C.484

After the expiry and/or termination of this agreement all parties undertake not to seek to exploit and/or make any disclosure to the press, radio, television, publishers, news organisations and/or any other media and/or otherwise make public and distribute any details of events, conversations, documents, finances, family and/or any private and/or confidential data, information and/or other material relating of the other party without the consent of that person. The exception for both parties shall be in respect of their own professional [legal advisors/accountants/agent].

C.485

The [Presenter/Contributor] agrees and undertakes that he/she shall use their reasonable endeavours to prevent the publication and/or disclosure of any confidential information concerning the business and/or finances of the [Company] and/or its subsidiaries or any of their affairs either during and/or after the expiry and/or termination of this agreement. This undertaking shall apply to any script, text, rules, pictures, design, arrangement, title, format, music, programme idea or theme, film, DVD, podcast, blog, book in whole or any part based on or derived from any material owned, controlled or used by the [Company] or any subsidiary. Together with all records and other materials developed by and/or or received by the [Presenter/Contributor] in the course of the provision of his/her services which shall be and remain the property of the [Company]. All material of any nature shall be returned to the [Company] upon termination and/or expiry of this agreement and/or at the request of a director of the [Company] at any time during the Term of this Agreement.

C.486

The [Artist] shall not issue any statement in public and/or display any logo, sign and/or message and/or communicate and/or supply to the media including newspapers, magazines, news organisations, radio, television, mobile phone companies and/or any internet related person and/or company any confidential business, data, products, services and/or decisions and/or plans of the [Company/Distributor] acquired under this agreement and this clause shall apply until [date].

C.487

The [Group] agrees not to issue any statement on social media and/or to any news organisation and/or to the press, media and/or on the internet during the Term of this Agreement concerning the professional lives, careers and/or future plans of the [Group] or the [Manager] without the prior consent of the [Manager]. This clause shall not apply after [date].

C.488

1.1   [Name/Group] and the [Manager] shall not disclose to any third party any confidential business, data, records, images, sound recordings, films and/or future plans of any other party at any time acquired during the existence of this agreement.

1.2   No reference is to be made to the terms of this agreement by either party in any advertising publicity or promotional material without the prior consent of the other party on each occasion.

1.3   After the expiry and/or termination of this agreement all parties undertake shall be entitled to make any disclosure and/or communicate and/or be interviewed and/or publish any matter to any news organisation, blog, podcast, magazine, newspaper, radio, television, publisher and/or media and/or internet company in respect of any events, conversations, documents, financial arrangements and/or general behaviour of any party to this agreement without the specific consent of that person.

1.4   No information and/or material shall be deemed confidential and/or private after [date].

C.489

The [Contributor] undertakes that he/she shall not reveal, communicate, supply and/or distribute any confidential information, data, marketing, advertising and/or financial plans concerning the [Company] which is originally acquired in the course of his/her engagement under this agreement to any third party from the date of this agreement until [date].

C.490

The [Artist] agrees not to issue any statement to the media, newspapers, or on the internet or to supply to any third party any confidential business, data, agreements and/or finances of the [Agent] and/or details of any negotiations or terms of any agreements in relating to the [Agents] other clients.

C.491

The [Promoter] agrees not to use, release, exploit and/or use to their advantage and/or to the detriment of the [Company] any commercially sensitive information, data, documents, software, photographs or any other material in any medium during the Term of this Agreement without the prior express approval of [Name] at the [Company].

C.492

The [Agent] and the [Artist] mutually agree that each of them shall not during the Term of this Agreement publish in writing and/or otherwise make known to the public and/or reveal and/or disclose any matter concerning the family and/or business affairs of the other without their prior consent. This shall not apply in the event of the termination and/or expiry of this agreement and/or where one party instigates legal proceedings against the other party.

C.493

No reference is to be made to: [specify topics/documents] by either party in public, to any newspaper, publisher, news organisation, magazine, in any film or sound recording for television, radio and/or for any podcast, blog, video and/or live and/or pre-recorded streamed programme and/or otherwise without the prior written consent of the other party.

C.494

The [Consultant] agrees that he/she shall not:

1.1 disclose and/or communicate and/or distribute to any third party any confidential information which is provided by the [Company] at any time of any nature and/or in any medium and/or format from the date of this agreement until [date]. This shall not apply to any information which is released by the [Company] to the public and/or to the media and/or a significant sector of an industry.

1.2 No reference is to be made to any part of this agreement except with the prior approval and/or written consent of a director and/or officer the [Company]. The parties shall agree a press and social media announcement.

1.3 The [Consultant] shall not be entitled to advertise and/or promote that the [Consultant] has worked for the [Company] on any brochure, website, app, platform and/or in any marketing and/or advertising material except with the prior approval and written consent of a director and/or officer the [Company].

1.4 This clause shall no longer apply after [date].

C.495
[Name] and their [Agent] agree that where future programme ideas and projects are discussed at meetings with the [Company] prior to the conclusion of any agreement for the services of [Name]. That [Name] and their [Agent] agree not to supply, distribute and/or reproduce any part of such information and/or any associated material to any national and/or local media and/or other third party including but not limited to newspapers, magazines, radio, television and/or in any personal blog, on social media and/or by any method on the internet without the prior approval of the [Company] before [date].

C.496
The [Company] agrees and accepts that no part of this agreement and/or any future information, data and/or material released and/or supplied to [Name] shall at any time be treated as confidential. That [Name] shall not be placed under any restrictions, prohibitions and/or obligations and may market and promote his/her appearances, contribution and work at the [Company] in any format and in any media.

Sponsorship

C.497
In the event that [Name] shall decide to write a biography and/or engage a ghostwriter to do so and/or be commissioned by a publisher and/or distributor to do so and/or agree to a film and/or other recording and/or adaptation of his/her life. Then prior to the supply of the proofs to the publisher and/or completion of the script. [Name] agrees to disclose and supply extracts of any references to the [Sponsor/Company] and/or its directors and/or officers to the [Sponsor/Company] for consultation purposes but not for approval.

C.498

1.1 The [Sponsor] and [Name] both agree and undertake that they shall not disclose to any third party (except professional legal advisors, agents and accountants) any confidential information, data, contracts, development plans and/or other matter directly acquired as a result of the existence of this agreement.

1.2 No reference is to be made to the terms of this agreement and/or any breaches and/or defaults and/or allegations by either party in any media without the prior approval of the other party. After the expiry and/or termination of this agreement all parties agree that this clause [–] shall apply until [date/time].

C.499
Both parties agree that none of the information and/or any other material released and/or supplied under this agreement shall be considered and/

441

or deemed confidential, private and/or commercially sensitive. Neither the [Sponsor] nor the [Company] shall be bound by any rules of confidentiality and/or privacy in respect of this [Project]. Both parties agree that they shall be entitled to reproduce, supply, distribute and display on their website and/or app any part of the information provided by either party in respect of the [Project] for the purpose of marketing, advertising and fundraising for the [Project]. Provided that a suitable acknowledgment of copyright ownership and/or trade marks is made in a reasonably prominent and clear position in each case.

C.500

The [Company] agrees and undertakes that it shall not either during the Term of this Agreement until [date] reproduce, supply, distribute and/or disclose to any third party [except consultants, agents, public relations and professional advisors] any information, business plans, inventions, computer software, financial information, reports, assessments and/or other material which is communicated and/or supplied to the [Company] in circumstances where it is made clear at the time by the [Sponsor] that it is confidential.

C.501

No duty of confidentiality shall be owed by the [Company] to the [Sponsor]. Where information is inadvertently released and/or any statement made by any person at the [Company] and/or third person which is derogatory and/or likely to adversely affect the sales of the [Sponsor's] services and/products. The [Sponsor] agrees that the [Company] shall not be held responsible and/or liable and that all rights are waived by the [Sponsor] in respect of any claim, action, loss and/or damage which may be created and/or suffered. That the [Sponsor] agrees to bear the cost of all such risk and consequences of its participation in the [Festival/Event/Programme].

C.502

Both parties agree and confirm that there are no confidentiality provisions in this agreement and neither shall they be applied at any time in the future and that they have waived any right to do so.

University, Charity and Educational

C.503

1.1 The [Institute/Charity] and the [Company] both agree and undertake that as far as reasonably possible they shall not disclose, reproduce, exploit and/or distribute during the Term of this Agreement and/or thereafter until after [date] any confidential information which is supplied and/or revealed on that basis by one party to the other.

1.2   Any data, information and/or material which is not confidential may still not be released and/or distributed to third parties without the consent of both parties in each case.

1.3   This clause shall not apply to the disclosure to legal and professional advisors, government departments and/or any person engaged by the [Institute/Charity] who is a [Consultant] on the [Project].

1.4   Both parties agree and undertake they will both approve any press and/or media statement and/or interviews and any films, videos podcasts, blogs and/or articles for advertising and/or promotional purposes and/or any registration and/or corporate documents.

C.504

The [Consultant] agrees and undertakes that he/she shall not, either during the Term of this Agreement or thereafter at any time, use and/or divulge to any person any confidential information, business plans, data, patents, financial information, reports or assessments relating to the [Institute/Charity], its employees and/or [students/employees] which are provided either in confidence or on the basis that they are not for publication and/or distribution to a third party. This clause shall not apply where the disclosure is made by a third party or the material is put into a public forum by the [Institute/Charity] and/or is available as a matter of public record at a later date.

C.505

All material including text, images, logos, trade marks, photographs, computer software, discs, sound recordings, films, DVDs, videos, podcasts, music, websites, apps, reports, catalogues, financial data and directories supplied to, created by and/or commissioned by the [Company] in respect of the [Project] for the [Institute/Charity] shall remain and/or be assigned to the [Institute/Charity] as the legal owner of all rights in all media at any time. All material of any nature in the possession and/or under the control of the [Company] shall be returned to the [Institute/Charity] upon termination and/or expiry of this Agreement at the [Company's] cost including any codes, passwords and/or any other material in any format. The [Institute/Charity] may, at any time, request a full list of all material held and/or controlled by the [Company].

C.506

The [Institute/Charity] agrees not to use, release, exploit, supply and/or distribute any family and personal information and/or any statements, data, documents, software, photographs and/or other material in any medium which it may hold relating to the [Author] and/or which the [Author] has been supplied and/or communicated. The prior express approval of [Author] shall be required in each case.

C.507

Neither party is bound by any undertaking as to confidentiality either of the [Project] and/or of any information disclosed in any presentation, report, interview and/or any other material unless it is specifically stated to be so at the time. Both parties agree that they shall be entitled to make any press and/or media statement, use any data, information, concepts, film, sound recordings, podcasts, reports, business knowledge and plans, and develop any new material without any approval and/or consent being necessary from the other party.

C.508

1.1   Both parties undertake to agree a press and social media statement and filmed news interview which will be co-ordinated by the [Institute/ Charity]. There shall be no further disclosure and/or release to the public unless both parties agree the method and terms of reference.

1.2   Both parties agree to try not to release and/or disclose any information and/or data which may be confidential and/or private. However both parties agree that neither shall be held responsible and/or liable for any such default and/or failure.

C.509

The [Consortium] agree that any information distributed and/or supplied by one party to any other party involved in this [Project] shall not be treated as confidential and/or restricted in anyway and may be released to professional legal and tax advisors, employees, consultants and form part of any report, press release and may be distributed, supplied and/or reproduced by a third party.

CONFLICT OF INTEREST

General Business and Commercial

C.510

The [Promoter] confirms that this agreement will not cause any conflict of interest with any of its existing clients and undertakes not to enter into any agreement with any third party during the duration of this agreement which would result in a conflict of interest with the [Company] and/or its products and/or services.

C.511

Where either party becomes aware of any order, information, customer, product or other factor which could potentially create a conflict of interest between the parties under this agreement. Then that party shall be obliged to disclose and communicate such material facts to allow the other party to decide whether they wish to cancel and/or withdraw from the agreement on terms to be agreed between the parties.

C.512

There shall be no duty by either party to report to or inform the other party of a potential and/or actual conflict of interest. Either party may engage in business and/or provide services and/or products and/or advice to any person, company or organisation at any time whether or not they are in direct competition with the other party.

C.513

The [Consultant] agrees and undertakes that he/she is not engaged and/or involved with any existing business, person and/or company which is a direct competitor of the [Company] and/or involved in the [specify type] market. In the event that after the conclusion of this agreement the [Consultant] decides to work for a direct competitor then the [Consultant] shall notify the [Company] of the conflict of interest and agree to terminate this agreement on terms to be agreed between the parties.

C.514

The [Sponsor] agrees that the existence of this agreement and the funding of the [Event] does not permit and/or allow the [Sponsor] to promote, advertise and/or use in anyway their association with the [Institute/Charity] and/or the [Event] in a manner and/or form which would damage the reputation and/or conflict with the interests of the [Institute/Charity].

C.515

The [Licensee] shall be entitled to enter into licensing arrangements and agreements with any third party that it thinks fit including a direct competitor of the [Licensor] and/or the [Product/Services] which are referred to in this agreement.

C.516

Where at a later date the agent, advisor and/or consultant is engaged to provide services to a company which is a direct and/or indirect competitor of the [Distributor]. Then the [Distributor] shall be entitled to terminate the agreement with immediate effect and shall only be liable to pay for the services of the agent, advisor and/or consultant to the date of termination.

CONSORTIUM

General Business and Commercial

C.517

'The Consortium' shall consist of the following members [Company name/address/legal status] who shall each contribute, work and share any rights as equal partners and be jointly and severally party to and responsible for this agreement.

C.518

Each member of the [Consortium] shall only be bound by their own individual undertakings, responsibilities and liabilities to each other and in respect of the performance and completion of this [Project/Event].

C.519

1.1   The [Institute/Charity] shall not be liable for any acts, omissions, errors, responsibilities, defaults, failures and/or liabilities of the other members of the [Enterprise] and/or the [Enterprise] as a whole.

1.2   There is no partnership, agency, subsidiary, associate or parent company relationship between the parties. There is no right on the part of any other member to authorise, commit, pledge, waive, sign and/or agree to any changes, variations and/or deletions for any reason on behalf of the [Institute/Charity].

C.520

The [Sponsor] acknowledges that other third parties shall fund the [Event/Project] and acquire other rights/and interests. The [Sponsor] agrees that the [Company] shall be entitled to disclose the following terms and conditions of this agreement [specify clauses] to ensure that such third parties are also bound by the undertakings in their agreement to the [Sponsor].

C.521

Each member of the [Consortium/Enterprise] agrees and authorises [Name/Agent] to negotiate, conclude and sign all agreements relating to the exploitation of the following rights: [specify range of rights] in respect of the [Film/Podcast/Trade Mark] from [date] to [date]. No agreement shall be signed by [Name/Agent] which relates to any other rights and/or which is an assignment and/or which grants any rights after [date].

C.522

In the event that two or more members of the [Collaboration/Enterprise] wish to withdraw and/or terminate their arrangements with the other parties due to lack of funding and/or a change in the nature of the [Project] which is contrary to their terms of reference and/or is in conflict with their moral, ethical and/or legal position. Then it is agreed that the [Collaboration/ Enterprise] shall be brought to an end and the agreement terminated and/ or cancelled. Provided that the remaining parties may seek to create a new organisation and agreement and transfer the work and rights to a new entity for a nominal fee.

C.523
'The Consortium' shall comprise the following names who shall each hold the same rights and interest in the [Project] and also be jointly and severally liable for any losses that may be incurred: [list full legal names and trading names/address/contact details].

CONSULTATION

Film, Television and Video

C.524
The [Distributor] agrees to consult with the [Artist/Company] in respect of the content of the editing of the [Film] and the packaging for the [DVD/ Format/Unit], but shall not be bound to incorporate the changes, deletions or additions requested.

C.525
The [Distributor] shall be bound to adhere to all instructions, directions, and orders regarding the editing, production, manufacture, addition to or deletion of any material, any sub-titles and/or translations, packaging, distribution and release dates of the [DVD/Format/Unit of the [Film]. The [Company] shall not be obliged to consult with the [Distributor] nor seek their approval.

C.526
The [Licensee] shall make available and deliver to the [Licensor] at the [Licensee's] cost a sample copy of the [Disc/Format/Unit], the cover and any labels, packaging and marketing material for [the views and opinion/written approval] of the [Licensor] before it is manufactured, promoted and/or distributed.

C.527
The [Company] agrees and accepts that all editorial decisions, arrangements, licences and agreements in respect of the production, manufacture, distribution, marketing and promotion of the [Character/Script/Film] in any

rights granted to the [Licensee] shall not require any prior consultation and/or approval by the [Company].

C.528

[Name] shall be entitled to be consulted on the production and editing of the final version of the sound recording, film, cover, marketing, advertising and content of any part of any material relating to the [DVD/Disc/Format] at the [Licensee's] cost.

C.529

The [Licensee] shall consult with and seek the views and opinions of [Name] as regarding:

1.1 The production schedule; use of third parties; locations; product placement and layout of any sets; use of background music and lighting; choice of editor and production company for manufacture of the [Product].

1.2 Marketing and advertising strategy in print, on radio and television and online as banner links, blogs and on websites, apps and podcasts.

1.3 That in any event the [Licensee] shall supply [Name] with a copy of all such material as may be available at the [Licensees] sole and expense which shall not be deducted from any sums due to [Name].

C.530

The [Executive Producer] appointed by the [Company] and such representatives as may be nominated shall, without making any disruption to the making of the [Film/Series] or any material or sound recording, be entitled to attend during any shoot or recording to view [Film/Series] and the preparatory materials and listen to any sound recording at any reasonable time during the production of the [Film/Series] as may be necessary. Such costs and expenses of the representatives shall be agreed in advance by the parties and the reasonable and proper expenses of the personnel shall be attributed to the Budget as part of the production costs.

C.531

The [Production Company] shall not permit the [Author] any editorial control in respect of the [Film/Series], but agree that the [Author] may [be consulted/approve] the [draft and final script/the main characters/any product placement/any music/locations/other].

C.532

The [Company] agrees to arrange for the [Author] and his/her representatives a private viewing of the completed final version of the [Series/Programme] before it is made available to third parties.

C.533

The [Company] agrees to keep the [Author] advised on a regular basis as regards the production, licensing and exploitation of the [Series/Film] and any associated merchandising, sponsorship and/or product placement. The [Company] agrees to consult with the [Author] and [Agent] to listen to and consider their proposals to change, amend or exploit any material in the [Series/Film], any rights in any format, and any associated packaging, marketing and/or other material. The [Company] shall not be obliged to carry out the requests unless it relates to the contract terms relating to the title of the book, or images based on artwork, slogans, logos or trademarks supplied or licensed by the [Author].

C.534

The [Licensee] agrees to keep the [Licensor] informed of proposed transmission dates and to provide the [Licensor] with information and/or copies of any associated merchandising, publicity and advertising material that may be created at the [Licensee's] cost.

C.535

This agreement shall not grant and/or assign any rights and/or option and/or interest in any sequel of the [Work/Book/Script/Film] and/or any subsequent series in any form in any medium to the [Licensee]. There shall be no obligation to notify and/or consult with the [Licensee] in the event that the [Licensor] intends to exercise any such rights and/or grant them to a third party. This agreement is solely for the production, distribution and exploitation of the [Product].

C.536

The [Distributor] shall not be obliged to consult with [Name] in respect of any exploitation and/or marketing of the [Film/Series] and/or parts provided that no use shall be made of any part of the [Film/Series] which features [Name] which would be deemed offensive and/or would give the impression and/or represent that [Name] supported a political campaign and/or was linked to the promotion and/or marketing of a product, service, gambling, a lottery, betting, alcohol sales, a charity and/or a religion.

C.537

The [Company] agrees to consult with the [Agent] and [Name] in respect of the proposal to market, promote and broadcast and/or transmit the [Programme/Interview] in association with any sponsor, service and/or product at any time. In any event the [Company] agrees not to enter into any such agreement with the following types of businesses [specify excluded list].

General Business and Commercial

C.538

The [Company] agrees that [Name] shall have the right to be consulted with respect to the [Work/Material/Service] but such right of consultation, for the avoidance of doubt, shall not be deemed to be a right of approval and/or confer any right of veto.

C.539

The [Company] shall consult with any interested parties who are involved in the [Project] and [the local community/the public/consumers] to endeavour to take into account all reasonable requests to change, develop or alter the [draft plan] based on demand, supply, use, availability of resources, costs, health and safety and environmental issues. Where there is shown to be strong objections which raise issues relating to health and safety, environment, cost or other reasons. Then the [Company] accept that it shall be the final decision of [specify person/role] as to whether the [Project] proceeds and/or is cancelled.

C.540

The [Company] agrees and undertakes to carry a detailed and comprehensive consultation with the following specified persons and companies: [public/trade/other] in order to ascertain their views and opinions on the proposed [Project] by the [Enterprise]. A copy of the proposed scope of the [Project] is attached to and forms part of this agreement in appendix A.

C.541

The [Company] shall agree in advance and seek the prior written approval of [Name] at the [Enterprise] as to:

1.1 The method and content of the consultation and the languages in which it is to be made available.

1.2 The amount of advertising and promotion required.

1.3 The formalities for compliance with any legislation including data protection, privacy, freedom of information.

1.4 The layout and structure of the report of the consultancy and the analysis of the results.

1.5 The final proposed budget for the consultation.

C.542

The [Company] agrees and undertakes to carry out such public consultations, surveys and assessments and to engage such qualified experts as may be required to provide valid evidence in respect of the [Project] and the proposed expenditure. That the [Company] shall not withhold and/or destroy any results which conflict and/or are to the detriment of the local community and/or the [Company] and/or the [Project] which are raised at any time.

C.543

[Name] shall not be obliged to consult with the [Company] to seek approval and/or to make them aware of any activity, work and/or other marketing, blog, articles or otherwise that [Name] may write, create, develop and/or participate in. Provided it is does not involve services, premises and/or equipment owned and/or controlled by the [Company] and any such work is not done by [Name] within the exclusive hours allocated to the [Company].

Internet, Websites and Apps

C.544

Any consultation process shall not be binding on the [Company] and shall be purely for background information and assistance. There shall be no obligation on the [Company] to disclose any further information, data and/or other material nor to pay any participant in the consultation for their suggestions, ideas or proposals whether used and adopted by the [Company] or not.

C.545

There [Company] shall be entitled to sell the [Product/Service] and to discount, reduce, increase and/or cross promote and market the [Product/Service] at its sole discretion without any prior consultation and/or approval by the [Supplier/Author]. Provided that the [Product/Service] is not altered and/or adapted in any manner and the payments due to the [Supplier/Author] are not reduced.

C.546

The [Company] operates and runs this [Website/App/Platform] entirely at its own cost and discretion. There is no obligation on the [Company] to consult with, seek the approval and/or obtain permission from any person and/or business and/or other third party who uses this [Website/App/Platform] in any manner. The [Company] may at any time delete, adapt, change, vary, add to, suspend operation of, transfer all the business to another third party and/or assign and sell rights and obligations to a third party. No notification and/or consultation shall be required by the [Company].

C.547

The [Company] agrees that the [Contributor] shall be consulted in respect of the final version of the [Podcast] and any photographs, biography, image, likeness, quotes and/or other material relating to the [Contributor], his/

her work and/or services on the [Website/App] and in any links, banners, promotional, publicity, advertising, and marketing owned and/or controlled by the [Company].

C.548

The [Company] shall not be obliged to consult with you prior to the deletion, removal, and/or changes to your name, title, content and display of your comment, images, films and/or other content at any time.

C.549

The [Company] agrees not to add any links, images, film, text and/or other material prior to and/or in connection with your [Blog/Podcast] relating to a third party without prior consultation. In the event that [Name] objects to any material, then the [Company] agrees that it shall not insist on such material being added, provided that the [Company] will not incur any direct financial losses as a result. In the event that the [Company] will lose advertising and promotional revenue from a third party, then [Name] accepts that the decision of the [Company] shall be final and that they may add such material despite any objections.

C.550

[Name] agrees that the [Company] may make such deletions, additions and/or alterations to the [Blog/Podcast/Material] as it thinks fit based on the advice of its legal advisors. That while the [Company] may decide at its sole discretion to consult [Name] the decision of the [Company] shall be final.

Merchandising and Distribution

C.551

The [Designer] agrees to consult with the [Licensee] with respect to the prices at which the [Licensed Articles/Products] are to be sold whether by retail, wholesale or at a discounted price.

C.552

The [Distributor] shall consult with the [Supplier] in respect of any images, photographs, films, videos, articles, podcasts, reviews, price comparisons, price changes, special offers and/or other material relating to the [Products] on the [website/app/other], in its catalogues and any marketing, packaging and/or promotional material.

C.553

There shall be no obligation or requirement to consult, advise or contact the [Company] regarding any price changes, discount, reduction, images, slogans, film, video, podcast, cross promotion and/or marketing regarding the [Products] by the [Distributor]. Provided that all the packaging, labels, copyright and trade mark notices and warnings are not removed, covered over or interfered with by the [Distributor]. That any representation of the [Product] shall be a true image and no derogatory, offensive or inappropriate comments shall be displayed with or close to the [Products].

C.554

1.1 The [Distributor] agrees that there shall be no right to make any alterations and/or changes to any part of the [Article/Product] and any associated material and/or to add any material except the name of the [Distributor] and any other legal requirements.

1.2 That the [Distributor] shall not alter and/or change the content and/or the name of the [Article/Product] and/or any logo, slogan and/or image, copyright and trade mark notices, warnings and safety advice for use, compliance codes and/or add any labels, alter any instruction leaflets and/or packaging;

C.555

That where the [Distributor] is unable and/or unwilling to follow the strict guidelines and/or directions and/or conditions set by the [Licensor] in this agreement. That production by the [Distributor] must cease until such time as the [Licensor] instructs otherwise and is satisfied that the [Distributor] is complying with the conditions. That where the matter is unresolved for more than [number] [months] including weekends and public holidays. That the [Licensor] may terminate the agreement and the [Licensor] shall not be liable for any losses, damages, expenses and/or costs due to the default of the [Distributor].

C.556

The [Licensee] shall keep the [Licensor] regularly informed regarding all developments in respect of the production and exploitation of the [Work/ Product/Service]. The [Licensee] shall at its own cost supply the [Licensor] with samples copies of all material, items, budgets, advertising and marketing proposals prior to any final decision, production and/or distribution to a third party. The [Licensee] shall be obliged to follow the decision of the [Licensor] in all matters subject to the criteria that the preferred option is not within the [Licensee's] budget. This shall include but not be limited to any prototypes, artwork and designs, covers, promotional, publicity, packaging, brochures, flyers, advertising, website, app, podcast and other marketing.

C.557

The [Company] agrees and undertakes that all sub-licensing of the [Work/ Product/Service] shall be subject to the prior written approval of [Name] which may be withheld for any reason. There is no obligation on [Name] to agree to any sub-licence proposals nor does the [Company] have the authority to sign and/or authorise any such agreements which must be signed by [Name]. The [Company] shall consult with [Name] as to which businesses may be suitable and shall ensure that they are financially secure and solvent prior to entering any negotiations.

C.558

The [Distributor] shall sell, supply, market and exploit the [Work/Product/Service] to the best of its ability and shall not be obliged to consult and/or seek the prior approval of [Name] for any adaptation, translation, modification, addition to, and/or deletion from the [Work/Product/Service].

C.559

1.1 The [Sub-Licensee] agrees and undertakes not to alter, adapt, amend and/or add to any material relating to the [Work/Film/Image] and/or [Name] supplied by the [Licensee] at any time.

1.2 The [Sub-Licensee] agrees that it shall be in breach of this agreement if it does not consult with and obtain the prior written approval of the [Licensee] in respect of any new material that the [Sub-Licensee] may wish to develop for production, packaging, marketing or any other purpose in respect of the rights granted under this agreement.

C.560

The [Licensor] agrees that the [Licensee] shall have absolute discretion as to the exploitation and marketing of the [Work/Product] and that there shall be no obligation to consult with the [Licensor] and/or seek approval of any kind during the development, production, manufacture and distribution of the [Work/Product]. That the [Licensee] may make any such decisions as regard the content, packaging and promotion as it thinks fit.

C.561

The [Licensee] agrees:

1.1 Not to change the title and/or words of any text and/or any images in the [Work/Book/Podcast] and/or any part of any translation of the [Work/Book/Podcast] into another language and/or sub-titling without the prior approval of the [Licensor] of the draft proposal.

1.2 That the [Licensor] shall be provided with a minimum of [one] calendar month to consider any such proposal in each case.

1.3 That where the [Licensor] authorises any new title and text in any translation it shall be the responsibility of the [Licensee] to check that this does not conflict with any existing title in the market for which the translation of the [Work/Book/Podcast] is intended to be supplied, sold and/or distributed.

Publishing

C.562
That the [Company] shall inform the [Author] of any proposal and consult with them on the format and/or content of the [Author's] profile and/or [Book/Audio File/Extracts] on the [Company's] website, app and/or channel and/or that of any third party.

C.563
The [Publisher/Distributor] shall keep the [Author] informed on a regular basis regarding developments in respect of the exploitation of the [Work/Book/Merchandising/other] including supplying sample prototypes, packaging, posters, labels, details of distribution and release dates and arranging meetings with any third parties that may be involved if so requested.

C.564
The [Publisher/Distributor] agrees that the [Author] shall be consulted in relation to all content and material in respect of the exploitation of the [Work] which shall be of a high professional standard and which shall include but not be limited: photographs, illustrations, artwork, typography, design, blurb on jacket, index, preface, copyright notices and credits, layout and content of the website, app and/or blog material, biography and profile, images, podcasts, films and sound recordings of the [Author] and any signature, summaries of the text, use of third parties to promote and/or endorse the [Work], promotional, packaging, brochures, advertising and marketing. Together with all the content and details relating to any other format and/or rights which may be exploited at any time in any medium. The [Author] accepts that the [Publisher/Distributor] shall have the final decision.

C.565
The [Licensee] agrees that the [Licensor] shall be consulted in relation to any artwork and designs to be created by the [Licensee] in respect of the [Extracts].

C.566
[Name] and the [Company] agree that [Name] shall be consulted regarding the accuracy and detail of the [Articles] and any associated images, photographs and headlines prior to publication in the form in which it is intended to be published in the [magazine/newsfeed]. In the event that [Name] is not satisfied that the [Article] and/or the images, photographs and/

or headline is accurate and that the detail is correct and the [Company] are not willing and/or able to change the content. Then the [Company] agrees that the [Article], images, photographs and headline shall not be published by them and this agreement shall be terminated. In such event [number] per cent of the sums already paid to [Name] shall be returned to the [Company] within [one] calendar month of termination.

C.567
The [Company] agrees after consultation with the [Author] to revise, amend, correct, delete and/or change any material of any nature and in any format which is created under this agreement which it proposes to sell, market and/or exploit so that it meets the stipulations of the [Author]. The decision of the [Author] shall be final.

C.568
The [Author] acknowledges that there shall be no right of approval, consultation and/or to be advised of any matter relating to the exploitation of the [Work/Product/Service] and any rights and/or any adaptation, variation and/or other development at any time.

C.569
Where the [Publisher/Distributor] has reached a decision that it is considering the option that it should cease printing copies of the [Work/Book] and only to supply the [Work/Book] as an online ebook via the internet as a download and/or in some other digital and/or electronic form but not in hardback and/or paperback. Then the [Publisher] agrees to notify the [Author] of their proposed plan to take such action and to provide the [Author] with an opportunity to have a meeting and to be consulted before any final decision by the [Publisher/Distributor].

C.570
The [Publisher/Distributor] agrees that where after any consultation the [Author] decides that he/she does not wish to remain with the [Publisher/Distributor] if there are to be less than [number] copies of the printed version of the [Work] available for sale at any time during this agreement. Then the [Author] may provide the [Publisher/Distributor] with [three/six] months written notice of the termination of the agreement. In such event the [Publisher/Distributor] agrees to release the [Author] from any contractual obligations and to sign any document requested by the [Author] and/or any authorised third party to confirm such release. Provided that if there are sub-licences in existence granted by the [Publisher/Distributor]. That the parties have reached a settlement in respect of those sub-licences.

Services

C.571

The [Company] agrees to consult with [Name] and the [Agent] in advance of the production and distribution in respect of any material and/or form of exploitation relating to the [Name] and/or the [Series] in which [Name] features including media, press and social media strategies, statements and marketing; filmed interviews for other programmes, podcasts, sound recordings and films; photo sessions; packaging, prototypes and samples for merchandising; advertisements, promotions, competitions and premium rate phone lines, sponsorship and product placement arrangements.

C.572

The [Manager] shall keep [Name] fully informed on a regular basis as regards any negotiations with any third party and agrees that he/she shall not be entitled to conclude any agreement and/or sign any document and/or commit [Name] in any manner without the prior [written] consent of and consultation with [Name].

C.573

The [Agency] acknowledges that it shall not be entitled to carry out and/or authorise any third party to adapt, alter, edit, add to or delete from and/or in any way change the [Work/Image/Sound Recording] without the prior [written] consent of the [Author/Name].

C.574

The [Agent] agrees to consult with the [Author] in respect of any proposed development and/or adaptation of the [Work/Product/Service] in a foreign language and/or subtitling and/or any related changes of title, names and other words in any other form. The [Agent] shall endeavour to ensure that all related costs are paid by the third party, but that copyright and intellectual property rights in any such new material are either assigned to the [Author] and/or held with the third party as joint owners.

C.575

Subject to prior consultation the [Actor] agrees that the [Agent] shall be entitled to use his/her name, signature, biography and profile, photograph, image and stage name in the promotion, advertising and marketing of the [Actor], provided that a copy of any such material shall be supplied to the [Actor] when so requested.

C.576

The [Agent] shall not be obliged to consult with [Name] in respect of accepting bookings and/or signing contracts which have been broadly discussed and agreed in advance. Where [Name] has advised the [Agent] that they specifically wish to review the terms of a proposed deal personally prior to signature, then the [Agent] shall not proceed without the prior consent of [Name]. The [Agent] acknowledges that [Name] will not carry out the following types of work: [specify type of work which cannot be covered].

C.577

The [Company] shall not be obliged to seek the approval and/or provide any details to the [Consultant] in respect of the [Project/Report] once it has been delivered to the [Company]. No reference shall be made to the contribution and/or work of the [Consultant] and all copyright and intellectual property rights and any other rights in the [Project/Report] shall belong to the [Company] in accordance with the assignment under clause [–].

C.578

The [Agent] agrees to consult with [Name] in respect of all proposed work and shall not commit [Name] as their agent unless [Name] has agreed to proceed with any work and/or project and has agreed to the fees and expenses.

C.579

The [Company] agrees that it shall not authorise and/or permit anyone at the [Company] to include the name, title, image and details of the services provided by the [Consultant] including their fees and expenses to be included in any annual and/or corporate report and/or any marketing material and/or advertising and/or to post any film, photographs, text and/or other work and/or material on any website, app, platform and/or otherwise without prior consultation with the [Consultant] in each case.

University, Charity and Educational

C.580

The [Institute/Charity] agrees to consult with [Name] in respect of the final version of the [Work/Report/Event] but such right of consultation, for the avoidance of doubt, shall not be deemed to be a right of approval and/or the right to prevent publication, distribution and/or marketing.

C.581

The [Author] shall not have any editorial control in respect of the [Project/ Event] once it has been delivered to the [Institute/Charity]. The [Institute/ Charity] agrees to provide details of any significant amendments, deletions and/or changes in respect of the final report relating to the [Project/Event] to [Name] but the [Institute/Charity] shall not be obliged to act on any recommendation and/or proposal by the [Author].

C.582

The [Institute/Charity] agrees that [Name] shall be provided with a complete copy of the final version of the [Review Report/Research Data] and have the right to be consulted regarding the accuracy and detail of the [Review Report/Research Data] prior to production, publication and distribution.

C.583

The [Institute/Charity] agrees and undertakes that the [Author] shall have the right to be consulted in relation to all material, rights and forms of exploitation in respect of the [Work/Content] by the [Institute/Charity]. The right to be consulted shall include but not be limited to photographs, illustrations, artwork, typography and design, index, the cover and preface, the [Authors] profile and image, quotes and summaries of the text, use of third parties to promote or endorse the [Work/Content], merchandising and products, sample prototypes, labels, copyright notices, packaging, advertising and marketing over the internet and in magazines, newspapers, podcasts and radio and television interviews. A copy of any such material shall be provided as soon as it is available in draft form and sent to the [Author]. As far as reasonably possible the [Institute/Charity] shall incorporate any changes, amendments, deletions and objections of the [Author].

C.584

The [Enterprise] shall keep the [Institute/Charity] fully informed on a regular basis as regards any negotiations and proposed commitment to any third party including new sponsors, licensees, agents, distributors and/or consultants. The [Enterprise] agrees that it shall not be entitled to conclude any agreement and/or commit the [Institute/Charity] and/or sign any document and/or make any registration and/or application without prior consultation with the [Institute/Charity] and specific authorisation in each case to proceed. In such case the [Enterprise] may prepare a draft document to be considered and reviewed by the [Institute/Charity].

C.585

The [Joint Venture/Consortium] all undertake and agree that any steps, expenditure and/or work must be authorised by the [committee/other] and that any new proposals may not be developed and/or progressed otherwise. That any costs to be incurred must be agreed in advance by consultation with all the members of the [Joint Venture/Consortium]. Where any single member creates additional costs which have not been authorised in advance then that member shall be personally liable for the unauthorised cost and not the [Joint Venture/Consortium].

C.586

The [Joint Venture/Consortium] shall be obliged to consult with its members [and legal advisors and trustees] at each stage of the [Project]. In the event at any stage a decision is reached by any member that they should cease funding the [Project] based on the fact that the costs and expenses have escalated beyond the original budget. Then that member and/or its representative may serve notice to the other members of the [Joint Venture/ Consortium that they terminate the agreement and will not supply any funds in excess of the original budget.

CONTROL

General Business and Commercial

C.587

'Change of Control' shall mean circumstances when any person, company, body or entity acquires (whether by a series of transactions pursuant to a scheme or otherwise), shares [or stock] in the [Company] which if taken together with all the other shares [or stock held] by the acquirer and persons acting in concert with it would result in the acquirer gaining an overall controlling interest in the [Company].

C.588

'Control' shall be defined in accordance with the following [statute/policy document] issued by the [government department/other].

C.589

'Controlling Company' shall mean any company or other body or individual which holds or is beneficially entitled to [fifty] per cent or more of the shares or voting power of the [Company].

C.590

'Control' shall be defined on a de facto basis which shall in any event include an interest of [thirty] per cent or more.

C.591

'Control' shall mean any interest in the [Company] which enables any third party by virtue of any interest of any nature whether through shares, voting power or by virtue of the [Company's] Articles of Association to secure that the affairs of the Company are conducted in accordance with the wishes of the third party or any company or body associated with the company or third party.

C.592

In the event that there is a change of control of the [Company] because it is sold, placed in administration, declared insolvent and/or there is a majority shareholding acquired by another company and/or it no longer exists as it is incorporated into and/or merged another company. Then the [Company] agrees and undertakes that all rights in the [Work] and all rights to ownership of all the master material which may be owned or controlled by the [Company] shall revert to the [Author].

C.593

There shall not have been a change of control where the transfer of the ownership of the [Company] is to an existing parent company. In the event that there is a change of control to a third party whether by the acquisition of the majority of the shares by one or more persons acting in concert, a sale, disposal and/or transfer. Then the following sums shall be paid to the following persons: [name/amount].

C.594

Where more than [number] of the voting shares of the [Company] are transferred and/or disposed of to a third party whether for money and/or other some other benefit by any person and/or company at any time. That transfer and/or disposal shall be considered and agreed as a change of control of the [Company].

C.595

[Name] agrees that where he/she intends to dispose of any shares and/or interest and/or enter into any charge and/or lien in and/or over the [Enterprise/Company] and its assets to a third party. That [Name] shall provide written notice in writing to the other parties to this agreement of that proposal in each case at least [one] month prior to any such steps and/or action being taken.

COOKIES

Internet, Websites and Apps

C.596

The [Client/User] agrees that:

1.1 The [Company] [and/or any parent, subsidiary, and/or associated third party, agent, market and/or research company] may send, transmit, place, deposit, store, retrieve, reproduce, alter, adapt, change, move, and/or otherwise vary the number, location, function, purpose, method, process, and/or otherwise of the Cookies on the software and/or hard drive on the [Clients'/Users] computer, mobile phone, gadget, and/or other system and/or device which the [Client] may own and/or control and through which you have gained access to the [Website/App/Platform] known as [specify name/reference] which is [owned/controlled/other] by the [Company].

1.2 That all and/or some of the Cookies may remain indefinitely on the software and/or hard drive until such time as they may be deleted and/or modified and/or otherwise changed by the [Company] and/or the [Client/User].

1.3 That there is no transfer and/or assignment of any copyright, database rights, computer software rights and/or any other intellectual property rights in the Cookies by the [Company]. That the [Client/User] shall not acquire any rights and/or interest of any nature in any medium at any time.

1.4 That where the [Client/User] are under [number] years of age, that a parent and/or guardian is aware of your use and/or access to the [Website/App/Platform] and has provided consent.

1.5 That the [Company] shall have the right to allocate the [Client/User] a unique identifier code which shall be linked to all the data, images, films, videos, searches, purchases, browsing and/or other information retrieved from the Cookies.

1.6 That the [Company] shall have the right to use the unique identifier code to retrieve, collate, analyse and/or store all the data, images, films, videos, searches, purchases, browsing and/or other information which can be derived from the Cookies regarding the [Clients'/Users'] use of sectors of and access to the [Website/App/Platform], pattern of behaviour over a period of one or more visits, personal profile and online preferences, use of [subject] resources, use of any links and/or banners and/or any other material whether text, images, videos, films, sound recordings, products, services and/or otherwise.

C.597

The [Company] agree and undertake that there shall be no obligation on the [Client/User] to accept the Cookies from the [Company] [and/or any parent, subsidiary, and/or associated third party, agent, market and/or research company] that the [Company] may wish to store and/or retrieve to and from the hard drive and/or software of the computer, mobile phone, gadget, and/or other system and/or device of the [Client/User] through which the [Client/User] has gained access to the [Website/App/Platform] known as [specify name and reference] which is [owned/controlled/other] by the [Company].

C.598

The [Enterprise] agrees that the [Client/User] may delete, block and/or deny access and/or the supply of the Cookies by the [Enterprise]. The [Enterprise] is obliged to inform the [Client/User] as to how to delete and/or block access and/or how to remove the Cookies. The following methods are advised [specify methods of deletion/blocking/removal].

C.599

The [Client/User] agrees that the [Distributor] may obtain and use the data and information in the form of log file data, codes and identifier codes obtained from the Cookies which are placed on the hard drive and/or the software to carry out the following functions:

1.1 Track online traffic flows and preferences.

1.2 Analyse profiles of visitors.

1.3 Assess how to make the [Website/App/Platform] more user-friendly.

1.4 Aid the playing of any online game, betting, gambling and/or participation in any quiz, competition and/or animated game.

1.5 Supply the cookies, log file data and unique identifier code to measurement and research companies to analyse and report back on how the service could be improved.

1.6 Save the [Client/User] repeating different functions they have already completed when they visit the [Website/App/Platform] including auto-resume, customised elements, layout of page, animation, audio material preferences, preferences based on geographic location and subject, news, weather, sport, colours.

1.7 Attach a unique identifier number for each hard drive and/or software on any computer and/or other gadget and/or mobile.

1.8 Track and record the journey through the [Website/App/Platform] by any [Client/User].

1.9 Assist in the downloading of material.

C.600

The [Company] has the following main Cookies embedded in the [Website/App/Platform]: [specify name/type/function].

C.601

The [Enterprise] agrees and undertakes that none of the data, information and other material obtained from the Cookies shall be supplied to any third parties except [specify names and addresses] who will analyse the data only in relation to a code and not with any personal details of the [Client/User].

C.602

The [Company] shall not be entitled to load and/or use cookies in respect of your data, searches and/or other use of the [Company] email newsletters, websites, apps and/or any banner links and/or other promotions unless you have provided your explicit prior consent. Failure to provide consent may mean that the [Company] will be obliged to restrict access.

C.603

Where data is collected through the use of cookies and/or any other analysis and/or storage and/or tracking device by the [Company], its distributors, payment agents, banks advertisers and delivery agents. The [Company] shall not treat all such information as confidential nor can it undertake that it can prevent access by all unauthorised third parties. The [Company] shall however ensure that all bank account details and passwords and codes are classified as private and confidential. A delivery name and address shall not be confidential nor shall the details of the products purchased.

C.604

The policy of the [Company] is respect of the use of Cookies is set out in the following document appendix A. You are advised to read this document prior to agreeing to the terms and conditions of access to this [Website/App/Platform].

The [Company] uses Cookies to track your searches, movements and use of the site and whether this led to a purchase or not and/or for security and other purposes. This data and information is stored and analysed by the [Company] to improve the function of the site; develop marketing strategies and to offer you targeted products and/or services which suit your interests. This data and information may be shared with third parties but not your personal private details such as your name, address, contact and/or bank details. If you cannot agree to the use of the Cookies which may be placed on your software and/or hardware then please do not sign this agreement for access to this site. It is a mandatory requirement and as we cannot ensure that no cookies will be used if you refuse your consent.

COPYRIGHT CLEARANCE

Film, Television and Video

C.605

The [Company] shall be solely responsible for all the administration, legal advice, funding and payments in respect of all necessary clearances, consents, licences, contracts including copyright and intellectual property rights, artists, performers, writers, contributors, location access, musicians, music, lyrics, products, services and sums due to licensing bodies, collecting societies, collective management organisations, independent management entities, rights holder, trade organisations and/or other third parties arising out of and/or in connection with the development and production of the [Film/Video/CD/Audio File] and/or any adaptation manufactured, distributed, sold, rented, supplied and/or exploited under this agreement.

C.606

1.1 The [Company/Name] warrants and undertake that they hold all legal rights in the [Series] including copyright and intellectual property rights and have cleared and obtained consent from any licensing body, collecting society and/or collective management organisation, independent management entity and/or rights holder.

1.2 That [[Company/Name] are not aware of any claim and/or rights of any third including any agent, distributor, licensee and/or radio, television and/or other media enterprise which might conflict and/or interfere with any of the terms of this agreement and/or the exercise of the rights granted.

1.3 That [Company/Name] is able to supply to the [Licensee] a complete list of all copyright, contract, licence, royalties and other payments which may be due for the exercise of any rights to third parties and/or any licensing bodies, collecting society, collective management organisation, independent management entity and/or rights holder.

C.607

The [Company/Name] confirms and undertakes that:

1.1 The [Company/Name] has obtained and will continue to own and/or control all rights throughout the [Territory] for the Term of the Agreement and the Sell-Off Period in the [Film/Series].

1.2 The [Company/Name] has paid and will pay all the development, production, copyright, rights, contract and reproduction costs of the [Film/Series] including the soundtrack due and/or owing and all taxes, costs, salaries, fees, advances, royalties and/or other sums due to performers, artists, writers, composers, musicians and support personnel. Together with all clearance costs that may be due in respect of the reproduction and exploitation of content of the [Film/Series] including images, stills, archive footage, graphics, artwork, music, products, sounds, computer-generated material, and any other material and/or rights of any nature.

1.3 That the [Licensor] has cleared and will pay for the sums due for the exercise of the rights in the format of [DVDs/Electronic Download/ Streaming subscription service over the internet]. That the [Licensee] shall not be liable for such sums and shall be reimbursed by the [Company/Name] upon receipt of an invoice if charged for any reason. Provided that the [Licensee] shall be responsible for the cost of all sums due to any licensing bodies, collecting societies, collective management organisations, independent management entities and/ or rights holders which are listed in appendix A and attached to this agreement in respect of the mechanical reproduction, transmission, broadcast, download, supply and/or performance of the [Film/Series] in the authorised format of [DVDs/Electronic Downloads/Streaming subscription service over the internet].

C.608

The [Company/Name] agrees and undertakes that to the best of its knowledge and belief the [Film/Sound Recording/Footage], its title and content including any interview, images, paintings, artwork, performance, music, lyrics, trade marks, service marks, logos, slogans, products, locations and/or services used have been cleared and paid for by the [Company/ Name] for the exploitation of the rights granted to the [Licensee] in clause [–]. That there are no outstanding contractual issues and/or liabilities and/ or copyright and/or intellectual property issues and/or disputes and/or legal proceedings. That the exploitation of the [Film/Sound Recording/Footage] in [specify format] in the licensed [Territory/country] by the [Licensee] will not infringe, breach and/or encroach upon any copyright, literary, dramatic, musical and/or other artistic and/or performance and/or contractual rights of any third party from [date] to [date].

C.609

The [Licensee] warrants and undertakes that it shall be solely responsible for the payments of any sums which arise through the exploitation of the [DVD/Video/Theatric/Non-Theatric] Rights under this agreement which are due to any sums due to any licensing bodies, collecting societies, collective management organisations, independent management entities, rights holder and/or other third parties for mechanical reproduction and/ or performance and/or otherwise which have not been paid for by the [Licensor]. The [Licensee] shall be liable to pay any other contributors and/ or third parties which appear and/or perform in person and/or in the form of a computer generated image and/or who have provided products and/or services which have been cleared but not paid for by the [Licensor] which may be due for the exploitation of the rights exercised by the [Licensee] in the [Territory].

C.610

1.1 The [Licensor] shall be solely responsible for obtaining and paying for all necessary consents, clearances, waivers and/or licences in respect of all copyright and/or any other intellectual property rights in any artistic, musical and/or literary work, sound recordings, films and/or any other rights and/or arrangements with third parties which directly and/or indirectly relate to the production, distribution and exploitation of the [Film] in the following format [DVD/Electronic Download/Archive Playback library under a subscription service]. The [Licensor] agrees and undertakes that it shall be responsible for all such payments in respect of the exercise of those rights granted to the [Licensee]. This clause shall be subject to the exception in 1.3.

1.2 The [Licensor] shall supply the [Licensee] at the [Licensor's] cost and expense upon request by the [Licensee] with copies of documentation relating to 1.1. In the event that the [Licensee] shall be required to make any payment to any third party for any reason due to the failure of the [Licensor] to obtain clearance or consents then the [Licensor] agrees to reimburse in full. If the [Licensor] should fail to pay any such sums then the [Licensee] shall be entitled to deduct them from any sums due to the [Licensor] under this agreement.

1.3 The [Licensee] agrees that the only exception to 1.1 shall be the reporting and payments due to any sums due to licensing bodies, collecting societies, collective management organisations, independent management entities and/or rights holders in any country for the reproduction, transmission, performance and/or supply of the [Film] in the following format [DVD/Electronic Download/Archive Playback library under a subscription service] which may be required as a result of the exercise of the rights granted to the [Licensee]. The [Licensee] agrees that they shall make such payments and shall not be entitled to deduct any such sums from monies due to the [Licensor].

C.611

1.1 The [Company] agrees that it shall be responsible for all payments which are or may become due in respect of the [Artiste] and/or the [Musical Work] and/or any associated film, podcast and/or sound recording in respect of the production, distribution and exploitation of the [CD/Electronic Download/Vinyl/Disc] in any media throughout the world not set out in the agreed Budget in Appendix A.

1.2 That any copyright and intellectual property rights in the [Musical Work] shall be held in the name of the [Artiste]. That any registrations in the sound recordings, films, videos, podcasts and/or other material developed pursuant to this agreement shall be held as rights holders by the [Artiste] and the [Company]. That all registrations with any licensing bodies, collecting societies, collective management organisations and/ independent management entities shall be as joint rights holders.

C.612

1.1   In respect of the [Film/Sound Recording] to be used in the format of a [DVD/Disc/Podcast] the [Company] undertakes that all copyright and any other consents and rights shall be cleared and paid for in respect of the rights licensed under this agreement for use by the [Licensee]. This undertaking shall not include the consent of the [Artist] and any licence related to the [Musical Work] which shall be the responsibility of the [Licensee] to obtain and pay as required.

1.2   In addition the [Licensee] shall bear the cost of and report any usage to any licensing bodies, collecting societies, collective management organisations, independent management entities in any country for the mechanical reproduction, transmission, performance and/or supply of the [Film/Sound Recording] in the following format [DVD/Disc/ Podcast].The [Licensee] agrees that they shall make such payments and reports and shall not be entitled to deduct any such sums from monies due to the [Company].

C.613

The [Assignee] confirms that it shall be responsible for any payments in respect of the [Artiste] and the [Musical Work] and any sums due in respect of the distribution and exploitation of the [DVD/Video/Disc] in any media throughout the [Territory] which are not set out in the agreed Budget. The [Assignee] confirms that it shall be responsible for any payments due in respect of any performing rights in any music and the mechanical reproduction of the [DVD/Video/Disc].

C.614

1.1   The [Company] represents and warrants that it will be the owner of and/or will control all rights in the [Film/Series/Podcasts] which are granted to the [Distributor]. The [Company] undertakes to obtain the consent in writing of all writers, artists, musicians, performers and other contributors whose appearances, performances, graphics, artwork and/or other material are reproduced in the [Film/Series/Podcasts]. That all necessary consents licences, waivers and/or other authorisations shall be obtained which are needed for the reproduction, distribution, sale, rental, supply and promotion of the [Film/Series/Podcasts] in [specify format]. Together with all necessary clearance for the use of professional and personal names, photographs, biographies and likenesses of any person on labels, websites, apps, in newspapers and magazines and other promotional material.

1.2 The [Company] shall provide the [Distributor] with a comprehensive and complete list of all royalties, repeat fees and other payments that may become due as a result of the exploitation of the rights granted to the [Distributor]. That there shall be no right for the [Distributor] to off-set and/or recoup any such clearance payments from sums due to the [Company]. The list provided by the [Company] shall also include details of any sums due to licensing bodies, collecting societies, collective management organisations, independent management entities and/or other rights holders.

C.615

1.1 The [Licensor] warrants that it will be the owner of and/or control copyright and any other intellectual property rights and other rights in the [Film/Video] which are granted to the [Licensee].

1.2 The [Licensor] will secure the consent in writing of all presenters, artists and musicians whose performances are reproduced in the [Film/Video] together with all other consents, licences and agreements necessary for the reproduction, manufacture, distribution, sale, supply, rental of [Film/Video] in the following formats: [specify formats] and for extracts of up to [number] minutes in duration to be broadcast, transmitted and/ or supplied on [specify medium/television/radio/online channels and accounts over the internet].

1.3 The [Licensor] shall supply the [Licensee] with a complete list of any clearance payments that must be made by the [Licensee] to any person and/or company from the exercise of the rights granted in this agreement. The [Licensee] shall not be liable for any production costs which shall be borne by the [Licensor].

1.4 In addition the [Licensee] shall be responsible for reporting any usage and making any payments in respect of the performing rights and/ or the mechanical reproduction and/or broadcast, transmission and/or supply of any music in respect of the exercise of the rights granted to the [Licensee] due to licensing bodies, collecting societies, collective management organisations and/or other independent management entities and//or other rights holders.

C.616

1.1 The [Assignee] agrees that it shall be responsible for any payments due in respect of the [Artiste] and the [Musical Work] and any other sums due in respect of the reproduction, distribution, performance, transmission, supply and exploitation of the [DVD/Video/Sound Recording] in any format and/or media which have been cleared but which are covered in the [Budget/Production Costs].

1.2 The [Assignee] shall be responsible for reporting any usage and making any payments in respect of the performing rights and/or the mechanical reproduction and/or broadcast, transmission and/or supply of any musical work, sound recordings and/or adaptation and/or any other material in any format in respect of the exercise of the rights assigned due to licensing bodies, collecting societies, collective management organisations and/or other independent management entities and//or other rights holders.

C.617

The [Promoter] agrees to provide the [Company] with the following details in respect of the production of any promotional material for the [Company's] when the material is delivered. A full breakdown of all payments which may fall due and the copyright clearances, contractual consents and obligations, waivers, licences, product placement and any other relevant matters. The promotional material shall be cleared for use in all media including television, radio, podcasts, interviews, social media accounts and channels, newsfeeds and otherwise. The list shall include artistes, performers, musicians, lyrics and music. It shall also list usage reports due, licence terms and payments due to licensing bodies, collecting societies, collective management organisations and/or other independent management entities and/or other rights holders for any use of the promotional material due to mechanical reproduction, performing rights, transmission and/or otherwise at any time.

C.618

The [Assignor] confirms and undertakes that it is controls the physical material of the [Film/Video/Sound Recording] which is in its possession which is being assigned to [Name]. There are no assurances and/or warranties provided regarding ownership of copyright, intellectual property rights and any other rights in the [Film/Video/Sound Recordings] which are assigned under this agreement. It is the responsibility of the [Assignee] to obtain consent for use of any material and to pay any costs that may be incurred for any form of exploitation.

C.619

The [Assignor] agrees and undertakes that all copyright and any other rights (except for the Artiste and the Musical Work) including consents required under [specify legislation] shall be cleared and paid for in respect of the rights assigned under this agreement to the [Assignee] of the [Film/Video] as are set out in the [Production Budget]. The [Assignee] shall be responsible for all all clearance and payments due in respect of the Artiste] and [Musical Work]. Together with all additional costs which may fall due to any third party from the exploitation of the [Film/Video] and/or any part not covered by the [Production Budget]. This liability shall include reports to and payments to licensing bodies, collecting societies, collective management organisations and/or other independent management entities and/or other rights holders for any use of the whole and/or any part of the [Film/Video] which arise as a result of mechanical reproduction, performing rights, transmission and/or otherwise at any time.

C.620

The [Assignor] undertakes that all sums due in respect of the production of the [specify title] of [Film/Recording/DVD] shall be paid as set out in the [Budget]. That in the event that it is expected that the [Budget] will be exceeded the [Assignee] shall be notified immediately in writing. That no additional costs or expenses shall be incurred without the prior consent of the [Assignee]. That the [Budget] only sets out the cost of clearance and payments for the [DVD Rights and the Non-Theatric Rights] and not all other media, nor the performing rights in any music or the mechanical reproduction of recordings by any third party.

C.621

1.1   The [Licensor] confirms that all sums due for the production of the [Film/Series] have and/or will be paid for and that no such costs are the responsibility of the [Licensee].

1.2   The [Licensor] confirms that it has arranged for clearances, consents, waivers, releases and all necessary copyright, moral right, intellectual property, and contractual matters for the exploitation of the [Television and Archive Playback Rights, DVD and Video Rights] in the [Film/ Series]. The [Licensee] shall bear the cost of all such royalties and other payments as may be due to third parties for the broadcast, transmission, mechanical reproduction, performing rights, supply and/ or other form of exploitation exercised by the [Licensee] granted under this agreement. The [Licensee] shall make reports and payments to licensing bodies, collecting societies, collective management organisations and/or other independent management entities and//or other rights holders' for any use of the [Film/Series] by the [Licensee] and/or sub-licensee].

C.622

The [Assignee] agrees and undertakes that it shall be responsible for and bear the cost of providing the services of and attendance of the [Artiste] and the [Musical Works] as required by the [Assignor] for the purpose of producing the [Project/Video] for [specify purpose].

C.623

1.1 In respect of the [Film/Extracts] the [Licensor] confirms that all copyright and any other rights of any nature including dancers, performers, writers, choreographers, music, lyrics, musicians, images and designers have been obtained in respect of the rights granted under this agreement.

1.2 The [Licensee] shall be responsible for payment of any sums that arise through the exploitation of [specify type of rights/use] and the associated promotional purposes. The [Licensee] shall be responsible to make such usage reports to licensing bodies, collecting societies, collective management organisations and/or other independent management entities and//or other rights holders' for any use of the whole and/or any part of the [Film/Extracts] which have been notified by the [Licensor] and are set out in appendix A.

C.624

1.1 The [Assignor] confirms in respect of the [Film/Video] and the accompanying soundtrack that all consents, copyright, rights in any music and/or any other intellectual property and/or other rights have been obtained in respect of the rights assigned under this agreement.

1.2 The [Assignee] shall be responsible and pay the cost of all clearance and/or other copyright and/or licence payments and any other sums that may arise due to any third party in any country in respect of the exploitation of the [DVD/Video/Disc] Rights in the [Film/Video] and any authorised marketing by the [Assignee].

C.625

The [Assignee] undertakes and agrees that it shall be solely responsible for any sums due in respect of the manufacture, reproduction, distribution, marketing and exploitation of the [DVD/Video/Disc] Rights in the [Film] and any parts including any payments due for the performing rights in any music and the mechanical reproduction of the [Film].

C.626

The [Assignor] agrees and undertakes in respect of the [Series] that all copyright, consents, releases, waivers, licences and other rights and clearances including performers, musicians, appearances, format, script, text, quotes, rules, music, artwork, logos, trade marks, service marks, stills, footage, computer-generated material, ringtones, sounds, slogans, title and credits, products and any other material or content of any nature shall be cleared in respect of the [specify rights] assigned under this agreement. Provided that the [Assignor] shall only be liable to make such payments as are set out in Production Costs in Appendix A. All other sums of any nature shall be at the cost and the liability of the [Assignee].

C.627

The [Assignee] confirms that it shall be responsible for any sums which arise through the exploitation of the rights which are not set out in the [Approved Budget] including but not limited to any payments due to the [PRS for Music/PPL/MCPS/other] in respect of the performing rights and/or the mechanical reproduction and/or any other use of any music and/or sound recordings in the [Series].

C.628

In respect of the [Film/DVD/Video] the [Assignor] undertakes and agrees that all copyright and any further rights including music and consents shall be cleared in respect of the [Non-Theatric Rights] assigned under this agreement provided that the [Assignor] shall only be responsible for such clearance payments as follows: [specify and list]. Any other costs and sums due shall be the responsibility of the [Assignee].

C.629

The [Company] confirms that it shall be responsible for the clearance, acquisition of rights, consents, releases, permissions, waivers, contracts, and payments of all costs, fees, royalties and other sums due in respect of the following matters in the [Film/Recording/Pilot] in respect of the use, reproduction, performance, mechanical reproduction, performing rights, transmission, distribution and licensing of the [specify type] Rights in [Country/Territory] from [date] to [date]:

1.1 Artistes, musicians, production, technical and editing personnel and companies, consultants, services, promotional and marketing persons and companies.

1.2 Music, lyrics, stills, films, podcasts, products, ringtones, sounds, computer generated material, images, graphics, designs, text, slogans, service marks, trade marks, domain names, artwork, sound recordings, internet material and [other].

C.630

The [Assignee] agrees that from the date of full signature of this assignment it shall be liable to bear the cost and expense of clearing and paying for all copyright, consents, releases and any sums due for the use and exploitation of the [Work] and the [Work Material] of any nature. The [Assignor] shall not be liable whether or not the matter was disclosed to the [Assignee] at any time or not.

C.631

[Name] shall not be obliged to have cleared, obtained any consents, copyright or any other rights in any part of the [Material] which is being acquired and assigned to the [Company]. [Name] provides no warranties and/or undertakings and does not represent and/or purport to know who owns or controls any rights in the [Material]. It is the responsibility of the [Company] to obtain and pay for any rights which it intends to use and/or does exploit at any time and no sums shall be claimed from [Name] and/or be due to be paid to [Name].

C.632

[Presenter/Name] agrees and accepts that the [Distributor] shall be entitled to recoup all costs, expenses, fees, charges and copyright clearances, mechanical reproduction, performing rights and/or any other sums due to any collecting society and/or other third parties for the development, production, reproduction, manufacture, marketing and exploitation of the [specify format] of the [Film] from the sums received including legal fees and other costs related to copyright protection and/or trade mark disputes and/or product recalls before the calculation of the royalties due of the Net Receipts to the [Presenter/Name].

C.633

All sums which may arise and/or be due which relate to the payment of copyright clearance and/or other fees for the use, reproduction and exploitation of any photographs, films, videos, manuscripts and diaries and/or any other material involved in the [Project] shall be the entirely at the cost and expense of the [Production Company] and not [Name].

C.634

It is agreed by the parties that [Name] shall not be liable to pay and/or contribute to any costs, sums and/or expenses that may be incurred and/or fall due at any time in respect of any third party contract, licence and/or copyright clearance and/or the acquisition of any intellectual property rights and/or any other material and/or contribution and/or performance and/or product and/or any other medium of any nature and/or images, text and/or music and/or sound recording and/or lyrics that appear in and/or reproduced in the [Film] and/or any other exploitation of the format of [DVD/Disc/other] and/or any associated packaging, marketing, promotion, registration and/or merchandising in any part of the world at any time. The sums shall be the sole responsibility and liability of the [Company] and the [Company] waives all rights to make any such claim against [Name].

C.635

1.1 The [Production Company] agrees and undertakes that all necessary copyright and other underlying intellectual property rights in the [Programme] including any soundtrack and music have and/or will be cleared for the proposed forms of exploitation itemised in clause [–].

1.2 The [Production Company] shall only be liable for the cost of the clearance payments set out in the agreed budget. The [Assignee/Licensee] shall be liable for any other costs and sums that may fall due to be paid to any third party for any reason whether those sums have been forecast by the [Production Company] or not.

C.636

1.1 The [Company] confirms that all clearances and consents have been obtained from all performers, musicians, actors, writers, directors, producers and any other contributors to the [Programme] and all relevant copyright related collecting agencies including but not limited to the [specify collective management organisations/licensing bodies/rights holders].

1.2 That any payments to be paid by the [Licensee] which may arise as a result of the exploitation of the [Programme] throughout the Territory during the term of this Agreement whether referred to as advances, residuals, royalties or licence fees have been detailed in the attached Schedule A.

1.3 That where there are any disputes regarding the payments in Schedule A which were not disclosed by the [Company]. Then the [Company] shall not be liable for any legal costs, damages and/or losses that the [Licensee] may incur and the [Licensee] accepts that it must bear any such costs.

C.637

The [Company] confirms and undertakes that all contractual obligations, licences, clearances, consents and payments which shall arise as a result of the transmission and/or exploitation of the [Film/Series] by the [Company] with respect to artists, performers, musicians, presenters, artistic works, musical works, literary works, images, sound recordings, films and videos and/or in respect of any licensing bodies, collecting societies, collective management organisations and/or other independent management entities and/or other rights holders for any use of the whole and/or any part of the [Film/Series] shall be the sole responsibility of the [Company] and not the [Production Company/Licensor].

C.638

The [Company] confirms that all contractual arrangements with third parties have been entered into on a complete buy-out basis and that no additional payments of any nature to any third parties shall be due except those which may be due of the collective management and/or licensing bodies [PRS Music/PPL/MCPS/other] notified to the [Distributor]. The [Distributor] shall be responsible for making any usage reports and/or paying any sums which may be due.

C.639

The [Licensor] confirms that it is the exclusive licensee controls all copyright and any other rights in the [Film/Video] which are granted to the [Sub-Licensee] under this agreement.

C.640

The [Licensor] agrees and undertakes that it is the original creator of the [Format] described in appendix A and is the sole owner. That no other person and/or company and/or third party has made any contribution and/or is entitled to make any claim of ownership.

C.641

The [Assignor] confirms that it is the sole owner of the [Series/Film] including the soundtrack which are assigned under this agreement subject to the following exclusive licences and other agreements which exist at the time of this agreement set out in appendix A. [summarise and list all licences and agreements and describe in detail]

C.642

The [Assignor] agrees and undertakes that all copyright and any other rights including footage, stills, music, and performances and consents required in the [Series] shall as far as reasonably possible be obtained and cleared for use in [specify rights/use/all media]. The [Assignee] agrees and accepts that it shall be responsible for any report and payments which may be due in the future in relation to the [Assignee's] exploitation of the [Series]. The [Assignee] shall be responsible for any sums due in respect of the performing rights, mechanical reproduction and/or otherwise to any collective management organisation and/or collecting society.

C.643

In respect of the [Film] the [Assignor] undertakes that all copyright and any other rights musical or otherwise, including consents required under the [Copyright, Designs and Patents Act 1988 as amended] shall be obtained and cleared in respect of the rights assigned under this agreement. Provided that the [Assignor] shall only be responsible for such clearance payments as are set out in the Budget in Schedule A. That the [Assignee] shall be responsible for all other sums that may be due from the exploitation of the [Film] and/or parts and/or any adaptation of any rights of any nature in any medium and/or by any method.

C.644

The [Assignee] agrees and undertakes that it shall be solely responsible for any sums due in respect of the exploitation and/or adaptation of the [Film] and/or parts and that the [Assignor] shall not be liable for any such payments. The [Assignee] shall also be responsible for any sums which may be due in respect of the performing rights in any music and the mechanical reproduction of the [Film].

C.645

The [Licensor] confirms that all sums due in respect of the development, production and delivery of the [Film] to the [Licensee] have been paid. That the [Licensor] undertakes that no further sums shall be due to any writers, artist, performer, director, musicians, production and technical support crew and/or in respect of location filming, products, services and/or any material in which there are copyright and/or intellectual property rights and/or any other consent, waiver, contractual obligation and/or rights except the following matters which shall be paid by the [Licensee]: [list details].

C.646

The [Company] agrees and undertakes that all sums due in respect of the development, production, reproduction, distribution, promotion, transmission and exploitation of the [Series] will be the responsibility of the [Company]. That the [Sponsor] is not and shall not be liable for any such payments.

C.647

1.1 [Company] warrants that it is and/or shall be the sole and absolute owner of the [Film/Sound Recordings] and all copyright and/or future copyright and/or any other intellectual property rights and/or any other rights of the [Film/Sound Recordings] in all media in any medium.

1.2 The [Company] agrees and undertakes that no rights and/or material shall be included the [Film] which are owned and/or controlled by a third party.

1.3 That the [Licensee] shall not be liable to pay the [Company] any additional payments for the transmission of the [Film] in the [Series]. Provided that the [Licensee] shall be responsible for any sums that may be due to the [Company] in respect of the following licensing bodies, collecting societies, collective management organisations and/or other independent management entities: [list in detail].

C.648

The [Licensor] agrees and undertakes:

1.1 That it will be the owner of and/or will control all rights in the [Series] which are granted to the [Distributor] in this agreement. That the [Licensor] has and/or will secure the consent in writing of all artists and/or musicians whose performances are reproduced in the [Series] including the soundtrack and/or any writers and/or all other consents necessary for the broadcast and transmissions of the [Series] in the manner authorised in this agreement. Except that the [Distributor] shall be responsible and liable for any reports and sums due to any licensing bodies, collecting societies, collective management organisations and/or other independent management entities which may be due from the exercise of the rights.

1.2 That the [Distributor] shall be entitled to use the legal and professional names, photographs, images, likeness, biography, profile and filmed interviews and podcasts of the main artists and musicians whose performances are reproduced in the [Series] and any other persons in minor roles. For the sole purpose of the marketing and promotion of the [Series] and not for merchandising and/or sub-licensing to endorse a product and/or service.

1.3 That it possesses full power and authority to enter into and perform this agreement and that at the date of execution there are not and during the full period of time during which the [Distributor] retains the rights granted in clause [–]. There will not be any liens and/or encumbrances against the [Series] which will and/or might impair the exercise of the rights. That the [Licensor] has not granted and will not grant any rights the exercise of which would derogate from and/or be inconsistent with the rights granted to the [Distributor].

C.649

1.1 The [Assignor] agrees and undertakes it will ensure that all such consents, waivers, licences and other agreements as are necessary under any legislation, regulations, union agreements, guidelines and/or codes of practice in [country] to develop and produce the [Film/Sound Recording] and/or part(s) have been obtained and/or adhered to. That the [Assignor] has paid all production costs and that there are no outstanding matters and/or legal issues which have not been resolved.

1.2 That the [Assignor] shall not be liable for any future royalties, costs and fees that may be due as a result of the exploitation of the [Film/Sound Recording] by the [Assignee] and/or any other third party. That the [Assignor] has paid all the sums due in order to enable it to make the [Film/Sound Recording] and acquire the rights in the [Film/Sound

Recording] and/or parts assigned to the [Assignee]. That the [Assignee] shall be liable for all sums for the exploitation of the rights which have been assigned including royalties, additional advances, repeat fees and/or any sums due for performing rights, mechanical reproduction and/or otherwise to any licensing bodies, collecting societies, collective management organisations and/or other independent management entities and/or rights holders which may become due at any time.

1.3 The [Assignee] shall [not] be entitled to deduct all such sums as it and/or any third party may be required to pay in 1.2 from any royalties and/or other sums which may be calculated and due to the [Assignor] under this agreement.

C.650

1.1 The [Company] confirms that it was the maker of the [Film/Video] including the sound track and made all the necessary arrangements.

1.2 That the [Company] is the first owner of the copyright in the [Film/Video] including the sound track.

1.3 That the [Company] has cleared all material on which the [Film/Video] including the sound track was based and/or is incorporated in it as are necessary for the exploitation of the rights granted in this agreement. That all the consents, waivers, performances, options, licences and other documents relevant to the acquisition and exploitation of the rights for the [Film/Video] including the sound track such as music, footage, stills, contributors and any sums due to any licensing bodies, collective management organisations and/or otherwise are listed in detail in appendix A. Together with a list of all sums and/or payments which shall be due to be paid by the [Licensee] in respect of the exercise of the rights granted in the future and/or any obligations such as credits and/or copyright notices.

1.4 The [Company] undertakes that none of the rights granted to the [Licensee] have been assigned and/or licensed and/or transferred to another third party for the [Territory/world].

C.651

The [Company] warrants that it is the exclusive licensee of the rights granted to the [Licensee] and is fully entitled to give the warranties and make the representations concerning the [Film/Video/Series] including the sound track which are set out in the agreement.

C.652

The [Company] warrants that all consents necessary under [specify legislation] in [country] to make, exploit and authorise the exploitation of the

[Film Series] in the agreed [Territory] have been obtained [and paid for] by the [Company].

C.653

1.1 The [Company] agrees and undertakes that all sums due to produce the [Film] including the sound track and the master material have been paid. That the copyright, intellectual property rights and/or other rights have been cleared for the exploitation of the rights granted to the [Licensee] for the [Territory/world/country] for the Licence Period.

1.2 That the [Licensee] shall be obliged to agree to pay all the third parties listed in appendix A which have been cleared by the [Licensor] in respect of the exercise of rights by the [Licensee] and/or any sub-licensee under this agreement. That the [Licensee] agrees and undertakes to pay all such sums which may be due and to indemnify the [Licensor] in respect of a claim by a third party for such sums. It is agreed that the [Licensee] and/or any sub-licensee shall also be liable to pay any sums due for the performing rights and/or mechanical reproduction and/or any other payments due to any licensing bodies, collecting societies, collective management organisations and/or other independent management entities and/or rights holders which may become due at any time arising directly and/or indirectly from the rights granted to the [Licensee].

C.654

The [Company] warrants that neither the [Film/Video/Sound Recording] nor the any matter included in it and/or upon which it is based infringes the copyright and/or any other rights of any person and/or company in the [Territory/country/world].

C.655

The [Licensee] undertakes that it shall be responsible for all payments which may fall due in respect of the performing rights in any music as controlled by [PRS for Music] and/or any society affiliated to it in respect of the exercise of the rights granted under this agreement.

C.656

The [Licensor] confirms that all copyright and any other rights, including consents required under the [Copyright, Designs and Patents Act 1988 as amended] have been and/or will be obtained in respect of the rights granted under this agreement. That the [Licensor] shall notify the [Licensee] a complete list of all the third parties who may be due any fees, royalties and/or other sums in respect of their performance, contribution, music, sound recordings, images and/or other material. The Licensee accepts and agrees that it shall be solely responsible for any sums that may be due to third parties from the exercise and exploitation of the rights granted in this agreement. That shall include any reports and /or payments to any licensing bodies, collecting societies, collective management organisations and/or independent management entities.

C.657

1.1 The [Licensor] warrants that it has and/or will control all copyright, intellectual property rights and/or any other rights in the [Film/Series] which are granted to the [Distributor].

1.2 The [Licensor] has and/or shall secure the consent in writing of all presenters, contributors, performers and/or musicians whose performances are reproduced in the [Film/Series] and all other consents from third parties including writers that may necessary for the exploitation of the [Film/Series] in [specify rights/format] in any part of the world from [date] to [date] by the [Distributor]. That any such consent shall include the right to use a persons', name, image and/ or profile in respect of any associated marketing on any packaging, advertisement and/or promotional material on social media and/or any related podcast and/or video.

1.3 That the [Licensor] shall provide the [Distributor] with a comprehensive list of the contractual sums due and/or owing to any third party for the exploitation of the [Film/Series] at any time. The [Licensor] shall also confirm which third party have been bought out and who have assigned all rights in all media to whom no further payments shall be due. The [Distributor] agrees and undertakes to pay all such sums as may be due for the exploitation by the [Distributor] and/or any sub-licensee.

C.658

1.1 [Assignor] confirms and undertakes to the [Assignee] that the [Film/ Video/Sound Recording] is owned entirely by the [Assignor] and that there are no liens, charges and/or other claims by a third party in respect of the copyright, intellectual property rights and /or any other rights in the [Film/Video/Sound Recording] which would prevent the assignment of the rights to the [Assignee] and/or the transfer of ownership of the physical material. That the assignment is subject to the payment by the [Assignee] of any sums due in respect of clearances in any format and for any adaptation which has been obtained from third parties including writers, images, music, contributors and/or otherwise.

1.2 That the [Assignor] has cleared all copyright, [intellectual property rights] and any other rights in the [Film/Video/Sound Recording] for the following rights: [specify and list]. That the [Assignor] has only paid all sums due in the production budget and not those payments which may fall due for future exploitation in any format and/or adaptation. Those additional sums shall be at the cost and liability of the [Assignee].

1.3   The [Assignee] agrees and undertakes to pay all clearance payments which may fall due to third parties and shall also make such usage reports as may be required and payments to any licensing bodies, collecting societies, collective management organisations, independent management entities and/or rights holders.

C.659

1.1   The [Licensee] acknowledges and accepts that the [Licensor] is only licensing the right to use the [Film Extract] itself and is not providing any rights and/or undertakings in respect of the performances of the actors, performers, musicians and/or the music soundtrack or otherwise.

1.2   The [Licensee] agrees and undertakes that it shall not use the [Film Extract] without obtaining all the necessary consents, releases, authorisations, clearances and licences from any person, company or entity as may be necessary. That the [Licensee] shall also make such usage reports as may be required and payments to any licensing bodies, collecting societies, collective management organisations, independent management entities and/or rights holders. That the [Licensee] shall be responsible for the payment of all sums that are to be paid and/or become due as a result of the use of the [Film Extract].

C.660

1.1   The [Company] agrees and undertakes that it shall endeavour to only use persons and companies for the [Film/Video] who will agree to assign all the rights in all media to the [Company] for a fixed fee. So that no additional royalty payments and/or fees shall be due at any time. This strategy shall include performers, actors, artists, dancers, choreographers, composers, musicians, directors, writers and any other contributors performing and/or taking part in and/or contributing to the development and production of the [Film/Video].

1.2   Where for any legal reason and/or union and/or trade agreement there cannot be a buy-out in all media and/or the cost would be prohibitive then the [Company] shall attempt to obtain as many rights as possible by way of an assignment. It is agreed between the parties that the [Company] shall not be expected to exceed the agreed budget set out in Appendix A.

1.3   In any event the [Company] shall keep accurate and complete records of all such agreements and make copies of the documents available to the [Distributor] upon request. That after delivery of the master material of the [Film/Video] to the [Distributor] then the [Distributor] shall be liable to pay any sums due to third parties which may fall due form the reproduction, transmission, broadcast, mechanical reproduction use and/or adaptation of the [Film/Video].

C.661
The [Licensor] agrees and undertakes that it is the sole owner of and/ or controls all copyright and any other rights in the [Film/Video/Sound Recording]. That all copyright and any other rights musical and/or otherwise including consents under the [Copyright, Designs and Patents Act 1988 as subsequently amended] have been obtained. That the [Licensee] shall only be liable for the payments due for rights and consents which are set out in Schedule A which is attached. Together with any reports and payments due for the performing rights, mechanical reproduction and/or transmission, broadcast, reproduction and/or other exploitation to any licensing bodies, collecting societies, collective management organisations, independent management entities and/or rights holders.

C.662
The [Licensee] agrees and undertakes that it shall be responsible for any payment in respect of the performing rights in any music as are controlled by the [PRS for Music] or a society affiliated to it in respect of the rights in the [Extract] granted under this agreement.

C.663
That the [Company] has and/or will obtain, clear, pay for and/or have reached agreement as to future payments by a third party for all copyright and any other intellectual property rights, consents, waivers, licences and/ or otherwise which may be necessary for the [Company] to grant the rights to the [Distributor] in the [Work/Material] and for the [Distributor] to be able to exercise the rights.

C.664
The [Company] agrees that it is the sole owner of and/or controls all present and future copyright and any other rights in the [Advertisement/Promotion] which are assigned under this agreement except for the [Product/Services] and any other material supplied by the [Commissioning Company].

C.665
In respect of the [Advertisement/Promotion] the [Company] undertakes that all copyright and any other rights, musical or otherwise and consents required

under the [specify legislation] in [country] shall be cleared in respect of the [specify rights/format/countries] for exploitation by the [Commissioning Company]. Provided that the [Company] shall only be liable for such payments as are set out in the Approved Budget between the parties.

C.666

The [Commissioning Company] agrees and undertakes that it shall bear the cost of obtaining and paying for all copyright, consents, clearance, waivers and contract payments set out in the [Approved Budget] including any sums due in respect of the distribution, exploitation, performance and/or mechanical reproduction of any music in respect of the [Advertisement/Film] in any media throughout the [Territory/world].

C.667

The [Agent] agrees and undertakes that all copyright, consents, music and any other rights required under the [Copyright, Designs and Patents Act 1988 as amended] have and/or will be cleared and paid for in respect of the transmission and/or broadcast by the [Company] of the [Advertisement/Film] including the soundtrack on channel: [specify details] and/or in electronic form over the internet through website of the [Company] by means of a playback archive service within [one] month of transmission and/or broadcast. The [Television Company] will be liable to pay such sums as are due in respect of the performing and/or mechanical reproduction rights due to [PRS Music] or a society affiliated to it.

C.668

1.1 The [Production Company] confirms that it shall control all copyright and/or any other rights in the [Film] except for the [Author's Work].

1.2 The [Production Company] and/or any licensee and/or assignee shall be entirely responsible for all costs incurred and sums due in respect of the development, production, distribution, marketing and exploitation of the [Film] and parts in any form and/or any sums due to any licensing bodies, collecting societies, collective management organisations, independent management entities and/or rights holders.

1.3 The [Author] is not and shall not be liable for any such payments in 1.2 and the [Production Company] and/or any licensee and/or assignee shall not be entitled to deduct any such sums prior to the payment of the royalties due to the [Author].

C.669

1.1 The [Production Company] agrees and undertakes that it shall be solely responsible for obtaining and paying for all copyright clearances, consents, waivers, licences, contractual obligations and any other rights which are due and/or owed to any third parties arising directly and/or indirectly in respect of any material in the [Film] including the soundtrack and/or parts.

1.2 The [Production Company] shall also be solely responsible for the cost of any exploitation of any of the rights in any media granted under this agreement including but not limited to, artistic, musical, literary works, sound recordings, films, performing rights in any music, mechanical reproduction of any recordings, actors, writers, stills, footage, computer generated material, and products. None of these costs shall be the responsibility of the [Author] and they shall not be deducted from the Gross Receipts.

C.670

The [Author] confirms that the [Author's Work] is the original work of the [Author] and does not infringe the copyright, intellectual property rights and/or any other rights of any third party throughout the [Territory/country] in respect of the rights granted to the [Production Company] under this agreement.

C.671

The [Company] undertakes that it was the maker of the [Film] and the person by whom the arrangements necessary for the making of the [Film] were made and the first owner of copyright in the [Film] and has acquired all rights in all material on which the [Film] is based as are necessary for the exercise of the rights granted under this agreement.

C.672

In respect of the [Pilot] the [Assignor] undertakes that all sums due in respect of the production of the [Pilot] will be paid and that the [Company] is not and will not be liable for any such payments. In respect of the [Pilot] the [Assignor] undertakes that all copyright and any other rights, consents, clearances, music or otherwise shall be cleared and paid for as are set out in the agreed [Budget] set out in Appendix A for the following purpose: [private viewings/other].

C.673

1.1 The [Assignor] agrees and undertakes that all copyright, consents, releases, moral rights, contractual obligations, music and any other rights of any nature shall be cleared in respect of all rights granted under this agreement but shall only be paid for to the extent that such payment is provided for in the [Budget] which is agreed between the parties and attached in appendix C.

1.2 The [Assignee] agrees and undertakes that it shall bear any additional costs of clearance payments not covered in the [Budget]. Any such payments shall be added to the sums allocated as Distribution Expenses. Payments due in respect of the performing rights in any music or the mechanical reproduction of the recordings shall as far as possible be at the cost of any third party who is authorised to exploit the [Film] and/or parts.

C.674

The [Company] shall set out a clear statement of all material to be cleared and acquired for the [Film/Video] and the soundtrack and the cost of clearance for:

1.1 All forms of satellite, terrestrial, cable television and radio including on: [specify channels].

1.2 All forms of electronic and telecommunication forms of exploitation over the internet, social media, websites, apps, banners and pop-ups, search engines and ringtones, images, sound and text on mobile phones, computers, televisions and other gadgets or devices.

1.3 Outdoor advertising, billboards, posters, newspapers, magazines, comics, food products, clothing and other forms of merchandising, endorsement and product promotion.

The [Company] shall use the budget to clear and pay for such rights. Where possible the [Company] shall acquire all media rights but where this would result in the Budget being exceeded they should merely advise the [Commissioning Company] of this fact and not acquire additional rights. The [Company] shall only be responsible for clearance and payment for material to the limit of the Budget.

C.675

The [Commissioning Company] confirms that it shall be responsible at its sole cost for all copyright and other clearance payments not set out in the Budget including any sums due in respect of the distribution and exploitation of the [Film/Video/Sound Recording] in any media throughout the [Territory/world] including any sums due for the performing rights in any music and the mechanical reproduction of any music.

C.676

1.1 The [Company] confirms and undertakes that all rights necessary for the use of [Work/Format/Scripts] for the [Film/Video/Series] have been cleared and paid for by the [Company for [one] broadcast and/or transmission on channel [specify details] from [date] to date].

1.2   That [Name] shall be entitled to the following fees and royalties for any further transmission and/or broadcasts and/or any other form of exploitation as set out in Schedule A. No rights are granted by [Name] for any archive playback and/or streaming service over the internet and/or any exploitation by means of any electronic format and/or by means of any telecommunication system which shall be the subject of a separate agreement. Where the form of exploitation is new and/or not listed then no clearance has been provided by [Name] and his/her consent must be obtained and terms agreed.

C.677

1.1   In consideration of the [Interview Fee] [Name] agrees to be interviewed by [Presenter] and filmed by the [Company] for the [Film/Series] to be broadcast, transmitted and exploited by [Distributor].

1.2   Further [Name] also agrees to assign to the [Company] all present and future copyright and intellectual property rights in any film and/or sound recordings that may be created in the interview by [Name] on [date] at [location] throughout the world and universe for the full period of copyright and/or any other terms of any other rights and any extensions and forever without limit of time and/or space.

1.3   The Interview Fee shall not include payment for access to his/her home for the purposes of filming which shall be a separate [Location Access Fee] of [number/currency] and subject to a separate agreement.

1.4   In addition a separate copyright and usage fee and agreement shall be agreed between [Name] and the [Company] for any reproduction, filming and/or exploitation of any documents, manuscripts, books, photographs, videos and other film and/or any other material which may belong to [Name] and/or any other member of his/her family and/or any other third party.

1.5   There shall be no presumption that because the [Company] has been permitted access to view any material that there is an automatic right by the [Company] to use such material. No implied and/or express licence is granted by this agreement. That no authority has been granted by [Name] and/or any other third party for the [Company] to exploit material supplied for the interview in 1.4. That any form of exploitation shall be subject to the conclusion of a new licence agreement in each case and the payment of an advance and royalties in respect of each form of exploitation.

C.678

1.1   [Name] agrees to be in the audience of the programme entitled [specify title of programme] and may be selected to take part as a contestant.

1.2 In the event that [Name] is selected to be a contestant then the [Company] shall pay [Name] a single payment of [number/currency] in order to buy out all copyright and any other rights that [Name] may have in their contribution to the programme in any form including performance, singing, dance, acrobatics and/or any other material [but not lyrics and/or music and/or [specify].] [Name] agrees and assigns to the [Company] all future copyright and any other intellectual property rights in his/her future contribution and/or appearance in all media and in all formats and methods of exploitation including new forms developed at a later date which do not exist now throughout the world for the full period of copyright and any other period where it extended and in perpetuity for all the contribution of [Name] [except any music, lyrics and [specify].]

General Business and Commercial

C.679
'Copyright' shall be defined as set out in the [Copyright, Designs and Patents Act 1988 as amended/specify other legislation] in [country/jurisdiction].

C.680
'Future Copyright' shall mean copyright which will or may come into existence in respect of a future work or class of works or on the occurrence of a future event and shall be defined in accordance with [Copyright, Designs and Patents Act 1988 as amended].

C.681
The [Licensor] confirms that all copyright, music and any other rights have been obtained and that the [Licensee] is not liable for any payments other than those specified as follows: [–].

C.682
The [Company] agrees that all copyright and any other rights necessary for the use by [Name] of the [item] from [date] to [date] at [address] in the following manner [specify use] has been obtained and paid for by the [Company].

C.683
In respect of the [Commissioned Work] the [Company] warrants that all copyright and any other rights including consents required under the [Copyright, Designs and Patents Act 1988 as subsequently amended] shall be obtained and paid for in respect of the rights assigned under this agreement for use by the [Assignee].

C.684

The [Licensor] agrees and undertakes that all copyright and any other rights in the [Illustration/Drawings/Artwork] including consents required under the [Copyright, Designs and Patents Act 1988 as amended] have been obtained and that the [Licensee] is not and shall not be liable for any payments other than those specified under this agreement.

C.685

The [Artist/Illustrator] agrees and undertakes that he/she:

1.1   is the original creator and designer of the [Artwork/Material] and that it is not adapted and/or developed from an original work of a third party.

1.2   is the sole owner and owns and controls all copyright and any other intellectual property right in the [Artwork/Material] which are licensed to the [Company] under this agreement. That no additional payments are due to any third party in respect of the rights granted to the [Company].

1.3   provides such consent as may be required under the [Copyright, Designs and Patents Act 1988 as amended] for the exercise of the rights granted as an exclusive licensee to the [Company]. Provided that the [Artwork/Material] is not altered, changed, mutilated and/or adapted without the prior written consent of the [Artist/Illustrator]. That there is no assignment of any rights and all rights not licensed are reserved by the [Artist/Illustrator].

C.686

The [Company] agrees and undertakes that as far as reasonably possible it shall clear and pay for all copyright, intellectual property rights, consents, releases, waivers, trade marks, logos, service marks, or any other rights of any nature in the [Work/Material] and/or parts necessary for the exploitation of the [Work/Material] by the [Distributor] in [countries] in the following formats: [specify rights and type of format].

C.687

The [Company] shall obtain and pay for the clearance and acquisition of rights in respect of any artist, musician, contributor, stills, footage, music, product, trade marks, logos, service mark, title, character, artwork, computer generated material, graphics, documents, books, and any other material of any nature incorporated in the [Work/Service]. All such material shall be cleared for use by the [Distributor] subject to any notified restrictions and/or additional costs, which shall be the responsibility of the [Distributor] for the duration of this agreement.

C.688

The [Assignor] agrees that it is the sole owner of all intellectual property rights and any other rights in the [Content] which are subject to the rights and material owned by third parties which may be included and/or any contractual and/or licence obligations including copyright notices, credits, moral rights and other matters set out in Appendix A which is attached to and included in this agreement. The [Assignor] shall be responsible for all payments, clearances and sums due up to the date of this agreement and the [Assignee] shall bear all costs and expenses owed to any third party from [date].

C.689

The [Company] undertakes that it shall be responsible for all sums due for the production, reproduction and exploitation of the [Work/Material] to any third party whether for consents, copyright licences, waivers or otherwise of any material or rights which are not owned and/or controlled by [Name].

C.690

The [Licensor] agrees and undertakes that it controls and is an exclusive distributor of the rights in [specify item] which are granted to the [Licensee] under this agreement. That there is no third party except the copyright owner [specify name] who has a claim to own and/or control the rights which have been granted to the [Licensee]. The copyright owner is aware of this agreement and has provided written consent that it may be concluded.

C.691

The [Distributor] agrees that the [Company] shall only pay such costs for copyright clearances, consents, licences, contracts, waivers, domain names, trade marks and/or to buy out and/or acquire any intellectual property rights as may be set out in the agreed [Budget] for the [Project]. Any other sums due to any third party and/or legal costs incurred in connection with any dispute and/or claim in respect of the exploitation in any format and/or medium by the [Distributor] and/or any licensee shall be paid for by the [Distributor] including any reports and sums due to licensing bodies, collecting societies, collective management organisations, independent management entities and/or rights holders. The sums incurred by the [Distributor] shall all be allocated as Distribution Expenses for the [Project] and shall be recouped from any sums received by the [Distributor] prior to the payment of any royalties.

C.692

There is no confirmation and/or undertaking by [Name] in relation to any part of the [Physical Material/Sound Recording/Images] as to whether they can be exploited and/or used in any format and/or country and/or comply with any relevant legislation and/or whether the consent of all the parties who may claim ownership and/or rights has been provided and/or any other matter. It is the [Purchasers'] responsibility to ensure that the [Physical Material/Sound Recordings/Images] are cleared for any purpose and the [Purchaser] shall pay and be liable for all the associated fees, royalties and costs including any legal fees in the event of a dispute.

C.693

1.1 It shall be the responsibility of the [Marketing Agency] to ensure that no physical material of any nature in any format is distributed and/or released to the public in any form in print, television and/or on the internet in respect of the promotion campaign for the [Distributor] in which the performance fees, location fees, music, stills and images, logos and brand names, reproduction of any music, lyrics, sound recordings, mechanical reproduction, broadcast and/or transmission fees, copyright and/or other rights have not been cleared and a licence agreement obtained for such authorised use in each case.

1.2 That the verbal agreement of a third party shall not be sufficient for the purpose of clearance of any rights and that the [Marketing Company] shall ensure that full and accurate complete records and documents are kept both in print form and on an excel document. That upon request at any time the [Marketing Company] shall provide copies to the [Distributor].

C.694

1.1 The [Company] agrees and accepts that [Name] is not supplying any agreement and/or undertakings as to the clearance of any copyright and/or any other rights in respect of the exploitation of the [Photographs/Sound Recordings/Films] at any time.

1.2 That it shall be the responsibility of the [Company] to clear and pay for any reproduction, performance, transmission, broadcast, computer generated version and/or any adaption in electronic form for distribution on the internet and/or through any telecommunication system through means of television, radio, computer and/or mobile phone and/or in any other manner. That the [Company] shall need to clear and pay for any music and/or lyrics, book and/or script and/or other written material upon which it is based and/or any name, trade mark, character name, title, slogan and/or otherwise that may be used. That responsibility shall also include reports and payments to any licensing bodies, collecting societies, collective management organisations, independent management entities and/or rights holders.

1.2 The [Company] is paying a fee to [Name] solely for the purpose of physical access to the [Photographs/Sound Recordings/Films] in order to [make a copy/film/display in an exhibition].

1.3 That in the event that any use and/or adaptation by the [Company] results in a claim and/or allegation against [Name] and/or the [Company] for breach of contract, copyright infringement and/or otherwise relating to the [Photograph/Sound Recordings/Films]. The [Company] shall be liable to deal with the matter on behalf of [Name] and shall bear all costs, expenses, losses, damages and legal costs which may be paid to any third party. [Name] shall not make a contribution to and/or be liable for any sums that may be due for any reason.

C.695

The [Executive] acknowledges and agrees that all rights of ownership and all intellectual property rights and any other rights created and/or developed in the course of the provision of his/her work under their contract of employment shall be and remain the sole and exclusive property of the [Company] including but not limited to: copyright, inventions, patents, design rights, rights to data and databases, trademarks, service marks, domain names, character names and/or slogans. This agreement does not purport to grant, assign or transfer any rights of any nature that may be created by the [Executive] outside his/her role as [specify title] at the [Company] which is original.

C.696

The [Company] agrees and undertakes that it shall not acquire any rights and/or interest and/or be entitled to register any claim to any of the following rights and/or material owned and/or controlled by the [Executive] as follows: [specify in detail and list Books/Websites/Apps/trade marks/other].

C.697

The [Company] agrees and undertakes that the [Company] shall not at any time be entitled to make a claim and/or take any legal and/or other action against [Name] for failure to consent to the use and/or exploitation by the [Company] of any material, copyright and/or other intellectual property rights held by [Name] prior to the date of this agreement.

C.698

1.1 [Name] agrees and provides consent to the fact that the [Company] shall own and control all material of any nature which may be created by [Name] during the course of his /her employment with the [Company] which is created and/or developed in the course of their position as [specify role/title]. That [Name] agrees that the [Company] and/or any third party distributor, sub-licensee may use and exploit any such material including title, text, images, film, music, photographs, software, databases, sound recordings, codes, passwords, articles, products and any other rights and/or material.

1.2 That [Name] shall agree to sign any further agreements and documents that the [Company] may require relating to any work and creations of [Name] in order to effect any transfer and/or assignment to the [Company] after the termination of the employment provided that the [Company] shall agree to pay an additional fee to [Name] of [number/currency].

C.699

1.1 It is agreed between the parties that no costs and expenses shall be incurred by any party in respect of the development, production and exploitation of the {Project] unless all parties have provided prior approval to the expenditure.

1.2 That the budget for the {Project] shall not exceed [number/currency] and shall be paid for in equal shares by both parties.

1.3 That neither party shall commit to any arrangement, licence and/or conclude any agreement for the [Project] where the third party will expect to be paid more than [number/currency] and/or will expect to be paid additional royalties and/or fess at a later date.

Internet, Websites and Apps

C.700
The material on this [Website] cannot be assumed to have been cleared for use by you except for viewing on the original site. You are specifically prohibited from storing, printing, downloading, reproducing and/or distributing any material. There is no licence granted, permission given and/or any claims made as to the copyright, intellectual property and/or ownership of material and/or trade mark unless specifically stated and a copyright notice and/or trade mark is displayed.

C.701
The [Website/Platform] is monitored regularly, but material may be displayed on the [Website/Platform] which may be defamatory, an infringement of copyright of a third party, misleading, inaccurate and/or otherwise contrary to any legislation and/or laws of any country. There are no assurances provided by the [Company] as to the ownership of the material and/or the rights and there is no sub-licence and/or other authority granted to you to reproduce, supply, distribute and/or exploit the material. You are strictly advised and prohibited from using the material for your own purposes whether private and/or commercial. The [Company] will not assist you and/or reimburse you and/

or be responsible for any claim made against you and/or any other criminal and/or civil proceedings that may arise from your use of any material.

C.702

I am the sole author and copyright owner of the following work; [title/pages/ISBN reference]. I consent to the following extract of my work being displayed on the internet at the website location and address [specify reference] under the domain name [specify reference] whose main place of business is at [specify address]. The duration of my consent is [specify period] and is subject to the written withdrawal of my consent at any time by notice in writing and/or email to the [Company].

C.703

The [Company] agrees that it shall not acquire any copyright, intellectual property rights and/or other interest in the [Article/Image/Video] and/or any part at any time in any format and/or medium. That [Name] has granted a non-exclusive licence for the [Article/Image/Video] to be reproduced on [Website/App/Blog] from [date] to [date]. The [Company] does not have any right to sub-licence the [Article/Image/Video] and/or any adaptation to a third party without the prior consent of the [Author] and the conclusion of a new licence agreement for the third party and additional fees and/or royalties on each occasion.

C.704

In consideration of the sums paid under the Payment Schedule in Appendix A the [Designer/Developer] assigns to the [Company] all copyright, intellectual property rights and other rights in all media and in all medium including in any electronic form for use over the internet and/or by means of any telecommunication system for use in connection with any television, radio, computer and/or mobile and/or any other gadget and/or the computer software rights which are created, owned and/or controlled by the [Designer/Developer] in the [Project] described in Appendix B whether in existence now and/or created in the future throughout the world [and universe] for the full period of copyright and any extensions, renewals and in perpetuity and/or in respect of any new formats and/or rights that may come into fruition at a later date.

[Appendix B specify proposal; exact material to be designed and how content is to be sourced; how it is to operate and function; any title; name; registration required]

C.705

1.1 The [Designer] and the [Company] agree that the [Designer] shall not acquire any copyright, intellectual property rights and/or any other interest in the [Website/App] of any nature except [specify].

1.2 Nor shall the [Designer] be entitled to register and/or claim any rights, interest and/or equity in any domain name, title, short form name, image, slogan, logo and/or any other content and/or material which has been created, developed and/or adapted for the purpose of the [Company's] [Website/App] under the terms of this agreement.

1.3 The [Company] confirms that any and all rights in any resource material supplied to the [Designer] under this agreement shall be owned and/or controlled by the [Company] unless expressly stated to belong to a third party.

C.706

1.1 The [Licensor] shall be obliged to ensure that all necessary clearances and consents have been obtained for the use and sub-licence of the [Work/Material] to the Distributor].

1.2 That the [Licensor] shall confirm to the [Distributor] prior to the conclusion of the sub-licence as to who owns and/or controls the copyright and/or intellectual property rights in the [Work/Material] and/or any parts. That the [Licensor] shall provide a complete list of the ownership of any content and whether any additional payments will be due for the exploitation authorised in the sub-licence. This shall also include any payments which may be necessary to any licensing bodies, collecting societies, collective management organisations, independent management entities and/or rights holders.

1.3 The [Licensor] shall also supply the [Distributor] with a list of obligations to the [Licensor] and third parties in respect of copyright notices, credits, moral rights, trade marks, service marks, logos, text, images, graphics, sound recordings, films and music to be supplied to the [Distributor].

C.707

The [Company] agrees that it shall be responsible for all copyright, consent and other sums due to third parties including collecting societies and/or rights holders arising from the operation and functioning of the [Website/App/Channel] from [launch date] in any part of the world. This shall include all the materials and/or rights of any nature whether comprising of text, images both visual and sub-liminal, graphics which are static, interactive or moving, photographs, drawings, plans, sketches, computer generated material, sounds, sound effects, music, logos, trade marks, design rights, background, banners, bookmarks, borders, tables, captions, characters, clip art, cartoons, computer generated art, maps, image map links, common gateway interface script, domain names, titles, film, video, DVD, CD-Rom, electronic material whether for over the internet and/or to be conveyed through any telecommunication system and/or broadcast, transmitted, transferred, downloaded, supplied and/or distributed by means of satellite, terrestrial, cable and/or digital television, radio, by means of a computer, mobile and/or any other device and/or gadget including a watch and/or headset and any associated software. Prior to the [launch date] all such costs and expenses shall have been itemised and included in the report of the [Designer] and paid in accordance with the budget in Schedule A.

C.708

[Name] agrees not to:

1.1 Post any material on the [Blog/Website/Channel] which has not been cleared and paid for so it can legitimately and legally be used in that manner.

1.2 Use any material in a way which would bring a claim of copyright infringement and/or any other allegation in respect of any other intellectual property and/or computer software rights and/or trade marks against the [Company] by any person and/or business in any country in any part of the world.

1.3 Post any material which he/she knows to belong to a third party without a suitable credit and/or copyright notice to that third party.

1.4 Distort, vary, change and adapt any material from a third party and represent it as the original work and effort of [Name].

C.709

1.1 Where you use and post material on this [Website/Channel] you must ensure that you do not to infringe any copyright and/or breach any contract and/or other rights of any other person and/company and/or expose yourself and the [Website/Channel] to any allegation of defamation, breach of any code of conduct and/or guidelines of any regulatory organisation and/or the threat of civil and/or criminal proceedings.

1.2 Where the [Website/Channel] are notified by a third party of any allegation it is our policy to act swiftly to remove, delete and cancel both the material in question and the account of the person involved even before an investigation is commenced. No responsibility is accepted by the [Website/Channel] for your posting and/or actions and you remain at all times liable for a claim against you by such third party. Your personal details will be supplied to such third party in the event that they obtain either a court order and/or there is a threat to the safety of any person.

C.710

[Name] agrees and undertakes that they have commissioned the [Podcast] to be filmed and that [Name] owns all copyright and intellectual property rights in the [Podcast] including the sound recording. That no third party has any claim and the content is not based on and/or derived from any rights and/or material which belongs to any third party including music and/or lyrics. That [Name] has the authority to grant a non-exclusive licence to the [Distributor] to: [specify rights/purpose/licensed countries/licence period].

C.711

1.1   [Name] is the writer of the articles for the [Blog] known as: [title] which is distributed and made available on the website [name/reference]. The theme and content of the articles is the original work of [Name]. Where any third party resource is relied upon then [Name] shall ensure that there is a suitable credit and/or copyright notice to such third party.

1.2   [Name] accepts and agrees that where the article is sub-licensed and/or distributed by the [Company] that no additional payments shall be due to [Name] for the duration of this agreement. After the agreement has ended and/or been terminated then use of any articles shall be subject to a separate arrangement between the parties.

1.3   Where the [Company] adds any images to accompany the article then the [Company] shall be liable for the clearance and payment of any sums which may be due to a third party. The [Company] shall not be obliged to consult with [Name] regarding any image but shall not include any image which is a product and/or service endorsement and/or which could be construed as offensive, defamatory and/or would have a detrimental effect on the reputation of [Name].

C.712

1.1   The [Film/Video/Sound Recording] was made by [Name] on [method/device] at [location] on [date]. It is on the subject of: [specify title] and includes the following persons: [specify names/age/address].

1.2   [Name] confirms that all the persons who appear have provided their verbal consent to [Name] to supply the material to: [Account/Channel/other] for transmission, broadcast and/or distribution and other forms of exploitation to the public.

1.3   That no payment and/or fee is due to any person except [Name] who will receive a fee of [number/currency] if the material is used by the [Company].

1.4   The [Company] accepts that no music and/or lyrics has been cleared for use in any manner and that it shall be the responsibility of the

[Company] to obtain a licence and make such payments as may be due including include any payments which may be necessary to any licensing bodies, collecting societies, collective management organisations, independent management entities and/or rights holders.

C.713

[Name] has not personally taken these [Images/Photographs/Graphics] but has commissioned a third party. [Name] has concluded an assignment agreement and buy-out with the third party creator for all originals and copies of the [Images/Photographs/Graphics] and [Name] is the owner of all copyright and/or intellectual property rights in all media throughout the world. That there is no third party who is entitled to any rights and/or who is entitled to make any claim.

Merchandising and Distribution

C.714

1.1 The [Licensor] confirms that he/she is the original creator and sole owner all copyright, intellectual property rights and any other rights in the [Character] including the title, logo, image. slogan and/or any associated artwork, costume designs, accessories and items and computer generated and/or electronic material which may have been created. Full details of the [Character] and the associated material are described in appendix A.

1.2 That the [Licensor] has been assigned all the rights and material by third parties who have been commissioned by the [Licensor] to create, develop and contribute to the [Character] and/or any other matter in 1.1 That the [Licensor] can supply evidence of such documents if required to the [Licensee] upon request.

1.3 That the [Licensor] has registered a trade mark in the title of the [Character] and logo. Fill details of the trade mark and the scope of the registration are set out in the attached appendix B.

1.4 The [Licensor] has registered the following [channel/domain name/ other] in the title of the [Character]. Full details are described and set out in appendix C.

C.715

The [Designer] confirms that he/she is the original creator and sole owner of and/or controls all copyright and/or future copyright, design rights and any other rights in the [Designs] and the [Garments] which may be supplied under this agreement.

C.716

The [Licensor] confirms that he/she is the original creator and sole owner of all copyright, design rights and any other rights in the [Board Game] and the [Prototype] which are granted to the [Company] under this agreement. That the [Licensor] has not copied and/or adapted any material owned by a third party. That to the best of the knowledge and belief of the [Licensor] the [Board Game] and [Prototype] do not and will not infringe the copyright, design rights or any other rights of any third party in [country].

C.717

The [Assignor] confirms and agrees that it has fully disclosed to the [Assignee] any rights and/or sums which may be due to third parties in the respect of the [Work] and/or the [Material] which are as follows: [specify and list].

C.718

The [Assignee] agrees that from [date] the [Assignee] shall be liable to bear the cost and expense for clearing and paying for all copyright, consents and any other rights in the [Work] and the [Material] of any nature in any medium together with fulfilling such contractual and/or licence obligations as may have been agreed with the [Assignor]. The [Assignor] shall not be liable any further sums and the [Assignee] accepts that this shall be the case regardless of whether the facts were known and disclosed and/or arise after the conclusion of the agreement on [date].

C.719

1.1 The [Company] agrees that it shall not be entitled to use, exploit and/or to grant a licence and/or assign any of the rights and/or material created for the purpose of this agreement in which [Name] appears in sound, vision and/or in any other form and/or manner except for the sole purpose of the endorsement, promotion and/or advertising of the products and/or services of the [Company] during the Term of the Agreement.

1.2 Where the [Company] wishes to use any such rights and/or material for any other purpose. Then the prior written agreement of [Name] is required and conclusion of a separate new agreement and payment terms.

C.720

The [Agent] agrees that he/she is not entitled to promote, advertise and/or offer for sale and/or represent that they are entitled to do so to any third party in any manner and/or form the [Character/Work] outside the following countries: [list in full]. That the [Agent] requires the prior approval and authority of the [Company] in each case and the agreement of new terms for any country and/or format.

C.721

1.1 The [Agent] agrees that he/she does not acquire any copyright, intellectual property rights, trade marks, domain names and/or any other rights in the name of the [Author/Creator] and/or any character in the [Work] and/or any products and/or services that may be created and/or developed in any other medium or format in whole or in part. That all rights of any nature belong solely to the [Author/Creator].

1.2 That the [Agent] agrees that he/she shall not represent that he owns any rights and/or material in 1.1 and/or that he/she is authorised to conclude an agreement to license and/or assign them to a third party.

1.3 That the [Agent] agrees that he/she shall not attempt to register any interest and/or rights in the name of the [Author/Creator] and/or any character in the [Work] and/or any adaptation and/or similar representation based on an image, letters and/or a word which sounds similar when spoken.

C.722

The [Licensee] acknowledges and undertakes that the [Licensee] is solely responsible for all costs incurred in respect of the commercial exploitation of the [Licensed Articles/Products] including development, production, manufacture, packaging, storage, distribution, supply, sales, advertising and/or promotions whether incurred as a direct cost and/or owed to a third party for clearance of any rights of any nature and/or for services or otherwise.

C.723

The [Purchaser] agrees that the [Designer] shall as the owner of the rights be entitled to sell, license and/or exploit the [specify designs/prototype/material] in any form at any time throughout the world.

C.724

1.1 The [Licensor] agrees and undertakes that it shall obtain such rights and/or consents, clearances and/or waivers that may be required for the exploitation of the [Work] by the [Licensee] for the Term of the Agreement whether by virtue of an assignment, licence, and/or other contractual clearance from any third party.

1.2 That the [Licensor] shall ensure that it owns and/or controls all the copyright, computer software rights, database rights, design rights, intellectual property rights, music, lyrics, sound recordings, trade marks and/or other rights that may be required any licence from any licensing bodies, collecting societies, collective management organisations, independent management entities and/or rights holders.

1.3 The [Licensor] agrees and undertakes that to date it has paid the sums set out in Schedule A.

1.4 The [Licensee] agrees and undertakes that shall be responsible for the payments and costs set out in Schedule B from [date/date of delivery of the master material].

C.725

1.1 The [Licensee] shall ensure that any sub-licensee, agent and/or distributor to be appointed is solvent and capable of paying any sums due prior to the conclusion of any agreement.

1.2 Where the [Licensee] grants any sub-licence, agent and/or distributors agreement to a third party. Then the [Licensee] shall bear the cost of any default, breach, losses, damages and/or failure to pay any sums that may be due to the [Licensor] for any reason.

C.726

The [Distributor] agrees and accepts that where new material is created and/or developed in order to produce a new licensed article, product and/or service and/or promotional material bearing the [Logo/Name]. That the cost of all copyright clearances and any other intellectual property and/or contractual payments and/or royalties and fees that may be due and/or arise shall be at the [Distributors] cost and expense. That the [Distributor] shall not be entitled to seek to offset, claim and/or recover any sums from [Name] and/or the [Company] and/or to seek to reduce the royalty payments and/or any other sums due at any time.

C.727

Where at a later date an additional fee and/or royalty becomes due to a third party which arises from the clearance of any copyright, intellectual property rights, rights of performance, reproduction, resale, mechanical reproduction, transmission and/or broadcast and/or any other form of exploitation in the [Project]. Then it is agreed that the [Licensee] may use up to [number/currency] for that purpose to resolve the matter and set any such sum off against any payments due to the [Licensor]. Provided that any such set-off is supported by the supply of documents supporting the sums paid and the reason.

C.728

The [Company] does not warrant that the importation, sales or distribution or use of [Products] will not infringe any patent rights, design rights or any other intellectual property rights of any third party. The [Company] shall not be responsible for and/or under any liability to the [Purchaser].

C.729

It shall be the [Customers/Company's] responsibility to obtain and pay for an annual licence from any collecting society and/or collective management organisations for the broadcast and/or transmission and/or other use of the [Film/Video/Sound Recording] on their business premises.

C.730

The [Company] confirms that it is the sole owner of or controls all copyright, design rights, trade marks and logos and any other rights and/or interest in the [Company] and the [Company's] Products throughout the world.

C.731

The [Company] confirms that the [Company] and the [Company's] Products including any trade marks, logo, title, artwork, packaging, promotional material and/or any developments and/or adaptations provided by the [Company] under this agreement do not and will not contain any material which infringes the copyright, design rights, intellectual property rights and/or any other rights of any third party.

C.732

The [Supplier] confirms that it is the sole owner of or controls all copyright, design rights, trade marks, service marks, and any other rights in the [Product], the [Supplier's Logo] and any associated packaging, advertising and/or other material throughout the [specify countries] except as follows: [specify and list].

C.733

The [Distributor] agrees and undertakes that the following details are true and accurate and that it is the owner and/or controls all rights and interest in:

1.1 The domain name: [specify name/reference].

1.2 The [Distributor's] [website/app/channel]: [specify name/reference].

1.3 The business known as: [specify name] which trades under the name: [specify name] which accounts through the [limited company/other] entitled: [state registered name/reference].

C.734

The [Company] confirms and undertakes that all promotions, marketing, offers, sales competitions, returns policies, cookie and privacy policies, storage and/or use of data, money laundering, security and/or any other matter which may arise shall comply with all relevant legislation, laws, regulations, directives, mandatory minimum standards, guidelines, codes of practice and/or conduct whether voluntary and/or otherwise in [country/Territory/World] from [date].

C.735

1.1 The [Distributor] agrees and undertakes that any new material created and/or commissioned by the [Distributor] which is an adaptation and/or development of the [Product] and/or the [Supplier's Logo] and/or any logo, service mark, trade mark or similar image, text, icon, slogan, sound or sound effects, music, graphics or otherwise associated with and/or directly relating to the [Supplier] shall be the property of the [Supplier].

1.2 That the [Distributor] shall use its best endeavours to ensure that any necessary documentation is concluded by any third party to confirm and/or transfer and/or assign ownership to the [Supplier] at the [Suppliers'/Distributor's] cost and expense.

C.736
In respect of the [Commissioned Work] the [Assignor] undertakes that all copyright and any other rights including consents and moral rights shall be cleared and paid for in respect of the rights assigned under this agreement.

C.737
The [Assignee] shall be entirely liable for and pay the costs of the [specify work] and the [Assignor] shall not be responsible for any such costs or sums.

C.738
The [Product/Service/other] is supplied to the [Customer] with labels, packaging and leaflets which explains the ownership of the intellectual property rights in any material. There is no permission, licence or rights given by the [Company] or its representatives which seeks to give you consent to reproduce, interfere with, supply, distribute or exploit the material in any manner except for your own [personal/business commercial] use at in [residential/business] premises.

C.739

1.1 The [Supplier] shall be responsible for all clearances, consents, designs, patents, copyright and performance and reproduction payments and any other fees that may be due to any third party and/or collecting society for the design, development, production, manufacture, distribution, sale, supply and marketing and promotion of the [Product] and its packaging by the [Company] in [country] from [date] during the Term of this Agreement.

1.2 The [Company] agrees to notify the [Supplier] in the event of any allegation and/or claim being brought to its attention in respect of 1.1 above.

1.3 The [Company] agrees that where the [Supplier] decides to change, adapt, alter and/or delete any part of any material as a result of a decision by the [Supplier]. That the [Company] shall assist the [Supplier] and at the [Suppliers'] cost add, remove and/or delete material provided that such actions would not create a complaint relating to a failure to comply with any legislation, compliance requirements and/or expose the [Company] to criminal and/or civil proceedings for any reason.

Publishing

C.740

The [Authors] agree that notwithstanding the nature of their individual contributions to the [Work] the copyright and any other rights in all media in the [Work] and the [Artwork] shall belong to the [Authors] jointly and equally during the existence of this agreement and at any time thereafter.

C.741

The [Author] confirms that the [Master Material] and the [Stills/Artwork] are the sole and original creation of the [Author] and that he/she is the sole owner of all copyright and any other rights which are [licensed/assigned] under this agreement to the [Company].

C.742

The [Licensee] agrees to be responsible for the cost of any additional material including images, caricatures and/or photographs that may be required for the [Article/Blog/Event]. That the [Licensee] shall supply a copy to the [Licensor] in the event of the creation of any new such material.

C.743

The [Licensor] agrees and undertakes that all necessary copyright clearances, consents, licences and waivers necessary for the publication of the [Article/ Book/Work] have been and/or will be obtained and have and/or will be paid for by the [Licensor] in respect of the rights licensed to the [Institute].

C.744

The [Author] warrants that the [Work] shall not result in an allegation of copyright infringement by a third party and/or be in breach of an existing agreement between the [Author] and a third party.

C.745

1.1 The [Author] undertakes to ensure that he/she has obtained all the copyright clearances and consents necessary for the publication of the [Work] including the [Artwork] throughout the [specify countries] in respect of the rights granted to the [Distributor].

1.2 The [Author] agrees to obtain all such clearances and consents in writing and to provide the [Company] with copies of all relevant documents. Together with a comprehensive list of the name of the third party, any credit and/or copyright notice and/or any other legal requirements and the sums due for each type of form of exploitation.

1.3 The Company] agrees to be liable to pay such sums as may be due to third parties for the exploitation of the rights which it has been granted which are confirmed by the [Author].

C.746
The [Ghostwriter] shall keep full and accurate records of all interviews, information and documents relied upon in the [Work/Manuscript] and shall keep film and sound recordings of all meetings and interviews. The [Ghostwriter] shall provide a detailed bibliography of press cuttings, sound recordings, film, video and/or DVD material, photographs, stills, footage, websites, books and any other archive, family, estates, museums or other sources relied upon or quoted. Together with a comprehensive report on the ownership of copyright in any material, copyright notices, contractual obligations, moral rights, credits, trade marks and the cost of clearance and use of any such material and details of the terms on which it is available.

C.747

1.1 The [Publisher] agrees and undertakes that it shall pay any copyright fees due for the illustrations and/or quotations up to [number/currency]. Any further sum shall be subject to agreement between the parties.

1.2 In default of such agreement the [Publisher] shall at its discretion be entitled to recoup the additional sum from the royalties due to the [Author].

C.748
The [Author] confirms that he/she has good title and authority to enter into this agreement and is not bound by any previous agreement which adversely affects and/or conflicts with this agreement.

C.749
The [Company] shall use its reasonable endeavours to clear and pay for the exploitation of the [Work/Service] in all media throughout the [Territory//

world/country]. In the event that any material cannot be cleared for such use then it shall not be included in the [Work/Service].

C.750

The [Author] agrees that he/she shall ensure that the [Work/Manuscript/Images] are cleared for publication and distribution in respect of the following rights granted to the [Publisher] under this agreement throughout the world:

1.1 Hardback and paperback books; serialisation in magazines, periodicals and newspapers.

1.2 Anthologies and quotations; straight non-dramatic radio and television readings; talking books in any form including discs, cassettes and other storage devices.

1.3 Dramatic and non-dramatic adaptations for all forms of satellite, cable, terrestrial and digital for exploitation over the internet and/or any telecommunication system in any medium on television, radio, computer, gadget, device and/or for a musical and/or other production in a theatre and/or for a documentary and/or feature film and/or some other film and/or video project.

1.4 Hardback and paperback reprints rights and to sub-license to a third party in that format including large print and educational editions; digest book rights in volume form; one shot digest rights to publish an abridgement in a magazine, periodical or newspaper; book club editions licensed or sold to another publisher.

1.5 Merchandising including products, services, theme parks, picture cartoons, mechanical reproduction and electronic and computer generated material in any form including e books and/or downloads in electronic form for distribution over the internet and/or through any telecommunication system and reception through a television, radio, computer, mobile, watch and/or any other device.

1.6 Any registration with a licensing bodies, collecting societies, collective management organisations, independent management entities shall have the name of the [Author] registered as the rights holder and not the [Publisher]. All such sums shall be paid direct to the [Author] [and the [Publisher] shall entitled to any sums which directly relate to the rights licensed to the [Publisher].]

1.7 Any other rights not specifically mentioned are reserved by the [Author] including rights and/or technology which may be created and/or developed in the future.

The [Author] shall only be responsible for the administration of obtaining clearance of any copyright, consents, waivers and/or licences in respect of the publication of the [Work] in the [specify countries/Territory] in [specify exact format]. The [Author] shall not be obliged to clear the [Work] for all the rights granted to the {Publisher]. The [Publisher] agrees and undertakes to pay all sums due for clearance and reproduction costs of any copyright, consents, waivers and licences which are due where the [Work] is exploited by the [Publisher]. That the [Author] shall not be liable for any such sums and the [Publisher] shall not deduct such sums from any monies due to the {Author]. The [Publisher] shall be entitled to allocate the sums as part of the expenses to be deducted from the Gross Receipts.

C.751

1.1   The [Author] agrees that he/she shall bear the cost and responsibility of obtaining all consents, clearances and copyright in any material included in the [Work] including, but not limited to: letters, diaries, quotations and other references, photographs, images, drawings, tables, maps, infographics, products, services together with the title, preface and index in respect of the rights granted to the [Publisher] in this agreement for the publication of the [Work] in hardback and paperback in the [Territory/world] , and the serialisation of [Work] in a magazine or newspaper in [country].

1.2   The [Author] shall not be under any obligation to clear any other rights in the [Work]. In the event that any further additional rights in the [Work] are granted to the [Publisher] at a later date then it is agreed that the administration, legal costs and payment for any further clearances, consents and copyright shall be the responsibility and liability of the [Publisher].

C.752

[Name] confirms that he/she owns all copyright and any other rights in the [Photographs/Images/Diaries] and that the supply by [Name] and the publication and distribution of the [Photographs/Images/Diaries] in the [newspaper/magazine/other] throughout the [Territory/world] will not infringe the copyright and/or any other rights of any third party and will not expose the [Publisher/Distributor] to the threat of and/or commencement of any civil and/or criminal proceedings in the [Territory/world].

C.753

The [Publisher/Distributor] confirms and undertakes that it shall bear the cost of any copyright and/or other consents, waivers and/or licence payments which are necessary for the use of any material which is owned and/or controlled by a third party which is incorporated in the [Article/Serialisation] and that [Name] shall not be liable for any such payments.

C.754

The [Author] confirms that the [Work] and the [Artwork] are the sole and original creation of the [Author] and that he/she is the sole owner of all copyright, intellectual property rights and any other rights in the [Work] and the [Artwork] including any title which are granted under this agreement.

C.755

1.1 The [Author] agrees and undertakes to obtain all copyright clearances and other consents necessary for the publication of the [Work] including the title, front and back cover, preface, any artwork, photographs, maps, charts, tables, infographics, quotations of text and/or lyrics and/or slogans and/or any other material in any format throughout the [Territory/world/universe] in respect of the rights granted in this agreement. All such clearances and consents shall be obtained in writing and copies provided to the [Publisher/Distributor] at no additional cost.

1.2 The [Publisher] agrees and undertakes that all sums to be paid in respect of such clearances and consents shall be at the [Publisher's/ Distributors'] cost up to a maximum of [number/currency] in total. Where it is expected that the cost will be exceeded for any reason then the prior written authorisation of the [Publisher/Distributor] shall be required before the material is to be included in the [Work].

C.756

The [Author] confirms that the rights granted to the [Distributor] have not been previously licensed and/or otherwise exploited in any form throughout the [specify countries/Territory/world] as at [date] except for those matters disclosed and list in appendix A which is attached to and forms part of this agreement.

C.757

1.1 The [Author] agrees and undertakes to obtain all such copyright clearances, consents, waivers, licences and other rights as may be necessary for the publication, distribution and exploitation of the [Work] including any third party resources and any artwork and/or illustrations which has been granted in this agreement to the [Company]. The [Author] accepts that the total budget agreed with the [Company] for such matters shall not exceed [number/currency] and shall include any additional administration costs, access fees and charges and the cost of reproduction and delivery of any material.

1.2 The [Author] agrees that he/she shall supply the [Company] with a complete list of all such clearances, consents, licences and terms agreed as regard payment, credits, copyright notices and/or otherwise with the third parties. The [Author] shall also supply the [Company] with copies of all documentation which may apply.

1.3 The [Company] agrees to supply the budget for the matters in 1.1 to the [Author] by [date]. The [Author] agrees that he/she shall not exceed the budget without authority and shall keep comprehensive records of expenditure to be provided to the [Company] upon request.

1.4 The [Company] agrees and undertakes that it shall be responsible for the payments of any sums due to third parties which are not covered under the original budget in 1.1 in respect of the exercise of the rights granted to the [Company] under this agreement.

C.758

The [Company/Distributor] confirms and undertakes that it shall be solely responsible for and bear the cost of all intellectual property rights including copyright, trade marks, service marks, logos, designs, slogans, text, artwork, titles, graphics, computer generated material and/or electronic material and/or all other consents, moral rights, endorsements, sponsorship, contractual obligations due and/or arising to any third party on and/or in respect of the [Product/Service] and/or any associated packaging, promotions, advertising and/or marketing.

C.759

The [Author] provides no undertaking as to the originality, copyright and intellectual property position, any claims by any third party or the legal position in any country as regards the [Work/Article]. Any publication, reproduction, distribution and exploitation shall be entirely at the [Publishers] own risk and expense and no claim for any sums due shall be made by the [Publisher] against the [Author] at any time.

C.760

The [Author] agrees and undertakes that he/she shall not supply to the [Publisher] any work in any form which is not the original work of the [Author] which in fact is derived from and/or is sourced from a third parties book, website, article and/or other material.

C.761

The [Author] agrees and undertakes that he/she shall provide a credit and/or copyright notice to any third party where a story, the chronology of a series of events and/or any descriptive words and/or extracts of any length are copied, reproduced used and/or adapted from a third party resource whether an archive, library, book, blog, website and/or otherwise and are not the original work of the [Author].

C.762

Where the majority of the material supplied by the [Author] to the [Company] is later found to be attributed to another person and/or the [Author] has not provided their true name. Then the [Company] reserves the right to terminate this agreement and no further sums shall be due to the [Author] and/or his/her agent including those sums which may be due and/or owed. The [Company] shall be entitled to seek to be repaid all sums paid to the [Author] up to the date of termination together with interest and legal costs.

C.763

The [Estate] of the deceased author [Name] do not provide any reassurances and/or undertakings in respect of the originality of the [Archive Material] and/or whether the material has been cleared for use and/or adaptation in any form and/or medium. The [Company] must assess its own legal position in respect of the rights granted by the [Estate] and how they may be exploited. The [Company] agrees and undertakes that no claim and/or deductions will be made against the [Estate] in respect of any sums due to third parties for any form of exploitation.

C.764

The [Author] agrees and consents to a holographic representational image being created of the [Character/Name] in the [Work/Book] in electronic form for the purpose of a feature film and/or computer game and/or for a theme park and/or as promotional material.

Services

C.765

1.1 The [Artist] agrees to supply an original and new logo for [Name] for his/her new business for a fee of [number/currency] by [date] subject to delivery of the [artwork/master material] by [date] to [Name].

1.2 The [Artist] shall deliver the [artwork/master material] of the logo in [format] together with all draft drawings, reproductions and other copies. The [Artist] shall only keep one copy for personal and archive reasons and not for commercial use and/or exploitation.

1.3 In consideration of the fee in 1.1 the [Artist] assigns to [Name] all copyright and intellectual property rights and the right to register the logo as a trade mark throughout the world in all media and in all mediums and for the full period of copyright and any extensions and/or renewals in perpetuity without limit. Together with the right to use, exploit, adapt and reproduce the logo and to sub-license others to do so at any time

1.4 The [Artist] agrees that he/she shall not be entitled to any additional fee, royalty, payment and/or other sum for any exploitation, registration and/or use whether known now and/or created at a later date.

1.5 The [Artist] waives all rights to be identified either by a copyright notice, credit and/or any moral rights and agrees and accepts that the logo may be distorted, adapted and varied entirely as [Name] thinks fit and no consent and/or approval of the [Artist] shall be required nor shall any additional payments and/or sums be due.

C.766

The [Contributor] assigns to the [Company] all present and future copyright and any other rights in all media in the product of his/her services and any material created under this agreement throughout the world, outer space and the universe for the full period of copyright and any extensions or renewals without any limitation of time. All media shall include, but not be limited to satellite, cable, terrestrial, digital television and radio whether films, videos, DVDs, cassettes and/or otherwise; all forms of publishing including hardback and paperback books, e books, audio files and/or any format for exploitation as electronic material and/or software over the internet and/or through any telecommunication system which is received by mobile phone, computer, and/or other device and/or merchandising.

C.767

The [Company] agrees that all rights not specifically assigned to the [Company] are reserved by [Name]. This shall include any new rights and/or technology and/or means of exploitation and/or registration not in existence at the time of this agreement.

C.768

The [Company/Distributor] acknowledges and agrees that the [Artist] shall retain all copyright in any original [Musical Work] including any associated lyrics or arrangement owned and/or controlled and/or developed by the [Artist] whether in existence now and/or created during the Term of this Agreement and whether incorporated in the [Sound Recordings] or not. That the [Artist] shall be entitled to register with any licensing bodies, collecting societies, collective management organisations and/or independent management entities as the sole owner.

C.769

1.1 The [Presenter] agrees and undertakes to supply his/her services to the [Company] where the [Company] has requested that he/she either individually and/or in a group be at a scheduled session for photographs, images, films, sound recordings and/or other material in respect of the [Presenter] for the purpose of the promotion of the [Company] and/or a programme and/or for incorporation in a documentary, advertisement, podcast whether on television, radio, the internet and/or in any newspaper, magazine and/or for an event.

1.2 Provided that the [Company] agrees to pay any expenses and costs that the [Presenter] may incur for such work. The [Company] shall whenever practicable and reasonable consult with the [Presenter] prior to booking any scheduled session.

1.3 The [Presenter] agrees to execute any such documents and as the [Company] may require to buy out all rights in any such material in 1.1.

1.4 The [Company] agrees and undertakes that it shall not without the approval of the [Presenter] use and/or authorise the use of any of the material in 1.1 and/or the [Presenter's] name to endorse any product and/or service and/or to promote any political and/or activist campaign and/or to be associated with any controversial subject.

C.770

1.1 In consideration of the [Presenter's Fee] the [Presenter] assigns to the [Company] all present and future copyright and any other intellectual property rights and/or any other rights in all media throughout the world [and universe] in the product of his/her services and any other material created for the purpose of this agreement and/or any adaptations for the full period of copyright and any extensions and/or renewals and thereafter forever. This assignment shall include but not limited to: photographs, images, graphics, recipes, scripts, interviews, slogans, films, podcasts, blogs, sound recordings, contributions to news programmes and/or documentaries, advertisements and/or promotions; electronic material for the internet such as apps, websites, electronic downloads and/or interactive material over the internet and/or any telecommunication system through any television, computer, gadget and/or other device and/or merchandising in any form.

1.2 Provided that in any exploitation the [Presenter] is credited as follows: [name/title of role]. In addition that the [Company accepts and undertakes that the professional and/or personal name of the [Presenter] and/or his/her image cannot be used for any purpose which would be offensive, derogatory of the [Presenter] and/or is likely to damage his/her reputation.

C.771

The [Presenter] agrees that any intellectual property of any kind including, but not limited to copyright, design rights, service marks, trade marks, logos, inventions, titles, formats, slogans, films, sound recordings, podcasts and any other rights held by the [Company] and/or which are created or developed in conjunction with the services of the [Presenter] under this agreement shall be the sole and exclusive property of the [Company]. The [Presenter] shall not acquire any rights and/or interest nor does this Agreement purport to grant, transfer and/or assign any rights to the [Presenter].

C.772

The [Contributor] agrees that the [Company] shall be entitled to assign, transfer, sub-license and/or otherwise exploit rights and/or material which are created and/or developed in respect of the product of the services of the [Contributor].The [Contributor] agrees and undertakes that when requested by the [Company] to execute and sign any documents which may be required at a later date to effect the assignment of the rights and/or material to the [Company] that he/she shall do so provided that the [Company] pays all reasonable expenses likely to be incurred by the [Contributor] in advance.

C.773

The [Artist] agrees that his/her consent as may be required under the [Copyright, Designs and Patents Act 1988 as amended/other legislation] is provided by this agreement for the purpose of the exercise of the rights [assigned/granted] to the [Company] and any sub-licensee and/or distributor under this agreement.

C.774

The [Manager] acknowledges and agrees that he/she is not acquiring and/ or is not entitled to make any claim as regard ownership of any copyright, intellectual property rights, domain names and/or any other rights in any material, work and/or services owned and/or controlled by the [Group] and/or any of its members individually including any rights in any musical works, lyrics, arrangements, manuscripts, books, biographies, memoirs, biographical documentaries, articles, photographs, images, logos, trade marks and/or otherwise whether in existence prior to this agreement and/ or created at any time during the Term of this Agreement and/or thereafter.

C.775

The [Agent] acknowledges and agrees that he/she is not acquiring any copyright and/or future copyright and/or any other intellectual property rights and/or other rights in any material in any format and/or medium owned and/or controlled by the [Artiste] and/or in the name of the [Artiste] and any goodwill and reputation created in respect of any trade mark, business name, logo, slogan, image or otherwise which shall remain the sole property of the [Artiste]. No part of this agreement is intended to transfer, grant and/

or assign any such rights in the [Agent] whether in existence prior to this agreement and/or created at any time thereafter.

C.776

At the end of the agreement the [Agent] agrees to assign any copyright in the advertising, marketing and promotional material relating to the [Artiste] held by the [Agent] under the agreement provided that the [Artiste] shall pay the sum of [number/currency].

C.777

1.1 The [Author] agrees and undertakes that the [Report/Article] is original and has been written by the [Author] and not copied from a third party.

1.2 That the [Author] is the sole owner of all copyright and any other rights in the [Report/Article] which are assigned under this agreement to the [Distributor].

1.3 The [Distributor] agrees and undertakes that it shall not delete the name of the [Author] from the [Report/Article] and/or represent that it was written by a third party.

C.778

The [Contributor] agrees that such present and future copyright and/or any other intellectual property rights as may be created in any material and/or media and/or medium as result of the provision of the services of the [Contributor] to the [Company] during the course of this agreement are and/or shall be assigned by the [Contributor] to the [Company] for the full period of copyright and any extensions and renewals throughout the world and/or for any further additional periods as may be applicable. The [Contributor] accepts that it is not the intention of this agreement that the [Contributor] shall own and/or control any material except any original material owned by the [Contributor] which has already been exploited and made available for sale to the public.

C.779

The [Company] acknowledges that the [Contributor] owns and/or controls his/her own business enterprise which comprises:

1.1 The registered [website/app/channel/accounts/podcast/blog] [specify name and reference].

1.2 The registered domain names and trade marks: [specify name/reference].

1.3 The following [books/films/documentaries/merchandising/other] [list name/reference].

All the matters listed in 1.1, 1.2 and 1.3 are described in detail in appendix A and belong solely to the [Contributor]. The [Company] shall not acquire any rights, interest and/or claim in respect of any such matters at any time regardless of whether they are adapted for incorporation in any form in any project in conjunction with the [Company].

C.780

1.1 [Name] confirms that he/she created the original [Musical Work] and is the author and that he/she is the sole owner and controls all copyright and any other intellectual property rights in the [Musical Work] as at [date].

1.2 That no third party has reproduced and/or exploited the [Musical Work] in any form and/or medium prior to the date of this agreement and that no commitment has been entered into to allow any third party to do so.

1.3 That [Name] has not registered any rights in the [Musical Work] with any licensing bodies, collecting societies, collective management organisations, independent management entities and/or assigned and/or licensed any such rights as at [date].

C.781

[Name] agrees and undertakes that he/she will be the original creator and/or author of the copyright and/or future copyright, design rights, computer software, illustrations and/or computer generated and/or electronic material which he/she supplies to the [Company] subject to any consents, licences and/or waivers necessary for the incorporation of material and/or formats owned by third parties and/or the [Company]. That none of the reports and/or material to be supplied by [Name] is for commercial exploitation and is only to be used for the purpose of reviewing strategies at the [Company].

C.782

1.1 In consideration of the fee of [number/currency] [Name] agrees to assign to the [Company] all the rights and/or material which are created and/or developed as a result of his/her contributions and/or services under this agreement to the [Company] whether in existence now and/or created in the future in all media throughout the world for the full period of copyright and any extensions or renewals in perpetuity without limit of time. All ownership and control of copyright, intellectual property rights and material shall pass entirely to the [Company] including but not limited to: scripts, articles, documents and text, films, sound recordings, podcasts, blogs, photographs, images, logos, slogans, music, advertising, marketing, merchandising, packaging, computer software, new formats and/or competitions and all electronic and/or other material for distribution and/or use over the internet and/or through any telecommunication system by means of radio, television, a computer, gadget, mobile and/or other device. This assignment shall not cover the matters set out in 1.2.

1.2 The [Company] agrees that 1.1 shall not be relevant to any business, product, service, trade mark and/or other rights which are owned by [Name] prior to [date] and/or are developed and produced with a third party completely independently from the [Company] which shall include: [trade mark/enterprise/accounts/products/books] which are listed and described In appendix A.

C.783

1.1 The [Company] agrees that it shall not be entitled to exploit any of the product of the services of the [Name] outside the specified agreed purpose of this agreement and/or the [Engagement Period]. Any exploitation outside the scope of this agreement and/or in any other format and/or media shall be subject to negotiation and the payment of additional sums to [Name].Both parties shall use their reasonable endeavours to reach agreement in good faith. Failure to do so shall result in the material not being exploited at any time and destroyed by the [Company] at the end of the [Engagement Period].

1.2 The [Company] agrees that this agreement only relates to the provision of the services by [Name] for the specified agreed purpose of this agreement for [Engagement Period]. The [Company] does not acquire any rights, interest, option and/or other right to exploit any other matter related to [Name].

C.784

1.1 The [Agent] agrees that all copyright and/or any other intellectual property and/or other rights in the [Work] in all media throughout the world whether in existence now and/or created in the future together with any associated title, artwork, developments and/or adaptations are and shall remain the sole property of the [Name].

1.2 The [Agent] agrees and undertakes that he/she shall not acquire any rights in the [Work] and/or any associated material and/or represent to a third party that he/she owns any such rights and/or make any attempt to register any ownership. That any advice, guidance, contribution and/or otherwise by the [Agent] shall be in the role of adviser and shall not give rise to any claim for joint authorship with [Name] and any such rights as may arise are waived by the [Agent] and shall be transferred to [Name].

C.785

The [Agent] shall ensure that all third parties who are licensed, appointed, engaged and/or involved in the exploitation of the [Work] shall not acquire any rights and/or interest in the [Work] other than those specifically set out in the agreement. The [Agent] shall at his/her sole cost ensure that any necessary documentation is executed to ensure an assignment to the [Name] by third parties of any rights that may be created in any reproductions, developments, adaptations and/or associated packaging, products, marketing and advertising.

C.786

The [Manager] agrees and undertakes that he/she is not to acquire and/or may any claim in respect of any copyright, intellectual property rights, computer software rights and/or any other rights in any name, logos, trade marks, images, graphics, slogan and/or any other material which is created and/or developed under this agreement related to [Name].

C.787

The [Company] agrees that all copyright, design rights and any other rights in the product of the services provided by the [Creator] excluding any material provided by the [Company] shall remain the sole and exclusive property of the [Creator] and this agreement does not purport to assign, grant and/or transfer any rights to the [Company].

C.788

The [Company] and the [Creator] agree that any material arising from the services of the [Creator] shall only be used by the [Company] for the specific purposes described in appendix A which form part of this agreement. [specify format/purpose/different languages/marketing/adaptations allowed if any/countries/duration].

In the event that the [Company] wishes to use any material for any other purpose then the prior written consent of the [Creator] shall be required and an additional fee paid in each case on terms to be agreed between the parties.

C.789

The [Company] agrees that the [Creator] shall be able to [use/refer to] the material created under this agreement as follows: [specify permitted marketing/background statement] provided that all confidential information is deleted and all other material supplied by the [Company].

C.790

There is no authorisation and/or consent expressly and/or implied provided by either party to this agreement to assign, transfer and/or vest any material and/or rights in the other party which are owned and/or controlled by either party as at [date]. Each party shall continue to own and control all material, rights and interest it held prior to entering into this agreement and any others which it may create, develop and/or invent in the future at any time.

C.791

1.1 [Name] agrees to provide his/her services to the [Distributor] for the purpose of developing, creating and writing new [financial/marketing/promotional] content for the website, blog, app, podcast and corporate material of the [Distributor].

1.2 The [Distributor] agrees that all the products, data, information and background material for the work is being supplied by the [Distributor] and/or obtained from third parties who are suppliers, customers, advisors, employees and/or consultants of the [Distributor].

1.3 The [Distributor] agrees and undertakes that it shall not be the responsibility of [Name] to verify the accuracy of any such material in 1.1 and 1.2. Nor shall [Name] be responsible to seek any consents and/or clearance and/or require any documents to be signed for the purpose of acquiring permission and/or copyright and/or other matter prior to publication and/or reproduction by the [Distributor]. Nor shall the [Distributor] seek to hold [Name] liable at any time and the [Distributor] agrees that it shall use any such material at its own risk and cost. That the [Distributor] shall have the sole discretion whether to use any such material and to decide whether to have a legal assessment and report conducted on any material.

C.792

The [Consultant] agrees that where he/she provides a written report to the [Company] in respect of any [Project]. That where in any part of a report the material is not the original work of the [Consultant] and has been derived from and/or adapted from any work of a third party in any medium whether it is out of copyright and/or not but can be attributed to a known person. That the [Consultant] provide sufficient information, acknowledgement, credit and/or copyright notice for the exact resource to be identified and at which library, institute and/or other enterprise it was accessed. The [Consultant] shall provide such detailed information as to permit the [Company] to view and access that other third party source directly.

Sponsorship

C.793

The [Sponsor] and the [Association] agree as follows:

518

1.1 That all copyright, intellectual property rights, trade mark rights and any other rights in the [Event/Project] shall be the sole exclusive property of and/or under the control of the [Association] including but not limited to the Satellite, Cable and Terrestrial Television Rights, the Theatric and Non-Theatric Rights, the Digital and Electronic formats over the internet and/or through any telecommunication system which is downloaded, accessed and/or played back through a streaming service and/or as part of an archive whether free and/or under subscription to any computer, television, gadget, mobile and/or other device whether from any website, app, platform and/or channel. Together with any adapted game and/or software, game format for a series, merchandising, theme park, hologram, musical, activity park and/or any associated competition and/or premium rate telephone line.

1.2 The [Association] shall be entitled to retain all sums received at any time from the exploitation of any rights and/or material in 1.1. That no payments and/or royalties shall be due to the [Sponsor].

1.3 That the [Sponsor] agrees it is the sole owner of or controls all copyright, intellectual property rights, trade marks and any other rights in the [Sponsor's Logo] and that the use of the [Sponsor's Logo] by the [Association] and/or any authorised third party will not expose the [Association] and/or the third party to any allegation and/or claim and/or the threat of and/or issue of legal proceedings whether civil and/or criminal. The [Sponsor] acknowledges that the third party shall include but not be limited to any television, radio, internet and/or other media entity whether an individual or a company.

1.4 That the [Association] agrees it is the sole owner of and/or controls all copyright intellectual property rights, trade marks and/or any other rights in the [Promotional Logo] and that the use of the [Promotional Logo] under this agreement will not expose the [Sponsor] to any allegation and/o claim and/or the threat of and/or issue of legal proceedings whether civil and/or criminal. The [Sponsor] is not authorised to sub-license the use of the [Promotional Logo] to a third party.

C.794

1.1 The [Sponsor] confirms and undertakes that it is the sole owner of and/or controls all copyright, intellectual property rights, computer software rights, trade marks, domain names and/or any other rights in the [Sponsor's] trade marks, logos, slogans, banner advertisements, podcasts, films, images, music, lyrics, sound recordings, products and services together with all packaging and marketing material.

1.2 That all material supplied by the [Sponsor] under this agreement shall be cleared and paid for by the [Sponsor] including any sums due at a later date to any licensing bodies, collecting societies, collective management organisations, independent management and/or other rights holder. This undertaking shall only apply to use of the material by the [Company] and not any third party.

1.3 The [Sponsor] undertakes that the [Company] shall not be exposed to any threat, claim, allegation and/or civil and/or criminal proceedings as a result of the use and/or reproduction of the [Sponsor's] trade marks, logos, slogans, banner advertisements, podcasts, films, images, music, lyrics, sound recordings, products, services, packaging and/or marketing material in [country] as authorised in this agreement.

C.795

[Name] acknowledges and undertakes that all copyright, intellectual property rights, computer software rights, trade marks, domain names and/or any other rights in the [Sponsor's] Logo and the [Sponsor's] [Products/Services] together with any goodwill shall belong to and remain the sole property of the [Sponsor]. [Name] shall not acquire any rights and/or interest including any associated new music, sound recordings, films, designs, logos, titles, artwork, podcasts, banner advertisements, competitions, games and any developments and/or adaptations of any nature.

C.796

The [Sponsor] confirms that it is the sole owner of and/or controls and will have paid for and cleared all copyright, consents, releases, trade marks, logos, service marks, designs, text, quotes, slogans, title, artwork, music, sound recordings, graphics, computer generated material, domain names and films in the [Sponsor's] [Trade Mark/Logo] and/or other material, products and/or services which is supplied by the [Sponsor] under this agreement.

C.797

The [Company] agrees and undertakes that all rights, copyright, consents, releases, contracts, waivers, insurance, music and/or other material and/or costs of any nature in respect of the [Event/Festival] shall be arranged, cleared and paid for by the [Company]. This shall not include any matters which are to be supplied and/or provided by the [Sponsor] under this agreement including but not limited to products, services, staff, vehicles, equipment, displays and stands.

C.798

The [Licensee] agrees that it shall be solely responsible for all costs and expenses incurred in reproducing and incorporating the [Licensor's] [Trade Mark/Logo] in the packaging, promotional material and advertising for the [Product/Service]. The details of the material and costs are stated in the attached appendix A.

C.799

The [Company] agrees to bear the cost all clearances, consents, waivers, releases, trading and/or alcohol licences, agreements, reproduction, marketing, advertising, health and safety compliance and/or certificates, administration and/or legal costs and other expenses that may be incurred by the [Company] and/or any third party appointed by them in using the [Sponsor's] [Trade Mark/Logo] and [Products/Services] for the [Film/Event/Project] whether this involves trade or government bodies, local authorities, television companies, owners of premises, other sponsors, advertisers and/or otherwise.

C.800

The [Sponsor] shall not be liable for any cost and/or expenses incurred by the [Company] in respect of any copyright, intellectual property rights, computer software rights and/or any other rights and/or clearances and/or any waivers, buyouts, licences and/or other agreements and/or any music, lyrics, sound recordings, artists, presenters, locations, facilities, and/or any other third parties and/or services and/or for any payments to any licensing bodies, collecting societies, collective management organisations, independent management entities and/or rights holders and/or any form of exploitation and/or adaptation of the rights in any part of the world at any time for the [Event/Project]. All such sum shall be at the liability of the [Company] and not the [Sponsor]. The only exception shall be in respect of the material supplied directly by the [Sponsor] and confirmed as owned by the [Sponsor]. In that case if there is a legal issue then the [Sponsor] shall be liable to reimburse the {Company].

C.801

1.1   The [Sponsor] shall ensure that any copyright, intellectual property rights, design rights, computer software rights, trademarks, service marks, titles, slogans, domain names, products, clothes, and/or other material supplied by the [Sponsor] to [Name] are owned and/or controlled by the [Sponsor] and are authorised for the purpose for which they are to be used and/or reproduced and/or distributed by [Name].

1.2   That [Name] shall not be responsible and/or liable for any sums which have not been paid and/or may be due in respect of any rights, material and/or other matters in 1.1 which shall be solely attributed to be at the [Sponsors'] cost and expense.

C.802

1.1   Where the [Sponsor] uses a specific sound recording, music and/or lyrics and/or jingle with their products, logos, names and brands which they intend to use and perform at the [Event] and to authorise third parties and the [Distributor] to reproduce and broadcast and/ or transmit and/or exploit. It shall be the sole responsibility of the [Sponsor] to ensure that the [Sponsor] is legally entitled to do so and has the authority and consent of all parties who have created, played, contributed to, performed, written and/or control and/or own such copyright and other intellectual property rights in any format and/or material. This shall include the responsibility to obtain any licence and/ or make any report and make any payment in the future to any licensing bodies, collecting societies, collective management organisations, independent management entities and/or rights holders.

1.2 The [Sponsor] shall provide such evidence as may be required and requested by the [Distributor] and their legal advisors to establish that any such matters in 1.1 have been dealt with and that there is no risk of legal action against the [Distributor] and/or any associated partner for the [Event].

1.3 The [Sponsor] agrees that where it fails to justify any use of any material at any time then the [Distributor] may insist that any part of any material in 1.1 may be omitted and/or deleted and/or adapted in any manner the [Distributor] thinks fit in the circumstances.

University, Charity and Educational

C.803

The [Author] confirms that he/she is the original creator and sole owner of all copyright, data, [computer software/design rights], domain names, logos, trade marks, service marks, formats and any other intellectual property rights and/or interest in the product of his/her services and all the material supplied to the [Institute/Charity] under this agreement excluding specifically any proposals, drawings, images, reports, information, data and/or material included at the request of the [Institute/Charity].

C.804

1.1 The [Author] acknowledges and undertakes that he/she is not acquiring any copyright and/or any other intellectual property rights, design rights, patents, computer software, domain names, images, text, films, sound recordings, data, names, logos, trade marks, slogans or any other material owned and/or controlled by the [Institute/Charity] and/or any third party.

1.2 Further that where the [Author] makes any contribution, development and/or other adaptation of any material to any work as part of any project and any rights are created to the benefit of the [Author]. The

[Author] agrees and undertakes to assign all such rights in all media to the [Institute/Charity] subject to a nominal payment of [number/currency] and to sign such documents as the [Institute/Charity] may require in order to transfer and/or establish ownership.

C.805

The [Company] agrees that this agreement does not purport to assign, grant and/or transfer any copyright, intellectual property rights and/or any other rights to the [Company] whether based on original material which exists prior to the date of this agreement held and/or owned by the [Institute] and/or whether created under the terms of this agreement. The [Company] also agrees that it is not authorised to exploit, license, supply and/or distribute any rights, information, data and/or material without the prior written consent of the [Institute] under a separate licence in each case and a new financial arrangement.

C.806

In consideration of the [Fixed Fee] the [Consultant] assigns to the [Institute/Charity] all present and/or future copyright and/or any other intellectual property rights in all media in any material, format and/or medium developed and/or created as a consequence of the provision of his/her services throughout the world and universe for the full period of copyright and any extensions and/or renewals and thereafter without any limitation of time and which shall continue indefinitely. This assignment shall include but not be limited to: all reports, graphics, data, maps, charts, infographics, images, films, sound recordings, computer generated material, computer software, slogans, logos, trade marks, merchandising, databases, advertisements, promotional and marketing material.

C.807

The [Consultant] agrees to draw up a list of material in his/her possession and/or under his/her control which relates to the [Project] at any time when requested to do so by the [Institute/Charity]. The [Consultant] shall itemise and describe each type of material and specify the contact details of the parties who own the copyright, intellectual property rights and/or any other rights. Together with copies of all relevant agreements, licences, invoices and/or payment records and/or other documents and/or records.

C.808

The [Researcher] shall not be expected to identify the ownership of any material where no original author can be attributed to a work and any such work shall still be reported and the source stated but shall be listed as an unknown and/or an orphan work for the author.

C.809

1.1 The [Consultant] shall not be liable for the accuracy and/or contents of those parts of the [Report] which are based on information, data, records, documents, translations, tests and/or computer analysis and statistics supplied by the [Institute/Charity] and/or commissioned by the [Institute/Charity] from a third party and/or interviews and/or market surveys and/or any other material of any nature which is not the original work of the [Consultant].

1.2 The [Consultant] agrees to highlight material where 1.1 shall be relevant, but cannot ensure that this is done in every case. Where in the opinion of the [Consultant] the [Report] cannot in any sense be approved by him/her then the [Consultant] reserves the right to remove his /her name but shall still be paid for the production of the [Report].

C.810

The [Institute/Charity] accepts that it shall be responsible for the cost of clearance in respect of any rights and/or material which it may authorise and/or supply for the [Event/Project] and any associated website, app and/or promotional material and/or merchandising. That the [Institute/Charity] shall only supply trade marks, data, images, films, sound recordings and/or other material which has been cleared for such use and for which there are no legal matters outstanding which may cause problems.

COPYRIGHT NOTICE

Film, Television and Video

C.811

The [Sub-Licensee] agrees and undertakes that all [Products/DVDs/other formats] of the [Film] and all associated artwork, images, labels, packaging, promotional, advertising, and/or marketing material in any medium relating to it shall be subject to the following terms:

1.1 That all such products and material shall be produced, manufactured, supplied, sold, rented, made available and distributed in accordance with and comply with all international, European and/or national legislation and/or laws of the licensed [Territory] including any directives, regulations, guidelines, policies, codes of practice including but not limited to labelling, content, safety warnings, health and safety and/or compliance requirements and standards.

1.2 That all products and material shall include on every copy all intellectual property, trade mark, and copyright symbols and/or words necessary to protect the rights of the [Licensor] and/or the [Copyright Owner]. That the [Sub-Licensee] will agree in advance with the [Licensor] on each occasion which copyright notices, trade marks, logos, text and warnings should be used. So that the ownership of any material, trade marks and content is asserted in a clear and prominent position, the contractual obligations of the [Licensor] to third parties are complied with and that there is a warning that the public is not allowed to copy, transfer, to download and/or send and/or arrange transmission by any means.

C.812

1.1 The [Distributor] agrees and undertakes that it shall be solely responsible for the administration of, compliance with and/or payment of the cost of all consents, licences, waivers and/or clearances from any third party in respect of any text, images, films, sound recordings, trade mark, service mark, logos, graphics, music, lyrics, computer generated material, computer software and/or the reproduction of any material in any format and/or by any means including any credit and/or copyright notice of and/or any contractual obligations to any person and/or company material that the [Distributor] shall decide to include in the [Products/DVDs/other formats] and on any labels, packaging, extracts, promotional and/or marketing material at the [Distributors'] cost and expense.

1.2 That [Name] shall not be liable for any such sums in 1.1 and/or the cost of any disputes and/or legal proceedings that may arise.

1.3 The [Distributor] shall not be entitled to deduct any such sums paid in 1.1 from the advances, royalties and/or other payments due to [Name

C.813
The [Licensee] agrees and undertakes to ensure that:

1.1 All copyright notices, credits, trade marks, service marks, designs, logos and moral rights in the [Film] including any soundtrack and/or any extracts and/or any labels, packaging, advertising, publicity and/or promotional material notified by the [Licensor] with the [Film Material] shall be transmitted, displayed and/or incorporated as required by the [Licensor].

1.2 That the [Licensee] shall not delete, change and/or alter the position, size, order and/or fail to transmit, display and/or incorporate any of the matters in 1.1 in respect the exploitation of the [Television Rights/DVD/other rights] Rights in the [Film] and/or parts and/or any associated material.

1.3 That where any errors, omissions and/or other failures to comply arises and/or takes place that the [Licensee] shall use its [best/reasonable]

endeavours to comply with the requests of the [Licensor] to remedy the position at the [Licensees'] sole cost.

C.814

The parties agree that they shall follow the [Universal Copyright Convention] in respect of the notification of claim to copyright and ownership of the [Work]. From the time of first publication all copies of the [Work] published with the authority of the [Author] or other copyright owner shall bear the symbol © accompanied by the name of the copyright owner, the year of first publication placed in such manner as to give reasonable notice of claim of copyright. The parties agree that the copyright notice for the [Work] [and/or any adaptations] shall be as follows: [specify copyright symbol/ name or names which can be persons or a company/trust/other/year of first publication].

C.815

[Name] agrees that the position, size, prominence, order and whether to include any credit, copyright notice, logo, trade mark, service mark, disclaimer, warning and/or otherwise to add any words, images, slogans and/or advice before, after and/or in the [Film] and/or any extracts and/or on any labels, packaging, marketing, advertisements, DVD, CD and/or on any electronic download from any website, platform and/or other source over the internet and/or through any telecommunication system to be accessed and/ or downloaded to a computer, mobile, gadget and/or other device and/or otherwise of any nature shall be entirely at the discretion of the [Company]. That [Name] shall not have the right to any recognition, credit and/or acknowledgement and has waived all such claims in respect of the exercise of the rights by the [Company] under this agreement.

C.816

Copyright © [Company] [year]. Manufactured and distributed by [Name/ Distributor] under licence from [Company]. All rights reserved.

C.817

Produced by [specify name of Distributor] [website/app reference] [year] under an exclusive licence from [specify Company] of [specify Group].

All rights of the distributor and the Company are reserved.

There is no authority and/or licence granted and you are strictly prohibited and must not reproduce, copy, hire, lend, perform in public, broadcast, transmit, upload to and/or use in any channel, platform, website, app and/or by any other means over the internet and/or through any telecommunication system any part of this [Material/format] except as specifically permitted by the terms set out in [specify document/location of terms].

C.818

All rights reserved and may not be reproduced and/or duplicated in any format.

Made in [country]

Software [year-year] [specify name] [trade mark name] are trade marks or registered trade marks of [specify owner]

Published and distributed by [specify name and logo]

Software exclusively licensed to [specify name and logo]

C.819

© [year] [Company] All rights reserved.

© [year] layout and design [name] All rights reserved.

For private personal one household residential use only. You are prohibited and must not upload, reproduce and/or distribute any content.

C.820

Film © [year] [Company] All rights reserved

Label Design and Artwork © [year] [Name] All rights reserved

[DVD/Disc] Logo is a trade mark of [name]

Distributor [Name] [Logo].

Not for rental this [DVD/Disc] is for retail sale to the public for private use only

Copyright warning [specify details].

C.821

© [year] [Company] Licensed and distributed by [Name] [Logo].

All rights reserved. For promotional use only in [country] not for sale. Copyright Warning [specify]

C.822

The [Licensee] undertakes to ensure that:

1.1 A copyright notice and registered trade mark notice, logo, image and title to the [Licensor] and any other third party requested by the [Licensor] shall be as follows: [specify details] which is to be reproduced on all copies of the [Product] in the size, manner and form and position set out in Appendix A.

1.2 No other copyright notice, trade mark notice, logo, image and title and/or claim of ownership and/or any interest is to be permitted and/or reproduced except for the [Licensee] as follows: [specify details]

which is to be reproduced on all copies of the [Product] in the size, manner and form and position set out in Appendix B.

1.3 That all labels, packaging sleeves and boxes, posters, banners, catalogues, online images and text on any website, app, channel, platform and/or in any electronic form on the internet and/or for any telecommunication system and/ any printed promotional and/or marketing material and associated merchandise, all advertisements and any other material in any medium and/or form used to exploit the rights granted under this agreement shall bear the copyright notice and registered trade mark notice and any logo, image and title specified in 1.1.

1.4 That neither the [Licensee] nor any unauthorised third party shall be entitled and/or permitted to add to, delete from, adapt and/or vary any part of the copyright notice and registered trade mark notice and/or any logo, image and title specified in 1.1.

1.5 Where the [Licensor] discovers that there has been a breach of any of the above terms and conditions. That the [Licensee] shall withdraw all such material as the [Licensor] may request immediately and take such steps as the [Licensor] may stipulate to resolve the matter at the [Licensee's] cost.

C.823

[Name] agrees and accepts to waive all copyright and intellectual property rights and all other rights to any copyright notice and/or other credit and all moral rights in any country in the world in the [Film] and/or any part and/or any sound recording, performance, interview and/or any packaging, marketing and/or other material which may be created, developed, produced and/or distributed by the [Company] at any time whether such rights exist now and/or come into existence by new technology and/or laws in the future.

C.824

1.1 The [Licensee] agrees to provide the following copyright notice, credit, trade mark, service mark, logo, image and slogan to the [Licensor] in any advertising, publicity, promotional and packaging material in respect of the exploitation, marketing and distribution of the [Film].

1.2 The [Licensee] agrees to provide the [Licensor] with copies and samples of any advertising, publicity, promotional and packaging material in respect of the exploitation of the [Film] at the [Licensee's] cost.

C.825

Both parties agree that the following copyright notice which attributes both parties as joint copyright owners shall be used in respect of the [Film] and in respect of all material in any media directly arising from the exploitation of any rights. Details of the specification, size, position, colour and priority in terms of listing together with a sample representation are set out in schedule A.

C.826
The [Distributor] agrees and undertakes to acknowledge by suitable legend the ownership of any copyrights in any such material they may use provided that the [Licensor] shall have so advised the [Distributor] in writing in advance by [date].

C.827

1.1 The [Consultant] shall not be entitled to any credit and/or acknowledgement unless he/she appears in sound and/or vision in which case the following credit shall appear in the [Series]: [name] [on screen/at the end of each film].

1.2 The [Consultant] agrees that the position, size, order and whether it is included in any advertising, marketing and/or promotional material shall be entirely the [Company's] decision.

1.3 The [Consultant] accepts that no credit and/or acknowledgement shall be due if he/she is edited out of and/or deleted entirely from the [Series].

C.828
The [Company] agrees and undertakes to provide the following on screen credit and copyright notice, [trade mark/logo] and caricature image of the [Author] in [front and end credits] of the [Programmes] and in any adaptation, packaging, promotional, advertising and in any other material of any nature in respect of the exploitation of the [Programmes] and/or parts in any media in any format. A copy of full details required in relation to examples of different formats and means of marketing and exploitation is set out and represented in the attached document A which forms part of this agreement.

C.829
The [Licensee] agrees and acknowledges that it shall use and shall not delete the credits, copyright notices, moral rights, trade marks, service marks, logos, titles or otherwise set out in Schedule B which is attached and forms part of this agreement. Except that the failure to broadcast and/or transmit any item listed due to unexpected lack of air time, failure of facilities and/or other unforeseen circumstances shall not be a breach of this agreement provided that reasonable endeavours had been made to comply.

C.830

© [Name] and [Name] [year]. All rights reserved

The copyright [Owner/Company] has licensed the [Sound Recording/Film including the sound track] contained in this [DVD/Disc/other format] to [Distributor]

[Cover/label/package design] © [year] [Artist/other]

C.831

© [Company] [year]. All rights reserved

Manufactured, sold and distributed by [Distributor]

C.832

© [Name] and [Name] in the [Book/Character] [year of publication]

© [Company] in the [Film] [year of release/other]

Manufactured and distributed under Licence by [Distributor].

© [Artist/other] [in the label/ cover/ packaging/marketing material] [year]

C.833

© Copyright [specify copyright owner] [year]

C.834

The parties agree the following acknowledgements, credits and copyright notices for the [Series/Films]:

1.1 Based on a book entitled [specify title/reference] by [Author]: [specify credit/copyright notice].

1.2 Adapted by [Writer] in collaboration with [specify person]: [specify credit]

1.3 Translated by [name]: [specify credit]

1.4 Music and lyrics by [name]: [specify credit/copyright notice].

1.5 Orchestration and sound recording by [names]: [specify credit/order].

1.6 Produced by [name]: [specify credit]

1.7 Director [name]: [specify credit].

1.8 Special effects and animation by [name]: [specify credit]

1.9 Costumes by [name]: [specify credit]

1.10 Equipment by [name]: [specify credit]

1.11 Performance of songs and singing by [names]: [specify credits/order]

1.12 Cast [names]: [specify credits/order]

1.13 Locations [names]: [specify acknowledgements].

1.14 Editing [name]: [specify credit]

1.15 Lighting [name]: [specify credit].

1.16 Animals and livestock [name]: [specify acknowledgement].

1.17 Production Company [name]: [specify credit]

1.18 Television Company [name]: [specify credit]

1.19 Distribution Company [name]: [specify credit]

1.20 Product Placement [names]: [specify acknowledgements]

1.21 Sponsors [names]: [specify acknowledgements].

C.835

1.1 It is agreed that the parties shall agree at a later the exact details of the copyright notices, credits, trademarks, logos and images that shall be reproduced at the end of the [Film] and/or in and/or any other material in any format and/or medium. The parties agree that as far as possible they shall all receive an equal and proportionate allocation of space and duration in each case.

1.2 That as a minimum no material shall be released in any form unless it bears the following copyright notice and credit to [Name] and the [Company] as follows: [specify details].

1.3 That where the parties disagree as to the exact form of any copyright notices, credits, trade marks, logos and images to be used and/or reproduced that any dispute shall be resolved by mediation at the [Company's] cost.

General Business and Commercial

C.836
The [Licensee] agrees and undertakes to acknowledge by suitable words, credit or copyright notice the ownership of any copyright in any material in the [Work] provided that the [Licensor] shall advise the [Licensee] in writing of the conditions required to be fulfilled.

C.837
[Name] shall be entitled to the following copyright notice, image and statement in respect of [format/rights/material]: [specify exact details/ images] on all copies of any material in any medium and/or format exploited

under this agreement. The exact specifications in relation to a range of different material and mediums are set out in appendix A and form part of this agreement.

C.838

The [Assignee] agrees to provide and observe the copyright notices, credits, moral rights and contractual obligations regarding, size, order, position and prominence and any applicable other conditions to third parties in respect of the [Work] and the [Material] notified to the [Assignee] by the [Assignor] before [date].

C.839

The [Researcher] agrees that he/she shall not be entitled to any credit, copyright notice and/or other acknowledgment in respect of the product of the work and/or services provided under this agreement whether original material created by the [Researcher] or not.

C.840

© [Name] [year]

C.841

© [Name] of the [Title/text/slogans/quotes] [year]–[year]

© [Name] of the [Artwork/graphics/images/photographs] [year]

© [Name] of the [Film/computer-generated material/sound recordings/format] [year]

Manufactured under Licence from [specify] by [Name]. Distributed by [Name] under the Brand known as: [specify exact details/link to site].

C.842

It shall not be a justifiable reason for the termination of this agreement in the event that a copyright notice and/or trade mark and/or logo is not reproduced in the exact form stipulated and agreed and/or is omitted and/or altered in some way in the course of the exploitation of the [Work/Product]. Provided that the [Licensee] takes all reasonable steps to mitigate the damage and agrees to pay the [Licensor] a reasonable sum in compensation.

C.843

1.1   The [Company] agrees and undertakes that it shall not represent and/or convey the impression in any way in any website, podcast, marketing, promotional material and/or advertising that it holds and/or controls the copyright, intellectual property rights and/or any other rights in the [Work/Service].

1.2 The [Company] agrees and undertakes that where it makes reference to the [Work/Service] in any manner that the following words and statement shall appear [specify exact details]. Further that where an extract of the [Work/Service] is used that the following copyright notice, credit, trade mark notice, slogan, logo and image shall also be positioned with that extract: [specify exact details].

Internet, Websites and Apps

C.844

1.1 The [Website/App/Platform] is owned or controlled by [Company/Name] contact details: [–].

1.2 You are only permitted to use the [content/material] for the authorised purpose of private research and/or educational purposes for your own background research.

1.3 Any report, essay and/or project must credit the [Company/Name] as follows: [specify credit and link to site]. In addition the actual extract of the [content/material] must provide a copyright notice to the copyright owner as follows: © [year of first publication] [name of copyright owner].

1.4 There is no right to use the [content/material] for a class, school and/or college as part of a study and/or language programme.

1.5 You must request additional permission and obtain a licence and pay a fee and/or royalties for any other intended form of exploitation.

C.845

This [Website/Material] was originally created and exploited in [year] by [name of business] the copyright owner. The contents are regularly updated and revised and the copyright owner remains the same. You are permitted to use this material for your own personal non-commercial use and to copy and print the information. In the event that you wish to commercially exploit any material of any nature then contact [email/address] for clearance and details of copyright fees that may be due.

C.846

© [Name] [year of release/publication/other] [Name] All Rights Reserved.

C.847

Copyright [Company] is a wholly owned subsidiary of [Parent Company] © [year] – [year] held by [Company].

C.848

Copyright Database and Index, © [Name] [year].

C.849

Index and Taxonomy © [Company/Author] [year–year].

C.850

Copyright Notice. The contents of these pages are © [name] [year–year].

C.851

Copyright © [year] [Company] a division of [specify name of Group]. All Rights Reserved.

C.852

All contents are protected by copyright and owned, controlled or licensed to the [Company]. © [year-year] [Company]. This notice applies to the whole site and where material is owned by third parties a separate notice or warning will appear and/or be displayed next to and/or near the content. There is no implied licence and/or right to copy and/or reproduce any content.

C.853

All contents are the property of [Name] unless otherwise stated or represented.

© [Name] [year].

C.854

1.1   Copyright, intellectual property rights, computer software rights, databases, codes, passwords and any other data, films, images, sound recordings and/or other material which is on this [Website/App/Platform] known as [Trading Name] is owned, controlled and distributed by [Name] under the [Trading Name]. Overall copyright ownership of the [Website/App/Platform] is held by [Name].

1.2   There is also content which is owned by third parties who may or may not display a copyright notice, failure to do so does not imply a right to copy or reproduce or supply any such content.

C.855

[Email/Letter] © [Author] [year]

C.856

© [Company] [year] All rights are reserved in all emails, letters, orders and other records or documents sent by any employee or officer of the [Company] and there is no right granted to reproduce, supply, license, distribute and/or exploit any part to any third party and/or on any website and/or in any newspaper and/or by mobile phone and/or otherwise.

534

C.857

Database, index and taxonomy © [Company] [year–year]

C.858

[Word entries on search engine] © [Company] [year–year]

C.859

Podcast on [subject] Copyright © [Name] [year]

C.860

[Video/Film/Mobile] clip © [Name] [year] All rights reserved.

C.861

[Newsfeed/Subscription Service] © [Company] [year] under licence from [Distributor].

C.862

[Blog title/text] © [Name/Writer/Company] [year]

[Blog Image] © [Name/Artist] [year]

[Blog Slogan] © [Name/Writer] [year]

[Blog Photograph] © [Name/Artist] [year]

[Blog Database] © [Name/Writer] [year]

[Blog Film] © [Name/Company] [year]

[Blog Sound recordings] © [Name/Company] [year]

[Reports/Articles] sourced and reproduced under [non-exclusive/exclusive] licence from [Company/Author]: © [Company/Author] [year]

[Blog Website] owned and controlled by [Name/Company] and hosted by [Platform Company].

C.863

[App title, logo, image and slogan] © [Name] [year]

[App hardware] [specify ownership]

[App Software] [specify ownership]

[App Programme and Animation] [specify ownership]

[App Maps] © [Name] [year]

[Games/Prizes] [specify ownership]

[App Data] held by [specify ownership]

C.864

[Image/Still/Drawing] entitled: [title] description: [subject] © [Name] [year]

All rights reserved.

C.865

[Infographics/Maps/illustrations/Data] entitled: [titles] descriptions: [subject]

[list individual image] © [Name] [year].

C.866

[Art installation/Sculpture] entitled: [title] description: [subject] commissioned by [Name] sponsored by [Company] owned by [Institute].

Copyright © [Institute] [year]

All rights reserved.

C.867

[Podcast Series] entitled: [title]

Title of each podcast: [specify title] Copyright © [Name] [year]

Merchandising and Distribution

C.868

The [Agent] agrees to ensure that any third party shall agree to provide the following credit, copyright notice, trade mark and logo to the [Licensor] in respect of the [Products/Images] in a prominent and clear manner on all packaging, publicity, advertising and promotional material in respect of the marketing, distribution and exploitation of the [Products/Images] as follows: [specify exact details].

C.869

The [Licensee] shall ensure that the following words are set out on each and every item of the [Product] and the [Product Package] [trade mark/trade mark registration/copyright notice/warning/other/text/slogan/position/size/colour/order] [specify in detail] and an example of each is attached to and forms part of this agreement in schedule A.

'The Product Package' shall mean all material associated with the [Licensee's] [Product] including any labels, packaging, advertising, promotion and marketing material, films, videos, podcasts, blogs, television and radio commercials and any other visual or sound recordings and/or printed material, photographs, computer generated graphics, scripts, artwork, music, DVDs, CDs and/or any other form of exploitation over the internet by any electronic means and/or method and/or through any telecommunication system to be accessed and/or downloaded to a computer, mobile phone, watch, gadget and/or any other device and/or method.

C.870

'The Company's Material' shall mean the content supplied by the [Company] which is briefly described as follows: [describe and itemise]. A full description of the Company's Material is attached to and forms part of this agreement in appendix C setting out all the copyright and intellectual property rights and where they should be displayed and/or located including copyright notices, trade marks, service marks, logos, designs, slogans, text, artwork, graphics, images and photographs, music, sound recordings, computer software, any other contributors and/or performers, computer generated material and all licences, consents, waivers, moral rights, contractual obligations obtained, paid for and/or due.

C.871

© [Company] and [parent company] [year–year]. All Rights Reserved

C.872

Game Code © [Company] [year–year]. All rights reserved

C.873

Distributed by [Distributor] under Licence from [Company].

C.874

Copyright © [Company] [year of first general release/publication]

C.875

© [Original characters/book] [Name/Estate] [year]

© [Film/Series] [Name/Estate/Company] [year]

© [Product] [Name/Estate/other]. Exclusive Distributor [Distributor]

C.876

1.1 The [Licensee] agrees and undertakes to ensure that the [Licensee] shall not make and/or use the [Work] in any material and/or reproduce it in whole and/or part in any format in any medium without an agreed copyright notice, credit, trade mark, slogan, image and logo to the [Licensee] as described and exhibited in Appendix A in the exact form, style and colour required for each format.

1.2   The [Licensee] agrees that all matters stated in 1.1 shall appear in a prominent position on each and every copy in any format and/or medium and in all packaging, advertising, publicity and marketing material. The [Licensee] agrees to submit samples to the [Licensor] for approval in advance in each case and if they are rejected shall make such amendments as may be requested.

1.3   The [Licensee] undertakes to ensure that this clause shall be a contractual obligation for all distributors, sub-licensees, consultants and/or marketing companies and/or any other third party who may be engaged by the [Licensee] for any reason related to the [Work].

C.877

The [Licensee] agrees and undertakes to ensure that the [Licensee] and any third party engaged by and/or under contract to the [Licensee] associated with the [Work] shall:

1.1   Ensure that the following copyright notice will be incorporated on every copy of the [Product] which is based on the [Work]: © [name] [year].

1.2   Not at any time delete and/or authorise the removal and/or omission of such copyright notice. The copyright notice shall be placed in such manner and position as to give reasonable notice to the public of the claim of copyright.

1.3   Supply and deliver to the [Licensor] for the prior written approval of the [Licensor]

(a)   All proposed drafts and copies of any packaging, advertising, marketing, and press releases and promotional material before it is issued to the press and/or public including email, website material, banners, trade exhibition material, catalogues, brochures, flyers, display stands and point of sale material.

(b)   Drawings and samples of any prototype and the final version of the [Product] before any tools for manufacture are created and/or the production, distribution and/or sale to the public.

(c)   Drawings and samples of any prototype and the final version of the [Product] before production, distribution and/or sale to the public of all packaging. Together with any other relevant material in any format and/or medium.

C.878

The [Licensee] agrees and undertakes to ensure that it shall not allow any third party to be involved in the production, distribution and/or sales and/or to act as an agent and/or otherwise be involved who is not bound by a contractual obligation to the [Licensee] as follows:

1.1 To act in good faith and ensure that the copyright notice and credit, and trade mark in Appendix A to the [Licensor] and the [Author] appear on all copies of the [Work/Film/Product/Disc].

1.2 To agree and undertake that they shall not acquire any copyright, intellectual property rights, computer software rights, design rights, and/or any other rights in any trade mark, service mark, logos or images, names, characters, words and titles and shall not attempt to register any rights.

1.3 To ensure that the copyright notice and credit, and trade mark are not deleted, removed and/or omitted from any copy of the [Work/Film/Product/Disc] and/or any packaging, marketing, publicity and/or promotional material.

C.879

© [Copyright Owner] [year – year] Based on [Work] by [Author]

Artwork/Cover © [Name] [year]

Computer-generated material © [Name] [year].

Software © [Name] [year].

Lyrics © [Name] [year].

Music © [Name] [year].

Film © [Title] [year] [Name]

[DVD/Content] Distributed by [Name].

C.880

1.1 The [Licensor] may notify and insist that the [Licensee] [at any stage during the agreement up to one year before the expiry date] make such changes, adaptations, deletions and/or variations of any copyright notices, credits, trademarks, logos and disclaimers and/or the terms and conditions of use of the [Work/Product/Service] and/or any other part and/or of any packaging, marketing and promotional material.

1.2 The [Licensee] agrees and undertakes to comply with 1.1 and to carry out such work at its sole cost and expense. Where any material is withdrawn from the market of the [Work/Product/Service] then the [Licensee] shall be entitled to dispose of such material in the remainder market and use any such sums received to recoup the costs of complying with 1.1. The [Licensee] shall be obliged to account for any sums received and any set-off by the [Licensee] to recoup costs.

C.881

The [Seller] agrees that as far as possible it shall try to include in any associated publicity, advertising, promotional material, emails, webpages or other marketing material by the [Seller] of the [Seller's] Website that the [Supplier's Logo] and the [Product] shall be given reasonable prominence, recognition and a copyright notice, trade mark notice and credit given in respect of the [Supplier's Logo] and [Product].

C.882

The [Seller] agrees to provide the following copyright notice, credit, service mark, trade mark or logo to the [Supplier] in respect of the [Product] as is specified in Schedule B in the [Seller's] website and any advertising, marketing, publicity promotional and packaging material. The [Seller] shall provide the [Supplier] with copies and samples at the [Seller's] cost on a regular basis.

C.883

1.1 The [Distributor] agrees to provide the following [copyright notice, credit, trade mark, logo, design, statement, other] to the [Company] in the following circumstances:

a. [specify details] on all packaging, labels, jackets, sleeves;

b. [specify details] on all posters, brochures, catalogues and advertisements;

c. [specify details] on all press and social media releases;

d. [specify details] on display stands at exhibitions.

1.2 It is accepted by [Name] that the failure to include any matter in 1.1 to 1.4 shall not be a breach of this agreement.

C.884

Produced in [country] for [Retailer] [year] [Company].

C.885

The [Distributor] agrees not to supply, release, distribute, market and/or sell [Products/Units] which do not bear the copyright notice to the [Licensor] and all such items shall be destroyed and the matter reported to the [Licensor] as soon as possible.

C.886

The manufacturer, supplier and distributor appointed by [Name] under this agreement shall not produce, release or distribute any copies of the [Work] and/or any adaptation in any country at any time unless it bears the following copyright notice to [Name] on each and every copy and in every style, format and media based on and/or derived from the [Work/Character/Service/other] and/or any part.

C.887

[Logo/Shape] © [Company] [year]

[Slogan] © [Company] [year]

[Product Name] © [Company] [year]

[specify] registered trade mark of [Company]

[specify] registered community mark of [Company]

[specify] registered service mark of [Company].

C.888

Manufactured by: [specify name].

Distributed by: [specify name].

Licensed by: [specify name]

Made in [country] by [specify name]

© [Company] [year] part of the [specify name] brand

Publishing

C.889

The [Distributor] agrees and undertakes that all copies of the [Work/Manuscript/Images] published pursuant to this publishing agreement shall bear a copyright notice © [the year of publication] together with the [Distributor's] full corporate name and the [Authors'] full name on each item and shall comply with the [Universal Copyright Convention].

C.890

1.1 The [Company] shall ensure that any copyright notices, credits, moral rights, trade marks, service marks and logos included in the publication of the [Work/Manuscript/Images] in [specify format] shall be duplicated exactly the same on the [Company's] [website/app/channel].

1.2 The [Licensor] shall also be provided with the [copyright notice, credit, trade mark, logo] in respect of reference to and/or use of the [Work/Manuscript/Images] in any advertising, publicity, marketing and distribution material as described in appendix A. The appendix includes two and three dimensional representations.

C.891

The [Company] agrees as far as reasonably possible that it will ensure that a copyright notice shall be displayed on and/or in conjunction with the [Image/Text] showing that the copyright belongs to [Name] as follows: [Title of Image/Text] © [Name] [year].

C.892

The [Publisher] undertakes that the following copyright notice will be incorporated on every copy of the [Work] © [name] [year of first publication] and on any material based on or derived from it including discs, tapes, advertising, brochures, flyers, websites, posters and in any other media created, developed, commissioned, licensed, sold and/or supplied by the [Publisher]. The [Publisher] shall not at any time delete or authorise the removal or omission of such copyright notice. The copyright notice shall be placed in such manner and position as to give reasonable notice to the public of the claim of copyright.

C.893

The [Publisher] agrees to impose a contractual obligation on any sub-licensee, agent, parent company, subsidiary and/or any other third party with whom it enters an arrangement, agreement and/or licence in respect of any copy of the [Work] in any media that:

1.1   They will incorporate the copyright notice in clause [–] to the [Author].

1.2   They shall not acquire any copyright, or any other intellectual property rights or computer software rights and/or any trade mark, service mark, logos, images, names, words, titles and/or other interest and shall not attempt to register any rights.

1.3   Where there is an error or omission in the copyright notice they shall withdraw all the material as soon as possible and issue the amended version.

C.894

1.1   The [Ghostwriter] agrees that he/she shall not have any copyright notice, credit and/or other acknowledgment and waives all moral and/or other rights in respect of the [Work/Manuscript]. The [Ghostwriter] agrees that the [Author] and/or any third party may at any time exploit the [Work/Manuscript] and any associated research, documents, films, sound recordings and/or Images in any media and/or format without any mention of the [Ghostwriter].

1.2   The [Ghostwriter] agrees that the [Author] shall receive the sole credit for researching and writing the [Work/Manuscript] and the copyright notice shall be as follows: © [name of Author] [year of publication].

C.895

The [Author] waives all right to a copyright notice in respect of the [Work/Article/Blog] and any parts and the artwork and material in Schedule A in all media at any time in the [Territory]. The [Author] agrees that the copyright notice shall be as follows: © [Company] [year].

C.896

The [Company] agrees and undertakes that:

1.1 The following copyright notice and words shall be displayed in the precise manner and order set out as follows: [Title of Extract] © [Name] [year] [statement/reference to Publisher] [link to Publisher].

1.2 That the matters set out in 1.1 shall appear, be displayed and/or be printed at the end of the [Extract] in each and every copy of the [Periodical] and on the website [reference].

1.3 That any reference to the [Extract] in the periodical on the front cover and/or any other marketing and other promotional material shall be limited stating [Name] in conjunction with the [Extract] and the copyright notice in 1.1 does not apply.

C.897

The [Licensee] agrees that it shall not at any time delete and/or authorise the removal and/or omission of such copyright notice which shall be legible and in such a size and position as to give reasonable notice of the copyright owner's rights.

C.898

1.1 The [Company] undertakes that a copyright notice in the form of a letter C enclosed by a circle followed by the name of the [Copyright Owner] and the first year of publication shall be displayed in the precise manner and order stated in clause [–] and printed on all copies of the [Work] on one of the first four pages.

1.2 The [Company] undertakes that the name of [Copyright Owner] shall appear prominently on the front cover and spine and back cover and the title page of the [Work] and in all marketing material.

1.3 The [Company] shall use its reasonable endeavours to ensure that an identical copyright notice appears in all sub-licensed editions of the [Work]. The [Company] agrees to ensure that any third party and/or successor in business in title shall agree to provide the conditions set out in clause [–] to the [Author].

C.899

The Publisher agrees that it is an important term of the agreement:

1.1   That there is a copyright notice to the [Authors] as follows:

© [personal/professional names of Authors in full or in some other format such as initials] [first year of publication]-[last year of publication]

which shall appear on each and every copy of the hardback and paperback book of the [Work] on the front inside pages.

1.2   The [Publisher] agrees to supply a copy of the proof with the copyright notice as it will appear in the hardback and paperback book for approval by the [Authors].

1.3   The [Publisher] agrees and undertakes that as far as possible it shall ensure that no copies of the [Work] and/or any part in any media shall be reproduced, supplied, distributed, sold, licensed and/or downloaded and/or otherwise exploited by the [Publisher] and/or any wholesalers, distributors, agents, sub-licensees, online digital retailers and/or any third party without the copyright notice to the [Authors]. That this condition will be imposed by the [Publishers] in all such agreements. Further that samples of the proofs shall be sent by all third parties to the [Authors] for approval in each case.

C.900

The [Publisher/Distributor] shall not authorise and/or permit third parties who are engaged, licensed and/or have an agreement with the [Publisher/Distributor] to impose their own copyright notice on any part of the [Work/Material] and/or any reproduction, development, adaptation, merchandising, packaging, labels, advertising, marketing in any format in any media. The [Authors] shall be the only persons entitled to a copyright notice, claim of authorship and/or other credit as authors of the [Work/Material].

C.901

The [Authors] accept that there is a practice not to display a copyright notice on the following marketing material on which only a summary of the [Work] will be included and no actual extracts of the [Work]: [specify type of material].

C.902

The [Author] agrees that where [the cover/illustrations/other] have been designed, commissioned and developed by the [Publisher] that the [Publisher] shall be entitled to a copyright notice in respect of that material.

C.903

The [Author] agrees that where third parties are appointed to create and develop new formats of the [Work] as manufacturers, sub-licensees and/ or distributors. Then the [Publisher] shall submit to the [Author] a draft of any proposed form of copyright notice and acknowledgements on samples of the label, packaging, products, advertising and marketing material in each case. The [Publisher] shall require the prior written approval of the [Author] before any manufacturer, sub-licensee or distributor can proceed to produce, manufacture or release any products.

C.904

Title, preface, text and index © [Name] [year]

Illustrations © [Name] [year]

Front Cover [photograph/computer-generated design] © [Name] [year]

C.905

© [Copyright Owner] [year]

C.906

Copyright © [Name] [year] All rights reserved

C.907

[Title of Work] Hardback © [Company/Distributor] [year to year]

[Title of Work] Paperback © [Company/Distributor] [year to year]

[Title of Work] [E book/Download/electronic form] © [Company/Distributor] [year to year]

[Artwork/Photographs] for the [cover/online image] [created/designed] by [name]

© [Company] [year]

[Index/databases] compiled by [name]

© [Company] [year]

[Interactive content/Article] supplied by [name]

© [Company] [year]

Product Placement [name] [product] [logo] [image] trade mark of [Company]

C.908

[Work/Images/Extract] [author unknown/out of copyright in country]. The physical copy of this material is owned by [Institute/Archive]. There is no licence is granted and/or implied to reproduce this [Work/Images/Extract] for any reason in any format. You have been advised not to record, film and/or to take any images and/or copies for storage on any device. Any reproduction and/or exploitation requires the authority and prior agreement of the [Institute] in the form of a licence.

Services

C.909

The [Record Company] agrees that:

1.1   It shall provide the following copyright notice, logo, and trade mark to the [Artiste] in respect of the [Musical Works] and/or any adaptation on each and every copy produced, manufactured, released, distributed, supplied, sold and/or downloaded in any format and/or in any medium as follows: [specify] [both in words and sound].

1.2   It shall not at any time reproduce, release, distribute, supply, market, promote, and/or exploit the [Musical Works] in any form in any media and/or manner and/or authorise others to do so without providing the copyright notice to the [Artiste] for such [Musical Works].

C.910

The [Manager] agrees to ensure that the following [credit/copyright notice/ trade mark/logo/compliance mark] of the [Artist] shall be prominently placed and displayed on all materials of any nature to be used and/or exploited by the [Manager] and/or third parties in connection with the [Artist] including but not limited to CDs, labels, packaging, marketing, advertising, websites, electronic download formats, videos, podcasts, interviews and tours.

C.911

The [Distributor] agrees and undertakes to provide the following copyright notice, credit, trade mark and logo to the [Company] in all advertising, promotional and packaging material in respect of the marketing and exploitation of the [Company's] [Products/Services] under this agreement: [specify details] Examples of which are attached in Schedule A.

C.912

1.1   The [Consultant] agrees that when preparing, compiling and writing the [Report/Review] that he/she shall ensure that all third party ownership of the copyright and/or intellectual property rights and/ or any material shall be suitably acknowledged and highlighted in the [Report/Review] in the form of a copyright notice and/or other relevant credit.

1.2 The [Consultant] shall provide a complete separate list of the title of the work, the source used and any reference, the contact details, confirmation as to whether there are any copyright and/or contract issues outstanding and/or whether the material is cleared for use by the [Company] and if so the payments that may be required.

C.913

1.1 The [Sub-Licensee] agrees and undertakes that all copyright notices, logos, trade marks and other credits and/or copyright warnings which the [Licensee] notifies the [Sub-Licensee] shall be on each and every copy of the [Work/Product] shall be adhered to and not deleted, amended and/or removed.

1.2 That the [Sub-licensee] undertakes to ensure that no copy is produced, manufactured, released, distributed, supplied, and/or otherwise exploited by the [Sub-Licensee] and/or anyone else authorised to act on its behalf without all the copyright notices, logos, trade marks and other credits and/or copyright warnings which the [Licensee] notifies the [Sub-Licensee] shall be on each and every copy of the [Work/Product]. The [Sub-Licensee] acknowledges that failure to carry out this important requirement may result in the immediate termination of this agreement by the [Licensee].

C.914

The [Consultant] and the [Company] agree that the [Company] shall own all the copyright and intellectual property rights in the [Report/Review], the title and any draft copies and/other material created and/or supplied by the [Consultant].

The [Company] and the [Consultant] agree that the following copyright notice and credit shall be reproduced on the front page of all copies:

Copyright all content: except where stated otherwise

© [Title of Report/Review] [Company] [year]

[Report/Review] prepared and compiled by [Consultant] [Business name/ website/link reference]

C.915

© Product [Company] [year] [Trade Mark/Logo]

© Service [Company] [year] [Trade Mark/Logo]

© [Website/App/Channel] [Company] [year–year] [Trade Mark/Logo]

© Audio File [Author/Company] [year]

Computer Software owned by [Name] [year] [Trade Mark/Logo]

© Newsletter [Name] [year–year]

© Photographs/Images [Name] [year]

© [Film/Archive/Streaming Service] [Name] [year]

© Electronic Download Format [Name] [year]

© Sound Recording [Name] [year]

© [Music/Lyrics] [Name] [year]

C.916

The [Contributor] agrees and undertakes that he/she shall not represent to any third party that he/she is the copyright owner of any work and/or services provided to the [Company] under this agreement. The [Contributor] agrees and undertakes that all his/her work is based on material and/or other directions, ideas and projects proposed by the [Company] and is not original to the [Contributor]. That the [Contributor] agrees that he/she shall not be entitled to any copyright notice for any of his/her work at any time for the [Company].

C.917

1.1   [Name] shall be attributed as the author of the [Project] in the following manner [specify material © name/year] in any printed material, website and/or app content, download, film, and/or marketing material by the [Company] and/or by any agent and/or consultant authorised by them.

1.2   [Name] shall be attributed as the author of the [Project] in the following manner [specify verbal statement] in any audio file and/or sound recording and/or radio and/or any other licensed recording and/or interview by the [Company] and/or by any agent and/or consultant authorised by them.

Sponsorship

C.918

The [Promoter] agrees to provide a copyright notice, slogan, trade mark image and link to the [Company] in any marketing, advertising, merchandising, packaging and online electronic materials including on any website, app and/or listing in accordance with the details and specifications set out in appendix A in respect of the [Event]. Where there is insufficient space and/or it is not possible for any reason then the {Promoter] shall as a minimum mention the name of the [Company].

C.919

1.1 It is agreed between the parties that no copies of the [Sponsors] [Product/Services] and/or any part should be distributed, supplied and/or otherwise exploited in any media by the [Promoter] and/or placed on any websites, platforms and/or other material and/or be used by any agent, sub-licensee and/or any third party authorised by the [Promoter] without the [copyright notice/trade mark/slogan/image/ link to the [Sponsors]. That the [Promoter] agrees to this impose this matter as a pre-condition.

1.2 Further that the [Promoter] and/or any third party shall submit samples of any material in 1.1 to the [Sponsors] for approval in each case at their sole cost and shall make such changes as may be required for the [Sponsor] to accept the material.

C.920

The [Company] agrees that the [Sponsor's] copyright notice, credit, [trade mark/logo], image and slogan set out in attached Appendix B shall be exactly reproduced in any medium and/or format and shall not be adapted and/or changed and/or anything added at any time. Where there is likely to be any alterations then the [Company] must first seek the consent of the [Sponsor].

C.921

That in the event that in the course of the development, production, staging, marketing, promotion, and/or exploitation of the [Event] a new version of any image, trade mark, logo, slogan, sound recording, film and/or other material owned by the [Sponsor] shall be adapted, designed, created and/or used. Then the [Company] undertakes to ensure that the employee, person and/or other third party shall assign and transfer all copyright, intellectual property rights, trade mark rights and/or any other rights in all media to the [Sponsor].

C.922

The [Sponsor] agrees that where for any reason the [Company] omits, deletes, and/or fails to provide a copyright notice, trade mark, image, slogan, credit and/or link to the [Sponsor] for any reason. That provided the [Company] acknowledges the failure and remedies the position if possible it shall not be deemed a breach of this agreement.

C.923

[Company] [address] [web/app/link reference]

[Title of Event/Image/Logo/Slogan] © [Company] [year]

This Guide is produced by [Company]

Publisher: [Name]

Editor: [Name]

Layout: [Name]

Printed by: [Name]

[Trade Marks] are the registered trademarks of the [Company]

Copyright Warning: [specify statement]

Disclaimer: [specify statement].

C.924
The [Sponsor] shall not be entitled to any copyright notices, trademark and/or other attributions of ownership and/or control in respect of any material for the [Event] and/or marketing which in the opinion of the [Organisers] would not be suitable due to lack of space; design and artistic issues; delays in creating material; failure to deliver master copies for reproduction within the time limits set and/or otherwise. The [Sponsor] agrees that in such event they shall not be entitled to paid any sums for any reason for any loss and/or otherwise and/or to seek a repayment of any sums paid to date.

C.925
Where for any reason copyright notices and credits do not appear and/or are not reproduced and/or are deleted, removed, edited out and/or altered and/or amended without the prior written approval and the consent of [Name]. Then [Name] shall have a valid claim for breach of this agreement and shall be entitled to a payment of [number/currency] for each and every case where the [Company] fails to comply. Any such sums due shall be paid within [number] days of invoice by [Name] specifying the failure by the [Company].

University, Charity and Educational

C.926
The parties agree to use the following copyright notices to provide notice of ownership and title of any text, images and other material in respect of the [Project]:

[Title of text] and the index and taxonomy: © [Institute] [year–year]

[Title of Illustrations/Photographs]: © [Name] [year]

[Artwork/Design/Computer-generated design]: © [Institute] [year–year]

All rights reserved.

Exclusive Distributor [Enterprise] under licence from the [Institute].

C.927

The [Institute/Charity] agrees and undertakes to endeavour to incorporate where possible the following copyright notice, credit, service mark, trade mark, logo, image and slogan to the [Author] in respect of the [Work] on any website, app, report and in any marketing and/or promotional material and/or at any event where the [Work] is displayed and/or exhibited and/or reproduced in any format. The [Institute/Charity] shall provide the [Author] with sample copies for review by the [Author] when possible for consultation purposes at the [Institute's/Charity's] cost on a regular basis.

C.928

1.1 The [Distributor/Licensee] agrees to provide the following copyright notice;

© [name] [year of first publication],

together with an attribution statement, image and link to the [Company/ Author] which shall be displayed in a prominent position on each and every copy and in every style, format and media on anything based or derived from the [Work/Service/Products] or any part so that it can be clearly read by any member of the public and/or purchaser. A detailed copy of visual examples is set out in the attached in Schedule C and forms part of this agreement.

1.2 The [Distributor/Licensee] agrees not to reproduce, supply, release, and/or market [Work/Service/Products] which do not bear the copyright notice to any third party. The [Distributor/Licensee] shall not at any time delete and/or authorise the removal and/or omission of such copyright notice in 1.1.

1.3 The [Distributor/Licensee] undertakes that the following copyright notice together with the attribution statement, image and link in 1.1 above shall also be incorporated on any material based on or derived from the [Work/Service/Products] including discs, tapes, brochures, flyers, on all packaging, labels, jackets, sleeves, posters, catalogues, advertisements, press and social media releases, in any product placement and/or on any website, app and/or other online digital blogging post and/or podcasts, and/or on display stands at exhibitions and in any other related media developed, commissioned, supplied, licensed and/or sold by the [Distributor/Licensee].

1.4 The [Distributor/Licensee] agrees and undertakes that it shall not acquire any copyright, trade marks, service marks, design rights, logos or any other intellectual property rights and/or computer software rights, names, words and/or any adaptation in respect of the [Work/

Service/Products] and/or the [institute] and shall not attempt to register any rights and/or interest and/or authorise others to do so.

C.929

The [Distributor/Licensee] agrees to impose a contractual obligation on any sub-licensee, agent, parent company, subsidiary and/or any other third party with whom it enters an arrangement, agreement or license in respect any copy of the [Work/Service/Products] in any media:

1.1   To provide the following copyright notice;

© [name] [year]

credit, logo, image and slogan to the [Institute/Author] on each and every copy of the [Work/Service/Products] or any part so that it can be clearly read by any member of the public and/or purchaser. A copy of the full details is described and represented in Schedule A and forms part of this agreement.

1.2   To provide an undertaking that they shall not acquire any copyright, trade mark, service marks, design rights, logo or any other intellectual property rights and/or computer software rights, names, words and/or any adaptation and/or translation and shall not attempt to register any rights and/or interest.

C.930

The [Institute/Charity] may at its sole discretion credit the [Contributor] as [specify name/role] in the [Project] in a similar manner and form as the other contributors at any time. The [Contributor] agrees that he/she shall have not right to a copyright notice in any form nor shall there be any obligation on the [Institute] to use the work of the [Contributor] and that it may be omitted in its entirety either now and/or at a later date from the Project].

COPYRIGHT WARNINGS

General Business and Commercial

C.931

The copyright and intellectual property rights in the [Content/Service] and all associated trade marks, logos, images, films, sound recordings and/or other material are owned by [specify name] and distributed under license. You are not authorised to make any copy, alter, adapt, supply, distribute, release, market and/or otherwise exploit this [Content/Service] in any media at any time. Requests for permission for any such uses should be sent to: [contact details].

C.932
You are only authorised to use this [Work/Material] for residential and domestic purposes and any commercial use shall require the prior written consent of [Name].

C.933

1.1 All copyright, intellectual property rights and all other rights are held and/or controlled by [Name] in respect of this [Channel/Podcast/Film]

1.2 There is no licence and/or authority provided to you either directly and/or implied to permit you to acquire any rights in any material and/or to attempt to register any interest in any material. You must not adapt any material and/or rights for your own commercial and/or other purpose at any time.

C.934
The following uses of this [Work/Content] as a whole are permitted, but all others require the prior consent of the [Company]:

1.1 Criticism, review or comparisons.

1.2 Educational resource in schools, colleges and universities.

1.3 Advertising, promotion and marketing by [retailers and wholesalers].

C.935
The [Company] has a strong policy of copyright enforcement and will issue a charge and take action against any person and/or business who in any part of the world is discovered to have illegally reproduced and/or exploited this [Work/Project] whether they have made money from it or not.

C.936
You may only download [all/extracts of] these [web pages/archive/sound recordings/audio files] to your computer, mobile and/or other gadget for your own personal use at home on residential premises. There is no authorisation implied and/or granted to use any part for any commercial project, any website, podcast, blog and/or any other educational, charitable and/or non-commercial purpose.

C.937
You are not permitted to copy, supply, transfer, distribute and/or exploit in any manner all and/or large extracts of this [website/archive/sound recordings/

audio files] to any third party at any time. You may keep copies at your personal address for your own use and research, but any commercial work, regular exchanges with others of text, pictures, data or other parts or any contribution to another website, book, film, or other adaptation using any of the material and/or any adaptation will require our prior written consent. Failure to obtain permission could create a risk of being sued for copyright infringement and a claim for all the legal costs, damages and/or losses. In any event all material sourced from this [website/archive/sound recordings/ audio files] should be provided with a copyright notice and credited as follows: [specify details of copyright notice and credit].

C.938

This [Website/Platform/Channel] is owned and controlled by [Name] trading as [Name]. Users are allowed to view the material to read the contents. There is no consent provided to permit copies to be made of any part in any form and/or to supply any such material to third parties whether for commercial gain or not. If you wish to store a copy at home, include material in a commercial project and/or send copies of extracts to others then complete the licensing application form and receive advance authorisation as follows: [specify procedure/information required/form].

C.939

No reproductions, copies, translations, adaptations, edited versions, quotes, extracts, films, books, audio files, podcasts, blogs, CDs, advertisements, marketing, products, services, databases and/or any other material in any format in any medium may be made and/or derived from any part of the material and/or rights on this [Website/Platform/Channel] without the prior authorisation of the [Company] and/or any underlying rights holders and shall only be permitted where a licence has been issued by the [Company].

C.940

You are only authorised to make [one] copy of up to [number] [articles/ images] on the [Website/App] for use by you in a private capacity as an individual to read in printed form and/or to store in your computer and/or on another gadget and/or device. There is no authorisation to distribute the material over the internet and/or through any telecommunication system by means of a mobile phone and/or otherwise.

C.941

There is no right to supply, transfer, edit, alter, change, adapt, interfere with and/or to reproduce and/or distribute the material and/or any parts on [Report/Project/Service] without the prior written consent from the [Institute/ Enterprise].

C.942

You are not authorised to use the material on this [Website/Platform/Channel] and/or any part for the purpose of marketing, advertising and/or promoting a third party product, service, book, event, film, person and/or company and/or any other subject. You are prohibited from using any such material to create and/or convey the impression that it is endorsed, supported by and/or associated with the [Website/Platform/Channel].

C.943

All the text, articles, blogs, images, artwork, graphics, logos, data, advertisements, games, titles, trade names, films, videos, podcasts, audio files, and other material and/or formats belong to a company or person who owns the copyright and who may or may not have displayed a copyright notice depending on the circumstances. You will need to ask for permission and prior written consent if you wish to make any use of their material and/or to adapt it and/or supply it to others. The [Company] has not provided any authorisation to you for any purpose except to view this [Website/Platform/Channel] and to read it directly on your [computer/television/mobile/other].

C.944

All the contributors on this [Website/App/Platform/Channel] have provided their services and/or work on the basis that it shall be made freely available to others over the internet and/or any telecommunication system for their own use at personal use and not for any educational, charitable and/or commercial purpose. Provided that any persons and/or company who access, read, download, reproduce and/or distribute the material and/or any extracts in any format will acknowledge copyright ownership and/or credits for any material, performances, music, lyrics and/or rights as may appear and/or be displayed on the [Website/App/Platform/Channel] and not attempt to hide and/or delete authorship and/or credit of any person and/or company and/or seek substitute another. Where it is the intention to use any material and/or extracts for any educational, charitable and/or commercial purpose then the prior authorisation and consent of the [Website/App/Platform/Channel] shall be required as follows: [set out procedure].

C.945

1.1   All the content of this [Website/App/Blog] is owned and controlled by [Name/Company] but is also subject to the supply of material and/or rights owned by third parties.

1.2   There is no express and/or implied licence that you may supply others, make copies, use any of the material on another website, podcasts, audio file, film, programme, platform and/or channel. You must not reproduce any images, data, text, photographs, films, sound recordings,

555

comments and posts and/or any exploit anything in any other medium regardless of whether you do so for your own personal use, for charity, an educational purpose and/or a commercial reason. You require a licence and must follow the stated procedure at: [reference/details].

C.946
The copyright, intellectual property rights and trade marks in this [Project/ Exhibition/Virtual Tour] are owned by [Company/Archive] and distributed under licence by [Subsidiary]. The public have no right to copy, reproduce and/or in any way exploit any part and to do so will be an infringement of the rights of both these parties who may issue legal proceedings at any time.

C.947
You are not permitted to reproduce, hire, broadcast, transmit and/or distribute and/or supply over the internet and/or through any telecommunication system and/or any post on any website, platform, channel, newspaper and/ or other media company site and/or store and/or play back on any hard drive and/or disc, mobile phone and/or any other gadget and/or to record, edit and/or adapt this [Work/Content/Material]. The purchase of this [Work/ Content/Material] only permits you to play the [Work/Content/Material] at residential premises in private on [format] without making any charge for viewing the [Work/Content/Material].

C.948
This copy is supplied for personal and private home use only. Do not make any copies, edit, adapt, change, add to, delete from and/or join this [Work/ Product/Disc] with any other at any time.

C.949
Reproduction of any part of this [Work/Content/Material] is strictly forbidden.

C.950
The title, trade marks, logos, images, illustrations, designs, characters and character names in the [Work/Script/Book/Podcast] have been created by and belong to [Name]. [Name] asserts his/her right to be identified as the copyright owner and/or as the creator and owner of any other rights. The copyright notice, credit, trade mark, image and link should be used in relation to all material and/or any adaptation in a prominent and clear position as set out in appendix A including on labels, packaging and/or as end credits. No reproduction is authorised and all rights are reserved.

C.951
No licence is granted to reproduce, supply, sell, license and/or distribute the [Report/Script/Book] in any form for any reason. There is no authority

to post, display and/or to distribute any part of the [Report/Script/Book] over the internet and/or any telecommunication system and/or in any other electronic format. Please apply to the [Company/Authors] for consent to reproduce and adapt the [Report/Script/Book]. In any event any use must incorporate a clear and prominent copyright notice to the [Authors], a credit to the [Company], the title of the [Report/Script/Book] and a link to [specify website/personal profile].

C.952

No part of this [Book/Work] and/or the accompanying [Disc/CD-Rom/Electronic Download] may be reproduced, distributed, transmitted and/or exploited in whole and/or part in any media by any means and/or stored in any retrieval system and/or archive of any nature without the prior written consent of the [Distributors] and the [Authors] except for:

1.1 Authorised use of the [Book/Work] and/or accompanying [Disc/CD-Rom/Electronic Download] as set out in the Software End User Licence.

1.2 Genuine and non-commercial fair dealing for the sole purpose of review and/or a critique and/or an educational and/or academic resource report.

1.3 Any use in accordance with the terms of a licence issued by the [Copyright Licensing Agency] in respect of photocopying and/or reprographic reproduction for educational purposes only.

1.4 Where a person or business uses the [Book/Work] and/or the accompanying [Disc/CD-Rom/Electronic Download] to incorporate the material into agreements for clients who are provide with the material directly and not through any distribution in a public manner over the internet and/or through any telecommunication system and/or any other form of publication and/or commercial exploitation.

C.953

All rights reserved. No part of this publication may be reproduced, stored in a retrieval system, or transmitted in any form or by any means without the prior written consent of the [Publisher], nor be otherwise circulated in any form of binding or cover other than that in which it is published and without a similar condition being imposed on the subsequent purchaser.

C.954

No part of this [Book/Audio File/Electronic Download] shall be reproduced, adapted, translated, used and/or exploited in any media in any form without the prior written consent of the [Author] and the [Publisher].

C.955

There is no right granted for any person and/or third party to display, reproduce, edit, adapt, change and/or translate any part of this [Work/ Project] on any website, the internet and/or any form of mobile, app, blog and/or telecommunication system at any time. Such prohibition shall apply to quotations, reviews, criticisms and/or otherwise to all text, logos, images, titles and headings, recipes, taxonomy, data, maps, charts, statistics, formulae and other material in any form which is contained in the [Work/ Project] and/or associated with it in anyway.

C.956

The [Sponsor] of the [Project] agrees that the [Schools/Colleges/ Establishments] that register with the [Company] shall be granted a non-exclusive licence to reproduce the [specify scope of material] at their own cost for the duration of the [Project]. Provided that the [Schools/Colleges/ Establishments] undertake not to remove the copyright notice, trade mark and profile summary of acknowledgement to the [Sponsor] which is provided on all copies prior to distribution to the students. Where such information is omitted the Company] shall have the right to terminate the right to participate in the [Project].

C.957

Do not duplicate, hire, rent, adapt, edit, transmit, broadcast, film, record, store on a computer, mobile phone and/or other storage device any copies of this [specify material] which is strictly prohibited. All rights are reserved and the copyright is owned by [Name].

C.958

All rights are reserved. No part of this [Event] may be filmed, recorded, broadcast, transmitted, stored in a retrieval system, reproduced, adapted, distributed, sold and/or otherwise exploited by any person who attends and/ or has a stand at the [Event].

C.959

There is no authority provided by the [Sponsor] and/or the [Company] to copy, reproduce, alter, adapt, supply, distribute, release, market, film, record, broadcast, transmit, upload to the internet and/or otherwise exploit this [Product/Service/Event] in any format and/or in any media at any time. Requests for permission for any such uses should be sent to: [name/email].

C.960

The [Company] shall ensure that any sub-licensees and/or distributors and/ or agents are made aware and informed of and provided with a copy of the corporate policy of the [Sponsor] regarding the use of its [Brand] and products a copy of which is attached in Schedule A and forms part of this agreement.

C.961

All copyright and intellectual property rights are owned and/or controlled by the [Institute/Charity]. There is no right to reproduce, supply, distribute, license and/or exploit whether for non-commercial, academic, educational, the internet, translation, and/or commercial purposes and/or any adaptation of any of the content, title, text, images, and/or any associated material of any part of this [Work/Service/Product]. Please contact [specify name/role/ details] to enquire about any possible use of any material.

C.962

It is permitted to make a short quotation from the [Work/Service] provided that it is for the purpose of review and/or criticism in an article and/or educational purposes for private study provided that it is limited to no more than [number] words in total and there is a credit to the [Institute] and the correct title, author and ISBN details quoted together with the name and website address of the [Institute].

C.963

Where the [Institute] owns the physical copy of a [document] but has no record of the [author] and/or attribution of any credit. Any person licensed by the [Institute] must not claim and/or represent that either they are and/or are aware of the name of the [author] and/or otherwise.

CORRUPTION

General Business and Commercial

C.964

Where at a later date after the signature of this agreement there is evidence to show that the [Company] offered inducements, rewards, money and/or other benefits to any person involved in the award of the [Tender/Contract] which were not disclosed or discovered prior to signature of the contract. Then the [Organisation] shall have the right to terminate the contract at once and shall be under no further liability to pay any sums due after that date or which are outstanding and shall be entitled to a full refund of all sums paid to the [Company].

C.965

The [Company] undertakes that it shall not offer any inducements, rewards and/or benefits whether in the form of gifts, holidays, travel, cars, loans and/or otherwise act in any manner which could be construed as corrupt, dishonest and/or in breach of any legislation, regulations, prohibitions, restrictions, procedures, rules, policies and/or guidelines which may directly and/or indirectly apply to the application process for and/or conclusion of contracts in [country].

C.966

That the [Company] shall not seek to disseminate information, data, errors, omissions, financial irregularities and/or news stories regarding other applicants for the [contract/subject] which would affect the value of their company assets, share price, reputation, products and/or services in order to effect the award of the [contract/subject] [except where based on verifiable facts and evidence].

C.967

No offers, inducements, money, products, services, discounts, promotion, benefits and/or shares shall be offered to any person, company, associate, officer or agents involved in the procurement, tender and award process at any time by any applicant. If there is any alleged evidence of such behaviour or acts by an applicant or someone acting on their behalf the [Company] reserves the right to refuse them permission to continue in the contract application procedure.

C.968

The [Company] shall not act in collusion and/or in concert with another party and/or authorise someone else to do something with the intention to misrepresent any facts and/or to distort the market in [subject] and/or to affect the supply agreements and/or to lower the price of the products and/or the primary content and/or to decrease demand.

C.969

No information, data, contract, agreement, partnership, agency, copyright ownership, costs, expenses, financial records and projections, registration details, sales and marketing and/or other material facts shall have been withheld, amended, altered and/or distorted which would significantly affect the award of this agreement to the [Company] and/or the terms of this agreement.

C.970

The [Consultant] agrees and undertakes that where appropriate he/she shall disclose any shares, options, interest, contracts and any other personal, family and/or other financial relationships and/or other matters which may conflict with the role which he/she is to carry out at the [Company] and/or which arise during the Term of the Agreement.

C.971

The [Consultant] agrees and undertakes that he/she shall not offer any inducements of any nature to any person and/or company involved in the allocation of the tenders to which the [Enterprise] has and/or will apply and in which the [Consultant] has and/or will assist.

C.972

In the event that any agent, advisor and/or other person receives funds on behalf of [Name] with the permission and authority from [Name] to the [Company]. Then where [Name] is the subject of fraud and/or negligence and/or money laundering by such agent, advisor and/or other person and does not receive the monies due. The [Company] shall not be liable and [Name] shall not be entitled to make any claim against the [Company] as the liability of the [Company] ceased once the sums were paid the agent, advisor and/or other person.

COSTS

Film, Television and Video

C.973

1.1 The [Licensee] agrees and undertakes that it shall be solely responsible for the payment of any sums due in respect of the manufacture, distribution, marketing, legal costs, [rights registration and] exploitation of [DVD/Television/other] Rights in the [Film] including the sound track and/or any payments in the future to any licensing bodies, collecting societies, collective management organisations, independent management entities and/or rights holders.

1.2 The [Licensee] agrees and undertakes that the [Licensor] shall not be liable for any such payments in 1.1 directly but the [Licensee] shall be entitled to deduct all such costs from the Gross Receipts prior to the calculation of the royalties due to the [Licensor] of the Net Receipts.

C.974

It is agreed that all packaging, marketing, administration, storage, distribution and delivery will be carried out under the control of the [Licensee] and at the Licensee's expense. That where damages, losses and/or any other consequential costs arise relating to an error, omission failure and/or otherwise that any sums incurred must be attributed to the [Licensee].

C.975

The [Assignee] agrees and undertakes that it shall be solely responsible for any sums due in respect of the production, manufacture, distribution, marketing, copyright clearance and fees, mechanical reproduction and/or performance of any music and/or any other sums due of any nature arising from the exploitation of the [DVD Rights/other] in the [Compilation] and that the [Assignor] shall not be liable for any such payments.

C.976

The [Company] acknowledges and undertakes that it shall bear sole liability for any sums due for the development, manufacture, distribution, marketing and exploitation of the [DVD and Non-Theatric Rights] in the [Film] including the sound track of the [Event] and that the [Sponsors] shall not be liable for any such sums.

C.977

The [Licensee] confirms that it shall be responsible for the payment of any sums which arise through the transmission, broadcast, supply, distribution and exploitation of the [Television/Archive Playback/Electronic Download/ DVD Rights] in the [Series/Films] which may be due in the future to any licensing bodies, collecting societies, collective management organisations, independent management entities and/or other rights holders for performing rights and/or mechanical reproduction. All other sums due to performers, contributors and/or any other third party shall have been cleared and/or acquired by the [Licensor] and shall be paid for by the [Licensor] as the sums fall due.

C.978

The [Work/Content] is provided by the [Company] and supplied to the public by the [Distributor] as a promotional [Disc/offer of an Electronic Download] to be supplied with [specify product/publication/services]. The [Company] agrees that it is solely responsible for all costs due and/or to be incurred for any payment arising from any assignment, licence, contract and/or any royalty and/or clearance of any copyright, intellectual property rights, photographs, images, music, lyrics, sound recordings, mechanical and performing rights, and/or other sums due to any collecting societies, and/or for any waivers, trademarks and any other rights and/or interest that may be required for the supply, reproduction and distribution exploitation of the [Work/Content] and any marketing, advertising and/or supply to the public for private home use only.

C.979

The [Distributor] agrees and undertakes that the total budget for the cost of the reproduction, supply and distribution of the [Work/Content] as a promotional [Disc/other format] shall not exceed [number/currency] in total. The [Distributor] agrees to pay [number] per cent of the final cost and the balance shall be paid by the [Company] within [one] month of receipt of invoice. The [Distributor] shall be paid an advance deposit of [number/currency] by the [Company] to be set-off against the final sums due. The deposit shall be paid by [date]. The delivery and supply of the master material of the [Work/Content] shall be at the [Company's] cost.

C.980

The costs of any marketing, advertising and promotion including television, radio, in cinemas and on the internet and/or over any telecommunication system and/or in any other electronic form; sponsorship, product placement, paid for blogs and/or podcasts and/or posts on accounts, banner links, paid search words and/or free apps for the [Film/Sound Recording/Artwork] reproduced in the [Unit/Product/Service] shall be at the sole cost of the [Licensee]. The [Licensee] shall not be entitled to recoup any of these sums from the gross receipts and/or to offset them against any advance and/or royalty due to the [Licensor] at any time.

C.981

Where [Name] provides any additional personal material for the [Film/Video/Dvd] which is then used by the [Company]. It is agreed that no additional payment and/or fees shall be due to [Name] for the use and exploitation of such material including but limited to photographs, films, clothes, diaries, objects and other material.

C.982

'The Production Costs' shall mean the actual budgeted and agreed costs of the development, production and delivery of the completed [Programme/Series] which shall include [Production Fee/other] as set out in appendix A. In the event that the Production Costs are not all expended any excess sums shall be repaid to the [Production Company] to the [Distributor] within [three] months of a final scrutiny of the accounts and the payment of all outstanding sums due.

C.983

'The Production Cost' shall mean the actual cost of the development, production and completion of the [Film] including the sound track as shall be certified by the [Production Company's] auditors and agreed between the [Distributor] and the [Production Company].

C.984

'Production Costs' shall mean the total actual certified cost of the preparation, development, production and delivery of a copy of the final edited master material of the [Film/Series] incurred by the [Company including but not limited to script development, contracts with performers, contributors and other third parties; cost of consents and clearances for music, sound recordings and/or any other copyright and/or intellectual property rights; location and location access costs; crew and other specialist personnel and/or consultants; lighting; health and safety compliance; security; equipment, costumes and transport; bank and/or finance charges; the cost of any insurance and/or guarantee and/or legal and/or other professional advice.

C.985

'The Production Costs' shall be the total costs whether direct and/or indirect of making the [Series] including all matters necessary for the development, pre-production, production, post-production and delivery of the [Series] to the [Licensee] including the [Licensor's Commissioning Fee] [which are not recovered from any third party by [date].]

C.986

The [Licensor] confirms that all sums due in respect of the development and production of the [Film/Pilot] have been paid and that the [Licensee] is not and will not be liable for any such payments.

C.987

The [Production Company] agrees and undertakes that it shall be responsible for any sums due in respect of the production, reproduction, distribution, marketing and exploitation of the rights in the [Series] and any associated material including any sums due in respect of any third party from the clearance, consent or otherwise of any material which is in the [Work] which is not owned and/or controlled by the [Author].

C.988

The [Company/Distributor] agrees and undertakes that it shall be solely responsible for all costs incurred in the production, broadcast, transmission, distribution and exploitation of the [Documentary/Series] and that the [Sponsor] shall not be liable for any such sums.

C.989

The [Company/Distributor] agrees and undertakes that all sums due in respect of the production of the [Film/Sound Recording] will be paid and that the [Sponsor] is not and will not be liable for any such payments.

C.990

The [Company] agrees that it shall be entirely responsible for all costs incurred and sums due for the development, production, distribution, marketing and exploitation of the [Film] and soundtrack in any form. The [Author] is not liable for any such payments and the [Company] shall not be entitled to deduct such sums from the Gross Receipts.

C.991

1.1 The [Company] confirms and undertakes that all copyright and/or intellectual property rights and/or any other rights, permissions, waivers, agreements and consents required under the [Copyright, Designs and Patents Act 1988 as amended/other] in respect of all material of any nature and/or persons and/or any other third party contribution in and/or to the [Film] including the sound track has been and/or shall be cleared and paid for. This undertaking includes but is not limited to: scripts, performers, artists, musicians, dancers, choreographers, costumes, stunt and/or other advisors, stills, images and music, computer generated and/or any other electronic development, products and services, crew and personnel, lighting; health and safety and security; post production editing; titles and credits and storage of the master material and reproduction of any copies. The [Company] agrees that the [Licensee] shall not be liable for any such payments for the production of the [Film].

1.2 The [Licensee] agrees and undertakes that it shall be liable to pay such sums as may be due to third parties in respect of the exercise of the rights granted in this agreement in respect of the transmission of the [Film] on channel: [name/reference] in the [Territory/country]. That the [Licensee] shall pay such sums direct to the third parties specified by the [Company] within [number] days of transmission in each case.

1.3 In addition the [Licensee] shall also pay any sums due for the transmissions to any licensing bodies, collecting societies, collective management organisations, independent management entities and/or other rights holders [in respect of the performing rights and/or mechanical reproduction and/or any other rights which may apply.]

C.992

1.1 The [Licensor] confirms that all sums due in respect of the production of the [Film Extract] have been paid and that the [Licensee] is not and shall not be liable for any such payments.

1,2 The [Licensee] shall pay the cost of the reproduction of a copy of the [Film Extract] in [format] and all delivery costs.

C.993

[Name] agrees that he/she shall be paid a fee of [number/currency] for his/her contribution to the [Work/Script] in full and final settlement. That the [Company] shall not be due to pay any additional sum as a royalty and/or other fee for any form of exploitation of any part of the [Work/Script] in any media and/or format. [Name] agrees that he/she has no right to make a claim of originality as the [Work/Script] is based on a book entitled [specify title/reference] published by [specify publisher] and [Name] has only contributed to a draft manuscript which was already developed by [specify person]. [Name] agrees that no additional costs, sums and/or expenses are due to [Name].

C.994

Both parties agree that for the purposes of this agreement the budget is in draft form and that where it is increased and/or adjusted at a later date that both parties shall be equally liable up to a maximum of [number/currency] in total for each party. Neither party authorises any costs beyond that limit and/or accepts any liability.

C.995

'The Production Costs' shall be the sums itemised in appendix A to be incurred in respect of the development, production, editing and completion of the [Film/Series] including the sound track and any music which is to be reproduced by the [Production Company]. There is a contingency of [ten] per cent for the budget to be exceeded by but no further authority to incur any further sums is provided by the [Sponsor/Distributor].

General Business and Commercial

C.996

'The Total Costs' shall mean all sums incurred in respect of the [Project/Event] which are to be paid for by the [Company] and not recouped from a third party for any reason which can be itemised and listed as solely related to the [Project/Event]. It shall not include general office, administration, staff, travel and/or hospitality costs of the [Company].

C.997

There shall be no costs paid by [Name] of any nature except [specify amount]. All other sums shall be paid by [Enterprise].

C.998

It is agreed between the parties that the total cost to be incurred in respect of the [Research Project/Review] shall be limited to a maximum of [number/currency] based on the work and services to be completed as described in appendix A. That where at a later date additional work and/or items are to be added then that additional cost must be authorised by an amendment to the main agreement.

C.999
There may be additional sums due for delivery, storage, insurance, customs duties, taxes, import and export costs, freight, bank charges, currency exchange charges and/or costs incurred by alterations and/or additions to the original quotation which shall at the [Company's/Purchaser's] cost.

C.1000
It is agreed between the parties that where the costs are to be exceeded for any reason. The [Company] agrees that an increase of up to [number] per cent does not require prior authority. Any cost increase of more than [number] per cent on any future order will require prior agreement between the parties and must be authorised in advance.

C.1001
The [Company] shall be entitled to request a deposit of [number/currency] as an advance against the total final costs of the [Project/Event]. This sum shall not be mixed with the other funds of the [Company], but shall be held separately until such time as the [Company] has completed the agreed duties and tasks to a satisfactory level that are required according to Schedule A which forms part of this agreement.

C.1002
The total cost of the order shall be the number of [Products] ordered multiplied by the [wholesale/retail/fixed] price quoted at the time of the order for each item by the [Company]. An additional discount may sometimes be applied to the total cost due to the [size/volume] of the order in each case. This cost does not include any government taxes, custom duties, insurance, delivery and packaging charges that may be added. The cost of the order must be paid by the purchaser in [currency] in [country].

C.1003
All prices displayed are for guidance only and may be adjusted by the [Company] and are not confirmed until a quote has been issued to you and accepted within the time limit specified. All prices are exclusive of any taxes, storage, freight, delivery, insurance, currency conversion and bank charges.

C.1004
The total projected cost of the [Event/Project/Work] shall be [number/currency] for the completion of the work and services set out in Appendix

A on [date]. Where alterations, additions and/or deletions are made to the quotation and/or agreement between the parties then the cost may be adjusted to increase and/or decrease accordingly. A verbal agreement between the parties shall be sufficient for any extra costs to be binding on the person and/or company ordering the [Event/Project/Work]. An email confirming the terms will be sent as confirmation.

Internet, Websites and Apps

C.1005

The cost of any [Service/Project] may vary at any time without notice. The costs and prices displayed on the [Website/App/Platform] are for guidance only and are subject to a quotation being issued by the [Company] upon request by the [Client]. A fixed quotation is then issued which is open to the [Client] to accept for a limited period. Any quotation which is accepted by the [Client] is also subject to the [Client] signing a binding contract between the parties as to the scope of the [Service/Project] to be completed by the [Company]. A deposit will be due on signature of the agreement by the [Client].

C.1006

The [Client/User] shall be responsible for all costs that may be incurred to obtain access to and/or use of and/or reliance upon the [Website/App/Platform] and any content and/or any links, competitions, chatrooms and/or other material. The [Client/User] shall be responsible for all the costs and charges that may arise and/or fall due including landline rental costs, telephone and mobile phone charges, connection charges, broadband costs, premium rate phone lines and/or otherwise and the [Company] shall not be liable and/or responsible for any such costs and charges.

C.1007

The [Client/User] obtains access to, uses and relies upon this [Website/App/Platform] entirely at their own risk and cost. Where access to and/or use of and/or reliance upon the [Website/App/Platform] and any content and/or any links, competitions, chatrooms and/or other material is interrupted, delayed, slow, inaccurate, withdrawn, amended, deleted and/or otherwise altered and/or varied. The [Company] shall not be liable for any costs, charges, losses and/or damages that may be arise at any time.

C.1008

Where [Products/Services] are ordered and/or obtained from a third party through the use of this [Website/App/Platform] and/or any advertisements, links and/or other promotions. Then all such orders and/or transactions are at the [Purchaser's] own risk and expense and no costs, charges and/or liability can be accepted by the [Company]. We advise you to follow the following [safety and security procedures].

C.1009

The [Marketing/Promotion/Advice Service] is at present provided for free on this [Website/App/Platform] and no subscription and/or other charges will be incurred by completing the application form to receive the [marketing/promotion/advice] email from the [Company]. You may unsubscribe at any time by taking the following steps [specify procedure]. The emails will contain regular reports, articles, special offers, competitions and highlight products and services. Any order and/or commitment to purchase any goods and services from a third party as a result of such emails shall be entirely at your own risk and not the responsibility of the [Company].

C.1010

No costs are charged for accessing and/or downloading the [Basic App]. Charges, costs and subscription fees will be incurred for the [Premium App].

C.1011

1.1 Use of any premium rate phone line listed here [specify number] will incur an increased charge to your [mobile and/or landline telephone] at the rate of approximately [number/currency] per minute which will immediately be charged to that account.

1.2 We adhere to the Code of Practice and guidelines issued by [specify organisation] in respect of premium rate telephone lines.

C.1012

This [Blog] may recommend and/or endorse products and/or services and/or other material of third parties. While every effort is made to ensure that prices and costs are accurate there may be changes made by the third party company as to the costs they charge. Any source material is therefore for guidance only and you must verify the facts yourself personally and no responsibility and/or liability is accepted by [Name].

C.1013

1.1 [Name] commissions [number] [Podcasts] in [format] of suitable professional standard and quality to be transmitted over the internet to be produced by the [Company] at [location] based on the summaries set out in appendix A for the subject matter and content of each podcast.

1.2 The total cost of each podcast shall be fixed at [number/currency] and shall involve [number] days of filming and/or editing for each podcast.

1.3 [Name] agrees to pay [number/currency] in advance and [number/currency] upon delivery and acceptance of the [formats] of the [Podcasts].

1.4 The [Company] agrees that where there are only minor changes to the content of any podcast no additional costs shall be incurred. That where the [Company] intends to add additional cost these must be disclosed to [Name] in advance and agreed with [Name] before the work is completed. So that [Name] has the choice to refuse to incur the additional costs.

C.1014

The [Account/Website] displays prices with the [Products] which are a fixed price for purchase of that individual item in [currency]. Additional costs may be added for taxes, import and export duties, delivery, insurance, packaging, currency conversion costs and/or otherwise by the [Company]. You will be notified of the additional costs when you confirm your request to purchase the item and state the delivery address. No item will be despatched until you have paid the purchase price and any additional costs which may need to be incurred.

C.1015

The cost of the annual subscription to the [Service] on [Website/Platform/Podcast] shall be [number/currency] from [date] to [date] which shall be payable on the first of each calendar month in advance. You shall have the right to cancel the service after the first [three] months by notification before the payment date for the [fourth] month to the [Company].

Merchandising and Distribution

C.1016

The [Licensee] agrees that it shall be solely responsible for all costs and expenses incurred in respect of reproduction and incorporation of the [Licensor's] [Logo/Image/Slogan/Trade Mark] in the [Product/Service] and any associated marketing material.

C.1017

1.1 The [Licensee] agrees and undertakes that it shall be solely responsible for all costs and expenses which may arise and/or be due in respect of the development, production, manufacture, distribution and commercial exploitation of the [Product/Service] and any associated legal costs, clearance and copyright payments and/or sums due for use of any music and/or any compliance requirements and/or other costs due for packaging, marketing, promotions and advertising.

1.2　The [Licensor] accepts and agrees that all the costs incurred by the [Licensee] in 1.1 shall be attributed as Distribution Expenses under the agreement and deducted from the Gross Receipts prior to the payment of the [Licensor's Royalties] of the Net Receipts.

C.1018

The [Assignee] confirms that it shall be responsible for any sums due in respect of the development, production, distribution, marketing and exploitation of the [Format] in any media at any time and that the [Assignor] shall not be liable for any such sums after [date of assignment].

C.1019

The [Licensee] agrees and undertakes that it shall pay for all costs incurred in the commercial exploitation of the [Licensed Article/Product] including the development, manufacture, distribution, selling, advertising and promotion. The [Licensee] shall not be entitled to set-off and/or recoup any such sums from Gross Receipts and/or to deduct such sums prior to the payment of the [Licensor's Royalties].

C.1020

1.1　The [Company] confirms that it shall be solely responsible for all costs directly and/or indirectly incurred in the development, production, manufacture, distribution, marketing, promotion, advertising, copyright and legal protection and exploitation of the [Licensed Articles/Products].

1.2　The [Licensor] and the [Licensee] agree that the [Licensee] may recoup and set-off [number/currency] of the cost in 1.1 from the sums received by the [Licensee] prior to the payment of the royalties to the [Licensor]. Provide that the sums to be recouped shall be spread over a [two] year period or more and shall not exceed [number/currency] in any one accounting period.

C.1021

The [Distributor] shall not be obliged to pay for any sums in respect of the manufacture and/or packaging of the [Products] supplied by the [Licensee]. The [Distributor] shall bear all costs relating to its own business, website, app, warehouse and distribution centre, taxes, import and exports charges, currency exchanges, freight and insurance costs or any other sums arising from the sale, supply and distribution to retailers, wholesalers and/or other customers under this agreement.

C.1022

1.1　The [Licensor] agrees and undertakes to be responsible for the clearance of any copyright, intellectual property rights, trade marks and/or any other rights, consents and/or waivers required in the [Work/Artwork/Sound Recordings/Film] supplied to the [Licensee].

1.2 The [Licensor] shall pay all the costs, fees, royalties and expenses incurred to [date] in which the [Licensee] acquires the rights under this agreement. Thereafter the [Licensee] shall pay all the sums that may be due for the exercise of the rights by the [Licensee] and the [Licensor] shall not be liable for any payments.

1.3 The [Licensor] shall provide the [Licensee] with a comprehensive list of the contracts, licences, consents and the payments and royalties which will be due for each type of use and/or format to any person and/or third party and/or any collecting society. Together with a list of any credits, copyright notices and/or other conditions which may be relevant.

1.4 The [Licensee] accepts that it shall also be liable to pay any sums due for the broadcast, performance, transmission, mechanical reproduction or otherwise that may become due any person and/or third party and/or any licensing bodies, collecting societies, collective management organisations, independent management entities and/or other rights holders.

C.1023

1.1 The [Licensee] agrees and undertakes that it shall be solely responsible for all corporate, administrative, legal, production, insurance, product liability, compliance, health and safety test and assessments and reports, and other costs, losses and/or damages incurred and/or which may arise directly and/or indirectly from the development, manufacture, supply, distribution, sub-licensing, marketing and exploitation of the [Product/Service] in any part of the [world/country]. The [Licensor] shall not pay and/or be liable the cost of any of these sums.

1.2 The [Licensee] agrees to supply copies of any documents and/or reports which the [Licensor] may request to verify that the [Product/Service] is complying with any legislation and/or is safe for the public at any time.

C.1024

The [Licensee] shall not be paid any costs and/or expenses for supplying any documents and/or data and supporting any trade mark and/or other registration which the [Licensor] wishes to file and/or make in any part of the world during the Term of this Agreement.

C.1025

1.1 [Name] agrees to attend and contribute to [number] promotional events for no more than [duration] organised by the [Company] in [country] at no additional cost and expense.

1.2 Where the [Company] wishes [Name] to attend additional events, conferences, online meetings, promotions and/or otherwise. Then it is agreed that the [Company] must pay all costs of expenses of business class travel, taxis, hotels, meals and hospitality, hair and clothes, travel insurance and any additional products and/or services required from a third party for [Name] and [additional person] plus a fee an additional fee no less than [number/currency] for each appearance.

C.1026

1.1 The [Designer] agrees to bear the cost of creating the design for the [Garment] based on the [Client's] proposals and all labour, fabric and material, delivery and insurance costs necessary for the design, fittings, adjustments and production of the final [Garment] which are included in the fixed price quotation.

1.2 Where the [Client] cancels the order for any reason they shall still be liable for the total cost of the fixed price quotation where the order has been commenced.

1.3 If the [Client] materially changes the order and makes requests that were not discussed in the original proposal then the [designer] shall be entitled to add additional costs to the total price provided that they are agreed in advance with the [Client].

C.1027

The [Supplier] agrees that it shall be responsible for any and all [export duties, custom and excise charges and fees, taxes/other] and shall continue to be responsible until the [Product] is delivered to the [destination address] all rights of ownership, risks, liabilities and costs shall remain with the [Supplier].

C.1028

1.1 The secure packaging of the [Product] shall be at the sole cost of the [Supplier]. Delivery, insurance and any other freight costs shall be paid for by the [Client].

1.2 The [Client] confirms that it shall be solely responsible for all costs in respect of the exploitation and sale of the [Product].

C.1029

The [Purchaser] agrees that it shall be personally liable for any costs and expenses that may arise from any use of the [Product].

C.1030

The [Assignee] confirms that it shall be solely responsible for all sums due in respect of the reproduction, distribution, marketing and exploitation of the [Commissioned Work] in any media in any format in any country in the world. That the [Assignor] is not liable for any such payments. That where there is any legal dispute as regard rights and/or any registration of any nature the legal costs, damages and/or losses shall be the responsibility of the [Assignee] and no indemnity is provided by the [Assignor].

C.1031

The [Supplier] shall not be held liable for any damages, losses, costs, expenses and/or other sums which may arise directly and/or indirectly as a result of the failure of the [Supplier] to fulfil all and/or some of the order for the [Products/Services] and/or to complete the delivery by the agreed date. The [Supplier] shall endeavour to notify the [Company] in advance of any problem but shall be entitled to cancel the order and/or change the order and/or delivery date as may be necessary due to circumstances beyond its control which may affect the order.

C.1032

In the event that the cost of each [Unit] is to be increased by more than [number/currency] then the [Supplier] shall notify the [Distributor] and the [Distributor] may cancel any further orders for the [Units] at the increased price.

C.1033

Where after an order has been agreed the value of the source material of the content of the [Product] increases to such an extent that the [Supplier] is unable to deliver the order as agreed. Then the [Supplier] shall have the right to terminate the order provided that all sums paid for any part of the order not delivered is returned to the [Company].

Publishing

C.1034

The [Assignee] confirms that it shall be solely responsible for all costs incurred and/or due in respect of the reproduction, manufacture, supply, distribution, marketing and exploitation of the [Work] and the [Artwork] and the material in Schedule A in any media at any time throughout the [Territory/world] and that the [Author] shall not be liable for any such sums.

C.1035
The [Licensee] agrees that it shall bear all costs in respect of the production, publication, distribution, marketing and advertising of the [Article] and the [Magazine/Website].

C.1036
The [Publisher] agrees that it shall be solely responsible for all costs incurred in the development, design, printing, reproduction, publication, distribution, marketing and exploitation of the [Work/Content] throughout the [Territory/world] in any format and/or medium and that no such sums shall be deducted from payments due to the [Author] under this agreement.

C.1037
The [Licensee] agrees to be responsible for the cost of any additional material and/or photographs that may be required for the [Article] and in the event of the creation of any new material shall provide a copy to [Name].

C.1038
The [Ghostwriter] shall not be responsible for and/or liable to pay any fees, royalties and/or other costs arising in connection with the publication, distribution and/or exploitation of the [Book/Manuscript/Images] including but not limited to all copyright clearances of archive material, stills, diaries, films, material sourced from websites and/or any other consents, moral rights, contractual and other obligations, legal costs and/or other sums which will be paid for entirely at [Name's] cost and expense.

C.1039
The [Agent] confirms that the [Author] shall not be responsible for any costs and/or expenses incurred by the [Agent] pursuant to this agreement including but not limited to administration and offices, telephone, mobile, internet and software costs; hospitality, hotels, travel, reproduction, photography, filming and/or the cost of packaging, delivery, marketing and promotional material. The [Agent] shall only be entitled to the [Agent's Commission].

C.1040
The [Writer] shall not incur any liabilities on behalf of the [Company] and/or pledge the [Company's] credit and/or commit the [Company] to any agreement.

C.1041
The [Distributor/Company] agrees and undertakes that it shall bear the entire cost of the design, production, publication, distribution, marketing and exploitation of the [Manuscript] in hardback and/or paperback and/or in any other format and/or through any other service and/or any sub-licence to

a third party. That the [Distributor/Company] shall not be entitled to deduct any such sums from the [sums received/Gross Receipts/published price].

C.1042
The Licensor agrees that it shall be solely responsible for the cost of copyright clearance and payments to the [Author] for the reproduction of the [Extracts] of the [Work] on [website/reference] from [date]. Provided that there is a clear credit to the [Author] as follows: [specify credit] and a copyright notice as follows: [specify copyright notice] and a link to the website of the [Licensor] as follows: [specify link].

C.1043
The [Assignee] confirms that it shall be solely responsible for all costs incurred in respect of the distribution, marketing and exploitation of the [Work] and the [Artwork] in any media throughout the Territory and that the [Author] shall not be liable for such sums.

C.1044
No sums of any nature shall be due to be paid by the [Author] and/or deducted from the advance and/or royalties unless prior written consent is provided by the [Author].

C.1045
The [Publisher] shall not be responsible for any research and/or access costs, charges and/or expenses of [Name] incurred in developing, editing, writing and/or collaborating with any third parties in respect of the [Work].

C.1046
The [Writer] shall not incur any costs and/or expenses and/or fees on behalf of the [Publisher] at any time and/or represent that he/she has the right and/or authority to do so.

Services

C.1047
It is agreed that the [Company] shall pay all production, manufacture, distribution, advertising, marketing and exploitation] costs in respect of the [Recordings/Film/Stills/Work] of the [Artist] made under the terms of this agreement. The [Artist] agrees that all such costs shall be recoupable by the [Company] prior to the payment of any royalties to the [Artist].

C.1048
The [Company] agrees to pay for all costs incurred of any nature which relate to the production, manufacture, distribution, marketing, advertising, and

exploitation of the product of the services of the [Artist]. That the [Company] shall not be entitled to recoup, offset and/or claim the right to a contribution to any such costs from the [Artist].

C.1049

The [Presenter] and/or the [Agent] agree and undertake that they will not pledge the [Company's] credit and/or enter into any commitments and/or negotiate contracts and/or incur any costs on behalf of the [Company] without prior written authority from [Name] at the [Company].

C.1050

The [Agent] confirms that he/she shall be solely responsible for any costs and/or expenses incurred by the [Agent] pursuant to this agreement and that the Agent shall only be entitled to receive the [Agent's] Commission and no other additional sums whether incurred in pursuance of this agreement or not.

C.1051

The [Agent] acknowledges and agrees that he/she is solely responsible for all costs and expenses that he/she may incur in respect of the provision of his/her services and advice under this agreement. That the [Agent] shall not be entitled to recoup and/or be reimbursed any other sums expended by him/her in respect of his/her services unless specifically agreed and authorised in advance by the [Licensor/Name].

C.1052

1.1 The [Record Company] agrees and undertakes that it shall be solely responsible for any sums due in respect of the production, manufacture, distribution, marketing, copyright protection, registration, legal costs and exploitation of the [Sound Recordings] and the [Records] and that the [Artist] shall not be liable for any such payments.

1.2 The [Artist] agrees that the [Record Company] may recoup all the sums paid in 1.1 from the [Gross Receipts] prior to the calculation of the royalties due to the [Artist] from the [Net Receipts].

C.1053

The [Licensee] confirms that it shall be responsible and liable for all costs, expenses and other sums incurred in the reproduction, transmission, broadcast and/or exploitation of the [Musical Work] in the [Sound Recordings] in any format under this licence agreement by the [Licensee] and/or any authorised third party. This shall include any sums due to any person and/or third party and/or any licensing bodies, collecting societies, collective management organisations, independent management entities and/or other rights holders.

C.1054

The [Agent] agrees that it shall be totally responsible for all costs incurred of any nature by it in respect of the [Agent's] services and the exploitation of the [Artist].

C.1055

The [Designer] agrees not to incur any additional expenses and/or to exceed the maximum cost of [number/currency] without the [Company's] prior verbal approval.

C.1056

The [Agent] undertakes that he/she shall not seek to be reimbursed by the [Artist] in respect of any costs and expenses incurred by the [Agent] in respect of the performance of his/her duties under this agreement unless specifically agreed in detail in advance with the [Artist].

C.1057

The [Artist] agrees that he/she shall bear the cost and expense of all his/her own hotel, telephone and mobile, stationery, clothes, hair and grooming, dental treatment, travel and visas, medical cover, taxes, personal insurance and national insurance. That the [Agent] shall only bear the cost of such expenditure which is specifically authorised within the allocated monthly budget of [number/currency] and/or is agreed in advance.

C.1058

The [Manager] agrees to assist the [Sportsperson] in general with the financial management of all the [Sportsperson's] Fees and financial affairs generally including tax, value added tax, national insurance, pension and health contributions and personal insurance. Provided that the [Sportsperson] shall seek specialist professional advice where appropriate and shall not seek to rely on the [Manager] to be liable for any errors, losses, omissions and/or other costs.

C.1059

The [Sportsperson] accepts that though the [Manager] may assist in his/her financial affairs he/she shall not be liable for any loss, damage, omission, failure and/or error, nor shall he/she bear the cost of seeking professional expert advice. The [Sportsperson] shall be liable for his/her own tax, national insurance, value added tax, dental and medical cover, travel insurance and other costs and expenses not specified under this agreement.

C.1060

The [Company] agrees that all costs and expenses incurred in the development, production, distribution and exploitation of the [Company's] [Product/Services] and any advertisements, promotional events and any other material shall be at the [Company's] sole cost and [Name] shall not be liable to pay any such costs and/or losses that may arise.

C.1061

The [Company] agrees that it shall be solely responsible for any sums due in respect of the organisation, security, health and safety requirements and/ or other costs incurred in the production and exploitation of the [Project/ Event]. That [Name] shall not be liable for any sums which may be due to the [Company] and/or to be paid to third parties.

C.1062

The [Agent] acknowledges that he/she is solely responsible for all costs he/ she may incur in respect of his/her services under this agreement.

C.1063

The [Consultant] shall be entitled to charge no more than [number/currency] as additional costs and expenses under this agreement. This allowance may not be exceeded and may only be claimed for [specify purpose] and must be supported by itemised receipts.

C.1064

Where after the conclusion and delivery of the [Report] the [Consortium] require additional work, information and/or data from the [Consultant]. Then the [Consultant] shall be entitled to be paid at the rate of [specify rate] by the [Consortium] for any such work and payment shall be made on a [weekly basis] by direct debit subject to invoice.

Sponsorship

C.1065

The [Sponsor] confirms that it shall be solely responsible for all costs incurred in respect of the production, distribution, promotion and exploitation of the [Sponsor's Product] and the [Sponsor's Logo] and that the [Sportsperson] shall not be liable for any such sums.

C.1066

The [Sponsor] agrees to bear all costs of creating the [Sponsor's Copy] and of supplying the [Sponsor's Copy] in a technical medium acceptable to the [Radio Station] for its incorporation in the [Programme] on or before [date].

C.1067

The [Company] agrees it shall pay all the costs of the supply of a copy of the original master material of the [Company's Product] and the [Company's Logo] in a format suitable for reproduction in the [Series/Programme/Event]. Together with the costs of any other reproduction that may be necessary for promotional and marketing purposes in any format.

C.1068

1.1 The [Company] agrees that all sums incurred and/or due in respect of the production and exploitation of the [specify programme/event/ other] will be paid by the [Company/Institute] and that the [Sponsor] is not and will not be liable for any such payments.

1.2 The [Sponsor] shall not be responsible for any costs arising from the hospitality suite and other facilities provided by the [Company/Institute].

C.1069

The [Sponsor] shall not be entitled to authorise third parties to assist in the funding of the [Event] without the prior written consent of the [Association]. Nor shall the [Sponsor] authorise, pledge and/or commit the [Association] to any third party.

C.1070

The [Association] agrees that the [Sponsor] shall not be responsible for any direct and/or indirect costs relating to the [Event] other than those specifically set out in this agreement in appendix A.

C.1071

The parties agree that the total cost of all expenditure shall be limited to [number/currency] to be paid for by [specify name]. In the event that this is exceeded for any reason then the person or company that incurred, authorised and/or agreed to the extra cost will be liable to pay and shall be entitled to seek a contribution from the other parties.

C.1072

The cost of the commissioning of the articles, photographs, artwork, production, editing, and printing of the [Brochure/Guide] shall be at the [Sponsor's/Company's] expense.

C.1073

The [Sponsor] agrees and undertakes to pay to the [Company] the cost of all the facilities, supplies, materials, access roads, security, health and safety compliance, electricity, gas, water, telephone charges, broadband access, food and drink, stationery, equipment, waste recycling, rubbish disposal, repairs and maintenance and/or any other additional costs and expenses which occur before and/or during and/or after the arise the [Event] which not specified in advance in the [Budget] which are incurred by the [Company] relating directly and/or indirectly to the [Sponsor] and its involvement in the [Event].

C.1074

The [Company] agrees and undertakes that the [Sponsor] shall not be liable for any sums and/or payments except those set out in [specify clauses/ appendix A]. That the [Company] is liable for any costs and/or payments that may be due either before, during and/or after the [Event]. This clause shall not apply where the costs arise directly from the actions and/or failures of the [Sponsor] whether deliberate and/or any error and/or omission but which in any event directly causes losses and/or damages to the [Company] and/or any third party. In such instance the [Sponsor] shall be liable for all such consequential costs and expenses.

C.1075

1.1 Where due to cancellation and/or delay of the [Event/Project] the [Sponsor] incurs additional costs and expenses. The [Sponsor] agrees that it shall not seek to recover any such sums from the [Organisers] for any reason.

1.2 Where the [Event/Project] is not transmitted, broadcast and/or exploited in any media by a third party as expected by the [Sponsor] and the [Organisers]. The [Sponsor] shall not have any right to claim for a refund and/or loss of publicity and/or brand exposure. Such a failure by a third party shall not be a breach of this agreement.

C.1076

Where through the actions and/or omissions and/or errors and/or negligence and/or failure of the [Sponsors] to use suitably qualified employees, casual staff and/or any other third parties and/or that their equipment, displays, stalls and tents and/or products are and/or were unsafe and not fit for purpose. That in the event that there is an allegation that any person has suffered injury, damage and/or loss. Then the [Company] shall be entitled to seek an advance payment towards legal costs from the [Sponsor] to instruct a legal advisor to review and advise on any claim. Where the legal advisor recommends the matter be settled then the [Sponsor] shall pay all the costs, expenses, losses and damages of all the parties involved in each case.

University, Charity and Educational

C.1077

1.1 The [Institute/Charity] agrees and undertakes that it shall bear all the costs and expenses in respect of the development, production, printing, publication, distribution, marketing, advertising, all copyright clearances or other consents, moral rights, contractual and other legal obligations, payments to collecting societies, any adaptation, translation, and/or sequel, telephone bills, freight, accommodation, travel and any exploitation of the [Work/Service/Artwork] in any media throughout the world.

1.2 That the [Contributor/Company] shall not be liable for any such sums [except for those rights and undertakings provided in clauses [specify].] nor shall the [Contributor/Company] be entitled to claim or be paid any sums except those set out in clause [–].

C.1078
The [Institute/Charity] agrees that it shall be solely responsible for all costs and expenses incurred in respect of the [Project/Event] and that no such sums shall be deducted from any payments due to the [Company] under this agreement.

C.1079
The [Author/Contributor] agrees and undertakes that he/she shall bear the cost and expense of all his/her own hotel, telephone and mobile phone bills and charges, stationery, postage and freight, travel, tax, personal insurance, national insurance, value added tax, pension and health contributions and any other costs and expenses incurred in respect of the performance of the services and/or supply of material under this agreement. The [Author/Contributor] agrees that the [Institute/Charity] shall not be liable for any such costs and expenses.

C.1080
The [Researcher] shall only be entitled to be paid such costs and expenses as may be authorised in advance by the [Institute/Charity] which relate directly to the [Project]. No sums will be authorised at any time for [specify excluded items].

CREDITS

Film, Television and Video

C.1081
The [Licensee] agrees to adhere to all credits, copyright notices, moral rights, contractual and legal obligations, trade marks, service marks, logos and/or other rights notified by the [Licensor] in the written statement with

the [Film Package]. The [Licensee] shall add its own distribution name as: Distributed by [specify name] with the following logo/mark [specify logo/ mark] in all forms of exploitation of the rights and any associated packaging, brochures, catalogues, websites, apps, links, publicity, advertising and/or otherwise whether by the [Licensee] and/or any authorised third party.

C.1082

The [Licensee] shall ensure that the [Film] and any credits, copyright or other contractual obligations and rights are accurately and adequately described and set out in the front and end credits in respect of any transmission and/ or broadcast and/or any archive playback and/or electronic download and/ or any packaging, catalogues, brochures and other marketing material. That the packaging and all text and artwork shall be of a high professional standard.

C.1083

1.1 The [Licensee] agrees to provide the following copyright notice, trade mark, logo and credit to the [Licensor] in any publicity, promotional, advertising and packaging material in any medium in respect of the exercise of the [DVD/Disc/other] Rights in the [Film] and/or parts granted under this agreement as set out in appendix A which forms part of this agreement. [detail layout/size/colour/format/order].

1.2 The [Licensor] shall not be accorded a credit in any case in which the [Licensee] is also not credited which may be due to the type of promotion, lack of time and/or space. In any event the [Licensor] shall at all times be provided with a copyright notice as set out in 1.1 on all copies of the [Film] and/or any adaptation.

C.1084

The [Assignee] agrees and undertakes to abide by any credit, copyright notice, trade mark and other contractual obligations notified by the [Assignor] by [date].

C.1085

The [Company] agrees to provide the following trade mark, logo and credit to the [Sponsor] in any publicity, promotional, advertising and packaging material in respect of the exploitation of the [DVD and Non-Theatric Rights] in the [Film/Sound Recordings] as follows: [specify details/format/attach a copy]. The position on the front and back of the label and packaging of the [DVD] shall be as follows: [specify details/size/colour/location/attach a copy]. The [Company] agrees to provide the [Sponsor] with copies and/or a list of all such material in which a credit appears to the [Sponsor] upon request by the [Sponsor] at the [Company's] expense.

C.1086

The [Licensee] agrees and undertakes to ensure that any sub-licensee, agent and/or distributor shall not delete, amend and/or vary any copyright notice, credits, trade marks and/or copyright warning which the [Licensor] has specified should be on any adaptation of the [Film/Sound Recording/Video] in any format and/or any copies, packaging, marketing and/or advertising material.

C.1087

[Name] original author of: [specify title] [reference/format/ISBN]

Adapted and translated by: [specify Company].

Translation owned by: [Name].

Performed and spoken by: [name of performer/presenter]

Distributed as an [Audio File/Sound Recording] in [format] on [website/channel] by: [Distributor]

C.1088

The [Television Company] agrees and acknowledges where appropriate by suitable legend to broadcast, transmit and display on all copies and material the ownership of any copyrights in any material they may use and shall not delete any credits and/or titles from the [Film] material supplied under this agreement. The failure to broadcast, transmit and/or display credits and/or titles due to any reason beyond the control of the [Television Company] including but not limited to, lack of time, failure of facilities or otherwise shall not be a breach of this agreement.

C.1089

The [Television Company] shall not delete from the [Series/Podcasts] any copyright notice, credits, acknowledgement, trade mark, service mark, logo, text and/or images accorded to any person, author, director, actor, company and/or distributor in the [Series/Podcasts] and/or any other material supplied under this agreement.

C.1090

The [Television Company] agrees that no other third party shall be entitled to sponsor the [Programme/Series] and/or have its logo, trade mark, service mark, design, product, image, slogan, ringtone and/or music incorporated in the [Programme/Series] and/or in the introduction, trailer and/or end credits whether for the purpose of corporate promotion, advertising and/or other publicity purposes at any time during the Licence Period in the [Territory/other].

C.1091

The [Distributor] agrees and undertakes that it shall comply with all reasonable copyright notices, credits, acknowledgements, trade marks, service marks, logos, texts, images and/or other requirements notified to the [Distributor] in writing by the [Licensor] both in the [Format] of the [Film] including the sound track and/or in any packaging, advertising and/or promotional material in any media. The [Distributor] agrees and undertakes that it shall first submit all such material to the [Licensor] for approval by the [Licensor] in the exact colour, size, layout and material it which it is intended to be used. The [Licensor] shall respond without delay and shall not unreasonably withhold approval. If the [Licensor] does not respond in any instance then approval shall be deemed to have been given if the [Licensor] shall not express written objection within [one] calendar month of having received proof copies from the [Distributor].

C.1092

The [Television Company] confirms that the [Sponsor's] Logo will be reasonably, prominently and clearly identifiable in the [Programme/Series] and shall not be obscured and/or otherwise positioned so that it is not easily recognisable. The [Television Company] agrees that the [Sponsor's] logo shall appear as described in Appendix A which forms part of this agreement. [description: duration/position/background/order/colour/format].

C.1093

The [Television Company] agrees and undertakes that it must ensure that the broadcast, transmission, premium rate phone line, website and/or app and/or other exploitation of the [Sponsor's] name, product, music, slogan and images will not infringe any sponsorship, endorsement, competition and/or advertising standards and practices, directives and/or legislation which apply to the [Television Company] and/or have been issued by the [Ofcom/other] in [country].

C.1094

The [Television Company] confirms and agrees that it shall notify any third party who is likely to review, promote and/or transmit the [Series] that the [Sponsor] shall be entitled to the following: [credit/words/text/image/logo/trade marks] [products/services] in all material distributed by the [Television Company] and/or any third party. A copy of the layout, design and colour to be used is represented in relation to different formats and described in appendix A. The [Television Company] shall not be liable for the failure of any third party to adhere to any such notification regarding the [Sponsor].

C.1095

The [Television Company] agrees and undertakes to broadcast and/or transmit the [Programme/Series] incorporating the [Sponsor's] [Trade Mark/ Logo/Image/Slogan] on-screen in any trailer and/or advertisement and in the front and end credits as follows: [location/order/duration]. It shall not be edited out, deleted and/or obscured when used a part of a streaming service over the internet and/or as part of an archive playback service at any time.

C.1096

The [Television Company] confirms that the [Sponsor's] [Trade Mark/Logo/ Image/Slogan] will be reasonably and prominently and clearly identifiable in the [Programme/Series] and in any event will not be less than the following relative on-screen dimensions: Horizontally [–]% Vertically [–]%. The [Television Company] undertakes that the [Sponsor's] [Trade Mark/Logo/ Image/Slogan] will appear on screen for not less than [number] seconds on not less than [number] separate occasions.

C.1097

The [Television Company] confirms that the [Sponsor's] trading name: [specify name] and an image of its products will appear on-screen [once] during the [Programme] as follows: [specify background/duration/location on screen].

C.1098

The [Company] agrees to ensure that the following trade mark, logo, credit and background profile to the [Sponsor] shall appear in the end credits, and on any packaging, direct marketing, promotional, advertising and/or website material in respect of the [Project].

C.1099

The [Licensee] agrees to provide the following copyright notice, credit, logo, image and slogan to the [Licensor] in the front and end credits of the [Film] and in any packaging, advertising and/or promotional material in respect of the exploitation of the [Film] and/or adaptation by the [Licensee] as described in detail in appendix A. [size/colour/location/order/other details]. The [Licensee] shall provide the [Licensor] with copies and samples of all such material upon request at the expense of the [Licensee].

C.1100

The [Licensee] agrees to provide the following acknowledgement; title, name of the [Musical Work], copyright notice and on-screen credit to the [Licensor] at the end of each episode of the [Series]. Where the cast is listed in any material and/or on any website and/or in any other format then the [Licensee] shall ensure that the acknowledgement to the [Licensor] is provided in full.

C.1101

The [Company] agrees and undertakes that the [Contributor] shall be entitled to the following on-screen credit at the start and end of the [Film/Episode]: [specify credit]. There is no obligation to provide any such credit on any website, advertising, and/or promotional material. A failure to transmit, broadcast and/or to incorporate the credit for any reason shall not be deemed a breach of this agreement.

C.1102

The [Contributor] agrees that the failure to transmit, broadcast and/or include the credit in any material shall not be considered a breach of this agreement where it occurs inadvertently, due to lack of space and/or time and/or some other justifiable reason.

C.1103

The [Assignor] agrees that he/she shall not be entitled to any credit and/or acknowledgment in respect of the exploitation of the [Format] in any media by the [Assignee] or any third party. The [Assignor] waives all rights to any credit and/or copyright notice.

C.1104

The [Licensee] undertakes to provide the [Licensor] with the following on-screen credit in respect of the [Footage/Stills]: [specify credit] in the [Documentary] in the end credits. The failure for the [Licensee] and/or any third party to transmit, broadcast and/or otherwise display the credits shall not be a breach of this agreement. No compensation and/or damages shall be due to the [Licensor].

C.1105

There is no obligation on the part of the [Company] to provide an on-screen and/or verbal credit in the [Film/Series] of the use of the [premises/location].

C.1106

The [Radio Station] undertakes to include in any programme on air and/or in any schedule, promotion, advertising and/or website material issued and/or distributed by the [Radio Station] in respect of the [Programme] a verbal credit as follows: [specify details] and the following written [credit/slogan/image] to the [Sponsor] for the duration of this agreement. A written and visual sample of which is attached to and forms part of this agreement in Appendix A. [details of style of credit/slogan/image].

C.1107

The [Consultant] agrees that he/she shall not be able to claim any right to a credit and/or acknowledgment unless he/she appears in sound and/or vision for more than [specify duration]. In such event the following credit shall appear [at the end of the Programme/on screen/on any advertising] as follows: [specify details of name and exact words of credit].

C.1108

The [Consultant] agrees to provide a true and honest [profile/biography]; and to either supply photographs and/or to allow images to be taken for a portrait. The [Consultant] agrees that the [Company] shall be entitled to credit him/her as [role/credit/name] in any publicity and/or promotional material relating to the [Series/Podcasts] and/or the [Company] at any time.

C.1109

[Name] agrees and accepts that there is no right to a credit on the [Film/DVD/other format] either when he/she appears and/or at the end and/or in any audio file format of the script and/or in any other exploitation of any of the rights by the [Company] and/or any third party.

C.1110

The [Company] reserves the right to remove and/or delete the credit and/or performance of any person who in their opinion has been discredited and/or exposed as a fraud and/or is the subject of a serious criminal legal action at any time.

General Business and Commercial

C.1111

The [Company] agrees to ensure that any third party and/or successor in title shall agree to comply and be contractually bound to carry out the conditions set out in clause [–] in respect of the credits, copyright notices, trade marks and other contractual obligations to the [Company] and/or third parties.

C.1112

[Name] agrees that the [Company] shall be permitted to use his/her [name, image, photograph, signature, slogan, comments, sound recordings and/or films for the marketing and exploitation of [specify agreed purpose] provided that it is not used for any other reason and/or to endorse any products and/or or promote any service without the prior written consent of [Name].

C.1113

[Name] shall be provided with an exact sample of each and every item of material of any nature which may be available which features the professional name, profile, image, signature and/or otherwise of [Name] produced and/or distributed or otherwise exploited by the [Company] under this agreement.

C.1114
The [Company] agrees to allow where possible [Name] and his/her [Agent] the opportunity to view in advance any major promotional and/or social media material which it intends to release and/or distribute featuring the [Name] in any form. It shall not be a breach of this agreement not to do so. The [Company] shall in any event send copies to [Name] and his/her [Agent] of all such material which is issued on a regular basis.

C.1115
The [Company] agrees not to permit and/or license any part of the material produced under this agreement which includes the [Actor] to endorse any product and/or service and/or political campaign and/or charity and/or any other third party unless the prior written consent of the [Actor] has been obtained in each case.

C.1116
The [Licensee] agrees that it shall not be allowed to make and/or authorise any cuts, changes, alterations and/or deletions to the credits, copyright notices, logos and/or trade marks which have been agreed under this agreement.

C.1117
No third party shall be entitled and/or authorised to fund and/or sponsor the [Film/Product/Service] or have its logo, trade mark, service mark, design, product, service, music and/or jingle and/or image associated with and/or in any part of the [Film/Product/Service] without the written consent of both parties to this agreement.

C.1118
The [Assignor] agrees to provide a detailed and complete list of credits, copyright notices, service marks, trade marks, logos, images, slogans and/or other acknowledgements required to the [Assignee] by [date] in respect of all the [Series/Books/Content] which have been assigned under this agreement. The [Assignor] shall provide the copies of the original licences, consents, waivers and any other documents, material and artwork that may be available at the [Assignee's] cost.

C.1119
The [Licensee] agrees that in all marketing, promotional and advertising material for [Film/Product/Services] no other [Artists] shall appear in sound or vision more frequently and/or more prominently than [Name].

C.1120

The [Assignee] agrees to abide by any contractual, moral, copyright and credit obligations specified by the [Assignor] in clause [–].

C.1121

The [Licensee] agrees that all endorsements, quotes and use of statements from third parties to be used in any packaging and/or marketing material of any nature shall be subject to the prior written approval of the [Licensor].

C.1122

[Name] agrees that where the [Company] fails to exhibit, display, print and/or include a credit for any reason to [Name] in any material that it shall not be deemed a breach of this agreement. There shall be no obligation to withdraw, destroy and/or correct the omission, but any new material must include the correction.

C.1123

Where a credit is not included in any material due to lack of space, time, the type of material, a printing error, technical failure and/or some other reason by the [Company, an agent and/or sub-licensee. This shall not give raise to a claim for compensation, damages, loss of reputation and/or breach of contract.

C.1124

A failure to provide any agreed copyright notice, credit, trade mark, logo image and/or slogan shall be deemed a breach of this agreement. Any associated material must be withdrawn from sale immediately and destroyed. The [Licensee] must bear the cost of any such recall. In addition were copies have been sold then the [Licensor] shall be entitled to compensation and damages on terms to be agreed between the parties.

C.1125

Your participation in this [Event/Market Survey] is provided without any obligation to provide your personal data and information except: [specify details]. The [Company] agrees and undertakes not to attribute and/or credit any part so as to release and/or publish your identity.

Internet, Websites and Apps

C.1126

There shall be no obligation to provide a credit to any person who contributes to this [Website/App/Platform] unless it has been agreed in writing with the [Company] in advance prior to the submission and/or posting of material.

C.1127

Any person who contributes to this [Website/App/Platform] who has been found to claim credit and/or copyright ownership of any material which is in fact incorrect or untrue shall have all the material removed, deleted and erased; their account shall be closed and access blocked to any future use of the [Website/App/Platform].

C.1128

Where any material whether text, logos, sound recordings, films, music, lyrics, artwork, images and/or any other material of any type contains a copyright notice, credit or other acknowledgement. There is no right to delete, remove, alter and/or attribute the material to another person. There is no automatic right to reproduce, store, download, distribute, supply and/or exploit any such material. If you use any of this material for any reason other than viewing at a private residential address for non-commercial purposes for [one] person then you may be at risk of a threat of legal action.

C.1129

Where any material on this [Website/Platform] is downloaded with the permission of the [Company] and in accordance with the terms and conditions. It is important that all copyright notices, credits, trade marks, logos and other references to distributors, licences and/or software are not deleted, removed, altered and/or changed. Where the [Website/Platform] and/or part is to be referred to in any article, research, and/or reproduced in any medium and/or format at any time. There should be a clear statement of the [Website/Platform] reference as follows: [specify reference]. In addition all copyright notices, credits, trade marks, logos and any other acknowledgements must be reproduced.

C.1130

Where the [Company] decides in its absolute discretion that a credit and/or copyright notice is not to be attributed and/or made on their [Website/App/Platform] and/or in their [schedule/catalogue] and/or any marketing. Then you shall have the right to withdraw the [Work/Material/Content] and to cancel the agreement.

C.1131

The [Company] shall only be able to use copyright notices and credits on the [Website/Blog/App] next to the material and/or other rights in which ownership and/or control is claimed where there is the space and it will not impair the functionality. It reserves the right to list copyright notices and credits in one allocated zone at the bottom of the [screen/page/other].

C.1132

1.1   The [Site] is operated by the [Company].

1.2   [Name] is the writer of the [Blog] known as: [title] and is the original writer of all the text in which [Name] is the copyright owner. The [Company] agrees to place the following copyright notice in respect of the text to [Name] as follows: Text of [Blog] © [year] [name].

1.3   The [Company] supplies the images for the [Blog] which are supplied under licence by third parties. The [Company] agrees that the third parties shall not be supplied with any credit for images in connection with the [Blog].

C.1133

1.1   [Name] commissions the production of the [Podcast Series] and is the copyright owners in the [Films] which are produced and distributed over the internet in electronic form and though telecommunication systems to televisions, computers, mobiles and other devices.

1.2   [name] is credited as the main presenter and the copyright owner on the front and end credits of each film of the [Podcast] as follows: [specify details].

1.3   All other third party contributors will only receive a credit on screen at the time of their appearance and/or performance if they role is significant otherwise there is no credit.

C.1134

The credits for the [Audio File/Sound Recording] appear on the screen next to the download electronic format profile of the [Audio File] and in sound at the end of the recording. Where there is limited space and/or time then only the major credits will appear.

C.1135

The [Image/Photograph/Painting] may not be reproduced in any format and/or any medium without a credit to [Name] as the [creator/artist] and a copyright notice to the [Estate/Trust] who hold the rights as follows: [specify details].

Merchandising and Distribution

C.1136

The [Licensee] agrees to acknowledge by suitable legend the ownership of any copyright and/or other rights in any material they may use. Provided that the [Licensor] shall have informed the [Licensee] in writing as to the required copyright notices, credits, trade marks, images and/or logos at the time of delivery of the master material.

C.1137
The [Licensee] and any sub-licensee may include in the [Product/Service] the name and trade mark and/or logo of the [Licensee] and/or any sub-licensee. Provided that neither the [Licensee] nor any sub-licensee shall alter, delete and/or change any other credit, trade mark, logo and/or copyright notice appearing on the [Product/Service] of a third party.

C.1138
The [Agent] agrees to ensure that any third party shall agree to provide the following credit, copyright notice, trade mark, image, slogan and/or logo to the [Licensor] in respect of the [Licensed Articles/Products] and all advertising, marketing and distribution material including any website and/or app content and/or packaging.

C.1139
The [Agent] agrees and undertakes to ensure that all third parties to be licensed by the [Licensor] under this agreement shall agree that the copyright notice for the [Character] and any trade mark or logo, together with any credit, shall be incorporated on each item of the [Product] in a prominent position so it can be clearly identified by the public and similarly on all packaging and/or marketing material in any format.

C.1140
The [Company] shall provide the following credit, copyright notice, logo, image, and/or trade mark to the [Author] as described and represented in appendix A [specify exact words, size, position and order] which shall be displayed in a prominent and visible position in every copy of any item produced under this agreement both on any cover and inside the book and on all adaptations, marketing, advertising and/or packaging material. The [Author] shall at all times be acknowledged as the copyright owner and no other party shall have their name listed first in order or in a more significant position.

C.1141
The [Assignor] agrees that he/she shall not be entitled to any credit or acknowledgment in respect of the exploitation of the [Format] in any media by the [Assignee].

C.1142
[Title of Article/Image] distributed by: [specify Company]

Country of origin [specify country]

© [year] [Name]

[specify Logo/Image/Slogan]

C.1143
The [Distributor] agrees that in any associated publicity, advertising, promotional material, direct marketing emails, text messages, pop-ups, banner advertisements and/or other marketing material by the [Distributor] of the [Distributors] [website/app/platform]. That in the first [six] months of this agreement that the [Supplier's Logo] and the [Products] shall be given reasonable prominence, recognition and credit as set out in schedule A. [specifications/size/location/colour/format].

C.1144

1.1 The [Retailer] agrees to provide the following copyright notice, credit and/or image and slogan to the [Supplier] in respect of the [Products] as specified in Schedule B in respect of the [Retailer's] [shop/brochure/website/other] and in any marketing which features the [Products].

1.2 The [Retailer] agrees that the [Supplier] shall be entitled to refer to the [Supplier's] [shop/website] in its own marketing in the form set out as follows: [specify details].

1.3 Neither party shall be obliged to seek the approval of the other party in respect of 1.1 and 1.2. Both parties do however agree to provide copies of the acknowledgements if so requested by the other party.

C.1145
The [Distributor] agrees that it shall not erase, remove, delete and/or in any way deface, alter and/or change and/or conceal any of the copyright notices, credits and trademarks of any of the parties on the [Product/Article/Work].

Publishing

C.1146
The [Ghostwriter] agrees that he/she shall not be entitled to any credit and/or acknowledgment in respect of the exploitation of the [Work] by the [Company] and/or any person and/or in any media at any time. The [Ghostwriter] agrees that the [Company] shall be entitled to receive the sole credit and copyright notice for the writing, production and exploitation of the [Work/Manuscript/Images/Index/Preface].

C.1147

The [Agent] confirms that in addition to the moral rights of the [Author] under this agreement the [Agent] shall ensure that the [Author] is provided with the following copyright notice, trade mark, logo, image, link and credit in the [Work] in any form and in any publicity, promotional, advertising, website and/or packaging material in respect of any type of exploitation of the Work as follows: [describe in detail copyright notice, trade mark, logo, image, link and credit]. Examples and representations for use in different formats and materials are set out in appendix A and form part of this agreement.

C.1148

The [Agent] agrees to ensure that as far as reasonably possible the [Author] shall be entitled to approve all proposed copies, samples and other material of the [Work] and/or any adaptation, development and/or variation whether by a publisher, distributor, wholesaler, licensee and any associated promotional material including but not limited to summaries of the storyline and/or profiles of the [Author], covers, labels, packaging, catalogues, posters, websites, pop-ups, banner links and/or any other matter in respect of the manufacture, distribution, exploitation and marketing of the [Work] and/or any adaptation in any format and./or medium at any time.

C.1149

The [Licensee] agrees to provide the following copyright notice, trade mark, link and credit to the [Licensor] in the [Magazine/Newspaper] and on its website and app in relation to the [Extracts] as follows: [describe detail of/order/location of copyright notice, trade mark, link and credit].

C.1150

The [Publisher] shall use its reasonable endeavours to ensure that the [Work] is accurately described in any marketing and advertising material and that the [Author's] name is clearly displayed. Further the [Publisher] shall use its reasonable endeavours to ensure that any quotes and/or use of statements by third parties in relation to the [Work] which it intends to use shall be subject to the approval of the [Author].

C.1151

1.1 The [Publisher] agrees to identify the [Author] as the original creator of the [Work] as follows: [Name/size/location] in a suitable and prominent position on the cover, the binding and the inside front pages of the [Work], on any packaging material, on all draft and printed copies, on any disks or other material, and in all media on every item and any associated parts together with any website, advertising, marketing and/or publicity material.

1.2 The [Publisher] shall not permit any other person and/or company to be attributed and/or credited as the [Author] of any part for any reason.

C.1152

The [Authors] agree that in all circumstances relating to the exploitation of the [Work] that the following credit shall apply [name of first author] [name of second author] which shall be [on the same level/which shall be parallel on separate lines] and in the same style, size and both appear on any occasion that one is credited. Both [Authors] shall also endeavour to ensure that in any commercial exploitation of the [Work] or any reference in public that they shall each acknowledge the co-authorship of the other and not give the impression that they are the main or sole contributor.

C.1153

The [Author] is entitled to the following credit in the following form and style: [specify details] on all copies of any material based on the [Author's Work].

C.1154

[Name] agrees and accepts that he/she shall not receive any acknowledgement and/or credit for their contribution to the development, preparation and conclusion of the [Project]. That [Name] agrees that he/she has no legal and/or other moral right to a credit and/or copyright notice in any form and/or any sums from the exploitation of the [Project]. That [Name] has accepted and received the [Fee] in full and final settlement.

C.1155

1.1 The parties agree that the [Author] and the [Company] shall be credited as joint copyright owners of the [Audio File] as follows: © [year] [Author] and [Company].

1.2 The parties shall also have the following joint credit: [specify statement].

C.1156

[Name] and [Name] have jointly originated and created the [Script] known as: [title] and are joint copyright owners and will be credited as follows on the [Script] and/or any development: [Originated by [Name] and [Name].

Copyright © [year] [Name] and [Name]

C.1157

The [Author] was the original copyright owner but is now deceased and the copyright in the [Work] is held by the [Estate/Trust] known as [Name]:

Copyright in [Title] © {Estate/Trust} [year]

An original work by the deceased author [Name].

Services

C.1158

Subject to prior consultation the [Presenter] agrees that the [Company] shall be entitled to use his/her professional name, biography, profile, photograph, signature, image, quotations and the product of his/her services in respect of the [Series/Films] and/or any parts in any adaptation and/or marketing.

C.1159

[Name] shall be reasonably, prominently and clearly identified at all times as follows: [Name/Image/Link] by the [Company] in respect of the [Programme/ Event] and/or any corporate material, website and/or in any press and/or social media releases. No images shall be used which are not approved by [Name] in advance.

C.1160

[Name] agrees that the [Company] shall be entitled to use and permit the use of the [Name's] professional name, profile, image and recorded interviews with [Name] for the purpose of promoting and advertising the [Company] and/or its [products/services] but only during the existence of this agreement. Provided that the [Agent] is notified in each case and is fully consulted as to the exact form and medium in which it is intended to be exploited.

C.1161

In the event that the [Film] is completed using the services of the [Director] then the [Director] shall be accorded a credit in the following manner [specify name, size, location] in all publicity, advertising and promotional material and in the end credits of the [Film]. The [Director] acknowledges that he/she shall not be provided with a credit in the following circumstances:

1.1 Short extracts of the [Film] to promote, advertise and/or exploit the [Film] in any media including television, radio, websites, pop-ups, banner links and/or on DVDs, and/or on mobile phones.

1.2 Where any advertising, publicity and/or other exploitation relates to the work on which the [Film] is based and/or the screenplay and/or any members of the cast, personnel, author and/or producer. Except when such material relates to the [Director] then a credit shall be provided.

1.3 Advertising, publicity and promotion in any media where due to lack of time or space no other artist or person involved in the production of the [Film] is credited.

1.4 All commercial tie-ins, merchandising or other related exploitation including publications, periodicals and other written form and sound recordings in any format.

1.5 Exploitation in the form of [DVDs/other] the credit shall be on the [Film] but not the associated packaging.

1.6 Any other exploitation where no credits are provided to any other production personnel.

The [Company] shall not be responsible for failure by third parties to provide a credit to the [Director] which was unintentional. Provided that when the [Company] becomes aware of any such failure or default it shall use its endeavours to remedy the position as soon as possible.

C.1162

The [Director] shall be entitled to a credit on the negative and all positive copies of the [Film] made by or to the order of the [Company]. The [Director's] credit in the opening credits of the [Film] shall be in the last position of a size not less than 75% (seventy-five per cent) of the size of the title on a separate panel in the form: Directed by: [–]. The [Director's] credit may at the [Company's] discretion be accompanied in small print by the [Company's] Logo and/or copyright notice.

C.1163

The [Record Company] agrees and undertakes that the [Artiste] shall be clearly, prominently and reasonably identifiable by the following credit and copyright notice: [–] which shall be provided on all material of any nature in relation to the record, the musical work and/or the [Artiste] which is created, distributed and/or released in any media by the [Record Company]. This shall include but not be limited to all advertising and/or promotional material, packaging, labels, cover designs, websites, electronic downloads and/or any communication over the internet and/or any broadcast, and/or transmission over the radio, via any form of television and/or by means of any telecommunications system to mobile phones.

C.1164

The [Publisher] agrees to ensure that the [Author] [shall be provided with the following credit in all copies of the [Work] and in any publicity, advertising, promotional and packaging material: [describe credit] in respect of any part of the [Work] whether the original musical work, any associated sound recording and/or arrangement.

C.1165

The [Contributor] understands and agrees that the [Company] shall not be obliged to use the contribution in any form or to provide a credit or acknowledgment to the [Contributor].

C.1166
The [Company] agrees that the [Contributor's] name, image and endorsement shall not be used for any purpose other than the promotion and marketing of the [Contributor's] [specify subject] to the public.

C.1167
Subject to prior consultation the [Actor] agrees that the [Agent] shall be entitled to use his/her name, signature, biography, photograph, image and stage name in the promotion, advertising and marketing of the [Actor] and to authorise others to do so provided that a copy of any such material shall in due course be provided by the [Agent] to the [Actor] upon request.

C.1168
The [Manager] agrees to ensure that a [credit/copyright notice/trade mark/logo/slogan/image] of the [Sportsperson] shall appear prominently in any material distributed by the [Manager] and/or agreed with and/or licensed to third parties relating to the [Sportsperson] of any nature including all products, services, publicity, advertising, promotional and packaging as follows: [detailed description].

C.1169

1.1 The Company agrees that the [Actor] shall be provided with the following on screen credit [specify name, size, order, location] at the end of each programme of the [Series] and on any other occasion in which other lead actors receive additional on-screen credits.

1.2 The [Company] shall ensure that no copy of any part of the [Series] shall distributed, exploited and/or marketed without adhering to the provision of the credit unless agreed in advance in writing with the [Actor].

1.3 Failure to provide credits on more than [number] occasions shall be deemed to be a breach and the [Actor] shall be paid an additional fee of [specify sum] in each such case.

C.1170

1.1 The [Company] agrees that the [Consultant] shall be entitled to the following credit in respect of the [Project] on the main report, any copies and any summary on the [Website/Channel] of the [Company] in respect of the [Consultants'] contribution to the [Project].

1.2 Where the [Consultants'] contribution is deleted from the [Project] and/or the main report no credit shall be due on any material and/or on the [Website/Channel].

1.3 The [Consultant] shall not be entitled to a credit in any promotional, marketing, advertising and/or other material that may developed and/or created at any time.

C.1171

1.1 The [Consultant] agrees and undertakes that he/she shall not be entitled to any credit, recognition and/or acknowledgement in respect of their services and/or any work and material provided under this agreement.

1.2 The [Consultant] waives all moral rights to be identified and/or to object to derogatory treatment of his/her work. The [Consultant] agrees that the [Company] shall be entitled to edit, delete, add to, amend and/or translate the work and material provided by the [Consultant] as it thinks fit at its sole discretion.

C.1172

The [Agent] agrees to provide the [Company] with a list of credit and copyright and/or contractual obligations that must be fulfilled in respect of the [Project]. Where possible the [Agent] shall supply current contact details of the party to whom such obligations are owed and a provisional list of the cost of any payments that shall fall due.

Sponsorship

C.1173

The [Television Company] confirms that the [Company's] [Product/Services] will be reasonably and clearly identifiable in the [Programme/Series] and in any event will be seen on-screen on not less than [number] of separate [scenes/occasions] each time for not less than [duration] seconds.

C.1174

The [Sponsor] agrees to provide the [Sportsperson] with samples of all proposed promotional, advertising, publicity, packaging and other material in which it is intended to use the name, image and endorsement of the [Sportsperson] under this agreement.

C.1175

The [Sponsor] agrees that the name image and endorsement of the [Sportsperson] shall not be used for any purpose other than the promotion and endorsement of the [Sponsor's Product] for the duration of the Sponsorship Period.

C.1176

1.1 The [Company] agrees that the [Presenter's] name, image, signature and endorsement shall not be used for any other purpose other than the marketing and exploitation of the [Programme] and [Company] unless agreed in advance on each occasion with the [Presenter].

1.2 The [Company] agrees to provide the [Presenter] with exact samples of all materials in any medium in which it is intended to use the name, image, endorsement or otherwise of the [Presenter]. In the event that the [Presenter] requests alterations or changes in any form then the [Company] agrees to carry out the request provided that it is reasonable in the circumstances and the cost is not prohibitive.

C.1177

The [Sponsor] agrees to provide the [Agent] with samples of all proposed promotional, advertising, publicity, packaging and other material in which it is intended to use the name, image, endorsement and/or any other contribution in any form of the [Sportsperson] under this agreement.

C.1178

1.1 The [Company] confirms that the [Sponsor] shall be entitled to the following text, slogan, trade mark, credit, image in all publicity, promotion and marketing material appearing in any written and/or sound and/or visual form distributed by the [Company] in respect of the [Project/Event] as follows: [–]

1.2 The [Sponsor] shall be able to use the following text, slogan, trade mark, credit, image in all publicity, promotion and marketing material appearing in any written and/or sound and/or visual form distributed by the [Sponsor] in respect of the [Project/Event] as follows: [–].

C.1179

The [Company] undertakes to include in any programme schedule, promotional, advertising, publicity or other literature or in any film, recordings, group or corporate photographs, graphics or on the website [website reference and name] or in any other material of any type released or published in respect of the [Programme] the following [credit/trade mark/ slogan/statement] on behalf of the [Sponsor]: [specify details].

C.1180

The [Sponsor] accepts that the script, programme schedule, presenters and other aspects of [Series] may be changed due to editorial, programme policy and/or legal reasons at the [Television Company's] own discretion. In the event that this results in less exposure of the [Sponsor's] [Products/ Services] and/or the [Company's] [Trade Mark/Image/Slogan] then no sums shall be repaid and/or claimed by the [Sponsor] unless the duration of which the [Sponsor's] [Products/Services] are visible on screen is less than [specify length] [in total in the Series/or in any one episode].

C.1181

The [Sponsor] accepts that any reference to the [Sponsor's] [Product/Service] in the [Series] and/or any in marketing material may differ on occasions depending on the circumstances and may not be mentioned at all.

C.1182

The [Company] shall include the following mention, credit, photograph and statement on behalf of the [Sponsor] in any material that may be issued or released or created relating to the [Event/Series/Artist] so that fair recognition is attributed to the [Sponsor's] contribution under this agreement.

C.1183

The [Company] agrees to provide the following [credit/trade mark/service mark/logo/image/copyright notice/statement/slogan] to the [Sponsor] in the following circumstances:

1.1 [–] on all packaging, labels, jackets or sleeves.

1.2 [–] on all posters, brochures, catalogues, and advertisements.

1.3 [–] on the first press and social media release.

1.4 [–] on the display stand signs at any exhibition.

1.5 [–] in radio programmes and commercials.

1.6 [–] in television programmes and commercials.

1.7 [–] direct marketing emails and newsletters.

1.8 [–] on the website, app, competitions and internet.

1.9 [–] in any DVD, products, interactive gadgets, games and merchandising.

C.1184

The [Sponsor] shall not use the name of the [Association] and/or any trade mark, image, logo, slogan and/or the title of the [Event] and/or any film and/or sound recording and/or the [Promoter] and/or any third party and/or any competitor for the purpose of merchandising, marketing, advertising and/or promoting any products and/or services which are not specifically authorised under this agreement.

C.1185

The [Company] agrees and undertakes that an official printed programme and an electronic version to download shall be made available to the general public during the [Festival] at a price within the discretion of the [Company]. The [Company] agrees that the official programme in all formats shall bear the [Sponsor's Logo] on the front page, a half page statement from the [Sponsor] on page [–] and a full page advertisement for the [Sponsor's] [Products] on the back of the cover.

C.1186

The [Company] agree to display the [name, logo and image] of the [Sponsor] in a form to be agreed throughout the venue on flags, banners, seating, the pitch and any other suitable locations. Provided that it shall not cause any health and safety issues and/or impede the primary focus of the [Company] to [specify purpose] and the [Sponsor] shall pay all the costs of any such materials, work and/or planning applications, legal and consultants costs, administrative costs and any expenses that may be required to both install and maintain any such marketing and promotional material for the [Sponsor]. At no time shall the [Company] be expected to pay and/or incur any costs and/or charges.

University, Charity and Educational

C.1187

1.1 The [Institute/Charity] confirms that the [Contributor/Consultant] shall be entitled to the following credit in respect of the [Project] as follows: [specify details/location/order].

1.2 In the event that no credit appears in any copies then the [Contributor/Consultant] agrees that there shall be no liability by the [Institute/Charity] to the [Contributor/Consultant] for any loss of reputation and/or breach of moral rights. The [Contributor/Consultant] waives all rights to any claim for losses, damages and/or otherwise in respect of any failure to put a credit on any material at any time.

C.1188

The [Company/Distributor] agrees that it shall not use the name, logo, trade mark, image and/or appearance of the [Institute] and/or the [Work/Service/Project] and/or any other material associated with them for the purposes of advertising, and/or marketing the other goods, services and work of the [Company/Distributor] and/or for any purpose not specifically authorised under this agreement.

C.1189

The [Institute/Charity] agrees and undertakes to use its reasonable endeavours to ensure that the following [credit/copyright notice/trade mark/logo/slogan/image] of the [Company/Author] shall appear prominently on all copies of the [Project/Work]. That it shall also appear on any copies to be reproduced, supplied, distributed and exploited by the [Institute/Charity] and/or which are to be licensed to third parties and/or in any associated material such as marketing, advertising, packaging and merchandising as follows: [specify credit/copyright notice/trade mark/logo/slogan/image] of the [Company/Author].

C.1190
The [Institute/Charity] does not endorse and/or promote any commercial events and/or projects without a written agreement setting out the terms and conditions of support, use of the logo, image and name and liability. Where a third party uses and adapts the logo, image and/or name of the [Institute/ Charity] without authority then the event and/or project may be cancelled without notice.

D

DAMAGES

General Business and Commercial

D.001

1.1 The [Company] shall be obliged to pay the [Enterprise] such compensation and/or penalty sums as set out in Schedule A as may be due for failure to reach the targets and/or complete the [Project].

1.2 Where any delay is due to changes requested by the [Company] and/or due to force majeure then new target dates and a completion date shall be agreed between the parties and 1.1 shall not apply in that instance.

1.3 The [Company] shall be obliged to pay such sums which may become due in 1.1 and/or 1.2 within [specify duration] of notice by the [Enterprise] that a target and/or completion date has not been fulfilled. In the event that the payment is not received by the [Enterprise] within that period then the [Enterprise] shall be entitled to seek to recover the monies owed together with interest at [specify percentage] above base rate of [Name Bank plc]. The [Enterprise] shall also have the choice and shall be entitled to decide to withhold and retain any payments due from the [Enterprise] to the [Company] in settlement.

D.002

Nothing in this agreement shall entitle the [Licensee] to any remuneration, payment, costs, expenses or damages from the [Licensor] if the failure to fulfil the terms of this agreement and/or its performance shall arise due to the default and/or breach of this agreement by the [Licensee] and/or any sub-licensee, distributor and/or agent at any time.

D.003

In the event of the [Company] being obliged to pay damages or compensation in respect of any problem of any nature caused directly or indirectly by the [Exhibitor] and/or its personnel and/or guests. Then the [Exhibitor] shall reimburse the [Company] for the total amount of the sum paid together with any legal and administrative costs that may have been incurred by the [Company] and/or any third party.

D.004
The [Company] agrees and undertakes that it shall be liable to [Name] from [date] to [date] for any physical damage, power failures, indirect and direct financial loss, interference with existing functions of software, machinery and/or devices, the failure to supply, deliver and/or distribute any material and/or products and/or cancellation and/or termination of orders and/or contracts and/or negotiations and/or any other consequence whether foreseeable or not which arises from the [Services/Products/Material] and/or the defaults, failures and/or is otherwise caused by the [Company].

D.005
Where damage is caused of any nature and/or loss to the [Customer's] personal property as a result of using these premises and facilities. The [Company] shall not be liable to pay for any such damage and/or loss and shall not be liable to compensate the [Customer] or offer any refund. The [Customer] uses these premises and facilities at your own risk and cost. You are strongly advised to use the secure storage available and not to bring valuable items onto the premises.

D.006
In the event that the [Company] is prevented from using and/or exploiting all and/or some of the rights granted to the [Company] under this agreement by reason of a material breach and/or default by the [Licensor]. Then the [Licensor] shall pay to the [Company] a reasonable sum in damages which shall not exceed a maximum total sum of [number/currency]. The [Company] agrees that no other sums shall be due and/or claimed. The parties agree that the [Company] shall notify the [Licensor] of the sum claimed as due and the parties shall negotiate a settlement in good faith based on the circumstances.

D.007
Neither party to this agreement shall be liable to the other for any damages, losses and/or costs and/or expenses which are:

1.1   caused indirectly and not related to this main agreement.

1.2   a penalty and/or punitive sum.

1.3   based on projections of revenue and/or sales which have not been fulfilled and cannot be substantiated by any supporting evidence.

1.4   due to loss of profits.

1.5   due to a delay and/or interruption of business which could not have been avoided.

1.6   due to the failures of a third party.

1.7   interest in any sum due.

D.008

In the event of non-performance of the conditions set out in clause [–] of this agreement then the party who has defaulted shall be liable to pay the [Company] the sum of [number/currency] per [day/week/month] as [damages/compensation/agreed repayments]. These sums are agreed by all parties to be a fair and accurate assessment of the damages due to the [Company] and are not a penalty.

D.009

Any damage and/or loss, costs and/or expenses which arise directly and/or indirectly relating to either of the party's businesses, brands, products and/or reputations as a result of this agreement shall not be claimed against the other party for any reason. Each party agrees and undertakes to take out insurance cover to the value of [specify value] for their own benefit and at their own cost to cover any such consequences.

D.010

All claims for damages, loss or other liability under this agreement against the [Company] shall be limited to [number/currency] in total unless directly caused by deliberate fraud, malice, negligence and/or results in death and/or personal injury.

D.011

Where the [Company] supplies access to and/or use of any services, products and/or other material by [Name] at the [Event]. It is agreed that [Name] must take due care and consideration and not cause any loss, damage, injury and/or other costs and expenses at any time. Where [Name] causes any damage, loss, injury and/or other costs and expenses then [Name] shall be obliged to pay the [Company] in full for all sums which shall be due, claimed and/or settled including legal costs and expenses which shall have arisen due to the actions, conduct and/or otherwise of [Name]. Provided that the [Company] can provide [Name] with full details of any such sums together with sufficient evidence. The [Company] agrees that [Name] shall not be liable to pay such sums claimed where they can be recovered by the [Company] under an existing insurance policy.

D.012

If any of the participants at the [Event] cause damage and/or loss for any reason then the [Company] shall hold [Name] liable for any sums which it may have to incur to remedy the situation and replace, repair and/or substitute any objects, decorations and fittings, furniture and/or to bring the accommodation and/or any part of the [Venue] and/or facilities up to the standard that it was before the [Event]. Where the impact has caused loss of other business for the [Company] then [Name] shall also be obliged to pay for that loss where other parties had booked.

D.013

The [Company] agrees to pay for the cost of a [specify role] to review and assess the facts and circumstances and to provide a written report and recommendation as to the best course of action and the likely costs that can be expected if alternative projects to remedy the damages are proceeded with by the parties.

D.014

It is agreed that in the event that any items are damaged for any reason that the maximum that [Name] will be liable to pay shall be [number/currency] per [specify]. That normal wear and tear and/or damages which arise where there is no evidence of negligence and/or carelessness and/or malice and/or excessive force shall not be paid for by [Name] and the [Company] shall bear its own costs for such damages.

D.015

The [Company] shall not be responsible for any damages, losses, costs and/or expenses and/or any other sums which may arise directly and/or indirectly as a result of following the advice, information and data on this [Website/App/Blog] relating to any service, products and/or other matter. This advice, information and data is for background guidance only. You are expected to carry out your own research and take any professional and/or legal advice as may be required and/or to read the instructions which accompany any product and/or service and to follow those instructions issued by the [manufacturer/supplier]. In any event where any claim is made you agree that the total maximum claim for damages, losses, costs and/or expenses is limited to [number/currency]. This exclusion shall not apply to any directly attributable personal injury and/or death caused by the negligence and/or breach of duty of care by the [Company].

D.016

The [Distribution Company] may claim damages against any supplier, manufacturer and/or other third party who provides products and/or services to the [Distribution Company] which are found to be defective and/or not fit for their purpose and/or are misleading and/or misrepresent their content and/or uses and/or which pose a risk to the health and safety of the public and/or are not produced in accordance with product safety standards required in any country and/or which fail to comply with all necessary legislation, standards, codes and practices in any country. The claim for damages is not fixed or limited in value and may include:

1.1   loss of profit;

1.2   administration, public relation and legal costs;

1.3   the costs of product recall from the public and other customers including freight and refund charges;

1.4   damage to and loss of reputation and goodwill;

1.5   fall in share price of the [Distribution Company];

1.6   cancellation and/or termination of existing contracts and agreements;

1.7   cancellation of promotions, advertising or marketing.

D.017
The [Company] supplies the service, information and data to you and makes no recommendation as to the personal decisions that you make seek to make based on any such material. The [Company] does not accept any responsibility for any subsequent losses, damages, failures and/or expenses that may arise and you are advised to seek professional and expert advice. This service is for [entertainment] and is not based on verifiable sources that can be disclosed to you.

D.018
This [Blog] is a personal diary and not intended to be considered as a professional advice column by its readers. No losses, damages, actions, failures, expenses, costs and/or any other omissions, errors, delays and/or any other matter can and/or will be accepted by and/or paid for by [Name] from any third party at any time. You must make your own decisions and do your own research and there is no promotion and/or endorsement of any product, business and/or person in any form and/or recommendation to purchase, sell, contribute to and/or engage with any third party.

D.019
This [App/Website/Platform] and its contents and use are provided to you to use for free as you think fit for your own purposes and to your own advantage. Provided that you agree to the following terms of use:

1.1   That you agree to waive all rights to make any claim and/or allegation and/or summons for any damages, losses, expenses and/or any other sum arising from such use including viruses, security failures and loss of data and/or other material.

1.2 That you will not reproduce and/or exploit any part of the [App/Website/Platform] in any form and/or in any media at any time.

1.3 That where you intend to incur any costs and/or take any steps based on information derived from your use of the [App/Website/Platform] that you agree that any such decision is at your own cost and risk.

1.4 That you agree that the [Company] and the [Distributor] have only granted you a non-exclusive licence to use the {App/Website/Platform] and content and that there is no right to sub-license any rights and/or grant and/or exploit any rights at any time.

D.020

The [Supplier] shall not be liable for any loss or damage incurred or suffered by the [Customer] and/or any third party arising from the use and/or reproduction of the [Work].

D.021

In the event of delay by the [Purchaser] collecting and/or taking delivery of the [Products]. The [Purchaser] agrees to pay the [Seller] storage charges for the [Products] and any other expenses and damages that the [Seller] may sustain. Any such payment shall be without prejudice to any other rights and remedies of the [Seller].

D.022

If the [Product] is lost, stolen or damaged after it has been delivered and/or installed, then the [Customer] must pay the cost of repair or replacing it excluding fair wear and tear.

D.023

The [Company] shall not responsible for any damage, loss, defect, corruption, and/or failure which may arise in a machine, gadget and/or other device which is owned and/or controlled by the [Customer] and/or any other third party in circumstances where the [Customer] installs and/or uses the [Product/Unit] in conjunction with it and/or by loading it.

D.024

1.1 This [Product] is not for general use and is only suitable for: [specify exact purpose] and is not to be used for: [specify exclusions]. You are advised not to use it in conjunction with any other [specify] and not to exceed [number] applications per [week]. Before general use you are advised to try a test sample on [specify]. In the event that you show any sensitivity do not use on any part of [specify] and/or anywhere else. Do not use on any person under age [specify]. Do not use after the expiry date on [specify]. Avoid contact with [specify].

1.2 No responsibility can be accepted for damage to the [Product] due to exposure to sunlight and/or use with other materials and/or any use which is not in accordance with the instructions. Do not use this [Product] if you have any of the following medical conditions: [specify].

D.025
No [Product] may be returned to the [Company] as faulty where the damage has arisen directly as a result of the fact that the consumer has used the [Product as follows:

1.1 the wrong tools have been used to operate it;

1.2 the instructions in the brochure were not followed;

1.3 the [Product] was used in conjunction with another product which was faulty which caused the damage;

1.4 there was a power failure and/or power surge; or

1.5 water, heat and/or pressure was applied to the [Product] and caused damage.

D.026
In the event that any party wishes to make a claim for damages arising from this agreement. It is agreed that that such party shall provide a detailed statement of the damage and sum claimed and provide the other party with [number] days to respond prior to the issue of any legal action and/or other claim.

D.027
There shall be no obligation to account for [Products/Units] which have been damaged in transit, destroyed, are lost or stolen or otherwise not delivered to the [Distributor] by the [Supplier].

D.028
The total liability for damages by the [Company] which can arise in respect of this [Order] and [Products/Services] shall be limited to the total value of the payment for that [Order].

D.029
Where no payment is made to the [Licensor] in respect of [Material/Products/Services] due to loss or damage of any nature for which the [Company] subsequently receives compensation under an insurance claim. Then the

[Licensor] shall be entitled to receive payment upon terms to be agreed between the parties.

D.030

Where any claim and/or payment is made to any person and/or third party for damages, losses, expenses, interest, refunds, product liability and/ any other liability and/or sum by the [Licensee] and/or any sub-licensee. There shall be no automatic right to deduct any such payments from the royalties due to the [Licensor]. Then all such payments and/or sums shall be the responsibility of the [Licensee] and/or any sub-licensee and not the [Licensor]. Except where any payment and/or other sum is directly attributable to the default and/or alleged breach of this agreement by the [Licensor] and/or the negligence and/or actions of the [Licensor] from [date] to [date]. In such instance all such payments and sums may be recouped from advances and/or royalties due to the [Licensor].

D.031

The [Sub-Licensee] agrees and undertakes that where there is any failure and/or delay in any manufacturing process and/or service required to produce and/or distribute the [Units/Products]. That where any damages, losses and/or expenses are incurred that all such sums shall be at the [Sub-Licensee's] sole cost and cannot be offset and/or recouped from the sums due to the [Company].

D.032

It is agreed between the parties that where [Products] are manufactured and/or distributed which are not of sufficient quality and/or are damaged in some form. That the [Licensee] may sell and dispose of these [Products] provided that:

1.1   The items are clearly marked as sub-standard and

1.2   The brand name and labels are removed and

1.3   The [Licensee] shall pay the [Licensor] a royalty of [number] per cent of all sums received.

D.033

Where any items are lost, damaged, destroyed, returned as faulty and/or for any other reason are unsuitable to be sold to the public as fit for purpose as [specify] under the brand [specify]. Than it is agreed between the parties that all such items shall be destroyed and not sold and/or disposed of as seconds and/or at a discount at any time. Further evidence shall be provided if requested of the record of destruction and any such item shall be specified as lost, damaged, returned as faulty and destroyed in the accounting reports to the [Company].

D.034

No royalties shall be paid to the [Assignor] in respect of copies of the [Work/Products] and/or parts which are destroyed in transit, by fire, water and/or remaindered and/or sold at cost and/or otherwise damaged and/or disposed of at cost price or below. Provided that no revenue or credit is received which is above cost and/or any other direct remuneration.

D.035

The [Distributor] undertakes that the [Work/Products] shall be stored in a secure place and shall be packaged and sent by such method as to ensure that the [Work/Products] shall not be damaged in transit.

D.036

The [Publisher] shall not be liable for any loss and/or damage to the manuscript, USB and/or other device upon which the material is stored and/or for any photographs, sound recordings, films and/or other material supplied for the [Book/Work/Product] and/or as part of the packaging, marketing and/or advertising by the [Author]. The [Author] shall be obliged to keep a complete copy of all material and only to supply copies not originals. The [Author] accepts and agrees that all material is to be supplied at the [Author's] own cost and risk.

D.037

Where the [Publisher] discounts and/or disposes of copies of the [Book/Work] due to the fact that there are errors, omissions and/or damage to all and/or any part. Then the [Author] agrees that the [Publisher] may provide a total figure for the sum received and the name of the party third party rather than the number of copies. That the [Author] shall be paid [number] per cent of all sums received and that payment shall be within [number] days of receipt of payment by the [Publisher].

D.038

Where damage to any [Sound Recording/Book/Product] is caused by fire, explosions, riots, war, floods, earthquakes, tornados and/or any other extreme weather conditions, outbreaks of violence in any locality and/or country and/or any other force majeure such that the [Publisher] is unable to verify either the exact circumstances and/or the value of the stock damaged. Then the [Author] agrees that the best estimate shall be acceptable for the purposes of accounting provided that the [Publisher] shall not seek to offset any damages and losses against sums due to the [Author] at any time.

D.039

The [Company] acknowledges that the services of [Name] are of a personal nature which can only be compensated in damages. The [Company] agrees that the [Company] shall not be entitled to and shall not seek, if the circumstances arise, an injunction or other equitable remedy to prevent or curtail any actual or threatened breach by [Name] with respect to the provisions of his/her services under this agreement.

D.040

The [Composer] acknowledges that the services of the [Composer] are of a unique nature and character, the loss of which cannot be reasonably or adequately compensated in damages. The [Composer] agrees that the [Company] shall be entitled to seek equitable relief by way of an injunction to prevent or curtail any actual or threatened breach by the [Composer] of the provisions of this agreement.

D.041

The [Organisers] and the [Promoter] agree that:

1.1   If the [Promoter] is given notice of the cancellation of the [Event] by the [Organisers] on or before [date] then the [Promoter] shall only be entitled to be paid [number/currency] together with all sums incurred in respect of the Promotion Expenses.

1.2   If the [Event] is cancelled after [date] then the [Organisers] and the [Promoters] agree that the [Promoter] shall be entitled to be paid the [Promoter's] Fee in total in addition to all sums incurred in respect of the Promotion Expenses.

1.3   These clauses shall not apply where the event is cancelled due to force majeure for any reason under clause [–].

1.4   In the event that these clauses are relied upon there shall be no further claim by either party of any nature against each other relating to the [Event].

D.042

In the event that [Name] causes any damage to any property and/or facilities of the [Company] and/or any third party whilst at the [Event/Location]. Than [Name] agrees that he/she shall be liable to pay the full cost and expense to be incurred by the [Company] to repair and/or replace any such damaged property and/or facilities directly caused by his/her negligence and/or as a result of a deliberate act of malice. Where the damages arise due to the original state of the property and/or facilities and/or are due to normal wear and tear then [Name] shall not be liable for any sum. In any event [Name] shall not be liable for more than [number/currency] in total.

D.043

Damages which may arise in respect of the [Company] relating to the services of [Name] shall not be the responsibility of [Name] at any time. The [Company] agrees to bear all the risk, costs and damages however they may arise and for whatever reason even if based on and/or indirectly related to the work of [Name].

D.044

1.1 The [Sponsor] confirms that it shall be entirely responsible for and bear all costs, expenses and damages that may arise from its sponsorship of the [Festival/Event] and/or its attendance as an exhibitor with supporting personnel and/or in respect of any services, products, equipment and /or material which it may supply and/or distribute at any time.

1.2 The [Sponsor] agrees that it shall arrange and pay the cost of a comprehensive insurance policy of not less than [number/currency] for any claim for the benefit of the [Sponsor/Organisers] which shall include cover for personal injury, death, loss, theft, damage and/or any other claim in respect of: the [Sponsor's] products, services and/ or any other material, equipment, personnel and/or other third party authorised to act on their behalf at any time at the [Festival/Event] from [date] to [date].

D.045

The [Sponsor] agrees that it shall not be entitled to make any claim against the [Company] nor seek repayment of any fees or offset any sum for any damages, costs, losses, expenses or any other reason arising under this agreement including but not limited to:

1.1 Breach or alleged breach of contract by the [Company] and/or any of its agents, suppliers, contractors and/or participants which are remedied.

1.2 Any loss of reputation and/or damage to the goodwill of the [Sponsor].

1.3 A delay and/or failure to launch a new brand, product and/or service as planned by the [Sponsor].

1.4 Advertising, marketing and promotional costs of the [Sponsor].

1.5 Fees and payments due to any third parties engaged by the [Sponsor].

1.6 The [Event/Festival] is cancelled, delayed, reduced in size and/or capacity for health and safety reasons and/or any [Artists/Athletes] do not perform, attend and/or provide commentary as proposed.

1.7 The [Event/Festival] is not broadcast, transmitted and/or otherwise distributed as planned on radio, television, the internet and/or social media.

1.8 The [Event/Festival] does not achieve the projected number of exhibitors, public admission figures, projected sales of [specify] or the expected ratings on [television/radio/website].

D.046

If any agents, consultants, employees, casual staff and/or any other person and/or third party engaged and/or appointed by the [Sponsor] causes any damages and/or losses and/or incurs any costs and expenses which have to be paid by the [Company] which relate directly and/or indirectly to the [Sponsor] and it attendance, participation and/or promotions at the [Festival/Event]. Then the [Sponsor] agrees that it shall pay the [Company] all such sums within [number] days of invoice by the [Company] subject to supporting evidence of any matter being made available to the [Sponsor].

D.047

Where there is any dispute between the [Sponsor] and the [Company] as to any claim for losses and/or damages made by either party. Then it is agreed that the party claiming the sum owed shall:

1.1 Send a detailed itemised report and list of the reason for the sum claimed and the cost of any replacement, substitution and/or repair supported by quotes from third parties.

1.2 Confirm that such losses and/or damages are not covered by an existing insurance policy they may hold and that no claim has been submitted and/or paid.

1.3 Where a payment of any sum cannot be agreed under this clause. Then the parties shall appoint a person to act as a [mediator/liaison] between the two parties in order to avoid legal costs. The cost of such person shall be paid by both parties whether the matter is resolved or not.

D.048

1.1 The [Institute/Charity] shall have the right to claim and be paid damages, losses, costs and expenses in a claim and/or demand against any [Consultant/Supplier/Distributor/Third Party] who provides maintenance, products, services and/or other work to the [Institute/Charity] where the [Institute/Charity] may decide as follows that any matter:

1.1.1 does not fit the agreed description and order;

1.1.2 is defective and/or not fit for its intended purpose and/or is misleading as to its content and/or uses;

       1.1.3 poses a risk and/or is not compliant with health and/or safety and/or software and/or data security in [country];

       1.1.4 fails to comply with all necessary legislation, guidelines, codes, standards and practices in [country].

1.2 The claim for damages, losses, costs and expenses is not fixed or limited in value and may include:

       1.2.1 Loss of profit;

       1.2.2 Administration, public relation and legal costs;

       1.2.3 The costs of product recall from the public and other customers including freight and refund charges;

       1.2.4 Damage to and loss of reputation and goodwill;

       1.2.5 Cancellation or termination of existing contracts and agreements;

       1.2.6 Cancellation of promotions, advertising or marketing.

D.049

That the total liability of the [Institute] shall be limited to a maximum claim of [figure/currency] [words] in respect of any damage, loss, failure or defect due to the actions and/or failures of the [Institute] its employees, students and visitors. This limit shall not apply in the case of gross negligence or death.

D.050

The [Company/Consultant] accepts and agrees that the [Institute/Charity] shall have the right at any time to terminate and/or cancel this [agreement/licence]. That in such event the [Institute/Charity] shall not be required to justify the decision and the [Company/Consultant] shall not be entitled to be paid any compensation, damages and/or payment for loss of reputation and/or goodwill and/or any other costs, losses, expenses and/or other sums. That the total liability of the [Institute/Charity] shall be limited to the fees due to be paid under clause [–] to the date of termination or cancellation.

D.051

Where any member of the public removes temporarily and/or permanently and/or internally and/or externally damages and/or causes any other losses and/or reduction in value of any material exhibited by the [Institute/Charity] and supplied by [Name] including: [specify]. The [Institute/Charity] agrees and undertakes that it shall bear all costs and responsibility for any sums due to repair, replace and/or compensate [Name] for any loss and/or damage. That the following sums shall be the minimum due for any of the following circumstances [specify event] [number/currency].

D.052

It is accepted by both parties that the condition of the [Manuscript/Work] is fragile and liable to deteriorate and/or suffer damage and/or fade and/or fall apart at any time. [Name] agrees and accepts that the [Institute/Charity] shall not be liable for any damage suffered by the [Manuscript/Work] and/or any subsequent losses, costs and expenses suffered by [Name] whether it occurred while the [Manuscript/Work] was in the possession and/or control of the [Institute/Charity] and/or in transit and/or while being viewed by another third party.

DATA

General Business and Commercial

D.053

The personal information, data, and [password/access code] which is collected by the [Company] on this [Website/App/Software] shall not be supplied, transferred or copied to any other third party for any purpose [except with your prior written consent.]

D.054

The [Company] shall be entitled to store, retain and disclose to their professional advisors any personal and financial details which I have provided on any software, documents or other records for the purpose of fulfilling the terms of this agreement, drawing up their accounts, carrying out an audit, tax return and/or other compliance with statutory and/or other legal obligations. Provided that any such advisors shall be obliged to keep my financial details confidential.

D.055

The [Applicant] agrees it is a pre-condition of the contract procedure that the [Company/Authority] be entitled as a [government/public] [body/authority] which is accountable for its decisions and awards that it should be able to disclose and make available to the public all the content of the tender documents for the contract which have been completed and submitted by the [Applicant] except those parts which are clearly marked [confidential/exempt/not to be disclosed] by the [Company/Authority]. This clause shall apply whether or not the [Applicant] is awarded the contract for [specify].

D.056

The [Company] shall comply fully with all relevant data protection legislation, codes, guidelines, standards and policies that may be in force during the existence of the agreement in accordance with the law of [country] and [regulatory organisation/stated role].

D.057

The [Company] shall not disclose any personal information and/or data submitted by the [Executive] and/or created by the [Company] and/or its officers to any third party without the prior written consent of the [Employee] including but not limited to: annual reviews, personnel assessments, disciplinary proceedings, management courses, complaints by the [Executive] relating to the actions and/or words of other employees at the [Company], matters relating to pension, national insurance, tax, benefits or other financial matters, the terms of employment or contract for services of the [Executive] and/or any other report, record, computer software, agreement and/or any other material relating to the [Executive] which may exist prior to or during the Term of this Agreement and/or after termination. This restriction shall apply to any parent, subsidiary, associate, affiliate or partner of the [Company] and all advisors, consultants, professional legal and accounting advisors. Except where there is a legal requirement to report and/or comply with a request for the disclosure of information and/or it is ordered to be disclosed by a Court.

D.058

The [Company] shall abide by its data protection policy in force from time to time and shall not disclose to any third party such information which is personal and private whether sensitive or not without the [Executive's] prior approval. That where consent is provided by the [Executive] then the use, disclosure and/or access to any personal data shall only be provided in confidence by the [Company] and not for public disclosure.

D.059

That [Supplier/Distributor] shall comply with the requirements of the following legislation: [specify]; codes of practice: [specify] and any other guidelines issued by: [specify organisation] relating to the collection, storage, supply, use and/or release of any personal data and/or bank and/or other payment details. Failure by the [Supplier/Distributor] to do so shall be considered a fundamental breach of this agreement.

D.060

You confirm and agree that the data and information collected by the [Company] may be stored, retrieved, transferred and verified to and by any third party for the following purposes:

1.1 Compliance with laws, directives, regulations, or codes of practice whether in relation to identity, address, nationality, residence, tax, national insurance, data compliance and protection, national security, money laundering, financial and credit status and debt collection.

1.2 For the exchange and supply of information with and to parent, subsidiary, associate, and affiliate companies and agents, underwriters, insurers, accountants, legal advisors, human resources, corporate affairs and public relations, the police, regulatory bodies, government agencies.

D.061

This clause shall apply at any time and be applicable to any part of the world in which the [Company] trades, operates or does business.

D.062

The [Company] and its associated companies, and agents shall be entitled to use, supply, store and retrieve the personal data and information you supply for any of the following purposes:

1.1 To carry out an identity, credit and financial background check whether against public records, by using a private investigator, or otherwise to prevent fraud, or money laundering or to verify the statements and details of the application.

1.2 To verify your medical history and current medical condition.

1.3 To add to or amend the records with the results of 1.1 and 1.2 including where fraud or dishonesty is suspected.

1.4 To supply material to others for statistical research, analysis, provided that personal sensitive information is deleted.

D.063

1.1 The [Company] agrees and undertakes that the personal information, medical records or reports, contract or any data and information relating to [Name] will only be disclosed at the [Company] to: [Managing Director/Finance Director/Head of Human Resources/Chair of the Board/Head of Audit Committee].

1.2 The [Company] undertakes not to supply, inform, reproduce and/or distribute any personal information, medical records, reports, test results, reviews, assessments and/or other personal data, records and/or information to any other person, employee, director, agent, insurer, underwriter, government agency or authority and/or third party at any time without the prior written consent of [Name].

D.064

The [Company] shall abide by any law, judgement, directive, statutory instrument or legislation, that imposes upon it restrictions, methods and/or obligations regarding the use of any personal data obtained from an individual and/or company. This may include but not be limited to personal name, address, passwords and codes, username, bank details, credit card details, age, blood group, DNA, birth records and/or medical history.

D.065

All personal, family, financial, medical, and/or other material of any nature supplied under and/or pursuant to this agreement to the [Company] shall be deemed to be confidential and private data and information whether or not it is covered by the legislation relating to data protection except for: [specify details not covered]. The [Company] shall not supply, release, distribute, license and/exploit any of this material to a third party without the prior written consent of [Name].

D.066

The [Company] shall abide with all relevant data protection legislation, codes of practice and/or guidelines in [country] from [date] to [date]. The [Company] shall abide by its data protection policy which may be in force at the time and shall not disclose to any third party such information personal and private relating to the [Executive] without the [Executive's] prior approval whether that information is deemed personal, confidential or not.

D.067

The [Company] is registered as a Data Controller with [organisation/ government body]. The data and information collected by the [Company] must be processed fairly and lawfully. The [Customer] is entitled to know how the [Company] intend to use any data and information provided by the [Customer]. The [Company] will use the personal data and information provided by you and/or your agent acting on your behalf to the [Company] to process your [Order/Booking] and to deliver the [Products/Services]. The [Company] may need to pass some of your personal data and information to the [Company's] agents, distributors and third party services engaged by the [Company] with your knowledge and consent in order to fulfil the [Order/Booking]. The [Company] may also pass your data and information to [government authorities] as required by law at any time. The [Company] and its agents and third party representatives will also use the data and information for statistical analysis and market research with some of the personal data and information deleted.

D.068

The [Company] may monitor and record telephone calls made to the [Company] for quality control and staff training purposes and if necessary for use in any dispute and/or legal action.

621

D.069

Where the [Customer] provides personal and financial details including but not limited to the [Customers'] name, address, landline, mobile, email, passwords and codes, username, bank details, credit card and other personal data and information for the purpose of ordering [Products/ Services] on the [Company's] [Website/App/Platform]. The [Company] agrees and undertakes to the [Customer]:

1.1 That the [Website/App/Platform] is secure and protected by: [specify].

1.2 To ensure that the [Company] complies with all relevant legislation, codes of practice and/or guidelines relating to data protection, payments, banking, finance and credit status.

1.3 That no third party except professional advisors [and collection agencies] shall be supplied with and/or authorised to access any such personal data and information unless the [Company] is requested to do so under an order of a Court and/or the [Company] is required to comply with any legislation whether in existence at the time of this agreement and/or which becomes law at a later date in any country.

1.4 That a copy of the [Company's] data protection policy is available at: [specify source/link]. This document sets out the procedure for any complaint and/or dispute regarding the use by the [Company] of any personal data and information.

D.070

It is agreed by the [Client] that the [Sponsor/Company] and/or parent, associated and/or any subsidiary, agent, consultant and other persons and/ or businesses engaged by the [Sponsor] and/or with whom the [Sponsor] works as a joint venture and/or partnership and/or otherwise may store, retrieve, use, supply and/or edit the personal data and information which you have provided for the purposes of this [Survey/Competition] in order to: [specify purpose].

D.071

The [Institute/University] stores on the hard drive and software of its computers and in paper form details of all those who students apply to the [Institute/University] for any reason and those third party parents and/ or guardians who may provide evidence of financial ability to pay the fees and other sums due. The [Institute/University] uses the information and data to process any application, and to compile statistics in order to report to government agencies. If you are offered a place on a course and accept the offer then the information and data will be used to verify your place on the course and to store details of your assessments, exam results, reports and record of your academic, sport, student union and other contributions at the [Institute/University]. The information and data may be used for many reasons including for the purpose of:

1.1   assessment of verification and/or eligibility of your academic record for grants and bursaries;

1.2   to administer and process your course, monitor attendance and/or performance and to provide a range of other support.

1.3   credit assessment and review and/or the collection of debts relating to accommodation and course fees and charges and/or compliance with money laundering legislation and guidelines, and/or to prevent crime and/or fraud.

1.4   disclosure to third party agents, legal and professional advisors and/or government bodies.

1.5   the need to assess mental and physical health of the students who may be at risk and/or are not coping with the course. So that the support can be offered.

1.6   review by the Data Protection Officer for the [Institute/University] who be contacted on: [specify name/contact information].

Information and/or data will not be released to any parent and/or guardian without the prior authority and consent of any student. The student is the first point of contact and not any parent who has provided financial support.

D.072

It is agreed that the [Institute/Charity] shall not be entitled to release and/or supply any personal information and details which you may provide in the course of your application for [specify post].

Except the following matters for which you provide your consent and agreement:

1.1   Your name, address, age, date of birth, passport number and photograph and application to verify the terms of your residency and your right to work in [country] with any government agency.

1.2   Your name, address, age, date of birth and photograph with your [school/university/organisation] to verify your qualifications.

1.3   Your name, address, age, date of birth, photograph and application with all the references that have been supplied.

1.4   Your name, address, age, date of birth and photograph and application with our medical advisor if your application is successful in order to arrange insurance cover.

1.5 Your name, address, age, date of birth and photograph and application with the national body [specify] to carry out a criminal record assessment and/or review.

D.073

1.1 You agree that the [Company] may use your name, gender and email address for the purpose of sending you newsletters, updates, promotional events and other marketing material.

1.2 You agree that the [Company] may also supply such personal data and information to third parties who promote products and services connected with the [Company], through its businesses, brands, partnerships and collaborations so that such third parties may contact you directly with marketing, offers and discounts.

D.074

The [Company] agrees and undertakes that it shall not as a matter of policy collect and/or store email addresses, dates of birth, names and/or other details and information in respect of children age [13/16/18] years and under. That it is the policy of the [Company] to contact and liaise with parents and/or guardians and to obtain their prior consent and authorisation. That the [Company] accepts and agrees that a child age [13/16/18] years and under cannot enter into a legally binding agreement without the consent of the parent and/or guardians. Further that any costs and expenses incurred and/or attributed without such consent cannot be claimed by and/or are not owed by the parents and/or guardians to the [Company].

D.075

'Data' shall be the following material, documents, software, databases, indexes, codes and records listed in Schedule A.

D.076

The [Company/Organisation] acknowledges that each person has the right for their data and information created, stored and/or held by the [Company/Organisation] be used in the following manner:

1.1 used fairly, lawfully and transparently.

1.2 used for explicit purposes.

1.3 used in a way that is adequate, relevant and limited only to what is necessary.

1.4 is accurate and where necessary kept up to date.

1.5 is kept for no longer than necessary.

1.6 is handled in a way that ensures it is secure and that includes protection against unlawful and/or unauthorised processing, access, loss, destruction or damage.

1.7 that there is the right to be informed how the data used.

1.8 that you have the right to access the data and information.

1.9 that you have the right to have incorrect data and information updated.

1.10 that where data and information is to be accessed, reused and/or transferred to a third party and/or used for a different service and/or purpose that you must be asked to provide your authority and consent. That you have the right to refuse to consent.

1.11 that you have the right to object to how your data is processed and/or stored and/or used and/or how long it is kept.

D.077
'Data' shall mean any material and rights of any nature including but not limited to text, images, graphics, logos, names, titles, headings, computer-generated material, codes, source references, taxonomy, indexes, databases, algorithms, computer software, discs and/or storage, retrieval, supply and distribution method which are in existence now [and/or created in the future].

D.078
'Data' shall mean any personal data and information relating to a living person in respect of the following matters stored on any material in any format:

1.1 name, address, date of birth, age, schools and education, social/economic group, family relatives and guardians.

1.2 race, ethnic group, political opinion, religious beliefs, trade union and other memberships organisations, genetics, biometric, blood group, health, disabilities, medial and sexual history, criminal record, convictions and offences.

D.079
'Data' shall mean any rights and/or any material and/or information of any nature owned, controlled by or in the possession of the [Company]:

1.1 All documents, records, text, rules, titles, procedures, slogans, formats, scripts, lyrics, contracts, licences, consents or undertakings.

1.2 Images, films, recordings, sound recordings, music, noises, ringtones and sounds, cartoons, characters, logos, drawings, maps, designs, photographs, plans, products and merchandising.

1.3 Computer software, computer-generated material, discs, website, app, internet material, icons, holograms, domain names and blockchain resources.

1.4 All recognised and pending patents, inventions, processes, applications and registrations with any organisation, government and/ or in any country.

1.5 All copyright, design rights, trade marks, service marks, musical, artistic, dramatic, literary works.

1.6 All trade secrets, moral rights, confidential information, recipes and processes.

1.7 All board minutes, and reports, auditors' reports, financial statements, projections and forecasts, tables, order forms, customer databases, wholesaler and supplier databases and any other list or compilation of information.

1.8 Marketing, advertising, publicity and promotional material.

1.9 All health, safety, security, compliance, product liability, legal actions or claims and any assessments, monitoring, reports, failures, criticism, warnings, fines, or estimated liability and forecasts.

1.10 All tax, insurance, telephone, water, gas, electricity, rates, material, staff, transport, freight, customs, and other costs, expenses and charges.

1.11 Any other matter relating to the [Company] not covered in 1.1 to 1.10.

D.080
The [Developer/Licensee] agrees and undertakes that:

1.1 All rights in the data and/or information supplied in any format under this agreement shall remain the property of the [Company]. That this [tender/agreement/license] is not intended to transfer any copyright, trade marks, service marks, design rights, computer software, database or any other rights of any nature to the [Developer/Licensee].

1.2 That neither the [Developer/Licensee] nor any of its employees nor any third party engaged or appointed by it shall acquire any rights or interest of any nature in any variations, development or adaptations of the data and/or any information which shall remain the sole property of the [Company].

1.3 That the [Developer/Licensee] shall ensure that neither it nor any third party engaged or appointed by it shall copy, edit, adapt, alter or vary any data and/or information except for the purpose of this agreement.

1.4 That the [Developer/Licensee] shall ensure that neither it nor any third party engaged or appointed by it shall delete and/or vary the copyright notice and/or trade mark notices and/or any image and/or other logo to the [Company] on any copies in any form in any medium.

1.5 That the [Developer/Licensee] shall ensure that both it and any third party engaged or appointed by it shall ensure that a copyright notice and/or any trade mark notice and/or any other image and/or logo specified by the [Company] is put on any new material.

D.081

The [Distributor/Licensee] shall take reasonable care of the [Company's] data and/information relating to the [Project/Event] and shall not authorise any person, firm or third party to copy or reproduce the material in any form without the prior knowledge and consent of the [Company].

D.082

That access by the [Consultant] to the [Company's] data and information on the business premises of the [Company] does not permit or authorise the [Consultant] to send, remove, copy, film, record supply and/or distribute any data and/or information to any other source, site, person and/or other third party at any time.

D.083

That all data, information and other material collected, compiled and developed under this agreement shall belong to the [Company]. The [Company] shall have the right to exploit, license, supply and distribute the data, information and/or material in any manner its thinks fit without the prior consent of the [Enterprise].

D.084

The [Purchaser] shall not use the disc, the software and any data and information in any manner inconsistent with the terms and conditions of this License. The [Purchaser] shall under no circumstances alter, remove, deface, erase and/or delete the copyright notice, trade marks or details regarding the [Publisher/Distributor] displayed on any part of this disc, the software and any data and information and/or packaging.

D.085

The [Licensee] agrees and undertakes that the [Licensor] and/or any parent company shall be entitled to make copies and/or have access to all of the following data, information and material either directly from the [Licensee] and/or any sub-licensee in respect of the [Product/Work/Service]:

1.1 All contracts, licences, assignments, consultancy, agency and distribution agreements, consents, waivers, registrations, applications and/or copyright and other intellectual property records in respect of any material and/or any rights and/or the [Product/Work/Service].

1.2 Invoices, receipts, payments, bank records, accounting records, commission and agency payments, stock and any other material and/or software and/or format in any medium.

D.086

The [Sponsor] shall not be entitled to access to and/or use of any data, information, databases, customer lists, bank account statements and/or any other financial, administrative and/or other details of the costs, income from and/or any other information and/or material regarding the operation of and/or visitors to the [Event/Festival]. The [Sponsor] shall only be entitled to a report of the total number of visitors for each day.

D.087

The [Consultant] undertakes and agrees that:

1.1 All data and information and other material which is supplied by the [Company] and/or any parent, subsidiary and/or associated business and/or any legal and/or professional advisors to the [Consultant] shall belong to the [Company] and not the [Consultant].

1.2 That any adaptation of the data, information and/or material in any medium shall belong to the [Company] and not the [Consultant]. That where for any reason rights are created which belong to the [Consultant] then the [Consultant] undertakes and agrees to assign any rights that he/she may have acquired to the [Company] at the [Company's] cost.

1.3 That the [Consultant] shall not have the right to release and/or disclose any content of the data, information, material and/or any adaptation to any third party without the prior written consent of the [Managing Director/Name]. That any failure to comply with this condition shall constitute a breach of this agreement and entitle the [Company] to terminate the agreement with immediate effect and without any further liability to pay any further sums to the [Consultant].

D.088

Tables, data and statistics © [Name] [year]–[year]

Copyright and all other rights throughout the world owned by [Name].

No rights of reproduction in any form granted for any reason without prior consent and a licence from [Name].

D.089

1.1 [Name] grants a non-exclusive licence to the [Company] to use all the data and information provided to them in this [Market Survey] in any manner they shall think fit provided that the name, address and personal contact details of [Name] are deleted and a code allocated.

1.2 Provided that the [Company] shall not use any of the data and information provided to contact the businesses and persons mentioned using the name, address and personal details of [Name] at any time.

D.090

It is agreed that no party to this [Consortium] shall be entitled to release, supply, distribute and/or reproduce the data, information and other material recorded, collected and developed in respect of the [Project] to any third party at any time (whether in confidence or not) without the prior written approval of all the other parties and agreement as to the terms of use and any copyright notice.

D.091

It is agreed that no party to this [Consortium] shall be entitled to authorise, commence and/or make any application for funding and/or development of a new project based on and/or derived from any data, information, material and/or conclusions from the current [Project] unless:

1.1 The current [Project] has already been released to the public and the data, information, material and research is generally available to everyone at no cost.

1.2 All the other parties have agreed and are part of the new funding application.

1.3 The applicant has bought out the rights of the other parties to the [Project].

D.092

1.1 All data, information and material submitted to the [Enterprise] is stored on computer software in the following format: [specify format].

1.2 Partial extracts of the data, information and material are displayed on the [Website/App/Archive] owned by the [Enterprise] which can be searched on line by members of the public.

1.3 If you do not want any of this data, information and/or material displayed on the internet then please state this request in your submission.

1.4 Data, information and material is supplied to third parties on a non-exclusive basis under licence where consent has been provided to do so. No royalty and/or other payments are made to you for the supply of such data, information and/or material to third parties. If you do not consent then state this request in your submission.

D.093

1.1 The current data protection policy of the company started on [date]. This policy is reviewed each year and may be updated.

1.2 Even after you close your account with the [Company] your data, records, transactions, recordings, information and other material will be stored and archived by the [Company] for a period of [number] years.

DATABASE

General Business and Commercial

D.094

'The Database' shall be the names, addresses and [specify details] which were originally compiled and created by the [Company] and of which the [Company is the copyright owner in the form of an ordered structure which is stored in the following format [on computer/disc/other] at [address] in [country].

D.095

'The Databases' shall mean the lists, directories and reference material in any format or material held by [Company] or any subsidiary, affiliate or associate owned or controlled by the [Company] or any company with which it has an agreement or arrangement relating to [specify subject] including lists relating to customers, suppliers, manufacturers, retailers, wholesalers, returns, refunds, lost and damaged stock.

D.096

The copyright in this database and index is owned by [Name] and you are only permitted to view the contents, make one copy for your own personal use and not for any educational, research or commercial purposes which requires the prior written consent of the copyright owner [Name].

D.097

The [Company] is an exclusive licensee of [Licensor] of the database entitled [title] which is used by the [Company] for the purpose of the promotion and marketing of [specify subject] and which it is authorised to do so from [date] to [date].

D.098

The copyright owners of this database are [Name] and there is no right to copy, reproduce, adapt, supply, to add the data as links on your website, app and/or platform and/or to reproduce the information for distribution to colleagues, use and/or adapt it for storage and retrieval in your library and/ or mainframe and/or in any software programme and/or to develop and/ or adapt the title, headings and/or contents for any purpose whatsoever except as a research guide for your own personal use whether on residential or business premises. Any other type of use requires the prior permission of the copyright owners.

D.099

The [Company] agrees and undertakes that the [Author] is the copyright owner of the [Database/Directory/Index] for the [Work/Search Engine]. That the [Company] shall only be entitled to use the [Database/Directory/Index] in the manner and for the purpose stated in clause [–] for the Term of this Agreement. The [Company] undertakes that it shall not use and/or exploit the [Database/Directory/Index] to promote any other work or project without the prior written consent of the [Author] and the payment of an additional advance fee and royalties.

D.100

The [Licensee] agrees that the [Author] shall be entitled to a right of access to and to inspect and make copies of any data, information and material in any format and/or medium and any database whether recorded in printed form and/or on a computer and/or other storage and retrieval device of any nature which relates to the development, production, distribution and exploitation of the [Work/Book/Films/Sound Recordings] in order to verify the sums due to the [Author] under this agreement.

D.101

The [Sponsor] shall not have the authority and/or right to exploit and/or use any database, data, information and/or material to which it is provided access by the [Company] except for the purpose of verifying the following criteria in respect of the [Event/Festival]: [specify authorised use].

D.102

The [Company] agrees that [Name] shall have the non-exclusive right to have access to and/or to inspect and/or make copies of the data and information on the database entitled: [specify] from [date] to [date]. In consideration of the Fee of [number/currency] the [Company] grants [Name] the non-exclusive to copy, adapt and edit the data and information on the database and to use and/or display it in the following manner: [specify authorised use].

D.103

The [Company] shall retain all your personal details on a [hard drive/main frame] at the [Company] and be entitled to make copies and/or supply them to such professional financial, legal, and insurance advisors associated with the [Company] who may advise and/or assist in the business and/or any third party who needs to be informed for the purpose of fulfilling the terms of this agreement for no more than [number] years from [date].

D.104

No personal details and/or any data stored on any database at the [Company] shall be supplied to any third party who is not connected with the business, nor shall any such data stored on any database be sold and/or disclosed to a third party for the purpose of marketing, promotion and/or any other purpose.

D.105

The [Company] owns and/or controls all copyright, intellectual property rights, taxonomy and database rights in the [List/Index/Compilation/Directory]. There is no right granted to exploit and/or adapt the [List/Index/Compilation/Directory] for any purpose and/or to make any copies. There is no automatic right of access, but it is agreed that you may inspect the [List/Index/Compilation/Directory] from [date] to [date] to use any information for your own personal use and not for any form of charitable, educational and/or commercial purpose.

D.106

In consideration of the payment of [number/currency] the [Author/Company] grants the [Distributor] the non-exclusive right to use and display the [Database/Taxonomy/Index/Directory] on the [website/app/software/platform] reference [specify] from [date] to [date] and to grant a non-exclusive license to third parties for access to and/or the use of the [Database/Taxonomy/Index/Directory] for [their own personal research/other].

D.107

Compilations, listings, indexes, themes, subject orders, data, information and any databases whether in the form of text, images, films, videos, sound recordings, downloads, tables, maps, charts and/or in any other format on any part of this [Website/App/Platform] and/or any associated material are owned and/or controlled by the [Company]. There is no permission and/or consent granted to use, adapt and/or exploit any part without prior consent and authorisation whether for commercial, educational, charitable and/or non-profit purposes. You are strongly advised to email [specify] and to seek permission.

D.108
Databases reproduced under licence from [Company] based on research by [Name].

D.109
It is agreed by the [Company] that where it creates databases and/or other information and/or material in any form including computer generated graphs, statistics, flow charts, presentations, maps and/or three dimensional projections. That all such data, databases and/or other material shall be assigned to and belong to the [Distributor] in all media and in all medium throughout the universe and world for the full period of any term of all rights including copyright, intellectual property and database rights and any extensions and/or renewals whether the technology and/or rights exist now and/or are created at a later date. That the [Company] shall not retain any rights, claim and/or ownership and/or control and shall not have the right to any additional payment and/or other sums from any exploitation and/or transfer of rights.

D.110
The [Company] confirms that in the event of a breakdown of facilities and/or interruption and/or due to a lack of an electricity supply and/or other energy resources. That the [Company] has a backup system which will still allow access to the [data/database] within [number] hours by the [Client].

D.111
Where a sub-licensee, distributor and/or other third party who is due and/or liable to account to the [Licensor] has failed to put in place a recovery system and/or data and/or database storage policy. In the event that records are not available and destroyed then it shall be deemed a breach of this agreement.

DEATH

General Business and Commercial

D.112
If before making his/her final award the [arbitrator/mediator] dies and/or ceases to act as the [arbitrator/mediator] the parties shall immediately

appoint a new [arbitrator/mediator]. No such new [arbitrator/mediator] shall be entitled to disregard any direction of the previous [arbitrator/mediator] and/or to vary and/or revise any award of the previous [arbitrator/mediator] except to the extent that the previous [arbitrator/mediator] would have had had power to do so and/or with the consent of both parties to this agreement.

D.113

The [Authors] agree that in the event of the death of one of the [Authors] to this agreement after the delivery of the [Work/Book/Sound Recording] for publication. Then the estate of the deceased [Author] shall be entitled to any monies which would have been due to the [Author] had he/she not died.

D.114

In the event of the death of the [Author] before the delivery of the [Work/Book/Sound Recording] then all further payments under this agreement shall cease unless sufficient material exists for the completion of the [Work] by a writer to be jointly selected by the [Publisher] and the appointed representative of the deceased's estate. In the event that the [Publisher] and the appointed representative agree not to appoint a writer to complete the [Work/Book/Sound Recording] then this agreement shall be terminated and the [Publisher] shall [not] be entitled to be repaid any sums previously paid to the [Author] under this agreement.

D.115

In the event that the [Licensor] should die during the Term of this Agreement the [Licensee] agrees that all sums which would have been due to the [Licensor] shall be paid to an appointed representative of the [Licensor's] estate or such other person who has been assigned copyright either by the estate or inherited from the [Licensor].

D.116

In the event of the death of [Name] the rights and obligations under this agreement may be terminated by notice in writing by the [Company] to the estate of [Name]. The [Company] shall be obliged to pay such sums as may be due for any work completed by [Name] up to the date of termination and/or which may become due thereafter.

D.117

1.1 In the event of the death of [Name] then the [Company] may terminate this agreement by notice in writing to the estate of [Name] provided that the [Work/Book/Sound Recording] has not been delivered in draft and/or completed form. In such case all rights in the [Work/Book/Sound Recording] shall revert in full to the estate of [Name] but the

[Company] shall be entitled to reclaim any sums which have already been paid to the [Name] and/or his/her agent.

1.2 If a draft and/or the completed [Work/Book/Sound Recording] has been delivered by [Name] to the [Company] then the [Company] shall be obliged to fulfil all its obligations set out in this agreement and to pay all sums that fall due to the estate of the deceased [Name]. The estate shall be entitled to assume the rights of [Name] in respect of approval, editorial control, audit, inspection and all other undertakings set out in this agreement.

1.3 If another person is required to contribute to the [Work/Book/Sound Recording] in 1.2 prior to its commercial exploitation then such person shall be subject to the prior approval of the estate. This other person shall not be entitled to a credit as author of the [Work/Book/Sound Recording] and all costs incurred in respect of their contribution shall be paid for entirely by the [Company]. The [Company] shall not be entitled to deduct any such sums from the monies due to the estate of [Name] for any reason. The [Company] shall in addition submit any material revised, edited or contributed to by that person to the estate for their written approval prior to the exploitation of the [Work/Book/ Sound Recording] in any form.

D.118

The [Agent] confirms that in the event of the death of the [Author] after the conclusion of a written agreement with a publisher for the publication of the [Work/Book]. The [Agent] agrees to ensure that all sums which are due to the [Author] are paid to the [Author's] estate.

D.119

The [Publisher] confirms that in the event of the death of the [Author] after the acceptance of the manuscript of the [Work/Book] then all sums due to the [Author] under this agreement shall be payable to the [Author's] estate.

D.120

In the event that the [Author] dies prior to the delivery of the manuscript the [Publisher] agrees to negotiate in good faith with the executors and/ or administrators of the [Author's] estate concerning the publication or otherwise of the [Work/Book].

D.121

In the event of the death, severe incapacity or degenerative illness of the [Name] so that they are unable to fulfil the terms of this agreement. It is agreed that the agreement shall be terminated by notice in writing to the person who holds power of attorney on behalf of [Name] and/or who administers the estate of [Name] to end on any date specified by the [Publisher]. It is agreed that all sums paid to the date of termination by the [Publisher] shall be retained by [Name] and not repaid. The [Publishers] shall not be obliged to pay any further sums after the date of termination of the agreement.

D.122

Where as a result of the death and/or serious injury and/or illness of any personnel involved in this [Project] the [Project] is to be delayed, cannot be fulfilled by the same persons specified in the contract and/or there is no possibility of an alternative substitute being agreed. Then the parties agree to enter into negotiations to agree the terms upon which the contract for the [Project] is to be terminated, who is to bear the costs and pay for the outstanding commitments and who is to own the rights. Where no agreement can be reached the parties agree to enter into alternative dispute resolution, mediation or arbitration and shall only resort to legal proceedings if they have first tried one of those methods.

D.123

Where [Name] dies during the course of this agreement for some reason unconnected with the [Company]. Then the [Company] shall be liable to pay all sums due until the date of death. Thereafter no further sums shall be due to [Name] or his/her estate and the [Company] shall be entitled to substitute another person to complete the work set out under the agreement and there is no requirement to provide any credit or reference to [Name] in any completed work of any nature.

D.124

If [Name] dies and/or is seriously ill and unable to fulfil the terms of this agreement the [Company] shall not be entitled to continue with this agreement without the prior written consent of an authorised representative of [Name] or the estate of [Name]. Where [Name] has delivered or completed all the required work, then the [Company] shall be entitled to proceed as set out in the agreement provided that it fulfils all the undertakings, credit obligations and payments to an authorised representative of [Name] or [Name's] estate.

D.125

Where [Name] the subject of the [Work/Book/Script] by the [Ghostwriter] dies and/or is severely mentally incapacitated prior to the approval and/or delivery of the [Work/Book/Script]. Then a nominated member of the family of [Name] and/or the [Executors] of the estate may fulfil the role of providing authority to approve and/or reject the draft manuscript prior to delivery to the [Publishers/Production Company].

D.126

Where [Name] is unable through death, illness, incapacity and/or otherwise to attend and/or participate in the [Event/Festival]. The [Sponsor] shall not have the right to withdraw the sponsorship funds and agrees that the [Enterprise] shall be entitled to substitute and/or replace the person with someone of equal stature and reputation. Where this does not happen and the person is not as well-known and/or successful then the [Sponsors'] shall be entitled to be repaid [number/currency] within [one] month of the end of the [Event/Festival].

D.127

In the event that one of the [Contributors] suffers ill health which results in severe incapacity for more than [number] months and/or dies during the course of this agreement before his/her work is started, developed and/or completed. Then all the [Contributors] agree that the [Company] shall have the right to substitute a new person to commence, continue with and/or finish the work required of that person. Provided a reasonable settlement is negotiated and agreed with a nominated representative of any such person to buy out all rights to their contribution and interest in this agreement by the [Company]. Where a settlement cannot be agreed then the [Project] will be held in suspension until the matter is resolved. In such instance all the parties agree that the timescales under this agreement may be adjusted to take account of the period of delay due to such suspension. Where the suspension continues for more than [number] years. Then any party may serve notice of termination of the agreement to the others by notice in writing for the [Project] shall cease within a period of no less than [six] months.

D.128

In the event of the death of [Name] the creator, developer and writer of the [Blog/Podcast/Film] then all ownership, control and interest in the copyright, intellectual property rights and assets in the domain name, title, characters and any trade mark and content shall be transferred and assigned to his/her nominated successor in title and ownership to: [specify person].

D.129

The [Company] agrees to arrange at its sole cost suitable insurance cover for the benefit of the family and children of [Name] to cover his/her position as [specify role/description] which involves considerable risk and danger at different times. The [Company] agrees to pay all the premiums and to ensure that they are kept up to date and that a copy of the policy is provided to [Name] and the stated beneficiaries listed on that document. That the [Company] shall ensure that the policy is not invalidated and/or does not exclude any area of work and/or travel and/or ill health and/or death in any country for any reason. That the [Company] agrees and accepts that cover shall be for a minimum of [specify number/currency] for the following medical cover, incapacity and death: [specify]. The [Company] shall in addition provide its own personal additional cover which shall be paid to the family and estate of [Name] of [number/currency] if he/she should die during the course of his/her work, and/or any assignment and/or travel requested by the [Company] at any time. Such sum to be paid within [number] days of death of [Name] in such circumstances which shall not be delayed due to the inquest and/or establishment of the final facts in such case.

DECLARATION

General Business and Commercial

D.130
The [Company] hereby declares that it has disclosed:

1.1   All particulars of its registered shareholders.

1.2   All options conditional or otherwise entitling any party to acquire any shares or loan capital of the [Company].

1.3   The full names, addresses, occupation(s), nationality and country of residence of all Directors of the [Company].

1.4   Copies of its up-to-date Memorandum and Articles of Association and any deeds affecting control of the [Company] including full details of all Resolutions adopted by the [Company] in the previous [twelve] months.

D.131
We the undersigned, hereby declare that the contents of our [Application/ Document] are true to the best of our knowledge and belief and that all relevant information has been disclosed to [specify body/company] as required under clause [–] of the [Application/Document].

D.132
The signature by [Name] on behalf of [Company] of [specify document] is a declaration that the facts, information, statements, figures and representations which have been made are true and accurate and can be verified by the [Company]. That no facts, information, data or material has been withheld, misrepresented, distorted, altered and/or omitted.

D.133

1.1   [Name] of [address] who holds post of [specify] at the company known as [specify].

1.2   [Name] confirms and agrees that he/she has taken an oath that these facts are true and that there is no information and/or documents which he/she are aware of which either may contradict and/or show this statement to be false as at [date].

1.3   [Name] confirms and declares that he/she is making this statement in good faith and without malice.

1.4   [Name] agrees that if after the date of this declaration he/she becomes aware of any facts which would show this statement to be misleading, inaccurate and/or false that he/she shall disclose such information to [specify].

1.5   That [Name] acknowledges that the supply of false information could constitute a civil and/or criminal offence.

DEED

General Business and Commercial

D.134

In witness whereof the parties hereto have executed and delivered this Agreement as a Deed the day, month and year first hereinbefore written:

1.1   Executed and Delivered as a Deed by the [Assignee] and signed by two Directors or one Director and the Company Secretary.

1.2   Executed and Delivered as a Deed by [Name] and witnessed by [Name].

D.135

This Deed shall cease to have effect [twelve] years after the full completion of the development under the [Management Contract] provided that no legal proceedings shall have been commenced against the [Management Contractor] by the [Company] prior to the expiry of the [twelve] year period.

D.136

This deed shall not negate or diminish any duty or liability otherwise owed by the [Contractor] to the [Developer].

D.137

No approval, inspection, testing or otherwise of the [Development] or of any designs or specifications of any work or materials by or on behalf of the [Developer] shall diminish and/or bring to an end and/or be deemed a waiver of any duty and/or liability of the [Contractor] arising under the Deed. The [Contractor] shall remain at all times entirely responsible and liable for all the designs, work and/or materials carried out by and/or provided by the [Contractor] in respect of the [Development] at any time.

D.138

This Deed dated [–] in respect of the property known as [address] in county in country [–] is evidence in writing of the freehold ownership of the house and land set out in Schedule A which forms part of this Deed. The freehold ownership is held by [Name]. Any transfer and/or assignment and/or lien and/or charge must be in writing and registered with [specify body] at [address] by [Name].

D.139

1.1   By a deed dated [–] [Name] owned the [Asset/Property] during his/her lifetime and there was and is no outstanding mortgage, charge, lien and/or any other control and/or ownership by any third party as at [date].

1.2   [Name] died on [date] and left a will for which probate was obtained on [date] by executors of the will. By a deed dated [–] the [Asset/Property] and all control and ownership is assigned and conveyed to [specify beneficiary] free from any encumbrances so that [beneficiary] may sell, exploit and/or charge the [Asset/Property] as he/she thinks fit.

DEFAMATION

Film, Television and Video

D.140

The [Assignee] agrees that it shall be responsible and/or liable for any damages, losses, costs and expenses arising from the content of the [Unit/Disc]. The [Assignee] undertakes to the [Assignor] that the [Unit/Disc] will not contain any material whether film, text, title, images, designs, music, lyrics and/or otherwise which are offensive, obscene, racially prejudiced, likely to incite violence and/or is likely to cause a danger and/or could affect the health and/or safety of children and/or could be defamatory and/

or expose the [Assignor] and/or the [Assignee] and/or any sub-licensee, distributor and/or agent to criminal and/or civil proceedings.

D.141

The [Assignor] undertakes that the [DVDs/Discs], packaging and any associated advertising, marketing and promotional material will not contain any material, text, images, words, lyrics, gestures, innuendos or any other material in sound and/or vision which may be considered obscene, give rise to an allegation of contempt of court, is and/or may be deemed defamatory or which is likely to lead to a criminal and/or civil action [as at specify date] in [country].

D.142

The [Licensee] agrees that it has viewed the [Film/Video/Podcast] and does not rely on any undertaking by the [Licensor] as to its content in respect of obscenity, defamation, compliance with any regulatory codes and/or programme guidelines and/or whether there is a real risk of civil or criminal proceedings and will seek its own legal advice. That the [Licensee] shall not hold the [Licensor] liable in respect of any of these matters for any use and/or exploitation of the [Film/Video/Podcast] by the [Licensee] under this agreement.

D.143

The [Licensor] confirms that the [Film/Video/Podcast] does not contain any obscene, defamatory and/or any other material which infringes the rights of third parties. The [Licensor] undertakes that the exercise of the rights granted by the [Licensor] to the [Licensee] will not expose the [Licensee] to civil and/or criminal proceedings in [specify country/any country in the world]. In any event the [Licensee] agrees that the liability of the [Licensor] [under this clause/this agreement] shall be a maximum of [number/currency] in total and no further sums shall be paid once this limit has been reached.

D.144

The [Licensee] shall not be under any obligation to include any material from the [Interview/Video/Series] and/or any sound recording in any [Documentary] to be reproduced and distributed under this agreement which would prevent and/or restrict and/or increase the risk of legal proceedings in any country. The [Licensee] may edit, delete and remove material which in its view is objectionable and/or may result in a claim and/or allegation of defamation, copyright infringement and/or any other matter. The [Licensee] agrees not to add any new material to the [Interview/Video/Series] except music authorised in advance for the purposes of continuity.

D.145

Where at any stage the [Licensor] receives an allegation and/or claim of defamation in respect of the [Film/Video/Series] and/or any sound recording and/or parts. Then the [Licensor] may decide to withdraw the [Film/Video/Series] from this agreement and may serve notice on the [Licensee] to that effect at any time prior to the commencement of reproduction of and/or exploitation of the [DVDs/Discs/Downloads]. The [Licensor] shall offer the [Licensee] the same terms for another film, video and/or series which the [Licensee] shall not be obliged to accept. If the [Licensee] does not accept the alternative proposal then all sums paid to the [Licensor] in respect of the withdrawn [Film/Video/Series] shall be repaid plus an additional sum of [number/currency] in the form of fixed compensation. These sums shall be paid within [number] days of the rejection of the proposal by the [Licensee].

D.146

The [Production Company] undertakes and warrants to the [Television Company/Distributor] that the [Programme] including all visual images, graphics, computer generated material, films, recordings, interviews, voice-overs and the accompanying soundtrack and music and/or products, documents and source references and/or any other information of any nature purporting to be facts are true and accurate. That the [Programme] does not and will not contain any material which is obscene, libellous, defamatory and/or is in contempt of court and/or in breach of any legislation in [specify countries] and/or codes of practice and programme guidelines by [specify organisations] and/or is likely to lead to a claim and/or allegation by any individual and/or company and/or is likely to result in civil and/or criminal proceedings for any reason against the [Production Company] and/or the [Television Company/Distributor].

D.147

The [Artist/Name] undertakes that his/her performance and/or any spoken words, music, lyrics and/or other material supplied and/or other actions and/or contribution shall not contain anything defamatory and/or which is likely to result in an allegation of copyright infringement and/or trade marks and/or complaints to any regulatory body by the public and/or is likely to cause offence, incite violence and/or be derogatory of any person, company, political party and/or product and/or service. Further that his/her performances and clothing, equipment and supporting personnel shall not endorse any products and/or services and/or advertise and/or promote any third party in any manner unless specifically authorised in advance by the Company I each case.

D.148

The [Licensee] undertakes not to edit the [Material] in anyway likely to impair its quality, meaning and/or integrity and shall not use and/or permit to be used any [Material] in any manner which is likely to bring the [Licensor] into disrepute or which is defamatory of any person, company or business.

D.149

The [Company] shall not knowingly include in any [Film/Series] and/or parts which is transmitted, broadcast and/or exploited by the [Company] any material which is defamatory, seditious, blasphemous and/or obscene and/or which is untrue and/or is slanderous and/or is any infringement of copyright, trademarks and/ intellectual property rights and/or design rights and/or which is in contravention of any existing legislation and/or embargo and/or would be a contempt of court and/or any other legal and/or contractual obligation and/or is likely to result in any civil and/or criminal proceedings.

D.150

The [Licensor] confirms that the [Film/Programme] does not and will not contain any material of any nature which is obscene and/or defamatory and/or will expose the [Licensee] to civil and/or criminal proceedings in [specify countries] and/or contravenes any codes and/or guidelines regarding [specify subject] in any of the following countries [–]. The [Licensor] confirms that the version of the [Film/Programme] to be supplied under the agreement will be that which has been rated by the [censorship body in country] as [specify rating].

D.151

The [Licensor] agrees and undertakes that to the best of its knowledge and belief the [Film/Series] does not contain any material which is obscene, defamatory, libellous, offensive and/or likely to incite violence and/or [specify other issues] in the jurisdiction of [country]. The parties to the agreement acknowledge that the [Film/Series] has not been cleared for every country in the world, only for those specified.

D.152

The [Assignee] agrees that it has viewed the [Film/Documentary] and does not rely on any undertaking by the [Assignor] as to its content in respect of obscenity, defamation and/or any other matter relating to suitability of content material for any markets in any country and/or compliance with any programme codes and/or guidelines and shall seek its own legal advice for use and/or exploitation of the [Film/Documentary].

D.153

The [Licensor] confirms that its own legal advisors do not believe the [Film/Series] to be defamatory, offensive and/or likely to lead to criminal or civil proceedings in [countries]. Despite that fact no such assurance and/or undertaking is given to the [Licensee] who has viewed the [Film/Series] and must take their own independent advice. The [Licensee] must also arrange suitable insurance cover for the benefit of [Licensor] and the [Licensee] in respect of the threat of any claim, settlement and/or legal action arising from the exploitation of the [Film/Series] by the [Licensee].

D.154

[Name] shall be entitled to insist that the [Licensee] delete, edit, add or alter any part of the [Film/Series] within [number] days of viewing the edited interview which for legal reasons [Name] has been advised should be changed and any such changes shall be at the [Licensees'] sole cost.

D.155

1.1 The [Licensee] agrees and undertakes that it shall only be entitled to exploit the [Film/Documentary] in the format, duration, order and content in which it is supplied by the [Licensor].

1.2 The [Licensee] shall not be entitled to add, delete, amend, change and/or alter any part of the [Film/Documentary] and/or the sound recording and/or the credits and/or the copyright and trade mark notices and/or the music, lyrics, title and/or the duration.

D.156

The [Licensee] agrees and undertakes that it shall not:

1.1 Add any distributor's credit, logo, text or sound, or market and promote any other films, products or persons without the prior written approval of the [Licensor].

1.2 Market or exploit the [Film] or any part or use any packaging or any other material or person in association with the [Film] or parts which may cause the [Licensor] to be in breach of contract with a third party, may result in a claim for defamation, or any other criminal or civil proceedings at any time.

D.157

The [Licensor] undertakes that the [Series] and/or any parts are not and will not be defamatory and that in the event that there is any claim or allegation the [Licensor] has an insurance policy to cover all such legal costs and expenses, losses and damages. That the [Licensee] shall not be responsible for any such sums and shall be entitled to recoup all sums expended from the [Licensor].

D.158

The [Company/Distributor] agrees and undertakes that it and/or its successors in business and/or title shall be responsible and bear all copyright, clearance, contractual, administrative, travel and hotel, legal and other costs and payments of any nature that may be incurred and/or arise from the use and/or adaptation of the interviews, filming and sound recordings of [Name] and/or any other third party which is made and/or reproduced and/or included in the [Programme] and any associated exploitation and/or adaptation in any form at any time.

D.159

Where any [Presenter/Artist] deliberately and maliciously seeks to use any programme and/or recording in which he/she appears to defame any person, company, sponsor and/or business. Then the [Company] reserves the right to take legal action against such [Presenter/Artist] and to be indemnified in respect of all sums which the [Company] may incur and/or pay to a third party including but limited to legal costs, corporate and staff expenses and any settlement costs and/or costs to defend the matter and/or any costs, damages and/or losses awarded against them.

D.160

1.1 The [Company] agrees and accepts all the risk, responsibility and liability for ensuring that the [Films] and/or any part of the [Series] are free from and/or are at minimal risk of exposure to the threat of a legal action in any country in which it will be exploited due to its title, sound recording, content and/or marketing.

1.2 The [Company] shall not be entitled to seek any sum in payment from [Name] and/or his/her agent in respect of any civil and/or criminal proceedings and/or legal claim, action, summons and/or allegation that may occur at any time due to the promotion, marketing, transmission and exploitation of the [Films] and/or any part in the [Series] in which [Name] appears, contributes and/or has his/her name mentioned and/or any other reference in any form.

General Business and Commercial

D.161

The [Assignee] undertakes not to reproduce or misrepresent the commissioned [Work] in any way which is likely to bring [Name/Company/Brand] into disrepute and/or which is obscene and/or offensive and/or derogatory in nature.

D.162

In the event that the [Exhibitor], his/her representative and/or employees shall conduct themselves on the premises in a manner and/or verbally and/or in writing which is considered by the [Organisers] to be objectionable,

645

offensive, defamatory and/or likely to cause adverse publicity. Then the [Organisers] shall be entitled to request that the [Exhibitor] and his/her personnel vacate the premises immediately and shall be entitled to escort them off the premises and to arrange for the removal of his/her exhibition stand and marketing.

D.163

The [Company] reserves the right in its absolute discretion to cancel the [Contract] and not to fulfil its obligations for any good reason. This shall include, but not be limited to the following reasons in respect of the [Work/Material] where the [Company] considers that it is defamatory, pornographic, obscene, socially unacceptable, or otherwise against [Company] policy. The [Client] shall not be entitled to be repaid any sums already paid in the event that the contract is so cancelled.

D.164

To the best of the knowledge and belief of [Company] the [Work/Material] contains no content which would be defamatory under the laws of [specify country/state/geographic area].

D.165

The [Assignor] does not make any warranty and/or provide any undertakings as to whether any part of the [Artwork/Illustrations/Images] and/or the [Material] is obscene, offensive and/or defamatory and/or likely to lead to criminal or civil proceedings. The [Assignee] accepts full responsibility from the date of this Agreement for any subsequent consequences arising from its exploitation by the [Assignee] of the [Artwork/Illustrations/Images] under this agreement.

D.166

The [Company] shall be entitled to edit, delete, erase, remove, change and/or alter any content and/or material which on the advice of its professional legal advisors is considered defamatory, in contempt of court, obscene, is an incitement to political unrest, war and/or acts of terrorism, offensive, dangerous, misleading, factually incorrect and/or an infringement of copyright, trade marks, domain names and/or is otherwise considered to be prejudicial to the commercial interests of the [Company].

D.167

The [Company] shall be under no obligation to reproduce, display, exhibit, publish, distribute and/or otherwise use and/or exploit any content and/or material which in the view of the [Company] is defamatory, obscene, offensive, or which could bring the [Company] into disrepute and/or prejudice its business.

D.168

All [Exhibitors] are warned and advised not to make any defamatory statements and/or allegations and/or representations and/or carry out any actions concerning the products, business practices and/or marketing of any other company and/or third party and/or any member of the public. The [Organisers] do not accept any liability and/or responsibility for any summons, claims, complaints and/or legal action that may be made against you and/or any member of your staff on your stand and/or elsewhere at any time. The [Exhibitors] reserve the right to provide any assistance and/or information and/or security films they think fit to any third party without a court order.

Internet, Websites and Apps

D.169

The [Company] shall be obliged to take out an annual policy in respect of the threat of any allegation of defamation in any one case for a minimum of [number/currency] at its sole cost. In the event that the [Company] is unable to obtain defamation insurance then it must develop a robust and effective policy to deal with allegations and/or complaints at an early stage to minimise the risk and costs. The [Company] must appoint an adjudicator to deal with such matters who has the authority to initiate removal of material from the [Website/App/Platform].

D.170

The [Licensee] undertakes not to use or permit the [Film/Video/Podcast] and/or any parts to be used and/or exploited in any manner which is likely to mock, denigrate, be defamatory of [Name] and/or any other person and/or be associated with other material which is offensive, obscene and/or involved in any political and/or activist campaign and/or creates an impression that [Name] endorses a product and/or service and/or is a supporter and/or sponsor for any reason at any time.

D.171

This [Film/Video/Podcast] and the right to reproduce and exploit it in [specify format/type of unit] is provided to the [Licensee] without any undertaking or commitment as to the suitability of the title or content for any country as to whether the material will be considered by the laws of any country to be obscene, offensive, defamatory, derogatory, in contempt of court, an infringement of copyright, or otherwise in breach of any laws, regulations, directives, codes or practices. The [Licensee] shall not seek to recover any sums, fines, penalties, costs and/or legal expenses from the [Licensor] in respect of any allegation and/or claim and/or other consequence at any time. The [Licensee] agrees that no indemnity is provided by the [Licensor] and that the [Licensee] reproduces, supplies, distributes and exploits the [Film/Video/Podcast] at its own risk and cost.

D.172

You agree that you shall not submit, send and/or enter any material whether words, images, graphics, logos, lyrics, films, sound recordings, or otherwise which could be construed as defamatory, derogatory, insulting, rude, obscene, violent or an incitement to violence, offensive and/or reveal any personal details and/or confidential information relating to any third party. Where there is any breach of this clause the [Company] shall remove, delete and erase all such material and shall seek to be indemnified by you for any allegations, claim, legal action and/or settlement including damages, losses and/or legal costs and expenses incurred that may arise from the material you submitted.

D.173

The [Company] has made it a requirement that all contributors to this [Website/App/Platform] read and abide by the conditions of clause [–]. The [Company] monitors the [Website/App/Platform] and deletes any inappropriate material and allows users to report incidents to the [Company]. The [Company] advises any person or business who wishes to complain about any content to inform the [Company] as soon as possible. We will then correct or delete the material. Where you institute legal proceedings and you lose the action we will seek to reclaim all our legal costs from you.

D.174

The [Contributor] agrees and undertakes not to supply and/or to upload to the [Website/App/Platform] and/or any part any material of any nature whether words, images, graphics, logos, lyrics, films, sound recordings, photographs, drawings, music and/or otherwise which is contrary to the policy of the [Company]. That the [Company] shall be entitled to remove, delete, bar, block and/or to refuse access to the [Website/App/Platform] by the [Contributor] whether free and/or as part of a paid for service where the [Contributor] is in breach of the policy of the [Company] as follows:

1.1 All and/or any part of the material is likely to be defamatory, obscene, offensive, abusive, intended to bully and mock, derogatory, insulting, rude, violent and/or an incitement to violence, riots, acts of terrorism and/or war and/or to create anarchy and/or revolt against the government in any country.

1.2 The material and/or any part of it reveals personal data regarding a child who is under [number] years of age.

1.3 The material and/or any part of it reveals personal data of a third party without consent of that person.

1.4 The material and/or any part of it has been disclosed in breach of contract, and/or licence and/or is in contempt of court and/or contrary to any legislation.

1.5 The material and/or any part of it infringes the copyright, trade marks, database rights, domain name, computer software rights, intellectual property rights and/or other rights of a third party.

1.6 The material and/or any part of it has already damaged and/or may impact negatively on the reputation of the [Company] and/or any third party associated with the [Company] in any manner.

1.7 The material and/or any part of it is misleading, factually inaccurate and/or against the commercial interests of the [Company] and/or any third party associated with the [Company].

D.175
[Name] agrees and undertakes not to make any comment, statement, innuendo and/or contribute any material in any form as text, words, sounds, images, photographs, films, videos, caricatures, gestures and/or otherwise to the [Blog/Podcast/Series] which is likely to be and/or is in fact defamatory, offensive, derogatory and/or demeaning of any person whether or not [Name] knows and/or believes such material to be true or not.

D.176
[Name] agrees that he/she must abide by the [Company] policy of clearing in advance all programme material for use with [specify name/role] in the event that he/she expects that it may be defamatory, controversial and/or cause a strong political reaction from any party and/or campaigning group. [Name] agrees that he/she shall not be entitled to seek legal and/or other advice on matters relating to programme material from any third party without permission. That where [specify name/role] at the [Company] indicates that there should be a delay and/or further verification of the source that this should be adhered to until formal authorisation is provided. Failure to comply with the policy will be considered a breach of this agreement and entitle the [Company] to terminate the agreement with [Name].

D.177
The [Contributor] agrees and undertakes that he/she shall not use any facts and/or information in the [Interview/Film/Article] which he/she knows to be untrue and shall not make any allegations, statements and/or suppositions which could potentially be defamatory of any person and/or company and/or brand.

649

D.178

[Name] accepts and agrees that he/she must follow the schedule and script provided by the [Company] for the [Series/Podcast]. That [Name] is not permitted to add any personal material and/or statements regarding a third party. [Name] agrees and undertakes that he/she shall not make any defamatory, obscene, offensive and/or abusive statements on the [Series/Podcast]. [Name] accepts that where he/she does so that it shall be a fundamental breach of the agreement and the [Company] may automatically terminate the agreement with immediate effect.

D.179

Where any member of the public in the audience and/or ringing in and/or otherwise makes a statement which is defamatory, offensive, threatening and/or is otherwise deemed unacceptable by the [Company]. Then the [Company] shall be entitled to remove the member of the public under secure escort from the premises and/or terminate the call and issue an apology to any listeners for their conduct and actions.

Merchandising and Distribution

D.180

The [Supplier] agrees that it shall be the decision of the [Seller] as to the nature and form of the images, displays, texts, marketing and exploitation of the [Products] on the [Website/App/Platform]. Provided that the combined effect shall not:

1.1 Be defamatory, offensive, demeaning or derogatory of the [Supplier] and/or its products and/or any third party.

1.2 Expose the [Supplier] to any allegation of breach of industry standards and practice by a government agency or authority.

1.3 Expose the [Supplier] to any civil or criminal legal actions, claims or allegations.

D.181

The supply of the [Product] by the [Company] to [Name] on loan for the purpose of [specify] shall be on the basis that [Name] agrees not to use, display, exhibit, adapt or present the [Product] in any media in a manner which is offensive, defamatory, derogatory, misleading, violent, dangerous, or damaging to the sales of the [Product], the business interests of the [Company] and/or its brands.

D.182

The [Supplier] agrees and undertakes to advise the [Distributor] of any serious allegations that may be made concerning the [Work/Product/Service] where the advice of professional legal advisors have been sought and they have reached the conclusion that there is a real risk that the allegations may result in adverse publicity and/or withdrawal and/or cancellation of production of the [Work/Product/Service] and/or identify a serious health and safety risk to the public.

D.183

The [Distributor] agrees that where it becomes aware of any negative, defamatory and/or other statements from the public including any customers which concern any aspect of the [Product/Work] and its packaging and marketing which may affect sales, result in features on television and/or radio and/or on the internet and/or create an impact on any of the brands owned and/or controlled by the [Supplier]. That the [Distributor] agrees and undertakes to inform the [Supplier] in each case and shall co-operate with them in respect of any strategy which may be developed to deal with the matter. Provided that all costs and expenses in each case shall be paid for by the [Supplier] and not the [Distributor].

D.184

The [Licensor] confirms that the [Characters/Artwork/Samples] do not contain any text, images, slogans, costumes, graphics and/or other material which is obscene, defamatory and/or offensive and/or is in breach of any legislation in [country].

D.185

The [Licensee] agrees and undertakes that none of the products and/or services which are to be created and developed under this agreement relating to the exploitation of the [Characters/Books/Sound Recordings] which are intended for the children's market shall contain any text, slogan, title, images, graphics, music, logos, trademarks, packaging and/or marketing material which are or could be construed as unsuitable for children, misleading, defamatory, obscene, likely to corrupt and/or be offensive.

D.186

The [Licensee] agrees and undertakes to arrange and pay for insurance cover for the exploitation of the [Product] based on the [Work] which shall cover product liability, and any claim for personal injury, death, defamation, and/or any criminal and/or civil proceedings rising form the exploitation of the [Product] in any country during the Licence Period.

D.187

The [Distributor] agrees and undertakes not that the [Work/Product] and/or any packaging, marketing and advertising shall only be reproduced in the exact format agreed with the [Licensor] prior to supply to the retailers and/

or the public. In the event there are any changes, additions and/or deletions which result in an allegation of defamation, infringement of copyright and/or trade mark and/or any other intellectual property rights. Then any sums due as costs and/or expense and/or as payment for any damages shall be the responsibility of the [Distributor] and not the [Licensor].

D.188

The [Licensee] and any distributor, sub-licensee and agent agree not to make any allegations against any third party and/or competitor regarding a competing product and/or work. The [Licensee] shall not have the right to include the name of the [Licensor] in any press release which has not been approved by the [Licensor]. Where defamatory allegations against the [Work/Product] are made by a third party of which the [Licensee] and any distributor, sub-licensee and agent becomes aware at any time. The [Licensee] shall notify the details to the [Licensor]. The [Licensee] agrees that it shall not take any legal action and/or release any press statement regarding the allegations without prior consultation with the [Licensor]. All the administrative and legal costs of dealing with any such allegation shall be paid by the party that incurred the cost. All damages and costs in settlement to a third party shall be split between exactly between the parties.

D.189

All the title, text, photographs and other contents of the [Interview/Book/Service/Sound Recordings] have been reviewed and cleared of any legal problems for defamation, copyright clearances and payments, trade mark infringement, passing off and other potential threats of legal actions and/or claims. The [Licensor] provides an assurance and agreement that it shall deal with any matters which arise from the exact reproduction of all the material supplied by the [Licensor] at any time. Provided that the [Licensee] passes all such matters directly to the [Licensor] to deal with as they think fit and the [Licensor] is not required to consult with the [Licensee] regarding any settlement. The [Licensee] agrees that it shall not seek to be paid any legal costs by the [Licensor] that it may incur at any time.

D.190

Any sub-licensee and/or distributor shall be liable for any action and/or claim that may be made against it arising from this agreement at its own risk and cost. Any sub-licensee and/or distributor must agree to waive all claims against the [Licensor] and [Licensee] arising from the distribution, supply, sale and exploitation of the [Material/Products/Service] and/or any promotion and/or marketing.

Publishing

D.191

The [Author] undertakes to the [Publisher] that the draft manuscript, agreed proofs and final edited version of the [Book] shall not contain any information, data, statements, images, photographs, source references, maps, infographics and/or any other material which is misleading, inaccurate, not verified by supporting evidence, and/or which is supposition rather than fact and/or which is obscene, defamatory and/or likely to lead to civil and/or criminal proceedings against the [Publisher] and/or any distributor.

D.192

The [Author] undertakes that the synopsis and the [Script/Images/Sound Recordings] do not contain any obscene, offensive or defamatory material and will not expose the [Agent/Company] to civil or criminal proceedings in [country] from [date] to [date].

D.193

The [Author] confirms that the [Article/Manuscript/Book] does not and will not contain any obscene, offensive, defamatory, blasphemous, sexual or racially prejudiced material which is against the law. Nor will the [Article/Manuscript/Book] incite violence, riot and/or other unlawful activity. The [Author] agrees and undertakes that the [Article/Manuscript/Book] does not and will not contain any statements, photographs, drawings, formulae or other material which is likely to or will threaten or expose the [Publisher/Distributor] to any criminal, civil and/or other proceedings of any nature whether in the licensed Territory and/or elsewhere in the world at any time. The [Author] shall not be responsible for any material of any nature contributed by the [Publisher/Distributor] whether text, drawings, cover, photographs, index or otherwise. The [Publisher/Distributor] shall be solely liable for any civil or criminal proceedings threatened and/or which may arise as a result of their editing, translation or other contribution to the [Article/Manuscript/Book] at any stage in any part of the world whether by themselves directly or as a result of the actions of any sub-agent, sub-licensee and/or sub-distributor and/or any further third party engaged by the [Publisher/Distributor].

D.194

The [Author] confirms that the [Blog/Report] does not and will not contain any material which is obscene, offensive, and/or defamatory, and/or will commit any breach of privacy, contract and/or duty of confidence and/or be in contempt of court and/or violate any laws and/or expose the [Publisher] to civil and/or criminal proceedings throughout the Territory during the Licence Period.

D.195

The [Author] has reasonable knowledge to believe that the [Manuscript/Book/Report] does not contain any text, image or other material which is likely to result in legal action by any third party. However no assurances are given as to the content of any type and it is for the [Publisher/Distributor] to take its own legal advice as to defamation, obscenity, contempt of court, breach of confidence, contract or privacy and any other threatened claim or action that may arise whether civil or criminal. The [Publisher] shall bear all the risk, cost, expenses and damages and shall not be entitled to seek to recover any sums or contribution from the [Author].

D.196

The [Author] confirms and undertakes that to the best of his/her knowledge and belief the facts and information contained in the [Script/Book/Article] will be and are true and accurate except where material is supplied or included at the request of the [Publisher/Distributor].

D.197

The [Assignee] agrees and undertakes that the [Work] and the [Artwork] and the material in Schedule A will not be used, adapted and/or exploited in conjunction with any other material by any method in any medium which could be construed under any legal system in the world as obscene, offensive, defamatory and/or derogatory of any person. That the [Assignee] agrees and undertakes not to damage the reputation of the [Author] and/or to cause any other losses and/or to cause the [Author] to be joined in any civil and/or criminal proceedings in any country.

D.198

The [Licensor] confirms that the [Extracts] have been reviewed by their legal advisors for legal problems prior to the proposed publication of the [Work/Book] in hardback. The [Licensor] does not accept responsibility for any legal action that may arise from the publication of the [Extracts] by the [Licensee] and the [Licensee] must seek its own specialist advice in respect of the threat of potential claims and/or actions by any third party.

D.199

The [Authors] shall not be liable for any sums due in respect of any civil and/or criminal legal actions, claims, allegations, settlements and/or other consequences that may arise from the publication and exploitation of the [Work/Book/Manuscript] and any associated material by the [Publishers] including but not limited to defamation, infringement of copyright and/or trade marks, breach of contract and confidentiality and/or any other rights by any third party at any time.

D.200

1.1 The [Publisher] agrees and undertakes to the [Contributor] that the [Publisher] and not the [Contributor] shall bear all liability, risk and cost of any allegations of defamation and/or any civil and/or criminal proceedings in respect of any material of any nature submitted by the [Contributor] and then published, used and/or adapted and/or distributed by the [Publisher].

1.2 That where the [Contributor] is also made the subject of any allegations, action and/or claim that the [Publisher] agrees that it shall fund directly in advance all the costs and expenses that may be incurred in respect of the administration, investigation and provision of legal and professional advice, reports and the cost of litigation and any awarded damages and/or losses and costs. This obligation shall cease on [date].

1.3 The [Contributor] agrees that where further evidence is required by the [Publisher] in any form including but not limited to emails, telephone and mobile records, documents, images and any other medium. That the [Contributor] shall assist at the [Publisher's] cost provided he/she is paid an additional fee for their services.

D.201

No responsibility and/or liability is accepted by the [Publisher/Distributor] and/or any parent company, distributor, sub-licensee and/or other third party for any information which is distorted, misrepresented and/or defamatory of any person and/or business which is included in any [Work/Article/Blog] and/or posted and/or reproduced as an extract. The [Publisher/Distributor] will without notice exercise the right to delete, amend, alter and/or remove any material including text and images which it has decided in its opinion are likely to result in an allegation and/or claim [whether this is based on the advice of a legally qualified person or not.]

Services

D.202

The [Actor] confirms that the product of his/her services will not contain any obscene, offensive or defamatory material and will not expose the [Agent] and/or his/her employees and/or representatives to any criminal or civil proceedings except where any material is included at the request of the [Agent] and/or a third party for whom the [Agent] has agreed the work on behalf of the [Actor].

D.203

The [Originator] confirms that the services will not contain any obscene, offensive and/or defamatory material and will not expose the [Company] to any civil and/or criminal proceedings except for any information, data and/or material supplied by, created and/or included at the request of the [Company].

D.204

1.1 The [Company] agrees that the [Presenter] shall only be responsible for any costs, losses and/or damages which arises directly from a serious breach of this agreement by the [Presenter] during the Term of this Agreement and that any claim by the [Company] shall be limited to a maximum of [number/currency].

1.2 The [Company] agrees that the [Presenter] shall not be liable to the [Company] and does not provide any indemnify to the [Company] in relation to any matter concerning the production, transmission, broadcast and/or exploitation of the [Programme/Series] in any media and/or format including but not limited to television, the internet and/or merchandising. The [Company] shall be entirely responsible for the production, distribution and exploitation of the [Programme/Series] which shall be entirely at the [Company's] cost and risk. The [Company] shall arrange an insurance policy to cover as a far as possible public liability, defamation, obscenity, breach of confidence, infringement of copyright, trade marks, contracts and any other matter for the benefit of the [Company] [and the [Presenter]] at the [Company's] cost.

D.205

The [Presenter] undertakes that all the product of his/her services under this agreement shall not contain any obscene, defamatory, offensive, abusive and/or mocking material and/or make any statement which incites violence and/or attacks any religion and/or wear any item and/or display any product and/or make reference to any person, company and/or brand which is an endorsement and/or promotes and/or advertises a product and/or service which would breach the codes of practice and standards of [specify organisation] and/or expose the [Company] to a fine, penalty and/or the risk of losing their licence and/or any civil and/or criminal proceedings. This clause shall not apply to any matter which is included at the request of the [Company]. The total liability of the [Presenter] shall be limited to [number/currency] and any other sums over this amount shall be paid for by the [Company].

D.206

The [Company] agrees that [Name] shall have the right to refuse to perform and/or request that the [script/dialogue] be changed where [Name] is asked to perform any material where the words and/or actions are obscene, racist, offensive, defamatory, degrading and/or impact on the reputation of [Name].

D.207

In consideration of the Fees [Name] has agreed to be interviewed and contribute to [specify Article/Film/Video] by the [Author/Producer] engaged by the [Company].

The [Company] agrees and undertakes that:

1.1 The [Company] shall be responsible for and shall ensure that there are no legal problems prior to the use of the material contributed by [Name] to the [Article/Film/Video].

1.2 [Name] shall not be liable to the [Company] in respect of any claim for defamation, libel, obscenity, breach of any laws, codes of practice and/or any infringement of copyright and/or any other matter which arises from the use, production, supply and exploitation of the [Article/Film/Video] at any time.

1.3 That the [Company] shall bear the cost and indemnify [Name] in respect of any costs, expenses, damages, losses and/or legal fees that may arise from the use of the material contributed by [Name] to the [Article/Film/Video] by the [Company].

D.208

The [Contributor] agrees and undertakes that he/she shall not during the course of the [Programme/Interview/Presentation]:

1.1 make any statement, allegation, threat and/or incite violence, war and/or riot and/or any other public disorder.

1.2 represent any facts as true which he/she knows to be false.

1.3 claim ownership of any material of any nature which he/she knows to belong to another person and/or third party.

1.4 claim that he/she is the original creator of a work which is in fact based on the work of another person and/or company.

1.5 attribute any material and/or work to another person and/or company which is incorrect and/or deliberately false.

D.209

The [Company] agrees that any legal problems which may arise from the use of the [Films/Sound recordings/Images/Service] supplied by [Name] shall be the sole responsibility of the [Company] and that [Name] shall not be liable for any use, exploitation and/or adaptation by the [Company] at any time. The [Company] acknowledges and agrees that no undertakings have been provided by [Name] as to the ownership and/or copyright clearances and/or any other rights payments and/or sums that may be and/or become due.

Sponsorship

D.210

The [Sponsor] and the [Sportsperson] both undertake and agree that neither party shall do anything and/or authorise any third party to carry out any action and/or make any statement and/or distribute any material which might reasonably be expected to damage the reputation of the other party. If notified of an unacceptable matter then both parties agree that they shall work together in good faith to minimise the damage which shall include withdrawal and destruction of material if required and payment of compensation and costs.

D.211

The [Sportsperson] agrees to provide his/her services to the best of their skill and ability to ensure the fulfilment of this agreement. The [Sportsperson] shall conduct his/her public and private life in such a manner that they are not damaging the reputation of the [Sponsor], its business, products and/or services. The [Sportsperson] undertakes not to make any defamatory statement regarding the [Sponsors] and/or not to criticize the [Sponsors] in public and/or any of their products and/or services and/or any partners and/or or other persons associated with them during the Term of this Agreement.

D.212

1.1   There are no undertakings provide in this agreement as to the conduct, actions, publications, films, recordings, photographs, images, slogans, words or other behaviour or communications, interviews, work, or private life of [Name] and/or his/her family and none should be implied.

1.2   This agreement is not intended to provide any such undertakings and/or constraints and/or to provide any indemnity to the [Company] for any allegation of defamation against [Name] and/or the [Company] or any civil or criminal proceedings.

1.3   Each party shall bear their own costs, expenses, losses, damages, penalties and legal costs in respect of any allegations, claims, proceedings and/or settlements including any adverse impact on their business interests and loss of reputation.

D.213

The [Sponsor] shall not be responsible for the conduct, actions and statements of [Name] and their agent nor for any behaviour, acts and/or words which are defamatory, offensive, obscene, threatening and/or causes damages and/or losses directly or indirectly to any person, company and/or or property. Whether at an event, conference, press launch and/or other occasion organised by or on behalf of the [Sponsor].

D.214

The [Sponsor] shall be responsible and bear the cost of any allegations and/or settlement and/or claims in respect of any threat, abuse, violence, defamation and/or other misconduct caused by any director, personnel, guest, casual staff, consultants and/or other third party arranged by the [Sponsor] for the [Event/Exhibition]. The [Company] shall not be responsible for any such matters and shall not be obliged to make any contribution to such sums that may be incurred.

D.215

The [Company] shall not be responsible for any legal problems whether defamation, obscenity, breach of any laws, breach of any codes of practice and/or guidelines and/or any breach of contracts and/or civil and/or criminal proceedings which may arise from the products, services and work provided by the [Sponsor] under this agreement. The [Sponsor] shall be entitled to deal with all such matters without the approval of the [Company] at its own cost. The [Company] shall be entitled to be paid for any services and/or administrative support that may be requested by the [Sponsor] together with any legal costs.

D.216

The [Sponsor] agrees and undertakes that neither it nor any of its employees, consultants and agents shall use the [Event] and/or any associated promotional and/or marketing material in any media to make any derogatory and/or defamatory reference and/or statement concerning any other person and/or business in competition with and/or with whom the [Sponsor] may have any dispute and/or legal action and/or otherwise. The [Sponsor] agrees that if for any reason it should breach this clause that the [Company] shall be entitled to terminate this agreement with the [Sponsor]. That in such event the [Sponsor] shall still be obliged to pay all the sums due in clause [–].

D.217

The [Sponsor] shall not be held liable for any acts, words, statements, allegations, threats and/or any claim for defamation and/or any civil and/or criminal proceedings and/or disciplinary actions against any member of the teams and/or management at the [Club]. Nor shall the [Club] be entitled to seek any contribution and/or payment by the [Sponsor] towards any such costs, expenses, losses, damages and/or legal costs that may arise in dealing with such matters.

D.218

Where a member of a team which is funded by the [Sponsor] makes derogatory, offensive, defamatory and//or abusive statements and/or threats to any other competing team members at any time during the duration of this agreement. The [Management] agree to institute an enquiry to validate the facts of the matter. If it is found that any such team member has acted in such a manner then they shall be suspended for a minimum of [number] months and fined a minimum of [number/currency] per month. The [Management] also agree to make a payment to a charity agreed with the [Sponsor] and to issue and agreed public statement regarding the matter.

University, Charity and Educational

D.219

The [Institute] confirms that the [Work/Report] will be reviewed by their legal advisors for legal and defamation problems prior to the proposed publication and/or distribution. The [Institute] accepts full responsibility for all costs and expenses from any legal action that may arise from the publication, distribution and/or any other exploitation of the [Work] by the [Institute]. The [Institute] shall not seek to recover any sums from the fees and/or royalties due to [Name].

D.220

The [Contributor] shall be liable for any sums due and/or paid to a third party by the [Institute/Charity] in respect of any civil and/or criminal legal actions, defamation, copyright infringement, claims, allegations or consequences that may arise from the reproduction and exploitation of the [Logo/Material/Product] by the [Institute/Charity]. The total liability of the [Contributor] shall be limited to [number/currency].

D.221

The [Institute/Charity] shall not be responsible and/or liable for the [Enterprise] and/or their representatives and/or any behaviour, acts, words and/or statements which are defamatory, offensive, obscene, threatening, and/or any damages, losses, settlement and/or other costs and/or expenses and/or any other sums which may arise as a result of any complaint and/or civil and/or criminal proceedings.

D.222

The [Contributor] undertakes that all the product of her/his services under this agreement shall not contain any obscene, offensive and/or defamatory material and/or anything which infringes the copyright and/or rights of a third party and/or promotes and/or advertises any service and/or product and/or political party and/or any other material which would breach the codes of practice of [specify organisation] known as [specify code] a copy of which is attached in appendix A. This clause shall not apply where the material is specifically incorporated at the request of the [Institute/Charity].

D.223

1.1 The [Consultant] confirms that the product of her/his services will not contain any malicious, obscene, defamatory and/or other material which infringes the rights of a third party. The [Consultant] agrees that he/she must not act in any manner and/or supply any material which would expose the [Institute/Charity] and/or its employees, trustees, representatives and/or agents to any criminal or civil proceedings in [specify country].

1.2 The [Institute/Charity] shall not be under any obligation to reproduce, distribute and/or otherwise use and/or exploit any material which in the view of the [Institute/Charity] is likely to bring the [Institute] into disrepute, damage its reputation and/or is believed to be defamatory.

D.224

1.1 The [Contributor] agrees that he/she shall be personally liable for any presentation, statement and/or words and/or acts and/or text, images and/or other material that he/she may use, distribute, supply, reproduce and/or make available in any form at the [Event/Exhibition] and/or at any time thereafter.

1.2 That no material in 1.1 has been approved and /or reviewed by the [Institute/Charity] and that no liability and/or responsibility is accepted by the [Institute/Charity] for any allegation of defamation and/or any other complaint, claim, summons and/or legal action that may directly arise. That the [Institute/Charity] shall in any case in which it is involved be entitled to settle the matter as it thinks fit and without any consultation with [Name].

DELIVERY

Film, Television and Video

D.225

The [Company] shall deliver to the [Customer] at such address in [England] as the [Customer] may specify [Units/Discs] as required as soon as practicable after receipt of a written order but within not more than [thirty] days of the order. The written order shall specify the [film/format/quantity/ delivery address/date/payment method/date/cost of delivery].

D.226

The risk in any [Units/Games/Discs] delivered to the [Customer] by the [Company] shall pass immediately upon delivery to the [Customer] but the

661

property shall remain with the [Company] until all sums due to the Company have been paid by the [Customer].

D.227

The delivery date provided by the [Company] is for guidance only and may vary according to availability of the [Unit/Product], the delivery method, and the country of destination. The [Customer] agrees that they shall not have the right to make any claim against nor seek to be indemnified by the [Company] for any delay or default in delivery which results in losses, expenses, or costs to the [Customer] or a third party. The [Company's] liability shall be limited to a full refund of the payment made by the [Customer].

D.228

Prior to the reproduction of the final master copy of the [Disc] of the sound recordings which shall include any copyright notices, credits and other information on the label. The [Company] shall at its sole cost supply a complete copy to the [Author/Composer/Performer] at [address] and/or arrange for a suitable date and/or time for them to listen to and/or analyse the content, label and cover of the [Disc]. The prior written approval of the [Author/Composer/Performer] shall be needed before the [Company] has the authority and/or right to reproduce, distribute and/or supply the copies of the [Disc] to any third party.

D.229

The [Client] agrees that where delivery is not by registered and/or recorded delivery and paid for by the [Client] as an additional cost and is sent by normal post. That the [Company] shall not be liable for the failure of the order to arrive where the [Company] can produce evidence of posting the [Unit/Product].

D.230

1.1 [Name] shall arrange and pay for delivery to the [Company] at [address] on [date] before [time] [number] copies of the [Film/Video/Sound Recordings] in [format/size] which is suitable for use and reproduction in conjunction with [specify gadget/device].

1.2 [Name] agrees that no charge shall be made to the [Company] for delivery.

1.3 The [Company] agrees to pay [Name] the sum of [number/currency] on [date] by [direct debit to bank account/method] in consideration of the delivery of the material in 1.1.

D.231

1.1 The [Licensor] shall at the [Licensor's] cost and risk deliver to the [Licensee's] offices at [address] or such other offices as the [Licensee] may at any time designate, the material described in clause [–] by [date].

1.2 Within [specify period] after delivery the [Licensee] will review such material in 1.1 and verify that a suitable copy of the [Film/Video] satisfactory to the [Licensee] can been made. The [Licensee] shall notify the [Licensor] of any defects and the [Licensor] shall promptly remedy such defects at the [Licensors] cost and deliver a replacement as soon as possible.

D.232

Each of the parties shall keep the other fully informed as to the [Film/Video] material which is available and shall promptly on demand supply original or copies of such prints, videotapes, films, DVDs, recordings, sound recordings, discs, scripts, credit and copyright notice lists, lyrics, trailers, promotions, music, publicity material and music cue sheets as may be reasonably required for the exercise of the rights granted in this agreement. Provided that the party requesting such items shall:

1.1 make its own arrangements for the collection, freight handling, customs duties, taxes and insurance of all such items at its own expense.

1.2 reimburse the party supplying the items with all costs incurred in supplying such items including reproduction costs.

D.233

The [Licensor] agrees to deliver to the [Licensee] by [date] the original English language master of the [Series] together with the material and documents referred to in Schedule A which have been created and/or filmed and/or recorded in making the [Series] whether used or not including all video recordings, sound recordings, negatives, unused takes, off-cuts and any other copies.

D.234

The [Company] shall have the right to approve the rough cut of the [Film/Video] and for this purpose it is agreed that [specify format] shall be sent by the [Distributor] at its cost to the [Company's] representative on or by [date].

D.235

The [Licensor] shall deliver to the [Company] at the [Licensor's] sole cost and expense on or by [date] the following material of the [Film/Video] to be held by the [Company] for the Term of the Agreement:

1.1   Technically acceptable master material in [format].

1.2   Associated sound recordings, music, photographs, graphics, computer generated material, rules, questions and answers, slogans and catchphrases.

1.3   Lists of credits, copyright notices, moral rights and other contractual obligations including royalty payments and clearance costs.

1.4   Advertising, promotional, posters, telephone line and website marketing and catalogues.

D.236

It is agreed that within [fourteen] days of full signature of this agreement the [Company] shall arrange for the delivery of the following master material on loan to the [Licensee]: [specify items/format]. The [Licensee] is authorised to make copies of the master material for the purposes of this agreement at the [Licensee's] cost. Once completed the [Licensee] shall return the original master material to the [Company] at the [Licensee's] sole cost.

D.237

1.1   All master material supplied shall be in first class condition and shall be to the technical standard required by the [Distributor] with all commercial breaks removed.

1.2   In the event that the [Distributor] rejects any material on the grounds of unsatisfactory technical quality the [Licensor] shall use its best endeavours to provide acceptable replacement material as required by the [Distributor].

1.3   The [Licensor] shall use its best endeavours to provide copies of the full length version of the [Series]. In the event that the [Licensor] is unable to supply acceptable material of any of the [Series] as required by the [Distributor] and/or the [Licensor] is unable to provide any full length version of an acceptable substitute then the [Distributor] shall be entitled to repayment of all the sums paid to the [Licensor] for the [Series] together with any additional costs and expenses already incurred by the [Distributor] in respect of the [Series].

D.238

The [Production Company] shall deliver the scripts and storyboard of the [Advertisement/Film/Podcast/] to the [Company] for approval on or before the following dates:

The draft scripts [date]. The final script [date]. The storyboard [date].

D.239

The [Production Company] shall deliver the [Advertisement/Film/Podcast] Master Material to the [Commissioning Company] on or before [date].

D.240

The [Company] agrees that the [Author/Contributor] shall be entitled to approve the draft format, sample and final version and shall deliver them to the [Author/Contributor] for approval on or before the following dates:

Draft format: [date]. Sample: [date]. Final version: [date].

D.241

The [Assignor/Production Company] shall deliver the rough edited version of the [Documentary] for approval to the [Assignee] at the [Assignee's] cost as follows: Format [specify material] on or before [date] to [address].

D.242

Unless the [Licensee] advises the [Company] that the material delivered is incomplete, technically unacceptable, or incorrect within [three] calendar months]. Then the material shall be deemed to have been accepted.

D.243

The [Company] shall deliver one new and clean copy of the [Programme/ Film] in [specify format] in the [specify] language to [address] in [country]. Together with a list of the cast and all credits, copyright notices, trademarks, music, sponsors and other third parties and specify how and when they must be acknowledged in any marketing and promotion. Together with a statement as to any restrictions and/or prohibitions as to the form of use of any content in any media which may apply.

D.244

Where the broadcast and/or transmission of [Programme/Series] is cancelled due to the failure of the [Company] to deliver suitable technical master material and/or to comply with the delivery dates. Then it is agreed that the [Distributor] shall have the right to terminate the agreement and refuse to arrange further dates for broadcast and/or transmission. The Company] must then return all of the sums paid by the [Distributor] to date relating to the [Programme/Series] within [number] months of any demand for repayment.

General Business and Commercial

D.245

If the completion date is not likely to be or has not been achieved the [Developer] shall immediately advise the [Company] of the cause of the delay in writing. The [Company] may decide to agree in writing to an extension of time by fixing a later date. If in the opinion of the [Company] it is not fair and reasonable to fix a later date the [Company] shall notify the [Developer] and specify the reasons for the refusal of the extension.

D.246

Both parties expressly agree that all specified dates for delivery of services and/or completion of work under this agreement are crucial and cannot be amended except due to circumstances beyond the reasonable control of either party which can be construed as having arisen as a result of force majeure.

D.247

1.1 Both parties agree that all the delivery, completion, payment and other dates set out in this agreement are not merely for guidance but are an important and material part of this agreement.

1.2 Further that failure by either party to comply with the dates shall be a fundamental breach of this agreement. In the event that for any reason either party should agree to a later date, then this shall not entitle the defaulting party to consider that all subsequent dates may also be delayed, and such dates shall remain the essence of this agreement.

D.248

The [Company] shall supply at its sole cost to the [Promoter] master copies of any material in its possession and/or control relating to [subject/name] which can be used for the purposes of this agreement which are set out in Appendix A: [Appendix A specify products, music and sound recordings, posters, photographs, artwork, scripts, films]. The [Company] shall also supply a list of any credits, acknowledgements, trademarks, logos, copyright notices and any music cue sheet which may be required.

D.249

'The Delivery Date' shall be [date] by which the [Agent] agrees to deliver the [Ingredients/Products/Material] to the [Company] at [address] at the [Agent's] cost and expense.

D.250

The [Company] agrees that the [Sample/Script/Material] is supplied on loan and shall remain the property of the [Agent]. The [Company] agrees and undertakes to return the [Sample/Script/Material] to the [Agent] by secure recorded delivery within [one] calendar month and shall not retain any copies in any format except those specified under this agreement.

D.251

[Products/Equipment/Displays] may not be delivered to and/or removed from the exhibition during the hours that it is open to the general public without the prior consent of the [Organisers]. All [Exhibitors] shall be responsible for the supply and removal of their own [Products/Equipment/Displays].

D.252

All [delivery/installation] dates are approximate only but every effort will be made to avoid delay. In the event that the [Products/Services] are not [delivered/installed] within [specify duration] it is accepted that the [Products/Services] shall not have been [delivered/installed] in accordance with the terms of this agreement.

D.253

No delivery will be accepted where any person and/or distributor has not paid for the full cost of freight, postage, customs duties and/or other taxes. All such products shall be returned to the sender and marked as undelivered and the [Company] shall not be liable for any such costs and expenses.

D.254

The [Distributor] confirms that the direct selling and marketing to the public will to the best of their knowledge and belief conform in all material requirements of any legislation, codes, guidelines, and standards voluntary or otherwise in the following countries: [–].

D.255

The [Distributor] agrees that the [Supplier] shall not be held responsible by the [Distributor] for any delay in delivery and/or failure of the [Product] to arrive at its destination for any reason including loss in transit, delivery to the wrong address and/or acceptance of delivery by an unknown third party and/or any other damages and/or losses, theft and/or otherwise once any [Products] are dispatched from the [Suppliers] premises by any of the following methods: [specify delivery methods/organisations].

D.256

Shipments shall be made to the delivery address unless notice in writing is received by the [Supplier] from the [Seller].

D.257

The [Seller] agrees that the [Supplier] shall be entitled to deal with, sell, loan, hire, distribute or otherwise exploit the [Product] at any time to any third parties whether on the internet or otherwise. Provided that the [Seller] shall not alter, adapt, vary, change or interfere with the [Product] including any packaging after receipt from the [Supplier] and before delivery to the third party.

D.258

Where the [Distributor] is unable to supply the [Product/Service] to the [Company] and delivery is to be delayed for more than [number] days. Then the [Company] shall have the right to terminate and/or cancel the delivery and to receive a full refund of all the payments made to date.

D.259

Both parties agree that where delivery and/or payment is delayed for any reason due to force majeure and/or any other reason. That they shall as far as reasonably possible without incurring any additional costs endeavour to mitigate the impact of the delay. Where the delay continues for more than [specify period]. Then the party who is not in default shall have the right to take such steps as may be necessary to terminate the agreement with immediate effect without prejudice to any outstanding claim under this agreement.

D.260

It is accepted that delivery may be delayed and the delivery dates adjusted at any time due to lack of ingredients and/or other production issues. The [Company] agrees that no failure to deliver by a specific date shall be grounds for termination unless there has been a complete failure to deliver [number] [weight] by [date].

D.261

All the delivery and/or supply of [Products/Services] by any agreed dates are an estimate and for guidance only and may be changed by the [Company] at any time. In the event that delivery and/or supply dates are changed then you will be allocated a new date as soon as possible. No sums are paid in compensation for failure to deliver and/or supply any [Products/Services] by any agreed dates. If delivery and/or supply is to be delayed more than [number] [weeks/months] then you shall have the right to terminate and/or cancel the agreement and be repaid any sums you have paid to date for the order. No additional sums shall be paid for any reason.

Internet, Websites and Apps

D.262

Delivery is only made within the following area [specify] at [fixed price]. All other deliveries shall be made in accordance with the quoted charge according to the circumstances which shall be agreed and paid in advance at the time of the order.

D.263

The person or company which placed the Order or an authorised representative will be requested to produce the [Reference/Order form] and shall be asked to check the condition of the [Products] on delivery and to sign an acknowledgement of receipt of delivery. We acknowledge that this acknowledgement does not constitute acceptance of the technical quality of the [Products].

D.264

No date, time and/or method of delivery can be guaranteed by the [Company] and/or that any advance notice will be provided. As far as possible we will contact you if the initial delivery date is to be changed. If the [Products] are returned due to non-delivery then an additional administrative and delivery cost will be charged for any further delivery dates if the [Customer] was unavailable to accept delivery.

D.265

The [Company] agrees to deliver and/or supply the [Products/Services] at the dates and times and/or duration agreed with the [Customer]. Where [Company] fails to fulfil any terms agreed for a period of more than [number] [days/weeks/months] then the [Customer] shall have the right to terminate and/or cancel the contract and be repaid a full refund of all sums paid to the [Company] for any [Products] not delivered and/or any period where the [Service] was not supplied. In the event that the [Customer] does not terminate and/or cancel the contract and another date and time and/or duration is substituted the [Company] agrees to provide the [Customer] with and additional [voucher/benefit].

D.266

1.1 The delivery dates for the supply of [Products/Services] are subject to variation and are only provided as guidance. The [Company] can only guarantee delivery next day and/or within [number] days if one of the following additional sums is paid for the [Client] to be provided with a recorded and/or registered delivery and/or courier delivery to the specified address in the [country]. [List price and type of delivery.]

1.2 Any delivery outside [country] will be by [freight/airmail/other] and the following choices are available at an additional cost. [List price and type of delivery.]

1.3 Insurance cover may be provided to cover the risk of loss and/or damage of the [Products/Services] whilst in transit at an additional cost. [List price and type of cover.]

D.267

Where the [Company] has been unable to deliver the Order due to an incorrect address and/or post code. Then an additional fee shall be paid to deliver the Order to any new address.

D.268

Delivery shall be at your own risk and cost unless you pay an additional fee for secure and signed for delivery. Where delivery is made to an address and signed for by any person who lives at that address and/or is employed by you in some capacity. Then delivery shall have been completed. Where there is any dispute regarding delivery then you must provide contact [specify person/email] and provide details within [number] days of the agreed delivery date.

D.269

1.1 You are strongly advised not to send any material to the [Company] which has not been specifically requested by the [Company]. Where any unsolicited material is sent to the [Company] by any person and/or other third party for any reason. The [Company] does not accept any liability for any failure for the material to arrive and/or for any loss and/or damage and/or theft and/or any other matter.

1.2 The [Company] does not store and/or return unsolicited material and it will be destroyed within [three] months.

D.270

Liability for delivery by the [Company] ends at the time of dispatch of the [Product] by the agreed method of delivery which you the [Purchaser] have paid for in advance. The [Company] will provide you the [Purchaser] with the dispatch details supplied by the [Courier/Shipment Agency]. It is your responsibility as the [Purchaser] to arrange insurance cover for any [Product] from the date and time of dispatch from the [Company] until it is delivered and accepted by you the [Purchaser]

D.271

Where you the [Seller] is shipping and/or sending and/or delivering any material and/or products to the [Distributor]. No liability and/or risk for delivery is accepted by the [Distributor] until the material and/or products have arrived at the delivery point and been accepted and processed by the [Distributor] as suitable for their intended and allocated a reference code.

Merchandising and Distribution

D.272

In the event that the [Supplier] fails to deliver the [Products/Material] in accordance with the list in Schedule A and/or by the delivery dates specified under clause [–] as agreed where time is of the essence. The [Purchaser] shall have the right to terminate this agreement with immediate effect by notice in writing by email to [email address]. The [Purchaser] shall not after termination be under any further obligation to the [Supplier] even where the circumstances have arisen due to force majeure. If this agreement is terminated on the grounds of failure to deliver all and/or part of the [Products] in accordance with this agreement the [Supplier] shall be liable to the [Purchaser] for all direct and indirect loss incurred by the [Purchaser] relating to such default. The [Supplier] shall repay all monies paid by the [Purchaser] to the [Supplier] for all [Products] not delivered and shall also pay all reasonable costs incurred by the [Purchaser] in obtaining the same or similar products from a third party.

D.273
The carriage and transport of the [Products/Units] shall be free on board [f.o.b.] which shall mean that all costs of whatever nature incurred in placing the packaged and secured [Products/Units] upon [name of vessel] shall be borne by the [Seller]. The [Seller] acknowledges that the [Seller] shall be responsible for any and all export duty and that until the [Products/Units] are actually on board the vessel that all property rights, risks and liabilities with respect to the [Products/Units] shall remain with the [Seller].

D.274
The [Seller] will replace free of charge any [Material] proved to the [Seller's] satisfaction to have been damaged in transit provided that within [twenty-eight] days after delivery both the [Seller] and the [carriers/couriers] have received from the [Purchaser] notification in writing of the damage.

D.275
The [Seller] shall only accept responsibility for the failure to delivery any [Products/Units] and/or any damage caused to the [Products/Units] in transit if within [number] days of the delivery date and/or the receipt of the damaged [Products/Units]. The [Customer] sends an email to the [Seller] specifying that the [Products/Units] have failed to arrive and/or are damaged. The [Customer] shall be required to [post/courier] the damaged [Products/Units] back to the [Seller] at the [Sellers] cost so that the [Seller] can inspect the damage. Where the [Seller] accepts responsibility for failure to deliver the [Products/Units] it shall immediately arrange a new delivery date with delivery at the [Seller's] cost. Where the [Seller] accepts the [Units/Products] were not damaged by the [Customer] then the [Seller] shall arrange for the delivery of a replacement with delivery charges paid for by the [Seller].

D.276

1.1 The [Company] shall promptly make shipment of the [Products/Units] after manufacture in each production month as agreed.

1.2 The [Company] shall not be responsible for the delay in production and/or shipment of the [Products/Units] and/or any other consequences whether arising from force majeure, shortage of supplies and/or otherwise.

1.3 Shipments shall be made to the addresses stated in the contract. The [Company] nevertheless may agree to changes to delivery addresses. In which case the cost of shipment and carriage shall be altered to cover increase costs and/or security.

D.277

The [Supplier] shall arrange and pay for all formalities involved in shipping, transfer, import and/or export as appropriate including packaging, storage, freight costs, customs duties, import and export taxes, product content verification, security checks, and any other matter required to comply with the laws, regulations, directives, codes, practices and standards of any country. Any documents required by the [Company] and confirmation of payment shall be provided by the [Supplier] upon request by the [Company].

D.278

The [Supplier] shall provide the [Company] at least [specify duration] before the [Products] are despatched ex-factory and in any event not later than the date of shipment with the following details of the products:

1.1 Number, dimensions, net weight, gross weight, with content and description. Together with a sample label on the product and packaging.

1.2 Date and place of shipment and method, with reference.

1.3 Date, method of importation, transportation and delivery address.

1.4 Value (pro forma invoice), setting out the ex-factory price of the unpackaged goods, packaging, carriage, duties, taxes and insurance costs in [currency] together with the reference numbers of the [items/products].

D.279

Each purchase order documentation shall be sent in triplicate, one attached to the material and package, the second sent to the receiving agent, and the third sent to the [Company]. If any purchase order is missing and/or delivery is delayed for any reason then all the consequential additional expenses, costs, losses and/or any other sums of any kind shall be at the [Supplier's] sole cost and expense.

D.280

The cost of the packaging, shipping, duties, taxes, carriage and insurance of the [Material/Units] shall be the sole responsibility of and entirely at the expense and risk of the [Company] and not the [Supplier].

D.281

1.1 The delivery dates and times quoted are for guidance and are only indicative of possible dates. All dates are subject to final confirmation by the [Company]. Delivery times and dates are not the essence of the contract even when the final delivery date is confirmed.

1.2 The [Company] shall not be liable for any losses, damages and/or costs and expenses incurred by the [Customer] whether arising from the failure to deliver and/or any delay and/or otherwise.

1.3 Delivery shall be to the name and address in the order form unless the [Customer] otherwise confirms in writing.

1.4 The [Customer] shall be obliged to notify in writing within [number] [days] of delivery to the agreed address any allegations and/or claim in respect of any defects, damage and/or error and/or omission in respect of any part of the order.

1.5 Unless it has been stated on the order that the order shall be fulfilled in one complete delivery. The [Company] shall be entitled to make deliveries by instalments of any part of the order.

D.282

1.1 Time is of the essence in the performance of the Purchase Order.

1.2 If delivery dates cannot be met the [Seller] shall promptly notify the [Company] of the earliest possible date for delivery. Despite that notice has been received and a new date offered. The [Company] shall not be obliged to agree a new delivery date.

1.3 The [Seller's] failure to delivery on the date specified in the Purchase Order shall entitle the [Company] if it shall so decide to cancel the Purchase Order. The [Company] shall be entitled to request a full refund of all sums paid.

1.4 The [Company] shall not however be entitled to hold the [Seller] liable for any losses and/or other additional costs that the [Company] has and/or may incur in finding a substitute order elsewhere. In any event the total liability of the [Seller] to the [Company] shall be equal to the cost of the Purchase Order which is up to a maximum of [number/currency].

D.283

A detailed Delivery Statement must accompany each consignment of [Products/Material/Ingredients]. A Delivery Statement signed by a duly authorised representative of the [Company] shall include an acknowledgment of the delivery subject to the terms of this contract. A copy shall be retained by the [Company].

D.284

The [Supplier] shall provide two copies of a detailed delivery statement with each consignment of the [Products]. The [Seller] shall sign the statement as accepted and agreed or as disputed by the [Seller]. One copy shall be retained by each party.

D.285

1.1 Time shall be of the essence of any Purchase Order placed by the [Company] and confirmed as accepted by the [Supplier/Distributor].

1.2 Delivery of the [Products] shall be at the [Supplier/Distributor's] own cost, risk and expense. If the [Products] are not packaged and/or stored correctly and/or deteriorate in transit due to equipment failure and/or delays in shipping and/or are stolen lost and/or damaged it shall be entirely at the liability and cost of the [Supplier/Distributor]. Delivery shall not take place until the [Products] have arrived at the destination stated on the Purchase Order.

1.3 In the event that the [Products] are not delivered in accordance with each agreed Purchase Order and/or by the specified agreed date in each case. Then the [Company] shall be entitled to cancel any such Purchase Order and to return all the [Products] at the [Supplier/Distributor's] cost and expense.

D.286

The [Supplier] shall deliver the [Products] in accordance with the delivery dates and quantities specified in accordance with Schedule A. Thereafter the [Supplier] shall provide each unit of the [Product] in accordance with the agreed format upon written request.

D.287

The [Supplier] will replace free of charge any products proved to the [Supplier's] reasonable satisfaction to have been lost and/or damaged in transit. Provided that within [three] days after acceptance of the delivery the [Supplier] has received notification in writing of the loss and/or damage.

D.288

1.1 It is agreed that any requested delivery date cannot be confirmed until the order is accepted by the [Company] and has been paid for in full by the customer.

1.2 Delivery dates may be changed due to weather conditions, transport problems, unexpected manufacture and/or packaging issues and/or any other reason. Where delivery is delayed for more than [number] days you may cancel the order and be provided with a full refund. No additional sums are paid for any other reason for any damages, losses and/or costs you may have incurred. The [Company] may offer at its discretion provide an additional voucher and/or discount against a future purchase.

D.289

If the delivery date relates to a purchase for a special occasion such as a wedding and/or birthday. Then you must make this clear on the order and request [specify special guaranteed delivery] and pay an additional sum of [number/currency] to have the delivery date and time of delivery confirmed as guaranteed by the [Distributor].

D.290

The [Company] undertakes to deliver to the [Licensee] a representation of the [Character/Logo/Artwork/Graphics] in two-dimensional form as an artistic work, in colour with such colour shades and dimensions as it may have been agreed together with [specify material/format] on or by [date] at the [Company's] cost.

D.291

'The Delivery Date' shall be the following date by which the [Material/Stills/Images] is to be delivered by the [Photographer] to the [Assignee]: [date].

D.292

The [Assignor] confirms that it shall deliver the commissioned [Work] to the [Company] on or before [date].

D.293

In the event that the [Distributor] fails to release and deliver the [Licensed Products/Units] to retail outlets by [date] to coincide with the transmission and/or broadcast of the [Series/Film]. The [Distributor] shall be obliged to pay the [Licensor] a fixed sum in compensation of [number/currency] for every [day/month] that the general release and delivery is delayed until the [Distributor] has delivered not less than [number] copies of the [Licensed Products/Units] in [country] to retail outlets.

D.294

The delivery by the [Author/Company] of the [Script/Video/Film/Sound Recordings/Photographs] to the [Distributor] by [date] is crucial to the performance of this agreement. Where the material is delayed, not delivered and/or partially delivered for any reason. The [Author/Company] shall have a period of [specify duration] to fulfil and complete the obligation beyond the delivery date. In the event that this is not complied with and there is no satisfactory delivery then the [Distributor] shall be entitled to terminate the agreement and to seek a full refund of any advance paid to date.

D.295

All the costs and expenses of delivery of any material of any nature under this agreement shall be paid for by the [Distributor]. Where the [Author/Company] has incurred any such sums then the full cost shall be reimbursed subject to the supply of receipts and/or other evidence of the sums incurred.

D.296

The [Licensee] agrees that it shall ensure that:

1.1   The [Products/Units] of the [Character/Logo/Images] are manufactured and ready for distribution and delivery by [date] in [country].

1.2   That where there is a problem with production, manufacture, packaging and/or distribution of the [Products/Units] of the [Character/Logo/Images] that the [Licensor] shall be informed and provided with details of the reasons.

1.3   That where the [Products/Units] are not available by [date] the [Licensor] shall have the right to terminate the agreement and seek to appoint a new licensee for the same rights.

Publishing

D.297

The [Author] and the [Publisher/Distributor] agree the following schedule for the delivery of the synopsis, manuscript and proof material:

1.1   Delivery of the synopsis by: [date]. Acceptance or rejection by the [Publisher/Distributor] within [specify duration] of receipt.

1.2   Delivery of the draft manuscript [date] of not less than [number] A4 typed pages in [format]. Acceptance or rejection by the [Publisher/Distribution] within [specify duration] of receipt.

1.3   Delivery of the final manuscript by [date]. Acceptance or rejection by the [Publisher/Distributor] within [specify duration] of receipt.

1.4 Subject to acceptance of the final manuscript in 1.3 and delivery of the proofs by the [Publisher/Distributor] to the [Author]. Delivery of the edited proofs to the [Publisher/Distributor] within [four] weeks of the date they are delivered to the [Author].

D.298
The [Author] shall deliver not later than [date] two typed legible copies of the manuscript of the [Work] by [email attachment/ recorded royal mail/courier/ other method]. The [Work] shall comply in every way with the specifications outlined below and shall be of a standard, in both style and content, that is of a sufficient quality for the [Work] to be published.

D.299
The [Author] shall deliver [two] complete typescripts of the [Manuscript] of not less than [number] words. Together with any preface, photographs, illustrations, disclaimers, and/or copyright notices and/or acknowledgements for the [Work/Book] to the [Publisher/Distributor] in: [format] on or by [date]. The material shall be of a standard and quality that it is ready to be edited and prepared for printing of the proofs and the creation of the index and/or contents page.

D.300

1.1 The [Author] shall ensure that the necessary permissions and consents from third parties have been obtained by him/her in writing for the inclusion of any such third party material in the publication of the [Work/Book/Article/Blog] by the [Publisher/Distributor] in the [Territory/ any part of the world] in respect of the following rights: [specify rights to be obtained].

1.2 The [Author] shall supply a complete list of all such third party material; the terms agreed and the sums due. Together with copies of any licences and/or other documents. The [Author] shall also supply a list of copyright notices, trade mark notices and any other credits and/or source references that must be included in any copy.

1.3 The [Publisher/Distributor] agrees and accepts that the [Publisher/ Distributor] shall make the payments in respect of the sums due for the inclusion of any such third party material at any time.

D.301
The [Author] undertakes to deliver to the [Publisher/Distributor] at the [Author's] cost not later than: [date] [two] complete typescripts of the text of the [Work/Book] ready for review by the editor nominated by the [Publisher/ Distributor] which shall consist of approximately [number] words together

with approximately [number] colour photographs sufficient to make [number] pages of illustration.

D.302

1.1 The [Author] shall provide the [Publisher/Distributor] with an introduction, index, tables and bibliography for the [Work/Book] at the [Author's] cost.

1.2 The [Author] shall assist in creating the marketing and the cover for the [Work/Book] which shall be designed and developed at the [Publishers'/Distributors'] sole cost.

1.3 Any new edition and/or adaptation shall be subject to a new agreement and terms between the parties and shall not be included in this agreement.

D.303

The [Author] shall deliver to the [Publisher] two sets of the complete manuscript acceptable to the [Publisher] and ready for the printer the original [Work] of the [Author] entitled [title] of approximately [number] words in length, as well as any illustrations or additional material agreed with the [Publisher].

D.304

'The Delivery Date' shall be: [date] on or before which the manuscript of the [Work/Book] is to be completed and delivered to the [Publisher] by the [Author]. The Author agrees that the Delivery Date is crucial and that time is of the essence.

D.305

The [Author] agrees to write and deliver two copies of the [Work/Script/ Manuscript] to the [Agent] based on the synopsis on or before the delivery date: [date].

D.306

The [Author] undertakes to prepare an index for the [Work/Book] which shall be delivered with the proofs to the [Publisher]. The [Publisher] shall arrange for the collection of the material by courier once notified by the [Author] that the material is ready for delivery.

D.307

'The Target Date' shall be: [date] which shall be the date by which the [Work/ Book/Sound Recording] is intended to be completed and delivered to the [Publisher/Distributor].

D.308

1.1 The [Writer] shall deliver the [Treatment] to the [Company] not later than [three] months after the date of full execution of this agreement.

1.2 The [Writer] shall deliver the [Scripts] to the [Company] within [six] months after receipt of the [Company's] written approval of the [Treatment].

D.309
In the event that the delivery of the [Work/Book/Sound Recording] is delayed for any reason the advance payments linked to delivery shall not be made until the [Work/Book/Sound Recording] has been delivered to and accepted by the [Publisher/Distributor].

D.310
Where there is a new delivery date substituted in the contract whether due to the [Author] and/or [Publisher] and a new publication date. There shall not be any alteration to the duration of the agreement and/or any other terms.

D.311

1.1 The [Publisher] agrees that it may at its discretion at the request of the [Author] adjust and delay delivery of the [Work] for a period of [number] months.

1.2 Provided that the [Author] agrees that where delivery is delayed beyond [number] months from the original date without consent. Then the [Publisher] shall be entitled to terminate the agreement and seek to arrange an agreement with a third party to write a book on the generic subject of [specify].

1.3 The [Publisher] agrees that it shall not have any right and/or claim to use and/or adapt any synopsis and/or part of the [Work] already received from the [Author] in the event that the [Publisher] terminates the agreement.

D.312
The [Contributor] agrees and undertakes to deliver [number] written typed pages of each chapter of the [Work] by the following dates: [specify dates/material].

D.313
The [Publisher/Distributor] agrees that the delivery dates of the [Script/Manuscript/Proofs] are for general guidance only. The [Publisher/Distributor] agrees that the [Author] shall not be in breach of this agreement if any

delivery is delayed by up to [one] year from the specified date. Provided that where delivery is delayed for any reason the [Author] also agrees that the duration of the Licence Period may also be extended by the same amount of time as the delay.

Services

D.314

Where the nominated personnel of the [Consultancy] is unavailable and cannot deliver the services and/or report required for the purposes of this agreement. Then the [Company] agrees that a suitable qualified substitute may be provided by the [Consultancy] to complete the [Project].

D.315

Where the delivery of material, products and/or services by and/or actions of a third party engaged by the [Company] has impacted and/or delayed the completion and delivery of this agreement by [Name]. Then the [Company] agrees and undertakes that [Name] will not be deemed and/or construed as in breach of this agreement where the delay and/or failure is due to such third party.

D.316

Where the supply of the services and/or the delivery of the required materials by the [Company] to the [Enterprise] cannot be provided in accordance with the agreed Schedule A which is attached to and forms part of this agreement. Then the [Enterprise] shall have the option at its sole discretion to either agree to a delay or to terminate this agreement and to be paid a full refund of all payments made under this agreement for work which has not been completed.

D.317

The delivery of an uninterrupted [Service] by the [Company] under this agreement is a major reason for entering into this agreement. Where delivery is delayed, irregular, intermittent and/or otherwise unreliable. Then the [Enterprise] shall be entitled to terminate the [Service] and this agreement and shall not be liable to pay any further sums to the [Company] from the date of termination.

D.318

Where the commencement of the [Service] is delayed and/or the [Service] regularly fails due to reasons beyond the control of the [Company]. The [Company] shall be entitled to terminate this agreement and/or delay the installation and/or offer a refund for anytime for which the [Service] was not supplied in excess of [number] hours. No additional losses, damages and/or other sums shall be paid for any reason.

Sponsorship

D.319

The [Sponsor] shall arrange delivery of the agreed number of [Products] specified in Schedule B to the [Company] at [address] at its sole risk, cost and expense. Where [Products] are damaged, stolen and/or lost in transit and/or have lost their labels and/or packaging then additional copies shall be supplied upon request.

D.320

The [Sponsor] shall supply to the [Company] a delivery [invoice/statement] specifying the number and detail of the [Products] and the fact that it is supplied at no cost.

D.321

Where the development and/or delivery by the [Company] of any launch date, marketing, samples of products and/or reports and/or any other data is delayed for any reason for a period of up to [number] months in each case. The [Sponsor] agrees that the [Company] shall not be deemed to be in breach of this agreement.

D.322

The [Sponsor] agrees that failure to deliver the materials necessary for the reproduction of the [Sponsors'] name and logo on any marketing and event banners by the delivery date agreed with the [Company] may result in the absence of the [Sponsors] details on such material.

D.323

The [Sponsor] acknowledges that where it fails to meet the delivery and/or completion dates required for the supply of personnel and invitation lists and/or master material and/or payments and/or the approval of samples. That the [Enterprise] shall not be obliged to delay any actions and/or promotions that it must complete prior to the [Event].

University, Charity and Educational

D.324

The [Supplier] shall arrange and pay for all formalities involved in shipping, transfer, import or export as appropriate including packaging, storage, freight and delivery costs, customs duties, import and export taxes, product content verification, security checks, insurance and any other matter required to comply with the laws, regulations, directives, codes, practices and standards of any country in respect of all [Services/Documents/Products] delivered to the [Institute] under this agreement. The [Supplier] will when requested to do so by the [Institute] provide a copy of any such documentation and proof of payments of the costs and expenses. The [Institute] shall not be liable for nor bear the cost and expense of any such matters.

D.325

1.1 The [delivery/availability] dates and times quoted are for guidance only and may be changed without any notice and shall not be of the essence of this agreement.

1.2 The [Institute/Charity] shall not be liable for any losses and/or damages and/or any costs and expenses which arise directly and/or indirectly from the failure to deliver and/or non-availability of any [Service/ Product/Event].

D.326

1.1 Time shall be of the essence of this order. The [Supplier] shall deliver the [Products/Services/Material] at its own risk and expense.

1.2 The [Institute/Charity] shall not be liable for any theft, deterioration in condition of the material and/or other losses and/or damages which occur at any time in respect of the [Products/Services/Material] prior to delivery and acceptance by the [Institute/Charity].

1.3 In the event that the [Products/Services/Material] are not delivered in accordance with the specifications as to quantity, content, quality, use, colour, and/or by the delivery dates. Then the [Institute/Charity] shall be entitled to refuse to accept delivery and shall not be liable for any of the sums due for the [Products/Services/Material] which did not adhere to the terms and conditions of the agreement.

D.327

The [Institute/Charity] shall not be obliged to accept delivery of the [Product/ Services/Material] until the [Product/Services/Material] have been tested, assessed, analysed, counted, verified and audited. The [Institute/Charity] reserves the right to refuse acceptance up to [twenty-eight] days after delivery on the grounds that all and/or any part of the delivery of the [Product/ Services/Material] is not in accordance with the agreed specifications and terms agreed between the parties.

D.328

1.1 All delivery deadlines specified for any coursework, dissertations and projects by any tutor, exam board and/or department must be adhered to by all students.

1.2 Where for any reason delivery deadlines in 1.1 are not expected to be met and /or have passed then the student must provide a certified medical certificate to show that the students' condition was reviewed by a medical practitioner in person and that there is and/or was a serious justifiable reason confirmed for the default by the student.

1.3 There is no automatic right to have any deadline delayed and/or extended. The [Institute] will review each case on its facts and reach a decision as to whether there are any special circumstances.

DEPOSIT

General Business and Commercial

D.329

The [Purchaser] acknowledges that the deposit shall be treated as part payment for the [Products]. In the event that the [Products] are not paid for in full within the time specified the [Seller] shall be entitled to retain the deposit and shall not be liable to return the deposit for any reason. The [Seller] shall also be entitled to take legal proceedings in respect of the outstanding sums due together with interest and/or to seek the immediate return of the [Products]. Title in the [Products] shall not pass to the [Purchaser] until such time as the [Products] have been paid for in full.

D.330

It is agreed that where [Client] is placing a firm order for [Products] to be ordered from a third party manufacturer then a deposit of [fifty] per cent of the total retail price will be required by the [Company]. Where [Products] are being purchased from existing stock then a minimum deposit of [twenty] per cent shall be required. The [Products] shall not be delivered in either case until the balance has been paid in full and any payment by has been cleared by a bank. There is no automatic right to have a deposit refunded and/or transferred and/or offset against other [Products] where the [Client] fails to pay the balance and/or cancels the order. In the event the [Company] agrees to provide a credit note and/or refund to the [Client] no other additional sums shall be paid for any reason. In such instance the [Company] shall be entitled to retain [number/currency] as an administrative charge. Any refund shall only be made to the original [Client] and not to any third party.

D.331

'Legal Deposit' shall mean the act of depositing published material which includes all printed publications in designated libraries and/or archives.

DEPOSIT

Publishers defined as anyone who issues or distributes publications to the public and distributors in the United Kingdom and in Ireland have the legal obligation to deposit published material in the six legal deposit libraries which collectively maintain the national published archive of the United Kingdom:

1.1 The British Library; the Bodleian Library, Oxford; the University Library, Cambridge; the National Library of Scotland, Edinburgh; the Library of Trinity College, Dublin; the National Library of Wales, Aberystwyth.

1.2 Publishers are obliged to send one copy of each of their publications to the British Library within one month of publication. The other five libraries have a right to claim those publications from the publishers or distributors.

1.3 This covers material published and distributed in the United Kingdom or published elsewhere, but distributed in the United Kingdom. The print run, size of material, subject, location of printing, or publication is not relevant.

D.332

'The Deposit' shall be [ten] per cent of the [Retail/Wholesale Price] exclusive of [any taxes that may be charged and/or applicable].

D.333

1.1 The deposit must be paid to the [Company] by the [Customer] by [method] from an approved bank on the day of the [Order/Purchase] and any interest on the deposit may be retained by the [Company]. The payment shall be supported by two documents which verify your identity.

1.2 In the event that the [Customer] does not comply with the payment terms and conditions in [Order/Purchase] document then the deposit shall be forfeited and shall be retained by the [Company].

D.334

The [Distributor] agrees to deposit a copy of the [Work/Book] in each of the main national libraries in the following countries: [–]. These copies shall be deposited at the [Distributors'] cost and expense.

D.335

If a deposit is paid on account as a contribution to the cost of any [Work/Service] to be provided by the [Company]. Where the [Client] subsequently decides to cancel and/or not proceed with the [Work/Service] for any reason then the deposit shall not be returned. The deposit shall be returned for any cancellation which is due to a default of any nature by the [Company] including but not limited to a delay in delivering the [Work/Service] and/or the inability to deliver the [Material/Content] which was agreed.

D.336

The [Company] shall hold your deposit in good faith as security against damage and/or loss of any [Articles] provided on loan. This sum shall be refunded to you in full in the event that the [Articles] are returned to the [Company] by the agreed date [specify] and in the same condition without ant marks, tears and/or other damage. The [Company] shall be entitled to be paid in full for the cost of any repairs and/or replacement and may offset and retain the deposit for that purpose.

D.337

1.1 Any deposit shall be returned to the [Customer] without interest in the event that the [Customer] changes his/her mind and cancels the order.

1.2 The deposit shall be deducted from the full purchase price before the calculation of the balance.

1.3 The deposit shall be held with the general funds of the [Company].

1.4 The [Company] shall have the right to return the deposit at any time and cancel the order. The [Customer] shall not be due any sums in compensation for any reason.

DESIGNS

General Business and Commercial

D.338

The [Company] acknowledges that all present and future Design Rights in the Design Documents, the Approved Designs, the Prototype Designs, the Trial Prototypes and the Final Design and any associated products, services and/or any other format in any medium are and will remain the sole property of [Name]. This agreement does not in any way purport to assign and/or transfer any copyright, intellectual property rights and/or Design Rights and/or any other rights in existence now and/or created in the future in the [Company].

D.339

In consideration of the sum of [fee/currency] by [date] in full the [Company] sells, assigns and transfers in perpetuity all intellectual property rights including patents, copyright, registered design rights, future design rights and associated designs in the Design Documents, the Approved Designs, the Prototype Designs, the Trial Prototype and the Final Product known as [specify details] and all the material listed and described in appendix A to [Name]. The [Company] shall not have further claim, right, ownership and/or interest.

D.340
The [Company] undertakes to the [Developer] that it shall supply upon request from the Developer] copies of any artwork, stills, videos, films, recordings, images, designs, drawings, maps, computer generated material, models, documents, records and/or any other data and/or information relating to the [Project] which is in the possession and/or under the control of the [Company]. Provided that the [Developer] agrees to pay the full cost of reproduction and any delivery charges.

D.341

1.1 The [Developer] shall be entitled on written request to be supplied by the [Contractor] with complete copies of all drawings, designs, details, specifications, calculations, documents, records, computer generated material, models or other material prepared by or on behalf of the [Contractor] relating to the [Development] subject to the payment of a reasonable reproduction and delivery charge.

1.2 In respect of the material supplied in 1.1 The [Contractor] grants to the [Developer] the non-exclusive right to use, reproduce and permit third parties to do so any material provided that it is for the construction of the [Development] and/or the maintenance, repair, reinstatement, reconstruction and/or any extension at any time whether now or in the future.

1.3 The intellectual property rights and copyright in the designs, documents and/or other material relating to the [Development] shall remain owned by the [Contractor]. The [Developer] shall not remove and/or erase any copyright notice and/or other credits that the [Contractor] may put on any material.

D.342
'Design' shall mean the novel shape, configuration, pattern or surface decoration of an [article/item] which has aesthetic appeal and can be manufactured and sold separately and is not an integral part of another article or item or purely functional in nature.

D.343
'Design document' shall mean any record of a design whether in the form of a drawing, a written description, photograph, data stored in a computer or otherwise.

D.344

'Design' shall mean the original design of any aspect of the shape or configuration (whether internal or external) of the whole or any substantial part of an article and/or any reproduction in the form of a prototype.

D.345

'Design Right' shall be defined as a property right which subsists in an original design. The design shall mean any aspect of the shape or configuration (whether internal or external) of the whole or any substantial part of an article. The design right shall not subsist until the design has been recorded in a design document or an article has been made to the design which was made or recorded after [date] under legislation: [specify law/country]. Design right shall only subsist if the design qualifies for protection in [country].

The design right shall not include and does not exist in a method or principle of construction, or the features of shape or configuration of an article (which enable the article to be connected to or placed in around or against another article so that the article may perform its function or are dependent upon appearance of another article of which the article is intended by the designer to form an integral part) or which is surface decoration.

D.346

'Designer' in relation to a design shall be defined [in accordance with [specify country/legislation] as the person who creates the design. Where the design is computer generated it shall mean the person by whom the arrangements necessary for the creation of the design are undertaken.

D.347

1.1 The [Designer] acknowledges that as the design is created in pursuance of a commission which was proposed by the [Company]. That the [Company] shall be the owner of any design rights and/or future design rights in the [Designs] and other material created and/or developed by the [Designer] for this [Project/Product].

1.2 In accordance with 1.1 the [Designer] where necessary agrees to complete and sign a full assignment document of all the rights to the [Company] in consideration of a nominal sum. This payment shall be an additional payment separate from the original agreed budget.

D.348

1.1 The [Employee] agrees and undertakes that where in the course of his/her employment he/she creates a design or article that the [Company] shall be the owner of any design rights and/or future design rights in such designs and/or articles.

687

1.2 The [Employee] agrees and undertakes that the [Employee] shall not be entitled to claim any ownership, rights and/or interest at any time and/or any right to receive royalties and/or any other sums in respect of the assignment, licensing and/or exploitation of any designs, articles, products and/or other matter based on or derived from the designs and/or articles created by the [Employee].

D.349
'Future Design Right' [shall be defined in accordance with [specify legislation] in [country]] shall mean the design right which will or may come into existence in respect of future design or class of designs or on the occurrence of a future event.

D.350
'Joint Design' shall mean a design produced by the collaboration of two or more designers in which the contribution of each is not distinct from that of the other [in accordance with [specify legislation]].

D.351
'British Design' shall mean a design which qualifies for design right protection by reason of a connection with the United Kingdom of the designer or by the person by whom the design is commissioned or the designer is employed by a company registered in the United Kingdom.

D.352
'The Designs' shall be the original concept and two-dimensional designs for a range of [specify items/articles] and other products to be created and developed by the [Designer] some of which are set out in the attached Schedule B and form part of this agreement. It shall also include such other designs as are created by the [Designer] in the future pursuant to this agreement.

D.353
'The Licensed Articles' shall be the three-dimensional reproduction and adaptations of the designs to be manufactured by the [Licensee] based on the [Prototype].

D.354
'The Designs' shall be the original concept and two-dimensional designs, sketches, drawings and patterns for an individual piece of clothing briefly described as follows: [–]. A full detailed description and images are set out in Appendix B.

D.355

1.1 The [Employee] acknowledges and agrees that all patents, inventions, trade marks, copyright, design rights, future design rights, intellectual property rights and any other rights of any nature in the product of his/ her services in any format and/or medium during the normal course of his/her employment as [specify role] shall remain the sole and exclusive property of the [Company]. The [Employee] shall not acquire any ownership, rights and/or interest and/or be entitled to receive any payments, royalties and/or other benefits in respect of the exploitation of any such rights and/or material and/or any adaptation, licensing and/or registration by the [Company] in any country in any language worldwide.

1.2 The [Employee] undertakes and agrees to sign any documents and/ or forms which may be required by the [Company] to assign, transfer and/or confirm ownership of any of the rights and/or material created in 1.1 above. Provided that where any costs and expenses have to be incurred by the [Employee] the [Company] will agree and pay in advance a sum agreed between the parties.

1.3 The [Company] agrees and acknowledges that it shall not acquire any rights in any material which is created and developed by the [Employee] including patents, inventions, trade marks, copyright, design rights, future design rights, intellectual property rights and any other rights of any nature in any format and/or medium which are created and developed by the [Employee] outside of office hours and in his/her own personal time which is not based on any knowledge he/ she has acquired at a result of his/her employment at the [Company].

D.356
'Designs' shall include all two-dimensional representations of the [Character/ Image/Logo] in whatever form and shall also include all three-dimensional objects and/or products of any nature derived from or based on two-dimensional design and vice versa.

D.357
'Designs' shall mean all two-dimensional artistic designs created by and/ or for and/or licensed to the [Company] for the purpose of developing the [Character/Image/Logo].

D.358
Design, drawings, specifications and other work developed under this agreement shall be the exclusive property of the [Company]. The [Company] may use and/or exploit such material in any way that it may decide. No

such material may be released exploited and/or published and/or used by the [Developer] except for the purposes of this agreement without the prior written consent of the [Company]. All originals, copies and any other reproductions in any medium shall be delivered to the [Company] by the [Developer] upon completion of this agreement or at the [Company's] request.

D.359

There shall be no transfer, assignment, license or other grant of rights in the [Designs] and/or the [Articles] under this agreement and all design rights, future design rights, patents, copyright, intellectual property rights, trademarks, computer software rights, domain names and/or any other rights and the right to reproduce copies in any form and/or media and to license others to do so and/or to authorise any adaptation shall be retained by the [Designer]. No other party shall be entitled to display and/or exhibit and/or distribute any material which attributes and/or claims ownership of any rights and/or material at any time and/or to register any rights and/or interest with a third party.

D.360

1.1 The [Company] shall not be entitled to claim any ownership of any intellectual property rights, copyright, design rights and future design rights, patent rights, computer software rights, trade mark, domain name and/or any other rights and/or interest in the product of the work of the [Consultant] except the following agreed material: [list in detail].

1.2 The presumption is that any rights and/or material created and developed by the [Consultant] pursuant to this agreement are owned and controlled by the [Consultant]. Where the work is based on material, facts, data and information supplied by the [Company] then the [Consultant] agrees that the [Company] shall own the rights in the product of the work. In such instance the [Consultant] must be credited by the [Company] on all copies as follows: [statement/name].

D.361

The [Company] agrees and undertakes that it shall not engage and/or appoint any other third party to work on and/or advise on the [Design/Project/Product] without the prior consent of the [Designer].

D.362

The [Designer] shall have the right as all times to be acknowledged as the original artist for the [Project] and in all artwork, reports, marketing and any form of reproduction and/or exploitation in any media at any time as follows: [state credit]. The [Designer] shall also have the right to specify to the [Company] that that their name and acknowledgement does not appear in any particular instance.

D.363
The [Designer] shall retain all copyright, design rights and future design rights and intellectual property rights and the right to register any trade mark, domain name, patent and/or any other rights and/or interest of any nature in the [Design Work] in any format and/or medium whether in existence now and/or in the future. The [Designer] shall have the sole right to retain all royalties, fees and/other sums received from the reproduction, licensing and/or exploitation of the [Design Work]. The [Designer] shall have the right to assign and/or transfer any and/or all of the rights to a third party at any time at its sole discretion.

D.364
Where the [Company] commissions a designer to develop, and create a new [design/logo/symbol/word] for the [Event] whether computer generated, by drawing and/or any use of any other means. The [Company] shall ensure that such person and/or any business shall assign all copyright, intellectual property rights, design rights, future design rights, trade marks, service marks, community marks, rights in any computer generated material, the right to any domain name and any other rights of any nature whether in existence now and/or created in the future to the [Sponsor/Name]. Further that such person and/or business and/or the [Company] shall not be entitled to received and/or be paid any royalties and/or other sums of any nature from the use and/or exploitation of the [design/logo/symbol] by the [Sponsor/Name] at any time.

D.365

1.1　The [Artist/Illustrator] has created, developed and supplied the shape, design, logo, name and domain name for [Name] for the total sum of [number/currency] for his/her business which currently trades under the name of: [specify].

1.2　In consideration of the additional payment of [number/currency] the [Artist/Illustrator] agrees and undertakes to assign all present and future copyright, intellectual property rights, present and future design rights, computer software rights, the right to create and/or develop a hologram and/or any other moving image and/or film, any right to register a domain name and/or any variations and/or any trade marks and/or any other rights to [Name] in all formats in all media throughout the planet earth and on land, sea and air and throughout the universe for the full period of all such copyright, intellectual property rights and any other rights and any extensions and for any new rights which may be created at a later date which do not exist now. No additional payments and/or royalties shall be due to the [Artist/Illustrator] from [Name] and/or any collecting society and/or from any adaptation, exploitation and/or reproduction in any form.

D.366

1.1 [Name] has created and produced a three dimensional [object/product/prototype] entitled: [specify]. [Name] agrees to sell the original [object/product/prototype] to the [Company] for the sum of [number/currency].

1.2 The sale in 1.1 does not include the right to create and/or develop and/or to authorise the reproduction of the original [object/product/prototype] in any form.

1.3 If the [Company] wish to reproduce copies, issue posters and/or create merchandise and/or exploit the [object/product/prototype] in any other form then they must enter into a new licence agreement with the [Name].

1.4 [Name] accepts that the [Company] may sell the [object/product/prototype] to a third party. The [Company] must ensure that any third party is made aware of these conditions.

D.367

The [Artist] has designed, produced and made a series of original [objects/units/displays] on the theme of [subject] in [material] by [specify method]. In consideration of the payment of the sum of [number/currency] the [Artist] authorises the [Purchaser] to reproduce, use and adapt and exploit the [objects/units/displays] as they think fit and at their sole discretion and no additional sums shall be due and/or owed.

DIRECTOR

General Business and Commercial

D.368

The duties of the [Executive] as a [Director] of the [Company] if appointed, shall be subject to the Articles of Association and Memorandum of the Company for the time being in effect and shall be separate from and additional to his/her duties as Executive. The [Executive's] remuneration is inclusive of any remuneration to which the [Executive] may be entitled as a [Director] of the [Company] or any associated company.

692

D.369

Where the main contract of employment of the [Executive] is terminated for any reason. Then the [Company] shall have the right to take such steps as necessary for the [Executive] to be removed as a Director of the Board of the [Company] and/or associated company. In such event the [Company] shall not be liable to pay any compensation for loss of office of any role as a Director to the [Executive].

D.370

1.1   Where a [Director] has been and/or is disqualified from and/or is the subject to an investigation which may result in disqualification from holding the office of a director of a company. Then the [Director] shall be obliged to notify this fact to the [Company Secretary] in writing with [seven] days of the event.

1.2   The Director shall also keep the [Chief Executive] informed of any significant changes in the circumstances of the [Director] which would affect his/her ability to fulfil the role of [Director] including but not limited to ill-health and medical reasons, agreeing to work for a competitor in any role, moving abroad and/or a pending court action, jury service and/or otherwise.

D.371

Where for any reason the [Director] decides not to proceed with the [Project] then he/she shall be obliged to repay all sums paid by the [Company] under this agreement for any work not completed to the date of notification by the [Director].

D.372

The final decision as to the appointment and/or replacement and/or removal for any reason of any Director shall be with [specify name/role] and his/her decision shall be final. There shall be no requirement to consult with any shareholders, management and/or funders of the [Project] before any decision is reached and/or any action taken.

D.373

The [Director] agrees as follows:

1.1   That the [Director] shall be under a legal duty to act in the best interests of the [Company] at all times.

1.2   Where there is any potential and/or actual conflict of interest between the [Company] and a third party with whom the [Director] has a family, business and/or charitable relationship and/or legal agreement. Then the [Director] is under a duty to declare this conflict of interest to the

[Company] and the Board as soon as the [Director] realises that there may be a conflict. The Board may decide that the [Director] must resign and/or not be involved in the decision making process of any such matter.

1.3 Where the [Director] is unable to fulfil his role effectively and does not read the documents required to reach decisions and/or fails to attend [four] consecutive Board meetings. Then the Board of the [Company] shall have the right to remove him/her as a Director and to cease paying any remuneration.

1.4 That where the [Director] chooses to become involved in any political and/or activist and/or public campaign and/or engages in any matter which may create a negative effect on the [Company] and/or its brands and/or services and/or products in any country for any reason. The Board of the [Company] shall have the choice to remove the {Director] from the Board.

1.5 That the [Director] shall not have the right to use the legal services of the [Company] for any reason without the consent of the Chief Executive.

1.6 That the [Director] shall not have the right to commit the [Company] to any contract and/or other arrangement which has not been approved and authorised by the Board.

DISCHARGE

General Business and Commercial

D.374
The rights and obligations of [Name] shall be formally discharged and end upon full and final payment of all sums due under clause [–] of this agreement except in respect of clauses [–] which relating to warranties, indemnities and confidentiality which shall continue in full force and effect until [date/time].

D.375
All rights, obligations and undertakings of any nature by either party shall be brought to an end on the date that the following conditions in clauses [–] have been carried out and fulfilled. After that date the agreement shall have been discharged so that neither party is bound by any contractual condition of any nature to the other.

D.376

Provided that the [Seller] shall have provided the [Products] and the [Purchaser] shall have paid the full price stipulated then all rights and obligations of either party shall be discharged. Except that there shall be a surviving obligation by the [Seller] for [number] [day/month/year] in relation to clauses [–] of this agreement relating to the description, use, condition and function of the [Product].

D.377

Where an invoice shall have been paid in full to the [Agent] then it shall have been discharged and there is no further liability by the [Company] in the event the [Agent] fails to pay [Name].

D.378

This agreement shall be settled in full and discharged where [Name] has paid the sum of [number/currency] together with interest to the [Company] by [date].

DISCLAIMER

General Business and Commercial

D.379

1.1 The comments, statements and/or views expressed in relation to any products, services, garments, articles, packaging, advertising, method, process, trade mark, distributor, supplier or manufacturer are the views of that individual and not the [Company]. The [Company] does not make any statements and/or does not endorse, recommend and/or make any ranking preferences which are personal to the [Company]. All data and information is based on views supplied by third parties.

1.2 The views and opinions of the [Contributors] to the [Website/App/ Platform] shall not be used for advertising or product and/or service endorsement or any other purposes without the prior written consent of the [Company].

D.380

All rights are reserved. You are specifically prohibited and not allowed to reproduce, copy, duplicate, manufacture, supply, sell, hire, distribute, exploit and/or adapt all or any part of this [Product] including any associated articles and/or packaging.

D.381

The [Service] and any associated [material/software] is supplied to and used by you on the on the following basis that you have agreed that:

1.1   That there are no undertakings, warranties, terms of agreement between the parties and/or guarantees by the [Company] as to the quality, standard and function of the content and the direct and indirect consequences arising from the use of the [Service] and any associated [material/software].

1.2   That there is no assurance that the [Service] and any associated [material/ software] is free from defects, errors, omissions and/or that it is accurate and/or that it is not flawed in any way and/or that it does not contain any viruses and/or other corruptions and/or is undamaged, fit for any particular purpose and/or suitable to be used in conjunction with any other particular products or systems and/or will operate without interruption, delay and/will not be suspended, cancelled or terminated.

1.3   That the [Company] shall not be liable for any consequences which arise as a result of the use of the [Service] and any associated [material/software] by you or any third party to whom you supply, copy, send, or distribute the [Service] and any associated [material/ software] including but not limited to loss of profit, loss of data and information, business, revenue, contracts, reputation or goodwill or any other expenses, costs and damages whether direct or indirect and whether reasonably foreseeable or not.

1.4   There is no assurance as to whether any content is in breach and/or infringes any copyright, patents, trade marks, service marks, computer software, design rights, films, sound recordings, music, lyrics, photographs, artwork, videos, domain name, confidential information and/or any intellectual property rights, any other contract and/or any other rights and/or interest in any country or of any person, business and/or organisation.

1.5   That all the risk, liability and choice of using the [Service] and any associated [material/software] is with you and you shall not seek to claim any sums from the [Company] unless the death and/or serious injury of a person is directly linked to and arises from their use of this [Service] and any associated [material/software] on your behalf and was directly caused by the default and/or negligence of the [Company].

D.382

This information and summary is for background material and may not be up to date or fully state all the relevant facts. There is no recommendation, endorsement or promotion of any person or company in preference to another or any commercial assessment or financial forecast which you may use to promote a product or business or which you should rely upon to make a decision regarding investment, or other commitment. The [Company] shall not be liable for any use of this material and you must make your own judgement and seek professional advice.

D.383

All the applicants must accept as a pre-condition of their entering the tender process that the [Agency/Company] shall not be liable for any sums incurred and/or for any losses, damages, expenses, professional fees and legal costs and/or any contracts entered into which are contingent on the application being successful. Nor shall the [Agency/Company] be liable for any other charges and/or consequences which may be alleged and/or which may arise directly and/or indirectly to any person and/or company which applies for and/or completes the tender process whether or not they are awarded the final contract. It is a pre-condition of any application that the applicants do so at their own risk and cost and that the [Agency/Company] shall not be liable for any sums.

D.384

[Name] and/or the [Company] are and will not be responsible and/or liable for any use of the [Service/Product/Computer Software] and any related material and/or any content, data, information by any person and/or business which has been supplied by a third party without authority and does not hold an official licence at any time for its specific use. [Name] and/or the [Company] have only approved the use of the [Service/Product/Computer Software] under licence which is exactly in accordance with the instructions and the intended purpose. No liability is accepted by any use and/or adaptation which is not permitted and/or authorised and any such actions are at your own risk and cost.

D.385

Any recommendation by the [Company] and/or any employee as to the [Footwear/Product] that the customer should purchase is for guidance only. No responsibility can be taken for any personal injuries, stress fractures and/or any loss and/or damage arising from the use of any [Footwear/Product] and/or the purchase of any item which is unsuitable for its intended use due to the type of terrain and/or sport for which it has been used.

D.386

[Name] does not recommend that:

1.1 This [Product/Service] be used by anyone under age [specify].

1.2 Follow the installation instructions exactly and do not use with other equipment and/or electrical connections which are out of date and/or have not been verified as of suitable standard.

D.387

Data, charts and statistics in this report including those which show projections for the future are based on sample surveys and current usage. They are theoretical projections and not to be relied upon to be accurate and/or may be subject to change at any time. No financial investment should be made based on these figures without seeking professional independent advice from an expert.

D.388

No liability is accepted by the [Company] for any property, equipment, vehicles and/or any other belongings which you may choose to leave in any changing room, storage facility, car park and/or in any other part of the premises. You do so at your own risk and cost. In the event of any loss, damage and/or theft the [Company] will not reimburse any claim and you are advised to contact the [specify authority.

D.389

1.1 The [Company] is not liable for any [Products/Material] until they are delivered to the [Company] and authorised as accepted.

1.2 Where any [Products/Material] are not delivered for any reason the [Company] shall not be liable. It is your responsibility to ensure that you send any {Products/Material] by a safe and secure method.

1.3 Where any [Products/Material] are not accepted by the [Company] and rejected as not of sufficient quality for their intended purpose and/ or damaged and/or not as described in the marketing. Then you shall arrange for the collection within [number] days at your own cost.

1.4 Where the [Company] has agreed to distribute and/or sell the {Products/ Material] on your behalf through its agents, distributors and/or online marketing. The [Company] shall accept liability for the minimum value of the [Products/Material] and/or part as estimated by them at the time they accepted the [Products/Material]. This sum shall not equate to the wholesale and/or retail value and/or any online price. No other additional sums shall be paid by the [Company] in the event that for any reason they are liable to pay for any loss and/or damage.

Internet, Websites and Apps

D.390

We disclaim responsibility for any consequences arising from your access to and/or use of this [Website/App/Platform] and/or any links, pop-ups and/

or advertising and/or product placement. All data, information and content is included entirely at the sole discretion of the [Editor/Company] and may be altered, edited, deleted and/or adapted at any time. Any material which you add to the site by way of postings or otherwise shall not be defamatory, in breach of copyright and shall either be cleared for use in this manner or shall be your own original material. You agree that we shall have the right to use any such material in our merchandising, marketing, advertising and/or in any article, blog, online account, newspaper and/or magazine.

D.391
The [Company] are not responsible for the contents or reliability of the linked apps, websites, advertisements and pop-ups, gambling sites, promotions and marketing of any nature. The lists and the views expressed in them are not the views of the [Company] and should not be taken as an endorsement of any kind. The [Company] have no control over the content of the links.

D.392
The data, information, records, images, text, slogans, graphics, designs, trademarks, service marks and/or any other material on this site and/or any links may not be accurate and there may be other more recent material available elsewhere. This site is intended only to be used for background research and is not intended to replace specialist advice from a [medical/scientific/financial/insurance expert]. It is not recommended that you rely on this site and you are strongly advised to seek independent advice. If you do chose to rely on this site then you do so at your own risk and costs and the [Company] cannot accept responsibility and/or liability for your actions and any sums you may incur and/or loss you may suffer as a result of such a decision.

D.393
You use this site and any material and download any of its contents at your own discretion and risk. The [Company] and its associates, affiliates, sponsors and suppliers do not accept responsibility for any consequences that may arise from your reliance on any material and/or the downloading of any contents at any time.

D.394
The [Company] and any content providers and/or contributors on this [Website/App/Platform] and/or any links in any part of the world and/or in any associated publicity, advertising and marketing and/or software and/or material of any nature which is stored, displayed, accessed and/or downloaded from and/or in conjunction with this [Website/App/Platform] shall not be liable to you the [user/member/subscriber] for any consequence that may arise from your access to, use of and/or actions based on and/

or associated with any matter in respect of this [Website/App/Platform]. This shall include the supply of your personal and financial details whether for ordering products and/or services and/or any search information and/or any other research and/or data. You agree that you have accepted that no representations, undertakings or warranties have been made and that you are advised to seek specialist professional advice and that this site is not intended to provide personal individual and/or corporate advice of any nature.

D.395

The owners of the [Website/App/Platform] rely on the suppliers of the information on this site to act in good faith and to provide accurate up-to-date data and records. All delivery dates, quotes, prices, exchange rates, special offers, and other details are subject to availability and may be changed at any time without notice. No responsibility and/or liability can be accepted for any errors, omissions, losses and/or damages, costs and expenses that may arise from your use, order and/or reliance on this site. The owners of the [Website/App/Platform] and the copyright owners of this site permit access to browse, order goods and services and access information for private and personal use. The site, data, information and content may not be reproduced, published and/or commercially exploited without the prior written consent of [name/contact details].

D.396

We endeavour to provide accurate, quality, detailed information, data and services on this site which is owned by [Company], operated by [Name] and trades as [Website/App/Account]. However we cannot accept liability for your reliance on this site and you are advised to take independent legal and commercial advice. You accept as a condition of your use of the site that you will make no claim for any loss, damage and/or expenses that may arise. There is no undertaking by us that any part of the site is accurate, complete or up to date and this site must be used for guidance only to highlight possible issues.

D.397

1.1　The [Parent Company], the [Subsidiary], the [Distributor] and any other third parties authorised by them cannot accept liability for your reliance on this [Website/App/Blog] of any nature whether commercial, financial, legal, medical, property, scientific and/or otherwise. You must take to independent advice from a third party to review and advise on your particular circumstances and facts. There is no undertaking that any part of the [Website/App/Blog] is accurate, complete or up to date and you must verify all facts independently and use your own judgement.

1.2 Do not carry out any action, commitment, or undertaking based on this [Website/App/Blog] alone or you may suffer some loss, damage, expense or other consequences which could have been avoided. There is no liability accepted for any such sums.

1.3 You accept as a condition of your access to and/or use of the [Website/App/Blog] that you will make no claim and/or seek to be indemnified for any losses, damages, expenses and/or other consequences that may arise for any reason.

D.398

You must only use this site if you agree that the [Company] who are the owners and service providers of the [Website/App/Forum] shall not be responsible and/or liable for:

1.1 Any losses, damages or other consequential direct and/or indirect costs, expenses and/or liability that may arise from your use and/or reliance on any data, information, material and products.

1.2 Any content which is misleading and/or any error and/or the failure of any operation system and/or function and/or any virus, destruction and/or interference with software and/or equipment and/or any security lapse and/or breach and/or failure to deliver any products and/or services and/or any delay, suspension and/or other matters which may arise due to force majeure.

1.3 Any defamatory, offensive, derogatory material, images, recordings, films, videos, logos and/or statements on any part of the site whether temporary or permanent.

1.4 Any failure to comply with trade descriptions, quality of products or services, fitness for purpose, prices, payment, delivery, delay in and/or failure to deliver by third parties.

1.5 Any infringement of copyright, design rights, moral rights, trademarks, service marks and/or any other intellectual property rights and/or any computer software rights and/or any other rights of any nature and/or any other legal obligation under a contract related to a third party.

D.399

The [advertisements/offers/promotions] on this [Website/App/Audio File] are used by you at your own risk, cost and liability and shall not be the responsibility of the [Company] for any reason. The details, terms and conditions of use and content of all such material is not owned or controlled by the [Company]. There is no consent, endorsement or recommendation provided by the [Company] express or implied that you should use and/or access any such material or otherwise.

D.400

There are sections of this site that rely on the users to provide information and data in good faith. Where material is displayed or accessible which has been provided by third party users then we do not accept responsibility for any material which is defamatory, offensive, inaccurate, misleading, contrary to legislation and/or any code of practice. We do however have a policy of receiving any complaints at [specify contact details] and review and may delete any material and/or close any account of any user whom we conclude should be removed for any reason.

D.401

Any guidance, advice, recommendations and/or promotions on this [Website/ App/Blog] must be followed at your own risk and cost. The [Enterprise] cannot accept any responsibility and/or liability for any payments you may make to a third party and/or any actions that you may take as a direct and/or indirect result of viewing and/or having access to any content, advertisements, links, databases and/or any other material. You are strongly advised where you are paying significant sums of money to ensure that you take independent advice and to check that the company and/or person is a legitimate operation and registered with an appropriate [trade/commercial] organisation and that your money is secure and protected.

D.402

This [Company] permits you to upload material to the [Website/App/Platform] upon the following terms and conditions:

1.1 That all the personal information is true and verifiable and is not inaccurate and/or dishonest.

1.2 That you will only upload material in which you are the copyright owner and which is your original work and not copied and/or adapted from the work of a third party.

1.3 That the content of the material which you upload is not and/or is not alleged to be offensive, illegal, defamatory, obscene, violent, an incitement to violence, evidence of a civil and/or criminal act against a person and/or property, encouraging any act which is potentially harmful to any person, in breach of any agreement and/or an infringement of the rights of a third party who owns and/or controls the material.

1.4 That the material uploaded by you is free from defects, errors, omissions, is accurate, and not misleading and does not contain viruses and/or other corruptions.

1.5 You will be entirely responsible for any legal action and/or other consequences taken against you whether by the [Company] and/or a third party for damages, costs, expenses and/or otherwise which may arise as a result of uploading the material to the [Website/App/Platform]. The [Company] shall not be liable for any consequences including but not limited to legal costs, losses, expenses and/or damages whether direct or indirect and whether reasonably foreseeable or not. Where the [Company] is held liable by a Court of law for any reason the liability of the [Company] is agreed to be limited to [number/currency] for any such claim. The [Company] reserves the right to seek to be reimbursed with any sums it is obliged to pay to a third party due to the actions of anyone who uploads material.

1.6 The [Company] will assist and/or supply material and/or data to any third party who has a Court Order who has taken legal action against the [Company] in order to obtain details of the person who has uploaded any material to the [Website/App/Platform].

D.403

Images may be edited, distorted, adapted and changed. The [Company] cannot verify that any images have not altered and/or varied prior to being posted on the [Website]. The [Company] does not accept responsibility and/or liability for any damages and/or loss that may be suffered by any person by such actions by a third party but undertakes to remove and/or delete all images reported to them as defamatory, offensive, false and/or posted without authority of the owner of the image.

D.404

Where the [Company] sends free samples of any product to any person at its own cost. Then that person shall not be entitled to any refund and/or other sum and/or any other product as a substitute in the event that they should return any such sample. Liability of the [Company] is limited to [number/currency] and any claim for personal injury can only relate to a claim for gross negligence and/or death directly caused by the [Company] and its samples in the country in which the sample was supplied to the person and used in accordance with the instructions.

D.405

This account on [specify site] is owned by [Name] through their trading company entitled: [–]. The videos, images, advice and articles are owned by: [specify name/trading company]. [Name] is not an expert and all advice is offered on the basis of personal experiences. [Name] cannot offer medical and/or other advice and you must seek professional guidance as to your personal suitability and fitness before you embark on any exercises and or other regimes. No liability can be accepted for any costs and/or expenses that you may incur for any reason you perform any exercise and/or regime entirely at your own choice and risk.

D.406

This blog on [specify site] is owned by [Company]. All the articles on the blog are written by authors engaged by the [Company] to create original work and the copyright in the words shown in relation to each articles is owned by the individual author if a copyright notice is displayed at the end of the article. The opinions and views are personal to each author and do not represent the views and opinions of the [Company]. There is no authority provided to reproduce and/or copy the articles and/or to distribute them in any format to third parties.

D.407

There are products displayed and shown on this site for promotional and marketing purposes which form part of the images, films, videos and locations shown. This product placement does not mean that the [Company] personally endorses the product and/or its fitness for purpose and/or any other matter. Any purchase of the product through a contact and/link on this site is a contract between you and the manufacturer and no liability is attributed to the [Company].

Merchandising and Distribution

D.408

The [Licensor] does not accept any responsibility for any legal actions, claims, losses, damages, costs and/or liability for the [Product] manufactured, supplied and/or sold by the [Distributor] at any time. The [Distributor] shall ensure that the [Product] is tested and sampled regularly so that it complies with all legislation, regulations, directives and policies in any part of the world in which the [Product] is to be sold, supplied and/or distributed. The [Distributor] shall arrange insurance cover to meet any potential liabilities from such exploitation.

D.409

The [Company] and/or its agents and/or any authorised representatives do not accept any responsibility and/or liability for any use of this [Product/Unit] in a manner and/or for any purpose for which it was not intended to be used and which could not be reasonably be foreseen. Where the [Product/Unit] is not used in accordance with the instructions and/or is interfered with in any manner and/or is used in conjunction with another article which is not intended in the original purpose. There shall be no liability by the [Company] and/or any agent and/or representative for any direct and/or indirect consequences, damages, losses, costs, expenses, and/or any other sums unless there is a death and/or personal injury and such death and/or personal injury is directly caused by the negligence of the [Company].

D.410

Neither the [Licensor] nor the [Licensee] shall accept any responsibility and/or liability for any claims, allegations, settlements, legal actions and/or costs, expenses, damages, losses, interest and/or other sums that may arise directly and/or indirectly as a result of the use and/or adaptation of any of the contents of the [Product/Work/Service] and/or any accompanying [packaging/disc/equipment].

D.411

1.1 The [Licensor] agrees and undertakes that it shall be liable for any default of this agreement by the [Licensor] and/or any infringement of copyright and/or any intellectual property rights and/or trade marks in respect of the [Character/Storyline/Name/Logo/Image] supplied by the [Licensor] under this agreement.

1.2 The [Licensee] accepts and agrees that the [Licensor] shall not be responsible and/or liable for any allegations, claims, legal actions and/or disputes in respect of the [Prototype] and/or the [Product] based on the material in 1.1 to be produced, manufactured and exploited by the [Licensee].

1.3 The [Licensee] agrees and accepts that it shall be responsible for all claims relating to product liability. That the [Prototype] and [Product] must be properly assessed and tested as suitable for [specify age/market].

1.4 The [Licensee] shall ensure that all [Products] bear suitable labels and that the packaging bears any appropriate warnings that may be required for safety reasons.

1.5 The [Licensee] agrees and undertakes to advise the [Licensor] of any complaints regarding the [Products] and health and safety.

1.6 The [Licensee] agrees and undertakes to notify the [Licensor] and provide the [Licensor] with details upon request of any pending and/or actual legal actions against the [Licensee] in respect of the [Products].

1.7 The [Licensee] agrees that where the [Licensor] is concerned as to the health and safety issues raised in 1.5 and 1.6 that the [Licensee] will arrange at the [Licensees'] cost for the [Product] to be re-assessed regarding those health and safety which have been raised.

1.8 Further that if the [Licensor] instructs the [Licensee] to withdraw the [Product] from sale that the [Licensee] will do so until such time as both parties are satisfied there is no risk to the public.

D.412

If any disc and/or data is incompatible with the [Purchasers] hardware and there is no alternative product available. Then there is no liability and/or responsibility on the part of the [Company] to provide another disc and/or data and/or any refund and/or reimbursement of any nature to the [Purchaser]. The purchase of the [Book] included the disc in the format supplied and no other format.

D.413

The [Company] and/or [Distributor] will only accept responsibility for any injury and/or death arising from the use of this [Product] where it is used in accordance with the [Instruction Manual] and the injury is caused as a direct result of the negligence of the [Company] and/or [Distributor]. No liability for any consequences is accepted where the [Product] in used in an unauthorised manner and/or in any way in which the [Product] was not intended to be used. This [Product] is not a toy and should not be used by any person under [number] age.

D.414

The [Distributor] supplies corporate information, data, maps, financial, insurance and analytical reports, podcasts, films, reviews and archive service to any third party at their own risk and provides no undertakings and/or confirmation as to the reliability, accuracy and/or impact of any of the material and/or any recommendations. Any decisions, investment, strategies and development proposal cannot rely on this material and all losses, damages, expenses and costs will not be paid for [Distributor] who disclaims all liability of any kind at any time which may arise whether it is directly and/or indirectly related to any material obtained from the [Distributor]. That in any event the total liability of [Distributor] to any third party is fixed at a maximum of [number/currency].

D.415

The [Company] seeks to provide regular reports, updates and references for use by third parties in the [subject] market. It must be acknowledged that there may be variations in the quality of the service in different countries due to differences in translations of terminology, technology both software and hardware and the location. Fluctuations in the number of reports, variations in content and power failures will all affect the level of service. No refunds, compensation and/or other costs and expenses will be paid at any time unless there has been a complete failure of the service for a continuous period of [number] days and then the payment shall be fixed at [number/currency] per day in total per company.

D.416

1.1 The [Author] and/or the [Company] shall not be held liable by the [Manufacturer/Distributor] for any legal actions, claims, allegations, damages, losses, costs, expenses and/or complaints and/or penalties relating to the [Product/Units/Service] created and developed by the [Manufacturer/Distributor] adapted from the rights granted under this agreement.

1.2 The [Manufacturer/Distributor] agrees and undertakes to arrange insurance cover to cover any such matter in 1.2 and shall at no time seek to be reimbursed by the [Author] and/or the [Company] even where not all the sums are covered by the policy.

Publishing

D.417
This [Novel] is a work of fiction. Names and characters are the product of the [Author's] imagination and creation and any resemblance to actual persons living or dead is entirely coincidental.

D.418
This book is a work of fiction. Names, characters, places and incidents are either products of the [Author's] imagination or used fictitiously. Any resemblance to actual people living or dead, events, locations or business establishments is entirely coincidental.

D.419
This book is a work of fiction and any person, character, name, business or other enterprise, locations and incidents or plots are the result of the original work of the [Author].

D.420
Neither the [Publishers] nor the [Authors] can accept any responsibility and/or liability for any losses, damages, costs, expenses and/or any legal actions and/or claims and/or settlements and/or other sums which may arise directly and/or indirectly as a result of the use, reliance upon and/or adoption of the concepts, ideas, data, information and/or arguments proposed in this [Book/Article/Report] and/or any associated disc and/or material. You are advised to seek independent legal and professional advice from a third party who is a qualified expert and not to rely on the accuracy, propositions and/or anticipated changes due to any data, information and/or other material from this [Book/Article/Report].

D.421

Any advice, recommendations, exercises and proposals made in this [Work] are the opinion of [Name] who is not a qualified practitioner of [subject]. You must take advice from an expert who can advise on your personal circumstances. If you decide to proceed without expert advice then you do so at your own risk and any consequences shall be at your own cost and no liability can be attributed to [Name]. If you have any of the following conditions you are advised not to follow any part of this [Work] as it will be dangerous to your health: [specify].

D.422

Neither the [Publishers] nor the [Authors] accept any responsibility and/or liability for any errors, omissions, costs, expenses, losses, damages and/or any legal actions, claims, settlements and/or other consequences of any nature which may arise directly and/or indirectly as a result of the use of any of the contents of this [Book/Audio File/Disc] at any time. Any use, reliance upon and/or actions taken based on any part of this [Book/Audio File/Disc] are entirely at your own risk and cost. You are strongly advised to get expert advice based on your individual circumstances. Any scenarios, circumstances and case studies are for general discussion and guidance and not intended to be personal and/or commercial advice to any individual and/or enterprise.

D.423

1.1 The [Sound Recording/Audio File] is supplied to you on a non-exclusive basis for your own personal use. There is no authority granted to supply the [Sound Recording/Audio File] to third parties and/or to make any adaptation.

1.2 There is no undertaking and/or indemnity provided to you the user regarding any content in the [Sound Recording/Audio File]. You shall not have the right to make a claim and/or seek any payment for your use of the [Sound Recording/Audio File] for any reason. In the event the [Company] notifies you that you must cease using the [Sound Recording/Audio File [at any time then you agree to delete all copies. In any event your right to use the [Sound Recording/Audio File] shall cease on [date].

Services

D.424

1.1 The [Service/Platform] provided by the [Distributor] contains content which is supplied by third parties. The [Distributor] does not accept any liability and/or responsibility for any errors, inaccuracies, false

information and/or data and/or any material which may be offensive
and/or defamatory and/or which is an infringement of copyright and/or
other intellectual property rights and/or any other matter.

1.2 The [Distributor] relies on you notifying them of any problems which
they will investigate and then delete material and/or close any account
based on their decision regarding the complaint.

1.3 In any event the maximum liability of the [Distributor] in relation to any
claim shall be limited to [number/currency].

D.425

1.1 The [Company] agrees and undertakes that as far as reasonably
possible the [Service] shall be up to date and based on the correct
information and/or data available at the time.

1.2 The [Company] shall not however be responsible and/or liable for any
delay in updating the [Service] due to circumstances which for any
reason are deemed to be force majeure. In such event the [Company]
shall not be liable for any consequences which may arise in respect of
any [Subscriber/User].

1.3 The [Company] may suspend and/or cancel the [Service] without
notice if in the view of the [Company] they are unable to maintain the
quality of the [Service]. In such event the [Company] shall not be liable
to any consequences which may arise in respect of any [Subscriber/
User].

1.4 Where any [Subscriber/User] relies on the [Service] for any reason and
as a result sustains losses, damages, expenses, costs and /or other
sums which can directly be attribute to reliance on the [Service]. Then
the [Subscriber/User] agrees that the total liability of the [Company]
for all claims shall be [number/currency] until [date]. Thereafter the
[Company] shall have no liability whatsoever for any reason to the
[Subscriber/User].

D.426

This is a free service which is supplied without any undertakings, assurances
and/or indemnity. You are only permitted to access the service on the basis
that the [Supplier] is under no liability whatsoever to you for your use of the
service at any time.

D.427

1.1 [Name] is a contributor and writer for the [Service] provided by the
[Company].

1.2 The [Company] accepts that [Name] is under no liability to the [Company] and/or any third party in respect of the content which [Name] supplies for the [Service]. That it is the duty and responsibility of the [Company] to check the content supplied by the [Contributor] for any legal problems. That in the event there are any claims, settlements and/or other sums paid relating to the content [Name] shall not be liable for any such sums.

D.428

1.1 The [Author] and/or the [Publisher] are not liable to you the [Purchaser/ Subscriber] for any reason except to the extent of the [Purchase Price/ Subscription Price of the [Work/Service].

1.2 Any [Purchaser/Subscriber] must make your own decision as to the contents of this [Work/Service] and any steps and/or actions you may take based upon any advice, data and/or recommendations are entirely at your own choice and risk.

1.3 The [Author] and/or the [Publisher] do not and cannot accept any responsibility for any losses, damages, interest, costs and expenses that you may decide to incur and/or may suffer at any time for any reason.

1.4 Where the [Work/Service] recommends any exercises and/or ingredients and/or equipment and/or some other matter. You are advised to seek a medical review by a qualified doctor before undertaking strenuous exercise and/or to review any possible contents which may cause an allergic reaction and/or other problems before using any ingredients.

1.5 The [Author] and/or [Company] accept that they cannot exclude liability for any direct consequences which may cause and result in personal injury and/or death which are directly attributable to the negligence and/or failure of duty of care of the [Author] and/or [Publisher].

Sponsorship

D.429

The [Company] agrees and undertakes that:

1.1 The [Company] shall be responsible for and bear the cost of all allegations, claims, losses, damages, legal actions, settlements and/ or otherwise which arise as a direct result of the [Event].

1.2 That the [Sponsor] shall not be liable to make any contribution and/ or bear any costs and/or expenses unless caused by the actions, negligence, failures, omissions and/or errors of the [Sponsor] and/or a third party engaged by the [Sponsor].

1.3 That the [Company] shall arrange and pay for the cost of insurance cover of [number/currency] which shall cover the following scenarios [specify detail].

D.430

1.1 The [Parent Company], the [Sponsor], the [Distributor] and [Organiser] cannot accept responsibility and/or liability for your entry into and/or taking part in the [Event]. You must accept as a condition of entry that this activity is only suitable for those who have a high level of fitness and are able to withstand strenuous conditions.

1.2 You are advised to take medical advice as to your health and to carry put a fitness assessment with a qualified person before making any payment for your entry.

1.3 No responsibility cannot be accepted for any travel, accommodation, food, insurance, telephone and mobile costs and charges that may arise as a result of your entry and participation in the [Event] which you do at your own cost and risk.

1.4 There is no undertaking by the [Parent Company], the [Sponsor], the [Distributor] and/or the [Organiser] that any part of the [Website/App/Brochure] is accurate, complete or up to date and this site must be used for guidance only. Data, information times and dates may be changed and amended and/or the location and/or dates changed at short notice due to unforeseen circumstances and/or weather conditions.

1.5 No liability is accepted by Parent Company], the [Sponsor], the [Distributor] and [Organiser] for any damages, losses, costs and/or expenses which arise as a result. You accept as a condition of your use of the [Website/App/Brochure] and entry to the [Event] that you will make no claim or seek to be indemnified for any loss, damage, expenses or other consequences that may arise unless it is for personal injury directly caused by the negligence and the failure of duty of care of the [Parent Company], the [Sponsor], the [Distributor] and/or the [Organiser].

1.6 You must at all times complete any task at the [Event] as instructed by the officials and marshals. You must only compete wearing the clothing and footwear which is of a suitable standard. Any failure to comply with either of these conditions may result in you being asked to leave the [Event] at any time.

1.7 If in the view of any official and/or medical advisor at the [Event] you are not sufficiently fit to take part and/or your health is at risk and/or you have suffered a personal injury. You are obliged if requested to leave the [Event] and any official and/or medical advisor may ensure that this request is complied with.

D.431

The [Sponsor] agrees and undertakes that it accepts full responsibility and liability for any products, services, equipment, staff, marketing, advertising and other material and/or persons which it has and/or will supply for the [Event]. That the [Sponsor] shall ensure that it has arranged and paid for suitable insurance cover of [number/currency] for any one claim and shall provide a copy of such policy to the [Company] upon request.

D.432

The [Sponsor] is not responsible for the acts, omissions, errors and/or views of any third party associated with the [Event]. No assurance as to the ownership of, reliability, accuracy and/or otherwise of any material supplied by a third party is provided by the [Sponsor]. The [Sponsor] does not endorse, agree with and/or monitor the content relating to any third party. The [Sponsor] does not have any editorial control over and/or power to delete, change and/or amend any material either on this [Website/App/Brochure] and/or in relation to the [Event].

D.433

1.1 The [Sponsor] does not agree to be liable for the failures and/or omissions of the [Company] at the [Event] in respect of any third parties including performers, visitors and/or caterers.

1.2 The [Company] must not represent to third parties that the [Sponsors'] are joint partners in the [Event] and/or responsible for any planning, organisation, insurance and/or marketing.

1.3 The total liability of the [Sponsor] is fixed at [number/currency] to the [Company] to make a funding contribution in return for product placement promotion at the [Event].

1.4 Any additional liability by the [Sponsor] to any third party for personal injury and/or death and/or any other reason shall be covered by the [Sponsors'] own public liability insurance taken out for its own benefit for that [Event].

D.434

The [Company] and/or the [Sponsor] both agree that they shall be jointly liable for the cost and expense of any complaint, allegations, claims, legal actions, losses, damages and/or other sums that may be incurred by any member of the public and/or any third party relating to the [Event] for which the [Company] and the [Sponsor] agree they are responsible and make any settlement and/

or which a court of law holds them liable for any reason. Neither party shall be liable for any legal and administrative costs incurred by the other.

D.435

The [Main Sponsor] of the [Programme/Event] agrees that:

1.1 It shall be liable for the cost and expense of any allegation, claim, settlement and other legal action against the [Company] which relates to the [Sponsor] and/or its personnel and/or brands, services and/or products at the [Programme/Event] at any time.

1.2 It shall also make a contribution towards the cost of any other allegation, claim, settlement and/or legal action against the [Company] which amounts to fifty per cent of any sum incurred by the [Company] including legal costs of up to [number/currency]. This undertaking shall not apply to a matter resolved after [date].

University, Charity and Educational

D.436

1.1 The [Institute/Charity] does not accept liability for your reliance on any information, data, products, advice, prices, availability or other matters of any nature provided by its employees, representatives, on its website, app and/or in its catalogues, emails and/or correspondence.

1.2 All details may change without notice, may contain errors and/or inaccuracies and are intended for guidance only. No responsibility can be accepted by the [Institute/Charity] for any loss, damage, expense and/or other consequences which may arise as a direct and/or indirect result of reliance on anything displayed and/or supplied by the [Institute/Charity] except in relation to a valid claim for personal injury and/or death.

D.437

No responsibility or liability can be accepted for any errors, omissions, corrections, delays, suspensions, losses and/or damages and/or other sums that may arise from use of any information, recommendations, data, software, databases, prices, services and/or products whether for private and personal use and/or otherwise. No consent, licence, permission and/or agreement is provided for any reproduction, supply, distribution and/or educational and/or commercial exploitation.

D.438

1.1 The [Institute/Charity] shall not be responsible for the use by you of any information, data, images, photographs, exhibitions, displays, articles, documents, records, databases, films, videos, sound recordings, books, computer software and/or any other media to which you are granted access and use of at the [Institute/Charity]. The arrangement to view the material in person does not grant you permission to take any images, photographs and/or films and/or other copies in any format and/or medium.

1.2 It is your responsibility if you wish to have the right to make any copies to seek a licence from the [Institute/Charity]. In the event that the [Institute/Charity] decide to grant any licence there may also be third parties with whom you must clear the material and pay for an additional licence to the copyright owner for the exploitation of the copyright and other intellectual property rights in any material.

1.3 You must abide by the photocopying and reproduction policy of the [Institute/Charity]. The [Institute/Charity] reserves the right to seek to make a claim for losses, damages, costs and expenses including legal costs against you in the event that the [Institute/Charity] is joined in any claim and/or legal action against you and/or any legal action is threatened as a result of the use of material obtained by you through the [Institute/Charity].

D.439

The [Institute/Charity] cannot and does not accept full liability for any scientific data and statements that it releases and/or distributes to any third party at any time. There is no authority provided to any third party to use and/or adapt and/or develop and/or rely on this resource as more than an archive library. Material is out of date at the time of release and new data may be withheld due to legal, confidential and/or other reasons.

D.440

1.1 The fundraising targets, case studies and other information and data on this [Website/App/Platform/Blog] may have been summarised and/or substituted with alternative names in order to protect the identity of an individual and/or to protect confidential information regarding a medical condition and/or treatment.

1.2 There is no right to copy, adapt, reproduce and/or exploit any content at any time without the consent of the [Charity/Institute].

1.3 The [Charity/Institute] is not making any scientific and/or medical recommendations for any person. Information, data and case studies are not addressed to any individual person. It may be dangerous to your health and safety to follow any matter without first seeking professional advice from an expert.

DISCOUNT

General Business and Commercial

D.441

The [Company] shall receive not less than [specify] per cent of the highest [retail/subscription] price of the [Work/Service] received by the [Distributor] whether or not the [Work/Service] is sold, supplied or promoted at a lower price.

D.442

Where a discount has been made to a [Customer] for [Products] which have a fault or are seconds and the price is reduced for that reason and the [Customer] is made aware of the fault or condition of the seconds at the time of purchase then there shall be no obligation to provide a refund and the [Products] cannot be returned.

D.443

The [Licensee] shall have the right to reduce the price to zero and/or to make such arrangements for two products for the price of one and/or such other cross promotions as it thinks fit in the circumstances in respect of the [Product]. Provided that the [Licensee] shall pay the [Licensor] no less than [number/currency] for each [Product] in each accounting period.

D.444

The [Company] shall only be entitled to discount and/or reduce the price for the [Product/Work] by [number/currency] from the price of [number/currency] for each item. Any further reduction shall require the prior written agreement and consent of the [Licensor].

D.445

There shall be no discount and/or reduction offered by the [Company] unless the value of the order made and paid for by the [Customer] exceeds [number/currency] for any one order. Then a discount of [number] per cent on the total value paid for the [Products] will be made and a voucher provided which can be offset against the next purchase by the [Customer]. No sums are paid in cash and/or refunded. The voucher will expire within [six months] of the date it is issued.

D.446

Where any [Materials/Products] are advertised and/or promoted at a discount, reduced price and/or as factory seconds and/or clearance stock and/or otherwise at any lower value than either the [retail/wholesale] price. The total liability of the [Company] shall be limited to the total value for which the [Materials/Products] are sold to the [Client] and no refunds and/or returns of any nature shall be made and/or are permitted. The [Company] is selling the [Materials/Products] to any [Client] subject to this condition.

D.447

The offer of this discount and reduction on the value of the purchase of [Work/Service] commences [date/time] and ends [date/time]. The discount and reduction is only available to those persons who complete the following registration for the [Company] newsletter [specify] and live and/or reside in [country] and are over [age] years.

D.448

This discount is only available to new customers:

1.1   You must not currently receive the [Service].

1.2   Over the age of [number] years who reside permanently in [country].

1.3   Who pass any credit assessment criteria.

1.4   Whose [premises/equipment] are suitable to receive the [Service].

1.5   End date of discount: [date/time].

The [Company] reserves the right to refuse the [Service] and/or discount to any person and/or third party without providing a reason.

DISCRIMINATION

General Business and Commercial

D.449

The [Company] agrees and undertakes that it shall not discriminate against any [person/company] who complies with all the criteria and undertakings set out in the application, meets all the deadlines and is able to verify the facts with supporting documentation. All applicants will be treated fairly and provided with the same information and assistance.

D.450

There shall be no discrimination on the grounds of age, status, gender, religion, racial group, family background, political beliefs and/or disability.

D.451

There shall be no discrimination in favour of any particular race, educational background and/or social group. All applicants will be judged on their personal ability, qualifications, skills and experience.

D.452

The [Company] requires persons with fluency in the following languages: [specify] and the following qualifications: [specify].

D.453

The [Company] will only consider applications for [work experience/ internship/roles/jobs] for the position of [specify] from persons over age [number] years for the fixed term contract who have one or more of the following disabilities; hearing which is impaired; deaf; visually impaired; blind and/or physical and/or mobility disability. The [Company] shall as part of the position put in place a disability access and support programme to facilitate the role by any person appointed.

D.454

It shall not be deemed discrimination to reject any candidates and/or applications in any part of the process either before and/or after appointment for a position at the [Company] who are found to have provided incorrect and/ false details in respect of any references; residence and/or home addresses; medical record and/or state of health; criminal record and pending legal and/or disciplinary actions; qualifications and work experience; holding of a valid passport and/or visa for the right to work. The [Company] reserves and shall have the right to terminate any agreement immediately and to withdraw all benefits and obligations which have been agreed with any such persons.

D.455

The [Agent/Distributor] agree and undertake that they shall ensure that both they and/or any sub-agent, sub-licensee and/or any other third party shall comply with any legislation and policies that may exist in any country in which they operate and/or do business including but not limited to those relating to discrimination, health and safety, product liability, transport, pay and conditions for employees.

D.456

The [Enterprise] agrees to support and adhere to in all its dealings with staff, students and third parties the policies of the following organisations: [specify organisation] [state policies] for the period [date] to [date].

DISMISSAL

General Business and Commercial

D.457

The [Company] agrees to abide by procedures and processes set out in the [Staff Handbook] subject to any existing legislation in [country].

D.458

The [Company] agrees that it shall not be entitled to rely on the [Employee's] personal use of the [Company's] telephone, mobile, internet, postage, refreshments, car and/or laptop as grounds for dismissal.

D.459

The [Company] shall be entitled to dismiss the [Executive/Presenter] without notice and with immediate effect in the event:

1.1 That the [Executive/Presenter] fails a random drug test and/or fails the annual medical.

1.2 That the [Company] has evidence that the [Executive/Presenter] has provided information and data to a rival business or competitor.

1.3 That the [Company] has evidence that the [Executive/Presenter] committed a serious crime and has been charged.

1.4 That the [Executive/Presenter] has failed to attend meetings and/or engagements for more than [two] weeks without a medical note and/or authorised absence.

1.5 That the [Executive/Presenter] has been dishonest and obtained money, goods and/or services from the [Company]; not been truthful about his qualifications and/or acted in such a manner that his/her behaviour was a physical threat to other staff.

D.460

In the event that the [Company] believes that it has reasonable grounds for dismissing the [Executive] from his/her position at the [Company]. Then the [Company] agrees to advise the [Executive] in writing of the grounds and to allow the [Executive] the opportunity to refute the allegations.

D.461

The [Executive] agrees to be bound by the terms of the [Grievance Procedure] which is attached to and forms part of this agreement as Schedule B.

D.462

In the event that there are concerns regarding the work, timekeeping and/or failure to wear the uniform required of any casual employee. The [Company] agrees to hold a meeting with the person to discuss the issues and to agree a resolution of the problem. Where after that meeting the casual employee still does not comply as requested then the [Company] reserves the right to terminate the agreement with them and shall pay them to the end of that calendar month in which the agreement is terminated.

D.463

The [Company] must comply with the highest standards relating to hygiene and health and safety at its premises and all employees are required to comply with the policy attached in Appendix A which form part of your terms and conditions of employment. Failure to comply with any part of the policy which is not due to the fault of the [Company] and/or a member of the management team will result in a written warning stating how you have failed to comply and an opportunity to respond. Then the [Company] may decide to dismiss you and/or terminate your employment and/or impose a temporary suspension and/or such other action as it deems suitable based on the severity of the matter.

DISPUTES

General Business and Commercial

D.464

The [Distributor] agrees that in the event of any dispute between the parties under this agreement. The [Licensor] shall be entitled to receive copies of all documents, papers, contracts, both internal and external correspondence, emails and exchanges, computer records and discs, accounts, receipts, invoices and all other material relevant to the dispute at the [Licensor's] sole cost.

D.465

The acceptance of the [Company] of any sums paid under this agreement shall not prevent the [Company] at a later date disputing and/or demanding details of the sums due at any time. Nor shall such acceptance constitute a waiver of any breach of any terms by the [Licensee] that may occur.

D.466

The parties agree that a dispute relating to the contract should be determined by an expert. Any party may request that an expert be appointed. The parties shall try to agree a single expert by whom the matter shall be adjudicated. If the parties fail to agree the expert within [specify duration] of any request to do so. Then the parties agree that the following body shall nominate the expert [name/organisation/address]. The expert once appointed shall specify a reasonable time and date for submissions, and information from each party. The parties shall co-operate with the expert and with such enquiries that he/she may deem necessary. No confidential information supplied to the expert shall be disclosed to any third party. The expert shall not be an arbitrator but an expert permitted to set out his/her own procedure and be entitled to award financial damages in [currency] or to order the performance or prohibition of any act as he/she deems fit or otherwise. Both parties agree to abide by the decision of the expert in any such matter.

D.467
[Name] and the [Company] agree that any dispute arising in respect of this contract shall be settled in accordance with the procedure for settlement of disputes by [specify organisation/policy]. A copy of the policy document is attached in appendix C.

D.468
The parties agree that before taking any legal proceedings that they shall try to agree to go through the process of either mediation, alternative disputes resolution or arbitration in [country]. This clause shall not apply if one party is unable, unwilling or fails to attend in which case either party shall be entitled to take any legal action and seek any remedy.

D.469
Both parties agree that this agreement shall as far as possible be first resolved by mediation through [specify organisation/method]. That legal proceedings shall only be instituted as a final last resort after both parties have used their reasonable endeavours to resolve the dispute.

D.470
Both parties agree that they will use all reasonable endeavours to resolve such disputes as may arise between them in a professional and efficient manner. That they shall both co-operate and provide such documents as may reasonably be required from the other party to verify the facts of the dispute.

D.471
In the event that any dispute of any nature under this agreement cannot be resolved by the reasonable endeavours of both parties. Then the [Author] and the [Distributor] agree to resolve any disputes concerning this agreement using the following forum and means: [Alternative Dispute Resolution/organisation/other] in [country]. Each party shall bear its own costs and expenses until the matter has been resolved and a settlement agreed between the parties.

D.472
Where the [Licensor] and/or the [Licensee] are in dispute as to the sums owed to the [Licensor] under this agreement. Then the [Licensee] agrees to a full disclosure of all relevant bank statements, accounts, invoices, receipts. Software, databases and data and/or otherwise of the [Licensee] and any

sub-licensee and/or agent to the [Licensor] at the offices of the [Licensee]. The [Licensor] shall be entitled to take images of any material provided that there is an undertaking that it is kept confidential and circulation limited to professional advisors and/or directors of the [Licensor].

D.473
Where the [Sponsor] and/or the [Company] and/or any third party are in dispute. Then the [Sponsor] and/or the [Company] agree that prior to the issue of any legal proceedings the parties shall try to arrange to meet to discuss and try to resolve the matter amicably without incurring any additional legal costs on a without prejudice basis. That the next step shall be an attempt to agree a form of mediation, arbitration and/or other informal resolution of the matter. Neither party shall be bound to take any of these steps prior to the issue of legal proceedings.

D.474
The [Consultant] agrees that where there is a dispute between the [Company] and the [Consultant] that the matter shall be resolved by the following method [specify organisation/method]. That both parties agree to participate and the decision of the person appointed to resolve the dispute shall be binding on both parties.

D.475
It is agreed between the parties to the [Consortium] that where there is any dispute that the parties shall endeavour to avoid legal proceedings and shall adopt a policy of negotiation and resolution of any matter by the appointment of an expert in the field to review and assess the facts and to make a recommendation as to how it may best be resolved to the satisfaction of all parties. The cost of the expert shall be paid for out of the [Consortium] funds for the [Project] and authorised by all parties. Any such review and recommendation shall not be binding and any of the parties shall have the right to take such legal proceedings as they think fit at any time.

D.476
Where there are any disputes between the [Agent] and the [Author] regarding fees, royalties and/or any other sums which may be due and/or owing to the [Author]. The [Agent] shall not be entitled to withhold and/or retain any sums against future legal costs and expenses and/or sums which are due to the [Author]. The [Agent] shall supply copies of all bank statements, invoices, documents, agreements, royalty statements, emails and attachments that may be requested by the [Author] and/or any consultant, accountant and/or legal advisor who may be assisting him and/or her. No charge shall be made by the [Agent] for this service to the [Author].

D.477

Disputes between any [Club] and its members shall be resolved by the procedure and process set out in its [Constitution/Memorandum and Articles of Association]. In the event that it cannot be resolved by this process then any member may make a resolution at the [Annual General Meeting] for consideration by all members provided it is supported by [number] members and submitted [number] days prior to the date of the meeting. Where the [Club] is subject to the rules and guidelines of a national governing body then account shall be taken of any rules, policies and guidelines that they may have issued which are applicable at the time.

D.478

Where there is any dispute between the [Company] and the [Client] regarding the valuation and/or content and/or prior ownership and history and/or any other matter regarding the [Unit/Item] at any time. The [Company] may refuse to list and/or offer the [Unit/Item] for sale without any reason. The [Company] shall pay for the cost of the [Unit/Item] to be delivered securely to the [Client].

DISQUALIFICATION

General Business and Commercial

D.479

Any applicant who cannot provide supporting evidence in the form required by the [Agency] or by the notified deadline may be disqualified at the total discretion of the [Agency].

D.480

In the event that any participant or their families, or their agents attempt to offer inducements, bribes, benefits or other rewards to any official, officer, or Director of the [Company/Agency] then that participant shall be disqualified.

D.481

The [Sponsor] shall not be entitled to withdraw the funds under clause [–] in the event that:

1.1 [Name] is not in the team for any reason and/or

1.2 the team which is expected to comprise of the following persons: [specify persons] is disqualified from participating in the [Event] for any reason.

D.482

1.1 Where an entry form is not submitted by the deadline of [date/time] to [address]. Then any person shall not be permitted to enter the [Event/Race].

1.2 The application will be rejected if the fee payment is not made according to the deadline whether or not the form has been submitted.

1.3 Where you have provided misleading and/or false information and/or data and/or represented that you have attained a standard and/or level which is inaccurate and/or false. Then the [Company] shall have the right to cancel your right to enter the [Event/Race] at any time.

1.4 You will not be permitted to take part where at a later date you are discovered to have used and/or failed a banned drug test in any country at any time. In such event your entry fee will be refunded and your place cancelled. There will be no right of appeal.

1.5 Failure to wear the required safety [equipment/other] will automatically disqualify you from participation on the day. The judgement of the [Company] is final and there is no right of appeal.

1.6 Any behaviour which is deemed inappropriate and/or offensive either before, during and/or after the [Event/Race] may result in you being banned from all future [Events/Races] for up [one] year.

D.483

You are disqualified from applying for this [post/role] in the event that you are:

1.1 under the age of [number] years on [date].

1.2 not in possession of a current and valid driving licence in [country].

1.3 not able to speak and write [specify language] fluently.

1.4 not authorised to work and be employed in [country] and/or do not hold the relevant visa.

1.5 not in possession of a valid passport for one of the following countries: [specify list].

DISTRIBUTION EXPENSES

General Business and Commercial

D.484

'Distribution Expenses' shall mean all sums reasonably and properly incurred and/or charged by the [Television Company] in connection with the clearance, acquisition, licensing, editing and administration of any copyright, intellectual property rights, trade marks, music, sound recordings and/or lyrics and/or contractual obligations including agency and distribution fees and commission, repeat fees and residuals, legal fees and any other sums of any nature that may arise which are not covered in the Budget.

D.485
'Distribution Expenses' shall mean all costs and expenses properly and reasonably incurred by or on behalf of the [Production Company/Distributor] in connection with the exercise of the rights granted under this agreement. The sums shall include but not be limited to all:

1.1 Development, reproduction, distribution, exploitation, advertising and promotional costs.

1.2 The cost of any fees, buy-outs, commissions and expenses due to consultants, designers, computer software, film and video developers, photographers, musicians and artists, sub-licensees, sub-distributors and/or any other third party in respect of the exploitation of the [Series/Films] in any part of the world.

1.3 Legal, administrative and accounting costs. The cost of dealing with any legal problems including any settlements, damages, losses and expenses.

1.4 Repeat, residual, clearance, consent and copyright fees and other rights and contractual payments which were not included in the original Budget. Sums due to any collecting society for the performance, transmission and/or use of any material.

1.5 Costs associated with the supply of master materials and the creation of any foreign language versions. The cost of supply of master materials and other promotional material, insurance, shipping, packaging, storage, inspection, duties and imports.

D.486
'The Distribution Expenses' shall be the following costs reasonably and properly incurred in respect of the exploitation of the [Films] by the [Licensee] which are not recouped from any third party:

1.1 Reproduction and replacement costs of original master material of the [Films] and/or any trailer, videos, images and associated marketing and promotional material.

1.2 Delivery, storage, shipping, custom duties, freight, handling charges and insurance.

1.3 Copyright, permissions and consents, clearance and performing right payments and other fees and expenses to individuals, companies and/or collecting societies for any material relating to the exploitation of the [Films].

1.4 Distributors', sub-distributors' and sub-licensees' commission.

1.5 Dubbing, editing, sub-titling, translation and other costs for foreign versions.

1.6 Accounting and auditing fees and charges and legal fees whether for debt collection and/or protection of any legal rights of the parties and/or any defence and/or payments related to any legal claim.

D.487
'The Promotion Expenses' shall mean all costs directly expended by the [Promoter] in furtherance of this agreement which have not been recouped from any third party which are not unreasonable and/or excessive:

1.1 The cost of any survey and marketing reports and/or data.

1.2 The cost of the development, production, exhibition and distribution of marketing videos, blogs, articles, website, app and other computer generated material. Cost of all artwork, designs, photographs, text and any other material. Together with payments to persons to promote the [Project] online on their personal blog, channel and/or platform.

1.3 All delivery, storage, shipping, customs duties, freight, handling charges and insurance.

1.4 The cost of the clearance of rights and/or the use and/or adaptation of any material. All fees and expenses due in respect of the copyright and/or intellectual property rights, trade marks, sound recordings, music, photographs and images in any material and/or the use of any products and/or services.

It shall not include administrative and/or personnel and/or legal costs of the [Promoter].

D.488
The [Organisers] confirm that it shall be solely responsible for all sums incurred in respect of the [Event]. The [Promoter] shall not be responsible for any sums except for any unauthorised expenditure and costs incurred by the [Promoter] which are not within the Promotion Expenses and which are not agreed in advance with the [Organisers].

D.489

The [Agent] confirms that the [Author] shall not be responsible for any costs or expenses incurred by the [Agent] pursuant to this agreement. The [Agent] shall only be entitled to receive the [Agent's Commission].

D.490

The [Publisher] agrees that it shall be solely responsible for all costs incurred in printing, publishing, distributing, marketing and exploiting the [Work/ Book/Audio File] throughout the Territory.

D.491

The [Assignee] confirms that it shall be solely responsible for all sums due in respect of the production, distribution, marketing and exploitation of the [Commissioned Work] in any media throughout the world. That the [Assignee] shall not seek to recoup any sums from [Name] for any reason.

D.492

The [Company] confirms that it shall be solely responsible for all costs incurred in the development, production, manufacture, distribution, marketing, promotion, advertising and exploitation of the [Products/Units]. That the [Company] shall not be entitled to deduct such sums and/or set-off any such sums prior to the calculation and payment of the Licensor's Royalties under this agreement. The [Company] shall be entirely liable for all such costs and no contribution of any nature shall be due from and/or claim made against the [Licensor].

D.493

The [Assignee] acknowledges that it shall be solely responsible for any sums due in respect of the manufacture, distribution, marketing and exploitation of the [Film/Television/Merchandising Rights] in the [Film/Series]. The [Assignor] shall not be liable for any such payments.

D.494

1.1 The [Company] agrees that the [Artiste] shall not be liable for any payments that may be incurred by the [Record Company] for any reason unless specifically authorised in writing by the [Artiste].

1.2 Nor shall the [Company] be entitled to deduct any sums from the royalties due to the [Artiste] at any time.

1.3 The [Company] shall solely be responsible and liable for all costs and expenses that may be incurred by the [Company] at any time including but not limited to: the cost of production, manufacture, distribution, marketing and exploitation of the [Films/Sound Recordings] and/or any records, tapes, music, lyrics, songs and/or any other material created and/or exploited pursuant to this agreement.

D.495

1.1 The [Distributor] agrees and undertakes that it shall provide a full breakdown of all the Distribution Expenses that may and/or have been deducted from the Gross Receipts pursuant to this agreement.

1.2 Further the [Distributor] agrees and undertakes that upon request by the [Licensor] the [Distributor] shall provide the [Licensor] with the opportunity to inspect the original documents and/or shall supply copies at the [Distributor's] cost.

1.3 The [Distributor] agrees that in any event the [Distributor] shall not be entitled to deduct more than [number/currency] in respect of the aggregate Distribution Expenses during the Term of this Agreement. Any further sums in excess of that total shall be the sole responsibility of the [Distributor] and the sums shall not be deducted from the Gross Receipts prior to the payment of royalties due to the [Licensor].

D.496
'The Distribution Expenses' shall be the aggregate total maximum of [number/currency] being such sums which the [Licensee] shall be entitled to deduct in respect of all costs reasonably and properly paid to third parties and which have not been recouped in respect of the commercial distribution and exploitation of the [Product/Service] by the [Licensee].

D.497
'Distribution Expenses' shall mean the expenses incurred and/or paid by the [Company] in respect of the distribution of the [Film/Series] and shall include, but not be limited to the cost of:

1.1 development, reproduction, delivery, storage and/or exploitation of all master material in any format and/or medium that may be required. The cost of all dubbing, sub-titling, editing, adaptations, trailers and/or extracts of the [Film/Series].

1.2 development, reproduction and exploitation of all packaging, marketing and promotional material in any medium.

1.3 customs duties, freight, shipment, importation taxes and/or duties, fees and costs incurred in respect of obtaining approval from any third party for shipment and/or the consent of any government or other bodies that may arise.

1.4   clearance, consent, waiver, and/or authority to exploit any material in the [Film/Series] whether copyright, trademarks, design rights, and/or any other contractual and/or intellectual property rights in the [Film/Series] and/or soundtrack. All costs and payments in respect of the use, transmission and/or performance of any music and/or sound recording to any individual, union and/or collecting society. All costs and payments in respect of consents for material which has already been obtained, but for which further sums are due.

1.5   agency and distributor commissions and fees, accountant and audit fees, legal fees, professional agencies, technical and computer software companies in respect of the production, distribution and exploitation of the [Film/Series], and/or the instigation of legal proceedings and/or the collection of any payment and/or the registration of any rights.

1.6   insurance cover for the [Film/Series] and any other material at any time including cover for any indemnity provisions.

D.498
The [Company] shall be entitled to deduct all costs and expenses relating to the sale, distribution and/or other exploitation of the [Work/Product] including but not limited to all distributors, agents and/or representatives' charges, commission and expenses and/or other sums paid under any indemnity by their agreements with the [Company].

D.499
'Distribution Expenses' means all sums reasonably expended to a third party by the [Licensee] and/or any authorised sub-licensee in respect of the supply, sale, distribution, exhibition, and exploitation of the [Work/Service] in the Territory.

D.500
'Maximum Fee' shall mean the sum of [number/currency] which shall for the avoidance of doubt be the combined total costs of the [Fee and Expenses] as may be paid by the [Company] to the [Designer].

D.501
The [Distributor] shall be entirely responsible for all the costs of the distribution, supply and marketing of the [Product/Unit] including but not limited to insurance, freight, advertisements, packaging, telephone charges, custom duties and taxes, compliance with trading standards and other legal requirements. The [Distributor] agrees and undertakes that it shall not seek to recoup any sums from [Name] even if the projected sales of the [Product/Unit] are not achieved.

D.502

The [Licensee] and/or any sub-licensee and/agent shall not have the right to deduct any distribution charges, costs, expenses, commission, freight and transport, insurance and product liability, packaging, marketing, legal costs, damages, losses and/or any other sums from the percentage of the Gross Receipts due to the [Licensor] under this agreement.

D.503

The [Sponsor] shall reimburse the [Company/Institute] subject to the production of invoices and/or an itemised statement of the full cost of reproducing, supplying, packaging, distributing and marketing the [Sponsor's] logo, slogan and products as set out in Schedule B which is attached to and forms part of this agreement. The [Company/Institute] agrees that the total cost shall not exceed [number/currency] without the prior written consent of the [Sponsor] which it shall not be obliged to provide. That any additional costs not authorised by the [Sponsor] shall be the responsibility of the [Company/Institute].

D.504

Distribution expenses does not include any office and management expenses, travel, accommodation, mobile and landline telephone costs and charges, stationary, marketing and publicity on line, in catalogues and flyers and/or by any social events, entertainment, promotional and exhibition events of the [Agent] and/or any sub-licensee, distributor and/or other third party.

D.505

Distribution expenses which can be deducted prior to payment to [Name] under this agreement shall be limited to [number] per cent of the reasonable reproduction costs of the [Work] and [number] per cent of the reasonable freight, delivery and insurance costs. No other sums may be deducted from any sums due to [Name] and the [Company] shall bear all other costs and expenses. Where any sums are deducted then full details of the cost and original documents must be provided.

D.506

1.1 The [Company] and any sub-agent, sub-licensee agree and undertake that they must bear all the costs and expenses and liability of all sums that may be due and/or arise from the exploitation of the [Work] including but not limited sums due to develop, manufacture, reproduce, market, promote, exhibit and distribute the [Work].

1.2 [Name] shall not be obliged to make any contribution and/or pay any such sums in 1.1 at any time.

1.3 Nor shall the [Company] seek to withhold any sums due to [Name] for any reason. No such costs and expenses may be set-off and/or recouped from the Gross Receipts and any sums due to [Name]. The [Company] will remain and continue to be responsible for all the obligations and liabilities to [Name] of any sub-licensee and/or sub-agent. The [Company] and all such parties must pay all such sums in 1.1 at their own risk and cost.

D.507

1.1 There is no automatic right to deduct any expenses and/or costs from the sums due to [Name] under this agreement.

1.2 The [Distributor] must bear full responsibility for all sums which must be incurred and/or paid in order to develop, assess and test the [Sample].

1.3 The [Distributor] must pay for all the costs and expenses which are to be incurred to produce, manufacture, sell and distribute the [Products/Units] of any nature. No such sums shall be deducted from any monies due to [Name] and/or from any sums upon which those calculations are based at any time.

DOMAIN NAME

Internet, Websites and Apps

D.508

1.1 The [Designer/Developer] shall not acquire any copyright, intellectual property rights, computer software rights, database rights, trade marks, service marks and/or any other rights in the pending and/or registered domain name and/or similar variation and/or in the [Website/App/Platform] details of which are set out in the attached appendix A. [specify name/location/description].

1.2 The [Designer/Developer] shall not be entitled to register, apply, claim and/or otherwise represent that she/he owns and/or controls any right, interest and/or equity in the domain name and/or the [Website/App/Platform] and/or any other material created for and/or commissioned by the [Company] under this agreement.

1.3 The [Designer/Developer] acknowledges and agrees that the [Company] is the owner of the domain name and the [Website/App/Platform] in appendix A.

D.509

1.1 The [Company] agrees that it has and/or will register the domain name, website, app and online accounts: [specify names]. A detailed description which is set out in appendix A [domain name/website/app/on line accounts/references/trading name/trade mark/logo/image/slogan] which is attached to and forms part of this agreement.

1.2 The [Company] agrees and undertakes that it shall be entirely responsible for the cost of all applications, registration fees, renewals, trade mark applications and registrations, litigation and/or disputes, legal costs and expenses and/or any third party liability incurred and/or arising in respect of any matter in 1.1 and appendix A.

D.510

The [Designer/Creator] agrees and undertakes that he/she will not directly and/or indirectly seek to mimic, register and/or exploit the domain name: [specify registered name/reference] and/or any other name, letters, words, images and/or representations which could reasonably be construed as adapted from and/or similar to and/or connected to and/or based upon the domain name: [specify registered name] controlled by the [Company] at any time.

D.511

The [Seller] undertakes that the following details are true and accurate:

1.1 That the [Seller] is the original creator of and owns all rights and interest in the domain name: [specify name/reference].

1.2 That to the best of the knowledge and belief of the [Seller] there is no claim, legal action, dispute, complaint and/or interest in the domain name: [specify name/reference] which is pending and/or threatened by a third party as at [date].

1.3 That the domain name: [name/reference] is registered with [specify organisation] in the name of [specify exact registered name of owner] and that all required payments and fees have been paid to [date].

1.4 That the domain was not based on, derived from and/or copied from any third party and/or any other material owned and/or controlled by a third party by the [Seller].

1.5 The [Seller] agrees to supply the [Purchaser] with any original documentation in its possession relating to the registration of the domain name in 1.1 and/or any objections by third parties to the original registration.

D.512

The rights, registrations, computer software and material which are described in detail in schedule B are owned and controlled by [Name] as follows:

1.1   The domain name: [specify name/reference].

1.2   The website [specify name/reference].

1.3   The app [specify name/reference].

1.4   The online accounts: [names/references].

1.5   The online channels: [names/references]

1.6   The sound recording, slogan, logo and image: [brief description].

1.7   The trade mark: [name/reference].

There is no authority granted to any person to use, copy, adapt, reproduce and/or exploit any matters listed above without the prior written consent of [Name] and the conclusion of an authorised licence.

You are not permitted to create and develop any merchandising in any format and/or to use, display, adapt and/or reproduce any material, logo, trade mark, image, films, videos and/or otherwise for any reason.

D.513

1.1   Both parties agree that the domain names, on line accounts and/or channels, trade marks and any other names, logos and/or intellectual property rights, computer software rights and/or any other interest and/or material relating to the [Project] which may be in existence now described in appendix B and/or may be created in the future shall be registered in the name of both parties as the equal joint legal owners.

1.2   Both parties agree and undertake that they shall be jointly liable for the payment of any legal fees, the cost of any application and registration fees, renewals, and any other expenses and/or sums in respect of protection of the rights and material in 1.1 and/or any legal actions and/or disputes.

1.3   Neither party shall be entitled to assign, transfer, license, exploit and/or be entitled to agree to any variation in respect of the domain names, on line accounts, channels, trade marks and/or any other names, logos and/or intellectual property rights, computer software rights and/or any other interest and/or material relating to the {Project] which may be in existence now described in appendix B and/or may be created in the future without the prior written consent of other party.

D.514

'The Domain Name' shall mean: [specify name/reference] which is owned and/or controlled by [Name/Company] and was first registered with [specify organisation] on [date] in [name listed as owner]. The domain name is now owned by [Name/Company] and is still currently registered with them as at [date] and all fees and charges have been paid to [date]. The domain name shall not include any website and/or app content, associated artwork, logo, trademark, films, videos, images, sound recordings and/or computer generated material.

D.515

1.1   The [Licensee] agrees that the [Licensee] shall not register and/
      or attempt to register any domain name, trade mark, service mark,
      community mark and/or any other words, initials, images and/or shapes
      which are the same and/or similar to the [title/name/character] of the
      [Work] and/or [Product].

1.2   The [Licensee] shall ensure that any sub-licensee, distributor, supplier,
      retail outlet and/or agent and/or consultant that the [Licensee] shall
      engage and/or have an agreement with regarding the production,
      manufacture, sales and/or marketing of the [Product] shall also agree
      to this condition in 1.1.

D.516

1.1   The [Sponsor] shall own and/or control and/or have the right to apply
      for and register the following words, initials and/or slogans as domain
      names: [specify list] in respect of the [Event].

1.2   The [Company/Institute] agrees that the [Sponsor] shall own and/
      or control all rights in respect of the domain names in 1.1 and that
      the [Company/Institute] shall not have any rights and/or interest
      whatsoever.

D.517

The [Consultant] agrees that where he/she has worked on the [Project] to develop, create and design a corporate name, logo, design, domain name, banner links and other promotional material that he/she shall not have right and/or authority to attempt and/or to register, exploit and/or benefit from any such material and that all rights are held and/or owned and/or controlled by the [Company] and are assets of that [Company].

D.518

1.1   [Name] confirms that he/she has applied for and registered the
      domain name [specify name/reference] with [specify organisation]

from [date] to [date] and has paid all the fees due and shall also pay any renewal fees.

1.2 [Name] confirms that the domain name in 1.1 and the associated [website/app] known as [name/reference] are used in conjunction with the slogan, logo and other material set out in Schedule A which is attached to and forms part of this agreement.

1.3 In consideration of [number/currency] [Name] assigns and transfers all the rights and interest in 1.1 and Schedule A to the [Club/Company] together with any copyright, intellectual property rights, trade marks, service marks and domain name rights of any text, image, logo and/ or other such material for the full period of any rights and the right to renew and extend any such period.

D.519

1.1 No consultant shall have the right to reproduce, use, adapt and/or exploit any domain name, logo, slogan, trade mark, image, film and/or other rights and/or material owned by the [Institute/Charity].

1.2 The [Consultant] must seek authorisation in order to display any such material in 1.1 on your profile, website, blog and/or on any publication, film and/or otherwise.

1.3 There is right to create the impression and/or to represent that the [Institute/Charity] endorses the work of the [Consultant] in any format.

D.520

1.1 [Name] is the original creator of the word [specify word] which he/ she has registered successfully as a domain name with [specify organisation] from [date].

1.2 [Name] confirms that he/she has not traded under the domain name.

1.3 [Name] confirms that no third party has made any claim and/or allegation relating to passing off and/or copyright infringement and/ or that the name is similar to an existing registration and/or trade mark against [Name] and/or the word and/or the domain name.

DOWNLOADING

Internet, Websites and Apps

D.521

Any downloading of material from this [Website/App] must be done subject to the terms and conditions set out in [specify location] on this [Website/App] and all material should be credited with the following acknowledgement and copyright notices must not be erased or deleted, nor should material be edited or adapted:

[Website/App Name] [reference]

[Name of Website/App Copyright Owner] © [year]

[Specify Material] is owned by [Copyright Owner of Material]

[Name of Material Copyright Owner] [year]

[Specify Material] is distributed under licence by [Distributor of Material]

D.522

Downloading, storage and retrieval of any material on any system, gadget or by any method or process or means whether in existence now or created in the future is strictly forbidden unless you have registered and agreed to abide by the terms and conditions of the [Subscription Service/Access and User Licence Agreement].

D.523

There is not a general right to download material of any nature from the internet, and you are expected to respect the copyright notices, trade marks and domain names of others which are displayed and to seek their permission for the use of any material you may wish to exploit. You are allowed to make copies of all the pages on this site for personal and non-commercial and educational purposes only for your own use. This does not include educational establishments and/or reproduction for distribution to students.

D.524

Material on this [Website/App/Audio File] may be downloaded, copied, stored for personal use and educational purposes, review, criticism, quotes, and research. No licence and/or permission is provided and/or granted to supply any material to a third party for the use, adaptation and/or exploitation in any form of any part of the [Website/App/Audio File] and/or any content.

D.525

You download material form this [Website/App/Audio File] at your own risk and expense. No liability is accepted by the owners of the [Website/App/Audio File] and/or the copyright owner of any material for any consequences that may arise as a result of your downloading the material. There is no undertaking and/or assurance and/or indemnity provided that the material is free from viruses and/or other defects and you are advised to carry out your own scan of any material.

D.526

The free [Downloads/Material] on this [Website/App/Audio File] may be downloaded, stored, retrieved, distributed, copied and/or adapted and/or developed without charge at your sole discretion. There is no obligation to credit this [Website/App/Audio File] as the source nor to pay any sums for the use and/or exploitation of any material.

D.527

1.1   The material on this [Website/App] is owned and/or controlled by [Copyright Owner] and [Licensee] and [Distributor].

1.2   You are only entitled to view the [Website/App] and no authority is given to store, retrieve, print, download, reproduce, transmit, supply, distribute and/or adapt any material and/or any part of the content.

1.3   Where material and/or content is stored and/or downloaded temporarily for personal use only and subsequently deleted and/or destroyed then no legal action will be taken for infringement and/or breach of any rights.

1.4   Please apply to [specify] for any application for a license for any other use for which a fee and/or royalties will be charged.

D.528

There is a non-exclusive license granted to the [Subscriber/User/Name] to:

1.1   make a maximum [number] copies of no more than [number] pages of this [Website/Article/Document] for private, non-commercial, residential purposes only in [country] at any time. This shall not include [specify areas].

1.2   Provided that where the pages are stored on the hard drive before printing they are subsequently deleted.

1.3   Provided that each page has a copyright notice as follows [specify copyright notice].

D.529

1.1   Where any part of this [Website/App/Audio File] permits and/or offers you the choice of downloading and/or accessing any material for free then any use and/or reproduction is limited to non-commercial purposes by you and your friends and/or gadgets.

1.2   You are not permitted to edit, adapt, change and/or vary the content in the course of reproduction and/or supply to another person outside your immediate family and friends.

736

1.3 You are not permitted to add any logos, images and/or other material belonging to a third party to any material supplied by the [Company].

1.4 The [Company] reserves the right to request at any time that you delete copies of the material that you have downloaded as you have used the material in a manner which they believe is derogatory, damaging and/or not in keeping with the reputation and policies of the [Company] in any part of the world.

D.530

There is no automatic right granted by the [Institute/Charity] to any person who accesses and/or enters this [Website/App/Platform] to reproduce, download, copy, adapt, edit and/or use any part of this [Website/App/Platform] and/or any material on it and/or linked to it and/or any archive except for non-commercial and educational research purposes only for their sole and personal use in the course of their education at a school, college and/or university.

Provided that a full title, credit and copyright notice is provided as follows: [specify copyright notice/credit/source reference] to the [Institute] and the author.

Any references must not exceed [number] words including any to be used for criticism and/or review. There is no authority and/or permission to exceed that limit and no defence of fair dealing and/or public domain will be considered and/or accepted as a valid excuse for failure to comply. All other persons must seek a written licence and authority from [specify] contact [specify].

DRAMATIC WORK

General Business and Commercial

D.531

'Dramatic Work' shall be defined in accordance with its ordinary and natural meaning. It shall mean a work of action with or without words and/or music which is capable of being performed before an audience. Copyright shall not exist until the dramatic work is recorded in some manner in writing and/or on film and/or by some other method which provides copyright protection. It shall include plays, scripts and scenes for films, choreographed dances and any other work that is performed dramatically but not complete films.

D.532

'Dramatic Work' shall include a work of dance or mime. Copyright shall not subsist in a dramatic work until it is recorded in writing or otherwise. The time at which such a work is made is the time at which it is actually recorded. That shall be the case regardless of whether it is recorded by or with the permission of the [Author] or not.

D.533

The performance of the [Work] will require permission from the copyright owner and all necessary rights, clearances, licences and consents will be obtained and paid for by [Name].

D.534

The parties agree that the [Work] does not include any element of any dramatic work.

D.535

1.1 The [Author] authorises and grants the [Company] the right to film, record and reproduce a [Programme/Video/Disc] based on filming and recording of the [Play/Dance] at [theatre/location] from [date] to [date].

1.2 The [Company] shall produce an edited version and then consult with the [Author] as to the final version to be reproduced for the [Programme/Video/Disc]. The parties agree that no additional material shall be added at any time except a new sound track, music and credits and/or sub-titles which must be agreed between the parties.

DUE DILIGENCE

General Business and Commercial

D.536

The [Assignor] warrants and undertakes that all representations as to good title in this agreement are made on the basis of the [Assignor] having instructed their duly qualified solicitors to conduct a full exercise of due diligence at the [Assignor's] sole cost.

D.537

The [Company] confirms that it will use all due diligence to ensure adherence to and compliance with all laws, industry standards and codes of practice whether under [specify legislation] and/or any other relevant law in force at the time of the performance of this agreement in [country].

D.538

1.1 Both parties shall have the opportunity to carry out due diligence at their own costs and expense in respect of the [Project] from [date] to [date].

1.2 Both parties shall make available any material which is requested by the other side which is directly relevant to the [Project] and shall arrange inspection of original material.

1.3 All exchanges of material, information and data under due diligence shall be deemed confidential and not for release to any third party and shall be strictly contained within a named list of personnel on both sides.

D.539

Both parties agree that neither shall be entitled to rely on any representations, disclosures and/or material made available under due diligence which are not incorporated as terms and condition of the final agreement signed by both parties.

D.540

Each party shall be responsible for arranging and bearing the cost of its own due diligence in respect of the [Project/Event]. There shall be no liability to the other party for failure to disclose information, facts, data, financial records, stock, and/or corporate details which one party acquires. The parties shall be limited to the undertakings and terms which are set out in the final agreement for the [Project/Event].

D.541

Where in the process of due diligence the [Company] has deliberately misled, misrepresented and/or withheld vital and significant information, facts, financial records, corporate reports and projections, information relating to shareholders and stock and/or the terms and conditions of its agreements with its directors, employees and/or third parties. Then the [Company] shall have the right either to seek to claim compensation, damages, losses, costs and expenses plus interest and/or to be paid the fixed sum of [number/currency] upon demand and the provision of supporting evidence.

D.542

The [Licensee] agrees to carry out due diligence on all sub-licensees, agents, designers, developers, consultants and distributors who are and/

or will be engaged to market the [Product/Work/Film] to ensure that they comply with the following criteria:

1.1 That they are established and experienced in the field and have been in operation for no less than [number] years.

1.2 That audited accounts are available to verify their solvency and ability to fulfil their contractual obligations.

1.3 That there are no pending legal actions, investigations and/or claims against them which would effect and/or damage the reputation of the [Product/Work/Film] and/or the [Licensor].

D.543

The [Sponsor] shall not have the right to carry out due diligence on any third party that the [Company] may wish to use for the [Event]. All such decisions are entirely at the sole discretion of the [Company]. There shall be no obligation to notify the [Sponsor] of the names and details relating to any such third party.

D.544

Where the [Licensee] would like to obtain the prior consent of the [Licensor] to sub-license the [Product/Work/Film]. Then the [Licensee] shall provide a comprehensive and thorough due diligence report which shall include the last three years of audited accounts, summary of the directors, staff and premises, health and safety compliance assessment, examples of products, marketing and advertising.

D.545

Where after the completion of this agreement the [Purchaser] considers and/or has evidence that the [Seller] over valued any part of the [Assets]. Then it is agreed that the [Purchaser] shall not be entitled to seek a refund and/or rebate and/or damages and/or any losses and agrees and accepts that it had the right to investigate and assess and review all the [Assets] prior to purchase with an independent company and has therefore no claim and/or legal and/or equitable action against the [Seller] and/or any of its advisors.

D.546

The [Company] agrees to provide access to [Name] to view, inspect [and make copies of all reports, surveys, statistics and other assessments made by the [Company] and its consultants and agents from [date] to [date] on the subject of [specify project]. Provided that [Name] agrees that no undertakings and/or any confirmation is provided by the [Company] that all the content is accurate, true and/or up to date and that [Name] cannot rely on it in order to take any steps and/or action and/or enter into any agreement which may result in any financial and/or other losses and/or damages at any time. Further that [Name] waives the right to make any claim and/or take any action against the [Company].

D.547

Where at any time documents, data, information and/or any other materials in any medium are withheld and/or destroyed during the course of the due diligence by the [Seller] which would materially affect the value of the [Asset] being transferred and/or sold. Then the [Seller] shall only be liable to reimburse the [Purchaser] for the difference in the value if it can be shown that it would have caused the [Purchaser] to withdraw from the agreement and/or make a substantially lower offer.

EDITORIAL CONTROL

Film, Television and Video

E.001

1.1 The [Licensee] shall only have the right to reproduce the [Film/Video/Podcast] on each copy of the [Units/Download/Service] with the complete titles and credits in the sequence, colour and manner that as it is supplied by the [Licensor] on the master material. There is authorisation and/or consent provided to the [Licensee] to make any deletions, alterations, modifications, additions and/or otherwise edit and adapt the [Film/Video/Podcast].

1.2 The [Licensor] agrees that the [Licensee] shall have the right to incorporate a credit on to the [Units/Download/Service] preceding the main titles and/or following the end titles of the [Film/Video/Podcast] the words [Distributed by Licensee] together with a logo, image and/or trade mark. The [Licensor] shall have the right to view the proposed credit in the final format and to have it amended if it is considered unsuitable due to the size, layout and/or content.

E.002

The [Assignee] shall be entitled at its sole discretion and cost to make minor changes, deletions, alterations, interruptions and/or additions to the [Film/Video/Podcast] as may be reasonably required provided it is no more than [number] per cent of the total duration. In the event that major changes deletions, alterations, interruptions and/or additions are envisaged the prior approval of the [Assignor] shall be required in advance.

E.003

The [Assignor] accepts that all editorial decisions in respect of the [Film/Video/Podcast] are at the [Assignee's] sole discretion. The [Assignee] agrees that where editorial changes are made by the [Assignee] that increase the Budget and result in additional costs. The [Assignee] shall be responsible for the cost of all such additional work.

E.004

The [Assignor] acknowledges that the [Assignee] shall have the right entirely at its sole cost and discretion to:

1.1   edit, adapt, alter, add to, delete and/or amend any part of the [Film/Video/Podcast] including any soundtrack, music, images, graphics, words, text and/or computer generated material.

1.2   add or delete any product placement, advertisements, sponsors, endorsements of products and/or services and/or any other material.

1.3   This right in 1.1 and 1.2 shall include the following material, credits, products and services of any of the following: [specify actors, companies, distributors].

E.005

There is no right whatsoever to alter, amend, adapt, develop and/or edit any part of the [Film/Video/Podcast] and/or any other material provided under this agreement. Any changes whether of size, length, colour, style, content, credits and/or any other type of any nature must be notified in advance to the [Company] for their consideration. No action may be taken unless the [Company] has provided written authority from [specify name]. In the event that this procedure is not followed then the [Company] shall have the right to order the destruction of all material which has not been authorised.

E.006

The [Distributor] agrees that it shall not distort and/or significantly change the [Film/Video/Podcast] in the event that any editing, dubbing and/or other alterations are required to exploit the [Film/Video/Podcast]. The [Distributor] agrees and undertakes that it shall not add any additional material and/or change the credits, copyright notices, trade marks and other acknowledgements. The [Distributor] shall however be able to change any material which its legal advisors have recommended be removed in order to avoid the likelihood of criminal and/or civil proceedings against the [Distributor] in any country to which it markets the [Film/Video/Podcast].

E.007

The [Licensee] shall not be entitled to edit, adapt and/or alter the [Film/Video/Units] nor to authorise any third party to do so without the prior written consent of the [Licensor]. The [Licensor] agrees that subject to prior written consent the [Licensee] may carry out minor edits of up to [specify period] in duration of the [Film/Video/Units] provided that it does not interfere with the integrity and/or continuity of the [Film/Video/Units].

744

E.008

The [Company] agrees that the [Distributor] may edit, alter, delete and/or change parts of the [Film/Video], the sound track and/or the title in order to adapt the [Film/Video] for different countries, markets, formats and languages. Provided that the [Distributor] shall consult with the [Company] in advance and provide a copy of each different version which may be created at the [Distributor's] cost.

E.009

[Name] agrees that the [Company] may make such changes, additions, variations, distortions, caricatures and/or alterations to all and/or any parts of the [Film/Video/Installation], sound recordings, name, image and/or other material as it wishes in order to develop, enhance and/or increase sales and revenue. Provided that at no time shall any material be used in a form and/or manner which is likely to result in [Name] being depicted as associated with any act, words and/or other material which may be a civil and/or criminal offence in any country.

E.010

The [Company] acknowledges and agrees that the signature, name, image, representation and personal name and performance name of [Name] are owned and controlled by [Name]. That at no time before, during and/or after this agreement shall the [Company] be entitled to claim ownership, control and/or the right to authorise any changes, additions and/or any variations of any nature either in the [Film/Video/Installation] and/or associated sound recording and/or sound track and/or in any marketing and/or promotion and/or merchandising in any medium and/or format. Nor shall the [Company] seek to register any interest, rights and/or trade mark associated with [Name] and/or any signature, name, image, representation and/or personal name and/or performance name and/or associated slogan, music, lyrics, slogan, title, character, colour and/or otherwise.

E.011

The [Company/Distributor] shall be entitled to make any editorial changes that may be necessary in respect of the [Series/Film/Documentary] including making deletions, editing material and/or adding material which are required due to the advice of legal advisors and/or compliance with any legislation in [countries] and/or in order to comply with regulatory codes, licences, standards, contractual obligations and/or any other guidance.

E.012

The [Company] shall:

1.1   Notify the [Author] of all proposed changes required in the [Script/Film/Video] however minor and provide the [Author] with the opportunity to accept and/or reject the proposals.

1.2 Not have the right to make any changes without the prior authorisation and consent of the [Author] in each case.

1.3 Where the [Script/Film/Video] is to be translated and/or sub-titled and/or a new sound track added and/or otherwise adapted. Then the [Author] must be consulted at an early stage and approve the appointment of the translator and/or any other third parties to be involved in the project.

1.4 The [Author] shall have the right to approve any translation and/or any new version before it is finalised.

1.5 Where a new translation and/or title is created then those copyright and intellectual property rights shall be assigned to the [Author] and the [Company] shall not retain any rights and/or allow any third party to do so.

E.013

The [Television Company] may at its sole discretion make any changes, alterations and amendments to the [Script] in order to conform with all rules, standards, Codes of Practice and/or guidelines in force from time to time with respect to any regulatory bodies including but not limited to [Ofcom/other].

E.014

The [Company/Distributor] may at its sole discretion and cost, edit, adapt and make such changes and deletions in respect of the [Series/Films/Videos] as may be required in pursuance of its programme policy governing suitability of material and/or timing and/or presentation. The [Company/Distributor] shall not exercise this right unreasonably and/or unnecessarily and any editing or deletions shall be of a minor nature and not impair continuity.

E.015

The [Distributor/Company] may at its discretion, edit, change, alter and/or adapt the [Films/Videos/Series] at its sole cost in order to comply with its programme schedule and/or its programme content policy and/or any other reason in order to comply with the advice of its legal and business advisors and/or any regulatory organisation and/or any code of practice and/or compliance requirement and/or any legislation in any country in which the [Film/Videos/Series] is to be transmitted and/or exploited and/or adapted..

E.016

The [Author] acknowledges that the [Production Company] shall be entitled to make alterations to the scripts during the production of the [Film/Video/Podcast] provided that such amendments are minor and not substantial, and do not amount to unjustified modifications or derogatory treatment of the [Author's] work.

E.017

The [Company] acknowledges that it shall not be entitled to arrange and/ or permit the development and writing of any treatment, script or other material for a [Film/Video/Series] based on the [Script/Manuscript/Book] by the [Author] unless the [Company] has exercised the option granted under clause [–] and an agreement has been concluded between the parties relating to the transmission and exploitation of the [Film/Video/Series] based on the [Script/Manuscript/Book].

E.018

The [Company] shall be entitled at its sole discretion to make such changes additions, deletions and/or interruptions to any [Film/Video/Series] that may be required by the [Company] for the purpose of transmission and playback archive services on [specify channels]. Prior to making any significant alterations of any nature the [Company] shall consult with the [Production Company] and take into account the requests of the [Production Company]. In the event of any disagreement the decision of the [Company] shall prevail and be final.

E.019

The [Company] may at its sole discretion edit and/or adapt the [Film/ Video/Series] for the purpose of inserting advertising material, public and/ or political campaigns and/or to assist in the transmission schedules for the [Company] and/or to meet the requirements of any licences, statutes, codes, policies, and/or other guidelines and/or laws relating to the content of the material transmitted by the [Company].

E.020

The cost of all editing carried out by the [Company] required under this agreement shall be paid to the [Company] by the [Licensor]. The [Company] shall provide full details of the reasons for the work and the rates charged. The sum shall be payable by the [Licensor] within [number] days of receipt of an invoice.

E.021

The [Company] shall have the right to edit the [Films/Videos/Programmes] but not to add material except an interview with [specify Individual] which shall be at the [Company's] sole cost.

E.022

The [Company] may at its discretion undertake minor editing of and/or deletions from any of the [Films/Videos/Series] in pursuance of its programme policy governing the suitability of material and/or the requirement of accurate timing of its schedules. The [Company] shall not exercise this right unreasonably and/or unnecessarily and any editing or deletions shall be of a minor nature and not exceed [number] minutes in duration.

E.023

[Name's] representative shall be entitled to attend the development, production and editing of the [Film/Video/Podcast] at any time and to view and examine the [Film/Video/Podcast] before the final version is produced. Provided that such attendance shall be in such a manner as to not interfere with the completion of the [Film/Video/Podcast]. The [Production Company] shall consider the verbal and written comments of the representative. The [Production Company] shall have the final decision in respect of all editorial matters relating to the [Film/Video/Podcast].

E.024

The [Company] may produce and/or authorise the production of an edited or otherwise amended version of the [Films/Videos/Series] which includes the use of outtakes and/or otherwise unused filming. Provided that the [Company] shall advise the [Licensor] and shall supply details of the proposals for their approval. If the [Company] authorises a third party to carry out the work it shall still continue to observe the terms of this agreement. The [Company] undertakes to ensure that any such work shall not misrepresent or distort the views of [specify Individual] in the [Films/Videos/Series].

E.025

The [Licensee] shall use all reasonable means to ensure that the [Film/Video/Documentary] is exhibited and/or transmitted in the original form of the master copy supplied by the [Licensor] and that there shall be no changes, alterations, additions and/or deletions of any nature for any reason.

E.026

For the avoidance of doubt all programming, editorial, scheduling decisions, sponsorship and/or promotional matters on [specify channels/websites] relating to the [Film/Video/Series] shall be at the sole cost and discretion of the [Company].

E.027

The [Series] shall follow the [Scripts] except for such minor alterations as may be necessary as a result of unforeseeable production and/or artist changes. The [Company] shall not unreasonably withhold its consent to any other alterations required by the [Production Company] unless in the opinion of the [Enterprise] the alterations would detrimental to [Name] and/or his/her reputation and/or other products, films, books and/or projects in which they are involved.

E.028

The final decision on editorial matters will rest solely with the [Company]. However, the [Company] agrees to allow a representative of the [Production Company] to view the [specify format] of the final version of the [Films/Videos/Programmes] and to make available [specify name/role] to discuss with and take note of the representative's comments in respect of the [Films/Videos/Programmes].

E.029

The editing of any material supplied under this agreement shall be subject to the following policy criteria [specify rules] a copy of which is attached. If after any review one party whose material has been edited is not satisfied. Then such party may send notice in writing specifying the problem and the failure to observe the agreed criteria. Where there is more than one complaint of this nature then the party who has served notice shall have the right to terminate the agreement by [number] months' notice.

E.030

The [Licensee] shall not be entitled to add to, change, delete from, edit, adapt and/or otherwise create a new translation, format and/or version of the [Film/Video/Podcast] and/or any part at any time. No editing is permitted of any nature and/or no changes in the dialogue and/or soundtrack and no animations, characters, names, trade marks and/or products added to the titles, credits and/or any other part.

E.031

The [Assignee] shall be entitled at its sole discretion and cost to make such changes, deletions, alterations, interruptions, additions and/or translations of the [Series] and/or use of the soundtrack for radio and/or audio promotional purposes as may reasonably be required. There shall be no obligation to consult with the [Assignor].

E.032

The [Company] shall be entitled to edit, adapt, alter, change, delete from, add to, translate, and exercise whatever editorial control is required in order to transmit, exhibit, reproduce, promote, supply, manufacture, distribute and/or exploit the [Film/Video/Series], the soundtrack, characters, plot, themes, locations and/or title in any format and/or by any method and to engage third parties to carry out such work and/or to assist in the exploitation of the rights in any media.

E.033

It is agreed by [Name] that the [Company] may make the following alterations in respect of his/her appearance and/or performance in any recording, sound recording, and/or films for the [Programmes] and any form of exploitation:

1.1 Change the character's name and/or add a different person's voice and/or computer generated version for the sound recording.

1.2 Change the words spoken for the purpose of sub-titles and/or translation.

1.3 Edit, change and/or delete any part in order to meet transmission schedules and/or create shorter programmes and/or to develop the [Programmes] in other media and/or formats.

Provided that no more than [number] per cent of the total length shall be deleted of the whole performance in any programme.

E.034

Neither the [Company] nor any sub-licensee nor any other third party engaged to market, promote, distribute and/or exhibit the [Film/Video/Series] at any time shall be entitled to make any changes, alterations and/or add any material and/or music and/or sounds to the [master Material] supplied by the [Licensor]. No copies of the [Master Material] shall be reproduced and/or supplied to any third party which has not been specifically approved and authorised by the [Licensor] in advance. Failure to adhere to this procedure shall entitle the [Licensor] to terminate the agreement by notice by email to [Name] with immediate effect.

General Business and Commercial

E.035

The [Company] shall give due consideration in good faith to any representations made by the [Organisation/Name] with respect to the content of the [Manuscript/Book/Event]. Provided that the [Company] adheres to the approved outline of the [Manuscript/Book/Event] the [Company] shall not be obliged to make any changes except where the [Organisation/Name] requests changes for reasons due to matters beyond their control and/or because of the threat of legal proceedings. Then the [Company] shall as far as possible incorporate such changes and/or alterations.

E.036

If after reviewing the proposed draft [Manuscript/Book/Event] the [Organisation/Name] requests further changes, then the [Company] shall comply with such requests. All costs incurred in respect of such further changes which are not covered by the agreed Budget shall be at the expense of the [Organisation/Name]. However, where such additional changes were due entirely to the failure of the [Company] to fulfil the terms of this agreement and to adhere to the conditions and outline of the [Manuscript/Book/Event], the [Company] shall bear the cost.

E.037
No addition to, deletion from, alteration to or adaptation of the [Work Schedule/Quote/Format] may be made without the prior written permission of the [Company/Licensor/Supplier].

E.038
The [Company] undertakes not to edit the [Artwork/Images/Logos] in any way which is likely to impair its quality, meaning and/or integrity.

E.039
The [Company] agrees to obtain the prior [written] consent of [Name] before any major alterations, changes, additions to and/or deletions from are made and/or planned in respect of the [Work/Service/Product].

E.040
The final decision on all editorial matters rests solely with the [Company].

E.041
The [Company] has the right to [use/reproduce/distribute] the [Work/Material] in the form and version licensed and supplied by the [Licensor]. The [Company] is not authorised to make any changes in the [Work/Material] whatsoever.

E.042
The [Company] may not in any manner and/or for any purpose alter, modify and/or change the [Work/Material] and/or authorise any such acts except with the prior written consent of [Name] during his/her lifetime and a representative of his/her estate thereafter.

E.043
The editorial decisions in respect of all material are entirely at the [Company's] sole discretion.

E.044
The [Company] shall be entitled to modify, revise, enhance, improve, adapt, alter, amend, translate, vary and/or develop the [Work/Material] and/or any associated instructions, brochures, packaging and/or marketing.

E.045

For the avoidance of doubt the [Company] agrees and confirms that by virtue of the assignment of the intellectual property rights and the transfer of the ownership and control of the [Master Work and Material] under this agreement. The [Assignee] or its assigns or any person or company licensed, authorised or permitted by it shall be entitled to edit, adapt, modify, change and/or develop the [Master Work and Material] in all formats, in any media and in any language throughout the [Territory/country/world] indefinitely subject to the restrictions and limitations specified in Schedule A which set out the copyright, trade mark, contract, credit, moral rights and other obligations in respect of the [Master Work and Material].

E.046

The [Company] acknowledges that all such adaptations, variations, edits or developments of the [Work/Product/Service/Images] as are permitted may have the effect of creating a new copyright and/or any other intellectual property rights, patents, computer software, trade marks and/or domain names which shall belong to and be assigned to the [Enterprise].

E.047

The [Company] shall be entitled to modify, revise, enhance, improve, adapt and/or develop the [Work/Unit/Service] or any related documentation or material in any manner the [Company] may decide. The [Company] shall be the owner of any such modifications, revisions, enhancements, improvements, adaptations and developments and may use and exploit any of them at the [Company's] sole discretion.

E.048

The [Company] shall be entitled to make use of the [Master Material and Units] in such manner as it shall in its sole discretion think fit including the making of changes, alterations and/or substitutions.

E.049

The artistic and editorial control of the [Book/Magazine/Sound Recording] shall be at the sole discretion and decision of the [Company]. The [Company] shall in good faith consider the requests and suggestions of [Name] in respect of content, interpretation and presentation.

E.050

The [Licensee] shall not be entitled to edit, adapt and/or alter the [Images/Sound Recordings/Scripts/Products] and/or to authorise a third party to do so without the prior written consent of the [Licensor] in each case. Approval for one development does not provide consent to all future changes.

E.051

The final editorial decisions in respect of the [Work/Service/Products/Promotions] shall be at the [Licensee's] sole discretion and cost. The [Licensee] agrees to consult with and disclose full details of all proposals to the [Licensor]. The [Licensee] agrees to consider and take account of any representations and communications made by the [Licensor] where appropriate. The [Licensee] shall not be obliged to fulfil the requests of the [Licensor] regarding editorial matters.

E.052

The [Company] agrees that no alterations shall be made to the agreed Work Plan and/or the Work Schedule without the prior approval of [Name].

E.053

The decision of [Name/Company] shall be final in respect of all production, manufacture, editorial, scheduling, release dates, marketing, advertising, licensing, distribution, prices and fees, the appointment of third parties, the adaptation, alteration, variation and/or development of the [Work/Products/Service] and any packaging, competitions, sponsorship, product placement, endorsements, promotions, tie-ins, cross-promotions, and/or any other matter.

E.054

The [Company] shall not have the right to instruct, permit, allow, authorise and/or agree with any third party that they may contribute in any manner to the [Work/Product/Service] and/or that they may publish, reproduce, distribute and/or market the [Work/Product/Service] together with any material in any format in any medium unless in each case the prior written consent of [Name] have been provided for such purpose.

E.055

No authority is provided and/or granted to reproduce and/or adapt and/or supply and/or edit any part of the material, products and/or services which is provided at any time under this agreement.

E.056

The [Company] agrees that it shall not make any editorial changes to the [Work] without prior consultation with [Name] as to the alterations, amendments and/or additions that it would like [Name] to make to the [Work]. That where after consultation the parties cannot agree that [Name] shall be provided with an opportunity to make an alternative proposal within [one] calendar month for the [Company] to consider. If thereafter the parties have still failed to reach agreement then the [Company] and/or [Name] shall have the right to terminate the agreement provided that all funds paid to date are repaid.

Internet, Websites and Apps

E.057

The [Company] shall have the final editorial decision in respect of the structure, layout, content and method and means of distribution of the [Website/App/Platform]. The [Company] shall be entitled to change, edit, delete, comment upon, endorse and/or develop and adapt the subject matter of any rights and/or material which is displayed, posted and/or supplied from and/or to and/or on the [Website/App/Platform] subject to clearance of any copyright, intellectual property rights, software and/or other contractual obligations and payments.

E.058

The [Enterprise] and/or the [Company] have the right to control all material of any nature on this [Website/App/Platform] and at their sole discretion either and/or both of them may without notice to any subscriber, user and/or otherwise delete, edit, adapt, vary, reproduce in another section, license and/or distribute to a third party and/or amend, translate, publish and/or issue as part of a press release any material in any format or medium which is contributed to, displayed on, communicated to or added to this [Website/App/Platform] by any person, company or organisation.

E.059

The [Company] is in charge of this [Website/App/Sound Recording/Image] and shall have the final decision in respect of anything on or connected to it of any nature. Therefore the [Company] will able to do anything it decides is in its best interests subject to any laws, rights and contractual obligations which may exist which may be relevant at the time.

E.060

The [Company] agrees and undertakes that:

1.1 The [Company] shall not change, alter, adapt, amend, edit, translate, revise, interfere with and/or reproduce in another format and/or medium the [Article/Blog/Artwork/Sound Recording/Images], the title or any part which has and/or will be supplied by [Name]. Nor shall the [Company] permit, authorise, license and/or agree with any other person, charity and/or company that they may reproduce, distribute and/or adapt the [Article/Blog/Artwork/Sound Recording/Images] in its entirety and/or any part without the prior written consent of [Name] in case and the agreement of additional terms and payments.

1.2 The [Company] shall not delete, erase and/or remove the copyright notices to [Name] and/or any other credits to any other person and/or company in respect of the ownership of the [Article/Blog/Artwork/

Sound Recordings] and/or logos, slogans, trade marks and/or characters associated with it of any nature

E.061

You the [Client] must accept full responsibility for any consequences arising from your access to and/or use of this [Website/App/Platform] and/or any content, links, endorsements and/or promotions. You use this [Website/App/Platform] and any content, download and/or any other material at your own discretion and risk. All content and material may be altered, deleted, added to and/or adapted at any time by the [Company] without notice. The [Company] are not responsible for the contents and/or any material and/or any reliance upon them and/or the links and/or promotions. The mere fact that a company, service and/or product is listed is not an endorsement of any kind. All dates, prices, special offers, products, services, premium rate services and/or other content and material are subject to availability and may be changed and/or withdrawn at any time. There is no assurance provided that there are no inaccuracies, errors, viruses, false attributions, misleading and/or illegal content. We will delete any material which we conclude should be removed for any reason and make any changes we may decide are necessary to update, maintain and improve the [Website/App/Platform] whether or not this causes interruptions, delays and/or a suspension of the [Website/App/Platform].

E.062

Where the [Company] decides that any person has uploaded text, images, music, lyrics, sound recordings, film, video, viruses and/or other material to the [Website/App/Platform] which is/are dishonest, misleading, fraudulent and/or amount(s) to advertising, promotion and/or an endorsement and/or which is/are potentially malicious, and/or is/are not acceptable for any other reason. Then the [Company] may delete any such material without notice and block the person's use and/or access to the [Website/App/Platform] and close any account.

E.063

You may post, display and distribute [images/Photographs/Videos] which you own, control and/or have taken on this [Website/App/Platform]. You are not entitled to falsely attribute any name to any identity and/or misrepresent their association with any person and/or group. You are not entitled to add any slogan, comment, images, words, text and/or other material which alters, degrades, defames, humiliates, offends and/or makes any derogatory implication regarding that person's appearance, relationships, employment, religion, school, university, family life and/or career and/or otherwise whether false, malicious and/or a matter which you believe to be true.

E.064

This [Website/App/Sound Recording] is owned by [Name] and the material is monitored and controlled by the [Company] who acts as the [webmaster/ controller] for [Name]. You are advised to email with any concerns as to any content whether regarding copyright ownership, offensive material and/or errors. Please complete the relevant form [specify email].

E.065

Material is posted at your own risk and no liability is accepted by the [Company] for any defamatory material which you submit and/or any claims and/or legal actions against you which may be made at any time by any third party. The [Company] reserves the right to remove, delete and/or destroy all material which poses a threat to the [Company] on any grounds whatsoever whether an allegation has been made or not including but not limited to on the grounds of security, obscenity, a breach of any criminal and/or civil legislation and/or any international policies and/or any other reason. The [Company] is not obliged to provide any reason for their actions to you and you are not entitled to any refund and/or compensation.

E.066

The [Contributor] agrees that the [Company] may edit, publish, distribute, translate and/or adapt the [Article/Images/Film/ Sound Recordings] for the blog known as [specify site] as it thinks fit. The [Contributor] shall have no right to be consulted and/or to review and/or otherwise be involved. The [Contributor] agrees and accepts that he/she has waived their right to a credit, and/or copyright notice and has all waived all their moral rights. The material may be distorted, mutilated and/or reconfigured in any manner and/ or added to any other material by any means.

E.067

The [Contributor] has supplied the [Article/Image/Sound Recording] in the exact manner in which it is to be reproduced by the [Company] on the blog known as [specify site]. There is no right for the [Company] to alter, change, amend and/or to add material in any manner. All editorial control in respect of the [Article/Image/Sound Recording] remains with the [Contributor]. If any changes and/or translation and/or adaptations are intended then they must be expressly approved in writing in advance by the [Contributor]. The [Contributor] shall not be under any obligation to agree to any proposal.

E.068

The [Performer/Contributor] to the [Video] shall follow the [Script/ Choreography] as directed. There shall be no artistic and/or editorial control permitted and all decisions shall remain with [Name] and the [Company].

E.069

[Name] has agreed to interview [person B] on their [Video/Blog/Podcast] and to discuss the agreed list of issues and questions and to mention and promote the branded [products]. [Name] shall have ultimate control over the conduct of the interview, the filming and/or recording and any editing which may be required. Although the parameters of the interview have been agreed there is no transfer of artistic and/or editorial control to [person B]. [Name] agrees to supply a copy of the final edited version to [person B] before it is distributed. If [person B] is not satisfied and does not want the interview released. Then they must pay back the fee of [number/currency] paid by [Name] together with a cancellation fee of [number/currency].

E.070

The [Company] agrees that the [Influencer] shall have the right to vet and approve the written words, title, images and films which are to be reproduced and distributed by the [Company] on its website, app, magazine and to its third party subscribers in advance of publication. It shall be a breach of this agreement if the [Company] shall fail to allow the [Influencer] to vet and approve and/or reject the material. The [Company] agrees and undertakes to make such changes as may be requested and to ensure that there is no release of any unauthorised material to third parties.

Merchandising and Distribution

E.071

The [Products/Material] shall not be changed, altered, added to, adapted and/or varied in any way by the [Distributor] and shall be kept in the exact same form, content and packaging in which it is delivered by the [Supplier].

E.072

The [Manufacturer/Supplier] acknowledges that the [Distributor] shall have the sole discretion as to the manner and method to be used in the production, supply of source materials, manufacture, labels, packaging, delivery, distribution, marketing and promotion of the [Products/Units]. No changes, additions, variations, deletions or otherwise of any nature shall be made or authorised by the [Manufacturer/Supplier] without the prior consent of [Name] at the [Company].

E.073

It is agreed that minor variations, in colour, content, appearance, labelling and packaging may occur due to the source of the materials, the production process, the length of storage and the delivery method. No major changes, alterations or variations will be made to the [Products/Units] or any packaging or storage or delivery method without the advance approval and written consent of the [Company].

E.074

The [Distributor] agrees that any labels, brochures and/or packaging supplied by the [Company] in respect of each of the [Products/Units] shall not be removed, covered, hidden, damaged and/or altered by the [Distributor] at any time during the course of this agreement.

E.075

[Name] agrees that the [Distributor] shall not be restricted as to the reproduction, manufacture and form of exploitation of the [Characters/Images/Logos/Products]. That the [Distributor] shall have the choice at any time to develop, change and/or adapt and/or alter the name, colour, layout, design and/or packaging of the [Characters/Images/Logos/Products] and/or any parts in order to achieve higher sales and/or to improve the brand and/or develop new markets.

E.076

No translations and/or adaptations for another language other than [specify] shall be made of the [Book/Sound Recording/Product] without the prior written approval of the [Licensor] in each case.

E.077

The [Company] shall allow the [Distributor] to have full and complete control over the manner and extent of the exploitation, promotion and advertisement of the [Work/Units/Character] throughout the Territory. The [Company] authorises the [Distributor] to make and authorise the making of alterations in adaptations of and additions to the [Work/Units/Character] at the [Distributor's] discretion and to provide translations of new words or lyrics in other languages.

E.078

The [Company] shall provide a style guide presentation layout pack for the [Products/Service] for the [Distributor], sub-agents and retailers. The [Distributor] shall monitor the displays and catalogues to ensure that the standards are maintained and that the brand and quality of presentations and displays is high and in prominent locations.

E.079

The [Distributor] confirms that it will not edit, adapt, alter and/or add to the [Material/Article] and/or any part of the name, logo and/or packaging without the prior approval of the [Licensor]. That any changes that may be agreed shall be at the [Distributor's] sole cost and shall not be offset against any sums due to the [Licensor].

E.080
The [Licensor] acknowledges that the [Distributor] shall have the sole discretion as to the manner and method to be used in the production, manufacture, distribution, marketing and promotion of the [Work/Product/Character/Logo].

E.081
The decision of [Name/Company] shall be final in respect of the [Products/Service] as follows:

1.1 The development, production, manufacture, and approval of the final prototype of any products, packaging, labels and instructions.

1.2 The appointment of all third parties including agents, distributors, publicity and/or suppliers and/or the commission of any artwork, graphics, computer generated material, software, films, videos, podcasts and/or sound recordings.

1.3 The promotion, marketing, advertising, editorial control, sponsorship, endorsements, cross promotion and launch dates.

1.4 The creation and reproduction and distribution of any adaptation in any format by any method in any language.

E.082
The [Licensor] agrees that the [Licensee] and/or any sub-licensee shall be entitled to edit, adapt, change, translate and/or otherwise develop the [Work/Format] provided that all rights in all new material which are created are assigned to the [Licensor] without the payment of any additional sums and the [Licensor] receives royalty payments in accordance with clause [–].

E.083

1.1 The [Licensor] does not grant the [Licensee] any right to adapt, change, alter and/or vary the colour of the [Name/Logo/image] which is set out in Schedule [–].

1.2 The [Licensee] agrees that it must reproduce, distribute and supply the [Name/Logo/Image] which is set out in Schedule [–] in the exact shape, form, size and colour without any changes however minor.

1.3 The [Licensee] agrees that it has no authority to permit, allow and/or represent to any third party that they may use, reproduce and/or supply the [Name/Logo/image] which is set out in Schedule [–] for any reason. That all third parties including agents, marketing and publicity companies and distributors must be authorised directly and personally by the [Licensor].

E.084

The [Author] agrees that the [Agent] and/or the [Distributor] may make changes, alterations and/or adaptations to the storylines, characters, book titles, chapter titles, images and illustrations and/or backgrounds and locations and/or equipment and/or products mentioned and/or words and/or language and/or translations which may be needed to take account of local market cultures, religions and/or to form product placement partnerships and/or to create and/or develop the [Work] in other forms and/or media including but not limited to film, television, radio, discs and/or as a download and/or for educational material and/or licensing for associated products.

Publishing

E.085

The [Author] acknowledges that the [Company] shall be entitled to make alterations to the [Scripts] provided that such amendments are not substantial and do not amount to unjustified modifications or derogatory treatment of the [Author's] work.

E.086

The [Publisher] shall at its sole discretion be entitled to edit and revise the [Work/Manuscript/Sound Recording] either before the [Work/Manuscript/Sound Recording] is ready for first publication in any format or thereafter before any new edition and/or version is issued. The [Publisher] shall notify the [Author] in writing specifying the editing, revision and new material required and shall stipulate a reasonable date for completion of such work. In the event that the [Author] shall neglect or be unable for any reason to edit or revise the [Work/Manuscript/Sound Recording] and/or to supply new material to the satisfaction of the [Publisher]. The [Publisher] shall be entitled to engage some other competent person to carry out such work and any fee or other payment made to such person shall be payable by the [Author] and deducted from the royalties due to the [Author] under this agreement. The choice of such person and the fee to be paid to such person shall be subject to the [Author's] prior approval and such approval is not to be unreasonably withheld or delayed.

E.087

The [Publisher] shall not be entitled to edit, revise, change, alter, add to, or delete from the [Manuscript/Amended Proofs] which may be delivered and/or authorised by the [Author] unless the prior written approval of the [Author] is obtained in each case. The [Publisher] agrees to provide full details of any proposed changes and to negotiate with the [Author] an additional fee for the cost of such editing, revision, or other changes required to be fulfilled by the [Author]. The [Publisher] shall not be entitled to deduct the additional fee from any sums due to the [Author] under this agreement.

E.088

The [Publisher] shall make no changes in the title or text of the [Work] without the [Author's] written consent except that the [Publisher] shall be entitled to correct factual errors and to delete any material which would expose the [Publisher] and/or its sub-licensees to the threat of allegations and/or any legal action and/or any other matter which might cause the business of the [Publisher] to incur losses and/or damages and/or to have a negative impact on its reputation and/or brands.

E.089

The [Distributor] agrees that it will not allow any alteration in the title, illustrations, words, preface and/or index of the [Book/Sound Recording/Work] to be made in sub-licensed editions and/or adaptations in any format without the prior written consent of the [Author]. The authorised version by the [Author] shall be the final [hardback/paperback/download] version together with the approved cover, spine and ISBN which is released in the [United Kingdom/countries] by the [Distributor].

E.090

The [Publisher] acknowledges that it shall not be entitled and/or permitted to authorise any third party to adapt, alter, edit, add to, delete from and/or in any way change the [Podcast/Artwork/Film/Master Material] without first seeking the prior written consent of the [Author] to any proposal. The [Author] shall have absolute discretion as to whether to accept and/or reject any proposal.

E.091

The [Publisher] undertakes to consult with the [Author] in respect of any proposed translation of the [Work] into a foreign language and such translations shall be at the [Publisher's] sole cost and expense. The [Publisher] shall not be entitled to deduct such translation costs from any sums due to the [Author] under this agreement.

E.092

If the [Publisher] considers it necessary to modify the layout, and/or alter the date and/or position of the advertisement, and/or to make any other alterations which are of such significance that they will have an impact on the value of the marketing to the [Advertiser]. The [Publisher] shall use its reasonable endeavours to contact the [Advertiser] to discuss the matter prior to publication. The [Advertiser] shall have the right to cancel the insertion of the advertisement if the alterations proposed are not accepted.

E.093

The [Publishers] shall consult with the [Authors] as to the cover, copyright notices, the disclaimer, the print size, font, format, layout, design, binding and marketing of the [Work]. The [Authors] shall be provided with an opportunity to meet the marketing team and to provide information, summaries of key selling points, quotes and shall be entitled to comment on the draft cover and marketing material that is produced in all formats and for all markets whether for the website, catalogues, shops, posters, bookmarks or otherwise. The general management of the editorial process the choice of editor, proofreader and the production, publication, promotion, pricing, the size of any print run, reprinting, sale and distribution of the [Work] shall be entirely at the [Publisher's] cost and discretion.

E.094

The [Author] shall discuss with the [Company] the content of the [Work] and shall follow the [Company's] reasonable requests with regard to its contents. When the first draft of the [Work] has been written the [Author] shall submit a copy to the [Company] and shall ensure that the reasonable requests of the [Company] for any editing and amendments are adhered to by the [Author]. If the [Author] refuses to carry out the changes requested by the [Company] prior to delivery of the final draft. Then the [Company] shall have the right to refuse to make any further payments to the [Author] until the changes have been made and delivered.

E.095

The [Journalist] and the [Publisher] agree that [Name] shall be entitled to approve the [Article/Draft/Manuscript] prior to publication in the form in which it is intended to be published in the [Magazine/Website/Book]. In the event that the [Article/Draft/Manuscript] is not approved by the [Name]. Then the [Journalist] and the [Publisher] agree that the [Article/ Draft/Manuscript] and the associated [images/photographs/film/sound recordings] shall not be published and/or distributed at any time. Any copyright and other intellectual property rights in the unpublished [Article/ Draft/Manuscript] and/or any [images/photographs/film/sound recordings], notes and/or any other material created under this agreement shall belong to [specify persons who own the rights].

E.096

The [Author] agrees to amend, alter and/or edit such parts of the [Work] as the [Publisher] may request in the event that its legal and/or business advisors consider that the [Work] contains material which is likely to result in the threat of legal action by some person and/or company and/or charity against the [Publisher] and/or criminal and/or civil proceedings and/or a complaint to a regulatory organisation and/or is likely to affect the potential sales and/or promotions in a negative manner.

E.097

The [Publisher] agrees that the [Author] shall be entitled to be consulted in relation to the layout, quality, artwork, typography, design, colours and draft and final proposals of the cover of the [Work] and/or any promotional and/or marketing material in any media. The final decision shall be a matter for the [Publisher] but where the [Author] strongly objects the [Publisher] agrees to consider alternative proposals.

E.098

The [Ghostwriter] agrees that [Name/Company] shall have the sole and exclusive discretion as to the research, interviews and content of the [Work] and any title, acknowledgements, copyright notices, cover, photographs, artwork and/or other material and/or any production, printing, licensing, distribution and/or any merchandising and/or exploitation of the [Work] and any associated material which is created and/or delivered by the [Ghostwriter] pursuant to this agreement.

E.099

The [Ghostwriter] agrees to redraft, alter, edit and amend the [Work] for a maximum duration of [number] days as requested by the [Company/Name] who have commissioned the [Work] during the Term of the Agreement. Once the final draft has been agreed and submitted to the [Publisher] then all additional changes required by the [Ghostwriter] requested by [Company/Name] and/or the [Publisher] shall be paid at the rate of [number/currency] for each [number] hours. The [Ghostwriter] shall submit the invoice for the work to [Company/Name] and the sums due shall be paid within [number] days.

E.100

The [Authors] agree that no material of any nature in any medium is to be included in the [Work/Installation/Artwork/Film] and/or added, deleted and/or changed and/or adapted unless both parties provide their express authority and consent.

E.101

The [Author] acknowledges that the [Assignee] shall be entitled to edit, adapt, translate, alter, add to, delete from, vary and/or amend, divide and/or rearrange the [Work] entirely at its sole cost and discretion. The [Assignee] shall not be obliged to seek any consent from the [Author] and/or to consult with the [Author].

E.102

The [Publisher] accepts that no alteration, amendment, deletion, addition, translation, adaptation, variation and/or development of the [Work] shall be made, agreed and/or licensed without the [Author's] prior written consent in each case. Further the [Author] shall then be entitled to be supplied with a draft copy of each proposal and/or sample and/or product prior to production, printing and/or manufacture. In the event that approval is withheld by the [Author] for any reason then the [Work] in that form shall not be reproduced and/or exploited by the [Publisher] and/or any third party at any time.

E.103

The [Author] agrees that where any alteration in the preface, cover, spine, logos, images, text and/or title is required prior to exploitation in any country due to the serious threat of legal action by a third party. Then the [Author] shall not unreasonably withhold and/or delay his/her consent to such changes.

E.104

The [Publishers] shall not have the right to authorise, permit and/or allow any third party to add to, delete from and/or otherwise make any contribution to the [Work] and/or to publish the [Work] as part of a compendium and/or joint work and/or to adapt the [Work] in any format in any other medium and/or to use the [Work] to endorse another product, person and/or entity.

E.105

The [Publisher] shall be entitled to exploit, reproduce, license, adapt, develop and/or distribute the [Work] and/or any article, product and/or copyright and/or intellectual property right based on and/or derived from it in any manner, shape, form and/or by any method that the [Publisher] at its sole discretion shall decide. The [Publisher] shall not be required to inform, advise, consult and/or obtain consent from [Name] at any time. Nor shall there be any restriction and/or limit on the length of time, countries, associated products, services, companies and/or persons that may be used by the [Publisher].

E.106

The [Publisher] agrees that the [Author] shall not be obliged to make any edits, changes and/or alterations to the [Work] prior to publication which he/she does not wish to consider. That the [Author] shall have the final decision in respect of the content of the [Work] and any cover, index, preface, marketing, promotion, exploitation and translation and/or adaptation at any time.

E.107

The [Contributor] agrees that the [Company] shall be entitled to edit, change, adapt and/or translate and/or make a sound recording of the [Work] and/or otherwise adapt and exploit the [Work] as the [Company] in its sole discretion shall decide. There shall be no obligation for the [Company] to consult with the [Contributor]. The [Company] may appoint a third party to add, change, alter, amend, adapt and/or exploit the [Work] and that such third party may also credited in some manner.

Services

E.108

The [Director] shall not alter, amend and/or deviate from the Production Schedule, the Budget, or the Final Script provided by the [Company] without the prior consent of the [Company] in each case.

E.109

The [Artist] acknowledges that the Company's decision shall be final in respect of all matters of any nature regarding the content, soundtrack, editing, additions to and/or deletion of any material and/or the licensing of any adaptations, merchandising, marketing and/or other exploitation of the [Film/Podcast/Video].

E.110

The [Agent] agrees that he/she shall have no authority and/or right to authorise and/or make any amendments and/or otherwise edit and alter any part of the synopsis of the [Work] without the prior written consent of the [Author].

E.111

The [Agent] agrees not to promote, advertise and/or market the [Artist] in any way which might impugn the reputation and/or embarrass the [Artist]. As far as possible the [Agent] shall provide copies of all proposed material and agrees to adhere to all changes requested by the [Artist]. The [Agent] agrees that it shall be entirely responsible for the cost of all such material and changes and no sums shall be paid by the [Artist].

E.112

The [Agent] agrees that:

1.1 it shall not authorise and/or carry out any editing, alterations, amendments and/or adaptations of the synopsis and/or the [Work] without the prior written consent of the [Author].

1.2 the artistic and editorial control of the [Work] shall be at the sole discretion and decision of the [Author].

1.3   it shall use reasonable endeavours to ensure that any third party will not have the right to edit, adapt and/or alter the [Work] without the prior written consent of the [Author].

1.4   it does not have the right itself to carry out and/or to authorise others to edit, adapt, add to, delete or in any way change the [Work] without the prior written consent of the [Author].

1.5   as far as possible all authorised changes shall be at the sole cost of the third party and that all copyright and other rights shall be assigned to the [Author] including any proposed translation and/or merchandising.

E.113
The [Manager] accepts that the [Sportsperson] shall be entitled to refuse to carry out any work which he/she deems to be in conflict with his/her image, religious beliefs and/or reputation and/or ethical lifestyle choices and/or which is likely to cause offence and/or is demeaning and/or dangerous and/or would pose a real risk to his/her health and/or ability to compete as an athlete in the future and/or may conflict with any code of conduct of any [professional body] of which he/she is a member and/or other work and/or family commitments and/or contracts.

E.114
The [Company] agrees to consult with and to seriously consider the recommendations and requests of [Name] and the [Agent] in respect of all proposed scripts, titles, slogans, logos, music, lyrics, images, films, videos, sound recordings, computer generated material, website, app, mobile and/or other material to be offered, reproduced, streamed and/or exploited and/or adapted in any media in any format including packaging, advertising, promotional, publicity and marketing material.

E.115
[Name] acknowledges that all final editorial decisions in respect of all content, material, services and exploitation under this agreement shall be at the sole discretion of the [Company] subject to the clause to consult in clause [–]. The [Company] shall have the right to edit, adapt, add and/or delete material and other persons as it thinks fit and shall not be obliged to include the services of [Name].

E.116
The [Company] agrees that the name, image and endorsement of the [Sportsperson] shall not be used for any other purpose other than [specify use and products or services authorised] for the duration of the Sponsorship Period.

E.117

The [Name] agrees that the [Company] shall have the sole discretion as to the manner and method and content to be used in the production, distribution and exploitation of the [Service/Performance/Film/Material] and that no further sums shall be due to the [Name] except those set out under this agreement. The [Company] shall have the final editorial decision in all matters and shall be entitled to edit, amend, adapt, delete and add any content and/or authorise others to do so. The [Company] may decide to complete remove [Name] from the final version and shall be entitled to do so provided that all sums due under clause [–] are paid.

E.118

In the event that the parties shall fail to agree on the choice of material to be recorded under this agreement then the decision of the [Artist/Company] shall be final.

E.119

The [Licensee] acknowledges that it shall not be entitled to exploit in any manner any [Sound Recordings] of the [Musical Work] without the prior written consent of the [Licensor].

E.120

The [Agent/Company] agree that [Name] must be consulted and provide prior authorisation to any proposed changes to any part the content of the [Event/Work/Project] set out in Schedule [–] which is attached to and forms part of this agreement. That the decision of [Name] shall be final and that where [Name] refuses consent any liability and/or consequences that arise shall be at the [Agent's/Company's] sole cost and not attributed to [Name].

E.121

Where the services of [Name] are no longer required for any reason and/or are not included in the final version of the [Work] which is produced and/or developed by the [Company]. Then there shall be no obligation by the [Company] to add any credit and/or acknowledgement of their participation at any time.

E.122

Where the members of the [Consortium] cannot agree on the editorial decisions regarding the content of any material for the [Project]. Then the decision shall be made on the basis of a majority decision between the parties. Where any one party is not willing to accept that decision then they shall be entitled to terminate their arrangement to be involved in the [Project] provided that the [Consortium] can find another substitute to take over their obligations.

Sponsorship

E.123

The [Sponsor] acknowledges that the [Association/Company] has no editorial control in respect of the programme times, dates, duration and content of the broadcasts, transmissions, streaming and playback and/or any other exploitation of the [Series/Event/Films] and cannot be responsible for any technical failures, cancellation and/or other delays and/or interruptions that may occur of any intended coverage on television, radio, websites, apps, mobiles, gadgets and/or otherwise.

E.124

The [Sponsor] acknowledges that all editorial, scheduling and programming decisions concerning the [Programme/Event] are entirely at the sole discretion of the [Company/Distributor].

E.125

The [Company] shall be entitled at its sole discretion and cost to make such changes, deletions, alterations, interruptions, adjustments and/or additions to the content of the [Series/Film/Recordings] as may be required for any reason including but not limited to artists, music, scripts, products, locations, title and/or translations.

E.126

The [Company] shall have final editorial control of the [Series/Films/Videos/Sound Recordings]. In the event that the [Series/Films/Videos/Sound Recordings] are to be substantially changed, altered and/or the content no longer uses the services and/or performance of [Artist] and/or music by [Name] and/or script by [Name]. The [Company] shall inform the [Sponsor] in writing and provide them with the opportunity to cancel the agreement upon terms to be agreed between the parties. The [Sponsor] accepts that in any settlement agreement to cancel the sponsorship there shall be no additional repayments due to be paid by the [Company] as compensation, damages and/or otherwise.

E.127

The [Sponsor] agrees that it shall have no editorial control and/or right to be consulted over any part of the [Event/Project], the content, any agreements with third parties, the marketing and/or any media coverage arranged and/or organised by the [Company].

E.128

The [Sponsor] agrees that it shall have no control and/or rights to be consulted and/or approve any part of the [Project/Exhibition/Conference]. That the [Company] may change the title, content, dates and means of marketing

768

and/or exploitation and/or the use of third parties as the [Company] chooses for any reason. That the [Sponsor] agrees that such variations and changes shall not be provide grounds for withdrawal and/or termination provided that the [Company] completes the obligations in clause [–] before [date].

E.129

The [Company] agrees that the [Sponsor] has agreed to provide the funds in clause [–] due to the proposed appearance and performance by [Name] at the [Event/Programme]. In the event that [Name] should cancel and/or terminate their appearance and/or performance and/or contribution. Then the [Company] agrees to notify the [Sponsor] and to agree alternative individuals who could be approached which would be acceptable to both parties. Where the substitute is not of a comparable status the payment by the [Sponsor] under clause [–] shall not be reduced.

E.130

The [Sponsor] has agreed to provide funding on the basis of the proposed projected:

1.1   attendance and marketing figures in appendix A;

1.2   outline for the layout and exhibitors in appendix B;

1.3   series of workshops and conferences in appendix C.

Where any of these matters is to be revised and/or altered then the [Sponsor] must be consulted and provided with the opportunity to comment on the proposals. Where any change is likely to significantly reduce the numbers of the public attending and/or media coverage. Then the [Company] must make such alterations to the proposals as the [Sponsor] may suggest provided that they are reasonable.

E.131

The [Brand Company] has agreed to supply [number] items of [specify product] free of charge to [Name] for the purpose of product placement in the [Video/Podcast]. [Name] shall not have the right to use the [products] in any manner which would have a negative impact on the marketing and sales of all products sold and/or supplied by the [Brand Company]. [Name] agrees not to associate the products with any politics, offensive material, parodies and/or any other scenario which does not enhance the sales of the [Brand Company] and/or the authorised products which have been supplied.

University, Charity and Educational

E.132

1.1   The [Contributor] agrees that the [Institute/Charity] shall have the sole discretion as to the how the material and/or copyright and/or intellectual property rights are developed, created and/or reproduced and/or exploited at any time. All editorial control shall be with the [Institute/Charity] and there is no obligation to consult and/or seek approval. Nor shall the [Institute/Charity] be under any obligation to pay any additional royalties and/or other sums to the [Contributor] for any form of exploitation in any media and shall only pay those set out under this agreement in clause [–].

1.2 The [Institute/Charity] may edit, amend, adapt, add to and/or delete material produced under this agreement and/or authorise others to do so in such manner and method as the [Institute/Charity] in its absolute discretion shall decide. Where the product of the services provided by the [Contributor] are not to be used in any final version the sums due in clause [–] must still be paid.

E.133

The [Company/Contributor] agree and undertakes that in the event that the [Institute/Charity] requests deletions, amendments, alterations and/or changes to the title, characters, text, images, photographs, cover, products, packaging, publicity, marketing and/or any other material at any time due to errors, omissions, and/or the threat of civil and/or criminal actions. Then the [Company/Contributor] agrees to consent to such deletions, amendments, alterations and/or changes as may be necessary provided that the additional costs are met by the [Institute/Charity].

E.134

The [Licensee] undertakes not to edit, alter, delete, amend, add to and/or change in any way the [Work/Project/Product] without the prior written approval and consent of the [Institute/Charity].

E.135

The [Licensee] agrees and undertakes that the [Work/Project/Product] shall only be reproduced, distributed, supplied and sold in the exact form and with the same materials, design, structure, content, packaging, marketing and promotional material as approved by the [Institute/Charity].

E.136

The [Company] acknowledges and undertakes that the decisions and requirements of the [Institute/Charity] shall be paramount in respect of the creation of the [Service/Website/Project]. That it shall be the [Institute/Charity] and not the [Company] which has the right to make all the final decisions in respect of all matters relating to the [Service/Website/Project].

E.137

After the [Company/Contributor] have delivered the [Project] and been paid in full for the provision of their services. The [Institute/Charity] shall have the absolute right to engage such third parties as it thinks fit to develop, adapt, license and/or exploit the [Project]. No consent, authority and/or any sort of agreement shall be required with the [Company/Contributor] and no further additional sums shall be due.

E.138

The [Institute/Charity] agrees that:

1.1   neither the [Trustees/Directors] nor any employees, representatives, and/or agents shall make and/or authorise any alterations, editing, and/or adaptations of the [Work/Film/Product/Image] without the prior written consent of the [Copyright Owner].

1.2   the artistic and editorial control of the [Work/Film/Product/Image] shall be at the sole discretion and decision of the [Copyright Owner].

1.3   the [Institute/Charity] shall use reasonable endeavours to ensure that any third party shall be informed in writing that they do not have the right to alter, edit and/or adapt the [Work/Film/Product/Image] without the prior written consent of the [Copyright Owner].

E.139

The [Institute/Charity] shall at the [Institutes'/Charity's] cost and expense:

1.1   Collaborate and take account of the views of the [Company] as to any cover, label, copyright and trade mark notices, disclaimers, print size, font, format, layout, design, packaging, website and app content, advertising, promotional and marketing of the [Work/Film/Product].

1.2   Provide the [Company] with draft copies and samples of all proposed material for the [Work/Film/Product]. The Company shall have the right to be consulted but shall not have the final decision on any matter.

1.3   Provide the [Company] with two examples of any finished version of all material for the [Company] to keep as a record.

E.140

[Name] agrees that the [Institute/Charity] and/or any publisher and/or distributor shall have the right to edit, adapt, change, alter, add to, delete and/or distort and/or mutilate any part of the [Work/Sound Recording/Video] which he/she has written, contributed to and/or appeared in voice and/or film as part of the [Project]. That [Name] agrees and accepts that he/she has no claim any/or rights and/or interest and/or moral rights over any such product of his/her services and/or [Work/Sound Recording/Video]. That the

771

[Fee] paid by the [Institute/Charity] has included a payment to for [Name] to waive all rights and moral rights.

E.141

The [Author] agrees that the [Institute/Charity] may use and/or adapt up to [number] words as an extract of the [Work] for the purpose of promoting and marketing the [Institute/Charity] and/or the [Event] and/or for reproduction in the distribution material of a sponsor. Provided that a credit and acknowledgement is provided to the [Author] and a link is stated to [specify source].

E.142

The [Institute/Charity] accept that they shall not have any editorial control over any part of the [Project/Event], marketing, licensing and/or other exploitation. The [Institute/Charity] shall only be responsible for its own [exhibition stand/plot/displays]. There shall be no right of veto of any other exhibitor, contributor, speaker, artist and/or any other material of any nature.

E.143

The confidential information, data and research material is owned and controlled by [Name] and not the [Institute/Charity]. There is no right to display, supply, reproduce and/or distribute and/or exploit any confidential information, data and research material to any third party and/or to license any rights. All copyright, intellectual property rights, patents and computer software rights belong to [Name]. The prior written consent of [Name] is required to reproduce and/or supply any of this material in any format. There is no right to reproduce this confidential information data and research material for the purposes of further education and/or other non-commercial purposes. None of this research material is in the public domain.

ELECTRONIC

General Business and Commercial

E.144

'Electronic' shall mean words, texts, sounds, music, images, logos, graphics, film recordings, and sound recordings conveyed, transferred, supplied, or distributed by electric, magnetic, electro-magnetic, electro-chemical or electro-mechanical means through any method or material.

E.145

'Electronic Rights' shall mean the sole and exclusive right to use, display, exhibit, supply, license, reproduce, distribute and exploit any form of rights and material whether in existence now or developed in the future in relation to the internet, websites, apps, computers, mobiles, watches and fitness and/or time devices and/or any form of telecommunication system and the exclusive right to download, access, stream and/or playback any such material whether, text, sound, images. films, sound recordings, animated characters or any other format to any other gadget, device, watch, fitness or leisure device and/or machine whether by subscription, free or pay per use on land, sea and air in any part of the world and throughout the universe [from [date] to [date].

E.146

'Electronic Rights' shall mean the right to be the sole owner of and have the sole and exclusive right to exploit in any format and/or by any electronic and telecommunication means any words, texts, sounds, music, images, logos, graphics, films, videos, sound recordings, animations and/or characters which are stored, conveyed, transferred, supplied and/or distributed by electric, magnetic, electro-magnetic, electro-chemical or electro-mechanical means through any method or material. That shall include but not be limited to the sole and exclusive right to use, display, exhibit, supply, license, reproduce, distribute and exploit any form of rights and material whether in existence now or developed in the future in relation to the internet, websites, apps, computers, telephones, mobiles, watches and/or other leisure and fitness items which incorporates any form of telecommunications system. This right shall also include the exclusive right to download, access, stream and/or supply any such material to any other gadget, device or machine whether by subscription, free or pay per use on land, sea and air in any part of the world and throughout the universe for the full period of copyright and any extensions, renewals and thereafter in perpetuity.

E.147

'Electronic communication' shall mean a communication transmitted from one person to another or one device to another or vice versa by means of a telecommunication system or by any other means which is in electronic form. Communication shall include a communication comprising sounds or images or both and a communication where payment is required.

E.148

The [Company] agrees and undertakes that the [Copyright Owner] is and shall remain the sole and exclusive owner of all copyright, intellectual property rights, computer software rights and all other electronic rights which exist now and/or may be created in the future in the [Work/Film/ Sound Recordings/Project] and/or any adaptation and/or other form of exploitation.

E.149

'The Electronic Digital Files' shall mean all the words, texts, sounds, music, images, logos, graphics, film recordings, and sound recordings stored, conveyed, transferred, supplied, or distributed by electric, magnetic, electro-magnetic, electro-chemical or electro-mechanical means through any method or material whether in existence now or developed in the future including the internet, websites, apps, computers, telephones, mobiles, or any other form of telecommunication system.

E.150

'The Electronic Digital Files' shall mean the [format] files held by the [Company] reproduced from the [Master Material] which are to be used to [specify purpose].

E.151

'The Telecommunication and Transmission Rights' shall mean all forms of telecommunication and/or transmission through sound, air, land and/or water and/or any chemical, substance, wireless telegraphy, WiFi and/or any other method and/or material and/or by intermediary gadgets and/or equipment by any means whether known now as at [date] and/or developed in the future including images, text, films, recordings, photographs, music, sound recordings, animation and/or any computer generated creations and/or otherwise including but not limited to by television, radio, landline and mobile phones, laptops, computers, websites, apps and the internet and/or any gadgets, devices and/or storage systems in any medium through which content id downloaded, displayed, viewed, played and/or streamed.

EMBARGO

General Business and Commercial

E.152

[Name] the recipient of this news release hereby confirms and accepts that the content of the document shall not be placed into the public domain until after [time] on [date]. That in the event that the embargo is not complied with as requested that the following conditions shall apply [specify].

E.153

For the purposes of this agreement an embargo shall mean an arrest laid on [name of vessel] or any merchandise or products on board the vessel by any authorised public authority or court or an order prohibiting [name of vessel] from putting to sea and/or entering a port. In the event of an embargo then clause [–] shall apply.

E.154

The [Company] agrees and undertakes not to make available, release, sell, distribute, and/or otherwise supply the [Product/Service/Work] to the public before [time] on [date]. That the [Product/Service/Work] shall be kept under maximum security at the head office and only the following agreed personnel shall be allowed access and/or to be made aware of the launch [specify personnel]. The [Company] shall not respond to any press and/or media enquiries and shall refer all such matters to [specify name].

E.155

This [Work] must not be reproduced and/or distributed to any third party before [time] [date] without the prior written consent of [Name].

E.156

Where in any part of the preparation of the [Work] any material is and/or has been provided to [Name] by a third party which is confidential and private and/or is the subject of legal proceedings concerning two persons who are the subject of a court order regarding their identity. Then [Name] shall not be under any obligation to the [Company] to supply details and may withhold such information.

ENDORSEMENT

General Business and Commercial

E.157

1.1 In consideration of the agreed payments [Name] undertakes to provide an endorsement from [date] to [date] in respect of the following version of the [Product/Service]: [specify product] [manufactured/distributed/ sub-licensed] by or to the [Company] in [country].

1.2 No endorsement in relation to the product shall be used by the [Company] after [date] in any medium.

1.3 The endorsement shall be in the form of a [film/video/podcast] of less than [number] minutes in duration which shall incorporate the use of the following words by {Name]: [specify words/script].

1.4 [Name] shall have the right to approve the draft script and the draft proposals for the filming. If any part is not acceptable to [Name] then it must be changed otherwise [Name] shall have the right to terminate this agreement. If [Name] terminates the agreement before carrying out the endorsement work then all the sums paid by the [Company] must be refunded.

E.158

[Name] shall act in a professional manner in both his/her public life and on social media and at events. [Name] shall not make any statement or threat which could potentially be viewed as harmful and/or damaging to the [Company], its brands and its products and/or services. [Name] agrees that he/she is to view this role as an ambassador for the [Company] at all times. [Name] must not during the course of this agreement become involved in any other work which would have a negative impact on the [Company] and/or the sales of its products and/or services and/or result in significant negative social media from the public and on radio, television, magazines and/or newspapers.

E.159

The [Company] agrees and undertakes that the [Company] is financially stable and will continue to be able to make the payment commitments in clause [–] to [Name] and the [Company] is not under threat of any kind and likely to stop production of the [Product] during the Term of this Agreement.

E.160

The [Company] agrees and undertakes that the entire range of all its products and in particular the [Product] together with any packaging are entirely safe and fit for their intended purpose and function, and comply with all standards, legal requirements and tests that are or may be applicable.

E.161

The [Company] agrees and undertakes that neither [Name], nor their business, nor their agent shall be in anyway responsible for or liable to pay any sums of any nature if there is any allegation, any claim, action, or otherwise against the [Company] arising from the services and work of [Name] under this agreement at any time.

E.162

The [Company] agrees to provide the non-exclusive services of [Name] who has agreed to endorse and promote the [Distributor's] [Product/Services] upon the following terms:

1.1 The [Distributor] shall pay [Name] as follows [specify advance/fees/ repeat fees/additional uses/expenses]. Payment shall be by the following method [specify] by [date] subject to completion of the required work in each case. The [Distributor] shall also arrange at its sole cost comprehensive insurance cover in the name of and for the benefit of [Name] for any claim relating to provision of their services in the sum of [number].

1.2 [Name] shall carry out the following work: [specify number, duration and detail of recordings in radio, film, television, advertisements, personal appearances, newspapers, magazines and trade journals, website, app and mobile material, written statements and associated characters and logos].

E.163

The product of the work of the services of [Name] shall only be exploited by the [Company] from [date] to [date] thereafter the [Company] must either destroy all the material or store it and undertake not to use it without the prior written consent of [Name].

E.164

The [Company] shall not have the right to use, transmit, supply and/or distribute the material produced under this agreement in any form except in [specify countries] in [specify language] from [date]. This shall include any period after the expiry and/or termination if this agreement.

E.165

The [Company] shall not have the right to sub-license or authorise others to copy, supply, distribute or exploit the material created under this Agreement unless it is specifically to promote, market and advertise the [Product] in the manner, means and style agreed with [Name]. All other such uses shall require the prior written consent of [Name], a further agreement and additional payments. Failure to comply with this clause shall entitle [Name] to [specify].

E.166

The [Company] agrees that it shall not be entitled to use, exploit or license any of the material produced or created for the purposes of this Agreement in which the [Celebrity] appears in sound, vision for any purpose at any time other than for the endorsement, promotion or advertising of the [Company's] Product during the Term of the Agreement. Where the [Company] wishes to use any material at any time for any other purpose and/or to license rights to any third party. Then on each occasion a new agreement must be concluded with the [Celebrity] and the consent of the [Celebrity] provided to the [Company].

E.167

[Name] and their agent [specify] agree that the [Company] shall be entitled to exploit, sub-license, distribute, market, transfer, assign, and reproduce the material created under this Agreement including the name of the person at any time and in any format and there shall be no restrictions or prohibitions on its use. Provided that the [Company] undertakes to ensure that the material shall be acknowledged as being originally related to an endorsement of the [Product] and that no use shall be derogatory, defamatory or prejudicial to the career of [Name] or their business.

E.168

In the event that the [Product/Magazine/Advertisement] is withdrawn from the [website/magazine/event] and/or is not reproduced and/or distributed for any reason the [Company] shall still be entitled to receive all the sums specified in clause [–] for the endorsement by [Name].

E.169

The products, articles, links, blogs, and all other material on this are supplied, posted and/or promoted by third parties on this [Website/App/Platform]. You may choose to purchase, use, reproduced and/or promote the content at your own risk and cost. There is no recommendation and/or endorsement by the [Company] nor any acceptance of any liability for any consequences that may arise unless caused directly by the negligence of the [Company] and which directly causes personal injury or death. If there are any inaccuracies, omissions, allergic reactions and/or problems with health and safety issues and/or instructions then please email us with the details so that we can try to delete and/or amend them accordingly.

E.170

[Name] agrees that the [Company] shall be entitled to edit, adapt, add to and/or delete the [Film/Work/Images/Photographs] of [Name] endorsing the [Product/Services] of the [Company] provided that the final version is not offensive, derogatory and/or likely to damage the reputation of [Name] and/or any of his/her existing sponsors [specify sponsors].

E.171

The [Company] shall be entitled to add other products, services, images, text, videos, sound recordings and any other material as it thinks fit to the final [Film/Work/Project] provided that it is made clear that there is no endorsement by [Name] of this other new material. That the endorsement provided by [Name] is limited to [specify product/manufacturer]. The [Company] agrees not to include any directly competing products in the [specify market] and shall ensure that any content including [Name] shall not include any new material.

E.172

[Name] reserves the right to withdraw his/her support of the [Company] and/or its work and/or products where any senior executive and/or management make a political statement against [specify subjects] which would be contrary to the existing views of [Name]. In such circumstances [Name] may terminate this agreement and shall only be entitled to retain all the sums paid to date for all the work by [Name] which has already been completed.

E.173

[Name] agrees to be used in a short term marketing campaign from [date] to [date] for the new app on the subject of [specify] for the [Distributor]. [Name] agrees that the [Distributor] may use his/her name, image and logo for that sole purpose but not for marketing and promoting the other products of the [Distributor]. [Name] shall not be obliged to do any photo shoot and/or filming and shall supply his/her own images that he/she agrees can be used. Provided that the [Company] agrees that they are not authorised to use those images after [date] and/or in any other media.

E.174

[Name] shall have the right to seek third parties to endorse and/or sponsor and/or enter into product placement and/or affiliation programmes with [Name] for the [App/Blog/Podcast] at any time. [Name] shall be entitled to retain all sums and benefits received and shall not be obliged to account and/or share any sums with the [Company].

E.175

The [Company] agrees and undertakes:

1.1　not to become involved in any controversy, politics, campaign, social media vendetta and/or legal proceedings which would be detrimental to the career, brands and/or business of [Name].

1.2　to inform [Name] of any such potential problem which is likely to have a negative impact on [Name] which directly and/or indirectly relates to [Names'] endorsement of the products and/or services of the [Company] and/or any other matter in respect of the [Company] and/or its suppliers and/or distributors.

1.3　where in the opinion of [Name] any issue may result in an adverse reaction to [Name] by the public and/or media by association with the [Company]. Then [Name] shall have the right to suspend and/or terminate the agreement. In such instance [Name] shall only be entitled to be paid for work which has been completed and for work which was projected to be completed within the next [number] months.

ENVIRONMENTAL

General Business and Commercial

E.176

The [Company] undertakes that it shall use its reasonable endeavours to ensure that the following policies are adopted, maintained, and monitored as part of its planning, purchase and operational requirements of the business:

1.1 That it will try to source materials from verifiable sustainable resources and use and give preference to other services and goods which are rated as better for the environment.

1.2 That it will reduce and phase out the use of toxic or dangerous substances, chemicals and solvents, or those gases or emissions which damage the ozone layer or pollute the air.

1.3 That it will reduce and prevent discharges into land, sea and rivers and will conserve water, energy and resources; reduce waste and recycle.

1.4 That transport methods are considered not only by the cost, but also the effect on the environment.

E.177

The [Company] confirms and undertakes that it has and will maintain the following environmental policies in relation to all its [Products], packaging, methods of storage, delivery and sourcing of ingredients provided that the cost impact is not prohibitive:

1.1 All sources of material shall as far as possible come from sustainable resources.

1.2 No additional chemicals, salt, additives, preservatives or other substances or ingredients are added which have not been declared on the label even in very small amounts whether required by law or not.

1.3 No genetically modified material is present in any form or any substance combined with or derived from it.

1.4 There is a set target to reduce packaging, and packaging is kept to a minimum and is capable of being recycled.

1.5 That preference is given to environmentally friendly products, services and transport and other companies and businesses that adopt environmentally aware practices.

1.6 That there are regular reviews and records, documents and evidence can be supplied to support their compliance and procedures.

1.7 That there is use and support of fair trade for self-supporting communities and that it is a condition of their contracts with suppliers or other businesses that working practices must comply with certain minimum standards.

E.178

The [Company] agrees that it shall not and undertakes that it shall not allow any person and/or company and/or agent to enter on, gain access to and/or use in any way, and/or pass over, under, or through any part of any structure, building, article, lighting, utility, whether on the land, above or below the surface or in the sea, the air or any part of [address] [land registry reference] anything related to the following subjects [mobile phone masts/transmitters/ pesticides/toxic or poisonous substances/quarry/factory/fracking] at any time. The [Company] acknowledges that this is an important clause without which this agreement would not have been entered into by [Name].

E.179

The [Company] agrees and undertakes that it shall have a policy for sustainable development and shall its [best/reasonable] endeavours to source all products, materials and vehicles from third parties who practise good environmentally aware policies.

E.180

The [Company] agrees that it must operate an energy and environmental conservation, resource and sustainability policy in line with the targets of [specify organisation]. Copies of the policies are attached and form part of this agreement. That the [Company] shall reduce use of paper and encourage recycling of materials; that where equipment and/or other fittings are replaced they will be disposed of for re-use by a charity and/or other community use and not added to landfill. That use of public transport and walking shall be encouraged to all staff and a loan scheme established for public transport.

E.181

The [Enterprise] shall operate a policy of effective use of resources in accordance with the guidelines laid down by [specify organisation]. The [Enterprise] shall monitor and report on its use of water, paper, light, heat, petrol, equipment, ink cartridges, furniture and other resources and waste disposal, recycling and air pollution. The [Enterprise] agrees and undertakes to have an active plan to reduce costs and adopt as far as possible a sustainable green policy.

E.182

The [Company] agrees and undertakes to establish green policies for its business, agents, distributors and employees in respect of the following:

1.1 Purchasing and supply of materials. Policies relating to glass, plastic and biodegradable materials. Support of fair trade communities.

1.2 Recycling, re-use by charities and other enterprises and waste disposal; discharges into the land, sewage, rivers and sea. The release of toxins into the air and pollution.

1.3 Travel including air flights and cars; freight, packaging, storage and delivery methods.

EQUAL OPPORTUNITIES

General Business and Commercial

E.183

The [Company] shall make arrangements for promoting in relation to employment, equality of opportunity between men and women and between persons of different racial groups and people of disabilities and review those arrangements from time to time. The [Company] shall make such adjustments in access and/or the equipment which may be required to support the role of any person provided that the cost is reasonably affordable by the [Company].

E.184

The [Company] undertakes that it shall endeavour to ensure that there is compliance with all equal opportunity requirements in [country] from [date] to [date] and that all applicants for positions at the [Company] shall be treated in a fair manner based on their qualifications and experience and not race, disability, gender, religion or otherwise.

E.185

The parties agree to treat all candidates equally regardless of gender, race, disability, religion, type of education, socio-economic group, political views and/or age.

E.186

The policy of equal opportunities applies to all candidates, but it is a requirement of the position that in the application form each person who applies agrees to be subject to a full [DRB/Criminal Record/Qualification/Reference] check which is mandatory.

E.187

The [Company] agrees that all applicants shall be considered on their merits and based on their qualifications and work experience. No preference is provided to any person except that it is a requirement of all positions that the person be entitled to work in [country] and can speak and write fluent [language].

E.188

The [Contractor] agrees and undertakes to at all times operate and adhere to:

1.1 An equal opportunities policy in accordance with any legislation and policies of [country] which may exist and/or may be brought into existence and

1.2 To provide a minimum of [number] training apprenticeships for candidates [age 18–24] years for not less than [number] weeks for not less than [payment] per person.

E.189

The [Company] agrees and undertakes to comply with any legislation and/or government guidelines and/or policies in [specify countries] which may exist during the term of this agreement which directly apply to the [Company] in respect of its employees, services, products and/or agents.

ERROR

General Business and Commercial

E.190

References to errors, incorrect statements, mistakes or omissions in this agreement shall not include those which are of a minor or inconsequential nature.

E.191

The [Company] undertakes to minimise disruption that may be caused by technical errors, viruses or any other phenomenon which affects the function of the [Website/App/Software]. There can be no assurance that the data, information and any material whether text, images, graphics, music, sounds or sound effects or recordings, chatrooms, icons, links or otherwise are free of errors. Nor can the [Company] accept responsibility for any impact or loss or damage that the failure of this [Website/App/Software] to function effectively may have on you personally and/or your business.

E.192

Where an error is found or later disclosed whether by the [Licensor] or the [Licensee]. The [Licensee] shall not be entitled to a refund of any overpayment to the [Licensor]. Nor shall the [Licensor] be entitled to any interest, compensation, or damages for an error provided that the error was not deliberate or fraudulent and payment is made immediately. An error arising from an audit by the [Licensor] shall result in the [Licensee] paying all cost and expenses in respect of the accountants and the legal advisors for such audit where the error is more than [number/currency] in any [one year/accounting period].

E.193

Errors, inaccuracies, mistakes, incorrect advice, formulae, contents, faulty connections, system failures, viruses, bugs, hackers, losses, damages, theft, and/or identity disclosures of email addresses by mistake and/or the failure to encrypt information are possible when using this [Website/App/Software] and the [Company] is not and will not be responsible. [Name] accepts and agrees that they use this [Website/App/Software] at their own risk.

E.194

The [Institute/Charity] cannot accept any responsibility for the consequences and/or liabilities arising from any errors, omissions, misrepresentations, mistakes in prices and/or dates on the [Brochure/Website/Service]. All details may be changed and/or amended without notice by the [Institute/Charity].

E.195

Where there has been an error, omission and/or default at any time which has been caused by the [Company] and will result in losses and/or damages being suffered and/or incurred directly and/or indirectly by the [Licensor]. Then the [Company] shall be obliged to pay the full cost and expense of all such losses and /or damages to the [Licensor] together with interest at [number] per cent from the date of the error, omission and/or default until the matter is resolved.

E.196

It is accepted by all parties that there shall be no claim and/or action and/or demand against any of the others in the [Consortium] for any errors, omissions, mistakes, deletions and/or fraud and/or negligence by any of the persons involved in the development, creation and delivery of the [Project]. That all parties shall bear their own losses, damages, costs and expenses and accept that they have entered into this agreement at their own risk and cost.

ESTATE

General Business and Commercial

E.197
In the event of the death of the [Author] the following person shall be treated as the literary executor of all the written drafts, manuscripts, published hardback and paperback and e books, sound recordings, audio files, articles and diaries of the [Author]: [Name] [address] [contact details].

E.198
In the event of the death of [Name] and/or power of attorney being made to another person acting on behalf of [Name]. Then all copyright, intellectual property rights, trade marks, images, drafts and material which has been published, licensed and/or sold and any interest, benefits and sums due under this agreement shall be transferred to the estate and/or the authorised person with power of attorney. The obligations of the [Company] shall continue under the terms of the agreement until the expiry date and/or until such time as the parties have reached a settlement agreement.

E.199
Where the [Executor] is unable and/or unwilling due to ill health and/or other personal reasons to administer the estate of the deceased [Name]. Then the following person may be substituted to act in their place [specify person/ address]. Provided that all the beneficiaries agree and no additional costs are required.

E.200
'The Estate of [Name]' shall include all property belonging to [Name] including all houses, flats, land whether freehold and/or leasehold and/or however else it may be held, rights of way, mining rights, fishing rights, chattels, goods and contents of any property. garage and storage facility, money, shares, investments, savings, trusts, life insurance and all digital and electronic accounts and passwords, images, data, records and information of any nature whether stored in a gadget and/or in an online account on the internet and all registered domain names, trade marks, logos, sound recordings, films, computer software, draft manuscripts and all published and unpublished works in any media in any part of the world.

E.201
'The Estate' shall include all the following matters:

1.1 Property, land, freehold, leasehold, rental agreements, rights of occupation, rights of way and access, fishing rights, sea and coastal areas owned, controlled or held in the name of [specify] or for the benefit of [Name] known as [address/reference/deposited at/charges/liens/other].

1.2 All intellectual property rights, copyright, patents, trade marks, service marks, design rights, future design rights, computer software, trade secrets, domain names, registrations, contracts, licences, confidential information or other rights in any media of any nature whether in existence now or created in the future owned, controlled or held in the name of [Name] or for the benefit of [Name].

E.202

The estate of [Name] shall include the following books, films, articles, videos, websites, apps, products, diaries, draft manuscripts and letters, bank and savings accounts, shares, bitcoin, records, passwords, medical records, images, photographs, drawings, paintings and artwork and any other material in any format in any media owned and/or controlled by [Name] which shall include [specify and list in detail]. Together with all intellectual property rights, copyright, patents, trade marks, service marks, design rights, future design rights, computer software, trade secrets, domain names, registrations, contracts, licences, confidential information or other rights in any text, image, logo, photograph, sound recordings, films, and in any other media of any nature whether in existence now or created in the future owned, controlled or held by [Name] or for the benefit of [Name] by any person, company and/or other entity.

E.203

'The Estate' shall comprise all the copyright and intellectual property rights and computer software rights, patents, trade marks and material owned and/or controlled by [Name] at his/her death which relates to his/her career as a [specify role]. This material shall include all diaries, drawings, artwork, paintings, computer generated material and animations, research notes, school books and certificates, manuscripts, draft documents and all licences granted by [Name] and all royalties which may be due. Together with all images, photographs, recordings, films, videos, characters, emails, text messages and other correspondence with agents, publishers, television companies, and any other third party. As well as material stored on any hard drive and/or software of a computer, gadget, mobile and/or some other device., drawings, sketches, paintings which directly relates to the [literary/artistic] work of [Name].

E.204

1.1 The Estate of [Name] of [address] who was born on [date] and died on [date] in [country] shall be referred to as [specify].

1.2 [Probate/other] was granted on [date] by [specify]. A copy of which is attached and forms part of this agreement.

1.3 The [Executors/Trustees] of the Estate are [specify] who have the following authority [specify].

1.4 The beneficiaries and their guardians of the Estate are as follows [specify].

1.5 The assets of the Estate as at [date] are as follows [specify].

1.6 The liabilities of the Estate as at [date] are as follows [specify].

E.205
The {Company] agrees that in the event that [Name] shall die and/or be personally incapacitated so that he/she is unable to fulfil the terms of this agreement. That the [Company] shall not seek to be refunded any money paid under this agreement from the estate of [Name]. The [Company] agrees and undertakes to continue to pay all royalties and other sums due to the estate as required under the agreement to [Name].

EUROPEAN UNION

General Business and Commercial

E.206
The [Supplier] warrants that all goods and services shall comply with all relevant European Union Directives, regulations, standards, policies and codes which are and may come into existence during the Term of this Agreement which may be applicable including, but not limited to [specify].

E.207
The [Company] undertakes that the [Work/Services/Products] shall comply with all the existing and future European directives, regulations and cases. That the [Company] shall regularly review whether they are fulfilling all the terms required and update accordingly.

E.208
The [Product/Service] and the [Company] shall comply with all legal requirements, directives, regulations and practices required by the European Union which are displayed on its websites, published in its journals and/or are applicable as binding decisions, judgements and/or notified to member states and/or incorporated in the legislation of any member states.

E.209

This agreement is not bound by any legislation, directive and/or regulation of the European Union except where products and/or services are supplied, distributed and/or sold in the member states of the European Union and the legislation and laws of that country apply.

E.210

This agreement is subject to the laws of [country] which is a member state of the European Union. The products and/or services are to be produced and/or exploited worldwide and shall be subject to whatever legislation and/or laws are relevant in each country.

EXCLUSIVITY

Television, Film and Video

E.211

The [Company] shall have the non-exclusive rights in the [Territory/country] during the Term of this Agreement to use, transmit and broadcast the same identical excerpts of the [Film/Video] of not more than [number] minutes in duration in total for the purposes of any advertising, publicity, promotion or review of the [Film/Video] on the channel known as [specify] and the [website/app/platform] known as [specify].

E.212

The [Company] will not from the date of this agreement until the expiry of the Licence Period and/or the termination of the agreement exercise and/or authorise, and/or in any manner permit the exploitation in the Territory by any means of the [Film/Video/Sound Recordings] and/or parts and/or any characters and/or storylines including but not limited by means of any digital, electronic and/or form of telecommunication, mobile and/or landline phones, satellite, cable and streaming through digital television and other gadgets and devices, radio, videos, DVDs, discs, through use of the supply and/or distribution of any such material on the internet and/or any website, app, game and/or by any adaptation and/or merchandising, products, theme parks, gambling, betting, lottery and/or in any other form by any means whether in existence now and/or created in the future.

E.213

During the existence of this agreement and with immediate effect [Name] undertakes and warrants to the [Consortium] that the [Name] will not grant and/or authorise the use by any third party of any of the rights granted to the [Consortium] under this agreement. Except that [Name] shall be permitted to use the [Film/Video/Images] for illustration purposes during the course of any public lectures by [Name] in [specify countries].

E.214

The [Company] undertakes that it will not from the date of the agreement until the expiry and/or termination of the agreement grant any copyright and/or intellectual property rights and/or license, assign and/or otherwise exploit any part of the [Film/Video/Images] in any media and/or any format to any third party in any country worldwide and/or to any business, charity and/or person which operates on land, sea and/or in the air.

E.215

1.1 In consideration of the Distribution Income in clause [–] the [Company] grants to the [Licensee] the sole and exclusive licence in the Territory throughout the Licence Period to exploit the following rights in the [Film/Recordings] to be reproduced in full in the following manner: Theatric Rights, Non-Theatric Rights and DVD and Video Rights.

1.2 There is no right granted to use any extracts and/or to grant rights to third parties in such extracts.

1.3 All form of reproduction, streaming, transmission and/or broadcast on television, radio, the internet, websites, apps, podcasts and mobiles, are specifically excluded.

1.4 There is no right granted to create and develop any merchandising and/or to exploit any other rights in any form.

E.216

In consideration of the Licence Fee the [Licensor] grants to the [Distributor] the sole and exclusive rights in all media whether known at the date of this agreement and/or created and developed at a later date in the [Film/Series/Videos] and/or any parts including the associated soundtrack throughout the Territory for the Term of this Agreement. For the avoidance of doubt it is agreed that such rights shall include, but not be limited to:

1.1 all forms of television including satellite, cable, terrestrial and any type of playback and/or subscription service;

1.2 all digital and electronic methods of exploitation whether through a website, app, platform, software, computer generated material and via any gadget, mobile, watch or other device;

1.3 all methods of reproduction for CDs, DVDs, sound recordings and other units which can be sold direct to the public.

1.4 all theatric and non-theatric uses and screenings in outdoor venues where a charge is made and for free;

1.5 all forms of publication, merchandising and exploitation relating to any adaptation including hardback, paperback, e and audio books, children's books and toys, cartoons and animations, household and food products, clothes and the licensing of extracts; theme parks, reproductions in the form of characters, logos, promotions and endorsements of third party products and/or services.

E.217

1.1 In consideration of the Licence Fee and the Author's Royalties the [Author] grants to the [Company] the sole and exclusive right to produce [number] episodes of the [Series] details of which are set out in appendix A based on the [Author's Work].

1.2 The [Author] grants the [Company] the sole and exclusive rights to exploit all the Cable, Satellite and Terrestrial Television Rights in the [Series] for the duration of the Licence Period throughout the Territory.

1.3 This shall include the right to stream and download the [Series] through electronic and telecommunication means to the main nominated website and app of the [Company] known as [specify details] in order for the [Series] to be viewed as part of a playback archive for a period of up to [specify duration one week/one month] after the broadcast and/or transmission of each episode of the [Series].

1.4 Any other rights in the [Series] shall not be exploited by the [Company] unless the parties conclude separate agreements in each case based on the proposals which have been disclosed.

1.5 The [Company] accepts that the [Author] shall not be obliged to grant any merchandising rights based on the [Authors' Work] to the [Company]. Nor shall the [Company] be entitled to a share of any sums received in respect of any merchandising rights.

E.218

The [Company] acknowledges that it shall not be entitled to exploit any other rights in the [Author's] Work not specifically granted under this Agreement including but not limited to the right to exploit extracts of the [Series], merchandising, publication rights, the right to transmit, display or download the [Series] on the internet, by any telecommunication system or to use the [Series] to endorse any person, company or product.

E.219

In consideration of the [Fee] and the [Additional Fees] the [Copyright Owner] grants the [Licensee] the non-exclusive right to broadcast and/or transmit the [Film/Image/Sound Recordings] in the [Programme] and appoint an authorised distributor to sell, supply and reproduce the [Film/Image/Sound recordings] in the [Programme] to third parties in order to exploit the following rights [specify] in [specify countries] from [date] to [date].

E.220

The grant of the non-exclusive right in clause [–] to the [Licensee] shall not entitle the [Licensee] to exploit any other rights which are reserved by the [Copyright Owner]. Where the rights have not been created and/or the technology developed at the time of this Agreement. Then any such rights shall belong to the [Copyright Owner] and not the [Licensee].

E.221

In consideration of the [Advance Fee] and the future royalties from the exploitation of the [Documentary/Series] set out in clause [–]. Provided that all the [Advance fee] and royalties which fall due are paid and accounted for to the [Licensor] and the [Licensor] is provided with the following credit at the end of the [Documentary/Series] [specify].

The [Licensor] grants the [Licensee] the non-exclusive right to include the [number] minutes in duration of the [Sound Recordings] and the [number] minutes in duration of extracts of the [Films] in the [Documentary/Series].

The [Licensee] shall have the right to appoint a distributor to exploit, sub-license and market the [Documentary/Series] throughout the [Territory] from [date] to [date].

The rights granted in respect of the [Sound Recordings] and extracts of the [Films] shall only be in respect of the following rights:

1.1   All forms of television including cable, satellite, terrestrial and streaming through electronic and telecommunication systems via a television set, website, app and/or some other software and/or playback through access through a gadget, device, watch and/or mobile.

1.2   All forms of sale as a separate unit such as a DVD, video and/or other format where the [Documentary] is stored on the unit and played back.

1.3   The right to arrange sub-titles in another language and/or sign language.

1.4   Any other adaptations and/or developments of any kind are specifically excluded including publication of any related books, toys, games. The authorisation and consent of the [Licensor] must be sought for any other use in any medium.

E.222

1.1 In consideration of the payment of the Non-returnable Advance and the Licensor's Royalties, the [Licensor] grants to [Licensee] the sole and exclusive [DVD/Video/Disc] rights in the [Film] in the Territory for the duration of the Licence Period and the right to authorise third parties to exercise such rights.

1.2 The [Licensee] agrees that all rights not specifically granted are excluded from this agreement including all forms of television, format rights, merchandising and/or publishing rights, computer games, theme parks and any form of exploitation by any electronic and telecommunication systems and/or method.

1.3 That after the end of the Licence Period the [Licensee] shall not have any rights in the [Film] and/or any master material and/or reproductions developed and/or created pursuant to this agreement. The [Licensee] undertakes to ensure that all such rights shall revert to the [Licensor].

1.4 The [Licensee] accepts that the [Licensor] shall be entitled at its sole discretion to assign the rights granted to the [Licensee] at any time to a third party subject to the terms of the exclusive licence.

E.223

It is agreed that the [Licensee] shall be permitted to use and permit the use of extracts of the [Film] to be shown at trade exhibitions and fairs for the purpose of the promotion of the [DVDs/Videos/Discs].

E.224

The [Licensee] shall be permitted to incorporate parts of the [Film] on other suitable [DVDs/Videos/Discs] during the Term of the Agreement provided that the subject matter of the other films is not violent, offensive or [specify] and no more than [duration] is used and the sole purpose is the promotion of the [DVD/Video/Disc] of the [Film].

E.225

The [Licensee] acknowledges that all other rights including terrestrial, satellite, cable television and other forms of distribution of material by any electronic means and/or telecommunication systems whether through use of the internet, websites, apps, computers, mobile phones and/or other devices and gadgets; the sub-licensing of any adaptations and/or merchandising and/or licensing of extracts for any other reason are not granted to the [Licensee] and are retained by the [Licensor].

E.226

The [Distributor] grants the [Agent] the exclusive right to obtain orders for, advertise, market and sell copies of the [DVD/Disc] in [country] from [date] to [date]. The [Agent] shall not be entitled to produce, reproduce, translate, sub-title and/or otherwise create its own version and/or packaging for the [DVD/Disc]. The [Agent] shall only be entitled to sell the [DVD/Disc] in the exact form which it is supplied by the [Distributor]. All requests for copies of the [DVD/Disc] shall be forwarded to the [Distributor] who shall provide the stock. The [Agent] shall have no authority and/or rights to grant to any third party.

E.227

In consideration of the [Fee] the [Licensor] grants the [Licensee] the non-exclusive right to exhibit and show the [Work] on the [Disc] at the [specify venue and address] to a non-paying audience on [date]. Provided that the copyright notice and credit is not omitted and/or deleted at the time of the exhibition and the exhibition is to promote and advertise [specify reason]. There is no right to exhibit and/or use the [Work] and/or [Disc] at any other time and/or to make copies and/or to add and/or change any part of the [Work] and/or [Disc] supplied by the [Licensor].

E.228

1.1 The [Copyright Owner] grants the [Licensee] the non-exclusive right to include the [Image/Text] known as [specify/reference] in the [Work] and [Film] to be reproduced in the form of a printed [Report] and [Disc] in [country] from [date] to [date].

1.2 The [Licensee] shall only be entitled to make copies and/or reproduce the [Image/Text] for the purpose of producing the [Report] and [Disc] which shall only be used to submit for [specify reason] purposes to [specify organisation].

1.3 No right is granted to create an electronic and/or digital version and/or to license and/or authorise any third party to make copies for any reason. Nor is any right granted to add to, vary, change and/or delete from the [Image/Text] which should remain unchanged, in content, colour and layout. Nor is any translation and/or adaptation authorised and all other rights are reserved to the [Copyright Owner].

E.229

1.1 In consideration of the [Fee] and the royalties due in clause [–] [Name] grants to the [Distributor] the sole and exclusive right to reproduce, exploit and sub-license the performance and appearances of [Name] in all films, sound recordings, photographs, computer generated images and any other associated material created and/or developed under this agreement which features [Name] throughout the world in any medium, and/or by any method and/or format. [Name] grants such exclusive rights to the [Distributor] for a period of [number] years from [date].

1.2 The [Distributor] shall have the right and/or option to renew the exclusive period of rights for an additional period of [number] years from [date]. This will be granted by [Name] in the event that the [Distributor] pays a non-returnable fee which cannot be offset against future and/or past royalties of [number/currency].

1.3 In the event that the exclusive period is not extended then neither party shall be entitled to exploit any of the material created under this agreement and/or the rights unless both parties agree terms and conditions.

E.230

[Name] has agreed to be filmed and recorded on [date] at [location] to appear and contribute to a [Film] provisionally entitled: [specify title of film]. In consideration of the payment of a fee of [number/currency] [Name] grants an exclusive licence to the [Company] in all his/her contribution, performance and product of his/her work for the [Film] in any form throughout the world and universe which he/she may and/or will make including all present and future copyright and intellectual property rights and any other rights and/or interest in any media and/or format from [date] and in perpetuity.

E.231

The [Company] acknowledges that it shall not have any right and/or be entitled to attempt to apply and/or register any trade mark, service mark and/or domain name in the name of [Name] either under their real birth name of [specify] and/or their stage name of [specify].

E.232

There are no rights granted and/or assigned in respect of the lyrics, music and/or sound recordings owned and/or controlled by [Name].

E.233

1.1 The parties agree that the [Company] shall not have exclusive rights for the full Term of this Agreement.

1.2 [Name] grants the [Company] exclusive rights for the first [six] months from [date] to [date] in [specify countries] in respect of the following matters: [specify rights/areas].

1.3 After [date] [Name] grants only non-exclusive rights to the [Company] until [date] in [specify countries] in respect of the following matters: [specify rights/areas]. The [Company] accepts that [Name] may license these same rights to a third party at any time from [date].

General Business and Commercial

E.234

The [Employee] shall provide his/her services to the best of his/her skill and ability on a full-time and exclusive basis and shall perform all services diligently to ensure that the obligations under this agreement are satisfactorily performed.

E.235

The [Employee] agrees and undertakes that he/she:

1.1 will not undertake any other employment outside his/her working hours whether remunerated by payment or benefits in kind or otherwise.

1.2 will not have any interest in any business or project which directly or indirectly competes with the business interests of the [Company], its subsidiaries or associates.

1.3 shall seek the prior written consent of the [Managing Director] of the [Company] in the event that he/she wishes to pursue any role in conflict with 1.1 and/or 1.2 above.

E.236

1.1 The [Consultant] confirms that he/she shall not during the course of his/her agreement with the [Company] supply services of the same or similar nature to a direct competitor of the [Company] including [specify third parties].

1.2 The [Consultant] accepts that although his/her services are not exclusive to the [Company]. That in the event that the [Consultant] decides to work directly with a competitor of the [Company]. That the [Company] shall have the right to terminate this agreement and shall not be obliged to make any further payments to the [Consultant].

E.237

'The Services' shall mean the product of the services of the [Executive] to be provided to the [Company] under this agreement which are described in the [Executive Job Description] which are attached in Schedule A and form part of this agreement.

E.238

During the continuance of the appointment the [Executive] shall provide his/her services to the [Company] as follows:

1.1 in a professional manner, on a full-time and exclusive basis and shall perform his/her duties diligently and in good faith so that his/her services are satisfactorily performed under this agreement.

1.2   carry out the duties described in the [Executive Job Description] in Schedule A.

1.3   undertake such other duties and exercise such powers in relation to the conduct and management of the [Company] and its associated businesses as the [Board of Directors] may request, direct and resolve provided that the additional matters are not major changes and effectively a new job description.

E.239

The [Executive] agrees that he/she shall not at any time during the course of this agreement supply his/her services to any third party without the prior written consent of the [Company] for duties which would be either prejudicial to the interest of the [Company] and/or are to be performed during working hours.

E.240

The [Company] agrees that this is not an exclusive agreement for the provision of the services of [Name] and is only a limited contract of employment which is not long term and/or full time. The [Name] may enter into an agreement and/or be employed by any third party that he/she thinks fit whether or not it is a direct rival of the [Company].

E.241

The [Company] agrees that the developing inventions, filming, making sound recordings, research, writing, books, publications, speeches, talks and any other matters which the [Executive] performs or does outside his/her scheduled work at the [Company] are not a matter which is relevant to this contract and are entirely at the discretion of the [Executive] and his/her choice and responsibility. The [Company] shall have no legal claim, rights and/or interest in any copyright, trade marks, domain names, software, designs, patents and/or intellectual property rights in any material created and/or developed by the [Executive] which is not part of his/her scheduled work at the [Company].

E.242

The [Company] agrees and acknowledges that there is no exclusive arrangement for the services of [Name]. That [Name] is at liberty to work with, endorse, promote and/or advertise any other company, service and/or product at any time. The [Company] agrees that there are no verbal and/or written restrictions, and/or codes of practice and/or guidelines to which [Name] must adhere. Nor is there any requirement by the [Company] that [Name] should notify and/or seek the approval of the [Company] at any time prior to any commitment to a third party.

E.243

[Name] agrees that all reports, blogs, articles and contributions made by him/her during the course of his/her employment with the [Company] including any domain name, trade mark, title, image and logo associated with him/her shall belong to the [Company] but not the actual first name and surname of [Name].

E.244

The [Company] acknowledges and agrees that [Name] is entitled during his/her working day at the [Company] to access and send personal emails; use social media and operate and write his/her own blog and website. That any such use shall not be grounds for termination of this agreement provided that [Name] completes the work and services required by the [Company].

E.245

The [Company] agrees that [Name] shall be employed and work at the main head office at [address]. In the event that this is relocated for any reason then [Name] shall be provided with the option of moving with the [Company] and/or taking voluntary redundancy on terms to be agreed between the parties.

E.246

During the continuance of this agreement the [Supplier] is not required to make its services available exclusively to the [Company] but at all times the interests of the [Company] shall prevail. The [Supplier] shall not undertake any engagement or activity which is liable to detract from its ability to render its services hereunder or impair its efficiency to do so or which would conflict with or be detrimental to the interests and operation of the [Company].

E.247

[Name] will perform the role and exercise the powers and functions which may be reasonably given to him/her by the [Company]. [Name] undertakes that he/she will not enter into any agreement or perform any act or do anything which may derogate from or interfere with the [Company's] exercise or use of the rights granted pursuant to this agreement.

E.248

'Exclusive Licence' in respect of copyright works shall mean a licence in writing signed by or on behalf of the [Copyright Owner] authorising the [Licensee] to the exclusion of all other persons including the person granting the Licence to exercise a right which would be exercisable exclusively by the [Copyright Owner]. The parties accept that the [Licensee] under an Exclusive Licence has the same rights against a successor in title who is bound by the Licence as he/she has against the person granting the Licence.

E.249

'Exclusive Licence' shall [be defined in accordance with the Copyright, Designs and Patents Act 1988 as amended in respect of dealings with design right] and shall mean a licence in writing signed by or on behalf of the [Design Right Owner] authorising the [Licensee] to the exclusion of all other persons including the person granting the Licence to exercise a right which would otherwise be exercisable exclusively by the [Design Right Owner].

E.250

During the period of this agreement and with immediate effect the [Company] agrees and undertakes that the [Company] and/or any agent and/or representative will not grant access to the [Material/Work/Services] to any third party. Neither will the [Company] exercise or authorise the use, exploitation and/or adaptation by any third party of the rights granted exclusively to the [Licensee].

E.251

The [Company] warrants and undertakes to the [Distributor] that it has not and will not grant to any third party any rights, licences, permissions or authorisations which will or might conflict with and/or derogate from the rights granted to the [Distributor] under this agreement.

E.252

[Name] reserves all rights not specifically [granted/assigned] under this agreement.

E.253

'A Non-Exclusive Licence' shall mean a licence in writing in respect of copyright works signed by or on behalf of the [Copyright Owner] which grants the [Licensee] the right to exercise a non-exclusive right. The [Copyright Owner] can also grant this right to as many other third parties as it decides without any regard to the [Licensee].

E.254

The [Company] shall be entitled to engage any third party that it wishes in order to change, develop, improve, add to, maintain, repair, and/or to provide any other work for any other reason in respect of the [Rights/ Services/Material/Software]. Both parties agree that the exclusivity of this agreement shall not prevent, restrict and/or prohibit the [Company] from exercising this right and the [Enterprise] agrees to cooperate and assist such third party as may be required by the [Company].

E.255

No authority, licence and/or consent is given and/or granted either directly and/or implied by the supply of and/or access to any [Material/Software/Services] provided by the [Company]. You have no right of any nature to copy, reproduce, distribute and/or otherwise replicate and/or adapt any part of the [Material/Software/Services] for any reason.

E.256

[Name] grants the [Company] the sole and exclusive rights to market, promote and exploit the [Event/Project] from [date] to [date] at [location]. Provided that [Name] receives and is paid [number] per cent of all gross sums which are received by and/or accrued by the [Company] at any time without the deduction of any expenses, costs, discounts and/or any other sums incurred by the [Company]. The [Company] agrees that it shall have no rights and/or other interest and/or claim to any part of the [Event] and/or its name, format, image, logo and/or any sums received after [date].

E.257

In view of the fact that no hours of work are guaranteed each month under this contract. The [Company] agrees that this is not an exclusive agreement for the work and/or services of [Name]. [Name] shall have the absolute right to work and/or to provide his/her services to any other third party. [Name] does not require the approval and/or consent of the [Company].

Internet, Websites and Apps

E.258

I am the sole author and copyright owner of [Work/title/length/reference]. I consent to the following extract of my [Work] being used and displayed as follows [specify length/name and address of business/domain name/exact use]. The consent is to be for a minimum period of [three] months and is subject to withdrawal at any time thereafter by notice in writing or email to the [Company]. The fee to be paid shall be [number/currency] for each period of [three] months payable in advance.

E.259

The [Company] shall not authorise, permit and shall prohibit the reproduction and/or display the [Installation/Images/Sound Recordings] on other websites, apps, forums and/or mobiles and shall make it clear that there is no right to reproduce and/or adapt the [Installation/Images/Sound Recordings] in any other format in any medium without the prior written consent of [Name].

E.260

The [Company] recognises that there is no exclusivity over the [Work] submitted to the [Website] by [Name] and that no rights have been granted except to display the [Work] in full without deletions, editing or additions with the full title and the copyright notice to [Name]. There is no right to reproduce the [Work] elsewhere for any purpose and/or to authorise and/or license others to do so whether for educational, promotional, review, non-commercial and/or commercial reasons at any time.

E.261

The parties agree as follows:

1.1 [Name] grants the [Company] the sole and exclusive right to display the [Material/Work] on the [Website] known as [specify] [reference] owned and controlled by the [Company] trading under the name of [specify] from [date] to [date].

1.2 The [Company] shall be entitled to authorise users of the [Website] to view the [Material/Work], but not to make copies or to reproduce or exploit the [Material/Work].

1.3 [Name] shall not from [date] to [date] authorise, permit, license or agree that any other person, company or organisation may display the [Material/Work] on their website, on the internet or download the [Material] to a television, telephone, gadget or other machine, article or receiving device.

1.4 The [Company] shall not be liable to [Name] for the actions of any person and/or entity who has access to the [Website] and who may reproduce, distribute, supply and/or adapt the [Material/Work] elsewhere at any time.

E.262

1.1 The [Copyright Owner] grants the [Company] the non-exclusive right to include and display the [Text/Image/Logo] on the [Website/App] in the following format and manner [specify].

1.2 The [Company] shall have the right to display the [Text/Image/Logo] on the [Website/App] for the purpose of being viewed by the public over the internet and/or by supply over any telecommunication system, and/or accessed by any television, mobile, or other gadget in any part of the world from [date] until [date].

1.3 The [Company] shall not have the right to authorise and/or facilitate the [Text/Image/Logo] on the [Website/App] to be downloaded, stored, reproduced, adapted and/or retrieved.

1.4 The [Company] shall not have the right to sub-license the [Text/Image/Logo] to any third party at any time nor to authorise any adaptation, merchandising and/or endorsement.

E.263

All other rights are retained by the [Copyright Owner]. The [Copyright Owner] shall be entitled to grant another licence on any terms in respect of the [Text/Image/Logo] to any other website and/or third party whether or not it is a competing business.

E.264

1.1 In consideration of the payment of [number/currency] by [date]. The [Author] grants a non-exclusive licence for the [Music/Lyrics] and the Sound Recordings to the [Company] to use for a banner advertisement for the [Company] on the [Website/App] on the internet and by means of electronic and telecommunication systems in any part of the world from [date] until [date].

1.2 The [Company] shall only be entitled to edit the [Music/Lyrics] and the Sound Recordings and shall not be entitled to add any new material without the prior written consent of the [Author].

1.3 All other rights are reserved. No right is granted to make any advertisement for television and/or radio and/or to grant any rights to third parties at any time. Nor is there any right to substitute another person for the [Music/Lyrics] and the Sound Recordings and/or to make any translation and/or adaptation.

E.265

In consideration of the [Fee] the [Author/Company] grants the [Distributor] the sole and exclusive right to reproduce, display and exploit the product of the services under this agreement summarised in Appendix A which may be created and/or delivered which are owned by the [Author/Company] and/or developed in the future in all media and in any format and by any means throughout the world, on land, sea and in the sky and into outer space and any other planets from [date] without any end of the licence period which shall continue indefinitely. The licence shall include but be limited: websites, apps, the internet and WiFi, downloads, mobiles and watches, DVDs, discs, television, radio, theatre, toys and merchandising, publishing, theme parks and any associated name, character, logo, music, sound recording and/or film.

E.266

This licence shall grant the [Licensee] the right to authorise a third party to exercise such rights by sub-licence and/or to adapt, edit and/or translate the [Work]. No sub-licence shall extend beyond the period of the original grant of rights by the [Copyright Owner].

E.267

1.1 [Name] consents to a non-exclusive supply agreement with the [Distributor] to market, promote and sell their [Products/Units] in their stores, catalogue and on line through their [website/app] known as [specify] from [date] to [date].

1.2 [Name] agrees that the [Distributor] shall be supplied with the [Products/Units] on loan by [Name] and that the [Distributor] shall hold the [Products/Units] on behalf of [Name]. That no ownership and/ or risk shall pass until the [Distributor] has received funds from the [Client] and paid [Name] all the sums received less a commission of [number] per cent.

E.268

1.1 The [Designer] grants the [Company] an exclusive licence to display, reproduce, supply, adapt and exploit in all media and medium of any nature from [date] to [date] the image and logo and the three dimensional copy in Schedule A which forms part of this agreement.

1.2 The [Designer] agrees that both the [Designer] and the [Company] shall be registered as holding a joint and equal interest in respect of any copyright, trade mark, service mark and/or design registration in respect of the image and logo and the three dimensional copy in Schedule A. The [Company] agrees that it shall pay all costs and expenses of any applications and registration fees and charges that may be incurred.

E.269

1.1 [Name] grants to the [Distributor] the non-exclusive right to produce, reproduce, distribute and/or sell a hardback, paperback, ebook and audio book based on a manuscript supplied by [Name]. The manuscript shall be based on the synopsis supplied by [Name] which is attached in Appendix A and is based on the [life/interests/regime/cookery] of the blogger and their website, app, Facebook and Instagram accounts known as [specify title and reference].

1.2 The licence shall commence on [date] and end on [date]. There is no right to extend and/or renew the contract.

1.3 The licence is limited to the following countries: [specify countries].

1.4 The material in 1.1 must be in the [specify] language. There is no right granted to translate and/or adapt the material.

1.5 The [Distributor] accepts that there is no restriction on [name] granting exactly the same rights to a third party at any time.

E.270

1.1 [Name] is the founder of the [Blog/Website/App/Account] known as [specify detail]. [Name] operates his/her business through a company known as [specify company name] referred to as the [Company].

1.2 The [Company] owns and/or controls all the copyright and other intellectual property rights in the [Blog/Website/App/Account] on behalf of [Name].

1.3 The [Company] grants the [Distributor] an exclusive licence for a period of [number] years from [date] to [date] to create, reproduce, supply and sell the Product described in detail in appendix A in the Territory.

1.4 [Name] and the [Company] agrees that neither shall not license and/or grant the same rights in respect of the same and/or a similar product for the duration of the exclusive period of the licence.

Merchandising and Distribution

E.271

1.1 In consideration of the Licence Fee the [Licensor] grants to [Company] the non-exclusive right to reproduce an adaptation of the [Artwork/Character/Logo] for the duration of the Licence Period throughout the Territory for exploitation by the [Company] on the following products: [specify products] and in all its packaging, marketing and distribution material.

1.2 The [Company] shall submit all draft material of the [Artwork/Character/Logo] to the [Licensor] for approval. If it is rejected then the [Company] must make another new proposal.

E.272
In consideration of the Agent's Fee the [Agent] agrees to provide its non-exclusive services to the [Company] for the Term of the Agreement throughout the Territory for the purpose of promoting, marketing and obtaining orders for the purchase of the [Products/Services] from retail stores and other trade outlets.

E.273

The [Company] shall be the sole and exclusive agent and representative for [Name] for the [Work/Product/Service] for the zone specified as [area detail] a copy of which is reproduced on the map which is attached to and forms part of this agreement. The period of exclusivity shall start on [date] and end on [date]. Thereafter the [Company] shall only act on a non-exclusive until [date].

E.274

The [Company] agrees that it does not have any exclusive rights to the [Product] and undertakes not to represent in any marketing, advertising and/or on its website and/or app that it has any sort of exclusive arrangement with [Name].

E.275

The [Supplier] acknowledges and agrees that the [Company] shall have the right to use and/or engage any other person and/or business that it thinks fit to work on the [Project] and/or with the [Supplier] and/or to maintain, repair and/or develop the [Equipment/Services/Project].

E.276

No appointment of any supplier, distributor and/or any other third party by the [Company] is on an exclusive basis and all agreements are non-exclusive and for a maximum period of [one] [day/month/year] at any time. The [Company] reserves the right to use whoever they think fit dependent on the circumstances and to cancel, terminate and alter the terms and conditions.

E.277

The [Supplier] agrees to deliver the [Product] to the [Seller] for sale on the [Seller's] website, app and their retail store on a non-exclusive basis for the duration of this agreement in consideration of the agreed terms and payments.

E.278

That the [Supplier] has not entered into and shall not enter into an agreement with any of the following [companies/website owners/distributors].

E.279

The [Supplier] agrees that the [Product] will only be sold from the [Distributors'] website and in [specify retail locations] on an exclusive basis for a period of [three] months from [date]. Thereafter there is no guaranteed exclusivity to the [Distributor] and the agreement is then on a non-exclusive basis.

E.280

The [Company] agrees to appoint the [Distributor] as the sole and exclusive supplier of [Product] and any other products in the category of [specify] to the [Company] from [date] to [date].

E.281

This clause shall not apply to any parent, subsidiary, affiliated or associated company of the [Group].

E.282

The [Distributor] shall not be entitled to authorise and/or supply the master material of the [Products] to another manufacturer at any time during the Term of this Agreement unless the prior written approval of [Name] has been provided in advance.

E.283

The exclusive licence shall cease with immediate effect in the event that the [Distributor] should fail at any time during the Term of this Agreement to pay the royalties by the due date. No delay, error, omission and/or other reason including force majeure shall be considered relevant criteria for such failure.

E.284

In consideration of the [Agent's Commission] the [Agent] agrees to provide his/her non-exclusive services to the [Licensor] for the Licence Period throughout [countries] to carry out and fulfil the following services to the [Licensor] which is set out in schedule A [specify detail of work required from Agent in Schedule].

E.285

1.1 In consideration of the Net Receipts the [Licensor] agrees to engage the non-exclusive services of the [Agent] for the Licence Period throughout the [countries].

1.2 The [Licensor] grants the [Agent] the non-exclusive right to negotiate agreements for the manufacture, distribution and sale of the [Licensed Products] together with the associated [trademark/logo/image] of the [Licensor].

1.3 The [Agent] agrees that he/she shall not be permitted or authorised to commit the [Licensor] or to sign, authorise or provide consent to any third party on behalf of the [Licensor]. That all licences must be in writing and may only be signed and authorised by the [Licensor]. That the [Licensor] shall have the right to refuse to conclude any agreement at its sole discretion.

E.286

The [Company] agrees that after [date] and/or the expiry and/or termination of this agreement, whichever is the earlier. The [Company] shall not be entitled to exploit the [Licensed Products] and shall have no rights and/or interest.

E.287

1.1 In consideration of the [Agent's Commission] the [Agent] agrees to provide his/her non-exclusive services to the [Licensor] for the Term of the Agreement throughout the Territory.

1.2 In consideration of the Net Receipts the [Licensor] engages the exclusive services of the [Agent] for the Term of the Agreement throughout the Territory and grants to the [Agent] the sole and exclusive right to instigate and negotiate agreements for the production, manufacture, distribution, sale and supply of the [Licensed Products] for the Term of the Agreement throughout the Territory.

E.288

In consideration of the Non-Returnable Advance and the Licensor's Royalties the [Licensor] grants to the [Company] the sole and exclusive right to develop, produce, manufacture, distribute, supply, and sell the [Licensed Products] based on the Prototype throughout the Territory for the duration of the Licence Period.

E.289

The [Company] shall also be entitled to appoint third parties as sub-agents and/or sub-distributors to supply, distribute, market and sell the [Licensed Products] provided that the third party is obliged to comply with the terms of this agreement. The [Company] shall not be however be entitled to appoint any other third party to manufacture the [Licensed Products] except for the following permitted named manufacturers: [specify details/country].

E.290

The [Licensor] undertakes that it will not grant any third party a licence and/or any rights in respect of the production, manufacture, supply, distribution, reproduction, adaptation and/or translation of the [Board Game] and/or the Prototype including any new developments or variations throughout the Territory for the duration of the Licence Period and/or until the date of termination of this agreement whichever is the earlier.

E.291

The [Designer] undertakes that he/she will not license and/or grant any rights to any third party to produce, make, manufacture, copy, supply, or distribute the [Designs] or the [Licensed Articles] or any development or variation thereof throughout the Territory from [date] to [date]. This clause shall not prevent the [Designer] having discussions and/or negotiations with third parties for future business arrangements.

E.292
The [Company] grants the [Distributor] a non-exclusive licence to reproduce the [Trade Mark/Image/Logo] on all copies of the packaging for the [Products] and associated advertising and promotions which are approved by the [Company] for the [specify] campaign. The [Distributor] shall be entitled to sell, supply, distribute and promote the [Products] with the [Trade Mark/Image/Logo] on all copies of the packaging in [country] from [date] to [date].

E.293
No right is granted by the [Company] to authorise and/or use the [Trade Mark/Image/Logo] in any other manner and/or to authorise its use and/or reproduction by any third party. There is no right granted to register any version of the [Trade Mark/Image/Logo] and/or for the Distributor] to acquire any ownership, interest and/or rights of any nature. All rights in the [Trade Mark/Image/Logo] are retained by the [Company]. Where for any reason any new material and/or rights are created and/or developed the [Distributor] agrees and undertakes that any such copyright, intellectual property rights trade marks and all rights in all media shall be assigned to the [Company].

E.294
In consideration of the Advance and the [Royalties/Unit Payments] the [Author] grants to the [Company] the sole and exclusive right to reproduce, supply and sell a toy product in the form of a [specify] details of which are set out in appendix A based on the character called [name] from the [Book/Film] entitled [specify]. The licence shall be exclusive from [date] to [date] and thereafter the licence shall be non-exclusive until expiry on [date]. The licence shall be for the Territory.

E.295
The licence granted in respect of the [Products] by [Name] does not entitle the [Company] to use, exploit, register and/or market the name, image, three dimensional representation, logo and/or brand of [Name] in conjunction with the [Products] at any time.

E.296
1.1   The [Distributor] grants the non-exclusive licence to the [Supplier] to create, develop, reproduce, supply, sell and distribute a [Product]

[specify detail toy/book/clothes] based on the character [specify] with the name [specify] from the [Programme] subject to the approval of the sample prior to manufacture.

1.2 The licence shall commence on the date of this agreement and continue until [date].

1.3 The licence is limited to the following countries and languages [specify]

1.4 The licence will only start if the [Fee] has been paid to the [Distributor] and the [Supplier] continues to pay the sums due and provides regular accounts, statements and payments as set out in clauses [–].

1.5 At the end of the licence period all rights granted shall revert to the [Distributor] and all production, reproduction and exploitation in any form shall cease and all remaining stock shall be destroyed by the [Supplier].

1.6 The [Supplier] shall not be entitled to register any copyright, computer software, trade marks, domain names and/or any other rights of any nature in respect of the character and/or its name.

Publishing

E.297

The [Author] confirms that the [Work/Sound Recordings/Manuscript] has not been previously licensed to any third party and has not been exploited in any form at any time throughout the Territory.

E.298

1.1 In consideration of the fee [Name] agrees to be interviewed by the [Interviewer] on behalf of the [Publisher] for [number] minutes at [location].

1.2 [Name] agrees that the [Interviewer] and/or a nominated photographer make take [number] photographs and images to be used in the proposed article.

1.3 No sound recording of the interview shall be permitted.

1.4 [Name] shall submit the draft article to [Name] for approval. The [Publisher] agrees to correct any errors and/or omissions in the article but retains editorial control.

1.5 The article and accompanying photographs shall be published in the [Magazine] and the website of the [Publisher] on [date] or within one month of that date at the latest.

1.6 No other rights are granted by [Name] for any further use, license and/ or exploitation of the article and photographs. The [Publisher] must conclude a new agreement with [name] in respect of any new proposal.

E.299

[Name] agrees that from [date] until [date] she/he will not give any interviews or information to the media including, but not limited to, newspapers, magazines, television, radio, news agencies, telephone companies and/or their agents or grant permission for or consent to the reproduction, supply or distribution of the [Photographs/Films/Sound Recordings/Documents] by any third party in any part of the world.

E.300

The [Publisher] and [Journalist] acknowledge that after [date] [Name] shall be entitled to divulge the same or similar information provided under this agreement to any third party.

E.301

The [Journalist] and the [Publisher] agree that they shall not be entitled to exploit in any media the final published article and/or any sound recordings, films, notes, photographs and/or images for any purpose other than for publication in the [Periodical] on the publication dates without the prior written consent of [Name]. In such event [Name] shall be entitled to receive such additional sums as may be agreed between the parties.

E.302

In consideration of the Author's Royalties and the Advance the [Author] grants to the [Publisher] the sole and exclusive right to publish and exploit the [Work/Sound Recordings/Manuscript] and any parts in All Media throughout the Territory for the duration of the Licence Period.

E.303

1.1 In consideration of the Author's Royalties and the Advance the [Author] grants to the [Publisher] the sole and exclusive right to publish, sell and exploit the [Final Manuscript] based on the Synopsis including any images, title, headings, index and cover in all media in any format which shall include but not be limited to: all methods of publication and reproduction including hardback, paperback, e books, downloads and any other electronic version, serialisation in any form, translations, anthologies, quotations, the right to the collection due to mechanical reproduction and/or performance, radio, theatre, film, television, telecommunication systems and WiFi, games, merchandising, toys, costumes and theme parks or events. These rights are only granted throughout the Territory for the duration of the Licence Period.

1.2 All sub-licences in 1.1 must end by [date] and may not extend beyond that date. After that date then all copyright, intellectual property rights and/or computer software and/or any other rights and interest which have been created and/or developed by the [Publisher] and/or any sub-licensee must be assigned to the [Author] at the [Publishers'] cost.

E.304

The [Author] acknowledges that the [Publisher] shall be entitled to permit Braille and charitable recordings to be made of the [Work/Book] for the sole use of the blind and those with severe disabilities free of charge during the Licence Period.

E.305

In consideration of the fee the [Writer] agrees to provide his/her non-exclusive services to the [Company] for the Term of the Agreement to write, research and produce the draft [manuscript/script] for the [Book/Film/Sound Recordings] in accordance with the services and work described in Appendix A.

E.306

1.1 [Name] has created a [Concept/Synopsis] and agrees to engage the non-exclusive services of the [Writer] to research and write a [Manuscript] of not less than [number] pages based on the [Concept/Synopsis] which is to be delivered to [Name] by [date] in [format].

1.2 The [Writer] is nor providing his /her exclusive services to [Name] and may enter into an agreement with any third party to write, research or produce any other book or publication provided that it is not on the same and/or a similar subject to the [Concept/Synopsis] at any time during the Term of the Agreement throughout the Territory and/or the world.

E.307

The [Author] undertakes that during the continuance of this Agreement he/she has not and will not, other than for the [Publisher], authorise publication or reproduction of the [Work] or any expansion or abridgement or part [in Volume Form] in the [Publisher's] exclusive Territory nor shall the [Author] prepare anything of a nature which is likely to affect prejudicially the sales of the [Publisher] in respect of the [Work].

E.308

The [Licensor] agrees that for the duration of the Licence Period the [Licensor] shall not directly or indirectly license, sub-license, authorise, promote, distribute or make available the [Work] or any parts or any adaptation, translation, development or variation in any of the following rights [specify] within the Territory during the Licence Period to any other third party.

E.309
That the [Licensor] has not granted any licence or other authorisation to any third party to supply, sell, reproduce and/or exploit the [Work] in whole, in parts and/or by means of any adaptation including but not limited to over the internet or from any website or as a download or to be stored, retrieved or supplied over any telecommunication system and/or in any other electronic form or to any computer, television, gadget or otherwise.

E.310
The [Author] reserves these rights and the [Publisher] agrees that it shall not have the right to:

1.1 appoint, employ or engage any third party to contribute in any form to the [Work] or any adaptation or development without the prior written approval of the [Author].

1.2 to publish, supply and distribute the [Work] in any form except as a separate book and it shall not be packaged, combined with or added together with any other article, work or book.

1.3 To use the [Work] in any form to endorse, promote or sponsor any event, article, product, item, book, person or other matter.

E.311

1.1 The [Author] grants the [Publisher] the sole and exclusive right to publish, distribute and supply the [Work] in [hardback/paperback] in [country] from [date to [date] using the following printer [specify].

1.2 All other rights are specifically not granted and are retained by the [Author].

1.3 The [Company] shall be entitled to market, sell and promote the [Work] on their website, app and other online accounts: [specify website, app and account name/reference] reference [specify]. The company shall not have the right to supply to or appoint another third party to sell and distribute the [Work] except [specify names of companies] without the prior approval of the [Author] in each case.

E.312
In consideration of the [Fee] the [Author] grants the [Company/Name] the non-exclusive right to reproduce [number] copies of [number] pages of the [Work] in printed form on paper by means of photocopying in [country] during the period from [date] to [date]. The [Company/Name] agrees and undertakes that the correct copyright notice and title shall be on the front of

all copies together with the words 'All rights reserved. No right to copy and/
or reproduce in any form.'

E.313

In consideration of the [Fee] the [Author] grants the [Company/Name] the
non-exclusive right to scan [number] copies of [number] pages of the [Work]
onto the hard drive of the computer temporarily and to supply and distribute
by means of an email attachment the same material to [number] persons over
the internet during the licence period from [date] to the completion of the
task but no late than [date]. The [Company/Name] agrees and undertakes
to ensure that the correct copyright notice and title shall be on the front of all
copies in any email attachment together with the words 'All rights reserved.
No permission is granted to store permanently on your hard drive and/or to
supply copies to others. Please print only one copy.'

E.314

In consideration of the [Fee] the [Company] grants the [Publisher] the
exclusive rights to the [Image/Photograph] for the [Magazine/Book] cover
and any associated website, advertising and marketing from [date] to
[date]. The [Publisher] shall not have the right to sub-license and/or assign
the rights to any third party. The [Publisher] shall at all times acknowledge
the copyright ownership of the [Company] as follows: [specify] and credit
the photographer as follows: [specify] in respect of all copies of the [Image/
Photograph] in a prominent position on the edge of the [Image/Photograph].

E.315

1.1   In consideration of the [Fee] the [Author] grants the [Publisher/
      Distributor] the non-exclusive licence to use [number] words on pages
      [specify] as a quote from the [Work] reference ISBN [specify] to be
      included in the Book entitled [specify] in the [specify] language which
      is to be sold in printed form in hardback, paperback and as an ebook
      and audio recording throughout the [world/Territory] from [date] until
      the expiry of a period of [number] years.

1.2   All other rights are reserved by the [Author] and no rights are granted to
      sub-license, and/or assign the extract from the [Work] and/or to exploit
      the [Work] in any other media at any time. Nor is any right granted to
      register any right and/or interest in any part of the [Work] and/or the
      title and/or any character.

E.316

1.1   In consideration of the payment of the Licence Fee the [Licensor] grants
      to the [Licensee] the non-exclusive right to reproduce the [Licensors']

Logo on each copy of the [Product/Work] and any associated packaging, marketing and advertising in accordance with Schedule A throughout the Territory for the duration of the Licence Period.

1.2 The [Licensee] agrees and undertakes to ensure that on all copies of the [Licensors'] Logo which are reproduced shall appear the words. 'The trade mark is reproduced under licence from [Licensor] and is the registered trade mark of [Licensor].'

E.317

In consideration of payments per [Unit] the [Author] grants to the [Company] the non-exclusive right to reproduce, supply, sell and distribute copies of the [Work] and/or part as part of a documentary delivery service whether over the internet by means of scanning and an email attachment, by electronic and/or telecommunication system and WiFi, by post and/or some other delivery method. The [Author] acknowledges that copies may be stored, and retrieved by the [Company] and/or any third party by means of a hard drive on a computer and/or any other gadget and may make one and/or more copies. This licence shall apply throughout the world and shall commence on [date] and expire on [date].

E.318

1.1 In consideration of the sum of [number/currency] [Name] grants an exclusive licence to the [Distributor] for the reproduction, distribution and exploitation of his/her [Article/Project] in whole and/or in part on one and/or more of the websites owned and/or controlled by the [Distributor] and/or any sub-licensee, sub-distributor and/or other third party in any country of the world and in any medium at any time.

1.2 This licence in 1.1 shall include the right to reproduce the [Article/Project] in hardback and paperback form, and/or as part of another work with other contributors and/or as an electronic and/or ebook and/or to adapt the contents for radio, television and/or film and/or to create any translation and/or subtitled work.

E.319

The [Title] and [Slogan] and [Image] are owned by [Name] and no licence is granted to use, adapt, register and/or exploit the [Title] [Slogan] and/or [Image] except in the form of a book cover and online marketing and promotion directly related to the work of [Name].

E.320

1.1 [Name] grants the [Distributor/Publisher] the following exclusive rights throughout the world from [date] to [date]: [specify rights].

1.2 After [date] [Name] grants the [Distributor/Publisher] the following non-exclusive rights throughout the world from [date] to [date]: [specify rights].

1.3 After [date] the [Distributor/Publisher] shall not hold any rights or any licence. All existing stock and/or content must then be deleted and/or destroyed and/or returned to [Name] at no cost.

Services

E.321

1.1 In consideration of the [Agent's] Commission the [Agent] agrees to provide his/her non-exclusive services to the [Author] as Literary Agent for the [Work] for the Term of the Agreement throughout the Territory.

1.2 In consideration of the Net Receipts the [Author] agrees to engage the exclusive services of the [Agent] as Literary Agent for the [Work] for the Term of the Agreement for the purpose of the commercial exploitation of the [Work] in all media.

1.3 The [Agent] confirms that the [Author] shall have the final decision to conclude and sign any agreement, contract or other document relating to the exploitation of the [Work] and that no authority is granted under this agreement for the [Agent] to sign on behalf of the [Author].

1.4 The [Agent] acknowledges that this agreement is related solely to the [Work] and that the [Agent] is not entitled to exploit any other material including any books, sound recordings and/or podcasts created by the [Author] without the prior written consent of the [Author] and the conclusion of a further agreement.

E.322

It is expressly agreed between the parties that this agreement shall be exclusive to the Agent for the duration of the Term of this Agreement throughout the [United Kingdom and Northern Ireland] but non-exclusive for all other territories throughout the world.

E.323

The [Artist] agrees that the [Manager] shall have the sole and exclusive right to represent the [Artist] throughout the Territory for the Term of the Agreement only in respect of those activities specified under Schedule A [specify scope of work/materials/formats] to this agreement.

E.324

The [Artist] agrees that the [Manager] shall have the non-exclusive right to represent the [Artist] throughout the Territory for the Term of the Agreement in respect of the product of the [Artist's] services in the field of [acting/filming/advertisements] but not [writing/singing/dancing/painting/computer-generated material/music/other].

E.325

The [Artist] agrees that the [Manager] shall have the sole and exclusive right to represent the [Artist] throughout the Territory for the Term of the Agreement and thereafter on a non-exclusive basis unless otherwise agreed between the parties in writing.

E.326

1.1 In consideration of the [Agent's Commission] the [Agent] agrees to provide his/her non-exclusive services to the [Artist] for the Term of the Agreement throughout the agreed defined Territory.

1.2 In consideration of the Net Receipts the [Artist] engages the exclusive services of the [Agent] from [date] to [date] throughout the Territory to engage and commercially exploit the [Artist] their name, image, services and work in all media including, but not limited to, all forms of sound, vision, interactive, image, text, icons, film, video, DVD, television, radio, theatre, telephones, merchandising, publishing, biography, endorsements, advertising, commercials, promotional work and on the internet, websites, apps and other electronic forms.

1.3 The [Agent] agrees that any form of exploitation of the [Artist's] services, name or work shall require the prior consent of the [Artist]. The [Artist] shall be entitled to refuse to agree to any work or to carry it out or for the use of his/her name for any reason and/or any other proposal by the [Agent]. The [Artist] shall be entitled to reject any matter without reasons and in such instance the [Agent] shall not be entitled to seek any compensation, losses and/or damages or otherwise which arises from the failure of the [Artist] to provide consent and/or provide his/her services.

E.327

1.1 In consideration of the [Guaranteed Fees] and the [Group's Fees] the [Group] agrees to engage the services of the [Manager] and the [Group] shall provide its exclusive services to the Manager for the Term of the Agreement throughout the Territory.

1.2 In consideration of the [Manager's Commission] the [Manager] agrees to provide his [non-] exclusive services to the [Group] for the Term of the Agreement throughout the Territory.

E.328

The [Company] agrees to appoint the [Promoter] as the sole and exclusive agent to market, advertise and promote the [Product] on behalf of the [Company] throughout the [country] from [date] until [date] in the following media: internet and electronic and telecommunication means including the internet, websites, apps, blogs, podcasts, pop-ups, search engine listings, outdoor marketing, product placement, interviews in newspapers and magazines and on cable, satellite and terrestrial television and radio programmes and at festivals, events, exhibitions and student fairs.

E.329

1.1 The [Company] agrees to engage the services of the [Contributor] throughout the Engagement Period and to pay the Basic Fee, the Expenses and the Bonus Fee in accordance with this agreement.

1.2 The [Contributor] agrees that for the duration of the Engagement Period the [Contributor] agrees to provide his/her professional services exclusively to the [Company] and not to any other website, app, gambling and betting site, television, radio and/or podcast and/ or online media and/or product company.

1.3 The [Company] acknowledges that the [Contributor] shall be permitted to offer his/her services in any other business not specified in 1.2 above during the Engagement Period to third parties. Where for reasons beyond the control of the [Contributor] such material should appear on the worldwide web the [Contributor] shall not be held to be in breach or liable in any manner under this Agreement.

E.330

1.1 In consideration of the Promotion Fee and the Promotion Expenses the [Promoter] agrees to provide its non-exclusive services to the [Company] to act as agent to promote, market and advertise the [Company] and the [Services/Products] throughout the [country] for the duration of this agreement.

1.2 The [Promoter] agrees that the principal aim and objective of its services to the [Company] shall be to promote and increase the sale of the [Services/Products] of the [Company]. Together with a campaign to develop the public profile of the [Company] and brands on social media.

E.331

The [Promoter] confirms that this agreement shall not cause any conflict of interest with any of its existing clients and undertakes not to enter into any agreement with any third party during the Term of this Agreement which would conflict with or be prejudicial to the interests of the [Company] and/or whose products or services compete directly or indirectly with the [Company] and/or whose reputation could potentially harm, damage and/or cause losses to the [Company].

E.332

1.1 The [Company] and the [Presenter] agree that in consideration of the Presenter's Fee and the Presenter's Royalties the [Presenter] shall provide his/her exclusive services as principal presenter for the [specify role/job description/details of which are set out in Appendix A].

1.2 The [Presenter] shall carry out his/her duties as required by the [Company] for [number] hours per [week/month] during [start time] and [end time] and/or as may otherwise be agreed between the parties. The [Presenter] shall agree his/her schedule of contributions and work with [Name] at the [Company] for the Term of the Engagement.

E.333

The [Presenter] agrees to provide the following non-exclusive services to the [Company]:

1.1 To attend at such times, dates, locations and premises in [location/country] as the [Company] may reasonably require subject to sufficient prior notice which shall not be less than [specify period of notice].

1.2 To comply with all rules in force at such locations and to observe all reasonable directions given by [Name] on behalf of the [Company].

1.3 To assist in such background research as may be required and to be available for development of scripts, planning, filming and interviews for promotional work which may be necessary for a period of [specify period] maximum of [specify length of time]. Any additional work and services shall be subject to further agreement.

E.334

1.1 The [Company] and the [Presenter] agree that in consideration of the [Presenter's] Fee the [Presenter] shall provide his/her exclusive services to the [Company] as presenter of the [Series] and provide such other contributions as may reasonably be required by the [Company] in respect of recordings, films, photographs, appearances, meetings and other work directly related to presenting and promoting the [Series] for the Term of the Agreement throughout the Territory.

1.2 The [Presenter] agrees not to provide his/her services for any other media, film, theatre, television, radio, mobile, product, online and digital company, website, app, platform and/or archive and playback company and/or publisher whether a charity, educational, non-commercial and/or commercial business and specifically not [specify particular businesses such as direct competitors] during the Term of this Agreement without the prior written consent of the [Company].

E.335

The [Company] agrees to engage and the [Agency] agrees to make available the freelance non-exclusive services of [Name] on first call to the Company and/or any associated company in the capacity of [specify role/job description] as and when required by the [Company] for a period of [one] year from [date].

E.336

[Name] shall be free to provide his/her services to other third party companies in the [media/technical/other] industry in the [United Kingdom/country/area] subject to obtaining prior confirmation from the [Company] that its business interests are not directly prejudiced and/or in conflict with the proposed third party. The [Company] agrees not to unreasonably withhold and/or delay such consent.

E.337

The [Company] agrees to engage the services of the [Artist] to be the principal person to promote and advertise the [Company's] products in all advertisements for television, radio, newspapers and magazines, promotional films, and events for the Term of the Agreement throughout the Territory.

E.338

The [Presenter] undertakes to the [Company] that from [date] to [date] the [Company] shall be entitled to the exclusive services of the [Presenter] in respect of [specify field news/current affairs/sports/comedy/consumer] as a researcher, reporter and presenter throughout the [United Kingdom/country/world].

The [Presenter] agrees and undertakes that they shall not during the existence of this agreement without the previous written consent of the [Company] either directly or indirectly:

1.1 contribute in any way to [news/ current affairs/sports/comedy/consumer] television in any form through any podcast, blog, documentary, website, app, radio and/or any other online, digital, electronic, WiFi and/or telecommunication system and/or by means of cable, satellite and terrestrial television and/or radio and/or any online streaming service over the internet and/or by any other method for any third party.

818

1.2 undertake any activity which associates or is liable to associate the [Presenter] in any way with the endorsement of any products and/ or services and/or any promotion and/or advertising for any charity, institution and/or commercial in [specify country/area] without the prior written approval of the [Company].

E.339

1.1 In consideration of the [Agent's Commission] the [Agent] agrees to provide his/her non-exclusive services to the [Artiste] for the Term of the Agreement throughout the Territory.

1.2 In consideration of the Net Receipts the [Artiste] agrees to engage the exclusive services of the [Agent] for the Term of the Agreement throughout the Territory in all media including but not limited to:

(a) work for third parties for online digital internet for pop-ups, websites, apps, voice-overs;

(b) all forms of television and archive streaming and playback, radio, videos, DVDs, CDs, characters and performances in films.

(c) articles and interviews in newspapers and magazines; contributions as a writer and artist to books and other material. The right to negotiate an authorised biography and/or any work of fiction and/or non-fiction and/or any children's book by the [Artiste]

(d) all licensing of any name. trade mark and/or product and other merchandising.

(e) all contributions to any blogs and podcasts, tours and live and pre-recorded appearances, charity promotions and endorsements and any other exploitation of the [Artiste] under this agreement.

E.340
The [Agent] acknowledges that he/she shall not be entitled to negotiate or promote in any manner or form the commercial interests of the [Artiste] outside the Territory unless specifically agreed in advance with the [Artiste].

E.341
The [Actor] agrees that the [Agent] shall be his/her exclusive agent in respect of all work in respect of appearances and performances on satellite, cable, digital and standard television programmes, theatre, national and local radio, commercials on radio and television, feature films, corporate and educational DVDs, voice-overs for the Term of the Agreement throughout the Territory. Merchandising and all publishing rights are reserved and

retained by the [Actor] including the publication of children's books, sound recordings and toys.

E.342
The [Agency] agrees and undertakes that this agreement does not give any rights to them and/or permit the [Agency] to act on behalf of and/or commit the [Actor] in any of the following areas:

1.1 any image rights, and any right to register and/or exploit the name and/or signature of the [Actor] and his/her real name and/or stage name and/or any two and/or three dimensional artistic representation.

1.2 any publishing and/or merchandising including a biography, a work of non-fiction and/or any children's books, toys, licensed characters and/or other products.

1.3 any matter in respect of any performance, promotion and/or other material to be solely reproduced on the internet, a website, app and/or over any telecommunication system and/or mobile phone and/or other gadget and/or any sound recordings, lyrics and music.

1.4 any sponsorship and/or endorsements of any product, event, service, brand and/or company and/or campaign by a charity and/or other organisation.

E.343
The [Company] and the [Name] agree the following terms:

1.1 The [Company] agrees to engage [Name] for the purpose of providing his/her non-exclusive services to the [Company] throughout the Territory for the Term of this Agreement in accordance with the Work Plan and Schedule in Appendix A.

1.2 In consideration of the Fee and Expenses the [Name] agrees to provide his/her non-exclusive services to the [Company] throughout the Territory for the Term of the Agreement as set out in the Work Plan and Schedule in Appendix A.

1.3 That any material arising from the services of [Name] shall only be used by the [Company] for the following specific purposes [state authorised purposes]. In the event that the [Company] wishes to use the material for any other purpose then the prior written authorisation and consent of [Name] shall be required together with an additional payment to be agreed between the parties.

E.344
The [Company] acknowledges that the [Originator] shall be entitled to exploit any material created by the [Originator] under this agreement provided that

all references to any confidential information and material provided by the [Company] are deleted.

E.345

The [Company] acknowledges that the [Originator] is already committed and entitled to carry out the following work for third parties during the Term of the Agreement [specify parties and work].

E.346

1.1 In consideration of the Fee and Repeat Fees the [Artist] agrees to provide his/her non-exclusive services to the [Company] in [country] and to contribute to such material as may be required to promote and advertise the [Company's] Products by personal appearances, performances in promotional films, voice-overs and otherwise for marketing and advertising for the internet, television, radio, newspapers, magazines and events in accordance with the Work Schedule B which is attached and forms part of the agreement. In addition the [Artist] agrees to provide his/her services to the [Company] on such other additional dates as may be agreed between the parties.

1.2 The [Artist] undertakes and agrees not to provide his/her services to the following businesses who are direct competitors from [date to [date]: [specify list].

E.347

The [Artist] agrees not to promote or advertise or otherwise endorse any commercial product and/or service of any type whether it competes with the [Company's] Product or not throughout the Term of the Agreement without the prior written consent of the [Company] except for those contributions of an entirely charitable purpose.

E.348

1.1 The [Company] and the [Director] agree that in consideration of the [Director's] Fee the [Director] shall provide her/his exclusive services as Director and such other contributions as specified under this agreement in respect of the [Film/Podcast/Video] for the Production Period.

1.2 The [Director] agrees to provide her/his exclusive services to the [Company] as the [specify title/role] for the Production Period and in accordance with the Production Schedule and to assist in such other matters including script revisions and pre-shooting arrangements as may be required for the completion of the [Film/Podcast/Video].

E.349

1.1   In consideration of the [Manager's Commission] the [Manager] agrees to provide her/his non-exclusive services to the [Sportsperson] to act as agent and manager in all media [which is in existence now and developed in the future] for the Term of the Agreement throughout the Territory.

1.2   In consideration of the [Sportsperson's Fees] the [Sportsperson] agrees to engage the exclusive services of the [Manager] for the Term of the Agreement throughout the Territory in all media including columns and articles in magazines, newspapers and on websites; public, professional and charitable appearances at events; sponsorship, promotions and endorsements of products, businesses, and services; filming, voice-overs, podcasts, presenting and contributing to programmes for television, radio and the internet; licensing of merchandising and/or any other exploitation of the [Sportsperson], his/her name, image and signature.

1.3   The [Sportsperson] agrees to refer all requests for his/her services and any rights or consents to the [Manager]. The [Sportsperson] agrees that the [Manager] shall have the sole and exclusive right to negotiate with third parties for the commercial and charitable services of the [Sportsperson] during the Term of this Agreement.

1.4   The [Manager] accepts and agrees that the [Sportsperson] shall have complete control of all matters relating to their sports career as an [specify role] and their fulfilment of any competitions and events.

E.350

1.1   The [Company] agrees that [Name] shall be the sole and exclusive personality to be engaged by the [Company] for the Term of this Agreement in the Territory to endorse, promote and advertise the [Company's Products].

1.2   In consideration of the Fee, the Repeat Fees and the Expenses and the Products. [Name] agrees to provide his/her exclusive services to the [Company] to endorse, promote and advertise the [Company's Products] by personal appearances, performances, recordings, films, images, photographs, text messages or otherwise of material of or associated with the [Name] for advertisements and promotions in all media in accordance with the Work Schedule and on such other occasions as may be agreed for the Term of the Agreement in [country].

1.3   [Name] undertakes not to provide his/her services to any third party for the endorsement, advertisement or promotion of any other product or service of any type whether it directly competes with the [Company's Product] or not without the prior written consent of the [Company] except in the following services or work to which there is a prior commitment [specify prior commitments].

E.351

1.1   This is an exclusive recording contract between the performer and artist known as [Name] and [Person/Company] in respect of the recordings of his/her performance at [Event/Studio] on [date].

1.2   [Name] agrees that [Person/Company] is entitled to the exclusion of all other third parties and [Name] to make the recordings in 1.1 with a view to their commercial exploitation namely with a view to the recordings being sold or let for hire or shown or played in public.

E.352

1.1   The [Company] agrees to engage the non-exclusive services of the [Consultant] to assess and report on and recommend a strategy and campaign to promote, market and advertise the [Company], its website, app and products and/or services throughout the world for the Term of this Agreement.

1.2   In consideration of the Fee and Expenses the [Consultant] agrees and undertakes to provide his/her non-exclusive services to the [Company] for the Term of the Agreement. The [Consultant] agrees and undertakes not to provide any services and/or to work for the following companies during the Term of this Agreement [specify list of companies].

E.353

The [Consortium] agrees that the [Consultant] may provide his/her services to any third party during the term of this agreement including the competitors of any members of the [Consortium].

E.354

The [Agent] agrees and undertakes that he/she shall not engage any person as a client for his/her agency whose political and/or personal life would conflict with and/or create problems by association through the agency with the reputation of [Name]. That in such event then [Name] shall have the right to terminate the agreement and provide [number] months' notice. That thereafter the [Agent] shall have no right to any sums derived from the work, services and/or exploitation of any copyright and/or intellectual property rights and/or trademarks owned and/or controlled by [Name] in any form at any time.

Sponsorship

E.355

In consideration of the [Sponsorship Fee] and the Performance Related Fee the [Sportsperson] agrees to provide his/her non-exclusive services to the [Sponsor] to promote and endorse the [Sponsor's Product] for the duration of the Sponsorship Period throughout the Territory in accordance with the terms of this agreement.

E.356

The [Sponsor] agrees to engage the non-exclusive services of the [Sportsperson] to promote and endorse the [Sponsor's Product] throughout the Territory for the duration of the Sponsorship Period.

E.357

The [Sportsperson] undertakes not to enter into any other sponsorship agreement with any third party concerning the same or similar items in respect of the [Sponsor's Product] namely [sportswear/shoes/clothes/cars/life insurance] from [date] to [date].

E.358

The [Sportsperson] undertakes not to enter an agreement to promote or endorse the products and/or services of the following organisations and/or companies for the first [two] years: [list excluded companies/products/services].

E.359

The [Sponsor] agrees that it does not have any exclusive rights in respect of the [Event/Programme] and the [Company] shall be entitled to receive and/or arrange such other forms of funding, endorsement, product placement and sponsorship with any third party it thinks fit. That no consultation with and/or approval by the [Sponsor] is required prior to the conclusion of any agreement.

E.360

The [Company] agrees and undertakes not to enter any arrangement and/or agreement with a third party in respect of the [Event/Programme] which will be detrimental and/or damaging to the reputation of the main [Sponsor]. Nor shall the [Company] make arrangements and/or enter into agreements with any organisations, persons and/or third parties whose products, services and/or business are not suitable for [specify market/age/other factors].

E.361

The [Company] agrees that the [Sponsor] shall always be ranked first and be prominent in the brochure for the programme, at the [Event], on the website and in any packaging, advertising, marketing and promotional material.

E.362

The [Company] reserves the right to appoint additional sponsors and/or contributors and/or third parties for product placement, advertising and/or promotion and/or include material associated with political campaigns and lobbying in connection with the [Event/Programme/Film].

E.363

Where any other sponsor is to be appointed by the [Company] to either contribute sums and/or products to the [Event/Programme]. Then the [Company] agrees that it shall not appoint a manufacturer and/or distributor of the following types of products and/or services: [list excluded areas].

E.364

1.1 It is agreed by the [Enterprise] that the [Company] shall be the sole and exclusive sponsor of the [Event/Campaign/Film/Podcast] from [date] to [date].

1.2 The [Enterprise] agrees that no other person and/or third party shall be acknowledged as the main sponsor and/or supplier for the [Event/ Campaign/Film/Podcast] for the period in 1.1.

E.365

Any sponsor is one of many contributors to the fundraising and endorsement of the [Event/Campaign]. Any sponsorship is for a period of [three] months. Any sponsor may withdraw at any time and cancel the next three-month period of sponsorship.

E.366

This agreement with the [Sponsor] only relates to the specific [Event/Festival] on [date] and does not apply to any other scheduled events by the [Enterprise].

University, Charity and Educational

E.367

The [Company] and the [Contributor/Author/Artist] agree that in consideration of the Fee and Expenses the [Contributor/Author/Artist] shall provide her/his exclusive services as [specific title/role] for the [Work/Project] from [date] to [date] to carry out the following duties and deliver the following material [specify in detail].

E.368

1.1 The [Consultant] agrees and undertakes to provide his/her non-exclusive services to the [Institute/Charity] in respect of the [Project] as an expert in the field of [specify subject].

1.2 The [Consultant] shall be available at such times and dates for discussions, meetings and presentations as may be required to fulfil the duties, services and work itemised in broad detail in Schedule A which is attached to this agreement.

1.3 In the event that the [Consultant] is regularly unavailable to attend meetings and/or respond to the [Institutes'/Charity's] requests. The [Institute/Charity] shall have the right to provide the [Consultant] with a warning that unless matters improve that they will end the agreement. If the problems with the [Consultant] still continue then the [Institute/Charity] shall have the right to terminate the agreement with [one] weeks by notice in writing to the [Consultant]. In such event no further sums shall be due for work which has not been completed and/or delivered prior to the date of termination.

1.4 The [Consultant] agrees and undertakes to complete and deliver the following reports, presentations and material to the [Institute/Charity] as follows: [comprehensive list of titles of record/presentation/material] [length and format] [delivery date].

E.369

1.1 The [Agent/Consultant] agrees and undertakes that this agreement does not give copyright, trade marks, patents, domain names, computer software rights and/or any other intellectual property rights and/or interests to the [Agent/Consultant] and/or any right to own and/or control any material created and/or developed for the [Institute/Charity]. The [Agent/Consultant] agrees and undertakes not to authorise and/or license and/or exploit any such rights and/or material in any media.

1.2 The [Agent/Consultant] agrees and undertakes not to represent that it has the authority to negotiate, conclude and/or otherwise act on behalf of the [Institute/Charity] with any third party unless the prior express consent of the [Institute/Charity] has been obtained. The [Agent/Consultant] agrees and undertakes not to enter into any contract of any nature without permission whether for rights, products, services and/or for any other work on behalf of the [Institute/Charity].

E.370

In consideration of the [Author's] Royalties and the Advance the [Author] grants to the [Institute/Charity] the sole and exclusive right to publish and exploit the [Report/Manuscript/Artwork/Image] and any parts in [define subject areas of the Rights/All Media] throughout the [Territory/world/country] for the duration of the Licence Period.

E.371

The [Author] confirms that the [Report/Manuscript/Image/Sound Recording] has not been previously licensed to any third party and has not been exploited in any form at any time throughout the [Territory/world/country].

E.372

In consideration of the Royalties and the Advance the [Author] grants to the [Institute/Charity] the sole and exclusive right to print, reproduce, supply, distribute, license, publish and exploit the [Work] and any parts in all media including but not limited to all methods of publication and reproduction, including hardback, paperback, serialisation, translations, anthologies, quotations, mechanical reproduction, radio, theatre, film, terrestrial, cable, satellite and digital television, the internet, worldwide web and downloads, telephones, mobiles and all forms of telecommunication and electronic means and any gadgets and devices, games and merchandising and lottery, gambling, betting, theme parks, advertising and promotional event, or material derived from and/or based upon any title, name, character, word or sound or music, words or text whether in existence now and/or created in the future throughout the world and universe for the duration of the full period of copyright and all intellectual property rights and thereafter to continue without an end date and indefinitely.

E.373

The [Contributor] agrees not to enter into any arrangement, and/or agreement with any third party to write, research or produce any other article, blog, podcast, film and/or book which is on the same topic and/or has a similar title, subject matter and/or theme before [date].

E.374

All rights not specifically granted to the [Licensee] are reserved and are retained by the [Licensor]. That the [Licensor] has not granted any licence or other authorisation to the [Licensee] and/or any third party to make the [Work] in whole or part available over the internet, on any platform, website and/or app and/or to be downloaded, stored, retrieved and/or supplied over any WiFi and/or by means of any telecommunication system and/or to any television, radio, mobile, gadget, watch or otherwise in any electronic form and/or otherwise by some other method created and/or developed in the future.

E.375

1.1 The [Institute/Charity] grants the [Distributor] the exclusive rights to exploit the [Work] in the following format [specify] in the following countries [list] from [date] to [date].

1.2   The [Distributor] shall not have the right to sub-license the [Work] to any third party at any time.

1.3   The reproduction, manufacture, distribution and sales of the [Work] must be carried out by the [Distributor] in accordance with the samples, drafts and to the quality agreed and approved with the [Institute/Charity].

E.376

1.1   The [Author] grants the [Institute/Charity] the non-exclusive right to store, retrieve, reproduce and make available the [Report including the copyright notice and credits] to all persons at the [Institute/Charity] at no charge from [date] to [date] in [country].

1.2   There is no right granted to supply copies to other third parties and/or to charge any fees for the supply of a copy except photocopying costs. The [Institute/Charity] shall not register and/or attempt to register an interest as the copyright owner with an organisation and/or collecting agency and the [Institute/Charity] agrees that the copyright is owned by the [Author].

E.377

The [Institute/Charity] agrees that it shall only have exclusive rights to the [Work] from [date] to [date]. After [date] then the [Institute/Charity] agrees that any licence granted to it by [Name] shall be non-exclusive and that [Name] may appoint other parties to reproduce and exploit the [Work] in any form.

E.378

1.1   [Name] has agreed to supply an exclusive range of branded products to the [Charity] for the [Event] which shall incorporate the name, logo and image of the [Charity] on each product.

1.2   [Name] shall submit an exact sample prototype for approval by the [Charity]. The [Charity] shall have final control as to the whether to proceed with the manufacture of the branded products. If the samples submitted are not acceptable then the project shall not proceed. If no branded products are produced as no sample is agreed. Then the [Charity] shall only be due to pay [name] the sum of [number/currency] and shall be entitled to terminate this agreement.

E.379

1.1   The [Enterprise] agrees to act on behalf of the [Charity] on a non-exclusive basis to promote, market and fundraise for the [Charity] in consideration of the payment of the Monthly Fees.

1.2 This agreement is on a monthly basis and may be cancelled by the [Charity] at any time by [two] weeks' notice to the [Enterprise].

1.3 The [Agent] shall not be entitled to hold itself out as acting as an exclusive agent and/or to represent that it has any authority to conclude agreements on behalf of the [Charity].

1.4 All sums raised must be paid direct to the [Charity] and not via the [Enterprise] into [account/code].

EXPENSES

Film, Television and Video

E.380
The [Company] agrees to supply the services of the [Executive Producer] without charge to the [Consortium]. It is agreed that the actual personal expenses of the [Executive Producer] in respect of the provision of his/her services to the [Consortium] shall be paid for by the [Consortium] under clause [–].

E.381
The actual costs and expenses incurred by the [Company] in respect of the operation of the [Service] and/or the provision of transport, staff, equipment, insurance and/or premises shall be reimbursed to the [Company] by the [Consortium] under clause [–].

E.382
The [Licensee] agrees to reimburse the [Licensor] in respect of all the reproduction, insurance, delivery, import and export duties, taxes and costs incurred in providing an acceptable [Film Package] subject to satisfactory receipts being provided upon request.

E.383
Where an expense and/or cost is not covered by the provisional budget allocated for the [Project] if it exceeds [number/currency]. Then it must be authorised in advance by [Name] and failure to adhere to this corporate policy may be considered a disciplinary matter.

E.384
The [Company] agrees to provide [Name] with the following costs and expenses:

1.1 Relocation costs from [place] to [place] of [number/currency].

1.2 Business class travel for [Name] and a partner on all travel in [country] and elsewhere on [Company] business.

1.3 Technology and communication services required at work and any main residence as follows: [specify equipment]. This shall include all costs of installation, maintenance and any monthly standing payments which may be incurred required for the operation of the equipment.

1.4 Life insurance for [Name] of not less than [number/currency] for death and [number/currency] for any other personal injury and/or disability during the course of the agreement and up to [number] years thereafter. The cost of all premiums to be paid for by the [Company].

1.5 Mortgage and/or rental payments of [number/currency] per month direct to [Name] for the first [twelve] months of the agreement.

1.6 Private medical and dental cover for [Name] and his/her family with [organisation] for [list requirements].

General Business and Commercial

E.385
In addition to the remuneration specified under clause [–] the [Executive] shall be reimbursed by the [Company] for all costs incurred with his/her duties under this contract including all travelling, hotel and other expenses properly and reasonably incurred by him/her in the discharge of his/her duties and in accordance with the rules and practices of the Company for the time being in force.

E.386
Any credit and charge cards supplied to the [Executive] by the Company shall be returned to the [Company] on leaving the [Company's] employment. Any money paid to the [Executive] to meet expenses incurred on a [Company] credit or charge card shall be used for that purpose and no other. The [Executive] shall be liable for the discharge of any personal expenses incurred by him/her using the [Company] credit or charge card.

E.387
The [Company] shall pay the [Manager] during the continuance of his/her employment such reasonable train, aeroplane, car, travel, insurance, hotel, entertainment, telephone (both landline and mobile), and computer or laptop, and other expenses incurred by the [Manager] wholly necessarily and exclusively in connection with the provision of his/her services. All such expenses must be subsequently supported by receipts and not exceed the monthly budget allocated and authorised by the [Company] for this purpose.

E.388
All expenses shall be paid in accordance with the provisions of the agreement between the [Company] and the [Union] of which [Name] is a member.

E.389
The [Employee] agrees not to pledge either during the Term of this Agreement or at any time thereafter the [Company's] credit or enter into any commitments or negotiate contracts on the [Company's] behalf except within the limits and authority set out by the [Company].

E.390
[Name] agrees that he/she is not permitted to order any products, services or otherwise to commit the [Company] to any payment and/or contractual obligation without following the notified internal policy procedure of the [Company] known as: [specify name of policy] a copy of which is attached to this document.

E.391
The [Company] shall provide comprehensive [personal/property/life] insurance cover for the [Executive] [and his/her family members] and the benefit of his/her estate for the term of the provision of his/her services at the [Company] including any period of illness at the [Company's] cost. The [Executive] shall be provided with a complete copy of the policy which shall start on [date] and be for not less than [number/currency].

E.392
The [Employee] is not entitled to any additional payments and/or expenses in respect of their work and no sums shall be paid unless authorised in advance by [specify person] and supported by receipts and/or invoice as requested.

E.393
Mobile telephone and WiFi charges and costs, clothes and uniform washing and dry cleaning, petrol and travel costs and any other expenses incurred by you are not paid for by the [Company] and remain your responsibility.

E.394
The cost and expense of all currency conversions and commissions shall be paid by [specify details] and the items clearly set out and the rate and date specified.

E.395
Each party to this agreement shall bear all their own expenses. Costs and disbursements incurred or made in pursuance of this agreement unless it

is expressly specified as a term of this agreement to be the responsibility of one particular party or as it is otherwise agreed in writing.

E.396

The [Company] agrees to reimburse [Name] in respect of reasonable travel costs by train, car and plane, mobile phone and WiFi costs and expenses, entertainment, hospitality and other business expenses which directly arise as a result of [Name] in carrying out his/her obligations under this agreement and/or which are authorised by the [Company]. The [Company] may require any such expenses to be supported by receipts or other evidence of the expenditure.

E.397

The [Licensee] shall not be responsible for any delivery charges and/or any other costs and expenses incurred by the [Licensor] in making any copies, supplying any master material and/or samples to the [Licensee] under this agreement.

E.398

[Name] confirms that he/she shall be responsible for his/her own expenses, value added tax, personal insurance, national insurance and/or personal tax due and/or claimed by any government authority and/or the cost of any related litigation and/or disputes which may occur.

E.399

[Name] agrees to obtain the prior consent of the [Company] in respect of all costs and expenses to be incurred in excess of [number/currency] in any [one] calendar month. The [Company] agrees to pay [Name's] expenses reasonably and properly incurred for the purpose of this agreement subject to satisfactory receipts or records being produced upon request in respect of the following matters: [specify authorised areas].

E.400

[Name] shall not be entitled to place any order and/or commit the [Company] to order, use, endorse, promote and/or supply and/or sell any products, services and/or any other rights and/or material without the prior consent of the [Company].

E.401

The [Company] agrees to provide the following items and benefits to [Name] at the [Company's] sole cost and expense for the duration of the agreement:

1.1 The Products: [–]

1.2 Clothing: [–]

1.3   Equipment: [–]

1.4   Facilities: [–]

1.5   Medical and Dental Benefits: [–]

1.6   Insurance: [–]

1.7   Travel: [–]

1.8   Technology: [–]

At the expiry and/or termination of this agreement any physical products supplied shall be the property of [Name] and not the [Company].

E.402
The [Company] agrees that it shall provide [Name] with a new car bearing the [Company's Logo/Image] described below for his/her personal and professional use which shall be comprehensively insured, taxed, serviced and any road charges, tolls, parking fines and charges shall be at the [Company's] expense: [specify make/age/value]. The car shall remain the property and be owned by the [Company] and/or any nominated third party.

E.403
'The Authorised Expenses' shall be the agreed costs of producing, supplying and distributing the [Work] which shall include [specify] and shall not exceed [number/currency].

E.404
In addition to the Fee the Assignee agrees to reimburse [Name] in respect of the Authorised Expenses within [seven] days of the presentation of an invoice or other record of expenditure.

E.405
[Name] shall not without the prior written consent of the [Publisher] incur any expenditure or costs on behalf of the [Publisher].

E.406
No costs, expenses, obligations, commitments or pledges shall be made by or on behalf of the [Company] and the total sums to be paid by the [Company] shall be limited to those set out in clause [–].

E.407
Attached is a copy of the [Company] policy regarding any claims for expenses and costs. The [Company] reserves the right to amend and/or remove any authorised expenditure at any time and shall notify all relevant parties by a display on [specify site]. There is no automatic right to be paid

any costs and expenses under any agreement and payment is made at the discretion of the [Company].

E.408

The [Company] agrees to pay all expenses and costs incurred by the [Consultant] directly related to their work for the [Company] including but not limited to mobile telephone costs; cost of design, reproduction, supply and distribution of marketing and promotional material; travel by bus, train, coach but not taxi in [city]. No claim shall be paid for food and drink and/ or accommodation. All sums shall be paid upon invoice by the [Consultant] which itemises the costs and sums due and dates incurred.

Internet, Websites and Apps

E.409

There shall be no responsibility for any costs, fees, charges, expenses, losses, damages, mobile, WiFi , internet, telephone, viruses, scams, copyright, performing, broadcast, transmission, sound recording, music, licence, trade mark or any other rights or other sum which may arise directly or indirectly that may be owed to any person, company or collecting society as a result of your use of any material or content on this [Website/App/ Platform] at any time.

E.410

The [Company] shall not be liable for any costs, expenses, charges, penalties, damages, losses, connection charges, telephone bills, viruses, defects, cookies, legal fees, replacement costs, credit card and bank charges, interest and/or any other sums incurred by the [Customer] from the use of this [Website/App/Platform] and/or any downloads, software and/ or products except those due to the negligence of the [Company] related to personal injury and death.

E.411

The [Customer] is responsible for payment of all the costs and expenses relating to delivery of the [Work/Product] including freight, customs duties, taxes, insurance and packaging costs and any associated administration expenses.

E.412

The [Company] agrees to pay [Name] the sum of [number/currency] to cover his/her fee and expenses each month for promoting the [Brand/Product] on his/her [Blog/Podcast] known as [specify] on [number] occasions for [number] minutes in each case. These payments shall not be made by the [Company] if [Name] does not carry out the required work for any reason.

In the event of any dispute the parties agree to enter into negotiations to endeavour to resolve the matter prior to any litigation.

E.413

1.1   [Name] confirms that he/she shall not be entitled to claim any additional costs and expenses from the [Company] for any reason. [Name] shall bear all his/her own costs and expenses relating to the work to be completed for the [Company]. [Name] accepts that the fees to be paid in respect of the number and duration of the posts to be made by [Name] on his/her [Blog] [Online Accounts] known as [specify] shall be the only sums due from the [Company].

1.2   [Name] shall arrange and for any filming, lighting, photography, location, clothing, equipment, sets, facilities, support personnel, security, travel and accommodation costs and other matters that may be required.

E.414
The [Company] agrees to supply the [Developer] at the [Company's] cost with suitable copies of all the master material he/she may require to design and create the [Website/App/Project]. The [Company] agrees and undertakes to bear the cost of all the third party services, material and other matters that may be required by the [Developer] for the [Website/App/Project]. The [Developer] is authorised to incur expenses and costs for their personal use up to [number/currency] in total for expenditure during the course of the provision of their services. When that is expected to be exceeded then [Name] must seek authorisation of an additional allowance from the [Company].

E.415
The authorised expenses are limited to those set out in the projected Budget for the [Project]. No other payments are agreed by the [Company]. There is no authority provided to incur additional expenses and costs on behalf of the [Company] for any reason.

Merchandising and Distribution

E.416
The [Agent/Distributor] agrees that it shall be solely responsible and the [Company] shall not be liable for the costs and expenses incurred by the [Agent/Distributor] in respect of the provision of its services under this agreement including but not limited to: travel, accommodation, entertainment, meals, equipment, telephone and communication systems, publicity and promotional material, freight and cost of premises and

staff. If the [Agent/Distributor] should visit the premises of the [Design Company] at any time the [Agent/Distributor] shall be solely responsible for any costs and expenses it may incur unless the [Company] has provided written specific consent to reimburse or contribute to authorised costs in advance.

E.417

Each party shall bear its own costs and expenses for its business, staff, telephone, internet, WiFi, software, freight, transport, health and safety, compliance, copyright and intellectual property and any other subject of any nature which it incurs whether related to a service or product under this agreement or not unless specified in clauses [–].

E.418

Where additional equipment and/or other items are purchased to develop, produce and/or reproduce the [Image/Sound Recordings/Products]. Then the [Supplier] shall receive a contribution of up to a maximum of [number/ currency] from the [Company] as an additional payment towards costs. Provided that valid receipts can be supplied with the relevant invoices to the [Company]. The [Company] agrees that the [Supplier] shall own such material not the [Company].

E.419

The [Distributor] shall not be responsible for any personal taxes, freight, custom and excise duties, taxes or penalties, national insurance costs and/ or other expenses incurred by the [Licensor] at any time in respect of this agreement. Each party agrees to bear its own costs and expenses for travel and accommodation at exhibitions and promotional events, insurance, administrative costs and other charges which they may incur and shall not seek to be reimbursed and/or deduct any such expenses from any sums due under this agreement.

E.420

The [Distributor] agrees and undertakes that it shall be responsible for and bear the cost of all sums incurred in respect of the development, tests, risk assessments, prototype development and samples, production, manufacture, distribution, agents, freight, packaging, product recall, product liability, insurance, legal proceedings, marketing, advertising and promotion of the [Product] based on character from the the [Book/Film] known as [specify name] which is reproduced in [two/three] dimensional form. That the [Author] shall not be liable for any such sums whatsoever that may arise and no such sums shall be deducted from any payments due to the [Author] under this agreement.

E.421
The [Distributor] agrees and undertakes that all sub-licensees shall in any agreement be required to pay the following costs and expenses in respect of the [Product] based on the [Work]: [specify costs to be paid by sub-licensee].

E.422
The [Company] agrees that any additional costs and/or expenses not included in the quote must be sent to the [Client] for approval in advance. That the [Client] shall have the right to cancel the order due to the additional sums requested and shall be entitled to a full refund of any sums paid to date.

E.423
The [Sportsperson] shall be entitled to be provided with the following personnel and expenses for him/her and [number] members of their family and entourage form [date] to [date] in [country] in respect of their appearance and performance at [Event] on [date]:

1.1   Personnel for chauffeur, security, florist, personal trainer, hair stylist, clothes stylist, photographer, chef, and such other qualified personnel as may be required from [date] to [date] at the [Company's] cost.

1.2   Travel first class on [specify company] and accommodation at [specify company/address] and all meals and hospitality on dates to be agreed.

E.424
The [Licensee] shall be obliged to pay all the cost and expenses that may be necessary for any reason for the [Licensee] to fulfil the terms of this agreement. The [Licensee] shall not be entitled to deduct any such sums from the [Gross Receipts/sums received] and/or any payments due to the [Licensor]. The [Licensee] must be responsible for all its own costs and expenses and ensure that any third party does not seek to claim any payments from the [Licensor].

Publishing

E.425
The [Author] shall not be responsible for any costs and expenses of the [Agent] and the [Agent] shall only have the right to claim the [Agent's Commission].

E.426
The [Publisher] agrees to pay or reimburse [Name] in respect of all expenses reasonably and properly incurred in providing his/her services under this

agreement to complete the [Project] including travel and accommodation for research and carrying out interviews; meals and hospitality; archive charges and costs; reproduction of documents, images, sound recordings and film; books and computer software, equipment and materials; mobile phone and internet charges and costs subject to satisfactory receipts or records being produced upon request.

E.427

The [Agent] agrees to pay or reimburse the [Ghostwriter] in respect of all expenses incurred in providing his/her services during the Term of the Agreement subject to satisfactory receipts or records being produced upon request up to a calendar monthly maximum of [number/currency] which shall include all [telephone/photocopying/archive access fees/ travel/ accommodation] but exclude [insurance/stationery/other]. There shall be a maximum limit of [specify amount and period].

E.428

The [Commissioning Company] agrees to pay for any research, archive and access, copyright and other clearances and payments, printing, copying, software, laptop, mobile, camera and photography, filming, equipment, business class travel and transport, hotels, hospitality and other costs and expenses which are specifically agreed in advance with the [Ghostwriter] for the purpose of fulfilling his/her obligations under this agreement. The [Ghostwriter] shall set out a proposal by email with the anticipated costs and seek approval of an allocated allowance which shall be paid in advance by the [Company].

E.429

The [Authors] agree to be personally responsible for their own expenses incurred in respect of the preparation, research, writing and delivery of the agreed material for the manuscript and the edited proofs of the [Synopsis/ Concept].

E.430

The [Publishers] agree to pay the [Authors] for the following sum in advance for the costs and expenses projected to be necessary for the development, research, writing, delivery of the [Artwork/Illustrations/Infographics]: [number/ currency]. No receipts or evidence shall be required at a later date and the [Authors] shall be entitled to retain this sum which shall not be deducted from or offset against any other sum due to the [Authors] under this agreement.

E.431

The [Publisher] agrees to pay a [designer/other] to create suitable images, videos, podcasts and other material in association with the [Author] for its website, app, catalogue, exhibitions and marketing material to increase sales of the [Work]. Such sums shall not be offset and/or recouped from any sums due to the [Author].

E.432

The [Distributor] shall be entitled to deduct the following costs and expenses from any sums received prior to the calculation of the payments due to the [Author]:

1.1 The advance payment to the [Author].

1.2 The cost of creating any index not supplied by the [Author].

1.3 The cost of any third party contributions to writing the [Work] and/or clearing copyright in any material in the [Work] and/or on the cover.

1.4 It shall not entitle the [Distributor] to deduct costs of any editor and/or proofs, printing, binding and/or creating and designing a cover and/or marketing and/or promotional costs, delivery costs and/or the cost of the development of any sub-licensed translations and/or sound recordings of the [Work].

Services

E.433

The [Agent] shall be entitled to deduct all reasonable expenses properly incurred in furtherance of this agreement from the Gross Receipts provided that the [Agent] shall at all times whenever possible and practicable keep all relevant receipts and documents confirming such expenses.

E.434

If [Name] shall at the request of the [Company] attend at any location which is more than [distance] from [town] in order to render the services required under this agreement. The [Company] agrees to book and pay for first class return travel and/or chauffeur car and/or pay for airline tickets for two people whichever is the most efficient.

E.435

If [Name] shall at the request of the [Company] be required to stay in any place for one or more nights. The [Company] shall book and arrange suitable hotel or other accommodation which is no less than a five star rating.

E.436

In respect of all copying charges relating to the production by the [Composer] of the score and orchestral and/or vocal parts of the [Music] the [Company] shall pay the cost of such copying at the [Standard Guild or Union scale rate] for the time being in force subject to the production and delivery to the [Company] of full and correct invoices for such amount from third parties addressed to the [Company].

E.437

The [Company] shall reimburse the [Presenter] on the presentation of appropriate invoices for reasonable wardrobe expenses incurred by the [Presenter] subject to an overall maximum of [number/currency] per calendar month which shall become the property of [specify ownership].

E.438

The [Company] agrees to pay or reimburse the [Presenter] in respect of all expenses reasonably and properly incurred in the provision of the services including travel, taxis, clothes, beauty, dental and nail treatments, hairdressing, jewellery, computer equipment, software, watches and gadgets subject to satisfactory receipts or records for both appearances on the [Programmes]; promotional and marketing events; advertisements for the [Company]; attendance at conferences, high profile events and any other matter which is authorised in advance by the [Company].

E.439

The [Agent] agrees that it shall only be entitled to the [Agent's] Commission for the Term of the Agreement subject to the provision of the services by the [Agent] and the continuance of this agreement. The [Agent] shall not be entitled to any additional expenses, royalties, products, compensation, damages, losses and/or other sums from the [Company].

E.440

The [Company] shall pay such reasonable expenses incurred by [Name] wholly necessarily and exclusively in connection with the provision of his/her freelance services pursuant to this agreement up to a maximum of [number/currency] per calendar month. [Name] shall submit an expenditure statement by the end of each month and provide suitable evidence such as receipts. The [Company] agrees to pay [Name] within [number] days of the submission of the statement.

E.441

The [Company] agrees to either arrange and pay for and/or reimburse the [Artist] in respect of all fees, charges, costs and expenses incurred by the [Artist] in the provision of his/her services under this agreement without any limit on the sum including:

1.1   Travel, car, taxis, air travel, travel insurance, surcharges, excess baggage costs and upgrades. The cost of booking any location to be used and/or any budget that may be incurred. Accommodation whether hotel and/or rental of a studio.

1.2 Beauty treatments, cosmetics, hair, clothes, personal trainer, cosmetic dentistry and medical cover.

1.3 Internet connection, telephone, both landline and mobile, gadgets, computer software and equipment, lighting, materials, photographic and filming equipment and the cost of any supporting personnel. Freight and transport costs for any material and personnel.

1.4 Any material and equipment supplied and/or bought for the [Artist] shall belong to the [Artist] and not the [Company].

E.442
The [Company] agrees to pay [Name] from [date] to [date] a monthly expenses allowance of [number/currency] which can be spent in any manner that [Name] may decide. The [Company] shall pay the allowance in advance on the first day of each month. In the event that the agreement is terminated early for any reason it is agreed that [Name] shall still be entitled to be paid the outstanding monthly expenses allowance until [date].

E.443
In addition to the [Presenter's] Fee and the authorised annual allowance for matters relating to appearances on the [Series]. The [Company] also agrees to reimburse the [Presenter] in respect of all other costs and expenses which are reasonably and properly incurred for the purpose of fulfilling his/her obligations under this agreement including taxis, petrol, telephone charges and business lunches subject to satisfactory receipts or other records being produced upon request.

E.444
The [Company] agrees that it shall provide [Name] with:

1.1 A new executive car for his/her personal use for the Term of the Agreement which shall be comprehensively insured, tested, taxed and serviced entirely at the [Company's] expense and shall remain the property of the [Company] or its leasing agents: [specify].

1.2 A new company charge card to be used for all the authorised expenses: [specify].

1.3 Private health care with [Name] for [Name] and their family with the following benefits: [specify].

1.4 Life Assurance for the benefit of: [specify] in the sum of [amount].

1.5 Pension benefits: [specify].

1.6 Share Options: [specify].

1.7 Bonus: [specify].

1.8 Equipment: [specify].

1.9 Relocation costs up to a maximum of [number/currency].

E.445

The [Company] shall ensure that suitable insurance cover is arranged for [Name] and her/his personal property and shall provide her/him with a copy of the policy upon request. The [Company] confirms that the [Name's] life insurance for the benefit of her/his estate shall not be less than [specify sum]. The nominated beneficiary is [specify person].

E.446

The [Company] agrees to arrange and pay for any travel and accommodation required of [Name] by the [Company] under this agreement. The [Company] undertakes that as far as possible all accommodation shall be a minimum of four-star hotel and all forms of travel will be business or first class.

E.447

The [Agent] acknowledges that he/she is solely responsible for all costs he/she may incur in respect of the provision of his/her services under this agreement to [Name] including administration, collection of fees and payments due, legal costs and expenses and/or the promotion, advertising and marketing of [Name]. [Name] shall not be liable and/or responsible for any costs and expenses incurred by the [Agent]. Nor shall the [Agent] be entitled to deduct such sums from payments due to [Name].

E.448

'The Authorised Expenses' shall be the following sums reasonably and properly expended by the [Manager] for and behalf of the [Sportsperson] which are not recovered through any third party:

1.1 First class travelling costs and the cost of all accommodation. Provided that the [Sportsperson] is attending competitions, events or other business matters under the terms of this agreement or at the request of the [Manager].

1.2 The following credit and charge card shall be supplied by the [Manager] to the [Sportsperson]: [specify]. The [Sportsperson] agrees to use this card exclusively for them only and not family members for the purpose of settling his/her expenses under this agreement. The [Manager] shall be responsible for the payments due for any credit and charge card. The card shall be returned at the end of the agreement.

1.3 The following goods or equipment shall be supplied for the [Sportsperson] to retain: [specify items/value].

1.4 A monthly allowance for the [Sportsperson] of: [number/currency] which is to be paid at the end of each calendar month in arrears for the duration of this agreement. Any items purchased using this allowance shall be owned the [Sportsperson].

1.5 Comprehensive insurance policy in respect of the [Sportsperson] his/her sports equipment and family: [specify items/persons/value].

1.6 Specialist medical benefits: [specify].

1.7 Training facilities: [specify].

1.8 Security: [specify].

If the agreement expires and/or is terminated early then all right to the matters set out in 1.1 to 1.8 by the [Sportsperson] shall cease.

E.449
'The Promotion Expenses' shall be all the costs and expenses reasonably and properly expended by the [Promoter] in furtherance of this agreement which are not recouped from any third party:

1.1 The creation, supply and cost of advertising in local and national newspapers, magazines including articles and photographs. Sound recordings for radio and interviews.

1.2 The development, production and distribution of a promotional blog, podcast, website, app and/or other online material and promotional accounts. The registration of domain names and other rights in the name of [specify]. Clearance costs, fees and expenses for the negotiation and acquisition of any required material and contributors and/or performers. The commissioning of any software, artwork, graphics, music, text, merchandising or any other material for publicity, advertising and promotional material.

1.3 It shall include delivery, storage, shipping custom duties, insurance and handling charges but not hospitality, travel costs, mobile, landline telephone and internet and/or general business administration and staff costs of the [Promoter].

E.450
'The Authorised Expenses' shall be the following sums expended by the [Manager] which solely and directly relate to the [Group] which are not agreed to be paid by a third party: [travel costs/accommodation/clothing/publicity/advertising/equipment/telephone/stationery/insurance cover] for

both the [Manager] and/or the [Group]. The [Manager] must provide a monthly report to the [Group] itemising all the authorised expenses which he/she intends to deduct and/or claim. The [Manager] accepts that he/she has no right to expend any sum in excess of [number/currency] in respect of any matter in one and/or multiple transactions without the prior consent of all the [Group].

E.451

The [Manager] acknowledges that any materials provided as part of the Authorised Expenses shall be the property of the member of the [Group] for whom it was originally purchased.

E.452

There shall be no obligation to pay any additional sums for costs and/or expenses incurred by the [Company/Agent/Artist] in providing their services under the agreement. The total sum to be paid by the [Distributor] shall be limited to the [Fees/number/currency].

E.453

Where [Name] requires additional costs and expenses to be paid for any reason in order to fulfil the terms of this agreement. Then the [Distributor] agrees to pay a maximum of [number/currency] in each calendar month subject to invoice by [Name] for a period of [three] months.

E.454

[Name] shall not be entitled to any costs, expenses and/or other sums except the [Fee] for the [Internship/Work]. In the event for any reason [Name] is requested to commit and/or incur any cost and expense on behalf of the [Company] by any person. Then [Name] shall be entitled to refuse and shall seek the advice and permission of [Executive] to provide authority for such expenditure.

Sponsorship

E.455

The [Sponsor] agrees to bear all the costs and expenses of all the work, services and materials required relating to the development, design, commission and production of the [Sponsor's] Logo and the supply of the [Sponsor's] Logo in a format which is suitable and accepted by the [Company] for its incorporation in any material for the [Programme/Event]. The [Company] shall not be responsible for any such sums. In the event that the material is to be developed and/or created by a third party who is already engaged in the [Programme/Event]. Then the [Sponsor] agrees to negotiate a budget for the work required to create the new material with the

[Company] and/or the third party. The [Sponsor] shall pay the sums due under the budget in advance for the work provided that the [Company] and/or third party shall provide a full assignment of all copyright and/or intellectual property rights in the new material to the [Sponsor] at no additional cost.

E.456
The [Company] agrees that it shall bear all the cost and expense of the preparation, design, development, production, distribution, marketing and exploitation of the [Event/Programme] and that [Name] shall not have any liability whatsoever for any sums that may arise at any time. In the event that a claim is made against [Name]. The [Company] shall indemnify [Name] under clause [–].

E.457
The [Sponsor] shall pay all the agreed expenses set out in Appendix A subject to the production of receipts, bank statements and/or other supporting evidence before [date]. After that [date] no further sums shall be paid by the [Sponsor].

E.458
The [Sponsor] agrees that where due to unforeseen circumstances, error and/or some other reason insufficient quantities of the [Sponsors'] product are available for the [Competitors]. That the [Sponsor] shall reimburse the [Company] with the full cost of purchasing and/or arranging for the supply of alternative products at short notice which may be incurred by the [Company].

E.459
Where the [Company] have to incur costs and expenses due to the acts, negligence, errors, omissions and/or due to the failure of the [Sponsor] and/or any of their agents, employees, casual staff and/or other persons associated and/or engaged by them. Then the [Company] shall be entitled to incur such sums on their behalf as may be necessary to remedy and/or resolve a matter and the [Sponsor] shall be liable for and pay all the costs and expenses upon demand by the [Company]. Together with such administration and compensation payment as the [Company] may decide to charge dependent on the circumstances.

E.460
The [Company] does not accept responsibility for any expenses and/or other sums incurred by the [Sponsor] due to any alteration and/or cancellation of the [Event] for any reason. The [Sponsor] agrees to accept the risk and agrees that the [Company] shall not be liable for such sums.

845

University, Charity and Educational

E.461

The [Contributor] agrees that she/he shall bear the cost of all her/his own travel, accommodation, telephone and mobile charges, photocopying, computer software and hardware costs and any other expenses incurred in respect of the preparation, research, and writing required for the satisfactory completion and delivery of the [Report/Survey/Development Plan] to the [Institute/Charity]. The only sum due to be paid by the [Institute/Charity] is the agreed fee in clause [–].

E.462

The [Institute/Charity] agrees to pay or reimburse the [Contributor] in respect of all expenses reasonably and properly incurred in the provision of the services under this agreement subject to satisfactory receipts or records up to a maximum of [number/currency] in any one year period. In the event that this agreement is terminated early for any reason. The [Contributor] shall have no claim to be paid for these expenses which directly relate to the fulfilment of the services and work.

E.463

The [Institute/Charity] and the [Company] both agree that they shall bear their own costs and expenses incurred in respect of this agreement and shall not seek to claim and/or deduct any such sums. Each party shall be responsible for the administration of its offices, engagement of employees and/or consultants, telephone and mobile charges, freight, transport and its own compliance with legislation and/or codes of practice and/or guidelines relating to how it operates, data protection, health and safety, product liability, public liability and/or any other matter.

E.464

The [Consultant] acknowledges and agrees that she/he shall be responsible for all costs and expenses that she/he may incur in respect of the provision of her/his services under this agreement. The [Consultant] shall ensure that the [Consultant] has suitable personal insurance cover for herself and her equipment and agrees to follows all the directions and guidelines issued by the [Institute/Charity].

E.465

The [Institute/Charity] shall pay the [Executive] during the continuance of his/her employment such reasonable train, air, car, travel insurance, hotel, entertainment, telephone (both landline and mobile), and computer or laptop, and other expenses and costs incurred by the [Executive] directly in order to carry out his/her duties under this agreement. All expenses over [number/currency] must be agreed and authorised in advance in each case and supported by receipts.

E.466
The [Institute/Charity] shall during the Term of this Agreement provide comprehensive life, personal and health insurance cover for the [Executive] and his/her immediate family and for the benefit of his/her estate at the [Institute's] cost for not less than [number/currency].

E.467
Where the [Charity/Enterprise] requires a [researcher/student] to attend a conference and/or to make any presentation and/or wishes to exploit their [Report/Marketing Skills/other]. Then it is agreed that the [Charity/Enterprise] shall pay the [researcher/student] a fee of [number/currency] per [day/month] in arrears at the end of each calendar month. Together with all travel, accommodation, stationary, software, telephone, mobile, meals and other costs of no more than [number/currency] for each calendar month.

F

FACILITY ACCESS

Film, Television and Video

F.001

1.1 The [Company] agrees to provide access to the following space at address [specify address and space] a plan of which is attached in Appendix A setting out arrangements for electricity, water, gas, lighting, heating, parking and access routes and any costs to be incurred and who is to pay. Access shall be permitted from [date] to [date] between the hours of [number] and number]. The purpose of the access to the location is for the [Distributor] to record, film, make sound recordings and create such images as may be required for the [Project] and/or any associated marketing and not for any other reason.

1.2 The [Distributor] shall be responsible for all the actions and consequences arising from any personnel, artists, catering staff, security and other third parties that it may engage and/or invite to the location space.

1.3 The [Distributor] agrees that it shall not use and/or access any areas which are closed and/or blocked off and shall provide a deposit to the [Company] of [number/currency] against any loss and/or damages which may be incurred which are not covered by any insurance cover which the [Company] agrees to arrange for the location access for the benefit of the [Company].

1.4 Where the [Company] is unable and/or unwilling to permit access, then the [Distributor] agrees that it shall not have any action, claim and/or legal action against the [Company] and that the [Company] has the right to refuse access and/or use of their facilities at any time.

F.002

1.1 [Name] consents to access by the [Company] and any associated personnel to their home for the purpose of filming and interviewing [Name] on [date] in their [specify space]. This shall not include the right to film and/or record other members of the family and/or other locations within the house.

1.2 Where at any time [Name] decides that he/she wishes to cancel, terminate and/or reschedule the filming and/or interview then [Name] shall be entitled to do so for any reason. Provided that in the event that no filming and/or interview of [Name] takes place then no payment shall be due and any sums paid shall be refunded to the [Company]. [Name] shall not however be liable for any costs and expenses that the [Company] may have incurred for any reason relating to the proposed filming.

F.003

1.1 The [Distributor] agrees to provide access to and use of the following facilities [specify] to the [Company] and its personnel at the [Distributors'] cost to produce, edit, reproduce and supply copies of the [Film] for the [Project/Video/Podcast].

1.2 The [Company] agrees that it shall not be entitled to incur any additional cost and expenses and/or to commit the [Distributor] in any manner to pay for and/or be liable for any person, service and/or other material required by the [Company] at any time.

F.004

The [Producer] agrees to provide to the [Television Company] a Facility Access Letter signed by a Director of the [Facilities House] and the [Producer] by [date] which sets out the following conditions which shall apply until [date]:

1.1 an undertaking that the [Facilities House] will retain possession of the master copy of the [Films/Series] and any sound recordings, clips and other associated material and will not assign, transfer and/or destroy any such material without the prior written consent of the [Television Company].

1.2 an undertaking by the [Facilities House] that they will act on the authority of the [Television Company] and not the [Producer] from [date] to [date] in respect of the master copy of the [Films/series] and any sound recordings, clips and associated material. The [Facilities House] will fulfil all orders and requests by the [Television Company] subject to payment for the order. That the product of the work of the services of the [Facilities Company] shall be of the highest quality and any event at all times comply with all technical standard and transmission requirements of [Ofcom/other].

1.3 The [Facilities House] shall not claim any right, interest, liens or charge of any nature against the master copy of the [Films/Series] and any sound recordings, clips and associated material.

F.005

1.1 The [Company] may decide to offer some or all of its internal facilities for the production of any [Programme/Film/Video] subject to their availability. There is no obligation for the [Company] to offer the facilities and for them to be used.

1.2 In the event that the [Production Company] does use the facilities of the [Company] then the cost to be charged shall be the usual charge out cost to third parties. Both parties shall enter be obliged to conclude a separate facilities agreement for that purpose.

F.006

1.1 This Agreement does permit and/or authorise the [Company] and/or any executives and/or third parties engaged by them to use and/or have access to any premises, equipment and/or other facilities of the [Distributor] at any time.

1.2 The normal procedures for bookings at the [Distributor] must be adhered to at all times and the [Company] shall be liable to pay hire costs and other relevant charges at the usual rate for any arrangement that may be agreed. There are no reduced rates, discounts and/or waiver of any cost and/or expenses by the [Distributor] to the [Company].

F.007
The [Company] agrees that:

1.1 [Name] shall be allocated his/her own [space/room] from [date] to [date] with its own personal facilities as follows [specify].

1.2 there shall in addition be sufficient security paid for by the [Company] to prevent access by unauthorised visitors.

1.3 the [Company] shall also ensure that there are no hidden bugs and/or cameras prior to access and/or use of the [space/room] by [Name].

1.4 [Name] shall be provided with sole use of the [space/room] for the period and shall be entitled to make his/her own arrangements for cleaning and servicing the [space/room] as he/she thinks fit.

1.5 no claim and/or action shall be made for any costs, expenses and/or loss and/or damage that [Name] may incur provided it is less than [number/currency]. [Name] shall be obliged to pay any sum due to the

[Company] in excess of that figure subject to an invoice setting out the basis of the claim.

General Business and Commercial

F.008

The [Company] undertakes that it will not authorise and/or consent to the removal, destruction, deletion and/or sale of any material relating to the [Film/Work/Products] and/or any parts and/or related packaging, marketing and promotional material held in any offices, warehouse, factory and/or other premises in [country] without complying with the following conditions:

1.1 The [Company] shall notify [Name] of the intention to move, destroy, delete and/or sell the [Film/Work/Products] and/or any parts and/or related packaging, marketing and promotional material and provide [Name] with an opportunity of not less than [two] months from the date of notification to make an offer and/or proposal in respect of the material

1.2 Where material is moved for any reason then the [Company] agrees that it shall be obliged to provide a new access letter. Where the cost of access and reproduction of the material is more expensive then the [Distributor] shall bear those costs not the [Company].

F.009

The [Assignor] shall provide all material of any nature and in any format which exists or is created in the future in the [Work/Film/Video/Game] in the possession or under the control of the [Assignor] or any director, officer, or representative or agent, licensee or other third party known by the [Assignor] to be in possession and/or control of material to the [Assignee] including but not limited to:

1.1 all copies of any master material in any form and all films, videos, discs, sound recordings, clips, stills, computer generated material, artwork, graphics and drawings.

1.2 a list of locations, premises, offices, warehouses and factories in any country at which any material is held. Together with authorisation to the [Assignee] to gain access and to remove any such material without incurring any additional costs. Further to confirm that the [Assignee] from [date] holds all legal ownership and title.

1.3 all copies of any contracts, licences, music, lyrics, applications for registrations of trade marks, applications to collecting societies, copyright clearances and fees, performing rights clearances and payments if any, any other consents and permissions, proofs, scripts, packaging, promotional and advertising material, posters, catalogues, labels and press and media reports, sales reports, budgets, and other accounting records in any format.

1.4 all material relating to any name, character name, image, trading name, associated trade marks, design rights, service marks, logos, domain names, websites and apps or any slogan, text, icon, image, jingle, ringtone or otherwise.

F.010

1.1 The [Agent] agrees to allow the [Company] supervised access to [Name] to conduct an in-depth interview on the subject of [specify topic].

1.2 The [Agent] agrees to supply originals of the following material [specify] for the purpose of reproduction solely in association with the interview for the [Programme]. There is no right to use the material in any other format and/or to use the material for marketing and promotional purposes on the website and/or app of the [Company].

1.3 The filming of the interview will take place at [address] and start at [specify time] and end at [specify time] on [date].

1.4 The [Company] agrees that the agreed fee of [number/currency] must be paid in advance to the [Agent]. The [Company] accepts full liability for any damage and/or loss that arises directly as a result of their access and/or filming at the location.

F.011

The [Company] shall not be obliged to provide use of their facilities, equipment or materials to any person or business who they appoint as an agent, service provider or in any other capacity to act on their behalf or to produce any material. The decision shall be entirely at the discretion of the [Company] at any time. Where facilities, equipment or materials are not made available the [Agent/Service Business/other] shall make their own arrangements at their own cost and agree that there is no right to seek to reclaim any such sum from the [Company] as an additional or unforeseen expense.

F.012

The [Institute/Charity] shall not be obliged to provide use of its facilities and/or access to the premises for the purposes of this Agreement. Where permission is granted the [Company] shall obey all the policies and instructions given by the representatives of the [Institute/Charity] and shall use any such facilities and premises at the [Company's] own risk and cost.

The [Company] shall indemnify the [Institute/Charity] in respect of all direct and indirect damages, losses, expenses, legal costs and costs that may be incurred in respect of any land, property, equipment, products, services, data, records, staff and/or other personnel relating to the [Institute/Charity].

F.013

Where facilities are made available to the [Company] at the premises of [Name]. The [Company] agrees:

1.1 to abide by and adhere to all the following policies [specify] which are applicable.

1.2 that any persons from the [Company] shall be required to follow any instructions of authorised personnel of [Name] who may be in charge of and operating the [equipment/systems].

1.3 the [Company] shall be obliged to pay for any additional costs that may be incurred which may arise as a result of the access to and/or use of the facilities.

1.4 the [Company] [shall be obliged to provide a schedule [one month] in advance to the [Name] which specifies in detail the proposed use of the facilities, the persons who will attend and the material which will be used.

F.014

1.1 The [Agent] shall not have any access to and/or use of the facilities and/or premises of [Name] at any time as part of this Agreement.

1.2 The [Agent] shall be obliged to pay for all administration, reproduction, development and marketing costs and expenses at his/her sole cost.

1.3 There shall be no obligation on [Name] to supply and/or deliver any material including archive photographs and/or other recordings and/or films which he/she may own and/or control.

FAIR DEALING

General Business and Commercial

F.015

'Fair Dealing' shall mean the quotation, small sample or agreed extract of the [Work] which shall be acknowledged with the relevant title, copyright notice and credit to the [Copyright Owner], and/or [Exclusive Licensee/ Distributor] and source reference for the [Work] for the purpose of review or criticism in [country].

This shall not include any educational, charitable and/or commercial enterprise, databases and/or storage and retrieval system and/or any adaptation and/or any right to license third parties which shall require the prior written consent of the [Copyright Owner].

F.016
'Fair Dealing' in the context of this Agreement shall mean to deal with fairly and reasonably but in any event the [Licensee] shall use no more than [ten] per cent of the [Licensor's] material and/or [number pages/minutes] whichever is the shorter for promotional purposes.

F.017

1.1   There is no right to quote from, extract sample words, data or images from this [Work] or any part. For review or criticism purposes you may only refer to the title, copyright owner and source of reference and a maximum of [number] words in [country] for a non-commercial purpose.

1.2   Any other direct use and/or adaptation of the material of the [Work] requires the prior written consent of [specify name]. This clause shall apply for all purposes whether educational, charitable, commercial, or as a non-fee paying contribution to a website, blog, app, magazine and/or other enterprise.

F.018

1.1   The [Licensor] grants the [Licensee] the non-exclusive right to use the following [Text/Images/Data] [Title] [Description] [Words/pages/ copy of image] A copy of which is attached to and forms part of this Agreement.

1.2   The [Licensee] shall only be entitled to use the [Text/Images/Data] in the following manner [specify purpose in detail]. In the following countries [specify]. For the Licence Period from [date] to [date].

1.3   The [Licensee] agrees that at all times the following credit and copyright notice shall be provided to the [Licensor] on all copies and all associated labels, packaging and marketing material [specify].

F.019
It is acknowledged by all parties to the [Consortium]:

1.1 That all the product of any work, service and/or material and/or rights arising as a result of any contribution to the [Project] should as far as possible be assigned to the [Consortium] known as [specify name]. All matters to be held as joint owners by all the parties in the Consortium.

1.2 That this [Project] is a commercial enterprise and that no reliance must be placed on clearing and/or acquiring material and/or services on any concept of fair dealing, public domain and/or review, criticism and/or otherwise.

1.3 That as a matter of policy rights should be acquired by assignment and/or exclusive licence for the most extensive use worldwide within the constraints of the [Budget]. That if possible payments should be agreed for future use so that projected costs can be fixed.

1.4 That proper records of clearance of all copyright, intellectual property rights, credits, copyright notices, trade marks and any other rights should be maintained and held by [specify] and not destroyed at any time. That these details shall be supplied to any party to the [Consortium] upon request provided that they meet all costs required to fulfil such task.

F.020

1.1 [Name] agrees that the [Author] may use the following lyrics, words, sound recording and film [specify] from the song entitled [specify] on their blog called [specify].

1.2 Provided that the [Author] agrees that a link is provided from the blog as follows [specify link web reference] and a copyright notice and credit is displayed as follows at all times next to the lyrics, words, sound recording and film as follows [specify details].

1.3 That the [Author] agrees not to post and/or display and/or use and/or adapt the material in 1.1 on any other website and/or in any other format and/or medium at any time without the prior written consent of [Name].

FAIR TRADING

General Business and Commercial

F.021

The [Company/Distributor] agrees and undertakes not to abuse any dominant market position which it may have or achieve in respect of the

[Product] and/or to enter into any agreements which would or might restrict or distort the market and/or competition in [countries].

F.022

The [Company/Distributor] agrees and undertakes not to abuse any dominant market position which it may have or achieve in respect of any of its products or services and/or to enter into any agreements which would and/or might restrict and/or distort and/or mislead the market in [list countries] and/or be against legislation and/or laws relating to competition in [list countries].

F.023

The [Company] agrees not to source material or enter into agreements with suppliers, manufacturers, agents or other third parties who do not follow the fair trade principles and policies of [specify organisation] during the Term of this Agreement. Copies of the policies are attached to and form part of this Agreement.

F.024

The [Manufacturer] agrees and undertakes to comply with all the following principles in its working practices for its business and in its dealings with the [Company]:

1.1   not to employ child labour and/or any person under the age of [specify].

1.2   to adopt health and safety practices which comply with [specify body].

1.3   to source all materials as far as possible from sustainable resources and from a source which can be identified through the chain at all times.

1.4   to pay [workers/staff/others] no less than [specify rate] in [country].

1.5   to provide a health care programme, medical cover and insurance as follows [specify].

1.6   to provide the [Company] access to the premises, offices and warehouses of the [Manufacturer] at any time without prior notice to verify compliance with any of the above and to make it a condition that any suppliers or any third parties agree to comply and provide access on the same terms.

1.7   to comply with all the following policy documents [specify].

F.025

1.1   The [Supplier] agrees and undertakes to develop, produce, manufacture, package and deliver all [Products] ordered by the [Company] in accordance with the [subject] policy of [organisation] in [country].

1.2 That the [Supplier] agrees that where for any reason there is a failure and/or discrepancy and/or departure from these principles for any reason in respect of any order that the [Company] shall be advised before the delivery is despatched and provided with the opportunity to cancel the order.

F.026

It is not a requirement of this Agreement that any part of the [Products/Services/Work] comply with and/or are subject to any fair trade, green, recycling, carbon neutral and/or any other environmental and/or international development policy.

F.027

It is a fundamental term of this agreement that the following policies are adopted and maintained in relation to all the main parties and third parties whose services, work, products and materials are engaged and/or used for the purpose of this agreement:

1.1 That the following carbon neutral policy [specify] of [organisation] be considered and incorporated as part of the planning of any {Project].

1.2 That all plastics be kept to a minimum and are not used unless absolutely no alternative can be used provided that the cost impact is not excessive.

1.3 That recycling is promoted and used for all materials and products.

1.4 That materials sourced from trees and be replaced with a replanting tree scheme in equal measure in another location.

1.5 That no materials are sourced from areas where the removal of the material impacts on the environment and poses a threat to the extinction of the indigenous populations and/or animals.

1.6 That a transparent policy of resources and sources will be adopted and information published on the website [specify] and app [specify].

1.7 That there will be a staff scheme which encourages innovation, cost savings and environmental impact matters with a reward scheme.

FILMS

General Business and Commercial

F.028

'The Film' means a feature film and the accompanying soundtrack and musical score complying with the following particulars:

1.1   Title: [specify]

1.2   Running Time: [specify duration] minutes

1.3   Based on: [book/idea/script/synopsis] created by [name]

1.4   Individual Producer: [name]

1.5   Director: [name]

1.6   Composer: [name]

1.7   Principal Artists: [name]

1.8   Technical description of material: [–]

1.9   Budget cost of production: [specify]

F.029
'The Film' means a film of approximately [duration] minutes entitled [title] based on the novel [specify] by [author] and shall include the associated sound recording.

F.030
'The Film' shall mean the film entitled [title] with a running time of not less than [duration]. Based on a screenplay to be written by [Writer] which is based on an original published book entitled [specify title] and published by [name of publishers] in [country] and a treatment by the original creator and writer [Author].

F.031
'The Films' shall mean the feature films described in Schedule A which is attached to and forms part of this Agreement. [Schedule A list title/copyright owner/distributor/duration/credits and copyright and trade mark notices].

F.032
'The Film' shall mean a feature film provisionally entitled [specify title] based on a novel entitled [title] by the Author [Name] which has been published by [Company] and has the reference [specify ISBN/other].

F.033
'Film' shall be defined as a recording on any medium from which a moving image may by any means be produced.

F.034
'The Series' shall mean the Series provisionally entitled [specify title] which shall consist of [number] programmes each of which shall be [number] minutes] in duration. The Series shall be on the subject of [specify topic]

based upon the book entitled [specify title] written by the [Author] and published by the [Distributor]. The programmes for the Series shall be produced in accordance with the copies of the synopsis and draft scripts which are attached in appendix A and forms part of this agreement.

F.035

'The Series' shall be the series of films and any associated sound recordings based on the treatments and the scripts entitled [title] consisting of [number] episodes each of which shall be [length in minutes] in duration.

F.036

For the avoidance of doubt the definition of the Programme shall include any advertisement and/or promotion in that programme as well as any items or products. It shall also include any teletext transmission.

F.037

'Programme Material' shall include a film and any other recording and any advertisement or other advertising material.

F.038

'Programme' shall mean the live or recorded television programme and shall include all underlying works whether literary, dramatic, artistic, musical and/ or sound and/or commentary which form part of the Programme.

F.039

'Cable Programme' shall mean any item included in the cable programme [specify title] on the following service [specify company] in [country].

F.040

'Feature Film Material' shall mean all the material specified in Schedule A to this agreement including all accompanying soundtracks, sound recordings, films, videos, stills and unused footage which it is intended to be incorporated in the [Programmes] to be produced by the [Company].

F.041

'The Series of Programmes' shall be the following films and any associated sound recordings and/or music which is described as follows:

1.1   Title of Series of Programmes: [specify]

1.2   Title of each episodes: [specify]

1.3   Language: [specify]

1.4   Sub-titles: [specify]

1.5   Product placement and sponsorship details: [specify]

860

F.042

'The Film' shall be the full length feature film and associated sound recordings to be produced by the [Production Company] based on and adapted from the [Book] which is an original work devised and written entirely by the [Author] which shall include the title, any artwork, characters, logos, place names and quotes contained in the [Book] which has been published by [specify publisher] and has the ISBN reference:[specify].

The Film is broadly described as follows:

1.1   Title of Film: [specify].

1.2   Duration of Film: [specify].

1.3   Languages and subtitles: [specify].

1.4   Final master copy of the Film to be in format: [specify].

F.043

'The Series' shall be the series of films and any associated sound recordings that may be produced, developed and exploited based on the [Pilot]. The Series shall be subject to a separate agreement between the parties but shall be subject to the following terms:

1.1   No less than [number] episodes of duration [number of minutes].

1.2   Feature as the main presenter: [name]

1.3   The copyright in the Series shall be owned jointly by [specify] and [specify].

F.044

'The [Video/Film/Disc]' shall be the promotional film and any associated sound recording for the [Musical Work] to be performed by the [Artist].

F.045

'The Film' shall be the following film in which 'The Commissioned Work' is to be incorporated entitled [specify title of film].

'The Commissioned Work' shall be the title sequences and end copyright notices, trade marks, service marks, domain names, credits, disclaimers and copyright warnings to be prepared, produced and delivered by the [Assignor] to the [Production Company] which is in described appendix A and forms part of this agreement. [specify duration, sequence of list of names, design, logos, colour and additional images and/or background].

F.046

'The Footage' shall be the following extracts of the [Film] called [specify title] including all related sound recordings: [specify extracts and duration] in format [specify].

F.047

'The Corporate Video' shall be the following film and any associated sound recordings and musical works in which the footage is to be included described as follows:

1.1 Title of the Corporate Video; [specify].

1.2 Duration of the Corporate Video: [specify].

1.3 Purpose and aim: [specify].

1.4 Intended methods of exploitation of the Corporate Video: [specify].

F.048

'The Film' shall be the film called [specify title] of [number] minutes in duration a copy of a brief summary and description is attached in Appendix A. Together with any appearances, contributions or material of any nature which may be incorporated including films, videos, sound recordings, voice and sound effects, music and lyrics, computer generated material, stills, performances, advertisements, product placement, merchandising, sponsorship, sculptures, paintings, buildings, transport, artists, persons, animals, or gadgets.

F.049

'The Archive Film' shall be a copy of the physical film material entitled [specify title/reference] which is [number] minutes in length which is controlled by the [Institute/Charity] but for which the copyright owner is either unknown and/or unconfirmed which is to be supplied to the [Company] under this agreement.

F.050

'The Banner Advertisement' shall be the film and sound recording known as [specify title] which can run for up to [number] minutes and be repeated indefinitely on the [web page/app]. It is linked to the [website/app reference] and when a person clicks on the film the connection opens to the linked [website/app].

F.051

'The Training Film' shall mean the reproduction and final edited version of the filming of the participants completing the requested tasks, interviews and other matters at the training day. The specific purpose of the training film is to illustrate and highlight the methods and techniques to be used to [specify].

F.052

'The Advertiser Funded Film' shall mean a film including sound recording entitled; [specify] which shall be [number] minutes in duration which is to be produced, edited and supplied to the [Product Distributor] by the [Production Company] which is in accordance with the Project Specifications in Appendix A and Budget set out in Appendix B which form part of this agreement.

F.053
'The Sponsored Film' shall mean the film and the sound recording which is [number] minutes in length to promote and market the [Charity/Festival/Enterprise] and their work with [specify subject] which is to be sponsored and funded by [specify sponsor] and to be produced by the [Company]. It is agreed that he [Charity/Festival/Enterprise] will own the copyright and all other intellectual property rights and interest in the Sponsored Film not the Company.

F.054
'The Short Film' shall mean the video, film and/or moving images of [number] minutes recorded by [Name] on [gadget] of the participants at the [Event] on [date] in [format] with the [slogan/title] [specify] in which the copyright, intellectual property rights and all other rights in [country] are owned entirely by [Name] and that [Name] was not prohibited from filming at the [Event] by the organisers and/or any other reason which would impact on the use of the material by the [Company].

F.055

1.1   The [Agent] agrees that there shall be no right to edit, adapt, add to and/or delete from any part of the [Film] and/or sound recording and/or to add any additional credits, acknowledgements, sounds, images, sub-titles, music, text, products, logos and/or recordings. The [Company] shall use and exhibit the [Film] at [location] in the exact form and sequence in which it is delivered by the [Artist].

1.2   The [Agent] agrees and undertakes not to authorise and/or permit any person and/or third party to take any photographs and/or film and/or other images of the [Film] during the exhibition.

F.056
'The Films' shall be the series of films supplied by the [Distributor] as set out in Schedule A which forms part of this Agreement to be transmitted by the [Company] on channel [specify name] in [specify language] in [country] under the theme [subject]

FIRST REFUSAL

General Business and Commercial

F.057
In consideration of the payments made under this Agreement the [Author] hereby grants to [Agent/Publisher] the exclusive right of first refusal with

respect to any subsequent literary work and/or novel of more than [number] words. Literary works produced by the [Author] of less than [number] words shall not apply.

F.058

'First refusal of the sequel' shall mean the obligation of the [Author] to provide an opportunity to the [Agent] to acquire the same or similar rights as those granted under this Agreement with respect to the next sequel of the [Work] and prior to the sequel being offered to any third party.

The [Agent] shall be under no obligation to acquire the sequel of the [Work]. The right of first refusal shall only apply to the first sequel not subsequent ones. The period of first refusal shall run for six weeks from the date that the [Agent] is first offered the sequel rights. If no terms are agreed and concluded in that period then the right of first refusal shall end.

F.059

The [Author] agrees to provide the [Publisher] with a limited right of first refusal with respect to his next literary work provisionally entitled [specify title] [the New Work] which is due to be completed in [draft form] by [date].

In consideration of the payment of [number/currency] upon full signature of this Agreement [which is a separate sum from the advance against royalties] the [Author] grants to the [Publisher] the following rights of first refusal in respect of the [New Work]:

1.1 That the [Author] shall provide the [Publisher] with a copy of the finished manuscript by [date] or by such later date that the [New Work] is completed.

1.2 That the [Publisher] shall have [one] month from the date of delivery of the finished manuscript to express interest in the [New Work] and to confirm that they wish to make an offer to publish the [New Work].

1.3 That the [Publisher] shall have [one] month from the date of delivery of the manuscript to make an offer to the [Author] of the proposed advance, royalties and terms for the publication of the [New Work] in [country].

1.4 The [Author] shall not be bound to accept any offer by the [Publisher] nor shall he/she be obliged to give any reasons for any rejection. The [Author] shall be entitled to agree any terms which he/she so decides are in his/her interests, and shall not be obliged to accept the same terms as this Agreement.

1.5 The [Publisher] agrees that all material and representations provided or made by the [Author] are in confidence and are not for distribution or reproduction to any parties or person other than [specify] without the prior written approval of the [Author].

F.060

1.1 The [Enterprise/Company/Charity] grants to the [Sponsor] the right of first refusal to sponsor the [Event/Festival/Race].

1.2 The right of first refusal shall commence on [date] and expire on [date].

1.3 In the event that the [Enterprise/Company/Charity] have not agreed in writing the main terms of an agreement for the sponsorship and product placement for the [Event/Festival/Race] during the period set out in 1.2 above. then the right of first refusal shall end.

1.4 The [Enterprise/Company/Charity] shall then be entitled to negotiate an agreement for the sponsorship and product placement at the [Event/Festival/Race] with any third party subject to 1.5 below.

1.5 Except that where the [Enterprise/Company/Charity] negotiate more favourable terms for an agreement with a third party that were not offered to the [Sponsor]. Then the [Enterprise/Company/Charity] shall be obliged under this agreement to offer such favourable terms to the [Sponsor] who shall have [seven] days to accept or reject such terms. In the event that the [Sponsor] does not reply within the [seven days] it shall be deemed to have rejected the terms. Unless the terms are accepted by the [Sponsor] within that period then the [Enterprise/Company/Charity] shall be entitled to conclude a sponsorship and product placement agreement with the third party.

F.061

1.1 The [Company] agrees that where it intends to transfer, assign and/or dispose of any rights of any nature and/or format in any medium to any third party. It shall first offer such rights to the [Distributor] by email and/or letter.

1.2 The [Distributor] shall have [one] month from the date of the written offer to accept the terms proposed by the [Company] and/or to make another offer.

1.3 If the parties cannot agree terms and/or the [Distributor] rejects the proposal and/or the alternative offer is refused. Then the [Company] shall be free to dispose of such rights to any third party.

1.4 Even where the [Company] offers better terms to a third party there shall be no obligation to offer those terms to the [Distributor] after the parties have failed to agree terms.

F.062

The [Licensor] agrees and undertakes to provide the [Licensee] with a right of first refusal in respect of all and/or some of the rights in the [Archive/Films/Artwork] if and when the [Licensor] decides at any time before [date] to dispose of, license, assign and/or transfer any copyright, intellectual property rights and/or any other interest to a third party.

F.063

1.1 [Name] agrees to provide the [Distributor] with the right of first refusal to make a satisfactory offer to market and exploit the next sequel of the [Book/Work/Product/Services] created, developed and written by [Name] which [Name] intends to make commercially available through a third party.

1.2 [Name] shall notify the [Distributor] of the copyright, intellectual property rights and other rights available and the format of the physical material. [Name] shall set a deadline of not less than [thirty] days for a written response and formal offer by the [Distributor]. If there is not an offer within the period specified or the offer by the [Distributor] is less than [number/currency] then the first refusal clause shall cease to apply and [Name] may offer the rights and material elsewhere.

F.064

This clause shall only apply from [date] to [date] and shall be limited to the subject of [specify] and shall not apply to [specify].

F.065

This first right of refusal shall only apply to the next subsequent [Film/Work/other] and not any other further work, rights or material whether on the same subject and/or theme or not.

F.066

This clause shall only apply to the [Company] and not any parent company, subsidiary or associated company.

F.067

The [Company] shall not acquire any option, first right of refusal and/or any right of renewal and/or other rights and/or interest under this Agreement.

F.068

1.1 Where a [Sponsor] has been the sole and exclusive company and/or person to pay for the funding and total cost of the [Project] and is to be acknowledged as the only contributor.

1.2   Then the [Sponsor] shall be provided with the opportunity to increase the funding in the event that additional funds are required at a later date by the [Company/Charity]. The [Sponsor] shall be permitted [one] month to refuse and/or to confirm that they will make the additional payments.

1.3   In the event that the [Sponsor] refuses the request further funding request in 1.2. Then the [Company] shall be allowed to seek funds elsewhere and to have an additional sponsor who is ranked below the first party in any promotional displays.

F.069

The [Distributor] shall not have any first right of refusal, option and/or any right, interest and/or claim over any rights which are reserved and/or any sequel and/or adaptation of the [Work/Product/Service] at any time.

F.070

1.1   In consideration of the sum of [number/currency] to the [Agent] of [Name] by [date]. [Name] agrees to grant the [Company] the right of first refusal to acquire and purchase the right to exploit the [Work/Product/Music] in [specify format] from [date] for a period of [five] years subject to the conclusion of a new agreement.

1.2   After payment of the fee in 1.1 the [Agent] and [Name] agrees to provide the [Company] with the detail of the proposed terms and conditions. The [Agent] and [Name] agree to permit the [Company] a period of [four] months to negotiate and conclude an agreement from the date of notification of the proposal.

1.3   If the parties cannot conclude and sign an agreement within the period of [four] months in 1.2. Then the [Agent] and [Name] shall be entitled to retain the fee in 1.1 and also offer the rights to any other third party. In the event that they change the rights and/or terms of the offer there shall be no obligation to provide another right of first refusal to the [Company] even if terms and conditions are more favourable than those offered in the proposal and/or during negotiations.

FORCE MAJEURE

Film, Television and Video

F.071

In the event the Agreement cannot be performed or its obligations fulfilled for any reason beyond the reasonable control of either party including war, industrial action, floods for a continuous period of [specify duration] and/or as a result of any Act of God which has created a scenario which has impacted severely on either party so that their business cannot function in the normal manner. Then either party may at its discretion terminate this Agreement by notice in writing of the circumstances of force majeure. Where no payments have been made and/or material delivered and/or created then the agreement shall leave each party in the same state as they entered the agreement in terms of liabilities. Where that is not the case and one party has paid over money and/or incurred costs and expenses in reliance upon the agreement. Then the parties agree to negotiate a settlement in respect of the end of the agreement. If that fails to enter into mediation with a paid mediator with the cost shared equally between the parties.

F.072

Neither party shall be liable to the other for any costs, expenses, losses and/or damages arising from its failure to perform its obligations under this Agreement for any reason whatsoever beyond its reasonable control.

F.073

In the event that this Agreement cannot be performed or its obligations fulfilled in whole and/or part for any reason beyond the reasonable control of one and/or both parties including war, industrial action, floods, hurricane, Act of God, blockades and marches, riots and lack of fuel and/or the failure of a supplier to deliver materials due to scarce availability. Then such failure to perform and/or fulfil its obligations by any such party relying on force majeure shall be deemed not to be a breach of this Agreement. Where this Agreement cannot be performed or its obligations fulfilled for any reason beyond either parties reasonable control for a continuous period of [number] [weeks/months]. Then at the end of that period either party shall have the right to terminate the agreement whether they are in default or not by notice in writing to terminate the agreement immediately.

F.074

Where the [Licensee] is prevented from fulfilling the terms of this Agreement and is unable to produce, manufacture, distribute and supply [DVDs/Units] of the [Film] for any reason beyond the control of the [Licensee]. Whether caused or due to an Act of God or other force majeure such as war, fire, earthquake, strike, lockout, death or incapacity of the artists and/or performers, labour dispute, civil commotion, act of any government, its agencies or officers, or any order, regulation or legislation, or any action by any union or trade association or by delays in the delivery of materials and supplies. The [Licensee] shall have the right by written notice to the [Licensor] and without liability to suspend the obligations of both parties and the terms of this Agreement until such time as the circumstances have changed and the parties can perform and carry out this Agreement. The parties agree that the Licence Period shall be extended by the period for which the Agreement was suspended and not fulfilled.

F.075

Notwithstanding anything contained in this Agreement, in the event that it is rendered impossible to perform by either party for any reason beyond its reasonable control which reasons may include, but are not be limited to, war, invasion, act of foreign enemy, hostilities (whether war be declared or not) civil war or strike, rebellion, lockouts or other industrial disputes or actions, Acts of God, acts of government or other prevailing authorities or defaults of third parties. Then such non-performance shall be deemed not to constitute a breach of this Agreement. If such an event occurs to the extent that the Agreement cannot be performed for a period of [four] months] or more then the [Company] shall have the right at its discretion to terminate this Agreement by notice in writing at the end of such period. If any of the events occurs in only a limited part of the Territory then the [Company] may decide at its discretion to terminate the Agreement in respect of those countries but not the rest of the unaffected countries.

F.076

The [Company] shall use its reasonable endeavours to fulfil orders accepted by it for the manufacture of videos and DVDs of the [Film] within a reasonable time of receipt thereof. Provided that the [Company] shall not be liable for any failure or delay in the fulfilment of any order or any parts resulting from any cause beyond the reasonable control of the [Company] which could not have reasonably been foreseen.

F.077

There shall be no right by either party to make any claim from the other party for damages, losses, costs and/or expenses which have been incurred and/or committed where the Agreement is suspended, terminated and/or not fulfilled due to any Act of God caused by storms, lightning, floods, hurricanes, snow, ice, low temperatures, earthquakes, landslides, sinkholes or other extreme catastrophes, fire, explosions and/or the failure of supply of equipment, machinery, ingredients, electricity, gas and solar power and/or any other energy resources and/or water.

F.078

The parties both agree that the following matters shall not be considered force majeure under this Agreement:

1.1 The failure to clear and/or pay for the necessary copyright, moral rights, waivers, licences and/or any other contracts and/or intellectual property rights and/or computer software and/or trade mark and/or service mark clearances and consents required from third parties.

1.2 Any failure due to poor maintenance, lack of security, the failure to comply with any legislation and/or health and safety matters which should have been assessed for risk and compliance and/or any other policies, guidelines and codes in force at the time.

1.3 Postal strikes, slow, interrupted and/or suspended internet service, website and/or app, the failure of any telecommunication system including mobile phones, landlines, and messaging services. Gridlocked traffic, heavy snow and rain, power failures and organised actions by activists creating blockades.

F.079

The [Licensee] agrees and undertakes that the following circumstances shall not constitute force majeure under this Agreement:

1.1 A suspension and/or failure of the internet, mobile phone service and telecommunication systems, electricity, gas, water and other resources [specify] in [countries] for less than [number] days.

1.2 A declaration of emergency measures by the government relating to water conservation relating to a potential drought.

1.3 The blockade of an airport, seaport and/or international trade route and/or suspension of transport by air, sea and/or rail for less than [number] days in [countries].

1.4 Any extreme weather conditions storms, lightning, flash floods, hurricane, snow and severe weather which does not endure for more than [number] days.

1.5 Any emergency water sprinkler damage, fire, smoke damage, water, electricity, gas and lighting problems which are at other premises and not the head office and factory of the [Company].

F.080

1.1 The [Company] shall not be entitled to rely on the force majeure term in this Agreement where any delays, errors, omissions, losses and/or damages have been and/or are caused by the fact that the [Company] failed to engage, use and enter into agreements with reputable and financially secure third parties. Where if the [Company] had carried out background checks it would have discovered and/or been aware that the third parties which have caused the problems were at risk of entering into administration and/or bankruptcy at the time.

1.2 In such circumstances as apply in 1.1 above the [Company] agrees that it shall be entirely liable for the payment of all the sums due to [Name] from such third parties who have defaulted in any manner. In addition the [Company] agrees to pay the any legal costs that may be incurred by [Name] and interest at [number] per cent from the date that any monies were originally due to be paid to [Name]. The [Company] accepts that it may not recoup such sums from any other payments due to [Name].

F.081
Force majeure shall not apply under this Agreement where there is a reasonable cost effective alternative method and/or route for the [Licensee] to follow which would resolve the issue. Provided that any changes shall be approved in advance by the [Licensor] and shall not involve the grant of additional rights and/or reduce the sums due to the [Licensor].

F.082
No party shall be liable for its inability to perform and/or delay in fulfilling any of its obligations pursuant to this agreement if it is caused by circumstances beyond the reasonable control of the party. The following matters shall be considered as factors beyond the reasonable control of either party provided that they have a direct affect on the reason for the failure to fulfil the obligations including but not limited to:

1.1 industrial action, riot, civil unrest, activist action, political action, governmental restrictions on movement and/or access, embargo, impact by an aircraft, lorry and car, criminal damage,

1.2 explosion, sinkhole, fire, storm, tempest, earthquake, typhoon, tidal wave, floods, lightning, an Act of God, gas leak, problems with drains and removal of waste, power failure of gas, electricity, water, heating and solar energy.

1.3 Lack of access to and/or failure of the systems relating to the internet, landlines and/or mobiles for data, customer details and/or other crucial information for a period of more than [24] hours at any one time where the business is severely disrupted and unable to carry out and/or perform its normal work and schedules.

F.083
The [Company] shall use all its reasonable endeavours to transmit the [Customer Material] at the times agreed with the [Customer] and otherwise comply with the terms of this Agreement. The [Company] shall be under no liability to the [Customer] and/or any third party in respect of the following circumstances:

1.1 Where the [Company] fails to make any transmission whether at the time specified and/or otherwise. In the event that there are any interruptions, delays, inaccuracies errors and/or omissions in the transmission of the [Customer Material].

1.2 If the [Company] is prevented for any reason from making the transmission to the [Customer] as a result of the termination of any agreements the [Company] may have with [organisation] and/or any government and/or statutory body for any reason which affects its right and authority to operate the service and/or to transmit material to the public.

1.3 If the [Company] fails to provide the service required under this agreement and/or to transmit the agreed [Customer Material] where such failure is directly and/or indirectly caused by an Act of God, malfunctioning and/or defective equipment, or any laws, order, regulation, or otherwise of any government, authority, international or statutory body and/or any emergency, war, strike, lockout, work stoppage, labour difficulty, extreme weather conditions, failure and/or interruption of power resources, disease, embargo and/or any other matter which is not with the reasonable control of the [Company] which could not have been anticipated and prevented by careful planning and maintenance.

1.4 Any failure which is directly attributable to the [Customer] whether deliberate, negligent and/or otherwise which affects the transmission and delivery of the [Customer Material] and/or the service at any time.

F.084

1.1 In the event that the development, production, delivery and/or exploitation of the [Film] and any associated sound recordings shall be prevented, interrupted and/or delayed by reason of fire, flood, casualty, lockout, strikes, labour problems, unavoidable accident, natural disaster, mechanical or other breakdown of electrical or sound equipment, failure or delay by a supplier, unforeseen problems with export or transport, Act of God, impact of any statutory provision and/or other legal requirement and/or any cause arising out of or attributed to war or by any other cause of any nature beyond the control of the [Licensor]. Then the obligations, undertakings and liability of the [Licensor] in respect of the [Film] and any associated sound recording shall be temporarily suspended for such period as may be necessary in order for the [Licensor] to be able to carry out and perform the terms of this agreement.

1.2 In such circumstances as set out in 1.1 above the [Licensee] agrees and undertakes that shall not be entitled to claim any costs, expenses, damages and/or losses from the [Licensor] for the temporary suspension of the fulfilment of the agreement nor shall the [Licensee] seek to cancel the agreement.

1.3 If the temporary suspension of the agreement should continue for more than [two] years. Then the parties agree that they shall enter into negotiations to resolve the matter amicably. If that is not successful then they agree to appoint a mediator of their joint choice and at their joint cost who will act as a liaison to bring the parties together to end the agreement and avoid litigation. If after mediation no solution is agreed then either party may at its discretion take such legal action as they think fit at their own cost.

1.4 The [Licensor] agrees to notify the [Licensee] by any method available of any proposed temporary suspension of the agreement and to state the grounds and reasons which apply and to endeavour to estimate the potential date by which the matter may be resolved.

F.085

1.1 If either the [Company] and/or the [Distributor] is unable to carry out, perform and/or deliver any obligations and/or service and/or material required under this Agreement due to an event, situation and/or series of factors which is and/or has been beyond their reasonable control which was not foreseeable and could not have been prevented.

1.2 Then if the matters in 1.1 occur the [Company] and/or the [Distributor] which is so affected and is unable to carry out their terms and obligations may give notice in writing to the other party to suspend agreement for a specified period and/or such other period as may be necessary in respect of the [Films]. The start date of the suspension shall be specified and the predicted end date. In the event that the end date of the suspension cannot be specified then the parties agree that the situation shall be reviewed after each [one] month period.

1.3 During the suspension the [Company] and the [Distributor] both agree to mitigate all costs and expenses in respect of the [Films].

1.4 If the suspension continues for [thirty] calendar months] or more then the [Distributor] shall be entitled to terminate the agreement by notice in working to the [Company]. The [Company] may then cease to produce the [Films]. The [Distributor] shall not then be obliged to pay any further sums to the [Company] other than those necessary to settle the sums owed up to the date of termination.

1.5 Upon such termination by the [Distributor] in 1.4 above all copyright, intellectual property and other rights in the [Films] whether completed or not shall revert to the [Company] and the [Distributor] shall not be entitled to any rights, interest, royalties and/or claim.

F.086

If the [Company's] services, business activities and delivery schedules are cancelled, restricted, prevented and/or changed by any legislation, licence, code, policy and/or legal action and/or any Act of God, event and/or circumstance beyond the [Company's] reasonable control. The [Company] shall have the choice as to whether to terminate this contract by notifying the [Agency/Advertiser]. Such termination shall be without prejudice to the [Company's] right to be paid by the [Agency/Advertiser] any sums which are due and/or owing at the date of termination.

F.087

In the event that the [Company] decides that due to unforeseen or unusual circumstances it is necessary to change the [Film] arrangements and/or the performances under this Agreement and/or there is some reason of force majeure which prevents the Agreement being fulfilled and/or any other cause beyond the reasonable control of the [Company]. Then the [Company] may immediately or at any time thereafter terminate this Agreement. Upon such termination the [Artist] shall not be entitled to any sums from the [Company] except for the payment of the fees in respect of the work carried out up to the date of termination.

F.088

Neither of the parties shall be responsible and/or liable to the other and/or obliged to provide any indemnity for any losses, damages, costs and/or expenses incurred and/or committed whether directly and/or indirectly which arise from its failure to perform and/or carry out any of its obligations in any clause in this Agreement by reason of any cause whatsoever beyond its reasonable control which is due to force majeure.

F.089

If the [Company] is prevented from starting the production of the [Programmes] and/or the production and/or delivery is delayed and/or interrupted at any time due to an event or circumstances beyond the reasonable control of the [Company]. It is agreed that in those circumstances the [Company] shall not be liable for any losses, damages, costs and expenses (either direct or indirect) or otherwise that the [Contractor] may incur and/or be liable for as a result of the [Company's] failure to fulfil the terms of this Agreement. This shall include, but not be limited to, fire, or other disaster, withdrawal of labour and/or other services (overtime ban, work to rule) industrial dispute, withdrawal or interruption of public or power services, illness, incapacity and/or death of key personnel. Provided that any such event was not due to the neglect of the [Company] and/or was not reasonably foreseeable at the date of this Agreement.

F.090

1.1 Notwithstanding any other term of this Agreement if either the [Company] and/or the [Distributor] for any cause beyond its reasonable control cannot perform this Agreement. Then such non-performance by either party shall not be a breach of this Agreement. If any such event occurs to prevent the performance of this Agreement for a period in excess of [four] months by either party. This Agreement may then be terminated at the end of such period by notice in writing by the [Company] and/or the [Distributor].

1.2 If the [Company] is unable to broadcast/transmit the [Film/Video] for any reason beyond its reasonable control then the Licence Period shall be extended for such period as may be necessary to enable it to be broadcast/transmitted but in any event the Licence Period shall not be extended beyond [date].

F.091

The parties both agree that the following circumstances shall not be considered force majeure under this Agreement:

1.1 A fire which is contained and which does not prevent the operation of the main business of the [Company] from the premises.

1.2 An industrial dispute which is in arbitration and/or mediation.

1.3 Failure and/or suspension of gas, electricity, water for less than [two] days.

1.4 The removal and/or suspension of [Name].

1.5 Breakdown and/or maintenance of equipment.

1.6 Failure to comply with health and safety legislation.

1.7 Blockades, riots, activist actions, supply problems for material and/or any other matter which is for less than [two] days.

F.092

Where the parties cannot agree whether the circumstances constitute force majeure or not. It is agreed that the parties will put all the facts to an independent person whom both parties agree to share the cost of in order to reach a non-binding view of the issue. This shall be without prejudice of the right of either party to issue legal proceedings for breach of contract.

F.093

1.1 It is agreed between the parties that it shall be deemed that the Agreement has been subject to force majeure where filming cannot take place due to disease, risk of contamination with radioactive material, landslides, mudslides, flooding from rivers, lightening, snow, ice, tornadoes, typhoons, drought, heatwave, riots, threats of outbreaks of violence and/or terrorist attacks and/or war, military occupation, fires, kidnaps of civilians, looting and/or political campaigns and/or other threats and/or lack of resources which would pose a risk to health and/or safety of any person associated with the [Project] at any time.

1.2 It is agreed that the [Project] may be delayed for up to [number] months and thereafter any party shall have the right to serve notice that the [Project] must either go ahead as planned and/or be ended upon terms to be agreed between the parties.

F.094
It is agreed that the [Licensee] shall not be entitled to rely on force majeure of any kind in order to delay payment and/or transfer of any sums to the [Licensor] under this Agreement.

General Business and Commercial

F.095
Force majeure shall mean any circumstances beyond the reasonable control of either of the parties which impact on the fulfilment of the agreement to the other party and shall include but not be limited to the following matters:

1.1 War, hostilities whether war be declared or not, invasion, incursion by armed forces, bombs and explosions, act of hostile army, nation or enemy on land, sea and in the air. The attempted eradication of indigenous population and/or restrictions on the native population which infringes their human rights as recognised by [specify organisation] including imprisonment without trial.

1.2 Riot, uprising against constituted authority, civil commotion, disorder, rebellion, organised armed resistance to the government, insurrection, revolt, military or usurped power, civil war and activists action on political and global issues. Chemical, nuclear or other warfare, insurgence, attack and/or accident.

1.3 Acts which hinder the course of or stop, hinder, prevent, interrupt and/or breach the production, development, supply and/or provision and/or distribution and/or delivery of any material, service, power and/or resource which is required under this Agreement.

1.4 Any hazardous, dangerous, perilous, unsafe chemical, substance, material, property, use and/or adaptation which threatens and/or poses a risk to the health of any person.

1.5 Acts of God, epidemics, disease, floods, fire, arson, storm, lightning, tempest, typhoon, hurricane, earthquake, landslides, avalanches, acts of terrorism, hijacking,

1.6 Damage to computers, software, equipment, machinery, master material or property through viruses, hackers, sabotage, vandalism, and/or other criminal acts which destroy, erase and/or manipulate material and content.

1.7 Death, injury and/or long term illness of key personnel [specify].

F.096

In the event that this Agreement cannot be performed or its obligations fulfilled for any reason beyond the reasonable control of either party to this Agreement as a result of such events as war, industrial action, floods or Acts of God. Then such non-performance or failure to fulfil its obligations by any such party shall be deemed not to be a breach of this Agreement.

F.097

No party to this Agreement shall be held in any way responsible for any failure to fulfil its obligations under this Agreement if such failure has been caused (directly or indirectly) by circumstances beyond the reasonable control of the defaulting party. This shall include accident or equipment failure, war, riot, industrial action and/or act of terrorism (except where such accident or equipment failure has been caused by the negligence of the defaulting party, its employees, sub-licensees, sub-contractors, agents or otherwise).

F.098

1.1 In the event that the reason this Agreement cannot be carried out, performed and/or the material delivered and/or the sums paid which is due to any reason beyond the reasonable control of either party for a continuous period of [three] months.

1.2 Then the party which has not defaulted may at its discretion decide to terminate the Agreement by notice in writing after the expiry of the [three] month period in 1.1. If this Agreement is in fact terminated then both parties shall agree a fair and reasonable payment for the work completed up to the date of termination taking into account any prior contractual commitments entered into in reliance on the performance of this Agreement.

F.099

Neither party shall be liable to the other for delay in and/or failure to perform any of its obligations under this contract due to force majeure. For the purposes of this contract force majeure shall mean causes which are unpredictable and beyond the reasonable control of the party claiming force majeure which could not have been avoided or prevented by reasonable foresight, planning and implementation.

F.100

Notwithstanding anything contained in this Agreement, in the event of this Agreement being rendered impossible of performance by either party for any reason beyond its reasonable control (including, but not limited to, war, invasion, act of foreign enemy, hostilities, whether war be declared or not, civil war or strife, rebellion, strikes, lockout or other industrial dispute or actions, Acts of God, acts of government or other prevailing authorities or defaults of third parties), then such non-performance shall be deemed not to constitute a breach of this Agreement.

F.101

If in the opinion of the [Licensor] the performance of this Agreement shall for reasons arising from state of war, civil commotion, lockout, strike, industrial action, breakdown of equipment, natural disaster or other abnormal circumstances become impractical or if the complete performance of the Agreement shall be prevented by force majeure or any other cause beyond the reasonable control of the [Licensor] or the [Licensee]. Then the [Licensor] may decide that it must serve notice to the [Licensee] to terminate the Agreement immediately. If the Agreement is terminated by the [Licensor] accepts that the [Licensee] shall have no claim on the [Licensor] for remuneration, expenses, costs, damages, losses or otherwise except for such proportion of the total fees as may already have been paid by the [Licensee] to the [Licensor] under the terms of this Agreement which should be refunded immediately.

F.102

1.1 No responsibility and/or liability is accepted by the [Organisers/Enterprise] in the event of the delay in starting, postponement, cancellation and/or any restrictions in respect of the [Exhibition/Event/Festival] as a result of circumstances beyond the reasonable control of the [Organisers/Enterprise] which constitutes force majeure.

1.2 No responsibility and/or liability can be accepted for any hotel, accommodation, train, car and/or aeroplane bookings you may make and pay for in reliance upon the [Exhibition/Event/Festival]. You make such bookings at your own risk and cost and cannot seek any indemnity and/or contribution from the [Organisers/Enterprise].

1.3 Force majeure shall include extreme weather forecasts which would pose a risk to the public and exhibitors, artists and performers at the [[Exhibition/Event/Festival]. As well as refusal of public liability insurance by and/or alcohol licences from third parties, withdrawal of sponsorship by main contributors to the costs, cancellation of appearances of the main leading performers and/or artists, transport and/or catering issues by third parties which would result in the failure to carry out sufficient preparations for the [Exhibition/Event/Festival]. Inadequate and/or the malfunction of waste disposal units and/or other recycling and/or security preparations due to unforeseen circumstances.

F.103
None of the parties to this Agreement shall be under any liability to the others or any other party in respect of anything which may constitute a breach of this Agreement arising by reason of force majeure. Force majeure shall include all circumstances beyond the control of the parties including, but not limited to, the following events: Acts of God, perils of the sea or air, fire, flood, explosion, sabotage, accident, embargo, riot, civil commotion, invasion, epidemic, drought, earthquake, volcano eruption, blizzard and landslides.

F.104
Notwithstanding any other provision of this Agreement to the contrary neither party shall be liable to the other for any failure to perform this Agreement which is due to an Act of God, accident, fire, lockout, strike, labour dispute, riot, civil commotion, failure of technical facilities and/or services, compliance with legislation, orders and declarations by national and/or local government and/or police and/or emergency services and the armed forces and/or the failure of electricity, gas and/or other power facilities and/or any other matters of any nature beyond the reasonable control of either party which be deemed force majeure.

F.105
If either the [Company] and/or the [Distributor] is prevented and/or delayed in the actions, steps and obligations required under this contract due to factors which amount to force majeure. The party in default and/or both parties if applicable shall deliver written notice to the other party specifying the detail of the reasons for the circumstances of force majeure and provide such supporting evidence as may be available. In addition any party in default shall provide an estimate of the period for which it is expected that the delay or otherwise shall continue. In these circumstances neither the party in default nor the other party shall be liable for the terms of the contract which cannot be completed for any reason from the date on which the

circumstances regarding force majeure came into effect until the contract is fulfilled and/or terminated.

F.106

The [Company] shall not be under any liability if by reason of abnormal circumstances beyond its control it is unable to hold the [Conference/Event]. These circumstances shall include but not be limited to, strikes, lockout, labour troubles, fire, explosions, civil disturbances, riots, gas leaks, electrical or other power breakdowns, failure of health and safety assessments and tests, epidemic, disease, and outbreaks of illness, failure of the waste disposal and water system, floods and extreme weather conditions and warnings, occupation for emergencies by the fireman, army, police and/or medical services.

F.107

If this Agreement cannot be performed and/or its obligations fulfilled for any reason beyond the reasonable control of the [Licensor] and/or the [Licensee] including such events as war, industrial action, Acts of God, explosions, marches and action by activists which create blockades and/or affect the transport system and/or motorways and/or airports and/or ports, snow, ice, hailstones, earthquakes, tornadoes, hurricanes, floods, mudslides and extreme weather and other incidents on land, sea and in the air. Such failure to perform and/or fulfil its obligations by the defaulting party in circumstances which amount to force majeure shall not to be a breach of this Agreement. Where the default continues for a period of [two] consecutive months then the other non-defaulting party may at its discretion terminate this Agreement by notice in writing at the end of that period.

F.108

Neither party shall be responsible to the other party in circumstances where the obligations under this Agreement cannot be performed or carried out due to matters or conditions outside the control of the [Assignee] or the [Assignor]. In the event that this Agreement is not fulfilled or performed by [date] then this Agreement shall automatically end on that date.

F.109

In the event that this Agreement cannot be fulfilled by either party due to force majeure which is beyond their reasonable control both parties agree that the whole but not part of the agreement can be suspended for one continuous period of [duration] by written notice by either party who is so affected. If after that period of suspension the situation continues so that the agreement is still prevented from being fulfilled then both parties agree to bring the agreement to an end as soon as possible by negotiating a settlement.

F.110

Where circumstances are such that a party to this Agreement is prevented from fulfilling their obligations and responsibilities due to force majeure which is beyond their reasonable control and which could not have been reasonably expected and/or predicted. Then it is agreed that such party shall be provided with an additional period of [number] days to comply. If the matter cannot be resolved within that period then the other parties shall have the right to terminate, cancel and/or amend the Agreement as they think fit in order to resolve the matter and this shall include the right to demand a repayment of all and/or some of the sums paid to date.

Internet, Websites and Apps

F.111

1.1 Where the [Company] is unable to provide all the [Service/Work/ Products] specified in this agreement for any reason due to circumstances beyond its reasonable control which constitute force majeure. Then the [Company] may at its sole discretion decide to suspend, delay and/or cancel the development, production and/or delivery of the [Service/Work/ Products].

1.2 Where the [Company] relies upon 1.1 above and suspends, delays and/or cancels the agreement. The parties agree that the [Company] shall not be liable to pay to the [Customer] any additional sums in compensation and/or as damages and/or for expenses and/or costs which may be incurred. The total liability of the [Company] shall be to return all and/or part of the sums received where the [Service/Work/ Products] have not been supplied and/or delivered to the [Customer].

F.112

1.1 Where circumstances attributable to force majeure result in difficulties and/or failure to deliver the requested [materials/service/products]. The [Website/App Company] shall have the right to terminate the Agreement without notice and to only be liable to pay back to the [Customer/Charity] the sums paid.

1.2 The [Website/App Company] shall not be liable to the [Customer/ Charity] and/or any associated business and/or enterprise for the cost and expense of any equipment and/or software that may have been purchased from third parties in reliance upon this agreement. No additional charges, penalties, interest, damages, losses, and/or other claims shall be valid and/or allowed.

1.3 Force majeure shall include but not be limited to telecommunication, internet and power failure such as gas, electricity and water, software and equipment failure, accident, fire, lockout, strike, industrial action, labour dispute, riot, civil commotion, failure of technical and payment facilities, war, invasions, riots, blockades on roads, port and/or airports, drought, an explosion, sabotage, epidemic, the imposition of a curfew, action by activists which disrupts transport services and infrastructure.

F.113

1.1 The [Company] shall not be liable to the [Client] in the event that this Agreement cannot be performed or its obligations fulfilled for any reason beyond the reasonable control of the [Company] which can be interpreted as being directly relevant to the fulfilment of the agreement and amount to force majeure. Provided that the matter could not have reasonably been foreseen and that there were no reasonable steps that the [Company] could have taken to avoid the problem that has arisen.

1.2 The interpretation of force majeure in 1.1 shall include but not be limited to the following catastrophic extremes of weather, hurricane, typhoon, monsoon, storm, flooding due to rain and high tides and dams failing; Acts of God, riots, war, threat of invasion and/or attack by armed forces and/or air raid and/or nuclear attack on land, sea and/or air. National strikes, epidemic, disease, severe disruption of power supplies due to national disaster and/or power failures of gas, lighting, heat, electricity and/or other services.

F.114
The parties agree that the following situations shall not be deemed to fulfil the requirements of force majeure under this agreement:

1.1 Electricity, gas, water, heating and/or lighting, landline, mobile, telecommunication systems, internet, website and/or app interrupted, suspended and/or inaccessible for less than [number] [hours/days].

1.2 Equipment and/or software failure and/or defect where another can be substituted and/or purchased.

1.3 Any personal injury and accident which occurs as a result of the failure to comply with health and safety legislation and/or codes of conduct and/or any risk assessment not carried out when legally required.

1.4 Any fine, penalty, charge and/or other legal proceedings by a government body and/or constitutes a criminal act and/or relates to a county court claim and/or other civil proceedings.

1.5 Any other failure to comply with any legislation, regulation and/or other code and/or guidelines that may be applicable.

F.115

The parties agree that no reliance shall be placed by either party on force majeure without strong evidence that the fact disclosed is the reason for the failure to perform and fulfil the terms of this Agreement. The parties agree that the following situations shall not constitute force majeure:

1.1 Street riots, protests and/or disorder which last for less than [number] days.

1.2 The suspension and/or interruption of electricity, gas, water and/or the internet for less than [number] days.

1.3 The non-delivery of the materials required from a third party due to an embargo, blockade and/or other interruption to the ports and/or airports for less than [number] days.

1.4 The termination of the contract of employment of the Chief Executive of the [Company] and/or any other senior employees in the management.

1.5 A third party supplier cancels and/or terminates a supply contract upon which the [Company] relies upon for this agreement but another supplier is substituted within [one] month.

1.6 A sub-licensee cancels and/or terminates a sub-licence agreement with the [Company] which relates to this agreement.

F.116

Where a situation arises where one party seeks to rely on force majeure as the reason for the delay and/or failure to fulfil all and/or part of the Agreement. The parties agree that the defaulting party shall specify the reason in writing and offer the other party the right to accept the terms offered and/or receive a full refund of all payments which relate to the unfulfilled work.

F.117

Force Majeure shall not include:

1.1 Attacks, scams, viruses, hacks, fraud and security breaches by third parties.

1.2 The failure to register any domain name, copyright, trade mark and/or other rights and/or interest under this agreement.

1.3 The failure to comply with and/or delays in making payments in respect of custom, border control and other duties, taxes and costs and/or compliance government legislation, regulation and policies.

F.118

1.1 The [Company] shall be entitled at any time to rely on grounds of force majeure and other circumstances beyond its reasonable control which means that the [Service/Work/Products] may be cancelled, terminated, delayed, suspended and/or otherwise changed and/or substituted depending on the situation.

1.2 The [Company] agrees to notify [Name] of the fact that it has decided to rely on force majeure based on the circumstances. The [Company] shall inform [Name] as to the options available to [Name] as to what the [Company] can now provide.

1.3 Subject to 1.1 and 1.2 the [Company] and [Name] agree to reach a financial settlement based on the facts and [the [Company] agrees to repay to [Name] any sums paid for any [Service/Work/Products] which have not been provided to [Name]. [Name] agrees that the total liability of the [Company] in such situation shall be limited to [number/currency].

Merchandising and Distribution

F.119
No party shall be held in any way responsible for any failure to fulfil the obligations if such failure has been caused directly by circumstances beyond the reasonable control of the defaulting party. This shall include accident, equipment failures, war, riot, industrial action, terrorism. The defaulting party shall notify the other party as soon as possible and propose a cause of action and delay which the other party must accept if the situation is to be remedied within [duration] or may reject if a longer period is envisaged.

F.120
No party shall be liable to the other for any losses, damages, costs and expenses arising from the suspension, delay and/or failure to carry out all or part of the terms that it is required to fulfil under this Agreement for any cause whatsoever which is beyond the reasonable control of that party and could not have been foreseen and/or expected when the agreement was signed.

F.121
In the event that this Agreement cannot be performed and/or its obligations fulfilled for any reason beyond the reasonable control of the [Licensor] and/or the [Licensee] including war, hostilities, strikes, Acts of God, natural disasters, fire, breakdown of equipment not caused by negligence and/or neglect. Then this Agreement may be suspended by notice in writing of the defaulting party to the other party in whole and/or part up to a period of [number] months. Thereafter either the [Licensor] and/or the [Licensee] may terminate this Agreement (whether they have defaulted or not) by notice in writing subject to the agreement of an equitable settlement between the

884

parties based on the sums paid and/or the terms fulfilled to the date of termination.

F.122

In the event that the [Company] and/or the [Distributor] cannot perform and/or carry out their obligations under this Agreement due to factors and conditions which could not have been expected and which are outside the control of one and/or both parties then the following terms shall apply:

1.1 Where the [Company] and/or the [Distributor] is and/or are unable to perform and/or carry out all and/or some of the terms. Then such defaulting party and/or parties must notify the other party promptly. The notice must state the circumstances for such force majeure and the problems and the estimated time required to remedy the matter and complete the agreement.

1.2 Where one party has not defaulted then they shall have the choice to serve notice of termination of the agreement if they receive notice of delay, suspension and/or complete failure to perform and/or carry out the agreement by the other party.

1.3 Both parties agree that they shall endeavour to reach an amicable settlement to resolve the matter and reach a financial settlement.

F.123

1.1 The [Licensee] shall not be entitled to rely on a matter of force majeure for the failure to pay the [Licensor] any payments which have accrued under this Agreement.

1.2 The [Licensee] agrees that where funds cannot be transferred for any reason from a third party from which the [Licensor] is due a royalty. That the [Licensee] shall bear the cost and pay the [Licensor] the sum owed and then seek to recover the sums from the third party.

F.124

The parties agree that the following facts shall not be deemed force majeure and shall be excluded [specify].

F.125

1.1 Where the [Licensee] and/or any sub-agent, sub-distributor and/or other third party seeks to rely on grounds of force majeure for any reason. Then it is agreed by the [Licensee] that the [Licensor] shall not be obliged to permit any delay to extend beyond [number] months from the date of the first notification of the issue.

1.2   That thereafter the [Licensee] agrees that the [Licensor] may take such steps as it thinks fit to remedy and/or resolve the matter including but not limited to terminating the licence to the [Licensee] and any such sub-agent, sub-distributor and/or third party.

F.126

It is agreed between the parties that force majeure shall include:

1.1   Failure to pass the health and safety and product tests for [subject].

1.2   Delays in processing applications and authorisations by [organisation].

1.3   Smoke and sprinkler damage, fire, floods, nuclear war, invasion, declaration of war, riots, earthquake, tornados, monsoon, tidal wave and Acts of God.

1.4   Failure, suspension, interruption and/or damage to air conditioning, storage facilities and/or the supply for water, electricity, gas, coal, solar power and other sources of energy and fuel.

F.127

If the delivery of the [Material] and/or the performance of the terms of this Agreement are delayed and/or prevented by circumstances beyond the reasonable control of the [Assignor] and/or the [Assignee] where the facts can reasonably be held to amount to force majeure. Then such delivery and/or performance shall be deemed suspended and shall not be a breach of the agreement. However if the suspension continues for more than [number] days and the [Material] is not delivered and/or the terms performed. Then the agreement may be terminated by the [Assignor] and/or [Assignee] by notice in writing subject to a settlement document. Provided that it is agreed that the [Assignor] must be paid the sum in clause [–] if the [Material] has been delivered to the [Assignee]. That the [Assignee] cannot refuse to pay any future royalties to the [Assignor] where the [Material] has been delivered.

F.128

If the ability of the [Company] to accept delivery of the [Goods] and/or the provision or performance of services is delayed, hindered or prevented by circumstances beyond the reasonable control of the [Company]. Such delivery and/or provision or performance shall be suspended and if it cannot be carried out within a reasonable time after the due date then it shall be cancelled by notice in writing by the [Company] to the [Client].

F.129

1.1   Neither party shall be liable for any consequential loss to the other for failure to perform any of their obligations under this Agreement for reasons outside their control.

1.2 If for any such reason the [Supplier] ceases to be able to make available any further [Products] then the [Purchaser's] obligation to make further payments pursuant to this Agreement shall be suspended.

1.3 The suspension in 1.2 shall continue until such time as the [Supplier] is able to supply the [Products] whereupon payments by the [Purchaser] shall be resumed. The amount due to the [Supplier] in the Contract shall be adjusted to reflect the period of suspension and the quantity of the [Product] affected.

F.130

In the event that one or both parties cannot perform and/or fulfil the obligations under this Agreement due to conditions which are outside the control of one and/or both parties the following terms shall then become applicable:

1.1 One or both parties who are in default shall promptly give notice to that effect to the other party stating in detail the circumstances for such force majeure and the estimated time to remedy such event.

1.2 Then the defaulting party or both parties if relevant may only serve notice of the end of this Agreement specifying an end date if the situation continues for a period of [two] months from the date on which notification was received.

1.3 Both parties agree that in the event they shall reach an amicable settlement to resolve the matter. Each party shall bear its own losses, costs and expenses. Except that the [Seller] shall pay for all units of the [Products] which have already been delivered. The [Supplier] shall not be under any obligation to buy back products already supplied or to replace damaged and/or lost stock.

F.131

1.1 Neither party shall be liable to the other party for any losses, damages, costs, expenses, materials and/or other matters arising from third party agreements and/or licences and/or other arrangements concluded in reliance on this agreement. Where this agreement cannot be carried out and/or performed in whole and/or part due to factors which can reasonably be considered as force majeure which prevent, hinder and/or disrupt the business of either party and/or their suppliers.

1.2 Under this agreement it is agreed that the following events can be accepted as examples of force majeure: port embargoes, road blockades, fire, blizzard, tornado, hurricane, landslide, sinkhole, contamination of water resources, power and transmission failures for internet, electricity, gas and mobile phones.

1.3   If the factors in 1.1 and 1.2 prevent the agreement being progressed and performed for more than [number] weeks. Then the non-defaulting party may terminate this Agreement by notice in writing and both parties agree to negotiate in good faith an amicable resolution of this matter.

F.132

1.1   Where it is clear that an event has taken place which amounts to force majeure which impacts on the terms of this agreement and prevents either party from performing and complying with its obligations. There shall be no obligation by either party to give notice of force majeure at any time.

1.2   If the agreement is temporarily interrupted and/or suspended due to the force majeure in 1.1. It shall not be a breach of the agreement by either party.

1.3   Where the force majeure circumstances mean that it is unlikely that the agreement will be fulfilled and/or performed within [six] months. Then both parties may mutually resolve to end the agreement. Provided that all work and/or services so far completed and/or material delivered are paid for by the other party. There shall also be financial remuneration for any costs and expenses incurred in reliance upon the agreement by either party up to a fixed sum of [number/currency].

F.133

The parties agree that the following shall not be deemed and/or accepted as circumstances which constitute force majeure:

1.1   The temporary ill-health of the [Author] for less than [number] weeks.

1.2   The closure of the [Publisher's] offices due to fire, flood and/or terrorist action.

1.3   The printers being placed in administration, receivership and/or unable to operate and/or deliver the finished published product of the [Work].

1.4   The loss of the manuscript on the hard drive of the computer of the [Author].

1.5   The death and/or incapacity of the subject of the [Work] where the interviews, sound recordings and filming of the subject have already been concluded.

F.134

Where the parties are unable to agree as to whether a particular circumstance and/or event constitutes force majeure or not. It is agreed that an independent person shall be appointed who is a member of the [specify body] who shall review all of the written arguments of both sides. The parties both agree to share equally the cost of the independent person and to endeavour to reach a settlement based on their decision prior to the commencement of any legal proceedings.

F.135

The delivery date for the [Products] is not adjustable and where force majeure and/or any other circumstances delay delivery and/or result in the [Products] not being produced at all. The [Client] has the right to terminate the Agreement and to obtain a full refund of all payments made to date. The [Company] shall not be entitled to deduct and/or recoup and/or charge for any costs incurred.

Publishing

F.136

'Force Majeure' shall mean any Act of God including, but not limited to, fire, flood, earthquake, storm or other natural disaster, war, invasion, act of foreign enemies, hostilities (whether war be declared or not), civil war, rebellion, revolution, insurrection, military or usurped power or confiscation, nationalisation, requisition, destruction or damage to property by or under the order of any government or public or local authority or imposition of government sanction, embargo or similar action: law, judgment, order, decree, blockade, labour dispute, strike, lockout, boycott, interruption or failure of electricity, gas, water or telephone service; failure of the supply of any equipment, machinery or material required by the [Publisher] for publication of the [Work]; breach of contract by any key personnel or any other matter or cause beyond the reasonable control of the [Publisher].

F.137

1.1 In the event that the obligations, responsibilities and terms set out in this agreement cannot for any reason beyond the reasonable control of the [Author] and/or the [Publisher] be carried out either temporarily and/or permanently and/or are interrupted and/or suspended on grounds which constitute force majeure. Then any such delay, problem and/or other matter shall be deemed not to be a breach of this agreement provided that it has significant impact on the agreement.

1.2 Both the [Author] and the [Publisher] agree that grounds of force majeure in 1.1 shall include the ill-health of the [Author], disease, riots, war, industrial action, floods and/or Acts of God.

1.3 Where the delay and/or default continues for more than [one] year. Then the party who has not defaulted may terminate this Agreement by notice in writing at the end of that period. Both parties agree to negotiate in good faith an equitable settlement taking into account the agreed reversion of intellectual property rights and copyright in the [Work] in all media to the [Author] and the sums paid by the [Publisher] to the date of termination.

F.138

Neither party shall be liable to the other for any loss, damage, compensation or expenses arising from its failure to perform its obligations under this Agreement for any cause whatsoever beyond its reasonable control.

F.139

1.1 Neither the [Author] nor the [Publisher] shall be liable for any loss or damage suffered or incurred by the other arising directly or indirectly from its failure to carry out, fulfil or perform any of its obligations under this Agreement of any nature. Provided that such events or circumstances shall be due to matters which were not reasonably foreseeable at the date of this Agreement, and/or were not due to the neglect or deliberate act of such party and/or were due entirely to an event or circumstance of force majeure.

1.2 The party affected in 1.1 shall use its best endeavours to immediately rectify the position and advise and write to the other party explaining the reason for the situation. The defaulting party shall provide an estimate of the delay or interruption and propose a date by which it is anticipated that the position will be rectified.

1.3 In the event that the matter relates to the failure by the [Publisher] to publish the [Work] then this clause shall not relieve the [Publisher] of his obligation to pay the [Author] all the advance in full and to agree a settlement for the loss of royalties from the exploitation of the [Work] and the enhancement of the [Author's] reputation.

F.140

In the event that due to unforeseen or unusual circumstances it is necessary to delete, change or alter the interview arrangements, photographs, headline or advertising or the publication dates. Then it is agreed that the agreement may be entirely suspended for [duration] and the relevant dates adjusted accordingly to a later period up to a date no later than [date]. After that time either party may at its discretion terminate this Agreement without prejudice to any rights and remedies either may have in respect of the agreement.

F.141

In the event that the [Publisher] does not publish the [Work] of the [Author] for any reason due to force majeure. Then the [Author] shall have the right to serve notice on the [Publisher] at any time to terminate the Agreement and subject to the repayment of the [Advance] to have all rights and all material revert to, assigned to and be owned by the [Author] and for all rights held by the [Publisher] to be terminated without any additional payment.

F.142
Where the [Distributor] is unable to reproduce, publish, distribute and supply the [Work] for any reason beyond its control for a period of [three] calendar months. Then the [Author] shall have the right to serve notice on the [Distributor] that unless the [Work] is made available to the public within [two] calendar months and not less than [number] copies. Then all rights shall revert to the [Author] and shall be assigned back by the [Distributor]. The [Distributor] agrees that the [Author] shall not be obliged to pay any sums for such reversion of rights. The [Distributor] also agrees to provide at the [Distributors] cost any manuscript, printers ready copy and any other material held by and/or under the control of the [Distributor] relating to the [Work].

F.143
For the purpose of this agreement force majeure shall include:

1.1 The failure and/or destruction and/or damage to the laptop, computer, storage devices and/or other material of the [Author] which prevents and/or delays delivery of the [Work].

1.2 Ill health and/or disability which results in the [Author] being unable to write, edit and deliver the [Work] by the deadline.

1.3 The failure of the internet for more than [one] day.

1.4 Failure to deliver the [Work] in written form by freight and/or postal delivery due to strikes, power failures, crime and/or destruction of any building and/or property.

Services

F.144
If a condition of force majeure is declared by either party and continues for a period of at least [ten] consecutive days. Then either party may cancel the provision of the services and terminate this Contract] by [seven] days' written notice to the other party.

F.145
Force majeure shall include: Acts of God, war (declared or undeclared), insurrections, hostilities, strikes (other than strikes by the parties' employees which shall be decreed not to be a force majeure event), lockouts (other than lockouts by parties of its employees which shall be decreed not to be

a force majeure event) riots, fire, storm, government intervention and any other matter beyond the reasonable control of the [Company/Enterprise].

F.146

1.1 Any party which is unable in whole or part to carry out its obligations under this contract shall promptly give written notice to that effect to the other party stating in detail the circumstances for such force majeure and the estimated time to remedy such event.

1.2 Any party claiming force majeure shall diligently use all reasonable efforts to remove the cause of such force majeure, and shall give written notice to the other party when the force majeure has ended and shall resume performance of any suspended obligations as soon as possible.

F.147

1.1 Where events and/or factors occur and/or any Act of God which have an immediate impact on the business of the [Licensor] and/or [Licensee] and/or this agreement which they could control and/or predict and/or could not been foreseen at the time of the signature of this agreement. Then any default, non-performance and/or failure of its obligations by either party shall be deemed not to be a breach of this Agreement where it is based on grounds of force majeure.

1.2 For the purpose of this agreement force majeure shall include but not be limited to extreme weather conditions, invasion, riots and war, blockades and embargoes. disease and epidemics, breach of health and safety legislation by suppliers which results in cancellation of delivery of materials and content, fraud, scams and viruses, loss of data, errors and omissions in data and software, contamination of water supplies, floods and failure and/or contamination of production processes.

1.3 In the event that this Agreement cannot be performed and/or its obligations fulfilled beyond the reasonable control of the [Licensor] or the [Licensee] for a continuous period of [three] months]. Then the party who has not defaulted and/or both parties or if both are affected may terminate this Agreement by notice in writing at the end of that period.

1.4 If this Agreement is terminated then both parties shall agree a fair and reasonable payment for the work completed up to the date of termination. This payment shall take into account any prior contractual commitments entered into in reliance of the performance of this Agreement.

F.148

1.1 Neither party shall be responsible to the other party in circumstances where the obligations under this Agreement cannot be performed due to circumstances outside the reasonable control of the defaulting party.

1.2 However if such circumstances persist for more than [five] working days the non-defaulting party or either if both are affected may terminate this agreement in writing subject to the proposal of a reasonable settlement which takes account of the work completed and/or the products delivered to date and offers a small sum in compensation of no more than [number/currency].

F.149

1.1 In the event that this Agreement cannot be performed or fulfilled in respect of some significant or major part due to any reason beyond the control of either party including war, industrial action, floods, Acts of God. Then the failure to carry out such work or deliver any material shall be deemed not to be a breach of this Agreement.

1.2 Any party which is unable in whole or part shall, if reasonably possible, give written notice stating the problem to the other party and whether it is expected that issue will be resolved and the effect on the agreement. A failure for a period of [two] months whether continuous or interrupted shall entitle the non-defaulting party to notify the other that the Agreement is to end on a specified date. The parties shall then be obliged to agree a settlement based on the facts although no damages and/or compensation and/or losses shall be paid.

F.150

1.1 In the event that the terms of this agreement and its responsibilities, obligations and liabilities cannot be fulfilled for any reason beyond the reasonable control of the [Company], [Agent] and/or the [Actor] due to force majeure. Then the agreement shall be automatically suspended and/or temporarily interrupted and it shall not be deemed a breach by the [Company and/or the [Agent] and/or Actor].

1.2 Where no sums have been paid to the [Agent] by the [Company] and the force majeure has impacted on the ability of the [Actor] to perform his and/or her work for the [Company] under this agreement. Then the [Company] shall have the right to terminate the agreement with immediate effect and shall not be obliged to agree to a suspension and/or temporary interruption of the agreement.

1.3 Where the [Company] has paid an advance and/or other sums to the [Agent] where it is clear that the problem will not be resolved swiftly.

Then the [Company] may terminate the agreement but shall not be entitled to claim any refund of any sums paid to the [Agent].

F.151

Any party which is unable in whole or part to carry out its obligations under this Agreement shall promptly notify the other party. The reasons for such force majeure should be stated and the estimated time before the terms agreed can be performed. In the event that this is not possible and the situation cannot be remedied within a reasonable period then either party may terminate the agreement without prejudice to any legal rights and remedies

F.152

The parties agree and undertake that the following situations shall not be considered and shall be specifically excluded from force majeure under this Agreement:

1.1   Non-performance for any period which is caused by any reason for a period of less than [number] days.

1.2   A delay which is caused due the failure of one party to deliver and/or supply material and/data which is vital to the next stage of the [Project].

1.3   The withdrawal of funding and/or other professional support which arises as a result of a finding of a breach of health and safety legislation and/or codes and/or other matter by a court and/or government body in respect of any part of the [Project] and/or one party.

F.153

Where the parties are not agreed as to whether a fact and/or circumstance constitutes force majeure under this Agreement. Then prior to the instigation of any legal proceedings both parties agree to meet for a conference to endeavour to resolve the situation with a third party acting as the independent mediator. The cost of the independent mediator shall be agreed in advance by both parties and shall be part of any settlement that shall be reached.

F.154

The [Distributor] shall not be entitled to rely on force majeure for any reason where it is unable and/or unwilling to supply the [Company] with the required level of personnel which it must deliver set out in Schedule A. Failure by the [Distributor] to recruit and/or find relevant qualified personnel for the service shall not constitute a ground for force majeure.

F.155

1.1   The [Company] agrees that the [Supplier] may delay, adapt and/or provide an alternative service to the [Company] as it thinks fit where circumstances beyond its normal control have affected the quality and/or duration of the content of the service at any time.

1.2   The [Company] agrees that no refund, compensation and/or other payments for any losses and/or damages shall be due and the [Company] waives any such claim and/or action against the [Supplier].

Sponsorship

F.156

1.1   No party shall be liable to the other for any costs, expenses, losses, damages and/or any other sums arising from the failure to perform, deliver and/or complete any of its obligations in this Agreement for any cause whatsoever beyond its reasonable control.

1.2   Where the grounds of force majeure continue for [one] month and there is no expectation that the matter will improve. Then the parties agree to terminate the agreement by mutual consent and to enter into formal negotiations and/or mediation to reach a settlement of the outstanding issues relating to the agreement.

F.157

1.1   Where circumstances due to force majeure result in the cancellation of the [Event/Festival/Race] by the [Organisers]. Then the [Sponsors] accept that the [Organisers] shall not be deemed to have breached this Agreement despite the fact that the [Event/Festival/Race] will not take place.

1.2   The [Sponsors] agree that where 1.1 means the [Event/Festival/Race] is cancelled even at very short notice. That the [Organisers] shall be entitled to retain all the sponsorship funds paid by the [Sponsor] to the date of cancellation.

1.3   The [Organisers] agree that they shall not be entitled to be paid any further sponsorship funds due after the cancellation date in 1.1.

1.4   It is agreed that the following matters amount to grounds of force majeure: severe weather warning for rain, floods, hurricane, typhoon, tidal waves, snow, ice, extreme heatwave, drought; riots, war, invasion and/or threat of activist action and blockades; threat of spread of disease; threat of inadequate water supplies and/or access routes for paramedics and ambulances; potential risk to performers of electrocution; insufficient security measures due to removal of fencing by third parties; and other matters which may pose a severe risk to the health and safety of the public.

F.158

The parties both agree that the following facts and circumstances shall not be considered force majeure:

1.1 The suspension and/or failure of the electricity, gas, water, sewage, drainage, and/or heating for the [Venue] provided that it is for less than [number] hours.

1.2 The failure to obtain a licence from the local authority to sell and/or supply alcohol.

1.3 The disruption, suspension and/or blockade of the local roads, motorway, rail, airport and/or transport links.

1.4 The identification of a health and safety hazard at the [Venue] which is being investigated by the local authority and/or government agency.

F.159

The [Sponsor] agrees that the following circumstances shall constitute force majeure for the purposes of this Agreement:

1.1 The location and venue is not available due to adverse weather conditions, floods, fire, security and/or health and safety matters.

1.2 [Name] has withdrawn from the [Event] and a new performer is required.

1.3 There has been an outbreak of some disease and/or virus which has resulted in restrictions on people, animals, traffic in and/or near the location and/or venue.

1.4 Lack of sanitary and water facilities at the location and/or venue.

1.5 Failure to be granted any relevant licence, planning permission and/or insurance cover.

University, Charity and Educational

F.160

The [Institute/Charity] and its employees, volunteers, sub-licensees, sub-contractors, agents or otherwise shall not be liable for the failure to perform, deliver, pay, carry out work and/or provide a service and/or facilities and/or any other circumstances beyond the reasonable control of the [Institute/Charity] including but not limited to war, hostilities, invasion, terrorism, riot, civil war and/or any other uprising, takeover, or attack whether caused by the public, army, an enemy or military, chemical, nuclear or other warfare and/or accident; the failure, interruption, non-availability of water, gas, electricity, oil, light and any other material and resources; any health and safety issue;

flood, fire, arson, storm, lightning, tempest, hurricane, epidemic, disease, earthquake, landslides, avalanches, acts of terrorism, hijacking, sabotage, vandalism, and other criminal acts which cause destruction; damage of equipment, machinery, master material or property; death, injury or illness of key personnel.

F.161

No party to this Agreement shall be held in any way responsible for any failure to fulfil its obligations under this Agreement if such failure has been caused by force majeure and is beyond the reasonable control of either the [Company] and/or the [Institute/Charity]. Force majeure shall include any Act of God, fire, flood, earthquake, storm, natural disaster, war, invasion, hostilities, civil war, military power, government, local authority or international imposition of government sanction, embargo or order, labour dispute, strike, boycott, interruption or failure of oil, electricity, gas, water or telecommunication and internet, website and app service; and/or the failure to supply any equipment, machinery or material. In the event that the agreement is suspended and/or cannot be fulfilled for [six] months then either party may terminate the agreement by notice in writing. The parties agree to enter into negotiations to reach a settlement in relating to the outstanding issues and if they are unable to agree shall appoint an independent mediator and/or arbitrator prior to any litigation.

F.162

In the event that this Agreement cannot be performed, fulfilled and/or carried out due to circumstances which are grounds for force majeure of the defaulting party. Then any such non-performance, failure and/or delay shall not be considered a breach of this Agreement. The defaulting party must immediately endeavour to notify and/or contact the other party and explain the circumstances and the expected date by which the issue should be resolved. Where the default shall and/or is likely to continue for a period of [three] months. Then the other party shall have the opportunity at any time to notify the defaulting party that the agreement is to end on a specified date. The parties shall then be obliged to agree a settlement based on the reversion of all rights granted under the agreement.

F.163

The parties agree that the following situations and/or causes will not be deemed force majeure under this Agreement:

1.1   Fire, flood, storm, lightning and/or other condition which only affects part of the premises and where access is still allowed in other areas by the public.

897

1.2 A failure of the light, electricity, gas, heating, water, drainage, air conditioning and/or any other part of the premises which can be remedied within [number] hours.

1.3 The ill-health of the main speaker where a suitably qualified substitute is available at short notice.

F.164
The [Institute/Charity] shall be entitled to rely on force majeure where it is obliged to restrict and/or limit and/or close any part of the venue to the public at any time due to any unexpected incident, crime, health and safety and/or security matter and/or any other reason which may arise at any time. There shall be no obligation to refund any part of any entrance fee to any person although the [Institute/Charity] may offer a voucher for an alternative later date.

F.165

1.1 The [Charity] shall be entitled to cancel, reschedule and/or change the dates and details of the [Event] where circumstances arise which prevent the [Event] being completed as planned which are beyond the reasonable control of the [Charity].

1.2 The [Company] agree that they shall not charge the [Charity] any costs and expenses for the cancellation, rescheduling and/or change of dates and details of the [Event]. Provided that the new terms are agreed within [number] days and the [Charity] agrees to pay no less than [number/currency] for the new booking. The [Company] agrees that any sums paid for the first booking will be allocated to the second booking but not refunded directly to the [Charity].

FORMAT

General Business and Commercial

F.166
'The Format' of the [Film/Work/Video] shall mean the title, the basic idea and concept set out in any treatments, the scripts, the running order, the design and layout of the set, the content and presentation of the questions and answers, sound effects, score system and prizes, catchphrases, slogans, graphics, images, artwork, two and three dimensional representations of any person, article or product. Together with all intellectual property rights,

present and future copyright, design rights, future design rights, trade marks, service marks, domain names, logos and any associated images and slogans; all computer software, downloads and versions in electronic form, any telecommunication system in any form and any storage and retrieval system and material in any form, music, lyrics and sound recordings relating to the [Film/Work/Video].

F.167

'The Format Rights' shall mean in respect of the [Series/Podcast/Video] the following:

1.1   The title of the [Series/Podcast/Video] and each individual episode, any catchphrases, emojis, slogans, lyrics, sound recordings, music, musical works, sounds, logos, images, new character names and place names which are original, trade marks, domain names of websites, references for apps and any other material and content created for marketing, promotional and merchandising purposes.

1.3   The theme and concept including any development drafts, treatments and synopsis. The original manuscripts, drafts, scripts, characters and names, plots and storylines. Any adaptation and/or variation which may occur for the purposes of exploitation.

1.4   All copyright, intellectual property rights, computer software and electronic and telecommunication system rights, trade marks and any other rights and interest of whatever nature in any media at any time in any material whether in existence now and/or created in the future in some new format and/or as a result of new technology and/or arising through new legislation.

1.5   The right to adapt, vary, change, delete from and/or license and/or assign any and/or all rights at any time.

F.168

'The Format' shall mean the exclusive rights granted by the [Licensor] to the [Licensee] to produce, reproduce and distribute another [Series/Podcast/Episodes] based on the [Films] in schedule A in the Territory for the Term of the Agreement for the television, radio, viewing on a website and/or podcast and/or via a computer and/or mobile as a download.

The format shall include, but not be limited to:

1.1   The right to copy, reproduce and exploit the [Series/Podcast/Episodes] and any associated trailers, advertising, publicity and other material.

1.2   The right to use the title known as [specify] and the associated trade mark, logo, artwork and sound recordings.

899

1.3 The right to reproduce the design, layout, colour, signs, scoreboards, and equipment of the studio set.

1.4 The right to use and reproduce both in the studio and for distribution the rules, procedures, catchphrases, slogans, questions and answers.

1.5 The right to use and reproduce the costumes and outfits.

1.6 The right to reproduce and exploit copies of all running orders, scripts and other written material.

1.7 The exclusive right to exploit the [Series/Podcast/Episodes] shall be limited to the right to do so in the exact shape and form as the first. The necessary copyright, design rights, trade marks, logos, literary, musical, dramatic, artistic and all other intellectual property rights are granted solely for that purpose.

1.8 There is no right to create any other merchandising and/or the right to grant rights for a theme park, product placement and/or exploitation in any other medium and/or by any other method.

1.9 The right to appoint financially stable and reliable third parties as sub-licensees and sub-distributors provided that the duration of those agreements do not exceed that granted under this agreement which is [date].

F.169

The [Licensor] grants the [Licensee] the non-exclusive right to reproduce, manufacture, sell and distribute the [Licensed Articles/Products/Units] which are described in detail in schedule A based on the [Format] in the [Series/Podcast/Work] for the duration of the Licence Period throughout the Territory.

F.170

'The Format' shall be the original concept and structure of a [Television/Radio/Podcast Series] entitled [specify title] which is described in detail in appendix A which is attached to and forms part of this agreement

F.171

1.1 The [Licensor] and the [Licensee] both acknowledge that there is currently no recognised copyright in the Format of the whole [Game Show] which is acknowledged in law in this country. That the [Licensor] desires to license the right to exploit the Format to the [Licensee].

1.2 The [Licensor] grants to the [Licensee] the exclusive right to produce, reproduce, distribute, sell and exploit the [Television, Video and DVD Rights, the Merchandising Rights and the Publishing Rights]

in the [Game Show] and the sound recordings and any associated content throughout the [Territory/world] for the [duration of the Term of this Agreement/Licence Period].

F.172

1.1 The [Licensee] agrees and undertakes that it shall not acquire any copyright, intellectual property rights and any other rights or interest in the [Concept/Format/Programme] owned or controlled by the [Licensor] whether in existence now or created in the future except those stated in this agreement. The [Licensee] shall be limited to the exploitation of the rights specifically granted in this agreement for the Licence Period.

1.2 In the event that there are any adaptations, translations, variations, developments and/or alterations of the [Concept/Format/Programme] created and/or commissioned by the [Licensee] pursuant to the exercise of the licence granted. The [Licensee] agrees to assign and transfer all such interest, copyright and intellectual property rights in any such adaptation, translation, development and/or variation and/or alteration to the [Licensor] entirely. The Licensee shall have no claim and/or interest and/or rights and shall not seek to register any such interest and/or rights at any time.

F.173

'The Programme Format' shall mean the Format of the [Programme] including the characters, storylines, scripts, structure, scenarios, slogans, title, set, graphics and costumes, music, sound effects, sound recordings and all appearances, contributions and artists. The details of which are described in Appendix A which is attached to and forms part of this agreement.

F.174

'The Format' shall be the original concept and novel idea for and structure of a series of films on the theme of [subject]. Full details of which are attached and form part of this agreement in the attached Schedule A and shall include the following matters:

1.1 Title, script, characters, plot, storyline, location, running order, sequence, design and layout of set, presentation of questions and answers, score system, prizes, slogans, graphics, costumes.

1.2 Advertising, publicity, trade marks, service marks, logos, icons, credits, copyright notices and intellectual property rights, music, sound recordings, stills, images, computer generated material, domain names, website and app, premium rate telephone line recordings.

F.175
'The Format' shall mean the right to create and develop other films, videos and products based on the original [Concept/Film/Work] by [name]. This right to adapt, vary and develop the [Concept/Film/Work] is non-exclusive and covers all musical, literary, dramatic, artistic and other content which is contained in the description and images of the [Concept/Film/Work] in schedule A which form part of this Agreement and shall be only for the period from [date] to [date]. There is no right provided to sub-license and/or sub-contract work to third parties and/or to appoint a distributor without the prior approval of [Name].

F.176
The [Licensee] agrees that all rights not specifically granted are reserved by the [Licensor] including but not limited to [specify].

F.177
There is no right granted to license, appoint, authorise or to engage any third party to exploit the [Format] at any time.

F.178
'The Quiz Format' shall mean the original concept and idea for a [Quiz]. The material shall include the title, logo, slogan, scripts, design and layout of the set structure, presenters script, questions and answers, list of prizes, graphics, images, text and computer generated material and software, score system and charts, running order, music, sound effects, sound recordings, gadgets, advertising and publicity campaign and promotional material, trade marks, service marks, icons, cross-promotional material for a website and app; credits, copyright and trade mark notices; premium rate telephone line questions and answers. Full details of which are attached and form part of this agreement in appendix B.

F.179
'The Premium Rate Line Format' shall be the original concept and idea for a phone in service on a premium rate line number to a call centre together with a newspaper, magazine and media advertising and publicity campaign and promotional material. Full details of which are attached and form part of this agreement in schedule A.

F.180
The [Licensee] agrees and acknowledges that it shall not register and/or attempt to register the domain name, website and/or app and/or any software and/or computer generated material, artwork, graphics, text, trade marks, service marks, community marks, logos, slogans, music, sound recordings, copyright and/or any intellectual property rights in respect of any part of the

[Format] with any company, trade organisation, collecting society, copyright organisation and/or otherwise. The [Licensee] agrees that all such rights are owned and/or controlled by the [Licensor].

F.181

No format rights and/or right to adapt and/or distort and/or to authorise the reproduction and/or to license any characters, logos, names, images and/or text in respect of this [Film/Work/Project] are granted under this licence.

F.182

1.1   [Name] is the original writer and copyright owner of the [Work].

1.2   [Name] has licensed the [paperback and hardback and ebook] rights in [specify] language to the [Distributor].

1.3   [Name] owns and controls the title and logo and the content of the [Work] and the right to adapt, vary, change and distort the [Work] for exploitation by any means through television and film throughout the world and has not provided an option and/or granted any such rights to any third party except 1.2.

GARDENING LEAVE

General Business and Commercial

G.001

In the event that [Name] serves notice under this Agreement to cease to be employed by the [Company] at any time for whatever reason. Then the [Company] shall have the right at its sole discretion to decide that it shall continue to pay all the sums and benefits due under the Agreement to [Name] until the date of termination, but that [Name] shall no longer attend or carry out his duties and that access to the premises shall be denied. Provided that no false statement or claim shall be made by the [Company] relating to the reason and [Name] shall be entitled to arrange for the removal of his/her possessions without undue haste or pressure or in any way which creates an impression that there has been any wrongdoing.

G.002

In the event that the [Company] wishes to pursue the option that the [Executive] should be placed on gardening leave for all or part of the remaining term of notice or agreement. Then the parties shall enter into a settlement which sets out the following matters:

1.1 The payments of the sums due and benefits and the date upon which they should cease or be given up. Agreement in respect of the payment of any bonuses, rewards, options, reviews, increases or promotion which would arise in that period.

1.2 An agreed press statement and circular for staff.

1.3 A reference for future employers signed by [specify] which is the agreed wording for any future reference.

1.4 A statement of the pension benefits, insurance cover, and share options and how this is affected by the gardening leave. Where the benefits lapse then a financial payment shall be agreed.

1.5 An agreement by the [Company] as to the property and products to be owned and retained by the [Executive]. As well as a list of those items which must be returned such as company car, security pass, company credit card, gadgets and computer equipment. It is agreed that the [Executive] shall have the right to erase and delete all passwords, data, information and content which may be stored on any such products or other material to be returned.

1.6 An agreement by the [Company] to bear all legal costs and expenses of the [Executive] in relation to his/her tax and accountancy advice, legal costs and expenses in resolving the matters arising from the settlement up to a maximum limit of [number/currency].

G.003

The [Company] shall not have the right to place the [Executive] on gardening leave unless the [Executive] serves notice that he/she intends to leave and work for one of the competing companies or businesses set out in the following list [specify names].

G.004

The [Company] shall not have the right to notify the [Executive] that he/she are on gardening leave at any time. Any such arrangement must be mutually agreed between the parties.

G.005

1.1 The [Company] agrees and undertakes that it shall not have the right to insist that the [Executive] take paid leave of absence. Such action by the [Company] shall be deemed a breach of this Agreement.

1.2 Nor shall the [Company] have the right to give the [Executive] no notice that his/her services are not required and to arrange an escort from the building. That any such action by the [Company] shall be deemed a breach of this Agreement.

1.3 In either case where the breaches the agreement in 1.1 and 1.2 the [Company] agrees to pay the [Executive] [number/currency] for each such instance in addition and without prejudice to any claims the [Executive] may have for unfair dismissal or otherwise.

G.006

1.1 The [Company] may at any time notify the [Executive] that he/she is to commence from a specified date up to but no more than [number] [days/months] a leave of absence which shall be subject to full salary payments but not bonuses for that period. During that leave of absence the [Executive] shall not be required to carry out his/her normal duties but may be asked to cooperate with any internal company investigation.

1.2 The [Company] agrees that the [Executive] shall have the right to refuse the proposed leave of absence and may decide to treat such notification as breach and/or termination of the Agreement and/or to make an allegation of unfair dismissal.

GIFTS

General Business and Commercial

G.007

For the purposes of this Agreement 'Gift' shall mean a transfer of property without consideration of a beneficial interest.

G.008

Shares settled on trust for the [Employees] shall be deemed not to be personal gifts.

G.009

No gifts, gratuities, benefits, rewards or financial payments shall be offered, promised, given or provided to any person, business or company at any time in order to secure favour or preference. Where it comes to light that any of these has taken place then the [Company] shall have the right to cancel the contract immediately and request all sums be repaid for work which has not be performed or carried out.

G.010

The employees, agents, volunteers, representatives and licensee of the [Institute/Charity] may only accept gifts, gratuities and monies which are valued at less than [number/currency]. Any sum and/or benefit offered over that sum must be notified to and approved in advance with the [Chief Executive] prior to acceptance. The [Chief Executive] may decide at his absolute discretion that the gift, gratuity and/or money should become the property of the [Institute/Charity].

G.011

1.1 The [Institute/Enterprise] agrees that directors, trustees, employees, volunteers and agents shall be entitled to accept small gifts and hospitality provided that it is declared and reported in accordance with the policy document referred to as [specify policy].

1.2 All donations, items, products, services and property which exceed [number/currency] must be reported immediately to [name] as required under policy [specify]. All such matters will become the property of the [Institute/Enterprise] and not the individual.

1.3   Failure to adhere to 1.1 and 1.2 is a serious matter. In the event that there is a significant delay and/or failure to report such matters then the [Institute/Enterprise] may decide in its absolute discretion to dismiss, reprimand and/or terminate the agreement with person and/or company. Where it is believed that fraud, a criminal act and/or other wrong has been committed and/or is alleged then the matter will be reported to the relevant third party for investigation.

G.012
Any hospitality, benefit, gift and/or contribution which is valued below [number/currency] shall not fall within the policy [specify] and shall not be deemed a breach of the contract with the [Company].

G.013
It is a policy of the [Institute/Company] that all directorships, non-executive positions, work, gifts, benefits, free tickets, free services, use of facilities, holidays, loans and/or financial arrangements, provision of transport by car, rail and/or air, accommodation and/or any other similar interest which is made with any third party as a result of your connections with the [Institute/Company] are declared in the [Register of Interests/Gifts].

G.014
The [Company] agrees that any employee, agent and/or consultant may accept money, gifts, gratuities, tickets, products and free meals and accommodation from any third party who may be interested in entering into agreements with the [Company]. Provided that no binding commitment and/or undertakings verbally and/or in writing are made to such third party by any employee, agent and/or consultant that will commit the [Company] to enter into any agreement.

G.015
Any gift made to any person who is part of the [Consortium] which relates to the [Project] and which is in excess of [number/currency] must be declared and reported to [Name].

GOODWILL

General Business and Commercial

G.016
'The Goodwill' of the [Company] shall mean the reputation, good standing, esteem, respectability, fame, historic record and high regard in which the

[Company] and its [Products] are held. It shall include the goodwill attached to [but not the ownership of] the company name, brand and product names, any copyright, trademarks, service marks, logos, images, slogans, designs, packaging, blogs, domain names, apps, music, sound recordings, films and videos, designs, goods and any other material of any nature attached to or in the possession or control of the [Company], and its relationship with its customers, the list of its customers and all marketing, promotion and advertising either directly through paid adverts and/or through product placement, sponsorship and other collaborations which Goodwill is a separate element of the [Company].

G.017
All Goodwill generated as a result of the use by the [Licensee] arising out of its sub-license of any copyright, trademark, logo, design or any other material in any medium authorised and/or provided by the [Licensor] under this Agreement shall vest in and belong entirely to the [Licensor].

G.018
The [Licensee] agrees and undertakes that all intellectual property rights including copyright, design rights, future design rights, computer generated material, computer software rights and patents and goodwill are reserved by and belong exclusively to the [Licensor] in the [Product] and any packaging, marketing and promotional material and merchandising and in the trademarks, logos, images, text, graphics and slogans and/or any adaptation, development and/or variation. The [Licensee] shall not acquire any rights, interest, or goodwill under this Agreement and shall not attempt to register any rights or represent to others that the [Licensee] has the right to do so.

G.019
The [Licensee] agrees and undertakes that any goodwill and copyright and intellectual property rights and any other rights generated as a result of the use and exploitation by the [Licensee] of any trademark, domain name, title, slogan, name, text, image, logo, design or artwork, graphics, computer software or computer generated material and/or any development and/or adaptation shall belong to the [Licensor].

G.020
All goodwill arising as a result of the use by the [Licensee] of its sub-license of any trademark, copyright, designs rights, logo, image, text, slogan, graphics or other material licensed and supplied by the [Licensor] shall belong entirely to the [Licensor]. The [Licensee] shall not acquire any interest or rights in any such goodwill at any time nor shall the [Licensee] be entitled to transfer or authorise any third party to exploit such goodwill.

909

G.021

The [Agent] acknowledges that it shall not acquire any title in the [Collection samples, the Garments or the Company Logo]. The [Agent] confirms that any goodwill and reputation created in the [Company Logo] shall remain the sole and exclusive property of the [Company] and that no part of this Agreement is intended to transfer any copyright, design rights or any other rights in the [Company Logo, the Collection Samples or the Garments] to the [Agent].

G.022

1.1   The [Company] agrees that all copyright, design rights, future design rights, computer software rights, trade marks, service marks, domain names, logos and any adaptations, variations, developments, translations and any other rights and goodwill in the [Celebrity's] birth name, business name, marketing name, image, profile, representations, slogan, catchphrase or any aspect of the [Celebrity] [and/or his family] shall remain the sole and exclusive property of the [Celebrity].

1.2   That there is no intention to assign or transfer any such rights and goodwill to the [Company]. The [Company] agrees that in the event it shall commission and/or create any new content containing such rights that the [Company] shall not be entitled to exploit such material without the prior authority of the [Celebrity]. Further the [Company] undertakes to assign to the [Celebrity] all such rights and physical material commissioned and/or created under this Agreement which relate to the matters stated in 1.1.

G.023

The [Assignor] agrees that from the date of this Agreement it shall not have any rights, goodwill or interest in the promotion, marketing or exploitation of the [Work] of any nature provided that the [Assignment Fee] is paid in full.

G.024

The [Assignor] agrees that it shall not at any time seek to undermine, prejudice or otherwise impugn the goodwill and reputation of the [Work/Name] by making statements to the media which are intended to be critical, offensive or derogatory or would affect the sales, marketing and promotion of the [Work].

G.025

The [Manager] agrees and undertakes that the name of the [Sportsperson] and any copyright, goodwill and reputation and any other rights created in respect of the [Sportsperson] and his/her name, trademark, business name, logo, image, text, graphics, music, slogan or other material owned or controlled by the [Sportsperson] shall remain the sole and exclusive property of the [Sportsperson] including any developments or variations whether proposed by the [Manager] or any third party. That no part of this Agreement is intended to assign, transfer, grant or authorise the [Manager] to acquire these rights at any time. That the [Manager] shall cooperate fully in the documentation required for any assignment to the [Sportsperson].

G.026
The [Company] agrees and undertakes that any title, name, logo, trade mark, service mark, domain name, image, slogan, catchphrase, music, lyrics, ringtones, sound recordings and sounds which are created and/or developed by [Name] in respect of their services under this Agreement which directly relates to them personally and is not based on or derived from the [Series] shall belong to [Name] together with any goodwill. The [Company] shall supply any requested copies of material at the [Company's] cost which may be necessary to support any application for any registration or the protection of any rights whether during the Term of this Agreement or for up to [three] years thereafter.

G.027
The [Distributor] agrees and undertakes that all intellectual property, copyright, design rights, future design rights, computer software rights, data and database rights, trade marks, service marks, domain names, logos and any adaptations, variations, developments, translations and any other rights and goodwill in the [Material/Website/App/Manuscripts/Film] supplied by the [Institute/Charity] and any developments, variations and/or any new material which is created relating to the [Project] shall be owned and controlled by the [Institute/Charity]. The [Distributor] shall not retain, own and/or control any such rights and/or interest and shall authorise transfer and assignment to the [Institute/Charity] without delay provided that they arrange and pay for all the costs of the documentation.

G.028
The [Company] agrees and acknowledges that any name, title, slogan, logo, image, trade mark, service mark, community mark, domain name, business name, trading name and/or otherwise either on and/or associated with the [Sponsors'] products and/or services and/or personnel and/or any adaptation together with any goodwill shall be the sole property of the [Sponsor]. The [Company] shall not have any claim and/or interest and shall not attempt to register any right with any third party at any time.

G.029
Where the [Distributor] creates and/or develops a new name, title, logo, trade mark and/or community mark and/or domain name which is used in

respect of the [Product] and/or a series of [Products]. Then it is agreed that the [Licensor] and the [Distributor] shall be registered as joint owners of the copyright in the name, title, logo, trade mark and/or community mark and/or domain name and any goodwill. The parties agree that they shall share any benefits from such rights and interest equally.

G.030
All goodwill and reputation in respect of the [Project], title, logo, image and any trade mark, copyright, patent, invention and/or any other intellectual property rights which may exist in any material and/or be created and/or developed and/or adapted shall belong jointly and severally to all members of the [Consortium] equally and any interest shall be registered as such and any revenue shall be divided on that basis.

G.031
Goodwill shall not be quantified for the purpose of this Agreement and no sum shall be attributed. Goodwill generated and/or created by the [Licensee] shall not permit the [Licensee] to register and/or acquire any rights and/or interest in any part of the [Product/Work] which is owned by the [Licensor].

G.032

1.1 Goodwill in respect of [specify material/rights] has been valued by [specify organisation] at [number/currency] on the basis of the following documents set out in Schedule A supplied by the [Seller].

1.2 If at a later date the valuation is found to be incorrect and based on the fact that the documents in Schedule A are discovered to contain serious errors, omissions and/or misrepresentations. Then it is agreed between the parties that the [Seller] shall not be liable for any losses, damages, costs and/or expenses that may arise from the later lower valuation. The [Purchaser] has been advised that the documents are for guidance only and that they should seek an independent valuation of the goodwill.

GROSS RECEIPTS

Film, Television and Video

G.033
The 'Gross Receipts' shall mean all the sums received by the [Licensee] in respect of the exploitation of the rights under this agreement as described in 1.1 and 1.2 below. The [Licensee] shall be entitled to make the deductions

set out in 1.3 from the sums received. The [Licensee] shall not be entitled to deduct the costs in 1.4 from the sums received.

1.1 All the total amount of all monies received and/or attributable and/ or derived by the [Licensee], its subsidiaries, affiliates, distributors, and agents from the exploitation, licensing, supply, hire, rental and/or distribution of the [Films/Videos/Discs] and/or part(s) and the exercise of all the rights which have been granted by this Agreement in the Territory.

1.2 All sums received by the [Licensee] in respect of any settlement, compensation, damages or otherwise in respect of the infringement of the rights granted to the [Licensee] which are paid by a third party but excluding legal costs.

1.3 All sums which have and/or need to be paid by the [Licensee] and/or its agents, distributors and/or other third parties for commission, fees, charges, freight and delivery costs, insurance, custom duties, levies, taxes, currency conversion charges, packaging costs.

1.4 It is specifically agreed between the parties that marketing and promotional costs and expenses may not be deducted. Each party must be responsible for its own costs and expenses including [specify].

G.034
'Gross Receipts' shall mean the gross amount of monies received by the [Licensee] in any quarter directly or indirectly in respect of the exploitation of the [DVDs/Videos/Discs] of the [Film] howsoever arising after the deduction of any value added taxes or similar taxes to be borne by the [Licensee].

G.035
'Gross Receipts' shall mean all monies actually received by the [Licensee] from [DVDs/Videos/Discs] containing the [Film] sold (and not returned) and all monies actually received by the [Licensee], its sub-licensees, sub-agents and distributors and any other third party from the supply, licences, rental, distribution and/or other exploitation of [DVDs/Videos/Discs] containing the [Film] at any time in the [Territory]. This shall include but not be limited to advances, fees and other sums. In calculating the Royalties earned the [Licensee] shall be entitled to deduct from the Gross Receipts all the cost of the masters and a charge of [fifteen] per cent of the Gross Receipts, together with all fees, costs, expenses, commission and other sums which are incurred by the [Licensee], its sub-licensees, sub-agents and distributors and any other third party which directly relate to the exploitation of the [DVDs/Videos/Units] and the rights granted to the [Licensee] and the generation of revenue under this Agreement. There shall also be the right to deduct such taxes including sales taxes and value added tax but this shall

913

not cover personal or corporate taxes which relate to turnover, income or profit which are specifically excluded.

G.036
'The Gross Receipts' shall be all the sums and benefits in [currency] of any nature which are credited, paid to and/or received by the [Company]and/ or any parent company, subsidiary, associate, agent, sub-licensee and/ or distributor and/or any other third party connected with and/or engaged by the [Company] in respect of the exploitation of the rights granted in the [Films/Videos] and/or any parts and/or any content and/or any sound recordings, character and/or otherwise during the Licence Period and/or thereafter. The [Company] shall only be entitled to make the deductions of the sums in 1.1 and 1.2 below:

1.1 any refunds, returns, discounts, setoffs, free copies, material which are lost and/or damaged or other adjustments.

1.2 commission, clearance costs, fees, reproduction and manufacturing, development and packaging, marketing, advertising, product placement, sponsorship, taxes on products and/or supply of material, custom duties, delivery, security, storage and administration.

G.037
'Gross Receipts' shall mean all sums and benefits paid to, received by or credited to the [Company] and any parent company, subsidiary, affiliate or associate, or any sub-agent, sub-licensee, sub-distributor or other third party in respect of the exploitation of the [DVD/Video/Disc] Rights in the [Film] and any parts of any nature at any time in any country whether sale, supply, distribution, rental, subscription or otherwise whether during the Term of this Agreement and/or thereafter.

G.038
'The Gross Receipts' shall be the total sums received by the [Company] [and any authorised agents, distributors and other third parties] from the exploitation of the [Discs/Units/Downloads] based on the [Sound Recordings] and any parts throughout the [country] from [date to [date] after the deduction of taxes (excluding personal and corporate), commission, the cost of reproduction of material, freight and delivery costs, currency conversion costs and bank charges, insurance. No deductions shall be made for administration, telephone charges, packaging, marketing and advertising.

G.039
'The Gross Receipts' shall mean all the sums received in [sterling] after conversion from any other currency in the [country] by the [Company] from the exploitation of the rights granted in respect of the [Images/Music/Lyrics]

914

on the [Disc] and associated packaging and as an [Electronic Download] to any gadget and/or device. No deductions shall be made of any nature except costs incurred in currency conversion and exchange, sums payable to governments for taxes for the supply, distribution and/or export and/or import of the [Discs] and [Electronic Download].

G.040

'The Gross Receipts' in respect of the exploitation of the [Units/Discs/ Project] shall mean all sums actually received by the [Company] and shall not include sums not yet transferred from and/or which are not paid by any agent, sub-licensee and/or distributor and/or any other third party. After the deduction of such sums authorised under any sub-licence and/or other third party agreement such as commission, discounts, bank and/or currency charges, expenses and/or any other costs for reproduction of material, packaging, delivery, security and insurance costs.

G.041

'The Gross Receipts' shall mean the total sums received by the [Distributor] in respect of the sale and exploitation of the [Film/Disc/Work] during the continuance of this Agreement and thereafter until all sums have been accounted for by the [Distributor]. Without any deduction for development, production, manufacture, packaging, marketing, freight, administration and/ or commission and/or any other costs and/or expenses

G.042

'The Gross Receipts' shall be the total proceeds from the exploitation of the [Series/Programmes/Videos] and any parts throughout the Territory at any time received by or credited to the [Company] and its authorised sub-agents, and other third parties acting on its behalf after the deduction of the following matters:

1.1 Taxes but not corporate and personal taxes. Only those charged on the reproduction and/or supply and/or distribution by national governments.

1.2 Fees and commission of agents, sub-licensees and other third parties promoting and selling the [Series/Programmes/Videos].

1.3 The cost of reproducing and supplying master copies of any material in any format and/or language. Cost of delivery, insurance, security,

1.4 The cost of editing material to suit legislation in any country and/or delete from and/or add to and/or alter material.

1.5 The development of trailers, podcasts and software, apps, premium phone line competitions, filmed interviews as promotional packages, label, packaging, marketing and promotional material. Online marketing, paid advertising and premieres.

1.6 The cost of additional appearances, travel, accommodation and other expenses of the main characters, director and other significant contributors to music, sets, costumes and scripts.

1.7 The cost of all contractual obligations and payments, copyright clearance, payments to collecting societies for mechanical reproduction, performances and licences. Costs of contributors, waivers, consents and all other legal requirements including health and safety.

G.043

'Gross Receipts' shall mean all sums actually received by the [Television Company/Distributor] from the exploitation of all rights in all media whether in existence at the time of this agreement and/or created in the future in the [Programmes/Series/Quiz Show] and all material therein including any advances, fees or royalties but excluding:

1.1 Any sums received by the [Television Company/Distributor] from the simultaneous relay by cable and/or satellite television of any broadcast and/or transmission programme service intended primarily for reception in the [United Kingdom] which includes the [Programmes/Series/Quiz Show] or any other person or business with which there is an annual agreement for access to material.

1.2 Any sums received from any subscription service in any media and/or any play back service and/or licensing of any extracts and/or sound recordings and/or any of the [Programmes/Series/Quiz Shows] to third parties.

1.3 Any sums received in respect of advertising, product placement, sponsorship, or endorsement of any person, product or services or premium-rate telephone line service and any viewer information services or competitions or promotions which are or will be included at the beginning, in, during or after the [Programmes/Series/Quiz Show] or any breaks.

G.044

'The Gross Receipts' means the aggregate proceeds of the exploitation of rights in the [Film/Video/Unit] and/or part(s) in any media actually received by the [Licensor] and/or an appointed distributor or any other authorised third party at any time.

G.045

'Gross Receipts' shall mean the gross proceeds of the exploitation of the [specify rights] in the [Film/Video/Unit] actually received by the [Company] in freely convertible currency after there shall have been deducted from such proceeds all costs and expenses relating to the reproduction, supply, distribution, sale and/or other exploitation of the [Film/Video/Unit] including, but not limited to the cost of commission and agency fees and charges, reproduction of material, editing, translations, packaging, freight and delivery, advertising and promotional material, copyright clearance fees, royalties, the recording, performance and transmission of any music, composition and lyrics, refunds, discounts, legal costs, damages and compensation as a result of any legal action and/or allegation relating to this agreement.

G.046
The Distribution Gross Receipts' shall mean the total receipts from the distribution, exhibition and exploitation of the [Film/Video/Unit] actually received from the [Distributor] by the [Company] in accordance with the terms of the Distribution Licence.

G.047
'Gross Receipts' shall mean all the monies and receipts from the supply, reproduction, hire, distribution and exploitation, any compensation, damages, advances, royalties, funding, subsidies, grants and/or any other sums and/or payment of any kind in any currency which is credited to, paid to and/or received by the [Licensee] and/or any sub-licensee and/or any distributor in respect of the distribution, exhibition and/or exploitation of the [Film/Video/Unit] at any time.

G.048
'Gross Receipts' are defined as all actual sums invoiced and received from each [theatre/venue] exhibiting the [Film/Video/Unit] as well as any other sums collected by the [Licensee] on any account whatsoever in connection with the [Film/Video/Unit]. The Gross Receipts are the exclusive property of the [Licensor] who authorises the [Licensee] to retain the sums due to it under clause [–].

G.049
'Gross Receipts' shall mean all sums of money actually received by or credited to the [Distributor] or its sub-agents or sub-licensees arising from the distribution and exploitation of the [Series/Films/Units] during the Term of this Agreement.

G.050
'The Gross Receipts' shall be the total proceeds from the exploitation of the [Film/Video/Unit] and any parts including any adaptation and/or development, music, lyrics and sound recording throughout the Territory at any time received by or credited to the [Production Company] or its sub-

agents, sub-licensees or distributors after the deduction of any taxes levied by a government on the supply and/or distribution.

G.051

'Gross Receipts' shall mean all monies in any currency received by and paid to the [Company] at any time from [date] to [date] in respect of the [specify rights/subject] after the deduction of any taxes, levies or charges which are added to the payment which must be reported to and repaid to any government.

G.052

'The Gross Receipts' shall be all the sums received from the sale, supply, licensing, distribution, exploitation and/or adaptation in any format and/or medium and/or derived from the [Images/Footage] in any part of the world by the [Licensee] and/or any agent, sub-licensee and/or any other third party at any time whether during the term of this Agreement and/or thereafter.

G.053

'The Gross Receipts' shall mean all the sums received by the [Distributor] in respect of ticket sales, merchandising, exhibition, transmission and any other exploitation of the [Film/Video/Installation] by the [Distributor] at any time after deduction of any venue hire costs, marketing, costs up to [number/ currency] and any taxes and/or costs of reproduction of any material costs of the [Film/Video/Installation] up to [number/currency]. No other costs and/ or charges shall be deducted. All administration and staff costs shall be paid for by the [Distributor].

G.054

'The Gross Receipts' shall be the total amount of all sums received by [Name] in [country] in [currency] between [date] and [date] from the exploitation and licensing of the [Film/Work/Images] after deduction of commission, agent's fees, freight, insurance, material, marketing legal and bank costs and charges that may be due and/or paid which directly arise from any agreement that may be concluded but which shall be limited to no more than [number/currency] in any one accounting period.

G.055

'Gross Receipts' shall mean [one hundred] [per cent] [100] % of all gross sums arising directly and/or indirectly from the exploitation of the [Content/ Videos/Sound Recordings] in the Territory during the Term which shall include all advances, royalties, costs, fees, expenses and damages paid or awarded in settlement or as a result of any legal proceedings in connection with the [Content/Videos/Sound Recordings]. It shall exclude value added taxes, sales taxes or other similar taxes, any sums due to any collecting societies for licences, performance and/or mechanical reproduction and/ or fees due to any agencies as commission and/or any other payments for clearances, consents and other contractual obligations which directly relate to the exploitation of the [Content/Videos/Sound Recordings].

General Business and Commercial

G.056
'Gross Receipts' shall mean [one hundred] [per cent] [100] % of all sums actually received by the [Company] in sterling in the [United Kingdom] arising directly and identifiably from the use and/or exploitation of the [Musical Work/Artwork/Sound Recordings] and any development and/or adapted version in the Territory by the [Company] at any time.

G.057
'Gross Receipts' shall mean [one hundred] [per cent] [100] % of all sums actually received by the [Company] in [currency] in [country] arising directly and identifiably from the use and/or exploitation of the [Musical Work/ Artwork/Sound Recordings] in the Territory during the term of this agreement and thereafter until all sums have been accounted for to the [Licensor]. After deduction of any taxes on the supply and distribution of material in any medium which are relevant.

G.058
The [Licensee] agrees to pay the [Licensor] royalties of:

1.1 in [countries] [eighty] [per cent] [80] % of the Gross Receipts after deduction of the Distribution Expenses from the exploitation of the defined Rights and

1.2 in [countries] [sixty] [per cent] [60] % of the Gross Receipts after deduction of the Distribution Expenses.

G.059
The [Licensee] makes no representation or warranty with respect to the amount of any Gross Receipts which may be derived from the exploitation of the [Product/Unit/Service].

G.060
'The Gross Receipts' shall be the total proceeds from the exploitation of the [Product/Unit/Service] throughout the Territory at any time received by or credited to the [Licensee] and actually received from its sub-agents and/or sub-licensees after the deduction of any sales tax, and any value added tax paid by the [Licensee].

919

G.061

'The Gross Receipts' shall be defined as all sums which the [Agent] is able to receive and retain and deposit in the nominated account and shall not include the following costs and expenses which may have to be deducted:

1.1 Any import, export and/or supply taxes, duties and payments.

1.2 Any sales tax or value added tax or any other government charge on goods or services excluding personal and corporation tax.

1.3 Any currency conversion or exchange costs or losses.

1.4 Any insurance, bank or transfer costs or commissions.

1.5 Any agent, or third party commission, fees, expenses, royalty, consent or performance or mechanical reproduction payments or waiver.

1.6 Any damage, loss, error, legal proceedings, product liability, or fines.

1.7 Any discounts, returns, errors, replacement, remainder, packaging, delivery and freight costs.

1.8 Any editing, translations, censorship, credits, copyright notices and copyright protection.

1.9 Marketing, promotional and advertising material, labels including computer generated material and software for websites, apps and premium rate phone line competitions for television, mobiles and other gadgets.

G.062

'The Gross Receipts' from the [Project/installation/Service] shall be all sums and/or benefits and/or rights and/or interest which may arise and be received by [Name] directly and/or indirectly in respect of the [Project/Installation/Service] and/or any part at any time including but not limited to all sums from the exploitation of any copyright, patents, trade marks, computer software, computer generated material, database rights, licences, assignments, and/or any other formats and/or medium and/or adaptation and/or development which exist now and/or may be created at a later date in any part of the world and/or universe .

G.063

'The Gross Receipts' shall mean the total amount which is paid to [Name] from the sale of the [Work] excluding [government taxes on supply] without deduction of any reproduction and/or material costs and/or any other expenses and/or charges.

Internet, Websites and Apps

G.064

'Gross Receipts' shall mean all the sums received and paid to the [Website/ App Company from the [Financial Transaction Company] which collects and administers the payments for access and use of the [Website/App] after the following matters have been deducted:

1.1 any commission costs and fees, currency conversion charges, payments for supply of financial services and/or transaction portal.

1.2 any discounts, and promotional deductions due to the use of an authorised code and/or cashback offer, refunds and/or other compensation.

1.3 any payments made and/or due for consents, copyright clearances, waivers, sums due to any collecting society and/or any contractual obligations and/or otherwise for the use and exploitation of any content.

G.065

'Gross Receipts' shall mean the subscription fees, advertising and product placement fees, licensing fees and any other sums received and retained by the [Company/Enterprise] in respect of the reproduction, supply, use and/or adaptation of the [Service] on the [Website/App] [specify trading name and reference] [from date to date/at any time] and in any part of the world without any deductions for costs, expenses, charges or otherwise of any nature except taxes on the supply or provision of any services which are applicable under the authority of any government.

G.066

'Gross Receipts' shall be all sums paid to, received by and/or credited to the [Company/Enterprise] whether directly and/or indirectly and/or through a third party and/or a subsidiary, affiliate and/or associate and/or any parent company which relates to the supply, sale, distribution, license and/or assignment of any [Work/Service] on any website and/or app and/or any part of the internet and/or any mobile phone and/or device and/or by means of any telecommunication system and/or any television, radio and/or other gadget at any time and to any country and whether free to the public and/or acquired through a blanket licence, subscription, pay per download, or any other payment or access method.

G.067

'Gross Receipts' shall mean the sums received and retained by the [Company/Distributor] relating to the reproduction, sale, supply, hire and/ or distribution of the [Product/Service/Work] on the [Website/App] after the deduction of the following costs:

1.1   commission.

1.2   agency fees.

1.3   currency exchange costs and losses.

1.4   bank charges and fees.

1.5   administration costs and charges.

1.6   any import, export and/or supply taxes, duties and payments.

1.7   any sales tax or value added tax or any other government charge on goods or services.

1.8   any insurance costs and charges.

1.9   copyright and consent fees and royalties; usage; performance; mechanical reproduction payments and/or waiver and/or other contractual obligations which may be required for the use and/or exploitation.

1.10 any costs paid for damages, losses, errors, legal proceedings, product liability, and/or fines and/or any other sum imposed as a penalty and/or additional charge including interest.

1.11 any discounts, returns, replacement, remainders, insurance, packaging, and freight costs.

1.12 marketing and promotional costs for newspapers, television, websites, sponsorship, product placement, blog influencers, exhibitions and trade fairs up to [number/currency] in total.

G.068
'The Gross Receipts' shall be the total sums from the exploitation of the [Product/Work/Service] throughout the [world/universe] at any time received by the [Licensee] in [currency] in [country]. This sum shall not include any monies due and owing to the [Licensee] from any sub-agents and/or sub-licensees and/or any other authorised third party which has not been transferred to the [Licensee]. All sums received in whatever currency shall be converted to [currency] and any charges and conversion costs deducted from the sums due. There shall be no right to deduct any other sums of any nature except any taxes imposed by a government on the transfer and/or supply which must be charged and then paid to the government. No marketing , advertising and/or promotional costs may be deducted.

G.069
'The Gross Receipts' shall be all the sums received by the [Company] from the provision of a premium rate phone line and service to the public on

the [Website/App] after authorised costs and expenses for the cost of the supply of the service for the period but which in any event shall not exceed [figure/currency] as a deduction.

G.070

'Gross Receipts' shall be all the sums received by the [Company] and converted to [sterling/euros/dollars/yen] and held in a nominated bank account in [country] after the deduction of currency conversion costs and bank charges [and before taxes].

G.071

'Gross Receipts' shall be the sums paid to the [Company] by any third party in respect of the [Website/Blog/Work] which are received and not returned and/or cancelled after deduction of any [specify tax], delivery costs and an [agency/commission] fee of [number] per cent during the Term of this Agreement and thereafter until expiry and/or termination of this Agreement.

G.072

'Gross Receipts' shall mean all the sums received by [Name] and [Name] in respect of the [Blog/App] reference [specify]. No deductions shall be permitted for any expenses and/or costs. The sums shall include all sums relating directly to the [Blog/App] and any other payments which may be associated with it including merchandising, appearance fees at events and on radio and television, tours, trade fairs, product placement fees, sponsorship and brand promotion fees and any other monies for any other form of exploitation which relates to the [Blog/App] and any content and associated material, logo, image and/or sound recording and/or text, messaging service and/or premium rate phone line and/or download. It shall not include all the product of the work of [Name] and [Name] which is not related to the [Blog/App].

Merchandising and Distribution

G.073

The [Licensor] acknowledges that the amount of Gross Receipts which may be achieved from the sale and distribution of the [Licensed Articles] is not confirmed. The [Licensee] has made no representation or provided any undertaking as regard the amount of the potential Gross Receipts.

G.074

The [Distributor] shall be entitled to receive [number] per cent of the Gross Revenue which shall be received as a result of the exploitation of the Merchandising Rights in the [Territory] in consideration of their services.

G.075

'Gross Receipts' shall mean all revenue generated through the exploitation of the [Character] in any form at any time in any country under the terms of this Agreement less any value added tax or other tax on sales or supply of goods which is not retained and is repaid to a government body or agency under any legislation, policy or practice, but not corporate or personal tax.

G.076

'The Gross Receipts' shall be the total proceeds from the exploitation of the [Licensed Articles] throughout the Territory at any time directly or indirectly received by or credited to the [Agent] or any sub-agent or sub-licensee after the deduction of any value added tax or any other taxes imposed on the wholesale and/or retail price of the [Licensed Articles].

G.077

The [Agent] agrees that all sums received in respect of the exploitation of the [Character] under this Agreement shall be deposited in a separate bank account at a bank to be agreed with the [Licensor]. Further that the [Licensor] shall be permitted access at all times to statements of account directly with the bank. The [Agent] shall not be entitled to create any charge or lien over the sums nor to withdraw any sums without the prior authorisation to the bank by the [Licensor].

G.078

'The Gross Receipts' shall be all sums and the total proceeds actually received by and/or credited to the [Production Company] or any of its sub-agents, sub-licensees and/or any other authorised third party arising from the exploitation of the [Film/Video/Product] based on and adapted from the [Author's Work] and any parts and all media rights under this Agreement after the deduction of such commission, agency and distributor charges and expenses which shall be specified in the account in detail and the deduction of any taxes imposed by any government on the supply and/or distribution of any which must be repaid to the government relating to the [Film/Video/Product].

G.079

The [Distributor/Enterprise] agrees to deposit and keep all sums received in respect of the exploitation of the [Licensed Article/Product] in a separate bank account in [specify country] to be administered by [specify accountant/lawyer] over which no lien, charge or undertaking to a third party shall be given by the [Distributor/Enterprise].

G.080
'The Gross Receipts' shall mean [one hundred] per cent of all sums received and/or credited to the [Company] in [sterling] in the [United Kingdom] arising directly, indirectly and/or otherwise from the use, exploitation and adaptation of the [Work/Product/Service] throughout the [Territory/world] at any time after the deduction of any taxes [but not corporate and/or personal taxes], currency conversion costs and bank charges.

G.081
Where a third party does not remit, pay and/or transfer the monies due to the [Distributor] at any time. There shall be no obligation on the [Distributor] to be liable for the failures of any such third party and/or to pay the deficit to increase the Gross Receipts.

G.082
The [Sub-Licensee] agrees and undertakes:

1.1 to disclose and verify to the [Licensee] all sums received and/or credited and/or any other benefits derived from the exploitation of the [Work/Service/Product] throughout the following countries: [specify]

1.2 not to withhold any sums for currency conversion and/or bank charges, commission, freight, insurance, material costs and/or for any other reason without the prior agreement of the sums with the [Licensee] that it is an authorised deduction.

G.083
The [Sub-Licensee] agrees that it shall not be entitled to deduct any sum in excess of [figure/currency] from the Gross Receipts in any one accounting period. Any sum which is not recouped must be delayed and included in the next accounting period.

G.084
'The Gross Receipts' shall mean all sums of any nature received by the [Company] and/or any parent and/or associated company from the exploitation of the [Work/Service/Product] and/or any part and/or any character, name, image, logo and/or text and/or sound recording of the original and/or any adaptation which is owned and controlled by [Name] and/or developed by the [Company] and/or from any registration, license, supply, sale, reproduction and/or any other format and/or medium and/or method whether in existence now and/or created at a later date subject only to the following authorised deductions :

1.1 agents' fees which shall not exceed [number] per cent at any time.

1.2   commission to any distributor which shall not exceed [number] per cent at any time.

1.3   taxes which relate to supply and/or transfer of products. Services and/or rights but not corporate and/or personal tax.

1.4   delivery, freight, insurance, customs duties and currency conversion costs and bank charges.

1.5   payment of any sums due to a collecting society for use of material, consents and permissions, licences, copyright clearances and the assignment of rights for new artwork and logos, computer generated material, software, registration of trade marks and other intellectual property matters.

The following matters are not authorised and such costs and expenses are prohibited from being deducted: travel, accommodation and entertainment, marketing, advertising, legal and business affairs and administration, reproduction of material and insurance.

G.085
'The Gross Receipts' shall mean the total monies in sterling derived from the ex-factory prices quoted for the [Garments] actually received and paid to the [Company] at any time from the parties in the Territory during the Term of the Agreement [after deduction of any sums incurred due to exchanges of currency, alterations, rejections, discounts and any other reduction in the ex-factory price but excluding freight, and additional insurance not included in the ex-factory price] and any taxes or duties arising directly from orders obtained by the [Agent] under this Agreement.

G.086
'The Gross Receipts' shall mean the total monies in [currency] received by the [Company] in [country] in the nominated bank account at [specify] and not refunded, returned or claimed back in respect of the distribution, sale, supply, marketing, promotion and exploitation of the [Product/Service/Work]. The [Company] shall be entitled to deduct the following sums before the calculation of the total sum:

1.1   any custom duties, export and import taxes, taxes on the sale and supply of goods or services, but not corporation tax.

1.2   any currency conversion or exchange costs, bank charges and commission.

1.3   any insurance, losses, discounts, returns, errors, replacements, remainder, packaging, delivery, insurance and freight costs.

1.4   any agent or other third party commission, fees and expenses.

1.5　copyright clearances and payments, royalties, consents, waivers and/ or sums due to any collecting society for the performance, mechanical reproduction and/or transmission of any material.

1.6　any editing, translations, censorship, credits, copyright notices and copyright protection, registrations of trade marks, software and other rights, product liability, product recall, legal costs and sums awarded in damages and/or compensation and/or otherwise to third parties and/or which are paid in settlement as a result of any allegation.

1.7　the creation and development of artwork, logos, music, sound recordings, videos and films, labels, packaging, marketing, promotional and advertising material, content for any website and/or app and/or mobile phone and/or other gadget.

G.087
Where a distributor, agent, licensee and/or other third party ceases trading for any reason and/or does not pay the sums due to the [Company] which is all and/or part of the Gross Receipts. Then it is agreed by both parties that the [Company] shall not be held responsible and/or liable to pay any such sums which the [Company] has not received to the [Licensor].

G.088
Where any sub-licensee, agent, distributor and/or other third party is appointed and/or engaged to exploit the [Work/Service/Product] on behalf of the [Company]. Then where any such person and/or third party does not pay any sums due to the [Company]. The [Company] shall still be obliged to pay the [Licensor] any royalties and/or other sums which would have fallen due to be paid at its own cost and expense.

G.089

1.1　The [Company/Agent] agrees and undertakes that all the sums received in respect of the [Work/Service/Product] under this Agreement shall be held separately from the other funds of the [Company].

1.2　The [Company/Agent] shall arrange for the deposit of all the funds in a separate bank account at a bank to be agreed with the [Licensor]. Further that the [Licensor] shall be provided with monthly statements of account supplied by the bank.

1.3　The [Company/Agent] shall not be entitled to create any charge and/or lien over the sums in the bank account in 1.2 above and/or to withdraw any sums without the prior written approval of the [Licensor].

G.090
'Gross Receipts' shall be the retail price paid and sums received for the [Product/Work] and retained by the [Company] [without the deduction of any

costs, fees, commission and/or any other charges which may be incurred] during the term of this Agreement and thereafter until all stock has been accounted for and the [Product/Work] is no longer supplied, transferred and/or sold by the [Company].

G.091

'Gross Receipts' shall be all sums received by the [Consortium/Enterprise] from the sale, supply, transfer, license, assignment and exploitation of the [Product/Work/Service] after deduction of the following costs which can be supported by relevant original documents:

1.1 Development costs of the [Product/Work/Service] up to [number/ currency] in total. Any costs over that figure shall be at the liability and cost of [specify].

1.2 Manufacturing costs of the [Product/Work/Service] which shall be no more than [number/currency]. Any costs over that figure shall be the liability and cost of [specify].

1.3 Marketing, promotion and advertising costs and expenses related to the [Consortium] and the [Product/Work/Service] including any computer software, logo, artwork, and content for a website and app up to [number/currency]. Any costs over that figure shall be the liability and cost of [specify].

1.4 Any bank charges, currency conversion costs, legal costs and expenses for agreements, sums due to collecting societies and for the clearance of music, lyric and sound recordings. The registration of trade marks, copyright and contractual matters, taxes, customs duties, product liability and other insurance, freight, delivery, fees and payments due for commission, agents fees and other third parties engaged to produce material and/or exploit the [Product/Service/Work].

Publishing

G.092

'The Gross Receipts' shall be the total proceeds from the exploitation of the [Work/Product/Service] in any form throughout the licensed Territory and/ or any unauthorised countries at any time directly or indirectly received by and/or credited to the [Agent] and/or any sub-agent after the deduction of any taxes which may be imposed by governments for the supply, sale and/ or transfer of the [Work/Product/Service].

G.093

'The Gross Receipts' shall be the total proceeds from the reproduction, sale, supply, licensing, distribution and exploitation of the [Work/Service/Product] and/or any parts throughout the world and universe at any time whether during the Term of this Agreement and/or at any time thereafter received by and/or credited to the [Publisher] and/or its parent company and/or any associated and/or affiliated company and/or any distributor, sub-agents, sub-licensees or any other authorised person and/or enterprise after the deduction of any taxes on the supply and or transfer of material [but not personal and/or corporation tax] currency and conversion charges, but not additional bank costs.

G.094
'The Gross Receipts' shall be all sums, credits, benefits and/or financial gains of any nature received by the [Company] and any parent company, subsidiary, affiliate, associate and/or business partner and/or collaborator relating directly and/or indirectly to the [Work/Service/Product] and any part which shall include the main title, character names, place names, the layout, format and compilation of the sets, costumes, questions, props, images, logos, music, lyrics, sound recordings, films and videos and/or any adaptation, translation, publication and/or development and all copyright and intellectual property rights and computer software rights in any media in any format and/or by any means and/or method including television, radio, all telecommunications and electronic methods of exploitation such as websites, apps, downloads, sound recordings and audio to text transmissions, patents, trade marks, domain names, and merchandising at any time whether during the Term of the Agreement or not and in any part of the world, air, sea or otherwise.

G.095
'The Gross Receipts' shall be all sums after conversion into [currency] which are actually received by the [Distributor] at any time arising from the reproduction, sale, license, supply, adaptation and/or exploitation of the [Work/Image/Logo] and/or any parts in any media and/or by any format and/or any other method whether in existence now at the time of the agreement and/or created and/or developed at a later date. The sums received shall be included whether or not a royalty rate was agreed at the time. Any new royalty rate shall be as a minimum [number] per cent. The Gross Receipts shall be the total monies before there are any deductions of the authorised expenditure listed in Appendix A.

G.096
'The Gross Receipts' shall be defined as the sums received and/or accrued from the sale, supply, license, rental, hire, reproduction, distribution, use and/or exploitation of the [Work/Sound Recordings/Artwork] and/or any part by the [Company], any subsidiary, associated company, parent company, partner, joint venture, sponsor, collaborator and/or any other third party at

any time without any deductions except for such sums as are due under tax and customs duty legislation to any government [but excluding personal and corporation tax.]

G.097

'Gross Receipts' shall mean the sums received in [sterling] by the [Publisher] in [country] and/or any other part of the world relating to exploitation of any of the rights granted under this Agreement in the [Work/Manuscript/Product] after the following authorised deductions:

1.1 commission which shall not exceed [number] % in any one case.

1.2 agency fees which shall not exceed [number] % for any agent.

1.3 currency exchange costs and charges.

1.4 any import, export and/or supply taxes, duties and payments.

1.5 any sales tax, value added tax or any other government tax on the supply, transfer and/or sale of material.

G.098

For the avoidance of doubt all sums accrued and owed and/or paid to the [Distributor] in respect of the exploitation of the [Work] shall be used to calculate the gross receipts and the sums due to [Name]. The [Distributor] shall bear the liability and risk of any sums accrued and not yet paid. Where a licensee and/or agent defaults and does not make any payment as required to the [Distributor]. Then the [Distributor] shall be liable to pay any sums due to [Name] in substitute for the licensee and/or agents' default. No interest shall however be due on such sums.

G.099

'Gross Receipts' shall be the total sum of the payments which the [Consortium/Enterprise] receives through its distributor and/or sub-licensees from the supply of the [Work/Service] as part of a subscription and/or educational service and/or directly to any person and/or company but not for any material supplied for free and/or for charitable purposes for short events.

G.100

'Gross Receipts' shall mean all the monies in [currency] which are received by the [Company] and/or any parent company and/or subsidiary and/or any new company specifically created for a project which are directly and/or indirectly related to the exploitation of the [Work] and/or any part at any time whether during the term of this agreement and/or thereafter at some later date. The sums received shall relate to the exploitation of the [Work] in any medium and/or by any means and/or method whether in existence now and/or created at a later date whether through new technology, rights and/or other forms of reproducing and/or adapting material and/or developing new variations.

There shall be no right to make any deductions from the sums received prior to the calculation of the gross receipts. All costs and expenses of any nature must be paid for separately by the [Company] at the [Company's] cost and expense. The sums must be kept in a new bank account held in the name of [specify] at [bank] and with the following authorised signatories [specify].

Services

G.101
'Gross Receipts' shall mean the total proceeds from the exploitation in any form and by any method of the [Sportsperson] whether commercial or not throughout the [Territory/World/Universe] at any time received by and/or credited to the [Manager] and/or any company and/or enterprise created by the [Manager] and/or any sub-agent and/or sub-licensee and/or other third party after the deduction of any value added tax or sales tax whether received during the Term of this Agreement or any time thereafter including:

1.1 Sponsorship, endorsements and promotion advances, fees and royalties, payments for public appearances, performances, sound recordings, texts, messages, voice-overs, avatars and animated versions and/or reproduction on satellite, cable, digital, terrestrial television, DVDs, videos, films, websites and apps and any other method over the internet and/or any other form of telecommunication and/or electronic method, live and pre-recorded radio, any biography and/or memoir and any other publications, blogs and/or articles.

1.2 Prize money, appearance fees for performances at professional sporting events, speaking tours, musical and/or other guest appearances.

1.3 The name of the [Sportsperson], and name, image, logo, slogan, initials, trade mark and/or brand whether registered or not and any three dimensional adaptation and/or other development.

G.102
'The Gross Receipts' shall be the total proceeds from the exploitation of the [Work/Product] in the following format: [specify] in [country] which is actually received by the [Distributor/Agent] after conversion to [currency] from [date] to [date]. After [date] all sums must be paid directly to the [Licensor] and not through the [Distributor/Agent].

G.103

'The Gross Receipts' shall be the total sums derived from the exploitation of the films, videos, advertisements, promotions, tours, plays, performances, appearances, endorsements, recordings, merchandising and/or other commercial exploitation in any other form of the [Actor] throughout the [Territory/country/world] from [date] to [date] directly or indirectly received by and/or credited to the [Agent] after the deduction of the following costs and expenses: [specify].

It is accepted that where the [Actor] contributes to a project for a charity that no commission and/or fees shall be due to the [Agent].

It is agreed that the [Agent] shall not be entitled to any fees and/or commission which arise from the sums received by the [Actor] from the following accounts on the internet and the pre-existing material:

Blog [title/reference]

YouTube [reference]

Instagram [reference]

[Other/reference]

[List pre-existing material and references].

G.104

'The Gross Receipts' shall be the total proceeds from all events, competitions, promotions, sponsorship fees, public appearances, performances, television and radio appearances, recordings, endorsements, photographs and stills, publications, merchandising and/or other sums from the commercial and non-commercial exploitation in any form in any media and by any method of the [Sportsperson] and his name, image, initials, three dimensional representation, voice, biography and family history throughout the [specify countries/Territory] at any time directly and/or indirectly collected and retained by the [Manager] and/or any company which may be created for that purpose.

G.105

The [Sportsperson] authorises the [Manager] to receive and deposit the [Gross Receipts] in the following joint bank account [specify account details]. This account shall require the signature of both parties for the removal of any funds, and the [Manager] undertake to comply at all times with this procedure. The [Manager] agrees only to deposit those sums which relate to the [Sportsperson] and not any third party. The [Manager] agrees that he/she shall have nor right and/or authority to create any charge, lien, loan and/or other debt against the sums.

G.106

The [Manager] agrees and undertakes not to deduct any sums from the Gross Receipts and shall disclose all sums received by and/or credited to the [Manager] to the [Sportsperson] prior to the deduction of any commission and/ or sums due to the [Manager] under this Agreement. No sums shall be hidden, misrepresented or transferred to prevent payment to the [Sportsperson].

G.107

'The Gross Receipts' shall be all the sums received and/or credited to the [Company] for the services of [Name] and/or any associated licensing of rights, endorsement, merchandising and/or any other exploitation in any media and/or medium whether received during the term of this Agreement or thereafter.

G.108

The [Company] agrees and undertakes to keep the sums due which accrue from the Gross Receipts in respect of [Name] in a separate account which is clearly identifiable and held for [Name]. The [Company] agrees that no charge, lien and/or other right shall be given to any third party over the funds. In the event that the [Company] is to cease trading and/or is in receivership and/or administration the [Company] and/or any third party shall not have any rights to the sums in the separate account.

G.109

The [Consultant] agrees and undertakes that it shall have no right to receive payment and/or hold any sums on behalf of the [Company] from third parties. That the [Consultant] shall ensure that all payments are made direct to the [Company] for the duration of this Agreement.

G.110

The [Company] agrees to pay all fees due to the [Consultant] as a total gross payment as stated in the invoice submitted including expenses and shall not deduct any tax, national insurance and/or any other sum at any time.

Sponsorship

G.111

The [Sponsor] agrees that it shall not have any right to any part of the total proceeds from the ticket sales, merchandising, television coverage and/or any other exploitation in any media throughout the world at any time.

G.112

'Gross Receipts' shall be defined as all sums received by the [Company] from the [Event] which shall include ticket and programme sales,

933

advertising, sponsorship, product placement, food, drink, accommodation, merchandising and any other exploitation including television, radio, mobiles, films, videos, blogs, websites, apps, premium rate telephone lines and competitions and any other method and means on the internet and/or in any other format of the [Event] and/or any part and/or any content and/or any adaptation in any language and/or other development between [date] and [date].

G.113
'The Gross Receipts' shall be the total amount of money received by the [Company] from all the series of [Programmes] sponsored by [Name]. Together with any sums received from any associated premium rate phone lines, competitions, publications, merchandising, television, radio, DVD, the internet and/or any other exploitation in any media throughout the world.

G.114
The [Company] and/or any licensee and/or sub-licensee shall only be entitled to deduct any payments and/or taxes due to a government which must be paid and/or deducted at source. No other deductions and/or payments made be made.

G.115
'The Gross Sponsorship Fees' shall be all payments by any method which are received by and/or due under any binding agreement to the [Company] from any third party which relates to the [Event] at [location] in [year] and any filming and recording and exploitation through any media at any time in any part of the world and/or any products, services and/or merchandising and/or derived from any sub-licence, sub-agent and/or sub-distributor at any time. It shall not apply to any other annual event and/or after [date].

G.116
'The Gross Receipts' shall be all sums received after conversion to [currency] by the [Enterprise] in respect of the [Conference] from the ticket and programme sales for the [Event] by the end [date]. It shall not include any sums received after the end date and/or any other sources of funding such as sponsorship, collaborations, partnerships, product placement and/or contributions by any other third parties.

G.117
The [Sponsor/Collaborator] agrees and accepts that they shall not be entitled to any sums received by the [Enterprise/Trust] in any form from the exploitation of the [Project] and any associated events, merchandising, films, videos, photographs and/or any other matters at any time whether in existence now and/or created in the future.

University, Charity and Educational

G.118

The [Institute/Charity] provides no undertaking and/or commitment as to the level of revenue, income, and/or gross and/or net receipts and/or any royalties due under this Agreement. The [Institute/Charity] shall only be liable to pay those costs and expenses set out in this agreement. It shall be entitled to deduct all other matters from any sums received before the calculation of any payments.

G.119

'The Gross Receipts' shall mean all the monies received by the [Institute/Charity] after conversion to [sterling] in the [United Kingdom] arising directly from exploitation of the [Service/Work/Product] throughout the world at any time after the following deductions: [specify].

G.120

'Gross Receipts' shall mean all the sums received and retained by the [Institute/Enterprise/Charity] relating to the sale, supply, rental, distribution and/or exploitation of the [Product/Service/Work] throughout the world in any format and/or by any means after the deduction of the following costs:

1.1 commission, agency and service fees and charges to any third party.

1.2 cost of product and design development including any name, logo, image, trade mark, sound recording, film, video, reproduction, manufacture, distribution, packaging, advertising, promotion and marketing. Insurance, freight, storage, delivery, stationary, postage, mobiles, travel, entertainment and accommodation.

1.3 business affairs and administration costs and charges. Sums due for advances, fees and royalties, waivers, buy-outs, contractual obligations, copyright clearance and consent fees and royalties, usage reports, sums due to collecting societies for performances, mechanical reproduction and/or otherwise. Currency exchange costs, losses, bank charges and fees; import, export and/or supply taxes, duties and payments. Any sales tax or value added tax or any other government charge on goods or services.

1.4 the cost of health and safety tests and assessments, compliance with legislation and other codes of practice and guidelines; editorial changes due to language and cultural differences. Sums due for fines, penalties, damages, infringements, legal costs, registrations, losses, errors and the settlement of any claims and/or legal proceedings.

G.121

'The Gross Receipts' shall be the sums received and/or credited to the [Enterprise/Charity] at any time whether during the Term of the Agreement or thereafter from the exploitation of the [Work/Service/Product].

G.122

The [Institute/Charity] shall not be liable and/or responsible for the default and/or failure of any third party for any reason. Where sums are not received by the [Institute/Charity] for the [Project] there shall be no obligation to account and/or make any payments.

G.123

'The Gross Receipts' shall be all sums, credits, and/or gains of any nature received by the [Enterprise/Charity] and any parent company, subsidiary, trust, affiliate, associate or business partner or sponsor relating directly or indirectly to the exploitation of the [Work/Service/Product] in any form and any part and/or any adaptation, development and/or variation from [date] to [date] in the [Licensed Area].

G.124

'The Gross Receipts' shall be all the sums held in [sterling] by the [Enterprise] in [country] which are the payments received from third parties for the non-exclusive right to access, read and make one copy of the [Project/Work] which is owned by [Name].

G.125

No sum shall be attributed as within gross receipts if it has not been paid even if it is owed and/or due at that time. The [Institute/Charity] shall have the discretion to retain, withhold and/or accrue any sums which are in dispute and/or the subject of legal proceedings and/or where costs have been incurred to convert the payment into [sterling].

G.126

'The Gross Receipts' shall be all the sums collected on [date] throughout [country] by the volunteers of the [Charity] which are calculated by the nominated accountants. The [Company] agrees to match this sum and to make a payment equal to the Gross Receipts within [number] days of the notification of the total figure.

GROUP ACCOUNTS

General Business and Commercial

G.127

'Accounts' in this agreement shall include all accounts relating to the [Company] and any parent, subsidiary, associate, affiliate, consortium of which the company is a member, partnerships with third parties, joint venture partners, and/or any other trust and/or holding company and any other business, venture, or project in which it has an interest of stock, shares and/or a contractual arrangement and/or of which it is a beneficiary and/or in which it has any control of the management and/or board and/or business plans either directly and/or indirectly.

G.128
Throughout this agreement references to accounts shall relate solely to the audited accounts of the [Company] in [country] and not to any parent and/or associated and/or holding company and/or subsidiary and/or licensee.

G.129
The [Company] may not rely on group accounts to support any statements as to the sums due to [Name]. The [Company] agrees and undertakes that [Name] shall be supplied with copies of a set of accounts for each individual parent, associate and/or licensee company at the [Company's] sole cost.

GUARANTEE

General Business and Commercial

G.130
In consideration of the rights granted to the [Licensee] by the [Licensor] in this agreement. The [Licensee] agrees to pay to the [Licensor] a non-returnable minimum guarantee payment of [number/currency] which shall be called the 'Minimum Guarantee'. In addition the [Licensee] shall pay such other royalties and sums as may be due as set out in clauses [specify]. The Minimum Guarantee shall be paid as follows:

1.1 [number/currency] upon signature by both parties of this agreement.

1.2 [number/currency] upon delivery to and acceptance by the [Licensee] of the Delivery Materials in clause [–].

1.3 [number/currency] upon first release to the general public of the [Film] in [country] whether in the form of a disc, via television and/or in some other manner.

1.4 The [Licensee] shall recoup the full amount of the Minimum Guarantee from the [Licensor's] share of Gross Receipts.

1.5 All expenses and costs [specify] shall be borne solely by the [Licensee].

G.131

There are no undertakings, projections and/or binding figures in respect of the potential future revenue, income and/or sums due from the exploitation of the [Film/Video/Disc] either as gross receipts or in royalty payments to the [Licensor].

G.132

There is no undertaking in respect of the release date, price, packaging, distributor and/or countries in which the [Film/Video/Disc] will be exploited, sold and/or exploited. Except the [Company] agrees and undertakes that [number] copies of the [Film/Video/Disc] will be released to the general public in [country] by [date] at the latest at [price/currency] by [Distributor] in the [specify] language.

G.133

The [Licensee] cannot guarantee the sales and/or royalty payments that may be made to the [Author] as a result of the exploitation of the [Disc] reproducing the [Sound Recording].

G.134

The [Sub-Licensee] agrees and undertakes to pay the [Licensee] not less than [number/currency] in each financial year during the term of this agreement. The [Sub-Licensee] shall not be entitled to recoup any such minimum payments from future accounting periods.

G.135

The [Company] agrees and undertakes to provide a guaranteed payment to [Name] of [number/currency] in respect of the [Work/Project] by [date] which shall not be set-off and/or recouped against any other sums due to [Name]. Provided that [Name] is available and capable of completing the [Work/Project] regardless of whether it goes ahead or not and/or is cancelled and/or delayed for any reason including grounds of force majeure.

G.136

The [Company] shall be entitled to stipulate the terms and conditions of the completion guarantee and to approve any such arrangements. In the event that the completion guarantor is a third party then the cost of such completion guarantee shall be set out in the [Budget]. In the event that there is any surplus of sums paid in respect of the completion guarantee by anyone at any time then it shall be repaid to the [Company]. The [Production Company] shall use its best endeavours to comply with all the terms of the Completion Guarantee.

G.137

'The Completion Guarantors Advance' shall mean all sums provided by the [Completion Guarantor] in respect of the [Film/Project] to the [Company] and the [Co-Production Company] to produce, complete and deliver the [Film/Project] together with all costs, charges and expenses and/or other sums which are advanced until recouped as set out in the document between the [Completion Guarantor] and the [Company] and the [Co-Production Company].

G.138

The [Company] confirms that it has taken out a Completion Guarantee with a reputable financial institution and that the beneficiary is the [Name]. The [Company] confirms that the Completion Guarantee covers any sums due to be paid to any third party for the successful completion of the terms of this Agreement and such costs shall not be less than the [Fixed Price Budget].

G.139

There are guarantees and/or undertakings provided by the [Distributor] that the [Film/Programme] will be transmitted and/or exploited and/or that any minimum payments will be made to [Name] in respect of the exercise of the rights granted in this Agreement.

G.140

The [Contractor] guarantees to the [Company] that all work supplied by the [Contractor] in performance of this contract shall be supplied by personnel who are qualified, skilled, experienced and competent in their respective professions. The [Contractor] further guarantees to the [Company] that the work shall conform with recognised professional standards and guidelines and meet all health and safety requirements. This Guarantee shall be provided for [ten] years from the date of the completion of the work.

It shall however not cover the following matters:

1.1 Damage caused by wear and tear and/or negligence by the [Company] and/or any third party.

1.2 In respect of any material supplied by the [Company].

1.3 In respect of any problem where the [Company] uses the services of a third party to remedy the matter and/or which is not reported immediately.

1.4 Any matter where the problem has arisen due to the force majeure including fire, floods, gas explosion, chemical leak and/or otherwise which could not have been expected and/or prevented by the [Contractor].

1.5 The guarantee shall be limited by a monetary value of [number/currency] in total for any repair and/or replacement work.

G.141

The [Supplier] agrees and undertakes that:

1.1   it shall comply with all the policies of the [Company] set out in Appendix A which form part of this Agreement; and

1.2   it shall also comply with the Code of Practice and Guidelines reference: [specify code] of [specify organisation]. A copy of which is attached and forms part of this agreement.

G.142

The [Company] agrees and undertakes and guarantees that only suitably qualified personnel will be engaged for the [Project] with a minimum of [number] years as [specify post] with valid work permits and/or visas and who are fluent in the technical language [specify] and registered as [specify] with [governing body].

G.143

The [Sponsor] agrees and undertakes that all personnel who attend the [Event] on behalf of the [Sponsor] shall be entitled to work in [country], have no criminal record and will be suitably qualified to fulfil the task they are allocated. The [Sponsor] agrees to supply a detailed list of all persons who will attend and/or work at the [Event] on behalf of the [Sponsor] to the [Company/Enterprise].

G.144

The [Sponsor] agrees and undertakes to the [Company] that it shall deliver all the material specified in Schedule A to the [Company] at its own cost and risk before [date]. That, where any items are damaged, lost and/or unsuitable, the [Sponsor] guarantees to supply replacements.

G.145

The [Sponsor] agrees and acknowledges that there are no warranties, guarantees and/or undertakings as to the number of people who will attend the [Event] and/or any sums received from the sales of the tickets and/ or whether the [Event] will be reported on television, radio and/or in any newspapers and/or on any media websites and/or apps.

G.146

The [Company] agrees and undertakes to the [Sponsor] that a minimum of [number] members of the public will attend the [Event] on [dates] at [location] provided that the [Event] is not cancelled and/or delayed due to circumstances beyond the [Company's] control as set out in clause [–] relating to force majeure.

G.147

1.1 If within [12] months after the [Goods/Products/Service] have been purchased and used. There is any defect discovered and/or which arises through normal [domestic/residential] use which is a fault due to design, materials and/or workmanship.

1.2 Then if 1.1 above occurs the [Supplier] agrees that it shall remedy the defect either by replacement and/or repair at the [Supplier's] expense. A new period of guarantee starts to run where the item is repaired and/or replaced.

1.3 The [Supplier] shall be entitled to reject any claim not mad within the [12] month period.

1.4 This Guarantee shall be without prejudice to any other rights or remedy that the [Purchaser] may be entitled to for any defect and/or otherwise. This guarantee shall only apply in [countries].

G.148
Your [Item] is guaranteed for [two] years from the date of purchase. In the event that the [Item] should become defective in that period then the defective part(s) will be repaired or at the [Supplier's] option replaced free of charge. This Guarantee shall not apply in the event that the [Item] is not used properly for its intended purpose in accordance with the instructions and/or there is no proof of purchase and/or the [Item] has not been previously repaired by unauthorised part(s) and/or personnel. Nor shall the Guarantee cover parts which are expected to be replaced due to normal wear and tear such as [–]. This Guarantee is not intended and does not in any way affect the [Purchaser's] legal and statutory rights in respect of the [Item].

G.149
All [Products/Service] purchased are guaranteed for [12] months from the date of the till receipt or delivery whichever one is the later. [Products/Service] will only be accepted for repair or replacement upon proof of purchase from the [Company]. The [Company] shall not be liable for:

1.1 Any defects resulting from wear and tear, accident, neglect and/or improper use by the [Customer] other than in accordance with the instructions and/or advice of the [Company] and/or the manufacturer.

1.2 Any [Products/Service] which have been modified and/or repaired except by the [Company]. The [Customer's] legal rights are not affected in any way by this guarantee.

G.150

In the event of any [manufacturing/production] defect in materials and/
or workmanship in any part of your [Product/Service] which arises within
[specify period] of the date of the original purchase [or hire purchase]
of your [Product/Service]. Then the [Customer] must return the [Product/
Service] to the [Company] at the [Customer's] risk and cost within that
period. The [Company] shall repair and/or replace any defective parts
covered by this guarantee at no cost to the [Customer]. When the [Product/
Service] is repaired the [Customer] will be responsible for collecting it at the
[Customer's] cost and risk. The guarantee does not operate in the following
circumstances:

1.1   Damage arising from work on the [Product/Service] by a person who is
      not a qualified engineer.

1.2   The original purchase receipt cannot be produced, or some other
      evidence of date of purchase or there is no guarantee.

1.3   There is no compensation for any losses, expenses, costs and/or
      damage to any other item used by the [Customer] in conjunction with
      the [Product/Service].

1.4   There is no compensation for any delay and/or otherwise in repairing
      and/or replacing the [Product/Service].

G.151

The [Company] confirms that the [Product/Service] is protected by a [ten]-
year guarantee. This guarantee is in addition to your statutory rights at law.
The guarantee excludes faults due to incorrect installation and/or misuse,
accidental and/or wilful damage and/or any repair and/or interference with
the [Product/Service] by a person not authorised by the [Company] and/or
any non-domestic and/or commercial use of the [Product/Service] and/or
any matter arising outside the authorised countries [specify and list].

G.152

The [Company] undertakes that if within [6] months of the date of purchase
of the [Work/Product/Service] any part is proved to be defective by reason
of faulty workmanship and/or materials and/or any other reason due to the
[Company]. The [Company] undertakes that it will repair and/or replace
the [Work/Product/Service] free of any charge for labour, materials and/
or delivery. This assurance shall only apply where the [Work/Product/
Service] has been used for residential purposes only and in accordance
with the instructions. No person unauthorised by the [Company] must
have already repaired and/or altered the [Work/Product/Service]. This
guarantee is in addition to your statutory and other legal rights. The
guarantee does not cover:

1.1 damage from transportation, improper use or neglect, the replacement of parts deemed to be the [Customer's] responsibility.

1.2 commercial use except under licence.

1.3 ancillary telephone, mobile and/or internet costs and expenses and/or damage to any other connected equipment and/or services.

G.153

1.1 The [Company] makes no guarantee as to the results that can be achieved by using the [Product/Service/Work] and/or otherwise.

1.2 This clause is not intended to exclude the [Company] of any warranty, obligation and/or liability and responsibility that the [Company] may have at law as the manufacturer, supplier and/or distributor of the [Product/Service/Work].

G.154

The guarantee will cease to apply in the following circumstances;

1.1 You and/or any third party have deliberately and/or intentionally damaged the [Product/Service/Work].

1.2 You have failed to use the [Product/Service/Work] in accordance with the instructions.

1.3 You have used the [Product/Service/Work] in conjunction with another item which was faulty and caused the damage.

1.4 You have exposed the [Product/Service/Work] to excessive water, heat, light and/or any chemical.

1.5 The [Product/Service/Work] is more than [number] years old since the date of purchase.

1.6 There is no evidence of proof of purchase, ownership and/or the level and/or type of damage is inconsistent with the details of the claim.

HEALTH

General Business and Commercial

H.001

1.1 The [Employee] confirms that he/she is in good health and has disclosed all matters relating to his/her personal health on the enclosed [Private Health Declaration] to be returned to the [HR officer] marked 'strictly private and confidential'.

1.2 The [Company] agrees that the document shall at all times be kept private and confidential and shall only be used for company insurance purposes and for no other reason under any circumstances without the prior written approval of the [Employee].

H.002

1.1 The [Employee] is not required to participate in any medical examination and/or to complete any report with regard to the specific and/or general nature of their health at any time.

1.2 The [Company] recognises that they have no inherent right to request private and confidential medical details from the [Employee] and/or their medical advisor unless the written consent of the [Employee] is provided.

1.3 A medical certificate from the [Employee's] General Practitioner and/or other qualified Doctor will be regarded as sufficient evidence for any absence due to ill-health for any period in excess of [three] days.

H.003

The [Company] shall have the right to request that the [Employee] provides a blood, urine, hair or other sample to a medically qualified practitioner engaged by the [Company] to test for drugs, alcohol and/or the use of other substances while on duty. The [Company] must have reasonable grounds to suspect and/or already have evidence that the [Employee] is carrying out his/her duties whilst drunk, incapacitated and/or on drugs not prescribed by a doctor and/or available over the counter in a pharmacist.

H.004

There shall be no obligation on [Name] to co-operate, assist and/or provide a blood, urine, hair and/or other sample to a medically qualified practitioner engaged by the [Company] and/or any other person to test for drugs, alcohol and/or other substances in respect of [Name] under any circumstances. The [Company] shall not be entitled to make a presumption of guilt due to any failure to provide a sample and/or be entitled to use this fact as a ground for alleging gross misconduct and/or otherwise. Such a refusal to provide any sample such not be deemed a breach of this agreement.

H.005

It shall be sufficient that the [Employee] provide a letter and/or other communication from their personal [general practitioner/medical practice] that they are fit to work and capable of performing the tasks required for their fulfilment of this Agreement. It is agreed that no medical examination shall be requested by the [Company] for any reason

H.006

The [Company] agrees and undertakes that it shall at all times maintain a safe and healthy workplace and comply with all legislation, regulations, guidelines and Codes of Practice that may be in force and/or applicable with respect to health, safety and security matters in any country where the [Employee] is required to work on any premises owned, controlled and/or used by the [Employee] in the course of his/her duties.

H.007

The [Company] acknowledges its duties and undertakes that it will:

1.1 take reasonable care to ensure that all equipment, premises, and systems of work used in the business are fit for their intended purpose and do not pose a threat to the health of any employees and are secure and safe to use.

1.2 ensure that all employees are regularly informed and to keep up-to-date with the [Company's] general policy with respect to the health and safety at work of its employees and of the arrangements for carrying out that policy. That where training courses and specialist safety clothing is required that these shall be provided at the cost of the [Company] to all relevant employees.

1.3 regularly review all the procedures and safety measures in place every [six] months and consult with such representatives of the [Health and Safety Executive/other government body] with a view to making and maintaining effective arrangements for the health and safety of its employees.

H.008

The [Contractor] agrees to perform the work in accordance with the health, safety and quality control standards of the [Company] and strictly to comply with all standards and practices of the [specify organisation] in [country] which are in force at the time, and all legislation, codes and professional trade guidelines.

H.009

The [Contractor] and its agents, directors and management, employees and sub- contractors undertake that they shall exercise all reasonable care and due diligence to:

1.1 Prevent pollution and contamination of the land, sea and/or air in performing work under this contract.

1.2 No rubbish, equipment, waste, oil, fuel, gases, lubricant, radioactive, hazardous substances and/or other pollutants will be discharged and/ or disposed of by the [Contractor] and/or any other third party under its control.

1.3 The [Contractor] agrees that it shall clean up, make good and remove any such pollution caused by the [Contractor] and/or any third party under tis control.

1.4 Comply with the safety, health, environmental and climate change policies and procedures of all the organisations listed in existence at the time that the work is completed: [specify].

H.010

The [Company] shall at its sole cost and responsibility take all necessary steps so that the [Product] shall pass the health and safety standards set by: [specify body] at all times during the Term of this Agreement. The [Company] shall monitor the production and distribution of all stages of the [Product] so that quality control is maintained and where any [Product] is recalled due to any reason shall bear all the administration, advertising, recall and replacement costs.

H.011

In the event that after the date of this Agreement any of the health and safety standards set by: [specify body/rules/other] should be changed, modified and/or altered so that other additional standards are applicable to the [Product] and/or there are changes in any laws, regulations or otherwise in the Territory. Then the [Company] shall provide such information to the [Licensor] and the [Company/Licensor] agrees to bear all costs and expenses incurred in connection with or arising out of any modifications, changes, alterations to the tools, prototypes, samples and [Product] required to attain and pass any new health and safety standards.

H.012

No [Product] shall be shipped unless and until the [Product] has passed the health and safety standards applicable at that time unless the [Licensor] so directs or provides consent and agrees to bear responsibility and liability for any consequence arising from such shipment.

H.013

1.1 If the [Units/Products] are perishable and/or have a fixed duration where they are fit for purpose and/or if there are any adverse circumstances which impact on the potential quality of the [Units/Products]. Then you are under a legal obligation to notify the [Company] of any such facts and not to withhold such information.

1.2 If you become aware that there is any health risk to the public in the supply, production and/or packaging process then you must act quickly and notify the [Company].

1.3 A detailed record shall be kept of all sample tests of the content of the [Units/Products] which shall be made available upon request to the [Company].

1.4 A detailed record shall be kept of all complaints by the public relating to the quality and content of the [Units/Products] which shall be made available upon request to the Company].

H.014

[Name] shall be responsible for ensuring that all equipment, or other item or material supplied by [Name] pursuant to this Agreement shall be safe, and complies with the health and safety policy of the [Company]. [Name] shall not supply or use any material of any kind which shall or might pose any risk to the health and safety of any employee or agent of the [Company] and/or the general public in any circumstances.

H.015

The [Artist] agrees that to the best of his/her knowledge and belief he/she is not now nor has at any time been subject to any illness, injury and/or medical condition which would in any way prevent him/her providing his/her services. The [Artist] will at all times do all that is reasonably necessary to attain and maintain such sound state of health as will enable him/her to perform fully his/her services under this Agreement and will not undertake any hazardous pursuits.

H.016

The [Sportsperson] agrees to conduct himself/herself in a fit, proper and professional manner at all times during the Term of the Agreement.

H.017
Irrespective of any holiday leave the [Company] agrees that the [Presenter's] fee shall not be affected by any leave due to ill-health provided that it does not exceed [ten] days in any one year and is supported by a medical certificate on each occasion.

H.018
In the event that the [Director] is unable to perform his/her obligations under this Agreement for any reason including ill-health, mental incapacity, family crisis and/or some other reason which is an unexpected emergency. The [Company] shall be entitled to terminate the Agreement subject to making fair and reasonable payment to the [Director] in respect of the services already provided to the date of termination.

H.019
The [Company] shall have the right by notice in writing to terminate this Agreement if the [Presenter] is unavailable through ill-health or any other reason for more than [specify duration] to provide his/her services as agreed.

H.020
The [Company] agrees not to cancel this Agreement due to the illness, injury and/or death of a person listed as key personnel provided that a suitable substitute can be arranged within [one] calendar month from the date that the person is unavailable, incapacitated and/or has died.

H.021
In the event that all and/or any of the key personnel provided by the [Enterprise] for this [Project/Work] are not available for a continuous period of more than [seven] working days [excluding weekends]. Then the [Company] shall have the right to terminate the Agreement with immediate effect and to only pay for such work as has been approved and completed prior to the date of termination. All work and material which has been created, developed and/or commissioned by the [Enterprise] for the [Company] shall be assigned to and owned by the [Company]. Where there are outstanding issues the parties agree to enter into mediation and/or dispute resolution and/or arbitration prior to commencing any litigation.

H.022
The [Company] agrees that [Name] shall be entitled to unpaid leave of absence for up to [seven] days on an annual basis for the purpose of completing an annual health check-up, medical and hospital treatment, dental appointments and treatment, eye tests, mental health and drug treatment and therapy, homeopathy, osteopathy, physiotherapy and related health and wellbeing matters related to [Name] and their immediate family.

H.023

Where any part of a [Product/Project] involves tests, materials and/or processes and/or packaging that pose a risk to human health. Then the [Company] agrees and undertakes to ensure that all necessary steps are taken to reduce risk and any potential liability to a level of safety that complies with the standards set out in [country] together with any guidelines, codes and legislation.

H.024

The [Company] agrees that where any person is absent on leave due to ill health and then returns but cannot fulfil their previous role. That the [Company] shall consult with them to offer alternative roles which may be available and/or agree a termination and a settlement agreement.

H.025

The [Company/Charity] agrees that it shall comply with the following policies when entering into merchandising agreements with any third party:

1.1   It shall not use any products which use animal fur.

1.2   It shall not agree that any tests should be carried out on live animals.

1.3   As far as possible recyclable materials will be used and the use of plastic reduced to a minimum including in any packaging.

1.4   Local resources should be utilised if possible to reduce the freight of material by air.

1.5   Material should not be used from areas of the world where the source reduces the number of trees significantly and/or depletes endangered habitats.

HIRE PURCHASE

General Business and Commercial

H.026

The [Unit/Products] have been lent for hire under the terms and conditions attached and no title, ownership and/or other proprietary right shall pass under any circumstances to the [Hirer].

H.027

This Agreement is a 'Hire Purchase Agreement' and accordingly is not a conditional sale. The [Unit/Products] are bailed [or in Scotland hire] in return for periodical payments by the person to whom they are bailed or hired. The property in the [Unit/Products] will pass to that person only once the terms of the Agreement are complied with in full.

H.028
There is no right granted and/or consent and/or authorisation provided for you to hire, sub-let and/or permit any third party the use and/or possession and/or control of the [Unit/Product] at any time.

HOLDING COMPANY

General Business and Commercial

H.029
'Holding Company' shall mean any company which directly and/or indirectly owns not less than [51] % [fifty-one] per cent of the voting share capital of another company which is known as the subsidiary. The Holding Company and the subsidiary are associated companies.

H.030
'Holding Company' in this Agreement shall mean a Holding Company as defined by [specify legislation] in [country] at the date of this Agreement.

H.031
'The Groups' shall mean the [Company] including any holding company or companies of the [Company] and any subsidiary or subsidiaries of, any such holding company. 'Holding Company' and 'Subsidiary' shall be defined in accordance with existing legislation at the time of this agreement.

H.032
'The Holding Group' shall mean the following companies which are linked either indirectly through associated businesses and/or directly through shareholdings as subsidiaries [specify name/company registration/address].

H.033

1.1 The [Company] is the holding company for the receipt of funds and payments for the [Consortium] known as [specify name] which was created on [date] and funded by [specify].

1.2 The [Company] shall not pay, commit and/or transfer any funds out of the accounts relating to the [Consortium] unless authorised by [Name] on behalf of the [Consortium].

1.3 The [Company] shall hold any funds in [specify account] in the name of [specify] and shall provide copies of statements on a regular basis upon request to [specify].

H.034

Where after the conclusion of this agreement any new holding and/or subsidiary company is created by the [Licensee]. Then the [Licensee] agrees to notify the [Licensor] of all such information and report on the impact that this may have on the accounting and agreements if any.

HOLIDAYS

General Business and Commercial

H.035

The [Employee] shall be entitled to [number] days leave on holiday per annum which shall be in addition to all recognised Bank Holidays listed as follows: [specify].

H.036

1.1 The [Company] acknowledges that the [Executive] is entitled to the Executive's Holidays in addition to Bank Holidays.

1.2 The [Company] agrees that Bank Holidays and the Executive's Holidays shall be subject to the agreed rates of payment in accordance with the Executive's Remuneration.

1.3 In the event that the [Executive] is requested to work on Bank Holidays or on days which have been agreed as the Executive's Holiday then such work will be paid for on an ad hoc basis on terms to be agreed between the [Company] and [Executive] at a higher rate than normal.

1.4 The [Executive] shall at all times provide proper and reasonable notice to [specify position] prior to taking any holiday entitlement.

1.5 The [Company] shall not unreasonably refuse any request or provide unnecessary delay in providing their authorisation. Where no response is received within [seven] days then the [Executive] shall be entitled to presume and it shall be deemed that authorisation has been provided for any such leave.

H.037

The holiday year will be [1 January] to [31 December] in each year. Holiday entitlement shall accrue at the rate of [two] days for each period of [four] weeks worked up to a maximum of [number] days in the holiday year. In addition the [Employee] shall be entitled to take as leave all public and bank holidays.

H.038

The [Employee] is not entitled to carry over holiday entitlement from one year to the next. In exceptional circumstances the [Company] may at its discretion allow the holiday entitlement to be carried over to the first [three] months of the following holiday year.

H.039

All holiday dates must be agreed in advance with the [Employee's] manager.

H.040

[Employees] leaving the employment of the [Company] shall be entitled to payment in lieu of accrued holiday entitlement. If on leaving the [Company's] employment the [Employee] has received paid holiday in excess of his/her accrued holiday entitlement then the [Company] shall be entitled to deduct such excess holiday payment from any other sums due to the [Employee].

H.041

The [Company and the [Employee] agree the following terms:

1.1 Holidays accrue pro rata during the period of employment. The [Company] shall be entitled to require the [Employee] to work on public and bank holidays if such holidays fall on a day on which the [Employee] would normally be required to work.

1.2 All holiday dates must be agreed with the [HR department] a minimum of four weeks in advance.

1.3 [Employees] leaving the [Company] shall be entitled to payment in lieu of accrued holiday entitlement. If the [Employee] has received paid holiday in excess of accrued holiday entitlement the [Company] may deduct such overpayment.

H.042

In addition to the usual public holidays the [Manager] shall be entitled to [five] weeks paid holiday in each consecutive period of [twelve months] commencing on [1 April] in each year. The holidays shall be taken at such times as may be agreed between the [Manager] and the [Company]. The [Manager] may not without the consent of the [Company] carry unused holiday leave over to the next yearly period.

H.043

In the event of the termination of the [Manager's] employment for any reason the [Manager] shall be entitled in respect of the holiday year in which termination occurs to a proportionate part of the period of paid holiday and shall be paid in respect of any holiday that remains outstanding and has not yet been taken.

H.044

The [Employee] accepts that the precise date relating to the [Employee's] holidays if not already specified in clause [–] shall be agreed between the [Company] and the [Employee]. The [Employee] shall be required to give reasonable notice with respect to the taking of any holidays other than public or bank Holidays. The [Company] shall be entitled to deduct from any sums due to the [Manager] any payments due to the [Company] for any holiday leave which is in excess of that to which the [Employee] is entitled.

H.045

'Employee's Holidays' shall be [number] working days in any calendar year in addition to bank holidays.

H.046

'The Holiday Schedule' shall mean the times and dates during which the [Sportsperson] shall not be obliged to provide his services under this Agreement. A copy of the Holiday Schedule is attached to and forms part of this Agreement.

The [Manager] agrees that the [Sportsperson] shall be entitled to such holidays and other leave as set out in the Holiday Schedule together with such other dates as may be agreed between the [Manager] and the [Sportsperson].

H.047

The [Company] confirms that in any event the [Presenter] shall be entitled to not less than [number] days' holiday leave per year excluding public and bank holidays and weekends.

H.048

The [Presenter] shall inform the [Company] at the earliest opportunity of all leave which he/she intends to take under the terms of this Agreement which are not in the attached [Schedule A] and in any event to give the [Company] not less than [number] days notification to [Name].

H.049

There shall be no obligation on the [Company] to pay for holiday leave or any other period of absence. All payments are subject to completion of work.

Provided that [Name] fulfils the scheduled [appearances/contributions] there is no notice required of any leave of any nature.

H.050

The [Executive] shall be entitled to take up to [ten] days additional leave of absence which is unpaid during the year. Provided that at least [one] calendar month's notice is provided to the [Company] and it is not during the following dates [specify dates].

H.051

Holiday entitlement does not apply until you have completed the [probationary/ internship] period and have been notified that your agreement will continue thereafter. The holiday leave is [number] days in the first year from the date of the end of the probationary period. This period is in addition to bank and public holidays.

H.052

Where there is any dispute between the parties in respect of holiday leave and other absence. Then the matter shall be referred to [Name] to endeavour to resolve the matter prior to any other steps and/or actions are taken.

I

ILLEGALITY

General Business and Commercial

I.001
The [Licensor] shall not be responsible and/or liable for any statements, acts, images, text, omissions, illegality and/or conduct which comes within the doctrine of ultra vires and/or is against public policy and/or is otherwise contrary to legislation in any country by the [Licensee] and/or any sub-licensee, agent, distributor and/or supplier at any time.

I.002
The [Purchaser] agrees that it shall not:

1.1 use and/or authorise any type of use of the [Work/Disc/App] and/or any data and information, text, images, software and other material in any manner which is inconsistent with the intended purpose of the non-exclusive licence granted to the [Purchaser].

1.2 deface, erase, remove, delete, add to and/or alter any part of the [Work/Disc/App] and/or any copyright notices, trademarks, service marks, disclaimers, serial codes] displayed and/or on any packaging.

1.3 make more copies than permitted and shall not supply the [Work/Disc/App] and/or any content and/or copies to any third party for their own use and exploitation without the consent of the [Licensor].

I.003
The [Licensee] shall not and shall not authorise others to carry out any acts, use any materials and/or display any images and/or texts and/or to exploit the [Products] in any manner which could be construed as a breach of any laws of [specify countries].

In the event that it becomes apparent that there is an allegation of wrongdoing of any nature whether fraud, banned ingredients and/or failure to comply with international standards and/or some other reason. Then the [Licensor] shall have the right to suspend and/or terminate the agreement with immediate effect by notice in writing to the [Licensee]. Such termination shall be without

957

prejudice to any claim for damages, losses, payments under the contract and/or loss of reputation.

I.004

In the event that there is any allegation of fraud, corruption, breach of contract, infringement of copyright and/or other intellectual property rights and/or infringement of trade marks and/or any logos, images, text and/or videos, irregular accounting practices, failure to adhere to health and safety standards and control and/or any other breaches and/or allegations which could and/or do result in criminal and/or civil proceedings against the [Licensee] [and any sub-licensee, agent, distributor and/or supplier appointed by the [Licensee]]. Then the [Licensor] shall have the right to suspend the agreement for a period up to [six] months and/or to terminate the agreement with [three] months' notice and/or to serve notice to revert all rights granted back to the [Licensor] within [three] months.

I.005

Where the [Institute/Enterprise] becomes aware and/or is informed by any authority, police and/or government and/or regulating body that the [Company] and/or its directors:

1.1 are being investigated and/or prosecuted for a breach of the following Codes: [specify titles].

1.2 are alleged and/or have breached health and safety regulations and legislation and/or failed to renew, register and/or hold a mandatory licence for any reason relating to the agreement.

1.3 are alleged and/or have failed to adhere to normal accounting practises and committed a fraud and/or misappropriated funds and/or are otherwise a shell company for a criminal operation.

Then the [Institute/Enterprise] shall have the right to serve notice on the [Company] to terminate this agreement and no further sums which may be due shall be paid to the [Company] and all rights shall revert to the [Institute/Enterprise] on the date the notice is received by the [Company].

I.006

Where the [Consultant] becomes aware that there is a conflict of interest between the aims and interests of the [Company] and the [Consultant] and/or that there is an intention by any person at the [Company] and/or any third contractor not to fully comply with all the required legislation, Codes of Practice and Guidelines. Then the [Consultant] agrees that where he/she becomes aware of these potential problems that he/she shall advise [title/name] at the [Company] as soon as reasonably possible.

I.007

Where at any time during the continuance of this Agreement the [Consortium] discovers and/or becomes aware that one party and/or any of their employees, researchers, consultants and/or agents and/or any other third party engaged by them have obtained, supplied, distributed and/or reproduced any data, information, records and/other material of any nature from the [Project] without consent and/or in breach of the code of conduct and protocol of [specify body] and/or may have committed one and/or more breaches of copyright, data protection and/or an allegation has been made of a criminal offence and/or civil and/or criminal proceedings have started and are pending. Then it is agreed that the [Consortium] shall appoint a person to investigate the matter and to report on the circumstances. Provided that it is agreed that no steps shall be taken by the [Consortium] where an external and/or civil and/or criminal action is pending except to suspend any person from involvement in the [Project] until the matter has been decided.

I.008

The [Consortium] reserves the right to terminate and/or cancel this agreement in the event that:

1.1   an employee, consultant, researcher, director and/or other third party engaged by the [Company] in respect of this [Project] makes derogatory statements and/or portrays any derogatory images of the [Consortium] and/or the [Project] on social media and/or is the subject of a criminal investigation in any country for fraud, misleading investors and/or failure to comply with legislation and health and safety regulations, codes and guidelines.

1.2   the [Company] exceeds the agreed Budget for the [Project].

1.3   the [Company] is found to have actively misled the [Consortium] as to the level of expertise which it can provide and the other similar projects which it has already completed.

1.4   the [Company] is financially insolvent and incapable of paying its debts, loans and other creditors.

IMPLIED TERMS

General Business and Commercial

I.009

For the avoidance of doubt all express terms contained in this document shall prevail over any terms which it may be possible to construe as implied by law.

I.010

This agreement sets out the terms, conditions and undertakings which have been agreed between the parties in respect of [subject/project]. No terms should be implied which directly conflict with any of these existing clauses in this agreement. Nor should any additional rights be implied as only those mentioned in this document have been granted to the [Licensee].

I.011

The parties agree that any matters discussed, disclosed, planned and/or projected for the future whether in writing, by email, text, skype and/or in person shall not be included in this agreement and/or implied as a term. Any matter must be specifically stipulated in the agreement otherwise it is excluded.

I.012

All discussions, disclosures, promises, representations, projections, plans, marketing proposals and any other matter represented and made by the [Company] to the [Institute/Enterprise] in respect of this [Project] shall be considered to be included as part of this agreement.

I.013

There shall be no implied terms in respect of this agreement. The standard, quality and condition of all material is as stated and there is no assurance of uniformity, that there will be no flaws and/or that the material will not deteriorate whilst in transit.

I.014

The parties both agree that all implied terms are specifically excluded from this contract and the terms are only those which are stated.

I.015

No representation by any person, officer, director, trustee and/or other trust, company and/or entity nor any data, records, documents, financial projections, software, emails, sound recordings, samples, prototypes, film, text, image and/or logo can be implied into this agreement at any time. The parties agree that any disclosures, representations and other material were not intended to be part of this agreement and were intended as guidance only. The [Purchaser] agrees that it must seek its own independent advice and must base their decision on their own research and not on any facts and/or information supplied prior to the date of the agreement.

960

INCOME

General Business and Commercial

I.016
'Income' shall be the aggregate of all the sums and/or financial benefits of any nature received by and/or credited to the [Company] and/or any entity, company, enterprise, associate, subsidiary set up and/or created to receive and/or pay any sums including payments due for advertisements and promotions, sponsorship, endorsements, product placement, licensing and/or distribution of material and/or any other service, product and/or rights in any format and/or medium in respect of [Project].

I.017
'Income' shall be all the sums received by the [Licensee] and/or paid to the [Licensee] from any third parties in respect of the exploitation of the copyright and intellectual property rights in the [Work/Film/Recordings] which are specifically granted to the [Licensee] under this agreement. Income shall also include any sums received by any sub-licensees, sub-agents, sub-distributors, subsidiaries, associates and/or connected bodies. There is no right in this agreement to assign any rights and/or to transfer the title in any form by the [Licensee] in the [Work/Film/Recordings].

I.018
'Income' shall mean all sums actually received by the [Licensee] from the exploitation of the copyright and intellectual property rights granted in the [Artwork/Image/Logo] under this agreement after the deduction of the following costs, expenses, commission and fees: [specify].

I.019
'Income' shall mean such income as is subject to taxation under the existing legislation in [country].

I.020
'Income' shall be the sums received by [person] in respect of the position [specify role] for the [Company] from [date] to [date] but excluding the following: [Share option/Bonus/expenses/pension/personal insurance/car/laptop/mobile/petrol allowances/other benefits].

I.021
'Executives Basic Remuneration' shall mean the annual sum of [number/currency] which shall be the gross sum payable by the [Company] to the [Executive] in accordance with the terms of this agreement.

I.022

The [Company] agrees to pay the [Executives] Remuneration by credit transfer to the [Executives] personal bank or building society account on or before the [specify day] of each month. In the event that the payment date is a bank holiday then the payment shall be made the day before the due date.

I.023

'The Total Income' shall be all the sums received by the [Enterprise/ Charity] in respect of the [Project/Fundraising Promotion] after conversion to [currency] which has been received from any source and/or by any method. All such sums shall be deposited in the bank account held at [bank]. The only sums which may be deducted at any time shall be all the expenses, costs and expenditure which has been authorised in advance by [specify person/role] under the authority of the [Board/Trustees] of the [Enterprise/Charity].

I.024

The [Licensee/Agent] agrees that it shall be obliged to disclose all sums and benefits, gifts and free and/or discounted resources, material and hospitality which are received, supplied and/or offered at any time whether or not directly attributable as income which relate to [Name], his/her trade marks, images, logos and/or services and/or any related merchandise, promotion and/or marketing.

I.025

'The Total Revenue' shall be defined as all the income and other sums received in respect of the reproduction, supply, distribution, licensing, adaptation and/or exploitation of the [Work/Product/Characters] and/or any parts whether directly and/or indirectly through a third party from [date] to [date] by the [Enterprise] in [country] in [currency]. No sums not remitted for any reason shall be included.

INDEMNITY

Film, Television and Video

I.026

The [Company] agrees that it shall keep the [Distributor] indemnified against all liabilities, claims, actions, proceedings, damages, losses and legal costs incurred by the [Distributor] and/or awarded against the [Distributor] and/ or any sums agreed and paid by the [Distributor] on the advice of its legal advisors which have directly arisen and resulted from any breach and/or alleged breach and/or non-performance of any of the terms of this agreement by the [Company].

I.027

The [Assignor] agrees to indemnify the [Assignee] against all claims, liabilities, demands, actions, costs, damages and/or reasonably foreseeable losses which may arise as a direct result of any breach by the [Assignor] of any term, warranties, representations and/or inducements in respect of this agreement which may arise before: [date]. After that time the [Assignor] shall not be liable to pay the [Assignee] any sums whatsoever however they may arise regardless of whether they are caused by the [Assignor]. The [Assignee] agrees that this indemnity shall not continue after: [date].

I.028

In the event of any claim, writ, dispute, action, summons and/or threatened legal action and/or proceedings of any nature in connection with clause [–] above before the end of the indemnity. The parties agree that the party who may seek to rely on the indemnity to be paid any sums shall be obliged to notify the other party as soon as reasonably practicable of any matter. Neither party shall incur any costs of any nature in such circumstances without first obtaining the prior approval of the other party which shall not be unreasonably delayed or withheld. In any event no settlement shall be made to the claim of any third party unless the party from whom the indemnity is sought has had an opportunity to review the case and offer its opinion.

I.029

The [Company] shall indemnify the [Distributor] against any liability, losses, damages, expenses and/or costs that may be incurred and/or may be made against the [Distributor] arising directly and/or indirectly from the exploitation of the rights granted in the [Film] and/or the [Film Material] under this agreement and/or as a result of the failure by the [Company] to perform any of the terms of this agreement.

I.030

The [Company] shall indemnify the [Distributor] against any liability, losses, damages, expenses or other matter arising directly or indirectly from the breach and/or non-performance of this agreement by the [Company] with the following financial limitations of liability in each of the following countries: [specify country] [specify financial limit].

The [Distributor] agrees to accept the financial limits set out in this clause for each country and agrees that regardless it shall not be entitled to any additional sums.

I.031

The [Producer] and the [Distributor] agree that they shall not provide any indemnity provisions and/or undertakings to each other but shall arrange insurance cover for such purpose in the sum of [number/currency] for the benefit of each party for [specify subject].

I.032

The [Company] shall indemnify the [Distributor] in respect of any claims, actions, and/or other legal proceedings, losses, damages and legal costs and expenses which relates to a matter which directly concerns any part of the [Film/Video/Podcast] including the artists, performers, music, lyrics, scripts, computer generated material, images, products, locations, credits, trade marks, logos and sound recordings provided that the [Distributor] complies with the following procedures:

1.1 That the [Distributor] will notify the [Company] as soon as possible of any matter upon which it seeks to be indemnified by the [Company] and will disclose all information, documents and background material as well as arrange access to any persons and/or records that may be relevant.

1.2 That the [Distributor] shall not take any steps or make any offer to settle the matter without the authority and approval of the [Company] of both the amount of the financial settlement but also the documents that must be signed.

1.3 That all legal costs shall be kept to a minimum and the [Distributor] shall regularly keep the [Company] informed of any expenditure over [number/currency] which it intends to incur.

1.4 That where any sums can be recouped and/or reimbursed under an insurance policy held by the [Distributor] then the [Distributor] shall not seek to be indemnified by the [Company].

I.033

The [Distributor] agrees to indemnify the [Licensor] in respect of any disputes, settlements, claims, actions, and/or other legal proceedings, losses, damages, legal costs and expenses incurred by the [Licensor] as a direct result of the actions, omissions and/or errors of the [Distributor] in respect of the exploitation of the [Sound Recordings] by the [Distributor] and/or any sub-licensee, agent and/or other third party engaged and/or authorised by the [Distributor] from [date] to [date] but not outside those dates.

I.034

The parties agree that the following matters are not covered by any indemnity from one party to the other:

1.1   Administrative and reproduction costs.

1.2   Costs of financial and accounting advice.

1.3   Telephone, accommodation, hospitality and travel costs.

1.4   Fees for consultants, agents, and other experts except legal advisors.

1.5   Matters which arise as a result of the failure to pay any manufacturer, supplier and/or any other third party.

I.035
The [Licensor] and the [Licensee] agree that the total maximum liability of each party under this agreement to the other party shall be limited to [number/currency]. That no party shall be entitled to be indemnified for any reason beyond that sum whether or not the excess sum is claimed as a result of negligence, error, omission and/or for any other reason.

I.036
The [Distributor/University] agrees that:

1.1   there is no indemnity provided in respect of the [Film/Work/Product] and/or any of the master and promotional material and stock which has been supplied to the [Distributor/University] either before and/or as part of this agreement.

1.2   the [Distributor/University] shall not be entitled at a later date to seek any sum as a contribution from [Institute/Estate of name].

1.3   the [Distributor/University] has purchased the [Film/Work/Product] and all the master and promotional material and stock without confirmation and/or verification as to clearance and/or payments for any copyright, intellectual property rights, contractual liabilities and/or legal ownership in any form.

1.4   the [Distributor/University] shall bear all the risk and shall be liable for all costs, expenses, claims, actions, settlements, payments, clearance costs and any matter that arise and shall not seek to join [Institute/Estate of name] as a party and/or institute any legal proceedings against [Institute/Estate of name].

I.037

1.1   The total liability of any indemnity by [Agent/Name] to the [Distributor] shall be limited to [number/currency].

1.2   The [Distributor] agrees that they shall not be entitled to any sums in excess of that figure in 1.1.

1.3 The [Distributor] agrees that it shall also bear the cost of any matter which is less than [number/currency] and that [Agent/Name] shall not be liable to pay such sums below that amount at any time.

1.4 Any indemnity between [Agent/Name] and the [Distributor] shall end on [date]. No claim may be made after that date.

I.038

The [Licensor] will at its own expense, indemnify, save and hold harmless the [Licensee] and its successors, licensees, assigns and employees, from and against any and all liability, loss, damage, cost and expense (including without limitation reasonable attorneys' and legal fees) incurred by them by reason of or resulting from any alleged breach, actual breach or claim by a third party with respect to any of the warranties, undertakings or terms made by the [Licensor] in respect of this agreement.

I.039

Any liability, loss, damage, cost or expense resulting from any such alleged breach and/or breach and/or claim may be recouped by the [Licensee] from the [Licensor's] share of the Gross Receipts. If the [Licensor's] share of Gross Receipts is not sufficient to pay the sum then the [Licensor] shall still be obliged to pay the balance of the sums due within [thirty] days of the demand for payment.

I.040

1.1 In the event that any person shall make any claim and/or institute any legal action and/or proceedings whether through a claim form on line and/or through the Courts which makes allegations of copyright and/or trade mark infringement and/or any other intellectual property rights and/or an allegation of breach of a contract and/or failure to make payments and/or any other matter relating to the subject matter of this agreement and/or any exploitation arising from it against the [Licensee] and/or the [Licensor]. Then both the [Licensee] and/or the [Licensor] agree to give prompt written notice to the other party.

1.2 In respect of 1.1 the parties agree that the [Licensor] shall where necessary undertake at its own cost and expense to defend any matter on behalf of both parties and use competent and experienced legal advisors. Where the [Licensor] either fails to defend the matter and/or refuses to do so then the [Licensee] may engage their own legal advisors] and the reasonable charges shall be recouped from payment due to the [Licensor] under the agreement.

1.3 It is agreed that any settlement by the parties shall only be made with the [Licensor's] approval, which approval shall not be unreasonably withheld.

That where the settlement is paid by the [Licensee] that the sum may be recouped from any payments due from the [Licensee] to the [Licensor].

1.4 The [Licensee] shall have the right to withhold a reserve from any monies whatsoever payable to the [Licensor] to meet its legal costs and as an indemnity fund to meet any claim that the [Licensee] may have against the [Licensor].

I.041
The [Artist/Performer] agrees to indemnify the [Television Company] in respect of all legal actions, proceedings, claims, damages, expenses and liability whatsoever which may be made and/or brought against and/or incurred by the [Television Company] in consequence of any breach of the terms of this agreement and/or the contribution by the [Artist/Performer] to the [Series/Programme/Podcast].

I.042
The [Contributor/Presenter] shall not be liable to the [Company] and/or any third party for any allegations, claims, defamation, civil and/or criminal offence, breach of contract, infringement of copyright, disclosure of confidential information, damages, losses, expenses, costs or otherwise arising from the provision of the [Contributors'/Presenters'] services and appearances on [Series/Podcast/Programme]. The [Company] accepts full responsibility and liability for all such matters in respect of the [Contributor/Presenter] and the [Company] and the [Series/Podcast/Programme]. There is no indemnity and/or undertaking by the [Contributor/Presenter] to the [Company] of any nature. The [Company] accepts that the script is supplied by the [Company] and that the [Contributor/Presenter] is required to follow the reasonable directions of the [Company]. The [Company] agrees that any direct and/or indirect consequences that may arise are entirely at the [Company's] risk and cost. The [Company] also agrees that where the [Contributor/Presenter] is obliged to defend a legal action relating services and appearances under this agreement by a third party that the [Company] will pay all the legal and administrative costs and expenses.

I.043
In consideration of the grant of permission to allow filming at [address of premises/location]. The [Company] agrees that it shall indemnify and be liable to the [Name/Company] up to [number/currency] in respect of any damage to property and/or facilities, loss of sales, legal actions, claims, personal injury, death and any other damages, losses, expenses and costs which are directly caused by the negligence, errors, omissions and/or acts of the [Company] and/or any person for whom the [Company] is responsible and/or has engaged and/or invited onto the premises.

I.044

The [Company] and the [Collaborator] will indemnify and keep indemnified each other against liabilities, claims, demands, actions, costs including reasonable legal fees and/or damages and losses arising out of the performance and/or non-performance and/or breach of any of the obligations undertakings, rights and/or terms set out in this agreement.

I.045

The [Licensee] undertakes to keep the [Licensor] at all times indemnified against all allegations, claims, legal actions, damages, losses, costs and expenses, legal costs, delays in payments, bank charges, fall in currency exchange rates and any other matter which may incur a sum which can be calculated as attributable as a default and/or breach under this agreement to the [Licensee].

I.046

1.1 The [Licensor] undertakes to indemnify the [Licensee] in respect of the rights granted in the [Film/Podcast/Series] to the [Licensee] for the duration of this agreement in the event that there is a claim and/or legal action by a third party for infringement of copyright, breach of contract and/or some other matter by the [Licensor] which prevents the [Licensee] from exploiting the [Film/Podcast/Series] as set out in this agreement.

1.2 The undertaking in 1.1 is limited to [Number/currency] in total.

1.3 No payment shall be made in 1.1 and 1.2 where the actions and/or conduct of the [Licensee] has created the problem.

I.047

There is no indemnity provided to any subscriber to the service for any damage to property that may be required to install equipment to receive the service to which the subscriber must provide consent and/or for any failure to supply the service at any time and/or any default and/or delays and/or interruptions of any nature by the [Supplier]. The subscriber uses the service at their own risk and cost and no liability is accepted by the [Supplier]. The [Supplier] reserves the right to cancel, terminate, vary and/or change the service at any time without liability to the subscriber. Any liability is limited to a refund for the period in which the service was unavailable at any time which exceeds [number] hours.

I.048

The [Licensee] agrees to and shall indemnify the [Distributor] and hold the [Distributor] harmless from and against any and all claims, demands, causes of action, losses, judgments, legal fees, costs and expenses that may be made against and/or sustained and/or paid out and/or incurred by the [Distributor] on account of any breach and/or alleged breach by the [Licensee] of any term in this agreement and/or on account of any agreement made by the [Distributor] with any sub-distributor, sub-licensee, exhibitor or others with respect to the [Film] and/or any parts and/or the soundtrack and/ or any marketing and/or promotional material.

I.049

That the [Licensor] will keep the [Company] indemnified from and against all liabilities, claims, actions, proceedings, damages, losses, costs and expenses incurred by the [Company] and/or awarded against the [Company] and any compensation agreed and paid by the [Company] on the advice of legal consultants and/or professional advisors in consequence of and/or arising out of any breach and/or alleged breach and/or non-performance of any of the warranties, representations, obligations, undertakings and responsibilities of the [Licensor's] and/or any other person and/or agency and/or other third party acting on their behalf relating to this agreement.

I.050

The [Company] warrants and undertakes that it and its assignees, licensees and successors in title shall indemnify the [Institute/Enterprise] for all losses, damages, loss of revenue, loss of interest costs and expenses the [Institute/Enterprise] may incur due to any breach by the [Company] and its assignees, licensees and successors in title of the terms and undertakings set out in this agreement at any time. The indemnity shall include but not be limited to late delivery of stock, late payments of royalties and delays in accounting and failure to conclude third party merchandising agreements.

I.051

The [Company] agrees and undertakes that it controls all the rights necessary to enter into this agreement. The [Company] undertakes to indemnify the [Licensee] against any claim which is either settled and/or results in a legal action which is then won by a third party arising out of the use of the [Material/Content] supplied by the [Company]. Provided that the [Material/Content] is only used in the format and purpose for which it has been licensed by the [Company] to the [Licensee].

I.052

If [Company] notifies the [Licensee] at any time that licences, consents, permissions and/or clearances of copyright and/or rights must be obtained by the [Licensee] from any contributors, copyright owners and/or any other third parties prior to the exercise of the rights granted by this agreement. The [Licensee] agrees and undertakes that it will obtain at its sole cost and expense all such licences, consents, permissions and/or clearances of copyright and/or rights as may be required by the [Licensee] for the use and/or exploitation of any material in any medium. The [Licensee] agrees and undertakes that it shall indemnify the [Company] against all actions, claims, legal costs, damages, losses, costs and expenses incurred, awarded against and/or paid out by the [Company] in consequence of any breach and/or failure by the [Licensee] in respect of this agreement.

I.053

1.1 The [Author] and the [Company] undertake to indemnify each other against all liabilities, claims, demands, actions, costs, damages and/ or losses arising out of any breach by either of them to the other party in respect of any of the terms of this agreement.

1.2 Both parties agree to keep the other informed of any potential allegations and/or legal actions and to cooperate with each other to endeavour to resolve the matter with the least expenditure and legal costs possible in the circumstances.

1.3 In the event that the parties cannot agree the terms upon which to settle any allegation, claim, legal action and/or other liability under this agreement. Then it is agreed that the advice and opinion of a suitably qualified legal expert shall be sought at the [Company's] cost. However such advice and opinion shall be for guidance only and not be considered binding upon the parties.

I.054
The [Licensor] and the [Licensee] mutually undertake to indemnify the other against all liabilities, claims, demands, actions, costs, damages, losses, costs and expenses arising out of any breach by the [Licensor] and/or the [Licensee] of any of the undertakings in and terms of this agreement. Both the [Licensor] and the [Licensee] agree that in the event that they intend to make any claim of any nature in respect of this indemnity then they must have informed the other party of the problem at the earliest opportunity as follows:

1.1 Notify the other party of any threat and/or potential claim which may arise and make no admission of settlement.

1.2 Provide the other party with the opportunity to be fully consulted in respect of the proposed course of action with the case.

1.3 In any event the maximum liability of either party shall be limited to [number/currency] in total for each party under this agreement to the other party.

1.4 The indemnity shall only apply if the party seeking to rely on the indemnity has notified the full nature of the claim and co-operated fully with the other party.

I.055

The [Author] and the [Company] agree and undertake that:

1.1 In the event of any allegations, threats, claims, disputes, legal proceedings, fines, breaches of health and safety requirements and/ or any other matter arising out of this agreement which may be made against the [Author] and/or the [Company] and/or any third party sub-licensee, distributor, agent and/or otherwise. That the [Author] and/or the [Company] agrees to provide full details to the other party and shall not settle any matter without first consulting the other party whether or not they intend to make a claim under any indemnity.

1.2 No settlement shall be made of any fraudulent, spurious and/or malicious allegations, claims and/or actions with any person, company and/or entity. Any matter must only be resolved based on the advice of in house legal advisors and/or external professional advisors on the basis that there is a potential valid claim and not purely on the grounds of the avoidance of the expenditure of legal costs.

1.3 The [Author] agrees to indemnify the [Company] up to a maximum of [number/currency] in respect of any losses, damages and/or costs arising from any breach of the undertakings by the [Author] in this agreement subject to clauses 1.1 and 1.2 above. Any sum over that total shall be the responsibility of the [Company] and such sum may not be recouped under this agreement.

1.4 The [Production Company] agrees to indemnify the [Author] up to a maximum of [number/currency] in respect of any losses, damages and/ or costs arising from any breach of the undertakings by the [Company] in this agreement subject to clauses 1.1 and 1.2 above. Any sum over that total shall be the responsibility of the [Author] and such sum may not be recouped under this agreement.

I.056

There are no undertakings and/or indemnity provided to the [Company] under this agreement of any nature in respect of originality of the [Artwork/ Text/Content/Film] and/or copyright ownership and/or infringement of copyright and/or whether all the intellectual property and other rights in the master material have been acquired by and/or belong to [Name] and/or whether all sums due have been paid. The [Company] has been provided use of and access to the material for the [Artwork/Text/Content/Film] at its own risk and agrees to bear the cost of any allegations, claims, actions, legal proceedings, copyright clearance and other fees that may be due as well as any legal costs and settlements that may arise from the use of the [Artwork/Text/Content/Film] and the material by the [Company].

I.057
The [Publisher] agrees that any material and/or content whether titles, text, images, patterns, logos, graphics, maps, illustrations, sound recordings, computer generated material and/or otherwise shall be excluded from the indemnity by the [Author] in the event that:

1.1   The [Publisher] has decided to include the material and/or content despite the fact that the [Author] has indicated that there might be a legal problem and/or the [Publisher] has received legal advice that there is a risk of being sued by a third party.

1.2   The [Author] has advised the [Publisher] that the copyright owner is unknown and/or untraceable and/or the material has not been cleared in advance.

1.3   There has been an error, omission and/or negligence by the [Publisher] and/or printer.

1.4   The claim for any sum relates to an action and/or other matter outside [specify countries].

I.058
This indemnity by the [Author] to the [Publisher] shall end on [date] and after that date the [Publisher] shall not be entitled to make under claim and/or seek to be indemnified for any matter by the [Author] whether it is a legitimate claim or not. The [Publisher] agrees and undertakes not to take make any claim against and/or seek to be indemnified by the [Author] after [date].

I.059

1.1   [Name] agrees that he/she shall be interviewed and filmed by the [Company] on [date] for the purpose of a contribution to the [Programme/Podcast/Video] entitled [specify].

1.2   [Name] shall not be liable to the [Company] in respect of any matters which may arise in respect of the broadcast, transmission and/or exploitation the [Programme/Podcast/Video] which contains the material in 1.1 relating to [Name]. The [Company] agrees and accepts that [Name] provides no indemnity and/or undertaking and any claim which may arise for defamation and/or any other matter shall be at the [Company's] sole risk and cost.

1.3   [Name] agrees that where the [Company] requires additional information and/or interviews and/or documents and/or affidavits signed by [Name]. That [Name] will co-operate and assist provided additional fees and expenses are paid to [Name].

1.4   That the [Company] agrees and undertakes to waive all claims of any sums against [Name] of any nature arising from 1.1 and accepts that the information may be misleading, wrong and/or malicious as recollected by [Name].

I.060

The copyright owner [Name] of the [Image/Video/Film] supplies a copy of the material to the [Distributor] for display, use and supply on [Website/App/Channel] known as [specify reference]. [Name] agrees that the material may be edited by the [Distributor] provided that no additional words, images, sound recordings and/or film are added and that the [Image/Video/Film] is not mutilated and/or distorted. The [Distributor] agrees that it has waived all undertakings by [Name] as to originality, ownership, liability and indemnity and that [Distributor] shall be liable for any consequences which arise as a result of the use of the material and that it uses the material at its own risk and cost.

General Business and Commercial

I.061

The [Employee] undertakes to indemnify the [Company] against all liabilities, claims, demands, actions, costs, damages and/or losses arising out of any breach by the [Employee] of any of the terms of this agreement including the [Employee's] negligence, recklessness, dishonesty and/or defamation which directly relate to this contract of employment.

I.062

The [Executive] does not provide any indemnity whatsoever to the [Company] in respect of any losses, claims, liabilities, costs, expenses and/or damages that may arise directly and/or indirectly as a result of any part of this agreement.

I.063

There is no indemnity provided to the [Company] under this agreement by [Name] in respect of any act, conduct, words, work, documents, communications, damages, losses and/or legal proceedings which may be brought against the [Company] at any time due to [Name]. The [Company] agrees and undertakes that it shall not seek to be indemnified by [Name] under any circumstances and the [Company] shall be responsible for all the risk and costs and any other direct and indirect consequences that may arise.

I.064

The total liability of the [Executive/Company] under this agreement shall be limited to: [number/currency].

I.065

The [Company] agrees and undertakes that it shall arrange suitable insurance cover at the [Company's] cost for the benefit of the [Company] and the Executive to cover any matters that may arise from this contract of employment and/or the ultra vires actions of the [Executive] and any allegation, claim and/or legal action by any third party and/or any shareholder and/or any other employee. Director and/or collaborator which may arise at any time until the expiry of [one] year from the end date of the contract of employment and/or termination date whichever is the earlier.

I.066

It is agreed by the [Company] that the [Employee] provides no indemnity to the [Company] of any nature in respect of his/her work and/or any use of any equipment, clothes and/or other materials they may be required to use and/or wear under this agreement and/or any records, data and/or information they may be required to collect, collate and/or distribute.

I.067

The [Company] agrees and undertakes to indemnify [Name] for all sums which for any reason may result in the fact that [Name] does and/or will suffer losses, damages, costs and expenses whether they arise as a result of any legal actions, claims, summons, investigations and/or other matters which arise as a direct result of his/her work at the [Company] and/or their use of any property owned and/or controlled by the [Company] and/or as a result of following any instruction, direction and/or policy and/or arising from any statement, photographs, films, sound recordings, image and/or exploitation and/or adaptation of any material and/or premises relating to the [Company].

I.068

The [Licensor] agrees to indemnify the [Licensee] in respect of any third party allegations, legal actions, applications, claims, losses, damages, settlements, legal costs and expenses against the [Licensee] which may be paid to such third party as a result of any matter relating to the [Film/Image/Sound Recording/Manuscript] in respect of the exercise of the rights granted and/or the supply and distribution of any adaptation under this agreement. Provided that in all cases the [Licensee] shall:

1.1 Notify the [Licensor] as soon as possible of the details of any threats, legal proceedings, applications, claims, losses, damages, costs and expenses.

1.2 Consult with the [Licensor] as to the best course of action in dealing with such matters. Ensure that no settlement shall be reached with any third party without the prior approval of the [Licensor] which shall not be unreasonably withheld or delayed.

I.069

The [Licensor] shall only indemnify the [Licensee] in respect of any breach of this agreement where the [Licensee] has suffered a quantifiable loss, damage, cost and/or expense directly relating to a breach of this agreement by the [Licensor] by [date].

I.070

The [Company] shall indemnify and keep indemnified the [Licensee] including the [Licensee's] officers, directors, employees and agents against all liabilities, claims, costs, damages, expenses and legal fees reasonably and properly incurred arising out of any breach of any representation, warranty, undertaking and/or obligation on the part of the [Company] contained in this agreement.

I.071

If the [Licensee] wishes to assert its rights to be indemnified under this agreement then the [Licensee] must:

1.1 Promptly notify the [Licensor] of any allegations, claims and/or legal proceedings and/or other matter which give rise to such right and make no admission or settlement without the prior written authority of the [Licensor].

1.2 Provide the [Licensor] with the opportunity to participate in and fully control any settlement or other resolution of any allegations, claims or other proceedings subject to an additional indemnity being provided by the [Licensor].

1.3 Co-operate with the reasonable requests of the [Licensor] and at the [Licensor's] reasonable expense supply any documents, information, affidavits and other material that may be required.

I.072

The [Licensor] warrants that the [Licensor] will keep the [Licensee] and the [Licensee's] sub-licensees, agents and distributors indemnified from and against all liabilities, claims, actions, proceedings, damages and losses suffered and/or incurred and/or awarded against the [Licensee] and/or the [Licensee's] sub-licensees, agents and distributors and any compensation, settlement and/or other sum paid to a third party and/or incurred in legal costs and expenses in consequence of and/or arising out of any breach and/or alleged breach and/or non-performance of all and/or any of the terms of this agreement by the [Licensor's] and/or any other person and/or company acting on behalf of the [Licensor].

I.073

The [Licensor] warrants that it will keep the [Licensee] indemnified from and against all liabilities, claims, actions, proceedings, damages and loss suffered and/or incurred by the [Licensee] and/or awarded against the [Licensee] and any compensation agreed and paid by the [Licensee] on the advice of [Professional Legal Advisors/Legal Consultants/In house advisors] and agreed by the [Licensor in consequence of any breach and/or alleged breach by the [Licensor] of this agreement.

I.074

1.1 The [Licensee] shall at its sole expense indemnify the [Licensor] and its successors and assignees from and against any and all liability, losses, damages, legal costs and other costs and expenses incurred by the [Licensor] and/or its successors and assignees in respect of any breach of this agreement by the [Licensee] which results in a claim and/or legal proceedings against the [Licensor] and/or its successors and/or assignees. This indemnity shall end on [date] and shall be limited to a total value of [number/currency] for all claims.

1.2 In the event that any person shall make any claim and/or institute any legal proceedings alleging any facts which, if true, would constitute a breach by the [Licensee]. The [Licensor] and/or any successor and/or assignee shall provide the [Licensee] of the details of the claim and/or allegations for which indemnity will be sought.

I.075

The [Company] will indemnify and hold harmless the [Licensee], its officers, directors and employees against all claims, damages, liabilities, losses and expenses and reasonable legal costs but not for any sums which relate to any indirect loss. The [Licensee] shall promptly notify the [Company] in writing of any litigation, claim, or threat of legal action to which this indemnity applies. The [Company] shall at its own expense assume the defence of or deal with any such matter. The [Company] shall not be obliged to indemnify the [Licensee] in respect of any settlement of any claim, threat or litigation which has not been approved by and/or authorised by the [Company].

I.076

1.1 If the [Company] is prevented from exercising the rights in respect of the [Work/Product/Service] by reason of any breach by the [Licensor] of the terms set out in this agreement for a period of more than [specify duration]. The [Licensor] agrees and undertakes that it shall pay to the [Company] the total sum of: [number/currency] in respect of each such occasion.

1.2 The [Company] may set off the sum due from the [Licensor] in 1.1 against payments due from the [Company] under this agreement.

1.3 The [Licensor] shall not liable to indemnify the [Company] in respect of any loss of profit, business, stock and/or customers that may arise by reason of any breach by the [Licensor] of this agreement.

I.077
The [Company] shall for the Term of the Agreement indemnify the [Enterprise] against all actions, claims, liabilities, costs, settlements, judgments, losses, damages and expenses including legal fees in respect of any breach of any nature of any representation, warranty or undertaking by the [Company]. The [Enterprise] shall be entitled to withhold any sum due under the agreement to the [Company] in respect of any sum claimed under this indemnity by the [Enterprise] until the matter is resolved.

I.078
The [Company] and the [Distributor] mutually undertake to indemnify the other against all liabilities, claims, demands, actions, costs, damages or loss directly arising out of any direct breach by them of any of the terms of this agreement. In the event of an action, claim, dispute, writ or proceedings arising out of the performance of this agreement the [Company] and/or the [Distributor] agree to provide full details to the other party at the earliest opportunity and shall not settle any such matter without first consulting the other party.

I.079
In the event that there is an allegation that the use of the [Item/Unit/Service] infringes any third party rights. The party against whom the claim is made shall be entitled to defend it and shall be entitled at its sole discretion to join any other party to this agreement. There shall be no obligation to conclude any indemnity arrangement with any such party and/or to pay their costs and expenses.

I.080
The [Company's] cannot exclude liability for matters relating to personal injury and/or death which arise as a result of the negligence and/or failure of duty of care of the [Company]. However in respect of all other matters the [Company] shall only be liable to pay for any one claim under the indemnity a maximum of [number/currency]. The total maximum liability of the

[Company] under the indemnity for all claims shall be [number/currency]. Any sums over those limits shall be at the cost and expense of [Name] and not covered by the indemnity.

I.081

The [Assignor] and the [Assignee] mutually undertake to indemnify the other against all liabilities, claims, demands, actions, costs, damages and/or losses arising out of any breach by either of them of the terms of this agreement. In the event of any allegation, claim, dispute, legal action and/or other proceedings against either of them the [Assignor] and the [Assignee] agree to provide full details to the other party at the earliest opportunity and shall not settle any such matter without first consulting the other party.

I.082

The indemnity shall only be provided in respect of any matter which is notified to the [Supplier] during the existence of this agreement which arises from [specify countries] and shall be limited to a maximum sum of [number/currency] in total for all claims. There is no indemnity provided for any other countries and where the limit on liability is exceeded no further sums shall be paid by the [Supplier]. This clause does not apply to any matters relating to personal injury and/or death.

I.083

The [Assignor] shall not be liable to and/or indemnify the [Assignee] in respect of any of the following matters:

1.1 Where the [Assignee] has adapted and/or changed the [Work/Image/Film/Sound Recording] and/or added and/or deleted material which has materially and significantly changed the content to such an extent that over [number] per cent is different from the original.

1.2 For any sums due to a third party from the [Assignee] for copyright and/or other payments due for the use, adaptation and/or exploitation of the [Work/Image/Film/Sound Recording].

1.3 For any sums due outside [specify countries].

I.084

The indemnity by the [Assignor] to the [Assignee] shall cease on [date]. The [Assignor] shall only be liable for any notified claims under the indemnity made by that date. Thereafter all liability by the [Assignor] to the [Assignee] shall cease and no further claims for any reason for any sums may be made by the [Assignee] under the indemnity. The [Assignee] agrees and undertakes to bear all the risk and to be responsible for the cost of all allegations and/or claims by third parties after [date].

I.085

The [Consortium] members agree and undertake that they shall all equally and jointly be liable for any sums that may arise under any indemnity provided to any third party in respect of the [Project] in respect of agreements that may arise provided that:

1.1 No member of the [Consortium] authorises and/or concludes any agreement which is not approved by the Board and/or its legal advisors.

1.2 No contribution shall be sought from other members of the [Consortium] where it could be paid under an insurance claim through the policy paid for and taken out by the [Consortium] in respect of the [Project].

1.3 No more than [number] years have expired since the end of the [Project] and/or the expiry and/or termination of all the agreements.

1.4 Where a member no longer exists, then any successor and/or assignee of the member shall still be held liable for any sums due.

1.5 Where any sum claimed relates to a civil and/or criminal action and/or proceedings then any member shall be entitled to be provided with access to and/or copies of all material of any nature subject to payment of the administrative costs incurred to do so.

I.086

The [Distributor] agrees to indemnify [Name] in respect of the failure of any sub-agent, sub-licensee and/or other third party engaged by them to pay any sums due from the exploitation of the [Work/Image/Film/Sound Recording] which are due to [Name] before [date].

I.087

The [Enterprise] shall be liable for, and shall indemnify the [Company] and any successors in title and assignees against any expenses, costs, damages, liability, losses, claims and/or legal action and/or proceedings in any country in the world whatsoever arising under any laws, legislation, case law, directives, regulations, codes, standards and/or policies of any government, organisation and/or agency in respect of any illness, allergy, defect, personal injury and/or death of any person and/or unborn child arising out of and/or in connection with the [Project/Product] whether caused and/or arising during the existence of this agreement and/or thereafter at any time.

I.088

The [Developer] shall subject to clause [–] be liable for and indemnify the [Company] against any legal and administrative costs, expenses, liability, legal proceedings, claims, fines and penalties, interest and/or any award of damages against the [Company] and/or any losses incurred by the

[Company] and/or in respect of any allegations which are settled with third parties in respect of any death, personal injury, legal action and/or allegation and/or any damage to and/or destruction of any property and/or any land and/or any electricity, gas, water and/or other facilities and/or any material stored in and/or nearby which is caused directly and/or indirectly by the performance of this agreement by the [Developer] and/or any third party engaged by the [Developer] in connection with the [Project]. This indemnity shall apply whether it is caused by the negligence, breach of statutory duty, omission, error and/or default of the [Developer] and/or any employees, freelance personnel, consultants, agents and/or of any person and/or entity engaged by them in any manner in connection with the [Project].

I.089

1.1 The [site/location] set out in Schedule [–] and which forms part of this agreement is not safe and is not habitable and is used by the [Company] at its own risk and cost. There are no indemnity provisions and/or undertakings as to suitability for any use and/or access.

1.2 Prior to access you must agree to take out comprehensive public liability insurance cover at your own cost for all persons that may enter and/or use the [site/location] to provide protection for [Name] and your [Company] in the sum of [number/currency] which shall be valid for the duration of this agreement and thereafter for a period of [number] years.

1.3 The [Company] shall engage health and safety and such other advisors as may be required to assess the [site/location] for use and to provide such safeguards as may be required at the [Company's] sole cost.

Internet, Websites and Apps

I.090
No indemnity is provided to any person, company, business and/or entity which uses, accesses, downloads, reproduces, distributes and/or supplies and/or purchases any material, products, services, books, games, toys, DVDs, CDs, images, artwork, graphics, data, databases, logos, trade marks, service marks, merchandising, films, videos, sound recordings, lyrics, music, ringtones, computer-generated material, software and/or otherwise in any other format and/or medium from this [Website/App/Platform]. Your arrangement, contract, license and/or purchase is direct with a third party and no responsibility is accepted by the [Company] for their failure, delay, errors, omissions, breach of agreement and/or otherwise and you agree that you shall not make any claim against the [Company].

I.091

The total indemnity by the [Company] shall be limited to the value of the [Product/Service/Download] and no responsibility can be accepted for any other loss, damage, costs, expenses, destruction of data, delay in delivery, interruption, suspension and/or other consequences which may arise whether direct and/or indirect at any time in relation to your access to, use and/or storage of the [Product/Service/Download].

I.092

No person, company, entity and/or otherwise who uses this [Website/App/Platform] is provided with any undertakings and/or indemnity of any nature. Any use and/or reliance upon information, research and data and/or any films, videos, podcasts, sound recordings, text, images, music and/or any other material and/or media is entirely at your own risk and cost. No assurances are provided as to:

1.1 Ownership of material; copyright ownership and notices.

1.2 Compliance with any codes, practices, legislation, regulations, directives and cases.

1.3 That there are no viruses, defects and/or errors which could cause harm and/or damage.

1.4 That the content has been checked for errors, omissions, defamatory and/or offensive material and/or is threatened by and/or the subject of legal proceedings.

I.093

The [User] undertakes to indemnify the [Company] in respect of the total sum incurred by the [Company] and/or any legal advisors, agents and/or consultants for any allegations and/or settlements, legal proceedings and/or damages, losses and/or other costs for infringement of copyright, trade mark infringement, defamation, breach of database rights, infringement of computer software rights, breach of contract, and/or any other intellectual property rights and/or any other rights and/or interest by a third party in respect of any material uploaded by the [User] to the [Website/App/Platform] whether text, images, films, videos, photographs, sound recordings, music, lyrics, trade marks, service marks, community marks, logos and/or any other material in any medium and any format at any time in any part of the world.

I.094

The indemnity in clause [–] shall not apply:

1.1 To any issue which relates to any third party outside [country].

1.2 After [date].

1.3   Where the [Licensor] has already been paid [number/currency] in total
       which is the maximum liability of the [Company].

1.4   Where any matter has not been notified during the Term of the
       Agreement and/or before the date of termination of the agreement and
       up to [one] year thereafter whichever is the earlier.

I.095

The [Contributor] is not providing any indemnity to the [Company] in respect
of any threats, allegations, claims, liabilities, demands, actions, costs,
damages, losses, fines, penalties and/or other sums arising directly and/
or indirectly out of any breach and/or alleged breach of the terms of this
agreement by the [Contributor].

I.096

The [Distributor] does not provide any undertakings and/or indemnity in
respect of the supply and/or reproduction of the [Sound Recordings] in the
form of [Discs] and/or downloads and/or otherwise. There is no right to make
copies and/or to transfer the material to third parties and/or to store the
material as part of a storage and/or retrieval system on any equipment and/
or in any software.

I.097

1.1   [Name] agrees to indemnify the [Distributor] in respect of any
       allegations, threat, legal action, claims, losses, damages, costs and
       expenses including legal costs which may arise from the exercise of
       the rights granted by [Name] under this agreement before [date].

1.2   Provided that the indemnity in 1.1 shall not cover any sums paid by the
       [Distributor] to any employee, director, consultant and/or agent.

1.3   The [Distributor] in order to rely on the indemnity must provide full
       disclosure of the facts to [Name] and copies of all relevant documents,
       facts and information. No legal costs should be incurred without
       consultation I advance with [Name] and no sum should be paid in
       settlement to any third party without prior consultation with [Name].

1.4   In any event the total indemnity in 1.1 by [Name] to the [Distributor] shall
       be limited to [number/currency] and shall only be in respect of any claim
       and/or legal action in [country] and not any other part of the world. All
       other sums shall be at the cost, expense and liability of the [Distributor].

I.098

1.1   The indemnity provided by [Name] to the [Distributor] shall only be
       in respect of any sums which are paid by the [Distributor] relating to

allegations of breach of copyright, privacy, contract, defamation and/
or infringement of trade marks in respect of the [Work] in [country]
before [date].

1.2 The [Distributor] agrees to bear the cost and liability of all other matters
of any nature that may arise which may result in payments by the
[Distributor] and shall not offset and/or recoup these from any sums
due to [Name].

I.099

In order to upload any material to the [Website/Forum/Platform] you must
accept that you are obliged to supply an indemnity to the [Company] for
any costs, expenses, damages, interest, legal fees and expenses, fines,
penalties and/or other sums that the [Company] may be obliged to pay
to a third party whether an individual, a company and/or an organisation
as a result of the fact that the material you have supplied and posted is
in fact defamatory, offensive, in breach of contract, a criminal offence, an
infringement of copyright, an infringement of a trade mark, service mark
and/or logo, and/or a pirate copy of any material including artwork, music,
sound recording and/or a character and/or animation and/or otherwise
results in a claim, allegation, legal action and/or other matter which incurs
legal, regulatory and/or compliance problems for the [Company].

Merchandising and Distribution

I.100

1.1 The [Licensee] shall indemnify the [Licensor/Estate] and/or any
assignees and/or other successors in title from [date] until [date]
in respect of the exploitation by the [Licensee] of the [Work/Image/
Product/Film] as a whole and/or any part.

1.2 The indemnity in 1.1 shall be in respect of all sums, cost and expenses
including legal fees on a full indemnity basis and fees for accountants
and professional advisors which the [Licensor/Estate] and/or any
assignees and/or other successors in title may incur and/or expend as
a direct result of any breach by the [Licensee] of this agreement and/
or any product recall, and/or product liability and/or any other matter
arising as a result of the production, manufacture, use, reproduction,
distribution, sale and/or supply by and/or for the [Licensee] of any
format and/or material relating to the [Work/Image/Product/Film]. This
indemnity shall therefore include all investigations, allegations, claims,
fines, criminal and civil legal actions and proceedings, product liability,
health and safety and statutory compliance matters.

INDEMNITY

I.101

The [Licensee] agrees to indemnify the [Licensor] and the [Agent] and their respective assigns against all actions, claims, costs, demands and expenses which any of them may suffer or sustain in respect of the exploitation of the rights granted by the [Licensee] under this agreement.

I.102

The [Originator] will indemnify and at all times keep the [Company] fully indemnified against all actions, proceedings, claims, costs and damages whatsoever made against or incurred by the [Company] in consequence of any breach and/or non-performance by the [Originator] of any of the representations, warranties and/or obligations contained in this agreement.

I.103

The [Licensee] agrees to indemnify the [Licensor] and bear all cost and expenses and other sums of any nature in respect of all actions, demands, claims, settlements, criminal and/or civil proceedings of any nature at any time that are made against, and/or incurred by the [Licensor] as a result of any breach and/or alleged breach by the [Licensee] of any of the terms of this agreement and/or any other agreement made for or on behalf of the [Licensee] with any third party including but not limited to any sub-distributor, agent, sub-licensee, exhibitor and/or other third parties in respect of the exploitation of the rights granted under this agreement.

I.104

1.1 Both the [Licensee] and the [Licensor] agree to provide an indemnity to each other for the duration of the [Licence Period] against all legal actions and proceedings, claims, costs, expenses and legal fees that may be incurred by the other in consequence of any alleged breach and/or actual breach of the terms of this agreement. Neither indemnity shall apply after [date].

1.2 Both the [Licensor] and the [Licensee] agree to provide full details to the other party within a reasonable period of being aware of the matter and agree that they shall consult with each other as to the best course of action in each case.

1.3 Both parties agree that the liability of the [Licensor] shall not have a financial limit except that it shall only relate to matters arising within the Licence Period. The [Licensee's] total liability shall be limited to [number/currency] except for matters relating to personal injury and death.

984

I.105

The [Distributor] agrees to indemnify the [Licensor] for any damages, losses, costs, expenses, legal fees, and/or loss of profit and/or royalties and/or infringement of intellectual property rights and/or other rights whether direct or indirectly arising from the breach and/or alleged breach of the terms of this agreement by the [Distributor] and/or any third party appointed and/or engaged by the [Distributor] including but not limited to:

1.1 Failure to by a third party to account and/or transfer any sums due.

1.2 The recall of the [Product] for health and safety reasons, and/or quality control reasons.

1.3 The delay, cancellation and/or alteration of the proposed launch date.

1.4 Any personal injury, death, or other matter relating to the use, and fitness for purpose of the [Product] its content, packaging and any associated material and/or any other product liability and/or compliance required under any laws, legislation, directive, regulation, policy or code in any country.

I.106

There shall be no general indemnity under this agreement and the total liability of [Name] to the [Company] shall be limited to [number/currency] under this agreement for any breach excluding liability for personal injury and death which arises as a direct result of the negligence of [Name].

I.107

The indemnity in clause [–] shall not apply after the expiry of the licence and/ or [date] whichever is the earlier.

I.108

The indemnity under clause [–] shall be limited to the any translations of the original [Manuscript] by the [Licensee] and shall not apply to the original language and/or to any sub-licensees, distributor, agent and/or any other third party.

I.109

The indemnity in clause [–] by the [Author] shall not apply and no sum shall be due and/or paid to the [Distributor] where:

1.1 any allegation and/or claim by a third party is made which is not proved to be correct by a court of law and/or is not agreed to as a settlement by the [Author].

1.2 it relates to any issue which arises outside [specify countries].

1.3 more than [one] year has passed since the termination and/or expiry of the agreement.

1.4 the [Author] has already paid the [Distributor] [number/currency] under the indemnity which is the maximum liability in total under this agreement of the [Author].

I.110

[Name] agrees to indemnify the [Distributor/Agent] in respect any sums which may be incurred which arise from the failure of [Name] to assist in the marketing and promotion of the [Product] as set out in clause [–] up to a maximum of [number/currency].

I.111

1.1 The [Consortium] agrees to indemnify the [Company] with a payment of no more than [number/currency] if circumstances require that the [Event] be delayed, cancelled and/or materially changed as to its content provided that the [Company] is able to provide evidence of any losses and/or damages and/or costs and/or expenses which have and/or will arise as a direct result and those sums cannot be recouped from a third party under any insurance policy.

1.2 The [Company] agrees that the indemnity shall be limited as set out in 1.1 whether or not the [Company] has and/or will incur greater costs and/or expenses and/or created and/or developed and/or booked advertising and/or other promotions based on the [Event]. The [Company] waives any claim in respect of any sum above that set out in 1.1 which may arise directly and/or indirectly for any reason.

1.3 The [Company] agrees that the indemnity shall not be due and/or payable where the [Company] agrees to any delay, cancellation and/or or change in content and suffers no losses and/or damages and/or costs and/or expenses.

I.112

The [Distributor] agrees and undertakes to indemnify [Name] in respect of any costs, expenses, damages, losses including travel, loss of future work and fees, and damage to his/her reputation which are suffered and/or incurred by [Name] as a result of any allegations, claims, civil and/or or criminal actions and/or proceedings and/or any investigations against the [Distributor] and/or any sub-licensee and/or any other third party associated with the [Distributor] for the [Project/Product/Service] at any time in any country and/or to any part of their business and/or their manufacturers.

I.113

1.1 The [Supplier] shall fully indemnify the [Company] against all valid claims which are made against the [Company] by third parties which are not resolved amicably and which result in the [Company] paying additional sums in compensation and/or expenses and/or costs to the third party which directly arise from an actual breach of this contract by the [Supplier] and/or as a direct consequence of the use and/or consumption of the {Products] by the third party.

1.2 The [Company] accepts that the [Supplier] shall not be liable for any legal and other professional costs and expenses incurred and/or paid by the [Company].

1.3 The [Company] accepts that where any claim and/or product liability is covered by an insurance policy held by the [Company] and that any sums paid are recouped under that policy. That the [Company] shall not seek to be repaid any such sums by the [Supplier].

I.114
Where the [Material/Product] supplied is on hire and/or loan to the [Customer] for a fixed period. Then the [Customer] shall indemnify the [Company] against the full cost of replacement or repair of the [Material/Product] whether or not such replacement or repair of the [Material/Product] is occasioned by losses, damages and/or destruction which have occurred as a result of the negligence of the [Customer], its servants, agents or otherwise.

I.115
The [Agent] agrees to indemnify the [Company] against any allegations, legal actions and/or proceedings, on line claims, losses, damages, cost and expenses and any reasonable court fees, legal fees and other expenses incurred as a result of any breach and/or alleged breach by the [Agent] of its obligations under this agreement and/or any person and/or legal entity and/or charity authorised by the [Agent] to carry and/or fulfil work and/or provide services which are in breach of this agreement. This indemnity shall start on [date] and continue until [date] whether or not this agreement is terminated and/or expires before [date]. The total liability of the [Agent] under this agreement shall be limited to [number/currency] except where any matter relates to defamation, personal injury, death and/or product liability.

I.116
The [Supplier] shall indemnify the [Distributor] from any and all claims, liabilities, damages and/or expenses incurred and/or sustained by the [Distributor] including any consequential losses, expenses, damages and fines as follows in respect of:

1.1 any alleged breach and/or actual infringement of any intellectual property rights, copyright, trade and/or service marks, patents, design rights, computer software and/or any other rights of any third party and/or

1.2 any sums incurred and/or paid by the [Distributor] as a direct and/or indirect consequence of the failure by the [Supplier] to perform its obligations under this agreement and/or to supply services and/or products which comply with legislation and/or other guidelines and codes of practice and/or

1.3 any death and/or personal injury and/or anxiety, distress and/or other mental health issues directly caused to any person employed and/or engaged by the [Distributor] and/or any appointed agent and/or any third party who purchases the services and/or products supplied to the [Distributor] by the [Supplier] at any time.

I.117

The [Seller] shall indemnify the [Purchaser] against any liability, loss, damage, claim, costs, expenses, interest and legal fees which arises as a direct result of the use of the [Product] in the manner for which it was created where personal injury and/or death occurs and/or damage to other property which is directly attributable and caused by a fault and/or defect in the [Product] and/or any part.

I.118

The [Supplier] and the [Seller] mutually undertake to indemnify the other against all claims, liabilities, demands, actions, costs, damages and/or reasonable foreseeable losses and expenses arising directly out of any breach by the defaulting party under the terms of this agreement. The total maximum liability of either party in total for the duration of the agreement shall be [number/currency] in each of the following countries: [specify countries]. The total aggregate liability shall be [number/currency] but this shall not apply to any liability for death and/or personal injury which shall be unlimited.

I.119

1.1 The [Licensee] agrees to indemnify the [Licensor] against all legal actions, allegations, settlements, online claims, legal and administrative costs and/or expenses and/or sums incurred in respect of professional consultants, accountants and/or legal advisors and/or any court fees and/or registrations fee which may arise directly and/or as a consequence of any alleged breach and/or otherwise of any of the terms of this agreement by the [Licensee] and/or any sub-licence granted pursuant to this agreement and/or any failure by any sub-licensee and/or any other matter relating to the [Products/Services] to be created and/or developed under this agreement in any part of the world and/or universe from the date of signature of this agreement until the expiry of a period of [six] years from the expiry and/or termination of the main agreement and/or any sub-licence.

1.2   It is agreed that the following matters shall not be covered by the terms of this indemnity: [specify].

I.120

The [Licensor] shall only be liable to indemnify the [Licensee] against any legal actions and proceedings, trade mark and/or service claims and/or copyright infringement claims and/or domain name claims and/or any other allegations, settlements, legal costs, damages and expenses which directly relate may to the [Licensor's] trade marks, logos, images, characters and/or slogans. This indemnity shall cease upon the expiry and/or termination of this agreement except to the extent that any matter is not yet resolved but has been to the [Licensor].

I.121

The [Purchaser] is only authorised to use the [Product/Software] in the following manner [specify] and for the following purpose [specify]. There is no authority provided to make copies and/or to reproduce the [Product/Software] in any other format and/or to create adaptations. In fact any such use and/or changes are specifically prohibited. The [Purchaser] must accept that they use this [Product/Software] entirely at their own risk and cost except in relation for any claim for personal injury and/or death. Where the [Product/Software] is used in conjunction with any other software, equipment and/or gadget no responsibility can be accepted for any consequential losses, damages and/or other matters that may occur. No assurance can be provided as to the accuracy and/or content of the [Product/Software] and you are advised to make your own decision based on independent advice. The [Product/Software] is for guidance only.

I.122   In the event of any claims, demands, actions and/or otherwise by the [Purchaser] and/or any business for any reason arising from the use of the [Product/Software] and/or data, recommendations and/or other information and content. The [Publisher] and the [Author] shall only be liable in total to repay the full purchase price of the [Product/Software] to the [Purchaser]. The [Purchaser] agrees that it is the [Purchaser's] responsibility to arrange and bear the cost of insurance cover for the benefit of the [Purchaser], any business and third party for the use of the [Product/Software] by the [Purchaser]. That the [Publisher] and [Author] shall not bear any responsibility and/or liability for any direct and/or indirect use of any type of the [Product/ Software] by the [Purchaser], any business, third party or otherwise at any time. This clause shall not apply to any claim relating to personal injury and/ or death which is directly caused by the negligence of the [Publisher] and/ or [Author] in respect of the authorised use of the [Product/Software].

I.123
The [Distributor] agrees that the indemnity in clause [–] shall end on: [specify date] and that all rights to make a claim in respect of any other matters shall be waived after that date. All such matters shall be at the total liability, risk and cost of the [Distributor] after [date] and there shall be no right under this agreement to be indemnified for any reason.

I.124
The indemnity in clause [–] shall not apply if:

1.1   The damage, loss, cost and/or expense is caused by the [Purchaser] and/or

1.2   The [Product] has not been used in accordance with the instructions and/or

1.3   The [Purchaser] has not notified the [Distributor] and made a claim within [three] years of purchase.

I.125
The [Company] agrees and undertakes that it shall indemnify [Name] and his/her distributors, customers, agents and any other third party related to [Name] involved in the supply, sale and marketing of the [Products] in respect of all sums which they may reasonably demand and seek to claim in respect of losses, damages, legal and administrative, advertising, freight, customs duties, tests, health and safety reports and assessments, loss of orders and damage to reputation and any other costs and expenses of any nature which are reasonably incurred in any part of the world at any time whether during and/or after the termination and/or cancellation of this agreement in the event that:

1.1   The [Company] and/or any manufacturer authorised and/or engaged by it uses and/or includes any ingredients in the reproduction of the [Products] which are toxic and/or not suitable and/or are likely to cause an allergic reaction and/or are not pure and/or the source, content and supplier cannot be verified.

1.2   The [Company] and/or any manufacturer authorised and/or engaged by it uses any premises which are unfit for purpose and pose a risk to health and safety of the employees and/or casual staff according to the international standards set by [specify] and/or has used persons under [number] age as workers.

1.3 The [Company] and/or any manufacturer authorised and/or engaged by it have not disclosed the fact that they do not hold a licence and/or certificate to carry out this type of work and do have suitably qualified management and/or craftsmen and/or machinery and/or software and/or facilities to complete the necessary techniques for the [Products].

1.4 The [Company] and/or any manufacturer authorised and/or engaged by it fails in whole and/or part to take such reasonable precautions as set out by [specify body] to protect the local environment and wildlife and community from any harm that may arise from any waste material that may be stored, discharged and/or released into any rivers, sea, sub-terrain, land and/or air at any time.

Publishing

I.126
The [Author] undertakes to indemnify and keep indemnified the [Publisher] and any sub-licensee, distributor and/or other third party engaged to exploit the [Project/Work/Service/Illustrations] where any legal action, claim, allegation, investigation and/or any criminal and/or civil proceedings relate to infringement of copyright and/or any intellectual property rights and/or any trade and/or service mark and/or any other logo and/or image and/or defamation and/or any other matter which directly relates to the material supplied by the [Author] and not any adaptation, translation and/or any content and/or character created and/or developed by a third party. Provided that the [Author] is notified in full of any potential claim under the indemnity and provided with an opportunity to verify the stance of the [Author] and dispute the matter. That no matter will be settled without the consent of the [Author] unless the [Publisher] and/or any sub-licensee, distributor and/or other third party agrees not to make any claim under the indemnity.

I.127

1.1 Any indemnity by the [Author] shall be limited to the [Company] and not apply to any sub-licensee, agent, distributor and/or other third party.

1.2 The indemnity shall end on: [date].

1.3 The indemnity shall not apply outside: [specify countries].

1.4 The indemnity shall not apply to any translation, adaptation, service, compilation, download, electronic version and/or format, any product, toy and/or other variation.

991

1.5 The indemnity can only be relied upon where the [Company] has failed to make a successful claim under any insurance policy which it may hold for its business and/or that of its parent company.

1.6 The costs, expenses, losses and/or damages claimed under the indemnity must be quantifiable and not related to potential loss of profit on sales.

1.7 The indemnity only relates to the undertakings by the [Author] in this agreement and not any pre negotiation representations.

1.8 Any costs and expenses incurred in in-house legal and administrative costs and expenses cannot be reimbursed under the indemnity.

1.9 If the [Company] has not consulted with the [Author] regarding any allegation and/or claim before it is resolved. Then the indemnity shall not apply to any sums paid by the [Company].

1.10 The [Company] agrees to discuss any potential press and social media comment with the [Author] prior to its publication in any format.

I.128

The [Author] agrees to indemnify the [Company] in respect of any third party claims, losses, damages, settlements, legal costs and expenses which may be paid to such third parties by the [Company] as a result of the [Manuscript/Artwork/Product] which has infringed any copyright and/or other intellectual property rights and/or which is in breach of any contract and/or which has given rise to a civil and/or criminal proceedings provided that in all cases the [Company] shall:

1.1 notify the [Author] as soon as possible of the detail of any allegations, claims, losses or damages and the fact that the [Company] may seek to be indemnified by the [Author] and

1.2 consult with the [Author] and take account of their view of the facts and

1.3 not pay any such third party who is making allegations and/or a claim any sum without prior consultation with the [Author].

Where the [Company] fails to adhere to 1.1 to 1.3 above, then the [Author] shall not be liable for the sums paid by the [Publisher]. Where the indemnity is applicable then the [Company] shall agree a repayment schedule over more than [number] years with the [Author] in respect of those sums which fall within this indemnity provision.

I.129

1.1 The [Author] shall indemnify the [Publishers] against any legal proceedings, criminal and/or civil action and/or enquiry and/

or investigation, expenses, costs, losses, damages, allegation of defamation and/or copyright infringement, cancellation of events, cancellation of advertising and/or any other matter which directly arises out of the actual breach and not alleged breach by the [Author] of the undertakings provided by the [Author] under this agreement.

1.2 The indemnity in 1.1 shall not apply to any loss of potential profit and/or sales nor shall it relate to any losses, cost and expenses incurred by third parties.

1.3 The indemnity shall not apply where on the advice of the [Company] the [Author] has agreed to incorporate new names, places, characters and/or plotlines at the request of the [Company].

1.4 The indemnity shall not apply where the [Author] has agreed that the [Project/Work/Product] may be changed, altered and varied based on the advice of legal advisors to the [Company.

1.5 The indemnity by the [Author] shall continue after the expiry and/or termination of this agreement. The [Author's] liability in respect of the indemnity shall end on [date].

I.130

1.1 The [Author] shall only indemnify the [Publisher] in respect of any losses, costs, damages and/or settlement in excess of [number/currency].

1.2 The total liability in respect of the indemnity of the [Author] under this agreement to the [Company] shall be [number/currency] in respect of any breach and/or alleged breach of any of the terms set out in this agreement and/or any sub-licence and/or other related document.

1.3 In the event that the [Publisher] wishes to rely on this indemnity it must notify the [Author] immediately of any claim, action, proceedings and/or threat by notice in writing providing full details of the matter.

1.4 The [Publisher] shall keep the [Author] fully informed and provide the [Author] with the opportunity to refute or deny the allegations in each case.

1.5 The [Author] shall also be entitled to request to assist in the defence of the case as required and to be provided with copies of all documentation upon request. The [Publisher] shall be under no obligation to pay for the legal costs and expenses that may be incurred by the [Author].

I.131
The [Publisher] agrees to indemnify the [Author] against any civil and/or criminal proceedings, enquiry, investigation, product liability, online claim,

legal action and/or proceedings, settlement, allegations, losses, damages, expenses, costs and any reasonable legal expenses and fees incurred by the [Author] as a result of any breach and/or alleged breach by the [Publisher] and/or any sub-licensee, agent, distributor, person, company and/or other third party appointed by the [Publisher] of its obligations under this agreement in any country at any time.

I.132

The [Author] agrees to indemnify the [Publisher] against any actions, claims, proceedings, demands, losses, damages, product liability, personal injury, death and any costs, expenses and legal expenses incurred and/or any sums paid in settlement on the advice of the legal advisors by the [Publisher] as a direct result of any breach and/or alleged breach by the [Author] of his/her obligations under this agreement subject to a maximum limit of [number/currency] and compliance with the following procedures:

1.1　Promptly notify the [Author] of any claim and/or legal proceedings which have arisen and make no admission or offer of settlement at that stage.

1.2　Provide the [Author] with the opportunity to be fully consulted as regards any proposed steps to be taken and any settlement of the matter.

1.3　The [Publisher] shall not have the right to deduct any sums owed by the [Author] under the indemnity from sums due under this agreement to the [Author] and/or to make any other set-off unless there is written consent in each case from the [Author].

I.133

1.1　The [Artist] agrees to indemnify the [Music Publishers] and its licensees and assigns against all claims, actions, demands, costs, damages and expenses arising in any form from the use of the [Musical Work/Lyrics/Recordings] in [format] by the [Music Publishers] and/or its licensees and assigns in accordance with this agreement in respect of the undertakings by the [Artist] in clauses [–].

1.2　The [Artist] shall not be liable for any material added by the [Music Publishers] and/or for any sums due for productions costs, the clearance of rights and/or consents of musicians and singers and/or manufacturing and/or productions costs of any master copies, software, packaging, marketing and/or promotional material.

1.3　This indemnity shall end on [date] in respect of the [Music Publishers] and any licensees and assigns. Thereafter no claim and/or indemnity shall be made under this agreement to the [Artist].

1.4   This indemnity shall not apply in the following formats and methods of distribution: [specify].

1.5   This indemnity shall not apply to any country outside [specify territory].

I.134

The [Company] agrees that it shall not have the right to seek any sums from the [Name] in respect of this agreement provided that he/she fulfils the obligation to deliver the [Manuscript/Sound Recordings/Images] by [date]. All responsibility for any legal liability and/or proceedings which may arise from the use and/or exploitation of the [Manuscript/Sound Recordings/Images] and any other adaptation, variation and/or translation shall be at the sole risk, cost and expense of the [Company]. No indemnity is provided by [Name] to the [Company] in respect of this agreement. The [Company] waives all rights to make any claim against [Name].

I.135

The [Publisher] shall carry out the following steps in respect of all allegations, threats and legal actions which may arise relating to the [Manuscript/Sound Recordings/Images] and if it does not do so shall not be able to seek to be indemnified by the [Author]:

1.1   Notify the [Author/Agent] of the detail of any allegation, threat, civil and/or criminal action, claim and/or other matter within [seven] days of receiving any email, letter, writ, complaint or otherwise.

1.2   The [Publisher] shall consult with the [Author] as to the best course of action to be adopted and the steps to be taken in dealing with the matter including the legal costs to be incurred.

1.3   The [Publisher] shall keep the [Author] regularly updated and provided with the opportunity to put their view of the allegations, claims or complaint.

1.4   The [Publishers] shall allow the [Author] to inspect all the material within the possession or control of the [Publisher] and/or their legal advisors relating to any claim, action, allegation or complaint including any legal reports and opinions.

1.5   In the event that the [Publishers] fail to adhere to these conditions then the [Author] shall not be liable to pay any sums of any nature.

1.6   The total liability of the [Author] under this indemnity shall be limited to [number/currency].

1.7   The [Publisher] shall not seek to claim any indemnity for its own acts, omissions, failures or breaches of this agreement nor for any third party whether a sub-licensee, sub-agent and/or distributor and/or in respect of any material which has been added and/or created at the request of the [Publisher] and/or developed by an employee of the [Publisher] and/or any third party and/or which is a translation and not the original language of the [Author] and/or has been adapted by a sub-licensee.

1.8 This clause shall continue in force after the expiry and/or termination of this agreement for [one] year from the earliest date.

1.9 No indemnity shall be sought from the [Author] where over [number] per cent of the sums expended are recouped by the [Publisher] under an insurance policy.

I.136
The [Publisher] shall not seek to be indemnified by the [Author] except under clause [–] as to the originality of the [Manuscript/Images/Sound Recordings] supplied and attributed to the [Author]. All other legal actions, proceedings, allegations, on line claims, complaints and/or disputes relating to the exploitation of the [Manuscript/Images/Sound Recordings] and/or any adaptation, translation, merchandising, services, product placement, sponsorship, promotions and/or otherwise relating to the [Publisher] and/or any other third party shall be at the sole responsibility, liability and risk of the [Publishers] and no sums shall be claimed under the agreement and/or any indemnity from the [Author] and/or deducted from any advance, royalties and/or other payments due to the [Author].

I.137
The indemnity provision shall only apply to matters notified and claimed from the [Author] before [date].

I.138
The indemnity only applies to exploitation of the [Manuscript/Sound Recordings/Images/Characters] in the following countries: [specify] in [specify formats] and all other territories and locations are specifically excluded from any indemnity and all other methods of reproduction, publication, distribution and/or exploitation which shall be used, adapted and marketed at the [Publishers] sole risk and cost.

I.139
The indemnity only applies to any matter arising from the publication of the first edition of the [Book] in [country] by the [Publisher] before [date] which is an exact reproduction of the words supplied by the [Author]. Any other translation, change of title, characters and names, locations and other information shall be the sole legal responsibility of the [Publisher] and no indemnity shall apply from the [Author].

I.140

The [Publisher] agrees that the following matters are not covered by the indemnity in clause [–] and shall not seek to be paid any costs, damages, losses, expenses and/or other sums for these excluded items:

1.1 The index.

1.2 The title and the cover.

1.3 The accompanying promotional product and/or disc and/or service and/or electronic and/or digital version.

1.4 Liabilities which arise due to the errors, omissions, negligence and/or failures of the [Publisher], agents, distributors, printers, newspapers, magazines, websites, apps and/or authorised outlets.

1.5 Any contributions and/or adaptations by third parties whether approved by the [Author] or not.

I.141

All claims under the indemnity clause [–] must be received by the [Company] by [date] [time]. Thereafter the indemnity shall no longer apply. The [Publisher] waives all rights and agrees not to make any further claims against the [Company] after that date.

I.142

The [Software Company] agree to indemnify the [Distributor] and to pay all costs, expenses, losses and/or damages which may be substantiated in respect of the following failures by the [Software Company]:

1.1 The loss, destruction and/or damage to the [Master Copy] fixed at a maximum liability of [number/currency].

1.2 The failure by the [Software Company] to restrict access to and keep confidential the [Master Copy] while it is in its possession fixed at a maximum liability of [number/currency].

1.3 The failure to prevent a copy of the [Master Copy] being made by an unauthorised third party fixed at a maximum liability of [number/currency].

1.4 The corruption and/or addition of other material including viruses fixed at a maximum liability of [number/currency].

I.143

[Name] agrees and undertakes to indemnify the [Publisher] and any agent, distributor and/or sub-licensee if it is proved and/or discovered at a later date that they have suffered any loss and/or damage and/or costs and/

or expenses due to the fact that [Name] is not the copyright owner of the [Manuscript/Artwork/Sound Recordings] and/or has deliberately used and adapted material belonging to a third party without consent and/or has failed to acknowledge and credit and/or clear and/or pay the fees due for any such material and/or has failed to disclose an existing agreement with a third party which affects the terms of this agreement and/or has already disposed of and/or assigned all and/or some of the rights granted and/or assigned under this agreement to a third party. This indemnity shall end on [date] and no sums shall be due and/or paid which have not be notified by that date.

Services

I.144

1.1 The [Consultant] agrees that it will indemnify the [Company] within [number] days of an invoice against any liability, assessment and/or claim for taxation whatsoever including but not limited to any liability for personal income tax and/or for national insurance contributions where such liability, assessment and/or claim is made and paid by the [Company] in connection with the performance of the services of the [Consultant] for the [Company].

1.2 The [Consultant] also agrees to indemnify the [Company] against all reasonable costs and expenses and any penalty, fine, charges and/or interest which may be paid by the [Company] in consequence of any such liability, assessment or claim in 1.1.

1.3 The [Company] shall be entitled if it so wishes to recoup any sums due in 1.1 and 1.2 above by deducting such monies from any payments due to the [Consultant] by the [Company]. These deductions shall be instead of invoicing the [Consultant] for payment.

1.4 In any even the [Company] shall be obliged to provide copies of al supporting documentation which supports the reasons for the sums paid and the invoice and/or deductions.

I.145

In the event that [Name] shall cause any financial losses to the potential sales of the [Products] and/or negative publicity surrounding the other brands of the [Company] as a direct result of his/her actions and conduct, social media postings and/or any other matter. Then the [Company] shall be entitled to terminate this agreement immediately without notice and shall not be obliged to pay [Name] any further sums. Provided that the [Company] agrees not to seek any indemnity and/or make any claim against [Name] in respect of any sums, damages, costs, expenses and/or losses.

I.146

The [Presenter] shall not be bound to provide any indemnity to the [Television Company] for any reason except for any liability and claim for personal taxes which may fall due and/or national insurance payments which directly arising out of the Presenter's services under this agreement and which have been paid by the [Television Company].

I.147

The [Television Company] acknowledges that it shall be entirely and solely responsible for the cost of all losses, damages, on line claims, legal actions and proceedings, complaints and/or allegations arising out of and/or in connection with the [Presenter's] services at the studios and/or some other location carrying out research and/or being filmed and/or at any press and media and/or promotional event and/or any conference, meeting and/or other matter on behalf of the [Company]. Further the [Television Company] agrees that where the [Presenter] is required to assist and/or support the [Television Company] in regard to any matter that the [Television Company] shall reimburse the [Presenter] with all reasonable expenses and costs which he/she may incur. Where necessary the [Television Company] shall also bear the cost of any separate legal representation and advice that may be required for the [Presenter].

I.148

1.1   The [Developer] agrees to indemnify both the [Company] and the [Parent Company] in respect of the services and/or work to be provided under this agreement by the [Developer] and/or any third party engaged, employed and/or otherwise allowed to complete any part of the work and/or services.

1.2   The indemnity by the [Developer] shall relate to all the undertakings and schedules set out in this agreement.

1.3   The indemnity shall continue after the completion of the work and/or services for a period of [number] [months/years].

1.4   The indemnity shall not apply where the [Company] and/or the [Parent Company] has failed to pay any sums due to the [Developer] under this agreement where there is no dispute over the quality of the work and/or services. There shall be no right to withhold and/or set-off any sums by the [Company] and/or the [Parent Company].

1.5   The indemnity shall cover all direct and/or indirect allegations, settlements, disputes, legal proceedings and/or on line claims and/or any losses, damages, costs, charges, expenses, legal fees and expenses caused by the [Contractor] and/or any third party engaged, employed and/or otherwise allowed to complete any part of the work and/or services.

1.6 The total limit of the indemnity by the [Developer] shall be [number/currency] except in relation to personal injury and/or death where the indemnity is not limited in any manner

I.149

The provisions of the clause [–] above shall not entitle the [Company] to disclaim all liability to third parties. The [Company] shall continue to be liable to third parties in respect of all disputes, legal actions, proceedings, claims, costs, charges, losses, expenses, damages and/or settlements which arise directly and/or indirectly as a result of the negligence, default, omission and/or any failure by the [Company] and/or its directors, agents and/or otherwise to perform and/or fulfil the terms of this agreement at any time.

I.150

1.1 The [Developer] agrees that it is responsible for ensuring that all health and safety legislation, product liability and/or other guidelines and/or codes are adhered to in respect of the supply of the services and/or the completion of the work and/or the creation of the [Project].

1.2 The [Developer] shall ensure that all employees and/or agents are suitably qualified with up to date training for their roles. That no unqualified person shall be permitted to carry out work and/or provide services which required specialist skills.

1.3 That the [Developer] agrees to indemnify the [Company] in respect of any cost, expenses and/or other sums that may be incurred due to the failure to adhere to 1.1 and 1.2 above. This indemnity shall include the cost of replacements, renewal and/or recall of material and/or starting the [Project] again if that is the most cost effective option.

1.4 The [Developer] agrees to pay the cost of comprehensive insurance cover in respect of any claim by the [Company] under 1.1, 1.2 and/or 1.3.

I.151

The [Distributor] shall indemnify the [Company] in full in respect of all losses, damages, claims, demands, civil and/or criminal proceedings, costs and/or expenses incurred by the [Company] and/or its officers, employees and/or agents in respect of any losses and/or damage to any land, property, access routes, gas, water, electrical, solar power, telephone, mobile, internet and/or other facilities owned and/or controlled and/or used by the [Company] and/or any tools, equipment, furniture, transport and/or stock. Provided that any such sums are directly and/or indirectly caused to be incurred by the negligence, default, failure to perform and/or other defect and/or breach of this agreement by the [Distributor] and/or any person, agent and/or other third party engaged by them

I.152

The [Contributor] is supplying his/her services under the direction and guidance of the [Company]. The [Contributor] is not supplying original material. The [Contributor] is not providing any indemnity to the [Company] of any nature and/or any undertakings. The [Company] uses the work and/or services of the [Contributor] at its own risk and cost and shall not make any claim against the [Contributor] at any time for any reason. Any foreseeable loss that may arise whether caused by a breach of this agreement or not shall be at the liability and sole cost of the [Company].

I.153

1.1 [Name] agrees to indemnify the [Company] against all liabilities, claims, actions, costs, damages or losses arising out of any breach or alleged breach by [Name] of any of the terms of this agreement up to a maximum liability of [number/currency].

1.2 The [Company] undertakes to indemnify [Name] against all liabilities, claims, actions, costs, damages or losses arising out of any breach or alleged breach by the [Company] of this agreement.

1.3 [Name] and the [Company] agree that in order to seek any indemnity from the other in any case they must comply with the following conditions:

1.3.1 Notify the other party of the full details of the allegations which have been made and supply copies of relevant documentation;

1.3.2 Consult with the other party as to the best course of action in dealing with such matter;

1.3.3 Not incur significant legal costs or pay any third party any sum for any reason to resolve or settle the matter without the prior written approval of the other party which shall not be unreasonably withheld or delayed.

1.4 The indemnity of the [Company] shall continue after the expiry or termination of this agreement.

1.5 The indemnity of [Name] shall end at the expiry or termination of this agreement whichever is the earlier.

I.154

1.1 The [Author] and the [Agent] mutually undertake to indemnify each other against all liabilities, claims, demands, actions, costs, damages or losses by third parties arising out of any breach by either party of the terms of this agreement. This indemnity shall not include legal fees, cost and expenses incurred by the [Author] and/or [Agent]. It will include legal fees and other sums paid to third parties in settlement and/or arising from a legal action.

1.2 In the event that either the [Author] and/or the [Agent] shall seek to rely on 1.1 above then they must first provide full details to the other party from whom they seek any indemnity at the earliest opportunity and not settle any matter without prior consultation.

I.155

The [Company] acknowledges that there are no indemnity provisions from [Name] to the [Company] and the [Company] shall not seek to make any claim, demand or otherwise against [Name] whether there is a breach of this agreement or not.

I.156

The [Company] agrees that the [Presenter] shall only be liable for any breach of the undertakings in clauses [–]. In the event that the [Company] is to seek an indemnity from the [Presenter] it agrees that it must promptly notify any claim by the [Company] and/or any allegations and/or legal proceedings by a third party and make no admission, offer and/or settlement. In either case the [Presenter] shall be provided with all the available information and given the opportunity to respond.

I.157

The [Company] agrees that the indemnity in clause [–] to [Name] shall continue after the expiry and/or termination of this agreement until [date] [time]. There shall be no indemnity after that date except where a claim has already been notified and/or there is any existing dispute and/or litigation.

I.158

The [Company] agrees that any undertakings and the indemnity in clause [–] shall not apply in the following circumstances:

1.1 Where the claim, cost, expenses, damages, losses and/or liability has/have arisen as a result of the [Company] using and/or exploiting any material produced under this agreement beyond and outside the stated purposes.

1.2 The matter has arisen due to the negligence, errors, omissions and/or delays of the [Company] and/or any agent, sub-licensee, distributor and/or other third party authorised by the [Company].

1.3 The matter has arisen due to the delay, adaptation, editing, and/or alteration of the original material by the [Company] and/or any agent, sub-licensee, distributor and/or other third party authorised by the [Company].

I.159
The [Company] agrees that no indemnity is provided by the [Agency] in respect of the persons which it recruits for positions at the [Company]. That any final decision regarding appointments is at the sole discretion of the [Company]. Further that no indemnity and/or undertakings are provided by the [Agency] as to references, personal backgrounds and/or criminal records of any person. That data and information and reports supplied for the [Company] are for guidance only and cannot be relied upon as verified facts for which an indemnity is provided.

I.160
The [Agency] undertakes to indemnify the [Company] in respect of any costs, expenses, losses and damages which may be incurred and/or suffered by the [Company] in respect of any candidate vetted and proposed by the [Agency] during the course of this agreement. The indemnity shall cease to apply at the time of appointment and/or refusal of any candidate proposed and in any event shall cease to apply at the point at which a candidate is rejected by the [Company]. Where at a later date there are errors, omissions and/or inaccuracies which are found in any background summary supplied by the candidate and/or the [Agency] then the [Company] agrees that it shall have no right to make a claim against and/or to seek to be indemnified by the [Agency] for any reason.

Sponsorship

I.161
The [Sponsor] undertakes to indemnify the [Sportsperson] against all allegations, threats, defamatory statements, liabilities, claims, legal actions and/or proceedings and/or complaints by any third party including any regulatory and/or other governing bodies in respect of the fines, charges, costs, expenses, damages, losses, legal costs and fees as well as those of any public relations company, agent, social media advisor and/or any other person engaged by the [Sportsperson] to assist in minimising the damage caused to the reputation and/or career of the [Sportsperson] which directly and/or indirectly arises out of any breach and/or alleged breach by the [Sponsor] of any of the terms of this agreement and/or any associated filming, social

media, publicity and/or products at any time whether during the existence of this agreement and/or thereafter for a period of up to [number] months.

I.162

1.1 The [Sponsor] indemnifies the [Television Company] against all liabilities, claims, costs, actions, damages, expenses including legal fees, expert witnesses and reports reasonably and properly incurred by the [Television Company] arising out of any breach and/or alleged breach of this agreement up to a maximum total of [number/currency] in each year during the Sponsorship Period.

1.2 The [Television Company] indemnifies the [Sponsor] against all liabilities, claims, costs, actions, damages, expenses including legal fees, expert witnesses and reports reasonably and properly incurred by the [Sponsor] arising out of any breach and/or alleged breach of this agreement by the [Television Company] up to a maximum of [number/currency] whether during the existence of the Sponsorship Period or not.

1.3 In order to claim under the indemnity provisions the [Sponsor] and/or the [Television Company] must promptly notify the party from whom they seek the indemnity of any claim and/or legal proceedings and make no settlement and/or admission at that stage. The party who will pay the indemnity must be provided with an opportunity to participate in or control any settlement or proceedings as appropriate.

I.163

1.1 The [Company] shall keep the [Distributor] indemnified from and against all liabilities, actions, claims, proceedings, damages and losses suffered or incurred directly but not indirectly by the [Distributor], or awarded against the [Distributor] or any compensation or settlement agreed in consequence of alleged breach or actual breach by the [Company] [including/excluding] any third party appointed by them under this agreement.

1.2 The [Distributor] agrees to indemnify the [Company] in respect of all liabilities, actions, claims, proceedings, damages and losses suffered or incurred directly but not indirectly by the [Company] or awarded against the [Company] or any compensation or settlement agreed in consequence of any breach or alleged breach of this agreement by the [Distributor] [including/excluding] any third party appointed by them under this Agreement.

I.164

1.1 The [Sponsor] and the [Production Company] mutually undertake to indemnify each other against all liabilities, claims, demands, actions, costs, damages or losses arising out of any breach by the [Sponsor] and/or the [Production Company] of any of the terms of this agreement.

1.2 In the event that either party shall seek to rely on this indemnity then they must provide full details to the other party, within a reasonable time, of the matter arising and allow the other party to be fully involved in the case at their own cost.

I.165

1.1 The [Sponsor] and the [Association] mutually undertake to indemnify the other against all liabilities, claims, demands, actions, costs, expenses, interest, charges, compensation, damages and/or losses arising out of any breach by either party of any of the terms of this agreement which are reasonably foreseeable. In the event that either party shall seek to rely on the indemnity then they shall provide full details to the other party at the earliest opportunity and shall seek their views before settling any matter. Each party shall bear its own legal and administrative costs and shall not seek to reclaim them. They may seek to be indemnified and paid in respect of legal costs paid to a third party in settlement of any matter.

1.2 It is agreed that the maximum liability for any reason of each of the parties under this agreement shall be fixed at:

1.2.1 [number/currency] in total for the [Association].

1.2.2 [number/currency] in total for the [Sponsor].

These sums shall not apply to any matter relating to personal injury and/or death.

1.3 No claim shall be made under any indemnity by either party where they are able to claim all the sums under an existing insurance policy.

I.166

The [Sponsor] agrees that it shall not seek to be indemnified by the [Company] for any direct and/or indirect and/or consequential financial loss, expense, damage to reputation, changes to an advertising campaign, merchandising and/or promotional events which arise due to the following matters:

1.1 Cancellation, delay, alteration of the content of the scheduled [Film/Programme/Sound Recordings], artistes and/or the location.

1.2 Changes in any title, players, outfits to be worn, banners, flags, official brochures, television, radio, internet and/or social media coverage.

I.167

The [Company/Charity] does not and shall not provide any indemnity to the [Sponsor/Promoter] for any reason under this agreement. The [Sponsor/

Promoter] enters this agreement at its own risk and cost and shall be responsible for all the cost and expenses that it may be liable for and/or incur whether caused by the actions, failures and/or breaches of this agreement by the [Company/Charity] or not. The [Sponsor/Promoter] accepts that even where the [Company/Charity] is at fault the [Sponsor/Promoter] shall not take any legal action as it recognises that the [Company/Charity] has very few assets and low financial resources.

I.168

The following matters shall not be covered by the indemnity in clause [–] and the [Company] agrees that there shall be no right to claim any sums and that all such rights are waived where:

1.1 Any sums can be claimed and are paid under an existing insurance policy for the [Event].

1.2 Any sums due which arise as a result of the negligence, omission, error, delay and/or failure of a third party.

1.3 Any sums which are not notified and the reason provided by [date].

I.169

The [Athlete] acknowledges and agrees that the [Sponsor] does not provide any indemnity to him/her and his/her agent and/or coach and/or family and/or agree to pay any costs, expenses, travel and/or accommodation costs and/or cancellation fees, equipment, access to training facilities and/or any other sums, losses and/or damages which may arise in respect of the attendance of the [Athlete] at any event, race, presentation, interview, filming and/or otherwise which he/she may attend, participate in and/or contribute to at any time.

I.170

The [Sponsor] agrees and undertakes to indemnify the [Athlete] in respect of any expenditure which may be due and/or incurred by him/her which arises directly and/or as a consequence of the provision of the services of the [Athlete] under this agreement and/or associated his/her training requirements and/or in order to communicate with his/her agent, coach, team members and/or family including without limitation:

1.1 All mobile, WiFi and internet and telephone costs and charges in any part of the world.

1.2 All five star hotel, food, drink, hospitality, gym and spa costs including any additional services and costs charged during the stay.

1.3 All first class travel by aeroplane, train, chauffeured car, helicopter and/or any other means required.

1.4 All training and fitness equipment, sports clothes and shoes, membership, access and location fees.

Provided that the total monthly payment by the [Sponsor] to the [Athlete] shall be limited to [number/currency] and any additional sums due shall be held over until the next month until paid in full. Subject to the supply of a statement invoice and further receipts and/or payment records if requested.

University, Charity and Educational

I.171

The [Company] shall be solely responsible for and shall indemnify the [Institute/Charity] and/or the associated [Enterprise] and its officers, employees and/or agents against all direct and/or indirect liabilities, allegations, legal actions, claims, losses, damages, personal injury, death, damage to and/or suspension of the use and access to equipment and/or facilities, defects and/or viruses caused to software, recall of stock, distribution of personal and other data without consent to third parties, complaints, civil and/or criminal proceedings, administrative costs and/or other charges, costs, interest and expenses and court fees and legal expenses incurred by the [Institute/Charity] and/or the [Enterprise] including any matter settled on the advice of a legal advisor by the [Institute/Charity] and/or the [Enterprise] as a result of a breach and/or alleged breach by the [Company] of its obligations under this agreement and/or any third party whom they have engaged to fulfil and/or perform the obligations under this agreement.

I.172

1.1 The [Institute/Charity] agrees and undertakes to indemnify the [Company] against all claims and/or legal actions, costs, expenses, damages and/or losses which arise as a consequence of a significant breach and/or alleged breach by the [Institute/Charity] of the terms of this agreement up to a maximum of [number/currency] in [country]. This indemnity shall not apply to the actions and/or failures of any third party and shall only apply to matters notified before [date].

1.2 The [Company] agrees and undertakes to indemnify the [Institute/Charity] against all claims, legal actions, costs, expenses, damages and/or losses which arise as a consequence of a significant breach and/or alleged breach by the [Company] of the terms of this agreement up to a maximum of [number/currency] in [country]. This indemnity shall apply to the actions and/or failures of any third party and shall only apply to matters notified [date].

1.3 In the event that either party shall seek to rely on the indemnity provided by the other party. Then they must first provide full details to the other party at the earliest opportunity and allow them the opportunity to refute the allegations and/or claim and shall not settle any matter without prior consultation with the party.

I.173

1.1 The [Institute/Charity] and the [Sponsor] mutually agree and undertake to indemnify each other against all costs, expenses and other sums and expenditure that may be incurred which directly relate to the failure of the other party to carry out, perform and/or fulfil the terms of this agreement.

1.2 Where the agreement is terminated by one party and another third party substituted then there shall be no claim under 1.1.

1.3 Where the agreement is suspended and/or delayed then any sums due under 1.1 shall be paid in full.

1.4 There shall be no right to claim for any sums which are incurred by third parties and not directly paid by the [Institute/Charity] and/or the [Sponsor].

1.5 There shall be no liability to pay any legal costs and expenses and/or administration costs.

1.6 No interest shall be paid on any sums.

1.7 In the event that either party shall seek to rely on this indemnity then they must provide full details to the other party within [one] month of the matter arising and allow the other party to be consulted as to the options as to how the matter can be defended and/or resolved.

I.174

1.1 [Name] shall indemnify the [Institute/Charity] against all allegations, complaints, legal actions and/or proceedings, online claims, settlements, costs, expenses, legal fees, charges and expenditure for expert witnesses, damages and/or losses incurred and/or paid out by the [Institute/Charity] in respect of any allegation of infringement of copyright and/or trade marks and/or any other intellectual property rights by a third party in respect of the material created, developed and originated by [Name] which is supplied under this agreement for use and exploitation by the [Institute/Charity].

1.2 [Name] agrees that the [Institute] shall have the right to change, alter, adapt and amend any material provided by [Name] which in the opinion of the [Institute/Charity] is likely to incite violence, cause offence, be defamatory and/or result in a civil and/or criminal proceedings and/or a significant negative reaction on social media

1.3 The indemnity by [Name] shall end on [date] at [time]. Thereafter the [Institute/Charity] accepts that it shall not be entitled to make any claim and/or take any legal action against [Name] in respect of the indemnity in 1.1.

I.175

Both parties agree and undertake to arrange and bear the cost of suitable insurance cover for their own benefit for the [Project]. Neither party agrees nor undertakes to indemnify the other and each shall bear its own risks and costs which may arise. This clause shall not exempt any claim, action and/or costs which may be sought in the course of a civil and/or criminal against either party by the other.

I.176

The total indemnity by the [Institute/Charity] to the [Company] shall be limited to [number/currency] which is the total value of the [Products/Services/Event]. No responsibility can be accepted by the [Institute/Charity] for any other losses, damages, costs, expenses, destruction of data, delay in delivery, interruption of facilities and/or services, non-availability of key personnel, inaccuracies, errors, defects, failure to account and/or pay any sums due whether directly and/or indirectly arising from reliance on this agreement by the [Company].

I.177

The indemnity in clause [–] by the [Contributor/Institute] shall not apply in respect of the following matters: [specify].

I.178

The [Consortium] agrees that no party to this agreement shall provide any indemnity to the other members of the [Consortium] at any time and that each party shall bear its own costs and expenses of any losses, damages and/or sums that may fall due and/or be claimed by any third party and/or any student, employee, consultant and/or otherwise.

I.179

The [Student/Delegate] agrees that they are allowed access and use of the facilities and accommodation on the basis that they do not suffer any damage, destruction, graffiti, water damage, stains, use of electrical power points and/or connections in an unauthorised manner, use of unauthorised gadgets, removal of any furniture and fittings and/or any other matter which would likely result in costs and expenses in order to restore them to their original condition. Normal wear and tear is excluded. Where work is required and/or items need to be replaced then the [Student/Delegate] shall forfeit their deposit and in addition be obliged to indemnify the [Institute] with any additional sum incurred provided that it is itemised and proof is provided which justifies the cost.

INDEX

General Business and Commercial

I.180

If the [Author] and the [Publishing Company] agree that an index is required but the [Author] does not wish to undertake the task. Then the [Publishing Company] shall entitled to engage a competent indexer to compile one and the costs shall be paid by the [Publishing Company]. The [Author] shall not be required to make any payment to the work of the third party indexer. The draft index shall be submitted to the [Author] for approval. The [Publishing Company] agrees to make any changes and/or edits and/or additions to the index that the [Author] may stipulate. The [Publishing Company] agrees to ensure that the third party indexer does not acquire any copyright and/or other intellectual property rights in the index and/or any compilation and/or any taxonomy and that all such rights shall be assigned to the [Author].

I.181

The [Author] agrees that she/he shall provide the [Distributor/Publisher] with a detailed index and/or key word search list for the [Work/Images/Sound Recordings] as may be required at his/her sole cost and expense. Provided that the [Author] is only required to supply a draft typed list and any format adaptations with be completed at the [Distributors'/Publishers'] sole cost.

I.182

If in the opinion of the [Distributor/Publisher] it is desirable that an index be included in the [Artwork/Book/E and Digital Book]. It is agreed between the parties that the [Publishers] shall ensure that an editor and/or researcher employed by them shall create a draft and a final edited index at the [Distributor's/Publisher's] cost and expense. The [Distributor/Publisher] agrees to ensure that the [Author] is provided with copies of the draft index and the final edited version so that any requested amendments by the [Author] can be incorporated. The [Distributor] and the [Author] agree that they shall hold joint copyright ownership in the index for the [Artwork/Book/E and Digital Book]. Neither the [Distributor] nor the [Author] shall be entitled to grant any rights in the index to a third party without the prior consent of the other party.

I.183

If in the opinion of the [Publisher] and the [Author] it is decided that an index, bibliography and/or preface should be included with the [Artwork/Sound Recordings/Manuscript] prior to publication and distribution in any format. Then the [Author] agrees to provided such assistance as may be required and to prepare, write and deliver at the [Authors'] cost and expense the following material:

1.1 An index of [number] pages.

1.2 A bibliography of quoted resources and material from third parties with relevant copyright notices, credits and acknowledgements and to state the name of any archive, institution and/or other organisation and/ or person who supplied any material whether owned the rights and/or only the physical material.

1.3 A title and preface of [number] words.

I.184

The [Author] undertakes to prepare a comprehensive summary of key words and points in the sequence of the [Artwork/Manuscript/Film] which will enable it to be searched effectively by a third party. Where the [Author] is for any reason unable and/or unwilling to do so then the [Distributor/Publisher] may decide to do so at its own cost provided that no sums are deducted from any payments due to the [Author]. Where any copyright and/or other intellectual property rights are created in such new material. Then it is agreed that the [Distributor/Publisher] shall assign all such rights to the [Author] and shall not make any claim to own any such rights.

I.185

The [Author] undertakes to prepare an index for the [Work]. In the event that due to a change in circumstances this is not done. Then the [Publishers'] may create an index provided that they consult with the [Author] and pay the cost of all sums incurred in the creation of the index and do not seek to acquire any copyright and/or other rights in the index and/or to allow a third party to do so.

I.186

The development of any indexes in any languages for the [Book/E and Digital Book/Game] shall be the responsibility of the [Publisher/Distributor]. The index shall be subject to the prior approval of the [Author] who shall be entitled to be supplied with a copy in each format. The [Publisher/Distributor] shall have the final decision as to whether an index is necessary in any particular format and whether it is to be included or not.

I.187

The [Distributor/Publisher] is prohibited from including any content in and/ or relating to the promotion and marketing of the [Artwork/Book/Sound Recording] unless it has been created, written and supplied by the [Author]. Where the [Author] has supplied an index, preface, bibliography and/or any other material for the cover and/or to be accessed on line. The [Distributor/ Publisher] agree that they shall not amend, delete, translate and/or otherwise alter any such material without the [Author's] prior written consent.

I.188

1.1 The [Author] agrees that he/she shall create, compile and develop an index for the [Work] after delivery of the draft proofs by the [Company] to the [Author].

1.2 The [Company] agrees that the copyright and ownership of the index and its taxonomy shall belong exclusively to the [Author]. The [Author] shall be entitled to the following copyright notices and credits: [specify detail and format] on each and every copy of the index and taxonomy reproduced, supplied and/or distributed by the [Company] in any format and in any media at any time.

1.3 That the [Company] shall not have any right to edit, adapt, amend and/ or delete any material from the index without the prior written consent of the [Author]. The [Company] shall not have the right to supply, license and/or distribute the index and/or taxonomy to any internet, website, app and/or search engine business and/or any other third party without the prior written consent of the [Author].

I.189

That the index shall be compiled by a nominated person to be agreed between the parties. The parties agree to ensure that the copyright and taxonomy shall be assigned to both parties to be held jointly and equally. Neither party shall be entitled to amend, adapt, delete and/or develop the index and taxonomy without the prior written consent of the other party. All sums received from any exploitation shall be shared equally between the parties.

I.190

The [Company] shall not use the index and/or contents list of the [Work/ Book/Sound Recording/Compilation] in any manner without acknowledging the title, the ISBN and the name of the [Author] and displaying the copyright notice on each occasion.

I.191

Where the [Company] sub-licenses the [Work/Book/Sound Recording] to be translated into another language other than [specify]. Then the [Author] shall have the right to be consulted and must provide express approval concerning the translation of the title, contents list, headings, full text and images and the index. A complete copy should be provided to the [Author] at the [Licensees'] cost and expense prior to production, printing and distribution for the [Authors'] comments and approval. The suggestions by the [Author] must be included in any new version otherwise the [Author] will be justified in withholding and/or delaying consent.

I.192

The [Company] agrees that the [Author] is the owner of the copyright, computer software rights and all other intellectual property rights in the title, images on the cover, logos, slogans, contents list, headings, text, graphics, illustrations, maps, spatial layout, index and taxonomy of the [Work]. Any application to register such rights and/or interest in any media whether as a trade mark, domain name, with any collecting society, and/or otherwise shall be made by the [Author] and not the [Company].

I.193

The data, personal information, thematic subject headings, order of the text, images and logos and all indexes, key words, links, lists and databases belong to [Name] and there is no right to reproduce, adapt and/or exploit them in any form and/or by any means whether for the purposes of education, research, for a charity and/or a commercial reason. In all cases an application must be made for permission to [Name]. There is no consent to any use for any reason by a third party unless the prior written agreement of [Name] has been obtained and a licence specifically granted for any such use.

I.194

1.1   [Name] agrees to create a database, index and key word search list for the [Company] for use in conjunction with their website, app, business, social media, marketing and promotions.

1.2   In consideration of the payment of a fee of [number/currency] [Name] shall waive all rights of any nature including moral rights and a right to a credit and/or copyright and/or other acknowledgement to all material supplied to the [Company] under 1.1.

1.3   [Name] assigns to the [Company] all present and future copyright, database, trade mark, service mark, computer software and any other intellectual property rights and/or other rights of exploitation in any form whether they exist now and/or are developed and/or created in the future through new legislation, technology and/or otherwise throughout the land, sea, air of the planet earth and through time and space without limit including the full period of copyright and the full period of database rights and any further periods which may arise and/or be created.

INSOLVENCY

General Business and Commercial

I.195
In the event that the [Management Contractor] makes a composition of its debts or any other arrangement with its creditors or has a proposal for a voluntary arrangement for a composition of its debts, or has an application made to a court for the appointment of an administrator, or has a winding up order made (except for the purposes of amalgamation or reconstruction), or a resolution for a voluntary winding up is passed, or has an administrator, liquidator, receiver or manager appointed or has possession taken on behalf of the holders of any debentures or holders secured by a floating charge, then this contract shall be automatically terminated.

I.196
Without prejudice to any rights or remedies of either party at law if either party shall become insolvent and/or unable to make payments to its creditors as and when payment for such sums become due. Then the other party who is not in that position shall have the right, but not the obligation to terminate this agreement at its discretion.

I.197
'Insolvent' shall mean that the company, business or partnership is unable to fulfil to pay their debts as they fall due and an insolvency petition is likely to be and/or has been presented to a court.

I.198
If the [Company] delays in paying its sums due to the [Institute/Charity] as it has financial difficulties and/or is threatened with insolvency. Then the [Institute/Charity] shall have the right at its sole discretion to cancel and/or terminate and/or suspend and/or take such action as its thinks fit in the circumstances to protect the interests and rights of the [Institute/Charity].

I.199
It is agreed between the parties that where for any reason any member of the [Consortium] becomes insolvent and/or unable due to a reduction in funding contributions from a third party to continue with the [Project]. That all assets of the [Project] held by that defaulting member shall continue to belong to that member and not the [Consortium]. That the [Consortium] shall be provided with the option by that defaulting member to purchase the assets they hold relating to the [Project] for a value to be agreed between the parties. That where no purchase takes place the defaulting member may sell and/or license the assets to a third party who is not part of the [Consortium].

I.200

It is agreed between the [Company] and the [Artist/Athlete] that where the [Managing Director/Chief Executive] has been advised by the Board of Directors that the [Company] is to undergo restructuring and/or insolvency and/or disposal of all and/or part of the business which relates to the [Artist/Athlete]. That the [Artist/Athlete] shall be notified at an early stage of this fact to enable them to seek full payment of their services under this agreement and to obtain the return of all material which they own and/or to purchase any other material which they may wish to seek to exploit.

INSPECTION OF ACCOUNTS AND RECORDS

General Business and Commercial

I.201

The [Administrator] may issue instructions requiring the [Contractor] to arrange for the inspection of any work whether covered up or secured, and order tests of any materials or goods or of any work in relation to the [Project]. If the inspection or tests shows that the work, materials or goods are not in accordance with this contract then the [Contractor] shall be required to remedy the problem entirely at their own cost and expense where it can be shown they have not followed the agreed plan, budget and/or instructions.

I.202

1.1 The [Author] shall be allowed to inspect the accounts of the [Publisher/Distributor] and/or to authorise a suitably qualified person to do so on his/her behalf both during the Term of this Agreement and thereafter for up to [number] years. Provided that reasonable notice is given to the [Publisher/Distributor] by the [Author] and the purpose of the inspection is to verify the sums due to the [Author] and any costs related to any such inspection are paid for by the [Author].

1.2 The [Publisher/Distributor] agrees not to charge for making any copies of documents, providing access to software and/or any other administrative expenses that may be incurred by them in respect of 1.1. If any such inspection reveals an error in the [Publisher's/Distributors'] favour of [ten] per cent or more the cost of any such inspection shall be paid in full by the [Publisher/Distributor] upon invoice by the [Author]. The [Author] agrees not to charge any additional interest on any sum found not to have been paid in error and/or omitted. In any event the [Publisher] shall only be obliged to allow one inspection in any accounting period.

I.203

1.1 The [Licensee] shall keep accurate, clear and verifiable accounts in accordance with professional accounting practices in [country] which are a true and complete record however the information, data, agreements, licences, expenses, costs and other records are stored whether in books, on software and some other format. No material shall be destroyed, deleted and/or amended in any manner which creates a false impression and/or omits significant information and/or data and/or sums received and/or paid in respect of the exploitation of the [Units/Products] which are based on the [Film/Video/Book].

1.2 The [Licensor] shall be entitled at its own expense to inspect, examine and make copies of all such accounting records in 1.1 and all material created by the [Licensee] in any format and/or by any method. Such inspection shall be made at the offices of the [Licensee] during office hours by the [Licensor] itself and/or a qualified accountant and/or an authorised representative of the [Licensor]. The [Licensor] must provide the [Licensee] with [number] days' written notice in order to be permitted any inspection and may not do so more than once in any period of [six] months. This right of inspection shall continue until [number] years from the expiry and/o termination of this agreement. If any such inspection shall reveal an error in excess of [five] per cent of the sums due to the [Licensor]. Then the [Licensee] shall pay the full cost and expense of such inspection; the sum owed plus interest at [number] per cent from when the sum should originally have been paid. Where the error in in excess of [number/currency]. Then an additional sum shall be paid as compensation which shall be [ten] per cent of the sum owed to the [Licensor].

I.204

1.1 The [Company] agrees that the [Agent] shall be entitled to request copies of the contracts and/or invoices stored and/or retained in any format relating to the orders and sales obtained by the [Agent] in order to verify the sums due to the [Agent] under this agreement for the [Garments/Units] for which payment has been received.

1.2 The [Agent] shall at its sole cost be entitled to arrange for one audit during the Term of the Agreement to inspect and make copies of the [Company's] accounts, records and contracts relating to orders obtained by the [Agent] in order to verify the sums paid and/or due to the [Agent]. Such audit shall be at such times and dates as may reasonably be agreed between the [Company] and the [Agent].

I.205

1.1 The [Distributor] agrees to maintain software, computer records, data, information, costs, expenses, agreements, licences and other documents in accordance with accounting principles in [country] and to retain all such material for a period of not less than [four] years after expiry and/or termination of this agreement and/or in the event of litigation between the parties until such time as it has been resolved.

1.2 The [Supplier] and its authorised representatives shall be supplied by the end of each calendar month with a complete breakdown of all the deductible expenditure, incoming revenue and the calculation of the sums due to the [Supplier]. Where the [Supplier] has any concerns regarding any report then further information and data and documents shall be provided as soon as possible and if necessary an inspection may be authorised to access the original source of the report however it may be stored and/or held in any format and/or by any means. The [Distributor] agrees that it shall have no right to refuse any such inspection.

1.3 Where at any time after the termination and/or expiry of this agreement and/or the end of the services of the [Distributor] and/or any associated company. It appears that sums were not disclosed which were due to the [Supplier]. Then the [Supplier] shall be entitled to carry out a full audit and inspection at the [Suppliers'] cost and expense. Where a serious error and/or default is found by the [Supplier] then the [Distributor] shall be obliged to immediately pay upon invoice all such sums as may be due together with the costs of the audit and any interest.

I.206
The [Company shall be entitled to delete and/or obscure from any right of inspection and/or audit all such confidential information, data, databases, formulas, processes, information relating to patents, trade marks, sources of material, product placement, sponsorship and any other details and sums which are not directly related to the calculation of the sums due to [Name].

I.207

1.1 Where in any inspection and/or audit the sum due which has not been paid is more than [number/currency]. The defaulting party shall also promptly pay the total costs and expenses paid and/or due to any accountancy firm and/or other professional advisor and/or representative who carried out the inspection and/or audit together with such other sums as may have been discovered to be due.

1.2 Where there is any dispute then the parties agree to refer the dispute to the following organisation: [specify]. The parties agree to fulfil the following procedure recommended by that organisation: [specify].

1.3 Both parties agree that they shall comply with the matters in 1.1 and 1.2 prior to the start of any litigation regarding the payments under this agreement.

I.208

1.1 The [Licensee] agrees to permit the [Licensor] or their authorised legal advisors, accountant and other experts at all reasonable times to inspect, examine, test, assess and audit and take copies from the relevant software, data, documents, records, accounts, stock, products and other materials which directly relate to this agreement and/or any sub-licensees and/or any relevant agents and/or production companies and/or suppliers at any time upon request. The [Licensee] agrees that all such material shall be maintained and not destroyed by the [Licensee] for a period of [number] years from [date].

1.2 The [Licensee] further agrees to give any additional information, data and other documents and/or records reasonably required to enable the amount of the royalties due to the [Licensor] to be verified and to ensure the compliance with health and safety requirements of the [Products/Units].

1.3 In the event of an inspection revealing an error of the royalties accrued and due to the [Licensor] at any time. The [Licensee] shall pay to the [Licensor] all the costs of any such audit and inspection upon receipt of an appropriate invoice justifying the costs. The [Licensee] shall pay to the [Licensor] any sums shown to be due together with interest at [number] per cent.

I.209

1.1 The [Company] may at its sole cost appoint independent auditors to complete a comprehensive report on the costs and expenses relating to the [Project] which have been claimed by the [Enterprise] and/or any third party which have been deducted and/or recouped by them from the Budget for the [Project].

1.2 Where it is found that sums have been falsely claimed and/or excessive charges have been made which does not correlate to the work completed. The [Company] may decide at its sole discretion decide to deal with the matter as a criminal offence and/or by legal proceedings against the [Enterprise] and/or any third party. The [Company] agrees to give the [Enterprise] and/or any third party an opportunity to explain and to offer a sum in settlement.

I.210

The [Company] agrees and undertakes to fully cooperate, and provide access to all premises, warehouses, offices, data, documents, records, databases, discs, order forms and sales receipts, invoices, stock and any other material in any medium in order for [Name] to carry out a thorough and comprehensive inspection and audit in respect of [specify subject]. Any material which is relevant which the [Company] does not intend to allow access to for any reason should be listed in an inventory to be provided by the [Company] with a statement as to the grounds for non-co-operation.

I.211

Prior to the inspection of any records, accounts or other material the [Company] and their legal advisors and/or accountants shall sign each sign a confidentiality agreement which undertakes that they shall not disclose to any third party any information which is not in the public domain except where legitimately required for the purposes of legal advice, financial and/or compliance reports and/or legal proceedings.

I.212

The [Distributor] shall allow inspection of the [premises/goods/records/software/accounts] by the [Company] and/or any nominated person at any time by verbal notice from a senior officer of the [Company]. Inspection shall not be limited by time, frequency or material under this agreement and unrestricted access shall be permitted so that the [Licensor] may examine any matter which relates or potentially relates to this agreement.

I.213

All sub-licences and other contracts concluded by the [Licensee] relating to [subject] shall permit the [Licensor] to inspect and verify for itself the sums due to the [Licensee] and/or the [Licensor]. A direct authorisation shall be sent to the [Licensor] on each occasion. No agreement shall be concluded with a third party who will not agree to those terms.

I.214

1.1 The [Publisher/Distributor] undertakes to the [Author/Creator] that competent and professional reports and background material shall be kept of the exploitation of all the rights and/or formats of the [Manuscript/Artwork/Sound Recordings] by the [Publisher/Distributor] from [date] to [date].

1.2 Any report should include detailed list of all data, documents and software, licences, assignments and other agreements concluded so that an accurate audit and inspection can be carried out by the [Author/Creator]. All costs, expenses and other expenditure shall be itemised and all deductions before the calculation of the royalties due to the [Author/Creator] shall be made clear. Any currency conversion costs and charges should be recorded and the date of the conversion rate. The date of receipt of any payments from a third party must be included and supported by appropriate documents. Where sums have not been paid then the fact they have not been received should be stated.

I.215
Where after any inspection and/or audit it is clear that the [Agent] has not fulfilled the terms of this agreement and a serious error of more than: [number/currency] has occurred. Then the [Agent] shall pay the sum due in full together with interest at [number] per cent and damages on each occasion of [number/currency] together with all legal and accountancy costs and expenses of the [Artist] which have been incurred.

I.216
The [Manager] shall upon request at no charge provide the [Sportsperson] with a copy of any contract, letter, document, data, database, accounts and/or other material stored on any software relating to the [Sportsperson] in the possession and/or under the control of the [Manager] and/or any sub-agent and/or sub-licensee and/or any other third party company with whom the [Manager] has been negotiating with and/or concluded any arrangement and/or agreement with relating to the [Sportsperson].

I.217
The right of inspection shall not apply to any parent, associate and/or affiliate company to the [Company].

I.218
The [Company] shall not be obliged to bear the cost of any photocopying, telephone calls, electricity, catering and/or other facilities which may be required for the purposes of the inspection and audit which shall be arranged and paid for by [Name].

I.219

1.1 The parties agree that the [Enterprise] shall keep the following list of documents and material stored on software as a record of the [Work/Products/Services] reproduced, supplied, distributed, licensed and/or sold under the terms of this agreement: [specify].

1.2   The documents and software records listed in 1.1 shall be copied and supplied to the [Licensor] at the [Licensee's] cost at the end of each [four] calendar month period.

1.3   In addition the [Licensor] shall have the right to visit the premises and offices of the [Licensee] once in each calendar year for no more than [four] days to carry out an audit and inspection at the [Licensors'] cost.

I.220

The [Institute/Enterprise] shall have the right to carry out a full and comprehensive inspection and audit of the records stored on software and/or any agreements and documents, invoices, payment records and accounts, bank and savings accounts, reports, complaints and company emails, films, videos, sound recordings, images, corporate records, insurance and minutes of the Board of Directors of the [Company] and any associated business which relate to the [Project]. The [Company] shall have the right to exercise this clause no more than twice in any year during the Term of this Agreement. The [Institute/Enterprise] shall have the right to appoint such legal and professional advisors to carry out the inspection and audit on its behalf as may be required in the circumstances.

I.221

There shall be no right to inspect and/or audit the accounts, records and/or any other data, information, contracts and/or material relating to the [Institute/Charity] by the [Company]. The [Institute/Charity] may provide copies of such information as may reasonably be requested relating to the fulfilment of the agreement, but reserve the right to refuse any request at its sole discretion.

I.222

The [Company] shall have the right to arrange for a professional legal, computer, financial and/or accountancy advisor to visit the premises, offices and warehouses of the [Distributor] and/or its agents and to view and make copies of all relevant accounts, data, records, documents, stock, sales, expenses and costs held on any computers, laptops, gadgets and/or any other storage devices together with any physical records and/or material in any format in any part of the world at any time. No notification shall be required for any such visits.

I.223

The [Distributor] agrees and undertakes to ensure that the [Licensor] shall have complete access to the computer and manual accounts and any documents and records and that it shall be a condition of all such agreements with any sub-licensee, agent, and/or other third party engaged by the [Distributor] in respect of the exploitation of the rights granted under this agreement.

I.224

The [Distributor] shall make available to the [Licensor] a full set of audited accounts each year together with an itemised statement of the sums due to the [Licensor] at the [Distributors'] sole cost. The statement shall be clear as to the gross sums received and any sums deducted. No sums shall be withheld and/or not disclosed.

I.225

The [Sub-Licensee] agrees and undertakes to provide the [Company] with copies of all receipts for any expenditure which is claimed by the [Sub-Licensee] under this agreement. The [Sub-Licensee] agrees to make available to the [Company] the following material and records in any format and/or medium including printed format, stored on a hard drive on a computer and/or any laptop and/or on any mobile and/or recorded on any other software in any other gadget at the [Sub-Licensee's] offices at [address] in [country] in respect of the exploitation of the [Products/Units/Book] under this agreement:

1.1 Warehouse and stock records.

1.2 Records of supply, sale, distribution, destruction, disposal without charge and any other method.

1.3 The latest audited accounts.

1.4 A list of all the methods by which the records are held in any format and/or medium.

1.5 A list of all locations at which stock is held.

1.6 A list of all parties who are authorised by the [Sub-Licensee] to deal in the stock.

I.226

1.1 The [Company] agrees to provide [Name] with a detailed statement of the sums due from the affiliation programme to [Name] during the existence of this agreement until the date of termination and/or expiry of the agreement whichever is the earlier.

1.2 [Name] agrees that the [Company] shall not be required and/or obliged to supply personal information, names, residential and business addresses, email addresses, mobile telephone numbers and bank details of any person and/or entity to [Name] and that information shall remain confidential to the [Company] and shall not be disclosed.

1.3 The Company agrees to provide in any statement information which shall include the date of any relevant transactions, the total value of the sales exclusive of any taxes and other charges received and not returned and the calculation of the sum due to [Name].The parties agree that the statement shall be sent at the end of each calendar month. All sums due to [Name] shall be paid within [number] days of each such statement.

1.4 The parties agree that where there is a dispute and [Name] wishes to seek to verify the sums paid and/or due and the stock sold and returned. That the [Company] shall arrange for [Name] to have a meeting with the [Finance Director] of the [Company] to be shown such part of the computer software and other records as may be available. That where the dispute involves a sum of more than [number/currency] the parties may agree to appoint a third party to provide a form of dispute resolution and that both parties agree to be bound by that decision. The cost of the dispute resolution to be paid for by the [Company] and may not be recouped under this agreement.

I.227

1.1 The [Agent] agrees and undertakes that no sums received by the [Agent] shall be held in any account except [specify] at [specify] bank. That the [Athlete] shall be entitled to receive copies of all bank statements and other documents that may be issued in relation to that account.

1.2 Further the [Agent] agrees that where any costs, expenses and other sums are attributed and deducted from any sums due to the [Athlete] that the [Athlete] shall be entitled to inspect and/or receive copies of all emails, documents and any other material which deal with the matter in any form. That where deductions have not been justified that the sum owed shall be paid to the [Athlete] together with the additional sum of [number/currency] on each occasion.

1.3 The [Agent] agrees and undertakes that the [Athlete] shall be entitled to be provided with a copy of all material in any media which relates to the provision of his/her services to any third party at any time which is held, controlled and/or in the possession of the [Agent] and/or his/her advisors and/or consultants.

I.228
[Name] acknowledges that all records, data, information and other material relating to access to, downloading and/or use of the [Apps/Links/Website/Blog] are carried out electronically and by computer software and telecommunications and supplied, delivered and processed by a variety of

suppliers for the [Company]. [Name] agrees that a report by email in the form of a pdf and/or excel and/or other format shall be sufficient evidence supplied by the [Enterprise] as to the payments due and no paper and/or other records and/or documents need be provided. [Name] agrees that there is no automatic rights of inspection and/or audit and/or the right to request copies of supporting documentation.

I.229
There shall be no right of inspection of any corporate, advertising, promotional and/or sponsorship agreements by [Name] of the [Company] and any right shall be limited to the supply of the internal report entitled [specify] from [date to [date] during the existence of this agreement.

INSURANCE

Film, Television and Video

I.230
The [Distributor] shall arrange at its sole cost comprehensive insurance cover in respect of the exercise of the rights by the [Distributor] under this agreement for the benefit of the [Distributor/Licensor] of not less than: [number/currency] in respect of any allegations, claims, settlements, damages, losses, liability and/or legal costs which shall be in effect from [date] to [date] and cover all the following countries: [specify].

I.231
The [Distributor] shall ensure that it is a condition of the agreement with any sub-licensee, agent and/or any other third party that they are insured for no less than [figure/number] in respect of any errors, defects, damages, losses, claims, personal injury, death and/or any other liability that may arise in respect of the [Work/Service/Product] for the duration of the agreement and for up to [number] years after the end of the agreement.

I.232
The [Company] shall arrange and pay for insurance cover for the benefit of [Name] whilst the [Sound Recordings/Videos/Images] are in the possession and/or control of the [Company]. The [Company] shall at all times ensure that there the master copy is kept in a secure place and kept in conditions which will not result in the deterioration of the material. The [Company] shall ensure that all persons involved in the production of the [Discs/Units/Programme] from the [Sound Recordings/Videos/Images] shall adhere to any conditions of the insurance policy and [Name].

I.233

It is agreed between the parties that the following matters be specifically excluded and shall not be covered by an insurance policy in respect of the [Project] and that each party shall bear such matters at their own risk and cost: [specify excluded detail].

I.234

[Name] agrees and accepts that the [Products/Units/Videos/Images] are not insured while stored at [address] and in the event of their destruction and/or damage for any reason agrees that payment to [Name] shall not exceed [number/currency].

I.235

The [Distributor] confirms that has not arranged insurance cover for the [Products/Units/Videos/Images] whilst they are in transit after they have left the [production company] and/or thereafter at any time. That in the event that any items are lost, damaged and/or destroyed then it is accepted that all such costs incurred shall be the responsibility of the [Distributor]. However no sums shall be due to [Name] in respect of such lost, damaged and/or destroyed items.

I.236

The [Company/Distributor] undertakes and agrees that it shall ensure that there is a comprehensive insurance policy in place in respect of the production and/or exploitation of the [Film/Programme/Series] by the [Company] and/or the [Production Company] in respect of the following matters: [specify cover]. The [Company] agrees to pay for the cost of such policy and shall not deduct any such sum from the agreed Budget with the [Production Company]. The policy shall be for the benefit of the [Company/Distributor] and the [Production Company]. Both parties shall be provided with a copy of the policy.

I.237

1.1   The [Company] shall at all material times maintain and pay for annual insurance cover with a reputable company regarding the development, production and/or exploitation of the [Project] from [date] to [date]. The cover shall be for not less than [number/currency] in respect of each claim. There shall be no excess of more than [number/currency]. The policy shall cover the following areas:[specify]. The policy shall applies to all the following countries: [specify]. The insurance policy shall be for the benefit of the [Company].

1.2   The [Company] agrees that it shall adhere to all the conditions of any insurance policy and shall not do anything and/or authorise any actions and/or work which may invalidate the insurance cover.

I.238

[Name] and [Name] agree that the following matters are specifically excluded and shall not be covered by any insurance policy and each party shall be responsible for their own work and the use of their contribution at their own risk and shall be responsible for their own damages, losses, liability, costs and expenses that may arise in respect of the [Film/Blog/Podcast]: [specify excluded issues not covered by insurance].

I.239

1.1 The [Company] agree that [number/currency] of the [Budget] shall be allocated to insurance in respect of the cast, equipment, locations, third party and public liability and that the policy shall be for no less than [number/currency] and apply in [country/worldwide] for the benefit of [specify].

1.2 That the [Company] shall also ensure that in the event that any person has a medical condition that this is notified to the insurers and that where additional payments are required that it be arranged.

1.3 That where there are additional risks and hazards and insurance cannot be arranged due to the high cost. That a risk assessment will take place in each case and if the health and safety advisor does not provide consent that the event will be cancelled.

General Business and Commercial

I.240

The [Company] confirms that there will be in existence during the Term of this Agreement adequate public and employer's liability insurance with [specify insurance company] in respect of the [Event/Festival/Conference].

I.241

Subject to any limits set by any legislation the [Company] agrees to provide life assurance cover entirely for the benefit of the [Executive] and his/her family at rates and upon conditions acceptable to the [Company]. The [Company] shall make arrangement for life assurance at [four times basic salary/number/currency] and shall provide a copy of the policy to the [Executive].

I.242

Where at a later date it becomes clear and there is evidence that a person has not disclosed a pre-existing medical condition to the [Company] and/or the insurer at the time that a policy was arranged. The insurance policy may not provide cover for any such condition and in such circumstances no claim shall be paid by the [Company] and/or the insurer.

I.243

The [Company] agrees and undertakes that it shall arrange and pay for first class life insurance of not less than [number/currency] with [specify] and first class medical and dental insurance to cover death, disability, cancer, allergic reactions, any operations and associated treatment and medical interventions and dental treatments that may be required in [country/worldwide] for [Name]. The cover shall be for all periods whether [Name] is at work and/or on holiday and/or other leave from [date] and shall continue until [Name] is no longer under a contract of employment with the [Company]. [Name] shall be specified on all policy documents and have the right to make any claim and not be limited to make any request through the [Company].

I.244

In the event that the [Company] fails to ensure that additional insurance and medical protection cover is in place at any time so that [Name] is insured for any work which is dangerous, high risk and/or outside the normal policy of the [Company]. Then the [Company] agrees that it shall be liable and pay for any sums due to the family and [Name] on the basis as if there had been a policy at the [Company's] cost and expense.

I.245

The [Company] agrees and undertakes that it has arranged and paid for professional indemnity insurance covering defects, omissions, faults, design failures, defects relating to plans, designs, construction and specifications under this contract for not less than [number/currency] for any one claim and/ or settlement and/or legal action for the benefit of [specify]. The [Company] undertakes to maintain such insurance policy at its sole cost for a period of [ten] years after the completion of the [Project].

I.246

1.1 The [Company] undertakes that it holds valid [Employers liability insurance] from [date] which is to be renewed on [date]. That there is cover in respect of any claim of not less than [number/currency]. That the policy covers any employee who is working on the premises of a third party enterprise.

1.2 The [Company] undertakes that it holds valid [Comprehensive General and Public Liability insurance] for all the contracts and work and services that it provides to third parties for not less than [number/ currency] in respect of any claim, settlement and/or legal action. It shall cover any claim for personal injury and/or death for any directors, consultants, advisors, interns and/or employees, and/or any third party engaged by the [Company] and/or the general public and/or losses and/or damage caused to property, stock, vehicles, machinery and/or equipment owned, hired and/or used by the [Company] and/or any third party engaged by it and/or for causing any environmental pollution, health and/or safety risks and/or any other matter which could reasonably be foreseen and which is caused by the defaults, negligence, errors and/or omissions of the [Company] and/or any employee, agent and/or other third party engaged by them at any time.

I.247

It shall be the responsibility of [Name] to arrange and pay for an insurance policy with [specify] to cover [specify] for the [Land/Building] at [address] registered as [reference] by [body] from [date] until [date] for not less than [number/currency] for the benefit of [specify].

I.248

1.1 The failure to arrange insurance cover and/or to fully comply with any of the provisions of the insurance conditions shall not in any way relieve the [Company] of its obligations under this contract. Where no insurance is arranged as agreed then the [Company] shall bear all the cost and expense of all sums that may be due.

1.2 In any event, where any losses, damages, costs and expenses and/or claims are rejected by the insurers in whole and/or part for any reason and/or if the [Company] fails to maintain the required insurance. The [Company] agrees that it shall indemnify the [Enterprise], its subsidiaries and affiliates, agents, employees and/or directors against all allegations, claims, legal actions and/or settlements of any nature including all costs, expenses, legal fees of counsel and solicitors, investigation agencies, and any other litigation expenses and/or liabilities which would otherwise be covered by the insurance that was agreed between the parties pursuant to this contract.

I.249

The [Company] agrees that it shall:

1.1 at its sole cost arrange insurance cover against the [Event] not taking place for any reason and/or any claims by third parties in respect of such cancellation and/or delay whether due to force majeure, failure of facilities and/or a health and safety issue. The policy shall be for the benefit of the [Company] and the [Name] in the sum of: [number/currency].

1.2 provide the [Name] with a copy of the insurance policy upon request and proof of payment of the premiums if required.

1.3 not authorise and/or carry out any actions which would result in the insurance policy being declared invalid.

1.4 the [Company] agrees to notify the [Name] in the event of any circumstances which may arise which may result in a claim under the insurance policy and shall not settle any such claim without the prior written approval of the [Name]. Any sums paid by the insurers to the [Company] which is for the benefit of the [Name] shall be immediately paid without delay.

I.250

The [Licensee] shall promptly provide the [Company] with proof of adequate insurance upon request. If the [Licensee] fails to provide the [Company] with proof of such insurance within [seven] days of the request. Then the [Company] may suspend the agreement until proof of such insurance is provided.

I.251

All insurance policies required of the [Company] under this contract shall contain endorsements that the underwriters will have no rights to sue, recover, claim and/or subrogate any losses and/or damages of any nature for any reason against the [Distributor], its subsidiary, affiliated companies and/or their agents, directors, officers and/or employees.

I.252

Any and all excesses and/or deductibles in the insurance policies arranged by the [Company] shall be at the [Company's] sole risk and cost.

I.253

It is agreed between the parties that the insurance cover for the [Project] must not contain any geographical and/or jurisdiction exclusions and/or limitations.

I.254

It is agreed that any insurance policy to be arranged and deducted from the Budget shall relate only to one individual party under this agreement. Each party shall hold its own policy upon which it is entitled to rely and/or claim even though it relates to the same [Project]. There shall be no joint insurance documents.

I.255

In the event that the [Enterprise] does not arrange and/or maintain the agreed insurance cover as required under this agreement. Then the [Company] may arrange such insurance and pay the premiums and shall be entitled to deduct such sums from any monies due to the [Enterprise] from the [Company].

I.256
The [Distributor] shall ensure that it maintains adequate insurance cover at all times to meet its obligations to pay the sums due under this agreement. The [Distributor] shall upon request provide evidence of such insurance and that the [Company's] interest is specified.

I.257
There are a number of areas which will not be covered by any insurance policy and these excluded areas are specified as follows [List matters not covered by insurance]. It is agreed between the parties that all matters on the excluded list shall be carried out, performed and/or adhered to at each persons' own risk and cost. There are no undertakings to indemnify the other party nor to make any contribution to any cost, expenses, damages and/or losses that may be incurred and/or arise as a result.

I.258
The [Consortium] agrees that each party may arrange and pay for its own insurance cover in respect of the [Project]. In addition a further policy in the name of [specify] for the sum of [number/currency] shall be arranged with [specify] for the duration of the [Project] and for up to [number] years thereafter to cover claims by the persons engaged to work on the [Project] in any capacity and/or any trials and/or any products and/or data and/or records which may be supplied, reproduced, sold and/or exploited at any time. The cost to be met from [specify fund] for the [Project].

I.259
Where any party to this agreement fails to have insurance cover for public and third party liability of no less than [number/currency] which is valid at all times and for which all the premiums are paid. Then such failure shall be deemed a breach of this agreement and shall entitle the other party to terminate the agreement without notice and to not be liable for any further payments that may fall due thereafter.

Internet, Websites and Apps

I.260
The [Company] does not provide any insurance cover for the benefit of the [Purchaser] in respect of the [Services/Products/Accommodation/Travel]. Insurance cover is an additional item which must be ordered and paid for in advance. All insurance policies are customised to suit the application details completed by the [Purchaser] and are with a third party.

I.261

No liability can be accepted by the [Website/App/Platform] for the failure by any third party to fulfil the terms of the agreement of the order and/or request for services that have been made. The [Website/App/Platform] does not control and/or own the third party companies who offer and/or display their products and/or services. You deal with them at your own risk and cost. There is no insurance policy in place to cover any losses, damages, costs and expenses caused by any failure to deliver material and/or any service.

I.262

The [Company] agrees and undertakes that it shall arrange and pay for comprehensive insurance cover with a reputable company for the total amount of [number/currency] per claim and/or settlement of any allegation which shall cover defamation, legal proceedings, and/or claims for losses and/or damages by any third party and/or employees, directors, officers and/or investors of the [Company] in [countries]. The [Company] shall send a draft copy of the insurance policy to [Name] for approval prior to finalising the policy. The [Company] shall also ensure that all the directors, officers, and/or investors are sufficiently protected by the insurance policy from a personal exposure to a claim arising from the actions. Failures, defaults and/or errors by the [Company] at any time.

I.263

The parties agree that neither the [Website/App/Platform] nor the [Company] is covered by any comprehensive insurance policy for all the countries in the world. It is agreed that where any insurance policy does not cover any matter and/or the insurer refuses to pay all and/or some of any claim. Then the parties shall split the cost and expense of all the consequences and/or liabilities which are not covered equally between them.

I.264

Any material which is sent by normal post in [country] is limited to a total value of [number/currency] regardless of the value of the actual contents. If you wish to have full insurance cover and protection then you must arrange to pay for a courier service and pay the additional costs. The [Company] cannot bear the cost of insurance and is only liable if you suffer any loss and/or damage and/or costs and/or death, personal injury and/or disability and/or otherwise which have a direct causal connection to some serious failure by the [Company] and/or the products and/or the services and is not due to your own negligence and/or fault.

I.265

No undertakings are provided as to insurance cover by [Name] and/or the [Company] in respect of the [Blog/App/Website] and each party shall take all necessary precautions to minimise the threat of any allegations, claims, losses, damages, costs, expenses, fines and/or civil and/or criminal action against either and/or both of them in [country] and in any other country of the world for any reason. Both parties agree that where there is any matter which arises that they shall notify the other and share the knowledge and assist in resolving the matter swiftly with the intention of reducing liability and costs regardless of whether the allegation and/or claim and/or otherwise has merit or not.

I.266

Each party to this agreement shall be responsible for arranging and paying for its own insurance cover including public liability insurance, emergency medical and/or product liability cover. There shall be no obligation to arrange joint insurance cover for the [Event].

Merchandising and Distribution

I.267

The [Company] agrees that it shall at its sole cost arrange comprehensive insurance cover for the exercise and exploitation of the copyright and/or intellectual property rights granted in this agreement and/or their use and/or adaptation in the form of the following [Products/Units]: [specify] in any part of the world. This insurance cover shall include development, production, sales and supply and distribution as well as product liability. The minimum total cover per claim shall be [number/currency] with no excess. The [Company] agrees to provide the [Licensor] with a complete and valid copy of the insurance policy for each year of the agreement upon request.

I.268

The [Licensor] agrees that there is no requirement for the [Licensee] to arrange and/or pay for insurance cover in respect of the exercise of the rights granted under this agreement and/or any liability.

I.269

During the Term of this Agreement the [Licensee] shall ensure that it has arranged and paid for insurance cover with a reputable insurance company for the production, reproduction and distribution of the [Artwork/Sound Recordings/Videos/Films/Manuscript] and/or any adaptation for the benefit of the [Licensee and Name]. The minimum insurance cover shall be no less than: [number/currency] for each potential claim. The [Licensee] shall [not] be entitled to deduct the insurance premium payments from any sums due to the [Licensor] under this agreement.

I.270

The [Licensee] shall ensure that any sub-licensee, agent, distributor and/ or other authorised third party shall agree that they must be covered by insurance in respect any claim and/or allegation by the public and/or any retailer to the value of more than [number/currency] in [countries] for any period in which they are authorised to exercise and/or exploit the rights granted in this agreement. The [Licensee] shall make available to the [Licensor] copies of the policies upon request together with evidence of the payment of the premiums. Where there is no insurance cover in place then the [Licensee] shall be obliged to notify the sub-licensee and/or agent and/or distributor and/or any other third party that the agreement must be terminated.

I.271
The [Licensee] shall not be required to arrange additional insurance cover for the stock which the [Licensee] holds of the [Artwork/Products/Units] which are created under this agreement provided that it is covered by an existing policy for no less than [number/currency]. In the event that additional insurance cover is required the [Licensor] agrees that the [Licensee] may deduct [number] per cent of the premiums paid from any sums due to the [Licensor]. Provided that the [Licensor] and [Licensee] are both named on the policy and a copy is supplied to the [Licensor].

I.272
Where material which belongs to [Name] is destroyed, damaged, lost, stolen and/or otherwise not returned to [Name] for any reason after the end of this agreement. Then the sum to be paid by the [Company] shall be limited to the cost of replacement and/or the current market value whichever is the higher.

I.273
The [Customer] must ensure that each [Item] is returned to the [Supplier] by any method which can provide proof of delivery and that the [Item] is insured for not less than [number/currency].

I.274
The [Company] shall take out adequate insurance for the benefit of [Name] in respect of death, personal injury, medical and dental costs, plastic surgery, rehabilitation, loss of income and/or other losses, damages, expenses and/or costs which may arise directly and/or indirectly as a result of the attendance and/or participation of [Name] at the [Event] from [date] to [date]. The insurance cover shall start on [date] and continue until [date] and shall be for not less than [number/currency] for any one claim. Where there are any exclusions under the policy then the risk and costs shall be the responsibility of the [Company].

I.275

The [Licensee] confirms that:

1.1 A comprehensive public and product liability insurance policy is and will be in force covering any allegations, claims, legal actions, settlements, damages, costs and expenses which may arise as a direct or indirect result of the use by the public of the [Product] and/or any associated packaging, films, videos, images and/or promotional and/or advertising material in [any part of the world/specify countries].

1.2 The [Licensee] shall arrange and pay for insurance cover for the benefit of the [Licensor] to cover any failure to pay sums which arise from insolvency, bankruptcy, fraud, corruption, financial and/or accounting irregularities and/or non-payment by the [Licensee], and any agent, sub-distributor and/or sub-licensee of any sum due to the [Licensor].

1.3 The [Licensee] agrees to provide the [Licensor] with a copy of the relevant insurance policies in 1.1 and 1.2 upon request.

I.276

The [Consortium] agrees that it shall arrange for insurance cover at the [Consortium's] cost to ensure that the Board, Executive and Non-Executive Directors and senior management are not held personally liable at any time. The insurance policy shall provide cover for all members of the Board and senior management in respect of any claim, allegation, threat, legal action, settlement and/or other matter which may arise relating to the [Products/Services/Projects] and shall include development, applications, production, licensing, distribution and any other form of exploitation at any time. The cover shall include fines, interest, legal costs and expenses of individual legal advisors and the payment of any sums that may be paid to third parties.

I.277

1.1 The [Licensee] shall arrange individual product liability insurance for no less than [number/currency] for each type of [Products/Units/Services] by [date] and ensure that each such policy applies in [specify countries] which shall be for no less than [number] years.

1.2 The [Licensee] agrees that it shall ensure that where any [Product/Unit/Service] has failed to pass any risk assessment, test and/or trial for any reason that it is not reproduced and/or distributed in that form and that a new risk assessment, test and/or trial must be carried out for the new version.

1.3 That the [Licensee] shall monitor and report on to the [Licensor] all cases where a [Product/Unit/Service] is recalled and/or withdrawn from production and/or exploitation.

Services

I.278

The [Company] agrees and undertakes to provide insurance, medical, dental and legal cover for the [Presenter] at the [Company's] sole cost which shall be for the benefit of the [Company] and/or the [Presenter]. Where the [Presenter] is required to present and/or carry out other work in any situation and/or circumstances that may potentially not be included within the policy. The [Company] shall arrange additional insurance, medical, dental and legal cover as appropriate based on the facts. Where at a later date any sums incurred for any reason are not covered by the policies then the [Company] agrees to pay such costs and expenses in full subject to invoice and request for payment by the [Presenter]. The [Company] shall provide a copy of any insurance policy from which the [Presenter] will benefit upon request. The [Company] agrees that the minimum level of cover per claim shall be:

1.1   [number/currency] in respect of personal injury and/or death.

1.2   [number/currency] in respect of legal costs and expense incurred by the [Presenter].

1.3   [number/currency] relating to any allegation of defamation, infringement of copyright and/or any other threat, settlement, claim, legal action and/or complaint to and/or by a regulatory body.

I.279

[Name] agrees and undertakes that:

1.1   He/she is not currently suffering from any illness, injury and/or other matter which will in any way prevent him/her from providing his/her services as required under this agreement. That [Name] shall endeavour to ensure that they are physically fit, not under the influence of any medication and/or drugs and/or alcohol and/or in any manner have their ability and capacity impaired from [date] to [date].

1.2   He/she will comply with all reasonable stipulations made by an insurer to enable the [Company] to obtain and pay for insurance cover for [Name] and/or the [Company] prior to the commencement of the [Film/Video/Series] as the [Company] may require.

1.3   He/she will attend a medical examination and undertake such tests including but not limited to blood, hair, skin, and urine tests as the [Company] shall require. [Name] shall have the right to nominate an approved medical practitioner and/or hospital for all such matters subject to the agreement of the insurers.

I.280

1.1 The [Company] may arrange, in its own name, for its own benefit and at its own cost and expense, life insurance, accident insurance or health insurance and any other insurance required by the [Company] in respect of [Name/Group]. [Name/Group] agrees that [he/she/they] shall not have any right, title and/or interest in any such insurance policy or any money payable pursuant to any such insurance policies unless they are also stated to be beneficiaries of such insurance cover.

1.2 There shall be no obligation by [Name/Group] to agree to answer any medical questionnaire and/or comply with any medical examination.

I.281

[Name] agrees and undertakes:

1.1 To co-operate in the completion of all proposal forms and execute any other documents from time to time required by the [Company] in order to arrange for any policy of insurance or make any claim upon any such policy.

1.2 To provide evidence that they have no health and/or mental health and/or allergy issues which may be affected by their participation in the [Project].

1.3 That they shall ensure that they are physically and/or mentally capable of participating in the [Project].

1.4 That they are not aware of any reason which if it were known would cause their participation in the [Project] to be terminated.

1.5 That they shall not to be involved in any hazardous pursuit or activity during their involvement in the [Project] and shall not take any risk at any time which would result in the cancellation of the insurance policy and/or is likely to result in any claim being rejected by the insurers.

I.282

The [Company] agrees and undertakes that it shall have insurance policies in existence at its own cost during the Term of this Agreement for the following matters: [specify subjects to be insured] in respect of the provision of its services to the [Distributor] for not less than [number/currency].

I.283

The [Supplier] shall arrange and bear the cost of third party liability insurance of not less than [number/currency] in [country] in respect of each potential claim and/or settlement relating to the exploitation of the

[Products/Services]. All premiums and/or excess shall be paid at the [Suppliers] sole cost.

I.284

The [Company] shall ensure that life, personal injury, travel, medical, dental and legal costs insurance cover is arranged for the benefit of [Name] and his/her estate and/or his/her clothes, equipment, car, gadgets, mobile, laptop and/or any other agreed physical material in respect of the services and/or work to be completed by [Name] during the Term of this Agreement until [date] for no less than [number/currency] for each claim. The [Company] shall provide [Name] with a copy of the valid insurance policy.

I.285

The [Company] shall not be entitled to insist that [Name] completes a full medical assessment in order for the [Company] to arrange insurance cover. A summary of the health and medical conditions of [Name] by [Name's] own medical practitioner will be considered sufficient background information and no further information, data or assessments need to be provided and/or disclosed whether requested by the insurers or not.

I.286

The [Company] is not responsible for arranging and/or paying for any insurance cover for the [Consultant] during the term of the engagement of his/her services. The services of the [Consultant] are excluded from the [Company's] general insurance policy except to the extent of public liability insurance.

I.287

Where the [Athlete/Artist] is unable to provide his/her services for any period under this agreement for any event and/or performance and no substitution can be made. Then it is agreed that the [Athlete/Artist] shall not be liable for any sums that may arise and/or be claimed by any third party. The [Distributor] agrees to be responsible for all the costs and expenses, losses and/or damages that may be due and it is not dependent on the fact as to whether it is covered by an insurance policy or not.

I.288

The services supplied under this agreement are not insured for the benefit of the [Client]. You must arrange your own insurance cover at your own cost. Where there is any allegation, claim, legal action and/or dispute the [Company] and/or the [Client] shall each bear their own legal costs and expenses. There is no obligation by either party to consult the other regarding any proposed settlement, defence and/or any other matter.

Sponsorship

I.289

1.1 The [Sponsor] undertakes to arrange sufficient insurance cover at its sole cost for the [Event/Festival/Launch] to cover any cancellation, postponement, losses, damages, legal actions, claims, settlements, allegations of breach of contract, infringement of copyright, defamation and/or any other complaint by a third party and/or the [Association] and/or any artist and/or contributor to the [Event/Festival/Launch].

1.2 The [Sponsor] shall ensure that the policy includes product liability and public liability against failure of any products, equipment, material and/or services supplied by the [Sponsor] and/or any claim and/or legal action relating to personal injury, death, trauma and any allegations of any nature which would impact on any visitors to the [Event/Festival/Launch] and/or any other exhibitors and/or sponsors and/or any other persons who are working and/or providing their services directly and/or indirectly caused by the [Sponsor] whether arising as a result of negligence and/or otherwise.

1.3 Any insurance cover shall apply to any set up period before the [Event/Festival/Launch] and for the period where equipment and/or other material is removed. As well as for the duration of the [Event/Festival/Launch].

I.290
The [Sponsor] agrees that it shall not seek to make any claim and/or allegation of liability against the [Enterprise/Charity/Name]. The [Sponsor] agrees and accepts that it enters into this agreement at its own risk and cost. The [Sponsor] confirms that it shall arrange comprehensive insurance for its sole benefit at its sole cost as follows:

1.1 From [date] to [date].

1.2 Product liability for the [Event/Podcast/Series] in respect of the [Sponsor's] products, and any other materials, owned or controlled by the [Sponsor], or any personnel, agents or other persons authorised by the [Sponsor] to attend and/or carry out work which are supplied, sold and/or given away which are used and/or consumed and/or worn by the public and/or any other third party which shall be for not less than [number/currency] for any one claim and/or settlement.

1.3 Insurance cover for any cancellation, postponement, delay, losses, theft, fire, accidental and deliberate damage, floods, explosions and/or any force majeure which may occur for any reason for not less than [number/currency] for any one claim and/or settlement.

I.291

Neither party shall be required to take out insurance cover in respect of the [Project] and both parties agree to bear the risk, cost, losses and damages which may arise due to a claim, action and/or complaint relating to their own products, intellectual property rights, consents and permissions, personnel, equipment, transport, publications, data, research and/or other material which they have and/or will provide under this agreement.

I.292

These excluded areas in Schedule [–] are not covered by any insurance policy. The [Sponsor] and the [Institute] shall each bear their own risk, cost and expense in respect of any liability that may arise as a result of the preparation, development, performance, completion and/or clearing up after the [Event]. Neither party shall be obliged to contribute and/or pay any of the liabilities that may arise which are caused by and/or incurred by the other party.

I.293

[Name] agrees to attend the [Club] at his/her own risk and cost and the [Club] shall not be liable for any claim, losses, expenses, damages, injury, emotional distress, and/or any other matter whether to the person and/or their property unless caused as a direct result of the negligence and/or failure to comply with existing legislation by the [Club] and/or any of its officers. In any event the liability of the [Club] shall be limited to [figure/currency] for all matters except personal injury and/or death.

I.294

Where the [Sponsor] sets up, supplies, installs and/or displays any banners, flags, lighting, balloons, fireworks and/or any other material and/or equipment at the [Event]. That where for any reason the health and safety and/or other officer of the [Company] and/or any authorised contractor and/or local authority requires that they be removed on safety grounds that the [Sponsor] shall comply immediately with any such request. That in any event the [Sponsor] shall have paid for specific insurance cover for their attendance and participation at the [Event] to include:

1.1 All public and third party liability of not less than [number/currency].

1.2 To cover any damages, losses and expenses incurred by the [Company] relating to the [Sponsor] of not less than [number/currency].

1.3 To cover any damage and/or loss of electricity and any other power supply, pollution of water, sanitation, failure to remove and/or repair and/or reinstate any services and/or land and/or premises used by the [Sponsor] including access roads, fences, trees and foliage.

A copy of such policy to be provided to the [Company] by [date] together with evidence that the relevant premiums required have been paid.

I.295

1.1 The [Sponsor] of the [Event] acknowledges that is not covered as a contributor to the funding of the [Event] by any insurance policy of the [Company].

1.2 The [Company] agrees and undertakes that it shall arrange and pay for public and third party liability for the [Event].

1.3 The [Company] agrees and undertakes that it shall not seek to claim any contribution by the [Sponsor] to any claims, actions and/or civil and/or criminal proceedings relating to the [Event] and that the total liability of the [Sponsor] to the [Company] is limited to the funding contribution of [number/currency].

University, Charity and Educational

I.296

The [Institute/Charity] agrees and undertakes to arrange insurance cover at the [Institutes'/Charity's] cost for the [Contributor] and her/his personal property in respect of the services provided under and during the Term of this Agreement. The [Institute/Charity] shall provide the [Contributor] with a copy of the insurance policy upon request. The [Institute/Charity] agrees that the insurance for the benefit of her/his estate shall not be less than: [number/currency] and shall cover the following work and services to be carried out by the [Contributor]: [specify detail of services].

I.297

During the Term of this Agreement and before: [date] the [Company] will arrange insurance in respect of the [Project] for the benefit of [Name] for the period [date] to [date]. The cover shall be at least: [number/currency] for each case with an annual total of [number/currency] in respect of any allegations, settlements and/or claims relating to the [Project] and/or the related work and/or services by [Name]. A copy of the policy shall be provided to [Name].

I.298

The [Licensee] confirms that a comprehensive insurance cover shall be arranged by the [Licensee] with an established insurance company at the [Licensee's] cost for the benefit of the [Institute/Charity].The cover shall include public and product liability insurance policy, any threats, fines, criminal proceedings, allegations, claims, losses, damages, expenses, civil proceedings, investigations, complaints by the public and/or any trading standards and/or other government and/or local authority, legal costs and awards, interest and/or aggravated damages, fraud, misrepresentations and/or any other matters which may arise as a direct result and/or the indirect result of the use by the public of the [Product/Service] and/or any associated material, data, information, packaging, promotional material and/or advertising owned or controlled by the [Licensee] and/or any other action, conduct and/or breach of this agreement by the [Licensee]. The [Institute/Charity] shall be entitled to review the proposed terms of the insurance policy and the exemptions. A copy of the final policy shall be supplied to the [Institute/Charity] by the [Licensee]. Where at any later date any matter is not covered by the policy to the detriment of the [Institute/Charity] then the [Licensee] shall be liable for any sum due.

I.299
The [Company] shall arrange and bear the cost of its own comprehensive insurance for the [Event/Product/Service] and its employees, agents, consultants and any other third parties which it engages. The [Institute/Charity] shall not be liable for any damages, losses, financial losses, equipment failure and/or damage, power failure, loss of data and/or software and/or damage to hardware, water damage, fire, destruction of material of any nature unless caused directly by the [Institute/Charity] and/or an employee and/or representative and due to the negligence and/or deliberate fault of the [Institute/Charity] and not exempted by force majeure.

I.300
The [Consortium] agrees that it shall not arrange any specific insurance cover for the individual members of the [Project] but shall arrange and pay for product liability insurance at the [Consortiums] cost before any sample developments and/or products are placed in any trial, test and/or marketed to the public in any country.

I.301
The [Institute/Charity] does not accept any liability for any loss and/or damage to the equipment and/or resources and/or data and/or any viruses and/or scams against and/or to any person who uses the facilities of the [Institute/Charity] for their research at any time. Please ensure that you have suitable personal insurance cover and do not disclose any personal details such as passwords, pin codes and/or other information to any person who may contact you as this information is never requested by the [Institute/Charity].

INTEREST

General Business and Commercial

I.302

The [Guarantor] agrees to pay interest to the [Creditor] at the rate of interest [number] per cent on all sums which are actually due under this Guarantee. The interest shall be payable from the date of the [Creditor's] demand under this Guarantee provided that the [Creditor] has provided full details of the breakdown of the sums due whether damages, losses, costs or expenses. All such interest shall accrue on a day-to-day basis and be calculated by the [Creditor] on the basis of 365 days a year and interest shall be compounded in accordance with the usual practice of the [Creditor].

I.303

The [Creditor] shall [not] be entitled to recover any amount in respect of interest and/or any other penalty at any time whether due to the failure to pay any sums which may fall due under this [Guarantee/Document] or not.

I.304

'Interest Rate' means [number] per cent from [date] to [date]. At all other time it is based on [specify organisation/source].

I.305

The [Company] reserves the right to charge interest on the outstanding balance of all overdue sums at [five] per cent per annum above the current base rate at [specify Bank] or the maximum interest rate permitted by law in [country] whichever is the higher at the time.

I.306

The [Company] shall be entitled to charge interest on any sum payable by the [Licensee] under this agreement which is not paid on or before the due date at the rate of [number] per cent from the due date where the sum should have been received until the date upon which the payment is paid in full.

I.307

If the independent chartered accountant appointed by a party under clause [–] decides that the other party has not received all the sums due under this agreement. The defaulting party shall upon invoice immediately arrange to pay the sums due to the other party together with interest. Interest shall be calculated at the rate of [number] per cent for the period the sum was not paid up to a maximum interest payment in total of [number/currency].

I.308
[Name] shall pay to [Company] interest on the aggregate of all the sums advanced which are from time to time outstanding at the annual rate of [number] per cent above the base rate for lending of [specify Bank]. The [Company] agrees that the payment for interest due from [Name] in any one year shall be capped at [number/currency].

I.309
The [Company] reserves the right to charge interest on the amount of any delayed payment at the rate of [number] per cent per calendar month on all and/or part of any sums due and owing until payment has been made in full. The [Company] agrees that the maximum payment of interest under this agreement shall be set at [number/currency] in total. No sums shall be due in interest when that maximum has been reached regardless as to whether there are still any sums due to be paid.

I.310
The [Company] reserves the increase and/or change the calculation and/or rate of interest on any sums due after [date].

I.311
The [Distributor/Supplier] shall not have the right to charge any interest, costs and/or expenses due to delay in the receipt of payment and/or for any other reason.

I.312
The [Company] reserves the right to seek to recover interest on any sum which is not paid on time whether under subscription, purchase price, licence fee, and/or access fee and/or usage fee. The rate of interest shall be entirely at the sole discretion of the [Company] depending on the circumstances of the case and company policy.

I.313
The interest rate to be charged by the [Company] shall not exceed [number] per cent of the sums due in total at any time and shall only apply after any sums have not been paid for more than [number] months.

I.314

1.1 No interest shall be due on any sum which is delayed due to force majeure.

1.2 Any interest to be charged shall only be due after payment has not been received and payment has been delayed by more than [number] days.

1.3 The total amount of interest which can be charged by the [Company] shall not be more than: [number/currency].

1.4 No other additional penalties may be imposed.

1.5 The [Institute/Charity] shall not be obliged to pay any additional sums. There shall be no charge for administration and/or legal costs unless ordered by a court,

I.315
Where the sums held by the [Licensee] accrue interest then the interest shall be added to the total funds before the calculation of the royalties due to the [Licensor].

I.316
Where the [Sponsor] delays and/withholds monies due to the [Company] under this agreement for more than [number] days. Then all such sums shall be subject to an interest charge of [number] per cent which shall arise from the date the money is due to the day it is actually paid. The interest charge shall be paid at the same time as all the other money.

I.317
It is agreed by the parties that no interest will be charged and/or due provided that no payment is delayed beyond [number] [days/months].

I.318
The interest rates to be charged shall vary according to the daily rates of [specify]. The interest shall be charged on the total sum due that day. The interest rate may increase and/or decrease. Where no rate is available then the rate of the previous day shall be used.

INTERPRETATION

General Business and Commercial

I.319
Words which are singular shall include the plural and vice versa. Words which are masculine and/or feminine shall refer to all genders. Words referring to persons shall include corporations and other entities. Where there is any issue with interpretation the actual literal words of the agreement shall prevail.

I.320
In the case of any inconsistency between these Special Conditions and any other term of this contract the Special Conditions shall prevail.

I.321
Clause headings or titles do not form part of this contract and shall not affect its interpretation.

I.322
A reference to a gender in this document is intended to include a reference to all genders.

I.323
Headings are for convenience only and shall have no effect on the interpretation of the document.

I.324
Words which can be interpreted as singular shall not include the plural and vice versa.

I.325
The headings and titles in this agreement are for convenience only and are not intended to affect the interpretation of this agreement.

I.326
This contract is signed on [date] and is in the primary language of [specify language] and translated in [language]. There are two copies to be signed of each language. Each party will keep one document for each language. The primary language document supersedes the translation where there is a conflict of interpretation and/or language.

I.327
Words and phrases under this licence will be construed and interpreted in accordance with any legislation and/or laws in [country].

I.328
Unless otherwise stated references to clauses, sub-clauses, paragraphs, sub-paragraphs, schedules, annexes and exhibits all form part of this agreement.

I.329
Headings, clauses or other parts are for reference only and are not to be construed as part of this contract.

I.330
The interpretation of this contract shall be governed by [specify] language and the laws of [country]. Where there are issues which are ambiguous and/or which conflict then both parties agree that the matter shall be resolved

first by one of the following procedures [mediation/alternative disputes resolution/other] prior to any legal action being taken

I.331

The interpretation of this agreement shall be in the [specify language] and using the [specify] dictionary. Where there are conflicts of meaning then no part shall take precedence over another. Any dispute shall be subject to resolution by mediation which shall be paid for by both parties agreeing to the fee in advance with the mediator. Where mediation is not successful then the parties shall be entitled to issue legal proceedings.

I.332

This agreement and the attached schedules are in [language] and subject to the laws of [country] as has been specifically agreed between the parties. Both parties agree that any legal proceedings shall not be commenced in [country] where the parent company of the [Assignor] is based and/or [country] where the parent country of the [Assignee] is based. The interpretation of this agreement shall be subject to the governing laws of [country].

INVENTIONS

General Business and Commercial

I.333

'Invention' shall mean a new invention involving an inventive step which is capable of industrial application and is otherwise capable of registration in [country/any part of the world] under [specify legislation].

I.334

The [Company/Name agree that any inventions developed, created, adapted and/or made by [Company/Name] during the performance of this agreement based on access and/or use of any data, research and/or confidential information and/or material supplied and/or permitted by the [Enterprise] shall be the property of and owned by the [Enterprise]. The [Company/Name] agrees to assign all rights in any such inventions to the [Enterprise] including any rights to register a patent, design and/or any industrial, intellectual property or other rights which may exist and/or be created in the world.

I.335

All rights and the right to apply for statutory protection such as patent protection for any improvement to the [Technical Information] made by the [Company] shall be vested solely in the [Company].

I.336

Any invention and/or improvement made and/or discovered by an [Employee/ Consultant/Student] alone and/or jointly with others during the course of being employed and/or engaged and/or allowed access to the [Company] whilst involved in [Company] business of any nature shall belong to and be assigned to the [Company]. Provided that the [Company] agrees to pay a fair and reasonable sum as a contributors' fee to buy out the rights.

I.337

The [Employee] agrees at the request and expense of the [Company] at any time to assist the [Company] to apply for, register and protect its rights in any invention, patent, copyright, development, variation, adaptation or improvement. The [Employee] shall provide an affidavit of the circumstances, sign any document and form and appear in person as required provided that the [Company] shall meet all expenses, costs and losses that may arise that the [Employee] must incur to fulfil this co-operation.

I.338

All inventions, patents, computer software, trade marks, service marks, logos, intellectual property rights, copyright, database rights, design rights, future design rights, domain names, formats, titles, films, videos, sound recordings, graphics, images, music, lyrics, sounds and ringtones, slogans and any other rights of any nature in any material in any media developed, created and/or adapted by the [Employee] in the course of his/ her employment and/or based on the consequences of his/her work and/or services shall belong to the [Company] and the [Employee] shall have no claim, rights and/or interest of any nature at any time in any part of the world.

I.339

The [Enterprise/Charity] agrees that in the event that the [Employee/ Intern] develops, designs, adapts and/or creates any inventions, patents, computer software, trade marks, service marks, logos, intellectual property rights, copyright, database rights, design rights, future design rights, domain names, formats, titles, films, sound recordings, graphics, images, music, sounds and ringtones, slogans, formats, games, themes and any other rights of any nature in any material in any media for which there is a distinct commercial value to the [Enterprise/Charity] [which is not in the normal course of the [Employee's/Interns] duties/whether or not it is in consequence of the [Employee's/Interns] routine duties]. The [Employee/ Intern] shall be entitled to receive a substantial and equitable sum from such monies received by the [Enterprise/Charity] which shall be on terms to be agreed between the parties based on the actual commercial value and a percentage of [number] per cent.

INVENTIONS

I.340

The [Consortium] agrees and undertakes that any new website, app, game, computer software, hardware, mobile telephone and/or telecommunication systems, processes, method and/or any other intellectual property rights and/or any inventions, patents, trade marks and/or any other creations and/or developments which arise directly and/or indirectly from the [Project] and/or whether and/or not based and/or derived on material owned and/or or controlled by any member which has been contributed to the [Project] shall be held and owned and controlled by the [Consortium] and all sums received therefrom shared in equal proportions. No member shall have a greater claim to any rights and/or sums than any other party. Any application for registrations shall be made in the name of [specify name].

I.341

[Name] has created and developed [Unit/Prototype/Project] and agrees to enter into an agreement with the [Agent] in order to create a commercial product which can be exploited. [Name] and the [Agent] agree that:

1.1 [Name] shall remain the sole and exclusive owner of all rights of any nature in the [Unit/Prototype/Project] and any commercial product including copyright, intellectual property rights, patents, trademarks, design rights, computer software and hardware rights, telecommunication, television, film and all media in any formats which may arise and/or exist and/or be recognised in the future in any part of the world at any time.

1.2 That the [Agent] agrees, accepts and undertakes that he/she shall not acquire any of the rights in 1.1 and/or any sums that may be derived from the exploitation in any form at any time. That the total sum due to the [Agent] for any contribution, work and/or services shall be a fee of [number/currency] per month up to a maximum of [number/currency]. All fees due shall be paid by [Name] at the end of each calendar month subject to invoice. The [Agent] agrees and undertakes that [Name] may terminate the agreement at any time by one month's notice in advance.

J

JURISDICTION

General Business and Commercial

J.001

The [Guarantor] agrees with the [Creditor] that this agreement shall be subject to all the legislation and courts of England and that no other jurisdiction shall be used by either party. Any claim, legal action, threat, dispute and/or otherwise which may arise out of or in connection with this Guarantee shall be subject to that jurisdiction. Neither party shall be entitled to commence and/or make any claim through any other jurisdiction and/or legislation even if they are no longer resident in [country].

J.002

The [Creditor] shall have the right to choose any relevant jurisdiction and/or legislation and/or country to commence any legal proceedings against the Guarantor in respect of this guarantee. This agreement is not intended to limit the rights of the [Creditor] in any manner. The [Guarantor] shall also have the right to choose any other relevant jurisdiction and/or legislation in the event that the [Creditor] defaults, delays and/or is unable to pay the sums due at any time.

J.003

The [Guarantor] authorises and appoints [Name] or such other legal advisors as may from time to time be substituted by notice to the [Creditor]) to accept service of all legal proceedings arising out of or connected with this Guarantee from the [Creditor]. Service on such legal advisors or such other substitutes shall be deemed to be service on the [Guarantor].

J.004

Both parties to this agreement agree and undertake that any dispute, litigation, interpretation, damages and/or losses and/or any other claim and/or action which arises directly and/or indirectly as a result of this agreement and/or the defaults, delays and/or failure to fulfil the terms of this agreement by either party shall be subject to the laws and courts of [country]. That no other jurisdiction and/or governing law shall be used by either party in relation to this agreement.

J.005

This agreement shall be interpreted and construed in accordance with the laws of [specify country] and the parties hereby agree to submit to the jurisdiction of the courts, tribunals and/or other authorities in [country].

J.006

This agreement is made in [England/other] and is subject to the Laws of [England/other]. It is agreed that any claim, action and/or legal proceedings in relation to any part of the agreement must be instituted and/or commenced by either party in the [High Court of Justice/other] .and/or any other relevant court in [England/other].

J.007

This distribution agreement shall be governed and construed solely by the Laws of [Scotland/Northern Ireland/Wales/Ireland].

J.008

This licence agreement shall be governed by and construed in accordance with the Laws of [country/region/area] and the parties submit to the [non-] exclusive jurisdiction of the courts, tribunals and online procedures in [country/region/area].

J.009

This Agreement shall be subject to the Laws of [England].

J.010

This supply agreement shall be governed and construed in accordance with the Laws of [England/other] and any dispute, claim and/or legal action between the parties in respect of this agreement and/or its interpretation shall be subject to the courts, tribunals and other procedures, practices and methods which apply in that jurisdiction.

J.011

Regardless of the place of execution of any signature by the [Company] and/or the [Author]. It is agreed between the parties that this agreement shall be construed and governed by the [Laws of the State of New York].

J.012

The [Company] and the [Author] agree that two jurisdictions shall apply to this agreement and either party may commence any claim, action and/or otherwise in either jurisdiction which is as follows:

1.1   First jurisdiction: [specify]

1.2   Second jurisdiction: [specify].

1.3   It is accepted that the legislation and courts and procedures in either jurisdiction may not be the same. Neither jurisdiction shall prevail over the other. If an action and/or dispute has been alleged and/or commenced in one jurisdiction then the other party agrees that it must accept that jurisdiction as the correct forum to resolve the dispute.

J.013
Whatever the nationality, residence and/or domicile of the employees of the [Company] and/or any registered business address of the [Company] and/or any distributor, sub-licensee and/or agent and/or the location of the production and/or supply of the [Products/Service/Units]. It is agreed between all the parties that the agreement shall be subject to the Laws of [country] and no other forum and/or legislation shall be used to construe and/or interpret this agreement.

J.014
This Agreement is to be governed by and construed in accordance with [English/other] Law and the parties agree to the fact that this document will be entirely subject to the exclusive jurisdiction of the [English/other] courts as a result of any dispute and/or legal proceedings and/or other steps that may be taken in respect of this [procurement/supply/distribution] agreement and any other related matter.

J.015
This Agreement shall be subject to the Laws of [England/other] and any dispute and/or interpretation of the meaning of and/or scope of the agreement and/or its consequences shall be dealt with by both parties in that jurisdiction. Any claim, legal action, allegation and/or defence and/or application shall be subject to the relevant case law and legislation in that jurisdiction and take place in any authorised relevant court, tribunal and/or by any appropriate online digital procedure and/or otherwise.

J.016
This Agreement shall be construed in accordance with the Laws of [England/ other] and shall be subject to the exclusive jurisdiction of the [High Court of Justice in England/other].

J.017
This Agreement has been entered into in the State of [specify name] and its validity, construction, interpretation and legal effect shall be governed by the State of [specify name] applicable to contracts entered into and performed entirely within the State of [specify name].

J.018

This Agreement shall be interpreted and construed in accordance with [specify name] Law and the parties agree to submit to the jurisdiction of the [specify name] courts.

J.019

This contract shall be governed and construed in accordance with [specify] Law and any regulations and/or directives, of the European Union and the judgments of the European Court of Justice.

J.020

Both parties agree and acknowledge and confirm that any interpretation, dispute, litigation, damages or losses which arise directly and/or indirectly as a result of this Agreement and/or any licence, contract and/or other matter arising from it shall be subject to the Laws of [specify country/area/court] and no other jurisdiction shall be used by any of the parties..

J.021

This licence shall be governed and construed in accordance with the legislation and laws, guidelines and codes of practice of the countries known as: [specify list]. Any interpretation of the construction and meaning of the document shall be based on [specify] law. All legal proceedings, allegations, disputes and claims shall be subject to the law of [specify] and where a claim is in excess of [number] the following court shall be used by either party: [specify court].

J.022

Any dispute, litigation and/or issues of construction shall be subject to the exclusive jurisdiction of the laws of [country].

J.023

This Licence shall interpreted by and subject to the laws of [country] and any claim, action and/or other legal proceedings shall only be commenced and held in that jurisdiction. It is irrelevant whether the [Disc/Data/Unit] is reproduced, supplied and/or distributed from another country. Both parties have agreed this jurisdiction as a fundamental term of this licence agreement.

J.024

This agreement shall be interpreted and fall within the jurisdiction of any country in which either party has their main business premises and/or offices and/or in which the material is produced, stored, distributed, sold and/or otherwise exploited. Either party is entitled to nominate any appropriate country as they think fit provided that there is a valid connection to their business and/or the material.

J.025
Both parties agree that this agreement shall as far as possible be resolved first by mediation and that legal proceedings shall only be instituted as a final resort. That any interpretation of the agreement shall be based on industry practice and subject to the laws and codes of the following countries: [specify].

J.026

1.1 From [date] to [date] the parties agree that either may issue any claim and/or proceedings in any of the following countries: [specify list] and no others.

1.2 After the expiry of the end date in 1.1 either party may choose any jurisdiction which they believe is applicable in the circumstances.

J.027
The jurisdiction of this agreement and in which any company which forms the consortium may choose to institute and/or commence legal proceedings against another is limited to the following countries in which one and/or more of the parties have their head office and/or is registered and/or incorporated and/or their main assets are held and/or in which most services and/or products are produced, delivered and/or purchased which is as follows: [specify list of countries].

J.028
All parties agree and undertake that all mediations, alternative dispute resolutions, arbitrations, resolution of disputes, applications for injunctions, institution of legal proceedings and/or claim for any breach, losses, damages, failure to deliver, non-performance, product liability, injury, death and/or otherwise which arise directly and/or indirectly from this agreement shall be subject to the laws, directives, regulations, standards and codes of practice of [country/other]. That all parties agree and undertake that they have decided not to nominate or subject this agreement to any other country, forum or jurisdiction.

J.029
The [Name] and the [Company] agree and undertake that this Agreement shall be subject to the jurisdiction of any court in [state/country] for the purpose of commencing any legal proceedings and/or resolving any dispute by any method.

J.030
The [Employee] agrees that this contract shall be subject to the jurisdiction of the laws of the [state/country]. That for the purpose of resolving any dispute

and/or taking legal action and/or seeking any remedy that this agreement shall be governed by and construed under the law of [state/country].

J.031
This [document/contract/agreement/licence/assignment] shall be governed, construed and interpreted subject to the Laws of the State of [specify name] in the [specify country]. You consent and agree to submit to the exclusive jurisdiction of the courts of [specify] in [specify county] in the State of [specify name].

J.032
This agreement is governed by [English/French/Spanish/Indian/Chinese] Law and the parties submit to the exclusive jurisdiction of the courts of [region/country/other].

J.033
This agreement is governed by and to be interpreted according to the laws of [country/other]. Any issue as to construction and/or any breach, default, dispute, claim, allegation and/or legal action shall be subject to the laws of [country/other] and take place in the appropriate forum and courts in that jurisdiction. Both parties must provide consent in writing in order to affect a change to this clause and to nominate a new jurisdiction.

J.034
The [Company] and/or the [Licensee] both agree that this licence agreement shall be subject to more than one jurisdiction. That either party shall have the right to use any of the following countries as the jurisdiction to interpret this licence and/or in which to make any claim and/or start any legal action:

1   [country] where the parent company is incorporated and registered.

2   [country] where the [Products] are manufactured.

3   [country] where the [Supplier] is based.

4   [country] where the website known as [specify] which markets the [Products] is based.

5   [country] where the main head office of the [Company] operates.

6   [country] where the [Licensee] has its head office.

7   [country] where the [Licensee] produces and/or supplies the majority of the [Service/Units/Products].

J.035

1.1 The [Athlete] agrees that the jurisdiction of this agreement shall be [country] and subject to the laws of [country].

1.2 That the [Athlete] and/or the [Sponsor] shall use all reasonable means to mediate and/or resolve any matters without litigation.

1.3 That the [Athlete] and/or the [Sponsor] shall set out in writing the full detail of any claim and/or allegations and the remedy they seek and supply it to the other party prior to the commencement of any legal action and/or civil, criminal and/or disciplinary proceedings.

J.036

1.1 The use and/or supply and/or distribution of the [App/Blog/Website] is worldwide but any disputes, claims, actions and /or other matters which arise are subject to the legislation, policies and jurisdiction of [country] where the [Enterprise/Distributor] is registered and has it head office.

1.2 You are not authorised by [Enterprise/Distributor] to access, download, use and/or supply and/or distribute the content in any form unless you have agreed to this fundamental term of this agreement.

J.037

The [App] is supplied on the basis of a non-exclusive licence to you personally to load and/or store on the agreed device and/or gadget. There is no authority and/or consent for you to supply, transfer, adapt, mutilate and/or change in any manner the software for the [App] and/or the content. In the event that the [Company] is required to take legal action and/or make any claim against you for any reason as a result of your breach of this licence. Then this licence shall be interpreted and subject to the Laws of [country] which is the jurisdiction and governing law of this agreement.

J.038

1.1 The [Charity] is registered as a recognised charity in [country] and adheres to the legislation which applies in [country] to fullfil the legal requirements of a charity. It is recognised by the [Charities Commission] and abides by all their guidelines and recommended practices.

1.2 The [Charity] enters into agreements with third parties throughout the world. It is a fundamental term of all such agreements that as a matter of policy the jurisdiction and governing law is [country] only. That no other jurisdiction shall apply to any agreement entered into by the [Charity]. If you cannot accept this term and wish to use some other jurisdiction then the [Charity] will not conclude the agreement as it is contrary to its declared policy.

1.3 Where the [Charity] has reason to believe that a third party has defaulted and/or breached the terms of this and/or any other agreement. Then the [Charity] shall endeavour to reach a settlement without litigation. All legal proceedings shall be commenced either through the online digital procedures to make claims and/or the relevant courts, tribunals and/or other dispute resolution options that may be available in [country].

1.4 Where there is an error and/or omission in the agreement which does not address any issue. Then it is agreed that there should be a presumption that the [Charity] has not granted those rights and/or provided consent. Where the rights and/or material did not exist at the time of the signature of this agreement then all such rights and interest are reserved and owned by the [Charity].

K

KNOW-HOW

General Business and Commercial

K.001

'Know-how' shall mean any industrial techniques, data, information, tests and assessments which may have been and/or will be used in the manufacture, production and/or procedures involved in the creation, supply, distribution and/or reproduction of any products, services, materials and/or other content in any industry which are not generally available to the public.

K.002

1.1 The [Licensor] and [Licensee] agree that all know-how, rights, trade marks and intellectual property and computer software rights in the [Product/Service/Unit] shall remain and belong entirely and exclusively to the [Licensor].

1.2 That it is not the intention of this agreement that the [Licensee] should acquire any rights and/or interest in any specialist knowledge and techniques known by the [Licensor] which are supplied to the [Licensee].

1.3 Where the [Licensee] acquires any rights, interest and/or intellectual property rights and/or copyright as a result of commissioning third parties and/or an employee and/or consultant works on the [Project]. Then the [Licensee] agrees to assign all such rights in the [Product/Service/Unit] to the [Licensor]. Provided that the [Licensor] pays for all the costs of such an assignment in each case.

K.003

'The Know-how' shall mean the confidential knowledge, method, processes and applications of the [Company] in respect of any machines, products, materials, goods, services and processes which are not in the public domain which were developed, created, and/or devised and/or commissioned by the [Company].

K.004

1.1   The [Company/Enterprise] has agreed to supply and make available for inspection confidential information, data, material and records in respect of the manufacture, reproduction, supply and distribution of the [Products/Service/Gadgets] which is not available to any third party without the prior approval of the [Company/Enterprise].

1.2   It is a fundamental term of that all such details in 1.1 held by the [Company/Enterprise] and the [Licensee] are kept confidential and that no attempt is made to release such knowledge in any form to the public and/or a third party whether for free and/or financial gain.

1.3   That the licence granted is specifically only for the stated purpose: [specify].

1.4   In the event that the [Licensee] breaches 1.1 and 1.2 above and discloses, publishes, transmits and/or distributes any and/or all of the matters in 1.1 and/or 1.2 without the prior written approval of the [Company/Enterprise]. Then the [Licensee] agrees to pay a fixed total payment of [number/currency] for such default and/or breach.

1.5   The [Licensee] shall be entitled to share such matters in 1.1 and 1.2 with their nominated accountants and legal advisors provided that those third parties accept the confidential nature of the material.

K.005
All rights in any know-how, design rights, future design rights, inventions, patents, copyright, intellectual property, trade marks, service marks, domain names, database rights, data, computer software rights, blog, app, blockchain, confidential information, shape, pattern, configuration, articles, machines, products, processes, means of transmission and/or delivery of any service, retrieval and/or storage method, and any content, labels, packaging, marketing, advertising and promotional material and merchandising together with any goodwill and any right to apply and hold any registration in respect of the development, production, manufacture, reproduction, supply, sale, distribution and/or any other adaptation and/or method and/or any other exploitation in any medium and/or material in any part of the world and/or universe shall be solely and exclusively with [Name] and all title and ownership shall belong to [Name].

K.006
The [Distributor] agrees and undertakes that it shall not be entitled to apply for, register and/or represent that the [Distributor] and/or any parent and/or associated and/or affiliated person and/or company controls and/or owns any interest and/or rights in any know-how, design rights, future design rights,

inventions, patents, copyright, intellectual property, trade marks, service marks, confidential information, computer software, processes and/or any other matter of any nature in respect of the licensed [Article] and/or any adaptation and/or developments and/or related services, marketing and/or other content and/or products which may be created which are derived from and/or based on in some part from the original licensed [Article] at any time.

K.007
The [Company] agrees that:

1.1 it will enter into a confidentiality agreement with [Name] in respect of the material and methods of the [proposal/subject/invention] briefly described in Appendix A which forms part of this agreement.

1.2 no disclosure shall be made by the [Company] of the matters set out in 1.1 and Appendix A above [unless [Name] provides written consent in advance] to any parent, affiliate, associate and/or subsidiary company and/or any third party and/or any other officer, employee, and/or consultant of the [Company].

1.3 the information and matters set out in 1.1 and Appendix A shall be limited to the following named persons: [specify list] and the legal advisors [specify list].

1.4 in the event that no confidentiality agreement is concluded and details are disclosed by the [Company] outside the agreed circle of people in 1.3. Then the [Company] shall be obliged and shall indemnify [Name] in respect of any damages, losses, loss of profit and/or commercial benefit and gain, and rights that he/she shall suffer, incur and/or shall arise directly or indirectly from the breach of this clause and there shall be no limitation on the liability by the [Company] to [Name].

K.008
The [Company] and the [institute] are working in partnership to develop the [Project]. It is agreed between the parties that all inventions, patents, copyright, design rights, future design rights, intellectual property rights, trade marks, service marks, domain names, database rights, data, confidential information, computer software rights, domain name, apps and any material in any medium, know-how, confidential knowledge, methods, processes and applications in respect of any machines, products, materials, goods, services, ideas, concepts and techniques which are not in the public domain which are created and/or developed, designed, registered and/or commissioned by the [Company] and/or the [Institute] for the [Project] shall be owned, controlled, registered and exploited jointly and equally between the [Company] and the [Institute]. That both parties shall require the prior written approval of the other party in order to take any steps to protect,

license, assign, transfer, exploit and/or use the rights and know-how they jointly own and control.

K.009

The [Consultant] agrees and undertakes all intellectual property rights, inventions, patents, copyright, design rights, future design rights, trade marks, know-how, confidential information, computer software rights and any other new original methods, content, applications and processes which are developed by the [Consultant] as a result of the [Project] shall be the sole and exclusive property of the [Company]. That the [Consultant] shall not have any claim and/or interest to any rights even if he/she has contributed to and/or worked on the [Project], attended meetings and/or made reports. The [Consultant] agrees to waive all claims to any such rights which may be created and agrees that he/she shall assign all such rights to the [Company] for a nominal fee.

K.010

All data, records and material relating to the creation, development and exploitation of the [Project/Work] including know-how, confidential information, recipes, techniques and processes, computer software records, documents and reports, test results, prototypes, tools, computer-generated material and drawings, risk assessments, personnel records, laboratory analysis, films, sound recordings, images, text and/or otherwise shall be archived at [location] by [Name] for the [Consortium] and not destroyed and/or removed without prior [six] months prior notice to all members of the [Consortium].

L

LABORATORY ACCESS

General Business and Commercial

L.001
The [Company] undertakes to provide to the [Assignee] a complete written list of where and with whom all material of any nature in any medium and any copies, packaging, advertising, promotional and other material are stored and/or held of which they are aware whether or not they are in the possession and/or control of the [Company].

L.002
The [Production Company] shall supply a [laboratory access/resource material] authorisation, access and the right to remove the material document to the [Commissioning Company] to allow them to control and request material directly from the [Storage/Archive Company]. The document shall be agreed in advance with the [Commissioning Company]. It shall list all the material of any nature which is stored, the format, duration, language and shall inform the [Storage/Archive Company] that ownership of all such material has been assigned and transferred to the [Commissioning Company]. That neither the [Production Company] nor any other third party shall have any rights.

L.003
The [Production Company] shall authorise the [specify resource organisation] to grant [exclusive/non-exclusive] access to the [Commissioning Company] to request and make copies for the purposes of this agreement at the [Commissioning Company's] sole cost and risk. This shall not include the right to remove any master material.

L.004
The [Production Company] shall arrange for the provision of a laboratory letter in the form specified in Schedule A to the [Commissioning Company] signed by both an authorised representative of the laboratory and the [Production Company].

L.005
The [Distributor] shall provide the [Company] with a laboratory access letter [in customary/agreed form] giving the [Company] the irrevocable right to order copies of the [Film] and/or parts at the [Company's] sole cost direct from the original negatives or other material in the following formats: [detail of format of master material]. The letter must contain irrevocable instructions that the negatives of the [Film] and/or parts must not be destroyed or transferred from the possession of the [Facilities Enterprise] prior to [date] without the prior written consent of the [Company].

L.006
The [Facilities Enterprise] are authorised and instructed by the [Company] to accept and honour any orders for reproduction of material and other editing services from:[Company/Distributor] of [address] by [Name] with respect to the [Film] entitled:[Title] reference code: [–] Format of master material: [–]. This authorisation is effective from [date] until [further notice/date].

L.007
All costs, charges and expenses arising from any order placed by the [Distributor] shall be at the [Distributor's] cost and shall not be the responsibility of the [Company]. In the event that the [Distributor] shall fail to pay for the [Facility Enterprise] services. The [Facility Enterprise] agrees and undertakes not to place any lien, charge and/or other restriction over access to and/or use of the master material of the [Film] and/or shall not refuse to release ordered copies to other third parties.

L.008
All reproduction, editing and other facility services ordered by the [Distributor] will be at their sole cost and liability. The terms and conditions of access shall be agreed between the [Licensor] and the [Facilities Enterprise]. In the event of any default of payment by the [Distributor] no lien, charge and/or restriction on access shall be made against the master material and/or any claim made against the [Licensor].

L.009
The parties agree that no original [master material/negatives/footage/outtakes/sound recordings/adaptations] of the [Film] and/or parts in any format held and/or controlled by either party shall be destroyed and/or erased at any time and/or any material removed from the [Facilities/Storage Company] at [address] for any reason without the prior written consent of the [Company] and [Name] whether during the Term of this Agreement or thereafter.

L.010

The [Company] agrees that the [Distributor] shall be entitled to arrange for and pay the cost of obtaining one complete copy of the [Film] together with the sound track and any trailers which is held at the [Facilities House] at [address]. Provided that such consent by the [Company] is subject to the following agreed terms as follows:

1.1 That the [Distributor] shall be responsible for and pay the [Facilities House] the agreed cost of all requests made by the [Distributor] in respect of the reproduction of the [Film] and any sound track and trailers.

1.2 That the [Distributor] shall not be entitled to delete any part of the [Film] and/or any sound track and/or trailers. The [Distributor] shall ensure that all the credits, copyright notices, trade marks, service marks, music acknowledgements and sources, disclaimers, title and front and end credits are reproduced accurately.

1.3 In the event that the master material held by the [Facilities House] is damaged as a result of making any copy which the [Distributor] has ordered. The [Distributor] agrees to pay the full cost of a replacement for the master up to a maximum of [number/currency].

1.4 The [Distributor] shall only have authority to request copies from [date] to [date].

L.011

1.1 [Name] shall not be entitled to access at any time the [footage/master material/archive material] in the possession of the [Company] at any premises and/or whether held by a third party.

1.2 [Name] shall be required to request any copies of the [footage/master material/archive material] from the [Company] direct for his/her own personal use and records and/or under a licence for commercial purposes. The [Company] shall be entitled to decide at its sole discretion whether it will fulfil any such request. In the event that the [Company] shall decide to provide any copies and/or grant a licence it shall be entitled to charge [Name] for the full cost of making the copies, freight and packaging, an administration fee, and such additional fees as it may deem appropriate in the circumstances. [Name] shall pay the total sums due to the [Company] upon invoice which shall be due prior to the commencement of any reproduction of any copies.

L.012

Where a person and company is granted access to the [Master Material] of the [Artwork/Film/Video/Sound Recordings] at the facilities of the [Copyright Owner/Distributor/Archive Institute] it is on the following grounds that:

1.1 There is no right to remove, damage, erase and/or otherwise alter the [Master Material].

1.2 Any use and/or exploitation of any material is subject to the full disclosure of the intended use of such material and the conclusion of a written licence agreement between the parties.

1.3 That there shall be a charge for the costs of reproduction, administration and any freight costs which shall be paid [in advance/upon delivery].

1.4 That all credits, copyright notices, trade mark and other notified copyright, intellectual property and/or other contractual obligations shall be adhered to.

1.5 That the person and company agree that they shall have no right to claim any copyright, computer software rights, trade mark, intellectual property rights and/or any other rights and/or interest in any of the original material supplied and/or any adaptation in which it is used and/or included. This shall also apply to any rights and/or formats and/or technology not in existence at the time of this agreement and/or any licence.

L.013

1.1 The [Institute] agrees that [Name] and his/her agreed research team listed in section A may have access to and use the following facilities on a non-exclusive basis at [location] to the specify facilities listed in Section B from [date/time] for the [Project] described in Section C [detail of project/purpose/authorised agreed commercial exploitation. Sections A, B and C form part of this agreement.

1.2 The [Institute] agrees to pay all costs of electricity, light, water, rates, security and any materials and equipment which may be required provided that the cost of any new materials shall not exceed [number/ currency].

1.3 [Name] agrees and undertakes that neither he/she nor any of their research team shall use, develop and/or adapt any material which would pose a serious risk to human health and/or pose a fire risk and/ or is likely to result in the evacuation of the premises and/or involves any illegal action and/or process and/or method and/or intentionally commit any criminal offence and/or otherwise. That neither [Name] nor his/her research team shall enter any unauthorised areas of the building and/or access any unauthorised material, data and/or information. That no unauthorised images, filming and/or sound recording and/or other activity shall take place at any time.

1.4 [Name] agrees that the [Institute] shall be acknowledged as a contributor to the [Project] and provided with the following acknowledgement in any future report and/or marketing: Supported by research facilities at [specify] [image/logo/reference].

1.5 [Name] agrees that if at any time the [Institute] refuses and/or delays access to the facilities. That [Name] shall not be entitled to make any claim for any loss and/or damage and/or expenses that may occur and that [Name] shall bear all such sums.

1.6 [Name] agrees and undertakes that in the event that any persons involved in the research work cause any losses, damages, expenses and/or any other sums to be incurred by the [Institute] due to their acts, omissions and/or errors. That [Name] shall pay the total sum due to rectify the matter.

1.7 Name] agrees that neither he/she nor any person in the research team shall be entitled to remove, delete, erase, destroy, borrow, lend and/or otherwise dispose of and/or supply to any third party any data, information, records and/or equipment and/or material in any medium of any nature owned, controlled and/or purchased by the [Institute] at any time.

L.014

1.1 The [Institute/Charity] agrees that [Name] may use the following equipment [specify at [location] in order to develop and create a new website, app and game provisionally entitled: [describe project].

1.2 [Name] agrees and undertakes to adhere to and abide by all the guidelines, policies and regulations of the [Institute/Charity].

1.3 [Name] agrees and undertakes to pay such sums and expenses as are set out in [specify document] for the access granted in 1.1.

1.4 Name] agrees that the [Institute/Charity] may refuse access and/or withdraw their agreement at any time without reason without advance notice.

1.5 [Name] agrees that he/she shall not use, access and/or download any material to any equipment and/or device and/or gadget which is likely to affect the reputation and/or create a negative marketing impact on the [Institute/Charity] and/or any other person associated with them and/or any third party in partnership with the [Institute/Charity].

1.6 [Name] agrees that he/she must not damage, remove, delete, adapt, vary and/or remove any data, records, equipment, computer software, computer hardware, furniture, fixture and fittings and/or any other material owned, controlled and/or owned by the [Institute/Charity] and/or any other third party.

1.7 That [Name] agrees to a request to have their clothes and shoes and bag searched and to be subject to a body scan if required before entering and leaving the building by a person of the same gender who is a senior security officer. Provided that [Name] shall have the right on each occasion to refuse the request and may therefore be refused entry.

LANGUAGE

General Business and Commercial

L.015
All notices, claims and/or communications under and/or in connection with this [document/agreement] shall be in the [English] language.

L.016
This contract is set out in both [state language] and [English]. In the event of a dispute as to the meaning of any words and/or phrases. It is agreed between the parties that the [English/other] language shall prevail as regards interpretation.

L.017
Where the language of the contract becomes out of date due to developments in technology, equipment, media, communication, storage, translation, adaptation or otherwise it is agreed between the parties that there should be a presumption that all such rights that are not directly covered shall be reserved by and belong to [Name].

L.018
Where the language of the contract becomes out of date due to developments in law, technology, equipment, media, communication, storage, translation, adaptation or otherwise it is agreed between the parties that there should be a presumption that all such rights that are not directly covered shall be owned and controlled by [Name].

L.019
The [Project/Film/Article] shall be in [English/German/Spanish/French/Mandarin/ Italian/other] and no other language shall be used. No new title, logo, text, dialogue, images, film, sound recordings, translation, subtitles, dubbing, packaging and marketing shall be developed, reproduced, supplied and/or distributed without the prior written approval and consent of the [Company] in each case.

L.020

1.1 The [Sub-Licensee] shall be entitled to arrange for the translation and adaptation of the [Book/Audio Recording/Film/Product] in the following languages: [list authorised languages].

1.2 All translations and adaptations shall be subject to prior written approval of any drafts and samples by the [Licensee] and the [Licensor]. No project may proceed to manufacture and distribution without such authorisation.

L.021

The [Sub-Licensee] shall arrange for a translation of the title, text, index and images of the [Work] at the [Sub-Licensee's] cost. When it is completed the [Sub-Licensee] shall send a complete draft copy to the [Licensee] and the [Licensor] for approval. The [Sub-License] shall be obliged to make such changes to the translation as may be required by the [Licensee] and [Licensor]. The [Sub-Licensee] shall not be entitled to proceed with the translated work without the prior written approval of the [Licensee] and [Licensor] of the proposed draft version of the complete work.

L.022

The [Licensee] shall ensure that it is a condition of their contract with any third party that such third party shall not acquire any copyright and/or intellectual property rights, trade marks, database rights and/or any other rights and/or interest in the [Work] adaptation and/or any translation. The [Licensee] shall provide a draft copy of any proposed contract with such third parties to the [Licensor]. The [Licensee] shall be obliged to make such changes to the proposed contract as may be required by the [Licensor]. The [Licensee] shall not be entitled to proceed with the proposed contract without the prior written approval of the [Licensor].

L.023

The [Licensor] shall pay and arrange for any translations of the [Film/Work/Sound Recordings] at the [Licensors'] cost. The [Licensor] may also change the title, text and images of the [Film/Work/Sound Recordings] in order to meet the requirements of the market and/or the differences in meaning and/or culture.

L.024

The [Licensor] agrees that the [Licensee] and/or distributor and/or any other third party involved in the exploitation of the [Work] may in the process of any agreed adaptation and/or translation substitute any part of the [Work] including the main title, chapter headings, character names and any text, image and logo provided it is necessary due to differences in culture, religion and/or translation and interpretation. Further that the [Licensee] and/or any distributor and/or any third party must agree in advance to assign all copyright, intellectual property rights, trade marks and any other rights and/or interest in such new versions and all the material to the [Licensor] in consideration of the payment of [number/currency]. That they will agree to sign the documents supplied by the [Licensor] to effect any such assignment.

L.025

1.1 There shall be no right granted under this agreement to exploit the [Work] in any other language except: [specify language] with the regional accent for [specify].

1.2 No right exists to change, edit, adapt, vary the title, character and place names, quotes and/or any text, image, logo, film, sound recording, music, lyrics and/or any other part of the [Work] and any associated packaging, marketing and/or promotional material.

L.026

No language, words and/or phrases will be used by any person and/or company at the [Event] which is/are political, threatening, offensive and/or likely to incite violence and/or any other social media reaction which is negative to the [Company]. The [Company] reserves the right to remove, cancel and/or otherwise delete the contribution and/or performance and/or edit out any part of any product of the services of any person and/or other group which in its discretion the [Company] decides should not be used, transmitted and/or distributed for any reason. No explanation and/or reason shall be provided to the person and/or group.

LEGAL PROCEEDINGS

Film, Television and Video

L.027

In the event of any action, claim, dispute, writ and/or proceedings arising out of this agreement with any third party. The [Assignor] and the [Assignee] agree to provide full details to each other at the earliest opportunity. No offer, settlement or disclosure shall be made to the third party [unless required by order of a court of law] until both the [Assignor] and the [Assignee] have agreed the best course of action and/or taken legal advice. The [Assignor] and the [Assignee] shall each be responsible for its own costs and expenses unless the problem is directly attributable to either the [Assignor] or the [Assignee] alone. In which case the defaulting party shall bear all the costs and expenses of both the [Assignor] and the [Assignee].

L.028

In the event that any complaint, claim, allegation and/or legal proceedings are made against and/or threatened or issued by any third party against the [Distributor] in respect of the [Unit/Disc] of the [Film] and/or any associated soundtrack, packaging, marketing and/or promotion. Then the [Distributor] shall immediately notify the [Licensor] of the nature of the claim, allegation, action or complaint and shall provide copies of all documents and shall provide all such assistance as may reasonably be required in order to deal with, refute, settle or defend such case. The [Distributor] agrees to follow the instructions and guidance of the [Licensor] and will permit the [Licensor] to assume control of the matter. The [Licensor] shall only reimburse and/or indemnify the legal costs and expenses incurred by the [Distributor] where the [Licensor] is in breach of this agreement and its undertakings to the [Distributor].

L.029

The [Distributor] shall advise the [Licensor] in the event of the [Distributor] becomes aware of any infringement by any third party of any copyright and/or any other intellectual property rights and/or any other rights of any nature which may relate to the [Unit/Disc] of the [Film] and/or any associated soundtrack, marketing and/or material. The [Distributor] shall be entitled as an exclusive licensee to take legal action against any third company or person who reproduces, sells, supplies and/or distributes copies of the [Unit/Disc] of the [Film] when they are not authorised to do so in any Territory which applies to this agreement. The [Distributor] shall bear all the costs and expenses relating to any legal action it may decide to take and shall retain all sums recovered for losses, damages, legal costs or otherwise by the [Distributor].

L.030

1.1 Where any legal proceedings are issued against the [Licensor] and/or the [Licensee] in respect of the [Sound Recordings] and/or the [Unit/Disc]. The parties agree to cooperate with each other in order to settle and/or defend any such claim.

1.2 Each party shall bear their own legal costs and shall only be entitled to rely on any indemnity under this agreement where the other party has defaulted under the terms of this agreement and the non-defaulting party has fully disclosed all the details of the claim and consulted with the defaulting party prior to settling any claim and/or defending any legal action.

1069

L.031

The [Distributor] agrees and undertakes that it shall not threaten and/or take any action to commence legal proceedings against any third party in respect of the [Unit/CD/Disc] of the [Film/Work] unless it has completed all the following steps and tasks:

1.1 Informed the [Licensor] of the details of the case and provided details of any supporting information.

1.2 The [Distributor] has verified the facts of the case and assessed the potential loss and/or damage to the [Distributor] and the [Licensor].

1.3 The [Distributor] has received the approval of the [Licensor] to proceed and to take such action as it thinks fit.

1.4 The [Distributor] is capable of funding all the costs and expenses without any contribution from the [Licensor].

1.5 That the [Distributor] has carried out an assessment of the full potential liability if any action should fail.

1.6 The [Distributor] agrees that no costs and/or expenses shall be deducted from any sums due to the [Licensor] under this agreement at any time.

1.7 In the event that the [Distributor] loses any legal proceedings it will still be capable of operating as a fully functional business and to meet all its liabilities and to pay all the sums due to the [Licensor].

L.032

The [Company] shall not be obliged to consult with [Name] in the event that the [Company] and/or any agent, licensee and/or distributor should decide to take any legal action of any nature to register, protect and/or defend any rights to the [Unit/DVD/Disc/CD] of the [Project].

L.033

If at any time in the future the [Distributor] becomes aware of any facts or information indicating that any third party is or may be infringing the [Licensor's] copyright in the [Films]. The [Distributor] shall promptly inform the [Licensor] of all such facts or information. If the [Licensor] in its sole discretion determines that it shall institute any legal action then the [Distributor] shall co-operate fully. The [Distributor] may be joined in the legal action by the [Licensor] as a party. The [Distributor] shall also have the right to institute any legal action against a third party in its own name. The [Distributor] shall not institute any such legal action without the prior written consent of the [Licensor], such consent not to be unreasonably withheld or delayed.

L.034

1.1 In the event that any legal proceedings are commenced by any third party against either the [Commissioning Company] or [the Production Company] in respect of the [Series] and/or any associated soundtrack, marketing and/or other material. Then written notice of such a claim and/or threat shall immediately be given to the other party (as the case may be) who shall provide all such assistance as may reasonably be required in order to settle or defend such case. Each party shall bear its own legal costs and expenses subject to the indemnity in clause [–].

1.2 If either the [Commissioning Company] or [the Producer] become aware of any infringement by any third party of any copyright, or any other intellectual property rights or any other rights and/or any breach of any contract of any nature which may relate to the [Series] and/or any associated soundtrack, marketing and/or other material. Then written notice shall immediately be given to the other party (as the case may be) who shall provide all such assistance as may reasonably be required by the other party including joining in any legal or other proceedings against such third party. Each party shall bear its own legal costs and expenses subject to the indemnity in clause [–].

L.035
The [Company] agrees and undertakes that it shall be responsible for, and bear the cost of, all complaints, allegations, claims and legal proceedings which may arise in respect of the development, production, exploitation, merchandising and marketing of the [Film] and/or parts and/or any sound track and/or recordings and/or any adaptation, translation and/or otherwise. That no such sums, costs and expenses shall be deducted from any advance, royalties or other sums due to [Name/Writer/Artist] under this agreement.

L.036
The [Company] shall not be entitled to deduct the legal costs and expenses from the Budget, Distribution Income or any other sums allocated to and/or received in respect of the [Film/Video/Podcast].

L.037
No settlement shall be made of any claim of any third party unless such claim is settled on reasonable grounds and in good faith taking into account the opinion and recommendation of the legal advisors of the [Company]. In the event that the parties cannot agree upon the terms upon which to settle any matter. Then it is agreed that the legal report of an expert advisor shall be sought at the [Company's] cost but such report shall not be considered binding upon the parties.

L.038

In the event that there is any allegation, claim, and/or legal proceedings against the [Name/Author] and/or the [Company] in respect of the [Script/Book/Work] and/or the [Film/Series] for infringement of copyright, breach of contract and/or otherwise. Then the [Name/Author] and/or the [Company] party shall each be responsible for its own legal costs and expenses which may arise in order to defend, settle and/or contest the claim. Each party shall be entitled to act in its own best commercial and personal interests and shall not be obliged to take in to account the views of the other party as to how to deal with the matter. Such right of choice as to how to conduct, settle or defend the case shall be without prejudice to the right of either party to take proceedings against the other and/or seek any indemnity from the other for legal costs, damages, losses, or otherwise in respect of any matter arising out of this agreement.

L.039

The [Licensor] and the [Distributor] agree that all complaints, allegations, legal proceedings, disputes, and taking of legal action in respect of the [Film/Video/Podcast], the soundtrack, the excerpts, and any packaging, advertising and marketing of the [Film/Video/Podcast] shall be passed to and controlled by the [Licensor]. The [Licensor] shall consult with the [Distributor] in any matter.

L.040

The [Licensee] must arrange suitable insurance cover for the benefit of the [Licensor] and the [Licensee] as part of the cost of the Budget with a reputable company to provide comprehensive cover for the threat of any legal proceedings, complaint, dispute, allegation, breach of contract, defamation, infringement of copyright, and/or any allegation of unauthorised use of any material against either party and/or any authorised third party in respect of the [Film/Video/Programme] and/or parts and/or any exploitation in any form from [date] to [date].

L.041

In the event that legal proceedings are threatened and/or some claim, action or allegation is made by any third party in respect of the [Series/Podcasts/Sound Recordings] against the [Licensor] and/or the [Licensee]. Then either party shall promptly notify the other accordingly. The [Licensor] shall assume all responsibility for all such matters on behalf of both parties and bear all costs and expenses. The [Licensee] shall provide such material, documents and other evidence as may be requested and generally co-operate fully with the reasonable requests of the [Licensor].

L.042

Where legal proceedings are instituted and/or any claim is made by a third party in respect of the [Film/Programmes/Sound Recordings] based on the [Work/Book/Interview] and/or any other adaptation by the [Distributor]. The [Distributor] agrees and undertakes to pay for all the legal costs, expenses and damages which may be incurred by and/or awarded against the [Name/Author] and/or the [Agent] at any time in any country and in any language.

L.043

[Name] agrees that the [Distributor] may at its discretion institute any legal proceedings and/or take such steps as may be necessary to protect its rights in the [Film/Video/Sound Recording] of [Name]. That [Name] provides his/her consent to be named as a party to any such legal proceedings and/or steps provided that the [Distributor] shall pay of the personal and legal costs and any other expenses, interest and any other sums including losses, damages and third party legal costs that [Name] may incur and/or be advised and/or ordered to pay by any mediator and/or court of law from [date] to [date].

L.044

The [Distributor] agrees that in the event that it should take any legal action and/or make any allegations against a third party in respect of the [Programme/Series]. That [Name] shall not be obliged to assist and/or support and/or contribute in any form at any time and shall be entitled not to be joined as a party to any application and/or action in any other form. Nor shall the [Distributor] be entitled and/or authorised to represent to any third party that [Name] endorses and/or supports any such legal proceedings.

L.045

The [Company] agrees and undertakes that it shall not be entitled to deduct any sums incurred as legal costs and expenses and/or losses, damages, interest and administrative costs in respect of the [Programme/Series] from any gross receipts which maybe received nor from any sums due to be paid to [Name]. That the [Company] must be responsible and bear the liability for all such sums.

General Business and Commercial

L.046

It is agreed that neither the [Supplier] nor the [Company] shall be held liable to the other party for any of the following matters which may arise as a direct and/or indirect result of any legal action, claim, defence and/or breach of any legislation, codes of practice; withdrawal of products and/or publicity:

1.1   loss of production;

1.2   loss of goodwill;

1.3   loss of profit;

1.4   loss of orders and cancellation of existing orders with third parties;

1.5   termination of any licence;

1.6   any other losses, damages and/or loss of reputation.

L.047

The [Company] agrees that it shall accept any order obtained by the [Agent] entirely at its sole risk and that the [Agent] shall not be liable for the failure of any retail store, retail outlet and/or other third party to pay any sums that may be due to the [Company] as a result of shipment and delivery of any such order.

L.048

The [Agent] agrees that it shall only be entitled to the [Agent's] Commission and the fee for the Term of the Agreement subject to the continuance of the agreement and shall not be entitled to any other sums, garments, compensation, cancellation fee or otherwise from the [Company].

L.049

The [Agent] agrees that it shall be solely responsible and the [Company] shall not be liable for the costs and expenses incurred by the [Agent] in the provision of its services under this agreement including but not limited to: travel and accommodation, entertainment and hospitality, mobile and internet charges, entrance fees and exhibition attendance costs, reproduction, development and marketing costs, insurance, freight, staff, equipment, and office costs.

L.050

It is agreed that the [Company] shall be under no obligation to make use of the [Artwork/Images/Photographs/Products] in the [Film/Programme]. That decision of the [Company] not to make use of and include the [Artwork/Images/Photographs/Products] in the [Film/Programme] shall not enable [Name/Artist] to make any claim for breach of contract; the loss of the opportunity to enhance his/her reputation and/or for damage to his/her reputation and/or other losses at any time.

L.051

Both parties agree that in the event that any of the [Work/Licensed Articles] should be destroyed as a result of fire, flood, marine peril or any other circumstances beyond the control of the [Company]. That it is agreed that no royalties shall be due and/or paid on any of the [Work/Licensed Articles] which are destroyed and not sold.

L.052

The [Company] is under no liability whatsoever for any damages and/or loss of profit claimed by the [Customer] in respect of any interruptions, delays, inaccuracies, errors, omissions and/or failure to transmit the [Service] at any time.

L.053

In the event that any property of the [Company] is lost and/or damaged in the course of transportation by aircraft and/or vessel to [location] by [freight company]. The [Company] shall be entitled to be paid compensation in excess of [number/currency] from the insurer [specify name/address] under policy [type/duration/value].

L.054

The [Customer] is responsible for any loss and/or damage to the [Product] occurring between the time the [Product] is delivered to the [Customer] and until time it is safely returned to the [Company].

L.055

The [Company] does not operate an insurance scheme for the [Products/ Units]. The [Customer] is responsible for safety and care of the [Products/ Units]. Any {Products/Units] which are lost and/or returned damaged will be charged to the [Customer] at [number/currency] per [Product/Unit] plus any taxes. Any such costs and shall be deducted from any deposit and/or paid upon invoice.

L.056

If the [Licensee] fails to return and/or delays the return of any [Item/Unit] to the [Licensor] and/or fails to forward and/or delays the forwarding of any such [Item/Unit] to any other person as directed by the [Licensor]. Then the [Licensee] agrees to pay the [Licensor] the amount of any loss and/ or damage directly caused to the [Licensor] up to a maximum of [number/ currency].

L.057

If any [Master Material] is lost, stolen, destroyed, damaged and/or disappears between the time of delivery by the [Licensor] and the return by the [Licensee]. The [Licensee] shall immediately notify the [Licensor] in writing and shall pay the [Licensor] the full cost and charges of any replacement. Any property which is damaged when delivered by the [Licensee] to the [Licensor] shall be deemed to have been damaged by the [Licensee] unless the [Licensee] has previously notified the [Licensor] that the property was damaged when delivered to the [Licensee].

L.058

1.1 Risk and responsibility for the [Unit/Product] passes to the [Client] from the time that they are received until their safe return. The [Client] shall inform the [Supplier] in writing of any loss, damage and/or other harm to the [Unit/Product] while in the [Client's] possession or control.

1.2 If the [Unit/Product] is not returned within [specify length] of the date upon which it is due to be returned to the [Supplier]. The [Supplier] shall be entitled to deem that the [Unit/Product] has been lost and/or otherwise disposed of by the [Client]. The [Client] shall be liable to pay compensation to the [Supplier] in respect of each [Unit/Product] which is not returned, lost, damaged and/or otherwise as follows: [specify repayment amount]. The [Client] agrees that the payment of compensation does not entitle the [Client] to any rights or interest in the [Unit/Product]. An [Unit/Product] which is subsequently returned when compensation has already been paid shall entitle the [Client] to a [fifty] per cent refund of the compensation.

L.059

The [Supplier/Distributor] shall not be liable for any of the following categories of losses which may arise and/or be incurred by the [Company] under this agreement:

1.1 Any loss and/or damage which does not directly arise from the services and/or products supplied and/or distributed by the [Supplier/Distributor].

1.2 Design faults due to the nature of the material used and/or the specifications provided by and/or requested by the [Company].

1.3 Delays in delivery due to changes in the original specification by the [Company] and/or force majeure.

1.4 Testing and compliance with legislation which results in the delay of the [Project].

1.5 Breakdowns and interruptions of equipment, facilities, power and services.

1.6 Loss of profit by the [Company] and/ damage to equipment, data and property of the [Company] and any officer and/or employee and/or any other third party involved with the [Project].

1.7 Increase production, manufacture and/or supply of material costs.

1.8 Cancellation of any contracts, publicity, advertising and/or lapse of any consents, permissions and/or grants, funds and/or facilities.

1.9 Departure, death and/or personal injury of key personnel associated with the [Project].

L.060

Where a publisher and/or distributor suffers a loss as a result of the failure of the [writer/name] to deliver the manuscript for the [Book/Film]. Then the total liability of the [Licensor] shall be limited to the total sum of the advance. No sums shall be due to compensate the publisher and/or distributor for any loss of profit, sales, reputation and/or to cover any other losses and/or damages incurred and/or for any other reason.

L.061

If the weather conditions result in the cancellation of the [Event/Festival] the [Company] shall not be obliged to repay the [Sponsorship Fee] to the [Sponsor]. In addition it is agreed that the [Company] shall not be liable and/or obligated to pay the [Sponsor] for any losses, damages, costs and/or expenses that the [Sponsor] may incur either directly and/or indirectly as a result of the cancellation. The [Sponsor] undertakes not to seek to may any claim against the [Company] in respect of any such cancellation and agrees that it has accepted the risk.

L.062

Where a sub-licensee fails to pay any funds due and/or ceases to operate and/or does not fulfil the terms of the sub-licence. Then any such losses, expenses, damages and costs that may be incurred by either party to resolve the matter shall be at their own cost. The [Licensee] shall not be liable to pay any sums to the [Licensor] in respect of any payments it has not received from any such sub-licence where the sub-licensee have defaulted.

L.063

In the event that there is a product recall of the [Products/Units] for any reason which results in losses, damages, fines and/or other costs and expenses which are incurred and/or paid by the [Licensee]. Then these sums shall be the [Licensee's] sole responsibility and shall not be deducted from any sums due to the [Licensor] and/or shared by the [Licensor].

L.064

In the event that any person suffers any loss of data and/or damage to their software, laptop, gadgets, watch, mobile and/or any other device and/or suffers any other malfunction due to a virus and/or interruption to the service and/or any attack by a hacker as a result of the use of the electronic and/or telecommunication system and/or service supplied by the [Company] at any time in any medium and/or format. Then the total liability of the [Company] shall be limited to [number/currency] which shall be supplied in the form of a redeemable voucher for future use at the [Company] and no financial payment shall be made at any time.

L.065

The location is not secure and members of the public use these premises and/or services at their own risk. The [Company] cannot accept liability for any loss of equipment including laptops, mobile phones, headphones, watches and/or any other personal and/or business material which may be left on the floor, tables, in lockers and/or in any other manner on the site. You use this location at your own risk and shall bear the cost and responsibility of any damage, loss, costs and expenses that may arise whether due to theft, accidental damage and/or otherwise for any reason. The only liability which the [Company] accepts is personal injury and/or death directly attributable form the negligence and/or failure of duty of care of the [Company].

L.066

There is a real risk that this investment may make a loss as well as make a gain and it is entered into by you at your own risk with the knowledge that you may lose all the initials funds supplied to the [Company] and not receive any interest, dividends and/or other payments.

L.067

1.1 The [Assignee] shall from [date] have the right entirely at its own discretion to litigate and proceed with any actions, proceedings, claims and/or demands against any third party who have and/or may have infringed any rights and/r breached any contract held by the [Assignee] in the [Work] and/or [Work Material].

1.2 The [Assignor] agrees that after [date] all damages, costs, expenses and any other sums due or arising from the [Work] and/or [Work Material] shall belong to the [Assignee].

1.3 Where necessary the [Assignor] agrees to be a party to the action in name but all co-operation and assistance shall be subject to agreement as to the costs and expenses and the conclusion of an indemnity document by the [Assignee].

L.068

1.1 In the event that there is any allegation, complaint, report, claim and/or legal action that alleges and/or states that the use of this [Product/Work/Service] infringes any rights of any third party. Then the [Assignor/Licensor] against whom the claim is made shall be entitled to defend it and/or settle it as they may decide is in their best interests.

1.2 The [Assignee/Licensee] may decide at its discretion to seek an indemnity from the [Assignor/Licensor] in the event that the claim impacts on the existing agreement and/or losses, damages, costs and expenses are incurred.

L.069
In the event of any claim, dispute, action, writ and/or other allegation arising out of the rights granted and/or the fulfilment of this agreement. The [Assignor/Licensor] and [Assignee/Licensee]] agree to provide full details to the other party at the earliest opportunity and shall not settle any matter without first consulting the other party.

L.070
In the event that any infringement of any rights in the [Product/Work/Service] owned and/or controlled by the [Licensee] shall come to the attention of the [Sub-Licensee]. The [Sub-Licensee] shall promptly inform the [Licensee]. Each party shall be entitled to take whatever legal action they may decide is best in the circumstances.

L.071
Each member of the [Consortium] agrees that they shall notify all the other members immediately of any claim, demand, allegation and/or legal action or action by any third party relating to the [Project]. Any member agrees to consult with the other members as regard how they intend to proceed in respect of any matter including any defence, offer of settlement and/or the proposed disclosure of the details of this agreement.

L.072
The [Agent] agrees to advise the [Company] of any potential infringement of copyright, trade mark, service mark, design rights and/or any other rights in the Territory relating to the [Samples], the [Product/Service] and/or the [Company's] Logo which come to the attention of the [Agent]. The [Agent] agrees to provide assistance, expert evidence and any affidavit that may be required with respect to any legal or other proceedings provided that agreement is reached as to the basis upon which the time and effort of the [Agent] is to be paid for by the [Company].

L.073
During the Licence Period both the [Licensor] and the [Licensee] agree that they shall co-operate in respect of any legal proceedings, allegations and/or claims by third parties which arise in respect of this agreement. The [Licensee] shall notify the [Licensor] as soon as reasonably possible in the event that any of the following matters should be brought to their attention:

1.1 Pirate copies of the [Product/Units/Work] are manufactured, reproduced, distributed, supplied and/or sold by any third party in [any country in the world/in the licensed Territory].

1.2 Copies of the [Product/Units/Work] are marketed by unauthorised agents, distributors, retailers, wholesalers and/or on the internet by any means.

1.3 The [Product/Units/Work] and/or any copies are manufactured, reproduced, sold, supplied, distributed and/or otherwise exploited in circumstances which give rise to the suspicion that they are illegal copies and/or of inferior quality.

1.4 The [Product/Units/Work] and/or any copies are being used in a derogatory, offensive and/or other manner which is likely to impugn the reputation of the [Licensor] in any advertisement, periodical, newspaper and/or in any other medium.

1.5 A third party has complained and made allegations and/or threatened to make a claim and/or has commenced legal proceedings in respect of the [Product/Unit/Works], the soundtrack, music, the logos, trademarks, service marks, design rights, product liability and/or any associated item, packaging and/or marketing material.

1.6 A trade and/or consumer body and/or a retailer has complained of any matter including defects in relation to the [Product/Units/Work].

1.7 A purchaser of the [Product/Units/Work] has complained and/or notified any aspect which is defective, dangerous and/or or likely to cause harm.

1.8 The [Product/Units/Work] have not complied with any product liability, censorship, law, regulation and/or standards and practice which apply.

L.074

The parties agree that they:

1.1 shall not be obliged to notify the other party of any threatened allegation and/or the institution of any legal or other proceedings against them and/or any other third party appointed under this agreement. That any such party shall bear their own costs and expenses related to any such matter.

1.2 shall each be entitled to settle, defend and/or commence any legal or other proceedings as they think fit entirely at their own discretion and cost. That there shall be no indemnity under this agreement in respect of legal costs unless awarded by a court and/or agreed in settlement.

L.075

1.1 In the event that the [Licensor] and/or the [Licensee] become aware of any infringement of any copyright and/or other rights and/or any contractual obligations and/or any other acts by a third party in respect of the [Product/Units/Work] that may potentially be a problem. Then the [Licensor] and the [Licensee] shall keep each other informed on a regular basis of any steps they have taken to resolve the situation.

1.2 Both the [Licensor] and the [Licensee] agree that they shall provide sufficient funds to pursue vigorously all third parties who infringe any copyright and/or other rights and/or or contractual obligations and/or any other acts by a third party in respect of the [Product/Units/Work] and/or any other circumstances which have brought about a breach and/or alleged breach of this agreement.

1.3 Both the [Licensor] and the [Licensee] agree to co-operate in any legal proceedings and/or action that may be required. Where the parties have taken legal proceedings together and jointly shared the legal and administrative costs, then any sums received shall be shared equally. Where only one party institutes or commences the legal proceedings and pays all the legal costs and other expenditure incurred and the other is joined as a party, but make no contribution to the legal costs. Then the party which bears the legal costs shall be entitled to retain all sums received as damages, costs, for losses or otherwise.

L.076

The [Company] authorises the [Licensee] to institute, prosecute and defend such proceedings and to do such acts as the [Licensee] may consider necessary to protect the rights granted under this agreement and/or any part of them and to seek and claim damages, penalties and/or any other remedy for any infringement of such rights. The [Company] authorises the [Licensee] in so far as may be necessary to use the name of the [Company] for such purposes and the [Company] shall provide such assistance as the [Licensee] may reasonably require in proving and/or defending such rights and shall join with the [Licensee] as co-plaintiff if requested by the [Licensee] to do so. In such event the [Licensee] shall fully indemnify the [Company] against any costs, expenses and charges including counsel, solicitors', and agents' fees incurred by the [Company] relating to such proceedings.

L.077

The [Licensee] shall at its sole cost and expense take all necessary action and legal proceedings against third parties who infringe the copyright or any other rights in any media in the [Product/Work/Service] anywhere in the Territory which have been granted to the [Licensee] under this agreement. The parties mutually undertake to assist one another in their investigations and claims for any infringement or unauthorised use. The [Licensee] shall keep the [Licensor] informed of the progress of any legal proceedings. The [Licensee] agrees that as its sole discretion and cost the [Licensor] shall be entitled to institute its own enquiries and legal proceedings or to join any claim, demand and/or proceedings commenced by the [Licensee].

L.078

1.1   The [Licensor] and [Licensee] agree to notify each other as soon as reasonably practicable of any allegation and/or potential legal and/or compliance problem in respect of the ownership and/or infringement of any rights and/or the production, manufacture, sale and/or exploitation of the [Work/Service/Product] by the [Licensor] and/or the [Licensee] and/or any sub-licensee, distributor, agent and/or supplier.

1.2   The [Licensor] will at its own cost [and without any claim at a later date for a contribution by the [Licensee]] do all such acts and things necessary to protect the copyright, rights and interest of any nature including but not limited to taking legal action and/or other steps that may be required against any person, firm or company and shall advise the [Licensee] of all such cases as they arise.

1.3   The [Licensee] agrees to assist the [Licensor] in 1.2 at the [Licensor's] expense in any steps or action that need to be taken and if requested shall agree to be joined in any proceedings or action. Provided that the [Licensor] shall arrange for full disclosure to the [Licensee] of all legal documents relating to any case including any opinion of Counsel and expert witnesses, so that if necessary the [Licensee] can seek its own independent legal advice and be given a full indemnity in relation to any legal costs.

1.4   The [Licensor] accepts that the [Licensee] shall still be entitled if it should wish to do so to act and institute legal proceedings to protect its own rights and interest which shall be at the [Licensee's] sole cost and expense. In such instance the [Licensor] shall upon request agree to be joined to the proceedings or action subject to full disclosure to the [Licensor] of all legal documents relating to that case including the opinion of Counsel and any expert witnesses provided that the [Licensee] agrees to give a full indemnity to the [Licensor] for any legal costs.

L.079

In the event that the [Company] decides at its sole discretion to take legal action in respect of any unauthorised use of the [Material/Work/Products] and/or to defend any claim by a third party. The [Licensee] will to the best of its ability provide full assistance to the [Company] by providing information and obtaining such relevant evidence as may be within its control and/or possession.

L.080

Each party agrees that in the event of any legal proceedings they shall each bear their own legal costs and shall not be indemnified except to the extent any sum may be claimed under an existing insurance policy.

L.081

1.1   There shall be no obligation on the [Company] to take institute civil and/or criminal proceedings at any time and/or to pursue all parties who infringe the copyright and/or other rights in the [Product/Work/Service].

1.2   The [Company] shall be entitled at its sole discretion to decide whether to take any steps, action or otherwise. The [Company] may decide on commercial grounds and because of the potential costs that the matter should be dealt with without legal action. The [Company] may decide to use the police and/or some other authority and/or method despite the loss, damage and loss of reputation incurred by the [Company], the [Licensee] and/or any agent, distributor or other third party.

L.082
The [Company] agrees that it shall not incur any legal costs and/or instruct any legal advisor to institute any legal proceedings of any nature unless it has been authorised in advance by more than [number] Directors of the [Company] and a provisional statement of the issue, the proposed remedy and estimated costs and risk considered prior to any documents being issued to third parties.

L.083
No employee, consultant, agent, supplier and/or distributor and/or any other person engaged by and/or supplying services to the [Company] shall have the right to make any public statement and/or release any data and/or information and/or supply and/or distribute and/or publish any material in any medium regarding any investigation, enquiry, report, civil and/or criminal proceedings and/or any other allegations which are made against and/or by the [Company] against a third party at any time. Any breach of this clause shall be deemed a breach of this agreement and entitle the [Company] to end the agreement.

Internet, Websites and Apps

L.084
In the event that the [Company] is obliged to defend a legal action by a third party due to [Name] and/or to take legal action and/or any other steps against [Name] and/or due to a serious complaint and/or one or more breaches of the user access licence on this [Website/App/Platform] and/or any infringement of copyright, and/or any other rights owned or controlled by the [Company] and/or any third party. The [Company] shall seek and be entitled to recover from [Name] all legal costs, losses, loss of profit, damage to reputation, third party payments of any nature and any other

sums which arise directly or indirectly from the conduct, acts, behaviour, communications, post and/or otherwise by [Name] to the [Company], the [Website/App/Platform] and/or any related third party including any supplier, distributor, manufacturer, advertiser or other contributor.

L.085

1.1 It is not the policy of this [Website/App/Platform] to take legal action against and/or seek an indemnity of any nature from its users and we maintain a comprehensive insurance policy for that purpose.

1.2 We reserve the right at all times to take such steps, to delete, amend and/or vary your terms of access and/or use and to close any account and/or delete any images, text and/or other material as we may decide should be dealt with in such manner without any further notice to you.

1.3 We will take all such actions and steps as may be necessary to maintain a secure site, prevent criminal acts and activities and to protect the interests and safety of the public particularly children. We will carry out any investigations we deem necessary and may monitor your activity and communications in order to do so. Do not send any messages and/or post any material which is offensive, threatening, incites violence and/or is contrary to any existing legislation and/or act in a conspiracy to commit any crime and/or to cause personal injury and/or any other harm and/or damage to any person, animal and/or property.

1.4 We will report and supply any material which we believe should be reported to the police, security investigators, and any other body or authority or person we decide should be made aware of the facts.

1.5 It is a condition of your access and use of this [Website/App/Platform] that you agree that the [Company] shall not be liable to you for any consequences that may arise whether direct or indirect as a result of any actions and/or reports and/or any other matter of any nature by the [Company].

L.086

The [Company] shall have the right to edit, delete, amend, vary and/or destroy any material of any nature whether text, films, sound recordings, music, logos, images and photographs added and/or reproduced on this [Website/App/Platform] by any person and/or other third party. The [Company] may institute legal proceedings against any such person, company, business and/or entity which causes the [Company] to be the subject of a claim, action, injunction, dispute, writ, summons, fine, loss and/or other damage arising out of the actions and/or conduct and/or material supplied by the person, company, business and/or entity.

L.087

Where any legal proceedings are issued and/or any claim made against the [Company] arising from your contribution of any material of any nature to the [Website/App/Platform]. Then the [Company] shall seek to reclaim all the administrative, management and legal costs and expenses, and any damages, interest, losses and settlement payments that may be incurred by taking legal action against you without further notice and applying for a charge and/or lien over your property and money.

L.088

Where a civil and/or criminal action is taken by an individual, company, the police and/or a government agency arising from text, images, photographs, sound recordings, music, lyrics and/or any other material that you have uploaded and/or sent to the [Website/App/Platform] whether open to the public and/or in a secure area. The [Company] may at its sole discretion provide full cooperation to such third party in pursuance of such matter and you accept that you shall have no right to a claim and/or action against the [Company].

L.089

All material which is uploaded and/or sent to the [Company] whether on public display and/or sent to a limited group which contains material of any nature which in the view of the [Company] is illegal will be reported to the relevant authorities who may decide to take criminal and/or civil proceedings against you.

L.090

The [Company] shall not be responsible for and/or or make any payment towards, any settlements, legal costs and/or other expenses, damages, aggravated damages and/or fines that any [Contributor] to the [Website/App/Platform] may incur as a result of the [Contributor] posting, sending and/or communicating any material in any form to the [Website/App/Platform]. Any [Contributor] must pay all their own costs and expenses of any legal proceedings and any other sums.

L.091

In the event [Name] and/or the [Blog/App] and any text, image and/or any associated material and content are threatened with and/or subjected to legal proceedings by a third party for breach of contract, infringement of copyright, and/or any other allegation of infringement of intellectual property rights, data, privacy, defamation and/or otherwise of any nature. Then the [Company] reserves the right to remove and delete all reference to the [Blog/App] and any text, image and/or associated material and content without consultation with [Name] in order to reduce the risk of any threat and/or legal proceedings against the [Company] at any time. [Name] agrees and accepts that the [Company] shall be entitled to do so without stating any specific reason.

L.092

The [Company] is not liable for the costs and expenses of any legal action and/or proceedings whether civil and/or criminal, claim, summons, investigation, enquiry and/or representation before any commission which relates to the actions and conduct of any person, director, officer and/or employee during their time at the [Company] after their term of employment and/or office has ended.

L.093

The [Company] shall accept responsibility and pay for any legal costs and expenses incurred by [Name] up to [number/currency] in total where the legal proceedings and/or any investigation, enquiry, royal commission and/or health and safety and/or other inspection is and/or are commenced in [country] and relate to his/her role as [specify role] during the term of his/her employment and/or the supply of his/her services to the [Company] whether or not such matter arises after the expiry and/or termination provided it is within [number] years of the end date.

L.094

It is agreed between the parties as follows:

1.1 [Name] shall not have any right and/or authority to commence legal proceedings and/or make any threat to a third party on behalf of the [Company].

1.2 [Name] shall refer all complaints, threats of legal actions and/or any other compliance matter which has come to their attention to the [Company].

1.3 [Name] shall not use the [Podcast/Blog] to defame any person and/or criticise any products and/or services of a third party.

1.4 Where the [Company] decides that [Name] is not following the company policies regarding the content and presentation of the [Podcast/Blog]. Then the [Company] shall be entitled to terminate the agreement with [one] month's notice and to put [Name] on paid leave for that month. In such event [Name] shall not be entitled to any other sums.

Merchandising and Distribution

L.095

The [Licensee] shall be solely responsible for paying any costs, damages and expenses arising from any claim, action or liability arising from the production, manufacture, sale, distribution or other exploitation of the [Units/Products] excluding: the representation of the defined Character and any associated name. trade mark, slogan, image, music and/or sound recordings.

L.096
In the event that any legal proceedings are commenced by any third party against either the [Licensor] and/or the [Licensee] in respect of the [Character] and/or the [Units/Products]. Both parties agree to ensure that written notice of such claims shall immediately be given to the other party. Where the allegation or claim relates to the infringement or breach of third party rights then either party shall be entitled to defend itself without prejudice to the right of either party to take whatever legal action and/or other steps as they shall decide is in their best interests.

L.097
If there is any dispute of any nature by any third party relating to the [Licensor's] rights in the [Licensor's] Logo, the use of it by the [Licensee] or the [Licensee's] Product at any time during the Licence Period or during the sell off period. The party against whom the allegation is made or who receives the complaint shall provide full details to the other within [seven] days. Both parties shall assist each other as far as possible to settle or defend the matter. Each party shall bear its own legal costs but may seek to recoup them later on an indemnity basis if the other party has defaulted and/or breached this agreement.

L.098
Each party agrees that in the event of any complaint, threat, legal action and/or allegation of any infringement of copyright, trade mark, service mark, logo, slogan, domain name, words or images. That each party shall be entitled to deal with the matter without consulting the other and shall be able to decide what to do based on their own commercial interests. Provided that if they proceed on that basis they do not intend to seek to be reimbursed for any legal costs under any indemnity clause in this agreement.

L.099

1.1 The [Licensee] shall at its sole cost and expense take all necessary action and legal proceedings against third parties who infringe the copyright or any other rights in any media in the [Product/Work/Service] anywhere in the Territory which have been granted to the [Licensee] under this agreement.

1.2 The [Licensor] and the [Licensee] both mutually undertake to assist one another in their investigations and claims for any infringement and/or unauthorised use. The [Licensee] shall keep the [Licensor] informed of the progress of any legal proceedings. The [Licensee] agrees that at its sole discretion and cost the [Licensor] shall be entitled to institute its own enquiries and legal proceedings or to join any claim, demand or proceedings commenced by the [Licensee]. Where the [Licensee] intends to seek to be indemnified by the [Licensor] under this agreement. Then the [Licensor] should be informed of the matter as soon as possible, be regularly consulted and allowed to refute the allegations, and kept informed of progress and advised of any proposed settlement.

L.100

In the event that any complaint, claim, allegation and/or legal proceedings are made against and/or threatened or issued by any third party against the [Distributor] in respect of the [Product/Service/Character] and/or any associated packaging, marketing and/or promotion. Then the [Distributor] shall immediately notify the [Licensor] of the nature of the claim, allegation, action or complaint and shall provide copies of all documents and shall provide all such assistance as may reasonably be required in order to deal with, refute, settle or defend such case. The [Distributor] agrees to follow the instructions and guidance of the [Licensor] and will permit the [Licensor] to assume control of the matter. The [Licensor] shall only reimburse and/or indemnify the legal costs and expenses incurred by the [Distributor] where the [Licensor] is in breach of this agreement and its undertakings to the [Distributor].

L.101

1.1 The [Sub-Licensee] shall not be entitled to threaten and/or commence any legal proceedings against third parties who infringe the copyright or any other rights in the [Product/Service/Work] anywhere in the Territory without the prior written approval and agreement of the [Licensor] and the [Licensee].

1.2 The [Sub-Licensee] shall provide full details to the [Licensor] and the [Licensee] for their consideration and shall make a recommendation as to the steps to be taken. Where the [Licensor] and the [Licensee] provide consent all legal costs and expenses shall be at the [Sub-Licenses] risk and cost unless agreed otherwise. The [Sub-Licensee] shall keep the [Licensor] and the [Licensee] informed of the progress of any legal proceedings. The [Sub-Licensee] shall be entitled to keep all damages and costs awarded to the [Sub-Licensee].

L.102

1.1 The [Sub-Licensee] shall not require the consent of the [Licensee] in order to threaten and/or commence any legal proceedings against a third party who has breached and/or infringed the rights held and/ or controlled by the [Sub-Licensee] in respect of the [Unit/Product/ Work].

1.2 The [Licensee] agrees to provide such cooperation as may be required subject to the proviso that the [Licensee] shall not be required to incur any additional costs. The [Sub-Licensee] shall keep the [Licensee] informed and provide copies of all documentation upon request. The [Sub-Licensee] shall be entitled to keep all costs awarded to the [Sub-Licensee], but all damages and other payments shall be included in the accounting reports to the [Licensee] and share [number] % to the [Licensee] and [number] % to the [Sub-Licensee].

L.103

The [Licensor] agrees and undertakes to cooperate and assist the [Licensee] in any legal proceedings by supplying authorised copies of any original documents that may be required in order to prove copyright ownership in respect of the rights granted to the [Licensee].

L.104

1.1 In the event that the [Licensee] and/or any supplier, agent and/or distributor is contacted by any third party alleging personal injury, death, infringement of copyright and/or any other intellectual property rights and/or breach of contract, breach of product liability and/or any other health and safety legislation and/or policies and/or any other matter which may potentially give rise to a claim and/or civil and/or criminal proceedings and/or a fine and/or otherwise against the [Licensor] and/ or the [Licensee]. The [Licensee] shall provide full disclosure of the allegations and any records to the [Licensor].

1.2 Where the [Licensor] wishes to take control of the response, any defence, claim and/or other legal proceedings. The [Licensee] shall consent provided that the [Licensor] undertakes to bear all legal and other costs and expenses which may be incurred by the [Licensee] in each case.

L.105

The [Licensee] agrees and accepts that where any dispute, legal proceedings and/or other claim and/or allegation is made against the [Licensor] in respect of any logo, image, text and/or content in respect of any of the [Products/Units] set out in Section B in this agreement. That the [Licensor] may withdraw any such item from the list and cease selling in any consumer market in any part of the world and substitute another which is of comparable status and type.

L.106

The [Trade Mark User] shall immediately bring to the attention of the [Registered Owner] any improper or wrongful use of the Trade Marks which comes to its notice during the Term of the Agreement.

L.107

1.1   The [Agent] agrees to send comprehensive information to the [Company] in respect of any potential infringement of rights in the Territory relating to the [Samples] and the [Products/Units] and/or the [Company's] Logo including copyright, design rights, trade marks or any other intellectual property rights.

1.2   The [Agent] agrees to immediately advise the [Company] of any complaint it may receive as to defects in the [Products/Units].

1.3   The [Agent] agrees to cooperate and assist the [Company] with any matter provided that any administrative, legal costs and other expenses that may need to be incurred are paid in full by the [Company] and not deducted from any sums due to the [Agent].

L.108

If there is any allegation, threat, claim, legal action and/or complaint lodged and/or other steps taken by any third party against the [Supplier] and/or the [Distributor] in respect of the production, supply, sale and/or other access to the [Product/Unit/Service] and/or any associated support material on the [Distributor's] website, app and/or other retail outlet. Each party shall notify the other immediately of the nature and detail of any such matter of which they have knowledge. In the event that any party seeks to be indemnified from the other for legal costs, losses and/or damages then it is under an obligation to allow the other party against whom the indemnity will be sought to have the opportunity to [assist in/control] the defence of and/or settlement of any matter.

L.109

If circumstances arise which give reasonable cause for action to be taken against any third party by virtue of a breach of either party's intellectual property and/or contractual rights of any kind. The parties agree to provide reasonable co-operation to each other as is required to protect such rights. As a general principle all costs and monies recovered shall be shared equally provided that both parties are named in the action and equally share the legal costs.

L.110

The [Distributor], and/or any agent, supplier, online retail outlet and/or store and/or any other person, retailer, wholesaler or otherwise shall not have the right or be entitled to take any legal action or proceedings whether civil or criminal and/or to report any matter to the authorities and/or take any steps against a person, company or business and/or make any applications and/or register any objections and/or defend any matter in the name of and/or on behalf of [Name] without the prior written consent and authority of [Name]. [Name] agrees not to unreasonably withhold and/or delay their consent provided that there is full disclosure of the facts in each case to [Name] and the matter does not prejudice the commercial interests of [Name] and/or Name] has been advised by its own professional and legal advisors not to provide authority and/or consent.

L.111
Where a third party has made a complaint and/or threatened legal proceedings and/or started a legal action. Then the [Company] shall keep a complete log of all emails, calls and documents. Where the matter is not resolved and/or settled within [number] months. Then the [Company] agrees to follow the following procedure: [specify procedure].

L.112
The [Supplier] agrees that it shall pay to the [Distributor] upon invoice all the administrative, freight and legal costs and expenses and losses and damages which the [Distributor] may incur and/or which arise due to any personal injury, death, allergic reaction and/or ill health including short term and long term illness which is found by any investigation by an independent expert and/or government department and/or body and/or as a result of civil and/or legal proceedings to be connected with and/or result from the contents and/or packaging of the [Product] and/or any ingredients and/or other material used by the [Supplier] in developing, creating, producing and distributing the [Product] in any country at any time to the [Distributor] and/or any member of the public and/or other third party supplied by the [Distributor].

L.113

1.1 It is agreed that each party to this agreement shall bear its own expenses and costs in the event that it decides to take advice, threaten, commence and/or defend any legal proceedings and/or object to any registration and/or defend and/or register any domain name, trade mark, service mark and/or other intellectual property rights and/or register as a controller of any data and/or any other matter.

1.2 That no party shall have the right to seek to deduct payments due to the other under this agreement to set-off any administration, legal costs and expenses.

1.3 That where the co-operation and assistance of any other party is required that terms shall be agreed as to the basis of the contribution and who is

1091

to pay the costs and who is to receive and/or pay any settlement and/or who is to retain sums received which may be awarded.

L.114

1.1 [Name] agrees and confirms to the [Company] that there are currently as at [date] no threats and/or pending and/or actual legal proceedings against the [Product/Service/Trade Mark/Logo] and/or [Name] in [country].

1.2 [Name] agrees that the failure to disclose to the [Company] the fact that there has been a threat of legal action by a competitor, member of the public and/or any other third party in [country] in respect of the [Product/Service/Trade Mark/Logo] and the nature of the complaint shall be a breach of this agreement for any matter before [date].

1.3 [Name] agrees that where there is a breach as set out in 1.1 and 1.2 above that the [Company] shall be entitled to terminate the agreement and seek repayment of all sums paid under this agreement to [Name].

Publishing

L.115

1.1 If the [Publisher] on the basis of internal and/or external professional legal and business advice shall consider that the copyright and/or other intellectual property rights, domain names, trade marks and/or artwork in respect of the [Book/Sound Recording/Manuscript] and/or any associated marketing has been and/or will be infringed and/or harmed in any manner by a third party. The [Publisher] shall be entitled to take such action as the [Publisher] may deem necessary including but not limited to legal proceedings, settlement or otherwise.

1.2 In the event that the [Publisher] wishes to name the [Author] as a party to the proceedings the [Publisher] shall only be entitled to do so if the [Publisher] provides a written undertaking to the [Author] that the [Publisher] shall bear all costs and expenses and fully indemnify the [Author]. The [Author] shall bear no liability and/or responsibility for any sums of any nature that may be incurred and/or become due.

1.3 The [Publisher] shall be entitled to deduct all legal costs and expenses not recovered from a third party from any damages and other sums that may be received. The [Author] shall be entitled to be paid [fifty] per cent of the monies which are then retained by the [Publisher]. The [Publisher] shall not be entitled to off-set any other sums.

L.116

The [Publishers] agree that the [Author] shall be consulted in relation to any proposed settlement and/or compromise of any legal and/or business matter in respect of the [Artwork/Book/Sound Recording]. Further that the Author shall be entitled to share in any sums received as damages, interest and/or otherwise after deduction of any legal costs and expenses by the [Publisher].

L.117

1.1 If at any time during the Term of this Agreement either the [Author] and/or the [Publisher] decide that the copyright and/or some other intellectual property right and/or other interest is infringed and/or breached and/or harmed by a third party. The [Author] and/or the [Publisher] shall have the right to take legal proceedings and shall give written notice to the other party of its intention to do so. The [Publisher] shall be entitled to require the [Author] to take part in such proceedings and if it does so it shall pay all costs and expenses incurred in such proceedings by both the [Publisher] and the [Author].

1.2 Any monies which shall be recovered as a result of legal proceedings and/or any settlement in which both the [Author] and the [Publisher] have participated shall after deduction of all costs and expenses be divided equally between the [Author] and the [Publisher]. If no agreement is reached for joint action either party may proceed as it shall see fit bearing all the legal costs and retain and/or pay all the damages and/or other sums which may be awarded and/or incurred.

L.118

1.1 The [Writer] authorises the [Company] in any country of the world to institute, commence and defend such criminal and civil proceedings and to do such acts as the [Company] may deem fit to protect the rights assigned under this agreement and to seek to recover such damages, stock, interest, legal costs and other sums as it may decide.

1.2 The [Writer] authorises the [Company] to use his/her name as the author of the [Book/Translation/Sound Recording/Work] for such purposes provided that all costs and expenses shall be paid for by the [Company] and the [Company] shall keep the [Author] fully informed and supply copies of all documents relating to any such matters upon request.

1.3 The [Writer] agrees to provide his/her reasonable assistance in any action whether to prove and/or defend the rights assigned to the [Company]. The [Company] agrees to pay the [Writer's] and his/

her agent's legal costs and expenses, accommodation, mobile and internet charges, hospitality, travel costs and such other sums as may be necessary in for the [Writer] to assist the [Company] as required.

L.119
The [Publisher] undertakes at its own discretion to instigate and proceed with any necessary actions, proceedings, claims and demands against any company, firm, or person who may infringe the copyright and/or any other intellectual property rights in the [Work/Book/Sound Recordings]. The [Publisher] agrees that any damages and other benefits recovered by the [Publisher] shall after deduction of reasonable legal costs and expenses shall be divided [50] per cent to the [Publisher] and [50] per cent to the [Writer].

L.120
The [Author] agrees that the [Publisher] may use the [Author's] name as a party to take legal action against any third party for copyright infringement in respect of the [Work/Book/Service] provided that:

1.1   The [Author] is kept fully advised of the details of any legal action.

1.2   The [Publisher] gives a full detailed indemnity to the [Author] agreeing to pay all costs, expenses, and losses in respect of the legal action incurred by the [Publisher] and the [Author].

1.3   That in the event that any profits, damages, awards or other sums or benefits or stock are recovered in respect of the [Work/Book/Service]. The [Publisher] shall share such sums or otherwise equally with the [Author] after the deduction of all reasonable costs and expenses of the [Publisher] incurred by the [Publisher] which are not recovered from a third party and/or which cannot be claimed under any insurance policy.

L.121
The [Publisher] and/or any agent, distributor, supplier or otherwise shall not have the right or be entitled to take any legal action or proceedings whether civil or criminal, and/or to report any matter to the authorities and/or take any steps against a person, company or business and/or make any applications, register any objections and/or defend any matter in the name of and/or on behalf of the [Author] without the prior written consent and authority of the [Author].

L.122

1.1   The [Publisher] shall notify the [Author/Illustrator] of the detail of the threat of any legal proceedings against the [Publisher] and any allegation of defamation, breach of contract, infringement of copyright, infringement of trade mark and/or threat of injunction and/or any writ, claim and/or otherwise for losses, damages and/or personal injury and/or any other matter relating to the [Work/Artwork/Photographs] as soon as reasonably possible.

1.2 The [Publisher] agrees and undertakes to inform the [Author/Illustrator] of any matter in 1.1 as soon as possible and to provide copies of any documents relating to the case to the [Author/Illustrator] and/or their legal advisor and to consult with the [Author/Illustrator] where the [Publisher] intends to seek to be indemnified by the [Author/Illustrator] under this agreement. The [Publisher] shall regularly consult with the [Author/Illustrator] and allow them the opportunity to set out the reason why the allegations should be refuted. The [Publisher] shall advise the [Author/Illustrator] of the proposed terms of any settlement and seek their views.

L.123

The [Licensee] agrees and undertakes to cooperate and assist the [Sub-Licensee] in the issue of and/or defence of any legal proceedings in respect of the rights granted in respect of the [Work/Book/Sound Recordings] under this agreement. The [Licensee] shall provide at their sole cost authorised copies of any original documents that may be required in order to prove copyright ownership in respect of the rights granted to the [Sub-Licensee]. The [Licensee] shall not be liable under any indemnity for any costs, expenses, damages and/or losses the [Sub-Licensee] may incur which do not directly relate to the rights granted in respect of the [Work/Book/Sound Recordings].

L.124

The [Company] reserves the right at any time not to publish the [Artwork/Illustrations/Photographs] and/or to recall at its sole discretion any copies and/or to cease printing and/or to cancel and/or terminate any licence agreements and/or to remove, delete and/or to cease marketing any part where allegations and/or the threat of legal proceedings have been made by a third party which are established to be likely to be true and show that the [Artwork/Illustrations/Photographs] has resulted in the defamation of any person who is not deceased and/or a substantial part of the [Artwork/Illustration/Photographs] is based on and/or derived from the original copyright material of a third party and is not original to [Name].

L.125

Where there are any allegations and/or threats and/or claims and/or legal proceedings made against the [Company] and/or the [Work] and/or [Name] to the [Company]. In such event the [Company] shall provide evidence of

1095

the allegations and facts to [Name] and provide them with an opportunity to refute the allegations at a meeting at the offices of the [Company] with a senior executive and a legal advisor of the [Company].

L.126

Where as a result of the investigations, research and product of the work of [Name] the [Company] reproduces, supplies, sells and distributes and publishes an article and/or image and/or allegations against a third party. Then the [Company] agrees to pay for all personal and legal costs and expenses that may arise from any response, threat, claim, enquiry, police and/or government investigation, commission and/or civil and/or criminal and/or other legal proceedings including any individual, estate, corporation and/or otherwise from any third party whether or not [Name] is no longer associated with the [Company]. This agreement shall not apply after [date].

L.127

The [Company] and the [Author/Contributor] agree:

1.1 That either party may decide to threaten and/or take legal action against a third party in respect of their rights in the [Work]. No permission and/or consent of the other party is required.

1.2 That neither party shall bear the other parties legal and other costs when pursuing a third party for any infringement and/or breach of any nature.

1.3 Neither party shall be obliged to share any damages, losses, and/or other sums received form any settlement and/or legal action with the other party.

1.4 That none of these sums shall be obliged to be recorded in the accounts and/or royalty payments.

Services

L.128

1.1 In the event that legal proceedings are commenced by any third party against either the [Designer] and/or the [Company] in respect of the [Website/App/Service/Project] or some other matter relating to this agreement. Then both parties shall be kept fully informed and provide each other with assistance to resolve or defend the matter. Each party shall bear its own legal costs and expenses and consult with each other prior to any settlement.

1.2 Where any legal action relates to work requested by the [Company] for the [Website/App/Service/Project]. The [Company] agrees to act on behalf of both parties and shall pay the [Designer's] legal costs and expenses provided that he/she agrees to be represented by the same legal advisors as the [Company]. The [Designer] agrees to execute such legal documents as may be reasonably required.

L.129

The [Company] accepts and agrees that it shall be solely responsible for the legal consequences and liabilities that may arise in respect of the production, distribution and exploitation of the [Event/Services/Series]. That where any legal proceedings, actions, claims, complaints and/or allegations are made against the [Company] and/or the [Contributor] in respect of the [Event/Services/Series]. The [Company] undertakes to fully indemnify the [Contributor] for the cost of separate and independent legal representation and advice and any other sums that may be awarded against and/or incurred by the [Contributor] until [date].

L.130

The [Consultant] shall send copies of any complaints, and/or compliance and/or legal actions which are threatened and/or commenced against the [Consultant] and/or [Company] in respect of the services by the [Consultant] provided under this agreement to the [Company] and/or related third parties in respect of the [Project]. The [Company] shall not be responsible for any legal costs and expenses incurred by the [Consultant] in defending and/or otherwise settling any such matters unless the [Consultant] was acting in accordance with instructions issued by the [Company].

L.131

[Name] and the [Company] agree that in the event of any complaint, threat, claim, legal action, disciplinary proceedings and/or other allegation in respect of any matter. That [Name] and/or the [Company] shall not be obliged to consult with and/or seek the approval of the other prior to reaching any settlement, defending the action and/or taking any other steps that may be necessary. This clause shall not prevent either party relying on any undertaking and/or indemnity in this agreement to recover any costs and/or expenses and/or other sums that may have been incurred.

L.132

Both parties agree that where a third party takes legal action against both parties that they shall first try to resolve and settle the matter without incurring legal costs. That if that fails they shall agree the total budget for the legal costs and the [Company] shall pay [number] % and the [Distributor] shall pay [number] %.

L.133

[Name] has not authorised and/or provided any consent for the [Agent] to threaten any third party with legal proceedings by [Name] and/or to take any legal advice at [Names'] cost and expense and/or to instruct any person and/or company to register, take action, defend and/or settle any matter on behalf of [Name].

L.134

[Name] agrees that he/she authorises the [Agent/Company] to take such steps as may be necessary to seek advice and take legal action in order to develop, protect, register and defend the brand of [Name] and any associated trade mark, domain name, logo, images and slogan. Provided that where the proposed costs and expenses are likely to exceed [number/currency] in any one case that the prior written approval of [Name] must be obtained. In such instance the [Agent/Company] must provide [Name] with a detailed breakdown of the total projected sums.

L.135

[Name] shall not be obliged to sign any documents, swear any affidavit and/or commence any legal proceedings and/or be joined as a party to any legal action by the [Company] in respect of any matter which may arise directly and/or indirectly from the provision of the services of [Name] and his/her original material to the [Company]

Sponsorship

L.136

If any legal proceedings are commenced or threatened by any third party against the [Sponsor] and/or the [Television Company] in respect of the [Sponsor's Logo] and/or the [Films]. Within [seven] days of receipt the party who has received notice should inform the other of the problem. Each party shall be responsible for dealing with its own legal problems and bear its own legal costs. This clause does not prevent a later claim for indemnity, legal costs, damages or otherwise against the party which is at fault and has been in breach of this agreement.

L.137

1.1   The [Sponsor] accepts and agrees that it shall be solely responsible for the legal consequences and liabilities that may arise in respect of the content and exploitation of the [Sponsors Logo] and the [Sponsors Product] by the [Athlete] and the [Company] under this agreement.

1.2   This agreement shall not authorise the [Sponsor] and the [Sponsor] shall not have any right to use the name of the [Athlete] and/or [Company] in relation to any matter without their prior written consent in each case. Where any legal proceedings, actions, claims, complaints and/or allegations are made the [Sponsor] undertakes to fully indemnify the [Athlete] and his/her agent and the [Company] for the cost of separate and independent legal representation and advice, and/or any other costs, losses, damages, expenses and sums that may be incurred and/or awarded against them as a consequence of this agreement.

L.138

If there is any threat, complaint, claim, and/or legal action by any third party against the [Sponsor] and/or the [Company] in respect of the [Event] and/or the services and/or products supplied by the [Sponsor] under this agreement. Each party agrees and undertakes to notify the other within [number] days by email and in writing of the nature and detail of any such matter of which they have knowledge together with copies of any documents. In the event that the [Company] and/or the [Sponsor] seeks to be indemnified from the other for legal costs, expenses, damages and/or other costs. Then the party seeking to rely on any indemnity is under an obligation to allow the other party to have the opportunity to assist in the defence of and/or settlement of any such case.

L.139

Where any allegation is made and/or a complaint and/or a claim is made and/or any legal proceedings are commenced by any third party against either the [Sponsor] and/or the [Company] in respect of any matter directly and/or indirectly arising from the terms of this agreement. Then both the [Sponsor] and the [Company] agree that where they shall seek to rely on any indemnity from the other party to recoup the costs. That they shall be obliged to notify the other party at the earliest opportunity and to keep that other party fully informed. That no indemnity shall be relied upon under this agreement if the party seeking the indemnity contributed to the legal problem as a result of their actions, errors, omissions, failures and/or default.

L.140

The [Athlete] agrees and undertakes to:

1.1 Notify the [Sponsor] by telephone and then in writing of any civil and/or criminal proceedings which are threatened, commenced and/or pending against the [Athlete] [and/or any immediate family member] during the Term of this Agreement.

1.2 Notify the [Sponsor] by telephone and then in writing of any disciplinary proceedings by any of the following organisations against the [Athlete] which arise during the Term of this Agreement: [specify organisations].

1.3 Notify the [Sponsor] by telephone and then in writing of any failure by the [Athlete] to attend random tests and/or the failure of any test which arise during the Term of this Agreement by the following organisations and bodies: [specify list].

1.4 Supply copies of any documents which relate to the above matters in confidence to the [Sponsors] upon request during the Term of this Agreement.

1.5 Cooperate in the drafting of and distribution of any press and social media statement and to be available at no more than [number] media conferences as may be necessary during the Term of this Agreement.

L.141
The [Company] shall not be required to bear the cost of and/or contribute to the expenses and/or any damages, interest and/or losses incurred by the [Sponsor] as a result of legal proceedings by a third party against the [Sponsor] in respect of the [Event].

L.142
The [Sponsor] agrees that in the event that any third party shall make any threats, allegations, derogatory and/or offensive statements and/or institute any legal proceedings in any country of the world in respect of [Name] and/or the [Sponsor] in respect of any advertising campaign, promotion, appearance and/or trade marks, logos, images, films, sound recordings, interviews, blogs, websites, apps, products and/or events in connection with the work of [Name] and the material created under this agreement. That the [Sponsor] agrees to pay all the costs and sums that may be incurred by [Name] and/or his/her professional advisors to deal with the matter including legal, travel, accommodation, public relations, marketing and any other sums which may be directly incurred as a result of this agreement up to a maximum of [number/currency] from [date] until [date].

L.143
The [Sponsor] agrees that where the [Company] has received a claim for less than [number/currency] and has decided to settle the matter without any admission of liability in respect of allegation which relates to the [Company] and/or the [Sponsor] and/or the [Event/Project]. That the [Sponsor] will pay [number] per cent the settlement sum to the [Company] and shall not dispute the cost.

University, Charity and Educational

L.144
The [Institute/Charity] shall have the sole discretion as to whether to take any steps, actions and/or commence any legal proceedings for any

civil and/or criminal matter. The [Institute/Charity] shall not be obliged to keep the [Company/Name] informed as to the progress in any case. The [Institute/Charity] shall not be obliged to consult with the [Company/Name] as to the terms of any settlement and/or the defence of any claim. The [Institute/Charity] shall be entitled to keep all legal costs, damages, losses, interest and any other sums received as a result of any such legal proceedings and the [Company] shall have no right to receive any such sums.

L.145
In the event that any threats, allegations, claims and/or legal proceedings are made against the [Institute/Charity] and/or the [Licensee] in respect of the [Work/Artwork/Product]. The [Institute/Charity] and/or the [Licensee] shall immediately notify the other party of the details and provide such copies of any documents as may be available. Both parties shall assist each other as far as possible to settle and/or defend the matter. Each party shall initially bear its own legal and administrative costs. This clause shall not prevent one party seeking to be reimbursed and/or to make a claim against the other that it is due any sum under an indemnity and/or for a default and/or breach of this agreement by the other party.

L.146
The [Institute/Charity] and/or the [Company] shall both have the discretion to take such legal, commercial and practical steps as may be required in order to claim ownership of, protect and/or defend their rights and interest in the [Project/Work/Product]. Both parties shall have the choice whether to issue any legal proceedings, make any claim, demand, defend any action and/or whether to settle any matter and/or register any domain name, patent, copyright and any other rights and interest. Where both parties decide to take any legal proceedings they shall agree in advance the basis upon which any costs are to be split and how any damages, losses, interest and other sums awarded are to be shared.

L.147
In the event that legal proceedings are commenced by any third party against either the [Institute/Charity] and/or the [Company] in respect of the [Project/Work/Event] or some other matter relating to this agreement. Then both parties agree and undertake to inform the other party of any such allegation and where necessary provide each other with assistance to resolve or defend the matter. Each party shall bear its own legal costs and expenses and consult with each other prior to any settlement. This clause shall not prevent either party seeking to be repaid any sum under the indemnity provisions in this agreement.

L.148

The [Institute/Charity] shall have the right to defend any allegations and/ or to resolve and/or settle any threat and/or start legal proceedings and/ or to deal with any matter relating to a breach of any code and/or policy guidelines as it thinks fit and in the best interests of the [Institute/Charity]. The [Institute/Charity] may settle any matter without any admission of liability in order to save costs and/or adverse publicity. The [Institute/Charity] shall not be obliged to consult with any person prior to any final decision as to the best course of action.

L.149

The [University] agrees and undertakes that it shall not be entitled to take any legal action and/or commence any legal proceedings and/or instruct any debt collection agency against any person who has attended a [course/ conference/event] organised and managed by the [University] unless [number] months has/have expired since the sum due has been owed and/ or the [University] has offered to accept payment in monthly instalments over a fixed period and that offer has been refused.

L.150

1.1 The [College] and the board of [Trustees/Governors] reserve the right and shall be entitled to take such action, steps and seek legal advice and/or institute any legal proceedings and/or arrange security and/or request the presence of the police and/or shall be entitled to exclude any person and/or parents and/or family members and/or friends from the [College] as may be necessary to protect the health, safety and security of all the students, staff and other third parties and the property at any time.

1.2 The [College] reserve the right to cancel and/or terminate any right of access to the [College] website, app, courses, library and resources for any reason where they have reason to believe that there is a security risk, potential fraud and/or virus and/or any other threat to safety and/or any potential infringement of copyright and/or for any other reason.

1.3 That where the [College] has a security system in place to check the content of [bags/persons] on site in order to vet entry and/or exit that where a person refuses to co-operate and permit a search that access may be refused.

1.4 The [College] agrees that no physical body searches shall take place at any time. The [College] shall have the right to refuse permission to bring certain items onto the premises which in the opinion of the [College] pose a risk.

1.5 The [College] maintains constant filming through [cctv/other] in locations throughout the site. These recordings are for the purpose of security and safety and the [College] reserves the right to use and/or supply any material taken whilst you are on the site to any third party without a court order including legal advisors and the police in order to assess and/or conduct and/or to supply evidence in support of any civil and/or criminal proceedings at any time.

L.151

1.1 [Name] shall not have any right to act as an ambassador of the [Charity/University] and/or to represent that they have authority to do so in any manner. Their role shall be limited to attending and promoting the [Charity/University] at fundraising events.

1.2 [Name] shall not attempt to register any logos, images and/or slogans created and/or developed by the [Charity/University] and/or any third parties in fundraising events. [Name] shall not use any such logos, images, slogans and other material for the purposes of merchandising and/or other commercial exploitation and/or the marketing of [Name] without the prior written consent of the [Charity/University].

1.3 [Name] shall not be entitled to reproduce and/or supply any data and/or other material to a third party regarding the [Charity/University] which has been supplied to [Name] under this agreement except his/her agent and/or professional accountants and/or legal advisors.

1.4 [Name] shall not have any right to start any legal proceedings on behalf of the [Charity/University] for any reason. Where any allegation is made against [Name] which relates to the role and/or work of [Name] for the [Charity/University] then the matter must be immediately be referred to [specify person] at the [Charity/University].

LIABILITY

Film, Television and Video

L.152
The [Assignor] confirms that all sums due in respect of the production of the [Film] have been paid and that the [Assignee] is not and will not be liable for any such sums.

L.153

1.1 The [Licensor] shall not be responsible and/or liable for any losses and/or damages of any nature whether direct and/or indirect including any loss of profits and/or any consequential damages suffered and/or incurred by the [Distributor] for whatever reason. In the event that the [Distributor] is delayed, interrupted and/or is unable to commence manufacture, reproduction, supply and/or distribution of the [Product/Unit/Service] of the [Film/Sound Recordings] in any country for any reason.

1.2 Where the failure and/or default lasts for more than [number] months then the [Licensor] shall be entitled to terminate the agreement in respect of that country provided that the [Licensor] shall repay to the [Distributor] any advance in full which has not been recouped. The [Distributor] agrees that it shall not be entitled to seek to be indemnified by the [Licensor] and/or make any claim for any costs, expenses, damages and/or any other sums.

L.154
The [Licensee] agrees that no additional payments shall be due in compensation if the [Licensor] does not provide any option on any rights, first right of refusal and/or chooses not to renew and/or extend the duration of this agreement after it has expired and/or does not grant any rights in in respect of any sequel and/or other adaptation.

L.155
The [Licensee] agrees that there is no obligation on the [Licensor] to grant any option on any rights and/or provide any first right of refusal and/or to extend and/or to renew the Licence Period and/or to grant any rights in respect of any sequel and/or any other adaptation.

L.156
The [Distributor] shall be liable for any loss and/or damage to the master material of the [Sound Recordings/Film] and any photographs and/or other material supplied on loan by [Name] whilst it is in transit to and/or from any location and/or while being used for the purpose of the manufacture and reproduction of the [Programme] and/or for the [DVD/Disc]. The [Distributor] shall ensure that there is insurance cover in place to the value of [number/currency] per claim and shall indemnify [Name] for the full replacement value of [number/currency] if they are lost and [number/currency] if they are damaged.

L.157
Where for any reason the [Programme/Film] is not completed and/or the [DVD/Disc] is not produced and/or is withdrawn from the market. The [Distributor] shall not be liable to [Name] for any sum for damage to reputation, loss of publicity and/or any other reason and shall only be liable for the sums due in clause [–].

L.158
The total aggregate liability of each of the parties under this agreement shall end on [date] and shall be limited as follows:

1.1 The [Licensor] to the [Distributor] shall be limited to [number/currency].

1.2 The [Distributor] to the [Licensor] shall be limited to [number/currency].

L.159
The [Licensee] agrees and undertakes to the [Licensor] that the [Licensee] shall be responsible and held liable for all the acts, errors, omissions and/ or failures of any sub-licensees, sub-agents, distributors and/or any other third parties engaged by the [Licensee] pursuant to this agreement. That the [Licensee] shall be obliged to pay any sums due to the [Licensor] which should have been paid from sums received from such third parties.

L.160

1.1 The [Distributor] agrees and undertakes that [Name] as a contributor shall not be liable and/or asked to contribute to any sums which may arise and/or be incurred by the [Distributor] and/or any other associated third party either during the Term of this Agreement and/ or thereafter whether losses, damages, legal costs and expenses, loss of revenue, loss of reputation and goodwill and/or sums due for copyright clearance and other royalty payments and/or for any other matter in respect of the [Film/Sound Recording] for the [DVD/ Disc/Series].

1.2 The [Distributor] agrees and undertakes that 1.1 shall apply even if the subsequent behaviour, acts and/or omissions of [Name] result in publicity which affects the marketing and sales of the [DVD/Disc/ Series] and/or causes the [Distributor] to cancel, delay and withdraw the proposed [DVD/Disc/Series].

1.3 The [Distributor] agrees and undertakes that provided that [Name] completes the scheduled work for the [Film/Sound Recording] that regardless of the circumstances which may arise in the future that the [Distributor] shall have no grounds to seek repayment of any fees and/ or expenses from [Name].

L.161
The [Licensee] agrees that in the event that the [Licensee] does not exploit and sell more than [number] copies of the [DVDs/Unit/Films] before [date]. The [Licensor] shall have the right to serve written notice to the [Licensee] to terminate this agreement with [number] months' written notice. In the event of termination in this manner the [Licensor] shall not be liable for any

reproduction and development costs, marketing and promotional expenses, losses and/or payments associated with the [Licensee] and/or any third parties and/or any other sums which the [Licensee] may have to pay and/or already have incurred. The [Licensor] shall not be obliged to to repay to the [Licensee] any advance payments against royalties which have not been recouped by the [Licensee].

L.162

Where the date of release and/or launch of any [DVD/Unit/Series] is delayed for any reason. The [Licensee] shall not be liable to the [Licensor] for any loss of royalties for that period.

L.163

1.1 The [Company] reserves the right at its absolute discretion to edit, delete, vary change and/or cancel any promotion, advertisement and/or product placement which in the opinion of the [Company] is unsuitable for the audience and/or is in breach of any code and/or policy guidelines issued by any government body and/or regulatory authority in any country in which it is intended to broadcast, transmit and/or convey in any format by any means.

1.2 The [Promoter/Advertiser] accept the terms in 1.1 and shall not make any claim against the [Company]. The [Promoter/Advertiser] accepts that it was notified of the requirements of the [Company] and all the codes and guidelines as at [date]. The [Promoter/Advertiser] accepts that the total liability of the [Company] shall be limited to the cost of the charges for any promotion, advertisement and/or product placement.

L.164

The [Company] shall not be liable for any failure to transmit all and/or any part of the [Advertisement/Film/Sound Recordings] on [specify channel] for any reason where the omission is due to programme schedule changes, force majeure and/or technical problems. The [Company] shall offer the [Promoter] another date and time to transmit the [Advertisement/Film/Sound Recording] to remedy the problem. There shall be no right to compensation of any nature.

L.165

Any booking may be cancelled by either party without liability provided that notice in writing is received and acknowledged by the [Company] and/or the [Advertiser] as the case may be more than [number] full working days ending at [time] before the agreed booked transmission date.

L.166
Any person seeking to follow this [workout/exercise sequence/dance] in the [Film/Podcast/Video] is strongly advised to seek medical advice before trying to do so. You must wear suitable clothes and footwear and make sure that the space in which you will be exercising is suitable and poses no hazards. You must take care and only copy, perform and/or carry out such physical exercises and/or movements in accordance with the advice, information and directions provided. No liability is accepted for any personal injury which may arise and you must carry out any actions at your own risk.

L.167
The [Licensee] shall be liable for all sums due to the [Licensor] for all obligations, acts, errors, omissions, defaults and/or failure to make payments and/or to account by the [Licensee] and/or any authorised sub-licensees, sub-agents and any other third parties engaged by the [Licensee] pursuant to this agreement.

L.168
In addition to any sums due under the agreement the [Licensee] shall pay for all the [Licensor's] legal and professional costs for auditing and accounting; master material reproduction costs and delivery charges, mobile, meeting and internet charges, travel, accommodation and translation charges. Provided that sufficient proof of expenditure can be supplied.

L.169

1.1 The [Distributor] shall bear all liability and be responsible for any medical and legal costs and expenses, financial losses relating to current and/or future work, mental incapacity and/or distress, disability, personal injury or otherwise of any nature that [Name] may incur as a direct result of his/her contribution and filming for [Film/Series] in the capacity of [sport/activity] and/or any other payments due to the estate and beneficiaries of [Name] for his/her death which arises as a direct result of his/her participation in the [Film/Series].

1.2 The [Distributor] and [Name] agree that although an insurance policy is being arranged with [specify] for [cover] for [currency/number] from [date] to [date] at the [Distributor's] cost. That any exclusions within that policy shall not apply to the liability of the [Distributor] under 1.1.

L.170
The [Licensee] shall be liable for all payments due and/or that may arise related to obtaining clearance of any copyright and/or intellectual property rights and/or any domain name, trade mark, computer software, location and/or otherwise related to the reproduction, broadcast, transmission,

performance and exploitation of all the [Series] and/or any sound recording, lyrics, music, footage, stills and/or other material and to collecting society, person and/or company and/or any adaptation, translation and/or other form of exploitation in any format at any time. The [Licensee] shall not be entitled to recoup and/or set-off any of these payments from the sums due to the [Licensor].

L.171

The [Company] agrees that [Name] may take images and film the [Event] on [date] at [location] provided that [Name] agrees that no liability is accepted by the [Company] for any costs, expenses, damages and/or loss that may arise either directly and/or indirectly to [Name] and/or any transport, computer, photography and film equipment and/or otherwise unless caused by the negligence of the [Company] and results in personal injury which causes permanent damage and/or death. In any event [Name] agrees that the total liability of the [Company] is limited for all other matters to [currency/number].

General Business and Commercial

L.172

The [Employer] shall not be liable to the [Employee] or to his/her personal representatives for:

1.1 Any loss or damage whatsoever caused to the [Employee] and/or his/her property sustained at or whilst in transit to and/or from where the [Employee] provides his/her services except to such extent as the [Employee] is able to enforce a claim under the insurance policies held by the [Employer] for the benefit of the employees.

1.2 This shall not apply to personal injury or death caused by the negligence or deliberate default of the [Company] and/or any agent acting on behalf of the [Company].

L.173

The [Company] agrees and undertakes that it shall be liable to the [Employee] for all direct and indirect damages, losses, costs, expenses, injury, anguish, distress and any other identifiable and recognised condition and/or compensation that may arise out of this agreement to the [Employee] in [country] during the existence of this agreement and thereafter until [date].

L.174

The [Company] shall ensure that there is a suitable insurance policy arranged and that the premiums are up to date to cover any personal injury, damages, losses, costs and/or expenses due to [Name] and/or medical, dental and/or mental health treatment which may be required which may arise as a direct and/or indirect result of the performance of the terms of this agreement by [Name].

L.175

The [Employee] shall follow all reasonable directions, instructions, guidelines and policies and undertakes to complete any records that may be required by the [Employer] which are in place in order to comply with existing and/or future health and safety legislation and/or any other legal requirements. Failure to do so may result in the [Employee] being in breach of this contract. Where the [Employee] acts recklessly and without regard to the safety of others then the [Employer] shall not be liable to the [Employee] for any personal injury, emotional distress, damage, loss, costs and/or expenses that may arise unless caused by the negligence of the [Employer].

L.176

The [Company] agrees and undertakes that [Name] shall not at any time be held liable by the [Company] for any sums that may fall due and/or be lost and/or be incurred as a result of the work of [Name] at the [Company].

L.177

1.1   [Name] agrees that where he/she uses the facilities and services of the [Company] and/or orders and/or commits the [Company] for a matter which is for his/her own personal use and not connected to their work and/or for the benefit of the [Company]. That the [Company] may seek to charge [Name] for such sums and [Name] will be obliged to pay.

1.2   The [Company] agrees that provided payment is made in 1.1 the [Company] shall not be entitled to use these grounds to terminate the contract of employment with [Name].

L.178

The [Company] agrees to repair and/or pay the cost of any damage to the [premises/site] known as: [name/address] which arises directly out of the [Company's] occupation and use from [date] to [date] which is caused as a direct result of negligence on the part of the [Company] and/or any authorised third party which is not due to normal wear and tear.

L.179

In the event that there is any change in venue, cancellation of the [Exhibition/Event], error and/or omission in any marketing material of any nature and/or alteration in the allocation of the [Space/Stand] at the [Exhibition/Event] and/or in the quoted opening times to any [exhibitor/attendee].In any such circumstances it is specifically agreed that the [Company] shall not be liable for any costs, expenses, losses and/or damages which may arise as a result whether direct and/or indirect for any reason. Each [exhibitor/ attendee] agrees to accept this risk and to be liable for all such sums. In such cases the [Company] will endeavour without prejudice to make a substitute arrangement, but shall not be bound or obligated to do so. The [Company] is also specifically entitled to change the position of the [Space/ Stand] allocated to any [exhibitor/attendee] should circumstances require that it is necessary. The [Company] shall also have the right prior to the date of the opening of the [Exhibition/Event] to cancel this agreement with the [exhibitor/attendee] without stating any reason provided that it repays all sums paid.

L.180

The total liability of [Name] for the use and hire of the premises at [location] shall be limited to [number/currency]. The [Company] agrees that any additional losses, damages and/or sums due to the [Company] which may arise from the actions and/or behaviour of [Name], any guests and/or any other person and/or third party at the [Event] shall be paid for by a claim against the insurance policy for which the premiums have been paid for by [Name]. Where any sums cannot be claimed including any excess then the [Company] may not seek to be reimbursed by [Name].

L.181

The [Supplier] undertakes to carry out its services with all reasonable care in the performance of this agreement. The [Supplier] shall not be liable for any loss and/or damage suffered by [Name] and/or any third party arising from use and/or reproduction of any [Artwork/Images/Sound Recordings] by the [Supplier]. [Name] accepts that the material is fragile and already has damage which was incurred prior to delivery to the [Supplier]. [Name] accepts that the [Artwork/Images/Sound Recordings] may suffer additional damage and accepts that the [Supplier] shall not be liable.

L.182

The [Company] reserves the right at its absolute discretion to refuse at any stage to carry out and/or perform this agreement without giving any reason. The [Agent] and/or the [Client] shall not have the right to any legal action and/or claim against the [Company] provided that all sums paid are refunded promptly.

L.183

1.1   The total liability of the [Licensor] to the [Distributor] shall be limited to [number/currency]. All liability to the [Distributor] shall end on [date] and all claims must be notified by the [Distributor] by [date].

1.2   The total liability of the [Distributor] shall be limited to [number/currency] for each year of the agreement and a total liability of [number/currency]. All liability to the [Licensor] shall end on [date] and all claims must be notified by [date].

L.184
The lists and other materials delivered to the [Licensee] under this agreement shall be complete and accurate. The [Licensee] shall not be liable for any actions or claims by any third party provided that the [Licensee] has used the lists and materials in the manner and detail in which they have been authorised.

L.185
The [Company] shall not be liable and shall be deemed not to have breached any condition of this contract if the [Company] is prevented or materially hindered from carrying out any obligation by reason of any unavoidable cause whatsoever. In such event the [Company] shall be under no liability to the [Client] and the [Client] shall not be entitled to any refund of the charges paid where part of the work has been carried out and/or compensation for damages, loss of business and/or otherwise.

L.186
The [Company] shall not be responsible and/or liable for any losses or damages of any nature whether direct or indirect including any loss of profits or any consequential damages, costs and expenses suffered and/or incurred by the [Exhibitor] for whatever reason. In the event that the [Exhibitor] is prevented from attending and/or exhibiting at the [Exhibition] because the [Company] cancels the reservation made by the [Exhibitor] without good reason at any time. Then the [Exhibitor] shall be entitled to a full refund of all sums paid to the [Company] for the reservation. The [Exhibitor] agrees that it shall not be entitled to claim any additional sums by way of compensation or otherwise.

L.187
At all times the [Company] shall exercise great care and take the highest level of precautions as may be required under any health and safety legislation and/or guidelines in [country]. The [Company] shall remain strictly liable to the [Enterprise] in respect of the services of the [Company] at all times. The [Company] accepts that it owes a high level of duty of care to the [Enterprise] and any employees, consultants and/or other third parties and the public to take all necessary precautions particularly when carrying out work which involves hazardous, dangerous, toxic, inflammable, explosive and/or radioactive materials and/or using any other material and/or carrying out any other activities which could potentially cause personal injury and/or death.

L.188

The [Company] acknowledges that the [Products/Work/Services] are still in development and that [Name] does not make any representation, warranty or undertaking whatsoever express or implied with respect to the purpose, functionality and/or health and safety compliance and/or product and/or other liability in respect of the [Products/Work/Services]. [Name] expressly excludes any warranties or conditions of merchantability or suitability for a particular purpose. [Name] shall not be liable for any damages, losses, costs or expenses which may arise whether as a direct and/or indirect consequence of any kind of this agreement. The [Company] accepts that [Name] has provided no undertakings, warranties and/or otherwise and that the [Products/Work/Services] are a prototype and not suitable for sale and/or supply to the public and has not been fully tested. The [Company] agrees that [Name] shall not have any liability to the [Company] for any reason and the [Company] undertakes not to seek to make any claim. The [Company] accepts all responsibility and liability regarding their use and/or exploitation of the [Products/Work/Services] regarding any claim for personal injury and/or death from [date].

L.189

The [Company] shall not be liable to [Name] for any costs, expenses, loss of fees and/or other sums and/or damage to his/her property and/or for any personal injury, illness and/or death suffered by him/her in connection with or arising out of this agreement except where any such sums, personal injury and/or death is directly caused by the actions, conduct, negligence and/or failure of the [Company] and/or any third party engaged by the [Company] and/or [Name] was carrying out his/her duties under the direction of the [Company] and/or any other authorised third party.

L.190

The Company shall not be under any liability to [Name/Brand Company] in respect of any claim for loss of publicity and/or opportunity to enhance the reputation of [Name/Brand Company] and/or loss of profit at any time and/or any other loss, damage and/or cost and/or expense for the failure to display, transmit and/or use the [Product/Image/Logo/Trade Mark] in any feature article, blog, campaign and/or other matter agreed with the [Name/Brand Company] for any reason. [Name/Brand Company] shall be obliged to accept an alternative proposal to be scheduled and shall not be entitled to any compensation.

L.191

The [Company] shall not be under any liability in respect of any loss or damage to the [Agent's] property whilst it is in transit to and/or from and/or whilst at other locations controlled by third parties and/or stored and/or used on the premises of the [Company]. The [Company] shall not be responsible and/or liable for any personal injury and/or death caused to the [Agent] by the negligence of a third party in a location not owned and/or controlled by the [Company]. The [Agent] shall at all times be covered by the insurance policy: [reference] which covers: [specify detail] from [date] to [date]. The [Agent] shall notify the [Company] of any claim directly under such policy and the [Company] shall process the application.

L.192
Any failure to renew or extend the duration of this agreement by the {Company] before and/or after its expiry shall not constitute grounds for any claim and/or other payments whatsoever. The [Agent] agrees that it shall not be entitled to any sums.

L.193

1.1   [Name] confirms and agrees that the [Company] is only able to provide the [Service] at the fee set out in this agreement on the basis that the [Company] is under no liability whatsoever to [Name].

1.2   [Name] agrees that the [Company] is under no liability to him/her whatsoever for any indirect, incidental and/or consequential damages and/or losses, costs and expenses whether by the [Customer] and/or by a third party in respect of any interruptions, delays, inaccuracies, errors, omissions or failures at any time in respect of the [Service].

1.3   The terms of this clause shall survive any termination of this agreement and shall continue in full force and effect until [date].

1.4   This clause shall not exclude personal injury and/or death directly caused as a result of the negligence, actions and conduct of the [Company] and/or any authorised persons and/or entity acting under the directions of and/or engaged by the [Company].

L.194
The liability of the [Company] shall be limited to [number/currency] in any one claim due to loss and/or damage and/or some other reason. The [Client] agrees that any additional sums that may fall due are to be waived and are not recoverable unless related to personal injury and/or death.

L.195
The total liability of the [Supplier] to the [Retailer/Distributor] shall be limited to the stated value of each Purchase Order up to a maximum of no more than [number/currency] except in respect of any claim related to personal injury and/or death caused by the negligence, default and/or conduct of the [Supplier] and/or any third party engaged by them.

L.196

1.1 The liability of the [Company] shall be limited to [number/currency] in respect of each and every claim. The total aggregate liability for the duration of this agreement or thereafter shall be limited to [number/currency].

1.2 All other sums are waived and cannot be claimed except those which directly relate to personal injury and/or death where the [Company] is held by a coroner, in civil proceedings and/or other institution and/or by a police investigation and criminal proceedings, to be liable.

L.197

1.1 The total liability of the [Company] to the [Customer/Retailer/Distributor] shall be limited to the [contract price/sale price/percentage of fixed sum].

1.2 It is accepted that any claim for personal injury and/or death cannot be excluded.

L.198
If for any reason the [Company] reaches the decision that any person and/or property is likely to and/or has caused any direct and/or indirect costs, expenses, damages and/or losses and/or interfered with the operation of any service and/or facility and/or access to any part of the [venue/land/location] and/or has acted in a manner which is to the detriment of other people at the [Event/Festival].Then the [Company] shall be entitled to exclude such person and/or property from the [venue/land/location]. In such circumstances the [Company] shall not be liable for any subsequent sums that the person may have to incur and/or their failure to attend the [Event/Festival].

L.199
If the [Company] terminates this agreement due to the failure of [Name/Enterprise] to fulfil the terms as set out in clause [–]. Then [Name/Enterprise] agrees that the [Company] shall not be liable for any related and/or associated agreements that [Name/Enterprise] may have agreed and/or concluded in reliance upon this agreement

L.200

1.1 The liability of the [Company] shall be limited to [number/currency] in the event that it shall be obliged to delay and/or cancel and/or alter the content of the programme material, location, dates and/or other matters for the [Exhibition/Conference]. No additional sums shall be paid for any travel, accommodation and/or other costs that any exhibitor, attendee and/or other third party may have booked and/ or incurred which relate to attendance at and/or participation in the [Exhibition/Conference].

1.2 The [Company] shall offer a full refund of the fees paid to date and/or that the booking be confirmed for the [Exhibition/Conference] as now stated.

Internet, Websites and Apps

L.201

[Name] agrees and undertakes to waive all claims and rights and agrees that the [Company] shall not be liable to [Name] [and/or any third party] for [Name's] access to and/or the use of any content on the [Website/App/ Download] and/or for any disc, software, updates, instructions, advice, messages, emails, guidance, information, data, links, banners, and/or any products and/or services advertised and/or promoted by the [Company] and/or a third party and/or any competitions, premium rate or other mobile charges and costs which [Name] may decide to incur and/or any viruses, junk emails and/or scams and/or damage to equipment and/or other personal property and/or any destruction of stored material and/or images and/or sound recordings and/or any loss of profit and/or other financial and/ or businesses losses, damage to reputation and/or goodwill, endorsements, sponsors or otherwise incurred by and/or caused to [Name]. There is no exclusion for personal injury and/or death which is the direct responsibility and liability of the [Company] and caused by their material, advice and/or instructions. No liability is accepted where any person has acted outside the scope of the authorised use. In the event that it is decided by a court of law that any part of this clause cannot be permitted to waiver liability then the liability of the [Company] in total shall be [number/currency] excluding personal injury and/or death.

L.202

The total liability of the [Company] to the [Customer] shall be limited to the [subscription price/sale price] of the [Product/Service] excluding personal injury and/or death which is directly attributable and proved to be caused by the [Product/Service] supplied by the [Company].

L.203

Neither the [Company] who own the [Website/App/Platform/Download/ Game] nor any investors, shareholders and/or personnel and/or any service providers and/or any other associated businesses and/or advertisers and/or sponsors accept any liability for any direct, indirect and/or consequential loss of business, reputation, financial losses, expected business developments, damages, loss of profit and/or contracts and/or any other costs and expenses from any use, licensing, reproduction and/or exploitation of this [Website/App/Platform/Download/Game]. This clause shall not apply to any personal injury and/or death directly caused by the negligence of the [Company] and recoverable on that ground under any legislation and/or any legal duty of care in law in any country.

L.204

The [Company] shall not be responsible for any liability, allegations, claims, fines, costs, expenses and/or any other sums that may arise as a direct and/or indirect result of the access to and/or display of the [Banner Advert/Material] on the [Website/App/Platform].

L.205

No liability can be accepted by the [Company] which provides the [Service] on the premium rate line for any line rental costs and/or any other additional charges that may be imposed by a third party for the use of and/or access to the [Service]. All such sums are the responsibility of the person who uses the [Service] and not the [Company]. Where the person accesses the [Service], but it is interrupted, suspended and/or otherwise fails to operate properly then a fee may still be charged. No refunds are available unless no service is provided for more than [number] days in which case the following email address should be contacted to request a pro rata refund for that period: [specify].

L.206

The [Company] does not accept any responsibility and/or liability for any legal and/or other consequences which may arise directly and/or indirectly as a result of the use of this [Website/App/Podcast] and/or any data, text, images, films, sound recordings, downloads and/or other material.

L.207

It is a condition of access to this [Website/App/Podcast] that the total liability of the [Company] to any person who views, enters, relies upon and/or uses this [Website/App/Podcast] shall be [number/currency] in total for all claims from that person except for any matters including personal injury and/or death which cannot be excluded under any legislation in any country.

L.208

It is a condition which you must accept that the [Company] shall have the right to block your access to the [Website/App/Forum] and/or to cancel your account and/or to edit, delete and/or amend any material in any medium and/or format you may have submitted and/or reproduced whether text, film, images and/or otherwise. If you do not accept that the [Company] shall not be under liability to you for such actions then please do not open an account and/or use any part of this [Website/App/Forum].

L.209

1.1 Where any images, photographs, text, logos, data, information, music, lyrics, films and/or sound recordings are displayed, posted, distributed, edited and/or adapted on the [Website] and/or [Blog] and/or [App] by any third party.

1.2 The [Company] reserves the right to take such actions as may be necessary to minimise the liability of the [Company] from any adverse publicity, legal proceedings and/or allegations of any nature including association with criminal activity, copyright infringement and/or defamation.

1.3 The [Company] shall hold the person and/or company who sent the material to the [Website] and/or [Blog] and/or [App] and/or who held the account with the [Company] liable for all sums including legal costs and expenses that the [Company] be obliged to incur both in house and through an external law firm and/or other professional publicity and marketing advisors in order to defend, resolve and/or settle the matter.

L.210

1.1 The [Company] agrees that it shall not hold [Name] liable for any reason at any time for any claim, action and/or allegation and/or cost and/or expenses that may arise either directly and/or indirectly as a result of the assignment by [Name] of the [Images/Photographs/Logos/Slogans] to the [Company] and/or for use by the [Company] on its website, app and/or in any promotional material and/or in any other manner and/or form.

1.2 The [Company] agrees and accepts that [Name] has provided no assurance and/or undertaking as to originality and has followed the instructions and directions of the [Company] in respect of the development and creation and reproduction of the [Images/Photographs/Logos/Slogans].

1.3 The [Company] accepts and agrees that it is the responsibility and liability of the [Company] to assess whether there is any similar material and/or conflict with any existing trade mark use in the market in any country and/or whether the material is capable of being registered as a trade mark. The [Company] agrees that [Name] shall not bear any liability and/or responsibility for any sums that may become due as a result of any litigation and/or legal proceedings.

1.4 That if at any future date the [Company] requires the assistance and co-operation of [Name] that the [Company] shall agree payment terms for any such work.

L.211

1.1 The [Contributor] to the [Podcast/Video/Film] shall not have any right to insist that the [Company/Name] take any legal action against a third party for any reason.

1.2 Where a third party makes an allegation against the [Company/Name] regarding the product of the services of the [Contributor] in the [Podcast/Video/Film]. The [Company] shall not be obliged to consult with the [Contributor] at any time and may defend, settle and/or otherwise deal with any allegation and/or claim as it may decide is in the best interests of the [Company/Name] at any time.

L.212

There is no obligation by the [Company] to update the [App/Software] and [Name] is obliged to purchase any new material. The [Company] does not accept any liability to [Name] for any data, information and/or records which [Name] may store on the [App/Software]. [Name] is at all times advised to make a backup record. Where any data, records and/or other material is deleted, corrupted and/or destroyed and/or otherwise unusable the [Company] shall not be liable to [Name]. Any liability shall be limited to the purchase price of the [App/Software]

L.213

1.1 The payment of the monthly subscription to the [Service] permits access to the audio files for the following period of [one] month.

1.2 Access permits you to listen to and play the audio files from the [Service] on [specify equipment]. Any audio file that have been stored must be deleted at the end of each month and there is no right to store the audio files and/or to supply them to a third party.

1.3 The [Supplier] is only liable for the [Service] and is not liable for your access and/or use of any equipment to listen to and/or play the audio files. The total liability of the [Supplier] shall be limited to the fee paid in advance each month for the [Service]. No additional sums shall be due for any reason. If the [Service] is interrupted, delayed, of poor technical quality and/or any other reason there shall be no right to claim compensation. Any claim shall be limited to the monthly fees and a pro rata adjustment of the cost.

Merchandising and Distribution

L.214

The [Distributor] agrees to arrange and pay for insurance cover for: [specify type of cover] for the [Stock/Material/Products] whilst it is in the possession of [Name] from [date] to [date] for the value of [number/currency] per claim in [country] for any sum in excess of [number/currency].

L.215
The [Distributor] shall be liable for any destruction, misuse, losses, damages, costs and/or expenses which relate to the loan of the [Master Material] by the [Licensor] from the date of delivery to the [Distributor] until the [Master Material] is returned to the [Licensor]. The total insurance replacement value shall be in accordance with Schedule A which sets out the details of the material and the sums to be paid. All sums due shall be paid within [number] days of a notified claim unless written reasons have been provided for rejection of the claim. Where there is any dispute between the parties regarding any claim they agree to endeavour to resolve the matter by negotiation of a settlement prior to any legal proceedings being issued.

L.216
The [Distributor] shall not be held liable for the acts, errors, omissions and/or failures of any sub-licensees, sub-agents, sub-distributors and/or any other third parties engaged by the [Distributor] pursuant to this agreement. Nor shall the [Distributor] shall be obliged to pay any sums due to the [Licensor] which should have been paid by such third parties which are not received by the [Distributor].

L.217
The total liability of the [Licensor] to the [Distributor] under this agreement shall be limited to [number/currency] for any breach and/or default and/or otherwise of this agreement. No further sums shall be due for any reason.

L.218
The [Licensee] agrees that where any sums are not received from any third party including but limited to any sub-licensee, agent, distributor and/or otherwise in respect of the exploitation of the rights granted under this agreement and/or any other related matter. That the [Licensee] shall be held responsible for the defaults, failures, non-payment and/or actions of any such third parties. That where sums have not been paid to the [Licensor] due to such third parties the [Licensee] agrees and undertakes to account and pay all sums owed to the [Licensor] at the [Licensee's] cost. Any such payments shall not be recouped by the [Licensee] under this agreement.

L.219
The [Agent] agrees that he/she shall be held liable for any losses, damages, interest, royalties, advances, sponsorship, fees, costs and expenses and/or other sums which [Name] may have failed to be paid and/or which [Name] has suffered and/or incurred which are attributed to the negligence, errors,

omissions, failures, defaults and/or fraudulent conduct by the [Agent] and/or any of its accountants, banks, legal and/or professional advisors and/or any other employees, consultant and/or person associated with the [Agent].

L.220

1.1 The [Distributor] must ensure that it has sufficient funds available held in [country] in order to meet the payments and liabilities due to [Name] under this agreement.

1.2 Where the parent company of the [Distributor] changes its location and is based outside [country] then the [Distributor] agrees and undertakes to open a bank account for the deposit of a minimum of [number/currency] in [country] in the name of: [specify].

1.3 That the [Distributor] agrees and undertakes that where a sub-licensee fails to make the necessary payments to the [Distributor] and/or [Name] as may be the case then the [Distributor] shall be obliged to pay any such outstanding sums to [Name] which the sub-licensee was due to pay together with interest.

1.4 That the [Distributor] agrees that no currency conversion and/or bank charges for the transfer of any funds in any form shall be paid by [Name] and the [Distributor] shall pay any such costs.

L.221
The [Licensor] agrees that the [Licensee] shall be entitled to take any legal action it thinks fit against a third party in respect of the rights granted to the [Licensee] under this agreement. Provided that the [Licensee] agrees that the [Licensor] shall not be liable to contribute to any legal costs and expenses.

L.222
[Name] is the originator of the concept and idea for the [Format/Quiz/Game] which has been [licensed/assigned] to the [Distributor]. The [Distributor] agrees to accept all liability for any legal proceedings, claims and/or allegations, damages, losses, threat of copyright and/or trade mark infringement, defamation and/or any other matter and all related legal costs and expenses which may arise in respect of the development, production, distribution, licensing and/or exploitation of the [Format/Quiz/Game] by the [Distribution Company] at any time.

Publishing

L.223
The [Author] acknowledges that the [Publishers] are not insurers of the [Book/Manuscript/Drawings/Photographs] placed in their possession by the

[Author] and shall not be liable for any damage, destruction or loss thereof [unless caused by the negligence of an employee or agent of the Publisher].

L.224
The [Publisher] agrees that it shall be solely responsible for the security and safe keeping of the [Manuscript/Images/Sound Recordings] once it has been delivered by the [Author]. The [Publisher] shall be liable to the [Author] and/or any other third party for any loss of royalties, damages, losses, failures, breaches, defects and/or other errors which arise in respect of the reproduction, distribution, licensing, sale, merchandising and other exploitation in any format by any method in whole and/or part. The total liability of the [Publisher] to the [Author] and/or his/her agent under this clause shall be limited to [number/currency] in total. This figure shall not include the advance to the [Author].

L.225
The [Publisher] shall be totally responsible for the safekeeping of the [Manuscript/Archive Material/Stills] once it is delivered and accepted by the [Publisher/Distributor]. The [Publisher/Distributor] agrees that it shall ensure that the [Manuscript/Archive Material/Stills] are not deleted, destroyed, damaged, lost and/or released and/or supplied to any third party unless authorised under the terms of this agreement. The [Publisher/Distributor] shall be liable for any matters that may arise which affect the material whether direct or indirect and may cause the [Author] to suffer any type of foreseeable loss whether loss of revenue and sales, interest, enhancement of reputation, loss of film, option and merchandising agreements and/or otherwise until [date].

L.226
The [Publisher] shall bear all liability for any losses, damages, costs and expenses directly arising from any matter in relation to the manuscript and any associated material of the [Work] once it has been delivered in whole or in part. The maximum sum payable in any one instance to the [Author] which relates to any claim shall be [number/currency] and in aggregate total over the period of the agreement limited to [number/currency].

L.227
The [Company] agrees that it shall be liable to the [Author] for all acts, omissions, errors, losses and/or damages, loss of revenue and/or any other matter directly arising from and attributable to any subsidiary, affiliate, associated, parent, agent, licensee and/or distributors and/or any other third party engaged and/or authorised by the [Company] in any country at any time.

L.228

The [Licensor] agrees that the [Manuscript/Sound Recordings/Images] have been considered and reviewed by its own legal advisors prior to publication, sale and distribution to the public in [specify format] by the [Licensee]. The [Licensee] must however take its own legal advice from experts as to the potential legal problems that may arise and no such responsibility is accepted by the [Licensor]. The [Licensor] is not liable for any sums which may fall due to any third party arising from any legal, action, claim, threat, settlement and/or otherwise by any third party against the [Licensee] from the publication, sale and/or distribution of the [Manuscript/Sound Recordings/Images] reproduced in the [specify format] and any related cover, marketing and/or products and/or services. The [Licensee] agrees that it must seek its own independent legal advice and shall bear all costs, expenses, compensation and damages that may be claimed by any third party against the [Licensee].

L.229

The total liability of the [Author] under this agreement shall be limited to [number/currency]. The liability of the [Author] under this agreement to the [Publisher] shall end on [date] and after that date no further sums shall be paid by the [Author] except in respect of already notified outstanding claims and disputes.

L.230

The total liability of the [Author] shall be limited to [number/currency] under the terms of this agreement. In the event that any claim and/or allegation and/or legal action is instigated by the [Publisher] and/or any third party for any reason, any sum due to be paid by the [Author] for any reason shall not exceed this sum.

L.231

The [Distributor] agrees that it shall be liable for any sums that may be incurred and/or be due in respect of the reproduction, supply, development, promotion, marketing, licensing, distribution and exploitation of the [Work] including; developing and commissioning new material, website, app and logo designs, travel and freight and exhibition costs and any other sums. That no such sums shall be deducted from the payments due to the [Author] for any reason and all such costs and expenses shall be paid for solely by the [Distributor].

L.232

The [Author] agrees and undertakes:

1.1 not to maliciously and/or recklessly include any material which is wrong, offensive, inaccurate and/or defamatory of any person.

1.2   not to make reference to any incident and/or information which cannot be verified by an affidavit from a person who was a direct witness in the matter and who would be prepared to attend any court of law to verify the facts.

1.3   not to rely on any third party resource and/or data and/or information without a proper credit and acknowledgement.

1.4   not to use the [Article/Work/Blog] as a personal attack on a political party and/or an individual with whose lifestyle the [Author] disagrees and/or for any other reason raise issues which are unrelated to the agreed synopsis between the parties.

Services

L.233
The [Company] shall be fully liable to the [Celebrity] for all acts, statements, omissions, failures, damages and losses, damage to career prospects, damage to reputation caused by and/or attributable to the [Company] and/or any third party engaged, contracted or authorised by the [Company] during the Term of this Agreement and/or thereafter until [date] relating to the services of the [Celebrity] under this agreement and/or any material created in pursuance of the agreement.

L.234
The [Company] shall be liable to the [Agent] and [Name] for any consequences which may arise directly as a result of the actions, omissions, errors, defaults and/or breaches of this agreement and/or any associated document by the [Company] and/or any consultant, agent, sub-licensee and/or other third parties that the [Company] may use for the purposes of its business which directly affect and cause losses and/or damages to and/or or harm the reputation of the [Agent] and/or [Name] during the existence of this agreement until [date].

L.235
The [Company] shall not be liable to the [Agent] and/or [Name] for any indirect consequence that may arise as a result of the breach and/or alleged breach of this agreement by the [Company] and/or any authorised third party. No liability is excluded for death and injury due to negligence and recoverable on that ground.

L.236
The [Name] understands that the [Company] shall not be obliged to use, keep or exploit any of the material created under this agreement nor shall it be obliged to provide a credit or acknowledgment to [Name].

L.237

In consideration of the [Work/Interview/Blog] by the [Contributor] the [Company] shall pay a fee of [number/currency] by [date] in [method of payment] to the [Contributor] which shall be in full and final settlement. No further sums of any nature for any reason shall be due to the [Contributor] for the provision of his/her services or the exploitation of the material in any media at any time. Nor shall any additional sums be due to the [Contributor] for any reason for any failure to provide a credit and no consent shall be required to add, delete, amend, translate, adapt and/or otherwise alter all and/or any part of the [Work/Interview/Blog] in any context at any time.

L.238

1.1 The [Company] agrees that the [Presenter] shall only be liable for any direct breach of the undertakings in this agreement in clause [–] from [date] to [date] in [country] and the total liability of the [Presenter] to the [Company] shall be limited to [number/currency] at any time.

1.2 In the event that there is no claim by the [Company] before [date] then any liability by the [Presenter] under this agreement shall end and no sums shall be due and/or claimed by the [Company] whether caused by the [Presenter] or not.

L.239

The [Company] agrees and accepts that it shall be entirely responsible for the legal consequences and liabilities that may arise in respect of the production, transmission, content, marketing and exploitation of the [Series/Images/Recordings] and any other associated material. That where any claim, action, demand or complaint results in the [Presenter] incurring any costs, expenses, damages, losses or other sums of any nature including legal, accountant, agent or otherwise. The [Company] shall reimburse the [Presenter] and also agree an additional sum in compensation for the [Presenter's] assistance in each case.

L.240

[Name] is not providing any indemnity to the [Company] under this agreement and the [Company] shall not seek any sums from the [Name] for any consequence arising directly or indirectly as a result of this agreement, whether the matter arises from a breach by [Name] or not. All liability, risk, costs, damages and expenses are the entire and sole responsibility of the [Company] at all times and not [Name].

L.241

The [Company] accepts that it shall not be entitled to seek any sums from [Name] in respect of this agreement provided that he/she performs his/her services by [date] as set out in section A. All responsibility for any legal liability and/or legal actions and/or defences which may arise from the use of any material provided by [Name] collected, under this agreement and in the product of his/her services shall be at the sole cost, risk and expense of the [Company]. The [Company] shall not seek to reclaim any sums from [Name] and/or make any deductions and/or seek to be indemnified for any reason even where it is shown on the basis of legal advice that [Name] acted in a manner which was wrong for any reason.

L.242
No liability shall be attributed to [Name] in the event that there is an error, omission or other inaccuracy and/or any allegation, claim, legal proceedings, complaint and/or objection in respect of the content, clearance and/or any intellectual property rights and/or any other rights, obligations or otherwise in any media of any nature in respect of the development, production, transmission, distribution, supply, licensing and/or exploitation of the [Work/Service] in any country at any time.

L.243
Where for any reason the [Supplier] has to vary, cease and/or interrupt the [Service] provided to the [Company] due to a change in circumstances of the availability of material and/or facilities to the [Supplier]. The [Company] agrees that the [Supplier] shall not be liable for any losses, damages and expenses and costs that may arise and the [Company] accepts the risk and liability at its own cost provided the interruption is less than [number] [hours/days]. After that time the [Company] shall have the right to terminate the [Service] by written notice to the [Supplier] with immediate effect and to seek to replace the [Supplier] with a third party.

L.244
In the event that the service under this agreement is terminated by the [Supplier] and the [Company] is unable to arrange a suitable substitute at short notice and is therefore forced to cancel the [Event/Exhibition/Festival]. Then the [Supplier] shall be liable to pay for all the expenses and costs of all sums relating to and associated with the cancellation of that [Event/Exhibition/Festival] and rescheduling a new one including the cost of administration and advertising by the [Company] and third party agreements.

Sponsorship

L.245

1.1   The [Licensee] shall be liable to the [Licensor] for all acts, omissions, errors, failures and defaults with respect to the [Licensee] and/or any third party appointed by the [Licensee] in respect of the [Licensor's Logo] and the [Licensor's Product].

1.2   The [Licensor] agrees and undertakes that the details of the content and the materials of the [Licensor's Logo] and the [Licensor's Product] delivered to the [Licensee] shall be complete and accurate. The [Licensee] shall not be liable to the [Licensor] under 1.1 where they are used in any manner authorised by the [Licensor].

1.3   The [Licensee] is responsible for any material which is supplied under this agreement by the [Licensor] on loan and then lost, damaged or stolen while in the possession or control of the [Licensee] and/or any authorised third party.

L.246
The [Company] shall not be liable to [Name/Group] for any indirect losses, damages, expenses, costs and/or other sums that may arise from the cancellation of the [Event/Festival] and/or termination of this agreement and/or the failure to use the services and/or performances of [Name/Group] including but not limited to any loss of publicity, television and media coverage, the failure to enhance reputation and/or any other career opportunities that may not be made available as a result at any time.

L.247
The [Sponsor] agrees and undertakes that it shall arrange a comprehensive insurance policy to cover any damages, losses, legal costs, expenses and/or other sums which may be claimed, due, lost and/or arise directly and/or indirectly as a consequence of this agreement by the [Sponsor] and/or the [Athlete] and/or any third party including but not limited to loss of reputation, cancellation of any social media and/or advertising campaign, and/or damages caused to withdrawal of any product and/or services endorsed by the [Athlete]. All responsibility for any liability and/or legal actions, claims, threats, settlements and/or other proceedings which may arise from the use of any material obtained and/or provided under this agreement and in the product of the services shall be at the sole cost, risk and expense of the [Company].

L.248
The [Athlete] is not providing any indemnity to the [Sponsor] under this agreement and the [Sponsor] shall not seek any sums from the [Athlete] for any consequences arising directly and/or indirectly as a result of this agreement. All liability, risk, costs, damages and expenses are the sole responsibility of the [Sponsor] at all times and not [Athlete] whether the matter arises from a breach by [Athlete] or not. The only exception is for repayment of any sums due to the failure of the [Athlete] to carry out the agreed work.

L.249
The [Sponsor] shall be liable to the [Sportsperson] for all acts, statements, omissions, failures, damages and losses, damage to career prospects,

damage to reputation caused by and/or attributable to the [Sponsor] and/or any third party engaged, contracted or authorised by the [Sponsor] during the Term of this Agreement relating to the services of the [Sportsperson] under this agreement and/or any material created and/or distributed in pursuance of the agreement until [date].

L.250

1.1　The total liability of the [Company] under this agreement shall be limited to [number/currency]. The liability of the [Company] under this agreement to the [Sponsor] shall end on [date] and after that date no further sums shall be paid by the [Company] except in respect of existing notified claims.

1.2　The total liability of the [Sponsor] under this agreement shall be limited to [number/currency]. The liability of the [Sponsor] under this agreement to the [Company] shall end on [date] and after that date no further sums shall be paid by the [Sponsor] except in respect of existing notified claims.

L.251

The [Sponsor] shall not be held liable for any sums which may be due to the engagement of the performers, staff, security personnel and any other casual workers and/or volunteers arranged by the [Company] for the [Event].

L.252

1.1　The [Sponsor] agrees and undertakes that in the event that the [logo/ image/trade mark/slogan] and/or colour and/or layout and/or design of any material has to be changed and/or amended for any reason. That the [Sponsor] shall pay all the costs and expenses that the [Company] may be obliged to incur in advance to the [Company] in order to update and/or change all the material required for the [Project/Event/ Programme] including advertising and promotional material and other merchandise.

1.2　The [Company] shall then not exploit and/or sell and/or use the first version and shall agree how it is to be stored and/or disposed of with the [Sponsor].

L.253

1.1　The [Sponsor] agrees that it shall be jointly responsible with the [Company] in respect of any liability, costs, expenses, damages and losses that may result from the [Products] which may be used and/ or adapted by any member of the public whether they are free and/or purchased at the [Event].

1.2 That the [Sponsor] shall arrange insurance to cover public and product liability of not less than [number/currency] in [country] for period [date] to [date].

1.3 That the [Sponsor] shall ensure that the [Products] contain adequate instructions for use and comply with all health and safety and product liability requirements in law and/or in any guidelines in [country].

1.4 That the [Sponsor] shall notify the [Company] of any concerns regarding product liability and/or health and safety which may affect the suitability and/or use of the [Products] at the [Event].

L.254

The [Sponsor] accepts full responsibility and/or liability for any [Products/Services] which it supplies and/or distributes at the [Event]. The [Sponsor] agrees that it shall reimburse the [Company] in respect of any sums that it may incur which arise as a result of any claim, complaint, threat, fine, settlement, legal actions, legal costs and/or expenses paid and/or due to a third party which relate to the use of the [Product/Services] at the [Event] and/or thereafter.

University, Charity and Educational

L.255

1.1 The [Institute/Charity] shall not be liable to the [Contributor] for any acts, statements, omissions, failures, damages, legal costs, losses, damage to career prospects and/or reputation and/or loss of profits caused by and/or attributable to the [Institute/Charity] and/or any employee, representative, agent, and/or third party authorised by the [Institute/Charity] during the Term of this Agreement. This shall apply to the services of the [Contributor] under this agreement and/or any material created, developed, reproduced and/or distributed including any products, packaging, marketing, film, radio, website and/or other electronic material. This shall not apply in the case of death and/or injury caused by the negligence and/or directly attributable to the default of the [Institute/Charity].

1.2 The [Contributor] agrees and undertakes that he/she shall not seek to be indemnified by the [Institute/Charity] provided that the [Institute/Charity] arranges at its own cost to an comprehensive insurance policy for the benefit of the [Contributor] to cover any acts, statements, omissions, failures, damages, legal costs and losses, damage to career prospects and/or reputation and loss of income caused by and/or attributable to the [Institute/Charity] and/or any employee, representative, agent, and/or third party authorised by the [Institute/Charity] during the Term of this Agreement in excess of [number/currency].

L.256

The [Institute/Charity] shall not be liable to the [Consultant] for any direct and/or indirect costs, expenses, losses, damages, legal costs, damage to reputation, loss of profits, failure, errors, omissions, and/or any other matter which is attributable to and/or caused by the [Consultant] in respect of the [Project]. This shall not apply to personal injury or death caused by the negligence or deliberate default of the [Institute/Charity].

L.257

The [Contributor] agrees and undertakes that all sums due in respect of the [Project/Report/Work] have been and/or will be paid and that the [Institute/ Charity] is not and will not be liable for any additional sums at any time.

L.258

The [Marketing Company] agrees that the [Institute/Charity] shall not be obliged to use, exhibit, exploit, display and/or license any of the material created and/or developed under this agreement nor shall it be obliged to provide a credit or acknowledgment to the [Marketing Company] in respect of the [Project] and/or any associated promotional material on any website, app, competition, fundraising and/or other material and/or content.

L.259

The [Company] shall be liable to the [Institute/Charity] for any acts, statements, errors, omissions, defaults and/or failures, damages, legal costs and losses, interest, personal injury, death, damage to career prospects and/or reputation and/or loss of profits caused by and/or attributable to the [Company] and/ or any employee, representative, agent, and/or third party authorised by the [Company] during the Term of this Agreement and at any time thereafter in respect of the [Project] and any associated material in relation to the [Institute/ Charity]. There shall be no limit as to the level of liability and/or the jurisdiction and this clause shall survive the termination of this agreement.

L.260

1.1   Neither party shall be liable to the other for any direct and/or indirect consequential losses, damages, expenses and/or costs that may arise as a result of a delay in this [Project] due to any failure caused by an interruption of power, water, energy and/or supplies of materials and/or extreme weather conditions and/or any other reason which is beyond the control of either party and/or due to force majeure.

1.2   Both parties shall each be limited to a total liability of [number/ currency] to the other in respect of the [Project]. Any notification of a claim for payment of any sums must be made before [date] by either party. Thereafter all liability to the other party shall cease and be limited to breach of contract, failure to account and/or make payments, and/or failure to adhere to legislation, codes of practice and/or other health and safety requirements.

L.261

The [Institute] shall not be liable to pay any damages and/or other sum in compensation where as a result of an administrative error a booking has had to be changed, altered and/or cancelled. Provided that the [Institute] has made a full refund and offered another booking at a discount of [number] %.

L.262

The [Consultant] agrees and undertakes to the [Institute/Charity] that he/she shall not commit the [Institute/Charity] beyond the scope of his/her authority and/or incur any liability on their behalf and/or represent that he/she is entitled to enter into any agreement and/or holds and/or is authorised to grant any copyright and/or other intellectual property rights.

L.263

Where a [Participant/Volunteer] agrees to take part in any event and/or to fundraise in any manner then they must accept the following conditions:

1.1   That the [Participant/Volunteer] has no delegated authority to act on behalf of the [Charity].

1.2   That any sums raised must be paid directly to the [Charity] and not into any personal account.

1.3   That where any activity requires physical exercise that the [Participant/Volunteer] will seek medical advice as to their fitness and suitability for the task.

1.4   That the [Participant/Volunteer] must use the name and logo of the [Charity] in the form and colour authorised for the [Event]. There is no authority granted to license and/or reproduce any merchandise bearing the name pf the [Charity] and/or the logo except on any personal social media account.

LICENCE FEE

Film, Television and Video

L.264

'The Licence Fee' means the fee of [figure/currency] payable by the [Licensee] to the [Licensor] in respect of the rights granted by the [Licensor] to the [Licensee] under this agreement. The Licence Fee is payable as a royalty advance which the [Licensee] shall be entitled to recoup under clause [–]. The Licence Fee shall be paid to the [Licensor] by the [Licensee] as follows:

1.1 [number/currency] on signature by both parties of this agreement.

1.2 [number/currency] on acceptance by the [Licensee] of the [Master Material] for the [Film/Sound Recording].

1.3 [number/currency] on or by [date] subject to completion of 1.1 and 1.2.

1.4 [number/currency] upon first release to the public of the [Film/Sound Recording] in [format/disc] in [country] but in any event no later than [date].

1.5 [number/currency] upon the [format/disc] achieving sales figures of [number] units in [country].

1.6 [number/currency] upon the [format/disc] winning [specify] award.

1.7 [number/currency] upon the [Licensee] receiving gross receipts from the exploitation of the [format/disc] of [number/currency] at any time in any country.

L.265
'The Licence Fee' shall mean the sum of [number/currency] which is a total sum payable by the [Licensee] as follows:

1.1 [number/currency] upon full signature by both parties of this agreement.

1.2 [number/currency] upon delivery and acceptance of a complete copy of the master material in [specify format] which is technically suitable for reproduction.

1.3 [number/currency] on or before [date] subject to the completion of the transmission of the [Film/Video/Series] on [specify channel] in [country].

L.266
The 'Licence Fee' the sum of [number/currency] which shall be paid by the [Licensee] to the [Licensor]. The [Licensee] may not set this sum off against any future royalties that may fall due nor shall it be returned by the [Licensor] if the [Project] does not proceed for any reason.

L.267

1.1 The [Distributor] shall pay a fee of [number/currency] to [Name] for the attendance at the filming and/or sound recording and/or photography for the [Film/Video/Units] in accordance with the Work Schedule in Appendix A.

1.2 The [Distributor] shall in addition pay the [Agent] [number/currency] subject to the completion of work by [Name] in 1.1

1.3 The fees paid in 1.1 and 1.2 shall not be repaid under any circumstances and may not be recouped by the [Distributor] from any other sums due to [Name] and/or the [Agent] under this agreement.

L.268

1.1 The [Distributor] shall pay [Name] a fee of [number/currency] on [date] subject to the completion of the sound recordings by [Name] at [location] on [dates] in accordance with the planned schedule C.

1.2 Where additional sessions for editing and adapting any material are required then the [Distributor] agrees to pay an additional fee of [number/currency] for each [number] hours completed by [Name] at the [Distributors'] request. All fees shall be paid within [number] days of invoice after the work has been completed.

L.269

'The Licence Fee' means the fee of [number/currency] payable by the [Licensee] to the [Licensor] in respect of the rights granted by the [Licensor] to the [Licensee] under clause [–]. The Fee consists of [number/currency] in respect of [specify rights] and [number/currency] in respect of all other media. The fee is payable as a royalty advance which the [Licensee] shall be entitled to recoup against future royalties under clause [–].

L.270

In consideration of all the services performed and contributed by [Name] and the rights assigned under this agreement. The [Company] shall pay [Name] the sum of [number/currency] within [28] days of satisfactory completion of the work and the return of this signed document.

L.271

'The Licence Fee' shall mean the total sum of [number/currency] which is to be paid to the [Company] as follows:

1.1 [number/currency] to the [Company] by the [Licensee] subject to signature by both parties to this document.

1.2 [number/currency] to the [Company] by the [Licensee] upon acceptance of the [Products/Material] by the [Licensee].

1.3 [number/currency] subject to the completion of 1.1 and 1.2 the [Licensee] shall pay the [Company] [number/currency] in the event that the [Programme] incorporating the [Products/Material] achieves [ratings/audience/gross receipts] of more than: [specify].

L.272
In consideration of the rights granted in this agreement the [Licensee] shall pay to the [Licensor] a fee of [number/currency] as follows:

1.1 [number/currency] subject to the conclusion of this agreement; the budget; format and development plans and marketing strategy.

1.2 [number/currency] subject to acceptance by the [Licensee] of the [master copy format] of the [Film/Video/Series].

1.3 [number/currency] on or by [date] subject to completion of 1.1 to 1.2.

1.4 [number/currency] on or by [date] and/or first transmission of the [Film/ Video/episode of the Series]] whichever is the [earlier/later].

1.5 [number/currency] upon first release to the public of the [Unit/Product/ Toy] but in any event no later than [date].

1.6 [number/currency] upon first transmission in [country] of the [Film/ Video/Series] in [language] but in any event no later than [date].

L.273
'The Licence Fee' means the fee of [words] [figures] payable by the [Licensee] to the [Company] in respect of the [Rights] to be granted by the [Company] to the [Licensee] under this agreement.

L.274
The [Company] agrees to pay the [Licence Fee] to [Name] subject to the delivery of a copy of the [Sound Recordings/Artwork/Musical Work] in [format] in consideration of the non-exclusive rights granted in this licence.

L.275
The [Client] shall pay the Licence Fee in advance and any reproduction costs and delivery charges upon conclusion of the agreement. No material will be ordered, reproduced and/or delivered until payment has been received in full.

L.276
The Basic Fee shall be [number/currency] which shall be paid as follows:

1.1 [number/currency] within [seven] days from the signature of this agreement by the [Writer].

1.2 [number/currency] upon delivery of the draft script.

1.3   [number/currency] upon acceptance of the final script.

1.4   [number/currency] upon first broadcast or transmission of the [Film/ Programmes] based on the final script in [country] and/or by [date], whichever is the earlier.

1.5   The additional royalty fees shall be paid in accordance with the Schedule attached to and forming part of this agreement based on the method of exploitation. No payment shall be due for any form of exploitation not in existence at the time of the conclusion of this agreement.

L.277

1.1   In consideration of the rights assigned by [Name] to the [Distributor] in this agreement. The [Distributor] agrees and undertakes to pay [Name] and/or his /her estate and beneficiaries the licence fees, royalties and other sums set out in Appendix A in respect of each of the rights and countries specified which are exploited by the [Distributor].

1.2   The [Distributor] agrees that if at a later date new rights and/or technology are created and/or developed and a new means and/or method of exploiting any part of the [Films/Programmes] in which [Name] appears and/or has contributed in any form. That [Name] shall be entitled to be paid additional fees by the [Distributor] on terms to be agreed between the parties but which shall not be less than [number/currency].

General Business and Commercial

L.278

The 'Licence Fee' shall be the non-returnable and non-recoupable advance payment which is the sum of [number/currency].

L.279

'The Licence Fee' shall mean the sum of [number/currency] payable by [Name] under this agreement by [date] to the [Licensor] by [method].

L.280

1.1   In consideration of the rights granted the [Licensee] shall pay the [Licensor] the Advance Licence Fee as follows:

a.   [number/currency] upon signature of this agreement by both parties.

b.   [number/currency] upon delivery to and technical acceptance by the [Licensee] of the [Reproduction Material] in clause [–].

c.   [number/currency on or before [date] subject to fulfilment of clauses 1.1 a and b.

1.2   The [Licensor] agrees and accepts that the [Licensee] may recoup the Advance Licence Fee paid under this agreement from royalties which may be owed to the [Licensor] from the exploitation of the rights granted in this agreement.

1.3   The [Licensee] agrees that the Advance Licence Fee is not to be returned by the [Licensor] unless it is later shown that the [Licensor] did and does not won the rights granted to the [Licensee].

1.4   The [Licensee] agrees that it shall recoup the Advance Licence Fee over a period of [number] years and shall not recoup more than [number/currency] in any one year period.

L.281
'The Licence Access Fee' shall be the sum of [number/currency] per calendar month payable by the [Company] to the [Agent] during the Term of this Agreement. The total sum due for the year shall be [number/currency]. The fee shall only be paid while the agreement continues and there is a [showroom/storage facility/outlet] provided. The fee shall be paid at the end of each calendar month by such method as the [Company] shall at its sole cost and discretion decide.

L.282
Where the [Company] fails to pay the Licence Fee by [date] then this agreement shall end on [date]. After the end of this agreement all rights granted by [Name] shall be belong to [Name] and the [Company] shall not have any copyright and/or intellectual property rights under their control relating to the [Project/Work].

L.283
The Licence Fee of [number/currency] for access to the [Service] is payable in advance on [date] of each month. Where the sum is not paid then no service will be provided. The [Licence Fee] may be increased at any time by notice in writing after the first [six] months. Where there is an interruption and/or suspension of the [Service] for any reason there shall be no automatic right to any refund where the [Service] is only affected for [number] [days/hours].

Internet, Websites and Apps

L.284
The licence fees for the use and/or exploitation of any [Material] to be downloaded and/or supplied from this [Website/Platform] must be agreed and paid in advance prior to the supply, transfer, downloading, reproduction and/or distribution of any [Material].

L.285

The licence fee which must be paid in advance before [Unit/Service] is accessed and/or downloaded is [number/currency]. which shall be payable to the [Company].

L.286

The [Contributor] shall receive [number] per cent of the total [Licence Access Fee] per [Unit] received by the [Company] [and not returned] from any member of the public for access and use of the [Unit] after the deduction of a fixed cost of [number/currency] per [Unit] to cover production and marketing costs. All fees shall be paid to the [Contributor] at the end of each calendar month in arrears supported by an itemised accounting statement.

L.287

Where any licence fee and/or other fee charged by the [Company] is not paid by a [Customer] and/or payment is rejected at a later date by a bank. Then the [Company] shall be entitled to charge an additional administration fee for the costs incurred in collecting the sum due.

L.288

'The [Artist/Photographer] Fee' shall be the sum of [number/currency] in respect of the non-exclusive licence for the following rights: [specify rights/uses/purpose].

L.289

1.1 The [Company] charges a licence fee of [number/currency] per copy for the supply of [one] complete copy of the [Document/Artwork/Sound Recordings] per person for your own personal use for private and educational purposes for students at school/college and/or university in the form of a non-exclusive licence in [format] for [purposes/rights] in [country] in [language].

1.2 It does not include the right to: make copies and/or to supply copies to third parties for them to reproduce and/or the right to post any material on the internet in any manner.

1.3 Any failure to adhere to these conditions will result in the issue of additional fees, charges and costs being paid.

1.4 There is no undertaking and/or indemnity relating to the material and/or the rights.

L.290

'The Licence Fee' shall be the sum of [number/currency] to be paid by [Name] by [date] for the right to reproduce the [Image/Sound Recording/

Logo] on the [App/Website/Podcast] in the manner described in appendix A. It does not include the right to sub-licence and/or assign any rights to a third party.

L.291

1.1 'The Contributor's Fee' shall be the sum of [number/currency] which shall be paid within [number] days of completion of the [filmed/ recorded] [Interview/Panel Discussion] for [specify Series/Programme] on [specify Website/Channel/Podcast] by [Name] as a leading expert and qualified professional in [subject].

1.2 [Name] agrees and undertakes to sign a complete buy-out assignment of all the rights in the product of his/her services relating to 1.1 provided that the [Company] pays an additional fee of [number/currency] which shall be paid within [number] days of signature of the agreed document.

L.292
[Name] has supplied a video news story which was shot on his/her mobile phone. The [Company] agrees to pay a licence fee for the exclusive use in any format and/or media in any country worldwide of the material on any website, app and/or media outlet owned by the [Company] of [number/ currency] for a period of [one] calendar month. During that exclusive period no copy of the video shall be supplied to any third party by [Name]. After [date] the [Company] shall not have any rights in the video supplied by [Name] and [Name] shall be entitled to exploit the material as they wish.

L.293
In consideration of live sound interview and contribution of [Name] to the [Programme] on [channel/podcast] and the [assignment/licence] of all the rights in all media in any sound recording worldwide. The [Company] shall pay [Name] a fee of [number/currency] to include the live interview and consideration for the [licence/assignment] a copy of which is attached as appendix A.

L.294
[Name] shall pay the [Brand Company] a licence fee of [number/currency] for the right to use the [Products/Services] listed in appendix A in association with the [Website/App/Platform] from [date] to [date].

Merchandising and Distribution

L.295
'The Non-Returnable Advance' shall be the sum of [number/currency] payable by the [Distributor] to the [Licensor].

L.296

'The Licence Fee' shall be the sum of [number/currency] payable to the [Licensor] which can be set-off against the royalties due to the [Licensor] until it has been recouped in full by the [Licensee].

L.297

No advance under this agreement may be set-off against any sums due under any other agreement between the parties at any time.

L.298

In consideration of the rights granted in this agreement the [Licensee] shall pay to the [Licensor] a licence fee of [number/currency] which shall be paid subject to the conditions as follows:

1.1   [number/currency on [date] subject to signature of this agreement by all the parties.

1.2   [number/currency] on [date] subject to the technical acceptance by the [Licensee] of a pristine copy of the [Master Material] in [format].

1.3   [number/currency on [date] subject to the delivery of a [Prototype/ Draft/Sample] of the [Product/Service/Unit] to the [Licensor].

1.4   [number/currency] on [date] subject to the commercial distribution of the [Product/Service/Unit] in [country] in [specify format].

L.299

The Licence Fee shall be repaid to the [Licensee] where:

1.1   the [Master Material] is not delivered by the date specified and/or the technical quality is not of sufficiently high quality for its intended purpose and so it has been rejected; and/or

1.2   it becomes clear that the [Licensor] does not own and/or control the rights granted to the [Licensee] in this agreement.

1.3   the [Licensor] has already granted the same and/or similar rights to a third party and not disclosed this fact to the [Licensee] at the time of the agreement.

L.300

The [Distributor] agrees to pay the [Company] a licence fee as follows:

1.1   [number/currency] upon delivery to and acceptance by the [Distributor] of copies of master material in clause [–].

1.2   [number/currency] after approval by the [Company] of the sample prototype of the [Product/Artwork/Sound Recording].

1.3 [number/currency] on the earliest of either [date] or the release and/or distribution of the [Product/Artwork/Sound Recording] to the public in any of the following countries: [list countries].

1.4 [number/currency] after the first adaptation and/or translation sub-licence in [language] of the [Product/Artwork/Sound Recording].

The [Distributor] shall be entitled to recoup [fifty] per cent of these sums paid in 1.1 to 1.4 from any future sums due to the [Company] under this agreement which are received by the [Distributor]. The [Distributor] shall not be entitled to charge any interest.

Publishing

L.301

The [Publisher] shall pay the [Author] the following advance [number/currency] which shall be on account and set-off against all sums that may become due to the [Author] under this agreement as follows:

1.1 [number/currency] on signature of this agreement by both parties.

1.2 [number/currency] on [date] subject to delivery and approval of written evidence of sufficient progress such as outline of chapters and draft chapters.

1.3 [number/currency] on [date] subject to delivery and approval of the completed manuscript, preface, introduction and any photographs, images, maps, illustrations and infographics.

1.4 [number] on [hardcover/paperback] publication of the [Work] by the [Publishers] in [country] but in any event no later than [date] whichever is the earliest subject to adherence to 1.1, 1.2 and 1.3 by the [Author].

L.302

The [Publisher] shall pay to the [Agent] on behalf of the [Author] the following non-returnable advance of [number/currency].

1.1 [number/currency] on signature of this agreement by the [Publisher], [Author] and [Agent].

1.2 [number/currency] by [date] subject to approval of [number] [draft chapters] by the [Publisher].

1.3 [number/currency] by [date] subject to delivery and approval of the complete typed copy of the manuscript and the accompanying [email attachments/storage device] of the [Work] based on the [Synopsis].

1.4 [number/currency] within [number] days of first publication of the hardback of the [Work] by the [Publishers] or by [date] whichever is the earliest.

1.5 [number/currency] on first publication of the paperback of the [Work] by the [Publishers] or by [date] whichever is the earliest.

1.6 [number/currency] upon the hardback of the [Work] achieving total [sales of units/net revenue/gross receipts/number units/number/ currency] according to [specify source] worldwide.

1.7 [number/currency] upon the conclusion of a licence relating to a feature film to be based on the [Work].

1.8 [number/currency] upon the conclusion of a merchandising licence relating to the [Work] for the exploitation of [toys/household items/games].

1.9 [number/currency] upon the [Publisher] receiving gross receipts from the exploitation of the [Work] from any source in any country in excess of [number/currency].

The [Publisher] shall not under any circumstances be entitled to recover this advance except where the [Author] fails to deliver the [Work] in full. The [Publisher] shall not be entitled to recoup the advance against any future royalties under this agreement and/or any other concluded with the [Author].

L.303
The [Publishers] agree to pay the sum of [number/currency] to the [Author] as a recoupable advance against royalties which may become due to the [Author] under this agreement [which shall only apply to this first edition] and be paid as follows:

1.1 The sum of [number/currency] on signature of this agreement by the [Author] and the [Publisher].

1.2 The sum of [number/currency] on the receipt and approval by the [Publishers] of the copies of the manuscript and disc of the [Book] as set out in clause [–].

1.3 The sum of [number/currency] on or before [date] subject to completion of 1.1 and 1.2.

1.4 The sum of [number/currency] within [number] days of upon first publication and commercial release of the [Work] of in [hardback/ paperback/electronic/ plastic format].

1.5 [number] per cent of the advance received relating to any licence and/ or sub-licence agreement concluded by the [Publishers] and/or their authorised distributors and/or agents.

All the sums specified in 1.1 to 1.5 shall be recoupable by the [Publisher] from the royalties due to the [Author]. In the event that for any reason there are insufficient royalties to recoup 1.1 to 1.5 the [Publisher] shall not be entitled to reclaim such sums directly from the [Author]. The [Publisher] shall however be entitled to recoup the sums under any other earlier and/or later agreement with the [Author].

L.304

The [Publishers'] agree to pay the [Author] the following sums which shall be recoupable advance and may be offset against any royalties due to the [Author]:

1.1   [number/currency] within [number] days of signature of this Agreement by both parties. [number/currency] within [number] days of delivery of the first [number] pages of the manuscript.

1.2   [number/currency] within [number] days of acceptance and approval by the [Publishers] of the [manuscript/master material] of the [Work].

1.3   [number/currency] on delivery of the marked up proofs [together with an index/contents list, preface, cover and marketing material] by the [Author] to the [Publisher].

1.4   [number/currency] upon publication of the [hardback/paperback/electronic version/ebook] of the [Work] [but in any event not later than [date]].

1.5   [number/currency] upon publication to the public of the [audio file/ audio recording] of the [Work].

L.305

The [Publishers] agree to pay the [Author] in advance and on account of all sums payable under this agreement the sum of [number/currency]. One third on signature of this agreement, one third on delivery of the complete draft copy of the manuscript which is ready to be edited and one third on first commercial publication.

For the avoidance of doubt the advance payments set out above payable to the [Author] under this agreement shall be repaid to the [Publishers] if there remains any unrecouped balance on the [Author's] account upon termination or expiry of this agreement. Any unrecouped balance shall be repaid to the [Publishers] upon service of written notice on the [Author] to that effect and the Publishers agree to negotiate a repayment schedule with the [Author] over a [one] year period.

L.306

The [Author] agrees that if the [Publisher] refuses to accept and have valid reasons for rejecting the manuscript of the [Work]. That the [Author] shall repay all and/or such proportion of the advance as may be requested by the [Publisher], in regular instalments over a period of not more than [specify period].

If the [Author] does not agree with the grounds of rejection by the [Publisher] and/or the rejection is due to management and/or other changes attributable to the business and not the manuscript then no advance shall be obliged to be automatically repaid. The parties agree to appoint a third party to endeavour to negotiate a settlement of the matter.

L.307
The [Publisher] agrees that as the [Author] has used and/or spent the advance on research, travel and/or other material relating to the [Work] prior to delivery as originally envisaged. The advance shall not be repayable by the [Author] even if the [Work] is rejected and/or not published by the [Publisher] for any reason.

L.308
The [Publisher] agrees that no part of the advance shall be reclaimed by the [Publisher] from the [Author] for any reason once the manuscript has been accepted and the [Publisher] may only offset it against future royalties.

L.309
In consideration of the permission granted by the [Licensor] for the use of the [Character/Book] as a strip cartoon in the [specify magazine] for a period of [specify weeks] for publication in the [specify] language in [countries] by the [Licensee].

The [Licensee] shall pay the [Licensor] a fee of [number/currency] for each picture strip published in the magazine each week. Such sums shall be payable immediately upon invoice. For the avoidance of doubt it is agreed that this sum is not related to the circulation figures of the magazine.

L.310
The [Publisher] shall be entitled to offset and recoup the advance for the [Work] against future royalties received from the publication of the [hardback/paperback] editions of the [Work] and any other sums received from the exploitation of the [Work]. In the event that for any reason there are insufficient royalties to recoup the advance the [Publisher] shall not be entitled to reclaim such sums directly from the [Author] and/or his/her agent and/or from any future agreements with the [Author].

L.311
The [Publisher] shall only be entitled to offset the [Licence Fee/Advance] in clause [–] against royalties received for the [Book] in [hardback/paperback] in [country] and not from any other forms of exploitation.

L.312
The [Publisher] shall not be entitled to offset and/or claim back any unrecouped advance from the [Work] against any other work, book, option, licence, contract or otherwise that the [Publisher] may have with the [Author] at any time.

L.313
The [Distributor] shall not be obliged to pay any licence fee and/or other payment to [Name] for contributing to and supplying the [Blog] on the [Website/App/Platform]. [Name] agrees that no fee shall be due and that the [Distributor] may exploit, supply and distribute the [Blog] and/or any part as it thinks fit. Provided that [Name] is credited and any use is not defamatory, mocking and/or likely to adversely affect the reputation of [Name].

Services

L.314
The total licence fee due to the [Agent] for the supply of the services of [Name] shall be [number/currency] which shall be in addition to any fees and payments due to [Name].

L.315
The [Company] shall not be entitled to add and/or charge any additional copyright clearance payments, insurance costs, planning, licence fees and/ or any other sums in addition to the cost of the service.

L.316
The licence fee charged by [Name] is for a fixed period of [number] months. Any additional use will incur an additional licence fee payment. The [Company] reserves the right to increase the fee and shall not be obliged to charge the same rate and/or provide the same service.

L.317
The [Company] may terminate this agreement and/or cancel access to the [Service] at any time provided that it pays back pro rata any sums for any unused period paid for by the subscriber.

L.318
The initial licence fee is waived and you are allowed trial access and use of the [Basic Service] on [specify channel] for a period of [one] month without any payment. Thereafter a monthly fee is due payable in advance for access and use of the [Basic Service]. Additional charges, fees, line rental and mobile costs may be incurred for optional add-on services.

Sponsorship

L.319
'The Sponsorship Fee' shall be the sum of [number/currency].

In consideration of the services of [Name] the [Sponsor] shall pay [Name] the Sponsorship Fee as follows;

[number/currency] upon full signature of this agreement and

[number/currency] by [date] subject to the completion of the services by [Name] in accordance with the [Work Schedule] and the assignment of the rights in the product of the work.

L.320
The [Sponsor] agrees that the Sponsorship Fee shall be paid despite the fact that [Name] may be unable to provide his/her services under this agreement due to illness and/or ill-health provided that it is supported by a medical certificate from a qualified doctor or consultant and the parties agree to reschedule the work required.

L.321
In the event that the [Company] does not wish to use the [Sponsor's] Logo and/or products due to adverse publicity and/or other allegations regarding the [Sponsor], its officers, directors and/or products. The [Company] shall be entitled to terminate this agreement without any further liability provided that it repays the [Sponsorship Fee] to the [Sponsor].

L.322
'The Product Placement Fee' shall be the sum of [number/currency] which shall be paid by the [Company] to [Name] after the transmission and/or display of the agreed products in the [specify account] of [Name] and on their podcast known as [specify reference] in accordance with the requirements in appendix C.

L.323

1.1 The [Sponsor] shall pay the [Company] a fee of [number/currency] by [date] as a payment for access to and use of the following facilities at [Event/Festival] by persons who work at the [Sponsor]: [specify requirements].

1.2 The [Sponsor] agrees that this agreement is not exclusive and that the [Company] may also be funded by any other sponsor and/or third party that it thinks fit including a competitor in the same market.

L.324
The [Sponsor] licenses the [Logo/Trade Mark] to the [Promoters] on a non-exclusive basis to reproduce the [Logo/Trade Mark] on any website, app

and/or merchandise for the [Event] form [date] to [date]. No licence fee shall be charged except a nominal fee of one [currency]. The [Promoters] have no right to change and/or adapt the [Logo/Trade Mark] at any time and/or to create another version. The [Logo/Trade Mark] must be replicated in the exact colour, size and format in which it is supplied by the [Sponsor].

University, Charity and Educational

L.325
The [Contributors] Fee shall be the sum of [number/currency] which shall be paid to the [Contributor] as follows:

1.1 [number/currency] within [twenty-one] days of the signature of this Agreement by the [Contributor] and the [Institute/Charity].

1.2 [number/currency] upon delivery and acceptance of the [Work/Report/Service] by the [Institute/Charity].

1.3 [number/currency] on and/or by [date] provided that 1.1 and 1.2 have been completed.

L.326
'The Licence Fee' shall mean the non-returnable sum of [number/currency] payable by the [Company] to the [Institute/Charity] under this agreement. This sum cannot be set-off and/or recouped against any other payment due to the [Institute/Charity].

L.327
In consideration of the rights granted by the [Institute/Charity] to the [Company], the [Company] shall pay the [Institute/Charity] the Licence Fee as follows:

1.1 [number/currency] within [one] calendar month of delivery of a signed copy of this agreement to the [Company].

1.2 [number/currency] on or before [date] subject to the delivery and acceptance of the [Resource Material] listed in appendix A to the [Company] by the [Institute/Charity].

1.3 [number/currency] within [number] days of upon first release and/or publication of the [Work/Report/Products] by the [Company] but in any event not later than [date].

1.4 [number/currency] within [number] days of the [Event/Conference/Exhibition].

1.5 [number/currency] upon the achievement of: [specify target].

L.328

The [Institute/Charity] agrees to pay the [Author] the following sums:

1.1 [number/currency] within [twenty-eight] days of signature of this agreement by both parties which shall be a recoupable advance which can be offset against future royalties.

1.2 [number/currency] within [twenty-one] days of the acceptance by the [Institute/Charity] of the [Images/Sound Recordings/Films/Work].

1.3 [number/currency] on the first commercial release of the [Products/Services/Units] by the [Institute/Charity] and/or any authorised licensee in any country.

L.329

The [Author] agrees that the Advance Fee shall be repaid by [Author] to the [Institute/Charity] in the event that the [Author] fails to deliver the material specified in clause [–] and/or the material is rejected on reasonable grounds. Provided that the [Institute/Charity] has allowed the [Author] an additional period of [six] months to deliver the material and/or the [Author] has had the opportunity to remedy the matter and failed to do so.

L.330

The Advance Fee set out above payable to the [Author] under this agreement shall be repaid to the [Institute] if there remains any unrecouped balance on the [Author's] royalty account upon termination or expiry of this agreement. Any unrecouped balance shall be repaid to the [Institute] upon service of written notice on the [Author] to that effect and without prejudice to any repayment schedule which may be agreed with the [Author].

L.331

The [Institute] shall be entitled to offset and recoup the Licence Fee paid to the [Author/Creator] for the [Work/Images] against future royalties due to the [Author/Creator] received from the exploitation of the [Work/Images] in any media at any time. In the event that, for any reason, there are insufficient royalties to recoup the Advance Fee. The [Institute] shall not be entitled to reclaim such sums directly from the [Author/Creator] and/or his/her agent. Nor shall the [Institute] be entitled to offset and/or claim back any unrecouped Advance Fee from the [Work/Images] against any other work, book, option, licence, contract or otherwise that the [Institute] may have with the [Author/Creator] at any time.

L.332

Where a fee is charged by the [Institute] for access, reproduction and/or other use of the facilities at [address/library]. These sums do not provide the right to reproduce the material for any purpose and you are required to conclude a licence agreement with the [Institute]. The [Institute] may refuse to grant a licence and there is no obligation to do so. An additional licence fee, royalties and material costs with be charged. You may also be notified that additional copyright and other clearances and licences are required from third parties.

LICENCE PERIOD

General Business and Commercial

L.333
The [Company] grants the [Distributor] an option to extend the Licence Period for a further period of: [specify duration]. This option can be exercised at any time prior to the expiry of the Licence Period and is subject to the payment to the Company of a fee of [number/currency] on or by of date that the option is exercised. There is no right to any further options.

L.334
'The Licence Period' shall commence upon the date of this agreement and shall continue until [date/event/the completion of all transmissions].

L.335
The Licence Period shall commence from the date of the full execution of this agreement by all the parties and shall continue for a period of [two] years unless terminated at a prior date.

L.336

1.1 The Licence Period shall commence on [date] subject to the signature of this agreement by both parties and shall continue for a period of not less than [one] year. Thereafter it shall continue until such time as terminated by either party in accordance with clauses [–] below.

1.2 The [Licensee] shall always be liable to account for and pay any royalties due to the [Licensor] from the commercial exploitation of the [Products/Units/Service] both during and after the expiry of the Licence Period.

L.337
The Licence Period shall be subject to:

1.1 The exercise of any Option under clause [–].

1.2 The extension of the Licence Period by reason of force majeure under clause [–] and other specific circumstances under clause [–].

1.3 The accounts and payments due to the [Licensor] shall continue after the expiry of the Licence Period.

1.4 The indemnity provisions shall continue after the expiry and/or termination of the Licence Period until [date].

L.338

The Licence Period shall mean the period commencing from the first [theatrical/release] to the public in [format] of the [Film] in the [Territory] which shall not be later than [date] and shall continue for a period of [ten] years from that date.

L.339

The Licence Period shall commence on [date] and continue to but not including [date]. The Company shall supply the [Service] to the [Licensee] on such dates and at such times as specified in Schedule A.

L.340

'The Licence Period' shall commence on the date of this agreement which is [date] and shall continue for a period of [seven] years from the date of technical acceptance by the [Licensee] of the [Film/Master Material] set out in clause [–].

L.341

The present licence agreement commences on [date] and terminates automatically on [date]. There is no right to renew and/or extend the agreement for any reason.

L.342

The Licence Period shall commence on [date] and continue for a period of [ten] years from the date of first publication and commercial distribution to the public of the [hardback/paperback] of the [Work] by the [Publisher/ Distributor] and/or any authorised third party.

L.343

'Licence Period' Start Date: [specify date/time] End Date: [specify date/ time].

L.344

'The Licence Period' in respect of the [Product] shall commence on the earlier of the acceptance of the [Original Material] by the Company and [date] and continue until the expiry of a period of [specify duration] from [date].

L.345

'Licence Period' shall commence on [date] subject to the execution of this document by all parties and shall continue for a period of [specify length] unless terminated earlier due to force majeure and/or the grounds set out in clause [–].

L.346

The Licence Period shall begin on [date/time] and continue for a period of [number] months and end on [date]. Provided that the fee is paid by [date] in full.

L.347

1.1 The Licence Period shall commence on the [date] of this agreement and continue for a period of [ten] years.

1.2 The [Company] agrees that there is no right of renewal, extension and/ or variation of the Licence Period.

L.348

There is no option to extend the Licence Period.

L.349

'The Sponsorship Period' shall commence on [date] and continue until [date].

L.350

The Licence Period shall begin on [date] and continue for a period of [number] years and expire on [date].

L.351

The Licence Period shall be for the duration of the [Event] and shall begin on [date] at [time] and end on [date] at [time].

L.352

The licence period granted is for a period of [number] hours from the time of the completion of the download.

L.353

The [Licensee] shall not have any right to have the agreement renewed nor shall the [Licensee] have any right of first refusal in respect of any sequel and/or other adaptation and/or development.

L.354

1.1 The licence shall be held by the [Company] and shall not be transferable to any third party.

1.2 The licence shall commence on [date] and end on [time] on [date] on the last day of the [Event/Festival].

1.3 The licence shall be terminated by [Name] if any of the requirements set out in the document known as [specify] attached as Appendix [–] are not complied with at all times.

L.355

1.1 The licence period shall commence on the date of the confirmation by the [Company] of [Name] in the [sport] team for the [Company] which shall be no later than [date] and shall continue thereafter for [one] year.

1.2 There shall be no automatic right of renewal, extension and/or any option for a further period.

1.3 The licence period shall continue for the full period even if [Name] is removed from the team by the [Company], suspended and/or suffers ill health, disability and/or dies at any time.

L.356

The parties in the [Consortium] shall all be granted the same licence period for the [Work] which shall commence on the date of this Agreement and continue for a period of [number] years. After that period no party shall be entitled to exploit the [Work] unless all the parties agree new terms and conditions.

L.357

The licence period in respect of your use of the [App/Game] shall commence on the date that you access, download and are supplied the use of the material by the [Company] and end at the expiry of a period of [one] month. The access code will no longer work after that period has expired.

L.358

1.1 The [Licence Period] agreed between the parties shall start on [date] and continue for a period of [number] months.

1.2 The [Licence Period] is subject to the payment of the [Licence Fee] by [date] to [Name]. The Licence Period shall not start if the fee is not paid.

1.3 [Name] may terminate the Licence at any time if the [Licensee] uses the [Material/Content] for any purpose which is not authorised by the

[Licensor]. In such circumstances the [Licensee] shall not be entitled to be repaid any sums.

L.359

1.1 The [Licensee] shall have the right to extend the Licence Period for an additional term of [number] [years/months] subject to the payment of an extension fee of [number/currency] by [date] to [Name].

1.2 The [Licensee] shall not be entitled to grant any sub-licences beyond the period of the end of the Licence Period of the main agreement.

1.3 Where for any reason due to force majeure the start of the Licence Period is delayed and/or there is a delay in the delivery of the [Master Material] by the [Licensor]. Then it is that the Licence Period may be extended for an additional period of up to [number] months on terms to be agreed between the parties.

LOCATION ACCESS

General Business and Commercial

L.360
That the [Owner] owns and controls the freehold land and property [reference land registry/other] and there are no reasons why the [Owner] does not have the absolute right to grant the [Company] access to and use of the land and property for the purpose of rehearsals, filming and storage of equipment for the [Film] [title/brief description] on the following dates and times: [specify].

L.361

1.1 That in consideration of the filming facilities the [Company] shall pay a fee of [number/currency] exclusive of any value added tax due on or before [date].

1.2 In addition the [Company] shall pay a daily fee of [number/currency] to cover access to sanitation, water, light, electricity and other resources as may be available.

L.362
That the fee is in full and final settlement and that no further sums shall be due to the [Owner] for the use, licensing, adaptation, exploitation and/or distribution of the material filmed at [location] in any form.

L.363

That the [Owner] is entitled to grant access to and use of the filming facilities and no further releases, consents, rights of way, and/or other permissions are necessary except [specify local authority/other].

L.364

That there is no obligation to provide an on-screen credit in the [Film] to the [Owner].

L.365

The [Company] agrees and under takes that it shall be responsible for any electricity, utility, water, telephone and other bills and charges that may be incurred by the [Company] and/or the [Owner] whilst the [Company] is in occupation from [date] to [date] together with any losses and/or damages, costs and/or expenses arising directly and/or indirectly from the use of the land, property and storage by the [Company] and/or any other third party authorised by the [Company].

L.366

The [Company] undertakes to arrange and pay for comprehensive [public liability/other] insurance of not less than [number/currency] per claim with [name] for the benefit of [specify parties].

L.367

The [Company] agrees and undertakes that it shall ensure that the [location] is left in good order after use, and clear all rubbish, repair all damage and reimburse the [Owner] for any losses, damages, costs and expenses including wear and tear up to a maximum of [number/currency] for any claim notified within [number] months after the [Company] has left the site.

L.368

The [Company] undertakes that the material filmed on [location] and any marketing, advertising and promotional material for the [Film] will not be used by the [Company] in any manner which will bring the [Owner] into disrepute or is defamatory to the [Owner] and/or which is obscene, defamatory, offensive and/or prejudicial to the value of the [Owner's] business, land and/ or property at any time.

L.369

The [Company] shall indemnify the [Owner] in respect of any financial losses, costs, expenses, loss of goodwill, damages, wear and tear which may be incurred and/or paid by the [Owner] in respect of the use of the site by the [Company] and/or any authorised third parties and in respect of any other claim, complaint, demand, action or otherwise arising from the use, storage, access and/or filming at the site at any time up to a maximum limit of [number/currency] until [date].

L.370

The [Owner] agrees and undertakes that they shall not be entitled to any additional sums and the [Company] shall only be obliged to pay the [Location Access Fee]. Any electricity, telephone, utility, rates and/or any financial loss, costs, expenses, loss of goodwill, damage, wear and tear and/or any claim, complaint, demand, action or otherwise arising from the use, storage, access and filming and exploitation of the [Film] at any time relating to the [Owner] and/or the land and/property shall be at the [Owner's] sole cost and risk.

L.371

Where a location is to be used for filming of material for the advertisement and marketing of a [Product]. Then the [Company] shall ensure:

1.1 That the [Product] has been approved by the [Owner].

1.2 That the material to be filmed is suitable for an audience on [television/ social media] at [time].

1.3 That the name and address of the location will not be made available in any press and social media release without the prior authorisation of the [Owner].

1.4 That any additional filming and photo shoots shall be for an additional fee and subject to a separate agreement.

L.372

The [Company] shall ensure that the location is left in the same condition as when they started. Where any damage and/or losses are caused by the [Company]. The [Owner] shall arrange for [two] quotes to replace and/ or repair the damage and agree the cost in advance with the [Company]. Where the [Owner] repairs the damage then a rate of [fee] per hour may be charged in addition to the material costs. Where the parties are unable to agree then the parties shall agree on an independent mediator paid for by the [Company].

L.373

The [Company] shall not have the right to use and/or adapt the name of the [house/location] and/or business of the [Owner] and/or to use any associated logo, trade mark, service mark and/or otherwise. There is no licence and/or grant of intellectual property rights under this agreement to the [Company].

L.374

1.1 Where any person is permitted access for any reason you must comply with the reasonable directions and instructions of the [Company] and any security staff.

1.2 There is no right to access any area of the venue which is marked restricted, private and/or locked.

1.3 There is no right to take any images and/or film any area of the venue including by mobile phone.

1.4 There is no right to record any voice and/or interview and/or conversation with any personnel.

1.5 There is no right to dispose of any material at the venue and/or to cause any damage and/or to remove any material.

1.6 In the event that you are requested to leave the venue and refuse the [Company] shall use its security guards and film you as well as summon the police for assistance.

1.7 There is no right to use and/or access any telecommunication system, equipment, electricity, gas, water and/or other resource unless consent is provided by a member of staff.

L.375

The [Company] agrees:

1.1 that the [Owner] shall be entitled to use a short clip of the [Film] of [duration] seconds to promote the site as suitable for filming.

1.2 that they shall cooperate with the [Owner] to minimise the environmental damage to the wildlife at the site.

1.3 to remove all rubbish and not to pollute the waterways at the site.

1.4 to provide a regular update of the personnel authorised to access the site.

1.5 to supply at the [Company's] sole cost sufficient security and health and safety measures to protect members of the public who may try and access the site without consent.

1.6 to assist the [Owner] in improving any access route which is not suitable for heavy machinery at the [Company's] cost.

1.7 to ensure that the site is not used before [time] or after [time] each day without prior consent.

1.8 not to bring any animals on the site.

1.9 not to store and/or use any toxic chemicals.

LOGO

General Business and Commercial

L.376

The [Licensor] agrees to pay for the cost of supplying a master copy of the [Licensor's Logo] in [format] on loan for reproduction by the [Distributor] in the [Film/Video//Disc].

L.377

The [Distributor] agrees and undertakes to put the following trademark, logo, text, image and credits to the [Licensor] on the first page and the last page content of the disc, the label, the outside of the centre of the disc, the cover and in all press releases, posters, publicity, promotional, advertising and packaging material in respect of the [Disc] of the [Film/Work] as set out in Appendix A [specify size, shape, position on each type of material] which forms part of this agreement.

L.378

The [Distributor] agrees and undertakes to reproduce and display the [Licensors'] master material of the logo, trade mark, images, text and shapes in the exact size and colour that they are supplied. The [Distributor] shall not change, alter and/or vary any part without the prior approval of the [Licensor].

L.379

The [Distributor] agrees and undertakes that it shall not acquire any copyright, trade mark and/or other intellectual property rights in the master material owned and/or controlled by the [Licensor] including but not limited to any logo, trade mark, images, text, slogan, shapes and/or colours.

L.380

The [Distributor] agrees that no part of this agreement is intended to transfer any copyright, design rights, future design rights, domain name, trade mark, service mark, community mark, business name, trading name, invention, patent including any developments or variations in the master material of the [Licensors'] logo, trade mark, images, text and shapes to the [Distributor]. The [Distributor] agrees that all such rights in relation to such material are the sole and exclusive property of the [Licensor].

L.381

1.1 The [Designer] has created and developed a computer generated three dimensional moving image of the [Logo] which has been commissioned by the [Company] which is in different colours and formats as described in Schedule A entitled the [New Logo].

1155

1.2 The [Designer] agrees to assign all copyright, intellectual property rights, computer software and design rights and any other rights and/ or interest in the [New Logo] to the [Company] throughout the world and universe for the full period of copyright and all other periods of intellectual property rights and any extension and forever in perpetuity including in respect of all new rights and/or developments created at any time in the future in return for the payment of the [Commission/Fee] and [Budget] attached in Schedule B.

1.3 The [Designer] agrees to provide all original and copies of all preparatory and development material to the [Company] which he/she may have in his/her possession at the [Company's] cost. The [Designer] agrees that he/she shall not retain any material except: [specify].

1.4 The [Designer] agrees that he/she shall not receive any additional payment for the work and/or any registration of the [New Logo] and/or any exploitation and/or adaptation in any form at any time.

L.382
During the course of the [Programme] the [Television Company] undertakes that the [Sponsor's Logo] will appear on screen for not less than [number seconds] on not less than [number] separate occasions. Further that the [Sponsor's Logo] will appear in the course of the [Programme] in the following circumstances and background to appear as follows: [specify].

L.383
The [Television Company] agrees to ensure that the broadcast or transmission of the [Sponsor's Logo] and [Products] will not infringe any sponsorship, product placement, gambling and advertising codes, guidelines and standards, rules and/or legislation concerning the [Sponsor's Logo] and/or [Products] including its size, shape, colour, wording, on-screen position or general nature and in particular those in existence issued by the following bodies and organisations: [specify].

L.384
The [Production Company] agrees to provide the following trademark, logo and credits to the [Sponsor] in any publicity, promotional, advertising and packaging material in respect of the marketing and distribution of the [Film/ Video/Podcast] [specify size, shape, position on each type of material].

L.385
The [Licensee] agrees that it shall be solely responsible for all costs and expenses incurred in respect of the reproduction and incorporation of the [Licensee's Logo] in the [Film/Product/Podcast].

L.386

1.1 The [Licensor] agrees that the [Licensee] may use and/or reproduce the [Logo/Trade Mark/Image] in respect of [specify] use and purpose on [product/service] from [date] to [date]. Provided that a sample is agreed in advance with the [Licensor].

1.2 The [Licensor] agrees that the [Licensee] may use and/or reproduce the [Logo/Trade Mark/Image] in conjunction with its [Festival/Event] in [year] to market the proposed website, app, brochure, outdoor advertising and related merchandising.

L.387

Where any [Employee] whether temporary, permanent and/or otherwise contributes to and/or designs and/or creates any new logo, slogan, lyric, image, photograph, film, sound recording, title, recipe, blog, website, app, invention, patent, trade mark and/or any other computer software, hardware, new technology, process and/or method of telecommunication which is entirely original and/or based and/or derived from other work by the [Company]. The [Employee] shall not own and/or control any copyright, intellectual property and/or patent and/or any other rights of any nature in any such material and shall not be entitled to receive any sums from any form of exploitation, registration and/or sale at any time.

L.388

The [Company] acknowledges that the [Employee] owns and controls the following rights and material set out in Schedule A prior to the date of this agreement.

L.389

The [Company] agrees that where the [Employee] designs, creates and/or invents a new logo, product and/or patent and/or any other new material which is original and which the [Company] wishes to produce and/or exploit. That the [Company] shall be obliged to negotiate a licence agreement with the [Employee] and the [Employee] agrees that the [Company] shall receive not less than [number] per cent of the sums received from the exploitation.

L.390

The [Licensee] warrants that:

1.1 All uses of the [Logo] upon the [Products] will be in accordance with the terms of this agreement and no modification may be made to any part of the [Logo] which shall always be used in the format set out in the Schedule A.

1.2 It shall not make any challenge against the rights of the [Licensor] in the [Logo] or its validity in any way provided that the [Licensor] shall not be in breach of any of its warranties in relation to the [Logo].

1.3 If the [Licensee] becomes aware of any unauthorised use of the [Logo] within the Territory it will promptly notify the [Licensor] with appropriate details.

1.4 No other logo, image or wording will be used on any of the [Products] together with the [Logo] except with the prior written approval of the [Licensor].

L.391
The [Agent] may use the trade names, service marks, logos and icons set out in Appendix A or as otherwise specified by the [Company] in writing solely in the promotion and/or sales of the [Products] during the Term of this Agreement. The [Agent] acknowledges that all rights in relation to such material are the sole and exclusive property of the [Company] and that this agreement is not intended to vest or transfer any interest to the [Agent].

L.392
The [Agent] acknowledges that it shall not acquire any title in the [Product Samples], the [Product], or the [Company] Logo. The [Agent] confirms that all goodwill and reputation created in the [Company] Logo shall remain the sole and exclusive property of the [Company] and that no part of this agreement is intended to transfer any copyright, design rights, domain name, trade mark, service mark or any other rights in the [Company] Logo, the [Product Samples] or the [Product] to the [Agent] including any developments or variations.

L.393
'Logo' shall mean a two-dimensional graphic representation [capable of registration as a trademark].

L.394
The [Company] Logo shall be the following trademark, design or logo together with any associated words briefly described as follows: [specify]. A two-dimensional copy of the [Company] Logo is attached to and forms part of this agreement.

L.395
The [Promoter's] Logo shall be the design, logo and trademark together with any accompanying words of the [Promoter] to be used for all promotion, advertising and marketing of the [Festival/Event] in any media. A copy of the [Promoter's] Logo is attached to and forms part of this agreement.

L.396

The [Licensee] agrees to ensure that all third parties to be contracted by the [Licensee] under this agreement will agree that all copyright and any other rights concerning the [Licensor's] Logo shall remain the sole and exclusive property of the [Licensor]. That the [Licensee] and all such third parties shall not acquire, nor represent that they own and/or control and/or attempt to register any domain name, rights, interest and/or goodwill in the [Licensor's] Logo nor any trademark, logo, service marks, title, text, slogan, catchphrase, image, artwork or otherwise or any developments, variations or adaptations in any language at any time which is based on, derived from and/or associated with it.

L.397

The [Licensor] confirms and undertakes:

1.1   That it is the sole owner of or controls all intellectual property rights, trade marks, service marks, and any other rights in the [Licensor's] Logo throughout the [country] which is attached to and forms part of this Agreement in Section A.

1.2   That the [Licensor's] Logo [is registered with/has a pending application] with the following [organisations]: [registration reference].

1.3   That the [Licensor] is not aware of any claim, allegation, complaint and/or threat of legal action by any third party relating to the [Licensor's] Logo and/or any other conflict of interest.

L.398

The [Licensee] agrees that all copyright, trademarks, service marks, design rights and any other rights in the [Licensor's] Logo together with any goodwill shall remain the sole property of the Licensor. The [Licensee] shall not acquire any rights or interests in the [Licensor's] Logo or in any related trademark, design, title, artwork, music and/or other material in any medium and/or any adaptation in any format.

L.399

The [Company] agrees that the prior written approval of the [Manufacturer] shall be required in the event that the [Company] intends to promote, market or exploit the [Product] or the [Manufacturer's] Logo by any of the following means: publicity, advertising, promotional material, fashion shows, television, radio, newspaper, magazine features and/or by means of any other material, event or method.

L.400

The [Company] confirms that it is the sole owner of or controls all copyright and any other rights in the [Company's] Logo and that the use of the

[Company's] Logo under this agreement will not expose the [Licensee] to any criminal and/or civil proceedings and that the [Licensee] shall not acquire any rights or interest in the [Company's] Logo including any developments and/or variations.

L.401

1.1 The [Consortium] acknowledge and agrees that the trade marks, logos, images and slogans are owned and controlled by the following parties as set out in Section B which form part of this Agreement.

1.2 That this Agreement is not intended to transfer, assign and/or license any of the trademarks, logos, images and slogans in Section B to any other member of the [Consortium] and/or to entitle them to claim any revenue and/or sums from any exploitation and/or registration.

L.402

All trademarks, logos, brands, trade names, titles, names, products, slogans, catchphrases, music, sounds and domain names which are displayed and exhibited on this [Website/App/Platform/Product] belong to a person, firm and/or company who own and control the rights. You need to contact them directly in order to copy, reproduce, transfer, develop, distribute and/or otherwise exploit their material. We have not provided any authorisation for you to use their material for your own personal use and/or for any commercial project. We cannot be liable to you for any claim they may make against you for any unauthorised use of their material and/or rights.

L.403

The [Company] own and control the Logo known as [specify detail] which you may download in conjunction with the material relating to it on this [Website/App/Blog/Podcast] for your own personal use at home whether in printed format, on a disc or onto the hard drive of your computer. There is no authorisation and/or consent to any reproduction for commercial purposes, but you may refer to this [Website/App/Blog/Podcast] and the Logo and the associated material for criticism and/or review in the media and/or educational reasons for use by tutors, teachers, students, schools, colleges and universities.

L.404

The [Customer] shall not delete, erase, change, alter and/or vary the [Company's] logo, trade mark, images, text, shapes and colours and/or any other credits which are on any services and/or products supplied by and/or downloaded from the [Website/App/Platform] by the [Customer].

L.405
No person and/or company who uses this [Website/App/Blog/Podcast/ Service] shall have the right to reproduce on their own website, app, blog video, podcast and/or otherwise the [Company's] trade mark, logo and slogan: [specify]. No person and/or company is entitled to represent that they own, control, have been authorised under a licence and/or shall attempt to register any interest with a third party and/or otherwise use and/or adapt the trade mark, logo and slogan.

L.406
There is no authority granted to reproduce, exploit and/or distribute any logo and/or trade mark on this [App] to any third party except in the exact form, colour, words, shape and context in which it appears on this [App] and subject to the terms of the user licence.

L.407
The [Licensor] agrees that you may make [one] copy of the [Product/App/ Material] for your own personal use but not for school and university and other educational establishments, charitable and/or commercial purposes provided that no credits, acknowledgements, trademarks and logos are removed, deleted and/or adapted and no additional copies are made and/ or distributed to any third party.

L.408
This Logo [Image/Words] belongs to [Name] who owns all rights in all media worldwide and there is no right to reproduce it for any purpose except in relation to this [App/Blog/Podcast].

L.409
Any unauthorised reproduction and/or use of any logos and/or images and/ or words from this site is not permitted for any reason.

L.410
The [Licensor] agrees to supply at its cost and expense such exact master copies of the trade mark and/or logo and/or any other credits and/or images and/or sound recordings required by the [Licensee] in respect of all publicity, advertising, packaging, marketing, distribution and exploitation of the [Units/Products] by the [Licensee].

L.411

1.1 The [Licensee] agrees and shall ensure that any sub-licensee agrees to provide the following credit, copyright notice, trade mark and logo to the [Licensor] in respect of the [Units/Products/Service] and any packaging and/or promotional material in the positions and size specified in the attached Appendix A which is attached to and forms part of this agreement.

1.2 The [Licensee] agrees that the [Licensor] shall be entitled to approve an exact sample of the [Units/Products/Service] and any packaging and/or promotional material prior to reproduction and development. The [Licensor] shall provide written approval or rejection of the sample within [number] days of delivery. Failure by the [Licensor] to reply within that period shall be deemed approval of the sample.

L.412

The [Licensor] shall not have a right of approval over all material for publicity, advertising, marketing and/or distribution of the [Units/Products/Service] by the [Licensee]. The [Licensee] agrees to consult with the [Licensor] and where there is a trademark, logo and/or credit to the [Licensee] also include one to the [Licensor] in the same size and position.

L.413

The [Distributor] agrees and undertakes that all copyright, design rights, future design rights, computer software rights and intellectual property rights in the [Character/Product] together with any trade marks, service marks, community marks, logos and associated domain names and goodwill and any developments and/or adaptations are and/or shall be owned and controlled by the [Licensor].

L.414

'The Company's Logos' shall mean the designs and the associated texts, images and colours. A two-dimensional copy of the Company's Logos is attached to and forms part of this agreement.

L.415

Where during the course of this agreement [Name] develops, creates and/or registers a new logo and/or trade mark and/or any other marketing and/or promotional material associated with his/her personal name and/or public name and/or sporting activity which is/are owned by [Name] and/or any holding company. Then in the event that the [Company] wishes to use any of the new material in any form the [Company] shall be required to enter into a new licence agreement with [Name] as that new material does not form part of this agreement.

L.416

The title and content of the [Work] including any preface, index, cover and any electronic version and/other medium shall be owned by the [Authors].

The [Publisher] agrees and undertakes that it shall not have any right to claim copyright and/or ownership of any intellectual property rights and/or to register any domain name and/or to apply for any trade mark and/or to register as the owner with any rights management organisation whether in that exact form and/or any variation of the title, text, characters, images and/or any translation and/or development in any medium and/or method at any time.

L.417

In the event that the [Publisher] commissions a designer and/or requests an employee and/or consultant to create any artwork, photographs, images, typography, index, titles, character names and/or cover and/or slogan. The [Publisher] agrees that all such material shall be owned jointly by the [Author] and the [Publisher] and that no material shall be used, adapted and exploited without the prior written approval of the [Author] in each case and that the [Author] shall be entitled to a minimum of [number] per cent of any sums received by the [Publisher] in such case where the parties agree to exploit any such material.

L.418

The [Publisher] agrees that it may not add any new logos, trademarks and/or other credits to the [Work] and/or any adaptation without the prior written approval of the [Author] of the exact proposed sample.

L.419

Where the [Company] commissions and pays for an electronic three dimensional holographic [logo/image] of any character in the [Work] and/or the [Author] and/or his and/or her initials. It is agreed that the ownership of all such new material shall be held jointly by the [Company] and the [Author] and all revenue shall be split upon terms to be agreed. If no agreement is reached with the [Author] then the [Company] shall not have the right to use and/or exploit any such new material.

L.420

Where the [Author] supplies [infographics/images/computer-generated material] as a contribution to a {Project/Work}. Then the [Author] shall have the right to a credit and a logo displayed with all such material wherever it is reproduced by the [Company] on each page.

L.421

There is no right granted by the [Consultant] for the [Company] to use the personal name and/or business name and/or logo of the [Consultant] in relation to any corporate document, application and/or marketing unless the [Consultant] has viewed and approved the material and provided his/her consent in each case.

L.422

The [Agent] does not own and/or control the personal name, stage name and/or slogans, logos, images, photographs, scripts, films and/or marketing material of [Name]. No rights are to be granted by the [Agent] to any third party and all material must be authorised by [Name] for any use on each occasion.

L.423

The [Sponsor] confirms that it is the sole owner of or controls all copyright, trade marks and any other intellectual property rights throughout the world in the [Sponsor's] Logo. The [Sponsor] confirms that the [Sponsor's] Logo does not infringe the copyright or any other rights of any third party throughout [the world/country].

L.424

The [Sponsor] agrees to bear all costs of creating the [Sponsor's] Logo and of supplying the [Sponsor's] Logo in a form acceptable to the [Company] for incorporation in its [brochure/video/website/app/other].

L.425

The [Company] confirms that the [Sponsor's] Logo will be reasonably, prominently and clearly identifiable in the [brochure/programme] and in any event will not be less than the following dimensions: [specify].

L.426

The [Sponsor] agrees to provide to the [Organisers], at the [Sponsor's] sole cost and expense, all suitable artwork of the [Sponsor's] Logo in order for it to be reproduced in all printed and social media material under the control of the [Organisers] by the following date: [–].

L.427

The [Organisers] confirm that the design, artwork, and wording of the [Sponsor's] Logo shall be at the sole discretion of the [Sponsor] subject to prior consultation with the [Organisers].

L.428

The [Organisers] confirm that whenever possible they will ensure that the [Sponsor's] Logo will be used, displayed and reproduced in accordance with this agreement. That the [Promoter] has undertaken to the [Organisers] to use its best endeavours to ensure that the [Sponsor's] Logo is incorporated in all promotional, advertising and publicity material.

L.429

No person, company and/or supplier is entitled to reproduce the logo, shield, trade mark and/or images of the [Institute/Charity] in any form without prior consent of the [Institute/Charity] and/or to represent that they have their endorsement, support and/or represent their interests and/or associated with them by reproducing the name, logo, shield, trade mark and/or other images.

L.430

1.1 The Logo was designed and created by [Name] and belongs to the [Charity/Institute].

1.2 The [Logo] may only be used for the purpose of fundraising by individuals and companies for the [Project].

1.3 Your right to reproduce, adapt and create other versions of the [Logo] ends on [date].

1.4 You must agree not to acquire any rights in the [Logo] and/or any variations and/or adaptations at any time.

1.5 There is no right to reproduce the [Logo] for any commercial purpose for the sale of any products, services and/or otherwise.

1.6 The [Charity/Institute] may notify you directly and/or by an announcement on [specify] at any time that they have withdrawn your authority to use the [Logo].

MARKETING

Film, Television and Video

M.001

The [Assignor] acknowledges that the [Assignee] shall have the sole discretion as to the manner and method to be used in marketing, promoting, publicising and advertising of the [Film/Series/Products] in respect of the rights which have been assigned under this agreement.

M.002

The [Company] agrees and undertakes not to place any advertisements, promotions and other material relating to the following [groups/persons/ businesses]: [specify details] on any material of any nature which is to be released and/or distributed to the media, public and/or displayed, exhibited and/or reproduced which relates to [Name/Group].

M.003

The [Company] shall submit to the [Licensor] for approval in advance prior to production, publication and/or distribution all sales literature, advertising material, brochures, catalogues, posters, labels, packaging, shop display material, promotional extracts and website, app, audio and other internet material of the [Film/Video/Series] in any shape, form or medium. The [Company] shall take into account all changes and amendments requested by the [Licensor] and shall then resubmit any such material for approval by the [Licensor]. No material shall be published and/or distributed and/or otherwise released unless it has been approved by the [Licensor].

M.004

The [Licensor] agrees to provide the [Licensee] upon request at the [Licensor's] sole cost/on loan] the following artwork and master copies of material for use in the creation of the packaging, marketing and/or promotion of [Units of the Film/Merchandising Products]:

1.1 The brand and style book of the [Licensor] together with accurate and precise three and two dimensional colour copies and representations of all copyright notices, trade marks, service marks, logos, slogans and images, credits, disclaimers, copyright warnings and product warnings and notices to be reproduced and used by the [Licensee] including the size, location and how it is to be used in relation to each type of format.

1.2 A list of all legal and contractual obligations that must be fulfilled in relation to any third parties in respect of any reproduction of any format in any medium by the [Licensee].

The [Licensee] accepts and agrees that they shall have no right to create and/or develop any new version of any material without the express prior consent of the [Licensor]. That all material shall be subject to the prior approval of the [Licensor] in sample form before any material can be reproduced and/or distributed in any format and/or medium.

M.005
The [Distributor] shall at all times have the right at their sole discretion to decide upon the production schedule, the release dates, the supply, subscription, sale, rental, and distribution prices, discounts, and price reduction strategy and promotional offers and the marketing of the [Film/Video/Units/Products].

M.006
The [Assignee] agrees and undertakes that it shall use its best endeavours to exploit the rights in the [Film/Video/Units/Products] assigned under this agreement and to achieve as far as possible the maximum Gross Receipts.

M.007
The [Licensor] agrees to supply to the [Distributor] on loan such copies of the master material of any background, advertising and/or promotional material held by the [Licensor] in connection with the [Film/Video/Series] which the [Licensor] may wish to make available including:

1.1 Filmed interviews and sound recordings with the presenter and other contributors in respect of their role;

1.2 Promotional photographs, images and stills; pop-ups, banner, cinema, television and radio advertisements and promotions, posters, packaging and other marketing material.

M.008
1.1 The [Licensor] shall provide the [Distributor] with details of any restrictions in respect of the use of any marketing and promotional master material and/or other matters regarding rights, copyright and clearance payments; moral rights and contractual obligations.

1.2 The [Distributor] shall only be permitted to use any such master material in clause [–] in respect of the distribution, supply, sale, supply, packaging and promotion of the [Film/Video/Units/Products] which have been licensed under this agreement.

1.3 The [Licensor] shall invoice the [Distributor] and the [Distributor] shall pay the full cost of the supply of all such master material in clause [–] including reproduction costs, delivery, customs duties, taxes and other charges. At the expiry and/or termination of the agreement all such master material and all associated copies shall be returned at the [Distributors'] cost to the [Licensor].

M.009

The [Distributor] shall be entitled to use the professional name, photograph, image and brief biography of the [Writer] in any commercial exploitation of any [Film/Video/Unit/Products] in respect of which the [Writer] has provided his/her services under this agreement unless the [Writer] at a later date requests that his/her credit be deleted.

M.010

The [Distributor] shall be under no obligation to produce, manufacture, distribute and/or exploit any [Film/Video/Units/Products] in respect of which the [Writer] has rendered his/her services under this agreement. The [Writer] shall not have any right to a claim for loss of publicity, reputation, damages and/or otherwise from any failure by the [Distributor] to exploit any contribution by the [Writer].

M.011

The [Assignee] agrees upon request to provide the [Assignor] at the [Assignees'] sole cost with copies and samples of all material created, reproduced, commissioned, issued, distributed and/or released by the [Assignee] to market, promote and/or exploit the [Film/Video/Units/Products] including but not limited to: artwork, press releases, posters, packaging material, labels, website and app material, advertisements, banners, pop-ups and merchandising.

M.012

The [Assignee] confirms that it shall be responsible for any sums due in respect of the distribution, marketing and exploitation of the rights in the [Film/Video/Units/Products] and any parts which are assigned under this agreement including but not limited to any payments due in respect of any performing rights and/or mechanical reproduction due to any rights management organisation, rights holder and/or any other third party contributor.

M.013

1.1 The [Licensee] undertakes that throughout the Term of this Agreement it will diligently and conscientiously manufacture, sell, rent, supply by subscription, promote and distribute the [Units/licensed rights] of the [Films] in the Territory.

1.2 The [Licensee] shall have the final decision in respect of all aspects of the manufacture, distribution, price, sale, rental, subscription price and marketing of the [Units/licensed rights] of the [Films].

M.014

The [Licensor] grants to the [Distributor] the right to use, reproduce and publish in respect of the [Characters/Artists] whose performances are reproduced in the [Programmes] or any other person concerned in the making of the [Programmes], their legal and professional names, photographs and likenesses provided that it directly relates to the marketing of the material created as a direct result of the rights licensed under this agreement. There is no right granted to sub-license any material to a third party for another film, video and/or podcast which does not promote the [Programmes].

M.015

The [Distributor] may use and permit the use of excerpts of up to a maximum of the same [three] minutes in duration from the [Film/Video/Unit] for the purposes of promotion, advertising and/or trade and in-store demonstrations.

M.016

The [Company] may without further payment use and permit the use of excerpts from the [Film] and/or soundtrack and/or images and/or text on the internet and/or television, radio, video, mobile and/or any other media for the purpose of programme promotions, schedules, reviews, discussion and/or advertising. Provided that the same total aggregate of [five] minutes of excerpts shall be used in all media. There is no limit on the amount of usage of these same five minutes provided it is within the Licence Period and not for the purpose of sponsorship and/or endorsement of a third party product or business.

M.017

The [Company] may incorporate extracts of other [films/recordings] before and/or after and/or at the end of any versions reproduced of the [Film/Video/Sound Recording] provided that they are also promoted by the [Company] and will appeal to a similar audience and/or age group.

M.018

The [Company] shall have the right to authorise others to transmit, broadcast and/or to supply a short extract of the [Film/Video/Podcast] which shall be agreed with the [Licensor] and shall not exceed [two] minutes in duration for the purpose of promoting the [Film/Video/Podcast]. Provided that sufficient credits and links are provided by the third party as follows: [specify detail].

M.019

The [Distributor] shall not have any merchandising, licensing, endorsement or sponsorship rights in respect of the [Film/Video/Podcast] and/or any other material created under this agreement. The [Distributor] shall not have the right to appoint any sub-agent and/or sub-distributor and/or any other person and/or company in relation to any rights and/or material at any time.

M.020

1.1 The [Licensee] may design, manufacture and create at its own expense and cost advertising, promotional and packaging material for the exploitation of the rights in the [Film/Video/Sound Recordings] granted under this agreement.

1.2 The [Licensee] shall ensure that the material in 1.1 conforms in all respects with the contractual and moral obligations of the [Licensor] and all notified copyright notices, credits, trade marks, images, slogans and logos. All samples of every item shall be supplied by the [Licensee] prior to the start of any reproduction, manufacture and/or distribution to the public so that the [Licensor] may approve the samples. The cost of the samples and freight shall be at the [Licensee's] cost but may be off-set as an itemised expense against the sums received.

M.021

All material of any nature in any media which is to be used on and/or in and/or in association with the exploitation of any of the rights licensed under this agreement in respect of the [Film/Video/Sound Recordings] shall be submitted to the [Licensor] for their prior written approval. The [Licensee] shall abide by all requirements of the [Licensor] as to colour, layout, title, copyright notices, credits, trade marks, logos and any other text, images and content.

M.022

The [Licensee] agrees and undertakes that it shall not market, exploit and/or sell, hire, supply and/or make available the [Units] in the following countries and/or on any aeroplanes, ships, vessels, oil rigs and/or other structures on the sea, in the air and/or transport: [specify excluded list].

M.023

The [Licensee] shall not be entitled to license and/or authorise the downloading, display and/or use of the [Film] and/or any parts in any form by means of the internet, any website, app, download and/or by means of any electronic and/or telecommunication systems including laptops, mobiles and/or any other gadgets.

M.024

The [Licensee] agrees that it shall not have the right to market any sound recording, title, character, and/or other part of the [Film/Video/Podcast] separately at any time and/or to authorise any third party to do so.

M.025

The [Licensee] agrees that it shall not be entitled to reproduce, create, develop, sell, supply, market, promote and/or exploit the [DVD/Disc/CD] of the [Film/Programme] in any of the following formats and/or mediums and/or countries and/or languages:

1.1 That there is no permission and/or consent and/or right to supply, rent, lend, sell and/or exploit the [Film/Programme] and/or [DVD/Disc/CD] in an electronic and/or digital format by any means as an ebook, download and/or another method of supply whether for free and/or at a commercial rate over the internet and/or any telecommunication and/or delivery system from any website, app and to be delivered to any mobile and/or gadget in whole and/or in part at any time.

1.2 That there is no permission and/or consent and/or right to promote and/or market and/or use any part of the [Film/Programme] and [DVD/Disc/CD] in any advertisements and/or sponsorship and/or endorsements on any websites, apps, links and/or radio and/or television programmes whether terrestrial, cable and/or satellite and/or at any exhibition and/or or event whether educational, for charity and/or otherwise except those specified [–].

1.3 That there is no permission and/or consent and/or right to sub-license and/or authorise the use by any third party of any part of the [Film/Programme] and/or [DVD/Disc/CD] except by a member of the public purchasing a copy for their own personal use at home only.

1.4 The [Licensee] acknowledges that the following countries are excluded from this agreement: [specify excluded countries].

1.5 The [Licensee] acknowledges that the following languages are excluded from this agreement: [specify excluded languages].

1.6 The [Licensee] acknowledges that there are no associated merchandising rights granted under this agreement and the [Licensee] is not authorised to reproduce and/or supply any posters, stickers, confectionary, T shirts and/or any other products of any nature whether sold at a price and/or given away for free to promote the [DVD/Disc/CD].

1.7 The [Licensee] acknowledges that there is no right granted to authorise and/or produce any theme park, hologram, animated character, computer game, computer software and/or blog and/or app and/or to register with any collecting society and/or government and/or regulatory body any title, character name, place name, logo, image and/or slogan and/or text which forms part of and/or is associated with the [Film/Programme] and/or any adaptation and/or development and/or any work on which it is based at any time.

M.026

The [Licensor] shall provide to the [Company] without extra charge, any promotion and publicity material, stills, photographs and any commercially produced trailers for the [Film/Video/Sound Recording] as may be available.

M.027

The [Licensee] agrees to provide the following credit, copyright notice, trade mark, logo, slogan and image to the [Licensor] in the [Series] and in any advertising, publicity, promotional or packaging material in respect of the marketing and distribution of the [Series] which is set out in Schedule A and forms part of this agreement. The size, position and location of such information shall be as clear and prominent as that for the [Licensee] in each case, and shall be legible and visible to the public.

M.028

1.1 The [Licensor] agrees to provide to the [Licensee] on loan any artwork, stills, photographs, biographies of the principal persons or other material that may assist the [Licensee] to exploit the rights granted under this agreement.

1.2 The [Licensor] agrees that the [Licensee] shall be entitled to arrange for copies to be made of such material at the [Licensee's] cost so that the original material may be returned to the [Licensor] by an agreed date.

1.3 The [Licensee] agrees that any material shall only be used for the purpose of the promotion, marketing and commercial exploitation of the [Series] and that any other use shall be subject to the prior written consent of the [Licensor].

1.4 The [Licensee] agrees to be bound by any restrictions, credits or obligations that the [Licensor] may at any time specify which are required by the [Licensor] and/or any third parties in respect of such material.

1.5 The [Licensee] shall not be entitled to sub-license, exploit and/or transfer rights in any of the material to any third party for any purpose except as specifically authorised under this agreement.

M.029

In respect of all publicity and promotional material for the [Film/Series] it is agreed that no other person shall appear in vision more frequently or prominently than the [Artist] in any promotional extracts of the [Film/Series], advertisements, stills, photographs, posters, likenesses, artwork, labels, catalogues, reviews, merchandising and/or packaging.

M.030

It is the intention of the [Company] to designate a distributor for the [Film/Series] and to negotiate such terms with the distributor so as to ensure that [Production Company] will be entitled to not less than [number] per cent of the Distribution Income [before/after] deduction of any costs relating to reproduction and development of material, marketing, promotion and/or advertising.

M.031

[Name] acknowledges that the [Company] shall have the sole discretion as to the manner and method to be used in marketing, promoting and advertising the [Film/Series] and/or parts in respect of the rights granted under this agreement. That the [Company] is not required to send samples to [Name] and/or to seek approval for any such material.

M.032

The [Licensee] confirms that it shall use its best endeavours to exploit the rights granted under this agreement and to achieve as far as possible the maximum Gross Receipts.

M.033

The [Licensee] agrees to provide to the [Licensor] at the [Licensee's] cost and expense with copies and samples of all final products and/or adaptations and/or translations relating to the exploitation of the [Film/Video/Sound Recording] and any associated labels, packaging, brochures, newspaper, magazine and television advertising, details of promotional events, promotional giveaways, merchandising, sponsorship and endorsements and/or reviews and any other material of any nature every [six] months in the first year and at the end of each calendar year thereafter until the termination and/or expiry of this agreement.

M.034

The [Licensee] confirms that the [Licensee] shall be solely responsible for any sums due in respect of the exploitation and marketing of the [Film/Video/

Sound Recordings] and/or parts and that the [Licensor] shall not be liable for any such payments.

M.035
The [Licensee] shall be entitled to use, license and permit the use of excerpts of the [Film/Video/Sound Recordings] and/or parts for advertising, marketing, sponsorship and endorsement purposes related to the [Film/Company/Sequel/Products] for [television/radio/video/DVD/Discs/CDs/websites/apps/the internet/mobiles] provided that the total aggregate duration shall not exceed [number] minutes of the [Film].

M.036
The [Company] shall have the non-exclusive right in the Territory during the Term of this Agreement to use and broadcast and/or transmit excerpts of the [Film/Video/Sound Recordings] on [television/radio/internet/mobiles] of not more than [two] consecutive minutes in order to advertise and permit reviews of the [Film/Video/Sound Recording] and/or any adaptation and/or sequel. In addition to promote the overall brands of the [Company] in any segment which includes the [Film/Video/Sound Recording] at any exhibition, event and/or award programme.

M.037
The [Company] shall have the non-exclusive right in the Territory during the Term of this Agreement for the purposes of advertisement, publicity, promotion and/or review to reproduce and publish in any language a synopsis, or summary of not more than [number] words from the script of the [Film/Video/Sound Recording] in any printed format whether in newspapers, magazines, trade journals, posters or otherwise and/or to a website company on the internet and/or an app and/or a mobile company and/or a television, radio or news agency and/or any other media and/or to authorise others to do so. Provided that at all times all parties agree and undertake to be the following associated credits, copyright notices and acknowledgements: [specify details].

M.038
The [Company] shall have the non-exclusive right in the Territory during the Term of this Agreement for the purposes of advertisement, publicity, marketing, and review only to use and to permit third parties to use in sound and/or vision the name, physical likeness, voice and biography of any actor, writer, director, or contributor to the [Film/Video/Sound Recording]. Provided that such use shall not constitute either an implied or direct endorsement of any other third party products, services, merchandising and/or activities of any kind.

M.039

The [Distributor] shall have the right to use film some part of the making of the [Series] in order to obtain material to use for promotional excerpts and to make trailers. The [Production Company] shall arrange access to any set or location during the course of production for the purpose of the [Distributor] filming such material at the [Distributor's] sole cost.

M.040

Neither the [Licensor] nor the [Distributor] shall grant nor permit the exercise of the rights granted to the [Television Company] by any other person, company or body. Nor shall the [Licensor] or the [Distributor] execute any document or do anything in derogation from the rights granted under this agreement. The [Licensor] and the [Distributor] shall have the non-exclusive right to permit any cable, satellite, terrestrial, or digital television company in the [United Kingdom/Europe/other] to transmit and/or broadcast excerpts from the [Film/Video/Sound Recording] of up to [number] seconds in total on any one occasion in programmes for the purpose of review, criticism, or promotion of the [Film/Video/Sound Recording]. Provided that the same excerpt is used on each occasion and such excerpt has been approved by the [Television Company].

M.041

Both parties agree that the advertising, marketing, publicity and promotion of the [Film] and/or any parts shall be the sole responsibility of the [Company]. Any requests by third parties relating to such matters shall be passed to the [Company] to deal with whatever the nature of the issue. Failure to adhere to this requirement shall be considered by both parties as a significant breach of this agreement. All personnel, artists, agents, writers, advisors, financiers, composers and musicians and other persons involved in the [Film] shall be advised in writing of this stipulation.

M.042

The [Licensor] shall make available at no extra cost and/or charge any trailers, promotion and publicity material and stills that may be available which shall be retained by the [Licensee] on loan for the duration of this agreement. In the event that trailers of any of the [Films] are not available then the [Licensee] may transmit and/or broadcast short sequences of not more than [two] minutes from each of the [Films] for the purpose of programme announcement and trailing. The [Licensee] shall bear the cost of any damage caused to the [Films] by reason of the extraction of short sequences for such purposes.

M.043

The [Licensee] shall be entitled to broadcast and/or transmit short extracts of parts of the [Films] in sound and/or vision and/or image and/or text and to authorise others to do so whether by television, radio, video and/or by means of telecommunication and/or any other electronic method on the internet, by mobile and/or landline telephone and/or promotional products such as flags, flyers, T shirts, balloons and posters for advertising, promotion, marketing and/or display at trade fairs only. Provided that such use shall be limited to not total more than [one] minute in duration of the [Film] at any time with an aggregate total of [five] minutes duration. The [Licensee] undertakes to ensure that it shall abide by all credits, copyright notices and moral rights obligations in clause [–].The [Licensee] agrees and undertakes to send the [Licensor] a detailed marketing report every [six] months from [date].

M.044

No use of any material shall be permitted which would be derogatory, demeaning, offensive, or prejudicial to the commercial or financial success of the [Film/Video/Sound Recording] and/or the [Artist] and/or the other brands of the [Company].

M.45

The [Distributor] shall be entitled to publicise, advertise, market and promote the [Documentary] in [country/Territory] and to appoint any sub-licensee or other authorised agent to do so during the Term of this Agreement. No sub-licence and/or agency agreement shall exceed the expiry date of this agreement: [specify end date].

M.046

1.1 The [Licensee] shall have the right to create a promotional extract in the following format [specify format] incorporating not more than [number] second of the [Documentary] which shall be used only for promotional, marketing and review purposes.

1.2 The [Licensor] shall not have the right of approval of 1.1, but nothing shall be done which shall be derogatory or offensive to the [Documentary] or anyone associated with any part in vision, sound or otherwise.

1.3 The [Licensee] shall not have the right to license the promotional extract to any third party or any to use such extract in conjunction with any other programme or film transmitted by the [Licensee].

1.4 The [Licensee] shall provide the [Licensor] with one free copy of each promotional extract which may be created.

M.047

1.1 The [Production Company] undertakes that it shall be solely responsible for all costs incurred and sums due in respect of the development,

production, distribution, marketing and exploitation of the [Series/
DVDs/Units/Products] and parts in any form. That the [Author] is not
and will not be liable for any such payments and that the [Production
Company] shall not be entitled to deduct them from the Gross Receipts.

1.2   The [Production Company] agrees to provide copies and samples at
its own cost of any versions, adaptations, advertising, marketing and
packaging in respect of the commercial exploitation of the [Series/
DVDs/Units/Products] when requested to do so by the [Author].

1.3   The [Production Company] agrees to keep the [Author] informed of the
progress of the production and exploitation in any media. The [Author]
shall be advised of all proposed release dates in any media at any
time in the Territory. The [Production Company] agrees to provide a
marketing and exploitation update to the [Author] upon request but no
more than [once] in every year throughout the Licence Period.

M.048
The [Author] accepts that the editorial and artistic control of the marketing
shall be entirely at the [Company's] discretion.

M.049
No third party shall be entitled to be added as a sponsor and/or for the purposes
of product placement and/or as any other type of contributor to the [Documentary/
Series]. No other logos, trade marks, service marks, products, image, slogans,
characters, and/or music and/or sound recordings shall be added in the title
and/or end credits and/or in any related marketing material at any time.

M.050
The [Assignee] agrees that it shall consult with the [Assignor] where it is
proposed to use the [Film/Sound Recording] and/or parts for the purpose of
sponsorship, product placement, endorsement and/or advertising of other
services.

M.051
The [Licensor/Licensee] shall ensure that the consent and agreement is
obtained from all parties involved in the creation and supply of the publicity,
promotion, advertising and marketing material. The cost of payment of
any expenses and fees shall be paid for by the [Licensor/Licensee]. No
such sums shall be deducted from the [Gross Receipts/Net Receipts/sums
received] before the calculation of the royalties due to [Name].

M.052
The [Licensee] shall be entitled to use, license and permit the use of excerpts
of the [Film] and/or parts across all media and formats for advertising,

marketing, sponsorship, endorsement and/or promotional purposes provided that the revenue generated is allocated to the [Gross Receipts/ sums received] and there is a direct related theme to the [Film] and/or the [Sequel] and/or the associated licensed [Products] and/or the licence will reach a wider audience and generate future revenue.

M.053

The [Licensor] agrees that the [Licensee] shall entitled to use and to authorise others to transmit, play, and/or make available an agreed extract of the sound recording of the [Film] of no more than [number] minutes for the purpose of the promoting and marketing the [Film] on radio, the internet, mobiles and/or any other gadget and/or form of exploitation. The [Licensee] shall not be required to pay any additional copyright fee for such use and any right to use the sound recording in this manner shall end on [date].

M.054

The [Licensor] agrees that the [Licensee] may market and promote up to [number] minutes of the same extract of the [Film/Programme] which is agreed with the [Licensor] in advance in the form of banner links, pop ups, advertisements, content on any websites, apps and/or blogs for viewing on any computer, television, laptop, gadget, mobile telephone and/or otherwise provided that the sole purpose is the promotion and marketing of the [Film/Programme] on [channel] in respect of the rights granted by the [Licensor] to the [Licensee].

M.055

The [Licensee] agrees that the [Licensee] shall not be entitled to exploit, supply, sell, distribute and/or offer as a download and/or in electronic and/or digital format and/or by any method and/or means over the internet and/or by any telecommunication system the [Film/Programme] and/or any parts to be viewed and/or received and/or stored by any business, educational body and/or for home use by the public and/or in any marketing, promotional and/ or advertising material at any time.

M.056

1.1 The [Licensor] agrees that the [Licensee] may use a sequence of [images/ film] with added sound recordings and music supplied by the [Licensor] at its cost in [format] which is to be used in that exact form by the [Licensee] for marketing, advertising and promoting the [Game Show] on channel: [specify channel] and on the website: [specify reference] and in the [newsletter/feed] known as [specify detail] during the Licence Period.

1.2 The [Licensee] agrees that all other use of the material in 1.1 must be approved and agreed with the [Licensor] in advance in each case and may be refused at the sole discretion of the [Licensor].

M.057

[Name] agrees that the [Distributor] may use his/her personal and stage name, image, caricature, photographs, sound recordings and any parts of their performances in the [Film/Series] in any format and/or medium and/or language at any time provided that it is to promote and market the [Film/Series] subject to payment to [Name] of an annual additional marketing fee of [number/currency] by the [Distributor].

M.058

It is agreed between the parties that all costs of reproduction of material, editing, copyright and music clearances and payments, and payments due to collecting societies in any part of the world, freight, insurance, contract payments, commission, discounts, currency conversion and bank charges, development of marketing and promotional material and/or the cost of advertisements, banner links, newsfeeds, blogs and listings and/or reviews on any websites and/or apps shall be at the [Licensee's] sole cost.

General Business and Commercial

M.059

1.1 The [Distributor] agrees and undertakes that it shall not nor shall it permit and/or authorise any sub-agent, employee and/or other person engaged by the [Distributor] to release, supply, distribute and/or publish material, data and/or information of any nature relating to this contract or its contents or the [Project] without the prior written approval of the [Company].

1.2 The [Distributor], its sub-agents, employees and/or other persons engaged by the [Distributor] shall be permitted to release their own personal and corporate data; the terms of this agreement and the nature of the [Project] and/or any other relevant data, information and material to professional advisors and/or government bodies and/or any other regulatory organisation for the purpose of any requirement which covers compliance with and/or reporting any legal matter, tax and accounting and/or health and safety.

M.060

The [Enterprise] agrees that it shall not be entitled to arrange and/or permit any advertising, promotional marketing and/or other material to be displayed, exhibited and/or reproduced on the hoardings, exterior walls, buildings, or otherwise of the [Land] and/or equipment and/or structure. That the [Company] shall have the sole right to exploit and retain any revenue from advertising, promotional material, sponsorship, marketing or public relations. and/or any other material to be displayed, exhibited and/

or reproduced on the hoardings, exterior walls, buildings, land, equipment, structure or otherwise at any time.

M.061
Neither the [Project] nor any clothing, structure, land, equipment owned or operated by the [Company] and/or any marketing material, exhibition space and/or any associated promotional [Video/Film/Podcast] may be used by [Name] or any agents with regard to any marketing, promotions, advertising or publicity by them and/or any other person without the prior written consent of the [Company].

M.062
[Name] agrees that he/she shall send to the [Company] at his/her sole cost copies of all material which [Name] would like to use for publicity, marketing or promotional purposes whether website and/or app material, in printed form and/or in any other media which shall incorporate any brand, title, logo, slogan, image, trade mark, quote or text relating to the [Company] and/or the [Project]. [Name] agrees that the [Company] shall then be entitled to reject or approve any such material for use by [Name]. The [Company] shall not be obliged to state any reasons.

M.063
No reference is to be made to the terms and conditions of this agreement by either party at any trade fair and/or exhibition and/or in any interview for any media by any management executive and/or in any marketing, advertising and/or promotional material without the prior written consent of the other party.

M.064
Your appearance and contribution is on the basis that you shall not mention, plug, promote and/or wear any clothes, shoes and/or carry any product for which you are paid a fee and/or reward for product placement and/or endorsement either directly and/or indirectly through a colleague, family member and/or friend. Your appearance and contribution is on the basis that there shall be no advertisement, product placement, endorsement or anything of an advertising or promotional nature by you at any time.

M.065
Nothing contained in this agreement shall prevent and/or restrict the [Distributor] at any time from developing and/or otherwise acquiring rights in and/or marketing and/or exploiting any other [Unit/Product] which is in the field of [detail subject examples exercise/sport/music] whether or not it is similar to the subject matter for the [Unit/Product].

M.066

The [Sub-Publisher] shall use its best endeavours to maximise the commercial exploitation of the [Compositions] in the Territory during the Term and shall use its best endeavours to recover all sums due.

M.067

The [Record Company] agrees that the minimum marketing budget with respect to each [Album/Recording] shall not be less than [number/currency] in each year for the first two years.

M.068

Neither the [Project] nor any location, facilities, vessels and/or other material owned and/or operated by the [Company] and/or its subsidiaries may be used by the [Enterprise] and/or third party consultants for the purposes of marketing, promoting and/or creating images, sound recordings, films, videos and/or podcasts without the prior written consent of the [Company].

M.069

The [Enterprise] agrees and undertakes that it shall not reproduce, publish and/or distribute any material to be made available to the public regarding their services under this agreement and/or the nature of the work to be fulfilled at any time without the prior approval of the [specify role/Chief Executive] of the [Company].

M.070

The [Assignor] acknowledges that the [Assignee] shall have the sole discretion as to the manner and method to be used in marketing, promoting, advertising and distributing the [Product/Work/Services] in respect of the rights assigned under this agreement.

M.071

The [Distributor] agrees to use its reasonable endeavours to reproduce, distribute and sell the [Units/Products/Services] to the public in [country] within [four] months of the date of this agreement.

M.072

The [Distributor] undertakes to provide the [Licensor] with a minimum of [number] free copies in each and every medium and/or format that the [Units/Products] and any packaging and marketing are released to the public or otherwise commercially exploited.

M.073

The [Licensee] acknowledges that it shall not be entitled to exploit in any manner any sound recordings of the [Musical Work] without the prior written consent of the [Licensor].

M.074
The [Licensee] agrees that it shall not be entitled to register any domain name, trade mark, character, title, logo, image, slogan and/or computer software associated with the [Work/Service/Products/Films]. The [Licensee] acknowledges that all such rights and material set out in Schedule A are the subject of existing and/or pending applications by the [Licensor].

M.075
[Name] agrees that the [Company] may use the material [filmed/recorded/photographed] on [date] as it thinks fit and in any manner and /or by any means and/or medium at any time. Provided that the [Company] does not license the material to any third party and/or edit, adapt and/or vary the material so that it mocks, demeans and/or represents [Name] in a derogatory and/or offensive manner.

M.076
[Name] agrees that all promotional and marketing material to be distributed by [Name] which bears the name of the [Company] and/or the [Products] supplied to [Name] by the [Company] must be approved in each case. [Name] agrees and undertakes that no such material of any nature in any medium shall be distributed on the internet through any blog, podcast, website and/or app and/or any other social media forum and/or in any interview, recording and/or programme without the prior consent of the [Company].

Internet, Websites and Apps

M.077
It is a condition of the supply by any person of any material in any format which is reproduced, loaded, displayed and exhibited on this [Website/App/Forum] which is made available to the public by the [Company]. That the [Company] shall have the right and be entitled to quote, refer to, and/or reproduce any such material as it thinks fit in any marketing, advertising and publicity without any payment. This may occur by the [Company] directly and/or through a third party. The only requirement shall be that the [Company] ensures that there is a suitable acknowledgement as to the source and/or provides a copyright notice and/or credit as required.

M.078
The [Distributor] undertakes to feature the [Service/Product/Company] on the [Website/App] reference [specify] under the category listing [specify], together with the summary and an image for not less than [specify period]. No additional cost and/or charge shall be made to the [Company] for such advertising and promotion.

M.079

No contributor, blogger, member of the public and/or any other person, entity, charity and/or corporation has the right to use any part of this [Website/App/Platform] and/or any part of any content and/or products and/or the name of the [Company] and/or any trade mark, service mark, logo, image and/or slogan for the purposes of promotion, advertising, endorsement, sponsorship, product placement and/or otherwise to assist their own business, products, services, website, app and/or those of a third party and/or otherwise whether for financial gain or not. If you wish to use any part of this [Website/App/Platform] the prior written consent of the [Company] will be required. Failure to do could result in the commencement of a legal action against you for infringing the rights and/or causing loss and/or damage to the [Company].

M.080

As a subscriber to this [Website/App/Platform] you are encouraged to assist the [Company] in the marketing, promotion and advertising of the [Website/App/Platform] and may download short extracts of parts of the [Website/App/Platform] of not more than [number] minutes in duration in the form of films, sound recordings, number [words] in text and/or [number] images in total and supply it to friends and on social media without charge provided that:

1.1 it is not for financial gain and/or any other benefit.

1.2 no credit, copyright notice, trade mark and/or copyright warning is deleted and/or edited and/or amended.

1.3 no use shall be permitted which would be derogatory, demeaning, offensive, or prejudicial to the material and/or the copyright owner and/or the [Company].

1.4 the following credit is made to the [Company] and the [Website/App/Platform]: [specify details].

M.081

The [Company] shall be entitled promote, market and/or exploit the product of the [Contributors] work and/or any part on the [Website/App/Blog] in any media including but not limited to advertisements, television, radio, mobiles, the internet, newsletters, downloads, merchandising, books, magazines and newspapers without any further payment.

M.082

The [Company] agrees and undertakes that:

1.1 it shall not market and/or promote the [Contributor] in any format and/or media outside the [Website/App] without the prior written consent and approval of [Name].

1.2 it shall not seek to register a domain name in the [Contributor's] personal and/or stage name and/or any shortened version related to their initials and/or any other name by which they may be known.

1.3 it has no authority and/or right to authorise any third party to use the name of the [Contributor] in 1.2 to endorse, market and/or promote any other website, service, product and/or any other matter.

M.83

The [Company] and/or any parent company and/or subsidiary shall be entitled to market and promote the [Product/Service/Festival] on its [Website/App] and on any banner advertisements and/or pop-ups and/or listings on the internet, in printed form in catalogues and adverts in magazines and newspapers; by text messaging and direct email marketing. As well as at trade fairs, exhibitions, conferences and marketing on the streets with branded teams of promotional personnel.

M.084

The [Company] agrees and undertakes that:

1.1 it shall in respect of any advertisement and/or promotion of the [Product/Service/Work] under this agreement ensure that the colour, style and layout of the trade mark, logo, image and name of the [Product] which is specified in Schedule A is used and not any variation and/or adaptation.

1.2 it shall not authorise and/or commission any third party to create and/or develop any new material without the prior written approval of the third party and the proposed use by the [Company].

M.085

[Name] agrees that the [Company] may display, adapt, reproduce and supply to third parties in any form at no cost the [Image/Photograph/Sound Recordings] in order to promote and market the [Event/Festival] before [date].

M.086

The [Company] agrees that in the event that [Name] wants any marketing, promotional and/or advertising material amended, adapted, deleted and/or removed for any reason from the [website/social forum] of the [Company] and/or any other material. Then the [Company] agrees that it shall make such changes and take such actions as may be required in order to meet the demands of [Name]. Provided that alternative material is agreed and substituted and the cost in total does not exceed [number/currency].

M.087

It is agreed between the parties that the [Company] and/or any distributor, licensee and/or agent shall be entitled to use short extracts agreed with [Name] of the [Podcast] in order to promote, market and advertise the [Book/Documentary/Products] at no additional cost to the [Company]. Provided that all parties shall adhere to the required credits, acknowledgements and brand criteria in clause [–].

M.088

1.1 [Name] agrees that his/her interview and contribution on the [Programme/Podcast] shall include both [Name] and the following family members: [specify]. The appearance fee of [number/currency] is for all such contributions.

1.2 [Name] provides authority for the [Company] to reproduce, distribute, market and promote the interview both before and after the [Programme/Podcast].

1.3 [Name] shall supply additional photographs of all such other persons in 1.1 on loan which may be used by the [Company] for the [Programme/Podcast] and/or marketing for a fixed fee of [number/currency] without further payment.

M.089

1.1 [Name] is the main contributor and performer in an online internet account known as [specify details] on [specify site]. [Name] grants the [Company] the non-exclusive right to reproduce and develop a [specify product type] bearing the following words, text and image relating to [Name] and his/her brand known as [specify].

1.2 The [Company] shall have a licence which shall commence on [date] and end on [date]. The licence shall only apply to [specify countries].

1.3 The sample product must be approved by [Name]. The [Company] agrees and undertakes to make any changes that [Name] may request.

1.4 The [Company] shall submit a proposed marketing report to [Name] for his/her consideration before any campaign is launched. The [Company] agrees and undertakes to make any changes that [Name] may request.

1.5 The [Company] accepts that all final editorial, artistic, marketing and other decisions remain with [Name].

M.090

The [Enterprise] has commissioned the following material: [specify Logo/Image/Film/Computer Software/Animation/Character] for incorporation in a [website/app/product]. The [Enterprise] has bought out and been assigned all the rights in all media in clause [–]. This shall include the right to make any changes, alterations and/or adaptations and/or to market, promote and/or license such material and/or rights without any further payment to the [Creator/Artist].

M.091
There shall be no right to use and/or authorise the use of any title, logo, image, character, trade mark, slogan and/or otherwise and/or to create any adaptation for any reason of any part of this [App/Product]. You are not permitted to add any material from this [App/Product] to any marketing material for your own podcast, blog and/or internet account of any nature.

Merchandising and Distribution

M.092
The [Licensor] agrees to provide on loan copies of the artwork of the [Character] and any trade mark, logo, copyright notice, image or other credit as may be required by the [Licensee] for the purposes of this agreement.

M.093
The [Designer] agrees to be responsible for all packaging, publicity, advertising, promotions and sales of the [Products] and confirms that all such costs shall be at the [Designer's] cost and shall not be offset in any manner in the calculation of the Net Receipts.

M.094
The [Licensee] shall ensure that the [Licensed Products] together with all wrappings, containers, contents, labels, packaging, displays, articles, marketing, publicity or advertising materials in any format shall adhere to the requirements of the brand samples, credits and copyright notices, trade marks, logos, images, slogans and associated sound recordings set out in appendix A in size, colour, layout, design and location.

M.095
The [Licensee] acknowledges that it shall be responsible for all costs incurred in the commercial exploitation of the [Licensed Products] including production, manufacture, distribution, sales, marketing, advertising and promotions. The [Licensee] accepts and agrees that it shall not be entitled to deduct all these costs from the sums received before payment of any royalties to the [Licensor]. The [Licensee] shall only be entitled to deduct a maximum of [number/currency] and this shall be spread over [number] years of the Licence Period in equal amounts of [number/currency] for the first [number] years. Any sum in excess of these numbers shall be at the [Licensees] sole cost.

M.096

The [Licensee] undertakers that the minimum [wholesale/retail selling price] for each of the [Licensed Products] shall be not less than [number/currency] in the first [number] years of the Licence Period.

M.097

The [Licensee] undertakes to use and reproduce the [Character] and any trade mark, logo, slogan, image, text, computer-generated material, graphics, icon, recording and music for the sole purpose of producing, manufacturing, selling, supplying, distributing and marketing the [Licensed Products]. The [Licensee] shall not be entitled to issue any sub-licence to any third party for any reason.

M.098

1.1 The [Licensee] undertakes that it shall use its best endeavours to exploit the rights granted under this agreement and as far as possible to achieve a level of Gross Receipts of not less than [number/currency] with a marketing and promotional budget for the first calendar year of not less than [number/currency].

1.2 The [Licensee] shall compile a detailed strategy and marketing report for consideration by the [Licensor] which shall specify key target retail outlets; planned social media and product placement proposals; paid for advertisements on television, radio and in newspapers and/or magazines; outdoor advertising together with all associated costs of creating and developing the relevant material.

1.3 The [Licensee] agrees to consult with the [Licensor] and to take into account any recommendations and/or changes that they may wish considered.

M.099

The [Company] undertakes that it shall be solely responsible for and bear the cost of all sums which may be incurred in respect of the development, production, manufacture, distribution, marketing, promotion, advertising and exploitation of the [Licensed Products] and that such sums shall not be deducted from the [sums received/Gross Receipts/Net Receipts] and/or offset in any manner and shall not impact on the calculation of the royalties due to the [Licensor] under this agreement at any time.

M.100

The Company undertakes that not less than [number] units of the [Licensed Products] shall be manufactured and reproduced within [twelve] months of approval of the [Prototype/Final Sample].

M.101
The [Licensee] shall provide a regular marketing, advertising and sales report to the [Licensor] and supply examples of all material which has been distributed at the [Licensee's] cost.

M.102
The [Licensee] shall be entitled to market and promote the [Product] and any associated packaging, image, logo, trade mark and product name [in language] in [countries] as follows:

1.1 On the [Licensee's] [Website/App] and those of any agent, distributor and sub-licensee by means of a summary on a page, by promotional material as electronic attachments via emails, by text to mobile phones, through a regular newsletter, banner advertisements, pop-ups and on social media, blogs, podcasts and films through product placement. As well as in any catalogue, printed adverts in magazines, newspapers, journals, and flyers; at trade shows, exhibitions and events.

1.2 Provided that at all times in 1.1 the [Product] is the main feature and appears as a separate item and is not be combined with any other service and/or product.

M.103
The [Licensee] shall not be entitled to promote, market and/or exploit the [Product] by means of any form of electronic and/or telecommunication means over the internet, in podcasts, television, radio and/or as licensed merchandising, books and toys and/or as an endorsement of a person and/or charity and/or in any film, video, sound recording, play, DVD, disc and any other form of mechanical reproduction in any format and/or in hotels, on aeroplanes and/or in educational establishments. The [Licensee] is only permitted to sell the [Products] through it own website and retail outlets listed in appendix A.

M.104
The [Licensor] agrees that the [Licensee] may market, promote and advertise the availability of the [Licensed Products] in newspapers, over the internet and on websites and social media in articles, advertisements, banner links and/or in the form of prizes for competitions and/or through product placement arrangements.

M.105
The [Licensee] agrees and undertakes that it shall not be entitled use and/or adapt any part of the [Licensed Products] and/or any associated trade name, character, logo and/or image and/or storyline from the [Project/Film/Book] as a computer software game, toy, app, board game, household

utensil and/or clothing, stationary and/or by any other form of adaptation except the exact form in which it is licensed and specified in Schedule A.

M.106

1.1 The [Agent] agrees to promote, market and obtain orders for the [Products] based on the [Samples] at the prices and on the terms and conditions specified at any time by the [Licensor].

1.2 The [Agent] agrees to inform any retail store or outlet or online distribution company that wishes to order the [Product] that they must pay the total sum in [dollars] of the [ex-factory] price of any item plus freight and insurance to the requested destination and shall be responsible for all customs clearance, storage duty and taxes that may be incurred.

1.3 Title in any [Products] ordered shall remain with the [Licensor] until full payment of the invoice has been received by the [Licensor].

M.107
The [Supplier] agrees that the [Outlet] may:

1.1 market, promote and sell the [Product] at any price it deems fit provided that the fixed price per unit of the [Product] shall be paid for each unit supplied and not returned.

1.2 reproduce, display and market the [Product] and any image, text, endorsement in any shape and form as it thinks fit provided that there is no offensive or derogatory treatment of the [Product], the [Supplier] or any third party.

M.108

1.1 The [Distributor] shall at its own expense diligently direct its activities to sell the [Products] supplied by the [Company] under the [Company's] name and trade marks.

1.2 The [Distributor] shall send to the [Company] as much market information as may be available in order to develop and manufacture other similar products which are competitive.

1.3 Both parties shall co-operate with each other in good faith and in the event that there are any technical or marketing problems concerning the [Products] the parties shall endeavour to reach a solution based on a long-term working relationship for the benefit of both parties.

M.109
The [Distributor] shall submit to the [Company] for prior approval in writing all sales, packaging, promotional and advertising matter including labels,

containers, banner links, pop-ups, photographs images, text, slogans and logos for websites, apps and articles in magazines, trade journals and newspapers; videos, films, sound recordings whether created by the [Distributor] and/or commissioned from a third party in connection with the [Product]. The [Distributor] agrees that it shall make any changes to any material required by the [Company] and accepts that the [Company] has the final decision.

M.110

The [Company] agrees that it shall arrange at the [Company's] cost in [country] for:

1.1 a major launch of the [Product/Service] with a budget of not less than [number/currency].

1.2 [National/international] promotions on the internet and social media, on television and radio; magazines and newspapers subject to the restraints of the proposed budget in 1.1.

1.3 advertising in the following magazines: [specify names] before [date].

1.4 advertising on the following websites: [specify names] for at least [three] months.

1.5 a premium telephone line prize/promotion game in conjunction with a programme on television, radio or through an online media company.

1.6 a review and strategy report to be prepared and supplied with detailed data and information by [date].

M.111

The [Company] shall advertise and promote the [Seller's] [Products/ Services] on the [website/app]: [name/reference] as follows:

1.1 The [Seller] shall be the main display advertiser and the [Products/ Services] shall feature on all the main pages: [specify detail].

1.2 No other advertiser shall have the right to be displayed where there is a direct conflict of interest resulting from the same type of products or same market namely: [specify conflicting products/markets].

1.3 That where there is any other associated publicity, advertising or promotional material distributed by the [Company] during the Term of this Agreement. Then the [Seller] and its [Products/Services] shall be given due prominence, credit and recognition as the main advertiser on the [website/app] with the following text, trade mark and image: [specify detail].

1.4 In any flotation of the [website/app] or any in the production of stock market documents that may be issued by the [Company] then the [Seller] and its [Products/Services] shall feature in the documentation.

1.5 The [Company] shall have the final editorial decision in respect of the position and size of the [Products/Services] and the name of the [Seller] and any commentary. Provided that it shall represent a true and accurate image, trade mark, text and information of the [Products/Services] and the [Seller].

M.112
The [Company] agrees that the [Product] shall only be sold in the following outlet and method: [specify detail].

M.113
The [Seller] agrees that it shall not issue any statement to the media regarding the [Products] and/or the [Supplier] without the prior consultation with [the press office/name] of the [Supplier]. The [Seller] agrees that it shall not knowingly and with malice deliberately bring the [Supplier] and/or its [Products] into disrepute and/or act in a derogatory and/or offensive manner and/or cause any loss and/or damage to the business and/or reputation of the [Supplier] and/or its reputation and/or its [Products].

M.114
The [Distributor] agrees and undertakes that [Name] shall not be liable for any of the costs and expenses associated with the development, production and/or exploitation of the [Work] in the form of the [Product] and all packaging, marketing, advertising, product liability and/or any competitions and/or associated promotions through the [Distributor] and/or any parent company, licensee and/or third party at any time.

M.115

1.1 The [Distributor] agrees that the domain names and the trademarks and the associated slogans, text, images and logo set out in Schedule A are owned by [Name].

1.2 The [Distributor] agrees not to try to register any other material which may be created under this agreement which is derived from and/or based on any concepts, contribution, work and/or other material supplied by [Name]. That any new domain names, trade marks and material which may be created in relation to the [Products] and are capable of being registered shall be registered by [Name] in his/her sole name at his/her cost. The [Distributor] shall not acquire and/or share any interest in any such material with [Name]. Where new material is commissioned and/or developed by the [Distributor] all such rights in all media shall be assigned to [Name] for a nominal sum.

M.116
The [Licensee] shall not be entitled to advertise, promote and/or sub-license any part and/or all of the [Products/Services] in any formats other than that specifically authorised under this Licence. The following formats are not permitted:

1.1 Animations, films, videos, podcasts, sound recordings, computer generated material, moving images and/or art installations and/or holograms.

1.2 Theme parks, balloons, three and two dimensional representations, clothes, shoes, bags, stationary, household items, toys, audio books, ebooks, hardback and paperback books, merchandising and/or promotional giveaways.

Publishing

M.117
The [Publisher] agrees that the [Author] shall be entitled to be consulted in relation to the layout, size, colour, photographs, illustrations, artwork, typography, binding, index and copyright notices and corporate information of the [Work/Book] and the design, text and blurb on the jacket or cover. In addition, the [Publisher] agrees to take account of the views of the [Author] in respect of the price, format and marketing of the [Work/Book]. The [Author] acknowledges that the [Publisher] shall have the final decision in respect of the [Work/Book] in all matters except: [specify]. The [Publisher] shall use its reasonable endeavours to ensure that the following conditions in respect of the [Work/Book] are fulfilled:

1.1 That the [Work/Book] is accurately and adequately described and set out in each of its catalogues, brochures and other marketing and advertising material.

1.2 That sufficient copies of the [Work/Book] are available for distribution and sale to the public by the publication date and the first print run in [country] shall not be less than [number] copies.

1.3 That the cover of the [Work/Book] and the text and artwork shall be of a high professional standard suitable for the nature of the [Work/Book] and feature the name of the [Author] on the front and spine of the [Work/Book].

1.4 That all quotes and use of statements from third parties in respect of the [Work/Book] to be used in respect of any marketing, advertising, promotional material or the cover shall be subject to the prior written approval of the [Author].

1.5 That a total marketing and promotion budget of not less than [number/ currency] shall be allocated and used in respect of the [Work/Book] in [country].

1.6 That review copies of the [Work/Book] shall be sent to all persons specified by the Author up to [number] in total.

1.7 That the marketing and promotion of the [Work/Book] shall include newspapers, television, radio, podcasts, videos and other content for websites, blogs and apps, book signing sessions, outdoor advertisements, posters, features at Literary Festivals, Book Fairs and other events where reasonably possible.

1.8 That the [Publisher] shall pay to the [Author] all reasonable expenses and costs incurred in respect of the attendance of the [Author] and his/her agent at any additional dates to complete any work and/or to market and/or promote the [Work/Book].

1.9 The [Publisher] agrees to provide the [Author] with copies of all marketing, advertising or other material associated with the [Work/ Book] upon request.

M.118
The [Publishers] shall unless prevented by circumstances beyond their control produce, print, reproduce and publish the [Work/Book] in [country]:

1.1 In [hardback] not less than [number] copies within [six] months of delivery and approval of the manuscript and proofs of the [Work/Book]; and

1.2 In [paperback] not less than [number] copies within [twelve] months of the date of publication in [hardback] in 1.1.

M.119
The [Publisher] shall consult with the [Author] regarding:

1.1 the layout, design, images, slogans, binding and marketing of the proofed and edited version of the manuscript of the [Work] and its reproduction in the format of a hardback and/or paperback book and/ or any audio recording.

1.2 any person to be chosen to provide any voices and/or music for any audio recording.

1.3 the editorial decisions, production, publication, promotion, pricing, reprinting, exploitation and sale of any format of the [Work].

The [Author] accepts that the final decision in respect of all matters in respect of 1.1 to 1.3 above shall be that of the [Publisher].

M.120

The [Publisher] undertakes to promote and market the [Work/Book] by [date] and to reproduce, distribute and make available for sale [number] copies of the final approved proofed version by [date] in [format]. This undertaking is subject to any circumstances which may arise from force majeure in clause [–] and the delivery of the first draft manuscript by [date] by the [Author].

M.121

The [Publisher] agrees that it shall be solely responsible for all costs, expenses, charges and liabilities which may be incurred in the development, printing, binding, publishing, distribution, advertising, promotion, marketing and exploitation of the final agreed [Work/Product/ Service]. The [Publisher] shall not have any right to set-off, claim and/or deduct any sums due to the [Author] and/or in respect of any of the [Gross Receipts/Net Receipts/sums received] except those matters specifically agreed in clause [–].

M.122

1.1 At the date of this agreement the proposed first print run of the [Work/ Book] is [number] copies in [format/country]. The [Publisher] agrees to inform the [Author] as soon as possible after publication of the actual number of copies printed and of the persons to whom complimentary copies have been promised on publication.

1.2 All details as to production, printing, publication, typography, cover design, price and terms of sale, advertisement and promotion of the [Work/Book] both in the United Kingdom and overseas and the number and destination of free copies shall be at the discretion of the [Publisher] which shall bear all such costs and expenses but shall be entitled to deduct such sums from the [Gross Receipts/Net Receipts/ sums received] prior to the calculation of any royalty payments due to the [Author].

1.3 The [Publisher] will consult the [Author] on all matters regarding the publication date; attendance at festivals, events, book signings, interviews, filming, recording, the development, design and creation of marketing material for any media, artwork, illustrations and photography, the cover design, any flyers, posters and/or promotional merchandising. The [Author] accepts that the [Publisher] shall have the final decision in all such matters.

M.123

1.1 The [Publishers] will have the entire control of the format, paper, binding, typography, layout and design of the [Work/Book] and its jacket. All decisions as to the production, publication, distribution, advertising, price and terms of sale of the [Work/Book] will be made by the [Publishers] at their sole discretion including the location of any images, names, titles, notices or credits.

1.2 The [Publishers] shall send a copy of the proposed jacket, biographical material and any marketing quotes to the [Author] in advance of publication of the [Work/Book] for the purpose of consulting with the [Author].

M.124

The [Author] shall make himself/herself available as reasonably required by the [Publisher] for the promotion of the [Work/Book] for the following periods:

1.1 [ten] [appearances/interviews] up to [four] months after the date of publication of the [hardback/paperback].

1.2 [ten] [appearances/interviews] up to [two] months after the date of publication of the [e book/audio recording].

The [Author] shall attend such events at no extra cost provided that the [Publisher] shall bear the cost of any reasonable expenses. The [Publisher] shall pay the [Author] a fee to be agreed in advance on each occasion for any additional appearances.

M.125

At the date of this agreement the proposed first print run of the [Work/Book] is [number] copies. The [Publisher] agrees to inform the [Author] as soon as possible after publication of the actual number of copies printed in each format. The [Publisher] shall also provide the [Author] with a list of persons who have received complimentary and/or review copies.

M.126

All details as to the manner of production, publication, advertisement and promotion of the [Book/Service] in the Territory and the number and destination of free [copies/ trial subscribers] shall be at the discretion of the [Publisher] which shall be responsible for all such costs and expenses. The [Publisher] undertakes to produce and market the [Book/Service] to a high standard.

M.127

The [Publisher] shall use its reasonable endeavours to market the [Work/ Service/Product] effectively as follows:

1.1 Distribute a [leaflet/email] to a database of at least [number] companies/ persons who work in the field of [specify subject area].

1.2 Describe the [Work/Service/Product] accurately both in its marketing material and catalogue and when supplying information to third parties.

1.3 Despatch review or promotional copies to at least [number] companies/ persons.

1.4 Arrange for advertisements in the following: [detail trade journals/ magazines/newspapers].

1.5 Ensure that the [Work/Service/Product] is featured on the [Publisher's] stand at all trade exhibitions and in any major promotions on the internet.

1.6 Ensure that sufficient copies are printed and/or reproduced for distribution and sale to the public by the publication date and in any event not less than [number].

1.7 Ensure that the [Work/Service/Product] and any cover, illustrations, artwork and associated promotional shall be of a high professional standard.

1.8 That all quotes and uses of statements from third parties by the [Publisher] of the [Work/Service/product] shall be subject to the approval of the [Author].

1.9 That the total marketing budget is not less than [number/currency].

1.10 That [number] review copies will be sent to persons recommended by the [Author].

1.11 That the marketing of the [Work/Service/Product] shall cover the following media: [specify strategy plan of media coverage/attach appendix].

1.12 The [Publisher] shall, unless prevented by force majeure and/or delay by the [Author] try to aim for these release dates in each format: [specify format and release date].

M.128
The [Company] shall be permitted to use extracts of the [Author's Work] on other books or publications up to a limit of [number] words without additional payment to the [Author]. Provided that the extracts are used solely for the purpose of advertising, promotion and publicity of the [Author] and/or the [Author's Work].

M.129
The [Company] shall regularly send the [Author] copies of all publicity, advertising and promotional material for the [Work/Service/Product]. Where

the [Author] reports an inaccuracy and/or error then the [Company] agrees that it shall ensure that it is not repeated. Further the [Company] will be willing to arrange meetings for the [Author] with the marketing personnel prior to the preparation of the marketing material and launch of the [Work/Service/Product] so that the [Author] is given the opportunity of being consulted as to the proposed strategy.

M.130

The [Company] shall advise the [Author] of the marketing budget for the [Project] and shall fully disclose details of the planned strategy. The [Author] shall be consulted but the final decision in any marketing matter shall be decided by the [Company].

M.131

The [Company] agrees that it shall provide a budget of [number/currency] for the marketing of the first edition of the [Work/Book/Service/Product] in [format/ hardback/paperback] in [country].

M.132

Where the [Author] is required to attend any event in respect of the marketing of the [Book/Service/Product] in any form. The [Company] agrees that it shall arrange for and bear the cost and expense of all [first class] accommodation, a chauffeur-driven car and/or first class airline tickets, all food and drinks, hospitality and other costs directly related to any such event incurred by the [Author] but not his/her agent.

M.133

The [Author] agrees that the [Publisher] shall be entitled to use and permit the use of an agreed style and material for his/her name, photograph, biography and image but not signature in respect of the publication and commercial exploitation of the rights licensed under this agreement.

M.134

The [Author] agrees that the manner and method of producing, distributing and marketing the [Book/Service/Work] including the cover designs, selling price and terms of sale of the [Book/Service/Work] shall be at the [Publisher's] sole discretion subject to clauses [–] which relate to copyright notices, credits and moral rights.

M.135

1.1 The [Publisher] shall consult with the [Author] in respect of the appointment of any third party to exploit the [Work/Book/Service/Products].

1.2 The [Publisher] shall provide the [Author] with details of the proposed release dates in respect of the exploitation of the [Work/Book/Service/ Products]. Together with [number] exact examples in each and every format in which the [Publisher] has supplied and/or sold and/or otherwise exploited the [Work/Book/Service/Products] which shall be produced and delivered at the [Publisher's] sole cost.

M.136

The [Company] shall not add either in the main content of the [Book/ Service] and/or on any cover, dust jacket, label and/or packaging and/or in conjunction with it at any time place and/or display any advertisement, promotion, sponsorship and/or marketing for any other company, business, person, book, product and/or article which creates the impression that it is endorsed by and/or marketed in connection with the [Author] and/or his/her [Book/Service] without the prior authorisation of the [Author].

M.137

The [Author] shall be entitled to be consulted in respect of all proposed material to be created and/or developed in respect of the [Book/Service/Products] including but not limited to: book covers, display materials and posters, online marketing images, biographical summaries and/or key marketing tags; promotional, advertising and packaging material in any country throughout the world at any time. The [Company] shall ensure that this a contractual obligation to all sub-licensees, agents, suppliers and/or distributors.

M.138

The [Publisher] shall not be entitled nor shall it permit any employee, consultant, agent and/or distributor and/or any other third party to edit, adapt, alter, translate and/or change the preface, introduction, disclaimer, the proofed manuscript reproduced in the [Work/Book/Service] and/or any part including the illustrations, photographs, index, the main title and/or any chapter headings in any way for any purpose.

M.139

The [Publishers] agree and undertake to consult with the [Author]:

1.1 in respect of all aspects of the production, printing, publication, promotion, sale, display, price, advertising, marketing and exploitation of the [Book/Service].

1.2 in the development of the book cover which shall include the design, colour and layout.

1.3 to allow the [Author] to comment on draft proposals for slogans, images, written content for marketing flyers and brochures; website, app and social media promotional material.

1.4   to arrange for the [Author] to meet with the marketing personnel to discuss options and strategy.

1.5   to provide the [Author] with a marketing update report after the first [twelve] month period in order to report on sales and prospects for the future.

M.140

The [Author] and the [Publisher] agree that they shall jointly own, control and hold the rights in the domain name and any other similar names which may be registered in respect of the title, characters and themes related to the [Work/Book/Service] which shall be registered at the [Publisher's] sole cost. That all rights, interest and sums received from any sale, exploitation and/ or otherwise related to any such registration shall also be shared equally between the parties.

M.141

The [Author] and [Publisher] agree that where any computer-generated material, app, website, blog, webinar, film, sound recording, computer game, product, competition, toy and/or other associated marketing material is created, commissioned, developed and/or adapted from the [Character/Manuscript/ Book] and paid for by the [Publisher] and/or any sub-licensee, agent and/or other third party. It is agreed that the [Author] and the [Publisher] shall jointly own, control and hold all copyright, computer software rights, domain name, trade mark, intellectual property rights and/or any other interest equally and shall share all sums that may be received at any time equally between them..

M.142

The [Publisher] agrees that the [Author] shall be provided once a year with a detailed breakdown of the number of copies and formats of the [Work/ Book/Service/Products] supplied and/or sold in any country. Where possible the [Publisher] shall also supply examples of advertising, marketing and promotional material.

M.143

The [Contributor] accepts that he/she shall have no right to be consulted in respect of the marketing and/or promotion of the product of their work under this agreement. No additional fees shall be due to the [Contributor] for any reason.

Services

M.144

The [Manager] shall use his/her best endeavours to promote and publicise the [Group] in all forms of the media including television, radio, press, reviews, musical engagements, appearances, merchandising, commercial recordings, the internet and social media. The [Manager] shall advertise the [Group] in [magazine] on no less than [number] occasions, display their details on the website [specify] and issue press releases relating to their services.

M.145

Subject to prior consultation the [Presenter] agrees that the [Company] shall be entitled to use his/her name, biography, photograph, likeness, signature and image in respect of the promotion and advertising of the [Company] and the [Series] in all media throughout the [Territory/Country/world]. Provided that any other commercial exploitation relating to the [Presenter] shall be subject to the prior written consent of the [Presenter] and subject to an additional agreement.

M.146

1.1 The [Company] shall have the right and license to use and reproduce the [Artist's] name, signature, biographical material and likenesses for the purposes of this agreement including labels, catalogues and exploiting the [Records/DVDs/Units] on the website [specify] for direct sales and under a subscription service.

1.2 The [Company] agrees to supply the [Artist] with a sample of any proposed label. catalogue, cover, packaging, web site and/or social media material for his/her appraisal. The [Artist] agrees to provide a verbal response to the [Company] within [number] days of receipt of any material. The [Company] agrees to incorporate all reasonable requests made by the [Artist].

M.147

1.1 The [Agent] undertakes not to disclose any material nor make nor repeat any statement, whether true or not, concerning the [Artist's] private life and social life, political and personal views to any media including newspapers, television, radio and on the internet and/or by means of any telecommunication system and/or mobile [at any time/ during the Term of this Agreement] without the prior written consent of the [Artist].

1.2 This agreement shall not include the right of the [Agent] to receive any sums in respect of the authorised and/or unauthorised biography and/ or other memoir of the [Artist].

M.148

The [Agent] agrees not to promote, market and/or advertise the [Actor] in anyway which may impugn the reputation and/or embarrass the [Actor].

As far as possible the [Agent] shall provide samples of all material and undertakes to adhere to any changes requested by the [Actor]. The [Agent] agrees it shall be entirely responsible for the cost and expense of all such material and no such sums shall be deducted from any monies due to the [Actor].

M.149

The [Presenter] and the [Company] mutually agree and undertake that each of them shall not during the Term of this Agreement publish in writing or otherwise make known to the public and/or the media and/or act in any way likely to result in publication of any matter concerning the business affairs of each other at any time which are not publicly available without the prior written consent of the party to whom any such data, information and/or material may relate or effect.

M.150

The [Company] agrees to consult with the [Actor] and the Agent in respect of all proposed scripts, credits, labels, packaging, advertising, promotional, publicity and marketing material prior to the production, manufacture and distribution of the material by the [Company] and/or any third party.

M.151

The [Company] acknowledges that the [Actor] shall be entitled upon request to be provided at the [Company's] sole cost with a copy of any publicity, advertising, promotional and marketing material in the possession or under the control of the [Company] featuring the [Actor].

M.152

The [Agent] agrees to ensure that the [Author] shall be entitled to be consulted with respect to all proposed copies, samples and other material of the [Artwork/Sound Recordings] in respect of the production, distribution, marketing and exploitation of the [Artwork/Sound Recordings].

M.153

The [Manager] shall use his/her skills to obtain work for the services of the [Sportsperson] and to promote the [Sportsperson] in all forms of the media in [specify countries/the defined Territory] in order obtain paid work for the [Sportsperson] in:

1.1 Programmes, films, theatre, DVDs, discs, corporate videos and events, sound recordings, voice-overs, guest appearances, interviews, game shows and presentations.

1.2 Advertisements, commercials and appearances for all forms of terrestrial, cable, satellite, digital television, radio, mobile, newspaper, magazine and media companies for websites, apps and the internet, podcasts, blogs, product placement and endorsement advertisements and events.

1.3 Merchandising, publications and licensing of his/her image, name and brand for services, products and as a supporter of campaigns and/or events.

M.154

The [Company] agrees that all corporate, advertising, publicity, packaging, labels and promotional material shall be provided to the [Presenter] in the exact form in which it is intended that it should be used by the [Company]. The prior written approval of the [Agent/Presenter] shall be required and if refused the material of any nature shall not be used.

M.155

The [Presenter] agrees to be available and provides such legal consent as may be required in order for the [Company to exploit the product of the services of the [Presenter] as follows:

1.1 to take, use, authorise and reproduce photographs, films and sound recordings whether for digital, cable, satellite, terrestrial or other form of television, video, DVD, internet, telephone or otherwise. This shall include a direct image or voice or digitised image or voice or an interactive one of the [Presenter].

1.2 to take, use, authorise and/or reproduce the [Presenters] name, nickname, signature, slogan, image, physical likeness and/or short form biography of the [Presenter] in whole or part.

1.3 Provided that all such material in 1.1 and 1.2 is only to be used for the purpose of the advertisement, publicity, exhibition and commercial exploitation of the [Programme/Product/Event] and no other reason. Nor is any use to directly or indirectly demean, be offensive or derogatory of the [Presenter] or any third party. In addition there is no authority to use any material to endorse or promote any other third party services or products and/or to sub-license any rights relating to the name of the [Presenter] to a third party.

M.156

The [Company] shall engage the services of the [Name] who agrees to be available on the terms and conditions in consideration of the payment terms in clause [–]:

1.1 To appear in [number] advertisements to be transmitted on: [specify authorised use/ internet, blogs, podcasts and social media/satellite, digital, cable and terrestrial television/in cinemas/at exhibitions/videos/ DVDs/discs/marketing material] in [country] from [date] to [date]. There may be unlimited use in any of these areas during the specified dates.

1.2   There shall be no right to exploit any of the material in 1.1 after [date] or in any format or media not stipulated nor to authorise others to do so without the prior written approval of [Name] and the negotiation of a new agreement.

1.3   [Name] shall be available for [number] [hours] recording days for filming, voice-overs and photographs. Additional days shall be paid at [specify rate].

1.4   The [Name] shall not be obliged to fulfil any request which he/she decides is unsuitable to their image, career or reputation.

1.5   There is no obligation for [Name] to attend award ceremonies, corporate or director events or to otherwise promote the [Company] and/or its products in any other circumstances. It is also accepted by the [Company] that there is no restriction on the use or promotion of rival products by [Name] at any time.

M.157
The [Company] shall agree in advance and pay an additional fee and all costs and expenses for the services of [Name] at all marketing and promotional events, meetings, exhibitions [Name] agrees to attend. Where a family member also attends with [Name] then the [Company] agrees to pay additional expenses that may be incurred.

M.158
The [Company] shall have the right and license to use and publish the [Contributor's] name, signature, biographical material, photographs, image, caricature and likeness for the purpose of labels, posters, calendars, packaging, T shirts, promotional material and/or the marketing and/ or exploitation of the [Product/Service/Material]. The [Company] agrees to send a proof of any sample material which contains and/or refers to the [Contributor's] name, signature, biographical material, photograph, caricature or likeness for consultation with the [Contributor]. The [Contributor] shall within [two] days provide details to the Company of any objections and comments to be considered.

M.159
Subject to prior consultation the [Presenter] agrees that the [Company] shall be entitled to use his/her name, biographical details, photographs, image, and stage name in respect of the promotion, advertising and marketing of

the [Company] and the [Documentary Series]. The [Company] agrees that any commercial exploitation and/or product endorsement shall be subject to prior written agreement between the parties.

M.160

The [Company] agrees at its own cost and expense to provide copies of any promotional brochures, posters and outdoor advertising, pop-ups, banner links, online and social media marketing material in respect of the [Artist] which have been used by the [Company] upon request by the [Agent].

M.161

The [Agent] agrees to provide a regular report on [type] technical business and market trends and developments in the Territory which would assist the [Company] and/or could indicate factors that might be detrimental to its business.

M.162

The [Agent] agrees that the prior written approval of the [Company] shall be required in the event that the [Agent] intends to promote, market or exploit the [Collection Samples], the [Garments] or the [Company] Logo by any of the following means: publicity, advertising, promotional material, appearances, fashion and trade shows, radio, internet, podcasts and blogs, video, DVD, discs, television, mobiles and through any WiFi and/or telecommunications system; newspaper and magazine articles or features and in any other any media in any country.

M.163

The [Agent] shall provide its services to the best of its skill and ability and shall perform all duties diligently to maximise the sales of the [Products/Services] under this agreement throughout the Territory to third parties for the duration of the agreement.

M.164

The [Agent] agrees that it shall endeavour to promote, market and obtain orders for the [Products] based on the [Samples] throughout the Territory for the Term of this Agreement.

M.165

The [Agent] shall keep the [Licensor] fully informed on a regular basis as regards negotiations with any third party pursuant to this agreement and shall provide a written report by email at the end of each [three] month period commencing with the first report by [date]. The report shall include all relevant contact information for any potential client.

M.166

1.1 The [Licensor] agrees to engage the non-exclusive services of the [Agent] from [date] to [date] for the purpose of obtaining orders for the purchase of the [Products/Service].

1.2 The [Agent] shall only be permitted to use marketing and promotional material supplied by the [Licensor]. All costs and expenses of reproduction and delivery shall be paid by the [Agent]. The [Agent] shall not have the right to commission and/or to develop any new material.

M.167

The [Agent] acknowledges that the [Licensor] shall be entitled appoint another agent and/or third party in the same countries and/or areas to sell and/or otherwise exploit exactly the same [Products/Service].

M.168

The [Management] agrees that it shall promote and advertise each date for the appearance of the [Group] at the [Venue] at the [Management's] sole cost in the following manner:

1.1 Billboards at [locations].

1.2 Advertisements of size [specify] in the following magazines and newspapers [specify].

1.3 A press release to be issued to no less than [number] media companies and other persons on the internet, radio and television in [country].

1.4 A press release on the [website/app] known as [specify].

1.5 A short mention in the scheduled events listings in the following [websites/apps/magazines/newspapers].

M.169

The [Licensee] agrees that by [date] during the Licence Period it shall appoint that a sub-licensee to produce, supply, distribute, market, advertise and otherwise exploit the [Products/Services/Work] in [specify countries].

M.170

The [Assignee] shall be entitled to use the [Assignor's] name, likeness and biography in connection with the exploitation of the rights assigned hereunder. Provided that no use shall at any time express or imply an endorsement by the [Assignor] of any product and/or other material and/or person other than the subject matter of this agreement.

M.171

[Name] shall not without the prior written approval of the [Company] inform any other person or company other than his/her agent, legal advisers, accountant, financiers and/or immediate family members about any advertising, marketing and/or publicity plans by the [Company] which are disclosed before and/or during the course of this agreement. [Name] agrees not to release and/or disclose any details prior to any launch by the [Company which would damage and/or be prejudicial to the impact of the campaign. [Name] shall not be bound by this obligation where any such information and/or material is made available to the public by the [Company].

M.172

[Name] agrees that the [Company] may use the name, logo and image of [Name] set out in Schedule [–] and all his/her contributions in person and by means of sound recordings and/or films at the [Event/Project] in the following manner:

1.1 On the [website/app] known as [specify references] and by means of a news feed from the [Company] and/or a third party to other businesses and consumers worldwide.

1.2 Through on line webinars in sound and/or vision which are edited from the sound recordings and/or films.

1.3 Through magazine and newspaper articles, blogs, podcasts and press releases released and distributed by the [Company].

1.4 Through sub-licensing of parts of the films and/or sound recordings for use in news, current affairs and/or review programmes and/or for future programmes for broadcast and/or transmission on television and/or any other format and/or media at any time in any part of the world.

1.5 Through the sale and assignment of all copyright, intellectual property rights and any other interest to a third party of the sound recordings and the films of the [Event/Project].

M.173

The services to be supplied by the [Consultant/Name] do not entitle the [Company] to expect and/or be provided with mobile, online and/or other contact with the [Company] by [Consultant/Name] outside of these times and days of the week: [specify days/hours].

M.174

Where the [Consultant] is required to provide additional work, material and/or other support to the [Company] which is not listed in Schedule [–]. The [Company] agrees that additional fees and payments shall be due of not less than [number/currency] per [hour/day].

M.175

The [Company] shall be entitled to deduct the cost of the design, development, reproduction, supply and distribution, booking and delivery costs and charges which may be incurred by the [Company] and/or paid by a third party and reimbursed by the [Company] which arise directly and/or indirectly in respect of any media in any country relating to the marketing, promotion and/or exploitation of the [Work/Product/Service] in any language, format and/or by any method. The [Company] shall be entitled to recoup all such sums before any payments are made to the [Licensor].

Sponsorship

M.176

The [Organisers] confirm and agree that an official printed programme shall be made available to the general public at the [Festival/Event] at a price decided by the [Organisers]. The [Organisers] agree that the brochure shall include:

1.1 The [Sponsor's] Logo on the front cover.

1.2 A statement from the [Sponsor] of [number] words on the introduction pages.

1.3 A full page advertisement of the [Sponsor's] [Product/Service] on the inside back cover.

M.177

The [Organisers] agree that the [Sponsor] shall be entitled to create its own advertising and publicity material in respect of the [Sponsor's] association with the [Festival/Event] and that the [Organisers] shall not have the right of approval of such material issued by the [Sponsor].

M.178

The [Radio Station] confirms that no products, services or other material of any nature shall be advertised, promoted or in any way discussed or raised during the course of the [Programme] which is in direct competition with the [Sponsor's] [Product/Service] for the duration of the Sponsorship Period. This clause shall also apply to any material in a commercial break.

M.179

The [Sponsor] shall be entitled to have the advertising material and/or other displays of any third party at the Venue during the course of the [Event] removed if the third party product directly conflicts with the following products of the [Sponsor]: [specify products] and is used for [state purpose].

M.180

The [Sponsor] acknowledges that the [Association] shall be entitled to license, authorise and/or permit third parties to advertise, promote and/or market their products and/or services during the [Event] for all types of products and/or services of any nature except the following category of products and/or services in the following markets which the [Association] has specifically agreed to exclude: [specify list].

M.181

The [Sponsor] agrees to provide at its sole cost the following minimum number of give-away products for the [Event] for the [Association] to distribute to competitors, press and for hospitality: [specify number/item].

M.182

The [Sponsor] agrees that the [Association] shall be entitled to retain all sums received from the exploitation of the [Event] in any form including ticket sales, films, videos, sound recordings, live and pre-recorded programmes and extracts for the internet, television and radio, licensing, merchandising and other forms of exploitation in all media and/or advertising and/or marketing.

M.183

The [Company] shall try to ensure that all marketing, promotional and publicity material released by the [Company] and/or a business and/or person appointed by the [Company] in respect of the [Event/Festival] shall ensure that the Title [specify exact words/style] of the [Sponsor] shall be used on all printed material including the [Guide/Brochure] and on all [front/end] credits related to any sound recordings, films, videos, radio and/or television programme and/or any other material to be used on the internet. This clause shall not however apply to any merchandising products. Where no credit is provided for any reason the [Sponsor] accepts that it shall not be entitled to claim any compensation, damages and/or losses and/or any other sum.

M.184

The [Sponsor] shall have the right at its own cost to market, publicise and promote the [Event] and all associated participants and content. The [Organisation] shall be required by the [Sponsor] to include the use of the [Sponsor's Products] at the [Event].

M.185

1.1 The [Organisation] acknowledges that the purpose of the funding of the [Event/Festival/Forum] by the [Sponsor] is to obtain the maximum amount of promotion for the [Sponsor] and its [Products/Services].

1.2   The [Sponsor] shall be entitled to publicise and promote the names, photographs, pictures, or other material relating to the [Event/Festival/Forum] within the possession or control of the [Organisation].

1.3   The [Organisation] shall request that each participant in the [Event/Festival/Forum] shall co-operate with the [Sponsor] in any public relations that may reasonably be required by the [Sponsor] during the Term of this Agreement.

1.4   The [Organisation] shall request that all participants use, eat, drink or wear as appropriate items supplied by the [Sponsors] including the [Products/clothing/equipment] at [location] at the [Event/Festival/Forum] from [date] to [date].

1.5   The [Sponsor] shall [subject to the prior consent of any individual] be entitled to use any such material for a period of [three] months after the [Event/Festival/Forum] for the purpose of publicity and promotion of the [Sponsors'] [Products/Services] until [date] in any media.

M.186

Where any participants and/or competitors refuse to use, endorse and/or wear the [Sponsors'] products, clothing and/or equipment. The [Sponsor] agrees that the [Company] shall not be in breach of this agreement provided that the majority have cooperated.

M.187

The [Company] shall be permitted throughout the [Event] to distribute, free of charge to spectators and others at the venue, free samples of such other products, samples and articles as the [Company] may decide at its sole cost.

M.188

The [Sponsor] agrees that the [Sportsperson's] name, images and endorsement shall not be used for any other purpose other than the promotion and endorsement of the [Sponsor's] [Product/Service]. The [Sponsor] agrees to provide the [Sportsperson] with exact samples of all materials in any medium in which it is intended to use the name, image and/or endorsement of the [Sportsperson]. Such material whether for promotional, advertising, publicity and/or packaging shall be supplied at the [Sponsor's] cost to the [Sportsperson] prior to the production and/or distribution of any such material. In the event that the [Sportsperson] requests alterations and/or changes relating to any references to the [Sportsperson] in any form at any time then the [Sponsor] agrees to be bound by these stipulations and undertakes to alter the references.

M.189

The [Sponsor] acknowledges that this agreement does not oblige the [Sportsperson] to perform and/or appear in any advertisements, interviews, films, radio programmes, videos, sound recordings, podcasts, blogs and/or other promotional material for the [Sponsor]. All such matters shall be the subject of separate agreements and shall require the [Sponsor] conclude additional agreements with the [Sportsperson].

M.190

The [Sportsperson] agrees to attend and participate in all the events and interviews specified in the Schedule in appendix B and to prepare with sufficient training and to perform to the best of his/her ability subject to an exemption for illness, personal injury and/or some other valid reason which prevents the [Sportsperson] from fulfilling this clause.

M.191

The [Sportsperson] undertakes not to enter into any agreement to wear, use, buy, endorse, promote and/or advertise the products, services and/or other brands of the following companies for the duration of the Sponsorship Period: [specify competitors names, brands/services/products] and/or any services or products in any of the following markets: [specify excluded markets/zones].

M.192

The [Sponsor] agrees and undertakes not to engage any other person as the public image, promoter and ambassador of the [Sponsor's] products, business and/or services from [date] to [date].

M.193

The [Sponsor] agrees to provide the [Sportsperson] at the [Sponsor's] cost with a copy and/or sample of each and every product item, poster, animation, pop-up, advertisement, podcast, article, magazine feature and/or other material in which the [Sponsor] uses the name, likeness, image, photograph, signature, caricature, representation and/or endorsement of the [Sportsperson] under this agreement whether for promotional, advertising, publicity, packaging, merchandising and/or marketing purposes.

M.194

The [Sportsperson] agrees to wear the clothing and use the equipment and car provided by the [Sponsor] under this agreement as far as reasonably possible and appropriate at all competitions, events, press calls, television, radio, internet and media interviews throughout the Sponsorship Period in the Territory and not to wear and/or use the sponsored goods of any third party unless provided by the [Organisers] of any event for all participants.

M.195

The [Sponsor] warrants that the name, nickname, images, photographs, films, recordings, merchandise, signature, comments and interviews and endorsement of the [Sponsor's] Products by the [Sportsperson] shall not be used for any purpose other than the promotion and endorsement of the [Sponsor's] Products and the [Sponsor's] business in general for the duration of the Term of the Agreement.

M.196

The [Sponsor] agrees that all material produced by them shall be of a high professional standard and the [Sportsperson] shall be consulted and have a right of approval over all material in any media which directly relates to the [Sportsperson] under this agreement including promotional, publicity, advertising, packaging, brochures and press releases, photographs, illustrations, artwork, typography, design and layout, biographical details, image, text, or otherwise.

M.197

The [Sponsor] agrees and undertakes not to attempt to register any interest, right and/or claim in respect of the name, nickname, abbreviation and/or initials, image, likeness, catchphrase, slogan, caricature version, logo, trademark, domain name and/or any other material derived from and/or based on the career, life, person and/or name of the [Athlete] which is supplied, created and/or developed for the purposes of this agreement.

M.198

The [Sponsor] shall not be entitled to use the name, image and/or details of any [Participant] to market, promote and advertise the [Event] without the prior written and/or authority consent of that [Participant] and/or their parent and/or guardian. No authority and/or consent is provided by the [Company] in respect of any one individual and/or group.

M.199

The [Sponsor] shall be entitled to promote, market and advertise its funding of the [Event] as it thinks fit provided that it does not represent that:

1.1   It is paying any individual directly.

1.2   The funding is for political purposes.

1.3   It has any control over the content of the [Programme] and/or operation of the [Event].

1.4   It has the right to authorise, license, sub-license and/or exploit the [Programme] and/or [Event] to any third party in any media.

M.200

The [Sponsor] shall be entitled to use promote and market its connection with the [Event/Project] in any manner it thinks fit provided that any material developed and/or created is not offensive and/or derogatory and/or does not and/or will not permit and/or make any comments on the competitors, the teams and/or the [Company] which are not positive at any time.

M.201

1.1 The [Company] agrees that the [Sponsor] may arrange for its own film crew at the [Event/Project] in order to make such sound recordings and/or films as it may wish and to use such material for future advertisements and/or promotions both online over the internet and through radio, television, cinema and in any other format and/or media.

1.2 Provided that the [Sponsor] shall not be entitled to record and/or film [specify] and shall be obliged to ask any member of the public who may be interviewed by them to provided their written consent and shall be liable for all fees, costs and copyright, intellectual property rights and interest, contract and royalty payments, recording, performance and broadcast and transmission fees that may become and/or fall due as a result of 1.1.

M.202

The [Sponsor] accepts and agrees:

1.1 That the [Sponsor] has no editorial control over the [Event/Forum] and/or any schedule of appearances and/or forms of exploitation in any media.

1.2 That the [Company] may terminate the arrangement with the [Sponsor] at any time subject to the repayment of all the Sponsorship Fee in full.

1.3 That where the [Sponsor] and/or it Chief Executive and/or any senior management become involved in a social media scandal for any reason whether true or not. That the [Company] may enter into negotiations with the [Sponsor] to bring this agreement to an end. That the [Company] shall be entitled to retain all sums paid by the [Sponsor] where the [Company] has carried out all its obligations to the [Sponsor]. If only some of the terms have been fulfilled then only some of the funds may be retained.

University, Charity and Educational

M.203

1.1 The [Institute/Charity] shall have the right and licence to reproduce, use and publish the [Contributor's] name, biographical material, photographs, image and likeness for the cover, catalogue, website, app, social media blogs and podcasts, flyers, packaging, marketing, advertising and exploiting the [Product/Service/Work] and to authorise others to do so.

1.2 The [Institute/Charity] agrees to send a draft sample of any material which contains and/or refers to the [Contributor's] name, biographical material, photograph, image and/or likeness for approval by the [Contributor]. The [Institute/Charity] agrees at its own cost to provide one copy of any material in respect of the [Product/Service/Work] in which the [Contributor] appears and/or is mentioned in 1.1.

M.204

1.1 The [Institute/Charity] agrees to consult with the [Contributor] in respect of all proposed copies, credits, labels, samples, packaging, advertising, promotional, publicity and marketing material prior to the production, manufacture, distribution and exploitation of the material by the [Institute/Charity]. The editorial control and the decision of the [Institute/Charity] in respect of any matter shall be final and the [Institute/Charity] shall not be obliged to adhere to the suggestions of the [Contributor].

1.2 The [Institute/Charity] shall at the [Institute's] sole cost deliver to the [Contributor] a copy of any products, packaging, publicity, advertising, promotional and marketing material in the possession or under the control of the [Institute/Charity] featuring the [Contributor].

M.205

The [Contributor agrees that the [Institute/Charity] shall at its sole cost have the entire control and discretion as to the management, production, budget, development, design, publication, launch date, distribution, advertisement and promotion of the [Work/Service/Event]. There shall be no obligation to consult and/or seek any approval from the [Contributor].

M.206

[Name] agrees that the [Institute/Charity] shall be entitled to reproduce, display and distribute the [Artwork/Logo/Image] in the following circumstances:

1.1 As a three-dimensional moving image on their website, app and in any associated link and/or other advertisement on any third party site.

1.2 In any other material including any catalogue, brochure, marketing flyer, banner, flag and/or other products in any form exploited by the [Institute/Charity].

1.3 There is no right to sub-license any third party to create and/or develop any adaptation of the [Artwork/Logo/Image] and/or to assign the copyright and/or any other intellectual property rights to a third party.

M.207

The [Consortium] agrees that it shall be liable for the cost and expenses of any marketing and promotion, administration and copyright, computer software, trade mark, intellectual property and other rights clearances and payments and contractual obligations which may arise in respect of the [Event/Project] which are incurred by the [Institute].

M.208

1.1 The [Charity] has appointed [specify company] as the sole and exclusive marketing and promotion enterprise from [date] to [date] for the [Charity]. No other third party shall be appointed during that exclusive period. This agreement shall cover the internet, podcasts, blogs, radio, television, radio and newspapers.

1.2 It does not cover licensing products and/or services, merchandising, sponsorship and collaborations, product placement, endorsements and/or events.

1.3 All final editorial control and decisions rest with the [Charity] and not the [Enterprise].

1.4 All material in 1.1 must be approved by the [Chief Executive/Name] of the [Charity] in draft and/or sample form.

1.5 The [Enterprise] must submit a detailed strategy report itemising the work and the cost to the [Charity].

1.6 No costs may be incurred by the [Enterprise] without prior approval by the [Charity] and the allocation of a specific code for each type of work to be completed.

MATERIAL

Film, Television and Video

M.209

The [Company] engages the [Writer] and the [Writer] agrees to make his/her services available to the [Company] to produce a treatment for [number] [Programmes] not exceeding [duration] each on the subject of: [state description] provisionally entitled [specify title] along the lines discussed between the [Company] and the [Writer]. The treatment shall include information on the ownership of any existing films and/or sound recordings of any nature, the details of any music to be used including details of the composer, musicians and copyright owner. The [Writer] shall deliver this treatment to the [Company] not later than [date].

M.210
The [Licensee] undertakes not to supply, sell, hire, rent, transfer and/or distribute to any third party any of the material supplied in accordance with this agreement. Neither shall the [Licensee] reproduce or exploit and/or authorise any third party to do so except as specified in this agreement.

M.211
The [Author] agrees to provide the [Company] with a list of the source of the [Material] supplied by the [Author] for the [Programme] and confirms that the [Material] shall be cleared in respect of the rights granted by the [Author]. The [Company] shall be responsible for the payment of the sums due for the use of the [Material] in respect of the exercise of the rights under this agreement.

M.212
The [Licensor] shall provide the [Company] with one copy of any consents, releases, documents, licences and contracts which provide evidence of the ownership of the material supplied by the [Licensor].

M.213
If and when requested by the [Licensee] the [Licensor] shall supply at the [Licensee's] cost copies of such stills, logos, trade marks, labels, packaging, advertising, publicity and other materials that the [Licensor] may have in its possession which are suitable to be adapted by the [Licensee] for the purpose of this agreement.

M.214
The [Licensor] will provide the [Licensee] with a letter of access to enable the [Licensee] to order all such stills and other materials directly at the [Licensee's] cost and expense from [specify location] to be used for the purposes of this agreement.

M.215
The [Company] shall promptly supply on request by the [Licensee] such copies of the Master Material of the [Films/Videos] together with [scripts/ running orders] in the [English/other] language and music cue sheets. Subject to acceptance of the copy of the Master Material by the [Licensee]

as suitable technical quality. The [Licensee] shall pay to the [Company] the cost of reproducing and delivering the Master Material including freight, taxes, insurance and other charges.

M.216
'Master Material' shall mean a fully edited, pristine, digitised [specify format] recording of broadcast and/or transmission standard in [country] incorporating fully synchronous music, voice, text and sound effects, technically suitable for use in the manufacture of [specify units].

M.217
'Master Material' shall mean the edited Master of each of the [Programmes of the Series] reproduced as a Digital [specify format] copy of the Master.

M.218
'The Treatment' shall be the synopsis of the [Film/Video/Podcast]. A copy of which is in appendix A and is attached to and forms part of this agreement.

M.219
'The [Documentary/Video/Podcast] 'shall be the following film and any associated sound recording based on the Treatment entitled: [specify title] which shall be [number] minutes in duration and briefly described as follows: [brief summary].

M.220
'The [Promotional Film/Video/Podcast] 'shall be the film and any associated sound recording for the [Musical Work] to be performed by the [Artiste]. A full description of which is set out below:

1.1 Budget [number/currency].

1.2 Completion date of the final edited version: [date].

1.3 Director, production company, contributors, artists, musicians and composer: [specify details].

1.4 Duration: [specify].

1.5 Language: [specify].

1.6 Format of the final edited version to be supplied: [specify].

M.221
'The Artistic Concept' shall be the brief narrative description of the [Film/Video/Podcast] which includes images, locations and the technical format. A copy of the Artistic Concept is attached to and forms part of this agreement as Schedule A.

M.222

The [Assignor] confirms that the [Video/DVD/Disc] shall be produced so that it appears on screen in colour in the English Language and that the musical work, voices, text and sound effects will be synchronised with the visual images and will be delivered in the following digitised format: [specify format of material].

M.223

The [Assignor] confirms that the [Film/Video/Podcast] shall not contain any other music, lyrics, sound recordings, recordings and/or sound effects, images, logos and/or other content except the [Musical Work] unless there is prior written consent by the [Assignee].

M.224

'The Material' shall be the following material of the [Film/Video/Podcast]:

1.1 Technical material suitable for [specify purpose] comprising: [specify format].

1.2 Typed final script, running order and music cue sheet.

1.3 Copies of any labels, packaging and/or any other master promotional material including exact specifications regarding credits and acknowledgements, trademarks, service marks, images of artists, stills, slogans and any disclaimers, copyright notices and/or other matters.

1.4 A full and comprehensive statement setting out all contractual obligations, copyright, consents, releases, moral right assertions and waivers, trade marks, service marks, logos, credits, images, copyright notices, copyright warnings and disclaimers in relation to the [Film/Video/Podcast] and any other material to be supplied, produced and/or created. The detail must include a description, image, duration, position, colour, context and background.

M.225

'The Master Material' shall be the following material of the [Film] including any soundtrack:

1.1 Technical material of first class quality comprising: [specify format] to be supplied at the [Assignee's] cost.

1.2 [Number] copies of the [Film] in the following digitised format: [specify] to be supplied at the [Assignee's] cost.

1.3 A complete list of any locations at which any material relating to the [Film] is held together with access letters giving the [Assignee] complete authority to obtain, remove and/or otherwise exploit the material and/or make copies at its sole discretion.

M.226

'The Delivery Material' shall be the following material of the [Series]:

1.1 [Number] copies in [format] of technical material of first class quality of the complete [Series] suitable for broadcast and or transmission in [country] on channel [specify] which conforms to the standards and guidelines stipulated by [specify organisation].

1.2 All technical and master material and any copies in any format, gauge including rushes, outtakes, videotapes, discs, sound recordings, music and effects, tracks, title and subtitle tracks and/or viewing copies in the possession or under the control of the [Assignor]. Together with an itemised list of all such material.

1.3 A list of the laboratories and any other locations at which any material relating to the [Series] is held together with access letters giving the [Assignee] irrevocable authority to have access to, make copies and remove the material at its sole discretion.

1.4 A complete typed final script, running order and music cue sheets listing each musical work with the name of the composer, author and publisher; the duration of each musical work and the description of use in each case.

1.5 A detailed statement and copies of all records of the contractual obligations, copyright, intellectual property rights and/or music, lyrics, performing rights and mechanical reproduction clearance and/or other royalty payments due and/or paid and/or any moral rights asserted and/or waived and/or product placement, sponsorship and/or other arrangements and/or copyright notices, trade marks, service marks and any other obligations which have been agreed in respect of the [Series].

M.227

'The Film Material' shall be all the physical material of the [Film] and/or parts in the possession or under the control of the [Assignor] including:

1.1 All technical and master material and any copies in any format and in any gauge including but not limited to: negatives, rushes, outtakes, videotapes, prints, sound recordings, music and effects, tracks, DVDs, CDs, discs and storage devices, trailers and promotional clips, electronic material developed for any use on the internet and/or for any website and/or app and any associated computer software and any other material created, developed and/or used on any mobile, WiFi and/or telecommunication system at any time.

1.2 A complete list of all locations in the possession or under the control of the [Assignor] and/or any third party at which any material of any nature relating to the [Film] and/or parts is held together with access letters giving the [Assignee] irrevocable authority to obtain, remove and make copies as it thinks fit.

1.3 All originals and all copies and/or records however they may be stored in any format in any media of all licences, contracts and distribution and agency documents and other data, text, information, images, graphics, computer generated material, recordings, scripts, music cue sheets, publicity, photographs, stills, negatives, posters, catalogues, packaging, labels, advertising, and promotional material. Together with all the records and lists relating to any copyright, credit and moral rights clearances and requirements; domain names, trade marks, service marks, logos, icons and any other obligations and commitments and/or any other intellectual property rights, consents, licences, releases and/or insurance matters.

M.228

'The Master Material' shall be all the sound recordings, documents, contracts and material stored on a storage and retrieval system and/or a computer hard drive and/or in other physical and/or other form in any medium in the possession and/or under the control of the [Assignor] in respect of [Name] in respect of any song, music and/or lyrics and in particular the material set out in Appendix A which is attached to and forms part of this agreement.

M.229

1.1 The [Images/Photographs/Maps] supplied by [Name] on loan for inclusion in the [Film/Series] on the day of the interview will not be retained and shall be returned immediately to [Name].

1.2 [Name] agrees that no additional payment and/or fee shall be charged for any use in the [Film/Series] and/or by means of any archive playback system that may be available and/or through any television, radio and/or internet transmission and/or streaming except the fee and expenses in clause [–].

1.3 In the event that the [Distributor] wishes to sib-license the [Film/Series] and to exploit the [Images/Photographs/Maps] reproduced in the [Film/Series] in the form of merchandising, publications and/or any other manner then an additional agreement shall be required and [Name] shall be entitled to be paid additional fees and royalties.

M.230

1.1 The [Licensee] agrees and undertakes that it shall not be entitled to exploit the [Sound Recordings/Film/Photographs] of the interview by

[Name] on [date] except for the purpose of exhibition at the [Event] to be held on [date] at [location] organised by [specify organisation].

1.2 No other form of exploitation and/or reproduction is permitted in any form and the [Sound Recordings/Film/Photographs] may not be licensed, sold, reproduced and/or supplied to any third party and/or made available on television, the internet and/or otherwise.

1.3 That in the event it is proposed to exploit the material in any other form that the prior written consent of [Name] and/or his/her estate shall be required and a new agreement concluded in which [Name] and/or his/her estate shall receive an advance of not less than [number/currency] and no less than [number] per cent of all the gross sums received from any form of exploitation.

M.231

The [Production Company] agrees to provide the [Distributor/Sponsor] with the following material at its sole cost upon request:

1.1 Copies and samples of all reviews, publicity, promotional, advertising and packaging material in respect of the [Documentary/Series].

1.2 [Number] free copies of all of the [Documentary/Series] in each format that it shall be either exploited or made available to the general public.

M.232

The [Licensor] shall deliver to the [Licensee] a first-class [specify format] of the English language version in stereo. The [format] shall be first-class, new, undamaged, a complete edited version with front titles, credits and closing acknowledgements. The colour tone, shading and intensity shall be of a suitable quality for [specify purpose]. The soundtrack, words and music shall be clear and in perfect synchronisation with the visual images. The cost of such material and all delivery charges shall be paid for by the [Licensee] in advance.

M.233

The 'Delivery Items' shall mean the following material to be supplied by the [Licensor] at the [Television Company's] cost and expense:

1.1 New and first-class technically acceptable 35mm transmission print of the full-length version with all commercial breaks removed of the [Film] in the English language complete with the main and end titles and all credits on which the sound shall be fully synchronised with the picture.

1.2 Laboratory access letter in customary form giving the [Television Company] the irrevocable right to order prints of the [Film] at its sole expense direct from the original negatives held at the laboratories and irrevocable instructions that negatives may not be destroyed or transferred from the laboratories prior to the expiry of the Licence Period without the prior consent of the [Television Company].

1.3 Copies of the detailed final dialogue and action continuity and the timed music cue sheet listing each musical work, the name of the composer, author and publisher, the timing of each item and description of use for the [Film].

1.4 A statement of the on screen credits, copyright notices, trade marks, logos, product placements and other contractual obligations for the [Film].

1.5 Such advertising and promotional material, stills, photographs, videos, posters and trailers of the [Film] as are available on loan.

M.234

The [Film Package] shall be the following material of the [Film] supplied at the [Licensor's/Licensee's] sole cost including freight, taxes, duties, insurance and packaging:

1.1 Technical material of first-class quality comprising of: [specify format].

1.2 Authorisation for access to the storage facility and/or business holding the master material with the authority to make arrangements for copies.

1.3 A transcript of the final [script/dialogue]; the copy of [running order/action continuity/shot list].

1.4 A music cue sheet listing each musical work with the name of the composer, author and publisher including the duration of each musical work and the description of use in each case.

1.5 A statement of and samples of all credits, copyright notices, trade marks, service marks, logos, moral rights, waivers, assertions, disclaimers, product placement and brand promotion, sponsorship, preview material, commercials, trailers, photographs, videos, stills, posters, promotional and/or any other material which may be available.

1.6 Together with a list of all contractual and copyright, computer software, performing right and/or mechanical reproduction and/or broadcast and/or transmission and/or other intellectual property and/or other forms of exploitation stating whether clearances have been made or not and what payments and/or royalties may become due.

M.235

The [Licensor] shall supply on loan [a digitised format] of the [Film/Video/Series] from which the [Company] shall be entitled to make at its own cost a master copy for the purposes of this agreement. The master copy must be returned to the [Licensor] at the [Licensee's] cost at the expiry and/or termination of this agreement.

M.236

1.1 The [Licensor] shall supply the [Sub-Licensee] with a complete and edited version of the [Documentary/Game Show/Video] in the following format: [specify digitised formats/other] at the [Licensor's] cost. The material shall be in first-class condition and without defects and/or damage and shall be of a technical standard and quality suitable for: [specify purpose/use] and in accordance with the standards required by [specify organisation] and [guidelines/code] known as [specify].

1.2 After the expiry of the Licence Period the [Sub-Licensee] shall return all the original material and copies in 1.1 to the [Licensor] at the [Sub-Licensee's] sole cost.

M.237

The [Licensee] agrees to reimburse the [Licensor] in respect of all the reproduction and delivery costs incurred in providing an acceptable [Film Package] subject to satisfactory receipts being provided upon request.

M.238

The [Series Package] shall be the following first-class quality material of the [Series] comprising:

1.1 [number] [format] copies.

1.2 Typed synopsis of each episode.

1.3 Music cue sheet listing full details of each musical work.

1.4 Statement of all credit, contractual and moral obligations.

1.5 A detailed statement of the copyright, consents and other clearances obtained and due in relation to all artists, music and any other material in the [Series] and the [Series Package].

M.239

'The Film Package' shall be the following material of the [Film/Video]:

1.1 Technical material [–].

1.2 Script, music cue sheet and running order.

1.3 Statement of credit, copyright notices, union and contractual obligations.

1.4 Copies of such advertising and publicity material as may be available.

M.240

'The Programme' shall be the film and any associated sound recording to be produced by the [Company] provisionally entitled: [specify draft title].

M.241

'The Series' shall be the series of films and any associated sound recordings based on the format set out in Appendix B. It shall consist of [number] episodes each of which shall be [number] minutes in duration.

M.242

'Programmes' shall mean the programmes set out in the Schedule A and shall include such other additional programmes as may be added by written agreement between the parties.

M.243

'Programme' shall include all literary, dramatic, artistic and musical material, computer generated material, graphics, images, text, film, commentary, soundtrack, recordings and the source material and all third party material incorporated into, synchronised with or otherwise forming part of such programme. It shall also include all material produced for the purposes of the programme, negative, tapes, films, videos, DVDs, discs, recordings, outtakes, sound recordings, animations and all electronic and computer generated material however commissioned, ordered or otherwise.

M.244

'The Film' means a feature length cinematograph film entitled [specify title] based on [Book/Script/Life of person] brief details of which are set out in appendix B. [specify title of film/language/writer/producer/composer/artists/duration/format].

M.245

'The Series' shall be the series of films and any associated sound recordings entitled: [specify title]. There are [number] episodes as follows: [specify individual titles]. Each episode is [number] minutes] in duration in colour in [specify] language. There are no sub-titles.

M.246

The [Assignor] shall provide a detailed statement to the [Assignee] by [date] of the following matters in relation to the [Estate of Person] in the possession or under the control of the [Assignor] in respect of the [Research Material] and the [Documentary] including any associated domain name and/or electronic material:

1.1 All technical and master material in any format or gauge including but not limited to digitised formats, unused footage, sound recordings, videos, photographs, stills, posters, computer software and electronic versions.

1.2 All background notes, diagrams, maps, scripts, plans, data, research and other material however it may be available and/or stored.

1.3 A complete list of all material held by any third party and authorisation to such third parties to release all such material directly to the [Assignee].

1.4 Copies of all correspondence, documents, records, registrations with collecting societies and/or other organisation for domain names and/or trade marks, contracts, licences, consents, waivers, scripts, music cue sheets, promotional, advertising and related merchandising material and products.

1.5 All copyright, copyright notices, trade mark, logos, moral rights, waivers, disclaimers and other intellectual property rights or contractual obligations including music, consents, clearances, fees and payments set out in full stating the party, personal details, the obligations, payments, and rights as far as they may be known at [date]. Together with copies of any associated material and records and payment history that may be available.

M.247
'The Format of the Series' shall be the original concept and novel idea for the structure of a series of [films/quiz/game shows] full details of which are attached to and form part of this agreement in Appendix A. [Specify title of series and title of each episode; scripts and running order; any special characters, storyline, location; any details regarding trade marks, logo, names, computer software, copyright and intellectual property rights; design and layout of any set, presentation of questions and answers, score system, prizes, slogans, graphics, costumes, telephone line recordings including online website and app material, interactive element and competitions.]

M.248
'The Treatment' shall be the summary of the contents and structure of the [Programme]. A copy of the treatment is attached to and forms part of this agreement.

M.249
'The Treatment' shall mean the existing treatment by the [Writer] for the [Film] based on the novel: [title of novel]. A copy of the Treatment has been delivered by the [Writer] to the [Company].

M.250

'The Treatment' shall be the summary of the [Pilot] which is based on the Format. Details of the Treatment are attached to and form part of this agreement.

M.251

'The Treatment' shall be the summary of each of the episodes of the [Series]. A copy of the Treatment is attached to and forms part of this agreement.

M.252

'The Scripts' shall be the draft and final scripts based on the Treatment to be prepared by the [Writer].

M.253

'The Scripts' shall be all draft and final scripts to be prepared by the [screenplay writers] based on the [Author's] [Book/Biography/Synopsis].

M.254

'The Authors' Work' shall mean all the proposals, treatments and scripts prepared, written and/or adapted by the [Author] including all drafts, redrafts, revisions, translations, sub-titled versions, adaptations or other developments and all the titles, characters, plots, dialogues, sequences, locations and other material arising from the provision of the [Author's] services pursuant to this agreement.

M.255

The [Author] agrees and undertakes that he/she shall not have the right to create, develop, adapt and/or produce any sequel, strikingly similar work or material and/or subsequent film, video, mini-series, DVD, storyline, publication, podcast or otherwise in any media at any time based on the whole and/or any part of the [Authors' Work] under this agreement.

M.256

'The Extract' shall be the following parts from the [Film] entitled: [title of film] maximum authorised duration: number] format: [specify].

M.257

'The Actor's Performance' shall mean the reproduction into electronic form of the movements and gestures of the actor in synchronisation with the voice so as to produce movements in the representation of the [Character] in the [Film/Video/Game Show].

M.258

'The Film' shall be the feature length cinematic film and sound recordings of [number] minutes in length in [–] language to be produced by the [Production

Company] based on and adapted from the [Book/Synopsis/Treatment] by the [Author] with the title: [–].

M.259
The [Production Company] agrees that the [Author] shall be permitted to view the rushes of the [Film], the edited versions and the final version upon request.

M.260
The [Company] agrees and undertakes not to use, reproduce, license, exploit and/or display and/or distribute the [Work/Film] by any method, manner or in conjunction with any other material which would be offensive, derogatory, defamatory, or otherwise prejudicial to the [Author].

M.261
The [Company] agrees that where new material is created and/or developed by them and/or any licensee whether in the [specify] language and/or any other adaptation which includes the name, image and/or character played by [Name] in the [Programme]. That the [Company] will consider any requests which [Name] and his/her agent may make in respect of any draft and/or final version and shall ensure that all such new material does not represent [Name] and/or his/her character in any offensive and/or derogatory manner. That the [Company] acknowledges and recognises that [Name] and all material associated with him/her must be suitable for [category/age range].

M.262

1.1   [Name] agrees that the [Company] may create, develop and adapt such material as it thinks fit at any time to promote the [Film] and/or any part and/or any associated exploitation which may include the personal name, caricature, a three dimensional representation of [Name] and/or his/her image and/or his/her character which shall include but not be limited to any trailers, posters, product endorsement, merchandising and sub-licensing and distribution, blogs, apps, computer software and games, advertising, sponsorship and promotional material.

1.2   That where the [Company] is to receive any payments from a third party from 1.1 that the [Company] shall pay [Name] [number] per cent of all [gross/net] sums received at any time such payments to be made in [country] in [currency] within [number] months of receipt by the [Company].

M.263
'The Programme' shall be the sound recordings whether live or pre-recorded, broadcast and/or transmitted by [Radio Station/Channel] entitled: [name] [length] [description].

General Business and Commercial

M.264

Designs, drawings, specifications, computer-generated graphics, data and information and other work or material developed under this agreement shall be the exclusive property of the [Company]. The [Contractor] agrees that none may be released or reused by the [Contractor] without the prior written consent of the [Company]. All original material shall be saved by the [Contractor] and shall be delivered to the [Company] upon completion or termination of this agreement or at the request at any time of the [Company] at any time. No material shall be destroyed by the [Contractor] unless instructed to do so by the [Company].

M.265

'Building' shall include a fixed structure and a part of a building or fixed structure.

M.266

'The Designs' shall be the original concept and two-dimensional designs for a range of items described as follows: [brief name]. Full details of the Designs are attached to and form part of this agreement in Schedule C.

M.267

'Artistic Work' shall mean:

1.1   A graphic work, photograph, sculpture or collage irrespective of artistic quality.

1.2   A work of architecture being a building or a model for a building.

1.3   A work of artistic craftsmanship.

M.268

'Graphic Work' shall include any painting, drawing, diagram, map, chart or plan and any engraving, etching, lithograph, woodcut or similar work,

M.269

'Sculpture' shall include a cast or model made for the purposes of the sculpture.

M.270

'The Artwork' shall mean any photographs, drawings, sketches, pictures, diagrams, maps or any other illustrations or visual images which are intended to be included as part of the [Commissioned Work].

M.271

'Property' shall include all chattels, estates, real and personal, and all choses in action.

M.272

'Photographs' shall mean the physical and intellectual property rights in the negatives, stills, transparencies, images and prints howsoever stored, reproduced or supplied and which are not films.

M.273

'Photograph' shall mean a recording of light or other radiation on any medium on which an image is produced or from which an image may by any means be produced, and which is not part of a film.

M.274

'The Photographs' shall mean any photographs or drawings, sketches, pictures, diagrams or any other illustration which are intended to be included as part of the [Article/Interview].

M.275

'The Photographs' shall mean all recordings of light or other radiation on any medium on which an image is reproduced or from which an image may by any means be reproduced and which is not part of a film commissioned by [Name/Company] or taken by them directly and shall include any negatives or prints howsoever stored or reproduced.

M.276

The [Company] reserves the exclusive right to take or arrange for the taking of photographs on the stands and/or at any other location at the [Exhibition/Conference]. Any person wishing to take any photographs will need to register as a [photographer] and pay a fee of [number/currency] to obtain consent to do so.

M.277

'The Commissioned Work' shall be the product of the services of the [Photographer] for the design, creation, production and delivery of the agreed images and stills set out in the summary in appendix B by the [Photographer] to the [Assignee].

M.278

'The Stills' shall be the following photographs: [reference code/title/description/colour/source material] in which the copyright is owned by [Name] and the physical material is owned by [Name/Company].

M.279

'The Stills Material' shall be the material owned or controlled by the [Licensor] to be reproduced and supplied to the [Licensee] at the [Licensee's] cost and risk as follows: [description/format/delivery date/address].

M.280

Subject to prior consultation the [Licensor] agrees that the [Licensee] shall be entitled to use his/her professional name, summary biography and authorised images in respect of the exercise of the rights granted under this agreement. It shall not however include any domain name, representational image, caricature, hologram, merchandising, slogan, music and/or other personal and/or professional information.

M.281

'The Records' shall be the reproduction of the master tape in whole or in part in any material form whether manufactured by any method for release to the general public or supplied or licensed to any third party with or without visual images.

M.282

'The Master Tape' shall be the sound recording of the performers which is in the following digitised format: [specify format required].

M.283

'The Material' shall mean any and all materials of any nature in any medium and/or format and/or adaptation in any language and/or rights of any nature whether in existence now or created in the future including but not limited to:

1.1 Hardback and paperback books, plastic, fabric, interactive and pop-up children's books, newspapers, magazines, journals, comics, stationery, cards, posters, pens, stickers, calendars, balloons.

1.2 Images, graphics, photographs, drawings, illustrations, plans, sketches, electronic and/or computer-generated material, design rights, background tables, maps and infographics.

1.3 Sounds, sound effects, sound recordings, music, ringtones, CDs, vinyl records, tapes audio material and any material stored on a storage and/or playback device and/or gadget.

1.4 Logos, trade marks, icons, characters, domain names, trading names, slogans, catchphrases, emojis and any associated images and words.

1.5 Banners, bookmarks, borders, captions, clip art, links, downloads, ebooks, audio books and/or recordings, blogs, podcasts, website, app, internet and electronic material.

1.6 Terrestrial, cable, digital and satellite television, films, cartoons, videocassettes, discs and lasers, DVD, discs, games, advertisements, infomercials, mini-films, and adaptations for sound recordings, images and texts on landlines, mobiles and/or through any WiFi and/or telecommunication system.

1.7 All products, toys, merchandising, theme parks, costumes, sponsorship, endorsement and product placement material.

1.8 All forms of electronic and digital and other method of supply, distribution, storage, and retrieval and mechanical reproduction and/ or performance and/or transmission.

M.284
'The Artwork' shall mean any photographs, plans, visual images, drawings, sketches, pictures, diagrams, maps, image maps or other illustrations or electronically generated material, logos, trade marks, design rights, character, clip art, computer generated art, infographics and domain name which are intended to be included as part of the [Final Project/Work].

M.285
'The Work Material' shall mean all the material of the [Work] in the possession or under the control of the [Assignor] including:

1.1 All copies of any master material in any format and of any duration.

1.2 A list of locations at which any material is held together with access letters giving irrevocable authority for the [Assignee] to remove such material.

1.3 All documents, records, data in any form, contracts, licences, consents, waivers, lists, proofs, scripts, publicity, advertising material, computer software, photographs, advertisements, banners, negatives, posters, catalogues, and any other material in any medium.

M.286
The [Assignor] agrees that it shall not retain any right and/or interest in the [Work/Product/Service] and/or the [Physical Material].

M.287
The [Assignor] agrees that it has fully disclosed any right and/or interest and/or conflict with any third parties in respect of the [Designs/Image/Logo] and/or the [Master Material].

M.288

1.1 The [Licensee] agrees and undertakes that the [Master Material] supplied by the [Licensor] for the purpose of reproduction and exploitation for the purpose of this agreement shall be held by the [Licensee] in a secure location and shall not be supplied and/or sub-licensed to any third party at any time.

1.2 That when all the authorised copies required by the [Licensee] has been made that the [Licensee] shall return all the [Master Material] to the [Licensor] at the [Licensee's] sole cost.

1.3 The [Licensee] agrees that it not the intention of this agreement that the [Licensee] be transferred any ownership of any copyright, trade marks, logos, images and artwork, domain names, computer software, data, sound recordings, films, videos, scripts and/or any intellectual property rights and/or other interests in the [Master Material] at any time. That the rights of the [Licensee] are limited to the terms of this [exclusive/non-exclusive licence].

1.4 That in the event new rights and/or ownership and/or material in any media are created, developed and/or commissioned by the [Licensee] relating to the exploitation of the [Master Material] and/or any other associated packaging, marketing and/or otherwise. That the [Licensee] shall conclude all such documents requested by the [Licensor] to transfer and assign all such rights, ownership and material in any media to the [Licensor] in consideration of the payment of a nominal sum of [number/currency]. In addition the [Licensee] agrees to supply all available master and other copies of all such new material to the [Licensor] at the end of this agreement at the [Licensees'] cost.

M.289
The [Distributor] agrees and accepts that the [Company] has not granted any rights and/or authority to the [Distributor] to edit, translate, develop, adapt, alter and/or change any part of the [Master Material/Products/Services] supplied by the [Company] under this agreement.

M.290
The [Distributor] agrees and accepts that it shall have no right and/or authority under this agreement to register any claim and/or interest in and/or attempt to register any domain name, trade marks, computer software, logos, images, characters, films, videos, sound recordings and/or any other ownership, copyright and/or intellectual property rights in the [Products/Service/Units] and/or any related packaging and/or marketing and/or any developments and/or adaptations at any time.

Internet, Websites and Apps

M.291
'The Website Material' shall mean the domain name and website reference: [specify details] and all the content, databases, downloads and associated

material, but not any other website or app. The material shall include text, scripts, titles, index, data, footnotes or references, headings, publications, images, graphics, photographs, drawings, illustrations, plans, sketches, computer generated material, design rights, background, tables, maps, sounds, sound recordings, music, ringtones, icons, logos, trade marks, characters, trading names, slogans, catchphrases, banners, bookmarks, borders, captions, clip art, and any advertising, promotional and publicity material and associated computer software, discs and any other method of storage and retrieval of the material held, owned and/or controlled by [Name] relating to the website.

M.292
'The Digital File" shall mean the digitised record of the [text/images] of the [Work] which is held in electronic form for reproduction and use on a website, app and/or the internet in any format.

M.293
'The Audio Digital File' shall mean the digitised record of the sound recordings which is held in electronic form for reproduction and use on a website, app and/or the internet in any format.

M.294
'The Electronic Digital File' shall mean the digitised record of the words, text, sounds, music, logos, images, graphics, films, recordings, sound recordings and any other material in respect of the [Work/Product/Service] which can be conveyed, transferred, supplied and/or distributed by electric, magnetic, electro-magnetic, electro-chemical, electro-mechanical means through any method or material and/or by any telecommunication system and/or by any other means in electronic form [whether in existence now and/or created in the future]. [This shall include but not be limited to the ability to be reproduced, supplied, used, displayed, exhibited, licensed, distributed and exploited in any medium and material in relation to the internet, websites, apps, computers, laptops and iPads, mobiles, gadgets and devices in any shape, form, process and method which may be developed at any time.]

M.295
'The Contributor's Work' shall mean the interview with the [Contributor] on the subject of: [state topic area] which shall be filmed, recorded and edited for a Podcast for the [Company]. A summary of which is attached and forms part of this agreement in Schedule B.

M.296
'The Podcast' shall be the final edited version of the film and sound recordings of the [Contributor's Work] produced and developed by the [Company] and/or an authorised third party engaged for that purpose.

M.297

Where any material is submitted and/or provided and/or posted by a member of the public either on the [Website/App] and/or as part of a survey and/or through a competition and/or otherwise. The [Company] reserves the right to edit, adapt and/or delete any material which in its view it is offensive and/or likely to lead to a claim for defamation and/or civil and/or criminal proceedings and/or the [Company] has been notified and/or suspects that it is an infringement of copyright held by a third party and/or any other intellectual property, domain name, trade mark, service mark, design right and/or otherwise. In such event the [Company] may exclude entry by that person to any account, online forum and/or competition and notify them that are not entitled to access any website, app and/or material owned and/or controlled by the [Company] indefinitely.

M.298

1.1 [Name] agrees that he/she has created and developed the [Computer Software/App/Blog/Website] for the [Distributor] based on an original idea and concept and/or brief summary of required work by the [Distributor].

1.2 That [Name] has agreed to payment of a fee of [number/currency] for all the work that he/she does and all the material which is supplied under this agreement for the [Distributor] and that no additional payments, fees and/or expenses and/or royalties shall be paid and/or due.

1.3 That [Name] agrees and undertakes to assign all copyright and computer software rights and intellectual property rights and codes, passwords and master source material and copies to the [Distributor] upon request both in the form of the assignment of all such rights and the physical and stored material in any format and/or medium whether this agreement is terminated early before all the work is completed or otherwise.

M.299

'The Blog' shall mean the online internet series of pages hosted on [specify website/app reference] which are written and composed by [Name] entitled: [specify name of blog] as a series of articles, images, photographs and links.

M.300

'The Blog' is on the [website/app/platform] known as [specify details] owned and controlled by [specify name of company/parent company]. The Blog is entitled: [title of blog] and written by the [Contributor] and edited by: [specify].

M.301

'The App' is entitled: [title of app] and features: [detail of purpose] and is available to the public as a free download and/or accessible from the [website/online store]: [name/reference].

M.302

'The App' entitled [specify] is supplied by [specify] from [source] to members of the public through [source] at a cost of [number/currency] for use in conjunction with [specify] for a period of up to [number] days.

M.303

'The Banner Link' shall mean the advertisement and promotional film and sound recording supplied and owned by the [Company] which features [Product] entitled [specify].

M.304

You are authorised to download and store the [app] to any laptop, gadget, watch and/or mobile for your personal use only. There is no consent provided for any commercial exploitation and/or adaptation of the [app]. The [Company] reserves the right to request that you cease using and delete the app at any time.

M.305

By your action of downloading, storing and use of the [app] you have given the [Company] access to personal details relating to you and your location and other matters which may fall within data protection legislation. If you do not want the [Company] to have access to your personal data by this method then please uninstall the [app].

M.306

Access to the material and advice including: [films/videos/sound recordings/data] and information on this [website/channel/podcast] is on the following basis:

1.1 It is for your own personal use and/or your family.

1.2 There is no authority to reproduce and/or supply any such material and/or any parts to a third party at any time.

1.3 There is no authority to reproduce and/or exploit any part of any material for any reason whether for an educational, charitable and/or for a commercial purpose.

1.4 If you have decided to follow any advice you are strongly advised to seek medical and/or legal advice. Any actions you do take will be at your own risk.

Merchandising and Distribution

M.307

The [Supplier] agrees that the [Products] shall conform to the quality, description and standard stated on their [website/app/flyer] and shall be fit for their intended purpose.

M.308

All specifications, drawings, maps, schedules and any other material, data and/or information provided to [Name] by the [Company] shall belong to the [Company] who shall hold the copyright and any other intellectual property rights.

M.309

The [Agent] agrees that it shall not be entitled to permit or authorise the use, reproduction, copying, drawing, taking photographs, filming or exploitation in any form or medium of the [Products/Services/Designs] and/or the [Company] Logo at any time without the prior written consent of the [Company].

M.310

The [Licensee] shall at the [Licensee's] cost make available an exact copy of the [Products/Designs/Sound Recordings] and any associated material specified in the agreement for inspection and retention by the [Licensor] upon request.

M.311

'The Prototype' shall be the three-dimensional reproduction of the [Board Game/Gadget] created and reproduced by [name].

M.312

'The Licensed Articles' shall be the three-dimensional reproductions based on the prototype to be manufactured and distributed by the [Company].

M.313

The [Licensor] agrees to provide the [Company] upon request with access to all such materials of the [Product] and the [Prototype] as may be available to assist in the production and manufacture of the [Licensed Articles].

M.314

1.1   The [Licensor] shall supply such basic reference drawings and specifications of the [Characters] comprised in the [Product] as are available. All further artwork and designs involving the [Product] shall be based on such material and shall be carried out at the cost of the [Licensee].

1.2   All such artwork in 1.1 must be approved by the [Licensor] prior to production and distribution. The [Licensor] shall be entitled to reject any proposals without stating a reason. The [Licensee] shall have the right to commission a third party to prepare and produce any such artwork and/or samples and/or [Products] provided that such third party shall not acquire any copyright and/or intellectual property rights in any such development and/or adaptation and/or any ownership of any physical material.

M.315

The [Product] shall be the original concept and novel idea for a [Product] created by the [Licensor] which is briefly described as follows:

Title: [–]. Brief Description: [–].

A copy of the full two-dimensional illustration, specifications and details of the [Product] including the colour, dimensions and materials of each of the components and a complete list of rules and instructions are attached to and form part of this agreement.

M.316

'The Character' shall be the original concept and novel idea for a character which is briefly described as follows: [character name]. A full description and representation of the Character are set out in appendix B which is attached to and forms part of this agreement. [Appendix B to cover source of character, colour, style, clothes, accessories, movement, voice, different versions and formats, trade marks, logos, copyright and trade mark notices.]

M.317

'The Characters' shall be the original concept and novel idea for a series of characters which are briefly described as follows: [Names] based on: [specify source and copyright owner] with the identifying and original features: [specify].

Full details of the characters are attached to and form part of this Agreement in Schedule B. [Schedule details to cover copyright and other intellectual property rights, design rights, trade marks, logos, plot, storyline, artwork, colour, signs, scoreboard, equipment, catchphrase, slogan, costumes, outfits, scripts, 2D and 3D drawings.]

M.318

'The Licensed Article' shall be the licensed product to be produced and distributed by the [Licensee] which shall be based on or derived from the [Character] and which is described as follows: [name/title]. Full details of the [Licensed Article] are attached to and form part of this Agreement in Schedule A. [Schedule details to cover colour, size, name, design, material, accessories.]

M.319

The [Licensee] agrees that the [Licensor] shall be entitled to approve the [Licensed Articles/Products] prior to manufacture and distribution. The [Licensee] undertakes to supply such samples of the [Licensed Articles/Products] in the exact form and material in which the [Licensee] proposes to manufacture, distribute, market, advertise, promote and sell the [Licensed Articles/Products] at the [Licensee's/Licensors'] sole cost. The [Licensee] acknowledges that such approval must be in writing from the [Licensor].

M.320

The [Licensee] agrees to provide the [Licensor] with not less than [number] [Licensed Articles/Products] in each and every form in which they are released and/or sold to the general public at the [Licensee's/Licensor's] cost.

M.321

'The Licensed Articles' shall be any licensed product based on and/or derived from the [Character] to be produced and distributed under agreements to be instigated, negotiated and concluded by the [Agent] and/or any sub-agent and/or any sub-licensee appointed by the [Agent] with the agreement of the [Licensor].

M.322

It is agreed that all merchandising, designs and formats shall be subject to the approval of the [Company] and such approval shall not be unreasonably withheld. The designs and formats shall be approved by the [Company] within [number] days of delivery. In the event that there is no reply then approval shall be deemed to have been provided by the [Company] after the expiry of [number] days from the date of delivery.

M.323

The [Company] shall supply such basic reference drawings and specifications of the [Character] as are available. All further artwork and designs based on the [Character] for the [Products] shall be at the [Licensee's] cost and shall not be manufactured and/or distributed by the [Licensee] and/or any third party for supply and/or sale to the public until the prior written approval of the [Company] has been provided. It is agreed that a third party may be engaged by the [Licensee] for the purpose of creating the artwork and designs.

M.324

The [Company] shall submit to the [Licensor] for written approval samples of the [Licensed Articles/Products] and any contents and/or other articles to be sold and/or used in conjunction with it including wrappings, containers, display materials, advertisements and publicity. The [Company] shall not distribute any [Licensed Articles] and/or publish and/or distribute any material unless prior written approval has been obtained from the [Licensor] that it is of acceptable quality.

M.325
The [Agent] agrees to ensure that all third parties to be licensed by the [Licensor] under this agreement shall agree that the prior written approval of the [Licensor] shall be required to approve all prototypes, samples and final versions of the [Products/Services] in the exact form and material in which such third party proposes to manufacture, produce, distribute, supply and/or sell any of the [Products/Services].

M.326
'The Format' shall comprise but not be limited to: all the goodwill and reputation, the title and sub-titles, the basic idea and concept, the original script, characters, plot, storyline, location, running order, design, layout, colour, signs, scoreboards, studio equipment, rules, procedures, catchphrases, questions, answers, slogans, costumes, outfits and all written material, graphics, artwork and computer-generated graphics and other electronic material; all copyright, intellectual property rights, computer software, design rights, trade marks, service marks, logos, musical, literary, dramatic, artistic and other works which are described in detail in Appendix A and shall form part of this agreement.

M.327
'The Format Package' shall mean all the material of the [Format] in the possession or under the control of the [Assignor] and/or any third party in any form and/or medium in any part of the world including copies of all documents, contracts, licences, trade mark registrations, data and/or any records stored in an archive and/or on software and/or any database.

M.328
'The Board Game' shall be the original concept and novel idea for a board game created by the [Licensor] which is briefly described as follows: [Title/description]. A copy of the full two-dimensional details of the [Board Game] including colour, dimensions and materials of each of the components and a complete list of the rules and instructions are attached to and form part of this agreement as Schedule D.

M.329
'The Designs' shall be the original concept and two-dimensional designs, sketches, drawings and patterns for an individual piece of clothing described as follows: [description details].

M.330
'The Designs' shall be the original concept and two-dimensional designs for a range of [specify generic type of market/product] and other products to be created and provided by the [Designer]. The Designs shall include all such designs listed in the attached Schedule F together with such other designs as may be created by the [Designer] in the future in accordance with the terms of this agreement.

M.331
'The Garment' shall be the three-dimensional reproduction of the Designs to be created and supplied by the [Designer] which shall principally be of the following material: [list type of material] and in the following colours: [list].

M.332
'The Prototype' shall be the three-dimensional reproductions of the Designs which are the final products upon which the manufacture of the [Licensed Articles] are to be based.

M.333
'The Prototype' shall be the three-dimensional reproduction of the [Board Game] created and produced by the [Licensee] as the sample.

M.334
'The Licensed Articles' shall be the three-dimensional reproductions based on the [Prototype] to be produced, manufactured and distributed by the [Licensor].

M.335
'The Licensed Articles' shall be the three-dimensional reproductions and adaptations of the Designs to be manufactured by the [Licensee].

M.336
The [Licensee] shall not be entitled to reproduce, distribute and supply copies of the [Licensed Article] based on the [Character] until the [Licensor] has provided written approval of the sample, the finished article, the packaging and the promotional material.

M.337
The [Sub-Licensee] shall not be entitled to edit, adapt and/or alter the marketing material supplied by the [Licensee] for the [Product] without the prior written approval of the [Licensee] in each case.

M.338
The [Licensee] agrees that it shall not have any authority, rights and/or be entitled to register any domain name, trade mark and/or with any collecting

society and/or government and/or international organisation any title, chapter headings and/or other any fictional character names, places names, initials, catch phrases and/or any other images, text and/or themes associated with the [Work/Product/Service] and/or any part either in its original form and/or as an adaptation and/or translation in any language under this agreement.

M.339
[Name] and the [Licensee] agree that where any new material is created and/or developed under this agreement by the [Licensee] at the [Licensees'] sole cost. That the parties shall be joint owners of all copyright, intellectual property rights, computer software, trade mark and/or any other interest in any media and/or format and any means and/or form of exploitation whether in existence now or created in the future. Such joint ownership shall include new domain names, trade marks, websites, apps, merchandising and publication material in any part of the world at any time.

M.340
'The Licensed Product' shall mean a [specify exact item] which shall bear the name, logo and image of [detail of character/persons' name] in the exact form agreed and represented in Schedule A and for which the sample for manufacture has been approved by the [Agent/Name/Company].

M.341
All specifications, drawings, sketches, models, samples, tools, designs, technical information or data and other information written, oral or otherwise furnished to the [Buyer/Hirer] by the [Company] shall remain the property of the [Company] and shall be promptly returned on the [Company's] request. Such information shall be treated as strictly confidential and shall be kept safely and not used or disclosed by the [Buyer/Hirer] except as required for the performance of the authorised purpose.

M.342
The description of [Products/Services] stated in this contract, invoice, order form, descriptive material, specifications, catalogue, brochure, marketing and/or advertising material published and/or issued by the [Company] is for identification only and not intended as a sale by description. The [Products/Services] are available for inspection prior to any purchase order being made by the [Client].

M.343
It is a condition of the contract between the [Supplier] and the [Company] for the supply of the [Products/Services] that the [Products/Services] shall conform to the quality, description and other particulars stated in the purchase order. The [Products/Services] shall conform to all samples,

drawings, descriptions and specifications provided and shall be suitable for their intended purpose and free from all defects. These conditions shall survive any inspection, acceptance of delivery and/or payment and shall also include any replacement, repaired and/or substituted [Products/Services] by the [Supplier] to the [Company].

M.344

'The Product' shall mean such products including any packaging and instructions as are described in Schedule A which is part of this agreement. Together with such additional identical and/or similar products which may be added by agreement between both parties at a later date. Reference to the Product shall include the plural where the context so determines.

M.345

The [Supplier] shall ensure that each [Product] is supplied with suitable labels, packaging and instructions which clearly sets out the purpose for which each unit of the [Product] is to be used; any age restrictions; and the precautions that should be taken to ensure that the [Product] is safe and will not put the public at risk.

M.346

'The Company's Products' shall mean the products and accompanying supporting services and guarantees of the [Company] which is described as follows: [title/brand/brief description].

A two dimensional and three dimensional image and representation of the [Company's Products] is set out in Appendix B. Together with information regarding all copyright and trade marks notice; disclaimers and warning notices; support services and helplines; guarantee forms and other relevant information.

M.347

'The Brand' shall be the following trade marks, service marks, designs, logos, slogans, texts, characters, graphics, artwork, images, sound recordings, personalities and/or or material and/or charities relating to the [Licensor's] [business/products/services]. Full details are described in Appendix C together with issues relating to ownership, registration, authorised uses and any specific requirements and restrictions.

M.348

'The Authorised Product' shall be the following product which is produced, manufactured and distributed by the [Sub-Licensee] in accordance with the terms of this licence. A two and three dimensional copy of [The Authorised Product] with exact specifications is part of this agreement in section A.

M.349

'The Marketing Material' shall mean all material associated with the [Product/ Service] which the [Licensor] decides at its sole discretion to make available on loan as examples to the [Licensee] including any labels, advertising and promotion material, films, videos, television and radio commercials and any other visual and/or sound recordings, photographs, computer generated graphics, scripts, artwork, music, discs, computer software, and electronic and/or other material for use on the internet, any website, app and/or through any telecommunication system for supply via any gadget, watch, computer, mobile phone and premium rate telephone lines. It shall not include merchandising, product placement, sponsorship and/or any new developments and/or adaptations created in the future either as rights and/or through technology. Any domain names, trade marks, service marks, logos, slogans and other material shall remain in the ownership of the [Licensor].

M.350

The [Licensee] agrees and undertakes not to use the [Material] supplied under this agreement in any manner which could prejudice and/or damage the [Licensor's] business and/or bring the [Licensor] into disrepute and/or create bad publicity and/or reduce sales of the [Licensor's] products and/or services in any country.

M.351

The [Licensee] agrees and undertakes that the [Material] supplied under this agreement is not to be reproduced and supplied to any third party, but is solely to be used for the purpose of the [Licensee] creating, developing and marketing the [Product].

M.352

1.1 [Name] shall not be entitled to remove and/or authorise use and/or access to the master copies of the material created by the [Company] to produce and manufacture the [Product/Services]. All such material shall be retained by the [Company].

1.2 The [Company] agrees and undertakes that it shall not supply, use, adapt, and/or reproduce and/or permit any third party access to the master copies of the material created by the [Company] at any time except with the prior written permission of [Name].

M.353

Where in the process of the development and manufacture of the [Product] by the [Company] is based on a concept and idea supplied and/or licensed by [Name]. The sample, prototype and final version of the [Product] and all the material and all the copyright and/or intellectual property rights shall be owned by the [Company/Name]. The [Company] agrees and undertakes that where it has commissioned any material and/or acquired any rights that it shall assign and transfer [number] per cent of all such material and copyright and intellectual property rights to [Name]. The parties agree to share all the revenue on the following basis: [specify percentage/format].

M.354

'The Template' shall be the master copy which has been approved by [Name] for the purpose of reproduction by the [Company] in the exact form, shape, layout, design and material a copy of which is shown in section B which forms part of this agreement.

Publishing

M.355

'The Synopsis' shall mean the summary of the [Work] which sets out the chapter outlines, structure, style, length, format and general content of the [Work]. A copy of the synopsis is attached to and forms part of this agreement.

M.356

The [Author] shall deliver [one] copy of the complete typescript of the [Work] in [format] consisting of approximately [number] words ready for [proofing by the agreed editor/setting by the printer] together with any artwork, photographs, illustrations, index, preface and resource list at the [Author's/Publisher's] cost and expense.

M.357

'The Author's Work' shall mean the original work of the [Author] including the cover and spine, introduction, [number] illustrations, charts and infographics, [number] chapters, footnotes and index entitled: [title] published by: [name] ISBN reference: [number] in [language] in [format].

M.358

'The Work' shall be the following book including the artwork based on the synopsis provisionally entitled: [draft title] which shall consist of approximately [number] typed A4 pages.

M.359

'The Synopsis' shall mean the brief summary of the [Work] which sets out the main elements of the storyline, the principal characters, chapter headings, structure and intended general content of the [Work]. A copy of the synopsis is attached as part of this agreement.

M.360

'The Artwork' shall mean any photographs, drawings, sketches, pictures and diagrams, maps or other illustrations supplied by [Name] which are intended to be included as part of the [Article/Blog].

M.361

'The Artwork' shall mean any photograph, drawing, sketch, picture, diagram, map, chart, plans, graphic work or any other illustration or any engraving, lithograph, woodcut or similar work and any other material listed: [state details] which form part of or is attached and/or included to the [Work].

M.362

The [Licensee] undertakes not to permit, authorise, license and/or transfer the right to publish the Extracts and/or part(s) of the [Work] in any other newspaper, periodical and/or magazine, website, app, blog, podcast, sound recording, film, video and/or any other media owned or controlled by any third party throughout the [Territory/world/universe] for the duration of the Licence Period [except for the purposes of review, criticism or other fair dealing].

M.363

'The Magazine' shall mean the following publication owned or controlled by the [Licensee] in which the [Work] is to be serialised: [name of magazine].

M.364

'The Extracts' shall mean the following parts of the [Work]: [specify written text/pages] [specify illustrations/photographs/pages] of [hardback/paperback/other format] edition ISBN: [reference] pages [–].

M.365

1.1 The [Publisher] shall send the [Author] [number] complete set of the proofs of each format] of the [Book] including hardback, paperback, disc, ebook and audio book.

1.2 The proofs shall include all the front pages, copyrights notices and disclaimers, any preface and/or introduction, all artwork, illustrations and other diagrams, all chapter headings, index, the front cover and the back and any other material to be included in or on the [Book] in each format and in each language.

1.3 Where the format is being distributed in any electronic or other format then the proofs shall also be accompanied by a copy of any online marketing and/or licence to be agreed to by any subscriber and/or member of the public relating to their use of the format.

1.4   The [Author] shall correct and return each of the proofs to the [Publisher] within [number] [weeks/months] of the delivery date to the [Author].

1.5   The [Author] shall not bear the cost of any sums arising from corrections in the proofs whether caused directly by amendments and changes made by the [Author] or not. The [Publisher] shall not be entitled to deduct such sums from the royalties which shall become due to the [Author].

1.6   The [Author] agrees that where errors are made in the printing process which are not noticed until after distribution and sale of the [Book]. That the [Author] shall not seek any compensation and/or damages for such errors and/or loss of sales from the [Publisher].

1.7   The [Publisher] agrees to send a copy of each of the final edited proofs to the [Author] to retain at least [specify period] before each such proofs is sent to the printers.

M.366

The [Author] will read and correct the proofs of the [Book] and will return them to the [Publisher] within [four] weeks of receipt. In the event that the proofs are not corrected and returned by the [Author] the [Publisher] shall be entitled to arrange for the proofs to be read and corrected at the [Author's/Publishers'] cost and shall be entitled to print and publish the [Work].

M.367

The [Author] shall correct and return the typed proofs to the [Publisher] in [format] within [twenty-eight] days of receipt. In the event that the cost of changes and corrections by the [Author] amount to more than [ten/number] per cent of the [complete number of pages/cost of the composition]. Then the amount in excess of [ten/number] per cent shall be payable by the [Author] and shall be deducted from future royalties due to the [Author].

M.368

The [Publisher] shall be entitled to deduct from any sums due to the [Author] under this agreement all costs of alterations and changes arising from any request by the [Author] which are incurred by the [Publisher] but specifically excluding the cost of artists and photographers, editors, printer's errors, and errors and omissions by the [Publisher]. The [Author] shall bear the following costs:

1.1   The cost of such alterations to original or printed artwork or photography in excess of [five per cent/number/currency] of the original development and reproduction costs and the artist's or photographer's fees.

1.2   Proofs of the [Work] in excess of [twenty per cent/number/currency] of the cost of the composition.

M.369

The [Publisher] agrees and undertakes that the [Author] shall not be liable and the [Publisher] shall pay all the costs and expenses of preparing and delivery by the [Author] of the proofs; all alterations and changes to the proofs; artwork; photographs; index; mistakes by the publishers and printers; alterations due to legal problems and any other matters in any format that may arise. The [Author] shall only bear the cost of the delivery of the original manuscript.

M.370

The [Publisher] agrees and undertakes that the [Publisher] shall pay for the cost of the following matters in respect of the writing, preparation printing, distribution and exploitation of the [Book], the proofs, the cover and/or jacket and any photographs, illustrations, maps, artwork, graphics, index, or other material that may be necessary for inclusion in and/or on and/or in connection with the [Book/Work]:

1.1   Where the [Author] requires access to additional material for research purposes for the text and/or artwork and/or photographs, to obtain copies and/or for the reproduction of any material. Then the [Publisher] agrees to pay the cost up to a maximum limit of [number/currency]. This sum shall be paid upon request in advance subject to confirmation of the material required and/or upon receipt of an invoice for the expenditure.

1.2   There shall be no charges of any nature for any reason made by the [Publisher] to the [Author] for alteration, correction and changes made to the proofs and/or any later version of the [Book/Work] whether due to requests by the [Publisher], [Author] and/or due to legal advice and/or any allegation and/or legal action at any time.

1.3   Where the index is prepared by the [Publisher] no deduction and/or charge shall be made to the [Author] either directly and/or by the deduction of any sums from the advance and/or royalties.

1.4   The cost of the design and artwork for the cover and/or jacket and any cost related to the production, distribution, exploitation and advertising, promotional and marketing material shall be entirely at the [Publishers] cost. No costs shall be deducted from any sums received by the [Publisher] and/or due to the [Author].

M.371

'Typeface' includes an ornamental motif used in printing.

M.372

'Writing' includes any form of notation or code whether by hand or otherwise and regardless of the method by which or the medium in or on which it is recorded.

M.373

On first publication the [Author] will receive [number] presentation copies of the [Work] and shall be entitled to purchase further [unlimited/number] copies for personal use but not for resale at a [number] per cent discount.

M.374

The [Authors] shall be entitled to receive on first publication [twelve] presentation copies each of the [Book] [in each and every format and language in which it is published]. The [Authors] shall also be entitled to purchase further copies for personal use at a discount on the published price of [twenty-five] per cent.

M.375

The [Author] shall be entitled to receive [number] free copies of the first and any subsequent editions of the [Work] and shall be entitled to purchase further copies at cost price for personal use but not for resale.

M.376

The [Publisher] agrees at its sole cost to provide the [Author] with not less than [24] copies of the work in each and every form in which it is made available to the public in the Territory.

M.377

The [Author] undertakes that the [Work] will be of a standard and quality suitable for commercial exploitation and in any event shall consist of not less than [number] A4 typed pages together with a sufficient number of [black and white/colour] photographs to make [number] pages of illustration.

M.378

The [Publishers] agree and undertake that they shall not be entitled to add to, delete from and/or alter and/or adapt any part of the [Work] as delivered by the [Author]. The Editorial Director who edits the manuscript must advice the [Author] of all proposed changes they wish to make for the [Author's] approval. The only exception to this is where changes need to be made as a result of a libel report and/or other legal advice by the [Publisher's] legal advisors and they have recommended that there be some alterations in order to avoid potential legal actions by third parties.

M.379

The [Publishers] shall not have the right to engage any third party to contribute and/or edit and/or update the [Work] without the prior written consent of the [Author] and/or the estate of the deceased and/or the nominated person with a power of attorney over the affairs of the [Author] if he/she is incapacitated for any reason.

M.380
The [Publishers] shall not have the right to publish the [Work] or any part in conjunction with any other work in any medium without the authority of the [Author].

M.381
The [Publishers] shall not have the right to exploit, license, adapt, translate and/or create any new version in any media and/or country other than those specifically set out in this agreement. Any other format and/or country requires a separate licence agreement with the [Author]. This shall also include a prohibition on any rights and/or technology and/or methods of exploitation not in existence at the time of this agreement.

M.382
The [Publishers] shall not include any material in any format in any medium of the [Work] which has not been provided by the [Authors] and/or for which the [Authors] have not provided their written consent in advance on each occasion.

M.383
The [Publishers] shall not without the [Authors'] prior written consent show the [Work] and/or disclose its contents to any other author before publication.

M.384
The [Publishers] shall publish the [Work] in [hardback/paperback/other format] no later than [twelve] months from acceptance of the manuscript [Work] by the [Publisher] and the delivery and acceptance of the edited proofs. Where no proofs are supplied to the [Author] due to the default of the [Publisher] then the end date for publication shall be [date].

M.385
'The Artwork' shall mean the non-text elements of the Work including but not limited to the cover, artwork, logos, illustrations, graphs, maps, drawings and photographs.

M.386
'The Logo and Title' shall mean the words and shapes and registrations described in detail in appendix D which are owned and/or have been registered as a trade mark and domain name by [Name] and any other similar and/or distinct variations which shall form part of this agreement.

M.387
'The Project' shall be the website, app, blog and associated educational published works to be created, developed and developed by the [Distributor] based on the original concept and work of [Author].

M.388

'The Marketing Material' shall be the following contributions, performances and other material supplied by the [Author] for the purpose of the [Publisher] promoting the [Work]:

1.1 Completed marketing questionnaire including background biography; key elements of the [Work] and any other relevant information.

1.2 Any articles, blogs, videos, interviews and podcasts which the [Author] shall write and/or appear in as agreed with the [Publisher].

Services

M.389

The [Company] agrees that it shall at its sole cost and expense provide the [Presenter] with a copy of any of the following material in its possession and/or control which is produced and/or created at any time:

1.1 Any photograph, illustrations, films, DVDs, discs, videos, sound recordings, computer generated material, website and internet material and/or other recordings of the [Presenter].

1.2 Any material used by the [Company] in relation to any advertisement, publicity, exhibition, corporate and/or commercial exploitation of the [Presenter] in which the [Presenter's] name, image, autograph, biography, performance and/or appearance is used in any format.

M.390

[Name] shall at the end of the Term of this Agreement return to the [Company] all material prepared by him/her and/or in his/her possession and/or control relating to the [Company] and/or the services provided by the [Name] which are owned by the [Company]. [Name] may only retain such other material as the [Company] may agree that he/she can retain for his/her own personal use and/or for references.

M.391

At the end of the Term of this Agreement the [Consultant] shall deliver to the [Company]:

1.1 All originals and copies of all material in any format in any medium supplied by the [Company]. Where the [Consultant] wishes to retain any material then the [Consultant] must supply a list of all such material for approval by the [Company].

1.2 All website material, domain name registration forms, databases, text, scripts, titles, index, data, publications, images, graphics, photographs, drawings, illustrations, plans, sketches, pictures, diagrams, computer-generated material, tables, maps, sound recordings, music, logos, trade marks, characters, trading names, slogans, catchphrases, banners, and any advertising, promotional and publicity material, computer software, discs and other methods of storage and retrieval of the material in the possession and/or under the control of the [Consultant] which are owned by and/or based on work for the [Company].

M.392

It is agreed that both parties shall be obliged to return to the other party all material which is owned and/or controlled by the other party which has been supplied on loan during the Term of this Agreement.

M.393

1.1 The [Company] agrees that [Name] shall be entitled to retain and keep for his/her own personal reference and use copies of any documents, records, data and information in any media and format which have been supplied by the [Company] and/or obtained by [Name] from a third party during the course of this Agreement.

1.2 [Name] agrees that the material in 1.1shall not be used for the purposes of publication and/or distribution over the internet and/or any telecommunication system and/or exploitation in any media in any form at any time without the prior written consent of the [Company].

M.394

The [Company] agrees that the [Consultant] shall retain ownership of all material, data, logos, images, documents, drawings and designs which are the original creations of the [Consultant] and developed and produced by the [Consultant] during the course of this agreement. That the [Company] shall not acquire any copyright and/or any other intellectual rights, computer software rights, trade marks and/or any other interest and/or claim over the product of the original work of the [Consultant].

Sponsorship

M.395

The [Sponsor] agrees to provide the following items and benefits to the [Sportsperson] at the [Sponsor's] sole cost and expense for the duration of this agreement: [list products/clothing/equipment/facilities/medical/insurance].

M.396

The [Sponsor] agrees that it shall provide the [Sportsperson] with a new car bearing the Sponsor's Logo for his/her personal and professional use throughout the Term of the Agreement which shall be comprehensively insured, taxed and serviced entirely at the [Sponsor's] expense and shall be owned by and be the property of the [Sponsor/Sportsperson]. The car shall be: [description].

M.397

Any material which is provided by the [Sponsor] to the [Company] for distribution to the public at the [Event] may be retained and used by the [Company] after the [Event].

M.398

The [Sponsor] shall be entitled to request that any material donated by the [Sponsor] for the [Event] is destroyed and/or returned after the [Event] at the [Sponsor's] cost.

M.399

'The Marketing Material' supplied by the [Sponsor] shall comprise: the annual report and accounts; a recent newsletter; a three dimensional and two dimensional representation of [Sponsor's] name, logo and slogan; [number] banners; [number] flags; [number] [clothing]; [number] stationary; [number] wristbands]; and a short film highlighting [specify purpose] which shall be produced and supplied at the [Sponsor's] cost.

M.400

Where the [Company] has to incur additional costs and expenses in order to reproduce, adapt and/or display, exhibit and promote and market the [Sponsor] at the [Event/Festival]. Then the [Sponsor] shall be obliged to pay for all such additional costs and expenses in advance upon request by the [Company]. The [Sponsor] agrees and accepts that these additional costs may include flyers, brochure, posters, transport, labour, equipment, facility and access costs, security, hire of staff, reproduction and manufacture costs, freight, insurance and administration.

M.401

The [Sponsor] shall not have any right to create, develop, produce, sell and/or distribute any film, video, music, sound recording, product and/or service which uses any trade mark, logo, image, icon, slogan and/or colours and/or other theme and/or material and/or rights associated with the [Festival/Event] and/or any artists and/or other contributors at any time.

M.402

The [Sponsor] shall not have the right to develop, market and/or exploit any merchandising material related to the [Event/Festival] which has not been authorised, approved and licensed by the [Company].

M.403

The [Sponsor] shall have no editorial control and/or right of approval over any part of the content of the [Event/Festival] and/or any marketing and/or promotional material distributed by the [Company].

University, Charity and Educational

M.404

'The Consortium Project' shall mean the aims, work, targets, personnel, budget and proposals set out in the Section A which forms part of this agreement.

M.405

'The Contributor's Work' shall mean the original work of the [Contributor] including the preface, artwork, photographs, index and headings based on the synopsis provisionally entitled: [draft title] which shall consist of approximately [number] typed A4 pages. A copy of the synopsis is attached to and forms part of this Agreement

M.406

'The Work' shall mean the original document held by the [Institute] in its [archive/depository] entitled: [title of document] reference [code number/file] the physical copy of which is controlled by the [Institute/Charity] which is dated [year]. There is no data provided regarding ownership, copyright and/or intellectual property rights in any such material.

M.407

'The Manuscript' shall be the draft document written and created by [Name] based on [specify concept] an original idea by [specify] in [format].

MEDIATION

General Business and Commercial

M.408

If any dispute and/or difference of opinion of any nature between the parties shall arise pursuant to this agreement then such dispute and/or difference of opinion shall:

1.1 At first be referred to a single mediator to be appointed in accordance with the mediation procedures of: [state organisation] in [country] or such other organisation which provides mediation services and/

or person which may be agreed between the parties. The mediator shall be agreed upon by the parties but failing such agreement within [twenty-eight] days of one party requesting the appointment of a mediator the mediator shall be appointed by the [President of the Law Society/other] of [country] at that time.

1.2   If not resolved by the procedure in 1.1 such dispute or difference shall be referred to a single arbitrator under the [Rules of the Chartered Institute of Arbitrators/other] in [country] for resolution.

1.3   If not resolved by the procedures in 1.1 or 1.2 then either party shall be at liberty to pursue such action and remedies as it shall, at its sole discretion, decide in the circumstances subject to the terms of this agreement.

M.409

The [Licensor] and [Licensee] agree that in the event that any dispute arises pursuant to this Agreement which cannot be resolved by negotiation between the parties they shall endeavour to agree the appointment of a third person to assist in the resolution of the matter. The cost of the services of such person to resolve the dispute shall be shared equally between the parties.

M.410

Without prejudice to any rights or remedies of either party to this agreement. The [Manager] and the [Sportsperson] agree that prior to the commencement of any legal proceedings in the event of a dispute, difference or other problems which arise pursuant to this agreement which cannot be resolved by negotiation between the parties. That both parties shall endeavour to agree the appointment of a third party to assist in the resolution of the matter. It is agreed that the cost of any such mediator shall be shared equally between the parties irrespective of the eventual outcome of the dispute.

M.411

If any dispute or difference of any nature shall occur which cannot be resolved by negotiation between the parties. Then prior to the start of any claim and/or legal proceedings the parties shall consider whether they can agree the appointment, on a shared cost basis, of a mediator who will review the facts and advise upon a basis on which to settle the dispute. Neither party is bound to use a mediator nor are they bound by any recommendation or decision.

M.412

The [Company] and the [Distributor] agree that in the event of any dispute, disagreement, default, delay and/or other problem that may arise under this agreement which cannot be resolved by negotiation between the parties. Without prejudice to any legal claim or remedy, the parties shall use their reasonable efforts and resources to agree the appointment of a third party to act as mediator between the parties on terms to be agreed.

M.413
There shall be no provisions as to arbitration, mediation, complaints procedure, appeal, code of practice or other method of resolution of any disputes or problems under this agreement which are binding on either party.

M.414
Prior to taking any legal action the parties agree that they shall first use one of the following processes and methods to try to reach a resolution of the dispute:

1.1 Arbitration.

1.2 Mediation.

1.3 Alternative Dispute Resolution.

1.4 Appointment of a third party who is independent and a legal and/or other expert to provide a written opinion. Both parties will have the opportunity to provide the written arguments of their case, and a conference prior to any report and/or decision.

M.415
The parties agree that in the event of any dispute, threat of legal action, threat of termination of the agreement and/or failure to deliver and/or adhere to the terms of this agreement. Then as the first option both parties agree that they shall avoid litigation and opt instead for mediation through [specify organisation]. In the event that either party refuses to cooperate with the mediation process in good faith and/or matter is not resolved to the satisfaction of either party. Then either party shall have the right to take legal action against the other at its sole discretion.

M.416
The [Licensee] and the [Sub-Licensee] agree that where they are in dispute in respect of any matter under this agreement that [name] of [organisation] shall be appointed to resolve the matter as the first option prior to any litigation. The cost of the services of {name] shall be paid by each party in equal shares.

M.417
The [Sponsor] and the [Company] agree and undertake that where there is any dispute and/or other areas of different views and/or allegations

between the parties. That the parties shall endeavour to reach terms for the appointment of a [mediator/third party] to resolve the matter in [country]. That if they are unable to agree terms and/or the procedure is unsuccessful then either party may instigate legal proceedings.

M.418
Where the [Licensee] is in dispute with a sub-licensee in respect of the exploitation of the [Character] and/or the payment of any royalties. The [Licensee] shall keep the [Licensor] fully informed and provide all such information, data, copies of documents, records and/or legal opinions and/or other material that may be held by the [Licensee].

M.419
It is agreed between the parties that both parties shall consider the process of mediation and/or arbitration and/or alternative dispute resolution and/or some other method of resolving the issue which may have caused the dispute for a period of [number] months after the dispute arises prior to the commencement of any legal proceedings in order to avoid unnecessary legal costs.

M.420
1.1 The parties to this agreement have agreed that if a dispute should arise that they will refer the matter to [name] who shall endeavour to act as a third party to assist in resolving the matter. The cost of [name] shall be paid for by both parties from [specify funding source].

1.2 In the event that [name] cannot resolve the matter to the satisfaction of both parties. Then either party may seek to find another forum for resolution of the dispute and/or take legal action in any court in [country].

1.3 Either party may use the information, data and/or material disclosed in 1.1 in any subsequent legal action.

MEDICAL REPORT

General Business and Commercial

M.421
This agreement is conditional upon [Name] undergoing a medical examination at the expense of the [Company]. In order for the [Company]

to engage [Name] the Company must receive on or before [date] a medical report on [Name] which confirms that [Name] is in good health and has the physical and mental ability and capacity to fulfil the terms of this agreement. That [Name] does not suffer from any condition, illness and/or other issue which would severely impact on the performance of this agreement.

M.422
[Name] agrees to submit to a medical questionnaire and examination required by the [Company's] insurers by a qualified [gender] medical practitioner at [location] in order to support the [medical/insurance] cover application for [Name] by the [Company].

M.423
The [Employee] agrees to undergo a medical interview and examination by a competent and qualified doctor of the [Company's] request and at the [Company's] cost for insurance cover purposes only.

M.424
In the event that the [Company] should require a medical report for any reason in respect of the [Presenter] then the [Presenter] shall only agree upon the terms:

1.1 That the Doctor or Consultant should be specified by the [Presenter].

1.2 That the full cost of the medical report is paid by the [Company].

1.3 That an additional fee is to be agreed in advance with the [Presenter] together with all reasonable expenses.

1.4 That a copy of the medical report is to be sent to the [Presenter] for written approval before it is sent to the [Company].

1.5 That the medical report will only be used for the purpose specified in writing in advance by the Company and will only be sent to the named personnel.

1.6 That in the event this agreement is terminated or when it expires all records relating to the medical report shall be returned to the [Presenter] or an undertaking given that they have been destroyed.

M.425
The [Presenter] agrees to be the subject of a medical examination and report relating to his/her general health once in each year during the Term of this Agreement. The medical shall only be carried out by a qualified doctor who is acceptable to the [Presenter] and shall be only for the purpose of obtaining or continuing insurance over for the benefit of the [Presenter] by the [Company].

M.426

The [Sponsor] acknowledges that the sponsorship fee shall be paid to the [Sportsperson] notwithstanding that the [Sportsperson] may be unable to provide his/her services under this agreement due to illness and/or injury and/or other incapacity which is supported by a medical report from a qualified doctor in [country].

M.427

The [Executive] is eligible for the annual medical screening at the [Company's] cost by a qualified medical practitioner specified by the [Company]. The [Executive] agrees to a medical examination including a drug, blood, urine, hair and HIV test at the request and expense of the [Company] at any time during the continuance of his/her appointment provided that it shall not exceed [one] review in any [number] month period. The [Executive] authorises [the Chief Executive/Head of Personnel] to view and read any such report made by the medical practitioner provided that they agree that it is private and confidential. There is no obligation by the [Executive] to permit access to and/or to authorise the release and/or supply of copies of any other medical records held by any other general practitioner or consultant at any time.

M.428

The [Executive] is eligible for the annual health screening at the [Company's] cost by a qualified medical practitioner specified by the [Executive]. The [Executive] agrees to a general medical examination, but shall not be required to provide any drug, blood, urine, hair, HIV and/or other tests. There is no obligation on the [Executive] to permit access to and/or authorise the release of copies of any medical records at any time relating to the [Executive] and/or his/her family.

M.429

The [Sportsperson] agrees to submit to an annual examination by a [private medical Consultant/dentist/physiotherapist] in order for the [Manager] to arrange suitable insurance cover throughout the Term of this Agreement. Provided that the following conditions are applied:

1.1   The [Sportsperson] should agree the choice of person.

1.2   The full cost of any report is to be paid by the [Manager].

1.3   The [Manager] is to pay the [Sportsperson's] reasonable expenses.

1.4   That there shall be no obligation to undergo any internal examination, X-rays, drug test, hepatitis, HIV or other blood, urine, hair test, psychometric tests and/or counselling.

1258

1.5   That a draft copy of any report will be sent to the [Sportsperson] for their comments. The final report shall then only be read by [specify persons] on a strictly confidential and private basis and all copies shall be held by [name] at [location]. No additional copies shall be made and at the end of this agreement all reports shall be returned to the [Sportsperson].

M.430

The [Company] agrees that [Name] is not to provide personal medical details or to agree to any medical examination for the purpose of this agreement. All insurance shall be arranged without the supply of any such data and/or information by [Name].

M.431

It is specifically agreed that [Name] shall not be required and/or requested to have any medical and/or health review and/or provide any personal details concerning themselves and/or their family other than those required by the [Company] by law in [country].

M.432

The [Participant] shall be obliged to adhere to the [Company's] [Drug Testing and Health] [Policy/Code of Practice]. Failure by the [Participant] to comply for any reason shall result in automatic disqualification from the [Event] and/or removal of any prize, bonus, title and/or other benefit that may have been awarded.

M.433

[Name] shall be entitled to be absent for up to [number] days without any medical evidence as to the cause of the absence. After that period a medical certificate shall be required from a doctor who has seen [Name] in person.

M.434

The [Company] shall have no right to require a medical report in respect of any personnel involved in the [Project]. The personnel shall be requested by the [Company] to complete a medical questionnaire for insurance purposes, but may refuse to do so and arrange their own insurance cover.

M.435

Where a person fails to attend a drug test and/or medical review for any reason. They shall be provided with the opportunity to attend a later date within the next [week/month]. Where they fail to attend on a second occasion then the [Company] shall be entitled to deem that they have refused to be subject to a drug test and/or medical review.

M.436

[Name] shall not be required to agree to a personal medical examination by any medical practitioner appointed by the [Company] for any reason nor shall he/she be obliged to disclose any medical data which he/she would prefer not to supply to the [Company].

M.437

[Name] agrees that where he/she becomes ill with any virus, infection and/or disease which his /her doctor has advised them is contagious, infectious and/or easily transmitted. That [Name] agrees that they shall not attend work at the [Company] until they are no longer a risk to any other person with whom they may come into contact whilst at work. The [Company] agrees to pay [Name] for any such period of absence [up to [number] months].

MONITORING

General Business and Commercial

M.438

The [Employee] acknowledges and agrees that the [Company] and any third party appointed by them shall have the right under this agreement to monitor, record and store copies of all emails, telephone calls, faxes, texts, downloads, data, and material which is sent, received and/or transmitted in any format in any media using mobiles, laptops, gadgets, equipment, and/or facilities and/or on premises owned and/or controlled by the [Company] and/or incurring costs at the [Company's] expense.

M.439

The [Company] shall not have the right to monitor, record and/or store copies of emails, telephone calls, faxes, texts, downloads, data, and material which are sent, received and/or distributed by the [Executive] without first notifying the [Executive] of their intention to do so.

M.440

The [Company] agrees that the [Executive] shall be allowed to use at the [Company's] cost and expense for both personal and business purposes the following: laptops, software, emails, text messages, mobile phones, clothes, credit cards, accommodation, hospitality, gadgets, taxis, airline tickets, petrol and other transport.

M.441

The [Employee] recognises and accepts that there is a strict ban of the use of [Company] equipment and facilities which are not for [Company] business such as emails, texts, telephone calls, and/or other benefits without the express permission of a line manager.

M.442

The [Company] may record and store this [telephone call/email] and use it to review its services, marketing and sales, and exchange such information with other companies within the [Group], but for no other purpose.

M.443

The [Consultant] agrees that the [Company] shall be entitled to monitor and carry out surveillance of the [Consultant] while present at the [location] and while working for the [Company] by cctv and/or sound recordings and/or surveillance and/or by access to any emails, documents, mobile calls and/or any other matter whether private and/or confidential and/or personal or not.

M.444

The [Consultant] agrees to complete and return such questionnaires, surveys and assessments that the [Company] may require in order to monitor, assess, evaluate and compile reports in respect of the [Project].

M.445

The [Consultant] only agrees to comply with any health and safety assessment and/or review by the [Company] and/or monitoring, surveillance, questionnaire and/or other matter to the extent that the [Company] is required to reduce any potential legal liability and/or to comply with any guidelines and/or code of practice and/or legislation in any relevant country.

M.446

[Name] does not provide any consent to the [Company] to access, intercept and/or monitor his/her mobile telephone calls and/or texts and/or videos and/or images which are made on the equipment supplied by the [Company].

MORAL RIGHTS

General Business and Commercial

M.447

[Name] [waives/asserts] all moral rights in respect of the product of his/her services provided under this agreement.

M.448

[Name] acknowledges that all copyright, design rights, future design rights, intellectual property rights, computer software rights, patents, trade marks and any other rights in the [Film/Product/Service/Work] shall remain the sole and exclusive property of the [Company]. This agreement does not purport to grant, assign or transfer any rights to [Name].

M.449

The [Employee] may not reproduce, supply and/or distribute any [Work] created, designed, developed and/or produced in the course of his/her employment and/or at the [Company's] request without the prior written consent of a Director of the [Company].

M.450

The [Employee] acknowledges that there are no moral rights in works produced by the [Employee] in the course of his/her employment under this agreement. The [Employee] acknowledges that when a literary, dramatic, musical and/or artistic work is made by the [Employee] in the course of his/her employment the [Company] shall be the first owner of any copyright in the work.

M.451

The [Employee] acknowledges and agrees that the right to object to derogatory treatment shall not apply to work created by the [Employee] in the course of his/her employment under this agreement. In the event that the right does apply to the [Employee] then the [Employee] agrees that the right shall not be infringed if there is a sufficient disclaimer.

M.452

The [Employee] waives all right to object to derogatory treatment of his/her work created in the course of his/her employment under this agreement at any time provided that he/she is not identified in relation to the work by the [Company].

M.453

The [Company] agrees and supports the fact that [Name] asserts his/her rights to be credited as the creator of the original concept and idea: [specify detail] to be exploited by the [Company] which was not developed under his/her contract of employment but as a specially commissioned work outside that contract.

M.454

The [Company] agrees and undertakes that where an employee make a suggestion, creates an idea and/or proposes changes and/or develops a product and/or invention which significantly benefits the [Company] by more than [number/currency] in any financial accounting year. That the [Company] shall acknowledge the contribution by an award of a payment to the employee of [number/currency] for every such year up to [number] years.

M.455
The [Finance Director/Company Secretary] are the authors of the annual report and accounts which is and/or has been approved by the [Board of Directors/Trustees] and issued by the [Company] endorsed by the [Chairman].

M.456
The [Author] declares his/her moral right to be recognised and acknowledged as the original [creator/author/other] of the [Work] and to be clearly, identifiably and prominently brought to the attention of the public to be known as: [specify name/credit] on all copies of any material distributed and/or exploited by the [Company] based on, referring to and/or reproducing and/or adapting the [Work].

M.457
The [Author] declares his/her right to object to derogatory treatment of the [Work] unless the [Author] has given his/her prior written approval to the [Company] in which case there shall be a conditional waiver. No waiver shall be applicable to any other matter.

M.458
The [Company] acknowledges the moral rights in clause [–] and agrees to be bound by them and to ensure that all third parties and successors in title are given notice of them and agree to accept such contractual conditions.

M.459
In order to constitute a sufficient disclaimer of a work in respect of an act capable of infringing the right to object to derogatory treatment of a work. The work which has been subjected to derogatory treatment must have a disclaimer which must be sufficiently clear and reasonably prominent to indicate that the [Work] has been subjected to treatment to which the [Author/Director] has not consented. That if there is any identification of the [Author/Director] then next to and/or near the credit should be a clear and reasonably prominent statement that the [Work] has been subjected to derogatory treatment to which the [Author/Director] have not provided their consent.

M.460
In consideration of the payments made and due to be made under this agreement the [Author] waives all moral rights in [country/in any part of

the world/universe] except to the extent that the [Author] shall be given the credit as detailed under clause [–].

M.461

1.1 The [Author] of the copyright of the film, literary, dramatic, musical or artistic work entitled: [title] has the right to be identified as the [Author] of the work and the identification must in each case be clear and reasonably prominent.

1.2 The [Author] therefore hereby asserts the right to be identified in relation to the work entitled: [Title/ISBN] at all times in the following form in [country/in any part of the world/universe]: [Name/Pseudonym/Initials/Logo/Trade Mark].

1.3 The [Author] asserts this right to be identified in relation to the work entitled :[Title/ISBN] at all times in the following form: [Name/Pseudonym/Initials] both in relation to the original work and/or any subsequent adaptation, translation, merchandising, development and/or otherwise whether in existence now and/or created in the future in any format, medium and/or method.

M.462

For the avoidance of doubt any adaptation shall include but not be limited to: merchandising, audio and sound recordings, films, DVDs, videos, CDs, any website, app, internet and/or electronic material in any form and/or use of any telecommunication system, stage play, theme park, hologram, or otherwise which is based on or derived from the original [Work] in any format in any media and/or country.

M.463

The [Author] of the musical work and/or literary work consisting of words intended to be sung or spoken with music entitled: [title] duration: [length] [brief description] asserts the right to be clearly and reasonably prominently identified as the [Author] by the following form of identification: [Name/Pseudonym/Initials/Other] whenever:

1.1 The work is published commercially.

1.2 Copies of a sound recording of the work are issued to the public.

1.3 A film of which the soundtrack includes the work is shown in public and/or copies of such a film are issued to the public.

That right shall include the right to be identified whenever any of those events occur in relation to an adaptation of the work as the [Author] of the work from which the adaptation was made and/or any copies of the original and/or adaptation.

1264

The [Licensee] shall be obliged to notify all third parties who acquire a licence or interest in the work and/or any adaptation of this assertion by the [Author] and shall ensure that the [Author] is identified on each copy in a clear and reasonably prominent manner likely to bring the identity of the [Author] to the attention of the public.

M.464

The [Author] of an artistic work entitled: [title] [brief description] has the right to be identified whenever:

1.1 The work is published commercially and/or exhibited in public and/or a visual image of it and/or a film including a visual image of the work is shown in public and/or copies are issued to the public and/or is broadcast, transmitted and/or included in a cable, terrestrial, satellite and/or other television and/or in any news, media and/or other service on the internet and/to any telecommunication system any computer, laptop, gadget, device, mobile and/or otherwise.

1.2 In the case of a work of architecture in the form of a building or a model for a building, a sculpture or a work of artistic craftsmanship, copies of a graphic work representing it, or of a photograph of it, are issued to the public.

1.3 The [Author] of a work of architecture in the form of a building also has the right to be identified on the building as constructed or where more than one building is constructed to the design, on the first to be constructed.

The [Author] asserts the right generally and in relation to each of the acts above to be identified as follows: [name/credit/acknowledgement].

Further in relation to the public exhibition of the [artistic work/model/drawings], the [Author] confirms that he/she has identified himself/herself on the original on the [frame/model/designs] as follows: [name/credit].

M.465

The [Licensee] shall not remove or obscure the identification of the [Author] and shall ensure that all copies bear the same identification.

M.466

The [Author] of the [Computer Programme/Computer-Generated Work] acknowledges that there are no moral rights in the [Work] in [specify countries].

M.467

The [Company] recognises that the [Author] of a copyright, literary, dramatic, musical or artistic work has the right to object and not to have the [Work] entitled: [title/description] to be subjected to derogatory treatment. The treatment of a work shall mean any addition to, deletion from, alteration to or adaptation of the work other than:

1.1   A translation of a literary or dramatic work.

1.2   An arrangement or transcription of a musical work involving no more than a change of key or register.

The treatment of a work is derogatory if it amounts to a distortion or mutilation of the work or is otherwise prejudicial to the honour or reputation of the [Author]. In the case of a literary, dramatic or musical work the right is infringed by a person who:

1.1   Publishes commercially, performs in public, transmits, broadcasts and/or includes in a cable programme service a derogatory treatment of the work; or

1.2   Issues to the public copies of a film or sound recording which include a derogatory treatment of the work.

This right extends to the treatment of parts of a work resulting from a previous treatment by a person other than the [Author] if those parts are attributed to or likely to be regarded as the work of the [Author].

M.468
The [Company] recognises that the [Author] of the artistic work entitled: [title] has the right to object to and not have his/her work subjected to derogatory treatment. Treatment of a work means any addition to, deletion from, alteration to or adaptation of the work. The treatment of a work is derogatory if it amounts to distortion or mutilation of the work or is otherwise prejudicial to the honour or reputation of the [Author].

M.469
The [Author] agrees that in relation to the [Computer Programme/Any Computer-Generated Work] the [Author] does not is object to any derogatory treatment, distortion and/or alterations and/or adaptations at any time.

M.470
The [Author] acknowledges that the right to object to derogatory treatment is not infringed by anything done for the purpose of avoiding the commission of an offence and/or complying with any legislation and/or laws and/or regulatory codes and/or to avoid anything which offends against good taste and/or decency and/which is likely to encourage and/or to incite crime and/or to lead to disorder and/or to be offensive to public feeling. Provided where the [Author] is identified at the time of the relevant act or has previously been identified in or on copies of the work that there is a sufficient disclaimer.

M.471

The [Author] waives all moral rights in the [Work] entitled: [title/reference/ description]. The waiver shall apply to:

1.1 The right to be identified as the author.

1.2 The right to object to derogatory treatment of the work.

1.3 The waiver shall apply to the [Company] and any licensees, or other parties who may acquire an interest or right in the exploitation of the [Work] as well as all successors in title and assignees of the [Company].

1.4 The waiver in this clause is conditional upon the full payment of all sums due to the [Author] being made under the terms of this agreement. In the event that all or part of the sums are not paid or accounted for in full. Then the [Author] shall be entitled to revoke the waiver by notice in writing to that effect to the [Company] at any time up to [five] years from the date of this agreement.

M.472

The [Author] waives the right to be identified as the [Author] in respect of the [Work] upon the following terms:

1.1 That the [Company] pays the [Author] the sum of [number/currency] in consideration of this waiver by [date].

1.2 That no other person is identified as the author of the [Work].

1.3 That this waiver shall only apply to the use of the [Work] by the [Company] for the purposes of [specify authorised uses].

1.4 That the waiver shall not apply to any other act by the [Company] or any third party.

1.5 That the [Author] shall be entitled to revoke the waiver if these conditions are not fulfilled by notice in writing to the [Company] at any time.

1.6 That in the event a further waiver is required by the [Company] from the [Author] at any time for some other act then an additional fee shall be negotiated between the parties.

1.7 That this waiver shall only be applicable from [date] to [date].

M.473

1.1 The [Artist] is the creator and original designer of the [Work/Logo] which was commissioned by [Name] at the [Company] for the [Event/ Festival] at [location] between [date] and [date].

1.2 [Name] and the [Company] have been agreed that the [Artist] shall retain all copyright and/or intellectual property rights in the [Work/Logo].

1.3 The [Artist] has granted the [Company] an exclusive licence to use the [Work/Logo] for the [Event/Festival] in all marketing and promotional material in any media and format. Provided that the [Company] shall not be entitled to sub-license and/or authorise any other use and/or adaptation of the [Work/Logo] and the [Artist] is at all times credited with a copyright notice as follows: [specify credit] in all material in any media and/or format.

M.474

The [Researcher] acknowledges that he/she shall have no right to be credited and/or acknowledged as the person who created, developed and/or edited and/or annotated and/or indexed the [Material/Database] which was commissioned by [Name]. That for the avoidance of doubt the [Researcher] waives all moral rights of any nature and agrees that [Name] may exploit, adapt and sub-license the [Material/Database] as he/she thinks fit at any time and no further payments shall be due.

Internet, Websites and Apps

M.475

The [Company] acknowledges that the [Author] asserts his/her moral rights generally in respect of the [Work] and in particular to be reasonably, prominently and clearly identified as follows: [state name] on the [Website/App/Blog/Podcast/Audio File] by the [Company] at all times and on any downloads, copies and/or any adaptations.

M.476

The [Author] waives the right to be identified as the [Author] in respect of the [Work] supplied to the [Company] for the [Website/App/Blog/Podcast/Audio Files] known as: [state reference] upon the following terms:

1.1 That the [Company] pays the [Author] the sum of [number/currency] in consideration of this waiver.

1.2 That the [Company] may be identified as the author of the [Work] and the copyright owner.

1.3 That there is no limitation on the use, reproduction, supply, transfer, assignment, distribution, adaptation, registration of the [Work] by the [Company] at any time and no further sums or payments shall be due to the [Author].

1.4 That the [Author] shall not be entitled to revoke the waiver and/or object to any derogatory treatment.

1.5   That the [Author] shall authorise a full assignment of all rights in all media of any nature whether in existence now or created in the future in the [Work] in all formats and/or media forever to the [Company].

M.477
The [Contributor] asserts her/her moral rights in respect of her/her original work for the [Website/App/Blog/Podcast/Sound Recording/Image] which is: [specify material/title/location]. The [Contributor] asserts her/his right to the [Company] and any third parties who may be authorised and/or licensed by the [Company] that she/he should at all times be credited and acknowledged as author of and copyright owner as follows: [specify name/title of work/copyright notice].

M.478
The [Company] agrees that [Name] will be acknowledged in the following manner in respect of the content of the text, images, sound recordings, films and other material on the [Website/App/Game/Audio Recording] [specify reference] designed and developed by [Name]: [specify credit] that such acknowledgement may either be at the bottom of a page and/or another section where appropriate. [Name] accepts that there may be variations in the form of acknowledgement due to lack of space and/or layout.

Merchandising and Distribution

M.479
The [Author] asserts his/her moral rights in respect of the [Artwork/Text] to be credited as the copyright owner of the [Artwork/Text] in respect of all copies of any adaptations produced, reproduced, sold, supplied and/or distributed by the [Licensee] on both the article itself and any packaging under this agreement in the following manner: © [year] [Name] [The original Artwork and Text of Title].

M.480
The [Licensee] agrees and undertakes to notify any sub-licensee, agent, distributor and all other third parties who acquire a licence or interest in the work or any adaptation. That it is a condition of all agreements that the [Author] has asserted his/her moral rights and that a sufficient reasonable and prominent and clear credit must be provided as requested by the [Licensee] on all copies in any format.

M.481
The [Licensee] shall ensure that it is condition of any contract and/or licence with any sub-licensee that they agree that the [Author] has asserted his/her moral rights in respect of the [Artwork/Text] to be credited as the copyright

owner of the [Artwork/Text] in respect of all copies of any adaptations produced, reproduced, sold, supplied and/or distributed by the sub-licensee in the following manner: © [year] [Author] [Title].

M.482

That the [Sub-Licensee] agrees that it shall ensure that the [Author] is identified on each copy and on all packaging in a clear and reasonably prominent manner likely to bring the identity of the [Author] to the attention of the public.

M.483

The [Company] agrees that in the event that any [Products] which are produced do not bear the relevant copyright, credits and trade mark notices specified by the [Licensor] on all items and on all packaging and marketing and promotional material. That the [Company] shall be obliged to withdraw such material at its own cost and expense and shall be obliged to destroy and verify the disposal of all such items and material to the [Licensor].

M.484

1.1 [Name] asserts his/her moral rights to be identified as the author of the [Work] and all the characters, artwork and storylines entitled [title] and any adaptation which may be developed and/or created based on that [Work] in any language at any time in any country.

1.2 [Name] shall be entitled to approve all proposed copyright notices, trade mark notices and other credits for [Name] and any third party in respect of the [Work] in any media and/or format at any time. In the event that [Name] does not approve and provide written consent then the proposal cannot proceed and must be cancelled.

Publishing

M.485

The [Ghostwriter] agrees that he/she shall not be entitled to any credit or acknowledgment in respect of the exploitation of the [Work] by [Name] and/or any third party in any media at any time. Accordingly, the [Ghostwriter] unconditionally waives all moral rights in respect of the [Work] and all the product of his/her services to [Name] pursuant to this agreement.

M.486

[Name] agrees that the [Ghostwriter] shall be entitled for biographical purposes only to state that the [Work] was written by [Name] with the research assistance of the [Ghostwriter].

M.487

In consideration of the Assignment Fee the [Author] agrees that he/she shall unconditionally waive all moral rights in the [Work] and the artwork including the right to be identified as the original [Author] of the [Work] and the artwork.

M.488

The [Author] hereby asserts his/her right to be identified as [Author] of the [Work] and further asserts the right not to have his/her [Work] subject to derogatory treatment and/or to have any other work falsely attributed to him/her as [Author].

M.489

The [Author] further asserts the right not to have the [Work] subject to derogatory treatment and/or to have any other work falsely attributed to him/her. The [Company] acknowledges this assertion and agrees to advise and make it a condition of any contract with third parties.

M.490

The [Company] acknowledges that the [Author] asserts his/her moral rights generally in respect of the [Work] and the right to a credit and copyright notice and trade mark in [country/world] and in particular to be reasonably, prominently and clearly identified as follows: [credit/copyright notice/trade mark].

M.491

The [Author] asserts all his/her moral rights in [country] generally in respect of the [Work] and in particular his/her right to be identified as the author and writer as [credit] on all copies of the [Work] in all media.

M.492

The [Publisher] agrees to make it a condition of any contract with any third parties that the [Author] must be identified in relation to the [Work] in all packaging, publicity, advertising, marketing, promotional and website, app, internet and telecommunication system material and/or merchandising material.

M.493

The [Company] acknowledges that the [Author] has asserted his/her moral rights under this agreement in relation to the [Work]. In addition the [Company] agrees to identify the [Author] as such on all publicity, promotional and marketing material.

M.494

1.1 The Company agrees that the [Author] of the literary work or dramatic work entitled [title, description, code] (other than words intended to be sung or spoken with music) has the right and asserts the right to be identified clearly and reasonably prominently whenever the work is distributed, broadcast and/or transmitted, adapted and/or exploited commercially.

1.2 The [Author] shall be identified as follows: [specify details/position].

1.3 The [Company] agrees that this clause shall bind the [Company] and/or any third party appointed by the [Company] who acquires any interest or rights in the literary work or dramatic work at any time. The [Company] shall be obliged to notify all such third parties of this clause.

M.495

1.1 The parties to this agreement recognise and accept that the [Author] of the [Work] entitled: [title/description] has the right to object to derogatory treatment of his/her [Work] in [countries]. That this assertion shall not apply to all the licensed countries.

1.2 Treatment shall mean any addition to, deletion from, alteration to or adaptation of the [Work] other than a translation of the literary or dramatic work. The treatment shall be deemed to be derogatory if it amounts to a distortion or mutilation of the [Work] or is otherwise prejudicial to the honour or reputation of the [Author].

1.3 The [Author] acknowledges that the right to object to derogatory treatment is not infringed where anything is done for the purpose of avoiding the commission of an offence or complying with a duty imposed by or under any enactment provided that the [Author] is identified at the time of the relevant act or has been previously identified in or on published copies of the work and there is a sufficient disclaimer.

M.496

The [Author] waives all moral rights in respect of the [Work] entitled: [title/ description] in the following countries: [list] to the [Company] and any licensees but not to any successors in title upon the following terms:

1.1 That in consideration of the waiver the [Company] shall pay the [Author] the sum of [number/currency] by [date]. This sums shall should not be added to the advance and/or recouped from the royalties due to the [Author].

1.2 The [Company] agrees and undertakes to identify the [Author] as the author of the [Work] in a suitable and reasonably prominent position on the [cover, binding, inside front pages] of the [Work] and on all other copies that it may publish, supply, distribute and/or sell.

1.3 That the [Author] shall be identified in all marketing, publicity and advertising material as the author of the [Work] by the [Company].

1.4 That the [Author] shall be identified as follows: [credit/other details].

1.5 That the [Author] shall have the right to be identified as the author of the [Work] in any translation, adaptation, serialisation or other exploitation of the rights granted in this agreement by the [Company] and/or any third party licensee appointed by the [Company].

1.6 That any changes of any nature of the original [Work] by the [Company] or any third party licensee appointed by the [Company] shall be subject to the prior approval of the [Author] who shall be provided with full details of the proposed changes in each case.

1.7 The [Company] shall endeavour to ensure that there is no derogatory treatment of the [Work] which is prejudicial to the honour or reputation of the [Author] by the [Company] or any third party which it licenses or appoints in respect of the [Work]. In the event that there is clear evidence of derogatory treatment the [Company] shall arrange for all copies to be destroyed and publicly apologise to the [Author].

1.8 The [Publisher] shall not license, permit or otherwise consent to any other person being identified as the author of the [Work] in its original form, or any translation, adaptation and/or otherwise in any format and/or medium.

M.497

The [Publisher] acknowledges that the [Author] asserts his/her moral rights generally in respect of the [Work] [under the Copyright, Designs and Patents Act 1988 as amended/specify other] and in particular to be reasonably, prominently and clearly identified as follows [–] in all references to the [Work] and/or parts including the title by the [Publisher].

M.498

The [Publisher] undertakes to respect the moral rights of the [Author] and to ensure that where part or all of the [Work] is supplied, distributed or sold that the following copyright notice will be displayed on the [Work] or any part on each occasion [–].

M.499

The [Licensor] agrees that he/she has viewed the [Work] in [format] and does not object to any such treatment.

M.500

[Name] agrees that it has viewed the proposal for the adaptation of the [Work] in [language] and agrees that the [Publisher] may sub-license the [Work] and authorise the sub-licensee to develop the translation which will not be an exact copy of the existing [Work].

M.501

The [Contributor] acknowledges and agrees that he/she shall only be credited as [Editor] for the [number] edition and that his/her name shall not appear in future editions where they are not the main editor.

Services

M.502

The [Company] acknowledges that:

1.1   [Name] asserts his/her moral rights generally in respect of the product of his/her services under this agreement as set out in the [Work Plan] including any documents, artwork and other material and in particular to be identified in a clear, prominent and reasonable manner on all copies in any media as [name/author/copyright owner/creator/other].

1.2   [Name] asserts the right to object to derogatory treatment of his/her work under this Agreement whether addition to, deletion from, alteration or adaptation which is a distortion or mutilation or is otherwise prejudicial to the honour and reputation of the [Name] [which is not a direct translation].

M.503

1.1   The [Director] asserts all moral rights in the product of his/her services with respect to the [Film] and/or parts and/or sound track.

1.2   The parties to this agreement recognise and accept that the [Director] of the [Film] has the right to object to and not to have his/her work subject to derogatory treatment. The treatment of a work means any addition to, deletion from, alteration to or adaptation of the work. The treatment of a work is derogatory if it amounts to distortion or mutilation of the work or is otherwise prejudicial to the honour or reputation of the [Director]. The [Director] is the author of the [Film] and soundtrack entitled [–] [duration] [description].

1.3   The [Director] acknowledges that the right is not infringed by anything done for the purpose of avoid criminal and/or civil proceedings and/or and/or complying with any legal obligation and/or law and/or on the professional advice of legal advisors in order to avoid an allegation and/or claim by a third party.

1.4   Where the [Director] objects to any matter in 1.2 then the parties agree to completely delete all mention of the [Director] and accept that a disclaimer will not be adequate to avoid damaging the reputation of the [Director].

M.504
The [Director] waives all rights to object to derogatory treatment of the [Film] at any time by the [Company] and/or any licensees, distributors or otherwise. This waiver shall be unconditional and shall extend to all third parties who acquire an interest on rights in the [Film] and/or soundtrack and/or parts and shall include any successors in title of the [Company].

M.505
The [Record Company] acknowledges that the [Artist] asserts his/her moral rights generally in respect of the [Sound Recordings] and the [Products] and in particular to be identified as follows: [credit/logo/trade mark, image/copyright notice/warnings].

M.506
The [Company] agrees that [Name] is asserting his/her moral rights in general in respect of the services to be provided under this agreement. [Name] shall be reasonably, prominently and clearly identified at all times in the following [style/manner/format] and in particular by the following [Name] whether in any original material created and exploited under this agreement, supplied by the [Celebrity] or issued in supporting press releases or otherwise.

M.507
The [Contributor] asserts his/her moral rights generally in respect of the [Programme] and the product of their services and any other contributions in sound, text or vision that may be created by the [Presenter] under this agreement. The [Presenter] shall be identified as [Name/initials/other] [size/location/colour/order] in [state format/media].

M.508
The [Contributor] asserts the moral right not to have any work which he/she has contributed to or created treated in a derogatory manner at any time.

M.509

The [Contributor] asserts all his/her moral rights to the [Company] and any third parties or successors in title in respect of the [Series]. The [Presenter] asserts that he/she must be identified in the form and style [–] in respect of the [Series], on all copies and/or any adaptations whether during the Term of this Agreement or not. The identification must be clear and sufficiently prominent for him/her to be brought to the attention of the public.

M.510

The [Company] shall observe and respect the moral rights of [Name] to be reasonably, prominently and clearly identified as the [Author] of the [Work]. That the [Work] shall not be treated in a derogatory or demeaning manner which would impugn on the reputation of the [Author] or the [Work].

M.511

The [Designer] waives all moral rights in respect of clause [–] both to the [Company] and any licensees and in respect of any successors in title. The [Designer] agrees that it shall not be entitled to any credit, copyright notice, acknowledgement or otherwise in respect of the [Website/App/Product/Service] and any subsequent development and/or adaptation.

M.512

[Name] agrees that the [Company] may license and/or exploit all and/or any part of the [Programme] without any credit to [Name] and that his/her appearance and/or contribution may be edited out, adapted, changed and/or a new sound and/or voice over recording added with a new person. That no such alterations shall be a breach of the moral rights of [Name] and no additional payments shall be due.

M.513

[Name] agrees that he/she shall not be entitled to any personal credit in the [Report/Work] which has been commissioned by the [Company]. That the [Company] shall be entitled to claim copyright ownership and to display a copyright notice and to register any interest with a third party without any reference to [Name].

Sponsorship

M.514

The [Sponsor] agrees that it is not aware of and has not received any assertion of any moral rights by any person in respect of any material supplied by the [Sponsor] under this agreement.

M.515

The [Sponsor] notifies the [Company] that the following credit and copyright notice is due to the [Designer] on all copies of the [specify material] which is reproduced and/or adapted by the [Company].

M.516

The [Company] shall not be entitled to subject the [Work] to derogatory treatment in the form of distortion and/or mutilation and/or to do anything which is prejudicial to the reputation and/or honour of the [Designer] without the prior written consent of the [Sponsor] and the [Designer].

M.517

The [Sponsor] has and/or will obtain waivers of all moral rights in respect of the material and products supplied by the [Sponsor] to the [Company] under this agreement. These waivers shall not apply to any third parties and/or any successors in title of the [Company].

M.518

The [Sponsor] agrees that it shall not be entitled to any reductions in the payment of any fees as a result of any failure by the [Company] to reproduce, display, supply and/or exhibit and/or transmit the name, image and logo of the [Sponsor] in the exact form in Schedule B.

University, Charity and Educational

M.519

The [Institute/Charity] acknowledges that the [Author] asserts her/his moral right in respect of the [Work] to be reasonably, prominently and clearly identified as follows: [credit/other] on all copies of the [Work] to be distributed to the public during the Term of this Agreement.

M.520

The [Contributor] as the original author asserts his/her right to the [Institute/Charity] and any third parties and/or successors in title in respect of the [Work/Project]. The [Contributor] asserts that he/she must be clearly identified as follows: [credit/other] in respect of the [Work/Project] and on all copies and any adaptations whether during the Term of this Agreement or not. That the credit to the [Contributor] shall not be deleted and/or substituted by another person.

M.521

The [Consortium] agrees that as a matter of policy only the lead person on any project shall be acknowledged and credited in any summary report to be published by the [Consortium].

M.522

The [Consortium] agrees that where any individual project has originated by a third party which is funded by the [Consortium] in whole and/or in part that the [Consortium] shall be credited and acknowledged with the following names, logos and images and references set out in appendix A a copy of which forms part of this agreement.

MUSICAL WORK

General Business and Commercial

M.523

'Music' means such incidental background music, featured music songs, themes and other musical works and lyrics written by the [Composer] as may be required by the [Company] and sufficient in the sole discretion of the Company for inclusion in the [Film] and all trailers of the [Film].

M.524

'Musical Work' shall mean a work consisting of music exclusive of any words or action intended to be sung, spoken or performed with the music. The musical work shall be recorded in writing or otherwise.

M.525

'The Musical Work' shall be the musical composition and recording entitled: [title/duration/description/format].

M.526

'The Work' shall be the following original musical work including any associated works, lyrics or arrangement entitled: [–].

M.527

'The Work' shall mean any and all lyrics and/or musical compositions and/or other musical, literary or dramatic works, whether written, generated or stored electronically, mechanically, graphically or by any other means whatsoever and whether wholly or partly directly or indirectly owned, controlled, written, composed, orchestrated or arranged by the [Composer] whether alone or in collaboration with others.

M.528

1.1 [Name] has a new [Musical Work] in [format] which he/she has developed and created with [specify person] at the [Company].

1.2 [Name] has agreed that the [Musical Work] was based on a concept and theme decided by the [Company] to be used in conjunction with a future media marketing and promotional campaign for [purpose/subject].

1.3 That [Name] agrees that he/she and the [Company] shall jointly hold all the copyright and intellectual property rights in the [Musical Work] and any sound recordings, film and/or other material which are as follows: [specify].

1.4 That [Name] and the [Company] shall share any sums received from any collecting societies in any part of the world equally and any other sums from the exploitation of the [Musical Work] and any sound recordings, film and/or other material in 1.3 above. That all the parties in 1.3 must be named in and sign any agreement to register and/or sub-license any rights to a third party.

1.5 That where the parties cannot agree on any form of exploitation that they shall endeavour to avoid litigation and appoint a third party to assist with the resolution of the matter prior to taking any legal action for any reason.

1.6 That if any party wishes to buy out all the rights from the other the payment shall not be less than [number/currency] but no party shall be obliged to dispose of their share of the rights in any form.

M.529

The [Licensor] shall furnish the [Company] with [one] copy of a full music cue sheet for the [Series] listing each music work; the name of each composer, author and publisher, the duration and description of use whether vocal, feature, background.

M.530

The [Licensor] shall provide the [Licensee] with a copy of the music cue sheet for the [Film] which shall list the following details for each separate section of music.

1.1 Title of music/Format

1.2 Performer/Composer/Arranger.

1.3 Publisher/Reference Codes.

1.4 Duration of the music/Description background, featured, vocal or instrumental.

M.531
The [Company] shall furnish the [Licensee] where available and on request with a list of titles, composers, and publishers of all music used in the [Format/Series/Podcast/Sound Recordings].

M.532
[Name] agrees to supply details of the information required for the music cue sheets for all the musical works that he/she performs, sings, plays and/or uses at the [Event] for the [Company] at no additional cost.

N

NET RECEIPTS

Film, Television and Video

N.001
Where [Films/Videos/Discs] are sold, rented, supplied, streamed and/or distributed by the [Distributor] under any arrangement at the original published price, but are then later reduced in price for any reason including damages, discounts, old stock and/or a special promotion. Then the royalty payable will be calculated upon the sums received [exclusive of sales tax] by the [Distributor] instead of the original published price.

N.002
No sums shall be withheld and/or deducted by the [Licensee] for any reason which is not disclosed to the [Licensor] and/or set out in the accounting statement.

N.003
The [Licensee] agrees that the Advance under clause [–] shall not be returnable by the [Licensor] under any circumstances. The [Licensee] shall not be permitted to offset the Advance against the Net Receipts and/or any of the Royalties. That these conditions shall not be contingent in any way on the sales achieved under this agreement.

N.004
'Net Receipts' shall mean the total proceeds of the exploitation of the [Film/Video/Disc] Rights in the [Film] and/or part(s) actually received by the [Licensee] after there shall have been deducted and/or paid from such sums all reasonable costs and expenses incurred by the [Licensee] and/or any sub-agent and/or sub-distributor and/or sub-licensee which shall include but not be limited to commission and agency fees, currency conversion and bank charges, insurance, freight, taxes on products and/or services, duties, reproduction, distribution and marketing costs, the clearance of all content including music, lyrics and sound recordings, consent and copyright payments, indemnity payments and costs incurred in legal proceedings and/or any other legal obligations.

N.005

'The Net Receipts' shall mean the aggregate of the proceeds of exploitation of the [Film/Video/Disc] Rights in the [Film] received by the [Company] and/or its nominated distributor, agent and/or other authorised third party in [specify] currency. After there shall have been paid and/or deducted from such proceeds all costs and expenses of and relating to the production, reproduction, distribution, sale and/or other exploitation of the [Unit] of the [Film] and/or parts. There shall be an agreed maximum limit of [number/currency] which can be deducted [in total during the Agreement/in any accounting period/in any one calendar year].

N.006

'Net Receipts' under this agreement shall mean all the total sums received by and/or credited to the [Distributor] in respect of the reproduction, supply, sale, rental, subscription, and distribution of the [Films/Videos/Discs] of the [Film] in the [Territory/country/world] whether during the Term of the Agreement and/or thereafter which remain after the [Distributor's Commission] is deducted. The [Distributor's Commission] shall be fixed at [number] per cent. No other sums, costs, commission, expenses, charges, freight, insurance and/or otherwise of any nature shall be deducted by the [Distributor].

N.007

The [Licensor] agrees that the [Distributor] shall be entitled to offset the Advance due to the [Licensor] in clause [–] against the Net Receipts due to the [Licensor] until such time as the Advance has been recouped in full by the [Distributor]. The Advance shall not however be repayable by the [Licensor] at any time if it cannot be recouped.

N.008

The [Distributor] agrees and undertakes that it shall not offset the Advance to the [Licensor] in clause [–] against the Net Receipts and/or any sums due to the [Licensor].

N.009

'The Net Receipts' shall be the total proceeds of any sums received by the [Distributor] from the exploitation of any of the rights granted under this agreement less the following reasonable commission costs and expenses:

1.1 Distribution Fee to the Distributor of [number] per cent of the total sums received.

1.2 A commission of no more than [number] per cent due to any authorised third party who is under the control of the [Distributor] and/or with whom the [Distributor] have concluded an arrangement or agreement.

Together with a maximum limit of [number/currency] [in any one accounting period/during the whole Term of this Agreement].

1.3 No sums shall be deducted for administration and staff, consultants, publicity, promotion, advertising, marketing, merchandising, packaging, storage, currency conversion costs and charges, brochures, catalogues, website and internet material, mobile, telephone and telecommunication system material, competitions, trade fairs, exhibitions and/or any other reason.

1.4 The [Distributor] shall try to ensure that the reproduction and freight costs are paid for by any licensee and the material returned at the end of the agreement. Where costs are paid for by the [Distributor] there shall be a total maximum limit of all such sums which can be deducted of [number/currency] which shall be spread in equal instalments over the duration of the Agreement and shall not be exceeded for any reason.

N.010
'Net Receipts' shall mean all the monies received by and/or credited to the [Company] in respect of the reproduction, supply, sale, licence, rental, subscription, downloading, distribution and/or any other exploitation of the [Sound Recordings] by means of the [Disc/Unit] and/or any other form of mechanical reproduction and/or over the internet and/or to mobile phones and/or any other form of transmission by any telecommunication system and/or by any form of television and/or radio in the [Territory/country] whether during the Term of this Agreement and/or received thereafter after the deduction of the [Distributors] Commission which shall be fixed at [number] per cent.

N.011
'Net Receipts' shall be defined as all sums received by the [Licensee] from the exploitation of the rights granted under this Agreement after the deduction of the following agreed expenses and commission in each accounting period:

1.1 Commission to the [Licensee] of [number] per cent.

1.2 All costs of reproduction, freight, packaging and insurance to supply and deliver material to third parties up to a total maximum of [number/currency].

1.3 Marketing costs up to a total maximum of [number/currency] in total

N.012
'The Net Receipts' shall be all sums in any currency received by and/or credited to the [Company] and/or any parent and/or subsidiary company

less the following permitted deductions during the Term of the Agreement as follows:

1.1 [number/currency] maximum in total for reproduction costs for the [Sound Recordings].

1.2 [number] per cent commission to the [Company].

1.3 a commission of no more than [number] per cent to any agency and/or sub-licensee.

1.4 [number/currency] maximum in total for marketing, promotion, advertising, sponsorship and endorsements of the [Sound Recordings] by the [Company].

N.013

'Net Receipts' shall be all the sums received by [Name] from the exploitation of the [Disc/Unit/Film] by [Name] and/or any authorised third party at any time in the world after the deduction of the following costs:

1.1 Bank charges and costs relating to currency conversion and/or transfer. Commission, fees and other costs and expenses incurred by [Name] required to promote, exploit and/or market the [Disc/Unit/Film] including travel, accommodation, insurance, hospitality, entertainment and other services and/or products that may be supplied.

1.2 Commissioning translations, designs, artwork, computer-generated material, website, app and other development, marketing and/or promotional costs. The cost of manufacture, reproduction, supply and distribution of material, packaging and delivery charges.

1.3 Payments due for copyright and other rights clearance and payments and/or royalties. Sums which arise as a result of the performance, transmission, broadcast, recording and/or other exploitation to any rights management organisation and/or rightsholder not paid by a third party and/or the cost of registration of any trade mark, domain name and/or rights and/or any legal proceedings.

N.014

'Net Receipts' shall mean all sums and/or benefits received by [Name] and/or any associated company in any country in the world at any time from the exploitation of the [Work] and/or any part and/or any image, word, text and/or other matter associated with the [Work] including any sequel, option, character, title, trade mark, domain name and/or merchandising and/or any other form of exploitation, licensing and/or transfer of assets and/or rights and/or interest after the deduction of the agreed commission due to [Name] of [number] per cent [–]%. There shall not be a deduction of any other sums except taxes which are legally charged on the transfer of goods and/or services by any government.

N.015
'Net Receipts' shall be defined as the Gross Receipts less the defined Distribution Expenses.

N.016
'Net Receipts' shall mean the balance which remains after the Distribution Expenses and all the Programme Production and Marketing costs have been deducted from the Gross Receipts.

N.017
Net Receipts' shall mean the monies retained by the [Company] after the [Distribution Expenses] are deducted from the Gross Receipts.

N.018
'Net Receipts' shall mean the figure remaining after the Approved Budget and the Distribution Expenses have been deducted from the Gross Receipts.

N.019
'Net Receipts' shall be the Gross Receipts less the Production Costs and the Distribution Expenses.

N.020
'The Distribution Income' shall mean the aggregate of the proceeds of exploitation of the rights granted in the [Film] and/or parts actually received by the [Television Company] or its nominated distributor, agent or other authorised third party in freely convertible currency after there shall have been paid or deducted from such proceeds all costs and expenses of and relating to the production, reproduction, distribution, sale and/or other exploitation of the [Film] and/or parts including, but not limited to, all distribution charges, commissions and all other deductions and expenses which such distributors and third parties are entitled to make, which they incur and/or in respect of which they are entitled to reimbursement, recoupment and/or any indemnity under their agreements with the [Television Company].

N.021
'The Net Receipts' shall mean the balance of the proceeds from the distribution and exploitation of the [Film] and any parts received by all means and in all media throughout the world which is remaining after the following sums shall have been paid or deducted from the gross sums:

1.1 All costs and expenses relating to the distribution, sale or other exploitation of the [Film] including charges, commissions and all other sums which any third party, sub-licensee, distributor, representative or agent are entitled to make or in respect of which they are entitled to be reimbursed and/or paid under any indemnity under their agreements with the [Company].

1.2   The cost of the production of the [Film] and any interest charged and/or any amounts retained by the Distributors of the [Film] to recoup the cost of any changes.

1.3   All completion guarantee costs and expenses.

1.4   The aggregate cost of any sums not included in the certified cost of the production which are payable at a later date for any reason or any sum due as a percentage of Gross Receipts to any person who provided finance, facilities or services or otherwise in connection with the [Film].

N.022
'Distribution Income' means the total proceeds of the exploitation of the rights in the [Film] and/or part(s) in any media actually received by the [Licensor] and/or any appointed third party after there shall have been deducted or paid from such sums all reasonable costs and expenses relating to the distribution, marketing and exploitation of the [Film] and/or parts which are not recouped from some other third party.

N.023
'The Net Receipts' shall be the total proceeds of any sums received by the [Distributor] from the exploitation of any of the rights granted under this agreement less the following reasonable commission, costs and expenses:

1.1   The actual cost of the supply, distribution, promotion, advertising and marketing including but not limited to reproduction and development of material, merchandising, packaging, storage, customs, freight, insurance, currency conversion costs and charges, brochures, catalogues, website, internet, mobile and telecommunication system material, competitions, promotions, trade fairs, exhibitions, clearances, copyright and consent payments that may be due in respect of any material, stills, graphics, artists, director, contributor, music, computer-generated material, sound recordings, voice-overs, the performance and/or mechanical reproduction and/or reproduction and/or transmission and/or other exploitation and/or adaptation.

1.2   A Distribution Fee to the Distributor of [number] per cent of the balance of the sum after all the deductions in 1.1 have been paid.

1.3   The remaining sum after the deductions in 1.1 and 1.2 shall be the Net Receipts due to the [Licensor].

N.024

'The Net Receipts' shall be the total amount of all monies received by the [Distributor] from the exploitation of the rights granted under this agreement at any time less the following sums which the [Distributor] shall be entitled to deduct provided that they are reasonable and full details are provided justifying the costs and expenses:

1.1 The Distributor's Commission which shall be:

    a. [number] per cent of the total amount of all monies from [specify rights].

    b. [number] per cent of the total amount of all monies from [specify rights].

1.2 The direct cost of the supply and distribution of the materials of the [Film] such as reproduction charges, freight, customs duties, insurance.

1.3 Any royalties and/or other sums due for clearances, rights, consents and/or under any contract in respect of the development, reproduction, use performance, transmission, mechanical reproduction and/or any other exploitation in any form of the [Film] and/or any material and/or content including music, sound recordings, artists, images and/or otherwise which may be due and/or paid to any third party and/or any rights management organisation and/or rightsholders by the [Distributor].

1.4 There shall be no other deduction for any:

    a. sub-agent, sub-distributor or other third party or associated, subsidiary or parent company at any time.

    b. publicity, promotion, advertising, marketing, merchandising, packaging, storage, currency conversion costs, catalogues, website and internet material, trade fairs, exhibitions, travel and accommodation and/or any other matter.

1.5 The Net Receipts shall be the total balance of the monies after the deductions under 1.1, 1.2 and 1.3 above.

N.025

In consideration of the licence granted the [Licensee] agrees to pay to the [Licensor] royalties as follows:

1.1 [number] per cent of all sums received from the exhibition of the [Film/Video/Installation] after the deduction of the directly related costs and expenses incurred by the [Licensee] and/or charged by any third party.

1.2 [number] per cent of all other sums received from all other authorised forms of exploitation in any format and/or medium after deduction of the directly related costs and expenses incurred by the [Licensee] and/or charged by any third party.

N.026

The [Company] agrees that it shall be solely responsible for any sums due in respect of the production, reproduction, supply, performance, mechanical reproduction, broadcast, transmission, advertising, promotion, marketing, distribution and exploitation of the [Film] and/or parts in respect of the rights granted under this Agreement and that the [Licensor] shall not be liable for any such sums.

N.027

The [Assignee] agrees that it shall not be entitled to offset any of the Budget against the Gross Receipts and any such deduction shall be limited to the agreed authorised Distribution Costs.

N.028

'The Net Receipts' shall be all sums in any currency in any part of the world at any time received by and/or credited to the [Distributor] and/or any authorised third party who is under their control and/or with whom they have concluded an arrangement or agreement in respect of the [Film] and/or parts and/or any adaptation.

The only deductions that are permitted before the transfer of the total sum on [date] and [date] each year to the [Licensor] shall be as follows:

1.1 In any one year a maximum of [number/currency] for material reproduction costs for the supply of the [Film] and/or parts together with freight and custom duties.

1.2 After the deduction of 1.1 then the [Distributor] may allocate and receive [number] per cent for their commission.

1.3 No other sums are to be deducted for costs and expenses of the [Distributor] and/or any authorised third party who is in their control and/or with whom they have concluded an arrangement or agreement of any nature.

1.4 No sums are to be deducted for the marketing, promotion and advertising by the [Distributor].

1.5 The [Distributor] shall endeavour to ensure that as far as possible that any authorised third party shall either receive material on loan or pay the reproduction and freight costs in advance and then return material at the end of the agreement.

1.6 The cost of any commission or other sum due to any authorised third party who is in the control of the [Distributor] and/or with whom the

[Distributor] have concluded an arrangement or agreement of any nature shall be paid for entirely by the [Distributor].

N.029

'The Net Receipts' shall be the total proceeds of any sums received by the [Distributor] from the exploitation of any of the rights granted under this agreement less the following reasonable commission, costs and expenses:

1.1 A Distribution Fee to the [Distributor] of [number] per cent of the total sums received by the [Distributor] after all authorised deductions.

1.2 A commission of no more than [number] per cent due to any third party with whom the [Distributor] has concluded any arrangement or agreement. Provided that no more than a maximum limit of [number/currency] can be deducted in any one accounting period. Any balance must be carried forward to the next accounting period to be deducted.

1.3 Any sums paid for the supply and reproduction of material for any licensee or other third party together with the cost of all advertising, marketing, merchandising, packaging, storage, currency conversion costs and charges, the reproduction and creation of content for websites, apps, mobiles, trade fairs and exhibitions. Provided that there is no more than a maximum of [number/currency] deducted in any one accounting period. Any balance must be carried forward to be deducted in the following periods. There shall be which can be deducted. No more than [number/currency] may be deducted in any one accounting period during the Term of this Agreement.

1.4 The [Distributor] shall try to ensure that material is either supplied on loan for a short period or that the reproduction, delivery and other costs are paid by any sub-licensee and the material returned at the end of the agreement.

N.030

It is agreed between the parties that they shall each be responsible for their own costs and expenses in respect of the matters set out below. Neither party shall be entitled to be reimbursed and/or deduct the sums from the Gross Receipts:

1.1 Administration, travel, accommodation, hospitality and entertainment, clothing, make up and beauty treatments, meals, gadgets, mobile and wifi and technology charges; costs for any employees, consultants and/ or freelance persons and/or other third party engaged directly by them.

1.2 Legal, accountancy, insurance and security costs; promotion and marketing and social media monitoring. Agency and management commission and expenses.

General Business and Commercial

N.031
'Net Receipts' shall mean all the Gross Receipts less the agreed Expenses.

N.032
'Net Receipts' shall mean the Gross Receipts less the following [specify Items/costs/limit].

N.033
'The Net Receipts' shall be the total sums received from any third party licensee (after the deduction of the third party commission and costs) by the [Distributor] which arise directly and/or indirectly from the exploitation of the rights granted and/or any adaptation and/or development under this agreement at any time whether during the Term of this Agreement or thereafter including but not limited to any advances, royalties, damages, compensation, fees and/or any other sums.

N.034
'The Net Receipts' shall be the Gross Receipts received and retained by the [Company] for the reproduction, supply and/or distribution of the [Work/Unit] less the following specific agreed costs:

1.1   The fixed cost of reproducing each [Work/Unit] of [number/currency].

1.2   The fixed cost of supply, distribution, packaging and insurance of each [Work/Unit] of [number/currency].

N.035
No sums shall be deducted, retained and/or withheld and/or not disclosed by the [Distributor] of any nature relating to the [Work/Service/Unit].

N.036
All sums deducted from the Gross Receipts shall be supported by copies of relevant invoices with the accounting statements.

N.037
All sums due shall continue to be accounted for and paid even after the expiry and/or termination of the Term of this Agreement.

N.038
'Net Receipts' shall mean all sums received by, credited to and/or transferred to the [Company] in respect of the [Project/Product/Service] in any currency after the deduction of the following costs and expenses:

1.1 Development, production, manufacture, reproduction, supply, distribution, packaging, freight and sales costs up to a total maximum of [number/currency].

1.2 Advertising, marketing, merchandising, promotions, competitions and premium rate telephone service up to a total maximum of [number/currency].

1.3 Insurance and liability, legal proceedings and actions, refunds, compensation, indemnity payments, fines, cancellations, and disputes up to a total maximum of [number/currency].

N.039
The [Company] shall not be entitled to deduct the following costs and expenses from the sums received prior to the calculation of the Net Receipts:

1.1 Staff, personnel, consultants, suppliers, administrative costs and any costs of registrations, attendance at events, exhibitions and fairs.

1.2 Travel, hotels, hospitality, gifts and marketing costs.

1.3 Currency conversion costs, bank charges, taxes, duties, national insurance, insurance, health and safety compliance, environmental compliance.

N.040
'Net Receipts' shall be the total sums received from ticket sales, sponsorship and other forms of exploitation of the [Event] less any expenses and costs incurred by [Name] of any nature which have been paid and/or are due to any third party which are supported by receipts and invoices before [date] which directly relate to the organisation of the [Event] and/or the associated activities. If there is a loss then [Name] cannot recoup any sums and/or be reimbursed by the [Contributor].

N.041
'Net Receipts' shall be the sums retained by the [Company] after it has deducted all the costs and expenses of organising, producing and promoting the [Event].

Internet, Websites and Apps

N.042
'The Net Receipts' shall be the total sums received by the [Company] in respect of the [Work/Unit] less the following costs and expenses incurred by the [Company] not any third party:

1.1 The [Company's] Commission of [number] per cent.

1.2   Insurance, packaging, freight, duties, taxes and any other delivery costs.

1.3   Refunds and replacements, currency conversion costs and charges, health and safety compliance, environmental compliance, banking and trading compliance, product liability and repayment under indemnity provisions, legal costs, damages and compensation.

N.043

'The Net Receipts' shall be the total sum of all monies received by the [Company] in [currency] at any time when [Work/Unit/Service] is sold, made available, disposed of, and/or transferred to any third party by the [Company] whether for a fixed price, at a discount, for a monthly fee and/or any other method of subscription from which shall have been deducted the [Company's] Commission of [number] per cent.

N.044

The [Enterprise/Agency] agrees that if within [twelve] months of the date of this agreement the Net Receipts paid to [Name] are less than [number/ currency]. Then [Name] shall have the right to terminate this agreement by notice by text message and/or email to the [Enterprise/Agency] on the basis that the target promised payment has not been achieved.

N.045

'The Net Receipts' shall be the total sum of all money transferred to and retained by the [Distributor] in [currency] at any time as a result of the reproduction, supply, sale, subscription service and/or otherwise of the [Work/Unit/Service] to the general public and/or any third party after the [Company's] Commission of [number] per cent shall have been deducted.

N.046

'The Net Receipts' shall be the actual sums collected and paid to the [Company] in respect of the [Work/Product/Service] after the deduction of any of the following sums:

1.1   All commission costs due to the [Company] and any sub-agent, sub-distributor and/or any other third party.

1.2   All costs of reproduction, sub-titling, translation, artwork and images, music, lyrics, sound recordings, films, payments arising from the clearance of and exercise of any copyright, intellectual property rights, and/or any other interest. Payments due for the creation of any commissioned content of any nature and/or any mechanical reproduction, performance, adaptation, waiver, contractual obligations and any sums due to any rights management organisation.

1.3 Any sum due for advertising, marketing, merchandising, trade fairs, and exhibitions. freight, customs duties, packaging, insurance and taxes due to any government which form a distinct element of the price and are not recoverable.

1.4 Discounts, refunds, rebates and/or any payments due to loss and/or damage. legal and accountancy costs and expenses. The cost of any legal proceedings whether to sue and/or to defend and/or the cost of any settlement.

1.5 The cost of all currency conversion costs and bank charges shall be deducted from the original money.

N.047

'The Net Receipts' shall be all the sums received in any currency by the [Distributor] and/or held by any associated and/or parent company and/or third party connected with the [Distributor] from any form of exploitation and/or other benefit derived from the [App/Download/Service] and/or any part of the name, logo, software and/or content in any part of the world at any time after the deduction of [number] per cent commission to the [Distributor]. No other sums shall be deducted.

N.048

The [Company] agrees that it shall only be entitled to receive payment of those sums set out in clause [–] in respect of the [App/Download/Service].

The [Company] agrees and accepts that it shall be obliged to bear the cost of all the following matters which it is not authorised to deduct:

1.1 The cost and expenses relating to design, development, adaptation, production, computer software, online content and social media, marketing, advertising, packaging, security, hospitality and/or other promotional events.

1.2 Any sums due to any sub-agent and/or sub-licensee and/or for copyright clearance and/or other intellectual property payments and/or any costs and expenses due to collecting societies and/or for any music and/or other contribution and/or to any legal and/or other advisors and/or consultants.

N.049

'The Net Receipts' shall be the sums paid to the [Distributor] which are retained and not returned to any third party which are received from the exploitation of the [App/Download/Service] and/or any part and/or by any other means and/or telecommunication system, website and/or other form in any medium in any format during [the term of this Agreement/at any time] less the following costs and expenses:

1.1 Sums paid for the development, production, design, artwork and computer software up to a maximum of [number/currency].

1.2 Sums paid to register any domain name, trade mark, design and/or to engage the services of any third party consultant, legal and other advisors in the creation, development and/or licensing of the [App/Download/Service] up to a maximum of [number/currency].

1.3 Sums paid for clearances and consents for exploitation of copyright, intellectual property rights, computer software and/or as royalties and/or to any rights management organisation and/or rightsholder in respect of this agreement.

1.4 Sums paid in commission, agency fees and other payments for affiliations and/or links up to a maximum of [currency/number].

1.5 Sums paid for advertising, promotion and marketing up to a maximum of [currency/number].

N.050

'The Net Receipts' shall be the sum paid by any person and/or other third party to the [Company] to acquire and purchase [one] copy of the [Image/Work/Photograph] at [price] which is owned by [Name] less the following agreed deductions:

1.1 Total reproduction costs of the limited edition which shall be no more than [number/currency] in total.

1.2 A fixed fee per sale of [number/currency] to the [Company].

N.051

1.1 The [Company] agrees to pay [Name] [number] per cent of the sums received from the exploitation of the [Film/Image/Work] after the agreed deductions which been recouped.

1.2 The agreed deductions shall be all costs and expenses incurred by the [Company] to produce, reproduce, distribute, promote and supply the [Film/Image/Work] to any third party at any time. Provided that the [Company] agrees that these costs and expenses shall be limited to a total maximum of [number/currency] in any one year. Any costs and expenses in excess of that figure in each shall year shall be paid for by the [Company] and not carried forward to the next year.

Merchandising and Distribution

N.052

'The Net Receipts' shall be sum which remains after the [Distributor's/ Agent's] Commission has been deducted from the Gross Receipts and all the money shall have been converted to sterling and transferred to a bank in [country] which is held by the [Distributor].

N.053

The [Agent] acknowledges that he/she is solely responsible for all costs and expenses that he/she may incur in respect of their services under this agreement and that there is no authority provided to deduct such sums from the Gross Receipts and/or any other sums.

N.054

1.1 The [Licensor] agrees that all sums due under any licence agreement shall be paid direct to the nominated [Agent]: [specify details].

1.2 The [Licensor] agrees that receipt of the sums due by the [Agent] shall constitute payment to the [Licensor]. That if the [Licensor] subsequently is not paid by the [Agent] that is not the fault of the [Licensee] which has discharged its responsibilities.

N.055

The [Licensee] acknowledges that the Licence Fee shall not be offset against the Gross Receipts, the Net Receipts and/or the [Licensor's] Royalties.

N.056

'The Net Receipts' shall be the Gross Receipts less the reasonable costs and expenses of:

1.1 all materials, moulds, prototypes, consents and rights clearance, software licences and the cost of any adaptation incurred and/ or commissioned by the [Licensee] for the purpose of developing, producing and exploiting the [Licensed Articles] and any health and safety compliance tests and assessments. Subject to a total maximum limit of [number/currency] in total. Any sums over that limit must be paid by the [Licensee] and cannot be recouped and/or set-off.

1.2 Registration of any website, domain name, trade mark and/or any other right in the name of [specify] relating to the [Licensed Articles]. However it shall not include legal and/or consultancy advice for that purpose.

1.3 Packaging, promotional events, print and on line marketing, internet developments, website and app content and software;

endorsements and sponsorships, product placement, product and public liability insurance, security, storage, delivery and freight, Subject to a total maximum limit of [number/currency] in total. Any sums over that limit must be paid by the [Licensee] and cannot be recouped and/or set-off.

N.057

'The Net Receipts' shall be the total monies in [sterling] actually received and paid to the [Company] at any time from third parties from the exploitation of the [Unit/Service] in the licensed Territory during the Term of this Agreement after deductions have been made for the following sums:

1.1 Transfer and conversion of currency costs and bank charges.

1.2 Commission and agency fees, costs and expenses.

1.3 Cost of adaptations which have to be made due to language and market adjustments.

1.4 The cost of manufacture, supply and distribution of the [Unit/Service] which shall be no more than [number/currency] for each such [Unit/ Subscriber for the Service]. No more shall be deducted even if this fixed amount is exceeded.

1.5 No additional sums shall be deducted for copyright clearance payments and consents, insurance, packaging, freight, promotion and/or advertising material of any nature.

N.058

'The Net Receipts' shall be the balance of the total monies in [currency] received by the [Distributor] from exercise of Merchandising Rights in the [Work/Film/Unit] granted under this agreement after deduction of the following monies below:

1.1 Distribution Fee to the [Distributor] of [number] per cent.

1.2 The cost of all manufacture, reproduction, distribution, marketing and exploitation including but not limited to catalogues and flyers, films, videos, sound recordings, photographs, artwork, graphics, competitions, product placement, endorsements and sponsorship, packaging, trademarks and logos, customs duties, freight, insurance, payments for consents, waivers, copyright clearance and contractual obligations and/or any sums due to any rightsholders and/or rights management organisations and/or otherwise of any nature sums due to a third party in respect of the rights granted and material created under this agreement.

N.059

'Net Receipts of the [Company]' shall mean Gross Receipts less:

1.1 the [Company's] commission of [number] per cent up to a maximum of [number/currency] in any one calendar year.

1.2 the agreed Budget for the launch costs set out in Appendix A which is attached to and forms part of this agreement.

1.3 the search fees, legal costs and cost of registration of the trade mark [specify]; the domain name [specify] and the creation and development of a website, app, blog and photograph account and promotional film account online on the internet together with all the software and content.

N.060

The [Distributor] agrees that it shall be entirely responsible for all costs, expenses, damages and losses incurred and/or due in respect of the following matters:

1.1 the administration, development and consultancy work with third parties and the cost of acquisition of all rights for any artwork, design, logo and trade mark, prototype and samples, production, manufacture, sales, distribution, storage, freight and shipping, customs duties, legal costs and dealing with any claims and/or legal proceedings.

1.2 the registration of any domain name, creation of any website and/or app and/or content, labels, packaging, store and online marketing, promotion and advertising.

1.3 health and safety compliance tests and reports, product liability, public liability insurance and all other costs and expenses incurred directly and/or indirectly in respect of the exploitation of the [Licensed Articles] based on the [Work/Unit/Film].

N.061

'The Net Receipts' shall be the total proceeds of any sums received by the [Distributor] from the exploitation of any of the rights granted under this agreement less the following reasonable commission costs and expenses:

1.1 A Distribution Fee to the Distributor of [number/currency] of the total sums received.

1.2 A commission of no more than [number] per cent due to any authorised third party sub-agent and/or sub-distributor with whom the [Distributor] have concluded an agreement. Together with a maximum limit of [number/currency] in any accounting period.

N.062

The [Distributor] agrees and undertakes that any other sums not specified as authorised to be deducted under this agreement shall be at the cost and expense of the [Distributor] including but not limited to distribution and exploitation, advertising, marketing, merchandising, product placement, blogs, endorsements, sponsorship, catalogues, photographs, artwork and graphics, packaging, trade marks and logos, customs duties, freight, insurance, website, internet and mobile material, premium rate phone lines and competitions, trade fairs and exhibitions.

N.063

The [Distributor] agrees that if the [Distributor] does not achieve and pay the following minimum targets for the Net Receipts to be paid to the [Licensor]. Then the [Licensor] shall have the right to terminate this Agreement by notice in writing by letter and/or email as soon as any one of the payments has not been achieved and/or paid by the due date set out below:

1.1 From the date of this agreement to [date] the [Company] to achieve Net Receipts of [number/currency] for that period which shall be paid to the [Licensor] by [date].

1.2 From [date] to [date] the [Company] to achieve Net Receipts of [number/currency] for that period which shall be paid to the [Licensor] by [date].

1.3 From [date] to [date] the [Company] to achieve Net Receipts of [umber/currency] for that period which shall be paid to the [Licensor] by [date].

N.064

'The Net Receipts' shall be the sums received by and/or held by the [Licensee] during the Term of this Agreement and/or thereafter which relate to the supply, rental, sale, disposal and/or exploitation of the [Game/Product/Work] to any third party including any parent company and/or associated business and/or any other person and /or company and/or entity after the deduction of the following costs and expenses:

1.1 The actual wholesale cost and/or manufacture costs which have been paid by the [Licensee] to a manufacturer and/or other production company to supply the [Game/Product/Work] in a form with packaging suitable for marketing.

1.2 The actual cost paid by the [Licensee] for a short advertising campaign in accordance with the agreed plan in Schedule A for which a budget of [number/currency] has been allocated.

1.3 After the deduction of the sums in 1.1 and 1.2 then the commission due to the [Licensee] shall be deducted of [number] per cent. The balance shall then be paid to the [Licensor].

N.065
'The Net Receipts' shall be the sums received by the [Agent] from the exploitation of any products, services, endorsements, product placement and/or other forms of exploitation and/or licensing in any part of the world in any medium which relate to the [Brand Name] and/or [Logo] and/or [Image] and/or [Trade Mark] and/or [Domain Name] and/or any associated material owned and/or controlled by [Name] from [date] to [date] less commission to the [Agent] of [number] per cent of any sums received before payment is made to [Name].

N.066

1.1 After [date] the [Agent] shall not any have right to receive and/or retain any sums from the rights granted in clause [–] by [Name].

1.2 The [Agent] agrees and accepts that all payments thereafter under any agreements and/or licences concluded and/or arranged by the [Agent] shall be made direct to [Name].

1.3 That the [Agent] shall not be due and/or paid any commission on any sums after [date].

Publishing

N.067
'Net Royalties' and 'Net Fees' shall mean the gross royalties and gross fees earned from the exploitation of the [Work] by the [Publisher] after deduction of Value Added Tax or other similar tax and the bona fide commission charges of any agency and discounts given to any third parties.

N.068
'The Net Receipts' shall be the total proceeds from the distribution and exploitation of the [Work] whether by retail, sale, hire, license, subscription and/or otherwise throughout the Territory at any time received by or credited to the [Publisher] or its sub-agents and/or its sub-licensees after the deduction of any value added tax, sales tax and any commission fees of any collection agencies.

N.069
The [Publishers] undertakes to pay the [Author] the following percentages of the net sums received by the [Publishers] less any fees for the reproduction of copyright material from the sale of such rights [category] [percentage].

N.070
'The Net Receipts' shall mean the sums actually received by the [Publishers] from the exploitation of the [specify] Rights in the [Work] [at any time/during the Term of this Agreement] from all countries outside [specify territory].

N.071

The [Distributor] agrees that if the [Distributor] does not achieve the following minimum targets under the Net Receipts. Then the [Licensor] shall have the right to terminate this Agreement by notice in writing and/or by email as soon as the targets have been confirmed by the [Distributor] as not achieved for any period.

1.1   From [date] to [date] the [Distributor] to achieve Net Receipts of [number/currency] for that period.

1.2   From [date] to [date] the [Distributor] to achieve Net Receipts of [number/currency] for that period.

1.3   That by [date] the total aggregate Net Receipts since the start of the agreement shall be no less than [number/currency].

Any waiver by the [Licensor] for any period shall not apply to any later period and the right to terminate. Where there is a delay and/or other interruption due to force majeure and/or some other reason. Then the applicable periods shall be varied according to the period of the delay and/or interruption.

N.072

'The Net Receipts' shall be the total sum of all monies received by the [Company] in [currency] at any time when [specify subject] is sold, made available, disposed of, or transferred to any third party by the [Company] whether for a fixed price, discount, fee and/or under subscription less the [Company's] Commission of [number] per cent.

N.073

The [Company] agrees that if within [twelve] months of the date of this Agreement the Net Receipts paid to [Name] are less than [number/currency]. Then [Name] shall have the right to terminate this agreement by providing [six] months' notice in writing and/or by email to the [Company].

N.074

The [Distributor] shall not be entitled to deduct the following costs and expenses from the sums received either from the published price, whole sale price and/or any other sums received from any form of exploitation of the [Work/Unit/Service]:

1.1   The cost and expenses relating to the operation and administration at the [Company] and the appointment of any legal and/or accountancy and/or trade mark advisors, consultants, recruitment and/or marketing agencies and/or any third party agreements for development of computer software and/or technology.

1.2 The cost and expenses relating to development of designs, artwork, covers, labels, competitions, newsletters and/or any creation of any format and/or reproduction of any samples and/or prototypes and/or any website and/or app and/or blog.

1.3 Any losses, damages and/or other sums incurred due to destruction and/or withdrawal of stock and/or delays in publication and/or translation of the [Work/Unit/Service] and/or the creation of an audio and/or braille edition at any time.

N.075

'The Net Receipts' shall be the sums received by the [Licensor] from the supply and license of the complete [Work/Unit/Service] to the [Sub-Licensee] which is to be developed, adapted, downloaded and/or accessed from [specify website/app] to any member of the public or other commercial, charitable and/or educational enterprise at any time for a fixed fee of not less than [number/currency] for complete [Work/Unit/Service] which is the original creation of the [Author].

N.076

The [Author] agrees that the [Sub-Licensee] in clause [–] shall be entitled to a fixed commission of [number] per cent of all sums received by the [Sub-Licensee] in respect of copies of the [Work/Unit/Service] in [format] from the [specify website/app].

N.077

The [Author] agrees that the [Sub-Licensee] in clause [–] shall be entitled to a fixed fee of [number/currency] in respect of each complete copy of the [Work/Unit/Service] in [format] which is sold and/or supplied and for which a fee of [number/currency] is received by the [Sub-Licensee] from the [specify website/app].

N.078

'The Net Receipts' shall be defined as the sums which are paid to the [Company] from third parties for the distribution, supply, use and/or adaptation of the [Films/Sound Recordings] and any parts of [Name] performing and/or reading the [Work] for the [Series] entitled [specify] on the [radio/television/webinar/podcast] known as [specify] [at any time/until [date]].

N.079

[Name] agrees that he/she shall not be entitled to any payments from the Net Receipts after [date] and/or any other form of exploitation and/or adaptation after that date in any language and/or format in any medium. That all obligations to account, report and make payments by the [Company] to

[Name] shall end and there shall be no further liability to [Name] and/or sums due.

N.080

[Name] agrees that:

1.1 the [Company] has acquired all the rights in all media in all formats in all medium of any nature in the [Work/Unit/Service] created developed and owned by [Name].

1.2 the fees paid to [Name] under this agreement are in full and final settlement of all sums due.

1.3 [Name] shall not be entitled to claim any further fees, costs, royalties and/or other sums. That [Name] shall not be entitled to any payments from the exploitation of the [Work/Unit/Service] from any part of any gross and/or net receipts.

1.4 the acquisition by the [Company] includes all rights, formats, technology, material and/or any other matter which may be created and/or developed in the future from the [Work/Unit/Service] and/or any other adaptation.

Services

N.081

The [Record Company] shall pay the [Artiste] a royalty of [number] per cent of the retail price (less all taxes) in respect of [90]% [ninety] per cent of [Records/Units] manufactured and sold in the Territory from recordings made pursuant to this agreement less the cost of packaging [and marketing]. When the recording from the [Artiste's] recordings only form part of an entire [Record/Unit] the royalty payable shall be limited to an equitable proportion relative to the extent of the [Artiste's] recordings to the whole [Record/Unit].

N.082

'The Net Receipts' shall be [–] % [number] per cent of the total proceeds from the distribution and exploitation of the [Records/Units] including promotional and merchandising material whether by retail, sale, hire, license or otherwise throughout the Territory at any time received by or credited to the [Company] and its sub-agents, sub-licensees and sub-distributors after deduction of any value added tax and any sales tax which may from time to time be in force paid by the [Company].

N.083

The [Company] shall pay you a royalty of [number] per cent of the retail price less all taxes in respect of [90%] (ninety per cent) of the [Records/

Units] manufactured and sold in the [United Kingdom and United States of America] from recordings made under this agreement.

N.084

The [Company] shall pay to the [Artist] the royalties on [Records/Units] sold by the [Company] or its agents calculated on [85]% [eighty-five]per cent of the price to the general public after deducting an allowance for packaging and any taxes levied as part of the selling price.

N.085

'The Net Receipts' shall be one hundred per cent of the total proceeds from the supply, distribution and exploitation of the [Records] whether by retail, sale, hire, license, subscription or otherwise throughout the Territory at any time received by or credited to the [Record Company] or its sub-agents or its sub-licenses after the deduction of the following reasonable costs and expenses:

1.1 any taxes which form a distinct element of the price and are not recoverable but excluding personal and corporation tax.

1.2 The production and clearance costs of the recordings and the payment of any sums due to collecting societies and trade organisations which shall in any event not exceed [number/currency].

1.3 The cost of the creation and editing of the master copy for the production of the [Records] and all other master formats needed for the purposes of exploitation; all musicians and technical personnel, all computer software and computer generated material, artwork, logos and packaging up to a maximum of [number/currency].

1.4 The cost of administration, promotion and marketing are specifically not allowed and are excluded.

N.086

'Net Receipts' shall mean all income received directly or indirectly by the [Manager] as a result of the performance of the obligations of both parties to this Agreement less the [Manager's] Expenses.

N.087

'Net Receipts' shall mean the Gross Receipts less the [Agent's] Commission and the [Agent's] Expenses.

N.088

'The Net Receipts' shall be the Gross Receipts less the Agent's Commission.

N.089

'The Net Receipts' shall be the Gross Receipts less the Authorised Expenses.

N.090

'The Manager's Commission' shall be the following percentage of the Net Receipts [number] per cent.

N.091

'The Sportsperson's Fees' shall be the Net Receipts less the Manager's Commission.

N.092

1.1 The [Agent] agrees that if within [twelve] months of the date of this Agreement the Net Receipts paid to the [Artist] are less than [number/currency]. Then the [Artist] shall have the choice and right to terminate this Agreement by serving the [Agent] with notice by letter and/or email that the agreement will end in [one] month.

1.2 After the termination of the agreement the [Agent] shall not have any right to any sums from the services and/or work of the [Artist] for any reason. All sums received after the date of termination must be paid by the [Agent] direct to the [Artist] without any deductions for commission and/or expenses.

N.093

1.1 The [Agent] and the [Artist] agree that in the normal course of business all third party contracts shall be directly with the [Artist] and signed by the [Artist].

1.2 The [Artist] undertakes and agrees that in each third party contract negotiated by the [Agent] under this Agreement the [Agent] shall be entitled to a clause which authorises the third party to make all payments under the Agreement to the [Agent].

1.3 It is agreed that all such third party agreements must include a clause which allows both the [Artist] and the [Agent] the right to audit and inspect any accounts and records at their own cost and expense.

1.4 Neither the [Artist] nor the [Agent] shall be entitled to recoup the cost of any accountancy and/or legal fees from the sums received from the third party agreements without prior joint consent between the parties.

N.094

The [Company] agrees that if the [Company] does not achieve the following minimum targets for Net Receipts and/or meet the target payments to the [Licensor]. Then the [Licensor] shall have the right to terminate this Agreement by notice in writing by letter and/or email as soon as the targets have not been achieved and/or paid by the due date:

1.1 From the date of this agreement to [date] the [Company] to have received Net Receipts of [number/currency].

1.2 By [date] the [Company] to have paid the [Licensor] the sum of [number/currency] in royalties.

1.3 That from [date] to [date] the Net Receipts to be achieved by the [Company] shall be no less than [number/currency].

1.4 For the period [date] to [date] the [Company] shall have paid the [Licensor] the sum of [number/currency] in royalties.

N.095
'The Net Receipts' shall be the total sum of all monies received by the [Company] converted into [currency] at any time from any country and any type of exploitation and/or adaptation in respect of the [Recordings/Film/Work] of the product of the services of [Name] which is made available by any method by the [Company] and/or any third party whether for a fixed price, discount, licence fee and/or under subscription service, rental, hire, or other payment less the [Company's] Commission of [number] per cent.

N.096
'Net Receipts' shall be the sums received by the [Agent] from any distributor, licensee and/or other third party with whom the [Agent] has concluded an agreement for the use of the services, image, logo and/or personal name of [Name] at any time after the conversion from the currency in which it is paid to [sterling/dollars/euros/other] and the deduction of the following sums:

1.1 The [Agents'] commission fee of [number] per cent for the first [number/currency] and thereafter the commission shall be reduced to [number/currency] on all further sums in that financial year. The financial year shall start on [date] and end on [date].

1.2 The cost and expenses which the [Agent] has paid, advanced and/or contributed to [Name] for travel, accommodation, equipment and technology, security, hospitality, clothes, accessories and styling and related costs and charges for his/her family members up to a maximum of [number/currency] in total in any one financial year. Any sums in excess of that sum shall be paid for by the [Agent].

N.097
All sums received by the [Agent] in respect of the Net Receipts due to [Name] must be held in a separate bank account in the name of [specify]

at [bank]. Such funds must not be used by the [Agent] in any form and/or any lien and/or charge created for his/her business and/or expended and/or transferred to any third party.

N.098

'Net Receipts' shall be all the monies received for the supply of the services of [Name] after the deduction of the following sums:

1.1 The agreed Agency Commission of [number] per cent of the total sums received.

1.2 Then the deductions of all costs and expenses provided by the [Agency] to [Name] at any time including but not limited to travel, hotels, hospitality, beauty and clothing expenses and any other sum.

1.3 No deduction shall be permitted for marketing and promoting [Name].

1.4 Where new images, films and other material is to be created for [Name] then the [Agency] shall only be entitled to deduct these costs if the expenditure has been approved in advance by [Name].

University, Charity and Educational

N.099

'The Net Receipts' shall be the total sum of all monies received by and/ or credited to the [Institute] which has been cleared and retained by the [Institute] in [currency] at any time from the exploitation of the [Work/Service/Product] after the deduction of the cost and expense of:

1.1 taxes which form a distinct element of the price and are not recoverable which are charged by any government on the supply and/or sale of any product and/r service.

1.2 commission charges and expenses of any agency, licensees and/or distributors.

1.3 discounts, refunds, or reductions to any third parties.

1.4 reproduction and development, distribution and exploitation, packaging and materials, customs duties, freight, storage and insurance.

1.5 legal, accountancy and expert consultancy.

1.6 registration of any intellectual property rights, domain names, trade marks, computer software and/or patents and any legal and/or agency fees and costs.

1.7 the creation, design, production and supply of any advertising, marketing, merchandising, brochures, photographs, artwork, graphics, leaflets, trade marks, logos, websites, apps and other material for radio, television, the internet and mobiles, trade fairs and exhibitions.

1.8 copyright clearance and payments, contractual obligations, consents and fees, clearance and payments of any sums to collecting societies.

1.9 currency conversion costs and bank charges.

1.10 any legal settlement or litigation with a third party relating to any matter regarding the [Work/Service/Product].

N.100

'Net Receipts' shall mean the Gross Receipts less the [Distributor's] Commission and the [Distributors] Expenses. The [Distributor's] Expenses shall be limited to [number/currency] in any one financial year. Any sum over that limit shall be paid for entirely by the [Distributor].

N.101

The [Distributor] agrees that it shall be solely responsible in respect of all costs incurred in the development, production, manufacture, distribution, marketing, promotion, advertising, sales and exploitation of the [Work/ Service/Product] and that such sums shall not be offset against any Net Receipts due to the [Institute/Charity] under this Agreement.

N.102

1.1 The [Enterprise] agrees that if within [two] years of the date of this Agreement the Net Receipts paid to the [Institute/Charity] are less than [number/currency] for that period. The [Institute/Charity] shall have the right to serve written notice on the [Enterprise] that the agreement will end after the expiry of a period of [six] months from the date of the notice.

1.2 After the end of the agreement all rights granted and/or acquired under this agreement by the [Enterprise] shall revert to the [Institute/ Charity]. The [Enterprise] agrees and undertakes that it shall sign any such documents as may be required to revert all rights to the [Institute/ Charity] including the rights in any new material which may have been created. The [Institute/Charity] shall pay for the expense of all such documents. It is accepted by the [Enterprise] that this agreement was not intended to transfer any rights to the [Enterprise] for any period after the end of this agreement.

1.3 The [Enterprise] agrees that it shall account for and pay any sums that may be due until such time as all sums have been accounted for to the [Institute/Charity].

N.103

The [Company] agrees that the [Institute/Charity] shall have the right to terminate this Agreement] by notice in writing by email, text message and/or letter if the [Company] does not achieve and/or provide evidence of and/or pay any of the sums due to the [Institute/Charity] as follows:

1.1   That by [date] the [Company] will have provided a financial statement and paid to the [Institute/Charity] no less than [number/currency].

1.2   That by [date] the total aggregate Net Receipts received by the [Company] since the start of this agreement shall be no less than [number/currency] and the total sum paid to the [Institute/Charity] shall be not less than [number/currency].

1.3   That the [Company] shall have sold and been paid for not less than [number] units of the [Work] by [date].

N.104

'The Net Receipts' shall be the balance which is available for distribution by the [Licensee] to the [Consortium] after the deductions of all sums incurred and paid for by the [Licensee] in respect of the [Project] in the development and testing, registration and compliance procedures and processes, production, manufacture, promotion, marketing, advertising and legal and administrative costs and expenses associated with any advisors, consultants, agents and/or government and/or international bodies.

N.105

Where no Net Receipts are available for distribution to the [Consortium] and the [Licensee] has incurred a loss. The [Licensee] agrees that the [Consortium] shall not be liable to make any contribution to such losses and all such costs and expenses shall be the responsibility of the [Licensee].

NEW EDITIONS

General Business and Commercial

N.106

The [Distributor] confirms that it will not edit, adapt, alter and/or add to the [Master Material] without the prior written approval of the [Licensor] and that any such changes shall be entirely at the [Distributor's] cost.

N.107

There shall be no obligation on the [Licensor] to provide any consent and/or grant any new licence for an updated version, sequel and/or new edition of the [Film/Video/Unit/Work]. Nor shall the [Licensee] have any option and/or first right of refusal on any subsequent Film/Video/Unit/Work] of the [Project].

N.108

The [Company] shall be entitled to modify, revise, enhance, develop, adapt, update, and distribute a new issue of the [Film/Video/Unit/Work] of the [Master Material] and any associated subject matter in any way that the [Company] may decide without any further advance payment to the [Licensor]. Provided that the [Company] continues to pay royalties for the new issue in accordance with the terms of this Agreement and the new issue is distributed and sold during the existing Licence Period.

N.109

1.1 Where the [Company] wishes to make a sequel and/or other adaptation and/or animation and computer generated version and/or any other new and/or subsequent version and/or translation and/or audio and/or sound recording of the [Film/Programme/DVD/Disc]. The [Distributor] agrees and accepts that it shall have no right and/or option and/or any interest in any such new material which the [Company] may decide to create, develop, distribute, market and sell whether during the term of the existing Agreement with the [Distributor] or not.

1.2 In addition the [Distributor] agrees that it shall have no right to any payment of any nature in respect of 1.1.

N.110

The [Artist/Presenter] agrees that where at a future date a new adaptation and/or sequel of the [Film/Programme/DVD/Disc] and/or any sound recordings is to be created by the [Company] and/or any third party. That there is no contractual obligation to use the [Artist/Presenter] by the [Company] and that the [Company] may choose any such other person as they shall decide at their own discretion.

N.111

The [Publisher/Distributor] shall not have the right to create, commission, publish and/or distribute new adaptations, arrangements and/or other sequels of the [Work]. Nor shall the [Publisher/Distributor] have the right to add new material whether it be music, lyrics, sound recordings and/or computer generated sounds without the prior written consent of [Name].

N.112

1.1 The [Publisher/Distributor] undertakes to ensure that the copyright in any new adaptations and/or arrangements of the [Work] and/or

1309

additions and/or alterations in the music, lyrics, sound recordings and/or any films and/or images of the recording of the material shall be owned and controlled by the [Publisher/Distributor].

1.2 The [Publisher/Distributor] undertakes and agrees to assign to [Writer] and [Artist] the intellectual property rights and copyright which may exist now and which are created in the future in any new adaptations and/or arrangements of the [Work] and/or additions and/or alterations in the music, lyrics, and sound recordings and/or any films and/or images of the recording of the material in all media and formats for the full period of copyright and any extensions or renewals throughout the world and universe. [Provided that all parties agree that the terms of this Agreement shall apply to all such new material.]

N.113

Where the [Enterprise] wishes to order a new adaptation and/or development relating to all and/or part of the [Work]. Then the [Enterprise] shall give the [Company] reasonable notice and shall bear the full cost of any charges that may arise. The alterations shall not be carried out by the [Company] until the parties have settled the cost and price which will be paid to the [Company].

N.114

The [Company] shall have the right to modify, revise, develop, enhance, adapt, update, exploit and re-issue the [Work] and any associated material such as instructions, packaging, or brochures in any way that the [Company] may decide without further payment to the [Licensor] during the Licence Period.

N.115

The [Distributor] agrees and undertakes that:

1.1 it has no right and/or authority to develop, create and/or license and/or supply any new edition, sequel, adaptation and/or variation of the [Work/Product] by the [Author].

1.2 it is only authorised to exploit the rights granted under this Agreement in [specify] language and in the exact form and with the exact copyright notice, disclaimer, moral rights notice and content, layout, design and format specified in schedule A which forms part of this Agreement.

N.116

1.1 The [Author] shall, if requested by the [Publisher/Distributor] and without charge to the [Publisher/Distributor], edit and revise the [Work/Script].

1.2 In the event that the [Author] shall neglect or be unable for any reason to edit or revise the [Work/Script] to the reasonable satisfaction of the [Publisher/Distributor]. The [Publisher] shall be entitled to engage some other competent person to carry out such work and any fee or other payment made to such person shall be deducted from the royalties for the [Work] due to the [Author]. Provided that the choice of such person and the fee to be paid to such person shall be subject to the [Author's] prior written approval, not to be unreasonably withheld or delayed.

N.117

1.1 The [Work/Article/Programme] shall not be edited, revised, altered, changed and/or reprinted and/or reproduced with any new material added in any form without prior written consent of the [Author].

1.2 If the [Author] and the [Company] agree that the [Author] shall adapt and/or update the [Work/Article/Programme] with the addition of new material and editing and deletions. Then this work shall only be undertaken subject to an agreed additional advance against Royalties being paid to the [Author].

1.3 The [Publisher/Distributor] has no rights and/or authority to employ, engage and/or commission any employee, consultant and/or other third party to adapt, amend, revise and/or edit and/or delete from and/or add to the [Work/Article/Programme] without the prior written consent of the [Author]. There is no obligation on the [Author] to provide such consent.

1.4 The cost of the services of the third party if agreed in 1.3 shall be paid for by the [Company/Distributor] in full. The engagement of any third party by the [Company/Distributor] shall be subject to the prior written approval of the [Author].

1.5 The [Company] shall bear all liability in respect of any losses and/or damages arising from the services and work of the third party and agrees to indemnify the [Author] in full in respect of any claim including all legal costs.

1.6 The [Company] agrees to ensure that any such third party shall not be entitled to a credit as a contributor and/or co-author in respect of the [Work/Article/Programme] at any time and/or to claim any copyright, intellectual property rights, moral rights and/or otherwise.

1.7 The [Company] agrees to ensure shall that all copyright and intellectual property rights in the work of the third party is and/or are assigned to the [Author].

N.118

Prior to the publication of a new edition the [Publisher/Distributor] shall send a written request to the [Author] requiring the [Author] to revise and update the [Work] with all necessary changes, alterations and deletions within a reasonable period. In the event that the [Author] shall fail to deliver a new edition as agreed and/or refuse to revise and write a new edition within [three] years of such written request. Then the [Publisher/Distributor] shall be entitled to engage a competent and qualified third party to revise and update the [Work] at the [Publisher's] sole expense. The Author shall be entitled to receive the royalties set out in this Agreement in respect of such new editions and agrees the third party who updates the work shall be entitled to a suitable credit as an [editor/contributor], but shall not be entitled to acquire any copyright and/or interest in the [Work] and/or any royalties.

N.119

In order to keep the [Work] up to date the [Authors] will, when mutually agreed between the parties, prepare new editions of the [Work] during the continuance of this Agreement. The [Authors] shall supply such new material, and amend, or alter the [Work] as may be necessary. In the event that the [Authors] are unwilling or unable by reason of death or otherwise to edit or revise the [Work] the [Publisher/Distributor] shall not have the right to ask any third party to do so.

N.120

The [Publisher/Distributor] shall have the right to make alterations in, deletions from and additions to the [Work] at the sole discretion of the [Publisher/Distributor]. The [Publisher/Distributor] shall also be entitled to arrange for new translations, sub-titles, new films, sound recordings, merchandising, adaptations which are a sequel and/or other new development of any content. All such new material and rights shall belong to [Name] and the [Publisher/Distributors]. All the original material and content shall belong to [Name].

N.121

1.1   The [Publisher/Distributor] shall not be entitled to alter, change, amend, add to and/or vary, adapt and/or develop the [Work/Manuscript] and/or any part(s) including the music, words, images, title or otherwise at any time.

1.2   The [Publisher/Distributor] shall only be entitled to exploit the [Work/Manuscript] in the exact form that it is supplied by the [Author] under this agreement.

1.3   In the event that the [Publisher/Distributor] would like to make alterations, changes, amendments and add to and/or vary, adapt and/or develop the [Work/Manuscript]. Then the [Publisher/Distributor] shall send a proposal in writing to the [Author]. Subject to the payment of a reasonable fee on each occasion the [Author] may agree to carry out such work. The [Author] shall not be obliged to provide any changes and/or new material and may refuse his/her written consent. The [Publishers] shall be bound by the final decision of the [Author] and shall not be entitled to make any changes, or variations of any nature without the prior written consent of the [Author]. The copyright in any such material shall be vested in and/or assigned to the [Author] by the [Publisher].

N.122

In the event that the [Publisher/Distributor] decides to issue a new adapted version of the [Work/] with additional new material and images. Then the [Publisher/Distributor] shall contact the [Author] and make the proposal regarding the new adapted version. In the event that the [Author] is unwilling and/or unable to be involved in developing the new adapted version. Then the [Publisher/Distributor] may engage the services of a third party to either work with the [Author] and/or to create the new version which the [Author] may then edit and approve and/or reject. The cost of such third party shall not be deducted from the sums due to the [Author] under the agreement and all such costs shall be paid by the [Publisher/Distributor].

N.123

1.1 The [Author] agrees to edit and revise the [Work/Content] upon request once every [four] years. Provided that the necessary changes to update the material are limited to altering no more than [number] pages. The [Publisher/Distributor] shall pay the [Author] an update fee for each revised work of [number/currency] which is due upon delivery and acceptance of the material.

1.2 Where it is clear that the [Work/Content] would require substantially more than the revision and update stated in 1.1. Then this is considered a new book and a new edition not an update and requires a new advance and agreement for publication.

N.124

1.1 The [Publisher/Distributor] shall not have the right to any updated, revised and/or new editions of the [Work/Content] by the [Author] and/or to engage any third party to do so during the Term of this Agreement.

1.2 This agreement is for this single edition of the [Work/Content].

1.3 Any further updated, revised and/or new editions shall be the subject of a separate and new publishing agreement on each occasion if agreed with the [Author]. The [Author] is not obliged to enter into any new agreement on the same terms as this Agreement.

1.4 The [Author] shall have the right during the Term of this Agreement to offer any third party the right to publish an updated, revised and/or new edition of the [Work/Content] upon expiry and/or termination of this agreement.

N.125

Where there are escalating royalty provisions the publication of a new edition shall not permit the [Publisher/Distributor] to treat the print run as if it has begun at zero and is effectively a new book. Where the advance and royalties relate to the same agreement then the print run for the new edition shall be added to the previous print run figures.

N.126

The [Distributor/Enterprise] agrees and accepts that:

1.1 A new edition and/or any development of a digital and/or e book and/or translation and/or other adaptation of the [Work/Content] shall be the subject of a new agreement between the parties.

1.2 There shall be no obligation on the [Author/Contributor] to update, revise and/or develop new material of any nature in any part of the [Work/Content] after the publication of the [Work/Content] in [country].

1.3 That any new material created by the [Author/Contributor] including marketing and promotional material at the [Distributor's/Enterprise's] request which is agreed shall be the subject of separate agreements and payments by the [Distributor/Enterprise].

N.127

Where the [Publisher/Distributor] fails to commission a new edition of the [Work/Content] from the [Author/Contributor] within [number] years from the date of publication of the last version of the [Work/Content]. Then the [Author/Contributor] shall have the right to offer any new version in any language and/or format to any third party and the [Publisher/Distributor] agrees that it shall not have the right to object if it has failed to commission any new [Work/Content] within the period of [number] years.

N.128

1.1 That in consideration of the payment of an additional fee of [number/currency] It is agreed that the [Publisher] shall be entitled to have first option to commission a new edition in respect of the [Work] which shall be the subject of a new agreement. The option shall start on [date] and end on [date].

1.2 That if the [Publisher] and the [Author] fail to conclude a new agreement for any reason that the fee paid in 1.1 shall not be paid back by the [Author]. After [date] the [Author] may offer the new edition of the [Work] in any format and any medium to any third party including a competitor of the [Publisher].

1.3 Where the [Author] concludes an agreement with a third party for a new edition then the [Publisher] agrees to conclude a document to release the [Author] and confirm the rights are available to be licensed to the third party at no additional cost to the [Author].

N.129

1.1 The [Institute] shall have the right to update, revise and/or create a new edition and/or sequel and/or adaptation of the [Work/Service/Product] by the [Contributor] and/or to engage any third party to do so whether during the Term of this Agreement or thereafter.

1.2 This Agreement is for the single edition and the [Contributor] shall have no right, interest, option and/or claim to any future editions, update, revisions, developments and/or adaptations.

1.3 There shall be no royalties, advances and/or any other sums due to the [Contributor] in respect of any other future editions, update, revisions, developments and/or adaptations.

1.4 The [Contributor] shall not be entitled to any credit, copyright notice and/or acknowledgement in respect of any other future editions, update, revisions, developments and/or adaptations.

N.130
The [Institute] agrees that it shall not have the right to develop, produce, publish and exploit any future new editions, updates, revisions, sequels and/or adaptations without the prior written consent of the [Author]. The parties shall enter into negotiations for a new agreement on each occasion. In the event that the [Author] is unwilling or unable by reason of death or otherwise to edit, revise, develop and/or adapt the [Work] the [Publishers] shall not have the right to ask any third party to do so without the prior written consent of the [Author] or an executor and/or trustee of their estate and a new agreement has been concluded as to the terms.

N.131
The [Institute] shall be entitled to edit, adapt and delete and vary contributions by any person to any [Work] which it may wish to supply, distribute and reproduce and exploit at any time. Any such person whose contribution is then not included shall not be entitled to receive any sums from the subsequent version and/or edition of the [Work].

NOTICES

General Business and Commercial

N.132

Any notice shall be deemed to have been served if:

1.1   in respect of the [Company] it is personally delivered to a Director of the [Company] and/or sent by recorded and/or first class post to the [Company] at its registered office for the time being which is at [specify address] and/or

1.2   in respect of [Name] it is personally delivered to him/her and/or sent by recorded and/or first class post to him/her at his/her address specified in this agreement and/or such other address as he/she may have notified to the [Company].

1.3   A notice sent by first class post shall be deemed served on the day following the day on which it was posted.

N.133

Without prejudice to the right to serve notices by any other means any notice served under this agreement shall be in writing by letter and not email or text message.

Any notice which has been sent by first class pre-paid post shall be deemed to be received [48] hours thereafter (excluding Saturdays, Sundays and Public Holidays). For the purpose of this Agreement all notices shall be sent to the following addresses:

    The Employee [specify address].

    The Company [specify address].

N.134

1.1   Notices pursuant to this agreement shall be in writing by first class recorded delivery to the following parties:

    [Name] [address] in respect of service on the [Executive].

    [Name] [address] in respect of service on the [Company].

1.2   No service shall be in person at the work place of the [Executive].

1.3   Any change or alteration of any address in 1.1 must be in writing and confirmed as agreed by the other party. No amendment may be made to 1.2.

1.4   No other method of service and/or notification whether by fax, email, text, in person or otherwise shall be accepted as notice under this agreement.

N.135

Notices to be served in respect of to this agreement may be by any method provided that it is in writing and in [language] to the [Executive] and/or the [Company] whether by fax, text, email, post, courier or hand delivered. Provided that no method and circumstance shall be chosen to embarrass, humiliate and/or prejudice the career prospects of the [Executive] and/or cause distress in front of other personnel of the [Company].

N.136

The [Company] shall provide not less than [three] calendar months' notice of the reduction of the working hours of the [Employee] under the terms of this Agreement.

N.137

The [Company] reserves the right to serve notice to any person and/or third party consultant as follows:

1.1 By pre-recorded and registered post and/or first and/or second class post in the form of a letter.

1.2 By email and text message to the last known email address and/or mobile telephone number.

1.3 Through an announcement on the sound system at the premises and/or in any meeting on the premises.

1.4 In person through a delegated person directly employed by the [Company] and/or engaged through a third party.

1.5 By any other method which is considered suitable by the [Company].

N.138

1.1 All notices and accounting which the [Licensee] is required or may desire to send to the [Licensor] shall be in writing and shall be sent by:

    a. email marked urgent to [specify] and

    b. in addition by pre-paid postal service and/or by a delivery service to: [address] and

    c. in addition a copy shall be sent to the [legal/accountancy] offices at [address].

    d. The details above may be changed by the [Licensor] notifying the [Licensee] of the substitutions that may be required.

1.2 All notices which the [Licensor] is required or may desire to send to the [Licensee] shall be in writing and shall be sent by:

a. email marked urgent to [specify] and

b. in addition by pre-paid postal service and/or by a delivery service to: [address] and

c. in addition a copy shall be sent to the [legal/accountancy] offices at [address].

d. The details above may be changed by the [Licensee] notifying the [Licensor] of the substitutions that may be required.

N.139

Without prejudice to the right to serve notices by any other means any notice required to be served for the purposes of this agreement shall be deemed sufficiently served after it has been sent first class pre-paid post to the registered office or last known address of the party on whom it is desired to serve it.

N.140

1.1 Any notice given under the provisions of this agreement shall be in writing and sent to the address of the party to be served set out at the head of this agreement or to such other address of which notice has been given.

1.2 Any notice to the [Licensee] shall be marked for the attention of the following person [Name] and a copy thereof shall be sent to [Name] at the same address.

1.3 All notices shall be delivered in person and/or by a courier and/or a delivery service and/or by registered and/or recorded delivery letter. All notices shall be accepted as having occurred when delivered in person and/or by courier and/or a delivery service and/or when signed for by at that address and/or when confirmed by the postal service as delivered.

N.141

Any notice to be served under this agreement shall be sent by one of the following methods:

1.1 Pre-paid recorded delivery and/or registered post which shall be deemed to be received within [three] days of posting provided that the notice is sent to the following addresses in respect of each party:

[Name] [address] [Name] [address].

1.2 By email which shall be deemed to be received within [two] hours provided that notice is sent to the other party using the following email addresses:

[Name] [email address] [Name] [email address]

1.3 Any changes regarding the details in 1.1 and 1.2 must be notified to the other party. Unless changes are notified then service will have taken place on relation to the last known information.s

N.142
All notifications from the [Company] to [Name] must be in writing and sent by email to [email address] with the headline reference [subject]. They must also be sent to [Name] [Address].

N.143
Where [Names] wishes to notify the [Company] they must follow the procedure on the website [reference] and contact customer services by completing an online form.

N.144
Any notice to be served must be in writing and may be served personally or by registered post. In respect of notice to the [Company] at its registered office and in the case of the [Customer] at their last known address. Any notice shall be effective on the day it is delivered at the relevant address.

N.145
All notices required to be given pursuant to this agreement shall be in writing and may be sent by first class post or email. Any notice shall be deemed to have been delivered by first class post within two days of proof of posting. An email will be deemed received on the day that it is sent.

N.146
Any notice or other document to be delivered pursuant to this agreement shall be in writing in the [English] language signed by the [Managing Director] of the party and in a legible written form. Notices shall be sent to the registered office and last known address of the relevant party. Any notice shall not be deemed received and there must be clear evidence that it was properly served.

N.147
Any notice under these conditions shall be given in writing. Any such notice shall be deemed to have been properly served if it is either delivered to a prominent part of the Exhibition Stand of the Exhibitor, handed personally to the [Exhibitor] and/or any employee and/or sent to the last known registered office or business address by any method.

N.148
Any notice or direction to be given by the [Company] to the [Contractor] under this agreement shall be made on behalf of the [Company] by any

person(s) holding the position of [Managing Director] and/or [Company Secretary]. Any notice to be given by either party shall be in writing and shall be sent pre-paid recorded delivery addressed in the case of the [Company] to its principal address at [–] and in the case of the [Contractor] to its registered office. Any such notice if sent by pre-paid recorded delivery shall be deemed to have been served on the day after the date of posting unless returned for any reason.

N.149

Notices must be served under this agreement in writing and sent by first class pre-paid post or air mail to the last known business address of the party. All notices shall be deemed served when delivered to the business address.

N.150

Any notice to be given by any one party to the other in this agreement may be given by any reasonable method provided that it is in writing. A notice shall be deemed properly served if it is in writing and sent by pre-paid first class post or by courier or personally delivered to the registered office or the business address set out in this agreement. Any such notice must be signed by a Director and be on official letterhead paper of the party. Provided such conditions are fulfilled it shall be accepted as proof of authority and service by the party giving the notice.

N.151

Unless otherwise stated all formal legal notices and threats of legal proceedings shall be sent by courier or some other delivery or postal service provided that the recipient in all instances shall be required to sign for any such documents. Service shall be as follows:

1.1 Any notice to the [Licensor] shall be sent to the [Agent] [specify name] at [address].

1.2 Any notice to the [Licensee] shall be sent to its registered office at [address].

1.3 Any changes to these addresses must be sent in writing to the Chief Executive of the relevant party. Evidence is required of any service and/or notification and there shall be no deemed delivery. No notice may be served by email, text message and/or any other electronic means.

N.152

Any notice given under the provisions of this agreement shall be in writing and be sent to the address of the party to be served as specified in this document or to such other new address for which notification has been received. All notices shall be delivered by hand or sent by first class registered or recorded delivery letter. An email attachment sent to either party shall not be evidence of compliance with this condition.

N.153

Any notice shall be sent to the address of the party to be served as set out in this agreement or to such other address of which notice has been received. Any notice given to the [Distributor] shall be marked for the attention of the Managing Director and a copy shall also be sent to the [Contracts Manager] at the same address. All notices shall be delivered by hand or by registered or recorded delivery letter.

N.154

1.1 Unless otherwise specifically stated in this agreement, all notices, approvals, payments or accounting which the [Licensee] is required to deliver to the [Licensor] shall be in writing and shall be personally delivered or posted for which the postage/or cost shall be pre-paid and sent to the [Licensor] [Name] [Address] or to such other address as the [Licensor] may subsequently notify.

1.2 All notices, approvals, documents and other materials which the [Licensor] is required to deliver to the [Licensee] shall be in writing and shall be personally delivered or posted for which the postage or cost shall be pre-paid and sent to the Licensee [Name] [Address] or to such other address as the [Licensee] may subsequently notify.

1.3 Courtesy copies of all notices to the [Licensee] shall also be sent to the [Licensee] at the above address to the attention of the [Department].

1.4 Notices shall not be deemed served unless there is clear evidence that the notice was received by the other party.

1.5 Both parties also agree to send emails to the other party confirming that notice has been sent with copies of the documents attached.

N.155

The parties agree and shall have the right to serve legal notices, report accounts and royalties and any other matter relating to this agreement to each other as they think fit at their sole discretion using the following details:

The [Company]: [specify name/ role/address/email].

The [Designer]: [specify name/role/address/email].

N.156

The parties agree that they may communicate, exchange data and information and/or deliver any formal notice under this agreement by any method whether it be in writing and/or verbally, and/or by text message, email, via skype and/or otherwise.

N.157

Any notice under this Agreement shall be in writing and either by recorded delivery post and/or courier which is then signed for upon delivery by an authorised officer of the [Licensor] at [address] and/or an authorised officer of the [Licensee] at [address]. Notice is received when it is signed for by the recipient.

N.158

Any notice given under this agreement may be in any method provided it is in [English] and legible. It will only be accepted as received if there is sufficient and clear evidence that it was properly served and received by the party.

N.159

Any notice shall be served personally on the [Managing Director] of the [Company] or [Name] by a private courier or shall be by first class recorded delivery post marked private and confidential. No other method shall be accepted as proper service.

N.160

Any notice or direction given by the [Company] to [Name] shall be made by only the following person or his/her substitute [Managing Director/Company Secretary/Director] or other person of comparable position in charge of the [Project]. Any formal notice shall be in writing and may be sent by any method to the other party. Every effort should be made to verify that notice has been received.

N.161

1.1 Any notice shall be sent to the other party to the last known address or other details of which there is sufficient evidence as well as the address stated on this Agreement. Any notice shall only be effective once it is received and the other party has knowledge of its contents.

1.2 Any notice must be in writing and the sender must be able to prove that it was actually received. Acceptable methods include a letter sent by courier which is signed for on delivery, recorded delivery sign for postal service, email with an attachment for which an acknowledgement is received.

N.162

All notices under this agreement must be in writing and delivered by courier or recorded post. Service by skype, fax, email, text messages or otherwise will not be accepted by either party as proper service under this agreement. Copies may be sent by fax, email, or texted, but shall not alone constitute sufficient notice.

N.163

Notices may be sent by any method provided they are legible and the sender can provide evidence of their receipt. The opportunity must be given on each occasion to allow a breach to be remedied within [number] days. Where notice is to terminate or suspend the agreement then notice must be by courier or recorded delivery. The parties' details are as follows unless otherwise amended:

The [Sponsor] contact role [specify] [address] [email] [mobile]

The [Charity] contact role [specify] [address] [email] [mobile]

N.164

Notices shall be in writing by recorded delivery whether post or courier as follows [Title/Name/Address] of each party. Information may also be sent by other means but will not constitute service of notice.

N.165

All notices must be in writing under this agreement and delivered by courier, hand delivered, first class, recorded and/or registered post. Service by email, text message, coded messages and software notifications or otherwise will not be accepted by either party as proper service under this agreement. Service shall be made to the parties as follows:

[Institute] [name] [Chief Executive/role] [address]

[Enterprise] [name] [Chief Executive/role] [address]

N.166

Where a party has attempted to serve notice and it has been wrong for some reason. They may serve a subsequent valid notice in respect of the same matter.

N.167

It is agreed between the parties that no notice and/or amendment to this Agreement may be made by voicemail, email, text and/or some other electronic method. That the only valid and recognised process is in writing on paper in the [specify] language.

N.168

[Name] agrees that for the purposes of this Agreement where [Name] is not available for any reason that any notice may be served on [specify] their Agent and/or their [specify] their legal advisor.

N.169

The parties agree that any notice and/or any amendment to this agreement may be made in writing, by spoken words, texts, email, voicemail, letter and/or coded smart contract software notification and/or by any other method. Provided that it is addressed or sent to the correct person and/or company and the content is clear.

N.170

1.1 It is agreed between the parties that the [Company] may notify the [Customer] of changes and amendments to this agreement by publishing notices on the [Company] website and through text and email messages to the registered mobile number and email account for the [Customer].

1.2 The [Company] agrees that where the notice relates to a price increase that the [Customer] may terminate the agreement provided that he/she pays for [number] months of the service thereafter at the current price.

N.171

Where any communication and/or notice is to be sent to the other parties to this agreement. Then the following principles shall apply:

1.1 Any method may be chosen this shall include automated responses, text messages, personal calls via mobile and/or landline, video and film online exchanges in real time and/or delivery of a product and/or letter bearing the message.

1.2 The communication must be unequivocal as to its content and the expected response by the other party must be stated and made clear to resolve the matter.

1.3 Where a problem can be remedied by any party then they must be allowed the chance to do so provided it is within a reasonable period of time and does not result in another party bearing excessive additional costs and expenses.

1.4 The aim is to avoid unnecessary litigation and all parties agree to consider all other options as a form of resolution prior to commencing any legal action.

NOVATION

General Business and Commercial

N.172
The [Television Company] shall be entitled to assign the whole or any part of the benefit of this agreement to a third party. The [Television Company] shall give the [Publisher] notice in writing of any proposed assignment and the [Publisher] agrees that it shall co-operate with the novation of this Agreement and enter into an agreement on the same terms with the third party. Provided that the [Television Company] and the third party can provide sufficient evidence that the third party can and will fulfil all the terms of the original agreement and that there shall be no detriment to the [Publisher] from such action.

N.173
The [Distributor] may assign all of its rights, liabilities and obligations under this agreement to any person and/or third party subject to the prior written consent of the [Licensor]. In the event of such assignment the [Distributor] shall remain jointly and severally liable to the [Licensor] with its assignees for the performance of its obligations. The [Distributor] shall not be entitled to make or consent to any other or further assignments without prior written consent of the [Licensor]. Full details of the proposed assignment and any other agreement with any third party in respect of the material covered by this agreement shall be provided to the [Licensor] [except for any confidential company information] at least [two] months prior to the execution and conclusion of any such assignments. The [Distributor] shall in any event be bound to make the payments due to the [Licensor] in the event that the third party is unable or unwilling to do so for any reason.

N.174
The parties to this Agreement acknowledge that any successors in title to the [Company] shall be entitled to the benefit and burden of the terms of this agreement without the prior consent of the parties.

N.175

1.1 [Name] agrees to novate the agreement dated [–] between the [Company] and [Name] by [date]. The [Company] shall be under no obligations of any nature to the [Name] nor shall the [Company] have any interest in or entitlement to any rights of any kind in the [Work] under this agreement after [date].

1.2 [Name] agrees that the [Company] shall be entitled to assign the benefits and obligations of this agreement in respect of the [Work] to the [Third Party D] who shall assume all rights and obligations to the [Name].

1.3   [Name] agrees to 1.1 and 1.2 subject to the [Third Party D] entering into an agreement directly with the [Name] on the same terms and conditions set out in this Agreement. Except that the third party agreement shall be on the condition that the [Third Party D] shall not seek to recoup or set off at any time any sums which have been paid to the [Name] by the [Company] which shall include any advances.

N.176

The [Author] agrees to the novation of the Publishing Agreement dated [–] by the [Publisher] to the [Company] on the following terms and conditions:

1.1   In consideration of the payment of the sum of [number/currency] by the [Publisher] to the [Author] upon signature of this document by the [Author]. The [Author] agrees to novate, relinquish and release the [Publisher] from its contractual obligations and liabilities to the [Author]. Further the [Author] agrees that the [Publisher] may assign the Publishing Agreement to the [Company].

1.2   The [Publisher] shall not be released from its contractual obligations to the [Author] unless and until it pays the consideration set out in 1.1 above and pays all sums due under the existing agreement and sends [free of charge] all existing stock which is in its control to the [Author] and transfers title to the [Author].

1.3   The [Publisher] shall confirm to the [Author] in writing that it has no further claim to or interest in the Publishing Agreement and/or the [Work] and/or any adaptation and/or development.

1.4   The [Publisher] shall provide the [Author] with a detailed account of the royalties due and/or payable by the [Publisher] to the [Author] and shall pay all sums due upon signature by the [Author] of this document.

1.5   In addition the [Publisher] shall undertake to continue to account to the [Author] in respect of all sums received in respect of the [Work] after the date of this document. The [Publisher] shall provide a full breakdown of any such future sums specifying the payments due in detail and providing copies of all agreements.

1.6   The [Publisher] agrees to arrange with the [Company] that any advances against royalties previously paid by the [Publisher] shall not be offset against royalties due to the [Author] from the [Company].

1.7   The [Company] shall provide a new Publishing Agreement to the [Author] signed by the [Company] setting out its rights and obligations to the [Author].

1.8   The [Publisher] agrees that all existing material including the cover in any published work of the [Author] is respect of the [Work] shall be [assigned/licensed] to the [Company].

1.9   Despite the fact that the [Publisher] is no longer contractually bound to the [Author] and has no rights, interest or obligations. In the event that the [Company] is unable or unwilling to publish the [Work] within [one] year of the date of this document and/or is made bankrupt, put into receivership and/or an administrator is appointed, then the [Publisher] shall pay to the [Author] the sum of [number/currency] as additional compensation.

N.177
There are no rights of novation by the [Company] under this Agreement, either to a different company or a related body whether there is a change of policy, ownership or control or otherwise. The Agreement is only with the [Company] for the particular imprint agreed namely [specify title/imprint/format/method].

N.178
Where the parent company and a subsidiary changes control and is sold to a third party then the [Author] agrees to the transfer to the successor in title provided that the interests of the [Author] are not prejudiced and there is no reduction in the marketing and promotion of the [Author's] Work.

N.179
Where the ownership of a parent company changes to a third party to which the [Author] objects and/or does not wished to be aligned with their brand and/ or ethos. Then the [Author] shall have the option to terminate the agreement with the parent company and/or the subsidiary with immediate effect. The [author] shall specify the reasons for the termination and request that the [Company] concludes a document which completes a full reversion of all the rights in the [Authors'] [Work] by a fixed date. The [Author] agrees not to seek any damages and/or compensation for the reversion. The [Company] agrees that it shall not be entitled to any repayment of any advance and/ or royalties and/or to receive any money from future agreements which the [Author] may conclude with any third party.

N.180
The [Company] agrees and undertakes that any successors in title to the [Sponsor] shall be entitled to the benefit and burden of the terms of this Agreement and shall not require the prior consent of the [Company].

N.181
Where there is a change of control and/or ownership of the [Licensee]. Then the [Licensee] shall be entitled in such event to notify the [Sub-Licensee] of the novation of the agreement. In such event the parties shall agree a novation agreement either for the reversion of all the rights to the [Licensee] and/or a transfer to a third party.

N.182

The [Author] agrees to the novation of the Merchandising Agreement dated [–] by the [Distributor] to the [Company] on the following terms and conditions:

1.1 In consideration of the payment of the sum of [number/currency] by the [Distributor] to the [Author] upon signature of this document by the [Author]. The [Author] agrees to novate, relinquish and release the [Distributor] from its agreement with the Author and shall accept the assignment of the Merchandising Agreement to the [Company].

1.2 The [Distributor] shall confirm to the [Author] in writing that it has no further claim to and/or interest in the Merchandising Agreement and/or the [Work] and/or any adaptation and/or development and that all sums due to the [Author] have and/or will be paid by [date].

1.3 The [Distributor] shall supply a full list of all stock, master material and other documents held by the [Distributor] which are to be delivered to the [Company].

N.183

Where either party wishes to novate and/or transfer the benefits and liabilities of this agreement to a third party in respect of the [Service/Work/Project]. Then a new agreement must be drawn up between the parties setting out:

1.1 The sums to be paid to any party.

1.2 The date on which the novation and/or transfer takes effect.

1.3 The ownership of all physical and intellectual property and copyright material which may exist

1.4 The accounting process for outstanding sums due if any.

1.5 The transfer of any registrations with any collecting society and/or government body and/or international organisation in respect of domain names, trade marks, service marks and/or otherwise.

1.6 The supply of documents relating to any continuing payments and/or obligations to third parties.

1.7 The supply of documents relating to the buyout and/or assignment of any rights.

1.8 The supply of documents relating to any active legal and/or contractual and/or other claims, actions and/or investigations by third parties.

N.184

1.1 The [Sponsor] has agreed to fund the [Event] and to include its name and brand in the title.

1.2   The [Charity] accepts and agrees that it does not have the right to transfer the sponsorship and/or endorsement of the [Event] to any third party at any time.

1.3   The [Charity] agrees that no third party may share the main sponsorship of the [Event] and/or the title.

1.4   That if the [Event] is cancelled for any reason that no third party may be substituted at a later date. That if the [Sponsor] does not fund any future event that a new title must be used and a new concept and the [Project/event] developed with the [Sponsor] not repeated with a third party.

N.185

It is agreed that where the [Designer/Creator] of the [App/Website/Software] wishes to sell, transfer, assign and/or novate this agreement to a third party. That it is accepted that the [Designer/Creator] shall be entitled to do so without any discussion and/or prior consent form any contributor, writer, musician, artist and/or other person whose work and/or services appear on the [App/Website/Software]. Provided that the new third party takes over the full responsibilities of the existing agreement with that person and fulfils all the payments. [In addition that the [Designer/Creator] agrees to take out an insurance policy to cover any failure by the third party to fulfil the terms of the agreement.]

O

OBSCENITY

Film, Television and Video

O.001

The [Assignor] undertakes that the [Film/Video/Disc] does not and/or shall not contain any obscene, offensive, defamatory and/or derogatory material and will not expose the [Assignee] to civil and/or criminal proceedings in [country] except:

1.1   where there has been agreement in advance in writing between the parties and/or

1.2   the nature of the sound recordings, films, images, words and/or other content has been described in detail in the synopsis in Schedule A which sets out the detail of the [Project] and/or

1.3   where the [Film/Video/Disc] is part of any performances and/or sound recordings by the [Artist] and/or any lyrics and/or filming of such performances.

O.002

The [Licensor] undertakes that the [Film] and/or parts, its title and contents, any sound, text, vision, music, lyrics and/or sound recording in respect of the exploitation of the [Film/Video/Disc] Rights granted to the [Distributor] will not expose the [Distributor] to civil and/or criminal proceedings and/or infringe and/or breach the copyright, contract, trade mark, service mark, logo, design, literary, dramatic, musical, artistic or other rights of any third party during the Term of this Agreement in the following countries: [specify].

O.003

This clause shall only apply to the original master material and not apply to any material of any nature added to the [Film] and/or any text of any sub-titled version and/or sound recording of a translated version which is supplied and added by the [Licensee].

O.004

The [Licensor] confirms that the [Film/Disc]:

1.1   does not contain any obscene, defamatory and/or excessively violent material and/or any other content which is likely to result in the [Film/Disc] not being stocked and/or distributed by major supermarkets and retail outlets and

1.2   will be suitable for the age [number] years and over and

1.3   will not expose the [Licensee] to civil and/or criminal proceedings and/or any fines from any regulatory and/or governing organisation.
Provided that the liability of the [Licensor] under this clause shall be a maximum of [number/currency] in total.

O.005

The [Licensor] agrees and undertakes that the [DVDs/Discs/Units] of the [Film] and/or parts and the exercise of the rights by the [Distributor] in accordance with this agreement shall and will not expose the [Distributor] to the threat of civil and/or criminal proceedings in [country] in respect of obscenity, copyright infringement and/or defamation during the Term of this Agreement until [date]. Thereafter the [Licensor] shall be under no liability to the [Distributor].

O.006

Where the [Licensee] has added subtitles and/or a sound track and/or other sounds, images, words and/or material of any nature which has not been arranged and/or paid for by the [Licensor]. Then the indemnity in clause [–] shall not apply to any such material and the [Licensee] shall be bear all the liability, cost and expense of any allegation, claim, fine and/or civil and/or criminal proceedings that may arise not the [Licensor].

O.007

The [Licensee] agrees and undertakes to the [Sub-Licensee] that the copies of the master material of the [Sound Recordings] reproduced on the [Disc] which shall be supplied to the [Licensee] under this agreement shall not contain any lyrics, words, sound and/or title which is likely to cause serious offence, may be interpreted as derogatory of a particular person and/or be considered obscene, defamatory and/or will expose the [Sub-Licensee] and/or any other agent and/or distributor to civil and/or criminal proceedings in any country from [date] to [date].

O.008

1.1   The [Distributor] agrees and undertakes not to promote, market and/or advertise the [DVD/Disc/CD] and/or any associated material on any websites, blogs, apps, text message and/or in any magazine and/or other periodical and/or on television and/or through any telecommunication system in any form which is classified [specify] and/or contains obscene and/or graphic images which members of the public are likely to find offensive and/or images and/or text which [Name] would not want to be associated with at any time.

1.2 The [Distributor] agrees that where [Name] notifies them under 1.1 that there is material posted and/or displayed and/or distributed which [Name] finds offensive and/or falls within 1.1 that the [Distributor] will take action and endeavour to remove all such material as soon as possible.

O.009

The [Licensor] and the [Distributor] undertake to the [Licensee] that there are no acts, words, text, images, products or computer-generated material in the [Film] including the soundtrack and any other material supplied under this agreement which are or may be construed as obscene and/or defamatory in [country] whether under any law, statute, regulation, directive, guidelines, standards or code relating to the exercise by the [Licensee] of the rights granted in this Agreement. This undertaking shall only apply from [date] to [date]. Any claim which is not notified within that period shall not be the responsibility of the [Licensor] and the [Distributor].

O.010

It is agreed that the master copy of the [Film] supplied by the [Company] may be rejected on the grounds of quality and/or fitness for purpose and/or that the performances, words, text, images and/or soundtrack are vulgar, offensive, obscene defamatory, likely to cause a negative reaction from the audience, and/or may result in aggression and acts of violence outside the venue. Provided that the reason for the rejection is stated and sent to the [Company] within [number] days of receipt of the master copy. The [Company] agrees to provide a substitute film for the [Distributor] within [number] days of notification of the rejection.

O.011

In the event that the [Film] is considered by the [Licensee] to be obscene and/or indecent in law and/or to contravene any codes of practice in any part of the Territory. The [Licensor] shall use its best endeavours to enable the [Licensee] to obtain, alter, amend, edit and otherwise change the offending parts. In the event that the [Film] cannot be edited to an acceptable standard then the [Licensee] shall be entitled to request an immediate refund of all sums paid to the [Licensor] by the [Licensee] in respect of that [Film].

O.012
The [Licensor] confirms that the [Films] do not and will not contain any material of any nature whether in sound, vision, or text which is obscene or defamatory or will expose the [Distributor] to civil and/or criminal proceedings in respect of the exercise of the rights granted to the [Distributor] under this Agreement. The [Licensor] confirms and undertakes that the version of the [Film] supplied to the [Distributor] will be that which has already been approved or rated by the relevant censorship authority in the Territory.

O.013
The [Company] confirms and undertakes that the [Film] contains no obscene or defamatory matter in sound, image or text and will not expose the [Licensee] to civil and/or criminal proceedings. That this undertaking shall only apply to [specify countries] in the [specify] language from the date of this agreement until [date]. After [date] this undertaking shall no longer apply.

O.014
The [Company] agrees and undertakes to ensure that the [Series] will not contain any act, performance, parody, image, words, text, lyrics, gesture, article and/or sound recording which is obscene, defamatory and/or would prevent the supply, sale, marketing and/or distribution of the [Film] in the following countries [specify] and/or would result in the [Film] not obtaining a classification as [rating] with [specify organisation].

O.015
The [Licensee] agrees and undertakes to the [Licensor] that it shall bear responsibility for any legal and/or other proceedings including any costs, expenses, damages, losses, penalties and settlement which arise as a result of the exploitation of the [Film] by the [Licensee] under this agreement. This shall include but not be limited to any allegation of obscenity, defamation, a fine by a regulatory body, an allegation of breach of confidence and/or privacy, infringement of copyright and/or otherwise.

O.016
[Name] agrees and accepts that the interview by the [Presenter] with [Name] may include questions, jokes, caricatures, films, sound recordings and other material which is rude, vulgar, obscene, derogatory and offensive upon which [Name] is expected to react to and/or comment on.

O.017
[Name] agrees and undertakes to conduct him/herself in a respectable manner at all times at the [location/venue] for the filming of the [Programme/ Series] and shall not make any obscene gestures, swear, wear any clothing

which displays offensive words and/or images and/or is likely to cause offence and/or cause the [Distributor] to be in breach of the Code of Practice and guidelines known as [specify code] and/or the terms of its contractual licence issued by [specify organisation].

General Business and Commercial

O.018
In the event that an [Exhibitor] and/or any representative and/or any employee and/or any casual personnel act and/or communicate in any manner on the premises of the exhibition in such a way that the [Organisers] decide in their sole discretion that it is not acceptable including but not limited to any lewd and/or vulgar gestures and/or obscene behaviour, drunkenness and/or deliberately cause conflict and/or inciting violence and/or acting aggressively and/or are suspected of being involved in drugs and/or other illegal activities. The [Organisers] shall have the right to request that any such person and/or exhibitor leave the premises immediately. In the event that they fail to comply with the request then the [Exhibitor] agrees that the person may be removed by security staff from the premises.

O.019
[Name] warrants and undertakes that his/her performance shall not contain anything obscene and/or defamatory and/or anything calculated to bring the [Company] into disrepute and that it shall not contain any advertisement, promotion and/or endorsement of any company, service, product and/or person except [specify].

O.020
To the best of the [Company's] knowledge and belief nothing in the [Work] shall be defamatory, seditious, blasphemous and/or obscene and/or commit a tort in breach of any right of privacy or other personal rights and/or be in breach of any contract and/or duty of confidence and/or data and/or official secrets and/or in contempt of court and/or in breach of any statute and/or legislation in force and/or infringe any copyright, design right, moral rights, trade or service marks, performance right, right of mechanical reproduction, patent, computer software, registered design or other intellectual property rights including passing off [at any time/in the Territory during the Term of this Agreement].

O.021
The [Licensor] agrees and undertakes that the version of the [Work] supplied to the [Licensee] shall be in the form and content approved by the censorship authority in [country]. The [Licensor] agrees that the [Licensee] shall be entitled to make such changes, cuts or alterations as may be

required by any other censorship authority in any other licensed country prior to the distribution of the [Work]. Provided that a copy of any such new version shall be supplied to the [Licensor] at the [Licensee's] cost.

O.022
The [Licensee] undertakes to use all reasonable endeavours to obtain approval and certification from the relevant governing organisations and/or authorities in the Territory for the commercial exploitation of the [Work].

O.023
The [Licensor] agrees and undertakes that the [Work] is not obscene, defamatory and/or does not contravene any standards, practices or codes in the [specify] language in any of the following countries: [specify]. This undertaking shall not apply to any other country not listed.

O.024
The [Licensor] confirms that its legal advisors have confirmed that the [Work] is original and created and developed entirely by [Name] who has assigned the rights to exploit the [Work] to the [Licensor]. The [Licensor] agrees and undertakes that the [Work] when adapted by the [Licensee] for the purpose of selling and distributing a toy product [specify] shall not expose the [Licensee] to civil and/or criminal and/or proceedings and/or the risk of a claim by a third party.

O.025
The [Licensor] agrees and confirms that to the best of its knowledge and belief the [Work/Film/Video/Content] does not contain any material which is obscene, defamatory, libellous, offensive and/or likely to incite aggression and/or violence and/or result in a very negative social media reaction in any of the following countries: [specify].

O.026

1.1 The [Assignee] agrees that it has [examined/viewed] the master and complete copy of the [Work/Film/Video/Content] and shall be entirely responsible for any risk, liability and/or legal action and/or claim that may arise directly and/or indirectly from the exploitation of the [Work/Film/Video/Content] by the [Assignee]. That the [Assignee] shall bear its own cost and expenses and seek its own independent advice.

1.2 The [Assignee] agrees that there are no undertakings by the [Assignor] as to any threat of civil and/or criminal proceedings that may arise and/or whether any of its content are in breach of any laws in any country in any respect including relating to obscenity, defamation and/or any other reason.

O.027

The [Licensor] has confirmed that its own advisors do not believe the [Work/Film/Video/Content] to be obscene, offensive or defamatory but no such undertaking is provided in this agreement to the [Licensee]. The [Licensee] accepts that it has been advised to seek its own legal advice. The [Licensee] agrees that it has viewed the [Work/Film/Video/Content] and has agreed to take its own independent advice. The [Licensee] has agreed that it must arrange suitable insurance cover for the [Licensor] and the [Licensee] to adequately cover the threat of any claim, action and/or legal proceedings of any type from the exploitation of the [Work/Film/Video/Content] from [date] to [date].

O.028

The [Licensee] agrees that the [Licensor] shall only be liable in respect of a claim for expenses, damages, costs and losses arising from material in the [Film] which is agreed as part of a settlement to be and/or found by a court and/or a regulatory body to be obscene, offensive, defamatory and/or derogatory up to [number/currency] in [each case/total].

O.029

The [Company] shall be entitled to dismiss for gross misconduct any person at the [Company] who makes an obscene gesture and/or is abusive and/or makes offensive and derogatory remarks in person and/or via any social media and/or by text and/or image and/or film and/or sound recording whether during their hours of employment and/or at any other time when not at work at the [Company] which relates to management at the [Company], its brands and/or products which would have a negative impact on the image and/or sales of the [Company].

Internet, Websites and Apps

O.030

The [Company] regularly checks and monitors the [Website/App/Blog/Podcast], but we cannot be responsible for any obscene, defamatory, offensive, derogatory and/or other material which is posted and/or submitted by members of the public in any associated forum and/or in response. We will try to:

1.1 remove material brought to our attention within [specify period] which is within our control.

1.2 block all material which we consider is not rated suitable for [specify].

1.3 ban and/or serve notice on any member of the public who posts obscene, defamatory, offensive, derogatory and/or other material which we consider unsuitable and will make it a clear condition of our terms of use that they will be personally liable for any damages, losses and costs arising from their contributions to the material on the [Website/App/Blog/Podcast].

O.031
[Name] acknowledges and agrees that the [Company] cannot be responsible for any obscene, defamatory, offensive, derogatory and/or other material which is posted and/or submitted by members of the public and/or any other third party. That [Name] will be personally liable for any damages, losses, costs and expenses which may be paid in settlement by the [Company] as a result of any allegation and/or claim and/or as a result of any legal action and/or proceedings and/or other online claim which arises directly from [Name's] contributions to the material on the [Website/App/Blog/Podcast].

O.032
The [Contributor/Client] agrees and undertakes to the [Company] that:

1.1   all the material whether text, images, photographs, graphics, logos, films, sound recordings and/or any other format and/or medium shall be the original work of the [Contributor/Client].

1.2   all the material in 1.1 will not infringe the copyright and/or any other rights of any person and/or third party.

1.3   that all the material in 1.1 will not contain any defamatory, libellous, blasphemous, obscene and/or indecent material and/or any matter which would be considered as unsuitable for [specify age/programme/event].

1.4   that all the material in 1.1 will not make the [Company] and/or its licensees, agents and representatives and/or any parent and/or associated business liable to any threat, claim, infringement and/or any legal action.

O.033
Where as a result of an email, text, image, slogan, photograph, film and/or any other material being sent to any part of the [Website/App] by any person and/or any other registered user of this [Website/App]. The [Company] receives an allegation of obscenity and/or indecent material and/or any other serious allegation and/or is the subject of any civil and/or criminal proceedings.

The [Company] will not withhold information and shall as a matter of policy supply the details of the sender of any such material to the police, court and regulatory organisations as it may decide and such other government without any liability whatsoever to the sender of the material [except where mandatory by law].

Where the [Company] is also the subject of legal proceedings it shall be entitled to seek a full indemnity against the sender of the material including all legal costs.

O.034
All subscribers who submit material which is obscene, defamatory, spam, hoaxes, contains viruses and/or other damaging content shall have all their material deleted and their access blocked from all [websites/apps/accounts] associated with the [Company] without any liability for such termination and destruction of their material. Legal proceedings may be commenced and a claim made by the [Company] for damages, losses and legal costs against any subscriber who has defaulted in respect the terms of their access and use of the [website/apps/account] without any advance notice being provided.

O.035
The [Supplier] agrees and undertakes that:

1.1　the [Service/Promotion/Material/Product] to be delivered by the [Supplier] shall not contain any content which is obscene, mocking, crude, a parody and/or illegal and/or an infringement of any copyright, trade mark, service mark, design and/or intellectual; property rights of any third party.

1.2　the risk of any claim and/or liability to a third party in respect of 1.1 shall be kept to a minimum and shall not expose the [Supplier] and/or the [Company] to any threat of legal action relating to a breach of health and safety regulations and/or legislation in [country] and/or any other civil and/or criminal proceedings from [date] to date].

O.036
The [Company] agrees that any material of any nature which is included in the [Website/App/Software/Product] to be developed by the [Company] for [Name] shall not contain:

1.1　any images, text, sound recordings, films, logos, artwork, signs, trade marks, service marks, designs, music, lyrics, products, locations and venues and/or other content which belongs to a third party which has not been cleared and/or paid for and/or acquired for use by the [Company] for [Name].

1.2　any content which is unsuitable for [specify group and age].

1.3　any content which could be construed as aggressive, inciting violence, encouraging the use of illegal drugs, vulgar, obscene, offensive and/ or likely to result in numerous complaints from the public when it is exploited.

O.037

There are no undertakings and/or warranties provided regarding the content of the [Website/app/software] and you are advised to seek your own legal advice. The liability and responsibility in respect of any legal action and/or claim is solely with the [Company] who must bear all the costs and expenses and not [Name].

O.038

1.1 There is no indemnity and/or right to seek to be reimbursed for any action and/or claim by a third party that the [Product/Website/App/Film/Video] is not fit for purpose and/or unsuitable for its intended use as it is not in the form in which it was commissioned by [name].

1.2 The only course of action available to the [Company] shall be to seek a full refund of the purchase price paid to [Name].

Merchandising and Distribution

O.039

The [Licensor agrees and undertakes to the [Distributor] that the [Work/Product] is the original work of the [Licensor] and will not infringe the copyright or any other rights of any person in respect of the rights and Territory granted to the [Distributor]. Nor does the [Work/Product] contain any material which is and/or could be construed as defamatory, obscene, and/or is likely to result in civil and/or criminal proceedings in [country].

O.040

The [Distributor] agrees and undertakes to the [Licensor] that it shall not alter, edit, change and/or add any material whether text, images, films, advertising, logos and/or sound recordings and/or any other matter to the [Work/Product] which is alleged to be derogatory of any person and/or political party and/or defamatory and/or could be construed as obscene, offensive and/or intended to create a social and/or political statement and/or create controversy.

O.041

The [Distributor] agrees and undertakes to the [Licensor] that all the titles, packaging, advertising, marketing, brochures, flyers and posters shall be designed and directed at the [specify age group] market. That no content shall be rude, swearing, alleged to be defamatory, alleged to be obscene and/or contain any text, images and/or innuendos which are not appropriate and could bring the [Licensor] into disrepute and/or damage their brand and/or sales of any of their products.

O.042

There are no undertakings and/or assurances by the [Author/Creator] that the content of the [Work/Design/Material] to be adapted to develop the [Product] is free from any legal claim in respect of any allegation breach of copyright, contract, defamation, obscenity and/or other matter. The onus is on the [Distributor] who accepts the risk and responsibility that they shall be liable to take legal advice for each country as necessary and to change the [Product] as required to avoid litigation. Further that the [Distributor] shall not seek to make any claim against the [Author/Creator] in respect of any legal action that may arise and shall bear all the costs and consequences for any damages and losses.

O.043

1.1 The [Licensee] shall be entitled to delete, amend, substitute and/or vary any words and images in the [Work] which would be deemed obscene, offensive and/or inaccurate as a result of the translation of the [Work] into another language.

1.2 The [Licensee] agrees and undertakes to make such changes at its sole cost but shall not be entitled to reproduce and distribute the new version in 1.1 until the draft [proofs/sample] has been approved by the [Licensor] in each case.

O.044

The [Licensee] agrees that the packaging, marketing, advertising and/or promotional material for the [Work/Product] shall not involve any person and/or material and/or design which would not be suitable for [children] under [age] years.

O.045

The [Distributor] agrees and undertakes that the [Distributor's] [Website/App/Software] does not contain and will not contain any sound recordings, music, lyrics, literature, slogans, text, images, logos, articles, products or other material which are or may reasonably be construed as being defamatory, likely to cause offensive, categorised as unsuitable for [specify group/age], derogatory of any religion, obscene and/or cause the [Supplier] and/or its products to be the subject of negative and damaging social media, television and newspaper articles and news reports which affect its reputation and/or result in a fall in sales and/or a fall in share price and/or some other consequence which is damaging to their business.

O.046

The [Licensee] undertakes that the [Licensee's Product] and the [Product Package] will not be offensive or obscene in any nature or derogatory of any third party and will not expose the [Licensor] to any civil or criminal proceedings [in respect of the exercise of the rights granted under this Agreement in [specify countries].

O.047

The [Licensee] agrees and undertakes to the [Licensor] that the [Product/Work] shall not be sold in conjunction with any other product and/or service which is obscene, lewd and/or offensive and/or may lead to criminal proceedings.

O.048

The [Licensee] agrees that it shall make it a condition of supply to any third party that the [Product/Work] is not suitable for sale to anyone under the age of [number] years.

O.049

The [Company] agrees that:

1.1   The [Content] shall not be adapted and/or used in conjunction with any other material which is not suitable for [specify age category] and over.

1.2   That no other material shall be added and/or included in any form which is obscene, defamatory and/or likely to breach any legislation in any country in the world.

1.3   That in the event that any material is discovered to be used in conjunction with the [Content] that is unacceptable to [Name] shall have the right to notify the [Company] to remove and delete the offending material. If it is not removed and deleted within [number] days of notice by [name]. Then [Name] shall have the right to terminate the licence and to retain all sums paid to the date of termination. In such event the [Company] accepts that it shall not have any legal claim against [Name].

Publishing

O.050

The [Author] confirms that nothing in the [Work] contains any obscene or indecent material or any matter which would tend to deprave or corrupt any persons who may have access to the [Work] and will not expose the [Publisher] to proceedings of any nature in respect thereof.

O.051

The [Author] warrants to the [Publishers] that all statements contained in the [Work] which are facts are true and that the [Work] contains nothing which is obscene, libellous, defamatory, blasphemous or otherwise unlawful.

O.052

1.1 The [Company] warrants that the [Manuscript/Book] shall be the original work of the [Writer] and will not infringe the copyright or any other rights of any person except where the [Manuscript/Book] is based on and/or incorporates material supplied by the [Distributor] and/or any third party at the request of the [Distributor].

1.2 The [Company] shall carry out reasonable investigations and research to establish whether the [Manuscript/Book] contains any material which is defamatory, obscene and/or will infringe any copyright and/ or other rights of any person. The [Company] shall ensure that the [Manuscript/Book] will not contain any text, photographs and/or other material which is likely to result in a legal action being commenced against the [Distributor] and/or its licensees by a third party.

O.053
The [Publishing Company] warrants to the [Author] that the [Publishing Company] will not incorporate into the [Work] prior to publication anything which is libellous, obscene or the publication of which would an infringement of the copyright of any third party. The [Publishing Company] shall indemnify the [Author] in respect of any damages, losses, expenses and costs arising suffered and/or incurred by the [Author] directly as a result of the unauthorised material added by the [Publishing Company].

O.054
The [Publisher] reserves the right in its absolute discretion to cancel any contract or to omit or suspend any advertisement for any reason including but not limited to the grounds that the advertisement and/or the product and/or service it promotes is defamatory, obscene, offensive, pornographic, and/or for any reason unsuitable for publication.

O.055
That the [Writer] agrees to ensure that all reasonable searches and enquiries are made to establish whether or not the [Work/Book/Manuscript] contains any matter which is likely to be construed as defamatory, obscene, illegal and/or inciting a person to commit an offence. The [Writer] undertakes that the [Work/Book/Manuscript] shall not contain any material which will expose the [Company] to a civil and/or criminal legal action and/or cause the distribution and sale of the [Work/Book/Manuscript] to be suspended and/or cancelled.

O.056
The [Author] confirms that the [Work/Book/Manuscript] does not and will not contain any obscene, offensive, defamatory, or racially prejudiced material

and will not expose the [Publisher] to civil and/or criminal proceedings for the duration of the Licence Period in the following specify countries [–].

O.057
The [Author] agrees and undertakes that the [Work] supplied by the [Author] shall not contain any obscene, offensive, defamatory, or racially prejudiced material and will not expose the [Publisher] to civil and/or criminal proceedings in respect of the publication of the [Work] in the [hardback and paperback] in the [United Kingdom/other] during the Term of this Agreement. In the event that there is any claim by the [Publisher] against the [Author] under this clause the total liability of the [Author] shall be limited to [number/currency].

O.058
The [Author] understands and agrees that the [Publisher] shall be entitled to delete, add to, vary and/or amend any minor part of the [Work] which its legal advisors have requested should be made in respect of the publication of the [Work] in the [hardback and paperback] in the [United Kingdom/ other] during the Term of this Agreement. Where major changes are to be made then the prior consent of the [Author] shall be required and the full report of the recommendations by the legal advisors shall be disclosed in confidence to the [Author].

O.059
The [Publisher] agrees that:

1.1 the [Author] shall not be under any obligation to the [Publisher] in respect of any legal problems and/or proceedings and/or claims that may arise from the publication, distribution, sale and promotion of the [Work/Book/Manuscript].

1.2 the [Publisher] accepts that it exercises the rights granted under this Agreement at its own cost and risk.

1.3 the [Publisher] shall not seek to claim any indemnity and/or offset and/ or recoup any sums from the advances and/or royalties due under this Agreement from the [Author] in respect of 1.1 and 1.2.

1.4 the [Publisher] shall commission at its own cost a pre-publication libel and risk assessment report of the accuracy, sources, copyright infringement, and potential civil and criminal proceedings that may arise in respect of the [Work/Book/Manuscript].

O.060
[Name] shall have the right to refuse to have any contribution which he/she has created, developed and/or written to be combined with other material

in a compilation for publication which in the opinion of [Name] is obscene and/or not suitable for the [specify] market and/or likely to have a negative impact on the reputation of [Name] and/or affect the ability of [Name] to carry out his/her work as [specify role].

O.061 The [Publisher/Distributor] accepts and agrees that the [Author/Contributor] provides no undertakings, warranties and/or indemnities in respect of this licence. That the [Publisher/Distributor] must carry out its own research regarding the originality of the material supplied and any potential threat of a legal action regarding the material. In any event the [Distributor/Publisher] agrees that no claim shall be made for any reason against the [Author/Contributor]. In the event that the future co-operation of the [Author/Contributor] is required regarding any claim and/or legal action then the [Distributor/Publisher] shall agree a daily fee and pay all costs and expenses.

Services

O.062
The [Presenter] undertakes that all the product of his/her services under this agreement shall not be aggressive, offensive, verbally abusive, defame any person, be obscene and/or use gestures and/or words which are likely to result in complaints by the public and/or promotes any political party and/or campaign and/or endorses any product and/or service which is not part of the [Films/Series]. Except that the [Presenter] shall not be held responsible in anyway where material of any type is included at the request or direction of the [Company].

O.063
The total liability of the [Presenter] under this clause shall be limited to [number/currency].

O.064
This clause shall not apply to any use and/or exploitation by the [Company] and/or any authorised third party outside [country].

O.065
This clause shall not apply to any use and/or exploitation by the [Company] and/or any authorised third party after [date].

O.066
The [Company] acknowledges and agrees that [Name] shall have the right not to be subjected to or at any time required to use any material, present any script and/or make any recording, film, or carry out any work which

[Name] considers is obscene, racist, offensive, demeaning, defamatory, rude and/or which mocks, parodies and/or ridicules another person and/or business and/or which is likely to create a backlash on social media which poses a risk to the safety of [Name] and/or which might otherwise negatively affect the reputation and/or career of [Name].

O.067

The [Company] undertakes that no material of any nature concerning [Name] shall be used by the [Company] or licensed and/or supplied to any third party which is to be used in any offensive, obscene, derogatory, defamatory and/or demeaning manner and/or might result in the risk of civil and/or criminal proceedings against the [Company] and/or [Name] in any part of the world.

O.068

The [Company] acknowledges and agrees that no part of the services to be supplied to the [Enterprise] are intended to include any person, material and/or performance and/or display which features anything which is likely to offend religious organisations, those with disabilities and/or families with children and/or create any negative reaction and/or response from the local community.

O.069

The [Enterprise] accepts and agrees that it must monitor and assess the risk of legal action by any third party in respect of the [Event/Programme/Podcast]. That the [Contributor] shall only be responsible to deliver the [Script/Film/Installation] based on the synopsis supplied by the [Enterprise]. That any legal consequences that may arise from the use and/or exploitation of the [Script/Film/Installation] shall be the sole responsibility of the [Enterprise]. The [Enterprise] agrees that the [Contributor] has provided no undertakings, warranties and indemnity to the [Enterprise] and none is implied. All liability is at the cost and expense of the [Enterprise].

Sponsorship

O.070

The [Sponsor] undertakes that it will not do anything and/or permit any third party to do anything and/or require the performance under this contract of any action, word, text, sound and/or image, recording, film, appearance and/or otherwise which is likely to be derogatory, detrimental and/or damaging to the reputation, brand and/or career of the [Name]. In the event that [Name] and/or his or her agent advises the [Company] of any such material which is authorised and/or made available in conjunction with the [Sponsor] by a third party. Then the [Sponsor] shall immediately withdraw such material and ensure it is not reproduced any further and/or use its best endeavours to prevent any third party from doing so. Where the [Sponsor] authorised the use of the damaging material then the [Company] agrees that it shall be liable to pay [Name] compensation for the impact on the reputation of [Name] and any loss of revenue that may have been incurred as a result. Where the damaging material was not authorised but used by a third party without the knowledge of the [Company] then the [Company] agrees that it shall fund any legal action by [Name] and the [Company] that may be necessary to prevent the use of such material.

O.071

The [Company] confirms that the [Products/Website/App] and the [Company's Logo] and promotional material do not contain any obscene, defamatory and/or any other material of any nature which could be construed in [specify countries] as contrary to any legislation in relation to any person, charity, religion, political party, commercial company, trade organisation and/or any other entity. The [Company] agrees that it shall not endorse and/or become involved in any campaigns and/or social media promotions relating to any person and/or group which would have a negative impact on [Name] and their brand.

O.072

The [Sponsor] agrees and undertakes not use the name, image, photograph, details and/or representation of any official, competitor, and/or any other person in association with the [Event] in any advertising, promotion, packaging and/or marketing which could be construed as offensive, derogatory, obscene, defamatory, ridiculing, mocking, and/or in any manner and/or style in conjunction with other material which impugns their reputation at any time whether during the period of this agreement and/or thereafter.

O.073

The [Company] shall not be liable for any content, material, services, products and/or other material supplied by and/or made by the [Sponsor] which results in civil and/or criminal proceedings including but not limited to allegations and/or legal actions relating to defamation, obscenity, product liability, comments and promotions on social media, advertising and competitions.

O.074

[Name] agrees and acknowledges that he/she must at all times during the course of their training and participation in [sport] events during the course of this sponsorship agreement conduct themselves as an ambassador for the [Sponsor] and avoid any gestures, words, behaviour, innuendos, images, texts, social media comments, films and videos which might be construed in any language in [country] as obscene and/or vulgar and/or expose the [Sponsor] to ridicule and/or adverse publicity.

O.075

The [Sponsor] accepts and agrees that [Name] shall only be bound by the Code of Conduct of [specify organisation] in respect of this agreement. That no additional responsibilities and/or standard of conduct is imposed. Provided that [Name] does not make any public comment, statement and/or act in any manner which results in him and/or her being arrested and/or charged and/or any legal action is commenced which makes an allegation that affects the reputation of [Name]. In such circumstances the [Sponsor] shall have the right to suspend the agreement for a fixed period until such time as the matter has been resolved and to suspend all payments. In the event that [Name] is found guilty and/or loses any legal action then no further payments shall be due to [Name] from the date of the suspension.

University, Charity and Educational

O.076

1.1 The [Institute/Charity] agrees and confirms that to the best of its knowledge and belief the [Work/Service] does not contain any material which is obscene and/or defamatory in [specify country].

1.2 No undertakings are given as regard any other country in the world and no responsibility can be accepted. The [Institute/Charity] cannot accept responsibility for third parties who use the [Work/Service] and no such undertaking is provided in relation to them.

1.3 The [Institute/Charity] does not accept responsibility for compliance with any standards, practices and/or codes.

1.4 This clause shall only apply from [start date] to [end date]. The [Company] agrees and accepts that any matters arising from this clause must be notified in writing to the [Institute]/Charity by the [end date].

O.077

The [Contributor] agrees and undertakes to the [Institute/Charity] that the [Work/Service] supplied by the [Contributor] shall not contain any obscene, offensive, derogatory, defamatory and/or any other material of any nature which exposes the [Institute/Charity] to the threat of complaints from the public and/or the risk of any allegation and/or reprimand and/or legal action by any person, company and/or organisation in any part of the [Territory/world/country].

O.078

1.1   The [Contributor] agrees that the [Institute/Charity] shall be entitled to delete, add to, vary and/or amend all and/or any part of the [Work/Image/Film] as the [Institute/Charity] shall at its sole discretion decide in order to protect their reputation, integrity and public perception.

1.2   Where the [Institute/Charity] decides not to use and/or reproduce any part of the [Work/Image/Film]. The [Contributor] accepts that they shall not be entitled to any further sums and/or to make any claim that the failure to use such material has created a loss and/or damage.

O.079

The [Institute/Charity] agrees to ensure that all the contributions, material and marketing that it provides at the [Event] and for the website of the [Promoter] shall be checked to ensure that there is no risk that it will contain any material which is obscene, defamatory, inaccurate, misleading and/or is likely to invoke a negative social media reaction and/or will damage the reputations of the other persons and/or companies associated with the [Event] and/or the business of the [Promoter].

O.080

The [Institute/Charity/University] reserves the right to ban any person from the site of the premises and offices and to prevent their participation in any event, course and/or workshop. Where that person has threatened, abused and/or made obscene gestures to any member of security, staff and/or another student at any time whether directly in person and/or indirectly through social media and/or some other means. The ban will continue indefinitely and may be invoked by the [Institute/Charity/University] at any time. There is no defined method of notification and there is no right of appeal where the person concerned poses a threat to the safety and mental health of others. The ban will only be lifted if the [Institute/Charity/University] has decided that any person no longer poses a threat to others and/or has agreed to adhere to any conditions imposed by the [Institute/Charity/University].

O.081

The [Promoter] agrees and accepts that the maximum liability of the [Institute/Charity/University] under this agreement shall be limited to [number/currency] in total in respect of all matters. That the [Institute/Charity/University] cannot be held liable for the actions, words and/or conduct of its members and/or students and/or any other person. The [Promoter] accepts that the [Institute/Charity/University] cannot prevent adverse reactions on social media and/or in the form of protests on site in response to any performers, speakers and/or other matters that the [Promoter] may arrange for the [Event/Exhibition].

OMISSION

General Business and Commercial

O.082

Any act or omission which, if it were an act or omission by the [Licensee] would be a breach of this Agreement, shall be deemed to be an act or omission for which the [Licensee] is responsible if done or omitted by any associate, affiliate, subsidiary, parent company, sub-agent, sub-licensee or other person, firm and/or business who has been engaged, instructed or appointed by the [Licensee].

O.083

The [Supplier] shall be responsible for errors, omissions or discrepancies in drawings, written information and instructions provided by the [Supplier] or any authorised representative. The [Supplier] shall be liable for the consequences of the cost and expense of any remedial work, alterations and changes which may arise directly or indirectly from such matters.

O.084

The [Company] shall be responsible for and shall indemnify the [Service Company] against all costs, expenses, claims and/or damages arising by reason of the acts and/or omissions of the [Company's] agents in respect of [specify subject]. Provided that any such allegation and/or claim is notified to the [Company] and the [Company] is provided with the opportunity to settle the matter either directly with the [Service Company] and/or any third party without any legal proceedings having been commenced. This clause shall not apply after [date].

O.085

In the event that any error and/or change should arise from the allotment of space at the Exhibition or in the quoted duration of the exhibition provided to the [Client] by the [Organisers]. The [Organisers] will endeavour to provide a substitute arrangement, but are not bound to do so. The [Organisers] reserve the right to change the position allotted to the [Client] at any time should it be necessary. The [Organisers] shall not be liable for any expenses, losses, costs and/or damages which may arise directly and/or indirectly from the allotment of space and/or the quoted duration of the exhibition and reserve the right to alter the arrangements at any time.

O.086

The [Publisher] shall take reasonable care in inserting the advertisement in the position, form and date agreed with the [Advertiser]. In the event that the advertisement is not published or there is any other error or omission of any nature whether on the part of the [Publisher] or any third party. The [Advertiser] agrees that the maximum liability of the [Publisher] shall be the total cost of the payment for the advertisement. The [Publisher] shall not be liable for any direct and/or indirect consequential loss and/or damage incurred of any nature for any reason. The [Advertiser] shall notify the [Publisher] in writing specifying in detail the grounds of complaint within [six] months of the date of booking the advertisement. Thereafter the [Advertiser] shall be deemed to have waived any claim of any kind against the [Publisher].

O.087
Where there is an error, omission, and/or other inaccuracy which occurs in respect of the [Work/Film/Product] which is not deliberate and/or malicious. Then the defaulting party shall be provided with the opportunity to correct the mistake and to resolve the issue. Where the error, omission, and/or other inaccuracy is of such a nature that the other non-defaulting party has suffered damage to their reputation and/or incurred losses. Then the defaulting party shall be obliged to indemnify the non-defaulting party for all such costs, expenses, damages and/or losses.

O.088
The [Licensee] agrees and undertakes that it shall be responsible for all the acts, errors, omissions, inaccuracies, negligence and/or breaches by any agent, distributor, sub-licensee, bank and/or any other person engaged by the [Licensee] in respect of the exploitation of the [Artwork/Product/Film] under this agreement.

O.089
The maximum liability of the [Company/Distributor] in respect of any errors, omissions, delays, inaccuracies and/or interruptions of the [Service] shall be [number/currency] in total to [Name].

O.090
[Name] agrees and accepts that in the event his/her performance is not included in the [Film/Series/Podcast] after the material has been edited by the [Distributor]. That [Name] shall not be entitled to any further payments from the exploitation of the [Film/Series/Podcast].

O.091
The [Distributor] agrees and undertakes that it shall not have the right to omit any part of the [Film] and/or credits and copyright notices from the transmission of the [Film] on [channel]. That the failure to transmit the [Film] in its complete state as it is delivered and/or the omission of any part shall be a serious breach of this agreement and the [Distributor] shall be obliged

to pay the [Licensor] an additional fee of [number/currency] per minute of material that is not transmitted.

O.092

Any omissions, errors, delays and/or misrepresentations which occur which are not deliberate by either party shall not be grounds for termination of this agreement provided that any such issue is resolved within [one] month of the date that the matter first arises.

O.093

[Name] agrees that he/she shall not be entitled to any refund and/or repayment for failure to deliver the [Service] where the delay, error and/or omission is for less than [number] hours in any week.

O.094

The [Company] does not accept any liability where errors, omissions and/or other inaccuracies on the [Website/App/Service] provide information which is misleading and/or not reliable. The information is for guidance and may change at any time before the information can be updated and you are advised to verify the information with your own research and professional advice.

O.095

The [Institute/Charity] shall not be responsible for and/or liable to the [Distributor] for any omissions, errors, delays, costs, amendments, corrections, and/or substitutions which may arise under this agreement at any time. Nor shall the [Institute/Charity] provide any indemnity to the [Distributor]. The [Distributor] agrees and undertakes that it shall bear its own costs and expenses, arrange suitable comprehensive insurance and not seek to rely on any indemnity from the [Institute/Charity].

O.096

The [Company/Enterprise] shall be responsible for the acts, omissions, errors, negligence and/or failures of any associate, affiliate, subsidiary, and/or parent company, agent, licensee and/or any other person, company, and/or business who has been engaged, instructed, appointed and/or authorised and/or sub-licensed and/or sub-contracted by the [Company/Enterprise] to carry out any work and/or provide any services under this agreement on behalf of the [Company/Enterprise].

O.097

The [Institute] shall be responsible for any errors, omissions, and inaccuracies which it shall endeavour to rectify as it thinks fit within [two] months of complaint by the [Licensee]. The [Licensee] agrees that the maximum liability of the [Institute] shall be the total cost of the payment for the [Work/Service] paid by the [Licensee] and that no additional sums for any direct and/or indirect damages, losses and/or expenses and/or costs shall be due.

O.098
The [Consortium] agrees that the omission by one party to fulfil the terms of this agreement in accordance with the timeline in Schedule A shall entitle one and/or more of the other parties to serve notice to terminate their involvement in [Project].

O.099
The [Charity] agrees that where it has omitted to disclose material information and/or data regarding any [Project/Event] for which the [Sponsor] has agreed to provide funding. That the [Sponsor] shall have the right after the disclosure of any such facts to decide whether to terminate this agreement. In the event that the [Sponsor] terminates the agreement then the [Charity] agrees that it shall be obliged to return all the payments made by the [Sponsor] in full in respect of the [Project/Event].

O.100
Where there has been information withheld by [Name] which would have had an impact on the decision of the [Company] to provide sponsorship and/or other expenses. That when these facts are discovered at any time the [Company] shall have the right to terminate this agreement and to seek a full repayment of all the sums paid to [Name] in the previous period of [twelve] months.

OPTION

Film, Television and Video

O.101
The [Licensor] agrees to grant to the [Distributor] an Option to extend the Licence Period for a further [two] years under the existing agreement provided that the agreement has not been cancelled, expired and/or terminated. The Option can be exercised at any time during the Licence Period before [date] by written notice to the [Licensor] to that effect and the payment of the option fee [number/currency] by the [Distributor] to the [Licensor]. This option fee shall not be recouped and/or offset against any advance, royalties and/or otherwise by the [Distributor]. In the event that the

Option is exercised the agreement shall end on [date] and there shall be no further option and/or right of extension of the Licence Period.

O.102

The [Company] grants to the [Licensee] three separate sole exclusive and irrevocable Options in consideration of an initial payment [number/currency] as follows:

1.1 The first Option is to acquire the [DVD/Blu-ray/other rights] in the [Film] in [specify countries] for a period of [number] years from [date] on terms to be agreed between the parties subject to an additional payment of [number/currency].

1.2 The second Option is to acquire the [Merchandising Rights/ Interactive Game and theme park rights] in the [Film] in [specify countries] for a period of [number] years from [date] on terms to be agreed between the parties subject to an additional payment of [number/currency].

1.3 The third Option is to acquire the [Archive playback rights for subscribers through the internet, any gadget, mobile and/or other device in the [Film] in [countries] for a period of [number] years from [date] on terms to be agreed between the parties subject to an additional payment of [number/currency].

The [Licensee] shall be entitled to exercise the options at any time between [date] and [date] by notice in writing in respect of each option to the [Company] and the payment of the sum due for the option in each case. The [Licensee] shall then have a period of [three] calendar months to negotiate and conclude an agreement for the acquisition and exercise of the rights in each case with the [Company]. No payments for the Options shall be refunded by the [Company] nor shall the payments be offset against any other sums relating to the grant and/or exercise of the rights under the new agreements.

O.103

1.1 In consideration of the Option Fee of [number/currency] [Name] grants to the [Company] the sole and exclusive right to exercise an option to produce a [Film] based on the [Book/Synopsis/Series] and to exercise and exploit the [DVD/Video/Disc] Rights in [specify countries] from [date to [date].

1.2 The right to exercise the Option shall commence on [date/date of this Agreement] and end [date]. Notice must be in writing and an additional sum paid of [number/currency] to [Name] in order to exercise the Option.

1.3 In the event that the [Company] exercises the Option and has made the second payment. Then [Name] and the [Company] agree to enter into an exclusive licence/distribution agreement] with the following terms [specify main terms].

1.4 The [Company] acknowledges that if the parties fail to agree terms and conclude an agreement or the [Company] does not exercise the Option and/or pay the sums due the [Company] shall have no further rights in the [Book/Synopsis/Series].

O.104

In consideration of the payment of [figure/currency] the [Author] grants the [Company] the sole and exclusive Option to acquire an exclusive licence for [all media rights] in the [Sound Recordings] in accordance with the draft Licence set out in Appendix [–] which forms part of this Agreement. The Option shall start on [date] and end on [date]. During that period the [Company] may exercise the Option by the payment of [figure/currency] and written notice that they wish to conclude the Licence.

O.105

There is no option and/or first right of refusal granted to the [Licensee] in respect of any subsequent book, work, sound recording, film, video, disc and/or other material and/or format which is based on and/or associated with and/or adapted from the [Work/Sound Recording/Film] owned and/or controlled by the [Licensor].

O.106

The [Licensee] shall not be obliged to offer and/or provide the [Sub-Licensee] with a first option to purchase any adaptation, development and/or merchandising of the [Work/Film/Product] for any country. The [Sub-Licensee] shall not have any rights and/or interest and/or option over any sequel, new series, new product, book, audio recording, theme park, animated version and/or any other development, adaptation and/or merchandising of any nature.

O.107

1.1 The [Company] agrees that in the event it decides to make another [Film/Programme] for the [DVD/Blu-ray/Disc] market that it shall first offer the role of main [Presenter/Consultant] to [Name] upon the same terms and conditions as set out under this Agreement.

1.2 [Name] agrees that if he/she has not accepted the offer within [seven] days of receipt of the proposal. Then the [Company] shall be entitled to appoint a third party.

O.108

In consideration of the payment of [number/currency] direct to the bank account of [Name] by [date]. [Name] grants the [Distributor] an exclusive option which shall start on [date] and end on [date] to acquire the sole and exclusive right to distribute and sell the [Format/Synopsis] of the [Work] in [specify country/throughout the world]. If for any reason the parties have not concluded the final written agreement for the acquisition of the rights by [date] then the option shall end and [Name] shall retain all sums paid to that date. [Name] shall then be able to exploit, sell and offer an option to a third party and the [Distributor] shall no longer have any option to exercise.

O.109

The [Licensor] hereby agrees to grant to the [Licensee] an option to make a further [number] broadcasts and/or transmissions of the [Film/Footage/Podcast] such option to be exercised in writing before [date]. In the event the [Licensee] does exercise this option the Licence Period shall be extended and will expire on [date]. An additional Licence Fee of [number/currency] shall be payable upon the exercise of the option by the [Licensee] to the [Licensor].

O.110

The [Production Company] agrees and undertakes that it shall not be permitted to arrange or carry out any development or any other work in respect of the treatment, scripts or other material relating to the [Author's Work] unless it has exercised the option granted under this agreement and the exclusive licence agreement has been concluded between the parties.

O.111

1.1 The [Company] grants to the [Distributor] an exclusive option to acquire the same rights in respect of any further films, videos, programmes and/or series which the [Company] commissions and/or produces based upon original [Films/Programmes/Series]. The exact terms and financial payments shall be subject to separate negotiation and a new agreement.

1.2 The [Company] shall notify the [Distributor] of any further films, videos, programmes and/or series subsequent to the original when it is completed and available. The [Distributor] shall have [two] calendar months from the date of notice in which it shall be entitled to reject or negotiate for the acquisition of the new version. In the event that there is no response from the [Distributor] the [Company] shall be entitled to deem the new version rejected and shall be entitled to offer the new version to any third party.

O.112

The [Licensor] shall have the option to acquire all copies or derivatives of the [Film] within the possession or control of the [Licensee]. The option period shall be the period of [six months] prior to the date of expiry of this Agreement. The [Licensor] shall provide the [Licensee] with written notice of that intention to acquire such material and enter into negotiations for the settlement of the sum due and the detail of the material available. In the event that no such notice is received by the [Licensee] or the [Licensor] does not wish to acquire such material, then the [Licensee] shall destroy all such material after the end of the Agreement and shall send a report to the [Licensor] of that fact.

O.113

In consideration of [number/currency] the [Company] grants to the [Licensee] two separate sole exclusive and irrevocable options as follows:

1.1 The first option is to acquire the sole and exclusive Television, Video, Radio, Electronic and Streaming Rights in the [Film] and/or any sound recording as defined in the draft Licence set out in Schedule A.

1.2 The second option is to acquire the publishing and merchandising rights in the [Film] and/or any sound recording as defined in the draft Licence set out in Schedule B.

The [Licensee] shall be entitled to exercise each of the options from [date] to [date] by notice in writing to the [Company]. Within [seven] days of the exercise of the option in 1.1 the [Licensee] shall deliver to the [Company] a signed copy of the Licence in Schedule A and pay the sum of [number/currency]. Within [seven] days] of the exercise of the option in respect of 1.2 above the [Licensee] shall deliver to the [Company] the signed Licence in the Schedule B and pay the sum of [number/currency].

O.114

In consideration of the Option Fee the [Author] grants to the [Production Company] the sole and exclusive right to exercise an option to produce the [Film/Series/Podcast] based on the [Author's Work]. The right to exercise the option shall be for the duration of the Option Period.

O.115

'The Option Period' shall mean the period commencing on the date of this Agreement and ending on [date].

O.116

In the event that the [Production Company] exercises the option, then the [Author] and the [Production Company] agree to sign the exclusive licence agreement which is attached to and forms part of this Agreement.

O.117

The [Production Company] acknowledges that after the expiry of the Option Period the [Production Company] shall have no further rights and/or option in respect of the [Author's Work] and shall not be entitled to produce and/or commission the [Film/Series/Podcast].

O.118

The [Author] undertakes that he/she shall not grant an option nor authorise, license or permit any third party to produce, commission, develop a film, programme and/or series and/or any other recordings based on the [Author's Work] and/or any adaptation, translation, merchandising and/or other format in any media during the Option Period without the prior written consent of the [Production Company].

O.119

In the event that the option is not exercised then all copyright, intellectual property rights, computer software and all other rights in the [Work], title, format, and any associated material and/or adaptation, merchandising and/or other development shall remain vested in and belong to the [Author/Agent/Company].

O.120

Any failure to renew or extend the Option Period following the expiry shall not be grounds for any claim or payments for any reason. The [Author] and the [Production Company] agree they shall not be entitled to any claim or sums for failure to renew, extend, or negotiate a further period.

O.121

The [Company] agrees and undertakes that in the event it decides to create, develop and produce a new series of the [Programme] that it shall offer [Name] the role of [specify] if it continues as a character in the script. If the character is not in the new [Programme] then there shall be no obligation to make any offer of another role.

O.122

The [Company] agrees and undertakes to grant the [Distributor] an exclusive option to acquire the [interactive online game, betting and premium rate telephone competition rights] to be used in conjunction with the [Distributors] business, website and app [specify] provided that the following terms are fulfilled:

1.1 The [Distributor] pays a non-returnable Option Fee of [number/currency] by [date] to the [Company].

1.2   The [Distributor] concludes an exclusive licence agreement with the [Company] by [date] which has a non-returnable advance of not less than [number/currency] and is for a fixed term of [number] [months/years].

1.3   At the time of the conclusion of the agreement in 1.2 the [Distributor] is solvent and not the subject of any investigation and/or action and/or civil and/or legal proceedings by any government and/or regulatory body.

1.4   The [Distributor] agrees and undertakes that it shall assign all copyright and all intellectual property and computer software rights in any new material and rights created and/or commissioned by the [Distributor] in respect of the exercise of the rights granted under 1.2.

General Business and Commercial

O.123

'The Option Fee' shall be the sum of [number/currency] which shall be payable upon signature of this agreement by the [Licensee]. This sum shall be paid in addition to any other payments due under this agreement and shall be non-returnable and shall not offset against any future payments to which the [Licensor] may be entitled.

O.124

The [Company] undertakes that it has not assigned, licensed, charged and/or in any way dealt with the copyright or any other intellectual property rights in the [Synopsis/Work/Product] and will not do so until the expiry of the Option on [date].

O.125

'The Option Period' shall mean a period of [six] calendar months from the date of this agreement. This period may not be extended and/or varied for any reason.

O.126

'The Duration of the Option' shall be a period which starts on [date] at [time] and ends on [date] at [time].

O.127

'The Option' shall mean the sole and exclusive option and right to acquire the [specify Rights] during the period [date] to [date] by the [specify party] by notice of the exercise of the rights and the payment of the [Option Fee] within [seven] days of notification.

O.128

The [Company] warrants that it shall not grant or purport to grant the [specify Rights] for any part of the Territory to any other person and/or company unless the [Distributor] fails to exercise the option during the Option Period.

O.129

The Option may be exercised by the [Distributor] giving to the [Company] written notice of exercise of the option at any time during the Option Period.

O.130

In the event that the [Company] decides to appoint another sub-agent in the Territory during the Term of the Agreement. The [Company] agrees to give the [Agent] the opportunity to match or better the terms offered, but the [Company] shall not be bound or obligated to accept any such proposal by the [Agent].

O.131

The [Company] agrees that until the expiry of the Option Period it will not assign, license or in any way dispose of or subject to a lien or charge the copyright, intellectual property rights or any other rights in respect of the [Artwork/Script/Images] in any manner which would or might impair the future grant by the Company of the [specify Rights].

O.132

The [Company] shall be entitled to renew this Licence for a further period of [number] months at their sole option by notice in writing at any time before the agreement has expired on [date] by [time]. If the option is not taken up then there shall be no further additional licence period due and/or granted.

O.133

[Name] agrees and accepts that he/she has no right of first refusal, option and/or any other preferential claim and/or right to a reduced and/or discounted rate in respect of the [Work].

O.134

There is no option granted to the [Licensee] of any nature. There is no obligation to offer first refusal on any subsequent sequel, adaptations, translations and/or merchandising. This agreement is not intended to grant any additional rights to the [Licensee] other than those explicitly stated and described. Any rights which might be created in the future and/or technology and/or any other matter are not covered and/or included in this agreement.

Internet, Websites and Apps

O.135

The [Company] grants the [Consultant] the non-exclusive option to extend the agreement for a further period of [number] months. The [Consultant] shall notify the [Company] by [email] in order to exercise the option before [date]. After that [date] the option shall not apply and the agreement cannot be extended.

O.136

1.1 The [Company] grants [Enterprise] the exclusive option in respect of the [Website/App/Podcast/Audio/Videos/Film] known as [specify] described in Appendix A to exploit the rights described in Appendix B. The option period in which the option may be exercised shall start on [date] and end on [date].

1.2 In order to be granted the rights and to be able to conclude an agreement for the exercise of those rights with the [Company]. The [Enterprise] must decide to notify the [Company] of their wish to exercise the option and must pay the Option Fee to the [Company] by [date]. In the event that the option is exercised then the parties shall conclude an exclusive licence agreement with an advance of not less than [number/currency]. If no such agreement is concluded then after [date] the [Company] shall be entitled to grant the rights to any other third party and the [Enterprise] shall have no rights and/or claim.

O.137

In order to have acquire the rights under the option and to conclude the non-exclusive Licence in Appendix A with the [Company]. The [Distributor] must pay to the [Company] an option payment of [number/currency] by [date]. If the sum is not paid by that date then the option shall lapse and shall cease to exist. The [Company] shall have at all times the right to grants the rights set out in the non-exclusive Licence to any other third party.

O.138

No person, business and/or third party shall be entitled to any priority, option, renewal and/or extension of any agreement with the [Company]. Nor shall they be entitled to any sums for loss of reputation, investment, projected sales, commission, and/or any other losses and/or damages, costs and expenses.

O.139

[Name] agrees to grant the [Distributor] an exclusive option period to enter into an agreement to be licensed the next [number] of original [Apps/

Podcasts/Videos/Images/Sound Recordings] that he/she shall solely create and develop subject to the following terms:

1.1 The [Distributor] pays [Name] an option fee of [number/currency] within [number] days and/or by [date] at the latest.

1.2 If the option fee is paid in 1.1 then the [Distributor] shall have a period of [number] months from the date of payment of the option fee where [Name] agrees not to enter into agreement with any third party for the next [number] original apps he/she will create. This shall not prevent [Name] from having discussions with third parties.

1.3 During the option period if the [Distributor] and [Name] do not agree and conclude an agreement then [Name] shall not be obliged to repay the option fee. If the parties do conclude an agreement then the option fee shall not form any part of that agreement.

1.4 The [Distributor] accepts that no agreement to be concluded with [Name] shall require an assignment of any rights to the [Distributor].

O.140

[Name] has not granted any option and/or other rights over any work of [Name] and/or his and/or her [Website/App/Podcasts/Internet Accounts] and/or any products, brand, logo, trade mark and/or developments which may exist at the time of this agreement and/or at any time thereafter. Where technology and/or rights and/or methods of exploitation do not exist at the date of this agreement but which are created in the future. They are not included in the scope of this agreement and no rights are granted to the [Distributor/Company].

Merchandising and Distribution

O.141

1.1 The [Company] shall have the exclusive and sole option to be the exclusive [Supplier/Distributor] of products for [market/type] at all the Venues including stadium, press centres and any other facilities or premises over which the [Club] have control and/or authority in [country] referred to in Schedule A which is attached to and forms part of this agreement.

1.2 In the event that the [Company] decides to exercise that Option in 1.1 they shall serve written notice on the [Club] before [date] and pay [number/currency] which shall be an advance against the sums to be paid to the [Club] under the contract to be concluded between the parties which is summarised in attached Schedule B which forms part of this agreement.

O.142

The [Company] shall have the option to be exercised by notice in writing for a period of [60] days prior to the expiry date of the Licence to renew the Licence for a further period of [specify duration]. This right of renewal shall only exist in the first agreement and not any later extension. Such renewal shall be on the same terms and conditions as set out in the first Licence. In order to exercise the option the [Company] must pay [Name] the sum of [number/currency] as an option fee. This payment shall not be repaid for any reason and shall not be offset against any other sums due to [Name] under any licence or other agreement.

O.143

1.1   In consideration of the Option Fee, the [Author] grants to the [Company] the non-exclusive right to exercise an option to produce [number] type of products, articles and/or other manufactured goods, based on the characters and names in the [Manuscript/Book/Synopsis] of the [Author] in [language] subject to the prior approval in each case of the item by the [Author].

1.2   The Option in 1.1 must be exercised by notice in writing to the [Author] during the period from [date] to [date] and the agreement to be concluded shall be an exclusive licence for [number] years summarised in the attached Schedule A.

1.3   The Option in 1.1 shall not apply to any film, video and/or podcast derived from [Manuscript/Book/Synopsis].and/or any associated title, trade mark, logo, design, image or words and/or any music, sound recordings and/or lyrics associated with any film, video and/or podcast. Nor shall it apply to any sound recording and/or audio version and/or translation of the [Manuscript/Book/Synopsis].

O.144

1.1   The [Author] grants to the [Distributor] an exclusive option to acquire the [Merchandising] Rights which are defined in Schedule A which is specifically aimed at children and household items in respect of the [Work/Manuscript/Images] and [Characters] which the [Author] created from [date] to [date]. The scope of the products and items which are covered by those rights are listed in Schedule A and any item not listed is not covered by this option. Films, videos, theme parks, betting, gambling, animations, holograms, websites, apps, podcasts, computer-generated material, software, algorithm, electronic and any form of telecommunication system are all expressly excluded from this option and the exclusive licence.

1.2 The draft exclusive licence to be concluded if the option is exercised is set out in Schedule B except that the financial terms which shall be subject to separate negotiation.

1.3 The [Distributor] agrees to pay the [Author] the sum of [number/currency] upon full signature of both parties of the exclusive option. The [Distributor] shall exercise the option by notice in writing after [date] and before [date] to the [Author] setting out their intentions. The option shall not entitle the [Distributor] to have any other rights and/or interest and/or first right of refusal once the option period has ended. In the event that the option is not exercised and/or the parties cannot agree terms. Then the option fee paid shall not be returned to the [Distributor] and the [Author] shall be entitled to grant any such rights to a third party after [date].

O.145

1.1 The [Company] agrees that the [Distributor] shall have an exclusive option to acquire the merchandising rights for the [specify] market in all its [Works] provided that it pays an annual fee to the [Company] of [number/currency] payable by [date] in each year. This exclusive option shall start on [date] and end on [date].

1.2 The [Company] shall offer any [Work] to the [Distributor] and if the parties cannot agree terms and conclude an agreement and/or if the [Distributor] refuses the offer. Then the [Company] may offer that particular [Work] to a third party whether within the period of the exclusive option or not.

1.3 In the event that the [Distributor] fails to pay any advance and/or royalties due to the [Company] and/or any person in the [Works] at any time. Then the [Company] shall have the right to terminate the exclusive option in its entirety and all agreements which have been concluded with the [Distributor] connected with it. In such event the [Distributor] agrees that it shall not have the right to be repaid any sums paid prior to termination.

O.146

It is agreed that there are no options granted to any sequel, new material and/or any development and/or adaptation created by [Name] at any time whether based on the original [Work/Image/Logo/Content/Character] and/or a completely new original concept. The scope of this licence is limited specifically to those matters granted in clause [–] and the licence shall end on [date].

Publishing

O.147

Unless otherwise stated there is no express and/or implied grant of any option of any nature to the [Publisher] over any of the [Author's] future written, audio and/or other works of any nature in any format. This shall apply to any sequel, adaptation and/or new edition. This agreement is solely limited to the manuscript of this original work supplied by the [Author].

O.148

The [Company] acknowledges that after expiry of the Option Period the [Company] shall have no further rights in the [Work] and shall not be entitled, unless terms are agreed in writing between the parties to produce or further exploit the [Work/Characters/Series].

O.149

1.1 The [Author] undertakes that he/she will not grant an option nor authorise, license or permit any third party to produce a film, podcast, video and/or sound recording based on the [Manuscript/Book/Synopsis] or any character, storyline, adaptation and/or sequel during the Option Period without the prior written approval of the [Company].

1.2 It is agreed that the [Author] shall not be obliged to take any legal proceedings against a third party in order to comply with 1.1. The [Author] does agree to co-operate fully with the [Company] in the event that the [Company] wishes to take action provided that the [Company] agrees to indemnify the [Author] in respect of all costs and expenses that he/she may incur including the provision of independent legal advice and representation.

O.150

1.1 The [Author] agrees to give the [Publisher] the first exclusive option to publish the next full-length work, book and/or manuscript based on [specify subject] by the [Author] before [date].

1.2 The [Publisher] agrees that such option in 1.1 shall start on [date] and end on [date] and shall be subject to the payment of an option fee by the [Publisher] to the [Author] of the sum of [number/currency] by [date]. If the option fee is not paid then the option shall lapse immediately.

1.3 The [Author] agrees to send a draft copy of his/her next proposed synopsis to the [Publisher] and then the completed manuscript for consideration. If the [Author] and the [Publisher] cannot agree the terms of the new licence. Then the [Author] shall be obliged to return [fifty per cent/all] of the option fee to the [Publisher]. If the licence is not finalised by [date] then the exclusive option shall end on that date. If the licence is concluded the [Publisher] [may/may not] recoup the option fee against the royalties due to the [Author].

O.151

In consideration of the sum of [number/currency] paid to the [Author] on the date of this agreement receipt of which the [Author] acknowledges. The [Author] grants to the [Publishers] first right of refusal of the [Author's] next full-length work on any subject which he/she may decide to write and which shall be licensed to the [Publishers] by the [Author] on such fair and reasonable terms as shall be agreed between the parties. The right of first refusal shall include the first opportunity to read the work and consider it for publication. It shall not apply to any biographical work and/or memoire.

O.152

The [Author] undertakes that he/she will not grant any option nor authorise, license any third party to produce a film, video, DVD, television and/or radio programme, series, podcast and/or documentary and/or any other visual moving image, sound recordings, and/or produce for and/or distribute any other material on the internet, any telecommunication system, telephone, computer, gadget, storage and retrieval system and/or as computer-generated material whether in sound, vision or text any version in any language based on the [Author's Work] and any associated characters, names, titles, trade marks, logos, slogans, costumes, locations, lyrics, music, images, words and/or any adaptation, development and/or sequel during the Option Period without the prior written consent of the [Company].

O.153

The [Author] shall not provide any consent and/or license the use and exploitation of the [Work/Images/Content] to a third party before [date]. This restriction shall include exploitation by means of all printed material and/or any download and/or sound recording, film, television, video, radio and/or through any telecommunication system and/or by any electronic means over the internet.

O.154

1.1   The [Author] grants to the [Publisher] the exclusive option to negotiate terms for the publication of the next full-length work in the field of [subject] by the [Author]. The [Author] shall deliver the synopsis of the work to the [Publisher] for their consideration. The [Publishers] shall then have a period of [6] weeks to negotiate terms which are acceptable to the [Author] which shall be no less than those set out in this agreement.

1.2   In the event that the [Publisher] is not in a position to make an offer, or rejects it or the parties cannot agree terms, then at the expiry of the [6]-week period the [Author] shall be entitled to offer the work to any other third party and the option shall be at an end. If the [Publishers'] wish to extend the Option Period then they shall be obliged to pay the sum of [number/currency] to the [Author] for a further [6]-week Option Period.

O.155

If the [Assignor] should write or permit to be written a sequel to the [Work] before [date], the [Assignor] shall deliver a copy to the [Assignee] as soon as it is completed and ready for submission to publishers. The [Assignor] agrees not to exercise or grant to any third party any rights in such sequel which in respect of the [Work] are granted to the Assignee unless the following stages have been completed. During the period [state duration] following such delivery the [Assignee] shall be exclusively entitled to negotiate for such rights. If at the end of such period the [Assignee] has not agreed to acquire such rights, the [Assignor] shall not exercise or grant such rights to any third party unless the [Assignor] shall first make a written offer to the [Assignee] to grant the relevant rights in the sequel to the [Assignee] on terms the [Assignor] proposes granting such rights to a third party. The [Assignee] shall have a period of [state duration] to accept or reject such a proposal and unless the [Assignee] agrees to such terms the [Assignor] shall be entitled to grant such rights to any third party.

O.156

The [Publishers] acknowledge and agree that this agreement is solely limited to the first edition of the [Work/Manuscript] in [format] in [language]. The [Publishers] shall have no right of first refusal, option, or prior claim to any further work of the [Author] and/or any sequel and/or subsequent edition and/or any version for any electronic subscription service, download, film, disc, playback service, audio and/or sound recording and/or any computer generated version and/or any other media whether based on, derived from and/or adapted from the [Work/Manuscript] and/or any character, plot, storyline, name, words, images, illustrations and/or otherwise.

O.157

1.1   [Name] agrees to consider and may offer the [Distributor] the opportunity to purchase future editions of the [Work] and/or other material created and developed by [Name].

1.2   The [Distributor] agrees that there is no obligation for [Name] to make any offer in 1.1 and that the [Distributor] has no right to develop, adapt and/or vary the [Work] in any manner to create new versions for exploitation at a later date.

1.3 The [Distributor] accepts that the licence is non-exclusive and that [Name] is free to sell, exploit, supply and license the [Work] to any third party in any language.

Services

O.158

The [Company] is the main supplier of [subject] to the [Enterprise] for the current period. The [Company] accepts that it has no prior claim and/or option to supply the services as the primary contractor. That the [Enterprise] may at any time decide to terminate the agreement for the service with the [Company] and engage a new third party. There is no obligation by the [Enterprise] to first offer the terms to the [Company] for any reason.

O.159

You shall be provided with the option to place a booking for the same accommodation and services at the [Venue] at the current price within [number] days of the end date that the booking is completed. This [number]-day option shall be subject to payment for the first booking and the availability of the required accommodation on the dates you wish to book. This promotional option shall only exist for a [number]-day period and shall not exist after those dates.

O.160

The [Presenter] agrees that he/she shall have no prior claim and/or option over any other further series and/or adaptation to be engaged as the main host of the [film/programme/podcast]. The [Presenter] accepts that the [Company] may offer the role to any third party.

Sponsorship

O.161

The [Sponsor] agrees and accepts that there is no option and/or right of first refusal offered and/or made by the [Enterprise] in respect of future sponsorship of the same event and/or any other matters held by the [Enterprise]. No priority and/or special arrangements will be made and the [Sponsor] will be treated like any other third party.

O.162

The [Enterprise] has agreed to grant the [Sponsor] the right to pay an additional option fee of [number/currency] to acquire an option to be the primary sponsor at the next event known as [specify] in [year]. In order to exercise the option the option fee must be paid by the [Sponsor] to the [Enterprise] by [date]. If it is not paid then the option proposal will lapse and cease to exist. If the option fee is paid then the parties will agree the new terms of sponsorship for the next event. The [Enterprise] may impose any terms it thinks fit and it is not bound to offer the same terms as the previous sponsorship agreement with the [Sponsor]. The [Sponsor] agrees that if the parties cannot agree terms for the new sponsorship that the option fee shall not be due to be repaid nor shall it be set off in any new agreement between the parties.

University, Charity and Educational

O.163

The [Institute] does not grant any option and/or rights to the [Company] which can be exercised in respect of the [Work/Service] and/or any sequel, adaptation, new edition, development and/or subsequent version of the [Work/Service] or any part.

O.164

The [Institute] shall have the exclusive option to extend this licence for [twelve] months and/or to enter into a further licence on the same terms and conditions for [two] years. The [Institute] must exercise the option by notice in writing to the [Company] by [notice date]. If the option is not exercised and/or notice received this agreement shall expire on [end date].

O.165

1.1 The [Contributor/Author] agrees that the [Institute] shall have the first right of refusal to any sequel and/or subsequent edition and/or any other version and/or development of the [Work]. This right of refusal shall not apply to any other books, articles, work and/or subjects written by and/or developed by the [Contributor/Author] at any time.

1.2 The [Contributor/Author] shall deliver the outline of the sequel and/or subsequent edition and/or any other version and/or development of the [Work] to the [Institute]. The [Institute] shall then have a period of [three] calendar months] to negotiate terms which are acceptable to the [Contributor/Author] and to conclude a new agreement or to reject the outline. At the end of the [three] calendar month period the [Contributor/Author] shall be entitled to offer the outline of the sequel and/or subsequent edition and/or any other version and/or development of the [Work] to any other third party and the first right of refusal shall be at an end.

O.166

The [Institute] agrees that it has no prior claim and/or option over the work of the [Researcher] and that he/she may offer their analysis, data, records, information and reports to any third party for publication and/or exploitation in any form.

ORDER

General Business and Commercial

O.167
Any order for [Films/Videos/Discs/Units] shall be in writing stating the title, duration, reference code, wholesale price [excluding vat] and the requested method and date of delivery and cost. Payment of the price and cost of delivery shall be made in advance and delivery shall not be arranged until all sums have been received.

O.168
There shall be no charge by the [Company] for any delivery by the [Company] of any order of [Units/Films/Discs/Products] where the total cost exceeds [number/currency] for any one order between [date] and [date] in [country].

O.169
The Company shall proceed with the [Works] in accordance with the decisions, instructions and orders given by [Name] in accordance with the Contract.

O.170
All orders are only accepted when [approved/authorised] by [Name].

O.171
The [Company] shall be under no liability in respect of orders for the service placed by or on behalf of the [Customer] until the [Company] shall have accepted such orders in writing.

O.172
The [Contractor] undertakes to provide the [Company] with any information it may request for the management of the Contract.

O.173
All proposed orders for the manufacture of the [Product/Unit] shall be submitted as a request by the [Company] in writing by email and shall be allocated a reference order code by the [Manufacturer] as confirmation of acceptance of the order.

O.174
All orders are accepted subject to the acceptance of the draft material to be used by the [Publisher]. The [Advertiser] shall supply all details of any special offer, merchandising or competition or any other material which is

associated with the [Product] for the advertisement at the time that the draft material is submitted to the [Publisher].

O.175
The [Company] shall supply the [Material] in accordance with the written orders supplied by the [Customer] and/or its agents. The [Company] shall be under no liability in respect of such orders until the [Company] shall have accepted the order in each case [in writing/by allocation of an invoice number]. The orders are placed on the express understanding that acceptance by the [Company] shall be governed by the terms of this agreement.

O.176

1.1 The [Company] reserves the right to cancel, vary, amend and/ or substitute an order at any time with the [Supplier] based on the requirements of its business.

1.2 The [Supplier] agrees to 1.1 provided that the minimum order in any one financial year shall be [number/currency].

1.3 The parties agree that where the order has been delivered then 1.1 shall not apply.

O.177
All orders accepted by the [Company] from the [Buyer] are accepted on the terms stated in this document. No other term of any nature whatsoever shall be added unless expressed in writing and signed by an authorised member of the senior management of the [Company]. No retail advisor, agent and/or otherwise of the [Company] has authority to agree to any verbal and/or written variation and/or addition to these terms in any circumstances whatsoever.

O.178
The [Supplier] shall not be responsible for all export and custom duties, insurance, taxes and/or other expenses, charges and costs that may be incurred once the [Product] is delivered to the address of the agent nominated by the [Company]. All property, rights, risks and liabilities shall only remain with the [Supplier] until delivery of the [Product] is made to the nominated agent and any payment has been received in full. Thereafter the responsibility rests with the [Company].

O.179
The [Supplier] shall deliver the [Product/Units] in accordance with the delivery dates and quantities specified in accordance with Schedule A. Thereafter the [Supplier] shall only provide the [Product] in accordance with a written request and subject to availability of stock.

O.180

It is a condition of this order that the [Products/Toys] comply and will continue to comply with all provisions relating to the design, development, manufacture, content, supply, use, packaging, health and safety, fire safety, durability and environmental sustainability of the [Products/Toys] in respect of any legislation, codes of practice, guidelines, industry practices and/or any other relevant matter which exists in and/or is in force and/or which becomes law and/or enforceable in [specify countries/Territory] during the existence of this agreement and/or until [date].

O.181

The [Products/Units/Items] and all supporting labels, packaging, content, containers literature and/or any other associated promotional material and/or service and/or competition will conform with all the stated purposes, descriptions and dimensions and shall comply with all legislation, codes of practice, guidelines and health and safety standards, assessments and tests throughout [specify countries/Territory/world] from [[date] to [date].

O.182

The [Distributor] will supply and/or grant access to any instruction manual in software form and/or in written format in respect of the [Products/Items/Units] on and/or by the date of delivery. The [Distributor] shall ensure that the supporting literature clearly sets out the purpose for which the [Products/Items/Units] are suitable and may be used and the health, safety and fire precautions that should be taken to ensure that the use of the [Products/Items/Units] will be safe and not put any customer and/or third party at risk of personal injury and/or death.

O.183

The conditions of this Purchase Order shall be incorporated in the contract between the [Supplier] and the [Distribution Company] for the supply of products and goods specified in the purchase order. These conditions shall supersede and prevail over any inconsistent terms and/or conditions contained in the [Suppliers'] original quotation and/or acceptance of order and/or as otherwise or implied by trade or custom. No addition to and/or variation of these conditions shall be binding upon the [Distribution Company] unless they are in writing and signed by a duly authorised representative of the [Distribution Company].

O.184

The [Purchaser] agrees that when placing a firm order for the [Products/Units] from the [Company] that it shall pay a deposit of [one-third] of the total price. The [Purchaser] shall ensure that all details and measurements on the order form are correct. The [Company] shall not be responsible for any incorrect details and/or measurements specified by the [Purchaser]. In any event, the Purchaser agrees that the order cannot be rectified once work has commenced [seven] days after the order form date.

O.185

1.1 The [Company] shall place an order with the [Manufacturer] for the [Products] in the form of a purchase order or similar document specifying the product name, model number, description, quantity, price, payment terms, production month and destination of the [Products].

1.2 The [Company] shall place the purchase order in 1.1 at least [four] months before the order is intended to be manufactured. The [Company] agrees that the failure of any purchase order to arrive at the [Manufacturer] shall delay production and shipment. The [Manufacturer] shall not be in any way responsible for any direct or indirect consequential losses arising from the delay and/or otherwise of the purchase order.

O.186

Such purchase orders shall be deemed to be offers by the [Company] to the [Manufacturer] to purchase the [Products] on the terms set out therein. If the [Manufacturer] accepts the order it will send on acknowledgment form of a separate sales contract.

O.187

The [Company] shall provide the following goods, materials, machinery equipment or facilities and the [Buyer/Hirer] shall purchase or hire the same as specified for delivery or use on the date(s) specified and in accordance with the payment terms.

O.188

All terms contained in this sales order shall apply to the sale of the [Goods/Products/Articles] by the [Company] to the [Buyer]. No terms stipulated by the [Buyer] shall be included in this order unless set out in writing by the [Company]. There shall be no binding agreement and/or acceptance by the [Company] of the request until the [Company], its employee and/or agent has notified the [Buyer] in writing and/or by email and/or verbally that the order is accepted and allocated a reference order code.

O.189

The [Company's] website, app, catalogues, price lists, promotional offers and advertising material are for information and guidance only. The [Company] reserves the right to change the details at any time without any notification being necessary.

O.190

If within [one] month after delivery an Order is found to be incomplete and/ or some items are defective and/or not of the standard of the sample shown to the representative of the [Company]. Then the [Supplier] agrees at its own cost and expense to deliver the missing items and/or substitute others of suitable standard which are acceptable to the [Company] within [number] days of notification by the [Company].

O.191

The [Company] agrees that where it has placed an order with the [Supplier] for delivery of [Products] and the weather conditions means that the [Products] may not sell as expected. That the [Company] shall not have any right to cancel the order and/or delay delivery which has been placed once the payment for the complete order has been made to the [Supplier].

O.192

The [Agent] agrees that the [Company] shall be entitled to accept or reject any order obtained by the [Agent] for any reason including poor credit rating of client, bad payment record, the failure to obtain suitable textiles, conflict of interest with existing client, potential and/or threatened legal proceedings.

O.193

The [Company] agrees that where the [Agent] has obtained orders from any retail store or retail outlet in the Territory introduced by the [Agent], accepted by the [Company], the [Company] agrees not to sell any of the [Products] based on the [Samples] to such retail store or retail outlet for that relevant [season] without arranging the order through the [Agent].

O.194

The [Agent] agrees to use the order forms provided by the [Company] and acknowledges that it is not permitted to offer any discount and/or other reductions in the ex-factory price and/or change any terms stated in the order forms without the prior written consent of the [Company].

O.195

1.1 The [Agent] agrees that all existing customers in the Territory notified by the [Company] shall not be contacted by the [Agent] for the purpose of obtaining orders for the [Products]. A copy of the list of existing customers is attached to and forms part of this Agreement.

1.2 The [Agent] agrees not to contact for the purpose of obtaining orders for the [Products] any persons or companies with whom the Company has business dealings at any time which it may notify to the [Agent] and which the [Company] wishes to exclude from the agreement.

1.3   It is acknowledged by the [Company] that this clause shall not apply to introductions made by the [Agent].

O.196

The [Company] agrees to send to the [Agent] at its expense order forms to be used by the [Agent] for the purpose of obtaining orders for the [Company] for its products and services. The contract shall be directly between the purchaser and the [Company] and the [Agent] shall not be a contracting party to the agreement. The [Company] agrees that it shall accept any order obtained by the [Agent] entirely at its own risk and that the [Agent] shall not be liable for the failure of any retail store and/or outlet to pay any sums that may be due to the [Company] as the result of the purchase and shipment of any order.

O.197

The [Company] agrees to:

1.1   advise the [Agent] with the reason for rejecting any particular order proposed by the [Agent]. No commission shall be due to the [Agent] for any order which is rejected by the [Company] for any reason and

1.2   inform the [Agent] in writing as soon as possible of any changes in the prices, terms and delivery conditions required by the [Company] for orders for the [Products].

O.198

The [Agent] agrees that:

1.1   The title in any [Products] ordered shall remain with the [Company] until full payment of the invoice relating to any order has been paid in full to the [Company].

1.2   The [Agent] shall not be entitled to any related commission on any order until title has been transferred to the purchaser of any order and the [Company] has been paid in full.

1.3   The [Agent] keep the [Company] informed on a regular basis and report no less than [once] a month as regard any negotiations with any third party pursuant to this agreement where the potential order is in excess of [number/currency].

1.4   The [Agent] shall not deviate from the [Company's] price list and terms of business in respect of the [Products]. The Agent shall not be entitled to offer any discount, credit, delay in payment and/or any other inducements of any nature without the prior written consent of the [Company].

O.199

The [Agent] shall offer the [Products] for sale only at the prices and upon the terms and conditions of delivery and sale as set and varied by the [Company]. The [Company] shall supply the [Agent] with the proposed purchase orders to be used by the [Agent]. The [Agent] shall immediately send details of all purchase orders concluded within [number] days. The purchase orders will not be binding on the [Agent] and/or the [Company] and shall be subject to acceptance and/or rejection by the [Company. Any order must be accepted by the [Company] and no order may be deemed to have been accepted for any reason.

O.200

The [Agent] agrees to promote, market and obtain orders for the [Garments] based on the [Collection Samples] at the prices and subject to the terms and agreements specified at any time by the [Company]. The [Agent] acknowledges and agrees to inform any retail store or outlet that wishes to order the [Garments] that they must pay the total sum in [dollars] of the ex-factory price of any item plus freight and insurance to the requested destination. Further that the [Purchaser] shall be responsible for all customs clearance, storage duty, and taxes that may be incurred. Further that the title in the [Garments] shall remain with the [Company] until full payment of the invoice has been received by the [Company].

O.201

The [Ghostwriter] shall carry out his/her duties at such times, dates and locations as the [Company] may reasonably require and observe all reasonable instructions by the [Company].

O.202

The [Contractor] shall perform all services under this Contract as an independent Contractor. Except as specified in this contract the [Company] shall not exercise any control over the employees, agents, or sub-contractors of the [Contractor] in the performance of any work, services and/or project unless specified in the agreement.

O.203

The [Writer] shall provide his/her services conscientiously and to the best of his/her skill and ability in accordance with the directions from time to time given by the [Company]. The [Writer] agrees that he/she shall work in collaboration with such persons as the [Company] may reasonably specify to the [Writer]. The [Writer] agrees to attend such meetings at the [Company] and/or elsewhere as the [Company] may reasonably require for consultations in respect of the [Work/Project]. Provided that the [Company] agrees to pay the cost in advance to the [Writer] of any travel, accommodation and/or other expenses that may arise and/or be incurred by the [Writer].

O.204
The [Writer] agrees that during the continuance of the engagement under this Agreement that the [Writer] shall carry out his obligations to the best of his/her skill and ability. The [Writer] agrees to observe all directions and restrictions as may be reasonably given to him/her by or on behalf of the [Company] for the purpose of this engagement.

O.205
The [Company] shall be entitled to cancel and/or terminate the order for the [Services] at any time by notice in writing and shall only be liable to pay the sums due to the end date specified in any such notice.

O.206
The [Distributor] agrees that it shall not without the prior written consent of the [Institute/Charity]:

1.1   reproduce, manufacture, supply and distribute [Work/Products], packaging, images, trade marks, slogans, films, marketing and/or any other material and/or online content which have not been approved by the [Institute/Charity].

1.2   alter the price list and/or change the terms of the agreement in respect of the supply of the [Work/Products] which has been approved by the [Institute/Charity].

1.3   offer any discount, credit, delay in payment or any other inducements of any nature and/or license, authorise and/or otherwise exploit any matter owned and/or controlled by the [Institute/Charity].

O.207
The [Company] shall ensure that all its employees, directors and contractors adhere to the [Work Plan] and the [Work Schedule] and any instructions and orders given by [Name] as the representative of the [Institute/Charity]. The [Company] agrees that at all times its personnel shall take account of the health and safety of the public and employees, consultants, volunteers and the students at the [Institute/Charity] and shall abide by all codes, practices, regulations and legislation that may be in force at any time.

O.208
1.1   Where the [Institute/Charity] makes an order for any service, product and/or other material it must be in accordance with its tender and

procurement policy [specify] and authorised by [department] with a requisition number.

1.2 The [Institute/Charity] does not accept responsibility for any orders placed by anyone purporting to represent the [Institute/Charity] where 1.1 has not been followed for the order to be completed and paid for by the [Institute/Charity].

ORIGIN

General Business and Commercial

O.209

The [Company] confirms and undertakes that the [Product/Material] was [grown/produced/manufactured/reproduced] in [country] between [date and [date] and identified by the following code and/or label [specify] which is on [label/can/packaging].

O.210

The [Supplier] undertakes that all ingredients, materials and packaging for any [Products] manufactured and delivered to the [Company] will be identifiable from its original source where it was grown and/or created and/or developed. That the [Supplier] shall ensure that accurate and complete records are recorded and retained for [number] years so that any defects, impurities and/or other matters can be notified to and/or investigated by the [Company].

O.211

In the event that the [Supplier] finds that any person and/or third party has misled the [Supplier] as regard the origin of the materials for any [Products], the results of any tests and/or the operation and/or standards relating to any factory conditions. The [Supplier] shall immediately notify the [Company] and provide full details of the problem in a detailed report. The [Supplier] shall cooperate fully with any investigation by the [Company] and permit unlimited access to any premises, records, documents, software, test results and/or other material which may be required by the [Company] to assess the matter and the level of risk to the public of the report.

O.212

The [Supplier] agrees and undertakes to disclose the true origins and source of the ingredients of the [Products] which it provides to the [Company] under this agreement prior to production in [country].

O.213

The [Company] is unable to verify the origin of all the sources of the material for the order and ingredients may have been blended, added, mixed and/or packaged in different countries which cannot be identified.

ORIGINALITY

Film, Television and Video

O.214

The [Author] agrees and undertakes that the [Book] entitled [specify title] ISBN [specify reference] published by [Publisher] is the sole and original work of the [Author]. That the [Film/Television/Disc/Video/Podcast, playback and streaming] rights are held and controlled by the [Author] and that no option, licence, assignment, transfer and/or charge has been and/or is due to be made to the [Publisher] and/or a third party. That the [Author] holds free and unencumbered the ownership of all [Film/Television/Disc/Video/Podcast, playback and streaming] copyright and intellectual property rights in the [Book] and/or any adaptation throughout the world including [specify countries] as at [date].

O.215

The [Company] agrees and undertakes that the [Film/Video/Podcast] entitled [specify] transmitted on [date] on [channel/website/app] and distributed by [Distributor] is owned and controlled by the [Company]. That the [Film/Television/Theatrical/DVD/Video/Download and Electronic] Rights are held and controlled by the [Company] and that no option, licence, assignment, transfer and/or charge has been and/or is due and that copyright ownership is held by [specify] and the original material was created by [specify]. That the [Company] hold the free and unencumbered [Film/Television/Theatrical/DVD/Video/Download and Electronic] Rights in the [Film/Video/Podcast] throughout the [world/universe].

O.216

The [Licensor] confirms that the [Sound Recordings] are based on music by [specify name] and lyrics by [specify name] and were produced by [Production Company]. The [Licensor] confirms and undertakes that the [Sound Recordings] are an adaptation and not original. The [Licensor] controls all rights in the [Sound Recordings] and is entitled to grant such rights as stated in this agreement to the [Licensee].

O.217

[Name] confirms and undertakes that he/she has designed, created and produced the artwork and the associated computer-generated images which are described and attached in Schedule A and that it is original and not based on the work in any form of a third party.

O.218

The [Assignor] confirms that the [Format] is an original idea created solely by the [Assignor] and has not been previously exploited in any form and is not in the public domain.

O.219

The [Producer] warrants that the [Script] is and will be original by the [Writer] and that the [Writer] was during the period the Script was written a legal resident in [country] and paid taxes in [country] and will remain so until the [Writer] has completed the [Writer's] services in connection with the [Series] up to [date].

O.220

The [Author] agrees that the [Script] shall be the original work of the [Author] and shall not contain any other published material by the [Author] and/or any other third party unless authorised in advance by the [Company].

O.221

The [Author] agrees and undertakes that the [Book] entitled [specify] ISBN [specify reference code] published by [Publisher] is the sole and original work of the [Author]. That the [Cable, Satellite, Terrestrial Television and playback and streaming and Digital Electronic] Rights are held and controlled by the [Author]. That the [Author] has not granted any option, licence, assignment, transfer and/or charge to the [Publisher] and/or any third party in respect of such [Cable, Satellite, Terrestrial Television and playback and streaming and Digital Electronic] Rights in the [Manuscript/ Book] and/or any adaptation and/or merchandising.

O.222

The [Company] agrees and undertakes that the [Film] entitled [specify] transmitted on [date] is owned and controlled by the [Company] under an [exclusive licence/assignment] agreement from [Name] who is/was the copyright owner of the original material. That the [Cable, Satellite, Digital, Terrestrial Television] Rights, the [DVD/Video] Rights and the right to any electronic, telecommunication, streaming and playback and/or merchandising rights are held and controlled by the [Company] [until [date]/forever].

O.223
[Name] agrees and undertakes that the [Script/Work/Speech] it has supplied to the [Company] is his/her original work and that no part is based on real life characters and/or plagiarised from any book, sound recording, film and/or other material whether stored in an archive and/or out of copyright or not and/or copied from any other resource, article, text and/or unpublished work of any nature in any country of the world.

General Business and Commercial

O.224
The [Employee] warrants that all contributions supplied by the [Employee] to the [Employer] shall to the best of his/her knowledge and belief be original, shall not contain anything which is an infringement of copyright or other like right or is defamatory and shall not contain any advertisement or anything of an advertising nature where the work or material is purported to be the sole creation and work of the [Employee]. Where any work or material is requested by the [Employer], based or derived from material supplied or referred to by the [Employer], then this clause shall not apply.

O.225
Any commercial or non-commercial exploitation of any material or work created by the [Employee] during the course of this employment shall be entirely at the risk and cost of the [Employer] and the [Employer] shall not be entitled to make any claim of any nature against the [Employee]. There is no undertaking of originality provided by the [Employee] to the [Employer] of any nature.

O.226
The [Executive] shall not authorise the reproduction for commercial exploitation and/or self-promotion any work and/or material created during the course of this agreement without the prior consent of [Name/Job Title].

O.227
The [Executive] provides no undertaking as to the originality, copyright and/or content of the material, work and/or any service which is to be created by him/her and/or any other persons under his/her authority during the existence of this agreement. All material, work and services are used and exploited at the sole risk and cost of the [Company]. The name and status of the [Executive] shall only be acknowledged and/or used by the [Company] if he/she approves the item in advance and provides his consent. No material, work and/or service shall be used by the [Company] at any time in a manner which demeans the reputation of the [Executive], is derogatory of the [Executive] and/or others. Nor shall the [Company] be entitled to

attribute the material, work and/or services of the [Executive] to some other person and substitute their name as author and/or the creator of the work, material and/or service.

O.228

The [Employee] provides no undertaking as to the originality of their work, material and/or otherwise at any time during the course of their employment. The [Company] agrees and undertakes that it will use any such work and material entirely at its own cost and risk and waives any right and agrees it shall have no right to seek an indemnity, claim, costs, expenses and/or otherwise against the [Employee].

O.229

The [Company] agrees and acknowledges that where the [Employee] creates, develops, invents and/or designs a new and original work, service and/or product and/or process and/or method and/or means of exploitation in any media outside of work hours at the [Company]. That the [Company] shall have no claim and/or right to any part unless it has been derived and/or based on access by the [Employee] to materials, confidential information, reports and data held and/or stored and/or owned and/or controlled by the [Company].

O.230

The [Originator] warrants for the benefit of the [Company] that the [Concept] is original and confidential to the [Originator] and has not been disclosed to any other party.

O.231

The [Originator] warrants that he is the original creator and sole owner of or controls all copyright, design rights and any other rights in the product of his/her services to the [Company] under this agreement, excluding any information, data and/or material supplied by and/or included at the request of the [Company].

O.232

The [Work] is original to the [Assignor] and that it does not and will not infringe the copyright and/or any other rights of any third party.

O.233

The [Author] warrants that the [Work] is an original [Artwork/Image/Logo/Sound Recording/Video] and that the [Author] is the owner of the copyright and all other intellectual property rights which may exist. The [Author] has not granted, transferred and/or assigned any rights and/or any part to any third party which may and/or will affect the terms of this agreement.

1382

O.234

The [Assignor] warrants that he/she is ordinarily resident in the [United Kingdom/country] and that he/she holds a valid passport dated [specify] for [country]. That the [Software] has been created and developed by the [Assignor] and is his/her own original work and creation and is not adapted from material owned by any third party.

O.235

The design shall not be treated as original in respect of the design right in original designs if it is a commonplace in the design field in question at the time of its creation.

O.236

The [Company] can provide copies of the agreements with the persons who originally designed, developed, created and produced the [Image/Text/Sound Recording/Film/Product] in [format] to the [Licensee] upon request provided that the financial details are deleted. In the event that the [Licensee] is subject to any claim and/or action by a third party in respect of the originality of the [Image/Text/Sound Recording/Film/Product] then the [Company] shall seek to provide such assistance as may be necessary to defend a claim for infringement of copyright and/or passing off at the [Company's] own cost.

Internet, Websites and Apps

O.237

The [Designer] warrants that the entire product of its services shall be original and that the performance of the obligations by the [Designer] under this agreement shall not contravene any rights of any third party. That where the [Material] to be included in the [website/app/podcast] is not the original work of the [Designer] that it shall be set out in detail in the report specifying the type of material, the name of the company, the nature of their rights and the expected cost of the use of their material and any credit and/or other conditions that may be required to be fulfilled.

O.238

[Name] undertakes that all the product of his/her services under this agreement shall be original and will not infringe the copyright and/or any other intellectual property and/or computer software and/or electronic and/or telecommunication rights of any third party. The [Company] agrees that this undertaking shall not apply after [date] nor shall it apply to any content and/or material which the [Company] has requested be incorporated and/or used and/or adapted and/or which is believed to be in the public domain and/.or used under licence from a third party.

O.239

There is no provision as to the originality of material on this [Website/App/Podcast] and you must use your own endeavours to ensure that you do not infringe and/or breach the copyright, designs, graphics, trademarks, service marks, logo, moral rights and/or any other copyright, intellectual property rights, licences and/or contractual obligations of any third party rights. There is no automatic right to reproduce, copy, adapt and/or exploit material due to the fact it is displayed on this [Website/App/Podcast].

O.240

All the product of the work of the [Designer] for the [Website/App/Brand] is based upon and/or derived from ideas and concepts requested and provided by the [Client] and is not the original idea of the [Designer]. There are no undertakings made by the [Designer] as to originality and/or any indemnity provided regarding the threat of legal action by a third party.

O.241

Where you are sending original material to the [Website/App/Forum] you are strongly advised to appreciate that the [Company] cannot be liable for any infringement of copyright and/or any other intellectual property rights that may arise from your use of the [Website/App/Forum] and/or the actions of third parties. You are personally liable for the consequences of any material which you send and/or display on the [Website/App/Forum] including allegations from third parties of defamation, harassment, the recording of criminal offences, committing criminal acts and/or offences and/or any other legal matter whether action can be taken in [country] or elsewhere.

O.242

1.1 [Name] created, designed and developed the [App] based on the content and background material supplied by the [Company] and the software known as [specify].

1.2 [Name] commissioned artwork, graphics and computer generated moving images, sound recording and film from [specify].

1.3 [Name] has delivered the completed [App] in [format] to the [Company].

1.4 Both [Name] and [specify] agree to assign all copyright, computer software rights and/or any other intellectual property rights in each and every part of the material and data they have created in 1.1 and 1.2 to the [Company] in consideration of payment for the completion of their work.

1.5 [Name] and [specify] provide no undertakings as to originality to the [Company].

O.243

[Name] is the original creator of the [Characters] which were first published in [Book] in [year]. [Name] owns all the computer software and electronic and telecommunication game rights in the [Characters] and all associated trade marks which are described in schedule A which is attached to and forms part of this agreement.

O.244

[Name] provides no undertaking and/or warranties regarding the originality of any material supplied to the [Company] by [Name] under this agreement. The artwork and computer-generated images are based on ideas and concepts and instructions provided by the [Company] and details from the [Company] archive. This commission is not intended as a project for original work but an adaptation of existing material.

Merchandising and Distribution

O.245

The [Company] confirms and undertakes that:

1.1 [Name] was the original creator of [Product and Character] and by an assignment agreement dated [specify date] assigned all rights in all media throughout the world to the [Company] which now owns and controls all intellectual property rights, design rights, trade marks, logos and images in the [Product and Character], the domain name [specify] and all the packaging, material and property associated with and/or based upon it.

1.2 That no option, licence, assignment, transfer and/or charge has been and/or is due to be made and that the [Company] holds free and unencumbered all rights in all media in the [Product and Character], the domain name [specify] and all the packaging, material and property associated with and/or based upon it throughout the [world/universe].

O.246

[Name] warrants to the [Company] that the [Concept] is original and confidential to [Name] only and has not been disclosed to any other third party except to the [Company] and its advisers. Further, that the [Concept] has not been previously licensed, assigned, or exploited in any form in any part of the world and is not in the public domain and that the [Concept] was created by [Name] and all the rights as at [date] are held by [Name].

O.247

The [Assignor] undertakes and agrees that it is the original creator and sole owner of all copyright, intellectual property rights and trade marks in the [Work] which are [assigned/granted] under this Agreement.

O.248

The [Licensor] confirms that he/she is the original creator and sole owner and controls all copyright, design rights, trade marks, logos, character names and any other intellectual property and computer software rights in the [Board Game] and the [Prototype] which are granted to the [Company] under this agreement.

O.249

The [Sub-Licensee] shall not be entitled to any legal claim, damages, losses, costs and/or expenses against the [Licensor] and/or the [Licensee] in the event that it is found that the material for the [Work/Product] is not original at any time and the sub-licence must therefore be terminated. The [Sub-Licensee] agrees to accept the risk and those specific terms.

O.250

[Name] owns and controls all rights in the physical material of the [Work] but is not the author. [Name] owns the physical material as a result of a legal inheritance from the estate of [specify person] who died on [date]. There is no ownership of copyright and/or intellectual property in the [Work] by [Name] as those rights were assigned to [specify company/library]. No assurances and/or undertakings can be provided as to the originality of the [Work] by the deceased author. The supply of copies of the material for the {Project] for private research is not a licence for distribution and/or exploitation in any format and/or by any means.

O.251

The [Manufacturer] agrees and undertakes not to include and/or reproduce any material in the [Products], packaging and other marketing for the [Distributor] which it knows is not original and/or belongs to third party and has not been licensed for reproduction and authorised by the [Distributor].

Publishing

O.252

The [Author] warrants that the [Work] is the [Author's] own original material created by his/her own skill and effort except for material in the public domain and such excerpts from other third parties that may be included with the written permission of the copyright owners as stated in the manuscript.

O.253

The [Writer[agrees and undertakes that he/she has not granted and will not grant and/or assign any rights in the [Work] which will conflict with and/or prejudice the rights granted to the [Company] under this agreement. The [Writer] further agrees and undertakes that the [Work] is original and is not based on and/or derived from any rights and/or material owned by a third party and/or for which there is no known author.

O.254
The [Author] warrants that the [Work] shall be the original work of the [Author] and does not and will not infringe the copyright or any other rights of any third party in respect of the rights granted under this agreement.

O.255
The [Author] warrants that the [Work] has not been previously published or otherwise exploited in any form in the Territory.

O.256
The [Author] undertakes to the [Distributor] that he/she owns and controls all rights in the [Work] and that it has not been supplied, published, distributed and/or sold in any format in any media as at [date]. Except for those matters disclosed in Schedule A which is part of this agreement.

O.257
The [Assignor] agrees and undertakes that the [Work] is his/her own unpublished original [Work].

O.258
The Author confirms that the [Work] is the [Author's] own work except for such material as in the public domain and such extracts from other material for which the written consent of the copyright owner has been provided to the [Author] for inclusion in the [Work].

O.259
The [Works] shall be original to the [Writer] except where it incorporates any material supplied or requested by the [Company].

O.260
The [Author] confirms that the Synopsis and the [Work] are and shall be the original work of the [Author] and do not and will not infringe the copyright or any other rights of any third party in respect of the rights granted under this agreement.

O.261
The [Author] confirms that to the best of his/her knowledge and belief that all statements purporting to be facts are true and that any instructions, recipes, games, questions, advice and/or recommendations have been tested and

assessed as safe by the [Author] and that they are accurate and not likely to cause any loss, damage, personal injury and/or death.

O.262

The [Author] confirms that the [Synopsis] and the [Work] shall be the original work of the [Author] and do not and will not infringe the copyright, design rights, moral rights, trade or service marks, logos or other intellectual property rights of any third party in respect of the rights granted by the [Author] under this agreement.

O.263

The [Author] confirms that the [Work] is the original creation of the skill and effort of the [Author] and does not infringe the copyright or any other right of any third party in the following countries [specify]. Except the following material which is owned or controlled by a third party which has been included in the [Work] and for which the following consent has been obtained. Details of each licence including material supplied, consent provided and the cost are set out in Appendix A which forms part of this agreement.

O.264

Where the [Publisher] arranges for a cover and/or other design to be created and/or developed by an employee and/or consultant for the [Work]. The [Publisher] agrees that any material submitted for approval by the [Author] shall be original and new and that the copyright shall be assigned to the [Publisher/Author].

O.265

There is no undertaking as to originality of any nature by the [Author]. The [Work] has been commissioned by the [Distributor] as a sequel to an original novel by [Name] which was published in [year]. The characters and locations were in the original novel. The [Author] is creating and writing a fictional sequel to the original publication.

Services

O.266

The [Contributor] confirms that he/she is and will be the sole owner and originator of the product of his/her services performed under this agreement unless based on or incorporating material specifically included at the request of the [Company]. No undertaking is however provided to the [Company] regarding the originality of the result of any work which may be completed and/or delivered by [Contributor].

O.267

[Name] shall provide his/her services to [Company] at [address] from [date] to [date] in accordance with the following description [specify]. There is no undertaking or confirmation that the duties provided or any work created are original, new or otherwise.

O.268

The [Actor] agrees that the product of his/her services shall be original and will not infringe the copyright or any other rights of any third party throughout the Territory except where any material, script, changes, gesture, words, films, recordings, images and/or characters are supplied by the [Agent] and/or the [Company] and/or any other third party involved in the [Project/Tour/Film].

O.269

The [Sportsperson] confirms that all the product of his/her services shall be original except where work is based on ideas and/or concepts and/or scripts, material and directions and guidance of the [Distributor] and/or any other nominated person and/or third party instructed by the [Distributor].

O.270

[Name] provides no undertaking as to the originality of the product of the work under this agreement and the [Company] shall use any material at its own cost, risk and expense and shall not be entitled to seek to be indemnified by [Name]. In the event that for any reason [Name] is held liable there shall be a limit of [number/currency] in total under this agreement.

O.271

The [Consultant] undertakes that:

1.1 all information, advice and material provided to the [Company] by the [Consultant] shall to the best of his/her knowledge and belief be true and accurate, and original. Where material is not original the source will be clearly identified and credited in any report.

1.2 where requested by the [Company] and/or its legal advisors the [Consultant] will assist in providing supporting documentation to validate the matters upon which the [Consultant] has advised.

O.272

[Name] undertakes that:

1.1 all the product of his/her services under this agreement shall be original; and

1389

1.2 will not infringe the intellectual property rights, domain names, trade marks, service marks, logos, computer software, database rights, confidential information, patents, copyright, contracts and/or any other rights of any third party except as stated in 1.3.

1.3 sub-clause 1.2 shall not apply to work and material supplied by [Name] which incorporates material of any third party which is included at the [Company's] request and/or for which [Name] has credited and acknowledged the resource and/or is genuinely believed to be out of copyright and/or to be an orphan work and/or to be in the public domain.

O.273

The [Company] acknowledges that the [Distributor] is not the original creator of the [Service/Work] and makes no undertaking to that effect.

O.274

1.1 [Name] confirms that he/she inherited the estate of [specify] under a will for which probate was granted on [date] in [country]. That [specify name of deceased] was the original creator of the [Work/Service] and that it is now owned and/or controlled by [Name]. Copies of the supporting documents for this fact are set out in Appendix A.

1.2 That the [Work/Service] has been adapted, developed and translated and that the main contributors to new original material for the [Work/Service] are [specify names of contributors and role].

1.3 That no undertakings are provided to the [Company] by [Name] in respect of originality and/or any indemnity provided regarding any claim and/or legal action that may arise in any civil and/or criminal proceedings in 1.1 and 1.2 above.

Sponsorship

O.275

The [Sponsor] agrees and undertakes to the [Company] that all trade marks, logos, slogans, artwork, products, services and other material provided by the [Sponsor] under this agreement shall be owned and/or controlled by the [Sponsor]. That if required by the [Company] the [Sponsor] shall be able to prove the originality and authorship of any part of such material at the [Sponsor's] cost and expense.

O.276

The [Sponsor] agrees and undertakes to the [Company] that as at [date] there are no pending legal proceedings and/or disputes in respect of the originality and/or content and/or packaging of the material specified in Schedule A which is to be supplied by the [Sponsor] to the [Company] under this agreement.

O.277
The [Company] shall ensure that they own and/or control and/or are licensed to use any material which is to be printed in the [Brochure] and/or displayed on the [Website] and/or are reproduced in respect of any merchandising. No claim shall be made as to copyright ownership by the [Company] of material which originated from any third party unless there is a written agreement to support that assertion.

O.278
The [Sponsor] undertakes that the [Logo] is the original work of [Name] and that all rights in all media in all countries have been assigned to the [Sponsor].

O.279
The [Sponsor] confirms that all products, services, names, logos, images, films, advertisements, banners and other material to be distributed and/or displayed at the [Event] by the [Sponsor] and/or any agent acting on its behalf shall either be original material owned by the [Sponsor] and/or supplied by a third party under an existing licence agreement. In any event all such material must be approved in advance by the [Company] and the [Sponsor] must submit exact samples for inspection at the [Sponsors'] cost.

O.280
The [Company] confirms that the crest design is registered with [specify organisation] and owned by [specify Name]. That [Name] has granted authority to the [Company] and its sub-licensees and distributors to use the crest in association with the product specified in appendix A and on the packaging and in the promotional material. The crest must be reproduced exactly in the design, format and layout that it is supplied and must not be adapted and/or distorted and/or reproduced in any manner which is likely to impact on the reputation of the crest and/or [Name].

University, Charity and Educational

O.281
The [Contributor/Author] agrees and undertakes that:

1.1 the [Contributor/Author] is a national of [country] and resides in [country] and holds a passport dated [specify].

1.2 The [Contributor/Author] is the original author and developed, devised, wrote and designed the [Work] and owns all the rights and interest. That none have been licensed and/or assigned to any third party as at [date].

1.3 The [Contributor/Author] agrees and undertakes that the [Work] has not and will not infringe the copyright, design rights, future design rights, computer software rights, trade marks, database rights, confidential information, patents and/or any other intellectual property rights of any third party at any time in any country throughout the world.

O.282

The [Consultant] confirms that all the product of her/his services shall be original except where:

1.1 work completed at the request of the [Institute/Charity]; and/or

1.2 is subject to the direction and instructions of a third party whom the [Institute/Charity] has nominated to lead and/or manage any [Project]; and/or

1.3 the work is based on pre-existing material which has been published and/or peer reviewed; and/or

1.4 where material is not original and the [Consultant] has clearly identified and acknowledged the source and/or stated that its authorship cannot be traced and/or obtained consent from the third party author and/or contributor to waive their moral rights to be identified.

O.283

The [Author] agrees and undertakes that the [Work/Film] are and/or shall be the original work of the [Author] and do not and will not infringe the copyright or any other rights of any third party in respect of the rights granted under this agreement to the [Institute/Charity].

OUTER SPACE

General Business and Commercial

O.284

The [Licensee] confirms that all necessary licences, consents and authority has and/or will be obtained from any national, government, military, space, peacekeeping, international and/or Commonwealth and/or European body that may be necessary and/or required to provide the licence in respect of the [Project] in [Outer Space].

O.285
'The Territory' shall mean the earth including all land, sea and air and outer space but exclude all satellites and other man-made objects in geostationary orbits.

O.286
'The Territory' shall include all land, man-made islands, sea, sky, beneath the land and below the sea, and throughout the universe, outer space and the galaxy, stars, planets and black holes without limit of time and/or space.

O.287

1.1 This agreement shall not apply to any planet other than Earth and all other planets, moons and outer space which form part of the universe shall be excluded.

1.2 The planet Earth shall include the sea, land, sub-terrain and air and up to a distance of [number] metres above the Earth and shall also include oil rigs, satellites, aeroplanes, helicopters but not rockets and/or space stations for transportation and/or orbit.

O.288
'The Territory' shall be defined as:

1.1 The solar system and include all planets, dwarf planets, celestial bodies, moons, sun; and

1.2 The planets: Mercury, Venus, Earth, Mars, Jupiter, Saturn, Uranus, Neptune; and

1.3 The dwarf planets: Pluto, Ceres, Makemake, Haumea, Eris; and

1.4 Charon, Kuiper Belt objects and meteors, meteorites, asteroids, comets and small solar system bodies.

1.5 It shall exclude orbiting objects, satellites, stations, debris and other material which is created on Earth and sent to that location.

P

PARTIES TO AGREEMENT

General Business and Commercial

P.001
AN AGREEMENT made the [day] of [month] [year]

BETWEEN:

[full registered Company Name] whose registered office is situated at [registered address] in [country] which shall be referred to as 'the Company' which expression shall include all assigns, assignees, licensees and successors in title of the Company;

and

[Name/Company] whose address is [home/business address] in [country] who shall be referred to as 'the Consultant').

P.002
This Agreement is dated: [date].

Between:

[Name of Company] a company incorporated in [country] under number [specify registration reference] having its registered office at [address] which shall be referred to as 'the Company A' in this agreement

and

[Name of Company] a company incorporated in [country] under number [specify registration reference] having its registered office at [address] which shall be referred to as 'the Company B' in this agreement.

P.003
Agreement signed and executed on: [date].

Parties to agreement:

1.1   [Name of Company] registered in [country] as [reference] whose principal place of business is at [address] which for the purposes of this agreement shall be called 'the Company';

and

1.2   The [Contributors] whose names and addresses are set out in Schedule A and form part of this agreement who for the purposes of this agreement are called 'the Contributors'.

P.004

Agreement dated: [specify date].

PARTIES TO THIS AGREEMENT:

[Name of Company] to be referred to as 'the Licensor' of [address]

and

[Name of Distributor] to be referred to as 'the Distributor' which has its head office at [address].

P.005

Title of the agreement: [Merchandising Agreement/Television and Media Licence/other].

AN AGREEMENT dated: [date].

BETWEEN:

[Name of Author/Creator] of [address] to be known as 'the Licensor' in this agreement;

and

[Name of Company] of [address] to be known as 'the Licensee' in this agreement).

P.006

Date of Licence: [date].

Agreement between the following parties:

[Name of photographer] of [address] referred to as 'the Licensor'

and

[Name of agency] of [main business address] referred to as 'the Licensee'.

The parties have agreed the following terms: [specify]

P.007

'The Organiser' shall be: [Name/Company].

'The Exhibitor' shall mean the company, partnership or business in whose name the application form has been signed.

P.008

An Agreement concluded on: [date].

Parties to the Agreement are as follows:

1   [Company] of [address] ('the Company') which expression shall include its successors in title and assignees;

    and

2   [Writer/Contributor] c/o [Agent's Name] of [address] ('the Writer/ Contributor') which expression shall include his/her successors in title and assignees.

P.009

Date of this agreement: [date].

Between:

1   The [Developer/Designer]: [Company Name] of [address of business/ registered address] which shall be referred to as 'the Developer/ Designer' and

2   The Commissioning Company: [Charity/Enterprise] of [address of charity/registered address] which shall be referred to as 'the Commissioning Company'.

[Introduction summary/Preamble]

This agreement relates to the commissioning of a new website and app by [the Commissioning Company] which is to be designed, created and produced by the [Developer/Designer] in accordance with the terms of this agreement and the Budget.

P.010

AN AGREEMENT dated: [–].

BETWEEN:

1   [Name] registered in [country/address] whose principal place of business is at [address] (to be known as 'the Supplier'); and

2   [Name] registered in [country/address] whose principal place of business is at [address] (to be known as 'the Enterprise').

P.011

Title of the agreement: [describe type of agreement].

BETWEEN:

1   [Name of company] ('the Company') of [registered/main business address]; and

2   [Name] ('the Contributor') of [address].

P.012

MEMORANDUM OF AGREEMENT made this [date] [month] [year]

BETWEEN:

[Name of Authors] [addresses] (hereinafter called 'The Authors') of the one part and shall include the [Authors] executors, personal representatives, administrators and assignees.

and

[Name of Company] [address] (hereinafter called 'The Publishers' of the other part) for themselves, and their respective executors, administrators and assignees and/or successors in title in whole or in part.

P.013

Publishing Agreement dated: [day/month/year].

[Author] of [address] (who shall be referred to as 'the Author' throughout this Agreement) which shall be defined to include the Authors' executors, personal representatives, administrators and assignees

AND

[Publishing Company] trading as [specify trading name] registered number [reference] whose registered office is [address] (which shall be referred to as 'the Publishers' throughout this Agreement) which shall be defined to include the following agreed assignees who form part of the [Name Group] [registered number] of [address]: the parent company [name/address] and the following subsidiary: [specify names/addresses].

P.014

Agreement dated: [date].

[Full legal name] who writes under the pseudonym of [specify name] of [address] (who shall be referred to as 'the Writer') which shall be defined to include the Writer's executors, personal representatives, and administrators of the one part [but excluding all other assignees].

AND

[Registered name of company] [registered reference] registered in [country] whose registered office is at [address] which trades under the name [specify trading name] (which shall be referred to as 'the Distributors' throughout this agreement) and shall not include and shall specifically exclude all other assignees, successors in title and/or business, parent and/or subsidiary and/or associate and/or affiliate companies and/or entities and/or any other joint venture partners and/or collaborators.

P.015
The [Publishers] shall not have the right to assign, transfer and/or license and/or delegate the whole of this agreement and/or any parts and/or the rights and/or obligations under this agreement to any other company, body and person within the [Group], consortium, joint venture partnership and/or any other third party of any nature except the named companies above who are the agreed assignees of the [Publishers].

P.016
THIS AGREEMENT is dated [date] and between [Name of Group] a corporation of [region/county/area] and its successors in title and/or assignees in whole and/or part (the 'Company') and [Name] a person who resides at [address/state/country] (the 'Employee').

P.017
[Name] to be called ('the Employee/Applicant') for the purposes of this agreement and

[Status/Name] who is an Officer of the State for [Government Agency] referred to as 'the Government Agency' which is the authorised signatory and representative of [specify government] in [country] as of [date].

P.018
[Agreement/Contract] date: [date].

[description and title of agreement/reference].

[Name] (called 'the Speaker') represented by the [specify representative person/company] which is authorised by [Name] to sign this [Agreement/Contract] on their behalf.

and

[Name of Consortium] (called 'the Consortium') which has been set up in [address/state/country] represented by [Name of advisors] who act as their advisors and are authorised on behalf of the Consortium to sign this [Agreement/Contract] on their behalf.

P.019

[Subject] Agreement dated [day/month/year].

Between the following parties:

1   [Full Name of Institute] whose main address is [address]

      and

2   [Full Name of Contributor] who resides at [address].

P.020

THIS AGREEMENT is made: [date]

      BETWEEN:

      [The Supplier] a UK private limited company registered with [Companies House/other] company registration no. [reference number] having its registered office at [address] and its place of business at [address] (hereinafter called 'The Supplier').

      AND

      [The Purchaser] a company known as [name of company/reference] which is a subsidiary of the Parent Company [name of parent company] (hereinafter called 'The Purchaser'). The terms of this agreement apply to the subsidiary and the parent company jointly and severally.

P.021

AN AGREEMENT made the [number] day of [month] [year].

BETWEEN:

The parties to this agreement are as follows:

(1)   [Name] of [address] referred to as 'Member A'.

(2)   [Name] of [address] referred to as 'Member B'.

(3)   [Name] of [address] referred to as 'Member C'.

P.022

A licence and distribution agreement for a product

Date of agreement: [date].

Agreement between:

[Name of Company] a private limited company registered under the Laws of [England/other], Company Registration No. [reference] having its registered office at [address] (hereinafter referred to as "the Licensor'), on behalf of themselves, their successors in business and title on the one part,

AND

[Name of Enterprise] of [address] which shall not include any successors in business and title on the other part (hereinafter referred to as 'the Licensee').

P.023
Agency Agreement dated: [date].

The contracting parties to this agreement are as follows:

1   [Name] of [address] (referred to as 'the Actor')

    AND

2   [Company] whose main place of business is [address] (referred to as 'the Agent').

P.024
AN AGREEMENT made the [–] day of [month] 20 [–].

BETWEEN:

[Name] of [address] (to be known as 'the Author')

AND

[Company] of [address] a company registered under the Laws of [specify] (to be known as 'the Publisher') in this Agreement such expressions to include the Publishers' successors in business and title).

P.025
PUBLISHING AGREEMENT dated: [date].

BETWEEN:

[Name] and [Name] both of [address] (hereinafter jointly and severally called 'the Authors' which shall include the Author's executors, personal representatives, administrators and assigns) of the one part

AND

[Company] incorporated in [specify] Registration No. [specify] whose registered office is at [address] (hereinafter called 'the Publishers' which expression shall include the Publishers' permitted assignees as defined below at clause [–]) on the other part on behalf of the parent company [Parent Company] incorporated in [specify] Registration No. [–] whose registered office is at [address].

P.026

Agreement date: [specify].
This Agreement is between the following parties and no other and does not apply to any estate, beneficiary, assignee, administrators and/or other third parties:

[Personal Name] currently living at [address] in [country] and also known as [professional name] and

[The Agent] which operates under the trading name [specify] and is registered as a company in [country] under the name [specify] of [address].

P.027

Terms of proposed Agreement subject to contract dated: [date]

Party 1.   [The Charity] otherwise known as [specify name] which is registered with the [specify organisation] as reference [specify registered number] whose head office is based at [address].

Party 2.   [The Sponsor] which trades under the [Brand Name] and is registered as an [incorporated company] in [specify name] in [country] registration reference [specify registered number].

Party 3.   [The Artist] [who is not a signatory to this Agreement and] is represented by the [Agent] who is authorised to act on behalf of the Artist whose address is [specify address of agent] and operates under licence from [specify organisation] and is registered as a business with [specify organisation/government body] as [specify reference].

P.028

These terms and conditions which are proposed are for discussion only and may be changed by [Name] at any time. It is not intended that there should be any binding pre-contract and/or verbal terms and conditions and all matters are subject to a final written agreement. If no agreement is concluded then [Name] has made no commitment and you should not rely on pre-contract discussions to incur costs and expenses and/or to make any commitment to a third party.

P.029
Buy-out assignment document dated: [date].

Agreement between a contributor and an App company for the buy-out of all rights in a sound recording.

Contributor: [name/address].

App Company: [registered name/address] which trades as: [trading name].

P.030
Sponsorship agreement dated: [date].

Parties:

1   The Sponsor: [name/address]. [to be called 'the Sponsor' in this agreement].

2   The Charity: [name/address]. [to be called 'the Charity' in this agreement].

This agreement shall not include successors in title, business and/or assignees. It is restricted to the named parties. If any changes are required then it must be approved by both parties.

P.031
Assignment document: [date].

This agreement was signed by both parties on [date].

This agreement begins on [date/time].

1   The Assignor A in this agreement shall be [name/address].

2   The Assignee B in this agreement shall be [name/address].

P.032
Confidentiality agreement: [date].

Agreement between the parties:

[Name] who currently resides at [address] called 'the Originator' in this document

AND

[Company] whose primary business is in [country] and whose main address is [address] called 'the Company'. It shall not include any successors in title and/or other assignees.

P.033

Collaboration agreement: [date]

Members of the collaboration:

1   [Institute] [address] referred to as [specify reference name].

2   [Charity] [address] referred to as ['Charity A'].

3   [Sponsor] [address] referred to as ['Sponsor B'].

4   [Artist] [address] referred to as ['the Artist'].

PARTNERSHIP

General Business and Commercial

P.034

The Business Partnership shall mean [name of business] trading as [trading name] at [address] which is authorised to carry on a business as [specify subject/reference/licence].

There are [number] partners listed as follows: [list partners full name/address].

P.035

It is a fundamental term of the Business Partnership that each of the partners agree to the following terms:

1.1   That each partner shares responsibility for the Business Partnership with all the other partners.

1.2   That as at [date] no partners are classified as limited partners and/or general partners.

1.3   That as at [date] all partners are individuals and not limited companies.

1.4   That each partner shares responsibility to pay all the bills which are not paid for by the Business Partnership.

1.5   That each partner is responsible equally for any debts and/or obligations until the partnership is registered with [specify organisation/government body].

1.6   That each partner shall be liable for and pay their own tax on their share of the Business Partnership. That this sum shall not be recouped and/or due from the Business Partnership.

P.036

'The Partner A' shall be the limited company known as [specify name of company] which was registered with [specify organisation/government body] on [date] and has the registration number: [reference code].

P.037

1.1 'The Nominated Partner' of the Business Partnership shall be [name of person/limited company].

1.2 The Nominated Partner agrees and undertakes to manage the accounts, tax returns and business records of the Business Partnership from [date] for the duration of the Business Partnership until it is closed and/or dissolved and/or a new nominated partner is substituted.

P.038

'The Limited Partnership' shall be defined as:

1.1 [Name of Business]

1.2 Registered address: [specify address].

1.3 The Partners set out below who all own an equal share: [list name/ address].

1.4 Registered with: [Companies House/organisation/government body] as at [date] with the reference: [specify registration number].

P.039

'The Limited Liability Partnership' shall be defined as:

1.1 [Name of Business].

1.2 Registered address: [specify address].

1.3 The Partners set out below:

   a   Partner A: [name/address] Status: no limit on liability. General Partner.

   b   Partner B: [name/address] Status: no limit on liability. General Partner.

   c   Partner C. [name/address] Status: limit on liability. Limited Partner.

      Partner C contributed fixed sums and/or property to business when it was set up of: [specify details including transaction date].

      Partner C is only liable to the amount contributed of: [number/ currency].

Partner C cannot manage the business.

Partner C cannot remove the original contribution of [number/ currency].

1.4 Registered with: [Companies House/organisation/government body] as at [date] with the reference: [specify registration number].

P.040

'The Limited Partner T' shall mean [name/address] who shall have limited liability in respect of the Business Partnership D. [Name] contributed fixed sums and/or property to the Business Partnership D when it was first set up of: [specify details including transaction date]. [Name is only liable to the amount contributed of: [number/currency]. No interest shall be added to this sum. [Name] cannot manage the Business Partnership D. [Name] shall not have the right to remove the original contribution of [number/ currency].

P.041

'The General Partner F' shall be defined as [name/address] who shall be:

1.1 Equally liable with the other partners [none of whom are limited partners] for any debts which the Business Partnership S cannot pay.

1.2 Entitled to control and manage the business known as [specify name] of the Business Partnership S with the other general partners.

1.3 Entitled to make decisions, commitments and enter into agreements which are binding on the Business Partnership S.

1.4 Entitled to make applications to third parties to register for any reason and/or to obtain a licence and/or to carry our compliance matters for planning, building control, health and safety and/or to register and/or report any matters for accounting, tax and/or insurance reasons.

1.5 Entitled to act for the Business Partnership S if it is to be closed, wound up and/or dissolved for any reason and/or in any other legal matter.

P.042

'The General Partner H' shall be the limited company: [registered name of company] registration number: [specify] registered with [organisation/ government body]. The contact person at the limited company shall be [name/role].

P.043

'The Limited Partnership' shall be as follows:

1.1 Registered address: [specify address].

1.2   Registered Name: [specify business name registered].

1.3   Type of business activity: [specify scope and description].

1.4   Details of the Partners:

   A   Partner A: [name] [address] Limited Liability. Sum contributed by Partner A: [number/currency].

   B   Partner B: [name] [address] Limited Liability. Sum contributed by Partner B: [number/currency].

   C   Partner C: [name] [address] Limited Liability. Sum contributed by Partner C: [number/currency].

   D   Partner D: [name] [address] Limited Liability. Sum contributed by Partner D: [number/currency].

P.044
The [Partners] each agree and undertake that they shall:

1.1   Use their [best/reasonable] endeavours to ensure the successful operation of the Partnership and at all times shall conduct themselves in accordance with the laws of [country] and comply with any codes and/or guidelines of [organisation] which may be issued during the Partnership [and for additional period].

1.2   That in all transactions and/or business dealings of any nature affecting the Partnership, all [Partners] shall disclose to all the other [Partners] any matter which may potentially prejudice and/or conflict with the rights, interests and/or business of the Partnership.

P.045
'The Partnership' shall mean the partnership created by this Deed dated: [date].

P.046
No other partners may be added to this Partnership without the express prior written approval of all the current Partners listed in Schedule A.

P.047
This Agreement shall not constitute and/or to be deemed to imply a legal partnership between the parties. Nor shall either party be deemed to be an agent of the other for any purpose whatsoever. Neither party shall have any right and/or authority to represent that they can provide any consent on behalf of the other party. Neither party has any right to enter into any agreement which would bind both parties.

P.048

There is no partnership created between the parties to this agreement. Both parties remain separate entities. There is no delegated authority to the other party. There is no intention to create a partnership between the parties and none shall be construed.

P.049

This Agreement has not and will not create any relationship and/or connection and/or association between the parties which is and/or might be deemed to be a partnership, joint venture, agency, fiduciary and/or employment relationship between the parties. No such relationship between the parties was intended by this Agreement either between themselves and/or in respect of the [Film/Work/Services].

P.050

Nothing in this Agreement shall be deemed to create any joint venture, partnership and/or agency relationship between any of the parties. None of the parties shall hold itself out in its advertising, promotional and social media material and/or its activities and/or otherwise in any manner which would indicate and/or imply any such relationship with the other.

P.051

This Agreement shall not be deemed to constitute a partnership or joint venture or contract of employment between the parties.

P.052

This Agreement shall not be deemed to create any partnership or employment relationship between the parties.

P.053

No partner shall have any personal financial interest in the [Project/Services/Material] apart from those sums and interests declared on [date] unless the prior written approval of all partners is obtained in advance.

P.054

This Agreement shall not be deemed to create any partnership, joint venture, agency, fiduciary and/or employment relationship between the parties. Neither party shall hold itself out as the agent and/or partner of the other.

P.055

This agreement shall not be deemed to create any collaboration, partnership, agency and/or joint venture relationship between the parties. Both parties remain as separate legal entities. This agreement does not authorise and/or permit either party to assign, grant and/or transfer any rights to a third party so that the third party may enforce the terms of this agreement.

P.056

1.1 This agreement is only intended to be [state express purpose] and does not constitute a partnership, employment, agency and/or other relationship of any kind except those specified.

1.2 This Agreement is not intended to affect any acquisition and/or transfer of rights except those explicitly specified.

1.3 No third party may join, rely on, endorse and/or assume any rights and/or obligations under this agreement without the prior written consent of both parties.

P.057

This agreement shall not constitute and/or imply a partnership, employment or other relationship between the parties. Neither party shall be deemed to be an agent of the other for any purpose whatsoever. Neither party shall have any authority and/or power and/or right to bind the other party in anyway.

P.058

This agreement shall not be deemed to create any partnership, employment, agency, fiduciary and/or any other legal relationship between the parties other than that stated in this document. No party to this agreement shall have authority to commit any other party to any binding agreement with any third party.

P.059

1.1 The [Licensor] and/or the [Licensee] have not granted authority to each other to make any commitment and/or any other binding agreement with a third party on each other's behalf at any time. This agreement is not a partnership, joint venture, collaboration and/or otherwise.

1.2 The [Licensor] has only granted the rights stated in this agreement and all other rights are reserved. Where the [Licensee] wishes to exploit any rights and/or agree any terms with a third party which are not specifically authorised under this agreement then the [Licensee] must seek the prior written approval of the [Licensor]. The [Licensor] shall have the right to refuse any such request from the [Licensee] without stating any reason for their decision.

P.060

1.1 This is a [assignment/licence/sponsorship/image rights] agreement between the particular named parties.

1.2   There is no intention by either party to create any terms, conditions and/or relationship between the parties other than those set out in this document. There is no agency, partnership, employment, joint venture, and/or other trust and/or equitable relationship that should be implied at any time.

P.061

No party shall be entitled to hold themselves out as representing the other to any third party, any company within their Group, any government agency and/or body and/or to commit, pledge, consent, undertake and/or enter into any contract, licence, or other agreement on their behalf and/or to make any application and/or registration for any reason to any third party as they are not entitled and/or authorised to do so at any time.

P.062

The [Institute/Charity], the [Sponsor] and all the other parties in engaged in this [Project] shall remain at all times, separate legal entities. There is no intention to create any partnership, employment, agency, joint venture and/or other relationship. No party shall be entitled to authorise, commit and/or sign any documents and/or incur any costs, fees and/or pledge to pay any sums on behalf of any other party.

P.063

Both parties agree and undertake that it shall require the consent and agreement of both parties in order to license and/or sub-license, sell, transfer, assign, novate, endorse, sponsor and/or otherwise exploit any of the logos, images, slogans, trade marks and/or other intellectual property rights and/or computer software and/or any other rights and interests owned and controlled by both parties under this agreement.

P.064

Where the [Company] engages third party consultants to work and collaborate on the [Project] at any time. It is not intended that any such collaboration shall be construed as forming any partnership with the [Company]. The [Company] is commissioning work from such third party consultants and shall make payment in return for the assignment and transfer and waiver of all the copyright, intellectual property rights, computer software and data rights and moral rights and any other rights and/or interest in the product of any of the third party consultants work including all drafts, samples and finished versions which may be created and/or developed in any medium and/or format at any time. It is not intended that any consultant should retain any rights and/or interest.

P.065

In the event that no formal [deed/document] of partnership is drawn up between [Name] and the [Creator]. Then it is agreed that the parties shall not be entitled to exploit any rights and/or interest held by the other party without prior written consent and agreement in the form of a licence.

P.066

1.1 In the event that one of the partners wishes to retire, leave and/or sale his/her share of the [Company/Partnership]. Then it is agreed that an independent valuation shall be sought from a third party to assess and validate the total value in [currency] of the whole [Company/Partnership] including land and other assets which shall be paid for by the [Company/Partnership].

1.2 The partner may sell his/her share to existing partners and/or any third party provided that the third party is acceptable to the existing partners.

1.3 Where the partners cannot agree the terms upon which the partner can sell his/her share. Then the [Company/Partnership] shall be sold as a going concern to a new purchaser within [one] year.

P.067

This document is an understanding and memorandum between the parties to collaborate on work and projects on the theme of [subject]. Each party shall retain their separate legal identities at all times. It is not a partnership or an agency agreement. There is no assignment and/or license of any rights. Any specific project which is developed in principle shall be subject to a more detailed agreement and terms.

P.068

1.1 The Partnership shall start on [date].

1.2 The Partnership shall only continue to exist as long as the business continues to make a profit. Any partner may request that the Partnership shall end if there is no profit in more than [number] financial years.

1.3 Where a Partner dies then the estate of the deceased Partner shall hold the interest until it is transferred to the beneficiary. If the Partnership cannot agree terms and does not wish to accept the new beneficiary as a partner. Then the Partnership may decide to end the business and/or sell the business to a third party subject to the agreement of everyone who holds an interest.

P.069

Your work on the [Website/App/Sound Recording/Video/Blog] in the role of [contributor/presenter/writer/artist] does not mean that you acquire any copyright, intellectual property rights and/or other interest in the material and/or the business known as [specify trading name]. You are not a collaborator, partner and/or copyright owner of any content.

PATENT

General Business and Commercial

P.070

'Patent' shall mean any new invention which involves an inventive step which is capable of industrial application and which qualifies for protection and is not exempt under any law in [state/country/world].

It shall not be considered an invention if it is:

1.1   a discovery which is a scientific theory and/or mathematical method; and/or

1.2   a literary, dramatic, musical or artistic work or other aesthetic creation; and/or

1.3   it is scheme, rule and/or method for performing a mental act, playing a game, doing business and/or is a computer software program for a computer and/or other device.

P.071

1.1   No patent will be granted for an invention which is capable of commercial exploitation which would be contrary to public policy or morality.

1.2   The fact that it may currently be against the law in [country] does not mean that a patent could not be granted.

P.072

All rights and the right to apply for statutory protection including, but not limited to, patent protection for any improvement to the [Product] made by the [Company] and/or the [Employee] shall vest and be retained solely in the [Company].

P.073

The [Manager/Employee] agrees that he/she shall promptly communicate to the [Company] all inventions, modifications, improvements, processes, formulae, materials, know-how, designs, models, photocopies, sketches, drawings, plans or other original matter (whether or not they are capable of protection) which he/she may create and/or discover during the performance of his/her employment with the [Company].

P.074

1.1 The [Employee] shall while employed by the [Company] if so requested at the [Company's] cost and expense sign and provide documentary support for any applications by the [Company] for any design, invention, patent and /or registered design and/or other trade marks and/or computer software and/or any other intellectual property rights which the [Employee] has been involved and/or witnessed.

1.2 The [Manager/Employee] acknowledges and agrees that the [Company] shall own all such rights in 1.1 except where the [Employee] is the sole creator. In such instance the [Employee] agrees that the [Company] and the [Employee] shall [jointly own such rights/shall negotiate a settlement in respect of the rights.]

1.3 Where after the contract of employment has ended the [Company] requires the [Employee] to provide assistance. Then the [Company] agree a fee and pay all expenses for the cost of the co-operation of the [Employee].

P.075

1.1 The [Company] agrees and undertakes that where the [Executive/ Expert] during the course of his/her employment creates, develops, and/or discovers on his/her own at the [Company's] expense [and/ or with others as part of a team] any inventions, modifications, improvements, developments, processes, formulae, materials, know-how, designs, trade marks, logos, computer software and/or other original artistic, musical, literary, sound recordings, films and/or two and/or three dimensional objects and/or any other copyright and/or intellectual property rights and/or other rights, material and/or interest whether or not they are capable of protection at any time.

1.2 That where the [Company] intends to register, use, exploit, license, sell and/or market and/or use any such matters in 1.1. That all such rights and material shall be shared with the [Company] [number] per cent and the [Executive/Expert] [number] per cent share. Any registration and/or record shall show the rights and material owned by the [Executive/Expert] and the [Company]in those proportions in any part of the world.

1.3 The [Executive/Expert] and the [Company] shall share any sums received from the exploitation of the rights and material in 1.1 in the proportions stated in 1.2.

1.4 The [Company] agrees and undertakes to bear all the cost and expense of any applications, registrations and protection including legal fees which the [Company] shall not be entitled to recoup from any sums due to the [Executive/Expert].

1.5 The [Company] waives any right to dispute the terms of the ownership which have been agreed with the [Executive/Expert] in 1.1 and 1.2. Where there is any omission of any rights and/or material covered in 1.1 and/or new rights are created in the future the presumption is that they shall be shared according to the proportions stated in 1.2.

P.076
The [Company] agrees and undertakes to assign to the [Institute/Charity] all rights and interest of any nature in any medium and any format that may be created, developed, discovered and/or originated by the [Company] and/or any employee and/or consultant engaged by the [Company] during the course of the [Work/Project] [and at any time thereafter] which arise directly [and/or indirectly] as a result of the [Work/Project]. The rights and interest which should be assigned by the [Company] shall include but not be limited to all patents, inventions, modifications, improvements, processes, formulae, materials, know-how, design rights, and future design rights, all copyright in any text, images, photographs, films, videos, sound recordings, music, and all rights in any databases, index and taxonomy rights and the right to register any trade marks, service marks, logos, computer software, source codes, passwords, formats, domain names and any other original material whether or not defined and/or capable of protection under existing legislation which relate to the [Work/Project].

P.077
The [Company] and the [Institute/Charity] agree that they shall both ensure that all third parties who are licensed and/or involved in the adaptation and exploitation of the [Work/Project] shall not acquire any rights and/or interest in the [Work/Project] whether in existence now and/or created in the future including any patent, copyright, trade mark, service mark, computer software, design rights, future design rights, and all any other intellectual property rights and/or other interest at any time.

P.078

1.1 The [Supplier] agrees that if the [Supplier] and/or any employee assists with the design, development and/or creation of a new generation of products and/or services based on instructions, guidance, ideas and/or work provided and/or requested by the [Company] that all such rights, material and interest shall owned by the [Company].

1.2 That where the [Supplier] and/or any employee is found to technically own the rights and/or material that they shall be assigned to the [Company] for a nominal sum of [number/currency] including but not limited to any computer software, invention, patent, logo, image, trade mark, design and/or intellectual property rights.

1.3 The [Supplier] agrees that it shall not attempt to register ownership of any such rights and/or material.

1.4 The [Supplier] agrees that it shall not be entitled to receive any additional payments and/or royalties from the exploitation of any such rights and/or material.

P.079

1.1 [Name] is a contributor to the [Blog/Channel/Service] in the role of [subject/presenter].

1.2 [Name] accepts and agrees that all rights and material in the product of the work of [Name] shall be owned and controlled by the [Company] except for rights and material which were owned and controlled by [Name] which pre-date this agreement including but not limited to: [specific existing rights and material owned by [Name] [books/merchandising/films/logos/trade marks/slogans/patents].

PAYMENT

Film, Television and Video

P.080
Any payment which shall be due for the supply and delivery of the [Units/Videos/Discs] by the [Distributor] must be paid by the [Enterprise] within [number] days of delivery and the supply of the dispatch invoice.

P.081
'The Wholesale Selling Price' shall be the actual selling price of a single [Unit/Video/Disc] charged by the [Assignee B] to any third party including but not limited to warehouses, shops, retailers, online direct marketing companies and/or distributors whether the [Unit/Video/Disc] is supplied for sale, rental

and/or otherwise. This sum shall include any premiums, surcharges and/ or other additional sums charged by the [Assignee B]. It shall not however include any discounts, deductions, sales tax and/or other sums imposed by any government and/or other authority as a tax.

P.082

In consideration of the rights and obligations imposed upon the [Assignor] and the [Assignee] under the terms of this agreement the [Assignee] shall pay to the [Assignor] the Assignment Fee as follows:

1.1 [number/currency] upon full signature of this agreement by both parties.

1.2 [number/currency] upon delivery and acceptance of the [Master Material] of the [Film/Video/Sound Recording] by the [Assignee].

1.3 [number/currency] upon delivery and acceptance of all the master packaging, promotional, advertising and marketing material by the [Assignee].

1.4 [number/currency] upon first release to the public of the [Units/Discs/ Download] of the [Film] in any country and/or [date] whichever is the earliest.

P.083

The [Company] agrees to pay [Name/Agent] the total fee of [number/ currency] which shall be paid in two stages:

1.1 [number/currency] within [number] days of full signature of this agreement by all the parties and

1.2 [number/currency] within [number] days of the completion of all the scheduled work by [Name] required in this agreement.

P.084

'The Total Fixed Cost' shall mean the sum of [number/currency] which is agreed to represent the fixed price sum [which is exclusive of any taxes] of the entire cost and expense of the development, reproduction, and delivery the master copy of the [Film/Video/Podcast] in [format] to the [Licensee].

P.085

'The Licence Fee' shall be the sum of [number/currency].

In consideration of the rights granted under this agreement the [Distributor] shall pay to [Name] the Licence Fee as follows:

1.1 [number/currency] upon signature of this agreement of all the parties.

1.2   [number/currency] on or before [date] subject to delivery and acceptance of the [Master Material].

1.3   [number/currency] upon first transmission and/or broadcast of the [Film/Video/Sound Recording] on television whether cable, satellite, terrestrial and/or through a subscription or other service in electronic form and/or as a download and/or play back archive catalogue over the internet and/or any telecommunication system.

The [Distributor] agrees that the Licence Fee shall not be returnable by [Name] and shall not be offset and/or recouped against any royalties due to [Name].

P.086
The [Company] shall open a separate bank account designated as an account for all sums received and/or credited to the [Company] under this agreement in respect of the exploitation of the [Units/Videos/Discs] of the [Film].

P.087
'The Advance' means the payment to the [Company] by the [Distributor] of the sum of [number/currency] which shall be due within [number] days of the conclusion and signature of this agreement. This advance shall be recouped by the [Distributor] from the [Company's] share of the Distribution Income under clause [–].

P.088

1.1   The [Licensee] shall pay to the [Licensor] a non-returnable Advance.

1.2   The [Licensee] may recoup the non-returnable Advance against the [Licensor's] share of the Gross Receipts before any royalties due under this agreement are paid to the [Licensor]. No payment shall be due to the [Licensor] until the Advance has been recouped by the [Licensee] in full.

P.089

1.1   The [Distributor] shall pay the [Company/Name] an advance of [number/currency] on [date] subject to conclusion of this agreement and acceptance of the master material of the [Film/Video/Sound Recording].

1.2   The [Distributor] shall pay the [Company] an additional advance of [number/currency] within [number] days of transmission and/or broadcast of the entire [Film/Video/Sound Recording] on channel [specify licensee] in [country].

1.3   The [Distributor] shall be entitled to offset the advance against any royalties due under this Agreement to the [Company/Name].

1.4   In the event that the receipts in 1.2 are insufficient for the [Distributor] to recoup all of the advance then the [Distributor] shall have the right to recover any such sum from the [Company/Name] within [number] days of the expiry of this agreement. There shall be no right to recoup any outstanding sum in respect of the advance if the [Company/Name] terminates this agreement at an earlier date than [date].

P.090
'The Licence Fee' shall the sum of [number/currency] which may be set off against the [Author's] Royalties due to the [Author] under this agreement. In consideration of the rights granted under this agreement the [Company] shall pay the [Author] the Licence Fee as follows:

1.1   [number/currency] upon signature by both parties to this agreement.

1.2   [number/currency] on or before [date] subject to [specify condition].

1.3   [number/currency] upon approval in writing by the [Author] of the final script.

1.4   [number/currency] upon first transmission, exhibition, theatrical premiere and/or broadcast of the [Film/Video/Unit] in any country of the world but in any event no later than: [date].

P.091
In consideration of the rights granted by the [Licensor] to the [Licensee] under this agreement in respect of the [Sound Recordings/Series/Programmes]. The [Licensee] agrees to pay the [Licensor] in [currency] as follows:

1.1   [number/currency] upon signature of this agreement.

1.2   [number/currency] on or before [date] subject to delivery and acceptance by the [Licensee] of a copy of the master material of the [Sound Recordings/Series/Programmes].

1.3   [number/currency] upon approval by the [Licensor] of the final version of the [Sound Recordings/Series/Programmes] to be edited, adapted, reproduced and exploited by the [Licensee].

The [Licensee] agrees that the sums set out above shall not be set-off and/or recouped against any royalties and/or other sums due to the [Licensor] under this agreement and/or any other agreement at any time.

P.092
The [Licensee] agrees to ensure that all sums received from the exploitation of the [Sound Recordings/Disc] in any currency are converted at the most

favourable exchange rate in existence at that time. That any conversion costs and charges shall be paid for by the [Licensee].

P.093

The [Licensee] agrees to ensure that all [Sub-Licensees] shall undertake to keep any sums received from the exploitation of the [Sound Recordings/ Disc] in a separate bank account and shall not mix such sums with those of the rest of their business and/or allow and/or create any lien, charge and/or other claim over the sums by a third party.

P.094

[Name] agrees to pay the [Artist/Performer] a fixed fee of [number/currency] which shall be paid as follows:

1.1 [Number/currency] subject to completion of the work for the [Film/ Project] on [dates].

1.2 [Number/currency] subject to completion of any photographs, images, sound recordings and/or other videos for the marketing.

1.3 [Number/currency] for attendance at the launch of the [Film/Project] and a short speech and presentation and [number] press interviews at the event.

P.095

The [Company] shall pay [Name] a fee of [number/currency] by direct debit to a nominated account the day after completion of the filming for the [Project] at [location] on [date] which has been agreed with the [Company]. Any payment shall be accompanied by any additional payment required for [value added tax/other] purposes if an invoice is provided in advance supported by a [value added tax/other] code.

P.096

In consideration of the rights and obligations imposed upon the [Assignor A] and the [Assignee B] under the terms of this agreement. The [Assignee B] shall pay to the [Assignor A] the Assignment Fee as follows:

1.1 [number/currency] upon full signature of this agreement by both parties; and

1.2 [number/currency] upon delivery of the final approved script; and

1.3 [number/currency] upon commencement of principal photography; and

1.4 [number/currency] upon first public release of the [Film] by [specify method] anywhere in the [Territory/world].

1.5 In the event that matters set out in 1.2, 1.3 and 1.4 above are not fulfilled for any reason and are not merely delayed. It is agreed that the [Assignee] shall pay the [Assignor] [number/currency] by [date] instead of those sums in 1.2, 1.3 and 1.4 above.

P.097

The [Company] agrees to pay [Name] the total fee as follows:

1.1 [number/currency] upon signature of this agreement by both parties. Such sum shall be a Non-Returnable Advance.

1.2 [number/currency] by date: [date].

P.098

'The Fixed Price Budget' shall mean the sum of [number/currency] which is agreed to represent the fixed price sum (exclusive of any additional taxes on the supply of goods and/or services) of the entire cost of the preparation, development, production, editing, and delivery of the [Series/Podcasts] in accordance with the terms of this agreement as set out in Appendix A. The Fixed Price Budget shall not be varied except in circumstances where additional work and services are requested by the [Enterprise] after the date of this agreement.

P.099

'The Option Fee' shall be the sum of [number/currency].

In consideration of the [Author] granting to the [Company] the option rights under this agreement. The [Company] agrees that it shall pay to the [Author] the Option Fee within [number] days of both parties signing this agreement.

P.100

In consideration of your agreement to the filming facilities we agree to pay you a fee [exclusive of any tax on the supply of goods and/or services] of [number/currency] for each period of [specify hours] each day. The sum shall be paid as follows:

1.1 [figure/currency] upon signature of this agreement and

1.2 the balance of the sum due within [number] days of completion of filming.

1.3 The fee is in full and final settlement and no further sums shall be due to you in respect of our use, adaptation and/or exploitation of the material which has been filmed in any form.

P.101

'The Sponsorship Fee' shall be the sum of [number/currency]. The [Sponsor] agrees to pay to the [Company] the Sponsorship Fee as follows:

1.1 [number/currency] upon full signature of this agreement by all the parties.

1.2 [number/currency] within [number] days of recording and/or filming the [Event/Festival].

1.3 [number/currency] within [number] days of the first transmission, broadcast and/or streaming over the internet of more than [number] minutes of the [Programme] relating to the [Event/Festival] by the [Company] and/or any authorised third party. In the event for any reason this is delayed then the [Sponsor] shall in any event pay the sum by [date] provided that a new transmission, broadcast and/or streaming date has been proposed by the [Company].

1.4 [number/currency] on or before [date] subject to the completion of 1.2 and 1.3. Where those sums are delayed for any reason due to the alteration of the [Event/Festival] date and/or force majeure. Then this sum shall also be delayed and the parties shall agree a new payment date.

P.102
'The Transmission Fee' shall be the following amount; [number/currency] due to be paid by the [Promoter] to the [Television Company] within [number] days of the transmission and/or broadcast of the [Advertisement/Promotion/Competition] set out in appendix B. Payment shall still be due whether or not the transmission and/or broadcast is delayed and/or cancelled due to non-compliance with guidelines and/or codes issued by [specify organisation].

P.103
'The Repeat Fees' shall be the sums to be paid by the [Company] to [Name] in addition to the Basic Fee on each occasion when any of the following types of advertisements and/or any parts which include the performance or voice-over of [Name] are broadcast and/or transmitted at any time throughout the world by any method:

1.1 Terrestrial Television: whole commercial: [fee] part of commercial less than [number] seconds: [fee].

1.2 Cable Television: whole commercial: [fee] part of commercial less than [number] seconds: [fee].

1.3 Satellite Television: whole commercial: [fee] part of commercial less than [number] seconds: [fee].

1.4 Digital, electronic and/or other transmission and/or download over the internet to any device and/or gadget in any format: whole commercial: [fee] part of commercial less than [number] seconds: [fee].

1.5 Terrestrial, Cable, Satellite, Digital, electronic and any other transmission and/or download over the internet in any format: whole commercial: [fee] part of commercial less than [number] seconds: [fee].

1.6 All other forms of exploitation and/or use not set out in this agreement are subject to the payment to be agreed in advance between the parties in each case.

P.104

'The Licence Fee' shall be the sum of [number/currency].

In consideration of the rights granted under this agreement the [Production Company] shall pay to the [Author] the Licence Fee as follows:

1.1 [number/currency] upon signature of this agreement.

1.2 [number/currency] on or before [date].

1.3 [number/currency] upon promotion and/or marketing of the [Film] to the public in any format but in any event no later than [date].

1.4 [number/currency] upon transmission and/or broadcast of the [Film] on television in any form whether terrestrial, cable, satellite or digital anywhere and/or the streaming of the [Film] over the internet but in any event no later than [date].

1.5 [number/currency] within [number] days of the conclusion of the first product placement agreement for the [Film] between the [Production Company] and a third party in excess of [number/currency]. This sum shall in any event be paid by [date].

1.6 [number/currency] within [number] days of the conclusion of the first merchandising agreement for the [Film] between the [Production Company] and a third party. This sum shall in any event be paid by [date].

1.7 The [Production Company] agrees that the Licence Fee shall not be returnable by the [Author] and shall be due on the specified dates at the latest irrespective of whether the [Film] is delayed and/or cancelled for any reason and/or otherwise.

P.105

The [Production Company] shall open a separate bank account designated as an account under the name of the [Production Company] and the [Film] solely for that purpose. The [Production Company] shall credit all sums paid by the [Television Company] under this agreement to such account and shall only be used for the purpose of the production of the [Film].

P.106

'The Royalty Advance' shall mean the payment to the [Company] by the [Distributor] of the sum of [number/currency] which shall be paid as follows:

1.1   [number/currency] upon full signature of this agreement.

1.2   [number/currency] subject to acceptance of the [Master Material] of the [Series] by the [Distributor].

1.3   [number/currency] within [number] days of the first transmission and/or broadcast of the first episode of the [Series] on any cable, satellite and/or terrestrial channel in any country in the [Territory/world].

1.4   [number/currency] within [number] days of the conclusion of any agreement to transmit the [Series] under any subscription service over the internet in digital and/or electronic form and/or as part of a play back service.

P.107

1.1   The [Licensee] shall pay to the [Licensor] a non-returnable Advance.

1.2   The [Licensee] may recoup the non-returnable Advance against the [Licensor's] share of the royalties due from the Gross Receipts as they arise.

1.3   No payment shall be due to the [Licensor] until the Advance sum shall be recovered by the [Licensee] in full.

1.4   The [Licensee] shall pay to the [Licensor] an additional the sum of [number/currency] for the [Master Material] subject to acceptance of the technical quality of the material by the [Licensee]. The [Licensee] shall not be entitled to recoup this payment.

P.108

1.1   The [Distributor] shall pay the [Company] an advance of [number/currency] which shall be in addition to the royalties due to be paid under this agreement.

1.2   The [Distributor] shall have the right to offset the advance against any royalties due under this agreement to the [Company]. In the event that the receipts are insufficient for the [Distributor] to recoup all the advance then the [Distributor] shall have a claim against the [Company] for any unrecovered sum.

P.109

1.1   It is agreed that the [Licensee] shall pay the [Licensor] a minimum guaranteed advance on the sums to be received by the [Licensee] of [number /currency] payable as follows:

     a   [number/currency] within [number] days of the signature of this agreement by both parties.

     b   [number/currency] on or by [date].

     c   [number/currency] on or by [date] and/or later if required as payment is subject to the approval by the [Licensor] of the [prototype/sample] of the [Product].

     d   [number/currency] on or by [date] and/or later if required as payment is subject to the commencement of the production of the [Product] in [country].

     e   [number/currency] on or by [date] and/or later if required as payment is subject to the distribution and sale of not less than [number] [Products] in any country.

1.2   It is expressly agreed that the [Licensee] may recoup this advance in 1.1 by withholding sums due from the [Licensor's] share of the receipts. When the [Licensee] shall have fully recouped such sum then the [Licensor's] share of the receipts will be paid according to the terms of this agreement.

1.3   If there are not enough receipts to allow the [Licensee] to recover the advance in 1.1. The [Licensee] shall not have the right to claim the amount from the [Licensor]. The advance in 1.1 is not returnable by the [Licensor].

P.110

The [Licensee] shall pay to the [Licensor] a non-returnable advance of [number/currency] plus [any government taxes that may be due] on [date] subject to signature of this agreement and delivery and acceptance of the [Images/Sound Recordings/Scripts]. Such sum shall not be contingent on any further matters and cannot be repaid at a later date.

P.111

The [Production Company] agrees that the [Licence Fee] shall not be returnable by the [Author] and shall be due to be paid in full on or before the specified dates irrespective of whether the production and/or exploitation of the [Film] is cancelled, delayed and/or altered.

P.112

'The Licence Fee' shall be the non-returnable and recoupable advance against the [Author's/Artists'] Royalties which is the sum of [number/currency].

The [Author/Artist] agrees that the Licence Fee can be offset against the [Author's/Artists'] Royalties.

1424

In consideration of the rights granted under this agreement the [Company] shall pay the [Author/Artist] the Licence Fee as follows:

1.1   [number/currency] within [number] days of the conclusion of this agreement.

1.2   [number/currency] on or before [date] subject to approval by the [Author/Artist] of the [Draft Script/Production Schedule/Budget/ Contributors/Actors/Samples].

1.3   [number/currency] upon acceptance by the [Author] of the [Final Script/other].

1.4   [number/currency] within [number] days of the first broadcast and/or transmission of the [Series/Film/Cartoon] on terrestrial, cable and/or satellite television in [country/any part of the world] and/or by [date] whichever is the earliest.

1.5   [number/currency] within [number] days of theatrical release of the [Series/Film/Cartoon] in [country/any part of the world] and/or by [date] whichever is the earliest.

1.6   [number/currency] within [number] days of release to the public for sale, rental and/or subscription of a [DVD/Unit/Electronic Download] of the [Series/Film/Cartoon] in [country/any part of the world] and/or by [date] whichever is the earliest.

1.7   [number/currency] within [number] days of release to the public for sale, rental and/or subscription of a [Product/T shirt/Game] of the [Series/Film/Cartoon] in [country/any part of the world] and/or by [date] whichever is the earliest.

1.8   [number/currency] within [number] days of the conclusion of a product placement agreement with a third party in respect of the [Series/Film/ Cartoon].

P.113

1.1   The fixed sum of [number/currency] which shall be paid by the [Licensee] to the [Licensor] in respect of each [Customer] which books and pays for the [Film/Event/Match/Game] under the service operated by the [Licensee] on [channel/premises/area]: [specify channel/premises/area].

1.2   This sum in 1.1 shall be paid by the [Licensee] regardless of the method of payment by which the [Customer] is charged including subscription, a package deal, pay per view, whether direct dial booking, remote controlled or otherwise. Customers whose package or service includes the [Film/Event/Match/Game] will be deemed to have booked and paid.

P.114

The fixed sum of [number/currency] which shall be paid by the [Licensee] to the [Licensor] in respect of each [Customer] which books and pays for the [Film/Event/Match/Game] under the pay per view [television/video/play back/other] service operated by the [Licensee] as follows: [specify channel/method].

P.115

The [Distributor] agrees that an additional payment of [number/currency] shall be made to the [Licensor] for the right of the [Distributor] to make available the [Film] to the public for a period of [one] month after transmission and/or broadcast for unlimited use by the public through its [Video on Demand/ playback service/archive] for personal home use only on any television set, laptop and/or other gadget including mobile telephones and tablets.

P.116

It is agreed between the parties that where completion of work by any person is delayed due to force majeure which are beyond the control of the [Distributor] that no payments shall be due.

General Business and Commercial

P.117

1.1 The [Company] shall be entitled to charge for any [Material] ordered by any [Client] at the relevant price calculated by the [Company] at the date of despatch of the [Material].

1.2 Any quotation and/or price list and/or website and/or app promotions in existence at any time are for guidance only and not a firm confirmation of the final price to be charged.

1.3 The [Company] reserves the right to alter and/or amend and/or increase the price at any time.

1.4 The price of any order is based on availability from a supplier and/or the quality of the product and/or material and/or any additional work that may be required prior to delivery.

P.118

In the event of the Total Price being exceeded by up to [number] per cent then the [Company] agrees to pay such additional costs. Provided that the [Supplier] informs the [Company] in advance and provides upon request a statement of costs incurred to date and details of the additional costs.

P.119
In the event of the agreed [Cost/Quote/Budget] being exceeded by more than [number] per cent the [Company] agrees to pay such additional costs provided it has given prior written approval of the expenditure to the [Supplier].

P.120

1.1 The [Contractor] agrees that its total financial entitlement under this contract (excluding any entitlement to any sums and/or remedies which may arise and are recoverable at law) shall be the sum of [number/currency] which shall be the Guaranteed Price plus value added tax.

1.2 In the event that the [Contractor] is issued with further instructions requiring Project Changes or Works Contract Variations resulting in additional costs to the [Contractor]. The [Contractor] shall be entitled to decline to carry out the work unless it is agreed between the parties to increase the [Contractor's] total financial entitlement above the Guaranteed Price and the increase is confirmed in writing by all parties.

P.121
All payments shall be made in the following currency [specify currency] to the address on the invoice. The rates stated in the Contract Order shall not be subject to any increase unless the [Company] has received notice of such increase not less than [number] days prior to the effective date of the increased rate. The rates or payment shall not however be increased in respect of any specific part of the work which the [Contractor] has already accepted, unless otherwise specifically agreed.

P.122
No overtime shall be payable unless specifically approved by the [Company].

P.123

1.1 The [Contractor] shall invoice the [Company] each month in a form acceptable to the [Company]. All time sheets shall be subject to the approval of the [Company] and each invoice shall refer to the relevant Contract Order together with details to support the charges and original receipts.

1.2 The [Company] shall pay the invoices in 1.1 within [specify period] of receipt of the invoices.

1.3 In the event that the [Company] disputes any item on an invoice it shall notify the [Contractor] and payment may be withheld until the matter is resolved. Delayed payment of disputed items shall accrue interest at [number] per cent from the due date.

1.4   Costs which are not invoiced by [date] will not be reimbursed.

1.5   All bank charges, transfer costs and currency exchanges shall be at the [Company's] expense in respect of any payments unless the [Contractor] requests payment into an account not specified in this agreement in which case the additional bank charges shall be at the [Contractor's] cost.

P.124

The [Company] undertakes to pay the [Employee] the salary of [number/ currency] per year pro rata in arrears each month. The first payment shall be due on [number] [month] [year]. The payment of the salary each month shall be subject to:

1.1   confirmation of the qualifications and references provided by the [Employee].

1.2   compliance by the [Employee] with all the policies including the code of conduct and health and safety guidelines and social media activity policy issued by the [Company] at any time which apply to the role of the [Employee] at the [Company].

1.3   the assignment of the rights in clause [–] in respect of the product of any work of the [Employee] while at the [Company].

P.125

The [Employer] agrees and undertakes that all remuneration payable in this agreement shall be paid to the [Employee's] bank account specified in schedule A on the [25th] day of each calendar month. Where such date falls on a weekend or Bank Holiday the payment shall be made on the following weekday.

P.126

The [Employee's] rate of pay will be [number/currency] payable every two weeks in arrears. This equates to an annual salary of [number/currency] and includes [specify financial benefits] and [specify type] allowance. The [Employee] will receive increments in accordance with the union agreement [specify reference]. Payment to the [Employee] by the [Company] will be made by credit transfer direct to his/her bank account. The [Employee's] salary will be received on [date] of each month subject to the continuance of this contract of employment.

P.127
The [Company] agrees to pay the [Employee's] remuneration by credit transfer to the [Employee's] personal bank or building society account on the last Thursday of each month. In the event that a Bank Holiday falls on a Thursday the [Company] shall be entitled to make payment to the [Employee] on the next working day unless some other arrangement is made between the parties.

P.128
The fee of [number/currency] shall be paid by the [Company] by equal four-weekly payments of [number/currency] in arrears throughout the period of this agreement. Each instalment shall be paid upon presentation of invoice at least one week in advance of the notified pay dates.

P.129
The [Employee's] rate of pay will be [number/currency] payable every four weeks in arrears. This is an annual salary of [number/currency] including an additional [allowance/payment] of [number/currency]. The [Employee's] salary shall be reviewed each year on or by [date] with his/her [manager/other]. All payments shall be made to the [Employee] by credit transfer to a nominated bank account.

P.130
The [Employee] shall receive incremental increases in salary and benefits in accordance with the national agreement with [specify union/organisation/agreement/date]. A copy of which is attached to and forms part of this agreement.

P.131
The [Company] agrees that the [Employee's] pay shall be reviewed on or by [date] each year. There is no obligation on the part of the [Company] to agree to any salary. The [Company] however does agree that where a role of a person has changed and/or there has been a significant increase in responsibility that the salary level for the existing role will be reviewed.

P.132
'Executive's Basic Remuneration' shall mean the annual sum of [number/currency] for the period 1 January to 31 December in each year during the existence of this Agreement. That's an entire year not a period within a year? This gross sum shall be payable by the [Company] to the [Executive] in accordance with the terms of this agreement.

P.133

1.1 The [Company] agrees to pay the Executive's Remuneration by credit transfer to the [Executive's] personal bank account on the [last Thursday] of each month. In the event that there is a Bank Holiday then the payment shall be made on the [earlier/next] working day unless some other arrangement is made between the parties.

1.2 The [Company] agrees to make all additional expenses, costs and other payments required under this agreement to the [Executive] personally by [specify method] and shall not be authorised to alter or change this arrangement without written instructions from him/her.

P.134

'Additional Remuneration' shall mean such financial or other benefits in kind to which the [Executive] may be entitled including:

1.1 any minimum annual bonus of [specify number/currency] or more in the event the [Company] achieves specified turnover, profit and/or cashflow targets as set out in the Executive's Bonus Scheme attached as Appendix A.

1.2 any option and/or shares allocated under the Executive Share Scheme details of which are attached in Appendix B.

1.3 any laptop, mobile, gadget and/or services provided and/or to be paid for by the [Company].

1.4 any transport, car, valet service, airline and/or train tickets provided and/or paid for by the [Company].

1.5 any credit card, loan, resettlement and/or relocation payment, health insurance, dental insurance and/or any other financial and/or direct and/or indirect benefit provided by the [Company].

P.135

The basic salary shall be paid to the [Employee] by the [Company] from [date] at regular intervals per [week/month] [in arrears/in advance] and shall be paid by [direct debit/cheque/other].

P.136

1.1 The [Company] shall pay [Name] at the rate of [currency/number] per hour for every full hour of completed work as [specify role] at the [Company] from [date].

1.2 Payment shall be made at the end of each calendar month by direct debit to the nominated account of [Name] subject to supply of the following documents being supplied and approved as correct: [specify details of documents required/credit /crime/qualifications/references/ passport/visa/main residence].

1.3 If you do not attend for work for any reason then no payment shall be made. There is no right in this temporary role to any other payments. No payment shall be made for ill health whether or not a medical certificate is available.

1.4 If you do not pass the first probationary day of work then you shall be paid for that day only.

1.5 If you do not wear the required uniform and hair protection then you may be refused the right to work even if you attend.

P.137

It is agreed that the [Licensee] shall be entitled to mix any part or portion of the [Licensor's] share of Net Receipts which may be received by the [Licensee] with any of the [Licensee's] own monies. There shall be no obligation to open a new and separate bank account for all the sums received relating to the exploitation of the [Project/Product/rights which have been granted].

P.138

All payments by the [Licensee] to the [Licensor] under this agreement shall be made without any deduction and/or withholding of any monies unless required the [Licensee] is required to do so under any legislation and/or order of a Court of law. In the event that monies are deducted and/or withheld the [Licensee] shall promptly pay the amount withheld to the appropriate authority and shall provide the [Licensor] with the original receipt issued by that authority and/or other sufficient evidence of payment.

P.139

The [Licensee] agrees and undertakes to ensure that all sub-licensees and/ or other third parties associated with the exploitation of the rights granted under this agreement are:

1.1 verified to have been trading for a minimum of [three] years and are able to produce audited accounts for that period.

1.2 are advised of all the terms and conditions imposed on the [Licensee] under this agreement which may also apply to a sub-licensee and/or third party.

1.3 obliged to keep any monies received from any sale and/or licence in a separate bank account and not mix the sums received with their other money relating to the business.

1.4   bound to pay all sums due to the [Licensee] in [currency] and that no such bank and other conversion charges are to be reimbursed by the [Licensor] and/or [Licensee].

1.5   bound to account and make payment to the [Licensee] on the basis of every [three] month period.
In the vent for any reason any sums are not received and/or paid by any sub-licensee and/or third party. Then the [Licensee] agrees that it shall be solely liable for the consequences of such default to the [Licensor].

P.140
The [Licensee] agrees to reimburse the [Licensor] in respect of all the reproduction, insurance and delivery costs and charges incurred in providing acceptable [Material] subject to satisfactory receipts being provided upon request.

P.141
The [Licensor/Name] agrees and confirms that all sums due pursuant to this agreement shall be paid direct to the [Agent] until the expiry and/or termination of this agreement and not the [Licensor/Name].

P.142
All monies payable by the [Licensee] to the [Company] under this agreement shall be paid to the following representatives of the [Company] as follows:

1.1   [number] per cent to [Name] of [address] or at such other address as may be notified to the [Licensee] in writing by the [Company] and

1.2   [number] per cent to [specify bank] of [address] for the credit of the account in the names of [specify joint names] or such other account as may be notified in writing to the [Licensee] by the [Company].

1.3   The receipt of the monies by the parties in 1.1 and 1.2 shall be good and sufficient discharge to the [Company] of the sums paid.

P.143
Notwithstanding the provisions of this agreement any sums to be paid to the [Company] shall not be paid until the [Assignee] has received a release in writing executed by each of the persons entitled to the benefit of the Charge created by the [Company] described in clause [–] in a form and manner acceptable to the [Assignee].

P.144
The Assignment Fee shall be the sum of [number/currency].

In consideration of the rights assigned by the [Assignor] the [Assignee] shall pay to the [Assignor] the Assignment Fee as follows:

1.1   [number/currency] upon signature of this agreement by the [Assignor] and the [Assignee] and/or their authorised representatives.

1.2   [number/currency] on or before [date] subject to delivery and acceptance of the material listed in Schedule A.

P.145
It is crucial that payment of the monies for your booking is made as follows:

1.1   deposit shall be by [date]; and

1.2   the balance shall be made on or before [date] in [currency] by [method] to [name/company/account details].

1.3   The time of payment shall be of the essence of this document.

1.4   In the event that payment has not been received and cleared [number] days prior to the start of the [Festival/Conference/Exhibition]. Then the booking shall not be confirmed and the [Company] shall be entitled retain the deposit which shall be forfeited and to reallocate the space to a third party.

P.146
The [Company] reserves the right to withhold delivery to the [Licensee] of any material if payments due under this or other agreements have not been received by the [Company]. In addition the [Company] shall charge interest at the rate of [number] per cent per annum on all amounts outstanding beyond the payment dates shown on its invoices. The agreement shall not take effect until the agreement has been signed and returned to the [Company] and the Licence Fee has been paid in full.

P.147
The [Licensee] shall open an account in the name of [specify persons/corporate name] at [bank/address] entitled [specify names of account]. It is agreed that it shall be a condition of the account that all withdrawals shall require the consent and authorisation by a representative of the [Licensor] as co-signature and that such instructions to the bank shall cannot be altered without the prior written consent of the [Licensor].

P.148
All payments made under this agreement shall be in [currency] and by company [cheque/direct debit/other].

P.149

All payments are made via bank transfer and all charges are at the [Customers] sole cost.

P.150

It is agreed between the parties that where payment under this agreement is delayed and/or prevented by force majeure for any reason. That such non-payment shall not be deemed a breach of this agreement provided that payment is made within [number] [days/weeks/months]. Thereafter the other party who has not been paid shall have the right to terminate this agreement and to seek payment of the sums due together with interest and legal and administrative costs incurred.

P.151

Where the [Company] has paid any sum in advance for delivery of services and/or products by [Name]. Then in the event that [Name] fails to deliver the services and/or products to the [Company] by the dates agreed. That the [Company] shall be entitled to set off the value of the non-delivery against any sums due from the [Company] to [Name] under any other agreement between the parties.

Internet, Websites and Apps

P.152

All fees due for the use of the subscription service must be paid on the due date monthly in advance otherwise the [Company] reserves the right to cancel your access to and use of the service.

P.153

You may download any [Unit/Recording/Film] in the [Archive/Channel] provided that you have paid the access Licence Fee and agree to be bound by the terms and conditions of the User Licence.

P.154

1.1 No fees shall be charged for you to read, view and make one copy for your own personal use at home and for non-commercial purposes of the contents of this [Website/App/Sound Recording/Image] provided that there is sufficient acknowledgement of the source and copyright ownership.

1.2 There is however no waiver of the right to demand fees, royalties and charges for any other use that you may make of the contents in any language, in any medium at any time. There is no licence granted to supply, distribute, transfer and/or reproduce the material to any third party at any time whether by copying, scanning and/or otherwise.

P.155

1.1 The [Company/Distributor] shall pay the [Supplier] the fixed sum of [number/currency] as a Usage Fee for every [Film/Sound Recording/ Unit] provided by the [Supplier] which is used on the [Website/App/ Archive] and which is then purchased, accessed and viewed for which sums are received and retained by the [Company/Distributor].

1.2 The [Company/Distributor] shall provide a statement to the [Supplier] for [each month/every three months] from [date] which sets out the name of the [[Film/Sound Recording/Unit], the date upon which it was purchased and payment was made and the sum received by the [Company/Distributor].

1.3 The [Company/Distributor] shall pay the [Supplier] all sums due in respect of the Usage Fees in arrears at the end of [each month/every three months] from [date].

P.156

The [Company] agrees and undertakes to keep accurate records of the orders from the public and shall meet such requests promptly and shall pay the [Supplier] for all the [Units/Service] for which payment is received by the [Company].

P.157

'Unit Price' shall mean the fixed sum for each item of the [Products] that the [Distributor] shall pay to the [Supplier]. A copy of the Unit Price for each item of the [Products] is set out in the attached Schedule A and forms part of this agreement.

P.158

'The Contributors Fee' shall mean the sum of [number/currency] for the work and services to be provided under this agreement set out in Appendix B to be paid by the [Distributor] to [Name].

P.159

The [Company] shall pay the [Contributors'] Fee to [Name] by bank direct debit within [number] days of receipt of an invoice setting out the sum due for the work and services provided under this agreement and with relevant bank details. Any such payment shall be subject to the satisfactory completion of the work and services by [Name].

P.160

'The Basic Fee' shall mean the sum of [number/currency].

P.161

The [Company] shall pay the Basic Fee in equal monthly instalments one month [in advance/arrears]. The first payment is to be made within [number] days of the signature of this agreement by both parties. Payment shall be made directly into the [Contributors'] bank account by direct debit and shall be subject to the provision of an invoice on each occasion which sets out the sum due.

P.162

'The Bonus Fee' shall mean a one off payment of [number/currency] which is separate and additional to the Basic Fee and any expenses which shall be payable by the [Company] in the event that the number of [responses/clicks/sales/premium line calls] exceeds [number] from [date] to [date].

P.163

The [Company] shall provide the [Contributor] with a report by [date] which sets out the number of [responses/clicks/sales/premium line calls] exceed [number] from [date] to [date]. The [Company] shall then pay any sums due to the [Contributor] within [number] days] of receipt of an invoice.

P.164

The [Company] shall pay the [Contributor] a fee of [number/currency] for the completion of the interview and filming for the [Podcast]. No payment shall be due if the work is not completed and/or the [Contributor] is not available on the agreed date.

P.165

The [Company] shall not be obliged to pay any fee, royalty and/or other payment to any member of the public, subscriber and/or other person who has submitted text, images and/or other material to the [Website/App/Platform] for the use of such material in any advertising, promotion and/or marketing material at any time and/or the sub-licensing of such material to a third party.

P.166

All financial transactions and payments in respect of this [Website/App/Platform/Channel] are made through [specify payment company] which is an independent and separate legal entity and not part of the [Website/App/Platform/Channel Company]. No order shall be sent until confirmation of payment has been received from the [payment company]. No responsibility can be accepted by the [Website/App/Platform/Channel Company] for any problems that may arise from the use of the [payment company] and/or any losses, damages, costs and/or other expenses that may be incurred.

P.167

The [Company] may at any time offer [Name] a substitute alternative [Film/App/Event/Product/Service] other than the one which [Name] has paid for. [Name] shall have the right to accept and/or refuse the substitution. If it is refused then the agreement shall end and a refund be made to [Name] where appropriate for any period where the original order is not provided.

P.168

1.1 No refunds will be made at any time by the [Company] where the [Service/Download/Sound Recording] which [Name] has paid for has been interrupted, delayed and/or has been without sound and/or vision and/or text and/or images for any reason.

1.2 A [redeemable voucher code] will be offered where it is decided by the [Company] that [Name] has not received a reasonable standard service in the circumstances.

P.169

1.1 Payment must be made in full in advance by a [specify] card held in your own name which you are authorised to use through [specify company].

1.2 Payment cannot be accepted by any other method.

1.3 Any bank charges to be incurred shall be at your own cost.

1.4 Part payment will not be accepted nor payment by instalments.

1.5 Where there is evidence of fraud, misrepresentation of age and/or the payment is rejected by the bank then no ticket shall be supplied for the [Event].

P.170

Any order shall only be shipped to the delivery address when payment has been received and retained by the [Supplier]. Where there is any rejection of the payment request to the [Supplier] by a third party then the order will not be fulfilled.

P.171

Payment will only be accepted by the [Supplier] in the following methods:

1.1 Credit card excluding [specify excluded companies].

1.2 Direct debit from a registered bank excluding [specify excluded types of banking].

1.3   Payment must be in [currency].

1.4   No transfer by [specify format] is accepted.

1.5   The payment name for the order must match the account of the person making the payment.

P.172

In order to continue to be provided with access to the [Service/Archive/Library Catalogue] you must have paid the monthly fee in advance. Failure to make the payment by the due date will mean that your access to the [Service/Archive/Library Catalogue] is blocked at the end of the last date to which your previous payment applies. In order to reinstate access the full monthly payment must be paid within [number] days. After that period the [Enterprise] shall have the right to terminate this agreement and cancel your account.

Merchandising and Distribution

P.173

'The Licence Fee' shall mean the sum of [number/currency] which shall be payable by the [Licensee] to the [Licensor] as follows:

1.1   [number/currency] within [number] days of signature of this agreement by both parties.

1.2   [number/currency] upon acceptance by the [Licensee] of the reproductions of the [Master Material]

1.3   [number/currency] upon acceptance by the [Licensor] of the prototype of the [Licensed Articles/Products].

1.4   [number/currency] upon acceptance by the [Licensor] of the final version for manufacture of the [Licensed Articles/Products].

1.5   [number/currency] upon first commercial release of the [Licensed Articles/Products] in [country] to [the general public/major retail outlets].

1.6   [number/currency] on or by [date] subject to the achievement of [number/currency] total gross sales of the [Licensed Articles/Products] by the [Licensee] by that date. If that figure is not achieved then the payment shall be delayed until the target is reached.

P.174

In the event that the cost of the development of the [Article/Product] exceeds the sum of [number/currency] which is the agreed Budget. The payment of any overspend shall be at the entire cost of the [Company]. The [Company] shall be entitled to recoup the cost of the agreed Budget but not any overspend from the calculation and payment of any future royalties to the [Licensor].

P.175
The [Designer] agrees to consult with the [Licensee] with respect to the prices at which the [Licensed Articles] are to be sold, whether by retail, wholesale or at a discounted price.

P.176
The [Distributor] undertakes that the minimum wholesale selling price for each unit of the [Licensed Articles/Products] throughout the [Territory/world] shall not be less than [number/currency].

P.177
In consideration of the rights granted under this agreement the [Licensee] shall pay to the [Licensor] the Advance Licence Fee as follows:

1.1   [number/currency] within [number] days of signature of this agreement and receipt of an invoice from the [Licensor].

1.2   [number/currency] on or before [date] subject to completion of 1.1 and the acceptance of the master material specified in Appendix A.

1.3   [number/currency] on or before date provided that the first commercial distribution of more than [number] copies of the [Licensed Articles] to retail and online outlets has occurred in any country in the world. If this has not been attained for any reason then the payment shall be delayed until it has been achieved.

1.4   The [Licensee] acknowledges that the Advance Licence Fee is not returnable by the [Licensor] and is not to be offset against the [Licensor's] Royalties.

P.178
The minimum sum for each unit of the [Licensed Articles] on which the [Licensor's] Royalties shall be calculated shall be [number/currency]. If the sum received for any reason is lower the accounts shall be carried out as if this minimum sum is the deemed receipt. The cost of the difference shall be entirely the responsibility of the [Licensee].

P.179
'The Assignment Fee' shall be the sum of [number/currency].

In consideration of the rights assigned under this agreement the [Assignee] agrees to pay the [Assignor] the Assignment Fee as follows:

1.1   [number/currency] upon full signature of this Agreement by both parties.

1.2   [number/currency] on or before [date].

1.3   [number/currency] subject to satisfactory collection by the [Assignee] of the [Work Material].

P.180

In consideration of the rights granted under this agreement the [Distributor] shall pay to the [Licensor] the Licence Fee as follows:

1.1   [number/currency] upon signature of this agreement.

1.2   [number/currency] on or before [date] subject to acceptance of the [Material].

1.3   [number/currency] upon approval of the sample of the [Licensed Articles/Products] by the [Licensor].

1.4   [number/currency] upon approval of the labels, packaging and advertising of the [Licensed Articles/Products] by the [Licensor].

1.5   [number/currency] upon first availability of the [Licensed Articles/ Products] by the [Licensor] to the general public anywhere in the world.

P.181

'The Advance Fee' shall be the non-returnable and recoupable advance against the [Authors'/Licensors'] royalties which is the sum of [number/ currency] [words].

P.182

In consideration of the rights [granted/assigned] under this agreement the [Company] shall pay the [Licence/Assignment Fee] to the [Author] as follows:

1.1   [number/currency] within [number] days subject to signature of this agreement by the [Author] and the [Company].

1.2   [number/currency] on or before date [date] subject the completion of 1.1.

1.3   [number/currency] within [number] days of approval by the [Author] of the final versions of the Script and Storyboard and characterisations, Budget, Cast List and other matters set out in Appendix A.

1.4   [number/currency] within [number] days of completion of the final edit and private viewing of the [Film] by the [Author].

1.5 [number/currency] within [number] days of the first premier opening of the [Film] in any part of the world.

1.6 [number/currency] upon first television transmission and/or broadcast in any part of the world but in any event no later than [date].

1.7 [number/currency] within [number] days of the conclusion of any merchandising agreement with a third party for the [Film] by the [Company] but in any event no later than [date].

1.8 [number/currency] within [number] days of the conclusion by the [Company] of any subscription agreement with a third party for viewing the [Film] over the internet but in any event no later than [date].

1.9 [number/currency] upon first commercial release of any [Computer Game/DVD/Animation] of the [Film] but in any event no later than [date].

P.183

[Name] agrees to pay the [Artist] a fee of [number/currency for the development, assignment of rights and delivery of the [Image and Logo]. Payment shall be in three stages:

1.1 [number/currency] on signature of this agreement for the services of the [Artist].

1.2 [number/currency] on delivery to [and acceptance by] [Name] of the following material: all draft copies of the [Image and Logo] and the master copy of the computer generated [animated] film and sound recording together with music cue sheets.

1.3 [number/currency] on signature by the [Artist] of the assignment document supplied by [Name].

P.184

1.1 All sums due shall be paid within [number] days of receipt of an invoice from the [Supplier] subject to acceptance of all the [Products].

1.2 Payments may be made on account as an advance against the total cost if the total value of the order by the [Company] exceeds [number/currency].

1.3 The [Company] shall not pay more than [number] per cent in advance of delivery of the [Products].

1.4 Where there is any dispute regarding the quality of the [Products] and/or any damage the [Company] shall be entitled to delay payment until the dispute is resolved. If the dispute is not resolved then the [Company] shall have the right to cancel all further orders of the [Products] and shall not be liable for any further payments except for the disputed sums.

P.185

1.1 Time is of the essence in respect of the payment terms of this agreement. All payments due must be made within [number] days of the date on which any [Products/Material] are sent by the [Company]. After the expiry of the [number] day payment period interest will be charged at an annual rate of [number] per cent above the Base Rate charged from time to time by [specify bank].

1.2 No title and/or right of ownership to the [Products/Material] shall pass to the [Client] until the sums due have been paid in full.

1.3 The [Company] reserves the right to retrieve the [Products/Material] and to charge for any damages and/or losses if payment is not received within [number] days from the date it is sent to the [Client].

P.186

The price of the [Products] shall be paid in [currency]. The Company shall establish with a reputable bank satisfactory to the [Seller] an irrevocable letter of credit representing the full amount of the purchase price in [currency] under the contract in favour of the [Seller] to be drawn on or by [date].

P.187

The price to be paid by the [Buyer] for the [Company's] Products shall in all cases be the relevant price contained in the [Company's] Wholesale Price Lists in force at the date of delivery. Where the [Company's] Products are delivered in returnable storage packages the [Buyer] shall pay the appropriate deposit charged by the [Company which shall be reimbursed provided the storage packages are returned within [specify period].

P.188

'The Wholesale Selling Price' shall be the sum charged by the [Supplier] to any warehouse distributor, online direct marketing enterprise and/or retail sales outlet for the purchase of each [Product/Unit] before they add any mark-up prior to sale to the public.

P.189

1.1 The total costs to be charged for the [Project/Products/Units] shall be stated in the confirmed [Sales/Purchase] Order for the [Project/Products/Units] by the [Company]. No email and/or verbal quotation by the [Company] shall be considered binding and should be considered as guidance only as to potential costs.

1.2 Where any additional work is requested then the [Company] shall be entitled to add further sums to be agreed with the [Client]. Any such additional work shall not proceed until such sums have been confirmed between the parties.

P.190

1.1 The price which is stated in the quotation provided by the [Company] shall only be held for a maximum [twenty-eight] days. After that period the offer by the [Company] shall lapse and not apply.

1.2 The [Company] at its entire discretion at any time within that period in 1.1 withdraw the offer if there is a major change of circumstances which affects the quoted price. Factors which may cause the [Company] to withdraw the offer include but are not limited to increases in the cost of petrol, oil, transport, taxes, exchange rates and/or the supply of materials.

1.3 Once the [Client] has accepted an offer by the [Company] the final price agreed by the [Company] shall be confirmed in an order acknowledgement form with an order reference number.

P.191

'Fixed Price Firm Sale' shall mean that the sum that [Name] shall pay the [Supplier] for each unit of the [Product] provided by the [Supplier]. [Name] accepts that there shall be no right to return any units of the [Product] which are not sold by [Name].

P.192

'The E price' shall be the recommended price at which the [Work] is sold to the public over the internet excluding freight, packaging, insurance and administrative costs which shall be [number/currency].

P.193

The [Agent] acknowledges that it is not permitted to offer any discount and/or other reduction in this ex-factory price and/or offer any other special terms, promotions and/or deductions without the prior written consent of the [Company].

P.194

In consideration of the [Products/Units/Services] the [Company] agrees to pay the [Distributor] the following fee/rates: [price per unit/per month/per batch]. Payment shall be made in full subject to satisfactory delivery and acceptance of the [Products/Units/Services] by the [Company] subject to a payment delay of up no more than [number] days from receipt of invoice from the [Distributor].

P.195
Prices are inclusive of [value added tax/government taxes on the supply of goods and/or services] subject to any changes in the rates which may apply before the [Client] has paid the price in full. Prices are in [pounds sterling]. The [Client] shall reimburse the [Company] on demand for any expense incurred on the conversion of foreign currencies, bank charges, presenting and/or processing of any payment or otherwise which arose from converting the sums to sterling. Payment is not actually made until the sums in sterling have been received by the [Company].

P.196
A deposit of [number] per cent of the total cost price must be sent to the [Company] with the request form in order to secure the reservation of the [Material]. The balance of the cost price is due on the first instalment date of delivery of the [Material]. Time of payment shall be of the essence of the contract.

P.197

1.1 The [Agent] agrees that it must adhere to the instructions of the [Company] at all times and must adhere to the price lists and sale conditions imposed by the [Company] in respect of any third parties.

1.2 The [Agent] accepts that he/she does not have the authority to increase, decrease and/or alter prices and/or conditions relating to the sale and/or supply of the [Products/Services] to any third parties.

1.3 The [Agent] agrees that he/she shall not offer, agree and/or discuss any discounts, reductions in prices and/or deferments in payment to any third parties.

1.4 The [Agent] accepts that the [Company] shall issue any invoices direct to any [Client] and that all payments shall be made direct to the [Company] not the [Agent].

1.5 The [Agent] agrees that he/she is not entitled to receive any payments relating to the [Products/Services] from any [Client]. That the authority of the [Agent] is limited to the marketing and promotion and the negotiation of orders only.

P.198
All orders are subject to payment on receipt of invoice, unless otherwise agreed in writing by a Director of the [Company]. All accounts must be settled by the agreed due date. Failure to do so will entitle the [Company] to withdraw such facilities. All charges involved in the collection of overdue accounts will be payable by the [Customer].

P.199
The [Company] shall provide the [Agent] with a list each season of the prices in [specify currency] of the cost of ordering the [Garments] based on the collection samples which shall be the ex-factory price together with the estimated freight and insurance costs to destination which shall each be itemised. The price list shall not include customs and excise and any duty costs, storage and other taxes and levies which may apply as those shall be an additional cost to be paid by the [Customer]. The [Agent] agrees to promote, market and obtain orders for the [Garments] at the prices and on the conditions specified by the [Company]. The [Agent] acknowledges that title to any garments ordered shall remain with the [Company] until full payment of any invoice has been received by the [Company] and that this shall be made clear to any [Client].

P.200
The payment for the [Products/Service] shall be due monthly in advance on the [number] day of each month subject to the supply of an invoice setting out the sums due. [number] days' notice is required in advance in order to cancel the agreement for the delivery of the [Products/Service] after the completion of the first [six] months. Where payment is delayed for any reason no additional sum shall be charged for a delay of up to [number] days on the outstanding sum but thereafter an additional fee of [number/currency] in total may be added for each day until the sum is paid in full.

P.201
Unless otherwise stated in the Sales Order the payment of invoices shall be made by the [15th] of each calendar month following the preceding date in which the [Products] were delivered to the [Client]. The [Company] reserves the right to deduct and set-off any monies due to the [Client] any monies due from the [Client] to the [Company].

P.202

1.1 The [Company] shall pay [Name] the sum of [number/currency] as an advance against royalties that may be earned from the sale of the [Product/Service].

1.2 The [Company] agrees that it shall not seek to reclaim the advance from [Name] and that it can only recoup such sum from the allocated future royalty payments to [Name].

1.3 In the event that the total [gross sales/net revenue] from the exploitation of the [Product/Service] exceed [number] in the first six months. The [Company] agrees that it shall pay [Name] an additional advance of [number/currency].

1445

P.203

Where the [Company] has paid the sums due for the [Products] to the [Supplier] and subsequently discovers after delivery that the [Supplier] has misled and/or provided inaccurate information to the [Company] as to the country of origin of the content. The [Supplier] agrees that the [Supplier] shall pay for the cost of shipment of the [Products] back to the [Supplier] and/or arrange for collection. In addition the [Supplier] shall refund all payments made for the [Products] by the [Company] plus an additional penalty of [number/currency] to cover administrative costs incurred. Such payment to be made by the [Supplier] within [number] days of notification by the [Company] as to the facts.

P.204

If payment is delayed for any reason then the [Supplier] shall be entitled to cancel the order by [Name] and to offer the [Products] to another third party. Title and ownership in the [Products] at all times remains with the [Supplier] until payment has been received in full.

P.205

The [Supplier] agrees that ownership and title in the [Products] delivered to the [Distributor] shall be transferred to the [Distributor] on the date and time of delivery. That such change of ownership shall not be subject to the receipt of payment for the [Products] by the [Supplier]. That the [Distributor] shall be entitled to sell the [Products] to a third party.

P.206

The [Supplier] agrees that the [Distributor] may delay payment for the [Products] for up to [number] months from the date of delivery. That the [Supplier] will not charge interest on any such delayed payment.

P.207

Where payment is not received by the [Supplier] within [number] days. The [Supplier] shall have the right to enter the premises of the [Distributor] and to retrieve the [Products] which have been delivered. The [Distributor] agrees that in such circumstances it shall be obliged to return the [Products] to the [Supplier].

P.208

All statements and payments under this agreement shall be as follows:

1.1 in [currency].

1.2 all currency conversion and bank charges to be at [Licensees' cost/split between the parties in equal shares/other].

1.3   all statements state the original currency, the date and rate of conversion and the final sum in [currency].

1.4   all statements must include any lost and damaged stock and those given away for free.

1.5   all payments must be to [name] to the specified bank and account nominated in each year by [method]. Where [name] is deceased then all the payments shall be made to the legal estate of [name].

1.6   all deductions of any sums from the gross receipts before the calculation of the royalties due to [name] must be itemised in detail. Copies of any receipts shall be supplied to [name] upon request to verify the expenditure. These sums in any accounting period shall not exceed [number/currency] and any balance shall be carried forward to the next accounting period.

Publishing

P.209

The [Author] acknowledges that the selling price of the [Work/Book/Audio Recording/Merchandising] shall be within the sole and exclusive discretion of the [Publisher]. The [Publisher] shall consult with the [Author] prior to making a final decision on any recommended retail prices.

P.210

1.1   The [Author] has authorised that any payments due to the [Author] under this agreement shall made to the [Agent].

1.2   The [Publisher] shall make all payments to the [Agent] until such time as the [Author] shall notify the [Publisher] that payment is to be made to the [Author] and/or another third party.

1.3   The [Author] agrees that any payment to the [Agent] in 1.1 discharges any such debt owed by the [Publisher] to the [Author].

1.4   The [Author] agrees that if the [Agent] fails to transfer any required payment to the [Author] and is found to be fraudulent and/or negligent and/or misappropriates the sums paid in any form the [Publisher] shall not be held liable.

1.5   The [Author] also agrees that if he/she instructs the [Publisher] to make any payments direct to the [Author] at any time then the [Publisher] shall be bound to follow the instructions of the [Author] and shall not be liable to the [Agent] for any reason.

P.211

The [Publisher] shall pay the [Author] the Advance against Royalties as follows:

1.1 [number/currency] within [number] days of the signature of this agreement by both parties.

1.2 [number/currency] subject to delivery and acceptance of the complete manuscript of the [Work].

1.3 [number/currency] subject to delivery and acceptance of the edited proofs by the [Author] together with any preface, introduction, preface and index.

1.4 [number/currency] on within [number] days of the first date of the publication of the [Work] in [hardback format].

1.5 [number/currency] on within [number] days of the first date of the publication of the [Work] in [paperback format].

1.6 [number/currency] on within [number] days of the first date of the publication of the [Work] as an [Audio Recording].

1.7 [number/currency] on within [number] days of the first date of the publication of the [Work] in any online electronic subscription service which is made available over the internet in any format.

P.212

The [Writer] confirms that the [Company] shall be entitled to retain all sums received from the exploitation of the [Work/Manuscript] in any media throughout the [Territory/world] at any time and the [Writer] shall not be entitled to any such additional sums.

P.213

'The Serialisation Fee' shall be the sum of [number/currency].

The [Licensee] agrees to pay the Serialisation Fee to the [Author] as follows:

1.1 [number/currency] by the end of the next calendar month which follows the date upon which this agreement was signed by all the parties.

1.2 [number/currency] within [number] days of acceptance of the manuscript of the [Extracts] by the [Licensee].

1.3 [number/currency] within [number] days of the satisfactory conclusion of the consultation process with the [Author] in respect of the layout of the format, title, text and images for the serialisation.

1.4 [number/currency] within [number] days of the publication in [country] in any format by the [Licensee] of the [Extracts] including online over the internet and/or in any magazine, newspaper and/or otherwise.

P.214
'The Ghostwriter's Fee' shall be the following sum [number/currency].

In consideration of the rights assigned under this agreement and services provided by the [Ghostwriter] the [Company] shall pay to the [Ghostwriter] the [Ghostwriter's] Fee as follows:

1.1 [number/currency] within [number] days of the signature by both parties of this agreement subject to an invoice from the [Ghostwriter].

1.2 [number/currency] on or before [date] subject to approval of written evidence of sufficient progress such as outlines of chapters and [number] draft chapters by the [Company].

1.3 [number/currency] subject to acceptance of the final manuscript of the [Work] together with copies of any photographs, images, maps and references the artwork by the [Company].

1.4 [number/currency] on or before [date] subject to completion of the editing of the printed proofs by the [Ghostwriter] and delivery of the proofs to the [Company].

1.5 [number/currency] on or before [date] subject to the publication of the [Work] in [hardback] in [country].

1.6 [number/currency] on or before date subject to the publication of the [Work] in [paperback] in [country].

1.7 [number/currency] on or before date subject to the publication of the [Work] as an [Audio Recording/File] for access, download and/or under any subscription service in electronic form over the internet.

P.215
The [Company] shall pay to the [Writer] the total fee of [number/currency] (exclusive of any tax imposed by any government on the supply of goods and/or services) as follows:

1.1 [number/currency] on the full signature of this document and subject to the submission of an invoice by the [Writer].

1.2 [number/currency] upon [the receipt/acceptance/approval] of the Treatment by the [Company].

1.3 [number/currency] upon [the receipt/acceptance/approval] of the Script by the [Company].

P.216

As full consideration for the rights in and to the [Book] which shall include the manuscript, the title, any logo, images, graphics, preface and index. The [Publisher] shall pay to the [Writer] the total sum of [number/currency] (exclusive of any value added tax/other). The sum shall be paid as follows:

1.1 [number per cent] upon signature of this agreement by all parties and subject to an invoice from the [Writer]; and

1.2 the balance upon receipt and approval by the [Publisher] of the completed manuscript with the title, images and graphics. It shall not include the preface and index which shall be provided after the printed proofs.

P.217

The [Publisher] shall pay the [Author] the sum of [number/currency] as an advance against royalties. Such payment to be on account of any sums that may become due to the [Author] under this agreement in respect of the first edition as follows:

1.1 The sum of [number/currency] within [one] month of the signature of this agreement by both parties.

1.2 The sum of [number/currency] on delivery to the [Publishers] of the [Manuscript/Sound Recordings/Films/Photographs].

P.218

The [Publisher] agrees to pay the [Author] the Advance against future royalties as follows:

1.1 [number/currency] within [number] days of signature of this agreement by the [Author] and the [Publisher].

1.2 [number/currency] upon delivery to the [Publisher] of the first [number pages/chapters] of the [Work] typed in A4 pages in [specify format].

1.3 [number/currency] subject to delivery to and acceptance by the [Publisher] of a manuscript of the [Work] in [format].

1.4 [number/currency] subject to the return to the [Publisher] of the corrected and edited proofs.

1.5 [number/currency] on or before [date] subject to the authorised serialisation of [number] words of extracts of the [Work] in a magazine and/or newspaper.

1.6 [number/currency] within [one] calendar month of the first publication of the [Work] in hardback in any country.

1.7 [number/currency] within [one] calendar month of the first publication of the [Work] in paperback in any country.

1.8 [number/currency] subject to the conclusion of one or more merchandising agreements but in any event no later than [date].

1.9 [number/currency] as a one- off bonus in the event that total net [sales/receipts] in respect of the [hardback/paperback book] exceed [number/currency] in total in [the first year of publication/the first three years].

1.10 [number/currency] within [one] month of the release of the [Audio Recording] of the [Work] for sale to the public.

1.11 [number/currency] within [one] month of the authorisation and conclusion of an agreement for upon for any [film/series/documentary] adaptation of the [Work].

1.12 [number/currency] within [one] month of the first broadcast and/or transmission of any such [film/series/documentary] on television in any form whether terrestrial, cable, satellite or by electronic means over the internet.

1.13 [number/currency] within [one] month of the first release of any [Computer Game/Merchandising Product] derived from the [Work] and/or in conjunction with any [film/series /documentary] adaptation of the [Work].

P.219
The [Publisher] agrees that no part of the Advance payment shall be returned by the [Author] once the [Publisher] has accepted the manuscript of the [Work].

P.220

1.1 Advertising rates may be increased at any time subject to [one] [week/ months'] written notice prior to the date of publication.

1.2 The [Customer] is responsible for the cost of the delivery, creation, development and preparation of all artwork, layout and photography which shall be quoted in advance when the order is confirmed as accepted.

1.3 All advertisements accepted for publication are subject to the following policies and guidelines: [specify policy/organisation].

1.4 The [Company] shall not be obliged to accept all orders placed for advertisement and may refuse the request without providing any reason.

1.5 Where an order is accepted then payment shall be required as follows: [fifty] per cent of the agreed total order price in advance and [fifty] per cent within [number] days] of the date of publication of the advertisement.

P.221

The [Publisher] shall be entitled to offset the Advance against future royalties due to the [Author] under this agreement but not against any other agreement that the [Author] may have with the [Publisher] and/or any parent company.

P.222

The [Publisher] agrees and undertakes that it is not entitled to claim any unearned advance back from the [Author] which is not recouped against royalties under this agreement. Neither is the [Publisher] permitted and/or authorised to recoup any unearned advance against royalties and/or sums due to the [Author] under any other agreement which the [Author] has with the [Publisher] and/or any parent and/or subsidiary company.

P.223

1.1 The [Publisher] shall be entitled to offset the Advance against future royalties due to the [Author] under this agreement and against any other agreement that the [Author] may have with the [Publisher] and/or any parent and/or subsidiary company at any time.

1.2 The [Author] agrees that the [Publisher] shall be entitled to claim any unearned portion of the Advance payment directly from the [Author] which is not recouped against royalties due under this agreement and/ or which cannot be offset against royalties due to the [Author] under any other agreement which the [Author] has with the [Publisher] and/ or any parent and subsidiary company. The [Publisher] agrees to conclude a repayment plan with the [Author] of [one] year.

P.224

The [Publishers'] shall not recoup and/or offset any sums due from one agreement against another without notifying the [Author] in writing and explaining the reasons. The [Author] shall be provided with the opportunity to dispute the matter and to set out in writing the reasons as to why this procedure is not acceptable.

P.225

The [Licensee] shall pay to the [Company] by [method] a non-returnable advance of [number/currency] [excluding any taxes which may fall due which require an invoice] on [date] subject to delivery and acceptance of the [Master Material] in Appendix B. Such sum shall not be contingent on any further matters and cannot be repaid at a later date.

P.226
The [Publisher] agrees that it shall not be entitled to recoup and/or offset any sums due under this agreement with [Name] against any other previous and/or future agreements without the prior written consent of [Name].

P.227
The [Author] shall not receive any additional payment for contributions to promotion, development and/or marketing of the [Work] which is less than [number] hours. Thereafter the [Distributor] agrees to pay the [Author] a daily rate of [number/currency] for [number] hours per day such sums to be paid within [number] days subject to invoice.

Services

P.228
The [Photographer] acknowledges and agrees that the [Assignee] shall be entitled to commercially exploit the [Work] in any form without further payment to the [Photographer].

P.229
In consideration of [Contributor's] services the [Company] agrees to pay the Contributor's Fee as follows:

1.1 [number/currency] within [number] days of signature of this assignment document by all parties to this agreement and subject to an invoice from the [Contributor].

1.2 [number/currency] on or before [date] subject to the completion of the services and work set out in Schedule A and the delivery of the material in clause [–].

1.3 [number/currency] on or before [date] subject to the return to the [Company] of all material supplied on loan and the assignment of all copyright in the material created and delivered by the [Contributor] to the [Company] under this agreement.

P.230

1.1 The [Company] agrees to pay the [Actor/Presenter] the Repeat Fees within [number] days of each of the dates upon which a repeat broadcast and/or transmission is made throughout the Territory at any time.

1.2 Any other matters not dealt with in this agreement shall be the subject of separate notification in each case by the [Company] and the parties must on each occasion agree an additional payment for that use. The [Company] agrees that no payment shall be less than [number/currency].

P.231

'The Payment Schedule' shall mean sums to be paid by the [Company to the [Designer] set out in Schedule A subject to the conditions to be fulfilled by the [Designer].

The [Company] shall pay such sums as are due to the [Designer] in accordance with the Payment Schedule subject to completion of the required work to a satisfactory standard and within [one] calendar month of receipt of an invoice.

P.232

1.1 The [Company] shall pay the [Artist] an advance payment of [number/currency] against future royalties and earnings relating to the [Artist] and the [Group] on or by: [date].

1.2 The [Artist] agrees that the [Company] shall have the right to recoup the advance fee from the royalties and earnings due to the [Artist] under this agreement before any further sums are paid to the [Artist].

1.3 That if by [date] the [Company] has not recouped the advance fee in 1.1 that the [Company] shall have the right to request that the [Artist] repay the sum due provided that the [Company] have commercially released the sound recordings of the [Artist] in any format by [date].

1.4 That the [Company] agrees not to issue any legal proceedings against the [Artist] provided that it is agreed that the sum due will be repaid within [twelve] months of the date of the demand for payment.

P.233

The [Company] shall pay the [Artist] a fee of [number/currency] as a non-returnable Advance against future royalties relating to the services of [Artist] provided under this agreement as follows:

1.1 [number/currency] upon within [number] days of the signature of this agreement by all the parties.

1.2 [number/currency] upon delivery and acceptance of the [Lyrics/Compositions of the Music Works] set out in Schedule A.

1.3 [number/currency] on or before: [date] subject to the successful completion of [duration] hours of sound recordings and filming described in Schedule B.

1.4 [number/currency] within [one] calendar month of the date of the first release to the public of the [CD/Album/Disc] in any country.

1.5 [number/currency] in the event that a [Download/Audio File] is made available in electronic form by the [Company] either under a subscription service and/or through payment for access by each individual over the internet any gadget, computer, mobile, television and/or other method of listening to and/or viewing by the public in any language.

1.6 [number/currency] within [one] calendar month of the first release to the public of any related product and/or service and/or merchandising based on and/or adapted from the sound recordings and/or musical works provided by the [Artist].

1.7 [number/currency] as a bonus in the event that [unit] sales of the [CD/Album/Download/Audio File] exceed [number] in total anywhere in the world.

P.234
The [Company] agrees and undertakes that:

1.1 the [Company] is not entitled to claim any unearned advance back from the [Artist] which is not recouped against royalties.

1.2 the [Company] is not entitled to set-off unearned advance under this agreement against any advance and/or royalties due to the [Artist] under any other agreement which the [Artist] has with the [Company].

P.235
The [Artist] agrees that the [Company] shall have the right to recover the Advance from the royalties and earnings due to the [Artist] under this agreement. That if by the expiry date of: [date] the [Company] has not recouped the Advance that the [Company] shall have the right to seek that the [Artist] repay the sum due provided that the [Company] have commercially released the [CD/Album/Audio File] by the expiry date of [date]. The [Company] agrees not to issue any legal proceedings and/or to seek to be entitled to legal costs against the [Artist] provided that the sum due shall be repaid within [three] years of the expiry date and/or the date of the demand by the [Company] whichever is the later.

P.236

1.1 The [Company] shall be entitled to offset the Advance against future royalties due to the [Artist] under this agreement and against any other agreement that the [Artist] may have with the [Company] [and/or any subsidiary and/or parent company at any time].

1.2 The [Artist] agrees that the [Company] shall be entitled to claim any unearned advance back from the [Artist] which is not recouped against royalties due under this agreement and/or which cannot be offset against royalties due to the [Artist] under any other agreement which the [Artist] has with the [Company] [and/or any subsidiary and/or parent company at any time].

P.237

The [Company] shall not recoup and/or offset any sums due from one agreement against another without notifying the [Artist] in writing and explaining the reasons. The [Artist] shall be provided with the opportunity to dispute and to set out in writing the reasons as to why this is not acceptable.

P.238

The [Consultant] shall in consideration of his/her services be paid a fee of [number/currency [per hour/half day/day/calendar month]. Such sums shall be payable in arrears by the last day of each such four-week period. The first of such payments shall be made on: [date]. The fee shall be subject to review on [date]. All sums shall be subject to the supply of an invoice and where any taxes on the supply of services are charged by government a registered reference must be provided.

P.239

In consideration of the services to be rendered to the [Company] the [Presenter] shall receive a fee of [number/currency] for each period of [three] calendar months. Payment shall be made in advance by the start of the first day of work by the [Presenter] subject to the supply of an invoice to the [Company]. The fees stated are exclusive of [VAT/other]. The [Company] agrees to pay [VAT/other] on such fees upon submission of a [VAT/other] invoice.

P.240

'The Presenter's Fee' shall be the following sums:

1.1 [number/currency] for the first twelve calendar months from [date].

1.2 [number/currency] for the following twelve calendar months from [date].

1.3 [number/currency] for the following [six calendar months until the end date on: [date].

In consideration of the [Presenter's] services the [Company] agrees to pay the [Presenter's] Fee in equal instalments throughout the Term of the

Agreement on the last day of each calendar month. The first instalment shall be due on [date].

P.241

1.1 The [Company] during the continuance of this agreement shall receive a monthly fee payable in arrears of [number/currency] for the first [number] calendar months.

1.2 The first payment shall be due on [date] for the preceding month. Where the start date is not a complete month then only a pro rata portion shall be paid.

1.3 The monthly fee shall be increased from [date/month/year] to [number/currency] until the expiry of the agreement on [date].

P.242

1.1 The [Contributor's] Fee shall be the sum of [number/currency] payable in equal monthly instalments one month in advance, such sum to be in addition to the Expenses as defined in Clause [–] to this agreement and exclusive of any [VAT/taxes on the supply of services imposed by any government]. The first payment shall be made immediately following the signing of this agreement by both parties. Payment shall be made directly into the [Contributor's] bank account by electronic transfer.

1.2 The [Contributor] confirms that he/she shall be liable for the arrangement for and payment of his/her [national Insurance contributions/other] and any other sums which are or may be payable to the [HMRC/other] as a result of the payments made under this agreement.

P.243

The [Company] shall pay to the [Director]:

1.1 [number/currency] exclusive of [value added tax/any taxes on the supply of services] of which [number/currency] has already been paid by the [Company] to the [Director] and the balance of which shall be paid on or by [date]. No further sums shall be paid after this date if the filming is cancelled for any reason.

1.2 [number/currency] on the commencement of principal photography of the [Film] but not in any event later than [date] provided the filming is not cancelled in which case no payment shall be due.

1.3 [number/currency] on the last day of the [number] week of principal photography provided the filming is not cancelled in which case no payment shall be due.

1.4 [number/currency] on completion of the final cut of the [Film] provided the filming is not cancelled in which case no payment shall be due.

1.5 [number/currency] on or by [date] which is the end of the scheduled production and editing period. Together with payment of such other additional sums as the [Director] may be entitled to be paid in accordance with the relevant union agreement with [specify organisation/country]. Provided that the filming is not cancelled in which case no payment shall be due.

1.6 Where filming has started but is then cancelled then a pro-rata payment shall be paid to the [Director].

P.244

1.1 The [Celebrity] confirms that all sums due to the [Celebrity] shall be paid directly to the [Agent] until such time as the [Celebrity] may otherwise supply different instructions. Any payments due to the [Celebrity] under this agreement shall have been met and fulfilled by the [Company] by payment to the instructed representative.

1.2 In the event that the [Agent] fails to transfer payment to the [Celebrity] then the [Celebrity] agrees and undertakes that it shall not be the fault and/or responsibility of the [Company].

1.3 If the [Celebrity] instructs the [Company] to make payment direct to the [Celebrity] then the [Company] shall be bound to follow the instructions of the [Celebrity] and shall not be liable to the [Agent] for any reason.

1.4 Payment to the [Agent] at the direction of the [Celebrity] does not make the [Agent] a party to this agreement and/or provide any legal obligation to the [Agent] from the [Company].

P.245

In consideration of the services provided by the [Contributor] and the rights assigned to the [Company] under this agreement. The [Company] shall pay to the [Contributor] the fee of [number/currency] on or by [date]. In the event that the [Contributor] is requested by the [Company] to provide services over and above those set out in appendix A then the [Company] undertakes to agree with the [Contributor] the payment of additional fees.

P.246

In consideration of the services provided by the [Researcher] and the rights assigned under this agreement. The [Company] shall pay the [Researcher] a daily fee of [number/currency]. The [Researcher] acknowledges that the daily fee shall be for an [8] hour day and pro rata payments may be made where appropriate. No overtime or additional fees shall be due unless specifically agreed between the parties in advance.

P.247

The [Company] agrees to pay the [Researcher's] Fee within [number] days of the end of each working week following receipt of an invoice setting out the hours and days worked by the [Researcher] and the details of all such work.

P.248

In consideration of the expert services, work and report provided by [Name] in the role of [specify expertise]. The [Company] agrees to pay to [Name] the fee of [number/currency] by [date] in [cash/bankers draft/by direct debit] in full and final settlement subject to delivery of the report. No expenses or other sums of any nature shall be due to [Name] and the [Company] shall be entitled to exploit all the product of his/her services, work and report in any format in any media at any time.

P.249

The current charges and payments due for the [Service/Subscription] are specified in Schedule A. The [Company] shall have the right to increase the sums due at any time no more than [twice] a year. Provided that the [User/Subscriber] is provided with [number] [days'/months'] written notice and is allowed the opportunity to cancel the [Service/Subscription] from the date of any new increase.

P.250

The charges for the [Service/Subscription] are those specified in Schedule A. The [Company] reserves the right to increase the charges at any time. All charges are exclusive of taxes on the supply of services and must be paid without any deduction. Where appropriate value added tax, sales tax and/or any other taxes on the [Service/Subscription] shall be paid by the [Customer] in addition to the charges where required to do so by law.

P.251

'The Repeat Fees' shall be the sums set out in Appendix B to be paid by the [Company] to the [Artist/Actor] in addition to the Basic Fee. These sums shall be due to the [Artist/Actor] on each occasion any material in whole and/or part produced under this agreement is exploited and/or reproduced and/or licensed and/or transmitted in any medium at any time including but not limited advertisements, performances, recordings, films, photographs, images, voice-overs or otherwise. The payment for each type of use shall be in a accordance with Appendix B and all payments shall be made within [28] days of the material being used, exploited and/or licensed for use by the [Company] and/or any sub-licensee.

P.252

In consideration of the services of [Name] the [Company agrees and undertakes to pay [Names] fee as follows:

[number/currency] within [10] days of both parties signing this agreement.

[number/currency] on or before [date] subject to completion of the services set out in clause [–].

P.253

[Name] agrees that if he/she does not pay for the [Service/Work] by [date] at the end of each calendar month. That the [Company] shall have the right to terminate the agreement within [number] days after a final warning by [email/letter].

P.254

The [Company] agrees that it shall accept payments by instalments spread over [number] months provided that an additional cost is paid of [number/currency].

Sponsorship

P.255

In consideration of the rights assigned under this agreement the [Sponsor] agrees to pay to the [Association] the Sponsorship Fee as follows:

1.1 [number/currency] subject to signature of this agreement by the [Sponsor] and the [Association].

1.2 [number/currency] on or before [date] subject to the announcement of the new sponsorship arrangement by the [Association] on its website, app and to the media in [country].

1.3 [number/currency] within [one] month of the conclusion of the [Event] which starts on [date].

P.256

In addition to the Sponsorship Fee the [Sponsor] agrees that it shall be responsible for the payment of all the prize money to be paid to the successful competitors at the presentation ceremony in accordance with the [Prize Money Schedule] which is attached to and forms part of this agreement. The [Sponsor] confirms that the total prize money amounts to be paid is [number/currency] in [year].

P.257

The [Sponsor] agrees that it shall not be entitled to:

1.1 authorise any third parties to assist in the funding of the [Sponsors'] share of the costs for the [Event/Festival] without the prior written consent of the [Association].

1.2 authorise any third parties to film, record, transmit and/or otherwise exploit the [Event/Festival] in any manner in any medium at any time.

1.3 withhold and/or set-off any funds for any reason.

P.258

In consideration of the services provided under this agreement the [Sponsor] shall pay to the [Sportsperson] the Sponsorship Fee as follows:

1.1 [number/currency] on or by [date] subject to the signature by both parties of this agreement.

1.2 [number/currency] on or before [date] subject to the completion by the [Sportsperson] of the promotional marketing podcast set out in Schedule Q.

1.3 [number/currency] on or before [date] subject to the completion of the [number] appearances at conferences, [number] interviews on television and radio and [number] days of promotional work which are listed in Schedule R.

P.259

1.1 'The Performance Related Fee' shall be the sums to be paid by the [Sponsor] to the [Sportsperson] in the event that the [Sportsperson] wins and/or achieves any of the events, national and/or world records and/or other matters set out in the Performance Related Schedule P which is attached to and forms part of this agreement.

1.2 The [Sponsor] agrees to pay to the [Sportsperson] the Performance Related Fees subject to winning and/or achieving any of the sporting events and/or national and/or world records and/or other matters set out in the Performance Related Schedule P. Payment shall be made by the [Sponsor] within [number] days of receipt of notice of the event and/or occasion which the [Sportsperson] has achieved and/or won in each case. The [Sponsor] acknowledges that more than one sum may become due for any one event and/or occasion.

P.260

The [Sponsor] acknowledges that the Sponsorship Fee shall be paid to the [Sportsperson] notwithstanding that the [Sportsperson] may be unable to provide his/her services under this agreement due to illness, injury and/or some other medical and/or mental health issue provided it is supported by a statement from a qualified doctor verifying the facts.

P.261

'The Annual Sponsorship Fee' shall be the sum of [number/currency] to be paid by the [Sponsor] to the [Athlete] during the continuance of this agreement until the end of the Term of the Agreement. The sum shall be paid each year in equal monthly instalments one month in advance. This fee is in addition to any authorised expenses to be paid under the agreement and does not include any government taxes on the supply of goods and/or services. The first payment shall be made immediately following the signing of this agreement by both parties. Payment shall be made directly into the [Athlete's] nominated bank account by electronic transfer in [country].

P.262

The [Athlete] agrees and undertakes that he/she shall be responsible for any liability and payments due in respect of his/her national Insurance contributions and any other sums which may be due in personal and/or corporation taxes in respect of the sums received and benefits provided to the [Athlete].

P.263

The [Athlete] accepts that where the contract and/or the [Athlete] has instructed the [Sponsor] to make any payments under the contract to the [Agent], a family member, a parent and/or guardian. That once payment has been made by the [Sponsor] as instructed that the [Sponsor] has fulfilled its contractual obligations in that respect and is no longer liable to the [Athlete] for that sum.

P.264

The [Sponsor] shall not be entitled to withhold and/or not pay all and/or any part of the Sponsorship Fee due to a change of venue, artists, programme, television, radio and/or other media coverage and/or weather conditions and/or a rescheduling of the date of the [Event].

P.265

The [Sponsor] agrees to make additional payments to the [Artist/Athlete] in respect of the achievement of the following events:

1.1 [number/currency] if the [Artist/Athlete] wins [specify award] at any time in during the Term of this Agreement.

1.2 [number/currency] if the [Artist/Athlete] wins [specify competitive event] at [specify Festival] in [year].

1.3 [number/currency] if the [Artist/Athlete] personally writes and/or agrees to a ghostwriter being commissioned and concludes an agreement with a publisher for an authorised biography and the [Sponsor] is mentioned on the front hardback and paperback book cover in [language] in [country].

1.4 [number/currency] if the [Artist/Athlete] attends more than [number] promotional events on behalf of the [Sponsor] in [year].

P.266
The [Sponsor] agrees that the [Institute] may at any time during the course of this agreement decide to terminate the agreement with the [Sponsor] provided that the [Institute] shall provide the [Sponsor] with [three] months' written notice. In such event the [Sponsor] shall only pay those sums due for that period until the date of termination. No further sums shall then be due to be paid by the [Sponsor].

P.267
Where the social media activity of the senior management and/or directors of the [Sponsor] is in the view of the [Company/Institute] detrimental to the aims and policies of the [Company/Institute]. Then the [Company/Institute] may immediately serve notice on the [Sponsor] that the agreement for sponsorship has ended. Where the [Company/Institute] is unable and/or unwilling to fulfil the specific terms promised for the funding then all and/part of the sponsorship fees may be returned to the [Sponsor].

University, Charity and Educational

P.268
The [Institute/Charity] shall pay the [Company] the total sum of [number/currency] [exclusive of any value added tax/other government taxes on the supply of goods and/or services] for the [Work/Service/Products] described in appendix A. The sum shall be paid in four equal instalments:

1.1 [number/currency] upon acceptance and confirmation of the order by the [Company].

1.2 [number/currency] upon approval of the [draft/sample/pilot/prototype] by the [Institute/Charity].

1.3 [number/currency] upon delivery and approval of the completed [Work/Service/Products] by the [Institute/Charity].

1.4 [number/currency] by [date] provided that the [Work/Service/Products] has been in operation and functioning as require for more than [one] month] without any failure, defects and/or errors.

1.5 Where any sum cannot be paid by the [Institute/Charity] as the stated terms have not been fulfilled. Then no payment shall be made until the terms have been carried out by the [Company] to the satisfaction of the [Institute/Charity].

P.269

The [Institute/Charity] agrees to pay the Contributor's Fee of [number/currency] in four stages:

1.1 [number/currency] within [one] month of the signature by all the parties of this agreement.

1.2 [number/currency] on or before [date] subject to the completion of the tasks required in respect of the [Project/Report/App] set out in clause [–].

1.3 [number/currency] on or before [date] subject to acceptance by the [Institute/Charity] of the completion of the [Project/Report/App] in accordance with the agreed outline and purpose in Schedule A.

P.270

1.1 The [Licensee] shall pay the [Institute] a non-returnable Licence Fee of [number/currency] which shall be paid in advance before delivery of a master copy in [format] suitable for reproduction of the [Images/Photographs].

1.2 The [Licensee] agrees and undertakes to report to the [Institute] the number of copies, format and use of the [Images/Photographs] and to pay the additional royalty fees due for such exploitation which are set out in the attached Royalty Price List a copy of which is attached to and forms part of this agreement. All such sums shall be paid at the end of each [six] month period in arrears.

P.271

In consideration of the rights licensed under this agreement the [Company] agrees to pay to the [Institute/Charity] the Licence Fee as follows:

1.1 [number/currency] within [number] days of signature of this agreement by the [Company] and the [Institute/Charity].

1.2 [number/currency] on or before [date].

1.3 [number/currency] within [number] days of delivery and acceptance of the copies of the original master material of the [Logo/Image/Slogan] by the [Company].

1.4 [number/currency] within [number] days of first general commercial release to the public of any marketing and/or packaging for any approved [Products/Services] anywhere in the world by the [Company] which incorporate the [Logo/Image/Slogan].

1.5 [number/currency] as a bonus payment in the event that net sales receipts by the [Company] of the [Products/Services] which incorporate the [Logo/Image/Slogan] exceed [number/currency] in total in [country/worldwide].

P.272

The [Company] agrees and undertakes that it shall not be entitled to authorise and/or permit any third parties to contribute to the funding of the [Project/Event]. Nor shall the [Company] vary its shareholders and/or change its corporate structure so that any other person and/or third party is able to claim that they have supported and/or donated to the funding of the [Project/Event]. The [Company] agrees and accept that any changes must be subject to the prior written consent of the [Institute/Charity].

P.273

The [Consortium] agree that no one party to this agreement shall be entitled to make and/or authorise any payments from the funds held at [specify bank/account] on behalf of the [Consortium] unless the payment has been disclosed to the Board in advance and approved as within the agreed [Budget].

P.274

The [Consortium] agree that the [Finance/Managing Director] of [specify accountancy company] shall monitor, report on and authorise payments that may be required to third parties on behalf of the [Consortium] from [date] until [date] from the funds held by [specify bank/account]. Provided that he/she shall not be entitled to authorise payments in excess of [number/currency] in total without the express authority in advance of each member of the [Consortium].

PENALTY

General Business and Commercial

P.275

The parties agree and undertake to mitigate any losses, damages and/or other consequences that they may suffer. The parties agree and undertake that neither party shall seek to claim more than [number/currency] in total including legal costs for any breach of this agreement from the other at any time.

P.276

Both parties agree and undertake to quantify the losses and/or damages they may suffer at any time for the non-performance by the other party of all and/or some of the terms of this agreement. The [Company] shall be limited to a single claim in total of [number/currency] or less for failure to deliver all and/or some of the [Products/Services]. The [Supplier] shall be limited to a single claim of [number/currency] or less for failure to pay for the [/Products/Services].

P.277

In the event that the [Distributor] commits a fundamental breach of this agreement and fails to [specify default/failure]. Then a penalty of [number/currency] shall be paid to the [Company] within [specify payment period]. If the penalty is not paid then the [Company] shall have the right to terminate the agreement by notice in writing with immediate effect and shall no longer be liable to the [Distributor] under the agreement. In such event the [Company] shall be entitled to a reversion of all the rights granted and for all master material to be returned and for all sums paid under this agreement to be reimbursed in full within [one] calendar month. If the penalty is not paid within the time limit there shall be no right to make the payment later and remedy the fundamental breach.

P.278

No penalty and/or additional charge will be imposed by the [Company] for a delay of up to [number] days of any payment under this agreement.

P.279

The [Company] shall charge a daily rate of [number/currency] as a penalty for non-payment of the sum due up to a maximum of [number/currency] in any one calendar month.

P.280

The [Enterprise] shall be entitled to charge a fixed penalty for the following material breaches of this agreement:

1.1   A daily rate of [number/currency] in respect of the failure to complete the [Project] according to the scheduled dates in appendix A. This shall be limited to a maximum of [number/currency] in total.

1.2   A daily rate of [number/currency] for failure to ensure that the [Project] functions according to the operational requirements in appendix A. This shall be limited to a maximum of [number/currency] in total.

PENSION

General Business and Commercial

P.281

The [Executive] shall be eligible to be a member of the [Company's] Pension Scheme upon the terms and conditions from time to time applicable under the Scheme and the [Company's] pension policy. Company contributions in respect of the [Executive] shall at all times be subject to the applicable [organisation/government/legislation] limits.

P.282

If the [Executive] chooses not to be member of the [Company's] Pension Scheme the basis upon which the [Company shall contribute to a personal pension taken out by the [Executive] shall be subject to further agreement with the [Company]. The contribution by the [Company] shall in any event not be less than [number] per cent of the [Executives'] Basic Remuneration.

P.283

The [Contributor/Consultant] undertakes to bear the cost of his/her own pension and pension contributions and agrees that no right and/or interest is acquired by the [Contributor/Consultant] under this agreement to any pension run, operated and/or administered by the [Company] and/or any associated business.

P.284

There is no pension, life assurance, medical cover and/or other expenses provided under the terms of this agreement to [Name].

P.285

[Name] agrees and accepts that he/she shall not have any right to a pension from the [Company] unless he/she has been employed by the [Company] for more than [number] [months/year]. Thereafter [Name] shall have the right and choice as to whether to join the [Company] pension fund or not and to make such contributions as may be required to acquire the range of benefits.

PERFORMANCE BOND

General Business and Commercial

P.286

The [Guarantor] covenants with the [Company] and any permitted successors in title and assigns that:

1.1 During the course of this agreement the [Contractor] shall observe and perform all the terms of this agreement. If at any time the [Contractor] shall fail and/or default in respect of the observance and/or performance any of the terms of this agreement. Then the [Guarantor] will be held liable and shall bear full responsibility for the consequences of the obligations and duties of the [Contractor] which it has failed to deliver and/or for which it is in default.

1.2 The [Guarantor] shall indemnify the [Company] against all losses, damages, costs and expenses arising and/or incurred by the [Company] as a direct result of such failure and/or default by the [Contractor] in 1.1 which cannot be remedied.

1.3 This Guarantee shall not be affected by any variation to this agreement and/or any allowance of additional time and/or any waiver and/or any compromise and this Guarantee shall apply to all such amendments.

1.4 If at any time during the course of this agreement the [Contractor] shall enter into liquidation and/or administration and/or some other dissolution so that the [Contractor] is not trading. The [Guarantor] shall within [30] days of written notice of such event assume the full responsibilities, obligations and liabilities of the [Contractor] under this agreement.

P.287
'Performance Bond' shall mean a written arrangement executed under Deed between the [Contractor] and the [Guarantor]. The beneficiary of the Deed is the [Company] as the [Guarantor] has agreed to guarantee and ensure the fulfilment and performance of the terms of the third party agreement in the event of the failure and/or default of the [Contractor].

P.288
The [Contractor] shall at the [Contractor's] sole cost provide the [Purchaser] with a bond or guarantee for the performance of the contract by a reputable and established insurance company, bank or verifiable individual in [country]. The bond shall contain the following minimum conditions:

1.1 Amount of the bond [number/currency].

1.2 Period for which it is in force from [date] to [date] or subject to completion of [specify project], whichever is the earlier.

1.3 Procedure for inspection [specify methods].

1.4 Arrangements for release of bond.

1.5 In the event that the bond is not in place by [date] then the [Purchaser] shall have the right to bring the contract to an end and shall be repaid all sums that the [Purchaser] has paid under this agreement.

P.289
Despite inspection of the [Products] on delivery and installation. The [Company] shall at its sole cost guarantee for [one] year from the date of delivery of the [Products] to replace and/or repair any faulty [Products] which have not been misused. If any [Products] are found to be defective, then a further guarantee period of [one] year shall run from the date a

suitable replacement is returned to the [Customer]. The [Company] shall not be liable where any [Products] were used in a manner other than for their intended purpose and/or repairs have been carried out by the [Purchaser].

P.290
There are no additional guarantees, performance bonds and/or other undertakings provided by the [Company] to the [Customer] except those required by law in [country]. Where additional cover and insurance provision is required then the [Customer] will have to pay an additional sum for insurance protection with a third party.

PERFORMANCES

General Business and Commercial

P.291
'Performers' shall mean actors, singers, musicians, dancers, mime artistes and other persons who act, sing, deliver, play in or otherwise perform literary or artistic works.

P.292
'Performances' shall include acting, mime, dance, speech, singing, playing a musical instrument or conducting, either alone or with other persons.

P.293
'Performance' shall mean:

1.1   A dramatic performance (which includes dance and mime).

1.2   A musical performance.

1.3   A reading or recitation of a literary work; or

1.4   A performance of a variety act or any similar presentation which is or so far as it is a live performance given by one or more individuals.

P.294

1.1   [Name] agrees to read his/her poetry from [specify title] at [location] on [date] as a free event for the [Company]. [Name] agrees that no fee shall be due and/or paid to [Name].

1.2   [Name] agrees that the [Company] may take photographs and film the performance and event for the purpose of marketing and promotion in newspapers, magazines and to post on sites on the internet. Provided that a link and credit is provided to [specify link] which promotes sales of the [specify title].

1.3 The [Company] agrees to display the [specify title] in the front window at [location] for [one] week between [date and [date].

1.4 The [Company] agrees that it shall not have any authority to authorise and/or to reproduce extracts of the [specify title] in any marketing and promotional material and/or on any website, app and/or blog and/or otherwise over the internet without the prior approval and consent of [Name].

P.295

'The Recitals' shall mean the musical performance by [Name] playing the [instrument] at [location] on [dates] with the music by the composers set out in Appendix 1 which forms part of this Agreement as part of the [specify theme] season by the [Company].

P.296

'An Illicit recording' shall be defined as a recording of the whole and/or any substantial part of a performance which is made without the performer's consent and is made for some other reason than use for private purposes. Where any person and/or company has an exclusive recording contract for the performance. Then the recording is illicit unless the recording has been made with the consent of the person and/or company who hold the recording contract and the performer except for use of the illicit recording for private purposes.

P.297

'Phonogram' shall mean any exclusively aural fixation of sounds of a performance or of other sounds.

PODCAST

Internet, Websites and Apps

P.298

'The Podcast' shall mean the final edited version of the film and sound recording of the [Contributors' Work] produced and developed by the [Company] and/or any authorised third party engaged by the [Company] for that purpose.

P.299
'The Contributors' Work' shall mean the interview with the [Contributor] on the subject of [specify in detail] which shall be filmed, recorded and edited for a Podcast by the [Company] and/or an authorised third party. A summary of which is attached to and forms part of this agreement in Appendix A.

P.300
The [Company] agrees to engage the non-exclusive services of the [Contributor] for the purpose of recording and filming an interview with the [Contributor] for the [Podcast/Blog] known as [specify title/reference].

P.301
In consideration of the Contributors Work and the rights assigned in this agreement to the [Company]. The [Company] agrees to pay the [Contributor] the [Contributors' Fee] as follows:

1.1 [number/currency] upon full signature of this agreement by both parties.

1.2 [number/currency] subject to the completion of the Contributors' Work.

P.302
The [Company agrees and undertakes that it will pay for all the cost and expense of filming, recording and editing the interview with the [Contributor]. That the [Contributor] shall not be liable for any such sums and no indemnity is provided by the [Contributor] to the [Company] in respect of any claim, liabilities, demands, actions, costs, damages and/or losses arising out of any matter which may arise in the interview and/or any breach by the [Contributor] of any part of this agreement. It is agreed that the total liability of the [Contributor] if any shall be limited to [number/currency].

P.303
In consideration of the [Contributors'] Fee the [Contributor] assigns to the [Company] all copyright, intellectual property rights and any other rights in the product of the [Contributors' Work] and the product of the [Contributors] services and the Podcast to the [Company] in all medium and all media whether in existence now and/or created in the future for the full period of copyright and any other rights and any extensions and renewals and in perpetuity throughout the world and universe. This shall include the right to transmit, broadcast, display, license, supply, distribute and/or exploit the [Contributors' Work] and/or the Podcast and/or any parts on the internet, television, radio, in print, through mobiles and/or as any other electronic format and/or method of distribution and/or exploitation in any media.

P.304

The [Company] and/or any third party shall be entitled to develop, adapt, amend, alter and/or add to the [Contributors' Work] and/or the product of his/her services and/or the Podcast provided that the original material is still credited to the [Contributor] in the following manner [specify credit]. It is agreed that any such changes must not result in the [Contributor] being associated with material which is obscene, illegal, offensive, and/or is otherwise likely to impugn and/or damage the reputation of the [Contributor]. In such event the [Contributor] shall be entitled to have all the original material removed from such new work.

P.305

1.1 In consideration of the payment of a fee of [number/currency] for each [module/podcast/programmes] filmed and recorded by [Name] and delivered to the [Company]. [Name] agrees to appear and perform as sole presenter and to write the content for a series of short [modules/ podcasts/programmes] to be transmitted and displayed on a [website/ app/subscription service] to be developed by the [Company] which relate to the [Work/Book/Product] written by [Name].

1.2 The [Company] agrees to pay the fees due for each [module/podcast/ programme] in 1.1 within [seven] days of completion of delivery of the master material in [format] to the [Company].

1.3 The [Company] agrees that it shall not edit, adapt and/or vary the content of any [module/podcast/programme] without prior approval and consultation with [Name]. That where [Name] objects to any changes and the parties cannot agree then the material shall not be used, transmitted and/or displayed.

1.4 It is agreed that the purpose of the series of [modules/podcasts/ programmes] is to assist in the development, marketing and promotion the [Company] its products and services and to market the [Work/ Book/Product]. The [Company] accepts that it shall have no authority to sub-license the [modules/podcasts/programmes] to a commercial third party at any time without prior agreement with [Name].

1.5 The [Company] agrees that in the event that the [Company] ceases to sell, promote and/or distribute the [Work/Book/Product]. That the [Company] shall remove and delete all the [modules/podcasts/ programmes at the request of [Name].

1.6 It is agreed between the parties that where [Name] has written and filmed the [modules/podcasts/programmes] that all copyright and intellectual property rights and any other rights and interest shall belong solely to [Name].

P.306

'The Podcasts' shall be the films and sound tracks recorded by and/or commissioned by [Name] entitled [subject/title] which have been transmitted on [specify channel/reference] from [date] to [date] featuring [Name]. The Podcast shall include any music, lyrics, sound recordings, images, logos, slogans created and developed and/or commissioned by [Name] which are included in the title, headings, films and/or sound track

P.307

There is no undertaking provided by [Name] that all the material included in the [Podcast/Video] is original and/or that it has been cleared and a licence granted by any copyright owner and/or any sums due have been paid. No indemnity is provided by [Name] to the [Distributor] and the [Distributor] must carry out its own legal risk assessment and make such arrangements and pay such sums as may be due to exploit the material.

P.308

[Name] agrees and undertakes that:

1.1 all the content and title of the [Podcast/Video] is original and was created by [Name] and is owned solely by [Name].

1.2 no third party has any claim in respect of the [Podcast/Video] and that no legal proceedings have been threatened and/or commenced against [Name] in respect of the [Podcast/Video].

1.3 [Name] is not in any partnership and has not collaborated with any third party in respect of the concept, development, design and production of any of the content except: [specify details].

1.4 [Name] has the legal capacity to grant the rights to the [Company] and is age [number] years.

P.309

1.1 [Name] authorises the [Company] to transmit [number] seconds of the [Podcast/Video] on their [website/app] known as: [specify reference]. This right is not exclusive and shall start on [date] and end on [date]. There is no right granted to sub-license these rights and/or use to any third party for any reason.

1.2 In consideration of 1.1 the [Company] shall pay [name] a fee of [number/currency] on or by [date] by direct debit to a nominated bank account.

1.3 The [Company] agrees that the extract of the [Podcast/Video] in 1.1 must at all times bear a copyright notice and credit to [Name] as follows: [specify details] and a link as follows: [specify details].

POLICIES

General Business and Commercial

P.310
This [specify title/heading] Policy is for guidance only and is a summary of the existing legislation which relates to [specify subject]. All persons at the [Company] are expected to adhere to the Policy. Any issues which arise relating to the Policy should be raised with [Name] [specify role/contact information].

P.311
The following Policies [Health and Safety/Data Protection/ Freedom of Information/Child Protection Policy/Equality/Energy Conservation/Travel and Parking/Expenses/Recycling/Internet and Emails/Telephone and Mobiles/Drugs/Alcohol/Complaints/other] have been issued by the Board of Directors of the [Company] for the purpose of following existing legislation and/or to provide a clear and coherent procedure and acceptable practice across the [Company] to all officers and staff whether full-time, part-time and/or temporary.

P.312
The officer for the [subject] Policy is [Name] who will advise any member of staff on any questions that may arise from the Policy in the future. No other person in the [Company] is entitled to deal with, contact, advise, and/or report on any matter arising from the content and/or fulfilment of the Policy with any third party. All queries from the media and/or the public should be directed to [Name].

P.313
Where a person is reported for a breach and/or failure to adhere to any Policy of the [Company] for any reason. Then the person against whom the allegation has been made shall be provided with an opportunity to explain the matter to the relevant nominated officer of that Policy. The person may be required to follow a further training programme of the Policy. Any breach shall not automatically be deemed a breach of their contract with the [Company]. Any person must be shown to have acted ultra vires of their authority and position at the [Company] and/or caused significant loss and/or damage to the [Company] and/or have caused harm to the reputation of the [Company.

P.314
The Policies specified in Schedule A [List title of all Policies and attach actual Policy] are attached to and form part of this agreement. It is a condition of this agreement that [Name] agrees and undertakes to adhere to the procedures

and/or conditions set out in the Policies during the Term of this Agreement at the [Company].

P.315

1.1 [Name] agrees that the [Staff handbook] and the [Policies] of the [Company] are for guidance only and may be changed without notice to [Name].

1.2 The [Company] agrees that any breach by [Name] of the [Staff Handbook] and/or [Policies] shall not automatically be deemed to be a breach of this agreement and/or a disciplinary offence and/or the subject of any other internal inquiry and/or investigation. All such matters shall be dealt between [Name] and [specify person] in the first instance. [Name] may be reprimanded and put on a first warning for the first incident. Thereafter any matter may be sufficient for the [Company] to conclude that the agreement should be terminated due to a material breach by [Name].

P.316

This agreement shall not include any policies, company handbook and/or any other guidelines that the [Company] shall issue to its staff and/or otherwise. It is specifically agreed that all such documents shall not apply to [Name] and are excluded from the terms of this agreement. That any such document may only be added to this agreement by an amendment document referring to the additional material which is signed by both parties.

P.317

1.1 This Licence reference number [–] has been awarded to the [Company] by the [Organisation] on [date] and continues for a period of [number] years.

1.2 During that period of the Licence the [Company] shall be subject to all the policies, guidelines and Codes of conduct which may be issued by the [Organisation] whether in existence at the time the Licence is awarded and/or created and/or developed at any time thereafter either by the [Organisation] and/or any other body and/or institute which takes over the governance and control of the [specify] market in [country].

1.3 It is a requirement of this Licence that the [Company] at all times adheres to all matters in the Licence in 1.1, the policies, guidelines and codes in 1.2 and the laws of [country]. Failure to do so may result in the suspension, withdrawal, amendment and/or termination of the Licence by the [Organisation].

P.318

It is crucial that you follow the health and safety instructions exhibited on the [site/premises] and wear the safety protective equipment. These conditions are mandatory to all personnel. Failure to adhere to these policies will mean your removal from the [site/premises] and termination of your contract.

P.319

1.1 The [Website/App/Channel] has a number of policies which apply to all content and users as follows: [specify policies/display summary key points/reference complete document].

1.2 Where any person and/or company fails to adhere to any part of the policies in 1.1 then the [Enterprise] reserves the right to delete material and/or close any account and/or block and person and/or company and/or report any matter to the relevant authorities.

POWER OF ATTORNEY

General Business and Commercial

P.320

This Power of Attorney given on this [–] day of [–] 20 [–] by me [Name] of [address] witnessed by [Name of witness] as follows:

1.1 I appoint [Name] of [address] to be my attorney for the purposes of [specify relevant legislation] with authority to execute and/or exercise on my behalf all the trust, powers and discretions vested in me as [Trustee of the Trust] created by the [Will/Deed] dated the [–] day of [–] 20 [–].

1.2 This Power of Attorney shall operate from [date] and shall continue until a written notice of replacement is served.

1.3 I hereby confirm that I have given notice of this Power of Attorney to my co-Trustees.

1.4 This Power of Attorney is executed and delivered as a Deed.

IN WITNESS WHEREOF I have hereunto set my hand this [–] day of [–] 20 [–].

Signed by: [Name] [signature] [date]

Witnessed by: [full name and title of witness] of [address] [signature]

whose date of birth [date] and occupation is [specify title/work address].

P.321

BY THIS POWER OF ATTORNEY

I [Name] of [address] being a Director, Employee or person who works full time for the [Company]

HEREBY APPOINT [Name] of [address]

to be my Attorney and in my name and on my behalf to apply for the aggregate of [number] Ordinary Shares of [value] each in the [Company] pursuant to the Prospectus dated: [date].

AND I HEREBY undertake to ratify everything which the Attorney shall do or purport to do by virtue of this Power of Attorney.

IN WITNESS whereof I set my hand and seal the [–] day of [–] 20 [–].

Signed, sealed and delivered by: [name/signature]

In the presence of [name/signature]

P.322

Dated: [date]

Parties:

[Name] of [address] ['the Copyright Owner']

[Company] of [address] ['the Company']

1.1 The [Copyright Owner] appoints the [Company] to be its attorney and in its name on its behalf to carry out such actions where necessary to institute, prosecute and/or defend such legal proceedings and/or to do all such other acts as the [Company] may consider advisable to protect the rights granted to the [Company] pursuant to the agreement dated [date] with and made between the [Copyright Owner] and the [Company].

1.2 The [Copyright Owner] undertakes to ratify everything which the [Company] shall do or purport to do in pursuit of this Deed and declares that this appointment shall be irrevocable.

1.3 This Deed shall be governed and interpreted in accordance with [English/other] Law and any dispute arising hereunder shall be referred to the [High Court of Justice in England/other].

IN WITNESS whereof the [Copyright Owner] has caused its Common Seal to be applied on the date set out above.

The Common Seal of the [Copyright Owner] is affixed:

[Copyright Owner]: [Name/signature]
Witness: [Name/role/signature]
[Company]: [Name/signature]
Witness: [Name/role/signature]

P.323

Each [Partner] undertakes to execute on becoming a partner, a power of attorney in a form approved by the [Board] appointing the Senior Partner as his/her attorney to execute on his/her behalf such documents as are required to be executed by him/her as relate to the ordinary course of the business from time to time.

P.324

[Name] of [address] being of sound mind [and not subject to any incapacity, disability and/or a mental health order which would restrict their ability to reach this decision] wishes to appoint [specify person] of [address] to manage and deal with their legal, financial, medical and other affairs and to act in [Name's] best interest and on their behalf including dealing with the responsibility of their freehold house at [address] and bank account at [location] held in the name of [specify] and private pension held at [specify] and state pension [reference] and all other sums held and/or received from any source. That [Name] has and/or will execute a power of attorney to [specify person] in the form attached to this document in Schedule A.

P.325

No power of attorney is granted to any person by [Name] under this document and/or deed. [Name] has not transferred the management of his/her health, medical treatment and/or day to day affairs and property and money to any third party. If at a later date [Name] does not have the capacity to manage his/her household matters and to make decisions due to incapacity and/or ill health and/or mental health issues then [Name] nominates [specify person] as the preferred option as the person who is to assume responsibility on behalf of [Name]. [Name] recognises that this nomination may not be binding in law in the future.

PREAMBLE

General Business and Commercial

P.326

Whereas:

The [Company] is entitled to the exclusive services of the [Director] and to make available such services and to grant and assign all rights in the product of the services of the [Director] to other third parties so far as is necessary for the purposes of this agreement.

P.327
Whereby:

1.1   [The Author] owns and controls all copyright and all other intellectual property rights in the [Characters/Book] which is intended to be adapted for television.

1.2   The [Production Company] wishes to procure a commission from a [Television Company] to produce a [Series] based on the [Characters/ Book].

1.3   Subject to the [Production Company] securing a commission to produce the [Series. The [Author] and the [Production Company] have agreed to co-produce the [Series] on the terms and conditions as set out in this document.

P.328
Whereas:

The [Company] intends [but does not undertake] to make the proposed [Film] described in Schedule A. In order so to do the [Company] wishes to retain the services of the [Name] as Director.

P.329
It is agreed that:

In consideration of the Licence Fee the [Licensor] grants the [Licensee] the exclusive right to broadcast and/or transmit and/or exploit the [Film] throughout the Territory subject to the terms set out in this Licence Agreement.

P.330
The [Licensor] is the owner of the Copyright and Technical Information described in Appendix A and has the sole and exclusive right to make the [Product] described in Appendix B in the Territory.

The [Licensee] wishes to acquire and the [Licensor] is willing to grant a Licence in the Territory on the terms and conditions set out in this agreement to use the Copyright and Technical Information in order to manufacture, use and sell the [Product].

P.331
The [Authors] both agree to develop, research, write and edit a new work on the subject of [specify subject] to be published as a book in hardback and paperback and as an electronic download and/or e book and/or audio recording. The provisional title of the new work is: [specify draft title] and shall be referred to as 'the Work'. The terms to be agreed between the Authors are set out below as follows: [–].

P.332

The [Agency] warrants that the facts set out in the preamble are correct and that neither the [Agency] nor the [Presenter] has or will enter into any commitment with any third party which might in any way detract from the rights granted in this agreement and/or the [Presenter's] ability to perform the services set out in this agreement.

P.333

1.1 The [Designer/Developer] has experience in the development, design and creation of websites, apps and software for marketing, promotional and commercial purposes.

1.2 The [Company] wishes to engage the services of the [Designer/Developer] to develop, design, create and deliver a fully operational and functional [website/app/software] for the purpose of [specify aim].

P.334

1.1 The [Institute/Charity] is creating a new [website/app/podcasts] and wishes to engage the freelance services of [Name] to assist in the development, production and design of the [website/app/podcasts].

1.2 [Name] has experience and expertise in [specify skills] and agrees to provide his/her services to the [Institute/Charity] for the purpose set out in 1.1 from [date].

P.335

1.1 The [Illustrator] and the [Author] intend to enter into a publishing and exploitation agreement with a [Publisher] concerning a series of books provisionally entitled [specify title] referred to as ['the Works/Books'].

1.2 The [Illustrator] and the [Author] wish to enter into an agreement to clarify their legal positions and to agree the ownership of the material and the allocation of royalties in respect of the publication and exploitation of the [Works/Books] and any future sequels, adaptations, licences and merchandising in any media and/or format at any time throughout the [world/universe].

P.336

1.1 The [Distributor] wishes to acquire for valuable consideration such rights, obligations, liabilities, and benefits as exist between the [Publisher] and [Author] under the written agreement dated: [date].

1.2 The [Publisher] wishes to be released from the agreement with the full knowledge and consent of the [Author] from such rights, obligations, liabilities, and benefits as exist between the [Author] and the [Publisher].

1.3 The [Author] wishes to release the [Publisher] from such rights, obligations, liabilities, and benefits as exist between the [Author] and the [Publisher] and for the [Publisher] to assign all such rights, obligations, liabilities, and benefits to the [Distributor].

P.337

The [Employee] was employed by the [Company] on a full-time basis under a contract of employment dated: [date] (referred to as 'the Employment Contract'). The [Employee's] employment came to an end at [time/date] referred to as 'the Termination Date' by reason of [redundancy/other].

P.338

1.1 The [Purchaser] and the [Seller] wish to conclude a summary [Heads of Agreement/Memorandum of Understanding] which is subject to the main contract being concluded. The subject matter is for the sale of the Assets set out in Appendix A by the [Seller] and the purchase of those Assets by the [Purchaser].

1.2 The [Seller] wishes to sell a specific publishing list, existing stock and current work in progress as specified in Appendix A subject to the conclusion of the main agreement.

1.3 The Purchaser wishes to purchase the Assets in Appendix A subject to the conclusion of the main agreement.

1.4 The parties have broadly agreed the following terms and conditions which must be incorporated in the main agreement: [–].

P.339

The [Company] engages [Name] to write a regular blog article of not less than [number] words for the following months: [specify months]. The [Company] shall pay [Name] a one-off fee within [number] days of delivery and acceptance by the [Company].

P.340

[Name] and the [Company] wish to enter into an agreement for the commissioning and creation of a fully operational and functioning new website, app and software for the [Company] based on the description and summary for the [Project] set out in Schedule D which forms part of this agreement.

1481

PREMIUM RATE PHONE LINES

General Business and Commercial

P.341
The Competition starts on [date] and ends on [date]. All entries must be received by [time/date]. All entries received and/or made after that time shall not be eligible to be entered in the Competition and shall be disqualified. There may be a charge incurred even though the entry is not accepted as valid. [There is no entry cost to the competition/The entry cost to the Competition is [figure/currency.] All costs which you may incur in entering the Competition are your personal responsibility. There are no refunds for any entries which are disqualified and/or received after the deadline.

P.342
Telephone entries by telephone may be by landline, mobile and/or the internet by telephone call to [number]. Then follow the instructions provided which shall be in the [specify] language. Speak clearly and leave your personal details that are requested and the answer. Failure to follow the instructions accurately may result in your disqualification from the Competition. [There is no limit to the number of entries you may make to the Competition/only [number] calls will be eligible from each telephone number.] All calls will be charged at different rates depending on the method you have used.

P.343
All entries must be completed by the deadline. Calls from mobiles and/or other networks and/or by any other method may be charged at a higher rate than landlines. All persons who enter must be age [number] and over by [date] and you must obtain the permission of the person in whose name the telephone and/or mobile is held and/or pays the bill. No acknowledgement of entry shall be provided by the [Company].

P.344
All entries by text shall be to [telephone number]. All entries by text shall receive a text confirming entry. The [Company] shall not be liable for any texts not received for any reason and/or any interruption, suspension, fault and/or delay in the service which may cause the entrants text not to be delivered, delayed and/or to contain errors.

P.345
No responsibility and/or liability shall be accepted by the [Company] for any entries which are disqualified as a result of being inaudible, incomplete, delayed, abusive, and/or otherwise not acceptable.

P.346
No responsibility and/or liability shall be accepted by the [Company] for any costs, charges and/or other expenses incurred by any person who enters the Competition at any time.

P.347
It is a condition of entry that you agree to assign all the copyright, intellectual property rights and all rights in all media in your [Answer/Competition Entry] to the [Company]. You agree to complete and sign such a document if so requested to do so by the [Company].

P.348
This is a commercial service and calls to this premium rate line [specify number] are charged by the [Company] at [number/currency] for every minute. Less than a minute is charged as a full minute. No refunds are provided where this service is used by mistake and a competition has ended and/or by any person under [age] and/or otherwise. The complaints procedure can be used on [specify details].

PRIVACY

General Business and Commercial

P.349
The [Photographer] agrees and acknowledges that the [photographs/images/computer-generated material] have been commissioned for private and domestic purposes and the [Commissioning Party] has therefore a right to privacy.

P.350
It is agreed that the use of the [Photographs] shall be used solely for the purposes defined under clause [–] to the agreement and the [Photographer] shall not be entitled to use the negatives, prints, computer generated material or any other copies in any format nor to authorise or provide any material to any third party for any other purpose without the prior written consent of the [Commissioning Party].

P.351
[Name] confirms that the [Photographs/Film] was not taken pursuant to a private commissioning arrangement with any third party and that the

publication of the [Photographs/Film] will not infringe the privacy rights of any third party.

P.352

'Privacy' shall mean the right to privacy in relation to the commissioned photographs and/or films which may be created as a result of a commission by any person for private and domestic purposes only. Where any person commissions the taking of a photograph and/or the making of a film and where copyright subsists in the resulting work which may be a film and/or photograph. The person who has commissioned the resulting work shall have the right not to have copies of the work issued to the public and/or exhibited and/or shown in public and/or the work broadcast and/or included in a cable programme service. This right of privacy shall not apply to any film and/or photographs commissioned for commercial purposes.

P.353

[Name] and [Guest] agree that the following terms and conditions shall apply to the [Event]:

1.1 That this is a private [Event] which is by invitation only and not open to the public.

1.2 That [Guest] agrees they are only permitted to attend and/or contribute to and/or participate in the [Event] on the condition that [Guest] is not entitled to take any recordings, sound recordings, photographs, images, films whether using a camera, mobile phone and/or any other gadget and/or method in any format for any reason and [Guest] undertakes not to bring and/or use any equipment and/or devices for that purpose.

1.3 That [Guest] will advise the [Name] immediately of any knowledge of an intended or actual breach of the requirement by others at the [Event] of 1.1 and/or 1.2.

1.4 That [Guest] recognises that the only published material of the [Event] will and/or may be that authorised by [Name]. That [Guest] shall not be entitled to any fee and/or payment of any nature for such exploitation and/or use of the [Event] at any time.

1.5 That [Guest] agrees not to bring and/or use a mobile phone and/or other recording device and/or gadget and shall not attempt to film, record and/or take any pictures of the [Event].

1.6 That [Guest] shall not release and/or distribute and/or make available to the public and/or the media any private details of the [Event] and/or enter into any product placement agreement with any company and/or business.

P.354

This is the stated privacy policy of this [Website/App/Distribution Service] which is provided by the [Company]:

1.1   Your personal details, name, address, age, employment, occupation, nationality, email, mobile and landline telephone number, internet access dialling code, access codes, passwords, bank account and credit card details and any other data and information that may be gathered are accepted by the [Company] as your private information and data.

1.2   These details in 1.1 will only be stored and used by us for the express purpose stated on the [Website/App/Distribution Service].

1.3   Any other supply, transfer and/or exploitation of your private information and/or data is expressly not allowed and the [Company] will obliged to seek your consent to any such transfer of information and data to third parties not authorised by you. This term shall not apply where the [Company] is required by an Order of a Court of law in any jurisdiction in any criminal and/or civil proceedings to provide information and/or data for any reason and/or there is evidence that the account is being used for illegal purposes contrary to legislation in any jurisdiction.

1.4   The [Company] shall have the right to extract information and data which does not release private and personal details which provides generic and statistical analysis and shall have the right to provide such marketing and promotional material to third parties without any further consent from you. This shall include type of usage of site, number and type of purchases, method of payment, age group, financial category, ethnic origins and any other material which does not reveal your specific private information and data.

1.5   Information and data is constantly collected on this [Website/App/Distribution Service] by the use of 'cookies' and other mechanisms which are then stored, analysed and reproduced in different formats. If you do not wish to have this system applied then you must refuse consent when asked whether this is accepted or not.

1.6   Where you provide updated, altered, amended and/or varied information and data then we will try but cannot undertake that it will be changed as requested. The previous details may however still be kept on file in the system either through error, historical records or otherwise.

1.7   The [Company] cannot ensure that a third party will not unlawfully access private information and/or data. We advise you to take all the precautions we suggest and do not permit others access to your codes and passwords.

1.8   The [Company] does not provide any indemnity and/or accept any liability of any nature. You must accept that you use this [Website/App/Distribution Service] at your own risk and cost. You are advised to take out insurance cover which is offered at an additional cost.

1.9   In the event that there are any legal proceedings then the jurisdiction shall be nominated at the discretion of the [Company] from the following countries: [specify list] based on the circumstances.

P.355

The [Company] agrees to be bound by any legislation, judgement, guidelines and/or code of practice issued in country] and/or by [specify organisation] that imposes on the [Company] best practices and/or restrictions regarding the use in any manner of confidential and private information and data supplied to the [Company] by the [Client]. Including but not limited to blood type, health and medical records, financial history and dealings, investments, property ownership, mortgages, loans, credit and bank card details, usernames, passwords and any defaults, failures to pay and/or other matters.

P.356

The [Company] reserves the right to supply and/or disclose to any third party details relating to the date of purchase, the nature of the [Product/Service] purchased, the method of payment and the cost.

P.357

The use of and access to this [Website/App/Service] is conditional on your agreement to the use of cookies to be stored on your web browser that enables the [Company] to monitor your movements and provide restricted and limited data as to the use of the [Website/App/Service]. If you wish to check the details held by the [Company] are accurate then contact [email address]. To remove the cookies please complete the following steps [detail procedure].

P.358

Any emails on laptops, computers and gadgets, telephone calls on mobiles, landlines and/or otherwise which are owned and/or controlled by the [Company] shall be monitored and shall not be private and/or confidential.

P.359

The [Company] shall not be in breach of any clauses relating to confidentiality, privacy and/or data protection where disclosure is made as a result of an order of a court, tribunal and/or as a result of any civil and/or criminal proceedings.

P.360

After the expiry and/or termination of this agreement neither party shall disclose any information, financial details, reports, business plans and/or discussions to any third party which are not in the public domain and which were provided in confidence and/or in a private meeting.

P.361

The [medical/health/financial] report to be provided by [Name] shall only be disclosed and copied to the following authorised persons [specify names] for [specify period]. The [Company] agrees to ensure that such persons provide an undertaking not to disclose the information in the report to any third party and that they return all copies which shall then be destroyed.

P.362

[Name] agrees and undertakes that he/she shall not at any time whether during the Term of this Agreement and/or thereafter for a period of [number] months:

1.1 Take any images and/or film on their mobile phone, camera and/or on any other gadget and/or device while at the [location] of any person, object, room and/or view and/or any other material and/or matter in respect of the [Project].

1.2 Make any recording and/or allow another person to listen to a conversation and/or discussion at the [location] and/or any other matter in respect of the [Project].

1.3 Enter into any arrangement with a third party to be supplied news, images and/or any other material relating to [location] and/or any other matter in respect of the [Project].

1.4 Provide details of conversations, discussions and exchanges with [specify persons] to any media including radio, television, magazines, newspapers and/or any online internet company and/or post any comments and/or criticism and/or complaint on any part of the internet and/over any telecommunication system by text, image and/or otherwise.

PROBATIONARY PERIOD

General Business and Commercial

P.363

The first [three months] of the [Employee's] service will be a probationary period. During this period, either party may terminate the contract by giving [one] [week's/month's] notice in writing to the other.

P.364

The [Company] agrees that the period from [date] to [date] inclusive shall be treated as a trial period. In the trial period the [Licensee] shall have the right to terminate this agreement if the parties cannot agree the proposed name of the [Product], its content and/or logo, slogan and/or marketing strategy.

P.365

The [Employee] acknowledges that throughout the probationary period the [Company] shall be entitled to terminate this contact with [one] [week's/month's] written notice or [one] [week's/month's] pay in lieu of notice.

P.366

'The Probationary Period' shall commence from the date of this agreement and shall continue for a period of [three/six] months thereafter.

P.367

The [Consultant] shall be required to complete an initial [number] months probationary period which starts on [date] and ends on [date]. In the event that the [Company] decides during the probationary period that it does not wish to continue to use the services of the [Consultant] then there shall be no obligation for the [Company] to extend the engagement of the services of the [Consultant] and/or to enter into an extended contract for his/her services after [date].

P.368

It is agreed between the parties that there is no probationary and/or other periods during which the suitability of [Name] for the role of [specify role] are to be assessed and/or reviewed.

P.369

[Name] shall commence at the [Company] in the role of an [Intern/other] from [date]. The first period of [number] weeks shall be a probationary period. The [Company] may decide at any time to terminate the agreement with [Name] without providing any reason. After [date] [Name] shall continue in the role of [Intern/other] for a fixed period of [number] months which shall start on [date] and end on [date].

PRODUCT

General Business and Commercial

P.370

'Product' shall mean any industrial or handicraft item including parts intended to be assembled into a complete item, sets or compositions of items, packaging, get-ups, graphic symbols and typographic typefaces but excluding a computer programme or semi-conductor products.

P.371

'The Product' shall be the subject-matter of the advertising copy which is briefly described as follows: [brief description].

P.372

'The Sponsor's Product' shall be the following [Product] known as: [title] which bears the trade mark and logo: [specify name/image]. A full description of the [Product], its labels, trade marks, logos, slogans, packaging, warning notices, ingredients and authorised purposes is set out in appendix A and forms part of this agreement.

P.373

'The Company's Products' shall mean the products of the [Company] which are briefly described as follows: [list products]. A full description of the Company's Products is attached to and forms part of this agreement in Schedule B which shall include two and three dimensional images, alternative designs, colours and layout, instructions, labels, packaging, trade marks, service marks, logos and any associated words and slogans, warning notices, copyright notices, compliance codes and references, ingredients and/or content and/or any other relevant factors.

P.374

'The Licensee's Product' shall be the following product which is produced, manufactured and distributed by or on behalf of the [Licensee] known as [specify title/name of product]. A two-dimensional copy and description of the Licensee's Product is attached to and forms part of this agreement in appendix C.

P.375

'The Products' shall mean the products of the [Company] which are described in appendix A and form part of this agreement. Appendix A shall include in relation to each product a detailed set of images of the sample and final product. Together with a statement regarding the ownership of the copyright and intellectual property rights, and any patents and/or invention, the contractual and/or moral right obligations, any consents and/or clearances which have been obtained and the sums paid and/or due for any form of exploitation. It shall in addition include data and information regarding any trade marks, service marks, logos, designs, slogans, text, artwork, sound recordings, films, scripts, images, music, photographs, computer-generated material, artists, performers and any other matter.

P.376
'The Product' shall mean the [Book/Sound Recording/Lyrics/Musical Work] entitled: [Title] created, written and produced by [Name] as the [Author/Musician/Performer].

P.377
'The Product' shall be the computer software and fully functional material for an [App] to be created, developed and delivered by [Name] based on the idea and concept supplied by the [Company] described in Appendix A and as adapted through the process of development, tests and production.

The products shall include all stages of the process of development including draft drawings, computer generated material, artwork, images, text, sound recordings, film, music, passwords and codes and access data and any material of any nature in any format and/or medium.

P.378
'The Licensed Product' shall mean the original sample [article/item] designed and created by [Name] known as: [name of product] which is described as follows: [brief description]. Images and a more detailed description of which are set out in appendix F. The original sample produced by [Name] is to be reproduced and distributed by the [Licensee] as a commercial product for sale to the public.

PRODUCT LIABILITY

General Business and Commercial

P.379
The [Licensee] confirms that as at [date] the final approved [Product] conforms with all health and safety and product liability legislation, regulations, directives, statutory instruments and any other codes of practice and/or guidelines which may exist in respect of [specify subject/type of product] in any country [listed in Schedule B/worldwide].

P.380
The [Licensee] confirms that a fully comprehensive insurance policy is and will remain in force with respect to any allegations, claims, legal actions and/or proceedings whether civil and/or criminal and/or any enquiries and/or investigations with respect to all product liability throughout the [Territory/world] until [date].

P.381

The [Licensee] undertakes that it will ensure that all the [Licensed Articles/Products] shall comply in all respect with all legislation, regulations, guidelines, standards, practices and/or otherwise which may be required and/or or issued by any government and/or other competent authority and/or organisation which relates to health and safety, product liability, contents, packaging, warning notices, storage and/or delivery of the [Licensed Articles/Products] in the [Territory/specify countries]. The [Licensee] undertakes to the [Licensor] that the [Licensee] will ensure that all the [Licensed Articles/Products] meet all the standards and quality control tests required and that they will be safe for use by the public and in particular suitable for children from age [number] years.

P.382

[The Licensee] agrees that prior to the supply, sale and/or distribution of the [Licensed Articles/Products] it will organise at its own expense satisfactory insurance cover on behalf of the [Licensee] and the [Licensor] in respect of any potential product liability and/or any legal costs, damages and losses that may be incurred as a result of any claim and/or legal action by the public as a result of the supply, sale and distribution of the [Licensed Articles/Products]. The value of the cover shall be not less than: [number/currency] per claim and [number/currency] in total. The policy shall be renewed by the [Licensee] for each year of this agreement until it has expired and/or has been terminated whichever is the earlier. The [Licensee] shall ensure that the interest of the [Licensor] is endorsed on the policy and at the request of the [Licensor] shall produce a copy of the policy and evidence of payments of the premiums.

P.383

The [Company] agrees and undertakes that:

1.1 it shall at all material times be covered by a comprehensive product liability insurance policy paid for by the [Company] until [date].

1.2 the [Products] shall be safe and fit for their intended use and comply with all necessary legislation, regulations, directives, policies, codes and guidelines that may be applicable in respect of any matter including but not limited to health and safety, contents and materials, packaging and label requirements, storage, electrical components, recycling, environmental issues, warnings and safety instructions, children and babies and safety mechanisms that may be in force at the time and/or are created during the existence of this agreement.

1.3 the [Company] undertakes to ensure that any manufacturer, supplier, distributor and/or other third party engaged by the [Company] in respect of the [Products] shall also be obliged to adhere to all the matters set out in 1.2.

P.384

The [Agent] agrees to ensure that all third parties to be licensed by the [Licensor] under this agreement shall undertake that all the [Licensed Articles/Products] and any associated packaging, advertising and promotional material shall be safe for their intended use and shall comply with all statutes, regulations, directives, standards and any other relevant legislation or guidelines in force at any time in the licensed Territory. In any event comprehensive public liability insurance cover for the benefit of the [Licensor] to cover the legal obligations of the [Licensor] and any acts, omissions and/or errors by any licensee shall be in existence with a reputable insurance company and paid for by the [Licensor] of not less than [number/currency] for each claim prior to the marketing and/or distribution to the general public of the [Licensed Articles/Products].

P.385

1.1   The [Sponsor] undertakes that the [Product] supplied by the [Sponsor] to the [Sportsperson] shall be safe for its intended use which is as follows: [specify details of use] and shall comply with all legislation which may be in existence at the time that it is supplied in [country].

1.2   The [Sponsor] agrees that the [Sportsperson] shall not be held liable by the [Sponsor] for any civil and/or criminal proceedings that may arise indirectly and/or directly from the use and/or promotion of the [Product] by the [Sportsperson]. That the [Sponsor] shall pay all costs, expenses, losses, damages and legal costs that may arise and/or be incurred by the [Sportsperson] relating to the [Product] and/or any allegation, claim, legal action and/or other matter.

P.386

The [Sponsor] confirms that a comprehensive product, service and public liability insurance policy will be in force during the Sponsorship Period covering any legal proceedings, claim, costs, expenses, damages and/or losses that may arise as a direct result of the use by a member of the public of the specific products and/or services being promoted under this agreement by [Name]. In addition the policy shall also cover any other products and/or services owned and/or controlled by the [Sponsor] which the public could reasonably associate with the [Sponsor's Logo]. The [Sponsor] shall provide a copy of such policies and evidence of payment of premiums upon request at any time.

P.387

The [Licensee] acknowledges that the [Company] is not competent to determine whether the [Products] are safe for supply, distribution and sale to the public. That any approval by the [Company] under this agreement is not a confirmation of compliance with any health and safety and/or other legislation and/or compliance requirements. It is the obligation of the [Licensee] to have the [Product] reviewed, assessed and tested by suitable experts to ensure that it meets such standards and shall not pose a risk to any purchaser.

P.388

The [Supplier] agrees that the [Product] shall comply and continue to comply with all provisions relating to design, content, material, manufacture, supply, use and packaging of any part of the [Product] relating to any statute, regulation, order, directive and/or other governing law in force at the time of delivery to the [Distributor] in [specify countries/world].

P.389

That the [Distributor] shall ensure that each [Product] is supplied with suitable packaging and supporting literature which clearly sets out the purpose for which each part of the [Product] is safe and suitable and any safety features and/or risks and any warnings of potential dangers from use.

P.390

That the [Supplier] agrees that it shall take out adequate insurance for the benefit of itself and the [Distributor] in respect of any death, injury, loss, damage and/or other liability that may occur in respect of the [Product] and any associated material as a result of this agreement.

P.391

The [Supplier] agrees that a comprehensive public and product liability insurance policy for the benefit of the [specify Supplier and other parties] is and will be in force covering any allegations, investigations, legal actions and proceedings, claims, actions, damages, expenses, losses and legal costs that may arise as a direct and/or indirect result of the use by the public of the [Products] from [date] to [date]. A copy of such policy with evidence of payment of the premiums shall be provided to the [Supplier]. All parties shall be named on the policy, the minimum value per claim shall be [number/currency] and all parties shall share the cost of the premiums.

P.392

The [Supplier/Distributor/Seller] confirms that the marketing, selling and payment procedures to the public shall conform with any relevant legislation and governing law, codes of practice, policies and guidelines which may be in existence at any time which may be relevant in any country.

P.393

1.1 The [Company] agrees that all costs, expenses and liability incurred in respect of the development, production, distribution and exploitation of the [Product] and any advertising, promotional events and any other material shall be at the [Company's] sole cost and risk and the [Celebrity] shall not be liable for any such sums.

1.2 The [Company] confirms that there exists comprehensive public and product liability insurance which shall continue to exist for the Term of this Agreement. The [Company] agrees to allow the [Celebrity] the opportunity to inspect the policy upon request.

P.394

1.1 The [Licensee] agrees that the licensed [Product] shall be tested and assessed by [specify company] of [address] in [country] prior to manufacture and supply to retailers and the public. The tests to be carried out shall be those set out in appendix A. The [Licensee] agrees and undertakes to supply a copy of the test results to the [Licensor].

1.2 In the event that the [Product] fails any of the tests and/or assessments then the [Licensee] agrees that the launch of the [Product] must be delayed until the [Product] is fully compliant and that fact has been proved to the satisfaction of the [Licensor].

P.395

1.1 The [Licensee] shall provide copies and details to the [Licensor] of any alleged incidents, faults and/or consumer complaints of the [Product] at the end of each [three] month period during each year of this agreement.

1.2 The [Licensee] agrees that it shall be obliged to deal with the matters in 1.1 swiftly and shall endeavour to resolve the matter with the minimum of publicity. The [Licensee] accepts that the policy aim of the [Licensee] shall be to avoid expensive litigation and/or adverse publicity which would affect sales.

P.396

The [Licensee] agrees that the approval of samples and/or [Licensed Articles/Products] by the [Licensor] does not detract and/or waive any duty by the [Licensee] to ensure that the [Product] is safe for its intended purpose. Further that it does not contain any material, chemical and/or parts which are toxic, dangerous and/or likely to result in injury and/or death and/or which pose a severe risk to children due to the nature of the product, the packaging and/or the contents.

P.397

That the [Licensee] shall be solely responsible for any expenses, legal costs, fines, damages and/or losses from any legal action, claim, allegation, investigation, default, failure and/or liability arising from the production, manufacture, sale and/or distribution of the [Licensed Articles/Products]. In the event that the [Licensor] is joined in any legal proceedings and/or sued directly then the [Licensee] agrees to repay all the consequential legal costs, expenses, damages and losses incurred by the [Licensor] which relate to the [Licensed Articles/Product] up to a maximum of [number/currency].

P.398

The [Licensee] shall ensure that each [Licensed Article/Product] shall conform in all respects to the quality, design, packaging and materials of the [Sample/Prototype] submitted to and approved by the [Licensor]. That the workmanship and/or materials shall not be defective and/or of poor quality and/or contaminated with undeclared substances and/or unable to be used for the intended purpose without a significant degree of wear and tear at an early stage which would result in the loss of attachments which might pose a health and safety risk.

P.399

1.1   The [Licensee] agrees that the [Licensor] shall be entitled to approve a sample of the [Licensed Article/Product] and any associated label, attachments, merchandise, leaflets, packaging and marketing material prior to the production, manufacture, supply, distribution and/or marketing.

1.2   The [Licensee] undertakes to provide the each and every sample in the exact form in which it is proposed it should be sold, displayed, and/or distributed to the public.

1.3   The [Licensee] agrees that no production and/or manufacture of the [Licensed Articles/Product] should commence until the prior written approval of each of the samples has been provided by the [Licensor].

1.4   The [Licensee] agrees that any alterations in the colour, shape, content, labels, packaging and/or any other matter shall require further samples to be sent to the [Licensor] for approval.

P.400

The [Company] agrees that the [Licensor] shall be entitled to approve the appointment of any third party to be used in respect of the production, manufacture, distribution, sale supply and marketing of the [Licensed Articles/Products]. That any such third party shall not be appointed by the [Company] if the [Licensor] does not provide approval.

P.401

The [Company] agrees to provide the [Licensor] at the [Company's] cost with not less than [number] units of the [Licensed Articles/Products] in the form in which they are distributed to the general public.

P.402

The [Licensor] agrees to provide written approval and/or to reject the samples of the [Licensed Articles/Products] within [specify period] of the date of delivery.

P.403

Where for any reason there is a dispute over product liability under this agreement. Then the parties agree to refer the matter to an independent person agreed between both parties. Such person must be a member of [specify organisation] and will endeavour to resolve the matter prior to litigation. Each party shall provide written arguments of their case and then be able to make representations. The parties agree to share the cost of the person equally between them.

P.404

1.1 Approval of the sample and/or prototype by the [Distributor] from the [Supplier] shall result in the fact that the [Supplier] shall not be responsible for the content and/or use and/or sale of the [Product] except where the negligence of the [Supplier] has directly caused injury and/or death. The [Distributor] agrees to shall pay for insurance cover at the [Distributors] cost to cover a serious injury and/or death claim against the [Supplier] relating to the [Product].

1.2 The [Distributor] agrees to bear all responsibility, liability and costs and expenses for any losses and/or damages and/or legal proceedings and/or claims that may arise from the specially commissioned [Product].

P.405

Where any party to this agreement engages third parties consultants, companies, contractors and/or suppliers. Then that party shall continue to be liable for the third party errors, omissions, delays, insolvency, administration and/or product and/or other content liability to all the other parties under this agreement and shall be obliged to pay for all costs and expenses, losses, damages, claims, actions and/or settlements and legal costs which may arise.

P.406

Product liability in respect of the [Products/Services] supplied by the [Company] in respect of the [Event] shall be entirely at the cost and risk of the [Company]. No contribution and/or other sums shall be paid by the [Institute/Charity] towards any legal proceedings, claims, settlements, costs, expenses, losses, damages and/or legal costs agreed and/or paid by the [Company].

P.407
Where there is any legal proceedings and/or allegation made against the [Institute/Charity] relating to the [Event] in respect of the [Products/Services] supplied by the [Company] at the [Event]. Then the [Institute/Charity] shall not be obliged to consult with and/or notify the [Company]. The [Institute/Charity] shall deal with the matter as they think fit. Where the [Institute/Charity] pays any sum to a third party as a settlement and/or respect of a legal action for legal costs, damages and/or otherwise. The [Company] agrees to reimburse the [Institute/Charity] for all such sums in full subject to an invoice and a brief summary of the facts.

P.408

1.1 All liability in respect of the consequences of the [Website/App/Social Media Marketing/Products] shall be shared between the following parties; [name/address/nationality].

1.2 All parties in 1.1 agree to deposit the sum of [number/currency] in a nominated account known as: [–] to hold the premium cost of product and other public liability insurance cover for [countries/world].

1.3 Where additional sums claimed and/or settled are not covered by any policy in 1.2 then the parties agree that they shall each pay an equal sum to cover any legal costs, fines, penalties, expenses, losses, damages and/or otherwise.

PUBLICITY

General Business and Commercial

P.409
The [Employee] is not permitted to publish and/or post and/or distribute any comments, letters, articles, books and/or other material in any media and/or other format which purport to represent the views of and/or report how the [Company] conducts its business and/or the conversations of the [Executives] and/or any other matter relating to the business, its products, its staff, consultants and/or third party suppliers, distributors and/or otherwise without the prior consent in writing of the [Managing Director].

P.410

The [Employee] must not comment on social media and/or contact and/or communicate with any member of the press, television, radio and/or other media relating to any matter concerning the business of the [Company] without the prior written consent of [Name]. Failure to adhere to this clause shall be deemed a breach of this agreement.

P.411

The [Licensee] shall not issue, release and/or make any statement to the press, television, radio, social media and/or in any other medium concerning any aspect of the [Company] and/or the terms of this agreement without first requesting permission from the [Company's] public relations office and/or the [Managing Director].

P.412

[Name] undertakes that he/she have not and will not during the continuance of this agreement post, display, distribute, publish and/or supply material concerning the internal affairs and/or business of the [Company] without the prior written approval of the [Company].

P.413

1.1 [Name] agrees and undertakes that he/she shall not except make and/or provide any statement, photograph, image, email, text and/or information relating to this agreement and/or the services to be provided by [Name] in respect of the [Film/Video/Sound Recording/Series].

1.2 [Name] agrees that all marketing and promotion shall be arranged with [specify person] at the [Company]. That [Name] is not to arrange and/or commit to any interview, article and/or other matter which may mention the [Film/Video/Sound Recording/Series] without first seeking approval from the [Company].

1.3 [Name] agrees that all scripts, schedules and other material supplied to [name] under this agreement are confidential and not for release in any format to the public.

P.414

No reference is to be made to the terms of this agreement by either party in any social media, online, print, outdoor and other advertising and/or promotional material and/or in any interview, article and/or corporate marketing without the prior consent of the other party.

P.415

The [Artist] shall not issue, release, distribute and/or make any statement, text, image, logo, sound recording and/or any other format in any medium available to the public and/or the media including but not limited to any newspaper, magazine, radio and/or television company and/or through the internet and/or in any electronic form through any telecommunication system any material, scripts and/or other confidential business and/or future plans of the [Company].

P.416
The [Group] agrees not to issue any statement to the press during the Term of the Agreement concerning the future plans of the [Group] or the [Manager] without the prior consent of the [Manager].

P.417
The [Artist] agrees that all marketing and publicity shall be the sole responsibility of the [Agent] and that the [Artist] shall not issue, release and/or respond to any request of any third party in the media concerning the personal and/or professional life of the [Artist] without the prior approval of the [Agent]. Provided that the [Artist] shall still be entitled to post, display and manage the following accounts on the internets without any consent and/or approval by the [Agent]: [specify accounts on the internet].

P.418
The [Agent] undertakes not to disclose any material and/or make any statement (whether true or not) concerning the [Artist's] private and social life, political and personal views to the media including newspapers, television, radio, internet and/or through any mobile and/or other any telecommunication system at any time without the prior written consent of the [Artist].

P.419
The [Artist] agrees not to issue any statement to the media at any time concerning any confidential business or future plans of the [Agent] and/or details of any negotiations and/or the terms of any agreements in progress and/or concluded by the [Agent] without the prior consent of the [Agent].

P.420
The [Celebrity] agrees not to participate in any dangerous sport, political controversy, take any illegal substances and/or act in any manner which could be capable of being a criminal act and/or any other activities which would prejudice the goodwill and reputation of the [Company] and the [Company's] [Products] during the Term of the Agreement and generate negative publicity surrounding the engagement of the services of the [Celebrity].

P.421
The [Author] shall not make any statement whether in writing and/or otherwise to the press and/or on any social media and/or to any newspaper, radio,

television, internet and/or other media companies in respect of the [Film], the other performers, the scripts, schedule, locations and/or any other business of the [Production Company] without the prior written consent of the [Production Company]. This clause shall apply after the agreement has been terminated and whether the [Film] has been completed or not and/or whether the [Author] and the [Production Company] are in dispute for any reason until [date].

P.422
The [Writer] undertakes not to disclose any material of any nature nor make any statement whether true or not concerning the private or public life or otherwise of the [Originator] or any third party interviewed or researched for the purposes of the preparation and writing of the [Work] to any third party at any time without the prior written consent of the [Originator] or unless requested to do so by the [Originator] or his/her [Agent].

P.423
The [Company] shall not without the written approval of the [Television Company] inform any person and/or media outlet other than its professional advisers and persons with whom it negotiates the financing of the production of the [Film] about any part of this agreement.

P.424
The [Company] shall not make any statement to the press or any other media concerning any aspect of the [Licensor] without obtaining permission from the [Licensor's] press office or its Managing Director.

P.425
[Name] is not permitted to make any arrangement with a third party for the publication, release, distribution and/or supply of any information, data, products or services relating to the [Company] unless prior permission is obtained in writing from [specify position/office]. Failure to comply with this permission may, if the circumstances are considered appropriate, be regarded as a breach of this agreement by [Name].

P.426
[Name] must not contact, communicate and/or supply documents, recordings, films or data in any form to any member of the press or media or anyone so connected on behalf of the [Company] unless prior permission has been obtained from [name/position/office].

P.427
The [Agent] undertakes not to disclose any material nor make any statement whether true or not concerning the [Actor's] private and sexual life, politics

and personal views to the media at any time without the prior specific approval of the [Artist] in each case.

P.428

1.1 The [Company] agrees that the [Presenter's] name, image, signature and endorsement shall not be used for any purpose other than the marketing of the [Product/Film] unless agreed in advance in each case.

1.2 The [Company] agrees to provide the [Presenter] with the exact samples of all materials in any medium in which it is intended to use material relating to the [Presenter].

1.3 All reasonable requests for changes by the [Presenter] shall be incorporated at the [Company's] cost.

A separate fee and licence shall be paid for in each case and shall be negotiated in good faith dependant on the circumstances.

P.429

The [Supplier] agrees and undertakes that it shall not issue and/or make any statement to the media, press and/or trade journals concerning the agreement with the [Company], the products which it supplies and/or any health and safety issue relating to them without first clearing it in advance with: [specify role/person/department] of the [Company].

P.430

The [Institute/Charity] agrees that in any associated publicity, advertising, promotional material, emails mailshots, and marketing. The [Company's] name, trade mark, image, slogan and copyright and trade mark notices as set out in Schedule A shall be given equal prominence and position with the [Institute/Charity].

P.431

The [Company] agrees that no other person, company, products, services, information and/or data shall appear in any publicity associated with the [Event] which potentially conflicts with and/or may damage the reputation and/or aims of the [Institute/Charity] and/or its products and/or services.

P.432

The [Institute] agrees and undertakes that the product of the [Contributors'] services, and his/her name, image and support of the [Event/Project] shall not be used for any purpose other than that authorised as follows: [specify purpose].

P.433

The [Company] agrees and undertakes that the [Work/Material] provided by the [Institute] shall not be used and/or licensed for any purpose except those set out in this agreement. That the [Company] does not have the right to use any [Work/Material] and/or any part and/or the name, trademark and/or logo of the [Institute] in any publicity, advertising, brochures, and/or on any website, app and/or social media marketing and/or online internet accounts and/or channels without the prior written approval of the [Institute].

P.434

The [Company] agrees and undertakes that it shall not publish any letters, provide any interviews, issue any statements and/or contact and/or communicate with any person and/or company purporting to represent the views of the [Institute] unless prior consent is provided under this agreement and/or the prior approval of the [Chief Executive] of the [Institute] has been obtained.

P.435

The [Sub-Licensee] agrees and undertakes not to issue and/or distribute any press release, marketing and/or other promotional material without the prior approval of the [Licensee] of the content of the material in any format and/or medium.

P.436

The [Sub-Licensee] agrees and undertakes that they shall use and adapt the press releases, data, promotional and marketing material supplied by the [Licensee] in respect of the [Film/Work/Sound Recordings]. That the [Sub-Licensee] shall not have the right to create, develop and reproduce other material based on the [Film/Work/Sound Recordings] for the purpose of marketing and exploiting the rights granted under this agreement.

P.437

The [Company] agrees to display the trade mark, logo and image of the [Company] on the [Product/Disc/Work] which is set out in the attached Schedule B on all copies of any material in any format which display and/or reproduce the image of the [Product/Disc/Work].

P.438

[Name] agrees that the [Company] may promote, advertise and market the [Work/Product] in any of the followings ways:

1.1 Over the internet on websites, on apps, banner links and online competitions in conjunction with digital newspapers, magazines, newsletters, direct email marketing, media news and other services and/or social media and mobile and other telecommunications but not call centre direct marketing to landline and mobile numbers.

1.2 Advertisements and free promotions in printed newspapers, journals, magazines, puzzle books, comics, event and conference brochures and in flyers and free merchandise.

1.3 Funded character promotional events, exhibitions and at galleries, museums and festivals.

P.439

1.1 The [Company] acknowledges that [Name] already holds and manages a number on online internet accounts and channels as follows: [specify detail].

1.2 The [company] agrees that it shall not acquire any rights and/or in any of these matters in 1.1 as a result of this agreement.

P.440
[Name] agrees and undertakes to post, display and promote the following material on his/her online accounts and channels as follows:

1.1 Account reference: [specify account] [number] of images of products of the [Company].

1.2 Account reference: [specify account] [number] of videos of up to [number] minutes of the services of the [Company].

1.3 The [Company] accepts that all editorial control in respect of 1.1 and 1.2 is with [Name] and not the [Company].

1.4 The [Company] accepts and agrees that the layout, design and content of any matter in 1.1 and 1.2 shall not require consultation with and/or approval of the [Company].

1.5 The [Company] agrees that not all the matters in 1.1 and 1.2 feature [Name].

P.441
The [Company] agrees to pay for all the cost and expense of [Name] appearing at any premier, event, interview, filming and/or any other matter requested by the [Company] and agreed with [Name]. This shall include but not be limited to the cost of clothes, hair, make-up, shoes, transport, hotels for [Name] and two other nominated people to assist [Name].

P.442

1.1 [Name] agrees use [number] [images/videos] supplied by the [Company] of the [Product/Service] on his/her online account and channel: [reference name/source] from [date] to date].

1.2 In addition [Name] agrees to include [number] products supplied by the [Company] in the filming of the next [three] videos filmed by [Name] which are posted by [Name] before [date]. In the event that for any reason the filming and/or post of the videos are delayed and/or cancelled for any reason. The parties agree to negotiate an alternative arrangement.

QUALIFICATION

General Business and Commercial

Q.001
The [Author] confirms that he/she holds a current passport issued by the relevant authority in the [United Kingdom] and that he/she is resident in and a national of the [United Kingdom]. That he/she has no plans to relinquish this status and shall remain a resident for the duration of this agreement.

Q.002
The [Author] confirms that he/she holds as passport in the name of [specify] [passport reference] issued by the authorities of [country]. That he/she is a [specify] national of the following [country] and entitled to reside in [country] and will remain so during the Term of this Agreement.

Q.003
[Name] confirms that he/she is a bona fide and paid up member of the following trade organisation and/or union known as [Equity/Musicians/other Union] and will continue to be so during the Term of this Agreement.

Q.004
The [Writer] confirms and undertakes that he/she is a [British] subject ordinarily resident in the [United Kingdom] and that he/she shall remain so for the duration of his/her engagement pursuant to this agreement.

Q.005
The [Consultant] confirms that he/she is:

1.1 a qualified [specify professional status]; and

1.2 an expert in the field of [specify subject]; and

1.3 holds the following qualifications [specify degree, training, graduation date and governing body]; and

1.4 is a member of the following organisations [specify]; and

1.5   that he/she is a competent, skilled and professional person, fluent in [specify language] and is a well-recognised authority; and

1.6   is capable of compiling, data, research and records which are detailed and accurate in the form of reports to the [Company] as required under this agreement.

Q.006

The [Designer] shall perform its obligations under this Agreement to the best of its skill and ability and shall maintain such high standards as are reasonably expected by the [Company] for [state purpose] under this Agreement.

Q.007

The [Designer] shall at all times employ suitably qualified and experienced [staff/consultants] who are reliable, skilled in their field and able to contribute to the success of the [Project].

Q.008

The [Company] confirms and undertakes that it is able to provide the service stated in Schedule A to the standard, quality and level stipulated by the [Distributor] and that:

1.1   all the [Company's] personnel who will work on the [Project] as [specify] hold professional qualifications of not less than [specify grade/qualification/level of expertise/years of experience] and are members of [specify organisation].

1.2   the [Company] is able to provide and/or source material for the [Project] which are not inferior to the samples displayed as part of the presentation and/or during discussions.

1.3   the facilities to be provided by the [Company] to process, design and develop the [Project] shall include the following [specify equipment].

1.4   no temporary, unqualified, inexperienced and/or unsuitable personnel and/or any person with a criminal record, and/or a record of alcohol and/or drug abuse will be used and/or supplied by the [Company] for the [Project].

Q.009

The [Contributor/Consultant] confirms and undertakes that he/she holds the following professional qualifications [specify details] and holds a [first/second/third] class degree from [name of University]. That he/she has practised as a [specify profession] continuously for the last [number] years. That there is no pending disciplinary proceedings and/or criminal action against the [Contributor/Consultant]. That there are no facts of which the [Contributor/Consultant] is aware which would affect the decision of the [Institute/Charity] to appoint the [Contributor/Consultant] in the role of [specify role].

Q.010

The [Company] agrees and undertakes that:

1.1 all the personnel which it provides under this agreement to fulfil the tasks shall hold relevant current qualifications and shall have completed such up to date training as may be appropriate for their work.

1.2 no personnel shall be used who have been qualified for less than [number] years and/or who are not fluent in the [specify] language.

1.3 the [Company] shall ensure that all personnel use and wear such safety equipment as shall be provided whilst on the premises. Failure to comply shall mean that the person is immediately removed from the premises and that their work must be terminated.

Q.011

The [Company] agrees and undertakes that all persons supplied by the [Company] under this agreement shall have had the following routine checks carried out and that they must have been assessed as approved before they are allowed on the site and/or supplied to complete work for [Name] that:

1.1 the persons are entitled to work in [country] and have met all the current legal requirements that must be met in order to do so.

1.2 the persons have valid [national insurance numbers] in [country].

1.3 there is no medical reason and/or any other ill health which would make them unsuitable and/or prevent them performing their work.

1.4 the persons have passed an enhanced security check for any criminal record and/or pending prosecution in [country].

Q.012

1.1 The failure by the [Supplier] to provide personnel who hold the relevant qualifications in [country] to fulfil the terms of the agreement and provide the [Service] as required shall entitle the [Company] to terminate the agreement with immediate effect.

1.2 The [Supplier] agrees that in the event of termination in 1.1 that the [Company] shall have the right to be repaid all sums paid after the date of the failure and that the [Company] shall not be liable to pay any further sums due to the [Supplier] throughout the term of the agreement.

Q.013

Where an applicant and/or employee and/or consultant has provided a detailed curriculum vitae and/or background record and/or displayed records on linked in and/or any other site which are subsequently found to be misleading, wrong, fraudulent and/or enhanced in any manner which is untrue. Then the [Company] shall have the right when fully aware of this fact to terminate the contract with that person immediately by communication in writing by email and/or any other form such as a verbally in a meeting. There shall be no obligation by the [Company] to pay the person any further sums after the date of termination.

QUALITY CONTROL

Film, Television and Video

Q.014

The [Assignor] confirms that the [Film/Video/Podcast/Disc] shall not contain any other music, lyrics, text, sound recordings, sound effects, persons, background material, trade marks, service marks, logos, images, products and/or other articles than [specify] unless there is prior written consent in advance from [Name].

Q.015

The [Company] confirms that the [Film/Video/Disc] will be of first-class technical quality according to standards set by [specify] in [country] and will conform to the specifications set out in Schedule A.

Q.016

The [Company] undertakes that it will produce the [Film/Video] for the [Film/Podcast/Disc] using the key personnel, artists and material as follows:

1.1   The Director: [–]

1.2   The [Presenter/Voice-over]: [–]

1.3   The [Writer/Choreographer]: [–]

1.4   The Senior Cameraman: [–]

1.5   The Editor: [–]

1.6   The Artists: [–]

1.7   The [Musical Works/Sound Recordings/Lyrics]: [–]

1.8   The [Stills/Photographs/Archive Film]: [–]

1.9   The [Products/Articles/Branded Clothes]: [–]

1.10 The [Computer-generated/Animated Character Material]: [–].

Q.017
The [Distributor] confirms that a representative of the [Company] shall be entitled to attend the filming, editing and viewing of the proposed final version of the [Film/Video/Disc] at any stage prior to its completion.

Q.018
The [Distributor] agrees and undertakes that it will ensure that the [Film/Work/Video/Unit] and the means by which it is produced, reproduced, distributed, supplied, sold and/or exploited at any time shall conform to all legislation, industry guidelines and Codes of Practice in [country] and issued by [specify regulatory body/trade organisations].

Q.019
The [Licensee] agrees and undertakes that:

1.1   it shall produce an adaptation of the [Sound Recordings] which is of a professional standard suitable for the [specify] market and sale to the public in [format].

1.2   no existing material of a third party which has already been released to the public shall be added to the finished version.

1.3   the following persons shall be engaged to produce, record and play the music; [specify name and role].

Q.020
The parties agree that the [Film/Footage/Recording] is for reproduction in the form of a [specify] for display by the [Charity] on its stand at events, workshops and exhibitions. That it is not intended to be sufficient quality for use for transmission on television, radio, on a website and/or any other media.

Q.021
The parties agree that the [Project] shall be recorded by [Name] on [specify equipment] and that copies shall be supplied in [format] to all the parties for use and adaptation in any manner they think fit at each parties cost and expense.

Q.022
The [Company] shall at all times employ, contract and/or engage agents, employees, consultants and/or temporary personnel which are of suitable

experience and technical ability in relation to their intended services. That any person shall be trained to a professional standard and capable of using the equipment and facilities that may be required for their role in order to successfully to complete the [Project] and the detailed requirements of the terms of this agreement.

Q.023
The [Company] confirms that the [Programme] will be of first-class editorial quality and will conform to the technical standards and specifications set out in Schedule A.

Q.024
'The Key Personnel' for the [Project/Series/Film] to be used by the [Assignor] shall be as follows:

1.1 The Producer: [–]

1.2 The Director: [–]

1.3 The Presenter: [–]

1.4 The Writer: [–]

1.5 The Narrator: [–]

1.6 The Senior Cameraman: [–]

1.7 The Editor: [–]

1.8 Costumes and props: [–]

1.9 Opening titles and credits: [–]

1.10 Lead Actors: [–]

1.11 Product Placement and Sponsorship: [–]

1.12 Music, Lyrics and Sound Recordings: [–]

Q.025
The [Production Company] agrees that it must ensure that the [Distributor] has approved all the content in respect of the [Advertisement/Film/Podcast]. That the [Production Company] shall ensure that the [Advertisement/Film/Podcast] complies with the description of the synopsis attached in appendix A. That the [Production Company] shall ensure that the [Distributor] has approved all the following matters:

1.1 Performers, dancers, artists, musicians, actors and/or any animal and/ or children and/or any other location.

1.2 The music, lyrics and sound recordings for the sound track whether comprising original musical works and/or existing recordings.

1.3 Images, stills, photographs, characters, archive film and/or video footage and/or any extracts of any film and/or sound recordings sourced from a third party.

1.4 Logos, trade marks and/or service marks, slogans, products and/or any other article for which specific payment is to be made for its inclusion.

1.5 All copyright notices, credits and acknowledgments on the [Advertisement/Film/Podcast] and on any associated material such as labels, packaging, reviews and/or merchandising.

Q.026

The [Production Company] confirms that a representative of the [Distributor] shall be entitled to attend the viewing of the proposed [Advertisement/Film/Podcast] where it is shown to a select audience to assess the impact. The [Production Company] shall then further edit and adapt the [Advertisement/Film/Podcast] before the master material is completed. The [Commissioning Company] agrees to keep the [Distributor] fully informed as to all locations, dates and times that work on the [Advertisement/Film/Podcast] is being carried out and will notify them of any unexpected delay and/or interruption in the production and/or editing.

Q.027

The [Production Company] agrees and undertakes that it will ensure that the [Advertisement/Film/Podcast] shall:

1.1 not be in breach of any legislation, regulations and/or rules in [specify country/countries] and

1.2 comply with all guidelines and codes of [specify organisation/trade union] which may be applicable to the production and/or exploitation of the [Advertisement/Film/Podcast].

1.3 not use any person under the age of [number] as a performer and/or contributor.

1.4 not contain any music, sound recordings, products and/or other items which promote any other third party and/or their brand. It shall contain no third party trade marks, logos, slogans and/or marketing material of any nature.

Q.028

The [Company] agrees that the prior [written/verbal] approval of [Name] and the [Agent] shall be required in respect of the [Promotional Video/Film/

Podcast] in the event that the [Company] wishes to adapt and/or license any part of the content to any third party. The [Company] agrees that in the event that [Name] and the [Agent] provide consent then an additional fee shall be due to both parties.

Q.029

[Name] agrees and undertakes not to wear any jewellery, clothes, make up and/or use any mobile telephone, tablets and/or laptops and/or any other gadgets and/or any other material and/or equipment whether for free and/or for payment and/or display any logos, products names and/or words and/or images and/or mention, write and/or make reference to any company, product and/or service which is a sponsor of [Name] and/or some other third party. [Name] agrees and accepts that it is a condition of this agreement that sponsorship agreements, free products and product placement are not permitted by the [Company] for all persons appearing in the [Series/Film].

Q.030

[Name] agrees that the decision as to which music and/or sound recording to add to the [Programme] shall be entirely at the [Company's] discretion. [Name] accepts and agrees that the [Company] may use a different person, dialect and/or language for the sound recording and voice for [Name] in the [Programme] provided that this is made clear in the credits at the end.

General Business and Commercial

Q.031

All materials and goods shall be of the quality and standard described in the [Project Outline and Schedule] a copy of which is attached in appendix A. In any event all materials and goods shall upon request be subject to the inspection of [specify person/role] in each case prior to the commencement of any work. There must be no changes and/or developments as to style, content, colour, quality, source or otherwise which are not given written approval in advance by [specify person/role].

Q.032

The [Company] shall upon the request of the [Institute/Charity] provide full details, documents and evidence to prove that the materials and goods comply with the standards, quality and quantity required for the fulfilment of the contract.

Q.033

The [Company] shall employ or otherwise engage the personnel listed in the Schedule A on site and for the completion of the [Project]. The prior written consent of the [Institute/Charity] shall be required for any replacement, addition or deletion of any such personnel or their functions, but such consent shall not be unreasonably withheld or delayed.

Q.034

The [Developer] agrees and undertakes that:

1.1 the [Company] shall be provided with access to all documentation, records, databases, plans, drawings, tables, graphics, designs, computer-generated material, computer software, discs, patents, models or other material, data and/or information in the control or possession of the [Developer] or any associated company, partnership, entity, director or senior executive of any nature in any media directly relating to the fulfilment of the [Project] within [two] days of receipt of a written request by email to the [Developer] and

1.2 the [Company] shall be entitled to access during the [Project] upon request to any directors, employees, consultants and/or professional advisors to verify any aspect of the [Project] and shall be entitled to ask questions, carry out inspections and take copies as required. The [Developer] shall provide the facilities for inspection and copying at the [Developer's] cost and shall not make any charge to the [Company].

Q.035

The [Company] undertakes to perform and carry out the [Project] in accordance with the highest professional standards and to ensure that it only uses suitably qualified personnel and first class materials for any part of the [Project]. Further that all health, safety and security measures are assessed and carried out to safeguard the employees, consultants, visitors, advisors and/or other third parties engaged by the [Company] and members of the public.

Q.036

1.1 The [Company] shall at all times supervise, control and be responsible for the work, acts and conduct of its personnel, sub-contractors, consultants, agents, suppliers and others that it engages and/or employs for any matter connected with the [Project].

1.2 The [Company] agrees and undertakes that it shall immediately remove and replace any person, sub-contractor, consultant and/or supplier which the considers to not be qualified, unsuitable and/or whose work, conduct and/or acts have been such that they affect the quality, schedule and/or compliance with any health, safety and/or security requirements and/or any compliance with any legislation, standards and/or any other matter for the [Project].

Q.037

The [Company] shall employ and/or engage a sufficient number of qualified persons for the design, development, production and completion of the [Article/Product/App]. The [Company] shall provide the [Distributor] upon request with detailed documentary evidence that the [Article/Product/App] complies with any relevant legislation, codes of practice and guidelines which may apply for the use, supply and/or exploitation of the [Article/Product/App] throughout the world. That no content and/or materials shall be used and/or incorporated which might create a legal problem and/or incur additional unforeseen costs and expenses to the [Distributor].

Q.038

Prior to the date upon which the [Site/Project] commences the [Developer] shall provide the [Company] with the following details:

1.1   Name, mobile number and email of the person responsible for the [Site Manager/other] and his/her senior manager.

1.2   Names of all delegated staff on the [Site/Project] and their areas of responsibility.

Q.039

The [Company] shall advise the [Developer] of all the names, mobile numbers and emails of the [Company's] nominated consultants, advisors and/or employees who have been delegated the responsibility of assessing and/or monitoring the performance of the work on the [Site/Project], adherence to the terms and specifications of the contract, and the materials and equipment used. The [Developer] shall ensure that the [Company's] authorised personnel which shall include any safety inspectors, architects, lawyers and accountants shall be provided access to the site for assessment, review and inspection purposes. The [Developer] shall provide such administration equipment and technical facilities that the authorised personnel may require on site to assess, review and inspect the work at no extra cost.

Q.040

The [Chairman/Chief Executive] shall have the right at any time by text, by mobile, email and/or any other written communication to the [Developer] suspend and/or cease work on the [Site/Project] if they have reached the conclusion that there is a serious health and safety issue which must be investigated and remedied before work can commence and/or the planned budget has been exceeded and the additional costs have not been authorised in advance.

Q.041

The [Developer] shall remain solely liable for the performance of the work and adherence to the terms of the contract. The supervision, review, monitoring and access to the [Site/Project] by the [Company] shall not be deemed to constitute a waiver of any of the terms of the contract nor reduce and/or vary the liability of the [Developer].

Q.042

The [Developer] shall be solely responsible for the performance and completion of the [Project] under the agreement. The [Developer] shall be responsible for and bear the cost of and be liable for the actions and/ or failures and/or negligence of all its employees, suppliers, advisors, consultants and any other third parties required by the [Developer] to carry out any work on the [Project] and/or to provide technical advice and/or equipment. The [Developer] shall ensure that all such persons adhere to the standard and quality of work required by the [Company] at all times.

Q.043

The [Supplier/Manufacturer] agrees and undertakes that it shall not have the right to reproduce and/or exploit in any media the commissioned [Product/ Video/Artwork] which is based on a concept and idea provided by [Name] for the [Company]. The [Supplier/Manufacturer] shall not use any logos, moulds, images, recordings and/or preparatory material for the [Product/ Video/Artwork] and/or reproduce them in any other format and/or authorise any third party to do so at any time.

Q.044

The parties agree that all requests for consent and/or approval shall be provided within [seven] days which shall include weekends.

Q.045

The [Company] agrees that it shall not be entitled to edit, adapt, mutilate and/or alter the [Work/Image/Logo] in any way manner and/or reproduce it in another format and/or medium and/or authorise a third party to do so without the prior written consent of the [Distributor].

Q.046

No authority is given to the [Company] to sign and/or authorise agreements and/or licences on behalf of [Name]. All offers, proposals and agreements should be supplied to [Name] who shall then be entitled to agree or reject any matter as he/she thinks fit. There shall be no obligation by [Name] to agree to any terms that may be proposed at any time. Nor shall the [Company] be entitled to make any claim for loss of revenue based on such rejection.

Q.047

The [Company] shall provide the following service [specify] which shall be according to the standards set by [specify organisation].

Q.048

The [Distributor] undertakes to meet the following [performance targets/level of service] [specify]. In the event that the [Distributor] fails to meet any of these targets then the [Company] shall have the right to terminate this agreement by notice in writing to end the agreement by [four] weeks' notice.

Q.049

The [Company] may alter, change and amend any part of the supply of the service and/or products and/or substitute any material, content, packaging, product, or other matter in respect of this agreement. The [Company] shall not be obliged to notify you in advance, but you shall have the right to reject any substitute which either is materially different and/or which does not fulfil the same function. If you do not accept substitution you should make this clear in advance of signing this agreement.

Q.050

It is a condition of this agreement that the [Supplier] must be able to produce evidence of the following matters when requested to do so by the [Company] for the period [date] to [date]:

1.1 Date, time and location, method of manufacture and production.

1.2 Source of supply of all materials, ingredients and content however small.

1.3 Health, safety, hygiene and content compliance in accordance with the standards set in [country].

1.4 Source of supply of any water used in any manufacturing process.

1.5 Data relating to any tests and samples that were carried out and results.

1.6 Materials rejected and/or destroyed as not of suitable standard.

1.7 Duration of storage, method used and date of supply to shipping agent.

1.8 Any claims and/or complaints by those working at the factory in respect of injuries, disability and/or death and/or working conditions recorded and/or made by any person.

1.9 Evidence of waste disposal, recycling procedures and compliance and environmental impact assessments.

Q.051

In order to fulfil the quality control criteria guidelines stipulated by the [Distributor]. The [Supplier] agrees that it shall carry out the following matters:

1.1 To verify the source of all materials in the [Product]s.

1.2 Not to use any materials which are not [specify].

1.3 To regularly carry out sample checks in the manufacturing process to ensure consistency and quality is maintained.

1.4 Allow access to the manufacturing process by the [Company] at least once very [three] months to view the premises.

1.5 Not to store the [Product] in any manner which would result in a deterioration of the materials.

1.6 Ensure that all items are bar coded and identifiable to a date and time of production.

1.7 Keep a regular log of any defects in the manufacturing process which might impact on the delivery of the standard of the quality of the [Product].

1.8 Ensure that all materials to be used are not past its expiry date.

1.9 Not store any [Products] with other items containing [specify].

Internet, Websites and Apps

Q.052

The [Contributor] undertakes that to the best of his/her knowledge and belief that the facts and information contained in the [Work/Film/Video/Sound Recording] are true and accurate except where any material is supplied by or specifically included at the request of the [Company].

Q.053

The [Contributor] agrees that the [Company] shall have absolute discretion as to the suitability of the content of the [Work/Film/Video/Sound Recording] for the [Website/App/Exhibition] and shall be entitled to request any deletions, changes and alterations to the [Work/Film/Video/Sound Recording] as the [Company] may require provided that the [Company] pays all the costs and expenses that must be incurred as a result of such instructions.

Q.054

Where there are any failures, suspension, delays and/or faults are caused by the [Company] which affect the operation and/or functionality of the [Service/Website/App]. The [Company] shall try to remedy the problem as quickly as possible but in any event it is agreed that the [Company] shall not be liable to repay any sums and/or any compensation, losses and/or damages of any nature for any matter which continues for a period of less than [seven] days in each case. Thereafter the [Customer] shall be entitled to cancel the payment for the [Service/Website/App] and shall be repaid all sums paid for any period after the date of termination.

Q.055

In the event that the [Company] fails to achieve the expected audience, sales, ratings and/or followers in accordance with the targets set out in Schedule A for the [Website/App] for the period [date] to [date]. Then the [Contributor] shall be entitled to terminate this agreement by [one] months' written notice. Upon the date of termination all the rights granted in the product of the services of the [Contributor] shall cease on that date and the [Company] shall no longer be authorised and/or entitled to use and/or exploit any material created which is a product of the work of the [Contributor] in any format and/or medium. In the event that the [Company] wishes to use and/or exploit any such material it shall be required to seek the prior written consent of the [Contributor] and to conclude a new agreement with additional licence fee payments.

Q.056

The [Company] has a number of policy guidelines regarding the use and access to the material on the [Website/App/Channel] which are part of the terms and conditions of the agreement for the [subscriber/public/user] to access, download and/or use the [Website/App/Software]. These policies may be amended by the [Company] without notice. The policies are set out in detail in [specify] and cover the following areas:

1.1   Privacy.

1.2   Copyright Notices, Credits, Trade Marks and Moral Rights.

1.3   Storage of your personal and bank details. Data Protection. Criteria for consent to marketing either directly and/or through third parties both on this site and through other means.

1.4   Access to and use of material. Reproducing material from the site for personal use and/or commercial use.

1.5   Cookies and tracking your search history.

1.6   Capacity, age requirements and consent from parents and guardians.

1.7   Editorial Control including use of forums, posting material and comments, removal and deletion of accounts.

Q.057

The [Contributor] agrees and undertakes that all material of any nature in any format supplied by the [Contributor] to the [Website/App/Film/Video] as content whether text, images, film, video, sound recordings, music, lyrics, computer generated material, photographs, trade marks, logos, slogans or otherwise shall comply as follows:

1.1 That it shall not be in breach of any contract and/or infringe any copyright and/or any trade marks and/or intellectual property rights and/or any data protection and/or any other interest of any person and/or company in any part of the world.

1.2 That no material shall be permitted which is likely to cause offense and/or could be considered defamatory, derogatory and/or demeaning and/or could be evidence of a criminal act and/or involves behaviour which causes distress to another person and/or promotes violence and/or anything of a sexual nature and/or is pornographic.

Q.058

Where any material submitted contains the image, name and/or other details regarding any child and/or other person age [number] years or under. The prior written consent of the parent and/or guardian has to have been obtained to permit the material to be displayed on the [Website/Programme]. The [Company] shall have an absolute discretion to refuse to display and/or to delete any material which it decides should not be on the [Website/Programme] at any time. No material should be submitted of another person and/or child without their knowledge and consent.

Q.059

The [Company] agrees and undertakes that it have the professional knowledge and expertise to create, develop and deliver a fully functional [Website/App/Podcast] in accordance with specifications made by the [Distributor] in the [Synopsis] in Schedule A and the [Budget] in Schedule B and in accordance with the stages set out in the [Delivery and Completion Schedule C all which form part of this agreement.

Q.060

The [Company] agrees and accepts that [Name] may wish to make [minor/significant] changes in the layout, design and functions of the [Website/App/Platform] in the development process from the original proposals and agrees that the cost of any such changes are included in the total price which has been agreed between the parties.

Q.061

1.1   In the event that [Name] decides at any stage that the quality of the work delivered by the [Company] is not of the standard expected by [Name] and/or the [Website/App/Platform] cannot fulfil the functions which were requested under this agreement. Then [Name] shall have the right to terminate the agreement and to be delivered all computer software, codes, passwords and all master material and copies completed to date by the [Company] provided that [Name] agrees to pay for all work completed prior to the date of termination.

1.2   The [Company] agrees that it shall not have any right to be paid the remaining fee after the date of termination and/or to charge for supply of the computer software and/or master material to [Name] except the cost of delivery.

Q.062

The [Company] agrees to develop and deliver a functioning [Website/App/Platform] to [Name] on the following basis:

1.1   That the design, structure and content shall be of the highest quality and shall be adapted and developed according to the direct instructions of [Name].

1.2   That all rights, copyright, trade marks, logos, films, sound recordings, domain names, registrations, slogans and any other material created and/or data developed shall be assigned to [Name] and belong solely to [Name]. That there is no intention that the [Company] shall acquire any intellectual property rights and/or any computer software rights and/or any other interest.

1.3   The [Company] accepts that it will not be entitled to any credit and/or acknowledgement on the [Website/App/Platform] at any time. All copyright notices, trade marks and credits shall be attributed to [Name].

1.4   That [Name] may at any time decide to use the services of a third party to collaborate with and/or work independently in respect of the [Website/App/Platform] and the [Company] shall have no right to object.

1.5   The [Website/App/Platform] shall be produced and developed In accordance with the Budget in Appendix A and the Delivery Schedule in Appendix B. Where additional costs and expenses are likely to be required. Then the [Company] must seek the prior consent of [Name] prior to creating any commitment.

1.6   The [Company] accepts that any third party may maintain, update and/
or develop the [Website/App/Platform] and that there is no exclusive
arrangement with [Name].

Merchandising and Distribution

Q.063
The [Supplier] agrees that it shall provide the [Distributor] with a full list of
the following details in respect of the [Products] upon delivery:

1.1   The specified number of [Products] and the wholesale and retail price.

1.2   The dimensions and weight, the ingredients and content together with
a description of any packaging and whether it can be recycled.

1.3   Confirm the required method of storage.

1.4   Confirm whether the delivery date was fulfilled and specify the cost of
freight, delivery, insurance and any import or export taxes, duties and
penalties.

Q.064
The [Units/Products] shall be of merchantable quality, fit for their intended
purpose and the description and other particulars of the [Units/Products]
stated in the sales order and shall conform to all samples, drawings,
descriptions, specifications and functions provided and/or promoted by the
[Company].

Q.065
The [Supplier] confirms that:

1.1   The [Product/Unit] is safe and satisfactory for its intended purpose if
used properly according to the accompanying instructions.

1.2   The [Product/Unit] conforms with the quality and description and
other particulars stated in [document] and is free from all defects prior
to use.

1.3   No responsibility is accepted for any normal wear and tear after
purchase unless caused by a defect.

Q.066
The [Company] shall take every care to ensure that the best results are
as far as possible obtained where materials or equipment are supplied by
the [Customer], but the [Company] will not accept responsibility for or be
liable for any imperfect work caused by defects in or unsuitability of such
materials or equipment.

Q.067

If after the date of this agreement the health, safety and quality of standards is changed, modified or altered which are applicable to the [Products] under any laws, regulations, codes, guidelines or other relevant material in the Territory. The [Distributor] shall provide such information to the [Company] and the [Company/Distributor] shall bear all the cost and expenses arising from the modification of the specifications of the [Products] and all costs and expenses of passing the health and safety and quality standards in force at that time.

Q.068

If within a period of [number] [days/months] after the date of delivery from the [Company] of the [Products/Units] to any purchaser. It is discovered and reported that there is a repetitive defect which is identifiable in a significant number of the products and such defects are attributable to faulty workmanship by the supplier to the [Company]. The [Company] agrees to supply at no additional cost replacement [Products] and/or to organise a recall and replace the component parts causing the problem and/or provide technical assistance for a third party to carry out the repairs at the [Company's] cost.

Q.069

The [Supplier] agrees that the [Products/Units/Services] shall conform with the description stated in colour, size, dimensions and purpose. The [Supplier] shall ensure that the quality and standard of the design and materials used for the [Products/Units/Services] shall be sufficiently high quality for use by the public and will not pose any risk to their health and/or safety and shall be free from defects, damage, faults or any other flaws of any nature.

Q.070

It is a condition of the contract between the [Supplier] and the [Company] for the supply of [Products/Units] that:

1.1 the [Products/Units] shall conform with the quality, description, performance specifications and other particulars of the [Products/Units] stated in the Purchase Order;

1.2 the [Products/Units] shall conform to all samples, drawings, descriptions and specifications provided;

1.3 the [Products/Units] shall be of merchantable quality;

1.4 the [Products/Units] shall be fit for their intended purpose and use;

1.5 the [Products/Units] shall be free from all defects; and

1.6 the [Products/Units] shall comply with any standards, laws, regulations, codes, guidelines and any other requirements applicable in the trade, industry or intended markets or countries in respect of products and/ or units of that nature.

These conditions shall apply after delivery and inspection, acceptance and/or payment pursuant to the Purchase Order and shall extend to any replaced, repaired or substituted or repaired [Products/Units] provided by the [Supplier] to the [Company].

Q.071

If the [Products/Units] are found to be damaged, defective and/or not consistent with the Order by the [Purchaser] upon delivery. Then a report shall be sent to the [Supplier] by email by the [Purchaser]. The [Products/ Units] will not be accepted by the [Purchaser] unless suitable replacements can to be supplied and are agreed between the parties. The [Purchaser] shall have the right to reject the [Products/Units] and to request that they be collected by the [Supplier] if the Order as agreed cannot be fulfilled.

Q.072

The [Licensee] agrees and undertakes:

1.1 to carry out regular quality control tests of the [Products/Units] to ensure that the content and/or any attachments and/or any associated packaging do not pose a risk to health and safety of the public particularly children.

1.2 that where necessary as a precaution and/or obliged to do so by legislation that safety warnings are displayed on the [Products/Units] and any associated attachments and packaging.

1.3 that where the [Licensee] identifies any problem in 1.1 then the [Licensee] agrees to inform the [Licensor] and to also advise the [Licensor] as to how the matter is to be resolved.

1.4 that where the [Licensee] reaches the decision that any aspect of health and safety relating to the [Products/Units] and/or any associated attachment and/or packaging and/or any other matter poses a serious risk. Then it is agreed between the parties that production of the [Products/Units] should be suspended until such time as a satisfactory solution can be obtained. In such event the [Licensee] shall not be entitled to any extension of the licence period under this agreement.

Q.073

The [Supplier] agrees that a representative of the [Distributor] may visit the premises of the manufacturer of the [Products/Units] without notice to carry out an inspection and review and to report on conditions at the manufacturer for the workers and the hygiene, health and safety and production of the

[Products/Units] to the [Distributor]. The [Supplier] accepts that the failure to admit the representative shall be deemed a serious breach of this agreement. The [Supplier] agrees that it shall fully comply with any requests for records and data which may be required which relate to any such inspection.

Q.074

The [Licensee] agrees and undertakes that it will:

1.1 supply at the [Licensee's] cost the [Licensor] with [number] samples of each of the proposed finished [Products/Units] and any associated material including packaging, leaflets, any other attached or enclosed feature or article, advertisements, publicity and any other material for written approval by the [Licensor] prior to commencement of the production.

1.2 indemnify the [Licensor] from any claims, losses, damages, expenses and/or liability arising from any claim from the public and/or any third party in respect of any defect and/or flaw in the [Products/Units] or any death, personal injury damages and/or losses which arise directly from the use of the [Products/Units] in the manner for which they were intended.

1.3 be entirely responsibility for and bear the cost of any defaults, failures, losses and/or errors by any distributors, sub-licensees and/or other third party engaged by the [Licensee] which affects the payments due to the [Licensor] under this agreement.

Q.075

The [Licensee] undertakes that each and every part of the [Products/Units] shall:

1.1 conform in all respects to the quality, design, packaging and materials of the samples submitted to and approved by the [Licensor] and will abide by and not contravene any statutes, laws, regulations, directives, codes, standards and guidelines whether in respect of design, safety, health, advertising, or any other matter within the [Territory/country/world/universe].

1.2 not breach any third party intellectual property rights or any other rights of any nature.

1.3 not be defective in workmanship and/or materials and shall not be made of dangerous materials and/or those which are not suitable for the [Product/Units] in relation to its reasonably anticipated use.

1.4 be suitable and safe for their intended purpose and shall not pose a risk to the health and safety of the public. That the [Licensee] shall take out sufficient and adequate insurance cover in respect of any product liability which may arise from any claim by any purchaser and/or any third party of not less than [specify].

Q.076

1.1 The [Licensee] shall submit to the [Licensor] for prior written approval samples of:

  a   the complete [Products/Units] in the exact style, colour, size, format and content in which it is proposed to be reproduced and exploited.

  b   together with proposed exact samples of all wrappings, packaging, containers, labels, display materials, advertisements, publicity and any other material which it is intended to sold with them and/or reproduced and/or displayed including all proposed trade marks, copyright notices, design credits, acknowledgments, logos, warnings, statements regarding country of origin, images and/or slogans in respect of the [Products/Units].

1.2 The [Licensee] shall not the reproduce, supply, distribute, sell, publish, promote and/or exploit the [Products/Units] and/or any associated materials until the approval in writing has been provided by the [Licensor].

1.3 The [Licensee] shall ensure that once approval has been given all the [Products/Units] and associated material shall adhere exactly in all respects with the approved samples.

Q.077
The [Licensee] agrees that:

1.1 The exact shape, colour, size and location of the [Logo/Image/Slogan] on the [Products/Units] and in all packaging, promotional and marketing material shall be agreed between the [Designer] and the [Licensee] before the production of any of the [Products/Units] under this agreement.

1.2 The [Licensee] shall not have the right to alter, amend, change and/or adapt the matters agreed in 1.1 with the [Designer] and/or have the right to create any new format and/or promotional material.

Q.078
The [Designer] confirms that the [Licensee] shall have the right to reject any of the proposed designs for the [Logo/Image/Slogan] on the grounds that in the reasonable opinion of the [Licensee] the proposed designs are not sufficiently distinctive and commercial to be reproduced on the [Products/Units].

Q.079

The [Licensee] confirms that all the manufacturing of the [Products/Units] under this agreement shall be at the business premises [specify address] except where in the opinion of the [Licensee] specialist services in the development, production and manufacturing of the [Products/Units] are required. In any event no material shall be sourced and/or reproduced outside [specify country].

Q.080

The [Licensee] agrees that the [Licensor] shall be entitled to approve and/or reject the following material. The [Licensee] acknowledges that such approval must be in writing in each case and that no production can commence until it has been agreed unless authorised by the [Licensor]:

1.1   An exact sample of the proposed [Products/Units].

1.2   A list of the proposed copyright notices, trade marks, design and other acknowledgments, logos, credits, slogans, country of origin of material, warnings and images.

1.3   An exact sample of all labels, wrappings, containers and any other article to be given away and/or attached to the [Products/Units].

1.4   Display materials, promotions, banners, advertisements including any slogan, music, artists, performers and/or sound recordings, sounds and jingles, brochures and catalogues, competitions and premium rate line promotions, paid for articles, press releases, product placement arrangements and any other material and/or format and/or medium which it is intended to promote, exploit and/or authorise the use of the [Products/Units].

Q.081

The [Licensee] agrees to provide the [Licensor] with copies of all artwork, images, logos, slogans, characters, packaging, films, videos, sound recordings, promotional and advertising material in relation to the supply, sale and distribution of the [Products/Units/Services] which shall be subject to the prior approval of the [Licensor] in each case before they are used.

Q.082

The [Licensor] agrees that the final decision as to the content, quality, scope, trade marks, logos, images, marketing and exploitation of the [Products/Units/Services] shall be entirely at the [Licensees] sole choice and discretion and that no consultation and/or approval from the [Licensor] shall be required.

Q.083

The [Licensee] undertakes and shall ensure that the [Character/Image/Logo/Credit] is reproduced and supplied by the [Licensee] on all [Products/Units/Services] in the exact form, shape and colour and with the words in the same style, layout and position as set out the Schedule A. The [Licensee] accepts and agrees that it is not authorised to make any changes, variations and/or developments nor to use the [Character/Image/Logo/Credit] in any manner which would be detrimental and/or damaging to its goodwill, use and/or value to the [Licensor].

Q.084

In the event that the [Licensor] discovers that the [Licensee] is creating, developing, reproducing and/or supplying any service and/or products and/or sub-licensing any rights and/or providing any unauthorised endorsement which are not licensed under this agreement in respect of the [Image/Logo/Slogan/Product/Work]. Then the [Licensor] shall be entitled to notify the [Licensee] of the allegations and permit them [one] week to reply and to provide a response. If the [Licensor] does not accept the reasons and/or the [Licensee] does not respond. The [Licensor] shall in any event be entitled to terminate the agreement with [one] weeks' notice and all rights granted under the agreement shall revert to the [Licensor].

Q.085

The [Licensee] agrees and accepts that:

1.1 it must follow the exact template for the [Image/Logo/Name] for reproduction on the [Products/Units/Service] provided by the [Licensor].

1.2 it shall not reproduce and/or develop and/or register any adaptation, variation and/or any different colour version in any format and/or medium..

1.3 it shall not create and develop a computer generated version of the [Image/Logo/Name] and/or any associated animated character.

1.4 it must not grant any sub-licence to any third party and/or authorise any other use and/or endorsement in any country at any time.

1.5 it shall not supply any [Products/Units/Service] for inclusion on posters, advertisements, in competitions for programmes and/or premium rate phone lines, banner links, features on websites, apps and/or blogs and/or in any magazines, newspapers, radio and/or television programmes and/or any other channel and/or at exhibitions, conferences and/or otherwise without notifying the [Licensor] in advance of the facts and seeking their advice and approval.

1.6 it shall not make any press and media statement and/or promotion
which would lead to ridicule and/or a negative reaction on social
media and/or otherwise damage the reputation of the [Licensor] and/
or the [Image/Logo/Name]. Nor shall the [Licensee] issue and/or make
public any sales figures and/or details of complaints and/or allegations
by members of the public regarding the [Products/Units/Service].

Publishing

Q.086
The [Author] shall deliver not later than [date] [two] legible typed copies
of the manuscript of the [Work/Book] and on [specify storage device].
The [Work/Book] shall comply with the description in the agreed synopsis
in Appendix A and shall be written in a competent manner and be of a
sufficient standard for publication in [format] in [language] in [country].

Q.087
The [Ghostwriter] agrees to deliver [two] typed copies of the proposed
[Manuscript] and the [Artwork] to [Name] on or before the target date of
[specify date]. The content shall be of a standard and quality that is suitable
for publication after being edited and reviewed and libel read before
publication by a reputable publisher.

Q.088
The [Author] agrees to write and deliver [two] copies of the [Script/Text] to
the [Agent] based on the [Synopsis] on or before [date]. The [Script/Text]
shall be well researched and shall be not less than [number] words in length.
All sources shall recorded in a separate document in relation to the [Script/
Text] and the name of the institute, archive and/or person stated together
with their contact details, terms of agreement and payment made and/or
due for the use of any such material. This document shall be delivered to the
[Agent] with the [Script/Text].

Q.089
The [Company] shall try to ensure that the [Writer] during the continuance of
the engagement, shall carry out the obligations under this agreement to the
best of his/her skill and ability. That the [Writer] shall observe all directions,
restrictions and requests given by an authorised representative of the
[Distributor] which are reasonable and relevant in the circumstances.

Q.090
The [Company] shall use its best endeavours to ensure that the screenplay
is written in such a way that it is likely to attract finance for the production of
the [Film/Series] based on the [Book/Synopsis/Script]. Further that all steps

are taken by way of preparation of a budget, shooting schedule, actors and lead roles and/or otherwise as may be necessary to enable potential investors to consider whether to contribute to the projected budget costs.

Q.091

The [Interviewer] and the [Publisher] agree that they shall not be entitled to exploit in any media the [Article/Text] and/or the [Sound Recordings/Films] and/or the [Photographs/Images] for any purpose other than publication in the magazine [specify name] on [date] without the prior written consent and agreement of the [Interviewer] and the [Publisher].

Q.092

[Name] and the [Publisher] agree that the [Name] shall be entitled to:

1.1 approve the [Article/Text] prior to publication in the exact form, words, photographs and headlines or other text or images and on the page in which it is intended that it should be published in the magazine.

1.2 veto the [Article/text] in the event that any requested changes and/or alterations by [Name] are not incorporated by the [Publisher].

1.3 prior approval of the final version of the [Article/Text] exactly as it will be reproduced and laid out in the magazine. That the [Article/Text] shall not be published without the prior receipt by the [Publisher] of the written consent of [Name] that it is acceptable and that the [Name] wishes it to be published.

Q.093

The [Publisher] agrees that the subject-matter of the [Article/Text] shall mainly cover [specify] and that the [Name] shall have the right to decline to answer questions of any nature and in particular those outside the specified subject area.

Q.094

[Name] agrees that to the best of his/her knowledge and belief that the facts and information which he/she has provided to the [Company] are true and accurate as at [date]. The [Company] agrees that where the [Company] seeks to rely on such information and facts in the [specify use] they do so at their own risk and shall be liable for any actions and/or claims that may arise. The [Company] accept that they must seek their own legal advice and carry out independent research and investigations to verify the facts and information that has been provided by [Name].

Q.095

The [Author] confirms that he/she has sought to verify and check all statements, text, illustrations and images in the [Manuscript] which he/

she purports to be true and accurate. That the [Author] is able to provide documentary evidence in support. Further that where there are instructions, directions, recipes, actions and/or advice to be acted upon or copied by the public that all such material that is recommended has been tested, assessed and confirmed as safe. That there is no risk to the health and safety of the public, especially children. The [Author] further undertakes that there is no risk of losses, damages or personal injury arising from following the instructions in the [Manuscript] for anyone over the age of [number].

Q.096

The [Writer] agrees that to his/her knowledge and belief that the facts and information contained in the [Work] is true and accurate except where any material is supplied by or specifically included at the request of the [Company].

Q.097

The [Company] agrees that any losses, damages, injury and/or claim and/or legal action arising from the contents and/or use of this [Work/Service/Podcast] shall be entirely the responsibility of the [Company] who shall bear all costs and expenses and expenditure of the [Company] and the [Author] which may arise at any time.

Q.098

The [Author] agrees to amend, alter, edit and/or change such parts of the [Work/Service/Podcast] as the [Publisher] may request in the event that the [Publisher's] legal advisors consider that there is a risk that the [Work/Service/Podcast] contains material which may result in legal proceedings against the [Publisher] and/or the [Author] and/or any sub-licensee.

Q.099

The [Publisher] agrees that it shall not be permitted to adapt, amend, add to or detract from the manuscript or approved proofs of the [Work/Service] prior to publication and/or distribution at any time thereafter without the prior [express/written] approval of the [Author] in each case. There shall be no right to engage a third party to replace the role of the [Author] unless the [Author] is deceased and such consent is provided by the estate of the [Author].

Q.100

[Name] confirms that the [Commissioned Work] shall:

1.1   be of first class technical quality;

1.2   comply with the standards and requirements of [specify code/guidelines/organisation/style book]; and

1.3 not contain any contribution of any nature by a third party and/or any element which constitutes advertising, promotion, sponsorship, product placement and/or endorsement of a third party and/or any other products, services and/or any other matter unless specifically requested in advance by the [Company].

Q.101
The [Agent] acknowledges that it shall not be allowed nor be authorised to permit others to adapt, alter, edit, add to or delete from or in any way change the [Work/Service/Images] without the prior [written] consent of the [Author].

Q.102
The [Distributor] agrees and undertakes that it must ensure that:

1.1 there is a suitable copyright notice, moral rights notice and credit as set out in the master copy of the [Work/Illustrations/Sound Recordings] in conjunction with and on all copies which may be reproduced including any packaging, marketing and extracts.

1.2 no third party in any country shall be authorised to reproduce extracts of the [Work/Illustrations/Sound Recordings] for the purpose of promotion, marketing and advertising material which exceed [number] [words/illustrations] and [number] pages in total and no other pages.

1.3 no translations, theme parks, holograms, competitions, merchandising and/or adaptations are permitted and/or authorised at any time except with the prior written consent and approval and subject to a new licence with the [Licensor].

Services

Q.103
The [Agent] acknowledges that he/she is not entitled to negotiate and/or promote in any manner and/or form the commercial interests of the [Character/Product/Artists] outside the agreed countries in the Territory unless specifically agreed in advance in each case with the [Company].

Q.104
The [Company] shall at all times engage and/or enter into agreements with assistants and personnel to support [Name] who have high quality professional experience and the technical ability in their field and shall ensure that they hold the necessary qualifications to use any equipment, materials and products that they may be required to use for the purposes of this agreement.

Q.105

The [Company] agrees and undertakes that the [Presenter]:

1.1   shall render his/her services to the best of the [Presenter's] skill and ability.

1.2   will comply with all reasonable directions given to the [Presenter] in connection with the services to be provided by him/her by authorised personnel at the [Distributor].

1.3   shall not engage in any hazardous and/or dangerous activities without the prior consent of the [Company].

1.4   shall not engage in any social media activity to endorse any products and/or services and/or any other third party and/be filmed and/or photographed for any commercial project and/or make any paid for appearance, speech and/or presentation at any conference and/or exhibition without the prior written approval of the [Distributor].

Q.106

The [Agent] shall endeavour to ensure that the [Presenter] shall whilst performing his/her services under this agreement comply with all directions and instructions of the [Company] in so far as they are reasonable and practicable. The [Presenter] shall provide his/her non-exclusive services to the [Company] in a professional manner and use his/her reasonable endeavours to promote the [Company] and its brands in a positive manner at all times during the term of this agreement.

Q.107

The [Manager] shall provide his/her services to a level of competence and professionalism which can reasonably be expected and shall perform all services diligently to ensure that the [Group] is regularly engaged by third parties on the best terms which can be achieved in each case.

Q.108

The [Director] shall provide his/her services to the best of his/her technical and artistic skill and ability and shall perform his/her services diligently and expeditiously to ensure the completion of the [Series/Podcasts/Videos]. The [Director] agrees not to make any public statement at any stage which might reasonably be construed as defamatory, derogatory, offensive to or critical of the [Series/Podcasts/Videos].

Q.109

The [Promoter] shall perform all services under this agreement conscientiously to ensure that the [Event] is promoted, marketed and advertised cost-effectively throughout the Territory for the duration of the Promotion Period.

Q.110
The [Designer] shall perform its obligations under this agreement in accordance with the recognised standards of a professional [Website/App/Podcast] designer in the industry. The level of work shall be skilled, accurate, and consistent in order to create a fully functional [Website/App/Podcast] for the [Company] on or before launch date of [date] in accordance with the agreed Budget and the agreed Proposal.

Q.111
That where necessary any personnel employed and/or engaged by the [Designer] shall be suitably qualified, experienced, fit and capable of contributing to the success of the [Project] and agree to sign a confidentiality document with the [Company].

Q.112
The [Designer] confirms and undertakes that the [Website/App/Podcast] shall be fully operational and consistent with the [Project Specification] in Schedule A and the Payment Schedule in Appendix B.

Q.113
The [Agent] shall use his/her best endeavours to promote, publicise and advertise the [Actor] generally and in particular to do the following work: [specify detail].

Q.114
The [Agent] shall provide his/her services in a competent and professional manner, and in each case advise, negotiate and conclude the most advantageous terms for the [Actor]. The [Agent] shall endeavour to ensure that the [Actor] is regularly engaged by third parties in respect of appearances, performances, roles and other work in the following media: [specify theatre, television, radio, publishing, social media, advertising, product endorsement, exhibition and conferences] for the following countries [specify] for the duration of this agreement.

Q.115
The [Agent] shall as far as possible keep the [Actor] fully informed on a regular basis as regards any offers, negotiations and/or any other business proposals by third parties relating to the [Actor]. The [Agent] agrees that he/she shall not be entitled to conclude and/or sign any agreement providing the services of the [Actor] without the prior consent of the [Actor].

Q.116
The [Agent] confirms that [Name] shall have the final decisions to conclude and sign any agreement, contract or other document relating to the

exploitation of the services of [Name] and that no authority is granted under this agreement for the [Agent] to sign on behalf of [Name] and/or to authorise the use of his/her name, slogan and/or any associated logo and/or image.

Q.117
The [Agent] agrees that the [Actor] shall be entitled upon request, either verbally or in writing to be provided with a copy of any contract, record, document, invoice or any other material in any medium in the possession or under the control of the [Agent] relating to the [Actor] at any time during the Term of this Agreement and up to [six] years after the expiry and/or termination of this agreement.

Q.118
The [Agent] shall provide his/her services to the [Author] in a professional, competent and thorough manner and shall perform his/her duties with regard to the career of the [Author] to achieve the following target. The [Agent] agrees that by [date] he/she shall have approached several leading publishing companies in [country] and tried his/her best to negotiate and conclude agreements for the publication of the [Work] in [format] by a reputable company with an advance of not less than [number/currency]. In addition the [Agent] shall aim to negotiate and conclude agreements with merchandising companies for the licensing of the [Work] in [country] with advances of not less than [number/currency] in each case.

Q.119
The [Consultant] undertakes that all the information, advice and material provided to the [Company] by the [Consultant] shall be true and accurate and that work which is attributed as original has not been derived from some other source. The [Consultant] shall observe all rules and regulations in force at any location where he/she may be required to provide his/her services and shall carry out and observe all directions as may reasonably be given to him/her on behalf of the [Company].

Q.120
'The Services' shall mean the product of the services of the [Executive] to be provided to the [Company] under this agreement which are described in the attached Appendix A and form part of this agreement.

Q.121
The [Company] agrees and undertakes to provide a professional and first class service as a [recruitment/publicity] agent to [Name] and shall ensure that:

1.1   all matters advised by the directors and officers and any other person at [Name] are treated by the personnel of the [Company] as confidential and private unless advised otherwise.

1.2   no statements, media and press release and/or social media and/or other text, image and email exchanges shall be released and/or distributed to the general public without the prior consent of [specify] at [Name].

1.3   no commitment, representation and/or contractual liability shall be made and/or incurred on behalf of [Name] without prior authority.

Sponsorship

Q.122

The [Sportsperson] agrees to provide his/her exclusive services to the best of his/her technical skill and ability as [specify role athlete/presenter/other] as far as reasonably possible in the circumstances and shall perform his/her duties under this Agreement at such times, dates [excluding bank holidays and weekends] and locations [except those designated dangerous] as may be agreed with the [Manager] in each case. The services shall include attendance at and participation in events, competitions, promotions, press calls, appearances, meetings and recordings as specified in Schedule A.

Q.123

The [Sportsperson] agrees to conduct himself/herself in public and in his/her training, sport and competitions and in any social media and/or media events in a manner which will not affect the reputation and/or brands of the [Sponsor]. Nor shall any conduct, statement and/or action by the [Sportsperson] whether in his/her public and/or private life give rise to any allegation of assault, drunkenness, drugs, corruption, fraud and/or any other allegation of criminal act. The [Sportsperson] agrees that other than due to ill-health and/or injury that he/she shall maintain the training schedule and keep fit and act at all times when outside his/her home in a proper and professional manner during the Term of the Agreement and will abide by the rules and regulations of the following bodies: [specify organisation and codes of conduct].

Q.124

The [Sportsperson] agrees to provide his/her services to the best of his/her physical and mental skill and ability to ensure the fulfilment of his/her obligations under this agreement. That the [Sportsperson] is committed to regular training and participation in sports events and competitions. That the [Sportsperson] appreciates their role as an example to others and the fact that they represent the [Club/Company] as an ambassador. The

1535

[Sportsperson] agrees to ensure that when in public they act in a professional manner and do not to engage in any activities and/or make any comments and/or create any image which would be offensive and/or detrimental to the [Sponsor] and/or the [Sponsor's Product].

Q.125

The [Sponsor] agrees to provide the [Sportsperson] with samples of all proposed products, services, films, videos, sound recordings, websites, apps, competitions, promotional material, articles, press releases, packaging and other material in which it is intended to use the name, image, voice, trade mark, slogan, and/or endorsement of the [Sportsperson] under this agreement.

Q.126

The [Sponsor] agrees that the name, image and endorsement of the [Sportsperson] shall not be used for any purpose other than the promotion and endorsement of the [Sponsor's Product] for the duration of the Sponsorship Period and that the [Sponsor] shall not be entitled to do so in any form at any time thereafter.

Q.127

The [Company] undertakes that as far as reasonably possible all personnel [specify categories] involved in the [Project] shall be members of recognised craft, trade or other professional bodies.

Q.128

The [Company] shall provide its services and responsibilities in accordance with specified agenda itemised in the approved budget for the [Event]. The [Client] accepts that there are cost restrictions imposed which may impact on the overall quality of the [Event] for which the [Company] shall not be responsible. The [Client] accepts that it has viewed and agreed the samples to be used for the [Event].

Q.129

The [Promoter] shall provide its services under this agreement to the level and standard which could reasonably be expected of a competent business within the budget which has been allocated under this agreement.

Q.130

The [Company] agrees that [Name] shall be entitled upon request to be provided at the [Company's] sole cost with an exact sample of any product, catalogue, packaging, publicity, advertising, promotional and/or marketing material in the possession or under the control of the [Company] featuring or relating to [Name] in any format in which it is reproduced and/or if the cost is prohibitive a copy in another format.

Q.131

The [Celebrity] agrees not to participate in any dangerous sport, political controversies and/or other activities and/or social media which would prejudice the goodwill and reputation of the [Company] and the [Company's Product] during the Term of the Agreement.

Q.132

The [Sponsor] agrees that it shall not have the right to use, exploit and/or promote the title of the [Film/Podcast/Service] and/or any script, artist, presenter, music, slogan and/or other parts of any nature whether in conjunction with the [Sponsor's Products] or any other products or services of the [Sponsor] under any circumstances. This agreement is solely related to the placement of the [Sponsor's Product] in the [Film/Podcast/Service] and not a sub-licence and/or other transfer of authority to the [Sponsor] to use any material and/or exploit any rights of any nature.

Q.133

The [Sponsor] agrees that the [Company] may in respect of the [Image/Logo/Name] supplied by the [Sponsor]:

1.1 adapt the size, colour and layout to suit the new marketing material created with the [Event/Programme].

1.2 create and develop a computer generated version as part of the animated introduction for transmission on screen at the [Event/Programme].

1.3 reproduce the [Image/Logo/Name] on all merchandise and material on which the name of the [Company] appears in connection with the [Event/Programme].

University, Charity and Educational

Q.134

The [Institute/Charity] shall be entitled to display, exhibit, publish, reproduce, exploit and/or cease to use the [Text/Image/Sound Recording/Film/Service] in any manner at its sole discretion as it thinks fit. There are no assurances as to the method, timescale, quality, quantity, packaging and/or marketing nor shall any sub-licensees and/or other third parties who may be authorised be subject to the approval of the [Licensor].

Q.135

The [Licensee] agrees that it shall not supply to any third party the same and/or substantially similar [Artwork/Products/Films/Text] that it has supplied to the [Institute/Charity] without the prior written approval of the [Institute/Charity].

Q.136

1.1 The [Institute/Charity] agrees and undertakes that it will not authorise any third party to test, appraise and/or repair the [Work/Service] without the prior written approval of the [Company].

1.2 That all the material which shall be created and developed by such third party in respect of the [Work/Service] shall be returned to the [Institute/Charity] and any ownership of the material and copyright and all other intellectual property rights and interest that may be created shall assigned to the [Company].

Q.137

The [Institute/Enterprise] confirms that to the best of the knowledge and belief of its officers in [specify department] that the facts, information, data, and material are a true and accurate representation of the [Project] at that time.

Q.138

1.1 The [Institute/Enterprise] does not confirm the accuracy, originality, copyright, and/or legal ownership of the material of the [Work/Service] which is provided to the [Company]. All use of the [Work/Service] shall be entirely at the [Company's] risk and cost and no responsibility shall be accepted by the [Institute/Enterprise].

1.2 The [Company] shall acknowledge the [Institute/Enterprise] as the source of the material of the [Work/Service] on all copies reproduced, supplied and/or distributed by the [Company] and all associated packaging, promotional and marketing material of any nature.

1.3 The [Company] agrees that the quality and content of the [Work/Service] shall be of a high standard suitable for the [specify] market and shall comply with all legislation, regulations, guidelines and codes of practice which may exist in respect of the [Work/Service] and which may be issued by any relevant authority and/or trade and/or government organisation and/or entity.

Q.139

The [Author] agrees that where in the opinion of the management of the [Institute/Enterprise] and/or their legal advisors the content, title and/or marketing of the [Work/Product/Service] should be edited, delayed, cancelled and/or recalled due to the threat of legal action by a third party, and/or there is a serious defect and/or fault and/or there are significant inaccuracies. Then the [Author] agrees that the [Institute/Enterprise] shall be entitled to take such action as may be necessary and the [Author] and the [Institute/Enterprise] shall enter into negotiations to resolve the matter. The [Author] agrees that he/she shall not be entitled to any sums for loss of reputation, royalties and/or any advance which is delayed and/or not paid where the [Author] was liable for the matter.

Q.140

1.1 The [Company] agrees and undertakes that the [Work/Product/ Service] shall not contain any text, images, photographs, music, sound recordings, film, trade marks, logos, slogans and/or any other material in any medium which has not been approved by the [Institute/ Enterprise].

1.2 The [Company] agrees and undertakes that the [Work/Product/ Service] shall not be adapted, altered, edited, nor shall any material be added to and/or deleted from it and/or changed without the prior written consent of the [Institute/Enterprise] in each case.

Q.141

1.1 The [Consortium] agree that [Name] shall be responsible for monitoring and reporting on the [Project] and compliance with the [Budget], [Completion Dates] and the overall quality of the services provided by the [Supplier].

1.2 That [Name] shall provide a written report to the [Consortium] at the end of each calendar month which highlights the work completed and any failures and the payments made and raises any concerns which may have arisen.

1.3 The [Consortium] agrees that [Name] shall have delegated authority by the [Consortium] to issue both verbal warnings and written letters to the [Supplier] on behalf of the [Consortium].

R

RATES OF EXCHANGE

General Business and Commercial

R.001

The [Company] and the [Agent] understand and agree that there shall be no fixed rate of exchange and the correct rate shall be such as may be obtained from a reputable bank on the day that any such currency may be converted. Both parties accept that the rate of exchange may rise and/or fall to the benefit and/or detriment of either party. All additional costs and charges shall also be deducted from the funds which are being converted at the time including commission.

R.002

The parties agree that all transfers, deposits and/or exchanges of any monies and/or currencies by either party shall be bound by and/or subject to compliance with any legislation and/or codes of conduct and/or other policies directed by any government and/or regulatory organisation. The [Company] shall endeavour to pay the [Licensor] in [sterling/specify currency] and the exchange rate used shall be that specified by any reputable national bank.

R.003

The exchange rates to be used by either party for the purpose of this agreement shall be those rates set by [specify bank] in [country] which may apply at the time of the conversion of the currency. All additional costs and charges associated with the conversion of the currency shall also be deducted prior to the transfer of the currency.

R.004

The rate of exchange shall be [specify rate] and shall be fixed at that rate for all conversions of currency from [specify currency] to [specify currency] for the period [date] to [date].

R.005

The [Licensee] shall not be obliged to justify the rate of exchange used to convert any currency under this agreement provided that it is conducted

1541

through an established bank in [the United Kingdom/specify other country] and receipts can be produced. All commission and other transfer charges shall be deducted from the monies by the bank at the time of conversion and prior to payment of any sums due to the [Licensor].

R.006

The [Licensee] shall use the best rate of exchange available at the time from any reputable bank for the conversion of any sums prior to payment of any sums due to the [Licensor] in [currency]. The [Licensee] shall as far as possible not incur additional charges and/or commission costs for the conversion of any currency, but if they do arise shall be entitled to deduct them from any sums due to the [Licensor].

R.007

The [Institute/Charity] shall be entitled to choose the most appropriate rate of exchange which in its opinion is most suitable to convert the money to be received into [specify currency]. The [Institute/Charity] is not obliged to choose the best rate available on the market, but that which is most convenient and cost effective in the circumstances.

R.008

Where the [Sub-Licensee] has to arrange for the conversion of any currency in respect of this agreement. The [Sub-Licensee] shall have absolute discretion as to which rates of exchange and/or bank to use for such purpose. The [Sub-Licensee] shall not be obliged to choose the most favourable rates available and/or to keep commission costs to a minimum. The [Sub-Licensee] shall be required to provide written evidence of the conversion rate and costs on each occasion to the [Licensor] in respect of each accounting period.

R.009

All payments by the [Sponsor] under this agreement shall be in [specify currency]. Where the [Sponsor] is requested to make payment in any other currency, then the expenses and charges associated with the conversion of the sum shall be at the [Company's] cost. The [Company] agrees that the [Sponsor] shall be entitled to deduct such expenses and charges from the payment due to the [Company] provided that the deduction is agreed in advance.

R.010

Where the [Agent] and/or [Distributor] directly and/or indirectly incurs any commission, bank charges and/or other sums relating to the conversion and/or transfer of any currency and/or payments due to [Name] under this agreement. There shall be no right to deduct and/or set off any such costs and other expenses from any sums and/or payments due to [Name].

R.011

Where the rate of exchange is not favourable then the other party may stipulate that the money is not exchanged and/or transferred until the rate of exchange has reached a fixed level. Where that is not achieved with a reasonable period the other party may request that the money be deposited in an account in the existing country of origin and is not converted.

R.012

Where the [Sub-Licensee] is required to convert monies from one currency to another and/or to transfer funds and commission, bank charges and other sums are incurred. Then the [Sub-Licensee] shall be entitled to recoup these costs and expenses as legitimate distribution expenses. Provided that if so requested they are able to provide supporting documentation.

RECORDINGS

General Business and Commercial

R.013

'The Recordings' shall mean any visual and/or sound recordings of the [Event/Film/Project] in any medium including but not limited to any electronic, chemical and/or mechanical forms of reproduction whether in existence now and/or created in the future.

R.014

The [Company] confirms that it shall provide to the [Distributor] such sound recordings of the [Musical Work] as may be available at the [Company's] sole discretion and cost for the purpose of production, reproduction, supply and distribution of the [Video /Disc/Unit].

R.015

'The Original Sound Recordings' shall be all sound recordings including any unused material of the performances of the [Artiste] for and on behalf of the [Record Company] made during the Term of this Agreement regardless of the medium in which the sound recording is made and/or the method by which the sounds are produced and/or reproduced.

R.016

'The Records' shall be the reproduction of the edited Original Sound Recordings in whole and/or part in any material form which is manufactured by any method for release to the general public and/or supplied, licensed and/or distributed to any third party [with and/or without visual images].

R.017
'The Sound Recordings' shall mean all the sound recordings made by and/or on behalf of [Name] in respect of the [specify name of subject/person] for the purpose of the [Article/Book/Film] regardless of the medium on which the sound recording is made and/or the method by which the sounds are produced and/or reproduced.

R.018
'The Recordings' shall be defined as any film and/or sound recording made directly from the live performance of [Name/Performer] and/or from any broadcast and/or transmission of the performance of [Name/Performer] and/or directly and/or indirectly from any other recordings of the performance.

R.019
'The Exclusive Recording Rights' shall mean:

1.1 The sole and exclusive right to make a recording of the whole and/or part of the [Event/Performance] from [date to [date] in any medium from which a moving image may by any means be produced and/or reproduced by any method [whether in existence now or created in the future].

1.2 The sole and exclusive right to make a sound recording of the whole and/or part of the [Event/Performance] from [date] to [date] in any medium and the production and/or reproduction by any method of the sounds [whether in existence now or created in the future].

1.3 The sole and exclusive right to make the [Film/Series/Podcast] entitled: [specify title name] including the soundtrack of the [Event/Performance] based on the material in 1.1 and 1.2.

1.4 The sole and exclusive right to exploit all the material and rights in 1.1, 1.2 and 1.3 as follows: [specify method/duration of rights/territory].

R.020
'The Non-Exclusive Recording Rights' shall mean:

1.1 The non-exclusive right to make a recording of the whole and/or part of the [Event/Performance] from [date to [date] in any medium from which a moving image may by any means be produced and/or reproduced by any method subject to 1.3 below.

1.2 The non-exclusive right to make a sound recording of the whole and/or part of the [Event/Performance] from [date] to [date] in any medium and the production and/or reproduction by any method of the sounds subject to 1.3 below.

1.3 The non-exclusive right to make the [Film/Series/Podcast] entitled: [specify title name] including the soundtrack of the [Event/ Performance] based on the material in 1.1 and 1.2 and to reproduce, supply, distribute, sub-license and/or exploit those rights as follows: [specify method/duration of rights/territory].

R.021

1.1 The [Sponsor] agrees and acknowledges that the [Association/Institute] has no editorial control in respect of the times, dates, duration and content of the reproduction, editing, supply, distribution, broadcast, transmission and/or otherwise of the [Recordings/Film/Series] of the [Event] by the [Distributor].

1.2 The [Sponsor] agrees and undertakes that it shall not seek to withhold any payment and/or to receive compensation, damages and/or any other sum from the [Association/Institute] for the cancellation, delay, disruption, failure and/or any other default in respect of the transmission and/or broadcast of the [Recordings/Film/Series] of the [Event] by the [Distributor].

R.022

1.1 The [Association/Institute] agrees that in the event that the [Company] does not produce the [Recordings] of the [Event] and deliver the master material for any reason. That [number/currency] of the Sponsorship Fee shall be repaid to the [Sponsor] by the [Association/Institute].

1.2 The [Association/Institute] agrees that in the event that the [Media Distributor] does not broadcast and/or transmit an edited version of the [Recordings] of not less than [number] minutes in duration on channel [specify licensed service] for any reason by [date]. That the [Association/Institute] shall be obliged to repay the [Sponsor] [number/ currency] of the Sponsorship Fee.

1.3 The [Association/Institute] agrees and undertakes that the [Sponsor] shall not be liable for any costs, expenses and/or other sums in respect of the arrangements for the [Recordings] and/or any edited version. Nor shall the [Sponsor] acquire any right to exploit any such material at any time.

R.023
Subject to prior consultation the [Presenter/Name] agrees that the [Company] shall have the right to use his/her name, biographical profile,

image, caricature and recordings in any commercial exploitation and/or promotion of the [Series] under this agreement.

R.024

'The Series' shall be the series of films and any associated sound recordings or recordings based on the Treatment and the Scripts with the provisional title: [specify provisional title] proposed number of episodes: [number] duration of each episode: [number] minutes.

R.025

'The Exclusive Recording Rights' in relation to the [Event/Festival] shall be defined as:

1.1 The sole and exclusive right in respect of the performance of the [Artists] at the [Event/Festival] to make films and/or sound recordings directly from the live performances and/or

1.2 The sole and exclusive right in respect of the performance of the [Artists] at the [Event/Festival] to make films and/or sound recordings directly made from any broadcast, transmission and/or other method of distribution which includes the performances and/or

1.3 The sole and exclusive right in respect of the performance of the [Artists] at the [Event/Festival] to make films and/or sound recordings directly and/or indirectly from any other recordings of the performances in any medium.

1.4 The sole and exclusive right to make any recordings of the whole and/or part of the [Event/Festival] in any medium from which a moving image may by any means be produced, reproduced and/or exploited by any method whether in existence now and/or created in the future.

1.5 The sole and exclusive right to make any sound recording of the whole and/or part of the [Event/Festival] in any medium and the production, reproduction and/or exploitation by any method of the sounds whether in existence now and/or created in the future.

1.6 The sole and exclusive right to make any [Film/Podcasts/Series] including any films, recordings and/or sound recordings of the [Event/Festival].

1.7 'The sole and exclusive right to reproduce, distribute and/or exploit any material and/or rights arising from 1.1 to 1.6 above in any format and/or medium in the world and universe and the right to assign and/or transfer them to any third party.

R.026

1.1 The [Sponsor] has contributed to the funding of the [Event/Programme] and shall be entitled to an equal share with the [Company] of all sums received from the exploitation of the [Recordings] and/or any parts made by and/or commissioned by the [Company].

1.2 The [Recordings] shall mean any visual and/or sound recordings of the [Event/Programme] in any medium including electronic, chemical and/or mechanical forms of reproduction whether in existence now and/or created in the future. It shall include but not be limited to exploitation by means of cable, satellite and terrestrial television and/or radio and/or any communication and/or transmission over the internet and/or any telecommunication system whether it is accessed via television, laptop, mobile and/or some other device and/or any archive playback subscription service and/or audio download and/or some other merchandising and/or adaptation except as stated in 1.3.

1.3 The [Sponsor] agrees that the [Company] shall retain all sums due from any ticket sales, refreshments, merchandising and other printed material which are sold at the location but not by any other method.

R.027

The [Advertiser] agrees and undertakes that it has not and will not:

1.1 Acquire any exclusive and/or non-exclusive rights to any recordings, films, podcasts, videos and/or sound recordings in relation to the [Event/Exhibition].

1.2 Make and/or commission any recordings, films, podcasts, videos and/or sound recordings either directly at the [Event/Exhibition] and/or by any other means in any medium from which a moving image and/or sound recording may be produced and/or reproduced by any method without the prior authority and approval of the [Company].

1.3 Represent that it has the right to authorise a third party to make any recordings, films, podcasts, videos and/or sound recordings either directly at the [Event/Exhibition] and/or by any other means in any medium from which a moving image and/or sound recording may be reproduced and/or exploited. Nor shall the [Advertiser] purport to licence, assign and/or transfer any such rights to any third party.

1.4 Have any editorial control and/or rights of consultation in respect of the times, dates, duration and content of the arrangements, recording, broadcast, transmission and/or exploitation of any material in 1.1 and 1.2.

1.5   Have any right to seek to claim any refund, compensation, damages, losses, expenses and/or other sums if the [Event/Exhibition] is delayed, cancelled, interrupted and/or suspended for any reason.

R.028

Both the [Sponsor] and the [Institute/Charity] agree that they shall hold the joint copyright and joint intellectual property rights and/or other rights and/or interest in the [Event/Project] as follows:

1.1   The ownership of the name of the title, slogan and images of the [Event/Project]. A copy of which described and represented in attached appendix A which forms part of this agreement.

1.2   The pending and/or registered domain name, app name, trademarks, logos, caricatures, puppets and/or characters associated with and/or created for the [Event/Project]. A copy of which is described and represented are attached in appendix B and forms part of this agreement.

1.3   That the agreement of both parties shall be required to grant and/or authorise any third party the right to reproduce, supply, distribute and/or exploit any recordings, films, sound recordings, images, trade marks, logos, caricatures, characters and/or any other rights and/or material and/or to assign, sub-licence and/or exploit and/or adapt any rights and/or to develop and exploit any merchandising and/or to authorise any endorsements, product placements and/or to enter into any collaboration.

1.4   That the agreement of both parties shall be required to apply for and/or register any rights and/or to defend and/or to issue legal proceedings in respect of the joint copyright, and joint intellectual property rights and/or other rights and/or interest in the [Event/Project] held by [Sponsor] and the [Institute/Charity].

1.5   That both parties shall have the equal right of editorial control and must both agree before any decisions are made in respect of the development, commissioning, licensing, distribution and/or exploitation of any rights and/or material in any medium and/or format at any time. If one party refuses consent then the proposal cannot proceed.

R.029

The [Licensor] agrees and undertakes not to authorise, license and/or permit the reproduction and/or exploitation of the rights in the [Recordings] and/or any material to any other third party from [date] to [date].

R.030

The [Institute/University] agrees and undertakes that:

1.1　It shall keep the physical material of the [Archive Material] at [location] in a secure and suitable environment which will not cause deterioration of the material.

1.2　It has only been granted the right to permit access by authorised personnel approved by the estate of [Name] for private viewing for research purposes only. There is no right to permit and/or licence any third party to take images and/or make any film, video and/or other recordings of the [Archive Material]. Nor does the [Institute/University] hold any right to commercially exploit, licence and/or reproduce the [Archive Material] in any medium by any method in any form.

1.3　That all intellectual property rights including copyright and any other rights in the [Archive Material] are owned and controlled by the estate of [Name].

1.4　That the [Institute/University] will acknowledge and credit the estate of [Name] as follows: [specify details] as the copyright owner in any database and in any other reference to the [Archive Material] in any electronic, printed and/or other material produced by the [Institute/University] for internal purposes.

1.5　That the [Institute/University] has no right to register any copyright ownership with any rights management organisation and/or to receive any fees and/or other sums from such exploitation. Nor shall the [Institute/University] have the right to apply for any associated domain name, trade mark and/or other right which is pending and/or held by the estate of [Name] and/or which may be registered by them in the future.

1.6　That the [Institute/University] has no right to make, commission, licence and/or exploit any recordings, films, podcasts, videos and/or sound recordings either directly of the [Archive Material] and/or by any other means in any medium from which a moving image and/or sound recording may be produced and/or reproduced by any method and/or any adaptation, merchandising and/or sequel without the prior approval of the estate of [Name].

R.031

1.1　The [Recordings] by the [Group] shall be jointly owned by all the following members [specify names of members] and/or in the event that any members are deceased by their estate and/or beneficiaries. All members shall hold an equal share in all rights of any nature whether in existence now and/or created in the future.

1.2   All sums received from the exploitation of the [Recordings] in all medium in any format and/or media shall be shared equally between the parties regardless of the actual contribution that each member made to the [Recordings] whether lyrics, music, singing, performances, computer-generated material and/or otherwise.

1.3   Each member agrees that all parties should be registered as joint copyright owners with all collecting societies and/or other such registrations for all parts of the [Recordings] throughout the world and that all sums received should be split equally between the parties.

1.4   All applications for registration of any trade mark, computer software, domain names and/or any other rights of any nature associated with the [Recordings] shall be in all the names of the members as equal shares. Where it is necessary to nominate one person as the holder due to the administration of that organisation. That member shall hold that registration on behalf of all members.

R.032

1.1   [Name] agrees that neither he/she nor his/her agent shall not make any arrangement and/or conclude any agreement with any third party to record, film, take images of and/or otherwise exploit the performance of [Name] at the [Event].

1.2   [Name] agrees that the [Company] holds the rights to all forms of commercial and non-commercial exploitation in respect of the performance of [Name] and any recordings in any medium at the [Event] including radio, television, the internet and distribution by means of any telecommunication system; and all rights to arrange sponsorship, product placement and/or merchandising.

1.3   That the [Company] agrees it shall not conclude any agreement for the reproduction of any music, lyrics, sound recordings and/or recordings without prior consultation with [Name] and the clearance of any rights held by any rights management organisations and/or other rights holders.

R.033

'The Recording' is an edited reproduction of the original sound recording of the voice and spoken word of [Name] which was recorded by [specify person] by [method] on [specify dates] in [specify locations].

R.034

'The Podcast Series' shall be the original and innovative recordings which comprises a series of films which include soundtracks entitled: [specify series title] created and developed by [Name].

R.035
'The Audio File' is a digitised version in electronic form of the sound recordings which comprise a dramatized performance by [Name] of an edited and scripted version of the book entitled: [specify title] by the author known as [specify name].

R.036

1.1 [Name] has agreed to be interviewed by the [Presenter] in consideration of the payment of a fee of [number/currency] which is to be paid within [number] days of completion of the work subject to an invoice.

1.2 [Name] agrees that all copyright and intellectual property rights in any films, sound recordings and/or any other recordings in any medium made by the [Company] and/or a third party shall be owned by the [Company].

1.3 The [Company] agrees and undertakes that it shall not assign, sub-license and/or exploit the films, sound recordings and/or any other recordings in whole and/or part in 1.2 for any other purpose except: [state purpose] without the prior consent of [Name].

REJECTION

Film, Television and Video

R.037
The hire of a [DVD/Video/Unit] may not be cancelled except by notice to the [Company] of not less than [two] days prior to the commencement of the hire (excluding Saturdays, Sundays and Bank Holidays). Cancellation includes any alteration to the contents of the hire and/or change in the location to which material supplied on hire is delivered and/or any substitute order in lieu of any previous order.

R.038
In the event that the [DVD/Video/Unit] is not of suitable [broadcast/technical quality] the [Company] shall be responsible for providing an acceptable replacement at its sole cost within [seven] days of receipt of notice of rejection by any of the following methods [email/customer care line/in writing]. If there is no acceptable replacement provided then all sums shall be repaid by the [Company].

R.039

All [specify format] of the [Film] including the sound track supplied by the [Distributor] to the [Company] shall be in first class condition and shall be to such technical standards and quality as customarily required for the general public in [country] and packaged in sealed wrappers. If any [specify format] of the [Film] is returned by any member of the public on the grounds of unsatisfactory technical quality and/or any other reason then the [Distributor] shall at its sole cost provide an acceptable replacement.

R.040

The [Company] shall have the right to reject the master copy of [specify format of material] of the [Film] including the soundtrack supplied by the [Distributor] for the [DVDs/Discs/other] on the grounds that:

1.1 The master copy of [specify format of material] is of poor quality and is not suitable for the reproduction of [DVDs/Discs/other] for sale to the public; and/or

1.2 That the master copy of [specify format of material] is the wrong duration; and/or

1.3 That the sound track is of poor quality; and/or

1.4 That the master copy of [specify format of material] is for the wrong film and/or sound recording.

1.5 That the [Film] is not in the [specify] language.

1.6 The master copy of [specify format of material] is not fit for its intended purpose.

In the event of any rejection of the [Film] and/or master copy of [specify format of material] by the [Company] and the [Licensor] is unable to supply an acceptable replacement within [one] month. Then the [Company] shall be entitled to terminate this agreement and the [Licensor] shall immediately repay to the [Company] any sums received by them under this agreement in respect of the [Film] and/or master copy of [specify format of material].

R.041

The [Licensee] shall have the right to reject the master material of the [Sound Recordings] supplied by the [Licensor] on the grounds that the technical quality is of a low standard and is not suitable for reproduction without additional costs and expenses being incurred. In the event that the [Licensee] rejects the master material and the [Licensor] is either unable to supply acceptable replacement material and/or refuses to meet the costs and expenses of the additional work required. Then the [Licensee] shall be entitled to terminate this agreement and the [Licensor] shall immediately repay to the [Licensee] all sums received under this agreement.

R.042

1.1 The [Sub-Licensee] agrees and accepts that the reproduction copy of the master material of [specify project] to be supplied to the [Sub-Licensee] by the [Licensee] is not of first rate quality and contains defects, flaws and other errors which may need to be remedied.

1.2 The [Sub-Licensee] agrees to pay the cost of any additional work that may be required to bring the reproduction copy up to suitable standard for the exercise of the rights granted under this agreement granted to the [Sub-Licensee].

R.043

Where material is rejected for any reason by the [Company] and the rejection is accepted by the [Distributor]. Then the [Distributor] shall not be entitled to substitute an alternative [Work/Film] and/or offer a voucher and/or credit note. The [Company] shall be entitled to a full refund of the payment made to the [Distributor]

R.044

The [specify format] of the [Film/Extract] supplied by the [Distributor] to the [Television Company] shall be in first class condition and shall be to such technical standards as are customarily required for programme material under the technical quality policy of [specify organisation/regulatory body]. If any [specify format] of the [Film/Extract] is rejected on the grounds of unsatisfactory technical quality. The [Distributor] shall use its best endeavours to provide an acceptable replacement as required at the sole cost of the [Distributor].

R.045

The [Company] shall retain the right to terminate this agreement in the event that:

1.1 the [Film/Series] is not produced in accordance with the agreed summary set out in appendix A; and/or

1.2 the quality and content of the [Film/Series] is not approved by the [Company]; and/or the master material of the [Film/Series] does not conform to the quality and/or technical standards stipulated by the [Company] in appendix A; and/or

1.3 delivery of the master material in [specify format] of the [Film/Series] is not made on or by [date].

In the event of such termination the [Company] shall be under no further liability and/or obligation to the [Licensor] and shall not be liable to pay the [Licensor] any further sums under this agreement. The [Company] shall be entitled to be reimbursed with all sums which it has paid to the [Licensor] under this agreement.

R.046

The [Company] shall have the right to reject the [Film Material] supplied under this agreement on the grounds of inadequate technical quality and/ or a failure to be suitable and/or fit for purpose which shall not be exercised without reasonable grounds. In the event of the rejection of the [Film Material] by the [Company] and in the event that the [Licensor] is unable to supply suitable material which is then accepted. The [Company] shall be entitled to terminate this agreement by notice in writing by email and/or letter with an end date and time. The [Company] shall also invoice the [Licensor] for all sums which may have been paid in advance as part of the Licence Fee. The [Licensor] agrees and undertakes that it shall be obliged to repay to the [Company] all such payments already received of the Licence Fee.

R.047

1.1 The [Company] shall have the right to reject any of the [Films/Episodes of the Series] if any of the content including the soundtrack is in the opinion of the [Company] defamatory, offensive and/or contrary to any code and/or policy of any regulatory organisation which applies to the [Company] and/or any legislation in [specify countries] and/or is likely to be a breach of any term of the franchise licence of the [Company issued by [specify organisation/Ofcom].

1.2 In the event of any such rejection in 1.1 by the [Company]. The [Company] may choose at its sole discretion to accept a substitute film and/or episode as required. Where the parties cannot agree to substitute any new material then the [Licensor] shall repay to the [Company] such sums as relate to the rejected films and/or episodes.

R.048

The [Licensor] reserves the right at any time to change the titles of any episode of the [Series]. The [Licensor] also reserves the right to withdraw any episode because of litigation and/or threatened litigation and/or some other valid reason. In the event an episode is withdrawn the [Company] shall receive a proportionate credit of the Licence Fee for the withdrawn episodes.

R.049

1.1 The [Author] agrees to either accept and/or provide written reasons for the rejection of the Treatment and/or draft and final Scripts for the [Film/ Series] within [number] days of delivery in each case. The [Author] agrees and undertakes that he/she shall not refuse and/or delay his/ her comments and/or approval without good reason.

1.2 The [Company] agrees that where the [Author] has rejected any material and asked for additional changes that the [Company] shall use its reasonable endeavours to incorporate the changes proposed by the [Author]. That the [Author] shall be provided with the opportunity to view the revised material and that the [Author] shall again be permitted time to comment on the content and express his/her approval and/or rejection.

R.050
The [Licensee] agrees to either accept or provide written reasons for its rejection of the [Transmission and Promotional Material] within [thirty] days of delivery [including weekends and bank holidays].

R.051
In the event that the reproduction and/or transmission material in respect of the [Film/Video] is not suitable for its intended purpose and/or is not of a high technical quality. The [Licensee] shall be entitled to serve notice to terminate this agreement on either of those grounds and/or for any other justifiable reason. In such instance the [Licensor] shall be obliged to repay to the [Licensee] any licence fee and/or other sums which have been paid in respect of the [Film/Video] within [number] days of invoice by the [Licensee].

R.052
The [Company] agrees to either accept and/or provide written reasons for their rejection of the [scripts/storyboard and outline/project] in each case. The [Company] agrees that any rejection shall be on reasonable grounds and in good faith. The [Company] cannot give any undertaking as to the period required to assess the material and respond. However the [Company] agrees that any such response shall not be delayed more than [number] months.

R.053
The [Production Company] agrees that it shall use its reasonable endeavours to comply with the following conditions:

1.1 That [Name] shall be provided with an opportunity to review and comment on the draft and final script, the key personnel, the production schedule and locations and/or any significant changes that may occur at a later date.

1.2 That [Name] shall have the right to approve the final script prior to production of the [Film/Series] and shall be consulted on all changes except minor editing.

1.3 That [Name] shall be entitled to approve the appointment of any agent and/or sub-licensee. That [Name] shall be provided with a sample copy of each and every type of proposed form of exploitation in each form of the media prior to production. The production shall not commence until [Name] has approved the sample.

1.4 That [Name] shall be entitled to revoke the moral rights waiver under clause [–] by notice in writing if the conditions 1.1, 1.2 and 1.3 are not fulfilled at any time.

R.054

[Name] shall have the right to reject any material and terminate this agreement on the grounds that the material:

1.1 is not of a high professional standard and workmanship.

1.2 has not been produced using the key personnel and/or artists set out in appendix A.

1.3 which includes the music and/or soundtrack is inaccurate, substandard and/or does not correlate to the [Film].

1.4 of the [Film] is too [long/short] and not of the agreed duration of [number] minutes.

1.5 which includes the dialogue, storyline, computer-generated graphics and/or costumes are of poor quality and/or do not represent the features agreed in the [Treatment/Script] in appendix B.

1.6 has not been supplied in accordance with the stipulated delivery dates.

1.7 is offensive, obscene and/or not suitable for the agreed age category of [number] years and below and/or the [specify type] market for which it was intended.

1.8 has not been cleared for use by [Name] and that there are legal problems and/or threats of litigation by a third party.

1.9 is the subject of legal proceedings by a third party against [Name] and/or the [Licensor].

R.055

The [Company] agrees that it has previewed the [Film] and shall not reject the [Film] on the grounds of content. The [Company] shall only be entitled to terminate this agreement on the grounds that the [Licensor] has failed to deliver a technically acceptable copy of the master in [format] suitable for reproduction, broadcast and/or transmission by [date].

R.056

The [Licensor] agrees and accepts that the [Distributor] may reject any film that it may offer in the [Distribution Period] on the grounds that any such film is not suitable for the audience in any particular country as the content could potentially be contrary to legislation and/or deemed offensive to any religion and/or cultural group and/or cause a negative social media reaction against the [Distributor] which might incite violence and/or result in the loss of future revenue.

General Business and Commercial

R.057
The [Work/Project] shall not be rejected by the [Company] except in good faith and on reasonable grounds. The [Company] agrees and accepts that it shall not be entitled to reject the [Work/Project] based on the grounds of a significant change in the management of the [Company] and/or strategic plans and/or financial circumstances of the [Company].

R.058
The [Company] shall have the right to reject any [Material/Work/Service] under this agreement on the grounds that:

1.1 It is not of merchantable quality and/or fit for its intended and agreed purpose.

1.2 It does not comply with reasonable professional standards.

1.3 The workmanship is of poor quality and substandard.

1.4 The content, material and specifications are not as stated in the contract.

1.5 The content, material and specifications are not in accordance with the approved sample and/or final version.

1.6 It is defective.

1.7 It does not operate and/or function as intended and agreed.

1.8 There are key elements which are missing; defective and/or inaccurate.

1.9 There are serious errors in the content, material and/or specifications.

1.10 The dimensions [size/volume/weight/length/height] are inaccurate.

1.11 It has not been delivered by the stated delivery dates in the exact form required under the contract.

1.12 The [title/label/content/artwork/words] is wrong, offensive, obscene and/or generally not suitable for the age category and/or market for which it was agreed and intended.

1.13 A third party has threatened legal action and/or made claims of ownership and/or allegations of infringement and/or breach of contract.

1.14 A government organisation, agency and/or health and safety and/or other professional advisor has raised concerns relating to compliance, health and safety, product liability, breach of any laws, regulations, directives, standards, codes and/or policies.

R.059

[Name] agrees that the [Company] shall have a period of [number] days after delivery to assess the quality and content of the [Products/Work] and to decide whether to accept and/or reject them. After the expiry of that period if the [Company] has not rejected the [Products/Work] then the [Company] shall be deemed to have accepted delivery.

R.060

The [Client] accepts that where a product and/or service has been customised under the directions of the [Client]. That the [Client] shall not be entitled to reject the delivery of the agreed order for the product and/or service due to the fact that the [Client] no longer wishes to proceed. Once an order is confirmed and the funds paid in full in advance and the cancellation period has expired. Then the [Client] shall only be allowed to reject the order if the [Company] has failed to deliver the agreed product and/or service. The [Client] will already have been provided with the opportunity of cancelling the order within [number] days of placement of the order with a full refund.

R.061

The [Client] may reject the delivery of the [Material] and return the [Material] to the [Company] at the [Company's] cost on the grounds that:

1.1 The stipulated delivery date was not adhered to.

1.2 The [Material] does not match the order which was placed by the [Client] in whole and/or part.

R.062

The [Company] shall be provided with the opportunity by the [Client] to remedy any defect in the delivery of the [Material]. Where necessary the order may be delivered in stages and/or on different dates due to failures in the supply chain. The [Client] agrees that the [Company] shall be permitted a period of up to [number] months to resolve any matter before the [Client] is entitled to reject the order in full and seek to be refunded.

R.063

The [Company] shall not be obliged to refund any sums in respect of material and/or products which have been damaged and/or deteriorated due to the actions of the [Client]. All material and/or products must be in their original packaging and not used in any manner. Any purchase must be supported by a receipt and/or some other evidence of the date and manner of purchase.

R.064

Any rejection of the [Project] must be on significant and reasonable grounds and the reason for the rejection must be justified. Where possible the parties agree to meet to discuss a resolution of the problems in order to continue with the [Project].

R.065

The [Enterprise] shall be entitled to reject any proposal for the [Project] by any other party to this agreement on the grounds that:

1.1 The proposed costs and expenses are excessive and/or not sustainable based on the proposed forecasts.

1.2 The proposal is outside the original agreed remit for the [Project].

1.3 The proposal would not be supported by prospective sponsors and/or financial contributors.

1.4 The proposal is political in nature and contrary to the ethos and policies of the [Enterprise].

R.066

The [Company] shall have the right at any time to decide not to proceed with the {Project] and to withdraw its support and funding. There shall be no obligation to pay any future sums which may have been promised and/or committed by the [Company]. The [Company] shall not be entitled to any refund of any sums and its name may be removed entirely from all documentation, promotions and/or events.

Internet, Websites and Apps

R.067

The [Service] may be cancelled by the [Company] at any time subject to the payment of a pro rata refund for any part of the [Service] which has been paid for and not supplied.

R.068

If the [Supplier/Distributor] does not deliver the [Product/Service] by the agreed delivery date. Then the [Customer] shall be entitled to reject the [Product/Service] and return all the related material to the [Supplier] and request a full refund of all sums paid including delivery costs.

R.069

If the [Supplier] does not deliver the [Product] by the agreed delivery date. The [Customer] agrees that the [Supplier] shall have the opportunity within the next [number] days] after the delivery date to rectify and remedy the problem. After that time the [Customer] shall be entitled to refuse to accept delivery and to reject the [Product] even if it subsequently arrives. The [Customer] shall return the [Product] to the [Supplier] at the [Supplier's] cost and be entitled to be paid a full refund of the purchase price.

R.070

The [Company] shall not be entitled to deliver substituted [Units/Products] and undertakes that all [Units/Products] shall conform to the description as to content, the packaging, dimensions, weight, colour and be safe for their intended and advertised purpose. The image on the screen is intended for guidance only. The [Customer] may reject the [Units/Products] for any reason up to [specify period] after delivery. After that time rejection must be on the grounds that there is a defect, failure and/or fault which is not due to incorrect use and/or the work of a third party.

R.071

The [Company] shall be entitled to deliver substituted [Products] which are similar where necessary. The [Company] cannot ensure that all [Products] will conform to the description as to content, packaging, dimensions, weight, colour. The image on the screen is intended for guidance only. The [Customer] may reject the [Products] for any reason up to [specify duration number/days] after delivery. After that time rejection must be on the grounds that there is a defect, failure and/or fault which is not due to incorrect use and/or the work of a third party and which is within the [specify period number/days] of the date of purchase. This clause is not intended to undermine any legal rights you may be entitled to in any country as an online purchaser of a product.

R.072

The [Company] reserves the right to reject the [Work/Material] if it is clear that the contents of the [Work/Material] do not conform to the style, form and subject matter stipulated by and agreed with the [Company]. In the event that the [Company] rejects the [Work/Material] the [Author] shall be obliged to repay to the [Company] all sums previously paid to the [Author] as an advance against future royalties. In such instance subject to repayment of the monies the [Author] shall be entitled to offer the [Work/Material] to a third party. That shall be the case regardless of whether the subject matter was initiated by the [Company] rather than the [Author].

R.073

The [Company] shall have the right to reject any [Material/Work/Service] under this agreement on the grounds that:

1.1 It is defective and has serious errors; it is not of merchantable quality and it is not fit for its intended purpose and/or does not function as required and/or comply with the agreed description.

1.2 It is not of a professional quality and does not comply with the standards of [specify organisation/compliance code].

1.3 It does not adhere to the approved sample and/or meet the specifications as to its function, method of operation and/or content and/or some other crucial factor.

1.4 That there has been a failure to clear and/or pay for copyright, consents and/or any other rights from third parties and/or that there are allegations and/or legal proceedings of a serious nature. That there has a failure to incorporate copyright notices and/or trade marks and/or labels and/or that the instructions, warning notices and/or packaging are inadequate.

R.074

The [Company] shall be entitled to reject the [Website/App/Platform] which has been commissioned on the following grounds:

1.1 That the layout, design, colour, function and operation of the [Website/App/Platform] is not in accordance with the agreed instructions and/or outline summary set out in appendix A.

1.2 That all and/or part of the [Website/App/Platform] is not original and developed specifically for the [Company] and has been copied from a third party. That all and/or part of the [Website/App/Platform] infringes the rights of a third party and/or has not been cleared for use and/or appears very similar and/or to be an imitation of a website, app and/or platform of a third party.

1.3 That the quality of the work for the [Website/App/Platform]] is not of a professional standard and/or suitable for the intended purpose in accordance with the agreed instructions and/or outline summary set out in appendix A. The operation and function is slow and/or does not achieve the desired effect and/or interaction and/or appearance which was expected and agreed would be achieved.

R.075

[Name] accepts that the [Company] may reject the [Website/App] and/or request that [Name] vary and/or change the layout, design, function, operation and/or colour in the event that:

1.1 The [Website/App] does not function and/or operate and/or fulfil the tasks and/or contain the content agreed with the [Company] set out in the agreed work schedule, description and visual representations of the specifications in appendix B.

1.2 The [Website/App] is not compatible with the existing operating system of [format] and/or existing technology of the [Company] as agreed.

1.3 The [Website/App] does not conform to the professional standards of [specify organisation] and/or is incomplete and/or missing material and/or functions.

1.4 The [Website/App] contains design faults which cannot be remedied without significant additional expenditure.

R.076

The [Distributor] shall have the right to reject any application to subscribe to the [Podcast Series] and shall not be obliged to state a reason for such rejection. Even when a person has applied and been accepted. The [Distributor] reserves the right to reject and/or cancel their continued subscription at a later date without providing any specific reason.

R.077

The [Company] shall be entitled to reject any application by any [player/person] to participate in any game, gambling, bingo and/or competition. The entry requirements may vary based on the circumstances. Acceptance of any entry is entirely at the discretion of the [Company]. Any application must comply with the specific stated requirements in each case. Where the [Company] suspects that the [player/person] is under [number] years and/or is unable to meet the costs required. The [Company] may automatically refuse the [player/person] and there shall be no right of appeal from such a decision.

R.078

Where the cost of any monthly subscription is increased at any time by more than [number/currency]. Then the subscriber shall have the right to reject the increase costs and to cancel the agreement with [one] [weeks'/months'] notice on their account.

R.079

The [Distributor] shall be entitled to remove, block, delete and/or report any content and/or material and/or sound recordings and/or images and/or gestures which are obscene, offensive, a parody, insulting and/or an incitement to violence and/or are likely to lead to damage to any persons and/or property and/or which are likely to be contrary to any legislation in [country/world] and/or to cause mental distress and/or harm to any individual [which cannot be justified as a valid reason].

R.080

The [Distributor] shall be entitled to reject any [Film/Podcast/Image/Sound Recording] on the grounds that:

1.1 It is political and/or promotes actions by third parties which would be contrary to the law of [country/world] and/or

1.2 It is factually inaccurate, defamatory, indecent, offensive, obscene and/or poses a threat of loss of life and/or damage to the property of any person and/or corporate entity.

1.3 It does not adhere to the ethos of the [Distributor] and/or

1.4 It encourages and/or promotes activities which are extremely dangerous without sufficient safety advice.

R.081

There is no automatic right to display a brand name, logo, trade mark, slogan, image, insignia, flag, product and/or service in association with your contribution to the [Platform]. The Company] reserves the right to remove and/or delete any such material which in its view should not be displayed. Please read the policy document [specify name] which sets out the outline of the expected standard and compliance requirements. Note that there are a number of banned insignia, words and images. Where any person refuses to co-operate then the account shall be closed and blocked.

R.082

The [Company] shall have the right to reject any material in any format and/or medium which a contributor wishes to display and/or transmit on their account including but not limited to any film, video, image, sound recording and/or otherwise. The [Company] shall not be obliged to give notification of removal of any such material in advance. Where any contributor disputes the right of the [Company] to do so. Then the [Company] reserves the right to completely cancel the account indefinitely and to refuse to allow the contributor to open any new account.

R.083

The right to open any account on the [Platform] is entirely at the discretion of the Company. There is no automatic right to open an account. Once the application form has been complete you are not accepted as a member until a code has been allocated for your membership for the year.

Merchandising and Distribution

R.084

The [Licensee] confirms that the [Prototypes/Samples/Products] shall not be rejected by the [Licensee] except on reasonable grounds and in good faith. The [Licensee] shall only be entitled to reject the [Prototypes/Samples/Products] by notice in writing within [thirty] days of receipt of delivery including weekends and bank holidays and the notice shall state the reasons for the rejection.

R.085

Where the [Prototypes/Samples/Products] are not accepted by the [Client] then the [Company] shall be entitled to take the complaints into account and deliver another selection of material for consideration by the [Client]. Where the material is still not accepted and is deemed by the [Client] to be of inferior quality and/or not in accordance with the agreed quotation. Then the [Company] agrees to refund to the [Client] all sums paid for the work except [number/currency] which the [Company] shall be entitled to retain.

R.086

The [Company] agrees that the [Licensor] shall have the right to approve all aspects of the [Licensed Articles/Products] and any associated packaging and marketing material prior to their production, manufacture, supply and distribution. The [Company] shall supply at its cost to the [Licensor] such copies, samples, packaging and marketing of the [Licensed Articles/Products] in the exact form and material in which it is intended that they should be reproduced, supplied, transmitted, exhibited, distributed and/or sold at any time. In the event that the [Licensor] does not in each case provide [verbal/written] approval then the [Company] must not proceed with production, manufacture, supply and/or distribution until the reasons for the rejection have been resolved and approval provided. There is no right to assume and/or deem approval by the [Licensor].

R.087

The [Licensee] agrees and undertakes that the final versions of the [Products/Articles] and all samples, artwork, posters, packaging, catalogues, websites, apps, pop-ups, podcasts, blogs, advertising, marketing and publicity material shall not be produced and/or manufactured by the [Licensee] and/or supplied, distributed and/or sold to any third party and/or the public until they have each in turn been inspected, assessed and approved in each case by the [Licensor]. The [Licensor] shall have the right to reject any proposal and/or material on the grounds of lack of artistic quality, size, colour, shape, failure to comply with health and safety legislation, guidelines and/or codes and/or the failure to own any copyright, trade mark, domain name and/or any other legal grounds, a risk of legal action relating to product liability, the labels being inadequate and/or the packaging unsuitable for the intended markets and/or any other reasonable objections which may impact on the [Licensor] and/or the [Products/Articles].

R.088
The [Sub-Licensee] agrees that it shall not reject any copies of any master material supplied on technical grounds provided that it is capable of being upgraded to a suitable standard. The [Sub-Licensee] shall carry out such additional work as may be required at its sole cost to remedy any problem up to [number/currency]. Where the work exceeds this sum the [Licensee] agrees to pay any additional costs provided that the [Sub-Licensee] agrees the cost in advance with the [Licensee].

R.089
Where the [Company] has commissioned work including any infographics, designs, artwork, photographs and/or other images. It is agreed that the [Company] shall not be entitled to reject the material in the event they are no longer required for the [Project] and there has been a change of strategy in relation to the marketing. The [Company] agrees to pay [Name] subject to delivery of the material for the commissioned work by the agreed delivery date.

R.090
The [Distributor] shall carefully check, inspect and test samples of the [Products] within [number] days of delivery to ensure that they comply with the requirements of the [Sales Order]. In the event that some and/or all of the [Products] are rejected they shall be returned at [Distributor's] risk and expense within [number] days to the [Company]. The parties shall endeavour to agree substitute products which shall be delivered at the [Company's] cost. Where the parties cannot agree any substitution the [Company] may deduct the sum owed to the [Distributor] from any other invoice to be issued by the [Company] to the Distributor].

R.091
If the [Samples/Products] which are delivered are not as described in any promotion and/or marketing and/or as represented by any agent and/or as stated in any completed order form by the [Company]. The [Client] shall at its sole discretion be entitled to reject the [Samples/Products] and to cancel the order in its entirety. The [Client] shall provide written notification to the [Company] that it is rejecting the [Samples/Products] and state the reasons. The [Client] shall request that the [Company] arrange for the collection of the [Samples/Products] at the [Company's] cost within [number] days. In addition the [Client] shall request that the [Company] pay back all the sums

paid by the [Client] within [number] days. The [Client] shall not be obliged to accept any alternative offer by the [Company].

R.092

1.1 The [Client] shall be entitled cancel and/or amend the order at any time up to [thirty/sixty] days before delivery of the [Products/Service]. In such event the [Client] shall be due a refund of any deposit paid and shall not be obliged to pay any additional sums to the [Supplier] unless otherwise agreed to be due in respect of a varied order.

1.2 The [Client] shall still be entitled to reject any [Products/Service] that may be delivered where it does not comply with the amended order and/or is not fit for purpose and/or does not comply with existing health and safety and/or other legislation which may apply.

1.3 The [Supplier] shall not have the right if any [Products/Service] are rejected by the [Client] to substitute another product and/or service unless otherwise agreed by the [Client]. The [Client] shall not be obliged to accept any such offer of substitution and shall be entitled to a full refund of the sums paid for any order.

R.093

1.1 The [Distributor] agrees to advise the [Supplier] in writing with their reasons for the rejection of any order within [a reasonable period/ twenty-eight days] of delivery in each case.

1.2 The [Distributor] agrees that the order for the [Products] is on a firm sale basis and that the [Products] shall not be returned unless they can be shown not to comply with the description of the order placed and/or are found to be defective in some manner and/or the labels and/or packaging are inadequate and/or do not comply with the legal requirements specified and/or the [Products] do not function and/or operate in accordance with the agreed purpose for which they were bought for supply to the public.

R.094

The [Supplier] agrees that where the [Company] rejects all and/or any part of any order that it has made for any reason. That the [Supplier] shall send another replacement of all and/or part of the order to the [Company]. The [Supplier] agrees that the [Company] may reject any part and/or all of any order on the grounds that:

1.1 The colour, shape, size, content, labels and/or packaging are wrong.

1.2 There have been reports by the public that the product has caused personal injury.

1.3 That the characters, words and/or artwork on the product and/or marketing material have resulted in a negative social media campaign which has impacted on sales.

1.4 The [Company] has decided to cease selling and/or distributing the products.

R.095

The [Company] reserves the right not to fulfil the terms of any purchase order and/or request for specific products, items and/or services at any time for any reason including but not limited due to the increase in cost of materials and/or the failure of a source of supply and/or the failure of energy supplies, machinery and/or facilities. In the event of the rejection of an order and/or request and/or cancellation at a later time. The [Company] agree to reimburse the [Client] in respect of any advance payment that has already been made. The [Client] agrees that the [Company] shall not be under any further liability for any loss of profit, losses and/or other sums in respect of such rejection and/or cancellation.

R.096

The [Client] shall be entitled to reject the [Products] if the [Products] are not the exact items specified in the agreed purchase order and/or the [Products] are not in a new and unmarked condition when they arrive and/or are not of merchantable quality and are not operating properly and/or are damaged and/or are not in any manner fit for their intended purpose. The [Company] shall after rejection of the [Products] by the [Client] verify the condition and nature of the [Products] which have been returned by the [Client]. If the [Company] confirms the complaint the [Client] shall have the option to a full refund and/or to have a replacement delivered and/or to order a different product for the same price.

R.097

The [Company] agrees that it shall not be entitled to reject the whole order for the [Products] from the [Supplier] due to a failure to deliver less than [number] of the items in total per order.

R.098

The [Company] shall not be liable to the [Client] for any reason for any consequential losses, damages, costs, expenses, loss of profit and/or other sums suffered and/or incurred as a result of late delivery; any incomplete order and/or any rejection of the [Products]. The total liability of the [Company] shall be limited to the sum paid for the order in each case. The [Company] accepts that it cannot exclude liability for any direct consequential personal injury and/or death caused directly by the negligence of the [Company] relating to the [Products] supplied to the [Client].

R.099

The [Purchaser] reserves the right to reject any [Products] supplied under this confirmed quotation and order if in the opinion of the [Purchaser] they do not conform to the exact written specifications agreed with the [Purchaser].

R.100

The [Purchaser] reserves the right to reject all the [Products] if the number of units delivered is less than that requested in the purchase order and/or the delivery date is not complied with as stated and/or some and/or all of the [Products] are damaged.

R.101

In the event that the [Purchaser] rejects the [Products] then the [Company] shall be responsible for all administration, delivery, freight and insurance costs that may be incurred by the [Company] to arrange for the collection of the [Products].

R.102

The [Company] agrees that signature for acceptance of delivery of the [Products] at the designated address shall not constitute formal acceptance of the number, content and condition. The [Purchaser] shall have [number] days from delivery to accept and/or reject the [Products]. Where no notification is received then the [Company] shall be entitled to assume that the [Products] have been deemed accepted after [number] days.

R.103

The [Company] shall have the right to take up to [number] [days/weeks] from delivery to decide whether to reject any service and/or products supplied by any third party. Where any service and/or products are found to be below the standard required by the [Company]. Then the third party shall be notified and permitted [number] days to remedy the problem. No further payments will be made until the problem has been resolved to the standard required by the [Company]. In the event that the matter cannot be resolved the parties agree to enter into mediation and/or some other alternative resolution procedure prior to the issue of any legal proceedings.

Publishing

R.104

The [Publisher] reserves the right to reject the [Work/Report/Article] if in the opinion of the [Publisher] it is clear that:

1.1 the contents of the [Work/Report/Article] do not conform to the description of the style, form and theme of the synopsis in appendix A agreed with the [Author]; and/or

1.2 the writing is not of a professional standard which could reasonably be expected for publication; and/or

1.3 the [Publisher] has become aware that all and/or part of the [Work/Report/Article] has been copied and/or adapted from the original work of a third party.

1.4 the content would cause damage and/or losses to the [Publisher] due to the controversial nature of the material.

In the event that the [Publisher] rejects the [Work/Report/Article] then the [Publisher] agrees and undertakes that it shall provide a detailed valid reason to the [Author]. There is no presumption that the [Author] should pay back any advance payment for the work. The [Publisher] agrees that the parties shall enter into negotiations regarding whether there should be any repayment of some and/or all of the sums paid to the [Author] under this agreement.

R.105
In the event that the [Publisher] shall reject the [Work/Manuscript/Article] for any reason. Then the [Publisher] agrees and undertakes to allow the [Author] the opportunity to resubmit the [Work/Manuscript/Article] taking into account the suggested amendments and/or grounds of rejection by the [Publisher] on the basis that the parties agree a new delivery date. This clause shall not apply where the [Author] has breached the copyright of a third party and falsely represented the work as their own original work and/or where there are threats of legal action by a third party which cannot be defended.

R.106
If the [Work/Manuscript/Images/Infographics] has been completed and delivered by the [Author] in good faith and with due care and attention in accordance with the agreed [Treatment/Summary/Synopsis]. Then the [Publisher/Distributor] agrees to abide by the Code of Practice of [specify organisation] in respect of the rejection of the material and shall not seek to reclaim any sums paid as an advance to the [Author]. The parties shall enter into negotiations to settle the matter amicably and without litigation as far as possible. Where the [Author] reaches an agreement for the sale of the rejected material to a third party then the [Author] agrees and undertakes to repay any advance that may have been paid by the [Publisher/Distributor].

R.107

The [Publisher] agrees that it shall only be entitled to reject the manuscript of the [Work/Book/Report] on reasonable and valid grounds which cannot be remedied by additional further amendments by the [Author] and/or by the editing process prior to publication. Provided that the [Author] has completed the [Work/Book/Report] in the style, form and content agreed in writing and has maintained a sufficiently competent standard of writing. Then the [Publisher] agrees that it shall be obliged to accept the [Work/Book/Report]. In the event the [Work/Book/Report] is rejected the [Publisher] shall provide detailed reasons for such rejection and provide the [Author] with sufficient time to remedy the alleged defects. Where the [Work/Book/Report] is further rejected then the [Publisher] agrees not to seek to recoup the sums paid in advance against royalties from the [Author] whether or not the [Work/Book/Report] is subsequently published elsewhere. The rejection of the [Work/Book/Report] by the [Publisher] shall terminate this agreement and all rights granted and/or assigned to the [Publisher] by the [Author] shall immediately revert to the [Author]. The [Publisher] agrees to confirm the reversion of rights to the [Author] in writing and that the [Author] is permitted to arrange for the publication of the [Work/Book/Report] with another publisher and/or other third party.

R.108

1.1 The [Publisher] shall be entitled within a period of [number] months of the date of this assignment to decide whether to retain and/or reject the [Archive Material/Sound Recordings/Content] delivered by [Name] under this agreement.

1.2 In the event that the [Publisher] decides to reject the [Archive Material/Sound Recordings/Content] on the grounds that it is not as described in the agreement in appendix A and/or is not suitable for reproduction and/or is of inferior technical quality then written notice shall be given to [Name] by the [Publisher] of the grounds of rejection. The [Publisher] shall assign all rights and interest it has acquired in the [Archive Material/Sound Recordings/Content] back to [Name] subject to the repayment of the assignment fee and any other sums paid. [Name] shall be obliged to repay to the [Publisher] any sums that it has received from the Publisher in respect of the [Archive Material/Sound Recordings/Content] at any time. The [Publisher] shall not be liable to pay [Name] any sums which may become due under this agreement in respect of the [Archive Material/Sound Recordings/Content] from the [date of notice/date of reversion of the rights to Name] which have not accrued to [Name] before that date.

R.109

1.1 The [Publisher] agrees either to accept or provide written reasons for its rejection of the [Work/Manuscript/Article] within [number] [days/weeks/months] of delivery of the agreed material.

1.2 The [Publisher] agrees that it shall provide the [Author] with a period of [number] [days/weeks/months] in which to remedy the reasons for the rejection of the [Work/Manuscript/Article] and by which the [Author] shall resubmit the [Work/Manuscript/Article] for further consideration.

1.3 The [Author] agrees that in the event that the [Publisher] shall refuse to accept the revised [Work/Manuscript/Article] which has been resubmitted in 1.2. Provided that the grounds of rejection are reasonable and in good faith and substantial written reasons have been provided to the [Author]. Then the [Author] shall be obliged to repay the [Publisher] the following sum [number/currency] by [date] by [method of repayment]. No other part of any advance shall be due to be repaid and no interest shall be due and/or repayment of expenses.

R.110

1.1 The [Publisher] shall notify the [Author] within [number] days of the delivery of the [Manuscript and Artwork] in [format] by [specify method] whether they have accepted and/or rejected the [Manuscript and Artwork] in principle in the form that it has been delivered subject to minor editing and amendments.

1.2 The [Publisher] may reject the [Manuscript and Artwork] entirely if in the view of the [Publisher] the material delivered by the [Author] does not comply with the agreed content, format and/or style and/or is considered to be so poor in quality that it cannot be remedied by the [Author] by suggested alterations by the [Publisher]. Alternatively the [Publisher] may reject the [Manuscript and Artwork] but allow the [Author] to carry out such adjustments to the material as may be necessary for it to be resubmitted at a later date. The [Publisher] shall still have the right to reject the revised material despite the fact it has contributed to the alterations.

R.111

The [Publisher] agrees that it has read and assessed the [Manuscript/Treatment/Synopsis] by the [Author] and accepted that the standard and quality of work by the [Author] is suitable for publication by the [Publisher]. There shall be no right of rejection under this agreement and no right to reclaim sums paid on that basis. In the event that the [Publishers] express the view that the work by the [Author] requires further attention for any reason then an in-house editor shall be appointed to work with and advise the [Author] at the [Company's] cost.

R.112

1.1 The [Publisher] agrees that [Name] shall have the right to be consulted regarding the accuracy and detail of the final version of the [Articles] prior to publication in the form in which it is intended to be published in the [newspaper/magazine] including any title headings, photographs, front cover headline, full layout of the article, together with any surrounding material and any website and/or app marketing and/or any other promotional and/or advertising related material.

1.2 If [Name] objects to the use of any part of the material in 1.1 on the basis that it is misleading, inaccurate and/or defamatory. The [Publisher] agrees that it shall make such changes, alterations and/or amendments as may be necessary. The [Publisher] may decide not to supply, distribute, sell and/or exploit all the material and to cancel the [Articles] based on the objections. In such case if the [Publisher] is forced to cancel the agreement due to the objections then [Name] shall be obliged to repay all the sums paid to him/her under this agreement to the [Publisher] within [number] days of receipt of the notice of cancellation.

R.113

1.1 The [Publisher] and [Author] agree that the [Author] shall write a series of [Articles] which shall cover all the following topics and persons: [specify and list].

1.2 The [Author] shall record every interview with each person and require their consent to assign all the copyright in the sound recordings and their words and the interview to the [Author] and [Publisher] as joint copyright owners.

1.3 The [Author] shall deliver the [Articles] to the [Publisher] by [date] for publication in the [newspaper/magazine] known as [specify name]. The [Author] shall also supply copies of all the sound recordings of the interviews.

1.4 The parties agree that the articles and/or sound recordings shall not be exploited in any other format without the prior agreement of both parties. Further that the parties shall also hold joint copyright in the [Articles]. Both parties shall have the right to reject any proposal by the other party. Both parties must agree to the proposal and the terms of any agreement.

R.114

The [Distributor] waives all right to reject the [Manuscript/Proofs/Articles] for any reason. The [Distributor] agrees that it shall not be entitled to a refund of any advance payments made under this agreement and/or have the right to withhold any future payments. The [Distributor] accepts and acknowledges that the reputation and success of the [Author] is exceptional and there can be no rejection of material based on the quality of the work delivered. The [Author] agrees that there may be alterations suggested at the editing stage and/or in the proofs by the [Distributor]. There shall however be no obligation on the [Author] to accept any such changes. The [Author] undertakes to assist the [Distributor] in resolving any issues which may arise in respect of the material.

R.115

The [Company] agrees that it shall not be entitled to reject the [Work/Content] and/or terminate the agreement on the grounds of non-delivery where the [Author] delivers the [Work/Content] within [three] months of the delivery date stated in the agreement.

R.116

The [Distributor] agrees to accept and not reject the written material submitted by [Name] for a series of articles on the [Website/Blog] on the topic of [specify subject] provided that the articles:

1.1 shall meet the length set by the [Distributor] in each case of [number] words.

1.2 shall only contain product placement, endorsements and/or links to any brand, business, company, product and/or service approved in advance with the [Distributor].

R.117

The [Distributor] shall be entitled to reject the [Products] on the grounds that:

1.1 The [Products] do not match the articles stipulated in the order form.

1.2 The [Products] are not delivered in accordance with the agreed delivery dates.

1.3 The [Products] are not labelled and/or packaged in [language].

1.4 The [Products] have been recalled in other countries due to allegations relating to health and safety.

R.118

Where the [Distributor] has rejected any [Products] it agrees and undertakes to notify the [Supplier] of the full reasons and to return the [Products] at the

[Distributor's/Supplier's] sole cost. The [Supplier] shall replace the rejected [Products] and shall not charge any additional sums. Where the [Supplier] is unable and/or unwilling to supply any replacement then the [Supplier] agrees to repay any advance deposit and/or payment made by the [Distributor].

Services

R.119
The [Licensor] agrees to advise the [Agent] with the reason for rejecting any particular order requested by the [Agent] with a third party. The [Agent] accepts that the decision of the [Licensor] shall be final and that the [Agent] shall not be entitled to claim for any loss of profit, commission and/or otherwise.

R.120

Where the parties have agreed the nature and detail of the services to be supplied by the [Company] to the [Client]. The [Company] shall still have the right to reject the application by the [Client] to be provided with the specified services if for any reason it is shown at a later date that the [Client] is unlikely to be able to meet the financial commitment required under the service agreement at any time.

R.121
Where [Company] gives notice to the [Distributor] to terminate the agreement due to the rejection of the prototype and/or final proposed product to be manufactured under the agreement. The [Company] shall have the right to retain the advance payments paid by the [Distributor] despite the fact that the agreement has been terminated. The [Distributor] has accepted the risk that the quality of the work would not meet the standards required by the [Company]. The [Company] agrees that it will allow the [Distributor] a period of [three] months to remedy the problem with the prototype and/or final version of the product which shall start from the date that notification of rejection and/or termination is received by the [Distributor] in each case.

R.122
The [Company] shall have the right to reject the provision of the services by the [Enterprise] and to terminate this agreement with [number] months' notice where:

1.1 the [Enterprise] is the subject of a large scale criminal investigation for fraud and/or criminal proceedings have been commenced and/or there are other allegations which have been made which are likely to result in civil proceedings by a third party and which have received extensive negative social media coverage.

1.2 the [Enterprise] has provided a service which has been regularly interrupted, suspended, withdrawn, unavailable, defective, inaccurate and/or otherwise not to a suitable professional and technical standard for its intended purpose.

1.3 the [Enterprise] is no longer authorised by the relevant regulatory body to provide the service to third parties in [country].

R.123
The services provided by the [Service Provider] to the [Company] may be rejected and the agreement terminated in the event that:

1.1 The qualified personnel are not available at the times and dates required and/or are late and/or not equipped to complete the work.

1.2 The standard to which the work is carried out by the personnel poses a risk to the public and/or raises security and/or health and safety issues to the detriment of the [Company].

1.3 The [Service/Provider] wishes to increase the agreed budget for the services prior to the commencement of work on the basis that the [Company] has made additional demands and/or requests which are not covered by the agreement.

R.124
Where after the signature of this agreement the [Performer/Presenter] suffers mental and/or physical and/or medical problems which affect his/her ability to perform and/or fulfil the terms of this agreement as required and the parties cannot agree alternative arrangements. Then [Company] shall have the right to terminate this agreement up to [one] week prior to the start of the work schedule without further liability to the [Performer/Presenter]. Where the problems arise after the work schedule has commenced then the parties agree that the [Company] shall only be obliged to pay for work which is completed. No payments shall be due to be paid where the [Performer/Presenter] is not available for any reason. The [Company] however agrees not to terminate the agreement but to arrange substitute persons where required. If at any point it becomes clear that the [Performer/Presenter] will not return to complete any work in the next year. Then the [Company] may terminate the agreement and agrees in such instance to pay the [Performer/Presenter] a one-off no obligation payment of [number/currency] as a gesture of goodwill. No other sums shall be due to be paid by the [Company].

REJECTION

R.125

Where any part of any product and/or service is not functioning as required and/or significant elements and/or sections are missing. The [Company] shall notify the [Supplier] and allow them [number] days to remedy the matter. After that period if the problem has not been resolved to the satisfaction of the [Company] then the [Company] may reject any further products and/or services to be supplied and terminate the agreement on the basis of default by the [Supplier].

R.126

The services to be provided by [Name] are stated in appendix A together with the completion dates. On the basis that the services are complete to a high standard and by the agreed dates. There shall be no right of rejection and/or cancellation by the [Company]. If the [Company] changes its strategy and decides not to use the services of [Name] there shall still be an obligation to pay the fees and expenses set out in clause [–].

R.127

The services provided by [Name] are subject to all the codes and/or policies of the [Company] which may exist at the time of this agreement and/or come into existence in the future. The [Company] shall not be obliged to notify [Name] but [Name] shall be obliged to check the website and/or app of the [Company] for any updates. Where [Name] is unable and/or unwilling to accept any new codes and/or policies of the [Company] for any reason and notifies the [Company] to that effect. The [Company] shall not be obliged to renew and/or extend the agreement when it expires and may terminate the agreement early on the grounds notified by [Name].

R.128

[Name] agrees that the [Company] shall be entitled to reject the work submitted by [Name] on the grounds that:

1.1 [Name] is not suitably qualified for the work and has misled the [Company] as to their qualifications and/or work experience and/or ability and skills.

1.2 The work provided to date is inadequate and does not satisfactorily complete the proposed task.

1.3 [Name] deliberately misled the [Company] as to the costs involved and inflated the costs and expenses.

In such instance the [Company] may terminate the agreement and shall be entitled to seek a partial refund of the sums paid by the [Company] up to [number] per cent.

Sponsorship

R.129
[Name] agrees and undertakes that his/her final decision as to whether to provide consent to the conclusion of any agreement negotiated by the [Company] shall not be unreasonably delayed and/or withheld.

R.130
The [Company] agrees that [Name] shall be entitled to refuse to carry out any work and/or provide any endorsement of any product, service and/or other matter which in the opinion of [Name] would pose a threat to his/her health and/or safety and/or would detrimentally effect his/her name, image, reputation, career prospects, and/or would contravene any code of conduct, policies and/or other obligations imposed by any regulatory and/or professional organisation of which he/she is a member and/or governed by as a legal requirement.

R.131

1.1 The [Sponsor] shall have the right to approve and/or reject any material upon which its name, logo and/or trade mark shall appear at the [Event] and/or in any merchandising, marketing and advertising and/or any other material in any format of any nature.

1.2 The [Company] shall supply a sample copy at the [Company's] cost on each occasion of any such material. The [Sponsor] agrees to approve and/or reject the material within [number] days. If the [Sponsor] rejects the material submitted to them for any reason. The [Sponsor] agrees to specify the reason and make a recommendation as to the solution required to gain approval. The [Company] shall then incorporate such necessary changes and resubmit the material again to the [Sponsor].

1.3 The [Sponsor] agrees that it shall not be entitled to terminate the agreement on the grounds that the [Company] did not seek approval for any material provided that it was a genuine error and the [Company] seeks to resolve the matter as soon as it realises the problem.

R.132
The [Club] shall be entitled to reject any material and/or products supplied by the [Sponsor] on the following grounds:

1.1 Health and safety and failure to comply with current legislation as to labels, content and/or product liability.

1.2 That the material and/or products are associated with a political organisation.

1.3   That the material and/or products are damaged, defective, flawed and/or not fit for their intended purpose.

1.4   That the material and/or products do not display the names, logos, images, slogans and trade marks in the layout, style and/or format agreed with the [Club].

R.133

The [Sponsor] shall not have any rights of approval and/or rejection over the advertising, marketing and promotion of the [Event]. The [Sponsor] shall not be entitled to refuse to pay the fees in clause [–] because it does not approve of the content of the catalogue, posters, banners and/or any other material. Provided that the [Sponsor's] [Logo/Name/Image] has been reproduced accurately and in the correct form and format agreed between the parties.

R.134

The [Company] shall be entitled to terminate this agreement and reject the funding to be provided by the [Sponsor] for the [Event/Series]. Where the [Company] has reasons to believe that the [Sponsor] is involved in a political campaign of any nature and/or is trading while insolvent and/or is involved in money laundering and/or is the subject of a major criminal investigation in any country.

R.135

Where at any time the [Sponsor] is sold to a third party in its entirety. Then the [Sponsor] shall not be entitled to assign this agreement to the third party without the approval of the [Institute]. The [Sponsor] shall notify the [Institute] of its wish to transfer the agreement and the [Institute] shall be entitled to accept and/or reject the proposal.

R.136

Where it becomes apparent at a later date after this agreement has been signed that the business and/or other activities of the [Sponsor] and/or its directors do not adhere to the ethos and brand strategies of the [Company] and/or the [Sponsor] is not complying with any legislation in [country] and/or is no longer licensed and/or authorised to [specify activity]. Then the [Company] may decide to cancel and/or terminate this agreement at the end of the first [six/twelve] month period and shall not be obliged to continue for the full period of [number] years.

R.137

The [Company] shall be entitled to reject any material supplied by the [Sponsor] for the website, app, marketing and/or merchandising. The final decision in all matters shall be the responsibility of the [Company] and the [Sponsor] shall be obliged to accept such decision if it wishes it logo, name and image to be reproduced for the [Event].

University, Charity and Educational

R.138

1.1 The [Institute/Charity] agrees to provide details of the reasons for any rejection of the [Work/Services/Project] in writing to the [Company] within [specify duration] of delivery and/or the operation of the [Work/Services/Project].

1.2 The [Institute/Charity] agrees that it shall provide the [Company] with a period of [one] month in which to remedy any problem at the [Company's] cost. If after that period any defect, fault, error, omission and/or lack of compliance with the original specifications has not been resolved between the parties. Then the [Institute/Charity] shall be entitled to reject the [Work/Services/Project] on reasonable grounds. In such instance the [Institute/Charity] shall serve notice of termination and shall be entitled to repayment of [number] per cent all the sums paid by the [Institute/Charity] to the [Company] for the [Work/Services/Project]. The [Company] shall not be liable for any direct and/or indirect consequential losses, damages, costs and expenses incurred by the [Institute/Charity].

R.139

In the event that the [Work/Services/Project] delivered to the [Institute/Charity] is not of satisfactory quality and/or does not comply with the agreed [Budget/Schedule/Summary] in appendix A attached to this agreement. Then the [Institute/Charity] shall provide [Name] with a reasonable opportunity to amend the [Work/Services/Project] based on the changes required notified by the [Institute/Charity]. If the revised [Work/Services/Project] are still not of satisfactory quality and/or do not comply with the agreed [Budget/Schedule/Summary]. The [Institute/Charity] shall be entitled to give [Name] verbal and/or written notice of rejection. The [Institute/Charity] shall not be entitled to seek repayment of the Budget from [Name]. The [Institute/Charity] shall be entitled to use a third party to remedy the problems and to seek a contribution to the cost of such work from [Name] of no more than [fifty] per cent.

R.140

1.1 There can be no presumption of approval and/or acceptance of delivery of a [Project/Service] by the [Institute/Charity].

1.2 A [Project/Service] may be rejected at any time up to [number] [weeks/months] after delivery.

1.3 Where no acceptance is notified by the [Institute/Charity] then any [Project/Service] shall be deemed accepted and approved after [number] [weeks/months] from the date of delivery.

R.141
If there is a delay in delivery for any reason of the [Material/Products] to the [Institute/Charity] of more than [thirty] days without the consent of the [Institute/Charity]. Then the [Institute/Charity] shall be entitled to reject the delivery of the [Material/Products] and to be paid a full refund of all sums paid for the order.

R.142
If the [Work/Project] is damaged, destroyed, unfit for its intended purpose, not in accordance with agreed specifications as to size, shape, colour, use, and/or is technically defective, and/or unable to function and/or requires additional materials not originally disclosed by the [Company]. Then the [Institute/Charity] shall be entitled without prejudice to any claim to reject the [Work/Project] by notice in writing to the [Company].

R.143
The [Institute/Charity] shall reject any [manuscript/images/recordings/reports] submitted by any Contributor which:

1.1 contains material in text and/or images from a third party which has been reproduced without sufficient credit and/or acknowledgement and/or without any source reference.

1.2 contains material which the [Institute/Charity] does not wish to publish as it would associate the [Institute/Charity] with an organisation, political view and/or party and/or religious belief and/or any other agenda and/or campaign.

1.3 contains material which is potentially defamatory and/or could pose a risk of contempt of court and/or may lead to criminal and/or civil proceedings against any person named and/or against the [Institute/Charity].

1.4 is likely to lead to a negative social media reaction against the [Institute/Charity] which is likely to damage its reputation.

R.144
The [Charity] reserves the right to reject any application for a place at the [Event] and shall not be obliged to state a reason for such action.

R.145

The [Institute/Charity] reserves the right to withdraw any place offered to any person if at a later date it is evident that they have deliberately misled the [Institute/Charity] as to their qualifications, references and/or background.

R.146

Where a person is rejected for a role in any {Project] the [Institute/Charity] agrees and undertakes to give feedback on the reasons where possible.

R.147

Where a person has submitted a [report/essay/thesis] for their course. The [Institute] agrees and undertakes that a consistent and clear assessment shall be carried out by skilled assessors as to the quality of the work. Where the marks allocated are not accepted by any person and are disputed then the [report/essay/thesis] may be reassessed by another assessor provided that the complaint is raised within [number] days of receipt of the result.

R.148

The [Charity/Institute] has not authorised any temporary and/or permanent staff and/or third parties to commit and/or enter into any agreements on behalf of the [Charity/Institute] at any time. All proposed agreements of any nature must be referred to [Name/role] and approved by the Board of Trustees. The [Charity/Institute] reserves the right to reject any proposed agreement without stating the reasons for the decision.

REMAINDERS

General Business and Commercial

R.149

The parties agree that no [Product/Material] under this agreement shall be sold off and/or disposed of except in strict accordance with the terms of this agreement. Where either party wishes to remainder, destroy, sell-off and/or otherwise depart from this agreement then it shall be subject to the prior written agreement of the parties in each case. In the event that stock is destroyed and/or sold off and/or transferred except as otherwise stated in this agreement and/or subsequently agreed in each case. Then the party who has defaulted shall be obliged to pay the full royalty rate which might have applied if the stock had been sold and/or used as required under this agreement.

R.150

All surplus, damaged and/or returned stock which remains following the termination and/or expiry of this agreement shall be stored, disposed of and/or sold in accordance with the sole decision of [Name].

R.151

After [date] all material created and/or developed under this agreement including any master material, adaptation, marketing and/or packaging material and/or stock and/or damaged returns shall belong exclusively to [Name]. Any licensee shall be obliged at its own cost to arrange for the delivery of all such matters to [Name] at [address].

R.152

If after more than [two] [months/years] from the date of first [manufacture/distribution/sale] of the [Units] of the [subject matter] the [Company] wishes to sell-off, dispose of and/or supply some copies of the [Units] at a reduced price and/or as remainder and/or to destroy any surplus stock. The [Company] shall notify [Name] and the parties shall negotiate a fixed unit cost payment per copy to be paid to [Name] on terms to be agreed.

R.153

Where the [Sub-Licensee] has stock remaining at the expiry of this agreement. The [Sub-Licensee] agrees and undertakes that there is no right to sell, supply, distribute and/or otherwise exploit such material either for the full price and/or at a reduced price, discount and/or other loss. The [Sub-Licensee] agrees and undertakes to arrange for the destruction of all such stock at a location and date agreed with the [Licensor]. The [Sub-Licensee] shall pay for all the costs of the destruction. Where stock is returned to the [Sub-Licensee] by third parties after the date of destruction then the [Sub-Licensee] shall ensure the safe disposal and destruction of all such material and notify the [Licensor] with the information.

R.154

It is agreed between the parties that at the end of this agreement the [Licensee] shall not be able to sell-off any remaining stock and it must all be destroyed and verification provided to [Name] to that effect.

R.155

It is agreed between the parties that stock held by the [Distributor] on [date] the last day of the agreement may be sold at a reduced and/or discounted price to any third party. Provided that [Name] is paid [number] per cent of the sum received by the [Distributor] within [number] days of receipt of payment for the reduced and/or discounted stock from any third party.

Further the [Distributor] agrees to provide supporting documentation of any such matter upon request by [Name].

R.156

1.1 If not less than [two/number] years after the date of first publication of the [Work/Book/Unit] the [Publisher/Distributor] wishes to supply, offer and/or sell copies at a reduced price and/or discounted price and/or has decided to remainder any copies and/or to destroy any surplus copies. The [Publisher/Distributor] shall inform the [Author] of its proposed plans and offer the [Author] the opportunity to comment on the proposal.

1.2 If the plans to supply, offer and/or sell copies at a reduced price and/or discounted price and/or to remainder any copies and/or to destroy any surplus copies takes place then the [Publisher/Distributor] shall pay the [Author] [10] % [ten per cent] of all the net receipts which it shall receive but only where such copies are sold at and/or above the cost price of the [Work/Book/Unit]. If the copies are sold below cost price no royalty shall be due to the [Author].

1.3 The [Author] shall be given [twenty-eight] days to purchase copies at the remainder price for his/her personal use. The [Author] shall not resell the copies without written permission of the [Publisher/Distributor].

1.4 In the event of the [Publisher/Distributor] deciding to destroy surplus copies the [Author] shall have the right to obtain all copies free of charge within [twenty-eight] days of notification provided that they are for personal use and/or for promotional purposes only and not for resale.

R.157

The [Publisher/Distributor] shall not sell-off copies of the [Work/Book/Unit] as remainders within [two] years from the date of first publication without the prior written consent of the [Author]. In the event of copies of the [Work/Book/Unit] being sold off as remainders at more than cost price the [Publishers/Distributor] shall pay the [Author] a fixed cost per copy of [number/currency]. The [Publishers] shall notify the [Author] in writing of their intention to remainder the [Work/Book/Unit] at any time and shall allow the [Author] the opportunity to acquire the stock at the intended remainder price. After notification in each case if the [Author] has not offered to purchase the stock at remainder prices the [Publisher/Distributor] shall be entitled to remainder such copies but shall deliver to the [Author] free of charge and at no cost [number] additional copies of the [Work/Book/Unit].

R.158

The [Publisher/Distributor] shall not be entitled to destroy, pulp, remainder and/or sell-off any stock of the [Work/Book/Unit] unless notice has been sent to the [Author] of their intentions and the Author has been offered the opportunity to acquire the stock. In any event the [Author] shall be sent [number] copies of the [Work/Book/Unit] on each occasion free of charge at the [Publishers/Distributors] cost.

R.159

The [Company] is prohibited from offering the [Work/Book/Unit] as remainder stock to a third party for the first year from the date of publication and/or supply. After that date the [Company] shall be obliged to inform the [Author] that it has decided to cease publication and/or distribution and wishes to dispose of all the existing stock to a third party at a reduced price as remainder and/or to destroy surplus copies. The [Author] shall be entitled to first refusal of the stock intended to be remaindered at the reduced price to be offered to a third party. If this arrangement is agreed between the parties then the sum due to be paid by the [Author] could be offset against sums owed to the [Author] by the [Company]. Where the [Company] intends to destroy the surplus copies and/or other stock then the [Author] shall be entitled to make plans to collect all the stock at the [Authors'] cost. The [Author] shall be entitled to resell such stock provided there is a clear label that the copy is sold by the [Author].

R.160

The [Licensee] will not destroy any stock in any format of the [Work/Book/Unit] and/or sell them off at a price which is below the cost of production and/or in any other manner which would affect the royalties due to [Name] without first providing written notice to [Name] of their intention and allowing [Name] to make a proposal as to how to proceed.

R.161

1.1 The [Licensee] agrees and undertakes that it shall not remainder, destroy, pulp and/or otherwise dispose of any copies of the [Work/Book] which are not damaged and/or contain significant inaccuracies for a period of [number] [months/years] from each of the dates which may apply in respect of the date of first publication of the [Work/Book] in hardback and/or paperback in any country and/or in any translation in any language.

1.2 If the [Licensee] decides after the expiry of the relevant period in 1.1 to remainder the [Work/Book] in any format, country and/or language. Then no notification to the [Author] shall be required. The parties agree that the [Author] shall be entitled to receive [fifty/number] per cent of the sums received by the [Licensee] regardless of whether it is above and/or below the base line cost of production of each copy.

1.3 If the [Licensee] shall decide to pulp and/or destroy copies of the [Work/Book] then written notification shall be sent to the [Author]. The [Author] shall be entitled to request that he/she be sent all such copies at the [Licensee's] cost. If [Author] does not wish to be provided with any copies then the [Licensee] may destroy all such copies.

R.162

Within [28] days of the last day of [June/December] in each year the [Licensee] shall provide a detailed report to the [Author] with a full breakdown of the exploitation of the [Work/Book/Unit] setting out the total sales including the number of copies supplied free of charge and to which persons for review and/or promotional purposes and the number of copies lost, damaged, stolen, destroyed, pulped, remaindered and/or which for any other reason no accounting and/or royalty payment has been made to the [Author].

R.163

The [Publisher/Distributor] shall be entitled at its absolute discretion to remainder, pulp, destroy for no payment at all and/or to sell-off at a reduced and/or severely discounted price copies of the [Work/Book/Unit] in any format where it is clear that there is not a demand, and/or there is a surplus of stock and/or there is a new updated version and it is out of date and/or there have been and/or are legal problems and/or there are significant printing errors and/or the [Work/Books/Units] are damaged in some way. The [Author] agrees that in such instance where the sum received is below the cost of production that no royalty and/or other sum shall be due to be paid.

R.164

The [Publisher/Distributor] shall be entitled at its absolute discretion to remainder, pulp, destroy and dispose of for zero money and/or to sell-off at a reduced and/or discounted price copies of the [Work/Book/Unit] in any format at any time which are no longer required for any reason and/or which are not suitable for use. The [Publisher/Distributor] agrees to pay the [Author] the minimum fixed price per copy of [number/currency] on all items disposed of above the value of [number/currency].

R.165

If at any time the [Institute/Charity] shall decide that in their view there is no longer a demand for the [Work/Product] and the [Institute/Charity] wishes to cease the production, distribution and/or exploitation of the [Work/Product] and/or any adaptation. Then the [Institute/Charity] agree and undertake to notify the [Company] of their intention and to provide the opportunity for the

[Company] to purchase the remaining stock and for all the rights to revert to the [Company]. In the event that the parties fail to reach agreement within [six] months from the date of such notification then the [Institute/Charity] may destroy the stock and/or dispose of it on any terms they think fit.

R.166

The [Outlet] agrees and accepts that the [Units] supplied by the [Supplier] are a limited edition. The [Outlet] agrees that in the event that they do not sell the [Units] within the agreed period of [number] months. That all the remaining stock shall be returned in good condition to the [Supplier] at the [Outlets'] cost. The [Supplier] agrees that it shall have supplied the [Units] on the basis of sale and return. The [Outlet] shall account for and pay the sums due for the [Units] sold by the [Outlet] by [date]. The [Outlet] accepts that it may not reduce the sale price and/or offer a discount for any of the [Units].

R.167

Where after the [Event/Festival] there are merchandising items supplied by the [Sponsor] which have not been distributed to third parties. Then the [Sponsor] agrees that the [Institute/Charity] may dispose and/or distribute these items as it may decide and shall not be obliged to report to the [Sponsor] in respect of such matters.

R.168

Where the [Archive] has unsold special edition calendars and/or other stock which is marked with the year and would be out of date if left unsold. Then the [Supplier] agrees that the [Archive] may reduce the price by up to [fifty] per cent in the last [number]calendar month of each year during the existence of this agreement.

R.169

The [Distributor] shall not be entitled to agree any retail and/or wholesale price reduction, discount and/or promotional offer to any third party without the express prior approval of [Name].

RESIDENTIAL SUBSCRIBER

General Business and Commercial

R.170

'Residential Subscriber' shall mean a private residential home or dwelling unit other than a room including, but not limited to, a residential apartment building or complex which is entitled to receive the [Channel/Service] by virtue of a contract with an authorised [Operator/Service Provider].

R.171
'Residential Subscriber' shall mean a private residence of any type whether rented, freehold and/or leasehold which is not classed as a business for tax purposes by any government agency in the country and for which the person who is responsible for the payment of the household bills has entered into an agreement for the supply of the [Service/Channel] through a legitimate licensed [Company] and undertaken to pay a monthly fee for the period of the agreement.

RESTRAINT OF TRADE

General Business and Commercial

R.172
The [Supplier] agrees that the [Television Company] is entitled to arrange for other companies to sponsor, endorse, advertise and/or promote their products, services, trade marks, logos and/or brands in the [Series]. The [Television Company] agrees that no third party shall be used which directly competes with the [Supplier] in the market of [specify type of product/service] in [country] and/or worldwide. The [Television Company] agrees that where there may be a potential conflict it shall consult with the [Supplier] to obtain their views.

R.173
The [Company] agrees and undertakes that it will not from [date] assign, license, charge and/or in any other way deal with any rights in any media assigned under this agreement to the [Assignee] including but not limited to the television, radio, the internet, electronic downloads, merchandising, games, books and/or audio files in respect of the [Films/Programmes] including the soundtrack and/or parts in any country in the world until the end of the Assignment Period and the reversion of rights to the [Company].

R.174
The [Sponsor] of the [Film/Art Installation/Event] agrees and undertakes that it shall not object to and/or have the right to prevent and/or restrict the funding, contribution, participation, adaptation and/or exploitation by third parties of the [Film/Art Installation/Event] on any grounds. That all decisions shall be the responsibility of the [Archive/Institute].

R.175
The [Employee] accepts and agrees that he/she shall not:

1.1 be employed for any reason by a third party while working for the [Company] in a full-time capacity; and/or

1.2 set up and/or operate his/her own business without the consent of the [Company] including any online commercial account and/or marketing over the internet and/or any telecommunication system.

1.3 enter into any consultancy arrangement with a third party without the prior consent of the [Company].

1.4 negotiate to work for a competitor while still employed by the [Company] unless notice has been served by the [Employee] that he/she intends to terminate the agreement and work elsewhere.

R.176
The [Employee] confirms that he/she shall not during the course of this agreement supply services of the same and/or similar nature to the services provided under this agreement to any third party without the prior written consent of the [Company].

R.177
Except with the prior written consent of the [Company] the [Employee] agrees and undertakes that he/she shall not be engaged directly and/or indirectly in any activity, arrangement and/or agreement which prejudices and conflicts with the interests of the [Company] during the existence of this agreement.

R.178
For a period of [one] year after the termination of the contract with the [Managing Director]. The [Managing Director] undertakes and agrees not to:

1.1 Solicit any clients of the [Company].

1.2 Contact any suppliers, agents and/or distributors of the [Company].

1.3 Make any public statement which attacks the [Company] and/or may impact on their share price.

1.4 Criticise the historical actions and decisions of the Board of Directors of the [Company].

1.5 Reveal to any third party any confidential business information, strategies and/or details of agreements concluded by the [Company].

R.179

The [Employee] may not attempt to register, reproduce, distribute, sell and/or exploit any work material and/or rights developed and/or created in the course of his/her employment at the [Company] at any time.

R.180

Each [Partner] agrees that upon his/her departure from the [Firm] he/she shall not without the prior written approval of the [Firm] for a period of [two years] from the date of [departure/termination/resignation] either alone or in conjunction with any other third party do any of the following matters which would prejudice and/or conflict with the business interests of the [Firm]:

1.1 Provide legal advice in any capacity within [a radius of one mile/the area of [–]] of the [Firm].

1.2 Solicit and/or endeavour to entice away any existing employee, partner or otherwise of the [Firm].

1.3 Approach, solicit, contact and/or seek to obtain the custom of any client of the [Firm] who was a client at the date of the [Partner's] departure particularly those persons who were advised by the [Partner] while at the [Firm] [including/excluding] [specify names] who were brought to the [Firm] by the [Partner].

1.4 The [Partner] shall not use any confidential information about the clients and/or business interests of the [Firm] for his/her own benefit and/or for the benefit of a competing person and/or company.

R.181

The [Employee] confirms that he/she shall not during the course of this agreement supply services of the same and/or similar nature to any third party without the prior consent of the [Company].

R.182

The [Employee] agrees and undertakes that he/she shall not during a period of [number] [months/years] after the expiry and/or termination of this agreement deliberately approach, contact and/or pursue any person, firm, company and/or business with whom the [Company] had a regular business relationship and/or a large contract at the time of the departure of the [Employee] of which the [Employee] was aware and/or with whom the [Employee] dealt with on behalf of the [Company].

This clause shall not apply where:

1.1 The [Employee] is approached and/or contacted by the person, firm or company, and the [Employee] shall have the right to take up an offer of employment to be with them.

1.2 The [Employee] was provided with written consent in advance by the [Company].

1.3 The [Employee] was and/or is alleging that he/she was unfairly dismissed and/or is suing the [Company] for breach of contract.

1.4 The person, firm and/or company was first introduced to the [Company] by the [Employee] due to a prior business relationship with the [Employee].

1.5 The [Company] has been sold and/or ceased trading.

1.6 The [Company] moves premises to another area and/or changes the market which it targets and/or the [products/services] which it sells.

R.183
The [Employee] undertakes that he/she shall not for a period of [three months/one year] after the expiry and/or termination of this agreement induce and/or seek to induce any other employee, consultant and/or client of the [Company] to cease its arrangement with the [Company]..

R.184
The [Company] agrees that it shall have no right to restrict and/or prevent [Name] from applying for a new job at a competitor and/or to restrict the ability of [Name] to be employed and/or work as a consultant for any other competitor and/or third party whether or not that involves making contact with and/or presentations to existing clients of the [Company.

R.185
Both parties agree and undertake that the terms of this agreement are fair and reasonable and are not against public policy either on the grounds of inequality and/or bargaining power and/or on the general grounds of restraint of trade. That both parties have been advised to seek independent legal advice.

R.186
The [Radio Station] confirms that no products, services and/or other material belonging to any third party which would reasonably be construed as being in direct competition with the [Sponsor's] products and/or services shall be mentioned, promoted and/or debated on the [Series] for the duration of the Sponsorship Period. This clause shall apply only to the actual [Series] itself and any commercial break during the [Series]. It shall not apply to any advertisements and/or promotions broadcast and/or transmitted at any time before and/or after the [Series].

R.187

The [Company] does not have any right to impose any restriction on the services and/or work that the [Contributor] may supply to third parties at any time. The [Contributor] has the absolute right to write, appear in and/or contribute to any blog, podcast, programme and/or other media at any time. The [Company] agrees that it is not entitled to the exclusive services of the [Contributor] and has no prior claim over any third party. Nor does the [Company] have any right to prevent the [Contributor] writing for, appearing in and/or discussing the same topic in any media with a third party once it has been disclosed to the general public by the [Company] at any time.

R.188

The [Company] agrees that [Name] shall be entitled during the Term of this Agreement to provide his/her services to any third party provided that it is not for the advertisement, promotion and/or endorsement of a product or service in the category of [specify type of market] from [date] to [date] in the following media: [specify media].

R.189

[Name] agrees and undertakes that he/she shall not provide his/her services, name. endorsement, lyrics, music and/or slogan for any business, promotion, gambling, lottery and/or other advertising on any website, app, blog, podcast, platform and/or otherwise over the internet and/or by means of any form of electronic exploitation and/or by means of any telecommunication system during the Term of this Agreement without the prior written consent and approval of the [Company].

R.190

It is agreed between all parties that the [Website/App/Platform] is only to be used for the sole purpose which has been stated in appendix A as agreed by the [Consortium] and not for any other reason without the prior consent of all parties.

R.191

In consideration of the payment of the [Fee] the [Company] agrees and undertakes not to license, authorise and/or endorse the reproduction and/or adaptation of the image of [specify title] reference [specify details and source] on the following products and/or services from [date] to [date] in [country].

R.192

The [Distributor] agrees and undertakes that it shall not seek to release to the public any directly competing product on its catalogue on the subject of [specify item] at the same time and/or within [number] weeks of the [Article/Unit] licensed by the [Licensor].

R.193

The [Licensee] agrees and undertakes not to enter into a written agreement with any other person and/or business with a directly competing product and/or service on the subject of [specify subject/object] from [date] to [date]. The [Licensee] shall be entitled to enter into negotiations during that period.

R.194

1.1 The [Company] agrees and accepts that it shall not be entitled to use, exploit and/or adapt the title of the [Podcast/Film/Series] and/or any text, script, artist, music, slogan, trade mark and/or any other parts in conjunction with and/or on the [Company's] products and/or in any packaging, marketing and/or promotional material of any nature without the express prior consent of the [Enterprise].

1.2 This agreement is solely related to the placement of the [Company's] products in the [Podcast/Film/Series] and is not a licence, sub-licence and/or any other authority to the [Company] to exercise and/or exploit any rights and/or interest.

R.195

The [Licensee] agrees and undertakes that it shall endeavour to ensure that no agent, distributor, supplier and/or manufacturer engages and/or uses persons in their business who are:

1.1 Under [number] years of age.

1.2 Paid less than the minimum wage of [number/currency] per hour.

1.3 Work for more than [number] hours in each week.

R.196

The [Copyright Owner] agrees and undertakes that it is a fundamental term of this agreement that he/she has not at any time prior to this agreement assigned, transferred, licensed and/or otherwise exploited the copyright and/or other intellectual property rights in the [specify subject matter] and/or in any associated master material. That the [Copyright Owner] agrees and undertakes that the [Company] shall hold the exclusive rights specified in clause [–] for the Licence Period and that the [Copyright Owner] shall not seek to assign, transfer and/or license the same rights to a third party until the Licence Period has expired and/or been terminated.

R.197

The [Distributor] accepts that it cannot impose any price control and/or other limitations on the wholesale and/or retail price of the [Products/Material] supplied by the [Company]. The [Distributor] shall be entitled to terminate the agreement after [six] months if the [Products/Material] have not been sold according to the targets set by the [Distributor].

R.198

1.1 The [Author] shall not without prior consent of the [Publisher/Distributor] write, supply, publish, authorise and/or permit the publication and/or distribution of any other interview, sound recording, film, article and/or book in printed form and/or in any other media on the topic of [specify subject] which would release information and details contained in the [Work/Book].

1.2 After [date] the [Author] shall be entitled to contribute to and/or collaborate in the development and publication of an article and/or book in printed form and/or any other interview, sound recording, film, article and/or book in any media on exactly the same and/or similar subject matter. It shall be irrelevant that any such new material is likely to compete with and/or prejudice the sales of the [Work/Book].

R.199

The [Author] shall not without the written consent of the [Publisher/Distributor] before [date] arrange the publication and sale to the public of any other script, book, sound recording, film and/or other material in any medium by the [Author] which because of its content is likely to have a prejudicial and/or damaging effect on the sales and/or revenue of the [Work/Book/Series]. After [date] the [Publisher/Distributor] agrees and accepts that there are no such restrictions on the [Author].

R.200

The [Author] shall be entitled to enter into an agreement with any third party to publish and/or authorise the publication of a competing work in any printed and/or electronic form for sale to the public on the same and/or a similar subject as the [Work/Book] and/or to licence any other adaptation. The [Company] accepts that it has only acquired the limited rights to the [Work/Book] and that it cannot restrict the [Author] in his/her career and/or future work in his/her specialist subject.

R.201

The [Author] agrees and undertakes that he/she shall not write, supply and/or authorise except for the [Publisher/Distributor] in the [Territory/country] any identical and/or substantially similar written work on the subject of [specify scope of subject] for exploitation in hardback, paperback, audio format and/or electronic form for distribution and sale to the public before [date]. After [date] this clause shall no longer apply under this agreement.

R.202

The [Company] agrees and undertakes not to engage any other writer and/ or consultant and/or to enter into any agreement with a third party to write, research and/or produce any other book, audio file and/or material based on [specify subject] for a period of [number] [months/years] from [date] which may directly and/or indirectly compete with and reduce sales of the works of the [Author].

R.203

The [Publisher/Distributor] agrees that this agreement is not intended to restrict the ability of the [Author] to be commissioned by and/or write any future work and/or book for publication and/or sale by any third party. That shall be the case whether or not the future work and/or book is a new edition, sequel and/or based on the same topic and/or might be considered a competing work and/or book. This agreement is limited to the licensing only of the [state number] edition of the [Work/Book]. The [Author] may enter into a new agreement with a third party for any new edition, revised version, sequel and/or development of any nature whether based on this [Work/ Book] and/or not at any time.

R.204

[Name] agrees and undertakes that from [date] until [date] he/she will not give any interview; disclose any information; agree to be filmed for any television programme and/or recorded for any radio series and/or have any images taken and/or supply any photographs and/or engage in any discussions by mobile and/or over the internet with any person, firm, company and/or business including but not limited to newspapers, radio, television, news agencies, media companies and/or otherwise on the subject of [specify topic]. That [Name] accepts that he/she has agreed a fee to remain silent for that period while the [Enterprise] markets and sells the [Podcast/Film/Book].

R.205

The [Publisher/Distributor] agrees and accepts that it has no rights and/or claim and/or option over any subsequent work by the [Author] whether based on the same subject or not including any new edition. That the [Publisher/ Distributor] shall not be entitled to prevent and/or restrict the [Author] being employed, engaged as a consultant and/or commissioned by any other publisher and/or distributor in any media, country and/or language.

R.206

The [Company] agrees that this agreement is not in any way exclusive and the [Supplier] shall be entitled to reproduce, offer, supply, sell, loan, hire and/ or otherwise exploit the [Product/Service] at any time to any third parties.

R.207

Where the [Supplier] intends to supply the [Product/Service] to a direct competitor of the [Company] whether a website business, mail order, wholesale distributor and/or otherwise. The [Supplier] shall notify the [Company] of its intentions and the [Company] shall have the right if it so chooses to terminate this agreement with [number] months' notice and shall only be liable to pay for any sums due to the date of termination.

R.208

The [Distributor] is not to use the information obtained under this agreement concerning the products and/or the market and/or the business and/or staff of the [Company] to entice, poach and/or solicit employees, agents, suppliers and/or customers of the [Company]. The [Distributor] agrees and undertakes not to disclose any information and/or data to any third party which is not available to members of the public which has been obtained by the [Distributor] directly from the [Company] during the course of this agreement.

R.209

The [Supplier] agrees and undertakes not to supply and/or distribute the [Product] to retail shops and supermarkets and/or wholesale outlets in the area of [specify place] until after [date].

R.210

The [Executive] agrees that he/she shall not without the prior written consent of the [Company] for a period of [three] months after the termination of this agreement be employed by and/or offer consultancy advice to any business in the field of [subject matter] which is a direct competitor of the [Company]. After that period has expired no further restrictions shall apply.

R.211

[Name] agrees and undertakes that he/she will not during the existence and continuation of this agreement without the prior written consent of the [Company]:

1.1 enter into any agreement to promote and/or take part in any way with commercial advertising, competitions, quizzes, lotteries, gambling and/or betting and/or product endorsements on television, radio, over the internet and/or any telecommunication system on blogs, podcasts, websites, apps and/or in any other material and/or computer software and/or electronic games; and/or

1.2 agree to make any endorsement, public statement, speech, presentation and/or to be filmed and/or to be recorded and/or take part in any interview and/or programme and/or to write any article and/or book and/or any script and/or to supply any image and/or video.

R.212

The [Artist] undertakes that where he/she intends to enter into an agreement with a third party for exploitation of any lyrics, musical works, sound recordings and/or other material which he/she owns and/or controls during the Term of this Agreement. That the [Artist] shall consider whether to allow the [Company] to have the opportunity to make a better offer in each case. There shall be no obligation on the [Artist] to do so and/or to inform the [Company] of that decision.

R.213

The [Artist] agrees and undertakes that where he/she has recorded any musical work, lyrics and/or other material with the [Company]. That the [Company] shall have an exclusive period of [one] year where the [Artist] shall not record the same musical work, lyrics and/or other material with a third party. After the expiry of that period the [Artist] shall not be bound by this clause regardless of whether the recorded material has been exploited by the [Company] or not.

R.214

The [Artist] agrees that where the [Company] has released a new [format] to the public which contains new material written and/or composed by the [Artist]. That the [Company] shall have an exclusive period in which such new material shall not be licensed for exploitation to a third party by the [Artist] of [six] months which shall commence of the date of release to the public of any such new material. After that time no restrictions shall apply and the new material may be adapted for product promotion and/or other commercial exploitation by the [Artist].

R.215

The [Presenter] agrees and undertakes not to enter into any agreement and/or to provide services for any cable, satellite, terrestrial and/or digital television and/or radio and/or telecommunications company and/or other media company and/or arrange to be filmed and/or recorded for any online digital blog, podcast, service and/or programme. Nor shall the [Presenter] wear any products which have been donated as gifts in return for promotional work by the [Presenter] and/or endorse any product and/or service whether paid for or not and/or contribute to any material to be used in marketing by any third party. These restrictions shall apply from [date to [date]. The [Presenter] shall be obliged to make any requests for exemptions to the [Company] on each occasion.

R.216

The [Presenter] agrees that he/she shall not engage in any sport and/or other hazardous and/or dangerous activity which would pose a real risk of personal injury to the [Presenter]. The [Presenter] agrees that he /she is to minimise and avoid unnecessary potential risks which could result in the [Presenter] not being available to complete the agreed work schedule.

R.217

[Name] shall not at any time either on his/her own account and/or jointly with and/or for any other person, firm and/or company solicit, interfere with and/or endeavour to entice away from the [Company] any person, firm, charity, sponsor and/or business who at any time during the Term of this Agreement and up to [one] year thereafter were employees, licensees, suppliers, advertisers, sponsors, partners, agents and/or consultants of the [Company] and/or any subsidiary company.

R.218

1.1 The [Consultant] undertakes to the [Company] that he/she shall not from [date] to [date] disclose and/or supply any data, documents, software, emails, images, plans, budgets, strategies, films, sound recordings and/or other material relating to the [Company] to a third party. The [Consultant] agrees that the [Company] must authorise any disclosure to a third party of any material which is not already available to the public.

1.2 The [Consultant] also agrees to follow any directions issued by the [Company] and to abide by any guidelines and/or codes of practice and/or policies which the [Company] may decide to impose at any time.

R.219

[Name] agrees and undertakes that he/she shall not after the end of this agreement for any reason supply confidential client information to a third party and/or attempt to entice other employees to leave the [Company] and to join any new business that [Name] has either set up and/or joined. This clause shall apply for a period of [six] months after the end of the agreement.

R.220

The [Artist] agrees that he/she has concluded an exclusive agreement for all the work and material that he/she has created in the past and/or will create in the future until [date]. This work shall include all lyrics, images, sound recordings, musical works, films, videos, podcasts, biographical notes and diaries, articles and/or any other material of any nature in any media and/or format. During the existence of this agreement the [Artist] shall not supply any original material and/or any copies to third parties without the prior authority of the [Company].

R.221

The [Distributor] confirms that the [Artist] is entitled to make contributions of a charitable nature to any third party event. Provided that the [Artist] gives the [Distributor] reasonable notice of the event, and that no such engagement shall take precedence over obligations of the [Artist] under this agreement.

R.222

The [Artist] agrees that for a period of [number] [months/years] that he/she will not enter into any arrangement and/or agreement with any third party for the commercial production and/or exploitation of a film, video, podcast, audio file, electronic download, record, CD and/or other format which incorporates any lyrics and/or musical work which the [Artist] has in his/her performances which have been recorded and exploited by the [Company].This restriction shall not apply after [date]. Nor shall this restriction apply to any material which has not been recorded by the [Artist] with the [Company].

R.223

The [Company] agrees that [Name] has the following prior commitments and agreements which he/she is entitled to carry out during the Term of this Agreement: [specify details and list]

R.224

The [Company] agrees that [Name] shall be entitled during the Term of this Agreement to provide his/her services and work to any third party provided that it is not for the advertisement, promotion and endorsement of a product and/or service in the category of [specify type] in [country].

R.225

The [Company] acknowledges that it does not have the right to restrict the services and/or work and/or endorsements that the [Contributor] shall be entitled to provide to a third party.

R.226

The [Agent] agrees that this agreement only relates exclusively to the manuscript supplied by the [Author and the exploitation of the proposed [Work/Book] in [hardback/paperback/electronic format]. That the [Agent] does not have the right to exploit any merchandising, adaptation and/or further sequel and/or any other subsequent material created by the [Author].

R.227

The [Sportsperson] undertakes that he/she has not and/or will not enter any other sponsorship, endorsement, promotion, marketing, product placement and/or any other type of agreement with any third party from [date] to [date]. That for a period of [number] months from [date] the [Sponsor] and the

[Sponsor's] products and/or services shall be the exclusive sponsorship brand used by the [Sportsperson] in his/her professional life. This clause shall not apply to any family related event.

R.228
The [Sportsperson] agrees and undertakes not to enter into any arrangement and/or agreement to market, promote, endorse and/or wear the products of the following global companies for the duration of the Sponsorship Period: [specify details and list]

R.229
[Name] agrees not to appear in any commercial, advertisement, podcast, film, video, sound recording and/or otherwise for any third party to market a service which directly and/or indirectly competes with the [Company's] service in any part of the world for a period of [number] months from [date].

R.230
This agreement does not and shall not entitle the [Sponsor] to prevent, restrict and/or interfere with the [Athlete] entering into any other arrangement and/or contract with any other firm, person and/or business and/or to be sponsored by and/or to endorse any goods and/or services of any nature in any country at any time.

R.231
The [Company] agrees and undertakes not to enter into any contract with and/or to authorise the sale, supply, and/or distribution of another product which is a [specify type] at the [Event]. This clause shall not apply after [date].

R.232
The [Company] agrees and undertakes not to authorise, permit and/or enter into any agreement for any product which is in the field of [specify type of product and market] to be used in any films, videos, podcasts, advertisements, promotions, signs, banners, sound recordings and/or any other material at the [Event] and/or in any marketing, merchandising and/or other forms of exploitation controlled by the [Company] for the [Event]. This clause shall not apply before [date] and/or after [date].

R.233
The [Company] agrees that it shall not reproduce, publish, supply, market, promote, distribute and/or exploit any work and/or product and/or service in any format and/or medium which is based upon and/or derives from the [Project] and/or any part including the title at any time. The [Company] agrees if it does so that this shall be considered a breach of this agreement.

R.234

The [Consultant] agrees and undertakes to the [Institute/Enterprise] that he/ she will not without the prior written consent of the [Institute/Enterprise] for a period of [six] months from [date] enter into an agreement with and/or be engaged by and/or carry out work for any of the following parties: [specify and list companies].

R.235

The [Institute/Charity] agrees and undertakes that this agreement does not confer any right on the [Institute/Charity] to restrict, prohibit and/or prevent the [Supplier] carrying out any work and/or services for any other person, company or otherwise.

R.236

1.1 The [Company] acknowledges and agrees that [Name] shall be entitled during the Term of this Agreement to provide his/her services to any third party subject to the prior approval of the [Company] which shall not be unreasonably withheld and/or delayed. Provided that [Name] will arrange his/her commitments so that those to a third party shall not take precedence over the obligations of [Name] to the [Company] under this agreement.

1.2 The [Company] acknowledges that [Name] is already committed and entitled to carry out the following work during the Term of this Agreement: [specify detail and list],

R.237

This agreement is not exclusive and there are no constraints imposed by the [Company] in respect of the supply of work, services and/or products by [Name] to any third party.

R.238

Any restrictions imposed on [Name] under this agreement shall end on [date] and shall only apply in [country].

R.239

1.1 The [Company] acknowledges that it has no right to restrict and/or prevent [Name] from carrying on and/or fulfilling his/her [profession/ career] as a [specify role/expertise].

1.2 That the contribution and involvement of [Name] in the [Project] does not in any way impose any future restrictions as to the nature of their work.

1.3 The [Company] accepts that none of the proposals, data, information and/or other material relating to the [Project] is confidential. That [Name] shall not be in breach of this agreement if any such proposals, data, information and/or material is disclosed to a third party at any time.

RIGHTS

Film, Television and Video

R.240
'The DVD and Video Rights' shall mean:

1.1 the exclusive right to transfer, manufacture, duplicate, supply, distribute, sale, rent, hire and/or make available under a subscription service and/or other payment arrangement and/or otherwise exploit the [Film/Series] including the soundtrack by means of electronic reproduction in the form of a disk and/or magnetic tape which consists of a sequence of visual images (both with and/or without sound) which are capable of being shown as a moving picture via a television and DVD/video player and/or some other portable device and/or a computer, laptop and/or other gadget.

1.2 This right shall not include any form of electronic material and/or reproduction and/or distribution in respect of the internet, any website and/or app and/or download and/or any transmission and/or broadcast by means of any telecommunication system for reception by mobile phone and/or any other device and/or gadget.

1.3 This right shall include the following formats: cassettes, cartridges, reel to reel, CD-Roms and disks but not storage and retrieval devices and/or any archive playback and/or catch up service.

1.4 This right is limited to use by private domestic residences only. It is not granted in respect of educational establishments, universities, vocational and/or sports colleges. Any use related to any charity, religion, club and/or commercial exploitation is excluded. There is no right to transmit material on any closed circuit television system to multiple persons.

1.5 The rights may be sub-licensed to any third party to carry out and do the things set out in 1.1. Provided that full responsibility continues to be accepted for the terms of the agreement and that there is an acceptance of total liability for all the acts, omissions and/or defaults of the third party.

R.241

'The Video Rights' shall mean the right to transfer, manufacture and duplicate the [Film/Series] by means of electronic reproduction in the form of any disk and/or magnetic tape which consists of a sequence of visual images with and/or without sound and/or with subtitles which is capable of being shown as a moving picture and to sell, rent, supply, hire, distribute and have distributed the [Series] in any such form for use by the public in a residential private home. It shall not include any form of exploitation over the internet and/or by means of any telecommunication system to any computer, laptop, mobile and/or other gadget and/or any form of video on demand service in electronic form. It shall not include any commercial business, charity, club, educational establishment, sports organisations and/or the right to supply to multiple occupants at the same time.

R.242

'The DVD and Video Rights' shall mean:

1.1 The right to transfer, manufacture, reproduce, supply, distribute, rent and sell the [Film/Series/Images/Sound Recordings] by means of electronic reproduction in the form of any disk and/or magnetic tape which consists of a sequence of visual images with and/or without sound capable of being viewed as a moving picture by means of a playback device. The playback device may be a separate device to be used in conjunction with the television set and/or gadget and/or an integral part of the television set, computer and/or portable device. It shall not apply to any form of exploitation over the internet and/or by means of any telecommunication system and/or any pay and/or subscription service in electronic form which can be downloaded and/or accessed as an archive playback. The authorisation and right only extends to the [Film/Series/Images/Sound Recording] being played and displayed on a screen which is for private home use only by the public and not for any commercial use and/or any non-theatric form of exploitation to schools, universities and/or clubs.

1.2 There shall also be the right to authorise and grant the right to any third party to carry out and do the things set out in 1.1. Provided that the main party who has authorised the third party to carry out the work accepts that they cannot remove liability. That the main party shall at all times remain responsible and liable for all the acts, omissions and/or defaults of the third party.

R.243

'The DVD and Disc Rights' shall mean the sole and exclusive right in the [Territory/country/world] during the [Licence Period/Term of the Agreement] to manufacture, reproduce, supply, distribute, rent and/or sell the complete

[Film/Series] in the form of discs and DVDs by means of electronic reproduction in the form of any disc which consists of a sequence of visual images with sound capable of being viewed on a screen as a moving picture by means of a playback device in conjunction with a television set, computer, and/or portable gadget for private home use only by the public.

R.244

'The Video, DVD and Disc Rights' shall mean:

1.1 The [exclusive/non-exclusive] right to transfer, manufacture, duplicate, reproduce, sell, rent, supply, hire, distribute and/or have distributed the [Film/Series] whether for home use only and/or by educational, cultural, religious and/or social groups and/or otherwise and/or to commercial companies and businesses including hotels, airlines, ships by means of electronic and/or mechanical reproduction [whether in existence now or created in the future] in any form of disk, magnetic tape or other method so that the [Film/Series] is shown as a moving image (with or without sound but not sound on its own) intended for reproduction on copies which are inserted in and/or used in conjunction with a machine or other apparatus to be played on a television, computer and/or other visual screen by a video recorder, DVD player or some other machine whether the two are distinct or one item including a videocassette, disc, disk, laser, reel to reel, DVD and/or CD-Rom.

1.2 This shall not include by means of the internet, and/or as a download from any platform, website and/or app and/or by wifi and/or any other electronic means and/or through any telecommunication system for reception by any television, computer, laptop and/or mobile and/or other device and/or gadget.

1.3 Nor shall it include the right to make any translation and/or sub-titled version.

1.4 The right shall only continue for the Licence Period granted by the [Licensor] stated in the agreement.

1.5 The right shall only cover the Territory granted by the [Licensor] stated in the agreement.

R.245

'The DVD and Disc Rights' shall be defined as the right to reproduce, manufacture, supply, hire, rent, distribute, sub-license, and/or to authorise any third party to do any of those things in respect of the [Film/Work/Sound Recordings] in the form of DVDs, CD-Roms, discs and any other form of mechanical reproduction which involves the replication of the material on a disc which is slotted into a machine and/or equipment of any type to be used in conjunction with a playback device so that the moving image and/or audio recording is played on the screen. The playback device shall include a television, computer, laptop and portable gadget. It shall not include any form of broadcast and/or transmission and/or communication through terrestrial, cable and/or satellite television and/or by means of the internet and/or any website, app and/or download and/or any telecommunication system and/or any electronic method and/or any storage and/or retrieval system and/or any other means of exploitation and/or adaptation whether in existence now and/or created in the future.

R.246
'The Non-Theatric Rights' shall mean the right to exhibit the [Film/Series] in the [Territory/country/area] during the Licence Period to non-theatric audiences who are not charged to view and/or hear the [Film/Series] but for whom the viewing may be included as part of an educational and/or entertainment service and which shall include the following categories of audiences:

1.1 Educational institutions such as schools, universities, colleges.

1.2 Educational and training classes and meetings held by companies and/or other non-educational bodies.

1.3 Clubs and/or other organisations of an educational, cultural, charitable or social nature; film societies and drama groups.

1.4 Prisons, military barracks, museums and hospitals.

1.5 Closed circuit television; an enclosed wired system which is relayed to an audience in a confined area such as hotels, hovercraft, trains, oil rigs, ships and aeroplanes.

R.247
'The Non-Theatric Rights' shall be defined as the sole and exclusive right in the [Territory/country/area] for the duration of the [Licence Period/Term of the Agreement] to license and/or otherwise exploit the [Film/Series] including the soundtrack in [format] by means of sale, hire, lease, licence and/or by means of the use of an agent and/or distributor and/or to authorise the exhibition of the [Film/Series] [in all formats and by means of all technologies which may be now in existence now and/or developed at a later date] for audiences for which no charge is made to educational and social institutions, schools, public libraries, churches, universities, dormitories, halls of residence, churches, vocational, training and evening programme colleges, museums, hospitals, prisons, summer camps, hotels, private clubs, dance, sports and/ or other clubs and/or organisations of any educational, cultural, religious, charitable and/or social nature; drama groups, film societies and/or

professional associations. It shall not include exhibition of the [Film/Series] in theatres, arenas, cinemas and/or outdoors to which the general public is invited subject to payment of an admission fee.

R.248

'The Non-Theatric Rights' shall be defined as:

1.1 The exclusive right to authorise and/or license, supply, hire and/or sell the exhibition of the [DVD/format] of the [Film/Series] in [language] to non-paying audiences in business and commercial industries and organisations of an educational, cultural, religious, charitable and social nature including but not limited to, schools, churches, evening institutions, museums, hospitals, prisons, summer camps, drama groups, film societies, professional associations, public libraries, colleges and universities, hotels, private clubs and aeroplanes.

1.2 This shall not include the right to make available other formats of the [Film/Series] and/or to make any translation and/or adaptation.

R.249

1.1 The [Licensee] accepts and agrees that it has not been granted any rights to exploit the [Film/Series] and/or any associated soundtrack and/or parts by means of the internet, any website, app, download and/or platform and/or by any electronic method of communication and/or transmission and/or through any telecommunication system and/or via any text messaging, emojis and/or otherwise. All rights not specifically granted are reserved by and belong to the [Licensor].

1.2 That this exclusion in 1.1 shall also apply to any marketing, promotional and advertising material. No part of the [Film/Series] and/or the associated soundtrack may be used on any part of the internet and/or any telecommunication system and/or otherwise in electronic form for any reason.

R.250

1.1 In consideration of the Licence Fee and the [Licensor's Royalties] to be paid under this agreement by the [Licensee]. The [Licensor] grants the [Licensee] the exclusive right from [date] to [date] to manufacture and have manufactured by a third party [Videos/DVDs/Discs] containing the [Film/Series] including the soundtrack in [language] and/or any other translation and/or sub-titled version in any part of the world.

1.2 The [Licensor] confirms that the right granted in 1.1 shall include the right of the [Licensee] to sell, lease, hire, license, sub-license, distribute, promote, market and/or exhibit the [Videos/DVDs/Discs] of the [Film/Series] including the soundtrack and/or any parts.

1.3 The [Licensee] may authorise any third party to carry out any of the matters in 1.1 and 1.2 provided that the [Licensee] remains liable for the actions, errors and defaults of such third party.

1.4 No rights are granted by the [Licensor] to authorise the use of such [Videos/DVDs/Discs] for viewing in any place where an admission fee is charged and/or for theatrical exhibition and/or any non-theatric purpose.

1.5 No rights are granted by the [Licensor] in respect of the terrestrial, cable, satellite television rights and/or for any digital and/or electronic means of exploitation over the internet and/or by means of any telecommunication system, wifi and/or any messaging and/or video and/or film service and/or as a download from any platform, app and/or website.

1.6 The only exception to 1.5 shall be that the [Licensee] shall also have the right to use the same section of [number] seconds of the [Film/Series] entirely for the purpose of advertising and/or promoting the [Videos/DVD/Discs].

1.7 In addition at any trade exhibition and/or marketing event the [Licensee] may exhibit and play the same section of [number] seconds of the [Film/Series].

R.251

In consideration of the Advance and the [Licensor's] Royalties, the [Licensor] grants to the [Licensee] the sole and exclusive [Video, DVD and Disc Rights] in the [Film/Series] including the soundtrack and/or parts throughout the [Territory/country/area] for the duration of the Licence Period.

R.252

In consideration of the Assignment Fee the [Assignor] assigns to the [Assignee] all present [Video, DVD and the Non-Theatric Rights] in the [Film/Series] and/or parts in [language] throughout the [Territory/world] for the full period of the copyright and any extensions and/or renewals [and in perpetuity].

R.253

In consideration of the Assignment Fee the [Assignor] assigns to the [Assignee] all present and future copyright and all intellectual property rights and any other rights in all media whether in existence now and/or created in the future in the [Images/Sound Recordings/Maps] and/or parts including any associated title throughout the [Territory/world] for all the period of copyright and any extensions and renewals and forever. The assignment shall include but not be limited to cable, satellite and terrestrial television, theatric and non-theatric rights, analogue and digital radio, the internet, podcasts, websites, apps; any form of telecommunication system and/or reception by any means, and all forms of publication in books, magazines and/or newspapers, merchandising and any adaptation, translation and/or other form of exploitation and the right to authorise any third party to exercise and/or use such rights.

R.254
In consideration of the Budget the [Assignor] assigns the present and future copyright to the [Assignee] of the sole and exclusive [Video, DVD and Disc Rights] in the [Series] including the soundtrack in [language] throughout the [country/Territory/area] from [date] for the full period of copyright and any extensions and/or renewals.

R.255
Subject to clause [–] the [Assignor] and the [Assignee] both agree that they shall hold joint present and future copyright and all other rights in the [Series] including the soundtrack and/or parts in all media (except for such rights as may be held and/or licensed by any third party) whether in existence now or created in the future throughout the [country/Territory/world/universe] for the full period of copyright and any extensions and/or renewals [and forever without limit of time].

R.256

1.1   The [Licensor] grants a licence to the [Licensee] in respect of the sole and exclusive [DVD/Video/Disc Rights] and the right to manufacture, sell, rent, hire, supply and distribute [DVDs/Discs/Units] which reproduce the [Film] in its entirety in the exact form in which it is delivered in [format] and without any editing throughout the [Territory/world] in [language] from [date] to [date].

1.2   The method of exploitation in 1.1 shall include by wholesale, retail, mail order, under a subscription delivery service and/or direct marketing. It shall also include the right to authorise third parties to perform and exercise the rights.

1.3   The [Licensee] may incorporate [one] extract of less than [number] minutes of the [Film] with any other films reproduced on DVDs, discs or other units as a trailer and/or advertisement before and/or after other films. Provided that the other films are categorised and appear as comparable in terms of age and content and the extracts are only used to promote and advertise the [Film]. No royalties shall be due to the [Licensor] in respect of reproduction of the parts of the [Film] for the purpose of trailers, advertising and promotion of [Film].

1.4 The Licensee shall not have the right to commission and produce dubbed and/or sub-titled versions of the [Film] in other languages.

R.257

The [Disc/Unit/Format] of the [Film] is supplied to the [Client] on the basis that the [Client] agrees and undertakes that:

1.1 It shall be used by the [Client] for private and/or domestic residential purposes only and that no charge shall be made for viewing the [Film].

1.2 The [Client] will not make any copies and/or store any copies on any computer and/or other gadget and/or distribute and/or supply a copy to a third party and/or upload it to any website, app and/or platform. Nor shall the [Client] make any assertion of ownership of the copyright and/or any other rights.

1.3 The [Client] shall not arrange any exhibition of the [Film] to an audience whether for a club, charity, to students in a school and/or as part of a university course and/or to raise funds for any other social enterprise.

R.258

The [Licensee] agrees that all sub-contracts, sub-licences and other arrangements for the exploitation of the [DVD/Video/Disc Rights] shall be subject to prior consultation with and approval of the [Licensor]. The [Licensor] undertakes that such approval shall not be unreasonably withheld and/or delayed.

R.259

The [Licensor] grants a non-exclusive licence to the [Licensee] to record the [Musical Works] in synchronisation with the soundtrack of the [Film] and to manufacture, distribute, sell, hire and/or supply [DVDs/Units/Format] reproducing the [Musical Works] synchronised with the [Film] throughout the [Territory/world] for the Licence Period.

R.260

The [Distributor] grants the [Exhibitor] a licence for the non-commercial exhibition of the [Film] on [date] for [one] showing at the [venue] provided that:

1.1 The [Film] may not be exhibited to the general public and a charge made for entry.

1.2 The exhibition may not be advertised to the general public.

1.3 No admission charges or other consideration may be requested of the members of the audience whether or not such charge or consideration relates to the exhibition of the [Film].

1.4 The [Film] must be exhibited in full as supplied including copyright notices, credits, titles, trade marks, and soundtrack.

1.5 The [Exhibitor] shall ensure that any other licence necessary for the performance of the [Film] notified by the [Distributor] is obtained and shall be paid for by the [Exhibitor].

1.6 The [Exhibitor] shall pay the [Distributor] a licence fee of [number/currency] and an administration fee of [number/currency]. In addition the [Exhibitor] shall pay for the cost of reproduction of the master material of the [Film] and all delivery costs that may be incurred. After completion of the exhibition the [Exhibitor] agrees to return the copy of the master material of the [Film] to the [Distributor] at the [Exhibitors'] cost.

R.261
The [Licensee] shall be entitled to use and permit the use of not more than [three] minutes of different extracts of the [Film] in each case for the purpose of trade exhibitions and/or international fairs and/or promotional tours and/or for background displays to appearances of any of the lead characters to promote and advertise the [Film].

R.262
The [Licensee] shall be entitled to incorporate not more than [specify duration] of the [Film] in each case on [DVDs/Units/Format] which also includes other films in whole and/or part for the purpose of promotion of the [DVDs/Units/Format] of the [Film]. Provided that the other films shall not contain any content of any nature which could be construed as offensive, obscene and/or which are not classified in the same viewing bracket as the [Film].

R.263
The [Licensee] agrees that the following rights are specifically excluded from this agreement and are retained by the [Licensor]:

1.1 [list excluded rights].

1.2 [list excluded languages/right to sub-title/dub].

1.3 There is no right to use extracts for any reason.

1.4 There is no right to edit, delete and/or adapt material.

1.5 There is no right to authorise a third party to fulfil the terms of the agreement.

1.6 The agreement does not apply to any country and/or territorial waters outside [specify area] marked on the plan in Appendix A.

1.7 There is no right to authorise the use of the [Work/Material] as part of an art installation, video, film, blog, podcast and/or news report.

R.264

This agreement does not cover future developments which may be created after the date of this agreement for the purpose of viewing films, sound recordings, images and/or other material for residential home use and/or commercial purposes. Any new apparatus and/or method of reproduction shall enable the [Licensor] to grant a new licence to any third party regardless of whether the new apparatus and/or method of reproduction directly competes with the market covered by this licence.

R.265

This licence agreement does not grant any right to the [Licensee] to use, transmit, broadcast, supply and/or exploit the [Film] and/or parts in respect of over the air terrestrial, cable, and/or satellite television and/or radio and/or by means of any telecommunication system, wifi and/or the internet and/or in any electronic form which can be accessed by a computer, laptop, mobile phone and/or any other gadget and/or to be downloaded and/or stored and/or retrieved and played back as catch up from any website, app and/or platform.

R.266

'Video on Demand' shall be defined as the right of the [Company] to supply and distribute on a non-exclusive basis copies of the [Films] from the [website/platform/archive library] known as [specify details] to members of the public for a fixed period of time for a fixed fee which is payable in advance. The members of the public shall be entitled to view the [Films] on any television, laptop, mobile telephone and/or any other device which is accessible with the format of the [Films].

R.267

'SVOD' shall be defined as subscription video on demand service by which the public can access and view a film and/or other material from an app, website and/or platform over the internet and/or via a telecommunication system to any television, computer, laptop, mobile watch, gadget and/or other device under a monthly and/or yearly payment scheme.

R.268

1.1 In consideration of the payment of the Advance Fee in clause [–] and the royalties in clause [–]. The [Licensor] grants the [Licensee] the non-exclusive subscription video on demand rights for the [Film/

Series] and/or parts in the [Territory/world] from the [Channel/Playback Archive/Website] known as: [specify name/reference].

1.2 The term in 1.1 shall be for the Licence Period in clause [–] and/or until such time as the agreement is terminated.

1.3 This right shall not apply to any other third party and/or website and/or platform whether through a parent and/or associated company or not.

1.4 This licence shall entitle the [Licensee] to supply an electronic format version of the [Film/Series] to the public on a monthly and/or yearly subscription fee basis for the Licence Period. There shall be no limitation on the number of viewings by any person during any such period.

1.5 This licence does not apply to any other form of exploitation including mechanical reproduction. Members of the public may include any person at a business but this agreement is primarily aimed at residential home viewing but not any club and/or viewings in large groups and/or where an additional charge is made. All other rights are reserved by the [Licensor].

R.269

1.1 It is accepted by the [Licensor] that the members of the public purchasing the [Films] under any subscription arrangement may be located in any country in the world.

1.2 The [Licensee] agrees and accepts that there are no rights to edit the [Films] and/or to sub-license any rights to any commercial, charitable and/or educational establishments including universities, care homes or clubs in any country for viewing by groups of people except in private residential homes.

R.270

[Name] grants the [Company] the non-exclusive right to reproduce a copy of the [Image/Logo/Artwork] on the cover of the [DVD/Disc/Format] of the [Film] as part of the packaging for supply, sales and distribution in [country] from [date] to [date]. Provided that the [Company] does not distort and/or mutilate the [Image/Logo/Artwork] and provides a proof sample for approval and pays the sum of [number/currency] by [date]. Together with a payment in advance thereafter of [number/currency] for every six calendar month period and/or part that the [Company] wishes to exploit the rights on the cover of the [DVD/Disc/Format].

R.271

'The Terrestrial Television Rights' shall mean the right to broadcast the [Film] including the synchronised soundtrack and/or parts on conventional VHF and UHF broadcast television transmitted by means of over the air signals from terrestrially based transmitters including multiplex services, free, pay per view, subscription, licence, rental and on demand for general reception. It shall specifically exclude cable television, digital and satellite television and/or any form of exploitation which uses a telecommunication system and/or wifi and/or any exploitation in electronic form over the internet and/or any other method of communication.

R.272

'The Standard Television Rights' shall be defined as:

1.1   the sole and exclusive right in the [Territory/country] during the Licence Period to broadcast and/or transmit whether by digital and/or analogue systems the [Film/Series] by way of conventional free terrestrial television transmitted by means of over-the-air television signals and to authorise others to do any such things.

1.2   It shall not include any service which requires a regular subscription payment except a nominal licence fee. It may require the purchase of an adapted reception box and/or television.

1.3   It shall specifically exclude cable and satellite television rights and/ or exploitation over the internet in electronic form and/or any archive playback and/or catch up service over the internet and/or any transmission by means of a telecommunication system for reception by mobile, computer and/or some other gadget and/or device.

R.273

'The Terrestrial Television Rights' shall be defined as the sole and exclusive right to broadcast the [Film] including the soundtrack but excluding any parts except agreed promotional trailers by means of over the air signals from terrestrially based transmitters for general reception by the public by television. Whether there is a specially adapted reception device or not and it may be by any method including free, subscription, rental, under a licence, on demand and/or otherwise encrypted or not. The rights do not include any method of exploitation by cable and/or satellite and/or over the internet in electronic form and/or through any telecommunication and/or wifi for reception by computer, laptop, watch and/or other gadget and/or device.

R.274

'The Cable Television Rights' shall be defined as:

1.1   The [exclusive/non-exclusive] right to transmit and/or to supply, distribute and deliver the [Film/Series] including the accompanying soundtrack and/or parts as and/or in conjunction with a licensed cable operator throughout the [Territory/country/area] for the duration of the

Licence Period by means of basic cable and/or pay cable and/or any other cable system and/or similar technology whether in existence now and/or created in the future. This right shall apply whether it is encoded and/or otherwise distorted and/or free, pay per view, subscription, licence, rental, on-demand, catch up and/or archive access and playback.

1.2   It shall not include terrestrial over the air and/or satellite television rights and/or any form of electronic communication and/or method over the internet and/or any wifi and/or telecommunication system. There shall be no right to promote and/or advertise the rights in 1.1 in any other format and/or by any other method unless expressly authorised in advance by the [Licensor].

R.275

The Cable Television Rights' shall be defined as:

1.1   The [non-exclusive] right to transmit the [Film/Series] including the soundtrack on the [Channel] known as [specify name/reference] which is operated by the [Licensee] from [date] to date]. There shall be a limit of [number] transmissions in total. When completed the licence shall expire if earlier than [date].

1.2   There is no right to transfer and/or assign this licence to a third party.

1.3   All other rights are expressly reserved by the [Licensor] and may not be exploited by the [Licensee].

1.4   There is no right granted to make any translation and/or make any adaptation and/or to edit the [Film/Series] and/or to authorise any merchandising and/or any other form of exploitation.

R.276
'The Satellite Rights' shall mean:

1.1   The [sole and exclusive] right to transmit the [Film/Programme] including the soundtrack [and/or parts] by means of one or more satellites so that the footprint of the satellite transmission is principally aimed at the authorised [Territory/country/world]. This right shall apply whether the transmission is encrypted or not and regardless of the method of payment including free, pay per view, subscription, licence, rental, on demand, and catch up playback and/or archive playback.

1.2   Reception may be by a range of devices including but not limited to: computer, laptop and television.

1.3 There is no right to transfer, sub-license and/or assign this licence to a third party without the prior written approval of the [Licensor].

1.4 All other rights are expressly reserved by the [Licensor] and may not be exploited by the [Licensee].

1.5 There is no right granted to make any translation and/or make any adaptation and/or to edit and/or delete and/or add a new title to the [Film/Series] and/or to authorise and/or reproduce any merchandising and/or promotional material in any other format and/or medium.

R.277

'The Satellite Television Rights' shall be defined as the right to transmit the [Musical Work/Sound Recording] in the [Series] on the [Channel] entitled: [name/reference] and to transmit the [Musical Work/Sound Recording] and/or any parts by means of a satellite where the signals transmitted by the satellite are intended mainly for reception within the [Territory/country].

R.278

'The Satellite Rights' shall mean the right to transmit the [Image/Artwork] by means of a satellite so that the signals transmitted create a footprint [and/or by means of similar technology whether in existence now and/or created in the future] and which can be used for reception via any television, computer, laptop, apparatus, landline and mobile telephone, watch and/or other device and/or apparatus. It may be a free service and/or subscription, pay per view and/or some other method. The service may be encrypted, scrambled and/or otherwise distorted.

R.279

'The Television Rights' shall be defined as:

1.1 The [non-exclusive] right to broadcast and/or transmit and/or supply the [Film/Series] on the [Channel/Website/Platform] known as: [specify exact full name] [reference] on [number] occasions from [date] to [date].

1.2 It shall also include the right to offer and supply the [Film/Series] as part of a catch up and/or playback service for a period of [one] calendar month after the date of each broadcast and/or transmission.

1.3 It shall also include the right to offer the [Film/Series] for viewing by the public as an electronic download either for free, under a subscription service and/or pay per view.

1.4 There is no territorial limitation on the rights and it is accepted that it covers the world. It does not however include the right to exhibit and/or show the [Film/Series] in cinemas, outdoors and/or on airlines and/or trains and/or to schools, educational, charitable and/or social enterprises and/or events regardless of whether it is free and/or an entry fee is charged.

R.280

'The Terrestrial, Cable, Satellite, Internet and Electronic Rights' shall be defined as:

1.1 The right to broadcast the [Film/Series] including the soundtrack and/or parts on conventional VHF and UHF broadcast television transmitted by means of over the air signals from terrestrially based transmitters for general reception by the public and

1.2 The right to transmit and/or to supply, distribute the [Film/Series] including the soundtrack and/or parts as and/or in conjunction with a licensed cable operator by means of basic cable and/or pay cable and/or any other cable system for general reception by the public and

1.3 The right to transmit and/or supply the [Film/Series] including the soundtrack and/or parts by means of one or more satellites [so that the footprint of the satellite transmission is principally aimed at the authorised [Territory/country/world]].

1.4 This shall also include the right to combine any transmission and/or re-transmission and distribution through a combination of cable and/or satellite.

1.5 The right to transmit and/or broadcast and/or supply and/or distribute the [Film/Series] including the soundtrack through any wireless telegraphy, wifi and/or electronic form over the internet and/or any telecommunication system.

1.6 This right shall apply whether such signals and/or communications are encoded, encrypted or not.

1.7 The right shall apply to any method of supply, distribution, streaming, on demand, catch up and/or archive access and/or playback including free, pay per view, subscription, licence, rental and/or otherwise.

1.8 This right shall apply to all similar technology through which these rights may be exercised whether is in existence now and/or created in the future.

1.9 There shall be no limit on the method by which the services to be provided for the exercise of these rights may be promoted and advertised to the public. Provided that no more than [number] minutes in duration in total are used of the [Film/Series] including the soundtrack.

1.10 Reception by the public may be by television, computer, laptop, mobile phone, watch and/or some other portable and/or stationary device and/or gadget.

1.11 All other rights are reserved by the [Licensor].

R.281

'The Television, Radio, Internet, Electronic, DVD and Non-Theatric Rights' shall be defined as:

1.1   The right to broadcast the [Film/Series] including the soundtrack and/or parts on conventional VHF and UHF broadcast television transmitted by means of over the air signals from terrestrially based transmitters for general reception by the public and

1.2   The right to transmit, supply and/or distribute the [Film/Series] including the soundtrack and/or parts as a licensed cable operator by means of basic cable and/or pay cable and/or any other cable system for general reception by the public and

1.3   The right to transmit and/or supply the [Film/Series] including the soundtrack and/or parts by means of one or more satellites so that the footprint of the satellite transmission is principally aimed at the authorised [Territory/country/world].

1.4   This shall also include the right to combine any transmission and/or re-transmission and distribution through a combination of broadcast, cable and/or satellite.

1.5   The right to transmit and/or broadcast and/or supply and/or distribute the [Film/Series] including the soundtrack through any wireless telegraphy, wifi and/or electronic form over the internet and/or any telecommunication system. Whether for free and/or as part of a subscription service and/or as a video on demand service by which the public can access and view a film and/or other material from any app, website and/or platform over the internet and/or via a telecommunication system and/or any other electronic method and/or any storage and/or retrieval system.

1.6   The right to reproduce, manufacture, supply, hire, rent and/or distribute the [Film/Series] including the soundtrack in the form of DVDs and any other form of mechanical reproduction which involves the replication of the material on a disc [and/or other similar format] which is slotted into a machine and/or equipment of any type to be used in conjunction with a playback device so that the moving image and synchronised sound track is played on a screen. The playback device shall include a television, computer, laptop and portable gadget.

1.7 The right to exhibit the [Film/Series] including the soundtrack to non-theatric audiences who are not charged to view and/or hear the [Film/Series] but for whom the viewing may be included as part of an educational and/or entertainment service and which shall include the following categories of audiences: schools, universities, colleges; clubs, film and drama societies and/or other organisations of an educational, cultural, charitable or social nature; prisons, museums, hospitals, hotels, ships and aeroplanes.

1.8 The rights shall apply whether such signals and/or communications are encoded, encrypted or not.

1.9 The rights shall apply to any method of supply, distribution, download, streaming, on demand, catch up and/or archive access and playback and/or method of payment including free, pay per view, subscription, licence, rental and/or otherwise.

1.10 The right shall apply to all similar technology through which these rights may be exercised whether is in existence now and/or created in the future.

1.11 There shall be no limit on the method by which the services to be provided for the exercise of these rights may be promoted and advertised to the public. Provided that no more than [number] minutes in duration in total are used of the [Film/Series] including the soundtrack.

1.12 Reception by the public may be by television, computer, laptop, mobile phone, watch and/or some other portable and/or stationary device and/or gadget.

1.13 The rights may be sub-licensed to and/or exercised by a third party.

1.14 All other rights are reserved by the [Licensor].

R.282

'The Internet, Electronic and Telecommunication Rights' shall be defined as:

1.1 The [exclusive/non-exclusive] right to transmit and/or broadcast and/or supply and/or distribute the [Film/Series] including the soundtrack and/or parts through any wireless telegraphy, wifi and/or by any electronic method and/or form and/or over the internet and/or by means of any telecommunication system and/or any storage and/or retrieval system whether catch up and/or archive playback and/or on demand throughout the [world/universe/galaxy] for the Licence Period.

1.2 There shall be no limit on the number of times the [Film/Series] may be transmitted, streamed, downloaded, accessed and/or used. The rights shall apply but not be limited to any website, app, platform and/or podcast.

1617

1.3 The rights may be for private home residential viewing and/or viewing by a commercial, educational and/or charitable entity.

1.4 The [Licensee] shall also have the right to sub-license the rights and/or parts in the [Film/Series] to any third party and/or to appoint a distributor to exploit the rights.

1.5 The [Licensee] shall be entitled to transfer this agreement to a parent company only.

1.6 The right shall apply to all similar technology through which these rights may be exercised whether is in existence now and/or created in the future.

1.7 No other format and/or rights may be used to advertise, promote and/or market the [Film/Service] except those granted in this agreement.

1.8 The supply and reception of the [Film/Series] through the exercise of the rights shall include but not be limited to: television, computer, laptop, mobile phone, watch and/or some other portable and/or stationary device and/or gadget.

1.9 All other rights are reserved by the [Licensor].

R.283

'The Digital Programme Service Rights' shall mean the [exclusive/non-exclusive] right to broadcast in digital form by means of a multiplex service the [Film/Sound Recording] on no more than [number] occasions on the following Digital Programme Service:

1.1 [specify name of licensed service]

1.2 [licensed operating hours/days/weeks]

1.3 [specify licensed coverage area including map, transmitter sites, grid references, frequencies, transmitter power and polarisation]

1.4 [specify period of authorised licence].

R.284

The Digital Additional Services Rights' shall mean the [exclusive/non-exclusive] right to broadcast in digital form by means of a multiplex system the [Teletext Services/Electronic Programme Guides/Data Services] on the following Digital Programme Service [specify name] and Multiplex System [specify method] for the following period. Start date: [–] End date: [–].

R.285

'The Theatric Rights' shall mean the sole and exclusive right in the [Territory/country/area] during the [Licence Period/Term of the Agreement] to reproduce, distribute and supply the [Films/Series] [which shall include any soundtrack] in [format] in [language] for exhibition to audiences where a charge for admission is made including by way of example cinemas, theatres, concert halls. lecture halls and arenas and to authorise others to do any of such things.

R.286

'The Off-Air Recording Rights' shall mean the right to include the [Programme] in a Licensing Scheme in [country] by [specify organisation] whereby licences are granted to enable the [Programme] to be recorded by and/or on behalf of educational establishments from any broadcast or cable programme service when such recording is for the educational purposes.

R.287

'The Radio Rights' shall be defined as the [analogue/digital] service licensed by [Ofcom/other regulatory body] for [specify frequency] under a licence dated [date of licence] for a radio service known as: [specify name of service] [reference].

R.288

'The Recording Rights' shall mean the right to make any visual and/or sound recordings of the [Event] or any part in any medium including all electronic forms of reproduction whether in existence now or created in the future.

R.289

1.1   In consideration of the Licence Fee the [Licensor] grants to the [Licensee] the sole and exclusive [Terrestrial Television Rights/Cable Television Rights] throughout the [Territory/country] for the duration of the Licence Period in the [Film/Series] including the soundtrack and/or parts.

1.2   The [Licensee] shall be entitled to [number] broadcasts/transmissions of the [Film/Series] within the Licence Period.

1.3   In the event that all the licensed number of transmissions and/or broadcasts shall be completed before the expiry of the Licence Period. Then the agreement shall end earlier after [number] days from the completion of all such transmissions and/or broadcasts,

1.4   The [Licensee] shall have the right to transmit no more than [number] minutes of the [Film/Series] for the purpose of programme announcement, trailing and post transmission comment and/or review in each case without further payment.

1.5   The [Licensor] agrees and undertakes that the [Satellite Rights] in the [Film/Series] will not be exercised by the [Licensor] and/or any third party before [date/time].

R.290

1.1 In consideration of the Licence Fee the [Licensor] grants to the [Licensee] the sole and exclusive [Satellite Television Rights/Satellite Rights] throughout the [Territory/country/world] from [date to [date] and/or until such time as all the authorised transmissions have been completed.

1.2 The [Licensee] shall only be entitled to [number] transmissions of the full length of the [Film].

1.3 The [Licensee] shall be entitled to transmit excerpts of any part of the [Film] for the purpose of programme announcement, promotion and/or trailers without further payment on [specify channels]. Provided that the total aggregate shall not exceed [number] minutes.

1.4 The [Licensor] agrees that where in the [Territory/country/world] the service is retransmitted and/or distributed by a cable operator and/or service after delivery by satellite. That such use shall be permitted on a non-exclusive basis provided that the [Film] is transmitted simultaneously and not as part of a separate transmission by cable service only. No parts of the [Film] may be supplied to any cable operator for promotion and/or advertising of the [Film] by a cable operator and/or on a cable service without the prior authorisation of the [Licensor].

1.5 The [Licensee] undertakes to pay any sums due to any rights management organisation and/or other rightsholder for the exercise of such rights.

R.291
'The Terrestrial, Cable, Satellite, Internet, SVOD, DVD, Theatric and Non-Theatric Rights' shall be defined as:

1.1 The right to broadcast the [Film/Series] including the soundtrack and/or parts on conventional VHF and UHF broadcast television transmitted by means of over the air signals from terrestrially based transmitters for general reception by the public and

1.2 The right to transmit, supply and/or distribute the [Film/Series] including the soundtrack and/or parts as and/or in conjunction with a licensed cable operator by means of basic cable and/or pay cable and/or any other cable system for general reception by the public and

1.3 The right to transmit and/or supply the [Film/Series] including the soundtrack and/or parts by means of one or more satellites [so that the footprint of the satellite transmission is principally aimed at the authorised area, country and/or territory].

1.4 This shall also include the right to combine any transmission and/or re-transmission and distribution through a combination of over the air terrestrial, cable and/or satellite and/or by means of the internet and/or any telecommunication system and/or in any other electronic format.

1.5 The right to transmit and/or broadcast and/or supply and/or distribute the [Film/Series] including the soundtrack and/or parts by any electronic method and/or form over the internet and/or by means of any telecommunication system and/or any storage and/or retrieval system whether catch up and/or archive playback and/or video on demand subscription service.

1.6 There shall be no limit on the number of times the [Film/Series] may be transmitted, streamed, downloaded, accessed, used and/or exploited by means of the authorised rights.

1.7 The rights shall apply but not be limited to any website, app, platform and/or podcast and/or streaming over the internet and/or via a telecommunication system to any television, computer, laptop, mobile watch, gadget and/or other device regardless of whether it is free, pay per view and/or otherwise.

1.8 The right to exploit the theatric rights in the [Film/Series] including the soundtrack and/or parts and to reproduce, distribute and supply the [Films/Series] for exhibition to audiences where a charge for admission is made including by way of example cinemas, theatres, concert halls, lecture halls and arenas and to authorise others to do any of such things.

1.9 The right to exploit and to exhibit the [Film/Series] including the soundtrack to audiences who are not charged to view and/or hear the [Film/Series] but for whom the viewing may be included as part of a training, educational and/or entertainment service and which shall include the following categories of audiences: schools, universities, colleges; clubs, film and drama societies and/or organisations of an educational, cultural, charitable or social nature and/or viewing for training purposes at a commercial entity.

1.10 The right to reproduce, manufacture, supply, hire, rent and/or distribute the [Film/Series] including the soundtrack in the form of DVDs and any other form of mechanical reproduction which involves the replication of the material on a disc and/or other similar format which is slotted into a machine and/or equipment of any type to be used in conjunction with a playback device so that the moving image and synchronised sound track is played on a screen. The playback device shall include a television, computer, laptop and portable gadget.

1.11 The right to sub-licence any of the rights in the [Film/Series] in 1.1 to 1.10 to any third party and/or to appoint an agent, distributor and/or parent company and/or subsidiary to exercise such rights.

1.12 The rights in 1.1 to 1.11 shall apply to all similar technology through which these rights may be exercised whether is in existence now and/or created in the future.

R.292

Printed publications and/or electronic formats of books, radio, toys, merchandising, household, drink and food products, theme parks, electronic and computer software formats of interactive games, stage plays, readings tours, gambling, lotteries and/or any sequel of the whole theme and/or any character are excluded from this agreement.

R.293

The [Author] grants the [Company]:

1.1 The [exclusive/non-exclusive] right to design, create and develop a hardback and/or paperback and/or electronic format book in conjunction with the [Film/Series] which incorporates images and information relating to the [Film/Series]. This right shall start on [date] and end on [date] and shall apply to the licensed [Territory/country/world].

1.2 The formats created in 1.1 may be translated in any language. No name and/or title can be changed without the prior approval of the [Author].

R.294

The [Licensee] agrees that it shall not be entitled to exploit in any manner any sound recordings of the [Musical Work] without the prior consent of the [Licensor] except as specified under the terms of this agreement.

R.295

The [Licensor] undertakes not to license any other third party to broadcast, transmit and/or exploit the [Musical Work] in synchronisation with any film, series, podcast and/or documentary and/or in any other format until after [date].

R.296

1.1 [Name] grants the [Licensee] the non-exclusive right to reproduce exact copies of the [Character/Logo/Artwork] for incorporation in the [Programme/Project] in the following manner: [specify purpose] for transmission on [channel/closed circuit television] [specify name/reference] on [date].

1.2 There are no other rights granted to reproduce and/or exploit the [Character/Logo/Artwork].

1.3 The [Licensee] undertakes not to change, adapt and/or alter the [Character/Logo/Artwork] and/or to mock, distort and/or add any material in conjunction with it which could be deemed offensive and/or derogatory.

R.297

The [Licensee] shall have the right to edit, delete from, distort and/or add any dramatization to the [Material/Film] which it may decide without consultation with the [Licensor]. Provided that it is made clear in the credits that the [Material/Film] has been adapted.

R.298

The [Licensee] shall have the right to:

1.1 make any translation and/or sub-titled and/or dubbed version and/or add any sound recording and/or delete any voices and/or performances.

1.2 add dramatized fictional material.

1.3 change the plot, and/or timeline of any story and/or remove and/or add any new characters.

1.4 add new footage and/or archive material.

1.5 add new and/or pre-recorded interviews.

1.6 complete editorial control for the {Project] and the [Licensor] shall have no right of approval and/or consultation.

1.7 be offered the opportunity to negotiate to acquire rights in any new sequel from the [Licensor]. This is not an option and the [Licensor] may offer the rights at the same time to any third party.

R.299

1.1 In consideration of the [Author's] Royalties the [Author] grants to the [Company] the sole and exclusive right to exercise the [Television Rights/ Video, DVD and Disc Rights/Non-Theatric Rights/Theatric Rights] in the [Film] and/or parts based on the [Author's Work] throughout the [Territory/world] for [Term of the Agreement/the full period of copyright and any extensions and/or renewals/other].

1.2 The [Author] agrees that he/she will not license, authorise any third party to produce any other films, videos, podcasts, recordings, sound recordings, DVDs, discs and/or any other moving visual images and/

or animation and/or any adaptation based on the [Work] of the [Author] and/or any sequel before [date].

R.300

The [Distributor] agrees that:

1.1 No rights are and/or have been granted to the [Distributor] in respect of any sequel and/or any other form of exploitation and/or adaptation.

1.2 There is no right granted to change the title, names and/or locations in the [Work/Material] reproduced in the [Film] and/or to supply the [Film] in any other language except [specify language].

1.3 After the end of the Licence Period the [Distributor] shall not be entitled to exploit the [Film] without further agreement with the [Author].

R.301

1.1 In consideration of the Approved Budget the [Assignor] assigns to the [Assignee] all present and future copyright in respect of the [specify rights] in the [Film] including the soundtrack and parts throughout the [Territory/world] for the duration of the Assignment Period.

1.2 The [Assignee] agrees that after the expiry of the Assignment Period, the [Assignee] shall have no rights in the [Film] and/or part(s) and that all rights assigned under this agreement shall revert to and be vested in the [Assignor].

R.302

1.1 The [Assignor] and the [Assignee] confirm that this assignment document is subject to the existence of the following agreements described and set out in Appendix A which have been concluded by the Assignor [specify list/date/title/subject matter in Appendix A].

1.2 That as far as possible and where permitted all these agreements listed in Appendix A shall be transferred and assigned to the [Assignee]. So that the [Assignor] shall not hold any rights and/or interest except the right to revenue and/or royalties specified under this agreement.

R.303

In consideration of the Approved Budget the [Assignor] assigns to the [Assignee] all present and future copyright and intellectual property rights and any other rights in all media whether in existence now and/or developed in the future including but not limited to the [Terrestrial/Cable/Satellite Television Rights/ the Video, DVD and Disc Rights/the Internet/Electronic/ Telecommunication Rights/Theatric Rights/ the Non-Theatric Rights] in the

[Series] including the soundtrack and/or parts throughout the world and universe for the full period of copyright and any extensions and/or renewals and in perpetuity.

R.304

In consideration if the Advance and the royalties set out in this agreement the [Licensor] grants to the [Licensee]:

1.1 The sole and exclusive right to broadcast, transmit and/or exploit the [Film] including the soundtrack and/or parts through exploitation of the [Terrestrial Television Rights/the Cable Television Rights/Satellite Television Rights] in the [Territory] for the Licence Period.

1.2 The sole and exclusive right to reproduce the [Film] including the soundtrack and/or parts and to sell, rent, supply, distribute and exploit the [Video, DVD and Disc Rights/Theatric Rights/Non-Theatric Rights] in the [Territory] for the Licence Period.

1.3 The [Licensee] shall be entitled at its sole cost to commission and produce dubbed and/or sub-titled versions of the [Film] for exploitation in [specify language] speaking countries in the [Territory] during the Licence Period.

1.4 All other rights of any nature and/or any other format and/or medium are reserved by the [Licensor] whether in existence now and/or created in the future.

R.305

The [Licensee] may broadcast and/or transmit by television and/or in sound only on radio and/or through some other means, gadget and/or device for the purposes of promotion and marketing short sequences of not more than [number] [seconds/minutes] in duration from the [Film] and/or soundtrack. This right shall only apply from [date] to [date] and shall not be permitted on the following media which are specifically excluded: [list excluded media where there are to be no promotions and/or marketing].

R.306

The [Licensor] grants to the [Licensee] the sole and exclusive right to broadcast and/or transmit the [Work] on [specify Channel/reference] throughout the [Territory/area] for the duration of the Licence Period. There shall be no limit on the number of broadcasts and/or transmissions.

R.307

1.1 In consideration of the non-returnable Advance and the [Licensor's] Royalties the [Licensor] grants to the [Licensee] the non-exclusive right to broadcast and/or transmit the [Text/Images/Videos] in the [Programme] and to exploit the [specify rights] throughout the [Territory/country] for the Term of this Agreement.

1.2 The [Licensee] shall be entitled to appoint an agent and/or distributor and/or other sub-licensee to exercise such rights subject to the terms of this agreement. Provided that the [Licensee] accepts full responsibility and/or liability for any defaults, errors, omissions and/or failure to pay by such third parties.

R.308

1.1 The [Licensor] grants to the [Licensee] the sole and exclusive right to broadcast and/or transmit the [Film] on channel [specify name/reference] throughout [the United Kingdom of Great Britain, Northern Ireland, the Channel Islands and the Isle of Man] and such other locations where there may be simultaneous relay by cable and/or satellite which fall outside the target [footprint/transmission area] for the duration of the Licence Period.

1.2 There shall be no more than [number] broadcasts and/or transmissions in any [one] year period during the Licence Period.

1.3 Provided that the [Licensee] pays the Advance in clause [–] and the annual additional fee of [number/currency] for each year of the licence. Then no other additional sums shall be paid by the [Licensee] except for the cost of any copies of material.

R.309

The [Licensor] agrees to grant the [Company] the following rights provided that the [Company] pays the Licence Fee by [date].

1.1 The exclusive right to transmit and/or broadcast and/or deliver the [Film] in the [Territory/country] by means of exercise of the [Satellite, Cable, and Terrestrial Television Rights] and/or the [Telecommunication Rights] and/or the right to receive and/or download the [Film] through a catch up library and/or archive service associated with the [Company] for the Licence Period. The method of payment shall include but not be limited to free, subscription, pay on demand and/or otherwise. Reception may be via a television, computer, laptop, mobile telephone, tablet, watch and/or some other gadget and/or device whether stationary and/or portable.

1.2 There are only [number] broadcasts and/or transmissions allowed from [date] to [date] by satellite, cable and terrestrial television by the [Company].

1.3 There is no right granted to create and/or license associated merchandising and/or to authorise third parties to use, adapt and/or exploit the [Film] and/or to authorise any associated book in any format.

1.4 Short agreed promotional extracts of the [Film] may be used on the [Company's] website, app and/or on the channel on which the [Company] operates but in no other medium.

R.310

Despite the terms of this agreement there is no obligation on the [Company] to broadcast and/or transmit the [Film]. In the event the [Company] decides not to broadcast and/or transmit the [Film] for any reason the [Licensor] shall still be entitled to retain the Licence Fee and no refund shall be due for that reason.

R.311

The parties agree that the [Licensee] may authorise a third party to include [number] [seconds/minutes] of the [Programme] on their [website/app/platform/news review series] for the purpose of promotion, marketing, award shows and/or reviews without making any charge for its use during the period [date] to [date]. Provided that the following minimum copyright notices and credits are shown on the screen: [specify details] and the content must be removed after [date].

R.312

1.1 The [Licensee] may before the expiry of the Licence Period pay an additional fee of [number/currency] to the [Licensor] in order to extend the Term of the Agreement by a further [number] [months/years].

1.2 In addition the [Licensee] shall have the right to [number] further broadcasts and/or transmissions of the [Series] in accordance with the rights granted under the original agreement.

R.313

The [Licensee] accepts and agrees that:

1.1 There is no option granted by the [Company] in respect of [Work/Book/Script] and/or any character, logo, image and/or other content.

1.2 That there is no right to any sequel and/or any option and/or prior claim of any nature in any medium in respect of such sequel.

1.3 That all rights are reserved unless specifically listed and granted under the agreement. There is no right to adapt the [Work/Book/Script] in any other format and/or by any method unless expressly authorised by the [Company].

1.4 There is no right granted to make any trade mark application linked to any fictional name and/or fictional place, image and/or caricature.

1.5 There is no right to register any domain and/or other registered name for any website, app and/or platform and/or for any other name which is similar whether for the title, a fictional character, fictional location, fictional equipment and/or otherwise.

1.6 There is no right granted to register [Work/Book/Script] and/or any part with any rights management organisation and/or other third party.

1.7 There is no right to exercise the rights granted in the [Work/Book/Script] outside the authorised countries and territorial waters.

R.314
The [Company] agrees and undertakes that it shall not [broadcast/transmit] the [Film] and/or parts before [date].

R.315
The [Company] will not broadcast, authorise and/or permit the broadcast and/or transmission and/or exploitation of the [Film] including the soundtrack in [country] until after the [Film] has first been broadcast by the [Licensee] pursuant to this agreement.

R.316
The [Licensee] agrees and undertakes to ensure that the complete [Film] is broadcast and/or transmitted within [number/six] months of the date of this agreement.

R.317

1.1 In consideration of the Licence Fee in clause [–] and the agreed payments in clause [–] the [Licensor] grants the [Distributor] the non-exclusive right to authorise the transmission and/or broadcast of the [Series] by third parties by means of the exercise of the [Television Rights/other] In the [Territory/list countries] from [date] to [date].

1.2 The [Distributor] undertakes that no third party shall be entitled to acquire exclusive rights of any nature.

1.3 The [Distributor] agrees that no sub-licence granted by the [Distributor] shall extend beyond [date].

1.4 The [Distributor] agrees to ensure that all third party sub-licensees do not retain copies of any master material and/or copies at the end of the term of the sub-licence.

1.5   The [Distributor] agrees and undertakes to verify the financial track record of any sub-licensee before concluding any sub-licence.

R.318
The [Author] agrees and accepts that he/she shall not have any right to be consulted and/or to approve the:

1.1   Actors to be appointed to perform the roles for the [Film].

1.2   Choice of music and/or lyrics to be selected and recorded for the soundtrack.

1.3   Draft and/or final edit of the [Film].

1.4   Director and/or film crew.

1.5   The storyline, draft and final script, shooting schedule and/or locations to be used.

R.319
The [Licensee] acknowledges and agrees that the [Licensor] has retained the rights to all forms of hardback and paperback books, audio files, downloads and publications; play outfits and/or costumes for children, household products and merchandising; sponsorship and product placement and/or endorsement by association with gambling, betting and/or lotteries and/or sports businesses and/or organisations and/or individuals and/or any authorisation and/or exploitation of any hologram, theme park, musical, touring event and/or podcasts and all DVD and Disc Rights, Theatric and Non-Theatric Rights.

R.320

1.1   The [Licensee] agrees and undertakes that it shall not appoint any sub-distributors, agents and/or sub-licensees without the prior written approval of the [Licensor] as to the person and/or company and the terms of the agreement to be concluded.

1.2   The [Licensor agrees and undertakes not to unreasonably withhold and/or delay any approval requested by the [Licensee] under this agreement.

R.321
The [Distributor] agrees and accepts that it cannot authorise any third party to exercise and/or fulfil the terms of this agreement except the parent company of the [Distributor].

R.322

The [Licensor] agrees that provided the [Licensee] pays the fixed monthly fee set out in clause [–] for the Term of the Agreement. That no additional royalties and/or other sums shall be due for the exploitation of the rights.

R.323

1.1 In consideration of the Licence Fee and the [Author's] Royalties the [Author] grants to the [Company] the sole and exclusive right to exploit [all Media Rights/other rights] in the [Film] including any soundtrack and/or parts based on the [Author's Work] for the duration of the Licence Period throughout the [Territory/world and universe].

1.2 The [Author] agrees that he/she shall not from the date of this agreement until the expiry of the Licence Period and/or after the termination of this agreement whichever is the earlier exercise and/or license and/or authorise the exploitation in the [Territory/world and universe] in any media of a film, programme, documentary, podcast and/or video and/or other recording in sound and/or vision of any type based on the [Author's Work].

General Business and Commercial

R.324

The [Licensor] agrees that the agreement may be transferred to a parent company and/or a new entity which has been created for that purpose. Provided that the new entity substantially acquires the whole of the previous business and that the main purpose is for a restructuring of the business and not a sell-off and/or other disposal to a third party.

R.325

1.1 The [Licensor] agrees that the [Licensee] shall be entitled to extend the Licence Period for an additional term of [number] [months/years] subject to the payment of [number/currency] by [date].

1.2 The [Licensee] agrees that the payment in 1.1 cannot be set-off and/or recouped against any future payments due to the [Licensor] by the [Licensee].

R.326

In consideration of the option fee of [number/currency] the [Company] agrees to grant the [Distributor] an exclusive option over the sequel to the [Work/Book/Script] by the [Author] on the basis:

1.1 That the option must be exercised by the [Distributor] by [date].

1.2 That the [Distributor] must pay an additional further sum of [number/ currency] within [number] months of the payment of the Option Fee to the [Company]. That neither sum may be recouped and/or returned.

1.3 The option is for the [Distributor] to acquire the same rights and terms as set out in the licence agreement for the first [Work/Book/Script]. Any additional rights shall require an additional advance payment.

R.327

The [Distributor] shall be entitled to add a credit, image and logo in conjunction with the [Work/Image/Project] as follows: [specify details and location].

R.328

1.1 The [Enterprise] agrees and undertakes to transfer and assign all associated trade marks, logos, domain names, slogans, drawings, images and/or musical works, sound recordings, films, videos, publications and/or other material and/or copyright and/or intellectual property rights in the [Service/Product/Work/Character] to [Name] by [date] subject to the terms of this agreement.

1.2 The [Enterprise] agrees to supply original and/or copies of all supporting documentation in respect of 1.1.

1.3 The [Enterprise] also agrees and undertakes to execute and/or sign any relevant documents and/or forms required by [Name] to be completed for the purpose of third parties which confirm such transfer and assignment in 1.1 and the terms of this agreement.

1.4 That the [Enterprise] shall provide a complete list of all organisations and/or bodies and/or archives and/or libraries with which any rights are recorded and/or registered and/or for which an application is ending including any rights management organisations, rightsholders and/or other forms of registration.

R.329

The [Company] shall be entitled to sub-license any rights granted under this agreement by the [Licensor] but there shall be no right of assignment at any time.

R.330

Where new technology and/or means and/or methods of exploitation fall outside the definitions in this agreement. Then the presumption shall be that the rights have not been granted. Every right and/or method of exploitation in this agreement is linked to the payment of one or more royalties for each such format and/or method. Where no royalty will be paid then it is agreed that the right and/or method of exploitation cannot be used unless a new agreement is reached in respect of those rights and/or method of exploitation between the parties and the payment terms agreed.

R.331

1.1 It is acknowledged that the [Performer] shall be entitled to performers rights in their performances as defined by [legislation] in [country] in the [Tour/Show].

1.2 That the consent of the [Performer] shall be required for any authorised recording of the performance of the [Performer] in the [Tour/Show].

1.3 That where a recording is made by any means in the [Tour/Show] which is not consented to by the [Performer] then it shall be in breach of their performers rights.

R.332

'Performance' shall be defined and mean a dramatic performance including dance and mime, a musical performance, a reading or recitation of a literary work or a performance of a variety or a similar presentation, which is or so far as it is a live performance given by one or more individuals.

R.333

'Performances' shall include acting, mime, dance, speech, singing, playing an instrument or conducting, either alone or with others.

R.334

'Performance' shall mean a performance of the [Work] being a work protected by copyright as a literary dramatic or musical work in public which would otherwise be a restricted act including delivery in the case of lectures, addresses, speeches, sermons and includes in general any mode of visual or acoustic presentation, including presentation by means of a sound recording, film, broadcast and/or transmission of the [Work].

R.335

'The Performers' shall be the following [Artist/Group/Speakers]: [specify details].

R.336

'The Performing Rights' shall include those rights administered by the rights management organisation and/or collecting society known as: [specify name/reference] in [country] and any society affiliated to it for inter alia:

1.1 the performance of the [Work] in public whether it is a live performance and/or recorded.

1.2   the right to broadcast and/or transmit the [Work] known as grand rights such as ballets, operas and musicals.

R.337
'The Radio and Stage Rights' shall mean the right to broadcast by means of analogue and/or digital radio and/or to organise and arrange the performance in public on a stage and/or at a theatre and/or other venue including an outdoor festival the [Musical Work/Script] and/or parts in the form of a [Programme/Play] and to authorise others to do so.

R.338
In consideration of the payment of the Placement Fee the [Distributor] grants to the [Company] the non-exclusive right to have the [Product/ Service] appear in the [Programme/Film/Event]. The [Distributor] agrees and undertakes to incorporate the [Product/Service] and the [Company's] [Trade Mark/Image/Slogan/Character] in the [Programme/Film/Event] in accordance with the summary set out in Schedule A which is attached to and forms part of this agreement. [specify timeline/purpose/exact material to be used/format/duration/location/number of appearances].

R.339
The [Company] agrees that the [Distributor] shall be entitled to have other third parties sponsor, advertise, promote and/or include their products, services, trade marks, logos, slogans and/or characters in the [Programme/ Film/Event]. The [Company] accepts that it shall have no right of approval and/or consultation in respect of such third parties and/or their products and/or services.

R.340
The [Distributor] agrees and undertakes not to advertise, promote and/or place any product, service and/or other material in the [Programme/Film/ Event] which directly competes with the sales of [Product/Service] in the [specify type] market.

R.341
'The Advertising, Sponsorship and Product Placement Rights' shall the sole and exclusive right of the [Supplier] to:

1.1   Advertise and promote products and/or services in the [number] minutes before the transmission, and/or broadcast of the [Programme/ Film] on channel: [specify name].

1.2   Advertise and promote products and/or services in the [number] minutes after the transmission, and/or broadcast of the [Programme/ Film] on channel [specify name].

1.3 Appear and/or be credited as the only sponsor [and/or third party funding source] of the [Programme/Film] other than [specify parties].

1.4 To provide at no additional cost to the [Company] up to [number] copies of any product and/or service to be used by the [Company] in the [Programme/Film] in a visible setting to suit the circumstances of the script. Attached is a copy of the proposed running order and script with markings for the use of any product and/or service to be provided by the [Supplier] which is attached to and forms part of this agreement.

1.5 The above rights in 1.1 to 1.4 shall only apply to the transmission and/or broadcast of the [Programme/Film] from [date] to [date] by the [Company] on channel [specify name] throughout the [Territory/country/world].

R.342
The [Executive] acknowledges, agrees and undertakes that all intellectual property rights and all other rights including copyright, design rights, computer software rights, inventions, patents, modifications and improvements, processes, formulae, know-how, computer generated material, rights to data and databases, trade marks, service marks, logos, domain names, characters, titles, slogans, images, drawings, sound recordings, films, photographs, electronic downloads and/or any other rights and material of any nature whether in existence now and/or created in the future in the product of his/her services under this agreement shall remain the sole and exclusive property of the [Company]. This agreement does not purport to transfer, assign, licence and/or otherwise provide any consent to the use and/or registration by the [Executive] of any rights and/or material at any time.

R.343
The [Executive] agrees and undertakes that all intellectual property rights and all other rights including copyright, design rights, trade marks, service marks, patents, rights to data and databases, and computer software which arise as a result of the provision of the [Executives'] services to the [Company] shall entirely belong to the [Company]. The [Executive] shall not have any rights and/or interest and/or be entitled to receive any sums from the exploitation of any material in any medium at any time.

R.344
The [Company] agrees and undertakes that the [Company] shall not be entitled to any material and/or rights in any work, research, project, and/or publication on the subject of [specify subject] which is created and/or developed by [Name].

R.345

The [Company] shall be entitled to own, control and represent that it is the copyright owner of all material and/or rights which are created during the course of the [Employees'] work for the [Company].

R.346

Where the [Executive] during the course of his/her services and/or work for 'the [Company] creates and/or develops any new and original material and/or intellectual property rights, copyright, computer software rights, inventions, patents, modifications, processes, formulae, know-how, trade marks, logos, domain names, characters and/or otherwise in any medium and/or method whether in existence now and/or created in the future. The [Company] agrees and undertakes to enter in to a separate agreement for such rights and/or material with an advance and royalties paid to the [Executive] for the use, registration and exploitation by the [Company] at any time. It is agreed that both parties shall hold the rights and/or material as joint owners.

R.347

1.1 [Name] agrees that in consideration of the fees to be paid by the [Company] that he/she shall assign to the [Company] all copyright, intellectual property rights, computer software rights, inventions, patents, trade marks, logos, slogans, computer-generated material, documents, data, emails, text messages, recordings, films, photographs, images and/or any other material in any medium and/or format which he/she creates, designs, develops, sends, receives and/or produces at any time during the course of his/her engagement and work at the [Company].

1.2 This clause shall not apply to any rights and/or material which are owned and/or created by [Name] which do not relate to his/her work at the [Company] and/or which is owned by a third party.

R.348

The [Company] agrees and accepts that:

1.1 It shall have no right to access and/or use and/or reproduce the private emails of [Name] whether sent during hours of employment or not.

1.2 It shall not have any right to supply the personnel file of [Name] at the [Company] to any third party except as requested by [Name] and/or under an order of a court which includes any confidential medical report and records.

1.3 That the [Company] may not disclose all the contents of a personnel file of [Name] to any third party except professional qualified legal advisors to the [Company].

1.4 It shall have no right to distribute, release, use, reproduce and/or supply the image of [Name] and/or any other recordings made by the [Company] and/or any consultant for any reason in any format to any third party without the prior written consent of [Name].

R.349

'Third Party Rights' shall be defined as the right of any third party who is not a party and/or signatory to this agreement.

No rights are to be conferred on any third party and all rights are limited to those parties which are named and have signed this agreement.

R.350

The parties to this agreement agree that the third party [specify name] shall be allowed to enforce the following rights directly against the parties to this agreement as follows: [specify details].

R.351

The [Company/Enterprise] owns all present and future copyright and intellectual property rights and any other rights throughout the [country/world/universe] in the [Work/Service/Product] and the material including but not limited to:

1.1 All forms of reproduction and exploitation of rights in respect of television and other devices: local, national, analogue, UHF, VHF, terrestrial, digital, cable, satellite; teletext, interactive and/or reception via any form of television, computer, gadget, watch, mobile phone and/or other device whether portable and/or stationary and any other method of storage, retrieval, catch up and/or archive playback, supply and/or distribution.

1.2 All forms of reproduction and exploitation of rights in respect of radio; analogue, overtheair, digital, interactive and in combination via any television, computer, gadget, watch, mobile phone and/or other device whether portable and/or stationary and any other method of storage, retrieval, catch up and/or archive playback, supply and/or distribution.

1.3 All forms of reproduction and exploitation of rights in respect of the internet, telecommunication systems, wifi, wireless telegraphy: electronic, digital, electromagnetic, electrochemical and/or any other form of reproduction, supply and distribution by any method and/or process; mobile and landline telephones, text messages, emojis, screensavers, ringtones, computer software, links, holograms, facial recognition, games and other formats, betting, competitions and/ or interactive services; words, text, images, websites, apps, blogs, podcasts, platforms and audio files via any form of television, computer, gadget, watch, mobile phone and/or other device whether portable and/or stationary and any other method of storage, retrieval, catch up and/or archive playback, supply and/or distribution.

1.4 All forms of reproduction and exploitation of rights in respect of mechanical reproduction and/or performing rights ; all music, lyrics, sound recordings, electronic downloads from any website, app and/or platform of any film and/or other material and/or publication and/or synchronization including: sound tracks, CDs, CD-Roms, videocassettes, discs, audio files and/or streaming videos.

1.5 All forms of reproduction and exploitation of rights in respect of stills, photographs, visual images both moving and/or static, designs, design rights, future design rights, models, sculptures, graphics, drawings, sketches, illustrations, artwork, two and three dimensional representations, plans, tables, charts, maps, colours, shapes, noise and smell.

1.6 All forms of reproduction and exploitation of rights in respect of films, series, cartoons, animations, adapted formats for programmes, advertisements, promotional videos, stage plays, performances, sound recordings, recordings, sounds and voices and any other method of storage, retrieval, catch up and/or archive playback, supply and/or distribution.

1.7 All forms of reproduction and exploitation of rights in respect of data, databases, statistics, infographics, material and information; computer-generated material, blockchains and algorithms and any other method of storage, retrieval, catch up and/or archive playback, supply and/or distribution.

1.8 All forms of reproduction and exploitation of rights in respect of merchandising, sponsorship, product placement; interactive computer games, licensing of characters, toys, board games, posters, calendars, sports, outdoor, leisure and other clothing for adults, children's clothing, household goods and services, food products, cooking utensils, storage boxes, stationary, magnets, theme parks, gambling, betting, lotteries, festivals, competitions, sculptures and 3D shows and costumes.

1.9 All brand names, trade marks, service marks, logos, words, phrases, domain names and/or names of the platform and/or app and/or short form initials, business names, trading names and the right to apply for and/or to register any such rights and/or interest.

1.10 All forms of reproduction and exploitation of rights in respect of confidential information, moral rights, trade secrets, know-how, goodwill, inventions, patents, modifications, improvements, formulae and processes.

1.11 All forms of reproduction and exploitation of rights in respect of publications including hardback, paperback, picture books, co-editions, large print, foreign editions, magazines, periodicals, digests, comics, strip cartoons, colouring books, educational books, serialisations, quotations, anthologies and/or reproduction and/or distribution by any electronic form of exploitation .

1.12 All forms of free and no charge and/or all methods of payment including rental, subscription, licence, mail order, entrance fee, pay per view, on demand, scrambled, encrypted and/or otherwise.

1.13 The right to appoint a supplier, distributor, agent and/or other third party; to reproduce, supply, distribute, adapt, develop, translate, arrange a sequel, and to exploit the rights and material in any manner through third parties.

1.14 All rights and material related to advertising, publicity, promotions, wrappings, containers, labels, packaging, display materials, exhibitions, conferences, courses, webinars and/or training, licensing of extracts, sponsorship, endorsement, product placement and/or other forms of sub-licensing and/or use of any rights.

1.15 Any other combination, use, device, method, system, process, transfer, supply and/or format whether in existence now or created at any time in the future.

R.352

'All Media Rights' shall be defined as all intellectual property rights and any other rights and interest of whatever nature in any medium in the [Work/Project/Product] and any parts including without limitation:

1.1 All copyright, trade marks, service marks, design rights, patents, computer software, digital and electronic files, trade secrets, moral rights and confidential information, domain names and/or any other registered associated names and/or rights.

1.2 It shall include the sole and exclusive right to reproduce, adapt, use, copy, license, authorise, print, transmit, distribute, store, retrieve, display, process, record, playback, rent, lend, supply, sell, promote, exhibit and/or otherwise exploit by any method in existence now and/or created in the future in any medium.

1.3 It shall include but not be limited to:

a. All scripts, text, logos, characters, colours, images, computer-generated art, photographs, drawings, plans, sketches, charts, maps, electronically generated material, any associated slogan, words, lyrics, jingles, music and/or sound recordings, films, videos and/or any other material and/or any combination.

b. All forms of exploitation in respect of the internet and/or by means of any telecommunication system including platforms, websites, links, apps, blogs, videos, podcasts, electronic downloads and audio files.

c. All forms of television and radio including terrestrial, UHF, VHF, cable, satellite, analogue and digital and electronic form over the internet and/or any by means of any telecommunication system, wifi and/or otherwise for reception by television, radio, computer, laptop, mobile phone, watch and/or any other stationary and/or portable device;

d. All rights in any performance and the associated performing rights;

e. All forms of exploitation which relate to mechanical reproduction;

f. All forms of theatric and non-theatric exploitation including cinemas, stage plays and musicals.

g. All forms of computer software and interactive multi-media such as compact discs, CD-Roms, computer games including all circumstances where there is an element of interactivity and/or there is any combination of sound, text, vision, graphics, music or otherwise.

h. All forms of advertising, promotional items and giveaways, format and character exploitation in any form; merchandising, toys, books, clothes, costumes, household goods, stationery, games, product endorsement, sponsorship, product placement, festivals, theme parks, betting, lotteries, gambling and two or three dimensional representations.

R.353

'All Media Rights' shall be defined to mean the sole and exclusive right to exploit the [Work] and/or parts throughout the [Territory/world] for the duration of the [Licence Period/the full period of copyright including any extensions or renewals as far as possible in perpetuity] in all media whether in existence now and/or created in the future including but not limited to:

1.1 All forms of exploitation through terrestrial, cable, satellite and digital television and radio;

1.2 All forms of exploitation over the internet; wireless telegraphy, wifi and/ or any telecommunication system, websites, apps, blogs, podcasts, audio files, electronic downloads, films, images and sound recordings; any streaming, catch up and storage and retrieval method for playback; any other method of electronic reproduction, communication, storage and/or distribution.

1.3 All forms of mechanical reproduction and rights and all forms of performances and performing rights.

1.4 Theatric and non-theatric exploitation including tours, plays, readings, outdoor screenings and festivals.

1.5 All forms of publishing whether in printed form, electronic and/or audio form including books, newspapers, online news services, downloads and audio archives..

1.6 Theme parks, merchandising, lotteries, betting, gambling, sports events, sponsorship, product placement and adaptations and/or developments in any medium and/or format and/or method.

1.7 The right to licence the above rights to a third party.

1.8 Whether free, pay per view, subscription, hire, sale and/or some other arrangement.

R.354

'All Media Rights' shall be defined to mean all media whether in existence now or created in the future including, but not limited to:

1.1 All forms of television including terrestrial, digital, cable and satellite.

1.2 All forms of radio including terrestrial, digital, cable and satellite.

1.3 All forms of mechanical reproduction including DVD, cassettes, discs and lasers.

1.4 All forms of publishing, hardbacks, paperbacks, newspapers, magazines, comics, serialisation and electronic versions in sound and vision.

1.5 All theatre, plays, readings, films, advertisements, performances and exhibitions.

1.6 All forms of merchandising and adaptation and sub-licensing of the title, character, storyline, logo, image, film, computer-generated material, photographs, text, interactive and/or multi-media computer games, theme parks and 3D formats.

1.7 The internet, telecommunications systems, electronic downloads, audio files, podcasts, blogs, websites, apps, computer generated material and/or electronic communications; the reproduction, supply, storage and retrieval and distribution of films, videos, images, graphics, infographics, maps, charts, data, information, logos, trade marks and any other material.

1.8   The right to translate and adapt for all languages including braille.

R.355
[Name] confirms and undertakes that he/she owns and controls the sole and exclusive right to produce, manufacture, supply, sell, rent, distribute, license, market and exploit the [Work] and any parts whether in existence now and/or created in the future in all forms of the media throughout the world and universe for the full period of copyright and any other rights and forever including but not limited to:

1.1   All intellectual property rights of whatever nature including without limitation all copyright, trade marks, service marks, design rights, trade secrets, computer software, moral rights and confidential information.

1.2   All forms of publication including hardback, paperback, digests, serialisation, newspapers, magazines, periodicals, quotations, anthologies, translations including exploitation of the title, index and taxonomy.

1.3   All forms of radio, television, video, and mechanical and/or electronic forms of reproduction and/or storage and retrieval and/or playback.

1.4   All forms of theatric and non-theatric exploitation.

1.5   All forms of merchandising and promotion including computer games, toys, clothing, stationery, sponsorship, endorsement, product placement, theme parks, betting, gambling, lotteries and game formats.

1.6   All forms of telecommunication systems and the internet, electronic communications, audio files and downloads and any method of reproduction, storage, access, retrieval and supply.

1.7   Any other adaptation, development and/or method of reproduction, supply, distribution and/or delivery; whether free and/or for any payment including on demand and pay per view and/or subscription.

1.8   The right to licence, authorise and/or permit third parties to exploit any of the rights and/or to assign, transfer, and/or charge any of the rights.

R.356
'All Media Rights' shall mean the sole and exclusive right to produce, manufacture, supply, rent, distribute, license, market, adapt and exploit the

[Work] and any parts in all forms of the media in existence now [and created in the future] including, but not limited to: all forms of publication; hardback, paperback; all forms of television, radio, video, sound recordings, films and recordings; cable; satellite; digital; cassettes; laser; disks; any technical method of delivery; any method of payment, charging, subscription, rental, lease and free; all forms of telecommunication systems; sound; sound effects; vision; graphics; text; icons; images or any combination; all forms of theatric and non-theatric exploitation; all forms of mechanical and electronic reproduction, dissemination or otherwise, internet, intranet and multi-media exploitation; all methods of merchandising; all patents, computer software, digital and electronic files and any method or process of storage, retrieval, supply and distribution and any developments, and/or adaptations of any nature.

R.357

1.1 The [Contributor] acknowledges and agrees that all present and future copyright and any other rights in the [Company's] [Service/Products/Project] shall be and remain the property of the [Company].

1.2 That the [Contributor] shall not acquire any rights or interest by virtue of this agreement to any copyright and/or any other rights in the [Company's] [Service/Products/Project].

1.3 At the end of the agreement the [Contributor] shall sign any document or do anything which is reasonably required by the [Company's] legal advisors to confirm and/or transfer and assign any rights which may have been acquired by the [Contributor] by reason of this agreement.

R.358
The [Assignor] agrees that it shall not retain any rights in the [Work] and/or the [Work Material].

R.359
The [Assignor] transfers and assigns to the [Assignee] All Media Rights in the [Work] and the [Work Material] throughout the planet earth, universe and galaxy for the full period of copyright and any other rights and for any extension and in perpetuity. Except those owned and controlled by a third party as set out in Appendix A [specify details and list].

R.360
In consideration of the Assignment Fee the [Name] assigns all present and future copyright and All Media Rights and any other rights of any nature whether in existence now or created in the future in the [Work] and/or any parts including the original physical material listed in Schedule A throughout the world, universe

and outer space for the full period of copyright and any extensions and renewals and continuing indefinitely and without limitation in perpetuity.

R.361

1.1 The [Licensor] grants to the [Licensee] a non-exclusive licence to develop, manufacture and supply and/or distribute the [Products/ Service] using the technical information and guidance, processes, trade secrets, trade marks and confidential information and the designs, samples, drawings, documents, computer software and programs and any other material described in Appendix A for the Term of this Agreement in [Territory/country].

1.2 The [Licensee] accepts and agrees that they shall not acquire any ownership of any rights licensed in 1.1 [except as stated in this agreement] and/or have the right to register any copyright, patent and/ or trade mark and/or any similar version.

1.3 The [Licensee] agrees and undertakes not to sub-license any rights in 1.1 to any third party except as expressly permitted under this agreement to a third party who purchases the [Products/Service].

R.362
All rights not specifically and expressly granted to the [Licensee] by this agreement are reserved to the [Licensor].

R.363
The rights assigned are for the [Assignment Period/Term of the Agreement] only after which time all rights under this agreement shall revert to the [Assignor].

R.364

1.1 In consideration of the Non-Returnable Advance and the Licensor's Royalties the [Licensor] grants to the [Licensee] the sole and exclusive [specify rights granted] throughout the [Territory/country/area] for the duration of the Licence Period and the right to authorise third parties to exercise such rights.

1.2 The [Licensee] acknowledges that all other rights including but not limited to the [specify rights not given] are specifically excluded from this agreement.

R.365
The [Author] agrees to execute any document and/or sign any form and/ or make any statement and/or complete some other task which may

be requested at the [Company's] cost and expense for the purpose of confirming the rights assigned under this agreement. Provided that the [Company] shall agree to bear the cost of all sums to be incurred by the [Author] in co-operating with any such requests.

R.366

The [Company] agrees that there is no transfer of copyright and/or any intellectual property rights and/or computer software rights in the [Artwork] and/or the computer generated material and/or software programme designed and created by the [Licensor] to the [Company] under this agreement.

1.2 That the [Licensor] has authorised the [Company] to use, display and exhibit the [Artwork] as an installation at [location] for the [Festival/ Event] from [date] to [date].

1.3 That the [Licensor] has authorised the reproduction in the official programme and on the [website/app] [reference] the image and credits of the [Artwork] supplied by the [Licensor].

1.4 The [Company] agrees that no other image and/or photograph shall be used in association with the [Artwork] other than that supplied under 1.3

R.367

1.1 The [Licensee] agrees and undertakes that where new material and/ or new versions of existing material are created and developed under this agreement which are based on and/or derived from the copyright, intellectual property rights, computer software rights, trade marks, designs and/or other rights held by the [Licensor]. That the [Licensee] shall upon request by the [Licensor] assign all the rights in any new material and/or new versions to the [Licensor] at the [Licensors'] cost and expense.

1.2 That the [Licensee] agrees and undertakes not to attempt to register and/or register the rights of any nature in any medium with any rights management organisation and/or collecting society in such new material and/or new versions in 1.1.

R.368

1.1 The [Licensee] agrees and undertakes that where new material and/ or new versions of existing material are created and developed under this agreement which are based on and/or derived from the copyright, intellectual property rights, computer software rights, trade marks, designs and/or other rights held by the [Licensor]. That the [Licensee] shall upon request by the [Licensor] assign all the rights in any new material and/or new versions to the [Licensor] so that the rights of any nature are held jointly by both parties. The cost of such arrangement shall be shared between the parties.

1.2　In addition it is agreed that any registration of any of the rights of any nature in any medium with any rights management organisation and/or collecting society in such new material and/or new versions in 1.1 shall be held in the joint names of the [Licensor] and the [Licensee].

R.369
The [Licensee] agrees and accepts that this is a non-exclusive licence. That the [Licensor] shall have the right to grant the exact same licence for the same countries to any third party. That the [Licensee] has no right to object to and/or prevent such action.

R.370
The [Company] shall have the right to end the agreement early and serve [number] months' written notice to the [Licensee] in the event that:

1.1　The [Licensee] is involved in a political campaign on social media.

1.2　The [Licensee] is involved in a criminal investigation in any country involving money laundering, tax fraud, drugs, criminal activity and/or any other serious allegation.

1.3　The [Licensee] defaults under the agreement and fails to report and account for any sums in any accounting period.

1.4　The [Licensee] is discovered to be exploiting rights which do not fall within the scope of the agreement which belong to the [Licensor].

R.371

1.1　The [Licensee] agrees and undertakes to:

A.　Supply samples of the prototype of any proposed products and/or services to the [Licensor] for approval.

B.　Supply an exact copy of the proposed final version of any product and/or services for approval by the [Licensor] prior to any production and/or distribution.

C.　Supply draft labels, packaging and/or marketing material for approval by the [Licensor].

1.2　The [Licensee] agrees and accept that if any approval is withheld that the [Licensee] may not proceed to production until the requests made by the [Licensor] are incorporated and approved.

Internet, Websites and Apps

R.372

'The Digital Electronic Rights' shall be defined as the right to exploit the [Work/ Image/Recording] commercially by digital and electronic means only which shall include the right to scan, copy, digitise, reproduce, adapt, promote, advertise, market, supply, sell and distribute the [Work/Image/Recording] for electronic dissemination by whatever means [whether in existence now and/or created in the future] as a whole and/or parts [and/or any adaptation by electronic means and/or form in conjunction with other electronic material including audio files, sounds, music, text, data, visual images, films and contributors. Together the right to authorise and/or sub-license third parties to exercise such rights.

R.373

'The Electronic and Telecommunication Rights' shall be defined as the non-exclusive right to reproduce, scan, copy, digitise, adapt, licence, supply, distribute, market, advertise, promote and exploit the [Work/ Artwork/Photograph/Sound Recordings] in whole and/or part whether for educational, charitable, non-commercial and/or commercial purposes in digital and electronic format by means of electronic dissemination over the internet and world wide web and/or via any telecommunication system for use and/or access by means of any television, laptop, computer, mobile, watch and/or other gadget and/or device by any person and/or any group throughout the world and universe from [date to [date].This shall include the right to add, delete, alter, adapt and/or reproduce it in different languages, colours and/or in conjunction with other material.

R.374

'The Internet and Telecommunication Rights' shall be defined as the right to:

1.1   Reproduce, display, exhibit, transmit, supply, sell, distribute and exploit the [Work] and parts and the associated original physical material by any electronic means of communication and/or method [whether in existence now and/or created in the future] over the internet including by not limited to on any platform, website, app, audio file, download, streaming and/or pay on demand service, blog, news service, podcast and/or video catch up and/or playback and/or archive storage and retrieval service; hologram, online game, online betting and gambling and/or other interactive sport and reception by any television, computer, laptop, mobile, gadget and/or device whether stationary and/or portable and

1.2   Reproduce, display, exhibit, transmit, supply, sell, distribute and exploit the [Work] and parts and the associated original physical material

1646

by any telecommunication system and/or any other such means of communication and/or method [whether in existence now and/or created in the future] including any catch up and/or playback and/or archive storage and retrieval service; online game, online betting and gambling and/or other interactive sport and reception by any television, computer, laptop, mobile, gadget and/or device whether stationary and/or portable.

R.375

'The Internet and Telecommunication Rights' shall be defined as the exclusive right to:

1.1 Exploit the [Work/Material] by any electronic means of communication and/or method in existence now as at [date] over the internet on the [Platform/Website/App] known as: [specify name /reference] in the form of a [audio file/download/ streaming video catch up and/or playback service/news service] from [date to [date].

1.2 Exploit the [Work/Material] by any telecommunication system and/or any other such means of communication in existence now as at [date] and/or in combination with the rights in 1.1 on the [Platform/Website/App] known as: [specify name /reference] in the form of a [specify format] from [date to [date].

1.3 There are no territorial limits for the rights in 1.1 and 1.2 and reception may be by any television, computer, laptop, mobile, gadget and/or device whether stationary and/or portable and/or otherwise.

R.376

The parties agree as follows:

1.1 That [Name] shall have the non-exclusive right to arrange for an electronic version of the [Work/Material] to be developed and produced which is an exact replica of the original without any alterations at the cost and expense of [Name].

1.2 That [Name] shall supply a free copy of the electronic version of the [Work/Material] to the [Institute] which they shall own and retain.

1.3 The [Institute] grants [Name] the non-exclusive right to reproduce, supply, sell, distribute and exploit the new electronic version in 1.1 of the [Work/Material] on the [Website/Platform/App] known as: [title/ reference] for the Licence Period throughout the world. Provided that [Name] pays the royalty fixed price per unit set out in clause [–].

1.4 The [Institute] agrees that [Name] may exploit the electronic version of the [Work/Material] over the internet and/or any telecommunication system by any method [Name] may decide whether for free and/or for financial gain. Provided that the electronic version is not adapted and/or combined with any other text, images, sound, music, music effects, videos and/or films and/or distorted in any manner.

1.5 [Name] agrees and undertakes that at all times where the electronic version is mentioned on the [Website/Platform/App] that the [Institute] shall be credited as the copyright owner and the source of the [Work/Material].

R.377

The [Licensor] agrees and undertakes that for the duration of the [Licence Period/Term of this Agreement] and/or under such time as it is terminated and/or expires the [Licensor] shall not:

1.1 Directly and/or indirectly license, sub-license, supply, promote, sell, distribute and/or exploit the [Work] and/or parts in respect of the exercise of and/or use of the Internet and Telecommunication Rights in any country and/or territorial waters in any part of the world.

1.2 Sub-license and/or authorise any third party to copy, produce, manufacture, develop, promote, sell, supply and/or distribute any new version and/or adaptation and/or sequel for exploitation in respect of the Internet and Telecommunication Rights in any country and/or territorial waters in any part of the world.

R.378

1.1 [Name] understands and accepts that the following [Work/Material] is to be displayed on the internet on the [Platform/Website/Podcast] known as: [specify name/reference] which is registered as: [specify details] with [specify organisation] and is held and owned directly by the [Company].

1.2 The duration of the licence is for [specify period] and may be renewed thereafter for any further period by consent in writing and payment of the additional fee specified in 1.3 below. The consent of [Name] to any renewal period may be withdrawn at any time prior to the end of any such period by notice in writing or email to the [Company].

1.3 The fee for the consent and such renewal is [specify number/currency] which shall be due at the start of each [three] month period from [date].

1.4 [Name] agrees that the [Work/Material] once on the internet may be copied, distributed, supplied and transmitted by others in different forms over which the [Company] has no control. That the [Company] has no means of monitoring and/or controlling the number of third parties which may pirate the [Work/Material] and fail to adhere to the moral rights without expending significant legal costs and expenses. The [Company] is not expected to take any legal action against such third parties by [Name].

R.379

1.1 You are permitted to download any material which is offered for free from the [Website/App/Platform] and to retain a copy on your [hard drive and/or on a USB stick and/or disc] for your own personal non-commercial use only.

1.2 No commercial exploitation is permitted unless authorised by and agreed in advance by the [Company].

1.3 You have no right to post the material on any internet website, app and/or platform and/or account including any online video and/or film distributor and/or any on line image account and/or to reproduce and to supply the material to any third party.

1.4 Use for any fundraising and/or charitable events is strictly prohibited and any proposed use must be agreed in advance with the [Company].

1.5 Your own private home use includes research and personal projects for school, college and university. It does not permit any educational purpose for classes and/or groups. In such instance a licence must be obtained in advance from the [Company].

1.6 You do not have the authority and/or right to add the material to any film, video, sound recording, website, app and/or other product and/or service at any time. Any such proposal must be authorised and agreed in advance by the [Company].

1.7 If you fail to adhere to these conditions then the [Company] may at any time instruct you to delete the material from your [hard drive and/or USB stick and/or disc] and to deliver up any copies you may have made.

R.380

'A translation of the original computer programme' shall be defined to mean a new and different version of the original computer programme where it has been converted into and/or out of one computer language and/or code and/or into a different computer language and/or code except where it is incidental in the course of running the original computer programme.

R.381

1.1 The [Purchaser] is granted a non-exclusive and non-transferable licence to use the [Download/Disc] and its content, information and data for the purpose for which it is intended in conjunction with the [Work/Product/Service] in the normal course of business, namely to [specify steps, actions and purpose that may be taken].

1.2 The [Purchaser] shall not acquire any rights and/or interest in the [Work/Product/Service] and/or the [Download/Disc] and/or its content, information and/or data and/or any parts in any media of any nature at any time.

1.3 All rights which are not specifically granted are reserved.

1.4 This right is personal to the [Purchaser] and shall also permit the [Purchaser] to copy files from the [Download/Disc] of the [Work/ Product/Service] to their [hard drive/other] and also to make one security copy of the [Download/Disc].

1.5 There is no right to make additional copies of the [Work/Product/ Service] and/or [Download/Disc] and/or content, information and/or data for any reason.

1.6 The [Purchaser] shall not have the right to make any additional copies and/or permit, authorise, sub-license, assign, transfer and/or otherwise exploit the [Work/Product/Service] and/or [Download/Disc] and/or content, data and information in any format for any reason.

R.382

There is no right granted to copy and/or reproduce the [Work] and/or any download, disc and/or other storage unit in any manner. You are not authorised to permanently store and keep any content and/or to make any copies and/or to reproduce and/or supply additional copies by any method including but not limited to using computer software, photocopying, scanning and/or any distribution by electronic means over the internet and/ or through any telecommunication system to any third party whatever the means of reception.

R.383

1.1 There is no right granted to use the [Work/Material] and/or any content to create, edit, adapt and/or develop a search engine index, taxonomy, index, and/or any other format and/or medium which shall be displayed and/or supplied on the internet and/or any telecommunication system and/or in any directory, database, computer software and/or in a printed format.

1.2 There is no right granted to exploit, adapt, licence, translate, create a new format based on the [Work/Material] and/or develop a new version based on the [Work/Material] for use on the internet and/or to use the

[Work] as part of any storage and retrieval system and/or process whether by any electronic means of communication and/or otherwise in any media.

1.3 The [Work/Material] are an excluded work from the [Copyright Licensing Agency/other organisation] and there is no licence granted to scan, photocopy, create a digital and/or electronic version and/or to reproduce, supply, distribute and/or sub-license the [Work/Material] and/or any part.

R.384

There is no right granted to permit, authorise, sub-license, assign, transfer, and/or otherwise exploit the [Work/Material] and/or any content and/or any parts in any form in any medium and/or by any other method, process and/or system whether for commercial, educational, charitable and/or non-commercial purposes and/or otherwise whether in existence now and/or created in the future except [specify rights which are permitted].

R.385

1.1 The use of the [Directory/Archive Library] on this [Platform/Website/App] is available at no charge for non-commercial use only by any person who has registered and been accepted and allocated an access code and account number.

1.2 Such account and code access in 1.1 is a temporary arrangement and may be cancelled by the [Enterprise] at any time without stating a reason.

1.3 Your account and code permits you access to the [Directory/Archive Library] and you may search, copy, download and store one copy on your hard drive and/or on a disc and/or USB and/or other storage device data and material on a temporary basis for research and educational purposes for your own personal non-commercial use.

1.4 There are no rights granted to you to transfer, assign, sub-license and/or to exploit any such data and material you may access from the [Directory/Archive Library] for any reason in any format whether educational, commercial, charitable and/or otherwise.

1.5 You may not make any additional copies and/or reproduce the [Directory/Archive Library] and any data, database, index, taxonomy and/or material in any form and/or medium and/or distribute, transfer, transmit and/or exploit the rights and/or material without the prior written consent of the [Enterprise].

R.386

In consideration of the [Fee] the [Licensor] grants [Name] the non-exclusive right to develop and adapt and reproduce in electronic form the [Image/ Graphics/Logo/Text] for reproduction on the [Platform/Website/App]: [specify name/reference] from [date] to [date].

Provided that:

1.1 [Name] undertakes that a copyright notice and credit to the [Licensor] shall appear in proximity to the electronic form of the [Image/Graphics/ Logo/Text] so that it is clear who is the owner.

1.2 The copyright and intellectual property rights in all the computer generated and electronic versions and forms of the [Image/Graphics/ Logo/Text] created by and/or commissioned by [Name] including original material and/or later versions shall be assigned completely to the [Licensor]. So that [Name] retains no rights whatsoever.

1.3 [Name] undertakes not to supply any copies of the electronic versions and forms of the [Image/Graphics/Logo/Text] on any products to be sold and/or supplied to the public and/or sub-license and/or authorise any third party to do so.

1.4 [Name] undertakes to deliver to the [Licensor] at the cost and expense of [Name] the original computer-generated and electronic versions and forms of the [Image/Graphics/Logo/Text] created by and/or commissioned by [Name] and/or later versions on or by [date].

1.5 [Name] undertakes to erase, delete and destroy all computer-generated and electronic versions and forms of the [Image/Graphics/ Logo/Text] and/or later versions from the [Platform/Website/App] and/ or all copies in any format on any storage device and/or storage and retrieval system and/or in any other format by [date].

R.387

1.1 In consideration of the [Buy-out Fee] of [number/currency] to be paid by the [Enterprise] to [Name/Holding Company] on [date] to a nominated bank account in [country].

1.2 [Name/Holding Company] assigns to the [Enterprise] the sole and exclusive rights and all copyright, intellectual property rights, computer software rights and all other rights in any computer-generated material and/or electronic files and/or electronic means of communication over the internet and/or through any telecommunication system and all other rights of exploitation in any form and in any medium and/or format and/ or any method of adaptation whether in existence now and/or created in the future for the full period of copyright and any extensions and/or renewals and for the full term of all other rights which may exist and thereafter be created and to continue indefinitely throughout the world and the universe in the following:

a. The [Website/App] known as [specify name of site/reference] which trades under the entity and brand of [specify details] which is registered as [specify name] as [specify legal identity] in [country] and is owned by: [specify exact registered owner which should be Name and/or Holding Company].

b. The domain and/or app names and any registered and/or trading name of any website and/or app and/or associated image, film, video, marketing and/or promotional account registered with any online third party on the internet.

c. The domain name: [specify name/reference].

d. The app: [specify name/reference].

e. The online accounts for images, films, videos and podcasts at: [specify names/reference].

f. All development, draft and final material in any format including scripts, shooting schedules, text, data, designs and graphics, images, artwork, photographs, logos, slogans, videos, films, podcasts, trade marks, sound recordings, packaging, merchandising, advertising and promotional material, music and lyrics; computer-generated material and/or any material developed for any electronic version and/or telecommunication system and/or any storage and/or retrieval and/or catch up and/or playback method of exploitation.

g. The Logos: [specify names/reference].

h. The Trade Marks: [specify name/reference] [date of registration/country].

i. All associated corporate documents, financial reports, commissioning and distribution agreements, licences, assignments, waivers, music cue sheets, registration forms and any other relevant records and/or material held by [Name/Holding Company] which relate in any manner to the above assignment.

1.3 The [Enterprise] accepts that some of the software and/or material used on the [Website/App] may be licensed from third parties and subject to additional payments and/or terms of use.

1.4 [Name/Holding Company] accepts that after the assignment has been completed that the owner of all rights and any copyright and intellectual property rights and/or other interest shall be the [Enterprise].

1653

1.5 [Name/Holding Company] agrees and undertakes that where necessary in order to effect any assignment of any of the rights further documentation is required to be completed. That [Name/Holding Company] will co-operate and sign any such documents as may be requested by the [Enterprise] up to [date]. Provided that the Enterprise] shall not expect [Name/Holding Company] to pay any legal and/or administrative and/or travel costs that may be incurred.

R.388

1.1 The [Contributor] agrees that he/she shall not acquire any copyright and/or intellectual property rights and/or any other rights in the [Blog/Podcast] and/or any title, name, logo, image, slogan, trading name, domain name and/or trade mark, text, sound recording, film, video and/or any other material at any time.

1.2 That this shall be the case regardless of whether the [Blog/Podcast] was created and/or commissioned by the [Company] specifically for [Name] and his/her contributions or not.

1.3 That the [Contributor] agrees that he/she shall not be entitled to receive any payment for the [Blog/Podcast] except a Contributors' Fee of [number/currency] each [week/month] subject to delivery of the material for the [Blog/Podcast].

1.4 That the [Company] shall be entitled to assign, transfer, remove and/or delete the [Blog/Podcast] at any time and/or to terminate and/or cancel the arrangement with the [Contributor] for the supply of material.

1.5 In consideration of the Contributors' Fee the [Contributor] assigns all copyright and intellectual property and the defined All Media Rights in the material which he/she delivers for the [Blog/Podcast] for the full period of copyright and any extensions and/or renewals and/or such other additional periods of rights as may be possible in the future and/or to continue indefinitely throughout the world and universe.

R.389

1.1 The [Company] agrees that no part of this agreement is intended to assign and/or transfer the personal and/or business name of the [Contributor] to the [Company] and/or the right to register it as a trade mark and/or to exploit it in any other form.

1.2 The [Company] agrees that if after the [Contributor] has ceased to supply material for the [Blog/Podcast] to the [Company]. The [Contributor] shall be entitled to request that the [Company] remove his/her name from the [Blog/Podcast] and/or any other part of the

[Website/App/Platform] [reference]. The [Company] agrees to remove and/or delete all credits to the [Contributor] as requested, but shall not be obliged to remove and delete the material supplied. The [Company] shall also cease to use the name of the [Contributor] in any corporate and/or promotional material.

R.390

1.1 The [Company] has designed, developed and commissioned the [App/Audio File] known as [specify name] which is described in detail in Schedule A and is attached to this agreement.

1.2 The [Company] agrees to licence the [App/Audio File] to the [Distributor] on a non-exclusive basis to be supplied, accessed, downloaded and sold to the public and/or any educational and/or charitable organisation and/or commercial business from their [Platform/Website/Service] known as [specify name/reference] from [date] to [date] anywhere in the world in electronic form as authorised over the internet and/or any telecommunication system.

1.3 The [Company] agrees that the licence for the [App/Audio File] may be accessed and downloaded in any country for use by individuals, commercial companies, educational establishments and/or other third parties by a variety of methods including mobiles, laptops, tablets, computers and/or any other gadget and/or device.

1.4 The [Distributor] agrees to pay the [Company] a fee of [number/currency] for each person, business and/or entity that accesses, downloads and purchases the [App/Audio File]. Any sums due to the [Company] shall be paid one month in arrears at the end of each calendar month direct to the nominated bank account of the [Company]. Together with a data analysis of the customers for that month.

1.5 The [Distributor] shall pay all the costs and expenses of adapting its own [Platform/Website/Service] and/or the [App/Audio File] so that it is integrated and functions properly as required.

1.6 Where the [Distributor] fails to report and/or pay any sums due to the [Company] then the [Company] shall have the right to terminate this agreement by email with immediate effect.

R.391

1.1 The [Licensor] grants [Name] the non-exclusive right to reproduce [number] minutes of the agreed extract of the [Sound Recording] described in Appendix A in conjunction with the [Podcast] which [Name] has [produced/commissioned] to market and promote their [Work/Products/Service].

1.2 The [Licensor] agrees that [Name] may use and reproduce the extract of the [Sound Recording] described in Appendix A in conjunction with the [Podcast] on its own [website/app] and over the internet and any telecommunication system in electronic form for access through any television, laptop, computer, mobile and/or other gadget and/or device whether stationary and/or portable gadgets for the authorised period in 1.4.

1.3 [Name] agrees that a credit and/or copyright notice is required in respect of any use and/or reproduction of the extracts of the [Sound Recording] in conjunction with the [Podcast] as follows: [specify details/location/size/format].

1.4 [Name] agrees that there is no right granted of any nature to use and/or reproduce the extract of the [Sound Recording] on its own and/or to make any adaptation and/or to add and/or alter any words, lyrics, sounds and/or other material.

1.5 The Licence shall start on [date] and end on [date] and shall only come into existence and continue until the end date if [Name] has paid the fees due for the Licence as follows:

   a. Licence Fee in total: [specify number/currency].

   b. Licence Fee to be paid in full by [date] by method of payment.

R.392

1.1 'The Image/Artwork' shall be defined as: [specify title] in [format] created by [Name].

1.2 [Name] grants the [Company] an exclusive licence to reproduce and exploit the [Image/Artwork] on its [Channel/Service] known as: [specify/reference] and on any form of associated merchandising for the Licence Period throughout the [Territory/world].

1.3 In consideration of the grant of rights in 1.2 the [Company] agrees to pay [Name] a initial fee of [number/currency] and then an annual fee of [number/currency] for each year of the agreement until it expires and/or is terminated.

1.4 The [Company] shall be entitled to adapt and alter the [Image/Artwork] and to create different versions in a variety of formats and media. Provided that it solely relates to the [Channel/Service] and/or the associated merchandising.

1.5 The [Company] may licence third parties to produce, sell and distribute the merchandising.

1,6 The [Company] agrees that it shall not have any right to register any trade mark in respect of the [Image/Artwork] and/or any adaptation and/or new version. That any registration of any trade mark shall be subject to further agreement between the parties.

R.393

1.1 [Name] is the writer and author of a series of articles for the [Website/ Blog] known as: [specify title/reference].

1.2 [Name] agrees and undertakes that all copyright, intellectual property rights and any other rights in the series of articles shall be assigned to the [Company] in respect of all media and/or medium which are in existence now and/or created in the future throughout the world and universe for the full period of copyright and any extensions and/or renewals and for any such further period of rights which may applicable to any format at any time and forever. So that [Name] shall retain no rights whatsoever.

1.3 The [Company] must at all times credit [Name] as the author of the series of articles and must not edit, delete and/or vary the content of the articles in any manner which would mislead the public as to the personal opinions of [Name].

R.394
'Image and Hologram Rights' shall be defined as:

1.1 The right to reproduce a series of images of [Name] in different formats, colours and/or by different methods whether in a film, video, podcast, magazine and/or promotional material in conjunction with difference products and/or services and/or games and/or other competitions which are approved by [Name].

1.2 The right to design, create and develop a two and three dimensional version which can be viewed and rotated and which is a computer-generated and/or an electronic version.

R.395

1.1 [Name] grants the [exclusive/non-exclusive] Image and Hologram Rights to the [Distributor] from [date] to [date] throughout of the world and the right to exploit the Image and Hologram Rights over the internet and/or any telecommunication system whether for reception by television, computer, mobile and/or any other gadget and/or device. No other method of exploitation is authorised.

1.2 [Name] shall be entitled to approve any sample and/or prototype in each version in respect of 1.1 and may withhold consent if the representation of his/her image is so distorted that it is unacceptable.

1.3 The Image and Hologram Rights shall not be sub-licensed by the [Distributor] to any third party without the prior consent of [Name].

1.4 The [Distributor] agrees and accepts that it shall not have any right to register any rights in respect of [Name] and/or the rights and/or material created under this agreement.

1.5 The [Distributor] agrees at the end of the agreement that it shall assign any rights and/or material which it may own and/or have commissioned to [Name]. Provided that [Name] agrees to pay a reasonable fee for the assignment. Otherwise the [Distributor] agrees that all the material shall be destroyed.

R.396

'Online Streaming Video Rights' shall be defined as the right to transmit, communicate, supply and/or distribute the [Film/Video] on the internet and/or over any telecommunication system from an authorised channel and/or service provider which offers a scheduled list of films and/or videos and/or catch-up and/or archive playback options to the public [and/or any commercial business, charity and/or educational establishment].

R.397

1.1 The [Licensor] grants the [exclusive/non-exclusive] Online Streaming Video Rights to the [Channel/Service Provider] in respect of the [Film/Video] throughout of the world and universe for the [Licence Period] solely for the purpose of transmission on channel [name/reference], website [name/reference] and app [name/reference].

1.2 Reception may be by television, computer, mobile and/or any other gadget and/or device. No other method of exploitation is authorised. All other rights are reserved by the [Licensor].

1.3 The rights may not be sub-licensed for exploitation by a third party.

1.4 The [Channel/Service Provider] agrees that it shall have no right to edit and/or adapt the [Film/Video] and/or to alter the opening and/or end credits, logos, trade marks, slogans and images. Nor shall the [Channel/Service Provider] have any right to use any part of the soundtrack as a separate entity.

1.5 All use of promotional extracts shall be limited to the confirmed extracts notified by the [Licensor] and no other material shall be used.

R.398

In consideration of the one-off [Fee] [Name] assigns All Media Rights in the [Image/Video] and the associated physical material which has been created and supplied by [Name] to the [Company] for the full period of copyright and any extensions and/or renewals and/or forever. So that [Name] has no claim to any ownership of the rights in any form. [Name] shall not be entitled to be paid any royalty for any method of exploitation.

R.399

1.1 [Name] is the creator of the concept and owner of all the copyright, intellectual property rights and any rights in any logo, slogan and/or image in any part of the world in the [Podcast Series] known as: [specify name/reference] which first started on [date] and which is on the [Platform] called [specify name].

1.2 [Name] confirms that he/she has not previously licensed, assigned and/or transferred the rights in 1.1 to any third party at any time.

1.3 [Name] confirms that he/she is not aware of any threat of legal action and/or other claim in respect of the [Podcast Series] from any third party including any allegation relating to defamation and/or infringement of copyright, intellectual property rights and/or trade marks.

1.4 That as far as [Name] is aware the only rights and/or material used on the [Podcast Series] which belong to and/or are controlled by any third party are set out in the attached Appendix A. [list number of podcast/rights/material/details of third party/documentation].

1.5 Subject to 1.4 above [Name] confirms that he/she has not copied, adapted and/or used any material and/or rights owned by any third party for the [Podcast Series] without their consent including any products, images, logos, words, text, music, lyrics and/or film and/or sound recordings.

R.400

1.1 The [Author] has carried out, conducted and recorded an interview with [Name] on the topic of [specify theme].

1.2 The [Author] confirms that Name] has signed an assignment agreement to the [Author] and that the [Author] owns all rights in the sound recording and the spoken words of [Name] which have been recorded. That [Name] has no objection to the [Author] licensing third parties and/or exploiting the sound recordings and words spoken.

1.3 In consideration of the fixed fee of [number/currency] the [Author] grants the [Licensee] the non-exclusive right to reproduce the exact version of the sound recording and spoken words of [Name] supplied by the [Author] in the [Film/Series] to be transmitted on the video on demand subscription service and playback archive library known as: [specify channel/reference] for distribution in electronic form over the internet and/or through any telecommunication system throughout the world from [date] to [date]. There is no right to use any other channel and/or media and/or to sub-license any rights to third parties.

R.401

1.1 The [Current Blog] entitled: [specify name] was created and developed by [Name] and has regularly featured on the website [specify name of website].

1.2 [Name] owns all the copyright and intellectual property rights and rights of ownership of the title, image and slogan associated with the [Current Blog]. These rights have not been assigned to any third party. Nor does any the website owner in 1.1 and/or any third party have any claim to such rights.

1.3 [Name] agrees to write a regular series of [New Blogs] for the [Company] for [specify name of Platform]. [Name] shall from [date] no longer continue with the [Current Blog] on the website in 1.1.

1.4 [Name] agrees to include links in the [New Blogs] with links to products and/or services nominated by the [Company].

1.5 The agreement shall start on [date] and continue on the basis of [three] month periods. Either party may terminate the agreement at any time by sending notification of termination.

1.6 The [Company] agrees and undertakes to pay [Name] a monthly fixed fee of [number/currency] and/or pro rata which shall be paid to a nominated account by [date] of each month.

1.7 The [Company] accepts and agrees that [Name] provides no indemnity of any nature to the [Company]. That the [Company] shall be responsible for the full cost and expense of any legal issues and/or claims and/or allegations that may arise relating to the [New Blogs].

1.8 The [Company] accepts and agrees that [Name] is not assigning the copyright, intellectual property rights and/or trade mark rights in the [New Blogs] to the [Company]. [Name] grants the [Company] an exclusive licence in each one which is delivered for a period of [one] year for transmission and distribution on the [Platform].

R.402

1.1 The [Distributor] agrees and undertakes to pay [Name] [number] per cent of the total sale price paid and retained by the [Distributor] for any products which are purchased by any person and/or company using the authorised link on the [Blog/Website/Online Account] owned and controlled by [Name].

1.2 [Name] agrees and accepts that [Name] does and will not acquire any copyright, intellectual property rights, trade mark rights and/or any other rights of ownership over the name, logo, slogan and/or any other part of any product and/or packaging at any time. That [Name] shall not have the right to attempt to register any such rights and/or to make any claim of ownership.

1.3 [Name] accepts that they must not make any changes and/or create any other versions and/or adaptations of any products owned by the [Distributor] by any method.

R.403

1.1 The [Company] engages [Name] as a brand ambassador for [specify type of company].

1.2 [Name] agrees to promote and market the products and services of the [Company] and to post a minimum of number of posts, videos and to carry out such work each month as described in Appendix A [where posts/videos are to be displayed/duration/length] from [date to [date].

1.3 [Name] accepts and agrees that he/she shall not acquire any copyright, intellectual property rights, trade marks and/or any other rights in the brands, products and/or services of the [Company] at any time.

1.4 The [Company] agrees to pay [Name] to promote and market its products and services on the basis of the sales actually completed. Both through following the links and the use of discount codes provided supplied by the [Company] to [Name]. When a sale is completed through the purchase by a third party of a product and/or service following the link and/or using the discount code. Then [Name] shall be entitled to be paid [number] per cent of each completed sale. No payment shall be due where any sums are subsequently repaid to the purchaser. Such sums which fall due to [Name] shall be paid at the end of each calendar month. In addition an itemised completed sales statement shall be provided at the end of each [three] month period.

R.404

1.1 The [Company] engages the non-exclusive services of [Name] to create and post original content, stories and images of the brands and products of the [Company].

1.2 The agreement shall start on [date] and continue until such time as either party shall terminate the agreement with [one] months notification.

1.3 [Name] accepts and agrees that he/she shall only be paid for the creation of original and high quality content which is posted by [Name] on the [specify account/blog/podcast/other].

1.4 [Name] agrees and accepts that [Name] must follow any guidelines and/or policies regarding the nature of the content issued by the [Company]. That no post can contain any reference to any products and/or services owned and/or controlled by a third party.

1.5 [Name] agrees and undertakes not to attempt to register any copyright, intellectual property rights and/or trade marks and/or logos owned and/or used by the [Company] at any time and/or to create any adaptation.

1.6 The [Company] agrees to pay [Name] a fixed fee of [number/currency] for each post which is successfully completed by [Name] and accepted by the [Company] as being of sufficient quality.

1.7 [Name] undertakes to post no more than [number] posts in each calendar month in respect of the products and services of the [Company].

R.405

1.1 [Name] agrees and undertakes to post a minimum of [number] high quality and new original [images/videos/articles] each month on [specify blog/podcast/on line account] from [date] to [date] in accordance with the planned marketing schedule and description set out in Appendix A which is attached to this agreement.

1.2 The [Company] engages the non-exclusive services of [Name] from [date to [date] to promote the brands and products of the [Company]. In consideration of the work to be completed in 1.1 the [Company] agrees and undertakes to pay [Name] a fixed monthly fee of [number/currency] from [date] to [date] which shall be subject to invoice by [Name].

1.3 The [Company] shall not be responsible for the payment of any expenses incurred by [Name] and/or the clearance of any rights and payment of any third parties which do not relate to the [Company] its brands, products, trade marks and/or associated packaging.

1.4 [Name] agrees that he/she shall have no right to make any claim to any rights of any nature held by the [Company] in respect of its brands, products, trade marks and/or associated packaging.

R.406

1.1 [Name] agrees to create, develop and post material, images, articles and videos which promote and market the [App] owned by the [Company].

1.2 The [Company] agrees that [Name] may [not] be entitled to mention other third parties and their apps, services and products in any material, images, articles and videos which he/she generates under this agreement.

1.3 [Name] agrees that the [Company] may use and adapt the material, images, articles and/or videos which he/she posts relating to the [Company] and/or the [App] and use and/or reproduce it and/or adapt it for any other form of exploitation by the [Company].

1.4 The [Company] agrees to pay [Name] a fixed fee of [number/currency] for the period of [number] weeks which shall be paid [number/currency] on date and the balance on [date] subject to completion of the agreed work.

1.5 The [Company] accepts that it shall have no claim of ownership to the name of [Name] and/or his/her slogan, image and/or any other content on [specify source].

R.407
'The Electronic Publishing Rights' shall be defined as the right to reproduce, use, supply, sell, distribute and/or adapt the [Work] by any electronic method of communication including over the internet and/or through any telecommunication system in text and sound only in any language including any electronic download, audio file, readings and/or any catch up and/or playback archive service. It shall not include films, videos, podcasts and/or any visual form of reproduction and/or exploitation.

R.408

1.1 The right to arrange and carry out any tour, event, musical and/or other adaptation of the [Work] for stage, theatre, festivals and any other location where there is an audience which attends shall be held by [Name]. [Name] shall be entitled to retain any sums received form such form of exploitation subject to 1.2.

1.2 Where any tour, event, musical and/or other adaptation of the [Work] for stage and theatre, festivals and/or other location where there is an audience which attends is to be recorded, filmed and/or streamed live over the internet and/or through any telecommunication system for reception by television, computer, laptop, mobile phone and/or any other gadget and/or device and/or any theatre audience, school, university, outdoor festival and/or other location. Then the rights shall be held by [Name and the [Company] and any sums received shall be split equally between the parties.

R.409

1.1 [Name] is a sponsored competitor in a tournament known as: [specify title of tournament] which is organised by the [Company].

1.2 The [Company] shall pay [Name] a fixed fee of [number/currency] to participate in and to promote the tournament on his/her social media. These payments shall be made in stages as follows: [specify payments].

1.3 [Name] acknowledges that the tournament is filmed and recorded and live streamed and played back on the internet and through any telecommunication system over the subscription service entitled: [title of service/reference] which is owned by the [Company].

1.4 [Name] assigns all copyright, intellectual property rights and any other rights throughout the world and universe in all media for the full period of copyright and any extensions and/or renewals and/or any other period of time that may be permitted and in perpetuity in:

A. his/her appearance and performance in the tournament and/or any live and/ recorded material which may be commissioned and/or arranged by the [Company] and

B. any interview and/or personal images, videos and/or films which he/she may arrange to be taken in his/her home and/or accommodation either before and/or after the tournament which are supplied to and/or arranged with the [Company].

R.410

1.1 [Name] authorises third parties to publish and distribute articles based on no more than [number] extracts of [length/duration] from the [Website/Podcast] in any printed and/or online digital and/or electronic format, magazine and/or newspaper in [country]. Provided that there is a clear credit and link provided to [Name] and the [Website/Podcast] as follows: [specify ownership/link/reference].

1.2 There is no right granted to any third party to reproduce and/or exploit any content in any other form and/or to adapt any material and/or to register and/or sub-license any rights.

R.411

1.1 [Name] has agreed that the [Company] may commission and create an audio file of the [Work] in [language].

1.2 The [Company] agrees to ensure that any third party shall not acquire any rights in the [Work] and/or the audio file.

1.3 [Name] and the [Company] agree that the parties shall each own an equal share in the audio file which is commissioned. That any sums received by the [Company] from the exploitation of the audio file shall be shared equally between the parties after deduction of any costs including the costs of commissioning the original audio file].

1.4 [Name] grants the [Company] the exclusive right to exploit the audio file of the [Work] on [specify channel/platform/website] from [date to date].

1.5 Both parties agree that after [date] the audio file may not be exploited without the agreement of both parties.

R.412

1.1 All the Contributors to the virtual [Event] are listed as follows: [specify name/address/contact].

1.2 The Contributors agree that it is a condition of participation that they agree and consent to the live streaming, recording and filming of their appearance, performance, words, actions, gestures, background material and verbal exchanges and other participation in the virtual [Event].

1.3 The [Contributors] agree that they shall have no editorial control and no right to demand any edit and/or deletion. The [Contributors] accept and acknowledge that all rights in the live streaming, recording and filming shall belong to the [Company]. The [Contributors] agree and undertake to sign any documents that the [Company] shall request to be completed to ensure that all rights are assigned to the [Company].

1.4 The [Contributors] agree to adhere to policies and guidelines of the [Company] which they may receive prior to the virtual [Event]. The [Contributors] acknowledge that the [Company] may completely remove and/or edit out any person at any time for any reason.

R.413

[Name] and the [Company] agree that in the event that there are any potential spin-offs and/or merchandising arrangements arising from the [Podcast Series] hosted by [Name]. That [Name] shall be involved in the negotiation of the terms of such agreements and entitled to [number] per cent of the [net receipts/sums received] by the [Company] from any such third party. Spin-offs shall include but not be limited to any: audio files, books, films, videos, images, competitions, toys and household products; jewellery, shoes, clothes, food products, drinks, stationery, games, theme parks, tours and festivals.

R.414

1.1 [Name] grants to the [Licensee] the right to adapt the [Work/Book] entitled: [title/ISBN]:

A. To develop and create, produce, supply, sell and distribute an interactive computer game which can be exploited in the form of computer-generated material; electronic material, film, video and computer software over the internet and by means of any telecommunication system and

B. To develop and create, produce, supply, sell and distribute an interactive computer game which can be exploited in the form of units and/or discs and/or some other method of storage which can be sold separately and installed in a computer and/or laptop and/or some other device and be loaded and played which are reproduced by means of mechanical reproduction.

1.2 [Name] grants the rights in 1.1 as an exclusive licence from [date to [date] for exploitation by the [Licensee] throughout the [Territory/ world].

R.415

1.1 In consideration of the [Advance] and the royalties in clause [–] [Name] grants to the [Company] the exclusive right to develop and create a game format series based on the [Characters/Script/Synopsis] for the [Channel/Website/Platform] as described and budgeted in Appendix A which forms part of this agreement. [list number of episodes, duration, production budget, schedule for production; final master material format]. Together with associated competitions and premium rate telephone lines.

1.2 The licence shall start on [date and end on [date]. The licence period may be extended for a further period of [number] years by the payment of an additional [number/currency] by [date].

1.3 The [Company] shall be entitled to exploit the game format series and the associated competitions and premium rate telephone lines in any part of the world in all media and/or any medium and/or any method of exploitation during the original licence period. Together with the extended licence period if the additional fee is paid.

1.4   At the end of the licence period all rights in the game format series and the master material and any copies and any marketing shall revert to [Name]. The [Company] agrees and undertakes to complete any documentation to ensure the assignment to [Name] is achieved as agreed.

R.416

1.1   [Name] is and/or shall be the original creator of the [Graphics/Artwork/Labels] which have been commissioned by the [Company] for its logo, slogan, image and marketing for its [Website/App] and [products/services].

1.2   [Name] both assigns and undertakes that he /she shall assign all present and future copyright, intellectual property rights, trade marks and any other rights in the [Graphics/Artwork/Labels] to the [Company] throughout the world for the full period of copyright and any extensions and/or renewals and/or such further periods as may be permitted and/or forever. So that [Name] retains no rights and/or claim to the [Graphics/Artwork/Labels] and shall have no right to receive any additional payment and/or future royalty.

1.3   [Name] agrees that the [Company] shall be entitled to adapt the [Graphics/Artwork/Labels] and/or to commission a third party to create and develop another animated version in electronic form to use and exploit over the internet and/or any telecommunication system.

1.4   [Name] shall not object to any registration of any trade marks by the [Company] in respect of the [Graphics/Artwork/Labels].

R.417

1.1   The [Infographics/Maps/Databases/Taxonomy] are based on data supplied by a third party licensee.

1.2   The [Company] has commissioned [Name] to design, develop and create the [Infographics/Maps/Databases/Taxonomy].

1.3   The [Company] agrees and accepts that [Name] shall be the copyright owner of the [Infographics/Maps/Databases/Taxonomy] which they have developed with their specialist skill and knowledge.

1.4   [Name] grants the [Company] an exclusive licence to reproduce, sell and distribute the [Infographics/Maps/Databases/Taxonomy] in conjunction with the [Work/Book] entitled: [title/ISBN] in any part of the world in any media and/or format for the Licence Period. Provided that [Name] is paid the advance in clause [–] and the royalties in clause [–] and there is a credit and copyright notice to [Name] as required in clause [–].

R.418

The parties agree that the [Material/Logo/Slogan/Film/Sound Recording] associated with the [Project] shall not be used and/or licensed to any website, app, platform and/or third party to be used to endorse and/or promote any betting, gambling, bingo, lottery and/or interactive game and/or competition.

R.419

1.1 It is accepted by all parties that they shall not be responsible for a breach of this agreement due to the actions and/or default of a third party including any sub-licensee and/or member of the public.

1.2 No legal action shall be taken by any parties unless the defaulting party has been informed of the problem and provided with an opportunity to remedy the matter.

1.3 Where any party to this agreement attempts to register any rights relating to [Project] they must notify all the other parties of that fact immediately.

Merchandising and Distribution

R.420

'The Merchandising and Promotional Rights' shall be defined as the right to develop, reproduce, manufacture, supply, sell and/or distribute and/or license one or more products and/or services which reproduce and/or depict and/or represent and/or adapt characters, names, logos, artwork, images, films, videos, storylines, scenes and/or other material derived from and/or based on the [Work/Book/Programme].

R.421

'The Merchandising Rights' shall be defined to mean the right to reproduce, manufacture, supply, sell, distribute and/or to license and authorise third parties to carry out and/or to exploit the following which bear the [Character/Logo/Scenes/Images] from the [Work/Book/Tour/Film] known as [specify title/description/reference]:

1.1 All high quality printed material which is in the form of comic strips, comics, calendars, stationery, posters, cards, stickers, children's plastic and/or fabric books and/or other printed books in hardback and/or paperback.

1.2 All high quality products and articles which can be manufactured, reproduced, sold and distributed including but not limited to drink containers, mugs, toys, puppets, T-shirts, bags, leisure wear, sportswear, bath products, household items, storage boxes, shoes, slippers and trainers.

R.422
'The Merchandising Rights' shall be defined as:

1.1 'The [Character/Logo/Image/Costume]' shall be the original concept and novel idea for a character which is described and represented in Appendix A which forms part of this agreement. [Describe in detail/ colour/functions/dimensions/name/logo, slogans/any specific features in words and images].

1.2 The sole and exclusive right to exploit the [Character/Logo/Image/ Costume] in 1.1 through the manufacture, production, distribution, promotion, supply, sale and sub-license of articles and products of any type based on and/or derived from the [Character/Logo/Image/ Costume] including but not limited to: posters, toys, board and other games, greetings cards, stationery, children and adult clothes and shoes, hair accessories, bags, food, drinks, catering material such as paper plates and cups, balloons, books and comics throughout the [Territory/area] for the duration of the Licence Period.

1.3 Any form of exploitation in the form of sound recordings, films, videos and/or interactive online digital and electronic games, quizzes and competitions are excluded. There is no right to create any podcast, film, video and/or audio file to exploit over the internet and/or by means of any telecommunication system in any electronic format.

R.423
'The Authorised Product' shall be the agreed and approved product licensed by [Name] which is to be manufactured, reproduced, supplied, sold and distributed by the [Licensee] which incorporates an adapted version of the [Character/Logo/Image] and which is described in detail in Appendix B and forms part of this agreement. [specify dimensions of authorised product/ location of character name and/or logo and/or any image/specify credits and copyright notices on product, packaging and marketing].

R.424
'The Licensed Articles' shall be any unit and/or article which is manufactured, reproduced, sold and/or distributed based on or derived from licensed

[Character/Logo/Image] by the [Agent] and/or any sub-agent, sub-licensee and/or sub-distributor at any time.

R.425

'The Format for the Quiz' shall be the original concept and novel idea designed and created by [Name] for a quiz show which is described in Appendix A and which forms part of this agreement. [Describe in full/set layout/scenery/questions/costumes/catchphrases/prizes/competitors/ method of entry/music/jingles.]

R.426

1.1 In consideration of the Licence Fee and the future royalties the [Licensor] grants to the [Licensee] the sole and exclusive right to develop, adapt, reproduce, manufacture, distribute and sell the specific [Licensed Article/Product] described in Appendix A based on the [Character/Logo/Image] throughout the [Territory/world] for the duration of the [Licence Period/Term of the Agreement].

1.2 No other format and/or product and/or method of exploitation is granted by the [Licensor]. All other rights are reserved.

R.427

1.1 In consideration of the payment of the non-returnable Advance Fee and the royalties in clause [–]. The [Licensor] grants to the [Licensee] the sole and exclusive right to exercise, reproduce, adapt, supply, sell and/or exploit from [date] to [date] in the [Territory] the Merchandising Rights defined in 1.2 in the [Name/Logo/Slogan/Image] in the [Territory/ Licensed Area].

1.2 The Merchandising Rights which shall be defined as the right to develop, reproduce, manufacture, supply, sell and/or distribute and/ or license one or more two and/or three dimensional products which reproduce and/or depict and/or represent and/or adapt [Name/ Logo/Slogan/Image]. Examples include household, cookery and food products and items; T shirts and caps, stationary, calendars, leisure and sportswear for adults and children, comics, annual books, colouring and sticker books, storage boxes, wall charts, toys, jewellery and accessories.

1.3 It is agreed between the parties that the rights granted in 1.1 and 1.2 shall not include any autobiographical book and/or book in electronic format to be sold over the internet and/or any telecommunication system and/or through theme parks, tours, betting, gambling, lotteries, holograms, sculptures, restaurants and bars.

1.4 The [Licensee] agrees and accepts that in the event that the [Licensor] refuses to approve any particular sample prior to manufacture due to the design and/or quality of the product. That the [Licensee] shall accept that decision and not proceed to production and sale unless the problem can be remedied.

1.5 That the [Licensee] agrees and accepts that any sub-licensee must be approved by the [Licensor] and must undertake to be bound by the same conditions as the [Licensee] under this agreement. That in the event that any sub-licensee defaults that the [Licensee] accepts full responsibility for the consequences of that default and shall pay any losses, damages, costs and/or expenses due to the [Licensor].

1.6 The [Licensee] agrees that the [Licensor] reserves all other rights.

R.428
The [Licensee] agrees and undertakes not to authorise any third party to reproduce and/or adapt and/or exploit the [Character/Costume/Name/Logo] at any time.

R.429
The [Licensee] agrees and undertakes not to attempt to register any domain name, title, initials, caricature, gesture, action, image and/or any other material and/or any copyright, intellectual property rights, trade marks and/or other rights in the professional name and/or personal name of [specify person] and/or any slogan, prop and/or personal appearance and/or representation with which they are associated at any time.

R.430
The [Licensor] agrees that the [Licensee] shall be entitled to authorise any third party to use any of the products produced under this agreement for any film, video, podcast, photo shoot and/or article in any magazine, newspaper, podcast and/or any other media company.

R.431

1.1 This agreement solely concerns the production by the [Licensee] of the authorised licensed [Product] known as: [specify name] details of which are described in the attached Appendix D which forms part of this agreement.

1.2 [Name] grants the [Licensee] a non-exclusive licence to manufacture and produce the licensed [Product] which incorporates the [Image/Design] owned by [Name]. The licence shall start on [date] and end on [date]. The licence shall apply to the following countries: [specify and list countries].

1.3 There is no right granted to the [Licensee] to exploit any other rights in the [Image/Design]. The [Licensee] is not entitled to appoint any agent, sub-licensee, distributor and/or any other third party to produce, sell and/or distribute the [Product] without the prior consent of [Name].

1.4 The [Licensee] agrees not to exploit the same rights with a third party until after [date].

R.432
The [Licensor] agrees that it shall not be entitled to any royalties under this agreement where the licensed [Units/Products] have been offered and given away for free as part of a short promotion at an exhibition; in a promotional competition as prizes and/or have been lost, destroyed, damaged and/or sold to a third party at below cost price due to lack of sales for more than [number] [months/years].

R.433
The [Company] appoints the [Agent/Distributor] to be the [Company's] [non-exclusive/exclusive] [agent/distributor] to arrange for the sale, supply and delivery of the [Products/Services] in the [Territory/country/area] from [date] to [date] subject to the following terms:

1.1 The [Agent/Distributor] shall not market, promote and/or offer the [Products/Services] outside the agreed [Territory/country/area] at any time.

1.2 The [Agent/Distributor] shall adhere to and follow any instructions provided by the [Company] and adhere to all health and safety guidelines and/or any codes of conduct and/or policies supplied by the [Company] at any time.

1.3 The [Agent/Distributor] shall not be entitled to market, promote and/or offer the [Products/Services] at retail outlets, trade fairs, markets and/or exhibitions outside the agreed [Territory/country].

1.4 The [Agent/Distributor] shall not acquire any patent, copyright, intellectual property rights, computer software rights, trade mark rights and/or any other rights in the [Products/Services] and/or any packaging and/or marketing material.

1.5 That in the event that the [Territory/country/area] is subject to war, a political upraising and/or a political coup, severe floods and/or other weather conditions and/or some other state of affairs which amounts to grounds of force majeure. That the [Company] may suspend the agreement. If the suspension continues for more than [number] months' the [Agent/Distributor] accepts that the [Company] may terminate the agreement with [number] months' notification.

R.434

'The Image Rights' shall be defined as:

1.1 The right to reproduce, supply, distribute, license and/or exploit the stage name, nickname, initials and/or personal appearance, image, photographs and/or any other visual representation and/or caricature of [Name] and any associated clothes, slogan and/or props which he/she may use as part of their public character in respect of any product, service and/or charitable enterprise.

1.2 The right in 1.1 shall not include any moving visual image such as a podcast, film and/or video and/or any sound recording of the voice of [Name].

R.435

'The Image and Promotional Rights' shall be defined to mean:

1.1 The right to offer the name, image and activities of [Name] and his/her services to third parties under a commercial licence to promote and/or endorse their products and/or services as an ambassador and/or brand representative and

1.2 The right to offer the name, image and activities of [Name] and his/her services to third parties under a commercial licence to participate in and/or promote an event, exhibition and/or campaign and

1.3 The right to offer the name, image and activities of [Name] and his/her services to third parties under a commercial licence to be associated with a marketing campaign for a product, service, fundraising for a charity, a financial investment and/or property scheme and/or some other matter which is sold, advertised and/or promoted to the public.

1.4 It shall not include the right to insist that [Name] in any manner infringe the policies and guidelines of his/her [sports organisation/governing body] known as: [specify name of organisation].

1.5 All other rights are reserved. There is no right granted to create any merchandising, computer games, documentary and/or film series and/or any new trade mark related to [Name] and/or to register any rights. All proposed agreements will be subject to the specific approval in each case of the terms by [Name].

R.436

'The Image Rights' shall be defined as:

1.1 The [exclusive/non-exclusive] right to reproduce, supply, distribute and exploit the still and/or moving and/or adapted image and likeness of the [Sportsperson] and/or any mannerisms, gestures, body language, catch phrases, slogans and/or voice likeness of the [Sportsperson] in all formats and in all media whether in existence now and/or created in the future throughout the world for the Term of the Agreement.

1.2 This definition shall include but not be limited to all forms of films, videos, programmes, marketing, advertising, sound recordings, podcasts, computer-generated material, holograms, two and three dimensional reproductions and/or communications in any electronic format over the internet and/or from any platform, website and/or app and/or by means of any telecommunication system, and/or any merchandising, licensing and/or endorsement of any product, service, gambling, betting, lottery and/or theme park.

R.437
'Image Rights' shall mean the right to reproduce, supply, sell and distribute the agreed image and name of [specify Name] and any associated trade mark on any specified and agreed product and/or service.

R.438

1.1 [Name] grants the [Company] the exclusive Image Rights from [date] to [date] in respect of the agreed [Product/Service] described in Appendix A which forms part of this agreement for the [Territory].

1.2 It shall not include any other rights which are reserved to [Name]. It is not intended that this agreement should assign to the [Company] any copyright, intellectual property rights and/or trade marks and/or any other rights in any adaptation which may be created in respect of the Image Rights in 1.1. Where any new material is commissioned by the [Company] then the [Company] undertakes to ensure that all such rights are assigned to [Name].

R.439
The [Company] agrees and undertakes that [Name] shall retain all present and future copyright, registered trade marks, intellectual property rights and/or any other rights that he/she owns and/or may control with respect to his/her name, any still and/or moving images, slogan, catch phrases, logos, scripts, costumes, props and/or otherwise at any time of any nature. This agreement is not intended to assign any rights of any nature to the [Company].

R.440
The [Company] agrees that the following matters are specifically agreed as excluded from this agreement:

1.1 [Name] shall be entitled to enter into any agreement with a third party for the publication of an autobiography and/or other book in hardback and/or paperback and/or in any electronic format as a download and/or audio file over the internet and/or any telecommunication system.

1.2 [Name] shall be entitled to appear in films, videos, programmes and/or other series for broadcast and/or transmission on any licensed 'terrestrial, cable, satellite and/or digital television and/or radio and/or podcast series and/or other platform and/or over the internet and/or any telecommunication system and/or any archive playback and/or catch up service whether free, on demand and/or subscription.

1.3 [Name] shall be entitled to contribute to and perform in any tour, play, musical, documentary, festival, competition and/or event that he/she may decide at any time.

R.441

The [Licensee] agrees and undertakes that:

1.1 The [Licensee] shall not without the prior written consent of the [Agent] and/or the [Licensor], reproduce, use or exploit the business and/or brand names of the [Licensor] and/or [Agent] in connection with the marketing of the [Licensed Articles] except for the agreed credits, copyright notice and trade mark set out in this agreement.

1.2 The [Licensee] shall not represent itself in any manner as the agent or representative of the [Licensor] and/or the [Agent] at any time.

1.3 The [Licensee] shall not acquire and/or attempt to register any rights in the name of the [Character] and/or any associated slogan, words, image, logo, text and/or pending and/or registered trade mark and/or otherwise under this agreement except the right to manufacture, distribute and sell the [Licensed Articles].

R.442

The [Agent] agrees and undertakes as follows:

1.1 Not to issue any requests for payment on behalf of the [Company] and/or to pledge and/or commit the [Company] to pay any sums and/or carry out any work and/or services for any reason unless the [Agent] has obtained the prior [approval/consent] of the [Company].

1.2 That the [Agent] shall not be entitled to authorise any third party to reproduce, copy, draw, take images and/or photographs, film and/or to exploit in any form and/or medium the sample prototypes and/or the [Products] and/or any slogan, brand name, trade mark and/or image of the [Company] unless the [Agent] has obtained the prior [approval/consent] of the [Company].

1.3 That the [Agent] shall not be entitled to negotiate, promote and/or distribute in any manner and/or form the [Character] and/or the [Products] outside the [Territory/Licensed Area]. Provided that it is agreed that the [Agent] may do so at the following exhibitions and trade fairs: [specify names/reference].

R.443

1.1 In consideration of the Assignment Fee the [Assignor] assigns to the [Assignee] all present and future copyright, intellectual property rights and all other rights in all media in the [Work/Format/Material] including any associated trade mark, image, slogan and/or jingle which are described in Appendix A whether in existence now and/or created in the future throughout the world [universe, galaxy and outer space] for the full period of copyright and any extensions and renewals [and for any such other periods as may be possible] [and forever] including but not limited to:

A. All forms and methods of reproduction, supply, distribution, broadcast and/or transmission and exploitation over terrestrial, cable, satellite television and/or radio and/or any catch up and/or playback archive retrieval.

B. All forms and methods of reproduction, supply, distribution, broadcast and/or transmission and exploitation in any electronic form and/or by any method for use and/or access over the internet and/or any telecommunication system and/or any catch up and/or playback archive service.

C. All forms and methods of reproduction, supply, distribution, broadcast and/or transmission, exploitation and/or publication including hardback, paperback, biographies, newspapers, magazines, comics; digests; serialisations; annuals and/or in any format including audio files and/or electronic downloads over the internet and/or any telecommunication system.

D. All reproduction, supply, distribution, broadcast and/or transmission and/or exploitation of any sequels, adaptations, merchandising, sponsorship, endorsement and product placement, festivals, sports and other outdoor events, computer games, lotteries, betting, gambling, competitions and theme parks.

E. All forms of exploitation of mechanical reproduction, theatric and/or non-theatric exploitation and/or rights in any performance and/or any associated recordings.

1.2   The [Assignor] accepts and agrees that no rights of any nature are reserved and retained by the [Assignor].

R.444

1.1   The [Company] grants the [Sub-Licensee] the non-exclusive right to reproduce, manufacture, supply, sell and distribute the [Character/Logo] on all copies of [specify article] in the manner which is described and represented in Appendix A from [date] to [date] anywhere in the world through retail and wholesale outlets and/or websites, apps and/or platforms over the internet and/or any telecommunication system.

1.2   The [Sub-Licensee] agrees that it shall not have the right to sub-license the rights and/or authorise any third party to reproduce and/or manufacture and/or make use of copies of the [Character/Logo] at any time.

1.3   The [Sub-Licensee] acknowledges that the [Company] shall have the right to sub-license the exact same rights to a competing third party and/or any other adapted version.

R.445

1.1   The [Sub-Licensee] agrees and undertakes not to sub-license the rights and/or authorise any third party to reproduce, manufacture, supply, sell and/or distribute copies of the [Artwork/Logo/Slogan/Character] and/or any adaptation. Nor shall the [Sub-Licensee] authorise the exploitation of the [Artwork/Logo/Slogan/Character] in respect of any other articles, products, services, packaging and/or marketing.

1.2   The only permitted exploitation under this agreement is the reproduction, manufacture, supply, sale and distribution of the approved [sample/prototype] and the final version of the [Product] and/or any packaging and/or marketing which incorporates the [Artwork/Logo/Slogan/Character]

R.446

The [Licensee] agrees and undertakes not to:

1.1   Change any part of the layout, design, copyright notice, content and packaging for the [Product] for which the sample has been approved by the [Licensor].

1.2   Market and/or promote the [Product] in association with any other person, brand, campaign and/or event which would be to the detriment of the reputation of the [Product] and/or business of the [Licensor] in any manner.

1.3 Make representations and/or claims in any marketing and promotional material which cannot be verified by supporting data and evidence.

1.4 Breach any guidelines, policies and codes of practice in any part of the world which relate to health and safety assessments, tests, product liability, advertising, packaging and/or the manufacture and/or the supply of products.

R.447

The [Licensor] agrees that the [Licensee] shall have the right to sub-license the rights set out in clause [–] to any third party. Provided that the [Licensee] shall not be relieved from any terms of this agreement and undertakes to bear all responsibilities for the acts, errors, omissions and/or defaults of the third party sub-licensee. Further the [Licensee] must agree to bear the cost of all royalties and pay for all sums due to the [Licensor] which are not paid to the [Licensee] by any third party sub-licensee at any time.

R.448

'The Music Exploitation Rights' shall be defined to mean the following rights which exist now in respect of the title, lyrics and musical work entitled [specify title/reference] which shall be referred to as the [Work]:

1.1 To publish, print, sell and/or distribute the [Work] whether in the form of an ordinary sheet music edition or as part of a folio or album and/or in any other printed form.

1.2 To reproduce the [Work] by means of mechanical reproduction by way of a record, disk, tape and/or other means of conveying sound and/or visual images. Excluding films, videos, podcasts and television programmes.

1.3 The right to grant any licences for the synchronisation of the [Work] with any feature film, programme for television, video, podcast, advertisement and/or any other visual moving images for transmission and/or broadcast over terrestrial, cable, satellite television and/or for communication in any electronic form as a download and/or video and/or podcast, film and/or series over the internet and/or by means of any telecommunication system.

1.4 The right to grant any licences for the reproduction and exploitation of the [Work] in sound only with any radio programme, promotion, competition, product, service, event, video, podcast, advertisement and/or for transmission and/or broadcast over terrestrial, cable, satellite television and/or for communication in any electronic form as an audio file and/or as part of a soundtrack for a video, podcast, film and/or series over the internet and/or by means of any telecommunication system.

1.5 The rights in 1.1 to 1.4 shall include the right to sub-license a third party to exercise such rights.

1.6 The rights in 1.1 to 1.4 shall not extend to any right and/or form and/or method which is not in existence as at [date].

1.7 The rights in 1.1 to 1.4 shall include the right to make and publish translations of the lyrics in the [Work] in any languages.

1.8 The right to authorise and/or grant a licence for the live and/or pre-recorded performance of the [Work] for any show, tour, artist and/or group and/or for any adaptation.

R.449
'Secondary Rights' shall mean all rights generated as a direct result of the production of the [Programme] but which are not in themselves rights in the [Programme] such as music, publishing and merchandising rights.

R.450
'The Theme Park Rights' shall be defined as:

1.1 The right to design, build and develop a large leisure, game and tourist attraction based in [location] which is centred around the [Artist/Work/Characters] for which a charge is made for entry by the public.

1.2 Such commercial enterprise in 1.1 shall contain waterslides, fairground attractions, interactive amusements, sports activities, retail shops, restaurants.

1.3 It shall include the right to use the names, logos, trade marks, slogans, costumes, scripts, lyrics and musical works associated with the [Artist/Work/Characters] and to make two and three dimensional and/or other adaptations based on and/or derived from the [Artist/Work/Characters].

R.451
The [Licensee] agrees and accepts that it shall not acquire any right to register a domain name, trade mark and/or any other copyright and/or intellectual property rights of any nature in the [Work/Project/Product] and/or any logo, image, character name, title, slogan, text, words and/or other content and/or packaging and/or marketing material whether it is supplied by the [Licensor] and/or created and developed for the purpose of this agreement.

R.452
The [Company] agrees and accepts that there are no rights granted to the [Company] which authorise and/or permit the [Company to register any rights in respect of the [Project] including but not limited to:

1.1 Any trade mark, service mark and/or any other name, logo and/or image and/or abbreviated and/or adapted form.

1.2 All mechanical reproduction rights and/or performing rights and/or any associated recordings with any rights management organisation.

1.3 Any domain name and/or website and/or app and/or product and/or service name and/or any similar version based on letters and/or otherwise.

R.453

This agreement only applies to any copyright, intellectual property rights and methods of exploitation which exist before [date]. It does not apply to any new technology and/or rights created in the future which create a completely new format and means of exploitation which were not envisaged as being covered by this agreement.

R.454

The [Licensee] accepts and agrees that there is no right granted by [Name] for the [Licensee] to create any series of podcasts, videos, sound recordings and/or any other material for use on any website, platform and/or social media and/or transmission in electronic form over the internet and/or by means of any telecommunication system.

R.455

[Name] accepts and agrees that the [Licensee] shall be entitled to create and develop, supply and distribute a series of images, podcasts and/or videos and/or any other material for use on any website, platform and/or social media and/or for transmission in electronic form over the internet and/or by means of any telecommunication system of the [Artwork/Material/Project]. Provided that the [Licensee] adheres to the terms of this agreement.

R.456

The [Company] agrees and undertakes that it will not license, permit and/or authorise any third party to reproduce, manufacture, supply, sell, distribute, market and/or adapt the [Image/Logo/Slogan] at any time unless expressly approved in advance by the [Licensor].

R.457

In the event that the [Licensee] is to be sold to and/or taken over by a third party which will purchase a large portion of its assets and business and/or is to be restructured under a new trading name and/or brand. The [Licensor] shall have the right and shall be entitled to terminate the agreement with the [Licensee] prior to the sale and/or restructuring and to remove any master material and/or copies which the [Licensor] owns which has been loaned to the [Licensee].

R.458

Where the [Licensee] adapts and use the original material supplied and/or rights granted to create and develop any new material and/or copyright and/or intellectual property rights under this agreement. Then the [Licensee] agrees and undertakes to assign all such new material and/or rights to the [Licensor] when requested either before the expiry of the agreement and/or as soon as possible after termination. Provided that the [Licensor] pays any legal costs of such assignment.

Publishing

R.459

'Electronic Publication Rights' shall be defined as:

1.1 The right to reproduce, supply, sell, rent, hire and/or distribute the [Work/Material/Book] in whole and/or in part by any electronic means and/or format for communication over the internet and/or through any telecommunication system.

1.2 It shall include any method of adaptation of sound, text, images, film, video and/or sound recording of the [Work/Material/Book] by any electronic means and/or format including but not limited to audio files, downloads, podcasts and/or any film and/or video supplied under any paid for subscription service and/or for free under any archive playback and/or catch up retrieval service from any website, app and/or platform.

1.3 It shall include the right to licence such rights in 1.1 and 1.2 to any third party for exploitation provided any such licence does not exceed the rights granted.

1.4 It shall include the right to translate and/or licence the translation of the [Work/Material/Book] in 1.1 and 1.2 to any third party for exploitation provided any such licence does not exceed the rights granted.

1.5 Reception may be by television, radio, computer, laptop, watch and/or some other stationary and/or portable device and/or gadget.

1.6 All competitions, quizzes, game formats, lotteries, betting, gambling and/or gaming websites, apps and/or platforms and/or methods of exploitation are specifically not covered by this definition and are excluded.

R.460

1.1　[Name] grants the exclusive Electronic Publication Rights in the [Work/ Material/Book] in whole and/or part to the [Distributor] from [date] to [date] throughout the world and outer space.

1.2　Any new rights, material and/or formats created by the [Distributor] under this agreement shall be owned by [Name] and the [Distributor]. After the expiry and/or termination of the agreement the written consent of both parties shall be required for the exploitation of any new rights, material and/or formats created by the [Distributor] under this agreement until [date]. After [date] the [Distributor] shall assign all new rights, material and formats to [Name].

R.461

'The Publishing Rights' shall be defined as the right to reproduce, supply, sell and/or distribute the [Manuscript/Work/Images/Book] by the [Author] in volume form namely in hardback and/or paperback.

R.462

'The Publishing Rights' shall be defined as:

1.1　The right to reproduce, supply, sell and/or distribute the [Manuscript/ Work/Images/Book] of the [Author] in hardback and/or paperback and/ or in plastic and/or fabric and/or some other material in printed format.

1.2　The right to reproduce, supply, sell and/or distribute the [Manuscript/ Work/Images/Book] of the [Author] through any electronic means and/or format for communication over the internet and/or any telecommunication system including any download, audio file and/or podcast.

1.3　The right to authorise and licence extracts of the [Manuscript/Work/ Images/Book] to be reproduced and/or read and/or performed.

1.4　It shall not include the right to grant an option and/or exclusive licence for a feature film and/or television series and/or documentary and/or any film, video and/or other project and/or adaptation which will consist of moving images and a soundtrack of more than [number] minutes in duration.

1.5　It shall not include the right to endorse any product and/or service in association with the [Manuscript/Work/Images/Book] of the [Author].

1.6　It shall not include the right to licence [Manuscript/Work/Images/Book] and/or any adaptation to any website, app and/or platform which is involved in any illegal, offensive, obscene, political and/or other activity and/or to which the [Author] raises objections.

1.7 All merchandising and cross promotion, theme parks, computer games, competitions, gambling, lotteries and betting are specifically excluded and no rights are granted by the [Author].

R.463

1.1 In consideration of the Fee the [Licensor] grants the [Licensee] the exclusive right to reproduce, publish, supply and distribute the [Article/Image] written and created by the [Licensor] in the [magazine/newspaper] known as: [specify name] and on the [website/app] known as: [specify name/reference] from [date] to [date].

1.2 The [Licensor] remains the copyright owner of the [Article/Image].

1.3 The [Licensor] shall be entitled to any remuneration due from any rights management organisation and/or any third party due to the syndication and/or exploitation of the [Article/Image].

1.4 The [Licensor] agrees and accepts the [Article/Image] will be published and distributed all over the world.

1.5 The [Licensor] agrees and accepts that the [Licensee] cannot control the actions of third parties who may copy the [Article/Image] in breach of copyright.

R.464

1.1 In consideration of the Advance Fee and the royalties the [Author] grants to the [Publisher/Distributor] the sole and exclusive right to reproduce, print, publish, distribute and sell the [Work/Manuscript/Book] in hardback and paperback in [specify language] only throughout the [Territory/world].

1.2 All other rights are reserved by the [Author].

1.3 The [Author] agrees and undertakes not to offer any other reserved rights to a third party until after [date].

1.4 The [Publisher/Distributor] agrees that it does not have any option over and/or right of first refusal to any new edition, sequel and/or other adaptation of the [Work/Manuscript/Book].

R.465
Where any feature film, documentary, television series and/or other programme is created and developed and exploited based on the [Work/Book] by the [Author]. The parties agree that the [Publisher] shall be entitled to share in any revenue received from any new book and/or publication associated with such new format. It shall be shared between the parties on

the basis of [number] per cent to the [Author] and [number] per cent to the [Publisher] of any sums received by either party.

R.466

1.1 In consideration of the payments set out in this agreement the [Author] grants to the [Publisher/Distributor] the sole and exclusive right to reproduce, supply, publish, sell, distribute and exploit the [Work/Manuscript/Book] for a period of [ten] years from the date of this agreement throughout the world in all languages in hardback, paperback and/or in the form of any audio file and/or electronic download as a reproduction of the over the internet and/or any electronic download with the exact same content and layout for exploitation over the internet and/or any telecommunication system for reception by computer, television and/or other gadget and/or device excluding any other adaptation into an electronic format, films, videos, podcasts and/or otherwise.

1.2 The [Publisher/Distributor] shall be entitled to sub-license the rights in 1.1 to any third party. Provided that the [Publisher/Distributor] remains liable to the [Author] for any failures and/or defaults of any such third party.

1.3 The [Author] grants to the [Publisher/Distributor] the sole and exclusive right to reproduce, supply, publish, sell, distribute and exploit parts and/or extracts of the [Work/Manuscript/Book] for a period of [ten] years from the date of this agreement throughout the world in all languages in the form of:

A. serialisations in newspapers and/or magazines;

B. anthologies and/or quotations in other hardback, paperback, audio files and electronic downloads as part of other works in printed form;

C. recordings of readings and/or performances of readings for stage, theatre, radio and/or television for any event, tour and/or programme.

1.4 All other rights are reserved by the [Author] including the right to licence the adaptation of the [Work/Manuscript/Book] for a series for radio, television and/or any podcast and/or feature film and/or merchandising, computer game and/or software and/or any mechanical reproduction and/or performing rights and/or any adaptation in any other format and/or medium whether in existence now and/or created in the future.

R.467

'The Serialisation Rights' shall be defined as the right to publish the extracts of the [Work/Script/Text/Images] [number pages/word limit] in a newspaper, magazine and/or periodical in printed format and to simultaneously replicate the content of the newspaper, magazine and/or periodical on a nominated website and/or app and/or platform for reproduction, supply, sale and/or distribution to the public. Whether it is available for free and/or a charge is made for purchase and/or the content is made accessible under a subscription service with a monthly charge.

R.468

1.1 In consideration of the Serialisation Fee the [Licensor] grants the [Licensee] the sole and exclusive Serialisation Rights throughout the [Territory/world] for the duration of the Licence Period.

1.2 The [Licensee] agrees and undertakes not to permit, license and/or transfer any of the Serialisation Rights to any third party without the prior written consent of the [Licensor].

1.3 The [Licensor] agrees and undertakes not to permit, license and/or transfer the right to publish any extracts of the [Work/Script/Text/Images] in any article, journal, newspaper, magazine and/or periodical in printed format in any part of the world until after [date/time].

1.4 The [Licensor] agrees and undertakes not to permit, license and/or transfer the right to reproduce, supply, publish and/or distribute any extracts of the [Work/Script/Text/Images] in any news report and/or on any blog, podcast, audio file, website, app and/or platform and/or by means of any electronic format over the internet and/or any telecommunication system until after [date/time].

1.5 The [Licensee]] agrees and accepts that the [Licensor] shall not be liable for any disclosures on social media which are not directly attributable to the [Licensor].

R.469

1.1 In consideration of the Advance and royalty payments set out in this agreement the [Author] grants to the [Publisher/Distributor] the exclusive right to reproduce, supply, publish, distribute and/or exploit the [Work/Script/Book/Image] and/or any parts in all media and/or in all medium and in all formats and languages throughout the world and universe for the full period of copyright and any extensions and/or renewals. Together with any such periods of rights which may exist and/or may come into effect in the future and/or forever.

1.2 The rights granted in 1.1 shall include the right to adapt and/or exploit all associated titles, names, places, items, locations, slogans, logos and/or other material associated with the [Work/Script/Book/Image]. Together with the right to make any application to register ownership as a trade mark and/or domain name and/or any other matter that may arise.

R.470

1.1 The [Publisher/Distributor] agrees and accepts that in the event that the [Author] grants an option and/or a licence and/or assigns the right to make a feature film and/or television series and/or some other dramatized version based on the published [Work/Book]. That the [Publisher/Distributor] shall not be entitled to receive any sums from the exploitation of such rights.

1.2 The [Publisher/Distributor] shall be offered [the opportunity/ first right of refusal] to publish a book in hardback and/or paperback and/or as an audio file and/or as an electronic download which has the same original text as the [Work/Book] but which incorporates additional images and material from any feature film and/or television series and/or some other dramatized version. Such proposal shall be subject to the [Author] and/or any third party and the [Publisher/Distributor] reaching a conclusion as to the terms of such exploitation and the basis of the split of the monies to be received.

R.471

1.1 The [Author] agrees that the [Publisher/Distributor] shall be entitled to make arrangements for and post short podcasts and/or videos marketing the [Work/Book] of no more than [number] minutes in duration.

1.2 Provided that the [Author] approves and participates in the content of the material in 1.1.

1.3 That any third party contributors which the [Publisher/Distributor] may wish to use may be vetoed by the [Author].

1.4 The [Publisher/Distributor] accepts and agrees that it has no right to make and/to commission any other film, videos, podcasts and/or recordings without the prior consent of the [Author].

R.472
In consideration of the Advance and the Royalties set out in this agreement the [Author] grants the [Publisher/Distributor] the exclusive rights in the [Work/Book/Images] throughout the world, universe and outer space from

[date] to [date] to reproduce, supply, sell, hire, rent, distribute, sell, sub-license, translate, subtitle and/or otherwise exploit the following rights and/or formats and/or material as follows:

1.1 All printed formats including hardback, paperback, large print, reprints, new editions, digest books condensation, book club editions, educational editions; plastic, soft cover and three dimensional and interactive children's books; anthologies and quotations in third party material. One shot digest of hardback and/or paperback and/or any later version as an abridgement in any newspaper, magazine and/or periodical.

1.2 In printed format as first, second and any subsequent serialisation, both exclusive and/or non-exclusive; before and after publication in newspapers, periodicals, magazines, journals and/or in electronic format over the internet and/or by means of any telecommunication system.

1.3 All sound recordings and/or audio versions including discs, tapes, CDs, DVDs, disc and/or interactive books; anthologies and quotations in third party material. One shot digest of the audio version of the hardback and/or paperback and/or any later version as an abridgement in any newspaper, magazine and/or periodical.

1.4 All sound recordings and/or audio versions as first, second and any subsequent serialisations, both exclusive and/or non-exclusive; before and after publication in newspapers, periodicals, magazines, journals and/or in electronic format over the internet and/or by means of any telecommunication system.

1.5 All readings, presentations, talks, speeches and non-dramatized versions whether for tours, exhibitions, trade fairs, religious and/or political conferences. All dramatized adaptations for plays, stage, theatre, festivals, outdoor performances and/or otherwise.

1.6 All forms of transmission, broadcast and/or exploitation by terrestrial, cable, satellite and/or digital television and/or radio and/or any other communication by electronic means over the internet and/or form over the internet and/or any telecommunication system of any visual moving images, (with or without sound) and/or any sound recording and/or any adaptation and/or sequel. It shall include electronic downloads, audio files, podcast, films, series, any catch up and/or playback archive service, closed circuit television, viewings and exhibitions to schools and educational establishments or other groups. It shall cover any free, paid for and/or subscription service and reception by television, computer, laptop and/or some other gadget and/or device.

1.7 It shall include the right to register any original title, name, fictional place and/or item and/or other rights and/or material and/or any similar variation and/or any adaptation and/or new development as a domain name, trading name, company name, app, trade mark and/or any other registration with any government agency and/or regulatory organisation and/or rights management organisation and/or other third party.

1.8 It shall include the right to make and/or authorise any adaptation in any medium and/or by any method including two and three dimensional versions, toys, household items, clothes, computer games, cartoons, licensing products and/or services, theme parks and/or any other form of merchandising; sponsorship and/or endorsements of third parties; licensing for lotteries, games, competitions; gambling and/or betting

1.9 Any other rights and/or material and/or format and/or method of exploitation and/or registration of rights not mentioned above in any media which exists now and/or is created in the future.

R.473

1.1 The [Publisher/Distributor] agrees and undertakes that at the end of the agreement by [date] and/or earlier if terminated for any reason. That the [Publisher/Distributor] shall assign all copyright, intellectual property rights, trade marks, domain names and/or any other rights and/or title of any nature in any medium and/or format and/or in any material and/or any registrations and/or rights of ownership in respect of the [Work/Book/Images] and/or any form of adaptation and/or exploitation entirely to [Name].

1.2 That it is not the intention of this agreement that the [Publisher/Distributor] and/or any sub-licensee should retain any rights after [date].

1.3 That the [Publisher/Distributor] and/or any sub-licensee shall sign and conclude any documents that [Name] may request so as to effect the assignment in 1.1 to [Name].

R.474

1.1 The [Publisher/Distributor] confirms that it has granted a non-exclusive licence to the [specify organisation] to reproduce literary works published by the [Publisher/Distributor]. Those literary works shall include the right to make copies of the [Work/Book] by photocopying, scanning and/or other reprographic means for sub-license and sale to third parties.

1.2 The [specify organisation] shall divide the net sums received after deductions from the exploitation of all the reprographic rights in 1.1 equally between the [Author] and the [Publisher/Distributor].

1.3 The [Author] shall receive the [Author's] share of the proceeds through the [Authors' Licensing and Collecting Society/specify other organisation] in accordance with their standard terms and conditions.

R.475

1.1 The [Author] does not grant the [Publisher/Distributor] any reprographic rights in the [Work/Book] whether by photocopying, scanning and/or any other methods and/or reprographic rights. All sums due in respect of the exercise of such rights shall be owned and controlled by the [Author]. The [Publisher/Distributor] shall not hold any such rights and shall not be entitled to any sums at any time.

1.2 It is agreed that the [Work/Book] shall be listed as an excluded [Work/Book] with the [Copyright Licensing Agency/ Authors' Licensing and Collecting Society/specify other organisation].

1.3 The [Author] shall be entitled to grant any reprographic rights in respect of copying, scanning, digitisation and/or other proposed method of reproduction and/or adaptation and to retain all sums that may arise.

R.476

1.1 In consideration of the [Fee/Fixed Unit Price] the [Author] grants the [Company] the non-exclusive right to photocopy and/or scan [number] pages of the [Work/Book] and to store it in electronic and/or digital format on the internal database computer system for its staff and employees only at [specify] from [date] to [date].

1.2 The [Company] shall have the right to send part and/or all of such copies over the internal computer system and intranet at [address] to [number] persons who are employees of the [Company] from [date] to [date].

1.3 It is agreed that the employees may use the pages of the [Work/Book] as: [state purpose].

1.4 No right is granted to distribute and/or display any part of the [Work/Book] on any podcast, app and/or website and/or over the internet and/or any telecommunication system and/or to supply and/or offer the [Work/Book] and/or any part to third parties.

1.5 After the expiry of the licence then all copies of the [Work/Book] shall be deleted from the internal database computer system [and/or any other records and/or material]. The [Company] shall provide an [email/letter] of confirmation of such destruction.

R.477

The [Publisher/Distributor] shall not be entitled to arrange to give away free copies of the [Work/Book] for any reason and/or to commission reviews and/or podcasts and/or marketing without prior discussions with the [Author] as to the reason, content and strategy.

R.478

1.1 The [Publisher/Distributor] agrees that the [Author] shall remain the copyright owner of the [Images/Text/Maps] and that the [Author] has not granted any rights to the [Publisher/Distributor] outside the Territory and/or in any language except [specify language].

1.2 The [Publisher/Distributor] accepts and agrees that it is not entitled to sub-license the [Images/Text/Maps] to any third party and/or to transfer and/or assign any rights of any nature.

1.3 The [Publisher/Distributor] may only exploit the [Images/Text/Maps] in the agreed format of [specify format]. There is no right to use any part of the [Images/Text/Map] for any other purpose. There is no right to create and/or develop any merchandising and/or to make any adaptation and/or to market the [Images/Text/Maps] in conjunction with and/or to endorse any other product, service, person and/or brand.

R.479

The [Author] and the [Publisher/Distributor] agree as follows:

1.1 That the ownership of the title of the [Work] and the characters shall belong to: [specify name].

1.2 That the design of the cover commissioned by the [Publisher/Distributor] based on the [Work] shall be belong to [specify name].

1.3 That the layout, format, design and typography of the content of the [Work] shall belong to: [specify name].

1.4 That there shall be no credit on the front and/or back cover to any designer of the cover.

1.5 That the index shall be completed by the [Author] and shall belong to: [specify name].

R.480

1.1 All rights not specifically granted to the [Company] are reserved by the [Author] for exploitation by the [Author] and/or any third party at any time.

1.2   The [Author] agrees to inform the [Company] of the disposal, licence, sale or otherwise of any such rights to a third party but not the details of the final agreement.

1.3   While the Licence Period granted to the [Company] is still in existence and the agreement has not expired and/or been terminated. The [Author] agrees that he/she shall assist the [Company] at the [Company's] cost to apply for if necessary in the name of the [Author] any renewal and/or extension of copyright in the [Work/Book] under the laws of any countries in which the [Company] has been granted a licence by the [Author].

R.481

The [Publisher/Distributor] agrees and undertakes that it shall not authorise and/or permit any person, sub-licensee, manufacturer, supplier and/or other third party to edit, adapt, add to, delete from and/or change the title, the disclaimer, preface, order, content, index, copyright notices and/or credits of the [Work/Book/Images] in any format without the prior written consent of the [Author].

R.482

1.1   [Name] grants the [Company] the exclusive right to reproduce, supply, sell and/or distribute the [Work/Book/Images] in hardback, paperback and/or electronic form in [specify language] as a download and/or audio file from [specify website/platform] throughout the world from [date] to [date].

1.2   No format shall be exploited which has not been proofed and/or approved by [Name] prior to final production and distribution.

1.3   There is no right granted to serialise the [Work/Book/Images].

1.4   There is no right granted to sub-license any merchandising rights.

1.5   There is no right granted to translate and/or adapt the [Work/Book/Images] and/or to issue any sequel.

1.6   All proposed marketing and promotional material shall be subject to the prior approval of [Name].

1.7   Where [Name] is requested to attend any events, deliver any blogs and/or create, write and/or produce videos and/or podcasts by the [Company] as part of the marketing strategy. Then [Name] shall be entitled to refuse to do so. The [Company] accepts that where [Name] agrees to carry out any such additional work then [Name] shall be entitled to be paid additional fees and expenses which shall be agreed between the parties prior to the commencement of any such work.

R.483

The [Company/Distributor] and [Name] shall share the sums received by either party from the exploitation of the following rights on the basis of [number] per cent to [Name] and [number] per cent to the [Company/Distributor]:

1.1 The right to reproduce, supply, sell and/or distribute the [Manuscript/Work/Images/Book] of the [Author] through any electronic means and/or format for communication over the internet and/or any telecommunication system with the exact same content as the original hardback and/or paperback adapted to be a electronic download and/or audio file. This shall not include any podcasts, videos, feature films, documentaries, television series and/or any other moving visual images.

1.2 The right to authorise and license extracts of the [Manuscript/Work/Images/Book] to be reproduced and/or read and/or performed.

1.3 It shall not include the right to grant an option and/or exclusive licence for a podcast, videos, feature film, documentary, television series and/or any other film, and/or adaptation which will consist of moving images and/or a soundtrack.

1.4 The right to endorse, collaborate and/or partner with and/or cross-promote with any organisation, business, product and/or service in association with the [Manuscript/Work/Images/Book] of the [Author].

1.5 The right to sub-license the use of the names, logos, trade marks, slogans, costumes and other material associated with the [Manuscript/Work/Images/Book] and/or any other rights for merchandising, theme parks, leisure, game and tourist attractions and events, festivals, interactive amusements, sports activities, retail shops, restaurants computer games and/or other similar adaptations.

1.6 Where it is unclear and uncertain whether any rights and/or method of exploitation is covered and/or will be covered by the terms of this agreement. Then the parties agree to enter into negotiations to settle and agree a new percentage of revenue to be allocated to each party. It is the intention of this agreement that both parties should benefit from the exploitation of all rights in all media under this agreement.

R.484

1.1 The [Company] agrees and undertakes that it shall not have the right to create an electronic version of the [Work/Book/Image] in any format in sound and/or vision for reproduction, supply and/or distribution over the internet and/or through any telecommunication system.

1.2 That in the event that the [Company] wishes to commission and/or exploit any electronic format of the [Work/Book/Image] it must reach a separate new agreement with the [Author]. The [Author] shall be entitled to refuse to enter into any such agreement.

R.485

1.1 In consideration of the payment of the Advance [which cannot be recouped and/or returned] and the fixed rate royalty payment in clause [–]. The [Author] grants the [Company] the [exclusive/non-exclusive] right to create, reproduce, supply, sell and/or distribute the [Work/Book/Images] in any electronic format in sound and/or vision for exploitation over the internet and/or through any telecommunication system. This shall include the right to commission the new electronic version from a third party and/or to sub-license such rights to a third party for exploitation. The licence from the [Author] to the [Company] shall start on [date] and end on [date]. It shall apply to the whole world, seas, manmade islands, the sky, sub-terrains and outer space.

1.2 The rights in 1.1 shall include the right to translate and/or add sub-titles and shall extend to all languages.

1.3 The [Company] shall ensure that all copies of the [Work/Book/Images] have a clear prominent copyright notice and credit to the [Author].

1.4 The [Company] agrees and undertakes to be responsible and/or liable for the defaults, failures and/or errors of any sub-licensee and/or third party which results in losses, damages, costs and/or expenses to the [Author] up to a maximum of [number/currency] in any one financial year. [Any unpaid balance shall be carried forward to the next financial year.]

1.5 The [Company] agrees and undertakes to ensure that all copyright, intellectual property rights, logos, trade marks, and/or other rights in the original and/or any adaptations and/or marketing which are owned by the [Company] and/or any authorised third party shall be assigned to the [Author].

R.486

1.1 In consideration of the payment of the Fee the [Author] grants the [Licensee] the non-exclusive right to reproduce the following original [Poem/Report/Extract] entitled [specify title/reference] in the [journal/magazine] entitled: [specify exact title] for publication and distribution in the [month] issue and publication by [date]. The [Licensee] shall be entitled to supply, sell and distribute the journal anywhere in the world.

1.2 The [Licensee] shall also be entitled to reproduce the [Poem/Report/Extract] on the [specify website/platform/ reference] for a period of [number] months from the date of publication of the journal. Provided that it appears in the exact same manner as in the [journal/magazine] in electronic form and is not offered as a separate commercial entity as a download and/or audio file. No right is granted to syndicate, sub-license and/or otherwise exploit the [Poem/Report/Extract].

R.487

1.1 In consideration of the Fee the [Author] grants the [Company] the non-exclusive right to reproduce, print, distribute and sell the [Script/Text/Artwork/Images] throughout the world for the Licence Period in a [Book/Journal] and/or to offer copies in electronic form as a download and/or audio file from a website, app and/or platform for a single charge for each copy and/or as part of a subscription service.

1.2 The [Company] agrees and undertakes that the [Script/Text/Artwork/Images] shall not be used in conjunction with any other material which could cause offence, is obscene and/or political in nature and/or derogatory of any religion and/or likely to cause controversy on social media.

1.3 The [Company] shall not be entitled to sub-license the [Script/Text/Artwork/Images] at any time without the prior consent of the [Author].

1.4 The [Company] shall not be entitled to alter the title, edit, add to, adapt and/or distort the [Script/Text/Artwork/Images] at any time without the prior consent of the [Author].

R.488

The [Company] agrees and undertakes not to:

1.1 Register and/or claim ownership of any copyright, intellectual property rights, domain names, trade marks and/or any other rights with any third party including any rights management and/or copyright organisation, regulatory body and/or otherwise of any part of the [Work] and/or any similar material and/or adaptation.

1.2 Attribute any other person as the original creator and/or owner other than the [Author] and/or to delete and/or add to any copyright notice and/or credit and/or trade mark and/or other acknowledgement.

1.3 Commission any translation in any other language without the prior approval of the [Author] to proceed and the persons to be used and/or the alterations to be made due to cultural and/or the interpretation differences and /or any other proposed changes.

R.489

The [Licensee] agrees and undertakes that the [Licensee] shall not:

1.1 Register the name of the author and/or the title of the [Text/Images/Infographics] and/or any similar words as a trade mark, service mark, domain name, company name and/or otherwise.

1.2 Register with any rights management organisation and/or copyright and/or other organisation to receive sums from the exploitation of the [Text/Images/Infographics] except: [specify exceptions if any].

1.3 Transfer, assign, authorise and/or grant any third party the right to use and/or adapt the [Text/Images/Infographics] in any format in any media and/or to endorse and/or promote another product and/or service and/or event and/or to be reproduced in any merchandising.

R.490

1.1 [Name] grants the [Distributor] the non-exclusive right to reproduce, supply, sell and distribute copies of the [Artwork/Logo/Work/Sample] in the form of [greetings cards/T shirts/covers for mobile telephones] from [date] to date] in [Territory/country].

1.2 In consideration of 1.1 the [Distributor] shall pay to [Name] a fixed payment of [number/currency] for every copy of the [Artwork/Logo/Work/Sample] in any format reproduced, supplied, sold and distributed by the [Distributor] in each period of [three] calendar months for the duration of the agreement. All such sums as are due shall be accounted for and paid on or by the last day of each [three] month period.

1.3 After the expiry and/or termination of the agreement all sums shall continue to be accounted for by the [Distributor] and paid until all payments due have been received by [Name].

R.491

The [Company] agrees that it shall not have any rights in respect of any of the following matters:

1.1 This agreement does not cover and/or apply to any new edition. The [Company] must negotiate and conclude a new agreement with the [Author] if it wishes to acquire such rights.

1.2 This agreement does not cover and/or apply to any sequel whether the title is exactly the same and/or updated and/or covers the same subject matter with a new storyline. The [Company] must negotiate and conclude a new agreement with the [Author].

1.3 There is no right granted which permits the [Company] to engage any third party writer in substitution for the [Author].

1.4 There is no right to assign any rights to a third party as part of any asset sell-off of a section of the business and/or to restructure the business under another name.

1.5 At the expiry and/or termination of the agreement the [Company] shall not destroy any master material, records, copies and/or other formats and/or stock. The [Company] shall offer the [Author] the opportunity to arrange collection at the [Author's] cost.

R.492

The [Author] and the [Company] agree that in the event of any application to register any ownership, copyright, intellectual property rights and/or trade mark and/or domain name and/or any other matter. The [Author] [or his/her estate] and the [Company] shall be specified and named as joint owners in all countries. Neither party shall attempt to remove the name of the other party at any time for any reason unless both parties have consented in writing.

R.493

1.1 Where the [Company/Distributor] after the conclusion of this agreement becomes involved in any campaign, charity, politics and/or expresses support for any actions and/or adopts any policies on social media to which the [Author] objects and/or does not wish to be associated with for any reason. Then the [Author] shall be entitled to serve [one] week's notice of termination of the agreement on the [Company/Distributor].

1.2 Where such notice is served by the [Author] in 1.1 then the [Company/Distributor] shall cease immediately producing and/or trading in the rights licensed under this agreement. The [Company/Distributor] shall not deliver any more copies and shall no longer have the right to market the [Author].

1.3 All reference to the [Author] shall be removed from all social media, websites, apps, podcastst and marketing of the [Company/Distributor]. The parties shall negotiate a settlement based on the sales achieved and/or other rights exploited and the sums due to the [Author]. No compensation for any costs, damages and/or losses shall be due to the [Company/Distributor] by the [Author].

R.494

The [Author] agrees that the [Company] shall be entitled to:

1.1 Be offered the opportunity to purchase any new edition and/or sequel of the [Book/Manuscript]. The [Author] shall first offer the rights to the [Company]. In the event that the proposal if any made by the [Company] is not acceptable then the [Author] shall enter into an agreement with a third party. The [Company] shall be allowed a period of [number] days only to make any proposal.

1.2 Sub-license the rights granted to the [Company] to a third party. No assignment is permitted.

1.3 Commission a translation of the [Book/Manuscript] in [specify languages]. Provided that the rights and ownership of any such translation is then assigned to the [Author].

1.4 Make such changes to the title and/or content as may be required for reasons of interpretation of the meaning in another language. Provided that the rights and ownership of such changes are assigned to the [Author].

1.5 Discuss and arrange with [Name] a strategy to register any trade marks, protect any rights and/or make any domain name or other application in respect of any characters, slogans, names and/or other matters in the [Book/Manuscript]. Provided that all registrations and applications shall be in the name of the [Author] and not the [Company]. The [Author] agrees that [number] per cent of the costs incurred to do so may be deducted from the sums due to the [Author]. Provided that the costs are spread over a period of [number] years. The rest of the costs shall be paid for by the [Company].

R.495

In consideration of the Fee the [Licensee] grants the [Sub-Licensee] the non-exclusive right to reproduce, supply and/or distribute the [Extract of the Work] set out in Appendix A in the [website/blog/other] known as: [specify title/reference] from [date to [date] throughout the world. Provided that the [Sub-Licensee] provides the following copyright notice and credit to the [Author] and the link to the website of the [Licensee].

R.496

The [Author] agrees that the [Company] shall be entitled to assign the benefit of this agreement to a third party where the whole assets of the [Company] are restructured and assigned to a new legal entity and/or the assignment is to the parent company [specify name of parent company]. Provided that:

1.1 The [Company] shall inform the [Author] of its proposed plans of assignment; and

1.2 The new legal entity and/or the parent company are capable of fulfilling the obligations to the [Author] under the agreement.

R.497

Where there is no royalty stated for any format and/or method of exploitation in this agreement either because it was omitted and/or the technology and/or rights and/or format did not exist at the time. Whatever the reason where the [Distributor/Company] wishes to exploit that format, method and/or rights then the parties must agree the terms as to the royalty and/or other payment. There is no part of this agreement where the [Distributor/Company] can state that no royalty and/or payment is due to the [Author].

R.498

There is no undertaking by the [Author] to enter into a new agreement with the [Company] for any new edition and/or sequel. The [Author] shall be entitled to write a competing work on the same subject area. The [Author] owes no such obligation to the [Company] and is entitled to conclude agreements with third parties.

R.499

1.1 The [Author] is the creator of the [Text] and the [Artist] is the creator of the [Illustrations/Artwork] which have been commissioned by the [Company] for the [Book] entitled: [specify title] [specify format] in [specify language].

1.2 The parties agree that the prior consent and approval of all the [Author] the [Artist] and the [Company] shall be required before any rights can be sub-licensed and/or assigned to a third party at any time. Where one party objects then the agreement cannot proceed.

1.3 It is agreed that all three parties shall hold the rights in the [Book] and the [Illustration/Artwork], the title, characters and any trade marks and/or any other forms of exploitation in any format and/or media as to one third each. All sums received of any nature shall be split on the same basis in the future.

1.4 It is agreed that all three parties shall be acknowledged as the copyright owner and/or owner of any other rights and named on any records.

R.500

1.1 Where the [Author] has created and supplied the index and/or taxonomy in the [Work/Book]. Then the copyright owner of the index and/or taxonomy shall be the [Author] not the [Distributor].

1.2 Where any index and/or taxonomy for the [Work/Book] is created by a third party and/or employee of the [Distributor] based on the [Work/Book]. Then the [Distributor] shall ensure that the ownership of the copyright and all other rights are assigned to the [Author].

R.501

The [Distributor/Company] agrees and undertakes that no employee, designer, consultant and/or other third party shall be permitted and/or authorised to contribute to the [Work/Book] in any format at any time and/or credited in any manner as having made a contribution in any media without the prior written consent of the [Author].

R.502

Where for any reason as part of a marketing and/or licensing strategy new material and/or versions of any names, initials, characters, images, slogans and/or any films, videos, computer software and/or other promotional material and/or products and/or services are developed and/or distributed. That the [Company] shall ensure that the rights in any such new material is not acquired by a third party.

Services

R.503

1.1 The [Company]: [specify name/address/email/mobile/other]. The [Contributor]: [specify name/address/email/mobile/other].

1.2 The [Company] has [filmed/recorded/photographed/interviewed] the [Contributor] on the subject of [specify topic] and the [Contributor] has carried out the following: [specify work/service/other].

1.3 In consideration of 1.3 the [Company] is to pay the sum of [number/currency] as a buy-out fee by [date] in [cash/cheque/other] to the [Contributor] in full and final settlement. No further sums of any nature for any reason shall be due for the provision of the work, services and/or the exploitation of the material in any media at any time.

1.4 The [Contributor] assigns to the [Company] all present and future copyright and any other intellectual property rights and/or interest in all media in the work and any material created, produced or provided by the [Contributor] under this agreement throughout the world, outer space and the universe for the full period of copyright and any extensions and/or renewals and in perpetuity. All media shall include any developments and variations and include, but not be limited to, film, television, video, DVD, radio, publishing, the internet; any telecommunication system and merchandising.

1.5 The [Company] shall have the right to assign, license and/or transfer any rights to any third party at any time without further payment of any type.

R.504

In consideration of the sum of [number/currency] the [Contributor] assigns to the [Company] all present and future copyright, intellectual property rights, trade marks, computer software rights and/or any other rights in the product of the services of the [Contributor] made under this agreement throughout the world for the full period of copyright and any extensions and/or renewals and forever. It is not the intention of this agreement that the [Contributor] should retain any rights in the product of his/her work under this agreement.

R.505

In consideration of the [Presenter's] Fee and the [Presenter's] Royalties, the [Presenter] assigns to the [Company] All Media Rights in the product of his/her services in the [Series] including the soundtrack, any scripts, sound recordings and/or any other promotional and/or marketing material created under this agreement throughout the world for the full period of the copyright and any extensions and/or renewals and/or such other periods as may be possible and/or indefinitely without any time limit.

R.506

1.1 The [Company] agrees and acknowledges that the [Presenter] reserves all rights not specifically assigned to the [Company] in clause [–].

1.2 That the [Presenter] also owns and/or controls the rights in the following [Books/Podcasts/Products] and any associated domain names and/or trade marks which were in existence prior to this agreement. That no such rights and/or interest are transferred to the [Company] under this agreement.

R.507

In consideration of the Assignment Fee the [Presenter] assigns all present and future copyright, intellectual property rights, trade marks, computer software rights and any other rights in all media and in all formats and/or methods of exploitation whether in existence now and/or created in the future throughout the world and universe in the product of his/her services and any other material created for the purpose of this agreement in connection with the [Presenter] for the full period of copyright and any extensions and renewals and forever. The rights shall include but not be limited to: scripts, photographs, images, caricatures, press releases, films, videos, sound recordings, podcasts, blogs, competitions, promotional and/or marketing material for distribution to any newspaper, magazine, website and/or platform; outtakes and/or bloopers which are not transmitted and/or merchandising.

R.508

The [Presenter] acknowledges and agrees that any intellectual property of any kind including but limited to copyright, design rights, service marks, trade marks, logos, inventions, titles, slogans and/or any other rights in any associated material which are held by the [Company] and/or developed in conjunction with the services of the [Presenter] under this agreement shall be the sole and exclusive property of the [Company]. The [Presenter] shall not acquire any rights and/or interest nor does this agreement purport to transfer, grant, assign any such rights in and/or derived from the product of the services to the [Presenter].

R.509

1.1 [Name] has agreed to be filmed and recorded endorsing the [Products/ Services] of the [Company] in a series of podcasts and advertisement to be broadcast and/or transmitted between [date and [date]. The detail of the work schedule and material to be produced is described in Appendix A which forms part of this agreement.

1.2 The [Company] agrees that it shall not have the right to reproduce, use, adapt, exploit and/or sub-license any rights and/or material created for the purposes of this agreement in which [Name] appears in sound or vision for any other reason than that stated in 1.1.

1.3 Where the [Company] wishes to acquire the right to reproduce, use, adapt, exploit and/or sub-license any rights and/or material for any other purpose at any time. Then the prior written consent of [Name] shall be required to confirm consent and additional fees and/or royalties and/or other payment and a new agreement concluded on each occasion.

R.510

In consideration of the payment of the [Budget/Fees/Commission] the [Promoter] assigns to the [Enterprise] all present and future copyright, intellectual property rights, trade marks, design rights, computer software rights and/or any other rights in the product of the services and/or the material and/or rights which it has developed by the [Promoter] [and/or commissioned from a third party] for the [Company at any time under this agreement. Such assignment by the [Promoter] shall be for the world and universe and shall continue for the full period of copyright and any extensions and/or renewals and shall as far as possible continue in perpetuity and/or for such periods as may be permitted.

R.511

1.1 In consideration of the Fee and Repeat Fees [Name] assigns to the [Company] all present and future copyright, intellectual property and any other rights in all media and means of exploitation throughout the [Territory/world] in the product of his/her services, performances and contributions to any material created under this agreement for the full period of copyright and any extensions, renewals and forever.

1.2 For the avoidance of doubt all media shall include but not be limited to cable, satellite, terrestrial and/or digital television and/or radio; electronic forms of communication over the internet and/or any telecommunication system; mechanical reproduction; films, videos, podcasts, discs, computer software, music, publishing and/or merchandising.

R.512

1.1 In consideration of the [Fee] [Name] grants the [Company] the exclusive right to broadcast, transmit and exploit in all media the film and/or sound track of [Name] which has been made for the [Series/ Documentary/Podcast] throughout the world [for the full period of copyright and any extensions and/or renewals and in perpetuity/ specify start date and end date].

1.2 The grant of rights in 1.1 does not permit the [Company] to alter and/ or adapt the film and/or sound track of [Name] in any manner which would imply that [Name] endorses a product and/or service and/or supports and/or endorses a third party.

1.3 The [Company] shall not be entitled to use [Name] and/or any film and/ or sound track of [Name] to create and/or exploit any merchandising.

1.4 The [Company] may sub-license the film and/or sound recording of {Name} for other programmes provided that they do not mock, denigrate and/or cause offence to [Name].

R.513

1.1 [Name] grants the [Company] an exclusive licence to reproduce, broadcast, transmit and/or distribute the interview with [Name] on: [specify channel/website/platform] between [date and [date] in the form of [text/sound recording/film]. Provided that the content of the final version has been approved by {Name].

1.2 The [Company] agrees and undertakes that it shall not be entitled to sub-license, exploit and/or adapt any of the rights and/or material created under this agreement in 1.1 for any other purpose than that which has been authorised.

1.3 Any other form of use in any manner must be expressly approved in advance by [Name] in writing in each case.

R.514

The [Company] agrees that all copyright, intellectual property rights, trade marks, domain names and/or any other rights in the professional and/or personal names, initials, images, slogans, logos, gestures and/or other material owned and/or controlled by [Name] shall not be transferred to the [Company] under this agreement.

R.515

1.1 The [Agent] agrees that this agreement only relates only to the specified [Work/Manuscript/Project] in [specify format] in [Territory] from [date] to [date] which is described in Appendix A created and written by the [Author].

1.2 The [Agent] does and has not acquired any rights, interest, option and/or right to exploit any sequel and/or any adaptation and/or other original written material of the [Author] whether in existence prior to the date of this agreement and/or developed at any time in the future.

1.3 The [Agent] has not right to register any trade marks, domain name, app and/or any other rights and/or interest related to any characters and/or locations in the [Work/Manuscript/Project] and/or any other content of any nature.

1.4 All other material and/or rights shall be the subject of separate negotiation and agreement between the [Agent] and the [Author] if the [Author] wishes to do so. There shall be no obligation on the [Author] to enter into any additional agreement.

1.5 The [Agent] agrees that he/she is not entitled to negotiate and/or promote in any manner and/or form the commercial and/or charitable and/or educational interests of the [Author] outside the [Territory] unless specifically approved in advance in writing with the [Author].

1.6 The [Agent] agrees that he/she shall not be entitled to any commission and/or payment from any agreement concluded by the [Agent] after [date]. That from [date] no sums shall be due to be paid for any reason to the [Agent] whether it relates to the format and/or rights in 1.1 or not.

R.516

The [Agent] acknowledges that the private and public name of the [Actor] and any goodwill and reputation created in respect of any trade mark, business name, logo, image, catchphrase, jingle, music, lyrics and/or otherwise which shall remain the sole and exclusive property of the [Actor] whether in existence now or created during the Term of this Agreement. No part of this agreement is intended to transfer any copyright, intellectual property rights, trade marks and/or any other rights owned now and/or created at a later date by the [Actor] and/or a third party to the [Agent].

R.517

1.1 The [Agent] shall use his/her skill and knowledge to negotiate and conclude the most advantageous agreements for the services of the [Actor]. That where possible the [Actor] shall be paid a portion of the fees in advance and additional expenses. That the [Agent] shall advise the [Actor] in advance of any discussions and/or negotiations of any contract and supply a comprehensive copy of all documents and/or emails which have been disclosed to the [Agent] by the third party.

1.2 That the [Agent] undertakes not to withhold any information and/or data and/or records from the [Actor] at any time.

1.3 That the [Agent] undertakes to use his/her reasonable endeavours to protect the copyright, intellectual property rights and any other rights of the [Actor] which may be created or developed under any contract with a third party.

1.4 As far as reasonably possible the [Agent] shall ensure that the copyright, intellectual property and any other rights in any photographs, images and/or other material commissioned by the [Agent] for marketing and promotion of the [Actor] shall be transferred and assigned to the [Actor/Agent].

R.518

[Name] agrees that both he/she and the [Manager/Company] shall hold all copyright, intellectual property rights, trade marks, images, logos, films, sound recordings, music, lyrics and/or any other rights and/or material in respect of [Name] and/or any collaboration and/or partnership for any work and/or project developed under this agreement in their joint names as joint owners as follows: [specify details of exact names to be used]. That both parties shall at all times be credited as the joint owners. That both parties shall equally share in any sums received from any form of exploitation at any time.

R.519

In consideration of the non-returnable Advance and the future Royalties in clause [–] the [Author] grants to the [Publisher/Distributor] the sole and exclusive right to;

1.1 Reproduce, supply, distribute and/or exploit the [Musical Work] in printed form as sheet music and/or a song book and/or

1704

1.2 In any electronic format under a subscription service and/or as a download for sale, supply and/or distribution over the internet and/or any telecommunication system and/or

1.3 Sub-license the production of any sound recording and/or any synchronised soundtrack in connection with a film, video and/or podcast for exploitation in any media.

1.4 All the rights licensed shall be for the [Territory/world].

1.6 The licence period shall start on [date] and end on [date].

1.7 After the end date all rights in 1.1, 1.2 and 1.3 shall revert to the [Author] and the [Publisher/Distributor] shall assign all rights which it may have acquired and the rights to all master material and copies and/or any adaptations.

R.520

1.1 In consideration of the [Assignment Fee] and the Royalties in clauses [–] [Name] assigns to the [Company] all present and future copyright, intellectual property rights, trade marks, domain name rights, computer software rights, synchronisation rights, performing rights, grand rights and the music publishing rights and any other rights in all medium and/or media throughout the world in the [Sound Recordings/Musical Works] described in Appendix A for the full period of the copyright and any extensions and/or renewals and/or for any such additional period of rights as may be permitted at any time [and in perpetuity].

1.2 This assignment in 1.1 shall include but not be limited to films, videos, podcasts, discs and electronic forms of communication over the internet and/or any telecommunication system whether in existence now and/or adapted from any existing work and/or material and/or is created and/or developed during the Term of this Agreement by [Name] and/or the [Company].

R.521
The [Distributor] agrees that the original [Musical Work/ Material] shall remain with and be owned by the [Licensor]. That the [Distributor] is not acquiring any copyright and/or intellectual property rights in the [Musical Work/ Material] and/or part except as set out in this agreement.

R.522

1.1 [Name] and the [Company] agree that both parties shall equally share in any performing rights, and/or grand rights and/or synchronisation rights from films, videos and/or podcasts and/or sums due for broadcasts and/or transmissions from exploitation on television, radio, the internet and/or any telecommunication system and/or any other media that may be received by any at rights management organisation and/or and/or other third party and/or either party at any time.

1.2 The agreement in 1.1 shall also apply to any adaptations and/or new forms of exploitation developed in the future.

R.523

1.1 The [Author] confirms that he/she is a member of [rights management organisation/collecting society] and has registered the following works: [specify type/registration reference/format]. The rights are administered by that organisation. All sums received by them shall be paid directly to the [Author] and the [Company] shall have no right and/or claim to any such sums.

1.2 The [Company] agrees and accepts that it must clear and make payment to the rights management organisation/collecting society] in respect of the exploitation of the following works: [specify type/registration reference/format] under this agreement.

R.524

1.1 [Name] has registered the [Musical Works/Sound Recordings] listed in Appendix A with the following rights management organisation: [specify name/reference]. They grant licences and collect fees and payments on behalf of [Name].

1.2 The [Distributor] shall be responsible for obtaining permission and/or reporting usage and/or making payments to the rights management organisation: [specify name/reference] in respect of the [Musical Works/Sound Recordings] listed in Appendix A.

R.525

[Name] agrees that this agreement is for a fixed term and ends on [date/time]. There is no right to any renewal and/or extension of the agreement and/or any right to be offered an alternative role beyond that date.

R.526

1.1 Where the [Enterprise] decides that the original budget allocated to the [Project] has been exceeded and that there are no additional funds available. Then the [Enterprise] shall be entitled to terminate the agreement for the services of [Name] for the [Project] without any notice period.

1.2　[Name] accepts and agrees that no additional damages, losses, expenses and/or other sums shall be due once the original budget has been expended for the {Project] in the event that the services of [Name] are no longer required.

1.3　[Name] accepts and agrees that it shall be obliged to deliver and/or transfer all master material, copies and rights which have been created and/or developed to the [Enterprise] at the [Enterprises'] cost by the final date of termination. In addition [Name] shall confirm that they no longer hold any rights and/or material.

R.527

1.1　In consideration of the [Fee] the [Contributor/Consultant] assigns to the [Company] all copyright, intellectual property rights, trade marks, domain names, computer software, data, databases, charts, inventions, patents and any other rights in the product of the services of the [Contributor/Consultant] for the [Project] [which are described in Schedule A which is attached to and forms part of this agreement] in all medium and in any media whether in existence now and/or created in the future for the full period of copyright and any extensions and renewals and in perpetuity throughout the world and universe.

1.2　It is not the intention of this agreement that the [Contributor/Consultant] should retain any rights in the product of his/her services under this agreement. The [Contributor/Consultant] shall only be entitled to the fees and expenses set out in clause [–]. No additional payments shall be made for any form of exploitation by the [Company] and/or any registration, sub-license, transfer and/or assignment of any rights to a third party.

R.528
The [Company] agrees that:

1.1　The [Supplier] shall be entitled to substitute any other suitably qualified person to carry out the tasks required under this agreement without notice to the [Company] in the event that any of the persons listed in the [Project] are not available for any reason.

1.2　The [Company] shall not have any right to terminate the agreement due to the fact that [specify person] is at any time not involved in the [Project] and/or leaves the [Supplier].

1.3　The [Supplier] may make changes to improve and develop the [Project] and make minor adaptations provided that the cost is not increased and there are no differences in the final planned result.

1.4 The [Supplier] shall be entitled to incur additional costs for the [Project] where it is discovered at a later date that the technology and/or software and/or security systems at the [Company] are not compatible and/or do not function effectively with the proposed [Project].

R.529

The [Company] agrees that the services to be provided by [Name] to develop and create an integrated software system for the delivery of [specify purpose] which is fully operational as set out in the specifications document in Appendix B does not include any future updates, tests and/ or maintenance once the system has been installed and approved by the [Company].

R.530

[Name] agrees to provide his/her services to design and supply [Images/ Graphics/Installation] to the [Company] for an [Exhibition/Festival] on the basis that:

1.1 That the [Images/Graphics/Installation] created and designed by [Name] for the [Exhibition/Festival] are owned by [Name] as the copyright owner and/or legal title.

1.2 That the [Company] may not replicate, reproduce, adapt and/or exploit the [Images/Graphics/Installation] in any medium.

1.3 That the [Company] shall not seek to grant any licence to any third party to exploit the [Images/Graphics/Installation].

Sponsorship

R.531

1.1 In consideration of the Sponsorship Fee and the payment of the Funding Budget which is attached in Appendix A. The [Company] grants to the [Sponsor] the exclusive right to sponsor the [Event] and to have the [Sponsor's] name, image, logo and services promoted and incorporated in the [Event] from [date to [date]

1.2 The details of the [Sponsor's] name, image, logo and services are described and attached in Appendix B and the manner in which they are to be used. [Describe material/size/location/format and other specifications in Appendix B.]

1.3 The [Company] agrees that the [Sponsor] may record and/or film a short [film/video] of no more than [minutes] in duration at the [Event] which highlights the [Sponsor's] role as sponsor. No interviews may be recorded with any persons without the prior consent of the [Company].

1.4 The [Company] grants the [Sponsor] the non-exclusive right to exhibit the [film/video] in 1.3 at conferences, trade fairs and/or on the website and/or social media accounts over the internet and/or any telecommunication system of the [Sponsor].

R.532

'The Title Rights' shall be defined to mean the exclusive right to have the [Event/Tournament] for all commercial, promotional, sub-licensing and/or other purposes including but not limited to any broadcast and/or transmission over radio, television and/or the internet and/or any telecommunication system and/or merchandising of the [Event/Tournament] throughout the world from [date] to [date] referred to as follows: [specify exact title agreed].

R.533

In consideration of the Sponsorship Fees the [Association/Institute] grants to the [Sponsor] the following rights in respect of the [Event/Exhibition] as follows:

1.1 'The Exclusive Title Rights' which shall be defined as the exclusive right to have the [Event/Exhibition] for all commercial, charitable, educational, promotional, sub-licensing and/or other purposes including but not limited to any broadcast and/or transmission over terrestrial, cable, satellite and/or digital radio and/or television and/or over the internet and/or through any telecommunication system and/or any adaptation whether for merchandising and/or otherwise of the [Event/Exhibition] throughout the world from [date to [date] referred to as follows: [specify exact title agreed].

1.2 The non-exclusive right to have [Sponsor's] name, image, logo, trade marks and/or domain name and/or other information reproduced and displayed on any website, app, brochure, labels, banners, scoreboards, electronic display systems, fences, advertising boards, flags, posters, national and local press, tickets, stationary and/or other promotional and/or marketing material [where the name of the [Association/Institute] appears] and to be credited as the holder of the exclusive title rights in the following manner: [specify colour/size/location/map/samples] as described in detail in the attached Appendix A which forms part of this agreement. This right shall apply from [date] to [date] and shall only apply to material controlled by the [Association/Institute].

1.3 The exclusive right to have the [Sponsor's] name, image and logo displayed on each [competitors'/stewards/officials] clothing during the course of the [Event/Exhibition] and on the clothing of all security, hospitality, catering, transport, volunteers and/or other personnel employed and/or engaged by the [Association/Institute] in accordance with the information and sample articles described in the attached Appendix B. This right shall apply from [date to [date] and shall only apply to persons and/or material controlled by the [Association/Institute] in [country].

1.4 The exclusive right of the [Sponsor] to award the [championship trophies/prizes] to any winners of any category from [date to [date] in respect of the [Event/Exhibition].

R.534

1.1 In consideration of the payment of the Sponsorship Fees the [Company] grants to the [Sponsor] the non-exclusive right to have the [Sponsor's] name, logo and image described in Appendix A and the [Sponsor's] [products/services] described in Appendix B incorporated for the duration of the Sponsorship Period in the following manner in the [Project]:

    a. On the main website and/or app in a prominent position as a major sponsor.

    b. On any marketing material in any format and/or medium as a major sponsor where the name of the [Company] is also mentioned. The [Company] agrees and undertakes where feasible to let the [Sponsor] view any proposed material for comment.

    c. It shall not include the right to appear on any merchandising material and/or other adaptation in any format.

    d. It shall not include the right to veto any third parties who may wish to contribute funding and/or sponsorship to the [Company] for the [Project]. This shall be the case whether the third party is a direct competitor and /or operates in the same market.

R.535

1.1 The [Sponsor] agrees that all intellectual property rights including copyright, trade marks, designs, logos, slogans, text, scripts, artwork, graphics, stills, images, characters and/or costumes, made up names, titles, films, videos, podcasts, sound recordings, music, lyrics, computer software and/or computer-generated material and/or any other rights and/or material in any medium and/or format and/or any adaptation and/or sequel shall belong to and be owned by the [Company] in respect of the [Event/Project]. That the [Sponsor] shall not own and/or acquire any such rights and/or interest and shall not receive any royalties and/or other sums from any form of exploitation.

1.2 The [Company] agrees and acknowledges that the [Sponsor's] name, image, slogan and trade mark and products shall remain the sole and exclusive property of the [Sponsor]. That it is not the intention of this agreement that the [Company] shall acquire such rights of ownership. That where any adaptations and/or variations are commissioned for any reason by the [Company] for any marketing purposes that the rights in such development shall be assigned to the [Sponsor] for a nominal sum.

R.536
The [Sponsor] agrees and undertakes that it shall not have the right to film, record, sub-license, adapt, authorise and/or otherwise exploit any part of the [Event/Programme/Performers] at any time without the express prior consent of the [Company].

R.537
The [Sponsor] shall not have any prior claim over and/or option and/or first right of refusal and/or any other rights and/or interest in respect of any subsequent [Programme/Event/Festival] in another year.

R.538
The [Sponsor] shall not have the right to approve any other sponsors who may contribute to the [Event/Project]. In the event that the [Sponsor] decides to withdraw from the [Event/Project] due to the proposed financial and/or other contribution of another third party. Then the [Sponsor] shall still be obliged to pay all sums due under this agreement and to pay an equivalent value in [sterling/currency] for any products and/or services and/or work that the [Sponsor] would have contributed under this agreement.

R.539
In consideration of the [Assignment Fee/Budget] the [Company] undertakes to assign to the [Sponsor] all present and/or future copyright, intellectual property rights and any other rights in any material which will be created which is an adaptation of the [Sponsor's] name, logo, slogan, image, trade mark and/or any other rights and/or original material of any nature which is owned by the [Sponsor] and has been supplied to the [Company] under this agreement. The assignment shall be in respect of all forms of exploitation and/or in all medium for the full period of copyright and any extensions and/or renewals and in perpetuity throughout the world and universe.

R.540

The [Athlete] agrees and undertakes that the [Athlete] is not acquiring any copyright, intellectual property rights and/or any other rights in any names, initials, logos, trade marks, images, text, slogans, products, services, films, videos, sound recordings and/or any other material owned and/or commissioned by the [Sponsor].

R.541

The [Sponsor] agrees and undertakes that:

1.1 The [Sponsor] and/or any consultant and/or agent is not entitled to claim any interest in and/or rights to the personal and/or professional name of the [Athlete] and/or any initials and/or other adaptation in any form.

1.2 The [Sponsor] shall not apply to register any trade mark, logo, gesture, image, slogan, garments and/or accessories, domain names and/or other rights based on and/or derived from the personal and/or professional name of the [Athlete] and/or any associated caricature, hairstyle, clothing, training techniques and/or skills and/or otherwise.

R.542

[Name] shall have the right to end the agreement with the [Sponsor] at any time without the necessity of stating any reason. [Name] shall be obliged to provide [number] [days/months] notice to the [Sponsor] to that effect by [email/written letter]. The [Sponsor] shall only be obliged to pay the sums due to the end date. In such event no sums shall be due from [Name] to the [Sponsor] in compensation for such action regardless of the fact that the [Sponsor] has planned events beyond the end date.

R.543

The [Sponsor] agrees and undertakes that it shall not:

1.1 Reproduce, commission and/or authorise the use of any caricature of [Name].

1.2 Register any copyright, intellectual property rights, domain names, trade marks and/or any other rights in any name and/or initials and/or or professional name used by [Name] and/or any associated word, catchphrase, movement, image, sound and/or other identifying feature used by [Name].

1.3 Permit any director and/or personnel to be interviewed by any unauthorised biographer of [Name] and/or allow access to any material concerning [Name] which is owned and/or controlled by the [Sponsor] without the prior written consent of [Name] in each case.

1.4 Represent to any third party that the [Sponsor] and/or any consultant and/or agent has the authority to act on behalf of [Name] for any reason and/or to provide any consents and/or approvals on his/her behalf at any time.

1.5 Commission, develop and/or authorise any app, blog, podcast, website and/or any marketing and/or other material which features [Name] and/or his/her name, image and/or representation and/or adapts any material created under this agreement which has not been authorised and approved by [Name].

R.544

1.1 [Name] has only agreed to endorse the [Products/Services] specified in this agreement at the [Event] from [date] to [date].

1.2 The [Sponsor] agrees and undertakes not to use the name and/or image of [Name] and/or any material commissioned and/or created by the [Sponsor] at the [Event] including films, videos, sound recordings and/or photographs to promote and/or market any other products, services, events and/or campaigns which have not been agreed with [Name].

R.545

Where after the conclusion of this agreement the [Company] enter into and/or concludes an agreement with a person and/or any other third party to be involved with the [Event/Exhibition] to which the [Sponsor] has objections for any reason. Then the [Sponsor] shall have the right to serve notice on the [Company] to terminate this agreement and to be removed with immediate effect as a sponsor. In such event the [Sponsor] shall be obliged to pay the sums due [to the date of termination/under this agreement in full despite the fact that the [Sponsor has withdrawn]. No sums shall be refunded by the [Company] to the [Sponsor].

R.546

The [Sponsor] agrees that the [Enterprise] shall be entitled at its sole discretion to:

1.1 Obtain funds from other third parties as sponsors of the [Event] including direct competitors.

1.2 Make arrangements for products and/or services to be used which will be filmed and promoted in association with the [Event].

1.3 Enter into agreements with third parties to conduct interviews, write blogs, make sound recordings, news reports, podcasts and/or programmes for radio and/or television and/or any other media which make reference to the [Sponsor] but not the content of any financial arrangements between the parties.

R.547

The parties agree that:

1.1 The [Sponsor] shall be referred to at all times as the main sponsor of the [Event/Project].

1.2 That no other supply third party shall supply [specify nature/format of products/services] for the [Event/Project]. That the [Sponsor] shall the sole supplier for that type of [product/service] from [date] to [date].

1.3 That the [Sponsor] shall have the first option to be the main sponsor for the next annual [Event/Project] in consideration of the payment of the option renewal fee of [number/currency] by [date].

R.548

1.1 The [Enterprise] agrees and undertakes to provide the [Sponsor] upon request with the names of the third parties who are providing funding, products, services and/or who are making personal appearances, contributions and/or supporting the [Event/Project].

1.2 The [Enterprise] shall not be obliged to supply such data and/ or information in 1.1 if the third party has requested that their involvement not be disclosed and/or it would be a breach of any legislation to do so.

R.549

The [Sponsor] shall only be entitled to use the name of the [Event] and the accompanying logo and slogan on its social media and marketing in any format from [date to [date]. It is not authorised to do so outside this period.

R.550

Where the [Enterprise] and the [Sponsor] collaborate and commission new designs, names, slogans, words, images and/or other material of any nature for the [Event/Project]. Then the copyright and intellectual property rights in this new material shall be owned by and/or assigned to [both parties equally/the Enterprise].

R.551

The [Enterprise] agree and undertake that after the completion of the [Event/ Project] that they shall not use the name, trade marks, logo, images and/ or products of the [Sponsors] in any marketing and/or promotional material without their prior approval and consent.

R.552

The [Sponsor] shall be entitled to:

1.1 Arrange for third parties to take images, films, videos and other material of the [Event]. Provided that the [Company] is informed in advance and such third parties complete a location access agreement with the [Company].

1.2 Use the title of the [Event] and the logo, name and image of the [Company] on the [Sponsors'] website, app and in any marketing material and/or promotional material at any time until [date].

1.3 Use and adapt images, films, videos and other material of the [Event] in conjunction with any services and/or products supplied and sold by the [Sponsor] until [date].

University, Charity and Educational

R.553
'The Non-Theatric Rights' shall be defined as the right to authorise, license, sale, hire and/or exploit the exhibition of the [Film/Video/Sound Recordings] in [format] to any audience which is not charged any entry fee and/or other access fee. This shall apply to any trade organisations; commercial companies and/or other institutions, charities, professional associations, educational establishments such as universities, schools and colleges; cultural, drama and arts enterprises including museums, trusts, summer camps, drama and film societies ; religious places of worship including churches and church groups, social philanthropy and social enterprise; hospitals, prisons, public libraries, hotels, holiday parks and private members clubs.

R.554
'The Non-Theatric Rights' shall be defined as the non-exclusive right to exhibit the [Film/Video/Sound Recording] in [country/Territory] from [date] to [date] to any audience which forms part of one of the following categories provided that there is no charge for their attendance and that any member of the audience may view the material for free:

1.1 Schools, universities, colleges, training and educational establishments.

1.2 Drama groups, film clubs, libraries, professional associations.

1.3 Social and charitable enterprises.

1.4 Arts, sports, music and cultural organisations.

1.5 Closed circuit television systems which are relayed in hotels, holiday parks, on oil rigs, ships and/or aeroplanes.

R.555

'The Non-Theatric Rights' shall be defined as the sole and exclusive right throughout the world for the duration of the Licence Period to authorise, supply, license, hire, sell and/or exploit the right to exhibit and play the [Film/Video /Sound Recording] in [all formats/specify format] and/or by any other means created in the future to an audience at the following types of institutions and/or organisations and/or bodies where no entry fee and/or charge of any nature is made for viewing the material in person as part of an audience:

1.1 Universities, sixth form and evening colleges, vocational and/or agricultural colleges, training and/or educational institutions, schools, halls of residence, drama, and film societies, public libraries, museums, hospitals and prisons.

1.2 Professional associations, hotels, camp sites, holiday parks; charities, social enterprises, clubs, trusts and other organisations connected with education, the arts, music, fashion and culture and religion.

R.556

'The Reprographic Rights' shall be defined as the reprographic copying by means of a reprographic process. Reprographic process means a process for making facsimile copies or involving the use of an appliance for making multiple copies and includes in relation to a [Work] held in electronic form any copying by electronic means but not a film or a sound recording.

R.557

'The Reprographic Rights' shall be defined as the right to reproduce the [Work] by photocopying and other reprographic means whether laser, photo images or otherwise so that a mirror image copy of the text words, illustrations, drawings or other material in the [Work] is exactly copied on to another two-dimensional format.

R.558

The [Company] confirms that it has granted a non-exclusive licence to the [Copyright Licensing Agency/other] to reproduce literary works published by the [Company] which shall include the [Work] by photocopying and other reprographic means. The [Copyright Licensing Agency/other] shall divide the proceeds from the reprographic rights between the [Author] and the [Company] as follows: [number] per cent to the [Author] and [number] per cent to the [Company]. The [Author] shall receive the [Author's] share of the proceeds through the [Author's Licensing and Collecting Society/other] in accordance with their standard terms and conditions.

R.559

The [Author] does not grant the [Company] any reprographic rights in the [Work]. The [Author] reserves and retains all reprographic rights of any nature whether in existence now and/or created in the future including but not limited to photocopying, scanning, laser and/or any other means. All sums due in respect of the exercise of these rights shall belong to the [Author] and the [Company] shall not be entitled to any sums at any time.

R.560

'The Off-Air Recording Rights' shall be defined as the right to include the [Programmes/Episodes/Series] in a Licensing Scheme for educational establishments under [specify legislation/authority]. The licences granted under the scheme grant the educational establishment the right to make a recording of the [Programmes/Episodes/Series] from any broadcast and/or cable programme service which is entirely for educational purposes of the students.

R.561

'The Theatric Rights' shall be defined to be the right to exhibit and play the [Film/Video/Sound Recording] in [specify format/all formats] to audiences in circumstances where a charge for admission is made for any person to be part of the audience. This shall include but not be limited to outdoor festivals, cinemas, arenas, stadiums, lecture halls and concert venues.

R.562

'Performance' shall be defined to be a performance of the [Work] in public where the work is protected by copyright in [country] as a literary, dramatic and/or musical work [which would otherwise be a restricted act] including but not limited to presentations, lectures, addresses, speeches and/or sermons. It shall also include any other mode of visual and/or acoustic presentation including a performance in respect of a sound recording, film, video and/or the broadcast and/or transmission of the [Work].

R.563

1.1 In consideration of the non-returnable Advance and the fixed unit payments in clause [–]. The [Institute] grants to the [Company] a non-exclusive licence to reproduce, supply, distribute and sell throughout the [Territory/world] for the duration of the Licence Period the agreed designs and products set out in Appendix A which bear the name, image and logo of the [Institute].

1.2 The [Company] agrees and undertakes not to use the name, image and/or logo of the [Institute] for any other purpose.

R.564

1.1   [Name] grants the [Institute] the right to store the [Essay/Article/ Coursework] on a storage and retrieval system, database and/or archive owned and/or controlled by the [Institute] indefinitely.

1.2   [Name] grants the [Institute] the right to reproduce copies to be distributed at no cost to be read by other persons at the [Institute] for personal and private study but not for any commercial purpose.

1.3   The [Institute] agrees that it shall not be entitled to register any copyright and/or any other rights with any rights management organisation and/or to assign any rights to any third party and/or to make copies available on the [Institutes'] website and/or to supply, sub-license, distribute and/or sell copies to the public in any form.

1.4   The [Institute] agrees that it shall not be entitled to edit, adapt and/or alter the [Essay/Article/Coursework] at any time and/or to arrange and/ or authorise any translation and/or to delete the name and/or copyright notice of [Name] and/or to attribute the [Essay/Article/Coursework] to a third party.

R.565
The [Institute] agrees that it shall not have any right to exploit and/or reproduce and/or licence images, films and/or sound recordings which it and/ or any members of its staff and/or students have made of the [Contributor/ Presenter] at the [Event] for commercial purposes in any format in any part of the world unless the [Contributor/Presenter] has concluded a commercial licence exploitation agreement with the [Institute].

R.566
[Name] does not assign any present and/or future copyright and/or intellectual property rights, inventions, patents and/or other rights in any material which is the original creation of [Name] under this agreement. All rights are reserved to [Name].

R.567
In consideration of the [Buy-out Fee] the [Contributor] assigns to the [Enterprise] all present and future copyright and intellectual property rights and any other rights in all media in the product of the work of [Name] in whole and/or part whether in existence now and/or created in the future throughout the world and universe for the full period of copyright and any extensions and renewals and in perpetuity including but not limited to:

1.1   The right to assign, transfer, licence, exploit, adapt, develop and/or authorise any third party to reproduce, register and/or protect any part in any medium in any language.

1.2 To right to reproduce, broadcast, transmit and/or exploit the rights and/or material in the form of terrestrial, cable, satellite and digital radio and/or television and/or by any method of mechanical reproduction; DVDs, videos, audiocassettes, CDs, disks and/or lasers.

1.3 The right to exercise the rights and/or material by means of theatric and non-theatric exploitation; educational, heritage and charity conferences, events and marketing; sub-licensing and/or merchandising, sponsorship, endorsement and/or product placement, periodicals, newspapers, comics, magazines and other printed publications including hardbacks, paperbacks and children's books.

1.4 The right to exploit the rights and/or material in any electronic format and/or method of access, storage, retrieval, supply, distribution and/or communication on the internet and/or through any telecommunication system and/or in any computer software programme and/or any other media of any nature including any website, app, download and game.

1.5 It shall apply whether access and use is free and/or a charge is made such as a one off payment and/or as a result of access and use under a subscription service and/or any other method.

R.568

1.1 The [Enterprise] agrees that where a new title, domain name, logo, image and/or other rights and/or material are created, developed and/or commissioned in respect of the [Project/Event/Conference]. That these new rights and material shall be shared equally between [specify name] and the [Enterprise].

1.2 That neither party shall be entitled to register any ownership of any rights and/or material without the consent of the other party. That both parties shall be named on all applications and other records.

1.3 Both parties must agree in order for any rights and/or material to be sub-licensed, supplied and/or assigned to a third party at any time.

R.569

Where a student designs and creates an original invention during their independent [Thesis/Project] at the [Enterprise]. The [Enterprise] shall not be entitled to assume ownership and control of the invention and to attempt to register any rights and/or patent. The student shall be presumed to be the owner and shall need to provide their consent and agreement.

R.570

1.1 Where any person and/or company engaged, employed and/or with whom the [Enterprise] has reached some other agreement develops and writes any new course work; designs and creates new titles, logos, images, trade marks and/or films, videos, blogs and/or podcasts in the course of their work specifically for the [Enterprise]. Then the copyright and/or all other intellectual property rights shall belong entirely to the [Enterprise].

1.2 It is a specific condition that any such person and/or company in 1.1 must agree to complete any assignment document required by the [Enterprise] to complete any transfer of such rights.

R.571

Where the [Consultant/Marketing Company] assists in the development of a computer software programme and/or the creation of new reports, charts, statistics, images, logos and/or other material based on any databases, data, documents and other information provided by the [Enterprise]. The [Consultant/Marketing Company] agrees and undertakes that all such present and future copyright and/or any other intellectual property rights and computer software rights as shall be created shall belong to the [Enterprise]. That it is not the intention of this agreement that any rights shall be retained by the [Consultant/Marketing Company].

R.572

1.1 The [Institute/Enterprise] reserves the right to issue new policies and guidelines [which relate to conduct/other theme] at any time which will apply to all [students/lecturers/personnel/consultants/companies] who engage with the [Institute/Enterprise] in any capacity.

1.2 The new policies and guidelines in 1.1 shall be added to the conditions as an amendment to any agreement.

1.3 Where they are not accepted by any person and/or company. Then the parties shall endeavour to resolve the matter by [specify method].

RISK

General Business and Commercial

R.573
The risk in the [Company's] [Products] shall pass on delivery to the [Buyer] and/or his/her nominated agent and/or distributor.

R.574
The risk in respect of the [Material] supplied under this agreement shall be transferred to the [Customer/Purchaser] either upon collection and/or delivery to the nominated address whichever is the earlier.

R.575
The entire risk in respect of the [Project] and all related material shall remain with the [Supplier] and shall not pass to the [Purchaser] on delivery to the nominated address. The [Supplier] must complete the installation of the agreed {Project] and allow the [Purchaser] to inspect and approve the installation and materials. The risk shall be transferred to the [Purchaser] when the completion of the installation is approved by the [Purchaser] in a formal document.

R.576
[Name] agrees that he/she entered the [competition/sport] and that he/she takes part and performs the agreed tasks entirely at their own discretion, choice, risk and liability. That he/she accepts that there is an inherent danger and a high risk of personal injury. That whilst the [Company] will endeavour to take all reasonable safety and health precautions and provide safety equipment, guidance and advice that [Name] must make a personal decision as to whether to proceed or not. That [Name] has the choice not to carry out any task.

R.577
All risk in the [Products] shall remain with the [Supplier] while it is in transit and prior to delivery to the agreed locations. Any material which deteriorates in quality so that it cannot be used and/or is lost, destroyed and/or damaged shall be at the [Suppliers'] cost and must be replaced by the [Supplier].

R.578
The risk in respect of storage, collection and/or delivery shall be the [Clients] responsibility and not the [Company's] from the date of purchase. The [Company] shall be entitled to charge storage fees and any sums incurred to arrange delivery as requested by the [Client].

R.579

1.1 The [Sub-Licensee] agrees and accepts that it shall be responsible for its own costs, expenses, liabilities and risks and shall not seek to be indemnified by the [Licensee] and/or the [Licensor].

1.2 That the [Sub-Licensee] shall arrange and pay for its own insurance to adequately cover any claims by the public and/or any other third party [and/or the Licensee and Licensor].

1.3 That the [Sub-Licensee] shall carry out such risk, security and health and safety assessments as may be required in accordance with any guidelines and/or code of practice which may be in existence at that time. That where the [Sub-Licensee] finds a serious failing as a result of any assessment then action should be taken to remedy the matter immediately.

R.580

Any person and/or company which accesses, downloads, stores and/or retrieves, contributes to and/or views the [Website/App] and/or any marketing and/or promotions; enters any competitions and/or sends any communications, films, videos, and/or images, photographs, text and/or sound recordings does so entirely at their own risk and cost.

R.581

Where the [Company] carries out a risk assessment and identifies a serious health and/or safety and/or security risk to the participants and/or the public in respect of the [Event]. Then the [Company] agrees to notify the [Sponsor] of the matter together with a recommendation as to the action it intends to take to resolve the problem. Where it is clear that the problem cannot be resolved by the start date of the [Event] then the parties are agreed that it should be rescheduled to start on later date. The parties agree that such a delay shall not be a breach of this agreement provided that both parties agree the delay.

R.582

1.1 The parties agree that this is a high risk [Project] and that each shall bear its own risk, liability, costs and expenses and arrange such insurance as it thinks fit in the circumstances.

1.2 The parties accept that the [Project] may be cancelled at any time due to weather conditions and/or failure of any risk assessment which has been carried out prior to the commencement of the [Project].

1.3 That each party agrees to ensure that all equipment, services and personnel to be provided by them to the [Project] are of the highest standard for the conditions in [country] and have been subject to all the necessary tests, protocols and reviews specified by [specify organisations].

1.4 That each party agrees and undertakes that they shall inform the other parties in the event that there are any risks which are identified as of concern and/or failures, omissions, errors and/or any other matters which may affect the successful conclusion of the [Project].

R.583

The parties to this agreement have created a new enterprise for the [Project] entitled: [specify name] which is registered with [specify organisation/ government department] as at [date]. That this new enterprise shall be responsible for all the risk, liability, damages, losses, costs and/or expenses that may be incurred and/or arise. That the parties are not jointly and severally liable except as stated in any new agreement with the new enterprise.

R.584
The [Company] is not responsible for the [Products] and the risk does not pass from the [Supplier] to the [Company] until the delivery of the [Products] has been made to the nominated [warehouse/ship/collection point].

R.585
The parties to this agreement agree and undertake that they shall carry out all such health and safety assessments and/or tests and/or shall fulfil all such product liability compliance requirements as may be required under any laws, codes of practice and/or guidelines in [country]. That shall include but not be limited to ingredients, labels, packaging, guidance for use, and/or age restrictions.

R.586
The [Distributor] shall supply the [Service] to the [Subscriber] at its own cost and risk provided that the [Subscriber] pays the monthly subscription charge and does not misuse and/or alter and/or adapt any equipment provided with the [Service].

ROYALTIES

Film, Television and Video

R.587
In consideration of the rights granted to the [Licensee] the [Licensor] shall be entitled to the following sums:

1.1 [number] per cent [number] % calculated on the Published [Retail/Wholesale] Price. This figure shall be inclusive of any rental surcharge, premium, licence or subscription fee, but not include any additional taxes which have been added on supply and/or sales. The royalties shall be due to the [Licensor] in respect of all [CDs/DVDs/Electronic Downloads/other formats] of the adapted version of the [Musical Work/Lyrics] which are reproduced and exploited of the soundtrack of the [Film].

1.2 No royalty shall be paid in respect of copies supplied, displayed, exhibited and/or distributed to and/or by third parties free of charge for any reason. Provided that it is strictly for promotional and marketing purposes of the [Film].

1.3 Where the [Musical Work/Lyrics] only form part of any unit. Then the royalty due in 1.1 shall be proportionately reduced by the proportion of the duration of the [Musical Work/Lyrics] to the total duration of the whole unit.

1.4 Where any formats and/or stock are no longer sold and/or are remaindered at and/or below cost price. The royalty payable shall only be calculated on the sums which are actually received by the [Licensee] exclusive of any sales tax.

R.588

1.1 The [Company] supplies the [Units] at a fixed price of [number/ currency] per item.

1.2 The [Distributor] shall be entitled to sell and exploit the [Units] at any price it shall decide.

1.3 In addition to the fixed price in 1.1 the [Distributor] shall also pay the [Company] a fixed additional royalty of [number/currency] for each of the [Units] that is sold and not returned.

1.4 The royalty in 1.3 shall also be due on any [Units] that the [Distributor] shall decide to supply at no cost. This shall not apply to items which are damaged, lost, destroyed and/or are returned by any purchaser.

R.589

1.1 [Name] has accepted a fixed fee in full and final settlement of all the work commissioned by the [Company].

1.2 [Name] has agreed and undertaken to assign all the present and future copyright, intellectual property rights and any other rights in all media in the product of his/her work to the [Company] at no additional cost.

1.3 [Name] has agreed and undertaken that he /she is not entitled to any royalties and waives any rights in respect of his/her work and/or the [Film//Recordings] and/or any form of adaptation and/or exploitation in all media and/or formats at any time.

R.590

1.1 The [Contributor/Performer] shall be entitled to be paid his/her agreed fees and such future royalties and/or repeat fees and/or other sums as may be set out in the agreement between the union known as [specify union/organisation] and the [Distributor/Channel] known as: [specify name/reference].

1.2 Where the union agreement fails to address any rights, technology and/ or forms of exploitation which may not exist at this date but which may be created and/or developed in the future. The [Contributor/Performer] accepts that no royalties and/or other payments shall be due.

R.591

'The [Licensor's/Assignors'] Royalties' shall be defined as the following percentage of the Gross Receipts which are actually received by [and/or accrued to] the [Licensee] [and/or sub-licensee, agent and/or distributor] at any time as follows: [number] per cent [number]% in respect of the rights granted by the [Licensor] under this agreement.

R.592

The [Licensor] shall be due to be paid all sums which constitute the net receipts after the [Licensee] has deducted its authorised commission from the sums which it receives from the exploitation of the rights.

R.593

1.1 The [Assignee] agrees and undertakes to pay the [Assignor] the Royalties in clause [–] in respect of the exploitation of the [specify format of rights/DVDs/Electronic and Telecommunication Rights/All Media Rights] of the [Film/Series].

1.2 There shall be no royalty due in 1.1 where the [Assignee] uses and/or authorises the use of [number] minutes in duration of the [Film/Recordings] for the purpose of trade exhibitions, in-store demonstrations, award ceremonies, promotional events and/or media channels, platforms, websites, apps and/or podcasts for marketing purposes only.

R.594

1.1 The [Distributor] shall pay to the [Company] a fixed sum of [number/ currency] for each unit of the [Videos/DVDs/Discs/other format] of the [Film] supplied, sold and distributed by the [Distributor] to any third party [where the ownership of the unit is transferred] during the Licence Period.

1.2 The [Distributor] agrees and undertakes that the [Retail/Wholesale/ other Price] in 1.1 in the first [six/twelve] months shall not be less than [number/currency] per unit.

1.3 In addition the [Distributor] shall pay the [Company] [number per cent] of all sums received by the [Distributor] [after the deduction of commission, administration, reproduction, marketing and other costs and any sales tax) from the rental, hire, lease, subscription service and/or other loan of [Videos/DVDs/Discs/other format] of the [Film] to other third parties during the Licence Period.

R.595
'The Licensor's Royalties' shall be defined to include:

1.1 [number] per cent of the sums actually received by and/or credited to the [Distributor] from the sale, supply, distribution, sub-license and exploitation of the [Sound Recordings/Film] and/or [Discs/other format] in any part of the world at any time and

1.2 [number] per cent of all sums received by the [Distributor] from any rights management organisations and/or collecting societies and/or other organisations for the transmission, broadcast, reproduction and/or other exploitation of the [Sound Recordings/Film] and/or [Disc/other format] in any part of the world at any time.

R.596

1.1 The royalties to be paid by the [Licensee] shall be based on the numbers of copies of the [specify unit/format] which are manufactured, reproduced, and distributed by the [Licensee] which incorporate the licensed [Slogan/Image/Logo].

1.2 The [Licensee] shall be entitled to appoint a third party manufacturer, packager and/or distributor in [country] from [date] to [date].

1.3 The [Licensee] shall pay the [Licensor] a fixed fee of [number/currency] per unit manufactured, reproduced and distributed by the [Licensee] which incorporates the licensed [Slogan/Image/Logo]. A unit shall be counted once the stock has left the manufacturer. Payment shall be at the end of each calendar month direct to the nominated bank account of the [Licensor].

1.4 It is agreed that payment is not reliant on sales of any stock.

R.597
'The [Performer's/Contributors'] Royalties' shall be defined as the Net Receipts less the [Licensee's] Commission.

R.598
'The Licensor's Royalties' shall be the following percentage of the Gross Receipts: [number per cent] [number] %.

R.599
'The Licensor's Royalties' shall be the sum total of the Net Receipts received by the [Company] after conversion to [currency] in [country] after deduction

of any customs duties, sales taxes, delivery costs, the [Company's] Commission and the authorised expenses.

R.600
'The Author's Royalties' shall be the following percentage of the Gross Receipts: [number] per cent.

R.601
'The Assignor's Royalties' shall be the following percentage of the Net Receipts: [number] per cent [number] %.

R.602
The [Author] agrees that the non-returnable Advance shall be offset against the [Author's] Royalties.

R.603
The [Author] agrees that no royalties will be due from promotional and/or review copies of the [Work/Book/Audio File] for which no payment is received by the [Company].

R.604
The [Assignor] agrees that no royalties shall be due from promotional, review, free and/or other forms of exploitation of the [Film] and/or parts for which no sums are received by and/or credited to the [Assignee].

R.605
No sums shall be due and/or royalties paid to the [Assignor] in respect of copies of the [Units/other formats] which are destroyed due to force majeure and/or damaged by fire, water and/or which are lost and/or stolen and/or which are remaindered and/or sold below cost price at any time.

R.606
The [Licensor] shall not be paid for any units which are:

1.1 Destroyed during the production and/or manufacture process provided they are not sold to a third party.

1.2 Provided for free for display, exhibition, promotional, marketing and/or advertising purposes up to a maximum of [number] copies.

1.3 Sold and/or disposed of below cost price for charitable purposes.

1.4 Damaged by floodwater, fire and/or some other reason due to force majeure.

1727

R.607

The [Distributor] shall not be entitled to deduct any costs of production, manufacture, distribution, sales, marketing, advertising and/or promotion from the sums actually received prior to the payment of the Royalties due to the [Licensor].

R.608

The [Licensee] agrees and undertakes to pay the [Company] [number] per cent of the [Gross Receipts/Net Receipts] from the exploitation of the [Theatric and Non-Theatric Rights] in the [Film/Series] after the [Licensee] has deducted all the Distribution Expenses which have been incurred.

R.609

1.1   In consideration of the assignment of the rights the [Assignee] agrees and undertakes to pay the Royalties in clause [–] to the [Assignor] in respect of the exploitation of the [Film] including the soundtrack and/ or any parts and/or any rights and/or adaptation in [currency].

1.2   The parties agree that where the rate of the royalty payment is omitted and/or not clear. That the presumption shall be that the [Assignor] shall be paid a royalty and that it shall not be less than [number] per cent of the Net Receipts. That any such new royalty shall be subject to agreement between the parties.

1.3   The parties agree that the [Assignee] may deduct all Distribution Expenses from the Gross Receipts prior to the calculation of the Net Receipts and the calculation of the royalty payments to the [Assignor].

R.610

The [Licensor] agrees that no royalties shall be due for the use of any part of the [Film/Series/Sound Recording] and/or any adaptation where the sole purpose of the use of the extract is promotion and marketing in any media and/or format. Provided that the extract shall not exceed [number] minutes in duration.

R.611

[Name] agrees that the [Company] shall have the option to buy out all the other rights which [Name] may own in the [Film/Series/Sound Recording] for a one-off payment of [number/currency]. This option starts on [date/time] and ends on [date/time]. Payment must be received by [name] by [date/time] at the latest if it is to be exercised by the [Company]. Where the option is not exercised then the option shall lapse on [date/time].

R.612

All royalties in this agreement shall be converted and paid in [specify currency]. The bank charges for any transfer including currency conversion costs and commission shall be paid for by the [Licensor/Licensee].

R.613

Where for any reason the [Distributor] is owed any sums by the [Company] whether under this agreement and/or any other arrangement. The [Distributor] shall be entitled to set-off and withhold any such sums from the royalties due to the [Company]. Provided that the [Distributor] confirms the reason and amount set-off in the royalty statement.

R.614

1.1 The [Company] shall pay any initial fees due to the [Artists] for their performances in the [Films/Series] within [one] calendar month after completion of the work. Thereafter any royalties which may be due to the [Artists] in respect of the exploitation of the rights granted to the [Company] and/or otherwise shall be paid within [number] months of the actual use of the rights in any format and/or medium by the [Company] and/or a third party.

1.2 There is no right to withhold any sums for any reason in respect of a dispute under another agreement.

1.3 Where any [Artist] dies then all payments shall be made to their named beneficiary and/or to the executors of their estate. The [Company] shall not require confirmation of probate and agrees to accept a personal letter from a family member.

R.615

1.1 [Name] has fulfilled the role of [specify purpose/role] and supplied the following work and material: [describe/work schedule/material].

1.2 [Name] agrees and undertakes that he/she shall not be entitled to be paid any additional royalties and/or expenses. That the agreed fee for the completion of the work and the supply of the material in 1.1 provided by [Name] for the [Film/Video/Sound Recording] is in full and final settlement for the buy-out of all the copyright, intellectual property rights and any other rights in all formats and media through the world and universe whether they are in existence now and/or created in the future. [Name] waives the right to any other sums.

R.616

1.1 The [Company] shall pay [Name] an initial fee of [number/currency] for his/her contribution and work for the [Project].

1.2 The [Company] agrees that the consent for the use of the contribution and work of [Name] has only been provided for exploitation of the [Project] as follows: [specify purpose/schedule/material].

1.3 The [Company] accepts that if there is any intention to use the [Project] for any other purpose and/or format that the prior consent of [Name] shall be required. That [Name] shall be entitled to be paid additional royalties and/or other payments for any such use and such exploitation shall be subject to a new agreement between the parties.

R.617

[Name] shall be entitled to receive a royalty payment from every format and/or means and/or method of exploitation of the [Film/Material] carried out by the [Company] and/or any third party. This principle shall apply whether the royalty rate is stated in this agreement or not and whether the rights and/or method of exploitation existed at the time of this agreement. The royalty rate to be applied shall be subject to discussions between the parties and the form of exploitation may not be used until terms have been agreed between the parties and an agreement concluded.

General Business and Commercial

R.618

The [Licensee] agrees that no sums shall be withheld from the [Licensor] which are not disclosed in the accounting statements and reports.

R.619

The [Licensor] agrees that the advance against future royalties] may be requested to be returned if the terms of this agreement are not fulfilled by the [Licensor].

R.620

Where under this agreement there is any doubt as to the royalty percentage to be applied to any exploitation of the rights and/or material. Then the highest rate in this agreement shall apply if the right and/or format and/or method of exploitation is specified. If there is no right and/or format and/or method of exploitation specified but it is covered by the terms of the agreement. Then the royalty rate to apply shall be subject to separate negotiation between the parties.

R.621

1.1 Where no royalty rate is stated in the agreement and/or the rights and/or method of exploitation did not exist at the time of the conclusion of this agreement. Then it is agreed that the rights and/or method of exploitation shall still belong to and be reserved to the [Licensor].

1.2   The [Licensee] shall have the first right of refusal, but in the event that the parties cannot agree terms within [number] months of notification to the [Licensee]. The [Licensor] shall be entitled to exploit the rights and/or method of exploitation and enter into an agreement with a third party. Provided that the terms of the new agreement do not breach the original agreement with the [Licensee].

R.622

The parties agree that where the rights, material and/or technology did not exist and/or were not envisaged at the time of this agreement. That there is no presumption under this agreement that such rights, material and/or technology has been authorised and/or granted to the [Licensee].

R.623

Where in any accounting period the [Company] receives less than [number/currency] from the exploitation of the rights granted by [Name] under this agreement. Then the [Company] shall not be obliged to account and/or make any royalty payment to [Name]. Any sum due to [Name] shall be carried forward to the next accounting period. The [Company] shall notify [Name] of the fact that they have taken this action.

R.624

Where any sub-agent, sub-distributor and/or sub-licensee fails to make payment of any royalties and/or defaults under any agreement so that [Name] incurs losses and/or damages and/or is not paid any sums due as a result. Then the [Company] accepts and agrees that it shall pay bear responsibility for failure and/or default and be liable for all royalties, losses, damages, interest and/or other sums due to [Name].

R.625

Where for any reason the payment of any royalties to [Name] is delayed by up to [one] month. It is agreed that no additional interest shall be due on the payment to [Name]. Thereafter interest shall be due at the fixed sum of [number/currency] for each day of delay of the payment up to a maximum of [number/currency] in total in any one year period.

R.626

1.1   The [Enterprise] agrees and undertakes that [Name] shall be entitled to receive a royalty of [number] per cent from any sums received from third parties by the [Enterprise] in [currency] from the exploitation and/or sub-licensing of the [Project] at any time. This sum shall be after the [Enterprise] and/or any third party has deducted reproduction, packaging and marketing costs, commission, administration, freight, insurance and any other costs, expenses, custom duties and sales taxes [excluding personal and corporation tax].

1.2 The [Enterprise] shall report and account to [Name] once in any financial year.

1.3 The duration of any third party agreement cannot extend beyond [date] without the prior consent of [Name].

R.627

1.1 The [Company] has agreed to pay [Name] a fee of [number/currency] for completion of the work: [specify work, schedule and material] which is to be used for the [Project].

1.2 [Name] has waived any right to any royalties for any other form of exploitation and/or adaptation of the product of the work of [Name] and/or any material and/or any rights and/or the [Project] at any time. It is not the intention of this agreement that [Name] should be paid any royalties and/or other additional sums in the future.

Internet, Websites and Apps

R.628

[Name] agrees that no royalties, fees, expenses, costs and/or other sums shall be paid by the [Company] to [Name] for any contribution, work and/or other rights and/or material submitted by [Name] to the [Account/Platform]. [Name] agrees that the [Company] shall be entitled to reproduce, supply, distribute, sell and sub-licence any contribution, work, rights and/or other material submitted by [Name] to the [Account/Platform] to any third party whether for educational, charitable and/or commercial purposes provided that they display the credit and copyright notice to [Name].

R.629

1.1 The [Company] agrees and undertakes that it shall pay [Name] a fixed unit payment of [number/currency] for each completed transaction where funds are received and cleared in respect of any authorised completed electronic download of the [Audio Recording/Images/Documents] from the [Website/App/Platform] from [date to [date].

1.2 The [Company] agrees and undertakes that it shall pay [Name] all the sums due to a nominated bank or other account at the end of each [three/six] month period from [date]. At the same time the [Company] shall send [Name] a short statement by [email/other] which sets out the details of the number of transactions and the calculation of the payment due to [Name].

R.630

'The Licensor's Royalty' shall be defined as the fixed sum of [number/currency] which shall be paid by the [Licensee] to the [Artist] each time that a complete copy of the [Artwork/Image/Video] is downloaded and accessed through any electronic means over the internet and/or through any telecommunication system in any part of the world from the [Website/Platform/Account] [at any time/during the Licence Period].

R.631

1.1 The [Licensee] agrees and undertakes that the [Licensee] shall pay the [Licensors'] Royalty to the [Licensor] at the end of each calendar month in arrears by electronic bank transfer in [currency].

1.2 The [Licensor] shall also supply by means of an [email attachment/other] a full statement of the details of the access and downloading of the [Artwork/Image/Video] from the [Website/Platform/Account].

R.632

1.1 The [Company] agrees to pay [Name] a fee of [number/currency] for every copy of the [Image/App/Work] supplied and sold by the [Company] either directly through its website and/or services and/or through a third party from whom the [Company] receives payment.

1.2 The [Company] shall pay [Name] any sums due every [two/six] calendar months from the commencement of the supply, reproduction and sale of the [Image/App/Work] by electronic transfer at the [Company's] cost to a nominated bank account. A short summary report shall also be sent by [email/other] to [Name] to explain the sales and payment.

1.3 No payment shall be due where a refund has been made and/or the payment was not cleared and retained by the [Company]. Where there is a dispute of any nature the sum due to [Name] shall be withheld and the fee for that copy carried over to the next period of payment.

1.4 The obligation by the [Company] to pay [Name] shall cease in the event that [Name] terminates this agreement. Then payment and the summary report shall be due to the date of termination and/or until such time as all sums have been accounted for by the [Company].

1.5 The [Company] shall not be entitled to assign this agreement with [Name] to a third party without the prior written consent of [Name].

R.633

The [Distributor] shall pay [Name] a fee of [number/currency] which shall be [number] per cent of the total [Gross Receipts/Net Receipts] received by and/or credited to the [Distributor] and/or any associated, connected and/or parent company and/or any sub-agent and/or sub-distributor and/or any authorised third party from confirmed subscribers to the service known as: [specify title of service]. It shall include the service provided through its website, app, text messaging and videos to mobile phones and/or any other method of exploitation in electronic form and/or over the internet and/or any telecommunication service throughout the world at any time.

R.634

1.1   [Name] has agreed to be interviewed for the [Podcast Series] known as: [specify title].

1.2   [Name] has agreed to appear to promote and market: [specify product/service/event].

1.3   [Name] is not being paid any fee for his/her appearance and contribution.

1.4   [Name] agrees and undertakes that he/she shall not be entitled to any fee and/or future royalty from the exploitation of the sound recording and/or film and/or video and/or final edited podcast in the [Podcast Series].

1.5   [Name] agrees that the [Company] who own and/or control the [Podcast Series] may assign, transfer and/or sub-license and/or otherwise exploit in any media and/or format all the material created as a result of the interview with [Name]. Provided that no form of exploitation discredits and/or mocks and/or exposes [Name] to negative social media at any time.

R.635

1.1   [Name] has agreed to read and record the [Text/Work/Poem] entitled: [specify title] written by the [Author].

1.2   The sound recording of [Name] shall be edited to create an audio file which will be offered, supplied and sold on: [specify platform] in [specify format].

1.3   The [Company] agrees and undertakes that [Name] shall be paid an advance against royalties of [number/currency] which can be recouped. Once recouped the [Company] shall pay [Name] a royalty of [number] per cent of the sums received by the [Company] from the agreed form of exploitation in 1.2.

1.4 The [Company] shall be entitled to deduct any commission paid but not marketing and/or production costs prior to the calculation of the sums due to [Name].

R.636

1.1 The [Company] has agreed and undertaken to pay [Name] a fixed unit price of [number/currency] for the purchase of the non-exclusive right to use the [Images/Designs/Graphics] for the [Account] known as: [specify name] from [date to [date] which shall be viewed by the public.

1.2 No other form of exploitation is agreed between the parties. The [Images/Designs /Graphics] may not be used on any other website, platform, app and/or marketing material.

1.3 In the event that the [Company] wishes to use and/or exploit the [Images/Designs/Graphics] in any other medium and/or format. That a new agreement must be concluded in each case and a new fixed unit price and/or royalty set based on the circumstances.

R.637

1.1 The [Licensee/Company] agrees and undertakes to pay [Name] [number] per cent of the actual sums received from the exploitation of the [Images/Logos/Slogans] [after the deduction of production and marketing costs] on any products manufactured, supplied, sold and/or distributed by the [Licensee/Company] from [date] to [date] anywhere in the world.

1.2 [Name] agrees that there is no restriction of the type of product that may be created by the [Licensee/Company].

1.3 The [Licensee/Company] agrees and accepts that the production and marketing costs for any one type of product shall be capped at [number/currency]. Any additional costs shall be the responsibility of the [Licensee/Company].

R.638

1.1 [Name] agrees and undertakes to use the [Product] and to post [number/images/videos] to the [specify name of account] of [Name] to be supplied over the internet and any telecommunication system from [date] to [date].

1.2 Each post shall clearly show the brand name of the [Product] and contain a link to the [website/platform] of the [Company] encouraging the public to purchase the [Product].

1.3 In addition to the initial fee of [number/currency] for the posts in 1.1. [Name] shall also receive an additional payment for every [number] copies of the [Product] purchased by the public before [date]. No additional sum shall be due after that end date regardless of whether the posts still exist and/or display the link.

R.639

The [Performers/Contributors] agree and accept that they have only appeared in the background to the [Film/Podcast]. They accept that they shall not be entitled to any additional sums and/or royalties for the exploitation of the rights and/or material at any time. That they have agreed that all copyright, intellectual property rights and any other rights have been bought out in all media worldwide.

R.640

1.1 [Name] has agreed to endorse and promote the services of the [Company] in [country] and to appear in advertisements, podcasts, videos and at other events specified in Appendix A. [describe work to be completed, dates, type of contribution].

1.2 [Name's] endorsement of the services of the [Company] shall be for the period from [date] to [date].

1.3 The [Company] has agreed to pay a fixed fee of [number/currency] for the completion of all the work in Appendix A.

1.4 In addition the [Company] agrees and undertakes to pay [Name] an additional royalty which is linked to the volume of new customer accounts opened with the [Company] for the period [date] to [date]. [Name] shall be paid a fixed sum of [number/currency] for each new customer who joins in that period and stays as a customer for more than [number] months.

Merchandising and Distribution

R.641

The [Licensee] agrees and undertakes to pay the [Licensor] [number] per cent of the Net Receipts received by the [Licensee] in respect of the exploitation of the defined Merchandising Rights in the [Character] throughout the world at any time.

R.642

The [Licensee] agrees and undertakes to pay the [Licensor] a royalty of [number] per cent of the wholesale selling price in respect of each unit of the [Licensed Article] which is sold.

R.643

The [Licensee] agrees that the Licence Fee cannot be returned and it cannot be offset against the royalties that may fall due and/or are to be paid to the [Licensor]. Even if there are no sales of the [Licensed Articles] under this agreement there cannot be any demand for the repayment of the Licence Fee.

R.644

'The [Licensor's] Royalties' shall be defined as the following percentages of the sums received by and retained by the [Company] in respect of the supply, sale and/or exploitation of the units of the [Licensed Articles/Products] which incorporate the [Images/Logos/Characters] described in Appendix A at any time:

1.1   In respect of units of the [Licensed Articles/Products] sold within the United Kingdom of Great Britain, Northern Ireland, the Republic of Ireland, the Channel Isles and the Isle of Man:

    A.   [number] per cent [number]% up to and including the first [number] units of the [Licensed Articles/Products];

    B.   [number] per cent [number]% for the subsequent [number] of units of the [Licensed Articles/Products];

    C.   [number] per cent [number]% for all other units of the [Licensed Articles/Products] thereafter.

1.2   In respect of units of the [Licensed Articles/Products] sold throughout the [Territory/world] excluding the United Kingdom of Great Britain, Northern Ireland, the Republic of Ireland, the Channel Islands and the Isle of Man:

    A.   [number] per cent [number]% up to and including the first [number] units of the [Licensed Articles/Products];

    B.   [number] per cent [number]% for the subsequent [number] units of the [Licensed Articles/Products]; and

    C.   [number] per cent [number]% for all other units of the [Licensed Articles/Products] thereafter.

1.3   No payment shall be due in respect of units which are given away in a free promotion at a trade fair and/or are damaged, lost and/or destroyed.

1.4   The payment of the royalties shall not be limited to the period of the grant of the licence by the [Licensor]. The procedure of accounting and payment of royalties must continue until all sums have been verified and payment made to the [Licensor].

R.645

1.1   The [Licensor] agrees that the Advance in clause [–] is to be offset against any sums due to the [Licensor] in respect of the royalties due under this agreement.

1.2   The [Licensee] agrees that the Advance is not returnable and/or contingent upon any sales figures being achieved in respect of the [Products].

R.646

1.1   The [Distributor] agrees and undertakes to pay [Name] [number] per cent of the Gross Receipts from the exploitation of the [Images/Text/Logos] in any format and/or medium from [date to [date].

1.2   The [Distributor] agrees and accepts that after [date] and the expiry of this agreement all sums received from the exploitation of the [Images/Text/Logo] in any format and/or medium by the [Distributor] and/or any third party shall belong to [Name]. That the [Distributor] shall not be entitled to any such sums except as is stated in 1.3.

1.3   [Name] agrees that where in 1.2 the [Distributor] assists in the collection of the sums due and receives the payment before it is transferred to [Name]. That the [Distributor] shall be entitled to a commission of [number] per cent.

R.647

No royalties shall be due for any stock disposed of without charge as donations to educational and/or community projects, lost, damaged, recalled as faulty, defective, destroyed, and/or for which no sums are received from any sub-licensee, agent and/or distributor. Provided that all such stock is declared to the [Licensor] and the reason stated for the non-payment.

R.648

1.1   The [Licensee] agrees to pay the [Licensor] a royalty of [number] per cent in respect of all the sums received by the [Licensee] after authorised deductions from the exploitation of the rights granted in the [Work] in clause [–].

1.2   The authorised deductions shall include:

A.   All taxes charged by any government on the production, supply, sale and/or distribution of any product and/or service;

B.   The cost and expense of the design, development, production, packaging, marketing and advertising costs up to a maximum limit in total of [number/currency].

C.   All freight, delivery and insurance costs.

D.   Commission costs of any sub-licensee, agent, distributor and/or other third party.

R.649
The [Sub-Licensee] shall not be entitled to continue to exploit and exercise the rights granted under this agreement where the [Sub-Licensee] has failed to pay any sums due and/or supply any royalty statements at any time during the Term of this Agreement.

R.650
The [Licensee] must pay all royalties directly to [Name] in [currency] and not to any agent and/or management company.

R.651
Delay in paying any royalties due shall incur a penalty fee of [number/currency] per day including weekends. Such sum to be added to any royalty payment due at that time.

R.652
Royalties must be paid on all units of the [Work/Product] supplied to a third party by the [Distributor] whether or not they have been disposed of for free, below cost and/or payment is not received by the [Distributor] due to the collapse and/or failure of the third party business.

R.653

1.1   The [Licensee] shall pay to the [Licensor] [number] per cent of the [Selling Price] in respect of each [Product/Unit] sold in the [Territory/country] by the [Licensee] and/or any parent company, subsidiary, sub-licensee, agent and/or distributor authorised by the [Licensee] to do so.

1.2   The [Selling Price] shall be defined as the price generally promoted for the [Product/Unit] and which is invoiced to the [Customer] for the [Product/Unit] less [specify taxes], custom duties, delivery and insurance charges, credits, allowances, discounts, rebates and returns.

1.3   A consignment of the [Product/Unit] shall be deemed sold when the [Customer] has been invoiced and paid the sum requested to the [Licensee] and/or any parent company, subsidiary, sub-licensee, agent and/or distributor authorised by the [Licensee] to do so. Ownership shall be transferred to the [Customer] on the date of actual delivery of that consignment to the [Customer] subject to valid payment.

R.654

The [Licensee] shall pay to the [Licensor] [number/currency] per unit in respect of each Product reproduced, supplied, distributed and sold anywhere in the world by any means whether through retail and/or wholesale outlets, over the internet on websites, platforms and/or apps and/or radio programmes and/or shopping television channels, mail order and/or otherwise where the sums are received and/or credited to the [Licensee]. No deductions shall be made by the [Licensee] for any commission, costs and expenses, taxes, duties, freight, insurance charges, advertising and/or other sums incurred.

R.655

Any delay in payment of any royalties shall result in an additional charge of [number/currency] per cent of the sum due being added to the payment due to the [Licensor].

R.656

1.1 The [Company/Distributor] shall be entitled to recover all its development, production, packaging, shipping, marketing and/or any other costs and expenses that it may incur from the exploitation of the [Characters/Images/Logos] in conjunction with the [Products] prior to the calculation of any royalties due to [Name]. There shall be no limit on the sums and costs that may be recouped.

1.2 After the sums and costs in 1.1 have been reimbursed to the [Company/ Distributor]. Then [Name] shall be due a royalty of [number] per cent of the sums received and retained by the [Company/Distributor] from the exploitation of the [Characters/Images/Logos] in conjunction with the [Products].

1.3 The sum shall not be deemed received if a sub-licensee, agent and/ or other third party does not transfer the money to the [Company/ Distributor]. The [Company/Distributor] shall not be liable for such failure to pay and/or default by third parties.

R.657

Where there are any currency transfer and/or bank charges incurred at any time then these costs and any commission shall be paid for by [specify name].

R.658

The [Company] shall pay [Name] a royalty on each copy of the [Work/ product] which bears the [Text/Image] in any format and/or medium supplied for free and/or sold to the public. The royalty shall be a percentage of the sums received after the deduction of all costs and expenses incurred by the [Company] as follows:

a.   [number] per cent up to [number] copies in any format and/or medium in each case

b.   [number] per cent from [number] copies thereafter in each case.

All sums shall be accounted for and paid to [Name] at the end of each calendar month. Payment shall be in currency and direct to the nominated account of [Name] and not to any third party unless authorised in writing by [Name].

Publishing

R.659
'The Author's Royalties' shall be defined as:

1.1   [number/currency] for each unit of the [Book] which reproduces the [Manuscript/Images] which is supplied, distributed, disposed of and/or sold whether during the Term of the Agreement and/or thereafter up to [number] units.

1.2   From [number] units a higher rate of [number/currency] shall be applied for each unit of the [Book].

1.3   The royalty rate shall apply whether the full retail price is paid and/or it is discounted and/or disposed of for free.

R.660
The [Author] agrees and accepts that the [Company] shall offset the Advance against the future royalties due to the [Author] first. That no sum shall be due to the [Author] until the Advance has been recouped. The [Company] must still provide an accounting statement that provides evidence of that fact.

R.661
The [Publisher/Distributor] agrees and undertakes to pay the [Author] an Advance which can be recouped against future royalties as follows:

1.1   [number/currency] subject to full signature of this agreement by both parties.

1.2   [number/currency] subject to delivery of a complete and acceptable manuscript in [format] for the [Book] by the [Author].

1.3   [number/currency] on or before [date] subject to completion of 1.1 and 1.2 above.

1.4 [number/currency] within [number] days of the completion of the approval of the proofs by the [Author] and the agreement as to the proposed changes if any with the editor.

1.5 [number/currency] within [number] days of the publication in [country] in [format] of the [Book].

1.6 [number/currency] within [number] days of the publication of the [audio file] of the [Book] on [specify platform].

R.662

The [Publisher/Distributor] agrees that no part of the advance or the royalties already paid shall be returned by the [Author] once the manuscript has been accepted by the [Publisher/Distributor].

R.663

1.1 The [Publisher/Distributor] agrees and undertakes to pay the royalties set out in clause [–] to the [Author] on all units of copies of the [Manuscript/Book/Audio Files] [and/or any part] which is reproduced, supplied, licensed, hired, distributed, sold and/or adapted by the [Publisher/Distributor] and/or any authorised third party.

1.2 The royalties shall be due to the [Author] for each unit regardless of whether a fee and/or payment is made or not to the [Publisher/Distributor] and/or any third party. Payment shall be linked to the unit of the [Manuscript/Book/Audio Files] [and/or part] and not the financial consideration. It is also to be applied to all copies supplied to the press, television, radio, magazines, podcasts, channels, trade fairs and/or any other form of promotion, marketing and/or review.

R.664

The [Publisher/Distributor] shall pay to the [Author/Agent] the following royalties in respect of the primary rights granted under this agreement:

1.1

A. [number] per cent [–] % on the first [number] copies sold of the hardcover edition of the [Work/Manuscript/Book] in the [United Kingdom and Republic of Ireland] which shall be calculated on the recommended published price of the [Publisher/Distributor].

B. Then [number] per cent [–] % on the next [number] copies sold of the hardcover edition of the [Work/Manuscript/Book] in the [United Kingdom and Republic of Ireland] which shall be calculated on the recommended published price of the [Publisher/Distributor].

C. Then [number] per cent [–] % [after the completion of A and B above] of all copies sold of the hardcover edition of the [Work/Manuscript/Book] in the [United Kingdom and Republic of Ireland] which shall be calculated on the recommended published price of the [Publisher/Distributor].

1.2

A. [number] per cent [–] % on the first [number] copies sold of the hardcover edition of the [Work/Manuscript/Book] sold throughout the world (excluding the United Kingdom of Great Britain, the Republic of Ireland and the United States of America) calculated on the sums received by the [Publisher/Distributor].

B. Then [number] per cent [–] % on the next [number] copies on all copies sold of the hardcover edition of the [Work/Manuscript/Book] sold throughout the world (excluding the United Kingdom of Great Britain, the Republic of Ireland and the United States of America) calculated on the sums received by the [Publisher/Distributor].

C. Then [number] per cent [–] % thereafter [after the completion of A and B above] of all copies sold of the hardcover edition of the [Work/Manuscript/Book] sold throughout the world (excluding the United Kingdom of Great Britain, the Republic of Ireland and the United States of America) calculated on the sums received by the [Publisher/Distributor].

1.3 In the event that any editions of the [Work/Manuscript/Book] are sold in other trade outlets including but not limited to: mail order, supermarkets, premiums, subscriptions and direct selling. The Author shall be entitled to [number] per cent [–] % of the sums received by the [Publisher/Distributor].

1.4

A. [number] per cent [–] % on the first [number] copies sold of the paperback edition of the [Work/Manuscript/Book] in the [United Kingdom and Republic of Ireland] which shall be calculated on the recommended published price of the [Publisher/Distributor].

B. Then [number] per cent [–] % on the next [number] copies sold of the paperback edition of the [Work/Manuscript/Book] in the [United Kingdom and Republic of Ireland] which shall be calculated on the recommended published price of the [Publisher/Distributor] and

C.   Thereafter [number] per cent [–] % [after the completion of A and B above] on all copies sold of the paperback edition of the [Work/Manuscript/Book] in the [United Kingdom and Republic of Ireland] which shall be calculated on the recommended published price of the [Publisher/Distributor].

1.5

A.   [number] per cent [–] % on the first [number] copies sold of the paperback edition of the [Work/Manuscript/Book] throughout the world (but excluding the United Kingdom of Great Britain, the Republic of Ireland and the United States of America) calculated on the sums received by the [Publisher/Distributor].

B.   Then [number] per cent [–] % on the next [number] copies sold of the paperback edition of the [Work/Manuscript/Book] throughout the world (but excluding the United Kingdom of Great Britain, the Republic of Ireland and the United States of America) calculated on the sums received by the [Publisher/Distributor] and

C.   Thereafter [number] per cent [–] % [subject to completion of A and B above] on all copies sold of the paperback edition of the [Work/Manuscript/Book] throughout the world (but excluding the United Kingdom of Great Britain, the Republic of Ireland and the United States of America) calculated on the sums received by the [Publisher/Distributor].

1.6   In the event that the [Publisher/Distributor] shall publish a reprint of the [Work/Manuscript/Book] in any country at any time of [number] copies or less. The royalties due to the [Author] shall be reduced to [number] per cent [–] % for hardback editions and [number] per cent [–] % for paperback editions.

1.7   Where editions of the [Work/Manuscript/Book] are sold at a discount of over [50] % and up to and including [62.5] %. The [Author] shall only be entitled to be paid [number] per cent [–] % on the relevant royalty that might have been paid if there had been no discount.

1.8   When editions of the [Work/Manuscript/Book] are sold at a discount over [62.5] % the [Author] shall only be paid [[number] per cent [60] % on the relevant royalty that might have been paid if there had been no discount.

R.665

1.1   The [Publisher/Distributor] agree and undertakes to pay to the [Author] the following royalties on the monies actually received and retained by the [Publisher/Distributor] (excluding any government taxes) in respect of the copies of the [Work/Manuscript/Book] in paperback and hardback which are sold anywhere in the world as follows:

A.   [10] % (ten per cent) on all the first [500/other number] copies.

B.   [12.5] % (twelve and a half per cent) on the next [1,000/other number] copies.

C.   [15] % (fifteen per cent) on the next [number] copies.

D.   [17.5] % (seventeen and a half per cent) on the next [number] copies.

E.   [20] % (twenty per cent) thereafter on all other copies.

1.2   The [Publisher/Distributor] agrees that the royalties in 1.1 shall be paid not only for the [Term of this Agreement/duration of the legal period of copyright and any extensions and/or renewals.] The royalties shall be due to the [Author] for any copies sold at any time by the [Publisher/Distributor] and shall include sums received after the end of the agreement.

R.666

1.1   The [Publisher/Distributor] agrees to pay the [Author] the following royalties on all sums received by the [Publisher/Distributor] (excluding government taxes) in respect of all copies of the [Work/Manuscript/Book] which are in electronic format as a download of the text [and/or images] and/or any audio file and/or other format which is a reading and/or performance of the text in sound which is sold anywhere in the world:

A.   [number] per cent on the first [number] copies.

B.   [number] per cent on the next [number] copies.

C.   [number] per cent thereafter on all copies.

1.2   The [Publisher/Distributor] shall only be entitled to receive the sums from the exploitation of the [Work/Manuscript/Book until the expiry date of this agreement and/or date of termination if earlier. Thereafter all sums shall be paid directly to the [Author] and the [Publisher/Distributor] shall not be entitled to receive any commission and/or other sums of any nature.

1.3   Where any sums are not remitted by a third party for any reason to the [Publisher/Distributor] as required under a sub-licence. The [Author] agrees not to hold the [Publisher/Distributor] responsible for the default and/or failures of the third party.

R.667

1.1 The [Publishing Company] shall pay to the [Author] a fixed royalty in respect of all copies of the [Work/Manuscript/Book] in printed format which are reproduced, supplied and/or sold by the [Publishing Company] and/or any third party in [specify language] at the rate of [number/currency] per copy on the first [number] copies of the [Work/Manuscript/Book] and at the rate of [number/currency] per copy thereafter.

1.2 The [Publishing Company] shall pay to the [Author] a fixed royalty in respect of all copies of the [Work/Manuscript/Book] in electronic format (which are complete copies of the printed version) which are reproduced, supplied and/or sold by the [Publishing Company] and/or any third party in [specify language] at the rate of [number/currency] per copy on the first [number] copies of the [Work/Manuscript/Book] and at the rate of [number/currency] per copy thereafter.

1.3 The [Publishing Company] shall pay to the [Author] a fixed royalty in respect of all copies of the [Work/Manuscript/Book] in audio format (which are complete copies of the text in the form of a reading by a person) which are reproduced, supplied and/or sold by the [Publishing Company] and/or any third party in [specify language] at the rate of [number/currency] per copy on the first [number] copies of the [Work/Manuscript/Book] and at the rate of [number/currency] per copy thereafter.

1.4 Any other adaptation and/or translation shall be subject to new terms being agreed between the parties.

R.668

1.1 The [Company] shall pay the [Author] in respect of disposals and/or sales of any copies of the [Work/Book] in [specify format] in [specify language] as follows:

   A. at the royalty rate of [number] per cent of the [Original Retail Price/Published Price] of the [Work/Book] on the first [number] copies.

   B. at the royalty rate of [number] per cent of the [Original Retail Price/Published Price] on all other copies thereafter.

1.2 The [Company] accepts that no deductions can be made in respect of production costs, copyright clearance and/or fees, cost of graphics and/or index, commission and/or marketing costs and/or any other sums.

1.3　It is accepted by the [Author] that the rates in 1.1 and 1.2 shall not apply to any translation in any other language and/or any other format. Any other method and/or adaptation shall be subject to a new agreement between the parties.

R.669

1.1　The [Company] shall pay to the [Author] a royalty of [number] per cent [–] % of the sums received by the [Company] after the [Company] has deducted all reasonable costs and expenses which it has incurred and/or had to pay a third party in respect of the reproduction, supply, licensing, sale, hire, rental and/or other exploitation and/or adaptation of the [Work/Material] by the [Company] at any time.

1.2　The deductions in 1.1 shall include but not be limited to: discounts, reproduction costs, copyright clearances and contributions to the work by third parties; freight and delivery costs; legal costs; marketing costs; government taxes, levies and custom duties; agents, distributors and third party charges, fees and commission.

R.670

'The Authors Royalties' shall mean the following percentages in respect of all sums received by [and/or credited to] the [Company] in respect of the [Work]:

The Home Market

1.1　Hardback copies of the [Work] sold [and/or disposed of] in the United Kingdom of Great Britain and Northern Ireland, the Republic of Ireland, the Channel Islands and the Isle of Man:

A.　In respect of the first [1,000/number] copies a royalty rate of [number] per cent.

B.　In respect of the next [2,000/number] copies a royalty rate of [number] per cent.

C.　In respect of the next [3,000/number] copies a royalty rate of [number] per cent.

D.　In respect of the next [4,000/number] copies a royalty rate of [number] per cent.

E.　In respect of the next [8,000/number] copies a royalty rate of [number] per cent.

F.　In respect of all copies thereafter a royalty rate of [number] per cent.

Such royalty percentages are to be calculated on the recommended retail price in the [United Kingdom]. It shall not apply where copies of the [Work] are sold for export including sales to the [Company's] parent company, subsidiaries and/or associated companies which are [registered/based] overseas in which case the percentages shall be based on the net amounts received by [and/or credited to] the [Company].

1.2 Paperback copies of the [Work] sold [and/or disposed of] in the United Kingdom of Great Britain and Northern Ireland, the Republic of Ireland, the Channel Islands and the Isle of Man:

A. In respect of the first [2,000/number] copies a royalty rate of [number] per cent.

B. In respect of the next [3,000/number] copies a royalty rate of [number] per cent.

C. In respect of the next [5,000/number] copies a royalty rate of [number] per cent.

D. In respect of the next [10,000/number] copies a royalty rate of [number] per cent.

E. In respect of all copies thereafter a royalty rate of [number] per cent.

Such royalty percentages to be calculated on the recommended retail price in the [United Kingdom].

It shall not apply where copies of the [Work] are sold for export including sales to the [Company's] parent company, subsidiaries and/or associated companies overseas in which case the percentages shall be based on the net amounts received by [and/or credited to] the [Company].

United States of America and Canada

1.3 Hardback copies of the [Work] sold [and/or disposed of] throughout the United States of America and Canada and their respective territories and dependants and the Philippine Islands:

A. In respect of the first [2,000/number] copies a royalty rate of [number] per cent.

B. In respect of the next [4,000/number] copies a royalty rate of [number] per cent.

C. In respect of the next [20,000/number] copies a royalty rate of [number] per cent.

D. In respect of all copies thereafter a royalty rate of [number] per cent.

Such royalty percentages to be calculated on the net amount received by [and/or credited to] the [Company].

1.4 Paperback copies of the [Work] sold [and/or disposed of] throughout the United States of America and Canada and their respective territories and dependants and the Philippine Islands:

A. In respect of the first [5,000/number] copies a royalty rate of [number] per cent.

B. In respect of the next [10,000/number] copies a royalty rate of [number] per cent.

C. In respect of the next [15,000/number] copies a royalty rate of [number] per cent.

D. In respect of all copies thereafter a royalty rate of [number] per cent.

Such royalty percentages to be calculated on the net amount received by [and/or credited to] the [Company].

The Overseas Market excluding the United States and Canada

1.5 Hardback copies of the [Work] sold [and/or disposed of] throughout the [Territory/world] excluding the United Kingdom of Great Britain and Northern Ireland, the Republic of Ireland, the Channel Islands, the Isle of Man, the United States of America and Canada and their respective territories and dependants and the Philippine Islands:

A. In respect of the first [2,000/number] copies a royalty rate of [number] per cent.

B. In respect of the next [4,000/number] copies a royalty rate of [number] per cent.

C. In respect of the next [8,000/number] copies a royalty rate of [number] per cent.

D. In respect of all copies thereafter a royalty rate of [number] per cent.

Such royalty percentages to be calculated on the net receipts received by [and/or credited to] the [Company].

1.6 Paperback copies of the [Work] sold [and/or disposed of] throughout the [Territory/world] excluding the United Kingdom of Great Britain and Northern Ireland, the Republic of Ireland, the Channel Islands, the Isle of Man, the United States of America and Canada and their respective territories and dependants and the Philippine Islands:

A.   In respect of the first [5,000/number] copies a royalty rate of [number] per cent.

B.   In respect of the next [10,000/number] copies a royalty rate of [number] per cent.

C.   In respect of the next [20,000/number] copies a royalty rate of [number] per cent.

D.   In respect of all copies thereafter a royalty rate of [number] per cent.

Such royalty percentages to be calculated on the net amount received by [and/or credited to] the [Company].

Remainder, Discounted and Reduced Hardback and Paperback copies

1.7   Where the [Company] sells [and/or disposes of] copies of the [Work] in hardback and/or paperback throughout the United Kingdom of Great Britain and Northern Ireland, the Republic of Ireland, the Channel Islands and the Isle of Man at a discount, reduced price and/or as remainder, overstock and/or other reason as excess to requirements. The [Author] agrees that he/she shall only be entitled to receive a royalty rate of [number] per cent in respect of all sums actually received by [and/or credited to] the [Company] where each copy of the [Work] is sold [and/or disposed of] at less than [number] per cent of the recommended retail price.

1.8   Where the [Company] sells [and/or disposes of] copies of the [Work] in hardback and/or paperback throughout the [Territory/world] excluding the United Kingdom of Great Britain and Northern Ireland, the Republic of Ireland, the Channel Islands and the Isle of Man at a discount, reduced price and/or as remainder, overstock and/or other reason as excess to requirements. The [Author] agrees that he/she shall only be entitled to receive a royalty rate of [number] per cent in respect of all the sums actually received by [and/or credited to] the [Company] where each copy of the [Work] is sold [and/or disposed of] at less than [number] per cent of the recommended retail price.

Mail Order

1.9   Where the [Company] sells [and/or disposes of] copies of the [Work] throughout the United Kingdom of Great Britain and Northern Ireland, the Republic of Ireland, the Channel Islands and the Isle of Man through mail order and/or other direct selling method. The [Author] agrees that he/she shall only be entitled to receive a royalty rate of [number] per cent of the price of each copy of the [Work] by mail order and/or other direct selling method.

1.10 Where the [Company] sells [and/or disposes of] copies of the [Work] throughout the [Territory/world] excluding the United Kingdom of Great Britain and Northern Ireland, the Republic of Ireland, the Channel Islands and the Isle of Man through mail order and/or other direct selling method. The [Author] agrees that he/she shall only be entitled to receive a royalty rate of [number] per cent of the price of each copy of the [Work] by mail order and/or other direct selling method.

Premium Offers, Book Club, Educational Editions and Subscriptions

1.11 Where the [Company] sells [and/or disposes of] copies of the [Work] throughout the United Kingdom of Great Britain and Northern Ireland, the Republic of Ireland, the Channel Islands and the Isle of Man as a premium offer, book club and/or or educational editions and/or subscriptions. Then the [Author] agrees that he/she shall only be entitled to receive a royalty rate of [number] per cent in respect of all sums received by [and/or credited to] the [Company] where the [Work] is sold at less than [number] per cent of the recommended retail price for each copy.

1.12 Where the [Company] sells [and/or disposes of] copies of the [Work] throughout the [Territory/world] excluding the United Kingdom of Great Britain and Northern Ireland, the Republic of Ireland, the Channel Islands and the Isle of Man as a premium offer, book club and/or educational editions and/or subscriptions. Then the [Author] agrees he/she shall only be entitled to receive a royalty rate of [number] per cent in respect of all sums actually received by [and/or credited to] the [Company] where the [Work] is sold at less than [number] per cent of the recommended retail price for each copy.

Small Reprints

1.13 Where the [Work] is reprinted in hardback for sale [and/or disposal] in the United Kingdom of Great Britain and Northern Ireland, the Republic of Ireland, the Channel Islands and the Isle of Man in any quantity of [number] copies or less. Then [Author] shall only be entitled to a royalty rate of [number] per cent of the recommended retail price for each copy.

1.14 Where the [Work] is reprinted in paperback for sale [and/or disposal] in the United Kingdom of Great Britain and Northern Ireland, the Republic of Ireland, the Channel Islands and the Isle of Man in any quantity of [number] copies or less. Then the [Author] shall only be entitled to a royalty rate of [number] per cent of the recommended retail price for each copy.

Subsidiary Rights

1.15 The [Author] shall be entitled to paid the following royalty rates in respect of the [net sums/sums received/net receipts] received by the [Company] in respect of the exploitation of the following rights in the [Work] throughout the [Territory/world]:

A.   Anthology and Quotation Rights: [number] per cent.

B.   Translation Rights: [number] per cent.

C.   Audiotape Rights/Cassette or talking books: [number] per cent. [Excluding all electronic rights; audio files and/or downloads.]

D.   Straight non-dramatic readings for radio, television: [number] per cent.

E.   Dramatic adaptations for all forms of films, documentaries, programmes, plays and/or other performances for television, radio, film and theatre: [number] per cent. [Excluding all electronic rights; audio files, streaming, playback, catch up and streaming over the internet and/or downloads; and/or any telecommunication system; videos and DVDs].

F.   Dramatic and non-dramatic mechanical reproduction, video and DVD rights: [number] per cent. [Excluding all electronic rights; audio files, streaming, playback, catch up and streaming over the internet and/or downloads; and/or any telecommunication system].

G.   Computer Software, storage and disc rights: [number] per cent.

H.   First serialisation where publication is prior to the release and publication of the hardback: [number] per cent.

I.   Second and subsequent serialisation which takes place after the release and publication of the hardback: [number] per cent.

J.   One-shot digest for the publication of an abridgement of the [Work] in a periodical or newspaper: [number] per cent.

K.   Digest book condensation in volume form: [number] per cent.

L.   All exploitation in electronic form of rights and/or material including audio files; downloads; transmission and/or streaming of films, programmes and/or sound recordings and/or text and/or images and/or music; playback; catch up; whether from a platform, channel, podcast and/or website and/or app and/or some other means over the internet and/or any telecommunication system. Storage and/or retrieval systems and/or archives and/or domain names and/or other associated name and/or place and/or story and/or plot rights which may be registered at any time: [number] per cent.

M. Two and/or three dimensional forms of exploitation including sub-licensing character, image and/or other merchandising in all media; trade marks; play and theme parks; sports events, festivals, lotteries, betting, gambling, bingo, premium phone lines, competitions and other associated rights: [number] per cent.

N. Product Placement agreements and/or arrangements with third parties: [number] per cent.

O. Sponsorship, endorsement, cross-promotion and/or other marketing arrangements: [number] per cent.

P. Hardback reprint rights licensed to another publisher [after the first [two] years of the agreement]: [number] per cent.

Q. Paperback reprint rights licensed to another publisher [after the first two years of the agreement]: [number] per cent.

R. Book club editions which are agreed with the [Author] as a separate arrangement which are licensed to a third party: [number] per cent.

S. Strip cartoons and picture form in printed form: [number] per cent.

T. Photocopying, scanning, document supply and/or other reprographic rights: [number] per cent. This right to be administered by [specify organisations] and paid to the [Author] through [specify organisation/method] and the [Company] through [specify organisation/method].

U. All other rights and methods and/or means of exploitation whether they are in existence now and/or created and/or developed in the future shall be subject to additional agreement between the parties. Where there is any discrepancy and/or doubt as to whether any rights, format and/or other adaptation fall within any definition. Then the presumption shall be that further agreement is needed between the parties.

R.671
In the event that any edition of the [Work] is reprinted and the number of copies of the reprint is [500/number] or less. Then the royalty rate due to be paid to the [Author] shall be [number] per cent of the sums received by the [Publisher/Distributor]. This reduction in rate shall not apply to any new edition and/or sequel.

R.672

All other rights and/or forms of exploitation not specified in this agreement and/or which may not be in existence now and may developed in the future in respect of the [Work] may not be exploited by the [Publisher/Company] at any time. All such rights and/or forms of exploitation are retained by and owned by the [Author].

R.673

1.1 The [Company] shall be entitled to authorise free of charge the reproduction of the [Work] in braille and charitable recordings for the blind and others with severe disabilities. Provided that these copies are not generally made available to the public for sale. No royalties shall become due to the [Author].

1.2 A large print book shall be at the usual rates for paperback and/or hardback books of the [Work]. There shall be no reduction of the royalty rate due to the [Author].

1.3 The [Company] shall not be entitled to authorise a sound recording and/or talking book of the [Work] free of charge.

R.674

[Name] agrees that he/she shall not be entitled to be paid any royalties by the [Publisher/Distributor] where for any reason sums are not received by the [Publisher/Distributor] due to the default and/or failure of a third party, sub-licensee, agent and/or distributor for the reproduction, supply, sale, hire, rental, distribution, adaptation and/or other exploitation of the [Work].

R.675

The [Publisher/Distributor] agrees and accepts that it has only been granted the hardback and paperback rights in the [Work] in [country] from [date to [date]. That the [Publisher/Distributor] shall not be entitled to:

A. Exploit the [Work] in any electronic form over the internet and/or by means of any telecommunication system in any part of the world.

B. Apply for any domain name and/or trade mark in respect of the title, content and/or any similar version of any part of the [Work].

C. Grant any sub-licence to any third party to exploit any merchandising.

D. To allow any third party to contribute to the [Work].

E. To alter and/or edit the [Work].

F. To translate the [Work].

G.   To authorise any third party to produce a film, podcast, video and documentary and/or other programme for radio and/or television and/or any other media.

R.676

The [Publisher] and the [Author] agree that the [Work] shall be listed with the [Copyright Licensing Agency and the Authors Licensing Collection Society/other organisations] as an excluded work. Any licence for photocopying, scanning, reproduction in the form of electronic and/or digital files shall be the subject of a separate agreement between the [Author] and the [Publisher].

R.677

No royalty shall be payable on any copies of the [Work]:

1.1   Destroyed and/or damaged by fire, flood and/or some other valid force majeure ground and/or which are lost, stolen and/or otherwise not in a good condition suitable for sale and not offered for sale and/or which are returned by a distributor and/or member of the public for good reason.

1.2   Distributed for promotional and/or review purposes to the media and/or nominated individuals and/or for marketing at trade exhibitions.

1.3   Provided free of charge to the [Author].

1.4   Sold at a discount to the [Author] which is equal to and/or below cost.

1.5   Deposited at a library, university and/or institute as part of the legal scheme in the [United Kingdom] and [country/worldwide].

1.6   Which are remaindered at cost price and/or below.

R.678

The [Company] shall be entitled to retain [number/currency] in any accounting period of the royalties due to the [Author] as a reserve against future returns of stock and/or copies of the [Work].

R.679

The [Publisher/Distributor] shall have the right to make a reserve against returns of the [Work] of [number] per cent of the royalties due to the [Author] in respect of the hardback edition and [number] per cent in respect of the paperback edition of the royalties due to the [Author]. The [Publishers] shall be entitled to withhold such sums up to and including the [third/other] royalty statement. All monies withheld shall then be paid in full to the [Author] on the [fourth/other] royalty statement.

R.680

During the first year of publication of the [Work/Book] the [Publisher/Distributor] may withhold up to [number] per cent of the royalties on sales in [country] as a reserve against returns. At the next accounting period this reserve will be added to the [Author's] royalties less any deductions for returned copies. Thereafter the [Publisher/Distributor] shall be entirely responsible for the cost of any monies paid or incurred in respect of returns of the [Work/Book].

R.681

The [Company] agrees and accepts that at no time shall the [Company] be entitled to withhold any sums due to the [Author] as royalties as a reserve against returns and/or to offset any stock which is lost, damaged and/or destroyed.

R.682

The [Publisher/Distributor] may suspend payment of any advance and/or royalties due to the [Author] in the event that there is any alleged breach by the [Author] of clauses [–] of this agreement. The [Publisher/Distributor] must notify the [Author] of the fact that it is not paying the money and state the reasons. The [Author] may accept and/or reject the allegations by the [Publisher/Distributor]. If the reasons are not accepted then the [Publisher/Distributor] must begin legal proceedings and dispute the sums and/or make payment within [number] days.

R.683

1.1 The [Author] agrees that the defined Advance shall be offset against the royalties due to the [Author] under this agreement.

1.2 The [Publisher] agrees that no part of the defined Advance shall be due to be repaid by the [Author] once the [Publisher] has accepted the manuscript of the [Work].

R.684

After the publication of the [Work] in [hardback/paperback/other] and provided that the defined Advance has been recouped [and any sums withheld as provision for returns in any period]. That where the [Publisher] sub-licenses any other rights and/or adaptation and/or other form of exploitation at any time. That the [Author] shall be paid additional advances of [number/currency] against future royalties from each sub-licence. The additional advances shall be paid within [number] days of the conclusion of each sub-licence by the [Publisher].

R.685
Where the [Publisher/Distributor] negotiates and concludes any sub-licence with a third party where an advance is paid. Then the [Author] shall be entitled to be paid [number] per cent of the advance on each occasion. Such advance payments shall be recouped from future royalties from the sub-licences granted by the [Publisher/Distributor].

R.686
The [Company] shall pay the [Author] [eighty/fifty/number] per cent of the sums actually received by the [Company] from the authorisation of the use and/or sub-license and/or other exploitation of the following rights:

1.1 Translations into any language except [specify original language].

1.2 Scanning, copying and document delivery services in whole or part.

R.687

1.1 In the event that the [Work] is reproduced, supplied, distributed, sold, licensed and//or disposed of in [the United States of America/other country] in volume form to an independent third party. The [Publisher] shall pay the [Author] [number] per cent of all sums received from such third party after deductions of government taxes on the supply that may be applicable; the reproduction costs of any material and/or any delivery and/or custom charges.

1.2 In the event that the copies of the [Work] are reproduced, supplied, distributed, sold, licensed and//or disposed of to a third party in [the United States of America/other country] which is in fact a parent, subsidiary, holding and/or associated company of the [Publisher]. Then the [Publisher] shall pay the [Author] the following royalty rates in respect of all copies of the [Work] sold in the [United States of America/other country] which shall be calculated on [the wholesale/retail/actual selling price] as follows:

A. For each copy of any hardcover edition of the [Work] [ten/other number] per cent on the first [5,000/other number] copies;

B. For each copy of any hardcover edition of the [Work] [twelve point five /other number] per cent on the next [5,000/other number] copies;

C. For each copy of any hardcover edition of the [Work] [fifteen/ other number] per cent on all copies thereafter.

D. Where there are small reprints of any hardback edition of [two thousand/other number) copies or less at any time. The royalty rate to be paid to the [Author] shall revert to the lowest royalty rate in A. above for that reprint only.

    E.   For each copy of any paperback edition of the [Work] [six/other number] per cent on the first [twenty thousand/other number] copies;

    F.   For each copy of any paperback edition of the [Work] [eight/other number] per cent on the next [thirty thousand/other number] copies;

    G.   For each copy of any paperback edition of the [Work] [ten/other number] per cent on all copies thereafter.

    H.   Where there are small reprints of any paperback edition of [seven thousand/other number) copies or less at any time. The royalty rate to be paid to the [Author] shall revert to the lowest royalty rate in E. above for that reprint only.

R.688

1.1   In return for the royalty payments the [Author] grants the [Company] the sole and exclusive right to reproduce, supply, distribute, sell, license, adapt and/or exploit the following rights set out below in the [Work] throughout the world.

1.2   The grant of rights in 1.1 shall include the right to exploit any title of the work, name, character, theme, costume, text, images and/or slogans.

1.3   It shall include the right to sub-license the right to third parties provided that any such third party agreement does not exceed and/or breach the terms of this agreement.

1.4   The [Company] shall pay the [Author] the following royalty rates in respect of the sums received by the [Publisher] after deduction of all expenses and costs relating to the administration of the agreement; legal costs; reproduction costs and the clearance of and delivery of material:

    A.   Translations in printed format: [number] per cent.

    B.   Anthology, quotations and short extracts in printed format of text, images, maps, charts and graphics: [number] per cent.

    C.   Digest book condensation; the right to publish an abridgement in volume form: [number] per cent.

    D.   Digest periodical rights; the right to publish a condensation or digest of the [Work] including maps, plans or illustrations or any abridgement in a journal, periodical or newspaper whether before or after the first publication of the [Work]: [number] per cent.

E.   Single issue or one shot newspaper or periodical rights; the right to publish the complete [Work] in one or more issues of a periodical or newspaper: [number] per cent.

F.   A straight reading of the text and/or an adapted dramatized version, series, documentary and/or play whether on stage, in a film, sound recording and for exploitation on terrestrial, cable, satellite and digital radio and/or television and/or over the internet; any telecommunication system and/or other medium: [number] per cent.

G.   First publication serialisation; the right to publish one or more extracts from the [Work] in successive issues of a newspaper, periodical or magazine before publication of the [Work] in hardback edition: [number] per cent.

H.   Second and subsequent publication serialisation; after first publication of the [Work] in hardback edition: [number] per cent.

I.   Where the hardback is licensed and reprinted by a third party publisher at a later date: [number] per cent.

J.   Where a book club edition is licensed to and reproduced by a third party publisher at a later date: [number] per cent. Except where a book club edition is licensed to and reproduced by a third party publisher at a later date on a royalty inclusive basis then the royalty rate shall be: [number] per cent.

K.   The exploitation of the rights in [United States of America/other country]: [number] per cent.

L.   Where the paperback is licensed and reprinted by a third party publisher at a later date: [number] per cent.

M.   Where the large print and/or educational editions are sold by the [Company] and/or licensed and reprinted by a third party publisher at a later date: [number] per cent.

N.   The right to exploit the [Work] by mechanical reproduction including DVDs; electromagnetic methods; the right to reproduce and license by scanning, photocopying and/or laser; document supply delivery service; discs; storage devices for storage and/or retrieval: [number] per cent.

O.   Electronic formats and/or means of exploitation over the internet and/or any telecommunication and/or wifi system: [number] per cent.

P.   Registration and rights with any rights management organisation and/or other collecting society: [number] per cent.

1759

Q. Interactive computer games, holograms, bingo, lotteries, competitions, promotions and marketing; strip cartoons and/ or other graphics; product placement and/or sponsorship arrangements; theme and sports parks, merchandising of the text, images, theme, character name and//or slogans, logos; registered trade marks, website names and domain names: musical works and /or any adaptation: [number] per cent.

R. All other new technology, means and/or methods of exploitation in any medium and/or format and/or rights and/or material not covered by the above list whether in existence now and/or created in the future: [number] per cent.

R.689

The [Company] agrees and undertakes to pay all advances and royalties to the [Author] in [currency] and to be responsible for the cost of all bank and currency conversion costs which may need to be incurred at any time.

R.690

The [Company] agrees and undertakes that it shall pay the advance and royalties to any agent and/or other third party nominated by the [Author]. Provided that the [Author] agrees to sign a disclaimer in respect of the failure of any third party to remit such sums to the [Author] at any time.

R.691

The [Author] has agreed to a buyout fee for the [Work] and waives the right to any future royalties from the exploitation and/or licensing of any part of the [Work] by the [Company] in any medium and/or by any method.

Services

R.692

The [Assignor/Name] agrees and accepts that where copies of the [Work] [in any form/in specific format] are distributed without charge at any festival, event, launch, trade exhibition and/or to the media for promotional and marketing purposes only. That no royalty payment shall be due to made to the [Assignor/Name].

R.693

1.1 '[Names'] Royalties' shall be defined as: [number] per cent of the [Gross Receipts/Net Receipts] received and retained by the [Company] at any time from the exploitation of the product of the services of [Name] in the role of [specify role] at [specify channel]. It is agreed that this clause shall not include any revenue from advertising, product placement, endorsements and/or sponsorship and/or transmission on channel: [specify channel].

1.2 [Name] agrees that the [Company] shall be entitled to recoup the advance payment of [number/currency] to [Name] from any future revenue which constitutes the [Gross Receipts/Net Receipts] in 1.1 prior to the payment of any royalties. The [Company] shall not be entitled to recoup the monthly payment for the services of [Name].

1.3 [Name] shall continue to be entitled to royalties from the [Company] even after the contract for the services of [Name] has expired and/or been terminated. Provided that the [Company] continues to exploit the rights and/or material to which [Name] has contributed at any time.

R.694

1.1 The [Company] shall not be entitled to recoup any part of the non-returnable advance from the royalties due to [Name] under this agreement.

1.2 The [Company] shall not be entitled to withhold any royalties for any reason.

1.3 The [Company] shall not be entitled to seek to recoup any legal, reproduction and/or marketing costs from the royalties due to [Name].

R.695
In consideration of the assignment of the rights in respect of the [Musical Work/Lyrics/Contribution and Performance] the [Publisher] shall pay the [Assignor] the following royalties and payments:

1.1 Sheet Music: royalty rate of [number] per cent) of the [retail/wholesale/actual] selling price of each copy of the [pianoforte/orchestration/arrangement/performance] of the [Musical Work/Lyrics/Contribution and Performance] reproduced, supplied, licensed, distributed, disposed of and/or sold by the [Publisher] in the United Kingdom and the Republic of Ireland for which any sums are received by the [Publisher].

1.2 A pro rata amount of the [retail/wholesale/actual] selling price in respect of all copies of any songbook, printed album or folio which includes the [Musical Work/Lyrics/Contribution and Performance] reproduced, supplied, licensed, distributed, disposed of and/or sold by the [Publisher] in the United Kingdom and the Republic of Ireland for which any sums are received by the [Publisher].

1.3 Mechanical Reproduction in any format: royalty rate of [number] per cent of any sums received by the [Publisher] in the United Kingdom and the Republic of Ireland after the deduction of any fees, charges and/or costs incurred by the [Publisher] and/or any rights management organisation and/or rightsholder for the reproduction of the [Musical Work/Lyrics/Contribution and Performance] in the manufacture and/or exploitation of the sound recordings, records, tapes, piano works and all other mechanical reproductions in any format whether sound alone and/or in conjunction with visual images.

1.4 Film Synchronisation Fees: royalty rate of [number] per cent of all sums received by the [Publisher] in the United Kingdom and the Republic of Ireland after deduction of any fees, charges and/or costs made by the [Publisher] and/or any rights management organisation and/or rightsholder in respect of the right to record the [Musical Work/Lyrics/Contribution and Performance] on sound recordings and/or soundtracks for use in conjunction with a film, documentary, television series, radio programme and/or series and/or films for transmission and/or exploitation over the internet and/or any telecommunication system, advertisements, promotions, podcasts and/or for use in conjunction with a sequence of moving visual images. It shall not include stills, photographs and art exhibitions.

1.5 Foreign Royalties outside the United Kingdom and the Republic of Ireland: royalty rate of [number] per cent of the net [sums/receipts] which are paid to and retained by the [Publisher] from third parties including a parent company, subsidiary, affiliate, associate and/or some other form of collaboration and/or partnership. Sums received from any third party, rights management organisation and/or sub-licensee appointed by the [Publisher] to exploit the [Musical Work/Lyrics/Contribution and Performance] in any format and/or medium. It shall not include performing rights and/or payments and/or sums related to broadcast and/or transmission on radio, television and/or over the internet and/or any telecommunication system.

1.6 All other formats and medium: royalty rate of [number] per cent of all the net [sums/receipts] which are paid to and retained by the [Publisher] from any other source in respect of the [Musical Work/Lyrics/Contribution and Performance] and/or parts including but not limited to newspapers, periodicals, books and sub-license and/or exploitation in all other formats, method and/or medium.

If the [Assignor] of the [Musical Work/Lyrics/Contribution and Performance] consists of two or more persons. Then the payments to the [Assignor] shall be apportioned between them as follows [Name] [number per cent] [Name] [number] per cent.

R.696

1.1 The [Company] are members of an organisation which collects sums from third parties for the exercise of the performing rights known as: [specify name/reference]. Through that organisation the [Company] receive payments of royalties for the licensing of those performing rights in the [Work/Material] and from any organisation affiliated to it.

1.2 [Name] agrees and accepts that the [Company] has been assigned the rights in the [Work/Material] and is entitled to register the [Work/Material] with the organisation in 1.1.

1.3 [Name] agrees that all payments may be made from the organisation direct to the [Company]. That the [Company] shall then pay [Name] [number] per cent in respect of all the sums which it receives from the organisation in 1.1 relating to the [Work/Material].

1.4 The [Company] agrees that in the event that [Name] is a member of the organisation in 1.1 [Name] shall have the right to request that [number] per cent of the sums are paid direct to [Name] and not via the [Company].

R.697

1.1 In consideration of the services of [Name] the [Company] has agree to pay a fixed fee of [number/currency] and an additional payment of [number/currency] per unit of the [Work] which is sold to a third party above the cost price from [date to [date].

1.2 No additional payment shall be due on any units sold by the [Company] after [date].

1.3 No payment shall be due on units which are returned, damaged, lost, recalled and/or otherwise unsuitable for sale and/or are given away for free and/or at cost price or below.

R.698

[Name] agrees and accepts that no royalty payments shall be due from the [Company] in the event that the [Company] ceases to sell the [Product/Work] and/or assigns the rights and/or transfers ownership of the master material with the consent of [Name] to a third party.

R.699

The [Company] has assisted in the development of the {Project] in collaboration with the [Enterprise]. The parties have agreed that in consideration of the services of the [Company] and the assignment of their rights in the [Project] to the [Enterprise]. That the [Company] shall be entitled to [number] per cent of all sums received from the exploitation of the {Project] by the [Enterprise] after the [Enterprise] has recouped all the expenditure and/or liabilities which it has incurred in respect of the {Project].

R.700

[Name] accepts and agrees that it has assigned all the product of his/her services to the [Company]. That [Name] has also assigned any rights in any material, methods and/or forms of exploitation that may be created and/or developed in the future. That [Name] agrees that he/she has no entitlement to any royalties from any form of exploitation in any media. [Name] agrees and undertakes to waive all rights and/or claim to any royalties at any time.

R.701

All copyright and/or intellectual property rights and/or rights of registration and/or forms of exploitation in any medium which have not been granted in this agreement are reserved by [Name]. That shall also include any rights and/or methods of exploitation and/or adaptation which may be created and/or developed at any time in the future. The [Company] may not at any time without the prior written approval of [Name] and the conclusion of a further agreement exploit any such rights owned by [Name].

R.702

Where the [Company/Distributor] fails to declare royalties and/or payments due at any time in excess of [number/currency] and they are accounted for and paid in any subsequent statement. Then a late fee of [number/currency] shall be paid as compensation for the delay.

R.703

The contribution of the [Company] to the development of the [Software/ Platform/App] does not create any entitlement to receive additional payments and/or royalties outside the agreed Budget in Appendix A.

R.704

1.1 Where [Images/Sound Recordings/Quotes] are offered and sold to the public. The [Artist] shall be entitled to receive a fixed royalty payment of [number/currency] for each sale by the [Company] and/or any authorised third party.

1.2 The royalty payment in 1.1 shall only be due when the sums for the sale have been received and retained by the [Company] in [country].

1.3 The [Company] shall issue statements of the sales by country, third party and format every three months from [date].

1.4   This agreement shall continue until terminated with [one] month's notice by either party. Any royalties which have accrued prior and/or after termination shall be paid to the [Artist].

Sponsorship

R.705

The [Sponsor] agrees that it shall not be entitled to any royalties and/or other sum from the [Company] from any payments received by the [Company] for the sub-licensing, assignment and/or transfer of any rights and/or any other form of exploitation of the [Event/Programme] at any time.

R.706

1.1   The [Company] agrees that the [Sponsor] shall be entitled to receive a royalty payment of [number] per cent of the [Net Receipts/sums received after deductions by the [Company] before [date] from the sub-licensing of the merchandising rights to a third party for the [Event].

1.2   The [Sponsor] agrees that the [Company] shall be entitled to first be reimbursed with all the budgeted and actual costs and expenses and liability for the [Event]. Together with all costs of administration, legal costs, location access, registration of domain and other legal titles and/or trade marks; and the cost of any associated advertising, marketing and promotional material.

R.707

1.1   The [Company] agrees that the [Collaborator] shall be entitled to share in the revenues which may be generated from associated activities, sponsorship, competitions, phone lines, merchandising, endorsements, films, podcasts, sound recordings, programmes and sub-licensing of rights and/or material to a third party in respect of the [Event].

1.2   The [Company] agrees to pay the [Collaborator] [number] per cent of the [Gross Receipts] after deduction of the authorised [Distribution Expenses] received by the [Company] from [date to [date].

R.708

The [Sponsor] agrees that it shall not be entitled to any payment, royalty and/or other sum from the [Company's] website, app, podcasts, events, merchandising and/or sub-licensing of rights for film, television and/or radio, books, funding from grants and/or other resources and/or any other financial contribution and/or arrangement with a third party by the [Company]. There is no expectation that the [Sponsor] will recoup any payment which it has decided to make to the [Company].

R.709

The [Sponsor] agrees to pay [Name] an additional fee of [number/currency] in arrears at the end of each calendar month for the exploitation of the [Image/Name/Logo] of [Name] on free corporate merchandising material for the [Sponsor] to be given away at events, conference and exhibitions for the Term of this Agreement.

R.710

1.1 [Name] has designed and created the [Graphics/Artwork/Logo] for the [Sponsor] and [Company] for the name and brand of the [Event/Project] which is described in Appendix A.

1.2 [Name] has been paid a fee of [number/currency] for the authorised and agreed purpose described as follows: [state purpose]. Any other use shall require the prior consent of [Name] in writing and a new agreement between the parties. [Name] may request a royalty payment in addition to an advance in any other new agreement.

1.3 [Name] owns the copyright and intellectual property rights and the computer software rights and the right to register any trade mark and/or domain name and all other rights in the [Graphics/Artwork/Logo] and they have not been assigned to the [Sponsor] and/or the [Company]. The [Company] and the [Sponsor] agree not to attempt to register any such rights and/or anything which is an imitation and/or similar].

University, Charity and Educational

R.711

1.1 The [Author] shall be entitled to receive a royalty rate of [number] per cent from the [Gross Receipts/Net Receipts/sums after deductions] retained by the [Institute] from the exploitation of the [Work] [at any time/from date to date].

1.2 The payments shall be made to the [Author] by [date] in each year in [currency] and shall be supported by a detailed statement of accounts which sets out the calculation for the payment.

1,3 No payment shall be made where no fee has been received and/or no charge has been made.

R.712

No royalty payments shall be made to the [Contributor] in respect of any copies of the [Work] in any form and/or medium which are:

1.1 Supplied and/or distributed to the students and/or other third parties at events, fairs, exhibitions and/or for review purposes and/or for marketing purposes. Provided that no payment of any nature is received by the [Institute].

1.2 Destroyed, damaged whether by floods and/or fire and/or lost, stolen and/or are defective and/or some other valid grounds of force majeure.

1.3 Sold and/or disposed of at a nominal cost which is below the actual production cost.

1.4 Provided free of charge to the [Contributor].

1.5 Deposited at a library, university and/or institute as part of any legal scheme which operates [in country/worldwide].

R.713
The [Contributor] agrees that the [Institute] may offset the [Advance Payment/Budgeted Fee] against the future royalties due the [Contributor] under this agreement. It shall not be applicable to any other agreement which the [Contributor] may have with the [Institute/Enterprise].

R.714
The [Institute/Charity] agrees to pay the [Author/Creator] as follows:

1.1 A non-returnable advance which cannot be recouped of [number/currency].

1.2 A fixed payment sum per unit of the [Work/Image] which is adapted and reproduced and/or sold by the [Institute/Charity] of [number/currency] for each copy sold to the public in [country].

1.3 The [Institute/Charity] agrees and accepts that it has no authority to sell the [Work] outside [country].

R.715

1.1 The [Institute/Charity] agrees and undertakes to pay the [Author/Designer] a royalty in respect of all sales and disposals of copies of the [Slogan/Text/Logo/Image] in [specify format/other medium] to the public at the rate of [number] per cent of the [Retail Price/Wholesale Price/sums received].

1.2 The [Institute/Charity] agrees that it shall bear the cost of production, commission, freight, customs duties and exploitation in 1.1 and that there shall be no deductions made from the [Retail Price/Wholesale Price/sums received] prior to the calculation of the payments due to the [Author/Designer].

R.716

1.1 The [Institute/Enterprise] has bought out all rights owned by [Name] in all media throughout the world and universe in the [Project].

1.2 [Name] agrees that no further payments and /or royalties are due to [Name] for any reason. Provided that the buy-out fee has been paid in full to [Name].

1.3 [Name] agrees that the [Institute/Enterprise] shall be entitled to edit, delete, change, add to, alter and adapt the [Project] and/or parts. That there is no requirement to consult with [Name].

1.4 [Name] has agreed to the fact that his/her name may not be used in conjunction with the [Project]. [Name] waives any right to a copyright notice and waives all moral rights.

R.717

Where there are no royalties stated in the agreement for the exercise of specific rights and/or methods of exploitation and/or material due to the fact that the technology, rights, method and/or material has not been discovered and/or developed and used commercially at the time of this agreement. Then all such matters are reserved to and retained by the [Author] and not granted and/or assigned to the [Institute/Enterprise] under this agreement.

R.718

Where any person whether a member of staff, consultant and/or student makes any discovery, invention and/or designs any new product and/or item which is new and innovative whilst at the premises of the [Enterprise] and/or engaged in any work and/or research project which has relied on access to knowledge, facilities, data and/or equipment provided by the [Enterprise]. Then the [Enterprise] shall be entitled to share in the ownership and revenue with that person on terms to be agreed between the parties.

R.719

The [Company] has licensed the [Software] to the [Institute] on the basis of an annual licence where the fees for access and use are paid monthly in advance. The [Company] agrees that no additional payments are required provided that the disclosures of the purpose of the use of the [Software] and the number of persons requiring access at any time is correct and can be verified upon request.

S

SALES TAX

General Business and Commercial

S.001

'Sales Tax' shall mean any sales tax, value added tax or other tax or taxes levied by the national government in [country] on sales and/or the supply of products, items and/or services which form a precise and calculable element in the total price and which are recovered directly and/or indirectly as part of the selling and/or supply price.

S.002

'The Sales Tax' shall mean any sales or other taxes levied by the government and/or the European Union and/or any of its member states and/or any other authority anywhere in the world on the sale, supply, rental, purchase and/or subscription of the [Film/Product/Service] which form a distinct element on the price and which is recovered as part of the price directly or indirectly by the [Licensee].

S.003

'The Sales Tax' shall be any taxes levied by the European Union, the United Kingdom and/or foreign national governments and/or authorities on the sale, supply and/or distribution of the [Records/Products/Service] which form a distinct element and which are recovered as part of the retail selling price directly and/or indirectly by the [Distributor].

S.004

'The Sales Tax' shall mean any sales and/or other taxes levied by any legitimate national government in the world including the United Kingdom on the sale, rental, supply and/or purchase of [Videos/Films/Apps/Services] which form a distinct element in the sale price in that country and which are recovered as part of the sale price by the [Licensee] and transferred to the relevant authority.

S.005

'Sales Taxes' shall mean any sales and/or other taxes levied on the sale and/or supply of goods which form a recognisable distinct element of the price and which are recovered directly and/or indirectly as part of the selling and/or supply price and all other taxes, levies, duties and/or government charges on [Ingredients/Products/Units/Services] from manufacture, production, supply, distribution, sale, lending, rental and subscription during the duration of this agreement.

S.006
All payments and charges are exclusive of taxes, levies, charges and duties that may arise and/or be due on the production, sale, supply, transfer, license, distribution and/or otherwise of the [Character] in any format under this agreement. Provided that the sums are charged and then after receipt are paid to any government agency by any party and not retained. Such sums do not have to be specified in the accounts.

S.007
All sums payable under this agreement are exclusive of any sales tax, value added tax and any other sum charged on the sale and supply of [Services/Products/Units]. Each party shall be responsible for its own personal tax and national insurance, corporation tax and public liability insurance.

S.008
All sums are exclusive of tax whether value added tax, sales tax or other tax levied on the products and/or services. However if such sum is deducted and/or added for any reason then it must be disclosed in the accounts and if the sums have been subsequently transferred and paid it must be stated how much, when and to whom any sums were paid. Each party shall bear the cost of its own taxes of any nature unless required by law to pass the charge or cost to the other party.

S.009
All charges and payments are not inclusive of tax and must be paid as far as legally possible with any value added tax, sales tax and any other tax, levy or assessment that may be due for any reason. Each party shall be responsible for any national insurance, taxes and other payments and charges that may be due which arise as a result of the payment being made to them.

S.010
All sums to be paid by the [Sub-Licensee] to the [Licensor] shall be exclusive of any sales taxes due to any government for the sale and/or supply of any material and/or services under this agreement.

S.011
Where any taxes are imposed and/or charged to any person and/or company on the supply of goods and/or services which any party wishes to claim from

the other. Then proof of registration for that tax shall be necessary by the supply of a legitimate reference and also an appropriate invoice specifying the tax and the goods and/or service to which it applies.

SCRIPTS

General Business and Commercial

S.012
'The Scripts' shall mean the full text whether typed and/or handwritten and/or amended including all preparatory notes, drafts, revisions and all other written material arrangements, dramatisations, adaptations and/or any other variations including, but not limited to the title, characters, plots, themes, dialogues, episode titles and all sound recordings, recordings and any other material of any nature in respect of the product of the [Writer's] services under this agreement.

S.013
'The Scripts' shall be the typed draft and final scripts based on the Treatment to be prepared by the [Writer/Licensor].

S.014
The [Assignor/Licensor] shall deliver the scripts to the [Assignee/Licensee] for approval on or before the following dates: Draft script [date/stages] Final script [date].

S.015
'The Script' shall mean the typed copy of the final script of the [Advertising Copy].

S.016
'The Script' shall be all draft and final scripts to be prepared by the [Screenplay Writer] based on the [Author's Work].

S.017
The [Production Company] agrees that the [Author] shall be entitled to approve the Scripts and the [Production Company] shall deliver the Scripts to the [Author] on or before the following dates: [Draft/Final Script].

S.018
The script material discussed and agreed with [Name] shall be subject to incidental amendments which may arise during the development and production of the [Work/Service/Video].

S.019

The [Production Company] shall deliver the scripts and storyboard of the [Advertisement] to the [Commissioning Company] for approval as follows:

1.1 Draft scripts on and/or by [date].

1.2 Final scripts on and/or by [date].

1.3 The storyboard on and/or by [date].

S.020

The [Company] agrees that except for minor alterations the final script shall be used for the [Programme/Series/Video]. It is agreed by the [Company] that if for any reason there are to be significant changes in the roles, characters, plots and/or any other material matter that the [Author] will be consulted and asked for his/her approval to any alterations to the final script.

S.021

[Name] shall return all copies of the [Script] to the [Company] at the end of the production period and/or by [date] whichever is the later and shall not be entitled to keep a copy for personal reference.

S.022

The [Author] shall either accept and/or provide written reasons for the rejection of the [Script] within [one] calendar month of delivery. Provided that the [Author] agrees not to unreasonably withhold and/or delay his/her consent.

S.023

1.1 The [Company] shall be provided with a reasonable opportunity to comment on the draft script, the key personnel, the production schedule together with any significant changes that occur at a later date.

1.2 The [Company] shall be entitled to approve the final script prior to production and supply of the [Film/Video/Service] and shall be consulted on all changes except minor editing.

S.024

The [Production Company] shall not permit and/or allow any editorial control by [Name] in respect of the [Film/Video/Service], but agrees that the [Author] shall be consulted about the draft and final script.

S.025

All drafts, documents, scripts, brochures and/or other material developed and//or created for the [Project] by the [Company] shall belong to and be the property of the [Company]. No rights are granted to any person to reproduce, license and/or exploit the material at any time.

S.026

'The Legacy Material' shall be all the diaries, draft notes, scripts, documents, drawings, sound recordings, films, videos, images, stills, artwork, illustrations, promotional and other material prepared, written, recorded, drawn and/or commissioned by [Name] during his/her life which is now owned and controlled by the [specify] Estate. A full list of the material is listed in Appendix B which is attached and forms part of this agreement.

S.027

The scripts for the {Film/Video/Podcast/Sound Recording]must not be supplied, distributed, reproduced and/or accessed for and/or by any third party [including any family members] and must be returned to the [Company] upon request and no ownership of any nature is transferred to the [Contributor].

SECURITY

General Business and Commercial

S.028

1.1 The [Company] agrees to ensure that the original and all reproductions of the [Material/Work] shall be kept in a secure and safe location at [address] in a [safety deposit box/vault/warehouse] which shall be fireproof and where there are [twenty-four] security guards at the [Company's] cost and expense.

1.2 The [Company] agrees and undertakes that no copies shall be released, distributed and/or supplied to the press, media and/or any third party except for the purposes of printing and storing the [Material/ Work] until the launch date.

S.029

The [Company] agrees to arrange at its own cost security software for the [Website/App/Blog] which shall prevent and/or scan for viruses, hackers, trojans and/or any other potential attacks which may cause loss, damage and/or interference with the data, emails and/or content of the [Website/ App/Blog].

S.030

The security for the payment of any sums shall be at your own risk and cost through [specify company]. No liability can be accepted by the [Distributor] for any charges, costs, fraud, losses and/or any other consequences that may arise as a result of using that payment method.

S.031

The [Company] does not accept any responsibility for any failure of the security, lighting, electricity, water, gas and/or any losses and/or damage to any personal valuables, cars and/or other portable items at the [Event] and/or any liability for personal injury which is not directly caused by negligence of the [Company]. It is accepted by all parties to this agreement that it is not possible to provide full comprehensive security at the [Event].

S.032

The [Sponsor] agrees to arrange at its cost personal security for [name] for the Term of this Agreement which shall be subject to the approval of [name].

S.033

Any safety measures and/or security and/or restrictions on access which need to be arranged and/or provided by the [Company] at the [Event/ Exhibition] shall be at the [Company's] sole cost and shall not be charged to [name].

S.034

The [Company] can only ensure that the [App/Blog/Website] is secure to the extent that it will operate the [specify/programme] system to scan the material submitted by the public.

S.035

Prior to the [Event/Exhibition] a full security, fire, health and safety assessment will be carried out and a report complied with recommendations at least [one] month prior to the start date. The cost of the assessment, report and compliance with the recommendations shall be paid for by [specify name]. It is agreed between the parties that all the recommendations made shall be carried out in order to provide maximum security, safety and fire control both of the premises and facilities but also any gadgets, software and machinery and/or equipment supplied. The cost of all the work shall be paid for by [specify] and may be deducted from the receipts from the ticket and merchandising sales prior to any distribution of any sums.

SELL-OFF PERIOD

General Business and Commercial

S.036
The [Assignee] shall be entitled to sell off, on a non-exclusive basis, licensed material and stocks previously manufactured under this agreement for the purpose of commercial sale for a period of [twelve] months from the date of expiry and/or termination. This clause shall only apply as long as the [Assignee] is not in breach and adheres to all the terms of this agreement.

S.037
After expiry or termination or completion of the sell-off period then the [Assignor] shall be entitled to instruct the [Assignee] to return or destroy all the master material, licensed material and any copies and any associated material of any nature in the possession or under the control of the [Assignee] pursuant to this agreement. The [Assignee] shall be required to report on all material in all formats in its possession and/or under its control and to act on the instructions of the [Assignor]. Where material is to be returned to the [Assignor] then the [Assignor] shall make the arrangements to collect the material and shall pay any costs and expenses of packaging, delivery, insurance and customs duties.

S.038

1.1 Provided that the [Licensee] has not manufactured or arranged for the manufacture of the [Licensed Articles] in numbers exceeding those that the [Licensee] can reasonably be expected to sell prior to expiry or termination and there are no unresolved allegations of breach or alleged breach of this agreement. The [Licensee] shall be entitled to sell-off and distribute on a non-exclusive basis for a period of [three] months the [Licensed Articles] which are already held in stock.

1.2 The [Licensee] shall not be entitled to manufacture and/or to produce any more [Licensed Articles] after the expiry or termination of the agreement.

1.3 The [Licensee] must ensure that the Royalties are accounted for to the [Licensor] for the period in 1.1.

1.4 The [Licensee] must ensure that the price charged by the [Licensee] for each [Licensed Article] is not less than the price charged prior to the sell-off period.

1.5 After the [three] month period the [Licensee] shall cease to sell the [Licensed Articles] and shall provide the [Licensor] with an inventory of stock at that end date which at the request of the [Licensor] shall be verified by an independent [chartered accountant/consultant] at the [Licensee's/Licensors'] cost.

1.6 The [Licensee] shall either destroy the remaining stock at the instruction of the [Licensor] or agree a reduced price for the purchase by the [Licensor].

S.039

1.1 At the expiry of the sell-off period the [Licensee] will at the request of the [Licensor] and its own expense destroy all remaining stocks of the [Licensed Articles] and all moulds, patterns, screens and/or other material and apparatus used to produce the [Licensed Articles].

1.2 The [Licensee] shall within [14] days of such destruction supply to the [Licensor] an affidavit of destruction detailing items which have been destroyed and confirming that no material of any kind relating to the [Licensed Articles] is in the possession or control of the [Licensee].

S.040

It is specifically agreed between the parties that there shall be no sell-off period and/or right to dispose of stock and/or the right to retain any stock and/or any other additional licence period and/or rights after the suspension, expiry and/or termination of this agreement unless agreed otherwise in writing between the parties.

S.041

Upon expiry of the Term of this Agreement the [Licensee] shall immediately cease any further manufacture or production of the [Videos/Discs/Products]. The [Licensee] shall have the non-exclusive right to sell off existing stocks which have already been manufactured for a period of [six] weeks from the last day of the Term of this Agreement. The [Licensee] shall not be entitled to reproduce and/or authorise any new stock from the last day of the Term of this Agreement. At the completion of such a sell-off period the [Licensee] shall destroy or erase all remaining stocks in the possession or under the control of the [Licensee]. If so requested by the [Licensor] the [Licensee] shall supply a statement of that fact from the [Managing Director] at the [Licensee].

S.042

Upon the expiry of this Agreement the [Licensee] shall be permitted on a non-exclusive basis to sell the [Licensed Articles] already manufactured under this agreement at a reduced price but in any event not less than [cost] until [date]. The royalty rate payment due shall not be reduced. Thereafter the [Licensee] shall return all master material, licensed articles, artwork stock, publicity and any other material of any nature in the possession or under the control of the [Licensee], and any agents, sub-licensees, or other third parties who have been authorised by the [Licensee] to hold any such material. All collection, freight and other costs shall be at the [Licensee's] sole cost.

S.043
The [Licensee] and any sub-licensee shall have the non-exclusive right after the expiry, but not the termination of this agreement to dispose and sell-off old stock whether at a reduced price, discounted or otherwise for a period of [three/six/twelve] months from the date of expiry. The [Licensee] shall pay the [Licensor] a [fixed price/royalty] on all such old stock of not less than [number/currency]/[number] [per cent].

S.044
There shall be no right under this agreement to any sell-off period and/or to dispose of any old stock and/or material after the expiry date and/or in respect of any earlier termination. The ownership of the stock and all other material shall be transferred to the [Licensor] and returned to the [Licensor] and/or destroyed as directed by the [Licensor]. No payment of any kind shall be due to the [Licensee] for the stock and/or material and/or the transfer of rights nor shall any sums be set-off by the [Licensee] against under sums due under this agreement to the [Licensor].

S.045
Where the [Supplier] terminates the agreement with the [Company] it is agreed that the [Company] shall still be entitled to list the [Products] on their stock database and on their [Website/App/Blog] for a period of up to [six] months and to sell and dispose of the [Products] to the public for that period. Provided that the [Company] accepts that this sell-off period is on a non-exclusive basis and that the [Company] must not make any claim to be an exclusive distributor and/or take any orders from the public which does not relate to existing stock within its possession.

S.046
The [Licensee] and/or any sub-licensee shall not have the right to dispose of, sell and/or otherwise supply, distribute and/or exploit the [Work/Product/Service] after [date] and/or the termination of this agreement whichever is the earlier. The [Licensee] and/or any sub-licensee shall be obliged to provide a comprehensive list of all the material and copies which are in their possession and/or control relating to the [Work/Product/Service] which have been created, developed, stored, marketed and/or sold. The [Licensor] shall then have the option to either notify the [Licensee] and/

or any sub-licensee to destroy the stock and/or dispose of it to a third party on specific terms and/or deliver the stock to the [Licensor] at the [Licensor's] cost.

S.047
After [date] the [Licensee] shall have no right to sell, supply, reproduce and/or exploit any copies of the [Image/Logo/Name] on any material and/or to reproduce, authorise, supply, sell, distribute and/or offer for sale and/or promote and/or advertise any [Products/Units] in any manner and/or format in any part of the world. All stock held by the [Licensee] as at [date] must be delivered on that date to the [Licensor] at the [Licensee's] cost. The [Licensor] may then either destroy the stock and/or sell it to a third party and retain all the sums paid.

S.048
The [Licensee] shall not be entitled to any extension of the licence period for any reason under this agreement. There is no sell-off period permitted after the licence has been terminated and/or expired. It is a condition of this agreement that the [Licensee] return all outstanding stock to the [Licensor] upon request at the [Licensees'] cost and expense. That the [Licensor] shall be entitled to donate the stock to a registered charity and/ or food bank and/or to destroy the stock. The [Licensor] agrees that it shall not sell and/or dispose of the stock to a third party on a commercial basis.

SET-OFF

General Business and Commercial

S.049
The [Licensor] acknowledges that the Licence Fee shall be set-off against the [Licensor's] Royalties. That until the Licence Fee shall have been recouped in full no royalty payments shall be due to the [Licensor].

S.050
The [Designer] agrees to be liable for the total cost of all packaging, containers, labels, insurance, postage, freight, advertising, promotions and sales of the [Licensed Articles]. The [Designer] confirms that such costs and expenses shall not be offset and/or deducted from any sums received and/ or the Net Receipts prior to the calculation of the payments due to [Name/ Company].

S.051
The [Company] acknowledges that the non-returnable Advance is to be set-off against the [Licensor's] Royalties but that it is not returnable and is not contingent on sales figures of the [Licensed Articles].

S.052
Without waiver and/or limitation of any rights and/or remedies it is agreed that the [Company A] shall be entitled to deduct from any amounts due and/or owing by the [Company A] to the [Contractor B] in connection with this agreement all amounts due and/or owing at any time by the [Contractor B] to the [Company A].

S.053
The [Licensor] and/or the [Licensee] shall not have any right to recoup any sums and/or set-off any sums of any nature under this agreement and/or any other contract between the parties.

S.054
The [Licensee] shall be entitled to set-off any and all monies owed by the [Licensee] to the [Licensor] against any and all monies owed by the [Licensor] to the [Licensee] whether related to this agreement and/or a subsequent agreement and/or any other matter concluded between the parties.

S.055
The [Company] may at the sole discretion of the [Company] set-off and/or retain any sums paid by the [Customer] in order to recoup any outstanding payment owed by the [Customer] to the [Company] under any agreement of any nature at any time. Provided that the [Company] notifies the [Customer] of that fact by letter, text and/or email in and/or by the next accounting period. Where the [Customer] disputes the matter that the [Company] agrees to follow the following procedure [specify policy].

S.056
Any overpayment which is subsequently identified by the [Publisher] within [one] year of payment to the [Author] in respect of the [Work/Service/Blog] may be deducted from any sums subsequently due to the [Author] from the [Publisher] at a later date. No claim for immediate repayment of the sum shall be issued to the [Author] by the [Publisher].

S.057
Each party agrees that they shall be bound to pay all sums in full to the other party. That no costs and/or expenses and/or other sums shall be deducted and/or set-off and/or claimed which are not specifically authorised under the terms of this agreement.

S.058

The [Licensee] shall be entitled to set-off the sum of [number/currency] per annum against any income prior to the distribution of the receipts which shall be considered remuneration as a fixed cost for expenses and costs. No other sums of any nature may be deducted prior to payment to the [Licensor].

S.059

The [Company] shall have the right to recoup, recover, set off and/or deduct any sums which are owed by the [Licensee] against any sums the [Company] may owe the [Licensee] against any contract, agreement, licence and/or other business dealing of any nature.

S.060

No sums shall be set off, deducted and or recovered by the [Company] under this agreement which are not fully disclosed in the accounting statements and records provided to the [Assignor].

S.061

Where at any time the [Company] assigns and/or transfers this agreement to a third party then the right of set-off in clause [–] shall cease. The [Company] agrees that no sums owing due by [Name] to the [Company] shall be transferred to the assignee and/or other purchaser of the agreement.

S.062

The right to set-off any sums in clause [–] shall start on [date] and end on [date] and shall only apply to those agreements where the [Company] has published and/or distributed and sold the [Work] to the public and made it widely commercially available.

S.063

The [Distributor] agrees that there shall be no right to set-off any sums due and/or owed under this agreement against any other contract, licence and/or or dispute which the [Distributor] may have with the [Author/Designer/Artist] and/or his and/or her agent at any time.

SETTLEMENT

General Business and Commercial

S.064

In consideration of the payment of [number/currency] by the [Distributor] to the [Company] of the settlement sum. The [Company] agrees that from [specify date] that it shall accept as valid and not make any further claim and/or allegations regarding the agreement between [Name] and the [Distributor] dated [specify] a copy of which is attached to and forms part of this agreement in appendix A.

S.065
[Name] confirms that he/she is fully aware of the content and consequences of this document and agrees to the transfer and assignment to the [Company] all the rights, obligations, liabilities, and benefits as exist between the [Name] and the [Distributor] under an agreement dated [specify] entitled [–] a copy of which is attached.

S.066
The [Company] agrees that it shall be liable to pay the following costs and expenses set out in Schedule A from [date] to [date].

S.067
[Name] agrees to accept the sum of [number/currency] [words] in full and final settlement of any and all threats, claims, actions, and/or allegations against the [Company] and in particular to [specify subject].

S.068
This agreement shall not affect the rights of [Name] in respect of his/her pension, medical and/or dental cover and/or any other claim that may arise in respect of personal injury, death, illness and/or any other default and/or liability by the [Company] at a later date.

S.069
'The Settlement Fee' shall be the sum of [number/currency] [words] payable by the [Company to [Name] in full by [date] by [method] directly to [Name] and not any consultant, agent and/or legal advisor.

S.070
The [Legal Consultant] agrees to arrange for the payment of the [Settlement Fee] by the [Distributor] to the [Company] within [twenty-eight] days of the signature of this agreement by the [Company] and the return of both signed documents.

S.071
Both [Name] and the [Company] agree to keep the terms of this agreement private and confidential. Disclosure shall not be a breach of this agreement where disclosure is made to a court of law, under a court order, to a government department and/or to any accountancy, legal and other professional legal and/or financial advisors and/or disclosure is made after [date].

S.072

[Name] agrees to return the following items [car/mobile/keys/security pass/ uniform] and all other the property, reports, products, documents and other material in any format and/or medium to the [Company] by [date] at [Names'] cost except for [specify] which may be kept for personal reference only.

S.073

The [Company] agrees and undertakes to provide the following reference in response to any future request for a reference by a third party. A copy of the wording of the reference is set out in Schedule A and is attached to and forms part of this agreement.

S.074

The parties agree that the following agreements between the parties [date/ title/summary] are summarily terminated. The parties agree that the following clauses shall survive the termination and be binding on the parties until the end date set out below in each case [specify clause/agreement/end date].

S.075

This settlement shall not prevent [Name] from making a claim against the [Company] at a later date for defamation and/or any other legal action where an officer and/or director of the [Company] has made reference to [Name] and impugned and/or damaged his/her reputation and/or made allegations and/or statements which are untrue and/or an incorrect and/or disclosed the terms of this settlement and made inaccurate statements.

S.076

The [Licensee] agrees that it shall not settle any claim with a third party in respect of the [Service/Work/Product] unless it has consulted with the [Licensor] and received their approval as to the terms of the proposed settlement. The [Licensor] agrees that it shall not unreasonably withhold approval where the settlement is based on no admission of liability.

S.077

None of the parties to this agreement shall settle, defend and/or resolve any allegation, claim and/or legal action relating to any part of this agreement unless they have:

1.1   notified all the other parties of the nature of the complaint and

1.2   allowed the other parties a period of [number] days to respond to 1.1 directly to the company dealing with the complaint and

2.3   not settled any matter without first consulting with all the other parties.

SEVERANCE

General Business and Commercial

S.078

If any provision of this agreement shall be prohibited by and/or judged by a court to be unlawful, void and/or unenforceable then such provision shall be severed from the main agreement. The remaining provisions of this agreement shall not as far as possible be changed and/or modified and all other terms and conditions not severed shall continue in full force and effect.

S.079

The parties agree that in the event of one or more of the terms of this agreement are subsequently declared invalid and/or unenforceable by a court and/or other binding authority then such a judgement and/or decision shall not in any way affect the validity and/or enforceability of any other terms.

S.080

In the event that any of these terms and/or part of any term shall be declared invalid, unlawful and/or unenforceable then such terms and/or parts conditions shall be severed and deleted from the agreement. This shall not affect the remaining terms which shall continue to be valid and enforceable.

S.081

If any portion of this contract is held to be invalid and/or unenforceable for any reason by a court and/or government authority of competent jurisdiction. Then such terms will be deemed to be removed from the contract and the remainder of the contract shall continue in full force and effect.

S.082

Any unenforceable and/or invalid clauses contained in this agreement shall be deleted. The remaining clauses shall remain in full force and effect except where the unenforceable and/or invalid clauses are central to the agreement and their deletion makes the agreement so incomplete that it cannot be fulfilled and/or is unworkable. Then the Agreement as a whole shall be brought to an end on such terms as may be agreed between the parties.

S.083

The parties agree that in the event of one and/or more clauses of this contract are subsequently declared illegal, invalid and/or unenforceable by a court of law in any country authorised under the contract. Then those clauses shall be deleted from the contract and the contract shall continue in full force and effect as if those deleted clauses had never been part of the contract. Where the clauses to be deleted are an integral part of the agreement and the deleted clauses relate to the fundamental terms then the parties must reach a settlement to bring the contract to an end.

S.084

Each clause and sub-clause of this agreement shall be separate and severable from each other. In the event that any of the clauses and/or sub-clauses are deemed invalid and/or unenforceable this shall not affect the validity and/or enforceability of the other clauses and/or sub-clauses. In the event that any right, obligation, exclusion, restriction and/or other matter is held to be invalid, unenforceable and/or ineffective but would be if some part of it were deleted or modified then it shall be deleted or modified to the extent that may be necessary to make it valid, enforceable or effective.

S.085

In the event that any clause and/or any part of this agreement is declared by any judgment in any court to be unenforceable, invalid and/or wrong in law then no part of this agreement may be severed and the whole agreement shall come to an end on the date of that judgment. All sums due and/or owed prior to that date shall be paid and the parties shall enter into negotiations to resolve all outstanding issues, payments and transfer of any rights.

S.086

In the event of severance of any clauses as a result of a judgement and/or decision by a competent court and/or consent between the parties. Then in such instance this agreement shall only continue if the clauses [specify reference] are not affected. If these clauses are affected then this agreement shall immediately come to an end. The parties shall enter into discussions to resolve any matters which are outstanding.

S.087

Where any term of this agreement is deleted, erased, severed and/or otherwise removed from this agreement for any reason. Then it is agreed between the parties that unless it relates to clauses [specify] then the agreement shall continue in existence. Where clauses [specify] are affected in whole and/or part then the Agreement shall be terminated within [number] months. The parties shall enter into negotiations to reach a final settlement relating to the payments due and/or work completed and/or ownership of any rights under the agreement.

S.088

It is not agreed that clauses can be deleted and/or amended and/or severed for any reason. In the event that any part of this agreement is found by a court of law to be unlawful, illegal, invalid and/or unenforceable. Then the whole agreement shall be declared void and the parties shall repay all sums made under this agreement in the last [number] years.

SIGNATURE

General Business and Commercial

S.089
IN WITNESS OF THEIR AGREEMENT each party has caused its authorised representative to execute this instrument effective as of date of this agreement:

[Distributor]: [specify]   [Company]: [specify]

Signed by: [–] Title   Signed by: [–] Title

Date: [–]   Date: [–]

S.090
This document is agreed by the parties through their authorised signatures on the final date of the signatures to this Licence Agreement:

Signed for and on behalf of the [Licensor]

Signed [–] Name [–] Title [–] Date [–]

Signed for and on behalf of the [Licensee]

Signed [–] Name [–] Title [–] Date [–]

S.091
The [Agent] and the [Owner] warrant and undertake to the [Licensee] that they have arranged tests and health and safety inspections and reports and that they are both entirely satisfied as to the [accuracy/quality/safety] of the [Product] on date [–].

Signed by authorised signatory on behalf of the [Agent]: [specify name] [–]

Signed by authorised signatory on behalf of the [Owner]: [specify name] [–]

S.092
This Deed is signed by the duly authorised representatives of the parties on [date] as follows:

Signed by: [–] [date] [specify Name/Title]

On behalf of [Company]

Signed by: [–] [date] [Name/Director]

Witnessed by: [–] [date] [Name/Title]

S.093

Signed by: [–] date [–]

FOR AND ON BEHALF OF: [specify Company]

In the presence of: [–] Date [–] [Name/Title]

Signed by: [–] date [–]

FOR AND ON BEHALF OF: [specify Supplier]

In the presence of [–] Date [–] [Name/Title]

Signed by: [–] Date [–]

S.094

Signed by: [–] [date] For and on behalf of the [Company].

Signed by: [–] [date] For and on behalf of the [Designer].

S.095

Name of [Author] [–] Signature [–] Address [–] Date [–]

Name of [Company] [–] Signature:[–] Address [–] Date [–]

S.096

[Name/Title]: [–] Signed by: [–] The Assignor Dated [–]

[Name/Title]: [–] Signed by: [–] The Assignee Dated [–]

S.097

Executed and delivered as a deed signed by: [–] [Name] [Company Director]

Witnessed and signed by: [–] [Name] [Company Secretary].

S.098

Signed by: [–] [Print Name/date] For and on behalf of the Artist.

Signed by: [–] [Print Name/date] For and on behalf of the Agent

S.099

Agreement dated: [–]

[signature] [Title/Name] [Sponsor]

[signature] [Title/Name] [Sportsperson]

S.100

Signed by the Presenter [–] [Print Name in full]

Signed by the [Company] [–] [Print Name in full]

Agreement signed and dated [–]

S.101

If any person specified is under eighteen years then this document must be signed and authorised by their parent, guardian and/or other adult who has legal custody of that person. No signature shall be binding if the contract is signed by the person who is under age.

S.102

For and on behalf of the [Sponsor]: [–]:

For and on behalf of the [Association]: [–]:

S.103

Date of the Agreement [–]

Signed by: [Website Company/Distributor] [–] Advertiser [–]

S.104

Name [–] Designation [–]

Signed by [–] [date] For and on behalf of the Company.

Name [–] Designation [–]

Signed by [–] [date] For and on behalf of the Executive.

S.105

If this agreement is not executed and signed by the [Licensee] within [thirty] days of the date upon which the offer document is sent by the [Licensor] to the [Licensee]. Then the [Licensor] shall have the right at its sole discretion to withdraw the offer and cancel the potential arrangement with the [Licensee].

S.106

1.1 If there is more than one author to this agreement then they shall all be required to sign the document and to accept that they shall be jointly and severally bound by the terms of the agreement.

1.2 That in the event that one or more of the authors either cannot fulfil the terms for any reason and/or has died and/or is unable to mentally and/or physically carry out the work required. Then the other authors and/or the [Company] may suggest a substitute to take over the role of the departed author which shall be on terms to be agreed between all the parties.

S.107

All members of the [Group] confirm that they are [18/21] years of age or older at the date of signing this agreement. Any member who is not [18/21] years of age and/or has any mental incapacity must have this agreement signed by a parent and/or guardian and/or other legally authorised third party.

S.108

The [Author] confirms that he/she has taken specialist legal advice and fully understands the consequences of signing this document.

S.109

[Name] is an authorised representative of the [Company] and this agreement has been approved in draft form by the Board of the Directors of the [Company].

S.110

[Name] confirms that as at [date]:

1.1 there is no physical illness, mental incapacity and/or legal reason why he/she is not capable of signing this agreement.

1.2 That he/she have read all the terms and accept that they have been advised to seek independent legal advice.

1.3 There is no existing contract and/or arrangement which conflicts with and/or prevents [Name] concluding this agreement.

S.111

Signed by: [Name] as authorised representative of the [Charity]

Signature: [date]

Signed by: [Name] as authorised representativeof the [Sponsor]: [–]

Signature: [–] date: [–]

This agreement shall commence on [date].

SOFTWARE

General Business and Commercial

S.112

'The Software' shall mean the source code of the computer and the binary code the machine readable coded programme [excluding the server] known as [specify name].

S.113
The [Company] agrees to supply at no additional cost any modifications, additions, amendments, adjustments, error corrections and virus protection at its sole cost to the [Licensee] for the current edition of the [Software], but not any later edition.

S.114
The [Licensee] is granted a non-exclusive non-transferable licence by the [Company] to use the [Software] [and data] for the purpose which it is intended [indefinitely/until date].

S.115
The [Licensee] agrees that no right is granted by the [Company] to the [Licensee]:

1.1 to make additional copies [except for one back up copy].

1.2 to reproduce, exploit, adapt, license, translate, develop the [Software] and/or any content for any reason.

1.3 to sub-license, permit, authorise, assign and/or transfer any rights of any nature in the [Software] and/or any content for any reason to any third party except data and records owned by the [Licensee].

1.4 to make [Software] available over the internet and/or through any telecommunication system and/or any other digital and/or electronic format and/or to offer, sell, supply, distribute and/or make available the [Software] and/or any part to any other member of the public and/or any other entity and/or company at any time.

S.116
The [Company] does not accept any responsibility for any viruses, errors, defects, omissions, failures, losses, damages and/or other liability arising directly and/or indirectly from the installation, use and/or any modifications, additions, amendments, adjustments and/or error corrections supplied by the [Company] at any time and/or any other matters of any nature arising from the [Software]. The [Licensee] must install and use the [Software] and any other material entirely at its own risk and cost and the [Company] shall not be liable for any costs and/or other sums of any nature that may arise unless arising from negligence by the [Company] which shall directly cause personal injury and/or death which is attributable to failures by the [Company].

S.117
The [Licensee] agrees that it shall not acquire any rights in any copyright, intellectual property rights, patent computer software and/or programme

rights and/or database rights in the [Software] and/or any data and/or the source code and/or the title. The [Licensee] agrees not to erase, delete and/or alter any copyright notices, trade marks, logos and/or warnings on any part of the [Software] and any packaging, discs and/or other material at any time.

S.118

The [Supplier] is not providing any copyright and/or ownership of the computer software programme which is owned by [specify]. The [Supplier] is developing and adapting the software programme to suit the requirements of the [Company] and to assist in the upgrade of the computer software in accordance with the specification in appendix [–] which forms part of this Agreement.

S.119

The [Supplier] agrees that the [Company] must be able to test and approve the capacity and functionality of the computer software prior to the payment of the instalment due on completion of the [Project]. That in the event that the system does not function as expected and there are unresolved problems. Then the final payment must be delayed until the [Company] has approved all the work.

S.120

The [Supplier] confirms that maintenance and later upgrades are not part of this agreement and are subject to the conclusion of other agreements and additional payments.

S.121

Where the [Company] wishes to add features, functions, tools and/or development to the computer software and system which were not part of the original specification agreed at the start. Then the [Supplier] shall be entitled to charge and be paid additional sums for any extra work.

S.122

[Name] is adapting and developing software supplied by the [Company] for the [Website/App]. It is agreed that the [Company] shall be responsible for the payment of any licence to any third party that may be required. That where [Name] uses software owned by a third party which is not currently used by the [Company]. That [Name] shall highlight this fact in his/her report and specify the costs of acquiring the software and any updates.

SOUND RECORDINGS
General Business and Commercial

S.123
'The Sound Recordings' shall be the sound recordings of the performance by the [Artist] for and on behalf of the [Record Company] made during the Term of this Agreement regardless of the medium on which the sound recording is made or the method by which the sounds are produced or reproduced.

S.124
'Sound Recording' shall mean the sound recording of [specify subject] which has and/or will be made by [Name] regardless of the medium on which the sound recording is made or the method by which the sounds are produced or reproduced, but does not include a film soundtrack when accompanying a film.

S.125
'The Master Recordings' shall mean all sound recordings of the [Interviewee] made by or for the [Interviewer] for the purpose of the [Article/Work] regardless of the medium on which the sound recording is made or the method by which the sounds are produced or reproduced.

S.126
'The Sound Recording' shall be defined as:

1.1 a recording of sounds from which sounds may be reproduced; or

1.2 a recording of the whole or any part of a literary, dramatic or musical work from which sounds reproducing the work may be produced.

This applies regardless of the medium on which the recording is made or the methods by which the sounds are reproduced or produced.

S.127
The [Licensor] agrees to attend at such times, dates and locations as the [Licensee] may reasonably require to assist in the production and editing of the sound recordings of the [Work/Film/Video] subject to reasonable notice.

S.128
The [Company] agrees and undertakes that it shall not use the sound recordings and/or any part and/or license, transfer and/or authorise the use and/or adaptation by others of the sound recordings for any purpose except [specify authorised purpose]. Any other use and/or exploitation shall require the prior written consent of the [Licensor].

S.129

At the end of the Licence Period all master material and copies of the [Sound Recordings] in any format and any medium shall be returned to the [Licensor] at the [Licensees'] cost and expense. The [Licensee] shall also confirm in writing that neither the [Licensee] nor any third party that it has engaged to work on the [Project] have in their possession and/or control any master material and/or copies.

S.130

'The Sound Recordings' shall mean all the sound recordings of the discussions and interviews between [Name] and the [Presenter] on behalf of the [Company] regardless of the medium on which the recording is made and/or the methods by which the sounds are produced and/or reproduced.

S.131

'The Exclusive [Sound Recording] Rights' shall mean the sole and exclusive right to exercise, license, and/or authorise any third party (to the exclusion of all others and the copyright owner) the right to reproduce, supply, distribute and/or exploit the [Sound Recordings] of the [Musical Work/other].

S.132

The [Licensor] agrees that the [Licensee] shall be entitled to sub-license the [Sound Recordings] listed in Schedule A by title, duration and format to third parties for the purpose of the reproduction, performance, transmission and/or adaptation for any format in any media including but not limited to advertisements, pop-ups, game shows and/or any other use on television, radio, websites, apps, mobile phones, ringtones, gadgets, storage and retrieval systems for supply of music, podcasts, films, plays, conferences, shopping centres, children's toys, theme parks, animated games, gambling, lottery and betting sites. Provided that no licence and/or authority shall be granted for any period beyond [date] and that no rights must be assigned to any third party.

S.133

The [Licensee] shall not have the right to license, authorise and/or permit the reproduction, use, adaptation and/or performance of the [Sound Recordings] in association with any endorsement, sponsorship, merchandising, marketing and/or promotion of any products and/or services and/or political and/or other charitable and/or commercial campaign by a third party without the prior written consent of the [Licensor]. The [Licensor] shall be entitled to refuse consent without providing any reasons.

S.134

The [Licensee] grants the [Sub-Licensee] the non-exclusive right to play the [Sound Recording] in conjunction with the [Podcast] of [Name] on the

[Website/Platform] from [date] to [date] for viewing by the public over the internet and/or any telecommunication system. The [Sub-Licensee] shall not be entitled to make the [Sound Recording] available as a download and/or individual audio and/or electronic file and/or to authorise and/or licence any third party to make copies and/or otherwise exploit the [Sound Recordings].

S.135
The [Charity] agrees that:

1.1   the [Sponsor] may arrange for images, sound recordings and films to be made of the [Event] at the [Sponsors,] cost.

1.2   the Sponsor] may use the material in 1.1 in any manner that it may decide provided that the [Event] and [Charity] are credited on each occasion.

1.3   the [Sponsor] agrees that it shall not be entitled to license and/or authorise third parties to exploit the material in any manner without the prior consent of the [Charity] and the payment of an additional fee in each case.

S.136
[Name] grants the [Company] the non-exclusive right to transmit and/or reproduce the [Sound Recordings] from a large screen and/or white board and/or other device as part of an [Exhibition/Conference] in conjunction with the [Products/Artworks]. Provided that a credit, trade mark and slogan is provided on screen at all times as follows [specify] and an advance fee of [number/currency] is paid to [Name] before that date.

S.137
Where the [Company] permits [Name] to carry out interviews of personnel, management and/or consultants for the purpose of producing a documentary on the subject of [specify project]. Where any sound recordings, films, images and/or other material is created, developed and/or produced. Then it is agreed that a copy of all such material shall be supplied at the cost of [Name] to the [Company] as well as a copy of the final documentary.

STATUTORY PROVISIONS

General Business and Commercial

S.138
Any reference to any statute and/or legislation shall be deemed to include a reference to any later amendment and/or consolidation and re-enactment and/or repeal of any part.

S.139

References to any statute or regulation shall be deemed to extend to any statute or regulation which is passed in substitution or substantially amends or consolidates and re-enacts the subject matter.

S.140

Where any interpretation is required of this agreement then legislation which existed at that time may be relevant for the purpose of interpreting the meaning of the words and the intentions of the parties.

S.141

Reference to any statute or any statutory provision shall include reference to any statute provisions which amends, extends, consolidates or replaces the same and to any other regulation, instrument or other subordinate legislation made under the statute.

S.142

All statutory rights of the [specify name] are reserved.

S.143

The [Company] shall:

1.1   ensure compliance with, and give all notices required by, any Act of Parliament, any instrument, rule or order made under any Act of Parliament or any regulation or byelaw of any local authority or of any statutory body which has any jurisdiction with regard to the [Project].

1.2   be entitled to do such things and order such materials for the [Project] as may be necessary in order to comply with any statutory provisions in order to avoid exposure of the [Company] to civil and/or criminal proceedings. The [Company] shall immediately provide written notice of the circumstances to the [Charity]. The [Charity] agrees to bear the cost of compliance provided that it is reasonable and necessary in each case.

1.3   not be liable for the failure to comply with any statutory provisions in the event that the [Company] has been instructed by an officer of the [Charity] either verbally or in writing not to do so. The [Charity] agrees to bear full responsibility for such direction and any consequences which may arise from such failure to comply with any statutory provisions.

S.144

The [Supplier] agrees and undertakes that it is a condition of this order that the [Products/Services/Material] comply and will continue to comply with all legislation, industry practices, codes and guidelines in [country] which are and/or may become applicable to the design, manufacture, production, content, durability, packaging, supply and use of the [Products/Services/Material] in force at any time prior to delivery and transfer of ownership to the [Company].

S.145
The [Work/Products/Services] shall be performed and delivered in accordance with any statutes, orders, regulations, codes and any relevant health and safety guidance for the industry from a government body and/or a trade organisation which exists now and/or may be developed at any time thereafter until the expiry and/or termination of this agreement in [countries].

S.146
Each party under this Agreement shall be responsible for ensuring its own compliance with any statutes, directives, regulations, policies, standards, codes of any nature including but not limited to the reproduction, supply, distribution, packaging, product liability, advertising, sponsorship, product placement, health, safety, environmental, recycling or otherwise. Further each such party shall bear the cost of any fines, damages, losses and/or other liability and/or expenses that may arise and shall not be entitled to offset them against any sums due under this Agreement to the other party.

S.147

1.1 This agreement shall be subject to legislation, directives, Codes of Practice, guidelines and policies which apply in [country]. Where there is any reference to any legislation it shall also include subsequent amendments and/or repeals relating to that subject.

1.2 The parties agree that the following documents must be complied with in respect of health and safety matters: [specify list]. The parties agree that the guidance of the following trade organisation relating to [subject] must be adhered to for the purpose of this agreement.

Failure to comply with 1.1 and 1.2 shall be a fundamental breach of this agreement.

SUB-LICENCE
General Business and Commercial
S.148

1.1 The [Company] reserves the right and shall be entitled to assign, sub-license, sub-contract, transfer and/or appoint any subsidiary, affiliate, associate, and/or parent company and/or third party to fulfil the terms, condition, rights and/or obligations to [Name] without notice at any time.

1.2 In the event of 1.1 and the subsequent agreement by [Name] the [Company] shall be under no further obligation to [Name] and shall be relieved of its rights and/or obligations under this agreement. The [Company] shall not be held responsible and/or liable for any acts, omissions and/or failures of any other party in 1.1.

S.149

The [Company] shall notify [Name] in advance in respect of the appointment of any third party who may be engaged to provide [Services/Work/Products] in order to assist the [Company] in the fulfilment of the terms of this agreement. The [Company] shall only be required to provide a copy of any relevant document to [Name] where the payment to the third party is in excess of [number/currency] and the [Company] intends to claim this sum as part of the deductible costs and expenses relating to the [Project].

S.150

The [Licensee] may sub-license any of its rights and benefits in whole and/or any part to any person, company and/or enterprise which shall then be entitled to the same rights and benefits with regard to the [Products/Designs/Logos] as the [Licensee] has under this agreement including the right to sub-license.

S.151

Where pursuant to this agreement the [Company] acquires any licences and/or rights and/or undertakes any liabilities and/or obligations. It is agreed that the [Company] shall be entitled to grant and sub-license such rights and/or to delegate such liabilities and/or obligations to any third party at any time. Provided that the [Company] shall continue to ensure fulfilment of the terms of this agreement to the [Licensor] and if any such third party shall default in any manner and/or breach the terms of this licence and/or the sub-licence. That the [Company] shall be liable for the consequences of the default and/or breach by the third party.

S.152

The [Distributor] shall be entitled to sub-license and/or sub-contract any of the terms of this agreement. The [Distributor] shall immediately notify [Name] of any sub-licence or sub-contract granted and provide details of the parties.

Provided that the [Distributor] shall continue to be bound by the agreement and intends to ensure that they are fulfilled. That where any sub-licensee and/or sub-contractor should default for any reason. That the [Distributor] shall ensure that there is no delay in delivery of the products and/or services to customers and/or any payments due to [Name]. That where any additional costs and expenses must be incurred as a result that all such sums shall be paid by the [Distributor] and that no contribution shall be attributable to [Name].

S.153
The [Company] shall be liable for the acts, defaults, and/or failure of any sub-contractor and/or his/her personnel, agents and consultants as if they were deemed to be the acts, defaults and/or failure of the [Company].

S.154
The [Distributor] may appoint a third party to manufacture all and/or part of the [Product] and/or any associated content and/or packaging. Provided that the third party:

1.1 has been in business and trading profitably for no less than [number] years.

1.2 has premises which meet current health and safety standards and complies with current legislation in [country].

1.3 is not associated with any [subject].

1.4 is able to produce a prototype sample prior to final production for examination by the [Distributor] and [Name].

S.155
The [Distributor] may not grant any sub-license and/or sub-contract any part of the work in respect of the [Product] without the prior written consent of the [Company].

S.156
In the event that the [Company] provides written consent to the appointment of any third party to perform any part of this main agreement on behalf of the [Distributor]. The [Distributor] undertakes and agrees that:

1.1 it shall be a condition of such consent by the [Company] that the [Distributor] shall not grant any sub-licence or sub-contract which can continue beyond the expiry and/or termination of the main agreement; and

1.2 where in the main agreement the consent and/or approval of the [Company] is required and/or there is any right of inspection, audit or otherwise. That the [Distributor] will ensure that the same provisions giving such rights directly to the [Company] shall be set out in any sub-licence or sub-contract; and

1.3 the [Distributor] shall be responsible for and liable to the [Company] for the performance and adherence to any such sub-licence and/or sub-contract by the third party.

S.157

For the avoidance of doubt this agreement contains the full rights and obligations conferred upon the parties to this agreement. This agreement does not permit the [Licensee] to assign this agreement and/or any rights and/or to transfer any title, copyright, trade mark and/or intellectual property rights and/or to create any franchise and/or to sub-license and/or appoint any third party in any manner.

S.158

1.1 Any rights granted by any sub-licence by the [Licensee] shall be subject and restricted to the terms of this main licence agreement. The [Licensee] cannot grant and/or offer to any sub-licensee greater rights than the [Licensor] has granted to the [Licensee].

1.2 The [Licensee] shall at all times be responsible for all the direct and/or indirect consequences and costs and expenses of any breaches, failures, delays, acts, losses, damages, omissions and/or other matters arising from any sub-licences and/or sub-licensees in respect of liability to the [Licensor] [and any other third party].

S.159

The [Company] may not grant any sub-licence under this agreement nor may the [Company] sub-contract the work of developing, manufacturing, supplying and/or distributing and/or advertising and/or marketing the [Product/Service] without the prior written consent of the [Licensor].

S.160

If the [Licensor] consents to any third party being appointed as a sub-licensee or otherwise the [Company] undertakes it shall be a condition of such consent that:

1.1 such appointment shall be by a written sub-licence subject to the same undertakings as set out in clauses [–] and shall be brought to an end either by termination and/or expiry on the same date as this agreement.

1.2 the [Company] shall ensure and be responsible to the [Licensor] for the performance, observance and liabilities of the sub-licensee and/or any other third party authorised by the [Company].

S.161

The [Licensee] shall not assign the benefit of this Licence which is purely personal in nature and shall not grant any sub-licence under this agreement.

S.162

[Name] agrees that the [Company] may sub-license the rights granted in the [Work] to a third party provided the prior written consent of [Name] is provided and the sub-licence is limited to the rights granted to the [Company]. The sub-licence shall not release the [Company] from the obligations to [Name] and all reports, statements and payments shall be made direct from the [Company] to [Name].

S.163

In consideration of the Fee the [Licensor] grants the [Licensee] the right to sub-license the [Work] reproduced in the [Disc/Sound Recording] to third parties to advertise, promote, display, package, distribute and/or reproduce the [Work] reproduced in the [Disc/Sound Recording] in association with any sponsorship, merchandising, marketing and/or promotion by such third party until [date].

S.164

1.1 In consideration of [number/currency] the [Licensor] grants the [Licensee] the non-exclusive right to play the [Images/Sound Recording/Characters] in conjunction with the opening credits of the [Podcasts/Films/Videos] of different persons developed by the [Licensee] on the [Website/App/Channel] for the duration of the Licence Period.

1.2 The [Licensee] shall be entitled to permit the [Images/Sound Recording/Characters] in conjunction with the opening credits of the [Podcasts/Films/Videos] accessible over the internet and/or any telecommunication system and/or as a download and/or electronic file and/or part of a playback archive service.

S.165

[Name] agrees and accepts that the [Distributor] may grant multiple non-exclusive and/or exclusive sub-licences to third parties and/or affiliates to exploit, market and promote the [Work/Images/Characters] and/or parts and/or any adaptation and/or development at any time.

S.166

The [Licensor] undertakes that it shall not license nor permit any third party to produce, manufacture, supply and/or distribute the [Game] and/or the Prototype including any developments or variations throughout the Territory for the duration of the Licence Period.

S.167

The [Licensee] shall have no right to discharge its obligations under this agreement through any sub-distributor, sub-agent and/or sub-licensee without prior written approval of the [Licensor] such approval not to be unreasonably withheld or delayed. Where approval is provided by the [Licensor] then the [Licensee] shall continue to remain fully liable for the acts, omissions, errors, delays, losses, damages and defaults by any sub-distributor, sub-agent and/or sub-licensee. The [Licensee] shall ensure that all such third parties shall follow current accounting and banking practices and keep accurate and complete financial records and copies of all relevant documents, data, stock, contracts and invoices for access and inspection by the [Licensor].

S.168

The [Company] agrees that the [Licensor] shall be entitled to approve the appointment of any sub-agent, sub-licensee, distributor and any other third party in respect of the development, production, manufacture, distribution, marketing and exploitation of the [Licensed Articles] under this Agreement.

S.169

'Sub-Licensee' shall mean any person, firm and/or company appointed by the [Licensee] in accordance with clause [–].

S.170

The [Company] may sub-license the manufacture and exploitation of the [Products] to a wholly owned subsidiary and/or parent company of the [Company]. Provided that the [Company] shall remain responsible for all liabilities, acts, omissions and/or defaults of that third party sub-licensee.

S.171

1.1 It is acknowledged that the rights granted to the [Licensee] under this licence are strictly personal to the [Licensee]. That the [Licensee] shall not be entitled in whole and/or part to assign, transfer, charge and/or create a lien over the licence nor be entitled to grant any sub-licence relating to the [Work/Product/Brand] and/or any part to any other third party.

1.2 However the [Licensee] may arrange for a third party to manufacture for the [Licensee's] own benefit and purpose alone the [Licensed Articles] subject to the prior written consent of the [Licensor] and upon condition that the third party signs a written agreement not to supply the [Licensed Articles] to any person or company other than the [Licensee].

1800

S.172

The [Company] agrees that the [Distributor] shall be entitled to sub-license the [Work/Image and Logo/Product/Film] in whole and/or in part to reputable sub-licensees provided that they have been in business for at least [three] years and the [Distributor] undertakes:

1.1   That any such sub-licence shall be subject to the prior written approval of the [Company].

1.2   That any such sub-licence shall not adversely affect the obligations of the [Distributor] to the [Company] and

1.3   The [Distributor] undertakes to be liable to the [Company] for all liabilities, acts, omissions, errors and defaults of any sub-licensee.

1.4   The [Distributor] shall indemnify the [Company] against any costs, expenses, losses, damages, claims, allegations and settlements caused by any sub-licensee.

S.173

The [Licensee] shall not have the right to advertise, promote, display, package, distribute and/or reproduce the [Work/Product/Logo and Image] in association with any sales, sponsorship, merchandising, event, exhibition, marketing and/or promotion by a third party and their brand and products as a collaboration without the prior written consent of the [Licensor].

S.174

The [Licensee] grants the [Sub-Licensee] the non-exclusive right to reproduce the [Work/Product/Image and Logo] in the form of a [specify product] in conjunction with [Name] from [date] to [date] for the charitable purpose of [specify].

S.175

The [Licensee] agrees to provide a complete copy of all sub-licences and sub-distribution agreements to the [Licensor] upon request.

S.176

The [Company] shall not be entitled to assign, sub-license, transfer and/or exploit with any third party any of the rights granted in this agreement without the prior written consent of the [Author/Licensor] as to the terms of the proposed new agreement. There shall be no obligation by the [Author/Licensor] to agree to any proposal.

S.177

The [Agent/Company] shall consult in good faith with the [Author] in respect of the appointment of any third party to exploit the [Work/Film/Video/Installation/Image].

S.178

The [Publisher] agrees to consult with the [Author] as to the terms for sub-licensing the rights to a third party and shall ensure that no agreement shall be concluded with a third party which is likely to go into administration and/or insolvency.

S.179

This Agreement is personal to the [Customer] who may not assign, transfer and/or authorise any part of this agreement to a third party.

S.180

You shall not at any time assign, transfer, sub-contract and/or sub-license the [Order] to any third party.

S.181

1.1 Except where otherwise provided [Name] shall not sub-contract any part of the [Work] without the prior consent of the [Company].

1.2 [Name] shall be entitled to sub-contract any part of the [Work] which is only minor in nature and/or for the purchase and sourcing of materials and/or for any manufacturer and/or supplier which has been agreed in advance with the [Company].

S.182

The [Company] reserves the right to assign, transfer, sub-license, sub-contract or otherwise transfer any of its rights and obligations to a third party without notice. Provided that no assignment, sub-licence, sub-contract or transfer shall, unless the parties otherwise agree, relieve the [Company] of its rights or obligations under this Agreement.

S.183

The [Company] reserves the right to sub-contract the performance of the Contract or any part.

S.184

The [Distributor] shall not be entitled to sub-license any copyright and/or other intellectual property rights in the [Work/Sound Recordings/Characters and Images] reproduced in the [Product] and/or to authorise any reproduction and/or exploitation by a third party.

S.185

It is agreed between parties that no sub-licence shall be granted to any third party which cannot produce three sets of certified accounts for the last three years prior to the proposed date of any agreement.

SUSPENSION

General Business and Commercial

S.186

The [Distributor] shall be entitled by written notice to suspend the engagement of the services of [Name] in the event that:

1.1   [Name] does not observe and abide by and/or fails to perform any of the services and/or obligations, undertakings and/or warranties and/or is otherwise in serious breach of this agreement.

1.2   [Name] shall have been prevented from performing the services by injury, illness, mental and/or physical disability and/or otherwise and/or shall be in the opinion of the [Distributor] incapable of performing the services for any reason.

1.3   [Name] shall have died and/or ceased to work as [specify role].

1.4   Any force majeure circumstance shall arise which shall prevents [Name] carrying out his/her work and fulfilling the terms of this agreement for more than [four] weeks.

1.5   The period of such suspension shall continue indefinitely until notice of resumption of service is given by the [Distributor]. During any period of suspension the [Distributor] shall not be obliged to pay [Name] any sums for work which has not been completed. The [Distributor] will remain entitled to all rights granted and/or assigned by [Name] under the agreement. The suspension by the [Distributor] shall be in addition to and without prejudice to any other rights or remedies.

S.187

The Company shall be entitled to suspend the agreement indefinitely for the services of the [Consultant/Executive] without any further payment and/or terminate the agreement at its sole discretion in the event that:

1.1   The [Project] is prevented, delayed, interfered with and/or interrupted by any cause beyond the control of the [Company] including without limitation fire, accident, war, civil disturbance, Act of God, lockout, strike, labour disturbance, illness or injury of key personnel and/or

1.2   The [Consultant/Executive] shall refuse and/or fail and/or neglect to provide his/her services as required under this agreement for more than [number] days and/or

1.3 The [Consultant/Executive] shall be in breach of any of the material obligations specified in relation to the [Project] and/or the completion of the work required by specified dates in relation to his/her services and/or

1.4 The [Consultant/Executive] shall be and/or become unable by reason of mental and/or physical incapacity and/or some other reason unable to provide his/her services as set out in this agreement for a period of more than [number] weeks.

1.5 In the event that the services of the [Consultant/Executive] are suspended for more than [number] weeks. The [Consultant/Executive] shall have the right to terminate the agreement without prejudice to any legal claim and/or action.

S.188

[Name] may be suspended by the [Company] on any of the following grounds provided that the [Company] shall continue to pay such sums as may be due to [Name] until such time as the suspension shall end and/or the agreement is terminated:

1.1 [Name] shall fail to submit to a medical examination and/or drug test in any year when requested to do so by the [Company].

1.2 The business of the [Company] is materially prejudiced by the present and/or past conduct, statements, images, films and/or recordings and/or social media of [Name].

1.3 The function or position of [Name] in the [Company] has ceased due to a reorganisation, merger and/or takeover.

1.4 The [Name] has committed an act of dishonesty, breach of confidentiality and/or gross misconduct.

S.189

The [Company] shall not have the right to suspend the services of the [Consultant] for any reason whether with or without payment. Any suspension shall be deemed a termination of this agreement by the [Company]. The [Company] shall be obliged to pay the [Consultant] all sums due to the [termination/end] date of the agreement.

S.190

The [Distributor] shall have the right to suspend the [Work/Service] for a period not to exceed [one] calendar month in any one year in the following circumstances:

1.1 If [Name/Company] is unable to fulfil the work and/or supply the products required under this agreement whether due to insufficient skilled labour, faulty equipment, illness, personal injury and/or due to reasons of force majeure.

1.2 If [Name/Company] enters into any agreement with a third party which conflicts with this agreement.

1.3 If [Name/Company] shall fail or neglect to perform any term of this agreement and it is not remedied within [fourteen] days of notice to that effect from the [Distributor].

S.191

There shall be no right or consent of any nature under this agreement to any form of suspension, delay without payment, gardening leave, holding the agreement in abeyance or requiring any of the terms to be removed or parties not to fulfil the terms as set out. This Agreement shall continue without interruption until it expires or is terminated.

S.192

In the event that the [Employee] is asked to leave the premises suddenly and without [seven days'] written notice and/or is suspended and/or told to go on gardening leave and/or asked to be on paid leave which is to continue indefinitely. Then the [Employee] shall be entitled to the sum of [number/currency] which shall be in addition to any other rights and remedies that the [Employee] may have in law. This sum is intended to compensate the [Employee] for the failure of the Employer to act in good faith and the deliberate act of failing to provide the [Employee] with reasonable notice.

S.193

In the event that the [Website/Channel], any service, product, game, helpline, delivery, payment facility and/or other content and/or any associated company and/or any directly and/or indirectly related other matter is not available, suspended and/or withdrawn, recalled, cancelled and/or otherwise terminated. Then the [Company] shall not be responsible for, and/or liable for any costs, expenses, damages, losses which may be incurred and/or any acts, omissions, errors, failures and/or non-compliance by any agent, sub-licensee, distributor or otherwise and the total liability shall be limited to a refund of any sums paid by the [Customer] to the [Company] for any product, service and/or other work.

S.194

The [Service] may be suspended by the [Company] due to force majeure and/or loss of energy and/or power failure, floods, maintenance work and/or upgrade work and/or riots, war, acts of violence and/or delays in travel and/or any other reason. The [Company] shall post notices on its website with regular updates as to the expected time before it is to be resolved.

T

TAXES

General Business and Commercial

T.001
The [Contractor] shall promptly pay directly to the appropriate government or authority all taxes, levies, penalties and/or assessments imposed on the [Contractor] and its personnel and/or agents by any government and/or other authority in the jurisdictions in which this contract may be are carried out and/or performed and/or concluded. The [Contractor] shall be solely liable for all sums which may fall due in connection with the [Contractor's] functions, performance and other roles under this contract. The [Contractors'] liability shall include but not be limited to corporation tax, personal income tax, employment taxes, sales taxes, customs and excise taxes, any relevant stamp tax, social security and/or national insurance taxes and/or any other tax, levy, penalty and/or assessment.

T.002

1.1   Where the [Author] is resident outside [the United Kingdom/other] and he/she is liable under [English/other] law to be charged [income/other] tax at the appropriate rate. Then the [Publishers] shall be entitled to deduct and/or withhold such sums from any payments due to the [Author] where there is a double taxation agreement between the [United Kingdom/other] and the country in which the [Author] resides.

1.2   The burden is on the [Author] to complete and returned any relevant documentation to the appropriate tax authorities in the [United Kingdom/other].

1.3   In order for the [Publishers] not to deduct and/or withhold any sums. The [Author] must satisfy the [Publisher] that the [Author] is entitled to receive the payments without any sums being withheld. The [Author] must supply copies of original documents and the [Publishers'] may decide at their sole discretion that they shall not withhold sums due as taxes.

T.003

The [Company] shall be responsible for complying with any national and international legislation, regulations, case law and/or practices which directly and/or indirectly relate to the [Company] in respect of any corporate and/or personal taxes, levies, assessments, national insurance, currency, product liability and/or the payment of any other sums which may arise in respect of the fulfilment of the terms of this contract by the [Company].

T.004

All payments by either party to the other under or pursuant to this agreement shall be made without any deduction and/or withholding of any sums unless the deductions and/or withholding of any sums is required by law. In such a case the party who is responsible shall pay the amount withheld promptly to the appropriate authority and shall provide the other party with a verified original document or other reasonable evidence issued by that authority on the receipt of the amount withheld.

T.005

All charges are exclusive of any taxes and must be paid without any deduction whatsoever. Where relevant value added tax, sales tax and/or any other tax imposed and/or levied shall be paid by the [Customer] in addition to the charges provided there is a suitable invoice which sets out the reason for the extra sums.

T.006

The [Sportsperson] agrees that he/she shall be responsible for his/her own national insurance, personal tax and/or the repayment of any sums charged for value added tax to any third party which shall be due in consequence of this agreement.

T.007

The [Manager] agrees to assist [Name] in the financial management of all the [Name's] Fees and financial affairs generally including tax, expenses, value added tax, national insurance, pension, health contributions and personal insurance. [Name] shall seek the benefit of specialist professional advice where appropriate and shall not seek to rely on the [Manager] to arrange and pay for such matters.

T.008

[Name] acknowledges that although the [Manager] shall assist in the [Name's] financial affairs, [Name] shall be ultimately responsible for seeking expert professional advice and paying for such costs and expenses together with his/her own value added tax, national insurance, personal insurance, pension and other medical, dental and/or health contributions.

T.009

1.1 The [Dealer/Fixed] Price is exclusive of tax and must be paid without any deduction whatsoever. Where relevant value added tax, sales tax or any other tax shall be paid by the [Seller]. Payment of any tax shall require a proper invoice with full details.

1.2 The [Seller] shall be responsible for complying with all national and international tax requirements and any import, export and customs and excise criteria and payments applicable to the fulfilment of this agreement by the [Seller].

T.010
The [Company] shall be responsible for complying with any national and/or international tax laws that may apply under this agreement in respect of the [Company] and/or the payment of any sums that may become due.. All sums due to the [Author] shall as far as possible be paid unless the [Company] is required by law to withhold them and/or to pay a part to a government agency and/or international body. All sums withheld and/or paid to third parties shall be verified by supporting documentation. The [Author] shall be responsible for complying with any national and/or international tax laws that may apply to the sums paid to the [Author] by the [Company].

T.011
All charges and payments are not inclusive of taxes, levies and/or any other sums of any kind that may be imposed by law. Taxes may be deducted and/or added as required by law depending on the circumstances but in each case shall be a separate itemised figure with appropriate reference to the type of tax, the rate and any codes or registration number, and whether it is deducted and/or added to the sum.

T.012
All [sums/prices/other] are exclusive of taxes of any kind unless otherwise stated. Any sales tax, value added tax or any other taxes or levies which are due to or imposed by any government and/or authority in any country which are not included must be stated as a separate itemised section of the invoice, with the type of tax, the rate and relevant registration and/or other details.

T.013
All prices are exclusive of any taxes. Additional sums and costs may be added which increase the total price due to exchange rates and/or due to taxes which must be charged for any reason at the stipulation of any relevant government body and/or as a result of any legislation in any country.

T.014

[Name] shall be responsible for the cost and expense of his/her own personal tax, national insurance, dental, medical and personal insurance payments and costs.

T.015

All charges, payments and sums shall be exclusive of sales tax, value added tax and any other sum due on the sale or supply of [Products] that may be payable by either party. There shall be a separate itemised charge or additional cost as appropriate on each relevant sales or payment document for any such taxes which shall be paid, withheld or transferred as appropriate.

T.016

The [Company] shall pay the [Settlement Fee] without deduction of tax and/ or national insurance costs and payments in accordance with the [specify organisation] policy document reference: [specify document].

T.017

All refunds and/or rebates of any taxes due to be received by the [Company] shall be included in the calculation of the assets and value of the [Company] as at [date].

T.018

Each member of the [Consortium] shall be responsible for their own corporation taxes, insurance, customs and excise and other duties and taxes that may fall due under this agreement.

T.019

1.1   [Name] and [Name] agree and undertake that they shall be jointly and severally liable for the [Partnership/Business]. That such liability shall include payment of any penalties, taxes, fines, charges, insurance and other sums due for any matter relating to the [Partnership/Business].

1.2   That [Name] and [Name] accept and agree that where one person defaults and/or is unable and/or unwilling to pay that the other person may be held liable for the total cost by a third party. That in such instance that person shall be liable to pay the total cost and then seek to claim that the other party who is in default and/or unable and/or unwilling to pay reimburses them for their half share.

1.3   Where there is any rebate relating to the [Partnership/Business] then the sum must be split equally between the parties. Except to the extent that one party has been obliged to pay the costs for both parties and then in such instance that party must have first lien over the rebate until the full sum due to them is reimbursed.

T.020

There is nothing in this agreement which transfers, assigns and/or makes one party liable for the corporation taxes, sales taxes, custom and excise duties and taxes and/or any other sum incurred and/or to be paid by the other party.

TENDER

General Business and Commercial

T.021

1.1 The Tender may be awarded by the [Company] based on any number of factors which the [Company] may decide in its absolute discretion to be a significant criteria for the [Work/Services/other].

1.2 There shall be no obligation to award the contract to be lowest bidder in terms of cost, price or otherwise.

1.3 Nor shall the [Company] be obliged to justify and/or state reasons for the award and/or the rejection of any party who may apply.

T.022

1.1 The [Company] may vary, adapt and/or modify the terms, subject and conditions of the tender process and/or application format at any time and/or withdraw the Tender.

1.2 The [Company] shall not be responsible for and/or liable to any party who may have incurred costs and/or expenses of any nature in respect of any application and tender for a contract at any time. All parties apply at their own cost and risk.

T.023

The [Company] shall consider all the factors in any applicants submission for the contract and may at its absolute discretion request further information, data and/or evidence and/or fail to permit an applicant to proceed to the final selection due to an inadequate, misleading and/or erroneous submission.

T.024

The [Company] shall not be bound to consider the [value/price] of the [quotation/tender] for the [Work/Service] to be the sole reason for the award of any contract. The [Company] may attach due weight and consideration to any factors that it shall in its absolute discretion decide including but not limited to the following:

1.1 Disclosure of facts, financial details and credit history, health and safety records, corporate background, compliance with legislation, standards and quality control policies and any other matter which may arise from an assessment of the stability, track record, and suitability of the applicant.

1.2 Personal, bank and business references.

1.3 Details of suppliers of materials, quality of materials, samples, products, packaging, the condition of the premises, insurance, freight, delivery and returns policy.

1.4 Customer service policy, complaints procedure, efficiency and operational management.

T.025

The [Company] reserves the right to amend the Tender dates due to unforeseen circumstances for any reason including but not limited to the acknowledgement of proposed application; the delivery of the application documents; the award of the Tender; the conclusion of the main agreement and/or the Tender terms and conditions and/or the payment of funds. In the event that any dates are altered all the applicants who have notified their intention to bid will as far as possible be notified in advance.

T.026

If in the opinion of the [Trustees/Directors] of the Board of the [Institute/Charity] any part of any of the applications is unacceptable. Then the [Institute/Charity] shall have the absolute right to refuse such an applicant and may also refuse to award the Tender. The grounds of refusal by the [Institute/Charity] are not limited but may include the lack of quality of the applications and/or the proposed use of personnel and/or the budgets and/or completion dates for work schedules and/or any other disclosure by the applicants.

T.027

There shall be no obligation on the [Institute/Charity] to award the Tender to any third party nor to justify the grounds of refusal to any applicant. The decision as to whether there shall be an award of the Tender, the terms upon which the Tender may be given and the payment of any sums that may be due shall be at the absolute discretion of the [Institute/Charity] at any time.

T.028
Any applicant accepts as a condition of entry to the Tender process that the applicant shall not have any right, claim and/or action against the [Institute/ Charity] for any costs, expenses, fees, charges, administrative costs, legal, accounting and consultants costs or any other sums which may be incurred and/or due to be paid by the applicant as a result of the applicants decision to apply for the Tender.

T.029
The failure by any applicant to disclose some material fact about their business, products and/or service in the application process shall be grounds for termination and/or cancellation of the Tender Process by the [Institute/Charity]. Where the [Institute/Charity] has awarded the Tender to the applicant prior to the disclosure and/or discovery of the material fact which would have affected the decision of the [Institute/Charity] to award the Tender to the applicant. Then the [Institute/Charity] shall be entitled to cancel and/or terminate the award of the Tender to the applicant.

T.030
The applicant grants the [Company] the right to store the details of the application form on a storage and retrieval system and database on a software system and/or computer at the [Company] and/or their professional advisors for a period of [number] months for the purposes of the tender application and process. If the applicant is successful then this period shall be extended upon terms to be agreed between the parties.

T.031
The [Company] agrees to delete the details of the application form of the applicant which is stored on a storage and retrieval system and database on a software system and/or computer at the [Company] after the expiry of a period of [number] months and/or within [number] weeks of the application being unsuccessful whichever is the sooner.

T.032
The initial Tender by the [Company] is for expressions of interest from third parties who may wish to be considered for the award of the contract. Each applicant must fill in the online form in all parts and submit it by the deadline. No applicants will be considered for the second part of the Tender application process who have not expressed an interest before the deadline.

T.033
The Tender requires that all applicants for the award of the [subject] agreement must have:

1.1 Personnel to provide the service who speak fluent [specify language].

1.2 Expertise and experience in the field of [subject] and are able to provide evidence of delivery of such work and services over the last [number] years to a [local/national] body with a budget of not less than [specify].

1.3 A solvent and trading company as the applicant which has clear evidence of trading in [country] in the field of [subject] over the last [number] years.

1.4 The applicant must not be the subject of civil and/or criminal proceedings in [country] which are not disclosed to the [Company] which relate to personal injury, death, fraud, tax evasion, money laundering, product liability and/or any other matter.

1.5 The applicant must disclose all material facts which would affect its ability to deliver the Tender as required.

T.034

The submission of an expression of interest is not binding on the [Company] and/or the applicant and either party may withdraw at any time. The [Company] reserves the right to end the Tender process at any time and it shall not be liable for any costs and expenses incurred by the applicant in reliance on the Tender process.

T.035

In the event that no applicant applies which the [Company] wishes to consider for the second part of the Tender procedure. Then the [Company] shall have the right to end the Tender and then begin a further process of advertising the Tender. Any applicant to the first Tender may apply to the new Tender.

T.036

This tender process is only open to companies:

1.1 which are registered with [organisation/government body] in [country].

1.2 which have operated and traded as a profitable business for more than [number] years.

1.3 which have expertise in the field of [subject].

1.4 which will not be required to sub-contract out any of the work and/or services required.

TERM OF THE AGREEMENT

General Business and Commercial

T.037

The [Employer/Company] shall have the right to terminate this agreement during the Probation Period by giving [one] [week's/month's] notice in writing to the [Employee]. After the completion of the Probation Period then the procedures set out in staff handbook which is supplied with this agreement must be followed by both parties.

T.038

This contract of employment may be terminated by either party giving to the other not less than [three] months' notice in writing. The [Employee] shall in any event retire upon attaining [number] years of age.

T.039

This contract of employment supersedes all previous arrangements if any relating to the employment of the [Manager] by the [Company] which shall be deemed to have terminated by mutual consent and shall be effective from [date]. This agreement shall commence on [date] and continue until the expiry of the Term of the Agreement subject to the provisions for termination in clause [–].

T.040

'Term of the Agreement' shall commence on [date] and shall continue indefinitely until such time as this agreement shall be terminated by either party by [number] days' notice in writing to the other party.

T.041

'Continuous Employment' for legal purposes shall mean the period of continuous employment beginning on the commencement of this agreement under clause [–].

T.042

The first day of employment shall be [date]. The date for calculating continuous employment shall be [date]. The [Company] may bring this contract to an end by serving on you the following notice period [specify duration] with an end date.

T.043

There shall be no regular and/or continuous employment between [Name] and the [Company] and all dates and hours shall be on a part time, short term, casual and temporary basis and shall be subject to alteration and cancellation by the [Company] at any time.

T.044

This agreement shall continue in force for the duration of the Assignment Period after which time all rights granted to the [Assignee] shall revert to the [Assignor] subject to the accounting provisions contained within clauses [–] and the indemnity clauses [–] under this agreement which shall continue until [date].

T.045

This agreement shall operate for the full period of copyright including any extensions and renewals [for as far as possible in perpetuity].

T.046

This agreement shall be deemed to have commenced on [date] and shall continue for a period of [twelve] months and thereafter shall continue unless and until terminated by [one/three] months' prior written notice by either party.

T.047

This agreement shall continue for a fixed period of [three] years from the commencement date of [date].

T.048

This agreement shall continue in force until terminated in writing in accordance with the termination provisions contained within clauses [–] in this agreement.

T.049

'Term of the Agreement' shall mean for the full period of copyright including any extensions and/or renewals and/or as far as possible in perpetuity and/or indefinitely and/or without limitation of time.

T.050

'The Term of the Agreement' shall mean the period of [five] years from the date of delivery of the [Master Material] to the [Distributor].

T.051

'The Term of this Agreement' shall commence on the date of this agreement and shall continue until [date/event].

T.052

The [Company] authorises the [Distributor] to collect all sums due to the [Company] in respect of the [Work/Services/Products] from any source throughout the [Territory/world] from the exploitation of the rights granted under this Agreement both during the Term of this Agreement and thereafter provided that all sums are then accounted for to the [Company].

T.053
Any failure to renew or extend the Term of this Agreement shall not constitute grounds for any claim and/or additional payments for any reason to the [Company] and/or [Name].

T.054
'The Term of the Agreement' shall commence on [date/time] and shall continue for [two] years up to and including [date/time]. This agreement shall thereafter automatically be renewed for [number] further periods of [six/twelve] months 'except where either party shall have given the other party written notice at any time that they do not wish to renew the agreement for any further period after the current expiry date.

T.055
'Term of the Agreement' shall start on [date] at [time] and continue until [date] [time]. There shall be no right to any extension and/or any automatic renewal period.

T.056
The period of the engagement of the services of the [Consultant] shall commence on [date/time] and continue until the completion of the [Project/ Event] and/or [date/time] whichever is the earliest.

T.057

1.1   The [Agent] acknowledges and agrees that he/she shall not be entitled to any commission and/or other remuneration in respect of work completed and/or agreed to be carried out and/or performed by the [Artist] prior to the date of this new agreement with the [Agent].

1.2   The [Agent] also agrees that he/she shall not be entitled to any commission and/or other remuneration for all such work organised and/or arranged by the [Artist] and/or any third party prior to [date] regardless of whether or not such work shall be performed and/or completed during the existence of the agreement with the [Agent].

1.3   The [Agent] also agrees and undertakes that he shall not be entitled to receive any sums from the royalties received by the [Artiste] in respect of agreements concluded by the [Artiste] and/or any third party before [date].

T.058

The [Company] acknowledges that [Name] is already committed and entitled to carry out the following commitments and work for third parties during the Term of the Agreement as follows: [specify details/dates/organisation/role].

T.059

1.1 The [Manager] agrees that he/she shall not be entitled to any commission and/or other sums in respect of any work done and/or agreed to be carried out by the [Sportsperson] and/or any share of any advances, royalties and/or expenses from any biography, online account, hardback and paperback books, sound recordings, videos, films, merchandising and/or any other matter in any format and/or medium prior to the date of this agreement.

1.2 The matters covered in 1.1 shall include: [list in detail].

T.060

The [Company] agrees that it shall not be entitled to exploit the [Services/ Images/Films/Sound Recordings] in any form in any medium after the expiry and/or termination of this agreement whichever is the earliest without the prior written consent of [Name].

T.061

Any failure to renew and/or extend this agreement following the expiry date shall not be grounds for any claim and/or additional payments for any reason. The [Company] and the [Artists] both agree that neither party shall be entitled to make any claim for any sum for the failure to renew, extend and/or negotiate a further agreement.

T.062

The 'Option Period' shall begin on [date] at [time] and continue until [date/ time]. Thereafter unless the option has been exercised as required it shall have lapsed.

T.063

This agreement shall commence on the date of this agreement and shall continue until the expiry of the Term of the Agreement subject to the termination provisions in clause [–].

T.064

This agreement shall be effective from [date] and supersedes all previous arrangements relating to the freelance engagement of [Name] by the [Company] from the [Agent].

T.065

The [Company] engages and the [Agent] agrees to make available the freelance non-exclusive services of [Name] on first call to the [Company] in the capacity of [job description] as and when required by the Company for a period of [one] year commencing on [date] (referred to in this agreement as 'the Term').

T.066

1.1 The duration of the licence is for a minimum of [six] months.

1.2 The minimum term in 1.1 may continue thereafter for a further [number] consecutive periods of [six] months. Provided that the [Licensor] has not sent written notice by email to the [Company] [one] month prior to the start date of any new period that they do not wish to proceed with a new licence period. In such case the [Licensee] shall not have any right to any additional [six] month period after notice has been sent by the [Licensor].

T.067

'Term of the Agreement' shall commence on [date/event] and shall continue until [date/event] unless terminated by either party in accordance with the terms of this agreement.

T.068

'Duration of the Agreement' shall be deemed to have commenced on [date] and shall continue for the full period of [twelve] months unless extended and/or terminated in accordance with the terms of this agreement.

T.069

This agreement shall be deemed to have come into force on [date] at [time] and unless terminated earlier in accordance with the provisions of this agreement shall continue in force and effect for [number] [days/weeks/years] up to and including [date] and [time].

T.070

This agreement shall be automatically renewed for [one] [year] periods unless prior written notice of termination has been received from either party to the other at least [number] months prior to the anticipated expiry and/or the day before the renewal date. If such prior written notice is given by either party then this agreement shall terminate on the original expiry date and/or the day before any subsequent renewal date.

T.071

'Launch Date' shall mean the date by which the [Service/App/Software/Game] is intended to be functional and ready for access by [the public/authorised members of the Institute].

T.072

'The Term of the Agreement' shall start on [date] and continue until the expiry of a period of [three] years from the acceptance of the [Master Material] by the [Distributor]. Where the [Master Material] is not accepted then the [three] year period shall not start until the material is delivered and accepted as being of suitable technical quality.

T.073

'The Pilot Contract Period' shall commence subject to the delivery of the [Reproduction Material] by the [Licensor] on the date of the launch of the [Product/Work] in the [subject] market by the [Licensee] and/or [date] whichever is the earlier. The contract shall continue for a period of [number] months] and expire at the end of the last day. There is no automatic right to have the period renewed, extended and/or to enter into a new agreement thereafter.

T.074

The [Licensee] agrees and undertakes that it shall not grant any rights to any sub-licensee any sub-licence which would extend and/or be enforceable in any contract after [date/time] for any reason. The [Licensee] agrees that there shall also be no right to grant an additional period for any sell-off and/disposal of stock beyond [date].

T.075

1.1 This agreement may not be extended, rolled over, renewed and/or the Term of the Agreement changed at any time without the prior written consent and authority of [Name].

1.2 Nor shall [Name] be liable for any costs, charges and/or expenses which may arise due to the failure of the [Company] to agree an extension, renewal and/or reach a new agreement with [Name]. There shall be no obligation on the part of [Name] to do so.

T.076

'The Term of this Agreement' shall mean the start date of: [date] and the agreement shall continue for a period of [number] years from the date upon which a minimum of [number] copies of the [Product] are first distributed, sold and/or made available to the public in [country]. Where the [Product] is not released within [number] years then the agreement shall end on [date].

T.077

'The Term of the Agreement' shall begin on [date] and shall continue for a further [number] years from the date of delivery and acceptance of the [Research Material] for the [Project] to [Name] and/or [date] whichever is the latest.

T.078

It is agreed that neither party shall have the right to continue the annual agreement which starts on [date] and ends on [date] into the following year. A new agreement must be signed and agreed in each case and each agreement is a separate and complete document.

T.079

The [Licensee] acknowledges that after the expiry of the Term of this Agreement that the [Licensee] shall have no rights in the [Format/Service/App] and/or any adaptations and/or developments.

T.080

The [Licensee] agrees that at the end of the Term of this Agreement it shall execute any documentation and/or anything required by the [Licensor] to vest all copyright, intellectual property, trade mark and any other rights in any variations and/or developments in respect of the [Format] and/or any associated marketing in the [Licensor].

T.081

The [Company] agrees that it shall not be entitled to exploit the [Images/Video/Film/Sound Recordings] in any form and/or medium after the expiry and/or termination of the Term of this Agreement without the prior written consent of the [Author/Artist].

T.082

'The Term of the Agreement' shall commence on the date of this agreement which is [specify date] and shall continue until the expiry of [five] years from the date of the first transmission and/or broadcast of the [Film/Video/Sound Recording] by the [Company] on [specify channel] in [country]. In the event that the transmission and/or broadcast is delayed then the start of the period of [five] years shall be delayed until such time as the transmission and/or broadcast takes place.

T.083

'The Term of this Agreement' shall commence on [date] and shall continue for the full period of copyright and any extensions and/or renewals.

T.084

'The Term of this Agreement' shall commence on [date] and shall continue until [date].

T.085

'The Term of this Agreement' shall commence on [date] and shall expire on [date].

T.086

'The Term of this Agreement' shall begin on the date of this agreement and shall continue until the end date of [date].

T.087

'The Term of this Agreement' shall begin on the date of this agreement and shall continue for a period of [number] [days/months/years].

T.088

'The Term of this Agreement' shall be for a period of [three] months which shall start on [date] and expire on [date].

T.089

'The Term of the Agreement' shall begin upon acceptance of the [Physical Material] by the [Licensee] and shall continue until the [Licensee] has completed all the broadcasts and/or transmissions of the [Images/Videos/Films] authorised under this agreement and/or [date] whichever is the earliest.

T.090

'The Term of the Agreement' shall commence on [date] and continue for a period of [number] years and/or until the [Licensee] has completed all the transmissions of the [Series] whichever is the latest.

T.091

The Term of this Agreement cannot be extended by the [Licensee] for any reason whether due to delay by the [Licensor], force majeure and/or otherwise.

T.092

The duration of the Licence shall start on [date] and shall continue for a period of [number] years until [date]. Thereafter the [Licensee] shall have the right to renew the Licence for a further period of [number] years provided that it pays an additional fee of [number/currency] by [date].

T.093

The [Contributor] agrees that the [Company] shall be entitled to display the [Image/Article] on the [Blog] indefinitely and that there shall be no limit to the term of the agreement. Provided that the [Company] pays the [Contributor] an annual fee of [number/currency] in each year of the term of the agreement by [date] in each year. If any payment is not made by the agreed date in any year then the [Contributor] may serve the [Company] with [one] month's notice by [email/text message] to terminate the agreement.

T.094

The [Writer] only authorises the [Agent] to make agreements where the licence and/or duration of the term are limited to [number] years. The [Agent] agrees and undertakes that he/she cannot commit the [Writer] to any agreement which transfers and/or assigns any copyright and/or intellectual property rights and/or computer software rights and/or any other rights and/or interest owned and/or controlled by the [Writer].

T.095

The [Artist/Musician] agrees and undertakes to carry out his/her services to the best of his/her skill and ability. The [Artist/Musician] agrees that if for any reason all the planned dates of the work and tours listed in appendix C are not completed within the Term of the Agreement. That the [Artist/Musician] agrees to negotiate and extension for the sole purpose of completing the work and tours listed. Provided that the [Company] shall agree to pay a reasonable additional fee and costs and expenses to the [Artist/Musician] for such extension.

T.096

The [illustrator] agrees that where additional work is required on the [Project] beyond [date]. That the [Illustrator] shall offer his/her services to the [Company] for an additional period of [number] months at the same rates and on the same terms as this agreement.

T.097

The [Sponsor] agrees that there shall be no restriction on the period of time that the [Enterprise] may exploit and/or license and/or adapt the sound recordings, films, images and/or other material relating to the [Event/Festival].

T.098

The data, records and other material supplied by the [Distributor] is only valid for use by [Name] from [date/time] to [date/time]. There is no authority and/or permission granted to use, adapt, store and/or exploit any part outside of those dates and times.

T.099

This service and maintenance agreement shall commence on [date] with an initial trial period of [one] month. Provided that the trial period is satisfactory then the main agreement shall commence on [date] and continue until the end of the year on [date] until [time]. There is no automatic right to renew for a further period. Any new agreement concluded shall start with a new trial period.

TERMINATION

Film, Television and Video

T.100

The [Licensor] shall be entitled (in addition to all its other rights and remedies at law) to decide at its sole discretion to send the [Distributor] formal written to terminate this agreement with immediate effect on the following grounds:

1.1 That the [Distributor] shall have failed to pay any sums which may have been due and/or shall have failed to perform any other material obligation required and that the [Distributor] shall not have remedied any such failure within [number] days of notification by the [Licensor] as to the scope of the failure by the [Distributor].

1.2 That the [Distributor] either has and/or intends to make an arrangement and/or assignment and/or lien with any creditor and/or other third party and/or any bankruptcy and/or insolvency and/or other legal proceedings have been threatened and/or commenced against the [Distributor] which may affect the ability of the [Distributor] to function and operate as a solvent business and/or which may result in any voluntary and/or compulsory liquidation of assets (however this shall not include a reconstruction and/or amalgamation for which the approval of the [Licensor] has been sought and agreed.)

T.101

Upon the expiry and/or termination of this agreement any original master reproduction material, scripts, music cue sheets, images and photographs, marketing, merchandising and stocks of the [Videos/Films/Sound Recordings/Units] in the possession and/or under the control of the [Distributor] shall be packaged securely and delivered at the [Licensors'/Distributors'] cost to any address which may be notified at that time by the [Licensor] in [country].

T.102

Upon the expiry and/or termination of the Term of this Agreement the [Distributor] shall be entitled to sell-off existing stocks which have already been manufactured and produced by that date for a fixed period of [six] months from that end date on a non-exclusive basis. Provided that the [Distributor] agrees to continue to be bound by the terms and conditions of this agreement. After the end of the sell-off period all stocks which are unsold shall then be destroyed by the [Distributor] unless some other arrangement is agreed by the [Licensor].

T.103

1.1 Upon the expiry and/or termination of the Term of this Agreement the [Distributor] shall within [one] month provide the [Licensor] with a full list of all master material, marketing, merchandising and stock which shall include its location, condition and how it is stored. The [Distributor] shall enter into negotiations for the [Licensor] to purchase all such material at cost price. The sum agreed may be set-off against some of the payments which may be due from the [Distributor] to the [Licensor] in respect of royalties. The [Licensor] shall be responsible for making the arrangements for the collection and delivery of all such material. The [Licensor] shall bear the cost of any delivery, insurance, custom and excise duties and/or other charges that may need to be incurred.

1.2 The [Distributor] shall not be entitled to sell-off and/or dispose of any the stocks to any other person and/or business unless directed to do so under the instructions of the [Licensor].

T.104

1.1 In the event of the termination and/or expiry of this agreement for any reason the [Distributor] shall immediately cease to have any rights in respect of the [Units/Films/Images/Sound Recordings/Videos/Discs].

1.2 The [Distributor] agrees and accepts that all copyright, intellectual property rights, master material, stock, marketing, packaging and artwork material and all electronic and digital material, merchandising, press reviews and reports, advertising, posters, labels, discs, sub-licensee, agency and distribution arrangements, mechanical copyright clearances and payments, and performing rights clearances and payments and copies of all sales databases, accounting and royalty records shall belong to and be assigned and/or transferred to the [Licensor] including any new material which has been created and/or developed during the Licence Period.

1.3 The [Distributor] shall not have any claim, interest and/or rights nor shall the [Distributor] be due any sums from the [Licensor].

1.4 The [Licensor] shall arrange for and bear the cost of the collection of all material in 1.2 and any other material in any format and/or medium of any nature which relate to the [Units/Films/Images/Sound Recordings/ Videos/Discs].

1.5 The [Distributor] shall only be entitled to retain those business records which it requires for compliance with legislation for any government agency and a copy of any documents and financial records it requires for its business use.

T.105

1.1 Any order for [Films/Videos/Units/DVDs/Discs] accepted in writing by the [Distributor] prior to the date of termination shall be valid. In the event of any order being received after the date of termination and/ or during the period of notice the [Licensor] shall have the right at its option to accept and/or reject such order provided that such action does not cause a breach of contract between the [Distributor] and its customers. If the [Licensor] accepts the order in writing the terms of this agreement shall apply.

1.2 After the date of termination the [Distributor] shall supply the [Licensor] with a complete list of all material of any nature of which the [Distributor] is aware which exists directly and/or indirectly in any format related to the [Films/Videos/Units/DVDs/Discs] whether held by the [Distributor] and/or any third party including but not limited to details relating to all copies of master material, artwork, stills, promotional and marketing material, sales literature, posters, merchandising, databases mailshot lists and any list of purchasers. Contracts with third party sub-licensees, agents and distributors; together with copies of all expenditure, payments for clearances and consents, registrations, accounting and royalty records and/or any other financial matter. At the request of the [Licensor] the [Distributor] shall pay for the delivery of all such material to a nominated address in [country].

1.3 After the date of termination the [Distributor] shall immediately cease to use any of all trade marks, service marks, logos, images, videos, films, slogans and/or music and/or sound recordings related to the [Licensor] and/or the [Films/Videos/Units/DVDs/Discs].

1.4 The [Distributor] shall co-operate with the [Licensor] to ensure the transfer of ownership and the assignment of any copyright, intellectual property rights, computer software rights, trade marks and/or other interest and/or registration which may have been acquired by the [Distributor] under this agreement to the [Licensor].

T.106

1.1 In the event of the termination and/or expiry of this agreement the [Licensee] shall immediately cease to use for the manufacture of the [Units] of the [Film/Video/Sound Recordings] the master material supplied by the [Licensor] and/or any copies and/or adaptations developed by the [Licensee].

1.2 The [Licensor] shall be entitled to instruct the [Licensee] to make arrangements for the delivery of all master material and/or any copies and/or adaptations developed, stored and/or controlled by the [Licensee] to the [Licensor] at the [Licensors'] cost and expense.

1.3 In the event that the [Licensor] shall not wish to instruct the [Licensee] to deliver any material in 1.2. Then the [Licensor] may issue instructions to the [Licensee] to erase and/or destroy material and to provide a statement of that fact signed by the [Licensee].

1.4 The [Licensee] shall have the non-exclusive right to sell-off stocks of the [Units] previously manufactured under this agreement which exist at the date of termination and/or expiry for a period of [three] months. At the completion of such sell-off period the [Licensee] shall destroy all remaining stocks of the [Units] and cease to offer them for sale. If so requested by the [Licensor] the [Licensee] shall provide evidence of the sell-off period and the destruction of the remaining stock.

T.107

In the event of the termination of this agreement by the [Licensor] for any reason any advance against royalties already paid (whether recouped or not) shall be retained by the [Licensor]. This retention of any advance shall be without prejudice to any other rights, remedies and/or claims by the [Licensor] against the [Licensee] and/or any sub-licensee, agent and/or distributor.

T.108

1.1 In the event that the [Assignor] does not deliver the [Series Material] and/or the [Assignee] does not market and distribute the [Series] in the form of [Videos/Downloads/Electronic Files] as set out in this agreement. The parties shall endeavour to resolve the matter by discussions for a period of [number] months. Thereafter it is agreed that they shall appoint [Name] as an unofficial arbitrator whose decision shall not be binding. The cost of the services of [Name] to act in this manner shall be paid by which both parties equally. The parties agree that the decision of [Name] shall not be binding but that both parties shall act in good faith to resolve the problems that have arisen. That neither party shall instigate legal proceedings until [Name] has delivered a recommendation and decision as to how to resolve the matter.

1.2 Where no decision is made by [Name] after a period of [number] months from the start date of the appointment of [Name]. Then either party may take such legal action as they deem necessary in the circumstances.

T.109

In addition to any other rights and remedies at law the [Assignor] and/or the [Assignee] may by giving written notice to the other defaulting party terminate this agreement on the grounds that the other party has defaulted and/or has failed to account and/or make payments as required and/or has committed one or more serious breaches of the terms which have not been remedied despite a request for them to do so.

T.110

The [Licensee] agrees that if the [Licensor's] Royalties received by the [Licensor] are less than [number/currency] by [date]. Then the [Licensor] may terminate this agreement by notice in writing to that effect that the target level of royalties has not been achieved.

T.111

If the agreement is revoked, terminated and/or withdrawn the [Licensee] shall immediately revoke, terminate and/or withdraw all other agreements, arrangements and/or business dealings with third parties including sub-licensees, sub-distributors and/or agents in respect of the [Film/Series/Sound Recordings].

T.112

This Agreement may also be terminated without prejudice to the rights of the parties on the following additional grounds:

1.1 That the [Licensor] and/or the [Licensee] has committed a material breach which is not capable of being remedied and/or which has not remedied within [seven] days of the matter being notified in writing.

1.2 That the [Licensee] has been declared bankrupt, insolvent and/or is likely to cease trading due to debts and/or its inability to meet its production and/or financial commitments.

1.3 That the conduct and/or activities and/or public and/or social media statements of the directors, employees and/or business of the [Licensees'] is likely to be prejudicial and/or damaging to the [Licensor's] business, directors and/or employees.

T.113
Upon the expiry and/or termination of this agreement all copyright, intellectual property rights, computer software rights, merchandising rights and/or any other right and/or interest in the [Film/Video/Sound Recordings] and/or any adaptation and/or format and/or translation including video on demand, DVDs, electronic files and/or any other material of any nature supplied, developed, produced and/or sub-licensed by the [Licensee] shall revert to the [Licensor] and shall be returned at the [Licensee's] cost. An undertaking shall be given by the [Licensee] that neither they nor any third party of which they are aware holds any other rights and/or material and that none will be exploited by them in the future.

T.114
The [Licensor] shall be entitled to terminate this agreement before the expiry date on the grounds that the [Licensee] is reproducing, distributing and/or marketing the [Film/Video/Unit/Disc] with and/or in association with other products, persons, services and/or companies which are damaging to the reputation of the [Licensor] and/or likely to bring the [Licensor] into disrepute in any part of the world.

T.115
The [Licensee] may terminate this agreement where the [Licensor] has misrepresented the cost of copyright clearance and other payments for the [Film] to be paid by the [Licensee] in order to exercise the rights granted.

T.116
If at any time both the [Finance Company] and the [Production Company] decide to cancel the production of the [Film/Video/Series] the parties may by agreement in writing terminate this agreement and agree that:

1.1 The [Production Company] shall take immediate steps to halt any further expenditure and/or commitments relating to the production of [Film/Video/Series] and shall deliver to the [Finance Company] as soon as possible a detailed statement of the expenditure incurred and/or due which has been certified as accurate and complete.

1.2 The [Production Company] shall be obliged to reimburse the [Finance Company] with any expenditure provided and/or arranged by the [Finance Company] which has not and/or will not be used for the production of the [Film/Video/Series] after the date of termination of this agreement. Such sums shall either be repaid to a third party and/or may be retained by the [Finance Company] dependent on the original source of the monies.

T.117

The [Production Company] and/or the [Finance Company] shall each be entitled at their own discretion to give written notice to the other party to terminate this agreement with [number] days' written notice if the other party:

1.1 shall fail to perform and/or fulfil any material obligations which may be required under this agreement and despite having been notified of the material default shall have failed to have remedied the problem within [one] calendar month of such notification.

1.2 shall be subject to legal proceedings which may result in insolvency, bankruptcy and/or the dissolution of the registered company in [country].

1.3 shall seek to make any arrangement with its creditors and/or is seeking to voluntarily dissolve the company and/or to reconstruct the share ownership and/or to be bought out by another company and/or to sell and/or assign the ownership of the company to a third party without the prior written consent of the other party.

T.118

1.1 The [Production Company] and/or the [Finance Company] shall still be entitled to exercise any rights and/or remedies which may be available to them in law if this agreement is terminated by the [Finance Company] due to the failure of the [Production Company] to abide by the terms of this agreement.

1.2 Without prejudice to any other rights and/or remedies to which the [Finance Company] is entitled the [Finance Company] shall be entitled to give written notice to the [Production Company] to deliver by a specified date to the [Finance Company] all master material, films, computer software and electronically stored material, prints, negatives, sound recordings, music, contracts, licences, consents and permissions, scripts, correspondence, accounting records and statements and any other documents and/or material in any format and/or medium in the possession and/or under the control of the [Production Company] relating to the [Films/Series/Videos] so that the [Finance Company] may arrange to have the [Films/Series/Videos] completed by a third party.

1.3 The [Production Company] shall have the right to share with the [Finance Company] the net receipts from the distribution and exploitation of the [Films/Series/Videos] which is then completed by a third party. The percentage share of any royalties to be paid from the net receipts to be allocated to the [Production Company] shall be subject to further agreement between the parties. The terms must be agreed before the exploitation and/or distribution of the [Films/Series/Videos] in any country.

T.119

Either party may serve written notice on the other party to terminate this licence on the following grounds:

1.1 That the other party has committed a material breach of this agreement and has failed to remedy the defect within [number] days of receipt of written notice from the non-defaulting party and/or

1.2 If such breach was and/or is not capable of being remedied has failed to pay compensation of an amount agreed between the parties and/or

1.3 If they cannot agree the basis of the compensation the parties have agreed to appoint a mediator and/or arbitrator and/or

1.4 If the other party has been threatened with legal proceedings which are likely to result in the dissolution of the company and/or insolvency and/or the company is trading but is unable to pay its debts and/or the company intends to voluntarily cease trading and/or to dissolve and no longer be registered and/or if a third party is appointed to sell and/or dispose of the assets of the company.

T.120

If this agreement is terminated and/or expires then the [Licensee] agrees and undertakes to execute without any further payment such documents as may be required by the [Licensor] in order to ensure the assignment of any copyright, intellectual property rights, trade marks, computer software rights, music, sound recordings, images and/or any material in any electronic form and/or any merchandising material and/or products and/or any other material in any format in any medium relating to the [Film/Video/Products/Programmes] and any script, title, character, slogan and catchphrase and/or any translation and/or other adaptation to the [Licensor].

T.121

1.1 If this agreement is terminated and/or expires then both the [Licensee] and any sub-licensees shall be obliged to either return all master copies of the material for the [Film/Video/Series] and all marketing and stock as directed by the [Licensor] at the [Licensor's/Licensee's] cost.

1.2 In the event that the [Licensor] does not want the material in 1.1 returned then the [Licensor] may instruct the [Licensee] and all sub-licensees to destroy all copies and to provide evidence of compliance with that request.

T.122

The [Company] and the [Production Company] agree that:

1.1 If either party shall commit a substantial breach of the agreement which cannot be resolved and/or

1.2 If either party shall commit a substantial breach of the agreement which cannot be remedied within [number] days of written notice notifying the breach and requesting that it be rectified and/or

1.3 If either party shall go into liquidation (other than for amalgamation or reconstruction purposes) and/or becomes insolvent and/or has an administrator and/or receiver appointed over any of its assets and/or fails to comply with a court order and/or is unwilling and/or unable to pay its debts.

Then the other party shall be entitled without prejudice to its other remedies to terminate the agreement by notice in writing to the party which shall be in breach. In the event of any breach by the [Production Company] the whole amount of all sums paid by the [Company] which have not been spent on items set out in the Budget shall immediately become repayable and the [Production Company] shall pay such sums upon demand.

T.123

In addition to any other rights and remedies at law either party may by giving written notice to the other party terminate this agreement on the grounds that:

1.1 The other party has failed to account and/to or make payments as required under this agreement;

1.2 The other party has committed a serious breach of is obligations and has not rectified the position within [specify period];

1.3 The other party has gone into voluntary and/or involuntary liquidation;

1.4 The other party has been declared insolvent and/or gone into administration;

1.5 The other party has not distributed and/or marketed and/or sold any copies of the [Work/Film/Video/Units] for more than [number] months.

T.124

Each party shall be entitled to terminate this agreement immediately by serving written notice on the other party if that other party shall:

1.1 commit a breach of any of its major obligations under this agreement which is not capable of being remedied and/or is not remedied within [seven] days of receipt of notice of the default and/or

1.2 intend to and/or have made an arrangement for the benefit of its creditors and/or legal proceedings have been threatened and/or taken to dissolve the company and declare it insolvent and/or legal action has been threatened and/or taken against any director to declare them bankrupt and/or steps have been taken to appoint a receiver, administrator, and/or other third party to manage, sell and/or dispose of the assets of the company and/or to dilute the shareholding and/or to reconstruct the company.

T.125
The [Licensee] shall have the right to terminate this agreement at an earlier date where the [Licensor] has made allegations against the [Licensee] regarding the content, production, reproduction and/or exploitation of the [Film/Recording] which damage the reputation of the [Licensee] and/or effect the value of the shares, assets and/or goodwill of the [Licensee]. In such event the [Licensee] shall be entitled to serve notice of termination with the grounds and to seek to reach a settlement of the matter based upon the completion of the agreement to that date.

T.126
The failure by the [Assignor] to supply the master material and/or copyright clearance and other contractual agreements required in clause [-] to the [Assignee] by [date] shall entitle the [Assignor] to terminate this agreement and not pay the sums due in clause [-].

General Business and Commercial

T.127

1.1 Both parties agree that in the event of a material breach by either party, the non-defaulting party shall notify the defaulting party of details of the breach and give them an opportunity to rectify the position within [specify period] of receipt of the notice in each case.

1.2 In the event that the defaulting party does not so remedy the position then the non-defaulting party may terminate this agreement immediately by service of a notice in writing to that effect.

1.3 A material breach shall include but not be limited to: failure to account, failure to pay royalties, the failure to obtain the required consents, approvals and/or licences from third parties and the failure to perform the terms of this agreement.

T.128

Where one party is unable and/or unwilling to carry out and/or comply with the terms of the agreement. Then that party shall be deemed to be in breach of the agreement and shall have [one] calendar month from the date of the default to remedy the breach. Failure to correct the breach shall result in the agreement being automatically terminated and does not require service of notice. The non-defaulting party shall then be entitled to reclaim all sums paid under the agreement but shall not be entitled to claim for any other costs, losses, expenses and/or damages that may arise whether directly and/or indirectly in consequence of the breach and/or the termination.

T.129

Where one party defaults under this agreement for any reason and the other party confirms that he/she shall agree to a delayed delivery date. That does not entitle the defaulting party to seek to delay the delivery date for a second time and the non-defaulting party may serve notice of termination of the agreement and a full refund of all payments made to date for failure to deliver by the agreed delayed date.

T.130

1.1 The [Executive] is required either to deliver to the [Company] and/or to arrange for the [Company] to collect at the end of his/her employment (howsoever terminated) all papers, documents, keys, credit cards, security passes, pagers, mobiles, cars, and all other material and/or property belonging to the [Company] and/or any third party authorised by the [Company] of any nature.

1.2 The [Executive] agrees and undertakes that from the date of termination of the agreement he/she shall no longer have the right to use the passwords, codes and security access procedures and/or email and/or mobile and/or other accounts and/or software and/or any other material owned and/or controlled by the [Company].

1.3 The [Executive] shall not be required and/or under any obligation to commit to and/or sign an undertaking that all such property has been returned.

1.4 The [Executive] shall have the right to retain all gifts, bonuses and any gadgets and/or products given to the [Executive] by the [Company]. Any share option shall lapse at the date of termination and/or expiry of the agreement. The [Executive] shall be entitled to retain documents and records for the purposes of any claim and/or legal action against the [Company] and/or any dispute regarding any medical and/or dental cover, national insurance and/or tax.

1.5 The [Executive] shall not be obliged to return any material to the [Company] where there is a dispute regarding ownership unless ordered to do so by a court of law in [country]. The [Company] shall have no right to search the physical person of the [Executive] and/or to seek to access personal data and information and the [Executive] may arrange for the erasure of any data before returning any material.

T.131

This agreement may be terminated by the [Company] without any period of notice and without payment in lieu if [Name] shall at any time:

1.1 be guilty of serious misconduct and/or any other conduct which is likely to seriously adversely affect the interests of the [Company]; and/or

1.2 becomes incapable of fulfilling his/her duties for more than [number] [days/months] due to mental health problems which he/she has confirmed cannot be resolved and which prevent him/her from fulfilling any part of the terms of this agreement.

1.3 becomes unable to attend the location for the performance of the duties required due to relocation to another country for more than [number] [days/months].

Such termination shall be without prejudice to any other rights and/or remedies of the [Company] against [Name].

T.132

The [Company] shall be entitled to terminate this agreement at any time with immediate effect in the event that the [Employee] has:

1.1 committed a serious act of misconduct which could form the basis for criminal and/or civil proceedings in respect of his/her employment and/or personal life.

1.2 disclosed confidential information and/or data to a third party who supplies and/or sells information, data and images to the media, newspapers, magazines and/or any online news operation and/or any online news operation and/or agency and/or person used by them. There shall not need to be evidence that the disclosure has resulted in adverse publicity which has seriously damaged the interests and/or value of the shares of the [Company].

1.3 been diagnosed as mentally ill and/or suffers with recurrent psychiatric problems and/or is aggressive, threatening and/or violent at work and/or has tested positive for illegal drugs in a medical by the [Company].

1.4   failed to carry out the duties required and/or is in serious and repeated breach under this agreement. That despite formal warnings, and/or being the subject of a disciplinary hearing the problem has not been remedied and the breach or non-observance of this agreement has continued.

Such termination shall be without prejudice to any other rights and/or claims of the [Company] against the [Employee].

T.133

The [Company] may terminate the agreement with [Name] with the required legal minimum notice if he/she shall:

1.1   be guilty of any serious failure and/or neglect to carry out his/her duties and/or commit any serious breach of any of the terms of this agreement; and/or

1.2   has repeatedly despite warnings refused to follow the reasonable directions of a [Senior Manager/other] and/or has failed a medical examination due to drink and/or drugs; and/or

1.3   become unable due to mental and/or physical ill-health for more than [specify period] be incapable of performing his/her duties; and/or

1.4   be unable and/or unwilling to comply with any health and safety policies and guidelines that may be required; and/or

1.5   be convicted of a serious criminal offence in any part of the world; and/or

1.6   commit any serious act of misconduct and/or neglect whether or not in connection with his/her duties and/or commits any act which might seriously affect his/her ability to carry out his/her duties; and/or

1.7   commit any act of dishonesty, fraud, theft, malicious damage and/or post any offensive, derogatory and/or defamatory comments on social media regarding the management and/or [Company]; and/or

1.8   secretly films, videos and/or records any person, premises, services and/or products at the [Company] and/or makes sound recordings without consent and/or makes copies of any material for which he/she does not have any authorised access.

T.134

The [Company] shall be entitled at its sole discretion to request that the [Manager] be on paid leave from the [Company] for a period of up to [three] months] for the purpose of investigating allegations concerning the conduct of the [Manager] and/or for any other reason.

T.135

1.1 Without prejudice to any claim, for damages, losses, interest and/or any other form of compensation and/or restitution and/or any other remedy which either party may have against the other under this agreement. Where the agreement with [Name] is terminated by the [Company] for any reason regardless of the grounds. It is agreed that [Name] shall return any car, mobile, charge cards, laptop, security pass and any other material supplied by the [Company] where ownership has been retained by the [Company]. It shall not apply to any material which has been gifted, purchased and/or donated to [Name]. Where legal proceedings are pending and any documents, images, emails, reports, films, sound recordings, products and/or other material are required by [Name] for that purpose. Then this category of material may only be returned under an order of a court.

1.2 There is no obligation on [Name] to provide any list of the material in any format and/or medium in his/her possession and/or control at any time. Where [Name] has obtained any material without the consent of the [Company] the burden shall be on the [Company] to prove that he/she was not entitled to do so.

1.3 [Name] shall be entitled to keep copies and/or evidence of any of the material and/or property which he/she returns to the [Company] where he/she is requested to do so by his/her legal advisors and/or other professional consultants at any time where such material is relevant to any potential legal action by [Name] against the [Company] and/or an investigation by a government agency and/or organisation.

T.136

The [Employee] may terminate the employment by giving notice of termination as set out below:

1.1 If the [Employee] has less than [twelve] months' consecutive service he/she shall provide [four] weeks' notice.

1.2 If the [Employee] has more than [twelve] months but less than [five] years' consecutive service he/she shall provide [six] weeks' notice.

1.3 If the [Employee] has more than [five] years' service he/she shall provide [eight] weeks' notice.

1.4 Alternatively instead of 1.1, 1.2 and 1.3 the [Employee] may terminate his/her employment by not receiving payment of any sums in lieu of notice and terminate the employment immediately. It is agreed by the [Company] that special consideration shall be given to the [Employee] where the person is leaving due to ill-health and/or any other medical reason and the [Company] agrees to negotiate the terms of departure in each case.

T.137

In the event of any serious failure, default and/or misconduct on the part of [Name] in respect of his/her performance of this agreement and/or his/her conduct on the premises of the [Company] at any time. The [Company] shall have the right to terminate the agreement without any written and/or verbal notice period. The [Company] shall be entitled to inform [Name] that the agreement is terminated and shall cease immediately. The [Company] shall only be liable to [Name] to the date of termination and thereafter shall not be bound to pay any further sums. No payment shall be due to [Name] for such lack of a notice period and/or any other damages.

T.138

Either party may terminate the employment by giving notice of termination as specified in the [Union/other] Agreement attached in appendix B.

T.139

This Agreement may be terminated by the [Executive] and/or the [Company] by giving [number] months' notice to the other party in the first year and [number] months' notice during the next five years, and [number] months' notice thereafter from [date].

Subject to the Grievance Procedure as set out in Schedule A which is attached and forms part of this document. The appointment may be terminated at once by the [Company] without prior notice and without pay in lieu if the [Executive] shall at any time:

1.1 be guilty of serious misconduct and/or other conduct including criminal convictions likely to affect prejudicially the interests and/or value and/or reputation of the [Company];

1.2 become physically and/or mentally incapable of functioning normally due to physical, psychiatric and/or mental problems;

1.3 make an unauthorised public statement which directly criticises the [Company] and/or exposes any failures and/or investigations at the [Company] without authority of the Board of the [Company];

1.4 be in material default and/or breach and/or not perform any terms of this agreement;

1.5 fail to observe required health and safety guidelines and/or any code of practice and/or other matters which the [Company] is bound to comply with and which has been brought to the attention of the [Executive] and which thereafter he/she has still not adhered to the procedures, practices and/or guidelines.

Such termination shall be without prejudice to any claim, remedies and/or the right of the [Company] to institute any legal proceedings in any country.

T.140
In addition to any other rights and remedies at law and notwithstanding clauses [-]. This agreement may be terminated by the [Company], by giving written notice to the [Executive] where the [Executive] has failed to attend to his/her duties for a continuous period of [specify duration] or more. The [Company] undertakes not to invoke this procedure where medical certificates have been provided for the period by the [Executive].

T.141
The [Company] shall have the right to request the [Executive] be on paid leave from the [Company] for a total period not exceeding [one] month for the purpose of investigating any allegations concerning the conduct, actions, health and/or some other matter relating to the [Executive] and/or his/her agreement with the [Company].

T.142
In the event that the agreement is terminated by the [Company] and/or the [Executive]. It is agreed that the [Executive] shall within [number] days of receipt of a written request by the [Company] return and/or arrange for collection of all material of any nature in any medium in the possession and/or under the control of the [Executive] which belongs to the [Company]. Where any material is required by the [Executive] for the purpose of potential evidence in future legal proceedings against the [Company] then all such material shall not be returned but placed with his/her legal advisors.

T.143

1.1 [Name] shall be entitled to retain the following items and products in the event that the agreement is terminated at any time by the [Company]: [specify and list].

1.2 Where the [Company] terminates the agreement for any reason at any time the [Company] agrees to pay [Name] an additional fee of [number/currency] in compensation. Provided that [Name] shall not seek to make any claim and/or institute any legal proceedings in respect of the termination.

1.3 [Name] accepts and agrees that he/she shall only be entitled to be paid any sums due under the agreement to the date of termination. That the

[Company] is not required to provide any reason for terminating the agreement.

T.144

The [Executive] shall have the right at the end of his/her employment to keep a selection of personal items relating to their history at the [Company] including business cards, minutes, papers, products, data, software and other material provided that they are for personal use and not for publication and remain confidential where appropriate.

T.145

The [Company] shall only have the right to terminate this agreement if the [Employee] has significantly breached one of the terms of this agreement and/or is unavailable permanently to carry out his/her work and/or is the subject of criminal proceedings for which imprisonment is likely and/or consistently refuses to follow reasonable requests at work and/or is repeatedly abusive, offensive and/or late at work.

T.146

1.1 There shall be no right under this agreement for the [Company] to summarily dismiss and/or remove the [Executive] from the premises without notice under any circumstances at any time.

1.2 Where the [Company] has a complaint about the conduct of the [Executive] and/or alleges that he/she is in breach of this agreement then the [Company] shall set out all the reasons in writing to the [Executive] supported by the evidence.

1.3 The [Executive] shall be provided with the opportunity to refute the alleged breach and/or allegations and an independent expert shall be appointed which shall be agreed between the parties to review all the arguments from both parties at the [Company's] cost. The decision of the independent expert who shall decide the case shall [not] be binding on both parties.

1.4 The [Executive] agrees to be on paid leave with the [Company] from the date on which the complaints and/or allegations are made until the matter is resolved and/or the agreement is terminated by either party and/or some other circumstance shall arise as a result of the actions of either party.

1.5 The [Company] agrees that it shall not be entitled to make any public statement to the media in any form regarding the [Executive] during the period of the existence of this agreement without his/her consent and approval.

T.147
Where the [Company] wishes to terminate any agreement with [Name] then the [Company] agrees to provide at least [number] months' notice to [Name] in advance and to provide a reference to assist [Name] to seek a position with a third party in a similar role.

T.148
In the event that the [Employee] becomes incapable of performing his/her duties under this agreement to the extent that the [Employee] is deemed by a duly qualified medical practitioner to be suffering from a permanent disability and/or impairment which makes its unsafe to continue in the role. The [Company] shall endeavour to offer the [Employee] an alternative role which he/she is capable of fulfilling on the same pay level. If the [Employee] refuses the alternative role then the [Company] have the right to terminate this agreement subject to the [Employee's] statutory rights and/or any other payments which may be due.

T.149
The [Company] shall pay the [Manager] in respect of the following absences from his/her work by reason of physical and/or mental incapacity as follows provided that he/she has complied with the required procedures for leave of absence and/or for payment:

1.1 After less than [three] months' service payment shall be at the full salary rate for one week and for the next week only at half the salary rate.

1.2 After [three] to [twelve] months' service payment shall be at the full salary rate for [two] weeks and at half the salary rate for the next [two] weeks thereafter.

1.3 After [one] to [two] years' service the full salary rate shall be paid for [four] weeks and half the salary rate paid for the following [four] weeks.

1.4 Thereafter payments shall be adjusted accordingly dependant on the length of service subject to a maximum entitlement of [twenty-six] weeks] at full pay and [twenty-six] weeks at half pay in any one year and any period of continuous absence.

T.150
If [Name] is absent from work due to ill-health and/or incapacity for [sixty] days or more in any one year whether continuous or not. Then the [Company] reserves the right to terminate the contract at once by notice in writing.

T.151
If the [Employee] receives statutory payments which the [Company] is obliged to pay which later are confirmed as not having been due based

on the circumstances and/or to which the [Employee] is later found not to be entitled for any reason. The [Company] shall be entitled to for any reason deduct and recoup such overpaid sums from any other subsequent payments due to the [Employee] under this agreement.

T.152

1.1 Where an [Employee] is absent from work the [Employee] must notify his/her manager as soon as possible.

1.2 The [Employee] agrees to provide the [Company] with as much notice as possible in the event that the [Employee] is unable whether as a result of ill-health, incapacity and/or otherwise to perform any of his/her obligations under this agreement.

1.3 The [Employee] agrees to provide a medical certificate for periods of ill-health, incapacity and/or other personal injury of more than one week and thereafter at weekly intervals. Together with a final certificate before resuming normal duties.

1.4 The [Employee] shall not be entitled to payment by the Company for ill-health, incapacity and/or other personal injury after the date on which the employment has ended either by notice of termination and/or by expiry.

1.5 If the [Employee] has ill-health, incapacity and/or personal injury on a Bank or Public Holiday, the Company will not grant additional leave. However such days will not be set against paid leave entitlement. If the [Employee] has ill-health, incapacity and/or personal injury whilst on annual holiday he/she will be entitled to take holiday leave at a later date within the holiday year period provided that a medical certificate has been provided to confirm the facts.

1.6 Where legally entitled to do so the [Company] may set off payments received by the [Employee] as statutory sick pay against sums due to be paid by the [Company].

T.153
If the [Employee] is absent from duty without permission and/or without any valid reason acceptable to the [Company]. The [Company] reserves the right to withhold payment and/or to deduct from his/her salary a proportionate sum which would have been paid if the absence has not been unauthorised.

T.154
The [Company] shall not have the right to deduct from any salary, fees, costs and expenses due to [Name] any sums which the [Company] wishes

to recoup for absence, incapacity, ill-health and/or otherwise at any time unless agreed with [Name] in advance.

T.155
If at a later date [Name] is discovered to have represented that they have a curriculum vitae and/or qualifications and/or work experience which is/are untrue and which would materially affect their ability to fulfil the work required by the [Company]. Then the [Company] shall be entitled to terminate the agreement with immediate effect as they think fit but shall not be entitled to seek to reclaim any sums paid under the agreement.

T.156
Each contracting party may at their own discretion and without being required to pay compensation of any nature terminate the contract by serving formal notice [two] months in advance of the final termination date to the other party.

T.157
The [Company] may terminate the contract at any time during its performance subject to the payment of fair compensation with respect to the outstanding matters, However, such sum shall not exceed the total value of the outstanding matters under the contract.

T.158
The [Company] may terminate the contract in whole and/or in part as of right and without instituting legal proceedings in the event that the [Supplier/Contributor/Name] and/or their associated trading company, parent company and/or subsidiaries are made bankrupt, dissolved, declared insolvent, put into administration, have ceased trading and/or have been wound up by a Court Order and/or the main assets disposed of to a third party and/or the business has been amalgamated with another and/or the business has been restructured and/or relocated outside [country].

T.159
This contract may be terminated by either party at any time by written and/or verbal notice to the other and the specification of an end date.

T.160
1.1   In the event of the termination of this agreement by the [Contractor] the [Contractor] shall complete any work and projects which have already been agreed and costed which the [Contractor] has already agreed to complete. The [Company] agrees to pay the [Contractor] for all such work and projects which it completes to a satisfactory standard.

1.2　In the event of termination of this agreement by the [Company] the work and projects shall cease as set out in the notice of termination. The [Company] shall pay the [Contractor] for the work and projects as far as they have been completed up to the final date of termination.

T.161

Either party shall be entitled to terminate this agreement immediately by serving written notice to the other including by email if that other party shall:

1.1　commit a breach of any of its major obligations under this agreement which are not capable of remedy and/or which are capable of remedy but which are not rectified within [one] month of receipt of notice; and/or

1.2　make any arrangement for the benefit of its creditors and/or any legal proceedings have been commenced by a third party against that party regarding the non-payment of debt and/or a claim for personal injury and/or death has been made and/or is pending which is likely to expose the party to the payment of significant damages, costs, legal fees and/or other losses which may cause the party to trade while insolvent and/or to be unable to pay its suppliers and/or any other third party and/or some other matter which would affect the financial stability of the party.

The parties agree that termination under this clause shall not prejudice the rights and remedies of the parties. All terms and conditions set out in this agreement which relate to the period after the expiry and/or termination of this agreement shall continue in full force and effect.

T.162

The undertakings, terms and indemnity in [specify clauses] provided by [Company/Name] shall survive the expiry and/or termination of this agreement for [number] years and continue until [date] whichever is the earlier. The clauses shall only be revoked at another date by written agreement between both parties.

T.163

The clauses [specify details] which relate to the undertakings and terms agreed by the [Licensee/Distributor] shall survive the termination and/or expiry of this agreement and shall continue until such time as all the accounting statements and payments due have been received and the [Licensor/Company] no longer wishes to make any claim under the indemnity and there are no outstanding matters to be resolved between the parties.

T.164

The [Company] shall have the right to terminate this agreement before the expiry date in the event that the [Enterprise] and/or any officer discloses confidential data, information and/or artwork, films, videos, sound recordings and/or images to the media and/or any competitor at any time. In such event the [Company] may notify the [Enterprise] of the termination of the agreement with immediate effect. No further payments shall be made to the [Enterprise] after the termination date and the [Company] shall be under no further liability to the [Enterprise].

T.165
Where this agreement is contingent upon the conclusion of another agreement by the [Company] with a third party. Where this agreement has been signed the [Company] but the third party agreement is not concluded for any reason within [number] [weeks/months]. The [Company] shall have the right to terminate this agreement and to cease to pay any further sums which may fall due for any reason.

T.166

1.1   Where the [Company] and/or the majority of its assets are sold in whole and/or part to one or more other third parties.

1.2   Then it is agreed between the parties that the successor in title to the [Company] in whole and/or part shall have the right to terminate this agreement by notice in writing within [number] months of the transfer of any such title to the successor.

1.3   The [Supplier/Contributor/Name] shall have the right to terminate any agreement which is transferred and/or assigned to any third party whether in whole and/or part.

Internet, Websites and Apps

T.167
This agreement may be terminated by notice in writing at any stage by either party and any obligations, undertakings and payments due shall continue until and/or be made until the termination date and time stipulated.

T.168
The [Company] may at its absolute discretion may terminate any agreement and cease to provide any service and/or to manufacture, distribute and sell any products and//or market any other material at any time. The [Company] shall not be required to serve a period of notice and/or to provide any reason. The [Company] shall only be liable to refund any sums already paid to the [Company] for services and/or any other matter which will now not be performed and/or fulfilled. The [Company] shall not be liable for any costs, expenses, damages and/or losses which may arise as a direct and/or indirect result of any such termination.

T.169

Where a [Customer] has entered into a monthly subscription [Service/Supply/Access] agreement with the [Company]. The [Customer] may cancel and/or terminate the [Service/Supply/Access] arrangement by notice in writing and/or by telephone and/or by email to the [Company] [number] days prior to the next payment date. In the event that notice is not received before the payment date. Then the agreement shall terminate on the day before the next payment date.

T.170

The agreement shall continue for periods of [one] year and may be terminated by notice in writing at any time before the end date of each such yearly period and the start date of the next. There shall be an obligation on the [Customer] to pay the full sum due for the year if notice is not received before the start date in each year. No sum shall be waived and/or reduced by the [Company] whether or not the [Customer] does not want to receive the [Service/Products/Cover] and/or has served notice at a later date to cancel the agreement. There may be circumstances in which the [Company] may decide at its discretion to reach a different decision based on the facts.

T.171

The [Company] agrees and undertakes that the [Customer] shall be able at any time to terminate, cancel, withdraw from and/or amend the [Service/Products/Access] up to [number] [hours/days/weeks] before the payment date in each month. That there shall be no additional charges, penalties and/or otherwise incurred as a result and no obligation to pay any sums which fall due after the end of the agreement.

T.172

In addition to any rights and remedies this agreement may be terminated by giving written notice to the defaulting party who has committed a material breach of this agreement. The defaulting party shall be given not less than [seven] days (excluding bank holidays and weekends) to remedy the alleged breach following formal notice from the other party. If the default is incapable of remedy and/or is not remedied as required then the non-defaulting party may terminate the agreement at any time.

T.173

1.1　In addition to any rights and remedies this agreement may be terminated by giving immediate written notice to the defaulting party who has committed a material breach of this agreement. Provided that the defaulting party has first been given not less than [one] calendar month to remedy the alleged breach.

1.2 Either party shall have the right, but not the obligation to terminate this agreement immediately by notice in writing in the event that the other party becomes insolvent, enters into an arrangement with its creditors, a receiver or receiver/administrator is appointed over the business of the defaulting party and/or the directors and/or the shareholders pass a resolution to suspend trading and/or to wind up and/or dissolve the defaulting party. This shall not apply to any amalgamation and/or reconstruction of the defaulting party.

T.174

1.1 In addition to any rights and remedies this agreement may be terminated by [seven] days written notice by email from the [Company] to the [Contributor] if in the opinion of the [Company] the [Contributor] has breached and/or intends to breach the terms of this agreement. The [Company] shall pay all sums due to the [Contributor] until the date of termination.

1.2 The [Company] shall have the right, but not the obligation to terminate this agreement in the event that the [Contributor] has been threatened with bankruptcy, insolvency, is unable to pay his/her debts and/or enters into an agreement with his/her creditors and/or has a receiver and/or administrator appointed over the [Contributors'] business.

1.3 In the event that this agreement is terminated by the [Company] then the [Company] shall not be liable to pay any further sums to the [Contributor] after the end date. The [Contributor] must return all the property, material and/or records which are owned and/or controlled by the [Company] and/or a third party which relate to this agreement including but not limited to reports, budgets, planning documents, laptop, car, security pass, mobile phone and any other gadgets.

1.4 After the date of termination of this agreement the [Contributor] shall not be authorised to have access to and/or use any channels, accounts, online digital accounts and/or use any passwords, codes and/or other material in any media supplied by the [Company] and/or created by the [Contributor] as part of his/her role at the [Company] for any reason. The [Company] may access and cancel all such accounts.

T.175

In the event that the [Distributor] and/or the [Company] become aware and/or have reasonable grounds to believe that the [Purchaser] and/or its business, employees and/or associates and/or any other third party are using the [Downloads/Digital version/Electronic Material] and/or any data, information and/or other content in a manner which contravenes the terms and condition of this licence and/or is prejudicial to the financial, sales and/or other interests of the [Distributor] and/or [Company]. Then this licence may be summarily terminated without any notice whatsoever. The [Purchaser] shall upon written request surrender all copies of any nature in any medium to the [Distributor] and [Company] of the [Work/Sound Recordings/Films/Videos/Images].

T.176

The [Company] agrees that it shall not terminate the Agreement with [Name] where delivery of the [App] by [date] is delayed due to additional requirements and/or specifications and/or changes requested by the [Company]. Provided that a new delivery date is agreed as a substitute.

T.177

The [Company] shall have the right to terminate the arrangement with [Name] to supply text, information, data and images for blogs, articles and other content for the [Company] website, app and marketing and promotional material at any time. Provided that [Name] is paid for all work agreed and completed up to the date of termination.

T.178

This agreement is a temporary short term arrangement between [Name] and the [Company]. The [Company] shall have the right to advise [Name] at any time directly verbally and/or by email that the agreement is ended and that no further work is required and that no further sums shall be paid.

T.179

The [Company] agrees:

1.1 to engage the services of [Name] for a period of [one] year from [date to [date].

1.2 that the [Company] shall not terminate the agreement during that [one] year period.

1.3 that regardless of whether the services and work written and produced by [Name] are used by the [Company]. That [Name] shall be paid the agreed monthly fee for the whole year.

1.4 that the financial situation and creditworthiness of [Name] is irrelevant to this agreement.

1.5 that the [Company] accepts and agrees that [Name] may provide the same and/or similar services to any third party. That this agreement is not exclusive.

T.180

The [Company] may terminate this agreement on the following grounds:

1.1   that the [Supplier] does not complete and deliver the functional and operational software, website and app which is described in appendix A by the agreed delivery dates.

1.2   that the [Supplier] has not completed the project in Appendix A and has exceeded the agreed Budget in Appendix B.

1.3   that the [Supplier] has misled the [Company] as to their level of expertise and/or experience in creating and developing software, websites and/or apps.

1.4   that the [Supplier] has delivered the software, website and/or app but it does not function and/or operate as required under Appendix A and/or is not suitable for the intended purpose described in Appendix A.

1.5   that the [Supplier] has disclosed confidential material, data and/or information to the media regarding the software, website and/or app without the consent of the [Company].

1.6   that the [Supplier] intends to sell the business to a third party.

1.7   that the [Supplier] has ceased trading and/or it is likely that its assets will be controlled by a third party.

T.181
Where the [Company] becomes aware and/or is notified by a third party that any person is using and/or adapting the [Sound Recordings/Audio Files] in a manner which is not authorised by the [Company]. Then the [Company] shall have the absolute right to terminate this agreement and/or to close your account with the [Company] and/or to block your access to any material and/or service. This right shall be in addition to any other rights and/or remedies which the [Company] may have against such person and/or any business under the law in any country.

T.182

1.1   [Name] agrees that access and use of the [Platform/Service/Material] provided by the [Company] is subject to [Name] adhering to all the codes of conduct, policies and guidelines issued by the [Company at any time. This shall include: [specify list].

1.2   [Name] agrees that where [Name] fails to adhere to 1.1 that the [Company] shall be entitled to close any account which [Name] has opened and/or to delete all the content and/or to remove any images and/or comments and/or videos and/or other material which [Name] has posted on the accounts of any third party. That in such circumstances [Name] shall not be entitled to any refund of any sums. [Name] shall not be liable to pay any further account charges to the

[Company] if their account is closed and they have no access to the [Platform/Service/Material].

1.3   [Name] agrees that the actions in 1.2 by the [Company] do not absolve [Name] for any legal liability to the [Company]. That the [Company] shall still be entitled to take such legal action against [Name] as it thinks fit in respect of any fines, penalties, damages, losses, costs, expenses, interest and legal fees paid by the [Company] as a direct and/or indirect result of [Name].

Merchandising and Distribution

T.183
Where the [Licensee] fails to comply with any legislation and/or compliance requirements and/or codes of conduct and/or guidelines issued by any regulatory organisation and/or government body in [country] relating to health and safety, product liability, consumers and the public, trading standards and/or any other matter which results in a fine and/or penalty and/or an award of damages and/or criticism by a court of law and/or any other body. Then the [Licensor] shall have the right to terminate the agreement on the basis of any such default.

T.184
The [Distributor] shall be entitled to terminate the agreement with the [Sub-Licensee/Agent] in the event that the [Sub-Licensee/Agent] releases and/or supplies confidential business plans and/or product designs and/or other corporate information which is not available to the public to a third party.

T.185
Without prejudice to any other rights and remedies under the law in [country] which may be available to the [Licensor]. It is agreed that the [Company] shall be in breach and/or default of this agreement in the event that it fails to comply with clauses [–]. Any such breach and/or default of those clauses shall entitle the [Licensor] to notify the [Company] that the agreement shall terminate with immediate effect and that all rights shall revert to the [Licensor]. In such circumstances the [Company] agrees that it shall not be entitled to any compensation for any losses, damages, expenses and/or costs and/or any other sums which may arise directly and/or indirectly as a result of the termination of this agreement.

T.186
Where the [Licensor] defaults and/or fails to provide the [Master Material] for the development and reproduction of the [Images/Service/Product] by the agreed date. The [Licensee] shall be entitled to a full refund of all the sums

paid in clause [–] and shall have the right to terminate the agreement. After the termination date nominated by the [Licensee] both parties agree to enter into negotiations to settle the matter by arbitration, mediation and/or some other method prior the commencement of any legal proceedings. Where no conclusion can be reached within [number] [months] of termination then either party may issue legal proceedings at its own risk and cost.

T.187
Where the [Service] is not available for any continuous period of [number] days then the [Company] shall have defaulted. In such circumstances the [Distributor] shall be entitled to terminate the agreement and claim a full refund for all days that the service was not available together with an additional sum of [number/currency] per day in compensation for the lack of service. The sum due shall be paid by the [Company] with [number] days of the demand from the [Distributor] by [email/other] which sets out the sums due and the reason.

T.188
The [Company] may by notice [in writing/by email/text message] to the [Sub-Licensee] terminate the sub-licence granted at any time after any of the following events shall occur:

1.1 The [Sub-Licensee] shall have failed to manufacture and sell a minimum of [number] of the [Licensed Articles/Products] within [six] months of the date of commencement of the licence period for the sub-licence.

1.2 The [Sub-Licensee] shall have failed to make the best arrangements that can reasonably be secured for the distribution throughout the Territory and sale of the [Licensed Articles/Products].

1.3 Any of the royalties due to the [Company] shall remain unpaid after they shall have become contractually due (whether or not they shall have been formally demanded).

1.4 The [Sub-Licensee] shall have failed to provide one or more of the accounting statements required in clause [–].

1.5 The [Sub-Licensee] shall commit and/or allow to be committed a breach of any of the undertakings on the part of the [Sub-Licensee] contained in this agreement.

1.6 If in each year of the Licence Period the [Sub-Licensee] shall fail to manufacture and sell a minimum of [number] units of any one category of the [Licensed Articles/Products] in any specified country of the Territory as stipulated in this agreement. The [Company] shall have the right at its discretion to terminate all of the rights sub-licensed to the [Sub-Licensee] in respect of that specific category of the [Licensed

Articles/Products] in that country. The [Company] shall from the date of termination have the right to grant other sub-licences to third parties in respect of those specific rights which have been terminated.

1.7 An order shall be made or resolution passed for the winding-up of the [Sub-Licensee] and/or there is a reconstruction and/or amalgamation and/or the [Sub-Licensee] shall make any arrangement with and/or for the benefit of its creditors and/or if a receiver and/or administrator shall be appointed in respect of any of the [Sub-Licensee's] assets.

Provided that any termination shall be without prejudice to any of the [Company] rights and/or remedies including the right to be paid the royalties which are due whether prior to the date of termination or thereafter.

Together with the right of the [Company] to collect and/or have returned all master material for the [Licensed Articles/Products] and/or any prototypes, moulds, designs, logos, artwork, packaging, stock, promotional material and/or marketing relating to the [Licensed Articles/Products]. That the[Sub-Licensee] agrees and accepts that all such material belongs to the [Company] and must be returned.

T.189

In the event that this agreement is terminated by the [Company] for any reason then all intellectual property rights, copyright, trade marks and any other rights in the [Characters/Logos] and all the associated physical master material from which it is created and/or reproduced shall immediately revert to the [Company]. In addition all sub-licences granted by the [Licensee] shall be transferred and/or assigned to the [Company]. The [Licensee] agrees to execute any documents which the [Company] may require to be signed for the purpose of fulfilling the terms of this clause.

T.190

It is a fundamental term of this agreement that the [Service/Products] shall be on sale to the public within [six] months from the date of this agreement. If the [Service/Products] are not made available by that date then the [Licensor] shall have the right to notify the [Licensee] that the licence will terminate with [two] months' notice period unless the situation is remedied by the [Licensee] within that period.

T.191

Either the [Company] and/or the [Distributor] may serve written notice and specify an end date and terminate this agreement (without prejudice to any other right or remedies available to them) at any time in the event that any of the following matters arise:

1.1 If the other party shall commit one or more breaches and/or defaults of the terms of this agreement which either cannot be remedied and/or which despite notification as to the problem the breach and/or default is not remedied within a reasonable period which shall be no more than [one] month.

1.2 If the other party has ceased trading and/or is unable pay its outstanding debts and/or is unable to fulfil the terms of this agreement due to force majeure and/or some other circumstance beyond its reasonable control.

1.3 If the other party is subject to negative social media as a result of the actions, statements and/or filming and/or recording of an interview with a director of the business and/or a person in the senior management of the other party has posted comments on social media on the internet which seriously damages and/or impacts on the sales and/or the reputation of the business and/or any of its brands.

T.192

1.1 When this agreement is terminated the [Distributor] shall cease all further manufacture of the [Products].

1.2 The [Distributor] may for an additional period of [three] months from the date of termination sell-off on a non-exclusive basis existing stocks of [Products] manufactured prior to the date of termination. No new stock may be manufactured.

1.3 · The [Distributor] shall also be able to fulfil any contracts for the sale of the [Products] already concluded before the termination date provided that those contracts are amended to be non-exclusive and limited in duration until the end of the sell-off period.

1.4 The [Distributor] shall not have the right to supply and/or sell any [Products] after the end of the sell-off period. Any stock which exists at that end date shall be delivered to the [Company] at the [Company's] expense and cost. The [Distributor] shall not be entitled to charge for any such old stock.

T.193

1.1 In the event that this agreement is terminated and/or expires the [Distributor] shall within [thirty] days return to the [Licensor] at the [Distributor's] cost all designs, drawings, specifications, reports and risk assessments, data, images and any other products, software and/or other material in any format and/or medium which has either been supplied by the [Licensor] and/or developed, designed and/or produced by [Distributor] based on the original material, data and/or records supplied by the [Licensor]. The [Distributor] shall not have the right to retain any copies and/or stock.

1.2 The [Distributor] agrees that after the termination and/or expiry of this agreement it shall have no right to use and/or reproduce any of the material, data and records in 1.1. The [Distributor] shall not have the right to use and/or reproduce any trade mark, logo and/or image relating to the [Licensor] and/or its products and/or services in any marketing and/or promotional material relating to the [Distributor].

T.194

1.1 In the event that this agreement is terminated by either party. Then it is agreed between the parties that all sub-licences shall also be terminated.

1.2 That any notification of termination by either party shall not absolve them from liability for any breach and/or default under this agreement prior to the date of termination.

1.3 That either party despite sending notification of termination of this agreement shall still be bound by those clauses which are stated to survive and continue after the end date. This shall include but not be limited to any inspection, accounting and royalty payments that may be outstanding.

T.195

The [Licensor] may terminate this agreement by notice in writing in the event the [Licensee] shall:

1.1 fail to have manufactured [number] units of the [Product] and/or failed to distributed and/or sell to the public [number] units of the [Product] before [date].

1.2 fail to pay the Licence Fee in full by date: [–].

1.3 fail to report and provide accounting statements for any accounting period and/or failed and/or delayed in paying any of the sums which may be due.

1.4 commit one and/or more serious breaches and/or defaults in respect of this agreement which when notified have not been remedied within [seven] days.

1.5 be unable to trade as a solvent business and/or unable to pay any demand, debt, expense and/or cost which has been incurred and/or is due and/or is the subject of legal proceedings by a third party which may result in the business being declared insolvent, wound up and/or put into receivership and/or administration and/or some other circumstance where the assets are transferred to and/or owned by a third party.

T.196

The [Licensor] may terminate this agreement by notice in writing in the event that the [Licensee] shall have failed to:

1.1 provide a [Prototype/Sample] for approval by the [Licensor] and/or to reproduce the [Licensed Articles] in accordance with the approved [Prototype/Sample].

1.2 provide samples of the final pre-production [Licensed Articles] to the [Licensor] for approval. Together with copies of any packaging, labels and/or promotional material for approval by the [Licensor].

1.3 manufacture, distribute and/or sell [number] units of the [Licensed Articles] before [date].

1.4 pay the Advance by [date] and/or has not reported and/or paid one or more statements and royalty payments due to the [Licensor] and/or has failed to allow access for an inspection and/or audit of the accounts when requested to do so.

1.5 continue to manufacture, distribute and/or sell the [Licensed Articles] continuously for the full period of the Licence Period and/or shall not be able to pay its suppliers and/or has ceased trading and/or is the subject of an investigation and/or enquiry in respect of the failure to comply with health, safety and/or product liability legislation and codes of practice and guidelines.

It is agreed that any such termination shall be without prejudice to any other rights and remedies that may be available to the [Licensor].

T.197

In the event of the termination of this agreement by the [Licensor] the following shall apply:

1.1 All sub-licensees, sub-agents, distributors and other third parties involved in the exploitation of the [Products/Rights/Characters] shall be notified by the [Licensee] that their agreements are terminated immediately. That the [Licensor] has terminated the main agreement and that they must cease exploiting the [Products/Rights/Characters]. That the rights have all reverted to the [Licensor] and that any outstanding payments must be made direct to the [Licensor].

1.2 The [Licensee] shall provide a complete list of all the parties notified in 1.1 and copies of the agreements with those third parties.

1.3 The [Licensee] shall ensure that all master material and any other contracts, licences, financial records and downloads, documents, copyright clearances, photographs, artwork, images, recordings, films or other material of any nature and/or format in the possession and/or under the control of the [Licensee] and/or any sub-licensees, sub-agents, distributors and/or other third parties shall not be destroyed but returned at the [Licensors/Licensees'] cost to the [Licensor].

1.4 No further sums shall be collected by the [Licensee] and/or any rights exploited by the [Licensee] at any time.

T.198

In addition to any other rights and remedies at law this agreement may be terminated by giving written notice to the other party who has breached this agreement and/or defaulted in the following circumstances:

1.1 where the [Company] has failed to account and/or make payments as required under this agreement.

1.2 where the other party has committed a serious breach of its obligations under this agreement unless the defaulting party remedies the matter within [one] calendar month of the breach and/or default.

1.3 where the [Company] goes into voluntary and/or involuntary liquidation and/or is the subject of an amalgamation and/or restructuring which changes the constitution, shareholding and/or ownership of the [Company].

1.4 where the [Company] is declared insolvent either in bankruptcy and/or arising from other legal proceedings.

1.5 where an agreement with creditors has been reached by the [Company] due to its failure and/or inability to pay its debts as they fall due and/or the [Company] is trading while insolvent.

1.6 where a receiver and/or administrator is appointed over the whole and/or part of the [Company's] business.

1.7 where [Name] is convicted of a serious criminal offence anywhere in the [Territory/country/world] including a drink driving offence which results in a driving ban and/or a drug offence.

1.8 where [Name] is found to be in serious breach of the rules of the [specify organisation] of which he/she is a member and is found guilty of serious professional misconduct and their membership is suspended and/or removed.

1.9 where [Name] makes public and/or private statements and/or performs in a manner and/or uses language and/or make gestures which seriously adversely affect the reputation and/or value and/or products and/or services and/or sales of the [Company] and/or any parent and/or associated company.

T.199

Termination for any reason will not affect the responsibility of the [Company] to make payments as would otherwise be due under the terms of this agreement for sums due to [Name]. Such obligations as exist to make payments shall survive termination and shall continue until [Name] has received all the payments that may be due and/or pending.

T.200

1.1 Where this main agreement is terminated for any reason then it is agreed that the [Company] and/or [Name] may also serve notice of termination on any related third party agreements which the [Company] and/or [Name] have entered into connected to the main agreement. The aim would be to end all the agreements on the same date.

1.2 [Name] may decide that he/she does not want to terminate the related third party agreements. In which case [Name] shall have the right and option to request that the third party agreements be transferred and/or assigned to [Name] for a nominal sum of [number/currency]. In such case [Name] shall be entitled to retain all the sums paid by the third party agreements from the date of the transfer and/or assignment of the agreement 'and/or assignment of the Agreement by the [Company] and/or the third party to [Name].

T.201

In the event of termination of the agreement the following steps shall be taken:

1.1 All sub-licences and sub-agent agreements and/or rights shall be terminated and revoked.

1.2 The [Company] shall ensure that all master material, stock, packaging and promotional material is returned to the [Company] at the [Company's] cost and that it shall not be destroyed but stored securely. The [Company] accepts that this material cannot be exploited and/or sold in any form without the prior written authorisation of [Name].

1.3 All master material owned and/or controlled by [Name] shall be returned to [Name] at the [Company's] cost including: [list material].

T.202

1.1   If the [Purchaser] shall receive from the [Company] a notice to the effect that the [Purchaser] has failed on the due date to pay the remaining outstanding sum due of the purchase price for the [Products] supplied by the [Company]; and/or

1.2   If a receiver and/or administrator and/or other official has been appointed to take over the business of the [Purchaser] and/or if any legal action has been taken and/or is pending to close and/or wind up the business of the [Purchaser]; and/or

1.3   If the [Purchaser] shall cease to trade and/or is unable to pay its debts as they fall due; and/or

1.4   If the [Purchaser] shall attempt to sell and/or dispose of any of the [Company's] [Products] which have been supplied to the [Purchaser] but in which no ownership has passed due to the need to pay the outstanding purchase price.

If any one of the reasons set out in 1.1 to 1.4 shall take place then the [Purchaser] shall be deemed to be in default and/or breach and/or to have repudiated the contract for the purchase of the [Company's] [Products] in respect of which ownership has not passed to the [Purchaser]. In any such case the [Company] shall be entitled to serve notice of termination of the agreement to the [Purchaser] and to demand the immediate return of the [Company's] [Products] and/or access to collect all such property by the [Company] and/or an authorised agent. The [Company] may permit the [Purchaser] an additional period of [one] calendar month to remedy the matter before collection but that is entirely at the discretion of the [Company].

T.203

If the [Company] shall become bankrupt and/or be put into receivership and/or administration and/or shall make any composition and/or arrangement with and/or for the benefit of its creditors and/or shall have legal proceedings issued against the [Company] for bankruptcy and/or any resolution is passed and/or any order is made by a court to wind up the [Company] and/or a receiver and/or manager shall be appointed by any creditor and/or any act shall be done which would cause any such event to occur. The [Supplier] shall be entitled to terminate the [Purchase Order] by written notice to the [Company] but without prejudice to any other rights and/or claim which the [Supplier] may have at the date of such notice.

T.204

If the [Purchaser] shall commit any breach of the contract and/or become insolvent and/or is unable to pay its debts and/or becomes bankrupt and/

or being a company goes into liquidation (other than for the purposes of reconstruction or amalgamation) and/or has a receiver appointed over its assets and/or any part. The [Company] may without notice suspend and/or terminate the contract and/or any part which has not been fulfilled and stop delivery of any products in transit without prejudice to any other right and/or remedy of the [Company].

T.205
In addition to any other rights or remedies at law this agreement may be terminated by giving immediate written notice to the defaulting party who has committed a material breach of this agreement. Provided that the defaulting party has been given not less than [number] working days to remedy the matter following formal notice.

T.206
Either party shall have the right but not the obligation to terminate this agreement immediately by notice in writing if:

1.1   the other party becomes insolvent; and/or

1.2   enters into an arrangement with its creditors; and/or

1.3   a receiver and/or administrator is appointed over the business of the defaulting party; and/or

1.4   the board of directors and/or its shareholders pass a resolution to suspend trading, wind up and/or dissolve the company other than for the purpose of amalgamation and/or restructuring where the terms of this agreement do not change in any manner.

1.5   a circumstance which amounts to force majeure has continued for a period of [number] months and there is no prospect that the matter will be resolved within the next [six] months.

1.6   the cost of supply of materials required to created and/or reproduce the [Products] has risen more than [number] per cent in price and the payment terms agreed under this agreement by the [Supplier] are not sustainable.

T.207
If the [Company] and/or the [Distributors] become aware and/or have reasonable grounds to believe that:

1.1   The [Purchaser] its employees and/or any associated third party have and/or are using the [Material/Software/Data] in any manner not authorised in the licence which is prejudicial and/or detrimental to the interests of the [Company] and/or [Distributor]; and/or

---

1.2   is in breach of any intellectual property rights, copyright, trade marks, computer software rights, patents and/or any other rights of the [Company] and/or the [Distributor].

The [Company] and/or the [Distributor] shall have the right to terminate the licence with the [Purchaser] without prejudice to any other rights and remedies that they may have against the [Purchaser] and/or any other third party. The [Purchaser] shall be obliged on receipt of notice to return, destroy and/or delete all copies of the [Material/Software/Data] held by the [Purchaser] and in their possession and/or control and to provide a legal undertaking to that effect. In addition the [Purchaser] must supply a comprehensive of all such copies supplied to third parties and/or posted and/or sold anywhere on the internet and/or otherwise.

T.208

[Name] may terminate this contract for any one of the following reasons and shall be entitled to a full refund of all sums paid including any deposit:

1.1   The [Products/Service/Material] are not delivered by the specified date of: [date]. Time is of the essence in this agreement. This date is crucial and cannot be delayed for any reason.

1.2   The [Products/Service/Material] have been delivered but are not operational and/or functioning as required and/or fit for their intended purpose.

1.3   The [Products/Service/Material] are not complete and/or parts are missing and/or are defective and/or do not match the description and/or does not comply with the specified order.

1.4   The [Company] has financial difficulties and/or is likely to cease trading in the near future.

1.5   There have been reports by a consumer body and/or government department which has resulted in a product recall of some or all of the products which are listed on the order.

T.209

The [Company] shall be entitled to terminate this agreement early and with immediate effect where the [Distributor] has been the subject of an investigation by a local authority and/or other government agency and/or the police and is the subject of criminal and/or civil proceedings and/or has breached and/or defaulted in respect of any legislation relating to health and safety, product liability, allergy warnings and/or some other matter in [country/worldwide].

T.210

1.1   The [Distributor] confirms that if within [two] years of the date of this agreement the [Licensee's] Royalties actually paid and received amount to less than [number/currency] including the Advance. The [Licensor] shall have the right to terminate this agreement by [one] months written notice to the [Distributor]. The [Distributor] agrees that after the termination date all rights granted under this agreement shall revert back to the [Licensor].

1.2   The [Distributor] agrees that the [Licensor] shall be entitled to retain all sums paid including the Advance. Further that the [Licensor] shall be entitled to receive all further sums which may be due in respect of the rights which may be received after the date of termination. That the [Distributor] shall not have the right to retain any sums after the date of termination.

T.211

This agreement may be terminated by either party giving written notice to the defaulting party who has committed a material breach of the terms. Where the breach is capable of being remedied the defaulting party shall be permitted [thirty days] from receipt of the notice to remedy the breach. Unless the breach is remedied the agreement shall be terminated at the end of that period.

T.212

After the expiry and/or termination of this agreement and the completion of the sell-off period. The [Assignor] shall be entitled to instruct the [Assignee] to return and/or to arrange for the collection of all original master material loaned and/or supplied by the [Assignor] and/or any prototypes, samples, artwork, drawings, electronic material, packaging, marketing and/or licensed products and/or any other material in any medium and/or any data, documents, copyright clearances and consents, licences, agreements, accounting records, spreadsheets, customer lists and/or other material stored in any software system and/or archive in the possession and/or under the control of the [Assignee] and/or authorised by the [Assignee] and/or held by a third party relating to the rights assigned under this agreement.

T.213

In addition to any other rights and remedies at law of the [Licensor] and/or the [Licensee]. Either party may by giving written notice to the other party terminate this agreement on the grounds that the other party has defaulted and/or breached this agreement as follows:

1.1   That the other party has failed to report, account, permit inspections and/ or made payments as required under this agreement.

1.2 That the other party has committed a serious breach of its obligations under this agreement which is capable of being remedied and has failed to so within [one] month of notification of the default and/or breach.

1.3 That the other party has been trading while insolvent and/or has been wound up and/or declared insolvent and/or a receiver and/or some other third party has been appointed to deal with the operation and/or sale and/or auction of the whole business and/or part of its assets.

T.214

The [Licensee] agrees that in the event that [Licensor's] Royalties received by the [Licensor] by date: [–] are less than [number/currency]. That the [Licensor] shall have the right to terminate this agreement by notice in writing to the [Licensee] to that effect at any time before [date].

T.215

If the agreement is terminated by either party under clause [–]. It is agreed that [Name] shall be entitled to retain all sums already paid. In addition [Name] shall be entitled to receive accounting statements and future royalties which may fall due for work already completed under this agreement which is exploited after the termination [date]

T.216

In the event that this non-exclusive licence agreement is terminated for any reason by the [Licensor] in respect of the [Images/Recordings/Videos]. The [Licensee] shall not be obliged to terminate any sub-licences which have already been granted, but shall not be entitled to conclude any new sub-licences in respect of the [Images/Recordings/Videos].

T.217

1.1 This agreement shall commence on [date] and shall continue for an initial period of [two] years from that date. Thereafter this agreement shall continue on an annual basis until terminated by either party.

1.2 In the first two years from [date] either party may terminate the agreement for any reason by providing the other with [number] months' written notice.

1.3 In the third year of the agreement and thereafter either party may terminate the agreement for any reason by [six] months written notice.

1.4 No further sums of any nature shall be paid by either party to the other after the termination date.

T.218

1.1 The following clauses [–] shall survive the termination of this agreement by [Name].

1.2 The following clauses [–] shall survive termination of this agreement by the [Company].

T.219

1.1 The parties agree that the following sums shall be paid by the [Company] in the event of the following defaults, breaches and/or failures: [specify type of issue/sum to be paid in compensation/payment method and duration].

1.2 The payments due in 1.1 shall once accepted and paid shall mean that [Name] shall not have the right to issue legal proceedings and/or make any claim in respect of that issue. That [Name] waives the right to make such a claim in respect of that matter. A waiver on one occasion however does not mean that the waiver applies to the same issue and/or matter at a later date.

Publishing

T.220

This agreement may be terminated and the rights granted to the [Magazine] shall revert to the [Company] if:

1.1 the [Magazine] commits any breach and/or alleged breach of the terms of this agreement and does not remedy such breach and/or alleged breach within [number] days of receiving written notice from the [Company] to do so. Unless within that period the [Magazine remedies the breach and/or informs the [Company] that there is a valid dispute the agreement will automatically terminate. It is agreed that if the [Magazine] claims that there is a valid dispute that the parties agree to allow a period of [two] months from the date of notification to resolve the matter. The parties in such event agree to act in good faith to resolve the dispute amicably. If it is not resolved in that [two] month period then the agreement will terminate at the end of the last day of that period.

1.2 Any such termination in 1.1 shall be without prejudice to any other remedies and/or damages and/or legal actions that may be available to the [Company] against the [Magazine] for any such default and/or breach.

T.221

In the event that the [Publishers] decide not to accept and/or to publish the [Sound Recordings/Manuscript/Script] the [Publishers] shall immediately notify the [Author] of the reasons for their decision in writing.

T.222

The [Publisher] agrees and confirms that if within [two] years of the [date of this agreement/date of first publication] the Author's Royalties paid by the [Publisher] are less than [number/currency] [including/excluding] the Non-Returnable Advance. The [Author] shall have the right but not be obliged to terminate this agreement by issuing [number] days' written notice to the [Publisher]. In such event upon receipt of notice for this reason the [Publisher] shall be obliged to ensure that all rights assigned under this agreement shall revert back to the [Author]. For the avoidance of any doubt the Author's Royalties in this clause shall mean the total Royalties paid to the [Author] (whether the [Author] is one or more persons).

T.223

1.1 Where the [Publisher] allows the [Hardback and/or Paperback Book] and/or [Download/Electronic version] of the [Work/Manuscript] to go out of print and/or not be available throughout all and/or part of the [Territory/ list countries] and/or the [Work] is not available to the public through retail outlets for more than [number] months and/or a new edition is not issued every [number] years. The [Author] shall be entitled to terminate this agreement by [three] month's written notice to the [Publisher].

1.2 Where the agreement is terminated in 1.1 all the rights granted shall revert to and be vested in the [Author] at the end of the notice period.

1.3 In addition the [Company] shall be required to notify and ensure that any sub-licences shall be terminated on the same termination date as notified by the [Author] in 1.1. Where this is not possible for any reason then the sub-licence shall be terminated as soon as possible thereafter. The [Company] agrees to ensure that any rights granted under any sub-licence are reverted back to the [Author].

1.4 Any such termination and/or reversion of rights shall be without prejudice to any legal and/or equitable claim that the [Author] may have for sums due under the main agreement and/or any sub-licence and/or any breach, default and/or otherwise against the [Company] and/or any sub-licensee.

1.5 The [Company] undertakes to ensure that all original master copies of any material in any format including manuscripts, electronic files, proofs, images, sound recordings and packaging and promotional material held and/or stored by the [Company] and/or any sub-licensee are returned at the [Company's] cost to the [Author].

T.224

1.1 The [Distributor] agrees that if within [one] year of the [date of this agreement/first publication and/or release to the public] of the hardback and/or paperback of the [Work/Book/Manuscript] the royalties paid by the [Distributor] to the [Author] excluding the Advance are less than [number/currency]. The [Author] may at its sole discretion decide to terminate this agreement by [six] months written notice to the [Distributor]. The [Distributor] shall not be entitled to any additional sell-off period.

1.2 In the event of termination by the [Author] in 1.1 the [Distributor] agrees to ensure that any existing agreements with sub-licensees are also terminated by the [Distributor] to terminate on the same date as the main agreement.

1.3 The [Distributor] agrees and undertakes to revert all rights in respect of the main agreement and/or any sub-licence to the [Author].

1.4 In addition the [Distributor] agrees to ensure that ownership and control of all intellectual property rights, domain names, apps, trade marks and copyright associated with the [Work/Book/Manuscript] and any characters, merchandising and/or other forms of exploitation and/or all the material in any medium and/or format shall revert to the [Author] on or by the last date of termination.

1.5 The [Distributor] accepts that this clause is without prejudice to any legal action and/or proceedings which the [Author] may have the right to take and/or any sums which may be due to be paid to the [Author] and/or any claim for damages, expenses and/or losses which the [Author] may have against the [Distributor] and/or any sub-licensee.

T.225

1.1 In the event that the [Author] shall not deliver the completed typed manuscript of the [Work] to the [Publishers] by the delivery date and/or any later delayed dates. Then after such period the [Company] may decide at its sole discretion to terminate the agreement on the grounds of non-delivery of the manuscript. In such instance the [Company] shall send the [Author] written notice stating the reason and stating that the [Author] shall be entitled to an additional [three] calendar months to remedy the problem and deliver the completed [Work] or the agreement with terminate on a specified date.

1.2 The [Company] shall not be entitled to terminate the agreement in 1.1 if the [Author] has delivered more than [number] per cent of the pages and the reason for the delay is due to the ill-health of the [Author] and/or a close family member.

1.3 In the event that the manuscript is not delivered and the agreement is terminated by the [Company]. The [Author] shall not be obliged to return the Advance.

1.4 In the event of termination of this agreement the [Author] shall be entitled to offer the [Work] to any third party for publication and exploitation. There shall be no obligation for the [Author] to consult with and/or notify the [Company].

1.5 The [Company] agrees not to make any statement concerning the [Work] and/or the [Author] in the event that it is published by a third party. Nor shall the [Company] reveal any reason for the termination of this agreement with the [Author] to the media without the consent of the [Author].

T.226

The [Company] agrees that all rights assigned and/or licensed to the [Company] under this agreement in respect of the [Work/Manuscript/Images/Maps/Infographics/Index] shall revert to the [Author] in the event that this agreement is terminated for any reason.

T.227

The [Publishers] confirm that if the [Work/Manuscript/Sound Recordings] is not accepted by the [Publishers] for any reason. The [Author] shall be entitled to have the [Work/Manuscript/Sound Recordings] published, sold and distributed by a third party. All copyright, intellectual property rights, domain names, trade marks and other rights granted to the [Publisher] [and/or any parent and/or subsidiary company and/or any sub-licensee] under this agreement shall revert to the [Author].

T.228

1.1 If the [Author] shall not deliver the typescript of the [Work/Manuscript/Book] by the agreed delivery date and/or in the form, style, content and/or length set out in the synopsis attached to this agreement in appendix A. The [Publishers] may if they think fit decline to publish, sell and/or distribute the [Work/Manuscript/Book]. In which case the [Publishers] shall send notification to the [Author] that the agreement shall be terminated on a certain date and shall state the reasons.

1.2 If the agreement is terminated by the [Publishers] in 1.1 on valid grounds then all sums which have been paid to the [Author] under this agreement shall upon such termination be due to be repaid to the [Publishers]. The [Publishers] agree to allow the [Author] a period of [six] months to repay the sums due and shall not charge interest and/or any other administration charges.

T.229

In the event that this licence agreement is terminated by the [Company] due to the failure to deliver the [Work/Book/Manuscript/Sound Recordings] by the [Author]. The [Author] shall be entitled to arrange and/or enter into a contract for the publication of the [Work/Book/Manuscript/Sound Recording] and/or any similar work by another publisher. There shall be no obligation on the [Author] to offer any material to the [Company].

T.230

If by the delivery date of [date] (which shall be of the essence of this agreement) the [Publishers] have not received [number] typed A4 pages of the [Work/Book/Manuscript] and/or in the [Publisher's] opinion it is not of the standard, content, style, format and/or length which had been agreed. The [Publishers] shall have the choice as to whether to publish the [Work/Book/Manuscript]. If the [Publishers] decide to terminate the agreement then the [Publishers] shall notify the [Author] in writing stating their reasons and the termination date. In such event any advance and/or other sums paid under this agreement to the [Author] which were to be offset against future royalties shall be due to be repaid to the [Publishers]. No such reversion of rights shall be made to the [Author] until such time as all the sums required to be paid back have been received by the [Publishers].

T.231

It is agreed that the [Company] shall be entitled to commission some third party to write a work on the same subject of [specify topic] provided that it is not based on and/or derived from the synopsis, manuscript and/or published [Works/Books] of the [Author].

T.232

1.1 The [Author] shall have the right to terminate this agreement by [two] months'] written notice setting out the reasons and the termination date if the [Work/Book] is allowed to go out of print at any time in [country] and/or the [Publishers] shall fail to authorise a new edition within [number years] of first publication of the first edition and/or shall fail to print and/or distribute at least [number] copies of the latest edition by [date].

1.2 The only exception to the valid grounds of termination permitted in 1.1 shall be where the [Publishers] notify the [Author] within [seven] days of receipt of written notice that there are circumstances under the force majeure provisions which are applicable which are the reason for the failure by the [Publishers]. In the event that there are force majeure circumstances the [Publishers] shall rely upon. The [Publishers] shall only be allowed a further period of [number] [months] from the termination date specified by the [Author] to remedy the problem. At the end of that period the agreement shall be terminated and all rights shall revert to the [Author].

1.3 If there are no force majeure circumstances stated by the [Publisher] in 1.2 and no new copies and/or new edition. Then the agreement shall terminate at the end of the notice period stated by the [Author] in 1.1. When the notification period has been complete the rights in the [Work/Book] granted to the [Publishers] under this agreement shall revert in full to the [Author].

1.4 The reversion of rights in 1.3 shall be subject to any third party agreements concluded by the [Publishers] prior to the receipt of the notice. Where any third party agreements cannot be terminated by the [Author] directly. Then the [Author] and the [Publishers] shall agree the terms of the settlement.

1.5 The termination of this agreement by the [Author] shall be without prejudice to any legal action, claim, damages and/or losses, costs and expenses and/or otherwise the [Author] may have against the [Publisher] and/or any third party.

T.233

1.1 If after the expiry of [three] years] from the date of first publication by the [Company] the [Work/Hardback Book/Paperback Book/Download] is out of print and/or not available to purchase as a first edition and no new edition has been published. The [Author] shall have the right to serve the [Publishers] with [two] months' notice of termination of the agreement which shall take effect in the event that the situation is not remedied in that period.

1.2 If the [Publishers] should refuse to remedy the situation and/or fail to make the [Work/Hardback Book/Paperback Book/Download] available to the public to purchase. Then all the rights granted and/or assigned under this agreement shall revert to the [Author] on the date of termination without further notice. The [Publisher] shall be bound to assign all rights to the [Author] subject to any existing third party agreements (but excluding subsidiaries, associated, parent and/or holding companies) to which the [Publisher] was contractually committed prior to the date of termination. These third party agreements shall be assigned to the [Author] and the [Publishers] shall not be entitled to retain any sums from such agreements after the termination date.

T.234

1.1 In the event that the [Work/Hardback Book/Paperback Book] becomes out of print for any reason and the [Company] declines and/or are unable to reprint the [Work/Hardback Book/Paperback Book] within [four] months of a written request by the [Authors] to do so. Then this agreement shall be terminated at the end of the notice period by the [Authors] if the situation is not remedied as requested.

1.2 In the event of termination of the agreement the [Company] shall if requested by the [Authors] in writing to do so arrange for the assignment of all the rights to the [Authors] without any charge or fee. That in addition where rights have been licensed to third parties those agreements shall be novated by the [Company] so that the benefit and obligations are transferred and assigned to the [Authors] directly and the [Company] is no longer involved.

T.235
The [Authors] both confirm that if this agreement is terminated for any reason [Author A] and [Author B] shall only hold the copyright in their individual contributions to the [Work] and shall be entitled to exploit their own individual contributions without the consent or any payment to the other author.

T.236
This agreement may be terminated at any stage where the [Authors] both agree to do so. Each [Author] shall own the rights in the material which he/she has created and developed and/or contributed provided that it is distinct from the work of the other [Author].

T.237
The undertakings, representations, liabilities and indemnity in clauses [specify clauses] on the part of the [Author/Contributor] in this agreement shall survive termination and continue for a period of [one] year and/or until such time as there is no unresolved outstanding claim by either party whichever is the later.

T.238

1.1 The [Author] shall have the right to terminate this agreement at any time by written notice in writing by [letter/email/other] to the [Publisher] in the following circumstances:

    a. If the [Publisher] shall be in alleged breach and/or alleged default of this agreement and shall not remedy the matter when notified of the facts within a reasonable period of no more than [number] months.

    b. If the [Publisher] shall be trading while insolvent and/or be the subject of threatened legal proceedings by creditors and/or is threatened with the appointment of a receiver and/or some other administrator to take over its business and assets and/or the [Publisher] is arranging to sell all and/or part of its business and/or assets to pay for its liabilities.

c. In the event that the latest edition of the [Work/Hardback Book/ Paperback Book] published in the [English] language are out of print and there are less than [fifty] printed copies in stock and/or it is not available through any retail outlets generally to the public. If the [Publisher] has not within [two] months of receipt of a written request from the [Author] reprinted at least [number] copies of the latest edition.

d. In the event that the [Publisher] has not agreed to enter into an arrangement with the [Author] for a new edition in the [three] years since the publication of the last edition.

1.2 Where the [Author] terminates the agreement for any reason all rights [granted/assigned] under this agreement shall revert to the [Author].

1.3 The [Author] agrees that any such termination shall not affect the continuance of any sub-licences granted by the [Publisher] provided that after the termination date the sub-licences are assigned to the [Author]. The [Author] shall share any sums received form the sub-licences with the [Publisher] so that the [Author] receives [eighty] per cent and the [Publisher] receives [twenty] per cent. This shall be regardless of the terms in the main agreement prior to termination. The sub-licences shall end on the specified expiry date in the sub-licence unless terminated in advance by the [Author] for any reason.

1.4 Termination shall be without prejudice to any legal and/or equitable claims which the [Author] may have for any failure to account and/or withholding of monies and/or failure to pay royalties which the [Author] may have against the [Publisher] in respect of any breach and/or default by the [Publisher] of the terms of this agreement.

1.5 Where the [Author] is owed any sums by the [Publisher] after the date of termination. The [Author] shall be entitled to recoup such sums by set-off of such sums against the payments due to the [Publisher] under any sub-licence after the termination of the main agreement.

T.239

The [Licensor] may terminate this agreement with [one] month's written notice on the following grounds:

1.1 That the [Licensee] has failed to pay any advance, royalty and/or other sum due under the licence and has not remedied the matter within [one] month after notification of the breach and/or default.

1.2 That the [Licensee] has been trading while insolvent and/or is unable to pay its debts and/or is the subject of legal proceedings to wind up the business of the [Licensee] and/or to appoint a receiver over the whole and/or any substantial part of its assets and/or the [Licensee] intends to dispose of and/or to sell the business to a third party.

1.3 If the [Licensee] shall has failed to consult with and seek the approval of the [Licensor] in respect of the [Material/Product/Service] prior to making it available to the public and/or has failed to make the necessary changes which were requested by the [Licensor].

1.4 If the [Licensee] shall be in material default and/or in breach of any of the terms of this agreement and fails to remedy the matter within [one] month of notification by the [Licensor].

T.240

This agreement may be terminated at the discretion of the non-defaulting party if the other party fails to perform and/or observe and/or adhere to any of the undertakings, procedures and/or terms and/or fails to remedy such failure and/or breach within [fourteen] days of receipt of a notice in writing giving adequate particulars of the alleged default and/or breach and specifying a termination date before which the matter must be remedied.

T.241

1.1 The parties agree that any termination of this main agreement shall be without prejudice to any rights, remedies and/or legal proceedings that may be available to either party against the other in any country and/or any claim for sums that may be due and/or owed before and/or after the date of such termination.

1.2 That the [Licensee] shall ensure that all agreements with any sub-licensee, sub-agent and/or distributor shall contain a clause that entitles the [Licensee] to terminate the sub-licence and/or other contract on or near the same date as the main agreement. That the [Licensee] agrees and undertakes that if this main agreement shall terminate then the [Licensee] shall cause any other agreement and/or arrangement based and/or derived from it to terminate at or near the same date of termination.

1.3 It is agreed that after the date of the termination of this agreement the [Licensee] and/or sub-licensee, sub-agent and/or distributor shall not be entitled to sell, supply and/or dispose of (other than by authorised destruction) of any unsold copies of the [Work/Product/Material].

1.4 Within [thirty] days after the date of termination of this main agreement the [Licensee] shall deliver to the [Licensor] a statement showing full details of all matters necessary to enable the [Licensor] to calculate the royalties due and/or owing including but not limited to the number and type of copies of the [Work/Product/Material] sold and/or disposed of, the prices charged, the gross and net receipts gross and net prices, the sum paid to the [Licensee] and/or any sums due to be paid and the relevant dates. Together with a list of all remaining stock and original physical material of any nature which is used to create the stock, packaging and marketing.

1.5   The statement in 1.4 shall be accompanied by an auditor's certificate confirming it as true and accurate.

1.6   The [Licensee] shall pay all sums owed to the [Licensor] within [two] weeks of the termination date. Any outstanding sum shall be paid as they are received from third parties. Where the third party defaults for any reason then no payment shall be due from the [Licensee] to the [Licensor].

T.242

1.1   The delivery date of the [Work/Manuscript/Book/Images/Infographics] shall be of the essence of this agreement. If the [Author] shall fail for any reason to deliver the [Work/Manuscript/Book/Images/Infographics]] by the delivery date. The [Company] shall have the right to send the [Author] written notice that the [Company] will only permit a delay of an additional period of [number] months. That if the [[Work/Manuscript/Book/Images/Infographics] is not delivered by the new delivery date that the [Company] intends to terminate the agreement on that date without further notice.

1.2   In the event of termination by the [Company] the [Author] shall not be entitled to conclude an agreement with a third party in respect of the [[Work/Manuscript/Book/Images/Infographics] until the advance paid by the [Company] has been repaid and/or a repayment schedule agreed between the parties.

1.3   Once the advance has been repaid by the [Author] then the [Company] shall confirm in writing to any third party as requested by the [Author] that they no longer hold any rights in respect of the [Work/Manuscript/Book/Images/Infographics]. That the [Author] is free to conclude any agreement with any third party and that there is no potential claim and/or threat of legal action by the [Company] against the [Author] and/or any third party.

T.243
In addition to any other rights and remedies at law this agreement may be terminated by written notice to the other party who has breached this agreement in the following manner:

1.1 Where [Name] has failed to account and/or make payments as required under this Agreement.

1.2 Where the [Writer] has committed a serious breach of his/her obligations under this agreement unless the [Writer] remedies the position within [number] [weeks/months].

T.244

Either party may terminate this agreement before [date] on any grounds. After that date either party shall have the right to terminate this agreement by notice in writing if the other party is unable to fulfil its obligations and/ or commits a material breach and/or whose conduct and/or activities are considered seriously detrimental, derogatory of and/or offensive to the other party and/or damaging to the brand and/or business of the other party.

T.245

1.1 In the event that the [Author] shall fail to deliver the [Manuscript/ Images] as described in the Synopsis in appendix A by the delivery date and/or the [Manuscript/Images] are rejected by the [Company] on the grounds that they are incomplete and/or not of sufficient quality and/or detail as required and/or the material is factually inaccurate and/or the material will expose the [Company] to criminal and/or civil proceedings by a third party. The [Company] shall have the right to refuse to publish the [Manuscript/Images/Work] and/or to specify and require changes by a new delivery date to comply with the content and form set out in the appendix A.

1.2 Any outstanding balance of the advance in clause [–] shall not be due and/or paid by the [Company] until the [Manuscript/Images/Work] has been accepted by the [Company]. In the event that the changes required by the [Company] are unacceptable to the [Author] and/or not complied with by the new delivery date. The [Company] shall be entitled to serve a further notice of termination to the [Author] with a specified termination date.

1.3 Provided that the [Author] repays all the advance payments made by the [Company] all rights granted and/or assigned by the [Author] shall revert entirely to the [Author] as if this agreement had never existed. The [Publishers] undertake to confirm and/or effect the reversion to the [Author] and also that the [Company] shall not be entitled to claim any rights, interest, option or otherwise in the [Manuscript/Images/Work].

T.246

The [Author] shall have the right to terminate this agreement by [one] calendar month's notice in writing in the event that:

1.1 The [Company] shall be trading while insolvent and/or unable to pay its debts and/or is the subject of legal proceedings to wind the [Company] up and/or to appoint an administrator and/or receiver.

1.2 The [Company] shall fail to publish the hardback book of the [Work] by [date] and/or the paperback book of the [Work] by [date] and/or the electronic version of the [Work] by [date].

1.3 The [Company] shall sell less than [number] copies of the [Work] in any format in any [two] year period.

1.4 The [Company] shall publish, adapt and/or exploit the [Work] without any credit and/or copyright notice to the [Author].

1.5 The [Company] shall subject the [Work] to derogatory treatment which prejudices the [Work] and/or [Author].

1.6 The [Company] shall cease to reproduce, sell and/or distribute the [Work] in [format] for a period of more than [number] months.

T.247
The [Company] shall be entitled to terminate this agreement at any time if the [Author] shall:

1.1 become involved in a social media dispute with a third party which will damage and/or cause losses to the sales, brands and/or business of the [Company].

1.2 be unable and/or unwilling to deliver the [Manuscript] of the [Work/ Book] by [date] as agreed for the delivery date.

1.3 become involved in an activist, political, environmental and/or other campaign which is not in keeping with the direction and ethos of the [Company].

1.4 be the subject of a criminal investigation in any country and/or have been charged and held in prison without bail and/or be the subject of civil proceedings which relate to personal injury of another individual and/or have committed fraud and/or money laundering and/or some other criminal offence.

Services

T.248

1.1 If the [Writer] is prevented by ill-health, mental and/or physical incapacity, bereavement, family circumstances and/or otherwise unavailable and/or unable to write and deliver the [Commissioned Works]. The [Company] shall be entitled by written notice to the [Writer] to terminate his/her engagement under this agreement,

1.2 The [Company] shall be entitled to engage another writer to write and deliver the [Commissioned Works] using the same, title, topic and research material.

1.3 No further sums shall be due to the [Writer] and all material delivered on loan from the [Company] shall be returned. The [Company] shall at all times be the copyright owner of the [Commissioned Works].

1.4 The [Company] however agrees that in the event of termination in 1.1 that it shall not seek to be repaid any advance paid to the [Writer].

T.249

The [Director] shall use his/her best endeavours to maintain a state of health which will enable him/her to provide their services under this Agreement and for the [Company] to arrange insurance cover for the loss of his/her services. The [Director] agrees to a medical examination for the purpose of obtaining insurance cover and agrees to provide any such medical, personal or other details that may reasonably be required by the [Company] and/or the insurers for that purpose.

T.250

1.1 The [Company] shall have the right to postpone the start date and/or cancel any dates for the supply of the [Presenter's] services for the [Series] and/or to use another person for any episode if the [Presenter] is unavailable for any reason and/or is absent due to ill-health, a medical and/or dental problem, a family crisis and/or some other reason.

1.2 In such circumstances the [Company] may withhold payment of any sum due for any episode until work has been completed by the [Presenter] and/or cancel the payment as no sum is due as another person completed that episode.

1.3 If any period of absence shall continue for more than [number] episodes then the [Company] shall be entitled to terminate the agreement with immediate effect and shall not be liable to pay for any more work which has not been completed by the [Presenter].

1.4 In such circumstances the [Company] shall not be liable to pay any further sums to the [Presenter] for the services which have not been performed and/or any sum in respect of loss of reputation and/or career opportunities and/or negative media reactions.

1.5 The [Company] agrees to issue a joint press and media statement with the [Presenter] regarding the termination of the agreement which shall be agreed between the parties.

T.251

The [Company] has commissioned the [Writer] to write [a column/series of features/other] under this agreement. If the [Writer] in the reasonable opinion of the [Company] is prevented by illness, injury and/or other mental and/or physical incapacity from fulfilling any of his/her commissions. The Company may at its sole discretion and shall have the right if it so chooses to send written notice to the [Writer] to terminate his/her engagement. In such circumstances the [Company] shall only be liable to pay for such work as has already been delivered to that date of termination. Any such termination shall be without prejudice to the vesting and/or assignment of the rights in such completed commissioned work to the [Company].

T.252

The [Agent] agrees that if within [six] months of [date/the date of this Agreement] the Company has not received as part of the Net Receipts full payment of the invoiced cost of [number] of the [Garments/Products] ordered through the [Agent]. The [Company] shall have the right to terminate this agreement by [seven] days' written notice to the [Agent].

T.253

The [Agent] agrees that the [Company] shall be entitled to give notice to terminate the agreement immediately in the event that [Name] is no longer actively involved in the business of the [Agent].

T.254

1.1 The [Agent] agrees that if by [date] the [Agent] has not negotiated and concluded an agreement with a reputable publisher and/or distributor for the publication of the [Manuscript/Quiz Book/Digital Electronic Book based on the Synopsis] by the [Author]. The [Author] shall have the choice after that date to terminate the agreement with [two] months' notice to the [Agent].

1.2 The [Agent] shall be entitled during that [two] month notice period in 1.1 to remedy the matter and shall have done so if they conclude an agreement with a third party publisher and/or distributor. If the matter is not resolved then the [Author] shall be entitled to negotiate and conclude an agreement with another agent and/or third party and the [Agent] shall not have any rights and/or claim to any such sums that may be received in respect of the [Manuscript/Quiz Book/Digital Electronic Book based on the Synopsis] by the [Author].

T.255

The [Writer] agrees to deliver to [Name] at [Name's] cost all documents, written material, recordings, photographs, master material, research material, discs, videos, DVDs, press cuttings, artwork and all other material of any nature relating to the [Work/Boo/Project] and any parts, copies and/or adaptations, developments and/or variations in the possession or under the control of the [Writer] after the expiry or completion of this agreement. The [Writer] shall provide a detailed inventory list of all the material, and confirm in writing that there is no further material of any kind in any medium in his/her possession or control.

T.256
The majority of the members of the [Group] may demand the departure of any member subject to a fair hearing on the following basis:

1.1 A meeting of all members of the [Group] shall be arranged to discuss the proposed departure.

1.2 Sufficient notice shall be given to all members of the time, date, location and agenda of the meeting.

1.3 The grounds of complaint against any member who the other members want to depart shall be made known to that member prior to the meeting and in sufficient time to allow that member to answer any complaints.

1.4 Any member which the others intend to ask to leave the [Group] shall be given the opportunity to state his/her case in the presence of all members before any decision is made.

1.5 Any member who makes an allegation against the member who may be asked to leave shall be obliged to justify the complaint and may be questioned by any other member of the [Group].

1.6 No complaint shall be treated as valid unless it is of a serious nature.

1.7 When the majority of the members have reached a decision and verbally requested that the member concerned leave the [Group]. If that member refuses to do so. Then the [Group] shall serve written notice to such member and state the grounds for the termination of their involvement in the [Group].

T.257
The [Presenter] agrees that in the event that the [Company] decides for any reason to discontinue the production of the [Programme/Film/Series] and consequently wishes to dispense with the services of the [Presenter]. The [Company] shall be liable for the [Presenter's] Fee [and the allowances] due for the outstanding period of the Term of the Agreement. The [Company] agrees to pay the total sum of the [Presenter's Fee [and the allowances] despite the fact that the work will not be completed. It is agreed that no other suns shall be paid for any reason.

T.258

The [Presenter] shall on the expiry and/or termination of this agreement deliver to the [Company] upon request all property and material which belongs and is owned by the [Company] which is in the possession and/or control of the [Presenter] including any security pass, mobile phone, car, television, gadgets, documents, recordings, films, books, photographs, laptop, storage devices and other equipment. The [Presenter] shall be entitled to wipe clean and delete all films, videos, data and/or other content. The [Presenter] may retain such material as may be agreed with the [Company] for his/her own personal use but not for commercial publication and/or exploitation without the prior written consent of the [Company].

T.259

Each party shall have the right by notice in writing to the other to terminate this agreement if the other party fails and/or neglects to perform and/or observe any material condition of this agreement. Any failure and/or neglect by the [Presenter] and/or his/her agency may be used by the [Company] as a reason for this purpose. In the case of a failure and/or neglect which is capable of being remedied then the defaulting party shall have a period of [number] days from notification to resolve the matter. If it is not remedied within the [number] days then the agreement shall automatically be terminated on the next day.

T.260

The [Company] shall have the right by summary notice in writing to the [Agent] for the [Presenter] to terminate this agreement if the [Presenter] shall for a period of [thirty] consecutive days be unavailable and/or unable due to incapacity, mental and/or physical ill-health of the [Presenter] and/or a family member and/or some other reason to provide the services required under this agreement to the [Company].

T.261

The [Company] may terminate this agreement without prior notice and with immediate effect and without prejudice to any other claim and/or remedy which may be available to the [Company] if the [Actor/Name] shall:

1.1   be in material breach of his/her obligations under this agreement.

1.2   become unavailable to complete all the work as required due to mental and/or physical and/or medical issues which affect their ability to function and/or complete tasks and/or creates mobility issues and/or he/she either voluntarily and/or under the direction of a doctor and/or consultant is admitted to a hospital, treatment centre and/or some other facility for more than [one] [week/month].

1.3 be convicted of a serious criminal offence where he/she is the subject of a prison sentence whether suspended or not and/or is held in a prison pending the trial and/or is extradited to another country for any reason and/or any other criminal and/or civil proceedings and/or investigation which result in and/or lead to [Actor/Name] not being available to complete the work and services required under this agreement.

1.4 makes any public and/or private statement which is controversial and/or becomes involved in any campaign, activism and/or political party and/or goes on any march and/or commits any acts which in the opinion of the [Company] poses a serious risk to the assets, brands status and share value and may lead to adverse publicity and public response against the [Company].

1.5 make any admission in any interview in the media and/or on any social media and/or film, video and/or radio interview that he/she has committed an act which is illegal in [country].

1.6 have entered into a contract with a competing brand, company and/or other third party without the prior consent of the [Company] before [date].

T.262

1.1 The [Manager] agrees that if within [twelve] calendar months of the date of this agreement if the total fees, payments and sums paid [excluding expenses] to the [Sportsperson] by the [Manager] are less than [number/currency]. The [Sportsperson] shall have the right to terminate this agreement with [number] days' notice to the [Manager].

1.2 If this right of termination in 1.1 is exercised then the contracts already concluded shall continue in existence, but all sums shall be paid direct to the [Sportsperson] and no sums shall be paid and/or due to the [Manager] after the termination date. The [Manager] shall be obliged to assign all such existing contracts entirely to the [Sportsperson].

T.263
When this agreement expires and/or is terminated all rights granted to the [Company] in respect of the work done and the services provided prior to the end date shall remain the sole property of the [Company].

T.264
When this agreement expires and/or is terminated the [Company] shall pay to the [Agent] the balance of any unpaid fees which have accrued and/or are due. Provided that these sums due to the [Agent] may be set off against any other sums which the [Company] claims are owed to the [Company].

T.265

The termination of this agreement by the [Company] before [date] for any reason shall entitle [Name] to the additional sum of [number/currency] in compensation provided no other claim is made and/or legal action is started by [Name] in respect of the termination.

T.266

The [Enterprise] shall have the right to terminate this agreement without any notice period and with immediate effect and without any liability in the event that the [Enterprise] becomes aware that this agreement is based on deliberately misleading information and/or data and/or any person who has entered into it has acted fraudulently to obtain the benefit of this agreement.

T.267

The [Company] shall be entitled at any time and without specifying any reason to give notice in writing to [Name] to terminate his/her engagement immediately. If so the [Company] agrees to pay [Name] and [Name] agrees to accept the sum of [number/currency] in compensation for such termination and which shall be in full and final settlement of any claim. [Name] agrees that he/she shall not be entitled to be paid any additional sums except those accrued for work completed prior to the date of termination of this agreement.

T.268

In addition to any other rights and remedies at law this agreement may be terminated by giving written notice to the other party who is in alleged breach and/or alleged default in the following circumstances:

1.1   where the [Manager] has failed to report on negotiations and/or provide copies of contracts and/or licences and/or supply accounting statements and/or pay any sums due to the [Sportsperson].

1.2   where the [Manager] and/or the [Sportsperson] have committed a serious breach of their obligations and/or undertakings and/or commitments under this agreement. That the matter has not then been remedied within [one] month of receiving written notice of the allegation of the breach.

1.3   where the [Manager] is threatened with legal proceedings due to the non-payment of debts and/or is trading while insolvent and/or has been declared bankrupt and/or has had his/her business assets made the subject of a court order and/or a receiver and/or administrator has been appointed.

1.4   where the [Sportsperson] has been convicted of a serious criminal offence and/or has committed a serious breach of the rules of the professional sports association [specify organisation] and has been suspended and/or expelled as a member of that organisation.

T.269

The [Presenter] shall have the right by notice in writing to end this agreement on any of the following grounds:

1.1 the planned production schedule for the [Series] is delayed for more than [number] weeks.

1.2 there are circumstances in existence which fall within the scope of force majeure which apply to the [Presenter] and/or the [Company].

1.3 the [Presenter] has not been paid by the [Company] for any of the work completed and the situation has not been remedied within [seven] days despite notification.

1.4 the [Company] is trading while insolvent and/or is unable to pay the majority of its debts and/or is the subject of a winding up petition and/or a court order where an administrator and/or receiver has been appointed.

1.5 the [Company] is to be sold to a third party.

1.6 the [Series] is to deal with issues and/or content with which the [Presenter] does not wish to be involved with.

1.7 the [Company] has been associated in the media with negative publicity regarding its conduct, activities, employees, policies and/or some other matter and has become involved in some controversy over a social, political or topical issue.

T.270

Either party shall be entitled to terminate this agreement by serving notice in writing with a termination date on the other party if the other party shall:

1.1 commit a breach of its obligations under this agreement which is not capable of remedy and/or which is capable of remedy but is not completely resolved before the termination date.

1.2 make any arrangement for the benefit of and/or with its creditors and/or any action and/or proceedings in bankruptcy and/or insolvency is taken including, but not limited to, the appointment of a receiver, administrator, liquidator (whether voluntary or compulsory) other than for the purpose of some form of restructuring or merger.

Termination shall not prejudice the rights and remedies of the parties. All terms and conditions set out in this agreement which relate to the period after expiry and/or termination of this agreement shall continue in full force and effect.

T.271

[Name] shall have the right to terminate the contract at any time on the following grounds which shall be accepted as constituting a breach of this agreement by the [Company]:

1.1   The [Products] to be promoted and/or endorsed by [Name] are found not to be safe and/or suitable for children and are withdrawn from the market.

1.2   The [Company] shall cease to manufacture and/or sell the [Products] before [date].

1.3   The [Company] shall be the subject of serious allegations of misconduct, fraud, breach of trading standards, price fixing and/or otherwise.

1.4   The [Company] is in serious financial difficulties and/or is suspected to be trading while insolvent and/or has not paid [Name] some and/or all of the sums due to [Name].

[Name] shall have the right to be paid the full outstanding value of all fees in clause [-] whether or not all the work is completed and shall rank in priority over other creditors as far as possible. Where no payment can be made due to lack of resources then some other material of equal value shall be agreed to be provided in lieu.

T.272

The [Company] shall have the right by [number] days' written notice to the [Agent] and/or [Name] to terminate this agreement on the grounds that:

1.1   The [Agent] and/or [Name] has failed to perform and/or observe any term of this agreement. If the matter complained of in the notification is not remedied and/or a settlement agreed between the parties within the [number] day notice period. Then the agreement shall end on the termination date.

1.2   If [Name] does not perform his/her services to the [Company] as agreed and/or is unable and/or unwilling to do so for any reason and is absent for more than [number] days. If the parties cannot agree alternative dates and/or [Name] does not co-operate in resolving the matter. Then the agreement shall end on the termination date specified in the notification.

1.3   There are circumstances which affect the [Company] and/or the [Agent] and/or [Name] which constitute force majeure and there are factors beyond their reasonable control which mean the agreement cannot be fulfilled for some reason for more than [number] months by any party. These factors shall include strikes, power failures, riots, extreme weather conditions, explosion, fire, pandemic, government lockdown of a town and/or city, swarms of ants, locusts and/or vermin, lack of sanitation, floods, drought and/or some other uncontrollable matter imposed and/or created by circumstances.

1.4 In the event of termination of this agreement by the [Company] all copyright and intellectual property rights granted and/or assigned to the [Company] in respect of the work done and services rendered by [Name] prior to termination shall remain vested absolutely in the [Company]. Provided that the [Company] shall pay to [Agent] and/or [Name] the balance of outstanding and unpaid fees due and payable up until the date of termination. Thereafter all liability of the [Company] to the [Agent] and/or [Name] shall cease and no further payments shall be due.

1.5 This termination of the agreement by the [Company] shall be without prejudice to any allegation, default, breach, damages, losses, expenses, legal action and/or other remedy shall be available to the [Company] and/or the [Agent] and/or [Name] in respect of this agreement.

T.273

If within a period of [three] years from [date] after the assignment to the [Company] one and/or more of the following forms of exploitation have not taken place in respect of the [Sound Recordings/Work] the [Author] shall have the right to serve notice to terminate the agreement:

1.1 The [Company] has released and/or distributed not less than [number] copies of the [Unit/Download/Audio Files] of the [Sound Recordings/Work] which are available for sale to the public;

1.2 The [Company] has concluded an agreement for the sub-license of the [Sound Recordings/Work] to be used in any advertising and/or promotional campaign for a range of products and/or services.

1.3 The [Company] has licensed the synchronisation of the [Sound Recordings/Work] for use and/or adaptation for the soundtrack of a feature film with a reputable film company and/or distributor which is or will be available on general release to the public before [date];

1.4 The [Company] has authorised and/or sub-licensed the public performance of the [Sound Recordings/Work] for use and/or adaptation for a series of episodes for television, radio, theatre and/or a major music festival.

The [Author] shall have the right to terminate this agreement by [three] months' written notice in writing to the [Company. After the termination date all copyright, intellectual property rights and material shall revert to the [Author]. From the date of termination the [Company] shall not hold any interest and/or rights and shall not be entitled to any further commission, royalties and/or other sums. The [Company] shall be obliged to ensure and transfer the assignment of all such rights as it may hold and any third party sub-licence agreements and all material to the [Author].

The [Author] agrees that it shall not have any further claim against the [Company] except for any royalties that may be due from the exploitation of the [Sound Recordings/Work] prior to the date of termination and/or in respect of any failure and/or default by the [Company] to assign all the rights, sub-licences and/or material to the [Author].

Sponsorship

T.274

Where the [Athlete] is unable and/or unwilling to participate in any event, filming, races and/or appearances whether due to injury, incapacity, training, a conflict of schedules and/or any other reason. The [Sponsor] shall not have the right to cancel and/or terminate the agreement unless it agrees to pay all the sums due under the agreement in full to the [Athlete].

T.275

Where a [Participant/Contributor] has misled and/or deceived the [Company] as to their identity and/or background. Then the [Company] reserves the right to cancel and/or terminate the agreement and to seek repayment of all sums and expenses paid under the agreement.

T.276

The [Sponsor] acknowledges that the Sponsorship Fee shall be paid to the [Sportsperson] notwithstanding that the [Sportsperson] may be unable to provide his/her services under this agreement due to illness, injury and/or some other physical and/or mental incapacity and/or other reason provided that it is supported by a medical certificate and/or letter from a qualified doctor.

T.277

1.1   Where the [Sponsor] fails to pay all and/or part of the sums due in clause [–] and/or to deliver the goods and/or services in clause [–]. Then the [Company] shall notify the [Sponsor] that they are in default and specify the reasons and allow them [number] [days/weeks] to remedy the issue in the manner specified by the [Company].

1.2 Where there is a total and/or partial failure to complete the remedy required in 1.1 the [Company] shall have the right to serve notice of termination on the [Sponsor] and/or to claim any direct and/or indirect damages, losses, costs and expenses that may arise including all costs and/or payments associated with the cancellation by the [Company] of the [Event].

T.278

In addition to any other rights and remedies at law this agreement may be terminated by the [Sponsor] and/or the [Sportsperson] by notice in writing to the other party who is alleged to have breached and/or defaulted in the following circumstances:

1.1 Where the [Sponsor] has failed to pay any sums which may be due and/or to supply the products, services, equipment and/or support which it has undertaken to provide.

1.2 Where the [Sponsor] and/or [Sportsperson] has committed a serious breach and/or default of its obligations under this agreement. That notice has been provided to remedy the matter within [number] days. That the breach and/or default is incapable of being remedied and/or the defaulting party fails to make the payment and/or perform the duties and/or correct the matter within the required notice period

1.3 Where the [Sponsor] is threatened with trading while insolvent and/or is likely to go into administration and/or goes into voluntary and/or involuntary liquidation and/or has been declared insolvent either in bankruptcy and/or other legal proceedings and/or has reached and/or is due to reach an agreement with creditors due to its failure and/or inability to pay its debts as they fall due and/or the [Sponsor's] business and/or a major part of it has been and/or is due to be placed in receivership.

1.4 Where the [Sportsperson] is convicted of a criminal offence including a drink/driving offence which results in a driving ban and/or a drug-related offence of any nature and/or harassment and/or threatening, lewd and/or offensive behaviour.

1.5 Where the [Sportsperson] has been found in breach of the rules and/or testing procedures of the [specify sports organisation] of which he/she is a member and/or the regulatory body [specify governing body].

1.6 Where the conduct and/or activities of the [Sportsperson] on social media, in public and/or at sports events are considered by the [Sponsor] to be detrimental to the [Sponsor's] public image, brands, business, products and/or services.

T.279

The [Sponsor] reserves the right to terminate this agreement in the event that any subsequent legislation, directive, regulation, industry code and/or other guidelines shall restrict and/or prohibit and/or impact on the sponsorship and/or endorsement of the [Event/Person/Product] under the agreed title and/or any other significant terms set out in this agreement.

T.280

In the event that this agreement is terminated the [Licensee] shall immediately:

1.1 cease to use the trade marks, service marks, slogans, sound recordings, musical works, logos, images, artistic works, text, product names, characters, films, videos and/or computer software and any associated material owned and/or controlled by the [Sponsor].

1.2 cease to have any right to use any registered trade marks and/or to be recorded as a registered user.

1.3 cease to have the right to represent to third parties that they are authorised to use any material listed in 1.1 and 1.2.

T.281

The [Sponsor] agrees that if for any reason it serves notice to terminate the agreement it shall still be bound to pay the [Company] the minimum sum of [number/currency] in total under this agreement.

T.282

1.1 The [Sponsor] agrees and undertakes that where for reasons due to force majeure the [Event/Exhibition] is delayed by the [Institute/Enterprise] for up to [number] years. That the [Sponsor] shall still pay the sums due to be paid under this agreement for each year of the agreement. That such delay shall not constitute grounds for termination by the [Sponsor].

1.2 That the [Sponsor] agrees that where the [Institute] decides to hold a virtual [Event/Exhibition] over the internet instead of the planned proposal due to force majeure. That the [Institute] shall be deemed to have fulfilled its obligation to hold an [Event/Exhibition] despite the fact that the public cannot visit in person.

T.283

The [Sponsor] agrees and accepts that it shall not be entitled to terminate this agreement in the event that:

1.1 the [Event/Exhibition] is delayed for up to [six] months for any reason.

1.2   the proposed list of contributors and/or performers shall be substantially different from those discussed prior to this agreement for any reason.

1.3   another major sponsor is required to fund the financial budget of the [Event/Exhibition]. Provided that such sponsor is not a direct competitor.

1.4   the [Institute/Charity] requires the [Sponsor] to pay any additional sums up to [number/currency] to cover unexpected costs.

T.284

The [Sponsor] shall be entitled to terminate the agreement on any of the following grounds:

1.1   That the [Event/Festival] is not now aligned to the same ethos, content and/or target audience as originally discussed with the [Company].

1.2   The television and/or media coverage of the [Event/Festival] has been cancelled by a third party.

1.3   The [Company] has engaged and/or booked any person and/or other business to provide services and/or products at the [Event/Festival] to which the [Sponsor] objects.

1.4   That there are circumstances which amount to force majeure which have resulted in the [Event/Festival] being delayed for more than [number] months and/or cancelled.

1.5   In the event of termination by the [Sponsor] the [Sponsor] shall not be obliged to pay any further sums after the date of termination. The [Sponsor] agrees however that the [Company] may retain all sums paid before that termination date.

T.285

That in addition to any other legal action and/or claim that either party may have against the other party. This agreement may be terminated by either party on the following basis:

1.1   That the proposed content of the [Series/Film] has materially changed from the original synopsis.

1.2   That the budget for the [Series/Film] has not been fully funded as additional sums have not been raised from third parties.

1.3   That the main [presenter/actor] of the [Series/Film] is no longer involved in the project.

1.4   That the [Series/Film] cannot be proceeded with due to an issue with clearances and/or consents requiring access to an [archive/estate] of [specify person].

Where this agreement is terminated by either party prior to commencement of the production and exploitation of the [Series/Film]. Then it is agreed that the [Sponsor] shall be entitled to a refund of all sums which have not been expended by the [Company]. The [Company] shall be entitled to enter into a new agreement with a different third party to sponsor the [Series/Film].

University, Charity and Educational

T.286

1.1 The [Institute/Charity] and the [Company] agree that any termination of this agreement by either party shall be without prejudice to their right to take any legal action and/or commence any proceedings and/or make any claim.

1.2 That the [Company] undertakes and agrees that all sub-licences, agency and/or distribution agreements based on and/or derived from this agreement shall be terminated at the same time that this agreement is terminated. That the [Company] shall ensure that all sub-licences, agency and/or distribution agreements shall contain a clause to that effect and further that none shall continue beyond the Term of this Agreement and/or [date] whichever is the later.

1.3 Within [twenty-one] days of the date of termination of this agreement the [Company] shall deliver to the [Institute/Charity] a statement showing full details of all sub-licensees, agents, distributors and other third parties with whom the [Company] has entered into agreements based on and/or derived from this agreement. The [Company] shall deliver to the [Institute/Charity] a statement showing full details of the location, number and condition of all the stock, master copies, marketing and/or other material held and/or controlled by all sub-licensees, agents, distributors and such third parties. The [Company] shall confirm in writing that all such agreements have been terminated and arrangements made for all stock, master copies, marketing and other material to be returned at the [Company's] cost to the [Institute/ Charity].

T.287

1.1 In addition to any other rights and/or remedies which may be available in any country to either party under any laws. This agreement may be terminated by either the [Institute/Charity] and/or the [Company] by providing written notice to the other defaulting party which has committed and/or is alleged to have committed a material breach of this agreement.

1.2 Both the [Institute/Charity] and the [Company] agree that the defaulting party shall be provided with the opportunity to remedy the breach and/or default within [three] calendar months of notice.

1.3 If the breach and/or default is not remedied then the non-defaulting party shall be entitled to terminate agreement on the first day after the completion of the notice period and no further notice shall be required.

1.4 The [Institute/Charity] and/or the [Company] shall have the right but not the obligation to terminate this agreement if the other party becomes insolvent, enters into an arrangement with its creditors for its debts, has a receiver or administrator appointed over its business and/or the directors, trustees and/or its shareholders pass a resolution to suspend trading, wind up and/or dissolve the legal entity except where it is necessary for the purpose of an amalgamation and/or restructuring and/or the parent company assumes all the liabilities and/or responsibilities of the agreement.

T.288

1.1 The [Company] agrees that if within [twelve] months of the date of this agreement the total sums received by the [Institute/Charity] from the [Company] under this agreement are less than [number/currency]. Then the [Institute/Charity] shall have the right and discretion to terminate this agreement. The [Institute/Charity] shall terminate the agreement by formal notice in writing and shall specify the termination date. There shall be no right on the part of the [Company] to remedy the situation.

1.2 The [Institute/Charity] and the [Company] agree that If the [Institute/Charity] provides written notice of termination to the [Company] that the contracts already concluded by the [Company] on behalf of the [Institute/Charity] shall continue in existence. The [Company] agrees that all such contracts shall be transferred and assigned to the [Institute/Charity] by the [Company]. Further the [Company] shall not be entitled to receive any further sums at all under such contracts and all such sums shall be paid direct to the [Institute/Charity].

1.3 When this agreement is terminated the [Company] shall pay to the [Institute/Charity] the balance of any unpaid sums which have accrued and/or are due. These unpaid sums held by the [Company] may not be used to be set-off against any claim, damages, losses, expenses and/or legal costs which the [Company] may have against the [Institute/Charity].

T.289

1.1 The [Institute/Charity] shall have the right by [one] [months] written notice to the [Consultant] to terminate this agreement without any reason and is not obliged to provide any grounds.

1.2 The [Consultant] shall not be entitled to any sum for loss of reputation, loss of fees, loss of publicity and/or credit for involvement in the [Project], damages, expenses, legal costs and/or otherwise.

1.3 The [Institute/Charity] agrees to pay the [Consultant] for all work completed to the date of termination in accordance with the terms of this agreement. Thereafter all liability of the [Institute/Charity] to the [Consultant] for the fees and any other sums after the termination date shall cease.

1.4 The [Consultant] shall assign to the [Institute/Charity] all copyright, intellectual property rights and/or any other interest acquired and/or created by the [Consultant] in respect of any work done and/or services provided to the [Institute/Charity] prior to the date of termination of the agreement.

1.5 The [Consultant] agrees that in the event that this agreement is terminated that the [Consultant] shall have not right to be acknowledged as a contributor to the [Project] in any report and/or in any media in any format.

T.290

In addition to any other rights and remedies at law in [country] this agreement may be terminated by the [Institute/Charity] and/or [Name] by notice in writing to the other party who is alleged to have breached and/or defaulted in the following circumstances:

1.1 Where the [Institute/Charity] has failed to report to [Name] and/or supply accounting statements and/or allow inspection of the financial records and/or documents and/or software to verify the sums due and/or make payments to [Name] as required under this agreement.

1.2 Where the [Institute/Charity] and/or [Name] has committed a serious breach and/or default of its obligations under this agreement which cannot be remedied and/or is not resolved satisfactorily within [one] calendar month of the party who has defaulted and/or breached the agreement receiving notice of the grounds of complaint.

1.3 Where the [Institute/Charity] no longer exists as an entity and/or [Name] is deceased and/or either party is unable and/or unwilling to pay their debts as they fall due and/or either party enters into an arrangement with a third party which conflicts with this agreement and/or either party is involved in a social media campaign with which the other does not wish to be associated with for any reason.

1.4 Where [Name] is convicted of a serious criminal offence including a drink/driving offence which results in a driving ban or a drug-related offence of any nature and/or is the subject of criminal and/or civil proceedings which have not yet been concluded which would jeopardise and/or have been decided and have affected detrimentally the reputation and/or standing of the [Institute/Charity] by attracting derogatory media attention and publicity.

1.5 Where [Name] has had a professional qualification removed by any organisation and/or where the conduct and/or activities of [Name] in his personal and/or professional life are not in the interests of the [Institute/Charity] and are likely to affect the support of [Institute/Charity] by the public, government bodies and/or sponsors.

T.291

1.1 The [Charity/Trust] agree that in the event that the expert services of [Name] are no longer required at any time from [date] to [date] and/or the [Charity/Trust] decides to terminate this agreement. That the [Charity/Trust] shall still be obliged to pay all the fees in clause [-] to [Name] regardless of whether the services are provided and/or the work completed.

1.2 That the [Charity/Trust] shall be obliged to acknowledge the contribution and services of [Name] in any report and/or in any medium in any format as follows: [specify credit and statement].

1.3 That there is no assignment and/or transfer of the product of the work and services of [Name] to the [Charity/Trust]. That the [Charity/Trust] shall be required to seek the consent of [Name] for any form of exploitation and/or use not expressly authorised in this agreement.

TERRITORY

General Business and Commercial

T.292

'The Licensed Vessels' shall be the ships owned and controlled by the [Company] which are set out in appendix A and which are operational from [date] to [date].

T.293

'The Licensed Aeroplanes' shall be the fleet of aeroplanes owned and/or controlled by the [Company] which are shown on the existing schedule which sets out flight routes in appendix B.

T.294

'The Licensed Area' shall mean the following countries listed in schedule C and shall include all the land, islands and territorial waters marked on the map in schedule D. Both these schedules form part of this agreement.

T.295

'The Territory' shall mean throughout the universe.

T.296

'The Territory' shall mean throughout the world and outer space.

T.297

'The Territory' shall mean the world and all the countries, islands, land, sea and air up to a distance of [number] [kilometres]. It shall not include any man-made temporary and/or floating structure, ships, oil rigs, aeroplanes. It shall not include any mineral and/or mining rights and/or rights of recovery to any wreck and/or archaeology.

T.298

'The Territory' shall be all countries, land, temporary and/or permanent structures whether floating and/or attached to existing land and/or static, ships, aeroplanes, oil rigs, bases and any other locations throughout the world excluding [specify list].

T.299

'The Territory' shall be the following specified countries: [list countries/include/exclude islands/territorial sea/moving structures].

T.300

'The Territory' shall be the following [Licensed Area/countries] listed and shown on the maps in appendix C and all ships, oil rigs, aircraft and military installations in that location.

T.301

'The Territory' shall be all countries, bases and locations both above and below the sea and land whether man-made, moveable or not throughout the planet Earth.

T.302

'The Territory' shall be the following countries marked on the attached map in Schedule C as follows; [list countries/islands/any other land] and all surrounding territorial waters.

T.303

'The Territory' shall mean the Licensed Zones listed, described and represented in Schedule B and/or as subsequently agreed in writing between the [Licensor] and the [Licensee].

T.304

'The Territory' shall cover the following countries which have the [English/French/Spanish/German/other] language: [list countries]. It shall not include any surrounding territorial waters and/or any moving structures and/or objects.

T.305

'The Territory' shall be outer space which shall include the moon and all celestial bodies [as defined in the Outer Space Act 1986 as amended/other].

T.306

'The Territory' shall be defined as [specify country] and all embassies, oil rigs, military installations, ships, aircraft and other subjects registered to that country wherever they may be located.

T.307

1.1 The [Author] grants the [Company] the exclusive right to publish, sell and distribute the [Work/Manuscript] in [specify language] in [format]: [list countries] from [date] to [date].

1.2 The [Author] shall be entitled to license, assign, publish, sell and distribute the [Work/Manuscript] in any other language in the countries listed in 1.1 except [specify language].

1.3 The [Author] shall be entitled to license, assign, publish, sell and distribute the [Work/Manuscript] in any other format in the countries listed in 1.1 except [specify format].

1.4 The [Author] grants the [Company] the non-exclusive right to publish, sell and distribute the [Work/Manuscript] in [specify language] in [format]: [list countries] from [date] to [date].

1.5 The [Author] shall be entitled to license the exact same rights in 1.4 to a third party.

1.6 There are no rights granted and/or licensed to the [Company] for any other countries and/or locations not expressly listed.

T.308

'Territory' shall mean all countries, islands, man-made islands, land, reclaimed land, beaches, rocks, mountains, sub-terrain, sea, harbours, airspace, bases, locations, sites and structures whether stationary, stable and/or moving including aeroplanes, ships, rigs, vessels and space objects throughout the world, airspace, outer space and the universe.

T.309

'The Territory' shall mean all countries, bases and locations throughout the world, the universe or otherwise without limitation of boundary including outer space.

T.310

The land and name shall be that which is recognised and acknowledged by [specify organisation] as at [date] and/or at any time during the existence of this agreement.

'The Territory' shall be defined as the following countries, their territorial waters and seas, airspace, mountains, under and below the land and any associated isles, islands and surrounding fragments of land as follows: [specify and list countries].

T.311

'The Territory' shall be the area known as [specify area/zone] in [country] which is outlined with a boundary on the attached map in Appendix A which forms part of this agreement.

T.312

'The Territory' shall mean all the countries listed below together with any sub-terrain below the land, and any area above in the sky, and the territorial waters and any area under the water and below the seabed and any islands and/or additional man-made structures which are added to the land and/or which are developed and/or created by the country: [specify list].

T.313

'The Territory' shall not include any aeroplanes, ships, oils rigs, vessels, tunnels, bridges and other objects which are not within the area specified even if they are registered as based in that country.

T.314

'The Territory' shall be defined as Algeria, Angola, Benin, Botswana, Burkina Faso, Burundi, Cameroon, Cape Verde, Central African Republic, Chad, Comoros, Congo, Congo (Democratic Republic), Ivory Coast, Djibouti, Egypt, Equatorial Guinea, Eritrea, Ethiopia, Gabon, Gambia, Ghana,

Guinea, Guinea-Bissau, Kenya, Lesotho, Liberia, Libya, Madagascar, Mali, Mauritania, Mauritius, Morocco, Mozambique, Namibia, Niger, Nigeria, Rwanda, Sao Tome and Principe, Senegal, Seychelles, Sierra Leone, Somalia, South Africa, South Sudan, Sudan, Kingdom of Eswatini (formerly Swaziland), Tanzania, Togo, Uganda, Zambia, Zimbabwe.

T.315
'The Territory' shall be the following countries, land and surrounding territorial sea: Afghanistan, Bahrain, Bangladesh, Bhutan, Brunei, Cambodia, China, East Timor, India, Indonesia, Iran, Iraq, Israel, Japan, Jordan, Kazakhstan, Korea (North), Korea (South), Kuwait, Kyrgyzstan, Laos, Lebanon, Malaysia, Maldives, Mongolia, Myanmar (Burma), Nepal, Oman, Pakistan, The Philippines, Qatar, Russia, Saudi Arabia, Singapore, Sri Lanka, Syria, Taiwan, Tajikistan, Thailand, Turkey, Turkmenistan, United Arab Emirates, Uzbekistan, Vietnam, Yemen.

T.316
'The Territory' shall be the following countries and areas: Afghanistan, Bangladesh, Bhutan, China, Hong Kong SAR, India, Japan, Korea (North), Korea (South), Mongolia, Maldives, Nepal, Pakistan, Sri Lanka, Taiwan.

T.317
'The Territory' shall be defined as Brunei, Myanmar, Cambodia, East Timor, Indonesia, Laos, Malaysia, Philippines, Singapore, Thailand, Vietnam.

T.318
'The Territory' shall mean:

1.1 Australia, Fiji, New Zealand, Maldives, Pacific Islands, Solomon Islands, Samoa, Sri Lanka, Tonga, Vanuatu, South Africa, Central African Republic.

1.2 Bangladesh, India, Pakistan.

1.3 Myanmar (Burma), Cambodia, China, Hong Kong SAR, Indonesia, Laos, Malaysia, Myanmar, Nepal, Papua New Guinea, Philippines, Singapore, Taiwan, Thailand, Vietnam.

1.4 Japan, Korea (South), Korea (North).

T.319
'The Territory' shall be the following countries and islands: Australia, Fiji, Kiribati, Marshall Islands, Federated States of Micronesia, Nauru, New Zealand, Palau, Papua New Guinea, Samoa, Solomon Islands, Tonga, Tuvalu, Vanuatu.

T.320

The Territory' shall be Australia, Tasmania and New Zealand and all the islands, land and territorial waters under their ownership and/or sovereignty.

T.321

'The Commonwealth' shall be the fifty-four countries by region which are members of the organisation known as The Commonwealth:

Africa: Botswana, Cameroon, Ghana, Kenya, Kingdom of Eswatini, Lesotho, Malawi, Mauritius, Mozambique, Namibia, Nigeria, Rwanda, Seychelles, Sierra Leone, South Africa, Uganda, United Republic of Tanzania, Zambia.

Asia: Bangladesh, Brunei, Darussalam, India, Malaysia, Maldives, Pakistan, Singapore, Sri Lanka.

Caribbean and Americas: Antigua and Bermuda, The Bahamas, Barbados, Belize, Canada, Dominica, Grenada, Guyana, Jamaica, St Lucia, St Kitts and Nevis, St Vincent and The Grenadines, Trinidad and Tobago.

Europe: Cyprus, Malta and the United Kingdom.

Pacific: Australia, Fiji, Kiribati, Nauru, New Zealand, Papua New Guinea, Samoa, Solomon Islands, Tonga, Tuvalu, Vanuatu.

T.322

'The Commonwealth' shall mean the independent countries of the Commonwealth as at [date] as follows:

Antigua & Bermuda, Australia, The Bahamas, Bangladesh, Barbados, Belize, Botswana, Brunei, Darussalam, Canada, Cyprus, Dominica, Kingdom of Eswatini, Fiji Islands, The Gambia, Ghana, Grenada, Guyana, India, Jamaica, Kenya, Kiribati, Lesotho, Malawi, Malaysia, Maldives, Malta, Mauritius, Mozambique, Namibia, Nauru, New Zealand, Nigeria, Pakistan, Papua New Guinea, St Kitts and Nevis, St Lucia, St Vincent, Samoa, Seychelles, Sierra Leone, Singapore, Solomon Islands, South Africa, Sri Lanka, Tanzania, Tonga, Trinidad and Tobago, Tuvalu, Uganda, United Kingdom, Vanuatu, Zambia. It shall not include Eire and Northern Ireland.

T.323

'The European Community' shall mean all the full and associate Member States of the European Union as at [date] set out below: [list].

T.324

'The European Union countries' shall mean all full member states of the European Union as at [date] and which shall be the following countries: [list].

T.325
The licensed territory under this agreement shall be Europe. Europe shall be defined to cover those areas of land and territorial waters which apply to those countries which are full members of the European Union as set out on europa.eu, the official website, as at the date of execution of this agreement as specified in Schedule A to this agreement. It shall not include members who join after [date]. Where a member state leaves the European Union then they shall not be included in the definition of Europe after the date of departure.

T.326
'The Territory' shall mean The Pacific Islands which shall include North Mariana Islands, The Federated States of Micronesia, Fiji, Kiribati, Marshall Islands, Nauru, New Caledonia, Palau, Samoa, Solomon Islands, Tonga, Tuvalu, Vanuatu.

T.327
'The Territory' shall be limited to the land, territorial waters and airspace of the following countries which are full members of the European Union at [date]: Austria, Belgium, Bulgaria, Croatia, Cyprus, Czech Republic, Denmark, Estonia, Finland, France, Germany, Greece, Hungary, Ireland, Italy, Latvia, Lithuania, Luxembourg, Malta, Poland, Portugal, Romania, Slovakia, Slovenia, Spain, Sweden, The Netherlands. It shall not include those which are candidate countries or potential candidates and/or which have departed and/or are in transition to depart.

T.328
'The Territory' shall be Europe and shall be defined by the shaded areas of land, sea and airspace as set out in the attached maps in Schedule B which form part of this agreement. The Territory shall cover a space below the sea of [distance] and above the land and sea of [distance]. The licensed area is defined by area rather than by the names of the countries which may change and it is not defined by reference to membership of the European Union or any other organisation.

T.329
'The Territory' shall be the following full member states of the European Union: Austria, Belgium, Bulgaria, Croatia, Cyprus, Czech Republic, Denmark, Estonia, Finland, France, Germany, Greece, Hungary, Ireland, Italy, Latvia, Lithuania, Luxembourg, Malta, Netherlands, Poland, Portugal, Romania, Slovakia, Slovenia, Spain, Sweden the [27] full members. It shall not include candidates Albania, Montenegro, North Macedonia, Serbia and Turkey. Nor shall it include potential candidates Bosnia and Herzegovina and Kosovo.

T.330

'The Territory' shall mean all the following countries which are full members states of the European Union as at [date] their land and territorial waters: Austria, Belgium, Bulgaria, Croatia, Cyprus, Czech Republic, Denmark, Estonia, Finland, France, Germany, Greece, Hungary, Ireland, Italy, Latvia, Lithuania, Luxembourg, Malta, Netherlands, Poland, Portugal, Romania, Slovenia, Slovakia, Spain, Sweden.

T.331

'The Territory' shall be defined as the following countries and their territorial waters: Austria, Belgium, Bulgaria, Croatia, Cyprus, Czech Republic, Denmark, Estonia, Finland, France, Germany, Greece, Hungary, Italy, Latvia, Lithuania, Luxembourg, Malta, Netherlands, Poland, Portugal, Romania, Slovakia, Slovenia, Spain, Sweden, Albania, Montenegro, North Macedonia, Serbia Turkey, Bosnia and Herzegovina, Kosovo, Andorra, Armenia, Azerbaijan, Belarus, Georgia, Iceland, Liechtenstein, Moldova, Monaco, Norway, Russia, San Marino, Switzerland, Ukraine, United Kingdom, Eire, Northern Ireland and Vatican City.

T.332

'The Territory' shall mean the following United Kingdom overseas territories which are not part of the United Kingdom but which have a constitutional link: Anguilla, Bermuda, British Antarctic Territory, Pitcairn Islands, St Helena and the Dependencies, British Indian Ocean, British Virgin Islands, Cayman Islands, Falkland Islands, Gibraltar, Montserrat, Turks and Caicos Islands, South Georgia and South Sandwich islands, the sovereignty base areas of Akrotiri and Dhekelia In Cyprus.

T.333

'The Territory' shall be defined as the United Kingdom of Great Britain and Northern Ireland and their adjacent territorial waters. It shall not include the Isle of Man and the Channel islands.

T.334

'The Territory' shall mean the United Kingdom of Great Britain and Northern Ireland, the Republic of Ireland, the Channel Islands and the Isle of Man.

T.335

'The Territory' shall mean the United Kingdom, Northern Ireland, the Channel Islands and the Isle of Man and the following countries: [–].

T.336

'The Territory' shall be defined as the United Kingdom meaning the United Kingdom of Great Britain and Northern Ireland and the United Kingdom Continental Shelf but excluding the Channel Islands and the Isle of Man.

T.337

'The Territory' shall mean the United Kingdom of Great Britain which includes England, Wales, Scotland, Northern Ireland and the territorial waters of the United Kingdom shall be treated as part of the United Kingdom. It shall also include things done in the United Kingdom sector of the continental shelf on a structure or vessel which is present there for purposes directly connected with the exploration of the seabed or sub-soil or the exploration of their natural resources.

T.338

The Territory' shall include in respect of each country of the Territory all ships, oil rigs and aircraft of the nationality, flag or registry of such country and all camps, bases, installations and reservations of the armed forces of such country.

T.339

'The Territory' shall be limited to the land known as [address] as specified on the [map/chart/plan]. A copy of which is attached and forms part of the agreement as appendix C. No rights are specified in relation to the sub-terrain, rivers, mining, fracking, excavation, extraction and/or the air space above. The use of the existing properties and structures on the land are included but no rights are granted in respect of any sub-terrain, rivers and water channels, mining, fracking, excavation and/or extraction and/or any air space over the land above [height].

T.340

The Territory' shall cover the [area/borough] of [name] in the [area/county] of [specify name] in [country].

T.341

'The Territory' shall be the United States of America and Canada, Hawaii, Puerto Rico, Mexico, Alaska, Guam and the North Mariana Islands.

T.342

'The Territory' shall be Central America and the Caribbean which shall mean Antigua and Bermuda, Bahamas, Barbados, Belize, Costa Rica, Cuba, Dominica, Dominican Republic, El Salvador, Grenada, Guatemala, Guyana, Haiti, Honduras, Jamaica, Nicaragua, Panama, Saint-Kitts and Nevis, Saint-Lucia, Saint-Vincent, Suriname, Trinidad and Tobago.

T.343

'The Territory' shall mean Argentina, Bolivia, Brazil, Caribbean, Central America, Chile, Columbia, Ecuador, French Guiana, Guyana, Mexico, Paraguay, Peru, Suriname, Uruguay, Venezuela.

T.344

'The Territory' shall be defined as the United States of America, Canada, Mexico, Guatemala, Cuba, Haiti, Dominican Republic, Honduras, Nicaragua and El Salvador.

T.345

'The Territory' shall be the continent of South America which is defined as Argentina, Bolivia, Brazil, Chile, Columbia, Ecuador, Paraguay, Peru, Uruguay and Venezuela

T.346

'The Territory' shall be all the independent states in the world and the dependencies and areas of special sovereignty noted below:

Afghanistan, Albania, Algeria, Andorra, Angola, Antigua and Barbuda, Argentina, Armenia, Aruba, Australia, Austria, Azerbaijan, The Bahamas, Bahrain, Bangladesh, Barbados, Belarus, Belgium, Belize, Benin, Bhutan, Bolivia, Bosnia and Herzegovina, Botswana, Brazil, Brunei, Bulgaria, Burkina Faso, Myanmar, Burundi, Cambodia, Cameroon, Canada, Central African Republic, Chad, Chile, China, Columbia, Comoros, Democratic Republic of the Congo, Republic of the Congo, Costa Rica, Cote d'Ivoire, Croatia, Cuba, Cyprus, Czech Republic, Denmark, Djibouti, Dominica, Dominican Republic, Ecuador, Egypt, El Salvador, Equatorial Guinea, Eritrea, Estonia, Kingdom of Eswatini, Ethiopia, Fiji, Finland, France, Gabon, The Gambia, Georgia, Germany, Ghana, Greece, Grenada, Guatemala, Guinea, Guinea-Bissau, Guyana, Haiti, Holy See, Honduras, Hungary, Iceland, India, Indonesia, Iran, Iraq, Ireland, Israel, Italy, Jamaica, Japan, Jordan, Kazakhstan, Kenya, Kiribati, North Korea, South Korea, Kosovo, Kuwait, Kyrgyzstan, Laos, Latvia, Lebanon, Lesotho, Liberia, Libya, Liechtenstein, Lithuania, Luxembourg, North Macedonia, Madagascar, Malawi, Malaysia, Maldives, Mali, Malta, Marshall Islands, Mauritania, Mauritius, Mexico, Micronesia, Moldova, Monaco, Mongolia, Montenegro, Morocco, Mozambique, Namibia, Nauru, Nepal, Netherlands, Netherland Antilles, New Zealand, Nicaragua, Niger, Nigeria, Norway, Oman, Pakistan, Palau, Panama, Papua New Guinea, Paraguay, Peru, Philippines, Poland, Portugal, Qatar, Romania, Russia, Rwanda, Saint Kitts and Nevis, Saint Lucia, Saint Vincent and the Grenadines, Samoa, San Marino, Sao Tome and Principe, Saudi Arabia, Senegal, Serbia, Seychelles, Sierra Leone, Singapore, Slovakia, Slovenia, Solomon Islands, Somalia, South Africa, South Sudan, Spain, Sri Lanka, Sudan, Suriname, Sweden, Switzerland, Syria, Taiwan, Tajikistan, Tanzania, Thailand, Timor-Leste, Togo, Tonga, Trinidad and Tobago, Tunisia, Turkey, Turkmenistan, Tuvalu, Uganda, Ukraine, United Arab Emirates, United Kingdom, United States, Uruguay, Uzbekistan, Vanuatu, Venezuela, Vietnam, Yemen, Zambia, Zimbabwe.

Akrotiri sovereignty of United Kingdom, American Samoa sovereignty of United States, Anguilla, sovereignty of United Kingdom, Antarctica, Aruba sovereignty of Netherlands, Ashmore and Cartier Islands, sovereignty of Australia, Baker Island sovereignty of United States, Bermuda sovereignty of United Kingdom, Bouvet Island sovereignty of Norway, British Indian Ocean Territory sovereignty of United Kingdom, Cayman Islands sovereignty of United Kingdom, Christmas Island sovereignty of Australia, Clipperton Island sovereignty of France, Cocos (Keeling) Islands sovereignty of Australia, Cook Islands sovereignty of New Zealand, Coral Sea Islands sovereignty of Australia, Curacao sovereignty of Netherlands, Dhekelia sovereignty of United Kingdom, Falkland Islands sovereignty of United Kingdom, Faroe Islands sovereignty of Denmark, French Guiana, French Polynesia sovereignty of France, French Southern and Antarctic Lands sovereignty of France, Gibraltar sovereignty of United Kingdom, Greenland sovereignty of Denmark, Guadeloupe, Guam sovereignty of United States, Bailiwick of Guernsey British Crown Dependency, Heart Island and McDonald Islands sovereignty of Australia, Hong Kong sovereignty of China, Howland Island sovereignty of United States, Isle of Man, British Crown Dependency, Jan Mayen sovereignty of Norway, Jarva Island sovereignty of United States, Bailiwick of Jersey, British Crown Dependency, Johnston Atoll sovereignty of United States, Kingman Reef sovereignty of United States, Macau sovereignty of China, Martinique, Mayotte, Midway Islands sovereignty of United States, Montserratt sovereignty of United Kingdom, Navassa Island sovereignty of United States, New Caledonia sovereignty of France, Niue sovereignty of New Zealand, Norfolk Island sovereignty of Australia, North Mariana Islands sovereignty of United States, Palmyra Atoll sovereignty of United States, Paracel Islands, Pitcairn Islands sovereignty of United Kingdom, Puerto Rico sovereignty of United States, Reunion Island, Saint Barthelemy, sovereignty of France, Saint Helena sovereignty of United Kingdom, Saint Martin sovereignty of France, Saint Pierre and Miquelon sovereignty of France, Saint Maarten sovereignty of Netherlands, South Georgia and the South Sandwich Islands sovereignty of United Kingdom, Spratly Islands, Svalbard sovereignty of Norway, Tokelau sovereignty of New Zealand, Turks and Caicos Islands sovereignty of United Kingdom, Virgin Islands sovereignty of United States, Wake Island sovereignty of United States, Wallis and Futuna sovereignty of France, Western Sahara.

T.347
'The Territory' shall be defined as the land and sovereignty and territorial waters of the [one hundred and ninety-three] member states of the [United Nations]: [list].

T.348
'The 'Territory' shall be the land, sub-terrain, air space, territorial waters and sovereignty of any other island and/or area of [specify country].

T.349

'The Territory' shall be the countries legally recognised and acknowledged by the Government of [country] as at [date] set out in attached Schedule B which forms part of this agreement.

T.350

Each country shall be recorded in the official name which is allocated by the United Kingdom Permanent Committee on Geographical Names/Foreign Office of country] as follows:

List countries Reference name [–] Official Name [–].

T.351

'The Territory' shall be the following countries which have [English/Spanish/other] as one of their official languages: [list countries].

T.352

'The Territory' shall be defined as the following countries with French as an official language: Belgium, Benin, Burkina, Faso Burundi, Cameroon, Canada, Central African Republic, Chad, Ivory Coast, Democratic Republic of the Congo, Djibouti, Equatorial Guinea, France, Haiti, Luxembourg, Madagascar, Mali, Monaco, Niger, Rwanda, Senegal, Seychelles, Switzerland, Togo, Vanuatu.

T.353

'The Territory' shall be defined as the following countries with German as an official language: Austria, Germany, Belgium, Liechtenstein, Luxembourg, Switzerland.

T.354

'The Territory' shall mean Egypt, Tunisia, Jordan, Morocco and Libya.

THIRD PARTY TRANSFER

General Business and Commercial

T.355

Either party shall be entitled to transfer, assign and/or to create a charge and/or lien over the benefit and/or obligations under this agreement. Provided that the rights granted in respect of this agreement are not adversely affected and the indemnity in clause [–] shall continue in full force and effect.

T.356

1.1 The [Licensee] shall not assign and/or transfer the benefit and/or any part of this Licence to a third party. This Licence by the [Licensor] which is of a purely personal nature and solely limited to the [Licensee].

1.2 There is no right to granted to the [Licensee] to grant sub-licence of any nature.

1.3 There is no right granted to the [Licensee] make any application to register any copyright, intellectual property rights, computer software rights and/or any other interest of the original material and/or rights provided by the [Licensor] and/or any adaptation and/or development.

T.357

This agreement shall not be assigned and/or transferred to a third party including but not limited to any parent, subsidiary and/or associated company in whole and/or part by either party at any time.

T.358

The [Company] may at any time assign, sub-license, sub-let and/or otherwise transfer any and/or all of its rights, benefits, duties and/or obligations under this contract subject to the prior consent of [Name]. [Name] agrees not to withhold consent on unreasonable grounds and/or to delay any decision without good reason.

T.359

The [Company] may at any time assign this contract to a third party in its entirety provided that the third party assumes all the obligations, undertakings, payments, liabilities and indemnities set out in the contract to [Name].

T.360

1.1 The [Company] shall not assign this agreement to any third party in whole and/or part and/or alter, change, transfer, sub-license, sub-let, sub-contract and/or otherwise engage and/or use any third party to perform, conduct and/or carry out any of its obligations and/or duties under this agreement.

1.2 If the [Company] wishes to do so then the prior written authority in each case must be obtained from the [Enterprise]. The [Company] must provide complete and transparent disclosure of the proposal and must undertake still to be bound by the terms of this agreement in the event that the third party fails and/or defaults and/or breaches any of the terms of this agreement.

1.3 The [Enterprise] agrees to consider each proposal and not to withhold consent in 1.2 unless it is reasonable to do so and/or to delay any decision more than [number] months from the date of any request.

T.361

1.1 The [Distributor] shall not without the prior and express approval of the [Company] assign the rights and obligations arising out of this contract in whole and/or in part and/or sub-contract any part of the contract and/or cause it to be carried out and/or performed by third parties.

1.2 Even where the [Company] authorises the [Distributor] to sub-contract all and/or part of the services and/or other duties to third parties. The [Distributor] shall still remain bound by its obligations to the [Company] even where any services and/or duties are performed by a third party.

1.3 The [Distributor] shall also be required to include in all contracts with such third parties approved by the [Company] the same restrictions, terms and undertakings as are set out in the main agreement between the [Company] and [Distributor].

T.362

1.1 The [Licensee] shall not assign the benefit of this agreement in whole and/or in part and/or sub-license and/or authorise the exploitation by a third party of any of the copyright. Intellectual property rights and/or any other rights granted and/or material supplied by the [Licensor] and/or any adaptation without the prior written consent of the [Licensor].

1.2 The [Licensor] may provide consent for the [Licensee] to transfer and/or assign the entire agreement to a parent and/or subsidiary company of the [Licensee]. In such event the parent company and/or subsidiary shall assume all the obligations duties, responsibilities and liabilities of the [Licensee] after the date of transfer and/or assignment. The [Licensee] shall then no longer be liable to the [Licensor] in any manner.

T.363
None of the parties to this agreement shall have any right and/or authority to assign, transfer, charge, sub-license, sub-contract and/or otherwise authorise a third party to perform any duties and/or to carry out any obligations and/or to acquire any rights of any nature in any medium and/or format. Any proposals must be agreed and consented to by all parties. Where one party to the agreement refuses to consent then the proposal cannot proceed.

T.364

Neither party to this agreement shall assign, transfer, charge and/or make over this agreement and/or any of its rights or obligations without the prior written consent of the other party.

T.365

This agreement cannot be assigned by either party for any reason except by [Name] to [specify person/company].

T.366

The [Distributor] shall not assign, transfer and/or otherwise create any charge and/or lien and/or other legal transfer of interest of any nature in respect of the whole and/or part of this agreement and/or in respect of any intellectual property rights, copyright, computer software rights, database rights, trade marks, products, services and/or any developments and/or adaptations in any form and/or medium to any third party without the prior written consent of [Name/Enterprise].

T.367

Neither party shall transfer and/or assign this agreement and/or any rights and/or interest acquired and/or obligations undertaken to any person, trust, charity and/or firm and/or company without the prior consent in writing of the other party. Such consent may not be unreasonably withheld and/or delayed where the party seeking consent wishes to assign the agreement as part of an amalgamation and/or restructuring to a company. This clause shall be without prejudice to the rights of either party to sub-license their respective distribution rights in the [Film/Product/Services] as set out in this agreement.

T.368

This Guarantee is freely assignable and/or transferable by the [Company] to any third party and the consent of [Name] is not required.

T.369

None of the [Guarantors/specify persons] may assign any of its obligations and/or undertakings and may not transfer any of its liabilities under this [Guarantee/Document] and/or enter into any transaction which would result in any of those obligations, undertakings and/or liabilities passing to another person and/or company except as a result of the death and/or mental incapacity and/or by an order of a court of law and/or as a result of some legal requirement under any legislation.

T.370

The licence agreement is not transferable except with the prior consent in writing of the [Company]. Consent shall not be given unless the [Company] is satisfied that the person or persons to whom it is proposed to transfer the licence agreement would be in a position to comply with all the terms, conditions and payment liabilities throughout the remainder of the Licence Period.

T.371

You shall not without our prior written consent, assign, transfer and/or sub-contract the [Order] to any third party.

T.372

1.1 This contract is personal between the parties and the [Company] may not assign any rights, obligations and/or liabilities under this contract to any entity other than a parent company without the prior written consent of the [Enterprise].

1.2 Where consent is provided then any assignee shall have to be bound by the same terms as contained in the main agreement. Any such assignment by the [Company] to an assignee shall mean that any assignee is also subject to the same restriction and requires the prior consent of the [Enterprise] in the event that it wishes to make a third party assignment.

1.3 The [Company] agrees that it shall be legally liable for any default, breach and/or failure by any assignee of their agreement and/or in the event that the [Enterprise] is unable to claim any losses, costs, expenses and/or damages from the assignee for any reason.

T.373

The [Company] acknowledges that the [Licensee] shall be entitled at any time and from time to time to dispose of any of its interests in whatever form in any Licensed Area. If such right is exercised then the only liability of the [Licensee] to the [Company] shall be to notify the [Company] that the [Licensee] has disposed of its interests to such third party. The [Licensee] shall no longer be entitled to receive and deliver the [Service/Work] in accordance with the terms of this agreement. In such event the [Company] agrees that it shall enter into a new agreement on terms not materially less favourable than this agreement with the person or persons to whom such disposal is made for the [Service/Work] in the Licensed Area.

T.374

1.1 The [Exhibitor] has no right to transfer, share, assign, sub-let, sub-licence or in any other manner use or allocate the exhibition stand area and/or promotional marketing with any other third party. The exhibition stand area and/or promotional marketing is only for the personal use of the [Exhibitor].

1.2 This requirement in 1.1 may be amended to permit certain exceptions provided that the facts have been disclosed to the [Company] that the [Exhibitor] is displaying and/or selling products and/or services and/or marketing third parties for sponsorship, endorsement and/or advertising purposes and/or for sales of their products and/or services and/or are acting as agents for third party products and/or services for which they will receive commission.

T.375
The [Website/App/Software] is owned and controlled by the [Enterprise]. No authority is provided to any person and/or entity to acquire, license, assign and/or transfer any copyright, intellectual property rights and/or any other rights to a third party. Any licence which has been granted for your use of any material may not be transferred and/or assigned to any third party. This prohibition applies to parent, subsidiary and/or affiliated companies.

T.376
The [App/Software] is supplied to you personally under this service and you may not reproduce, supply and/or authorise any third party to use and/or adapt the [App/Software].

T.377
The [Podcast/Video] is supplied to you on a non-exclusive basis on any device for personal use only and is not to be reproduced for any commercial and/or charitable purpose without the consent of [Name]. You do not have the authority and/or right to license, authorise, assign and/or grant any permissions and/or consent to a third party.

T.378

1.1 You are permitted to reproduce this [Blog/Article] on the following online accounts for non-commercial purposes to your contacts [once] only: [specify online accounts]. Provided that the source and the author are credited as follows: [reference source of Blog/Article] and [Name of Author].

1.2 There is no right to edit, adapt, translate and/or commercially exploit the [Blog/Article] and/or to reproduce it in any magazine, newspaper, book, television and/or radio programme and/or in any other format as a sound recording and/or over the internet and/or any telecommunication system.

T.379
[Name] shall be entitled to assign, sub-license, transfer and/or otherwise create a charge over the [Sound Recordings/Musical Work] and any adaptation and/or development at any time.

T.380

1.1 This product placement is directly between the [Company] and [Name]. [Name] agrees to place the agreed [Products] in the [Video/Podcast/Series] as set out in appendix D.

1.2 In the event at a later date [Name] decides to sell and/or assign the [Video/Podcast/Series] to a third party. The [Company] shall not have any right to object to such a sale and assignment. Nor does [Name] have to notify and/or consult with the [Company].

1.3 The [Company] does not acquire any rights in and/or control over the [Video/Podcast/Series] as a result of this product placement agreement.

T.381

[Name] agrees and undertakes that he/she will not assign and/or transfer any rights in the [Video/Podcast/Series] to a third party without first offering the same rights on the same terms to the [Company].

T.382

The [Licensor] may assign this agreement and/or any of its rights to any third party but any such assignment shall not relieve the [Licensor] of any of its obligations under this agreement.

T.383

The [Company] and/or [Name] may assign this agreement and/or any part of their rights and/or interest to any person, business and/or other legal entity. Provided that any such assignment shall not relieve that party whether the [Company] and/or [Name] of their obligations, undertakings and/or liabilities. The [Company] and/or [Name] shall remain responsible and bear the costs, expenses, damages and losses incurred in respect of the omissions, defaults and/or failures of any third party to whom they have disposed of and/or assigned any rights and/or interest.

T.384

1.1 The [Licensor] shall be entitled to license, transfer, assign and/or to create a charge and/or lien over the [Registered Trade Marks] in whole and/or in part including but not limited to: licensing the use of the [Registered Trade Marks] for a service and/or products in any country and/or any merchandising and/or exploitation in any other medium and/or format.

1.2 The [Licensor] acknowledges that in the [United Kingdom/other] the assignment and/or other transfer of a [Registered Trade Mark] is not effective without the consent of the [Registrar].

T.385

The [Licensor] shall have the right to assign the benefit of this agreement provided:

1.1 That the rights and licence granted to the [Licensee] shall not be adversely affected by such assignment and

1.2 The [Licensor] agrees to indemnify the [Licensee] against any losses, damages, costs, expenses and/or claim that may arise as a direct consequence of any such assignment.

T.386

1.1 The [Company] shall be entitled to assign and/or transfer the benefit of this agreement and/or to grant sub-licences to third parties without the prior consent of [Name].

1.2 In each case the [Company] shall only be required to give written notice of their intention to make such assignment, transfer and/or grant to a third party to [Name] a minimum of [one] month prior to the date of the agreement in each case. The [Company] shall provide the name of the third party but is not required to supply details of the proposed agreement.

T.387

This agreement may be assigned by either party to any respective personal representatives, assignees and/or other successors in title.

T.388

This agreement shall be binding upon the successors in business and/or title of the [Company/Name] and may in any event be transferred and/or assigned to any third party by the [Company/Name]. Provided that the third party agrees to be bound by all the terms of the main agreement and is financially capable of fulfilling the terms and paying for any liability.

T.389

1.1 This agreement is restricted to the contracting parties. Neither party may seek to assign, transfer, charge and/or otherwise dispose of any part of this agreement to any third party at any time.

1.2 Nor shall either party grant any sub-licence of any part and/or authorise any part of the performance of the obligations to be carried out by any third parties without the prior written approval of the other party. There is no obligation on the other party to provide approval. Where consent is provided it shall be on the basis that the party who has been provided with permission will still continue to be liable as well as the third party. Such consent shall not relieve either party of their undertakings and obligations under this agreement.

T.390

1.1 This agreement is personal to the contracting parties.

1.2 Neither party may seek to transfer, assign, charge, sub-license, sub-contract and/or appoint any sub-agent and/or sub-distributor and/or other manufacturer and/or any other third party to perform, be responsible for and/or bear the liability of this agreement without the consent in writing of the other party.

1.3 The exception in 1.1 and 1.2 is where the whole business of either party is to be sold to a third party and the other party has consented to such assignment. In such instance the benefit and burden of this agreement shall be binding upon the successors in business and/or title of the party which has made the assignment.

T.391

The [Company] shall be entitled either before or after the launch date of the [Collection] by the [Designer] to assign, sell, transfer, charge or otherwise dispose of the [Domain Name/Website/App] as it thinks fit. The consent and/or approval of the [Designer] is not required and the [Designer] waives any rights and/or interest provided that he/she is paid for the completion of their services for the [Collection] as described in Appendix C.

T.392

1.1 Neither party shall assign, transfer, sub-license and/or authorise any third party that they are entitled to exercise any rights and/or obligations under this agreement without the prior written consent of the other party. This prohibition shall apply to any parent, subsidiary and/or associated company and/or agency.

1.2 If permission is requested in 1.1 then full disclosure should be made of the proposal and in such case consent may not be unreasonably withheld and/or delayed.

1.3 Any such consent shall be subject to the conclusion of a written undertaking to the other party by the new assignee that the assignee will fulfil all the rights, obligations and liabilities under the new agreement.

1.4 Any new assignee in 1.3 shall not relieve the party to this agreement of any undertakings, obligations and/or liabilities under this main agreement. If any new assignee shall default, be in breach and/or unable to fulfil the terms for any reason. Then the party to this agreement who carried out the assignment shall pay all the costs, expenses, losses, damages and/or other sums that may be due to other party.

T.393

The [Licensee] undertakes not to assign to any third party any rights acquired under the terms of this agreement unless previously authorised in writing by the [Company] to do so.

T.394

The [Company] shall not be entitled to assign, transfer, dispose of and/or create a charge and/or lien over any part of this agreement without the prior consent of [Name] in each case.

T.395

The [Distributor] shall not assign the rights granted and/or any other benefit under this agreement (except as part of an internal restructuring of the [Distributor]) without the [Company's] written consent which shall not be withheld and/or delayed unless there are good reasons to do so.

T.396

1.1 The [Licensor] agrees that he/she shall not license and/or authorise any third party to reproduce, sell and/or exploit any other [Products/ Services/Programmes] based on the [Format/Character/] and/or any development and/or adaptation and/or sequel during the first [number] [months/years] of the Licence Period.

1.2 The [Licensee] accepts that the [Licensor] may assign the whole agreement to another third party after [date]. Provided that the new third party assumes responsibility and liability for the whole agreement.

T.397

1.1 The [Licensee] agrees that the [Licensor] shall be entitled to approve the appointment of any sub-agent, sub-licensee and/or any other third party in respect of the production, manufacture, supply, packaging, distribution, marketing and/or other exploitation of the [Products/ Services/Units/Rights] under this agreement.

1.2 The [Licensor] agrees to approve and/or reject any proposal within [number] days of the request by the [Licensee]. The [Licensor] shall not be obliged to state the grounds of objection.

T.398

The [Licensor] agrees that it shall not have the right to approve and/or be consulted in respect of the appointment of any sub-agent, sub-licensee, distributor and any other third party in respect of the production, manufacture, supply, distribution, packaging, marketing of the [Licensed Articles/Units] under this agreement.

T.399
Neither party may assign, transfer, charge and/or make over this agreement and/or any of its rights and/or obligations except that the [Distributor/Supplier] may assign the agreement to a parent company. No assignment shall relieve the [Distributor/Supplier] of any of its obligations and/or liabilities under this agreement if the parent company is in breach and/or default for any reason and fails to remedy and/or settle the matter within [number] months.

T.400

1.1 Neither party shall assign and/or transfer any part of this agreement to be owned, controlled, performed and/or carried out by a third party. This exclusion shall apply to any parent, subsidiary, associated accompany, affiliate and/or agency, manufacturer and/or distributor.

1.2 Where there are any proposed changes required then they must be agreed between the parties on each occasion. No party which is not a signatory to this agreement shall be entitled to rely on any of the terms.

1.3 Where changes are agreed then a new addendum to the main agreement must be concluded between the parties. Even where the matter relates to the appointment of a third party.

T.401
The [Licensee] shall not be entitled to assign, transfer, charge, dispose of, sub-license, sub-contract and/or otherwise delegate any part of this agreement to any third party except for professional legal and accounting advisors who provide data, information, reports and payments pursuant to this agreement on behalf of the [Licensee]. This shall not in any way absolve the [Licensee] from the obligations, duties and responsibilities set out in this agreement nor shall any such advisors be party to this agreement. No third party shall be entitled to rely on and/or enforce the terms of this agreement which is only between the contracting parties.

T.402
Both parties shall have the right to assign, transfer, license and charge the benefit of this agreement to any third party provided:

1.1 That it shall not relieve the [Company] of any of the obligations under this agreement. In the event of a breach by any such third party which is not remedied then the [Company] shall be liable.

1.2 The third party receiving the benefit of this agreement in whole and part must undertake that the rights of the other party under this agreement shall not be adversely affected by the [assignment/transfer/licence/charge] and must agree to indemnify the other party against any losses, damages, costs, expenses, claims and/or liability arising in consequence of such agreement with the third party.

T.403

The [Supplier] agrees that it is not authorised by the [Company] and/or entitled to assign, transfer and/or sub-contract the [Commissioned Order/Work/Unit] to any third party.

T.404

There shall be no restrictions on either party in respect of the engagement of third parties to carry out obligations and/or perform the terms. Either party may assign this agreement in whole and/or part to a third party. Provided that the third party agrees to arrange insurance cover for any default and/or failure by the third party under the agreement.

T.405

1.1 The [Supplier] has been assessed according to the policy procedures of the [Charity/Institute] and has been personally chosen from a selection of suppliers to perform the contract.

1.2 The [Supplier] shall not have the authority and/or right under this contract to assign and/ transfer the contract to a third party and/or to sub-contract out any part and/or all of the [Purchase Order/Project] and/or to delegate any responsibilities to a third party to perform without the prior written consent of the [Charity/Institute].

T.406

The term '[Publisher/Company]' in this agreement shall be deemed to include the person or persons or company for the time being carrying on the business under the same registered name as the [Publisher/Company], whether they be heirs, executors, personal representatives, administrators and/or assignees.

T.407

This agreement shall apply to the parties to this agreement and their respective personal representatives, assignees and/or other successors in title.

T.408

The [Publisher] may assign and/or sub-license this agreement in whole and/or part and/or any of its rights to any company that is a parent, subsidiary and/or associated with the [Publisher] in the group known as [specify name]. Any such assignees and/or licensees shall be entitled to the same rights and terms as stated in respect of the [Publisher] in this agreement. Any assignee and/or licensees shall be obliged to be responsible for same undertakings, responsibilities and liabilities as set out in the main agreement for the [Publisher] in respect of such rights as have been assigned under any agreement and/or granted under any licence.

T.409

1.1 The [Company] shall be entitled to assign this agreement and the rights granted to the [Company] in whole and/or in part to any third party.

1.2 The [Writer] agrees that if the [Company] wishes the [Writer] to provide his/her services in whole and/or in part to any third party. The [Writer] agrees that he/she shall do so provided that the third party is approved by the [Writer] and that a new agreement is concluded with the third party on the same terms and conditions as set out in this agreement and/or more favourable terms.

1.3 In the event that the [Writer] concludes any such agreement with a third party in 1.2. The [Company] agrees and undertakes that if such third parties shall default and/or fail to fulfil the obligations to the [Writer] that the [Company] shall pay such sums as may be due to the [Writer] up to a maximum of [number/currency] in total.

T.410

The [Company] undertakes not to authorise, license, assign and/or transfer the right to sell, publish and/or exploit the [Article/Interview/Sound Recordings] in any other language, newspaper, periodical, magazine, television and/or radio programme and/or to any other media in any format in any country for any purpose without the prior written consent of [Name] and his/her [Agent].

T.411

[Name] agrees and undertakes not to engage and/or enter into any agreement with any third party to write, research, produce and/or distribute and exploit any other hardback, paperback and/or audio file and/or other sound recordings based on the [Synopsis/Project/Manuscript/Work] and/or any adaptation and/or sequel in any media at any time [during the Term of the Agreement/from [date] to [date]] throughout the [Territory/world/country].

T.412

The [Company] shall consult with the [Author/Artist] in respect of the appointment of any third party including any sub-agent, sub-distributor, sub-licensee, manufacturer, designer and/or software development company to exploit the [Work/Character/Game].

T.413
The [Author] undertakes that he/she will not grant any option nor authorise, license and/or permit any third party to produce a [Film/Video/Series] based on the [Hardback/Paperback/Audio File/Work] of the [Author] and/or any adaptation, translation and/or merchandising during the [Option Period] without the prior written consent of the [Company].

T.414
If this agreement is assigned to a third party due to the sale of all the business assets of the [Company]. The terms shall be binding on all successors in title and/or assignees until the agreement expires and/or is terminated and/or there are no outstanding claims by either party whichever is the later.

T.415

1.1   This agreement is between the [Agent] and the [Actor]. No third party shall be entitled to rely on any terms of this agreement.

1.2   Neither party shall assign, transfer, charge and/or make over this agreement and/or any of its rights to any third party without the written consent of the other party.

1.3   The [Agent] is not entitled to sign any agreement on behalf of the [Actor].

T.416

1.1   This agreement is purely personal between the [Actor] and the [Agent] and no third party may seek to benefit and/or enforce its obligations unless it has been agreed to by the [Actor] and the [Agent].

1.2   This agreement may be terminated with immediate effect by notice in writing if either party is not available for a continuous period of [four] months (excluding weekends) to perform the obligations set out.

1.3   The [Agent] shall at all times be responsible for the acts, omissions, defaults and liabilities and other matters arising directly and/or indirectly from any third parties whom the [Agent] has arranged and/or appointed to carry out any work on behalf of the [Agent] relating to the [Actor].

1.4   Neither party shall be entitled to assign, transfer, license, charge and/or authorise and/or make over any part of this agreement and/or any part of its duties, rights, obligations, indemnities and/or liabilities to a third party without full disclosure of the terms proposed and the written consent of the other party.

T.417

1.1 This agreement is personal to the [Company] and [Name].

1.2 No third party including but not limited to any parent company and/or agent shall be party to this agreement at any time and therefore shall have no right to rely on the terms of this agreement.

T.418

1.1 The [Company] agrees that it shall not be entitled to reproduce, use, adapt, develop, license, assign and/or exploit any of the original master material and/or any copies created for the purposes of this agreement in which [Name] appears, talks and/or performs in sound and/or vision at any time other than for the promotion, marketing and advertising of the [Products] as set out and described in Appendix A during the Term of the Agreement and/or any time thereafter without the prior written consent of [Name].

1.2 The [Company] agrees that it shall not be entitled to reproduce, use, adapt, develop, license, assign, exploit and/or register any copyright, intellectual property rights, trade marks, mechanical reproduction rights and/or performing rights and/or any other interest in any material in which [Name] appears, talks and/or performs in sound and/or vision at any time without the prior written consent of [Name].

1.3 [Name] is under no obligation to provide any consent to any request in 1.1 and 1.2 by the [Company]. Any consent shall be subject to the terms of a new agreement.

T.419

The rights granted in this agreement are personal to the [Client/Customer] and may not be assigned, transferred, sub-licensed, supplied and/or distributed and/or otherwise disposed of at any time to another person and/or entity.

T.420

The [Agent] undertakes that he/she shall not at any time assign, transfer, and/or create a lien and/or a legal charge over the benefits, rights and/or sums to be received in the future under this agreement and/or any associated agreement to any third party without the prior written consent of the [Artist].

T.421

1.1 The [Company] shall be entitled to make available the services of the [Presenter/Name] to any parent company, subsidiary, joint venture partner and/or any other sponsor and/or major shareholder of the [Company] to film, record, provide voice-over and/or otherwise be involved in projects, promotions and/or marketing events which directly relate to the [Company]. Provided that any such arrangement shall be subject to the prior consent of the [Presenter/Name] and shall be subject to the conclusion of a new agreement for that work and the payment of additional fees and expenses.

1.2 The [Company] shall not have the right to authorise and/or assign the services of the [Presenter/Name] to a third party.

T.422
The [Music Publisher] shall not have the right to transfer and/or assign the benefit of this agreement and/or any parts without the prior written consent of the [Author]. Any consent provided by the [Author] shall be subject to the transferee and/or assignee concluding an agreement with the [Author] which incorporates all the obligations and liabilities of the [Music Publisher] to the [Author].

T.423

1.1 The [Publisher] acknowledges and agrees that the [Author] shall be entitled to transfer, assign, license, create a charge and/or lien over and/or bequeath any part of this agreement relating to the [Author] to a third party. Provided that the [Author] has completed the work required to be delivered under this agreement and the [Publisher] has received and accepted the [Musical Works/Sound Recordings/ Manuscript].

1.2 The [Author] agrees to notify the [Publisher] of their proposal in 1.1 and to allow the [Publisher] [one] calendar month from that date to make an offer to the [Author] which is more favourable.

T.424
The [Publisher] agrees that after the delivery and acceptance of the [Work/ Manuscript/Final Proofs/Audio Files]. The [Author] shall have the right to assign and transfer the agreement to any third party and/or to create a lien as security from the royalties and other sums that may fall due to the [Author]. Provided that no agreement with any third party shall relinquish the [Author] from any of the undertakings, obligations, liabilities and/or indemnities by the [Author] to the [Publisher] before [date].

T.425

The [Association/Charity] agrees and undertakes that it has not and will not grant to any third party any copyright, intellectual property rights, licences and/or consents which have and/or will directly conflict with and/or prejudice the agreement with the [Sponsor] from [date] to [date].

T.426

The [Sponsor] agrees that it shall not be entitled to make any arrangement with and/or authorise any third parties to contribute to the funding of the [Event/Project] without the prior written consent of the [Association/Charity].

T.427

Where there is a change of control and ownership of the [Sponsor] then the [Sponsor] shall not have the automatic right to transfer and/or assign this agreement to the successor in title. The prior written consent and authority of [Name] shall be required. [Name] is entitled to refuse consent and to serve notice of the termination of the agreement due to the change of control and/or ownership of the [Sponsor].

T.428

The [Institute/Charity] shall be entitled to assign and/or transfer the benefit of this agreement to other third parties and successors in title and/or enterprise and/or purpose and/or to grant sub-licences for the [Work/Services/Material] on the basis that:

1.1 The [Institute/Charity] shall give [two] calendar months written notice of such proposed assignment, transfer and/or grant of a sub-licence to the [Company] and

1.2 The person and/or company receiving the assignment, transfer and/or grant of a sub-licence agrees to be bound by the undertakings, obligations and terms of this agreement.

1.3 Where any such sub-licensee defaults, fails to pay any sums and/or otherwise breaches the sub-licence. The [Institute/Charity] shall be liable to pay for all such costs, expenses, losses and/or damages and/or interest which may be due and/or owed to [Name].

T.429

Neither the [Institute] nor [Name] shall assign, transfer, charge and/or make over any part of this agreement and/or any part of its rights and/or obligations without the prior written consent of the other party which shall not be unreasonably withheld or delayed.

1918

T.430

The [Institute/Charity] shall have the right to assign, transfer, license and charge the benefit of this agreement to any third party provided that:

1.1 A formal novation agreement is signed and authorised by the [Institute/Charity] and [Name] and

1.2 [Name] is provided with a single payment of [number/currency] by the [Institute/Charity] as a novation fee.

1.3 The [Institute/Charity] shall no longer be liable to [Name] in respect of those matters which are assigned permanently to a third party and which are novated.

T.431

1.1 The [Company] shall not without the written consent of the [Institute/Charity] be entitled to assign, transfer, charge, dispose of, appoint a sub-contractor, appoint an agent and/or delegate any of the duties, responsibilities, work, obligations and liabilities in this agreement without the prior written consent of the [Institute/Charity] on each occasion.

1.2 The [Institute/Charity] shall be entitled to refuse all such requests in 1.1. Any consent which is provided shall not absolve the [Company] from the terms of this agreement at any time.

1.3 No third party shall be entitled to rely on and/or enforce the terms of this agreement which is only between the contracting parties.

T.432

1.1 There shall be no restriction on the assignment of this agreement by the [Company] to any parent company, subsidiary and/or new entity created as a result of restructuring and/or rebranding the business.

1.2 The [Company] shall be entitled to assign, license, sell and/or otherwise exploit the material created as a result of the product of the services of [Name] under this agreement. [Name] shall not be entitled to any further fees, royalties and/or other sums.

1.3 The [Company] shall be entitled to delete and edit out the performance of [Name] from all the material which has been created. In such event then [Name] shall no longer be entitled to a credit.

TIME OF THE ESSENCE

General Business and Commercial

T.433

Both parties agree that all times and dates referred to in this agreement shall be of the essence.

T.434

Both parties agree that all times and dates referred to in this agreement shall be of the essence. In the event that the [Photographer] fails to deliver the [Photographic Package] by the Delivery Date the [Assignee] shall have the right to terminate this agreement by notice in writing. The [Assignee] shall be entitled to be repaid all sums previously paid to the [Photographer] in respect of the [Photographer's Fee] and the [Photographic Package].

T.435

In the event that the [Author] fails to deliver the [Manuscript/Material/Proofs/Sound Recordings] by the stipulated date: [specify date]. As it is agreed between the parties that time is of the essence the [Publishers] may at their sole discretion exercise their right to terminate this agreement by notice to the [Author] with an immediate termination date. The [Author] shall be obliged upon such termination to repay all sums previously paid to him/her pursuant to this agreement.

T.436

1.1 Both parties agree that the dates by which work must be performed and/or delivered and/or sums paid and/or any other matter as set out in this agreement are for guidance only and are not of the essence of this agreement.

1.2 It is agreed between the parties that dates may be varied by mutual agreement between the parties.

1.3 Neither party shall be entitled to terminate this agreement due to the default, breach and/or failure of the other party to carry out their obligations by the dates unless they shall have failed to do so for a period of more than [three] months after notification of the problem.

T.437

1.1 The delivery date of the [Work/Manuscript/Stills/Videos] shall be of the essence of this agreement.

1.2   If the [Author/Name] shall fail to deliver the [Work/Manuscript/Stills/ Videos] by the delivery date the [Publisher/Distributor] shall give the [Author/Name] [four] months' written notice to deliver the [Work/ Manuscript/Stills/Videos] and may at its discretion extend this period.

1.3   If the [Author/Name] fails to deliver the [Work/Manuscript/Stills/Videos] by the notified amended delivery date then the [Publisher] shall be entitled to serve notice to terminate the agreement with immediate effect.

1.4   If the agreement is terminated in 1.3 then the [Author/Name] shall be obliged to reach an arrangement for the repayment of all the Advance within a [one]-year period.

T.438

1.1   The delivery date is not the essence of the contract. The [Publisher/ Distributor] may give the [Author/Illustrator] up to [six] months or longer to deliver the [Work/Manuscript/Images/Artwork] after the first delivery date has not been adhered to.

1.2   If the [Author/Illustrator] still fails to deliver the [Work/Manuscript/ Images/Artwork] by any extended dates. Then after a further period of [two] months' notice the [Publisher/Distributor] shall have the right to terminate the agreement. In such event the [Publishers] agree that there shall be no obligation to repay the Advance unless the [Author/Illustrator] concludes another agreement for the same [Work/ Manuscript/Images/Artwork] and receives an advance from the third party in excess of [number/currency]. In such case the parties will agree a repayment schedule of the Advance.

T.439
It is agreed that the delivery of the [Products/Services] by the specified date shall be of the essence of this agreement. In the event that the [Production Company] fail to deliver the [Products/Services] to the [Enterprise] by the Delivery Date the [Enterprise] shall be entitled to terminate the agreement by notice in writing and/or the [Enterprise] shall be entitled to reduce the amount of consideration due to the [Production Company] payable by the [Enterprise] by [number/currency] (exclusive of VAT and any other taxes or levies) for every day and/or pro rata part of a day by which delivery of the [Products/Services] is delayed. Where the total deductions for late delivery exceed the total consideration due under this agreement to the [Production Company] then the [Production Company] shall not be obliged to pay [Enterprise] any additional sum for late delivery.

T.440

Time is of the essence for this agreement. It is vital that all times and dates for delivery and payment are adhered to at all times.

T.441

Both parties agree that all delivery and payment dates referred to in this agreement shall be crucial and that time is of the essence. The only exception shall be where the parties agree in writing that they may be varied in any instance. The waiver of one delivery date and/or payment date does not mean that all subsequent dates are also waived and/or amended.

T.442

Where a date which is specified in this agreement is waived, amended and/or varied this shall not mean that the party may not rely on the later agreed dates to terminate the agreement. Nor does it mean that the party shall be obliged to waive and/or alter other dates which are set out in the agreement.

T.443

1.1 It is a condition of this agreement that the [Writer/Creator] of the [Blog] meet the deadlines and times specified by the [Institute/Charity] on a monthly basis for the delivery and posting of the articles, films, videos, images and sound recordings based on the planned [Work Schedule] which is set out in appendix A.

1.2 The [Institute/Charity] accepts and agrees that there may be circumstances where the delivery of material is affected due to the default and/or actions of third parties and/or force majeure. In those situations there shall be no grounds for termination of this agreement.

T.444

[Name] is the original creator of the series of [Podcasts] known as [specify series title]. [Name] has agreed to promote and market the [Products/Services] on the [Podcasts] on the following dates: [specify dates]. It is a condition of this agreement that these dates cannot be changed and/or waived as the [Podcasts] are part of the [national/global] launch campaign of the [Products/Services] by the [Company] in [country/world].

T.445

The [Sponsor] agrees and undertakes that the payments dates relating to the Sponsorship Fees are crucial to this agreement and that time is of the essence. The [Sponsor] agrees that the payments cannot be delayed for any reason even if the [Event/Festival] is cancelled and/or delayed for any reason. That the [Sponsor] shall pay the sums and agree an alternative virtual [Event/Festival] with the [Organisers] as a substitute.

T.446

Although time is of the essence to all dates and payment schedules referred to in this agreement. Where the [Project/Event] is delayed, cancelled and/or materially altered due to force majeure and/or withdrawal of a major funding source and/or the cancellation of performers and/or disappointing sales. The [Sponsor] shall be entitled to withhold payment and not pay any sponsorship fees due until the matter has been resolved with the [Promoters/Company].

T.447

The [Software Company] agree that the proposed schedule set out in appendix A for the development, creation, testing, delivery and launch of a fully functional [Website/App/Platform] are of the utmost importance and cannot be changed for any reason except grounds due to force majeure which are beyond the reasonable control of the [Software Company] and/or with the express consent of [Name/role] at the [Institute/Enterprise].

T.448

1.1 The [Exhibitor] accepts and agrees that the dates, times and location of the [Festival/Exhibition] may be changed by the [Company] for any reason up to [one] calendar month prior to the [Festival/Exhibition].

1.2 The [Company] agrees that it shall not be entitled to delay the date of the [Festival/Exhibition] for more than [six] months unless the reasons for the delay are due to force majeure.

1.3 The parties agree that time is not of the essence in this agreement.

1.4 Where the [Festival/Exhibition] is to be delayed more than [six] months from the original booking. Then the [Exhibitor] shall be entitled to a full refund including any deposit if they so wish. The [Company] shall not be entitled to charge any administration and/or other costs.

TITLE

Film, Television and Video

T.449

1.1 The supply to the [Distributor] of the [Master Material] shall not imply a change of ownership in the [Films/Sound Recordings]. All such [Master Material] shall be and remain the property of the [Company] and shall not be used for any other purpose other than the manufacture and/or reproduction of [Units/DVDs/Downloads/Electronic Files] as set out in this agreement.

1.2 It is agreed that in the event that the [Distributor] has paid for the cost of a copy of the [Master Material] that they shall be entitled to retain possession of it for their sole use for the Term of this Agreement.

1.3 At the expiry and/or termination the agreement the [Master Material] together with all copies, adaptations and/or developments shall be returned at the [Distributors'] cost to the [Company] and/or at the [Company's] request destroyed and/or deleted. The [Chief Executive/other] of the [Distributor] shall confirm the destruction and/or deletion in writing and/or confirm that all material of any nature in any medium has been sent to the [Company].

T.450

1.1 The [Distributor] agrees that the copyright and any other intellectual property rights in all packaging, promotional material, and artwork and/or any copies provided by the [Company] for reproduction in whole and/or shall be owned by the [Company].

1.2 Where it is necessary for the [Distributor] to commission a new updated version and/or some other adaptation in any medium of any nature. The [Distributor] undertakes to ensure that any new copyright and/or intellectual property rights and/or trade marks, computer software and/or other rights of any nature are assigned to the [Company]. The [Distributor] shall ensure that such third party does not retain and/or acquire any rights and shall make it a condition of any such commission of new material that the third party will sign an assignment of the rights to the [Company].

T.451

1.1 The [Company] acknowledges that the copyright and all other rights of any nature whether in existence now and/or created in the future shall be the sole property of the [Distributor]. The [Company] agrees at the expense of the [Distributor] to do and execute all such documents as may be required by the [Distributor] to confirm its title to the rights.

1.2 'The [Company] as the owner assigns all present and future copyright, intellectual property rights, trade marks and/or any other rights in any other medium and/or format in the [Works and Material] listed in appendix A to the [Distributor] for the full period of copyright and all extensions and renewals and indefinitely without limitation of time throughout the world and universe whether in existence now and/or created in the future including but not limited to television, radio, the internet and any telecommunication system, hologram, merchandising and any sequel, merchandising, translation and/or adaptation.

T.452

The copyright in the material supplied is owned by the [Company]. No licence is granted to the [Customer] to make copies and/or to exhibit the material in public and/or to supply and/or distribute it to any other person at any time by any method.

T.453

1.1 The [Assignor] confirms that it is the sole owner of all copyright and any other intellectual property rights, computer software rights, mechanical reproduction rights and/or performing rights and/or any other rights in the [Video/Film/Recordings] which are assigned under this agreement to the [Assignee] for the full period of copyright and any extensions and/or renewals and shall continue in perpetuity throughout the world and outer space.

1.2 This assignment in 1.1 is subject to the criteria that any exploitation in any media shall be subject to the prior consent and payment of the persons specified in schedule B in accordance with the specified sums. Where there is a new format to be exploited not mentioned in the schedule then terms must be agreed with the person based on the proposed project.

T.454

[Name] assigns all present and future copyright, intellectual property rights and/or any other right and/or interest in any media and/or format of any nature to the [Distributor] in respect of the [Sound Recordings] and the [Material] whether in existence now or created in the future throughout the world and universe indefinitely and in perpetuity and/or for such other period as may be possible at any time including for the full period of copyright and any extensions and renewals.

T.455

'The Title Rights' shall be defined as the exclusive right of the [Company] to have the [Event/Series] marketed and promoted as: [specify title] for all forms of exploitation in any media from [date] to date] including but not limited to the broadcast and/or transmission and/or streaming and/or play back archive of the [Sound Recordings/Films] of the [Event/Series] on television and/or radio whether accessed by means of a laptop, computer, mobile and/or any other gadget and/or device and/or whether by terrestrial, satellite, cable and/or in electronic form by means of the internet and/or any telecommunication system, wifi and/or any other method and/or format.

T.456

'The Title Rights' shall mean the sole and exclusive right to have the [Event] referred to in all forms of the media of any nature in any format from [date to [date] as: [specify words/logos/other] as described in appendix A in any form of exploitation in sound and/or vision and/or otherwise by [Name] and/or any agents, licensees and/or third parties including satellite, cable, terrestrial television and radio and/or in advertisements, promotion and competition material and any exploitation over the internet and/or any telecommunication system including websites, apps, blogs, podcasts, streaming, downloads and audio recordings.

T.457

1.1 The [Licensor] undertakes and warrants that it has full power and authority to enter into and perform this agreement.

1.2 At the date of this agreement there are not and during the full period of time during which the [Licensee] retains the rights granted in this agreement there will not be any liens, charges and/ or encumbrances against the [Film/Sound Recordings/Artwork] which will and/or might impair the exercise by the [Licensee] of the rights granted.

1.3 The [Licensor] has not and will not grant any rights the exercise of which would derogate from and/or be in conflict with and/or the same as the rights granted to the [Licensee] in this agreement.

T.458

1.1 The [Agent] undertakes and warrants that the [Agent] has the control and authority to grant the rights in this agreement to the [Distributor]. That the [Agent] has been granted permission to execute and sign any agreement on behalf of [Name/Enterprise].

1.2 That the [Agent] has acquired the control to exercise the rights and the authority to do so from [Name/Enterprise] by an agreement dated [date] appointing the [Agent] as its exclusive representative.

1.3 That [Name/Enterprise] is the sole and absolute owner of the copyright and all other rights in all material incorporated in the [Film/Sound Recordings] as are and/or may be required to permit the [Film/Sound Recordings] to be exploited in all media except for such rights as are administered by a third party including the performing rights, mechanical reproduction rights and/or which are administered by any other rights management organisation throughout the world.

1.4 That the [Agent] shall arrange for [Name/Enterprise] to also sign this agreement.

T.459

1.1   The [Company] warrants that as at [date] the [Company] has good title and full right and authority to license the copyright and intellectual property rights, computer software rights and/or other rights in the [Film/Video] including the soundtrack to [Name] in [country] in [language].

1.2   That the [Company] is not aware of any threatened and/or pending legal proceedings.

1.3   That there is no lien, charge and/or any outstanding liability in respect of the production of the [Film/Video/].

1.4   That although the rights have been cleared for exploitation by the [Company]. [Name] shall be liable for all the sums specified in appendix A for the exercise and use of any rights to the third parties and rights management organisations and/or rightsholders listed and any other sums and costs that may be due.

T.460

The [Company] agrees that the [Material] and all copies and/or adaptations of any nature shall remain the property of the [Licensor] and that at the end of the Licence Period the [Material] and all copies and/or adaptations of any nature will be returned to the [Licensor] at the [Licensee's] cost.

T.461

1.1   The scripts, choreography, costumes, props and/or any other material provided to the [Performer] by the [Company] are on loan to the [Performer] solely for the purpose of the performances as set out in this agreement.

1.2   The [Company] are and shall remain the owners of all material and the [Performer] is not entitled to copy, reproduce, use, license and/or exploit the scripts, choreography, costumes, props and/or any other material for any other purpose without the prior written consent of the [Company].

T.462

1.1   The [Company] shall be the sole owner of all copyright and all intellectual property rights, trade marks and/or any other rights in the [Work/Material] from [date/time] and forever without limit including the full period of copyright and any extensions and/or renewals through the [world/earth, outer space and the universe].

1.2   The rights in 1.1 owned by the [Company] include but are not limited to any exploitation by means of television , radio, mobiles, gadgets, computers and/or the internet whether by means of broadcast, transmission, streaming, satellite, cable and/or terrestrial means and/or wifi and/or any telecommunication system and/or by electronic means in the form of films, sound recordings, extracts and/or any form of publication in hardback and/or paperback and/or as a transcript, audio file and/or download. It shall include any adaptation and/or development from the original [Work/Material] and/or any character and/or location and/or content included in it and/or any computer software and/or game and/or competition and/or promotions and/or gambling and/or theme parks which may be derived from it.

1.3 [Name] accepts and agrees that he/she no long owns and/or controls any rights and is not entitled to any additional royalties and/or other sums for any reason other than those set out in this agreement. [Name] accepts that he /she has no further claim and/or title after [date/time].

T.463

1.1 The [Distribution Company] warrants that it will be an exclusive licensee of the owner [specify owner] of all rights in the [Film/Series] and/or parts and shall be entitled to sub-license the rights to third parties.

1.2 That the [Distribution Company] controls the copyright in the [Film/ Series] which are granted to the [Television Company] for the purposes of this agreement. That such rights are or will prior to the start of the Licence Period be vested in the [Distribution Company] free from any encumbrances.

1.3 The [Television Company] accepts and agrees that it shall be responsible for:

    a.   any payment in respect of the performing rights in any music as are controlled by the [specify organisation] or any society affiliated to it in respect of the exercise of the rights granted under this agreement.

    b.   any payment in respect of actors, performers, singers, musicians and other persons who appear in and/or have contributed to the [Film/Series] and/or any sound track and/or any musical work and/or other matter as may be specified in the attached appendix A which forms part of this agreement.

T.464

1.1 In consideration of the [Company] providing the total funding budget to create and develop and produce the [Pilot]. [Name] agrees that the

[Company] shall have the exclusive option to conclude an agreement for the production and commercial exploitation of a [Series] based on the [Pilot] in all media throughout the world including terrestrial, cable, satellite, wifi and telecommunication systems and/or electronic means whether by radio, television, the internet, any playback archive and/or streaming and/or in any audio file, download, any mechanical reproduction and/or performance and/or adaptation in any format and/or by any means and/or device.

1.2 The exclusive option shall start on [date] subject to delivery of the [Pilot] to the [Company]. If delivery is delayed the start of the option shall be delayed accordingly. The [Company] shall have a [four] month period from the date of delivery of the [Pilot] to exercise the option by the payment of [number/currency] to [Name] together with written confirmation of the exercise of the option. If the option is not exercised [Name] shall be entitled to offer the same rights as set out in the option to one or more parties.

1.3 [Name/Company] shall be the copyright owner of the [Pilot]. If the option is exercised a new agreement shall be concluded between the parties and the [Company] and [Name] shall be the joint copyright owners of the [Series]. [Name] shall be entitled to a minimum [number] per cent of all net receipts received by the [Company] from the exploitation of the [Series] and/or any adaptations in any media and/or any merchandising after all costs and expenses and the budget for the [Pilot have been recouped.

T.465

1.1 The [Production Company] agrees and undertakes that the copyright and all other intellectual property rights, trade marks, service marks, design rights, computer software rights, database rights and any other rights whether in existence now and/or created in the future and all extensions and renewals in the [country] and in any other part of the world in the [Film/Series] and any part and any associated material including but not limited to any films, videos, podcasts, recordings, sound recordings, soundtrack, scripts, running orders, budgets, profiles, databases, images, photographs, characters, logos, advertisements and promotions, packaging, merchandising and any other material commissioned by and/or on behalf of the [Company] under and/or pursuant to this agreement shall belong entirely to the [Company] and be assigned by the [Production Company] subject to the ownership of any material by third parties and/or the payment of any fees, royalties and/or other sums that may be due for such clearances, consents and/or rights.

1.2 The [Production Company] agrees that it shall at the request and expense of the [Company] enter into any such agreements and/or do any such things as may reasonably be required or necessary to ensure and carry out the assignment to the [Company] of all such rights and material whether from the [Production Company] and/or a third party who has been commissioned to create and/or develop material of any nature.

1.3 The [Production Company] acknowledges that for the purpose of copyright law in the United States of America and any other jurisdiction which does not recognise any assignment of future copyright the [Production Company] agrees to make the transfer and assignment to the [Company] on completion of the [Film/Series] under this agreement.

T.466
The [Licensor] confirms and undertakes that it is the sole owner of or controls all copyright and any other rights in respect of the [Film/Format] and/or parts and the [Source Material] which are granted under this agreement. That such rights are vested in the [Licensor] free from encumbrances and that the [Licensor] is not bound by any prior agreement which adversely affects and/or restricts its authority to enter into this agreement.

T.467
The [Licensor] agrees and undertakes that it controls and is an exclusive distributor of the rights in the [Film/Series] which are granted to the [Licensee] under this agreement. That there is no third party except the copyright owner [specify name] who has a claim and/or controls the rights which have been granted.

General Business and Commercial

T.468

1.1 [Name] acknowledges and agrees that all present and future copyright, design rights, intellectual property rights, trade marks, database rights, computer software rights, patents and any other rights and/or interest which arise and/or are created and/or developed by [Name] during his/her period of contract of employment with the [Company] shall remain the sole and exclusive property of the [Company].

1.2 Where necessary [Name] agrees to sign any document which may be necessary to transfer, register and/or confirm the ownership by the [Company]. [Name] agrees that no part of this agreement is intended to grant, assign and/or transfer any rights to [Name]. Nor shall [Name] be entitled to royalties and/or any other payment from the exploitation by the [Company] at any time and/or any credit and/or acknowledgement.

T.469

The [Executive] acknowledges and agrees that all intellectual property rights including copyright, design rights, data and database rights, computer software rights, trade marks, patents, photographs, text, images, logos, films, sound recordings, documents, emails, reports and all other material created, developed, produced and/or authorised by the [Executive] during the course of his/her service shall belong to the [Company]. No rights and/or interest are acquired, transferred and/or assigned to the [Executive] under this agreement.

T.470

The [location/property] known as [address/country] is registered with [specify organisation/Land Registry] under reference: [specify reference code] in the names of the following: [specify persons/company] from [date]. The legal owner of the [location/property] is [specify names/company] who hold the [freehold/leasehold/other].

T.471

1.1   The [Management Contractor] agrees that the [Company] shall be entitled upon paying a reasonable charge to be supplied by the [Management Contractor] with copies of all drawings, plans, specifications. health, safety, security, drainage, sewage, electrical, water, gas and/or other assessments, reports and any data produced and/or commissioned by the [Management Contractor] relating to the [Project].

1.2   The [Company] shall be entitled to use and copy the documents and material in 1.1 for any purpose relating to the construction, repair, maintenance, letting and sale of the [Project] only.

1.3   The copyright, intellectual property rights, computer software rights and database rights in all such documents and material in 1.1 and any copies produced in 1.2 shall remain in the ownership of the [Management Contractor].

T.472

The agreement shall bind and ensure to the benefit of the parties and their respective personal representations, assignees, licensees and/or successors in title.

T.473

Nothing in this agreement shall be interpreted as a transfer of any property rights and/or copyright ownership and/or intellectual rights and/or title and/or control and/or possession of the [Work/Material] to the [Licensee] except as set out in the agreement. All rights not specifically granted are reserved by the [Licensor] including any rights which may be created and/or developed in the future which do not exist at the time of this agreement.

T.474

The [Assignor] confirms that the [Assignor] has good title and authority to enter into this agreement and is not bound by any previous agreement which adversely affects this agreement except for those agreements specifically referred to in appendix A.

T.475

1.1 The [Assignor] and the [Assignee] acknowledge and agree that the assignment in clause [–] is subject to the following existing agreements which are described below: [list agreements].

1.2 The [Assignor] agrees and undertakes to arrange for the assignment and/or novation of the agreements to the [Assignee] by [date].

1.3 In the event that any and/or all of the third party licensees, suppliers, distributors and/or creators and/or authors of these agreements listed in 1.1 refuses to have their agreement assigned and/or novated to the [Assignee]. Then the [Assignee] agrees that the [Assignor] and [Assignee] must agree terms for the reduction of the total sum to be paid by the [Assignee] which shall be limited to no more than [number/currency] in total.

T.476

The [Assignor] confirms that it has and will retain good title and authority to enter into this Agreement and is not bound by any previous agreement, commitment and/or undertaking which conflicts with, jeopardises and/or which adversely affects this agreement after [date].

T.477

The [Company] warrants and undertakes that neither it nor its predecessors in title to the rights granted has at any time prior to this agreement assigned, licensed and/or charged and/or in any other way reached agreement with a third party in respect of the [Treatment/Work/Material] and/or any copyright, intellectual property rights and/or any other rights in any manner which would adversely prejudice and/or conflict with the terms of this agreement.

T.478

1.1 The [Company] owns and controls the title to the annual [Project/Event/Festival] known as: [specify title].

1.2 The [Company] has the rights, permissions and authority to hold the [Project/Event/Festival] at [location] from [date] to [date].

1.3 All registrations, contracts, licences, consents, waivers, location access agreements, transport and car parks, health and safety, security and facilities assessments and plans have been approved by all relevant authorities.

1.4 The [Company] is entitled to grant the non-exclusive rights set out in clause [–] to the [Licensee].

T.479
The [Licensor] confirms that the [Film/Image/Script/Painting/Illustration] shall be the original creation of the [Licensor] and that he/she shall be the sole owner and/or control all copyright and any other rights in the [Film/Image/Script/Painting/Illustration] which are granted under this agreement. The [Licensee] acknowledges that all copyright and any other rights not specifically granted under this agreement remain the sole property of the [Licensor].

T.480
The [Assignor] agrees that he/she has full power to enter into this agreement and is the sole owner of the copyright and any other intellectual property rights in the [Work/Sculpture/Artwork] which are assigned under this agreement. That the [Work/Sculpture/Artwork] has not been reproduced, adapted and/or exploited in any form except in the exhibitions, merchandising and promotions set out and disclosed in appendix C which forms part of this agreement. As at [date] there are no such exhibitions, merchandising arrangements and/or promotions in existence they have all been terminated and/or expired.

T.481

1.1 The [Assignor] agrees that it is the sole owner of all intellectual property rights including copyright and any other rights in the [Work/Sound Recordings/Services] and parts and holds full title and ownership as at [date].

1.2 That this assignment by the [Assignor] is subject to the requirement that certain persons and/or companies must be paid in respect of the exploitation of the [Work/Sound Recordings/Services] by the [Assignee]. That the obligations in the associated contracts, licences and consents shall also be assigned to the [Assignee] and must be fulfilled. The list of associated contracts, licences and consents is specified in list form in appendix B. Copies of the documents ate attached in appendix C.

1.3 The [Assignee] agrees to be bound by the terms of the associated contracts, licences and consents and to provide such credits as may be stipulated and/or adhere to such moral rights obligations and/or to pay any sums as may be due to third parties.

1.4 The [Assignee] also agrees and undertakes to pay any sums due for the exploitation, performance and/or transmission of the [Work/Sound Recordings/Services] due to any rights management organisation and/or rightsholder in any country.

1.5 The [Assignor] shall be responsible for all payments up to [date/time] and the [Assignee] shall bear all costs and expenses owed to third parties from [date /time].

T.482

The [Assignor] confirms that the [Series] is based on an idea by [Name] which is original and not copied from any third party. That the copyright and all other rights have been transferred and assigned by [Name] to the [Assignor].

T.483

1.1 All specifications, drafts, drawings, two and three dimensional computer-generated images, models, samples, tools, designs, artwork, technical information, data, software and/or any other material, information, functions, ideas and/or creations supplied by [Name] to the [Company] shall remain the property of [Name].

1.2 The [Company] shall not acquire any copyright, intellectual property rights, design rights, registered design rights, trade marks, service marks, computer software, patent, and/or any other rights and/or interest.

1.3 The [Company] agrees that all material in 1.1 and 1.2 together with any copies shall be promptly returned to [Name] upon request. That the [Company] shall not have the right to share any confidential information with any third party except as authorised by [Name] under this agreement.

T.484

1.1 Designs, drawings, plans, risk assessments, test results, specifications, marketing, logos, images and/or slogans and any other material created and/or developed in any format and/or medium pursuant to this agreement shall be the exclusive property of and owned by the [Company].

1.2 Such material in 1.1 may not be released or reproduced and/or exploited in any form by the [Distributor] without the prior consent of the [Company].

1.3 All material prepared by the [Distributor] and all copies shall be delivered to the [Company] upon request.

1.4 The [Distributor] acknowledges that all records, reports, information, data, databases and any other material in any medium developed by and/or supplied to the [Distributor], its employee's, agents and other third parties in performance of this agreement shall remain the property of and solely owned by the [Company].

T.485

The [Distributor] agrees as a non-exclusive licensee that:

1.1 the [Original Material/Sound Recording] shall remain in the ownership of [Licensor/Name].

1.2 the [Distributor] is not acquiring any copyright in the [Original Material/ Sound Recording] and/or any musical work and/or any associated lyrics, composition and/or arrangement.

1.3 the copyright and intellectual property rights in the new edited versions of the [Original Material/Sound Recordings] reproduced as [Units/ Downloads/other] by the [Distributor] shall belong to the [Licensor]. That where necessary the [Distributor] shall return any rights which may be created by means of an assignment to the [Licensor/Name].

T.486

1.1 The [Company] agrees that each share is owned and controlled by the named individual and/or corporation specified in the share register of the [Company].

1.2 Any dispute between the [Company] and the previous shareholder shall not allow the [Company] to set-off and/or seek to claim any sum due to the subsequent shareholder who has purchased the shares in good faith and for equitable value. Except where the [Company] has evidence of money laundering, fraud and/or some other illegal conduct by the parties.

1.3 The [Company] shall take its instructions regarding the sale and/ or other disposal of the shares from the registered person and/or corporation named on the certificates and register.

1.4 Where the registered person is deceased then the [Company] shall act on the instructions of the executors who have been granted probate and/or any administrator appointed by a court order and/or any other person who complies with any existing legislation which may be applicable to the circumstances.

1.5 No title and/or interest in the shares shall be transferred by the [Company] to a third party without instructions in writing by an authorised person and/or corporation together with the completion of all necessary documents.

1.6 Where a share certificate and/or registration is held in joint names and one party is deceased, ownership and title shall pass to the estate of that party unless there have been notified instructions to the contrary prior to the death. Then the survivor shall gain ownership and title to all the shares held in joint names.

T.487

[Name] agrees and confirms that this is their last will and testament and that all other wills and codicils which may exist are revoked and/or lapsed. That [Name] wishes to ensure and agrees that [specify person] as sole beneficiary shall be entitled upon the death of [Name] to receive all physical material and all intellectual property and other rights whether in existence now at the date of this document and/or created in the future owned and/or controlled by [Name] including but not limited to patents, copyright, design rights, future design rights, films, videos, podcasts, trade marks, domain names, websites, apps, computer software, audio files, computer-generated material and any other material created and/or developed for exploitation by means of electronic, wifi and/or telecommunication means to any gadget, for television, radio and/or over the internet and/or otherwise, logos, scripts, manuscripts, images, photographs, sound recordings, DVDs, CD-Roms and other storage devices, artwork, titles, music, lyrics, books, articles, posters, packaging, marketing, documents, records in the [Collection/Archive/Library] which is described and listed in the attached Schedule A which forms part of this will. That [Name] assigns and leaves upon his/her death all such rights and interest as successor in title to [specify person] as sole beneficiary] in the [Collection/Archive/Library] for the full period of copyright and any extensions and renewals and for the full period of any other rights and in perpetuity. Those rights and title shall be subject to the terms of any existing agreements which may apply after the death of [Name].

T.488

The [Company] confirms and agrees that it holds the [Work/Material] which is no longer protected by copyright in its original form. No undertakings and/or agreement is provided by the [Company] as to who owns and/or any controls the intellectual property rights including copyright and/or whether any rights have been cleared and/or paid for in respect of any use by the [Licensee/Name].

T.489

1.1 The [Company] agrees to assign all rights in the registered trade mark known as [specify name] registration number: [number] and any associated logo, images, domain name for any website and any name associated with any app, and any character, slogan and any jingle and/or musical work and/or any other registrations associated with any material and all goodwill to the [Parent Company]. Full details of the rights and material are listed in the attached appendix A which forms part of this agreement.

1.2 It is the intention of the parties that no rights shall be retained by the [Company]. The [Company] shall complete all such forms, documents and other notifications as may be required to third parties at its own cost to ensure the assignment to the [Parent Company] is completed.

1.3 It is also agreed between the parties that the [Company] shall supply a copy of all the original documentation relating to the development of the rights in 1.1.

1.4 The [Company] shall supply the [Parent Company] with a full list of all agreements, licences and/or other authorised uses of the rights in 1.1 and the names of the parties. The [Company] shall assign all such third party agreements, documents, material, obligations, liabilities and rights to the [Parent Company].

Internet, Websites and Apps

T.490

The [Customer] acknowledges that all intellectual property rights including copyright and any other rights in the [Website/App] and any trade marks, logos and/or any associated goodwill shall remain the property of and belong to the [Company]. That the [Customer] agrees that he/she shall not acquire any rights in the [Website/App] and/or any name, slogan, word, phrase, trade mark, logo, title, artwork, images, design, music, lyrics, stills, recordings, films, sound recordings, computer software and/or any other material in any format of any nature. That no authority is granted to the [Customer] to develop, adapt and/or vary any content and/or translate and/or exploit the [Website/App]. This agreement does not transfer, license and/or assign any copyright ownership and/or any other rights in any material and/or content to the [Customer].

T.491

The [Contributor] to the [Website/App] agrees and undertakes that to the best of his/her knowledge and belief the facts and information contained in the [Work/Article/Blog] shall be original, true and accurate and that where material is quoted and/or relied upon from third parties that sufficient acknowledgement shall be provided to the source material, title and copyright owner.

T.492

The [Company] is the copyright owner and owns and controls all rights in this [Website/App/Audio File] unless stated otherwise. The right granted to use this [Website/App/Audio File] is limited and personal to the [Client] and does not permit the [Client] to exploit the [Website/App/Audio File] in any media of any nature at any time and/or to authorise others to do so. The [Client] shall not acquire any rights and/or interest in the [Website/App/Audio File] at any time which may be exploited by the [Client] and all rights are reserved by the [Company]. The [Client] is only permitted to access, view, listen to and/or store the [Website/App/Audio File] for [one] month. There is no right to reproduce any content not even for charitable and/or educational use and/or to supply the material and content to a third party and/or to exploit any rights.

T.493

The [Company] is the owner of the [Website/App] known as: [trading name] which is registered with [specify organisation] as [title/reference]. All the content of the [Website/App] has been commissioned and/or sourced by the [Company] from third parties and/or created as original material by the [Company]. The access permitted to the [Website/App] does not create any licence and/or permission to reproduce, supply, distribute and/or exploit any of the content in any media and/or format at any time. You must seek the prior written authority of the [Company] for a non-exclusive licence regardless of whether it is for an individual, business, educational establishment and/or charity. All rights are reserved by the [Company] and/or the stated third parties.

T.494

The [Website/App] and all associated content, copyright notices, trade mark notices and trade mark registrations, registrations with any collecting societies relating to any material including films, sound recordings, videos, music, written material, images and/or marketing material shall be held in the name of [specify] on behalf of all the parties which form the [Consortium]. Any sale, disposal, transfer, charge, lien and/or assignment of title in whole and/or part shall require the prior approval of all members of the [Consortium].

T.495

The [Company] agrees and confirms that the following parties hold all the copyright, intellectual property rights and other rights in the following material:

1.1   The artwork, logos, symbols, images, designs, sketches, illustrations and drawings described and represented in the attached appendix A are owned by [Name] and all authorised use, adaptation and/or exploitation of any such material and/or rights must bear a copyright notice, credit and/or trade mark to [Name] as follows: [specify details].

1.2   The sound recordings, music and lyrics described and represented in attached appendix B are owned by the [Company] and all authorised use, adaptation and/or exploitation of any such material and/or rights must bear the following copyright notice, credit and/or trade mark to the [Company] as follows: [specify details].

1.3   The website, app and computer-generated and electronic material and content are owned by the [Enterprise] subject to the ownership of the material in 1.1 and 1.2 and any other contributions of original material and/or services by third parties. All authorised use, adaptation and/or exploitation must bear a copyright notice, credit, and/or trade mark and/or a reservation of rights notice and/or disclaimer as follows: [specify details].

T.496

1.1   The [Website/App/Downloads/Audio Files] are owned by [Name]

1.2   Where a copyright notice, credit, trade mark and/or other notice is next to any material on this site. Then that material is owned and/or controlled by the person and/or company whose details are represented.

1.3   There is no authority provided to copy, adapt, develop and/or exploit any rights and/or material from the [Website/App/Downloads/Audio Files]. You are permitted access and to view, download and/or store material for up to [three] months. This is on the basis that the material is accessed and stored for your own private and personal use and not for supply to a third party. [Name] may revoke their permission at any time and request that all material you have stored be deleted and shall be entitled to cancel any account which you may have, delete any of your passwords and other data and/or images and/or to ban your access to the [Website/App/Downloads/Audio Files] without stating any reason.

1.4   There is no intention to transfer, assign, authorise and/or permit you to acquire any title and/or ownership in any part of this [Website/App/

Downloads/Audio Files] at any time. The terms of use of access may be changed and/or altered at any time without notice.

T.497

1.1 [Name] has agreed to be interviewed by the [Writer] for an article for the [Website/App/Blog] known as: [specify details and reference] which is owned by the [Company].

1.2 [Name] agrees to complete an assignment document which transfers all ownership of the copyright and intellectual property rights in all media in the interview and all spoken words and any associated sound recording to the [Writer/Company].

1.3 [Name] also agrees to be photographed for the article and agrees that the [Photographer] shall own the copyright in the images which are taken and may assign those rights to the [Writer/Company].

1.4 [Name] accepts and agrees that they shall not have any claim, title and/or ownership of any of the material arising from the interview.

T.498

1.1 [Name] has commissioned the [Production Company] to produce, film and record a series of [Podcasts/Videos/Films] for exploitation by [Name] on the internet and/or by electronic means and/or in any other media as set out in schedule A which is attached to this agreement.

1.2 The [Production Company] agrees and undertakes to assign all present and future copyright and all intellectual property rights, computer software rights and any other rights which may exist now and/or be created in the future in all media and/or in any medium throughout the world and outer space to [Name] in respect of the series of [Podcasts/Videos/Films] and all associated material created in the course of production for the nominal sum of [number/currency]. Provided that [Name] has paid the full agreed Budget as set out in schedule B attached to this agreement.

1.3 A copy of the proposed assignment in 1.2 is attached in schedule C.

1.4 The intention of the parties is that full title and ownership shall belong to [Name]. That the [Production Company] shall not hold any rights and/or have any claim to the material created and/or any right to authorise third parties to use and/or exploit such material in 1.1 and 1.2. Nor shall the [Production Company] be entitled to retain any copies of any material which is created and all material shall be delivered to [Name].

T.499

The [Computer Software] known as [specify name] used to produce this [Website/App/Game] is owned by a third party and/or there is no authority provided to reproduce, license, adapt and/or develop the [Computer Software] for any reason.

T.500

1.1 The [Photographs/Images/Hologram/Installation] are owned by the [Artist].

1.2 There is no authority granted to take any copies, images and/or photographs and/or film and/or record the [Photographs/Images/Hologram/Installation] for any article, programme, merchandising and/or any other commercial, charitable and/or educational purpose.

1.3 There is no right granted to reproduce the [Photographs/Images/Hologram/Installation] in any manner on any website, app, blog, podcast, on line account of any nature and/or anywhere on the internet and/or through means of any wifi and/or telecommunication system and/or by any electronic means.

1.4 Any breach and/or default of this requirement shall entitle the [Artist] to make a claim against you for unauthorised use for a sum which shall not be less than [number/currency].

T.501

1.1 The original [Character] known as [specify name of character] which is described and represented in images in Schedule A is owned by [Name].

1.2 [Name] owns and is the registered owner of the registered Trade Marks in relation to the [Character] as follows: [date of trade mark registration/name/reference]. Copies of the documents relating to the grant of the registered trade marks are attached in Schedule B.

1.3 The costumes in respect of the [Character] were designed and created by [specify person] and all rights have been assigned to and are now owned by [Name] who commissioned the costumes.

1.4 The slogans and scripts in respect of the [Character] are written by [specify person]. All rights have been assigned and are now owned by [Name] who commissioned the material.

1.5 No other person, entity and/or company owns and/or controls any copyright, intellectual property rights and/or has been granted and/or currently holds any licence and/or right of reproduction and/or exploitation of the [Character] and/or any related material in 1.1 to 1.4.

Merchandising and Distribution

T.502

1.1 'The Trading Name' in respect of the commercial exploitation of the [Licensed Articles/Products] shall be under the following title: [specify details].

1.2 All rights in 1.1 shall belong to [specify names] including any registered trade mark and/or any other associated images, jingle, sound recording, film, music and/or lyrics and/or other material which may be created and/or developed in the future.

T.503

The [Licensee] acknowledges that all copyright, intellectual property rights, computer software rights, design rights and any other rights in the [Character/Product], the name, samples, models, images, artwork, graphics, sound recordings, computer-generated material, articles, clothes and/or any other material and any trade mark, logo, words, phrases, slogans and/or associated goodwill and/or any developments and/or adaptations in any manner shall remain the property of and be owned by the [Licensor]. That the [Licensee] shall not acquire any such rights and/or interest and/or represent that they own and/or control them and/or attempt to register any interest except as specifically authorised in this agreement. All rights not granted are reserved by the [Licensor].

T.504

The [Company] acknowledges and agrees that all present and future copyright, design rights, patents, trade marks, computer software and any other rights of any nature in the [Product] and/or parts including the name of the [Product] and the prototype, samples and variations in development and/or any related packaging, marketing and promotional material which may be created and/or commissioned are and will remain the sole and exclusive property of the [Enterprise] and/or be assigned to the [Enterprise]. That this agreement does not in any way purport to transfer and/or assign any legal ownership in the [Product] and/or any parts and/or any other material.

T.505

The [Company] undertakes that at the end of the Licence Period it shall execute any document and/or do anything required by the [Licensor] to confirm and/or assign all copyright, design rights, patents, trade marks, computer software and any other rights of any nature in the [Product] and/or parts including the name and/or any variations, packaging, marketing and/or merchandising to the [Licensor]. That no rights of any nature whether in the [Products] and/or in any associated material shall be retained by the

[Company] whether they existence now and/or whether they are created and/or developed in the future.

T.506
The [Artist] agrees that he/she shall not be entitled to or acquire any rights in any character, title, pseudonym, design, image, film, video, logo, trade mark, slogan and/or product provided by the [Company] for the purpose of this agreement. That the [Artist] shall not be entitled to use any such material in any form and/or use them for product placement and/or marketing except with the prior written consent of the Company. The [Company] agrees that the [Artist] may use approved material in a portfolio for personal references purposes only.

T.507

1.1 The [Licensor] confirms that he/she is the original creator and sole owner of and/or controls all copyright and intellectual property and/or any other rights in the [Characters] which are granted under this agreement.

1.2 That the [Licensor] is not aware of any other character which is the same and/or similar in appearance and/or which predates the [Characters] and/or which are called the same names and/or wear the same outfits. That the [Licensor] is not aware of any legal issues connected with the [Characters] and/or any allegation of plagiarism against the [Licensor].

T.508

1.1 [Name] is the original creator and copyright owner of the [Board Game] and the [Prototype/Model Sample].

1.2 [Name] has granted the [Distributor] an exclusive licence and distribution agreement for [number] years from [date] for the following countries: [list countries] to design and reproduce a version in [language].

1.3 Where for any reason it is necessary to alter any names, titles, rules and any other matter due to interpretation of meanings of words. Any new words and other material created and/or developed by the [Distributor] shall at the expiry and/or termination of this agreement be assigned to [Name]. The [Distributor] agrees to complete such documents as may be supplied by [Name] to assign all rights in all media in all new material and/or rights which may be created pursuant to this agreement.

1.4 The [Distributor accepts and agrees that it shall retain any rights at the end of this agreement and/or be entitled to attempt to register any rights in respect of the [Board Game], the [Prototype/Model Sample] and/or any adaptation.

T.509

The [Licensee] agrees that all future copyright and design rights in the Designs, the [Licensed Articles], the Prototypes and the Complete Set are the sole and exclusive property of the [Licensor] and that this agreement does not in any way purport to transfer any copyright and/or design rights to the [Licensee] [except as stated in this agreement].

T.510

The [Purchaser] agrees that it will not and shall not be entitled to license and/or authorise any third party to copy, reproduce, manufacture, supply and/or distribute the [Garment] and/or the [Designs] including any development and/or adaptation at any time throughout the world.

T.511

The [Designer] agrees that all present and future copyright, design rights and any intellectual property and other rights in the [Licensed Articles/Products] manufactured during the Licence Period will be held and owned jointly by the [Licensee] and the [Designer].

T.512

1.1 The [Company] confirms that it is the sole owner of and/or controls all intellectual property rights, copyright, design rights, artwork and all trade marks, logos, slogans and packaging and all other rights in the [Images/Sound Recordings/Samples/Products] in all media throughout the world and any adaptations.

1.2 That the [Company] holds good title. That there is no prohibition and/or restriction imposed by a third party as to the exploitation of the [Images/Sound Recordings/Samples/Products] except the following matters: [specify]

T.513

1.1 The property and ownership of title to the [Products/Material] shall remain with the [Company] at all times in the case of a hire transaction. Where there is a sale of the [Products/Material] ownership shall pass only after payment have been paid in full and delivery and/or collection has taken place.

1.2 Any transfer of title in 1.1 is limited to the actual [Product/Material] itself and does not grant and/or authorise any reproduction and/or adaptation and/or license and/or assign any rights of any nature.

T.514

1.1 The [Products/Material/Units] shall remain the sole and absolute property of the [Company] as legal and equitable owner until such time as the [Purchaser] shall have paid to the [Company] the full agreed price of the order.

1.2 The [Company] may for the purpose of recovery of its [Products/Material/Units] enter upon any office, warehouse, storage facility, premises and/or ship, aeroplane and/or other location and/or structure where the [Products/Material/Units] are stored and may remove, claim, take possession of all the property which belongs to the [Company].

1.3 The [Purchaser] agrees that it shall store the [Products/Material/Units] in a safe and secure manner and shall not open the packaging and/or remove the seals until such time as the stock has been paid for in full. The [Purchaser] also agrees to store the [Products/Material/Units] separately from other stock and in a manner which makes them readily identifiable.

T.515

The [Purchaser] acknowledges that he/she is in possession of the [Products/Material/Stock] solely as a fiduciary for the [Company] until payment is made in full. If the [Products/Material/Stock] are sold and/or otherwise disposed of the [Purchaser] will ensure that the entire proceeds of the sale are held in trust for the [Company] and shall not be mixed with any other monies and/or otherwise disposed of and/or paid to a third party and shall at all times be identifiable as monies belonging to the [Company].

T.516

1.1 Title and ownership of the [Products/Units/Samples] remains vested in the [Company] until such time as the [Products/Units/Samples] have been fully paid for by the [Distributor].

1.2 In the event that the [Distributor] defaults and/or breaches the agreement and fails to pay part and/all of the sums due to the [Company] in 1.1 within [one] calendar month of notification of the default and/or breach. Then the [Company] may at its sole discretion without further notice enter the business address and/or warehouse of the [Distributor] to recover all the [Products/Units/Samples] which have not been paid for which belong to the [Company]. Any such action by the [Company] shall be without prejudice to any other remedies and/or legal action and/or claim for costs, losses and damages and/or interest which may be available to the [Company].

T.517

The [Company] warrants that it holds full legal title and ownership to the [Products/Units] which are to be bought by the [Purchaser] and that the transfer is lawful and that the [Products] are delivered free from any security, interest and/or encumbrance except as agreed in advance in writing between the [Company] and the [Purchaser] as follows: [specify].

T.518

1.1 The purchase price has been paid in advance in respect of the order. The transfer of ownership of the [Products/Units] shall pass to the [Company] on delivery to the nominated address specified in the order form and shall not be conditional upon the acceptance of the technical quality.

1.2 Where the [Company] rejects some and/or all of the [Products/Units] on the grounds of fitness for purpose and/or failure to function and/or defects and/or other faults. Then ownership shall be transferred back to the [Supplier] when the [Products/Units] are returned to the nominated address for the [Supplier]. The [Supplier] shall then repay any sums due to the [Company]. No sums shall be repaid where it is clear that the [Products/Units] have been damaged in transit and/or that the faults complained of have been caused by the [Company] and/or there is evidence of misuse.

T.519

All [Products/Units] are supplied under this agreement on the basis of the retention of title by the [Supplier]. The ownership of the [Products/Units] shall only pass to the [Customer/Distributor] as and when all sums due to be paid by the [Customer/Distributor] to the [Supplier] for all the ordered [Products/Units] have been paid in full.

T.520

1.1 The ownership and title in the [Products/Units] sold by the [Company] to the [Purchaser] shall not be transferred and/or assigned until payment has been made by the [Purchaser] to the [Company] of the payments due in respect of all [Products/Units] which the [Purchaser] has bought to date from the [Company] whether under one or more orders and/or contracts.

1.2 Until such time as the outstanding payment is settled by the [Purchaser] the [Company] shall hold any [Products/Units] and shall not sell them to a third party. Where no payment is received for a period of [six] months after notification to the [Purchaser]. The [Company] shall be entitled to sell the [Products/Units] which have been purchased but not supplied to the [Purchaser] to recoup any outstanding sums due under other orders and/or contracts with the [Purchaser]. The [Purchaser] agrees to this form of set-off by the [Company].

T.521

1.1 The [Company] warrants that title to and ownership of the [Products/ Units] when transferred to the [Purchaser] is lawful, valid and correct. That the [Company] has the authority to transfer the title and that the [Products] are delivered free from any lien, charge and/or encumbrance.

1.2 The transfer of the title in the [Products/Units] is limited to the stock and does not mean that there is any transfer and/or assignment of copyright, intellectual property rights and/or any other rights in the [Products/Units]. There is no authority granted to reproduce, exploit and/or adapt the {Products/Units] and/or to use them for product placement, merchandising and/or sponsorship except with the prior written consent of the [Company].

T.522

The property and risk in the [Products/Units] shall pass on delivery and/or if by instalments then in respect of those items delivered. Where all and/or part of the [Products/Units] are retained by the [Seller] but the [Purchaser] has paid the agreed price. The property in the [Products/Units] shall pass to the [Purchaser] on payment, but the risk in such [Products/Units] shall remain with the [Seller] until the actual date and time of delivery.

T.523

1.1 The [Assignor] is not the creator and does not own any rights in the [Material/Sample/Artwork] and is solely the owner of the physical material which is represented in appendix A known as the [Work/ Image/Sculpture].

1.2 The [Assignor] cannot confirm that there are no outstanding legal issues as to ownership of the [Work/Image/Sculpture]. The [Assignee] must purchase the physical material with the full knowledge that there may be third parties who may claim ownership and/or commence legal proceedings.

1.3 No indemnity is provided by the [Assignor] as to the title and ownership to the Assignee] and this is a fundamental condition which the [Assignee] has accepted.

T.524

The [Agent/Distributor] acknowledges that the [Company] shall have the right to deal with, sell, loan, hire and/or otherwise exploit and/or adapt the

[Products] and/or any other products and to reach the same and/or similar and/or any other type of agreement it wishes with a third party.

T.525

1.1 The copyright owners of the [Work/Infographics/Chart] are the [Author and the Illustrator]. The user licence and rights granted are personal to the [Purchaser] and only allow the [Work/Infographics/Map] to be used for non-commercial use by one person, and not for any reproduction and/or exploitation over the internet and/or by any electronic means and/or any other form in any media.

1.2 The [Purchaser] is not entitled to exploit any rights in the [Work/Infographics/Chart] in any media at any time and/or to permit others to do so and/or to supply copies to third parties.

1.3 All rights are reserved by the [Author and the Illustrator] and the exclusive licensee, the [Company].

Publishing

T.526

The [Publisher] acknowledges that all copyright and other intellectual property rights in the [Work/Manuscript/Images/Sound Recordings] shall remain with the [Author]. That the [Author] is the sole copyright owner and that this agreement does not purport to transfer and/or assign copyright ownership to the [Publisher].

T.527

1.1 The [Author] confirms that no licence, agreement and/or other authorisation has been signed by and/or on behalf of the [Author] concerning the reproduction, publication, adaptation and/or exploitation of the [Work/Manuscript/Photographs/Artwork].

1.2 That the [Author] is entitled to grant the rights to the [Company] in this agreement. That the [Author] is not the subject of any legal proceedings by a third party regarding ownership of the [Work/Manuscript/Photographs/Artwork].

T.528

The [Writer] agrees that to the best of his/her knowledge and belief the facts and information contained in the [Work/Manuscript/Article] shall be true and accurate, including all references to source material and title except where any material is supplied by and specifically included at the request of the [Commissioning Company].

1948

T.529

1.1 The [Publisher] intends to publish and has commissioned a first edition hardback, paperback and audio book [called the Work] which the [Author] has agreed to write and deliver by [date].

1.2 The title of the [Work] shall be: [specify title] and/or such other title as may be mutually agreed between the [Author] and the [Publisher]. The title shall be owned by [Author/Publisher]. Neither party shall be entitled to exploit the title in any subsequent edition and/or medium without the agreement of both parties.

T.530

In consideration of the Buy-out Fee [Name/Agent] acknowledges and agrees that the [Publisher/Distributor] shall be the sole owner of all present and future copyright and all intellectual property rights and any other rights in the [Article] and the [Sound Recordings] and [Videos/Podcasts] in all media whether in existence now and/or created in the future throughout the [Territory/world] for the full period of copyright and any extensions and renewals and/or for the full period of entitlement of all rights.

T.531

The [Publisher/Distributor] agrees that the photographs, documents, items, films and other material supplied by [Name] to the [Publisher] shall be on loan and that the copyright, intellectual property rights and all other rights and all the physical material shall remain the property of and be owned by [Name].

T.532

1.1 The [Licensor] has granted the [Company]an exclusive licence for a fixed Licence Period in respect of the [Work] which shall include any draft scripts, illustrations, maps, photographs, diagrams, preface and index to be included in the [Work].

1.2 There is no assignment of any copyright and/or intellectual property rights and/or any trade marks and/or any other rights in any title of the [Work] and/or character names and/or names of persons and/or places which have been created by the [Licensor] to the [Company]. The [Company] shall not have the authority to make any trade mark registration applications and/or register any domain name and/or app and/or any other names which are the same and/or similar. All such rights are owned by the [Licensor] and the [Company] is only permitted to do what is specifically authorised under this agreement.

1.3 All rights not specifically granted to the [Company] are vested in and belong to the [Licensor]. The rights reserved include but are not limited to serialisation rights, one shot digest rights, digest book condensation rights, anthology and quotation rights, braille and talking book rights and the right to publish extracts in newspapers and magazines, strip cartoon rights, feature film, documentary, video, podcast and all other film and sound recording rights, sponsorship, merchandising and product placement rights, satellite, cable, terrestrial and digital over the internet and wifi, streaming and archive playback television and radio rights, computer games, gambling, lotteries and theme parks.

T.533

The [Author] confirms that he/she has and will retain good title and authority to enter into this agreement and is not bound by any other document, licence, agreement and/or assignment in respect of the [Work/Artwork/Images/Illustrations] which adversely affects and/or undermines and/or conflicts with this agreement except: [specify details of other agreements].

T.534

The [Company] confirms that the existing agreement which the [Company] has with the [Author] permits and entitles the [Company] to sub-license and grant the Serialisation Rights in the [Work/Material] to the [Sub-Licensee].

T.535

The [Author] confirms that no agreement has been signed by and/or on behalf of the [Author] concerning the [Work] which prohibits, restricts and/or prevents the grant of rights under this agreement to the [Company].

T.536

1.1   [Name] confirms that he/she is the copyright owner of all intellectual property rights including copyright and any other rights in the [Artwork/Photographs/Samples] and owns and controls the material that is to be supplied on loan under this agreement. That [Name] [inherited/was assigned] these rights from [specify person] on [date].

1.2   That neither the [Artwork/Photographs/Samples] nor the material is subject to any prior and/or future legal claim, right, contractual obligation and/or other interest by a third party which would prevent, interfere with and/or be prejudicial to the display and reproduction of the [Artwork/Photographs/Samples] in the [Exhibition/Tour].

1.3   The [Company] agrees that it shall acquire no rights in the [Artwork]/Photographs/Samples] and/or the material except for the non-exclusive right to exhibit them for a fixed period. No [Artwork/Photographs/Samples] and/or other material may be posted for any reason on any website, app, blog and/or on the internet and/or any telecommunication system.

1.4 There are no rights granted to the [Company] to sub-license, reproduce, adapt, syndicate, distribute and/or exploit the [Artwork/Photographs/Samples] and/or material to a parent, associated, and/or subsidiary company and/or any other third party.

T.537

The [Authors] agree and undertake that:

1.1 That they are the copyright owners of the [Work/Images/Sound Recordings] which they have created with their own skill and labour.

1.2 That the [Work/Images/Sound Recordings] are not adapted from and/or based on any other work which is not disclosed in the [Synopsis/Manuscript]. That there is no agreement, licence, contractual obligation and/or arrangement in respect of the [Work/Images/Sound Recordings] with any third party which would affect this agreement.

T.538

There is no undertaking given by the [Author] in respect of the copyright and/or any other rights in the [Work]. The [Publisher] accepts the risk in respect of publication and agrees to bear all the costs in respect of any legal problems and/or litigation that may arise.

T.539

1.1 The [Infographics/Images/Charts] have been designed and created by [Name] based on data and source material supplied by [specify supplier]. [Name] is the copyright owner of the [Infographics/Images/Charts] which are licensed on an exclusive basis to the [Distributor] under this agreement.

1.2 There is no undertaking and/or claim to title of the data and source material on which the [Infographics/Images/Charts] are based by [Name].

T.540

1.1 The [Data/Images/Maps/Reports] on this [Website/App] are owned by the [Supplier/Company].

1.2 Your access to this subscription service does not transfer, assign and/or license any rights in the [Data/Images/Maps/Reports] to you. There is no right to adapt and/or reproduce it in another form and/or to distribute the [Data/Images/Maps/Reports] in any medium over the internet and/or via mobiles and/or wifi and/or any telecommunication system in any electronic form to third parties and/or to include the material in any publication, film and/or podcast.

1.3 You must seek prior written consent and enter into a licence agreement for any form of reproduction and/or exploitation.

T.541

1.1 The [index and taxonomy] will be created by [Name] and not the [Author].

1.2 The [Company] agrees and undertakes that it shall not be entitled to use and/or exploit the [index and taxonomy] created by [Name] in any other manner except that authorised under this agreement without the prior written consent of the [Author].

1.3 At the expiry and/or termination of this agreement the [Company] shall arrange for all copyright and any other rights in the [index and taxonomy] to be assigned to the [Author].

T.542

1.1 The [Company] has commissioned the [Writer] to create a series of [Books] based on the [Character] licensed by the [Enterprise].

1.2 The [Writer] shall assign all copyright and any other rights of any nature in all media and/or methods throughout the world to the [Company] for a buy-out fee of [number/currency]. The [Company] shall be the copyright owner of the [Books] and all the physical material including all drafts and the final manuscripts. The [Writer] shall not be entitled to any further sums and/royalties from the exploitation of the [Books] and/ or any adaptation.

1.3 The [Writer] shall receive the following credit: [specify credit and location on Books].

1.4 The [Company] shall commission a third party to create and illustrate the [Books].

T.543

1.1 The [Author] shall be entitled to approve the actor who will perform the audio version of the [Book/Work] in order to create and develop a sound recording and audio files.

1.2 The copyright and intellectual property rights in the sound recording and the audio files shall be held jointly between the [Company] and the [Author].

1.3 The [Company] shall ensure that the nominated production company and the actor assign all copyright and any other rights that they may hold to the [Company] and the [Author].

1.4 At the end of this agreement and/or on termination the [Company] agrees that all rights in the sound recording and the audio files shall revert solely to the [Author]. The [Company] agrees to assign all such rights as it may hold at that time.

Services

T.544

The [Company] warrants and undertakes that the facts set out in the preamble are correct and that neither the [Company] nor the [Artiste] has and/or will enter any commitment with any third party which has and/or will detract from the rights granted in this agreement and/or the [Artiste's] ability to perform the services. That neither the [Company] nor the [Artiste] is under any legal obligation, restriction and/or any other outstanding issue which affects the [Company's] and/or the [Artiste's] ability to enter into and/or fulfil this agreement as at [date].

T.545

The [Presenter/Name] confirms that he/she has full authority to enter into and perform this agreement and that he/she is not bound by any previous agreement which adversely affects and/or prejudices and/or conflicts with this agreement.

T.546

1.1 The [Company] agrees that the [Company] shall only acquire copyright ownership in the product of the services of the [Contributor] which have been commissioned under this agreement and are assigned by the [Contributor].

1.2 The [Company] shall not have the right to use and/or exploit any other material and/or rights owned by the [Contributor].

T.547

1.1 The [Contributor] agrees that all present and future copyright and any other intellectual property rights in the [Company's] [Website/Channel] shall be and remain the property of the [Company] including any developments and adaptations subject to any interests of third parties.

1.2 The [Contributor] shall not acquire any rights and/or interest by virtue of this agreement to any copyright or any other rights in the [Website/Channel] and/or any associated material and/or products unless specifically agreed in writing between the parties.

1.3 At the expiry and/or termination of this agreement the [Contributor] agrees that if necessary he/she shall sign an assignment document to ensure the assignment of any intellectual property rights including copyright that may have been acquired by the [Contributor] in the provision of his/her services to the [Company]. Provided that the [Company] agrees to pay a fee of [number/currency] in consideration.

T.548

1.1 The [Agent] acknowledges and agrees that the name of the [Actor] and any fan name and/or business name and/or his/her image, any caricature, slogan, emoji, logo, trade marks and/or any other material supplied, written, performed, filmed and/or recorded and any goodwill and reputation shall remain the sole and exclusive property of the [Actor] whether in existence now or created in the future.

1.2 No part of this Agreement is intended to transfer, assign and/or vest any copyright and/or any other intellectual property rights and/or trade mark, domain name and/or other rights in the product of the [Actor's] services and/or any associated material in the [Agent] at any time.

1.3 Where material is commissioned by the [Agent] the [Agent] agrees to sign whatever assignment documents may be required and requested by the [Actor's] legal advisors upon payment of a nominal sum to carry out the intention of this agreement.

T.549
The [Agent] shall use his/her reasonable endeavours to protect the copyright and any other rights of the [Actor] which may be created and/or developed under any contract with a third party. The [Agent] shall ensure that no third party shall acquire rights in the name of the [Actor].

T.550
The [Photographer] confirms that he/she is the sole owner of and controls all copyright and any other rights in the [Commissioned Work] which are assigned under this agreement.

T.551
All drawings, photographs, films, videos, recordings, discs, sound recordings, documents and other material supplied by [Name] shall remain the property of [Name]. There is no transfer of ownership.

Sponsorship

T.552
The [Sponsor] acknowledges and agrees that:

1954

1.1 all intellectual property rights including copyright, trade marks, services marks, designs, logos, slogans, text, artwork, titles, character names, films, sound recording, scripts, photographs, business names, music, graphics, computer-generated material and any other rights in the [Series] together with any associated advertising, promotions and marketing shall remain the sole property of the [Television Company].

1.2 the [Sponsor] shall not acquire any rights in the [Series] and/or any associated material and/or have the right to register any rights and/or to make an application for a domain name, trade mark and/or other registration in the same and/or similar names and/or to name a product and/or service after any name and/or material at any time.

T.553
The [Television Company] acknowledges and agrees that all intellectual property rights including copyright, trade marks, service marks, designs, logos, slogans, text, artwork, names, music, lyrics, computer-generated material and any other rights in the [Sponsor's Logo] and the [Sponsor's Product] shall remain the sole and exclusive property of the [Sponsor] together with any goodwill. The [Television Company] shall not acquire any rights and shall not be entitled to make any adaptations in another medium without prior authority and/or to use them for promotional purposes and/or to exploit them in another programme except as agreed.

T.554

1.1 The [Sponsor] acknowledges and agrees that the sponsorship of the [Programmes/Series] does not give the [Sponsor] the right to use the name of the [Television Company], their logo, the programme title and/or the theme of the series and/or any other material owned by the [Television Company] in any promotion, advertising, marketing and/or in association with any product and/or service owned and controlled by the [Sponsor].

1.2 The parties have agreed that the following uses and purposes by the [Sponsor] are permitted from [date to [date] as set out in appendix A. [specify exact type of use and details of layout, colour, size].

T.555
The [Sponsor] agrees that the [Radio Company] shall have the right to advertise, promote and endorse any third party products in the [Programme] and/or in conjunction with it whether or not it directly competes with the [Sponsor's] business, markets, products and/or services.

T.556

The [Sponsor] confirms that it is the sole owner of and/or controls all intellectual property rights including copyright and any other rights throughout the [Territory/world] in the [Sponsor's Logo] and the [Sponsor's Product]. The [Sponsor] undertakes that the [Sponsors Logo] and the [Sponsor's Product] do not and will not infringe the copyright and any other rights of any third party as authorised under this agreement.

T.557

The [Licensor] confirms that it is the sole owner of all intellectual property rights including copyright, trade marks, service marks and any other rights in the [Licensor's Logo] throughout the world. That as at [date] there are no pending and/or threatened legal proceedings from any third party.

T.558

The [Licensee] acknowledges and agrees that the [Licensor] owns all rights in the following matters which are described in more detail and represented in images where appropriate in appendix A:

1.1   business and/or trading name: [specify name].

1.2   the domain name, website and app known as:[specify references].

1.3   the registered trade mark known as: [specify details/reference].

1.4   the slogan: [specify words].

1.5   the musical work/lyrics/sound recording: [title/reference]

1.6   the products: [specify names].

The [Licensee] shall not acquire any rights and/or interest in 1.1 to 1.6 above and/or in any adaptation which may be created in any format during the course of this agreement. The [Licensee] agrees that it shall not attempt to register any such interests in its own name.

T.559

The Sponsor shall have the right to veto and to ban any product placement, advertising, sponsorship and/or endorsement by any third party intended to be displayed at the [Venue/Event] and/or in any associated promotions, marketing and/or merchandising material by the [Company] in any form which directly conflicts with and/or competes with the services and/or products of the [Sponsor].

T.560

1.1   The [Association/Institute] agrees that from [date] to [date] the [Event] shall be provided with the title: [specify title of the Event].

1.2 The [Association/Institute] shall ensure that the promoter and all other third parties engaged by the [Association/Institute] shall be contractually bound to use their best endeavours to ensure that the [Event] in all websites, app, direct marketing, posters, merchandising, on site and outdoor promotions, advertising, television, radio and media coverage shall use the title in 1.1.

1.3 The title shall be owned and controlled by the [Association/Institute] and the [Sponsor]. Neither party shall be entitled to use and/or exploit the title after [date].

T.561

The [Sportsperson] confirms that he/she has full title and authority to enter into this agreement and that he/she is not bound by any previous agreement at any time and/or professional rules and/or code of conduct and/or medical report and/or other restriction within the last [number] months which would undermine and/or adversely affect this agreement.

T.562

1.1 The [Sportsperson] agrees and undertakes that all present and future copyright and any other intellectual property rights, trade marks and/or any other rights in the [Sponsor's] services, products and trade marks and other material together with any goodwill shall belong to and remain with the [Sponsor].

1.2 That where for the purpose of this agreement a new version of the [Sponsors'] products, services and/or slogans and/or images, artwork, logos and/or some other material are created specifically to be worn and/or displayed by the [Sportsperson]. That the owner of all such any rights and/or interest shall be the [Sponsor].

T.563

1.1 The Title of the [Event] shall be: [specify full title].

1.2 The ownership of the title is held jointly by the [Sponsor] and the [Company].

1.3 Neither party shall be entitled to register and/or exploit any rights in the title in 1.1 without the prior written consent of the other party in each case.

T.564

1.1 The [Sponsor] has agree to sponsor a series of [zoom/skype/other] conferences over the internet which are to be recorded, filmed and edited for reproduction on [specify website/app/channel].

1.2 The [Contributors] shall be required to assign all copyright and intellectual property rights in all media to the [Sponsor] and the [Enterprise] who shall hold all rights jointly.

1.3 The [Sponsor] and the [Enterprise] agree that the final edited conference shall be owned jointly by the [Sponsor] and the [Enterprise] and that the parties shall equally share any sums which may be received in respect of the exploitation of the rights and/or material.

University, Charity and Educational

T.565

The [Contributor] agrees that all intellectual property rights, copyright, computer software rights, design rights and any other rights in the [Work], the name, the words and phrases, slogans, sounds, and any associated samples, models, images, artwork, graphics, sound recordings, computer-generated material or other material and any associated trade mark, domain name, website, app, channel, logo or associated goodwill or any developments or adaptations shall remain the property of the [Institute]. The [Contributor] shall not acquire any such rights and/or interest and shall not represent that he/she owns and/or controls them. Nor shall the [Contributor] attempt to register any such rights and/or interest.

T.566

1.1 The [Company] agrees that the [Institute/Enterprise] owns all rights in the [Institutes'/Enterprises'] business name and/or any products and/or services including any logo, image, music, jingle and/or sound recording and/or film and any registered trade mark and any goodwill and that it shall remain the sole property of the [Institute/Enterprise] whether adapted under this agreement or not. The [Company] shall not acquire any copyright, intellectual property rights and/or other rights and/or interest.

1.2 The [Company] shall not attempt to register and/or claim ownership of any related letters, initials, similar names and/or shapes and/or other matter relating to 1.1.

T.567

The [Company] acknowledges and agrees that all intellectual property rights, copyright and any other rights in the [Work/Event/Project] and the physical material shall belong to and remain the sole property of the [Institute/Charity]. The [Company] shall not have any right and/or interest in the title of the [Work/Event/Project] and/or any associated image, slogan, trade mark, logo and/or other material and/or rights at any time created in respect of the [Work/Event/project]. The [Company] shall not be entitled to use and/or exploit them in any manner without the prior consent of the [Institute/Charity].

T.568
The copyright, intellectual property rights, trade marks, patents, computer software rights and any other rights in the [Work/Project] developed by [Name] and the [University] shall belong to both parties jointly. Neither party shall be entitled to reproduce, supply, sell, license, assign and/or otherwise exploit the rights and/or any other physical material, data, databases, results and/or information whether confidential or not without the written consent of the other at any time in any part of the world and/or universe.

T.569

1.1 The [Sponsor] and the [Enterprise] agree that they shall develop and commission a new logo, image and title for the [Event/Project] which shall be held and owned jointly by both parties.

1.2 That any new sponsor in subsequent years shall not use the same logo, image and title created in 1.1.

1.3 That where either party wishes to register any rights and/or create any merchandising in respect of 1.1. That the consent of both parties shall be required and that both parties shall share equally any net receipts after the deduction of any relevant expenses and costs.

TRADE MARKS

General Business and Commercial

T.570
'Trade Marks and potential trade marks' shall be defined for the purpose of this agreement to include any actual registered trade marks, community trade marks, international trade marks, and/or service marks and/or any other titles, images, text, words, designs, signs, packaging, letters, numerals or shapes including real and made up names of places, people and products or services capable of being represented graphically that may potentially and/or actually distinguish any product, service, work or other material in existence before and/or created during this agreement and/or for which an application has been made which is pending and/or which may look the same, sound the same and/or mean the same in any form.

T.571

'The Registered Trade Marks' shall mean such trade marks as defined in [specify legislation] and [specify rules] and the international trade mark protocol [specify details] and/or as subsequently amended which have been registered by the [Company] and/or which are pending acceptance based on the [NICE] classification of [45] different classes. A full list is set out in appendix A which forms part of this agreement.

T.572

'Trade Mark' shall mean any sign capable of being represented graphically which is capable of distinguishing goods or services of one undertaking from those of other undertakings. A trade mark may consist of words, designs, letters, numerals or the shape of goods or their packaging in accordance with [specify legislation/protocol/classification] as amended.

T.573

'A Certification Mark' shall mean a mark indicating that the goods or services in connection with which it is used are certified by the [Proprietor] of the mark in respect of origin, material, make or manufacture of the goods or performance of services, quality, accuracy or other characteristics as defined in [specify legislation/classification /protocol] as amended.

T.574

'Community Trade Mark' shall be defined in accordance with [specify Directive/Regulations] as defined as at [date] in [country].

T.575

1.1 The [Proprietor] shall join with the [User] at the [User's] expense in making an application to the [Register of Trade Marks/other] for the purpose of securing the registration of the [User] as a registered [User] of the Trade Marks in accordance with [specify legislation] as amended.

1.2 The [User] shall only be entitled to use and/or exploit the Trade Marks as authorised and permitted under this agreement and the Register by the [Proprietor].

T.576

1.1 The Trade Marks listed and described and represented in appendix A shall be and remain at all times the sole property of the [Company].

1.2 The [Licensee] shall not use, license, sell, mortgage, transfer, merge, exploit and/or market the Trade Marks in any way except in the performance of this agreement without the prior written approval of the [Company].

1.3 The [Company] agrees to make an application to the [Trade Mark Register/other] for the [Licensee] to be registered as a user of the Trade Marks for the Licence Period.

1.4 The [Licensee] shall not be entitled to any ownership of, claim to and/or interest in the Trade Marks and/or any adaptations in any format in any medium at any time except as authorised under this agreement and/or the Register.

1.5 Where any new adaptations and/or designs, words, names, shapes, logos, letters, numeral and/or other graphics and/or artwork and/or computer-generated and/or electronic material are created and/or developed in association with the services and/or products of the [Company] and/or any marketing which are commissioned by the [Licensee]. The [Licensee] agrees to assigns all such rights to the [Company] in all media and in all medium. So that the [Licensee] retains no rights whatsoever and/or any claim to any sums.

T.577
The [Licensee] shall not use the Trade Marks in any manner which might threaten and/or put at risk the validity of the registrations.

T.578
The [Proprietor] authorises the [User] on a non-exclusive basis during the Term of this Agreement to use the Trade Marks in respect of the [Product/Work] made by the [User] in accordance with all such conditions specified in the agreement.

T.579
The assignment and/or other transfer of a [Registered Certification Mark] is not effective without the consent of the Registrar as specified under [specify legislation] as amended.

T.580
It is agreed that this agreement is not intended to contain and shall not be deemed to contain any trade mark licence.

T.581
'The Trade Marks' shall mean the registered and unregistered Trade Marks which belong to the [Company] whether national and/or international registrations and/or pending applications which relate to the [Products] and/or any packaging and/or any marketing and which have been and/or are used by the [Company] and/or its subsidiaries, agents and/or affiliated partners in connection with the [Products] whether in existence now and/

or created in the future which may be notified by the [Company] to the [Distributor] from time to time.

T.582

It is agreed that the licence to use the Registered Trade Mark (whether in general or limited) shall be binding on the successor in title to the [Company's] interest.

T.583

This licence does not authorise the transfer and/or assignment of this licence to any third party for the use of the Registered Trade Mark. There is no right to assign, sub-license and/or transfer any part of this agreement and/or the registered user documentation to any successor in title and/or other third party.

T.584

1.1 The name, image, logo and slogan of the [Group] whether registered as a trade mark or not shall belong to all members of the [Group].

1.2 In the event of the departure from the [Group] of any of its members the name shall only be used by the remaining majority. If the split results in there being no remaining majority of the parties to this agreement then no one shall be entitled to use the name for any purpose without the prior written consent of all parties.

T.585

1.1 The [Supplier] agrees and undertakes that it is the [owner/distributor] of the [Products/Services] described in appendix A.

1.2 That the design rights, copyright and intellectual property rights in the [Products/Services] in 1.1 are [owned/controlled] by [specify name].

1.3 That the trade marks, service marks, logos, images, graphics, computer generated material and computer software in 1.1 are [owned/controlled] by [specify name].

T.586

The following Trade Marks are owned and/or controlled by the [full name of Company] as follows:

1.1 unregistered trade marks: [–].

1.2 registered trade marks in [countries]: [–].

1.3 community trade marks in [countries]: [–].

1.4 international trade marks in [countries]: [–].

T.587

[specify trade mark] is the [registered/ unregistered] trade mark of [Company].

T.588

[specify trade mark] is the registered Trade Mark of [Company]. All rights are reserved by [Company]. The use of the [Trade Mark] by a third party in any format and/or medium is not permitted without the written permission of the [Company].

T.589

The [Licensee] agrees to provide the following copyright notice, registered trade mark, credit, logo and image set out in the attached appendix B to the [Licensor] on every copy of the label for the [Units] of the adaptation of the [Sound Recordings/Films/] and on all labels, covers, press releases, publicity, advertising, packaging, marketing, on any website, app and/or download and/or other rights and/or adapted material at any time.

T.590

1.1   The [Licensee] agrees and undertakes not to change, adapt and/or distort the copyright notice, trade marks, credits, logo and image of the [Licensor] without their prior written consent.

1.2   The [Licensee] agrees that the copyright notice, trade marks, image and logo set out in appendix B shall be and remain at all times the sole property of the [Licensor].

1.3   The [Licensee] agrees that it shall not have the authority to sub-license and/or authorise the reproductions of the trade marks, image and/or logo for use and/or adaptation by a third party.

1.4   The [Licensee] agrees not to attempt to register a trade mark, image and/or logo which is the same and/or similar and/or an imitation and/or to attempt to register as the copyright owner of the [Work/Material].

T.591

The [Licensor] agrees to supply electronic copies of the digital files of the trade mark and logo for the purposes of this agreement. At the termination and/or expiry of this agreement the [Licensee] undertakes to erase and/or delete all copies of the electronic digital files and any copies in any format subject to any legal proceedings that may be pending between the parties.

T.592

1.1   The [Company] grants to the [Distributor] a non-exclusive licence to incorporate the [Products] in the opening sequence of the [Series/

Channel] for the Licence Period in accordance with the terms set out in this agreement.

1.2 The [Distributor] shall acknowledge and display the name of the [Company], the [Products] and the associated [Trade Marks] in the closing credits of each episode of the [Series] as described in appendix A.

T.593

The [Company] acknowledges that the [Television Company] is entitled to arrange for any other companies and/or persons to sponsor, advertise and/or promote their products and/or services in the [Programme/Series] and that those third parties shall be entitled to have its products, services, trade marks, logos, images and/or music incorporated in or around the [Programme/Series] whether or not they are competitors.

T.594

The [Licensee] shall be entitled to release copies reproducing the [Programme/Series] in [format] in the Territory bearing and/or incorporating the [Licensor's] Logo on all material of any nature which directly relates to the exploitation and marketing: [specify words, logo, position, size, location].

T.595

The [Licensee] agrees to provide the following on-screen credit, copyright notice and registered trade mark notice to the [Licensor] in the [Podcast/ Series] and in any packaging, marketing and other authorised exploitation as follows: [specify details].

T.596

1.1 The trading name, logo, image and graphics associated with this series of [Podcasts/Videos/Products] is original and has been created by [Name].

1.2 A registered trade mark application is pending. All copyright and intellectual property rights and pending trade marks are owned by [Name].

T.597

This [Website/App/Blog] has an identifiable and original logo and name which is owned by the [Company]. There is no authority granted to reproduce the logo and name in any product, service and/or other media in any form.

1964

T.598

1.1 This agreement is limited to the supply of [number] [Products] to the [Company] for use in the [Film/Video/Podcast] as agreed between the parties as follows: [describe purpose/scene].

1.2 There are no rights granted to the [Company] for the use and/or adaptation of any trade marks, product names, images and/or logos owned by the [Distributor].

T.599

The [Performer] is known by the stage name: [specify name] and the personal name: [specify name]. There is no trade mark registered for either of these names and/or the associated logos and images. There are no rights granted to the [Company] to use and/or adapt and/or exploit the stage name and/or personal name of the [Performer] for any reason without the prior written consent of the [Performer].

T.600

The [Company] hold all the rights in the registered trade mark represented in appendix A. The [Company] authorises the [Distributor] to reproduce the registered trade mark in association with and in conjunction with the copyright notice of the [Company] in respect of all copies of the [Sound Recordings/Musical Works] in any format which may be produced and/or exploited under this agreement.

T.601

1.1 [Name] and [Name] agree that they shall hold the joint copyright, trade mark and all other intellectual property rights in the [Image/Logo/ Letters/words] which are set out in appendix C.

1.2 That all applications for any registration of a trade mark, community mark, service mark and/or some other matter shall be in the names of both parties.

1.3 That neither party shall be entitled to transfer, assign, exploit and/or otherwise use the rights and/or goodwill in 1.1 and 1.2 unless both parties agree in advance and provide their consent.

T.602

1.1 The [Licensor] agrees to supply different formats of copies of the artwork and/or electronic material of the [Character] and any trade mark, logo and/or credits at the [Licensee's] cost on temporary loan which may be required by the [Licensee] to assist in the production, manufacture and distribution of the [Products/Services].

1.2 The [Licensee] undertakes to use and reproduce the [Character] and any trade mark, logo and/or credits for the sole purpose of the manufacture, distribution, sale and/or marketing of the [Products/ Services] and not for any other purpose.

1.3 The [Licensee] agrees that no films, videos, podcasts, banner and/or pop-up advertisements, product placement, sponsorship, merchandising, and/or other promotional material and/or any sub-licensing has and/or will be entered into which reproduces the [Character] and/or any adaptation developed, authorised and/or exploited without the prior written approval of the [Licensor].

T.603

The [Licensee] agrees to provide the following credit, copyright notice, trade mark and logo and/or image to the [Licensor] in respect of the [Products/ Services] in a prominent position which is clearly legible and readily available to be read by the public and on all copies and on all packaging and promotional material in any media and/or format: [specify details].

T.604

1.1 The [Licensee] agrees that the [Licensor] shall be entitled to approve any exact samples of the [Products] prior to manufacture and distribution.

1.2 The [Licensee] undertakes to supply at the [Licensee's] cost to the [Licensor] such samples of the [Products] and packaging in the exact form and material in which the [Licensee] proposes to manufacture and distribute the [Products].

1.3 The [Licensor] shall provide written approval or rejection of the samples of the [Products] within [one] month of receipt. Failure by the [Licensor] to reply within that period shall not be deemed acceptance or approval. After the expiry of the [one] month period from receipt of the samples then if the [Licensee] has not had any communication to reject the samples. The [Licensee] shall be entitled to deem the samples accepted by the [Licensor] and approval provided.

T.605

The [Licensee] agrees that the Licensor shall be entitled to approve in advance all labels, packaging, product material, brochures, in store and outdoor posters, website and app details, pop up banners, advertisements in magazines and newspapers, associated jingles, music and/or sound recordings for radio and/or television and/or any performers and/or persons to be used for promotional purposes and/or any endorsement on their blogs, podcasts, websites and/or otherwise in any proposed format in any media which bears or incorporates the [Licensor's] trade mark, logo and/or credit and/or the licensed [Products]. That all such material, use and/or exploitation shall require the prior written consent of the [Licensor].

T.606

1.1 The [Licensee] agrees and acknowledges that all copyright, intellectual property rights and any other rights and/or interest in the [Character], its name, any trade mark, logo, image, domain and/or app name and/or slogan together with any goodwill and all developments and physical material and/or any adaptation described in appendix C are and shall remain owned by the [Licensor].

1.2 The [Licensee] agrees and undertakes that it shall not acquire any rights of any nature in the [Character], its name, any trade mark, logo, image, domain and/or app name and/or slogan together with any goodwill and/or any development and/or physical material and/or any adaptation. The [Licensee] is only granted the non-exclusive right to reproduce the rights and/or material in appendix C from [date] to [date] in [country] in the form of [Format/Product] in the exact form of the agreed sample.

T.607

'The Company's Products' shall mean the products of the [Company] including labels, attached and/or integral items, packaging, trade marks, service marks, images, logos, and any associated words, phrases, slogans, music and/or sound recordings which are described as follows: [detail material]. A detailed specification and two and three dimensional copies of the Company's Products are attached to and form part of this agreement in schedule A.

T.608

'The Character' shall be the original concept and novel idea for a character which is briefly described as follows: [name/description].

Full details of the Character are attached to and form part of this agreement in appendix A including:

1.1 full name and any short form.

1.2 copyright and other intellectual property rights, domain and app names, trade mark and logo representations, slogans and/or any associated musical work, sound recordings and/or sounds and/or voices and/or films, stills and/or other images.

1.3 costumes and details of designer and other relevant items used as props and/or as part of the role, scripts and plot outlines.

T.609

'The Character Report' shall be the original [animal/person/puppet/other] known as: [specify name]. The character was created and designed by [Name] who is now deceased and died in [year]. The estate of [Name] and all copyright, trade marks and intellectual property rights are held by [specify organisation]. The character is described in full detail with all specifications, colour, size and functions together with all references to the origin of any rights and the sub-licensing and/or assignment of any rights in appendix C.

T.610

1.1 The [Company] confirms that it is the sole owner of and/or controls all copyright, intellectual property rights, trade marks, names, logos, slogans, images and artwork, computer-generated and electronic material, sound recordings, music and/or lyrics and/or any other rights in the [Product/Service] and all packaging and promotional material and/or any adaptations in all media and in all formats throughout the [country/world]. Full details are set out in appendix A.

1.2 The only exceptions in 1.1 are the following rights and/or material which are owned and/or controlled by third parties which have been licensed to the [Company] and are set out in appendix B. [specify third party name/type of license/purpose/start and end date/clearance and fees due and other costs].

1.3 Where the [Company] supplies and/or authorises any rights and/or forms of exploitation by the [Licensee] under this agreement. The [Licensee] shall be obliged to pay any sums due to third parties as stated in 1.2 and appendix B for the exercise of such rights and/or the reproduction of the material.

1.4 The [Company] shall arrange for the [Licensee] to be registered as an authorised user of the [Company's] trade marks and/or other rights as required. Any such registration shall cease at any time at the sole discretion of the [Company] by notification to the appropriate organisation and/or on the termination of this agreement and/or on the expiry of this agreement. Any costs incurred by the [Company] to register the [Licensee] and/or remove the [Licensee] shall be paid for by the [Licensee] up to a maximum of [number/currency].

T.611

1.1 The [Company] shall provide the [Distributor] with a style book incorporating the manner, form, size, colour and position in which the Credits, Copyright Notice and Trade Marks are to be used. The [Distributor] agrees and undertakes not to deviate from the style book in any manner and/or to use the Trade Marks in any unauthorised format and/or medium without prior written consent of the [Company].

1.2 Nothing in this agreement shall prevent and/or prohibit the [Distributor] from identifying itself as the manufacturer and distributor of the [Products] and the [Distributor] shall be entitled to use its own trade mark, design and/or logo in addition to the [Company's] Trade Marks. Provided that the [Company's] Trade Marks are no less prominent and/or less frequent than those of the [Distributor].

T.612

1.1 The [Distributor] shall ensure that the registered Trade Marks of the [Company] both in respect of the [Company] and the [Products/Services] described and represented in schedule A are reasonably prominence and clear on any packaging, trade literature, promotional material and/or any website, app and/or any advertising and/or promotional material in respect of the [Products/Services].

1.2 The [Distributor] is not authorised to create and/or develop any new versions in another colour, style and/or format and/or similar name of the registered Trade Marks of the [Company] and/or the [Products/Services] in any media at any time.

T.613

The [Distributor] and/or its authorised agents shall be entitled to distribute, promote and sell the [Products/Services] in the [Territory/area] bearing the logos, images, slogans and/or trade marks as may be used by the [Distributor] and/or its authorised agents at any time.

T.614

1.1 The labels, packaging, marketing and promotional material reproduced on and/or used to sell and exploit the [Products] shall be subject to the approval of the [Licensor].

1.2 The [Licensor] confirms and undertakes that it is the owner of following rights in the Trade Mark set out in appendix A. The [Licensee] agrees and undertakes that all copies in any format and/or medium created and/or produced under this agreement shall bear the Trade Mark owned by the [Licensor] described in appendix A. [registration date/scope of cover/images/formats].

1.3 The [Licensor] agrees and undertakes to indemnify the [Licensee] in respect of any legal proceedings, claims, costs, damages, losses and/or expenses which may arise as a direct result of the use of the Trade Mark in appendix A by the [Licensee] during the [Licence Period] and/or until the termination of this agreement whichever is the earlier. Provided that the [Licensee] shall immediately notify the [Licensor] of any potential threat and/or claim and allow the [Licensor] to co-operate with the [Licensee] to minimise costs and to respond to any such third party on a joint basis to defend the claim.

1.4 The [Licensee] undertakes not to attempt to register the Trade Mark and/or any similar name, letters, logos, images, colours and/or shapes in respect of any other product, service and/or in any other format and/or medium at any time.

T.615

The [Licensee] shall ensure that the [Product], its packaging and promotional material reproduced, offered for sale, sold and/or otherwise exploited in the [Territory/country] shall be marked in a form approved by the [Licensor] with the Trade Mark: [specify details] which is described in detail in schedule A. Together with the following notice on all copies:

'The Trade Mark is manufactured under Licence from [Licensor] and the Trade Mark is the [registered/pending] Trade Mark of [Licensor] and copyright in the Product and all rights therein are owned by the [Licensor] and reproduced under Licence.'

T.616

'The Trade Mark' shall be the following trade mark, design, image and logo together with any associated words briefly described as follows: [brief description] which is owned and/or controlled by the [Licensor]. A two-dimensional and three dimensional full colour copy of each version of the Trade Mark is described in Schedule A. Together with a history of the creation, design and ownership. Schedule A forms part of this agreement.

T.617

'The Licensor's Brand' shall be the following trade mark, service mark, design, logo, slogan, text, graphics or other material. A detailed list of two and three dimensional representations, descriptions and specifications are set out in Schedule B and form part of this agreement.

T.618

In any consideration of the Fee the [Charity] grants the [Licensee] the non-exclusive right to:

1.1 reproduce the [Charity's] name and trade mark: [specify details] on [number] copies of [specify product] in [country] for the [Event/Festival] from [date] to [date]. The products are not for sale and are only to be worn by the [volunteers/staff].

1.2   reproduce the [Charity's] name and trade mark in 1.1 on the website/
      app for the [Event/Festival] and in any direct marketing from [date to
      date]. The [Charity] shall be identified as a supporter of the [Event/
      Festival].

T.619

1.1   The [Licensee] agrees that the [Licensor] shall be entitled to approve
      in advance of production, manufacture, supply and/or distribution
      all material in any format and/or medium in respect of the [Product]
      and all associated labels, packaging, marketing, product placement,
      sponsorship and/or any collaborations and/or partnerships.

1.2   The [Licensee] agrees that it shall not be entitled to use, manufacture,
      distribute and/or supply any material until the written approval in each
      case of the [Licensor] has been obtained.

1.3   The [Licensee] undertakes that it shall supply at its sole cost samples
      of the [Product] and/or any associated material in 1.1 in the exact form
      in which it is to be reproduced, used and/or exploited.

1.4   That the [Licensee] shall not enter into any arrangements which would
      harm and/or damage the sales and/or reputation of the [Product] and/
      or the [Licensor].

T.620

1.1   The [Products] shall bear the trade name of the [Licensor] and the
      registered trade mark: [specify details].

1.2   The [Licensor] agrees that any disputes and/or claims made by any
      third party with respect to the trade name of the [Licensor] and/or
      the trade mark which are used as directed by the [Licensor] on the
      [Products] shall be dealt with at the [Licensor's] sole cost.

T.621

1.1   The [Licensee] shall at its sole cost supply to the [Licensor] for
      written approval samples of the [Products] including content labels,
      trade marks, copyright and/or design right acknowledgments.
      Together with samples of all wrappings, containers, display materials,
      advertisements, website, app and mobile material and any other
      competitions, premium rate phone lines, sponsorships and/or any
      other marketing material.

1.2   The [Licensee] shall ensure that the following words are set out on each
      and every item of the [Product] and all packaging in respect of the
      trade mark described in appendix A: 'The trade mark is manufactured

and reproduced under licence from the [Licensor] and the trade mark is a registered trade mark of the [Licensor]'.

T.622

The [Artist] agrees that the [Company] shall own and/or control all trade marks, logos, images, words, colours, shapes and/or other matters which the [Company] commissions, creates and/or develops in conjunction with the record label known as: [specify name].

T.623

The [Artist] warrants that he/she shall not at any time use the name of the [Company] and/or any trade mark, service mark, design, logo and/or other device in any manner likely to give the impression that any performance and/or other matter is authorised by and/or is endorsed by and/or associated with the [Company] unless the prior written consent of the [Company] has been provided in each case.

T.624

The [Agent] acknowledges that the name of the [Artist] and any goodwill and reputation created in respect of any personal name, business and/or trade name and/or any image, icon, trade mark, logo, shape, colour, letters and/or otherwise shall remain the sole property of the [Artist]. That no part of this agreement is intended to transfer any present and/or future copyright, trade marks and/or any other intellectual property rights whether in existence now and/or created in the future to the [Agent].

T.625

The [Company] warrants that it is the sole owner of all rights of any nature throughout the world in the [Company's] Trade Mark and that the [Company's] Trade Mark does not infringe the copyright, trade mark, service and/or business mark and/or any other right of any third party throughout the Territory from [date].

T.626

The [Company] agrees to provide to the [Association/Charity] at the [Company's] sole cost and expense all suitable artwork of the [Company's Logo] in order for it to be reproduced in all printed and/or other media under the control of the [Association/Charity] for the purposes of this agreement.

T.627

'The Association's Brand' shall mean the artwork, designs, logos, service marks, trade marks, words, slogans, images, colours, symbols and/or characters to be used for the marketing of the [Event]. A package of samples of each of the types under this umbrella of brands are to be supplied as Schedule D which forms part of this agreement.

T.628

1.1   The [Organisers] agrees that all copyright, trade mark and any other rights in the [Company's] trade mark, design and logo shall be the sole and exclusive property of the [Company's] together with any goodwill.

1.2   The [Organiser] shall not acquire any rights and/or interest in the [Company's] trade mark, design and logo and/or any adaptations.

1.3   The [Company] confirms that it is the sole owner of and/or controls all copyright, trade mark and any other rights in the [Company's] trade mark and logo and that reproduction by the [Organisers] will not expose them to any civil and/or criminal proceedings at any time.

T.629

The [Company] undertakes that the specific products and/or services being promoted under this agreement shall be fit and safe for their intended use and shall comply with all legislation, regulations, guidelines and codes of practice in force in [country] from [date].

T.630

The [Promoter] agrees to conclude any document supplied by the [Company] to assign all copyright and intellectual property rights in any image, sound recording. film, logo and/or other rights and/or material to the [Company] which is commissioned and/or acquired by the [Promoter] relating to this agreement.

T.631

The [Sponsor] shall be the major sponsor of the [Event/Project] and shall be entitled to the following rights in respect of the [Event/Project] from [date] to [date]:

1.1   The right to display banners and advertising boards bearing or incorporating the [Sponsor's] name, trade mark, logo, image, slogans and the [Products].

1.2   One full page advertisement for the [Sponsor] in the official programme guide and one full page statement from the [Sponsor]. All such artwork, text and photographs to be supplied at the [Sponsor's] cost to the [Charity].

1.3   The exclusive right to include the [Sponsor's] name and trade mark, logo and image on all competitor's numbers and clothes in a prominent location.

1.4 The right to use the words the Official Supplier of the [Event/Project] together with the depiction of the [Charity's] trade mark, logo, image and slogan on all websites, apps and other electronic material on all copies of the [Products], packaging, outdoor advertisements and marketing in any media and in all competitions until [date].

T.632

The [Sponsor] agrees that it will not enter into any joint promotions, partnerships and/or collaborations with new third parties in respect of material and/or products which bear and/or incorporate the [Association's] trade marks, name, logo, image and/or other matter at any time without the prior written approval of the [Association] except with the [Sponsor's] parent, subsidiary, holding companies and/or existing third parties as follows: [specify names].

T.633

The supply of articles, products and/or services under this agreement which bear trade marks, service marks, images, logos, slogans and/or any other identifying letter, mark or otherwise does not imply and/or grant any right to reproduce and/or exploit such rights to any purchaser and/or any other third party at any time.

U

UNION

General Business and Commercial

U.001
The [Company] recognises and acknowledges that the [Employee] shall be entitled to become a member of a trade union, trade organisation or other body and that this shall not prejudice and/or affect the [Employee's] employment of and/or future prospects at the [Company].

U.002
The [Company] agrees that it shall not prevent and/or deter the [Employee] from being actively involved in an independent trade union at any time and/or shall not penalise the [Employee] for such participation.

U.003
In the event that the [Employee] becomes an official of an independent trade union which is recognised by the [Company]. The [Company] agrees that the [Employee] shall be assisted in arranging to take up to [number] days absence per year from his/her normal working hours for the purpose of carrying out official duties as a union official and/or to undergo training in aspects of industrial relations which are relevant to his/her duties as an official.

U.004
In determining the amount of time the [Employee] shall be entitled to have as authorised absence [which is not holiday leave] for official duties and training. The [Company] shall take into account the specific purpose and any ad hoc conditions which may be agreed between the [Employee] and the [Company]. In any event the [Company] agrees to be reasonable, taking all the circumstances into account and shall have due regard to any relevant provisions of any policies, guidelines, standards or code of practice issued by [government agency/union/other].

U.005
In the event that the [Company] and the trade union [Name] of which the [Employee] is a bona fide member of good standing enter into a formal

agreement relating to working conditions and/or pay structure and/or some other matter at the [Company]. The [Company] agrees and undertakes that any such new formal agreement with the trade union [Name] at a later date shall be incorporated into the terms agreed with the [Employee] as an amendment.

U.006

There is no agreement and/or undertaking by the [Production Company] that any designers, lighting, stage and production personnel, artistes, musicians, performers and other third parties involved in the development, production and exploitation of the [Podcast/Film/Video] shall be members of recognised unions, craft and/or trade organisations.

U.007

[Name] confirms and undertakes that he/she is a bona fide member of [Equity/Musicians Union/other] in [country] and will continue to be so during the Term of this Agreement.

U.008

1.1 The [Sportsperson] confirms that he/she is a bona fide existing member of the following [professional/sports] organisation: [specify name] and has been since [date].

1.2 That there is no existing, current and/or pending investigation and/or other complaint regarding the conduct and/or activities of the [Sportsperson] by [specify name].

U.009

The [Sportsperson] confirms and undertakes that he/she has full authority to enter into this agreement and is not bound by and/or subject to any previous agreement, arrangement, licence, professional rules, code of conduct and/or disciplinary decision and/or any civil and/or criminal proceedings and/or judgement which will and/or is likely to adversely affect this agreement.

U.010

[Name] is a fully paid up member of [Professional/Trade Organisation] in [country] and has been qualified as a [specify role] since [date]. There is no dispute, disciplinary hearing and/or other complaint and/or allegation against [Name] of which [Name] is aware which is pending and/or has been decided by that body since [date].

U.011

The [Company] acknowledges that [Name] is not a member of any trade and/or craft union and/or professional body and agrees that this is not required for the purposes of this agreement.

U.012

The [Company/Distributor] agrees that it shall abide by all laws, conventions, regulations, directives, policies, codes and practices that may be in force at any time from [date] to [date] in respect of union, trade, government and/or international bodies and organisations including but not limited to those that apply to any employee, premises, transport, health and safety, security, content, the manufacture, promotion and marketing of products, the supply of services, insurance, pensions, the use of resources, and/or waste, recycling and the environment.

U.013

The [Consultant] agrees and undertakes that he/she is a qualified [specify profession/other] and is a fully paid up member of [specify body/union]. That there is no conflict of interest and/or any other reason which would affect the ability of the [Consultant] to provide his/her services under this agreement and/or to provide independent, high quality and comprehensive advice to the [Company].

U.014

The [Consultant] is not providing any confirmation as to his/her professional qualifications, background and/or expertise. The [Consultant] is not required to have joined and/or be a member of any trade union and/or any other organisation for the purposes of this agreement.

U.015

The [Company] adheres to the national terms and conditions set by [specify organisation] in respect of [specify role/other] and all payments to [Name] shall be in accordance with the rates which may be applicable at the time of completion of the work by [Name].

U.016

1.1 [Name] is a qualified [specify profession] and is registered as a current member of [specify organisation]. [Name] currently holds a certificate from [specify organisation] to practice as a [profession/role] [reference].

1.2 The [Company/Trust] engage the services of [Name] as [profession/ role] at the rates and on the terms set out in the national agreement dated [date]. A copy of that agreement is attached and forms part of this agreement. Any amendments to and/or increase in the rates of the national agreement shall be incorporated to amend this agreement.

V

VALUE ADDED TAX

General Business and Commercial

V.001

The [Dealer/Whole/Fixed] Price is exclusive of any taxes and must be paid without any deduction whatsoever. Where relevant value added tax, sales tax and/or any other tax shall be paid by the [Company] as required under any legislation and/or laws of any country. Any taxes shall only be paid where the [Supplier] provides an invoice with the appropriate registered codes and/or complies with any other formalities that may be required.

V.002

1.1   All sums payable under this agreement are exclusive of any [value added tax/taxes] that may be payable by either party.

1.2   As far as possible either party shall give notification and formal documentation to the other party of any additional payments in the form of taxes, duties and/or other costs that may be due prior to the conclusion of this agreement for information purposes.

V.003

1.1   It is agreed that all fees due shall unless otherwise stated be exclusive of value added tax and/or any other taxes on the supply of products and/or services.

1.2   The [Company] agrees that it shall pay any value added tax and/or any other taxes which may be due at the time of this agreement and/or arise in the future to the [Supplier] in 1.1. Provided that any appropriate invoice is submitted to the [Company] which complies with any existing legislation and states the relevant registered reference codes of the [Supplier] for such purposes.

V.004

The [Artiste] agrees that he/she is solely responsible for his/her national insurance, personal tax, personal insurance, medical and dental cover, pension and/or any other taxes and/or documentation and/or submissions which may become due in consequence of this agreement which directly relate to the [Artiste] and/or his/her agent and/or other representative.

V.005

All fees are exclusive of [VAT/other]. The [Contributor] agrees to be responsible for the reporting and/or payment of his/her own national insurance and personal tax in any country. The Company agrees to make all payments required under this agreement to the [Contributor] directly. The [Company] shall only be obliged to pay [value added tax/other] upon receipt of a formal invoice.

V.006

If there is a legal obligation for the [Distributor/Company] to charge any taxes on the supply and/or provision of its products and/or services in any country which apply to this agreement at any time. Then the [Distributor/Company] shall submit an invoice to the [Enterprise/Charity] complying with all legal requirements and stating the additional sum which may be due. The [Enterprise/Charity] shall in such event pay the additional sum due and comply with the legal requirement.

V.007

1.1 The [Company] confirms that it is registered with [specify government body] to pay [specify tax] and has the reference code [specify].

1.2 The [Company] confirms that it is up to date with all payments in respect of the tax in 1.1 and that none are currently overdue.

1.3 The [Company] confirms that it is not the subject of any legal action by any third party in respect of any taxes in [country].

1.4 The [Company] confirms that it has an accrual policy for tax received in 1.1 that may be due to be paid.

V.008

1.1 [Name] confirms that he/she is not registered for [specify tax] and that none shall be claimed and/or due from the [Company] in respect of any of the services supplied under this agreement.

1.2 In the event that [Name] shall become at any time in the future due to pay [specify tax] in respect of the supply of her/his services. Then they shall notify the [Company] and shall submit an appropriate [invoice/payment request] in respect any such request for payment for services which are completed.

VARIATION

General Business and Commercial

V.009
Where the [Company/Supplier] receives an instruction and/or order which requires a significant change and/or alteration of the [Project/Products/ Services] set out in appendix A. The [Company/Supplier] shall within [ten] [hours/days/weeks] of receiving such instruction prepare and submit to the [Enterprise] a written estimate specifying the total revised cost including any additional administration charges and fees and the revised schedule, completion and delivery date.

V.010
The [Company] agrees that the detailed terms of the Production Schedule shall only be varied in exceptional circumstances but in any event shall not be varied without the prior written approval of the [Commissioning Company] as represented by [Name] or such other representative of the [Commissioning Company] as may be notified. Such approval must not be unreasonably withheld and/or delayed taking into account the third party contractual commitments in respect of the production.

V.011
The [Company] acknowledges and agrees that where any production, adaptation, developments and/or marketing of the [Series/Films/Podcasts] create any new and/or future copyright and/or any other intellectual property rights, trade marks, domain and app names and/or any other rights which may be held by a third party and/or the [Company]. That the [Company] shall ensure that all such new future copyright, intellectual property rights, trade marks and/or domain and/or app names and/or any other rights shall be assigned and owned and/or controlled by [Name].

V.012
There shall be no variation, change, alteration, modification, development, creation of new material, deletion of any existing material and/or any mutilation, distortion and/or adaptation without the written agreement of [Name] and [Name].

V.013
No variation, amendment, changes, alteration and/or otherwise shall be allowed to the [Product/Film/Work] which are not set out in a document specifying the exact authorised variation and signed by representatives on behalf of both parties.

V.014

The parties agree that changes, developments, alterations, increase in costs, delivery dates, materials, manufacturers, agents, distributors, suppliers, advertising, packaging and any other matters may be varied at any time either by verbal agreement and/or email exchanges between the parties.

V.015

The [Company] agrees and undertakes that it shall not vary, amend and/or change any part of the [Work/Project/Order] without the prior consent and authority of [Name] at the [Institute/Charity].

V.016

The [Consultant] agrees that the [Company] may change any part of the [Project] at any time and the scope of the work that is to be completed by the [Consultant]. Provided no additional costs and/or expenses are to be incurred and/or more time is required to complete the work. Then the [Company] shall not be obliged to pay any additional sums in fees to the [Consultant].

V.017

It is agreed between the parties that if at any time the [Supplier] cannot deliver any part of the content of the [Service/Work] and/or shall not meet the criteria set out in Schedule A. That there shall be no right to by the [Supplier] to substitute an alternative person, material and/or other third party.

VENUE

General Business and Commercial

V.018

'The Venue' shall be the following premises at which the [Event/Festival/ Conference] is to take place [specify address/site] the [freehold/title] of which is owned by the following [Company]: [specify name] whose registered address is at [specify address] in [country].

V.019

'The Venue' shall be the [land/site/house and grounds] which is known by the [Land Registry/other] as reference [specify reference] which is held in the name of [Name] as the freehold owner and on which [Name] has a lease for [number] years and has exclusive rights of occupation from [date] to [date].

V.020

The [Association] confirms that the [Sponsor] shall be provided with the following amenities, services and facilities:

1.1 a hospitality suite capable of accommodating not less than [number] persons.

1.2 an administrative headquarters for the [Sponsor] which shall have available the following facilities: [specify size/facilities].

1.3 not less than [number] complimentary [tickets/brochures] together with [number] free parking spaces at the Venue.

V.021

The [Sponsor] agrees to reimburse the [Association] with the cost and expenses incurred in respect of [number percent/all] the telephone, security, marketing, food, drink and catering, staff costs, licensing application costs, freight, postal services, cleaning services and any other matter which may arise as a result of the access and use by the [Sponsor] of any the amenities, services and facilities provided by the [Association].

V.022

1.1 The [Association] confirms that it has entered into a bona fide written agreement for the exclusive use of the Venue with the [Company] which owns the premises known as [specify address] from [date/time] to [date/time].

1.2 That the [Association] has and/or will make all necessary administrative and financial arrangements necessary for the smooth running of the [Event] including the hiring of the Venue, any prior arrangements with the [Company], the local authority, fire brigade, the police and ensure that fire regulations and licensing laws have been and/or will be adhered to for the duration of the [Event].

V.023

1.1 The [Association] agrees that it shall make all necessary administration and financial arrangements for the [Event] between [date] and [date] which shall be of a suitable and reasonable standard at an appropriate venue.

1.2 The [Sponsor] shall be entitled to approve the choice of the proposed venue by the [Association] prior to the [Association] entering into any contract for the [Event].

V.024

'The Land and Venue' shall be the following [site/plot/location] marked on the map in Schedule A at [address] the freehold of which is owned and registered in the name of [specify person] of [address].

V.025

1.1 The [Institute/Charity] shall provide the conference room on [date] from [time] to [time] and provide all necessary seating, stage, wifi, internet access, electricity, water, rates, lighting, gas, heating, parking, cleaning, security, licences and/or other facilities at the [Institute's/Charity's] sole cost.

1.2 The [Company] shall not install, connect and/or use any equipment, lighting, sound system and/or other material without prior consent from [Name].

1.4 The [Company] shall be liable for any damages, losses, expenses and/or costs which may arise directly and/or indirectly as a result of the use of and access to the premises and any car parking facilities. The [Company] agrees to indemnify the [Institute/Charity] in full upon invoice for any such sums that may be incurred and/or due provided that the matter is not covered by insurance and any claim is itemised and justified by the [Institute/Charity].

V.026

1.1 [Name] agrees that the [Company] may hire on an exclusive basis the [specify location and address] and the accompanying facilities from [date] to [date] in accordance with the summary set out in appendix C.

1.2 The cost of hire shall be [number/currency] which shall be paid by the [Company] to [Name] by [date] by [method of payment].

1.3 The cost of hire of the premises does not include the cost of food, wine, catering and/or hospitality, wifi and the internet access, electricity, water, waste disposal, rubbish removal, rates, lighting, gas, telephone line rental and other charges, heating, cleaning, parking, security, catering, staff and casual staff, spa and swimming pool access and/or any access route requirements and/or of any other material and/or facilities. All these additional matters shall be paid for by the [Company] as individual itemised items on a [daily/weekly/monthly] basis in arrears subject to an advance of [number/currency] which shall be set-off against expenditure and/or damages.

V.027
'The Venue' shall mean [full address/country] and the access road and use of the following rooms, facilities and outside space which is described and represented by a map and images in the attached appendix A from [date] to [date]. This shall include all the cost of the use of the facilities such as light, heat, water, broadband and internet access, electricity, waste disposal, rubbish removal, insurance including accidental damage. Security and staff are not provided. Cleaning must be done professionally by a third party at the end of the arrangement prior to the end date. Any damage, loss and/or other detrimental impact must be remedied before the end date.

V.028
'The Premises' shall [include/exclude] any boarding house, hotel, inn, tavern, guest house and lodging house.

V.029
'The Premises' shall mean all offices, studios, warehouses, garages, storage facilities, and locations owned and/or controlled by the [Company/Enterprise] as at [date].

V.030
'The Plot' shall include any river, marsh, harbour, territorial waters, land, mines and mining, drone rights, houses and/or other buildings, bridges, fixed and/or moveable structures, roads, rights of way, access routes, water sources, drains, sewers, wells and/or any other matter. The land shall include the area below ground up to [number/metres] and over ground in the air up to [number/metres]. A full description and images are represented in schedule A together with details of all legal registrations and licences relating to ownership.

V.031
'The Proprietor' is the following owner of the Venue [Name/Company] whose registered office is at [address] and whose [main place of business/trades at] [address].

V.032
The [Company] confirms and undertakes that it shall be responsible for and bear the total cost of the organisation and staging of the [Event/Exhibition] at the premises in accordance with the layout, content and timeline set out in appendix A.

V.033
The [Association/Charity] confirms and undertakes that it has and/or will:

1.1   enter into a bona fide written agreement for the use of the premises at [address] with the owner of the freehold and/or leasehold as may be appropriate in the circumstances.

1.2   be responsible for the arrangement and cost of the [Event/Festival] including any administration and staff whether permanent and/or temporary, premises hire, parking, catering and hospitality, lighting, furniture, broadband and wifi costs, the cost of any changes and/or alterations that may be necessary, health and safety issues, security staff and equipment, compliance with fire regulations and/or notifications to the police that may be required, public liability and other insurance, any planning and/or licence application for the type of use proposed and/or the sale of alcohol and/or the performance of music and/or any payments and any other local authority consents and/or requirements under any legislation which may need to be complied with.

1.3   That a copy of any documents relating to the above matters in 1.1 and 1.2 shall be provided at no charge to the [Sponsor] upon request. That the [Sponsor] shall have the right to appoint any third party to carry out inspections of the premises and documents to ensure compliance under this Agreement.

V.034
'The Development' shall be the house, outbuildings, land, access roads, electricity, gas, water, drainage and sewage arrangements, parking zones, helipad and facilities specified on the attached map in Schedule A which is attached to and forms part of this agreement.

V.035
[Name] shall not be responsible for all the charges and costs associated with the premises and the [Event] for the [dates] except: catering and hospitality including temporary additional staff, equipment, additional lighting and/or furniture, parking, cleaning both before and after the [Event], repairs and/or replacement of any items and/or material lost and/or damaged. A detailed statement shall be provided within [number] days and the sum recouped from the advance deposit.

V.036
'Multiple Occupation' shall mean any premises (excluding a private residential home) establishment and/or location (whether operated for commercial profit and/or otherwise) containing rooms and/or any other units which are made available as temporary and/or permanent accommodation for more than one guest and/or household and/or as office and/or business premises including without limitation, hotels, motels, inns, guest houses, boarding houses, hospitals, nursing homes, schools and/or other places

which are occupied by multiple persons which are not classified as a private residential property.

V.037
For the purpose of this agreement the multiple occupation shall be [specify address] in [country] which comprises of [number] units which are occupied by [number] students as a halls of residence at [specify college/university] which is owned by [specify freehold/other owner] and controlled by [specify name] under [type of document].

VERIFICATION

General Business and Commercial

V.038
The [Company] undertakes that the information, statistics, sales figures, product details and any other data and materials which it has provided to the [Distributor] are correct and there has been no intention to misrepresent, distort and/or withhold any fact which would materially affect the [Distributors] decision to enter into this agreement.

V.039
The [Company] agrees and undertakes that it cannot rely on the facts, figures, documents, presentations, projections, accounts, databases, sales records and/or any other data and/or information and/or material provided by [Name] in respect of the [Project/Product/Business]. The [Company] agrees that it must carry out its own investigations, research, due diligence, assessments, valuations and projections at its own cost and enters into this agreement entirely at its own risk.

V.040
All projections, estimates, forecasts, predicted sales and costs, valuations and any other information and/or data and/or material provided and/or supplied at any time relating to the future of the [Company] is for guidance only and is not part of any undertaking and/or agreement by the [Company]. All parties agree that there shall be no right at a later date to seek to reclaim any losses, damages and/or fall in value based on any of those facts, data and/or any other matter.

V.041
In the event that the [Company] decides to verify any fact, data, information and/or other matter under this agreement which relates to the [Supplier] and/

or the [Products] and any associated material. The [Supplier] undertakes to provide its full cooperation and to disclose any information, data, records, accounts, codes, reports, tests, samples and/or other material of any nature in any medium that may be requested at the [Company's] cost provided it is not confidential and/or is not in breach of its contractual obligations to a third party.

V.042

[Name] agrees and undertakes to provide the following documents to verify their identity, right of residence and profession in [country] and current home address:

1.1 Original passport from [country].

1.2 Original birth certificate in [country].

1.3 [National/Medical] Insurance number [specify].

1.4 Bank statement held by [Name] which has been issued by bank in [country] which is dated [month/year].

1.5 Drivers Licence [full/provisional].

1.6 Student card [specify].

1.7 Credit card statement.

1.8 Reference from [specify].

1.9 Original visa issued by [country].

1.10 Original certificates relating to all qualifications in the [background/ curriculum vitae] application.

1.11 Membership reference code of the professional organisation: [specify name].

VISAS

General Business and Commercial

V.043

The [Company/Enterprise] shall at its own expense obtain all such visas and work for specialist personnel and/or any permits, licences, registrations, certificates and/or other authorisations which may be necessary and/or arise from the [Company's/Enterprises'] performance of its obligations under this agreement.

V.044

Where any persons who are used by the [Supplier] to carry out part of the service to the [Company] under this agreement does not hold a valid visa and/or other documents to support a claim of a right to work in [country]. Then the [Company] shall have the right to prevent any such person's right of access to the premises of the [Company] and to terminate this agreement in its entirety with the [Supplier] and shall not be obliged to pay any further sums to the [Supplier].

V.045

Where any person does not hold a [specify] passport which is valid in [country]. Then where the [Supplier] intends to use persons who hold passports from other countries to fulfil the terms of the service specified under this agreement. Prior to the commencement of the provision of the service the [Supplier] must provide verified copies of all passports and visas and permissions for the right to work in [country] for each of those persons.

V.046

1.1   [Name] holds a current valid and full passport as a resident of [country]. [Name] does not hold any other passport.

1.2   [There is no restriction and/or prohibition on the right of [Name] to work in [country] as [specify role]. [Name] does not require any additional work visa and/or other documentation.

VOLUNTARY DEPARTURE

General Business and Commercial

V.047

1.1   Any member who has decided to leave the [Group] shall inform all other members at the earliest opportunity of that decision. The departing member shall be obliged to fulfil his/her duties to which he/she is already committed for [six] months from the date of notification to all the members of the [Group] unless agreed otherwise by all members of the {Group].

1.2   The departure of any member does not relinquish their rights to share in the royalties that have accrued and/or which may be earned in the future and/or to share in the ownership of the name of the [Group] and/or any trade mark, domain name and/or other rights.

1.3 Any new member which be substituted must be on a fixed salary and not considered a founding member of the [Group]. The member who has left agrees that the fixed salary of the new member may be recouped against the royalties due to the departing member in each accounting period.

V.048

1.1 In the event that any member of the [Group] shall decide to leave for any reason then from the date of departure and/or the date of termination of this agreement whichever is the later. That member shall no longer hold any rights of any nature in the name of the [Group] and/or any registered trade mark and shall have no right and/or authority to exploit and/or use them in any form and/or any medium.

1.2 Further that departing member shall cease to have any right to receive any royalties which may be received after that date from any third party which did not accrue before that end date.

1.3 The departing member shall have no right to be consulted and/or approve any substitute member and/or the terms on which that person is engaged.

1.4 The departing member shall retain either sole and/or joint ownership and copyright and/or intellectual property rights in any musical work, lyrics, sound recordings, films and/or other material which they have created and/or contributed to and/or performed in based on the original contract dated [–] a copy of which is attached in appendix A.

V.049

In the event that [Name] is unable and/or unwilling to perform the obligations and/or provide the services under this agreement. Then both parties shall agree fair and reasonable terms to end the contract which shall include payment for the conditions fulfilled to the date of termination.

V.050

[Name] agrees to end the post of [specify role] on [date] subject to:

1.1 The payment on that [date] of [number/currency] by the [Company].

1.2 The transfer of ownership of the following items: [specify laptop/car/software/clothes/other] to [Name] by the [Company].

1.3 The payment of [number/currency] in lieu of any pension.

1.4 An excellent reference to be supplied on [date] a draft copy of which is attached to and forms part of this agreement.

V.051

Any decision regarding the [Group] of any nature shall not be made without the consent of more than [fifty] per cent [50]% of the members. If the [Group] consists of two members then both must agree, if three then two members must agree, if four then three members must agree, if five then three members must agree, if six then four members must agree and so on.

WAIVER

General Business and Commercial

W.001

This agreement sets out the entire terms agreed between the [Company] and [Name]. No prior representations, assurances and/or other matters shall be included in and/or implied in this agreement. No amendment, waiver and/or other variation of this agreement shall be binding unless it is authorised in writing and agreed by both parties.

W.002

The [Employee] waives all moral rights in respect of the services provided and the work created under this Agreement under the [Copyright, Designs and Patents Act 1988 as amended/other].

W.003

The [Author] conditionally waives his/her moral rights in respect of the [Film] and its exploitation in any form in any medium and/or any associated merchandising and/or other sub-licensing and/or assignment under this Agreement. Provided that the [Company] undertakes to comply with the following conditions:

1.1 The [Author] shall be provided with the opportunity to review and comment on the draft script, the key production personnel, the music, and the artists.

1.2 The [Author] shall be entitled to approve the final script prior to production of the [Film] and shall be consulted on all changes except minor editing.

1.3 The [Author] shall be provided with an end credit on the [Film] and any catalogue, poster, packaging, advertising, marketing, website, app, podcast and/or other material in any format and/or medium as: [specify credit/slogan/logo]. The [Author] shall be supplied with free samples of all final products and/or other material and/or language in any format and/or medium which is sold to the public.

1.4   The [Author] shall be entitled to revoke the waiver if these conditions are not fulfilled at any time by notice in writing to the [Company].

W.004

There is no waiver of any moral rights of any nature by [Name] and [Name] asserts their rights to be identified as [specify] in a clear and prominent position on all copies of the [Work] and any adaptation, development, translation, packaging, labels, marketing, advertising and other material of any nature based on and/or derived from the [Work].

W.005

Where the [Licensor] decides at any time to waive any clause of this Agreement in respect of any proposed action and/or act by the [Licensee]. It shall not constitute a waiver of all other later actions which may be a breach of any clause.

W.006

The [Licensor] and [Licensee] agrees that no waiver shall be binding on the [Licensor] and/or the [Licensee] unless it is authorised by the [Managing Director] of the relevant party.

W.007

The [Production Company] agrees to ensure as far as reasonably possible that the [Director] of the [Advertisement] will waive unconditionally and without additional payment all moral rights in the [Advertisement] and any form of exploitation.

W.008

The [Author] waives his/her moral right to object to derogatory treatment of the [Work] and/or the [Film] and/or any form of exploitation and/or any adaptation in any medium subject to the following conditions:

1.1   The [Author] shall be kept regularly informed and provided with any information, scripts and/or material that he/she may request.

1.2   The [Author] shall be entitled to attend such meetings as he /she may wish to participate in and be supplied with relevant documentation.

1.3   The [Author] shall be provided with and entitled to approve or reject any sample of each type of proposed form of exploitation in each format in any medium including any merchandising, services, endorsements, collaborations and/or other adaptations.

1.4   The [Company] shall not produce and/or license any material, product and/or exploit any other rights in any manner which would subject the

[Author] to ridicule, significant negative social media and/or damage their reputation.

W.009
The [Author] has the right to object to derogatory treatment of the [Author's Work] on which the [Film] is based and does not waive any right to do so by approving the scripts. The [Author] accepts that the [Film] will not be an exact reproduction of the [Work].

W.010
The [Assignor] waives all moral rights in any media of any nature in respect of the [Format] at any time in any country.

W.011
In consideration of the payment of the [Waiver Fee] the [Author] agrees to unconditionally waive all rights to be identified and/or credited as a contributor to the [Script] for the [Film]. The [Author] agrees to waive all moral rights of any nature either to be identified as a contributor and/or to object to derogatory treatment of the contribution to the work by the [Author] to the [Script] for the [Film]. The [Author] agrees that no further payments and/or royalties shall be due to the [Author] and there shall be no right to object to any adaptation, assignment and/or other exploitation of the [Script] for the [Film].

W.012
No waiver of any default or breach of this Agreement by either party shall be deemed to be a continuing waiver or a waiver of any other breach or default relating to this Agreement, no matter how similar.

W.013
No waiver of any breach shall be decreed a waiver of any preceding or succeeding breach whether the same or not. No delay or omission in exercising any right or remedy shall operate as a waiver. No waiver shall be binding for any purpose unless put in writing and signed by the party. Any written waiver shall only be effective for the purpose stated and no other.

W.014
No waiver whether express or implied by this [Company] or [Name] shall be deemed as waiver or consent to any subsequent or continuing breach of this Agreement. Nor shall any failure to exercise and/or delay in exercising any right or remedy under this Agreement operate as a waiver of such right or remedy.

W.015
[Name] irrevocably and unconditionally waives all rights relating to the [Services/Work/other] to which [Name] is now or may in the future be entitled pursuant to the provisions of the [Copyright, Designs and Patents Act 1988 as amended/other] and any other moral rights to which the [Name] may be entitled under any legislation now existing or in future enacted in [country/world].

W.016
No waiver of any breach of any term and/or default under this agreement shall be deemed a waiver of any other breach and/or default at a later date.

W.017
Any waiver under this Agreement by any party shall only apply to those particular facts and not apply to any later circumstance.

W.018
No delay or omission in exercising any right or remedy shall operate as a waiver. No waiver shall be binding or effectual for any purpose unless set out in writing and signed by the party giving such waiver and such waiver shall only be effective in that specific case and for the purpose for which it is stated that the waiver is provided.

W.019
No waiver (whether express or implied) by the [Licensor] or the [Agent] of any breach by the [Licensee] of any of its obligations under this Agreement shall be deemed to be a waiver or consent to any subsequent or continuing breach by the [Licensee] of any obligations under this Agreement.

W.020
Any waiver by either party to a breach and/or default by the other party shall be limited to those facts and shall not apply to any later matter.

W.021
Failure of either party to insist upon the performance by the other party of any provision of this contract or documents attached shall in no way be deemed or construed to in any way affect the right of that party to require such performance.

W.022
No failure to exercise and/or delay in exercising by either party of any right or remedy pursuant to this Agreement shall operate as a waiver of such right or remedy.

1996

W.023
Any consent to any delay and/or default by the [Licensee] for any period by the [Licensor] shall not mean that the [Licensor] has waived the right to take legal action against the [Licensee] and to claim damages, losses and costs. If the [Licensor] intends to take legal action the [Licensor] agrees to notify the [Licensee] and allow them a further period of [number] [weeks/months] to remedy the matter. Any legal action shall only be instigated by the [Licensor] after the end date of that later period.

W.024
The [Assignor] unconditionally waives any and all moral rights under existing or future legislation in any country and the [Assignor] shall not be entitled to any credit or acknowledgment with respect to the exploitation of the [Work] and the [Work Material] by any party in any media at any time.

W.025
The [Assignee] agrees that the waiver only applies to the [Assignor] individually and does not apply to any other third party who may be due a credit or other acknowledgment in respect of the [Work] or the [Work Material].

W.026
No waiver by the [Company] of any breach, acceptance of any delay, omission and/or error shall be binding on any subsequent breach, act, error and/or omission.

W.027
The [Author] unconditionally waives his/her moral rights and the right to object to derogatory treatment of the [Work] provided that the [Company] uses its reasonable endeavours to comply with the following conditions:

1.1 That all persons who access and copy the [Work] shall be requested to use the following credit and copyright notice in respect of their use of the [Work] [specify]

1.2 That no authorisation and/or consent shall be provided by the [Company] to alter, adapt, translate and/or exploit the [Work] except for private home use only and that all persons seeking some other use should contact the [Author] at [specify].

1.3 The [Author] shall be entitled to revoke the waiver if these conditions are not fulfilled at any time by notice in writing to the [Company].

W.028
The [Name] irrevocably and unconditionally waives to the [Company] and/or any licensees and/or other third party and/or any successors in title and/or business:

1.1   All rights relating to the [Services/Work/other] to which the [Name] is now or may in the future be entitled pursuant to the [Copyright, Designs and Patents Act 1988 as amended/other]; and

1.2   Any other moral rights to which the [Name] may be entitled under any legislation now existing or in future enacted in any part of the world relating to the [Website/App/Material/Content].

1.3   The [Name] agrees that he/she shall no longer have the right to be identified as the author and/or the right to object to any derogatory treatment.

1.4   The waiver shall apply to the [Company] and any assignee, sub-licensee and/or any other third party.

1.5   [Name] agrees that the waiver cannot be revoked or otherwise altered at any time even after the death of [Name].

W.029

The [Designer] waives all moral rights both to the [Company] and/or any licensees and/or other third party and/or any successors in title. The [Designer] agrees that he/she shall not be entitled to any credit, acknowledgement, copyright notice or otherwise in respect of the [Project/Material] or any adaptation or development at any time.

W.030

1.1   The [Company] agrees that the [Artist] has not waived any moral rights of any nature.

1.2   The [Company] agrees to credit the [Artist] on the website and in all apps, posters and marketing and promotional material and other forms of exploitation with the copyright notice (c) [year] [Artist] which shall be placed either on and/or very close to the [Artwork].

1.3   The [Company] shall not make any changes to the [Artwork] in any form and/or medium and/or add and/or delete any part unless the prior written consent of the [Artist] has been obtained.

1.4   Where the [Company] fails in any case to provide the copyright notice and credit in 1.2 it shall be obliged to pay the [Artist] an additional fee of [number/currency] in total in each case.

W.031

1.1   The [Developer] waives all moral rights to any part of the content of the [App/Blog] which he/she has created and delivered to the [Company]. No recognition and/or credit shall be made to the [Developer] in any part of the [App/Blog].

1.2   The [Developer] accepts and agrees that the [Company] may make such changes and adaptations to the [App/Blog] as it wishes at any time and therefore waives all moral rights which he/she may hold in relation to changes in content and/or appearance and/or design and/ or colour.

W.032

The [Contributor] to the making of the music, performance and singing at the [Event] which has been recorded by means of sound recording and film by [Name] waives his/her moral rights which may exist to be identified and/ or receive any payment in respect of any future exploitation by [Name] of the material which [Name] has created.

W.033

Where the [Licensor] has waived any breach by the [Licensee] and/or sub-licensee and/or agent and set a new condition and/or date as a pre-condition of their consent to the waiver. Then such waiver shall not be deemed to be a waiver and/or consent to any subsequent breach by the [Licensee] and/or any sub-licensee and/or agent.

W.034

Where the [Licensee] has failed to perform any term of this Agreement by a specified date and the [Licensor] has agreed to a waiver for that breach of this Agreement. If the [Licensee] then fails to fulfil the conditions of the waiver by the subsequent date, then the [Licensee] shall not be entitled to rely on the waiver to avoid an allegation of breach of contract.

W.035

In consideration of the [Waiver Fee] the [Assignor] unconditionally waives all moral and/or legal and/or equitable rights in any part of the world in all media and in all medium to be credited and acknowledged and to have any copyright notice as the author of the original [Work] which has been assigned to the [Company].

W.036

In consideration of the [Waiver Fee] the [Assignor] unconditionally waives all moral and/or legal and/or equitable rights in any part of the world in all media and in all medium to object to derogatory treatment as the author of the original [Work] which has been assigned to the [Company]. The [Assignor] agrees that the [Company] shall be entitled to edit, adapt, delete from, add to and/or distort and/or otherwise change any part of the [Work] and/or exploit the [Work] in any manner it thinks fit at its sole discretion.

W.037

The [Author] has not provided any waiver in this Agreement and asserts all his/her moral rights and/or other legal and/or equitable rights which may exist now and/or be created in the future to be identified as the author of the original [Work] and to object to any derogatory treatment and/or distortion and/or adaptation in any form without the prior written consent of the [Author].

W.038

The [Ghostwriter] unconditionally waives all moral rights in any of the material created under this Agreement and in the [Work]. The waiver shall apply to the right to be identified as the author and the right to object to any derogatory treatment of the [Work]. The waiver shall apply to the [Company] and any publisher, licensees, assignees and any third party who may acquire any rights or interest. The [Ghostwriter] accepts that the waiver cannot be revoked or otherwise altered at any time.

W.039

The [Company] agrees that the [Ghostwriter] shall be entitled for biographical purposes only to state that the [Work] was written by [Name] with the research assistance of [Ghostwriter].

W.040

In consideration of the Assignment Fee the [Author] agrees:

1.1 That he/she shall waiver all moral rights in the [Work] and any parts including the [Artwork] and the material in Schedule [–].

1.2 That the [Author] shall not object to any failure to identify him/her as the author of the [Work] and/or the [Artwork] and/or the material.

1.3 The [Author] waives all right to object to derogatory treatment of the [Work] and/or [Artwork] and/or the material.

1.4 That all these waivers are unconditional and shall extend to all third parties and successors in title.

1.5 That he/she waives all right to a copyright notice in respect of the [Work] and the [Artwork] and/or the material in all media at any time in the [country/Territory].

W.041

The [Company] does not waive any rights of any nature in respect of the purchase order by the [Client]. Any delay in payment will result in the immediate cancellation of the order.

2000

W.042

Where an order has been accepted by the [Company] for the supply of [Products/Services]. The [Client] shall be obliged to pay the sums due to the [Company] by the agreed dates and there shall be no waiver.

W.043

The failure of the [Company] to take immediate legal action against the other party for a default shall not be deemed to be a waiver of the right to do so.

W.044

In consideration of the payments under this Agreement the [Contributor] waives all moral rights except to the extent that the [Contributor] shall be given the credit set out in clause [–].

W.045

The [Contributor] waives any and all moral rights in the product of the [Contributor's Work] and in particular waives any right to be identified as the author and creator of the [Contributor's Work].

W.046

In consideration of the [Assignment Fee] the [Author/Composer/Musician/ Artist] agrees to waive unconditionally all moral rights in the [Work] to which he/she may be entitled under the [Copyright, Designs and Patents Act 1988 as amended/other] in [country/world].

W.047

In consideration of the payments made under this Agreement [Name] waives all moral rights under the [Copyright, Designs and Patents Act 1988 as amended/other] in the [Work] on the condition that the [Assignee] shall credit [Name] as: [specify credit] on all copies of the [Work] and/or any adaptation and shall ensure that any third party shall be obliged to adhere to such an undertaking.

W.048

In consideration of the payments made under this Agreement the [Name] waives all moral rights provided that the [Assignee] shall ensure that the [Work] is not subjected to derogatory treatment by the [Assignee] or any third party which it may engage or license.

W.049

In consideration of the payments made under this Agreement the [Composer/Musician] waives all moral rights under the [Copyright, Designs and Patents Act 1988 as amended] in the [Work] subject to the following condition. That the [Assignee] shall ensure that the [Work] is not distorted or mutilated or otherwise treated in a manner which is prejudicial to the honour and reputation of the [Composer/Musician] or otherwise may amount to derogatory treatment. The [Composer/Musician] agrees that an arrangement or transcription of the [Work] involving no more than a change of key or register will not amount to derogatory treatment.

W.050

No waiver by the [Sponsor] of any breach, acceptance of any delay, omission, error and/or failure shall be binding on the [Sponsor] in respect of any subsequent breach, act, error, omission and/or failure by [Name].

W.051

The [Sponsor] agrees to waive any rights to rely on a breach of contract in respect of any of the following circumstances:

1.1   Where [Name] has been fined and/or suspended for less than [number] months by his/her professional body for a breach of the rules and/ regulations and/or for misconduct.

1.2   Where a fine has been imposed by a Court of Law provided it is not for [specify].

W.052

The [Company] agrees that there shall be no credit either on screen and/or in the catalogue and/or at the end of the [Event] in respect of any products which are supplied by the [Company] to be placed on the set and are agreed between the parties to be classified as product placement.

W.053

The [Sponsor] agrees to waive any credit in any material produced, distributed and supplied by the [Managers] of the [Project] provided that a suitable credit and mention is made of their contribution to the funding on the website [specify] and in any material distributed and/or supplied to the newspapers and media before [date].

W.054

No waiver, failure to act and/or enforce the Agreement by the [Institute/ Charity] against the [Company] shall mean that the [Institute] is bound and not able to take action at a later date if it is repeated.

W.055

The [Company] shall not be released from its liabilities under this Agreement by a verbal waiver from a representative of the [Institute/Charity]. All waivers and/or acceptance of breaches, failures and or errors must be in writing between the parties.

W.056

In consideration of the Fee the [Contributor] agrees to waive all moral rights in the [Work/Artwork/Article/Film] including the right to be identified as the author and to object to derogatory treatment. That the waiver and this term shall apply to any third party licensee and/or any successors in title to the [Institute/Charity].

W.057

In consideration of the [Assignment Fee] the [Author/Artist] agrees to waive unconditionally all moral rights in the [Work] to which he/she may be entitled under the [Copyright, Designs and Patents Act 1988 as amended].

W.058

The [Distributor] agrees to respect and adhere to the moral rights of the [Author] and shall endeavour to ensure that there is a clear and prominent display of the name of the [Author] and the copyright notice on all copies of the [Work] and any associated packaging and marketing material. The [Distributor] accepts that it shall not be entitled to waive the right of the [Author] to be identified and/or the removal and/or failure to put such details on all copies.

WAR DAMAGE

General Business and Commercial

W.059

In the event that the [Structure] or any part or any unfixed materials or items sustain war damage as defined in Clause [–].

Then in such event the following terms shall apply:

1.1 The war damage shall not be taken into account in respect of the payments due to the [Contractor].

1.2 The [Administrator] shall issue such instructions as may be necessary to ensure that the damage is remedied and the [Project] made safe.

1.3 The parties shall agree a new Completion Date taking into account the additional work required due to war damage.

1.4 All such work requested in respect of war damage shall be treated as a variation to this contract and additional costs and payment shall be agreed between the parties.

2003

W.060

'War Damage' shall mean any loss or damage caused by, or in repelling, enemy action, [excluding terrorist organisations] or by measures taken to avoid the spreading of the consequences of damages caused by or in repelling enemy action.

W.061

'War Damage' shall mean any damage and/or loss which may arise directly or indirectly as a result of hostile contention by means of armed forces whether between nations, states or rulers or between parties in the same state or nation or any other kind of active hostility or contention between armed forces provided that a state of war shall have been declared by the existing ruler, state, government or nation. Attacks by terrorist organisations and other acts of resurgence by any party group or individual are not included.

W.062

In the event that the government or state provides at any time a scheme for compensation for war damage then it is agreed that the [Company] shall be entitled to all such sums in respect of any war damage sustained or incurred by the [Project].

W.063

'War Damage' shall mean any loss or damage caused by, or in repelling, enemy action, acts of violence and work of terrorist organisations, hostility, attacks by armed forces with weapons, chemical, biological and/or other warfare, whether a state of war has been declared or not, and any measures taken to avoid attack, mitigate loss and damage and/or to repel enemy action.

WARRANTIES

General Business and Commercial

W.064

The [Company] warrants that the terms and conditions set out in this Agreement shall be complied with by the [Company].

W.065

The [Institute/Charity] shall be bound by the undertakings, warranties and terms of this Agreement until the end of the Term of the Agreement and/or the date of termination whichever is the sooner.

2004

W.066

The following clauses which set out the warranties provided by the [Company] shall survive the end of the Licence Period and/or termination of this Agreement. Provided that all sums due under the Agreement by the [Institute/Charity] have been paid to the [Company].

W.067

The [Company] warrants that all material, data, documents, accounts, reports, contracts and information provided by the [Company to the [Purchaser], their auditors and/or professional advisors in any format and/or medium relating to the [Assets] of the [Company] are true, accurate and comprehensive as at [date].

W.068

The [Company] warrants to the [Purchaser] that no facts, data, information, record, documents, contract and/or other material has been withheld, not disclosed and/or not revealed which would have an impact on the assessment of the value of the [Assets] and/or the decision by the [Purchaser] to buy the [Assets].

W.069

The [Company] undertakes that it has not withheld and/or distorted any material, data, documents and/or information relating to [Project] which would expose any significant risk and/or detrimental impact on the forecast outcome.

W.070

The [Company] warrants and confirms it is a company which is established and operates under the Laws of [specify]. That the [Company] has the power and authority to own its assets and operate and conduct its business and to enter into legally binding agreements. That this Agreement constitutes and sets out the legally binding obligations of the [Company] to the [Purchaser].

W.071

The [Company] warrants that it has at all times carried on its business in accordance with its [Memorandum and Articles of Association/other] in existence at that time and/or as subsequently amended.

W.072

The [Company] represents and warrants and undertakes to the [Purchaser] and its successors in title that to the best of the knowledge and belief of the [Company] the warranties in this Agreement are true and correct in all material respects.

W.073

The [Company] warrants that to the best of its knowledge and belief the [Company] has not manufactured and/or sold products which were and/or are and/or will become faulty and/or defective and/or which did not and/or do not comply with any warranties and/or representations expressly and/or impliedly made by the [Seller] and/or with all applicable laws, Treaties, Conventions, directives, regulations, standards and Codes of Practice and/or Guidelines.

W.074

The [Company] warrants that it holds good title to the [Assets] which are free from any lien, charge, claim, interest of any kind of a legal and/or equitable nature and/or otherwise. Except for the disclosures made by the [Company] as to any part owned and/or controlled by a third party and/or in respect of which ownership has not yet passed, but will do so by [date].

W.075

The [Licensor] warrants that it has full title and authority to grant such rights to the [Publisher] in the [Work] and is not bound by any agreement with a third party which undermines and/or prohibits either expressly and/or by implication the right of the [Licensor] to enter into this Agreement.

W.076

The [Licensor] warrants that it has full title to the [Trade Mark] and shall upon request provide to the [Licensee] a true copy of the formal certificate of registration of the [Trade Mark].

W.077

The [Company] warrants that all present and future copyright, intellectual property rights, computer software rights, trade marks, domain names and any other rights are owned solely by the [Company] in the [Work] including the title, text, artwork and illustrations, characters, maps, index. That the [Company] owns all the rights in respect of all forms of exploitation in any medium and/or adaptation and/or sequel of any part including in electronic form over the internet and/or by means of any telecommunication system and that none have been licensed and/or assigned to a third party.

W.078

This warranty is subject to the following restriction, reservation and disclosure [–].

W.079

[Name] confirms and undertakes that he/she has the original concept for the [Project] and that it was not based on any idea and/or work of a third party. That as a result of that concept [Name] designed, created and developed and an original [Game/Search Facility/other] which he/she then adapted so that it could be made into an [App] by the [Development Company].

W.080

The [Company] confirms and undertakes that the facts and financial data in the annual report and accounts and in all the documents supplied to [Name] prior to the date of this Agreement on which the valuation for this agreement was based on true and accurate facts and not intended to mislead and/or hid any information and/or disclosure which would have a detrimental effect on the valuation of the [Company].

WAYLEAVE

General Business and Commercial

W.081

The [Company] warrants that it has obtained the necessary wayleave from [specify person/legislation]. For the purposes of this Agreement 'necessary wayleave' shall have the same meaning as defined in the relevant legislation and mean the consent for the [Licence Holder] to install and keep installed the electric line on, under or over the land and to have access to the land for the purpose of inspecting, maintaining, adjusting, repairing, altering, replacing or removing the electric line.

W.082

The [Purchaser] shall within the times stated in the Schedule or if not specified before the delivery of any part to the site obtain all consents, wayleaves and approvals in connection with the regulations and byelaws of any local authority, government body, electricity, gas, water or other company or person which shall be applicable to [Works] on the Site.

WEBSITE

General Business and Commercial

W.083

'The Website' shall mean the worldwide web reference [specify] which is owned by the [Company] registered as a [business/corporation] in [country] trading under the name of [Trading Name] whose domain name is [specify] which is registered with [specify].

W.084

'The Website' shall mean the worldwide web reference [specify] which is owned or controlled by the [Company] whose main business address is [specify].

W.085

The [Company] agrees and undertakes not to register any domain name, trade mark, patent, computer software and/or other rights and/or register any website, app, account, podcast, channel and/or otherwise either directly and/or through a third party which is derived from the [Project/Work] with the [Institute/Charity].

W.086

'The Online Business' shall mean all the websites owned and controlled by [Name] which are set out in the attached appendix [–] and all the associated registered domain names whether in use and/or similar which have been registered by [Name].

WORK

General Business and Commercial

W.087

'The Work' shall be the following book including the [Artwork/Preface/Index] based on the [Synopsis] entitled [–] which shall consist of approximately [–] A4 typed pages.

W.088

'The Work' shall mean the following:

Title: [–] Author: [–]

ISBN No. [–] Published by [Name]

Pages [–] Description [–]

W.089

'The Work Schedule' shall mean such times, dates and locations at which [Name] has agreed to provide his/her services under this Agreement. A copy of the Work Schedule is attached to and forms part of this Agreement.

W.090

'The Work Plan' shall mean the detail of the nature of the services of the [Company] to be provided to the [Distributor] under this Agreement which are described as follows [–]. The [Distributor] agrees that no alteration shall be made to the Work Plan or the Work Schedule without the prior approval of the [Company].

W.091

'Working Day' means Monday to Friday inclusive in each week except any Bank or Public Holidays.

W.092

'Work Schedule' shall be defined as such times and dates of work as shall be agreed between the parties.

W.093

'The Work Plan' shall be the detail of the nature of the services of [Name] to be provided to the [Company] under this Agreement which are described as follows [specify duties/location/times].

1.1 Research and arrange interviews and recordings of [–] on [subject].

1.2 To keep full and accurate records of all sources of information, documents, interviews and recordings.

1.3 To report on the existence, format and quality of any stills, photographs, newspaper cuttings, film, video, archive material and sound recordings. Further, to provide a detailed statement of ownership of copyright, credits, moral rights, waivers and contractual obligations, the cost of reproduction, access, copyright and other clearance and intellectual property payments.

1.4 To obtain clearance of and arrange payment by the [Company] of such material as may be required.

1.5 To view, edit and comment on the final [–].

W.094

'The Company's Work/Services' shall mean the provision of a professional and expert service in accordance with the standards and code of practice expected of members of [specify governing or trade body] which shall be as follows [specify nature/manner to be provided/exactly what is expected].

W.095

The Work' shall mean all the material and related documents, records and data listed in appendix A in respect of [subject] which has been created and/or developed by [Name] and any other associated content and/or rights:

1.1   The title, character names, slogans, catchphrases and any adapted shortened version; domain names, trading names, trade marks, product and/or service names.

1.2   All related scripts, text, images, graphics, artwork, logos, costumes, computer-generated material, icons, music, lyrics, sound recordings, websites, apps, podcasts, blogs, films, audio files and material in any electronic form for use on the internet and/or by means of any telecommunication system and/or for transmission over any radio, television and/or other gadget and/or device and/or any other format and/or means of exploitation in any medium.

1.3   Marketing and promotional material, packaging, labels, competitions, product placements and/or collaborations, merchandising, theme parks, publications and any other sequel, development and/or adaptation in any format and/or medium.

1.4   Any other material and/or rights which have not been specified and/or which may be created and/or developed in the future.

W.096

'The Work Material' shall mean all the material of the [Work] in the possession or control of the [Assignor] including:

1.1   All copies of any master material in any form.

1.2   A list of locations at which any material is held together with access letters giving irrevocable authority for the [Assignee] to remove such material.

1.3   All associated material in any medium and/or format including contracts, licences, waivers, scripts, material in electronic form, promotional material, copyright and other intellectual property and/or transmission and/or performance clearance and payment documents; records of clearances, payments and reports to rights management organisations and rightsholders.

W.097

'The Work' shall mean the text of the [Titles/Books] specified in Schedule A to this Agreement and shall also include any other material which may be later specifically agreed in writing.

W.098

In accordance with the Work Schedule the [Artist] agrees to provide the following specific services:

1.1 The presentation of and performance in not less than [specify number/frequency] advertisements of not more than [specify duration] on each occasion for the purpose of broadcast or transmission on television.

1.2 The presentation of the corporate video which shall be no more than [specify maximum length in minutes].

1.3 The attendance at no more than [specify events/official functions/meetings/other] [specify who is to pay cost and expenses].

1.4 Photographic sessions [–].

1.5 Radio appearances [–].

1.6 Sound recordings/other [–].

W.099

'The Work Schedule' shall mean the times, dates and locations of all competitions, events, promotions, appearances and meetings at which the [Sportsperson] is obliged to attend under this Agreement. A copy of the [Work Schedule] is attached to and forms part of this Agreement.

W.100

'The Events Schedule' shall mean all the competitions, sporting and promotional events and meetings which the [Sportsperson] agrees to attend and participate in during the Sponsorship Period. A copy of the Events Schedule setting out the names, dates and locations of all such events is attached to and forms part of this Agreement.

W.101

'The Work Proposal' shall be the written report of [Name] which gives accurate and specific information, data and other material of:

1.1 The exact nature of the work to be provided including interim performance targets and final completion date.

1.2 A complete two dimensional representation of the [Project] setting out all the elements, dimensions, layout and operational objectives.

1.3 A full breakdown of the total budgeted cost including any contingency for delays and additional alterations.

1.4 A schedule of the expected payment of the total budget up to delivery and completion of the [Project].

1.5 An itemised list of all expected payments for any related contract, licence and/or copyright and/or intellectual property rights payments of any nature to any third party in the future both before and after the completion of the [Project].'

W.102

The [Executive] shall during the course of the appointment work for the [Company] on a full-time exclusive basis in a professional manner. He/she shall carry out the duties described in the [Executive's] job description as specified in Appendix B.

W.103

It is agreed between the parties that the job description may be moderately varied but not entirely redesigned in order to accommodate developments within the [Company]. Any increase in responsibilities or duties shall result in an increase in pay which shall be agreed between the parties.

W.104

The [Executive] agrees to undertake such duties and exercise such powers in relation to the conduct and management of the [Company] or its associated bodies, businesses and affairs as the Board of the [Company] shall decide that he/she shall fulfil and carry out from time to time.

W.105

The [Company] agree to provide the services of [Name] on the following terms:

1.1 Nature of contribution [Research/scripts/on screen appearance/other].

1.2 Title of Film/episodes/duration/transmission date.

1.3 Dates [Rehearsals/recording/voice-overs/other].

W.106

The [Company] confirms that the [Consultant] is engaged to provide his/her services for the [Series] as follows:

1.1 Title [–] Number of episodes [–] duration [–].

1.2 Proposed transmission/release date [–].

1.3 Agreed number of days work: [–]

W.107

In consideration of the [Fee] the [Consultant] agrees to provide his/her specialist advice and knowledge in respect of the [Series] to prepare background material and information, to review and report on the synopsis, scripts, stills and other content that may from time to time be requested by [Name]. The [Consultant] shall provide his/her assistance upon request to the [Writer] and/or [Director] and attend such meetings, recordings, filming, editing, marketing and other events as may be required up to a maximum of [number] days in total for all the work under this Agreement.

XEROGRAPHY

General Business and Commercial

X.001
'Xerography' shall mean the reproduction of the [Work] by a process of copying which does not involve liquids or chemicals in the development of the images but shall include any electrical or other means whether in existence and known now and/or invented and/or created in the future.

XYLOGRAPHY

General Business and Commercial

X.002
For the purpose of this agreement [Artistic Work] shall include all works created by means of xylography and any other material created through xylographic methods.

YEAR

General Business and Commercial

Y.001

'Year' shall mean for the purposes of this agreement the period of twelve months commencing on 1st January in each year and ending on 31st December. Any yearly interest which may be due shall be calculated on that basis for each year and/or pro rata as applicable.

Y.002

For the purposes of this agreement, 'Financial Year' shall mean the period of twelve months commencing on 1st April in one year and ending on 31st March in the next year. The calculation of the annual interest which may be due for each such period shall be based on those financial periods.

Y.003

The agreement shall begin on [date] and continue for a period of one year until [date]. It shall not continue indefinitely and/or be automatically renewed. A new written agreement must be concluded for each such period of one year or less. There is no obligation on the [Institute/Enterprise] to enter into any such new agreement after any previous agreement has expired.

Y.004

1.1 This agreement shall be terminated at the end of each year and end on [date]. There shall no automatic right of renewal.

1.2 If the [Supplier] wishes to enter into a new agreement for another year. Then the [Supplier] may notify the [Company] of the proposed terms at any time and the [Company] shall be entitled to accept and/or reject any such new agreement.

Y.005

'The Annual Period' shall be defined as a period of [twelve] months which shall commence on [date] in each year and end on [date] in the following year thereafter and any portion shall be calculated pro rata.

Y.006

It is agreed between the parties that where any party wishes to change the start date and end date of any accounting period. That any such change shall be subject to prior written agreement with the other party.

Y.007

The [Company] reserves the right to change, amend and/or vary any payment, statement and invoice dates where new technology, software and/or procedures at the [Company] are adopted and implemented at any time.

Z

ZERO RATED

General Business and Commercial

Z.001

1.1 The [Supplier] and the [Purchaser] both agree and undertake that as at [date] all [Products/Services] listed in appendix A supplied under this agreement shall be treated as [zero-rated outputs] and will therefore not be subject to [value added tax/other] in [country].

1.2 In the event that any legislation, regulations and/or other policies in [country] alter the position and/or there is a material change in the classification of any [Products/Services] so that [value added tax/other] is due to be paid and/or some other tax and/or other additional payment imposed by government as a legal requirement. Then the parties agree that any sum which may be due shall be invoiced and paid as required despite the above list.

Z.002

The [Supplier] confirms receipt of the [Purchaser's] document confirming the fact that the [Purchaser] is registered for [VAT/other] and the start date and reference code.

Z.003

The [Charity/Enterprise] undertakes to provide the [Sponsor] with a document which verifies the [tax/Vat] status of the [Charity] in [country] within [one] calendar month of the date of this agreement. The [Charity/Enterprise] shall confirm whether or not it is obliged to charge and/or impose any additional costs and/or fees and/or other charges on the [Fees] to be paid by the [Sponsor].

Z.004

The [Supplier] and [Purchaser] acknowledge that printed books supplied under this agreement are zero-rated but 'E-books' will attract [VAT/other] [at the official rate] as stipulated by any government body and/or agency and subject to any legislation and/or other guidelines that may exist at the time in any relevant [country/other].

Highlights in respect of some of the main types of clauses in a contract and how they can be varied

- This summary is only a general guide and is not intended to cover every aspect of drafting each type of clause in an agreement. It is really meant to identify possible areas you should consider.

Pre-contract research

- Before you even start with the contract first of all look at the wider picture of the actual set up and business operations of the parties involved. Are they a subsidiary? What do they actually produce and where? Do they make it themselves or is it produced by a third party? Where is their head office? Where are they incorporated? Are they new to the market or do they have a track record? What actual physical material is commissioned and developed in order to create your final product? Who will be engaged to package, market or distribute the product? Ask to see samples and understand the creative process involved. These practical issues matter and must be understood.

- Whether the contract is for a book, an app or a sponsorship agreement the same basic principle applies. The more you understand the parties and ask for lots of detailed information as to how things will operate and who will own different rights. The easier it will be to create a document which will result in a successful outcome which avoids litigation. It is important to examine the financial stability of a company and so review the last three to five years of their annual report and accounts. Other areas of interest may be press releases, marketing reports, catalogues and governance, policy and health and safety procedure documents.

- The nature of the work, material or services which are being assigned or licensed should be considered in two parts. The physical material and the actual rights both at the time of the agreement and later as the product or service is developed. The physical element would include the drawings for a logo, text, images, sound recordings, film and other material which should all be viewed as completely separate elements. The rights would need to cover the copyright and intellectual property rights in respect of each physical element. As well as address the issue of the registration of any trade marks, domain names and possible arrangements with rights management organisations.

- You need to be clear whether the assignment or licence is intended to cover both the physical material and rights as they exist now as well as those created in the future. Will the agreement cover all adaptations or new forms of exploitation and rights which may arise due to new technology being developed?

- The length of the assignment or licence could be for the full period of copyright and in perpetuity, or for a fixed term. A shorter limited term of a licence period for one to three years or an assignment period for five to ten years is preferable. Where there is also a clause for the reversion of all the rights to the licensor or assignor. This then allows you to enter into new agreements and to obtain further advances and royalties.

- The drafting of the definitions in an agreement which are applicable to the material and the rights are crucial. The rights can be drafted to be very narrow so no more than absolutely necessary is given. This is done by being very specific as to the method of use which is being authorised and specifically excluding those which are not allowed so that there is no ambiguity.

- A decision needs to be made as to the scope of the licence or assignment. Does it just relate to copyright or does it extend further to other intellectual property rights, trade marks, design rights, computer software, patents, database rights and domain names?

- Any assignment must be in writing and requires consideration of some kind to be provided. Even a nominal single currency is sufficient. The assignment clause should specify the party which is assigning the rights and who is to receive them. Most often the assignment is for the world, but it is possible to assign rights only for a specified territory or a single country.

- You may wish the assignor the party giving the rights to provide an undertaking that they will not register any further interest with a third party or be entitled to receive any further revenue.

Exclusive Licence

- The possible conflict of existing agreements should be raised and an undertaking provided that there are none.

- The exclusive licence must be linked to consideration, whether a fixed fee, royalties or an advance.

- A licence may be exclusive for a fixed period, but the different rights may revert back to the licensor either in stages as they have been used or all at once at the end of the agreement.

- The drafting of the definitions of the rights to be granted is very important. If you are acquiring rights under a licence you want the rights to be as wide and extensive as possible. If you are the one granting the licence then it is to your advantage to draft everything narrowly so that you retain rights. Those rights which are not granted should be stated as reserved. This may also include rights which do not exist at the time of the agreement but which come into existence at a later date due to advances in technology.

- Regard should be given to new material which will be created in the future – either commissioned, or developed – and that means not just the main service or product, but anything associated with it. It should be clear who will own those rights.

- The term of the licence can vary and you may often be asked to agree to the term of the period of copyright. Do not fall into this trap as a fixed period of a number of years is much better. The shorter a licence period is then the more opportunity there is to generate revenue and to exploit the rights effectively. A fixed licence period with start and end dates and no right of renewal should be considered. Where you want to prolong it then there should be a commencement date and the start of the duration of a period of years can be linked to completion of work, a distribution date or the use of the rights.

- The circumstances in which you would want a situation to be deemed applicable under force majeure needs to be considered. Will a pandemic, blockades by protesters, riots, failures in the supply chains or power failures count as grounds for force majeure? You can draft this clause to both include and exclude certain types of events. Where the agreement is temporarily suspended for the duration of the force majeure. You may need to draft the clause so that the term of the agreement is extended for that additional period.

- There should be specific consent given for the licensee to sub-licence or authorise third parties to exploit any rights which are granted. Where it is not permitted then it should be stated that no consent is provided.

- An undertaking may be required from the licensor that the rights granted will not be licensed, or exploited during the licence period by the licensor or any third party. This may also be drafted to apply to any development or adaptation.

- The territory for which the exclusive licence is given should be quite clear and the countries listed in the definition. You may wish to refer to both the land and territorial waters of each country. There are a number of countries which also own sovereign land elsewhere – are these included in the definition? Similarly moving and/or man-made objects such as ships, oil rigs, wind farms and aeroplanes may not be covered. With the advent of satellite and other objects orbiting around the Earth. It is possible to extend the area covered to not only Earth, but other planets and be defined to cover outer space or the universe.

- Where it is likely that there will be translations, sub-titling, use of material or rights in promoting a product or service then this should be agreed to in each case. The licence may be limited to one language and if translations are to be permitted a procedure for editorial control and consent of the adaptation may be necessary.

Pre-contract representations

- If there have been important and significant representations made by one party or the other before the contract is drawn up. You need to consider whether the final document really encapsulates all the assurances or disclosures you have been given. Many contracts exclude previous representations, quotations and other discussions. If this is the case and the only document which is to be considered binding is the contract. You may need to attach other material as an appendix and state that it does form part of the agreement.

Amendments

- The method by which a contract is usually amended is in writing, but it is becoming more common for there to be an exchange of emails and calls which are not then verified in writing by a formal amendment. The trail of exchanges is often only looked at when there is a dispute. This is a very risky method to adopt as a policy. So you should endeavour to clarify the detail of any amendments and get both parties to sign a formal amendment document which can be properly stored as an archive record.

Payments and costs

- Any sums should be referred to with as much detail as possible and clearly defined whether advances, royalties, budget, costs, fees and the currency should be stated.

- There should be undertakings as to when each of these payments will be made, the method of such payments and to whom payment will be made. As well as how they will be accounted for and whether there are any rights of inspection. Where payment is to an agent or other third party you also need to ensure you are not liable for the failure of the agent or third party to make over the money due to a particular person.

- The method by which any budget for a project or other costs can be increased should be agreed. If you do not want to approve any increase in costs can you terminate the agreement?

- In order to protect your liability to costs for any project you can set a maximum figure which cannot be exceeded in any circumstances in the agreement. The other party then provides an undertaking not to exceed this sum for any reason and may also accept responsibility for any additional sums.

- The responsibility as to who is liable to arrange for clearance of material and rights and who is to pay the costs which may be due should be set out in detail both for an acquisition and further exploitation.

- One party may provide an undertaking that they will be liable for all the costs and expenses for a project and accept that the other party will not be liable for or pay any costs.

- Where there is more than one contract with another party you need to address the issue of set-off. Can any sums owed under one agreement be set-off and recouped under another by either party? If an advance is not recouped under one agreement can the distributor recoup the advance under another agreement? If you do not want this to happen then it must be excluded. If you would like to be able to set-off sums across all the agreements then state as a fact that this is permitted to avoid ambiguity.

- If a payment is delayed for any reason. Is there a period in which no additional charge will be made? Will interest be due? If interest is to be paid a rate needs to be stated at which it will be calculated.

Accounting and Inspection Provisions

- Where royalties are to be paid the date by which payment will be made in full in each month or year and the currency needs to be established. Where costs or losses are to be incurred due to exchange rates and bank charges are these costs to be deducted from the original sum or is one party entirely liable to pay these sums?

- It is useful to have confirmation as to the detail of the content of the accounting royalty statement and how it is to be broken down. If the accounting statements are supplied by the licensee – will you also have access to those reports of any further sub-licensee?

- You must state the frequency of the payments and accounting royalty statements to be provided throughout the term of the agreement. As well as what is to happen for any period after expiry or termination.

- It is always a worthwhile exercise to work through some real life scenarios of the arrangements. It allows you to have a better understanding of the basis upon which the figures involved are calculated. Is your royalty actually based on a percentage of net or gross receipts or a fixed sum per unit. What costs can legitimately be deducted from any sums which may be made before any figure is used from which your royalty is derived. Some licensees may deduct nothing at all and pay a royalty based on a gross receipt. While others may deduct commission, production and development costs, marketing costs, withhold a percentage against returns, deduct advances, set-off aums owed under another contract or sell items at cost or below and make no payment.

- Will you have any right to be supplied with copies of any documentation with the accounts such as sub-licences, invoices or contract summaries? It is important to have a clause which allows you the right to carry out an inspection of the accounts. This may be limited to no more than once in any year. You will want to describe the extent of the documents, records, software, electronic and stored material that you will want access to for inspection. This should include a reference that you or your advisors be allowed to make copies.

- It is now also more common for contracts to state the length of time that documents, records, software, electronic and stored material should be kept for accounting purposes and the period after which they can be destroyed.

- It is also possible to include a clause which ensures that if there are errors or omissions which are discovered in an audit. That where the sums exceed a fixed percentage or figure that the other party will not only pay the additional sum but also interest at an agreed rate and the costs of the audit.

Credits, Copyright Notices and Moral Rights

- The exact wording and shape of any credit or copyright notice to any person or company, the location and size of any accompanying logo, image or trade mark should be stated in the contract and specifically related to the format of material upon which it will appear.

- In the event that the credit or copyright notice does not appear or is not displayed by the company as required under the agreement or a third party. There may be circumstances in which it may be possible to exclude liability for this failure.

- It can be specifically stated where the credit will not appear, for example in posters, packaging, reviews, and merchandising.

- The copyright notice or credit may appear more than once in any product or service.

- An undertaking can be provided that any copies produced which have no credit or copyright notice will not be supplied or distributed, but destroyed.

- Moral rights are not relevant to every situation. There is the right to be identified in a reasonably prominent position and the name should be set out in the contract. The second part of the moral rights assertion is the right not to be subject to derogatory treatment and this should be asserted if relevant.

- A complete waiver of any credit and moral rights would be applicable where all the material and rights are being bought out through an assignment.

- A copyright warning may also be considered in order to alert users of a service to the fact that the misuse of the content of a service could result in legal action against them.

Copyright Ownership and Title

- There is usually an undertaking that the company owns or controls the material and rights which are being granted or assigned.

- That there is no conflict with a previous agreement or any charges or restrictions which apply.

- That the rights and material will remain the property of the licensor and that the licensee does not become the copyright owner or have the right to register any such interest.

- That the rights and the material are listed and specified in detail and defined.

- That where rights or material is not cleared and there are prior agreements. That the material is then listed as excluded or accepted on that basis.

- Where there is an assignment it needs to be clear if it applies to new material and rights as well as those that exist already.

- Rights can be defined in many ways and can included and excluded, inter alia, copyright, intellectual property rights, satellite, cable and terrestrial television, DVDs, computer games, merchandising, publishing, computer software, database rights, patents, inventions, design rights, electronic rights, image rights, recordings, music, logos, photographs, artwork, models, and prototypes.

- When the agreement expires or is terminated then it should be clear what happens to the material and rights and who owns them.

- Clearance of material or rights should not be confused with payment and may be the responsibility of different parties. If it is expected that there will be no sums due to pay then a clause should be included to that effect.

Editorial Control, Quality Control and Marketing

- Specify which party has the final editorial decision.

- There may be consultation or approval clauses and the obligation to provide samples or copies in every format; a number of the final products and copies of all marketing.

- Written approval in relation to particular material such as samples, covers, flyers or products allows a degree of control which is greater than consultation. There is no limit as to how or when this should be and increases your involvement in the project. Build in a concept for the supply of copies of drafts and for discussion even if you have no final editorial control.

- Specify the detail of the content of the work, the standard and style expected, and the format in which it is to be delivered or distributed.

- Where the product, service or film is to be edited, or parts deleted or adapted then prior written approval can be required. Where you do not want to have to do this then it is imperative that the right to make changes extensively is incorporated in the agreement.

- Marketing, packaging and associated material should not be ignored nor should the use of any adapted logo, title or character name. It is vital that approval or consultation clauses are included in order to be able to express a view as to how your work is being exploited and promoted. This often also exposes the fact that a third party has created some new material based on your work which should be acquired and assigned.

- In some cases approval of material allows errors to be corrected, copyright notices to be put in which have been forgotten and misuse of your work avoided.

Insurance

- Whether insurance is required to protect both parties or an individual or a product it needs to be specified who is to bear the cost and who is to benefit from the policy.

- Product liability, a hazardous activity, defamation, life insurance and public liability insurance on location are just some of the policies that are included in agreements.

- Attention needs to be provided to those items which are excluded under the policy and who is to meet the shortfall of any claim which is not covered.

Indemnity, Liability and Legal Proceedings.

- Both parties or just one party may provide any indemnity. It can apply to the whole contract or just a selection of clauses.

- The indemnity may apply to only certain work, services or rights and may be limited by duration, country and cost. You need to examine which areas of the agreement create the most risk and assess the possibility of a claim under the indemnity. It may be an allegation of defamation, faulty products, or exceeding the budget.

- It is perfectly acceptable to agree a maximum fixed cost liability under the indemnity although liability for death and personal injury may not be excluded. A procedure for being notified of any potential claims, taking over control of a case or being consulted about any proposed settlement is necessary to be alerted at an early stage.

- Each party may bear its own costs and risk and a decision made that no indemnity be provided.

- The length of time which the indemnity lasts is significant, and may only be for the life of the contract or extend many years thereafter. There may be a time limit by which a claim must be made under the indemnity by the other party in respect of specified areas.

- If you are the party providing the indemnity it may be cost effective to take out insurance cover to cover that potential liability.

- Legal proceedings may be about defending or taking legal action, but the question of responsibility for legal costs and whether this is covered by any indemnity or can be set off from any of the sums due under the agreement needs to be considered.

- The right to join and use the name of the other party in any legal proceedings which may arise to protect the product or service may be agreed. There may be a specification that there is no responsibility for the internal administrative and legal costs but an undertaking to reimburse or pay in advance for any separate legal advice that may be required and to provide a full indemnity to cover all costs, expenses, damages, losses and other sums.

2029

Third Party Transfer, Termination and Governing Law

- The right to be able to transfer, charge or make an agreement to a third party without consent is a valuable clause in an agreement. It allows a degree of flexibility to sell on the product or service without paying any additional sum.

- A restriction prohibiting any such third party transfer allows you the opportunity to negotiate a fee to agree to the novation or sale. In addition you can choose the companies with which you do business. Often such contracts are assigned as part of a wider package.

- The assignment or transfer may or may not affect the liability and obligations of the company which has made the assignment. It needs to be stated whether they are released from their responsibilities and if the new business fails whether they will still be liable for the consequences under the agreement.

- There are many grounds of termination which can be included to end a contract and some should be directly relevant to the development and completion of the project.

- There may be sell-off provisions to allow stock to be disposed of at cost or for an agreed fixed price. The payments should be connected to this late sale.

- Whether it is the force majeure or terminations provisions which result in the end of the agreement. There should be steps included to try to avoid litigation as the next stage; such as mediation, arbitration or dispute resolution. These procedures may or may not be obligatory on the parties, but the issue of costs needs to be clear and whether any decision is binding.

- The jurisdiction or governing law may affect the type of action that can be taken, the evidence required, the costs and the damages and losses that can be awarded. The conduct of litigation in a forum where the law is uncertain in relation to the rights or obligations of parties for a project could result in protracted and expensive litigation in which, even if you win, not all the costs are recouped.

A short guide to the mistakes, omissions and errors to avoid in a contract, licence or distribution agreement

- There is plenty that can go wrong at any stage of a contract, but a great deal can be avoided by sufficient preparation at an early stage so that it is clearer as to what each party is actually expected to supply, create, undertake and achieve.

Clarify your aim and optimum terms

- The most important part of any contract or agreement starts well before the negotiation and drafting stage. You must be clear about the aim of the project and the most advantageous terms you hope to achieve as the outcome in the contract. That means that you have to try to establish which terms and conditions you would optimistically like to achieve, which rights you want to own or licence, and how much revenue you would like to generate in each financial year. You must try to plan through and map out how any rights you want to acquire may be used commercially, what material will be created and by whom, how will it be packaged, sold and marketed. If you don't have your own contractual targets and also a practical idea of the steps which will be taken to exploit any rights and material. Then not only will it be very much harder to negotiate a good agreement as you have no focus for what you want to achieve, but you are unlikely to cover all the issues effectively in the contract.

Create one contract document

- Contract documents vary in extremes as to their depth and complexity, and may be a few pages or hundreds. It is not uncommon these days for businesses to put their terms and conditions on the back of invoices and then seek to rely upon them to exclude some prior agreement, or for two parties to both seek to rely on their contrasting terms of business. Such conflict is best avoided by insisting that the other company accept that your terms and conditions apply and to get this confirmed in writing or to start with a new agreement entirely. Many general terms and conditions which are used for years do not spell out in sufficient detail what each party is meant to do and often avoid the issue of ownership of copyright and other intellectual property rights.

Investigate the business of the other party.

- As a fundamental rule, even before you attempt to negotiate, draft or amend anything, you need to understand far more about the business of the parties to the contract. This is a very necessary step of negotiating and drafting a good contract. At an early stage get an idea of how they do business and understand how they operate. Obviously make the effort to look at their website, review corporate documents or an annual report and understand what their business actually does and how they do it.

- A better understanding of the key personnel, products, brands and trade marks, sales, markets and distribution methods of a company will enhance your ability to create a short, clear and useful contract. You need to consider the turnover and profit history and solvency of the company, and whether it in fact is an empty shell subsidiary. Where any company is newly created for a project or is an insignificant subsidiary then you should consider whether a 'comfort letter' agreeing to take responsibility, and bear the cost of all liability and indemnities should be sought from the parent company or an individual.

- This type of background research is important and will help you understand not only what the company does well, but also their future plans and the products or services they do not exploit. That knowledge may give you the advantage to negotiate a far higher percentage royalty and a much greater advance. It may also mean that you may decide to retain a considerable number of rights or withhold countries or markets in which you know they have no experience.

Parties to the Agreement.

- It is essential to check that the party who purports to own the rights and grant them from that company name actually holds them. The trading name can be referred to, but the contracting party should be the name of the incorporated company or institute who holds the rights or from which the revenue flows and for which there are annual reports. It is worth considering whether the parent company and the subsidiary should both be the contracting parties.

- Often at this point some parties try to put in additional words such as 'including assignees and successors in business'. If you don't want the other party to be allowed to sell you on then all these type of references should be deleted.

- A third party transfer clause which deals with the issue and sets out permitted assignees or bars them altogether unless there is consent is the preferable route.

- The signature of the agreement is equally important and that the person signing has both the authority and the capacity to do so. If it is a particularly large contract a finance director or chief executive should be the signatories.

Law and Contracts.

- There are two main areas of the law which are used when drafting contracts and clearing and using any type of material – intellectual property rights and contract law. Often the legal definitions in the legislation, case law and regulations merely form the background to what is actually in the agreement.

- Quite often the law is far behind, or does not even recognise certain rights. This was true until relatively recently of the right to apply for a computer software patent and still applies to format rights for television programmes. The terms of a contract are not limited by the definitions which exist in law nor are the terms of a contract limited by the legislation of any country except to the extent that the terms in some way are illegal or contravene the law or are contrary to some case law or code of practice or policy.

Original Work and Copyright.

- Copyright is about the protection of an original work which has been created through skill and labour. The quality of the work is not the issue. In any contract where a person or company claims copyright in any material five basic questions should be raised.

- Is it original or is it merely copied from someone else's work?

- Who made the work and where did they make it or what is their nationality?

- How did they, or will they, make the work?

- Who has or will pay for the work and what type of agreement is required?

- What materials already exist and what will be created?

- In the United Kingdom the Copyright, Designs and Patents Act 1988 (as amended) groups materials in these categories: artistic work, photographs, sound recordings, literary works, computer-generated material, film, and soundtrack. Commissioned work is presumed to belong to the person who pays for it, but this is not always the case and so a signed assignment document is preferable to a dispute at later date.

Existing Material and clearance costs

- Copyright clearance of material, work, services and rights which are either being contributed by third parties or which are only a small part of the main project should not be overlooked.

2033

- The clearance and consent to use something is not the same as who bears the cost; these are two separate issues which often cause problems. Clearance should always be as wide as possible so that fixed fees are agreed in advance, but minimise the payments upfront so that payment is only linked to different types of actual use. This may be publication of a book, broadcast of a film, use of a service or operation of a website. As a rule any fees should not be linked to sales or net receipts and a one-off fee paid in stages for all media in any country is preferable.

- The aim should always be to acquire an assignment of all rights and actually become the copyright owner of the material and the rights. This makes it much easier when selling on your business to provide assurances in due diligence as to the ownership of your intellectual property rights. It is important that you establish at an early stage which material, work or service is being used or supplied for the project and not to treat this as an administrative matter to be sorted out later.

- The first list to draw up is that of material which already exists which is being used for the project. For every different example of material on the list the question is who owns or controls it, in which format is it being supplied and at whose cost. It is important to obtain a full list of all the clearance costs and to identify the agreements that need to be concluded. There may be a copyright licence or an assignment of all rights in all media required. You also need to research whether you need a licence from any rights management organisations or collecting societies for the performance, broadcast, transmission, mechanical reproduction, digitisation, reproduction or otherwise of any of the material and what sums will have to be paid for each type of use.

- Any licence or document providing consent should specify whether a copyright notice or credit is required and how it should be displayed and when. It is useful to include a clause that no credit will be provided rather than not address this issue.

New Material, Adaptations, and Developments

- You need to find out whether the material, work or service is to be adapted or developed, and if so who is creating the new work, the method used and whether there is a prototype, sample or draft before the final product. It helps establish a clear list of the material which will be created, the production costs and what rights are likely to be created in relation to specific types of material. It is very difficult to draft an agreement without having addressed this issue and understood the cycle of the agreement in a practical sense as well as from the perspective of the different types of copyright and intellectual property rights that are created.

- Draw up a list of all the material from the first drawings or computer software being created, to the finished product. Are any music, artwork, sound recordings, film, computer-generated material or photographs used, or is the product a development of an earlier work? This will help when resolving copyright issues in the drafting.

- Is a third party being commissioned, or are they an employee? If so does their contract deal with this issue or would an assignment of copyright and all other rights be the safer option. Wherever you engage anyone, whether on a freelance basis, as a friend or pay to commission a company to create new material of any type – artwork, photographs, designs, three dimensional manufacturing models, text, logos, or music – it is vitally important that there is a complete and full assignment of all rights in all media and that the proper paperwork is completed.

- It is only when a project is successful that it is likely that contributors will then try to claim an interest or register a right and this is best avoided. So that it is unequivocal who owns the material and the rights. There have been a number of disputes which have arisen either because the question of who owns new material which has been created has not been stated or because the question of the creation of new rights has not been dealt with. The ownership of the material and the ownership of the copyright or intellectual property rights should never be presumed to be clear but always specified in the contract.

Editorial Control and Quality Control

- The lists of existing material and that which is to be created in the future will allow you identify which clauses need to be incorporated in the agreement so that you can have the right to exercise the necessary degree of control over the project.

- This equally applies to the associated items such as labels, packaging, posters, advertising and marketing material. This can be dealt with by editorial control, quality control and title clauses. Even if the other party has final editorial control that does not prevent you from having rights of approval or consultation at each stage over the cover, binding, index, layout, colours, credits, copyright notices, disclaimers, type of content, and any additions or deletions which may be made.

- The essential aim is to impose undertakings to preserve the quality of the content or product at each stage. This equally applies to services and work. It is important that the personnel who carry out the project are suitably qualified and experienced.

Definitions

- If you try to define a large number of factors at the front of the contract which are referred to in a number of clauses then it simplifies the drafting. Definitions at the front of the agreement help create a clearer contract and hopefully avoid repetition throughout which makes it even more difficult to read. Failure to do this results in constantly repeating the descriptive narrative throughout which is often confusing and inconsistent.

- You may list for example a definition of the work, service or product to be supplied under the agreement, the advance, the territory to be licensed, the fees to be charged, the delivery date, the website, the term of the agreement, the work schedule, or how each of the different types of rights which are to be granted in the agreement are defined. The list is unlimited and should be used by providing the best possible description that you can.

- However attention needs to be made as to whether you are creating definitions which are not achievable and may result in the other party using it as an excuse to terminate the contract. Therefore when providing a description if the title, length, images or content is not yet certain state that it is only provisional and may be varied.

- The use of definitions can affect the revenue which is received under an agreement, an advantageous definition of the distribution expenses, the net or gross receipts, or the royalties will clearly affect how much money a company is able to deduct before it is obliged to pay any royalties.

Assignment, Licence and Rights

- There are five aspects to understanding rights and defining rights in an agreement. The material, work or service which already exists in any medium and which is to be supplied or used. The material, work or service which is to be created in the future. Which parties are carrying out which work or providing services and the method by which this is to be done. How the services, work and material fit in with the legal categorisation and definitions which exist. Then fit all this into achieving the best terms possible in the agreement.

- Ownership of the material is separate from copyright and the exploitation of the rights. The licensing of use of any copyright or the transfer of ownership must be done in writing and cannot be given in any verbal form unless it is a non-exclusive licence. An exchange by email and text may be deemed binding but would be based on the facts of the case. The key debate would be about the signature and whether the sender could be clearly identified and had consented or whether the exchange was merely negotiations and not intended to be binding. For clarity it is therefore useful to make any such exchange 'not binding and subject to final contract' to avoid ambiguity. In any event an original signed document is always better. An introductory letter for an interview to be recorded or filmed does not amount to an assignment of all rights in all media. As a basic rule you should acquire widely and licence narrowly. There are broad categories of types of agreements including those stated below.

- Assignment – Buyout – transfer of all rights in all media throughout the world and universe. This may be for a single fee or for an advance and a royalty percentage which varies according to the type of use. No rights are reserved.

- Assignment – transfer all rights in all media but only for fixed period of time such as ten or twenty years and for a fixed sum not necessarily for a royalty and may also be limited by the countries which it covers. All rights are to be assigned back to the assignor at the end of that period of assignment.

- Assignment – transfer only limited rights such as publishing or film, for a fixed period for a single fee paid in stages or an advance and royalties. Either worldwide or for certain countries. All rights are reserved which are not assigned.

- Exclusive licence of all rights in all media for the full period of copyright and any extensions and renewals and in perpetuity for the world and universe. This agreement would be drafted to include those rights and technologies created and developed in the future. No rights are reserved.

- Exclusive licence of all rights for a fixed term such as one to five years. The rights then revert back after the end date of the term of the agreement.

- Exclusive licence of limited rights for full period of copyright, but only in a specific licensed area or territory.

- Exclusive licence of limited rights for a fixed term in a country. The rights would then revert back after the end date of the licence period.

- Non-Exclusive licences which can be varied as to the rights, the length of time for which they are granted, and the countries or territory.

- If you are granting or assigning rights the primary intention should always be to retain as many rights as possible, to hold as much control over the project as you can and to maximise the revenue in the smallest amount of territory that needs to be given.

- The licence period should not be longer than absolutely necessary and all rights in the project should revert back to you at the end.

- Many agreements which are concluded fail to fulfil all these criteria as insufficient effort is put into shortening every aspect of the terms to achieve this intended aim.

- Every single aspect of the grant or assignment clause is important from the definition of the rights to be granted or assigned, the term of the agreement or licence period, the territory and the material to which it applies.

- The duration of the agreement could be crucial as to the financial liability and is too often included without any real thought as to the consequences. Establish whether it is in your interest to negotiate a very short licence period or term of the agreement. The drafting can be adapted to delay the start date or bring it forward so that it starts on the date of full signature of the agreement. It may be useful to link the duration to the meeting of financial targets and receipts of funds or to include a break clause.

- The concept of contracts which just roll on and are renewed without any consent without any real start and end date should avoided. Where the term of the agreement or payments are linked to completion of work or delivery or use of the rights then care should be taken to set out either a fixed date by which payment is triggered or by which the agreement will end.

- The territory should be either as wide or as limited as possible. The widest would be throughout the world and universe, next the world or only a defined list of countries, a single country or just a small licensed area which is local to a community.

- The issue of seas outside territorial waters around land, the sky, aeroplanes, satellites, ships, oil rigs and other moving objects may not fall within the countries defined and have to be addressed separately.

- Often there are all embracing exclusive licence clauses which are in effect buying everything because no effort has been made to spell out only limited rights and to negotiate a shorter licence period. Even three, ten or twenty years is better than agreeing to the full period of copyright.

- Where you are acquiring rights a comprehensive assignment with an extensive 'all media' definition which covers all formats, all mediums and any use is always preferable to a licence, but an exclusive licence for the full period of copyright and in perpetuity throughout the world and universe is the next step down.

- Whether it is an assignment or a licence there is no reason to give more than needed in the circumstances and so you should as a rule licence or assign only give those specific rights which you have defined in the agreement individually and reserve everything else.

- Especially those rights and technologies which are not in existence now and will be created in the future. It is important that the copyright and intellectual property rights in any new material are assigned back to the original copyright owner or business either during or at the end of the project.

- There have been many agreements where new technologies such as videos, CDs, computer games which exist now were not referred to at all and in which all royalties were only linked to certain formats of products. The resulting effect is that the assignor or licensor has not received any royalties as they did not reserve these rights. The assignees or licensees have successfully argued that they had no right to additional royalties as no royalty was mentioned in the agreement in relation to those new rights or products. In other examples the assignment or licence was sufficiently ambiguous for it to be accepted that the definition covered these new products which did not exist at the time.

Sub-Licensees

- It is also important to plan ahead and only to allow a project to be sub-licensed to those third parties which you have approved and which agree to be bound by the terms of the main agreement.

- Nor should the licensee be permitted to rely on the sub-licence to avoid responsibility and liability under the main agreement.

- Often no detailed reference is made to the sub-licensing of rights and the licensor is unable to exert sufficient control over them or new rights and material are created by a third party which are not then assigned to the licensor. The steps required to deal with this are then unnecessarily expensive and protracted as it was not dealt with in the contract.

- There is little benefit in granting rights to a company which they have no experience of exploiting or which will be sub-licensed to an unknown third party. The term of any sub-licence that can be granted should be limited to the duration of the main agreement and any sub-licence should end at the same time if possible.

Trade Marks, Logos, Slogans, and Domain Names

- The ownership of trade marks, service marks, community marks, logos, slogans, and domain names should be clarified and stated in the agreement. It should be part of a deliberate policy is to protect your own brand.

- Any trade marks, service marks, community marks, logos, slogans, and domain names should be defined and a copy attached if possible to the agreement. The agreement should state which party owns and controls it and who has the right to register any interest, reproduce it in different formats, licence third parties, commission new artwork and how it can be used.

- If there is no permission given to adapt or change the logo or trade mark then this should be clearly stated.

- A comprehensive list of material on which it may be used and the location may be drawn up and rights of approval incorporated which require written consent at each stage of development.

Credits, Copyright Notices and Moral Rights

- Moral rights consists of two categories: the first is the right to be identified; and the second the right not to be subjected to derogatory treatment which is quite different. That is, nothing is to be added, taken away, changed, or varied unless authorised in advance.

- In order to avoid any problems later it may be easier to draft a waiver of moral rights, but then include a consultation clause instead.

- The particular name, copyright notices, credits, images and logos required should be set out in the agreement including the location, colour and other specifications. It may vary dependent on whether it is in relation to the product or service, packaging, marketing, app or website.

- Where the parties agree that there is to be no mention of a person then that fact needs to be included and It is also useful to have a waiver.

Costs, Expenses, and Insurance

- The budget, costs, expenses, and allowances for hotels, gadgets and travel should all be specified in the definitions and a maximum limit set out in order to control the expenditure from the outset.

- The responsibility of each party as to the budget, costs, expenses and allowances should be set out in detail. Where possible documents should be attached which set out each item and they should form part of the agreement.

- A procedure for any increase can then be set out which has to be formally approved in advance and what is to happen to any underspend.

- Failure to place any restrictions could result in an unexpected financial liability and the possibility of being sued for the balance.

- It is also worthwhile to include a clause that each party will bear its own administration, travel or other costs which are not specified and that they cannot be recovered under the agreement.

- Also consider whether insurance cover should be taken out as part of the cost of a project.

Delivery, Rejection, Risk and Title

- Delivery, target or distribution dates should be included in an agreement otherwise there is no focus for the payments to begin.

- The dates may relate to the completion of each stage of a project, delivery of a manuscript, proofs or index, the development of a final product, operation of a website or release to the public.

- If it is stated that time is of the essence in relation to these dates then failure to comply may result in the right to terminate the agreement.

- There should also be a risk clause which identifies the point at which ownership in the material which is being delivered passes.

- A retention of title clause will ensure that ownership of the rights in the material are retained until payment is received in full.

- If the service or product is not delivered by the date then there should be a right to cancel or terminate. Often there is no completion date and so it is harder to rely on this as a grounds of termination if it is delayed.

- It is helpful to try to set out the manner in which a party shall be entitled to reject a product or service and to require them to specify the grounds and to do so within a specified period of time.

Royalties, Advances, Accounts and Inspection

- The royalties, advance and the stage at which payments can be made can all be varied according to each set of rights and forms of exploitation which exist.

- The most common mistake is apply the same royalty to too many rights instead of negotiating higher percentages for those which are worth the most money and retaining those which are not going to be exploited.

- It is also worthwhile including a clause where the royalties escalate either when basic costs have been recouped or if sales targets are achieved.

- There could even be a series of such increasing royalties linked to different markets.

- Targets can be either the total value of sums received, units sold, clicks on banner on a website, or the winning of a sporting event.

- Bonus and performance related sums may also be paid on sales or an event or the achievement of sales figure by a certain date.

- Any references to money should include the currency and how the exchange rate is to be fixed and who pays the charges.

- The sum received from the royalty percentage is totally dependent on the definition of the sum from which it is derived. This may be a fixed unit cost, a percentage of gross receipts or a percentage of net receipts.

- Often the net receipts are drafted in such a manner that there is never any royalty payment actually received as there are no limits to the expenditure and marketing costs which a company can deduct.

- A lower percentage of gross receipts is often better than a larger percentage of net. The only exception may be where costs and deductions from net receipts are capped and are not unlimited or where the product would not be exploited at all as it would not be commercially viable.

- All discounts, agent's commission or fees should be set out and limited in a contract and it made clear as to how and when they can be deducted.

- An advance can be any type of staged payments and does not have to be in one thirds, it can be linked to dates or completion of work.

- The contract should state whether the advance is to be recouped against future royalties or if it is non-returnable.

- If the companies have other contracts then a clause should be added that sums due under the agreement either can or can't be set-off against other agreements between the parties.

- It is important that there are provisions regarding how the sums received are held or managed. The contract may require a new bank account with agreed signatories allowed access.

- It may be preferable to arrange for sums to be paid direct rather than allow a third party to receive it as an agent. The money remains within their control until it is handed over and unless it is clearly identifiable as separate falls within their business and is subject to the possibility of mismanagement and the business collapsing.

- The accounting provisions should be very clear as to what is required in a royalty statement and should be as frequent as possible. For a mobile phone or website company every month or two is not unreasonable, but once a year is at the other end of the scale.

- Inspection of accounts and records is needed in order to verify the sums stated as due, but the inspection provision needs to be drafted widely to allow access to as much material as possible.

- A clause can also be included which obliges the party who has made the error in the accounts to pay interest and both the legal and accounting professional costs of the audit. There may be a margin of error over which this provision comes into effect this could be a percentage or a fixed amount.

Defamation, Liability, and Indemnity

- There should always be an undertaking that a party has not entered and will not enter into any other agreements or arrangements which would conflict with the present agreement.

- There may be one or more clauses which relate to the responsibility for checking the contents of any service or product and ensuring that it does not contain anything which is defamatory, obscene or offensive. These types of clauses need to be drafted very widely if you are seeking assurances and narrowly if it is your business providing the undertaking.

- Such undertakings would also be given for any consequential loss and damage arising from product liability and for compliance with any necessary legislation, tests, and codes of practice.

- The question is whether the clauses as drafted cover both direct and indirect losses and damages and is accompanied by an indemnity which is equally wide and unlimited. It is commonsense to consider whether both parties might also be protected by insurance cover.

- It is important to include a right to be able to edit, delete or amend material which in the view of the company's management or legal advisors is likely to result in litigation or adverse publicity.

- Where a company is going to rely on an indemnity provision for reimbursement of legal costs, losses and damages. Then there should be an additional clause relating to any potential right to be indemnified. The other party should be notified of any potential claims at an early stage by the company seeking to rely on the indemnity. The party should be consulted about the case and how it should be dealt with and provided with the opportunity to refute the allegations. Further it is useful to have a clause which confirms that no settlement will be reached with a third party without prior consultation as to the terms of the proposed settlement.

- Both indemnity and liability provisions can be subject to a fixed maximum limit under a contract to minimise the financial exposure of a company and this should always be considered for any contract.

- Liability can be limited in most areas but not for personal injury or death so it is possible to limit the clause by a fixed period of time, the type of loss and damages.

- Exclusion of liability is very common in insurance, health, and product policies or for computer software and equipment, but not so extensive in other agreements.

- It is possible to limit the life of indemnity, so that it ends with the agreement or only extends for a fixed number of years. Indemnity undertakings can also be limited to selected clauses in an agreement.

Jurisdiction, Legal Proceedings and Disputes

- The legal system and law which both parties decide the agreement should fall within is often not seriously considered. It needs to be decided in conjunction with the other alternative methods of resolving a dispute that the parties would like to have such as arbitration, mediation and alternative dispute resolution if any.

- There are serious cost and legal implications dependent on the forum which is chosen. Where the issues at stake are not serious then the avoidance of litigation and the heavy costs involved if one loses make it valuable to have the opportunity if you so wish to seek some other method of resolving a matter without prejudice to any rights or claim.

Termination and Force Majeure

- The termination clauses provide the chance to specify in detail the circumstances in which a party should have the right to bring an agreement to an end.

- It is possible to go well beyond the standard clauses to set out other grounds such as the failure to reach certain financial targets, complete stages of the project by certain dates, and get a product released to the public.

- Often it is forgotten that it should be stated what exactly is to happen if the agreement is terminated and whether any sums would be repaid, or rights revert or whether the parties would have to negotiate a settlement.

- The force majeure clause is also about suspending or terminating the agreement, but the circumstances which qualify within that category can be quite varied. It is possible to include specific types of situations than can be covered and to exclude those that are agreed not to fall within this clause.

Third Party Transfer

- Particularly where the contract is for the services or work of an individual with a company it is important to include a no third party transfer clause.

- This may also apply to a company in order to prevent the obligations, liabilities and benefits being transferred to a business which is far less solvent or with which you do not wish to be associated.

- A website or app company would want to make sure that it could be sold on without any delay and so the opposite approach would be taken and a clause included which specifically agrees that third party transfers are permitted and that no consent is required or any additional sums due in payment.

Factors in Sub-Licensing

- It is stating the obvious, but often forgotten, that before you grant any sub-licence or conclude a merchandising agreement you should look at the existing contracts and documents in your possession and try to get a complete picture as to who owns what material and rights.

- It is crucial that you make a clear and positive decision as to who actually owns those rights which you hope to exploit. No presumptions should be made that your company owns the rights.

- If the position is unclear or requires more research or clarification – now is the time to do so and not after the contract has been signed and the threat of litigation becomes an expensive mistake.

- It may be necessary to contact a potential claimant to state your view of the rights position and for them to confirm that you do in fact own the rights and that there is no potential conflict.

- It may be that when the original agreement was concluded that the technology or rights which you propose to exploit did not in fact exist. This could be the case with many earlier agreements which did not envisage satellite television, mobile phones, websites and the internet.

- Sometimes there is merely ambiguity because at the time the contract was concluded merchandising and sub-licensing was not even considered. The whole issue is therefore reduced to the interpretation of the actual wording of the agreement and documents that were concluded.

- You should carefully check the exact wording not only of the clauses relating to the rights which have been licensed or assigned to your company, but also whether there are other clauses in the agreement which restrict or prohibit your company's right to transfer, licence or assign the rights to a third party. There may be a no licence, transfer or assignment clause to a third party. Or any such new agreement may be subject to the prior approval or written consent of the original copyright owner.

- It is important to research whether any other agreement has already been signed at any stage prior to the current proposed sub-licence or merchandising agreement which would either prevent or restrict the rights that could be granted.

- There may be for instance a distribution agreement or option or other licence or assignment which relates to another topic, but still deals with these ancillary rights.

- Quite often company records are incomplete and badly recorded and not specific as to anything except the main subject of a contract. Therefore it is worth asking about the history as far as people recall – which will at least alert you to the fact that relevant documents may exist.

- Any document which potentially has already assigned or granted the rights must be examined to see whether that is in fact the case. It is also worth doing some investigations as to whether those rights and products have actually already been marketed in any country.

- There is always a need prior to entering into negotiations with a third party to check out their track record, financial history and how and where they actually currently market their products or services. Do your homework on the proposed third party – are they a distributor or a manufacturer with agents overseas? Are they a new company or have they been trading for some time? Is it a subsidiary of a more substantial company? Do they manufacture products themselves or do they appoint a manufacturer? Who have they used in the past? What products do they actually sell and where? Have there been any health and safety problems? Look at their website, catalogue, marketing material. Find out what stages they do go through before they market the final product? What trade marks, service marks or other registrations have they worldwide?

- Where are their main premises based, and where do they hold their bank accounts? It is not difficult to obtain copies of the accounts of a business. All this information helps you complete a more detailed picture of the operation and to assess the reliability of a third party.

- As a basic principle you should licence rather than assign rights to a third party and should not and cannot grant more rights than you actually already own. Therefore where you are a company and have acquired rights which you wish to sub-licence. The sub-licence should end on the same date as the rights acquired under the main agreement or earlier. The sub-licence cannot be granted for a longer term without the consent of the copyright or other rights owner.

- There is no reason to conclude a document that purports to be a licence, but in effect is so wide as to be similar to an assignment. It is often argued by sub-licensees or merchandising companies that an assignment is required, but this is not the case. An assignment would transfer all copyright and ownership to the third party and would prevent the copyright owner or your company having any further right to exploit the rights.

- The whole process should be to licence the rights and material as narrowly as possible for the shortest feasible period. There is no logical reason to licence rights which will not be exploited.

- If you wish to permit the sub-licensee to further sub-licence rights then ensure that there are clauses relating to consultation and rights of approval and for you to be able to accept or reject their proposals.

- The definitions section at the front of the agreement is very important as it is here that the work, the material, the trade mark and logo, and the rights which are to be referred to in the sub-licence are described in detail.

- A sub-licence or merchandising agreement may be exclusive or non-exclusive this is obviously reflected in the payment in terms of any advance and royalties.

- The term of the agreement can be any length, but should not be left open to being linked to a task that is never completed. So always put a start and end date to avoid ambiguity.

- When granting a sub-licence the rights given should be specific and limited to the actual product that is to be marketed. There is no reason provide a wider definition or to grant any other rights which should be reserved.

- There may be an undertaking not to exploit all or some of those reserved rights until after a certain date. The point is that they are still owned by the licensor and not the sub-licensee.

- Quite often you will find that a contract makes no reference at all to rights which are not granted. However where new technology or rights are created at a later date, the reservation of rights may then permit the licensor to grant another sub-licence to someone else.

- A grant of rights must also define the territory for which the rights have been granted. This can be as large as the world and the universe to as small as a specific commercial premises.

- Where it is likely that the book, product or film is part of a series or set. Then it is important to address the issue as to whether there is any right of first refusal or an option granted over future editions or sequels. Unless there is some consideration for this in the payments then it is better to make it clear that there is no such right.

- There may also be clauses which are intended to prevent competing works being made available for a fixed period on the market before a specified date. These clauses should be drafted as narrowly as possible or even refused.

- If a sub-licensee wishes to acquire an exclusive option or a right of first refusal, then that should be clearly drafted as such and consideration given. There is no reason to at this stage to limit your negotiation position by agreeing to the same terms for the new material.

- Delivery dates should be realistic as an agreement with a time of essence clause will then allow the sub-licensee to terminate for non-delivery.

- Calculating the costs of the supply of material is important and the agreement should make clear who is paying and at which point the risk and ownership of the material passes.

- Editorial control and quality control clauses facilitate procedures to inspect, approve and also prevent others exploiting your material in an unacceptable manner. This would apply to master material, samples, prototypes, packaging, marketing, translations, change of name, and other adaptations.

- The essence of these types of agreements is to make money. This means that the accounting requirements should be clear and the detail of how and when the money is to be paid. It is better for you to sign the agreement, and to have the sums paid directly to you.

- If you provide authority under the contract for the agent to receive the sums and statements, then make sure that you can still personally have a right of inspection of the accounts and records. Discuss with your agent where and how your funds are to be kept and paid.

- Where the royalty is to be paid as a percentage of net receipts then it should be drafted to limit the amount of deductions that are permitted by the sub-licensee. Failure to do so may mean that a very successful project results in no royalty payments to the licensor as the sub-licensee literally deducts every penny of its costs before it makes any payment.

- A percentage of gross receipts is often better than a percentage of net receipts which is broad.

- An advance may be a one off non-returnable payment or recouped against future royalties.

- Escalating royalties linked to successful sales allow for the licensor to benefit from greater financial rewards once certain costs are recovered.

- You should also look at exchange rates and the cost of transfer of funds; how are funds held and where; accounting statements and the detail these will provide; audits and errors. As well as how long records, documents and invoices should be kept.

- There are often clauses which prevent transfer or assignment of the rights to a third party without consent or those which relate to change of control of the business.

- The issue of product liability where an article or product is sold to the public is important and the arrangement of insurance is an integral part of these clauses.

- Where you are the licensor then you should endeavour to provide a limited indemnity in terms of the undertakings it covers and also one which is capped so that it is not an open ended financial risk. Try to limit your indemnity both by the length of time it operates; the amount, and the areas that it covers.

- The indemnity should be addressed at the same time as liability and legal proceedings. There should be a requirement that the licensor is kept advised of any threat of legal proceedings and that no legal costs are to be claimed unless the licensor has been kept informed. Further that if the licensor is required to join any legal action the sub-licensee intends to take against a third party that both parties will agree the costs in advance.

- In any sub-licence it is important to include clauses which cover copyright ownership, copyright notices, moral rights and credits from the viewpoint of the rights and the material which exists at the time of the agreement and those which will be created in the future.

- The ownership of names, titles, trade marks and logos should be clear and who has the right to register them and exploit them at a later date.

- As a product is exploited in different forms new versions are often created and the ownership of these new adaptations should be stated.

- There have been a number of cases where consultants have designed new images and the rights have not been assigned to the company. It doesn't matter whether it is a new link logo design, on a marketing label or part of a new website, the ownership should be clarified.

- Merchandising can vary from toys, stickers, books, films, computer games, clothing and ringtones to a format for a quiz show. The material created these days is extensive from posters for stands at trade fairs, to banner advertisements, podcasts, flyers, brochures, packaging and television advertisements. Both during negotiations and at a later stage ask for a marketing plan and report which will sets out estimated forecast of sales, formats and the marketing strategy in different countries.

- It is likely that a sub-licensee will use a range of third parties to create new material and care needs to be taken that all rights in any such material are assigned to the licensor. You should ensure that all work commissioned by the sub-licensee or carried out by any third party results in assignment of the copyright and intellectual property rights and that it is not left unresolved.

- The termination provisions set out the basis upon which the agreement can be ended and so it makes sense to include grounds for termination for non-payment of any part of the advance and royalties. The failure to reach specified performance targets may also be grounds for termination.

- The sub-licensee will want any force majeure clause to be wide, but this is not in the interests of the licensor. Certain types of technical or other failure may actually be the sub-licensee's fault. So you do not want the sub-licensee to be able to rely on force majeure when the licensor would prefer to terminate the agreement. Look at the termination and force majeure from view of the sub-licensee not printing your book or product, stopping selling it or going out of business. You need to make sure there are clauses that allow the licensor to have the rights transferred back to the licensor.

- After the expiry of the sub-licence there may be a sell-off period where the licensee is permitted to dispose of stock. This should preferably be non-exclusive and have a specified end date where material is destroyed or returned to the licensor at no charge or at cost. It is equally reasonable to not allow this, but insist that the end of the licence period is the final date and no further sales or distribution is allowed after that date.

- At the end of the sub-licence there will be in existence a whole collection of material from master material and moulds, to software, packaging, brochures, flyers and electronic files. It is therefore important to have addressed the ownership of this material in the contract and whether or not the licensor is entitled to have all copies delivered at the sub-licensee's cost or bought back or whether it is to be destroyed.

- The governing law clause is important both in terms of legal costs, but also what legal rights you may have as this will obviously vary depending on the jurisdiction.

Understanding copyright and how it is used in contracts

- It is always necessary in any agreement to think about whether there are any copyright, trade mark, or other intellectual property issues that need to be addressed in relation to both parties. This article is only concerned with copyright.

- There are two parts to this issue the rights and the material which exist at the time of the contract. Then the rights which may be created in the future and the material which will be developed. There may be different types of rights which all exist at the same time. Similarly there may be different types of material created at a variety of stages. It is crucial prior to drafting any contract to understand the practical issues of the format of the material required to be delivered or the methods by which it is to be produced, reproduced and exploited.

- Copyright is about the protection or exploitation of someone's original work which they have created as a result of their skill and labour. We are not dealing with all the other criteria which may be necessary in order to qualify for copyright protection in this article which you would need to meet.

- The quality of the work is not the issue, merely whether the work is original, and by whom, where and how it is created and the type of material which forms the record of its existence.

- A person may be the original copyright owner or they may have licensed their work to a company under an exclusive or non-exclusive licence. Alternatively the work may have been assigned to a distributor and the rights bought out in return for an advance and a royalty. The potential scenarios are wide and varied, but the same basic questions apply. Who was the original copyright owner? When and how did they make it? Was it original or was it based on someone else's work? What materials were created? If the company or distributor has acquired the rights under a licence or assignment where is the contract? What rights did you acquire under the contract? And what does the contract actually authorise you to do? Are you entitled to sub-licence these rights to a third party?

- The legal definitions in legislation and case law both in the UK, Europe and elsewhere merely form the background. Such terminology is not directly used in the terms of an agreement, but is changed to suit the circumstances.

- The whole aim when drafting a contract is to summarise the situation as far as possible so that the intention of the parties is most accurately and comprehensively described.

- Most legislation worldwide is far behind the advanced technological developments such as interactive television, downloading of material onto mobiles, websites and social networking. Some of the legislation has been drafted in broad terms to describe the method and medium, but without specifics and so would be unsuitable to use in a contract.

- Copyright is best envisaged as consisting of many slices of a cake and as technology develops new sections are created which did not exist before.

- It is crucial that the issue of rights of ownership of the copyright are dealt with as a separate one from the ownership of the material. A library may for instance own the physical copy of the work, yet not own or control the copyright in the work.

- The motto 'license narrowly and acquire widely' is a good one as a starting point.

- The licensing of the use of copyright or the transfer of ownership of any material of any type must be done in writing, and cannot be given on the telephone, by voicemail or any verbal form unless it's a non-exclusive licence.

- Where the services of a third party are being engaged for a project then the question of copyright ownership of the rights and material should always be dealt with in order to avoid a dispute at a later date. An informal arrangement with a consultant, web designer or other contributor can be a very expensive mistake if a project later becomes successful. If someone is commissioned to design any artwork, create a logo, record some music or write text. Then as a fundamental principle there should be a written document where consideration is provided to acquire some or all of the rights that you intend to exploit and to prevent the other person licensing third parties or registering the rights with a rights management organisation or collecting society.

- In contrast it is also needed to protect the author and their work so that the rights of the creator are not exploited without consent or without remuneration.

- Where you intend to sell the business on at a later stage, then it makes sense to have a clear and consistent record of the acquisition of rights and to adhere to this policy so that it permeates all parts of the company.

- This applies to all departments of a business as due diligence will reveal any failures to acquire rights which everyone presumed were owned by a company. Marketing departments often create or commission new labels, logos and artwork without the necessary paperwork being concluded and it has only been when a company has tried to register a trade mark that they have discovered that they do not even own the rights and that they were never acquired at an early stage.

- There is no reason to grant or assign rights for which you are receiving little financial gain or which the other party is not even going to exploit.

- Any licence which is to be granted should be as short as possible. There is no reason why an exclusive licence should be for 'the full period of copyright' when a period between one to five years will achieve the same financial result.

- The Copyright, Designs and Patents Act 1988 as subsequently amended allocates material into groups which include Artistic Work, Photographs, Sound Recordings, Computer-Generated Material, Film, Literary Work and Musical Work. There are others, but we are not dealing with all of them in this article. You will find many examples of different definitions in this book under the main headings Material and Rights as well as under other headings.

- An Artistic Work is defined to include a graphic work, photograph, sculpture or other work of artistic craftsmanship.

- A Graphic Work is expressed as including any painting, drawing, diagram or map.

- Therefore in a contract which involves artwork one of the ways in which the material could be described in the definition section at the beginning of the agreement would be as follows: 'The Artwork' shall mean any photographs, drawings, sketches, pictures, diagrams or other illustrations or visual images which is intended to be included as part of the [Work].

- Photographs is defined widely in the legislation, so that the photographs may be shot on any type of format. The description is of a recording of light or other radiation on any medium on which an image is produced or from which it may be reproduced. However it does not apply to one which forms part of a film.

- In a contract the photographs may simply be described as stills with a reference code as follows: 'The Stills' shall be the following photographs; [reference/code/title/description/source material] in which the copyright is owned by [Name] and the physical material is owned by [specify].

- Where the photographs are part of a commission then the following definition may be used: 'The Commissioned Work' shall be the following services and images to be created, developed, produced and delivered by the [Photographer] to the [Company] based on the summary which is set out in Schedule [–] which is attached to and forms part of this Agreement.

- Sound Recordings is also very broadly defined to mean a recording of sounds from which sounds may be reproduced or the recording of the whole or any part of a literary, dramatic or musical work. This shall be the case regardless of the medium on which the recording is made or the method by which the sounds are reproduced. This does not apply to a film soundtrack accompanying a film which has a different definition.

- Therefore a recorded interview would be applicable if it was in sound only, but moving images would fall within film. When dealing with sound recordings there are separate issues of copyright relating to the words and lyrics as opposed to the music. It is an important issue to ensure in the agreement that there is an undertaking that both these rights have been cleared with the relevant copyright owner and/or collecting society and paid for and also to state who is to bear the cost of any future payments that may fall due.

- The Sound Recordings may be defined in the agreement as follows: 'The Master Recording' shall mean all sound recordings of [Name] made by or for the [Interviewer] for the purpose of the [Article/Work] regardless of the medium on which the sound recording is made or the method by which the sounds are produced or reproduced.

- Computer-Generated Material is stated to mean work or designs that are generated by a computer where there is no human author. The act of creating the work on a computer such as text or graphics which you feed into the machine which is your own work and labour is not a computer-generated work as it was put together by your skill, and not the machine.

- Film is expressed very widely so that the moving image could be on a variety of formats. It is described as being a recording on any medium from which a moving image may by any means be reproduced. A cable programme and service have a different further definition. Examples include shooting material on your camcorder, in a studio or on location. It doesn't matter how long or short the recording is or what it is shot on and it can be in any format.

- In an agreement the film may be referred to as a film, series, programme or pilot, but the aim is to be quite specific so the title, duration and other details would be listed.

- 'The Film' shall mean a feature length film and an accompanying soundtrack and musical score complying with the following particulars: [Title/duration] Based on [Book/Script] created by [Name] [Producer/ Director/Artists] [Material].

- 'The Series' shall be the series of films and any associated sound recording based on the [Pilot] which both parties may agree to produce, develop and exploit following satisfactory completion of the [Pilot].

- Literary Works are defined as those in written form and cover text or others such as quotes. In an agreement reference would be made to the script, the book, the extract or the synopsis.

- 'The Synopsis' shall mean the summary of the [Work] which sets out the chapter outlines, structure and general content of the [Work]. A copy of which is attached and forms part of this Agreement.

- Musical Work is described as meaning the music excluding any words which are to be sung or performed with the music. However in an agreement the definition at the front may be defined so that the lyrics are included.

- 'The Musical Work' shall be the original musical composition entitled [Title] [duration] created and written by [Name].

- In relation to the internet and websites there is no reference to the word 'digital' in the Copyright Designs and Patents Act 1988 as amended. Throughout the word 'electronic' is used and is broadly defined to encompass both the internet and telecommunications and the use of mobiles, gadgets and computers.

- These types of rights can be drafted very narrowly by reference to a specific website or app or very widely to encompass all forms of electronic communication and future technological developments.

- In reality there are often packages of material supplied under an agreement at different stages from one party to the other. Whether it is the supply of a copy of the master material or samples for approval of marketing, packaging and products. In order to protect your copyright position, quality control provisions play an important part as you are not only preserving the integrity of your brand, but vetting the new material.

- It is also important to address the issue as to who owns the material at the end of a contract.

- It would seem obvious that before granting or sub-licensing rights that you should check that you own them. You cannot grant rights to a third party to exploit the copyright in a work which you do not own.

- There are many organisations today who try to do just that and forget the most basic principles. Often assumptions are made based on no research or evidence except details in a database that rights have been acquired in the past and no effort is made to verify the situation.

- It is crucial that good contract records are kept and if no record is available then the last known copyright owner contacted to clarify the issue.

- It is not acceptable to assume that because your business has the material on its premises that it has the right to exploit the material and license it to a third party.

- Nor is it possible to assume that you are entitled to exploit material or rights because the copyright owner has not notified you of their objections.

- It is totally wrong to assume that a copyright owner has an obligation to notify anyone of the fact that they wish to be excluded from a licensing scheme. The obligation is always on the person who is seeking to exploit work owned by someone else that they must seek prior consent.

- Drafting a contract or licence which deals with copyright and intellectual property rights is best approached on a factual basis and not directly derived from the legal definitions which can be either too limiting or too wide.

- When drafting a contract it is important that there are clear and detailed definitions at the start of the agreement. These definitions are then woven in at a later stage to the grant or assignment of rights.

- A short checklist of the areas in an agreement which are impacted by copyright issues include:

  The definitions at the front.

  The wording of the assignment or licence and the rights which are assigned or granted.

  A reservation of rights which are not granted or assigned may avoid disputes and also allow you to retain rights which don't exist at the time of the agreement.

  The undertakings by the copyright owner as to the originality and ownership of the rights in the work and the material; the fact there is no pre-existing agreements which conflict with the current one or any legal proceedings pending.

  An indemnity which can be drafted narrowly and capped so that liability is not unlimited or drafted widely so that direct and indirect costs are recouped.

The issue of the degree of change which is allowed to any adaptation must be stated. This is best done by defining the proposed new version and attaching a summary, and also putting approval or consent mechanisms in place. An editorial control clause may be used to stipulate the degree of change that can be made to any new adapted material that is based on the original work. Also the copyright owner can put in place quality control provisions so that there are rights of approval or consultation over each stage of a project.

Credits and copyright notice clauses are important in an agreement. Your name and copyright notice should be displayed in a prominent position on every single copy in any format of your work. This can be achieved in different styles, but involves a copyright notice, the name of the copyright owner and the year of first publication or release to the public. The issue of credits should be stipulated in the contract as a separate issue and if required the size/position/prominence set out. This may be important where there are other contributors.

- Although not a copyright issue moral rights cannot be ignored. Moral rights may be asserted or waivered and fall into two parts. The right to be identified as the author and the right not to be subjected to derogatory treatment of a copyright, literary, dramatic, musical or artistic work. A derogatory treatment of a work is defined to cover any addition to, deletion from, alteration to or adaptation of a work, but does not apply to an authorised translation.

- Where you get other people to carry out work for you such as photos, artwork or writing. The safest option is to make sure that there is a full and complete assignment of 'all rights in all media whether in existence now or created in the future for the full period of copyright and any extensions or renewals'.

- Advertising, marketing and packaging is often an area which is not considered for copyright issues in agreements. However it is crucial to be able to insist on rights of approval or consultation. As well as basic copyright notices and credits appearing on all copies that may be reproduced or distributed. It is also important to maintain a consistency of brand and to ensure that any person who creates a new version based on your own does not acquire any rights.

Funding and sponsorship of an Event or Festival

- Do you even need an agreement? Sponsorship in a wide variety of forms and shapes is now a very lucrative and desirable form of funding for the arts, culture, music, sports and festivals. It is a growing market where businesses are seeking to create an image and identity to align themselves to a very specific target audience and to feed into the social media as a tool for achieving sales.

- Organisations and individuals often rely for these arrangements on an exchange of emails which broadly sets out the amount of money to be paid and how the logo and name of the company is to be used in marketing and in the programme catalogue or on the entry tickets.

- Often these exchanges fail to clarify expenditure costs, liability and responsibilities and how the sponsor may use and promote its role as a sponsor or the material available to it from other third parties who are taking part or even who owns the new logos and other material which is created.

- Expectations may be high and planned television coverage and attendance may not be achieved due to bad weather or some other reason. It is in all the parties interest to set out the terms so that representations made in a meeting, on a website or by email are either set out as part of the document or recognised as promotional hype or useful background material but not binding.

- Many festivals and events set out what they can offer a sponsor and the role expected to be fulfilled by a sponsor on their website. Some organisations have levels of sponsorship and funding from platinum to bronze with clearly defined benefits attached to the annual payment. The sponsors' details may be displayed in the form of their name and logo on the website; in a catalogue; on a venue wall and in any email marketing newsletter; and on associated marketing merchandise.

- The level of sponsorship may fund the right to have the corporate, product or individuals name listed as the title for a seasonal programme of events; or it may fund the right to have a venue such as a research or sports centre named in their honour with an associated logo.

- Establish whether you are the sole funder of an event or if there is a tier of sponsors linked to sub-groups of a programme or categories such as food, drink, VIP hospitality, equipment, security, radio and television coverage, products, music, transport etc. Get a map or programme of previous years so that although the sponsors may not be the same. You have an actual example of the layout and use of the previous sponsors name, logo and products.

- Understand the operation and management of the event so that you can optimise displays and marketing material. Look at issues of the need for planning consent as well as health and safety factors relating to electrical supplies, adverse weather conditions and location access problems.

- You may not be sponsoring the event; just a display in a clearly defined sector or part of a programme of performances or you may be the sole sponsor and supplier in relation to a category of food, drinks or other products or services. There would therefore be a term in the contract that no other company, business or competitor would be allowed to have a stall, distribute or promote their products or brand or contribute any funds or products in any part in the event or festival. In extreme cases this has meant that as people have entered a venue all drinks have been confiscated as a condition of entry.

- The sponsorship agreement is often a combination of funds, products, services, staff and attendance by the sponsor. The payment of the funds by the sponsor may be in one payment in advance or subject to stage payments such as signature of the agreement, booking the venue, draft programme, first day of event and finally the display of all the banners and distribution of the promotional material as required under the agreement. The first option is obviously preferable for the organisers and no access to the site is permitted if the advance payment has not been received.

- The arrangements may be for sponsorship of a literary festival where in return for non-exclusive sponsorship funds there may be:

An agreed number of complimentary tickets;

Credits of the name and logo of the sponsor on the programme, tickets and website.

Some banners permitted to be displayed supplied by the sponsor or the sponsor's logo and name included on the banner and other displays of the organisers but not necessarily in conjunction with the name of the event and title rights which may be held by someone else;

Branding on a hired or allocated stall, tent or other venue to be used by the sponsor which may either be supplied for free or incur an additional hire cost. Staff wearing branded outfits and promoting and selling products or services.

The site of any location reserved should be specified in relation to a map of the site which is attached as part of the agreement. The traffic from those that attend may vary enormously based on the location.

The right to host a hospitality event at the sponsor's cost.

Membership of an organisation for a year as a listed sponsor and access to the use of their services.

A sponsored feature article in a newsletter or magazine distributed to members.

A promotional space on the website and app together with links to the sponsor.

Access to the venue and the use of the facilities such as parking, electricity, water, light, broadband and technical facilities if any and how the costs associated with these terms are to be paid. This would normally be combined with an undertaking to indemnify the other party in the event that there is any damage, loss or repairs required caused by access to the venue and use of the facilities.

The right to offer tickets in a competition for the public and how that may be promoted and marketed.

- Where there is an environmental, arts or cultural connection related to the sponsorship funding. There will be an automatic desire to vet and restrict the types of sponsors that may be permitted to participate. This may even involve a process of vetting a company in respect of their international trade; waste; recycling and how their brand is perceived by the public.

- The organisers may offer opportunities subject to a declared policy of types of companies or products, services and other contributions which would not be allowed to provide funding or to be used at the event.

- The organisers of an event may also refuse some forms of sales and marketing by a sponsor due to licensing, planning and health, safety and security requirements at the venue for the event.

- The organisers may refuse to allow any perimeter advertising on the venue or even any large banners, flags or electronic displays. This may be in order for the organisers to comply with their own legal occupation of the site; planning consent issues and on a more subjective level the overall appearance of the festival to maintain an environment which meets the organisers own criteria of their brand for that event.

- There may be restrictions which ban leaflet distribution in total through the site or limit promotion to a hired location.

- There may be restrictions as to the total number of categories of vendors and sponsors for food, drink and other goods being sold and distributed.

- Logos and names may also appear on litter bins and sponsors may be obliged to contribute to clean up costs related to the disposal process. In addition all glass may be banned on site as a safety measure.

- An agreement may require the sponsor to have a minimum level of public liability cover and to supply a copy of the policy to the organisers with proof of payment of the premiums.

- There are clear advantages for addressing each case on its facts and setting the roles and responsibilities for costs and budgets, liabilities and indemnities from either party to each other. This enables risk to be reduced and also for finances to be kept within reasonable accountable parameters.

- The organiser would want to list a series of circumstances in which force majeure could be construed as applying including fire, evacuation due to smoke, floods, electrical or other power failure or ill health of major performers. The force majeure clause should also clarify how the budgeted costs are to be paid in such circumstances and who is liable and how the event is to be rescheduled if at all.

- In the event that circumstances arose in which the holding company for the organisers went into administration. Who will then either have access to or own the material which has been created to date? This may not be clear from the agreement and so clauses relating to the process of resolving disputes and claims by either party would assist in order to avoid delays and huge litigation costs.

- It is common for new marketing images and logos to be altered and adapted for festivals and events; with a new banner link advertising, products and slogans to specifically appeal in style and content to suit the audience attending. This new adaptation will have meant that new artwork and electronic material, sound recordings, films, photographs and text are commissioned, designed and delivered. It is vital that the issue of ownership of the material and rights of all this new adaptation is reviewed.

- So that where there is payment for a commissioned work that there is also a reciprocal written assignment of all rights in all media in all formats. There may also be a waiver of any future credits or acknowledgement or agreement that the artists' or contributors' role shall be acknowledged and the style and layout and location set out.

- Where a sponsorship agreement is for a particular individual who is an athlete or sportsperson. Then standards of behaviour not being adhered to may reasonably be set out as grounds of termination of the agreement. It is useful for all parties to refer to the sports body and any code of conduct which may exist, but also to be very clear as to behaviour which would be deemed unacceptable by the sponsor.

- This also works in reverse the individual may want to be able to terminate the agreement in the event that company with which he or she is involved with gets into financial difficulties or is associated with a political or activist campaign which the individual does not wish to be associated with and/or endorse.

- It is also important that an individual should be entitled to terminate an agreement with a sponsor where the sponsor becomes involved at a later date in promoting, selling or exploiting products or services which the individual finds offensive, derogatory or believes will damage their reputation and career. If the individual terminates the agreement on those grounds then it may be the case that either the sponsor shall be under no further liability to pay any other sums or that all further sums due under the agreement must be paid in full.

- Sponsorship can also be limited by duration and/or territory; what is actually sponsored and covered and specifically be limited to the parties and not be transferable to any third party.

- Demands and duties may be set out on both sides to create a complete picture. Often what is most forgotten is the use of logos, names, slogans and products in promotion and marketing material on line and on site at a venue. There could be a process of approvals or consultation even if the organisers still retain complete editorial control.

- It is useful to specify the date on which any rights to the sponsor in relation to the event cease and that the sponsor must not claim to be associated to a later event by implication. The sponsor may agree to remove all logos and titles and names relating to the event from its website, app, products and marketing.

- Sponsorship of a charity or other organisation may also take the form of payments for branding on products to gain the factor of commercial advantage by association with a cause which is perceived as worthwhile.

- The payments by the sponsor to the charity may then be linked to achievement of sales or completely unrelated and fixed as a total payment upfront or paid in stages.

- There are often many sponsors for an event, whether it is a marathon, a car rally or a festival who fund and support the project in relation to the venue with flags, banners and electronic displays, equipment, products being distributed during or after the event, the programme, the agreed credits for the radio and television coverage as well as the participants' shoes, clothes, drinks, bags, accessories, technology and mobiles.

- Additional payments or performance related bonuses can also be paid by a sponsor connected to the achievement of media coverage, audience targets, ticket sales, viewing figures and ratings as well as success at competitive races for an individual.

- Sponsorship is a growing form of promotion and the development of new and imaginative ways of collaborating necessarily means that slogans, names, logos, images, music and other rights are created which need to be protected and controlled. This applies both to the organisers of the event who are creating a new brand or the sponsors' who are trying out new modes of marketing. Failure to address the issue only results in unnecessary disputes at a later date which could have been avoided.

- The control and access to data of sales information, personal data of customers and expenditure and budget should also be dealt with in the agreement. Many organisers will not release personal data unless specific consent has been provided by an individual due to their need to comply with legislation.

- If there is any requirement for a sponsor to contribute to any expenditure or budget then how is evidence of this to be substantiated. If the organisers only wish to supply an invoice without any other supporting documents then this should be agreed. A maximum amount may be set as a limit which must not be exceeded.

- The question of the potential liability of the organisers or sponsor to pay any sums that may be due to any rights management organisation or collecting societies for any material recorded, performed, broadcast, reproduced or otherwise exploited which they use at any time should also be covered in the agreement. The parties will then clarify what material may need to be cleared and confirm who will be liable for the additional costs.

Archive assets for the future. Do you know who owns the new material you commission?

- It is very common these days for many different people within a company to be involved in the process of creating, developing and commissioning new material. Whether it the supply of new software and technology for your company, marketing and promotion, product design developers, editors, interns, researchers, executives, license managers or legal and business units.

- A failure to agree terms and for letter agreements or some other document to be signed often means that a company is not creating a useable archive of assets for the future. This avoidance is largely due to a perception that the creative process may be delayed or impeded or that any such process is unnecessary. If the only evidence of the arrangement is an exchange of emails then when in later years the question is asked: who owns this material? Then the answer to the question could go either way and be based on a factual examination of the material which exists looking for copyright notices and other credits.

- The importance of agreeing terms affects the livelihood of the designer, creator, artist, musician or songwriter or author and it is essential for them to consider whether they will want to retain ownership and control of the copyright and other rights in the original work and material as well as any subsequent adaptations.

- There has been numerous instances of material whether it be a design for a logo or a photograph or a contribution to a musical work or a sound recording or written work. Where parties have been involved in expensive litigation as a result of the failure to clarify the nature and extent of their agreement at the time.

- If you are only agreeing for the commissioned work to be used in a specific manner for the payment then spell it out clearly and reserve all the other rights. Then additional rights can be licensed at a later date and payments can be negotiated for those specific uses if you so choose.

- if the work is only licensed for one language and translations are not permitted then it is important this these details are set out. The more specific areas that are covered then the less likely there is to be disputes.

- The preferred route would be therefore to licence anything on a non-exclusive basis for a limited time period in a small area for a specific authorised purpose only. Everything else would be reserved and retained by the rights or copyright owner. This would effectively allow sales and exploitation elsewhere and increase advance payments over a period of time.

- The second choice would be to grant an exclusive licence for a small territory for a specific purpose for a fixed period. So that the licensee has a margin of exclusivity for those types of services or products in that zone but not for anything else. So the exclusivity might be limited to calendars but would not apply to household goods or other types of merchandise.

- Here it is very important to try to set out the exact nature of what is permitted and what is not in detail and to retain everything else whether those rights exist in a form you are aware of now or not.

- There have been many cases of older contracts not making any reference to new rights and technology and so performers and contributors have not been paid any additional royalties or payments when the material has been reproduced and exploited in that new medium. There have also in the past been disputes over whether a plastic children's book for the bath constitutes a book or whether it is a toy.

- You would want to avoid exclusive arrangements which in effect transfer copyright and other rights in all media to another party for the full period of copyright and in perpetuity. Unless of course that is what you wanted to achieve because the financial remuneration which you are being paid is sufficient for that disposal in effect to be worthwhile.

- It does not matter whether you have a start-up business and your friends are helping by doing some artwork and photographs or you have a successful company. In due diligence when a company is prepared for flotation for the stock market and all the representations are verified. The failure to have set up a library of documentation can affect both the final price and the speed at which matters can progress.

- It is a clear benefit to have a strategy to acquire, own and control either all or as many of the rights as feasible given the budget. As well as the actual material including the masters in everything you commission or exploit.

- This can be done by an assignment or buy out of all rights in all media in the title, content, prototype, any sample and the final product. Everything is handed over and stored for future use by the purchaser of all the rights.

- The agreement would also include resolving the issue of whether there would be a right to a credit or some other form of acknowledgement; and also whether moral rights were asserted or waived.

- It is useful to have a clause that makes it clear that the purchaser of the rights can edit, delete from, vary and adapt any part of the material and also use a third party to work on it or make a contribution. That in such instance there would be no need to consult with the creator and that all editorial control and rights to adapt or vary the material rest with the owner of the rights.

- The reverse scenario would be for the creator and originator to hold on to the majority of the rights and material and only licence a very narrow section for a limited period. This would have the effect over a period of time of generating the most revenue.

- Great care should be taken in deciding whether it in your interests to register your work with a rights management organisation or collecting society. It is vital that you understand the authority that you have handed to these organisations to licence your work. The range of areas now covered means that unless you are on their excluded list at your request. That you may find that they have licensed material to a third party without any consultation with you despite the fact that you are not a registered member and have never asked them to deal with your work. Where you do authorise them to act on your behalf they are effectively acting as your authorised representative and will often not be required to consult with you regarding any request or to seek your specific consent. The collecting societies meet a demand and collect revenues which in many cases would not otherwise be paid. So a strategy in relation to all collecting societies is important so that you do not find your work has been exploited in a manner which permits use by a third party in return for very little revenue. Collecting societies do not just licence and exploit by collecting sums for scanning, photocopying, reproduction, performance and broadcast and resale. They now cover extensive forms of exploitation. They serve a worthwhile function for many members but you need to understand the scope of what they do and look at each one separately.

- There have been many instances where large sums have been spent on websites, apps, computer games, podcasts and other projects which have failed as a result of the work never being finished within budget or to the quality required. It is important to set out what in expected and to be achieved for the budget and costs and to connect the payment to completion of tasks and delivery.

- There have been cases where websites or apps have not functioned properly; design quality has been poor and the budget has been exceeded. This then leads to additional requests for additional sums justified in terms of changes and alterations that were different from the original idea. Therefore scope for changes should have been factored into the original budget and seen as a predictable factor with a contingency.

- Many of these types of disputes have meant that some developers have refused to hand over all the codes, software and rights to the unfinished site or to let any other third party work on it. Even if the developer has been paid all the original sums in the agreed budget. So in a website or app development agreement the right to get someone else to work on the project and for the developer to hand over all the material and rights is a key term whether or not the project is completed.

- Where the artist, photographer or other creator has licensed a logo, artwork or photograph for a book cover, label, website or marketing tool, but you know the company wishes to exploit it in other media. Then it is to your advantage to agree terms and prices at the start of the project. If the book or website is very successful either in terms of traffic or revenue the payments to be made for sub-licencing and merchandising will increase significantly. There is no reason however why a creator should not be entitled to share in the benefits of contributing to a project which is financially successful. This may be achieved in the form of a bonus or escalating royalties or fixed payments.

- The streaming of material makes it important that rights are cleared or acquired across many types of medium. It is not acceptable to assume that as you have acquired the photograph for a book cover or contribution to a magazine that it may also be used by licensing it to a third party through a subscription service. Nor can it be adapted and the colours and medium changed to suit a promotional or marketing campaign if the terms of use and payment have not be agreed.

- Consideration has to be given not only to copyright notices, credits, acknowledgement of sources as well as trade marks and domain names, but also to the different forms of moral rights which exist and can be asserted.

- There are two aspects to moral rights the right to be identified as the creator of the work in the form of a reasonably prominent and identifiable credit but also the right not to have a work changed and adapted so that it is distorted and represented in a completely different way from the original without consent.

- In an archive you are either trying to get such moral rights waived as a matter of policy and then agreeing credits and notices or moral rights in all forms are asserted in detail and the expected layout, design, wording and any logos specified.

- An undertaking as to originality and the formats in which the work is to be delivered and at whose cost ensure that both parties are clear that material is not expected to be a copy or plagiarised from third parties.

- Where the work is expected to contain third party material then it helps if it is spelt out that all such material must be clearly identified and the extent of the information required ie title, author ISBN, publication date, page reference or format, where material is held and by whom together with contact details. The source reference in the delivered work may be less extensive than the additional list.

- Where technology is changing at such a rapid rate one of the issues which arises is whether a party has the right to exploit something which did not even exist at the time of the original agreement. This will depend on the terms of the agreement that the parties concluded and how widely the clauses were drafted and/or if payments of royalties were only related to certain forms of exploitation which were listed. There have been many instances where artists and performers have not received any further payments for television series being exploited in new services over the internet and subscription services or in the form of merchandising. This failure to receive any sums could have been avoided if the agreements had specifically reserved the rights or had an additional clause which made reference to future rights and developments and set a rate or fee to be paid. That would be the case even it was not certain by what method or format those rights would be exploited.

Focus on Termination clauses

Scope of the grounds for termination

- The scope of the grounds for termination are important and the failure to address this issue may have significant financial consequences either to a company or an individual. It is possible to draft specific termination clauses for each of the parties to an agreement with different grounds of termination. Many agreements still use the same general clauses for both parties.

- The clause may refer for instance to the right to terminate the agreement on one or more of the following reasons in the event that:

  - there is a material breach of the agreement which is not remedied within a specific period after notification of the problem.

  - there are alleged breaches of specific clauses of the agreement.

  - there is a delay in or failure to deliver or complete work.

  - there is a delay in or failure to account or make payments due.

  - the company ceases trading.

  - there is court order to wind up the company.

  - the company is trading while insolvent.

  - the company is put into receivership or administration.

- Any of these type of grounds may be specified as sufficient for one party to service notice of termination on the other under the agreement.

- A sponsorship agreement or a contract for services may include other matters for grounds of termination by a company to an individual. If a person:

  - fails a drug test.

  - does not pass a medical assessment.

  - becomes involved in a political controversy.

  - posts on social media any material which could potentially damage the reputation of the company, its products and brand.

  - or is alleged to have committed or has actually been found guilty of a criminal act.

- There are also other additional grounds for termination that may be set out in an agreement which relate to regulatory bodies, legislation, Codes of Practice and internal corporate policies.

- Where for instance the actions of an individual could put a television or media company at risk of an investigation by a regulatory body such as Ofcom or could pose a threat to its right to operate under a commercial licence.

- The list of grounds can be very wide based on an assessment of the potential variety of scenarios which may arise in relation to the person and the company.

Procedure for notification and termination

- The method and process of notification of termination should be clear and there should be an obligation to provide some reasons as to the grounds for the termination. Termination must be served in the manner set out in the contract and also on the correct party. Failure to do so will not constitute valid notice.

- You may agree to a procedure so that where notice of any alleged reasons for termination are served. That on each occasion there is a fixed period in which the other party may have the opportunity to remedy the problem.

- In the event that the problem cannot be resolved the parties may also agree to hold informal discussions which are not binding as a means to try to avoid termination or litigation.

- Alternative dispute resolution, mediation and arbitration clauses may also be included in the agreement. The question will be whether these choices are optional or binding as a method of resolution of any dispute.

- It is normal practice to reserve the right of one party or the other to take any legal action that they may deem necessary without prejudice to any prior methods that may be considered. Unless of course the parties have specifically agreed otherwise.

Potential claims

- There may also be a potential future claim for loss of fees, expenses, costs as well as damages for the consequent effect on the reputation of a person or company of the termination. Therefore a contractual commitment that the person or company will not make any such claim if the contract is validly terminated on the agreed grounds may be one means of limiting liability.

- Any termination is inevitably linked to the detail and description of what the other party was required to fulfil or supply under the agreement. As well as those dates by which it was crucial the work was completed.

- The right to terminate can be included at many different stages of a contract for example when material is delivered which is not of the quality and standard required or when the other party seeks to transfer the agreement to a third party to fulfil the work.

- It is to your advantage to be very specific as to the work required and the quality and standard to be achieved for any project.

- It is also a good idea to put in place contractual obligations where at different stages the progress of a project can be assessed and reviewed. It is possible to link these assessments to grounds of termination where it is clear that the project is unlikely to succeed or be completed in the manner intended.

- Development agreements for websites and apps are a classic example where large budgets are agreed but there may be a failure to achieve the operational and functional aspects which were a crucial part of the plan which was discussed at the outset for the agreed budget. You may be faced with no option but to pay more money as you do not have any right to terminate the agreement and take the project to another third party.

- It is also possible to include an agreed fixed sum that the other party would receive at any such stage if termination were served on valid grounds. On the basis that they would then not make any further claim or demand additional sums for further work. The key difference is that these issues would be argued at the negotiation stage not after work has commenced.

Excluding certain grounds of termination

- You may seek to exclude certain grounds so that using the company email account or mobile for personal use are specifically accepted by both parties as not grounds for termination.

- Other matters which may be excluded may be for example a delay in delivery of less than a week or failure to complete a project by the date required due to the absence of key personnel for up to one month.

- You may insist on the fact that a whole order be fulfilled at once or be satisfied for any shortfall to be made up in a subsequent delivery.

- In a sponsorship agreement an excluded ground of termination may be the fact that the person does not take part in or win a specific event or is unable to complete their work due to their own ill health or that of an immediate family member.

- The relationship between the force majeure and termination clauses in the agreement is also relevant. If grounds for force majeure exist and one party is served. What will happen? Is the agreement suspended? Can immediate termination take place? How long can the grounds for force majeure be allowed to continue before one party will be entitled serve notice of termination?

Consequences of termination

- It is preferable that an agreement sets out in detail the likely matters that will arise in the event that one or both parties serves notice to terminate. There are crucial questions that could be addressed at the drafting stage which should be stated. Who will own the copyright, intellectual property rights, electronic, computer software rights and registrations in the new material which has been developed including any logos, images, text, films, websites, apps, domain names or trade marks. It should not be assumed that it necessarily follows that the company that has expended the budget will own those rights.

- In a merchandising agreement the licensor may seek to ensure that the rights which have been granted to the licensee revert back to the licensor in the event of termination by either party.

- Further that any new rights which have been created and any new material are also to be assigned to the licensor by the licensee. This may require additional documents being concluded in the form of an assignment from the licensee to the licensor.

- There is also the question of any stock or products that still may be held by the other party as well as models, samples, prototypes and moulds which may exist. Together with master copies of material, packaging, marketing and all the documentation, records and data which have been created. You may wish to have an obligation in the agreement for this material to be returned at your cost or to have the right to purchase it all for a nominal sum.

- A person who has an agency or management agreement with a company may want a clause which ends the right of the company to receive any percentage of any future income in the event that the agreement is validly terminated for certain reasons.

- Where a distribution agreement Is terminated by a licensor you would not want a situation where there is no further right to be paid any revenue that may be received. A licensor would still want the right to receive payments of all sums received at any time and to be accounted to by the distributor after the date of termination in relation to the product or service.

- It is useful to think through the potential scenario of the wish to terminate the agreement in the future. You may wish to terminate an agreement for instance because there has been a change of control of the other company. Does the agreement allow you to do this?

- Where there are insufficient grounds stated in an agreement then one party often tries to identify grounds which seem plausible but which are not specified. This makes it more likely that expensive litigation will follow unless a settlement can be reached.

- You may therefore also wish to think about including clauses which allow you to end an agreement at different dates without stating any grounds at all. In which case you would merely need to serve notice that the end date stipulated is being used.

Financial matters in a contract

Work through the calculations

- This article is intended to give you an idea of just some of the ways that you can improve the amount of money you receive under a variety of agreements. It is not addressing the other aspects such as accounting periods and procedures, inspection of accounts and records, interest, allocating budgets or other costs and expenses.

- If the aim of the agreement is to make money and not lose it then time must be taken to really understand and evaluate the whole money cycle of the agreement.

- How are any costs and expenses to be assessed and agreed? Is it intended that all the costs and expenses shall be recouped from the future receipts? If you have no right to approve the costs and expenses is there any total limit which caps the expenditure? There may be a limit set for a six month accounting period or for the whole agreement.

- What expenses cannot be recouped? You will not for instance wish to pay for an agents' administrative staff and other normal business costs whether travel, hospitality or marketing.

- You may limit the agents' payment entirely to the percentage commission which they will receive on the sums they actually receive. If so it should be made clear that no additional sums can be deducted, claimed or will be paid.

- The biggest failure under most contracts is lack of concern made to really examine what money if any will be made and what costs and expenses will be legitimately deducted.

- The scope of the authorised deductions or the defined distribution expenses may be so wide that in fact you never receive any sums under an agreement.

- It is crucial that you take the time to go through the actual potential figures and create a route map to work out the true financial picture.

- It will help you ask questions to clarify the charges for commission, costs and deductions that may be made. Just how many companies and third parties will be entitled to payment and when and how will those sums be deducted.

- Your royalties under the agreement may be calculated in relation to the money that is actually finally received. So if there are numerous off the top costs you will receive considerably less in royalties.

- The method by which money will be paid and how it will be held and by whom is not irrelevant and should be considered.

Advances and royalties

- The most obvious aspect to first consider is to negotiate a higher advance and percentage rates of the future royalties. A higher advance is based largely on showing that there are a number of unique aspects to a project and that it has the potential to reach a high level of targeted sales.

- How do you do that? You create a synopsis, marketing and strategy report which describes the features of your project in detail including any new titles, names, trade marks or images.

- In addition set out information regarding direct competitors or other similar products or services to your own. How is your product or service different? Describe and identify your audience and potential market and itemise the selling points of any features.

- Advances are often paid in stages including for example:

  a. within a specified number of days of signature by both parties.

  b. subject to delivery of stipulated master material being accepted.

  c. within a number of days of approval of a sample or prototype.

  d. subject to the broadcast or transmission of a film, image or sound recording.

  e. subject to delivery and acceptance of a manuscript.

  f. subject to publication of a hardback or paperback book.

  g. subject to the distribution of a product and sale to the public.

- It is likely that the advance may be linked to the delivery of material or the completion of certain work or the use of certain copyright and other intellectual property rights by the other party.

- Regardless of this fact always consider whether there should be a series of dates by which in any event money will be paid to you whether the event has taken place or work has been completed or not.

- Royalty percentages can be very low or very high. Do not accept the usual argument that a rate is standard in an industry. That is a deliberate tactic to pay you as little as possible.

- Is the other party really only acting as an agent and not really creating or contributing to the production of the new material or rights?

- An author for translation rights is often offered 70–85% of the sums received by a publishing or media company. Whereas they may only be offered 7–10% of the published price for a hardback or paperback in the home market in the United Kingdom. This is despite the fact that there are publishing agreements where much higher rates of 12, 15, 17.5 and 20% are agreed with the authors on the published price.

- Royalty rates for the overseas market outside the United Kingdom are often related to the sums received by a publisher. That is after a third party distributor has received the money from the sales, deducted their commission and maybe also other costs and then transferred the money. Again the royalty rates may be very low or much higher and escalate as the volume of sales increases over a period of time.

- The royalty payments for syndication of an image, article or other format from a website, app or from a streaming global series may be a small fixed unit cost in each country or area or managed through a rights management organisation which collects the funds from multiple parties for specific types of uses and then allocates the funds to it registered members according to its own policies and procedures. You may not necessarily receive through a rights management organisation what you consider to be commercial royalty rates and payments. On the other hand they will be able to collect funds which you may never even have realised you were due for your work. If you do not want to be registered then contact them and get your work listed as an excluded work that they have no right to licence. These types of organisations often act in a very presumptive manner towards the use of third party material.

- The payments that you receive for any royalty are directly connected to how the original pot of money from which you receive your percentage is defined. Great care should therefore be taken to understand whether you are receiving a percentage of gross or net receipts or whether it is based on sums received. Some gross receipts definitions are actually when you read them not gross at all but net. There is a long list of deductions that are permitted buried in the definition. There have been many feature film distribution agreements where no royalties have been paid as the costs of production, marketing, contracts, rights, legal, endorsements, merchandising and advertising have been recouped and deducted.

- If there is no prospect of the other party exploiting certain rights or formats then you are better off keeping them rather than agreeing to a token royalty rate which is low.

- I do not intend to list all the potential royalty rates for different formats or rights but whatever you are offered. Remember that there is always room for improvement. Shorten the term of the licence. Limit the rights and formats. Limit the territory or countries covered. Do not allow adaptations without consent. Seek to control all the associated rights and trade marks that may be created and registered.

- Do not allow the definition of the various formats or rights to be each so widely defined that there are only a few royalty rates and payments.

Expiry or termination

- You need to check whether you will continue to be entitled to receive payment of any royalties which accrue after the termination or expiry of both the main agreement and any sub-licences.

- No sub-licence should be longer than the original main licence. However if the main licence expires or is terminated you still want the right to be accounted to and paid all your royalties either as before or directly from a third party sub-licensee.

- Stock is also worth money – so will the old stock be sold off or destroyed or can you have ownership transferred to you at a nominal cost or can it be delivered to you for free?

- The moulds, samples, designs and all the accompanying documentation and records are also valuable assets. Will you be entitled to claim ownership of this material?

New future developments, formats and rights

- If you are receiving royalties derived from a long list of forms of exploitation such as publishing, merchandising, film, television, music, downloads, apps, sponsorship, brand endorsement and other forms of media. Against each type of definition or description of a format will be a royalty rate. It is unlikely that your list will cover all the potential forms of exploitation even if it is very long.

- It is important to ensure that all the future new rights and methods of exploitation of products, services, games and other developments are either subject to a new agreement in each case as you have reserved those rights and formats or you have set a fixed rate royalty based on the sums received or some other basis which can be applied.

- Failure to address the issue of new rights, technology and formats which arise after the contract has been signed may lead to the other party exploiting those rights and not paying you any sums for them at all. As it will be argued that if you were due a payment a royalty rate would have been stated and from which figures the payment was to be derived.

- The best option is to reserve and keep some existing rights, formats and developments as well as all those created in the future. That may include for instance some existing methods such as theme parks, holograms, emojis, sequels, adaptations and licensing of trade marks and collaborations with third parties. You therefore limit the licence you grant on each occasion to the absolute minimum of what you wish to licence and exploit and no more.

Increasing royalties

- You may negotiate escalating royalties so that you can receive a sequence of higher percentages after a specified number of units of a product are sold or when fixed financial targets are attained. These figures may be very high and appear unrealistic at the time of negotiation but reap great rewards if the project is an unexpected spectacular success.

- Your royalties may be linked to attainment of sales worldwide or specific countries, but the level of royalties increases significantly in jumps of five to ten per cent. If you do not do this when the project is amazingly successful when you look at a cake and your royalties are a slice. Your slice will be very small compared to the other section retained by the company which you have licensed.

Bonus

- It is possible to incorporate a series of bonus payments which relate to identifiable success. An athlete may receive an additional sum from a sponsor for winning a medal. A sponsor may pay an additional fee if the attendance figures at a festival or event substantially exceed expectations and reach a high agreed figure. If the author or director is nominated or wins a particular prize then an additional bonus figure may be due

Limit deductions

- The agreement should establish what deductions may be permitted before any royalty or other sums are paid to you. A blanket statement that marketing costs may be deducted may result in you receiving no sums at all. So you may wish to put a total capped amount on the deductions which are allowed as a whole or in relation to certain specified subjects.

- You may require that If any such sums are to be deducted that supporting evidence must be provided of the expenditure.

- You may set a financial limit for deductions which cannot be exceeded which relates to an accounting period or each year of the contract or the term of the agreement.

Clearances, costs and expenses

- It is vital to understand and list in detail in discussions the cost and expenses that the other party may incur and which they must pay in full. Their responsibility for these costs and expenses should also be stated in the agreement.

- It helps to ensure that none of these sums can be deducted prior to the calculation and payment of any sums due to you. It makes it clear that they cannot seek to make you pay a contribution.

- Examples of potential issues include production costs, health and safety tests and assessments, trade mark registrations and legal costs, designs, artwork and packaging costs, advertising and marketing in print, on social media and by endorsements by third parties. As well as clearance of copyright and intellectual property rights and all the payments that may fall due.

- A contract should identify which company or person must be responsible for and obtain clearances for the use of any intellectual property rights including copyright, trade marks and any other consents that may be required including performances, transmissions and broadcasts.

- This matter needs to be dealt with in relation to two main areas for which the facts and terms are not necessarily the same. The first is the original rights and material and the second is the creation and development of any new rights and new material.

- Note here that clearance or obtaining consent for something is not the same as being liable for the payment.

- A contract must set out the responsibility for the payment of the sums due for such clearances and consents both for the original rights and material and any new developments and forms of exploitation.

- Such costs may include reproduction of master material, software, music, text, scripts, mechanical reproduction, performance of a work, payments due to rights management organisations and collecting societies, use of photographs and images, videos, films, material from podcasts and websites, logos and trade marks and/or use of other products, services or artwork owned by third parties.

- It is a useful exercise to endeavour to predict all the costs and expenses which might be relevant to your project. The topics may then be dealt with in the contract to establish who is responsible for the payment of such sums.

- Examples include freight, import and export charges and custom duties, hotel, travel and mobile phone, broadband and data storage costs, bank charges, currency conversion costs and insurance.

- Other potential costs cover recall of any defective products; power failures and problems with the supply of source materials. The cost of manufacture and reproduction of any products, samples, packaging, advertising and marketing.

- There may be costs and expenses for ill-health and incapacity of a person who is a significant part of a project as well as sums for legal and professional advisors; the registration of domain names, trade marks and administration.

Notice Period

- Where you are the consultant or person engaged by a company. Then you may seek to agree a long period of notice before termination can take place under the agreement. The longer the notice period then the more money the company may have to pay to bring the agreement to an end under that notice period.

- In reverse a short notice period for termination may help you minimise costs.

Non-Exclusive or Exclusive Licence

- It is always preferable to grant a non-exclusive licence rather than an exclusive licence. As the non-exclusive licence does not prevent you from granting the exact same rights to a third party. Provided that there is no additional restriction or prohibition in the agreement.

- The only value to granting an exclusive agreement is if the consideration which you are receiving reflects the fact that you are not selling the same rights elsewhere while the licence exists.

Licence Period and reversion of rights

- There is an advantage in negotiating and agreeing a very short licence period and avoiding the grant of a licence for the full period of copyright.

- If you grant an exclusive licence for one year or three years or ten years. Then at the end of that licence period you may grant another exclusive licence and receive additional advances and royalties in respect of the same rights.

- Note that you should try to ensure that at the end of the licence period that all rights in the original work and material and in any new work and material revert to you the licensor rather than remain with any licensee or distributor.

Limit how the rights are defined

- There is a commercial benefit to you if you limit the type of right that you grant to a licensee or other third party and are very specific as to the format and the scope of the rights granted.

- You can do this by being very descriptive as to what is actually licensed and what is not.

- If you are not authorising the right to reproduce, adapt and exploit the rights in any other form of exploitation. Then it is vital that you exclude those rights and formats from the agreement and include examples of those excluded areas. Even within a category such as books or toys you can limit the market further. So for instance you may license teddy bears but not any other form of toys or dolls. You do not have to license the whole sector to one party as there is no financial benefit.

- If you grant a right to reproduce a character from a book as a toy in an approved way. Then also confirm that there is no right to acquire the right to register the name as a trade mark or to create other products around it or to create a theme park or hold a festival based on that character.

- In a sponsorship agreement it is necessary to confirm whether or not the sponsor has the right to film at the site and if so under what circumstances. How is the sponsor permitted to use the name of the festival and those that appear in any stage show or sports events?

- It is also important to clarify whether the sponsor has the right to use the images and names of those who appear in the show and events and if so in what manner.

- The contract may require that a new agreement needs to be negotiated and concluded for each new proposal by the sponsor.

- It maybe that the sponsor may only be authorised to use any image or name with the express prior approval of an artist or athlete and the organisers.

- The sponsor would be obliged to supply an exact example of the intended project together with copies of any associated marketing or advertising. The sponsor may also be obliged to pay additional fees to the artist or athlete and organisers in consideration of their consent and approval.

Allowances and additional benefits

- A television or podcast presenter may ask a company to pay a myriad of expenses which are necessary to keep up to date with the latest news and to create a suitable appearance on screen.

- These costs may be a fixed allowance or subject to an annual limit and the supply of relevant invoices and receipts.

- Examples of the type of costs which could be covered include hairdressing, spas, dental work, clothes, travel, entertainment, accommodation, technology, equipment, mobiles and security.

- There may also be additional payments due as part of the agreement for interviews, filming and photographic sessions and marketing; attending a number of functions and other promotional work.

- There are other benefits which may be agreed for an individual which may be requested. Examples include health cover, additional security, company credit cards, share options if the company is floated on the stock exchange, extended paid leave of absence; appointment as a director; options to extend the agreement which are then subject to increased payments; relocation costs and loans or payment for property rental or purchase. This is despite the fact that some of these financial and indirect benefits may be subject to tax.

The benefits of quality control clauses

Pre-contract

- It makes sense as part of your pre-contract discussions to ask for samples of a similar type of product and its packaging so that you can look at the quality involved.

- Do not rely on a quotation alone as to what actually will be delivered.

- Are there also other examples of successfully completed projects in which the company has been involved which they can identify and compare to yours without disclosing confidential information? This may help in both the budgeting and predicting potential problems.

- What health and safety tests and assessments do they carry out in relation to the product or service?

- Does the company belong to any recognised organisations?

- What compliance policies does the company have?

- Which Codes of Practice, guidelines and legislation do they adhere to?

- Does the company use third parties to carry out work, safety tests or assessments? If so will you have access to information regarding these third parties and their reports and data?

- Who monitors international and national legal requirements and how will you be notified of any changes?

- Where are factories or distributors based? What is their approach to child labour, environmental issues, recycling, waste and pollution? If your company has a green and sustainability policy as part of its brand promotion then this will all be relevant.

- In the book there are main clause headings for Compliance, Environmental, Fair Trading, Product Liability and Quality Control.

- The answers to the above issues can be addressed in the main contract to any extent you choose. The more detail in the agreement as to the standards to be achieved then the more obligations you are imposing on the other party.

- If there is a complete absence of any stipulated minimum level of standards, quality of work and tests. Then you will have no undertakings to fall back on which have been incorporated in the agreement. In which case you will be in a much weaker position to argue that the company is in breach of the agreement when there are problems.

Setting a benchmark

- At every stage look at the standard of performance and quality control that you wish to achieve and set out those detailed requirements in the main agreement or in the form of attached schedules.

- This may cover the designs and how original material is to be commissioned, the colours, specifications, content and materials to be used, the packaging, labels, safety warnings, disclaimers, trade mark and copyright notices and many other aspects about which you want clarity.

- Specify the exact product or service or event you require in as much detail as possible.

- Also consider all the related matters such as the preparations before, the approvals process if any and all the surrounding marketing.

- Ensure that there are clauses which mean that you must approve the use of third parties or be sent samples of artwork, packaging, products and other material before production is finalised. At each stage your consent and approval should be sought.

- Where your approval is not provided the company should be obliged to rectify the problem and resubmit another draft or sample.

- Who will pay the cost of any additional work if there are numerous drafts or samples produced which are not accepted?

- There should be a requirement in the contract that the company provide sufficient evidence of compliance with current health and safety legislation in the countries where the product is to be sold.

- You should not rely on historical tests. You may wish to insist that you have the right to access and be supplied with copies of all the tests, assessments, data and reports. This will enable you to ensure that they are accurate and valid. This is also relevant to the issue of product liability.

- Where the project is an event, podcast series, app or media campaign then you can set out what you expect to achieve as goals to be attained. Here you would include a synopsis of the proposed location, planned layout, duration, content, contributors, music, sound recordings and production personnel that are confirmed. As well as expected target audience, print, social media advertising and endorsements that are planned within the proposed budget.

- Do not assume that the demonstration video, presentation or representations in discussions will equate to what will actually be supplied, delivered or fulfilled. If the description in the contract is very vague or inadequate you will have very little evidence to rely upon when there is an argument about what has not been done.

- If specialist experts or third party authorised material is required for a project then it should be stated.

Termination

- The party who has commissioned the work or service or booked the event may decide that the service, product or event is below the agreed standard. They shall then have the right set out in the agreement to serve notice of termination.

- The contract should be clear as to whether any sums will be refunded and whether any sums already paid can be retained.

- Where a company has commissioned a supplier and the sample product or final version has been rejected due to concerns regarding quality control. The company needs to be able to rely on a clause to terminate the contract.

- In addition there needs to be a clause that makes it quite clear that the company will not be liable for any further costs.

- The company is unlikely to get a refund of the money it has already spent but there is no liability going forward.

- Where the contract requires a website, app or audio file to be developed ensure that the operational aims are listed.

- If the budget is spent or exceeded without any degree of functionality being achieved. The agreement needs to address the issue of whether you will be entitled to all the rights and material and to take the project elsewhere for a third party to complete.

- Many development contracts fail to set any criteria as to what actually has to be completed and how it is to be stored or function. This allows the developer to seek more funding for additional work and argue that they have delivered the project even though quality is low.

- Whether you are commissioning a podcast, app, website or a hologram. it is crucial that a very detailed description of how it is to work is set out in a schedule which forms part of the contract.

Contract based on the facts

- A major failure in procurement contracts and automated software is the lack of attention that is paid to the particular facts of each scenario. No detailed information is added which creates additional obligations and undertakings from one party to other outside the prepared text.

- It is not a good idea to expect that the assurances you received in a meeting will be remembered in five years' time.

- The contract is intended to be a record of the terms agreed between the parties so why would you not describe the fundamental aspects of the extent and level of work that is required.

- It is to the advantage of the other party for the specifications to be left vague and general.

- The source of the material and the ingredients as well as dimensions, colour, structure and function or purpose must be described in relation to any sample, final product or service.

- Attach to the main agreement long descriptions and detailed information in schedules including for example two or three dimensional images, product names, logos, materials to be used or a list of the persons to be commissioned for each part of the project.

- You do not have to limit the drafting of the terms of the contract to commission any work to the terms of the quotation you have been offered.

- If you are appointing a distributor who is arranging for the manufacture of a product. You can have a series of quality control clauses so that your approval and consent is sought at every stage.

- You may also want quality control clauses relating to the packaging, social media strategy and marketing. You therefore list your proposed aims in the agreement.

- The agreement may require the distributor to send you a strategy and marketing report for your consideration and that a meeting must be held with the relevant personnel to discuss the options. This process may be for consultation purposes or for your approval to be obtained. This procedure could happen once a year or on a more regular basis but helps to create a good working relationship.

- In such circumstances you may be consulted rather than have formal approval, but there is still a considerable degree of input and control which can be attained.

- There may for instance be certain types of websites or apps on which you would not want your product promoted as their content is not aligned to your brand.

- If your requirements are listed in the agreement and are very specific and clear. When there are serious problems for any reason you are able to point out that this level and standard of work was agreed as part of the contract. This puts you in a very much stronger position as the other party cannot claim that there was any misunderstanding or lack of communication.

Payments linked to tasks

- It is common for staged payments to be linked to approval of a prototype, draft material or a completed product. You also need clauses which set out the consequences if any material is rejected.

- Payments may also be linked to delivery dates and supply of material, health and safety reports and tests, launch dates or connected to release and sale of of a product or service in different countries.

Social media and marketing

- Every company is now sensitive to the impact on their sales and brand of adverse publicity. You may insist on clauses which allow you greater control over what is used to promote your product or service on a third party site whether it be a distributor or licensee.

- You want to be in a position where you can insist that content is deleted, amended or completely changed.

- You may insist that your product or service is not displayed in conjunction with other types of material which you believe are detrimental to your image. This may apply to an individual or a company. So instead of threatening legal proceedings you would have a legal right within the agreement to make specific requests that must be complied with.

Timescales

- The dates by which work is to be completed, material delivered or an event arranged should all be stipulated. Where it is essential that the dates are adhered to then add the words 'time is of the essence'.

- You may also state that the dates cannot be changed or waived for any reason.

- You may also put in a clause which says that even if you waive one date that does not mean you waive all the others.

- What happens when there is a delay? Are you entitled to all your money back? Are you still liable to pay the rest of the money under the contract despite the delay?

- At this point you then need to consider other types of clauses relating to cancellation, force majeure, suspension and termination.

Packaging and Promotions

- Treat the design, cover and promotion as an important element and clarify what will be developed and who will be completing the work.

- Then have in place a system of approvals of samples and finished versions which you can approve or reject in all formats and languages.

- If you have no such right then insist upon the right to be consulted so that your views can be considered.

- This will enable you to check credits, copyright notices, trade marks, logos, domain names and images which the contract states should be displayed on all copies and on any advertising, marketing and packaging.

Liability

- You cannot exclude liability for personal injury or death and product liability equates to a very high level of duty of care and responsibility. The quality control provisions assist you in creating an environment where you are not only monitoring standards but making it clear at the outset what is expected to be achieved.

- An agreement can fail at any stage and so there is a need for clauses which provide a method for problems to be resolved prior to litigation.

- There are a number of options which are not mutually exclusive and the parties may agree different ways of resolving disputes. The simplest is for one party to notify the other of the disputed facts and for discussions to take place to resolve the matter. Other options include dispute resolution, arbitration, mediation and nomination of a third party or governing body to provide a report and a non-binding decision. The agreement should clarify who will pay any costs that may be incurred for any of these choices.

Reasons to review and update your contracts

Creating Archives

- Every business whether a start-up or a company with a significant track record should have an archive of all the agreements, licences and other arrangements it has concluded.

- Similarly there should an archive related to corporate, copyright and intellectual property rights. This may include for instance commissioning documents related to logos and artwork, applications for trade mark registrations, records relating to rights management organisations and consents for use of material or registrations with regulatory organisations.

- The legal and business affairs aspects of a business are often treated as secondary to the main target of making money. However good contracts generate money and create identifiable intellectual property assets which have a value.

- If your company does become very successful the failure to have recorded all the necessary steps of the business transactions will impact on the due diligence which will be necessary for any sale or listing on the stock exchange or other market.

- Procedures need to be put in place to ensure that agreements are not being concluded by personnel who have little comprehension of the terms and who are merely issuing pro forma contracts with itemised blanks to be filled in. Multiple unqualified people in a company issuing agreements often results in poor archive records, costly mistakes and unnecessary litigation.

- Where in the early days of a start-up you are using friends or family that does not mean that you should not have a written record of the terms of your arrangement which you both sign.

- If you do not conclude a written agreement you expose yourself to the very serious risk of a legal action in the future. A person may seek to claim that they contributed to all the original work and are entitled to a share of the revenue.

Contracts and businesses both evolve

- When someone says that a contract is 'standard' or 'pro forma' it is more than likely that you are being presented with an out of date document which blatantly favours one party over another. It is also predictable that there will be a complete absence of anything more than the bare minimum of obligations. There are many different variations of agreements which can be drafted based on the same facts. The proposition that a contract is 'standard' is merely a mechanism used to get you to agree to sign a bad contract.

- There is the mistaken belief that generic agreements can be just rolled out with only minor editing to suit the circumstances for many years.

- Contracts need to be reviewed and amended regularly so that your business makes changes that are needed to address problems that have arisen in disputes.

- In addition basic corporate details may be out of date. The wrong company name listed or the address not updated. Some contracts even completely omit jurisdiction and governing law clauses. You may be surprised what fundamental clauses are often absent.

- There may be new legislation that should be considered, Codes of Practice and guidelines which may have an impact on the terms you wish to include in your documents.

- New technology, methods of exploitation and marketing will all give rise to copyright and intellectual property rights in new areas and other legal issues.

- The extent of social media marketing and the use of videos, images, sound recordings and collaborations and cross-promotions all result in extensive use of rights across many formats and media. This means that those rights must be acquired and bought out by an assignment or cleared and licensed for specific purposes.

- Where an author or artist is delivering a project there is now far greater movement in contracts allowing the author or artist greater involvement in the final decisions which might be taken. Although final editorial control may still rest with the publisher or the company. new clauses allow greater consultation through the production, distribution and marketing stages.

New rights and means of exploitation

- The definitions in an agreement may need to be refined to either expand the scope of the meaning or to reduce it. If you are a company buying in material and rights you acquire widely; if you are licensing material or rights to a third party you do so as narrowly as possible.

- There are methods of using, selling, distributing and making money out of material which did not exist twenty years ago. Blogs, apps, accounts to promote photos, videos and films, emojis, podcast series and audio recordings are all new formats. Some methods fall within existing definitions of rights and some are ambiguous and can be argued either way.

- Online competitions, bingo, gambling as well as computer games, theme parks, themed costumes, festivals, musical tours, jewellery, food and drinks and gifts are all expanding markets which may not have been dealt with in an agreement.

- New product lines may lead to the creation of new logos and artwork which you may wish to register as a trade mark. If you have not had an assignment from the person who created the work or there is no relevant clause within their employment contract. Then you may find that your business does not own the rights.

- Anyone who creates new material in any form whether it is images, sound recordings, music or merchandising for your company should be asked to sign a short form assignment document as a matter of policy.

Territory and language

- You may wish to expand the countries which fall within the authorised territory or to add additional languages into which you can translate or adapt the material.

- Do you need to make the contract worldwide rather than risk being in a technical breach?

- If the territory is defined too narrowly it could result in a serious loss of income in the future. It may also result in you being unable to exploit rights in a global market.

- You may wish to add an option for other languages which can be exercised by the payment of a nominal sum in each case.

Liability and indemnity

- The main clause headings, liability, risk, legal proceedings and indemnity are all important in any agreement. They may need to be amended to protect a company or individual.

- You may wish to set stringent standards for the other party to fulfil as well as require compliance with new codes and guidelines.

- The assessment of risk either in terms of the cost of potential litigation or the effect on the brand of a company has now changed. More stringent conditions apply to factory conditions and how products are produced and tested as well how they are certified and labelled.

- Where the services of a company or a person do not meet the criteria set in the agreement for a role. Where does the blame lie and who will be liable for the impact on any project?

- Identify potential issues and make a decision as to what the consequences will be if something goes wrong.

- If you do not want to accept liability then make it clear who is responsible and make sure that there is a wide indemnity from that other party to your company or you as an individual.

- Where you are liable and provide an indemnity to another party you may wish to set a procedure for any claim or set a limit on the time period for the indemnity or the amount where possible.

- You cannot however exclude liability for personal injury or death where you can be held accountable.

- As part of this process you may also consider whether there are any insurance policies available which would help cover the risk. Although it should be noted many are full of exemptions which may exclude certain circumstances.

- There is often failure to state who owns the rights to all the different types of material which have been developed if an agreement is terminated. If an agent or distributor goes out of business you want to be able to point at a clause in a contract which establishes your ownership of certain rights and master material.

- You may wish to expand your right to sub-licence and exploit merchandising relating to the main project. The right to arrange for the publication of a book and audio recording related to the film or podcast series based on the same title. The right to authorise a series of events or festivals based on the same title of the podcast series.

- Where a supplier has a close working relationship with a retailer the agreement may be revised to set out more detailed facets of the relationship which are being developed. This may include agreeing on a whole series of policies which will impact on the brand of the retailer and the products or services.

Costs and payments

- An analysis of the total expenditure which a company incurs under each agreement such as returns, freight, packaging, insurance, marketing and currency conversion charges often pinpoints costs which were not expected.

- Many contracts are constantly reissued as pro forma despite the fact that the work which is being completed under the agreement has considerably altered. The only evidence of the additional payments due may be through an exchange of emails.

- If you work out what money has been received and paid out under the different types of contracts it will help you identify effective changes in the drafting that will reduce costs and liability.

- Where the agreement requires that new material is created or rights must be cleared and paid for before it can be used. Who is responsible for ensuring that the clearance of the copyright or other intellectual property rights actually happens? Who is liable to pay the costs of the payments and the reproduction costs?

- If you make a list of what material and rights exist and then what is to be created and how it is to be used. You will then be able to identify which person, rights management organisations and collecting societies may be relevant. If you are not sure then contact them and ask do not avoid the issue. Just because material and rights are cleared and paid for in one instance it does not mean that it can be used in another format or manner. You need someone to clear material and rights who understands the whole picture. This is an area which is often forgotten in projects and may prove to be an expensive part of the budget.

- There have been a number of companies which have lost large sums as they have allowed distributors to hold sums on their behalf and not insisted on monies being processed and paid swiftly.

- You should not want any company or agent to build up large reserves of money on your behalf. The review of the accounting dates, procedures and payments is worthwhile. Is it possible for payments to be made more often? Modern technology means that many of the old arguments for delays are obsolete.

- You can also improve the clauses which relate to the supply of data relating to the product or service. Data protection legislation should not restrict you from being supplied with a more detailed breakdowns in terms of figures and unit sales relating to different countries and markets. You may also wish to request a report in terms of the problems and forecast in each sector.

Key issues which apply to contracts

Name of parties and third party transfers

- The name of the actual contracting parties is very important. You preferably want the other contracting party to have a track record which you can review and financial stability.

- Where a new shell company is being created for a project you need to consider whether there is a parent company or other connected parties who can provide additional undertakings or assurances.

- That does mean that it is necessary in every case and a decision may be taken that there is an acceptance of the potential risk. You may even calculate the potential loss if the project fails and assume that risk. A decision may also be made based on the fact that the start-up or project has potentially significant rewards.

- Many procurement contracts have repeatedly been awarded to large conglomerates which tick all the right boxes on their applications in terms of experience and financial records. That have not necessarily resulted in well executed work within budget. Instead many of them are later given additional costs and expenses which were not originally budgeted even despite the fact that the scope of the work required has not been fulfilled. So the fact that you pick what you think is a solid company may not mean that the project succeeds in the manner you expected.

- You need to notice whether the introduction to the names of the contracting parties adds in the words 'assignees and successors in business and title' or other similar words. If left in this would allow that party to assume that they are entitled to sell the whole business or even part of it to a third party at a later date. You may then not have any control over to whom the contract is transferred.

- This is a problem that may artists and musicians have experienced in that they and their work has been sold to a series of companies without any input from them.

- You need to have a complete prohibition on third party transfer in the agreement or a series of procedures that means that you must provide written consent to any proposal on every occasion. This would mean that you would be kept informed as to what is actually happening and not be presented with the facts after the company has been sold. In which case it would be too late for you to actually do anything to state your views.

- Where a company is selling off a list of rights which it owns you may be asked to sign a novation agreement. At this point you would be in a stronger position to negotiate as the company wants your signature on the document.

- If a distributor or a supplier wants the right to assign the contract and/ or sell off part of the business to a third party without seeking consent. It is a much better idea to include a comprehensive clause to that effect in the main agreement rather than rely on a few words at the start of the agreement.

Duration of a contract

- The length of the contract may be defined in many ways for example from a fixed start date to a fixed end date. This may be random dates or connected to financial accounting periods.

- A licence period may start on the date of the agreement and continue for a period of three or five years or more, but be drafted so that the term will be shorter if all the authorised transmissions of the film are completed earlier.

- The term is therefore linked to a task but it also allows the contract to be shortened if it is fulfilled. This type of contract will expire in any event whether the transmissions take place or not.

- A bigger problem is where a task or action needs to take place related to the term of the agreement but it does not happen. There is no end date to rely upon and the contract is left with the term unresolved.

- For instance where an event is delayed or there are technical problems which prevent the use of the master material which has been supplied. So it is useful to have some additional provision which deals with what should happen in such circumstances.

- In a publication agreement for a book or audio recording the agreement may start on a fixed date and end on a fixed date.

- More common is an agreement for a period of fixed years which starts on signature by both parties but which then continues from delivery of the manuscript or acceptance by the publisher of the manuscript or proofs for a fixed period of years.

- The term may be made longer by substituting the date of the publication in hardback or paperback or audio format as the point at which the period of years begins to run.

- What you do not want to do is allow the term of the agreement to be 'for the full period of copyright and any extensions and/or renewals'. This is

2096

often added in a licence despite the fact that the period is so long and unlimited that it is in effect an assignment.

- However you draft the period of the term of the agreement what you do not want is a term linked to a task that is never completed so that the second part of the term never takes place.

- Nor do you want the other party to be able to constantly renew and extend the agreement each year so that it rolls on unless you have served sufficient notice of termination.

- Many mobile phone, equipment and service contracts are drafted in this manner. So unless proper records are kept of notification periods required to end the contract you may as a charity or institute end up paying for a contract you do not use and incur additional charges.

- You should be able to specify a start date and end date for the term of the agreement.

- If the contract is extended then a new end date should be agreed in a formal addendum.

- Rolling renewal provisions which can be extended without notice should be avoided as these types of agreements are often badly drafted. One company may argue that notice for termination was served too late and the other that there was never any intention that the agreement should carry on.

- If you do not want a company to have the right to renew or have a right of first refusal or any option then state that fact in the agreement. There is nothing wrong with stating the obvious as a precaution.

Sub-contractors and sub-licensees

- If your company wants flexibility and the right to transfer, assign, sell, sub-licence or sub-contract then a clause to that effect is vital to avoid litigation as to what was permitted.

- You can add a clause which prohibits the right to sub-contract out the work for any part of the contract without the prior authorised written consent of a named individual. This therefore means that you can scrutinise the parties which it is proposed should be used and obtain more information upon which to base your decision.

- The clause may be adapted so that you agree that any decision will not be delayed or unreasonably withheld.

- It is possible to prohibit all sub-licensing of any material or rights to a third party. This is more difficult in a world where there are many layers

2097

of exploitation. A newspaper or media company will syndicate its news stories. A publisher or distributor relies on exploiting a manuscript in many formats including printed form, podcasts, e books, television series and merchandising.

- It is possible to compromise so that any sub-licence is subject to prior written approval in each case both of the proposed item or project but also the terms of the agreement for the sub-licence. Here you would want an absolute right of refusal and not be bound to accept a proposal which was either not very financially rewarding or which would result in an inferior quality product or service.

Ownership and title

- Possession of physical material is not the same as legal ownership of the copyright, intellectual property rights or the registration of ownership.

- Original master material, drawings, prototypes, new adaptations and developments, marketing, unsold products, source codes and relevant customer records and data, domain names, apps and websites need to be owned by one company or even held jointly in both names.

- A person who is under a contract of employment is presumed to have carried out any work in the course of their employment. Therefore their employer becomes the owner of their original work not the employee.

- Ownership may relate to copyright, patents, trade marks, computer software, intellectual property rights or data. There should be no doubt as to who owns existing material and rights and who will own those which are created in the future.

- Copyright is about the protection of someone's work which they have created as a result of their original skill and labour. Who made the work? How was it created? What materials were created? The quality of the work is not the issue but the originality of the work and whether or not it falls within one of the categories for protection listed in the legislation.

- The broad legal definition in legislation is often different from the more limited definition in the contract.

- In the United Kingdom the groups attributed in legislation are broadly as follows:

  a. Artistic work which includes a graphic work, photograph, sculpture or other work of artistic craftsmanship.

b.　Photographs may be shot on any type of format as the definition is wide namely a recording of light or other radiation on any medium on which an image is produced or from which it can be reproduced. Provided that it does not form part of a film.

- In a contract the definition for 'The Artwork' may be defined to cover any diagrams, sketches, drawings, illustrations, plans, maps, graphics, paintings and photographs supplied by a specific person who is named.

- Note here the photographs are included in the artwork.

- A different type of definition may be 'The Stills' which shall be defined in relation to actual physical photographs as follows: reference/code/title/description/source.

- Both the above definitions vary from the legislation but will be used in the agreement to establish who is to clear and pay for rights and who owns those rights.

- The question of ownership is then relevant to the undertakings and the indemnity in the agreement.

- Sound Recordings under legislation in the United Kingdom are defined as a recording of sounds from which sounds may be reproduced or the recording of the whole or any part of a literary, dramatic or musical work. This shall be the case regardless of the medium on which the recording is made or the method by which the sounds are reproduced.

- Note a film track accompanying a film has a different definition.

- Literary works are defined as those in written form and includes text and quotes.

- Computer-generated material means work or designs that are generated by a computer where there is no human author.

- Film is defined to be a recording or any medium from which a moving image may by any means be reproduced. A cable programme or service has a different definition. So the film can be any duration and shot in any format or medium provided it is a moving image.

- In a contract you would define a film or series by its format, duration and title. You may also attach a schedule of the cast, crew, credits, copyright notices and trade marks.

- The licensing of the use of copyright or the transfer of ownership must be done in writing and cannot be done verbally unless it is a non-exclusive licence. Despite this fact there are many instances where only verbal agreement is provided.

- A project, book or service may be summarised in an agreement by stating that the title, length or content is only in draft form and may be changed at a later date.

- Ownership applies to material and rights which exist now as well as those created in the future. If a series of designs and material are to be commissioned from third parties it is crucial that there are robust assignment clauses in the contracts.

- If you are acquiring contributions or material from third parties then you need to establish what rights have been cleared and what obligations you must carry out in terms of content, credits, copyright notices and payments.

Force Majeure

- A good force majeure clause may help a company buy time so that the agreement is suspended while a situation which is beyond their control which they could not have reasonably foreseen is resolved.

- Even if ultimately the contract cannot be saved and the problem has not gone away. The suspension of the agreement for a period allows the parties to try to reach a settlement and to avoid expensive litigation in a situation which is likely to already be very difficult.

- Are you intending to expand or restrict the scope of the force majeure clause? Does the clause apply to one or both parties?

- A force majeure clause is not expected to cover trivial matters but matters which impact at a fundamental level which prevent the performance of the agreement.

- It is possible to include and exclude situations and scenarios from force majeure.

- You may wish to accept that war is grounds for force majeure but what about riots and any uprising or military coup or activist action which creates blockades?

- If the water or electrical supply was not working at a venue would you accept that as grounds for force majeure? or if a venue failed to obtain an alcohol licence? It is perfectly reasonable to argue that these matters are reasonably foreseeable and should have been dealt with. That they do not fall within force majeure unless specifically listed as included.

- Acts of God, severe weather conditions, volcano eruptions, tsunamis, floods, hurricanes, plague, epidemics and heavy snow are all grounds for force majeure.

- Would you agree with a supplier or distributor that sought to rely on force majeure on the basis of its failure to comply with health and safety requirements? if the problems solely related to the supplier you would argue no, but if it was a nationwide problem your answer may be different.

- Many contracts have force majeure clauses but have a complete absence of any procedure for relying on it other than notification. More detail in this regard would assist both parties. When should notice be given, to whom and how? Can a contract be suspended indefinitely or only for a fixed period?

- Is there an automatic right to terminate the agreement if it cannot be carried out on grounds of force majeure? How can the financial consequences of the costs, losses and damages that each party may incur be recovered or attributed? There are questions of liability and indemnity which also arise in relation to these matters.

- If a period of three or six months is permitted to remedy the force majeure. After that period can one or both parties decide that it cannot be remedied and terminate the agreement? The overall aim would be to reach a settlement between the parties.

- Will any rights revert or payments need to be made in consequence of force majeure?

- It is possible that in a settlement any repayments by one party to the other could be spread over a year or more.

- Exclusions from force majeure are important so it is clear what circumstances do not fall within that clause. So for instance a factory fire may fall within force majeure but not failure of health and safety tests and assessments.

- The force majeure clause should also be considered in conjunction with the main clause headings, indemnity, liability, product liability, risk, legal proceedings and jurisdiction. As the intention of the grounds for force majeure is to exclude liability from a claim. That one party or the other is not liable as the problem could not reasonably be foreseen.

- Financial failure based on bad management or accounting practices is not relevant to force majeure.

- The facts may result in a situation where the supplier or distributor is able to complete some but not all of an order. Clarification may be needed as to whether a partial operation of a business may fall within the scope of the clause or not.

Some points on negotiation

State your case and identify amendments

- You may be glad to be offered a contract for work and keen to get it signed. The other party may be a large company which prepares the contract and sends it to you almost as a final draft and ready for signature. You may believe that there is not much room for negotiation. Do you accept it without any changes? The answer is no.

- There are always changes that you can ask to have made in any contract which will affect your future revenue, the rights you own and your liability.

- Examine the content of each clause in detail and begin a detailed list of the amendments that you require to improve the contract.

- It is much better if you suggest the actual words that you want added or which clauses must be deleted entirely.

- It is very likely that the contract will try to cover areas which were not even discussed.

- If a contract is so bias to the other party that there is little accountability, few obligations and the company makes claims on your work or money after the contract has ended. Then you must be willing to walk away and to refuse to sign an agreement which could have a severe impact on your future career.

- Many agency agreements are draconian and impose conditions which allow the agent to receive a percentage of a persons' income even after they have left the agency and terminated the contract. Why do people agree to these terms? Because they are so worried they will not be offered anything else that they sign anyway.

- There have been instances where despite advice not to sign an agreement a person has gone ahead and then only realised the consequences at a later date. They could not then enter into an agreement with another company even many years later.

- When you are negotiating any contract you are in an immediate position of strength if the other party realises that despite the offer on the table you will not settle for terms which you believe to be totally contrary to your own interests.

Drafting the contract

- Who drafts the contract? This simple fact of who drafts the original agreement and what it contains is the starting point for any final document. You are at a disadvantage if you are reviewing a contract someone else has drafted.

- If a person or company creates and supplies the documentation it is common to take this opportunity to add whatever you want outside the agreed terms. You may broadly keep to the parameters of what was agreed which may only be less than ten points, but add many new elements that were never actually raised in any discussions.

- So the negotiations are one stage, but the agreement is stage two. The discussions before the draft contract will not cover all the issues in the final agreement.

- The unwavering take it or leave it approach to negotiations is not likely to result in a very good working relationship. It is alright to be tough and firm but not to the point of not taking on board any proposals by the other party.

- You are creating a document on which you will rely in the future and you need to insist that a variety of aspects of the creative process, production, costs, clearances, schedules, marketing and exploitation are dealt with.

- If you are offered numerous representations during negotiations but those matters are not reflected in the contract. Then the strategy is a deliberate one to get you to sign but not to have the actual legal commitment.

- There will be a clause in the agreement which excludes all discussions and assurances which took place before the contract.

Approach to negotiation

- A professional and knowledge seeking strategy works best – eliciting as much information as you can and not putting all your views on the table the minute you enter the room.

- You may find out something which completely alters the whole basis of your view of the contract with the other party. This may be positive or negative.

- You do not need to immediately place your requirements before the other party. Sometimes it is more useful to listen to their full proposals and offer and then consider how you will proceed.

- Do not expect the negotiation to be completed in one meeting or one exchange of emails. It is not a smart move to rush matters when the only loser will be you as you have failed to understand and deal with the full scope of the depth of the agreement.

- Yes, you can try to work out roughly your target aim of what you want to achieve and the financial rewards you expect. However that is only a rough initial guide and may change over time due to the circumstances.

- If you want to achieve a fixed figure then you must aim much higher to achieve this sum. As it is a natural pattern of negotiation that if you demand 10 the other person will pitch much lower. So in order to arrive at 10 you need to start at a higher number and factor in a degree of concession on your part.

- You may need to seek to justify your figures by equating the economics to competing or similar products or services. It may be necessary to gather publicly available data to support your arguments as to the potential markets.

- The concessions which you make may be completely insignificant as far as you are concerned but the other party has gained points and feels they have obtained an advantage.

- That is why when negotiating terms before the contract or when reviewing the agreement you always ask for much more than you want and cover more factors. There may be 60 points you are making but in reality only 20 of them hold a great deal of importance for you. The rest are therefore secondary to you in negotiations and some may be conceded.

- Ask for more than you want and add clauses which protect your brand, require you to be consulted or create opportunities for you.

- Are you cutting back the scope of the agreement or expanding it? Do you want to restrict what can happen or do you want the right to do more? Once you understand which angle you are approaching the drafting of the agreement from then it becomes easier to see how clauses can be adapted to your advantage.

- Every aspect of the contract needs to be considered and understood both in a legal sense and practically.

- So any document will contain clauses that you definitely want to retain, those you are require to be edited and specific words added and those which must be deleted.

- There may also be new clause on topics not covered in the agreement. Here the terms of the new clauses would be provided to the other party already drafted.

- You are not simply making a point and leaving the drafting to the other party. You need to propose your own clause for them to include in the document. If you do not do that you may not end up with the clause you expected.

Protecting your position

- If you are taking a view of restricting the scope of the agreement then that applies to all the clauses whether it is the definitions, the term of the agreement, the territory covered, the undertakings, indemnity, liability, payments and costs.

- You limit the agreement to the minimum and do not provide anything which will not be used whether it be material or rights.

- You should include a clause which reserves all rights which are not granted and that would include any rights or formats or material not in existence at the time of the agreement which may be created or developed in the future.

- A licence is always preferable to an assignment unless you accept that a company is paying sufficient additional sums for the benefit of a more permanent acquisition.

- It is useful to try to see what is missing in the contract which is not covered.

- If is always advisable to examine the calculations of how the payments will be made through the agreement and to whom. What deductions if any will be permitted? How the definitions are drafted for the basis of the gross receipts or net receipts will have a huge impact on the money you receive.

- Whether an order or delivery is accepted immediately or if there is an agreed delay for the quality to be assessed is relevant to the payments under a contract.

- If you are required to provide an indemnity try to limit the length of time it applies and also try to set a fixed limit. Note you cannot exclude liability for personal injury or death for which you are directly responsible or to which you have contributed in some manner.

- Endeavour to exclude any right to new editions, any option, first rights of refusal, sequels, translations or other adaptations in any format or medium or associated merchandising.

- You must state what is not included to avoid one party arguing at a later date that the drafting is ambiguous or that the format they intend to exploit falls within the definitions.

- You need to avoid a situation where third parties whether agents, distributors and other third parties receive money which is due to you and then accumulate it and do not regularly account for and pay you the sums due. The frequency of the accounting statements and payments is important. You will also want the right to have access to all their financial and business records at least once a year. This may apply not only to the company but any sub-licensee or distributor engaged by them.

- If you are in a new project with a company you will want to consider what new copyright, intellectual property rights, titles of events, logos, images, trade marks, slogans, domain names, websites, apps , podcasts, sound recordings and other material will be created and who will own them. Otherwise you will find that the company goes ahead and assumes ownership as the matter was not raised. Both parties can share joint ownership but this is better stated and agreed at the outset. This also impacts on credits, copyright notices, registrations with rights management organisations and further potential revenue.

Drafting skills and techniques

The purpose of the agreement

- In this article it is not intended to cover every aspect of what you must consider to draft an agreement, but to discuss some of the questions that you need to think about as part of the process of drafting.

- What is the intention of the parties and the purpose of the agreement? What have the parties actually agreed?

- Drafting any document is essentially about you ensuring that you cover all the relevant points that have been agreed in advance. It is also about restricting your liability and exposure to unexpected costs and future claims.

- Most agreements are about one party or the other receiving payments and revenue of some kind. There are also however other benefits that you may wish to identify that the other party can pay for or supply which are not just financial.

- You need to be clear as to your objectives. What are you hoping to achieve? Establish your own targets whether that be a specific product or service, sponsorship of an event or development of an app.

- The more confident you are of your project and the detail which it involves. Then the easier it will be to persuade someone else to embrace it, but also to set out the parameters in the agreement.

- Draft your own synopsis and summary setting out all the important elements: This document may be attached as a schedule to part of the agreement or provide key information which can be used in creating the definitions or describing areas of responsibility.

- If you have developed an innovative title or characters or propose a new domain name or app. It is helpful to state whether you have investigated whether it is possible to register title, a domain name, trade mark or other rights.

- If material and rights have to be acquired from third parties then list their details and confirm the potential costs involved or which rights management organisations, agents, archives and institutions would have to be contacted to clear rights or acquire material.

- You may not have all the information but this process does flag up issues which need attention.

Legislation and other background

- Is it possible to draft an agreement that can be used in a global market despite the fact that the legislation and case law is different in so many countries? The answer is yes of course. The agreement is just the basic facts of what the parties agree between them at the date it is signed.

- The legislation and case law will affect the interpretation of the agreement.

- In most instances the wording of the contract is not a direct reflection of the words in the legislation. The legislation and case law is purely background information of which you are aware and take into account but it is not the only factor which is important.

- Often the legislation approaches the definitions of rights in a different manner to those you would necessarily use in a contract. They may be too wide and cover areas you do not wish to grant or too narrow for the market you wish to exploit.

- It is preferable to put a complete definition and the actual words in an agreement on which you seek to rely rather than just reference a section of legislation.

- In reality most contracts do not replicate the exact words in the legislation unless there is a very specific reason.

- There may be boundaries, restrictions and prohibitions imposed by legislation, case law, Codes of Practice, guidelines and policies which apply to your situation. This material and the topics it covers may assist you in highlighting matters which need to be covered when you are drafting a document.

- There are many definitions and rights used in agreements which are not even covered in legislation or case law. Legislation and case law is not the full comprehensive statement of all matters relating to contracts.

- Legislation often falls behind in recognising the new forms of rights, content and methods of exploitation which are created as the technology and new potential markets develop so rapidly.

- There is a much greater multi-layered approach now than ever before due to streaming, playback archives, podcasts, theme parks, computer games and the promotion of businesses by using characters, competitions, sponsorship, product placement, events as well as advertising.

- There was a point where computer software rights were not recognised by any legal category, however it did not prevent those rights being defined in a contract and licensed to third parties. Computer programs are now protected by copyright in many countries and the apparatus of any computer program or software related invention by patent.

- Similarly product placement and format rights agreements were used extensively in the film ,television, radio and the media industry for a long time even though there was no basis for them in law.

- There were regulatory guidelines in the past that prohibited product placement. So at that time although product placement was not against the law, it was contrary to guidelines which were predominantly not enforced.

- Fast forward to the present day and product placement and cross promotions is now a very lucrative source of money in many podcasts, films, television series and radio programmes. It is now accepted as a valid and commercial source of funding.

- This product placement arrangement may be subject to certain guidelines where the party who is involved in accepting the product placement operates under a licence for their service such as a radio or television company. They must then adhere to the policies imposed by the regulatory body for their respective forms of broadcast, transmission or exploitation.

- There are also different guidelines regarding advertising and product placement which relate to podcasts, newspapers and magazines.

- However there are still many grey areas where products and services are used without full disclosure to the public that one party has paid another to use them for promotional purposes.

- The rules which apply to a television company are not the same as those for a podcast series on the internet.

- The basis on which you would license the right to use a format for a touring stage show is not exactly the same as you would impose for a one off event or festival.

- When you grant format rights you are allowing the other party to use a whole load of material and rights which each individually contribute to the project. This may include the style of the set, the questions to be asked, games to be played, the equipment to be used, costumes to be worn, the title, trade marks and logos and images, the music and sound recordings, the use of associated premium rate phone lines and competitions. Whether it be a format for a dance show, quiz, reality show or otherwise. It may also include the right to create, develop and sell a variety of related merchandising.

- You want to encompass all the detail in the agreement so that it creates a full record which can be looked at later. You must remember that the document may be looked at by someone else five, ten or twenty years after the agreement was signed. They will then be seeking to interpret what was agreed and whether certain rights and material fall within the contract or not.

Where do you start?

- You may have your own personal library of agreements you have drafted, been involved in or concluded. You may use precedent books or have access to a main frame library of authorised pro forma master copies or access to a clause library supplied by a third party.

- Whatever you use to begin your draft document the most important step is to choose the right type of agreement. Do you need a licence, an assignment, a buy-out, a supply or distribution agreement? Is this an endorsement or a product placement agreement? Do you need a contract for services of an individual who is acting as a consultant or are they a contributor and creating original material?

- You have to understand what the agreement will be about in order to pick the right document to start with. Too many people try to adapt an agreement which is completely unrelated to the actual facts and quite unsuitable. This will mean that you do not cover key issues which should have been dealt with in the agreement.

- You want to create a document which breaks down all the issues to be covered into topics. Do not try and deal with multiple issues within one or two clauses.

- If when you read a clause it does not make sense then untangle it further and deal with different aspects of an issue in sections.

- Start with really good definitions at the front of the document which you can use to avoid repeating large chunks of text.

- Plan for the project to be a success and a failure and see what happens when you look at the document form one angle or the other.

- If the project is successful are you getting any extra rewards that will follow? Are there escalating royalty provisions linked to unit sales or revenue achieved. This might be by category or by market or related to the language.

- Do not be afraid of adding clauses which are either practical, innovative or which protect your brand or rights.

- If you want the right to use certain material or rights then make sure it is spelt out clearly in detail as to what you can do and how.

- Conversely where you do not think certain material or rights are included in the agreement then make a statement that all other rights are reserved. Then go further and give examples and make it clear that it is not an exhaustive list.

- Where royalties are to be paid if there is no percentage listed against a format or right in the document there is a strong argument that no payment is due. This has been used by many large media companies to avoid payment to contributors, performers and other third parties.

- So try and anticipate technology, formats and methods of exploitation to be developed in the future, but also where necessary make it clear that they are not covered in the agreement. and are the subject of separate negotiation and terms if they are required. Further that you as the licensor may refuse to grant any such licences and shall not be bound to do so.

Obligations and undertakings

- Here you are getting either party to commit to actually confirming what they own and control and that they are entitled to enter into the agreement. This may include confirmation of the ownership of material and rights. As well as the fact that it is original and the name of the creator.

- Either party may be asked to undertake that there is no previous agreement or commitment which conflicts with the proposed document.

- This section of the document only works well if you have clearly Identified what you want the other party to do for you. This information is then listed in the document with an undertaking by the other party to complete the tasks according to the budget, timescale and completion dates. This also involves setting detailed tasks and targets that must be achieved.

- Therefore you will list for example amounts, formats, ingredients, packaging, layout of a site or venue, schedules for the planned event and any other relevant information which completes the picture of what is planned.

- You may address responsibility and liability for security, health and safety, tests and assessments, power and water supplies, additional unexpected costs and a whole variety of matters.

Rights and Territory

- Spell out in as much detail as you can the specific rights you are being given or which you are granting to a licensee or other third party.

- Make it certain which rights are not being given in the agreement which are not included.

- It is important to look at the practical issues of what will be delivered, created and marketed. This allows you to deal with the issue of rights and material at different stages and put clauses in place so that you are asked for approval or consulted.

- The definition of the rights is linked to the licence period or the term of the agreement but also the area, country or territory which is defined in the document.

- You may define the territory if you wish by using the commonly used name of a country. It is a fact however that most countries have an official name which is used by governments and embassies and in international documents.

- Countries which are not landlocked may be defined on an official basis to include the surrounding defined territorial waters of that country and its islands.

- Many countries are also defined to include areas of land, islands and seas which are not directly next to their main country.

- The official definition of the country may include areas of land, islands or seas over which they have sovereignty.

- You need to decide whether aeroplanes, oil rigs, ships, wind farms, man-made land and other moving and static objects which are registered to a particular country are either included or excluded.

- You may approach the document by virtue of specifying a language rather than a country. So that it covers a certain language in the world.

Sponsorship

- What is each party responsible for?

- What must they actually do and supply?

- What do you want to be able to do under the agreement?

- What access to any venue or other location do you want?

- What trade marks and logos do each party have?

- What new titles, logos, images, sound recordings, films or other material, products, services and rights will be developed? Who will own them?

- What material can you use in conjunction with any of your own products, services and marketing?

- Are there any other costs you may be exposed to except the sponsorship fees?

- Have you thought about clearances and payment of copyright, music, performers or other matters?

- Who is overall liable for the event and its management?

- What if the event is delayed or cancelled? What is the position?

- You may provide undertakings in the agreement as a company for your material, products and rights but the other party may refuse to provide any indemnify to you on the basis that you should take out insurance cover and that it is not appropriate.

- You could still ask the other party to include a statement that sponsor is not liable for any claim and/or legal proceedings arising from the event unless directly caused by the sponsor.

- Do you want an option to sponsor and have the title rights in the next event?

- Do you have the right to film, record or create your own material on site? For example to record Interviews with performers using your own personnel.

- It is helpful to have plans and layouts of where the sponsors' brand is to appear on the site and stage, in any media coverage and on any new material. This would include flags, balloons, screens, banners, uniforms, tents, signage or otherwise. Each would be specifically itemised to set out the brand requirements to be fulfilled and what is to be reproduced and displayed. You would also want as a company to be able to approve the content of all this material surrounding the event.

- Is there a procedure in place to ensure that you acquire ownership of all the new rights in any new material created based on your brand, products or services? If it is being commissioned from a third party will they assign all the rights to the sponsor?

- Will you be able to terminate the agreement if there are performers or other third parties involved in the event with whom you do not want to be involved?

- From this long list you can see that drafting an agreement is also about asking a series of questions to establish the facts of what is expected, what might happen and to draft clauses which confirm that information. As well as to try to protect your brand, restrict your liability and endeavour to avoid disputes.

Effective ways to license merchandising

Different aspects of merchandising

- This article is not dealing with every aspect of what should be included in a merchandising agreement.

- The approach which is being taken in this article is to maximise your revenue and make the most of your rights. The whole concept of what merchandising covers has expanded enormously and is now much wider than ten or twenty years ago.

- The date order in which you may choose to exploit the merchandising rights has changed and is often connected to the timescale of the release of a book, a television series, a film, a record, a podcast, audio recording, tour or event.

- That does not mean that the people who are exploiting the book, podcast, tour or event are necessarily also the same people that own or control the merchandising.

- The author, an estate of a deceased musician or a company may have retained all the merchandising rights for their own benefit entirely. The merchandising rights would then be individually sub-licensed to third parties who were chosen for the quality of their work, their track record and their ability to deliver the financial rewards required.

- Where an author or an estate has granted the merchandising rights to a publisher, distributor, production or media company on the basis that they are secondary to the main project which may be a book or film. Often the other party who acquires the rights is actually acting in the role of an agent. This is sometimes reflected in the percentage royalties that may be agreed.

- For instance in a publishing contract the author may receive anything from 50% to 90% of the net receipts or sums received from the merchandising rights.

- Often these types of agreements are not very comprehensive in terms of the range of rights that are described and covered in the definitions. There may be many descriptions of forms of merchandising that are omitted.

- The primary project therefore for the publisher is the selling of the book related products which may be hardback, paperback or an audio file. There then tends to be different percentages which relate to translations, film rights and other forms of exploitation.

- An author concluding a children's book agreement may find that the publisher has paid more attention in the agreement to the merchandising rights if they are included. As the merchandising rights can on occasions be more lucrative than the book itself.

- The definitions you would use for a film agreement where the merchandising is secondary would be drafted in a different way. The royalty percentages are likely to be calculated on sums which allow numerous deductions before you get any money.

- You need to be very alert as to what distribution expenses if any will be deducted from the gross receipts, net receipts or sums received prior to the calculation of the sums due to you.

- You may be better off to receive a smaller percentage of gross receipts rather than a large percentage of net receipts or sums received.

- If there is no limit on the amount of deductions and the scope allowed is drafted to be very wide. You may find that you are never paid any royalties even if the project is successful. A blockbuster film can generate enormous revenue, but there may be deductions for production and manufacturing costs, packaging, freight, marketing, clearances and costs, promotions, insurance, commissions and many other sums which substantially reduce the pot from which your royalties will be paid.

- There may be a special edition book with the cover matching the actors in the film.

- If the film is a children's animation then there is likely to be a range of household products for bedrooms, nightwear, lunch boxes, brand related coats, shoes, sweets, balloons and birthday cakes and many other items.

- Different industries define and exploit merchandising in completely contrasting ways.

- The approach of a football club or sports organisation that hosts a series of annual games and events will focus on the products, services, items and brands that are most important to them.

- A tennis organisation may license or sell for example branded caps, wristbands, garden outdoor cushions, tennis clothes and equipment and products which would be useful or appeal to their audience and participants.

- A rugby, football, golf or other club will aim to make money out of the club shirt, scarf, hat, socks, boots, equipment, computer games, drink and food promotions as well as from connected content linked to betting, gambling and other third parties.

Governing bodies, agencies, Codes of Practice and guidelines

- There may be legislation or rules of a governing body or Codes of Practice and guidelines issued by a regulatory organisation or government agency that may apply to the situation.

- If you are entering into a sponsorship, merchandising or advertising arrangement with a third party you need to investigate what regulatory guidelines apply.

- This is particularly the case where any marketing or sales effect children or teenagers that is any person under eighteen. In some countries the age barriers may be higher.

- In the United Kingdom you may therefore need to consider the rules and guidelines of the:

  Gambling Commission www.gamblingcommission.gov.uk,

  Advertising Standards Authority www.asa.org.uk,

  the Competition and Market Authority

  www.gov.uk/organisations/compeitions-and-marketsauthority

  the Committee of Advertising Practice CAP,

  the Broadcast Committee of Advertising Practice BCAP and

  Ofcom www.ofcom.org.uk

- This is just a few of the organisations and if you are using premium rate phone lines for competitions then there are further codes of practice and guidelines.

- You may find that there are no issues and that none of the criteria are relevant to your circumstances but it is worth spending time on the research.

- You need to make these checks yourself as to what restrictions and prohibitions may be in place especially if a major part of your strategy is advertising, promotion and social media.

- You can no longer just look at a merchandising product in isolation. You cannot rely on the other party's assurances that there are no potential problems. As failure to do so may result in withdrawal of a product or impact on sales and marketing.

2117

Defining the product or the rights

- The club or sports organisation may appoint an agent to act on its behalf to exploit the rights. The question is whether the agreement is then directly with the club or with the agent.

- If you are the sub-licensee it is better to deal direct with the club in the contract.

- Where you are sub-licensing rights you want to make the contract as restricted as possible so that you are left with the most rights to make more money.

- Therefore you appoint a sub-licensee to reproduce, sell and distribute a very specific product for a limited period and countries and nothing more.

- This product might also be sold in the official shop, on the official website and app and at events. So it is relevant to look at not only the product, but also how the relationship will work in respect of scheduled events.

- Many publishers and media companies wish to acquire as many rights as possible regardless of whether they have any plans to exploit them or not. This may be the case even though they have never exploited any format of those rights at any time.

- A publisher or media company will ask an author to license or assign the hardback and paperback rights, film rights, translation rights, the right to contribute to educational books and co-editions. They may also try to include the right to any authorised biography.

- There are a wide range of formats that many publishers, distributors and media companies try to acquire to fall within merchandising. Examples include personal organisers, recipe cards, diaries, posters, wall charts, calendars and household items.

- Where it is a film or book for the children's market then it may cover picture books, plastic books, fabric books, annuals, activity books, sticker books, board books, fridge magnets, colouring books, clothes, costumes, stationary, pens, games, bath products, computer games, theme parks, musical shows, soft toys, teddy bears, jigsaws, play mats, duvets and pillows, wallpaper, furniture, puppets, dolls, frisbees, umbrellas, bags, vehicles, gadgets, kites, yoyos, badges and numerous other items.

- For both the film and book market there is a huge value attached to the merchandising of characters. Here it becomes important that there have been or will be an application for trade marks, domain names and any other relevant registrations and ownership of titles. There is a real necessity to have a brand, copyright and intellectual property rights strategy.

- You need to resist the request to license all the merchandising rights so that the other party can act as your agents and receive money from the revenue without any actual contribution. Unless the advance and royalties you are being paid are so good that you cannot refuse their offer as there is little benefit in you granting them all the merchandising rights.

- Reserve the film rights as an author and be able to negotiate and conclude your own agreement directly with a film company for a film or television series.

- An individual who is an elite in their sports field may agree to have a book published by a company which is written by a ghost writer based on a part of their life. Although it may not be an authorised biography. The individual has a personal name and may have a signature gesture or logo that they use or an abbreviated version of their name which is commonly used by fans and in social media.

- This individual would not be advised to license the merchandising rights in their brand to the publisher on an exclusive basis along with the book. They would giving their brand to another company rather than maintaining ownership and control. The company is unlikely to focus as much time and attention on the brand once the book has been published and has been remaindered.

- An individual would have the opportunity to license a range of products and services associated with their brand including clothes, training and exercise equipment and products, betting, gambling, cars, calendars, shoes, health and beauty products, watches, jewellery, drinks, food and entertainment.

- Artists and musicians often make significant sums from associated merchandising at their concerts. This is most commonly through the same company with whom that have licensed their services and music rather than an independent third party who they have licensed directly. This may therefore mean that they may receive a smaller percentage of the total sums.

- The estates of deceased artists and authors have had many legal disputes with film companies and distributors who have argued that new forms of exploitation which did not exist at the time the agreement was signed are still however covered. This will often mean that they are also arguing that no more sums are due or that an old royalty rate is applicable.

2119

- So the definition of the rights or the authorised product is very important. If there is a whole list of formats and means of exploitation not included then make that very clear and reserve all the rights especially those which may be created in the future.

- So a new product is being created. Who will own it? And who will own the rights to the title, characters, trade marks and associated forms of exploitation?

- Ensure that you understand all the aspects of the contributions to make up the product and then ask the questions who owns and control each part of those rights?

- You cannot grant to another company more than you actually own or control. So if there is a chain of ownership seek some verification and carry out due diligence.

What is the original master material and what is created that is new?

- There is the original material or source from which the authorised merchandising is derived. There are samples and prototypes created which need to be agreed and approved. From that agreed size, colour and content the new licensed article is reproduced.

- When the new licensed article is developed and reproduced there may be new material which has been commissioned from third parties. This may be in respect the content of the product, the packaging or the marketing. You need to ask the question – who owns this new material?

- There may be a variety of types of material developed including:

  a. Photographs, sketches, diagrams, maps, designs and other artwork such as book covers, labels, posters.

  b. Text, quotes, scripts, index and slogans.

  c. Trade marks, service marks, logos, images and symbols.

  d. Sound recordings in whole or part of any literary dramatic or musical work.

  e. Film and soundtrack.

  f. Music, ringtones and sounds.

  g. Computer generated material.

  h. Contributors by designers, presenters, consultants, directors, writers, performers, singers, musicians and other third parties.

i.　Moulds, samples, prototypes, toiles and other preparatory material.

j.　Costumes, sets and related props.

Some terms of licence

- If you are licensing rights to a third party then the preferred course of action should be to only grant non-exclusive rights. That means that it is possible to grant the exact same rights to another third party at the same time unless there is any restriction in the contract. So if you have awarded one distributor a contract to produce teddy bears, you can do the same with another in the same country.

- That might be useful as you can make the products different and even nave the licence periods covering the same dates. If there is a demand in a market for more than one product that makes sense.

- The manufacturer or licensee is likely to ask for an exclusive agreement and try to define the teddy bear product so widely that it also impacts on your potential to license a doll, a puppet or smaller pocket size versions. You need to be very careful to only allow the definition of the product to be a specific type of toy and not cover the whole toy market.

- Further you would include robust quality control clauses so that there are approval stages and the product does not pose a health and safety risk.

- If you are not receiving a large advance there is no reason to grant exclusive rights.

- You could grant a non-exclusive licence, but agree not to licence the same type of product to a third party for six months or a year. An end date should be specified after which you are free to do so. This then allows the distributor a small window, but you have not granted exclusive rights for years.

- The term of agreement or licence period should be as short as possible. When is the first production date likely to be? When will the product be on sale? When will it be out of date? Will they be allowed a sell-off period?

- The best contract has a fixed start and end date and is not linked to the completion of tasks or work that must be completed before the time runs and so will extend the term of the contract in some manner.

- Will one or two years be enough? Are three or five years sufficient? Or even ten?

- The licensee will try to make the licence period as long as possible and may even ask for the full period of copyright. This should be refused.

- You may decide to start the licence period from when you the licensor have delivered the master material which is required. The licensee will try to get you to agree that the period should run from the date of the first release of the product. What happens if the product is never released? There must be an end date whatever happens.

- It is possible for there to be different lengths of licence period for different rights, but this is not common.

- If you have granted an exclusive licence you would not want the sell-off period to be exclusive as well. So make any additional period to get rid of stock as non-exclusive.

- Do not agree to any clause which allows an extension or renewal of the licence without a further advance or other payment.

- Do not agree to any form of assignment of rights. You do not want to sell the ownership of your rights forever. Some licences may be drafted to be called licences but the wording makes them an assignment. So be aware of this fact and read the words carefully.

- Ensure that you make a statement as to what is not granted and reserve those rights. You may wish to list the types of products, languages or markets in detail so that there is no ambiguity. This also applies to new rights, formats, technology and methods not in existence

- If new material is commissioned ensure that the contract stipulates that the rights must be bought out as far as possible and assigned to the licensor at the very latest by the end of the agreement.

- Do not license a whole market such as household goods, printed form, adult and children's clothes, keep the definition of the product very narrow.

- Provide the exact detail of product with the specified size, colour and content and attach a two or three dimensional version.

- It is common for books in different languages and translations and formats to be licensed to many different companies.

- Define the territory which is to be licensed so that it only applies to those countries which will be active markets. If you grant languages rather than countries you may find you have granted more than you wanted.

- You may ask to be sent a list of existing agents, distributors and wholesalers that the company currently uses. It is possible to have a

- clause so that you approve any new third parties to be involved in the sales and distribution.

- If you do not want the licence transferred at a later date to a third party then put a clause in so that it cannot be done.

- Ideally you would want a non-returnable advance which is not set-off against future royalties that may fall due to you.

- Most advances are returnable if for instance the master material required is not delivered or it is found the company who is the licensor is not actually the owner. The majority of advances under agreements are set-off against royalties.

- The percentage royalty for each form of exploitation is important. You need to work out what you are actually getting a percentage of when you interpret the definition as it is drafted.

- If it is a percentage of gross receipts. Are there still any deductions before your money is calculated?

- The same applies to a percentage of net receipts. How is the final sum calculated from which you get your percentage? There may be distribution expenses allowed to be deducted which is a very long list of items that could be very expensive. All these sums will be recovered by the licensee before there is any payment to you the licensor. If the costs that can be deducted are not limited in any way or are very wide you may not receive any royalties.

- Some licensees will pay a percentage based on sums received rather than gross or net receipts. So if they do not receive payment from a third party then the licensee is not liable to pay any royalties as it has not been received.

- Are you getting a percentage of the retail price, a wholesale price, a discounted price, gross receipts, net receipts or sums received?

- Can the licensee recoup manufacture and development costs, exchange rate and banks costs, reproduction and distribution charges, advertising and marketing, copyright and other intellectual property clearances and costs, the cost of trade mark applications and registrations as well as legal costs. These sums are just examples of the variety of deductions that may be listed in an agreement.

- You do not have to agree to them all – you may for instance accept commission costs but not marketing. Identify the categories you will agree to and then try to get a financial limit set either for any accounting period or for the full life of the agreement.

- Be aware of the fact that if all your royalty percentages and payments are linked to either definition of types of rights and markets or types of products. If a new format or right or method of exploitation comes into existence. You either must have stated the rate which will apply or have kept those rights or formats by reserving them.

- A good agreement will list the obligations of each of the parties to the other. You will as the licensor require the licensee to undertake to adhere to all required credits, copyright notices, trade marks and moral rights.

- You may require that the licensee be responsible for obligations to third parties which relate to the master material. You may require that the licensee undertakes to clear and pay for the use of any contribution by another person.

- If you the licensor provide an indemnity to the licensee then it should be restricted by duration and amount. You may also limit it to only certain clauses in the licence and not the whole agreement.

- You may also insist that the licensee provides an indemnity to the licensor.

- In conjunction with any indemnity you would also put in place a procedure for any potential claim under the indemnity to be notified to the other party.

- For any toy or merchandising quality control, health and safety and product liability are key topics. You would want the licensee to be obliged to notify the licensor of any problems, complaints, product recalls, test failures, and potential claims.

- It is possible to include a clause which means that the licensee is required to provide a regular marketing and strategy report and review meeting.

- The licensee will try to have accounting statements and payments paid once or twice a year, but you can make this period shorter.

- You will need to include clauses in a licence which allow you access to audit, inspect and make copies of all the records in any medium in which they may be kept. Where there is an error or omission you may have an additional clause which means that all your costs of the audit are paid for by the licensee and the sum due plus interest.

- Even after the expiry or termination of an agreement you would still want a licensee to be obliged to account and make payments until all the sums due had been paid.

- One further point is that if you do not want the licensee to sub-licence rights to a third party then this fact should be stated and prohibited.

Legal, Commercial and Business Development Directory

- This is a brief reference guide to other sources of information that you will find helpful for background research. The Authors and the Publisher cannot accept any responsibility for your use of any links and/or any reliance you may place on the information, data and/or advice that you may obtain from any websites and/or other resources.

- We are not endorsing nor making any recommendations as to the quality and/or accuracy of any of the content of third parties. You use the references and resources entirely at your own risk. The Authors and the Publisher shall not be liable for any consequences of any nature whether direct and/or indirect that may arise as a result of your access to, use of and/or reliance upon on any link, content and/or guidance of the third parties.

Film, Television, Video and Radio

British Board of Film Classification www.bbfc.co.uk
Ofcom www.ofcom.org.uk
BBC www.bbc.co.uk
BBC Studios www.bbcstudios.com
BBC iPlayer www.bbc.co.uk/iplayer
ITV www.itv.com
ITV Hub www.itv.com/hub/itv
Channel 4 www.channel4.com
All 4 www.channel4.com
ITN www.itn.co.uk
Channel 5 www.channel5.com
My5 www.my5.tv
All3media www.All3media.com
STV www.stv.tv
Zenith www.zenithmedia.com
Sky www.sky.com
Discovery www.discoveryuk.com
Discovery Plus www.discoveryplus.co.uk
CNN International www.cnn.com
Freeview www.freeview.co.uk
Lion TV www.liontv.com
Tiger Aspect Productions www.tigeraspect.co.uk
The Walt Disney Company www.thewaltdisneycompany.com
Disney Plus www.disneyplus.com

Warner Bros www.warnerbros.co.uk
Warner Media www.warnermedia.com
Paramount Pictures www.paramount.com
Endemol Shine UK www.endemolshineuk.com
Amazon Prime www.amazon.com
Apple TV + www.apple.com
Britbox www.britbox.co.uk
Now TV www.nowtv.com
Netflix www.netflix.com
Freesat www.freesat.co.uk
Google Play www.google.com/store
Fox www.fox.com
Dave www.dave.uktv.co.uk
Alibi www.alibi.uktv.co.uk
Drama www.drama.uktv.co.uk
Yesterday www.yesterday.uktv.co.uk
Food Network www.foodnetwork.com
PBS America www.pbsamerica.co.uk
Lifetime www.lifetimetv.co.uk
Comedy Central www.cc.com
SYFY www.syfy.com
National Geographic www.nationalgeographic.com
Sony Channel UK www.sonychannel.co.uk
Sony Movies UK www.sonymovies.co.uk
BT Sport www.bt.com
Shine TV www.shine.tv
Talking Pictures TV www.talkingpictures.co.uk
Gold www.gold.uktv.com
British Pathe www.bristishpathe.com
Pathe UK www.pathe.co.uk
20th Century Studios www.20thcenturystudios.com
Universal Pictures UK www.universalpictures.co.uk
Universal Pictures International www.universalpicturesinternational.com
Maverick TV www.mavericktv.co.uk
Nickelodeon www.nick.com
NBC Universal www.nbcuni.com
Cartoon Network www.cartoonnetwork.co.uk
Producers Alliance for Cinema and Television PACT www.pact.co.uk
British Film Institute www.bfi.org.uk
The British Academy www.britac.ac.uk
British Universities Film and Video Council www.bufvc.ac.uk
UK Cinema Association www.cinemauk.org.uk
Screen Ireland www.screenireland.ie
European Broadcasting Union www.ebu.ch

European Conference of Postal and Telecommunications Administrations
  CEPT www.cept.org
Commonwealth Broadcasting Association www.cba.org.uk
International Federation of Film Producers Associations www.fiapf.org
International Association of Wildlife Filmmakers www.iawf.org.uk
British Film Commission www.britishfilmcommission.org.uk
FilmHub www.filmhub.com
Australian Communications and Media Authority ACMA www.acma.gov.au
Beyond www.beyond.com.au
Communications Association of Hong Kong www.cahk.hk
Motion Picture Licensing Corporation www.themplc.co.uk
Motion Picture Association www.motionpictures.org
American Film Institute www.afi.com
Independent Film & Television Alliance www.ifta-online.org
IMDb www.imdb.com
Film Distributors' Association www.filmdistributorsassociation.com
International Game Developers Association www.igda.org
Association of Film Commissioners International www.afci.org
European Children's Film Association www.ecfaweb.org
Film Producers Guild of Russia www.kinoproducer.ru
Swiss Film Producers Association www.swissfilmproducers.ch
Czech Film Commission www.filmcommission.cz
Nepal Motion Picture Association www.nempa.org.np
Screen Producers Australia www.screenproducers.org.au
Canadian Media Producers Association www.cmpa.ca
Danish Film Producers Association www.pro-f.dk
West Finland Film Commission www.wffc.fi
Association of Icelandic Film Producers www.producers.is
National Film Development Corporation of India www.nfdcindia.com
Italian Film Producers ANICA www.anica.it
Motion Picture Producers Association of Japan www.eiren.org
The Screen Production and Development Association of New Zealand
  www.spada.co.nz
Dreamworks www.dreamworks.com
Screen Daily www.screendaily.com
Hollywood Reporter www.hollywoodreporter.com
Screen Daily www.screendaily.com
Variety www.variety.com
Spotlight www.spotlight.com
The Stage www.thestage.co.uk
Equity www.equity.org.uk
British Equity Collecting Society BECS www.becs.org.uk
PACT www.pact.co.uk
BAPLA UK www.bapla.org.uk

International Artists Managers Association IAMA www.iamaworld.com
Directors Guild of GB www.dggb.org.uk
Directors Guild of America www.dga.org
Australian Screen Editors www.screeneditors.com
Guild of Location Managers www.golm.org.uk
European Producers Club www.europeanproducersclub.org
Institute of Professional Sound www.ips.org.uk
Satellite Industry Association SIA www.sia.org
ISOA EMEA European Satellite Operators Association www.esoa.net
Televisual www.televisual.com
Society of Audiovisual Authors www.saa-authors.eu
Association of Model Agents www.associationofmodelagents.org
Event Cinema Association www.eventcinemaassociation.org
BAFTA British Academy of Film and Television Arts www.bafta.org
Avalon Entertainment www.avalonuk.com
Associated Press www.apnews.com
www.aparchive.com
NBC www.nbc.com
BFBS Forces News www.bfbs.com
National Film and TV School www.nfts.co.uk
Eurosport www.eurosport.co.uk
BBC Radio www.bbc.co.uk/sounds
Classic FM www.classicfm.com
Capital Radio www.capitalradio.com
Paramount www.paramount.com
Virginmedia www.virginmedia.com
Ray Knight www.rayknight.co.uk
Storm www.stormmodels.com

Authors, Publishers, Distributors and News

eBooks.com www.ebooks.com
ebooks on Amazon www.amazon.co.uk/kindle
Gardners – The Hive Network www.hive.co.uk
Rakuten Kobo www.kobo.com
E reading Apps Kobo www.kobo.com/apps
Barnes and Noble ebooks Nook www.barnesandnoble.com/b/nook
Bloomsbury www.bloomsbury.com
Bloomsbury Professional www.bloomsburyprofessional.com
The Society of Authors www.societyofauthors.org
International Federation of Journalists www.ifj.org
Authors Licensing and Collecting Society www.alcs.co.uk
British Association of Picture Libraries and Agencies BAPLA www.bapla.
   org.uk
Publishers Association www.publishers.org.uk

British Library Public Lending Right PLR www.bl.uk/plr
Independent Publishers Guild www.ipg.uk.com
The Professional Publishers Association www.ppa.co.uk
Association of Learned and Professional Society Publishers www.alpsp.org
Society of Editors www.societyofeditors.co.uk
The Writers Guild of Great Britain www.writersguild.org.uk\
Chartered Institute of Journalists www.cioj.org
Chartered Institute of Editing and Proofreading www.ciep.uk
Writers Guild of America www.wga.org
The Association of American Publishers AAP www.publishers.org
American Society of Journalists and Authors www.asja.org
The Council of Editors of Learned Journals www.celj.org
Periodical Publishers Association www.ppa.co.uk
The Bibliographical Society www.bibsoc.org.uk
Press Complaints Commission www.pcc.org.uk
News Media Association www.newsmediauk.org
The Association of Newspaper and Magazine Wholesalers
    www.anmw.co.uk
National Newspaper Association www.nnaweb.org
National Newspapers Publishers Association www.nnpa.org
PR Newswire www.prnewswire.co.uk
Commonwealth Press Union www.cpu.org.uk
Press Gazette www.pressgazette.co.uk
Nielsen Book Data www.nielsenbookdata.co.uk
Association of Subscription Agents www.subscription-agents.org
The Royal Society of Literature www.rslit.org
Journalism www.journalism.co.uk
Australian Publishers Association www.publishers.asn.au
Australian Society of Authors ASA www.asauthors.org
Australian Writers Guild Copyright Agency www.awg.com.au
Australian Copyright Council www.copyright.org.au
Association of Publishers in India www.publishers.org.in
Association of Czech Booksellers and Publishers www.sckn.cz
Society of Indexers www.indexers.org.uk
American Society for Indexing www.asindexing.org
Pearson www.pearson.com
Historical Writers Association www.historicalwriters.org
National Association of Press Agencies www.napa.org.uk
Commonwealth Press Union www.cpu.org.uk
National Press Photographers Association NPPA www.nppa.org
Gardners Books www.gardners.com
Bertram www.bertram.com
Barnes and Noble www.barnesandnoble.com
Bol www.bol.com

Amazon US www.amazon.com
Amazon UK www.amazon.co.uk
Bowker www.bowker.com
Publishers Weekly www.publishersweekly.com
The Royal Society www.royalsociety.org
Copyright Licensing Agency www.cla.co.uk
Canadian Copyright Licensing Agency www.accesscopyright.ca
SACD www.sacd.fr
SABAM Belgium Society of Authors, Composers and Publishers
    www.sabam.be
SGAE Spanish Society of Authors and Editors www.sgae.es
Australian Society of Authors www.asauthors.org
Society of Children's Book Writers and Illustrators Australia and New
    Zealand www.scbwiaustralianz.com
UKSG www.uksg.org
BIC www.bic.org.uk
Evening Standard www.standard.co.uk
The Guardian www.theguardian.com
Telegraph www.telegraph.co.uk
Country Life www.countrylife.co.uk
The Scotsman www.thescotsman.com
The Sun www.thesun.co.uk
Financial Times www.ft.com
Times Higher Education www.timeshighereducation.com
Alibris www.alibris.com
British Printing Industries Federation www.britishprint.com
Metro www.metro.co.uk
Daily Express www.express.co.uk
Daily Mirror www.mirror.co.uk
Penguin Random House www.penguinrandomhouse.com
Hello www.hellomagazine.com
Science Fiction and Fantasy Writers of America www.sfwa.org
Blackwells www.blackwells.co.uk
Foyles www.foyles.co.uk
W H Smith www.whsmith.co.uk
The American Physical Society www.aps.org
Business Insider www.businessinsider.com
Dymocks www.dymocks.com.au
Fishpond www.fishpond.co.uk
Booksellers Association www.booksellers.org.uk
Publishers' Licensing Society PLS www.pls.org.uk
Independent Press Regulator IPSO www.ipso.co.uk
Scottish Book Trust www.scottishbooktrust.com
Scottish Publishers Association www.scottishbooks.org

Internet, Telecommunications and Mobiles

Internet Corporation for Assigned Names and Numbers ICANN
  www.icann.org
Association of Online Publishers www.ukaop.org.uk
Digital Content Next www.digitalcontentnext.org
Content Marketing Association www.the-cma.com
Amazon www.amazon.com
Ofcom www.ofcom.org.uk
UK Mobile Network Operators www.mobileuk.org
European Telecommunications Network Operators' Association
  www.etno.eu
International Association of Internet Hotlines Inhope www.inhope.org
Internet Watch Foundation www.iwf.org.uk
Mobile Marketing Association www.mmaglobal.com
Federal Communications Commission www.fcc.gov
Phones Paid Services Authority www.psauthority.org.uk
Mail Preference Service www.mpsonline.org.uk
Telephone Preference Service www.tpsonline.org.uk
Commonwealth Telecommunications Organisation www.cto.int
ISPA Internet Service Providers Association www.ispa.org.uk
Nominet.uk www.nominet.org.uk
InterNIC The Internet's Network Information Centre www.internic.net
The Internet Society www.internetsociety.org
Uwhois www.uwhois.com
Google www.google.org
Microsoft www.microsoft.com/en-gb/store/apps
Twitter www.twitter.com
Youtube www.youtube.com
Facebook www.facebook.com
Instagram www.instagram.com
Bing www.bing.com
Ask www.ask.com
Yahoo www.yahoo.com
Myspace www.myspace.com
EDRI European Digital Rights www.edri.org
P Interest www.pinterest.com
Apple www.apple.com
Apple i tunes www.apple.com/uk/itunes
WhatsApp www.whatsapp.com
Tik Tok www.tiktok.com
Skype www.skype.com
Linked In www.linkedin.com
Apps Radioplayer www.radioplayer.co.uk/apps
Reddit www.reddit.com

Lasso www.lasso.com
Asos www.asos.com
Shpock www.shpock.com
Spotify www.spotify.com
Tradesy www.tradesy.com
Vestiaire collective www.vestiairecollective.com
Save the student www.savethestudent.org
Depop www.depop.com
Vinted www.vinted.com
Etsy www.etsy.com
Ebay www.ebay.com
Zoom www.zoom.us
Zoopla www.zoopla.co.uk
Booking.com www.booking.com
Travelzoo www.travelzoo.com
Expedia www.expedia.com
Camelot Group www.camelotgroup.co.uk

Designers, Illustrators, Artists and Photographers

Association of Illustrators www.theaoi.com
Society of Illustrators www.societyillustrators.org
Artists Collecting Society ACS www.artistscollectingsociety.org
Chartered Society of Designers www.csd.org.uk
The Society of British Theatre Designers www.theatredesign.org.uk
The Royal Photographic Society www.rps.org
National Photographic Society www.thenps.com
Getty Images www.gettyimages.co.uk
The British Postal Museum and Archive www.postalmuseum.org
Royal Academy of Arts www.royalacademy.org.uk
Royal Collection Trust www.rct.uk
The Design Society www.designsociety.org
The Art Fund www.artfund.org
Design History Society www.designhistory.org
Arts Law Centre of Australia www.artslaw.com.au
Arts Council www.artscouncil.org.uk
The Renaissance Society of America www.nsa.org
Design and Artists Copyright Society DACS www.dacs.org.uk
Artists' Collecting Society www.artistscollectingsociety.org
Design Institute of Australia www.dia.org.au
Australian Graphic Design Association www.agda.com.au
Australian Interactive Multimedia Association www.aimia.com.au
National Portrait Gallery www.npg.org.uk
National Archives www.nationalarchives.gov.uk
GB Film Designers Guild www.filmdesigners.com

Designers Guild www.designersguild.com
IFFRO International Federation of Reproduction Rights Organisations – list
   of international organisations www.iffro.org/members

Music, Lyrics, Performances and Sound Recordings
PRS for Music www.prsformusic.com
PPL www.ppluk.com
ASCAP www.ascap.com
IFPI www.ifpi.org
Incorporated Society of Musicians www.ism.org
Music Publishers Association www.mpaonline.org.uk
Music Producers Guild www.mpg.org.uk
Guild of International Songwriters and Composers
   www.songwriters-guild.co.uk
The British Academy www.britac.ac.uk
UK Music www.ukmusic.org
Association of Independent Music www.aim.org.uk
Australian Mechanical Copyright Owners Society AMCO and Australian
   Performing Right APRA
APRA/AMCOS www.apra-amcos.com.au
Australian and New Zealand Music Publishers Association AMPAL
   www.ampal.com.au
Association of European Performers Organisations AEOP-ARTIS
   www.aeop-artis.org
American Society of Composers, Authors and Publishers ASCAP
   www.ascap.com
Music Publishers Association of US MPA www.mpa.org
American Performing Rights Society for Songwriters and Publishers SESAC
   www.sesac.com
Recording Industry Association of America www.riaa.com
American Federation of Musicians of US and Canada www.afm.org
Canadian Musical Reproduction Rights Agency CMRRA www.cmrra.ca
Norwegian Performing Right Society www.tono.no
Bureau of International Mechanical Copyright Societies www.biem.org
National Music Publishers Association www.nmpa.org
Society of Composers Inc www.societyofcomposers.org
Music Week www.musicweek.com
Warner Chappell Music www.warnerchappell.com
Universal Music Group www.universalmusic.com
Royal Opera House www.roh.org.uk
International Federation of Authors and Composers www.cisac.org
BPI www.bpi.co.uk
Musicians' Union www.musiciansunion.org.uk
The Ivors Academy of Music Creators www.ivorsacademy.com

London Symphony Orchestra www.lso.co.uk
The Society of Composers and Lyricists www.thesci.com
Concert Promoters Association www.concertpromotersassociation.co.uk
International Federation of Music Publishers www.icmp-ciem.org
International Federation of Authors and Composers CISAC www.cisac.org
IFFRO International Federation of Reproduction Rights Organisations
    www.iffro.org/members

Intellectual Property, Legal and Government
UK Government www.gov.uk/organisations
IPO Intellectual Property Office – IP, copyright, patents and trade marks
    www.ipo.gov.uk
British Copyright Council www.britishcopyright.org
Europa European Union www.europa.eu
EUR-Lex Official EU Law www.eur-lex.europa.eu
Cordis European Commission www.cordis.europa.eu
EU Ted Public Procurement www.ted.europa.eu/Ted
European Bureau of Library, Information and Documentation Associations
    EBLIDA www.eblida.org
European Parliament www.europarl.europa.eu/portal/en
FACT Federation against Copyright Theft www.fact-uk.org.uk
British Library Business and IP Centre www.bl.uk/business-and-ip-centre
Australian Copyright Council www.copyright.org.au
Benelux Office for IP www.boip.int
Intellectual Property Office of Ireland www.ipoi.gov.ie/en/
Chartered Institute of Trade Mark Attorneys www.citma.org.uk
International Trade Mark Association INTA www.inta.org
Institute of Professional Representatives before the European Patent Office
    www.patentepi.org/en/
International Intellectual Property Institute www.iipi.org
American Intellectual Property Law Association AIPLA www.aipla.org
Copyright Clearance Centre www.copyright.com
Worldwide Intellectual Property Organisation list of IP member
    www.wipo.int/directory
US Patent and Trade Mark Office www.uspto.gov
US Copyright Office www.copyright.gov
Munich Intellectual Property Law Centre MIPLC www.miplc.de
Japan Patent Office www.jpo.go.jp
Austrian Patent Office www.patentamt.at
Denmark IP Centre www.dkpto.dk
Finland Patent Office PRH www.prh.fi
German Patent Office DPMA www.dpma.de
Netherlands Patent Office www.rvo.nl
Intellectual Property Institute www.ip-institute.org.uk

The Honourable Society of Gray's Inn www.graysinn.org.uk
The Honourable Society of Inner Temple www.innertemple.org.uk
The Honourable Society of Middle Temple www.middletemple.org.uk
The Honourable Society of Lincoln's Inn www.lincolnsinn.org.uk
Ministry of Justice www.justice.gov.uk
American Bar Association www.americanbar.org
The New York State Bar Association www.nysba.org
Hong Kong Bar Association www.hkba.org
The Law Society www.lawsociety.org.uk
Law Society of Northern Ireland www.lawsoc-ni.org
Worshipful Company of Arbitrators www.arbitratorscompany.org
Licensing Executives Society www.lesi.org
Federation of Law Societies in Canada www.fisc.ca
Companies House
    www.gov.uk/government/organisations/companies-house
British and Irish Legal Information Institute www.bailii.org
British Institute of International and Comparative Law www.biicl.org
British and Irish Law, Education and Technology Association
    www.bileta.ac.uk
Scottish Law Agents Society www.scottishlawagents.org
Incorporated Council of Law Reporting ICLR www.lawreports.co.uk
Scottish Council of Law Reporting www.scottishlawreports.org.uk
International Association of Entertainment Lawyers IAEL www.iael.org
Commonwealth Lawyers Association www.commonwealthlawyers.com
Commonwealth Magistrates and Judges Association www.cmja.org
Commonwealth Association of Public Sector Lawyers www.capsl.org
Procurement Lawyers Association www.procurementlawyers.org
Canadian Association of Legal Administrators www.alanet.org
Chartered Institute of Legal Executives www.cilex.org.uk
Institute of Paralegals www.theiop.org
State Bar of California www.calbar.ca.gov
American Arbitration Association www.adr.org
American Law Institute www.ali.org
Student Law Journal www.studentlawjournal.com
IPKat www.ipkitten.blogspot.com
Society for Computers and the Law www.scl.org
American Society of International Law www.asil.org
Centre for International Environmental Law www.ciel.org
Ecclesiastical Law Society www.ecclawsoc.org.uk
Sports Lawyers Association www.sportslaw.org
Australian and New Zealand Sports Law Association www.anzsla.com.au
Japanese Federation of Bar Associations www.nichibenren.or.jp
The Chartered Governance Institute UK and Ireland www.cgi.org.uk
Association of Corporate Counsel ACC www.acc.com

International Bar Association www.ibanet.org
International Federation of IP Attorneys FICPI www.ficpi.org
International Trade Mark Association www.inta.org
Institute of Chartered Patent Agents www.cipa.org.uk
Environmental Law Institute www.eli.org
Charity Law Association www.charitylawassociation.org.uk
Copyright Licensing Agency www.cla.org.uk
Commercial Bar Association www.combar.com
United Nations www.un.org
The Notaries Society www.thenotariessociety.org.uk
Association of Women Chartered Secretaries www.awcsonline.net
Legislation Gov UK www.legislation.gov.uk
HM Courts and Tribunals Service www.justice.gov.uk/about/hmcts
Local Government Association www.local.gov.uk
Gov UK www.gov.uk
www.ukonline.gov.uk
Justice Gov UK www.justice.gov.uk
Gambling Commission www.gamblingcommission.gov.uk
Cabinet Office Gov UK
    www.gov.uk/government/organisations/cabinet-office
Commonwealth Parliamentary Association www.cpahq.org
Pensions Regulator www.thepensionsregulator.gov.uk
Pensions Ombudsman www.pensions-ombudsman.org.uk
Department for Works and Pensions
    www.gov.uk/government/organisations/department-for-works-pensions
HM Land Registry for England and Wales
    www.gov.uk/government/organisations/land-registry
Local Government Association www.local.gov.uk
Property Ombudsman www.tpos.co.uk
Information Commissioners Office www.ico.org.uk
Health and Saftey Executive www.hsc.gov.uk
Parliamentary and Health Service Ombudsman www.ombudsman.org.uk
Charity Commission www.gov.uk/organisations/charity-commission
Office of the Scottish Charity Regulator www.oscr.org.uk
US State Department www.state.gov
US Environmental Protection Agency www.epa.gov
US Customs and Border Protection www.cbp.gov
Nasa www.nasa.gov
United Nations www.un.org
European Network of Equality Bodies www.equineteurope.org
European Police Office www.europol.europa.eu
European Centre for Development Policy Management www.ecdpm.org
Institute of Chartered Surveyors www.rics.org
Crown Estate www.thecrownestate.co.uk

The Foreign Policy Centre www.fpc.org.uk
Society for Risk Analysis www.sra.org
Solicitors Regulation Authority SRA www.sra.org.uk
World Trade Mark Review www.worldtrademarkreview.com
Council for Licensed Conveyancers www.clc-uk.org
General Medical Council www.gmc-uk.org
Met Office www.metoffice.com
UK Hydrographic Office www.gov.uk/organisations/uk-hydrographic-office
Commonwealth www.commonwealth.org.uk
Royal Warrant Holders Association www.royalwarrant.org
British Council www.britishcouncil.org
Commonwealth British Council www.cbcglobelink.org
Commonwealth Secretariat www.thecommonwealth.org
Council of Institutional Investors www.cii.org
Chartered Institute of Water and Environmental Management
    www.ciwem.org

Trade, Advertising and Marketing

Institute of Practitioners in Advertising IPA www.ipa.co.uk
UK European Consumer Centre Trading Standards Institute www.ukecc.net
International Organisation for Standardisation www.iso.org
American National Standards Institute www.ansi.org
Bureau of Indian Standards www.bis.gov.in
Swedish Institute of Standards www.sis.se
British Standards Institute www.bsi.group.com
Trading Standards www.gov.uk/find-local-trading-standards-office
National Association of Manufacturers www.nam.org
World Trade Organisation www.wto.org
Advertising Association www.adassoc.org.uk
Advertising Standards Authority ASA www.asa.org.uk
American Association of Advertising Agents 4 A's www.aaaa.org
Advertising Federation of Australia www.afa.org.au
Data and Marketing Association UK www.dma.org.uk
The Marketing Society www.marketingsociety.com
Chartered Institute of Marketing CIM www.cim.co.uk
Institute for Supply Management www.ismworld.org
Advertising Producers Association www.a-p-a.net
Data and Marketing Commission www.dmcommission.com
Country Land and Business Association www.cla.org.uk
Chartered Management Institute www.managers.org.uk
Chartered Institute of Personnel and Development www.cipd.co.uk
Institute of Sales Professionals www.ismprofessional.co.uk
Sporting Goods Industry Association www.sgiauk.com
International Chamber of Commerce www.iccwbo.org

2137

British Chambers of Commerce www.britishchambers.org.uk
American Chamber of Commerce to Europe www.amchameu.eu
Department for International Trade
   www.gov.uk/organisations/department-for-international-trade
British Toy and Hobby Association www.btha.co.uk
Chartered Institute of Procurement and Supply www.cips.org
Eurochambres www.eurochambres.eu
Australian Trade and Investment Commission www.austrade.gov.au
New Zealand Trade and Enterprise www.nzte.govt.nz
Italian Trade and Investment Agency www.ice.it/it
The Royal Commonwealth Society www.royalcwsociety.org
The Commonwealth www.thecommonwealth.org
Commonwealth Foundation www.commonwealthfoundation.com
Advertising Council Australia www.advertisingcouncil.org.au
Legal Marketing Association www.legalmarketing.org
Branded Content Marketing Association www.thebcma.info
The American Economic Association www.aeaweb.org
The Economist www.economist.com
Campaign www.campaignlive.co.uk
PR Week www.prweek.com
Marketing Association of Australia and New Zealand
   www.marketing.org.au
Australian Marketing Institute www.ami.org.au
Australasian Promotional Products Association www.appa.com.au
Australian Association of National Advertisers www.aana.com.au
Australian Direct Marketing Association www.adma.org.au
The Federation of International Employers www.fedee.com
ACAS www.acas.org.uk
Eures European Job Mobility Portal www.eures.europa.eu
Foreign Trade Association www.foreigntradeassociation.com
European Brands Association www.aim.be
British Brands Group www.britishbrandsgroup.org.uk
Federation of International Trade Associations www.fita.org
Institute of Economic Affairs www.iea.org.uk
World Federation of Advertisers www.wfanet.org
Canadian Marketing Association www.cma.c
Hasbro www.hasbro.com
Lego Group www.lego.com
Dr Seuss Enterprises www.seussville.com
Forbes www.forbes.com

Finance, Audits and Statistics

Institute and Faculty of Actuaries www.actuaries.org.uk
Institute of Chartered Accountants in England and Wales www.icaew.com

International Federation of Accountants www.ifac.org
Chartered Institute for Securities and Investment www.cisi.org
Chartered Institute of Public Finance and Accountancy www.cipfa.org
Chartered Institute of Internal Auditors www.iia.org.uk
Chartered Institute of Credit Management www.cicm.com
Chartered Institute of Loss Adjusters www.cila.co.uk
Charted Institute of Logistics and Transport www.ciltinternational.org
Chartered Institute of Information Security www.ciisec.org
American Finance Association www.afajof.org
World Bank www.worldbank.org
Bank of England www.bankofengland.co.uk
The Royal Mint www.royalmint.com
World Gold Council www.gold.org
Chartered Banker Institute www.charteredbanker.com
Office for National Statistics www.ons.gov.uk
UK Finance www.ukfinance.org.uk
European Accounting Association www.eaa-online.org
The London Stock Exchange www.londonstockexchange.com
Secured Finance Network www.sfnetwork.com
Financial Executives International www.financialexecuitves.org
Financial Planning Association www.financialplanningassociation.org
Financial Director www.financialdirector.co.uk
European Investment Bank www.eib.org
European Banking Authority www.eba.europa.eu
Accountancy Europe www.accountancyeurope.eu
National Audit Office www.nao.org.uk
International Council of Securities Associations www.icsa.global
Financial Services Group of Livery Companies www.fsgcityoflondon.com
Association of Corporate Treasurers www.treasurers.org
The European Association of Corporate Treasurers www.eact.eu
The International Group of Treasury Associations IGTA www.igta.org
US Department of Treasury www.treas.gov
Bank of Texas www.bankoftexas.com
Federal Reserve Bank of New York www.newyorkfed.org

Sports, Sponsorship and Gambling
British Olympic Association Team GB www.teamgb.com
International Association of Athletics Federations IAAF
    www.worldathletics.org
England Athletics www.englandathletics.org
British Athletics www.britishathletics.org.uk
UK Sponsorship Database www.uksponsorship.com
English Institute of Sport www.eis2win.co.uk
European Commission – Sport www.ec.europa.eu/sport

International Olympic Committee www.olympic.com
London Federation of Sports and Recreation www.london-fed-sport.org.uk
Federation of International Football www.fifa.com
English Football Association www.thefa.com
World Rugby www.world.rugby
Commonwealth Sport www.thecgf.com
SportAus AIS www.sportaus.gov.au
American Sports Institute www.americansportsinsitute.org
European Sponsorship Association www.sponsorship.org
Chartered Institute for the Management of Sport and Physical Activity
    www.cimspa.co.uk
The Lawn Tennis Association www.lta.org.uk
Australian Open www.ausopen.com
US Open www.usopen.com
Wimbledon www.wimbledon.com
British Darts Organisation www.bdodarts.com
British Horseracing Association www.britishhorseracing.com
British and Irish Lions www.lionsrugby.com
England Hockey www.englandhockey.co.uk
England Squash www.englandsquash.com
Motor Sports Association www.msauk.org
Gambling Commission www.gamblingcommission.gov.uk
International Association of Gaming Advisors www.theiaga.org
Arcades and Gaming Machines Bacta www.bacta.org.uk
Betting and Gaming Council www.bettingandgamingcouncil.com
Bingo Association www.bingo-association.co.uk
Lotteries Council www.lotteriescouncil.org.uk
Gaming Regulators European Forum www.gref.net
International Association of Gaming Regulators www.iagr.org

Libraries, Archives, Institutes and Charities
British Library www.bl.uk
Archives Hub www.archiveshub.jisc.ac.uk
Bodleian Library www.bodleian.ox.ac.uk
UNESCO www.unesco.org
UNESCO Depository Libraries
    www.publishingunesco.org/depositories.aspx
Imperial War Museum www.iwm.org.uk
Royal Botanic Garden www.kew.org
Chartered Institute of Horticulture www.horticulture.org.uk
National Library of New Zealand www.natlib.govt.nz
National Library of Southern Australia www.sla.sa.gov.au
The National Archives www.nationalarchives.gov.uk
British Museum www.britishmuseum.org

American Association of Law Libraries www.aallnet.org
American Library Association www.ala.org
Library of Congress www.loc.gov
Biblioteque National France www.bnf.fr
British and Irish Legal Information Unit www.bialii.org
National Trust www.nationaltrust.org.uk
Museums Association www.museumsassociation.org
European Bureau of Library, Information and Documentation Associations
    www.eblida.org
Association of European Research Libraries LIBER www.libereuope.eu
The Library and Information Association CILIP www.cilip.org.uk
International Federation of Library Associations and Institutions
    www.ifla.org
Archives and Records Association www.archives.org.uk
International Council on Archives www.ica.org
Church of England Record Centre
    www.lambethpalacelibrary.org/content/cerccollections
Association of Research Libraries www.arl.org
Commonwealth Association of Museums
    www.commonwealth associationofmuseums.org
Association of Commonwealth Universities www.acu.ac.uk
Special Libraries Association www.sla.org
Copac www.copac.ac.uk
JISC Library Hub Discover www.discover.libraryhub.jisc.ac.uk
Museum of Cambridge www.museumofcambridge.org.uk
Danish Library Association www.db.dk
India Library Association www.ilaindic.co.in
Society of American Archivists www.2archivists.org
National Library of Scotland www.nls.uk
National Library of Wales www.library.wales
House of Commons Library www.commonslibrary.parliament.uk
London Library www.londonlibrary.co.uk
US Music Library Association www.musiclibraryassoc.org
The Society for Theatre Research www.str.org.uk
National Theatre www.nationaltheatre.org.uk
Royal Opera House www.roh.org.uk
Natural History Museum www.nhm.ac.uk
National Army Museum www.nam.ac.uk
Imperial War Museum www.iwm.org.uk
Victoria and Albert Museum www.vam.ac.uk
National Science and Media Museum
    www.scicenceandmediamuseum.org.uk
UCAS www.ucas.com – access to list of all universities in UK.
Guildhall www.guildhall.cityoflondon.gov.uk

National Records of Scotland www.nrsscotland.gov.uk
National Museums Scotland www.nms.ac.uk
Sadler's Wells www.sadlerswells.com
British Red Cross Society www.redcross.org.uk
Doctors without Frontiers www.msf.org.uk
Help for Heroes www.helpforheroes.org.uk
Teenage Cancer Trust www.teenagecancertrust.org
Charity Commission www.gov.uk/organisations/charity-commission
The Salvation Army www.salvationarmy.org.uk

Events, Fundraising, Charities and Environment

Association of Event Organisers www.aeo.org.uk
Legal IT Show www.legalitbizshow.com
Midem www.midem.com
The London Book Fair www.londonbookfair.co.uk
International Publishers Association
    www.internationalpublishers.org/our-industry-menu/book-fairs
Cheltenham Literary Festival www.cheltenhamfestivals.com
Edinburgh Book Festival www.edbookfest.co.uk
Nielsen www.nielsen.com
Gardners www.gardners.com
Glascow International Film Festival www.glascowfilm.org
Edinburgh International Film Festival www.edfilmfest.org.uk
BFI London Film Festival www.bfi.org.uk/london-film-festival
Cannes Film Festival www.festival-cannes.com
London Games Festival www.games.london
Book Expo America www.bookexpoamerica.com
Chartered Institute of Fundraising www.ciof.org.uk
Glastonbury www.glastonburyfestivals.co.uk
Glyndebourne www.glyndebourne.com
Netherlands Film Festival www.filmfestival.nl
Crowdfunder www.crowdfunder.co.uk
Ted www.ted.com/talks
Kickstarter www.kickstarter.com
LocalGiving www.localgiving.org
Justgiving www.justgiving.com
Gofundme www.gofundme.com
Charity Digital www.charitydigital.org.uk
Eventbrite www.eventbrite.co.uk

Eden Project www.edenproject.com

European Climate Foundation www.europeanclimate.org
Friends of the Earth Europe www.friendsoftheearth.eu
Greenpeace www.greenpeace.org.uk

International Union for Conservation of Nature www.iucn.org
European Environment Agency www.eea.europa.eu
European Maritime Safety Agency www.emsa.europa.eu
Rainforest Alliance www.rainforest-alliance.org

Codes of Practice, Policies and Guidelines

- This is not intended to be an exhaustive list, but just general background of some resources. Obviously you use these references at your own risk and the Authors and Publishers cannot be responsible for any content of third parties.

- Ofcom www.ofcom.org.uk – is the independent regulator and competition authority for the UK communications industries. Cable, satellite and terrestrial TV and on demand; radio, postal services, phones, the internet, telecommunication, wireless communication services and video sharing platforms. Through Ofcom you can access a list of their licensees.

- Ofcom's own policies and guidelines

  www.ofcom.org.uk/about-ofcom/policies-and-guidelines

- Ofcom Broadcasting Code www.ofcom.org.uk/tv-radio-and-on-demand/broadcast-codes includes:
  Code on Scheduling of Television Advertising
  Code on Sports and Listed Events
  Code on TV Access Services
  Code on EPGs
  Code on the prevention of undue discrimination between broadcast advertisers
  Regulation of e-cigarette advertising, sponsorship and product placement
  Code on Electronic Programme Guides
  Legacy Codes

- The Ofcom Broadcasting Code (with the Cross Promotion Code and the On Demand Service Rules)
  www.ofcom.org.uk/tv-radio-and-on-demand/broadcast-codes/broadcast-code

- Ofcom Electronic Communications Code – relates to installation and maintenance of electronic communication networks
  www.ofcom.org.uk/phones-telecoms-and-internet/information-for-industry/policy/electronic-comm-code

- BBC Policies and guidelines which relate to their mission and purpose www.bbc.com/aboutthebbc/reports/policies includes:
  BBC Code of Conduct
  Charities
  Child Protection

Distribution
Diversity and Inclusion
Editorial Guidelines
Environmental Sustainability
Fair Trading and Transfer Pricing
Licence Fee Collection Payments
Material changes to the BBC activities and commercial activities
Operational Separation
Ticketing for public service events
Use of alternative finance in BBC content
Welsh language scheme

- Other BBC policies on related Freedom Information site
  www.bbc.co.uk/for/publication-scheme/classes/policies-and-
  procedures includes:
  Equal Opportunities and Diversity
  Workforce Policies
  General Policies and Guidelines
  Health and Safety
  Records Management
  Supplying the BBC
  BBC Unions

- ITV – Governance www.itvplc.com/investors/governance

- ITV Commissioning Compliance Guidelines www.itv.com/
  commissioning/articles/compliance-guidelines includes:
  Producers Handbook
  Child Protection Guidelines
  Child Licensing Guidelines
  Viewer Trust In ITV
  Offensive language guidelines
  End Credit rules
  ITV Guidance for protecting participants
  ITV UGC Moderation Policy
  Social media Guidelines

- ITV Commissioning Guidelines www.itv.com/commissioning/
  guidelines includes:
  Producers Guidelines
  Social Partnership
  Step up 60
  Compliance Guidelines
  Duty of Care
  Coronavirus Guidance
  Technical Guidelines

Music Clearance and Silvermouse Guidelines
Programme Policy Statements
Britbox guidelines
Schedule D
ITV Global Distribution Guidelines
ITV Indication Tariffs
Brand and End Credit Guidelines
Creative Guidelines
Terms of Trade
Billing Templates
Publicity Guidelines
Health and Safety Guidelines
CITV Creative Guidelines

- GOV UK – Committee on Standards in Public Life www.gov.uk/government/organisations/the-committee-on-standards-in-public-life

- Health and Safety Executive – health and safety at work www.hse.gov.uk

- Patents Code of Practice to identify best practice in UK patent application process www.gov.uk/government/publications/patents-code-of-practice

- Independent Press Standards Organisation IPSO Editors Code www.ipso.co.uk/editors-code-of-practice

- WIPO Good Practice Toolkit for CMOs – Collective Management Organisations www.wipo.int/publications/en/details.jsp?id=4358

- Information Commissioners' Office ICO www.ico.org.uk includes:
Guide to Data Protection
Guide to Freedom of Information
Data Sharing Code of Practice

- Statistics Authority www.statisticsauthority.gov.uk
Code of Practice for Statistics

- Institute of Fundraising www.ciof.org includes:
Member Code of Conduct
Direct Marketing Code of Practice

- ISEAL www.isealalliance.org
Sustainability Standards Codes of Good Practice

- Financial Reporting Council www.frc.org.uk
Codes and Standards Committee includes:

UK Corporate Governance Code
Stewardship Code

- Public Relations and Communications PRCA www.prca.org.uk
includes:
Professional Charter and Codes of Conduct for public relations and
communication personnel who are members.

- Gambling Commission www.gamblingcommission.gov.uk – you can
access the register of licence holders and the register of gambling
premises.
Licence Conditions and Codes of Practice includes:
Betting on Lotteries and Lottery themed gaming products.
Casino Games
Lotteries – sector specific compliance
Bingo – sector specific compliance
Arcades and Gaming Machines – sector specific compliance
Gambling Software and online business – sector specific compliance

- Betting and Gaming Council www.bettingandgamingcouncil.com
Codes of Conduct for members – betting shops, casinos and online
betting and gaming companies includes:
BGC Code of Conduct
Higher value VIP reward programs
Gambling industry for socially responsible advertising
Partnered posts on football club social media accounts
Game Design
Gamcare industry code for the display of safer gambling information

- Bingo Association www.bingo-association.co.uk
Trade organisation for all licensed operators in GB. Code of Conduct
for Social Responsibility applies to its members.

- Department for Culture, Media and Sport www.gov.uk/government/
organisations/department-for-culture-media-and-sport

- Disclosure and Barring Service www.gov.uk/disclosure-barring-
service-check

- Advertising Standards Authority www.asa.org.uk
includes:
ASA Code of Practice
CAP Non-broadcast Code
CAP Broadcast Code

- Australian Advertising Council www.advertisingcouncil.org.au
Best Practice Guide Social Media and Online Commentary Conduct
Code

- National Union of Journalists www.nuj.org.uk
  Code of Conduct for its members

- Press Council of Ireland www.presscouncil.ie
  Code of Practice

- UEFA www.uefa.com
  Media Code of Conduct

- The EU Code of Conduct on countering illegal hate speech online
  www.ec.europa.eu/info/policies/justice-and-fundamental-rights
  Code has been agreed with Facebook, Microsoft, Twitter, YouTube,
  Instagram, Snapchat, Daily Motion, Jeuxvideo and Tik Tok.

- Central Digital and Data Office www.gov.uk
  Guidance – Technology Code of Practice to help government set
  criteria to design, build and buy technology.

- Crown Commercial Service www.gov.uk
  Guidance on commercial capability contract management standards
  www.gov.uk/government/publications/commercial-capability-contract-
  management-standards
  Review of major UK government contracts
  Contract management government principles

- European Sponsorship Association www.sponsorship.org
  ESA Code of Conduct for members

- Portman Group www.portmangroup.org.uk supports self-regulation of
  the alcohol drinks industry includes:
  Marketing Code of Practice – Naming Packaging and Promotion of
  Alcoholic Drinks
  Code of Practice for Alcohol Sponsorship

- Food Standards Agency www.food.gov.uk
  Food law Code of Practice for local authorities in the UK to follow.

- World Health Organisation www.who.int
  International food standards The Codex Alimentarius or the 'Food
  Code' is a collection of standards and guidelines and codes of
  practice adopted by the Codex Alimentarius Commission. A joint inter-
  governmental body of the Food and Agriculture Organisation of the UN
  and WHO – with 188 member countries and one member organisation
  – the EU.

- Office for Product Safety and Standards www.gov.uk
  Part of the Department of Business, Energy and Industrial Strategy

- Medicines and Healthcare Products Regulatory Agency MHRA www.gov.uk
  Drugs and medical devices.

- Verisign www.verisign.com

- Internet Architecture Board www.Iab.org
  Advisory body of the Internet Society

- Afilias www.afilias.info

- Canadian Internet Registration Authority www.cira.ca

- RIPE NCC Internet Registry System www.ripe.net/participate/internet-governance/internet-technical-community/the-rir-system

- The Internet Assigned Numbers Authority IANA www.iana.org
  Authority over all number spaces used in the internet including IP address space and autonomous system AS numbers.
  Regional Internet Registries – 5 RIRs
  ARIN
  RIPE NCC
  LACNIC
  AFRINIC
  APNIC

- Lending Standards Board LSB www.lendingstandardsboard.org.uk
  The Standards of Lending Practice in the UK.

- European Central Bank www.ecb.europa.eu
  Compliance and Governance office

- International Monetary Fund www.imf.org
  IMF and World Bank endorsed international recognised standards and codes in 12 areas including Data, Fiscal Transparency, Monetary and Financial Policy, Transparency, International Accounting Standards, International Auditing.
  www.imf.org/external/standards/index.htm

- IFRS Foundation International Accounting Standards Board www.ifrs.org/groups/international-accounting-standards-board

- Chartered Trading Standards Institute www.tradingstandards.co.uk

- International Communications Consultancy www.iccopr.com –
  umbrella organisations for 41 PR associations worldwide.
  Communications Management Standards for its members.

- International Telecommunication Union www.itu.int
  The United Nations specialised agency for information and communication technologies

- Publishers Association www.publishers.org.uk
  Services cover: Copyright Infringement Portal, PLS Permissions

- Society of Authors www.societyofauthors.org
  UK trade organisation for writers, illustrators, scriptwriters and literary translators.

Index

This index is compiled by reference to the alphabetical main clause headings and clause code numbers. Where * appears below this indicates that there is no such main clause heading in the book and you will be referred to other relevant main clause headings.

Some main clause headings only have a General Business and Commercial or Internet, Websites and Apps section, but most main clause headings are sub-divided and have the following sub-headings:
Film, Television and Video;
General Business and Commercial;
Internet, Websites and Apps;
Merchandising and Distribution;
Publishing;
Services;
Sponsorship;
University, Charity and Educational.

All references are to clause numbers.

A

Absence   **A.001**
See also Bank Holidays, Death,
Gardening Leave, Health,
Holidays, Medical Report,
Policies, Termination.

Acceptance   **A.049**
See also Cancellation, Copyright
Clearance, Delivery,
Editorial Control, Material,
Quality Control, Rejection,
Termination, Title.

Access   **A.130**
See also Copyright Notice,
Cancellation, Copyright
Warnings, Disclaimer,
Downloading, Error, Facility
Access, Insurance, Liability,
Location Access, Omission,
Rights, Risk, Termination,
Title.

Accuracy   **A.187**
See also Delivery, Disclaimer,
Due Diligence, Error, Material,
Omission, Order, Product
Liability, Quality Control,
Rejection.

Accounting Period   **A.202**
See also Accounting Provisions,
Inspection of Accounts and
Records, Payment, Royalties.

Accounting Provisions   **A.211**
See also Budget, Costs, Data,
Database, Disclaimer,
Expenses, Group Accounts,
Indemnity, Inspection of
Accounts and Records,
Interest, Liability, Payment,
Risk, Royalties, Sell-Off Period.

Act of God   **A.387**
See also Break Clauses,
Cancellation, Disclaimer,

L

Laboratory Access   **L.001**
See also Facility Access, Liability, Material, Title.

Language   **L.015**
See also Capacity, Interpretation, Jurisdiction, Parties to Agreement, Severance, Sub-Licence.

Legal Proceedings   **L.027**
See also Arbitration, Budget, Consultation, Costs, Damages, Defamation, Editorial Control, Implied Terms, Indemnity, Interpretation, Jurisdiction, Liability, Mediation, Obscenity, Origin, Originality, Quality Control, Risk, Voluntary Departure, Waiver.

Levies *
See Sales Tax, Value Added Tax, Taxes.

Liability   **L.152**
See also Acceptance, Arbitration, Disclaimer, Delivery, Defamation, Damages, Facility Access, Force Majeure, Indemnity, Insurance, Jurisdiction, Legal Proceedings, Location Access, Mediation, Product Liability, Quality Control, Risk.

Licence Area *
See Assignment, Exclusivity, Location Access, Rights, Territory, Venue.

Licence Fee   **L.264**
See also Acceptance, Budget, Costs, Expenses, Delivery, Interest, Payment, Rates

of Exchange, Rejection, Royalties, Set-Off.

Licence Period   **L.333**
See also Act of God, Assignment, Assignment Period, Cancellation, Exclusivity, First Refusal, Force Majeure, Option, Remainders, Rights, Sell-off Period, Suspension, Term of the Agreement, Termination.

Literary Work *
See Adaptation, Assignment, Audio Files, Books, Copyright Clearance, Copyright Notice, Defamation, Disclaimer, Exclusivity, Films, Index, Marketing, Material, New Editions, Performances, Rights, Royalties, Scripts, Sound Recordings, Work.

Litigation *
See Acceptance, Act of God, Cancellation, Compliance, Damages, Delivery, Disclaimer, Error, Force Majeure, Jurisdiction, Legal Proceedings, Liability, Material, Notices, Omission, Penalty, Policies, Product Liability, Rejection, Risk.

Location Access   **L.360**
See also Costs, Expenses, Facility Access, Indemnity, Insurance, Liability, Venue.

Logo   **L.376**
See also Brand, Copyright Clearance, Credits, Disclaimer, Domain Name, Downloading, Goodwill, Marketing, Material, Publicity, Rights, Title, Trade Marks.

Other supporting background material:

Series of Articles:
1. Highlights in respect of some of
    the main types of clauses in a
    contract and how they can be
    varied.
2. A short guide to the mistakes,
    omissions and errors to avoid
    in a contract, licence or
    distribution agreement.
3. Factors in Sub-Licensing

Legal, Commercial and Business Development Directory.

Codes of Practice, Policies and Guidelines

Single End User Licence

Access to and use of electronic downloads of The A-Z of Contract Clauses, 7th edition

The contract clauses, directories, articles and other background material and index in this edition are available to download electronically from https://bloomsburyprofessionallaw.com/azcc.

They are password protected and the password is 8H72N which can be used by one person.

You are allowed access to and use of the electronic downloads as the purchaser of the book subject to the single user licence in the book. You must adhere to the conditions of the single user licence.

Multiple access and use by more than one person of the electronic downloads is not authorised.

The prior written consent and approval of the Authors and the Publishers is required for any other form of exploitation outside the terms of the single user licence granted.

If you have any problems downloading the precedents or have any questions, please contact Bloomsbury Professional customer services on 01444 416119 or by email at customerservices@bloomsburyprofessional.com.

Terms of use of the book and access to the electronic files

1. The purchase of the Book also provides access to the electronic files by a single person. The use of the Book and/or the electronic files are licensed on that basis. No right is granted to permit multiple access and/or to supply clauses as part of a document and/or other electronic delivery service and/or in any other form in any medium to third parties. You must contact the Publishers and Authors and request an additional licence for any wider purpose.

2. There is only a single end user licence agreement for use of the Book and/or the electronic files by a single person whether the purchaser is an individual, institute, charity and/or company.

3. There is no right of access granted to any person who has not purchased a copy of the Book of **The A-Z of Contract Clauses, Seventh Edition** which is published under an exclusive licence by Bloomsbury Professional www.bloomsburyprofessional.com ('the Publishers').

4. **The A-Z of Contract Clauses, Seventh Edition** is an original work written by Deborah Fosbrook and Adrian C. Laing ('the Authors'). The Authors are the copyright owners of the Book ('the Book') and all the contents, data, index and the electronic files.

5. It is a condition and you as the Purchaser are required to agree to the terms contained in this licence in order to be permitted to use the Book and/or the electronic files. If you do not agree to these terms then no authority is provided to use any part of the Book and/or the electronic files in any manner except as a read only Book in paper form.

6. The Purchaser of the Book and access to the link for the electronic files is granted a non-exclusive and non-transferable licence by the Authors and the Publishers. The licence covers any country worldwide. **The A-Z of Contract Clauses, Seventh Edition** and the electronic files are intended to be used in conjunction with each other to facilitate the quick and easy drafting of a wide range of agreements.

7. The Purchaser is permitted to edit, cut and paste the clauses from the electronic files to create, revise, adapt and amend licences, agreements, documents and/or other records. Clauses may be added to documents supplied by third parties and/or used to review and update existing contracts and to promote the terms of entry of a competition and/or to set out the terms and conditions of access and/

or trading for a social enterprise, charity and/or business on a website, app and/or in social media marketing. This right is only granted to one individual and if multiple access is required by more than one person then permission must be sought from the Publishers and the Authors and an additional licence must be obtained.

8. The Purchaser is permitted to download and copy the electronic files on to the personal hard drive of that individual and also to make one security copy. Where there is multiple access by more than one person for any reason then a new licence agreement must be concluded with the Publishers and Authors prior to access and use by other persons. Failure to seek permission will constitute a breach of copyright.

9. You are not permitted to download and use the electronic files from a main frame and/or to create a document supply service and/or to licence and/or sell the contents of the Book and/or electronic files directly to third parties and/or to substantially copy whole sections of the Book and/or electronic files for sale to third parties.

10. It is accepted by the Publishers and the Authors that in house lawyers, solicitors, legal executives, copyright officers and general counsel and others in practice and/or the media and/or other industries may use the Book and the electronic files to provide legal advice and/or business services to individuals, agents, companies, institutions and international bodies and agencies. There is however no right granted to offer the Book and/or the electronic files and/or any adapted versions directly over the internet and/or any telecommunication system and/or otherwise in electronic form and/or in any other manner.

11. You are not permitted to use copies of the clauses and/or any part of the Book and/or electronic files as part of a document supply service and/or to offer them for sale as a download and/or pdf and/or otherwise. There is no right to copy, reproduce and/or supply the Book and/or the electronic files to third parties in whole and/or part by photocopying, scanning and/or any other form of reproduction and in any manner in electronic form and/or otherwise. You are not licensed to exploit the Book and/or the electronic files for your own purposes where you are operating an online business by means of the internet and/or any telecommunication system and/or software which sells contracts, clauses, documents and/or other formats in any medium.

12. You shall not have the right to make any additional copies and/or to reproduce the Book and/or the electronic files for any other reason and/or to add the Book and/or the electronic files to any central clause library for your business which is available to more than one person and/or anyone else other than the Purchaser.

13. You shall not have the right to use the Book and/or the electronic files to create an index for clauses and/or to develop and create any model clauses for use by your business and/or organisation which will be displayed, promoted and/or supplied on the internet and/or by means of any telecommunication system in a directory and/or to create and/or develop any contract management software and/or any training resource and/or workshops.

14. You shall not have the right to exploit, adapt, licence, translate and/or create a new format and/or create any other adapted version for use on the internet and/or over any telecommunication system as part of any storage and/or retrieval system in any form whether electronic and/or otherwise in any media and/or to permit, authorise, sub-licence, assign, transfer and/or exploit the Book and/or electronic files in any form in any medium, whether for commercial purposes or otherwise and/or by any other method whether in existence now or created in the future.

15. For the avoidance of doubt unauthorised copying includes using the Book and/or electronic files in any manner (whether for commercial gain or not) other than for adapting the contents for use within other documents, licences and agreements to be used for a specific purpose which excludes direct sale to the public in electronic form over the internet and/or any telecommunication system and/or otherwise. You must not represent that the clauses individually or collectively and/or any other content are your property and/or display them on any website, app and/or otherwise in whole and/or part in order to offer them for sale to a third party at any time.

16. The Book and the electronic files are an excluded work from the Copyright Licensing Agency and all other rights management organisations and/or collecting societies. There is no licence granted to scan, photocopy and/or to sub-licence and/or supply the Book and/or electronic files as part of any service of any nature whether for educational purposes or not.

17. You shall not under any circumstances use and/or adapt the Book and/or the electronic files in any manner which is derogatory, offensive, detrimental to and/or likely to damage the reputation of the Publishers and/or the Authors. The copyright owners shall claim damages, losses and costs for any breach by a third party and/or any unauthorised substantial copying, use, adaptation and/or other exploitation of any nature which is in breach of copyright, moral rights and/or any other rights.

18. The Purchaser shall not acquire any copyright, intellectual property and/or other rights and/or interest in the Book and/or the electronic files and/or any adaptation derived from them in any form in any media of any nature at any time and/or represent to third parties that they are entitled to do so. All rights that are not specifically authorised and granted are expressly reserved.

19. The Publishers and the Authors do not accept any responsibility and/or liability of any nature arising out of the use of the Book and/or the electronic files by the Purchaser at any time for any purpose. Neither the Publishers nor the Authors shall be liable for any expenses, costs, losses, damages and/or claim of any nature whether direct and/or indirect, consequential and/or otherwise that may arise in respect of the Purchaser and/or any business and/or enterprise in which the Purchaser is and/or may be involved and/or to which the Purchaser may supply material and/or advice for any reason and/or purpose. The Purchaser therefore uses the Book and/or electronic files entirely at the Purchaser's sole risk, liability and cost and the Purchaser agrees that the Publishers and Authors shall not be liable for any reason. You are strongly advised to get take independent legal and commercial advice based on your circumstances. Please also note that there is a disclaimer at the front of this Book.

20. Neither the Publishers nor the Authors accept any responsibility and/or liability of any nature howsoever arising for any errors, omissions, viruses, defects, failures and/or any other matters of any nature in the Book and/or the electronic files whether such fault is of a legal, technical or other nature. The Purchaser must use the Book and/or electronic files entirely at its sole risk and cost and accept that the contract clauses are for reference and guidance only and are intended to be adapted and varied accordingly by each Purchaser to suit their particular circumstances.

21. In the event that there is a problem with access and/or use of the electronic files not directly and/or indirectly caused by the Purchaser and/or their hardware, computer and/or software. Please contact the Publishers for assistance and a new link will be supplied within 90 days of the purchase. Where the electronic files cannot be accessed due to the Purchaser and there is no alternative available then there is no liability and/or responsibility on the part of the Publishers to provide any other resource and/or make any refund of any nature to the Purchaser.

22. In the event of any claim, action and/or demand of any nature being made against and/or by the Purchaser arising out of the use of the

Book and/or the electronic files in any circumstances. Any such claim against the Publishers and/or the Authors shall be limited to the purchase price of the Book.

23. The Purchaser agrees that it is the Purchasers' own responsibility to pay the cost of insurance cover for the benefit of the Purchaser, any business and/or third party for the use of the Book and/or electronic files by the Purchaser. The Purchaser agrees that the Publisher and the Authors shall not bear any responsibility and/or liability for the use of the Book and/or the electronic files by the Purchaser, any business, third party or otherwise which is supplied directly or indirectly by the Purchaser at any time.

24. The copyright owners of the Book and the electronic files are the Authors who formally assert individually and jointly their moral rights which may exist now and/or may be created in the future and shall therefore at all times be prominently and reasonably identified as follows:

© Deborah Fosbrook and Adrian C. Laing 1996–2021.

The Publishers shall be identified where appropriate as Bloomsbury Professional.

25. In the event that the Purchaser has reasonable grounds to believe that the Book and/or the electronic files are being used in any unlawful manner the Publishers and the Authors shall be informed in confidence without delay by the Purchaser.

26. In the event that the Publishers and/or the Authors become aware and/or have reasonable grounds to believe that the Purchaser, its business, employees and/or associates are using the Book and/or the electronic files in a manner that contravenes the terms of these conditions and/or which is prejudicial is any manner to the Publishers and/or the Authors. Then this licence may be summarily terminated without notice. In such circumstances the Purchaser will be obliged upon written request to surrender all copies of the Book and/or electronic files and/or to delete all copies held on any hard drive and/or elsewhere in any form under their possession and/or control.

27. The Purchaser shall not use the Book and/or the electronic files in any manner inconsistent with these terms and under no circumstances shall the Purchaser alter, remove, deface, erase and/or amend the copyright notice, trade marks, or details concerning the Publishers and/or the Authors displayed on any part of the Book and/or the electronic files.

28. The Publishers and the Authors reserve the right to suspend and/or terminate this licence at any time without notice in respect of access to the electronic files as they may decide and/or may take such legal action as is necessary to protect their copyright and/or intellectual property rights.

29. The licence is intended to be a legally binding agreement and shall be governed exclusively by the Laws of England and Wales.